Thanks for picking up this book. I appreciate the lift.

Hi! I'm Russ, the only guy foolish enough to spend a whole lifetime to write a computer book then update it 30 more times then rewrite it again to include tricks for living in the computer era.

Doubly delightful

This volume includes 2 books in one: it includes what would have been in the *The Secret Guide to Computers'* 31st edition and *Tricky Living*'s 3rd edition. Reviewers praised earlier editions for being the best computer & lifestyle books ever written, but this new edition is even better: it's updated, includes more topics, and expresses itself more wisely.

Unlike a "Dummies" book (which is written for dummies and keeps them dumb) and a "standard textbook" (shoved at overworked college students to bore them into snoring louder) and a "polemic book" (written by a crackpot whom you'd wish would shut up), this book throws you fast into the action of training you to be competent & wise. It explains how to buy a computer, use operating system & programs, write your own programs, and use tricks to enhance your life, fast!

Skippy?

Start at this book's beginning or skip to the parts that match your personality. (The *Tricky Living* part, which begins on page 346, is quite different from the rest.)

Free phone help

Whenever you have a question (about computers or anything else in your life), get free help by phoning me in my New Hampshire home at **603-666-6644**. Phone day or night (around the clock, 24 hours). I'm usually in, and I sleep just lightly. (If no answer, I'm out on an errand: try an hour later.)

I've answered hundreds of thousands of phone calls about computers (how to buy, use, fix, and program them) and how to handle careers and the rest of life (health, dating, other relationships, schools, foreign cultures, religion, and beyond).

I answer most questions directly. If your question's too tricky for a quick answer, I'll teach you how to find the correct answer yourself and which people and resources to use. I give you the path to the truth. Try me. I'm free.

When you phone, **begin by saying your name, city, how you got my number ("from the 31 edition"), and a one-sentence summary of your question**. Then we'll have a pleasant chat — unless I'm in the middle of another call or meeting, in which case I'll call you back free!

Here are the rules:

> For help about your computer, phone *when you're at the computer*. For help with your career or life, sob *before* calling, then tell me what facts you want analyzed. To handle many calls each day while juggling my other responsibilities as an author & publisher, I must keep the average call to 7 minutes (but I often go longer, and you can phone many times). If the answer's in this book, I'll tell you the page (since I can't read the book over the phone). I can't help you do inadvisable activities (such as taking illegal drugs, using pirated software, or bombing the USA).

If you're a kid, get your parents' permission to phone.

Come visit

When you visit New Hampshire, drop in and use my library, free. Drop in anytime: day or night! In case I'm having an orgy with my 40 computers, **phone first** to pick a time when we're cooled down.

You can also visit me in cyberspace at **www.SecretFun.com**, where you can read the latest news about us, click useful links, and read parts of this book online, free. I read all e-mail sent to **Russ@SecretFun.com**; but if you want me to chat and reply, *phone* me at 603-666-6644.

Please help me

I try to explain everything important about computers & tricky living, but that's as hard as catching a greased pig: whenever I think I've finally caught the truth, our culture bolts ahead in a weird new direction. Each time I finish an edition, I must start writing the next, in endless frustration. If you have suggestions for the next edition, please tell me.

I wish this book weren't needed. I wish computer companies would create pleasant hardware, software, and manuals. I wish the rest of the world would explain tricky living clearly. Until that happens, scribes like me are doomed to spend our lives explaining the world's mistakes.

Love your librarian

These details will save your librarian from getting fired:

Title:	*Secret Guide to Computers & Tricky Living*, 31st edition
Author & publisher:	Russ Walter at 603-666-6644 (24 hours, usually in)
Rating:	this is the top-rated book about computers & life
Copywrong:	end of 2011 by Russ Walter (for use in 2012)
ISBN:	Internat. Standard Book Number is 978-0-939151-39-4
Street address:	196 Tiffany Lane, Manchester NH 03104-4782
Internet addresses:	www.SecretFun.com, Russ@SecretFun.com

Elfish fun

I wrote most of this book myself, but over the years I've been helped by many elves, especially these:

> My wife (**Donna Walter**) wrote the "Donna's comments" section.
> Useful tidbits came from **Irene Vassos**, **Len Pallazola**, and **Lili Timmons**.
> **Priscilla Grogan and Kira Barnum** slavishly helped me for many years.
> **Thousands of readers** told me how to improve on earlier editions.
> **Family & friends** supported me when life got tough.

Don't read this

My editor told me to put this stuff in. You don't have to read it.

Dedication I dedicate this book to the computer, without whom I'd be unemployed.

Acknowledgment I'd like to thank:

> **my many friends** (whose names I've gladly forgotten)
> **my students** (who naturally aren't my friends)
> **my word processor** (which has a mind of its own)
> **all others** who helped make this book impossible

I'd especially like to thank:

> **God** (for influencing this book somehow)
> **Bill Gates** (for making software confusing, so I get paid to explain it)
> **Adolph Hitler** (for making my dad flee Germany and meet my mom)
> **buyers of previous editions** (for funding this stupidity)

Prerequisite This book was written for idiots. To see whether you can get through the math, take this test: count to ten but (here's the catch!) without looking at your fingers. To remove the temptation, cut them off.

What this book will do for you It'll make you even richer than the author! Alas, he's broke.

Apology Any original ideas in this book are errors.

Copyright Copying this book is all right! Make as many copies as you like, and don't pay us a cent. Just follow the "free reprints" instructions on page 9.

Forward because it's too late to turn back!

What's in this book?

The *Secret Guide to Computers & Tricky Living* is the world's only *complete* tutorial about computers & living in the computer era. It covers *everything* important about computers.

Feast your eyes on the massive table of contents, splashed across the next page. It reveals that the Guide includes all 9 parts of computer lifestyle lore: **buyer's guide**, **Windows**, **Internet**, **fixes**, **strange systems**, **word processing**, **tricky applications**, **tricky living**, **programming**, and **computer life**.

Buyer's guide

The Guide begins by explaining computer technology, computer jargon, and how to buy a great computer cheaply.

After giving you tricks for **using this book**, it explains **how to shop for a computer**. It analyzes each of the computer's parts (the **chips**, **disks**, **I/O devices**, and **software**) and tells you the best way to buy a **complete system**.

The Guide makes specific recommendations about which brands to buy and where to buy them. It explains the most common kind of computers (IBM-compatibles) and the fascinating competitors from Apple & others. It delves into each manufacturer's goodies and not-so-goodies and reveals nasty details that salespeople try to hide. It turns you into a German nun, who knows the difference between what's blessed and what's wurst.

Windows

Most computers use an operating system called **Windows**. The Guide explains the modern Windows versions: **Windows XP**, **Windows Vista**, and **Windows 7**.

Internet

Computers all over the world have joined forces, to form the international network called the "Internet". The Guide explains how to use all the popular **Web browsers**: Internet Explorer, Firefox, Chrome, and, in a later chapter, Safari. It explains how to use popular tools, such as **Google** and **YouTube**. It also explains popular **e-mail systems**: Outlook Express, Windows Mail, Windows Live Mail, Yahoo Mail, and Gmail.

Fixes

The Guide explains how to increase your computer's **security** (by fending off viruses & phishing schemes and making backups) and perform **maintenance** & **repairs**.

Strange systems

Instead of using Windows, some folks use strange systems, such as an **iPad** or the Windows imitation of **DOS**. The Guide explains how to use them and why they're popular.

Word processing

To write a nice-looking letter or report or book, you need a **word-processing program**. The Guide explains the most popular word-processing program (**Microsoft Word**, versions 2002 & 2003 & 2007 & 2010). Many computers come with **Microsoft Works** instead; the Guide explains that also.

Tricky applications

The Guide explores even the trickiest applications. You learn how handle **spreadsheets** (tables of numbers) by using Excel and Works; **pictures** by using PowerPoint and photo-editing programs, **movies** by using Windows Movie Maker and Pinnacle Studio, **desktop publishing** (newsletters and signs) using Microsoft Publisher, **Web-page design** (using Angelfire, HTML, and blogs), **databases** using Microsoft Access & FileMaker Pro & Works), **accounting**, **games**, and **humanity**.

Tricky living

There's more to life than just computers! This chapter explains everything *beyond* computers. It digs into issues of **health**, **daily survival**, **education**, **philosophy**, **psychology**, **math**, **science**, **art**, **music**, **film**, **writing**, **government**, **languages & cultures** (American, Canadian, German, Spanish, French, Japanese, and Chinese), **ethics**, **religion**, and **sex**.

> Its candid discussions of politics, religion, and sexual relations include comments from both sides of the aisle. Parents who wish to shelter their kids from exposure to life's difficulties should review this material before distributing it to the young. But it's no more controversial than what's discussed on TV and by high-school students every day.

Programming

Our world is split into three classes of people:

> **avoiders** (who fear and loathe computers and avoid them)
> **users** (who use computers but don't really understand them)
> **programmers** (who understand computers and can teach them new tricks)

The Guide elevates your mind to the heights of class 3: it turns you into a sophisticated programmer.

To program the computer, you feed it instructions written in a **computer language**. The Guide explains all the popular computer languages. For example, it explains all 3 popular versions of **Basic** (QBasic, QB64, and Visual Basic), both popular versions of **modern C** (Visual C++ and Visual C#), and both popular versions of **modern Java** (Sun Java 6 and JScript). I updated this chapter thoroughly, so it includes the newest versions of all those languages. It also compares oodles of other computer languages and gives you their history. Finally, to top it all off, you learn how to program by using the most common **assembler**.

Computer life

The Guide digs up the computer industry's **past**, counsels you to improve your computer career and **future**, and gives you helpful **resources** (an index and Secret Guide coupons).

Praised by reviewers

If you like this book, you're not alone.

Praised by magazines

All the famous computer magazines call Russ Walter the "computer guru" and praise him for giving free consulting even in the middle of the night. Here's how they've evaluated *The Secret Guide to Computers*.

PC World "Russ is a PC pioneer, a trailblazer, the user's champion. Nobody does a more thorough, practical, and entertaining job of teaching PC technology. It's a generous compendium of industry gossip, buying advice, and detailed, foolproof tutorials — a wonderful bargain."

PC Magazine "The Guide explains the computer industry, hardware, languages, operating systems, and applications in a knowledgeable, amusing fashion. It includes Russ's unbiased view of the successes & failures of various companies, replete with inside gossip. By reading it, you'll know more than many who make their living with PCs. Whether novice or expert, you'll learn from it and have a good time doing so. No other computer book is a better value."

Christian Computing Magazine "The Guide is the most comprehensive reference in the industry. What planet is Russ from? It must be populated with nice people. You'll learn more from his Guide than from any 10 computer books you've ever read. To say this book is 'comprehensive' is a staggering understatement: nothing else in the industry even comes close. It's worth triple what Russ charges for it."

Infoworld "Russ is recognized and respected in many parts of the country as a knowledgeable, effective instructor. His Guide is readable & outrageous and includes a wealth of info."

Scientific American "The Guide is irresistible. Every step leads to a useful result. Russ's candor shines; he clarifies the faults & foibles others ignore or are vague about. The effect is that of a private chat with a friend who knows the inside story. It reads like a talented disc jockey's patter: it's flip, self-deprecatory, randy, and good-humored. His useful frank content & coherent style are unique. He includes first-rate advice. No room with a small computer and an adult beginner is well equipped without the Guide."

Kiplinger's Personal Finance "Russ is a computer whiz whose mission is to educate people about computers. He lets strangers call him in the middle of the night for help with diagnosing a sick computer. His Guide covers all you ever wanted to know."

Computerworld "The Guide by unconventional computer guru Russ is informative, entertaining."

Computer Shopper "The Guide covers the entire spectrum. It's incredibly informative and amusing."

Barron's "Russ is an expert who answers questions for free and has been inundated by calls."

Esquire "The handy Guide contains lots of fact & opinion untainted by bias."

Classic magazines

Classic magazines The Guide's earlier editions were praised by the classic magazines.

Popular Computing: "Russ is king of the East Coast computer cognoscenti. His Guide is the biggest bargain in computer tutorials in our hemisphere. If CBS ever decides to replace Andy Rooney with a '60 Minutes' computer pundit, they'd need to look no further than Russ. His wry observations enliven his book. His Guide is the first collection of computer writings that one might dare call literature."

Personal Computing: "The Guide is bulging with information. You'll enjoy it. Russ's approach to text-writing sets a new style that other authors might do well to follow. It's readable, instructive, and downright entertaining. If more college texts were written in his style, more college students would graduate."

Creative Computing: "The Guide is fascinating, easy to understand, an excellent book at a ridiculously low price. We especially endorse it."

Byte: "The Guide is amazing. If you've had difficulty understanding computers, or must teach other people about computers, or just want to read a good computer book, get the Guide."

Computer Currents: "Your computer literacy will come up short unless you know something about Russ. He's a folk hero. He knows virtually everything about personal computers and makes learning about them fun. If you've given up in disgust and dismay at reading other computer books, get the Guide. It should be next to every PC in the country. PC vendors would do themselves and their customers a big favor by packing a copy of the Guide with every computer that goes out the door. The Guide deserves the very highest recommendation."

Abacus: "Russ provides the best current treatment of programming languages. It's irreverent, like the underground books of the 1960's. It's simple to read, fast-paced, surprisingly complete, full of locker-room computer gossip, and loaded with examples."

The Whole Earth Catalog in its "Coevolution Quarterly": "The personal-computer subculture was noted for its fierce honesty in its early years. The Guide is one of the few intro books to continue that tradition and the only intro survey of equipment that's kept up to date. Russ jokes, bitches, enthuses, condemns, and charms. The book tells the bald truth in comprehensible language."

Omni: "Guru Russ sympathizes deeply with people facing a system crash at midnight, so he broadcasts his home phone number and answers calls by the light of his computers, cursors winking. He's considered an excellent teacher. His Guide is utterly comprehensive."

Cider Press: "The Guide should be given to all beginners with the purchase of their computers."

Softalk: "The Guide fires well-deserved salvos at many sacred cows. It's long been a cult hit."

Computer Bargain Info: "The Guide is widely acclaimed by experts as brilliant."
Mac User: "It's an everything-under-one-roof computer technology guide."
Eighty Micro: "Theatrical, madcap Russ is a cult hero."
Interface Age: "The Guide is a best buy."
Enter: "It's the best book about computer languages."
Microcomputing: "Plan ahead; get the Secret now."
Compute: "Russ is an industry leader."

Praised by librarians

Librarians have called the Guide the best computer book ever written.

School Library Journal "The Guide is a gold mine of information. It's crystal clear, while at the same time Russ delivers a laugh a paragraph along with a lot of excellent info. It's accessible even to kids, who'll love its loony humor. Buy it; you'll like it."

Wilson Library Bulletin "The Guide is distinguished by its blend of clarity, organization, and humor. It cuts through the techno-haze. It packs more simple, fresh explication per page than anything else available."

BookLovers Review "It's the best computer intro you can buy, a miracle, a must-have tutorial & reference."

Net BookWatch "Many experts around the world agree this is the best single intro to computers. It's well organized, easy to understand, comprehensive, interesting, updated. Complex subjects are explained expertly. Every paragraph is easy to understand. With Russ as your guide, learning about hardware, software, and the Internet becomes pure fun. The Guide is essential reading for beginners and professionals."

Praised by computer societies

Computer societies, in their newsletters, newspapers, and magazines, have called the Guide the best computer book.

Boston Computer Society "The Guide is cleverly graduated, outrageous, funny. Russ turns computerese into plain speaking while making you giggle. He's years ahead of the pack instructing computer novices. His unique mix of zany humor & step-by-step instruction avoids the mistakes of manuals trying to follow his lead."

Connecticut Computer Society "Russ's books have been used by insiders for years. He's a special teacher because of 3 factors: his comprehensive knowledge of many computer topics, his ability to break complicated processes into the smallest components, and his humor. The Guide includes his valuable, candid comments about various computers & software. He's one of the few people able to review languages, machines, and software, all in a humorous, clear manner, with the whole endeavor set off by his sense of industry perspective, history, and culture. If you're ever struck with a computer problem, give him a call."

New England Computer Society "Russ is considered one of the few true computer gurus. His Guide is the world's best tutorial, the best present for anyone who wants to learn about computers without going crazy."

New York's "NYPC" "The Guide is the perfect book for any computer beginner because it covers a range of subjects otherwise requiring a whole reference library. It's even better for the experienced computer user, since it includes many advanced concepts, which one person could hardly remember. But one person apparently remembered them all: Russ. He's a fountain of computer knowledge and can even explain it in words of one syllable. His Guide reads like a novel: you can read simply for fun. It's recommended to anyone from rank beginner to seasoned power user."

Texas's "Golden Triangle PC Club" "Buy this book! You'll be glad! The marvelous Guide explains just about all computer topics in a way anyone can understand. In these days of having to use voice mail or email to reach tech support, it's amazing you can call Russ for help and he'll actually talk with you when you call. This book gives you extreme value for minimal cost. Russ is famous for his comprehensive knowledge of computers, his ability to simplify complicated processes, and his wry wit. Reading the Guide's a joy. He translates highly technical material into easily understandable language. He's the finest example of the preeminent computer professional. He's condensed so much material, in a way that never seems disorganized or cluttered. Anyone working with or interested in computers will find this book a must-have. The Guide stands above the crowd of computer books that just can't compete."

Sacramento (California) PC Users Group "The Guide is the best collection of computer help ever written. It includes just about everything you'd want to know about computers. You'll find answers for all the questions you thought of and some you didn't think of. No holds barred, Russ even tells you who in the industry made the mistakes & rotten computers and who succeeded in spite of themselves. The Guide is fascinating."

Tucson (Arizona) Computer Society "Wonderful stuff! Recommended. Very well done."

Praised around the world

The Guide's been praised by newspapers around the world.

Australia's "Sydney Morning Herald" "The Guide is the best computer intro published anywhere in the world. It gives a total overview of personal computers. It's stimulating, educational, provocative, a damn good read."

The Australian "The Guide's coverage of programming is intelligent, urbane, extremely funny, full of great ideas."

England's "Manchester Guardian" "Russ is a welcome relief. The internationally renowned computer guru tries to keep computerdom's honesty alive. His Guide's an extraordinary source of info."

Silicon Valley's "Times Tribune" "The Guide invites you to throw aside all rules of conventional texts and plunge into the computer world naked & unafraid. This book makes learning not just fun but hilarious, inspiring, addicting."

Dallas Times Herald "Easily the best beginners' book seen, it's not just for beginners. Its strength is how simple it makes everything, without sacrificing what matters."

Detroit News "Russ is a legendary teacher. His fiercely honest Guide packs an incredible amount of info. It's the only book that includes all. He gives you all the dirt about the companies and their hardware, evaluates their business practices, and exposes problems they try to hide. Phone him; you'll always get a truthful answer."

Chicago Tribune "The Guide is the best computer book. It's a cornucopia of computer delights written by Russ, a great altruist & dreamer."

Kentucky's "Louisville Courier" "Russ's Guide will teach you more computer fundamentals than the typical bookstore's thick books. The Guide gives his no-bull insights. The Guide's biggest appeal is its humor, wit, personality."

Florida's "Hometown News" The Guide is thoroughly entertaining. It brings intimidating tech issues down to everyday language. And boy, does it cover the topics! Everything from old systems to new modern workhorses is hit upon. If you're looking for a book that touches on just about every aspect of computers and is easy to read, the Guide's for you."

Philadelphia Inquirer "Russ is the Ann Landers for computer klutzes, a high-tech hero. His wacky, massive Guide is filled with his folksy wit."

New Jersey's "Asbury Park Press" "Most computer books, especially the good ones, are expensive — except the best one. The best computer book is the Guide. It's the only book that covers just about everything in computers."

New York Times "The computer-obsessed will revel in Russ's Guide. He covers just about every subject in the microcomputer universe. It's unlikely you have a question his book doesn't answer."

Wall Street Journal "Russ is a computer expert, a guru who doesn't mind phone calls. He brings religious-like fervor to the digital world. His students are grateful. His Guide gets good reviews. He's influential."

Connecticut's "Hartford Courant" "If you plan to buy a personal computer, the best gift for yourself is the Guide. It's crammed with info. It became an instant success as one of the few microcomputer books that was not only understandable & inexpensive but also witty — a combo still too rare today."

New Hampshire's "Hippo" "Very impressive."

Boston Globe "Russ is a unique resource, important to beginning and advanced users. His Guide is practical, down-to-earth, easy to read."

Boston Phoenix "Russ has achieved international cult status. He knows his stuff, and his comprehensive Guide's a great deal."

Experts

Experts love the Guide.

PC Week reporter "I write for *PC Week* and think the Guide is the *best* book of its kind. I'm sending a copy to my little brother, who's a budding byte-head." (Boston)

Math professor "I'm a math professor. The Guide's the best way in the universe to keep up to date with computers. People don't have to read anything else — it's *all* there." (New York City)

Diehard consultant "It's really neat! I've been a computer consultant for many years, and when your book came yesterday I couldn't put it down." (Cleveland Heights, Ohio)

Research center "Our research center uses and misuses gigabytes of computers. The Guide will improve our use/misuse ratio." (Naperville, Illinois)

Careers

The Guide's propelled many careers.

Land a first job "Last month, I bought your Guide. I've never seen so much info, packed so densely, in so entertaining a read. I was just offered a computer job, thanks to a presentation based on your Guide. I'm very, very, very happy I bought your book." (San Francisco)

Land a top job "Thanks to the Guide, I got an excellent job guiding the selection of computers in a department of over 250 users!" (New York City)

Found Wall Street "8 years ago, I took your intro programming course. Now I run the computer department of a Wall Street brokerage firm. I'm responsible for 30 people and millions of dollars of computer equipment. The Guide's always been my foremost reference. Thank you for the key to wonderful new worlds." (Long Beach, New York)

Consultant's dream "Inspired by your book, your love for computers, and your burning desire to show the world that computers are fun and easily accessible, I entered the computer field. Now I'm a computer consultant. Your ideas come from the heart. Thanks for following your dream." (Skokie, Illinois)

Kid who grew up "Years ago, I saw you sell books while wearing a wizard's cap. I bought a book and was as impressed as a 16-year-old could be. Now I've earned B.A.'s in Computer Science and English, and I'm contemplating teaching computers to high school students. I can think of no better way to plan a course outline than around your Guide." (Pennington, New Jersey)

Better late than never

Readers wish they'd found the Guide sooner.

1 year "I learned more from the Guide than from a year in the computer industry." (Redwood City, California)

5 years "I've fumbled for 5 years with computers and many books, all with short-lived flashes of enthusiasm, until I found your Guide. It's the first book that showed a light at the end of the tunnel, even for one as dull-brained as I." (Boise)

17 years "Though in a computer company for 17 years, I didn't learn anything about computers until I began reading the Guide. I love it! I always thought computer people were generically boring, but your book's changed my mind." (Hopkinton, Massachusetts)

Prince Charming arrives "Where have you been all my life? I wish I'd heard of your Guide long ago. I'd have made far fewer mistakes if it had been here alongside my computer." (White Stone, Virginia)

Hacker "Great book. I'm 14 and always wanted to hack. Thanks to your Guide, I laughed myself to death and look forward to gutting my computer. Yours is the friendliest, funniest book on computers I've seen. If I'd started out with the Guide, I'd have saved 5 years of fooling around in the dark." (Northport, Alabama)

Pass-alongs

Readers pass the Guide to their friends.

Round the office "Send 150 books. I passed my Guide around the office, and just about everyone who saw it wants copies." (Middleburg Heights, Ohio)

Coordinating the coordinators "Your book is amazing! I'm telling the other 50 PC coordinators in my company to be sure they're in on the secret. Bless you for your magnanimous philosophy!" (Morristown, New Jersey)

Hide your secrets "I thought the Guide marvelous and proudly displayed it on my desk. A friend from South Africa saw it and said our friendship depended on letting her take it home with her. What could I do? You've gone international. I'm ordering another copy. Should I hide the book this time?" (Cinnaminson, New Jersey)

Cries and anger "I made the mistake of letting several friends borrow my copy of the Guide. Each time I tried getting it back, it was a battle. (I hate to see grown people cry.) I promised to order them copies of their own. I delayed several months, and now I've got an angry mob outside my door. While you process my order, I'll try pacifying them by reading aloud." (Winston-Salem, North Carolina)

Round the house "Dad bought your Guide to help him understand my computer. It's become the most widely read book in our house. We love it!" (Boca Raton, Florida)

Squabble with Dad "I love the Guide. Dad & I squabble over our only copy. Send a second so I can finish the Guide in peace." (New York City)

Make your guru giggle "I showed the Guide to my guru. Between laughs, chuckles, and guffaws, he agreed to use it to teach his high-school computer class. He even admitted he'd learned something, and that's the most unheard of thing I ever heard of." (Arivaca, Arizona)

Advancing secretary "I'm ordering an extra copy for my secretary, to start her on the path to a higher paying and better regarded position." (Belleville, Illinois)

Compared with other publishers

The Guide's better than any other book.

Better than 10 "I learned more from your Guide than from a total of 10 books read previously." (Honolulu)

No big bucks "Your book is great! Its crazy style really keeps the pages turning. I appreciate someone who doesn't try to make big bucks off someone trying to learn. Thanks." (Vancouver, Washington)

Rip-off "If you can break even at your book's low price, lots of guys are ripping us off." (Choctaw, Oklahoma)

Who's the author?

This section reveals who wrote this book — even if you'd rather not know.

Interview with Russ

In this interview, Russ explains what's behind this book.

Why did you write the Secret Guide? I saw my students trying too hard to take notes, so I made my own notes to hand them. Over the years, my notes got longer. Each time I develop a new edition, I try to make it the kind of book I wish I had when *I* was a student.

What does the Guide cover? Everything about computers and life. Every topic is touched on, and the most important topics are covered in depth.

Who reads the Guide? All sorts. Kids read it because it's easy; professionals read it because it contains secret tidbits you can't find anywhere else.

Why do you charge so little? I'm not trying to make a profit. I'm just trying to make people happy — by charging as little as possible, while still covering expenses. Instead of "charging as much as the market will bear", I try to "charge so little the public will cheer".

Do you really answer the phone 24 hours? When do you sleep? When folks call in the middle of the night, I wake up, answer their questions, then go back to bed. I'm near the phone 85% of the time. If you get no answer, I'm out on an errand, so please call again.

Why do you give phone help free? Are you a masochist, a saint, or a nut? I give free help for 3 reasons: to be a nice guy, to keep in touch with readers (who suggest improvements), and to make callers happy enough so they'll tell their friends about me (so I don't have to advertise).

At computer shows, you've appeared as a witch? I've worn a witch's black hat and red kimono over a monk's habit and roller skates, while my white gloves caressed an African spear. Why? Because it's fun!

What's your background? I got degrees in math & education from Dartmouth & Harvard, taught at several colleges (Wellesley, Wesleyan, and Northeastern), and was a founding editor of *Personal Computing* magazine. But most of my expertise comes from spending many hours every day reading books, magazines, and Internet articles, discussing computer lifestyle questions on the phone, and analyzing computer life.

About the so-called author

Since the author is so lifeless, we can keep his bio short.

Birth of a notion The author, Russy-poo, was conceived in 1946. So was the modern ("stored-program") computer.

9 months later, Russy-poo was hatched. The modern computer took a few years longer, so Russ got a head start. But the computer quickly caught up. Ever since, they've been racing against each other, to see who's smartest.

The race is close, because Russ and the computer have so much in common. Folks say the computer "acts human" and say Russ's personality is "as a dead as a computer".

Junior Jews Russ resembles a computer in many ways. For example, both are Jewish.

The modern computer was fathered by John von Neumann, a Jew of German descent. After living in Hungary, he fled the Nazis and became a famous U.S. mathematician.

Russ's father was Henry Walter, a German Jew who fled the Nazis and became a famous U.S. dental salesman. To dentists, he sold teeth, dental chairs, and balloons to amuse kids.

The race for brains To try outsmarting the computer, Russ got his bachelor's degree in math from Dartmouth in yummy '69 and sadly stayed a bachelor for many years.

He got an M.A.T. in math education from Harvard. Since he went to Harvard, you know he's a genius. Like most genii, he achieved the high honor of being a junior-high teacher. After his classes showered him with the Paper Airplane Award, he moved on to teach at a private school for exclusive girls. ("Exclusive" means everyone can come except you.)

After teaching every grade from 2 through 12 (he taught the 2nd-grade girls how to run the computer but the 12th graders less intellectual things), he fled reality by joining Wesleyan University's math Ph.D. program in Connecticut's Middletown (the middle of Nowhere), where after 18 months of highbrow hoopla he was seduced by a computer to whom he's now happily married.

Married life After the wedding, Russ moved with his electrifying wife to Boston's Northeastern University, where he did a hilarious job of teaching in the naughty Department of "Graphic Science". After quitting Northeastern and also editorship of *Personal Computing*, he spends his time now happily losing money by publishing this book.

To provide company for his electronic wife, he bought her 40 computers, hid them in a van, and drove them around the country, where they performed orgies and did a strip tease, to show students a thing or two about computer anatomy. Banned in Boston, Russ and his groupies moved north, to Somerville, until it became an overpriced slumville in 1998, when they moved further north, to New Hampshire, called "the granite state", since Russ has rocks in his head.

That year, Russ became a bigamist: though still married to a computer, he also married a human, who's a Chinese philosopher even stranger than Russ. The couple is called "Russy-poo old and Egg-foo young."

Russ's body Here are Russ's stats, from head to toe:

head in the clouds, **hair** departing, **brow** beaten, **eyes** glazed, **lashes** 40, **nose** to the grindstone, **mouth** off, **smile** bionic, **tongue** bitten, **teeth** remembered, **cheeks** in a royal flush, **chin** up, **shoulders** burdened, **wrists** watched, **hands** some, **thumbs** up, **heart** all, **back** got everyone on it, **buns** toasted, **knees** knocked, **heeled** well, **arches** gothic, **toes** stepped on

He wears a stuffed shirt and sacramental socks — very holy!

Russ's résumé We told Russ to write this book because when he handed us this résumé, we knew he was the type of author that publishers long for: nuts enough to work for free!

Age: too. **Sex:** yes! **Race:** rat. **Religion:** Reformed Nerd.
Address: wear pants instead. **State:** distressed.
Father: time. **Mother:** earth. **Spouse:** Brussels.
Occupation: vegetable. **Career goal:** play dead.
Hobbies: sleep & cry. **Sports:** dodge tomatoes.
Greatest pleasure: hide under the sink. **Favorite food:** thought.
Humor: less.

About our headquarters

Come visit our Home Office, in Russ's home. It includes our Production Department, near or in Russ's bed. Russ gave birth to this book himself; nobody else would dare!

We do everything possible to make you happy....

Discounts

We give you a 20% discount for buying 2 copies of this edition, 40% for 4 copies, and 60% for 60 copies (so you pay just $10 per copy). To get the discounts, use the coupon on the back page.

Your gain, our pain: we lose money on shipping We're in New Hampshire. We ship books to the USA by standard mail for free. We usually ship promptly, so you get books fairly quickly. If you're in a rush, add $5 to your order to get your books a bit faster (we'll use a faster shipping method or move your order to the front of the line). If you want us to ship to a different country, add $8 per book, which gets you international airmail. Yes, we charge less than the post office usually charges us, but we don't mind losing money on shipping, since we're computer lifestyle missionaries who don't care about profit.

Use your past You're reading the 31st edition. To compute your discount, we count how many copies of the 31st edition you've ordered from us _so far_. For example, if you previously ordered 10 copies of the 31st edition and order 50 more, we say "Oh, you're up to 60 copies now!" and give you a 60% discount on the second order.

If you got a discount on the 30th _Secret Guide to Computers_ (or 2nd _Tricky Living_) because you bought many copies, we'll give you the same discount on the 31st edition even if you're buying just one copy.

To get a discount based on past orders, mail the coupon on the back page. Next to your name, write your phone number and "I'm taking a discount because of past orders."

Free reprints

You may copy this edition free. Copy as many pages as you like, make lots of copies, and don't pay us a cent!

Just **phone Russ first** (at 603-666-6644) and say which pages you're going to copy. **Put this notice at the beginning of your reprint:**

> Much of this material comes from _The Secret Guide to Computers & Tricky Living_, 31st edition, copyright 2011 by Russ Walter and reprinted with permission.
>
> Get **free literature** about the newest complete Guide, in 4 ways:
> - phone Russ at 603-666-6644 (day or night, 24 hours, he's usually in)
> - visit the official Secret website, www.SecretFun.com
> - send e-mail to Russ@SecretFun.com
> - mail a note to Russ Walter, 196 Tiffany Lane, Manchester NH 03104-4782

Then **send us a copy** of your reprint.

You may give — or sell — the reprints to anybody. Go distribute them on paper, on disk, by e-mail, or by your own Web postings. The Guide's been distributed by thousands of teachers, consultants, and stores and translated to other languages. Join those folks! Add your own comments, call yourself a co-author, and become famous! It's free!

Book on disk

You can order this edition printed on a CD-R disk instead of on paper. The disk includes files in several Microsoft Word formats and also in Acrobat PDF format. The CD will help you write your _own_ books and develop material to put on Internet Websites.

If you order this edition on CD, we recommend you order it on paper also, since the CD is more awkward to read than the printed book.

Internet

We're on the Internet! Visit our Secret Fun site, **www.SecretFun.com**. It reveals the newest secrets about our books & services & discounts, includes links to other secret fun Internet sites, lets you read parts of our books online free, and lets you send us e-mail. You can also send e-mail directly to **Russ@SecretFun.com**.

Get the classics

You're reading the 31st edition. To squeeze so many new topics into this edition, we had to leave out older topics, which you can still get in our **classic editions**. To let you get those lovely old classics easily, **we've dropped the price of all old editions to just $3**. At that low price, you can grab a whole bunch. Get some for yourself, your friends, schools on tight budgets, and your favorite charities.

Here are the biggest differences among the last five editions of _The Secret Guide to Computers_:

Topic	Editions
advanced DOS commands	27
Windows 3, 95	27 28 29
Windows 98	27 28 29 30
Windows 98SE, Me	28 29 30
Windows XP	28 29 30 31
Windows Vista	30 31
Windows 7	31
Internet Explorer 5	27 28 29 30
Internet Explorer 6	28 29 30 31
Internet Explorer 7	30 31
Internet Explorer 8, 9	31
Netscape Navigator	27 28
Firefox	30 31
Chrome, Safari	31
Outlook Express 5	27 28 29 30
Outlook Express 6	28 29 30 31
Windows Mail, Yahoo Mail	30 31
Windows Live Mail, Gmail	31
Apple Mac	27 28 29 30
Linux, Palm	28 29 30
Apple iPad	31
dBase, FoxPro, Q&A	27 28
WordPerfect, Quattro Pro	27 28 29
Microsoft Office 2003	29 30 31
Microsoft Office 2007	30 31
Microsoft Office 2010	31
Front Page	27 28 29
advanced HTML	28 29 30 31
JavaScript, JScript	29 30 31
blogs	30 31
advanced QBasic	27 28 29
Visual Basic 6	28 29 30
Visual Basic 2010, QB64	31
Visual C++ 6	27 28 29 30
Visual C++&C# 2010	31
Fortran, Cobol, Logo	27
Pascal	27 28
Java using Visual J++	27 28 29 30
Java using Sun Java 6	31
numerical analysis	27
dictionary of computer jargon	27 28
edit photos&videos	30 31
best advice on buying&fixing	31

Classic editions of _Tricky Living_ include thousands of other differences. For example, the first & second editions of _Tricky Living_ include a discussion of prostitution; the current book discusses the Bible instead.

To get classic editions, use the coupon on the back page.

Get more intense

We're developing more editions and events. Join our mailing list by using the back page's coupon.

Russ answers questions, quickly & free, by phone at 603-666-6644. He can also meet you anytime for intense face-to-face tutoring, counseling, consulting, and seminars, cheaply; phone for details.

How to shop

Here's how to shop for a computer — and deal with the jargon that's involved.

Kinds of computers

Up until 1940, computers were people. Dictionaries said a "computer" was "a person who computes." Astronomers hired many "computers," who computed the positions of stars.

People who computed were called "computers." Machines that computed were called "calculators."

After 1940, human "computers" were gradually replaced by gigantic machines, called **electronic computers**. Today the word "computer" means "a *machine* that computes." This book explains how to buy and use such machines.

During the 1950's, people realized that electronic computers can do *more* than compute.

Today's computers spend hardly any time doing math. They spend most of their time thinking about words and ideas instead. They ought to be called "thinkers" instead! Here's the modern definition of a computer:

A **computer** is any machine that thinks.

If you're bothered by that definition, which says an inanimate object can "think," use this alternative definition instead:

A **computer** is any machine that can seem to think.

If you're bothered even by *that* definition, which says a machine can be called a "computer" even if it seems to be just mumbling to itself, use this stronger definition instead:

A **computer** is any machine that can seem to do useful thinking.

Today's computers spend most of their time analyzing words & ideas — and very *little* time doing math. Even if you know just a *little* math, you can understand computers. If you know 5.2 is more than 5 and less than 6, you know enough math to master this book and get hired as a computer expert! Becoming a computer expert is easier than becoming an auto mechanic, and you don't get greasy!

Hidden computers

One kind of computer is called a **hidden computer**: it hides inside another device.

For example, a computer hides inside your digital watch; it computes how the time is changing. A computer also hides inside your pocket calculator, your cell phone, your videogame machine, your microwave oven, and your car's dashboard.

Though non-technical folks call such a computer "hidden," computer experts call it an **embedded computer** instead (since the computer is embedded in another electronic device) or, more commonly, an **embedded computer system** or an **embedded system**. So if you meet a person whose career is "**developing embedded systems**," that person invents computers that hide inside other devices.

Such a computer dedicates its entire life to performing just one task (such as "telling the time"), so it's also called a **dedicated computer**. Most such computers can be made for under $10 each — after the manufacturer has spent many thousands of dollars to research how to make them!

Visible computers

If a computer isn't hidden in another device, it's called a **visible computer**.

If the visible computer is used by just one person at a time, it's called a **personal computer (PC)**.

If the visible computer is used by many people simultaneously, it's called a **powerful server**: the powerful server manages many other computers and let them share info with each other. The typical powerful server is big. It sits in a corner of the room, or fills a whole room, or fills several rooms. Powerful servers are used by big organizations (such as the IRS, Social Security, banks, credit-card companies, and insurance companies) to manage your records and the people who want to use them.

A **standard desktop computer** is a personal computer that's too big to carry in one hand. It sits on a desk. It has 4 main parts:

A **keyboard** that lets you type commands to the computer.

A **screen (display)** that shows you the computer's answers.

A **mouse** that you roll across your desk, to indicate which part of the screen interests you.

The **system unit**, which is a box holding the computer's brain & memory.

In a standard desktop computer, each of those 4 parts is a separate device. Wires run out of the system unit to the keyboard, screen, and mouse, so the system unit can communicate with them. Here are 2 comments about the system unit:

If the system unit is taller than it is wide, it's called a **tower**. The typical system unit is a tower that's 15" tall and 15" front-to-back but just 7" wide.

If your desk is too small or too cluttered to include the system unit, put the system unit on the floor: put it under the desk (or next to the desk).

Here's how other computers differ....

In a **wireless desktop computer**, the keyboard and mouse communicate with the system unit by radio waves instead of wires.

In an **all-in-one computer**, there's no separate system unit; instead, the computer's brain & memory hide behind the screen, in the same case that includes the screen.

The term "**desktop computer**" is vague: it means "standard desktop computer or wireless computer or all-in-one computer".

In a desktop computer system, how big is the screen? If the system is modern, its screen size (measured diagonally, from corner to opposite corner) is between 18½" and 27"; the most common size is 20". If the system is older, its screen is smaller (between 12" and 18½").

A **laptop** computer is small enough to carry in one hand and use in your lap, though using it is more pleasant if you rest it on a desk. To let the laptop be carried in one hand, it's built using these tricks:

> The computer's brain & memory hide under the keyboard, in the same case that includes the keyboard.
>
> The keyboard is attached to the screen by a hinge, so you can pick the keyboard and screen up by a single handle. (Having a hinge is called a **clamshell design**: opening and closing the laptop is like opening and closing a clam's shell. Open the laptop to use it; close the laptop to transport it.)
>
> To indicate which part of the screen interests you, you don't have to use a mouse; instead, just rub your finger across a **touchpad** on the keyboard's surface. So the laptop doesn't require or include a mouse. (But since using the touchpad is awkward, you'll be happier if you buy a mouse to attach to the laptop.)

Modern laptops come in 2 sizes:

> If a laptop is about the size of a student's 3-ring-binder notebook, it's called a **notebook** computer.
>
> If the laptop is even smaller — small enough to fit in a woman's clutch purse — it's called a **netbook** because it's the minimum size needed to handle the Internet well (though the Internet is more pleasant if you use a bigger computer instead, such as a notebook computer or desktop computer).
>
> How big is the screen? For a notebook computer, the screen size is between 11½" and 17½", with 15.6" being the most common. For a modern netbook, the screen size is between 10" and 11½", with 10.1" being the most common. If the netbook is older, its screen is smaller (between 7" and 10").

The next size down is called a **modern tablet** computer. It's so small that you can use it while holding it in your two hands: you don't need a lap or desk to rest it on (though resting it on a desk can be helpful). To let the modern tablet be used without a lap or desk, it's built using these tricks:

> There's no mouse or touchpad. Instead of using a mouse or touchpad, you tap directly on the screen. (Such a screen, which can detect your taps and touches, is called a **touch-sensitive screen**.)
>
> There's no keyboard. Instead of having a real (**physical**) keyboard, the screen shows a *picture* of a keyboard, and you tap on the picture. The picture is called a **virtual keyboard**.
>
> The computer's brain & memory hide in the screen. So when you look at a modern tablet computer, you see just a screen: there's no mouse, no touchpad, no physical keyboard, and no separate system unit.

The modern tablet's screen size is between 7" and 10", with 9.7" being the most common. Of all the modern tablet computers, the most popular is the **iPad**, invented by **Apple** in 2010; its screen is 9.7". Now other companies are inventing competitors. If a tablet computer's main purpose is to read **electronic books (e-books)** copied from the Internet, the tablet computer is called an **e-book reader**:

> **Barnes & Noble** invented an e-book reader called the **Nook**.
>
> **Amazon** invented an e-book reader called the **Kindle**, but the Kindle is substandard: its screen isn't touch-sensitive, so the screen's case includes a tiny keyboard.

The smallest size of personal computer is called a **handheld computer** or **palmtop computer** or **pocket computer**, because it fits in the palm of your hand and in your pocket. It's about the size of a pocket calculator or a cell phone or a pack of cigarettes. Its screen size is under 7", with the most popular size being 3½". The typical handheld computer comes with programs that help you jot notes, store phone numbers, and keep track of appointments and to-do lists; that kind of handheld computer is called a **personal digital assistant (PDA)**. If the PDA also includes a built-in cell phone, it's called a **smartphone**. The fanciest smartphone is the **iPhone**, invented by Apple.

Any computer that can be carried in one hand is called a **portable computer**. A modern portable computer is therefore a laptop computer or modern tablet computer or handheld computer. (An older kind of portable computer, called a **luggable computer**, can be carried in one hand by using a handle but is too big to fit on your lap.) Each modern portable computer includes a rechargeable battery, so when unplugged from a wall socket it keeps running for several hours.

Traveling with a portable computer is called **mobile computing**, and the computer being transported is called a **mobile computer**.

During the previous century (the 1900's), computers were divided into 3 categories:

> A **maxicomputer** consumed a whole room and typically cost between $300,000 and $20,000,000.
>
> A **minicomputer** fit in a room's corner and typically cost between $10,000 and $300,000.
>
> A **microcomputer** fit on a desk (or lap or hand or was embedded in a tiny device) and typically cost between $1 and $10,000.

Maxicomputers were also called **mainframes**. The fastest maxicomputers were called **supercomputers**. But now microcomputers (which cost under $10,000) are fast enough to handle most calculations. If you need a computer system that's *extra*-fast, just wire several microcomputers together, to work as a team; that's cheaper than buying a maxicomputer. Hardly anybody buys maxicomputers or minicomputers anymore, and you'll hardly ever hear the words "maxicomputer" and "minicomputer" anymore.

If your employer bought a computer years ago (such as an old minicomputer or maxicomputer) and refuses to replace it with something more modern (because switching takes too much effort), the polite way to describe your situation is to say that you're stuck using a **legacy system**, because your employer's computer is a legacy handed down from the folks who preceded you; a **legacy system** is an outdated computer system.

Networks

Instead of buying a big computer, the typical big company buys many little computers and lets them communicate with each other, to form a **network**.

If the computers communicate with each other through cables of wires, the network is called a **hard-wired network**. If the computers communicate with each other by using radio waves instead, the network is called a **wireless network**.

If the network's computers all sit in the same office building, the network is called a **local-area network (LAN)**. If the computers are farther apart, the network is called a **wide-area network (WAN)**.

Each computer in the network is called a **node**.

A special person, called the **network supervisor**, manages the network by controlling the network's main computer, called the **server**. Ordinary folks (called **users**) sit at the network's lesser computers (called **workstations**), which all communicate with the server.

The most famous wide-area network is the **Internet**. It began in the 1950's as a small network (a few universities communicating with each other), but later it expanded dramatically, so now it includes *millions* of computers all over the world: most of the world's visible computers are part of the Internet. When you buy a typical computer, it communicates with the Internet **wirelessly** (by using radio waves) or through an ordinary phone line (called **dial-up**) or through a speeded-up phone line called a **digital-subscriber line (DSL)** or through a cable-TV line (called **cable**). An ordinary phone line (dial-up) is ridiculously slow; the other methods (wireless, DSL, and cable) are reasonably fast and called **broadband**. So if a computerist says "I want broadband," the computerist wants fast Internet access, not a band of female musicians!

You can mix technologies. For example, the typical notebook computer communicates with the Internet by sending a radio wave (wirelessly) to a little box, called a **wireless router** (usually pronounced so the "rou" rhymes with "cow"), which then passes the signal to the rest of the Internet by using cable or DSL, with the help of a converter box called a **modulator/demodulator** (**modem**, pronounced "Moe dem"). You can buy a wireless router (and modem) for your home or office.

When the wireless router is turned on (and attached to a modem), it creates a **wireless access point (WAP)**, which is also called a **hot spot**. While you're traveling with your laptop computer, you can use the hot spots that are in many coffeehouses, restaurants, public libraries, and other public locations. You can use them even while you're driving by in your car; that's called **wardriving**. While wardriving, keep your eyes on the road as well as on your laptop!

Desktop computer's parts

You already learned:

> A typical desktop computer's main part is the box called the **system unit**. The typical system unit is a tower that's 15 inches tall (and 15 inches from front to back) but just 7 inches wide.

Let's take a closer look.

7 cables Out of the system unit's rear come 7 cables.

One of those cables is the **power cord**. It goes to a source of electricity (the electrical outlet socket in the room's wall — or a power strip connected to that outlet). That cable feeds power to the computer.

One cable goes to the **keyboard**, which looks like a typewriter's keyboard. To send a message to the computer, type the message on the keyboard. A standard computer keyboard contains 104 keys, which let you type all the letters of the alphabet, all the digits, all the punctuation symbols, and other symbols too. Some of the keys are for editing: they help you edit what you typed.

One cable goes to the **monitor**, which looks like a TV set: it contains a screen that shows the words you typed, the computer's answers, and pictures.

One cable goes to the **mouse**, which is a small box about the size of a pack of cigarettes. If you slide the mouse across your desk, an arrow moves across your monitor's screen; so to move the screen's arrow, slide the mouse! To manipulate an object on the monitor's screen, slide the mouse until the screen's arrow moves to that object; then press the mouse's left button.

One cable goes to the **printer**, which is a box that prints on paper.

One cable goes to **stereo speakers**, so the computer can produce sound effects, play music, sing, and talk to you!

The final cable goes toward other computers (or a modem), to form a **network** (such as the Internet). That cable is called a **network cable**. If you're accessing the Internet by dial-up, the network cable is an ordinary phone line (which goes to your wall's phone jack); if you're accessing the Internet by broadband instead, the network cable is a fattened phone line, called an **Ethernet cable**, which goes to a modem.

If you're accessing the Internet by dial-up, you can add an optional 8th cable, to attach to an ordinary phone, so your computer and phone can share using the wall's phone jack.

Altogether, the typical desktop computer includes:

> the system unit
>
> a keyboard, monitor, mouse, printer, speakers, and cables from them to system unit
>
> power cords from wall (or power strip) to the system unit, monitor, and printer
>
> a network cable to let the computer communicate with other computers

Advertised price When you buy a computer, the advertised price includes most of those items: it typically includes the system unit, computer keyboard, mouse, and pair of stereo speakers. But **the printer is usually excluded from the advertised price: it costs extra.**

Does the advertised price include the monitor? To find out, read the ad carefully!

If you're lucky, the ad says "**monitor included**". If the ad says "**monitor optional**" instead, the monitor is *not* included in the advertised price and costs extra.

Extras If your computer is extra-fancy, 3 extra cables come out of the system unit:

> A cable goes to a **microphone (mike)**, which lets you feed sounds into the computer. If you talk and sing into the mike, the computer can make digital recordings of your speech and performance, analyze them, and react accordingly!
>
> A cable goes to a **scanner**, which is a box that you can shove a sheet of paper into; the scanner reads what's on the paper and tells the computer what the paper said. If you rip an article out of a newspaper and feed it into the scanner, the scanner will transmit the newspaper's article to the computer, so the computer can analyze what's in the newspaper's article and become a smarter computer! If you feed a photo into the scanner, the scanner will transmit the photo to the computer, and the photo will appear on the computer's screen.
>
> A cable goes to a **digital camera**, which takes photos and feeds them to the computer.

Summary In a typical desktop computer system, the main box is called the **system unit**, from which cables run out to other computer devices, called **external peripherals**, such as the keyboard, monitor, mouse, printer, speakers, and — if your system is fancy — a microphone, scanner, and digital camera.

Ports On the system unit's back wall, you'll see many sockets to plug cables into. Each of those sockets is called a **port**. Here's what the 11 most important ports look like (on a typical desktop computer):

Whose cable goes to port	Port's name	Port's appearance
keyboard	keyboard port	circle, with 5 round pinholes in it
monitor	video port	D shape, with 15 round pinholes in it
modern mouse	PS/2 mouse port	circle, with 6 round pinholes in it
traditional mouse	9-pin serial COM1 port	D shape, with 9 pins in it
modern printer, scanner, or camera	USB port	rectangular hole with 4 wires in it
traditional printer or scanner	parallel printer LPT1 port	D shape, with 25 round pinholes in it
phone on your desk	phone jack	square hole (4 wires in it) labeled "PHONE"
phone jack on room's wall	modem port	square hole (4 wires in it) labeled "LINE"
another computer or fast Internet	RJ-45 Ethernet port	slightly widened square hole (8 wires in it)
speakers	speaker jack	big round pinhole, next to loudspeaker picture
microphone	microphone jack	big round pinhole, labeled "MIC"

Traditionally, all those ports are on the system unit's back wall; but if your system unit is modern, some of those ports are on the system unit's front wall instead, so you can reach them more easily.

Unfortunately, the speaker jack has the same shape as the microphone jack. Make sure you don't mix them up! If you accidentally plug a speaker into the microphone jack, you'll hear a loud buzz!

The phone jack has the same shape as the modem port, but many computers still work even if you mix up those ports.

All the other ports are safer: they have different shapes to prevent mix-ups.

A **connector** (a **port** or a **cable's end**) that has pins sticking out of it is called **male** (because the pins look like little penises). A connector that has holes instead is called **female** (because it's eager to have a male connector plugged into it).

Setup Setting up the computer is easy! Just plug the cables into the components and ports, and you're done!

Notebook computer's parts

The typical notebook computer uses a **clamshell design**: it opens, like a clamshell, to reveal two parts:

The bottom part (¾" high) contains the main system-unit circuitry with a built-in keyboard, built-in pair of stereo speakers, built-in **touchpad** (square pad you rub with your finger instead of using a mouse), and built-in rechargeable battery.

The top part (½" thick) pries up to become a screen (made of the same materials used in screens of pocket calculators and digital watches).

The notebook computer can get power from its built-in battery; but if you plug the computer into a wall's electrical outlet, the computer will use the wall's power instead while the battery recharges.

Once the notebook computer gets electrical power, you can operate the notebook computer without attaching anything to it. But the notebook computer includes ports to let you attach optional extras. To its **USB ports**, you can attach a mouse (to use instead of the awkward built-in touchpad), printer, scanner, and digital camera. You can use the notebook computer's other ports to attach an **external keyboard** (to use instead of the awkward tiny built-in keyboard), an **external monitor** (to use instead of the awkward built-in screen), **headphones** (to use instead of the built-in speakers), and **network cables** (Ethernet cable or ordinary phone line).

Manufacturers

Who makes computers?

IBM The most famous computer manufacturer is **IBM**, which stands for **International Business Machines Corporation**.

Too often, it also stood for "Incredibly Boring Machines", "Inertia Breeds Mediocrity", "International Big Mother", "Imperialism By Marketing", "Idolized By Management", "Incompetents Becoming Managers", "Intolerant of Beards & Mustaches", "It Baffles Me", "It's a Big Mess", and "It's Better Manually". But those negative comments apply just to IBM's past: in the 1990's IBM switched; it became open-minded and friendly.

IBM is based in New York State.

During the 1950's, 1960's, and 1970's, IBM was famous mainly for selling huge computers (called **maxicomputers** or **mainframes** or **powerful servers**).

Later, IBM started selling small computers also. IBM's first successful small computer was a desktop computer called the **IBM Personal Computer (IBM PC)**. Then other companies made imitations, called **IBM-compatible computers** or **IBM PC clones**. Now most desktop and notebook computers are IBM-compatible.

Recently, IBM's stopped making cheap computers for consumers: instead, IBM sells just expensive computers (powerful servers) to big businesses. For example, IBM used to make a notebook computer called the **ThinkPad**, but IBM sold its ThinkPad division to a Hong Kong company called **Lenovo** (which is mainly in Hong Kong but recently created a headquarters office in North Carolina, to look American).

HP A California company called **Hewlett-Packard (HP)** makes more computers than any other company. It makes many kinds of computers: powerful servers, desktop computers, laptop computers, handheld computers, and hidden computers. Some of them are sold under the name "Hewlett-Packard"; others are sold under the name "**Compaq**", which is a company that Hewlett-Packard acquired; handheld computers are sold under the name "**Palm**", which is another company that HP acquired. Many of HP's computers are sold in chain stores such as **Staples** (which tends to have the lowest prices), **Best Buy**, and **Walmart**.

Dell A Texas company called **Dell** sold computers through mail-order but now also sells computers through chain stores (such as **Staples** and **Best Buy**). It mainly makes desktop computers and notebook computers, though it dabbles in other kinds of computers also. Dell used to have a reputation for high quality, but now Dell's computers are unexceptional.

Gateway An Iowa company called **Gateway** was famous for selling desktop computers through mail-order. Gateway acquired a company called "**eMachines**," which was famous for selling desktop computers cheaply through chain stores, especially Circuit City and Best Buy. Now Gateway and its eMachines division sell desktop & notebook computers through mail order & stores. Gateway moved from Iowa to South Dakota but now is headquartered in California. The entire Gateway company was bought by a Taiwan company called **Acer**.

Asian laptops Many companies in Asia make laptop computers. The most famous are **Sony** (from Japan), **Toshiba** (from Japan), **Acer** (from Taiwan), **Asus** (from Taiwan and means "Pegasus but let's begin with A"), and **Lenovo** (mainly from Hong Kong, though headquartered in North Carolina). Sony & Lenovo concentrate on high quality; Toshiba & Acer &Asus concentrate on low cost and give you the most amazing deals, especially when buy them through Staples or Best Buy.

White-box computers Many tiny computer stores build their own "generic" desktop computers by throwing together parts from many suppliers. Such an unbranded computer is called a **white-box computer**, since the system unit is a typically a plain white metal box that has no manufacturer's name written on it.

Apple A California company called **Apple** makes **Macintosh (Mac)** computers (desktops & notebooks), the **iPad** (a modern tablet computer), and the **iPhone** (a smartphone). They're all beautiful to look at, creatively designed, fun & easy to use, reliable, and come with good free help by phone. Apple's Mac computers are particularly popular among graphic artists and magazine publishers.

Unfortunately, Apple's computers cost a bit more than the competition, and Apple's computers aren't completely compatible with other computers: if you buy an Apple computer, you must learn to do things differently and buy different accessories for it.

What's popular? Here's the surprising truth.

> Of all the normal computers (not embedded, not tablet, not handheld) sold today **in the world**,
>
> 18% are by Hewlett-Packard (and its Compaq and Palm divisions),
> 12% are by Acer (and its Gateway and eMachines divisions),
> 12% are by Dell (which sells mainly by mail-order),
> 10% are by Lenovo (whose computers are especially popular in Hong Kong, China, and India),
> 6% are by Toshiba (whose notebook computers are especially popular),
> 4% are by Sony,
> 2% are by Asus,
> 2% are by Apple (and called "Macs"),
> 2% are by IBM (whose computers are mainly powerful servers),
> and the remaining 32% are by a wide variety of other manufacturers.

Since percentages bob up and down by 2% each month, I've rounded all those percentages to the nearest 2%.

In the U.S., different brands are stronger.

> Of all the normal computers (not embedded, not tablet, not handheld) sold today **in the U.S.**,
>
> 30% are by Hewlett-Packard (and its Compaq and Palm divisions),
> 22% are by Dell (which sells mainly by mail-order),
> 12% are by Acer (and its Gateway and eMachines divisions),
> 10% are by Toshiba,
> 10% are by Apple (and called "Macs"),
> 4% are by Asus,
> 4% are by Sony,
> 4% are by Lenovo,
> 2% are by IBM,
> and the remaining 2% are by a wide variety of other manufacturers.

Prices drop

On average, computer prices drop 3% per month. That price decline's been in effect ever since the 1940's, and there's no sign of it stopping.

Suppose for a particular computer item the average price charged by dealers is $100. Next month, that item's average price will probably drop 3%, to $97. After *two* months, its average price will have dropped about 3% again, so its price will be 97% of $97, which is $94.09.

Here's how the math works out:

> On the average, computer prices drop about 3% per month,
> 30% per year,
> 50% every two years,
> 90% every six years,
> 99% every twelve years.

Therefore:

> If a computer item's average price is $100 today, it will probably be $97 next month,
> $70 a year from now,
> $50 two years from now,
> $10 six years from now,
> $1 twelve years from now.

The typical computer system costs about $1000 (by the time you get done paying for all the extras & accessories). Here's what the math looks like for a $1000 system:

> If a computer system costs you $1000 today, it will probably cost you
> $970 if you buy a month from now,
> $700 if you buy a year from now,
> $500 if you buy 2 years from now,
> $100 if you buy 6 years from now,
> $10 if you buy 12 years from now.

Does that mean computer stores will be selling lots of computers for $10 twelve years from now? No! Instead, computer stores will *still* be selling computers for about $1000, but those $1000 systems will be much fancier than the systems sold today. By comparison, today's systems will look primitive — much too primitive to run the programs-of-the-future — so they'll be sold off as old, quaint, primitive junk in flea markets and garage sales.

Find that hard to believe? To become a believer in rapidly dropping prices, just try this experiment: walk into a flea market or garage sale today, and you'll see computer systems selling for $10 that sold for $1000 twelve years ago!

So the longer you wait to buy a computer, the less you'll pay. But the longer you wait, the longer you'll be deprived of having a computer, and the further behind you'll be in computerizing your life and becoming a computer expert.

Don't wait. Begin your new computerized life now!

Inside the system unit

The system unit is a magical box that you'll probably never need to open. But someday, you'll get curious about what's inside.

How to peek

Here's how to peek inside a desktop computer's system unit. Make sure the computer's turned off.

Remove the screws from the 4 corners of the system unit's back wall. Notice how big those screws are. Remove any other screws of that size from the back wall's edges.

Then remove the system unit's cover:

> If the unit's a **tower**, pull the cover back slightly, then lift it.
>
> If the unit's a **desktop**, slide the cover forward — or if it refuses, try sliding the cover back — then lift it slightly.
>
> **If the cover doesn't quite come off**, jiggle it slightly, and also double-check whether you've removed all the screws holding it in place.

Finally, peek into the system unit and admire the goodies within! To be safe, avoid touching them.

Circuit boards

Inside the system unit, you see several green plastic boards, called **circuit boards** (because they have electric circuits on them). On each circuit board, you see many black rectangular objects, called **chips**: each chip contains a miniature electronic circuit inside!

Mobo

The biggest circuit board is called the **motherboard** (or, more briefly, **mobo**). It's about the size of sheet of paper (8½" × 11"). In the typical desktop computer (which is a tower), the mobo is vertical, attached to the tower's right edge.

CPU

On the mobo, the biggest chip is the one that does most of the thinking. That chip is called the **central processing unit (CPU)**. It's also called the **microprocessor**. A standard computer uses a brand of microprocessor called a **Pentium**, manufactured by an intelligent California company called **Intel**.

Yes, in a microcomputer, most of the thinking is done by a single chip, called the microprocessor.

In older, bigger computers, the thinking is done by a gigantic collection of chips working together, instead of a single microprocessor chip. That collection is called the **processor**. The term **microprocessor** was invented by folks amazed that a processor could be made small enough to fit on a single chip.

Expansion cards

Besides the motherboard, the system unit contains smaller circuit boards (called **expansion cards**) that snap into slots in the motherboard.

The most important expansion card is the **video card**. It manages the monitor. It includes the video port, which attaches to the cable that comes from the monitor.

Another expansion card is the **sound card**. It manages the stereo speakers and microphone and attaches to the cables that comes from them.

Another expansion card is the **modem** (pronounced "mode em"). It manages phone signals and attaches to cables that come from the phone and the phone jack.

If your computer is part of a local-area network, your computer includes a **network interface card (NIC)**, which attaches to the network cable that comes from the network's other computers.

The keyboard does *not* have its own expansion card. Instead, the keyboard's cable plugs directly into the motherboard.

Memory

The three most popular kinds of memory are **ROM chips**, **RAM chips**, and **disks**.

ROM chips remember info *permanently*. Even if you turn off the computer's power, ROM chips continue to remember what they've been told. The most important ROM chips are on the motherboard.

RAM chips remember info *temporarily*. They're electronic scratchpads that the CPU uses to store temporary reminders. For example, they remember what problem the computer's working on at the moment. They get erased when you switch to a different computer problem or turn the computer off.

In an old computer, most RAM chips are on the motherboard, where the RAM chips are arranged in rows, 8 or 9 RAM chips per row. In a new computer, the RAM chips are instead on tiny expansion cards, which snap into tiny slots on the motherboard: each tiny RAM cards is called a **single in-line memory module (SIMM)** and holds 3, 8, or 9 RAM chips.

Disks work slower than ROM chips and RAM chips but can hold more info. Like ROM chips, disks can remember info *permanently*: unplugging the computer does *not* erase the disks. To use a disk, you must put it into a **disk drive**, which reads what's on the disk.

In a traditional computer, the system unit includes 3 disk drives, to handle 3 kinds of disks:

> A **CD-ROM disk** looks like a Compact Disk (CD) that music comes on, but a CD-ROM disk contain computer data instead of just music.
>
> A **floppy disk** is made of flimsy material but comes encased is a sturdy square jacket, which is typically 3½ inches on each side (though older disks come in 5¼-inch jackets instead). You can insert the floppy disk (including its jacket) into the floppy-disk drive. You can also remove the floppy disk (including its jacket) from the drive.
>
> The typical **hard disk** is made of hard material, hides in the hard-disk drive permanently, and never comes out, so you never see it.

Each of those three types has its own advantages:

> CD-ROM and floppy disks can be removed from their drives. The typical hard disk cannot.
>
> You can edit info if it's on a hard disk or floppy disk, but not if it's on a typical CD-ROM disk.
>
> The typical hard disk can hold lots of info. The typical CD-ROM disk holds less. A floppy disk holds even less.

The newest computers can also handle **DVD disks** (which hold movies and computer data) but don't bother handling floppy disks.

Power supply

The **power cord** comes from your office's wall and goes into the back of the system unit. Look inside the system unit, at the back wall, where the power cord goes in. There you see, inside the system unit, a big metal box, called the **power supply**.

> If you look in a *tower*, the power supply is usually at the top of the back wall.
>
> If you stand in front of a *desktop* computer and look down into it, so you see an aerial view, the power supply is usually in the back right corner.

The power supply is an **AC/DC transformer**: it converts the alternating current (coming from your office's wall) to the direct current that your computer requires.

The 3 wares

To build a complete computer system, you need **hardware**, **software**, and **liveware**.

Hardware

Computer equipment is called **hardware** because it's built from wires, screws, and other parts you can buy in hardware & electronics stores. Cynics say it's called "hardware" because it's hard to fix and because, when you try to buy hardware, you'll get screwed and go nuts.

I/O The info that the computer gives out is called the computer's **output**: it includes the computer's answers and reports. The info that the computer takes in is called the **input**: it includes your questions and commands.

The computer hardware that that handle input and output are called **input/output devices (I/O devices)**. The most popular I/O devices to buy are a keyboard, monitor, mouse, printer, microphone, modem (which connects to the phone system), and speakers.

3 types of hardware I said that a computer is "any machine that can seem to do useful thinking". For a computer to do "useful thinking", you must buy 3 types of hardware:

> The **processor** does the thinking itself; it processes info.
> The **memory** remembers the computer's thoughts; it includes RAM, ROM, disks.
> The **I/O devices** communicate those thoughts.

Each type is important and useful. A computer without memory is as useless as a person who says "I had a great idea but can't remember it." A computer without an input/output system is as useless as a person who says, "I had a great idea and remember it but won't tell you."

When you're buying a computer, check all 3 types and make sure they're good. This book explains how to judge them.

Software

The info that the computer deals with is called **software**, because you can't feel it: it flows through the computer's circuits as coded pulses of electricity.

The computer can handle two kinds of software: **data** (lists of names, addresses, numbers, words, and facts) and **programs** (lists of instructions that tell the computer what to do).

To feed the computer software (data and programs), you can type on the keyboard, or insert ROM chips or disks containing the software, or let the computer receive the software from another computer (by running wires between the computers or letting the computers chat with each other by phone).

If you feed the computer wrong software — wrong facts or wrong instructions — the computer will print wrong answers. Wrong stuff is called **garbage**. If you feed the computer some garbage, the computer spits out garbage answers.

If a computer prints wrong answers, the computer might not be broken; it might just have been fed wrong data or programs. If you tell a technician to fix it, the technician might reply, "Hey, the computer's fine! Don't blame the computer! It's *your* fault for feeding it garbage! If you put garbage in, you get garbage out!" That's called the principle of **garbage in, garbage out** (which is abbreviated **GIGO**, pronounced "guy go"). The technician will say, "it's just a case of GIGO".

Liveware

The person sitting at the computer is called the **liveware**, **operator**, **user**, or **meathead** — because the person's head is made of meat instead of wires.

The term **meathead** was first shouted publicly by that TV character from New York: Archie Bunker. The term **liveware** was invented in 1982 by Garry Trudeau, creator of the Doonesbury cartoons.

Summary

For a complete **computer system**, you need all 3 wares: the hardware (equipment), software (info), and liveware (people).

Beware of the 3 wares! You can spend lots to buy hardware (and repair it), buy software (and improve it), and hire helpers (and train them). Make sure you've budgeted for all 3 wares!

Congratulations! Now you know the 3 ways that buying a computer can suck up your money. Yes, buying a computer can really suck.

Subculture

Computers are like drugs: you begin by spending just a little on them but soon get so excited by the experience — and so hooked — that you wind up spending more and more to feed your habit.

Your first computer experience seems innocent: you spend just a little money for a cute little computer. You turn the computer on and suddenly the computer's screen shows dazzling superhuman colors that swirl hypnotically before you. You say "Wow, look at all those colors!" and feel a supernatural high.

But after two months of freaking out with your new computer, the high wears off and you wonder, "What can I buy that's new, exciting, and gives me an even bigger high?" So you buy more stuff to attach to your computer. Now you're in really deep, financially and spiritually. You're hooked. You've become addicted to computers. Each month you return to your favorite computer store to search for an even bigger high — and spend more money.

Look at me. I'm a typical computer junkie. I've already bought 50 computers, and I'm still going. Somebody help me! My computers have taken over my home. Whenever I try to go to sleep, I see those computers staring at me, their lights winking, tempting me to spend a few more hours in naughty fun, even if the sun's already beginning to rise.

Computerists use the same lingo as druggies: to buy a computer, you go to a **dealer**; and when you finally start using your computer, you're called a **user**.

As your addiction deepens and you search for greater highs, you squander even more money on computer equipment, called **hardware**. You stay up late (playing computer games or removing errors), so next morning you go to work bleary-eyed. Your boss soon suspects your computer habit, realizes you're not giving full attention to your job, and fires you.

Jobless while your computer bills mount ever higher, you run out of money to spend on computers, but your computer addiction still runs through your brain. To support your habit, you write or buy programs and try to resell them to friends. That makes you a pusher. You turn your friends into addicts too, and you all join the increasing subculture of computer junkies.

Drugs differ from computers in just one way: if you're into drugs, people call you a "washout"; but if you're into computers, people say you have a "wonderful career" — and they're right!

As a computer pusher, you can make lots of dough, but just if instead of calling yourself a "pusher" you call yourself a **computer consultant**. Yes, a computer consultant is a person who gives computer advice to other victims — and pushes them into buying more computers!

A computer consultant who gives free help seems kind, but the truth is revealed in these lines of Tom Lehrer's song, "The Old Dope Peddler":

> He gives the kids free samples
> Because he knows full well
> That today's young innocent faces
> Will be tomorrow's clientele.

Your marriage

The computer will fascinate you. It'll seduce you to spend more time with it. You'll fall in love with it. You'll start buying it presents: exotic foods (expensive programs to munch on) and expensive jewels (a printer and fancier speakers).

Then the computer will demand you give it more. While you enjoy an exciting orgy with your computer and think it's the most joyous thing that ever happened to you, suddenly the computer will demand you buy it more memory. It'll refuse to continue the orgy until you agree to its demand. And you'll agree — eagerly!

The computer's a demanding lover. You'll feel married to it.

Marrying a computer is much groovier than marrying a person: computers are good at "getting it on" (they make you feel all electric and tingly) and they never argue (they're always ready to "do it", except when they "have a headache").

I wanted to call this book "The *Sexual* Guide to Computers" and put a photo of my computer wife and me on the cover; but some communities still prohibit mixed marriages. That cover would be banned in Boston, which is where I've lived. So I had to play cool and say "Secret" Guide to Computers. But here's the real secret: this book's about sex.

If you marry a computer but already married a human, your human spouse will call you a "bigamist" and feel jealous of the computer. Your marriage to that human can deteriorate and end in divorce.

Several women got divorced because they took my computer course. Their husbands had two complaints:

> "You spend most of your time with the computer instead of with me. When you *do* spend time with me, all you want to talk about is the computer."

To prevent such marital problems, coax your spouse to play a game on the computer. Your spouse will get hooked on the game, become as addicted to the computer as you, enjoy blabbing about the computer with you, and encourage you spend money on your habit. Sociologists call that **technological progress**.

Why buy a computer?

The average American has three goals: to make money, have fun, and "become a better person". Making money is called **business**; having fun is called **pleasure**; and becoming a better person is called **personal development**. The computer will help you do all three: it'll improve your business, increase your pleasure, and help you grow into a better person.

The reasons why people buy computers are emotional:

Teenager: "Computers are a blast: sci-fi come true!"

Parent: "My kids must become computer-competent to survive! If I buy my kids a computer, they'll explore it (instead of sex & drugs), wonder how it's programmed, become programmers, get straight A's in school, become computer consultants, and make lots of dough, so they can support me in my old age and I can brag about them to my neighbors."

Grandparent: "The world's becoming computerized, and I don't want my grandkids to say I'm 'out of it.' I wouldn't blow money on this stuff myself, but my kids are giving me a computer so grandkids can send me mail and photos electronically, using the Internet. Those grandkids are so cute! Computers are so much fun!"

Kindergartner: "Grandma, I wanna computer for my birthday! And if you don't buy it, they say I'll never go to Harvard."

Social climber: "Damn! Now that big cars are passé, the computer's the only status symbol left. I'm sick of being intimidated by neighbors and bosses spouting computer jargon, and I'm tired of the guys at the bar bragging how big their computers are. I'm gonna learn that mumbo-jumbo myself so I can get back at those pompous asses and intimidate *them*!"

Worried worker: "My company is computerizing. If I don't master computers, they'll master *me* and steal my job! If I learn enough about computers, I can keep my job, get promoted, then quit and become a rich computer consultant!"

Middle-aged: "My life's a bore. I need a fun new hobby — a computer! I could fondle that cute toy when my company retires me, then start my *own* business, advertise on the Internet, and become internationally famous!"

Adventurer: "The computer's a challenge. If I can master it, that'll prove I'm not as stupid as people say!"

Wanting what's due: "I've been treated like shit all my life; I *deserve* a computer! I'm gonna get my hands on that mean machine and make it my personal slave."

Subversive: "If Big Brother has Big Blue watching me, I'll turn my computer into Big Mama and scramble their waves!"

Doctor: "Playing with the computer's anatomy is like playing God — and the computer could make my patients pay their bills!"

English teacher: "My students are hooked on computers. I'm gonna find out why then make computers channel the kids' excitement toward a higher good: poetry!"

Social-studies teacher: "The Internet is amazing! So much info is published there about current events and history and the future! I've gotta show it to my students, so they'll become part what this world is about! Then they'll do research by using the Internet, publish their *own* papers on the Internet, become internationally famous, and make *me* famous for being their teacher!"

Will your computer fulfill all those dreams? This Guide will help you find out!

Hassles

When you buy a new computer for your business, you'll have lots of hassles.

Repairs Since a complete computer system includes so many parts (CPU, ROM, RAM, disks, keyboard, screen, mouse, printer, stereo speakers, modem, microphone, scanner, network card, software, etc.), *at least one* of them won't work properly, and you'll need to fix it. Since the manufacturer or store typically provides free repairs during the first year, you'll lose nothing but your temper.

Manuals You won't completely understand the manuals for your hardware & software, so you'll ask your friends and me for help. You can also try getting help from the manufacturers and dealers; but if your question's long-winded, their answers will be curt.

If the dealer who sold you the computer is honest, he'll say, "I don't know how to run all the hardware and software I sold you. To learn how, read the manuals and buy books in bookstores. No, I haven't read them myself, because they're too long-winded, complicated, and vague. If you don't like the manuals, take our courses, which are expensive and won't teach you as much as you need but at least make you feel you're making *some* progress."

Most dealers are not that candid.

Programs If you try writing your own programs, you'll discover Murphy's law: no matter how long you think a program will take to write, it will take you longer. If you're wiser and try to buy a finished program from somebody else, you'll find the program works worse than advertised, its manual is missing or unintelligible, and you'll need to modify the program to meet your personal needs.

Data entry If you figure out how to use the program, your next torture is to type the data you want the program to process. The typing is sheer drudgery, but you must do it.

Worthwhile? Those headaches are just the _beginning_ of what can become an extended nightmare. Buying a computer starts by being exciting but quickly becomes nerve-racking.

Eventually, you'll pass that nerve-racking transition stage and be thrilled.

That painful transition is worth the effort if you plan to use the computer a lot. If you plan to use a computer just occasionally, you'd be better off not buying a computer at all: continue doing your work manually.

Promises Salespeople wanting you to buy fancy hardware or software say "it will be great", but computer stuff never turns out as good as promised.

For example, here's the tale of **the woman who was married 3 times but remained a virgin**:

> Her first husband, on his wedding night, discovered he was impotent; her second husband, on _his_ wedding night, decided he was gay; and her third husband was a computer salesman who spent the whole night saying how great it was going to be. Computer salesmen make great promises but don't deliver.

Here's the story of **the programmer who died and went to Heaven's gate**, guarded by St. Peter, who let the programmer choose between Heaven and Hell:

> The programmer peeked at Heaven and saw angels singing boring songs. He peeked at Hell and saw a beach full of beautiful bodies sunbathing and frolicking, so he chose Hell. Suddenly the beach vanished, and he was dragged to a chamber of eternal torture. When he asked "What happened to the beach?", the devil replied "Oh, that was just the demo."
>
> Though hot technologies look beautifully enticing, when you try to experience them you'll have a devil of a time!

Periodicals

To keep up-to-date about computers, read newspapers and magazines. They contain the latest computer news, criticize hardware and software, advise you on what to buy, and include ads for the newest products, services, and discount dealers.

Some ads and articles use technical computer jargon, which you'll understand by reading this book.

How to get periodicals

Visit your local computer stores, bookstores, and newspaper stands, and buy a copy of each newspaper and magazine that interests you.

After reading the periodicals you bought — or borrowed from your local library — subscribe to the ones you like best.

> Most periodicals come with a coupon that gives you a "special" discount off the subscription price "for new subscribers, if you hurry". Don't bother hurrying: the same discount is offered to practically everybody every year. And next year, when you renew, you'll be offered the same "special" discount, "for our loyal readers, if you hurry".
>
> Shortly after buying a one-year subscription, you'll receive a dishonest letter from the publisher warning that your subscription will "run out soon" and that "if you renew now, you'll get a special discount". Don't believe the letter; "run out soon" usually means "run out 8 months from now", and "if you renew now" means "if you renew sometime within the 8 months, or even later". Feel free to wait.

How to read reviews

Many computer periodicals review the newest hardware and software. Don't take the reviews too seriously: the typical review is written by just one person and reflects just that individual's opinion.

Some reviewers are too easy: they heap praise and say everything is "excellent". Other reviewers are too demanding: they say everything is "terrible". If one product gets a rave review, and a competing product gets a scathing review, the reason might be the difference between reviewers rather than the difference between products.

Giant conglomerates

Most computer magazines and newspapers are published by two giant conglomerates: **Ziff-Davis** and **IDG**.

> **Ziff-Davis** is a gigantic publisher in Manhattan. By the 1970's Ziff-Davis was publishing magazines about many hobbies. In 1982, when computers became a popular hobby, Ziff-Davis bought several computer-magazine publishers, so it's become a conglomerate of hobby-magazine and computer-magazine publishers. Ziff-Davis is usually called **ZD** or just **Ziff**. It's based in Manhattan. It was bought by a Japanese company called **Softbank**, which then resold it to a group of American investors.
>
> **IDG** (based in Framingham, Massachusetts) began publishing **Computerworld** in 1967. Later it bought up and published many other computer periodicals around the world. Now IDG publishes 270 computer periodicals in 75 countries.

Ziff and IDG have declared war on each other. For example, IDG refuses to publish articles by columnists who submit articles to Ziff. Each computer columnist must choose between either being a **Ziffer** or an **IDG'er**.

Mostly monthly

Most computer magazines are published monthly and let you buy individual issues (for about $6) or an annual subscription (for about $20).

General computer magazines

Here are the 3 best computer magazines for the general public:

Magazine	Publisher	Price	Pages	1 year	2 yr.	Editorial office	Toll free
PC World	IDG	$6.99	150	12 issues, $20	$25	CA 415-243-0500	800-825-7595
Maximum PC	Future US	$8.99	100	12 issues, $15	$30	CA 415-468-4684	800-274-3421
Smart Computing	Sandhills	$5.99	100	12 issues, $29	$48	NE 402-479-2104	800-733-3809

I've put the most important (PC World) at the top of the list, and listed the others in order of importance. That list shows each periodical's name, publisher, price (for a single issue), number of pages (rounded to the nearest 50), how many issues are printed per year, price of a 1-year subscription (using the discount card that's in the magazine), price of a 2-year subscription, editorial office's state and phone number, and any toll-free number for ordering a subscription.

To be fully aware of what's happening with computers, get all 6 of those magazines. If you can't afford all 6, start at the list's top and work your way down.

Topping the list is **PC World**. It's the best-balanced magazine.

> Of all the computer magazines, PC World does the best job of surveying readers to find out which computer brands are the most reliable and which computer companies are most helpful when answering phone calls. PC World publishes the survey results twice a year.
>
> Even if you buy just one issue of PC World, you can learn a lot from it, since each issue includes an updated list of the best brands of desktop computers, notebook computers, printers, video cards, and modems, with detailed ratings.

Maximum PC is the most youthful, exciting, and irreverent computer magazine. The writers aren't afraid to get cocky and trash the products they hate, using almost-four-letter words. They emphasize advanced hardware fiddling (explained from the ground up), computer games (and the graphics tricks underlying them), and other high-tech wow. Subscriptions cost just $15 per year. A single issue is expensive ($8.99) because it includes a CD-ROM disk (which is *not* included in the subscription price).

Of all the magazines, the easiest to read is **Smart Computing**.

> Since it's easy, it was called "PC Novice" but changed its name to "Smart Computing" to emphasize that it helps *everybody* who wants to become smarter, not just beginners.
>
> Each article is superbly crafted to explain even hard topics simply. If you want to understand how computers work, this is the magazine to get. Unlike other computer magazines, this magazine emphasizes "how computers work" rather than "which brands to buy". It also has the best "consumer complaint" department, where the Action Editor phones the companies that have screwed customers; the Action Editor usually succeeds in getting the companies to give refunds or exchanges.
>
> This magazine is the shortest — but sweetest!
>
> All other computer magazines are published in California or on the East Coast, but Smart Computing is published in Nebraska instead. Maybe that's why its writing is straightforward instead of strung out.

Mac magazines

Here are the best magazines about Apple's **Mac computers**:

Magazine	Publisher	Price	Pages	1 year	2 yr.	Editorial office	Toll free
Macworld	Mac Publishing	$6.99	100	12 issues, $20	$40	CA 415-243-0505	800-627-2247
Mac Life	Future US	$7.99	150+CD	12 issues, $20	$35	CA 415-468-4869	

The two serious Mac magazines used to be IDG's **Macworld** and Ziff's **Mac User**, but in 1997 those magazines merged into a combo called **Macworld**, It's published by a company called **Mac Publishing**, owned by IDG and Ziff working together. **Mac Life** is wackier and costs more because it comes with a CD.

Computer newsweeklies

Here are the best sources of weekly news about computers:

Newsweekly	Publisher	Price	Pages	1 year		Editorial office	Toll free
Computerworld	IDG	$5	50	51 issues, $100 or $0		MA 508-879-0700	888-559-7327
eWeek	Ziff-Davis	$6	50	51 issues, $195 or $0		MA 781-938-2600	888-663-8438

Each is published weekly (except the week after Christmas). **eWeek** (which used to be called **PC Week**) emphasizes the IBM PC and clones. **Computerworld** emphasizes bigger systems and management/social issues.

They're intended for computerists who buy lots of computers. To subscribe, you complete application forms asking how many computer purchases you make or influence yearly. If you answer acceptably, you get the newspapers free; otherwise, you must pay a lot.

That method of distribution — "specialists get it free, idiots pay through the nose" — is called **controlled circulation**. It assures advertisers that the readers are either influential or rich. Alas, it widens the gap between the "haves" and the "have-nots": if you're a low-income novice, this policy is guaranteed to "keep you in your place", unless you're lucky enough to find those magazines in your local library.

Daily newspapers

For today's news about computers, read the business section of your town's daily newspaper, or read national newspapers such as **USA Today**, **The Wall Street Journal**, and **The New York Times**.

Every Thursday is computer day. That's when **The New York Times** publishes its Circuits section (which is section E), and that's when **The Wall Street Journal** runs Walter Mossberg's computer column (on the first page of the Marketplace section).

Discount dealers

In computer magazines and newspapers, many ads offering big discounts. And if you buy from a dealer who isn't in your state, the dealer won't charge you sales tax.

Discount dealers change prices every month. Instead of asking them for catalogs (which might be out of date), examine their most recent ads. Then phone to confirm the prices. Usually, prices go down every month, but sometimes they rise.

Before buying, ask whether the product's in stock, how long the dealer will take to fill your order, and how it will be shipped. Ask what the dealer charges for shipping: many dealers overcharge! Ask whether there's a surcharge for using a credit card. Since products are improved often, make sure the dealer is selling you the *newest* version.

If the product you get is defective, the dealer or manufacturer will fix or replace it. But if the product is merely "disappointing" or doesn't do what you expected or isn't compatible with the rest of your computer system, tough luck!

Many discount dealers say "all sales are final." Other dealers let you return computers but not printers, monitors, or software. Some dealers let you return products but charge you a "restocking fee", which can be up to 25% of the purchase price!

So before you buy, ask questions about the product's abilities to make sure it will do what you expect. Tell the dealer what hardware and software you own, and ask the dealer whether the product's compatible with your system.

The typical product comes in a cardboard box. On the back of the box (or on some other side), you'll usually see a list of the **system requirements**. That's a list of what hardware and software you must already own to make that product work with *your* computer.

Use your credit card

Pay by credit card rather than a check. If you pay by credit card and have an unresolved complaint about what you bought, Federal laws say that the credit-card company can't bill you! Moreover, if the mail-order company takes your money, spends it, and then goes bankrupt before shipping your goods, the credit-card company gets stuck, not you!

The nicest credit cards (such as Citibank's) double the manufacturer's warranty, so a "one-year warranty" becomes a *two*-year warranty! Does *your* credit card give you that warranty extension? Ask your bank!

What's missing?

When buying computer equipment, find out what the advertised price does *not* include.

For example, the advertised price for a "complete computer system" might not include the screen. Ask! In a typical printer ad, the price does *not* include the cable that goes from the printer to your computer.

Read the fine print

When reading an ad, make sure you read the fine print at the bottom of the ad. It contains many disclaimers, which admit that the deal isn't quite as good as the rest of the ad implies.

Asterisk In the middle of an ad, next to an exciting price or feature or warranty, you'll often see an asterisk (*). The asterisk means: "for details, read the fine print at the bottom of the ad". That fine print contains disclaimers that will disappoint you. In long multi-page ads, the fine print is often buried at the bottom of just *one* of the ad's pages, far away from the page where the asterisk appeared, in the hope that you won't notice the fine print.

So if you see what looks like a great deal, but the deal has an asterisk next to it, the asterisk means "the deal is not really as great as we imply".

Fine-print phrases In many computer ads, the fine print contains these phrases....

"Monitor optional" means this price does *not* include a monitor. The monitor costs extra, even though the ad shows a photo of a computer with a monitor.

"Upgrade price" means you get this price just if you already own an older version of this stuff.

"With system purchase" means you get this price just if you're stupid enough to also buy an overpriced full computer system at the same time.

"Reflects cash discount" means you get this price just if you're stupid enough to pay cash instead of using a credit card. (By paying cash, you can't complain to a credit-card company if you get ripped you off.) If you use a credit card, the seller will charge you about 3% above the advertised price.

"Includes rebate" means you must pay more, then request a rebate from the manufacturer. (You'll probably never get that rebate, since you'll forget to ask for the rebate form, or you'll forget to mail the rebate form to the manufacturer, or the rebate form will have already expired, or you'll lose the receipt or code number you must mail with the rebate form to get the rebate, or you can't mail the receipt because you already used it to apply for a rebate on a second item you bought simultaneously, or the manufacturer loses your paperwork or is a jerk who waits many months to send the rebate or goes bankrupt.)

"Manufacturer's warranty" means that if the stuff breaks, don't ask the seller for help. Phone the original manufacturer instead (who'll probably ignore you).

"Factory serviced" means another customer bought this stuff, didn't like it, and returned it to the factory, which examined it and thinks it's good enough to resell (after jiggling it a bit), so now *you're* getting stuck with this lemon.

"For in-stock items" means that although the seller promised to ship immediately, the seller won't if you order stuff that's not yet in the warehouse.

"25% restocking fee" means that if you return the stuff, you won't get your money back. Instead, the seller will keep 25% of your money (as a restocking fee) and return just 75% to you.

Mail-order dealers

Back in the 1980's, two big mail-order dealers set the tone for the rest of the discount industry. Those dealers were **Telemart** and **PC Connection**.

When **Telemart** went bankrupt in 1993, its assets were sold to **Computer Discount Warehouse (CDW)**, which continued Telemart's tradition of low prices and wide selection. CDW also bought another competitor, called **Micro Warehouse**. Phone CDW in Illinois at 800-500-4CDW (for Mac goodies) or 800-454-4CDW (for IBM-compatible goodies).

PC Connection has the best reputation for service because it processes orders fast, charges little for shipping, handles hassle orders promptly and generously, and gives technical help on a toll-free 800 number.

> PC Connection began in a barn in the tiny town of Marlow, New Hampshire, then expanded to fill the inn across the street. Now PC Connection has become huge and is based in the city of Merrimack, New Hampshire.
>
> PC Connection has two divisions: IBM and Mac.
>
> The IBM division advertises in *PC World* (phone 800-800-0003 or 603-446-0003) and *PC Magazine* (phone 800-800-0004 or 603-446-0004). The Mac division calls itself **Mac Connection** in *Macworld* (phone 800-800-3333 or 603-446-3333). You can use the 800 numbers even if you're in Alaska, Hawaii, Puerto Rico, Virgin Islands, and Canada.
>
> Each division works round-the-clock, 24 hours daily. Your order's shipped immediately, even if you've paid by check. (Checks are cleared in less than a day.) Your order's shipped by Airborne overnight express so it reaches you the next day; if you order between 12:01AM and 3:15AM Eastern Time, you'll usually receive your order the *same* day (because the company built a warehouse next to Airborne's airport in Ohio).
>
> The IBM division is nice, the Mac division is even nicer! The IBM division's toll-free number is usually busy; the Mac division's toll-free number usually gets you a sales rep immediately. The IBM division offers fairly low prices (but not as low as other discount dealers); the Mac division offers rock-bottom prices, lower than almost any other Mac dealer.
>
> The company isn't quite as nice as before. For shipping, the company used to charge $5 or less, even if your order was huge, but now charges more. The company used to give a money-back guarantee but now gives no refunds for returned computers & printers and charges a 15% restocking fee for all other items.

Another competitor is Washington State's **Zones**.

> Like Micro Warehouse, it offers low prices on IBM and Mac goodies. Its IBM division, **PC Zone**, is at 800-258-2088. The Mac division, **Mac Zone**, is at 800-248-0800. For international calls to either division, phone 425-883-3088.

Stores

If you need hardware or software fast and can't wait for mail-order dealers to ship, go to the local computer stores that advertise in the business section of your local newspaper.

To encourage a store to give you a discount, mention low prices from competitors and agree to buy many items at once. Say that if you don't get a discount, you'll shop elsewhere. Many stores do **price-matching**: they'll match the price of any other local store, though not the prices of mail-order dealers. Some stores let salespeople give 10% discounts, which are subtracted from the salesperson's commission.

IBM and Apple give educational discounts to schools, teachers, and some college students. To find out whether *you* can get educational discounts, ask your school's administrators and your town's computer stores.

For low prices, visit a chain of huge superstores, such as **Micro Center**.

> It has 20 superstores (in Massachusetts, New York, New Jersey, Pennsylvania, Virginia, Georgia, Ohio, Michigan, Illinois, Minnesota, Kansas, Colorado, Texas, and California).
>
> It's the most pleasant place to browse, since the staff is friendly and the selection is huge: the typical Micro Center store contains 45,000 square feet displaying 36,000 products. A gigantic room is devoted to books, a gigantic room is devoted to Macs, a gigantic room is devoted to I/O devices (such as printers and scanners), etc. To find the store nearest you, phone 800-743-7537.
>
> Micro Center's salespeople are usually more knowledgeable than CompUSA's and make customers happier.

In California's Silicon Valley, visit a chain of superstores called **Fry's Electronics**, which has been a local favorite for many years. In New York City, visit a superstore called **J&R Music & Computer World**, which is run by Joe & Rachelle Friedman near Wall Street (15 Park Row, New York City NY 10038, 800-221-8180 or 212-238-9000).

For many computer items, the lowest prices are now at 3 chains: **Staples**, **Best Buy**, and **Walmart**. Check your Sunday newspaper for flyers advertising their weekly specials.

Computer shows

Another way to find low prices is at a computer show. The lowest prices are at small shows called **flea markets** or **swap meets**.

Many vendors at shows offer discounts, especially during the show's last three hours. When you buy at a show, jot down the vendor's name, address, and phone number, in case the goods don't work.

Beware: many vendors at those shows are like gypsies, traveling from show to show and hard to reach if you have a complaint. Many sell computers containing illegal copies of software that was never paid for and whose instruction manuals are missing. Make sure any software you buy comes with an official instruction manual (published by the company that invented the software), not just a book from a bookstore.

New computers cheap

On pages 61-68, I'll explain the *best* way to buy a complete new IBM clone cheaply.

Chips

The computer is full of chips. Let's examine them.

Chip technology

If you unscrew the system unit (the box containing the CPU and memory) and peek at the circuitry inside, you'll see a green plastic board, on which is printed an electrical wiring diagram.

Since the diagram's printed in copper (instead of ink), the diagram conducts electricity; so it isn't just a diagram of an electrical circuit; it *is* an electrical circuit!

The green plastic board — including the circuit printed on it — is called a **printed-circuit board (PC board)**. Each wire that's stamped onto the PC board is called a **trace**.

The typical computer contains several PC boards.

Motherboard & babies

In your computer, the largest and most important PC board is called the **motherboard** (or, more briefly, **mobo**). It lies flat on the bottom of the system unit.

The other PC boards are smaller. Those little baby boards (about the size of a postcard) are called **PC cards**.

The typical motherboard has several **slots** on it. Into each slot, you can put a PC card.

PCMCIA cards

If you buy a modern notebook computer, you'll see the case's right-hand wall has a special slot in it. You can shove a card into that slot without opening the notebook's case.

The kind of card that fits into that special slot is small and thin — the size of a credit card. That kind of card was invented by the **Personal-Computer Memory-Card International Assocation (PCMCIA)** and therefore called a **PCMCIA card**. That slot is called a **PCMCIA slot**.

People have trouble remembering what "PCMCIA" stands for. Cynics say it stands for "People Can't Memorize Computer Industry Acronyms". Since "PCMCIA" also stands for "Politically Correct Members of the CIA", computerists pronounce "PCMCIA" in two breaths: they say "PCM", then pause, then say "CIA".

Some PCMCIA cards are *very* thin. Other PCMCIA cards are thicker, so they can hold extra circuitry. A PCMCIA card and its slot are called **Type 1** if their thickness is 3.3 millimeters, **Type 2** if 5 millimeters, **Type 3** if 10.5 millimeters, **Type 4** if 18 millimeters.

Caterpillars

On each PC board, you'll see black rectangles. If you look closely at a black rectangle, you'll see it has tiny legs, so it looks like a black caterpillar. (Though farmers think it looks like a "black caterpillar", city folks think it looks more like a "yucky roach". Kids call it just "a black thingy with legs".)

The "caterpillars" come in many sizes. In a typical computer, the shortest caterpillars are three-quarters of an inch long and have 7 pairs of legs; the longest are two inches long and have more legs.

Though each black caterpillar has legs, it doesn't move. It's permanently mounted on the PC board.

Each leg is made of tin and called a **pin**.

Sadistic hobbyists play a game where they yank the caterpillars from a PC board and throw the caterpillars across the room. That game's called "tin-pin bowling".

Hidden inside the caterpillar is a metal square, called a **chip**, which is very tiny. The typical chip is just an eighth of an inch long, an eighth of an inch wide, and a hundredth of an inch thick! On that tiny metal chip are etched *thousands* of microscopic electronic circuits! Since all those circuits are on the chip, the chip's called an **integrated circuit (IC)**.

4 purposes

Each chip serves a purpose. If the chip's purpose is to "think", it's called a **processor chip**. If the chip's purpose is to "remember" information, it's called a **memory chip**. If the chip's purpose is to help devices communicate with each other, it's called an **interface chip**. If the chip's purpose is to act as a slave and helper to other chips, it's called a **support chip**.

So a chip is either a processor chip or a memory chip or an interface chip or a support chip — or it's a combination chip that accomplishes *several* purposes.

How chips are designed

To design a chip, the manufacturer hires an artist, who draws on paper a big sketch of what circuits are to be put onto the chip. It helps if the artist also has a degree in engineering — and knows how to use another computer to help draw all the lines.

After the big sketch is drawn, it's photographed.

Have you ever photographed your friend and asked the photography store for an "enlargement"? To produce a chip, the chip's manufacturer does the opposite: it photographs the sketch but produces a "reduction" to just an eighth of an inch on each side! Whereas a photo of your friend is made on treated paper, the tiny photo of the chip's circuitry consists of metal and semiconductors on treated silicon so the photo's an actual working circuit! That photographic process is called **photolithography** (or **photolith**).

Many copies of that photo are made on a large silicon wafer. Then a cookie cutter slices the wafer into hundreds of chips. Each chip is put into its own caterpillar.

The caterpillar's purpose is just to hide and protect the chip inside it; the caterpillar's just a strange-looking package containing the chip. Since the caterpillar's a package that has two rows of legs, it's called a **dual in-line package (DIP)**. That DIP's only purpose is to house the chip.

Computer hobbyists are always talking about chips & DIPs, and at parties serve chips & dips, and are called "dipchips".

Buying chips

If you ask a computer dealer to sell you a chip, the dealer also gives you the chip's DIP (the entire caterpillar). Since you've asked for a chip but also received a DIP, you might get confused and think that the caterpillar (the DIP) is the chip. But that caterpillar's *not* the chip; the chip hides inside the caterpillar.

The typical caterpillar-and-chip costs $3. You might pay somewhat more or somewhat less, depending on how fancy the chip's circuitry is.

If the circuits in a chip are defective, it's called a "buffalo chip". Folks who dislike that tacky term say "potato chip" or "chocolate chip" instead, like this: "Hey, the computer's not working! It must be made of chocolate chips!"

You can get chips from these famous mail-order chip suppliers:

JDR Microdevices
1850 S. 10th St., San Jose CA 95112
800-538-5000 or 408-494-1400

Jameco
1355 Shoreway Rd., Belmont CA 94002
800-831-4242 or 650-592-8097

ACP
1310 E. Edinger, Santa Ana CA 92705
800-FONE-ACP

The following chip suppliers are newer and often charge less:

Spartan Technologies
1500 E. Higgins Rd. #A, Elk Grove Village IL 60007
888-393-0340 or 847-364-9900

Chip Merchant
9541 Ridgehaven Ct., San Diego CA 92123
800-426-6375 or 619-268-4774

Memory Man
PO Box 11227. New Orleans LA 70181
800-MEGABYTE, 504-818-2717

How chips chat

The chip inside the caterpillar acts as the caterpillar's brain. The caterpillar also contains a "nervous system", made of thin wires that run from the brain (the chip) to the legs (the pins). The wires in the caterpillar's nervous system are very thin: each wire's diameter is about half of a thousandth of an inch.

If one caterpillar wants to send electrical signals to another caterpillar, the signals go from the first caterpillar's brain (chip) through the caterpillar's nervous system to its legs (pins). Each pin is attached to a trace (wire) on the PC board. The signals travel through those traces, which carry the signals across the PC board until the signals reach the second caterpillar's pins. Then the signals travel through the second caterpillar's nervous system to that caterpillar's brain (chip).

Binary code

To communicate with each other, the caterpillars use a secret code. Each code is a series of 1's and 0's. For example, the code for the letter A is 01000001; the code for the letter B is 01000010; the code for the number 5 is 101; the code for the number 6 is 110.

That's called the **binary code**, because each digit in the code has just *two* possibilities: it's either a 1 or a 0. In the code, each 1 or 0 is called a **binary digit**.

A **bi**nary dig**it** is called a **bit**. So in the computer, each **bit** is a 1 or a 0.

When a caterpillar wants to send a message to another caterpillar, it sends the message in binary code. To send a 1, the caterpillar sends a high voltage through the wires; to send a 0, the caterpillar sends little or no voltage through the wires.

So to send the number 5, whose code number is 101, the caterpillar sends a high voltage (1), then a low voltage (0), then a high voltage (1). To send those three bits (1, 0, and then 1), the caterpillar can send them in sequence through the same leg (pin); or for faster transmission, the caterpillar can send them through three pins simultaneously: the first pin sends 1, while the next pin sends 0 and the third pin sends 1.

The speed at which bits are sent is measured in **bits per second (bps)**.

The part of the computer that thinks ("the brain") is called the **processor** (or **central processing unit** or **CPU**).

In a maxicomputer or minicomputer, the processor consists of several chips, which are **processor chips**.

In a microcomputer, the processor is so small that it consists of just a single chip, called a **microprocessor**. It sits on the motherboard. Yes, in a typical microcomputer, the part that does all the thinking is just a tiny square of metal, less than ¼" on each side!

Intel's designs

In IBM-compatible PCs, the microprocessor uses a design invented by **Intel**. Intel has gradually improved that design by putting more circuitry on the chip:

Chip's name	Year invented	Transistors on chip
Intel 8088	1979	29,000 transistors
Intel 286 (also called 80286)	1982	134,000 transistors
Intel 386 (also called 80386)	1985	275,000 transistors
Intel 486 (also called 80486)	1989	1,200,000 transistors
Intel Pentium	1993	3,100,000 transistors

The Intel Pentium could have been called the "Intel 586", but Intel called it the "Pentium" instead so Intel can trademark the name and prevent companies from copying it. It's the first computer chip that sounds like a breakfast cereal: "Hey, kids, to put zip into your life, try Penti-yumms. They build strong computer bodies, 5 ways!"

The Intel 8088 was used in the original IBM PC and in a fancier computer called the **IBM PC XT**. Any IBM-compatible PC containing that chip is called an **XT-class computer**.

The Intel 286 was used in a computer called the **IBM AT**. Any IBM-compatible PC containing that chip is called an **AT-class computer**.

The 8088, 286, 386, and 486 chips are all outdated; they're no longer actively marketed. **All new IBM-compatible PCs contain Pentiums** — or imitations of it made by Intel's competitors.

Athlon

The most popular imitation of the Pentium chip is the **Athlon** chip, made by **Advanced Micro Devices (AMD)**. The Athlon chip tends to run faster than the Pentium chip and costs less: it's a better deal!

Requirements

Many new programs require you to have a Pentium-class chip (Pentium, Athlon, or similar imitation). Those programs won't run if your computer is so old that it contains an 8088, 286, 386, or 486.

Megahertz

In an army, when soldiers march, they're kept in step by a drill sergeant who yells out, rhythmically, "Hup, two, three, four! Hup, two, three, four! Hup, two, three, four!"

Like a soldier, the microprocessor takes the next step in obeying your program just when instructed by the computer's "drill sergeant", which is called the **computer clock**. The clock rhythmically sends out a pulse of electricity; each time the clock sends out a pulse, the microprocessor does one more step in obeying your program.

The clock sends out *millions* of pulses every second, so the microprocessor accomplishes *millions* of steps in your program every second!

Each pulse is called a **clock cycle**. The clock's speed is measured in **cycles per seconds**.

A "cycle per second" is called a **hertz (Hz)**, in honor of the German physicist Heinrich Hertz. A "million cycles per second" is called a **megahertz (MHz)**.

When Intel invented the Pentium chip in 1993, the Pentium's clock did 60 million cycles per second. That's 60 megahertz! Intel also invented a faster Pentium, at 66 megahertz, then even faster Pentiums at 75, 90, 100, 120, 133, 150, 166, 200, 233, 266, 300, 333, 350, 400, 450, 500, 550, 600, 650, 667, 700, 733, 750, 800, 850, 866, and 933 megahertz. For example, a 200-megahertz Pentium thinks twice as fast as a 100-megahertz Pentium.

1000 megahertz is called a **gigahertz (GHz)**. It's a billion hertz. Recently, Intel has invented faster Pentiums that go at 1, 2, 3, and even 3.6 gigahertz. For example, a 1-gigahertz Pentium thinks twice as fast as a 500-megahertz Pentium.

Slower than a Pentium

The Pentium is an amazing chip: while it thinks about one part of your program, it simultaneously starts getting the next part of your program ready for processing. That chip's ability to do several things simultaneously is called **parallel processing**.

The Pentium is smarter than earlier chips (the 8088, 286, 386, and 486): the Pentium can perform more tasks simultaneously; it performs more parallel processing.

Earlier chips seem slower: too often during a clock cycle in earlier chips, part of the chip "does nothing" while waiting for the other part of the chip to catch up. Those earlier chips therefore accomplish less useful work during a clock cycle than a Pentium.

During a clock cycle, a 486 accomplishes half as much useful work as a Pentium. We say the 486's **usefulness factor** is ½.

During a clock cycle, a 386 accomplishes a quarter as much useful work as a Pentium, so the 386's usefulness factor is ¼. A 286's usefulness factor is ⅕. An 8088's usefulness factor is ⅕.

You've seen that those early chips accomplish less useful work during a clock cycle than a Pentium. Moreover, they accomplish fewer clock cycles per second than a Pentium; they have fewer megahertz:

Chip	Megahertz	Usefulness
Intel 8088	4.77, 7.18	⅟₂₀
Intel 286	6, 8, 10, 12	⅕
Intel 386	16, 20, 25, 33	¼
Intel 486	20, 25, 33, 50, 66, 75, 100	½
Pentium	60, 66, 75, 90, 100, 120, 133, 150, 166, 200, 233, 266, 300, 333, 350, 400, 450, 500, 533, 550, 566, 600, 633, 650, 667, 700, 733, 750, 766, 800, 850, 866, 900, 933, 950, 1000, 1100, 1130, 1200, 1260, 1300, 1400, 1500, 1600, 1700, 1800, 1900, 2000, 2200, 2260, 2400, 2500, 2530, 2667, 2700, 2800, 3000, 3066, 3200, 3400, 3600	1

For example, suppose you buy an Intel 486 going at 100-megahertz. Since it suffers from a usefulness factor of ½, it accomplishes just ½ as much useful work per cycle as a 100-megahertz Pentium, so it acts about as fast as a 50-megahertz Pentium. A 20-megahertz 386, which suffers from a usefulness factor of ¼, acts about as fast as a 5-megahertz Pentium. A 10-megahertz 286, which suffers from a usefulness factor of ⅕, acts about as fast as a 2-megahertz Pentium.

The slowest chip is a 4.77-megahertz 8088. Since it suffers from a usefulness factor of ⅟₂₀, it acts about as fast as a 0.2385-megahertz Pentium. That's 14,256 times slower than the fastest Pentium, which goes at 3400 megahertz. Yes, the fastest IBM-compatible computers think over 10,000 times faster than the slowest ones! That's progress!

The "usefulness factor" is just an approximate average. During a cycle, for example, a 486 accomplishes about ½ as much useful work as a Pentium, *on the average*; but on certain tasks a 486 accomplishes *more* than "½ as much", and on other tasks it accomplishes less.

Variant chips

The Intel 8088 comes in two versions. One version (called simply the "8088") goes slightly slower than the other version (called the **8086**).

The Intel 386 comes in two versions. One version (called the **386SX**) goes slightly slower than the other version (called the **386DX**).

The Intel 486 comes in two versions. One version (called the **486SX**) goes slower than the other version (called the **486DX**). Moreover, the 486DX comes in three varieties: the original 486DX, the **486DX2**, and the **486DX4**.

Many Pentiums The Pentium comes in many versions. Here are the most popular, listed from slowest to fastest:

Version	Year invented (and comment)
Pentium classic	1993 (a variant called the "Pentium Pro" runs some programs faster, some slower)
Pentium MMX	1995 (understands 57 more instructions, called "MultiMedia eXtensions")
Pentium 2	1997 (resembles the Pentium MMX but about 30% faster)
Pentium 3	1999 (understands 70 more instructions, called "SSE")
Pentium 4	2000 (a variant called "Pentium 4M" uses less electricity, for mobile laptops)
Pentium D	2005 ("D" means "Dual"; the plastic caterpillar contains 2 chips)
Pentium Core Duo	2006 (it's 1 chip that includes 2 cores, so it acts like 2 chips, to go twice as fast)
Pentium Core 2 Duo	2006 (it's 1 chip that includes 2 cores, so it acts like 2 chips)
Pentium Core i3	2010 (it's 1 chip that includes 2 cores, so it acts like 2 chips)
Pentium Core i5	2010 (crude version was in 2009; now 2-core & 4-core versions are available)
Pentium Core i7	2010 (crude version was in 2008; now 4-core & 6-core versions are available)

To help low-income folks, Intel eventually decided to make cheaper Pentiums, called **Celeron**. They go slower.

The first Celeron, invented in 1998, was a cheaper, slower version of the Pentium 2.
The newest Celeron is a cheaper, slower version of the Pentium Core 2 Duo.

For *very* low-income folks, Intel makes a version that's even cheaper and slower, called the **Atom**. It's used in netbook computers.

What's available

Intel has stopped marketing old types of chips (8086 & 8088, 286, 386, 486) and old Pentiums (classic, 2, 3, 4, D, and Core Duo). **Your choices are now the Pentium Core 2 Duo, Core i3, Core i5 and Core i7 (and some Celerons and the Atom).**

Megahertz Here's how many megahertz are available:

Intel chip	Megahertz
8088	4.77, 7.18
8086	8, 10
286	6, 8, 10, 12
386SX	16, 20, 25, 33
386DX	16, 20, 25, 33
486SX	20, 25, 33
486DX	25, 33, 50
486DX2	50, 66
486DX4	75, 100
Pentium classic	60 up through 200
Pentium Pro	150, 166, 180, 200
Pentium MMX	166, 200, 233
Pentium 2	233, 266, 300, 333, 350, 400, 450
Pentium Celeron	266 up through 2930
Pentium 3	450 up through 1400
Pentium 4, etc.	1300 up through 3600

Prices Here are some prices:

Intel chip	Gigahertz	Price
Pentium Celeron D 325	2.53 GHz	$37
Pentium Celeron D 331	2.66 GHz	$47
Pentium Celeron E5400	2.7 GHz	$57
Pentium Core i3-530	2.93 GHz	$130
Pentium Core i3-540	3.06 GHz	$138
Pentium Core i3-2100	3.1 GHz	$144
Pentium Core i3-2120	3.3 GHz	$169
Pentium Core i5-650	3.2 GHz	$219
Pentium Core i5-2500	3.3 GHz	$248
Pentium Core i7-950	3.06 GHz	$318
Pentium Core i7-2600	3.4 GHz	$352

That chart shows the price charged by discount dealers (such as The Chip Merchant, JDR Microdevices, and Spartan Technologies) for a single chip when this book went to press in June 2010. By the time you read this, prices might be lower, since Intel drops prices frequently (about every 2 months). If you buy 1000 chips at a time directly from Intel, you pay even less.

Imitations

Intel's competitors have imitated Intel's chips. Some of the imitations go faster than Intel's originals!

Intel's chip	Imitations
8088 (4.77 or 7.18 MHz)	NEC's V20 chip goes faster: 10 MHz.
8086 (8 or 10 MHz)	NEC's V30 chip goes fast: 10 MHz.
286 (6-12 MHz)	Harris's 286 goes faster: choose 16 or 20 MHz versions.
386 (16-33 MHz)	AMD's 386 goes faster: 40 MHz.
486 SX (20-33 MHz)	Cyrix's 486SLC goes too slow (usefulness factor $\frac{1}{3}$ instead of $\frac{1}{2}$).
486 DX (25-100 MHz)	AMD's 486 goes faster: choose 66, 80, 100, or 120 MHz versions.
Pentium classic (60-200)	AMD's 586 and Cyrix's 586 go too slow (usefulness factor $\frac{2}{3}$ instead of 1).
Pentium 2 (233-450)	AMD's K6 (and K6-2) are slightly slow (usefulness factor $\frac{7}{8}$ instead of 1).
Pentium Celeron (266-2800)	AMD's Duron & Sempron goes about the same speed.
Pentium 3, etc. (450-3600)	AMD's Athlon, Athlon II, and Phenom II go about the same speed.

Here are the prices charged by discount dealers (such as The Chip Merchant, JDR Microdevices, and Spartan Technologies):

AMD chip	Cores	Gigahertz	Price
Sempron 2500+	1	1.6 GHz	$45
Athlon II X3 450	3	3.2 GHz	$100
Athlon II X4 640	4	3 GHz	$125
Phenom II X4 945	4	3 GHz	$182
Phenom II X4 955	4	3.2 GHz	$195
Phenom II X4 965	4	3.4 GHz	$221
Phenom II X6 1055T	6	2.8 GHz	$213

Half-assed systems

While a chip waits for your commands, the chip accomplishes nothing useful during the wait: it just mumbles to itself.

To make full use of a fast Pentium, make sure you know what commands to give the computer. To let the chip reach its full potential, buy lots of RAM, big disk drives, and a quick printer. Otherwise, the Pentium will act as idiotic as if it's in the army: it will just "hurry up and then wait" for other parts of the system to catch up and tell it what to do next.

A mind's a terrible thing to waste! To avoid wasting the computer's mind (the CPU), make sure the other computer parts are good enough to match the CPU and keep it from waiting.

If you get suckered into buying a computer that has a fast Pentium chip but insufficient RAM, insufficient disk drives, and a slow printer, you've bought a computer that's just half-fast: it's half-assed.

Total cost

When you buy a microcomputer, its advertised price includes a microprocessor, motherboard, and other goodies. Pay for the microprocessor separately just if you're inventing your own computer, buying parts for a broken computer, or upgrading your computer by switching to a faster microprocessor & motherboard.

Though the microprocessor is cheap, the computer containing it can cost many hundreds or thousands of dollars. That's because the microprocessor is just a tiny part of the computer. In addition to the microprocessor, you want memory chips, interface chips, support chips, PC boards (to put the chips on), I/O devices (a keyboard, screen, printer, speaker, and mouse), disks, and software.

Used-computer stores and garage sales get you IBM clones for these prices:

Chip	Complete computer
8088 or 8086	$5
286	$10
386	$15
486	$20
Pentium	$250

Those prices include nearly everything you need (such as the CPU, memory chips, disks, keyboard, and a screen displaying many colors) but do *not* include a printer or software. Those prices are approximate; the exact price you pay depends on the CPU's speed (how many megahertz or gigahertz) and on the other components' speed, quality, and size.

Notice that a 286 computer costs $10, which is $5 more than an 8086 computer. That's because a 286 computer includes a better CPU chip and also comes with a better keyboard, better screen, better memory chips, and better disks.

Math coprocessor

Each Pentium chip includes **math coprocessor circuitry**, which handles advanced math fast. That circuitry can multiply & divide long numbers & decimals and compute square roots, logarithms, and trigonometry.

Primitive chips — the 8088, 8086, 286, 386SX, 386DX, and 486SX — do *not* include such circuitry.

To make a primitive chip do advanced math, you must feed the chip a program that teaches the chip how to break the advanced problem down into a series of simpler problems. That program runs slowly — nearly 100 times slower than if a math coprocessor were present!

You'll be *very* annoyed at the slowness if you're a scientist trying to do advanced math — or an artist trying to rotate a picture, since the computer computes the rotated image's new coordinates by using trigonometry. For example, if you draw a 3-D picture of a house and then ask the computer to show how the house looks from a different angle, you need a math coprocessor to avoid a long delay.

But if you use the computer just as a souped-up typewriter (to record and edit your writing) or as an electronic filing cabinet (to record names and addresses on a mailing list), you'll never notice the lack of a math coprocessor, since you're not doing advanced math.

Each **486DX** chip (and 486DX2 and 486DX4) includes math-coprocessor circuitry; the **486SX** does not. So **here's the only difference between a 486DX and a 486SX: the 486SX lacks math-coprocessor circuitry.**

> Intel invented the 486DX, then later invented the 486SX by using this manufacturing technique: Intel took each 486DX whose math coprocessor was faulty and called it a 486SX. So a 486SX was just a defective 486DX.
>
> If you buy a 486SX now, you get a 486DX whose math coprocessor is either defective or missing.

If your CPU lacks math-coprocessor circuitry (because your CPU is an 8088, 8086, 286, 386, or 486SX), here's how to do math quickly: buy a supplementary chip, called a **math coprocessor chip**. Put it next to the CPU chip on the motherboard. It contains the math-coprocessor circuitry that the CPU lacks.

CPU	Which math coprocessor to buy
8088, 8086	Intel 8087
286	Intel 287
386SX	Intel 387SX
386DX	Intel 387DX
486SX	Intel 487SX

RAM

Although the CPU (the computer's brain) can think, it can't remember anything. It can't even remember what problem it was working on!

Besides buying a CPU, you must also buy **memory chips**, which remember what problem the CPU was working on. To find out what the problem was, the CPU looks at the memory chips frequently — millions of times every second!

You need two kinds of memory chips: **RAM** and **ROM**.

> The **RAM** chips remember info temporarily.
> The **ROM** chips remember info permanently.

Let's begin by looking at RAM chips. If a chip remembers info just temporarily, it's called a **random-access memory chip (RAM chip)**.

When you buy RAM chips, they contain no info yet; you tell the CPU what info to put into them. Later, you can make the CPU erase that info and insert new info instead. The RAM chips hold info just temporarily: when you turn the computer's power off, the RAM chips are automatically erased.

Whenever the CPU tries to solve a problem, the CPU stores the problem in the RAM chips, temporarily. There it also stores all instructions on how to solve the problem; the instructions are called the **program**.

If you buy more RAM chips, the CPU can handle longer problems and programs. If the computer doesn't have enough RAM chips to hold the entire problem or program, you (or a programmer) must split the problem or program into several shorter ones instead and tell the CPU to work on each of the short ones temporarily.

How RAM is measured

A **character** is any symbol you can type on the keyboard, such as a letter or digit or punctuation mark or blank space. For example, the word HAT consists of 3 characters; the phrase Mr. Poe consists of 7 characters (M, R, the period, the space, P, O, and E). The phrase LOVE 2 KISS U consists of 13 characters.

Instead of saying "character", hungry programmers say **byte**. So LOVE 2 KISS U consists of 13 bytes. If, in the RAM, you store LOVE 2 KISS U, that phrase occupies 13 bytes of the RAM.

RAM chips are manufactured by a process that involves doubling. The most popular unit of RAM is "2 bytes times 2 times 2 times 2 times 2 times 2 times 2 times 2 times 2 times 2", which is 1024 bytes, which is called a **kilobyte**. So **the definition of a kilobyte is "1024 bytes"**. It's about a quarter as many characters as you get on a typewritten page (assuming the page is single-spaced with one-inch margins and elite type).

The abbreviation for *kilobyte* is **K**. For example, if a salesperson says an old computer has a "512K RAM", the salesperson means the main circuitry includes enough RAM chips to hold 512 kilobytes of information, which is slightly over 512,000 bytes.

A **megabyte** is 1024 kilobytes. Since a kilobyte is 1024 bytes, **a megabyte is "1024 times 1024" bytes, which is 1,048,576 bytes altogether**, which is slightly more than a million bytes. It's about how much you can fit in a 250-page book (assuming the book has single-spaced typewritten pages). The abbreviation for *megabyte* is **meg** or **M**.

A **gigabyte** (pronounced "gig a bite") is 1024 megabytes. It's slightly more than a billion bytes. The abbreviation for *gigabyte* is **gig** or **G**.

A **terabyte** is 1024 gigabytes. It's slightly more than a trillion bytes. The abbreviation for *terabyte* is **T**.

In honor of the words "kilobyte", "megabyte", "gigabyte", and "terabyte", many programmers name their puppies Killer Byte, Maker Byte, Giggle Byte, and Terror Byte.

Rows of RAM chips

In a primitive microcomputer (such as the Commodore 64), the RAM is a row of eight chips on the motherboard. That row of chips holds 64K altogether. So it holds 64 kilobytes, which is slightly more than 64 thousand bytes (since a kilobyte is slightly more than a thousand bytes).

That row of chips is called a **64K chip set**. Each chip in that set is called a "64K chip", but remember that you need a whole row of those 64K chips to produce a 64K RAM.

The most popular style of 64K chip is the **TI 4164**. Although that style was invented by Texas Instruments, other manufacturers have copied it.

If your computer is slightly fancier (such as the Apple 2c), it has *two* rows of 64K chips. Since each row is a 64K RAM, the two rows together total 128K.

If your computer is even fancier, it has *many* rows of 64K chips. For example, your computer might have four rows of 64K chips. Since each row is a 64K RAM, the four rows together total 256K.

64K chips first became popular in 1982. If your computer is so ancient that it was built before 1982, it probably contains inferior chips: instead of containing a row of 64K chips, it contains a row of 16K chips or 4K chips.

During the 1980's, computer engineers invented 256K and 1M chips.

If your computer has very little RAM, you can try to enlarge the RAM, by adding extra rows of RAM chips to the motherboard. But if the motherboard's already full, you must buy an extra PC card to put the extra chips on. That extra PC card is called a **RAM memory card**.

Parity chip

The original IBM PC contains an extra chip in each row, so each row contains 9 chips instead of 8.

The row's ninth chip is called the **parity chip**. It double-checks the work done by the other 8 chips, to make sure they're all working correctly!

So for an original IBM PC (or imitations of it), you must buy 9 chips to fill a row.

Strips of RAM chips

If your computer is modern and you want to insert an extra row of RAM chips, you do *not* have to insert 8 or 9 separate chips into the motherboard. Instead, you can buy a strip (tiny memory card) that contains all 8 or 9 chips and just pop the whole strip into the computer's motherboard, in one blow.

If the strip is typical,
it contains a single row of chips, pops into one of the motherboard's slots,
and is called a **Single In-line Memory Module (SIMM)**.

If the strip is fancy,
it contains *two* rows of chips (one row on each side of the strip)
and is called a **Dual In-line Memory Module (DIMM)**.

If the strip is old-fashioned and weird,
it pops into a series of pinholes instead of a slot
and is called a **Single In-line Pin Package (SIPP)**.

Here's what SIMMs and DIMMs cost:

$3 for a SIMM that holds   8 megabytes
$4 for a SIMM that holds 16 megabytes

$6 for a DIMM that holds   64 megabytes
$7 for a DIMM that holds 128 megabytes
$8 for a DIMM that holds 256 megabytes
$10 for a DIMM that holds 512 megabytes
$21 for a DIMM that holds 1024 megabytes, which is 1 gigabyte
$39 for a DIMM that holds 2048 megabytes, which is 2 gigabytes
$69 for a DIMM that holds 4098 megabytes, which is 4 gigabytes

---

You can get those prices from discount dealers, such as:

Company	Phone
Spartan Technologies	888-393-0340 or 847-364-9900
JDR Microdevices	800-538-5000 or 408-494-1400
Chip Merchant	800-426-6375 ir 619-268-4774
Memory Man	800-MEGABYTE, 504-818-2717

Some computers use SIMMs containing a set of just 2, 3, or 4 chips. That set of special chips imitates 8 or 9 normal chips.

In old-fashioned computers,
each SIMM fits into a motherboard slot by using 30 big pins.

In computers that are more modern, each SIMM uses 72 big pins instead.

The typical DIMM uses 168, 184, or 240 big pins.

A **nanosecond** is a billionth of a second. The typical SIMM contains chips that are fast: they retrieve info in 60 nanoseconds. Some SIMMs and DIMMs contain chips that are even faster: 10 nanoseconds.

Dynamic versus static

A RAM chip is either **dynamic** or **static**.

If it's **dynamic**, it stores data for just 2 milliseconds. After the 2 milliseconds, the electrical charges that represent the data dissipate and become too weak to detect.

When you buy a PC board containing dynamic RAM chips, the PC board also includes a **refresh circuit**. The refresh circuit automatically reads the data from the dynamic RAM chips, then rewrites the data onto the chips before 2 milliseconds go by. Every 2 milliseconds, the refresh circuit reads the data from the chips and rewrites the data, so that the data stays refreshed.

If a chip is **static** instead of dynamic, the electrical charge never dissipates, so you don't need a refresh circuit. (But you must still keep the power turned on.)

In the past, computer designers used just static RAM because they feared dynamic RAM's refresh circuit wouldn't work. But now refresh circuits are reliable, and the most popular kind of RAM is dynamic.

Dynamic RAM is called **DRAM** (pronounced "dee ram"). Static RAM is called **SRAM** (pronounced "ess ram").

Faster circuitry

The circuitry on SIMM and DIMM cards has improved, to let a stream of data get from the memory card to the CPU chip faster. Such improvements have fancy names:

In 1987 came the first improvement, called **Fast Page Mode (FPM)**.
In 1995 came **Extended Data Output (EDO)**, which went even faster.
In 1996 came **Synchronous DRAM (SDRAM)**, which went even faster.
In 1999 came **Rambus DRAM (RDRAM)**, which went even faster.

In 2000 came **Double Data Rate SDRAM (DDR SDRAM)**,
which had 184 pins and went about as fast as RDRAM but cost less.

In 2003 came **DDR2 SDRAM**,
which has 240 pins and transfers data twice as fast as DDR SDRAM.
Early versions of DDR2 SDRAM didn't work well;
but at the end of 2004, DDR2 SDRAM improved enough to be practical.

In 2007 came DDR3 SDRAM,
which has 240 pins and transfers data twice as fast as DDR2 SDRAM.

Compatibility

If you want to buy an extra SIMM or DIMM to put in your computer, make sure you buy the same kind as what's already in your computer. Make sure the extra SIMM or DIMM has the same number of pins (30, 72, 168, 184, or 240?), the same number of chips on it (2, 3, 4, 8, 9, or more?), operates at the same number of nanoseconds (10 or 80?), and uses the same technology (FPM, EDO, SDRAM, RDRAM, DDR, DDR2, or DDR3).

Let your memory grow

Here's how much RAM you typically get altogether:

Computer's price	Typical quantity of RAM
$10-$30	64M (64 megabytes, 67,108,864 bytes)
$30-$50	128M (128 megabytes, 134,217,728 bytes)
$50-$100	256M (256 megabytes, 268,435,456 bytes)
$100-$200	512M (512 megabytes, 536,870,912 bytes)
$200-$300	1G (1 gigabyte, 1,073,741,824 bytes)
$300-$400	2G (2 gigabytes 2,147,483,648 bytes)
$400-$800	4G (4 gigabytes, 4,294,967,296 bytes)
$800-$2000	8G (8 gigabytes, 8,589,934,592 bytes)

IBM

The original IBM PC came with just 16K of RAM, but you could add extra RAM to it. Here's how much RAM the typical IBM-compatible PC contains now:

CPU	Typical quantity of main RAM
8088	512K or 640K
286	640K or 1M
386	2M or 4M
486	4M or 8M
Pentium	16M, 32M, 64M, 128M, 256M, 512M, 1G, 2G, 3G, 4G, 6G, or 8G

To run modern IBM PC software, you need at least 2G of main RAM; but many people still use old IBM PC software that can run on 1G, 512M, 256M, or even less RAM.

How RAM is divvied

For IBM-compatible PCs having at least 1M of RAM, here's how it's divvied up.

The first 640K of main RAM is called the **base memory** (or **conventional memory**). It's the part of the RAM that the computer can handle easily and fast. The next 384K is called **upper memory**. Those two parts (the conventional memory and the upper memory) consume a total of 640K+384K, which is 1024K, which is one megabyte.

The rest of the main RAM (beyond that first megabyte) is called **extended memory**. The first 64K of extended memory is called the **high memory area (HMA)** because it's just slightly higher than the base memory and upper memory.

ROM

If a chip remembers information permanently, it's called a **read-only memory chip (ROM chip)**, because you can read the information but can't change it. The ROM chip contains permanent, eternal truths and facts put there by the manufacturer, and it remembers that info forever, even if you turn off the power.

Here's the difference between RAM and ROM:

> **RAM chips** remember, temporarily, info supplied by you.
> **ROM chips** remember, forever, info supplied by the manufacturer.

The typical computer includes many RAM chips (arranged in rows) but just a *few* ROM chips.

What kind of info is in ROM?

In your computer, one of the ROM chips contains instructions that tell the CPU what to do first when you turn the power on. Those instructions are called the **ROM bootstrap**, because they help the computer system start itself going and "pull itself up by its own bootstraps".

In the typical microcomputer, that ROM chip also contains instructions that help the CPU transfer information from the keyboard to the screen and printer. Those instructions are called the **ROM operating system** or the **ROM basic input-output system (ROM BIOS)**.

IBM

In the typical IBM-compatible PC, the motherboard contains a **ROM BIOS chip**.

That chip contains the ROM BIOS and also the ROM bootstrap. If your computer is manufactured by IBM, that chip is typically designed by IBM; if your computer is manufactured by a company imitating IBM, that chip is an imitation designed by a company such as **Phoenix**. Such a chip designed by Phoenix is called a **Phoenix ROM BIOS chip**. Other companies that designed ROM BIOS chips for clones are **Quadtel** (which was recently bought by Phoenix), **Award** (which was recently bought by Phoenix), and **American Megatrends Incorporated (AMI)** (which remains independent).

How ROM chips are made

The info in a ROM chip is said to be **burned into** the chip. To burn in the info, the manufacturer can use two methods.

One method is to burn the info into the ROM chip while the chip's being made. A ROM chip produced by that method is called a **custom ROM chip**.

An alternate method is to make a ROM chip that contains no info but can be fed info later. Such a ROM chip is called a **programmable ROM chip (PROM)**. To feed it info later, you attach it to a device called a **PROM burner**, which copies info from a RAM to the PROM.

Info burned into the PROM can't be erased, unless the PROM's a special kind: **an erasable PROM (EPROM)**. You can buy 3 types of erasable PROMs:

> An **ultraviolet-erasable PROM (UV-EPROM)** gets erased by shining an intense ultraviolet light at it for 5 minutes (or leaving the chip in sunlight for 2 weeks). That technique erases the entire chip.
>
> An **electrically erasable PROM (EEPROM)** gets erased by sending it a 25-volt shock for a tenth of a second. That technique erases just one byte in the chip: to erase *many* bytes, you must perform that technique many times.
>
> **Flash memory** gets erased by sending it a 3-volt shock for 1 second. That technique erases a whole 64-kilobyte block at once, "in a flash". It's the most popular type of erasable PROM. It's used in digital cameras (to store pictures), cell phones, and reprogrammable BIOS chips. If the flash memory pretends to be an extra hard disk & drive, it's called a **solid-state drive (SSD)** and runs faster than a traditional hard disk & drive. A solid-state drive that plugs into the system unit's USB port is called a **USB flash drive** (and is about the size of your thumb); it costs $8 for 4 gigabytes, $12 for 8 gigabytes, $20 for 16 gigabytes, at Best Buy.

Those numbers (for erasure time, voltage, and block size) are typical; but for *your* chip the numbers might be different, depending on how the chip was manufactured. After you erase an erasable PROM, you can feed it new info.

If you're a manufacturer designing a new computer, begin by using an erasable PROM, so you can make changes easily. When you decide not to make any more changes, switch to a non-erasable PROM, which costs less to manufacture. If your computer becomes so popular that you need to manufacture over 10,000 copies of the ROM, switch to a custom ROM chip, which costs more to design and "tool up for" but less to copy.

Disks

Memory comes in three popular forms: RAM chips, ROM chips, and disks.

You already learned about RAM chips and ROM chips. Let's examine disks.

A computer disk is round, like a phonograph record.

Computers can handle 4 kinds of disks:

> A **floppy disk** is made of flimsy material. It's permanently encased in a sturdy, square dust jacket.
>
> A **hard disk** is made of firmer material. It typically hides in your computer permanently, unseen.
>
> A **CD** is the same kind of compact disk that plays music.
>
> A **DVD** is the same kind of digital video disk that plays movies.

Each kind has its own advantages and disadvantages.

> **Floppy disks** are the easiest to mail to your friends: just stick the floppy disk in an envelope, perhaps with some padding. Unfortunately, floppy disks work the most slowly, and they hold the least data: the typical floppy disk holds about 1 megabyte, while the typical hard disk or CD-ROM can hold *many hundreds* of megabytes.
>
> **Hard disks** work the fastest — over 20 times faster than the other kinds! But hard disks are also the most expensive. Moreover, they typically can't be removed from your computer and therefore can't be mailed to your friends.
>
> **CD**s and **DVD**s are the best value: they cost less than 1¢ per megabyte to manufacture. But they have a frustrating limitation: the info on those disks is to edit. A DVD can hold more megabytes than a CD and therefore costs more to manufacture.

Since each kind of disk has its own advantages and disadvantages, you'll wish you had all 4 kinds.

Computer experts argue about spelling. Some experts write "**disk**", others write "**disc**".

> Most manufacturers write "disk" when referring to floppy disks or hard disks, but write "disc" when referring to CDs and DVDs. That inconsistency annoys me.
>
> To be more consistent, I'll always write "disk", even when referring to CDs. Most computer magazines (such as *PC Magazine* and *PC World*) feel the same way I do: they always write "disk". The growing tendency is to always write "disk".

Floppy disks

A **floppy disk** (or **diskette**) is round but comes permanently sealed in a square **dust jacket**. (Don't try to remove the floppy disk from its square jacket.)

The floppy disk is as thin and flimsy as a sheet of paper but is protected by the sturdy, square jacket that encases it.

Three standard sizes

Floppy disks come in three standard sizes.

The most popular size is called a **3½-inch** floppy disk, because it comes in a square jacket that's about 3½ inches on each side. (Actually, each side of the jacket is slightly *more* than 3½ inches, and the disk's diameter is slightly *less*.)

An older size, used just on older computers, is called **5¼-inch**; it comes in square jacket that's exactly 5¼ inches on each side. An even older size, **8-inch**, is used just on ancient computers that are no longer built.

Those three sizes have nicknames:

> An 8-inch floppy disk is called a **large floppy**.
> A 5¼-inch floppy disk is called a **minifloppy**.
> A 3½-inch floppy disk is called a **microfloppy**.

Here's their history:

> **8-inch** floppies were invented in the **early 1970's** by **IBM**.
>
> **5¼-inch** floppies were invented in the **late 1970's** by **Shugart Associates**, which later became part of Xerox.
>
> **3½-inch** floppies were invented in the **1980's** by **Sony**. They've become the most popular size because they're the smallest, cutest, and sturdiest. They're small enough to fit in your shirt's pocket, cute enough to impress your friends, and sturdy enough to survive when you fall on your face. They're also easy to mail, since they're small enough to fit in a standard white business envelope and sturdy enough to survive the U.S. Postal System. Yup, nice things come in small packages!

Jacket colors

The jacket of a 5¼-inch or 8-inch floppy disk is usually black. The jacket of a 3½-inch floppy disk is usually black, blue, white, or beige (very light grayish brown). If you pay a surcharge, you can get jackets that have wilder colors.

Magnetized iron

The round disk (which hides inside the square jacket) is coated with rust, so it looks brown. Since the rust is made of iron, which can be magnetized, the disk stores magnetic signals. The pattern of magnetic signals is a code representing your data.

Drives

To use a floppy disk, you must buy a **floppy-disk drive**, which is a computerized record player.

If the drive is **external**, it's a box sitting near the system unit. If the drive is **internal**, it's built into the system unit. If your computer is standard, the drive is internal, but some Macs have external drives instead.

The drive has a slit in its front side. To use the drive, push the disk (including its jacket) into the slit.

When you push your disk into the slit, don't push the disk in backwards or upside-down! **Here's how to push the disk in correctly:**

> First, notice that the disk's jacket has a label on it and also has a big oval cutout. (If the disk is 3½-inch, the cutout is covered by a metal slider.) Insert the disk so that **the oval cutout goes into the drive before the label does**. If the drive's slit is horizontal, make sure the label is on the *top* side of the jacket; if the drive is vertical, make sure the label is on the *left* side of the jacket.
>
> If the disk is 5 ½-inch or 8-inch, you must the close the drive's latch, to cover the slit and hold the disk in place. (If the disk is 3½-inch, there is no latch.) Since the slit and latch act as a **door**, closing the latch is called **closing the door**.

Then disk drive automatically positions the disk onto the turntable that's hidden inside the drive. The turntable's called the **spindle**. It can spin the disk quickly.

Like a record player, the disk drive contains an arm with a "needle" on it. The needle is called the **read-write head**, because it can read what's on the disk and also write new info onto the disk.

To transfer info to the disk, the computer lowers the read-write head onto the disk. An electrical charge passes through the head. The charge creates an electromagnetic field, which magnetizes the iron on the disk's surface. Each iron particle has its own north and south pole; the patterns formed by the north and south poles are a code that stands for the info you're storing.

Tracks As the disk spins, the head remains stationary, so that the head draws a circle on the spinning disk's surface. The circle's called a **track**.

To draw the circle, the head doesn't use ink; instead, it uses a pattern of magnetic pulses. Since your eye can't see magnetism, your eye can't see the circle; but it's there!

When you start using a blank disk, the arm puts the head near the disk's outer rim, so that the head's track (circle) is almost as wide as the disk. That track's called **track 0**.

Then the arm lifts the head, moves the head slightly closer to the virgin disk's center, and puts the head back down onto the disk again. The head draws another circular track on the disk, but this new circular track is slightly smaller than the previous one. It's called **track 1**.

Then the head draws track 2, then track 3, then track 4, and so on, until the head gets near the center of the disk, and draws the last circular track (which is smaller than the other tracks).

To organize the info on a track, the computer divides the track into **sectors**. Each "sector" is an arc of the circle.

Single-sided versus double-sided drives A modern disk drive has two read-write heads. One head uses the disk's top surface, while the other head uses the disk's bottom, so that the drive can use both sides of the disk simultaneously. That's called a **double-sided disk drive**. The drive puts info onto the disk by first using track 0 of the main side, then track 0 of the flip side, then track 1 of the main side, then track 1 of the flip side, etc.

If a disk drive is so old and primitive that it has just *one* read-write head, it uses just one side of the disk and is called a **single-sided disk drive**.

Double-sided is also called **DS** and **2-sided** and **2S**. **Single-sided** is also called **SS** and **1-sided** and **1S**.

Capacity How many kilobytes can you fit on a floppy disk? The answer depends on which kind of drive you have.

The most popular kind of drive is called a **3½-inch high-density floppy drive**. Here's how it works:

> It holds a 3½-inch floppy disk. It writes on both sides of the disk simultaneously, since it's a double-sided disk drive. It writes 80 tracks on each side. It divides each track into 18 sectors. Each sector holds "512 bytes", which is half a kilobyte, ½K.
>
> Since the disk has 2 sides, 80 tracks per side, 18 sectors per track, and ½K per sector, the disk's total capacity is "2 times 80 times 18 times ½K", which is 1440K. So altogether, the disk holds 1440K. That's called **1.44M** (where an **M** is defined as being 1000K). That's why a 3½-inch high-density floppy drive is also called a **1.44M drive**. The kind of disk you put into it is called a **1.44M floppy disk** (or a **3½-inch high-density floppy disk**). Since it holds 1.44M (which is 1440K), and since a K is 1024 bytes, the disk holds "1440 times 1024" bytes, which is 1,474,560 bytes altogether. That's a lot of bytes!
>
> Although the disk holds 1440K, some of those K are used for "bureaucratic overhead" (such as holding a directory that reminds the computer which data is where on your disk). A Mac uses just 1 sector (½K) for bureaucratic overhead. An IBM-compatible computer uses 33 sectors (16½K) for bureaucratic overhead, leaving just 1423½K (1,457,664 bytes) for your data.
>
> When you buy a blank disk to put in a 1.44M drive, make sure the disk is the right kind. Make sure the disk is 3½-inch; and to get full use of what the drive can accomplish, make sure the disk is high-density! The abbreviation for "high-density" is HD. A high-density 3½-inch disk has the letters **HD** stamped in white on its jacket; but the H overlaps the D, so it looks like this: **HD**. Also, a high-density 3½-inch disk has an extra square hole cut through its jacket.

Old computers use inferior floppy drives, whose capacities are *below* 1.44M.

> A capacity below 150K   is called **single-density (SD)**.
> A capacity above 150M but below 1M is called **double-density (DD)**.
> A capacity above 1M   is called **high-density (HD)**.

Anything below high-density is called **low-density**.

Although the jacket of a high-density 3½-inch disk has "HD" stamped on it and an extra hole punched through it, the jackets of other kinds of disks can lack any distinguishing marks. Too bad!

Popular IBM-compatible drives For IBM-compatible computers, four kinds of floppy drives have been popular:

IBM drive's name	Capacity	Details
5¼-inch double-density	360K	40 tracks per side, 9 sectors per track
5¼-inch high-density	1200K(=1.2M)	80 tracks per side, 15 sectors per track
3½-inch double-density	720K	80 tracks per side, 9 sectors per track
3½-inch high-density	1440K(=1.44M)	80 tracks per side, 18 sectors per track

Each of those IBM-compatible drives is double-sided and has ½K per sector. They're manufactured by companies such as **NEC**, **Teac**, **Chinon**, **Epson**, and **Alps**. The fanciest drives (3½-inch high-density) used to be expensive, but now you can buy them for just $29 from mail-order discount dealers.

Mac drives For Mac computers, three kinds of floppy drives have been popular:

Mac drive's name	Capacity	Details
1-sided double-density	400K	1 side, 8-12 sectors per track
2-sided double-density	800K	2 sides, 8-12 sectors per track
high-density	1440K(=1.44M)	2 sides, 18 sectors per track

Each Mac drive is 3½-inch and has 80 tracks per side, ½K per sector.

On a disk, the inner tracks have smaller diameters than the outer tracks. Mac double-density drives puts fewer sectors onto the inner tracks and put extra sectors onto the outer tracks, as follows: the outer 16 tracks are divided into 12 sectors, the next 16 tracks into 11 sectors, the next 16 into 10, the next 16 into 9, and the inner 16 into 8.

Speed In the disk drive, the disk spins quickly.

> Low-density 5¼-inch disks revolve 5 times per second.
> 8-inch disks and high-density 5¼-inch disks revolve faster: 6 times per second.
> 3½-inch disks revolve even faster: between 6½ and 10 times per second.

Buying disks

When you buy a floppy disk, make sure its size matches the size of the drive. For example, a 3½-inch disk will *not* work in a 5¼-inch drive.

If your drive is single-density or double-density, it can*not* handle high-density disks at all.

Formatting the disk Before you can use a blank floppy disk, its surface must be **formatted** (divided into tracks and sectors). Buy a disk that's been formatted already, or buy an unformatted disk and format it yourself (by typing a command on your computer's keyboard or by using the mouse).

After the disk's been formatted, you can put whatever info you wish onto the disk. Do *not* tell the drive to format that disk again. If you accidentally make the drive format the same disk again, the drive will create new tracks & sectors on the disk by erasing all the old tracks & sectors and all your old data!

Remember:

> If a disk is blank, make sure it's formatted before you use it.
> If a disk already contains info, do *not* format it; it's been formatted already.

What's a disk worth? Although you can buy a blank floppy disk for under 50¢, a disk containing info costs much more. The price depends on how valuable the info is. A disk that explains to the computer how to play a game costs about $25. A disk teaching the computer how to handle a general business task (such as accounting, filing, or correspondence) usually costs about $100. A disk containing intimate, personal data about your business's customers, suppliers, employees, and methods is worth even more, perhaps *thousands* of dollars: to compute how much it's worth to you, imagine you've lost it or it fell into the wrong hands!

Protect your disks

Most parts of a computer system are sturdy: even if you bang on the keyboard and rap your fist against the screen, you probably won't do any harm. Just one part of a computer system is delicate: the disk! Unfortunately, the magnetic signals on a disk are easy to destroy.

One way to accidentally destroy them is to put your disk near a magnet; so **keep your disk away from magnets!** For example, keep your disk away from:

> paper clips that have been in a magnetized paper-clip holder
> speakers in your stereo, TV, and phone (because speakers contain magnets)
> electric motors (because motors generate an electromagnetic field)

So to be safe, keep your disk at least *6 inches* away from paper clips, stereos, TV's, phones, and motors.

Keep your disk away from heat, because heat destroys the disk's magnetism and "melts" your data. So don't leave your disk in the hot sun or on a sunny windowsill or in the back of your car on a hot day. If your disk drive or computer feels hot, quickly lower the temperature, by getting an air conditioner or at least a fan.

A 3½-inch floppy disk comes in a strong jacket. If you're using a 5¼-inch or 8-inch floppy disk instead, beware: its jacket is too weak to protect it from pressure; don't squeeze it; don't put it under a heavy objects (such as a paperweight or book); to write a note on the disk's jacket, don't use a ballpoint pen (which crushes the disk); use a soft felt-tip pen instead.

Keep the disk away from dust. For example, don't smoke cigarettes near the disk, because the smoke becomes dust that lands on the disk and wrecks the data.

Keep the disk dry. If you must transport a disk during a rainstorm, put the disk in a plastic bag. Never drink coffee or soda near the disk: your drink might spill.

To handle the disk, **touch just the disk's jacket, not the brown disk itself**. Holes in the jacket let you see the brown disk inside; don't put your fingers in the holes.

Write-protect notch When you buy a blank 5¼-inch or 8-inch floppy disk, the disk comes in a square black jacket. Since the jacket's square, it has four sides; but one of the sides has a notch cut into it. You can cover the notch, by sticking a plastic **tab** over it. The tab has a gummed back, so you can stick it on the disk easily and cover the notch. You get the tab free when you buy the disk.

(For a 3½-inch disk, the notch is different: it's a square hole near the jacket's corner but not on the jacket's edge. To cover it, you use a black slider instead of a tab. On old Apple Mac disks, the slider was red instead of black.)

Whenever you ask the computer to change the info on the disk, the drive checks whether you've covered the notch.

For a 5¼-inch disk, the normal situation is for the notch to be uncovered. For a 3½-inch or 8-inch disk, the normal situation is for the notch to be covered.

If the situation's normal, the computer will obey your command: it will change the info on the disk as you wish. But **if the situation's abnormal (because the notch is covered when it should be uncovered, or is uncovered when it should be covered), the computer will refuse to change the disk's info**.

Suppose your disk contains valuable info, and you're afraid some idiot will accidentally erase or alter that info. To prevent such an accident, make the situation abnormal (by changing whether the notch is covered), so that the computer will refuse to change the disk's info. It will refuse to erase the disk; it will refuse to add new info to the disk; it will refuse to alter the disk; it will refuse to write onto the disk. The disk is protected from being changed; it's protected from being written on. The disk is **write-protected** (or **locked**).

Since the tab affects whether the disk is write-protected, the tab is called a **write-protect tab**, and the notch is called a **write-protect notch**.

When you buy a disk that already contains info, the disk usually comes write-protected, to protect you from accidentally erasing the info. So if you buy a 5¼-inch floppy disk that already contains info, it might come with a write-protect tab already covering the notch, to write-protect the disk.

Instead of creating a notch and then covering it with a tab, some manufacturers save money by getting special disks that have no notch. The computer treats a notchless disk the same way as a disk whose notch is covered.

Backup Even if you handle your disk very carefully, eventually something will go wrong, and some of the info on your disk will get wrecked accidentally.

To prepare for that inevitable calamity, tell the computer to copy all info from the disk onto a blank disk, so that the blank disk becomes an exact copy of the original. Store the copy far away from the original: store it in another room, or — better yet — another building, or — better yet — another city.

The copy is called a **backup**. Use the backup disk when the original disk gets wrecked.

Making a backup disk is like buying an insurance policy: it protects you against disasters.

When you buy a floppy that already contains software, try copying the floppy before you begin using it.

> If you're lucky, the computer will make the backup copy without any hassles. If you're unlucky, the software company has put instructions on the floppy that make the computer *refuse* to copy the disk, because the company fears you'll illegally make copies to your friends. A floppy that the computer refuses to copy (and which is therefore protected against illegal copying) is called **copy-protected**. A floppy you can copy is called **copyable** (or **unprotected**).

Super-capacity floppies

A standard floppy disk holds up to 1.44M. **Super-capacity** floppy disks hold much more and come in three styles:

Type	Size	Capacity	Price
Zip disk	4"	100M	$89 drive by Iomega, $11 disk
Zip 250 disk	4"	250M	$187 drive by Iomega, $17 disk
LS-120 disk	3½"	120M	$100 drive by Imation, $10 disk

Super-capacity floppy disks used to be popular, but modern computers use editable CD disks instead, which cost less and hold more.

Hard disks

Hard disks are better than floppy disks in 3 ways:

> **Hard disks are sturdier than floppies.**
> Hard disks are hard and firm; they don't flop or jiggle.
> They're more reliable than floppies.
>
> **Hard drives hold more information than floppy drives.**
> The typical floppy drive holds 1.44 megabytes.
> The typical hard drive holds 500 gigabytes (which is 500,000 megabytes).
>
> **Hard drives work faster than floppies.**
> The typical floppy disk rotates between 5 and 10 times per second.
> The typical hard disk rotates between 90 and 167 times per second.

Hard drives cost more than floppy drives. The typical floppy drive costs $29; the typical hard drive costs about $55.

Unfortunately, the typical hard disk can't be removed from its drive: the hard disk is **non-removable**, stuck inside its drive permanently. (Hard disks that are **removable** are rare.)

Since the typical hard disk is stuck forever inside its drive, in one fixed place, it's called a **fixed disk**.

Though the typical floppy-disk drive holds just one disk at a time, the typical hard-disk drive holds a whole **stack** of disks and handles all the stack's disks simultaneously, by using many arms and read-write heads. For example, an 80-gigabyte hard drive holds a non-removable stack of disks, and the entire stack totals 80 gigabytes. Each disk in the stack is called a **platter**. If your hard drive is the rare kind that holds a *removable* stack of disks, the stack comes in a **cartridge** or **pack** that you can remove from the hard drive.

Back in 1977, the typical hard disk had a 14-inch diameter and was removable. The hard-disk drive was a big cabinet (the size of a top-loading washing machine), cost about $30,000, held 0.1 gigabytes, and required a minicomputer or mainframe.

Life's gotten smaller! Now the typical hard disk has a diameter of just 3½ inches, a height of just 1 inch, costs $55, holds 500 gigabytes, and fits in a desktop microcomputer. Some notebook computers use even smaller hard disks, whose diameter is just 2½ inches.

IBM drive letters

The typical IBM-compatible computer has both a floppy drive and a hard drive. The floppy drive is called **drive A**; the hard drive is called **drive C**.

> If the computer has *two* floppy drives, the main floppy drive is called **drive A**; the other floppy drive is called **drive B**.
>
> If the computer has *two* hard drives, the main hard drive is called **drive C**; the other hard drive is called **drive D**.

Copy between disks

When you buy a program, it usually comes on a floppy disk (or CD or DVD). Put that disk into its drive then copy the program from that disk to the hard disk. (To copy using an IBM-compatible PC, type the word "copy" or "install" or "setup" or use your mouse. To find out which to do and when, follow the instructions in the manual that came with the program.)

Then use just the copy on the hard disk (which holds more info and works faster than a floppy disk or CD or DVD).

Like floppy disks, hard disks are coated with magnetized iron. Floppy disks and hard disks are both called **magnetic disks**. Like floppy disks, hard disks are in constant danger of losing their magnetic signals — and your data!

Protect yourself! Every day, take any new info that's on your hard disk and copy it onto a pile of floppy disks (or CDs or DVDs or a USB flash drive), so you've created a **backup copy** of what was new on your hard disk.

To avoid giant disasters, avoid creating giant files. If you're writing a book and want to store it on your hard disk, split the book into chapters, and make each chapter a separate file, so if you accidentally say "delete" you'll lose just one chapter instead of your entire masterpiece.

How the head works

In a floppy drive, the read-write head (the "needle") touches the spinning floppy disk. But in a *hard* drive, the read-write head does *not* touch the spinning hard disk; instead, it hovers over the disk, very close to the disk (just a tiny fraction of an inch above the disk), so close that the read-write head can detect the disk's magnetism and alter it.

Since the head doesn't actually touch the disk, there isn't any friction, so the head and the disk don't suffer from any wear-and-tear. A hard-disk system therefore lasts longer than a floppy-disk system and is more reliable.

Winchester drives In all modern hard drives, the head acts as a miniature airplane: it **flies** above the disk.

It flies at a very low altitude: a tiny fraction of an inch. The only thing keeping the head off the rotating disk is a tiny cushion of air — a breeze caused by the disk's motion.

When you unplug the drive, the disk stops rotating, so the breeze stops, and the head comes to rest on a **landing strip**, which is like a miniature airport.

Such a drive is called a **flying-head drive**. It's also called a **Winchester drive**, because "Winchester" was IBM's secret code-name for that technology when IBM was inventing it.

The head flies at an altitude that's extremely low — about a ten-thousandth of an inch! That's even smaller than the width of a particle of dust or cigarette smoke! So if any dust or smoke lands onto the disk, the head will smash against it, and you'll have a major disaster.

To prevent such a disaster, the entire Winchester drive is sealed airtight, to prevent any dust or smoke from entering the drive and getting onto the disk. Since the drive is sealed, you can't remove the disks (unless you buy an extremely expensive Winchester drive that has a flexible seal).

Speed

Here's how the computer retrieves data from the drive.

First, the drive's head moves to the correct track.

> The time that the head spends moving is called the **seek time**. Since that time depends on how far the head is from the correct track, it depends on where the correct track is *and where the head is moving from*.
>
> According to calculus, on the average the head must move across a third of the tracks to reach the correct track. That's why the time to traverse a third of the tracks is called the **average seek time**.
>
> A **millisecond (ms)** is a thousandth of a second. In a typical hard drive, the average seek time is about 9 milliseconds. (In older hard drives that are no longer made, the average seek time was 28 milliseconds.)

After the head reaches the correct track, it must wait for the disk to rotate, until the correct sector reaches the head.

> That rotation time is called the **latency**. On the average, the head must wait for half a revolution; so the **average latency time** is a half-revolution. The typical cheap hard drive rotates 5400 times per minute, which is 90 times per second, so a half-revolution takes half of a 90th of a second, so it's a 180th of a second, so it's about .006 seconds, which is 6 milliseconds.
>
> If you add the average seek time to the average latency time, you get the total **average access time**. So for a typical cheap hard drive, the average access time = 9 milliseconds seek + 6 milliseconds latency = 15 milliseconds.
>
> For a higher quality hard drive, the rotation speed is 7200 rpm (instead of 5400), giving 120 rotations per second (instead of 90), an average latency of 4 milliseconds (instead of 6), and an average access time of 13 milliseconds (instead of 15).
>
> During the last few years, hard drive manufacturers have become dishonest: they say the "average access time" is 9 milliseconds, when they should actually say the "average seek time" is 9 milliseconds.

After the head finally reaches the correct sector, you must wait for the head to read the data. If the data consumes *several* sectors, you must wait for the head to read all those sectors.

Manufacturers

For many years, most hard drives for microcomputers were built by 4 American companies: **Seagate Technology (ST)**, **Quantum**, **Western Digital**, and **Connor**:

> **Seagate** was the first of those companies to make hard drives for microcomputers, and it set the standard that the other companies had to follow. New Seagate drives work fine, though Seagate's older models were often noisy and unreliable.
>
> **Quantum** became famous by building the hard drives used in Apple's Mac computers. Quantum also built drives for IBM PC clones. Quantum drives are excellent.
>
> **Western Digital** invented hard drives that cost less. They're popular in cheap clones and discount computer stores.
>
> **Conner** was the first company to invent hard drives tiny enough to fit in a laptop or notebook computer. Seagate had ignored the laptop/notebook market too long, and Conner's popularity zoomed up fast. Conner became the fastest-growing company in the history of American industry!

Other popular manufacturers of hard drives have been America's **Maxtor** & **Micropolis**, Japan's **NEC** & **Toshiba** & **Fujitsu** & **Hitachi**, and Korea's **Samsung**.

Companies have been merging:

> Seagate bought Connor's hard-drive business.
>
> Toshiba bought Fujitsu's hard-drive business.
>
> Maxtor bought Quantum's hard-drive business.
> Then Seagate bought Maxtor' hard drive business.
>
> Micropolis gave up: it went out of business.
>
> Western Digital is trying to buy Hitachi's hard-drive business.
> Seagate is trying to buy Samsung's hard-drive business.
> If those purchases are approved by monopoly regulators, the only hard-drive manufacturers left will be Western Digital (48% of all drives), Seagate (41%), and Toshiba (11%).

When buying a hard drive, you might also need to buy a **hard-drive controller**.

How many sectors?

How many sectors do you get on a track?

Early schemes Back in the 1980's, the typical hard-drive controller for IBM-compatible computers put 17 sectors on each track. That scheme was called the **Seagate Technology 506 with Modified Frequency Modulation (ST506 MFM)**.

An improved scheme, which squeezed 26 sectors onto each track, was called the **ST506 with Run Length Limited (ST506 RLL)**. A further improvement, which squeezed 34 sectors onto each track, was called the **Enhanced Small Device Interface (ESDI)**.

Squeezing extra sectors onto each track increases the drive's **capacity** (total number of megabytes) and also the **transfer rate** (the number of sectors that the head reads per rotation or per second).

All those schemes — MFM, RLL, and ESDI — have become obsolete.

IDE Now the most popular scheme is called **Integrated Drive Electronics (IDE)**. Like ESDI, it squeezes 34 sectors onto each track; but it uses special tricks to transfer data faster.

The original version of IDE was limited to small drives: up to 528M.

Western Digital invented an improved version, called **Enhanced IDE (EIDE)**, which could handle bigger drives. It also went faster: it transferred 16.6 megabytes per second. Seagate invented competing methods (called **Fast ATA-2** and **Fast ATA-3**), which also transfer 16.6 megabytes per second.

Those technologies (Enhanced IDE, Fast ATA-2, and Fast ATA-3) all got replaced by **Ultra**, which transfers twice as fast: 33.3 megabytes per second. The Ultra version of EIDE is called **Ultra IDE**; the Ultra version of Fast ATA is called **Ultra ATA**.

Then an even faster Ultra ATA was invented, called **Ultra ATA-100**: it transfers 100 megabytes per second instead of 33.3. Maxtor invented an even faster Ultra ATA, called **Ultra ATA-133**, transferring 133 megabytes per second.

All those ATA technologies (Fast ATA-2, Fast ATA-3, Ultra ATA, Ultra ATA-100, and Ultra ATA-133) are called **Parallel ATA (PATA)**. They're being replaced by an even faster type, called **Serial ATA (SATA)**. The first SATA controllers, called **SATA/150**, transferred 150 megabytes per second. Newer SATA controllers, called **SATA 2** or **SATA/300**, transfer 300 megabytes per second, 3 giga**bits** per second. The newest SATA controllers, called **SATA 3** or **SATA/600**, transfer 600 megabytes per second, 6 giga**bits** per second.

SCSI A totally different fast scheme is the **Small Computer System Interface** (or **SCSI**, which is pronounced "scuzzy"). For example, a fast version of SCSI, called **Ultra 160 SCSI**, transfers 160 megabytes per second.

During the 1980's and early 1990's, SCSI was used on most Mac hard drives and the biggest IBM-compatible hard drives, because IDE drives were too slow and held just a few megabytes. But during the late 1990's, IDE drives became faster, bigger and cheaper, so SCSI drives became unpopular.

IBM-compatible drives Modern, popular IBM-compatible hard drives cost **about 10¢ per gigabyte**. For example:

A 500-gigabyte drive costs about $50.
A 1000-gigabyte drive costs about $100.
A 2000-gigabyte drive costs about $200.
A 3000-gigabyte drive costs about $300.

Here are the prices charged by **Best Buy (BB)** and **Staples**:

Capacity	Speed	Cache	Controller	Brand	Model number	Price
320 gigs	5400 rpm	8M	SATA/300	Western Dig.	WD 3200 ANC	$50 BB
500 gigs	7200 rpm	16M	SATA/300	Seagate	ST3 500 641AS-RK	$60 Staples
1000 gigs	7200 rpm	16M	SATA/300	Seagate	ST3 1000 5N1A1AS	$80 Staples
1000 gigs	7200 rpm	32M	SATA/300	Western Dig.	WD 0010 HNC	$85 BB
2000 gigs	7200 rpm	32M	SATA/300	Western Dig.	WD 20000 LSRTL	$170 BB
3000 gigs	7200 rpm	64M	SATA/600	Seagate	ST3 3000 5N1	$300 BB

In that chart, "gigs" means "gigabytes". (When discussing hard drives, a "**gigabyte**" is defined to mean "1000 megabytes". A "**terabyte**" is defined to mean "1000 gigabytes".)

For Seagate drives, model number's main part is the number of gigs.
For Western Digital drives, the model number is 10 times the number of gigs.

Besides buying the hard drive, you must also buy a controller card to put in the computer's slot (unless your computer contains such a card already).

The drive's **cache** (or **buffer**) is RAM chips holding copies of the sectors you used recently — so if you want to look at those sectors again, you can read from the RAM chips (which are fast) instead of waiting for the disk to spin (which is slow).

Those were the prices when this book went to press in June 2011. By the time you read this book, prices might be even lower.

Western Digital also makes **Caviar Green** hard drives, which have many great characteristics (more megabytes, lower cost, and use less electricity) but rotate slower.

External drives A hard drive's price depends on whether the drive is **internal** (fits inside the computer) or **external** (comes in a separate box that you put next to the computer). Internal drives are faster; but if your computer is small or filled up, you must buy an external drive instead. The typical external drive plugs into a USB port.

When this book went to press in June 2011, here's what Best Buy and Staples charged for external USB drives:

Capacity	Manufacturer	Price
500 gigs	Verbatim	$55 at Staples
1000 gigs	Verbatim	$75 at Best Buy
2000 gigs	Seagate	$110 at Best Buy
3000 gigs	Western Digital	$150 at Best Buy

History During the last 20 years, hard-drive prices have dropped — and hard-drive capacities have grown — dramatically! Here's what size hard drive you could get for about $100, $200, $300, and $1000 each year:

Year	$100	$200	$300	$1000
1992		50 M (= .05 G)	90 M (= .09 G)	340 M (= .34 G)
1993		130 M (= .13 G)	250 M (= .25 G)	1 G
1994		340 M (= .34 G)	420 M (= .42 G)	1¾ G
1995		850 M (= .85 G)	1 G	4 G
1996		1 G	2 G	4 G
1997	1 G	3½ G	5 G	9 G
1998	2½ G	8 G	12 G	
1999	6 G	13 G	20 G	
2000	20 G	30 G	46 G	
2001	40 G	80 G		
2002	60 G	120 G		
2003	80 G	180 G		
2004	120 G	200 G		
2005	160 G	300 G		
2006	200 G	400 G		
2007	250 G	500 G		
2008	320 G	640 G		
2009	500 G	1000 G		
2010	1000 G	2000 G		
2011	2000 G			

Buy a big drive Buy a drive that holds many gigabytes. It will give you more peace of mind than a smaller drive, and it will also act faster.

For example, suppose you want to store 500 gigabytes of info, and you're debating whether to buy a 500-gigabyte drive or a 1000-gigabyte drive. Suppose each drive is advertised as having a 9-millisecond seek time. The 1000-gigabyte drive will nevertheless act faster. Here's why....
Suppose you buy the 1000-gigabyte drive and use just the first 500 gigabytes of it. Since you're using just the first half of the drive, the head needs to move just half as far as usual; so over the 500-gigabyte part that you're using, the effective average seek time is just half as much as usual: it's 4½ milliseconds!

RAID

If you need more than 500 gigabytes, attach several hard drives together, and make the drives all act simultaneously. The group of drives is called a **drive array** and acts as one huge drive. That technique is called **RAID** (which originally stood for **Redundant Array of Inexpensive Disks** but now stands for **Redundant Array of Independent Disks**).

Here are RAID's most popular versions:

RAID level 0, called **data striping**, is the fastest. It divides each long file into several **stripes**. A stripe's first part is put onto drive 1, second part onto drive 2, third part onto drive 3, etc., simultaneously, so that the stripe spans across all the drives. Each drive therefore has to handle just *part* of each stripe and just *part* of each file and finishes faster.

RAID level 1, called **data mirroring**, is the safest. It uses just two drives. It puts each file onto drive 1 and simultaneously puts a backup copy of the file onto drive 2, so that drive 2 always contains an exact copy of what's on drive 1. That way, if drive 1 ever fails, the computer can get the info from drive 2.

RAID level 3, called **shared data parity**, is more sophisticated: it's a clever compromise between RAID level 0 and RAID level 1. Like RAID level 0, it divides each long file into stripes, puts a stripe's first part onto drive 1, second part onto drive 2, third part onto drive 3, etc.; but onto the final drive it puts **parity info** instead, which is info that the computer uses to double-check the accuracy of the other drives.

RAID level 5, called **distributed data parity**, is the most sophisticated. It resembles RAID level 3; but instead of putting all the parity info onto the *last* disk, it puts the first stripe's parity info onto the *first* disk, the second stripe's parity info onto the *second* disk, etc., so that the parity info is distributed among *all* the disks, to prevent the last disk from getting overworked and bogging down the whole system.

Instead of buying a program on a floppy disk, you can buy a program on the same kind of **compact disk (CD)** that holds music.

A CD that holds music is called a **music CD** (or **audio CD**).
A CD that holds computer data instead is called a **computer CD** (or **data CD**). Since the computer data on it cannot be erased, a computer-data CD is also called a **CD read-only memory (CD-ROM)**.

To make your computer read the CD-ROM disk, put the disk into a **CD-ROM drive**, which is a souped-up version of the kind of CD player that plays music.

Like an ordinary CD player, a CD-ROM drive uses just **optics**. No magnetism is involved. The drive just shines a laser beam at the shiny disk and notices, from the reflection, which indentations (**pits**) are on the disk. The pattern of pits is a code that represents the data. So a CD-ROM drive is an example of an **optical disk drive**.

To put the disk into the drive, press a button on the drive. That makes the drive stick its tongue out at you! The tongue is called a **tray**. Put the disk onto the tray, so that the disk's label is face-up. (If the drive is old-fashioned, you must put the disk into a **caddy** first; but the most modern drives are **caddyless**.) Then push the tray back into the drive. Finally, use the keyboard or mouse to give a command that makes the computer taste what you've put on its tongue.

IBM drive letters

Here's how a modern IBM-compatible computer assigns the drives:

Drive A is a 3½-inch floppy drive (1.44M).
Drive B is a 5¼-inch floppy drive (1.2M).
Drive C is a hard drive (about 200G).
Drive D is typically a CD-ROM drive (or a drive that's even fancier).

If your computer has *two* hard drives, here's what happens instead: the first hard drive is C, the second hard drive is D, and the CD-ROM drive is the next letter (E).

If you bought just *one* hard drive but plan to buy a second hard drive later, you can leave "drive D" empty and make the CD-ROM drive be E.

Size

The standard CD-ROM disk has a diameter of 12 centimeters (which is about 5 inches) and holds 650 megabytes.

The CD-ROM disk is single-sided: all the data is on the disk's *bottom* side — the side that doesn't have a label.

The disk contains 2 billion pits, all arranged into a single spiral (like the groove on a phonograph record). If you were to unravel the spiral, to make it a straight line, it would be 3 miles long!

On a CD, each "song" is called a **track**; it can hold music or computer data. Each "song" (track) can be as long or as short as you wish. The CD can hold 99 tracks, totaling an hour of music (for an audio CD) or 650 megabytes (for a CD-ROM disk).

650 megabytes is a lot! It's about 450 times as much as a high-density 1.44M floppy! Yes, a single CD-ROM disk can hold as much info as a stack of 450 high-density 1.44M floppies!

Since a CD-ROM disk holds so much, a single CD-ROM can hold a whole library (including encyclopedias, dictionaries, other reference materials, famous novels, programs, artwork, music, and videos). It's the ideal way to distribute massive quantities of info! Moreover, a CD-ROM disk costs less than $1 to manufacture (once you've bought the appropriate CD-ROM-making equipment, which costs several hundred dollars).

CD-ROM disks store info differently than floppy & hard disks:

On a CD, each track is part of a spiral. On a floppy disk or hard disk, each track is a circle.
On a CD, different tracks have different lengths and hold a different number of bytes. On a typical floppy disk or hard disk, all tracks have the same number of bytes as each other.

Speed

When buying a CD-ROM drive, the most important factor to consider is the drive's speed.

Transfer rate The speed at which the drive spins is called the **transfer rate**. The higher, the better!

On the first CD-ROM drives that were invented, the transfer rate was the same speed as a music CD's: **150 kilobytes per second**. That speed is called **1X**.

Then came drives that could spin twice as fast (300 kilobytes per second). That's called **double speed** or **2X**.
Then came **3X** drives, then **4X**, then **4½X**, then **6X**, then **8X**, then **10X**, then **12X**. During the summer of 1997, most drives sold were 12X, which transfers "12 times as fast as 150 kilobytes per second", which is 1800 kilobytes/second.
Then came drives that were even faster. For example, you could buy a drive called **24X/12X** (or **24X maximum** or **24X max**), whose outer tracks are read at a maximum speed of 24X, though the inner tracks are read at just 12X.

Now you can buy drives that go much faster: **56X max**!

Seek time The average time it takes for the head to move to the correct track is called the **average seek time**.

The lower the average seek time, the better! In modern CD-ROM drives, the average seek time is 100 milliseconds or less.

Example The cheapest good CD-ROM drive is the **BenQ CD-656A**. It has a fast transfer rate (56X max), a fast seek time (just 90 milliseconds), a big cache (128K), and costs just $18 from discount dealers, such as CompUSA (a chain of discount stores, 800-Comp-USA, www.compusa.com).

That price is for an **internal drive**, which fit inside the computer's system unit. If your system unit is filled up and doesn't have any room left to insert an internal drive, you must buy an **external drive** instead, which sits outside the system unit and costs more.

Caring for your CD-ROM disks

A CD-ROM disk's main enemy is dirt.

Like a music CD, a CD-ROM disk comes in a clear square box, called the **jewel box**. To use the CD-ROM disk, remove it from the jewel box and put the disk into the drive. When you finish using the disk, put it back into the jewel box, which keeps the dust off the disk.
When putting the CD-ROM disk into or out of a drive, don't put your fingers on the disk's surface: instead, **hold the disk by its edge**, so your greasy fingerprints don't get on the disk's surface.
Once a month, gently **wipe any dust** off the CD-ROM disk's bottom surface (where the data is). While wiping, be gentle and don't get your greasy fingerprints on the disk. Start in the middle and wipe toward the outer edge.
For example, my assistant and I were getting lots of error messages when using a CD-ROM disk we bought from Microsoft. I was going to phone Microsoft to complain, but my assistant asked, "What about dust?" I flipped the CD-ROM disk over and sure enough, a big ball of dust was on the disk's bottom side. I wiped it off. That CD-ROM disk has worked perfectly ever since.

Don't put fluids on the disk. Fluids that clean phonograph records will *wreck* CD-ROM disks.

If you want to write on the disk, **use a felt-tipped pen** (not a ballpoint or pencil). Don't stick any labels on the disk.

The typical CD-ROM disk will last about 12 years. Then the aluminum on its surface will start to oxidize (corrode), and the CD will become unreadable.

CD-R

You can create your own CD's, in the privacy of your home, if you buy a **CD-Recordable drive (CD-R drive)**. It can write onto blank **CD-R disks**, which used to be expensive but now are cheap.

The cheapest way to get the CD-R disks is to look for sales at chain stores. For example, while I was writing this book in July 2007, Circuit City was having a sale where you get 100 CD-R disks for $12, making the disks cost just 12¢ each. **OfficeMax** (a chain of discount stores) sometimes has a deal where you get CD-R disks free, after rebate.

Although a CD-R drive can write onto a disk, it can*not* erase or edit what you wrote.

CD-RW

For more flexibility, you can buy a **CD-ReWritable drive (CD-RW drive)**, which can write onto a blank **CD-RW disk** and then edit what you wrote. CD-RW drives used to be expensive, but now they've become nearly as cheap as CD-R drives, so nobody bothers selling CD-R drives anymore.

Example An example of a cheap good CD-RW drive is the **Memorex 32023257**:

> It writes at a speed of **52X onto CD-R disks** (which cannot be erased) and **32X onto CD-RW disks** (which can be erased but cost more and act slowly; it **reads at 52X** (from CD-ROM, CD-R, or CD-RW disks), so it's called a **52×32×52 drive**. You can get it for $50 from discounters (such as CompUSA's Internet Web site at www.CompUSA.com or 800-CompUSA). It comes in a cardboard box that also includes a blank CD-R disk, a blank CD-RW disk, and a program called **Nero** (which helps you wrote onto CD-R and CD-RW disks).

During some weeks, there are discounts on other CD-RW drives. For example, when I was writing this book in May 2004, Circuit City was selling a 52x32x52 CD-RW drive (manufactured by **Lite-On**) for just $30 ($70 minus $40 rebates).

You can get blank CD-RW disks for 62¢ each if you buy 25 at a time from discount dealers such as **DiscountOfficeItems.com**. You get that price if you ask for the **Imation** brand of CD-RW disks. Like most CD-RW disks, they're officially rated just for 4X rewriting; faster-rated disks cost more.

Creating your own CD (by using a CD-R or CD-RW drive) is called **CD burning** (because the data is **burned into** the CD), so CD-R and CD-RW drives are called **CD burners**.

DVD

In 1997, the electronics industry began selling an improved kind of CD, called a **Digital Versatile Disk (DVD)**. It looks like a standard-size CD but holds more info.

Unlike a standard CD, which holds just an hour of music or 650M of data, a standard DVD can hold a 2-hour movie (including the video and sound) or 4.7G of data. Since it can hold a movie, some movie lovers call it a "Digital Video Disk", but it's more versatile than just that!

Improved DVD

A DVD can be recorded on just the bottom side (like a CD) or on both sides. (To use the second side, you must remove the disk from the drive and flip the disk upside down, like you'd flip a phonograph record.) A dual-sided DVD can hold 9.4G of data.

An improved technology, called **dual-layer DVD**, puts nearly *two* layers of data on each side, so you get 8.5G per side, 17G total.

A DVD that contains computer data (instead of a movie or music) is called a **DVD-ROM disk**. To use it, put it in a **DVD-ROM drive**, which costs just *slightly* more than a CD-ROM drive. Every DVD-ROM drive can read DVD-ROM disks and also standard CD-ROM disks. Unfortunately, just *modern* DVD-ROM drives can also read CD-R and CD-RW disks.

TigerDirect.com sells a DVD-ROM drive made by **Lite-On** for just $19. That drive is called "18X" because it rotates 18 times as fast as a plain DVD drive. The drive also acts as a 48X CD-ROM drive. Its seek time is 105 milliseconds for DVD, 95 milliseconds for CD. It includes a 198K cache.

Create your own DVD

To create and edit your *own* DVDs in your own home, buy a **DVD+RW drive**. It can write onto DVD+RW disks, DVD+R disks, CD-RW disks, and CD-R disks.

Get a DVD+RW drive, not a DVD-RW drive (which uses different disks, called DVD-RW disks), or get a **DVD±RW drive** (which can handle both DVD+RW and DVD-RW disks).

When this book went to press in December 2010, discount dealers (such as Staples, Best Buy, Office Max, TigerDirect.com, and DiscountOfficeItems.com) were offering these prices:

> a DVD±RW drive for $20
> blank DVD+RW disks for 71¢ each
> blank DVD+R disks for 20¢ each

I/O devices

To get info into and out of the computer, you need **input/output devices (I/O devices)**. Here they are....

Screens

The computer's **screen** is an ordinary TV (the same kind you watch Bill Cosby on) or *resembles* a TV. The screen shows what you typed on the keyboard and also shows the computer's responses. The computer's screen is also called the **display**.

Standard monitors

A standard computer uses a kind of screen that's called a **standard monitor**. A standard monitor resembles a TV but produces a sharper picture and costs more. It has no antenna and no dial for selecting channels: the only channel you get is "computer". Like a TV, it contains a picture tube. The picture tube (in a TV or standard monitor) is called a **cathode-ray tube (CRT)**.

Stand-alone versus built-in The monitor can be either **stand-alone** or **built-in**.

If your computer is standard, its monitor is **stand-alone**, which means the monitor sits separately from the system unit. Before buying a computer that uses a stand-alone monitor, ask whether the computer's price includes the monitor: the monitor might cost extra. The monitor's price includes a cable that runs from the monitor to the system unit.

Some Macs and other non-standard computers use a **built-in monitor**, which is a screen that's permanently screwed into the front of the computer's system unit. That included screen makes the system unit heavy and big so it's difficult for a thief to lift, hide, and steal. Built-in monitors are particularly popular in public schools in high-crime areas. Most other organizations prefer stand-alone monitors, which are easier to move (to a more convenient place on your desk or a more convenient room) and which are easier to replace (if you need repairs or you want to switch to a fancier monitor).

Colors versus monochrome When buying a TV, you ask for either "color" or "black-and-white". Similarly, when buying a computer monitor, ask for either **color** or **monochrome**. A color monitor displays all colors of the rainbow; a monochrome monitor displays just black-and-light.

Four kinds of monochrome monitors have been popular:

A	**paper-white monitor**	displays black and white.
An	**amber monitor**	displays black and yellow.
A	**green-screen monitor**	displays black and light green.
A	**gray-scale monitor**	displays many shades of gray.

But now monochrome monitors are all obsolete: standard computer use color monitors instead, which cost between $85 and $450.

How colors are produced On the monitor's screen, the picture shown is made of thousands of tiny dots. Each tiny dot is called a **picture's element (pixel)**.

In a color monitor, each pixel is made of three phosphors: one kind glows **red** if hit by an electron; another kind turns **green**, another kind turns **blue**.

Inside the monitor, 3 **guns** can shoot beams of electrons at the phosphors. The **red gun** can shoot electrons at the red phosphors (to make them glow red); the **green gun** can shoot at the green phosphors (to make them glow green); the **blue gun** can shoot at the red phosphors (to make them glow blue).

To make a pixel turn **red**, the computer tells the monitor's red gun to shoot at that pixel's red phosphor, so the pixel's phosphor glows red. To make a pixel turn **green**, the computer makes the monitor's green gun shoot at the pixel's green phosphor. **Blue** is similar.

To make a pixel be very bright, the computer makes the monitor's 3 guns all fire at the same pixel, so the pixel's red, green, and blue phosphors all glow simultaneously. That makes the pixel be very bright —a hot **white** flash.

To make a pixel be **black**, the computer makes *none* of the guns fire at the pixel.

To make the pixel be **cyan (greenish blue)**, the computer makes the green and blue guns fire simultaneously at the pixel. To make the pixel be **magenta (purplish red)**, the computer makes the red and blue guns fire. To make the pixel be **yellow**, the computer makes the red and green guns fire (which produces a color that's brighter and lighter than red or green alone).

That's how to produce 8 colors: red, green, blue, white, black, cyan, magenta, and yellow.

Although a primitive monitor produces just those 8 colors, a modern monitor can produce extra colors by varying the strength of the electron beams. For example, instead of the red gun being either "on" or "off", it can be "completely on", "partly on", or "off".

Here are the names for the different levels of monitors:

A **primitive RGB monitor** produces just **8 colors**. Its cable to the computer includes a red-gun wire, a green-gun wire, and a blue-gun wire. Each wire's current has 2 choices (on or off), so the total number of color choices is "2 times 2 times 2", which is 8.

A **Color Graphics Adapter monitor (CGA monitor)** can produce **16 colors**. Its cable to the computer includes a red-gun wire, a green-gun wire, a blue-gun wire, and an intensity wire. Each wire's current has 2 choices (on or off), so the total number of choices is "2 times 2 times 2 times 2", which is 16.

An **Enhanced Graphics Adapter monitor (EGA monitor)** can produce **64 colors**. Its cable to the computer includes 2 red-gun wires (generating a total of 4 levels of red-gun intensity), 2 green-gun wires, and 2 blue-gun wires, so the total number of choices is "4 times 4 times 4", which is 64.

A **Video Graphics Array monitor (VGA monitor)** can produce **over 16 million colors**. Its cable to the computer includes 1 red-gun wire, 1 green-gun wire, and 1 blue-gun wire, and each wire can handle 256 levels of intensity, so the total number of choices is "256 times 256 times 256", which is 16,777,216.

VGA has become the standard. Primitive RGB, CGA, and EGA monitors are obsolete.

For a VGA monitor, the cable to the computer includes 1 red-gun wire, 1 green-gun wire, 1 blue-gun wire, and several other wires to help administer the signals. Altogether, the VGA cable contains 15 wires.

CGA and EGA cables each contain just 9 wires. If you see a monitor whose cable contains just 9 wires, the monitor is either CGA or EGA. It's therefore obsolete.

Size The typical VGA color monitor's screen is **17-inch (17")**. That means the distance from the picture tube's top left corner to the picture tube's bottom right corner is 17 inches, measured diagonally.

Although the picture tube's diagonal size is 17-inch, you see just 16 inches, because 1 inch is hidden behind the plastic that makes up the monitor's case.

Most monitors are made by companies whose US headquarters are in California. Consumers complained to California's attorney general that such a monitor shouldn't be called "17-inch", since just 16 inches are viewable. California now requires all ads for "17-inch" monitors to include a comment, in parentheses, saying that the **viewable image size (vis)** is just 16 inches, so the ad looks like this:

17" monitor (16" vis)

Instead of buying a 17-inch monitor (which costs $85), you can buy a bigger one (19-inch or 21-inch) or a smaller one (15-inch or 14-inch). In each case, the viewable image size is about an inch less than the size of the tube.

A 14" monitor (13" vis) is adequate for most people and most software, but few companies still offer 14" monitors. 15" shows the same info as 14" but slightly magnified, so you can read "the fine print" on the screen more easily. 17", 19", and 21" monitors are much more pleasant; they're especially helpful if you're trying to create fine graphics (or ads) or many side-by-side columns (as in a newspaper, magazine, newsletter, textbook, or big table of numbers). **The newest programs (and many parts of the Internet) expect you to have at least a 17" monitor.** Big monitors are also helpful if you have poor eyesight (or you're sharing the computer with somebody who has poor eyesight).

Most folks buy 17" monitors. Richer folks buy 19" or 21".

Resolution Each position on the screen is called a **pixel**. The pixels are arranged in rows and columns, to form a grid. In a primitive VGA monitor, the screen is wide enough to hold 640 columns of pixels, and the screen is tall enough to hold 480 rows of pixels, so altogether the number of pixels in the grid is "640 times 480", which is written "640×480", which is pronounced "640 by 480". That's called the screen's **resolution**.

If you buy a big VGA monitor (such as 21-inch), the screen is big enough to hold *lots* of pixels. You can use such a screen in two ways: you can make the screen either show lots of tiny pixels or show a smaller number of fat pixels.

Here's how many pixels the typical screen can display:

If screen is 14" (13" viewable), it handles 640×480 well, 800×600 poorly.
If screen is 15" (14" viewable), it handles 800×600 well, 1024×768 poorly.
If screen is 17" (16" viewable), it handles 1024×768 well, 1280×1024 poorly.
If screen is 19" (18" viewable), it handles 1280×1024 well, 1600×1200 poorly.
If screen is 21" (20" viewable), it handles 1600×1200 well, 1800×1440 poorly.

Those resolutions have nicknames:

Resolution	Nickname	Alternative nicknames
640×480	**minimal VGA**	
800×600	**Super VGA (SVGA)**	**VGA Plus**
1024×768	**eXtended GA (XGA)**	**nice SVGA or Ultra VGA (UVGA)**
1280×1024	**Super XGA (SXGA)**	
1600×1200	**Ultra XGA (UXGA)**	

Refresh rate Here's how the red gun works:

It aims at the first pixel on the screen, decides how many electrons to fire at that pixel's red phosphor (depending on how red you want the pixel to be), and fires those electrons. Those electrons excite the first pixel's red phosphor and make the phosphor glow the appropriate amount. Then the red gun does the same thing for the screen's second pixel, then the third pixel, etc.
While the gun is dealing with later pixels, the gun is ignoring the first pixel's red phosphor, whose glow starts to fade. When the red gun finishes handling the last pixel, that gun hurries back to the first pixel and gives its red phosphor another shot of electrons, to refresh the phosphor's glow.

If the gun doesn't get back to the first pixel soon enough, that pixel's glow will have faded too much, and your eye will notice the fading and consider it an annoying flicker.

To avoid annoying flicker, the gun must get back to the phosphor fast, in less than an 85th of a second. That means it must refresh the phosphor at least 85 times per second. Instead of saying "the gun must refresh the phosphor at least 85 times per second," engineers say "the **vertical refresh rate** must be at least **85 hertz (85 Hz)**."

If the vertical refresh rate is less than 85 hertz, your eye might detect some flicker, which will annoy you. The flicker will be noticeable mainly if you look at the screen out of the corner of your eye, since your eye's peripheral vision is most sensitive to flicker.

85 hertz is excellent, flicker-free.
75 hertz is rather good. It's acceptable to most folks, annoying to some.
60 hertz is rather bad. It's annoying to everybody but still usable.
Below 60 hertz is terrible, unusable.

The typical cheap 17" monitor can show 1024×768 resolution well (at 85 hertz) but shows 1280×1024 resolution poorly (at 60 hertz). The ad for such a monitor typically begins by bragging that it can display 1280×1024 but then admits it handles that resolution poorly and should be used at just 1024×768; it says:

1280×1024 @ 60Hz, 1024×768 @ 85Hz

Trinitron In a traditional picture tube, each pixel is a trio of phosphor dots (red, green, and blue), arranged as three points of a triangle. That technique is called a **dot-trio shadow mask**.

Sony invented a more expensive kind of picture tube, called the **Trinitron**, using a technique called **aperture grille**: each pixel is a trio of vertical stripes (red, green, and blue), arranged side-by-side, like fence posts. That technique produces brighter colors and straighter vertical lines. But it makes diagonal lines look too bumpy; and if your eyesight is good, you'll notice an annoying grid of thin horizontal wires, which hold the vertical phosphors in place.

Dot pitch The distance from a red phosphor to the closest nearest red phosphor is called the **dot pitch**. On a standard monitor, the dot pitch is **.28 millimeters (.28mm)**. **The smaller the dot pitch, the better.** The best monitors have a dot pitch of .26, .25, .24, .23, .22, or .21.

Terrible monitors have a dot pitch of .31, .39, .42, or .51. Their screens are too blurry to let you read small characters.

On a Sony Trinitron monitor, the dot pitch is usually .25.

Flat screen In a typical monitor, the picture tube's surface is curved. If you pay slightly extra, you can buy a **flat-screen monitor** instead, whose picture tube's surface is flat. It has two advantages:

It displays horizontal and vertical lines more accurately (without curving).
It reflects light from fewer angles (so you see fewer annoying reflections).

Where to put the monitor According to researchers such as the government's **National Institute of Occupational Safety and Health (NIOSH)**, here's where you should put the monitor so you'll be comfortable while you're working at the computer....

Put the monitor slightly lower than your eyes, so you look *down* at the monitor (instead of looking up, which would strain your neck). When you're looking at the center of the monitor's screen, you should be looking down slightly (at an angle that's 15 degrees below horizontal).

Put the monitor a moderate distance from your face. NIOSH recommended that the distance from your eyes to the center of the monitor's screen be 17 inches; but that recommendation was made several years ago, when the typical monitor screen was just 12-inch. Now screens are bigger, so you need to sit farther from the screen to see the whole screen: a distance of 23 inches feels good to me.

Keep the room rather dark, to avoid having light reflected off the monitor's surface. **Put the monitor perpendicular to any light source**, so no light source shines directly onto the monitor's screen (which would create an annoying reflection) and no light source shines directly onto the monitor's back (since such a light source would also be shining into your eyes and create an annoying glare).

LCD screens

If your computer is tiny, it comes with a tiny screen, called a **liquid-crystal display (LCD)**. That's the kind of screen you see on digital watches, pocket calculators, handheld computers, and notebook computers.

Those computers use LCD screens instead of traditional picture tubes because LCD screens consume less electricity, weigh less, and are less bulky. Since an LCD screen uses little electricity, it can run on batteries. A traditional picture tube can*not* run on batteries. If your computer system runs on batteries, its screen is an LCD.

Desktop and tower computers use traditional picture tubes, for these reasons:

Big picture tubes cost less than big LCD screens.
The image on the typical LCD screen has poor contrast and resolution and responds too slowly to computer commands.

Kinds of LCD screens

A traditional LCD screen displays black characters on a white background. The screen consists of thousands of tiny crystals. Each crystal is normally white, but temporarily changes to black when an electrical charge passes through it. Newer LCD screens can display colors.

The main manufacturer of LCD screens is **Sharp**. Sharp's LCD screens are used in many brands of computers.

The price of a handheld or laptop computer depends on what kind of LCD screen it includes. You'll find color LCD screens on most of the modern handheld and laptop computers; you'll find monochrome screens just on the cheapest handheld computers and the oldest laptop computers.

Among color LCD screens, the old-fashioned kind is called **passive**; the next step up is **dual-scan passive**, which is brighter and works faster; the next step up is **high-performance addressing (HPA)**; the most expensive is **active-matrix**, which is the brightest and works the fastest.

Passive is also called **super-twist nematic (STN)**.
Dual-scan passive is called **double-layer STN (DSTN)**.
Active-matrix is called **thin-film transistor (TFT)**.

The newest laptop computers all have the best screens (color LCD active-matrix). Most are **widescreen**: that means the screen's width is 1.6 times as big as the height (instead of just 1⅓), so you can see the full width of a DVD movie (though such screens are not as tall as traditional screens).

LCD monitors

The typical LCD screen is built into a small computer (such as a handheld or laptop computer). A different way to get an LCD screen is to buy an **LCD monitor**, which looks like a monitor but includes an LCD screen instead of a CRT. You can attach an LCD monitor to a desktop or tower computer.

An LCD monitor is convenient because it consumes less desk space than a CRT and weighs less (so it's easier to move). LCD monitors used to be expensive but their prices dropped, so when this book went to press in July 2011 the prices were down to these:

Size	Resolution	Price
20" widescreen	1600×900	$100 at Staples & Best Buy
23" widescreen	1920×1080	$140 at Staples
24" widescreen	1920×1080	$200 at Best Buy
25" widescreen	1920×1080	$220 at Staples
27" widescreen	1920×1080	$250 at Best Buy

LCD projectors

An **LCD projector** resembles an LCD monitor but projects the image onto a huge movie screen (or your room's white wall), so the image is many feet wide and can be seen by a big audience in a movie theater (or big conference room).

Best Buy sells these:

Maker	Native resolution		Brightness	Contrast	Best Buy
Optoma	480p	(854×480)	50 lumens	800:1	$180
Vivitek	SVGA	(800×600)	2600 lumens	2300:1	$300
Vivitek	XGA	(1024×768)	2600 lumens	2300:1	$400
Optoma	XGA	(1024×768)	2800 lumens	3000:1	$575
Optoma	720p	(1280×720)	2500 lumens	4000:1	$700
Epson	WXGA	(1280×800)	2500 lumens	3000:1	$700
Optoma	WXGA	(1280×800)	2800 lumens	3000:1	$750
Optoma	1080p	(1920×1080)	1700 lumens	4000:1	$1100
Epson	1080p	(1920×1080)	2000 lumens	50000:1	$1300

TV sets

You can attach some computers to an ordinary TV set instead of to a monitor.

For example, here's how to attach an old primitive computer (such as an Apple 2 or Radio Shack Color Computer or Commodore 64 or Commodore VIC or Atari 800) to a TV set:

Look at your TV's antenna. Wires run from the antenna to 2 screws on the TV's back. Loosen those 2 screws, to detach the antenna from the TV. Instead of attaching the antenna's wires directly to those 2 screws, attach the antenna's wires to a **switchbox** (which is included in the price of such a computer), then attach the switchbox to the 2 screws on the TV's back, so the switchbox sits between the antenna and the TV. Finally, run an **RCA cord** from the switchbox to the computer's back.
The switch box has a switch on it. If you move the switch toward the antenna, you see normal TV shows; if you move the switch toward the computer's RCA cord, your TV's controlled by the computer so the computer can write messages on your TV screen.
To use the computer, move the switchbox's switch toward the RCA cord, then flip the *computer's* switch to channel 3 or 4, then turn your TV to the same channel. (Most of the primitive computers use channels 3 & 4, though some use channels 2, 10, 33, or 34 instead. To get a sharp picture on your TV screen, avoid the channel used by your local TV station, and adjust the TV's "fine tuning" knob.)

Keyboards

The usual way to communicate with the computer is to type messages on the computer's **keyboard**.

In 1981, IBM invented a keyboard containing **83 keys**. That keyboard is called the **XT keyboard**, because it was used on the original IBM PC and the IBM PC XT.
In 1986, IBM began selling a fancier keyboard, containing **101 keys**. It's called the **AT keyboard**, because it was used on the IBM PC AT.
In 1995, Microsoft began selling an even fancier keyboard, containing **104 keys**. It's called the **Windows keyboard**, because it contains extra keys for Windows.

Now **"104 keys" has become the standard**. Microsoft, IBM, and competitors all sell keyboards containing 104 keys.

The 104 keys are arranged like this:

Those 104 keys are for desktop computers. Notebook computers have fewer keys. Good notebook computers (such as the Hewlett-Packard G71-340US) have 101 keys, arranged like this:

Smaller notebook computers (such as the Compaq CQ5-110US) have just 86 keys, arranged like this:

Each keyboard can print all the letters of the alphabet (from A to Z), all the digits (from 0 to 9), and these symbols:

Symbol	Official name	Nicknames
.	period	dot, decimal point, point, full stop
,	comma	cedilla
:	colon	dots, double stop
;	semicolon	semi
!	exclamation point	bang, shriek
?	question mark	ques, query, what, huh, wildchar
"	quotation mark	quote, double quote, dieresis, rabbit ears
'	apostrophe	single quote, acute accent, prime
`	grave accent	left single quote, open single quote, open quote
^	circumflex	caret, hat
~	tilde	squiggle, twiddle, not
=	equals	is, gets, takes
+	plus	add
-	minus	dash, hyphen
_	underline	underscore, under
*	asterisk	star, splat, wildcard
&	ampersand	amper, amp, and, pretzel
@	at sign	at, whorl, strudel
$	dollar sign	dollar, buck, string
#	number sign	pound sign, pound, tic-tac-toe
%	percent sign	percent, grapes
/	slash	forward slash, rising slash, slant, stroke
\	backslash	reverse slash, falling slash, backwhack
|	vertical line	vertical bar, bar, pipe, enlarged colon
( )	parentheses	open paren & close paren, left paren & right paren
[ ]	brackets	open bracket & close bracket, square brackets
{ }	braces	curly brackets, curly braces, squiggly braces
<>	brockets	angle brackets, less than & greater than, from & to

For example, the symbol * is officially called an "asterisk". More briefly, it's called a "star". It's also called a "splat", since it looks like a squashed bug. In some programs, an asterisk means "match anything", as in a card game where the Joker's a "wildcard" that matches any other card.

In the diagram, I wrote the words "Shift", "Backspace", "LeftTab", "Tab", "Enter", "Windows", and "Menu" on some keys. To help people who don't read English, keyboard manufacturers usually put symbols on those keys.

The Shift key shows a fat arrow pointing up.
The Backspace key shows an arrow pointing left.
The Tab key shows arrows crashing into walls.
The Enter key shows an arrow that's bent (going down and then left).
The Menu key shows a diagonal arrow pointing up at a menu.
The Windows key shows a flying window (having 4 curved windowpanes).

Stare at *your* computer's keyboard and find these keys:

Key	Where to find it
Tab	the Tab key is left of the Q key
Backspace	104 keys: the Backspace key is left of the Insert key
	101 keys: the Backspace key is left of the Num Lock key
	86 keys: the Backspace key is left of the Home key
Shift	the left Shift key is left of the Z key
	the right-hand Shift key is right of the question-mark key
Enter	the Enter key is above the right-hand Shift key
Windows	usually, any Windows keys are next to Alt keys
	(if 86 keys but weird, the Window key is next to the Pause key)
Menu	usually, the Menu key is next to the right-hand Ctrl key
	(if 86 keys but weird, the Menu key is in the top-right corner)

The keyboard contains special keys that help you do special activities (such as moving around the screen while you type):

Key	Usual purpose
↑ or ▲	move up, to the line above
↓ or ▼	move down, to the line below
← or ◄	move left, to the previous character
→ or ►	move right, to the next character
Home	move back to the beginning
End	move ahead to the end
Page Up or PgUp	move back to the previous page
Page Down or PgDn	move ahead to the next page
Tab	hop to the next field or far to the right
Enter	finish a command or paragraph
Pause	pause until you press the Enter key
Print Screen or PrtSc	copy from screen onto paper or computer's clipboard
Shift	capitalize a letter
Caps Lock	change whether all letters are automatically capitalized
Num Lock	change whether keyboard's right side produces numbers
Scroll Lock or ScrLk	change how text moves up & down
Insert or Ins	change whether extra characters inserted in text's middle
Delete or Del	delete the current character
Backspace or BkSp	delete the previous character
Escape or Esc	escape from a mistake
Windows	show you Windows' Start menu
Menu	show you a shortcut menu
F1	get help from the computer
F2, F3, etc.	do special activities
Control or Ctrl	do special activities
Alternate or Alt	do special activities

The Caps Lock, Num Lock, Scroll Lock, and Insert keys are called **toggle keys**: they create special effects, which end when you press the toggle key again.

Shift Key

If a key has two symbols on it, the key normally uses the bottom symbol. To type the top symbol instead, press the key *while holding down the Shift key*.

Number Keys

To type a number easily, use the keys in the top row of the keyboard's main section. (For example, to type 4, press the key that has a 4 and a dollar sign.)

Numeric keypad On a desktop computer, the keyboard's far-right keys are in a rectangle called the **numeric keypad**, which begins with the NumLock key and includes all the numbers. **If you're a beginner, I recommend keeping your hands off the numeric keypad**: use the other number keys instead.

If you insist on using the numeric keypad, here's how it works:

The keys on the numeric keypad work normally (generating numbers) just while the Num Lock light glows. (The Num Lock light is usually near the Num Lock key and labeled "Num Lock", but on some computers the light is farther away and labeled "1".) Usually that light glows, and you should let it keep glowing. If you want to turn that light off (or turn it back on again), tap the Num Lock key. **When the Num Lock light is off, the keys on the numeric keypad don't generate numbers; instead, they imitate the edit keys** (Home, End, PgUp, PgDn, Ins, Del, and arrows).

Fn key

A notebook computer's keyboard includes an Fn key. While holding down the Fn key, you can tap another key. What happens? That depends on which computer you have.

For example, on my Toshiba Satellite 1115 notebook computer, here's what happens:

Keys	What the computer will do
Fn with F1	blank the screen (until you press a key and any password)
Fn with F4	change the volume of the low-battery alarm
Fn with F5	use (or stop using) external monitor instead of built-in screen
Fn with F9	turn off the touchpad (or turn it back on)
Fn with F10	turn on the numeric keypad's editing keys (or turn them back off)
Fn with F11	turn on the numeric keypad's number keys (or turn them back off)
Fn with F12	turn on the scroll lock (or turn it back off)

On my Compaq Presario 1200 notebook computer, here's what happens:

Keys	What the computer will do
Fn with F1	go to Compaq's main Internet Website
Fn with F2	go to Compaq's Internet Website shopping mall
Fn with F3	use (or stop using) external monitor instead of built-in screen
Fn with F4	sleep (until you press a key)
Fn with F5	decrease the screen's contrast
Fn with F6	increase the screen's contrast
Fn with F7	decrease the screen's brightness
Fn with F8	increase the screen's brightness
Fn with F9	play a CD
Fn with F10	stop playing a CD
Fn with F11	play the CD's previous track
Fn with F12	play the CD's next track

On my Compaq Presario CQ50-110US notebook computer, here's what happens:

Keys	What the computer will do
Fn with Esc	give details about your computer's hardware & software
Fn with F1	explain how to use the computer
Fn with F2	help you print onto paper
Fn with F3	run the Internet Explorer program (so you access the Internet)
Fn with F4	use (or stop using) external monitor instead of built-in screen
Fn with F5	hibernate (copy from RAM to hard disk then turn off computer)
Fn with F6	lock (hide the screen's info until a password is typed)
Fn with F7	decrease the screen's brightness
Fn with F8	increase the screen's brightness
Fn with F9	play (or pause the playing of) a music CD (or DVD movie)
Fn with F10	stop playing a music CD (or a DVD movie)
Fn with F11	play the previous track of a music CD (or DVD movie)
Fn with F12	play the next track of a music CD (or DVD movie)
Fn with Home	mute the speaker's sound (or turn it back on)
Fn with Pg Up	increase the speaker's volume
Fn with Pg Dn	decrease the speaker's volume
Fn with Scroll	turn on the numeric keypad (or turn it back off)
Fn with Insert	copy from screen to computer's clipboard

On my Hewlett-Packard G71-340US notebook computer, here's what happens:

Keys	What the computer will do
Fn with Esc	give details about your computer's hardware & software
Fn with F1	explain how to use the computer
Fn with F2	help you print onto paper
Fn with F3	run the Internet Explorer program (so you access the Internet)
Fn with F4	use (or stop using) external monitor instead of built-in screen
Fn with F5	sleep (blank the screen until you tap the power button)
Fn with F6	lock (hide the screen's info until a password is typed)
Fn with F7	decrease the screen's brightness
Fn with F8	increase the screen's brightness
Fn with F9	play (or pause the playing of) a music CD (or a DVD movie)
Fn with F10	stop playing a music CD (or a DVD movie)
Fn with F11	play the previous track of a music CD (or DVD movie)
Fn with F12	play the next track of a music CD (or DVD movie)
Fn with numeric keypad's +	increase the speaker's volume
Fn with numeric keypad's -	decrease the speaker's volume
Fn with numeric keypad's *	mute the speaker's sound (or turn it back on)

On my Acer Aspire 3623 notebook computer (model 3623WXCi), here's what happens:

Keys	What the computer will do
Fn with F1	explain what the Fn key does
Fn with F2	change startup and security
Fn with F3	ask whether to use less electricity (which would go slower)
Fn with F4	sleep (until you press a key)
Fn with F5	use (or stop using) external monitor instead of built-in screen
Fn with F6	turn off the screen's backlight (until you press a key)
Fn with F7	turn off the touchpad (or turn it back on)
Fn with F8	turn off the speakers (or turn them back on)
Fn with F11	turn on the numeric keypad (or turn it back off)
Fn with F12	turn on the scroll lock (or turn it back off)
Fn with ▲	increase the speaker's volume
Fn with ▼	decrease the speaker's volume
Fn with ►	increase the screen's brightness
Fn with ◄	decrease the screen's brightness

Missing Keys

If your keyboard is missing the Menu key and the two Windows keys, don't worry: those 3 keys are unimportant, since most folks prefer to use a mouse instead of tapping those keys. If you wish, you can substitute other keys instead:

Instead of tapping the Menu key, tap the F10 key while holding down the Shift key.
Instead of tapping a Windows key, tap the Esc key while holding down the Ctrl key.

If your desktop's keyboard is ancient, it has just 83 keys and you suffer:

Your keyboard is missing the Menu key and the two Windows keys.
Your keyboard is missing the F11 and F12 keys. (The F1 through F10 keys are arranged in two columns down the keyboard's left edge, instead of being spread out across the keyboard's top.)
Your keyboard is missing the second Ctrl key, the second Alt key, the second Enter key, and the second / key.
Your keyboard is missing the Pause key. (Instead, you must tap the NumLock key while holding down the Ctrl key.)
The PrintScreen key is labeled "PrtSc" and works just while holding down the Shift key. (If you don't hold down the Shift key, the PrtSc key acts as a second * key.)
Your keyboard is missing the 4 arrow keys and these 6 editing keys: Insert, Delete, Home, End, PageUp, and PageDown. (To perform those functions, you must press number keys after you've turned off the NumLock.)

83-key keyboards work just with outdated computers. If you're using an 83-key keyboard, that's proof your computer is outdated! Buy a new computer system!

Kinds of keyboards

When buying a keyboard, you have many choices. You can buy an **XT** keyboard (83 keys), **AT** keyboard (101 keys), **augmented AT** keyboard (101 keys plus an extra copy of the backslash key), or **Windows** keyboard (101 keys plus 3 special keys that help run software called "Windows"). You can buy a **standard-size** keyboard (with a ledge above the top row, for placing your pencil or notes), **compact** keyboard (which has no ledge and consumes less desk space), **foldable** keyboard (which folds in half, as if you're closing a book, so it consumes half as much desk space when not in use), or **split** keyboard (whose left third is separated from the rest, so you can have the comfort of typing while your forearms are parallel to each other). You can buy a **tactile** keyboard (which gives you helpful feedback by making a click whenever you hit a key), **silent** keyboard (which helps your neighbors by not making clicks), or **spill-resistant** keyboard (which is silent and also doesn't mind having coffee or soda spilled on it).

Pointing devices

If you feed the computer a picture (such as a photograph, drawing, or diagram), the computer will analyze the picture and even help you improve it. To feed the computer a picture of an object, you can use 4 methods.

Method 1: point a traditional **video camera** (or camcorder) at the object, while the camera is wired to the computer.

Method 2: take a picture of the object by using a **digital camera**, which contains a disk or RAM chips that record the image, then transfer the image to a computer.

Method 3: draw on paper, which you then feed to an **optical scanner** wired to the computer. Of the optical scanners that cost under $150, the best are Microtek's **X6** (which handles colors the best) and Visioneer's **One Touch** (which is much easier to use and reads words the best but handles colors less accurately).

Method 4: draw the picture by using a pen wired to the computer. The computerized pen can be a **light pen**, **touch screen**, **graphics tablet**, **mouse**, **trackball**, or **joystick**.

Let's look at method 4 more closely....

Light pens

A **light pen** is a computerized pen that you point at the screen of your TV or monitor. To draw, you move the pen across the screen.

Light pens are cheap: prices begin at $20. But light pens are less reliable, less convenient, and less popular than other graphical input devices.

Touch screens

A **touch screen** is a special overlay that covers the screen and lets you draw with your finger instead of with a light pen.

Graphics tablets

A **graphics tablet** is a computerized board that lies flat on your desk. To draw, you move either a pen or your finger across the board. Modern notebook computers include a tiny graphics tablet (called a **touchpad** or **glidepad**), stroked with your finger and built into the keyboard (in front of the Space bar).

Mice

A **mouse** is a computerized box that's about as big as a pack of cigarettes. To draw, you slide the mouse across your desk, as if it were a fat pen.

When you slide the typical mouse, a ball in its belly rolls on the table. The computer senses how many times the ball rotated and in what direction.

The mouse was invented at Xerox's **Palo Alto Research Center (PARC)**. The first company to provide mice to the general public was **Apple**, which provided a free mouse with every Lisa and Mac computer. Now a free mouse comes with each IBM PC and clone, too.

Microsoft Mouse The nicest mouse for the IBM PC is the **Microsoft Mouse**. Its first version was boring, but then came an improved version, nicknamed "**The Dove Bar**" because it was shaped like a bar of Dove soap. It felt great in your hand; but trying to draw a picture by using that mouse — or *any* mouse — was as clumsy as drawing with a bar of soap.

Then came a further improvement, nicknamed "**The Dog's Paw**" because it was shaped like a dog's lower leg: it was long with an asymmetrical bump (paw) at the end. It felt even better than The Dove Bar, if your hand was big enough to hold it.

The next improvement, nicknamed "**The Wheel Mouse**", looked like The Dog's Paw but added a wheel you could rotate with your fingers.

The newest version, nicknamed "**The Sneaker**" and officially called the **Intellimouse Pro**, resembles the Wheel Mouse but its left side is taller, like the raised arch of a fancy sneaker. It costs $65.

Mice from no-name manufacturers cost under $10. Microsoft made a cheap mouse too, called the **Home Mouse**, in the shape of a home, with the mouse's cord coming out of the chimney. Microsoft's newest cheap mouse is called the **Basic Mouse**; at $16, it's small enough to be used by kids, lefties, and short people.

Trackballs

A **trackball** is a box that has a ball sticking out the top of it. To draw, just put your fingers on the ball and rotate it. Some notebook computers have a trackball built into the keyboard.

Technologically, a trackball's the same as a typical mouse: each is a box containing a ball. For a trackball, the ball sticks *up* from the box and you finger it directly; for a mouse, the ball hides *underneath* and gets rotated when you move the box. The mouse feels more natural (somewhat like gripping a pen) but requires lots of desk space (so you can move the box).

The trackball was invented first. The mouse came later and has become more popular — except on notebook computers, which use trackballs and touchpads to save space.

Joysticks

A **joystick** is a box with a stick coming out of its top. To draw, you move the stick in any direction (left, right, forward, back, or diagonally) as if you were the pilot of a small airplane.

Sound

You can make the computer hear and produce sounds.

Speakers

To produce sounds, the standard computer includes **speakers**.

One tiny speaker hides inside the system unit. It's called the **internal speaker**. That speaker's main purpose is to beep at you if you make a mistake.

A pair of **stereo speakers** are bigger and can produce good, loud stereo music. Hey, baby, let's rock!

Those stereo speakers are usually separate boxes that sit outside the system unit. (Exception: some Compaq and Mac computers hide the stereo speakers in the monitor; most notebook computers hide the stereo speakers in the keyboard.)

If your computer is fancy, it includes a *trio* of stereo speakers: the third speaker is called the **subwoofer** and produces a big, loud, booming bass.

If your computer is extra-fancy, it gives you **surround sound**, where you're surrounded by 4 normal speakers (front left, front right, back left, and back right) plus a subwoofer, making a total of 5 speakers. Since that system includes 4 normal speakers plus 1 subwoofer, it's called a **4.1 speaker system**.

If your computer is even fancier (super-duper fancy), it gives you 5 normal speakers (front left, front right, back left, back right, and center) plus a subwoofer, making a total of 6 speakers. Since that system includes 5 normal speakers plus 1 subwoofer, it's called a **5.1 speaker system**.

Sound card

To handle the stereo speakers, a standard computer's system unit contains a **sound card**.

The most popular sound card is the **Sound Blaster**, made by a company called **Creative Technology**, founded by Mr. Sim Wong Hoo in Singapore. It's still run by him there, and he owns 35% of the stock, making him rich. Creative Technology is called "the Singapore surprise" because it surprises novices who think the best hardware companies are all based in the US & Japan. It was the first Singapore company to be listed on the Nasdaq stock exchange. Its US division is based in California and called **Creative Labs**.

Fancy computers speak words by including circuitry called a **speech synthesizer**.

Microphone

The newest computers come with a **microphone (mike)**. By using the mike, you can make the computer record sounds. For example, you can make the computer record the sound of your voice and imitate it, so the computer sounds just like you!

Printers

A computer usually displays its answers on a screen. If you want the computer to copy the answers onto paper, attach the computer to a **printer**, which is a device that prints on paper. The computer transmits your request through a cable of wires running from the back of the computer to the back of the printer.

A computer's advertised price usually does *not* include a printer and cable. The cable costs about $10; the typical printer costs about $100.

Printers are more annoying than screens. Printers are noisier, slower, consume more electricity, need repairs more often, and require you to buy paper and ink. But you'll want a printer anyway, to copy the computer's answers onto paper to hand to your computerless friends. Another reason to get a printer is that a sheet of paper is bigger than a screen and lets you see more info at once.

To get a printer cheaply, walk into chains of discount superstores, such as **Staples** (which sells all kinds of office supplies and some computer equipment) and **Office Max** (which resembles Staples but charges less for printers).

Kinds of printers

Three kinds of printers are popular.

An **inkjet printer** contains tiny hoses that squirt ink at the paper. It typically costs about $100.

A **laser printer** looks like a photocopier. Like a photocopier, it contains a rotating drum and inky toner. It prints faster and more beautifully than an inkjet printer. Like a photocopier, it's expensive: it typically costs about $400.

A **dot-matrix printer** contains tiny pins that put ink onto paper by smashing against an inked ribbon. It prints slower and uglier than the other kinds of printers, but it has one big advantage: its ink costs less. This kind of printer typically costs about $300.

Consumables

Besides paying for the printer, you must also pay for **consumables**: ink, paper, and electricity.

Ink After you've bought the printer and used it for a while, the ink supply will run out, so you must buy more ink.

In the typical **dot-matrix printer**, the inked ribbon costs about $5 and lasts about 1000 pages, so it costs about a half a penny per page. That's cheap!

In the typical **inkjet printer**, the ink cartridge costs about $20 and lasts about 500 pages, so it costs about 4 cents per page. That's expensive!

In the typical **laser printer**, the toner cartridge costs about $80 and lasts about 4000 pages, so it costs about 2 cents per page. That's moderate!

Those prices assume you're printing black text. If you're printing graphics or color, the cost per page goes up drastically. For example, full-color graphics on an inkjet printer cost about 50 cents per page.

If you use your printer a lot, you must buy ink often: every few months. The cost adds up: after a few years, you'll discover that the total cost of all the ink you've bought is more than the cost of the printer! If a printer is advertised at a low price, beware: the "almost free" printer is just a ruse to get you to spend lots of money on ink. (It's like buying an "almost free" razor, which is just a ruse to get you to spend lots on blades.)

Paper You must buy paper, which costs about 1 cent per sheet if you buy a small quantity (such as a **ream**, which is 500 sheets), or a half a cent per sheet if you buy a large quantity (such as a **case**, which is 5000 sheets). For low prices on paper, go to **Office Max**, **Sam's Club**, or **Staples**.

Electricity You must pay for **electricity** to run the printer; but the electricity's cost is negligible (much less than a penny per page) if you turn the printer off when you're not printing.

Warning: if you leave a laser printer on even when not printing, its total yearly electric cost can get high, since the laser printer contains a big electric heater. (You might even notice the lights in your room go dim when the heater kicks on.)

Inkjet printers

An **inkjet printer** contains tiny hoses that squirt ink at the paper. The hoses are called **nozzles**. They're in a device called a **print head**. The typical print head contains 144 nozzles.

When you use an inkjet printer, the print head moves across the paper, from left to right, its nozzles squirting ink at the paper, until it reaches the paper's right edge. Then the paper jerks up slightly, the print head moves back to the left again, and the process is repeated.

When using an inkjet printer, you hear the ink squirting at the paper, the print head moving across the paper, and the paper jerking up.

When you run out of ink, you're supposed to buy another **ink cartridge**, which is a tank containing ink.

Most inkjet printers can print in color. They mix together the three primary ink colors (red, blue, and yellow) to form all the colors of the rainbow.

3 main manufacturers The first popular inkjet printers were made by **Hewlett-Packard (HP)**. Later, **Epson** and **Canon** started making inkjet printers also.

The inkjet printers from all 3 of those companies are excellent. Each company makes a wide variety of inkjet printers, at prices ranging from about $25 to about $1000. Canon's inkjet printers are the best: all major reviewers rate Canon's **Pixma** printers tops, for printing color photos (and ordinary stuff, too) with high quality, inexpensively.

Each manufacturer has its own brand names:

HP's inkjet printers are called **Deskjets**. Epson's inkjet printers are called **Styluses**. Canon's old inkjet printers are called **Bubble Jets**; its new inkjet printers, which print photos better, are called **Pixmas**.

Most printers are designed for the IBM PC but can also handle the Mac.. Special Mac-only models are also available: HP's Mac-only models are called **DeskWriters**; Canon's Mac-only models, called **Stylewriters**, were marketed by Apple.

How does the ink get out of the nozzle and onto the paper?

In inkjet printers by HP and Canon, a bubble of ink in the nozzle gets heated and becomes hot enough to burst and splash onto the paper. Epson's inkjet printers use a different technique, in which the nozzle suddenly constricts and forces the ink out.

When using an inkjet printer, try different brands of paper.

Some brands of paper absorb ink better. If you choose the wrong brand, the ink will **wick** (spread out erratically through the strands of the paper's fiber). Start by trying cheap copier paper, then explore alternatives. The paper brand you buy makes a much bigger difference with inkjet printers than with dot-matrix or laser printers. Canon's printers are the best at tolerating paper differences, but Canon's ink is water-based and smears slightly if the paper or envelope gets wet (from rain or a sweaty thumb).

4 new competitors HP, Canon, and Epson are being attacked by 4 aggressive competitors (**Xerox**, **Brother**, **Lexmark**, and **Kodak**).

Lexmark printers cost the least but require expensive ink cartridges, so Lexmark printers are a good deal just if you print rarely.

Kodak is the opposite: Kodak printers cost the most but use the cheapest ink cartridge, so Kodak printers are a good deal if you print often.

Brother printers always offer good value (good quality at low prices).

Xerox was a dying company but has improved recently, so don't ignore it!

Dual-cartridge color Inkjet printers come in several styles. The most popular style is **dual-cartridge color**. If you buy this style of inkjet printer, you can insert two ink cartridges simultaneously, side by side.

One cartridge contains black ink. The other cartridge contains the color trio (red, blue, and yellow). The computer mixes together all 4 (black, red, blue, and yellow) to form all possible colors. That method is called the **4-color process**.

Epson's most famous such printer has been the **Stylus Color 777**, which costs just $89 from discount dealers. It prints precisely: the resolution is 2880 dots per inch vertically, 720 dots per inch horizontally, and the dots are squirted onto the paper neatly, without splatter. It prints fast: up to 8 pages per minute for black, 6 pages per minute for color. Those high speeds are obtained just while printing text in low resolution (360 dots per inch). To print a color photo in high resolution takes 1½ minutes for 4"×6", 3 minutes for 8"×10". It comes with a 1-year warranty. The cartridges are long-lasting: they'll print 600 pages of black text, 300 pages of color text; before the ink runs out and you must insert new cartridges. The black print head contains 144 nozzles; the color print head contains 144 nozzles (48 per color).

To compete against Epson, **Canon** offers several competitors. Canon's cheapest is the **Bubble Jet Color 2100 (BJC-2100)**. It lists for $100, but you get a $50 rebate, bringing the final cost down to just $50! That gets you 720×360 dpi, 5 ppm black, 2 ppm color, 1-year warranty. The price includes a cartridge containing all 4 colors. An all-black cartridge costs extra and is needed to achieve the "5 ppm black" speed.

HP offers these:

HP Printer	Black	Color	Duty cycle	Price
Deskjet 1000	16 ppm, 600 dpi, 5.8¢	12 ppm, 4800×1200 dpi, 14.9¢	1,000 pages/month	$30
Deskjet 3000	20 ppm, 600 dpi, 5.8¢	16 ppm, 4800×1200 dpi, 14.9¢	1,000 pages/month	$60

In that chart, "price" is the list price (discount dealers charge less), **duty cycle** is how many pages per month the printer can reasonably handle (without overheating and without "worn or loose" parts or "slow speed" making you curse excessively). The number of cents is the cost of the ink to print a typical page:

That cost assumes you play list price for an **extended-life (XL) cartridge** (which costs more than the standard cartridge but includes more ink). It assumes you cover just 5% of the page with black ink, or 30% of the page with colored ink, so most places on the paper remain white. That cost includes just the cost of the ink, not the cost of the paper.

Single-cartridge color A cheaper style is **single-cartridge color**. This category lets you insert either a black cartridge or a color cartridge, but you cannot insert both cartridges simultaneously.

If you try to print black while the color cartridge is in, the computer tries to imitate "black" by printing red, blue, and yellow on top of each other. That produces a "mud" instead of a true black, and it's also very slow. If you try to make such a printer reproduce a photograph, the image produced looks slightly "muddy", "washed-out", with poor contrast.

But the price is deliciously low!

The main such printer has been **Canon**'s **BJC-1000**. Here's why it costs little:

It comes in a box that includes one color cartridge (to get you started) but no black cartridge (which costs extra). The printer produces just 720×360 black, 360×360 color. The printer is very slow: just 4 ppm black, 0.6 ppm color. Its black print head contains just 64 nozzles; it color print head contains just 48 nozzles (16 per color).

It's been selling for $75, sometimes minus a $30 rebate (bringing the final cost down to $45), but it's being discontinued in favor of the BJC-2100, which costs just slightly more and is much better.

Lexmark's **Z-12 Color Jetprinter** is a single-cartridge color printer that's better than the BJC-1000. You can order it directly from Lexmark for $50 (plus tax and shipping) at Lexmark's Internet Web site (www.lexmark.com). Like the BJC-1000, its price includes a color cartridge but no black cartridge (which costs extra). Lexmark claims "1200 dpi" and "6 ppm black, 3 ppm color". Lexmark also includes discount coupons so you can get good software cheap.

Portable You can buy these portable inkjet printers, which are tiny and weigh little: Brother's **MP-21C** ($240, 2 pounds), Canon's **BJC-80** ($190, 4 pounds), and Canon's **BJC-50** ($305, 2 pounds, prints slower and more crudely than the BJC-80 but has the advantage of weighing less). They all work slowly, print less beautifully than desktop printers, and can't handle big stacks of paper.

Instead of buying a portable printer, consider buying Canon's BJC-1000. At 4.8 pounds, it weighs just *slightly* more than a portable printer and tends to work faster, print more beautifully, handle paper better, and cost less!

Wide-carriage Most inkjet printers handle just normal-width paper, which is 8½ inches wide. Canon, Epson, and HP all make expensive inkjet printers that To print colors on wider paper, get Canon's **BJC-4550** ($269, 11"-by-17" paper) or Epson's **Stylus 1520** ($449, 17"-by-22").

4-cartridge color Suppose you're printing a picture that contains lots of red but not much blue or yellow. When you use up all the red ink in a tricolor cartridge, you must throw the whole cartridge away, even though blue and yellow ink remain in the cartridge. What a waste! Canon's **BJC-3000** prevents such waste.

It uses 4 separate cartridges (a black cartridge, a red cartridge, a blue cartridge, and a yellow cartridge), so when the red ink runs out you can discard the red cartridge without having to discard any blue or yellow ink. It prints 9ppm black, 4ppm color. It costs just $99. Unfortunately, its cartridges are rather expensive.

HP offers these:

HP Printer	Black	Color	Duty cycle	Price
Officejet 6000	32 ppm, 600 dpi, 2.7¢	31 ppm, 4800×1200 dpi, 9.1¢	7,000 pages/month	$50
Officejet Pro 8000	35 ppm, 1200dpi, 1.6¢	34 ppm, 4800×1200 dpi, 7.2¢	15,000 pages/month	$90

Since the Officejet 6000 is a better deal than the Deskjet 3000, don't buy the Deskjet 3000.

Laser printers

A **laser printer**, like an office photocopier, contains a drum and uses toner made of ink. The printer shines a laser beam at the drum, which picks up the toner and deposits it on the paper.

LaserJet 5 For the IBM PC, the most popular laser printers are made by Hewlett-Packard (HP), whose laser printers are called **LaserJets**. After inventing its first LaserJet, HP invented a better version (the **LaserJet 2**), then an even better version (the **LaserJet 3**), then an even better version (the **LaserJet 4**).

Finally, in 1996, HP invented a truly great version: the **LaserJet 5**. I used it to print earlier editions of this book. It's terrific! Here are its specs:

> It can print 12 pages per minute (12 **ppm**). It can print 600 dots per inch (600 **dpi**); and it uses a trick called **Resolution Enhancement Technology (RET)**, which can shift each dot slightly left or right and make each dot slightly larger or smaller. That makes the printing nearly as beautiful as if there were twice as many dots per inch (1200 dpi).
>
> Its ROM contains the definitions of 45 **fonts** (typestyles). Each of those fonts is **scalable**: you can make the characters as big or tiny as you wish. You also get a disk containing the definitions of 65 additional scalable fonts: put that disk into your computer, copy those font definitions to your computer's hard disk, then tell your computer to copy those font definitions to the printer's RAM. So altogether, the printer can handle two kinds of fonts: the 45 **internal fonts** that were inside the printer originally plus **soft fonts** that are copied into the printer's RAM from the computer's disks.
>
> The printer contains 4 megabytes of RAM, so it can handle lots of soft fonts and graphics on the same page. Moreover, the printer uses a trick called **data compression**, which compresses the data so that twice as much data can fit in the RAM (as if the RAM were 8 megabytes).

Discount dealers were selling it for $988.

Cheaper LaserJets For folks who couldn't afford a LaserJet 5 at $988, HP invented a cheap **Personal version** (called the **LaserJet 5P**) and an even cheaper **Lower-cost version** (called the **LaserJet 5L**).

Afterwards, HP invented an improved 5P (called the **6P**) and an improved 5L (called the **6L**).

New LaserJets HP has stopped selling all those LaserJets (the LaserJet 1, 2, 3, 4, 5, 5P, 5L, 6P, and 6L). Now HP sells new LaserJets that are even better and cost less! These print just monochrome (black):

Printer	Resolution	Speed	RAM	Processor	Duty cycle	Price
LaserJet P1102w	600 dpi	19 ppm	8M	266MHz	5,000 pages/month	$100
LaserJet P1606dn	600 dpi	26 ppm	32M	400MHz	8,000 pages/month	$160
LaserJet P2035	600 dpi	30 ppm	16M	266MHz	25,000 pages/month	$200
LaserJet P2055d	1200 dpi	35 ppm	64M	600MHz	50,000 pages/month	$250
LaserJet P4014n	1200 dpi	45 ppm	128M	540MHz	175,000 pages/month	$600
LaserJet P4015n	1200 dpi	52 ppm	128M	540MHz	225,000 pages/month	$1200

These can print in color:

Printer	Black	Color	RAM	Processor	Duty cycle	Price
LJ CP1025nw	600 dpi, 17 ppm	600 dpi, 4 ppm	68M	400MHz	15,000 pages/month	$180
LJ CP1525nw	600 dpi, 12 ppm	600 dpi, 8 ppm	128M	600MHz	30,000 pages/month	$300
LJ CP2025n	600 dpi, 21 ppm	600 dpi, 21 ppm	128M	540MHz	40,000 pages/month	$375
LJ CP3525n	600 dpi, 30 ppm	600 dpi, 30 ppm	256M	515MHz	75,000 pages/month	$650
LJ CP4025n	1200 dpi, 35 ppm	1200 dpi, 35 ppm	512M	800MHz	100,000 pages/month	$1000
LJ CP4525n	1200 dpi, 42 ppm	1200 dpi, 42 ppm	512M	800MHz	120,000 pages/month	$1350

All those LaserJets are better than the charts imply, since they use RET (to make the resolution seem nearly twice as high as what's in the chart) and data compression (to make the RAM hold twice as much data as what's in the chart).

Those are the prices advertised by HP. Discount dealers charge less.

Duty cycle In that chart, **duty cycle** means how many pages per month the printer can print reliably (without overheating and without "worn or loose" parts making you curse excessively).

> If the duty cycle is under 20,000 pages/month, the printer "looks flimsy".
> If the duty cycle is between 20,000 and 60,000, the printer "looks solid".
> If the duty cycle is over 60,000, the printer "looks invincible, built like a tank".

Processor When your computer's system unit sends data to the LaserJet, the LaserJet handles that data with the help of a **printer processor chip**, which hides inside the printer. The charts show how fast the printer processor chip can think.

Paper size Each LaserJet printer in the charts can handle **letter-size paper** (8½ inches wide, 11 inches tall) and **legal-size paper** (8½ inches wide, 14 inches tall). If you want to handle **tabloid-size paper** instead (11"x17"), you must buy a **wide-format printer**, which costs more and goes slower.

Printer codes When your computer wants to give the printer an instruction (such as "draw a diagonal line across the paper" or "make that scalable font bigger"), the computer sends the printer a code.

HP's LaserJets understand a code called **Printer Control Language (PCL)**, invented by HP. The newest versions of PCL are **PCL 5e** (which is plain), **PCL 5c** (which can handle colors), and **PCL 6** (which can handle 1200 dpi). They're understood by the new LaserJets. Older LaserJets understand just older versions of PCL and can't perform as many tricks.

Most IBM-compatible laser printers (such as the ones by Epson, Panasonic, and Sharp) understand PCL, so that they imitate HP's laser printers, run the same software as HP's laser printers, and are **HP-compatible**. But most of them understand just *old* versions of PCL and can't perform as many tricks as HP's newest LaserJets.

Some laser printers understand a different code, called **PostScript (PS)**, invented by a company called **Adobe**.

Back in the 1980's, when PCL was still very primitive, Postscript was more advanced than PCL. The fanciest laser printers from HP's competitors used PostScript. The very fanciest laser printers were bilingual: they understood both PCL and PostScript.

Now that PCL has improved, it's about as good as PostScript. PCL printers cost less to manufacture than PostScript printers.

In PostScript, each command that the computer sends the printer is written by using English words. Unfortunately, those words are long and consume lots of bytes. In PCL, each command is written as a brief series of code numbers instead. Since PCL commands consume fewer bytes than Postscript commands, the computer can transmit PCL commands to the printer faster than Postscript commands, and PCL commands can fit in less RAM.

Some Apple Mac programs require a PostScript printer.

Most new LaserJet printers understand both PCL and PostScript.

HP's competitors HP has many competitors.

NEC's printers tend to go faster.

Lexmark's printers tend to go faster and print more dpi (to produce finer text and photographs).

Printers from **Panasonic**, **Brother**, and **Oki** tend to cost less; they're bargains.

Printers from **Kyocera** cost less to run, because their toner (ink) cartridges last longer & cost less per page.

But I recommend buying from HP, because people who own HP LaserJets are *very* happy, including me! HP LaserJets are more reliable than other brands, need repairs less often than other brands, cause fewer software headaches than other brands, cost just *slightly* more than other brands, and let you buy more toner from your local store more easily. The only exception to my "buy HP" advice is HP's Color LaserJets, which always get worse ratings than **Magicolor** laser printers, which are made by **Konica Minolta**. But you shouldn't buy a color laser printer anyway: color laser printers are too expensive; and they're much slower than black-only laser printers, even when printing just black! To get color, buy a nice, cheap color inkjet printer instead!

Dot-matrix printers

A **dot-matrix printer** contains a few **guns**, as if it were a super-cowboy whose belt contains several holsters.

Each gun shoots a pin at a ribbon that's covered with ink. When the pin's tip hits the ribbon and smashes the ribbon against the paper, a dot of ink appears on the paper. Then the pin retracts back into the gun that fired it.

Since each gun has its own pin, the number of guns is the same as the number of pins.

9-pin printers If the printer is of average quality, it has 9 guns — and therefore 9 pins. It's called a **9-pin printer**. The 9 guns are stacked on top of each other, in a column that's called the **print head**. If all the guns fire simultaneously, the pins smash against the ribbon simultaneously, so the paper shows 9 dots in a vertical column. The dots are very close to each other, so that the column of dots looks like a single vertical line. If just *some* of the 9 pins press against the ribbon, you get fewer than 9 dots, so you see just *part* of a vertical line.

To print a character, the print head's 9 guns print part of a vertical line; then the print head moves to the right and prints part of another vertical line, then moves to the right again and prints part of another vertical line, etc. Each character is made of parts of vertical lines — and each part is made of dots.

The pattern of dots that makes up a character is called the **dot matrix**. That's why such a printer's called a **9-pin dot-matrix printer**.

Inside the printer is a ROM chip that holds the definition of each character. For example, the ROM's definition of "M" says which pins to fire to produce the letter "M". To use the ROM chip, the printer contains its own CPU chip and its own RAM.

When microcomputers first became popular, most dot-matrix printers for them were built by a New Hampshire company, **Centronics**. In 1980, Japanese companies took over the marketplace. Centronics went bankrupt. The two Japanese companies that dominate the industry now are **Epson** and **Panasonic**.

Epson became popular because it was the first company to develop a disposable print head — so that when the print head wears out, you can throw it away and pop in a new one yourself, without needing a repairman. Also, Epson was the first company to develop a low-cost dot-matrix impact printer whose dots look "clean and crisp" instead of looking like "fuzzy blobs". Epson was the main reason why Centronics went bankrupt.

Epson is part of a Japanese conglomerate called the **Seiko Group**, which became famous by timing the athletes in the 1964 Tokyo Olympics. To time them accurately, the Seiko Group invented a quartz clock attached to an electronic printer. Later, the quartz clock was miniaturized and marketed to consumers as the "Seiko watch", which became the best-selling watch in the whole world. The electronic printer, or "E.P.", led to a better printer, called the "son of E.P.", or "EP's son". That's how the Epson division was founded and got its name!

Epson's first 9-pin printer was the **MX-80**. Then came an improvement, called the **FX-80**. Those printers are obsolete; they've been replaced by Epson's newest 9-pin wonders, the **FX-880** (which costs $250) and the **FX-1180** (which can handle extra-wide paper and costs $380). Epson's cheapest and slowest 9-pin printer is the **LX-300+** ($190). You can get those prices from discount dealers (such as Tri State).

For a 9-pin printer, I recommend buying the **Panasonic 1150** instead, because it prints more beautifully and costs just $149 from discount dealers. Too bad it can't handle extra-wide paper!

Besides Epson and Panasonic, four other Japanese companies are also popular: **NEC**, **Oki**, **Citizen**, and **Star**.

The most popular printers for the Mac were the **Imagewriter** and the **Imagewriter 2**. They were designed by Apple to print exact copies of the Mac's screen. They even print copies of the screen's wild fonts and graphics. Apple stopped selling them.

7-pin printers Although the average dot-matrix printer uses 9 pins, some older printers use just 7 pins instead of 9. Unfortunately, 7-pin printers can't print letters that dip below the line (g, j, p, q, and y) and can't underline. Some 7-pin printers print just capitals; other 7-pin printers "cheat" by raising the letters g, j, p, q, and y slightly.

24-pin printers Although 9 pins are enough to print English, they're *not* enough to print advanced Japanese, which requires 24 pins instead.

The first company to popularize 24-pin printers was **Toshiba**. Its printers printed Japanese — and English — beautifully. 24-pin Toshiba printers became popular in America because they print English characters more beautifully than 9-pin printers.

Epson and all the other Japanese printer companies have copied Toshiba. The best cheap 24-pin printers are the **Panasonic 2130** ($230 at Office Depot) and the **Epson LQ-590** (which is sturdier, easier to operate, and costs $280 at Office Max). The cheapest 24-pin printer that handles wide paper is the **Epson LQ-2090** ($460 at Office Depot).

24-pin printers print more beautifully than 9-pin printers but print slower, are less rugged, and don't bang hard enough to print multiple copies on thick multi-part forms.

In standard 24-pin printers, the even-numbered pins are slightly to the right of the odd-numbered pins, so you see two columns of pins. After firing the even-numbered pins, the print head moves to the right and fires the odd-numbered pins, whose dots on paper overlap the dots from the even-numbered pins. The overlap insures that the vertical column of up to 24 dots has no unwanted gaps.

In fancier 24-pin printers, the 24 pins are arranged as a diamond instead of two columns, so that the sound of firing pins is staggered: when you print a vertical line you hear a quiet hum instead of two bangs.

Beyond 24 pins The fastest dot-matrix printers use multiple print heads, so they can print several characters simultaneously.

Fights about printer technology

Now let's plunge into the technical details of printer technology....

Impact versus non-impact A printer that smashes an inked ribbon against the paper is called an **impact printer**. The most popular kind of impact printer is the dot-matrix printer. Other impact printers use daisy wheels, thimbles, golf balls, bands, chains, and drums. They all make lots of noise, though manufacturers have tried to make the noise acceptable by putting the printers in **noise-reducing enclosures** and by modifying the timing of the smashes.

A printer that does *not* smash an inked ribbon is called a **non-impact printer**. Non-impact printers are all quiet! The most popular non-impact printers are inkjet printers and laser printers.

Other non-impact printers are **thermal printers** (whose hot pins scorch the paper), and **thermal-transfer printers** (which melt hot colored wax onto the paper). Unfortunately, thermal printers require special "scorchable" paper; thermal-transfer printers require expensive ribbons made of colored wax.

Resolution If a printer creates characters out of dots, the quality of the printing depends on how fine the dots are — the "number of dots per inch", which is called the **print resolution**.

A traditional **laser printer** prints 300 dots per inch. That's called **desktop-publishing quality**, because it's good enough for printing newsletters. It's also called **near-typeset-quality**, because it looks nearly as good as a typesetting machine. (A standard typesetting machine prints 1200 or 2400 dots per inch. Those are the resolutions used for printing America's popular magazines, newspapers, and books.) **Most of the modern laser printers can print 1200 dots per inch.**

The typical **inkjet printer** can print 600 dots per inch. That's not quite as good as a modern laser printer but still adequate.

A **24-pin dot-matrix printer** prints just 180 dots per inch. That's called **letter quality (LQ)**, because it looks as good as the letters printed by a typical typewriter. It's good enough for writing letters to people you're trying to impress, though not as impressive as an inkjet or laser printer.

A **9-pin dot-matrix printer** is the ugliest of all: it usually prints just 72 dots per inch vertically. That's called **draft quality**, because it's good enough for rough drafts but not for final copy. It's also called **business quality**, because it's good enough for sending internal memos to your colleagues and accountant — and bills to your customers. If you make a 9-pin dot-matrix printer do 2 passes, it prints 144 dots per inch. That's called **correspondence quality**, because it's good enough for sending pleasant letters to your friends. It's also called **near-letter-quality (NLQ)**, because it looks *nearly* as good as the letters produced on a typewriter, though not quite! The typical 9-pin printer has a switch you can flip, to choose either 1-pass draft quality (which is fast) or 2-pass correspondence quality (which is slower but prettier).

Character width Like an old-fashioned typewriter, an old-fashioned printer makes each character a tenth of an inch wide. That's called "10 characters per inch" or **10 cpi** or **10-pitch** or **pica** (pronounced "pike uh"). Some printers make all the characters narrower so you get 12 characters per inch. That's called **12 cpi** or **12-pitch** or **elite**.

The typical dot-matrix printer lets you choose practically any width you wish. For example, the Epson LQ-850 can print 5, 6, 7½, 8 1/3, 10, 12, 15, 16⅔, and 20 cpi. The widest sizes (5, 6, 7½, and 8⅓ cpi) are called **double-width**, because they're twice as wide as 10, 12, 15, and 16⅔ cpi. The narrowest sizes (16⅔ and 20 cpi) are called **condensed** or **compressed**; they're 60% as wide as 10 and 12 cpi.

Modern printers can make each character a different width, so that a "W" is very wide and an "i" is narrow; that's called **proportional spacing**. It looks much nicer than uniform spacing (such as 10 cpi or 12 cpi). Modern printers let you choose either proportional spacing or uniform spacing. Uniform spacing is usually called **monospacing**.

Fonts You can make a capital T in two ways. The simple way is draw a horizontal bar and a vertical bar, like this: T. The fancy way is to add **serifs** at the ends of the bars, like this: T. A character such as T, which is without serifs, is called **sans serif**, because "sans" is the French word for "without".

The most popular **monospaced fonts** have been **Courier** (which has serifs) and **Letter Gothic** (which is sans serif). They were invented for typewriters. A new version of Courier, for computers, is called **Courier New**; a new version of Letter Gothic, for computers, is called **Lucida Console**.

The most popular **proportionally-spaced fonts** have been **Times Roman** (which has serifs) and **Helvetica** (which is sans serif). They were invented for typesetting machines. A new version of Times Roman, for computers, is called **Times New Roman**; a new version of Helvetica, for computers, is called **Arial**.

Printers — especially laser printers — can beautifully produce all those computer fonts: Courier New, Lucida Console, Times New Roman, and Arial. They can also produce other computer fonts that are more bizarre. Here are samples (each 8½ points high):

```
Here's Courier New. It's monospaced with serifs.
Here's Lucida Console. It's monospaced sans serif.
Here's Times New Roman. It's proportional with serifs.
Here's Arial. It's proportional sans serifs.
```

Paper Laser printers and most inkjet printers accept a stack of ordinary copier paper. You put that paper into the printer's **paper tray** (which is also called the **paper bin** and also called the **cut-sheet paper feeder**).

Some dot-matrix printers can handle stacks of ordinary copier paper, but most dot-matrix printers handle paper differently. To pull paper into the printer, dot-matrix printers can use two methods.

The simplest method is to imitate a typewriter: use a rubber roller that grabs the paper by friction. That method's called **friction feed**. Unfortunately, friction is unreliable: the paper will slip slightly, especially when you get near the sheet's bottom edge.

A more reliable method is to use paper that has holes in the margins. The typical dot-matrix printer has **feeder pins** that fit in the holes and pull the paper up through the printer very accurately. That method, which is called **pin feed**, has just one disadvantage: you must buy paper having holes in the margins.

If your printer uses pin feed and is fancy, it has a clamp that helps the pins stay in the holes. The clamp (with its pins) is called a **tractor**. You get two tractors: one for the left margin and one for the right. A printer having tractors is said to have **tractor feed**. Usually the tractors are **movable**, so that you can move the right-hand tractor closer to the left tractor, to handle narrower paper or mailing labels.

A **dual-feed** printer can feed the paper *both* ways — by friction and by pins — because it has a rubber roller and also has sets of pins. The printer's left edge has a lever: if you pull the lever one way, the paper will rub against the roller, for friction feed; if you pull the lever the other way, the paper will rub against the pins instead, for pin feed.

Most dot-matrix printers have dual feed with movable tractors.

Paper that has holes in it is called **pin-feed paper** (or **tractor-feed paper**).

Like a long tablecloth (folded up and stored in your closet), pin-feed paper comes in a long, continuous sheet that's folded. Since it comes folded but can later be unfolded ("fanned out"), it's also called **fanfold paper**. It's perforated so you can rip it into individual sheets after the printer has printed on it. If the paper's fancy, its margin is perforated too, so that after the printing is done you can rip off the margin and its ugly holes, leaving you with what looks like ordinary typing paper.

The fanciest perforated paper, called **micro-perf**, has a perforation so fine that when you rip along the perforation, the edge is almost smooth.

Most printers can use ordinary typing paper (or copier paper), which is 8½ inches wide. Pin-feed paper is usually an inch wider (9½ inches wide), so that the margins are wide enough to include the pinholes.

Some printers can handle pin-feed paper that's extra-wide (15 inches). Those **wide-carriage printers** typically cost about $130 more than standard-width printers.

Speed The typical printer's advertisement brags about the printer's speed by measuring it in **characters per second (cps)** or **lines per minute (lpm)** or **pages per minute (ppm)**. But those measurements are misleading.

Don't trust the speed of a **laser printer**:

To justify a claim of "8 pages per minute", Apple salesmen noticed that their Laserwriter 2 NT printer took a minute to produce 8 *extra* copies of a page. They ignored the wait of *several minutes* for the *first* copy! Like Apple, most other laser-printer manufacturers say "8 pages per minute" when they should really say: "¹⁄₈ of a minute per additional copy of the same page".

Don't trust the speed of a **dot-matrix printer**:

The advertised speed ignores how long the printer takes to jerk up the paper. For example the typical "80-cps" printer will print 80 characters within a second but then take an extra second to jerk up the paper to the next line, so at the end of two seconds you still see just 80 characters on the paper.

Epson advertised its LQ-850 dot-matrix printer as "264 cps", but it achieved that speed just when making the characters small (12 cpi) and ugly (draft quality). To print characters that were large (10 cpi) and pretty (letter quality), the speed dropped to 73 cps.

Panasonic advertised its KX-P1091 dot-matrix printer as "192 cps", but it achieved that speed just if you threw an internal switch that made the characters even uglier than usual!

So don't trust any ads about printer speed! To discover a printer's true speed, hold a stopwatch while the printer prints many kinds of documents (involving small characters, big characters, short lines, long lines, draft quality, letter quality, and graphics).

Interfacing

A cable of wires runs from the printer to the computer's main part (the system unit). The cable costs about $8 and is *not* included in the printer's advertised price: the cable costs extra.

One end of the cable plugs into a socket at the back of the printer. The cable's other end plugs into "a socket at the back of the system unit", which is called the computer's **printer port**.

If you open the system unit, you'll discover which part of the computer's circuitry the printer port is attached to. In a standard system unit, a cable runs directly from the printer port to the motherboard; but in some system units (such as the original IBM PC), the printer port is attached to a small PC card instead, called a **printer interface card**, which might not be included in the computer's advertised price.

When the computer wants the printer to print some data, the computer sends the data to the printer port; then the data flows through the cable to the printer.

Serial versus parallel The cable from the system unit to the printer contains many wires. Some of them are never used: they're in the cable just in case a computer expert someday figures out a reason to use them. Some of the wires in the cable transmit info about scheduling: they let the computer and printer argue about when to send the data.

If the computer's port is **serial**, just one of the wires transmits the data itself. If the computer's port is **parallel**, 8 wires transmit the data simultaneously.

A parallel port tends to be faster than a serial port, since a parallel port transmits 8 streams of data simultaneously. Unfortunately, a parallel cable is limited to shorter distances (about 12 feet instead of 50 feet), since it's hard to keep 8 signals strong and synchronized over long distances.

Classic cables Back in the 1970's, the typical serial cable contained 25 wires (1 of which transmitted the data). That cable was called the **recommended standard 232C serial cable (RS-232C cable)**. At that time, the typical parallel cable contained 36 wires (8 of which transmitted the data), using a scheme invented by a printer manufacturer called **Centronics** and called the **industry-standard Centronics-compatible parallel cable (Centronics cable)**.

IBM printer cable In 1981, when IBM invented the IBM PC, IBM decided that the 36-wire parallel cable was silly, since just 8 of the wires transmitted data; so IBM switched to a 25-wire cable instead; but to be compatible with the 36-wires printers that had already been invented, IBM glued a 36-pin connector/adapter to the printer's end of the cable; so the cable winds up with 36 pins on the printer's end but just 25 pins on the system unit's end. That weird cable is called an **IBM-PC compatible parallel printer cable (IBM printer cable)**.

If that cable is fancy enough to handle transmissions in both directions, it's called a **bidirectional IBM printer cable**. If it's even fancier and can handle transmissions *quickly* in both directions, it's called an **Institute of Electrical & Electronics Engineers standard 1284 cable (IEEE 1284 cable)**.

If the system unit's circuitry for handling the IBM printer cable is ordinary, you have a **standard parallel port (SPP)**. If that port's circuitry is faster, you have an **enhanced parallel port (EPP)**. If that port's circuitry is even faster, it's called an **extended capability port (ECP)**. It transmits data about 10 times as fast as SPP. Most of the new computers have ECP ports.

EPP was invented by Intel, Zenith, and Xircom. ECP was invented by HP and Microsoft. EPP and ECP have both been approved by IEEE and are part of the 1284 standard. To make full use of an IEEE 1284 cable, you need an ECP port and an ECP-capable printer. You also need software to control them: to use EPP or ECP, you or your dealer must inform the computer that you bought an EPP or ECP port; if you folks don't inform the computer, your printer will print slowly.

USB cable In 1988, when Apple invented the iMac computer, Apple decided that the 25-wire serial cable was silly, so Apple switched to a 4-wire serial cable instead, called the **Universal Serial Bus cable (USB cable)**. Recently, manufacturers of IBM-PC compatible computers have copied Apple's idea of using the USB cable for printing.

Printers for the iMac use the USB cable. Old printers for IBM-compatible PCs used the IBM printer cable; new printers for IBM-compatible PCs use the USB cable instead.

The USB cable can be used for many other purposes, too. For example, the USB cable is the most popular cable for attaching a scanner (to an iMac or an IBM-PC compatible computer). The iMac also uses the USB cable to attach the keyboard, mouse, and floppy-disk drives.

One nice thing about the USB cable is that it's **hot-swappable**: you can plug and unplug USB devices from the USB cable, even while they and the system unit are turned on, without damage. The system unit automatically figures out which USB devices are plugged into it at the moment.

The first version of USB was called **USB 1**. Later came faster versions, called **USB 1.1**, **USB 2**, and **USB 3**.

Software

The information stored in the computer is called **software**. Most software stays in RAM temporarily and is erased from RAM when you no longer need it. But *some* software stays in the computer's circuits *permanently*: it hides in the ROM and is called **firmware**.

To feed firmware to the computer, put extra ROM chips on the motherboard or insert a ROM cartridge. To feed other kinds of software to the computer, use the keyboard, disk, or tape: type the info on the keyboard, or insert a disk or tape containing the info.

You can feed the computer four kinds of software: an **operating system**, a **language**, **application programs**, and **data**. Let's look at them....

Operating systems

An **operating system (OS)** is a set of instructions that explains to the CPU how to handle the keyboard, the screen, printer, disk drives, and mouse.

BIOS versus DOS

In a standard IBM-compatible PC, the operating system is divided into two parts.

The operating system's fundamental part is in the motherboard's ROM chips and called the **Basic Input/Output System** (**BIOS**, pronounced "buy oss" or "buy us"). The operating system's advanced part is on a disk and is called the **disk operating system** (or **DOS**, which is pronounced "doss").

From MS-DOS to Windows

The first DOS for the IBM PC was invented by IBM and a company called **MicroSoft (MS)**. That DOS was called **IBM PC-DOS** or **MS-DOS**. It came on a floppy disk.

Version 1 came on a floppy disk and stayed there. **Version 2** came on a floppy disk but could be copied to a hard disk. (Version 1 couldn't handle hard disks.) **Versions 3, 4, 5, and 6** were even better: like version 2, they came on floppy disks and could be copied to the hard disk but could also be supplemented by a set of extra floppy disks, invented by Microsoft and called **Windows**, which let the computer perform tricks (such as dividing the screen into "windows of info" and letting you use a mouse instead of just a keyboard).

Windows' first version (**Windows 1**) and its early improvements (**Windows 2** and **Windows 3**) were just supplements to MS-DOS. To use them, you had to buy MS-DOS first. They were supplements (called **shells**) that tried to hide MS-DOS's ugliness (just like a clamshell hides an ugly clam); they made MS-DOS look prettier. People bought the ugly operating system (MS-DOS) plus the operating-system shell (Windows) to create a new **operating environment**.

Modern standard Windows

In 1995, Microsoft invented a better version of Windows, called **Windows 95**, which performed more tricks and was a complete operating system: it did *not* require you to buy MS-DOS first; it was *not* just a shell.

Windows 95 came on a floppy disk plus a CD-ROM disk. To use Windows 95, you (or the dealer) had to copy the floppy disk and CD-ROM disk to the hard disk.

After Windows 95, Microsoft invented further improvements. Here are the years:

In 1995 came **Windows 95**.
In 1998 came **Windows 98**.
In 1999 came **Windows 98 Second Edition (Windows 98 SE)**.
In 2000 came **Windows Millennium Edition (Windows Me)**.
In 2001 came **Windows eXPerience (Windows XP)**.
In 2006 came **Windows Vista**.
In 2009 came **Windows 7**.

Windows XP and the versions that came after it (Vista and 7) are called **modern Windows**. Earlier versions of Windows (Windows 1, 2, 3, 95, 98, 98SE, and Me) are called **classic Windows**.

Most computer programs require modern Windows: they require "Windows XP or later". Such programs refuse to run if you bought just classic Windows or MS-DOS.

Windows CE versus Palm

Microsoft invented a tiny version of Windows, for pocket computers and other electronic devices having a small RAM and small screen. That tiny Windows is called **Windows Compact Edition for Computers Embedded in Consumer Electronics (Windows CE)**. It fits completely into ROM chips and requires no disks.

It's used in handheld computers such as the **Compaq iPaq** and the **HP Journada**. It competes against an even smaller ROM operating system, called the **Palm Operating System (Palm OS)**, which is used in cheaper handheld computers such as the **Zire**, the **Treo**, and the **Sony Clié**.

Corporate versions of Windows

Big corporations running big networks used a fancy "corporate" version of Windows called **Windows New Technology (Windows NT)**, invented in 1993. The year 2000 brought an improved version, called **Windows 2000**. In 2001, Windows XP replaced them and made them obsolete, but later Microsoft invented another corporate version, called **Windows Server**.

Unix

AT&T's Bell Laboratories invented an operating system called **Unix**. It's pronounced "you nicks", so it sounds like "eunuchs", which are castrated men. (Be careful! A female computer manager who seems to be saying "get me eunuchs" probably wants an operating system, not castrated men.)

"Unix" is an abbreviation for "UNICS", which stands for "UNified Information & Computing System".

The original version of Unix ran just on DEC minicomputers used by just one person at a time. Newer versions of Unix can handle *any* manufacturer's maxi, mini, or micro and can even handle networks of people sharing computers simultaneously.

Linux A Finnish programmer named **Linus Torvalds** (whose first name is pronounced "lee nuss") invented a Unix imitation called "**Linu**s Uni**x**" or **Linux** (pronounced "lee nucks"). It's free!

It runs on 386, 486, and Pentium computers and also on Atari and Commodore Amiga computers. The most popular way to get it is as part of a **distribution** (which includes Linux plus extras), published by **Ubuntu** (pronounced "oo-BOON-too") or **Mandrake** or **Suse** or **Red Hat**.

Ubuntu's distribution, which comes from England, is free.
Mandrake's distribution, which comes from France, is cheap and nice.
SuSE's distribution, which comes from Germany and the USA, is the easiest and most pleasant.
Red Hat's distribution, which comes from the USA, includes the most features for setting up a network.

Solaris **Sun Microsystems** (which was recently bought by **Oracle**) makes **Sparc** minicomputers, which are used as graphics/engineering workstations and Internet servers. Sparc minicomputers use the **Solaris** operating system, which is a souped-up version of Unix.

Though Solaris is intended for Sparc minicomputers, you can get a version of Solaris that runs on microcomputers containing an Intel CPU.

Unix versus Windows Though many programmers adore Unix, it won't outsell Windows, since Unix is harder to learn and had its main features stolen by MS-DOS & Windows. But Unix networks are more reliable than Window networks and form the basis of the Internet.

Mac OS

The Mac uses its own operating system, called the **Mac OS**. To invent Windows, Microsoft copied many features from the Mac OS. Windows and the Mac OS are very similar to each other.

Versions 1-9 of the Mac OS were invented completely by Apple. Version 10 of the Mac OS is based on Unix instead: it's a version of Unix modified to resemble and surpass Mac OS 9. To emphasize OS 10's Olympic greatness, Apple writes it in Roman numerals (like this: **Mac OS X**), which Apple says to pronounce as "Mac oh ess ten". Apple will forgive you if you say "Mac oh ess ex", which sounds like "Mac — oh! — is sex!", since Mac OS X is the sexy operating system that makes the Mac gorgeously appealing.

iOS

Apple's small gadgets (the iPhone and iPad) use an operating system called **iOS**, whose newest version can handle touchscreens. To compete against iOS, Google invented an operating system called **Android**, whose newest version is **Android 3**, nicknamed **Honeycomb**.

Old computers

Old computers used old operating systems:

Apple 2 computers used **Apple DOS** or **Pro DOS**.
Radio Shack's TRS-80 computers used **TRSDOS** (pronounced "triss doss").
DEC's Vax minicomputers used an operating system called the **Virtual Memory System (VMS)**.
Ancient microcomputers used the **Control Program for Microcomputers (CP/M)**.

IBM maxicomputers use the **Multiple Virtual Storage (MVS)** system or the **Virtual Machine with Conversational Monitor System (VM with CMS)**.

Languages

Languages that humans normally speak — such as English, Spanish, French, Russian, and Chinese — are called **natural languages**. They're too complicated for computers to understand.

To communicate with computers, programmers use **computer languages** instead. The most popular computer languages are **Basic**, **Visual Basic**, **Java**, **JavaScript**, **C**, **C++**, **C#**, **Python**, **Perl**, and **PHP**.

Each is a tiny _part_ of English — a part small enough for the computer to master. To teach the computer one of those tiny languages, you feed the computer a disk (or ROM chips) containing definitions of that tiny language's words.

Of those 4 computer languages, Basic is the easiest to learn and the most practical for most purposes; JavaScript is the best for creating small but thoughtful programs on the Internet; Java is the best for creating deeper Internet programs (and animated Internet cartoons!); C++ is the hardest to learn but runs the fastest, consumes the least RAM and gives you the most control over the computer.

Although those languages have become the most popular, many others were invented.

Back in the **1960's**, the most popular languages were **Fortran** (which let computers do advanced calculations for engineering and scientific research) and **Cobol** (which let computers do accounting for big corporations).

During the **1980's**, most schools taught elementary-school kids to program in **Logo**, high-school kids to program in **Basic**, college kids to program in **Pascal**, graduate computer-science students to program in **C** (which was the forerunner of C++), and business students to program in **Cobol** (for maxicomputers) and **dBase** (for microcomputers).

This book discusses _many_ languages, so you become a virtuoso!

Internet

The **Internet** is an international network of computers that share info. You can make _your_ computer become part of the Internet too!

Web The most popular part of the Internet is the **World Wide Web (WWW)**, where people publish **Web pages** that everybody else using the Internet can view.

If you want to view the Web pages that other people have created, and browse through them, you need a program called a **Web browser**.

The most popular Web browsers are Microsoft's **Internet Explorer (IE)**, Apple's **Safari**, Mozilla's **Firefox**, and Google's **Chrome**. They're all free.

To invent and edit your own Web pages (so other people on the Internet can view them), get a **Web-page editor**. The fanciest is Adobe's **Dreamweaver**, which costs $399, but others cost less and are easier to learn.

Some Web pages let you copy software from the Internet to your own computer's hard disk. Copying from the Internet is called "**downloading** from the Internet." Copying _to_ the Internet is called "**uploading** to the Internet."

E-mail If you attach your computer to the Internet, you can send **electronic mail (e-mail)** to another computer on the Internet, if you have an **e-mail program**.

The most popular e-mail programs are **Windows Mail** (which is part of Windows Vista) and **Outlook Express** (which is part of older versions of Windows). Other e-mail programs are **Outlook**, **Windows Live Mail**, **Hotmail**, **Yahoo Mail**, and Gm**ail**.

Application programs

The computer will do whatever you wish — if you tell it how. To tell the computer how to do what you wish, you feed it a **program**, which is a list of instructions, written in Basic or in some other computer language.

To feed the computer a program, type the program on the keyboard, or buy a disk containing the program and put that disk into the drive, or buy ROM chips containing the program. But before buying the disk, make sure it will work with *your* computer. For example, if the disk says "for Windows", it will work with a modern IBM-compatible PC but not with the typical Apple Mac computer.

A person who invents a program is called a **programmer**. Becoming a programmer is easy: you can become a programmer in just a few minutes! Becoming a *good* programmer takes longer.

You can buy two kinds of programs. The most popular kind is called an **application program (app)**: it handles a specific application, such as payroll or psychotherapy or chess. The other kind of program is called a **system program**: it teaches the computer how to handle various kinds of hardware and various computer languages. An operating system (such as Windows or Unix) is mainly a collection of system programs, bundled together to form a nice package. Application programs are usually purchased separately, though a *few* applications programs are included in the operating system's price.

You'll want several kinds of application programs. Here are the most popular....

Word processing

A **word-processing program** helps you write memos, letters, reports, research papers, articles, and books. It also helps you edit what you wrote.

As you type on the keyboard, the screen shows what you typed. By pressing buttons (on the keyboard or the mouse), you can edit what's on the screen and copy it onto paper and onto a disk.

Most operating systems include a simple word-processing program.

MS-DOS	includes a simple word-processing program called **Edit**.
Classic Windows	includes a simple word-processing program called **Windows Write**.
Modern Windows	includes a simple word-processing program called **WordPad**.
Mac OS 6	includes a simple word-processing program called **TeachText**.
Mac OS 7, 8, and 9	include a simple word-processing program called **SimpleText**.
Mac OS X	includes a simple-word-processing program called **TextEdit**.

Those simple word-processing programs are very limited. For example, they aren't smart enough to correct your spelling.

Most businesses use a fancier word-processing program instead, called **Microsoft Word**. It can correct your spelling and perform many other tricks. It costs about $100. It works just if you've already bought Windows or the Mac OS. Its main competitor is **WordPerfect**, which costs less and is published by a company called **Corel**.

Instead of saying "word-processing program", it's shorter to say just "**word processor**", but beware: "word processor" can mean a program, a person, or a machine. Yes, "word processor" can mean 3 things:

"a word-processing program"
Example: "Does this computer's hard disk include a word processor, such as Microsoft Word?"

"a person who knows how to use a word-processing program"
Example: "I'd like to hire a word processor (such as Joan Smith) who'll type my book for $10 per hour."

"a computerized typewriter whose only purpose is to run a word-processing program"
Example: "Instead of buying a full computer, I want a cheaper machine, such as the Brother Word Processor."

Spreadsheets

To analyze a company, accountants examine the company's financial data (each month's expenses and revenues) and arrange all those numbers to form a huge "table of numbers", **spread** across a big **sheet** of paper. That's called a **spreadsheet**. A spreadsheet is a table of numbers, spread across a sheet of paper — or across the computer's screen.

A **spreadsheet program** lets you create a table of numbers on the computer screen. You can type any numbers you wish. For example, you can type amounts of money (for accounting) or scores (from sports or student exams) or measurements (from science-lab experiments or sociology surveys) or your ratings of members of the opposite sex.

The typical spreadsheet program is powerful. It can automatically do these things:

---

compute "the total, average, percentages, and other statistics" for each row & column

rearrange the data (to put the topics in alphabetical order or from "best" to "worse")

draw pretty graphs summarizing the results

copy all that to paper and disk

automatically change all the sums, averages, percentages, and graphs whenever you edit the original data

---

It's great for analyzing budgets, scientific experiments, statistics, and you!

Most businesses use a spreadsheet program called **Microsoft Excel**. It requires Windows or a Mac. Its main competitor is Corel's **Quattro Pro**, which requires Windows.

Danger: compulsive perfectionism

The most successful business programs are the ones that make work become fun, by turning the work into a video game. That's why word processing programs and spreadsheet programs are so successful — they let you move letters and numbers around the screen, edit the errors by "zapping" them, and let you press a button that makes the screen explode with totals, subtotals, counts, and other info.

Sometimes, word processing can be *too* much fun. Since it's so much fun to edit on a word processor, people using word processors edit more thoroughly than people using typewriters or pens. Word processing fosters **compulsive perfectionism**.

Word-processed documents wind up better-written than non-electronic documents but take longer to finish. According to a survey by Colorado State, people using word processors take about 30% longer to generate memos than people using pens, and the word-processed memos are needlessly long.

Danger: intimidation

Word-processing and spreadsheet programs can become weapons that mesmerize people into believing everything you say — even if what you're saying is wrong.

For example, suppose you want to submit a budget. If you scribble the budget on a scrap of paper, nobody will take you seriously; but if you put your data into a spreadsheet program that spits out beautifully aligned columns with totals, subtotals, percentages, bar charts, and pie charts, your audience will assume your budget's carefully thought out and applaud it, even though it's just a pretty presentation of the same crude guesses you'd have scribbled on paper.

Similarly, if you want to talk somebody into believing your idea, scribbling it on a scrap of paper won't impress anybody. Instead, print the idea beautifully, using a word processor to create headlines, footnotes, etc. That will make the idea seem carefully thought out, even if the thought is actually the same garbage.

Try it! If you're a kid, write a formal report on why your dessert tonight should be strawberry ice cream instead of vanilla. After submitting it to your Mom, submit it to an ice-cream company and watch yourself get praised, quoted, and hired! That's what marketing is all about: bad ideas, nicely packaged.

Pictures

A **graphics program** helps you create pictures that are pretty or bizarre or whatever else you want! You'll want to get several types of graphics programs.

One type is called a **paint program**. It lets you create pictures easily. These paint programs are the most famous:

Program	Characteristics
Mac Paint	the first paint program; ran on Mac OS; no longer marketed
Deluxe Paint	best early paint program; ran on Commodore Amiga and MS-DOS; no longer marketed
Paintbrush	came free as part of Windows 3, which is no longer marketed
Windows Paint	comes free as part of modern Windows (Windows 95 and later)
Corel Painter	fanciest paint program; imitates oil painting, charcoal, etc.; for Mac and Windows
Kid Pix	best paint program for kids; lots of fun; includes stars and many other kid shapes

Another type is called a **photo editor**. It lets you put a photo into the computer (by using a digital camera or scanner) and see the photo on the computer's screen. Then it lets you edit the photo: it lets you crop out the irrelevant parts, cover scratches and embarrassing details, improve the contrast and brightness and colors, remove red-eye (caused when eyes become accidentally red from the flashbulb), and add special dramatic effects. These photo editors are the best:

Program	Characteristics
Photoshop	performs the fanciest tricks, but hard to master; for Mac and Windows by Adobe
Photoshop Elements	a stripped-down version of Photoshop; easier to learn but reasonably powerful
Digital Image Suite	by Microsoft and even easier than Photoshop Elements

Another type is called a **drawing program**. It resembles a paint program but specializes in drawing straight lines instead of squiggles. It's best for drawing pictures of things that have straight lines, such as buildings, machines, and charts for technical illustrations. These drawing programs are the most famous:

Program	Characteristics
Microsoft Draw	included free as part of Microsoft Word and some other Microsoft products
Corel Draw	the fanciest drawing program for Windows
Adobe Illustrator	an old program; still the professional standard; expensive; for Mac and Windows

Another type is called a **computer-aided drafting & design program (CAD program)**. It resembles a draw program but does more math. For example, it can print mock blueprints, showing the lengths of all parts. It can compute the surface area (square feet) of any shape, so you can compute how much material to buy to build your structure and cover it. It lets you give fancy geometric commands, such as "draw a 37-degree angle, but make the point be round instead of sharp, so nobody gets hurt" or "draw a circle that goes through these three points" or "draw a line that grazes these two circles, so it's tangent to them". These CAD programs are the most famous:

Program	Characteristics	List
AutoCAD	the standard that professionals use; expensive	$3995
AutoCAD LT	a "light" cheaper version of AutoCAD, for students and experimenters	$899
TurboCAD Deluxe	much cheaper than AutoCAD and AutoCAD LT, but not as fancy	$150

Another type is called a **presentation program**. It lets you create a slide show, to accompany your speech. In the slide show, each slide can include photos, charts, and notes. These presentation programs are the most famous:

Program	Characteristics
PowerPoint	by Microsoft, for Windows and Mac
Freelance	by Lotus (which is part of IBM), for Windows
Corel Presentations	by Corel, for Windows

Movies

A **video editor** lets you edit the home movies your video camcorder creates. These video editors are the best:

Program	Characteristics
Adobe Premiere	performs the fanciest tricks, but hard to master; for Mac and Windows
Adobe Premiere Elements	a stripped-down version of Adobe Premier; easier to learn
Pinnacle Studio	even easier than Adobe Premiere
Windows Movie Maker	the easiest of all; comes free as part of Windows XP & Vista

Desktop publishing

A **desktop-publishing program** resembles a word-processing program but lets you more easily create newsletters, newspapers, magazines, posters, and signs, by letting you more easily include pictures, captions, multiple columns, and jumps (such as "continued on page 5"). These desktop-publishing programs are the most famous:

Program	Characteristics
PageMaker	the first desktop-publishing program, for Mac & Windows, expensive, by Adobe
InDesign	from Adobe, newer and better than PageMaker
Quark XPress	competed against PageMaker and became the most popular, but then InDesign beat it
Microsoft Publisher	cheap, easy to learn, the best for beginners, lacks advanced features, for Windows
Print Shop	cheap, easy; was popular in 1980's but too limited, beaten by Microsoft Publisher

Databases

A **database program** helps you manipulate long lists of data, such as names, addresses, phone numbers, and comments about your acquaintances (friends, customers, suppliers, employees, students, and teachers).

As you type the list of data, the database program automatically copies it to the hard disk. Then the program lets you edit that data. For example, you can insert extra data in the middle of the list. The program lets you view the data in any order you wish (such alphabetical order, ZIP-code order, or chronological order) and print that view onto paper.

The program can search through all that data and find, in just a few seconds, the data that's unusual. For example, it can find everybody whose birthday is *today*, or everybody who's blond and under 18, or everybody who lives out-of-state and has owed you more than $100 for over a year.

Most businesses use a database program called **Microsoft Access**. It requires Windows. Unfortunately, it's hard to master. You might be happier with an easier database program instead, such as **FileMaker Pro**, which is published by a division of Apple and runs on Macs and Windows. Other famous database programs are **Approach** (for Windows and published by IBM's Lotus division), **Oracle** (for large corporations), **Q&A** (for beginners using MS-DOS), **dBase** (for MS-DOS or Windows), and **FoxPro** (which resembles DBase but is fancier).

Office suites

Instead of buying a word-processing program, a spreadsheet program, and other programs separately, you can buy an **office suite**, which includes them all!

MS Office The best and most popular office suite is **MicroSoft Office (MS Office)**. The newest version, **MS Office 2010**, requires modern Windows (Windows XP, Windows Vista, or Windows 7). The list price is $500 because Microsoft wants rich people & companies to pay that, but Microsoft has invented many schemes to squeeze a few bucks out of normal folks too. Here are the schemes for you to take advantage of:

The $500 price is for the **Professional** edition, which includes 7 programs: Word, Excel, PowerPoint, OneNote (for organizing your materials), Outlook, Access, and Publisher. Just $280 gets you the **Home & Business** edition instead, which omits Access & Publisher, so you get 5 programs.

If you buy one of those editions, you're allowed to use it on **2 computers**: your desktop plus your laptop. But you must be the primary user on each: you're not allowed to copy the software onto a friend's computer.

Just $150 gets you the **Home & Student** edition, which resembles the Home & Business edition but omits Outlook (so you get just 4 programs), is licensed for any 3 computers (so 2 of your friends can copy it), but is illegal to use for anything serious: you're not licensed to use it for any business work, government work, non-profit work, or in schools; it's licensed just for doing homework & fun stuff at your home, though Microsoft doesn't have much ability to enforce that restriction.

Those prices get you a CD, which you (or your dealer) must copy to your hard disk. Some computers come with the **Starter** edition already installed. That edition includes just stripped-down versions of Word & Excel (so you get just parts of 2 programs) and forces you to watch ads.

To pay less, buy a **Product Key** instead of a CD. Here are the Product Key prices: $350 for Professional, $200 for Home & Business, $120 for Home & Student. After buying the Product Key (which is just a license number), you get it to work by either downloading the software from Microsoft's Website or telling the Starter edition to unlock the extra features. Unfortunately, when you buy the Product Key, it works on just one computer (not 2 or 3).

To pay nothing, you can download a **free trial version** of the Professional edition from Microsoft's Website. But after 60 days, the trial version won't let you edit further until you buy a paid version.

If you're a student who has an e-mail address at a college approved by Microsoft, you can buy an **academic version** of the Professional edition for just $80. It acts the same as the regular Professional edition but is to be used just by you.

All the prices I mentioned are the *list* prices. **Discount dealers** charge less, especially if you buy Microsoft Office at the same time as a computer. For example, many discount dealers often sell the Home & Student edition (which is the most popular) for just $100. If you join **Sam's Club** (by paying dues of $35 or $40 per year), you can buy the Home & Business edition there cheaply (the CD for $215, the Product Key for $169).

All those versions, editions, prices, and deals are for computer that use Windows. If you have a Mac instead of Windows, you must use MS Office's Mac version. The current version is **Microsoft Office 2011 for Mac**, which includes just Word, Excel, PowerPoint, and Outlook: Microsoft never invented a Mac version of Access, PowerPoint, or OneNote. The Mac's free trial version works for just for 30 days, not 60.

WordPerfect Office The main competitor to MS Office is Corel's **WordPerfect Office**. The newest version is called **WordPerfect Office X5**, costs $200, $130 for an upgrade, $100 for a Home & Student edition (which can be installed on 3 computers but isn't licensed for business use). You get the upgrade price if you own an earlier version of WordPerfect Office, Microsoft Office, or Microsoft Works Suite.

Open Office Another competitor to MS Office is **Open Office**, which is put together by volunteers who let you download it free from the Internet. It imitates an old version of Microsoft Office. It used to be called **Star Office** and was a commercial product, but now it's free.

Integrated programs

Instead of buying an office suite, you can pay less by getting a cute little program, called an **integrated program**, which does a little bit of everything!

The best integrated programs are **Microsoft Works**, **iWork**, and **Q&A**. Here's how they compare....

Microsoft Works This is **the best integrated program for handling word processing and spreadsheets**. It also handles databases.

Its Windows version is good. Its DOS and Mac versions are not.

Its newest Windows version, **Microsoft Works 9**, lists for $40. Many computers come with Microsoft Works 9 installed on the hard disk already, since Microsoft charges manufacturers just $10 per copy for permission to do that. (Microsoft has stopped selling a souped-up version called **Microsoft Works Suite**.)

Here's a trick: **buy Microsoft Works** (or a computer whose hard disk contains it) then use that as an excuse to get the upgrade price on other products. For example, **that gets you the upgrade price on MS Office 2007** and WordPerfect Office.

iWork This is **the best integrated program for handling desktop publishing**. It also handles word processing, spreadsheets, databases, presentations, painting, and drawing. It's published by Apple, which used to call it **AppleWorks** and **Claris Works**. It runs on Macs and costs $79.

Q&A This is **the best integrated program for handling databases**. It handles word processing poorly and doesn't handle spreadsheets at all, but its DOS version is great, and I still use it.

The Windows version is terrible, so I keep using the DOS version. If you've been using the DOS version but need to switch to Windows, try **Sesame Database Manager**, which imitates the database part of Q&A, runs in Windows & Linux, and can be downloaded from **Lantica Software** (in Pennsylvania at 800-410-6315) for $79.

Accounting

You can get a checkbook program. It helps you balance your checkbook, track your expenses (and categorize them so you can get tax deductions), manage your credit cards, track your investments (stocks, bonds, and bank accounts), and compute your net worth.

The first program to do that well was **Quicken**, published by **Intuit**. Then Microsoft invented a competing program, called **Microsoft Money**, which was easier, but recently Microsoft gave up trying to sell it. Quicken and Microsoft Money are fine for personal use or to run tiny businesses.

If your business has lots of employees, you'll want a program that's better at "paying your employees" and "billing your customers". The easiest powerful program is Intuit's **QuickBooks**, which is a souped-up version of Quicken. Other accounting programs, which is are even more powerful (and slightly harder to learn how to use) are **Peachtree Complete Accounting** and **Manage Your Own Business (MYOB)**.

Vertical software

Software that can be used by a *wide variety* of businesses is called **horizontal software**. Programs for word processing, spreadsheets, and databases are all examples of horizontal software.

Software targeted to a specific industry is called **vertical software**. Programs specifically for doctors, lawyers, and real-estate management are all examples of vertical software.

Vertical software is expensive because it can't be mass-marketed to the general public and isn't available from discount dealers. The typical vertical-market program costs about $1000, whereas the typical horizontal-market program costs about $100 from discount dealers.

Until the price of vertical software declines, use horizontal software instead. With just a few hours of effort, you can customize horizontal software to fit your own specific needs.

Viruses

Some nasty programmers have invented **computer viruses**, which are programs that purposely damage your other programs and can sneakily copy themselves onto every disk and e-mail message that you share with friends. To avoid catching a virus, protect yourself in 4 ways:

Be aware of the 6 kinds of common viruses, by reading this book's virus chapter.
Make sure all software entering your computer comes from reputable sources.
Keep your eyes open for suspicious behavior.
Get an **antivirus program**, such as **Microsoft Security Essentials** or **Norton AntiVirus**.

Data

The typical program comes on a CD-ROM disk. To use the program, put its CD-ROM disk into the CD-ROM drive. Then copy the program to your hard disk.

The CD-ROM disk containing the program might also contain lots of music, video, and other data. If the data is too big to fit on the hard disk, you must keep the CD-ROM disk in the drive while running the program, so the computer can access whatever part of the CD-ROM's data is needed at the moment.

Some programs let you create your own data, by typing the data at your keyboard. The computer stores that data on the hard disk. You should occasionally copy that data onto a floppy disk, as a backup copy, to protect yourself in case the hard disk gets damaged.

Software companies

Will your computer be pleasant to use? The answer depends mainly on which software you buy. Software companies will influence your life more than any hardware manufacturer.

The 13 dominant software companies are **Microsoft**, **Novell**, **Corel**, **IBM**, **Borland**, **Symantec**, **Oracle**, **CA**, **Intuit**, **Adobe**, **Autodesk**, **HM Rivergroup**, and **Electronic Arts**. Here's why....

Microsoft

The most important software company is **Microsoft**, which takes in about 62 billion dollars of revenue per year. It makes the most popular operating system (**Windows**) and the most popular office suite (**Microsoft Office**).

The company's main founder is **Bill Gates**.

Because of Microsoft's success, when he was 30 he became a billionaire and appeared on the cover of Time magazine. When he turned 40 (on October 28, 1995), he was worth 14.7 billion dollars.

At the beginning of 1997, he was worth 24 billion dollars. Seven months later, at the end of July, he was worth 40 billion dollars. Two years later, in mid-1999, he was worth 100 billion dollars! He was the richest person in the world.

100 billion dollars is a lot of money! For example, even if you earn 100 million dollars per year, you'd have to work 1000 years to get what Bill had. 100 billion dollars was enough to give $360 to each American, or $16 to each person on the planet. 100 billion one-dollar bills, if laid end-to-end, would stretch to the moon and back, 20 times. Programmers often measure their salaries in **microbills**, where a **microbill** is defined as being a millionth of Bill Gates' worth, so a microbill became $100,000.

Bill didn't have 100 billion dollars cash in his pocket, of course. Most of his billions were just on paper, invested in Microsoft stock: he owned 12% of Microsoft, whose stock was overpriced.

Bill said he planned to donate 95% of his wealth to worthy causes. To start that process, he and his wife Melinda created the **Bill & Melinda Gates Foundation**, which has given big grants to libraries, schools, and third-world health agencies. When I was writing this book in June 2010, Bill's worth had dropped to 56 billion dollars, because of the donations he made and because the stock market dropped. Now he's just the second-richest person in the world. (The richest is a Mexican, Carlos Slim Helú, who has 74 billion dollars and owns many companies, such as Latin America's biggest cell-phone service.)

Bill is semi-retired from Microsoft (which is now run by his friend Steve Ballmer), so Bill devotes full attention to giving his money away — by helping Melinda run their foundation.

Microsoft is the most diversified software company:

It has sold operating systems (**MS-DOS** and **Windows**), a word-processing program (**Microsoft Word**), a spreadsheet program (**Excel**), a desktop-publishing program (**Microsoft Publisher**), database programs (**Access** and **FoxPro**), an integrated program (**Microsoft Works**), a computerized encyclopedia (**Encarta**), programming languages (**Visual Basic**, **Visual C++**, and others), and a wide variety of other software. It's the main software publisher for the IBM PC and Mac. It also wrote the versions of Basic used by primitive computers (such as the Apple 2 family, Radio Shack TRS-80, Commodore 64, and Commodore Amiga).

It also sells hardware (such as **mice**, **keyboards**, and the **Xbox** game-playing system) and Internet services (such as **MSN**).

Microsoft continually develops new products because of pressure from competitors. For example, Microsoft was forced to improve Microsoft Word because of competition from WordPerfect and improve Microsoft C because of competition from Borland's C. Those continual pressures to improve keep Microsoft a vibrant, dynamically changing company.

Novell & Corel

Novell invented **Netware** & **Intranetware**, which are programs that help create computer networks.

In 1994, Novell bought **WordPerfect Corporation** (which made the most popular word-processing program, WordPerfect). Novell's purchase was natural, since both companies were in Utah. WordPerfect Corporation sold out to Novell because WordPerfect Corporation was having financial trouble, since many customers were switching to Microsoft Word, which has been improving dramatically.

In 1994, Novell also bought **Quattro Pro** (a top-rated spreadsheet program invented by a company called **Borland**). Borland sold Quattro Pro to Novell because Borland was having financial trouble competing against Microsoft.

Novell was founded by Ray Noorda. Novell's next CEO, Robert Frankenberg, tried to make the company smaller and more manageable, so in 1996 he sold WordPerfect and Quattro Pro to a Canadian company, **Corel**, which was famous for inventing a graphics program called **Corel Draw**.

In 2004, Novell bought a German company called **SuSE** (which made the nicest version of Linux, **SuSE Linux**).

Novell takes in about 1 billion dollars per year. Corel takes in about ¼ of a billion dollars per year.

Microsoft owns 25% of Corel.

Lotus & IBM

Lotus made the most popular spreadsheet program (which was **1-2-3**). For too many years, Lotus sat on its laurels, and customers gradually began to switch to competitors such as Microsoft Excel and Quattro Pro. We expected Lotus to die.

But during the 1990's, Lotus displayed good taste and made wise moves: it dramatically improved 1-2-3; it bought a company called **Samna**, which made the nicest word-processing program (**Ami Pro**), so Ami Pro became a Lotus product; it began selling an easy-to-use presentation-graphics program, **Freelance**; and it began selling a product called **Notes**, which helps people send electronic mail to each other and edit each other's documents.

In 1995, IBM bought Lotus, so now Lotus is part of IBM, which takes in about 100 billion dollars per year.

Borland & Micro Focus

Borland was started by Philippe Kahn, who grew up in France.

To study math, he went to a university in Zurich, Switzerland, where he got curious about computers and decided to take a computer class.

The university offered two introductory classes: one explained how to program using a language called **PL/I**, the other explained how to program by using a language called **Pascal** instead. Since Pascal was brand new then, nobody had heard of it, so 200 students signed up for PL/I and just 5 students signed up for Pascal. Philippe signed up for Pascal because he hated big classes. His professor was Pascal's inventor, Niklaus Wirth.

In 1983, Philippe went to California and started a computer company. Since he was an illegal alien, he tried to pretend he was thoroughly American and named his company **Borland**, in honor of the land that produced astronaut Frank Borman. His first product was **Turbo Pascal**, which he'd created back in Europe with the help of two friends.

Most other versions of Pascal were selling for hundreds of dollars. Philippe read a book saying people buy mail-order items on impulse only if priced under $50, so he charged $49.95. The book and Philippe were right: at $49.95, Turbo Pascal became a smashing success.

Later, Philippe improved Turbo Pascal and raised its price to $149.95. He also bought other software publishers and merged them into Borland, so Borland became huge.

Philippe occasionally experimented with dropping prices. For example, he dropped the price of Borland's spreadsheet program, **Quattro Pro**, to just $49.95, even though Quattro Pro was in some ways better than 1-2-3, which Lotus was selling for about $300. Microsoft's head, Bill Gates, said that the competitor worrying him the most was Borland, because he feared Philippe would pull another publicity stunt and drop prices below $50 again, forcing Microsoft to do the same.

During the 1980's, Borland bought two companies that invented wonderful database programs: **Reflex** and **Paradox**. Borland eventually stopped selling Reflex, but Paradox lives on.

Paradox's main competitor was **dBase**, published by a company called **Ashton-Tate**. Philippe decided to win the competition against Ashton-Tate the easy way: he *bought* Ashton-Tate, so now Borland publishes both Paradox and DBase. Philippe said he bought Ashton-Tate mainly to get his hands on Ashton-Tate's mailing list, so he could sell DBase users on the idea of converting to Paradox.

But Philippe paid too much for Ashton-Tate, whose products, employees, and mailing lists were all becoming stale. Since Ashton-Tate was bigger than Borland, Philippe had to borrow lots of money to buy Ashton-Tate, and he had trouble paying it back. Buying Ashton-Tate was his biggest mistake.

By 1994, he was having trouble competing against Microsoft's rapidly improving products and trouble repaying the money he'd borrowed to finance the takeover of Ashton-Tate. Financially strapped, he sold Novell his crown jewel, Quattro Pro, gave Novell the right to make a million copies of Paradox.

Novell's founder, Ray Noorda, said candidly he wasn't thrilled by Quattro Pro but wanted to buy it anyway, just as an excuse to give Philippe some money, so Philippe could stay in business and scare Microsoft, so Bill Gates would devote his energy to fighting Philippe instead of fighting Novell.

In 1995, Philippe stepped down from being the head of Borland. He spent most of his time running a start-up company called **Starfish Software**, which Motorola bought in 1998 then resold to Nokia, which makes cell phones using Starfish Software's patents.

Borland changed its name to "Inprise", then changed back to "Borland" again, then became part of **Micro Focus**, which takes in about ½ a billion dollars per year.

Why fight?

The heads of computer companies still act like a bunch of tussling toddlers. I'm waiting for their mama to say, "Boys, will you please stop fighting, shake hands, and make up!"

Why can't Bill Gates make peace with his competitors? Answer: they're all greedy — and Bill is brash. (For example, during an interview with CBS's Connie Chung, he walked out when she mispronounced "Dos" and asked a pointed question about a competitor.)

But Bill's actually somewhat glad at his competitors' successes, since Microsoft *needs* to have enough successful competitors to prevent the Justice Department from declaring that Microsoft's too big a monopoly. By letting several competitors invent new ideas and bring them all to market, we consumers get to choose for ourselves which ideas are best — and vote on them with our dollars — rather than kowtow to a single dictator.

Symantec

My favorite database program, Q&A, is published by **Symantec**.

Like Lotus, Symantec shows good taste in acquisitions: it bought two companies making good versions of the C programming language (**Lightspeed** and **Zortech**) and also bought two companies making **DOS utility programs** that fix DOS's weaknesses (**Peter Norton Software** and **Central Point Software**). Now Symantec takes in about 6 billion dollars per year.

Symantec tries hard to improve all those acquired products, but I wish it would improve Q&A instead! I'm sad to see Q&A, the world's best database program, be neglected and fall into obsolescence.

Specialized companies

Oracle and **CA** make software that runs on computers of all sizes: maxicomputers, minicomputers, and microcomputers.

Oracle's software handles databases. Oracle takes in 27 billion dollars per year. Oracle was founded by Larry Ellison, who still runs the company. Since he owns 24% of Oracle's stock, he's a multibillionaire, nearly as rich as Bill Gates, and yes, he's still single!

CA's software handles accounting (such as bill-paying, bill-collecting, inventory, and payroll). CA was founded by a Chinese immigrant on Long Island, New York: Charles Wang (pronounced "wong", not "wang"). Try saying this sentence fast: "wong" is right, "wang" is wrong. In August 2000, Charles Wang retired and turned the company over to another immigrant (Sanjay Kumar, who came from Sri Lanka when he was 14 years old). CA's software is so boring that consumers don't know it exists, but CA is huge, though shrinking: it used to take in 6 billion dollars per year but now takes in just 4½ billion. 25% of CA's stock is owned by a single rich man: Swiss billionaire Walter Haefner.

Intuit makes programs that handle accounting on microcomputers. Intuit's programs are cheap: under $100.

Intuit's most popular accounting programs are **Quicken** (which tracks expenses and balances your checkbook), **QuickBooks** (which handles all major business accounting), and **Turbo Tax** (which helps you fill in your 1040 income-tax form for the IRS). Turbo Tax used to be published by a company called **Chipsoft**, but Intuit bought Chipsoft in 1994.

In 1995, Microsoft tried to buy Intuit — and Intuit agreed — but Microsoft changed its mind when the Justice Department accused Microsoft of becoming too big a monopoly.

Intuit takes in 3½ billion dollars per year.

Adobe makes **Postscript** software (used in many laser printers), **Photoshop** (which edits photographs), and **Acrobat** (which does desktop publishing and lets you easily transmit the results by Internet). In 1994, Adobe bought **Aldus** (the company that invented the first desktop-publishing program, **PageMaker**). Adobe takes in 4 billion dollars per year.

Autodesk publishes **AutoCAD**, which is the fanciest program for handling computer-aided design (CAD). Autodesk takes in 2 billion dollars per year.

Electronic Arts (EA) makes excellent educational games and low-cost tools for budding young artists and musicians. It's also the world's biggest producer and distributor of video games for computers and for video-game machines (such as Sony's PlayStation and Microsoft's Xbox). It takes in 3½ billion dollars per year.

Buying software

You'll want 4 kinds of software: an operating system (which teaches the CPU how to handle the keyboard, screen, printer, and disks); a computer language (such as Basic); application programs (such as a word-processing program, a spreadsheet program, and a database program); and data.

When shopping for a computer, beware: its advertised price usually does *not* include all 4 kinds of software. Ask the seller which software is included and how much the other software costs.

The typical fancy program (such as a word-processing program, spreadsheet program, or database program) has a **list price** of $299. That's also called the **manufacturer's suggested retail price (MSRP)**. If you buy the program directly from the software's publisher, that's the price you'll pay. (You'll also pay about $7 for shipping & handling. If the publisher has a sales office in your state, you'll also be charged for sales tax, even if you're phoning the manufacturer's out-of-state headquarters.)

That list price is made ridiculously high as a marketing ploy, to give you the impression that the program is fancy.

But if you walk into a typical computer store, you will *not* pay $299 for the program. Instead, you'll pay $249. That's called the **street price** because it's the price you see when you walk down the street and peek in the windows of computer stores. (You'll also pay sales tax.)

Instead of charging $249, mail-order dealers charge slightly less: $229. That's called the **mail-order price**. (You'll also pay about $7 for shipping & handling, but you won't pay tax if the mail-order company is out-of-state.) Another way to get that kind of price is to visit a discount store, such as Best Buy or Staples, when that item is on sale.

Version upgrades

If you already own an older version of the program, you can switch to the new version cheaply, by asking for the **version upgrade**, which costs just $99. You can order the version upgrade at your local computer store, or from mail-order dealers, or directly from the program's publisher.

To qualify for the version upgrade, you must *prove* that you already own an older version of the program. You can do that in several ways:

If you're ordering directly from the program's publisher, the program's publisher will check its records to verify that you had sent in your registration card for the previous version. If you're ordering at a local computer store, bring in the official instruction manual that came with the old version: the store will rip out the manual's first page (the title page) and mail it to the publisher. If you lost that manual, you can instead give the store Disk 1 of the old version's set of disks. The store needs the *original* title page or disk; copies are not accepted. If you're ordering from a mail-order dealer, send the dealer the title page by mail or fax.

Some manufacturers (such as Microsoft) use a simpler way to qualify you for the version upgrade: when you install the new version, it automatically searches your computer's hard disk for the old version and refuses to run if the old version is missing.

If you bought the old version shortly before the new version came out, you can get the new version free! Just phone the publisher and ask for the **free version upgrade**.

> Here's how you prove you bought the old version shortly before the new version came out (where "shortly before" is usually defined as meaning "within 60 days"): mail either your dated sales slip or a "free version-upgrade certificate" that came in the old version's box. Though the upgrade is "free", you must pay an exorbitant charge for shipping and handling ($10 for just the disks, $30 for disks plus manuals).

Competitive upgrades

If you don't own an older version of the program, you can't get the version-upgrade price. Here's the best you can do:

> If you already own a competing program (such as a different brand of word processor that competes against the word processor you're trying to buy), ask for the **competitive-upgrade price**. It's usually $129, which is just slightly higher than the version-upgrade price. Get it from your local store, mail-order dealer, or directly from the publisher.

To prove you qualify for the competitive-upgrade price, provide the title page or Disk 1 of the competing program (or have Microsoft's software automatically scan for such programs).

Copying software

If you buy a program, you should make backup copies of the disks. Use the backup copies in case the original disks get damaged.

You're *not* allowed to give copies of the disks to your friends. That's against the law! If your friends want to use the program, they must buy it from the software publisher or a dealer, so that the programmer receives royalties.

If you give copies to your friends and become a lawbreaker, you're called a **pirate**; making the copies is called **piracy**; the copies are called **pirated software** or **hot software**. Don't be a pirate! Don't distribute hot software!

Some software publishers use tricks that make the computer refuse to copy the program. Those tricks are called **copy protection**; the software is **copy protected**. But even if the software publisher doesn't use such tricks, it's still against the law to make copies of the program for other people, since the program is still copy*righted*.

> If your friends want to try a program before buying it, don't give them a copy of the program! Instead, tell your friends to visit you and use the program while they sit at your computer. That's legal, and it also lets you help your friends figure out how to use the software.
>
> If you buy a version upgrade, you're *not* allowed to give the older version to a friend to use on a different computer. You must destroy the older version — or keep it just for emergencies, in case the newer version stops working.

Demo disks

Besides sitting at a friend's computer, another way to "try before you buy" is to phone the program's publisher and ask for a free **demo disk**.

Although some demo disks are just useless animated ads, the best publishers provide useful demo disks (called **trial-size versions**) that closely imitate the full versions. For example, the typical trial-size version of a word-processing program has nearly all the features of the full version, but it refuses to print memos that are more than a page long and refuses to copy your writing onto a disk.

Trial-size versions are nicknamed **crippled software**, because each trial-size version has one or two abilities cut off. Playing with crippled software is a great way to give yourself a free education!

Freeware

Software that you're allowed to copy and use freely is called **freeware**. For example, most demo disks and trial-size versions are freeware.

Most software invented by schools, government agencies, and computer clubs is freeware. Ask!

Shareware

Shareware is software that comes with a plea: although the author lets you copy the software and try it, you're encouraged to mail the author a contribution if you like what you tried.

The suggested contribution, typically $25, is called a **registration fee**. It makes you a **registered user** and puts you on the author's mailing list, so the author can mail you a printed manual and newer versions of the software.

Though most shareware authors merely "ask" for contributions, other shareware authors "demand" that you send a contribution if you use the software for longer than a month. Software for which a contribution is "demanded" is called **guiltware** — because if you don't send the contribution, the author says you're guilty of breaking the law.

To get shareware, copy it from a friend. If none of your friends own the shareware you want, buy the disks from a computer club or store for about $5 per disk; but remember that the $5 pays for just the disk, not the registration fee (which you're honor-bound to mail in if you extensively use the program).

Beta versions

After inventing a program, its publisher must **test** it, to make sure it works on many kinds of computer equipment and in many situations. At first, the publisher's employees test the program on their own computers: that's called **alpha testing**. Next, the publishing company lets *outsiders* try the still-not-quite-perfected program: that's called **beta testing**.

The outsiders who try it are called **beta testers**; the version being tested by outsiders is called a **beta version**. Beta versions are sometimes distributed for free or at a reduced price; but if you use a beta version, don't rely on it, since it hasn't been perfected yet.

Special deals

If your office wants many employees to use a program, ask the publisher for a **site license**, which permits your company to make copies for all employees in the office. Typically the employees are *not* allowed to take the copies home: the copies must all be used at the same site.

If you're in a school and trying to teach kids how to use a program, ask the publisher for a trial-size version or **academic version** or **educational site license**.

If you own two computers and want to put the same program on both, you must typically buy two copies of the program. For example, if you want to put Windows 98 on two computers, you must buy two copies of Windows 98 (to avoid piracy), unless both computers are on the same site and you have a site license. Microsoft and some other major software publishers permit this exception, called the **portable-computer rule**:

> If you're sitting at a computer, and you're the main person who uses that computer (so no other human uses it more than you), you're allowed to copy application programs from that computer to a portable computer (so you can work while you're traveling and take your work from office to home and to client sites); but just *you* are allowed to run that program on your portable computer (not other colleagues, not other family members, not friends). This rule lets you copy just application programs (such as Microsoft Word), not operating systems (such as Windows), not programming languages (such as C). Moreover, the application programs must have been purchased normally (not site-licensed).

Complete systems

Let's see how to put all the pieces together and create a complete system.

IBM's early computers

During the 1950's, 1960's, and most of the 1970's, all of IBM's computers were big. IBM ignored the whole concept of microcomputers for many years.

Eventually, IBM created microcomputers. But IBM's first microcomputers, the IBM 5100 and IBM System 23, weren't taken seriously — not even by IBM.

The IBM PC

When many IBM customers began switching to Apple 2 microcomputers to handle spreadsheets, IBM got alarmed, so IBM decided to develop an improved microcomputer, called the **IBM Personal Computer (IBM PC)**, which would be more powerful than Apple 2 computers.

To invent the IBM PC, IBM created 3 secret research teams who competed against each other. The winner was the research team headed by Philip "Don" Estridge in Boca Raton, Florida. His team examined everything created by the other microcomputer companies (Apple, Radio Shack, Commodore, etc.) and combined their best ideas, to produce a relatively low-cost computer better than all competitors.

Don's team developed the IBM PC secretly. IBM didn't announce it to the public until August 12, 1981.

The IBM PC was a smashing success: IBM quickly became the #1 microcomputer company — and Apple dropped to #2.

Improved versions

After inventing the IBM PC, IBM invented improved versions:

Month	Computer's long name	Short name	Nickname	Main new feature
1981 August	IBM Personal Computer	IBM PC	**PC**	many!
1983 March	IBM PC eXTended	IBM PC XT	**XT**	hard drive (instead of just floppy)
1984 August	IBM PC AdvancedTechnology	IBM PC AT	**AT**	faster CPU (286 instead of 8088)
1987 April	IBM Personal System 2	IBM PS/2	**PS/2**	better color video

After 1987, IBM invented many other improved versions.

While IBM was inventing improvements, IBM's competitors invented imitations called **clones**, which were often better than IBM's originals. Here's how they all compared....

Hard drive

The **PC** didn't have a hard drive. Here's what happened afterwards:

> The **XT** included a 10M hard drive.
> The **AT** included a 20M hard drive. AT clones typically included a 40M hard drive.
> **Modern computers** include hard drives that hold 2000 times as much: 80G or even more!

RAM

RAM has grown:

> The **PC** typically came with 64K, 128K, or 256K of RAM.
> The **XT** typically came with 256K, 512K, or 640K of RAM.
> The **AT** typically came with 512K, 1M, or 2M of RAM.
> The **PS/2** typically came with 1M, 2M, or 4M of RAM.
> **Modern computers** come with 512M, 1G, or 2G of RAM.

CPU

The **PC** and **XT** each contained an Intel 8088 CPU chip at 4.77MHz. Most XT clones ran twice as fast (and thus called **turbo** XT clones) because they contained an 8088-1 chip at 10MHz.

The **AT** contained an Intel 286 chip (which works more efficiently than an 8088) at 6MHz. In 1986, IBM switched to 8MHz. AT clones ran at 12MHz.

The **PS/2** came in many models: depending on how wealthy you were, you could choose an 8086 chip at 8MHz, a 286 chip at 10MHz, a 386SX chip at 16MHz, a 386DX chip at 16, 20, or 25 MHz, or several 486 models.

Modern computers contain an Intel Pentium chip or AMD Athlon chip. They run at about 2800MHz (which is 2.8GHz).

Keyboard

The **PC**'s keyboard contained 83 keys:

> 26 keys contained the letters of the alphabet.
>
> 10 keys (in the top row) contained the digits.
>
> 10 keys (on the keyboard's right side) contained the digits rearranged to imitate a calculator.
>
> 13 keys contained symbols for punctuation & math.
>
> 14 keys gave you control. They let you edit your mistakes, create blank spaces and capitals, etc.
>
> 10 function keys (labeled F1 through F10) could be programmed to mean whatever you wished!

The keyboard was designed by Don Estridge personally. To fit all those keys on the small keyboard, he had to make the Enter and Shift keys smaller than typists liked.

Above the top row of keys, he put a shelf to hold pencils. To make room for that shelf, he put the 10 function keys at the left side of the keyboard, even though it would have been more natural to put the F1 key near the 1 key, the F2 key near the 2 key, etc.

The **XT**'s keyboard was the same, but XT clones rearranged the keys to make the Enter and Shift keys be bigger.

The **AT**'s keyboard made the Enter and Shift keys be bigger and included 1 extra key (making a total of 84 keys). In January 1986, IBM began selling a bigger AT keyboard that included 101 keys and put the function keys in the top row (near the pencil ledge) instead of at the left.

Modern computers include 3 extra keys to handle modern Windows (making a total of 104 keys) and often include even more keys, to handle the Internet!

Removable disks

For the **PC**, IBM used 5¼-inch floppy disks holding just 160K. Then IBM switched to 180K, then 360K. The **XT** used 360K disks also. The AT used **1.2M** disks. All those disks were 5¼-inch.

The **PS/2** used 3½-inch disks instead, because they were sturdier, more reliable, easier to carry, and permitted the drive & computer to be smaller. Those 3½-inch disks typically held 1.44M. (Exceptions: the cheapest PS/2 models handled just 720K; some experimental models could handle 2.88M.)

Modern computers use CD and DVD disks instead of floppy disks.

Video

The PC's base price didn't include a monitor — or even a video card to attach the monitor to.

Color versus monochrome When IBM announced the **PC**, it announced two kinds of video cards. One kind attached to a color monitor and was called the **Color Graphics Adapter (CGA)**. The other kind attached to a monochrome monitor and was called the **Monochrome Display Adapter (MDA)**.

Which was better: CGA or MDA? CGA had two advantages: it could handle colors, and it could handle graphics. MDA had two advantages: it could produce prettier characters (though no graphics), and it could underline.

CGA could handle these display modes:

a graphic showing 4 colors,   at a resolution of 320×200
a graphic in black-and-white, at a resolution of 640×200
characters (each an 8×8 matrix, 80 characters per line, 25 lines per screen, one of 16 colors per character)

MDA could handle this display mode:

characters (each a 9×14 matrix, 80 characters per line, 25 lines per screen, one of 4 styles per character)

Hercules A company called **Hercules** invented the **Hercules graphics card**, which resembled the MDA but could also display black-and-white graphics on the monochrome monitor. Several companies made video cards imitating the Hercules card; those imitations were called **Hercules-compatible graphics cards**.

Hercules could handle these display modes:

a graphic in black-and-white, at a resolution of 720×350
characters (each a 9×14 matrix, 80 characters per line, 25 lines per screen, one of 4 styles per character)

EGA In September 1984, IBM invented the **Enhanced Graphics Adapter (EGA)** and an **EGA monitor** to go with it. That combination was better than CGA: it produced more colors and higher resolution. It could handle these display modes:

a graphic showing 16 colors, at a resolution of 640×350
characters (each an 8×14 matrix, 80 characters per line, 25 lines per screen, one of 16 colors per character)

Unfortunately, it was too expensive for most folks.

VGA The **PS/2** came with an even better color monitor, called a **Video Graphics Array color monitor (VGA color monitor)**, and a VGA chip on the motherboard to go with it. That combination produced even more colors and even higher resolution. It could produce many thousands of colors (262,144 colors!), though you could display just 256 of them simultaneously. IBM figured out a way to make the VGA chip cheaply, so it became popular. It could handle these display modes:

a graphic showing 16 colors, at a resolution of 640×480
a graphic showing 256 colors, at a resolution of 320×200
characters (each a 9×16 matrix, 80 characters per line, 25 lines per screen, one of 16 colors per character)
characters (each an 8×16 matrix, 80 characters per line, 30 lines per screen, one of 16 colors per character)

VGA downgrades For folks who were so impoverished that they couldn't afford the VGA chip, IBM invented an cheaper good chip, called the **Multi-Color Graphics Array chip (MCGA chip)**, which produced fewer simultaneous high-resolution colors. It could handle these display modes:

a graphic in black-and-white, at a resolution of 640×480
a graphic showing 256 colors, at a resolution of 320×200
characters (each an 8×16 matrix, 80 characters per line, 25 lines per screen, one of 16 colors per character)

For folks who couldn't afford a VGA color monitor, IBM invented a cheaper VGA monitor, which displayed shades of gray instead of colors.

VGA upgrades **Modern computers** come with better VGA monitors and chips, producing a resolution of 1024×768 or even higher.

Power supply

Inside the system unit, the **PC** contained a power supply, which transformed AC current to DC and could produce 63½ watts of power. It also contained a fan that acted as a farting ass: it sucked hot air from inside the computer and blew it out the computer's backside.

The **XT** contained a stronger power supply that could produce 135 watts, to help it handle the hard drive.

The **AT** contained an even stronger power supply: 192 watts. AT clones contained an even stronger power supply: 200 watts.

Modern computers use modern circuitry, which is more energy-efficient and doesn't require so much power. Some modern computers get by with just 135 watts. Tall towers containing extra circuitry sometimes contain bigger power supplies: 200 or 300 watts.

In modern computers, the power supply does *not* act as a farting ass. Instead, it pushes the air in the opposite direction. It sucks in air from outside the computer, so it acts as a nose: it breathes in fresh air.

Don't put your new computer back-to-back with an old computer. If you do, the new computer will breathe in the old computer's hot farts!

Bus

A computer's motherboard contains slots, to hold printed-circuit cards.

8-bit PC bus The **PC**'s motherboard contained 5 slots, to hold printed-circuit cards. The motherboard's 62 wires running to and through the slots were called the **bus**. Since it was in the PC, it was called the **PC bus**.

Of the 62 wires, just 8 carried data. The other 54 wires were "bureaucratic overhead" that helped control the flow.

Since just 8 wires carried data, the bus was called an **8-bit data bus**, its slots were called **8-bit slots**, and the printed-circuit cards you put into the slots were called **8-bit cards**.

The **XT**'s motherboard used the same PC bus but included 8 slots instead of 5.

16-bit AT bus The **AT**'s motherboard used a wider bus: 98 wires instead of 62. Of the 98 wires, just 16 carried data, so the bus was called a **16-bit data bus**. It was called the **AT bus**. That 98-wire technique was called the **Industry Standard Architecture (ISA, pronounced "eye suh")**. The bus was therefore also called the **ISA bus**, its slots were called **ISA slots**, and the printed-circuit cards you put into the slots were called **ISA cards**.

32-bit bus Later computers used an even wider bus: a **32-bit data bus**!

If you had a **PS/2** computer based on a 386 or 486 chip, it used a 32-bit bus called the **Micro Channel**. That technique was called **Micro Channel Architecture (MCA)**. Into its slots, you put **MCA cards**.

If you had a **clone** containing a 386 or 486, and the clone was fancy, it used a 32-bit bus technique called **Extended ISA (EISA, pronounced "ee suh")**. Its bus was called the **EISA bus**; into its slots, you put **EISA cards**.

If your computer is **modern** (containing a Pentium or Athlon or Sempron or Duron or K6), it uses a 32-bit bus technique called **Peripheral Component Interconnect (PCI)**. Its bus is called the **PCI bus**; into its slots, you put **PCI cards**. The nice thing about PCI cards is that the computer can automatically figure out what each card's purpose is, so you can just plug the card into the slot and start using the card immediately: that feature is called **plug and play**, though sometimes it works imperfectly (which is why cynics call it **plug and pray**).

**1-bit USB bus** If your computer is very **modern**, it contains a 32-bit PCI bus but also contains a second bus, called the **Universal Serial Bus (USB)**, which is a 1-bit bus that's slow but has three nice properties: all USB devices are **plug-and-play**, **external** (so you can install them without opening the system unit's case), and **hot-swappable** (so you can insert, remove, or swap the devices safely even while the power is still on). The typical modern computer has 1, 2, 3, or 4 USB slots, which are on the system unit's back wall and called **USB ports**.

Multimedia

The **PC**'s price included no mouse, no microphone, no modem, no speakers (except for a tiny internal speaker that just beeped), and no CD or DVD drive, because all those devices were too expensive then. The **XT**, **AT**, and **PS/2** had the same disappointments.

Modern computers come with a mouse, a microphone, a modem, stereo speakers (2 of them or 3 or 5!), and a DVD drive.

Computer prices

Here's how most computers are priced. (I'll show you the prices that were in effect when this book went to press in February 2011. Prices drop about 3% per month, 30% per year.)

$500 is the standard price for a "standard" computer. That's the cheapest kind of modern computer.

If you pay _more_ than $500, you get a computer that's fancier — a powerful "muscle machine" that will impress your friends. They'll be impressed by how much money you spent. (If you pay _much_ more than $500, they might also be impressed by how stupid you were to overspend.)

If you pay _less_ than $500, you get a computer that's old-fashioned. If you pay _slightly_ less than $500, the clone will still run most programs fine, though your friends might laugh at you for buying such a puny, quaint computer. If you pay _much_ less than $500, that's either because your computer will have significant difficulty running modern programs or you bought the computer at a special "sale" that restricts your benefits and options. But hey, if you can't afford $500, a substandard computer is better than no computer at all! If you buy a substandard computer, your next task is to figure out which software it can handle well; then buy just that kind of software.

Here are the details....

Search for perfection

I'd like to tell you about a company that makes reliable, powerful computers, charges you very little, and is a pleasure to call if you ever need technical help.

> That's what I'd _like_ to tell you, but I haven't found such a company yet! If you find one, let me know!
>
> Each month, I falsely think I've finally found my hero company. I give its name to folks like you who call me for advice. But my hoped-for hero eventually gets accused by my customers of degenerating into despicable behavior. How depressing! I've been writing this book for over 30 years and have yet to find a company I still feel proud about. I'm disgusted.

Hero companies rise but then fall because they suffer through this business cycle:

> When the company begins, it's new and unknown, so it tries hard to get attention for itself by offering low prices. It also tries to help its customers by offering good service.
>
> When news spreads about how the company offers low prices and good service, the company gets deluged with more customers than it can handle — and it's also stuck answering phone calls from old customers who still need help but aren't buying anything new.
>
> To eliminate the overload, the company must either accept fewer customers (by raising prices — or by lowering them slower than the rest of the industry), or offer less service per customer (by refusing to hire enough staff to handle all the questions), or hire extra staff (who are usually less talented than the company's founders but nevertheless expect high pay). In any of those cases, the company becomes less pleasant. Its heroism is relegated to history, and the company becomes just one more inconsequential player in the vast scheme of computer life.

What's in store for you

This chapter portrays the players.

> Warning: these portraits are anatomically correct — they show which companies are pricks.
>
> The computer industry's a soap opera in which consumers face new personal horrors daily. I wrote this in February 2011, but you can get the newest breathtaking episode of the computer industry's drama, _How the Screw-You Turns_, by phoning me anytime. I'll tell you the newest dirt about wannabe and were-to-be hero companies.
>
> So before buying a computer, **phone me at 603-666-6644** to get my new advice free. Tell me your needs, and I'll try to recommend the best vendor for _you_. Before phoning me, become a knowledgeable consumer by reading this chapter.

Walmart, Staples, Best Buy

To get the lowest prices for decent computers, buy from **Best Buy** or **Staples** or **Walmart**.

When this book went to press in June 2011, here's what those chains charged for notebook computers:

Type	Screen	RAM	Hard drive	Windows	CPU	Price
Netbook	10.1"	1G	250G	7 Starter	Intel Atom	$250
Modest	15.6"	3G	320G	7 Premium	AMD Dual-Core	$330
Standard	15.6"	4G	500G	7 Premium	Intel Core i3	$400
Upscale	17.3"	4G	640G	7 Premium	Intel Core i3	$500
Fancy	17.3"	6G	750G	7 Premium	Intel Core i7	$700

Here are examples of that pricing:

Maker	Screen	RAM	Hard	Windows	CPU	Price after rebate
Acer	10.1"	1G	250G	7 Starter	Intel Atom N570	$250 at Walmart
Toshiba	15.6"	3G	250G	7 Premium	Intel Celeron	$300 at Best Buy
HP	15.6"	3G	320G	7 Premium	AMD Athlon II Dual-Core P360	$330 at Staples
Samsung	15.6"	4G	320G	7 Premium	AMD Dual-Core E-350	$350 at Best Buy
Acer	15.6"	4G	500G	7 Premium	Intel Pentium Dual-Core P6100	$398 at Walmart
Gateway	15.6"	4G	640G	7 Premium	Intel Core i3	$450 at Best Buy
HP	17.3"	4G	640G	7 Premium	Intel Core i3-370M	$480 at Staples
HP	17.3"	6G	750G	7 Premium	Intel Core i7-2630	$700 at Staples

Here's what they charged for desktop computers:

Type	Screen	RAM	Hard drive	Windows	CPU	Price
Modest	18.5"	2G	500G	7 Premium	AMD Athlon II	$300
Standard	20"	3G	500G	7 Premium	AMD Athlon II	$400
Upscale	20"	4G	1T	7 Premium	AMD Athlon 640	$500
Fancy	23"	6G	1T	7 Premium	Intel Core i5	$650
Luxury	23" touch	6G	1T	7 Premium	Intel Core i5	$950

Here are examples of that pricing:

Maker	Screen	RAM	Hard	Windows	CPU	Price after rebate
eMachines	18.5"	2G	320G	7 Premium	Intel Celeron E3400	$299 at Walmart
Compaq	20"	3G	500G	7 Premium	AMD Dual-Core + printer	$380 at Best Buy
Asus	20"	4G	1T	7 Premium	AMD Athlon II X2 + printer	$500 at Best Buy
HP	20"	6G	1T	7 Premium	AMD Athlon 645 Quad-Core	$550 at Staples
HP	20" touch	4G	750G	7 Premium	AMD Athlon 645e Dual-Core	$600 at Staples
HP	23"	6G	1T	7 Premium	AMD Athlon 645 Quad-Core	$630 at Staples
HP	23"	8G	1.5T	7 Premium	AMD Phenom 960T Quad-Core	$730 at Staples
HP	23" touch	4G	750G	7 Premium	Intel Core i3	$850 at Best Buy

Acer, Gateway, eMachines

Acer, **Gateway**, and **eMachines** used to be 3 separate companies.

"Gateway" computers were sold mainly through mail-order.
"eMachines" computers were sold mainly through chain stores such as Best Buy and Circuit City.
"Acer" computers were sold mainly through small computer stores.

In 2004, Gateway bought eMachines. In 2007, Acer bought Gateway. So now Acer, Gateway, and eMachines are all under the same ownership, though the brand names and marketing strategies remain separate.

Here are the details….

eMachines

eMachines was the first major company that advertised modern computers for under $400 and let you buy them in many stores.

History Here's how the eMachines company began…

Tandy Corporation owned Radio Shack and also owned a chain of discount computer superstores called **Computer City**. Tandy eventually gave up trying to run Computer City and sold that chain to CompUSA. Computer City's president (Stephen Dukker) was dismayed at becoming a CompUSA vice-president, so he quit and started his own company, **eMachines**, which invented cheap computer systems (under $500) and sold them to retail stores such as CompUSA.

He started eMachines in September 1998, using money invested by two Korean companies: **Trigem** (which makes eMachines' computers) and **Korea Data Systems (KDS)** (which makes eMachines' monitors).

He was wildly successful. Nine months later, in June 1999, his company become the third-biggest seller of desktop&tower computers in retail stores: just Compaq and Hewlett-Packard sold more desktop&tower computers than he. In the next month, July 1999, he shipped his 1 millionth computer. In March 2000, eMachines went public, with stock selling for $8 per share. In September 2000, he shipped his 3 millionth computer.

But after that, eMachines fell on hard times. For example, in January 2001, eMachines' revenues (sales figures) were just half of the previous January's. That was because the prices of fancy computer decreased, so consumers decided to buy them instead of the crummy computers that eMachines sold.

Its board of directors got worried. In February 2001, the board fired Stephen Dukker and hired, as the new head, Wayne Inouye, who was Best Buy's senior vice president in charge of computer merchandising. In May 2001, the company was delisted from Nasdaq, because the shares were selling for less than $1 each. In November 2001, the board agreed to sell the whole company to KDS's owner, Lap Shun "John" Hui, and his private company, called **EM Holdings**, for $1.06 per share, 161 million dollars total.

By April 2002, eMachines had sold a total of 4 million computers since the company began. That's not much more than the 3 million sold by September 2000.

eMachines became number 2 in retail U.S. sales, far behind Hewlett-Packard (which sells the Hewlett-Packard and Compaq brands). Analysts worried that eMachines might go bankrupt; but in 2001, eMachines improved its computers (which had been miserable) and its tech support (which had been atrocious before Wayne Inouye spent 20 million dollars extra on tech support and customer service in 2001). Now eMachine computers are finally worth getting: they're good computers at rock-bottom prices. Consumer surveys show that computers from eMachines are more reliable and better serviced than computers from most other computer brands.

To guard eMachines from going bankrupt, the company accepted no returns from computer stores and kept few computers in stock: it kept waiting for small shipments to arrive by boat from its suppliers in Asia, so it occasionally ran out of computers.

When I went to buy a computer in 2001, I found myself buying an eMachines computer, because eMachines offered much lower prices than any other computer manufacturer. eMachines lived up to its new slogan, which was "the best computer and service little money can buy".

The computer I bought came with one "defect": whenever I moved the mouse, the computer made a buzzing sound. I finally figured it out: the eMachines company was too cheap to include a microphone and too stupid to remember to turn off the microphone jack, which picked up interference from mouse & monitor motions. The solution was to give the computer a command to disable the microphone jack.

eMachines work better now.

In 2003, the eMachines company's revenue was 1.1 billion dollars (a huge number!), even though eMachines had just 138 employees.

Prices eMachines computers are available at Walmart, Best Buy, and many other stores. The eMachines *con*tribution to the world of cheap computers is: *dis*tribution!

Here's what eMachines charged when this book went to press in February 2011:

Model #	AMD CPU	RAM	Hard	Price	Store
EL 1352G-41w	Athlon II 2.8GHz	2G DDR3	500G	$298	Walmart
EL 1333-21f	Athlon LE-1660	3G DDR2	500G	$330	Best Buy
EL 1333-23e	Athlon II 3.1GHz	4G DDR3	500G	$350	Best Buy
ET 1352G-03w	Athlon II X2 260u	4G DDR3	640G	$398	Walmart

The hard drive is fast (7200 rpm). Each computer also includes a 16X DVD±RW drive, keyboard, mouse (with 2 buttons and wheel), Ethernet connector (for connecting to the Internet or other high-speed network), Windows 7 Home Premium, Microsoft Office (Starter edition), and 1-year warranty.

Those prices do *not* include a monitor or speakers. eMachines advertises 2 monitors, which have built-in stereo speakers:

Model #	LCD widescreen	Resolution	Price
E 182 H Dbm	18.5"	1366×768	$140
E 202 H Dbmd	20"	1600×900	$160

So eMachines' cheapest computer with cheapest monitor costs a total of $298+$140=$438.

But wait! You can pay even less! Best Buy and Walmart **often have their own extra discounts**. Look in your local Sunday paper for the flyers from Best Buy and Walmart to find out what eMachine deals are available this week.

For example, when this book went to press, Best Buy was having a sale where you can get an EL 1850-01E computer (Celeron, 2G DDR2, 500G) and cheap monitor (E 182 H Dmbd) for a total price of just $400! That's how much you pay at the cash register; you don't have to wait for rebates. If you pay $50 more, Best Buy will give you the EL 1352-07E computer (Athlon II X2, 4G DDR3, 500G) instead of the EL 1850-01E.

Where to research For more info about eMachines, look at the eMachines Internet Web site, which is **www.e4me.com**. But don't buy computers directly from that Web site: buy from Walmart and Best Buy instead, to get the rebates.

"Free" computer Back in 1999, eMachines offered an extra $400 rebate if you'd sign a 3-year contract to make Compuserve your Internet service provider. The cheapest eMachines computer would cost you "$474 minus a $75 rebate minus a $400 Compuserve rebate", making the final price be about $0. Stores advertised it as being a "free computer". That kind of ad was popular in November 1999 and sold many eMachine computers.

Such ads neglected to mention that the price did not include a monitor and that you had to sign a 3-year Compuserve contract, at a cost of $21.95 per month, so the contract would cost you a total of "36 months times $21.95", which is $790.20. Those ads were declared "misleading" by many state governments in the year 2000 — and banned.

How Gateway arose

Gateway was the first company to sell lots of computers by mail. Gateway became the mail-order king — until Gateway stumbled and Dell zoomed ahead. Gateway's stumbling is what motivated Gateway to buy eMachines. Here are the details....

Gateway began because of cows. In the 1800's, George Waitt began a cattle company. According to legend, he got his first herd by grabbing cattle that jumped off barges into the Missouri River on the way to the stockyards. His cattle business passed to his descendants and eventually into the hands of his great-grandson, Norm, who built the Waitt Cattle Company into one of the biggest cattle firms in the Midwest. The company is on the Missouri River, in Iowa's Sioux City (where Iowa meets South Dakota and Nebraska).

Norm's sons — Norm Junior and Ted — preferred computers to cows, so on September 5th, 1985, they started the "Gateway 2000" company in their dad's office. They told him computers are easier to ship than cows, since computers can take a long journey without needing to be fed and without making a mess in their boxes.

22-year-old Ted was the engineer and called himself "president"; Norm Junior was the businessman and called himself "vice president". Their main investor was their grandma, who secured a $10,000 loan. They hired just one employee: Mike Hammond.

At first, they sold just parts for the Texas Instruments Professional Computer. Soon they began building their own computers. By the end of 1985, they'd sold 50 systems, for which customers paid a total of $100,000.

Gateway grew fast:

Year	Computers sold	Revenue	Employees
1985	50 computers	$100,000	2
1986	300 computers	$1,000,000	4
1987	500 computers	$1,500,000	8
1988	4,000 computers	$11,700,000	33
1989	25,000 computers	$70,500,000	176
1990	100,000 computers	$275,500,000	600
1991	225,000 computers	$626,700,000	1,300
1992	even more computers!	$1,100,000,000	1,876
1993	even more computers!	$1,700,000,000	3,500
1994	even more computers!	$2,700,000,000	4,500
1995	1,338,000 computers	$3,700,000,000	9,300
1996	1,909,000 computers	$5,000,000,000	9,700
1997	2,580,000 computers	$6,300,000,000	13,300
1998	even more computers!	$7,500,000,000	19,300
1999	even more computers!	$8,600,000,000	21,000
2000	even more computers!	$9,600,000,000	even more employees!

For each year, that chart shows how many computers were sold during the year, the total numbers of dollars that customers paid for them and for add-ons, and how many employees Gateway had at the year's end.

Here are highlights from the history of Ted Waitt and his employees during those years:

> In 1986, they moved to a bigger office in the Sioux City Livestock Exchange Building.
>
> In 1988, Ted began a national marketing campaign by designing his own ads and running them in *Computer Shopper* magazine. His most famous ad showed a gigantic two-page photo of his family's cattle farm and the headline, "Computers from Iowa?" The computer industry was stunned — cowed — by the ad's huge size and the low prices it offered for IBM clones. In the ad, Ted emphasized that Gateway was run by hard-working, honest Midwesterners who gave honest value. (At that time, most clones came from California or Texas; but Californians had a reputation for being "flaky", and Texans had a reputation for being "lawless"). Though cynics called Gateway "the cow computer", it was a success. In September, the company moved a few miles south to a larger plant in Sergeant Bluff, Iowa. Gateway's operations there began with 28 employees.
>
> In the summer of 1989, Gateway grew to 150 employees, so Gateway began building a bigger plant. To get tax breaks and business grants, Gateway built it upriver at North Sioux City, South Dakota, and moved there in January 1990.
>
> In 1990, Gateway became more professional. In 1989, the "instruction manual" was 2 pages; in 1990, it was 2 books. In 1989, the "tech support staff" (which answers technical questions from customers) consisted of just 1 person, and you had to wait 2 days for him to return your call; in 1990, the tech support staff included 35 people, and you could get through in 2 minutes. Gateway also switched to superior hard drives and monitors. In 1990, customers paid Gateway 275½ million dollars, generating a net profit of $25 million.
>
> By early 1992, Gateway was selling nearly 2,000 computers per day and had 1,300 employees, including over 100 salespeople and 200 tech-support specialists to answer technical questions. Not bad, for a company whose president was just 30! Since Gateway was owned by just Norm Junior and Ted, those two boys became quite rich!
>
> In March 1993, Gateway hired its 2000th employee. In April 1993, Gateway sold its one millionth computer. In December 1993, Gateway went public, so now you can buy Gateway stock and own part of that dreamy company, which by May 1995 had become so big that it answered over 12,000 tech-support calls in one day.
>
> On September 5th, 1995, Gateway's 6000 employees celebrated the company's 10th anniversary.

Now Ted own about 30% of Gateway's stock; Norm Junior owns very little.

Though Gateway became huge, with offices worldwide in France, Germany, Ireland, Australia, and Japan, it was still headquartered in North Sioux City, a small behind-the-times town that got its first 4-way stop sign in 1992, first McDonald's hamburger joint in 1994, and doesn't have any traffic lights yet.

Gateway gets along well with its neighbors: in fact, two former mayors of Sioux City became Gateway employees!

Gateway became a rapidly growing cash cow: moo-lah, moo-lah! But Gateway didn't lose its sense of humor. When you buy a Gateway computer, it comes in a box painted to look like a dairy cow: white with black spots.

Ben & Jerry's Ice Cream sued Gateway for copying the idea of putting cow spots on packages. Meanwhile, Gateway sued a shareware distributor called **Tucows** for using spotted cows to sell computer products. Those suits have been settled.

Gateway's ads

Gateway became famous because of the amazing photography in its ads.

> In early ads, the photos showed individuals in beautiful landscapes. Later ads showed hordes of Gateway employees dressed as Robin Hood's men in Sherwood Forest, top-hatted performers in Vegas cabarets, teenagers in a nostalgic 1950's diner bathed in neon glow, or movie directors applauding a ship full of pirates.
>
> The eye-popping photos, which seemed to have nothing to do with computers, grabbed attention. (Gateway's diner ad includes the only photo I've ever seen that makes meatloaf look romantic!) Then came headlines and florid prose that tried to relate the scene to Gateway's computers. Finally, after all that multi-page image-building nonsense, you got to the ad's finale, which reveals Gateway's great technical specifications (specs), great service policies, and low prices.
>
> That way of building an ad — fluff followed by stuff — worked wonders for Gateway! Idiots admired the photos, techies admired the specs, and everybody wanted to buy!

Gateway was the first big mail-order manufacturer to give honest pricing: the advertised price includes everything except shipping. The price even included a color monitor. And since all components were high-quality, a Gateway system was a *dream* system. With dreamy ads and a low price, how could you *not* buy?

Gateway also came up with a friendly slogan: "You've got a friend in the business."

How Gateway fell

On Millennium Day — January 1, 2000 — Ted Waitt decided to semi-retire: he turned the day-to-day operation of Gateway over to Jeff Weitzen, who had joined Gateway 2 years earlier after working at AT&T for 18 years. So Jeff became Gateway's President and Chief Executive Officer (CEO), though Ted remained Chairman of Gateway's Board of Directors.

Jeff was proud to be chosen as the man to take Gateway past the millennium. He had many inspired ideas — most of which turned out to be wrong.

He decided to move Gateway's executive offices to downtown San Diego, to attract executive talent who wouldn't put up with South Dakota's remoteness and harsh winters. Then Ted decided to move Gateway's executive offices again, to a San Diego residential suburb called Poway, so employees living in San Diego's suburbs wouldn't have to commute into the city. Meanwhile, manufacturing was still back in South Dakota, along with the cow-spotted boxes. The company was schizophrenic.

Another example of corporate schizophrenia was Jeff's decision to "think outside the box": sell not just a box full of hardware but also sell service.

> He called it the "beyond-the-box initiative". To accomplish that, he set up Gateway Country Stores in hundreds of cities — and also inside Office Max stores — so customers could walk in and get local service.
>
> But the Gateway Country Stores turned into sad jokes: customers there can stare at a few sample computers but typically can't walk out the door with them; classes are offered just rarely; and calling the store for "tech support" gets you a recorded message to call headquarters instead, since the store's "tech support" is mainly restricted to selling you upgrades and installing them.
>
> The cost of running the Gateway Country Stores forced Gateway to raise computer prices, so Gateway started charging even more than HP, Compaq, Dell, and IBM, especially since Gateway was wasting so much energy running stores that Gateway started lagging behind Dell in making manufacturing efficient.
>
> Gateway was no longer a low-priced discounter. Gateway had forgotten its roots.
>
> Gateway's new high prices and still-substandard tech support made Gateway a company to *avoid*. Why buy from Gateway, when Gateway was charging more than Dell and giving worse service than Dell?

Gateway's revenues plummeted, Gateway's profits suddenly started turning into huge losses, shares of Gateway stock became nearly worthless, and Ted Waitt became non-rich.

To be fair, you can't blame all of Gateway's problems on Jeff: the whole computer industry had a tough year in 2000, when consumers decided that the new computers weren't different enough from old computers to be worth upgrading to. But Jeff's moves were in the wrong direction.

In January 2001, a year after Jeff took over, he gave up — resigned — and Ted Waitt became the CEO again.

But it was too late. Gateway had lost its luster. The prince and king of mail-order had become a pauper. Upon becoming CEO again, Ted's first act was to run an ad bragging that Gateway would match the prices of 6 big competitors: IBM, HP, Compaq, Sony, Toshiba, and Dell. That ad was stupid. Gateway was supposed to be a mail-order discounter: all it can brag about is that's not more expensive than retail? The ad bombed. So did the company. In 2001, Gateway made no profit. In fact, it *lost* a billion dollars. That's a lotta moolah muck!

It's strange that the average mom-and-pop tiny business, which makes hardly any profit, nevertheless makes more profit than a huge company such as Gateway.

Here are Gateway's statistics:

Year	Revenue	Result
1999	$8,600,000,000	$428,000,000 profit
2000	$9,600,000,000	$241,000,000 profit
2001	$6,100,000,000	$1,034,000,000 loss

Afterwards, Ted started laying off employees, closing international sales offices, closing the Gateway Country Stores, making Gateway a tiny company, and reducing Gateway's reliance on mail-order computer sales: he tried to diversify into selling big-screen TV sets, digital cameras, and DVD players.

By July 2002, Ted had cut half the staff, so the number of employees was down to 12,000. In 2003, the company was even smaller: revenue was just $3,402,400,000, employees were just 7,407, and the company lost "just" $514,800,000. In March 2004, Gateway bought eMachines. In April 2004, all Gateway Country Stores were shut down, and the number of Gateway employees dropped to 4,000.

Here's my message to Ted:

Ted, I wish you luck. I also have a suggestion for you, which I'm sure you'll ignore. If Gateway wants to offer good service cheaply, why not just include tutorials from *The Secret Guide to Computers* in the cow box? This book's page 9 says reprints are free, and I give free tech support.

I feel sad about Gateway. I was one of the first journalists to recommend Gateway. I'm sorry to see Gateway go downhill.

The seeds of Gateway's downfall were already planted back in December 1993, when Gateway went public. That's when Gateway first lost sight of its roots, raised prices (to make the stockholders happy), and I stopped recommending Gateway: I switched to other, hungrier companies instead.

When Gateway bought eMachines in March 2004 (for 30 million dollars plus 50 million shares of Gateway common stock), the eMachines CEO (51-year-old Wayne Inouye) became the Gateway's CEO, replacing 41-year-old Ted Waitt (though Ted is still the chairman of Gateway's board of directors). That move was easy for Wayne, since Gateway's headquarters (in Poway, California) was just 50 miles from the eMachines headquarters (in Irvine, California).

Contacts

Here's how to reach Gateway — what's left of it.

800-GATEWAY, www.gateway.com

Executive offices	Manufacturing
14303 Gateway Place	610 Gateway Drive
Poway CA 92064	North Sioux City SD 57049
858-848-3401	605-232-2000

Acer

Acer is a huge consortium of Taiwanese computer companies.

It makes "Acer computers" and "Acros computers". They're particularly popular in Southeast Asia and Latin America. They've also been sold in the U.S., through computer stores and department stores.

In 2001, Acer split into 3 companies:

The main company is still called **Acer**.

The Communications & Multimedia Division is now a separate company called **BenQ**. It's Taiwan's biggest cell phone manufacturer. It also makes CD-RW drives, CD-RW disks, printers, scanners, and screens, under its own name and also secretly for Motorola & NEC. Its annual sales are 3 billion dollars.

The Design, Manufacturing, and Services Division is now called **Wistron**. It secretly designs, manufactures, and repairs computers for Dell, HP, Fujitsu, and Hitachi. Acer owns 40% of Wistron's stock.

After that split, Acer bought Gateway.

HP & Compaq

Hewlett-Packard (HP) and **Compaq** were two separate companies, but in 2002 HP bought Compaq. Here are the details.

How HP arose

Hewlett-Packard (HP) was started by two young Stanford University graduates — Bill Hewlett and Dave Packard — back in 1938, in a garage in Palo Alto, California, where they built their first product: an audio oscillator (electronic test instrument used by sound engineers), which they sold to several customers, including Walt Disney, who eventually used 8 of them to test the sound in movie theaters showing the movie *Fantasia*.

Those boys weren't sure whether to call the company "Hewlett-Packard" or "Packard-Hewlett", so they flipped a coin. Hewlett won. They formalized the partnership on January 1, 1939.

The company began to grow:

Year	Revenue	Employees
1939	$5,369	2
1940	$34,396	3
1941	$106,459	6
1942	$522,803	8
1943	$953,294	45

During World War 2, HP sold the U.S. Navy devices that generated microwaves and jammed radar. Later, HP started making other lab equipment, medical equipment, plotters, printers, minicomputers, and pocket calculators but was scared to enter the field of personal computers. HP developed a reputation for making equipment that was high-quality — and somewhat pricey.

How Compaq arose

The *first* company that made *high-quality* IBM clones was **Compaq**. Compaq began selling them back in 1983. (Before Compaq, the only IBM clones available were crummy.)

Compaq began in a restaurant. While eating at a House of Pies restaurant, two engineers drew on the paper placemat their picture of how the ideal IBM clone would look. Instead of being a desktop computer, it would be a luggable having a 9-inch built-in screen and a handle, the whole computer system being small enough so you could pick it up with one hand. Then they built it! Since it was compact, they called it the **Compaq Portable Computer** and called the company **Compaq Computer Corporation**.

They began selling it in 1983, helped by venture-capital funding from Ben Rosen. They charged about the same for it as IBM charged for the IBM PC.

They sold it just to dealers approved by IBM to sell the IBM PC. That way, they dealt just with dealers IBM said were reliable — and they competed directly against IBM in the same stores.

They succeeded fantastically. That first year, sales totaled 100 million dollars.

In 1984, they inserted a hard drive into the computer and called that souped-up luggable the **Compaq Plus**. They also built a desktop computer called the **Deskpro**. Like Compaq's portable computers, the Deskpro was priced about the same as IBM's computers, was sold just through IBM dealers, and was built well — a marvel of engineering, better than IBM's.

Later, Compaq expanded: it built IBM clones in all sizes, from gigantic towers down to tiny handheld computers. Compaq computers got the highest praise — and ridiculously high prices.

On many technological issues, Compaq was the first company to innovate: for example, when Intel invented the 386 chip, the first company to use it was Compaq, not IBM.

How Compaq cheapened

Compaq was founded by Rod Canion. Under his leadership, Compaq developed a reputation for high quality and high prices. Engineers said that Compaq's computers were **overdesigned**: they were built more sturdily than necessary for average use and were therefore too expensive.

Worried about Compaq's high prices, some Compaq employees went on a secret mission, without telling Rod: they sneaked into a computer show, pretended they weren't from Compaq, pretended they were starting a new computer company, and tried to buy computer parts from Compaq's suppliers. Compaq's suppliers offered them lower prices than the suppliers were offering Compaq — because Compaq had developed a reputation as an overly fussy company to do business with.

The secret missionaries went back to Compaq and reported their findings to the board of directors, who were becoming upset at Compaq's astronomically high prices; so in 1991 the board fired Rod and replaced him with a cost cutter, Eckhard Pfeiffer (from Germany). So Pfeiffer became the new **Chief Executive Officer (CEO)**.

He lowered Compaq's prices, so Compaq became affordable, and he gave up the idea that Compaq should have super-high quality. He began selling through a greater variety of dealers and through mail-order.

The low-price wide-distribution strategy worked well. More people bought Compaq computers. Sales zoomed, though Compaq's "quality reputation" declined. To compete against a company called "Packard Bell" (which sold junky computers cheaply through department stores), Compaq imitated Packard Bell: Compaq lowered its prices and its service.

In February 1995, Compaq started this nasty new service policy:

> If you phone Compaq for help, Compaq's staff asks for your credit-card number first, then listens to your questions. Unless your difficulties are caused by a mistake made by Compaq Corporation, you're charged $35 per question.

Eventually, Compaq dropped that nasty policy: tech-support calls are now free during the "initial period" (1 year on hardware questions, 3 months on software questions, longer if your Compaq was expensive): call 800-ok-Compaq, day or night (24 hours).

> After the "initial period" is over, help costs $40 per question (or $60 per year), billed to your credit card when you call 800-ok-Compaq; or call 900-RED-HELP instead, which charges just $35 per question on your phone bill.

Compaq is based in Houston, Texas. You can still reach Compaq by phoning **800-at-Compaq** or viewing Compaq's Internet Web site, **www.compaq.com**.

HP Pavilion

In 1995, HP began manufacturing an IBM clone called the **Pavilion**, sold through local computer stores, electronics stores, office-supply stores, and department stores. Here's why the Pavilion became popular:

> HP's Pavilion cost less than Compaq's desktop computers.
> HP's service was slightly better than Compaq's.

Compaq's reaction

Compaq started having financial difficulties, for 2 reasons:

> Compaq's CEO, Eckhard Pfeiffer, made Compaq buy Digital Equipment Corporation

> Compaq was having trouble competing against IBM clones priced under $700 (from companies such as HP and Packard Bell)

So in 1998, Compaq's board of directors fired Pfeiffer.

In 1999, the board finally decided to make Compaq's next CEO be Michael Capellas, a low-key friendly computer technician that everybody likes. Most important, he's liked by Ben Rosen (the venture capitalist who funded the Compaq's founder and was still chairman of the board).

Michael created computers that were low-cost but exciting. By the year 2000, **Compaq was selling more computers than any other manufacturer**. Yes, it was selling more computers than IBM, Gateway, HP, Dell, and the rest of the gang.

In July 2000, I had to buy a notebook computer for my stepdaughter. Since I'm supposed to be a "computer expert", I dutifully looked at all the ads in computer magazines and talked to my friends in the computer industry, trying to find the best deal. I thought the best deal would be some sort of mail-order company; but the best deal on a notebook computer turned out to be from Compaq! That notebook was the **Compaq Presario 1200-XL118**. It included lots of features but cost just $999 after rebates from Compaq and Circuit City — and I paid even less than that by using price-matching and further rebates from Staples. Compaq notebooks are even cheaper now!

Merger

The Compaq-versus-HP debate ended in 2002, when HP bought Compaq, with approval from Michael Capellas and Ben Rosen. The combo is called a "merger". The combined company is called "Hewlett-Packard", though Compaq lovers prefer to call it "Hewlett-paq" or "Hewpaq". So now you can get two kinds of computers from a single company, whose leader (chairperson and CEO) is a pleasant HP woman named **Carleton Fiorina**. (Her nickname is "Carly".)

Michael Capellas became Carly's assistant and got the title "President", but a few months after the merger he quit HP and took on a new challenge: becoming the new head of scandal-ridden WorldCom. WorldCom picked him because it wanted to be led by somebody who's really reputable!

Prices

Staples, Best Buy, and Walmart give rebates on HP and Compaq computers, so the final price you pay is just slightly higher than for eMachines — and the specs are slightly fancier.

Dell & Alienware

Though Compaq was the first company to make good IBM clones, its clones were expensive. The first company that sold fast IBM clones *cheaply* was **PC's Limited**, founded in 1984 by a 19-year-old kid, Michael Dell. He operated out of the bedroom of his condo apartment, near the University of Texas in Austin.

At first, his prices were low — and so were his quality and service. Many of the computers he shipped didn't work: they were **dead on arrival (DOA)**. When his customers tried to return the defective computer equipment to him for repair or a refund, his company ignored the customer altogether. By 1986, many upset customers considered him a con artist and wrote bitter letters about him to computer magazines. He responded by saying that his multi-million-dollar company was growing faster than expected and couldn't keep up with the demand for after-sale service.

In 1987, Dell raised his quality and service — and his prices. In 1988, he changed the company's name to **Dell Computer Corporation**.

Now he charges almost as much as IBM and Compaq.

His quality and service have become top-notch. They've set the standard for the rest of the computer industry. In speed and quality contests, his computers often beat IBM and Compaq.

In 1997 Dell officially became the top dog in the computer-quality wars: according to *PC World* magazine's surveys of its readers, Dell's computers were more reliable than any other brand, and Dell's tech-support staff did the best job of fixing any problems promptly.

Dell's ads bashed Compaq for having higher prices than Dell and worse policies about getting repairs — since Dell offered on-site service and Compaq doesn't.

For example, in 1991 Dell ran an ad calling Dell's notebook computer a "road warrior" and Compaq's a "road worrier". It showed the Dell screen saying, "With next day on-site service in 50 states, nothing's going to stop you." It showed the Compaq screen saying, "Just pray you don't need any service while you're on the road, or you're dead meat."

His ads were misleading. His prices were much lower than Compaq's *list* price but just *slightly* less than the discount price at which Compaq computers were normally sold. Though Compaq didn't provide free on-site service, you could sometimes get your Compaq repaired fast by driving to a nearby Compaq dealer.

Dell tried selling through discount-store chains but gave up and decided to return to selling just by mail. Though HP/Compaq is king of retail sales, Dell's become king of mail-order sales.

Dell computers used to come with this guarantee: if Dell doesn't answer your tech-support call within 5 minutes, Dell will give you $25! Dell doesn't make that guarantee anymore.

Dell gives lifetime toll-free technical support for hardware questions and usually answers its phones promptly. Unfortunately, Dell has reduced Windows technical support from "lifetime" to "30 days".

Dell's downfall

Though Dell's tech support used to be good, now it's terrible — because Dell's decided to save money by sending most tech-support calls to Bangalore, India, where your call is answered by a person whose English is hard to understand and who doesn't understand American slang and whose computer knowledge is minimal. After receiving many complaints from business customers, Dell's adopted this new policy: if you buy an expensive "business" computer from Dell, Dell will have your call answered in the USA; but if you buy a cheap "consumer" computer from Dell, Dell's gonna still treat you like dirt and have your call answered in India. All recent surveys show that consumers who buy Emachines or ABS computers are happier than consumers who buy from Dell. Stay away from Dell.

HP's CEO, Carly Fiorina, laughed at Dell and asks "Is Dell really a computer company?" since Dell doesn't really research, invent, manufacture, or service computers anymore: it just rebrands and markets computers manufactured by others and gives hardly any support. What a disappointment!

Alienware

Alienware is a company that makes high-speed computers, for use in playing high-speed action games and doing high-speed video editing. In 2006, Dell bought Alienware, so now Alienware is wholly owned by Dell.

How to get Dell

If you want a free Dell catalog or want to chat with a Dell sales rep, phone 800-BUY-DELL.

If you want to buy a Dell computer, don't react to the first ad you see: Dell sells the same computer at many different prices. For example, prices in Dell's catalogs, magazine ads, and Web sites are all different from each other. Consumers have discovered that the cheapest way to buy a Dell computer is often at **Costco** warehouse clubs. Another way to buy a Dell computer cheaply is at **Walmart**.

Other IBM clones

Here are other choices to consider....

Micro Express

Walmart, Best Buy, and Staples sell normal computers. If you want a fancier computer, consider **Micro Express**, which is a mail-order company that sells high-speed computers less expensively than Alienware. For example, Micro Express can sell you a computer that has a super-fast CPU chip (Intel Core i7 980X Extreme Edition), gigantic RAM (24G), and gigantic hard drive (2T). Micro Express sells cheaper computers also. Micro Express has a good reputation.

To configure your own favorite combination, phone Micro Express at 800-989-9900 or 949-460-9911 or write to Micro Express (at 8 Hammond Drive #105, Irvine CA 92618) or better yet, visit its Website at www.MicroExpress.net.

Micro Center

Though eMachines sells computers for under $500, the *first* major company to sell *good* computers for under $500 was **Micro Electronics Incorporated (MEI)**, which runs a chain of stores called **Micro Center**. It manufactures a computer called the **PowerSpec** and sells the system unit for $499.99. It also sells fancier versions at higher prices.

You can buy PowerSpec computers at a Micro Center superstore (a pleasant place to shop!) or mail-order (800-382-2390).

Industrial nuts

To get the lowest computer prices, many people have been phoning a secret group of amazing companies advertising in *Computer Shopper*. The group is called **the industrial nuts** because the employees are industrious, the prices are nutty, and the location is these two Los Angeles suburbs: "City of Industry" and "Walnut". The owners and employees seem mostly Chinese.

Recently, most of those companies shut down, but the following are still in business:

Company	Phone	Address	City	State	ZIP
ProStar Computers	800-243-5654, 626-854-3428	1128 Coiner Ct.	City of Industry	CA	91748
Sager	800-669-1624, 626-964-8682	18005 Cortney Ct.	City of Industry	CA	91748
HyperData Tech.	800-786-3343, 909-468-2960	809 South Lemon Ave.	Walnut	CA	91789

They sell mainly notebook computers.

These 22 industrial nuts have gone out of business:

> A+ Computer, All Computer, Altus, Atlas Micro Logistic, Bit Computer, Comtrade, Cornell Computer Systems, CS Source, Cyberex, Digitron, EDO Micro, Enpower, Multiwave, Nimble, PC Channel, Premio, Professional Technologies, Quanson, Royal, Syscon Technology, Tempest Micro, Wonderex, Zenon

Cleveland commandos

In 1997, *Computer Shopper* was deluged with ads from a horde of companies in Cleveland and its suburbs. Those companies offered low prices, nearly as low as the industrial nuts. Recently, most of those companies shut down, but the following are still in business:

Company	Phone	Address	City	State	ZIP
Adamant Computers	800-236-3550, 216-595-1211	4572 Renaissance Pkwy.	Cleveland	OH	44128
Americomp	800-217-2667, 440-498-0993	5380 Naiman Pkwy. #E	Solon	OH	44139
A2Z Computers	800-983-8889, 330-995-3355	325 Harris Dr.	Aurora	OH	44202

Those companies have advertised under alternative names:

Company	Alternative names
A2Z Computers	First Compuchoice, Computer King
Americomp	American Computech, Microvision

Those alternative names are no longer used.

These 15 commandos have dived to their death and gone out of business:

> American Micro, Amp Tech, Artcomp, ABC Computers, Cyberspace Computers, Digit Micro, Legend Micro, Magic PC, Micro Pro, Micro Pulse, Micro X, Micronix, New Age Micro, Odyssey Technology, PC Importers, Quickline Micro, Starquest, Unicent, United Micro

ABS

Earlier editions of this book praised ABS for selling high-quality computers.

Because of recent low-price competition from HP and Acer, ABS has given up trying to sell computers. Now ABS sells just high-quality computer *parts* (keyboards, headsets, cases, power supplies, and cameras), to make your own computer fancier.

Alternatives

In many towns, entrepreneurs sell computers for ridiculously low prices in computer shows and tiny stores. Before buying, check the computer's technical specifications and the dealer's reputation. If the dealer offers you software, make sure the dealer also gives you an official manual from the software's publisher, with a warranty/registration card; otherwise, the software might be an illegal hot copy.

For further advice, phone me anytime at 603-666-6644.

Apple

What's the most important computer company? IBM? Microsoft?

No! The most important computer company is actually **Apple**. That's the company that's had the greatest influence on how we deal with computers today.

Apple was the first computer manufacturer to popularize these ideas successfully:

> screens showing colors (instead of just black-and-white)
>
> 3½-inch floppy disks (instead of 5¼-inch, which are flimsy and less reliable)
> CD-ROM disks (instead of just floppy disks, which hold less data)
>
> using a mouse (instead of just the keyboard's arrow keys and Tab keys)
> using pictures (called **icons**) instead of just words
> pull-down menus (coming down from a menu bar, which is at the screen's top)
>
> laser printers (instead of just dot-matrix printers, which print in an ugly way)
> desktop publishing (instead of word processing, which can't handle beauty)
> pretty fonts (instead of typewriter-style fonts, which are monospaced and ugly)
> paint & draw programs (so you can create graphics easily, without math)

Apple didn't *invent* any of those ideas, but Apple was the first company to *popularize* them, make people *want* them, and thereby change our idea of what a computer should do.

> 3½-inch disks were invented by Sony. The first mouse was invented by the Stanford Research Institute. The first good mouse software was invented by Xerox. The first personal laser printers were invented by Hewlett-Packard. The first modern desktop-publishing program was invented by a software company, Aldus. But it was Apple's further product development and marketing that made those products *desirable*.

Though just 4% of the computers sold today are made by Apple, we all owe a big debt to Apple for how that company improved our world.

Here's how Apple arose and changed our lives....

Original Apple

The original Apple computer was invented by Steve Wozniak, who was an engineer at Hewlett-Packard. In 1975, he offered the plans to his boss at Hewlett-Packard, but his boss said Steve's computer didn't fit into Hewlett-Packard's marketing plan. His boss suggested that Steve start his own company. Steve did.

He worked with his friend, Steve Jobs. Steve Wozniak was the engineer; Steve Jobs was the businessman. Both were young: Steve Wozniak was 22; Steve Jobs was 19. Both were college drop-outs. They'd worked together before: when high-school students, they'd built and sold **blue boxes** (boxes that people attached to telephones to illegally make long-distance calls free). Steve & Steve had sold 200 blue boxes at $80 each, giving them a total of $16,000 in illegal money.

To begin Apple Computer Company, Steve & Steve invested just $1300, which they got by selling a used Volkswagen Micro Bus and a used calculator.

They built the first Apple computer in their garage. They sold it by word of mouth, then later by ads. The advertised price was just $666.60.

Like all computers of that era, the first Apple computer was primitive: it had *none* of the features for which Apple is now famous. (No color, no 3½-inch floppy disks, no CD-ROM disks, no mouse, no icons, no pull-down menus, no laser printers, no desktop publishing, no pretty fonts, no paint & draw programs.)

Apple 2

The original Apple computer looked pathetic. But in 1977, Steve & Steve invented a slicker version, called the **Apple 2**. Unlike the original Apple, the Apple 2 included a keyboard and displayed graphics in color. It cost $970.

The Apple 2 became a smashing success, because it was the first computer for under $1000 that could display colors on a TV. It was the *only* such computer for many years, until Commodore finally invented the Vic, which was even cheaper (under $300).

At first, folks used the Apple 2 just to play games and didn't take it seriously. But two surprise events changed the world's feelings about Apple.

MECC The first surprise was that the Minnesota state government decided to buy lots of Apple 2 computers, put them in Minnesota schools, and write programs for them. That state agency, called the **Minnesota Educational Computing Consortium (MECC)**, then distributed the programs free to other schools across America.

Soon, schools across America discovered that personal computers could be useful in education. Since the only good educational programs came from Minnesota and required Apples, schools across America bought Apples — and then wrote more programs for the Apples they'd bought. Apple became the "standard" computer for education — just because of the chain reaction that started with a chance event in Minnesota. The chain reaction spread fast, as teachers fell in love with the Apple's color graphics.

VisiCalc The next surprise was that a graduate student at the Harvard Business School and his friend at M.I.T. got together and wrote the first spreadsheet program, called **VisiCalc**. They wrote it for the Apple 2 computer, because it was the only low-cost computer that had a reliable disk operating system.

(Commodore's computers didn't have disks yet, and Radio Shack's disk operating system was buggy until the following year. Apple's success was due to Steve Wozniak's brilliance: he invented a disk-controller card that was amazingly cheap and reliable.)

The VisiCalc spreadsheet program was so wonderful that accountants and business managers all over the country bought it — and therefore had to buy Apple computers to run it on.

> VisiCalc was more nifty than any accounting program that had been invented on even the largest IBM maxicomputers. VisiCalc proved that little Apples could be more convenient than even the most gigantic IBM.
>
> Eventually, VisiCalc became available for other computers; but at first, VisiCalc required an Apple, and VisiCalc's success led to the success of Apple.
>
> In a typical large corporation, the corporate accountant wanted to buy an Apple with VisiCalc. Since the corporation's data-processing director liked big computers and refused to buy microcomputers, the accountant who wanted VisiCalc resorted to an old business trick: he lied. He pretended to spend $2000 for "typewriters" but bought an Apple instead. He snuck it into the company and plopped it on his desk. That happened all across America, so all large corporations had thousands of Apples sitting on the desks of accountants and managers but disguised as "typewriters" or "word processors".
>
> Yes, Apple computers infiltrated American corporations by subversion. It was an underground movement that annoyed IBM so much that IBM eventually decided to invent a personal computer of its own.

Apple 2+ In 1979, Apple Computer Corporation began shipping an improved Apple 2, called the **Apple 2+**.

Its main improvement was that its ROM chips contained a better version of Basic, called **Applesoft Basic**, which could handle decimals. (The version of Basic in the old Apple 2's ROM chips handled just integers.)

Another improvement was how the Reset key acted.

> On the old Apple 2, pressing the Reset key would abort a program, so the program would stop running. Too many consumers pressed the Reset key accidentally and got upset. On the Apple 2+, pressing the Reset key aborted a program just if you simultaneously held down the Control key.

Slots In the Apple 2+ and its predecessors, the motherboard contained eight slots, numbered from 0 to 7. Each slot could hold a printed-circuit card.

> Slot 0 was for a **memory card** (containing extra RAM).
>
> Slot 1 was for a **printer card** (containing a parallel printer port).
>
> Slot 2 was for an **internal modem** (for attaching to a phone).
>
> Slot 3 was for an **80-column card** (to make the screen display 80 characters per line instead of 40).
>
> Slot 6 was for a **disk controller**.
>
> Cards in slots 4, 5, and 7 were more exotic.

Apple 2e In 1983, Apple began shipping a further improvement, called the **Apple 2 extended, expanded, enhanced (Apple 2e)**. Most programs written for the Apple 1, 2, and 2+ also ran on the Apple 2e.

To improve on the Apple 2+ keyboard (which contained just 52 keys), the Apple 2e keyboard contained **11 extra keys**, making a total of 63.

> The extra keys helped you type lowercase letters, type special symbols, edit your writing, and control your programs.
>
> For example, the Apple 2e keyboard contained all four arrow keys (↑, ↓, ←, and →), so you could easily move around the screen in all four directions. (The ↑ and ↓ keys were missing from the Apple 2+ keyboard.)
>
> The Apple 2e keyboard contained a Delete key, so you could easily delete an error from the middle of your writing. (The Delete key was missing from the Apple 2+ keyboard.)

Unlike its predecessors, the Apple 2e **omitted slot 0**, because the Apple 2e didn't need a RAM card: the Apple 2e's motherboard already contained lots of RAM (64K).

The Apple 2e contained an extra slot, called **slot 3A**. It resembled slot 3 but held a more modern kind of video card that came in two versions: the plain version let your Apple display 80 characters per line; the fancy version did the same but also included a row of 64K RAM chips, so that your Apple contains 128K of RAM altogether.

The Apple 2e was invented in 1983 — the same year as the IBM XT. Which was better?

> An Apple 2e was generally worse than an IBM XT or an IBM XT clone. For example, the Apple 2e system had less RAM (128K instead of 640K), fewer keys on the keyboard (63 instead of 83), inferior disk drives (writing just 140K on the disk instead of 360K), and a crippled version of BASIC (understanding just 114 words instead of 178).
>
> Though worse than an IBM XT, the Apple 2e became quite popular in 1983, because **more educational programs and games were available for the Apple 2e than for any other computer**. That's because the Apple 2e still ran thousands of programs that were invented years earlier for its predecessors: the Apple 1, 2, and 2+. Fewer educational programs and games were being written for the IBM XT and clones, because the IBM XT cost more than schools and kids could afford. Although the IBM XT became the standard computer for business, the Apple 2e became the standard computer for schools and kids.

Apple 2c In 1984, Apple created a shrunken Apple 2e called the **Apple 2 compact (Apple 2c)**. Besides being smaller and lighter than the Apple 2e, it cost less. It also consumed less electricity.

But advanced hobbyists spurned the 2c — and stayed with the 2e instead — because the 2c didn't have slots for adding cards; it wasn't expandable.

> The typical consumer didn't need extra cards anyway, since the 2c's motherboard included everything a beginner wanted: 128K of RAM, 80-character-per-line video circuitry, a disk controller, and two serial ports. You could run cables from the back of the 2c to a serial printer, modem, second disk drive, and joystick.

When the 2c first came out, its ROM was fancier than the 2e's, so that the 2c could handle Basic and a mouse better than the 2e. But in February 1985, Apple began putting the fancy ROM chips in the 2e also, so every new 2e handled Basic and a mouse as well as the 2c.

Apple invented an improved Apple 2c, called the **Apple 2c+**, whose disk drive was 3½-inch instead of 5¼-inch. Apple's 3½-inch drive was technically superior to Apple's 5¼-inch drive but angered users, since most educational software still came on 5¼-inch disks and wasn't available on 3½-inch disks yet.

Apple 2GS In 1986, Apple created an improved version of the Apple 2e and called it the **Apple 2 with amazing graphics & sound (Apple 2GS)**.

> Its graphics were fairly good (better than EGA, though not as good as VGA).
>
> Its musical abilities were amazing. They arose from Apple's **Ensoniq chip**, which could produce 32 musical voices simultaneously!
>
> The computer contained an extra-fast CPU (the 65816), 128k of ROM, 256K of general-purpose RAM, and 64K of RAM for the sound synthesizer.
>
> To run the popular 2GS programs, you needed add an extra 256K of RAM, to bring the total RAM up to 512K. Many folks went further and bought 1M of RAM.
>
> Discount dealers sold the 2GS with 1M RAM for $800. That price did *not* include a monitor or any disk drives. To run the popular programs well, you had to buy a *color* monitor and *two* disk drives.

Apple 2 family All those computers resembled each other, so most programs written for the Apple 2 also worked on the Apple 2+, 2e, 2c, 2c+, and 2GS.

Apple has stopped marketing all those computers, but you can still buy them as "used computers" from your neighbors.

Clones Instead of buying computers built by Apple, some folks bought imitations, such as the **Pineapple**, the **Orange**, the **Pear**, and the **Franklin**. Such imitations were popular in the United States, Hong Kong, and especially the Soviet Union. Apple sued most of those companies (because they illegally copied Apple's ROM) and made them stop building clones.

Apple permitted one clone to remain: the **Laser 128**, because that clone's designer imitated the functions of Apple's ROM without exactly copying it.

> The Laser 128 imitated the Apple 2c. Like the Apple 2c, the Laser 128 included 128K of RAM, a disk drive, and a serial port. In three ways, it was *better* than an Apple 2c: it included a parallel printer port (so you could attach a greater variety of printers), a numeric keypad (so you could enter data into spreadsheets more easily), and a slot (so you could add an Apple 2c expansion card). It ran most Apple 2c programs perfectly. (Just 5% of the popular Apple 2c programs were incompatible with the Laser 128.)
>
> A souped-up version, called the **Laser 128EX**, went three times as fast.
>
> The Laser 128 and 128EX were built by the **Laser Computer** division of **VTech**, the same company that made IBM clones.

Apple 3

Back in 1980, shortly after the Apple 2+ was invented, Apple began selling the **Apple 3**. It was much fancier than the Apple 2+. Unfortunately, it was ridiculously expensive (it listed for $4995, plus a monitor and hard drive), it couldn't run some of the Apple 2+ software, and the first ones off the assembly line were defective. Few people bought it.

When the IBM PC came out and consumers realized the PC was better and cheaper than the Apple 3, interest in the Apple 3 vanished. Apple gave up trying to sell the Apple 3 but incorporated the Apple 3's best features into later, cheaper Apples: the Apple 2e and the Apple 2GS.

Lisa

Back in 1963, when Steve & Steve were just kids in elementary school, Doug Engelbart invented the world's first computer mouse. He was at the Stanford Research Institute. During the 1970's, researchers at **Xerox's Palo Alto Research Center (Xerox PARC)** used his mouse as the basis of a fancy computer system, called the **Alto**. Xerox considered the Alto too big and expensive to sell well but invited the world to see it.

In 1979, Apple employees nudged Steve Jobs to go to Xerox and see the Alto. Steve was impressed by the Alto and decided to invent a smaller, cheaper version, which he called the **Lisa**, because that was his daughter's name.

The Lisa changed the computer world forever. Before the Lisa, personal computers were awkward to use. The Lisa was the first affordable personal computer that made good use of a **mouse, icons, horizontal menus, and pull-down menus**.

> The Lisa's screen displayed cute little drawings, called **icons**. Some of the icons stood for activities. To make the Lisa perform an activity, you looked on the screen for the activity's icon. (For example, to make the computer delete a file, you began by looking for a picture of a garbage can.) When you pointed at the icon by using a mouse, and clicked the mouse's button, the Lisa performed the icon's activity.
>
> The Lisa also used **horizontal menus** and **pull-down menus**. (A horizontal menu is a list of topics printed across the top line of the screen. If you choose one of those general topics by using the mouse, a column of more specific choices appears underneath that topic; that column of specific activities is called a **pull-down menu**. You then look at the pull-down menu, find the specific activity you're interested in, click at it by using the mouse, and the computer immediately starts performing that activity.)
>
> Pointing at icons, horizontal menus, and pull-down menus is much easier to learn than using the kinds of computer systems other manufacturers had developed before. It's also fun! Yes, the Lisa was the first computer whose business programs were truly fun to run. And because it was so easy to learn to use, customers could start using it without reading the manuals. Everybody praised the Lisa and called it a new breakthrough in software technology.

Though the Lisa was "affordable", it was affordable by just the rich: it cost nearly $10,000. For the Lisa, Apple invented some special business programs that were fun and easy to use; but the Lisa could *not* run Apple 2 programs, since the Lisa had a completely different CPU.

> Independent programmers had difficulty developing their *own* programs for the Lisa, since Apple didn't supply enough programming tools. Apple never invented a version of BASIC, delayed introducing a version of PASCAL, and didn't make detailed manuals available to the average programmer. And though icons and pull-down menus are easy to use, they're difficult for programmers to invent.

Apple gradually lowered the Lisa's price.

Early Macs

In January 1984, Apple introduced the **Macintosh (Mac)**, which was a stripped-down Lisa. Like the original Lisa, the Mac uses a mouse, icons, horizontal menus, and pull-down menus. The Mac's price is low enough to make it popular.

The Mac is even more fun and easy than the Lisa! It appeals to beginners scared of computers. Advanced computerists like it also, because it feels ultra-modern, handles graphics quickly, and passes data from one program to another simply.

The original version of the Mac ran too slowly, but the newest versions run faster. They're priced nearly as low as IBM clones.

Since the Mac's so easy to use and priced nearly as low as IBM clones, many people have bought it. Lots of software's been developed for it — much more than for the Lisa.

To run Mac software well, you must buy a Mac. Since popular Mac software does *not* run well on the Lisa, Apple has stopped selling the Lisa and stopped selling a compromise called the **Mac XL**.

Let's take a closer look at the various early Macs....

Original Mac Apple began selling the Mac for $2495. The Mac's original version consisted of three parts: the mouse, the keyboard, and the system unit.

> The system unit contained a 9-inch black-and-white screen (whose resolution was 512 by 384), a 3½-inch floppy disk drive, and a motherboard. On the motherboard sat an 8-megahertz **68000** CPU, two ROM chips (containing most of the operating system and many routines for drawing graphics), rows of RAM chips, a disk controller, and two serial ports (for attaching a printer and a modem).

That Mac was called the **original 128K Mac** because it includes 128K of RAM (plus 64K of ROM).

Then Apple invented an improvement called the **512K Mac** because it included 512K of RAM. (It used two rows of 256K chips instead of two rows of 64K chips.) Apple wanted to call it the "Big Mac" but feared that customers would think it was a hamburger.

Mac Plus In January 1986, Apple began selling a new, improved Mac, called the **Mac Plus**. It surpassed the 512K Mac in several ways:

> It contains a bigger RAM (1 megabyte instead of 512K), a bigger ROM (128K instead of 64K), a better disk drive (double-sided instead of single-sided), a bigger keyboard (which contains extra keys), and a port that let you add a hard-disk drive more easily. The improved ROM, RAM, disk drive, keyboard, and port all served the same goal: they provided hardware and software tricks that let Mac programs run faster.

Like the 128K and 512K Macs, the Mac Plus included one floppy drive.

Mac SE In 1987, Apple introduced an even fancier Mac, called the **Mac SE**. It ran software 15% faster than the Mac Plus because it contains a cleverer ROM (256K instead of 128K) and fancier support chips. It was also more **expandable**: it let you insert extra circuitry more easily. The keyboard cost extra: you could buy the **standard keyboard** (which had 81 keys) or the **extended keyboard** (which had 105 keys and cost more).

Mac 2 When Apple introduced the Mac SE, Apple also introduced a luxury model, called the **Mac 2**. It contains a faster CPU (a 16-megahertz **68020**) and 6 slots for inserting printed-circuit cards.

Instead of sticking you with a 9-inch black-and-white monitor, it let you use any kind of monitor you wish: you could choose big or small; you could choose black-and-white or gray-scale or color. The monitor cost extra; so did the keyboard (standard or extended) and video card (which you put into a slot and attached the monitor to).

Since the Mac 2 let you choose your own monitor, the Mac 2 was called a **modular Mac**. When buying a modular Mac, remember that the monitor costs extra!

Performas versus Quadras In 1990, Apple stopped selling all the Macs that I've mentioned so far — the 128K Mac, 512K Mac, Mac Plus, Mac SE, and Mac 2. Apple switched to Macs that are more modern.

> Apple's first great modern Mac came in 1991. It was called the **Quadra**. It contained a **68040** CPU. It was called the **Quadra** because of the "4" in "68040". The **Quadra** was intended for folks smart enough to know that "quadra" is the Latin word for "4". It was intended to be sold by expert salespeople to expert customers.
>
> In 1992, Apple invented a "simplified Quadra", called the **Performa**, for beginners. It was intended to be sold by idiotic salespeople to idiotic customers, who think the word "performer" should be pronounced "performa".

Then customers could choose between the Performa (for beginners) and the Quadra (which was still available, for experts).

> Performa computers were sold mainly by idiots in office-supply stores (such as Staples & Office Max). Quadra computers were sold just by computer experts in computer stores (such as CompUSA).
>
> A Performa's price included lots of software — especially games and tutorials for beginners.
> A Quadra's price included very little software. You bought your own — or invented it yourself!
>
> For help with a Performa computer, you phoned "babysitters" at Apple's headquarters (800-sos-Apple).
> To repair a Quadra, you phoned the computer technicians at the computer store where you bought it.
>
> A Performa's price was simple: it included a keyboard, monitor, & fax/modem; no surcharges or choices!
> For a Quadra, you had to decide which keyboard, monitor, and fax/modem you wanted; they cost extra.

Though Performas were idiotic, they were the best values: you got more hardware and software per dollar when you bought a Performa than when you bought a Quadra. The Quadras were just for annoyingly fussy nerds who insisted on customizing the computers, making their own decisions about which keyboard, monitor, and fax/modem to use.

At first, the rule was simple: Quadras were sold just at computer stores; Performas were sold just at general stores. At the end of 1994, Apple began letting computer stores sell *both* kinds of computers (Quadras and Performas), to handle both kinds of customers (experts and idiots). Non-computer stores (such as Staples) were still restricted to selling to idiots: they sold just Performas.

Performas came in several varieties: you could choose a normal CPU (a **68030**), a faster CPU (a **68040**), or an even faster CPU (a **Power PC chip**).

Power Macs After watching the Performa-versus-Quadra war, Apple decided on a compromise: all new Macs would include a keyboard (like a Performa), but you can typically choose your own monitor (like buying a Quadra).

In 1994, Apple began selling powerful Macs, called **Power Macs**. Each contained a fast CPU chip (called the **Power PC**), but the advertised price did not include a monitor.

Mac clones In 1995, Apple's executives began letting other companies make clones of Macs. Those companies paid Apple a licensing fee. The most successful of those companies was **Power Computing**, whose clones ran much faster than Apple's originals! Clones were also made by **Radius**, **Motorola**, and **Umax**.

But in 1997, Apple had a change of heart and withdrew the licenses of all the clone makers except **Umax**. Apple restricted Umax to making just clones that are "junk" (priced under $1000).

Umax no longer bothers to make Mac clones.

iMacs

In 1998, Apple began selling simplified Macs, to help beginners use the Internet. Each simplified Mac is called an **Internet Mac (iMac)**.

Apple has sold it in 4 styles. Here are the details....

Classic iMac The **classic iMac** looks out-of-this-world!

It looks like an airplane's nose cone — or an ostrich egg from outer space. It's **translucent** — which means you can almost see through it, like trying to look through a frosted shower-stall door to see the sexy woman inside. Intriguing! Every reviewer who saw the classic iMac loved it, and so did Apple's customers. I bought one myself. It's great!

It includes a **15-inch CRT**, pair of stereo speakers, and fax/modem. The price also includes a keyboard, mouse, and software.

The translucent case is tinted in a wild color. The first iMac was in a color called **Bondi Blue** (named after Australia's Bondi beach); later iMacs were in colors called Blueberry, Strawberry, Grape, Lime, Tangerine, Blue Dalmatian (white spots on a blue background), Flower Power (a floral print inspired by the 1960's), Indigo (blue), Graphite (black) and Snow (white). Apple got lots of praise for creatively avoiding beige, and many hardware manufacturers imitated Apple's wild color schemes.

Though that classic iMac is wonderful, Apple has stopped selling it, because the eMacs and new iMacs are even more powerful.

The eMac The **eMac** is white. It resembles a classic iMac but has a bigger screen: a **17-inch CRT** instead of 15-inch. It was designed for schools ("eMac" means "educational Mac") and was originally sold just to schools, but Apple later let *everybody* buy it.

New iMac The **new iMac** looks totally different: even more out-of-this-world!

It's a **white hemisphere** (so it looks like a mound of mashed potatoes), with an arm coming out of its top. At the arm's end, instead of a hand, you get an **LCD** thin-screen monitor. (The original version's screen was 15-inch; Apple later offered 17-inch and 20-inch versions also.) The monitor hovers in front of the arm and hides the arm from your view, so the monitor seems to hover by itself mysteriously in the air, like a UFO propelled by aliens.

People who use the new iMac are said to "do the mashed potato", "play with their hovercraft", and "kiss aliens".

Since the new iMac looks so mysteriously intriguing, many IBM-clone manufacturers have copied Apple's idea of using a flat-screen LCD monitor. Those companies bought so many 15-inch LCD screens from suppliers that Apple could no longer get enough supplies for itself, and suppliers raised their prices, forcing Apple to raise its prices by $100. But eventually prices came back down.

Newest iMac **Apple has stopped selling the classic iMac, the eMac, and the new iMac.** Now Apple sells instead the **newest iMac**. It resembles the new iMac but has no white hemisphere; instead, all the system-unit circuitry hides inside the LCD monitor. The first version of the newest iMac was white plastic; the current version (introduced in August 2007) is aluminum instead.

Notebook Macs

Back in 1991, Apple began selling powerful notebook computers, called **PowerBooks**. Later, Apple began selling cheaper notebook computers also, called **iBooks**.

Apple has stopped selling all those notebook computers. Instead, Apple sells newer notebook computers, called **MacBooks**.

Modern Mac prices

Now Apple sells just 4 kinds of normal computers.

MacBook Apple sells a notebook computer called the **MacBook**. Here's how it was priced when this book went to press in June 2011:

Name	Screen		RAM	Hard	CPU type	GHz	Price
MacBook	13.3"	1280×800	2G	250G	Core 2 Duo	2.4 GHz	$999
MacBook	13.3"	1280×800	4G	250G	Core 2 Duo	2.4 GHz	$1099
MacBook	13.3"	1280×800	4G	320G	Core 2 Duo	2.4 GHz	$1149
MacBook Pro	13.3"	1280×800	4G	320G	Core i5	2.3 GHz	$1199
MacBook Pro	13.3"	1280×800	4G	500G	Core i5	2.3 GHz	$1249
MacBook Pro	13.3"	1280×800	4G	500G	Core i7	2.7 GHz	$1499
MacBook Pro	15.4"	1440×900	4G	500G	Core i7	2 GHz	$1799
MacBook Pro	15.4"	1440×900	4G	750G	Core i7	2 GHz	$1899
MacBook Pro	15.4"	1440×900	4G	750G	Core i7	2.2 GHz	$2199
MacBook Pro	15.4"	1680×1050	4G	750G	Core i7	2.2 GHz	$2299
MacBook Pro	17"	1920×1200	4G	750G	Core i7	2.2 GHz	$2499
MacBook Pro	17"	1920×1200	8G	750G	Core i7	2.66 GHz	$2699

Built into each MacBook you'll find a touchpad, a pair of stereo speakers, a microphone, a **SuperDrive** (DVD±RW drive) and the **iSight** video camera. The price also includes **OS X** (the operating system) and **iLife** (a suite of programs letting you edit photos, music, movies, DVDs, and Websites).

A variant, called the **MacBook Air**, has a flash drive instead of a hard drive (so it's thinner, weighs less, is easier to carry, and runs faster). Unfortunately, the flash drive doesn't hold as many gigabytes as a hard drive.

The iMac Apple sells a desktop computer called the **iMac**. It's an **all-in-one computer** (the system unit hides inside the screen). Here's how it's priced:

Screen		RAM	Hard drive	CPU type	GHz	Price
21.5"	1920×1080	4G	500G	Core i5	2.5 GHz	$1199
21.5"	1920×1080	4G	1T	Core i5	2.7 GHz	$1499
27"	2560×1440	4G	1T	Core i5	2.7 GHz	$1699
27"	2560×1440	4G	1T	Core i5	3.1 GHz	$1999
27"	2560×1440	8G	1T	Core i5	3.1 GHz	$2199
27"	2560×1440	8G	2T	Core i5	3.1 GHz	$2349
27"	2560×1440	8G	2T	Core i7	3.4 GHz	$2549

Each iMac's hard drive is fast (7200 rpm). The system unit hides inside the LCD screen; there's no separate tower case.

Built into each iMac you'll find a pair of stereo speakers, a microphone, and the iSight video camera. The price also includes the **Apple Keyboard**, the **Magic Mouse**, the SuperDrive, OS X, and iLife.

Mac mini The **Mac mini** is a system unit that's cheap because its price doesn't include a keyboard, mouse, screen, speakers, microphone, or video camera. If you already own a keyboard, mouse, and screen from an older Mac computer (or even from an IBM-compatible computer), you can attach them to the Mac mini to create a computer system.

Here's how the Mac mini is priced:

RAM	Hard drive	CPU type	GHz	Price
2G	320G	Core 2 Duo	2.4 GHz	$699
4G	320G	Core 2 Duo	2.4 GHz	$799
4G	500G	Core 2 Duo	2.4 GHz	$849
8G	500G	Core 2 Duo	2.4 GHz	$1049
8G	500G	Core 2 Duo	2.66 GHz	$1199

The Mac mini's price includes OS X and iLife. For $98 extra, you can buy a kit that contains an Apple keyboard and mouse, but that kit still doesn't include a screen, speakers, microphone, or video camera.

Mac Pro The **Mac Pro** is a big system unit that's expensive because it includes one or two CPU chips that are extra-fast. Its base price does not include a screen, speakers, microphone, or video camera; attach your own. The price includes everything else (SuperDrive, Apple Keyboard, Magic Mouse, OS X, and iLife).

Here's how the Mac Pro is priced:

RAM	Hard drive	CPU	Price
3G	1T	quad-core 2.8 GHz	$2499
6G	1T	quad-core 2.8 GHz	$2724
6G	1T	2 of quad-core 2.4GHz	$3499
6G	1T	2 of 6-core 2.66GHz	$4999
8G	1T	2 of 6-core 2.66GHz	$5149
8G	2T	2 of 6-core 2.66GHz	$5299
12G	2T	2 of 6-core 2.66GHz	$5599
16G	2T	2 of 6-core 2.66GHz	$5899

Monitor

The MacBook and iMac include a screen, but the Mac mini and Mac Pro don't. If you buy a Mac mini or Mac Pro but don't have a screen yet, you can get Apple's **Cinema Display**, which is an LCD monitor that's huge (27" widescreen, 2560×1440). It costs $999. Even if you have a screen already, you can add the Cinema Display so you have *two* screens!

Discounts

You can buy directly from Apple by phoning **800-MY-APPLE** or using the Internet to go to **store.apple.com** or visiting Apple's stores (which are in just a few cities). You can also buy Apple's computers from chain stores (such as **CompUSA**), local Apple dealers, and these mail-order dealers:

Dealer	Internet address	Phone number
Mac Mall	www.macmall.com	800-222-2808
Mac Connection	www.macconnection.com	800-800-2222

Mac Mall usually has more exciting ads, but Mac Connection usually charges less for shipping and installation.

I've been showing you Apple's list prices. Unlike IBM clones, whose prices drop each month, Apple's list prices stay constant for many months, then drop suddenly. But while Apple's list prices stay "constant", Apple secretly gives bigger discounts to dealers, who in turn give "deals" to customers. Here's what the "deals" usually involve:

You pay $5 less than the list price — the discount is just $5 because Apple gets angry if dealers advertise bigger discounts.

You get 512K of extra RAM for "free" — but just if you pay a $40 "required professional RAM-installation charge".

You get a "free" printer — but just if you pay $99 first, remember to mail the rebate forms, wait to receive rebate checks totaling $99, and put up with a below-average printer.

You get a special computer for $200 less than any of Apple's current prices — because the computer you're getting is an outdated model that Apple no longer sells, and the dealer is having a clearance sale.

You get rebates from Apple — but just if you buy Apple's most expensive computers or overpriced monitors.

Service

When you buy a Mac, you get **3 months of phone support** (so you can phone Apple for free help answering questions about how to use your Mac) and a **1-year limited warranty** (which says Apple will fix the hardware if it breaks during the first year and you carry your Mac to an Apple-authorized repair center).

If you wish, you can buy the **AppleCare Protection Plan**, which gives you phone support and warranty for **3 years**. That plan costs $149 for the Mac mini, $169 for the iMac, $249 for the Mac Pro, $249 for the 13.3" MacBook, $349 for the MacBook Pro. That plan covers the computer and also covers any Apple-brand screen, keyboard, or mouse that was bought at the same time. It covers OS X and iLife but not most other software.

Another option is to pay $49 per question. (That price is for questions about normal software. Questions about hardware or advanced software cost $199. Questions about networking cost $695.)

I recommend you do *not* pay for AppleCare, since most of your questions and difficulties will be during the first 3 months, when AppleCare is free. After the first 3 months, pay consultants and repair shops when necessary.

Should you buy a Mac?

When the Mac first came out, computer experts loved it and praised it for being easier than an IBM PC.

Then Microsoft invented **Windows**, which made the IBM PC resemble a Mac.

> The first version of Windows was terrible, much worse than a Mac. Nobody took that version of Windows seriously. But over the years, Microsoft gradually improved Windows.
>
> When **Windows 3.0** came out, it was good enough to be useable. Though still not as nice as a Mac, it became popular because it ran on IBM PC clones, which cost much less than Macs.
>
> When **Windows 3.1** came out, some folks even *liked* it.
>
> When **Windows 95** came out in 1995, the Mac became doomed. Most critics agreed that Windows 95 was *better* than a Mac. **Windows 98**, **Windows Me**, **Windows XP**, **Windows Vista**, and **Windows 7** were further improvements. Moreover, an IBM PC running Windows 7 costs *less* than a Mac. Apple's new operating system, OS X, looks lovely but is incompatible with a lot of old software and old hardware; for a while, Apple shipped OS 9 and OS X with each computer, making Apple's customers schizophrenic.

Apple faces a new problem: since practically everybody has switched to buying IBM clones (with Windows XP or Vista or 7) instead of Macs, most programmers aren't bothering to write Mac programs anymore. So if you have a Mac, you're stuck running old programs written long ago, in versions less pleasant than new IBM versions. As a result, the Mac has actually become *harder* to use than an IBM clone!

The big exception to Mac's downfall is the graphics-art community. Years ago, before Windows became good, the Mac became the standard for folks in the graphics-arts community (such as ad agencies, newspapers, magazines, artists, and companies running printing presses). They still use Macs.

Some universities standardized on Macs because Apple Computer Inc. gave those universities a discount. When the discounts expired, many of those universities shifted to buying IBM clones instead.

iPad

Apple's **iPad** is a tablet computer. The current version is the **iPad 2**. It includes a 9.7-inch screen (whose resolution is 1024-by-768), a 1 GHz dual-core CPU (invented by Apple and called the **A5**), 2 tiny video cameras, and the iOS operating system.

Its price depends on how much flash RAM is included. It costs $499 with 16G, $599 with 32G, $699 with 64G. There's no hard drive; since part of the flash RAM imitates a hard drive.

There's no mouse or touchpad. Instead of manipulating such a device, you swipe your finger across the touch-sensitive screen.

There's no physical keyboard. Instead, the touch-sensitive screen shows a **virtual keyboard** (a keyboard's picture you can type on).

Before using the iPad, you must install more software by attaching the iPad to a normal computer (using the iPad's USB cable). So before using an iPad, you must have another computer. The iPad can be your second computer but not your first.

Who runs Apple?

After being founded by **Steve Wozniak** and **Steve Jobs**, Apple's leadership changed.

Steve Wozniak got in an airplane crash that hurt his head and gave him amnesia, so he left the company and enrolled in college under a fake name ("Rocky Clark"). After he graduated, he returned to Apple Computer Company quietly. Steve Jobs managed the company.

Though Apple was successful, Steve Jobs' strategies upset some computerists.

For example, Apple's ads claimed that the Apple was the first personal computer (it was *not* the first!); Apple launched a big campaign to make businessmen buy Apple Pascal (though Apple Pascal didn't help the average businessman at all); Apple prohibited its dealers from displaying games (though Apple later relented); and Apple prohibited authorized dealers from selling Apples by mail order.

Apple Computer Inc. donated computers to schools for three reasons: to be nice, get a tax write-off, and lure schools into buying Apples (to be compatible with the Apples that the schools received free). But if Apple were *really* nice, it would have lowered prices to let low-income consumers afford them. Apple sold just to the "chic", not the poor.

Steve & Steve both left Apple and went separate ways.

Apple's next head was **John Sculley**, a marketer who used to be a vice-president of Pepsi. He made Pepsi the #2 soft drink (just behind Coke) and kept Apple the #2 microcomputer company (just behind IBM).

In 1993, he had Apple invent and sell a handheld computer called the **Newton**. Instead of including a keyboard, it included a tablet you could write on with a pen. The computer tried to read handwritten words but couldn't read handwriting accurately enough. Apple's board of directors ousted him for spending too much effort on the Newton and not enough on the Mac.

Apple's next head was **Michael Spindler**, an efficient German who dropped Apple's costs and prices. But in 1995, Apple's profits plunged for three reasons:

> Microsoft began selling Windows 95 (which let IBM clones become nearly as pleasant as Macs).
>
> Intel dramatically dropped prices on the Pentium chips used in IBM clones.
>
> Spindler guessed wrong about which Macs would sell well, so Apple got stuck with unsold inventory of some models, parts shortages for others.

In 1996, Apple's board of directors fired Michael and replaced him with **Gil Amelio**. To cut costs, Gil fired lots of employees. In 1997, the board fired *him* and put **Steve Jobs** back in charge. Steve is still there — and popular — though his pancreatic cancer and liver transplant have forced him to reduce his duties and take occasional leaves of absence.

Windows

Most computers use an operating system called **Windows**, invented by Microsoft.

Microsoft has improved Windows. Microsoft invented **Windows 1**, then **Windows 2**, then **Windows 3**, then **Windows New Technology (Windows NT)**, then **Windows 95** (in 1995), then **Windows 98** (in 1998), then **Windows 2000** and **Windows Millennium Edition (Windows Me)**. All those versions of Windows are obsolete; I explain them in this book's older editions (which you can get by phoning me at 603-666-6644).

Now I'll explain the three popular modern versions of Windows:

Version	Invented	Sold in stores
Windows eXPerience (Windows XP)	August 2001	October 2001
Windows Vista	November 2006	January 2007
Windows 7	July 2009	October 2009

When you buy a new computer, it typically comes with Windows 7 (or something better), but many people are still stuck using older computers that came with Windows XP or Windows Vista.

When you buy Windows, you can get the **normal edition** (which is intended for most folks) or a **special edition** (for people & companies who have different desires). Here are the details....

Windows 7 editions

Windows 7 comes in 4 editions:

The normal edition, **7 Home Premium** ($120), is for use in homes and small businesses.

A fancier edition, **7 Professional** ($200), is for big businesses that insist on more security (and more compatibility with old Windows XP programs).

An even fancier edition, **7 Ultimate** ($220), is for even bigger businesses that require even more security and more help handling foreign languages.

A stripped-down edition, **7 Starter**, is for low-income people outside the USA (and people in the USA who buy netbook computers lacking enough RAM to handle other editions).

My explanation of Windows 7 emphasizes the normal edition (Windows 7 Home Premium). Other Windows 7 editions are similar.

Windows Vista editions

Windows Vista comes in 6 editions:

The normal edition, **Vista Home Premium**, is for use in homes and small businesses.

A stripped-down edition, **Vista Home Basic**, includes just the *fundamental* parts of Vista Home Premium and looks ugly (like Windows XP).

A variant edition, **Vista Business**, is for big businesses that insist on more security than Vista Home Premium and don't need the fun parts of Vista Home Premium.

A fancy edition, **Vista Ultimate**, is for computer experts who want *everything* that's in all the other versions (the fun stuff and the serious stuff), plus even *more* security!

Microsoft also sold **Vista Starter** (just in low-income countries that can't afford even Vista Home Basic) and **Vista Enterprise** (just to huge international corporations).

My explanation of Windows Vista emphasizes the normal edition (Vista Home Premium). Other Vista editions are similar.

Microsoft has corrected Windows Vista's errors.

In 2008, Microsoft invented a slightly corrected Windows Vista, called **Windows Vista with Service Pack 1 (Windows Vista SP1)**. In 2009, Microsoft invented a further improvement, called **Windows Vista with Service Pack 2 (Windows Vista SP2)**.

If you have Windows Vista or Windows Vista SP1, you can upgrade to Windows Vista SP2, free.

Windows XP editions

Windows XP comes in 3 editions:

The normal edition, **XP Home Edition**, is good enough for most folks.

A fancy edition, **XP Professional**, can perform extra tricks that help businesses run computer networks easily and securely.

A different fancy edition, **XP Media Center Edition**, helps you use the computer as a media center (to play CD music, watch DVD movies, and attach the computer to your home's TV screen).

My explanation of Windows XP emphasizes the normal edition (XP Home Edition) and the XP Media Center edition. The XP Professional edition is similar.

Microsoft has corrected Windows XP's errors.

In 2002, Microsoft invented a slightly corrected Windows XP, called **Windows XP with Service Pack 1 (Windows XP SP1)**. In 2004, Microsoft invented a further improvement, **Windows XP with Service Pack 2 (Windows XP SP2)**. In 2008, Microsoft invented a further improvement, **Windows XP with Service Pack 3 (Windows XP SP3)**.

If you have Windows XP or Windows XP SP1 or Windows XP SP2, you can upgrade to Windows XP SP3, free.

RAM requirements

Here's how much RAM you need.

Version	Requirement
Windows 7	1G to run at all, 3G to run well
Windows Vista	most editions require 1G to run at all, 2G to run well Vista Home Basic can run in ½G Vista Starter can run in ¼G
Windows XP	64M to run at all, 512M (which is ½G) to run well

How to start

Here's how to start using your computer with Windows. (If you have difficulty, **phone me anytime for free help at 603-666-6644**.)

Set up the computer

When you buy a new computer, you must set it up.

Setting up a notebook computer

Here's how to set up a typical **notebook computer**: the HP G71-340US. (Other notebook computers are similar.)

**Unpack** The computer comes in a cardboard box. Open the box and put the contents on your desk (or table). The box contains packing material plus 6 items:

the **computer itself** (16 inches wide, 11 inches front-to-back, 1 inch thick)
a **battery** (8 inches wide)
a **power cord** (which can plug into your home's electrical outlet)
a **power adapter** (a box-with-cord that transforms DC power to AC)
a **cleaning cloth** (to help wipe away dirt and fingerprints)
instructions

Remove those 6 items from their plastic bags and boxes.

The computer's top is covered by a clear plastic protector sheet. Peel away that sheet and discard it.

Open the computer (by prying open one of its long edges). Discard the black plastic protector sheet inside, so you see the computer's screen and keyboard. Close the computer.

**Insert the battery** Flip the computer upside-down. You see an 8-inch hole in the computer's underbelly. Pop the battery into that hole. Then flip the computer right-side-up.

**Plug in** Plug the power adapter into the computer's side.

Plug the power cord into the power adapter. Plug the power cord's other end into an electrical outlet (in your room's wall or power strip or surge protector), and make sure the electrical outlet is on. A light on the computer's front side will glow.

**Power up** Open the computer, so you see the keyboard and screen.

On the keyboard, find the **power button** (which shows a circle having a line sticking up from it). That button is near the screen. It's above the F8 and F9 keys. Press that button. It lights up. The computer will say (on its screen) "Starting Windows."

Setting up a desktop computer

A **desktop computer system** typically comes in three cardboard boxes. Open them, and put the contents on your desk.

One box contains the monitor.
One box contains the printer.
One box contains the computer's main part (**system unit**), keyboard, mouse, speakers, and disks.
Each box also contains power cords, cables, and instruction manuals.

Here are exceptions:

If you bought a laptop computer, there is no monitor.
If you didn't buy a printer, the printer box is missing.

Into the back of the system unit, plug the cables that come from the monitor, printer, keyboard, mouse and speakers. Into your wall's electrical socket (or power strip), plug the power cords that come from the monitor, printer, speakers, and system unit. (On some computers, the cabling is different.)

**Turn on the system unit** On the system unit's front, find the **power button** (which shows a circle having a line sticking up from it). On a typical modern computer, that button is big, gray, and a third of the way up from the bottom.

Some system units are different:

If there are two similar buttons, make sure you press the one that shows a circle having a line sticking up from it, not the other button (which is the reset button).
If the system unit is old-fashioned, there might be a **power switch** instead of a power button. The power switch might be on the system unit's right side (instead of the front), might be red, and might say "1" and "0."
If the system unit is old-fashioned, there might be a power button on the front plus a power switch on the back. Put both on.

**Turn on the screen** Turn on the computer's screen (monitor).

After a few seconds, the screen will display some messages. (If you don't see the messages clearly, make sure the cable from the screen to the system unit is plugged in tightly, and adjust the screen's contrast and brightness knobs.)

The screen will eventually say "Microsoft Windows xp" or "Windows Vista" or "Windows 7".

Attach any printer

If you have a printer, make sure a cable runs from it to the computer, and turn the printer on.

Stare at your computer.

Examine the Keyboard

Test your powers of observation by staring at the keyboard. Try to find the following keys (but don't press them yet)....

Find the **Enter key**. That's the big key on the right side of the keyboard's main section. It has a bent arrow on it. It's also called the **Return key**. Pressing it makes the computer read what you typed and proceed

Find the **Backspace key**. It's above the Enter key and to the right of the + key. It has a left-arrow on it. You press it when you want to erase a mistake.

Find the key that has the letter A on it. When you press the A key, you'll be typing a small "a".

Near the keyboard's bottom left corner, find the **Shift key**. It has an up-arrow on it. Under the Enter key, you'll see another Shift key. Press either Shift key when you want to capitalize a letter. For example, to type a capital A, hold down a Shift key; and while you keep holding down the Shift key, tap the A key.

Find the key that looks like this:

```
!
1
```

It's near the keyboard's top left corner. That's the **1 key**. You press it when you want to type the number 1. Press the keys to its right when you want to type the numbers 2, 3, 4, 5, 6, 7, 8, 9, and 0. If you press the 1 key while holding down a Shift key, you'll be typing an exclamation point (!). Here's the rule: if a key shows two symbols (such as ! and 1), and you want to type the top symbol (!), you must typically hold down a Shift key.

Find the key that has the letter U on it. To the right of that key, you'll see the letters I and O. Don't confuse the letter I with the number 1; don't confuse the letter O with the number 0.

In the keyboard's bottom row, find the wide key that has nothing written on it. That's the **Space bar**. Press it whenever you want to leave a blank space.

Check Num Lock

If you have a desktop computer (instead of a notebook computer), be careful about this:

> Your keyboard has a **Num Lock light**. On a typical keyboard, that light is near the keyboard's top right corner and is labeled "Num Lock" or just "Num". (Exception: on the Microsoft Natural Keyboard, that light is in the keyboard's middle and labeled "1".) **Make sure that light is glowing.** If it's *not* glowing, make it glow by tapping the **Num Lock key** (which is near the keyboard's top right corner).

Try moving the mouse

The typical computer has a mouse. (If your computer does *not* have a mouse, buy a mouse: a mouse is much easier to use than a touchpad!)

Look at the computer's mouse. The traditional mouse has a **tail** (a cable that runs from the mouse to the computer); if your mouse is ultra-modern, it communicates with the computer wirelessly instead. The area where a tail meets the mouse is called the mouse's **ass**.

The mouse's underside — its belly — has a hole in it. Inside the hole is a ball (or ray of light).

Put the mouse on your desk and directly in front of your right arm. Make the mouse lie flat (so its ball rubs against the desk or its light ray shines on the desk). **Make the mouse face you** so you don't see its ass.

Move the mouse across your desk. As you move the mouse, remember to keep it flat and facing you.

On the screen, you'll see an arrow, which is called the **mouse pointer**. As you move the mouse, the arrow moves also.

> If you move the mouse to the left, the arrow moves to the left.
> If you move the mouse to the right, the arrow moves to the right.
>
> If you move the mouse toward you, the arrow moves down.
> If you move the mouse away from you, the arrow moves up.

Practice moving the arrow by moving the mouse. Remember to keep the mouse facing you at all times.

If you want to move the arrow far and your desk is small, move the mouse until it reaches the desk's edge; then lift the mouse off the desk, lay the mouse gently on the middle of the desk, and rub the mouse across the desk in the same direction as before.

Finish installing Windows

If nobody's used the computer yet (because it's new), the computer will say "Setup is preparing your computer for first use." That means you must finish installing Windows onto your computer.

To do that, practice using the mouse (or trackball), keyboard, and Windows on a different computer, then finish installing Windows onto your computer by getting help from the company that sold you the computer or from me at 603-666-6644 or by following a procedure such as the following (which works on the typical Windows 7 notebook computer):

> The computer will say "Choose a user name." Invent a name for yourself. For example, you can use your first name or nickname (such as "Russ"), but make sure the name differs from the name of other people using your computer or your home or office's network. Type the name then press the Tab key. Press the Tab key again.
>
> Invent a computer name (such as "HP-G71-Notebook" or "RussNotebook" or "BedroomNotebook"). To avoid difficulties, the name must be short (at most 15 characters), differ from your user name, contain at least one letter, and contain just letters, digits, and hyphens, without spaces. Type the name then press the Enter key.
>
> The computer will say "Set a password for your account." To save time, don't bother creating a password yet: just press the Enter key.
>
> Click both "I accept the license terms" boxes, then press Enter.
> Press Enter again.
>
> Click the "Time zone" box's down-arrow (which looks like a triangle pointing down), then click your time zone (such as "Eastern Time"). On the calendar, click the correct date. On the digits under the clock, click next to the hour, then click the up-arrow or down-arrow to adjust the hour, then press Enter.
>
> Make sure you've properly set up your room's wireless router (which lets a notebook computer communicate with the Internet), then click the router's name then "Start this connection automatically". Click "Next".
>
> If you're at home, click "Home network"; if you're at work, click "Work network" instead.
>
> The computer will say "Welcome" then "Preparing your desktop".
>
> If your computer says "WELCOME TO YOUR NEW HP COMPUTER", click "GO" and follow Hewlett-Packard's own registration process (or click "Register Later").

Use the Start menu

Eventually, the screen's bottom left corner shows the **Start button**:

In Windows XP, the Start button says "start".

In Windows Vista & 7, the Start button is colored windows in a blue globe.

The most important part of the mouse's arrow is its tip, which is called the **hot spot**. Move the arrow so its hot spot (tip) is in the middle of the Start button. When you do that, you're **pointing at** the Start button.

On the top of the mouse, you'll see 2 or 3 rectangular buttons you can press. **The main button is the one on the left.** Tapping it is called **clicking**. So to **click**, tap the left button.

While you're pointing at the Start button, click (by tapping the left button). That's called **clicking Start**.

When you click Start, you see the **Start menu**, which is your starting list of choices. Which choices does the menu offer you? That depends on which version of Windows you have:

Windows XP		Windows Vista		Windows 7
Internet	My Documents	Internet	Documents	Documents
E-mail	My Pictures	E-mail	Pictures	Pictures
	My Music		Music	Music
	My Computer		Games	Games
	Control Panel		Recent Items	Computer
	Set Program Access and Defaults		Computer	Control Panel
	Connect To		Network	Devices and Printers
	Help and Support		Connect To	Default Programs
	Search		Control Panel	Help and Support
	Run		Default Programs	All Programs Shut Down
All Programs		All Programs	Help and Support	
Log Off	Turn Off Computer			

Your computer might offer some extra choices also! If your Windows XP is outdated (before SP2) or weird or not completely set up, it might omit "Set Program Access and Defaults" and "Connect To."

How to shut down

Whenever you finish using the computer, do this:

Windows 7 Click "Shut Down".

Windows Vista Click the right-arrow (▸) that's at the Start menu's bottom-right corner. Then click "Shut Down".

Windows XP Click "Turn Off Computer" (which is the Start menu's last choice). Then click the red "Turn Off" button.

Then wait while the computer tidies the info on your hard disk. Finally, the computer will turn its own power off.

Programs menu

Make the Start menu appear on the screen.

In that menu, "All Programs" has the symbol " ▶ " next to it. That symbol means that if you choose "All Programs" from the Start menu, you'll see *another* menu.

Try it: point at "All Programs". Then you see this **Programs menu**:

Windows XP	Windows Vista	Windows 7
Set Program Access and Defaults	Default Programs	Default Programs
Windows Catalog	Windows Calendar	Desktop Gadget Gallery
Windows Update	Windows Contacts	Internet Explorer
Accessories	Windows Defender	Windows Anytime Upgrade
Games	Windows DVD Maker	Windows DVD Maker
Startup	Windows Live Messenger Download	Windows Fax and Scan
Internet Explorer	Windows Mail	Windows Media Center
MSN	Windows Media Center	Windows Media Player
Outlook Express	Windows Media Player	Windows Update
Remote Assistance	Windows Meeting Space	XPS Viewer
Windows Media Player	Windows Movie Maker	Accessories
Windows Messenger	Windows Photo Gallery	Games
Windows Movie Maker	Windows Update	Maintenance
	Accessories	Startup
	Extras and Upgrades	
	Games	
	Maintenance	
	Startup	

If you bought extra programs, the menu mentions them too.

If Windows Vista or 7 shows just *part* of the Programs menu, see the rest by using one of these methods....

arrow-click method: click the Programs menu's down-arrow (▾) or up-arrow (▴), several times

arrow-hold method: point at the Programs menu's down-arrow (▾) or up-arrow (▴), then hold down the mouse's left button awhile

wheel method (if your mouse has a wheel): point in the Programs menu's middle (without pressing the mouse's buttons) then rotate the mouse's wheel toward you (or away from you).

If your Windows XP is outdated (before SP2), it might say "StartUp" instead of "Startup," say "MSN Explorer" instead of "MSN," omit "Set Program Access and Defaults," and omit "Windows Movie Maker".

Accessories menu

From the Programs menu, choose "Accessories", by pointing at it. Then you see this **Accessories menu**:

Windows XP	Windows Vista	Windows 7
Accessibility	Calculator	Calculator
Communications	Command Prompt	Command Prompt
Entertainment	Connect to a Network Projector	Connect to a Projector
System Tools	Notepad	Getting Started
Address Book	Paint	Notepad
Calculator	Remote Desktop Connection	Paint
Command Prompt	Run	Remote Desktop Connection
Notepad	Snipping Tool	Run
Paint	Sound Recorder	Snipping Tool
Program Compatibility Wizard	Sync Center	Sticky Notes
Synchronize	Welcome Center	Sync Center
Tour Windows XP	Windows Explorer	Windows Explorer
Windows Explorer	Windows Sidebar	Windows Mobility Center
WordPad	WordPad	WordPad
	Ease of Access	Ease of Access
	System Tools	System Tools
	Tablet PC	Windows PowerShell

Test the calculator

The Accessories menu includes a "Calculator". To use the calculator, get the accessories menu onto the screen (by clicking Start then "All Programs" then "Accessories") and then click "Calculator". You'll see the **Calculator window**, containing a picture of a pocket calculator.

How to calculate

To compute 42+5, click the calculator's 4 button (by using the mouse to point at the 4 button and then clicking), then click 2, then +, then 5, then =. The calculator will show the answer, 47.

Instead of using the mouse, you can do that calculation a different way, by using the computer's keyboard. Try this:

> If you have a desktop computer (instead of a notebook computer), make sure the Num Lock light is on (by doing the "Check Num Lock" procedure on page 77).
> On the computer's keyboard, tap the 4 key, then the 2 key, then (while holding down the Shift key) the + key, then 5. Then tap the = key (or the Enter key). The calculator will show 47.

Try fancier calculations, by pressing these calculator buttons:

Windows XP&Vista	Windows 7	Meaning
+	+	plus
-	-	minus
*	*	times
/	/	divided by
=	=	show the final answer, the "total"
.	.	decimal point
C	C	clear the total, so it becomes zero
CE	CE	clear this entry, so you can retype it
Backspace	←	erase the last digit you typed
+/-	±	create (or erase) the total's minus sign

Standard versus scientific

You can choose two popular kinds of calculators. A **standard calculator** is small and cute: it does just arithmetic. A **scientific calculator** is big and imposing: it includes extra buttons, so you can do advanced math.

The first time you (or your colleagues) ask for the calculator, the computer shows a standard calculator (small and cute). If you want the calculator to be scientific instead, choose **Scientific** from the **View menu**. (To do that, click the word "View", then click the word "Scientific".) Then you'll see extra buttons, such as these:

Windows XP&Vista	Windows 7	Meaning
x^2	x^2	squared
x^3	x^3	cubed
n!	n!	factorial
pi	π	circle's circumference divided by diameter

If you click the 7 button and then say "**squared**" (by pressing the x^2 or x^2 button), the computer will multiply 7 by itself and say 49 (which is called "7 squared"). If you click the 7 button and then say "**cubed**" (by pressing the x^3 or x^3 button), the computer will do "7 times 7 times 7" and say 343 (which is called "7 cubed"). If you click the 7 button and then say "**factorial**" (by pressing the n! button), the computer will multiply together all the numbers up to 7 (1 times 2 times 3 times 4 times 5 times 6 times 7) and say 5040 (which is called "7 factorial"). If you click the **pi** or π button, the computer will say 3.1415926535897932384626433832795.

After making the calculator scientific, you can make it standard again by choosing **Standard** from the View menu.

Order of operations The calculator's answer to "2+3*4=" depends on whether you chose standard or scientific:

> If you said you wanted the calculator to be standard, the computer does 2+3 (which totals 5), then multiplies by 4, giving a final total of 20.

> If you said you wanted the calculator to be scientific instead, the computer does "2+3*4=" by doing the multiplication first, like scientists do: 3*4 is 12, and 2+12 gives a final total of 14 (not 20).

Tricky Keys

On the standard calculator, these 3 keys are tricky:

Button	Meaning
sqrt ("√" in Windows 7)	square root of the previous number example: "49 sqrt" is 7 (because 49 is 7*7)
1/x	divide 1 by the previous number example: "4 1/x" is .25 (because 1/4 is .25)
%	multiply the 2 previous numbers, then divide by 100 example: "2 * 3 %" is .06 (because it's 2*3/100) afterwards, click the C button (to clear the total)

Memory buttons

When a number (such as a total) appears on your screen, you can copy that number from your screen to the computer's memory. The calculator includes **memory buttons** to help remember the number:

Button	Meaning
MS	memory store copy from the screen to memory
MR	memory retrieve copy from memory to the screen
M+	memory add put memory+screen into memory
M- (just in Windows 7)	memory subtract put memory minus screen into memory
MC	memory clear erase what's in memory

Close

In the Calculator window's top-right corner, you see a red button with a white X on it. That button is called the **X button** (or the **close button**).

When you finish using the Calculator window, click that button. It **closes** the Calculator window, so the Calculator window disappears.

WordPad

When you buy modern Windows, you get a word-processing program free! That word-processing program is called **WordPad**. It's one of the Windows accessories.

WordPad basics

To use WordPad, get the Accessories menu onto the screen (by clicking Start then "All Programs" then "Accessories") and then click "WordPad." You'll see the **WordPad window**.

In the window's top right corner, you see the X button. Next to the X button is the **resize button** (which is also called the **maximize/restore button**) Clicking the resize button changes the window's size.

Try clicking the resize button: see the window's size change! Try clicking the resize button *again*: see the window's size change *again*!

If the window is small, clicking the resize button makes the window become huge so it consumes the whole screen. If the window is huge and consumes the whole screen, clicking the resize button makes the window become small.

If the window consumes the whole screen, the window is said to be **maximized**. If the window is smaller, the window is said to be **restored** to a small size.

Click the resize button if necessary, so that the WordPad window consumes the whole screen (and is maximized).

Now that the WordPad window consumes the whole screen, you can easily do word processing: you can easily type words and sentences. Try it! Type whatever sentences you wish to make up. For example, try typing a memo to your friends, or a story, or a poem. Be creative! Whatever you type is called a **document**.

Use the keyboard

Read the section called "Examine the keyboard," which is on page 77. Here are more hints to help you type….

Capitals To capitalize a letter of the alphabet, type that letter while holding down the **Shift key**. (One Shift key is next to the Z key; the other Shift key is next to the question-mark key. Each Shift key has an up-arrow on it.)

To capitalize a whole passage, tap the **Caps Lock key**, then type the passage. The computer will automatically capitalize the passage as you type it. When you finish typing the passage, tap the Caps Lock key again: that tells the computer to stop capitalizing.

Backspace key If you make a mistake, press the **Backspace key**. That makes the computer erase the last character you typed. (The Backspace key is in the top right corner of the keyboard's main section. It's to the right of the + key, and it has a left-arrow on it.)

To erase the last *two* characters you typed, press the Backspace key *twice*.

Word wrap If you're typing near the screen's right edge, and you type a word that's too long to fit on the screen, the computer will automatically move the word to the line below. Moving the word to the line below is called **word wrap**.

If you're using Windows XP, make word wrap work properly by doing this (unless you or your colleagues did so already):

> Click "View" then "Options" then "Rich Text" then "Wrap to ruler" then "OK."

Enter key When you finish typing a paragraph, press the **Enter key**. That makes the computer move to the line underneath so you can start typing the next paragraph.

Windows 7 automatically leaves a slight gap between the paragraphs, to separate them. If you want Windows 7 to leave a bigger gap between the paragraphs — or want Windows XP or Vista to double-space between the paragraphs — press the Enter key *twice* instead of once.

Tab key If you want to indent a line (such as the first line of a paragraph), begin the line by pressing the **Tab key**. The computer will indent the line a half inch.

Nudge a phrase To move a phrase toward the right, press the Tab key several times before typing the phrase. To move a phrase down, press the Enter key several times before typing the phrase.

Ctrl symbols On your keyboard, below the two Shift keys, are two Control keys, which say "Ctrl" on them. You can use them to type special symbols:

Symbol	How to type it
€	While pressing the Ctrl and Alt keys, type the letter "e".
ç	While pressing the Ctrl key, tap the "," key. Then type the letter "c".
ñ	While pressing Ctrl (and Shift), tap the "~" key. Then type the letter "n".
ô	While pressing Ctrl (and Shift), tap the "^" key. Then type the letter "o".
ü	While pressing Ctrl (and Shift), tap the ":" key. Then type the letter "u".
è	While pressing the Ctrl key, type the symbol `. Then type the letter "e".
é	While pressing the Ctrl key, type the symbol '. Then type the letter "e".

Alt symbols You can type these alternative symbols:

128 Ç	144 É	160 á	225 ß
129 ü	145 æ	161 í	
130 é	146 Æ	162 ó	227 ¶
131 â	147 ô	163 ú	
132 ä	148 ö	164 ñ	230 µ
133 à	149 ò	165 Ñ	
134 å	150 û	166 ª	241 ±
135 ç	151 ù	167 º	
136 ê	152 ÿ	168 ¿	246 ÷
137 ë	153 Ö	169	
138 è	154 Ü	170 ¬	248 °
139 ï	155 ¢	171 ½	249 •
140 î	156 £	172 ¼	250 ·
141 ì	157 ¥	173 ¡	
142 Ä	158 P	174 «	
143 Å	159 ƒ	175 »	253 ²

For example, here's how to type the symbol ¢, whose code number is 155. Hold down the Alt key; and while you keep holding down the Alt key, type 155 *by using the numeric keypad* (the number keys on the far right side of the keyboard). When you finish typing 155, lift your finger from the Alt key, and you'll see ¢ on your screen! Try it!

That chart skips numbers whose results are unreliable (producing different results on different printers and on different versions of Windows).

Windows copied that chart from DOS. But Windows goes beyond DOS by letting you also use this fancier chart:

0128 €		0192 À	0224 à
	0161 ¡	0193 Á	0225 á
0130 ‚	0162 ¢	0194 Â	0226 â
0131 ƒ	0163 £	0195 Ã	0227 ã
0132 „	0164 ¤	0196 Ä	0228 ä
0133 …	0165 ¥	0197 Å	0229 å
0134 †	0166 ¦	0198 Æ	0230 æ
0135 ‡	0167 §	0199 Ç	0231 ç
0136 ^	0168 ¨	0200 È	0232 è
0137 ‰	0169 ©	0201 É	0233 é
0138 Š	0170 ª	0202 Ê	0234 ê
0139 ‹	0171 «	0203 Ë	0235 ë
0140 Œ	0172 ¬	0204 Ì	0236 ì
	0173 -	0205 Í	0237 í
0142 Ž	0174 ®	0206 Î	0238 î
	0175 ¯	0207 Ï	0239 ï
	0176 °	0208 Ð	0240 ð
0145 '	0177 ±	0209 Ñ	0241 ñ
0146 '	0178 ²	0210 Ò	0242 ò
0147 "	0179 ³	0211 Ó	0243 ó
0148 "	0180 ´	0212 Ô	0244 ô
0149 •	0181 µ	0213 Õ	0245 õ
0150 –	0182 ¶	0214 Ö	0246 ö
0151 —	0183 ·	0215 ×	0247 ÷
0152 ˜	0184 ¸	0216 Ø	0248 ø
0153 ™	0185 ¹	0217 Ù	0249 ù
0154 š	0186 º	0218 Ú	0250 ú
0155 ›	0187 »	0219 Û	0251 û
0156 œ	0188 ¼	0220 Ü	0252 ü
	0189 ½	0221 Ý	0253 ý
0158 ž	0190 ¾	0222 Þ	0254 þ
0159 Ÿ	0191 ¿	0223 ß	0255 ÿ

For example, here's how to type the symbol ©, whose code number is 0169: while holding down the Alt key, type 0169 on the numeric keypad.

Scroll arrows

If your document contains too many lines to fit on the screen, the screen will show just *part* of the document, accompanied by two arrows at the screen's right edge: a **scroll-up arrow** and a **scroll-down arrow**.

In Windows Vista & 7, the scroll-up arrow is ▲; the scroll-down arrow is ▼.
In Windows XP, the scroll-up arrow is ∧; the scroll-down arrow is ∨.

To see a higher part of your document, click the scroll-up arrow (▲ or ∧).
To see a lower part of your document, click the scroll-down arrow (▼ or ∨).

Insert characters

To insert extra characters anywhere in your document, click where you want the extra characters to appear (by moving the mouse's pointer there and then pressing the mouse's button). Then type the extra characters.

For example, suppose you typed the word "fat" and want to change it to "fault". Click between the "a" and the "t", then type "ul".

(When you're using Windows, notice that you click *between* letters, not *on* letters.)

As you type the extra characters, the screen's other characters move out of the way to make room for the extra characters.

While you're inserting the extra characters, you can erase nearby mistakes by pressing the Backspace key or Delete key. The Backspace key erases the character that's *before* the mouse's pointer. The Delete key erases the character that's *after* the mouse's pointer.

Split a paragraph

Here's how to split a long paragraph in half, to form two short paragraphs.

Decide which word should begin the second short paragraph. Click the left edge of that word's first letter.

Press the Backspace key (to erase the space before that word), then press the Enter key. Now you've split the long paragraph in two!

If you want to double-space between the two short paragraphs, press the Enter key again. If you want to indent the second paragraph, press the Tab key.

Combine paragraphs

After typing two paragraphs, here's how to combine them, to form a single paragraph that's longer.

Click at the end of the first paragraph. Press the Delete key several times, to delete unwanted Enters and Tabs. Now you've combined the two paragraphs into one!

Then press the Space bar (to insert a space between the two sentences).

Movement keys

To move to different parts of your document, you can use your mouse. To move faster, press these keys instead:

Key you press	Where the pointer will move
right-arrow	right to the next character
left-arrow	left to the previous character
down-arrow	down to the line below
up-arrow	up to the line above
End	right to the end of the line
Home	left to beginning of the line
Page Down	down to the next screenful
Page Up	up to the previous screenful

On notebook computers (which have narrow keys), the Page Down key is labeled "Pg Dn" and the Page Up key is labeled "Pg Up".

Here's what happens if you press the movement keys while holding down the Ctrl key:

Keys you press	Where the pointer will move
Ctrl with right-arrow	right (to the next word or punctuation symbol)
Ctrl with left-arrow	left (to the beginning of a word or punctuation)
Ctrl with down-arrow	down to the next paragraph
Ctrl with up-arrow	up to the beginning of a paragraph
Ctrl with Page Down	down to the end of the screen's last word
Ctrl with Page Up	up to the beginning of the screen's first word
Ctrl with End	down to the end of the document
Ctrl with Home	up to the beginning of the document

Congratulations

You've mastered the basics of WordPad. Now let's explore WordPad's advanced features....

WordPad 7

The version of WordPad that comes in Windows 7 is called **WordPad 7**. Here are its advanced features. (If you have Windows XP or Vista instead, skip ahead to the next section, called "WordPad classic.")

Zoom slider

At the screen's bottom-right corner, you see a plus sign (+). Left of it, you see a minus sign (-). Between those signs, you see the **zoom slider**, which is a pentagon.

Try this experiment: **drag the zoom slider toward the right**. Here's how:

> Put the mouse pointer on the zoom slider. Then while pressing the mouse's main button (the left button), move the mouse toward the right.

If you drag the zoom slider toward the right, the screen's characters enlarge, so you can read them even if you're sitting far from the screen or have poor vision. It's like looking at the document through a magnifying glass: the document looks enlarged, so you can see the details of each word and character more clearly; but not as many words and characters fit on the screen. Use the arrow keys to see different parts of the page.

If you drag that slider toward the left, the screen's characters shrink, so they're harder to read but you can fit more characters and pages onto the screen.

When you finish playing with the zoom slider, put it back to its normal position (the middle), so the number left of the minus sign is "100%" (or a number close to 100%, such "98%"), by dragging the slider (or pressing the keyboard's arrow keys, which give you more accurate control).

All delete

Here's how to delete the entire document, so you can start over:

> While holding down the Ctrl key, press the A key. That means "all". All of the document turns blue.
> Then press the Delete key. All of the document disappears, so you can start over!

Quick Access Toolbar

At the screen's top-left corner, you see a gray bar (called the **Quick Access Toolbar**), which includes these **icons** (little pictures) called **buttons**:

> The **Save button** is a purple-and-white square that's supposed to look like a floppy disk (though it also looks like a TV set).
>
> The **Undo button** is an arrow curving toward the left. The arrow is blue (unless you haven't typed anything yet).

If you point at a button (by moving your mouse's arrow there, without clicking), the computer will tell you the button's name.

Here's how to use those buttons….

Save button To save the document you've been typing (copy it onto the disk), click the **Save button**.

If you haven't saved the document before, the computer will say "File name". Invent a name for your document. Type the name and press Enter.

That makes the computer copy the document onto the hard disk. For example, if you named the document "mary", the computer puts a document called mary.rtf into the Documents folder. If you wish, you can prove it by doing this:

> Click Start then "Documents". If you called the document "mary", you'll see mary is one of the files in the Documents folder. If you right-click mary's icon then click "Properties", you'll see the type of file is ".rtf", which means "Rich Text Format" (and "Rut The Fuck?", because documents in that format can look slightly fucked up). Finally, clear that proof off your screen (by clicking "OK" then the red X button).

Afterwards, if you change your mind and want to do more editing, go ahead! When you finish that extra editing, save it by clicking the Save button again.

Save often! If you're typing a long document, **click the Save button about every 10 minutes**. Click it whenever you get to a good stopping place and think, "What I've typed so far looks good!" Then if an accident happens, you'll lose at most 10 minutes of work, and you can return to the last version you felt good about.

Instead of clicking the Save button, you can use this shortcut: while holding down the Ctrl key, tap the S key (which stands for "Save").

Undo button If you make a mistake (such as accidentally deleting some text or accidentally inserting some useless text), click the **Undo button** (which is an arrow turning back). That makes the computer undo your last activity, so your text returns to the way it looked before you made your boo-boo. (To undo your last *two* activities, click the Undo button *twice*.)

Instead of clicking the Undo button, you can use this shortcut: while holding down the Ctrl key, tap the Z key (which stands for "Zap").

If you click the Undo button, the computer might undo a different activity than you expected. For example, it might even erase everything you typed! If clicking the Undo button accidentally makes the text look even worse instead of better, and you wish you hadn't clicked the Undo button, you can "undo the undo" by clicking the **Redo button** (which is next to the Undo button and shows a blue arrow curving to the right, so it bends forward).

Instead of clicking the Redo button, you can use this shortcut: while holding down the Ctrl key, tap the Y key (which stands for "Yes, I do want it, very much").

WordPad button

Near the screen's top-left corner, just below the Save button, you see the **WordPad button**. Click it. Then you see the **WordPad menu**:

```
New
Open
Save
Save as
Print
Page setup
Send in e-mail
About WordPad
Exit
```

From that menu, choose whatever you wish (by clicking it). Here are the most popular choices....

Save If you choose **Save** from the WordPad menu (by clicking the word "Save" after clicking the WordPad button), you get the same result as clicking the Save button that's on the Quick Access Toolbar.

Save as Suppose you've already saved a document then edited it some more, but you're not sure you like the new editing. Try this experiment....

Choose "**Save as**" from the WordPad menu (by clicking the phrase "Save as" after clicking the WordPad button); when you do that, make sure you click the phrase "Save as", not just the arrow next to it.

Then invent (and type) a new name for the document. At the end of the new name, press Enter.

The computer will copy the document's new, edited version onto the hard disk. That new, edited version will have the new name you invented.

The document's old original version will be on the disk also and keep its old original name. The disk will contain *both* versions of the document.

How to finish

When you finish working on a document, choose **Exit** or **New** or **a previous document** from the WordPad menu.

Exit Whenever you want to stop using WordPad, choose **Exit** from the WordPad menu (or click the WordPad window's X button).

New If you choose **New** (instead of Exit) from the WordPad menu, the computer will let you start typing a new, different document.

A previous document If you want to reuse a previous document you had saved, click the WordPad button. To the right of the WordPad button, you see a list of the **9 documents you used most recently**: that list starts with the most recent. Click whichever document you want to use. If you want to use a different document, which is not on that list of 9, do this:

> Choose **Open** from the WordPad menu (by clicking Open).
> The computer starts showing you a list of *all* documents in the Documents library. To see the rest of the list, either "click in that list then rotate the mouse's wheel toward you" or "repeatedly click the down-arrow that's to the right of that list".
> If you want to *use* one of those documents, **double-click** the document's name. (To double-click, tap the mouse's left button twice *quickly*, so the taps are less than .4 seconds apart. While tapping the left button twice, make sure the mouse remains still: don't let the mouse jiggle, not even a smidgen! Double-clicking is also called **opening**.) The computer will put that document onto the screen and let you edit it. If instead you want to *delete* one of those documents, click the document's name then press the Delete key then the Enter key; the computer will move that document to the Recycle Bin.

Didn't save? If you didn't save your document before doing those "how to finish" procedures, the computer asks, "Do you want to save?" If you click "Save", the computer copies your document's most recent version to the hard disk; if you click "Don't Save" instead, the computer ignores and forgets your most recent editing.

How to hide from the recently-used list To the right of the WordPad menu, you see a list of the 9 documents you used most recently. That list might annoy you, for two reasons:

> One of the documents might be embarrassing (perhaps because it's pornographic or a private letter), and you want to hide it from your colleagues and family.
>
> Even after you've deleted a document, that document's name might still be on that list.

If the **document list annoys you**, delete documents from it, as follows....

> The recently-used list shows just the names of *the last 9* documents you mentioned. Go use other WordPad documents; they'll go onto recently-used list and bump off the older documents.

Print

Here's how to print a document onto paper.

Make sure you've bought a printer, attached it to the computer, turned the printer's power on, and put paper into the printer.

If your computer has never used that printer before, do this:

> Get out of WordPad (by choosing Exit from the WordPad menu and answering any questions about saving a document). Then go back into WordPad. That resets WordPad, so it can find the new printer you just attached. Get onto the screen whatever document you want to print (by typing a new document or choosing an old document from the WordPad menu).

Choose **Print** from the WordPad menu (by clicking the word "Print" after clicking the WordPad button); when you do that, make sure you click the word "Print", not just the arrow next to it.

Press Enter. The computer will print the document onto paper.

Font group

To make sure your computer is acting normally, click the word "**Home**" (which is near the screen's top-left corner).

Then you see these 5 words: **Clipboard**, **Font**, **Paragraph**, **Insert**, **Editing**. Above each word, you see a **group** of icons. I'll explain how to use each group. Let's start with the **Font group**, which looks like this:

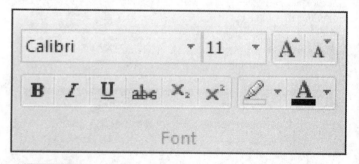

Underline Here's how to underline a phrase (like this).

Activate the **Underline button** (which says U on it) by clicking it. **Activating the button makes the button turn orange.** Then type the phrase you want underlined. Then deactivate the Underline button (by clicking it again).

Go ahead: try it now! Practice using the underline button before you progress to more advanced buttons!

Instead of clicking the Underline button, you can use this shortcut: while holding down the Ctrl key, tap the U key.

Bold Here's how to make a phrase be bold (**like this**). Activate the **Bold button** (which says **B** on it) by clicking it. Then type the phrase you want emboldened. Then deactivate the Bold button (by clicking it again).

Here's how to make a phrase be bold and underlined (**like this**). Activate the Bold and Underline buttons (by clicking them both). Then type the phrase. Then deactivate those buttons (by clicking them again).

Instead of clicking the Bold button, you can use this shortcut: while holding down the Ctrl key, tap the B key.

Italic Here's how to italicize a phrase (*like this*). Activate the **Italic button** (which says *I* on it) by clicking it. Then type the phrase you want italicized. Then deactivate the Italic button (by clicking it again).

Instead of clicking the Italic button, you can use this shortcut: while holding down the Ctrl key, tap the I key.

Superscript Here's how to make a phrase be tiny and raised (like this). Activate the **Superscript button** (which says x^2 on it) by clicking it. Then type the phrase you want superscripted. Then deactivate the Superscript button (by clicking it again).

The superscript button helps you type math formulas, such as the Pythagorean Theorem ($a^2 + b^2 = c^2$).

Subscript Here's how to make a phrase be tiny and lowered (like this). Activate the **Subscript button** (which says x_2 on it) by clicking it. Then type the phrase you want subscripted. Then deactivate the Superscript button (by clicking it again).

The subscript button helps you type math formulas, such as the Fibonacci Series ($F_{n+2} = F_n + F_{n+1}$) and the Slope Formula: $m = (y_2 - y_1) / (x_2 - x_1)$.

Strikethrough Here's how to make a phrase be crossed out (~~like this~~). Activate the Strikethrough button (which says ~~abc~~ on it) by clicking it. Then type the phrase you want crossed out. Then deactivate the Strikethrough button (by clicking it again).

The Strikethrough button helps you type semi-censored sentences, such as "You're ~~an asshole~~ showing little sympathy for the team's needs."

Font size Look at the **Font Size box** (which has a number in it). Usually that box contains the number 11, so you're typing characters that are **11 points** high.

Here's how to type characters that are bigger or smaller....

> Method 1: click the Font Size box. In that box, type a size number from 8 to 72. The number can end in .5; the number can be 8 or 8.5 or 9 or 9.5 or 10 or bigger. (Theoretically, you can pick a number even smaller than 8 or even bigger than 72, but those extreme numbers create ugly results.) When you finish typing the number, press the Enter key.
>
> Method 2: click the down-arrow that's to the *right* of the Font Size box. You see this list of popular sizes: 8, 9, 10, 11, 12, 14, 16, 18, 20, 22, 24, 26, 28, 36, 48, and 72. That list of popular sizes is called the **Font Size menu**. Click the size you want.
>
> Method 3: click the **Grow Font button** (which says A˄ on it). That makes the font be slightly bigger (the next popular size). To make the font grow even bigger than that, click the Grow Font button again.
>
> Method 4: click the **Shrink Font button** (which says A˅ on it). That makes the font be slightly smaller (the next popular size down). To make the font shrink even smaller than that, click the Shrink Font button again.

Any new characters you type afterwards will be the size you chose. (Characters typed earlier don't change size.)

The popular sizes look like this:

> This text is 8 points high, 9 points high, 10 points high, 11 points high, 12 points high, 14 points high, 16 points high, 18 points high, 20 pt., 22 pt., 24 pt., 26 pt., 28 pt., 36pt., 48pt., 72pt.

When you finish typing the enlarged or reduced characters, here's how to return to typing characters that are normal size (11 points high): click the down-arrow that's to the right of the Font Size box, then click 11.

Font You see a box saying "Calibri". That's called the **Font box**.

Next to that box is the symbol ▾. Click it.

You'll start seeing the **Font menu**, which is a list of fonts in alphabetical order. (To see the rest of the list, press the down-arrow key or rotate the mouse's wheel toward you.)

Click whichever font you want. Though Microsoft likes the font called "Calibri", the best fonts are "Times New Roman", "Tahoma", "Comic Sans MS", and "Courier New". Here's how they look:

This font is called "Times New Roman". It's the best for typing long passages of text, such as paragraphs in books, newspapers, magazines, and reports. It squeezes lots of words onto a small amount of paper but remains easy to read. You can make it plain or **bold** or *italic* or ***bold italic***.

If you make it big & bold, like this, it imitates an old-fashioned news headline.

This font is called "Tahoma". It's simple. It resembles Calibri and Arial but has several advantages, such as a better capital "I". You can make it plain or **bold** or *italic* or ***bold italic***. It's best for typing short phrases that attract attention. For example...

If you make it big & bold, like this, it's good for titles, signs, and posters.

If you make it small, like this, it's good for footnotes, photo captions, classified ads, telephone books, directories, and catalogs.

This font is called "Comic Sans MS". It resembles Tahoma but looks hand-drawn, like the words in a funny comic book. You can make it plain or **bold** or *italic* or ***bold italic***. It's best for typing short phrases that draw attention and giggles. For example...

If you make it big & bold, like this, it's good for funny titles, signs, and posters.

```
This font is called "Courier New".

If you make it 12 points high, like this, it
resembles the printout from a typewriter.

It makes each character have the same width: for
example, the "m" has the same width as the "i". It's
a good font for typing tables of numbers, since the
uniform width lets you line up each column of
numbers easily.

Choose plain, bold, italic, or bold italic.
```

After you've clicked a font, any new characters you type will be in that font. (The characters you typed earlier remain unaffected.)

When you finish typing in that font, here's how you can return to typing characters in the Calibri font: click the Font box's down-arrow then click "Calibri".

Text color Normally, the characters you type are black. Here's how to make them a different color, such as red.

Look at the **Text color button**, which has an underlined A on it. Notice the color of the A's underline. If it's the color you want, click the underline. If it's *not* the color you want, do this instead:

Click the down-arrow that's to the right of the A's underline. You see 30 colors.

If you like one of those colors, click it.

If you *don't* like any of those colors, click "More Colors", which shows you 48 colors: click your favorite then "OK".

Afterwards, whatever characters you type will be in the color you chose. (The characters you typed earlier remain unaffected.)

When you finish typing in that color, here's how to return to typing characters that are normal (black): click the down-arrow that's to the right of the A's underline, then click "Automatic" (which means "normal").

Text highlight color Normally, the characters have a white background, as if they were on plain paper. Here's how to make the background be a different color, such as yellow, as if you were using a yellow highlighting pen.

Look at the **Text highlight color button**, which is just left of the Text color button and shows a pen writing on paper. Notice the paper's color. If it's the color you want, click the underline. If it's *not* the color you want (if it's just white or pale blue), do this instead:

Click the down-arrow that's to the right of the pen. You see 15 colors. Click the color you want (such as yellow).

Afterwards, whatever characters you type will be highlighted in the background color you chose. (The characters you typed earlier remain unaffected.)

When you finish using that highlighter, here's how to return to typing normal characters (on a white background): click the Text color button's down-arrow, then click "No color" (which means "normal").

Select

Here's how to dramatically change a phrase you typed.

Point at the phrase's beginning. Then hold down the mouse's left button; and while you keep holding down that button, move to the phrase's end.

(Moving the mouse while holding down the left button is called **dragging**. You're **dragging** from the phrase's beginning to the phrase's end.)

The phrase you dragged across gets highlighted: its white background turns blue. Turning the phrase blue is called **selecting the phrase**.

Then say what to do to the phrase. For example, choose one of these activities:

To underline the phrase, activate the Underline button (by clicking it).
To make the phrase be bold, activate the Bold button (by clicking it).
To italicize the phrase, activate the Italic button (by clicking it).
To make the phrase be tiny and raised, activate the Superscript button (by clicking it).
To make the phrase be tiny and lowered, activate the Subscript button (by clicking it).
To make the phrase look crossed out, activate the Strikethrough button (by clicking it).

To prevent the phrase from being underlined, bold, italicized, superscripted, subscripted, or crossed out, deactivate those buttons (by clicking them again).

To change the phrase's point size, choose the size you want from the Font Size menu.
To change the phrase's font, choose the font you want from the Font menu.

To delete the phrase, press the **Delete key**.

To replace the phrase, just type whatever words you want the phrase to become.

Go ahead! Try it now! It's fun!

Other ways to select The usual way to select a phrase is to point at the phrase's beginning, then drag to the phrase's end. But sometimes other methods are faster!

To select a phrase, choose one of these methods....

Method 1: point at the phrase's beginning, then **drag** to the phrase's end.

Method 2: click the phrase's beginning; then while holding down the **Shift key**, click the phrase's end.

Method 3: by using your keyboard's **movement keys**
    (such as up-arrow, down-arrow, left-arrow, and right-arrow), move to the phrase's beginning; then while holding down the Shift key, use the movement keys to move to the phrase's end.

Method 4: to select just **one line**, click in its left margin.

Method 5: to select **several lines**, click in the first line's left margin;
    then while holding down the Shift key, click in the bottom line's left margin.

Method 6: to select just **one word**, double-click in its middle.

Method 7: to select just **one paragraph**, triple-click in its middle (or double-click in its left margin).

Method 8: to select **several paragraphs**, triple-click in the first paragraph's middle;
    then while holding down the Shift key, click in the last paragraph's middle.

Method 9: to select the **entire document** (all!), tap the A key while holding down the Ctrl key.

To select several phrases at once, do this procedure:

Drag across the first phrase. While holding down the Ctrl key, drag across the second phrase. While holding down the Ctrl key, drag across any extra phrases you wish to manipulate.

Then tell the computer what to do to all those phrases. For example, if you want to underline them all, click the Underline button.

Document vanishes While you're typing a document, if the whole **document suddenly disappears**, you accidentally deleted it. Here's why:

You tried to type a capital A, but instead of pressing the Shift key you accidentally pressed the Ctrl key. "Ctrl with A" tells the computer to "select the whole document", so the whole document becomes highlighted. The next character you type replaces the highlighted text, so the highlighted text is all lost.

Cure:

Immediately say "undo" (by clicking the Undo button or pressing Ctrl with Z). That undoes your last action. Say "undo" several times, until you've undone enough of your actions to undo the calamity.

Drag a phrase To move a phrase to a new location, just "select the phrase, and then drag from the phrase's middle to the new location." Here are the details:

First, select the phrase you want to move, so the phrase turns blue.

Then take your finger off the mouse's button. Move the mouse's pointer to the phrase's middle (so you see an arrow). Finally, hold down the mouse's button; and while you keep holding down the mouse's button, move the mouse slightly. You'll see a vertical line (red or black); drag that line to wherever you want the phrase to move. (Drag anywhere you wish in the document, or drag to the document's end. The computer won't let you drag past the document's end.)

At the end of the drag, lift your finger from the mouse's button. Presto, the phrase moves where you wished!

In that procedure, you drag the phrase to a new location then drop it there. That procedure is called **drag & drop**.

Clipboard group

In the Clipboard group, you see 3 choices: **Cut**, **Paste**, and **Copy**.

Cut and paste Here's another way to move a phrase to a new location.

Select the phrase (by dragging across it with the mouse, so the phrase turns blue). Click the **Cut button** (which looks like a pair of scissors). The phrase will vanish from its original location.

Click the new location where you want the phrase to reappear. Then click the **Paste button**'s picture of a clipboard (not the word "Paste"). The phrase will appear at that new location.

Here are shortcuts:

Instead of clicking the **Cut button**, you can press **Ctrl with X** (which means "X it out").

Instead of clicking the **Paste button**, you can press **Ctrl with V** (which stands for "Velcro").

Copy Here's another way to copy a phrase, so the phrase appears in your document *twice*.

Select the phrase (by dragging across it with the mouse, so the phrase turns blue). Click the **Copy button** (which looks like a pair of dog-eared pages). Click where you want the copy of the phrase to appear, and click the **Paste button**'s clipboard. The copy will appear at the new location, so the phrase will be in your document *twice*.

If you want the phrase to appear in your document a *third* time, click where you want that additional copy to appear, then click the Paste button's clipboard again. If you want the phrase to appear in your document a *fourth* time, click where you want that additional copy, then click the Paste button's clipboard again.

Here's a shortcut: instead of clicking the Copy button, you can press Ctrl with C.

Paragraph group

The **Paragraph group** looks like this:

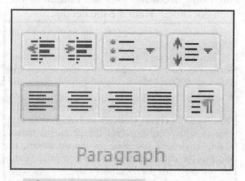

Alignment buttons While typing a line, you can click one of these **alignment buttons**:

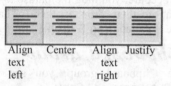

| Align text left | Center | Align text right | Justify |

Clicking the **Center button** makes the line be centered,

| like this line |

Clicking the **Align text right button** makes the line be at the right margin,

| like this line |

Clicking the **Align text left button** makes the line be at the left margin,

| like this line |

Clicking one of those buttons affects not just the line you're typing but also all other lines in the same paragraph.

Clicking the **Justify button** makes the paragraph be **justified**, so the paragraph's bottom line is at the left margin, and each of the paragraph's other lines is at *both* margins (by inserting extra space between the words),

| like   this   line |

When you click one of those alignment buttons, you're activating it. That button deactivates when you click a different alignment button instead.

When you start typing a new document, the computer assumes you want the document to be aligned left, so the computer activates the Align Left button. If you want a different alignment, click a different alignment button instead.

Examples:

> If you're typing a title or headline and want it to be centered, click the **Center button**.
>
> If you're typing a business letter and want it to begin by showing the date next to the right margin, click the **Align text right button**.
>
> If you're typing an informal memo or letter to a colleague or friend, and want the paragraph to look plain, ordinary, modest, and unassuming (like Clark Kent), click the **Align text left button**.
>
> If you're creating something formal (such as a newspaper or textbook) and want the paragraph to have perfectly straight edges (so it looks official, uptight, and professional, like Robocop), click the **Justify button**.

Clicking one of those alignment buttons affects the entire paragraph you're typing, but the paragraphs you typed earlier remain unaffected, unless you do this:

> To change the alignment of a paragraph you typed earlier, click in that paragraph's middle then click the alignment button you wish.

When you start typing a new paragraph, the computer gives that paragraph the same alignment as the paragraph above, unless you say differently (by clicking one of the alignment buttons).

Here's how to type a centered title:

> Press the Enter key twice (to leave a big blank space above the title).
>
> Next, click the Center button (so the title will be centered) and the Bold button (so the title will be bold). Type the words you want to be in the title and press the Enter key afterwards.
>
> Congratulations! You've created a centered title!
>
> Next, make the paragraph underneath the title be normal: make that paragraph be uncentered (click the Align text left button or Justify button) and make it be unbolded (deactivate the Bold button, by clicking it).

Here are shortcuts:

Instead of clicking the Justify	button, you can press Ctrl with J.
Instead of clicking the Align Text Left	button, you can press Ctrl with L.
Instead of clicking the Align Text Right	button, you can press Ctrl with R.
Instead of clicking the Center	button, you can press Ctrl with E (which stands for "Equidistant").

Line spacing While typing a paragraph, you can click the **Line Spacing button** (which has an up-arrow and down-arrow on it), which makes this menu appear:

>   1.0
> ✓ 1.15
>   1.5
>   2.0
> ✓ Add 10pt space after paragraphs

Clicking "**2.0**" makes the paragraph be double-spaced (so there's a blank line under each line). Clicking "**1.0**" makes the paragraph be single-spaced (without extra space under the lines). Clicking "**1.15**" makes the paragraph have a little extra space between each pair of lines; that's what the computer assumes you want if you don't say otherwise.

The computer assumes you want a 10-point-high blank space under the paragraph, to separate that paragraph from the paragraph below. If you don't want that space, remove the checkmark that's left of "**Add 10pt space after paragraphs**" (by clicking it).

Indentation Before typing a paragraph, you can press the Tab key. That makes the computer indent the paragraph's first line, half an inch.

If you want to indent *all* lines in the paragraph, do this instead of pressing the Tab key: while typing the paragraph, click the **Increase indent button** (which shows a right-arrow pointing at lines). That makes the computer indent *all* lines in the paragraph. (The paragraphs you typed earlier remain unaffected.)

When you start typing a new paragraph, the computer indents that paragraph if the paragraph above it was indented.

If you indented a paragraph by clicking the Increase Indent button but then change your mind, here's how to *un*indent the paragraph: click in the paragraph, then click the **Decrease indent button** (which shows a left-arrow pointing from lines).

For example, suppose you start typing a new document. Here's how to make just paragraphs 3, 4, and 5 be indented.

> Type paragraphs 1 and 2 normally (without pressing the Increase indent button).
>
> When you start typing paragraph 3, press the Increase indent button. That makes the computer start indenting, so paragraphs 3, 4, and 5 will be automatically indented.
>
> When you start typing paragraph 6, here's how to prevent the computer from indenting it: click the Decrease indent button at the beginning of paragraph 6.

To indent a paragraph you typed earlier, click in the middle of that paragraph and then click the Increase Indent button. To *un*indent a paragraph you typed earlier, click in its middle and then click the *Decrease* Indent button.

If you click the Increase indent button *twice* instead of just once, the computer will indent the paragraph farther. After typing that doubly indented paragraph, if you want the paragraph below to be unindented you must click the Decrease indent button twice.

Each time you click the Increase Indent button, the computer indents the paragraph a half inch farther. Each time you click the Decrease indent button, the computer indents the paragraph a half inch less.

Start a list Here's a different way to indent an entire paragraph: while typing the paragraph, activate the **Start a list button** (which is the third button in the Paragraph group) by clicking it. That makes the computer indent the paragraph and also put a **bullet** (the symbol •) to the left of the paragraph's first line. That's called a **bulleted paragraph**. The bullet symbol is indented a quarter inch; the paragraph's words are indented a half inch.

After you've typed a bulleted paragraph, any new paragraphs you type underneath will be bulleted also — so you're creating a list of bulleted paragraphs — until you request an *un*bulleted paragraph (by deactivating the Start a list button).

Here's how to request different symbols instead of the bullet symbol: instead of clicking the Start a list button, click that button's down-arrow. Then you see 7 popular choices:

> bulleted list
> numbered list (1, 2, 3)
> lettered list (a, b, c)
> capital-lettered list (A, B, C)
> Roman-numeral list (i, ii, iii)
> capital-Roman-numeral list (I, II, III)

Click the choice you want. Your choice affects the current paragraph. It also affects the paragraphs underneath that are part of the same list. It also affects each list you start typing in the future (until you choose different symbols instead or start a new document).

Editing group

In the Editing group, you see 3 choices: **Find**, **Replace**, and "**Select all**".

Find Here's how to make the computer search through your document to find whether you've used the word "love":

> Click where you want the search to begin. (For example, if you want the search to begin at the document's beginning, click in the middle of the document's first word.) Click **Find** (or press Ctrl with F). Type the word you want to find ("love"), and press Enter.
>
> The computer will search for "love". If the computer finds a "love" in your document, it will highlight that "love" so it turns blue. (If the Find window covers the part of your document that says "love", drag that window out of the way, by dragging the window's title, "Find".)
>
> If you want to find the next "love" in your document, press Enter; if you do *not* want to search for more "love", click the Find window's X (or press the Esc key).

Suppose you've written a history of America and want to find the part where you started talking about Lincoln. If you forget what page that was, no problem! Just put the cursor at the document's beginning, click **Find**, type "Lincoln", and press Enter.

Replace You can search for a word and replace it with a different word. For example, here's how to change each "love" in your document to "idolize":

> Click **Replace**. Type the old word you want to replace ("love"), then press the Tab key, then type the new word you want instead ("idolize"), then click the Replace All button. That makes the computer change each "love" to "idolize". Then press the Esc key twice.

The computer preserves capitalization. For example, if the document said —

> I love you. Love you! LOVE YOU! I want to kiss your glove!

the computer changes it to:

> I idolize you. Idolize you! IDOLIZE YOU! I want to kiss your gidolize!

Notice that when told to change "love" to "idolize", the computer unfortunately also changes "glove" to "gidolize".

The Replace command helps you zip through many chores:

> For example, if you write a letter that talks about Fred, then want to write a similar letter about Sue, tell the computer to replace each Fred with Sue.
>
> If you write a book about "How to be a better salesman" and then a feminist tells you to change each "salesman" to "salesperson", tell the computer to replace each "salesman".
>
> If you're writing a long ad that mentions "Calvin Klein's Hot New Flaming Pink Day-Glo Pajamas" repeatedly, and you're too lazy to type that long phrase so often, just type the abbreviation "Calnew". When you've finished typing the document, tell the computer to replace each "Calnew" with the long phrase it stands for.

Select all To select everything in the document (so the whole document is highlighted in blue), use one of these methods:

> Method 1: click "**Select all**".
> Method 2: while holding down the Ctrl key, tap the A key (which means "All").

Insert group

Here's how to make the computer type the date & time.

In the Insert group, click "Date and time". The computer will show a list of formats, like this:

> 12/25/2011
> 12/25/11
> 11/12/25
> 2011-12-25
> 25-Dec-11
> Sunday, December 25, 2011
> December 25, 2011
> Sunday, 25 December, 2011
> 25 December, 2011
> 10:59:20 PM
> 22:59:20

Double-click the format you want. The computer will type the date or time in the format you requested.

WordPad classic

The version of WordPad that comes in Windows XP & Vista is called **WordPad classic**. Here are its advanced features. (If you have Windows 7 instead, skip this section.)

Buttons

Near the screen's top, you see these buttons:

Here is each button's name:

Bold   Italic   Underline   Color   AlignLeft   Center   AlignRight   Bullets

If you forget a button's name, try this trick: point at the button (by using the mouse but *without* clicking), then wait a second. Underneath the button, you'll see the button's name; and at the screen's bottom-left corner, you'll see a short explanation of what the button does.

To use a button, **activate** it by clicking it with the mouse. Here are the details....

Underline Here's how to underline a phrase (like this). **Activate** the **Underline button** (which says U on it) by clicking it. **Activating the button changes its appearance:**

In Windows XP,	the button turns white and gets a blue border.
In Windows Vista,	the button darkens and gets a black border.

Then type the phrase you want underlined. Then deactivate the Underline button (by clicking it again).

Go ahead: try it now! Practice using the Underline button before you progress to more advanced buttons!

Instead of clicking the Underline button, you can use this shortcut: while holding down the Ctrl key, tap the U key.

Fancy formats Your version resembles WordPad 7, so **read these sections on page 85:**

"Bold"
"Italic"

Color Here's how to change a phrase's color.

Click the **Color button**. You'll see a list of 15 colors (plus "White" and "Automatic"). Click the color you want. Then type the phrase you want colorized.

Afterwards, click the Color button again and click "Black".

Alignment While typing a line, you can click one of these **alignment buttons**: **Center**, **Align Left**, or **Align Right**.

Clicking the **Center button** makes the line be centered,

like this line

Clicking the **Align Right button** makes the line be at the right margin,

like this line

Clicking the **Align Left button** makes the line be at the left margin,

like this line

Clicking one of those buttons affects not just the line you're typing but also all other lines in the same paragraph. When you click one of those buttons, you're activating it. That button deactivates when you click a different alignment button instead.

When you start typing a new document, the computer assumes you want the document to be aligned left, so the computer activates the Align Left button. If you want a different alignment, click a different alignment button instead.

Clicking an alignment button affects the entire paragraph you're typing, but the paragraphs you typed earlier remain unaffected, unless you do this:

To change the alignment of a paragraph you typed earlier, click in that paragraph's middle then click the alignment button you wish.

When you start typing a new paragraph, the computer gives the new paragraph the same alignment as the paragraph above, unless you say differently (by clicking one of the alignment buttons).

Here's how to create a centered title. Press the Enter key twice (to leave a big blank space above the title). Then click the Center button (so the title will be centered) and the Bold button (so the title will be bold), type the words you want to be in the title, and press the Enter key afterwards. Congratulations: you've created a centered title! Next, make the paragraph underneath the title be normal: make that paragraph be uncentered (click the Align Left button) and make it be unbolded (deactivate the Bold button, by clicking it).

Bullets While you're typing a paragraph, you can activate the **Bullets button** (by clicking it). That makes the computer indent the entire paragraph and also put a bullet (the symbol •) to the left of the paragraph's first line. That's called a **bulleted paragraph**.

After you've typed a bulleted paragraph, any new paragraphs you type underneath will be bulleted also — until you request an *un*bulleted paragraph (by deactivating the Bullets button).

Undo

If you make a mistake (such as accidentally deleting some text or accidentally inserting some useless text), click the **Undo button**, which is near the screen's top and shows an arrow curving back to the left. The arrow is blue (unless you haven't typed anything yet).

Clicking the Undo button makes the computer undo your last activity, so your text returns to the way it looked before you made your boo-boo. (To undo your last *two* activities, click the Undo button *twice*.)

Instead of clicking the Undo button, you can use this shortcut: while holding down the Ctrl key, tap the Z key (which stands for "Zap").

Font Size

Left of the Bold button, the screen shows a box containing the number 10. That's called the **Font Size box**. The 10 in it means the characters you're typing are **10 points** high.

If you change that number to 20, the characters will be twice as high (and also twice as wide). To change the number to 20, click in the Font Size box, then type 20 and press Enter. Try it! Any new characters you type afterwards will be the size you chose. (Characters typed earlier don't change size.)

You can make the font size be 10 or 20 or any other size you like. For best results, pick a number from 8 to 72. (If you pick a number smaller than 8 or bigger than 72, the result is ugly.) The number can end in .5; for example, you can pick 8 or 8.5 or 9 or 9.5 or 10.

Font

At the screen's left edge, you see a box saying "Arial". That's called the **Font box**. Next to that box is the symbol ▾. Click it.

You'll see the **Font menu**, which is a list of fonts in alphabetical order. (To see the rest of the list, press the up-arrow or down-arrow keys.)

Click whichever font you want. To avoid hassles, choose a font that has "TT" or "O" in front of it. (The "TT" means it's a **TrueType font**. The "O" means it's an **OpenType font**, which is even better.)

For most purposes, the best fonts are:

> Times New Roman (which is the best for most paragraphs and looks like this)
> Courier New (which is the easiest for tables of numbers)
> Arial (which is standard for short headlines and captions and looks like this)
> Tahoma (which resembles Arial but has a better capital "I" and looks like this)
> Comic Sans MS (which resembles Tahoma but is funny and looks like this)

All delete

Here's how to delete the entire document, so you can start over. While holding down the Ctrl key, press the A key (which means "all"). All of the document gets **highlighted**: its white background turns blue. Then press the Delete key. All of the document disappears, so you can start over!

Select

Here's how to change a phrase you typed previously.

Point at the phrase's beginning. Then hold down the mouse's left button; and while you keep holding down that button, move to the phrase's end.

(Moving the mouse while holding down the left button is called **dragging**. You're **dragging** from the phrase's beginning to the phrase's end.)

The phrase that you dragged across gets highlighted: its white background turns blue. Highlighting the phrase that way is called **selecting the phrase**.

Then say what to do to the phrase. For example, choose one of these activities:

> To underline the phrase, activate the Underline button.
> To make the phrase be bold, activate the Bold button.
> To italicize the phrase, activate the Italic button.
>
> To prevent the phrase from being underlined, bold, or italicized, deactivate those buttons (by clicking them again).
>
> To change how the phrase's paragraphs are aligned, click one of the alignment buttons.
> To change the phrase's point size, click the Font Size box then type the size and press Enter.
> To change the phrase's font, choose the font you want from the Font menu.
>
> To delete the phrase, press the **Delete key**.
>
> To replace the phrase, just type whatever words you want the phrase to become.

Go ahead! Try it now! It's fun!

Advanced selection Your version resembles WordPad 7, so **read these sections on page 87:**

> "Other ways to select"
> "Document vanishes"
> "Drag a phrase"

Extra buttons

Near the screen's top-left corner, you see these extra buttons:

New   Open   Save   Print   PrintPreview

Here's how to use them....

Save Here's how to **save** the document (copy it onto the hard disk). Click the **Save button**. Then invent a name for the document. The name can be short (such as "Joe") or long (such as "Stupidest Memo of 2011"). At the name's end, press the Enter key. Then the computer will copy the document onto the disk.

Afterwards, if you change your mind and want to do more editing, go ahead! When you finish that extra editing, save it by clicking the Save button again.

Save often! If you're typing a long document, **click the Save button about every 10 minutes**. Click it whenever you get to a good stopping place and think, "What I've typed so far looks good!" Then if an accident happens, you'll lose at most 10 minutes of work, and you can return to the last version you felt good about.

Instead of clicking the Save button, you can use this shortcut: while holding down the Ctrl key, tap the S key (which stands for "Save").

Print To print the document onto paper, click the **Print button**.

Print Preview If you're wondering what a page will look like but don't want to waste a sheet of paper to find out, click the **Print Preview button**. The computer will show you a **mock-up** of what the entire page will look like: **you'll see the whole page, shrunk to fit on the screen**, so the characters on the page appear very tiny. Those characters are too tiny to read, but you'll see the page's overall appearance: how much of the page is filled up, which parts of the page are blank, and whether the info on the page is centered. When you finish admiring that mock-up, click the word "Close".

Finishing When you finish working on a document, you can click the **New button** or the **Open button**. If you click the **New button** and then press Enter, the computer will let you start typing a new document. If instead you click the **Open button**, here's what happens:

> The computer will show you a list of the documents you saved earlier. **Double-click** the document you want. (To double-click, tap the mouse's left button twice *quickly*, so the taps are less than .4 seconds apart. While tapping the left button twice, make sure the mouse remains still: don't let the mouse jiggle, not even a smidgen! Double-clicking is also called **opening**.) The computer will put that document onto the screen and let you edit it.

When you finish using WordPad, click the X button (at the screen's top right corner). That closes the WordPad window, so the WordPad window disappears.

Before the computer obeys the New button, Open button, or X button, the computer checks whether you saved your document. If you didn't save your document, here's the consequence in Windows XP:

> The computer asks "Save changes?" If you click "Yes", the computer copies your document's most recent version to the hard disk; if you click "No" instead, the computer ignores and forgets your most recent editing.

Here's the consequence in Windows Vista:

> The computer asks "Do you want to save changes?" If you click the "Save" button, the computer copies your document's most recent version to the hard disk; if you click the "Don't Save" button instead, the computer ignores and forgets your most recent editing.

When you buy modern Windows, you get a graphics program free! That graphics program is called **Paint**. It's one of the Windows accessories.

Paint basics

To use Paint, get the Accessories menu onto the screen (by clicking Start then "All Programs" then "Accessories") and then click "Paint." You'll see the **Paint window**.

Make sure the Paint window consumes the whole screen. (If it doesn't consume the whole screen yet, maximize the window by clicking the resize button, which is next to the X button.)

Move the mouse pointer to the screen's middle. Then **drag** (move the mouse while holding down the mouse's left button). As you drag, you'll be drawing a squiggle.

For example, try drawing a smile:

> To do that, put the mouse pointer where you want the smile to begin (at the smile's top left corner), then depress the mouse's left button while you draw the smile. When you finish drawing the smile, lift the mouse's button. Then draw the rest of the face!

Paint 7

The version of Paint that comes in Windows 7 is called **Paint 7**. Here are its advanced features. (If you have Windows XP or Vista instead, skip ahead to the next section, called "Paint classic.")

Colors

When you start drawing, the computer assumes you want to draw in black.

At the screen's top, above the word "Colors", you see the 20 **main colors**, which have these names:

black	gray-50%	dark red	red	orange	yellow	green	turquoise	indigo	purple
white	gray-25%	brown	rose	gold	light yellow	lime	light turquoise	blue-gray	lavender

To draw in one of those colors instead of in black, click the color you want. Whatever you draw next will be that color. The computer will keep using that color until you choose a different color instead (or you exit from the Paint program).

If you don't like any of the 20 main colors, try this:

> Click "Edit colors".
> Below "Basic colors", you see 48 little colored blocks. On the right, you also see a big block containing a rainbow of other colors. Click your favorite color. If the color you clicked was in the big block, the vertical strip to the right will show variations of that color (from pale to dark); click the variation you want.
> When you've finished choosing your color, click "OK".
> The color you chose will appear below the 20 main colors. Whatever you draw next will be that color.

Warning: don't click the **Color 2 button**, until I explain later how to use it properly.

Eraser

If you drew a shape badly, erase it and try again! To erase, click the **Eraser button** (which is pink and above "Tools"). Then your mouse acts as eraser instead of a brush. Erase your mistake by dragging across your picture's bad part.

When you finish erasing, click the Brushes icon (which is above the word "Brushes") and try drawing better.

Undo

If you make a mistake, try clicking the **Undo button** (which is at the screen's top and shows a blue arrow bending back to the left). That undoes your last activity. For example, it can undo your last brushstroke or your last erasure. If you click the Undo button *twice*, it will erase your last *two* activities.

If you clicked the Undo button but wish you hadn't, you can "undo the undo" by clicking the **Redo button**, which is to the right of the Undo button and shows a blue arrow bending forward to the right.

The Undo and Redo buttons work just if their arrows are blue. While an arrow is gray, the button doesn't work.

All delete

Here's how to delete the entire picture, so you can start over:

> While holding down the Ctrl key, press the A key. That means "all". All of the picture is surrounded by a blue dotted line.
> Then press the Delete key. The entire picture disappears, so you can start over!

Change the brush

To change how thick the brushstrokes are, click "**Size**" then click the thickness you want.

If you click the **down-arrow under "Brushes"**, you see 9 different types of brushes:

Brush, which is plain & normal

Calligraphy brush 1, which thickens any diagonal line that's "falling" (heading toward the screen's bottom-right corner)

Calligraphy brush 2, which thickens any diagonal line that's "rising" (heading toward the screen's top-right corner)

Airbrush, to look like paint splattered out of a spray can by a vandal

Oil brush, to look like an oil painting

Crayon, to look like Crayola used by a toddler

Marker, to look like a Sharpie marker pen or a highlighter pen

Natural pencil, to look like a sketch drawn by a fine artist using a soft pencil

Watercolor brush, to look like a watercolor painting

Click the type of brush you want, then click "Size" and choose a thickness for that brush. If you're a beginner, choose the thickest size, so you can see clearly how that type of brushstroke looks.

If you click the **Pencil button** (which is above the Eraser button and looks like a yellow pencil), you'll draw with a hard pencil (instead of a softer tool). After clicking the Pencil button, click "Size" to choose the pencil's thickness. To switch from the hard pencil back to softer tools (such as brushes), click the icon above "Brushes" (to return to the same type of brush you were using before) or click the down-arrow under "Brushes" (to choose a different brush type).

Shapes

Above the word "Shapes", you see these 21 shapes:

The first 6 shapes are the most important. Here's how to use them.

Line To draw a line that's exactly straight, click the **Line** shape (which is the first shape). Then put the mouse pointer where you want the line to begin, and drag to where you want the line to end.

While dragging, if you hold down the Shift key, you'll force the line to be **perfectly simple** (perfectly vertical, perfectly horizontal, or at a perfect 45-degree angle).

Rectangle To draw a rectangle (box) whose sides are exactly straight, click the **Rectangle** shape (which is the fourth shape). Then put the mouse pointer where you want the rectangle's top left corner to be, and drag to where you want the rectangle's opposite corner.

While dragging, if you hold down the Shift key, you'll force the rectangle to be a perfect **square**.

Rectangle variants Instead of clicking the Rectangle shape, try clicking these variants:

> If you click the **Rounded Rectangle** (which is the fifth shape) instead of the Rectangle, you'll force the rectangle's corners to be rounded (instead of sharp 90-degree angles). If you hold down the Shift key while dragging out the rounded rectangle, you'll create a **rounded square**.
>
> If you click the **Oval** (which is the third shape) instead of the Rectangle, you'll force the rectangle's corners to be *very* rounded, so the rectangle looks like an oval (ellipse). If you hold down the Shift key while dragging out the oval, you'll create a perfect **circle**.

Polygon To draw a polygon (a shape that has many straight sides and corners), click the **Polygon** shape (which is the sixth shape). Then put the mouse pointer where you want the polygon's first corner to be, and drag to where you want the second corner. Click where you want the third corner, click where you want the fourth corner, click where you want the fifth corner, etc.

At the last corner, double-click instead of click. The double-clicking makes the computer complete the polygon: it makes the computer draw the final side back to the first corner.

Curve To draw a curve, click the **Curve** shape (which is the second shape). Then put the mouse pointer where you want the curve to begin, and drag to where you want the curve to end. Then take your finger off the mouse's button.

You temporarily see a straight line. To turn that line into a curve, bend the line's middle, by pointing at the line's middle and dragging that midpoint in the direction you want to bend it. (While doing that dragging, try wiggling the mouse in all four directions, until the line bends close to the way you want.) Then take your finger off the mouse's button.

To bend the line more, and even create a second bend (arc) in the line, drag again. (You get just two chances to bend the line.)

Other shapes If you click one of the other shapes (triangle, diamond, pentagon, octagon, arrow, star, or callout), here's what to do next. Imagine the shape is enclosed (embedded) in a box (rectangle). In your picture, put the mouse pointer where you want the box's top left corner to be, and drag to where you want the box's bottom right corner.

When you finish dragging, you'll see the shape is in your picture and temporarily enclosed in a blue box.

If the shape isn't yet exactly where you want it, move it by doing this:

> Put the mouse pointer in the shape's middle, then drag where you want the shape to move.

You can also adjust the shape by doing this:

> The temporary blue box's corners and edges have 9 **handles** (tiny squares you can drag). Tug at the handles (by dragging them with the mouse), until the shape is stretched and repositioned where you want it.

Afterwards, when you click elsewhere, the shape stays in your picture, though the temporary blue box vanishes.

Brushes for shapes To draw each of those shapes, the computer uses a normal brush unless you say otherwise.

To say otherwise, do this:

> Click the shape you want to draw. Click "**Outline**".
> You see this menu:
> ```
> No outline
> Solid color
> Crayon
> Marker
> Oil
> Natural pencil
> Watercolor
> ```
> From that menu, choose the brush you want. (Choose "Crayon" or "Marker" or "Oil" or "Natural pencil" or "Watercolor". Choosing "Solid color" gives you just a normal brush". Don't choose "No outline", which means "no brush".)
> Then choose a brush size, by clicking "Size" then the size you want. (If you're a beginner, click the thickest size.)
> Then put the shape onto your picture (by dragging across your picture).

To return to using a normal brush, click the shape again then "Outline" then "Solid color".

Pick color

Look at what you've created. In that picture, if you see a color you've used and like, here's how to use it again:

> Click the **Pick color button**. Click in your picture, where your favorite color is. Then draw more stuff; it'll be in the color you picked.

Save

To save the picture you've been creating, (copy it onto the disk), click the **Save button**. (It's at the screen's top, near the left edge. It's a purple-and-white square that's supposed to look like a floppy disk, though it also looks like a TV set.)

If you haven't saved the picture before, the computer will say "File name". Invent a name for your picture. Type the name and press Enter.

That makes the computer copy the picture onto the hard disk. For example, if you named the picture "mary", the computer puts a picture called mary.png into the Pictures folder. If you wish, you can prove it by doing this:

> Click Start then "Pictures". If you called the picture "mary", you'll see mary is one of the files in the Pictures folder. If you right-click mary's icon then click "Properties", you'll see the type of file is ".png", which is pronounced "ping" and means "Portable Network Graphics". Finally, clear that proof off your screen (by clicking "OK" then the red X button).

Afterwards, if you change your mind and want to do more editing, go ahead! When you finish that extra editing, save it by clicking the Save button again.

Save often! **Click the Save button about every 10 minutes**. Click it whenever you get to a good stopping place and think, "What I've drawn so far looks good!" Then if an accident happens, you'll lose at most 10 minutes of work, and you can return to the last version you felt good about.

Paint button

Near the screen's top-left corner, just below the Save button, you see the **Paint button** Click it. Then you see the **Paint menu**:

```
New
Open
Save
Save as
Print
From scanner or camera
Send in e-mail
Set ask desktop background
Properties
About Paint
Exit
```

From that menu, choose whatever you wish (by clicking it). Here are the most popular choices....

Save If you choose **Save** from the Paint menu (by clicking the word "Save" after clicking the Paint button), you get the same result as clicking the Save button that's at the screen's top.

Save as Suppose you've already saved a picture then edited it some more, but you're not sure you like the new editing. Try this experiment....

Choose "**Save as**" from the Paint menu (by clicking the phrase "Save as" after clicking the Paint button); when you do that, make sure you click the phrase "Save as", not just the arrow next to it.

Then invent (and type) a new name for the picture. At the end of the new name, press Enter.

The computer will copy the picture's new, edited version onto the hard disk. That new, edited version will have the new name you invented.

The picture's old original version will be on the disk also and keep its old original name. The disk will contain *both* versions of the picture.

How to finish

When you finish working on a picture, choose **Exit** or **New** or **a previous picture** from the Paint menu.

Exit Whenever you want to stop using Paint, choose **Exit** from the Paint menu (or click the Paint window's X button).

New If you choose **New** (instead of Exit) from the Paint menu, the computer will let you start creating a new, different picture.

A previous picture If you want to reuse a previous picture you had saved, click the Paint button. To the right of the Paint button, you see a list of the **9 pictures you used most recently**: that list starts with the most recent. Click whichever picture you want to use. If you want to use a different picture, which is not on that list of 9, do this:

Choose **Open** from the Paint menu (by clicking Open).
The computer starts showing you a list of *all* pictures in the Pictures library. To see the rest of the list, either "click in that list then rotate the mouse's wheel toward you" or "repeatedly click the down-arrow that's to the right of that list".
If you want to *use* one of those pictures, *double*-click the picture's name; the computer will put that picture onto the screen and let you edit it. If instead you want to *delete* one of those pictures, click the picture's name then press the Delete key then the Enter key; the computer will move that picture to the Recycle Bin.

Didn't save? If you didn't save your picture before doing those "how to finish" procedures, the computer asks, "Do you want to save?" If you click "Save", the computer copies your document's most recent version to the hard disk; if you click "Don't Save" instead, the computer ignores and forgets your most recent editing.

Print

Here's how to print a picture onto paper.

Make sure you've bought a printer, attached it to the computer, turned the printer's power on, and put paper into the printer.

Choose **Print** from the Paint menu (by clicking the word "Print" after clicking the Paint button); when you do that, make sure you click the word "Print", not just the arrow next to it.

Press Enter. The computer will print the picture onto paper.

If your printer doesn't have colored ink, it will print shades of gray instead.

Text

Here's how to type words in your picture.

Click the **Text button** (which is in the Tools group and looks like an **A**). In your picture, click where you want the first word's first letter to begin. Type the words.

The words will be surrounded temporarily by a blue box that's about 1.4 inches wide. If you type more words than the box can hold, the extra words will appear underneath, and the box will automatically grow taller, to hold the extra words.

On the box's edges, you see 9 **handles** (tiny squares you can drag). If you want to widen the box, drag any handle on the box's right edge: drag it toward the right.

While typing, you see the **Font group**, which resembles WordPad's: it lets you change the font and the font's size and create underlines, boldface, italics, and strikethrough.

When you finish creating and editing the text box, click "**Home**" (which is near the screen's top-left corner).

Select

Here's how to alter part of your picture.

First, say which part of your picture to alter, by using one of these methods....

Method 1: click the down-arrow under "Select", then click "**Rectangular selection**". Draw a blue rectangle around that part of your picture: to do that, put the mouse pointer where you want the rectangle's top-left corner to be, and drag to where you want the rectangle's opposite corner.

Method 2: click the down-arrow under "Select", then click "**Free-form selection**." Draw a loop around that part of your picture: to do that, put the mouse pointer where you want the loop to begin, and drag until you've drawn the loop. (The loop will temporarily turn into a rectangle, but don't let that bother you.)

Method 3: select the entire picture (by doing this: while holding down the Ctrl key, tap the letter A).

Then say what to do to that part of your picture. You have these choices:

> To **delete** that part of your picture, press the Delete key.
>
> To **move** that part of your picture, point at the rectangle's middle and drag that part of your drawing to wherever you want.
>
> To **copy** that part of your picture (so that part appears *twice*), point at the rectangle's middle and, while holding down the Ctrl key, drag that part of your picture to wherever you want the second copy to be.
>
> To **rotate** that part of your picture, click "**Rotate**", then click "**Flip vertical**" (to flip that part upside-down) or "**Flip horizontal**" (to see a mirror image of that part) or "**Rotate right 90°**" (to rotate that part clockwise) or "**Rotate left 90°**" (to rotate that part counterclockwise) or "**Rotate 180°**" (to stand that part on its end).
>
> To **enlarge** that part of your picture, click "Resize", then double-click in the "Horizontal" box, then type "200" (if you want that part to be twice as wide and twice as tall) or "300" (if you want that part to be 3 times as wide and three times as tall), and press Enter.
>
> To **crop** that part of your picture, click "**Crop**". The rest of the picture will disappear, so the part you selected will be all that's left, and the picture will probably be smaller.
>
> To **widen** that part of your drawing, press Ctrl with W. Type 200 (to make that part of your drawing twice as wide) or 300 (to make that part three times as wide) or whatever other percentage you wish. Click "OK".

Color 2

The computer can handle two colors simultaneously. The main color is called **Color 1**; the alternative color is called **Color 2**.

To draw, the computer normally uses color 1. To use color 2 instead, do this….

Click "**Color 2**". Then click a color you want to become color 2; for example, try clicking yellow.

To draw using color 2, drag while holding down the mouse's *rightmost* button instead of the left button.

When you erase (by using the Eraser button), the computer will make the erasure be Color 2 (instead of white).

Fill To make a shape's middle be color 2 (instead of transparent), do this:

> Click the shape you want to draw. Click "Fill" then "Solid color".
> Then put the shape onto your picture (by dragging across your picture). The shape's middle will be filled with color 2. So will all future shapes, until you turn that feature off (by clicking "Fill" then "No fill").

Changing color 1 again After you've clicked "Color 2", any color you click will become color 2. To change color 1 instead, click "Color 1" before clicking a color.

Zoom slider

At the screen's bottom-right corner, you see a plus sign (+). Left of it, you see a minus sign (-). Between those signs, you see the **zoom slider**, which is a pentagon.

Try this experiment: **drag the zoom slider toward the right**. That makes the picture appear bigger, so you can see it even if you're sitting far from the screen and have poor vision. It's like looking at the picture through a magnifying glass: the picture looks enlarged, so you can see the details of each brushstroke more clearly; but not as much of the picture fits on the screen. (To see the rest of the picture, drag the **scroll bars**, which are at the screen's right edge and bottom.)

When you finish playing with the zoom slider, drag it back to its normal position (the middle), so the number left of the minus sign is "100%".

The version of Paint comes in Windows XP & Vista is called **Paint classic**. Hare are its advanced features. (If you have Windows 7 instead, skip this section.)

Colors

When you draw, you're normally drawing in black. At the screen's bottom (in Windows XP) or the screen's top (in Windows Vista), you see 28 **colors**: red, yellow, green, etc. To draw in one of those colors instead of in black, click the color you want.

Toolbox

Near the screen's top-left corner, you see this **toolbox**:

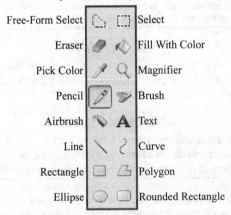

Free-Form Select	Select
Eraser	Fill With Color
Pick Color	Magnifier
Pencil	Brush
Airbrush	Text
Line	Curve
Rectangle	Polygon
Ellipse	Rounded Rectangle

As you can see, the toolbox contains 16 buttons. To use a button, activate it by clicking it.

When you start using Paint, the computer assumes you want to use the Pencil, so it activates the **Pencil button**. If you want to use a different tool, click a different button instead. Let's start with the most popular choices….

Brush

To draw a fatter squiggle, click the **Brush button**. Then put the mouse pointer in the screen's middle, where you want the squiggle to begin, and drag! Try it now!

Eraser

To erase a mistake, click the **Eraser button**. Then drag across the part of your drawing you want to erase. The part you drag across will become white.

Airbrush

To vandalize your drawing by using a can of spray paint, click the **Airbrush button**. Then put the mouse pointer where you want to begin spraying, and drag!

Line

To draw a line that's exactly straight, click the **Line button**. Then put the mouse pointer where you want the line to begin, and drag to where you want the line to end. While dragging, if you hold down the Shift key, you'll force the line to be **perfectly simple** (perfectly vertical, perfectly horizontal, or at a perfect 45-degree angle).

Ctrl key

While holding down the Ctrl key, you can tap the Z, S, P, N, or O key. Here are the details:

or O key. Here are the details:

> If you make a mistake, **zap** the mistake by press Ctrl with Z. That makes the computer zap (undo) your last action. To zap your last *two* actions, press Ctrl with Z *twice*. To zap your last *three* actions, press Ctrl with Z *three times*. Windows XP lets you zap the last 3 actions (but not the last 4 actions); Windows Vista lets you zap the last 10 actions.
>
> To **save** your painting (copy it onto the hard disk), press Ctrl with S. Then type whatever name you want the painting to have, and press Enter. Afterwards, if you edit your painting further, save that editing by pressing Ctrl with S again.
>
> To **print** your painting onto paper, press Ctrl with P. Then press Enter. If your printer doesn't have colored ink, it will print shades of gray instead.
>
> To start working on a **new** painting, press Ctrl with N.
>
> To **open** a painting (use a painting that you saved earlier), press Ctrl with the letter O. The computer will show you a list of the paintings you saved earlier. Double-click the painting you want. (To double-click, tap the mouse's left button twice *quickly*, so the taps are less than .4 seconds apart. While tapping the left button twice, make sure the mouse remains still: don't let the mouse jiggle, not even a smidgen!) The computer will put that painting onto the screen and let you edit it.

X button

When you finish using Paint, click the X button (at the screen's top right corner). That closes the Paint window, so the Paint window disappears.

Did you save?

Before the computer obeys Ctrl N, Ctrl O, or the X button, the computer checks whether you saved your painting. If you didn't save your painting, here's the consequence in Windows XP:

> The computer asks "Save changes?" If you click "Yes", the computer copies your painting's most recent version to the hard disk; if you click "No" instead, the computer ignores and forgets your most recent editing.

Here's the consequence in Windows Vista:

> The computer asks "Do you want to save changes?" If you click the "Save" button, the computer copies your painting's most recent version to the hard disk; if you click the "Don't Save" button instead, the computer ignores and forgets your most recent editing.

Advanced buttons

You've learned how to use the easy buttons (pencil, brush, eraser, airbrush, and line). Here's how to use the other buttons, which are more advanced.

Rectangle To draw a rectangle whose sides are exactly straight, click the **Rectangle button**. Then put the mouse pointer where you want the rectangle's top left corner to be, and drag to where you want the rectangle's opposite corner. While dragging, if you hold down the Shift key, you'll force the rectangle to be a perfect **square**.

Rectangle variants Instead of clicking the Rectangle button, try clicking these variants:

> If you click **Rounded Rectangle** instead of Rectangle, you'll force the rectangle's corners to be rounded (instead of sharp 90-degree angles). If you hold down the Shift key while dragging out the rounded rectangle, you'll create a **rounded square**.
>
> If you click **Ellipse** instead of Rectangle, you'll force the rectangle's corners to be *very* rounded, so the rectangle looks like an ellipse (oval). If you hold down the Shift key while dragging out the ellipse, you'll create a perfect **circle**.
>
> If you click **Text** instead of Rectangle, the rectangle will temporarily have dashed lines instead of solid lines. After creating that dashed rectangle, type whatever words you want inside the rectangle. Then click outside the rectangle. The dashed lines will disappear, so you won't see a rectangle, but you'll still see the words you typed.

Polygon To draw a polygon (a shape that has many straight sides and corners), click the **Polygon button**. Then put the mouse pointer where you want the polygon's first corner to be, and drag to where you want the second corner. Click where you want the third corner, click where you want the fourth corner, click where you want the fifth corner, etc.

At the last corner, double-click instead of click. The double-clicking makes the computer complete the polygon: it makes the computer draw the final side back to the first corner.

Curve To draw a curve, click the **Curve button**. Then put the mouse pointer where you want the curve to begin, and drag to where you want the curve to end. Then take your finger off the mouse's button.

You temporarily see a straight line. To turn that line into a curve, bend the line's middle, by pointing at the line's middle and dragging that midpoint in the direction you want to bend it. (While doing that dragging, try wiggling the mouse in all four directions, until the line bends close to the way you want.) Then take your finger off the mouse's button.

To bend the line more, and even create a second bend (arc) in the line, drag again. (You get just two chances to bend the line.)

Fill With Color After you've drawn a closed shape (a rectangle, square, rounded rectangle, rounded square, ellipse, circle, or polygon, or "a squiggle that forms a loop so it ends where it started"), here's how to fill in the shape's interior (middle), so the interior becomes colored instead of white:

> Click the **Fill With Color button**, then click your favorite color (from the 28 choices at the screen's bottom), then click in the shape's interior.

If you click outside the shape instead of inside, you'll be coloring the shape's exterior.

Pick Color Look at what you've drawn. In that drawing, if you see a color you've used and like, here's how to use it again:

> Click the **Pick Color button**. Click in your drawing, where your favorite color is. Then draw some more shapes; they'll be in the color you picked.

Select Here's how to alter part of your drawing.
First, say which part of your drawing to alter, by using one of these methods....

> Method 1: click the **Select button**. Draw a dashed rectangle around that part of your drawing: to do that, put the mouse pointer where you want the rectangle's top-left corner to be, and drag to where you want the rectangle's opposite corner.
>
> Method 2: click the **Free-Form Select button**. Draw a loop around that part of your drawing: to do that, put the mouse pointer where you want the loop to begin, and drag until you've drawn the loop. (The loop will temporarily turn into a rectangle, but don't let that bother you.)

Then say what to do to that part of your drawing. You have these choices:

> To **delete** that part of your drawing, press the Delete key.
>
> To **move** that part of your drawing, point at the rectangle's middle and drag that part of your drawing to wherever you want.
>
> To **copy** that part of your drawing (so that part appears *twice*), point at the rectangle's middle and, while holding down the Ctrl key, drag that part of your drawing to wherever you want the second copy to be.
>
> To **rotate** that part of your drawing, press Ctrl with R, then click "Flip vertical" (to flip that part upside-down) or "Flip horizontal" (to see a mirror image of that part) or "Rotate by angle" (to stand that part on its end). Click "OK".
>
> To **invert** the colors in that part of your drawing, press Ctrl with I. That makes black becomes white, white becomes black, yellow becomes blue, blue becomes yellow, green becomes purple, purple becomes green, red becomes greenish blue, and greenish blue becomes red.
>
> To **widen** that part of your drawing, press Ctrl with W. Type 200 (to make that part of your drawing twice as wide) or 300 (to make that part three times as wide) or whatever other percentage you wish. Click "OK".

Nifty features

Windows has nifty features. Here's how to use them.

Time

In Windows XP & Vista, the screen's bottom-right corner shows the time, like this:

8:45 PM

In Windows 7, the screen's bottom-right corner shows the time *and date*, like this:

8:45 PM
4/27/2011

Date in English

If you move the mouse's arrow to the time, the date in English will flash on the screen briefly, like this:

Wednesday, April 27, 2011

Calendar (in Windows Vista & 7)

To see a calendar, click the time. Then you see a calendar for this month, with today's date highlighted in blue.

The calendar also shows the end of last month and the beginning of next month. (If you want to see a calendar for *all* of next month, click the right-arrow.)

You also see the face of a traditional clock, with an hour hand, minute hand, and second hand that all move.

Date and Time window While viewing the calendar, you can click "Change date and time settings".

Then you see a bigger window, called the **"Date and Time" window**. It shows the traditional clock, the time zone (such as "Eastern Time"), and when Daylight Savings Time will begin or end.

If you want to change the time zone (because your computer traveled to a different time zone), do this:

Click "Change time zone". Press the keyboard's right-arrow key (or left-arrow key) several times, until your time zone is chosen. Press Enter.

Once you've chosen the correct time zone, the computer will automatically show the correct time, usually. (That's because, once a week, the computer synchronizes its internal clock with the Internet's clock.)

When you finish using the "Date and Time" window, click "OK".

Calendar (in Windows XP)

To see a calendar, double-click the time. Then you see a calendar for this month, with today's date highlighted in blue.

You also see the face of a traditional clock, with an hour hand, minute hand, and second hand that all move. You see the time zone, such as "Eastern Daylight Time".

If you want to change the time zone (because your computer traveled to a different time zone), do this:

Click "Time Zone". Press the keyboard's right-arrow key (or left-arrow key) several times, until your time zone is chosen.

When you finish using that clock/calendar window, click "OK".

Once you've chose the correct time zone and clicked "OK", the computer will automatically show the correct time, usually. (That's because, once a week, the computer synchronizes its internal clock with the Internet's clock.)

Taskbar

At the screen's bottom left corner, you see the Start button. At the screen's bottom right corner, you see the time. Across the screen's bottom, running from the Start button to the time, you see a box that's very wide (as wide as the screen) and about half an inch tall. In Windows XP, that box is blue; in Windows Vista, that box is gray; in Windows 7, that box is bluish gray. That box is called the **taskbar**. It includes the Start button (at the screen's bottom-left corner), the time (at the screen's bottom-right corner), and everything between them.

When you're running a task (program), the taskbar usually shows a button for that task. For example, while you're running WordPad, you see a WordPad button on the taskbar. While you're running Paint, you see a Paint button on the taskbar.

Experiment

Try this experiment!

Start running WordPad (by clicking Start then Programs then Accessories then WordPad). Now the taskbar includes a WordPad button. Since WordPad is a word-processing program, type a few words, so you've created a short document on your screen.

While WordPad is still on your screen, start running Paint (by clicking Start then Programs then Accessories then Paint). Now the taskbar includes a WordPad button and a Paint button, because WordPad and Paint are both running simultaneously: they're both in the computer's RAM memory chips. Paint is blocking your view of WordPad, but WordPad is still running also.

To see WordPad better, click WordPad's button on the toolbar. Then you'll see WordPad clearly, and WordPad will block your view of Paint.

Here's the rule: clicking WordPad's button lets you see WordPad better; clicking Paint's button lets you see Paint better. Both programs are in RAM simultaneously, until you close them (by clicking their X buttons).

Windows Vista lets you play this trick (if your edition of Windows Vista is at least "Premium"):

While you're running several programs simultaneously (such as WordPad, Paint, and Calculator), click the "Switch between windows" button. (That button is a blue square, on the taskbar, close to the Start button, and has many white windows on it.) When you click that button, the screen shows you all the programs simultaneously, in a stack of windows, rotated in 3-D. Click the window of whichever program you want to work on: then that window will expand to consume the whole screen.

Many tasks

You can run *several* programs simultaneously. For example, you can run WordPad, Paint, and Calculator all simultaneously, so you see all their buttons on the taskbar simultaneously. But if you try to run many programs simultaneously, the computer will tend to get confused and fail (especially if you bought too little RAM or your computer's been on for many hours in a row). To avoid headaches, run no more than two major programs at a time.

Clipboard

To copy data, you can use this 2-step process: first **copy** the data to the computer's invisible **Clipboard**, then stick the clipboard's data wherever you want it by using **Velcro**. Here are the details....

Ctrl with C

You can copy data from one document to another, even if the documents were created by different programs, and even if one "document" is a drawing and the other "document" contains mostly words. (For example, you can copy data that's a drawing, from Paint to WordPad.) Here's how:

> Get onto the screen the data you want to copy. Select that data, by dragging across it. (If that data's in Paint, click Paint's Select button before dragging.)
>
> Say "**copy**" by pressing **Ctrl with C**. That secretly copies the data to the **Clipboard** (a file you can't see).
>
> Get onto the screen the document you want to copy the data to. In that document, click where you want the data to be inserted.
>
> Say "**Velcro**" by pressing **Ctrl with V**. That sticks the Clipboard's data into the document.
>
> If you're sticking the data into a WordPad document, the computer sticks it where you requested. If you're sticking the data into a Paint document, the computer insists on sticking it at the painting's top-left corner; afterwards, drag the data where you want it.
>
> If you want to stick the Clipboard's data somewhere else also, click there and press Ctrl with V again.

Print Screen Key

Try this experiment: say **Print Screen** (by pressing a key labeled PrintScreen or PrtScr or PrtScn or PrtSc, or by pressing a key labeled fn then a key labeled prt sc). That makes the computer secretly take a snapshot of *your whole screen* and put that photo onto the clipboard.

If you want the computer to take a snapshot of *just one window*, do this:

> Click in that window. Then *while holding down the Alt key*, say Print Screen (by using the method above). The computer will put a snapshot of just that window onto the Clipboard.

After something's on the clipboard, stick it into a WordPad document or Paint document or some other document (by clicking there and then pressing Ctrl with V). Then, if you wish, edit the snapshot and print it on paper.

Snipping Tool

If you want to copy *part* of the screen to the clipboard, use Windows Vista or 7 and do this:

> Click Start then "All Programs" then "Accessories" then "Snipping Tool".
>
> Make sure the mouse pointer is a white cross. (If it's a different shape, make it a white cross by clicking the down-arrow next to "New" then "Rectangular Snip".)
>
> Draw a red box around the part of the screen you want to copy. To do that, put the mouse pointer where you want the box's top-left corner to be, and drag to where you want the box's opposite corner. If you drew the box wrong, click "New" then try again to draw the box.
>
> Click the Copy button (which looks like 2 sheets of paper with bent corners). Close the Snipping Tool window (by clicking its X button then clicking "No").

After you've done that, stick your clip into a WordPad document or Paint document or some other document (by clicking there and then pressing Ctrl with V).

Ball game

Windows XP & Vista include a ball game. I'll explain how to play. (Windows 7 lacks a ball game, so if you have Windows 7 skip ahead to the next section, called "Time".)

Windows Vista

In Windows Vista, the ball game is **InkBall**. You can access it in two ways.

> Method 1: click Start then "All Programs" then "Games" then "InkBall".
>
> Method 2: click Start then "Games"; maximize the window; double-click "InkBall".

Goal You see a blue ball and an orange ball, bouncing around, like billiard balls on a billiard table. To win, coax the blue ball into the blue hole, and coax the orange ball into the orange hole. (If the blue ball accidentally falls the orange hole — or the orange ball accidentally falls into the blue hole — you lose.)

Strategy To change the direction in which a ball moves, use your mouse to draw a black squiggle (by dragging, as if you were using Paint). The squiggle acts as a barrier: when a ball hits the barrier, the ball bounces off the barrier, and the barrier disappears.

For example, if the blue ball is getting too close to the orange hole, draw a barrier between the blue ball and the orange hole. If the blue ball is getting wonderfully close to the blue hole, nudge the blue ball into the blue hole by drawing a loop that contains the blue ball and the blue hole.

Speed You must be reasonably fast: the game has a 2-minute time limit. If you take more than 2 minutes, you lose. The window's red box shows how many seconds are left.

Game over If a ball falls into the wrong hole or you take more than 2 minutes, the computer says "Game over!" To react, press the Enter key; then the game will restart.

Winning If you get a ball into the correct hole, you get points. Your point total is written in white, in a black box. If you get *both* balls into the correct holes, you proceed to a more difficult round of the game, where you might encounter differently colored balls and differently colored holes. Gray holes are neutral: when a ball falls into a gray hole, you get no penalty but also no points.

How many points? When you correctly sink a ball into a hole, you get 200 points if the ball is orange, 400 if blue, 800 if green, 1600 if gold. When you successfully finish a round (by sinking both balls within 2 minutes), the computer notices how many seconds were remaining: those unused seconds are given to you as bonus points.

Close When you finish using InkBall, close its window (by clicking its X button).

Windows XP

In Windows XP, the ball game is **Pinball**. To access it, click Start then "Programs" then "Games" then "Pinball".

The computer will say "3D Pinball". After a few seconds, you see a fancy pinball machine with flashing lights and hear sounds of the machine reloading. It's much fancier than the pinball machines you see in video arcades and bars!

At the machine's bottom right corner, you see a ball (round bullet), and the computer says "Awaiting Deployment", which means the computer is waiting for you to fire the ball.

How to play Fire the ball, as follows:

> Hold down the Space bar for 5 seconds (while the ball's plunger retracts). Then release the Space bar (which makes the plunger fire the ball).

Then the ball goes zooming through the machine. Each time the ball bangs into something, you hear wild noises and get points.

Your goal is to keep the ball in play as long as possible, without letting the ball fall to the screen's bottom. To keep the ball in play, hit it up by using the flippers, which are near the screen's bottom.

> To raise the left flipper, press the Z key (near the keyboard's bottom left corner).
>
> To raise the right-hand flipper, press the slash key (which is near the keyboard's bottom right corner).

You get 3 chances to do all that (fire the ball and keep it in play). If the computer sympathizes with you (because you're amazingly good or pathetically bad), the computer gives you free replays, so you get *more* than 3 chances.

As you play, you see your score rise. When all your chances are used up, the computer says "GAME OVER".

High scores The computer keeps track of the 5 highest scores. If you have one of the 5 highest scores, you see the High Scores window: it's a chart showing the top 5 scores so far and who got them. Your score is temporarily called credited to "Player 1", because you haven't told the computer your name yet. Type your name and press Enter.

Play again If you (or a friend) want to play again, press the F2 key.

Bigger machine If you want to want the pinball machine to look bigger and fill the whole screen, press the F4 key. Unfortunately, that makes the menus disappear. Press the F4 key again to return to normal size and see the menus.

Pause If you want to pause (so you can go to the bathroom, wipe the sweat off your brow, catch your breath, order a pizza, tell your Mom you're doing your homework, or tell the boss you're doing accounting), press the F3 key. That makes the ball immediately stop rolling. As in a sci-fi movie, you've put the ball into a state of suspended animation!

When you're ready to resume, press the F3 key again, and the ball will come flying at you as fast as when you left off.

Close When you finish using Pinball, make sure the pinball machine is normal size, then close its window (by clicking its X button).

Play a music CD

Before 1980, music came on records or tapes. Nowadays, music comes on compact discs instead.

If you've bought a compact disc containing music, you can shove that disk into your computer's **CD-ROM drive** (or **DVD-ROM drive**) while Windows is running. Here's how....

Find the drive

Find your computer's **CD-ROM drive** (or **DVD-ROM drive**, which is a souped-up CD-ROM drive). It's in a desktop computer's front or a notebook computer's side.

If you're lucky, it's a 5-inch horizontal **slit**. If you're unlucky (which is more likely), it's a 5-inch-wide **drawer** you must open by pressing an **eject button** (which is on the drawer, or under the drawer's right-hand end).

Insert the disk

Grab the CD. Hold that disk horizontally, so its label is on the *top* surface. Don't touch its shiny underside.

Put that CD into the CD-ROM drive, as follows:

> If the CD-ROM drive is a **slit**, put the CD into the slit.
>
> If the CD-ROM drive is a **drawer**, open the drawer (by pressing the eject button) then drop the CD onto the drawer's tray then close the drawer).

Finish installing Media Player

If your computer has never played any CDs, it might ask you questions. Here's how to reply:

> If Windows Vista or 7 says "AutoPlay",
> click "Play audio CD using Windows Media Player".
>
> If Windows XP asks "What do you want Windows to do?",
> click "OK".
>
> If your computer says "Validate your copy of Windows", click "Validate" then "I accept".
>
> If your computer says "Welcome to Windows Media Player 10",
> press Enter thrice.
>
> If your computer says "Welcome to Windows Media Player 11",
> click "Express Settings" then "Finish".
>
> If your computer says "Welcome to Windows Media Player" with no number, click "Recommended settings" then "Finish".
>
> If the computer asks you to agree to legal stuff, click "I Accept".

Enjoy the music

The computer will play the CD as background music, while you continue your work.

Adjust the volume

On a desktop computer, do this:

> To adjust the music's overall volume, turn the **master volume knob**, which is typically on the front of the right speaker.
>
> (Some old systems put the master volume knob on the computer's back wall instead, below where the speaker's cable enters the computer. Some cheap systems have no master volume knob at all!)
>
> If you have a subwoofer (an extra speaker, to produce a booming bass), its front has a **bass knob**, which you can turn to boost the bass volume as much as you wish.
>
> If you have a 5-speaker system (2 stereo speakers plus 1 subwoofer plus 2 surround-sound speakers), you can boost the surround-sound speaker volume by turning the **surround knob** (which is next to the master-volume knob on the front right stereo speaker).

On most systems, the screen's bottom right corner shows a **Volume icon** (which looks like a blaring loudspeaker and is next to the time).

If you're using Windows XP but the Volume icon is missing, do this:

> In the middle of the toolbar (the blue bar across the screen's bottom), **right-click** (click the mouse's rightmost button). Click "Properties". You see some check boxes; if the bottom box ("Hide inactive icons") contains a check mark, remove the check mark (by clicking it). Then click "OK".
>
> That will probably make the Volume icon appear. If it doesn't appear yet, do the following.
>
> Click "Start" then "Control Panel" then "Sounds, Speech and Audio Devices" then "Adjust the system volume". Make sure the bottom check box ("Place volume icon in the taskbar") contains a check mark; if the box is empty, click it to make the check mark appear. Click "OK", then close all windows (by clicking their X buttons). That should make the Volume icon appear.

If you click the Volume icon, you'll see a slider. Using the mouse, drag the slider up (to raise the master volume) or down (to lower it).

For Windows Vista & 7, you can adjust the volume further by doing this:

> Click "Mixer" (which is at the slider's bottom). You'll see more sliders. To make sure you can get maximum volume, drag all those sliders up.

When you finish adjusting the slider window, close it by clicking its X.

Control what you hear & see

Here's how to control what you hear & see.

While the music plays, you see the **Windows Media Player window.** Make sure that window's top-left corner says "Windows Media Player" (or shows ▶). If you don't see that (because you're using an early version of Windows XP), make it appear by doing this: click the ◊ button (which is at the window's top left corner).

Maximize that window by clicking its maximize button (which is next to the X button).

At the window's bottom, you should see several buttons. (If you don't see them yet, make them appear by moving the mouse.)

Click the ‖ button to pause in the middle of a song. To resume, click that button again (which has changed to a big ▶).

Click ■ to stop back at the beginning of the current track (song). To begin playing there, click the big ▶.

Click ▶| or ▶▶| to skip ahead to the next track (song), |◀ or |◀◀ to hop back to the beginning of the previous track. (If you don't hear any music, click the big ▶ to remind the computer to play.) To skip to a far-away track, click those buttons repeatedly or double-click the track's number (or name) at the screen's right edge. (If the screen's right edge doesn't show the list of tracks yet, right-click the screen's middle then click "Show list". You'll see track names instead of numbers just if the CD is in the recording industry's database and you're connected to the Internet.)

As a song plays, you see a tiny object slide from left to right:

> In Windows Media Player 11 (which is part of Windows Vista and 7 and some versions of Windows XP), the object is a tiny blue bubble with a long blue tail.
>
> In Windows XP using Media Player 10, the object is a silver knob.

To fast-forward, use your mouse to drag that object farther to the right immediately. To reverse, drag that object back to the left.

As the music plays, you see the music's **visualization** (an animated abstract cartoon that thumps to the music's beat).

> In Windows Media Player 11 (which is part of Windows Vista and 7 and some versions of Windows XP), the most amazing visualization is called **Alchemy**: to choose it, right-click the screen's middle then click Visualizations then Alchemy then Random. Another amazing choice is Battery Randomization: to choose it, right-click the screen's middle then click Visualizations then Battery then Randomization.
>
> In earlier versions of Windows Media Player (which are part of early Windows XP), the most amazing visualization is called **Ambience Water**: to choose it, click View (at the screen's top) then Visualizations then Ambience then Water. While it thumps to your music, the screen's bottom left corner says "Ambience Water". A tiny ▶ points at that name; to explore other visualizations, click that tiny ▶ repeatedly.

When you tire of listening to that CD, click the eject button (which is the rightmost button on your CD-ROM drive), then remove the CD. If you wish, insert a different CD instead. If you don't want to listen to any CD now, close the Windows Media Player window (by clicking its X button).

Play a movie DVD

Videos used to come on videotape. Nowadays, a video come on **Digital Versatile Disk (DVD)** instead.

If you've bought a DVD containing a movie, you can shove that disk into your computer's **DVD-ROM drive** while Windows is running. Playing a movie DVD is similar to playing an audio CD. Here's how to do it.

Find the drive

Find your computer's **DVD-ROM drive**. It's in a desktop computer's front or a notebook computer's side.

If you're lucky, it's a 5-inch horizontal **slit**. If you're unlucky (which is more likely), it's a 5-inch-wide **drawer** you must open by pressing an **eject button** (which is on the drawer, or under the drawer's right-hand end).

Insert the disk

Grab the DVD. Hold that disk horizontally, so its label is on the *top* surface. Don't touch its shiny underside.

Put that DVD into the DVD drive, as follows:

> If the DVD drive is a **slit**, put the DVD into the slit.
>
> If the DVD drive is a **drawer**, open the drawer (by pressing the eject button) then drop the DVD onto the drawer's tray then close the drawer (by pressing the eject button again).

Finish installing Media Player

If your computer has never played any movie DVDs, it might ask you questions. Here's how to reply:

If Windows Vista or 7 says "AutoPlay",
click "Play DVD movie using Windows Media Player".

If Windows XP asks "What do you want Windows to do?",
click "Play DVD movie using Windows Media Player" then click "OK".

If your computer says "Welcome to Windows Media Player 10",
press Enter thrice.

If your computer says "Welcome to Windows Media Player 11",
click "Express Settings" then "Finish".

If the computer asks you to agree to legal stuff, click "I Accept".

Enjoy the movie

The computer will start playing the movie. (If the movie begins with a menu giving you a choice such as "play movie", click "play movie" with your mouse.)

Adjust the volume

To adjust the movie's overall volume on a desktop computer, turn the **master volume knob**, which is typically on the front of the right speaker.

Control what you see

If you move the mouse, the screen's bottom will show several buttons temporarily.

Move the mouse's pointer to the screen's bottom. That makes the buttons stay on the screen until you move the mouse's pointer back up.

While the buttons are on the screen, here's what you can do....

Click the ‖ button to pause the movie. To resume, click that button again (which has changed to a big ▶).

Click ■ to stop back at the movie's beginning. To begin playing there, click the big ▶.

While the movie plays, click ▶▶| to skip ahead to the next scene, |◀◀ to hop back to the previous scene.

As the movie plays, you see tiny blue bubble (with a long blue tail) slide from left to right. To fast-forward, use your mouse to drag that object farther to the right immediately. To reverse, drag that object back to the left.

Ending

When you tire of watching that movie, click the eject button (which is the rightmost button on your DVD drive). Then remove the DVD.

If you wish, insert a different DVD instead.

If you don't want to watch any more DVDs now, press the **Escape key** (which is at your keyboard's top left corner and says "Esc" on it). Then close the Windows Media Player window (by clicking its X button).

Explore your computer

What's in your computer? How much hardware and software do you have, and what type? Let's find out!

System properties

To find out what kind of computer system you have, do this....

Windows Vista & 7: click Start then "Computer" then "System properties".
Windows XP: click Start then "My Computer" then "View system information".

You'll see a message about your computer's properties.

Windows 7 When I bought a computer using Windows 7, its message said —

Windows edition
　Windows 7 Home Premium
　Copyright © 2009 Microsoft Corporation. All rights reserved.

System
　Manufacturer:　　　　　　Hewlett-Packard
　Model:　　　　　　　　　HP G71 Notebook PC
　Rating:　　　　　　　　　3.4 Windows Experience Index
　Processor:　　　　　　　Intel Core2 Duo CPU T6600 @ 2.20GHz
　Installed memory (RAM): 4.00 GB
　System type:　　　　　　64-bit Operating System

Computer name, domain, and workgroup settings
　Computer name: HP-G71-Notebook

Windows activation
　Windows is activated
　Product ID: 00359-OEM-8992687-00010

That means:

The computer is using Windows 7 Home Premium, invented in 2009 by Microsoft.

The computer is built by Hewlett-Packard and called an HP G71 Notebook PC. Its speed is rated 3.4. (You need a rating of at least 1 to run Windows 7 Starter, at least 3 is needed to run the most popular parts of Windows 7 Home Premium, at least 4 to run Windows 7's most luxurious features (such as handling 2 monitors simultaneously or handling HDTV). The computer's CPU chip is an Intel Core2 Duo T6600, whose speed is 2.2 gigahertz. The computer contains 4 gigabytes of RAM chips. The version of Windows 7 Home Premium is advanced (64-bit).

I named the computer "HP-G71-Notebook".

The copy of Windows 7 Home Premium on this computer has been **activated** (declared legitimate by Microsoft) and has serial number 00359-OEM-8992687-00010.

Windows Vista When I bought a computer using Windows Vista, its message said —

Windows edition
   Windows Vista Home Premium
   Copyright © 2007 Microsoft Corporation. All rights reserved.
   Service Pack 1

System
   Manufacturer: Hewlett-Packard
   Model: Compaq Presario CQ50 Notebook PC
   Rating: 3.6 Windows Experience Index
   Processor: AMD Turion Dual-Core RM-70 2.00 GHz
   Memory (RAM):   3.00 GB
   System type: 32-bit Operating System

Computer name, domain, and workgroup settings
   Computer name: Russ-PC

Windows activation
   Windows is activated
   Product ID: 89578-OEM-7332157-00061

That means:

The computer is using Windows Vista Home Premium, invented in 2007 by Microsoft but improved later by service pack #1.

The computer is built by Hewlett-Packard and called a Compaq Presario CQ50 Notebook PC. Its speed is rated 3.6. (You need a rating of at least 1 to run Windows Vista Home Basic, at least 3 is needed to run the most popular parts of Windows Vista Home Premium, at least 4 to run Windows Vista's most luxurious features (such as handling 2 monitors simultaneously or handling HDTV). The computer's CPU chip is an AMD Turion Dual-Core RM-70, whose speed is 2 gigahertz. The computer contains 3 gigabytes of RAM chips. The version of Windows Vista Home Premium is typical (32-bit).

I named the computer "Russ-PC".

The copy of Windows Vista Home Premium on this computer has been **activated** (declared legitimate by Microsoft) and has serial number 89578-OEM-7332157-00061.

Windows XP When I bought a computer using Windows XP, its message said —

System:
   Microsoft Windows XP
   Media Center Edition
   Version 2002
   Service Pack 2

Registered to:
   76487-OEM-0011903-00803

Manufactured and supported by:
   Hewlett-Packard Company
   Compaq Presario
   AMD Athlon 64 Processor
   3500+
   984 MHz, 960 MB of RAM

That means:

The computer is using Windows XP's Media Center Edition, invented in 2002 but improved later by service pack #2. The copy of Windows XP Media Center Edition on the computer is registered to me (Russ Walter) and has serial number 76487-OEM-0011903-00803.

The computer is built by Hewlett-Packard and called a Compaq Presario. The computer's CPU chip is an "AMD Athlon 64 3500+", whose speed is 984 megahertz. The computer contains 960 megabytes of RAM chips.

Your computer What message does *your* computer show?

When you finish admiring your computer's message, do this....

Windows Vista & 7: close the window (by clicking its X button).

Windows XP: click "OK" then close the My Computer window (by clicking its X button).

Disk drives

Each disk drive has a letter.

Drive A is the main floppy-disk drive (if you have one).
Drive B is the auxiliary floppy-disk drive (if you have one).
Drive C is the main part of the main hard drive.
Drives D, E, F, etc. are any extra disk drives (or parts of disk drives).

A typical computer has these drive details:

Drive A is the 1.44M 3½-inch floppy drive (if any).
Drive B is the 1.2M 5¼-inch floppy drive (if any).
Drive C is the hard drive's main part.
Drive D is the hard drive's recovery part (a copy of drive C's essentials).
Drive E is the main DVD drive (or DVD RW drive or CD-ROM drive).
Drive F is an extra DVD drive (or CD-RW drive).

Drive C is the most important: it's the main part of the main hard drive. Drive C holds Windows itself and the most important programs & documents.

Here's how the drives are named:

Drive A is called "**A:**" (which is pronounced "A colon").
Drive B is called "**B:**" (which is pronounced "B colon").
Drive C is called "**C:**" (which is pronounced "C colon").
Drive D is called "**D:**" (which is pronounced "D colon").

To find out what drives are in your computer and how they're lettered, do this....

Windows Vista & 7:   click Start then "Computer"
Windows XP: click Start then "My Computer"

You'll see the My Computer window. Make sure it consumes the whole screen. (If it doesn't consume the whole screen yet, maximize the My Computer window by clicking the maximize button, which is next to the X button.)

You'll see an **icon** (little picture) labeled "C:" (for the main part of your main hard drive) and icons for your other disk drives also.

The icons are labeled like this:

Hard Disk Drives
Local Disk (C:)   RECOVERY (D:)

Devices with Removable Storage
DVD RW Drive (E:)

If you're using Windows XP, do this....

At the screen's left edge, you see these headings: "System Tasks", "Other Places", and "Details". To the right of each heading, make sure you see the symbol ⌃. If you see a ⌄ instead, click it to make it become ⌃.

Drive C's files

To find out about drive C, do this:

Windows Vista & 7 Look at the screen. Below the "C:", you see a message about disk C, such as "255 GB free of 285 GB" (which means 255 GB are still unused & available, out of disk C's 285 GB total size). You also see a wide box, which represents the entire disk C: the blue part is what's used; the white part is what's unused (free). If you click the "C:" then "Properties" (which is near the screen's top), you'll see a pie chart with more details. When you finish admiring the pie chart, click "OK".

Windows XP Click the "C:" icon. Near the screen's bottom-left corner, you see messages about disk C, such as "Free Space: 135 GB" and "Total Size: 178 GB" (which means 135 GB are still unused & available, out of disk C's 178 GB total size). If you *right*-click the "C:" icon (by using the mouse's rightmost button) then click "Properties", you'll see a pie chart with more details. When you finish admiring the pie chart, click "OK".

To find out *even more* about your hard disk, **double-click the "C:" icon**. You'll see the **C window**, which lists files that are on disk C.

Make sure the C window consumes the whole screen. (If it doesn't consume the whole screen yet, maximize the C window by clicking the maximize button, which is next to the X button.)

If disk C contains more files than can fit on the screen, view the remaining files by pressing the ▾ and ▴ buttons, which are at the screen's right edge.

For each file, you see the file's name and a tiny picture (**icon**) representing the file.

Your computer can handle 3 kinds of files:

> If the file's a **document**, its icon typically looks like a notepad (or else a page whose top right corner is bent).
>
> If the file's an **application program**, its icon typically looks like a window.
>
> If the file's a **folder** containing other files, its icon looks like a yellow manila folder.

In the C window, you see a folder called "Program Files", a folder called "Windows" or "WINDOWS", and a folder called "Users" or "Documents and Settings".

Operating system	Disk C's main folders
Windows Vista & 7	Program Files, Windows, Users
Windows XP	Program Files, WINDOWS, Documents and Settings

Those folders are extremely important. You might also see some extra folders, documents, and application programs.

If you double-click a folder, a new window shows you what files are in the folder.

> Exception: if the files in that folder are dangerous to change, Windows XP might say "These files are hidden". If you insist on seeing those files anyway, click Windows XP's "Show the contents of this folder".

When you finish examining the new window, either close it (by clicking its X button) or go back to the previous window (by clicking the **Back button**, which is near the screen's top-left corner).

If you click a file's icon, here's what happens….

> **Windows Vista & 7:** the screen's bottom-left corner shows the file's name, the file's type (such as "Document", "Application", or "File Folder"), the date & time when the file was last modified, and (if the file's a document or application) the file's size & the date it was originally created.
>
> **Windows XP:** the screen's bottom-left corner (under the "Details" heading) shows the file's name, the file's type (such as "Document", "Application", or "File folder"), the date & time when the file was last modified, and (if the file's a document or application) the file's size.

Here's what happens if you double-click a file's icon:

> If the file's a **folder**, you see what's in the folder.
>
> If the file's an **application program**, the computer will try to run the program. Don't do that unless you've read instructions about how to run the program successfully!
>
> If the file's a **document**, the computer will try to use that document: the computer will try to run the program that created the document, but sometimes the computer can't correctly deduce which program created the document.

Here's how to find the documents you wrote using WordPad:

> **Windows 7** The Users folder contains a personal folder (having your name on it), which in turn contains the My Documents folder (containing the documents you wrote).
>
> **Windows Vista** The Users folder contains a personal folder (having your name on it), which in turn contains the Documents folder (containing the documents you wrote).
>
> **Windows XP** The "Documents and Settings" folder contains a personal folder (having your name on it), which in turn contains the "My Documents" folder (containing the documents you wrote).

**Views** While you're viewing icons, here's how to change their appearance.

For Windows 7, click the down-arrow near the screen's right edge, left of the question mark, then choose one of these 5 views.

> For most situations, click **Details** (or drag the slider there). That view is what the computer assumes you want anyway (unless you've said otherwise or the computer thinks you're in a picture-oriented folder). For each file, besides the filename you see a small icon and many details about the file.
>
> If you click **Tiles** instead of Details (or drag the slider there), the computer makes the icons easier to see (medium-size instead of small) but includes fewer details about the files.
>
> If you click **Content** (or drag the slider there), you see a compromise between "Details" and "Tiles".
>
> If you click **Large Icons** (or drag the slider there), the computer makes the icons large but omits any details about the files. If you drag the slider to Large Icons then drag further up (toward **Extra Large Icons**), the icons gradually grow even larger; if you drag the slider a bit down (toward **Medium** or **Small**), the icons gradually shrink.
>
> If you click **List** (or drag the slider there), the computer makes the icons small and puts them very close together, so many files can fit on the screen.

Here's a different way to express your desires: if you click the **Views icon** (which is left of the down-arrow) repeatedly, the computer will cycle among those 5 popular choices (from **Details** to **Tiles** to **Content** to **Large Icons** to **List** then back to **Details**).

For Windows Vista, click the down-arrow to the right of "Views", then choose one of these 4 views.

> For most situations, click **Details** (or drag the slider there). That view is what the computer assumes you want anyway (unless you've said otherwise or the computer thinks you're in a picture-oriented folder). For each file, besides the filename you see a tiny icon and many details about the file.
>
> If you click **Tiles** instead of Details (or drag the slider there), the computer makes the icons easier to see ("medium size" instead of "tiny") and includes different details about the files.
>
> If you click **Large Icons** (or drag the slider there), the computer makes the icons large but omits any details about the files. If you drag the slider to Large Icons then drag further up (toward **Extra Large Icons**), the icons gradually grow even larger; if you drag the slider a bit down (toward **Medium** or **Small**), the icons gradually shrink.
>
> If you click **List** (or drag the slider there), the computer makes the icons tiny and omits any details about files, so many files can fit on the screen.

Here's a different way to express your desires: if you click the word "Views" repeatedly, the computer will cycle among those 4 popular choices (from **Details** to **Tiles** to **Large Icons** to **List** then back to **Details**).

For Windows XP, click the word "View", which gives a **View menu**. The menu offer these choices:

> If you click **Tiles**, the icons will get as large and lovely as when you bought the computer.
>
> If you click **Icons**, the icons will get small, so you fit more of them on the screen.
>
> If you click **List**, the icons will get small and organized so you begin by reading down the left column.
>
> If you click **Details**, the icons will get small and accompanied by a comment showing each file's size, type, and the date & time when the file was last modified.
>
> If you click **Thumbnails**, you'll get an effect similar to Tiles, but you'll see a photo instead of a large icon for any file representing a photo (or a graphic similar to a photo).

Usually you'll be happiest if you choose "List".

New folder To create a new folder, do this:

Windows 7 Click "New folder" (which is near the screen's top).
Windows Vista Click "Organize" (which is near the screen's top-left corner) then "New Folder".
Windows XP Click "Make a new folder" (which is at the screen's left edge).

A new folder will appear. Type a name for it (and press Enter).

Close the C window When you finish examining the files that are on hard disk C, close the C window by clicking its X button.

CD-ROM files

The CD-ROM drive resembles drive C. (If your computer is modern, that drive can also create CD-R and CD-RW disks and handle DVD disks.)

Grab a CD-ROM disk that contains computer info, and put it in the CD-ROM drive. (To find out how, read "Find the drive" and "Insert the disk" on page 99.)

The computer will analyze that disk.

If it's a CD that contains music, the computer will automatically start playing the music (as I explained on page 99).

If it's a CD-ROM disk containing a program called autorun.inf, the computer will automatically start running that program, which typically makes the computer run another program, called setup.exe. If you don't want to continue running such programs, exit from them by clicking their X buttons or by clicking whatever "Exit" choices they offer you. Then if you want to find out what's on the disk, right-click the CD-ROM disk's icon (which is in the My Computer window) and click "Open".

If it's a CD-ROM disk that lacks an autorun.inf program, the computer will typically show you a list of files that are on the disk, with their icons. (If the computer doesn't show you that list yet, press Enter.)

When you finish examining any files that are on the CD-ROM disk, close the CD-ROM disk's window by clicking its X button.

Close

When you finish using the My Computer window, close it by clicking its X button.

Find a file's icon

To manipulate a file, the first step is to get the file's icon onto the screen.

If the file's a document you created using WordPad, here's the easiest way to get the file's icon onto the screen:

Make sure you saved the file and you're not in the middle of using it.
Run WordPad.
If you're using WordPad classic, click the Open button. If you're using WordPad 7, click the WordPad button then "Open".
Then you see a list of WordPad documents and their icons.

If the file's a painting you created using Paint, here's the easiest way to get the file's icon onto the screen:

Make sure you saved the file and you're not in the middle of using it.
Run Paint.
If you're using Paint classic, press Ctrl with O. If you're using Paint 7, click the Paint button then "Open".
Then you see a list of Paint's paintings and their icons.

If the file's on disk C, here's another way to get the file's icon onto the screen. *For Windows Vista & 7*, try this:

Click Start.
Begin typing the file's name — or whatever part of the name you remember. (You don't have to capitalize.) For example, if you want to search for WordPad, start typing "wordpad". If you want search for a file that might be called "Lovers" or "My love" or "To my lovely", you can start typing just "love". As you type, you see a list of files (and programs) that match what you've typed so far. The more of the file's name that you type, the more accurate the list will be. The list has an icon for each file.

For Windows XP, try this:

Click Start then "Search" then "All files and folders".
Type the file's name. At the end of that typing, press Enter.
The computer will show you icons for all such files, in a window. Maximize that window (by clicking its maximize button).

Another way to get a file's icon onto the screen is to go to the My Computer window and click icons for drives & files until you find the file you want.

Many programs put documents into a folder called Documents (or My Documents). Here's how to see what documents are in that folder....

Windows Vista & 7:	click Start then "Documents"
Windows XP:	click "start" then "My Documents"

The Paint program puts paintings into a folder called Pictures (or My Pictures). Here's how to see what's in that folder....

Windows Vista & 7:	click Start then "Pictures"
Windows XP:	click "start" then "My Pictures"

Some programs put music into a folder called Music (or My Music). Here's how to see what's in that folder....

Windows Vista & 7:	click Start then "Music"
Windows XP:	click "start" then "My Music"

Manipulate a file

Now I'll explain how to manipulate a file.

If you want to practice this stuff, use a file you don't mind wrecking. For example, create a WordPad document containing just once sentence (such as "I love you") and save it as a file called "Love".

To manipulate a file, find its icon (by using the tricks in the previous section) then do one of these activities....

Send to USB flash drive

Here's how to copy the file to a USB flash drive.

Close all windows (by clicking their X).

Plug the USB flash drive into one of the computer's USB ports. (To do that, you must first uncover the flash drive, if the flash drive had a protective cover.)

If the flash drive has a light, that light will flash awhile.

When any light stops flashing, you might see the AutoPlay window:

That window tells you the flash drive's letter (such as "E:" or "F:" or "J:"), which you should memorize. That window also asks whether you want to open a folder, but don't bother answering the question: just close that window (by clicking its X).

Which file to you want to copy to the flash drive? Right-click that file's icon, then click "Send to" then the flash drive's letter.

If the flash drive has a light, that light will flash. When the light stops flashing, the file's been copied.

Send to CD

Here's how to copy the file to a CD (or DVD) disk.

Windows 7 What CD do you want to copy the file to? Put that CD (which is blank or partially blank) into the drive.

If the CD has never been used before (or was totally reformatted), do this:

> Click "Burn files to disk". Invent a name for the disk. The name must be short (no more than 16 characters). Type the name (and press Enter).

If the CD is rewritable (CD-RW), the computer will say, "The format might take a long time"; to reply, press Enter then wait about 25 minutes.

The computer will say "Open folder to view files". Press Enter. You'll see the CD's folder.

Which file do you want to copy to the CD? Use any of these techniques:

> Method 1: Click the file's icon then "Burn". (This method works just if you see "Burn".)
>
> Method 2: Drag the file's icon to the CD's folder. (This method works just if you see the file's icon and the CD's folder simultaneously.)
>
> Method 3: Right-click the file's icon, then click "Send to" then "DVD RW Drive".

Copy more files that way, if you like.

When you finish copying files, click "Eject" (which is at the top of the CD's window). The computer writes final notes onto the disk then opens the drive's tray.

Remove the CD. Push the tray back in.

Windows Vista If you see "Burn" (at the top of the window where you saw the file's icon), click the file's icon then "Burn"; if you don't see that choice, right-click the file's icon then click "Send To" then "DVD RW Drive".

The computer will open the drive's door (tray). Put a blank CD or DVD disk onto the tray. Push the tray back in.

Invent a name for the disk. The name must be short (no more than 16 characters). Type the name (and press Enter).

If the CD is rewritable (CD-RW), the computer will say, "The format might take a long time"; to reply, press Enter then wait about 25 minutes.

The computer will copy the file to the disk. Then it will say "Files Currently on the Disc".

If you wish, copy another file to the disk (by clicking the file's icon then "Burn").

Press the drive's button (which is on the system unit below the drive's tray). The computer says "Preparing to eject". The computer writes final notes onto the disk then opens the drive's tray.

Remove the CD. Push the tray back in.

Windows XP Put the CD into the drive. (If the computer asks "What do you want Windows to do?", click "Take no action" then press Enter.)

Right-click the file's icon; click "Send To" then the CD's icon. That copies the file to a list called "Files ready to be written to the CD". Copy more files to that list, if you like.

Then copy that entire list to the CD, as follows:

> Click "You have files waiting to be written to the CD" then "Write these files to CD".
> Invent a name for the CD. Type the name (and press Enter).
> The computer will write onto the CD.
> Then the computer will eject the CD from the drive and say "You have successfully written your files to the CD". Press Enter.

Send to My Documents folder

For Windows 7, here's how to copy the file to your hard disk's My Documents folder (if the file isn't there already):

> Right-click the file's icon. Click "Send To" then "Documents". Then the computer copies the file to the My Documents folder.

For Windows Vista, here's how to copy the file to your hard disk's Documents folder (if the file isn't there already):

> Right-click the file's icon. Click "Send To" then "Documents". Then the computer copies the file to the Documents folder.

For Windows XP, here's how to copy the file to your hard disk's "My Documents" folder (if the file isn't there already):

> Right-click the file's icon. Click "Send To" then "My Documents". Then the computer copies the file to the "My Documents" folder.

Send to Desktop

To copy the file to your Desktop (which is the main screen), do this:

> Right-click the file's icon. Click "Send To" then "Desktop".

To save disk space, that technique copies just the file's icon to the Desktop. The file itself stays just in its original location.

On the Desktop, the file's icon's bottom left corner has a bent arrow, which means the icon is just a **shortcut** (which points the computer to the original location).

Here's how that shortcut icon is named:

> **Windows Vista & 7** That shortcut icon has the file's original name but with "- Shortcut" added afterwards. For example, if the file's original name was "Love", the shortcut icon's name is "Love - Shortcut".
>
> **Windows XP** That shortcut icon has the file's original name but with "Shortcut to" added in front. For example, if the file's original name was "Love", the shortcut icon's name is "Shortcut to Love".

If you double-click that shortcut icon, the computer will try to find the original file and run it. If the original file was on a floppy disk or CD, that works just if the file's floppy disk or CD is still in the drive.

Send to a different location

To copy the file to a different location (such as a folder on your hard drive), do this:

> Right-click the file's icon. Click "Copy". Right-click in any blank space (in any drive or any folder) where you want the copy to appear. Click "Paste".

Rename

To change the file's name, do this:

> Click the file's icon then the file's name. Type the new name (and press Enter).

If the file's on a hard disk or floppy disk, that procedure works fine. **If the file's on a CD, that procedure works in Windows Vista & 7 but not in Windows XP.**

Delete

To delete the file, try this procedure:

> Click the file's icon. Press the Delete key. Press Enter.

Does that procedure *really* delete the file? Here's the answer.

> If the file's on a floppy disk, that procedure really deletes the file.
>
> If the file's on a hard disk, that procedure just moves the file to the **Recycle Bin** (which holds hard-disk files you said to delete).
>
> If the file's on a CD, Windows XP usually refuses to delete the file.
>
> If the file's on a CD, Windows Vista & 7 analyze the CD: if the disk is **rewriteable** (CD-RW), the computer **deletes** the file; if the disk is just **CD-R** (which can't delete), the computer **hides** the file so it's inaccessible (though still taking up space on the disk); if the disk is a **plain CD** (which can't be altered at all), the computer **complains**.

**Peek in the Recycle Bin** To discover what's in the hard disk's Recycle Bin (which holds hard-disk files you said to delete), double-click the **Recycle Bin icon** (which is typically at the screen's left edge but might have moved elsewhere, such as to the screen's bottom right corner). You'll see the **Recycle Bin window**, which shows a list of hard-disk files you said to delete. (If you don't see a file list, the Recycle Bin is empty.)

To see lots of info about the files in the Recycle Bin, make sure the Recycle Bin window is maximized (so it consumes the whole screen). Make sure you're seeing the Details view, by doing this:

Windows 7 Click the down-arrow that's near the screen's right edge, left of the question mark, then click "Details".

Windows Vista Click the down-arrow that's to the right of "Views" then click "Details".

Windows XP Click "View" then "Details".

To see even more details about a certain file, right-click the file's icon and then click "Properties". When you finish admiring the details, click "OK".

If you change your mind and do _not_ want to delete a certain file, click the file's icon then "Restore this item". That makes the computer pull the file out of the Recycle Bin and put the file back to its original location on the hard disk.

If, on the other hand, you really _do_ want to delete a certain file, click the file's icon then press the Delete key then press Enter. The file will disappear.

To delete _all_ files from the Recycle Bin, click "Empty the Recycle Bin" (which is at the screen's _top_ in Windows Vista & 7 but at the screen's _left edge_ in Windows XP). Then press Enter.

When you finish admiring the Recycle Bin window, click its X button.

**Shift Delete** You've learned that to delete a file, the usual procedure is to click the file's icon, then tap the Delete key, then tap the Enter key. If the file was on the hard disk, that procedure moves the file into the Recycle Bin. Notice that the procedure involves tapping the Delete key. If instead you tap the Delete key _while holding down the Shift key_, the computer deletes the file immediately instead of moving it to the Recycle Bin.

Multiple files

To "delete" or "send" several files at once, highlight the files you want to manipulate. Here's how:

Method 1 Click the first file you want to manipulate. _While holding down the Ctrl key,_ click each of the other files you want to manipulate. That highlights all those files. (If you make a mistake and accidentally highlight an extra file, click it again while holding down the Ctrl key, to remove its highlighting.)

Method 2 Click the first file you want to manipulate. _While holding down the Shift key,_ click the last file you want to manipulate. That highlights the first file you want, the last file you want, and also all files in between.

Method 3 Click the first file you want to manipulate. _While holding down the Ctrl key,_ tap the A key (which stands for "all"). That highlights _all_ files in the folder.

Those methods work best while you're _not_ running a program. They do _not_ work while you're running a primitive program (such as WordPad). Those methods sometimes work while you're running a fancy program (such as Microsoft Word).

After highlighting the files, do this:

If you want to "delete" the files, press the Delete key then Enter.

If you want to "send" the files, right-click the first file and follow the rest of my instructions about how to send where you wish.

You'll discover that the other files magically "tag along" with the first file, because they're highlighted also.

Erase entire CD-RW

Here's how to erase an entire CD-RW disk:

Windows 7 Put the CD-RW disk into the drive. You see that disk's window. At the window's left edge, you see "DVD RW Drive"; right-click it. Click "Erase this disc". Press Enter. The computer will spend about a minute erasing all files from the CD-RW disk. Then the computer will say "You have erased the files on this disc." Press Enter.

Windows Vista Put the CD-RW disk into the drive. You see that disk's window. Click "Erase this disc". Press Enter. The computer will spend about a minute erasing all files from the CD-RW disk. Then the computer will say "You have erased the files on this disc." Press Enter.

Windows XP Put the CD-RW disk into the drive. In the My Computer window, right-click the CD-RW drive's icon. Click "Erase this CD-RW". Press Enter. The computer will spend about a minute erasing all files from the CD-RW disk. Then the computer will say "You have successfully erased the files on this CD-RW disc." Click "Finish".

Tricks

These tricks will make you a pro and amaze your friends.

Sample music

Windows comes with free samples of music.

**Windows 7** Here's how to hear 3 samples of music.

Click Start then "Music". Double-click "Sample Music". You see the names of 3 musical samples:

"Kalimba" (funky electronic by Mr. Scruff)
"Maid with the Flaxen Hair" (classical romantic orchestra by Debussy)
"Sleep Away" (smooth jazz piano by Bob Acri)

Each name begins with an icon of a musical note. Double-click whichever sample you want to hear. If the computer says "Welcome to Windows Media Player", click "Recommended settings" then "Finish".

**Windows Vista** Here's how to hear several types of music:

Click Start then "Music". Double-click "Sample Music". Maximize the window. You see the names of 11 musical samples; each name begins with an icon of a musical note. Double-click whichever sample you want to hear.

**Windows XP** Here's how to hear Beethoven or blues:

Click Start then "My Music". Double-click "Sample Music". Then double-click "Beethoven's Symphony No. 9 (Scherzo)" or "New Stories (Highway Blues)".

Here's how to hear David Byrne sing about what humans do:

Method 1 Click "Start" then "My Computer". Double-click "Shared Documents" then "Shared Music" then "music David Byrne".

Method 2 Click "Start" then "All Programs" then "Windows Media Player". Make sure you see "David Byrne" (near the screen's top left corner). Click the big "▶" (at the screen's bottom left corner).

Method 3 Your computer might have a shortcut way to start Windows Media Player. For example, if you see a "Windows Media Player" icon to the right of the "Start" button, click that icon; or if you see a "Windows Media Player" icon at the screen's left edge, double-click it; or if you click "Start" and then see a "Windows Media Player" icon, click it. Once you've finally started Windows Media Player, make sure you see "David Byrne" (near the top left corner). Click the big "▶" (at the screen's bottom left corner).

Sample video

Windows comes with free sample video.

**Windows 7** Here's how to see a sample video.

Click Start then "Computer". Click "Videos" (which is on the left). Double-click "Sample Videos" then "Wildlife".

Windows Vista Here's how to see 3 samples of video.

> Click Start then "Computer". Click "Public" (which is on the left). Double-click "Public Videos" then "Sample Videos". You see the names of 3 video samples ("Bear", "Butterfly", and "Lake"); double-click whichever video you want to view.

Windows XP Here's how to see a sample video.

> Click Start then "My Documents". Double-click "My Videos" then "Windows Movie Maker Sample File".

Recently used

The computer keeps track of what you've recently used.

When you click Start, you see a list of the programs you've used most often recently. That list appears at the screen's left edge, above "All Programs" but below the horizontal line under "E-mail".

> In Windows XP, that list shows 6 programs.
> In Windows Vista, that list shows 9 programs.
> In Windows 7, that list shows 10 programs.

Sleep

When you try to shut down the computer, the computer might take several seconds — or even several *minutes* — to do so. When you try to turn the computer back on, the computer might take several seconds — or several *minutes* — to do so. You might get annoyed at waiting for the computer to shut down and turn back on — especially during your lunch break!

Instead of telling the computer to "shut down" and then "turn back on", you can tell the computer to "**sleep**" and then "**wake** back up". The computer can go to "sleep" almost instantly and "wake up" almost instantly, so you don't have to wait.

While the computer sleeps, you can say it's "**napping**" and "**in standby mode**".

How to make the computer sleep
To make the computer sleep, try one of these 4 methods:

> Method 1: if your computer is a laptop or notebook, close its lid (so you don't see the screen).
>
> Method 2: if your keyboard has a Sleep key (which has a picture of a crescent moon or Z^Z on it), press it. Exception: if the Sleep key also has an F on it (such as F5), press the Sleep key *while holding down the Fn key*.
>
> Method 3: For *Windows 7*, click Start then the Shut Down button's right-arrow then "Sleep"; for *Windows Vista*, click Start then the on-screen Sleep button (which is brown, to the right of "Start Search", and shows a circle interrupted by a vertical line);. for *Windows XP*, click "start" then "Turn Off Computer" then the "Stand By" button;
>
> Method 4: don't touch the keyboard or mouse for 20 minutes.

Go ahead: try one of those sleep methods! It's okay to give one of those "sleep" commands anytime — even while you're running a program whose window is still open and whose work is still unsaved.

What happens during sleep
When you give a sleep command, the computer makes a note in its RAM about what you've been doing. On most computers, Windows Vista's sleep command does **hybrid sleep** (where the computer also copies its RAM to the hard disk, for extra protection).

Then the screen goes black and the computer takes a nap. While the computer is napping, it uses little electricity (about 5 watts) and its power light flashes.

If the computer is a laptop or notebook whose battery is running out and the computer isn't using hybrid sleep, Windows Vista will realize the emergency, copy the RAM's information to the hard disk, and put itself into a nearly powerless state called **hibernation**.

Waking
The best way to wake the computer from its nap is to tap the Shift key. Other ways, which usually work, are to tap any other key on the keyboard, or jiggle the mouse (or the table it's on), or press the mouse's button. If none of those techniques work, quickly tap the system unit's power button (which wakes the system unit from sleep and hibernation).

The computer will waken and make its screen show exactly the same image as when you put the computer to sleep, so you can continue your work where you left off. (Exception: if your computer has a password or several different users, the computer might ask you to identify yourself first.)

Is sleep good?
Sleep is fun, cute, consumes significantly less electricity than leaving the computer fully on, and happens fast enough to maximize your lunch break. But at night you should turn the computer off completely by giving the usual "Shut Down" command, which erases the computer's RAM and lets the computer start fresh the next day.

Run

Here's a different way to tell the computer to run WordPad:

> Click Start. (For Windows Vista & 7, then click "All Programs" then "Accessories".) Click "Run", then type "wordpad" (and press Enter).

To run Paint instead of WordPad, type "mspaint" instead of "wordpad". To run the Calculator, type "calc" instead. To play Pinball (which is included in Windows XP), type "pinball" instead.

When you buy a program, it typically comes on a disk (a floppy disk or a CD-ROM disk). The instructions for copying it onto your hard disk might say to run a program called "setup". To obey such instructions, do this:

> Put the floppy disk or CD-ROM disk into your disk drive. Click Start. For Windows Vista, then click "All Programs" then "Accessories".) Click "Run".
>
> If the program came on a floppy disk, type "a:setup". If the program came on a CD-ROM disk and your CD-ROM drive is called "D:", type "d:setup". If the program came on a CD-ROM disk and your CD-ROM drive is called "E:", type "e:setup".
>
> At the end of your typing, press Enter.

For some programs, the instructions say to type "install" instead of "setup".

Control Panel

To control your computer completely, go to the **Control Panel**. To do that, click "Start" then "Control Panel". Maximize the window.

You can see 2 **views**.

The **category home view** shows you these categories:

Windows XP	Windows Vista	Windows 7
	System and Maintenance	
Appearance and Themes	Security	System and Security
Network and Internet Connections	Network and Internet	Network and Internet
Add or Remove Programs		
Sounds, Speech, and Audio Devices	Hardware and Sound	Hardware and Sound
Performance and Maintenance	Programs	Programs
Printers and Other Hardware		
User Accounts	User Accounts and Family Safety	User Accounts and Family Safety
	Appearance and Personalization	Appearance and Personalization
Date, Time, Language, and Regional Options	Clock, Language, and Region	Clock, Language, and Region
Accessibility Options	Ease of Access	Ease of Access
Security Center	Additional Options	

(Windows Vista & 7 also show subcategories.)

The **icon classic view** shows you these icons instead:

Windows XP	Windows Vista	Windows 7
Accessibility Options		
Add Hardware	Add Hardware	
Add or Remove Programs		Action Center
Administrative Tools	Administrative Tools	Administrative Tools
Automatic Updates	AutoPlay	AutoPlay
	Backup and Restore Center	Backup and Restore
	Color Management	Color Management
		Credential Manager
Date and Time	Date and Time	Date and Time
	Default Programs	Default Programs
		Desktop Gadgets
	Device Manager	Device Manager
		Devices and Printers
Display		Display
	Ease of Access Center	Ease of Access Center
Folder Options	Folder Options	Folder Options
Fonts	Fonts	Fonts
Game Controllers	Game Controllers	Getting Started
		HomeGroup
Indexing Options	Indexing Options	Indexing Options
Internet Options	Internet Options	Internet Options
	iSCSI Initiator	
Keyboard	Keyboard	Keyboard
		Location and Other Sensors
Mouse	Mouse	Mouse
Network Connections	Network and Sharing Center	Network and Sharing Center
Network Setup Wizard		Notification Area Icons
	Parental Controls	Parental Controls
	Pen and Input Devices	
	People Near Me	
	Performance Information and Tools	Performance Information and Tools
	Personalization	Personalization
Phone and Modem Options	Phone and Modem Options	Phone and Modem
Power Options	Power Options	Power Options
Printers and Faxes	Printers	
	Problem Reports and Solutions	
	Programs and Features	Programs and Features
		Recovery
Regional and Language Options	Regional and Language Options	Region and Language
		RemoteApp and Desktop Connections
Scanners and Cameras	Scanners and Cameras	
Scheduled Tasks		
Security Center	Security Center	
Sounds and Audio Devices	Sound	Sound
Speech	Speech Recognition	Speech Recognition
	Sync Center	Sync Center
System	System	System
	Tablet PC Settings	
Taskbar and Start Menu	Taskbar and Start Menu	Taskbar and Start Menu
	Text to Speech	Troubleshooting
User Accounts	User Accounts	User Accounts
	Welcome Center	
	Windows Anytime Upgrade	Windows Anytime Upgrade
Windows CardSpace	Windows CardSpace	Windows CardSpace
	Windows Defender	Windows Defender
Windows Firewall	Windows Firewall	Windows Firewall
Wireless Network Setup Wizard	Windows Sidebar Properties	Windows Mobility Center
	Windows SideShow	
	Windows Update	Windows Update

(Windows XP's oldest versions omit Automatic Updates, Indexing Options, Network Setup Wizard, Security Center, Windows CardSpace, Windows Firewall, and Wireless Network Setup Wizard.)

Here's how to switch between those 2 views:

Windows 7 In the screen's top-right corner, click in the "View by" box. Then click "Category" or "Large icons".

Windows Vista In the screen's top-left corner, click "Control Panel Home" or "Classic View".

Windows XP In the screen's top-left corner, click "Switch to Category View" or "Switch to Classic View".

Pointer trails For your first experiment in Control Panel, play with pointer trails. Here's how.

Go to icon classic view.

For Windows 7, click the Mouse icon. For Windows XP & Vista, *double*-click the Mouse icon.

Click "Pointer Options".

Then if you put a ✔ in the "Display pointer trails" box by clicking it, you'll see a trail of mouse pointers whenever you move the mouse.

To make the trail be long and obvious, make sure the slider is dragged toward the right, to the "Long" position.

The long trail helps you notice the mouse pointer more easily. It's useful when you're giving a presentation to a group of people and want to make sure they always notice where the mouse is moving.

If you change your mind, stop the trails by clicking the "Display pointer trails" box again, so the check mark disappears.

When you finish experimenting with pointer trails, close the Mouse Properties window by clicking "OK".

Experimenting You can experiment by clicking (or double-clicking) any of the other icons in the Control Panel window, but be careful! If you tell the computer to use hardware you don't own, Windows will stop working! Before changing a setting, make a note to yourself of what the setting was, so you can get back to it! Be especially cautious about playing with the Display icon, since if you make a wrong choice your screen will be unreadable!

When you finish playing with the Control Panel window, close it by clicking its X button.

Notepad

Notepad is a stripped-down version of WordPad. Notepad is easier but does less.

Like WordPad, Notepad comes free as part of modern Windows.

Since WordPad does more than Notepad, most people prefer WordPad rather than Notepad. But sometimes WordPad is *too* fancy and *too* complex, and Notepad's primitive simplicity is appealing. Notepad is popular for writing "short notes", "computer programs", and "pages to put on the Internet". Notepad will confuse you less often than WordPad, since Notepad does less. It's retro; it's cool! Try it! Here's how....

To start using Notepad, click Start then "Programs" then "Accessories" then "Notepad". Make sure the Notepad window consumes the whole screen. (If it doesn't consume the whole screen yet, maximize the window by clicking the maximize button, which is next to the X button.)

Start typing whatever you wish, as if you were using WordPad. Here are the differences....

No formatting saved When you save the document (copy it to the hard disk), Notepad saves info about which characters you typed (which letters of the alphabet, digits, and symbols, and where you hit the Space bar, the Enter key, and Tab key); but it saves no info about the document's appearance. Notepad doesn't save any info about fonts, boldfacing, italics, underlining, font size, color, centering, justification, margins, or bullets; all those features are missing.

The document that's saved is called a **plain-text document**, since it contains just text, no formatting.

A stripped-down word-processing program (such as Notepad) that produces just pure text documents (and saves no formatting) is called a **plain-text editor**.

While you stare at your document (in the Notepad window), which font are you seeing? Here's the answer:

> The font is 10-point Lucida Console, unless you switch to a different font (by clicking "Format" then "Font" then choosing a different font then clicking "OK"). The font you choose affects Notepad forever (it affects how Notepad displays *all* documents), unless you switch fonts again.

But when you save your document, no font info is saved as part of the document.

Optional word wrap If you type near the screen's right edge, and you type a word that's too long to fit on the screen, WordPad automatically moves the word to the line below. Notepad does so just if you request **word wrap**.

Here's how to request word wrap:

> Click "Format". You see "Word Wrap". If there's no check mark before "Word Wrap", put a check mark there by clicking "Word Wrap".

No buttons Notepad has no buttons.

> Instead of clicking a Save button, click File then Save.
> Instead of clicking a Print button, click File then Print.
> Instead of clicking an Open button, click File then Open.
> Instead of clicking a New button, click File then New.

No drag & drop To move a phrase, WordPad lets you use drag & drop, but Notepad doesn't understand that; Notepad requires you to use cut & paste instead. So here's how to move a phrase in Notepad: select the phrase (by dragging across it), then say "cut" (by pressing Ctrl with X), then click where you want the phrase to be, then say "paste Velcro" (by pressing Ctrl with V).

Keyboard

A traditional keyboard contains 101 keys. If your keyboard is designed especially for modern Windows, it contains 3 extra keys near the Space bar, so you get 104 keys altogether (or more).

Two of those extra keys are the **Windows keys**: each shows a flying window. **If you press either of the Windows keys, the Start menu appears**. So pressing either of those keys has the same effect as if your mouse clicked the Start button. You can press *either* of the Windows keys: those two keys serve the same purpose as each other, except that one is nearer your left hand, the other is nearer your right. Your keyboard has two Shift keys, two Ctrl keys, two Alt keys, and two Windows keys.

The other extra key, called the **Menu key**, shows an arrow pointing at a menu. **If you press the Menu key, a shortcut menu appears.** For example, if you click an icon and then press the menu key, that icon's shortcut menu appears.

Property window Here are 4 ways to make an icon's property window appear....

> **Right-click method:** right-click the icon (so the icon's shortcut menu appears), then click "Properties"
>
> **Menu-key method:** click the icon, press the Menu key (so the icon's shortcut menu appears), then either click "Properties" or press the R key (which is the code for "Properties")
>
> **Alt-double method:** while holding down the Alt key, double-click the icon
>
> **Alt-Enter method:** click the icon; then while holding down the Alt key, tap the Enter key

Use whichever method you wish! My favorites are the right-click method (which feels the most natural) and the Alt-double method (which is usually the fastest).

Alt F4 While a window is open, try this experiment: while holding down the Alt key, tap the F4 key. That makes the computer click the window's X button, so the window closes.

Suppose your mouse stops working (because the mouse is broken or the computer gets too confused to handle the mouse). To get out of that mess, press Alt F4 several times. That starts the process of closing the windows and shutting down the computer. Finish shutting down the computer (as best as you can), then try again to turn the computer on.

Help

To get more help about using Windows, you can click Start then "Help and Support". You see the Help and Support window. Maximize it (by clicking its maximize button).

What topic do you want help about? To express your desire, do this —

> You see a list of the *major* topics. Click the topic you want. Then you see a list of subtopics; click the subtopic you want.

or do this:

> Click in the **Search Help box**. (That box is at the screen's top. In Windows XP; it's labeled "Search"; in Windows Vista & 7, it says "Search Help" and has a magnifying glass at its right edge.) Type any topic you can imagine. Your typing will appear in that box. Then press Enter.

If you want to go back to seeing the previous screenful of help, click the **Back button** (the white left-arrow at the screen's top-left corner).

When you finish using help, close the Help and Support window by clicking its X button.

Internet
Providers

A **computer network** is a group of computers (or computer terminals) that communicate with each other (by **phone** or other **cables** or **wireless** transmissions).

Now the most popular computer network is the **Internet**. It connects computers all over the world, by phone lines and by other communication methods that are faster. You can connect *your* computer to the Internet, so you can access computers all over the world, peek at their hard disks, and transfer their info to *your* computer. Now the Internet transfers games, news, photos, love letters, chitchat, ads, and globs of other info, public and private, to and from Barack Obama, David Letterman, and many *millions* of other workers, jokers, kids, and kooks across the country and around the world.

You can use the Internet to send and receive electronic mail. You can also use the Internet to browse through announcements posted by folks worldwide.

The Internet gives you a huge sea of info. You stand on its shore, watch its many waves come at you, and get high by joyously jumping into those waves. That's called **surfing the Net**, which means "browsing through the amazing info available on the Net".

You'll quickly get addicted to surfing the Net and spend many hours each day doing it. As you explore the Net, your electronic requests and their responses travel at electronic speeds around the world, on what Vice President Al Gore dubbed the **Information Superhighway (I-way)**, propelling you through **cyberspace** (the vast, surreal world where all info and people are represented by bits, bytes, and electronic signals, as opposed to the "real world", called **meatspace**, where people are composed of meat).

The Internet lets your mind fly around the world faster than a astronaut's. Your friends will call you an **infonaut** or **Internaut**. Cynics will call you an **Internut** or **Net-head**. But no matter what folks call you, you'll have fun, while learning more about the world than any pre-computer human could ever imagine.

The Internet lets you read facts & opinions contributed by many people. If you contribute *your* thoughts in a positive way, so they can be read by other people on the Internet and you've improved our world somehow, you're called a "good Internet citizen," a **netizen**.

Here's how the Internet arose — and how to attach yourself to it.

How the Internet arose

The Internet arose because of the Cold War. Here are the details....

Cold War research

Back in 1957, while the US was fighting the Cold War against Russia, the Russians launched the first satellite, **Sputnik**. That made the US military wake up and realize it was dangerously behind Russia in scientific research. In 1958 the US **Department of Defense (DoD)** reacted by creating the **Advanced Research Projects Agency (Arpa)**, which paid universities to do scientific research to help win the Cold War against Russia.

Arpanet

In 1969, Arpa created a clever computer network, called **Arpanet**, to let university computers send data over phone lines using a sneaky method that would work even if Russians bombed the phone lines.

The sneaky method was called **packet switching**.

> It divided each computer message into many little **packets** and sent the packets over the phone lines intelligently: if a packet couldn't reach its destination directly (because a phone line got bombed), the computer would sneakily switch that packet through different phone lines to different computers that would reroute the packet to its ultimate destination. At the ultimate destination, a computer would automatically make sure all the packets arrived, put them into the proper order, and make any lost (or damaged) packets be retransmitted.

At first, the Arpanet included just 4 computers: 1 at the University of Utah and 3 in California (at UCLA, UC Santa Barbara, and the Stanford Research Institute).

The next year (1970), Arpanet added 3 computers in Massachusetts (at MIT, BBN, and Rand). The next year (1971), Arpanet added more computers (in California, Massachusetts, Pennsylvania, Ohio, and Illinois), to make a total of 15 computers.

The next year (1972), Arpanet expanded to more parts of the country, so 2000 people were using Arpanet — and they were starting to have fun, since **electronic mail (e-mail)** was added to Arpanet that year. (Before that, Arpanet was just a big boring mass of technical documents & data.) The next year (1973), e-mail became so popular that 75% of all Arpanet transmissions were e-mails; and research institutions in **England** and **Norway** joined Arpanet, so Arpanet became international.

In 1979, the first **newsgroups** were created. (A newsgroup is a running discussion of facts and opinions, contributed by the newsgroup's readers, so it becomes a gigantic collection of "letters to the editor about the other letters that were written".)

On October 27, 1980, the entire Arpanet got shut down by a **virus** that was spread accidentally. Yes, a virus can accomplish what bombs cannot! Fortunately, the virus was eradicated.

Many universities around the world joined Arpanet because it was nifty, funded, and could be used for non-military purposes also, such as personal e-mail.

Split

Arpanet finally became too big to be managed simply, so in 1983 the military divided it into *two* networks:

> One network, called **Milnet**, was strictly for use by military personnel (at military bases).
> The other network, called "the new, smaller Arpanet", was for civilian use (at universities).

To let those two networks communicate with each other, an inter-network communication method was invented, called the **Internet Protocol (IP)**. That's how the Internet began!

IP came in several versions, the most popular being the **Transmission Control Protocol for IP (TCP/IP)**.

At the end of 1983, the Internet included about 600 **hosts** (computers that had permanent Internet addresses and could supply data to other computers). The Internet grew fast:

Year	How many Internet hosts at end of year
1981	200
1982	300
1983	600
1984	1,000
1985	2,000
1986	6,000
1987	30,000
1988	80,000
1989	200,000
1990	400,000
1991	700,000
1992	1,300,000
1993	2,200,000
1994	5,800,000
1995	14,000,000
1996	21,000,000
1997	29,000,000
1998	43,000,000
1999	72,000,000
2000	109,000,000
2001	147,000,000
2002	171,000,000
2003	233,000,000
2004	317,000,000
2005	394,000,000
2006	433,000,000
2007	541,000,000
2008	625,000,000

Let's see why it grew so fast....

National Science Foundation

In 1986, the **National Science Foundation (NSF)** wanted to let researchers share 5 supercomputers by using Arpanet, but NSF quickly changed its mind and decided to create its own network, called **NSF Net**. Like Arpanet, NSF Net used TCP/IP and was Arpanet-compatible, so NSF Net became part of the Internet. NSF Net ran faster than Arpanet (by running more phone lines between big cities, to form a strong Internet **backbone**), so universities switched to it from Arpanet. In 1990, Arpanet shut down permanently.

Arpa, which had created Arpanet, lived on but under its new name: the **Defense Advanced Research Projects Agency (Darpa)**.

Packet switching was practical

Though packet switching was invented as a way to avoid bombs, it turned out to have another advantage: it prevented any single user from hogging the Internet.

If a "bad guy" tries to hog the Internet by sending a long message, the Internet is smart enough to divide his message into many little packets. Other users are given a chance to squeeze their packets into the system without waiting for all the bad guy's packets to go through. Any overloaded phone lines are automatically bypassed by routing some packets through other phone lines managed by other computers.

Packet switching made the Internet be "free for democracy" in four senses:

free from destruction by bombs
free from overload by user hogs
free from censorship by governments
free from big start-up costs (because government already paid for the backbone)

You can still wreck a country's Internet if you're evil enough to bomb *all* phone lines or send *many* long messages or force *all* Internet computers to censor transmissions. Though misguided folks tried such tactics, the Internet outlasted them.

Web

The Internet was just a tedious collection of documents, data, and e-mails until 1990, when an Englishman named **Tim Berners-Lee** invented a nifty Internet feature called the **World Wide Web (WWW)**. To be briefer, folks call it just the **Web**. Here's how it works:

It lets you view a document on the Internet and, if a word in the document is underlined, you can click on that word to get "more info" about that word. The "more info" can be a whole page of info about that word and reside in a different file on a different hard disk in a different computer in a different country; so by just clicking that underlined word, you're suddenly accessing relevant info from a different computer in a different country. The person who invented the original document sets all that up for you, so by just clicking the underlined word you automatically access the info you want without needing to know what computer or country it's coming from.

The World Wide Web turns a whole world of documents into a unified system.

In that system, each page can contain *many* underlined words. Clicking an underlined word transports you to another page (on another computer) that contains related info and in turn has its own underlined words that you can click on to get to other related pages.

The underlined words are called **links**, because they link you to other documents.

To invent the Web, Tim was inspired by **Ted Nelson**.

Ted Nelson was a US visionary who in 1965 had predicted that text would someday be connected worldwide by underlined links and called hypertext. Ted Nelson's concept furthered what an earlier visionary, **Vannevar Bush**, had written in 1945.

Tim was the first person to take the ideas of Ted & Vannevar, apply them to the Internet, and make the whole system practical enough for humans to use.

Tim invented the World Wide Web while he was working in Switzerland at the **European Laboratory for Particle Physics**, which at that time was called the **Conseil Européen pour la Recherche Nucléaire (CERN)**. Afterwards, Tim moved to the **Massachusetts Institute of Technology (MIT)**, where he directs the **World Wide Web Consortium (W3C)**, which plans the Web's future.

War

The US's allies copied Internet technology — and so did the US's enemies:

In January 1991, during the Gulf War, the Internet's ability to defend itself against bombs was proved in a strange way: Iraq's own Internet helped Iraq's military command network withstand attack from US bombs!

In August 1991, the Soviet Union was paralyzed by a news blackout during the coup against Gorbachev, but the truth got out to the world by Internet transmissions from **Relcom** (a small pro-Yeltsin Internet service provider in the Soviet Union).

Mosaic

To use the World Wide Web, you had to use a program called a **browser**. When Tim invented the World Wide Web, he also invented his own browser, which was crude. The first *pleasant* browser was **Mosaic**, invented in 1994 by Marc Andreessen, an undergrad at the University of Illinois' **National Center for Supercomputing Applications (NCSA)**.

Since his research was funded by the National Science Foundation, everybody was allowed to copy Mosaic for free.

Later that year, he left NCSA and formed a company called **Netscape Communications Corp.**, which invented an improved Web browser (called **Netscape Navigator**) and sold it cheaply ($50 or less, per copy).

Mosaic and Netscape made the Web become much more popular. At the beginning of 1994, there were 600 **Web sites** (places on the Web that provide Web info); at the end of 1994, the number of Web sites shot up to 10,000; in later years, the number of Web sites continued to climb:

Year	How many Web sites at end of year
1993	600
1994	10,000
1995	100,000
1996	600,000
1997	1,700,000
1998	3,700,000
1999	9,600,000

Mass market

In 1995, these events made the Internet suddenly become more popular:

Netscape Navigator version 2 came out. It worked much better than version 1.

Windows 95 came out. It handled the Internet much better than Windows 3.11.

Microsoft invented Internet Explorer. Like Netscape Navigator, it was based on Mosaic and initially sold for $50 or less. Soon afterwards, Microsoft began giving Internet Explorer away for free.

The World Wide Web reached a critical mass: enough good Web sites had been created to make browsing worthwhile for the average consumer.

Many training schools began offering crash courses in how to use the Internet.

Yes, 1995 was the year that the general American public got excited about the Internet.

That year, the Internet got too big for the NSF to fund. The NSF stopped running NSF Net but gave grants to help universities buy Internet time from commercial networks that had sprung up, such as **Sprint**, **Alternet**, and **Performance Systems International (PSI)**. Consumers, sitting at home with their personal computers, could use the Internet by telling their computer modems to phone an **Internet service provider (ISP)**, which was part of the Internet. Many companies sprang up to act as ISPs.

Before the Internet became popular, several old companies had invented their *own* networks for consumers by using a clever trick: they took business networks (which were busy in the day but idle in the evening) and offered them to consumers at low evening rates.

The first two such companies were Compuserve (owned by H&R Block) and The Source (owned by Readers Digest). After The Source went out of business, two other big companies arose: Prodigy (which was owned by IBM & Sears but later became independent) and America OnLine (AOL). AOL is independent. It's bought Compuserve and now is merging with Time/Warner. When all those companies began, they expected consumers would want mainly online reference materials (computerized dictionaries, encyclopedias, and databases) but discovered consumers mainly just wanted to send e-mail and chat instead of doing "research".

When the Internet became popular (because it included so *many* e-mail addresses and so *many* Web sites), those old companies modified their networks to include access to the whole Internet.

Those old companies and new ISPs weren't sure how much to charge consumers. At first, they tried charging about $3 per hour. In 1996, a better standard developed: **unlimited access for about $20 per month**.

A few **discount ISPs** charged less. A few **business ISPs** charged more, for superior service. Later came **free ISPs**, which offered free Internet service in return for forcing consumers to watch ads while using the Internet; the advertisers pay for those free ISPs.

Who pays?

Here's who invented and paid for the Internet....

In the beginning, funding came from the **Defense Department** (ARPA) and the **National Science Foundation**. To invent the Internet, a lot of research was done by university **professors** (funded by government grants, student tuition, and alumni donations). A lot of research was also done by **student volunteers**, who wanted to be famous by being helpful.

When consumer ISPs became popular, many **consumers** paid $20 per month per household.

Many Web sites show ads, paid for by the **advertisers**. Those ad fees pay for the Web sites, the same way that ads pay for TV networks and newspapers.

Many **businesses** run their own Web sites, and pay for them in the hope that those sites will act as ads (to draw in new customers and make old customers buy more). The businesses also hope their Web sites will show lots of info online, so the businesses don't have to send brochures to customers and don't have to hire customer-service departments to answer customer questions.

Many Web sites are created by new startup companies who dream of becoming great. Those companies convince investors to buy stock in that dream. Some of those dreamy companies will succeed, and their stockholders will get rich; other dreamy companies will fail, and their stockholders will lose their shirts. All those **stockholders** pay for the Internet and hope to reap rewards in return. While the stockholders wait for results, the company's managers are paid high salaries (funded by stockholders), even though many of those startup companies haven't earned any profit yet and never will.

In 1999, many such startup companies began; and investors sunk many millions of dollars into them, hoping the managers wouldn't waste the money and would eventually turn a profit. A lot of jargon was invented to describe the situation:

A company whose Web site is its main fame is called a **dot com** (because its Web-site address ends in .com), and its employees are called **dot commers**. A Web site letting customers type credit-card numbers to place orders is said to do **electronic commerce (e-commerce)** and offer an **electronic shopping cart**.

A company selling mainly to consumers is called a **business-to-consumer company (B2C company)**. A company selling mainly to other businesses instead is called a **business-to-business company (B2B company)**. A company selling mainly to organizations who run Internet host computers (and helping those organizations improve their Internet computers and connections) is called an **Internet infrastructure company**.

An old-fashioned company (which ignores the Internet and runs just traditional retail stores in brick buildings) is called a **real-world company** and a **bricks-and-mortar company**. An ultra-modern company (which exists just on the Web and doesn't bother staffing any storefront buildings where customers could walk in to buy goods) is said to **exist just in cyberspace** and be a **pure-play Internet company**. A company doing *both* — having brick-like retail stores (or warehouses) and also selling on the Internet (by letting customers use mice to click on what they want) — is called a **bricks-and-clicks company**.

If a startup company lures investors by telling an enticing story about how it could be profitable someday — but the company has no customers yet — its stock is called just a **story stock**.

Many Web companies are in San Francisco, where the managers are freaky-looking snotty kids who are young (under 30), wear nose rings, drive fancy cars, and got rich by inventing a story that got investors to give them millions of dollars, even though their companies haven't made a profit yet and have hardly any customers yet and actually *lose* lots of money daily. Many of those Web companies have been buying office space in San Francisco (south of Market Street), encouraging landlords to jack up rents and kick out the poor people and non-profit organizations that were there before. People who resent those managers call them **e-holes**, **dot snots**, and **dot commies**.

Who uses the Internet?

When the Internet began, it was restricted to university scientific researchers, who were mostly men. But eventually the Internet grew, so people outside universities could get access. In the year 2000, women Internet users finally outnumbered men users, for 3 reasons:

The world contains more women than men.

The World Wide Web grew to become a big worldwide library. "Reading in a library" appeals to women more than men.

E-mail grew to be a powerful force. Sending e-mail is like passing a note. "Writing, reading, and passing notes" are activities that appeal to women more than men.

Modern providers

To access the Internet, you can choose from 5 kinds of service….

Dial-up service

Some people still use **dial-up service**. Here's how it works….

Make sure your computer contains a **modem**. (The fastest kind of modem is called a **56K modem**.) Unplug your home's phone cord from your phone, and attach the phone cord to your computer's modem instead, so your computer can make phone calls. Yes, you'll be using the **plain old telephone system (POTS)**. Tell your computer to phone a computer belonging to an **Internet service provider (ISP)**, which charges you **about $15 per month** for the service, billed to your credit card. You might have to also pay a $20 start-up fee.

The phone number that your computer calls is called an **Internet dial-up access number** or **point of presence (POP)**. Make sure the POP is a *local* phone number, so you don't pay any long-distance bills. To make *sure* it's local, ask your local phone company whether the POP's phone number is indeed a free call under your calling plan.

While your computer is using the Internet through this method, your computer is "tying up the phone line", so if any of your friends try to phone you they'll get a busy signal. You can solve that problem in 3 ways:

Solution 1: tell the phone company to install a **second phone line**, which will cost you about $25 per month (including taxes).

Solution 2: use the Internet just **late at night** (or early in the morning), when your friends don't try to phone you.

Solution 3: pay the phone company $4 per month for **voice messaging**, which makes the phone company create a voice-mail system that takes messages when your phone is busy — but then you have to call your friends back at your own expense.

Of all the standard-method Internet service providers, the one with the best reputation is **EarthLink**, based in Pasadena, California.

It was started in 1994 by a 23-year-old guy named Sky Dalton, who ran a West Los Angeles coffeehouse, worked for ad agencies & computer-graphics companies, and was repeatedly voted one of the most influential technologists in the Los Angeles area. Now EarthLink is national, affiliated with Sprint, and has POPs in Canada and all states except Alaska and Hawaii. Its POPs are in over 1000 cities! EarthLink recently bought excellent competitors (such as MindSpring, JPS Net, and OneMain.com) so now EarthLink is even bigger and better. To chat with an EarthLink human who will help you get started, phone EarthLink's sales department at 888-EarthLink.

Another big ISP is AT&T's **WorldNet**, which charges a monthly fee of just $15 but limits you to 150 hours per month (extra hours cost 99¢ each). Unfortunately, WorldNet is often overloaded, especially its technical-support staff. To find out about WorldNet, phone 800-WorldNet.

To save money, try a **discount service**. It's the same as the standard method, except you pay **just $10 per month** (plus a start-up fee) and get worse service: more busy signals, more disconnections, more errors (saying "not found" or "Incorrect password"), and more difficulty reaching the tech-support staff. For example, I use a discount ISP called **Galaxy Internet Services (GIS)**, which has POPs just on the East Coast (in NH, MA, RI, CT, NY, NJ, PA, MD, DC, VA, and GA). To find out about Galaxy, phone 888-334-2529 or 617-558-0900. Other discount ISPs are **NetZero** ($10 per month, phone 800-638-9376 for info) and **PeoplePC** ($90 per year, phone 877-947-3327 for info).

To pay no money at all, you can try an **ad-supported service**. It's the same as standard dial-up service, except you pay no monthly fee but must watch ads while you're using the Internet. The main ad-supported ISP is **Juno**, which is owned by NetZero and limits you to 10 hours per month; phone 800-879-5866 for info.

Cable-modem service

For faster transmission, try **cable-modem service**.

It's resembles dial-up service, except you use cable-TV wires instead of phone wires, get faster transmission (about 8 times as fast) and pay more (about $45 per month for the service, plus $25 for an **Ethernet card** (a network card that you put into your computer), plus about $50 for a **cable modem** (which attaches the Ethernet card to a cable-TV cord).

The cable-modem method has two advantages over the standard method:

It's **faster**. The cable wires can theoretically transmit about 12 megabits per second (which is nearly 240 times as fast as a 56K modem), but you're sharing those wires with many cable-TV-using neighbors, who clog the system (especially in the evening), so on the average the cable modem will download 9 megabits per second from the Internet to your computer and upload 3 ½ megabits per second from your computer to the Internet.

It **doesn't consume a phone line**; you do *not* need to get a 2nd phone line.

Since this method achieves its high speed by using a broad spectrum of frequencies for transmission, it's an example of **broadband transmission**.

Cable-modem service is available just if your neighborhood is wired for cable TV and your cable-TV service company is modern. To find out, phone your local cable-TV company or a local computer store (such as your local Best Buy).

DSL service

If your neighborhood lacks cable, try **DSL service**.

A **digital subscriber line (DSL)** is a broadband transmission method that resembles the cable method; but instead of using cable-TV wires, it uses ordinary phone wires and makes them handle many frequencies at once.

The most common type of DSL is **Asymmetric DSL (ADSL)**. It costs slightly less than the cable method: it usually costs between $30 per month. Usually, it works slightly slower than the cable method, but it's popular because it's more predictable: it's unaffected by your neighbors' usage. It's popular for businesses, who are in business districts that haven't been wired for cable-TV yet and therefore can't use the cable method. DSL works fastest if you're close to a telephone switching station; if you're more than 2½ miles from a telephone-switching station, DSL works so slowly that the phone company will refuse to install it. The main complaint about DSL is that service technicians delay several weeks before showing up to install it, and you must take a day off from work to wait for them, and often they don't show up on the scheduled day.

To find out about DSL, start by calling your local phone company. You can also order DSL service from dial-up ISPs, such as EarthLink (at 888-EarthLink) and Galaxy Internet Services (at 888-334-2529).

Satellite service

If you can't use cable or DSL, try **satellite service**. It uses a satellite-TV dish to communicate with the Internet. It's slower than cable or DSL.

How much does it cost? You start by paying about $200 (to buy a satellite dish and install it so it faces a satellite in the sky). Then you pay a monthly fee of $60 for unlimited use. You'll also want to buy a second phone line to avoid "tying up the phone line". This service is financially attractive if you already bought a satellite dish to watch TV.

The main source of this service is **HughesNet**, (800-428-9570), whose service you can also buy from resellers, such as **SatelliteInternet.com** (866-408-8926) and **Satellite Star Internet** (800-977-0020).

Free-group service

To pay nothing for the Internet, try **free-group service**. For example, if you visit your **local public library**, you can use the library's Internet-connected computers for free (though you might have to wait for other users to finish). While you're enrolled in a typical **college**, you can freely use the college's Internet-connected computers, which are in the college's computer labs, libraries, and dorms. Many restaurants and cafés include free **WiFi hotspots**, so you can bring your notebook computer and let it communicate wirelessly with the Internet.

Web

The most popular part of the Internet is called the **World Wide Web** (or just the **Web** or just **WWW**).

The World Wide Web sometimes runs slowly. You can spend lots of time waiting for it to respond to your commands. Cynics call it the "World Wide Wait".

To use the World Wide Web, you need a program called a **Web browser**.

The first good Web browser was **Mosaic**, invented by a University of Illinois undergrad, Marc Andreessen, in 1994. Later that year, he left the university and formed a company called **Netscape Communications Corp.**, where he invented a better Web browser called **Netscape Navigator** (or just **Navigator**).

In 1995, Microsoft invented a competing Web browser called **Internet Explorer (IE)**. Versions 1 & 2 of it were invented in 1995, version 3 in 1996, version 4 in 1997, version 5 in 1999, version 6 in 2001, version 7 in 2006, version 8 in 2009, and version 9 in 2011. Its recent versions (5, 6, 7, 8, and 9) are better than Netscape Navigator. They're free. They're included as part of Windows. **IE version 9 requires Windows Vista or 7**; if you're still using an older Windows (such as Windows XP), stay with an older version of IE (such as IE 8) or use one of IE's competitors instead.

In 1998, Netscape Communications Corp. gave up trying to compete against Microsoft: the company sold itself to AOL, which wrecked Netscape Navigator by putting lots of AOL ads into it. But a group of volunteers called **Mozilla.org** (helped by funding from AOL) invented an improved ad-free Netscape Navigator called **Mozilla** then invented further improvements: **Firefox 1** in 2004, **Firefox 1.5** in 2005, **Firefox 2** in 2006, **Firefox 3** in 2008, **Firefox 3.5** in 2009, **Firefox 3.6** in 2010, and **Firefox 4** in 2011. For many years, people considered Firefox to be better than IE; but IE 9 is a dramatic improvement over earlier IE versions, so it's about as good as Firefox.

Another popular Web browser is **Opera**. It was invented in 1994 by researchers at Norway's telephone company (**Telenor**), then spun off as a separate company (**Opera Software**) in 1995. It became famous for running faster than IE and Firefox and consuming less RAM. The current version is **Opera 11**. It's fast and consumes so little RAM that it can fit comfortably even in cell phones and the smallest videogame machines.

Apple's computers (the Mac and the iPad) come with Apple's own Web browser, called **Safari**. Microsoft used to make Mac versions of IE but stopped when Apple invented Safari. The current version is **Safari 5**.

In 2005, a company called **YouTube** started putting videos on the Internet. In 2006, **Google** bought YouTube but was frustrated that IE was handling YouTube's videos too slowly, so in 2008 Google invented its own Web browser, called **Chrome**, which handled videos faster. The current version is **Chrome 10.**

Though Firefox, Opera, Safari, and Chrome were each intended to improve on IE, most people still use IE, because it comes preloaded on most Windows computers. Moreover, IE's newest version (IE 9) claims to be fast and as good as those other browsers.

Here's what people actually use:

> **45%** of Web browsing is done by people using **IE**, because they're too lazy to switch.
> **30%** of Web browsing is done by people using **Firefox**, because they heard it's the best browser.
> **17%** of Web browsing is done by people using **Chrome**, because they heard it's new and exciting.
> **5%** of Web browsing is done by people using **Safari**, because they have computers built by Apple.
> **2%** of Web browsing is done by people using **Opera**, because they heard it's fast, compact, European.
> **1%** of Web browsing is done by people experimenting with other browsers.

This chapter explains the 3 most popular Web browsers: **IE**, **Firefox**, and **Chrome**. It explains the newest versions: **IE 6&7&8&9**, **Firefox 3.6&4&5**, and **Chrome 12**. (Later, in the iPad chapter, I'll explain the iPad's version of **Safari**.)

Install the browser

To use IE, Firefox or Chrome, you (or your dealer) must put it onto your computer's hard disk.

How to install IE

If you bought your computer in 1996 or afterwards, its hard disk probably contains IE already, since IE is included in all modern Windows versions (Windows 98, 98 SE, Me, XP, Vista, and 7).

To use IE, you might have to tell Windows about your **Internet service provider (ISP)** and your ISP's phone number. To find out how, read the instructions your ISP sent you. If you don't understand them, phone your ISP's technical-support number.

For example, if you're using Windows XP and want to use the IE 6 that it included, do this:

Click "start" then "Control Panel".
Click "Network and Internet Connections". (If you don't see that choice, make it appear by clicking "Switch to Category View".)
You see the **Network and Internet Connections window**.
Click "Set up or change your Internet connection". Press Enter. Press the Tab key. Type your area code (such as 603). Press Enter four times. Click "Set up my connection manually". Press Enter twice. Type **your ISP's name** (such as "Galaxy Internet Services") and press Enter. Type the **phone number of your ISP's computer** (such as 782-4447) and press Enter. Type the **user name** that your ISP agreed to assign to you (such as "poo"), press the Tab key, type the **password** that your ISP agreed to assign to you (you'll see black dots while you type it), press Tab, type the password again, remove the check mark from "Turn on Internet Connection Firewall for this connection" (by clicking there), and press Enter. Press Enter again.
Click "Internet Options" then "Connections" then "Dial whenever a network connection is not present" then "OK".
Close the Network and Internet Connections window (by clicking its X button). Close the Dial-up Connection window (by clicking its X button).

If you're using Windows 7 with IE 8, here's how to upgrade to IE 9:

Start using IE 8 (by clicking the "e" that's next to the Start button). Click in the address box. Type www.BeautyOfTheWeb.com and press Enter.
Click the orange "Download Now" button then the blue "Download Now" button. Close the IE 8 window (by click the X at the screen's top-right corner). The computer says "Setup needs to close these programs". Press Enter.
The computer says "Installing Internet Explorer 9" then "Set up Internet Explorer 9". Click "Use recommended security and compatibility settings". Press Enter.
The computer says "welcome to a more beautiful web". Close the IE 9 window (by clicking the X at the screen's top-right corner then clicking "Close all tabs"), so you can start fresh.

If you're using Windows Vista with IE 8, here's how to upgrade to IE 9:

Start using IE 8 (by clicking the "e" that's next to the Start button). Click in the address box. Type www.BeautyOfTheWeb.com and press Enter.
Click the orange "Download Now" button then the blue "Download Now" button.
If the computer asks "Do you want to run or save this file?" click the Run button. If the computer asks again "Do you want to run this software?" click the Run button again. If the computer says "A program needs your permission to continue" click "Continue".
The computer says "Internet Explorer 9 is now installed". Click "Restart now". Be patient: *after a pause,* the computer will shut itself down; *after another pause,* the computer will turn itself back on; *after another pause,* the computer's screen will return to the normal desktop.
Start using IE 9 (by clicking the "e" that's next to the Start button). Click "Use recommended security and compatibility settings". Press Enter.

The computer says "welcome to a more beautiful web". Close the IE 9 window (by clicking the X at the screen's top-right corner then clicking "Close all tabs"), so you can start fresh.

How to install Firefox

If you're using Windows 7 and IE 9, here's how to "upgrade" to Firefox 5:

Start using IE 9 (by clicking the "e" that's next to the Start button). Type "www.mozilla.com" (so your typing is in the address box) and press Enter. Click "Firefox Free Download".
If the screen's bottom says "Do you want to run or save Firefox" click the Run button. If the computer asks again "Do you want to run this software?" click the Run button again. If the computer asks "Do you want to allow the following program to make changes to this computer?" click "Yes".
The computer will say "Welcome to the Mozilla Firefox Setup Wizard". Press Enter twice. The computer will say "Ready to start installing Firefox".
Are you bold enough to make Firefox your main browser? If not (because you want IE to remain your main browser and want Firefox to be just your secondary browser), remove the checkmark from "Use Firefox as my default web browser" (by clicking the checkmark).
Press Enter four times.
If the computer says "Firefox is not currently set as your default browser", remove the checkmark (by clicking it) then click "No".
You'll see two windows (one for Firefox, one for IE). Close both windows (by clicking their X buttons) and click any "Close tabs" button, so you can start fresh.

How to install Chrome

If you're using Windows 7 and IE 9, here's how to "upgrade" to Chrome 12:

Start using IE 9 (by clicking the "e" that's next to the Start button). Type "www.google.com/chrome" (so your typing is in the address box) and press Enter. Click "Download Google Chrome".
Are you bold enough to make Chrome your main browser? If not (because you want IE to remain your main browser and want Chrome to be just your secondary browser), remove the checkmark from "Set Google Chrome as my default browser" (by clicking the checkmark).
Click "Accept and Install".
The computer will say "Choose a search engine". You can click Google's Choose button or Yahoo's Choose button or Bing's Choose button. For your first experiment with Google Chrome, I recommend you click Google's Choose button.
If the computer asks "Do you want to allow the following program to make changes to this computer?" click "Yes".
You'll see two windows (one for Chrome, one for IE). Close both windows (by clicking their X buttons), so you can start fresh.

Start browsing

Turn on the computer, so you see the Start button in the screen's bottom-left corner. Then choose one of these methods....

Method 1: double-click an icon saying "Internet Explorer" or "Mozilla Firefox" or "Google Chrome".

Method 2: click Start then either "Internet Explorer" or "Mozilla Firefox" or "Google Chrome".

Method 3: click the tiny Internet Explorer icon that's next to the Start button and has an "e" on it.

If the computer asks for your user name, type it and press the Tab key.
If Windows XP says "Password", do this procedure:

Put a check mark in the "Connect automatically" box (by clicking it), then click "Connect".

You'll see the Internet Explorer (or Mozilla Firefox or Google Chrome) window. Make sure it consumes the whole screen. (If it doesn't consume the whole screen yet, maximize it by clicking its resize button, which is next to the X button.)

If Chrome says "Google Chrome isn't your default browser", click "Don't ask again".

Show text labels

Here's how to make the browser easier to understand.

IE 6 Click "View" then "Toolbars" then "Customize". Make sure the "Text options" box says "Show text labels". (If it doesn't, click the box's down-arrow, then click "Show text labels".) Press Enter.

Firefox 3.6 Click "View" then "Toolbars" then "Customize". Make sure the Show box says "Icons and text". (If it doesn't, click the box's down-arrow, then click "Icons and text".) Press Enter.

IE 7&8&9 and Firefox 4&5 and Chrome The browser is already as easy to understand as possible, so skip this step.

Hide useless toolbars

Here's how to avoid having your screen cluttered with useless toolbars.

IE 9 Right-click the star (which is near the screen's top-right corner). Make sure you have a check mark in front of just "Lock the Toolbars", not in front of anything else.

IE 8 Right-click the word "Favorites" (which is near the screen's top-left corner). Make sure you have check marks in front of just "Compatibility View Button", "Command Bar", "Status Bar", and "Lock the Toolbars", not in front of "Menu Bar" or "Favorites Bar" or "Microsoft Live Search Toolbar" or anything else. (If the computer asks "Do you want to disable this add-on?" press Enter.)

IE 7 Right-click the gold star (which is near the screen's top-left corner) or any gray area across from it. Make sure you have check marks in front of just "Status Bar" and "Lock the Toolbars", not in front of "Links" or anything else (such as "McAfee VirusScan" or "Show Norton Toolbar" or "Yahoo! Toolbar" or "Google"). To add or remove a check mark, click its position.

IE 6 Click "View". Make sure you have a check mark in front of "Status Bar". (To add or remove a check mark, click its position.) Click "Toolbars". You see the Toolbars menu. On that menu, make sure you have check marks in front of just "Standard Buttons" and "Address Bar" and "Lock the Toolbars" (and "Google" if you see that choice), not in front of "Links" or anything else (such as "McAfee VirusScan" or "Acer eDataSecurity Management").

Firefox 3.6 Click "View". Make sure you have a check mark in front of "Status Bar". (To add or remove a check mark, click its position.) Click "Toolbars". You see the Toolbars menu. On that menu, make sure you have a check mark in front of just "Menu Bar" and "Navigation Toolbar", not in front of "Bookmarks Toolbar". (To add or remove a check mark, click its position.)

Firefox 4&5 and Chrome The toolbars are already as minimal as possible, so skip this step.

Address box

Click in the **address box**, which is the wide box near the screen's top-left corner. (In IE 6&7&9 and Firefox and Chrome, that box is white; in IE 8, that box is light gray. That box is also called the **address bar** or **location bar**.)

Any writing in that box turns blue. Then type the Internet address you wish to visit.

For example, if you wish to visit **Yahoo**, type Yahoo's **Internet address**, which is —

```
http://www.yahoo.com/
```

Yes, that's Yahoo's **Internet address**. It's also called Yahoo's **Uniform Resource Locator** (or **URL**, which is pronounced "Earl").

When typing an Internet address (such as "http://www.yahoo.com/"), make sure you type periods (not commas); type forward slashes (not backslashes).

The address's first part ("http://") tells the computer to use **HyperText Transfer Protocol**, which is the communication method used by the Web. The "www." emphasizes that you're using the World Wide Web. The ".com" means the service (Yahoo) is a commercial company.

Instead of typing "http://www.yahoo.com/", you can be lazy and type just this:

```
www.yahoo.com
```

That's because the computer automatically puts "/" at the address's end and puts "http://" before any address that doesn't contain ":" already.

In an Internet address, each period is called a **dot**, so "www.google.com" is pronounced "dubbilyoo dubbilyoo dubbilyoo dot yahoo dot com" by literate computerists; grunters say just "wuh wuh wuh dot yahoo dot com".

Notice that the typical address (such as "www.yahoo.com") begins with "www." and ends with ".com".

At the end of your typing, press Enter. (If you typed just "yahoo.com" and forgot to type the "www.", the computer will automatically do the "www." for you after a slight delay.)

Here's another shortcut: you can type just —

```
yahoo
```

but afterwards, instead of just pressing the Enter key, do this:

```
Hold down the Ctrl key; and while you keep holding down the Ctrl key, tap the Enter key.
```

That "Ctrl with Enter" makes the computer automatically type the "www." and ".com" for you.

Here's another shortcut: start typing "yahoo" (by typing "y" then "a" then "h") but look below where you're typing; if you see what you want (such as www.yahoo.com) because the computer successfully guessed what you wanted, click the computer's correct guess.

IE9 and Chrome have another shortcut: start typing "yahoo" (by typing "y" then "a") but notice that if it's something you typed previously, the computer will complete the typing for you: if you're satisfied with the computer's typing, just press Enter afterwards.

Using any of those methods, you'll eventually see the beginning of Yahoo's home page.

Seeing the rest of the page To see the rest of the page, click the scroll-down arrow (the ▼ or ∨ near the screen's bottom right corner) or roll the mouse's wheel (which is between the mouse's buttons) *toward* you. To see the page's beginning again, click the scroll-up arrow (▲ or ∧) or roll the mouse's wheel *away* from you.

Links

On Yahoo's home page, you see many topics to choose from. The screen's left edge shows these 18 **hot topics**:

```
mail, autos, dating, finance, games, health, horoscopes, jobs, Messenger, movies, omg!, real estate, Shine, shopping, sports, travel, updates, weather
```

The screen's center shows today's **news**. The rest of the screen shows extra topics.

Each topic is called a **link** (or **hot spot**). Click whichever link interests you.

> You can click anyplace where the mouse's pointer-arrow turns into a pointing finger. But for your first experiment, I recommend you **click an item from today's news** (in the screen's center), since the news is simpler to handle than the topics at the screen's edges.

As soon as you click — presto! — the computer shows you a whole new page, devoted entirely to the topic you linked to! Read it and enjoy!

While you're looking at that new page, you'll see its address in the address box. On that new page, you'll see more topics that are links: places where the mouse's pointer-arrow turns into a pointing finger. (The links are usually underlined or colored or bolded.) Click whichever link interests you, to visit a further page.

Back & forth

After admiring the new page you're visiting, if you change your mind and want to go back to the previous page you were looking at, click the **Back button** (which is near the screen's top-left corner and has a left-arrow on it).

Then you see the previous page. (On that page, any links you clicked might have changed color.)

After clicking the Back button, if you change your mind again and wish you hadn't clicked the Back button, click the **Forward button** (which is next to the Back button and has a right-arrow on it).

Back list To hop back several pages, you can click the Back button several times.

To hop back faster, do this:

> **IE 9 and Firefox 4&5 and Chrome** Right-click the Back button (or while pointing at the Back button, hold down the mouse's left button awhile). You see a list of pages you visited recently. The list is short: at most 9 pages in IE9, 14 pages in Firefox 4&5, 17 pages in Chrome.
>
> **IE 7&8 and Firefox 3.6** Click the ▼ next to the Back & Forward buttons. You see a list of pages you visited recently. The list is short: at most 9 pages in IE 7&8, 14 pages in Firefox 3.6.
>
> **IE 6** Click the ▼ near the Back button. You see a list of pages you visited recntly. The list is short: at most 9 pages.

Then click the page you want to go back to.

Home (useful just in IE & Firefox) Each time you launch IE or Firefox, the first page you see is called your **start page** or **home page** (because that's where life starts — at home). If you view other pages (by clicking links) and later change your mind, you can return to viewing the home page by clicking the Back button many times — or click the **Home button** once. (The Home button has a picture of a house on it. In IE 9, it's near the screen's top-right corner.)

History Here's how to see a list of pages you visited in the last few weeks.

For IE 7&8&9, do this:

> Click the Favorites button (which is a star) then the word "History". You see the History window.
>
> Decide which date's history you want to see: click either "Today" or a recent day or "Last Week" or "2 Weeks Ago" or "3 Weeks Ago". (Click once or twice, until you see that date's list of sites; then click a site once or twice, until you see that site's list of pages.) Click whichever page you want to visit.

For IE 6, do this:

> Click the History button (which is a clock with a green arrow curving back).

> You see the History window. Decide which date's history you want to see: click either "Today" or a recent day or "Last Week" or "2 Weeks Ago" or "3 Weeks Ago". (Click once or twice, until you see that date's list of sites; then click a site once or twice, until you see that site's list of pages.) Click whichever page you want to visit.
>
> The History window will stay on the screen until you close it (by clicking its X button).

For Firefox 4&5, do this:

> Click the orange "Firefox" button (which at the screen's top-left corner) then "History" (which is in the second column). You see a list of the last 10 pages you visited (including the current page). Either click one of those 10 page names (to visit that page) or click "Show All History", which gets you more choices, as follows....
>
> You see the History window. Decide how much history you want to see: for Firefox 4, click "Today" or "Last 7 days"; for Firefox 5, double-click "Today or "This month". You see a list of 15 pages: scroll down to see the rest of what you asked for. Double-click whichever page you want to visit.

For Firefox 3.6, do this:

> Click "History". You see a list of the last 10 pages you visited (including the current page). Either click one of those 10 page names (to visit that page) or click "Show All History", which gets you more choices, as follows....
>
> You see the History window. Decide which date's history you want to see: click either "Today" or "Yesterday" or "This Month" or an earlier month. (Click once or twice, until you see that date's list of pages.) The list of pages for that date is in alphabetical order. Double-click whichever page you want to visit.

For Chrome, do this:

> Click the **wrench** (which is near the screen's top-right corner, just below the X). Then click "History".
>
> You see a list of all pages you visited in the last few weeks. (To see the whole list, scroll down.)
>
> Click whichever page you want to visit.

Favorites If you're viewing a wonderful page, here's how to make the computer remember that the page is one of your favorites and bookmark it.

For IE 8&9, do this:

> Click the Favorites button (which is a star) then "Add to Favorites". Press Enter.
>
> In the future, whenever you want to return to your favorite pages, click the Favorites button (which is a star) then the word "Favorites" that's left of "Feeds": you'll see a list of your favorite pages. Click whichever page you want to visit (or delete a page from the list by doing this: right-click the page name you want to delete, then click "Delete").

For IE 7, do this:

> Click the "Add to Favorites" button (which is a green plus sign in front of a gold star). Press Enter twice.
>
> In the future, whenever you want to return to your favorite pages, click the Favorites button (which is a gold star) then the word "Favorites": you'll see a list of your favorite pages. Click whichever page you want to visit (or delete a page from the list by doing this: right-click the page name you want to delete, then click "Delete", then press "Enter").

For IE 6, do this:

> Click the word "Favorites" that's next to the word "View". Click "Add to Favorites". Press Enter.
>
> In the future, whenever you want to return to your favorite pages, click the word "Favorites" again: you'll see a list of your favorite pages. Click whichever page you want to visit (or delete a page from the list by doing this: right-click the page name you want to delete, then click "Delete", then press "Enter").

For Firefox 4&5, do this:

> Click the star *that's in the address box* (not the star at the screen's right edge). The star turns gold.
>
> In the future, whenever you want to return to that page, click the star *at the screen's right edge* then "Unsorted Bookmarks". You see a list of pages you created that way.
>
> Which page do you want to visit? For Firefox 4, click that page; for Firefox 5, *double*-click that page. (To delete a page from the list, right-click the page name you want to delete, then click "Delete".)

For Firefox 3.6, do this:

> Click "Bookmarks" then "Bookmark This Page". Press Enter.
> In the future, whenever you want to return to your favorite pages, click "Bookmarks" again: you'll see a list of your favorite pages. Click whichever page you want to visit (or delete a page from the list by doing this: in the list, right-click the page name you want to delete, then click "Delete").

For Chrome, do this:

> Click the **star** (which is near the screen's top-right corner). Press Enter.
> In the future, whenever you want to return to that page, click the "+" (at the screen's top): you'll see a list of your favorite pages. Click whichever page you want to visit (or delete a page from the list by doing this: right-click the page name you want to delete, then click "Delete").

Search box At the top-right corner of Yahoo's first page, you see a yellow "Web Search" button. To the left of that button is a white box, called the **search box**.

Try this experiment: click in the search box, then type a topic that interests you. For example, type:

> lincoln

Don't bother capitalizing: the computer ignores capitalization.

At the end of your typing, press Enter. Yahoo will find about 100 million Web pages mentioning Lincoln. Yahoo will begin by listing the 10 Web pages that Yahoo thinks you'll find the most useful, plus some ads. (Some of the ads have a pink background. Other ads are at the screen's right edge.)

For example, if you asked for "lincoln", Yahoo will list 10 Web pages about President Abraham Lincoln, Lincoln cars (made by Ford), Lincoln University (in Pennsylvania), Lincoln Electric (which makes welding machines), and the town of Lincoln (in Nebraska). To see all 10 of those Web pages, scroll down to the bottom of the page by using your mouse's wheel or the down-arrow near the screen's bottom-right corner.

Each Web page's name is underlined. Click whichever Web page you want — or click "Next" (at the bottom of Yahoo's page) to see a list of 10 more Web pages about Lincoln.

To be more specific, type more words in the search box. For example, if you're interested just in Abraham Lincoln, type:

> Abraham Lincoln

If you're interested in just Lincoln cars, type:

> Lincoln cars

If you're interested in just Abraham Lincoln's log cabin, type:

> Abraham Lincoln log cabin

Open something different

To switch to a completely different address, click in the address box again then type the Internet address you wish to visit.

For example, if you wish to visit **Google**, type this —

> http://www.google.com/

or type just this:

> www.google.com

At the end of your typing, press Enter. Then type a topic to search for (and press Enter). For example, if you type "lincoln", Google will find about 120 million Web pages mentioning Lincoln. It will begin by listing 10 pages about Abraham Lincoln, the Lincoln Memorial, Lincoln cars, Lincoln University, Lincoln Electric, Lincoln Industrial (which makes lubrication equipment), and the city of Lincoln (in Nebraska). The name of each Web page is underlined. Click whichever Web page you want — or click "Next" (at the bottom of Google's page) to see a list of 10 more Web pages about Lincoln. To be more specific, type more words in the search box, such as "Abraham Lincoln" or "Lincoln cars" or "Abraham Lincoln log cabin".

Yahoo and Google are called **search sites**, since their purpose is to help you search for other sites on the Internet.

They're also called **Web portals**, since their purpose is to serve as a grandiose door through which you pass to launch your journey across the World Wide Web.

Print

While you're viewing a page, here's how to print a copy of it onto paper.

IE 9:	while holding down the Ctrl key, tap the P key.
IE 7&8:	click the Print button (showing paper coming from a printer).
Firefox 4&5:	click the orange "Firefox" button then Print then OK.
Firefox 3.6:	click File then Print then OK.
Chrome:	click the wrench then Print then press Enter.

That makes your printer try to print the whole page — even the part of the page that goes below the screen's bottom edge and doesn't fit on the screen.

If the Web page is wider than your paper, the computer squeezes the Web page onto your paper by printing a shrunken image of the page. (Exception: IE 6&7 are too stupid to shrink the page, so they print just the page's left part and doesn't bother trying to print the page's rightmost part.)

If the Web page is very wide, make the printer rotate the page 90 degrees, so it fits on the paper. Here's how. For IE 9, do this:

> Click the Tools button (which is a bumpy-circle gear at the screen's left edge) then Print then Page Setup then Landscape then OK. Then while holding down the Ctrl key, tap the P key.

For IE 7&8, do this:

> Click the Print button's down-arrow then Page Setup then Landscape then OK then the Print button.

For Firefox 4&5, do this:

> Click the orange "Firefox" button. Put the mouse pointer on "Print" but don't click it. Click Page Setup (which appears in the second column) then Landscape then OK. Click the orange "Firefox" button again then Print then OK.
> Later, if you want to return to printing normally (without rotation), click the orange "Firefox" button then Page Setup then Portrait then OK.

For Firefox 3.6, do this:

> Click File then Page Setup then Landscape then OK. Click File then Print then OK.
> Later, if you want to return to printing normally (without rotation), click File then Page Setup then Portrait then OK.

For Chrome, do this:

> Click the wrench then Print then Preferences then Finishing then Landscape then OK then Print.

Simultaneous pages

Here's how to make your computer's RAM (memory chips) hold *two* Web pages simultaneously, so you can switch back and forth between those pages fast.

IE 7&8&9 and Firefox and Chrome While you're viewing a Web page, try one of these activities:

> Click a link *while holding down the Ctrl key*.

> While the mouse is pointing at a link, *click the mouse's wheel* (instead of the mouse's left button).

> In the address box, type an address and then, *while holding down the Alt key*, press Enter.

Near the screen's top, you see two wide **tabs**: each tab contains a Web page's name (title). To switch between the two Web pages, click their tabs.

When you get tired of having two tabs, here's how to have just one tab again:

> Decide which tab you don't want anymore. For Firefox and Chrome, click the X on that tab; for IE, click that tab then the X on it.
> That tab disappears, along with its Web page, so you see just the other tab.

IE 6 While you're viewing a Web page, do this:

> Hold down the Ctrl key; and as you keep holding down the Ctrl key, tap the N key (which stands for "new window").

You'll see a new window. It looks like the previous window (it shows the same Web page, and it completely covers the first window); but you can tell it's a *new* window, because at the screen's bottom center (to the right of the Start button) you now see *two* wide buttons about Web-page windows.

Suppose you change what's on the screen (by clicking a link, or entering a new Web address, or entering something new in a search box). That changes what's in the visible window; but the other window (which is hidden behind the visible window) remains unchanged. To view the window that's been hidden, click its wide button at the screen's bottom.

By clicking those two wide buttons at the screen's bottom, you can switch back and forth between the two windows.

When you get tired of having two windows, here's how to have just one window again:

> Click the X at the screen's top right corner. That deletes the visible window, so the RAM contains just the other window, which then appears on the screen.

Exit

When you finish using IE or Firefox or Chrome, close its window (by clicking its X button).

If you've been communicating with the Internet using old technology (IE 6, with an ordinary phone line instead of DSL or cable), press Enter.

3 ways to search

Here are the 3 popular ways to search for a topic on the Web.

Search-box method

In a search box, type the topic you're interested in, and then press Enter. That makes Yahoo (or Google or Bing) use its **search engine**, which searches on the Internet for pages about that topic.

Google has the best search engine. Here's how to use Google's search box. (Yahoo and competitors are similar.)

When you make Google search for a topic, Google typically finds *thousands* of pages about that topic. Google tries to guess which of those pages are the most relevant; Google begins by trying to show you a list of the most relevant pages (on a white background). That list is interrupted by some ads, which are marked "sponsored links" and have pastel colored backgrounds. The ads relate vaguely to the topic you requested, but you can ignore them. They're listed first because the advertisers paid for such listing.

What Google ignores Google ignores capitalization, so don't bother capitalizing. Typing "george washington" has the same effect as typing "George Washington".

In the search box, type just words separated by spaces. Google ignores commas, periods, question marks, and exclamation points.

Google usually ignores these common words:

> a, the
> be, is, are, was, will
> I, it
> of, for, about, in, on
> what, when, where, why, how
> and, or

Restricting your search The more words you type in the search box, the more restricted the search will be, since Google will show you a Web page just if the page includes *all* the words you mentioned.

If you type "bush", Google will list all Web pages that mention "bush". Google will guess that you're mainly interested in President George Bush, so it will begin by listing Web pages about George Bush the father, George Bush the son (even a page comparing his photos to a chimpanzee's), and their families. Google will also mention Web pages about Kate Bush (the singer), other people whose last name is Bush, a discothèque in Belgium called "La Bush", and eventually any plant called a "bush" and also pubic hair (for which the slang word is "bush").

If you're more specific, Google will mention fewer Web pages.

> For example, if you're interested in just Kate Bush the singer, type "Kate Bush" instead of just "Bush". Then Google will show you info about just Kate Bush.
>
> If you want info about plants that are bushes, type "bush plant". That gets you mostly Web pages about plants that are bushes but also includes a few jokes about President Bush being a plant and some comments about President Bush's opinions of nuclear power plants. You can also try "bush shrub" or "bush garden" (which includes info about gardens but also about a Japanese restaurant called "Bush Garden") or "bush landscaping".
>
> If you type "bush pubic", you get Web pages about shaving & combing pubic hair and a feminist protest against George Bush. Go try other combos that get closer to whatever kind of info you want to know about a "bush".

The more words you type in the search box, the more specific your request is, and the fewer Web pages will match. If you get too few Web pages, try different words instead.

Try variations. If you're interested in plants that are bushes, and you don't like what you get when you search for "bush plant", try searching for "shrub" instead, which will get you a different list: Web pages that mention the word "shrub".

Google notices your word order. If you say "bush plant", Google begins by listing Web pages that mention "bush" before "plant"; if you say "plant bush", Google begins by listing Web pages that mention "plant" before "bush".

Google searches for just the words you requested. For example, if you search for "airline", Google will list Web pages that contain the word "airline" but not Web pages that contain the word "airlines" instead. For complete listings, search for "airline" then search again for "airlines".

If you type quotation marks around a phrase (such as "to be or not to be"), Google shows just Web pages containing that exact phrase.

Which Web pages are important To determine which Web pages to show you first, Google considers how closely each Web page *matches* what you requested — but also considers how *important* each Web page seems to be. Google considers a Web page to be important if many other Web pages contain links to that page, and if the Web pages that link to it are themselves important also (by being linked to from other Web pages).

Feeling lucky? After you've typed some words into the search box, the usual procedure is to press the Enter key. That has the same effect as clicking "Google Search": it makes Google show you a list of relevant Web pages. Often, the first Web page in that list is the most relevant. If it is, congratulations: you're lucky! You found what you're looking for, fast!

If you think you're going to be that lucky, try this trick to go even faster: after typing words into the search box, click "I'm Feeling Lucky" (instead of pressing Enter). Google will take you immediately to the first Web page on the list, without having you wait for the whole list to be generated and having it wait for you to choose from the list.

Phone book In the search box, if you type a phone number (such as "603-666-6644"), Google will look through phonebook white pages and tell you who has that phone number (if the number is listed).

If instead you type a name (of a person or business) with a city and state (such as "Russ Walter Manchester NH"), Google will look through the phonebook white pages and tell you the phone number (if the number is listed), street address, and ZIP code. When you type a person's name, you must type at least the last name; do *not* type a middle name; type the first name or first initial if you know how it's listed in the phonebook white pages. Instead of typing a city and state, you can type a ZIP code if you know it.

Maps In the search box, if you type an address (such as "196 Tiffany Lane Manchester NH"), Google will show you a map of that address.

Pictures To search for a picture (instead of words), do this:

> Click "Images". In the search box, type what topic you want the picture to be about. Press Enter.
> You'll see tiny pictures about your topic. Click whichever picture you like. You'll see it enlarged.
> Click "Back" to return to Google. Google will assume you want all future searches to be about pictures, until you click "Web" instead of "Images" (or until you stop using Google).

Single site If you want Google to search through just one Web site, say so. For example, if you want to search for info about Windows Vista just on Microsoft's Web site (which is microsoft.com), say "Windows Vista site:microsoft.com".

Who links to you? To find all Web pages that link to your favorite Web page, type "link:" then your Web page's address, like this: "link:secretfun.com".

Censorship Google can censor the list of Web pages and pictures, so you don't see pornography.

To change how Google censors what you see, click "Preferences" (which is to the right of the search box) then choose complete censorship or no censorship or partial censorship (which censors pictures but not words), by clicking the appropriate circle under "SafeSearch Filtering". (If you've never expressed a preference, Google assumes you want partial censorship.) To confirm your choice, click the Save Preferences button (which is near the screen's top right corner), then press Enter.

Translation Google can translate English to & from 5 European languages (French, Spanish, Portuguese, Italian, and German). It can also translate French to & from Spanish & Portuguese.

For example, if you've been using English but Google finds a Web page in one of those 5 European languages, Google will translate the Web page to English if you do this: instead of clicking the Web page's name (in the list of Web pages), click the "Translate this page" nearby. Then Google will show you the Web page rewritten into English by Google's robots (which are computers). Google's robots make many translation mistakes but give you at least a rough idea of what the Web page is trying to say.

For further fun, try this:

> Click "Language Tools" (which is next to the search box), then click in "Translate text" box. Type some sentences in English or one of those 5 European languages. Click the down-arrow below that box. You see 14 choices of what languages to translate to and from (if you scroll to see the whole list): click the choice you want. Google's robots will translate what you wrote and put the answer in the top box.

Cached pages When Google shows you a list of Web pages about your topic, that list is based on info that Google collected several months ago about the Internet. The list might no longer be correct. When you click on one of the Web pages in the list, the Internet might give you an error message saying the page no longer exists, or the Internet might give you a page different from what you were expecting.

Fear not! Though the original Web page might have disappeared from the Internet, Google's kept a copy of that original Web page in **Google's cache**. To see the original, go back to Google's list of Web pages; but instead of clicking the Web page's name, click the word "Cached" that's below the page's name and description. Then you'll see the same original page that Google saw.

Experiment The Internet is huge. For a typical topic, Google will find thousands of pages about it. For the most popular topics, Google will find *millions* of pages.

If you try to fool Google by typing a short fake word (such as a nonsense syllable), you'll be surprised: Google will typically inform you that the word was already invented by others and will show you several pages about it (because it turns out to be the name of a rock band, or an organization's initials, or a word in a foreign language, or a word invented by a novelist to describe a splat-like sound). If you try to fool Google by typing several seemingly unrelated words or names (separated by spaces), Google will typically find a Web page containing them all (because the Web page is from a crazy novel or reading list or alumni list or dictionary).

Other search engines Here's a list of popular search engines:

> Google.com
> Yahoo.com
> Bing.com
> Ask.com
> MSN.com
> AltaVista.com
> AOL.com

Try them! Each gives slightly different results.

A **metasearch site** called **InfoSpace.com** runs 3 search engines simultaneously (Google.com, Yahoo.com, and Bing.com) and combines their results into a single list.

Search yippy The most advanced metasearch site was **Clusty.com**. It was invented by 3 scientists at Carnegie Mellon University in Pittsburgh. In 2010, it was sold to Yippy, which renamed it **search.yippy.com**. It shows you the combined list of results (based mainly on Bing.com and Yahoo.com) but also a list of clusters (categories that the results fit in).

For example, if you search for "Obama", the screen's left edge shows this list of clusters (which are also called "clouds") to choose from:

> + Re-election
> + Budget
> + Photos
> + Issues, Social
> + Articles
> + Sharpton
> + Barackobama
> + Michelle Obama
> + Answers
> + Policies, Candidates

Below that list, you see "all clouds"; if you click that, you see an even longer list of clusters (clouds).

If you click the "+" that's left of a cluster, you see a list of subclusters. When you find a subcluster you like, click it to see a list of Web pages about that subcluster.

Even if you search for a topic that's not nearly as famous as "Obama", search.yippy.com analyzes the results and invents clusters to organize them. For example, try doing a search on your own name (or the name of your organization, street, town, or favorite topic), and see how search.yippy.com invents clusters for your results. Amazing!

Subject-tree method

Go to **www.dmoz.org**. At that Website, called the **Open Directory Project**, you see this list of broad topics:

> arts, business, computers, games, health, home, kids & teens, new, recreation, reference, regional, science, shopping, society, sports

That list is called the **subject tree of knowledge** (because it's as tempting as the tree of knowledge in the Garden of Eden). Click whichever topic interests you (or click "World", which lets you read the site in 88 foreign languages instead of English.) Then you see a list of that topic's branches (subtopics). Click whatever subtopic interests you. Then you see a list of subsubtopics (twigs). Click whichever subsubtopic interests you. Keep clicking until you finally zero in on the very specific topic that interests you the most: it's the fruit of your search!

That site was created by 75,000 volunteers. It organizes 4 million of the Web's best sites.

Address-box method

Give your friends a sheet of paper and ask them to jot down the addresses of their favorite Web pages. (Or get lists of nifty Web addresses by reading computer books, magazines, newspaper articles, or ads.)

For example, here's a list of excellent Web sites:

Topic	Best Web site
news	yahoo.com
weather	weather.com
phone numbers	411.com
maps	maps.google.com
driving directions	MapQuest.com/directions
encyclopedia	wikipedia.org
health	InteliHealth.com
debunk rumors	snopes.com
classified ads	CraigsList.org
short movies	YouTube.com

(A more detailed list of Web sites begins on the next page.)

Type one of those addresses in the address box, then press Enter.

To understand how addresses work, consider the best driving-directions Web site, whose full address is:

> http://www.MapQuest.com/directions/

The address's first part ("http://") is called the **protocol**.

The address's next part ("www.MapQuest.com") is called the **domain name**; it tells you which computer on the Internet contains the info. The typical domain name begins with "www.", then has the name of a company (such as "MapQuest"). The domain name's ending (called the **top-level domain**) is typically ".com", which means "USA commercial company". Some addresses have different top-level domains:

Top-level domain	Meaning
.com	USA commercial company
.org	USA organization (typically non-profit)
.gov	USA government (typically federal)
.mil	USA military
.edu	USA educational institution
.net	USA network resource (typically ISP)
.us	USA other (typically local government)

.ar	Argentina
.au	Australia
.br	Brazil
.ca	Canada
.ch	Confoederacio Helvetica (Switzerland)
.cn	China
.es	España (Spain)
.fi	Finland
.fr	France
.de	Deutschland (Germany)
.dk	Denmark
.hk	Hong Kong
.ie	Ireland
.il	Israel
.in	India
.it	Italy
.jp	Japan
.kr	Korea (South)
.mx	Mexico
.nl	Netherlands (Holland)
.no	Norway
.nz	New Zealand
.ph	Philippines
.ru	Russia
.se	Sweden
.tv	Tuvalu (South Pacific islands)
.tw	Taiwan
.uk	United Kingdom (Britain & N. Ireland)

Recently, these new top-level domains were invented: .info, .name, .biz (for business), and .ws (for website).

The rest of the address (such as "/directions/") is called the **page name**; it tells which file on the computer contains the page you requested.

Type each address carefully:

> **While typing an address, never put a space in the middle.**
>
> **Watch your punctuation.** The typical address will contain a dot (.) and a slash (/). An address can also contain a hyphen (-) or squiggle (~). Addresses never contain commas, backslashes, or apostrophes.
>
> **For the typical address, type small letters (uncapitalized)**, since capitalized page names are rare. (The computer doesn't care whether you capitalize the protocol and domain name.)

Best sites

To enrich your life, go to the best Websites. Here they are....

Links

SecretFun.com is my own site. It contains info about *The Secret Guide to Computers* and my other book (*Tricky Living*). By clicking the links in the first pink box, you and your friends can read parts of *The Secret Guide to Computers* and *Tricky Living*, free, and you can also jump to the other sites recommended in this chapter.

General searches

Google.com finds the most topics on the Internet. If you type some words, then press Enter, you'll see a list of the main Web sites containing those words.

News

For news headlines and the stories behind them, go to **Yahoo.com**. At the screen's center, near the bottom, you see this menu bar:

News	World	Local	Finance

Click "News" for today's top articles, "World" for more articles about other countries, "Local" for articles about your region (after you tell Yahoo your ZIP code or city-and-state, or you click the down-arrow under "Local"), "Finance" for articles about the stock market, banks, and economy. You see headlines (after you scroll down); click a headline to see its story. Below each list of headlines, click "More" (or the words after it) to see a longer list of headlines. Instead of going to Yahoo.com and then clicking "More", you can use this shortcut: go to **Yahoo News (news.yahoo.com)**, which divides the news into these categories:

top stories, most popular, local news, world, U.S. news, politics, business, science, technology, health, entertainment, travel, sports, odd news, opinion

For details about today's stock market, go to Yahoo.com then click "Finance" (which is at the screen's left edge) or use this shortcut: go to **Yahoo Finance (finance.yahoo.com)**. Then, at the screen's left edge, click "Dow" or "Nasdaq" or "S&P 500" or "10 Yr Bond" or "Oil" or "Gold" to see a chart of how those indices changed in the last 24 hours.

For a bigger collection of news stories, try **Google News (news.google.com)**, which uses a computer (rather than humans) to decide which of the moment's news stories are the hottest. It shows you *thousands* of news stories, categorized and prioritized. The main categories are:

top stories, world, U.S., business, sci/tech, entertainment, sports, health, spotlight

Weather

To find out the weather, go to **Weather.com** (which is produced by The Weather Channel). Click in the box that says "Enter Zip, City, or Place" (which is at the screen's left edge).

Which place on earth do you want a weather report for? Type the ZIP code (or city-and-state or city-and-country or airport-and-state or landmark-and-state), then press Enter.

You see the current weather and the forecast for the next 36 hours (after you scroll down).

To customize your forecast, click one of these words on the menu bar:

Overview Hourly Tomorrow Weekend 5-Day 10-Day Month Map

You see a customized forecast.

To see more details, click whichever choice you see and prefer: "EXPAND WEATHER DETAILS" or "Details" or "Text" or "Video".

Time

Here's how to find the exact time.

For time in the U.S., do this:

Go to **Time.gov**, which is run by the U.S. government. You see a map of the U.S., showing the time zones. On the map, click the place whose time you want.

For time in other countries, do this:

Go to **TimeAndDate.com**. Click in the "Search for city" box (near the screen's left edge). Start typing the name of the city whose time you want. Below your typing, you see a list of cities that match what you've typed so far. (For example, if you type "Mos", the list will include "Moscow, Russia" and "Moss, Norway" and "Mossoró, Brazil" and "Mosul, Iraq".) Click the city you want.

After a brief pause, you'll see a digital clock. The clock tells you the exact time, to the nearest second, and updates itself every second. When you get tired of looking at the clock, go to a different Website instead.

Phone numbers

For info about who has what phone number, go to **411.com**. You see these tabs:

Find a business Find people Reverse phone Reverse address Area & ZIP codes

Do this:

Click "Find a business" if you know the business's name (and state) and want its phone number & address.

Click "Find people" if you know a person's last name and want the phone number & address — or you know an address and want names (and addresses and phone numbers) of all neighbors.

Click "Reverse phone" if you know a phone number and want to know what person or business has it.

Click "Reverse address" if you know an address and want to know what person or business lives there and the phone number.

Click "Area & ZIP codes" if you know a city and want to find its area code & ZIP code — or you know the area code or ZIP code and want to find which cities have it.

Then fill in the blanks and click the "Find" button next to them. You'll get free info. (If you get a list of too few or too many people, try again but for "first name" type just the first name's first letter.)

Then for more free info, click the person's name or the word "PHONE". (You'll also be offered the opportunity to buy a more detailed investigation of the person or business you're trying to research.)

To get you the answers, the computer uses several sources of info. Since the computer gets *most* of its info from phonebook white pages, it omits some folks whose numbers or addresses are unlisted or who have just cell phones or who moved recently.

To search for a person by typing the name, use these trick:

Since many people decline to list their full names in the phonebook, and since many people aren't sure whether to list their formal names or their nicknames, try typing the first name's first letter instead of the full first name — or leave the first name blank. If you think the person might have moved, leave the city blank (and type just the state).

Travel

The Internet lets you explore the whole world!

Maps The best way to see maps online is to go to **Google Maps (maps.google.com)**.

You see a map of the United States. (If you want to see a map of a different country, click in the map then rotate the mouse's wheel toward you, until you see a map of the whole world.)

To see more details about a spot on the map, do this:

Move your mouse until its pointer (which looks like a white hand) is at the spot on the map where you want more details; then rotate the mouse's wheel away from you (or double-click). If the map isn't centered the way you like, drag the map (by holding down the mouse's left button while you move the mouse). If you keep repeating that process, you'll eventually find a map showing the individual streets, unless you pick a rural area or third-world country. Another way to get a map of a location is to click in the white "Search Maps" box then type the location's address (or as much of it as you know) then press Enter.

If you click "Satellite" (which is near the screen's top-left corner), you see an aerial photo of that spot, taken from a satellite. Yes, you can even see a photo of your own house's roof! To use this feature pleasantly, you need a fast (broadband) Internet connection (cable or DSL). When you get tired of looking at the view from the satellite, return to a normal map by clicking the "Map" button (at the screen's right edge).

Driving directions The best way to get driving directions is to go to **MapQuest Driving Directions (MapQuest.com/directions)**.

Go ahead, have fun! See how MapQuest advises you to travel to your neighbors, your relatives, your job, and across the country. Mapquest's advice might surprise you: it might find a faster route you hadn't thought of.

Type the address where your trip starts (so it appears in the START box at the screen's left edge), then press the Tab key, then type the address where your trip ends (so it appears in the END box), then press Enter.

At the screen's left edge, below the words "Suggested Route," you see how many minutes and miles your trip will take. Below that, you see turn-by-turn directions. (Scroll down to see them all.) Next to each turn, you see how many miles you must drive to get to the next turn.

At the screen's right edge, you see a map showing your whole trip.

In the list of turns, if you click one of the turns then "Zoom to this Step", you see a close-up map of that turn.

The computer has found the route that's fastest, under normal traffic conditions. If you hate driving on one of those roads (because it's ugly or under construction or having a traffic jam or takes more distance & gas) and want to avoid it, do this:

Click in the list of turns where it says to turn onto that road. Then click "Avoid this Step". That forces the computer to find an alternative route.

To print the directions onto paper, do this:

Click "Print" (which is near the screen's top-left corner). If you want to add a close-up map of any of the turns, click that turn's "Show Map".

Click "Print Without Advertisement" (which is near the screen's top-right corner) then "Print Page as Shown" (at the screen's top-right corner). Turn the printer on. Press Enter. The printer will print the directions. Afterwards, close the window (by clicking its X), so you return to the previous window.

While you're driving, reset your car's mileage counter to 0 each time you make a turn, so you can use the directions about how far to drive before turning — or if you prefer, try using the cumulative mileages that your printer adds for you.

Warning: the directions might mislead you (because highway exit numbers have changed, or the directions accidentally say "turn left" when they should say "turn right", or construction makes you take a detour, or a vandal removed a street sign, or you didn't notice a turn), so give yourself extra time to backtrack, ask neighbors for directions, and try to bring along a traditional map!

MapQuest started as a division of a printing company (R.R. Donnelley), then became independent, then became part of AOL, so now AOL owns MapQuest.

Different countries The US Government has a branch called the "Central Intelligence Agency" (CIA), whose job is to spy on all the other countries. For a summary of what the CIA found out about each country, go to the **Central Intelligence Agency (CIA.gov)**, then click "World Factbook" (which is at the screen's right edge).

Click "Select a Country or Location". You see a list of all the world's countries and oceans. (Use that list's scroll arrow to see the whole list.) Click whichever country or ocean interests you.

Then you see a map and these 9 topics:

introduction, geography, people, government, economy, communications, transportation, military, transnational issues

For more details, click the map or whichever topic interests you.

Airplane flights If you want a cheap plane ticket and are flexible about what day you'll travel, try **Cheap Airline Tickets (cheapflights.com)**.

Of the major airlines, **Southwest Airlines (Southwest.com)** and **Jet Blue (JetBlue.com)** tend to have the lowest prices. For other airlines, try going to **Orbitz.com** (a consortium of 20 major airlines), though Orbitz doesn't handle Southwest, American Airlines, and Delta.

Reputable references

The Internet contains many reputable references, which you can use, free!

Encyclopedia **Wikipedia.org** is the world's biggest encyclopedia — and it's free! It includes over 3,562,000 articles written in English, 1,192,000 in German, 1,070,000 in French, 776,000 in Polish, 775,000 in Italian, 735,000 in Japanese, 723,000 in Spanish, 673,000 in Portuguese, 672,000 in Dutch, 664,000 in Russian, 387,000 in Swedish, 345,000 in Chinese, and many in 266 other languages, making a total of over 17 million articles.

To find an article, click in the empty white box, type the topic you want to search for, then press Enter (assuming your language is English). While you read the article, you can click any blue word to find a related article about that word.

The articles are written and edited by thousands of volunteers.

To edit an article yourself, click "Edit" (which is at the screen's top) while you're reading the article. (Exception: if the article is on a controversial topic that's often vandalized, such as "Obama" or "France" or "abortion", the article is locked so "Edit" is invisible.)

The edits you suggest will be reviewed by other editors, to make sure your suggestions are academically correct, appropriately footnoted, unbiased, and free of any sales pitches — and you're not a vandal. The computer keeps track of who did which editing.

Some articles begin with a warning that the article needs further editing.

Old-fashioned professors required students to write "term papers", but modern professors require students to write articles for Wikipedia instead.

The encyclopedia is based on the honor system: to keep it worthwhile, please edit responsibly!

Over 99% of Wikipedia's articles are correct. A few are misleading, so you can't trust Wikipedia completely and must double-check what you read there, but it's a good starting point for your research on any topic, especially since most of its articles on controversial topics give a balanced view.

Health For info about health, start at **InteliHealth.com**. It contains info that's reliable, easy to understand, and well organized. The Web site is owned by Aetna insurance company, but most of the info comes from (or is approved by) the Harvard Medical School and the University of Pennsylvania School of Dental Medicine, with additional input from the National Institutes of Health (a government agency).

More details from the National Institutes of Health (and the National Library of Medicine) are at **MedlinePlus (nlm.nih.gov/medlineplus)**.

Bogus health claims, from marketers of supplements and "natural cures," are called "quackery". To find out which health claims are bogus (false), go to **QuackWatch.com**.

Tutorials **About.com** includes easy-to-read articles that tutor you in over 70,000 topics.

Click in the white box that says "GO". Type whatever topic interests you and press Enter.

You'll see two lists of Web sites. Ignore the first list (titled "Sponsored Links"), which is just ads; use the second list (called "About.com Search Results"), which shows About.com's tutorials: click whichever tutorial you want.

Rumors Often you'll hear a strange rumor, from a friend or an e-mail. You'll wonder whether the rumor is true. To find out, go to **Snopes.com**, which analyzes pernicious rumors (just as William Faulkner's novels analyze the pernicious Snopes family).

To use the site, you can use two methods.

Here's the fun method....

> Click one of these rumor categories:
>
> autos, business, Cokelore, college, computers, crime, critters, Disney, embarrass, fauxtos, food, fraud & scams, glurge, history, holidays, horror, humor, inboxer rebellion, language, legal, lost legends, love, luck, media matters, medical, military, movies, music, old wives' tales, politics, pregnant, quotes, racial rumors, radio & TV, religion, risqué business, science, sports, toxins, travel, weddings, 9/11, Hurricane Katrina
>
> Then click an underlined subcategory. You'll see a list of rumors. Each rumor has a ball in front of it: if the ball is green, the rumor is true; if the ball is red, the rumor is false; if the ball has a different color, the rumor isn't simply "true" or "false".
>
> If you click the rumor's underlined word, you'll see the rumor's details.

Here's the researcher's method....

> Click in the Search box. Type the rumor's main words (then press Enter). You see a list of rumors containing those words. Click the rumor that interests you. You'll see the rumor's details.

For the rumor's details, you see a sample of the full rumor (usually from an e-mail) then an analysis of it by Barbara Mikkelson, the world's best investigative journalist!

Corporations To find out about any big U.S. company (such as Microsoft or IBM or General Motors or Exxon/Mobil), go to **Hoovers.com**. Click in the blank box at the screen's top right corner, type a company's name (such as "Microsoft"), and press Enter.

You'll see a list of companies related to what you typed. For each company, you see its headquarters city and annual revenue (how many dollars worth of goods or services they sold in a year). Click the name of whichever company you wish. Then you see the company's stock symbol (if any), address, phone number, and fax number.

Near the top, you see 4 topics about the company:

Overview	People	Competition	Financials

Click whichever topic interests you, then scroll down to read details about that topic. (You'll be invited to buy a subscription to see more details.)

Home values To find out the worth of your home (the home you're in now or any home you're curious about), go to **Zillow.com**, click in the box under "Find home values and listings", type the home's address, and press Enter. You'll see:

> a map or photo of the neighborhood
>
> Zillow's estimate (Zestimate) of what the home is worth (based partly on its assessed value and partly on what nearby homes have recently sold for); Zillow's estimate is close to what your home will sell for if your home is normal (not weird or recently altered) and your town has kept accurate property records
>
> your home's details (year built and number of bedrooms, bathrooms, and square feet); if you click the underlined address above those details, you'll see more details

Lawns For advice on caring for your lawn, go to a Web site run by the University of Illinois and called **Lawn Challenge (www.urbanext.uiuc.edu/lawnchallenge)**.

It lets you click on 8 lessons:

> 1. Know Your Lawn Grasses
> 2. Dealing with Shady Sites
> 3. Seeding and Sodding Lawns
> 4. Watering, Mowing & Fertilizing
> 5. Thatch and Lawn Renovation
> 6. Weed Problems
> 7. Grubs & Other Insect Pests
> 8. Managing Home Lawn Diseases

You're supposed to do the lessons in that order; so to become a complete lawn expert, start by clicking "Know Your Lawn Grasses".

Each lesson contains several pages of well-written text. (Click ">" at a page's bottom-right corner, to proceed to the next page.) The text is accompanied by photos of good and bad lawns. The lesson ends with a test on how well you understood the lesson.

The details apply to lawns in northern Illinois, but the general principles apply to all lawns. Next time you argue with your neighbors or family about your lawn, here's how to make them shut up: say "I took a college course on the topic and passed all the tests."

Government

You can reach your government through the Internet.

General site To explore the US government, start at **USA.gov** and follow the links.

Taxes For help with federal taxes, contact the **Internal Revenue Service (IRS.gov)**. To get a tax form or instructions, click one of the forms mentioned at the screen's left edge or do this:

> Click "Forms and Publications>>". You see a list of popular forms and publications. If you want one of them, click it; if not, click "Form and Instruction number (PDF)" then click in the Find box then type the number of what you want and press Enter then click the underlined item you want.

You see the tax form (or instructions) on your screen. To copy onto paper, click the Printer icon that's near the top of the screen's left edge then press Enter. When the printing has finished, click the Back button (which is at the screen's top-left corner and has a left arrow on it) so you can see and print other forms and instructions.

Post office For info about how to mail a letter, go to the Web site of the **United States Postal Service (USPS.com)**. It answers several questions....

What's the best way to write an address on an envelope? For example, if you live in the USA, what's the best way to write *your* address? What's your 9-digit ZIP code? What's the *best* way to write your street name, house number, apartment number, etc.? You might be surprised! To find out all that, do this:

> Click "FIND A ZIP CODE" (which is at the screen's top left corner). You see a form that has 5 empty boxes (called "Address 1," "Address 2," "City," "State," and "ZIP Code"). Fill in those boxes as best you can, then click "Submit".
>
> The computer will analyze what you typed, fix your mistakes, and write the address the way the post office prefers it. For example, the computer will put in the 9-digit ZIP code, abbreviate words such as "Road", "Lane", and "Highway", get rid of all punctuation, and capitalize everything, so your address will be written the way the post office prefers and junk mailers use.

How much postage should you put on your letter or package? To find out, do this instead:

> Click "CALCULATE POSTAGE" (which is at the screen's top). If the package is going to the U.S., click the "Go" below "Calculate Domestic Postage"; if the package is going to a different country, click the "Go" below "Calculate International Postage".
>
> The computer will ask you a series of questions then tell you the correct postage. (One of the questions is the package's weight; if you're not sure, give an approximation, and the computer will give you an approximate answer, which you'll need to double-check by going to the post office and using the post office's scale.)
>
> You'll be surprised at the range of prices and choices, depending on how fast you need the package to travel, what type of goods are inside the package, and how thick & long the package is.

Classified ads

Craig's List (CraigsList.org), which was started by Craig Newmark in San Francisco, is a list of classified ads that you can read — and you can create your own ad, free! The ads are highly organized, so you can find what you want fast!

Craig's List is very popular. Each month, Craig's List has:

> 50 million new classified ads (of which 1 million are job ads)
> over 50 million people reading the ads (making a total of 20 billion clicks)

To begin, look at the screen's rightmost column, where you see a list of locations: click whatever country, state, or city interests you. (The menus will let you choose from 700 locations.)

Then you see ads from that location, organized into 9 main categories —

> community, personals, housing, for sale, services, jobs, gigs, résumés, discussion forums,

and hundreds of subcategories. Click whichever subcategory you want. (Most subcategories are tame, but a few require you to be at least 18.)

For each ad in that subcategory, you see the ad's headline. Click a headline to see its ad. When you finish looking at the ad, click the Back button (the left-arrow at the screen's top corner), so you return to seeing the list of headlines.

While you're looking at a list of headlines, you can create your *own* ad by clicking "post" (which is at the screen's top-right corner). Posting your ad is free, except for therapeutic-services ads, apartment-broker ads in New York City, and job ads in these 17 markets:

> Atlanta, Boston, Chicago, Dallas, Denver, Houston, Los Angeles, Miami, New York, Philadelphia, Phoenix, Portland, Sacramento, San Diego, Seattle, San Francisco, Washington DC

Those few exceptions are how Craig's List gets funded.

Shopping

The computer can help you shop.

Banks To compare banks in your city, state, and across the nation and find out which offer the best rates, go to **BankRate.com**. You get each bank's official rates and phone numbers. But beware of these limitations:

> When Bankrate.com shows you a table comparing bank rates, it doesn't show you the best rates first. To see the best rates first, click the "APY" button, which makes the table be sorted by APY rate.
>
> Bankrate.com doesn't mention **promotional rates** (great temporary rates advertised to new customers for crazy-length terms, such as "7-month CD") and **negotiated rates** (where a bank helps its old customers by matching rates from competitors), so ask your local bank about better deals!

Cars If you want to buy a car (new or used), visit these car sites to get smarter: **MSN Autos (autos.msn.com)**, **AutoByTel.com**, **Edmunds.com**, and **CarsDirect.com**.

Housing To buy, sell, or rent a home, use the classified ads at **Craig's List (CraigsList.org)** but also look at the advice and listings at **MSN Real Estate (RealEstate.msn.com)**. To estimate what a house is worth, go to **Zillow.com**, click in the box under "Find home values and listings", and type the home's address.

Books To buy traditional books quickly and cheaply, go to **Amazon.com**. (But to buy *this* book quickly and cheaply, phone me at 603-666-6644 for better deals.)

Eyeglasses To buy eyeglasses cheaply, go to ZenniOptical.com.

> You pay just $6.95 for a complete set of glasses. That price includes high-index lenses with anti-scratch coating, UV protection, lens-edge polishing & beveling, frame, carrying case, and cleaning cloth. Add a shipping charge of just $4.95 per order (regardless of how many glasses are in the order). If you want special lens treatments or special frames, you pay a surcharge, but it's small. Before ordering, you must find out what kind of glasses you want (by getting a prescription or making your own crude measurements). The glasses are custom-made for you in China and shipped by air from China to California to you.

Jobs To get a job, look at the ads at **Craig's List (CraigsList.org)** but also visit **Monster.com** and **CareerBuilder.com**. Each of those 3 sites has a million jobs (plus advice), so you see about 3 million jobs altogether.

Buy a business Have you ever dreamed of being the boss and running your own business? But are you too chicken to start your own? Would you rather buy a business that's already successful, and have the pleasure of running it? If so, go to the Web to find out what businesses are available for sale. A good place to start hunting is **BizBuySell.com**, which has over 45,000 businesses for sale.

Arts

The Internet has lots of info about arts.

YouTube One of the most popular Websites is **YouTube.com**. It lets you watch thousands of movies (videos) that are very short (usually between 2 and 8 minutes long), contributed by amateur movie makers (mostly students in their dorm rooms). Many are hilarious. They're much more interesting, per minute, than the stuff that Hollywood churns out, and they're free!

To use that site, you need a fast (broadband) Internet connection (cable or DSL).

The site divides movies into these categories:

> entertainment, music, news & politics, film & animation, sports, how-to & style, science & technology, people & blogs, non-profits & activism, comedy, gaming

Two other categories are:

> most viewed (the movies watched recently by the most people)
> top favorited (the movies voted "favorite" recently by the most people)

Those are too many categories to fit on the screen, so you see just *some* of those categories.

Below each category name is a frame from a movie in that category. Either click one of those frames (to see its movie) or click a category name (to see many examples of movies in that category, then click the example you like) or click in the search box (then type a topic or category name and press Enter, to see many examples of movies that match, then click the example you like).

If you start watching a movie and don't like it, click a different movie instead (or click the Back button).

Most of the movies are tame. Some movies are raunchy but require you to register and confirm you're at least 18 years old. Once you register, you can copy movies that you've created to YouTube.com, free, so all your friends and the whole world can admire what you've created!

Each movie has an ID, which is 11 characters long. While you watch a movie, its ID appears in the address box after "www.YouTube.com/watch?v=". If you know a movie's ID, you can see the movie by doing one of these activities:

type its ID after "www.YouTube.com/watch?v=" and press Enter
type its ID in YouTube's search box, press Enter, then click the sample frame
type its title in YouTube's search box, press Enter, click a sample frame, then verify the ID
go to my Website (SecretFun.com) and find a link to the movie

For example, try one of these amazing movies:

Warning: "**l**" is lower-case L, "**1**" is the digit 1, "**I**" is capital I, "**0**" is the digit zero, "**O**" is capital O

ID	Title	Contents
v6iE2j-e6m8	Free Lunch	tale of a man who gets free lunches by dating
MW0l9PUFf60	Obama Silent Movie	silent movie about love, starring Barack & Michelle Obama
tSdELZxEnHY	Strangers Again	alas, a relationship goes through 6 stages then breaks up
sak-EW81qiU	Na Ponta dos Pés	ballet through a Brazilian slum
smDIBmeeWck	Hedgehog in the Fog	Russian tale of a hedgehog
nQ798THmR5Y	The Devil's Trill	baroque music played by sexy pop violist Vanessa Mae
gXagKiuaL_4	Mozart Files	young girls trying to play Mozart
rRgXUFnfKIY	Beethoven 5th	Beethoven's 5th symphony, illustrated with colored blocks
YXjrUGv5b94	The Competition	Beethoven's 5th piano concerto, abridged to 6 minutes
eG1Olvh7vCU	Chopin Ballade #1	pianist Horowitz plays Chopin ballade, while you see score
XhnRIuGZ_dc	Horowitz Plays	pianist Horowitz plays the same ballade, while you see him
gWrqtJTEmBk	The Minute Waltz	pianists play the both halves of Chopin's waltz simultaneously
LfSYwJuq3Vg	Dvorak Quintet pt 1	Bush's Secretary of State Condoleezza Rice plays piano
4Ytj-I28nt8	Dvorak Quintet pt 2	part 2 of Condoleeza Rice's performance
elQVmzhk2gA	Dvorak Quintet	same piece performed by 5 music teachers from 5 countries
smTbMMn1V0o	Second Waltz	André Rieu joyously plays Shostakovich's second waltz
k4RCpd2EIFo	Piano Quintet	frenzied musicians playing Shostakovich's Piano Quintet
jZ5EX4VF9EI	Red Violin Concert	violin orgasm, from the movie "Red Violin"
fYy2p_0DVMU	Hail Mary	song that made Pomplamoose a famous 2-person band
OvYZMqQffQE	My Favorite Things	Pomplamoose's creative version of "Sound of Music" song
vsMIuuV05uc	La Vie en Rose	Pomplamoose's creative version of Edith Piaf's French song
qrO4YZeyl0I	Bad Romance	Lady Gaga's song about destructive love (R rated)
l3WPKznFvfk	Lady Pasta	parody of Lady Gaga's "Bad Romance"
niqrrmev4mA	Alejandro	Lady Gaga's other song about destructive love (R rated)
nroUJEplPnY	Alejandro Translation	critique of Lady Gaga's "Alejandro"
UCVMuevcCvY	Zombie Love Song	song of a zombie who wants to steal your heart — and brains
LbkNxYaULBw	What song is this?	national anthem backwards, so "brave" sounds like "vayrb"
nonVj7odbmU	Homecoming Queen	song from 1984, when "guns in school" were just fun fantasy
zqfFrCUrEbY	My Generation	the elderly reinterpret The Who's "My Generation"
DMGlQvPBQE0	Ed Roll'D Trololo	on censored Russian TV, singer hides cowboy song's words
X2BEhk1fqZo	Je Suis Jalouse	French woman jealous when her boyfriend's ex-lover visits
Mg9APRGaUS0	HappySlip Jingle	"Jingle Bells" sung by a split personality
x-ihI5_Vg6A	Nixon on Jack Paar	Richard Nixon (Vice President then President) plays piano
Ym0hZG-zNOk	Beat It	Michael Jackson's video about avoiding fights
ZcJjMnHoIBI	Eat It	Weird Al Yankovic's scene-by-scene parody of "Beat It"
osSeY9Xx3Gg	Pancreas	Weird Al Yankovic's parody of Beach Boys style
JdxkVQy7QLM	Pachelbel Rant	the only good music video about hating music
1Lj_IUai3ZU	Children's Song	hey, kids, watch this fun video while mommy slits her throat

Movie database To find out details about famous movies, go to the **Internet Movie Database (IMDb.com)** then do this:

Click in the white box that's next to "go". Type your favorite topic (for example, type the name of an actor, actress, director, or movie) then press Enter. The computer will show you a list of underlined topics similar to what you typed; click the topic you want.

You'll see lots of info about that topic.

For example, if the topic's a famous movie, you'll see info about its actors, actresses, director, writers, plot, quotable lines, and mistakes. You'll also get lots of opinions (from ordinary folks) about whether the movie was any good. Those man-in-the-street opinions are much more emotional and to-the-point than the blather published by most movie "critics". Different people notice different things about a movie: after you've watched a movie, read these reviews to find out what you didn't notice! You can also add your *own* comments about the movie (if you register, which is free), and you can get and give a list of similar movies that are recommended.

The Website is extremely well linked. For example, if you look up a movie, you see links to each member of the cast and staff who created the movie; each such link takes you to a biography of that person. So if you're watching a movie and wonder "Where have I seen him before?" just click on his link to find out! You can link back: each person's biography contains links to all the movies the person was in.

Because of the good links and content, this Website is on everybody's list of "the best Web sites ever created".

Free music To hear your favorite music, you can use 3 free methods:

1. Go to **YouTube.com**, which has videos, and see whether anybody made a video about your favorite music.

2. Go to **GrooveShark.com**. In the "Search for Music" box (which is in the screen's middle), type the name of your favorite song, composition, performer, composer, or musical style (and press Enter). You see a list of relevant musical tracks; click the track you want then "Play Song". To switch to different music, click in the search box (which is now near the top-right corner and shows a magnifying glass), then type what you want.

3. Go to **Pandora.com**. Click in the "artist or song" box. Type the name of your favorite song, composition, performer, composer, or musical style (and press Enter). The computer will invent a radio station that plays music similar to what you requested. You'll hear the station's first song. If you want to skip to the next song, click ►►|. Under each song's icon, you see a thumbs-down button and a thumbs-up button; click one of those buttons (or click "menu" then "I'm tired of this song") to tell the computer whether you liked the song, so the computer learns what kind of songs you like most and adjusts the radio station to please you more.

Rap Dictionary When you listen to rap music, do you understand all the slang? If not, go to **The Rap Dictionary (RapDict.org)**, which defines about 5000 slang words. If you want the definition of a specific word, click in the search box (at the screen left edge), type the word, and press Enter. If instead you want to browse through the dictionary, click either "Dictionary" (which starts showing you the main dictionary) or one of these dictionary categories —

nouns, verbs, adjectives, interjections, gangs, geography

or "Artists" (which starts showing you the list of who's who in the rap biz) or one of these artist categories:

groups, labels, MCs, DJs, producers

Classic books Did you ever wish you could walk into a library and find the greatest classic books, all in one place? They're all together at **Great Books Online (bartleby.com)**.

You get the complete text of hundreds of famous classics: the Bible, Homer, Shakespeare, many more masterpieces from many countries, plus fairy tales (by Aesop & Andersen & Grimm), science classics (written by Darwin and Einstein), reference works (Bartlett's Quotations and the American Heritage Dictionary), and beyond. What a feast! Click one of the four tabs ("Fiction", "Nonfiction", "Verse", or "Reference") and browse!

Nearly everything your literature teacher said you "ought" to read is here. Indulge! It's all yours, free. You don't even need a library card, and you don't need to "return it by next Tuesday".

For more details about Shakespeare, his writing, and his times, go to **Mr. William Shakespeare and the Internet (shakespeare.palomar.edu)**.

Math

To solve a math problem, go to **WolframAlpha.com**. You see a wide, orange search box. Click in that box, then type a math problem. If you don't see the answer yet, press Enter.

For example, if you type—

2+3

the computer will immediately say:

2+3=5

If you enter instead —

3+x=10

the computer will solve that algebra equation and say:

Solution: x = 7

(To see that solution, scroll down.) Nearby, the computer will also show graphs about that equation.

If you enter a problem involving advanced algebra or advanced calculus, the computer will solve it, show you the exact answer using algebra & calculus symbols, calculate the answer as a decimal also, show you graphs of everything involved, and let you click "Show steps" to see how the computer figured out the answer — and so, by copying those steps onto your homework paper, you can trick your teacher into believing you figured out the whole thing yourself!

Besides knowing standard high-school and college math, the computer also knows the other important numbers in life. For example, if you enter —

How old was Queen Elizabeth II when Elvis Presley was born?

the computer will look up the birthdays of those famous people, realize the queen was about 8 years old when Elvis was born, and give the exact answer:

Result: 8 years 8 months 18 days

It can also convert units: inches & meters, quarts & liters, Fahrenheit & Celsius, dollars & euros (using today's exchange rates), and anything else you can dream of. For example, it can solve:

convert $5 to euros

It understands many topics. Way beyond being a calculator, it calls itself a "computational knowledge engine". If you click "EXAMPLES" (which is at the screen's top), you see this list of topics:

mathematics, statistics & data analysis, physics, chemistry, materials, engineering, astronomy, earth sciences, life sciences, computational sciences, units & measures, dates & times, weather, places & geography, people & history, culture & media, music, words & linguistics, sports & games, colors, money & finance, socioeconomic data, health & medicine, food & nutrition, education, organizations, transportation, technological world, Web & computer systems

For each topic, you also see a list of subtopics. If you click a subtopic, you'll see examples of how to type that subtopic's problems into the search box.

This Website is starting to change the way math is taught. Instead of getting bogged down in the details of algebra & calculus computations, teachers are telling students to let WolframAlpha do those details; students should concentrate instead on learning what the problems and answers *mean* and how to interpret them.

Humor

The world is funny, and the Internet reflects that.

Trivia For 3,000 strange but true facts about many topics, go to **Useless Facts (www.AngelFire.com/ca6/uselessfacts)**. The screen's left edge shows this list of 20 topics:

animals, bugs, celebrities, crimes, food, geography, history, inventors, medical, musicians, myths, plants, science, sports, strange laws, surveys, TV and movies, words, world records, other

Click whichever topic you wish. Then you'll see lots of strange trivia about that topic. Scroll down to see more. At the Web page's bottom, click "next" to see even more.

Political humor The best movies making fun of politics are at **Jibjab.com**. Go there, then click "ORIGINALS" (at the screen's top). You'll see a list of some political satires. Click one of them, or click "All JibJab Originals" (at the bottom) to see 3 pages more. These are the most polished:

Title	Year	Message
This Land	2004	2004 Presidential campaign was goofy
Big Box Mart	2005	Walmart is scary
Nuckin' Futs!	2006	2006 was scary — fuckin' nuts!
What We Call the News	2007	TV news is just fluff
Star Spangled Banner	2007	Presidential speeches are goofy
Time for Some Campaignin'	2008	2008 Presidential campaign was goofy
He's Barack Obama	2009	We want Obama to be Superman

For other political humor, go to **Political Humor (politicalhumor.about.com)**.

Black pride For a funny list of appliances invented by blacks, without which white folks would be miserable, look at **What If There Were No Black People (MuhammadSpeaks.com/Whatif.html)**.

Darwin awards Darwin believed in evolution, caused by "survival of the fittest". The Darwin awards are given each year to fools who proved Darwin's principle by accidentally killing themselves. To see how the fools killed themselves — and to be glad you're not as stupid as they — go to **DarwinAwards.com**. The Website says:

The Darwin Awards commemorate those who improve our gene pool by removing themselves from it.

Computer industry

For questions about the computer industry's dominant company (Microsoft) and its products, go directly to Microsoft's own Web site, **Microsoft.com**. Click a menu item, photo, or ad, or click the white box (at the screen's top-right corner) then type the specific topic you're interested in (and press Enter).

For info about Apple's computers & products, **go to Apple.com**.

Hassles

While you use the Internet, you'll experience several hassles.

Delays

The computer might take a long time to switch from one page to another. Near the Start button (at the screen's bottom-left corner), the computer prints messages about the switch.

How to stop

If the switch is taking a long time and you don't want to wait for it to finish, click the **Stop button**, which is near the screen's top *left* or *center*, not the top right!

IE9:	the Stop button is an *X* at the address box's end.
IE 8:	the Stop button is a *red X on a gray background.*
IE 6&7:	the Stop button is a *red X on a white background.*
Firefox 4&5:	the Stop button is an *X that appears at the address box's end.*
Firefox 3.6:	the Stop button is an *X that turns blue when available.*
Chrome:	the Stop button is an *X that appears left of the address box.*

Clicking the Stop button makes the computer stop the switching.

"Switching pages" is called **loading a new page**. When you click the Stop button, here's what happens:

If the computer has nearly finished loading the new page, the computer shows you most of the new page.

If the computer has *not* nearly finished loading the new page, the computer shows you the previous page.

How to try again

When you try to view a new page, the computer might get stuck because of a transmission error. To try again, stop the current transmission attempt (by clicking the **Stop button**) and then see what happens.

If you find yourself back at the previous page, try again to switch to the new page.

On the other hand, if you find yourself with most, but not all, of the new page on the screen, and you insist on seeing the entire new page, tell your ISP to try again to transmit the current page, by doing this:

IE 9:	Click the **Refresh button** (an arrow circling to the right).
IE 6&7&8:	Click the **Refresh button** (a pair of curved arrows).
Firefox and Chrome:	Click the **Reload button** (an arrow circling to the right).

Change the home page

When your computer gets IE or Firefox for the first time, here's what happens:

IE	makes the home page be the computer manufacturer's website.
Firefox	makes the home page be www.google.com altered for Firefox.
Chrome	makes the home page show a list of pages you'd like.

But you can change the home page. Make it be anything you want! If there's no particular page you want to always start with, you can even make the home page be blank.

Here's how to change the home page.

IE 9 If you want the home page to be just a blank page (and it's not a blank page yet), do this:

Click the Tools button (the bumpy-circle gear at the screen's right edge) then "Internet options" then "Use blank" then "OK".

If instead you want a particular page to become the home page, do this:

Get that page onto your screen (so you can admire it). Click the Tools button (the bumpy-circle gear at the screen's right edge) then "Internet options" then "Use current" then "OK".

IE 7&8 If you want the home page to be just a blank page (and it's not a blank page yet), do this:

Click the Home button's down-arrow then "Remove" then "Remove All" then "Yes".

If instead you want a particular page to become the home page, do this:

Get that page onto your screen (so you can admire it). Click the Home button's down-arrow then "Add or Change Home Page" then "Use this webpage as your only home page" then "Yes".

IE 6 If you want the home page to be just a blank page, do this:

Click "Tools" then "Internet Options" then "Use Blank" then OK.

If instead you want a particular page to become the home page, do this:

Get that page onto your screen (so you can admire it). Click "Tools" then "Internet Options" then "Use Current" then OK.

Firefox 4&5 Here's how to make a particular page become the home page:

Get that page onto your screen (so you can admire it). Click the orange "Firefox" button then "Options" then "General". Make sure the "When Firefox starts" box says "Show my home page"; if it doesn't, click the box's down-arrow then click "Show my home page". Click "Use Current Page" then OK.

If you want to avoid having Firefox start at a home page, do this:

Click the orange "Firefox" button then "Options" then "General". Click the "When Firefox starts" box's down-arrow. In the future, when you restart Firefox (by clicking "start" then "Mozilla Firefox"), what will you want Firefox to do? If you want Firefox to always begin with a blank page, click "Show a blank page" now; if you want Firefox to always begin by continuing where you left off in your previous session, click "Show my windows and tabs from last time" instead. Click OK.

Firefox 3.6 Here's how to make a particular page become the home page:

Get that page onto your screen (so you can admire it). Click "Tools" then "Options" then "General". Make sure the "When Firefox starts" box says "Show my home page"; if it doesn't, click the box's down-arrow then click "Show my home page". Click "Use Current Page" then OK.

If you want to avoid having Firefox start at a home page, do this:

Click "Tools" then "Options" then "General". Click the "When Firefox starts" box's down-arrow. In the future, when you restart Firefox (by clicking "start" then "Mozilla Firefox"), what will you want Firefox to do? If you want Firefox to always begin with a blank page, click "Show a blank page" now; if you want Firefox to always begin by continuing where you left off in your previous session, click "Show my windows and tabs from last time" instead. Click OK.

Chrome Don't bother changing the home page; it's already quite useful.

Cache

Whenever you view a page, the computer secretly puts a copy of it onto your hard disk, in a folder called the **cache** (which is pronounced "cash" and is a French word that means "hiding place"). Later, if you try to view the same page again, the computer checks whether the page's copy is still in the cache. If the copy is still in the cache, the computer puts that copy up onto your screen, because using that copy is faster than making your ISP retransmit the page.

When the cache gets so full that no more pages fit in it, the computer discards the pages you haven't viewed recently. Also, the computer tends to **clear the cache** (erase the entire cache) when you exit from the browser (by clicking the X box).

Whenever you tell the computer that you want to view a page, the page will come onto your screen fast if the computer uses the page's **cached copy**. If the computer can't find the page's cached copy (because the page was never viewed before or because the cached copy was discarded), the computer tells your ISP to transmit the page and you must wait awhile for the transmission to finish.

> Problem: suppose you want to check the latest news (such as the news about a war or an election or stocks). If you view a page that shows you news, you might be reading *old* news, because the computer might be using an old cached copy of the page. **To make sure you're reading the latest news, click the Refresh button** (which Firefox and Chrome call the "Reload button"). That forces the computer to get a new version of the page from your ISP.

Eat up your time

The Internet can eat up a lot of your time. You'll wait a long time for your modem, your ISP, and Web sites to transmit info to you. If you try search the Web for info about a particular topic, you'll spend lots of time visiting wrong Web sites before you finally find the site containing the gem of info you desire.

Along the way, you'll be distracted by ads and other seductive links to pages that are fun, fascinating, and educational. They don't directly relate to the question you wanted answered, but they broaden your mind and expand your horizon, o cybercitizen and student of the world! The Internet is the ultimate serendipity: it answers questions you didn't know you had.

Trust

Don't trust the info you read on the Internet. Any jerk can create a Web page. The info displayed on a Web page might be misleading, dishonest, or lies.

Unlike the typical book, whose accuracy is checked by the book's editor and publisher, the typical Web page is unchecked. An individual with unconventional ideas can easily create a Web page expressing those ideas, even if no book-publishing company would publish such a book.

Info on Web pages can be racist, hateful, sexist, libelous, treasonous, and deadly. Even though the Web page appears on your computer's screen, the info on the Web page might *not* have the good-natured accuracy that computers are known for.

Freedom of speech The United States Constitution's first amendment guarantees that Americans have freedom of speech and freedom of the press. The Internet makes that freedom possible, by letting anybody create a Web page that says anything to the whole world. The Internet is freedom unchained, uncensored. That's wonderful but frightening.

Dictators in many countries have tried to suppress the Internet, because the Internet lets people say and speak truths from around the world and band together to protest against dictatorship. Nice people in many countries have also tried to suppress the Internet when they see how many lies are printed on the Web.

Fringe groups The Web is an easy way for "fringe groups" to advertise themselves and make their voices heard. In a dictatorship, the "fringe groups" are those who want democracy; in a democracy, the "fringe groups" are often those who want to create their own little dictatorships.

Unreliable advice Use the Web as a way to broaden your mind to different ideas, but don't believe in them until you've thought about them and checked them against other sources. Some of the medical advice on the Web can kill you; some of the financial advice on the Web can bankrupt you; some of the career advice on the Web can land you in jail. About 90% of what's written on the Web is true, but beware of the other 10%.

Who's the source? When reading a Web page, consider its source. If the Web page is written by a person or company you trust, the info on that page is probably true. If the Web page is written by a total stranger, be cautious.

Errors If the Web page contains many spelling & grammar errors, its author might be a foreigner, an immigrant, a kid, or an idiot. Perhaps the ideas on the page are as inaccurate as the way they're expressed. When researching a topic on the Web, don't be surprised if one of the Web pages turns out to be just a copy of a term paper written by a kid whose teacher gave it an F because its info is all wrong.

Ads Even if a Web page is written by a reputable source, beware: it might include ads from other organizations whose motives are unsavory. When reading a traditional newspaper page printed on paper, you can usually tell which parts of the page are ads and which parts are articles, since the ads use different fonts; but when you're reading a Web page, it's not always clear which links are to "articles" and which links are to "ads", since the entire Web is a vast jumble of fonts.

Parental controls Many parents are afraid to expose their young kids to wild sex, wild violence, and wild hate groups. Many Internet pages contain lots of sex, violence, and hatred, either directly or through the ads they lead you to. Many parents don't want to expose their young kids to such Web pages. Many conservative religious people are afraid to expose *themselves* to such Satanic temptations.

You can get programs that censor the Internet. For example, you can get programs that stop your computer from displaying pages mentioning sexy words; but beware: a program stopping all references to "breast" will also stop you from researching "breast cancer" and "chicken breast recipes". You can get programs that limit kids to just pages that have been reviewed and approved by wise adults; but then the kids are restricted from reading any newer, better pages that haven't been reviewed yet.

E-mail

Here's another popular Internet activity: you can send **electronic mail** (**e-mail**). An e-mail message imitates a regular letter or postcard but is transmitted electronically so you don't have to lick a stamp, don't have to walk to the mailbox to send it, and don't have to wait for the letter to be processed by your country's postal system.

E-mail zips through the Internet at lightning speed, so a letter sent from Japan to the United States takes just minutes (sometimes even seconds) to reach its destination. Unlike regular mail, which the Post Office usually delivers just once a day, e-mail can arrive anytime, day or night. If your friends try to send you e-mail messages while your computer is turned off, your Internet service provider will hold their messages for you until you turn your computer back on and reconnect to the Internet.

Since sending e-mail is so much faster than using the Post Office (which is about as slow as a snail), the Post Office's mail is nicknamed **snail mail**. Yes, e-mail travels fast, takes just a few minutes to reach its destination, and is free; snail mail travels slowly, typically takes several *days* to reach its destination, and costs about 50¢ (for a stamp, an envelope, and paper to write on). So if your friend promises to send you a letter "soon", ask "Are you going to send it by e-mail or snail mail?"

An "e-mail message" is sometimes called just "**an e-mail**". Instead of saying "I sent 3 e-mail messages", an expert says "I sent 3 e-mails".

To use e-mail, you need an **e-mail program**.

The e-mail program is called **an e-mail client** if it's on your computer's hard disk. Here are the most popular e-mail clients:

Outlook Express	is part of Windows XP
Windows Mail	is part of Windows Vista
Windows Live Mail	is a free add-on to Windows XP&Vista&7
Outlook	is by Microsoft and part of Microsoft Office
Safari	is by Apple and part of Mac OS X
Thunderbird	is by Mozilla.org, for use with Firefox

The e-mail program is called **webmail service** if it's on a Website instead of your computer's hard disk. Here are the most popular webmail services for the general public:

Yahoo Mail	is at mail.yahoo.com,	which is owned by Yahoo
Gmail	is at www.gmail.com,	which is owned by Google
Hotmail	is at www.hotmail.com,	which is owned by Microsoft

Some ISPs (such as AOL and Comcast) have invented special webmail services for use by just their own customers.

Which is better to use: an e-mail client or a webmail service? An e-mail client has 3 advantages over a webmail service:

An e-mail client **runs faster** than webmail.

An e-mail client **understands more commands** than webmail.

A webmail service puts ads on your screen and in your outgoing messages; an e-mail client **doesn't force you to look at ads**.

But an e-mail client has 2 *dis*advantages:

Before you use an e-mail client the first time, **you must install it**.

If you've switch to a different computer (because you bought a new computer, or your building has several computers, or you're visiting a friend), you can't easily read your old messages: **your messages and e-mail privileges are restricted to one computer** (unless you fiddle a lot).

This chapter explains how to use these popular e-mail programs:

Outlook Express 6	(an e-mail client for Windows XP)
Windows Mail 6	(an e-mail client for Windows Vista)
Windows Live Mail 2011	(a newer e-mail client, for Windows Vista&7)
Yahoo Mail	(a webmail service)
Gmail	(a newer webmail service)

Simple e-mail

E-mail can be simple!

Start

Here's how to start using e-mail.

Yahoo Mail To use Yahoo Mail (which is a webmail service), use your Web browser (such as Internet Explorer) to go to mail.yahoo.com. The computer will say "Yahoo Mail".

If you have a Yahoo ID already, do this:

Type your Yahoo address (such as SecretGuide@yahoo.com) or just the part that comes before "@" (such as SecretGuide). Press the Tab key, type your Yahoo password, and press Enter.

If you *don't* have a Yahoo ID yet, do this instead:

Click "Create New Account". Click in the "First name" box. Type your first name, press the Tab key, type your last name, click the Gender box's down-arrow, click your gender ("Male" or "Female"), click "Select Month", click your birth month, and finish typing the date you were born (by typing in the Day and Year boxes).

The computer assumes you live in the United States. If you live in a different country, do this: click in the Country box, type your country's first letter, then click your country's name.

Click in the Postal Code box. Type your postal code (which in the United States is the ZIP code).

Click in the "Yahoo ID and Email" box. Invent your Yahoo ID. It must begin with a letter. It must have at least 3 more characters, which can include letters, digits, underlines, at most one period, no spaces, no special symbols. (For example, I invented SecretGuide.) Type what you invented. Click "Check".

If the computer says "This ID is not available", do this: click in the box, invent a different Yahoo ID, type it, then click "Check".

Click in the Password box. Invent a Yahoo password that's at least 6 characters long. Type it, press Tab, then type it again.

Finish filling the form. Click "Create My Account" (which you see when you scroll down).

The computer will say "Congratulations!" Click "Continue".

GMail To use GMail (which is a webmail service), use your Web browser (such as Internet Explorer) to go to www.gmail.com. The computer will say "Gmail".

If you have a Gmail account already, do this:

Type your Gmail address (such as TrickyLiving@gmail.com) or just the part that comes before "@" (such as TrickyLiving). Press the Tab key, type your Gmail password, and press Enter.

If you *don't* have a Gmail account yet, do this instead:

> Click "Create an account". Click in the "First name" box. Type your first name, press the Tab key, type your last name, and press the Tab key.
>
> Invent your Gmail account name. It must have at least 6 characters, which can including letters, digits, periods, no spaces, no special characters. (For example, I invented TrickyLiving.) Type what you invented. Click the "check availability" button.
>
> If the computer says "is not available", do this: double-click in the box, invent a different Gmail account name, type it, then click "check availability" again.
>
> Click in the Password box. Invent a Gmail password that's at least 8 characters long. Type it, press Tab, then type it again.
>
> Finish filling the form. Click "I accept. Create My Account" (which you see when you scroll down).
>
> The computer will say "Congratulations!" Click "Show me my accounts".

Outlook Express To start using Outlook Express, choose one of these methods….

> **Method 1** Click "start" then "Outlook Express".
>
> **Method 2 (works usually)** While you're running Internet Explorer 5, 5.5, or 6, click the **Mail button** (which is at the top of the screen). Click "Read Mail".

If the computer says "Internet Connection Wizard", do this:

> Type **your name** as you'd like it to appear in all e-mail messages you send (such as "Russ Walter"). Press Enter.
>
> Click in the "E-mail address" box. Type the **e-mail address** that your ISP agreed to assign you (such as poo@gis.net). Press Enter.
>
> Type the name of your ISP's **incoming mail server** (such as "pop.gis.net"). Press Tab. Type the name of your ISP's **outgoing mail server** (such as "smtp.gis.net"). Press Enter.
>
> Press the Tab key. Type the user password that your ISP agreed to assign to you. (While you type your password, asterisks or black circles will appear on your screen, to hide your password from any enemy who's looking over your shoulder.) Press Enter twice.
>
> If the computer asks you, type your password again (and press Enter).

Here's how to set up Outlook Express to work with Comcast's webmail service:

> Click "Set up a Mail account".
>
> Type **your name** as you'd like it to appear in all e-mail messages you send (such as "Russ Walter"). Press Enter.
>
> Click in the "E-mail address" box. Type the **e-mail address** that your ISP agreed to assign you (such as SecretGuide@comcast.net). Press Enter.
>
> Type the name of your ISP's **incoming mail server** (such as "mail.comcast.net"). Press Tab. Type the name of your ISP's **outgoing mail server** (such as "smtp.comcast.net"). Press Enter.
>
> Press the Tab key. Type the user password that your ISP agreed to assign to you. (While you type your password, asterisks or black circles will appear on your screen, to hide your password from any enemy who's looking over your shoulder.) Press Enter twice.
>
> Click Tools then Accounts. Double-click "mail.comcast.net" then Servers. Put a check mark in the "My server requires authentication" box (by clicking it). Click "Advanced". Type 587 and press Enter. Press Enter again.

You'll see the **Outlook Express window**. If it doesn't consume the whole screen yet, **maximize it** (by clicking its maximize button, which is next to the X button).

Windows Mail To start using Windows Mail, click Start then "Windows Mail".

If the computer says "Your Name", do this:

> Type **your name** as you'd like it to appear in all e-mail messages you send (such as "Russ Walter"). Press Enter.
>
> Click in the "E-mail address" box. Type the **e-mail address** that your ISP agreed to assign you (such as SecretGuide@comcast.net). Press Enter.
>
> Type the name of your ISP's **incoming mail server** (such as "mail.comcast.net"). Press Tab. Type the name of your ISP's **outgoing mail server** (such as "smtp.comcast.net"). Press Enter.
>
> Press the Tab key. Type the user password that your ISP agreed to assign to you. (While you type your password, black circles will appear on your screen, to hide your password from any enemy who's looking over your shoulder.) Press Enter twice.

> Click Tools then Accounts. Double-click "mail.comcast.net" then Servers. Put a check mark in the "My server requires authentication" box (by clicking it). Click "Advanced". Type 587 and press Enter. Press Enter again.

You'll see the **Windows Mail window**. If it doesn't consume the whole screen yet, **maximize it** (by clicking its maximize button, which is next to the X button).

Windows Live Mail Windows Live Mail is part of Windows Live Essentials.

If your computer doesn't have Windows Live Essentials yet, you can get it & install it by one of these methods:

> Method 1: Using your Web browser (such as Internet Explorer), go to explore.live.com. Click the biggest "Windows Live Essentials" then "Download now". Then follow the screen's instructions.

> Method 2: Click Start then "All Programs" then "Windows Update". Then follow the screen's instructions.

> Method 3 (requires Windows 7): Click Start then "Getting Started" then "Get Windows Live Essentials" then "Download now". Then follow the screen's instructions.

To start using Windows Live Mail (after it's been installed), click Start then "All Programs" then "Windows Live Mail".

You'll see the **Windows Live Mail window**. If it doesn't consume the whole screen yet, **maximize it** (by clicking its maximize button, which is next to the X button).

If the computer says "Sign in to Windows Live Mail", do the following….

If you have a Windows Live ID already, do this:

> Type your Windows Live ID password. Check the box marked "Remember me and sign me in automatically". Click the "Sign in" button.

If you *don't* have a Windows Live ID yet, do this instead:

> Click "Sign up". Click in the "Use your email address" box. Type the **e-mail address** that your ISP agreed to assign you (such as SecretGuide@comcast.net). Press the Tab key.
>
> The computer asks for a **Windows Live ID password**. You can invent a password; but to avoid confusion, I recommend you use the password your ISP assigned you. Type it, press Tab, type it again, press Tab again.
>
> Type your **first name** (or nickname) as you'd like it to appear in all e-mail messages you send (such as "Russ"). Press Tab, type your **last name**, press Tab again.
>
> Fill in the rest of the form. Click the "I accept" button (which you see when you scroll down).
>
> Close all windows, so you can start fresh (and avoid Microsoft's ads about Hotmail).
>
> Go back to the paragraph that begins, "To start using Windows Live Mail…".

If the computer asks "Set Windows Live Mail as your default email program?", click "Yes".

If your ISP is Comcast, do this (if you haven't done so already):

> Click "Accounts" (which is at the screen's top) then "Properties" then "Advanced". Type 587. Remove the check mark from "Leave a copy of messages on server" (by clicking). Press Enter. Click "Home".

If the computer says "Verify the email address", do this (if you haven't done so already):

> Click "Verify the email address". Then click the line below "Use this link to verify your account". Then follow the instructions. Then close the Web browser window, so you see the Windows Live Mail window again.

Incoming mail

Here's how to handle incoming mail.

At the screen's left edge, you see "Inbox".

> In Yahoo Mail & Gmail & Windows Live Mail, click the "Inbox" that's at the screen's left edge.

> In Outlook Express & Windows Mail, click the "Inbox" that's at the screen's left edge and below the word "Folders".

Now most of the screen is divided into 3 big white windowpanes, which I'll call "left", "top", and "bottom". (Exception: in Windows Live Mail", the "bottom" pane is actually to the *right* of the "top" pane instead of below.)

In addition to those big panes, you might see extras:

> Yahoo Mail shows ads at the screen's right edge.
>
> Windows Mail shows a calendar at the screen's right edge.
>
> Gmail shows a one-line ad at the screen's top.
>
> Outlook Express might show a tiny "Contacts" pane in the screen's bottom-left corner.

The top pane shows a list of all e-mail messages that other people have sent you. For each message, the list shows whom the message is **from** (the sender's name), the message's **subject** (what the message is about), and the time when the message was **received**.

> The first time Microsoft's Outlook Express or Windows Mail is used on your computer, the top pane shows you've received a message from Microsoft.
>
> The first time Windows Live Mail is used on your computer, the top pane shows you've received a message from the Windows Live Team. That message asks you to "Verify the email address".
>
> The first time Yahoo Mail is used with your Yahoo ID, the top pane shows you've received a message from Yahoo.
>
> The first time GMail is used with your Gmail account, the top pane shows you've received a message from the GMail Team.

After you've used the e-mail program awhile, you'll probably receive additional messages, from your friends!

Here's how to deal with a long list of messages:

> Each message is initially listed in bold type (and Outlook Express & Windows Mail & Windows Live Mail show a picture of a sealed envelope). If you look at a message's details awhile (at least 1 second in Windows Live Mail, 2 seconds in Yahoo Mail, 5 seconds in Outlook Express & Windows Mail), that message becomes unbolded (and Outlook Express & Windows Mail shows its envelope opened).
>
> If there are too many messages to fit in the pane, view the rest of the messages by pressing that pane's scroll-down arrow (the symbol ▼ or ∨ at the pane's bottom right corner).

In what order do the messages appear?

> **Gmail & Windows Live Mail** The computer puts similar messages together, to form a **conversation thread** of back-and-forth replies.

> **Outlook Express & Windows Mail & Yahoo Mail** If you click the word "Received" in Outlook Express & Windows Mail (or "Date" in Yahoo Mail), the messages are listed in the order received (chronological order). If you click the word "From" instead, the messages are listed by the sender's name (in alphabetical order). Clicking "Received" is typically more useful than clicking "From". When you click the word "Received" or "From", a triangle appears next to that word. If you click that same word again, the triangle flips upside-down — and so does the list. For example, suppose the triangle is next to the word "Received": if the triangle points down, the messages are listed from newest to oldest; if the triangle points up instead, the messages are listed from oldest to newest.

Look in the top pane, at the list of messages you received. Decide which message you want to read, and click the sender's name. Then you start seeing the complete message.

> **Outlook Express, Windows Mail, and Yahoo Mail**: the message appears in the bottom pane.
>
> **Windows Live Mail**: the message appears in the so-called "bottom" pane (which is actually to the *right* of the top pane instead of below).
>
> **Gmail**: the top pane shows the message, and its right edge shows ads relating to the message's words; when you finish reading the message & ads, click "Back to Inbox" to make the top pane return to normal.

If the message is too long to fit in its pane, you can see the rest of the message by press that pane's scroll-down arrow (the symbol ▼ or ∨ at the pane's bottom right corner).

Junk If a message seems to be junk, here's what happens:

> **Outlook Express** puts the message in the Inbox, like any other message.
>
> **Windows Mail** puts the message in the **Junk E-mail folder** instead of the Inbox. To see what's in the Junk E-mail folder, click "Junk E-mail". To see what's in the Inbox again, click Inbox.
>
> **Windows Live Mail** puts the message in the **Junk email folder** instead of the Inbox. To see what's in the Junk E-mail folder, click "Junk email". To see what's in the Inbox again, click Inbox.
>
> **Yahoo Mail** puts the message in the **Spam folder** instead of the Inbox. To see what's in the Spam folder, click the Spam button at the screen's left edge. To see what's in the Inbox again, click Inbox. Once a month, the computer erases the Spam folder's messages.
>
> **Gmail** puts the message in the **Spam folder** instead of the Inbox. To see what's in the Spam folder, click the Spam button at the screen's left edge. (If you don't see that button yet, make it appear by clicking the **more button**, which says "6 more" or something similar.) To see what's in the Inbox again, click Inbox. If a message has been in the Spam folder for more than 30 days, the computer erases it.

How to send mail

To write an e-mail message, perform 5 steps.

Step 1: get the window In Outlook Express & Windows Mail, do this:

> Click "**Create Mail**". You'll see the **New Message window**.

In Windows Live Mail, do this:

> Click "**Email message**" (which is near the screen's top-left corner). You'll see the **New Message window**.

In Yahoo Mail, do this:

> Click the **New** button (which is near the screen's top-left corner, next to "Check mail"). The top pane will say "**New Email Message**".

In Gmail, do this:

> Click "**Compose Mail**". The top pane will say "**To**".

Step 2: choose a recipient To whom do you want to send the message? To send an e-mail message to a person, you must find out that person's e-mail address. For example, if you want to send an e-mail message to me, you need to know that **my e-mail address is "Russ@SecretFun.com"**.

For the Internet, **each e-mail address contains the symbol "@", which is pronounced "at"**. For example, my Internet address, "Russ@SecretFun.com", is pronounced "russ at secret fun dot com".

To find out the e-mail addresses of your friends and other people, ask them (by chatting with them in person or by phoning them or by sending them snail-mail postcards).

If you send e-mail to the following celebrities and nuts, they'll probably read what you wrote. (But they might not have enough time to write back, and they prefer you use the feedback forms on their Websites instead.)

	Comment	E-mail address
Actors		
Clint Eastwood	rugged Westerner	RowdiYates@aol.com
Tom Hanks	plays nice guy in trouble	NY122@aol.com
Brad Pitt	heartthrob	CiaoBox@msn.com
Tom Cruise	heartthrob	AGoodActor@aol.com
John Travolta	black-jacket cool	JohnTravolta@EarthAlliance.com
Adam Sandler	childish adult	sandler@cris.com
Talk-show hosts		
David Letterman	CBS's "Late Show"	LateShow@pipeline.com
Jay Leno	NBC's "Tonight Show"	TonightShow@nbc.com
Oprah Winfrey	warm	harpo@InterAccess.com
Howard Stern	talks dirty on radio	SternShow@HowardStern.com
Politicians		
Barack Obama	President of USA	comments@WhiteHouse.gov
Joe Biden	Vice-President of USA	Vice_President@WhiteHouse.gov
Reporters & commentators		
Dave Barry	syndicated columnist	NoLowFlow@DaveBarry.com
Roger Ebert	movie critic, thumbs up	feedback@RogerEbert.com
Bill Nye	PBS's "Science Guy"	BillNye@nyelabs.com
Fictions		
Santa Claus	delivers presents	santa@NorthPole.com
Scott Adams	draws Dilbert cartoons	ScottAdams@aol.com
Computerists		
Bill Gates	Microsoft's chairman	BillG@microsoft.com
Russ Walter	nut, wrote this book	Russ@SecretFun.com
Pop singers		
Britney Spears	young	Britney@BritneySpears.com
Madonna	sexual	Madonna@wbr.com
Sports heroes		
Tiger Woods	golfer	Tiger@TigerWoods.com
Evander Holyfield	boxer had his ear bit	Evander@EvanderHolyfield.com

When you type an e-mail address, you don't have to capitalize. The computer ignores capitalization.

Never put a blank space in the middle of an e-mail address.

Warning: people often change their e-mail addresses, so don't be surprised if your message comes back, marked undeliverable.

Type the e-mail address of the person to whom you want to send your message. If you're a shy beginner who's nervous about bothering people, **try sending an e-mail message to a close friend or me or yourself**. Sending an e-mail message to yourself is called "doing a Fats Waller", since he was the first singer to popularize these lyrics:

> Gonna sit right down and write myself a letter,
> And make believe it came from you!

If you send an e-mail message to *me*, I'll read it (unless my e-mail address has changed) and try to send you a reply, but be patient (since I typically check my e-mail just a few times per day and don't check it when I travel) and avoid asking for computer advice (since I give extensive *advice* just by regular phone calls at 603-666-6644, not by e-mail).

At the end of the e-mail address, press the Tab key twice (just once in Gmail & Windows Live Mail), so you're at the line marked "Subject".

Step 3: choose a subject Type a phrase summarizing the subject (such as "let's lunch" or "I'm testing"). At the end of that typing, press the Tab key again.

Step 4: type the message Go ahead: type the message, such as "Let's have lunch together in Antarctica tomorrow!" or "I'm testing my e-mail system, so please tell me whether you received this test message." Your message can be as long as you wish — many paragraphs! Type the message as if you were using a word processor. For example, press the Enter key just when you reach the end of a paragraph. (If you're using Outlook Express or Windows Mail or Windows Live Mail, you can maximize the window you're typing in by clicking the window's maximize button, which is next to the X button.)

Step 5: send the message When you finish typing the message, click the **Send button**.

> **Outlook Express & Windows Mail** The Send button is above where you typed the e-mail address. It shows an envelope with a right-arrow.
>
> **Windows Live Mail** The Send button is left of where you typed the e-mail address. It shows an envelope with a right-arrow.
>
> **Yahoo Mail & GMail** The Send button is above where you typed the e-mail address.

If the computer says "Display name" (because you're using Outlook Express and haven't sent e-mails before), do this:

> Type **your name** as you'd like it to appear on all e-mail messages you send (such as "Russ Walter"). Press Enter.
>
> Type the **e-mail address** that your ISP agreed to assign you (such as "poo@gis.net"). Press Enter.
>
> Type the name of your ISP's **incoming mail server** (such as "pop.gis.net"). Press Tab. Type the name of your ISP's **outgoing mail server** (such as "smtp.gis.net"). Press Enter.
>
> Press the Tab key. Type the user password that your ISP agreed to assign to you. (While you type your password, black circles will appear on your screen, to hide your password from any enemy who's looking over your shoulder.) Press Enter twice.

In Outlook Express & Windows Mail & Windows Live Mail & Gmail, the window (or pane) you typed in will close automatically. In Yahoo Mail, this happens instead:

> If the computer says "Verification", type a copy of the big distorted characters you see (to prove you're a human who has eyes and a brain), then press Enter. (If the computer says "There was a problem", try again.)
>
> The computer will say "Message Sent". If the computer says "Recipients not in your Contacts", click the box marked "Automatically add new recipients to my Contacts".
>
> Click "OK".

When do messages transmit?

When you try to send or receive a message, when does the transmission actually occur?

Receiving a message from a friend When a friend tries to send you a message, the message goes from your friend's computer to your friend's **e-mail server** (such as Yahoo or your friend's Internet Service Provider), which passes the message on to *your* e-mail server. The message is stored on your e-mail server's hard disk.

Since your e-mail server is always turned on (day and night, 24 hours), it's always ready to receive messages your friends try to send you, even while your own computer is turned off.

When you try to examine your Inbox, your computer ought to contact your e-mail server and tell the e-mail server to transmit any new messages to your computer; but if your computer is lazy, it might not contact your e-mail server immediately to get the newest messages. Instead, your computer might decide to wait awhile before bothering your e-mail server. For example, your computer might contact your e-mail server just once every 30 minutes to check whether there are any new messages for you; or your computer might not contact your e-mail server until the next time you start running the e-mail program — which might be the next day.

Here's how to make your computer communicate with your e-mail server *now*, so all the messages you're trying to receive get transmitted to your Inbox *now*:

Outlook Express:	click the **Send/Recv button** (or press the F5 key)
Windows Mail:	click "**Send/Recv**" (or press the F5 key)
Windows Live Mail:	click envelopes above "**Send/Receive**" (or press F5 key)
Yahoo Mail:	click the **Check Mail button**
Gmail:	click "**Refresh**"

If you want Outlook Express & Windows Mail to check for messages more frequently (such as every 5 minutes), do this:

> Click "Tools" then "Options". Put ✔ in the box marked "Check for new messages" (by clicking). Put a small number (such as 5) in the minutes box (by clicking the box's down-arrow). Also, to make sure e-mails you create get sent immediately, do this: click "Send" (which is at the top of the screen); put ✔ in the box marked "Send messages immediately" (by clicking); click OK.

If you want Windows Live Mail to check for messages more frequently (such as every 5 minutes), do this:

> Click the **Windows Live Mail button** (which is left of "Home" and has a down-arrow) then "Options" then "Mail". Put a small number (such as 5) in the minutes box (by clicking the box's down-arrow). Press Enter.

Sending a message to a friend When you tell the computer to send a message to a friend, the computer typically transmits the message *immediately* to your e-mail server (which passes it on to your friend's e-mail server).

Printing

To copy a message onto paper, get the message onto the screen then do this:

Outlook Express & Windows Mail Click "Print". Press Enter.

Gmail Click "Print all" (which is near the screen's right edge). Press Enter.

Yahoo Mail Click "Actions" then "Print Email". Press Enter.

Windows Live Mail Click the Windows Live Mail button (which is left of "Home" and has a down-arrow) then "Print". Press Enter.

Acronyms

People often use these expressions and abbreviations when writing e-mail messages (and text messages on phones):

Expression	Abbreviation
I'm GRINNING!	<g>
I have a BIG GRIN!	<bg>
I have a VERY BIG GRIN!	<vbg>
Laughing out loud!	LOL
Lots of laughing out loud!	LOLOL
Lots & lots of laughing out loud!	LOLOLOL
Laughing my ass off!	LMAO
Laughing my ass off, on the floor!	LMAOOTF
Rolling on the floor, laughing!	ROTFL
Ha ha, only joking!	HHOJ
Tongue in cheek!	TIC

No problem!	NP
Way to go!	WTG
Too good to be true!	2GTBT
Good game!	GG
Great minds think alike.	GMTA
I love you.	ILY
Love you, miss you!	LYMY
Wish you were here!	WYWH
Hugs and kisses!	XOXO
Oh my God!	OMG
before	B4
later	L8R
real soon now	RSN
See you later!	CUL8R
Talk to you later!	TTYL
Ta-ta for now!	TTFN
Parent over shoulder!	POS
People are watching!	PRW
Best friend forever!	BFF
Thinking about you!	TAU
Be back later!	BBL
Be right back!	BRB
Be back in a flash!	BBIAF
Just a minute!	JAM
Back at keyboard!	BAK
Welcome back!	WB
Long time, no see!	LTNS
Thanks in advance.	TIA
No reply necessary.	NRN
in my opinion	IMO
in my humble opinion	IMHO
in my not-so-humble opinion	IMNSHO
off the top of my head	OTTOMH
I am not a lawyer.	IANAL
Trust me on this.	TMOT
Don't quote me on this.	DQMOT
Just kidding!	JK
for your information	FYI
frequently asked question	FAQ
waste of money, brains, and time	WOMBAT
Do it yourself.	DIY
Read the manual.	RTM
Read the f***ing manual.	RTFM
Oh, I see.	OIC
Still in the dark!	SITD
Are you OK?	RUOK
in real life	IRL
Been there, done that!	BTDT
Good luck!	GL
Good luck, have fun!	GL/HF
Shit out of luck!	SOL
by the way	BTW
as a matter of fact	AAMOF
for what it's worth	FWIW
before I forget	BIF
in any event	IAE
in other words	IOW
on the other hand	OTOH
Don't hold your breath.	DHYB
Laughing at your mamma!	L@YM
what the hell	WTH
what the fuck	WTF
Are you serious?	AYS
Oh, really?	O RLY
Yeah, really!	YARLY
No way!	NOWAI
Got to see you!	GTSY

Those abbreviations are called **acronyms**.

Acronyms can be ambiguous. For example, "LOL" can mean "laughing out loud" or "lots of love". If you receive an e-mail saying "LOL", you must guess whether the sender is laughing at you or laughing *with* you or loves you. Don't write an acronym unless you're sure the recipient will understand it.

Smiley's pals

Here's a picture of a smiling face:

☺

It's called a **smiley**. If you rotate that face 90°, it looks like this:

> :-)

People writing e-mail messages often type that symbol to mean "I'm smiling; I'm just kidding".

For example, suppose you want to tell the President that you disagree with his speech. If you communicate the old-fashioned way, with pencil and paper, you'll probably begin like this:

> Dear Mr. President,
>   I'm somewhat distressed at your recent policy announcement.

But people who communicate by e-mail tend to be more blunt:

> Hey, Prez!
>   You really blew that speech. Jeez! Your policy stinks. You should be boiled in oil, or at least paddled with a floppy disk. :-)

The symbol ":-)" means "I'm just kidding". That symbol's important. Forgot to include it? Then the poor Prez, worried about getting boiled in oil, might have the Secret Service arrest you for plotting an assassination.

The smiley, ":-)", has many variations:

Symbol	Meaning
:-)	I'm smiling.
:-(	I'm frowning.
:-<	I'm real sad.
:-c	I'm bummed out.
:-C	I'm *really* bummed out!
:-I	I'm grim.
:-/	I'm skeptical.
:-7	I'm smirking at my own wry comment.
:->	I have a devilish grin.
:-D	I'm laughing.
:-o	I'm shouting.
:-O	I'm shouting really loud.
:-@	I'm screaming.
:-8	I talk from both sides of my mouth.
:-p	I'm sticking my tongue out at you.
:-P	I'm being tongue-in-cheek.
:-&	I'm tongue-tied.
:-9	I'm licking my lips.
:-*	My lips pucker — for a kiss or pickle.
:-x	My lips are sealed.
:-#	I wear braces.
:-$	My mouth is wired shut.
:-?	I smoke a pipe.
:-}	I have a beard.
:-B	I have buck teeth.
:-[	I'm a vampire.

:-{}	I wear lipstick.
:-{	I have a mustache.
:-~)	My nose runs.
:-)~	I'm drooling.
:-)-8	I have big breasts.
:*)	I'm drunk.
:^)	My nose is broken.
:~I	I'm smoking.
:~j	I'm smoking and smiling.
:'-(	I'm crying.
:'-)	I'm so happy, I'm crying.
:)	I'm a midget.
;-)	I'm winking.
?-)	I have a black eye.
%-)	Dizzy from staring at screen too long!
8-)	I wear glasses.
B-)	I wear cool shades, man.
g-)	I wear pince-nez glasses.
P-)	I'm a pirate.
|-O	I'm yawning.
|^O	I'm snoring.
X-(	I just died.
O:-)	I'm an angel.
+:-)	I'm a priest.
[:-)	I'm wearing a Walkman.
&:-)	I have curly hair.
@:-)	I have wavy hair.
8:-)	I have a bow in my hair.
B:-)	My sunglasses are on my forehead.
{:-)	I wear a toupee,
}:-)	but the wind is blowing it off.
-:-)	I'm a punk rocker,
-:-(	but real punk rockers don't smile.
[:]	I'm a robot.
3:]	I'm your pet,
3:[	but I growl.
}:->	I'm being devilish,
>;->	and lewdly winking.
E-:-)	I'm a ham radio operator.
C=:-)	I'm a chef.
=|:-)=	I'm Uncle Sam.
<):-)	I'm a fireman.
*<:-)	I'm Santa Claus.
*:o)	I'm Bozo the clown.
<:I	I'm a dunce.
(-:	I'm a lefty.

The symbol for "love" is —

<3

because if you rotate it 90° in the opposite direction, it looks like a heart. So to say "I love you" just write:

I <3 U

To say "Lots of love!" just write:

<333

Since those symbolic pictures (icons) help you emote, they're called **emoticons** (pronounced "ee MOTE ee cons"). Technically, just the first one in that list is called a **smiley**, but some folks call *all* emoticons "**smileys**."

To understand those American smileys easily, you must turn your head 90°.

Japanese versions The Japanese have invented these **straight-on smileys**, which don't require you to turn your head — you can look at them straight-on:

Symbol	Meaning
(^_^)	I'm smiling.
(@_@)	I'm dizzy and giddy.
(*^_^*)	I'm smiling and blushing.
(^.^)	Smiling with my cute little-girl mouth!
(-_-)	I'm angry but trying to force a smile.
(T_T)	I'm crying. Tears run down my cheeks.
(p_-)	Trying to find secret, using magnifier!
(>_<)	Ouch! That was a painful failure!
(>_<)(>_<)	I deny it strongly, shake my head!
(._.?)	Are we confusing each other?
(._.)(._.)	What are you looking for?
(^_^;)	I'm stunned, break into a cold sweat,
(((((((^_^;)	and want to run outta here!
(^_^)V	Great! My hand makes the victory sign!
(^^)//	Great! My hands clap!
\(OoO)/	I'm wowed! My eyes bulge, arms flail.
(-_-)zzz	I'm going to sleep. Good-night!
QQ	I have tears in my eyes. I'm upset.

The Japanese call their straight-on smileys "**facemarks**", since they're marks that represent faces simply, without rotation.

Other body parts Analysts of American culture invented these **assicons** to illustrate slang:

Symbol	Meaning
(_!_)	regular ass
(!)	tight ass
(__!__)	fat ass
[_!_]	hard ass
(_)	half-assed
(_o_)	ass that's been around
(_O_)	ass that's been around even more
(_*_)	sore-ass loser
(_o^^o_)	wise ass
(_E=mc2_)	smart ass
(_?_)	dumb ass
(_zzz_)	tired ass
(_13_)	unlucky ass
(_jack_)	jackass
(_Y_)	ass that can't say no
(_x_)	kiss my ass
(_X_)	get off my ass
(_$_)	money coming out of his ass
(_#_)	take an ass pounding
(_~_)	Latin ass
(_/_)	Asian ass

Analysts of the female form have invented these **titicons** (which are also called **boobiecons**):

Symbol	Meaning
(o)(o)	regular tits
(O)(O)	big tits
(@)(@)	big, hairy tits
(.)(.)	tiny tits
{.}{.}	shriveled tits
(,)(,)	droopy tits
(')(')	perky tits
(.Y.)	curvy tits
($)($)	silicone tits

Leet

Youngsters sometimes write emails in a secret slang code called **Leet** (which stands for "élite"), so their parents won't understand — and neither will out-of-touch school administrators, employers, censors, and email filters.

To translate English to Leet, change the letters to similar-looking digits (or other symbols) or similar sounding expressions, like this:

English	Leet
the letter o or O	the digit 0
the letter i or I	the digit 1 or the symbol !
the letter s or S	the digit 5 or the symbol $
the letter z or Z	the digit 2
the letter b or B	the digit 8
the letter l or L	the digit 1 or 7
the letter t or T	the digit 7 or the symbol +
the letter a or A	the digit 4 or the symbol @
the letter g or G	the digit 6
the letter e or E	the digit 3
the letter h or H	the symbol #
the letter x or X	the symbol % or ><
the letter v or V	the symbols \/
the letter w or W	the symbols \/\/
the letter y or Y	the letter j
the letter f or F	the letters ph
the sound "ate"	the digit 8
the sound "are"	the letter R
the sound "you"	the letter U
the sound "and"	the symbol &
the sound "ant"	the symbol &

Examples:

English	Leet
boobs	80085
Leet	1337
shit	$#!+
ass	@$

To avoid too much confusion, make just *some* of those changes — just enough to confuse your parents without confusing your friends. For example, you can keep the b and t:

English	Leet
banned	b&
newbie (beginner)	n00b
Hooray! We won!	w00t (we own other team)

To further confuse parents and be cool, some kids purposely type letters in the wrong order or type a nearby letter on the keyboard:

English	Cool Leet
the word "the"	t3h (instead of th3)
newbie (beginner)	b00n (instead of n00b)
laughing out loud	OLO (instead of LOL)
the word "crap"	carp
the word "porn"	pr0n or n0rp
the letter "o"	p (which is next to o)
the word "own"	pwn
capital "O"	ZP (since Z is near Shift)
Oh, my God!	ZPMG

What did you send?

To check which messages you sent, do this:

Outlook Express & Windows Mail: in the left pane, click "**Sent Items**". Windows Live Mail: in the left pane, click "**Sent items**". Gmail: in the left pane, click "**Sent Mail**". Yahoo Mail: in the left pane, click "**Sent**".

You'll see a list of messages you sent. For each message, the list shows the address you sent it to, the message's subject, and when you sent it.

When you finish admiring that list, make the screen become normal again by clicking "Inbox" (which is in the left pane).

Reply

While you're reading a message that somebody's sent you, here's how to reply.

Click "**Reply**" (or use this Yahoo Mail shortcut: press the keyboard's R key). Then type your reply.

While you type, the computer shows a copy of the message you're replying to. In Outlook Express & Windows Mail & Gmail, the copy has a vertical bar ("|") in front of each line.

If you want to abridge that copy (so it doesn't clutter your screen), use your mouse: drag across the part you want to delete, then press the Delete key.

When you finish typing your reply, click the Send button. The computer will send your reply, along with your abridged copy of the message you're replying to.

Delete old messages

The list of received messages — and the list of sent messages — can become long and hard to manage. To reduce the clutter, delete any messages that no longer interest you.

To delete a message you received (or a copy of a message you sent), make the message's name appear in the top pane, then do this:

Outlook Express & Windows Mail & Windows Live Mail: click the name so it turns blue, then press the Delete key. **Yahoo Mail**: click the name so it turns green (or gray), then press the Delete key. **Gmail**: click the box that's left of the name so you see a check mark, then click "Delete".

That tells the computer you want to delete the message. The computer moves the message into a **Deleted Items** folder (which Yahoo Mail & Gmail call **Trash**). It resembles the Windows Recycle Bin.

To find out what's in that folder, do this:

Outlook Express & Windows Mail: click "Deleted Items". **Windows Live Mail**: click "Deleted items". **Yahoo Mail**: click "Trash". **Gmail**: if you don't see "Trash" yet, make it appear by clicking "more"; click "Trash".

You'll see what's in that folder: a list of the messages you said to delete.

Are you *sure* you want to delete all those messages?

If you change your mind, you can keep one of those messages. For Yahoo Mail, do this:

Find the message's name (in the top pane) and drag that name to where you want the message moved (the left pane's Inbox or "Sent").

For Gmail do this:

In the top pane, click the message's name then "Move to". You see a menu under "Move to". In that menu, click "Inbox".

For Outlook Express & Windows Mail, do this:

In the top pane, right-click that message's name (using the mouse's *right*-hand button). Click "Move to Folder". You see the Move window. In that window, double-click where you want the message moved ("Inbox" or "Sent Items"); if you don't see those choices, make them appear by double-clicking "Local Folders".

For Windows Live Mail, do this:

In the top pane, click that message's name then "Move to". You see the Move window. In that window, double-click where you want the message moved ("Inbox" or "Sent items").

When you're *sure* you want to eliminate *all* messages in the Deleted Items folder, do this:

Yahoo Mail Click the word "Empty" that's next to "Trash". Click "OK". **Gmail** While you're looking at the messages in the Trash, click "Empty Trash now". Click "OK". **Outlook Express & Windows Mail** Right-click "Deleted Items" (using the mouse's *right*-hand button). Click "Empty Deleted Items Folder" then "Yes". **Windows Live Mail** Right-click "Deleted items" (using the mouse's *right*-hand button). Click "Empty 'Deleted items' folder" then "Yes".

If you're using Windows Mail or Windows Live Mail or Yahoo Mail or Gmail, handle the Junk E-mail folder the same way as the Deleted Items folder.

Signature

At the bottom of your e-mail message, you can include a few lines that identify who you are. Those lines are called your **signature** (or **sig**).

For example, your sig can include your full name, address, and phone number. You can mention your *office*'s address & phone number, but be cautious about revealing your *home* address & phone number, since e-mail messages are often peeked at by strangers.

If you're employed, you might also wish to give your company's name, your title, and a disclaimer, such as "The opinions I expressed aren't necessarily my employer's." You might also wish to reveal your personality, by including your favorite saying (such as "Be creative" or "May the Lord bless you" or "Turned on by Twinkies"). But keep your sig short: any sig containing more than 7 lines of text is considered an impolite waste of your reader's time.

Don't bother putting your e-mail address in your sig, since your e-mail address appears automatically at the top of your message.

Here's how to put the same sig on all your e-mail messages easily. For Outlook Express & Windows Mail, do this:

> On the menu bar at the screen's top, click the word "Tools". Click "Options" then "Signatures" then "New".
> Press Enter (so your sig's top line will be blank). Then type whatever words and numbers you want to be in your sig; press the Enter key at the end of each line.
> Click "Add signatures to all outgoing messages". Click "OK". Then the computer will automatically put that sig at the bottom of each new message you write.

For Windows Live Mail, do this:

> Click the **Windows Live Mail button** (which is left of "Home" and has a down-arrow) then "Options" then "Mail" then "Signatures" then "New".
> Press Enter (so your sig's top line will be blank). Then type whatever words and numbers you want to be in your sig; press the Enter key at the end of each line.
> Click "Add signatures to all outgoing messages". Click "OK". Then the computer will automatically put that sig at the bottom of each new message you write.

For Yahoo Mail, do this:

> Click "Options" (which is near the screen's top-right corner) then "More Options" then "Signature" (which is at the screen's left edge).
> Click the button marked "Show a signature on all outgoing messages". Click in the box below "Show a signature on all outgoing messages".
> Then type whatever words and numbers and numbers you want to be in your sig; press Enter at the end of each line.
> Click "Save Changes". Then the computer will automatically put that sig at the bottom of each new message you write.
> Click "Back to Mail" (which is at the screen's left edge).

For Gmail, do this:

> Click "Settings" (which is near the screen's top-right corner). Scroll down until you see the word "Signature". Click the circle that's left of the white Signature box, then click in the white Signature box. Type whatever words and numbers and numbers you want to be in your sig; press Enter at the end of each line.
> Click the "Save Changes" button (which you'll see when you scroll down). Then the computer will automatically put that sig at the bottom of each new message you write.
> Click "Back to Mail" (which is at the screen's left edge).

While you edit a message, edit its sig! Customize its sig to match the rest of the message.

Finish

When you finish using e-mail, do this:

> **Outlook Express & Windows Mail & Windows Live Mail**: close the window (by clicking the X at the screen's top-right corner).
> **Yahoo Mail**: click "Sign Out" (which is at the screen's top).
> **Gmail**: click "Sign out" (which is at the screen's top-right corner).

Attachments

An e-mail message can have a file attached to it.

Send a file attachment

While you're writing a message, here's how to insert a file (such as a picture you drew in Paint, or a document composed in WordPad or Microsoft Word).
Click the **Attach button**, by doing this:

> Yahoo Mail: click the button that says "Attach"; it's next to the Send button.
>
> Gmail: click the button that says "Attach a file".
>
> Outlook Express & Windows Mail: click the button that says "Attach" and looks like a paper clip.
>
> Windows Live Mail: click the button that says "Attach file" and looks like a paper clip.

If Yahoo Mail says "Set up the easy attach tool", click the "I agree" box then "Continue" then "Run" then "Allow" then "Attach Files".
Which file do you want to insert? Make its icon appear on the screen. If its icon is not on the screen because the computer is showing a different folder, do this:

> **Windows Mail** Click the ∧ next to "Folders". Click the folder that the file is in.
>
> **Outlook Express** Click the ▾ or ∨ next to the folder's name. Click the hard disk's "C:" icon. Double-click the folders that the file is in.
>
> **Yahoo Mail & Gmail & Windows Live Mail** At the screen's left edge, you see a list of folders. (To see the whole list, scroll it up or down). Click or double-click the folder that the file is in.

When the file's icon is finally on the screen, double-click that icon.
Near the message you were writing, you should see your file's name. (Windows Mail & Outlook Express put the file's name into the Attach box, which is above the message. Yahoo Mail puts the file's name into the Attach pane, which is below the message. Gmail & Windows Live Mail put the file's name next to the paper clip, below the Subject box.)
Make sure the message and the file's name are correct.
Then click the Send button. That makes the computer send the message and attached file.

Receive a file attachment

Here's what to do if a friend sends you a message that includes an attached file.
Outlook Express & Windows Mail begin like this:

> While you're reading the message (in the bottom pane), you'll see a paper clip in that pane's top right corner. Click the paper clip.
> Under that paper clip, you'll see the attached file's icon. Click that icon.

Yahoo Mail begins like this:

> While you're reading the message (in the bottom pane), click the attachment's name. (The name is at the pane's top, next to a paper clip. The name is blue.) Click "Download Attachment".

Windows Live Mail begins like this:

> While you're reading the message (in the bottom pane), double-click the attachment's name. (The name is near the pane's top-left corner, below the word "To".)

Gmail begins like this:

> While you're reading the message, click "Download" (which is below the message).

If the computer asks "Do you want to open or save this file?", click "Open". (If the computer instead asks "What would you like to do with this file?", click "Open it" then "OK".)

If the computer says "A website wants to open web content", click "Allow".

If you're using Gmail (which shows a list of attachments), click the file's name.

The computer will try to show you the pictures and words that are in the attached file, by running the program that created the file. For example, if the file is a picture created by Paint, the computer will try to run Paint; if the file is a document created by Microsoft Word, the computer will try to run Microsoft Word. (If the file was created by software that your computer doesn't own and your computer doesn't know how to handle the file, your computer will gripe by saying "Open With".)

When you finish looking at the pictures and words that are in the attached file, close whatever program showed it (such as Paint or Windows Photo Gallery or Microsoft Word) by clicking that program's X button. (If you're using Gmail, also close the window that shows the list of attachments.) You'll return to seeing your e-mail program's screen.

Multiple people

An e-mail message can be sent to many people. Here's how....

Multiple addresses

Outlook Express, Windows Mail, Windows Live Mail, and Yahoo Mail:

> If you want to send a message to several people, put semicolons between their addresses. For example, if you want to send a message to the President of the United States (whose address is President@WhiteHouse.gov) and also to me (Russ@SecretFun.com), address the mail to:
> President@WhiteHouse.gov; Russ@SecretFun.com
> That little list of addresses is called the **mailing list**.
> The space after the semicolon is optional. If you accidentally type a comma instead of a semicolon, the computer will eventually turn the comma into a semicolon for you.

Gmail:

> If you want to send a message to several people, put commas between their addresses. For example, if you want to send a message to the President of the United States (whose address is President@WhiteHouse.gov) and also to me (Russ@SecretFun.com), address the mail to:
> President@WhiteHouse.gov, Russ@SecretFun.com
> That little list of addresses is called the **mailing list**.
> The computer automatically puts the space after the comma.

Carbon copies

Here's how to send a message *mainly* to the President of the United States but also send me a copy:

> In the main address box (called "To"), type the address of the main person you want to send the letter to (which is President@WhiteHouse.gov).
>
> In a box marked "**Cc**" (which stands for "Carbon copy"), type the address of the person you want to send a secret copy to (which is Russ@SecretFun.com). (If you're using Gmail, make the Cc box appear by clicking "Add Cc". If you're using Windows Live Mail, make the Cc box appear by clicking "Show Cc & Bcc".)

Here's how to send a message *mainly* to the President of the United States but also send me a copy, and make the copy be secret, so the President of the United States doesn't know the copy was sent to me:

> In the main address box (called "To"), write the address of the main person you want to send the letter to (which is President@WhiteHouse.gov).
>
> Make sure you see a **Bcc box**, just above the "Subject" box. ("Bcc" stands for "Blind carbon copy".) If you don't see a Bcc box yet, create it by doing this: for Gmail, click "Add Bcc"; for Windows Live Mail: click "Show Cc & Bcc"; for Yahoo Mail, click "Show BCC" (which is near the screen's right edge); for Outlook Express, click "View" then "All Headers".
>
> In the Bcc box, write the address of the person you want to send a secret copy to (which is Russ@SecretFun.com).

Replies

While you're reading a message you received, here's how to send a reply: click either "**Reply**" or "**Reply All**".

If you click "**Reply**", your reply will be sent to just the person who sent you the message. (Yahoo Mail permits this shortcut: instead of clicking "Reply", you can just tap the keyboard's R key.)

If instead you say "**Reply All**", your reply will be sent to the person who sent you the message and also to everybody else on that person's mailing list. Here's how to say "Reply All":

> **Outlook Express & Windows Mail**: click "**Reply All**".
>
> **Windows Live Mail**: click "**Reply all**".
>
> **Yahoo Mail**: click the Reply button's down-arrow then "Reply to All".
>
> **Gmail**: find the rightmost Reply button (which is near the screen's right edge); click that button's down-arrow then "Reply to all".

For example, if Bob sends a message addressed to a list of three people (you, Sue, and Jill) and you want to reply, click either "**Reply**" (which will send your reply just to Bob) or "**Reply All**" (which will send your reply to Bob and also to the other people on Bob's mailing list: Sue and Jill).

Type your reply, such as "Thanks for your email; you made me laugh" or "I love what you wrote and want to marry you" or "I think you're nuts and should be locked up".

Below your typing, the computer shows a copy of the message you're replying to. (If that copy is long, abridge it or delete it by using the keyboard's Delete key.)

Click the Send button. The computer will send what you typed, along with a copy of the undeleted part of the message you're replying to.

Forward

While you're reading a message you received, here's how to send a copy of it to a friend.

Click "**Forward**". Type your friend's e-mail address.

Press the Tab key several times, until you're in the big white box where you can type a message. Type a comment to your friend, such as "Here's a joke Mary sent me." Below your typing, the computer automatically shows a copy of the message you're forwarding.

Click the Send button.

 Fixes

I hate to admit it, but computers occasionally break. Have no fear: you can typically fix the computer yourself! The "**Repairs**" chapter explains how.

To avoid repairs, do what's in the "**Maintenance**" chapter. Even if your computer needs a repair, you can typically get the computer to fix itself if you do what's in the "Maintenance chapter.

If your computer acts so strangely that normal repair procedures don't fix it, the cause might be that a nasty person purposely screwed up your computer, by planting a virus inside the computer. The "**Virus**" chapter explains how viruses work and how to combat them.

After you read this stuff, you'll become smart enough so your neighbors will ask you to fix *their* computers too! You'll never rest.

Security

These tips will help keep your computer in good shape, so you'll have fewer problems and need fewer repairs.

Back up your work

When you're typing lots of info into a word-processing program (or any similar program), the stuff you've typed is in the computer's RAM. Every 10 minutes, copy that info onto the hard disk, by giving the Save command. (To learn how to give the Save command, read my word-processing chapter.)

That way, if the computer breaks down (or you make a boo-boo), the hard disk will contain a copy of most of your work, and you'll need to retype at most 10 minutes' worth.

Don't trust automatic backups

If your word-processor is modern, it has a feature called "automatic timed backup", which can make the computer automatically save your document every 10 minutes. Don't trust that automatic feature! It might be saving your latest error instead of what you want.

For example, if you accidentally wreck part of your document and then automatic timed backup kicks in, you've just replaced your good, saved document by a wrecked one, and the good one is gone forever. Give the Save command *manually*, so that *you*, not the computer, decide when and what to save.

Split into chapters

If you're using a word-processing program to type a long book, split the book into chapters. Make each chapter be a separate file. That way, if something goes wrong with the file, you've lost just one chapter instead of the whole book.

Make extra backups

Besides saving your work in the hard disk's main folder (which is typically called "My Documents"), make extra copies of your work also, in case you or colleagues wreck what's in My Documents accidentally — or an enemy or virus wrecks it maliciously.

While writing this book, I made several copies of it, to make sure I wouldn't lose what I wrote:

> I copied it **onto paper** (by telling the computer to "print" the document).
>
> I copied it **onto USB flash drive** (by doing the "Send to USB flash drive" procedure on page 104).
>
> I copied it **onto a CD** (by doing the "Send to CD" procedure on page 105).
>
> I copied it **onto a floppy disk** (by right-clicking the document's icon, then clicking "Send To" then "3½ Floppy").
>
> I copied it **into a folder called Safety** (by creating that new folder and then dragging the document's icon into that folder while holding down the Ctrl key).
>
> I **saved the document under a second name** (by doing this procedure: while viewing the words in the document, click "File" then "Save As", invent a second name and type it, then press the Enter key).

I did that copying each time I was at a good "resting point" (when I was confident of what I'd written so far but less confident of what I'd be writing next).

The easy forms of copying I did frequently (at many "resting points"). The harder forms I did less frequently (just at the "major resting points").

Copying is important

Computers work as you expect, 99.9% of the time. They're so reliable that you start to believe they work always, and you think backups aren't necessary. Then you don't bother making backups anymore. But someday, your document will eventually get wrecked (by a hardware failure or software error or your stupidity or a virus or other maliciousness). Then you'll feel devastated and swear you'll never forget to make backups again… but you *will* forget, and you'll be sorry again! It's human nature.

Protect your hardware

Here's how to protect your hardware.

Temperature

If possible, avoid using the computer in hot weather.

When the room's temperature rises above 93 degrees, the fan inside the computer has trouble cooling the computer sufficiently. Wait until the weather is cooler (such as late at night), or buy an air conditioner, or buy a window fan to put on your desk and aim at the computer, or use the computer for just an hour at a time (so that the computer doesn't have a chance to overheat).

Another problem in the summer is electrical brownouts, where air conditioners in your house or community consume so much electricity that not enough voltage gets to your computer.

Moving your computer

Some parts inside the computer are delicate. Don't bang or shake the computer! If you need to move the computer to a different location, be gentle!

Before moving the computer, make backups: copy everything important from the computer's hard disk onto floppy disks. For example, copy all the documents, spreadsheets, and database files you created. Unless you're using Windows Me or XP (which are solid), you should also copy AUTOEXEC.BAT, CONFIG.SYS, and COMMAND.COM.

Moving by hand If you must move the computer to a different desk or building, be *very gentle* when you pick up the computer, carry it, and plop it down. Be especially gentle when walking on stairs and through doorways.

Moving by car If you're transporting your computer by car, put the computer in the *front* seat, put a blanket underneath the computer, and drive slowly (especially around curves and over bumps).

> Do *not* put the computer in the trunk, since the trunk has the least protection against bumps. If you have the original padded box that the computer came in, put the computer in it, since the box's padding is professionally designed to protect against bumps.

Moving by air If you're transporting your computer by air, avoid checking the computer through the baggage department.

> The baggage handlers will treat the computer as if it were a football, and their "forward pass" will make you pissed.
>
> Instead, try to carry the computer with you on the plane, if the computer's small enough to fit under your seat or in the overhead bin. If the whole computer won't fit, carry as much of the computer as *will* fit (the keyboard, monitor, or system unit?) and check the rest as baggage. If you *must* check the computer as baggage, use the original padded box that the computer came in, or else find a giant box and put a *lot* of padding material in it.

When going through airport security, it's okay to let the security guards X-ray your computer and disks. Do *not* carry the computer and floppy disks in your hands as you go through the metal detector, since the magnetic field might erase your disks.

> For best results, just tell the guards you have a computer and disks, Instead of running the computer and disks through detection equipment, the guards will inspect your stuff personally.
>
> To make sure your computer doesn't contain a bomb, the guards might ask you to unscrew the computer or prove that it actually works. If your computer's a laptop and you need to prove it works, make sure you brought your batteries — and make sure the batteries are fully charged!
>
> Since airport rules about baggage and security continually change, ask your airport for details before taking a trip.

Beware of theft. Crooks have used this trick:

> A crook waits for you to put your laptop on the X-ray conveyor belt. Then the crook cuts in front of you and purposely gives himself trouble going through the metal detector (by having keys in his pocket). While he delays you and distracts security guards, his partner grabs your laptop off the conveyor belt and walks away with it.

Moving by mail Computer companies have discovered that FedEx handles computers more carefully — and causes less damage — than the post office and UPS.

Send e-mail cautiously

Remember this poem:

> Beware what messages you send.
> They may reach eyes you don't intend.

For example, suppose you send an e-mail message to Bob. Your message might be read by people other than Bob, for one of these reasons:

> Maybe Bob shares his e-mail address with his wife, kids, parents, and friends.
> Maybe Bob works for a department that shares just one Internet address.
> Maybe Bob's secretary reads all Bob's mail, to discard junk.
> While Bob shows a friend how to use e-mail, the friend can see Bob's e-mail.
> While Bob goes to the bathroom, a passerby can peek at Bob's screen.
> Whenever Bob receives interesting e-mail, maybe he forwards it to friends.
> Maybe you meant to reply to Bob but accidentally sent the reply to "All".
> Maybe your e-mail reaches a different guy named "Bob".

According to U.S. law, if you're an employee who writes an e-mail message by using the company's computer, the message becomes the company's property, and **your boss is allowed to look** at it. **Your message has no privacy.** Moreover, if your company is sued (by a competitor or customer), United States law can require your company to reveal all e-mail messages about the lawsuit's topic and about all the people involved in it: the cute joke you wrote can embarrass you when the judge makes you read it to the courtroom.

So **be especially careful about writing e-mails that contain sexual references** (such as "I love your body, so let's go out on a date and have sex!") **or anger** (such as "The boss is an ass and should be assassinated!"), since your e-mail might fall into the hands of the one person to whom you don't want to show that message. Here's the most important rule about e-mail messages:

> If you want to send a sexual or angry e-mail,
> wait an hour (to cool down) then read your draft and think again!

No "Undo"

When you tell the computer to send an e-mail message (by clicking the Send button, Reply button, or Reply All), the computer tries to transmit the message immediately. You can*not* cancel the transmission easily, since there's no "Undo button".

If you try to wreck the transmission (by unplugging your modem or turning off your computer's power), your computer will detect sabotage and overcome it: the next time you run your e-mail program, the computer will try again to transmit the wrecked message (by using a copy of the message that the computer keeps in your computer's **Outbox** folder).

Since e-mail transmissions can't be easily canceled, remember:

> Before you click **Send** or **Reply** or **Reply All**,
> check your **spelling** and **emotions**, or you'll all be appalled!

Beware of evil e-mail

You'll receive several kinds of e-mail messages. Some of those messages will help you (because they're written to you by your friends or business acquaintances, or because they're weekly or daily news bulletins that you requested from companies whose Web sites you visited).

But most of the e-mail messages you receive will be bad e-mail that's "a waste of your time to read" or "dangerous".

Get-rich-quick schemes

You'll get e-mails promising you'll get rich quick — if you pay the sender first. If you're stupid, you'll pay the sender — then realize you've become poorer, not richer, since the sender gives you nothing worthwhile in return.

For example, in what's called a **multilevel marketing (MLM)**, you'll be told you can get rich by selling products (such as pills or e-mailed reports) if you buy them first from the seller.

> After you stupidly buy the products, you realize you can't easily find other stupid people to buy them from you. That's because the products themselves are junk.
>
> The classic MLM scheme tries to get you to send $10 each to 5 people (for worthless "e-mail reports"), while you hope many people, in return, will be stupid enough to send $10 each to you. You'll soon discover than most people are *not* stupider than you, and just *you* are stupid enough to lose $50. Such a scheme is called a **chain letter** or **pyramid scheme**. The post office has ruled all such chain-letter pyramid schemes are illegal and constitute mail fraud, since the only way to get rich in such a scheme is to make hundreds of stupid people become poor. Most such schemes claim to be legal but aren't.

Another false road to riches is the **Nigerian scam**:

> You'll receive a letter begging your help in moving $30,000,000 out of Nigeria (because the money was secretly acquired by a slightly corrupt Nigerian official), and you'll be allowed to keep 30% of the money for yourself. The "catch" is that before the money is transferred to you, a "small" fee must be paid to lawyers, etc., to transfer the money. If you're stupid enough to believe the tale, you pay the fee (a few thousand dollars) — then find out you have to pay *another* fee, then another, then another, to get around "unexpected difficulties". You never receive a penny. All fees wind up in the pocket of the scammer (who pretends to be a lawyer).
>
> Thousands of Americans were stupid enough to fall for that Nigerian scam. The typical victim lost $50,000; the stupidest victims lost $300,000 per person. Several victims were stupid enough to go to Nigeria to get their money — and got murdered.
>
> The Nigerian scam is a more lucrative crime than anything the Mafia ever did. It brings in over $1,000,000 per day from all the victims. It's been imitated by other African countries and other constituencies. Example: "I'm a sinner who acquired $30,000,000 but I've mended my ways, and now I'd like to donate it all to your church, if you could please help me move it out of Sierra Leone." Some churches went broke believing that tale!

For a different scam, you'll be told you won $3,000,000 in the **Netherlands lottery** (though common sense should tell you that you can't win a lottery you didn't enter and never even heard of), and you just need to pay a "transfer fee" to get your winnings transferred to you.

> In a real lottery, there's no transfer fee; in this faked lottery, there's a transfer fee but no jackpot, except for the scammers who keep your transfer fee. At first, you'll be told the transfer fee is $5,000; after you've stupidly paid it, you'll be told that because of "difficulties" with the transfer, more fees will be necessary… and then more… and then more… until your bank account is empty.

The Nigerian scam and the Netherlands-lottery scam are both examples of **advance-fee scams**, where you're told you'll get rich if you pay a fee first.

For more details about scams, go to **www.crimes-of-persuasion.com**, then click on "Nigerian Scam" (or others).

Freebies

You'll receive e-mail offering you something for free (such as a free digital camera, or a free screensaver, or a free pornographic look at nude women, or free access to not-quite-legally downloaded music). You say to yourself, "What can it lose? It's free!" so you click yes.

That launches a barrage of ads upon you — through Web sites and through e-mails — trying to convince you to buy more. Many of the ads come in the form of **adware** and **spyware**. Page 144 explains how to cure them.

Oh yeah, about that "free" digital camera: you discover it's terrible, and it will be "free" just after you buy lots of other stuff first. Misleading, huh?

Some of the e-mails pretend to be surveys, such as "Who should the next President be?" The survey doesn't really care about your political opinion: it's just collecting (**harvesting**) your e-mail address and other personal data about you, to sell to advertisers.

Pornography

Most e-mails hawking **pornography** try to make you to visit a sexy Web site, full of nude women who try to get you to reveal your credit-card number and become a paying member. Other pornographic e-mails try to make you phone a sexy girl whose area code just happens to be in the Caribbean or Asia or Hong Kong or some other island that will give you a huge phone bill, whose profits go to a foreign phone company that secretly gives the scheme's manager a cut.

Phishing

You might receive an e-mail saying that the security department (of your bank, credit-card company, or employer) wants you to reenter your personal information (credit-card number, PIN number, social-security number, mother's maiden name, etc.) to protect against fraud. At the bottom of the e-mail is a button to click to go to the Web site, where you enter the info.

But that Web site's a fake: it's really run by a crook who's waiting for you to enter your personal info so he can steal your identity and credit-card info and buy things billed to you, then disappear before you realize you've been robbed and your credit history has been ruined.

Banks NEVER send e-mails asking you to reenter your account info. Such e-mails are always frauds.

> Those fake e-mails and fake Web sites are called **phishing**, because they're created by crooks who are "fishing" for suckers who'll tell the crooks all personal secrets. **Phishing expeditions** were first launched against customers of Australia and New Zealand banks, then spread to U.S. banks (such as Citibank) and beyond.

Spam

Unsolicited and unwanted e-mail is called **junk e-mail**. It's mass-produced and sent to millions of folks all over the world, using a technique called **bulk e-mail**. Junk e-mail is also called **spam** (because it spreads all over the Internet, just like Spam luncheon meat spread all over Europe during World War II). The person who sends it is called a **spammer** and said to be **spamming**.

> The typical spammer uses bulk e-mail to send spam to 3,000,000 e-mail addresses, all at once! 99.99% of the people who receive it will ignore it, but the other .01% keep the spammer in business: .01% of 3,000,000 people is 300 customers — and sending bulk e-mail costs nearly nothing!

In the USA, **90% of all e-mail is spam**.

Internet service providers (such as Earthlink and AOL) complain that most of their equipment is now just handling spam. They've sued spammers for "trespassing", and they've gotten some laws passed against spam. Remember:

> If you're a spammer,
> You'll wind up in the slammer.

If you're trying to advertise a business, you'll be tempted to send bulk e-mail (spam). It costs you nearly nothing, since Internet e-mail is free (unlike traditional mail, which costs 44¢ each, plus the cost of paper, plus the cost of putting labels onto all the envelopes). But since spam is associated with dishonest hucksters, sending spam can do your business's reputation more harm than good.

To avoid wasting time reading spam, some people (and their employers and Internet providers) use **spam filters**, which automatically erase spam (or dump it into a "Spam" folder or put the word "SPAM" in the subject line). To decide which e-mails are spam, spam filters use 3 techniques: **blacklists** (lists of known spammers), **whitelists** (lists of friends who are *not* spammers), and **Bayesian filters** (lists of characteristics of spam).

But spammers evade the filters and get their spam to you anyway, by using these tricks:

Spammers keep changing their e-mail addresses (to addresses that aren't blacklisted yet).

Spammers purposely misspell (they offer you "poorn" or "pOrn" or "p0rn" or "pron" instead of "porn") and add **word salad** (irrelevant words & sentences, often printed in white on a white background), so most of the e-mail doesn't seem to be about porn or Viagra or other spam topics.

Alas, spam filters reject valid mail that just *looks* like spam.

If you sent an e-mail to a friend, but your friend never saw it, that's probably because your e-mail looked too much like spam (you used too many spam-like words or fonts or graphics), so a spam filter hid your mail.

Hoaxes

A **hoax** is just an e-mail message that contains a scary incorrect rumor and warns you to "pass the message to all your friends".

The hoax is *not* a program; it's just a document. Though it theoretically does "no harm", actually it's as harmful as traditional viruses, since it wastes your time, waste your friends' time, embarrasses you (when you later discover the rumor is a lie and should be retracted), and creates a worldwide clogging of e-mail systems forced to transmit the rumor and retractions to millions of people.

Good Times In May 1994, people began sending each other e-mails spreading **a rumor that if you receive a file called "Good Times", don't download it**, because downloading it will erase your hard disk. The rumor was false: there is no "Good Times" virus.

The person who started the rumor knew it was false and started it as a prank. The rumor traveled fast and clogged e-mail systems all across the country, so the rumor *itself* became as annoying as a traditional virus.

The rumor gradually got wilder, and said that "Good Times" was an e-mail message, and just reading the message would erase your hard disk.

The rumor eventually became even more bizarre. Here's an abridgement of the rumor's current version:

"The FCC released a warning, last Wednesday, of major importance to any regular user of the Internet. A new computer virus has been engineered that's unparalleled in its destructive capability. Other viruses pale in comparison to this newest creation by a warped mentality.

"What makes this virus so terrifying, said the FCC, is that no disk need be inserted to infect a computer. The virus can be spread through Internet e-mail. Once a computer is infected, its hard drive will most likely be destroyed. If the program is not stopped, it will create a loop that can severely damage the processor if left running too long. Unfortunately, most novice users will not realize what's happening until far too late.

"Luckily, there's a way to detect what's now know as the 'Good Times' virus: the virus always travels to new computers in an e-mail message whose subject line says 'Good Times'. Avoiding infection is easy once the file has been received: don't read it.

"The program is highly intelligent: it will send copies of itself to everyone whose e-mail address is in a received-mail file or a sent-mail file. It will then trash the computer it is running on.

"So if you receive a file with the subject line 'Good Times', delete it immediately! Do not read it!

"Warn your friends of this newest threat to the Internet! It could save them a lot of time and money."

Again, there is no Good Times virus, but the *rumor* of the virus is itself a kind of virus!

Bad Times In December 1997, inspired by the Good Times virus hoax, Joe Garrick (and later others) published a rumor about a "Bad Times" virus. Here's the rumor's newest version (abridged):

"If you receive an email entitled 'Badtimes', delete it immediately. Don't open it.

"This one is pretty nasty. It will erase everything on your hard drive, delete anything on disks within 20 feet of your computer, demagnetize the stripes on all your credit cards, reprogram your ATM access code, screw up the tracking on your VCR, and scratch any CD you try to play.

"It will recalibrate your refrigerator so your ice cream melts and milk curdles, give your ex-lover your new phone number, mix antifreeze into your fish tank, drink all your beer, and leave dirty socks on the coffee table when company's coming over.

"It will hide your car keys, move your car randomly around parking lots so you can't find it, make you fall in love with a hardened pedophile, give you nightmares about circus midgets, and make you run with scissors.

"It will give you Dutch Elm Disease and Psittacosis. It will rewrite your backup files, changing all active verbs to passive and incorporating misspellings that grossly change the meaning.

"It will leave the toilet seat up and your hair dryer plugged in dangerously close to a full bathtub. It will molecularly rearrange your cologne, making it smell like dill pickles.

"It is insidious, subtle, dangerous, terrifying to behold, and an interesting shade of mauve.

"Please forward this message to everyone you know!!! Everyone deserves a good laugh."

E-mail tax In April 1999, a rumor swept across Canada, by e-mail, saying the Canadian government would start charging 5¢ for each e-mail ever sent, to reimburse the Canadian postal service, which was losing money because people were sending e-mails instead of regular letters. The rumor was false, a prank.

The next month, a U.S. variant began, which said "U.S." instead of "Canada".

Here's an abridgement of the rumor. [Brackets show where the Canadian and US versions differ.]

"Please read the following carefully if you intend to stay online and continue using e-mail.

"The Government of [Canada, the United States] is attempting to quietly push through legislation that will affect your use of the Internet. Under proposed legislation, [Canada Post, the U.S. Postal Service] will bill e-mail users.

"Bill 602P will permit the government to charge a 5-cent surcharge on every e-mail, by billing Internet Service Providers. The consumer would be billed in turn by the ISP. [Toronto, Washington DC] lawyer Richard Stepp is working to prevent this legislation from becoming law.

"The [Canada Post Corporation, US Postal Service] says e-mail proliferation costs nearly [$23,000,000, $230,000,000] in lost revenue per year. Since the average citizen receives about 10 e-mails per day, the cost to the typical individual would be an extra 50 cents per day, or over $180 dollars per year, beyond regular Internet costs.

"Note that this money would be paid directly to [Canada Post, the US Postal Service] for a service they don't even provide. The whole point of the Internet is democracy and non-interference.

"One [back-bencher, congressman], Tony Schnell, has even suggested a '20-to-40-dollar-per-month surcharge on all Internet service' beyond the government's proposed e-mail charges. Most major newspapers have ignored the story, the only exception being the [Toronto Star, Washingtonian], which called the idea of e-mail surcharge 'a useful concept whose time has come'.

"Don't sit by and watch your freedoms erode away! Send this e-mail to all [Canadians, Americans] on your list. Tell your friends and relatives to write to their [MP, congressman] and say 'No!' to Bill 602P. — Kate Turner, Assistant to Richard Stepp"

That rumor is entirely fiction. There is no "Bill 602P", no "Tony Schnell", no "Richard Stepp", and no desire by postal authorities or newspapers for a surcharge.

Viruses

A **computer virus** is a program that purposely does mischief and manages to copy itself to other computers, so the mischief spreads. Since computer viruses are **malicious malevolent software**, they're called **malware**.

People create viruses for several reasons.

Some people think it's funny to create mischief, by creating viruses. They're the same kind of people who like to play "practical jokes" and, as kids, pulled fire alarms.

Some people are angry (at dictatorships, at the military, at big impersonal corporations, at clients who don't pay bills, at lovers who rejected them, and at homosexuals). To get revenge, they create viruses to destroy their enemy's computers.

Some people are intellectuals who want the challenge of trying to create a program that replicates itself. Too often, the program replicates itself too well and too fast and accidentally does more harm that the programmer intended.

Some people want to become famous (or infamous or influential) by inventing viruses. They're the same kinds of people who, as kids, wrote graffiti on school walls and in bathrooms.

People who create viruses tend to be immature. Many are teenagers or disgruntled college students.

Different viruses perform different kinds of mischief.

Some viruses **print nasty messages**, containing four-letter words or threats or warnings, to make you worry and waste lots of your time and prevent you from getting work done.

Some viruses **erase some files**, or even your entire hard disk.

Some viruses **screw up your computer** so it prints wrong answers or stops functioning.

Some viruses **clog your computer**, by giving the computer more commands than the computer can handle, so the computer has no time left to handle other tasks, and all useful computer tasks remain undone.

The damage done by a virus is called the virus's **payload**. Some viruses are "benign": they do very little damage; their payload is small. Other viruses do big damage; they have a **big payload**. If a virus destroys your files, it's said to have a **destructive payload**.

Viruses

10% of all e-mail contains **viruses**. A **virus** is a malicious program that tries to wreck your computer and automatically spread itself to other computers. Even if the e-mail claims to come from a friend you know, the e-mail can contain a virus (because your friend doesn't know it contains a virus, or because the virus lied when it said it was from your friend — the virus could have just stolen your friend's name and e-mail address).

Many viruses come in e-mail attachments.

Don't open an e-mail attachment unless it comes with a cover letter that convinces you the attachment is really about something specific that you were expecting and that's specifically about you. For example, don't open an e-mail attachment that comes with a generic body saying just "open the attachment" or "look at these pictures" or "I'm shocked at what the attachment says about you" or some other depersonalized enticement. On the other hand, it's okay to open an attachment that says "Here are the pictures from the party I had with you and Sarah last Friday at 9PM", if you really *did* have a party with *that* person and Sarah last Friday at 9PM!

If the attachment's name ends in **.scr** or **.vbs**, the attachment is almost certainly a virus, since normal attachments don't have such names.

If the attachment's name ends in **.zip**, the attachment is *probably* a virus but might be innocent. Be *extremely* cautious.

If the attachment's name ends in **.doc**, the attachment is probably just an innocent Microsoft Word document; if the attachment's name ends in **.eml**, the attachment is probably just an innocent forwarded e-mail. But you can't be sure (since some viruses *pretend* to be ".doc" or ".eml"), so still keep your guard up. If you wish, phone or e-mail the sender and ask whether the sender really intended to send the attachment.

Propagation tricks

To propagate, viruses use two main tricks.

Trojan horse Homer's epic poem, *The Iliad*, describes how the Greeks destroyed Troy by a trick: they persuaded the Trojans to accept a "gift" — a gigantic wooden horse that secretly contained Greek warriors, who then destroyed Troy.

Some computer viruses use that trick: they look like a pleasant gift program, but the program secretly contains destructive warriors that destroy your computer. A pleasant-seeming program that secretly contains a virus is called a **Trojan horse**.

Time bomb If a virus damages your computer immediately (as soon as you receive it), you'll easily figure out who sent the virus, and you can stop the perpetrator. To prevent such detection, clever viruses are **time bombs**: they purposely delay damaging your computer until you've accidentally transmitted the virus to other computers; then, several weeks or months after you've been secretly infected and have secretly infected others, they suddenly destroy your computer system, and you don't know why. You don't know whom to blame.

How viruses arose

The first computer virus was invented in 1983 by Fred Cohen as an innocent experiment in computer security. He didn't harm anybody: his virus stayed in his lab.

In 1986, a different person invented the first virus that ran on a PC. That virus was called **Brain**. Unfortunately, it accidentally escaped from its lab; it was found next year at the University of Delaware. (A virus that escapes from its lab is said to be found **in the wild**.)

Most early viruses harmed nobody, but eventually bad kids started invented destructive viruses. The first destructive virus that spread fast was called the **Jerusalem virus** because it was first noticed at the Hebrew University of Israel in 1987. It's believed to have been invented by a programmer in Tel Aviv or Italy.

Most people still thought "computer viruses" were myths; but in 1988, magazines ran articles saying computer viruses really exist. Researchers began to invent **antivirus programs** to protect against viruses and destroy them. In 1989, antivirus programs started being distributed to the general public, to protect against the 30 viruses that had been invented so far. But then the nasty programmers writing viruses began protecting their viruses against the antivirus programs. Now there are over 50,000 viruses, though many are just **copycat viruses** that are slight variants of others.

Companies writing antivirus software are working as hard as the villains writing the viruses. Most antivirus companies release updates weekly.

Programs to protect you

To protect yourself against viruses, the first step is to make sure your Windows is up-to-date. Microsoft distributes updates often, especially on the afternoon of each special Tuesday (called **Patch Tuesday**, which is usually the 2nd Tuesday of each month). To make your computer check for updates and download them from the Internet, do this often (every few days): click **Start** then **All Programs** then **Windows Update**.

After making sure your Windows is up-to-date (so it includes the newest antivirus features), the next step is to supplement Windows by getting an antivirus program.

Norton The best antivirus program is **Norton AntiVirus**, which lists for $40. You can also get Norton Antivirus as part of **Norton Internet Security**, which lists for $70 and includes other utilities. Those prices get you a license for just one year, after which you must pay a yearly fee for updates.

> The Norton products are published by **Symantec** and sold in many stores, which usually charge about half of list price (after discounts and rebates). If you're in a rush and not near a store, phone PC Connection (a mail-order dealer at 800-800-0003), which charges just $5 for overnight shipping. (You can order late at night and still receive it in the morning!)

McAfee Another common antivirus program is **McAfee AntiVirus**, which comes in several versions. McAfee used to be an independent company but is now owned by **Intel**.

Freebies If your Internet Service Provider is Comcast, you can download Norton AntiVirus and other security software free, from **http://security.comcast.net**.

Windows Vista and Windows 7 each include Microsoft's **Windows Defender**, which is free and protects you against adware, spyware, and phishing (but not viruses). If you have Windows XP instead, you can download Windows Defender from **www.WindowsDefender.com**, free. Before downloading, that Website checks to make sure your Windows XP is legitimate (not a pirated copy) and has been updated (to include Service Pack 2 or Service Pack 3.

Better yet, get **Microsoft Security Essentials**, which is free and includes protection against every type of malicious software (adware, spyware, phishing, and viruses). Download it from **www.microsoft.com/security_essentials**.

Annoying detail: Microsoft Security Essentials is free for use on your home PC or on for a business having no more than 10 computers. If your business has more than 10 computers, Microsoft requires you to buy a fancier version, called **Microsoft Forefront Endpoint Protection**.

Instead of using Microsoft Security Essentials, some folks use other free protection, such as the free version of **AVG Anti-Virus** (downloadable from http://free.avg.com) and the free version of **Malwarebytes Anti-Malware** (downloadable from www.malwarebytes.org/mbam-download.php). But Microsoft Security Essentials has the advantage of being complete (no add-ons needed) and unobtrusive (no annoying messages).

Don't relax Even if you get an antivirus program, you can't completely relax, since new viruses keep getting invented. You must keep your antivirus program up-to-date, to make sure it can detect the newest viruses.

Some viruses are so powerful that they destroy antivirus programs. Some viruses even print their own fake messages saying "no virus found". Some viruses even pretend they are antivirus programs that found viruses on your computer — and they ask you to send money to complete the "cure" — and they block you from installing or updating true antivirus programs. Don't send money: it's wasted and goes to an international group of crooks.

Who gets viruses

The most common place to find traditional viruses is at schools.

> That's partly because most viruses were invented at schools (by bright, mischievous students) but mainly **because many students share the school's computers**. If one student has an infected floppy disk (purposely or accidentally) and puts it into one of the school's computers, that computer's hard disk will probably get infected. Then it will infect all the other students who use that computer. As disks are passed from that computer to the school's other computers, the rest of the school's computers become infected.
>
> Then the school's **students, unaware of the infection, take the disks home** with them and infect their families' home computers. Then the **parents bring infected disks to their offices** (so they can transfer work between home and office) and infect their companies. Then company employees take infected disks home and infect their home computers, which infect any disks used by the kids, who, unaware of the infection, then take infected disks to school and start the cycle all over again.

Anybody who shares programs with other people can get a virus. Most programs are copyrighted and illegal to share. People who share programs illegally are called **pirates**. Pirates spread viruses. For example, many kids spread viruses when they try to share their games with their friends.

Another source of viruses is computer stores, in their computer-repair departments.

> While trying to analyze and fix broken computers, the repair staff often shoves diagnostic disks into the computers, to find out what's wrong. If one of the broken computers has a virus, the diagnostic disks accidentally get viruses from the broken computers and then pass the viruses on to other computers. So if you bring your computer to a store for repairs, don't be surprised if your computer gets fixed but also gets a virus.

Occasionally, a major software company will screw up, accidentally get infected by a virus, and unknowingly distribute it to all folks buying the software. Even companies as big as Microsoft have accidentally distributed viruses.

The newest viruses are spread by Internet communications, such as e-mail, instead of by floppy disks. Internet-oriented viruses spread quickly all over the world: they're an international disaster!

History of viruses

Viruses fall into 6 categories: you can get infected by a **file virus**, a **boot-sector virus**, a **multipartite virus**, a **macro virus**, an **e-mail worm**, or a **denial-of-service attack**.

Here are the details....

File viruses

A **file virus** (also called a **parasitic virus**) secretly attaches itself to an innocent program, so the innocent program becomes infected. Whenever you run the infected innocent program, you're running the virus too!

Here are the file viruses that have been most common. For each virus, I begin by showing its name and the year & month it was first discovered in the wild. Let's start with the oldest....

Yankee Doodle (September 1989) This virus from Bulgaria **plays part of the song Yankee Doodle** on the computer's built-in speaker, at 5 PM every day. It infects .COM & .EXE files, so they become 2899 bytes longer.

Die Hard 2 (July 1994) This virus from South Africa infects .COM & .EXE files and makes them become exactly 4000 bytes bigger. It also wrecks .ASM files (programs written in assembler).

Chernobyl (June 1998) Back on April 26, 1986, radioactive gas escaped from a nuclear reactor in Chernobyl in the Soviet Union. To commemorate that event, the Chernobyl virus **erases your hard disk** on April 26 every year. A variant, called **version 1.4**, erases your hard disk on the 26th of every month.

If you get infected, you won't notice until the 26th; then your hard disk suddenly gets erased — and so do the hard disks of all your friends to whom you accidentally sent the virus!

The virus was written in Taiwan by a 24-year old guy named Chen Ing-Hau. Since his initials are CIH, the virus is also called the **CIH virus**.

The virus was invented in June 1998. At the end of 1998, three big companies (IBM, Yamaha, and Activision) got infected and accidentally spread the virus on disks distributed to their customers. The virus did its first damage on April 26, 1999. Computers all over the world lost their data that day. Most American corporations were forewarned and forearmed with antivirus programs; but **in Korea a million computers lost their data, at a cost of 250 million dollars**, because Koreans didn't use antivirus programs but did use a lot of pirated software.

Here's how the virus erases your hard disk:

> It starts at the disk's beginning and writes random info onto every sector, until your computer stops working. The data that was previously on those overwritten sectors is gone forever and can't be recovered.

The virus also tries to attack your computer's flash BIOS chips, by writing wrong info into them. If the virus succeeds, your computer will be permanently unable to display anything on the screen and also have trouble communicating with the keyboard, ports, and other devices, unless you bring your computer into a repair shop.

Here's how the virus spreads:

> Whenever you run an infected program, the virus in the program copies itself into the RAM memory chips, stays there (until you turn the computer off), and infects every other program you try to run or copy. To infect a program, the virus looks for unused spaces in the program's file, then breaks itself up and puts pieces of itself into unused spaces, so the file's total length is the same as before and the virus is undetected.

Before you use an antivirus program to delete the virus, you must boot by using an uninfected floppy. If instead you just boot normally from your hard disk, your hard disk's infected files copy the virus into RAM; then when you tell the antivirus program to "scan all programs to remove the virus", the antivirus program accidentally *copies* the virus onto all those programs and infects them all. Yes, the virus tricks your antivirus program into becoming a *pro*-virus program!

Boot-sector viruses

On a floppy disk or hard disk, the first sector is called the disk's **boot sector** or, more longwindedly, the disk's **master boot record (MBR)**. A virus that hides in the boot sector is called a **boot-sector virus**. Whenever the computer tries to boot from a drive containing an infected disk, the virus copies itself into RAM memory chips (even if the booting is unfinished because the disk is considered "unbootable").

Before hiding in the boot sector, the typical boot-sector virus makes room for itself by moving data from the boot sector to a "second place" on the disk. Unfortunately, whatever data had been in the "second place" gets overwritten and cannot be recovered.

The typical boot-sector virus makes the computer eventually **hang** (stop reacting to your keystrokes and mouse strokes).

The following boot-sector viruses have been most common....

Stoned (December 1987) This virus was invented in 1987 by a student at the University of Wellington, New Zealand.

If you boot from a disk (floppy or hard) infected with this virus, there's a 1-in-8 chance your computer will beep and display this message: "Your PC is now Stoned".

It was intended to be harmless, but it assumes your floppy disk is 360K. On higher-capacity floppy disks (such as 1.44M disks), it **accidentally erases important parts of the directory**.

It also **makes your computer run slower** — as if your computer were stoned.

Many other virus writers have created imitations & variants, called **strains**.

Form (June 1990) This virus from Switzerland is supposed to just play a harmless prank: **on the 18th day of each month, the computer beeps whenever a key is pressed**. But this virus is badly written and accidentally causes problems. For example, **if your hard disk ever becomes full, the virus makes the hard disk become unbootable**. And if the computer ever fails to read from a disk, the virus can make the system hang.

The virus's second sector contains this message, which never gets displayed:

> The FORM-Virus send greetings to everyone who's reading this text. FORM doesn't destroy data! Don't panic! Fuckings go to Corinne.

Michelangelo (April 1991) Inspired by the Stoned virus, this virus from Sweden sits quietly on your hard disk until Michelangelo's birthday, March 6th. Each year, **on March 6th, the virus tries to destroy all data on your hard drive**, by writing **garbage** (random meaningless bytes) everywhere. The overwritten data cannot be recovered.

To avoid damage from this virus, folks played this trick: on March 5th, before turning off their computers, they changed the computer's date to March 7th, skipping March 6th.

Monkey (October 1992) Inspired by the Stoned virus, this virus from the U.S. **encrypts the hard drive's partition table**, so **the hard drive is accessible just while the virus is in memory**. If you boot the system from a clean (uninfected) floppy disk, the hard drive is unusable. This virus is tough to remove successfully, since **removing the virus will also remove your ability to access the data**.

Parity Boot (September 1993) Every hour, this virus from Germany checks whether it's infected a floppy disk. If it hasn't infected a disk in the last hour, it says "PARITY CHECK" and stops the computer (makes the computer **hang**) until you press the Reset button.

Ripper (November 1993) This virus from Norway **randomly corrupts data being written to disk**. The chance of a particular write being corrupted is just 1 out of 1024, so the corruption occurs just occasionally and to just a few bytes at a time. You normally don't notice the problem until several weeks have gone by and the infection has spread to many files and your backups, too! Then it's too late to recover your data! That's why Ripper is a successful virus: its effects are so subtle you don't notice until you've infected your hard disk, your backups, and your friends! Then ya wanna die!

Anti-EXE (December 1993) This virus from Russia picks one of your .EXE files and waits for you to run that file. When you do, the virus corrupts the copy that's in the RAM (but not the copy that's on disk). While you run that corrupted copy, **errors occur, and the computer usually hangs**.

Anti-CMOS (February 1994) This virus from the U.S. **changes your system's CMOS settings**, as follows:

> Your hard drive becomes "not installed".
> Your 1.44M floppy drive becomes "1.2M".
> A 1.2M floppy drive becomes "not installed".
> A 360K floppy drive becomes "720K", and vice-versa.

To evade detection and give itself time to spread to other computers, it waits before doing that damage: it waits until you've accessed the floppy drive many times.

A variant virus, **Anti-CMOS.B**, generates sounds from the computer's built-in speaker instead of changing the CMOS.

New York Boot (July 1994) This U.S. virus's only purpose is to spread itself. But it spreads itself fast and often.

Multipartite viruses

You've learned that some viruses (called **boot-sector viruses**) infect the disk's boot sector, while other viruses (called **file viruses**) infect the disk's file system. If a virus is smart enough to infect the disk's boot sector and file system simultaneously, it's called a **multipartite virus**.

Yes, a multipartite virus hides in *two* places: the boot sector and also the file system. If you remove the virus from just the boot sector (or from just files), you still haven't completely removed the virus, which can regenerate itself from the place you missed.

If a virus is very smart, it's called a **stealth polymorphic armored multipartite virus (SPAM virus)**:

> A **stealth virus** makes special efforts to hide itself from antivirus software. For example, it tricks antivirus software into inspecting a clean copy of a file instead of letting it read the actual (infected) file.
>
> A **polymorphic virus** changes its own appearance each time it infects a file, so no two copies of the virus look alike to antivirus programs.
>
> An **armored virus** protects itself against antivirus disassembly.
>
> A **multipartite virus** hides in *two* places: the boot sector and also the file system.

One Half (October 1994) The most common multipartite virus is **One Half**, from Austria. It slowly **encrypts the hard drive**. Each time you turn on the computer, the virus encrypts two more tracks. The encrypting is done by using a random code. You can use the encrypted tracks while the virus remains in memory. When about half of the hard drive's tracks are encrypted, the computer says:

```
Dis is one half
Press any key to continue......
```

This virus is tough to remove successfully, since **removing the virus will also remove your ability to access the data**.

It's hard to detect, since it's polymorphic and uses stealth.

Macro viruses

A **macro virus** hides in **macros**, which are little programs embedded in Microsoft Word documents and Excel spreadsheets. The virus spreads to another computer when you give somebody an infected document (on a floppy disk or through a local-area network or as an e-mail attachment). During the past few years, e-mail has become prevalent, and so have macro viruses: they're more prevalent than all other viruses combined.

Here are the most prevalent macro viruses....

Concept (July 1995) This virus infects Microsoft Word documents and templates. When you load an infected document for the first time, you see a dialog box that says "1", with an OK button. Once you click OK, the virus takes over. It forces all documents to be saved as templates, which in turn affect new documents.

It consists of 5 macros: **AutoOpen**, **PayLoad**, **FileSaveAs**, **AAAZAO**, and **AAAZFS**. You can see those macros in an infected Word document by choosing "Macro" from the Tools menu.

Invented in 1995, it was historic:

> It was the first macro virus. It was the first virus that infects documents instead of programs or boot sectors. It was the first virus that can infect *both* kinds of computers: IBM and Mac!

Old antivirus programs can't detect it.

It was intended as just a harmless prank demonstration of what a macro virus could do (so it's also called the **Prank Macro virus**), but it spread fast.

In 1995, it became more prevalent than any other virus. Microsoft Word 97 was the first version of Microsoft Word to protect itself against the virus.

Wazzu (June 1996) Inspired by the Concept virus, this virus consists of a macro called **AutoOpen** that forces Microsoft Word documents to be saved as templates. Whenever you open a document, the virus also **rearranges up to 3 words and inserts the word "Wazzu" at random**.

Laroux (July 1996) This virus was first discovered in July 1996 in Africa and Alaska. It was the first macro virus that infected Excel spreadsheets (instead of Word documents). It does no harm except copy itself.

Tristate (March 1998) This macro virus is called **Tristate** because it's smart enough to infect 3 things: Microsoft Word documents, Excel spreadsheets, and PowerPoint slides.

Class (October 1998) This macro virus infects Microsoft Word documents. It just displays a stupid message on your screen occasionally.

> The original version (called **Class.A**) says "This is Class" on your screen, on the 31st day of each month.
>
> The most prevalent version (called **Class.D**) displays this message on the 14th day of each month after May: "I think", then your name, then "is a big stupid jerk!"
>
> The craziest version (called **Class.E**) says "Monica Blows Clinton! -=News@11=-" occasionally (at random, 1% of the time); and on the 17th day of each month after August, it says "Today is Clinton & Monica Fuck-Fest Day!"

Ethan (January 1999) When you use Microsoft Word, if you click "File" then "Properties" then "Summary", you see a window where you can type a document's title, author, keywords, and other items. When you close a document infected by the Ethan virus, this virus has a 30% chance of **changing the document's title to "Ethan Frome", the author to "EW/LN/CB", and the keywords to "Ethan".**

That's to honor *Ethan Frome*, a novel written by Edith Wharton in 1911, about a frustrated man — the kind of man who would now write viruses.

Melissa (March 1999) This macro virus infects Microsoft Word documents. When you look at (open) a document, if the document is infected, the virus tries to e-mail copies of the infected document to the first 50 people mentioned in Microsoft Outlook's address book (which is called the **Contacts folder**), unless the virus e-mailed to those people previously. Yes, **your document gets secretly e-mailed to 50 people**, without you knowing!

Each of those 50 people get an e-mail from you. The e-mail's subject says "Important message from" and your name. The e-mail's body says "Here is that document you asked for ... don't show anyone else ;-)". Attached to that e-mail is your document, infected by the virus.

This virus spreads fast just if your computer has Microsoft Outlook. In the typical large corporation, each computer *does* have Microsoft Outlook (which is part of Microsoft Office), so the virus e-mails itself to 50 people automatically, and each of those people passes the virus on to 50 other people, etc., making the virus spread fast.

The virus was invented by David L. Smith in New Jersey. He called it "Melissa" to honor a Florida topless dancer. Her name is hidden in the virus program. The virus spread all over the world suddenly, on March 26, 1999, when he put it in a message in the alt.sex newsgroup. His infected document, called LIST.DOC, contained a list of porno Web sites. In just a few days, 10% of all computers connected to the Internet contained the virus. It spread faster than any other virus ever invented. Since it created so much e-mail (from infected documents and from confused people denying they meant to send the e-mail), many Internet computers handling e-mail had to be shut down.

The FBI decided that the virus did over 80 million dollars of damage to business processes. David tried to hide his authorship of the virus; but the FBI did a thorough job of sleuthing, so on April 2, 1999 the New Jersey police arrest David. At first, he denied he distributed the virus; but he finally pleaded guilty and apologized. He was fined $5000 and sentenced to 20 months in federal prison plus 100 hours of community service plus 3 years of supervised release. He became cooperative and helped the FBI find the perpetrators of other viruses.

A TV cartoon show called "The Simpsons" has an episode called "The Genius", where Bart Simpson abruptly ends a Scrabble game by claiming he won with the word "Kwyjibo". The virus can put into your document this quote from him:

```
Twenty-two points, plus triple-word-score, plus
fifty points for using all my letters. Game's
over. I'm outta here.
```

The virus inserts that quotation just if you open or close the document at the precise minute when, on the computer's clock, the number of minutes equals the date. For example, on May 27th it will insert that quotation if the time is 1:27, 2:27, 3:27, 4:27, 5:27, 6:27, 7:27, 8:27, 9:27, 10:27, 11:27, or 12:27.

The virus runs just if you have Microsoft Word 97 or 2000. Those versions of Microsoft Word are supposed to protect again macro viruses, but the Melissa virus is smart enough to disable that protection.

Although the original virus's e-mail subject line said "Important message from", a new variant of the virus has a blank subject line, making the virus harder to notice.

Marker (April 1999) This macro virus infects Microsoft Word documents. On the first day of each month, it **tries to invade your privacy by copying your name (and your company's name and your address) to an Internet site** run by codebreakers.org. It copies the name & address you gave when you installed Microsoft Word. If it successfully uploads your info, it doesn't bother redoing it in future months.

Thus (August 1999) This macro virus infects Microsoft Word documents. It lurks there until December 13th, when **it erases drive C**. It's called "Thus" because its macro program begins with the word "thus".

Prilissa (November 1999) This virus imitates Melissa but displays different words:

> The e-mail's subject says "Message from" and your name. The e-mail's body says "This document is very Important and you've GOT to read this !!!". Instead of printing a quotation from Bart Simpson, the virus waits until Christmas then does this:
>
> 1. It says "©1999 - CyberNET Vine...Vide...Vice...Moslem Power Never End... You Dare Rise Against Me... The Human Era is Over, The CyberNET Era Has Come!"
>
> 2. It draws several colored shapes onto the currently opened document.
>
> 3. It changes your AUTOEXEC.BAT file so that the next time you boot, **the entire C drive will be erased** (by reformatting) and you'll see this message: "Vine...Vide...Vice...Moslem Power Never End... Your Computer Have Just Been Terminated By -= CyberNET =- Virus !!!".

E-mail worms

An **e-mail worm** is a malicious program that comes as an e-mail attachment and pretends to be innocent fun.

The following e-mail worms are the most prevalent....

Happy 99 (January 1999) This program, called HAPPY99.EXE, comes as an e-mail attachment. If you open it, you see a window titled "Happy New Year 1999 !!". In that window, you see a pretty firework display.

But **while you enjoy watching the fireworks, the HAPPY99.EXE program secretly makes 3 changes to your SYSTEM folder** (which is in your WINDOWS folder):

> 1. In that folder, it puts a copy of itself, and calls the copy SKA.EXE (which is why the Happy 99 worm is also called the **SKA worm**).
>
> 2. In that folder, it puts a file called SKA.DLL (by extracting SKA.DLL from HAPPY99.EXE).
>
> 3. It modifies that folder's WSOCK32.DLL file, after saving that file's original version as WSOCK32.SKA.

The modified WSOCK32.DLL file **forces your computer to attach the Happy 99 worm to every e-mail you send**. So in the future, whenever you send an e-mail, the person who receives your e-mail will also receive an attachment called HAPPY99.EXE. When the person double-clicks the attachment, the person will see the pretty firework display, think you sent it on purpose, and not realize you sent an e-mail worm virus.

To brag about itself, the virus keeps a list of everybody you sent the virus to. That list of e-mail addresses is in your SYSTEM folder and called LISTE.SKA.

An updated version, called **Happy 00**, comes as a file called HAPPY00.EXE. It says "Happy New Year 2000!!" instead of "Happy New Year 1999 !!".

Pretty Park (May 1999)
This virus comes in an e-mail. The e-mail's subject line, instead of saying "Important message", says just "C:\CoolPrograms\Pretty Park.exe". The e-mail's body, instead of containing sentences, says just "Test: Pretty Park.exe :)" and **shows a drawing of a boy wearing a hat**. The boy is Kyle, from the "South Park" TV cartoon show. The drawing is labeled "Pretty Park.exe". If you double-click it, you'll be opening an attachment called PrettyPark.exe, which is a virus.

Then you might see the 3D Pipes screensaver (which is one of the screensavers you get free as part of Windows 98). But secretly, **every 30 minutes, the virus peeks in Microsoft Outlook's address book and sends copies of itself to your friends listed there**. Every 30 seconds, it also tries to connect your computer to an Internet Relay Chat server computer, so the virus can invade your privacy by sending info about you and your computer to the virus's author or distributor.

This virus was first distributed in May 1999 by an e-mail spammer from France.

Explore ZIP (June 1999)
This virus destroys all your Microsoft Word documents (and all other file that end in .doc), **all your Excel spreadsheets** (and all other files that end in .xls), **all your PowerPoint presentations** (and all other files that end in .ppt), all your assembly-language programs (and all other files that end in .asm), and all files that end in .h, .c, or .cpp.

It destroys the files by replacing them with files that have 0 length. Since the file names still exist, you won't immediately notice that their contents are destroyed, and backup software won't notice which files are gone. It destroys those files on drives C, D, E, etc. For example, if your computer is part of a network, the virus destroys those files on your hard drive and also on the network server's hard drive.

It also **looks in your e-mail's Inbox** (created by Outlook Express or Outlook or Exchange), **notices any messages you haven't replied to yet, and replies to them itself!**

For example, if an e-mail from Joan with a subject line saying "Buy soap" hasn't been replied to yet, the virus sends a reply who subject is "Re: Buy soap" and whose body says:

> Hi Joan! I received your email and I shall send you a reply ASAP. Till then, take a look at the attached zipped docs. Bye.

The reply comes with an attachment called zipped_files.exe. If the recipient opens that attachment, zipped_files.exe starts running. To fool the victim, it displays a fake error message (which begins by saying "Cannot open file"). Then it puts a copy of itself into the SYSTEM folder (which is in the WINDOWS folder); the copy is called "Explore.exe" or "_setup.exe". It also modifies the "run" line in your computer's WIN.INI file so the program will run each time Windows starts.

Free Link (July 1999)
This virus finds people in Microsoft Outlook's address book and sends them an e-mail whose subject line says "Check this" and whose body says "Have fun with these links. Bye."

Clicking the e-mail's attachment makes the virus infect the computer and say, "This will add a shortcut to free XXX links on your desktop. Do you want to continue?"

If the recipient clicks "Yes", **the virus creates a shortcut icon pointing to an adult-sex Web site**. But even if the recipient clicks "No", the virus has already infected the computer and will use that computer to send e-mails, which will **embarrass the computer's owner when those e-mails reach the owner's friends**.

Kak (December 1999)
If your computer gets infected by this virus from France, every e-mail you send by using Microsoft Outlook Express gets infected. The virus infects by acting as an e-mail signature instead of an attachment, so **everybody reading your e-mail will get infected, even if the recipients don't look at any attachments**.

If your computer is infected, it will do this at 5PM on the first day of each month: it will protest against Microsoft by saying "Kagou-Anti-Kro$oft says not today!" and then the computer will shut itself down (as if you had clicked "Start" then "Shut Down" then "OK").

The virus is called **Kagou-Anti-Krosoft**, which is abbreviated as **Kak**. Its main file is KAK.HTM, which is put into your Windows folder. It temporarily puts a file called KAK.HTA into your Startup folder but erases that file when you reboot.

Love Bug (May 2000)
This virus comes in an e-mail whose subject line says "ILOVEYOU". The e-mail's body says "kindly check the attached LOVELETTER coming from me." and comes with an attachment called LOVE-LETTER-FOR-YOU.TXT.vbs. That attachment is the virus. When you activate it (by clicking the attachment), the virus infects your computer and does 3 dastardly deeds:

It sends a copy of itself to everybody in your Microsoft Outlook address book. This will embarrass you, when everybody in your address book gets an e-mail that says "ILOVEYOU". Your boss, assistant, colleagues, customers, friends, and ex-friends will all be surprised to get an e-mail saying you love them and sent them a love letter. (They'll be upset later when they discover the "love letter" is a virus you gave them!)

It wrecks graphics files and some programs. Specifically, it wrecks all files whose names end in .jpg, .jpeg, .vbs, .vbe, .js, .jse, .css, .wsh, .sct, and .hta. It wrecks them by renaming the files and inserting copies of itself into the files. Also, it hides music files (all files that end in .mp3 or .mp2), so you can't use those files until you "unhide" them. When looking for files to wreck or hide, it looks at your computer's hard drive and also the hard drives of any network server computers you're attached to.

It tries makes your computer download, from an Internet Web site in the Philippines, a program misleadingly called WIN-BUGSFIX.EXE. That program **tries to steal your passwords** by e-mailing them to a Philippines e-mail address called MAILME@SUPER.NET.PH. To that address, it tries to secretly send your Internet passwords, network passwords, your own name, your computer's name, and your Internet settings, so the virus inventor's computer can imitate yours and have all your Internet and network privileges.

This virus spread faster than all other viruses.

It began in the Philippines on May 4, 2000, and spread across the whole world in one day (traveling from Hong Kong to Europe to the United States), infecting 10% of all computers connected to the Internet and causing about 7 billion dollars in damage. Most of the "damage" was the labor of getting rid of the virus and explaining to recipients that the sender didn't mean to say "I love you". The Pentagon, CIA, and British Parliament all had to shut down their e-mail systems to get rid of the virus — and so did most big corporations. It did less damage in India (where employees are conservative and don't believe "I love you" messages) and the Philippines (where few people use the Internet because it's so expensive).

An international manhunt for the perpetrator finally led to a 23-year-old computer student in the Philippines city of Manila.

On May 11th (one week after the virus spread), he held a news conference. Accompanied by his lawyer and sister, he said his name was Onel de Guzman and didn't mean to do so much harm.

In the Philippines, Internet access normally costs 100 pesos ($2.41) per hour, and 100 pesos is a half day's wages! For his graduation thesis in computer science, he created a program that would help low-income Filipinos get free access to the Internet by stealing passwords from rich people. The university rejected his thesis because it was illegal, so he couldn't graduate. Helped by a group of friends called the Grammersoft Group (which was in the business of illegally selling theses to other students), he made his virus be fancy and distributed it the day before the school held its graduation ceremony.

The middle of the virus's program says the virus is copyright by "Grammersoft Group, Manila, Philippines" and mentions his college. The authorities found him by checking (and shutting down) the Philippine Web sites and e-mail addresses that the virus uses (to steal passwords), chatting with the college's computer-science department, looking for the Grammersoft Group in Manila, and comparing the virus with earlier viruses written by his friends.

But charges against him were finally dropped, since the Philippines had no laws yet against creating viruses.

It's called the **Love Bug** because it's a virus (bug) transmitted by a love letter. It's also called the **Killer from Manila**.

Copycats have edited the virus's program and created 28 variants. The original version is called **version A**. Here are examples of other versions:

Version A (the original version) says "ILOVEYOU" then "kindly check the attached LOVELETTER coming from me." It attaches "LOVE-LETTER-FOR-YOU.TXT.vbs".

Version C ("Very Funny") says "fwd: Joke" then has a blank body. It attaches "Very Funny.vbs".

Version E ("Mother's Day") says "Mothers Day Order Confirmation" then "We have proceeded to charge your credit card for the amount of $326.92 for the mothers day diamond special. We have attached a detailed invoice to this email. Please print out the attachment and keep it in a safe place. Thanks Again and Have a Happy Mothers Day! mothersday@subdimension.com". It attaches mothersday.vbs.

Version M ("Arab Air") says "Thank You For Flying With Arab Airlines" then "Please check if the bill is correct, by opening the attached file". It attaches ArabAir.TXT.vbs.

Version Q ("LOOK!") says "LOOK!" then "hehe…check this out." It attaches LOOK.vbs.

The following variants pretend to cure the virus but actually are viruses themselves:

Version F says "Dangerous Virus Warning" then "There is a dangerous virus circulating. Please click attached picture to view it and learn to avoid it." It attaches virus_warning.jpg.vbs.

Version G says "Virus Alert!!!" then a long message. This version also wrecks .bat and .com files.

Version K says "How to protect yourself from the ILOVEYOU bug!" then "Here's the easy way to fix the love virus." It attaches Virus-Protection-Instructions.vbs.

Version T says "Recent Virus Attacks — Fix" then "Attached is a copy of a script that will reverse the effects of the LOVE-LETTER-TO-YOU.TXT.vbs as well as the FW:JOKE, Mother's Day and Lithuanian siblings." It attaches BAND-AID.DOC.VBS. This version also wrecks many other files, and it totally deletes .mp3 and .mp2 files.

Version W says "IMPORTANT: Official virus and bug fix" then "This is an official virus and bug fix. I got it from our system admin. It may take a short while to update your system files after you run the attachment." It attaches "Bug and virus fix.vbs".

Version AC says "New Variation on LOVEBUG Update Antivirus!!" then "There is now a newer variant of love bug. It was released at 8:37 PM Saturday Night. Please Download the following patch. We are trying to isolate the virus. Thanks Symantec." It attaches antivirusupdate.vbs.

Life Stages (May 2000) Here's a famous comment about life stages:

The male stages of life:

Age Seduction line
Age	Seduction line
17	"My parents are away for the weekend."
25	"My girlfriend is away for the weekend."
35	"My fiancée is away for the weekend."
48	"My wife is away for the weekend."
66	"My second wife is dead."

Age Favorite sport
Age	Favorite sport
17	sex
25	sex
35	sex
48	sex
66	napping

Age Definition of a successful date
Age	Definition of a successful date
17	"Tongue!"
25	"Breakfast!'
35	"She didn't set back my therapy."
48	"I didn't have to meet her kids."
66	"Got home alive!"

The female stages of life:

Age Favorite fantasy
Age	Favorite fantasy
17	tall, dark, and handsome
25	tall, dark, and handsome, with money
35	tall, dark, and handsome, with money and a brain
48	a man with hair
66	a man

Age Ideal date
Age	Ideal date
17	He offers to pay.
25	He pays.
35	He cooks breakfast next morning.
48	He cooks breakfast next morning for the kids.
66	He can chew his breakfast.

The Life Stages virus tries to e-mail that comment, but the transmission is imperfect: the virus misspells "handsome" as "hansome" and makes other errors in spelling and punctuation.

The e-mail's subject is "Life stages" or "Funny" or "Jokes", with sometimes the word "text" afterwards, and sometimes "Fw:" beforehand. So there are 12 possible subjects, such as this: "Fw: Life stages text". (The computer chooses among the 12 at random.) By having 12 possible subjects instead of 1, the virus is harder for antivirus programs to stop.

The e-mail's body says "The male and female stages of life". Attached to it is a file that pretends to be just a simple text document called LIFE_STAGES.TXT, but actually it's a virus program called LIFE_STAGES.TXT.SHS. The **.SHS** means it's a **SH**ell **S**crap object program. When you open it, you see the comment about the stages of life. (You see it in a Notepad window.) While you read that comment, the virus secretly infects your computer, so your computer transmits the virus to 100 randomly-chosen people in your Outlook address book and to Internet chat groups.

After e-mailing the virus to your friends, the computer erases those e-mails from your Sent folder, so you don't know the e-mails were sent. To stop you from eradicating the virus by editing the registry, the virus changes the name of the computer's REGEDIT.EXE program to "RECYCLED.VXD" then moves it to the Recycle Bin and makes it a hidden file so you can't see it.

Snow White (September 2000) This virus **offers to tell you a naughty story about Snow White**.

It comes in an e-mail whose subject line tries to say "Snow White and the Seven Dwarfs — the REAL story!" and claims to be from hahahaha@sexyfun.net. The e-mail's body tries to send this message:

Today, Snow White was turning 18. The 7 dwarfs always were very educated and polite with Snow White. When they went out to work in the morning, they promised a HUGE surprise. Snow White was anxious. Suddenly, the door opens, and the Seven Dwarfs enter....

It sends that subject and message in slightly flawed English (for example, it says "Snowhite" instead of "Snow White") or in French, Spanish, or Portuguese: the virus is smart enough to analyze your computer to find out which language you seem to prefer!

To find out the rest of the sexy story, you're encouraged to open the attachment (which the English version calls sexyvirgin.scr, midgets.scr, dwarf4you.exe, or joke.exe). If you click that attachment, you'll launch the multilingual virus, which will infect your WSOCK32.DLL file and watch you forevermore! Whenever you send or receive an e-mail (or view a Web site that mentions an e-mail address), the virus will notice and, after a delay, send itself to that e-mail address; so if you try to send an e-mail to a friend, your friend will get *two* e-mails from you; the second is the Snow White story with virus.

The virus tries to communicate with a newsgroup called alt.comp.virus so it can send and receive new fancier versions of itself by swapping intelligence with copies that are on other computers. For example, one of the new fancy features **puts a spinning spiral onto your computer screen** once an hour (whenever your computer's clock says the number of minutes is 59). To drive you extra crazy, the spiral also appears all day on September 16 & 24. Another fancy feature copies the virus into all your .EXE files, which will still run but be infected, making the virus hard to remove.

The virus is also called **Hybris**, since the attachment includes a copyright notice saying the virus is called "HYBRIS (c) Vecna".

Magistrate (March 2001) This virus from Sweden, called **Magistrate** or **Magistr**, targets magistrates, judges, and lawyers.

After infecting your computer, it spreads to your colleagues by e-mail and networks then waits, still lurking in your computer.

If 2 months have passed, then on odd-numbered days **your desktop's icons will run away from the mouse pointer** whenever you try to click them.

If 3 months have passed, the infected file is deleted.

If you're a judge or lawyer, this virus is especially dangerous, because of this rule: if at least 1 month has passed and at least 100 colleagues were infected and at least 3 of your files contain at least 3 legal phrases (in English, French, or Spanish), **it wrecks your computer thoroughly**, by doing all this:

It deletes the infected file.
It erases your CMOS & flash BIOS chip (so you can't restart your computer).
It wrecks every 25ᵗʰ file (by changing it to repeatedly say "YOUARESHIT").
It deletes every other file.

It makes the screen say this:
Another haughty bloodsucker...
YOU THINK YOU ARE GOD,
BUT YOU ARE ONLY A CHUNK OF SHIT

It wrecks a sector on drive C (by putting different info there).

For example, here are the English legal phrases it looks for:

sentences you, sentence you to, sentences him to, ordered to prison
convict, found guilty, find him guilty, guilty plea, against the accused
affirmed, sufficiency of proof, sufficiency of the evidence
verdict, judgment of conviction, proceedings, habeas corpus
circuit judge, trial judge, trial court, trial chamber, ", judge"

The virus comes in a strange e-mail:

The e-mail's body is an excerpt from a .DOC or .TXT document that was on the sender's disk. The e-mail's attachment is an infected copy of an .EXE or .SCR program that was on the sender's disk. In the e-mail's return address ("From:"), the virus usually alters the second character, to prevent the recipient from replying to the sender and complaining about receiving a virus.

Sircam (July 2001) This virus **grabs a document you wrote and secretly sends it to somebody you never intended!**

This virus can get very embarrassing. For example, if you wrote a private note, to a friend, about how much you hate your boss, the virus might secretly send that note to your boss!

It sends e-mail to every e-mail address mentioned in your address book or your Web cache.

Each e-mail it sends has a 3-line body. The top line says:

Hi! How are you?

The middle line is one of these:

I send you this file in order to have your advice
I hope you can help me with this file that I send
I hope you like the file that I sendo you
This is the file with the information that you ask for

The bottom line says:

See you later. Thanks

Exception: if your computer uses Spanish instead of English, the 3-line message is sent in Spanish.

Attached to the e-mail is a document that you created by using Microsoft Word or WordPad or Excel or Winzip, and which the virus copied from your "My Documents" folder. The attached copy is infected with the virus; so while the recipient reads the document, the recipient's computer gets secretly infected. The document's name is used as the e-mail's subject.

If you're on a local-area network, the virus tries to spread itself to the rest of the network. The virus is supposed to also destroy some files; but the virus's inventor made a programming error, so the destruction never gets done.

Nimda (September 2001) If you spell "admin" backwards, you get "nimda", which is this virus's name. It spreads by e-mail and through networks. **Its main purpose is to attack a network's security**, by making every "guest" user get "administrator" privileges, so a hacker can log in as a guest and take over the whole network.

When transmitted by e-mail, the virus comes as an e-mail attachment called README.EXE, in **an e-mail that has a blank body and usually a blank subject.**

If you receive such an e-mail, you'll get infected even if you don't open the attached README.EXE file: **just staring at the e-mail's blank body will infect you**, since this virus uses a trick called "Automatic Execution of Embedded MIME type". That trick makes the virus spread fast.

To confuse you, the virus sends out the e-mails, then goes dormant for 10 days, the sends out e-mails again, then goes dormant again, alternating forever. During each 10-day dormancy period, it sends no e-mails, so you think you've been "cured"; you get annoyed and confused when 10 days later you get another burst of e-mails.

To make sure you don't erase the virus, it hides copies of itself throughout your computer's .EXE files and some .TMP files.

A variant called **Nimda.E** comes in an attachment called SAMPLE.EXE instead of README.EXE.

Klez (October 2001) This virus from China comes in 9 versions, called Klez.A, Klez.B, Klez.C, Klez.D, Klez.E, Klez.F, Klez.G, Klez.H, and Klez.I. The most common is Klez.H. Here's how Klez.H works.…

If your computer is infected, the virus looks all over your computer's hard disk for e-mail addresses then makes the computer send an e-mail to each address.

The virus uses a trick called **address spoofing**: the virus makes each e-mail message pretend to be from an **innocent bystander** instead of from you. In the e-mail's "From" field, instead of *your* return e-mail address, the virus inserts the e-mail address of an innocent bystander — an innocent uninfected person whose e-mail address happened to be on your computer's hard disk (such as your Inbox or Outbox). When the e-mail you sent reaches its victim, if the victim is using an antivirus program and notices the virus, the victim will blame the innocent bystander instead of you. You'll never be warned that you're spreading the virus, and you'll keep infecting more people, without you or your friends knowing you're the spreader.

Another trick: Klez.H often comes in an e-mail that **pretends to be protection** against Klez.E but actually contains Klez.H. The e-mail's subject is "Worm Klez.E immunity" and the body says the following (I've edited out some bad grammar):

> Klez.E is the most common worldwide spreading worm. It's very dangerous by corrupting your files. Because of its very smart stealth and anti-antivirus technique, most common antivirus software can't detect or clean it. We developed this free immunity tool to defeat the malicious virus. You only need to run this tool once, and then Klez will never come into your PC. Note: because this tool acts as a fake Klez to fool the real worm, some antivirus programs might complain when you run it. If so, ignore the warning and select "continue". If you have any question, please mail to me.

That e-mail is a lie: the e-mail itself contains the Klez.H virus.

Klez.H often comes instead in an e-mail containing an attached innocent document copied from the sender's computer. Klez.H borrowed that technique from Sircam.

Klez.H can also come in an e-mail pretending to be from your ISP's postmaster, saying you sent an e-mail that bounced and to look at the attached file.

Like Nimda, Klez.H can infect you even if you don't open the attachments. Klez.H contains routines to disable and destroy antivirus programs. Klez.H gives you a present: a second virus, called **Elkern**. Klez.H and Elkern try to corrupt all your computer's programs by inserting themselves into each program.

The virus is called "Klez" because it contains this message, which is not displayed:

> Win323 Klez V2.01 & Win32 Foroux V1.0
> Copyright 2002,made in Asia

Beagle (January 2004) This virus from Germany began as a program named **bbeagle.exe**, so it's called "Beagle", but some reporters made an error and **accidentally called it "Bagle"**. If you hear about a "Bagle" virus, it has nothing to do with bagels you eat for breakfast! As a joke, many virus experts now call it the "Bagle" virus.

The virus's first version, Beagle.A, was polite: it was invented on January 18, 2004 but was programmed to stop spreading itself on January 28, 2004. So after January 28, 2004, no more people would get infected by Beagle!

Beagle.A did no harm except spread itself. Its main symptom was that **it automatically turned on the Windows Calculator** program, calc.exe (which you'd otherwise run manually by clicking Start then Programs then Accessories then Calculator).

Unfortunately, many other versions of Beagle were invented afterwards: Beagle.B, Beagle.C, etc., up through Beagle.X. They're nastier and compete against the Netsky virus, described below.

Netsky (February 2004) A 17-year-old German high school student, Sven Jaschan, called himself **SkyNet** and invented a virus called **Netsky**. Then he wrote 27 more versions of it, plus a more powerful virus, called **Sasser**.

Those viruses, especially Sasser, screwed up millions of computers around the world and made people distrust the security of Windows XP. Microsoft offered a reward of $250,000 to discover who wrote those viruses. In May 2004, Sven's friends turned him in and collected the reward. He confessed. Since he distributed the virus on his 18th birthday, the German courts decided he was *under* 18 when he invented the virus, so he was tried as a minor and got off easy: no jail time and no fine! He just had to perform 30 hours of community service in a retirement home and pay about $3000 in damages to organizations that sued him.

His mom, Veronika, runs a computer consulting company called "PC Help" from her basement, and cynics think Sven wrote the viruses there to create more business for her, but probably his main goal was just to compete against the writer of Beagle. Newspapers call him the "world's most annoying teenager".

Here's how Netsky works. (I'll explain Sasser on the next page.)

Netsky's first version, called Netsky.A, came in this e-mail:

> Subject: Auction successful!
> Congratulations! You were successful in the auction. A detailed description about the product and the bill are attached to this mail. Please contact the seller immediately. Thank you!

If you got an e-mail like that, you'd be tempted to read the attachment, wouldn't you? The attachment contains the virus.

To further imply the e-mail is real, the e-mail's body includes an Auction ID number and a Product ID number (both fake), and the e-mail's address is spoofed (so it pretends to be from "EBay Auctions" or "Yahoo Auctions" or one of their competitors).

That's Netsky.A. Later came more powerful variants, called Netsky.B, Netsky.C, etc., up through Netsky.Z, then Netsky.AA, Netsky.AB, and Netsky.AC.

The most widely distributed version of Netsky is **Netsky.P**, which is smart: **it can generate many kinds of e-mail subjects and e-mail bodies**, by choosing them from a long list inside the virus. For example, here are some of the subjects and bodies it can send you:

Subject	Body
Re: Your document	You document is attached.
Re: Is that your document?	Can your confirm it?
Re: Question	I have corrected your document.
You cannot do that!	I am shocked about your document!
Sample	I have attached the sample.
Thank you!	Your bill is attached to this mail.
I cannot forget you!	Your big love, ;-)

Re: Old photos	Greetings from France, Your friend
Your day	Congratulations! Your best friend
Sex pictures	Here is the website. ;-)
Does it matter?	Your photo, uahhh... you are naked!
Protected Mail System	Protected message is attached.
Stolen document	I found this document about you.
Fwd: Warning again	You have downloaded these illegal cracks?
Administrator	Your mail account has been closed.
Hello	I hope the patch works.
Re: Hi	Please answer quickly!
Mail Delivery (failure)	Message has been sent as a binary attachment.
Re: Hi	I have attached your file. Your password is jk144563.
Re: Order	Thank you for your request. Your details are attached!
Spam	I have visited this website and I found you in the spammer list. Is that true?
Illegal Website	See the name in the list! You have visited illegal websites. I have a big list of the websites you surfed.
Re: Submit a Virus Sample	The sample file you sent contains a new virus version of Mydoom.j. Please clean your system with the attached signature. Sincerely, Robert Ferrew
Re: Virus Sample	The sample file you sent contains a new virus version of Buppa.k. Please update your virus scanner with the attached dat file. Best Regards, Keria Reynolds

At least one of those e-mails will make you curious enough to open the attachment, which contains the virus.

To encourage you to open the attachment, Netsky.P **pretends the attachment was approved by an antivirus program**. The body ends with a comment such as —

+++ Attachment: No Virus found
+++ McAfee AntiVirus — www.mcafee.com

or a similar comment mentioning one of the other 7 antivirus companies. The comment is a lie, written by the virus itself! **Even if you don't open the attachment, you can get the virus just by reading the body**.

Netsky.P erases some other viruses, to make Netsky.P be the remaining, dominant virus on your machine and SkyNet be acknowledged as the master of evil. (But Netsky.P will *not* erase the Sasser virus, which was created by SkyNet also! Netsky.AB pretends to erase the Sasser virus but doesn't.)

To taunt the competitor who wrote the Beagle virus (which is also called "Bagle"), Netsky.P contains this message (which is not displayed):

Bagle, do not delete SkyNet. You fucked bitch! Wanna go into a prison? We are the only AntiVirus, not Bagle. Shut up and take your butterfly!
— Message from SkyNet AV Team
Let's join an alliance, Bagle!

DoS attacks

Your computer can attack an Internet Web-site server computer (called the **target**) by sending so many strange requests to the target computer that the target computer can't figure out how to respond to them all. The target computer gets confused and becomes so preoccupied worrying about your requests that it ignores all other work it's supposed to be doing, so nobody else can access it. Everybody who tries to access it is denied service because it's too busy. That's called a **denial-of-service attack (DoS attack)**.

In the attack, the "strange request" asks the target computer to reply to a message; but when the target computer tries to reply, it gets flummoxed because the return address is a **spoof** (a fake address that doesn't exist). The target computer tries to transmit to the fake address and waits hopelessly for acknowledgement that the reply was received. While the target computer waits for the acknowledgement, the attacking computer keeps sending more such requests, until the target computer gets overloaded, gives up, and dies.

Denial-of-service attacks were invented in 1997. In March 1998, denial-of-service attacks successfully shut down Internet computers run by the Navy, the US space agency (NASA), and many universities.

Distributed DoS attacks In the summer of 1999, an extra-powerful denial-of-service attack was invented. It's called a **distributed denial-of-service attack (DDoS attack)**. Here's how it works:

A virus spreads by e-mail to thousands of innocent computers (which are then called **zombie agents** or **drones**). The virus waits in those computers until a preset moment, then forces all those computers to simultaneously attack a single Internet target computer by sending strange requests to that computer, to overload that computer and make it deny service to other customers.

The first DDoS attack viruses were **Trin00** and **Tribe Flood Network (TFN)**. Soon after came versions that were more sophisticated: **Tribe Flood Network 2000 (TFN 2K)** and **Stacheldraht** (which is the German word for "barbed wire").

Those viruses are flexible: you can teach them to attack any target. Though the inventors of those viruses said they were just "experiments", other folks used those viruses to attack Yahoo and many other Web sites in February 2000. The attacks were successful: they shut down Yahoo, CNN.com, Amazon.com, eBay.com, eTrade.com, Buy.com, Datek.com, and the FBI's Web site.

Blaster (August 2003) The Blaster virus tries to launch a DDoS attack against Microsoft, specifically against microsoft.WindowsUpdate.com. After Blaster was unleashed, Microsoft quickly reorganized its Web site (by stopping www.WindowsUpdate.com from redirecting people to microsoft.WindowsUpdate.com), so no lasting damage was done to Microsoft.

But Blaster has a nasty side effect:

While Blaster makes your computer try to attack Microsoft's Web site — and also send copies of Blaster to every other address on the Internet (by generating random Internet address numbers) — it **makes your computer reboot every 60 seconds**.

Blaster can spread through *any* Internet connection, not just through e-mail. **Whenever your computer is connected to your Internet Service Provider (ISP), you can get infected**, even if you're not using e-mail and not using the Web.

The virus is called **MsBlast.exe** and puts itself in your Windows folder.

Sasser (April 2004) Sasser is a Blaster variant invented by Sven Jaschan (the same kid who wrote the Netsky virus). Like Blaster, Sasser spreads to other computers by any ISP connection and **makes computers reboot**.

Sasser comes in 3 versions.

Sasser.A is called AvServe.exe.
Sasser.B and Sasser.C are called AvServe2.exe.

Blaster creates a DDoS attack (on Microsoft), but Sasser does *not* create any DDoS attack: it just spreads itself rapidly to computers all over the world.

Maintenance

These tips will help keep your computer in good shape, so you'll have fewer problems and need fewer repairs.

Clean your hardware

Eventually, your computer will get covered with dust, dirt, cigarette smoke, pollen, spilled drink, spilled food, dead insects, dandruff, and other unmentionable body parts.

Once a month, clean the computer, to increase the happiness of the computer and the people who see it (you, colleagues, customers, and visitors). To make cleaning easier, many companies prohibit employees from smoking, drinking, or eating near the computer.

Easy cleaning

Before cleaning the computer, turn its power off.

Just take a paper towel, dampen it with plain water, and wipe grime off the keyboard, the monitor's screen, the monitor's case, and the system unit's case.

Don't dribble water into the electronics. That would cause a short circuit and corrosion. Put water just onto the paper towel, *not* directly onto the hardware.

Don't use the computer until the water has dried. Don't open the monitor, since it contains high voltages even when "off".

Inside the system unit

If you wish to open the system unit's case, to remove dust from inside it, be careful not to give your computer a shock of static electricity. The computer's chips are delicate and can get destroyed by even the smallest spark. To avoid shocks, do this:

> Avoid working on the computer in the winter, when the air is cold and the humidity is low. Wait until summer, when the air is warm and the humidity is high.
>
> Avoid shuffling across the carpet in rubber-soled shoes. Remove your shoes and socks (so you look like a beach bum or hippie). Remove the carpet, or cover it with a plastic mat (or newspaper), or put anti-static spray on the carpet.
>
> While working on the computer, keep it turned off but still plugged into a 3-prong grounded socket. Keep touching the outside of the computer's case, which will be grounded. You can also keep touching other big metal objects in the room — so you'll shock them instead of your computer.
>
> Avoid directly touching the chips.

When fiddling inside the computer's case, make sure you don't loosen any of the cables inside, since if a cable gets loose you might forget which socket it belongs in and which direction it should be twisted in.

To remove dust, wipe it off — or just take a deep breath and blow, but try to avoid blowing spit.

Professional cleaning

That's how to clean your computer for free. Professional repair shops usually spend extra money:

> Instead of using water,
> they use **isopropyl alcohol**, which dries faster.
>
> Instead of using a paper towel,
> they use a **soft lint-free cloth**.
>
> Instead of blowing from their mouths,
> they blow from a **can of compressed air**, bought at Radio Shack.
>
> Instead of touching objects to dissipate static electricity,
> they wear an **electrostatic-discharge wrist strap (ESD wrist strap)**, which is a wrist strap that comes with a wire you can run from your wrist to a grounded metal object (such as the outside of a grounded computer case).

When cleaning a monitor's screen, do *not* use alcohol or traditional "glass cleaners", since they can harm the screen's antiglare coating.

Clean your mouse

Here's how to clean a traditional mouse (which contains a ball instead of shining a light):

> Turn the mouse upside down. Using your fingernail, scrape off any gunk you see. (Gunk tends to accumulate on the mouse's rubber strips or rubber feet.)
>
> In the mouse's belly, you typically see a rubber ball, whose purpose is to roll on your desktop (or on your mouse pad). Remove the ball's circular cover (by turning the cover counterclockwise or sliding it toward you). Remove the ball.
>
> On the ball, you'll probably see a little dust, dirt, hair, or food. Clean the ball by rubbing it against your clothes. (Oooooh! That felt Gooood!) If you prefer, you can clean the ball by using water, but do *not* use alcohol, which can shrink the ball and make it lopsided.
>
> Look inside the mouse, in the hole where the ball was. On the sides of that hole, you'll see two rollers (looking like rolling pins) that the ball is supposed to rub against. One of those rollers is for motion in the X direction (horizontal); the other roller is for motion in the Y direction (vertical). Dust and dirt are probably caked onto the middle of each roller. Scrape the dust and dirt off, by using your fingernail.
>
> Then put the ball back into the mouse and put its cover back on (by turning the cover clockwise or sliding it away from you).

Clean your software

For over 25 years, I've given free help to folks whose computers got messed up. That extensive experience taught me most computer problems can be solved by **software cleaning**: just remove any software routines that distract the computer from what you want to accomplish! If you remove those distractions, the computer can concentrate on accomplishing your goal. The computer's headaches — and yours — will disappear. The computer will run reliably — and faster.

Here's how to clean your software. To get free help using these methods and my other tricks (which are more bizarre), phone me anytime at 603-666-6644.

Windows 7

I'll start with the methods that are the simplest and most foolproof, then progress to methods that are more advanced and risky.

Shut down If the computer is on, try to shut it down properly:

> Click Start then "Shut Down". Wait while the computer tidies the info on your hard disk. Finally, the computer will turn its own power off.

If you can't do that shut-down procedure properly, give up and just turn the power off.

Wait for the computer to quiet down.

Start the computer again Turn the computer on. Wait for the Windows main screen to appear, so you see the Start button (a circle at the screen's bottom-left corner).

Stop the startup's pop-up windows When you turn the computer on, some windows might appear automatically without your asking for them. Here's how to stop them.

If the screen's top shows the **HP Advisor dock** (ribbon bar that begins with the words "HP Advisor") because you bought a Hewlett-Packard or Compaq computer), stop it (because it's distracting) by doing this:

> Click "HP Advisor" then "PC Dashboard" then "Settings" (which is at the window's bottom-left corner). Remove the check mark from "Launch Advisor PC Dock at every boot" (by clicking it). Click "Apply". Close the HP Advisor window by clicking its X. Close the HP Advisor dock by clicking the faint-or-white X that's to the right of the dock's top-right corner.
>
> (Here's how to see the HP Advisor dock in the future: click Start then "All Programs" then "HP Advisor".)

Stop the wallpaper When you're not in the middle of running a program, the computer's screen might show you **wallpaper** (a photo, or rays of colored lights, or your computer manufacturer's name & logo, peeking from behind all the icons). Though that wallpaper might cheer you up at first, after a month or two you'll find it distracting, and it makes the icons harder to see. Here's how to get rid of the wallpaper and change to a plain background:

> Right-click in the screen's middle, where there's no icon. Click "Personalize" then "Desktop Background". Near the screen's top, you see a box labeled "Picture location" (and it probably says "Windows Desktop Backgrounds" in it); click that box's down-arrow then "Solid Colors". Maximize the window. You see 33 big colored squares. Click the dark-blue square at the top of the 6th column (because that's the traditional restful color) or click whatever other color you prefer. Press Enter. Close the window (by clicking its X button).

(Here's how to see the wallpaper in the future: right-click in the screen's middle where there's no icon, click "Personalize" then "Desktop Background" then the Picture location box's down-arrow then "Windows Desktop Backgrounds"; scroll down to see all the icons; click the last icon (which is in the Windows category); press Enter; close the window by clicking its X.)

Do disk cleanup Click Start then "Computer" then the "C:" icon then "Properties". Click the **Disk Cleanup button**. **Put checkmarks in all the boxes.** Press Enter twice. The computer will erase the files. Then close all windows (by clicking their X buttons).

Do that disk-cleanup procedure often: once a week.

Windows Vista

Windows Vista includes many features that are cute but useless. When you buy a Windows Vista computer, leave it in its original state for the first two weeks, so you can admire the cuteness; but then erase that crap, so you can get your work done faster, with fewer cuties to distract you and the computer from your goals. If you're sharing the computer with friends or colleagues, get their permission before you clean.

Follow this step-by-step procedure to clean your computer….

Shut down If the computer is on, try to shut it down properly:

> Click Start. Click the right-arrow (▸) that's at the Start menu's bottom-right corner. Then click "Shut Down". Wait while the computer tidies the info on your hard disk. Finally, the computer will turn its own power off.

If you can't do that shut-down procedure properly, give up and just turn the power off.

Wait for the computer to quiet down.

Start the computer again Turn the computer on. Wait for the Windows main screen to appear, so you see the Start button (a circle at the screen's bottom-left corner).

Stop the startup's pop-up windows When you turn the computer on, some windows might appear automatically without your asking for them. Here's how to stop them.

If you see a window titled "HP Total Care Advisor — PC Health & Security" (because you bought a Hewlett-Packard or Compaq computer), stop it (because it loads slowly and is full of ads) by doing this:

> Click the Preferences button (which is at the window's top, near the right corner, and looks like a wrench). Remove the checkmark from "Launch HP Advisor automatically on start-up" by clicking there. Click "OK". Close the window by clicking its X button.
>
> (Here's how to see HP Total Care Advisor in the future: double-click the "HP Total Care Advisor" icon, or click Start then "All Programs" then "HP Total Care Advisor".)

If you see the **Welcome Center window** (which says "Welcome"), stop it (because you don't need it) by doing this:

> Remove the checkmark from "Run at startup" (which is at the window's bottom-left corner), by clicking there. Then close the window (by clicking its X button).
>
> (Here's how to see the Welcome Center window in the future: click Start then "Control Panel" then "Classic View", then double-click "Welcome Center".)

Stop the gadgets Along the screen's right-hand edge, near the screen's top, you might see **gadgets** (such as a clock, a slideshow, and a news feed) in an area called the **Windows Sidebar**. Though the gadgets are cute, they're distracting and also slow down your computer. Here's how to stop them.

> Find the green **Windows Sidebar icon.** (It's at the screen's bottom, near the right corner. If you don't see it yet, make it appear by clicking the right-arrow there.) Right-click the Windows Sidebar icon. Click "Properties". Remove the checkmark from "Start Sidebar when Windows starts", by clicking there. Click "View list of running gadgets". You see a list of running gadgets. Click the first gadget in the list, then the Remove button, then do the same for each other gadget in the list, until the list is empty. Click "Close" then "OK".
>
> (Here's how to use those gadgets in the future: click Start then "All Programs" then "Accessories" then "Windows Sidebar" then the plus sign near the screen's top-right corner; double-click "Feed Headlines" then "Slide Show" then "Clock" then any other gadgets you want to use; click the red X button to close the gadget window.)

Stop the wallpaper When you're not in the middle of running a program, the computer's screen might show you **wallpaper** (a photo, or rays of colored lights, or your computer manufacturer's name & logo, peeking from behind all the icons). Though that wallpaper might cheer you up at first, after a month or two you'll find it distracting, and it makes the icons harder to see. Here's how to get rid of the wallpaper and change to a plain background:

> Right-click in the screen's middle, where there's no icon. Click "Personalize" then "Desktop Background". Near the screen's top, you see a box labeled "Location" (and it probably says "Windows Wallpapers" in it); click that box's down-arrow then "Solid Colors". Maximize the window. You see 33 big colored squares. Click the dark-blue square at the top of the 6th column (because that's the traditional restful color) or click whatever other color you prefer. Press Enter. Close the window (by clicking its X button).
>
> (Here's how to see the wallpaper in the future: right-click in the screen's middle where there's no icon, click "Personalize" then "Desktop Background" then the Location box's down-arrow then "Windows Wallpapers"; scroll down to see all the icons; if you have a widescreen, click the last icon in the Widescreen category, otherwise click the last icon in the Vistas category; press Enter; close the window by clicking its X.)

Stop the screensaver The typical computer is set up so that if you don't touch the keyboard or mouse for 10 minutes, a screensaver comes on (which puts an animated cartoon on your screen); if you don't touch the keyboard or mouse for 15 minutes, the screen turns off; and if you don't touch the keyboard or mouse for 20 minutes, the computer goes to sleep. The 15-minute and 20-minute rules save electricity by having the computer partly shut down when you're not using it; but the 10-minute screensaver serves no purpose (it doesn't save electricity and doesn't protect your screen), so you should turn that feature off (unless you're in a hospital where the screensaver hides confidential patient data from passers-by). Here's how to turn off the screensaver:

> Right-click in the screen's middle, where there's no icon. Click "Personalize" then "Screen Saver" then the first down-arrow then "(None)". Press Enter. Close the window (by clicking its X button).
>
> (Here's how to reactivate the screensaver in the future: right-click in the screen's middle where there's no icon, click "Personalize" then "Screen Saver" then the first down-arrow then "Windows Logo". Press Enter. Close the window (by clicking its X button).

Stop the service ads Your screen shows icons that are ads for services. For example, if you buy a Compaq computer, your screen shows 7 icons that advertise: "AOL Sign-up", "Easy Internet Services", "eBay", "Get Vonage", "High-Speed Services", "MSN", and "Snapfish Photos — First 25 Prints Free". To remove one of those icons from your screen, do this:

> Click the icon, then press the Delete key then the Enter key.
>
> (Here's how to see those services in the future: double-click the "HP Total Care Advisor" icon then click "Internet Connection"; or click Start then "All Programs" then "HP Total Care Advisor" then "Internet Connection"; or click Start then "All Programs" then scroll down and click "Online Services" then "United States"; or use the Internet to go to www.aol.com, www.ebay.com, www.vonage.com, www.msn.com, or www.snapfish.com.)

Empty the Startup folder If you click Start then "All Programs" then Startup (which you'll see when you scroll down), you'll see what's in the Startup folder. (If you don't see anything, your Startup folder is empty.)

Each time you start running Windows, the computer automatically runs all the programs in the Startup folder. Some of those programs might even run continuously, until you turn off the computer.

The typical program in the Startup folder is junk you should remove. Here's how to remove programs from the Startup folder (after you get permission from friends who share your computer):

> Click Start (so you see the Start menu) then "All Programs" then "Startup" (so you see what's in the Startup folder). If you want to get rid of one of the programs, drag the program's name toward the right, toward the screen's middle, until the program's name is no longer in the menus. If the computer says "You'll need to provide administrator permission to move", click "Continue" once or twice until the computer stops griping.
>
> For example, you can move "Compaq Connections" (which sends you ads from Compaq twice a month), "Adobe Reader Speed Launch" (which lets Adobe Reader consume your RAM immediately), and "Adobe Reader Synchronizer" (which checks whether your computer contains the same document versions as other computers on your network): they're all junk that make your computer run slower.
>
> The next day or next week, when you've convinced yourself that the programs were indeed useless junk, delete their icons from your desktop screen by doing this to each one: click the icon once, then press the Delete key, then press Enter. That moves them to the Recycle Bin (unless their author protected them by making them read-only).
>
> (If you change your mind before you put them into the Recycle Bin, here's how to put them back into the Startup folder: click Start then "All Programs" then *right*-click "Startup" then click "Open" so you see the Startup folder's window, then drag the icons into that window, then close the window by clicking its X.)

Do disk cleanup Click Start then "Computer" then the "C:" icon then "Properties" (which has an orange check mark before it).

Click the **Disk Cleanup button** then "Files from all users on this computer" (if other users give you permission) then "Continue".

Put checkmarks in all the boxes. (To see all the boxes, you might have to scroll down by clicking the down-arrow repeatedly or rotating the mouse's wheel toward you.) **Exception: if your computer is a notebook, leave the "Hibernation File Cleaner" box blank** (so the hard disk will still have a hibernation file, which protects you if your battery runs out).

Press Enter twice. The computer will erase the files. Then close all windows (by clicking their X buttons).

Do that disk-cleanup procedure often: once a week.

Windows XP

I'll start with the methods that are the simplest and most foolproof, then progress to methods that are more advanced and risky.

Shut down If the computer is on, try to shut it down properly:

> Click Start then "Turn Off Computer" then "Turn Off".
> Then turn the power off.

If you can't do that shut-down procedure properly, give up and just turn the power off.

Wait for the computer to quiet down.

Start the computer again Turn the computer on. Wait for the Windows main screen to appear, so you see the Start button.

If the computer refuses to show you the Start button, go into **safe mode**. Here's how:

> Turn the computer's power on; then immediately hold down the F8 key, and keep holding it down. You'll hear some beeping.
> Take your finger off the F8 key; the computer will say "Windows Advanced Options Menu"; from that menu, choose "Safe Mode" (by pressing the Home key then the Enter key then the Enter key again). Eventually, the computer will say "To begin, click your user name". Click your name. Press the Enter key.
> Now you see the "Start" button, but all four corners of the screen say "Safe mode". While you're in Safe mode, you can repair your computer's software but cannot use fancy features: you cannot use the CD-ROM, printer, sound, fancy colors, or tiny icons (you see big icons instead).

Close whatever is open Get out of any programs you're in (by clicking their X buttons). Close any windows that are open (by clicking their X buttons).

At the screen's bottom, to the right of the Start button, you might see some other buttons.

> **Narrow buttons** (narrower than the Start button) **are okay.**
>
> If you see **a button that's wider than the Start button**, get rid of that button (by clicking it then clicking the X button that comes up).

Simplify the display Find a spot in the screen's middle where there's no icon yet. *Right*-click there (by using the mouse's *right*-hand button). From the pull-down menu that appears, left-click the bottom choice (which is "Properties"). You'll see the Display Properties window.

For Wallpaper, choose "None". Here's how:

> Look at the Theme box (which is below the word "Theme" and above the word "Sample". Make sure the Theme box says "Windows XP" or "Windows XP modified". (If it says something else, click the box's down arrow then click "Windows XP".)
> Click "Desktop". In the Background box, make "None" be highlighted (by pressing the Home key).

Click the "Screen Saver" tab (which is at the top of the window). Then **for Screen Saver, choose "None"**; here's how:

> Look at the Screen Saver box (which is wide but not tall). In that box, you should see the word "None". If that box doesn't say "None" yet, make it say "None" by pressing the Home key.

Although wallpaper and screensavers are cute fun, you should delete them (by choosing "none") because they consume RAM, slow down the computer, distract the computer, distract you, and are unnecessary (since all modern monitors are built well and don't need to be protected by screensavers).

Click the "Appearance" tab. Then **make the appearance be standard**. Here's how:

> Look at the "Windows and buttons" box. In that box, you should see "Windows XP style". If you see "Windows Classic style" instead, change it to "Windows XP style" by pressing the keyboard's down-arrow button.

Click the "Settings" tab. You have to decide how many colors and pixels to request. **For normal operation, you should request 1024-by-768 pixels and 16-bit color.** But you have these choices:

Pixels	Comment
800-by-600	best for 15-inch CRT monitors
1024-by-768	best for 17-inch CRT monitors, most programs, most Web sites
1152-by-864	best for 19-inch CRT monitors
1280-by-1024	the writing is too small, and the screen flickers or is unreadable

Colors	Comments
16-bit color	"16-bit color" means 2^{16} colors, which is 65,536 colors use this for most computers, most programs, most Web sites Windows XP calls this "medium quality"
24-bit color	"24-bit color" means 2^{24} colors, which is 16,777,216 colors accurate color, but slow intended just for artists & photographers fussy about color Windows XP calls this "high quality"
32-bit color	"32-bit color" means 2^{32} colors, which is 4,294,967,296 colors highest quality but too ridiculously slow intended just for the absolutely fussiest artists & photographers Windows XP calls this "highest quality" Windows XP omits this choice if your video card can't handle it

Suggestions:

> Switch to fewer colors if your computer is old (with a slow CPU chip or with little RAM on the video card) or having trouble.
>
> Switch to fewer pixels if your eyesight is poor or your monitor's screen is blank, fuzzy, or unreadable.

To choose the number of pixels, do this:

> Find the "Screen resolution" slider. Drag that slider towards the left or right.

To choose the color quality, do this:

> Find the "Color quality" box. Click that box's down-arrow, then click the color quality you want.

Click "OK".

If the computer says "Your desktop has been reconfigured", click "Yes" (before the image goes away).

Right-click in the screen's middle (where there are no icons). Then click "Arrange Icons By" then "Name".

Check your total RAM Windows XP requires 512M or RAM to run well. If you have less RAM, the main way you can make Windows run better is to buy more RAM.

To discover your total amount of RAM, click Start then "My Computer" then "View system information". Read the message on the screen. When you finish reading, close any windows by clicking their X buttons.

Clean up your hard disk Double-click the Recycle Bin icon. You see the Recycle Bin window, which shows a list of what's in the Recycle Bin. To see the list better, maximize the window (by clicking the box next to its X button).

That's the list of files you said to get rid of. If the list is not empty, deal with it as follows:

> Those files are still on your hard disk and consuming the hard disk's space, until you **empty the Recycle Bin**. If you're sharing the computer with friends, ask their permission before emptying the Recycle Bin.
> If you're sure you don't need any of those files anymore, empty the entire Recycle Bin (by clicking "File" then "Empty Recycle Bin" then "Yes"). If you want to erase just *some* of those files, click the first file you want to erase, then (while holding down the Ctrl key) click each additional file you want to erase, then press the Delete key then Enter.

Close the Recycle Bin window (by clicking its X button).

Next, **find out how full your hard disk is**. To find out, click Start then "My Computer". Right-click the hard drive's icon (which says "C:"), then click "Properties". You see a pie chart. **Make sure the amount of free space (colored red) is at least 10% of the disk's total capacity.** If your free space is less, you're in danger of having the computer gradually slow down or quit functioning, so you should delete some files. Later, I'll explain the best way to delete unused programs.

Do this:

> Click the **Disk Cleanup** button.
> The computer shows this list of file types:
> ☐ Downloaded Program Files
> ☐ Temporary Internet Files
> ☐ Offline Web Pages
> ☐ Recycle Bin
> ☐ Setup Log Files
> ☐ Temporary files
> ☐ WebClient/Publisher Temporary Files
> ☐ Compress old files
> ☐ Catalog files for the Content Indexer
>
> (If the list is too long to fit on the screen, see the rest of the list by using its scroll arrows.) Put a check mark in each type's box (by clicking) — except for "Recycle Bin" and "Compress old files", whose boxes should stay blank (since you dealt with "Recycle Bin" already, and "Compress old files" slows down your computer too much).
> Click OK, then press Enter. The computer will erase those files.

Close all windows (by clicking their X buttons).

Clean Outlook Express. Here's how (if you use Outlook Express 6):

> Start using Outlook Express (by doing the Outlook Express "start" procedure on page 131).
> Click "Inbox". You see list of incoming e-mail messages. Which of those messages do you want to delete? In that list, select the messages you want to delete, so they turn blue. (To select one message, click it. To select several messages, click the first and then, while holding down the Ctrl key, click the others. To select several adjacent messages, click the first and then, while holding down the Shift key, click the last. To select *all* message, tap the A key while holding down the Ctrl key.)
> Press the keyboard's Delete key. That makes the computer move the selected messages to the Deleted Items folder.
> Congratulations! You cleaned "Inbox".
> Click "Sent Items". Use that same technique to clean "Sent Items".
> Click "Drafts". Use that same technique to clean "Drafts".
> Right-click "Deleted Items". Click "Empty Deleted Items folder" then "Yes".
> **Click "File" then "Folder" then "Compact All Folders".**
> Close the Outlook Express window (by clicking its X button).

Delete unused programs. To do that, click "Start" then "Control Panel" then "Add or Remove Programs". You see a list of all programs that are on your hard disk and designed for modern Windows. (You see the list's beginning; to see the rest of the list, use the scroll arrows at the list's right side.) In that list, if you find a program that you're sure you'll never use again (such as a lousy game), here's how to delete it:

> Click the program's name. Click the Remove button (which might be labeled "Change/Remove"). Then follow the instructions on the screen. The computer will try to delete the program completely: the computer will delete the program's folder, the program's icons, and (hopefully) all references to the program.

Using that method, find and delete all programs that you're sure you'll never use again. Then close all windows (by clicking their X buttons).

Examine the task list Here's how to analyze what Windows is doing at any moment: **while holding down the Ctrl and Alt keys, tap the Delete key** (just once, not twice), then click "Processes".

You see the **task list**. That's a list of all tasks that the computer is running at the moment. The list of tasks is typically long, but don't worry: Windows XP can handle a long list okay.

Although you can end a task by clicking the task's name and then the "End Process" button, that ends the task just *temporarily*. To end the task *permanently*, so it won't resurface the next time you boot up the computer, try the following strategies....

Empty your StartUp folder If you click on Start, then Programs, then StartUp (yeah, it's there, keep looking), you'll see what's in the StartUp folder. Each time you start running Windows, the computer automatically runs all the programs in the StartUp folder. (That folder is the Windows equivalent of DOS's AUTOEXEC.BAT file.)

On a clean machine (such as mine), the StartUp folder should be empty (so your task list stays short). Microsoft Office tends to put two items into the StartUp folder ("Microsoft Office Fast Start" and "Microsoft Office Find Fast Indexer"), but if you eliminate those two items Microsoft Office will still run fine.

Here's how to remove items from the StartUp folder:....

> Click Start then Programs. Then *double*-click "StartUp".
> You'll see icons for all the programs in the StartUp folder.
> To remove a program from the StartUp folder, click that program's icon then press the Delete key then Enter. (To remove *all* programs from the StartUp folder, do this: tap the A key while holding down the Ctrl key, then press the Delete key then Enter.)

If you're not sure whether to remove a program from the StartUp folder, go ahead and try it (after getting permission from any friends who share your computer). Trying to remove a program from the StartUp folder is an experiment that's safe for three reasons:

> "Removing" an icon from the StartUp folder just sends the icon to the Recycle Bin, so you can restore the icon later if you change your mind. (To be extra-safe, tell your friends not to empty the Recycle Bin for several weeks, until you're sure your newly emptied StartUp folder makes you happy.)
>
> The icon you're sending to the Recycle Bin is just a *shortcut* icon (since it has a bent arrow on it) rather than the program itself.
>
> No items in the StartUp folder are ever needed to start Windows. In fact, Windows starts itself up before it bothers to look at the StartUp folder.

When you've finished, close all windows (by clicking their X buttons).

Remove unwanted networking Click "Start" then "Connect To" then "Show all connections".

You see a list of network components. Which ones do you need?

> The typical computer communicates with other computers by using just an ordinary phone cord and an ordinary Internet Service Provider. Such a computer needs just 2 network components: **Dial-Up Adapter** (which teaches the computer how to use the phone cord) and **TCP/IP** (which teaches the computer how to communicate with the Internet). So for such a computer, keep just those 2 components and remove any others. For example, you can remove **Client for Microsoft Networks**. If you're not sharing your computer with other people, or if you're sharing just with people who all have the same privileges as you (no separate passwords, no separate screen setups), you can also remove **Microsoft Family Logon**.
>
> If your computer is fancier, it needs more network components. For example, if your computer communicates with the Internet by using **America OnLine** (which is a non-standard Internet Service Provider), you must also keep a network component about **AOL**. If your computer communicates with the Internet by using a **cable modem** (which attaches to a cable-TV wire instead of a phone wire) or **DSL** (which attaches to a high-speed phone wire) or communicates with other computers by using an **Ethernet card** or **a local-area network (LAN)**, you must keep network components that teach the computer about those features.

Remove components you're not using; then your computer will run faster, stop asking for passwords to unused networks, and stop complaining about half-completed networks.

Here's how to remove a component:

> Click the component's icon, then press the Delete key.
> If the computer says "You cannot delete a connection while it is busy connecting", do this: press Enter then click "Disable this network device". (which is at the screen's left edge).

When you finish saying which components to remove, click "OK". (If the computer says "Your network is not complete", press Enter. If the computer asks you to restart, let it restart.)

Close any windows (by clicking their X buttons).

Improve your hard disk's structure Before trying to improve your hard disk's structure, you should typically **switch to safe mode**. (You can skip this switch if you're in safe mode already, or you're sure you're not running any antivirus programs or other hard-disk writing programs.) Here's how to switch to safe mode:

> Shut down the computer (by following the "Shut down" procedure on page 156).
> Go into safe mode (by following the procedure in page 156's second box).

Regardless of whether you switched to safe mode, click Start then "My Computer". Right-click the hard drive's icon (which says "C:"). Click "Properties" then "Tools" then "Check Now".

If you have the patience to wait through an hour-long thorough check, put a check mark in the box marked "Scan for and attempt recovery of bad sectors" (by clicking); otherwise leave that box blank.

Press Enter.

Then the computer will **run the ScanDisk program**, which analyzes your hard disk. While the computer analyzes, choose "Discard" whenever the computer lets you. That makes the computer discard useless files. At the end of the ScanDisk process, the computer will say "Disk Check Complete"; press Enter.

Next, **run the Defrag program**, by clicking "Defragment Now" then "Defragment". Then the computer will rearrange your hard disk's files, so you can access them faster.

After a long time (typically an hour), the computer will say "Defragmentation is complete". (If the computer takes several hours because the Defrag program keeps restarting, the real cause is that you forgot to do the "switch to safe mode" procedure in column 1, and you should go back and do that procedure.)

Close all windows (by clicking their X buttons). If you did the "switch to safe mode procedure", **return to normal mode** by doing this: shut down the computer (by following the "Shut down" procedure on page 156), then turn the computer back on.

Empty MsConfig A program called MicroSoft CONFIGuration (MsConfig) helps you configure Windows. Here's how to use it.

Click "Start" then "Run". Type "msconfig" and press Enter.

You see the System Configuration Utility window. Click "Startup" (which is near that window's top right corner). You see a list of programs.

If you want to widen any column, do this:

> Look at the column's heading.
> Look at the vertical line to the right of the heading.
> Drag that line farther to the right.

Every time you turn the computer on, the computer automatically runs all the programs in that list — unless you deactivate a program by removing the check mark from its box. (To add or remove a check mark, click the box.)

Programs get into that list because they were mentioned in the **StartUp folder** or the **Registry** or a file called **WIN.INI**. On a typical computer, you can deactivate most programs from the list, and the computer will still work fine.

Which programs should you keep, and which should you deactivate?

You can deactivate these:

> **PowerReg Scheduler** reminds you to register your software. **Billminder**, from Quicken, reminds you to pay bills today. **Works Calendar Reminder (wkcalrem)**, from Microsoft Works, reminds you of your appointments today. **Money Express** reminds you to try using the Microsoft Money program, which can balance your checkbook and compete against Quicken. You don't need those reminders, unless you want the computer to act as your tormentor and mother.
>
> Several programs put extra buttons at the screen's bottom right corner, in an area called the **tray**, next to the time. You don't need those buttons: they're redundant, since similar buttons already populate your screen's desktop (or in the programs menu or control panel). Although having a redundant button can occasionally be convenient (I admit liking the System Tray program, which puts the volume-control button into the tray), but I recommend you deactivate most such programs, to avoid cluttering your screen with useless buttons. Examples of redundant-button programs (which you should deactivate) are **AtiKey** (for ATI's video cards), **Aoltray** (for America Online and its Internet hookup), and **Igfxtray** (for Intel's video-chip graphics special effects).
>
> Microsoft has invented several programs that are supposed to make Microsoft Office run faster but actually make the Microsoft Office be *slower*. Deactivate them! These counterproductive devils are called **Microsoft Office StartUp Application (osa.exe)** and **Microsoft Find Fast (findfast.exe)**.
>
> **AtiCwd** is useful just if you have a TV attached to your video card.

To find out what some other program does, go to www.Google.com and type the program's name into the search box.

You can experiment by deactivating most of the listed programs: just get rid of their check marks. (You can see an even longer list of automatically run programs by clicking "Services".)

Then click "OK".

If you made changes, here's what happens next:

> The computer says "You must restart your computer". Press Enter.
> The computer automatically reboots.
> The computer says "System Configuration Utility"; to react, click the tiny square (at the window's bottom left corner) then click "OK".
> If you don't like the results of your efforts, run msconfig again and put the check marks back in.

Final steps Click "Start" then "Turn Off Computer" then "Turn Off". Then turn the power off.

Test your computer When the computer has quieted down, turn it back on and watch what happens.

Probably Windows will start fine (faster and better!) because of the software cleaning you did.

Probably **your DOS programs will work fine (even your DOS games!) if you start them the way Microsoft recommends:** click "Start" then "All Programs" then "Accessories" then "Command Prompt"; then if you see just a small black window, enlarge it by pressing Alt with Enter. If you start DOS that way, the mouse & CD-ROM will work even while you're running DOS software.

Someday, your computer will break down — or disappoint you. Here's how to fix the problem.

Strategies for repair

To repair a computer, follow these general principles….

Ask

Ask for help. Instead of wasting many hours scratching your head about a computer problem, get help from your dealer, your computer's manufacturer, your software's publisher, your colleagues, your teachers, your friends, and me. You can phone me day or night, 24 hours, at 603-666-6644; I'm almost always in, and I sleep only lightly.

Most computers come with a one-year warranty. If your computer gives you trouble during that first year, make use of the warranty: get the free help you're entitled to from your dealer. If your "dealer" is a general-purpose department store that doesn't specialize in computers, the store might tell you to phone the computer's manufacturer. For tough software questions, the dealer might tell you to phone the software's publisher.

Most computers come with a 30-day money-back guarantee. If the computer is giving you lots of headaches during the first 30 days, just return it!

Clean

Most repair problems can be solved by cleaning your software (as I explained on pages 154-158). Many other repair problems can be solved by cleaning your hardware (as I explained on page 153) or by getting rid of viruses (as I explained on page 144).

Chuck

If the broken part is cheap, don't fix it: chuck it! For example, if one of the keys on your keyboard stops working, don't bother trying to fix that key; instead, buy a new keyboard. A new keyboard costs about $25. Fixing one key on a keyboard costs many hours of labor and is silly.

If a 2-gigabyte hard disk stops working, and you can't fix the problem in an hour or so, just give up and buy a new hard disk, since 2-gigabyte hard disks are obsolete anyway. Today, 2 gigabytes aren't worth much; the price difference between an 8-gigabyte drive and a 10-megabyte drive is about $5.

Observe

Read the screen. Often, the screen will display an error message that tells you what the problem is.

If the message flashes on the screen too briefly for you to read, try pressing the computer's Pause key as soon as the message appears. The Pause key makes the message stay on the screen for you to read. When you finish reading the message, press the Enter key.

If you're having trouble with your printer, and your printer is modern enough to have a built-in screen, read the messages on that screen too.

Check the lights. Look at the blinking lights on the front of the computer and the front of the printer; see if the correct ones are glowing. Also notice whether the monitor's Power light is glowing.

Check the switches. Check the On-Off switches for the computer, monitor, and printer: make sure they're all flipped on. If your computer equipment is plugged into a power strip, make sure the strip's On-Off switch is turned on.

Check the monitor's brightness and contrast knobs, to make sure they're turned to the normal (middle) position.

If you have a dot-matrix printer, make sure the paper is feeding correctly, and make sure you've put into the correct position the lever that lets you choose between tractor feed and friction feed.

Check the cables that run out of the computer. They run to the monitor, printer, keyboard, mouse, and wall. Make sure they're all plugged tightly into their sockets. To make *sure* they're plugged in tight, unplug them and then plug them back in again. (To be safe, turn the computer equipment off before fiddling with the cables.) Many monitor and printer problems are caused just by loose cables.

Make sure each cable is plugged into the correct socket. Examine the back of your computer, printer, monitor, and modem: if you see two sockets that look identical, try plugging the cable into the other socket. For example, the cable from your printer might fit into *two* identical sockets at the back of the computer (LPT1 and LPT2); the cable from your phone system might fit into *two* identical sockets at the back of your modem (Line and Phone).

Strip

When analyzing a hardware problem, run no software except the operating system and diagnostics. For example, if you're experiencing a problem while using a word-processing program, spreadsheet, database, game, or some other software, exit from whatever software you're in. Turn off your printer, computer, and all your other equipment, so the RAM chips inside each device get erased and forget that software.

Then turn the computer back on.

If writing appears on your screen, and you can read it, your screen is working fine.

If you can make the hard disk show you what's on it (by by double-clicking "My Computer" then "C:" in modern Windows, or by typing "dir" in DOS), your hard disk is working fine.

If you can print something simple on paper (by typing "I love you" in WordPad and then printing that 3-word document), your printer is working fine. (On some laser printers, such as the Hewlett-Packard Laserjet 2, you need to manually eject the paper: press the printer's On Line button, then the Form Feed button, then the On Line button again.)

If your computer, monitor, hard drive, and printer pass all those tests, your hardware is basically fine; and so the problem you were having was probably caused by software rather than hardware. For example, maybe you forgot to tell your software what kind of printer and monitor you bought.

Relax

Don't get upset! Just relax. Stay, calm, cool, and collected while you analyze the problem. Have the attitude of Sherlock Holmes!

Perhaps you'd react to error messages more calmly if they were written as meditative poetry. In February 1998, an online magazine called **Salon.com** held a contest to turn each error message into a **haiku** (a Japanese meditative poem that has 5 syllables on the first line, 7 syllables on the second line, and 5 syllables on the third line). Here are the winning entries (as edited by me).

Missing Web pages

The Web site you seek
Cannot be located, but
Countless more exist.

You step in the stream,
But the water has moved on.
This **page is not here**.

Site moved, now secret.
We'd tell you where, but then we'd
Have to delete you.

Crashing

A **crash** reduces
Your expensive computer
To a simple stone.

Serious error.
All shortcuts have disappeared.
Screen. Mind. Both are **blank**.

Yesterday it worked.
Today it is **not working**.
Windows is like that.

The ten thousand things,
How long do any persist?
Windows, too, has gone.

Stay the patient course.
Of little worth is your ire.
The **network is down**.

Windows NT crashed.
I am the **Blue Screen of Death**.
No one hears your screams.

Lost data

Three things are certain:
Death, taxes, and **lost data**.
Guess which has occurred.

With searching comes loss
And the presence of absence:
"My Novel" **not found**.

Rather than a beep
Or a rude error message,
These words: **"File not found."**

Having been **erased**,
The document you're seeking
Must now be retyped.

A file that's so big?
It might be very useful.
But now it is **gone**.

Everything is gone.
Your life's work has been destroyed.
Squeeze trigger (yes/no)?

Starting over

Chaos reigns within.
Reflect, repent, and **reboot**.
Order shall return.

Seeing my great fault
Through darkening blue windows,
I **begin again**.

Aborted effort.
Close all that you have worked on.
You ask far too much.

Login incorrect.
Only perfect spellers may
Enter this system.

Server's poor response
Not quick enough for browser.
Timed out, plum blossom.

Errors have occurred.
We won't tell you where or why.
Lazy programmers.

To have no **errors**
Would be life without meaning:
No struggle, no joy.

Inadequate hardware

Printer not ready.
Could be a fatal error.
Have a pen handy?

The Tao that is seen
Is not the true Tao — until
You bring fresh **toner**.

No **keyboard** present.
Hit F1 to continue.
Zen engineering?

First snow, then silence.
This thousand-dollar **screen dies**
So beautifully.

Out of memory.
We wish to hold the whole sky,
But we never will.

I'm sorry, there's…um…
Insufficient…what's-it-called?
The term eludes me.

The code was willing.
It considered your request.
But the **chips** were weak.

You've reached a chasm
Of carbon and **silicon**.
No software can bridge.

Here's who wrote them:

Missing Web pages:	Joy Rothke, Cass Whittington, Charles Matthews
Crashing:	James Lopez, Ian Hughes, Margaret Segall, Jason Willoughby, David Ansel, Peter Rothman
Lost data:	David Dixon, Howard Korder, Len Dvorkin, Judy Birmingham, David Liszewski, David Carlson
Starting over:	Suzie Wagner, Chirs Walsh, Mike Hagler, Jason Axley, Rik Jespersen, Charlie Gibbs, Brian Porter
Inadequate hardware:	Pat Davis, Bill Torcaso, Jim Griffith, Simon Firth, Francis Heaney, Owen Mathews, Barry Brumitt, Rahul Sonnad

Common problems

Here's how to solve common computer problems.

Booting problems

Turning the computer on is called **booting**. When you turn the computer on, you might immediately experience one of these problems.

Unusual beeping When you turn the computer on, you're supposed to hear a single short beep. If **you hear unusual beeping** (such as *several* short beeps or a long beep), your computer's fundamental circuitry isn't working right.

If you hear *many* short beeps or a *very long* beep, your computer is having an electrical problem, so do this:

> Turn the computer off immediately. Perhaps the electrical problem was caused by a loose power cord: make sure the power cord is plugged in tight to the back of the computer and to the wall's outlet (or surge protector), not dangling loose. If the computer got damp recently (from a rainstorm or a spilled drink or dew caused by bringing the computer in from the cold), wait for the computer to dry thoroughly before turning it back on. If you moved the computer recently, perhaps a part got loose in shipment; if you wish, open the computer and make sure nothing major is loose; for example, make sure the PC cards and chips are firmly in their sockets (but before you touch any chips, reduce any static electricity in your fingers by grounding yourself, such as by touching a big metal object or the computer's power supply while it's still plugged into a grounded wall socket).

If you hear just a *few* short beeps or *several* long beeps or a *mix* of short and long beeps, your computer is complaining about a defective part. By listening to the computer's beeps, you can tell which part of the computer is ill. Lists of beep codes are on page 115 of the 30th edition.

Signal missing If the **screen says "signal missing" or "no signal"**, the monitor is not receiving any electrical signal from the computer. The monitor is complaining.

Look at the two cables coming out of the monitor's rear. One of those cables is a power cord that plugs into the wall (or into a surge protector). The other cable is the **video cable**, which is supposed to plug into the back of the computer, so the computer can send signals to the monitor. Probably, that video cable is loose. Tighten it. To make sure it's tight, unplug it from the back of the computer and then shove it into the computer's backside again, firmly.

If tightening the video cable doesn't solve the problem, maybe the computer is turned off. Make sure the computer is turned on:

> If the computer is turned on, lights should be glowing on the front of the computer and on the keyboard, and you should hear the fan inside the computer whir. If you don't see and hear those things, the computer is turned off. Try turning the computer on, by pressing its On switch or by turning on the surge protector that the computer's plugged into.

Another possibility is that the video card (which is inside the computer) is loose (because you recently moved the computer) or got fried (from a power surge caused by a thunderstorm) or got damaged (because you were fiddling with the computer's innards and you caused a shock or short or break). Make sure the video card is in tight; if a tight video card doesn't solve the problem, borrow a video card from a friend; if that still doesn't give you any video, maybe your whole motherboard is damaged, so give up and take your computer to a repair shop.

No video When you turn the computer on, the screen is supposed to show you words, pictures, marks, or at least a cursor (little line). If the **screen stays completely black**, probably your monitor is getting no electricity or no electrical signals.

Make sure the monitor is turned on. Make sure its two cables (to the power and to the computer's video card) are both plug... ...ght (... ... ...an easily come loose.) Make sure the m... ... with the knobs or butt... ...

If the monitor has a power-on light, check whether that light is glowing. (If the monitor doesn't have a power-on light, peek through the monitor's air vents and check whether anything inside glows). If you don't see any glow, the monitor isn't getting any power (because the on-off button is in the wrong position, or the power cable is loose, or the monitor is broken). If the monitor is indeed broken, do *not* open the monitor, which contains high voltages even when turned off; instead, return the monitor to your dealer.

If you've fiddled with the knobs and cables, and the power-on light (or inside light) is glowing but the screen is still blank, boot up the computer again, and look at the screen carefully: maybe a message *did* flash on the screen quickly?

If a message did appear, fix whatever problem the message talks about. (If the message was too fast for you to read, boot up again and quickly hit the Pause key as soon as the message appears, then press Enter when you finish reading the message.) If the message appears but does not mention a problem, you're in the middle of a program that has crashed (stopped working), so the fault lies in software mentioned in CONFIG.SYS or AUTOEXEC.BAT or COMMAND.COM or some other software involved in booting; to explore further, put into drive A your DOS disk (or Windows emergency recovery start-up boot disk) and reboot.

If absolutely no message appears on the screen during the booting process, so that the screen is entirely blank, check the lights on the computer (maybe the computer is turned off or broken) and recheck the cables that go to the monitor. If you still have no luck, the fault is probably in the video card inside the computer, though it might be on the motherboard or in the middle of the video cable that goes from the video card to the monitor. At this point, before you run out and buy new hardware, try swapping with a friend whose computer has the same kind of video as yours: try swapping monitors, then video cables, then video cards, while making notes about which combinations work, until you finally discover which piece of hardware is causing the failure. Then replace that hardware, and you're done!

SETUP Each modern computer (286, 386, 486, or Pentium) contains CMOS RAM, which tries to remember the date, time, how many megabytes of RAM you've bought, how you want the RAM used, what kind of video you bought, and what kind of disk drives you bought. A battery feeds power to the CMOS RAM, so that the CMOS RAM keeps remembering the answers even while the main power switch is off. If the **computer says "Invalid configuration specification: run SETUP"** (or a similar error message), your computer's CMOS RAM contains wrong info — probably because the battery died and needs to be replaced or recharged. In most computers, the battery is rechargeable; it recharges itself automatically if you leave the computer turned on for several hours.

To react to the error message, try running the CMOS Setup program, which asks you questions and then stores your answers to the CMOS RAM.

The CMOS Setup program hides in a ROM chip inside your computer and is run when you hit a "special key" during the bootup's RAM test. That "special key" is usually either the Delete key or the Esc key or the F1 key; to find out what the "special key" is on *your* computer, read your computer's manual or ask your dealer.

Once the CMOS Setup program starts running, it asks you lots of questions. For each question, it also shows you what it guesses the answer is. (The computer's guesses are based on what information the computer was fed before.)

On a sheet of paper, jot down what the computer's guesses are. That sheet of paper will turn out to be *very* useful!

Some of those questions are easy to answer (such as the date and time).

A harder question is when the computer asks you to input ...**rive-type number**. If your BIOS chip is modern ... ...rd drive is modern (IDE), you can make the computer automatically figure out the hard-drive-type number: just choose "auto-detect hard drive" from a menu. Otherwise, you must type the hard-drive-type number, as follows:

The answer is a code number from 1 to 47. If your hard drive is modern (IDE), choose 47 or "user"; if your hard drive is older, you must choose a lower number, which you must get from your dealer. (If your dealer doesn't know the answer, phone the computer's manufacturer. If the manufacturer doesn't know the answer, look inside the computer at the hard drive; stamped on the drive, you'll see the drive's manufacturer and model number; then phone the drive's manufacturer, tell the manufacturer which model number you bought, and ask for the corresponding hard-drive-type number.)

If you say 47 or "user", the computer will ask you technical questions about your drive. Get the answers from your dealer (or drive's manufacturer or by looking at what's stamped on the drive).

If you don't know how to answer a question and can't reach your dealer for help, just move ahead to the next question. Leave intact the answer that the computer guessed.

After you've finished the questionnaire, the computer will automatically reboot. If the computer gripes again, either you answered the questions wrong or else the battery ran out — so that the computer forgot your answers!

In fact, the most popular reason why the computer asks you to run the CMOS Setup program is that the battery ran out. (The battery usually lasts 1-4 years.)

To solve the problem, first make sure you've jotted down the computer's guesses, then replace the battery, which is usually just to the left of the big power supply inside the computer. If you're lucky, the "battery" is actually a bunch of four AA flashlight batteries that you can buy in any hardware store. If you're unlucky, the battery is a round silver disk, made of lithium, like the battery in a digital watch: to get a replacement, see your dealer.

After replacing the battery, run the CMOS Setup program again, and feed it the data that you jotted down.

That's the procedure. If you're ambitious, try it. If you're a beginner, save yourself the agony by just taking the whole computer to your dealer: let the dealer diddle with the CMOS Setup program and batteries for you.

Whenever you upgrade your computer with a better disk drive or video card or extra RAM, you must run the CMOS Setup program again to tell the computer what you bought.

In many computers, the ROM BIOS chip is designed by **American Megatrends Inc. (AMI)**. AMI's design is called the **AMI BIOS** (pronounced "Amy buy us"). Here's how to use the 4/4/93 version of AMI BIOS. (Other versions are similar.)

When you turn the computer on, the screen briefly shows this message:

```
AMIBIOS (C)1993 American Megatrends Inc.
000000 KB OK
Hit <DEL> if you want to run SETUP
```

Then the number "000000 KB" increases, as the computer checks your RAM chips. While that number increases, try pressing your keyboard's Del or Delete key.

That makes the computer run the AMIBIOS CMOS Setup program. The top of the screen will say:

```
AMIBIOS SETUP PROGRAM - BIOS SETUP UTILITIES
```

Underneath, you'll see this **main menu**:

```
              STANDARD CMOS SETUP
              ADVANCED CMOS SETUP
             ADVANCED CHIPSET SETUP
      AUTO CONFIGURATION WITH BIOS DEFAULTS
     AUTO CONFIGURATION WITH POWER-ON DEFAULTS
               CHANGE PASSWORD
             AUTO DETECT HARD DISK
              HARD DISK UTILITY
             WRITE TO CMOS AND EXIT
           DO NOT WRITE TO CMOS AND EXIT
```

The first and most popular choice, "STANDARD CMOS SETUP", is highlighted. Choose it (by pressing Enter).

The computer will warn you by saying:

```
Improper use of Setup may cause problems!!!
```

Press Enter again.

The computer will show you the info stored in the CMOS about the date, time, base memory, extended memory, hard drives, floppy drives, video card, and keyboard.

If that stored info is wrong, fix it! Here's how:

By using the arrow keys on the keyboard, move the white box to the info that you want to fix. (Exception: you can't move the white box to the "base memory" or "extended memory".) Then change that info, by pressing the keyboard's Page Up or Page Down key several times, until the info is what you wish.

When you've finished examining and fixing that info, press the Esc key. You'll see the main menu again.

If you're having trouble with a modern (IDE) hard drive, choose "AUTO DETECT HARD DISK" from the main menu (by pressing the down-arrow key six times, then pressing Enter). The computer will try to detect what kind of drive C you have, then it will say:

```
Accept Parameters for C: (Y/N) ?
```

Press the Y key then Enter. Then the computer will try to detect what kind of drive D you have and say:

```
Accept Parameters for D: (Y/N) ?
```

Press Y again then Enter. You'll see the main menu again.

When you've finished using the main menu, you have 2 choices:

If you're *unsure* of yourself and wish you hadn't fiddled with the SETUP program, just turn off the computer's power! All your fiddling will be ignored, and the computer will act the same as before you fiddled.

On the other hand, if you're *sure* of yourself and want the computer to take your fiddling seriously, press the F10 key then Y then Enter. The computer will copy your desires to the CMOS and reboot.

Non-system disk If the **computer says "Non-system disk or disk error"**, the computer is having trouble finding the hidden system files. (In modern Windows, the hidden system files are called IO.SYS and MSDOS.SYS.)

Those hidden system files are supposed to be on your hard disk. You can get that error message if those hidden system files are missing from your hard disk — because you accidentally erased those files, or a virus erased them, or your hard disk is new and not yet formatted, or when you formatted the disk you forgot to put a check mark in Windows format's "Copy system files" box).

A more common reason for getting that error message is: you accidentally put a floppy disk into drive A! When the computer boots, it looks at that floppy disk instead of your hard disk, and gripes because it can't find those system files on your floppy disk. Cure:

Remove any disk from drive A. Turn the computer off, wait until the computer quiets down, then turn the computer back on. If the computer still says "Non-system disk or disk error", find the CD-ROM disk that Windows came on and try again to install Windows onto your hard disk.

Slow If the **computer acts slower than before**, it's clogged with too many programs or too much data. Here are six possible reasons:

1. The hard disk is nearly full.
2. You have too many programs running in the RAM simultaneously.
3. Your computer is clogged with adware, spyware, or viruses.
4. You've left the computer on for too many hours, so fragments of programs you ran and abandoned are still in the RAM (because Windows is imperfect at erasing them from RAM).
5. The computer is in the middle of updating itself (by automatically running Windows Update and other updating software).
6. The computer is waiting for you to reply to a question, but the question is invisible because it's hiding behind a window.

Cure:

Walk away from the computer awhile (in case the cause is #5), then come back and try again. If you're still having a problem, shut down the computer, then turn it back on; that eliminates cause #6 and usually makes the computer faster (since you've eliminated cause #4). If the computer is still too slow, do the software-cleaning procedure (on pages 154-158), which helps eliminate causes #1 and #2. Get programs that protect you (on page 144) to eliminate cause #3.

Windows problems

If you're using Windows, you might experience the following problems....

Windows doesn't finish loading When the computer starts going into Windows, if the **Windows logo & clouds appear on screen but never go away** (so the computer seems stuck and you never see the Start button or icons), the computer is encountering a software conflict. Cure for Windows XP:

Turn the computer's power off. Go into safe mode, by following the instructions in page 156's second box. Finish the software-cleaning procedure, by reading from that box up through page 158.

Useless password request When the computer starts going into Windows, if the **computer unexpectedly asks you for a password**, you probably told the computer you're on a network (which requests passwords) or your computer is being shared by several people.

If you don't know any password, press Enter or the Esc key.

To prevent the computer from asking for passwords, follow the Windows XP procedure to "Remove unwanted networking" (on page 157-158). If that doesn't get rid of the password requests, look in the Control Panel window, then click "User Accounts".

Illegal operation If the **computer says "This program has performed an illegal operation and will be shut down"**, a program is trying to use a RAM section it's not allowed to. That RAM section is being used by a different program, with which your program is having a memory conflict. Cure:

Press Enter. Then do the software-cleaning procedure (on pages 154-158), which makes memory conflicts less likely to occur.

Start button in wrong corner The Start button is supposed to be in the screen's bottom left corner. If **your Start button is in a different corner**, you accidentally moved the Start button.

To move the Start button back, just "drag the taskbar to where you want it." Here's how:

One corner of your screen contains the Start button. Another corner contains the time. Running from the Start button to the time is a bar called the **taskbar** (which is blue in Windows XP & 7, gray in Windows Vista).

Point at the taskbar's middle, in a blank area where there are no buttons. While pressing the mouse's left button, drag to where you want the taskbar's middle to go: the middle of the screen's bottom. When you start dragging, you won't see the taskbar move yet; but if you drag the mouse pointer far enough, eventually the taskbar will hop. Then take your finger off the mouse's button.

Start button missing If the **Start button is missing and so is the time** (although the rest of the screen looks normal), you accidentally shrunk them.

The Start button and time are part of a bar, called the **taskbar** (which is blue in Windows XP & 7, gray in Windows Vista). The taskbar is supposed to stretch across the bottom of the screen and be about half an inch tall. You accidentally shrunk the taskbar.

To solve the problem, first close all windows (by clicking their X buttons).

If doing that makes the taskbar reappear, your problem is just that you accidentally set your taskbar to "Auto hide". Stop hiding the taskbar, by doing this:

Right-click "Start", then click "Properties" then "Taskbar".
Remove any check mark from "Auto hide" (by clicking).
Click "OK".

If closing all windows does *not* make the taskbar reappear, look at the screen's bottom.

If you see a gray (or light blue) line running across the screen's bottom, that line is your shrunken taskbar; make it taller by doing this:

Point at that line's top edge, so the mouse pointer becomes a black arrow (which has white edges and points upward). When pressing the mouse's left button, drag up about half an inch. Suddenly there, you'll see a gray (or red or yellow) line (or blue bar) stretch across the screen. Then take your finger off the mouse's button.

Icons missing If **some icons are missing from the desktop screen** (the main screen), they're probably just hiding behind other icons or past the screen's edge. To see them again, do this:

Close any windows (by clicking their X buttons). Right-click in the screen's middle, where there is nothing.
For Windows Vista, click "Sort By"; for Windows XP, click "Arrange Icons By".
Click "Name".

If that doesn't make the icons reappear, the icons might be in the Recycle Bin, so do this:

Double-click the "Recycle Bin" icon. If the Recycle Bin window shows one of the missing icons, right-click that icon then click "Restore".

Dialog box too big For the screen's resolution, you can choose "800 by 600" or "1024 by 768", by using a settings dialog box. If the **settings dialog box is too big to fit on the screen** (so the box's "OK" button hides below the screen's bottom), the computer is confused about what resolution you want. Instead of trying to click "OK", press Enter. If pressing Enter doesn't work, do this:

Close the dialog box (by clicking its X button), then recreate the dialog box again, then choose a resolution again, then try pressing Enter again.

Resolution refuses to increase If the computer refuses to let you choose more than "800 by 600" resolution, it's because the computer thinks your video card doesn't have enough RAM to handle such a high resolution.

Yes, the computer thinks your video card is inadequate or damaged!

But if your video card was working fine yesterday, the most likely "damage" is just that the video-driver *software* got corrupted. Here's the cure....

If you're using Windows 7, do this:

Click Start then "Computer" then "System properties" then "Device Manager". Click the triangle that's left of "Display adapters".

If you're using Windows Vista, do this:

Click Start then "Computer" then "System properties" then "Device Manager" then "Continue". Click the plus sign that's left of "Display adapters".

If you're using Windows XP, do this:

Click "start" then "My Computer" then "View system information" then "Hardware" then "Device Manager". Click the plus sign that's left of "Display adapters".

Indented underneath "Display adapters" you see the name of the video card that the computer thinks you have. Click that name. Press the Delete key.

The computer will warn you that you're going to uninstall that video-driver software. Though that warning looks scary, be brave and press Enter (because your computer secretly has an extra copy of that video-driver software).

Then just follow the instructions on the screen. The computer will recommend rebooting; let it. While the computer is rebooting, it will begin by thinking you have no video card, but then it will get surprised when it finds video-card hardware, and it will reinstall that video card, using a copy of the video-driver software that's still hiding on the computer. (When the computer asks where the video-driver software is, tell the computer to look just on the hard disk, not on a CD.)

The computer will find the video-driver software and finish booting. The screen's colors will look slightly better. To make the screen look exactly the way you wish, go to the display-settings dialog box again doing this:

Right-click any blank space in the screen's middle.

For Windows Vista, click "Personalize" then "Display Settings"; for Windows XP, click "Properties" then "Settings".

Then choose as many colors and as high a resolution as you wish. This time, your request will be obeyed!

Mouse problems

Mice can cause problems.

Mouse pointer lurches When you move the mouse, the mouse pointer (on the screen) is supposed to move also. **If the mouse pointer lurches erratically** (sometimes going fast, sometimes going too slow or not at all) **or moves in just one direction** (just horizontally, or just vertically, but not both), the mouse is dirty. Clean it by using the procedure on page 153; then the mouse will probably work well.

If the mouse doesn't work well yet, try this experiment:

Take the ball out again. Rub your finger against the X and Y mouse rollers, and see if the mouse pointer moves also. If the mouse pointer works fine using your fingers but not by using the ball, the ball isn't touching the rollers, probably because the ball's cover isn't locking the ball into the proper position. Reposition the ball and its cover.

If the mouse *still* doesn't work well, just buy a new mouse. You can buy a plain mouse for about $10.

Mouse pointer hard to see While moving the mouse fast, you might have **difficulty seeing where the mouse pointer went**, because the mouse pointer seems to become temporarily invisible.

That means your screen, video card, or eyes are too slow to keep up with you. That's probably because you're using a notebook computer that has the slowest kind of screen (passive-matrix). It could also be because your eyesight is poor or you're a beginner who feels lost. Like a magician, your hand is quicker than the eye or your screen.

To make the mouse pointer easier to see, create long "pointer trails" (by following the procedure on page 100) or buy a bigger monitor or a better notebook computer (having an active-matrix screen, which is faster than a passive screen).

Dead mouse If nothing happens on screen when you move the mouse, try these strategies....:

Perhaps you're just in the middle of a routine that doesn't use the mouse. Try these ways to get out of a routine:

> Press the Esc key twice (which might exit from a routine).
> If the mouse doesn't work yet, press Ctrl with C.
> If the mouse doesn't work yet, press the Alt key.
> If the mouse doesn't work yet, press the Alt key again.

If the mouse still doesn't work yet, maybe the task you've been performing has crashed, so end that task by doing this:

> While holding down the Ctrl and Alt keys, tap the Delete key. (If you're using modern Windows, then press Enter.)

If the mouse still doesn't work, maybe the mouse's cord is loose (tighten it!) or the mouse is dirty (clean it by following the procedure for "mouse pointer lurches") or it's a wireless mouse whose battery died (open the mouse and replace the battery) or the computer forgot what kind of mouse you have (reinstall the mouse-driver software that came with your mouse, or reinstall Windows) or just buy a new mouse.

Keyboard problems

Your keyboard might seem broken. Here's what to do.

Wet keyboard If **your keyboard got wet** (because you spilled water, coffee, soda, or some other drink), turn the computer off immediately (because water can cause a short circuit that can shock & burn the keyboard and computer and you). Unplug the keyboard from the computer.

Turn the keyboard upside-down for a few minutes, in the hope that some of the liquid drips out. Then let the keyboard rest a few hours, until the remaining liquid in it dries.

Try again to use the keyboard. It will probably work fine. If the keyboard doesn't work yet, do this:

> Unplug the keyboard again. Submerge and wash the keyboard in warm water (you can even put the keyboard into a dishwasher!) but use no soap. Dry off the keyboard. Wait a day for the keyboard to dry thoroughly. If still no luck, the keyboard has been permanently damaged, so buy another.

Dead keyboard If **pressing the keyboard's letters has no effect**, either the keyboard is improperly hooked up or the computer is overheating or you're running a frustrated program (which is ignoring what you type or waiting until a special event happens). For example, the program might be waiting for the printer to print, or the disk drive to manipulate a file, or the CPU to finish a computation, or your finger to hit a special key or give a special command.

Try getting out of any program you've been running. Here's how:

> Press the Esc key (which might let you escape from the program) or the F1 key (which might display a helpful message) or Enter (which might move on to the next screenful of info) or Ctrl with C (which might abort the program) or Ctrl with Break. If the screen is unchanged and the computer still ignores your typing, reboot the computer; then watch the screen for error messages such as "301" (which means a defective keyboard), "201" (which means defective RAM chips), or "1701" (which means a defective hard drive).

If the keyboard seems to be "defective", it might just be unplugged from the computer. Make sure the cable from the keyboard is plugged *tightly* into the computer. To make sure it's tight, unplug it and then plug it back in again.

If fiddling with the cable doesn't solve your problem, reboot the computer and see what happens. Maybe you'll get lucky.

Maybe some part of the computer is overheating. Here's how to find out:

> Turn the computer off. Leave it off for at least an hour, so it cools down. Then turn the computer back on. Try to get to a C prompt.
> After the C prompt, type a letter (such as x) and notice whether the x appears on the screen.
> If the x appears, don't bother pressing the Enter key afterwards. Instead, walk away from the computer for two hours — leave the computer turned on — then come back two hours later and try typing another letter (such as y). If the y doesn't appear, you know that the computer "died" sometime after you typed x but before you typed y. Since during that time the computer was just sitting there doing nothing except being turned on and getting warmer, you know the problem was caused by overheating: some part inside the computer is failing as the internal temperature rises. That part could be a RAM chip, BIOS chip, or otherwise.
> Since that part isn't tolerant enough of heat, it must be replaced: take the computer in for repair.

That kind of test — where you leave the computer on for several hours to see what happens as the computer warms up — is called **letting the computer cook**.

> During the cooking, if smoke comes out of one of the computer's parts, that part is said to have **fried**. That same applies to humans: when a programmer's been working hard on a project for many hours and become too exhausted to think straight, the programmer says, "I'm **burnt out**. My brain is **fried**." Common solutions are sleep and pizza ("getting some z's & 'za").
> When computers are manufactured, the last step in the assembly line is to leave the computer turned on a long time, to let the computer cook and make sure it still works when hot. A top-notch manufacturer leaves the computer on for 2 days (48 hours) or even 3 days (72 hours), while continually testing the computer to make sure no parts fail. That part of the assembly line is called **burning in** the computer; many top-notch manufacturers do **72-hour burn in**.

Sluggish key After pressing one a keys, if the **key doesn't pop back up fast enough**, probably there's dirt under the key. The "dirt" is probably dust or coagulated drinks (such as Coke or coffee).

If *many* keys are sluggish, don't bother trying to fix them all. Just buy a new keyboard (for about $20).

If just one or two keys are sluggish, here's how to try fixing a sluggish key:

> Take a paper clip, partly unravel it so it becomes a hook, then use that hook to pry up the key, until the keycap pops off. Clean the part of the keyboard that was under that keycap: blow away the dust, and wipe away grime (such as coagulated drinks). With the keycap still off, turn on the computer, and try pressing the plunger that was under the keycap. If the plunger is still sluggish, you haven't cleaned it enough. (Don't try too hard: remember that a new keyboard costs just about $20.) When the plunger works fine, turn off the computer, put the keycap back on, and the key should work fine.

Caps While you're typing, **if each capital letter unexpectedly becomes small, and each small letter becomes capitalized**, the Shift key or Caps Lock key is activated.

The culprit is usually the Caps Lock key. Probably you pressed it accidentally when you meant to press a nearby key instead. The Caps Lock key stays activated until you deactivate it by pressing it again.

Cure:

> Press the Caps Lock key (again), then try typing some more, to see whether the problem has gone away.
> If your keyboard is modern, its top right corner has a Caps Lock light. That light glows when the Caps Lock key is activated; the light stops glowing when the Caps Lock key is deactivated.
> If pressing the Caps Lock key doesn't solve the problem, try jiggling the left and right Shift keys. (Maybe one of those Shift keys was accidentally stuck in the down position, because you spilled some soda that got into the keyboard and coagulated and made the Shift key too sticky to pop all the way back up.)

If playing with the Caps Lock and Shift keys doesn't immediately solve your problem, try typing a comma and notice what happens. If the screen shows the symbol "<" instead of a comma, your Shift key is activated. (The Caps Lock key has no effect on the comma key, since the Caps Lock key affects just letters, not punctuation.) If pressing the comma key makes the screen show a comma, your Shift key is *not* activated, and any problems you have must therefore be caused by the Caps Lock key instead.

Perhaps the Caps Lock key is being activated automatically by the program you're using. (For example, some programs automatically activate the Caps Lock key because they want your input to be capitalized.) To find out, exit from the program, reboot the computer, get to a C prompt (in DOS) or WordPad (in modern Windows), and try again to type. If the typing is displayed fine, the "problem" was probably caused by just the program you were using — perhaps on purpose.

Printer problems

If you have trouble printing, try the following experiment. Shut down the computer and the printer (so you can start fresh). When the computer's become quiet, turn it back on; then turn the printer back on.

Go into WordPad (by clicking Start then "All Programs" then "Accessories" then "WordPad"). Type a document that contains three words (such as "I love you") and also the word "abcdefghijklmnopqrstuvwxyz". Print that document by doing this:

> For Windows XP & Vista, click "File". For Windows 7, click the WordPad button (which is left of "Home").
> Make sure your printer's name is highlighted. (If it's not, highlight it.)
> Click the "Print" button.

If the computer prints that document okay, all your hardware is okay. Any remaining problem is probably just software: for example, you forgot to tell your program or Windows what kind of printer you bought, or you told it incorrectly.

If the computer does *not* print that document okay, you're probably having a hardware problem (in your printer, your computer, or the cable connecting them); for example, make sure the cable connecting them is plugged in tight at both ends, and the printer is turned on and has enough paper & ink, correctly inserted.

Here's another possible reason for failure: you have a messed-up **printer queue** (your hard disk's list of documents waiting to be printed) because an earlier document was too complicated to fit in the printer's RAM. To solve that problem, empty the printer queue by doing this:

> Double-click the printer icon (which is at the screen's bottom, left of the time). You see the printer queue's window, which shows a list of documents waiting to be printed. Click "Printer" then "Cancel All Documents". Press Enter. Wait until the list of documents is empty. Close the printer queue's window (by clicking its X).

Here's info about special printer problems....

Incomplete characters When you look at the printed paper, you might see that **part of each character is missing**. For example, for the letter "A" you see just the top part of the "A", or just the bottom part, or everything except the middle. That means you're using an ink-jet or dot-matrix printer, and some of the ink jets or pins aren't successfully putting ink onto the paper.

If you're using an inkjet printer, probably one of the jets is clogged and needs to be cleaned.

> Follow the manufacturer's instructions on how to test and clean the ink jets. If cleaning doesn't solve the problem, try buying a new ink cartridge.

If you're using a dot-matrix printer and the bottom part of each character is missing, your ribbon is too high, so that the bottom pins miss hitting it.

> Push the ribbon down lower. Read the instructions that came with your printer and ribbon, to find out the correct way to thread the ribbon through your printer. If you're using a daisy-wheel printer, also check whether the daisy-wheel is inserted correctly: try removing it and then reinserting it.

If you're using a dot-matrix printer and some other part of each character is missing, probably a pin broke or is stuck.

> Look at the print head, where the pins are. See if one of the pins is missing or broken. If so, consider buying a new print head, but beware: since print heads are *not* available from discount dealers, you must pay full list price for the print head, and pay almost as much for it as discount dealers charge for a whole new printer!

Substitute characters When you tell the printer to print a word, the printer might print the correct number of characters but **print wrong letters of the alphabet**. For example, instead of printing an "A", the printer might print a "B" or "C".

That's probably because the cable going from the computer to the printer is loose, so do this:

> Turn off the printer. Grab the cable that goes from the computer to the printer, unplug both ends of the cable, then plug both ends in again *tightly.* Try again to print. If you succeed, the cable was just loose: congratulations, you tightened it!

If tightening the cable does *not* solve the problem, the cable is probably defective.

> To *prove* it's defective, borrow a cable from a friend and try again. If your friend's cable works with your computer and printer, your original cable was definitely the culprit.
> Once you've convinced yourself that the problem is the cable, go to a store and buy a new cable. It's cheaper to buy a new cable than to fix the old one. Make sure you buy the right kind: your printer might require an IEEE 1284 cable.
> If the new cable doesn't solve your problem, try a *third* cable, since many cables are defective!

If buying a new cable doesn't solve your problem, you have defective circuitry in your printer or in your computer's parallel-printer port.

> Get together with a friend and try swapping printers, computers, and cables: make notes about which combinations work and which don't. You'll soon discover which computers, cables, and printers work correctly and which ones are defective.

Extra characters When using a program (such as a word-processing program), the printer might **print a few extra characters at the top of each page**.

Those extra characters are special codes that the printer should *not* print. Those codes are supposed to tell the printer *how* to print. Your printer is misinterpreting those codes, because those codes were intended for a different kind of printer — or your printer cable is loose.

First, make sure the printer cable is tight.

Then try again to **tell your software which printer you bought**, by doing this....

> **Windows 7**: click Start then "Devices and Printers" then "Add a printer".
>
> **Windows Vista**: click Start then "Control Panel" then "Control Panel Home" then "Printer" then "Add a printer".
>
> **Windows XP**: click Start then "Control Panel" then "Printers and Other Hardware" then "Add a printer".

Then follow the prompts on the screen.

Misaligned columns When printing a table of numbers or words, the columns might wiggle: some of the words and numbers might be printed slightly too far left or right, even though they looked perfectly aligned on the screen.

That's because you're trying to print by using a proportionally spaced font that doesn't match the screen's font.

The simplest way to solve the problem is to **switch to a monospaced font**, such as Courier New or Lucida Console.

> Since those fonts are monospaced (each character is the same width as every other character), there are no surprises. To switch fonts while using Windows, use your mouse: drag across all the text whose font you wish to switch, then say which font you wish to switch to.

Unfortunately, monospaced fonts are ugly. If you insist on using proportionally spaced fonts, which are prettier, remember that when moving from column to column you should **press the Tab key, not the Space bar**.

> In proportionally spaced fonts, the Space bar creates a printed space that's too narrow: it's narrower than the space created by the typical digit or letter.
> If the Tab key doesn't make the columns your favorite width, customize how the Tab key works by adjusting the Tab stops. (In most word-processing programs, you adjust the Tab stops by sliding them on the layout ruler.)

Margins On a sheet of paper, all the printing might be too far to the left, or too far to the right, or too far up, or too far down. That shows you forgot to tell the computer about the paper's size, margins, and feed, or you misfed the paper into the printer.

Software makes assumptions:

> Most computer software assumes the paper is 11 inches tall and 8½ inches wide (or slightly wider, if the paper has holes in its sides). The software also assumes you want 1-inch margins on all four sides (top, bottom, left, and right).
> If you told the software you have a dot-matrix printer, the software usually assumes you're using **pin-feed paper** (which has holes in the side); it's also called **continuous-feed paper**. For ink-jet and laser printers, the software typically assumes you're using **friction-feed paper** instead (which has no holes).
> If those assumptions are not correct, tell the software. For example, give a "margin", "page size", or "feed" command to your word-processing software.

If you make a mistake about how tall the sheet of paper is, the computer will try to print too many or too few lines per page. The result is **creep**: on the first page, the printing begins correctly; but on the second page the printing is slightly too low or too high, and on the third page the printing is even more off.

> To solve a creep problem, revise slightly what you tell the software about how tall the sheet of paper is. For example, **if the printing is fine on the first page but an inch too low on the second page, tell the software that each sheet of paper is an inch shorter**.
> On pin-feed paper, the printer can print all the way from the very top of the paper to the very bottom. On friction-feed paper, the printer can*not* print at the sheet's very top or very bottom (since the rollers can't grab the paper securely enough while printing there). So on friction-feed paper, the printable area is smaller, as if the paper were shorter. Telling the software wrong info about feed has the same effect as telling the software wrong info about the paper's height: you get creep.
> So **to fix creep, revise what you tell the software about the paper's height or feed**. If the software doesn't let you talk about the paper's feed, kill the creep by revising what you say about the paper's height.
> If you're using a dot-matrix printer that can handle both kinds of paper (pin-feed and friction-feed), **you'll solve most creep problems by choosing pin-feed paper**.

If all printing is too far to the left (or right), adjust what you tell the software about the left and right margins; or if you're using pin-feed paper in a dot-matrix printer with movable tractors, slide the tractors to the left or right (after loosening them by flipping their levers). For example, **if the printing is an inch too far to the right, slide the tractors an inch toward the right**.

No sound

If **you don't hear sounds** (such as beeps and music), the problem could be caused by hardware or software.

Make sure the speakers are plugged into the computer. Make sure they're plugged into the computer's speaker jack tightly, not the microphone jack. If the speakers contain batteries, make sure the batteries are working. If the speakers need to be plugged into a wall socket or power strip, make sure they are. If the speakers have an ON button, make sure it's in the ON position.

Make sure all volume knobs are turned up:

> There's probably a volume knob on the front of the speakers. On the back of the computer, where the speakers plug into the computer, you might find a volume dial.

If you're still not hearing sounds, do software cleaning (by following pages 154-158), which reduces memory conflicts, because when the computer faces a memory conflict it gives up trying to produce sounds.

At the screen's bottom right corner, next to the time, you might find a Volume icon (which looks like a blaring loudspeaker). If so, do this:

> Click the Volume icon. You see a Mute box; make sure it's unchecked. You see a slider; drag it up to the top. Try clicking the slider; you should hear a bell sound, at the volume level you requested.
> For Windows XP, try this also.... Click "start" then "All Programs" then "Accessories" then "Entertainment" then "Volume Control". You'll see many sliders. Make sure each volume slider is dragged to the top, make sure each balance slider is centered, and make sure each Mute box is unchecked. Then close the window (by clicking its X button).

Click "Start" then "Settings" then "Control Panel". Double-click "Sounds". Make sure the Schemes box says "Windows Default". (If it doesn't, click that box's down-arrow, then choose "Windows Default" from the list.) Then do this test:

> In the big white box, scroll down to "Start Windows". Make sure the Name box says "The Microsoft Sound". Make sure the Preview box has a loudspeaker in it, instead of being blank. Make sure the triangle to its right is black, instead of being grayed out. If the Preview box is empty and the triangle is grayed out, the computer thinks you have no sound card. If you're lucky, and the triangle is black, click it: you should hear a long loud chord, accompanied by a background of synthesized outer-space new-age sounds. If you don't hear that chord, the computer thinks everything is fine, but everything isn't.

If you're still not having any luck, you can try having Windows redetect your hardware (click "Start" then "Settings" then "Control Panel" then double-click "Add New Hardware" then press Enter), but that's typically useless. An approach that's slightly more likely to succeed, if you have the patience, is to reinstall Windows. Phone me at 603-666-6644 if you want further help.

CD drive

If the **CD drive stops working**, the cause is probably dust, bad disks, a loose cable, or CD driver software.

First, get rid of dust. Dust off the disks and tray. Take a deep breath and blow air into the CD drive, but avoid spit. If you wish, buy a CD head cleaner at Radio Shack; it's a fake CD-ROM disk that has brushes on it, to brush dust off the CD lens.

If a CD has scratches on it, that disk might be damaged and never work. Try other disks instead.

If you're using a "homemade" CD-R or CD-RW disk created on another computer, the signals on that disk might be too weak to be detected by an old CD drive. Try disks created in other ways instead, or try using a different CD drive.

Open the computer and check the cable that runs out of the CD drive. Probably one end of that cable is loose and flimsy. Try to plug it in more snugly.

If you're using modern Windows and your screen's four corners say "Safe mode", you can't use the CD drive while your computer is in that mode: you must shut down the computer and restart in "Normal mode".

Strange systems

Instead of using the **Windows** operating system, some folks use a different operating system. This section explains how to use the **iPad** (which is made by Apple) and **DOS** (an old but beloved operating system, which Windows can imitate).

iPad

Apple makes a tablet computer called the **iPad**, which let you access the Web easily while you travel.

Start

Here's how to start using the iPad.

Unpack

The iPad comes in a white cardboard box. Open the box and put the contents on your desk (or table). The box contains packing material plus 5 items:

> the **iPad itself** (9½ inches tall, 7½ inches wide, and ¼ inch thick)
> a **power adapter** (white box, 1¾"x1¾"x1", to plug into an electric outlet)
> a **USB cable** (to connect your iPad to the power adapter or to a computer)
> **Apple decals** (so you can brag that you have an Apple product)
> **instructions**

Remove those 5 items from their plastic bags and boxes.

Prepare your computer

Before using the iPad, you must already have a normal computer (desktop or laptop, Windows or Mac) that contains a recent version of the iTunes program (which is a free download from www.itunes.com).

Set up the iPad

Plug the USB cable's big end into the iPad's bottom edge. Plug the USB cable's small end into your normal computer.

The computer will say "Installing device driver software" then "iPad Device driver software installed successfully".

Run the computer's iTunes program (by double-clicking the iTunes icon or doing this: click the Start button then "All Programs" then the iTunes folder then the iTunes program). If computer says iTunes Software License Agreement" (because you haven't run the iTunes program before), click "Agree" then "No".

You see the iTunes window. If it doesn't consume the whole screen yet, maximize the window (by clicking the box next to the X).

The computer should say "Welcome to Your New iPad". (If it doesn't say that yet, unplug the USB cable then plug it back in.)

For the moment, abridge the installation process by clicking "Register Later" then "Not Now" (which is at the screen's bottom).

The computer will say "iPad Software License Agreement". Click "I have read and agree to the iPAd Software License

Agreement" then "Continue" then "Done".

The computer will say "iPad sync is complete."

Disconnect the USB cable from the computer. Plug that cable into the power adapter instead. Plug the power adapter into your home's electrical outlet (after prying the power adapter's plug outward).

See the Home screen

Tap the iPad's **Home button**. (That button shows a rectangle with rounded corners. It's the only button indented on the iPad's glass surface. It's at the glass surface's bottom, near the USB cable.)

The iPad will say "slide to unlock". Put your finger on the right-arrow and **slide** (drag) it to the right.

If the iPad says "Edit Home Screen", tap "Dismiss".

You see the **Home screen**. The screen's top shows the time and how fully charged the battery is (as a percentage). The rest of the screen shows these 13 choices:

Calendar	Contacts	Notes	Maps
Videos	YouTube	iTunes	App Store
Settings			
Safari	Mail	Photos	iPod

Notes

For your first experiment, try using the iPad's built-in word processor, which is called **Notes**. To do that, tap "Notes".

You see a picture of a yellow blank sheet of paper. Tap the paper's middle; then you see a keyboard at the screen's bottom.

To type a note, type on the keyboard, using just one or two fingers.

> The iPad normally makes the letters be small (uncapitalized), but it automatically capitalizes the first word in each sentence & paragraph. To change how a letter will be capitalized, tap a **Shift key** (which shows an up-arrow) before tapping the letter.
>
> To erase a mistake, tap the **Backspace key** (which shows a white X).
>
> At the end of a paragraph, tap the **Return key**.
>
> To type a number or symbol, tap the **Number key** (which shows ".?123"), so you see numbers & symbols. Tap any numbers or symbols you want. (To see more symbols, then tap the **Symbol key**, which shows "#+=".) To return to the usual keyboard, tap the **Alpha key** (which shows "ABC").

Shortcuts

You can use these shortcuts:

> To type a period then a space, just **double-tap** the Space bar (by tapping the Space bar then quickly tapping it again).
>
> To type a long word, type its beginning. If the iPad shows the whole word (by guessing the word's ending correctly), tap the Space bar to confirm: that makes the iPad type the word's ending and a blank space after it.

Selections

To select a word to edit, double-tap it.

That makes the word have a blue background. You also see a blue dot before the word and another blue dot after the word. To make the selection include more words, slide (drag) the blue dots until the blue background includes all the words you want to select.

Then tell the iPad what to do to the selected words.

> If you want to **delete** the words, tap the **Backspace key**.
>
> If you want to **move** the words, do this: tap **Cut**, then tap twice the blank space where you want the words to appear, then tap **Paste**.

Accents

To type the symbol "é", rest your finger on the E key awhile. You'll see 8 kinds of "e", each having a different accent. Slide your finger to the "é" (or whatever other accented "e" you prefer).

Similarly, to type the symbol "ñ", rest your finger on the N key awhile. You'll see 3 kinds of "n", each having a different accent. Slide your finger to the "ñ" (or whatever other accented "n" you prefer).

These letters offer accents:

> A C E I L N O S U Y Z

Hide the keyboard

If you want to hide the keyboard, tap the **Keyboard key** (which is at the bottom-right corner). To make the keyboard reappear, tap the screen's middle again.

Scroll

If you type more lines than can fit on the screen, the screen will show just part of your note (document). To see the rest of the note, put your finger in the screen's middle and slide up (to see the note's beginning) or down (to see the note's end). Sliding the note is called **scrolling**.

Extra notes

To create an extra note, tap the "+" (which is at the screen's top-right corner). The iPad will say "New Note", show a blank sheet of paper, and wait for you to type a new note.

If you've created more than one note, you can switch from note to note by tapping the right-arrow or left-arrow. (You'll see those arrows at the screen's bottom, after you hide the keyboard.)

The right arrow shows the *previous* note. The left arrow shows the *next* note. (Yeah, I know that seems backwards.)

Another way to switch from note to note is to tap the word "Notes" (which is at the screen's top-left corner). Then you see a list of all your notes. Tap whichever note interests you.

Delete a note

To delete an entire note, get that note onto the screen, then tap the **Trash Can** (which you'll see at the screen's bottom, after you hide the keyboard) then "Delete Note".

Return to Home

When you finish writing and reading your notes, press the Home button (at the screen's bottom), so you see the Home screen again.

Tricks

Using the iPad can be tricky.

Sleep & wake

The iPad will go to **sleep** (make the screen be all black and use very little electricity) if you don't touch the iPad for 5 minutes (or if you **tap** the **Sleep/Wake button**, which is on the iPad's top edge, at the right).

To wake the iPad back up, tap the Sleep/Wake button again (or the Home button) then slide the arrow to the right. That makes the iPad continue where you left off. For example, if you'd been writing a note when the iPad went to sleep, the iPad's screen will show that note again upon awaking.

Turn off & on

To turn the iPad off completely (so it consumes no electricity at all), hold down the **Sleep/Wake button** (which is on the iPad's top edge, at the right), until you see a white right-arrow (on a red background). Drag that arrow to the right.

Here's how to turn the iPad back on:

> Hold down the Sleep/Wake button until you see a white apple. Then release your finger.
>
> 14 seconds later, the iPad will beep. Then the screen's bottom will say "slide to unlock".
>
> *Immediately*, put your finger on the right-arrow and slide it to the right. (If you delay more than 8 seconds, the screen will go black and you must press the Home button to try again.)
>
> You'll see the Home screen.

Portrait versus landscape

Normally, the iPad lies flat (horizontally) on your desk (or table).

Try this experiment: lift the iPad's top edge off the desk, until the iPad is vertical instead of horizontal. Then rotate the iPad clockwise, 90 degrees, so the iPad looks wider and not as tall. When you do that, all the writing on the screen rotates 90 degrees counterclockwise to compensate, so you can still read what's on the screen without turning your head.

When the iPad is wider than it is tall, you're in **landscape mode**; the **orientation** is landscape (and good for viewing a painting of a landscape).

To return to normal (which is called **portrait mode**), lift the iPad's top edge off the desk again then rotate the iPad counterclockwise, 90 degrees, so the Home button is at the iPad's bottom again. Then the iPad is taller than it is wide, you're in **portrait mode**; the **orientation** is portrait (and good for viewing a portrait of a person).

Calendar

When you're looking at the Home screen, you see the word "**Calendar**". Above that word, you see the day of the week (such as "Monday") and the date (such as "31").

If you tap the word "Calendar", you see a calendar for an entire month.

Make the calendar normal

To make sure the calendar consumes the whole screen, tap the word "**Month**" (which is near the screen's top). To make sure the calendar includes today, tap the word "**Today**" (which is at the screen's bottom-left corner).

Different months

After you've admired the current month, here's how to see a different month instead: tap whichever month or year you want (using the list of months & years at the screen's bottom).

Return to Home

When you finish using the calendar, press the Home button (at the screen's bottom), so you see the Home screen again.

Web

Here's how to access the Web from the iPad.

Safari

When you're looking at the Home screen, you see the word "Safari". To use the Internet, tap the word "Safari".

If the computer says "Select a Wi-Fi Network" and shows you a list of your neighborhood's wireless routers, tap the name of the router you want to use.

At the screen's top, you see two white boxes. Tap in the left box. A keyboard appears. Using the keyboard, type the Web address you want to visit. For example, if you want to visit www.yahoo.com, type:

www.yahoo.com

At the end of your typing, tap the keyboard's "Go" button.

After viewing several Web pages, you can go back to the previous Web page by tapping the **Back** button (the "◄" near the screen's top-left corner).

If a Web page (such as www.yahoo.com or www.NyTimes.com) shows several columns of type, try **double-tapping** a column. That magnifies the column, so it fills more of the screen (and you don't see the other columns as much.) To make that column return to its normal size, double-tap it again.

If a Web page (such as www.NyTimes.com or www.SecretFun.com) is too long to fit on the screen, here's how to see the page's bottom. Put your finger in the screen's middle, then **slide** up (or, to move faster, **flick** your finger up, as if you were flicking an insect off your screen). To return to the Web page's top, **slide** down or **flick** your finger down or **tap** the Web page's **title** (which is near the screen's top, immediately under the time and above the www).

Bookmarks If you find a Web page that you like a lot, do this while you're viewing it: tap the "**+**" (which is near the screen's top, left of the www) then "Add Bookmark" then "Save". In the future, whenever you're using Safari and want to return to that Web page, tap the **Bookmark** icon (which is just left of the "+" and looks like an opened book); you see a list of **bookmarked** Web pages; tap the Web page you want.

If you change your mind, you can remove that Web page from the bookmarked list by doing this: tap the Bookmark icon (so you see the list of bookmarked Web pages), then tap "Edit" then the page's minus sign then "Delete".

In the list of bookmarked Web pages, you see the Web pages you bookmarked plus these 4 Web pages, which Apple has already bookmarked for you:

Apple	www.apple.com
Yahoo!	www.yahoo.com
Google	www.google.com
iPad User Guide	help.apple.com/ipad/mobile/interface

Ending When you finish using Safari, press the Home button (at the screen's bottom), so you see the Home screen again.

YouTube

When you're looking at the Home screen, try this experiment: tap "**YouTube**". That gets you a version of YouTube, customized for display on the iPad screen.

Choose a video At the screen's bottom, you see these choices:

Featured	Top Rated	Most Viewed	Favorites	Subscriptions	My Videos	History

Tap "**Featured**" (to see 12 videos that YouTube wants to emphasize) or "**Top Rated**" (to see 12 videos that people voted the best) or "**Most Viewed**" (to see 12 videos that people looked at most often).

The screen is big enough to show 12 at a time. To see beyond the first 12, **scroll down** by doing this: touch the screen's middle, then slide your finger up the screen.

When you've decided which video to view, tap it. The video will play. Enjoy the show!

Alter the play While the video plays, try these experiments:

> Use the **volume button.** (It's the tall black button on the iPad's right-hand edge.) To increase the volume, press the volume button's top. To decrease the volume, press the volume button's bottom.
>
> Switch to landscape mode (by lifting the iPad's top and rotating 90 degrees clockwise). That makes the video look bigger.
>
> Tap the video's middle. That makes you see more controls.

Ending If you want to switch back to the previous screen (because the video has ended or you're tired of watching it), tap the screen's top-left corner. To return to the Home screen, press the Home button.

Peculiarities YouTube's iPad version gives you a different list of favorites than YouTube's normal version.

Unfortunately, YouTube's iPad version never shows YouTube's CC button. (On normal computers, YouTube's CC button can give you closed captions and French-to-English translations.)

Maps

When you're looking at the Home screen, try this experiment: tap "Map". That gets you a version of Google Maps, customized for display on the iPad screen.

Zoom in You see a map of part of the world. If you want to zoom in (so you see more details), use one of these methods....

> **Double-tap** method: double-tap where you want to zoom in.
>
> **Stretch** method: put two fingers where you want to zoom, then **stretch** (slide your fingers apart).
>
> **Address** method: tap "Search" (at the screen's top-left corner) then the address box (the wide white box near the screen's top-right corner) then an X at the box's right edge (if you see an X); type a location (such as "196 Tiffany Lane, Manchester NH" or "Los Angeles airport" or "White House"); at the end of your typing, tap the keyboard's Search key.

Zoom out If you want to zoom out (so you see fewer details but see a bigger part of the world), shrink the map by doing this: **pinch** your fingers (by putting two fingers on the screen then sliding the fingers toward each other).

If you do that several times, you'll see the whole world on your screen. (For best results, switch to landscape mode, to let your world map include the Pacific countries: New Zealand, Australia, Japan, and Korea.)

Map types If you tap the screen's bottom-right corner, you see this list of **map types**:

Map type	Meaning
Classic	a drawing of the streets
Satellite	an aerial photo (taken by a satellite)
Hybrid	an aerial photo (taken by a satellite), with streets labeled
Terrain	a drawing of the streets & hills

Tap whichever map type you prefer.

Ending When you finish using Maps, press the Home button (at the screen's bottom), to return to the Home screen again.

DOS

If you have an IBM-compatible computer, it understands DOS commands — even if your computer comes with Windows. This chapter explains how to give DOS commands.

DOS commands are worth learning because they give you total control over your computer. They solve the difficulties caused when Windows acts strangely or conks out.

DOS commands are trustworthy: when you give a DOS command, you know exactly what will happen. When you give a Windows command, you can't be sure of the consequences: Windows is flaky and full of unfortunate surprises. Technicians repairing computers rely on DOS.

DOS runs well and fast even on computers that are old, decrepit, or broken, where Windows runs slowly or erratically or not-at-all.

This chapter explains the DOS commands that are included in Windows. It also explains DOS jargon, which Microsoft often uses in Windows error messages!

Versions of DOS

The original draft of DOS was invented by Tim Paterson in 1980. He called it the **8086 Disk Operating System (86-DOS)**. He also nicknamed it the **Quick and Dirty Operating System (QDOS)**.

In 1982, he sold all rights to **MicroSoft (MS)**, for $75,000. Microsoft began reselling it to IBM and other computer manufacturers.

Now DOS comes in many versions. Old versions for the IBM PC are called **PC-DOS**. Old versions for computers built by Compaq are called **Compaq DOS**. All other versions of DOS are called **MS-DOS**.

Versions 1, 2, 3

Microsoft gradually improved DOS's abilities.

> **DOS 1** handled just the original IBM PC and its 5¼-inch floppy disks. That version wrote on just one side of each disk and put 8 sectors on each track, so each disk held 160K.
>
> **DOS 1.1** could write on *both* sides of each disk, so each disk held 320K.
>
> **DOS 2** could also handle the IBM PC XT and its 10M hard disk. That version also squeezed more data onto each floppy disk: onto each track, it put 9 sectors instead of 8, so the floppy disk held 360K instead of 320K.
>
> **DOS 2.1** could also handle the IBM PC Junior.
>
> **DOS 3** could also handle the IBM PC AT, its 20M and 30M hard disks, and its high-density 5¼-inch floppy disks (which held 1.2M instead of 360K).
>
> **DOS 3.1** could also handle networks.
>
> **DOS 3.2** could also handle the IBM PC Convertible and its 3½-inch 720K floppies.
>
> **DOS 3.3** could also handle the IBM PS/2 and its 3½-inch 1.44M floppies.

DOS 3.3 worked well. Earlier versions were severely limited:

> DOS 1&1.1 couldn't handle hard disks at all.
> DOS 2&2.1 made errors when handling hard disks bigger than 16M.
> DOS 3&3.2 were invented hastily and made lots of errors.
> DOS before 3.2 couldn't handle 3½-inch floppies.
> DOS 3.2 handled 3½-inch floppies, but just if they were 720K, not 1.44M.

Compaq DOS version 3.31 resembled PC-DOS version 3.3 but included easier commands for handling hard disks bigger than 30M.

Versions 4, 5, 6

In 1988, Microsoft and IBM began selling **DOS 4**. Like Compaq DOS version 3.31, it could handle big hard disks easily. Unfortunately, it consumed too much RAM and was incompatible with some older programs.

In 1991, Microsoft and IBM began selling **DOS 5**, which fixed DOS 4's problems and included many exciting new commands. In 1993 they began selling **DOS 6**, which was even fancier.

Afterwards, Microsoft and IBM parted company and competed against each other:

> IBM invented and sold **DOS 6.1**, without involvement from Microsoft. Then Microsoft fought back by inventing and selling **DOS 6.2**. Then IBM retaliated with **DOS 6.3** and **DOS 7**.

DOS 5 & 6.2 worked fine, but other versions were limited:

> DOS 6.1, 6.3, and 7 were too weird: they weren't invented by Microsoft and didn't accept standard Microsoft commands.
>
> DOS 6 worked acceptably just if you avoided using its 3 fancy routines (Double Space, Smart Drive, and Mem Maker), which were disastrously unreliable. DOS 6.2 included fixed versions of those routines.

DOS 6.2 came in three variants, called **6.20**, **6.21**, and **6.22**; here's why:

> A company called **Stac Electronics** sued Microsoft for putting Stac's ideas into Double Space. In 1994, Stac won the suit. The judge ordered Microsoft to pay Stac and stop selling DOS 6.0 and 6.20, so Microsoft came out with **DOS 6.21** (which omitted Double Space) and **DOS 6.22** (which included a Double Space clone called **Drive Space**). But Stac said Microsoft wasn't removing copies of versions 6.0 and 6.20 from store shelves fast enough, so Microsoft squashed the problem by paying Stac more and buying 15% of the Stac company itself, so the two companies became buddies.

DOS W

In 1995, Microsoft invented **Windows 95**, which included a DOS version I'll call **DOS W**. (Microsoft sometimes called it "DOS 7", but I'll say "DOS W" to avoid confusion with IBM's DOS 7.) Then Microsoft invented improved versions of Windows 95 (called **Windows 98** and **Windows Me**), which still included DOS W.

Modern DOS imitation

Then Microsoft invented **Windows XP**, which includes an *imitation* of DOS. The imitation is a program called **Command Prompt**, which is stored in a file called **cmd.exe**. (The Command Prompt's first version was invented by Therese Stowell when she was working with preliminary versions of Windows XP, called **Windows NT** and **Windows 2000**.)

The Command Prompt program is also in later Windows versions (**Windows Vista** and **Windows 7**).

This chapter

This chapter explains how to use the Command Prompt program in Windows XP, Windows Vista, and Windows 7. (For information about older versions of DOS, get older editions of this book by phoning me at 603-666-6644.)

To use DOS, you put your fingers on the keyboard and type a DOS command or equation. The popular DOS commands are explained on these pages:

Command	What the computer will do	Page
`attrib +r Mary`	make the Mary file be read-only	178
`attrib +h Mary`	make the Mary file be hidden	178
`c:`	make drive C be the current drive	176
`cd \`	show the standard C prompt	175
`cd Windows`	make Windows be the current folder	175
`cls`	hide what was in the DOS window	172
`color 1`	make the DOS window's characters be blue	172
`copy con Mary`	copy from keyboard to a file called Mary	177
`copy Mary con`	copy from the Mary file to your screen	177
`copy Mary Sue`	make copy of file Mary; call the copy "Sue"	177
`d:`	make drive D be the current drive	176
`date`	show today's date	172
`del Mary`	delete a file called Mary from the disk	178
`dir`	show a directory of files	172
`dir *.sys`	show a directory of files that end in ".sys"	174
`dir /a`	show directory of all files, even hidden ones	173
`dir d:`	show a directory of drive D's files	176
`dir p*`	show a directory of files that begin with "p"	174
`dir Windows`	show a directory of files in Windows folder	174
`echo wow`	show the word "wow" on the screen	171
`@echo off`	hide the batch file's commands	179
`help`	list other DOS commands you can give	179
`md Sarah`	make a new folder, called Sarah	177
`rd Sarah /s`	delete a folder called Sarah from the disk	178
`ren Mary Lambchop`	rename the Mary file; change to Lambchop	178
`time`	show the current time	172
`title DOS World`	make the DOS window's title 'DOS World'	172
`type Mary`	show, on the screen, what's in the Mary file	178
`ver`	say which Windows version is being used	171
`xcopy \S \T /e/h`	make copy of folder S; call the copy "T"	177

Get to standard C prompt

To start giving DOS commands, turn on your modern Windows computer then click Start then do this:

Normal method (recommended for beginners): click "All Programs" then "Accessories" then "Command Prompt".

Shortcut method in Windows Vista & 7: type "cmd" (and press Enter).

Shortcut method in Windows XP: click "Run" then type "cmd" (and press Enter).

You see the **Command Prompt window**. Maximize it (by clicking its maximize button, which is next to the X button). That makes the window taller (though not wider).

In that window, the first line says "Microsoft Windows" and tells you the version number. The next line says "Copyright" and tells you the year it was invented.

The next line says "C:" (which is pronounced "C colon" or "C drive"). It means the computer is examining the disk in drive C.

That line also says "Users" and mentions your user name. (Windows XP says "Documents and Settings" instead of "Users".)

For example, if your user name is "Joan", you see this line:

Windows version	What you see
Vista & 7	`C:\Users\Joan>`
XP	`C:\Documents and Settings\Joan>`

That line is called the **command prompt**.

To simplify your first experience, please **type "cd \"**. When you type that, make sure you type the symbol "\" (which is a **backslash** and above the Enter key), not "/" (which is a forward slash). Your typing appears to the right of the command prompt, so your screen looks like this:

Windows version	What you see
Vista & 7	`C:\Users\Joan>cd \`
XP	`C:\Documents and Settings\Joan>cd \`

When using the Command Prompt window, **you must press the Enter key at the end of each command you type**; so

after typing "cd \", press the Enter key.

Now your screen looks like this:

```
C:\>
```

That line is called the **standard C prompt**. Notice it consists of 4 characters: a **capital C**, a **colon**, a **backslash**, and a **greater sign**.

Now you can give standard DOS commands, simply!

I'll show you DOS commands. (Whenever you get tired of playing with DOS commands, close the Command Prompt window by clicking its X button.)

Simple commands

After the C prompt (which is "C:\>"), the computer waits for you to type a **DOS command**. When typing a DOS command, remember these principles:

Type the command after the C prompt. Remember that the C prompt is typed by the computer, not by you.

If you type a command wrong, press the Backspace key, which is above the Enter key and has a left-arrow on it.

When you finish typing a command, press the Enter key. That key makes the computer read what you typed.

Start by trying these simple DOS commands....

Version (ver)

After the C prompt you can type "ver", like this:

```
C:\>ver
```

(When you finish typing that command, remember to press the Enter key.)

The "ver" command makes the computer remind you which VERsion of Windows you're using, like this:

Windows	What the computer says
XP	`Microsoft Windows XP [Version 5.1.2600]`
Vista	`Microsoft Windows [Version 6.0.6002]`
7	`Microsoft Windows [Version 6.1.7600]`

Echo

The computer's your obedient slave: it will say whatever you wish!

For example, here's how to make the computer say "wow". After the C prompt, type "echo wow", like this:

```
C:\>echo wow
```

Remember to press the Enter key at the end of that command. Then the computer will say:

```
wow
```

The computer will do that by just displaying "wow" on the screen. (DOS is too stupid to know how to say words out loud.)

If you want the computer to say it loves you, type this:

```
C:\>echo I love you
```

That command makes the computer say:

```
I love you
```

If you want the computer to say it likes strawberry ice cream, type this:

```
C:\>echo I like strawberry ice cream
```

Then the computer will say:

```
I like strawberry ice cream
```

Notice that the echo command makes the computer act like a canyon: whatever you say into the computer, the echo command makes the computer echo back.

Clear screen (cls)

Suppose you make the computer say "I love you" (and other things that are even wilder), and then your boss walks by. You might be embarrassed to let your boss see your love messages. Here's how to hide all messages in the Command Prompt window.

After the C prompt, type "cls", like this:

```
C:\>cls
```

The "cls" command makes the computer CLear the Screen, so all messages in the Command Prompt window are erased and the window becomes blank. The only thing that will remain in the window is —

```
C:\>
```

so you can give another command.

Date

To use the computer's built-in calendar, type "date" after the C prompt, like this:

```
C:\>date
```

That makes the computer tell you the date.

For example, if the computer's clock was set correctly and today is Sunday, December 25, 2011, the computer will say:

```
The current date is: Sun 12/25/2011
```

Afterwards, the computer says:

```
Enter the new date: (mm-dd-yy)
```

Ignore that line: just press Enter.

Time

To find out what time it is, type "time" after the C prompt, like this:

```
C:\>time
```

That makes the computer tell you the time.

For example, if the computer's clock was set correctly and the time is 2.71 seconds after 1:45PM, the computer will say:

```
The current time is: 13:45:02.71
```

Afterwards, the computer says:

```
Enter the new time:
```

Ignore that line: just press Enter.

Color

In the Command Prompt window, you normally see white characters on a black background. To change to different colors, use these color codes:

0 = black	8 = gray
1 = blue	9 = bright blue
2 = green	a = bright green
3 = aqua	b = bright aqua
4 = red	c = bright red
5 = purple	d = bright purple
6 = yellow	e = bright yellow
7 = white	f = bright white

For example, to make all the window's characters suddenly become blue (instead of white), type "color 1" after the C prompt, like this:

```
C:\>color 1
```

To make all the window's characters suddenly become bright green, type "color a", like this:

```
C:\>color a
```

To change the background as well as the characters, **type the background code then the character code**. For example, to make the background be blue (color 1) and the characters be bright green (color a), type "color 1a", like this:

```
C:\>color 1a
```

If you don't type the background code, the computer assumes you want the background to be black.

Have fun playing with different color combinations! Go wild! Amaze your friends!

To make the window return to normal (white characters on a black background), type "color 7", like this:

```
C:\>color 7
```

Title

If you got to the Command Prompt window by using the normal method (instead of a shortcut method), the Command Prompt window's top says "Command Prompt". That's the window's **title**.

You can change the title. For example, to make the title say "The Wonderful World of DOS", type "title The Wonderful World of DOS", like this:

```
C:\>title The Wonderful World of DOS
```

Directory (dir)

After the C prompt you can type "dir", like this:

```
C:\>dir
```

That "dir" command makes the computer show you a directory of the files that are stored on the hard disk.

The directory looks like this sample:

```
05/01/2010   05:53  PM    <DIR>        Intel
07/13/2009   10:20  PM    <DIR>        PerfLogs
11/06/2010   02:47  AM    <DIR>        Program Files
11/06/2010   02:47  AM    <DIR>        Program Files (x86)
05/22/2010   06:20  PM    <DIR>        SwSetup
05/01/2010   04:47  PM    <DIR>        Users
11/12/2010   07:33  PM    <DIR>        Windows
```

That's how the directory looks on my computer that has Windows 7. On *your* computer, the directory might look slightly different, depending on what your hard disk contains and which version of Windows you're using.

In that sample directory, one line says:

```
11/12/2010   07:33  PM    <DIR>        Windows
```

Here's what that line means:

```
The hard disk has a file whose name is "Windows".
That file was last updated on November 12, 2010, at 7:33 PM.
That file is a folder (which has its own DIRectory).
```

In that sample directory, another line says:

```
11/06/2010   02:47  AM    <DIR>        Program Files
```

Here's what that line means:

```
The hard disk has a file whose name is "Program Files".
That file was last updated on November 6, 2010, at 2:47 AM.
That file is a folder (which has its own DIRectory).
```

Summary statistics Below the directory, the computer shows summary statistics:

```
             0 Files(s)
             7 Dir(s)   263,582,044,160 bytes free
```

That means:

```
The directory showed 7 folders (DIRs).
The directory showed no simple files (since it showed just folders).
On the directory's disk (which is disk C), over 263 billion bytes (263 gigabytes) are still unused.
```

Change the order The "dir" command shows the files in alphabetical order (from A to Z). To see the files in chronological order (from oldest to newest), say "dir /od" instead (which means "**dir**ectory **o**rdered by **d**ate"), like this:

```
C:\>dir /od
```

Change the time The "dir" command shows when each file was updated. To see when each file was originally created instead, say "dir /tc" (which means "**dir**ectory showing **t**ime **c**reated"), like this:

```
C:\>dir /tc
```

Hidden files A file can be marked "visible" or "hidden". The "dir" command shows just the files that are marked visible. To see *all* the files, even the ones that are marked "hidden", say "dir /a" instead (which means "**dir**ectory of **a**ll"), like this:

```
C:\>dir /a
```

For example, when I type that command on my Windows 7 computer, I see this:

```
05/01/2010  05:09 PM   <DIR>          $Recycle.Bin
08/15/2009  04:40 AM   <DIR>          boot
07/13/2009  08:38 PM        383,562   bootmgr
07/14/2009  12:08 AM   <JUNCTION>     Documents and Settings [C:\Users]
11/22/2010  08:30 PM    3,144,880,128 hiberfile.sys
10/15/2009  03:52 AM   <DIR>          HP
05/01/2010  05:53 PM   <DIR>          Intel
10/25/2010  11:56 PM   <DIR>          MSOCache
11/22/2010  08:30 PM    4,193,177,600 pagefile.sys
07/13/2009  10:20 PM   <DIR>          PerfLogs
11/06/2010  02:47 AM   <DIR>          Program Files
11/06/2010  02:47 AM   <DIR>          Program Files (x86)
11/22/2010  08:30 PM   <DIR>          ProgramData
05/01/2010  04:49 PM   <DIR>          Recovery
05/22/2010  06:20 PM   <DIR>          SwSetup
11/22/2010  08:41 PM   <DIR>          System Volume Information
05/01/2010  04:49 PM   <DIR>          SYSTEM.SAV
05/01/2010  04:47 PM   <DIR>          Users
11/12/2010  07:33 PM   <DIR>          Windows
             3 Files(s) 7,338,441,290 bytes
            16 Dir(s)  263,582,044,160 bytes free
```

That shows the computer has 15 normal folders (DIRs), 1 special folder (a JUNCTION), and 3 simple files (bootmgr, hiberfile.sys, and pagefile.sys). The 3 simple files consume 7 gigabytes. Many of those items are hidden, so they're not mentioned if I type "dir" instead of "dir /a".

A file can be hidden in two ways: it can be **H hidden** or **S hidden**.

To see a list of all files that are H hidden, say "dir /ah".
To see a list of all files that are S hidden, say "dir /as".

Files that are S hidden are called **system files**. A file can be both H hidden and S hidden, to make double-sure beginners and evil people don't normally see it and don't try to manipulate it.

Read-only files Another way to protect a file is to make it **read-only**, which means it can't be edited or deleted. To see a list of files that are read-only, say "dir /ar".

What's a switch? A **switch** is a comment that begins with a **slash**. You've learned about these switches:

/od	/tc	/a	/ah	/as	/ar

To type the slash, make sure you press the **forward slash** key, which says "/" on it. Do *not* press the key that says "\", which is a **backslash**.

If you wish, you can put a blank space before the slash. The blank space is optional. For example, you can say either "dir /a" or "dir/a".

You can combine switches. For example, if you want the directory to show all files and also be in order of date, say "dir /a /od".

The computer doesn't care which switch you type first: typing "dir /a /od" does the same thing as typing "dir /od /a".

Fundamental file The fundamental file is this:

Version of Windows	Fundamental file's name	What the name means
Vista & 7	bootmgr	boot manager
XP	ntldr	new-technology loader

When you turn on the computer (by pressing its power button or reset button), the computer obeys the instructions in the fundamental file, which tells the computer how to begin. To prevent people from wrecking that file, it's H hidden and S hidden and read-only.

What else is on the hard disk Besides all the files mentioned by "dir /a", the hard disk also contains these 2 special items:

the **master boot record (MBR)** reminds the computer to look at the fundamental file
the **master file table (MFT)** tells the computer where to find each file on the hard disk

Since those 2 special items aren't called "files", they aren't mentioned when you type "dir /a".

What's NTFS? When a disk is organized by using the MFT, the disk is said to use the **New-Technology File System (NTFS)**. It's used by modern Windows (such as Windows NT, Windows 2000, Windows XP, Windows Vista, and Windows 7).

A less sophisticated file structure, called the **File Allocation Table (FAT)**, is used instead of MFT on:

earlier versions of Windows (such as Windows 95, Windows 98, and Windows Me)
earlier versions of DOS
smaller disks (such as floppy disks)
smaller storage devices (such as digital-camera memory cards).

Extensions Notice that a file's name (such as "pagefile.sys") can include a period then an **extension** of 3 characters (such as "sys"). The period separates the main part of the filename from the extension.

That period is called a **dot**. So if you're chatting with another computer expert about "pagefile.sys", pronounce it "pagefile dot sys".

Though the typical extension has 3 characters (such as "sys"), an extension can be longer (such as "docx") or shorter.

The computer can handle many different types of files. Each type has a different extension:

Extension	What the file contains
.exe	a program you can EXEcute
.txt	TeXT you can read easily (by using Notepad or a word processor)
.rtf	text in Rich Text Format (written by WordPad or copied by using Ctrl with C)
.doc	a DOCument written by an old version of Microsoft Word (which is a word processor)
.docx	a DOCument eXtended, written by a new version of Microsoft Word
.wps	a document created by the Microsoft Works Word-Processing System
.pdf	a document written by Adobe Acrobat (in Portable Document Format)
.hlp	messages that HeLP you learn how to use a program
.xls	an old Microsoft EXceL Spreadsheet (table of numbers)
.xlsx	a Microsoft EXcel Spreadsheet (table of numbers) in modern (eXtended) format
.ppt	a slideshow created by an old version of PowerPoinT
.pptx	a slideshow created by PowerPoinT in modern (eXtended) format
.pps	an old PowerPoint Slideshow, modified to be easy to view
.ppsx	a PowerPoint Slideshow, modern (eXtended), modified to be easy to view
.bmp	a picture stored as a BitMaP, created by an old version of Windows Paint
.png	a picture in Portable Network Graphics, created by a new version of Windows Paint
.jpg or .jpeg	a picture in the format invented by the Joint Photographic Experts Group
.wav	music soundWAVes
.mp3	music in the format invented by the Moving Picture Experts Group, version 3
.htm or .html	an Internet Web page, written in HyperText Markup Language
.dat	DATa that's used by a program
.tmp	TeMPorary data, which the computer will use and then erase
.ini	data to INItialize a program, so the program starts properly
.sys	data that's part of Windows (which is the operating SYStem)
.db	a DataBase (table of data)
.idx	an InDeX to help find data in a database
.log	a LOGbook (a record of the times when files were created or altered)
.dll	part of the Dynamic Link Library (which helps a program manipulate devices)
.zip	a file that's ZIPped up (compressed to consume less space on the hard disk)
.bak	a file's BAckup version, kept just in case the file's other versions have difficulties

Wildcards The symbol "*" is called an **asterisk** or a **star**. To type it, tap the 8 key while holding down the Shift key.

Try this experiment: type "dir p*". (That command is pronounced "dir pee star".) That makes the computer print an abridged directory, showing info about just the files whose names begin with p. For example, when I type that command on my Windows 7 computer, I see this:

```
07/13/2009  10:20 PM    <DIR>          PerfLogs
11/06/2010  02:47 AM    <DIR>          Program Files
11/06/2010  02:47 AM    <DIR>          Program Files (x86)
```

(I also see the summary statistics.)

The symbol "*" means "anything". That's why saying "dir p*" makes the computer show a directory of anything that begins with p.

To see *all* the p files (even the ones that are marked hidden), put "/a" at the end of the command, so the command becomes "dir p* /a".

To see a directory of files whose names begin with w, say "dir w*". When I type that command on my Windows 7 computer, I see this:

```
11/12/2010  07:33 PM    <DIR>          Windows
```

To see a directory of all files whose names end in ".sys", even the ones that are marked hidden, say "dir *.sys /a", like this:

```
C:\>dir *.sys /a
```

A symbol (such as "*") that "matches anything" is called a **wildcard**.

Notice that in the word "Windows", the second letter is "i". To see a directory of files whose second letter is "i", ask for all files that begin with "a character followed by i", like this "dir ?i*". The "?" means "a character". My computer will say:

```
11/12/2010  07:33 PM    <DIR>          Windows
```

The symbol "?" is a wildcard that matches one character. To match *two* characters, use "??". For example, to see a directory of files whose third character is n, say "dir ??n*". My computer will say:

```
11/12/2010  07:33 PM    <DIR>          Windows
```

What's in a folder? To find out what's in a folder, say "dir" then the folder's name. If the folder's name includes a space, put the folder's name in quotation marks.

For example, to find out what's in the Windows folder, say this:

```
C:\>dir Windows
```

The list of files in the Windows folder is called the **Windows directory**.

To find out what's in the Program Files folder, say this:

```
C:\>dir "Program Files"
```

You must put "Program Files" in quotation marks because "Program Files" contains a space. The list of files in the "Program Files" folder is called the **Program Files directory.** To see even the hidden files, put "/a" at the end of the command, like this:

```
C:\>dir "Program Files" /a
```

Saying just "dir" shows the list of files that are *not* in folders. That list is called the **main directory** (or **root directory**).

So to see the root directory, just type "dir" after the C prompt, like this:

```
C:\>dir
```

The other directories (such as the Windows directory and the Program Files directory) are called **subdirectories**.

DOS commands don't care about capitalization. So instead of typing "dir Windows", you can type "dir windows": you get the same result.

Window too short?

If the Command Prompt window isn't tall enough to show everything you want to see, try these tricks:

Trick 1 Make sure the Command Prompt window is maximized (by clicking the button that's next to the X button, once or twice).

Trick 2 When giving a "dir" command, put "/p" at the command's end, like this:

```
C:\>dir "Program Files" /p
```

That makes the computer **p**ause at the end of each screenful, wait for you to read the screenful, and wait for you to press the Enter key to continue.

Trick 3 Roll your mouse's scroll wheel away from you. That lets you see the writing that disappeared from the screen's top. When you've finished reading that writing, roll the mouse's scroll wheel toward you.

Trick 4 Below the Command Prompt window's X button, you see an up-arrow. Using the mouse, point at that arrow, then hold down the mouse's left button awhile. That lets you see the writing that disappeared from the screen's top. When you've finished reading that writing, point at the window's down-arrow (which is at the window's bottom-right corner) then hold down the mouse's left button awhile.

Trick 5 While you stare at the C prompt, try pressing the up-arrow key. That makes the computer retype for you the command you typed previously. If you do indeed want to give that command again, press Enter. If you prefer, edit the command before pressing Enter. If you want an earlier command instead, press the up-arrow key a few more times, until you find the command you want; then press Enter.

Change directory (cd)

Here's how to examine your folders more closely....

Windows folder You've learned that you can find out what's in the Windows folder by saying "dir windows" after the C prompt, like this:

```
C:\>dir Windows
```

Here's a better way to find out what's in the Windows folder....
Say "cd Windows". (The "cd" means "change directory".) That makes the computer think about the Windows folder. The computer changes the prompt to this:

```
C:\Windows>
```

That means the computer is thinking about drive C's Windows folder. If you type "dir" after that prompt, the computer will print a directory of the files in drive C's Windows folder; but since the directory is too long to fit on the screen, you can see it better by typing "dir /p" instead.

When you finish using the Windows folder, you should **return to the standard C prompt by saying "cd \"**. (Make sure you type a backslash \, not a forward slash /.) Then the computer will print a standard C prompt again:

```
C:\>
```

Program Files folder Here's the best way to explore what's in the Program Files folder.

First, make sure the screen shows a standard C prompt, like this:

```
C:\>
```

Then say "cd Program Files". That makes the computer think about the Program Files folder, so the computer changes the prompt to this:

```
C:\Program Files>
```

To find out what's in that Program Files folder, say "dir /p", which makes the computer show a directory of the files in the Program Files folder.

When you finish using the Program Files folder, return to the standard C prompt by saying "cd \". Then the computer will print a standard C prompt again:

```
C:\>
```

Users folder Windows Vista & 7 have a Users folder. (Windows XP has a "Documents and Settings" folder instead.) To see what's in that folder, make sure the screen shows a standard C prompt, then say this...

Windows version	What to say
Vista & 7	`cd Users`
XP	`cd Documents and Settings`

Then analyze what's in that folder, by saying "dir". When you finish analyzing that folder, return to the standard C prompt by saying "cd \".

Folders in folders A folder can contain folders. For example, try this experiment. Make sure the screen shows the standard C prompt: "C:\>". Then say "cd Windows". That makes the computer think about the Windows folder, so the computer changes the prompt to this:

```
C:\Windows>
```

Then find out what's in the Windows folder, by saying "dir /p", which makes the computer print a directory of the files in the Windows folder. You'll see one of the files in the Windows folder is another folder, called System32. Yes, System32 is a folder that's inside the Windows folder! (Windows XP doesn't capitalize the S.)

To find out what's in the System32 folder, say "cd system" after the prompt, so your screen looks like this:

```
C:\Windows>cd System32
```

That makes the computer think about the System32 folder inside the Windows folder, so the computer changes the prompt to this:

```
C:\Windows\System32>
```

Then if you say "dir", the computer will show a directory of the files in the Windows System32 folder. On most computers, the System32 folder contains over 2000 files! To see them **a**ll, and make the computer **p**ause after each screenful, say "dir /a /p".

Parents When a folder is inside another folder, the situation resembles a pregnant woman: the inner folder is called the **child**; the outer folder is called the **mommy** (or **parent**). For example, the System32 folder is the child of the Windows folder.

When you finish using the System32 folder, you have a choice. **If you say "cd ..", those two periods make computer return to the mommy folder** (Windows) and say:

```
C:\WINDOWS>
```

If instead you say "cd \", the backslash makes the computer return to the root directory and say:

```
C:\>
```

Saying "cd .." is therefore called "returning to mommy". Saying "cd \" is called "returning to your roots". Whenever you feel lost and scared, return to mommy or your roots!

Pointer files Socrates warned, "Know thyself." Freud warned, "Be prepared to tell me about your mother."

To obey their warnings, each folder contains a Socrates file and a Freud file. The Socrates file, called ".", reminds the folder of what files are in the folder. The Freud file, called "..", reminds the folder of who the folder's mother is, so the computer will know what to do when you type "cd ..".

That's why, when you're in the middle of a folder and say "dir", the first two files you see in the directory are called "." and "..". They're called **pointer files** because they point to the folder's inner self and mommy.

Short cut Suppose the computer says:

```
C:\Program Files>
```

That means the computer is thinking about the Program Files folder. To make the computer think about the Windows System32 folder instead, you can use two methods.

The normal method is to say "cd \" (which makes the computer leave the Program Files folder and return to the standard C prompt), then say "cd Windows", then say "cd System32".

The shorter method is to combine all those cd commands into this single command: "cd \Windows\System32". In that command, make sure you type all the backslashes.

Backslash versus forward slash Don't confuse the backslash (\) with a forward slash (/).

```
Type a backslash (\) when you're discussing folders,
such as "cd \Windows\System32".

Type a forward slash (/) when you're giving switches,
such as "dir /a /p".
```

Different drives

If your computer has a floppy-disk drive, that drive is called **drive A**.

If your computer has *two* floppy drives, the main floppy-disk drive is called **drive A**; the other floppy-disk drive is called **drive B**. In most such computers, drive A is on *top* of drive B or to the *left* of drive B.

The main part of your computer's main hard drive is called **drive C**. If your computer has more than one hard drive, or its hard drive is **partitioned** into several parts, or you have a CD-ROM drive or DVD drive or USB flash drive or your computer is wired to other computers on a computer network, those additional memory surfaces are called **drive D**, **drive E**, **drive F**, etc.

For example, your computer probably has a drive D (which is probably a partition of your hard drive and called "RECOVERY" and contains a backup copy of the files that came with your computer when you bought it).

To find out what's on drive D, type "dir d:". For example, if you type that after the standard C prompt, your screen looks like this:

```
C:\>dir d:
```

To type the colon ":", make sure you hold down the Shift key.

If you're lucky, the computer will reply by printing a directory that lists the files on drive D's disk.

If you're *unlucky*, the computer will give you one of these gripes:

```
Gripe:   The system cannot find the path specified.
Meaning: Your computer doesn't have a drive D.

Gripe:   The device is not ready.
Meaning: Drive D is supposed to hold a CD or DVD,
         but you haven't inserted the disk yet.

Gripe:   File not found
Meaning: The files on drive D are all marked as hidden,
         so to see them you must say "dir d: /a" instead.
```

Change drive To find out what's on drive D, you've learned to say "dir d:" or "dir d: /a", but now I'm going to show you a better way....

When the computer is waiting for you to type a DOS command, the computer normally shows this prompt:

```
C:\>
```

That's called the **standard C prompt**. It means the computer is thinking about the disk in drive C.

To change the prompt, so the computer will think about drive D instead of drive C, type "d:", so your screen looks like this:

```
C:\>d:
```

When you press Enter after the "d:", the computer changes the prompt to "D:", so you see this:

```
D:\>
```

That's called the **D prompt**. It means that the computer is thinking about drive D.

After the D prompt, try saying "dir", so your screen looks like this:

```
D:\>dir
```

Because of the A prompt, that "dir" makes the computer print a directory of drive D (instead of drive C). Better yet, to make sure you see *all* of drive D's files (even the files that are hidden), say "dir /a", so your screen looks like this:

```
D:\>dir /a
```

When you finish analyzing drive D and want to return to drive C again, make the computer return to a standard C prompt. Here's how. After the D prompt, type "c:", so your screen looks like this:

```
D:\>c:
```

When you press Enter at the end of that line, the computer will change the prompt back to this:

```
C:\>
```

The drive the computer thinks about is called the **current drive** (or **default drive**). If the computer says "C:\>", the default drive is C; if the computer says "D:\>", the default drive is D.

So to make D become the default drive, say "d:" (and press Enter). To make C become the default drive again, say "c:" (and press Enter).

Edit your disks

Here's how to edit the info on your disks.

Make directory (md)

Let's create a new folder on your hard disk.

First, get a standard C prompt, so your screen looks like this:

```
C:\>
```

Then invent a name for your folder. Pick a short name, such as Sarah or Tony or Junk or Poetry or Fiddling. (The name must not contain a slash or backslash. To keep things simple, the name should not contain a blank space.) Type "md" then the name.

For example, **to Make a Directory called Sarah, say "md Sarah"** after the C prompt, like this:

```
C:\>md Sarah
```

At the end of that line, press the Enter key. (If the computer says "A subdirectory or file sarah already exists", your disk *already* contained something called Sarah, and you must pick a different name instead.)

Then the computer will say "C:\>" again, so you can give another DOS command.

To prove the Sarah directory was created, say "dir Sarah". The computer will show that Sarah contains two files: Socrates (.) and Freud (..).

Go ahead! Create a folder named Sarah and other folders!

Cd Suppose you've created a Sarah folder. If you wish, you can go into the Sarah folder by saying "cd Sarah", which means "change directory to Sarah". That makes the computer say:

```
C:\Sarah>
```

Then if you say "dir", the computer will show you the Sarah directory's two files. To return to the root directory, say "cd \".

Copy

The Jewish religion prohibits Orthodox Jews from eating ham. That's why Mary had a little lamb:

```
Mary had a little lamb,
'Cause Jewish girls can't eat no ham.
If Mary were a Hindu now,
Mary couldn't eat no cow.
Religions all are fine and dandy,
Even my dentist's, which says "No candy!"
But Ma's religion makes me shiver.
That's why mine says "Ma, no liver!"
```

Copy from console To put that poem onto your hard disk and call it Mary, start by doing this:

Windows XP Type "copy con Mary" after the C prompt, like this:
```
C:\>copy con Mary
```

Windows Vista & 7 Your version of Windows prohibits you from putting your own file at "C:", so you must create a *folder* to hold the file. Create a folder (by saying "md Sarah") and go into it (by saying "cd Sarah"), as I explained in the previous section (called "Make directory"), so your computer says:
```
C:\Sarah>
```
After that prompt, type "copy con mary", like this:
```
C:\Sarah>copy con Mary
```

Underneath that typing, type the poem.

(If your hard disk *already* contains a file named Mary, the computer asks "Overwrite Mary?" after you type the first line. To reply, press the Y key then Enter, then go on to type the second line.)

If you don't like that poem, make up your own! If you're a slow typist, make up a poem that's shorter to type, or type just the first two lines.

Underneath your poem, press the F6 key then the Enter key. The computer will automatically copy your poem onto the hard disk and call it Mary.

To prove that your computer put the poem onto the disk, look at the hard disk's directory, by typing "dir". You'll see that one of the files in the directory is Mary.

Your computer's **console** consists of the keyboard and screen. Saying "copy con Mary" tells the computer that you want to copy from the console (keyboard and screen) to a disk file named Mary.

Copy to console Suppose your disk contains a file called Mary. To find out what's in Mary, say "copy Mary con". That makes the computer copy Mary from the disk to your console's screen. For example, if Mary was a poem, the poem will appear on your screen.

Filenames When you create a file, give it a short name, such as Mary or Lambchop. The name must not contain a slash or backslash.

At the end of the filename, you can put a period and an **extension**. For example, you can name a file "Lambchop.yum". In that example, the "Lambchop" is called the **filename**; the "yum" is called the **extension**.

To keep things simple, don't put a blank space in the name. For example, the name shouldn't be "Tasty lambchop.yum." If you *insist* on including a blank space, you must put the whole name in quotation marks every time you mention it, like this:

```
copy con "Tasty lambchop.yum"
```

Many ways to copy After you've created a simple file called Mary, here are many ways to copy it.

Goal	What to say
copy Mary to your screen	copy Mary con
copy Mary to drive D	copy Mary d:
copy Mary to the "Tony" folder	copy Mary \Tony
copy Mary to drive D's "Tony" folder	copy Mary d:\Tony
make a copy of Mary, and call the copy "Sue"	copy Mary Sue

To copy all simple files from the Sarah folder to the Tony folder, say:

```
copy \Sarah \Tony
```

To make an exact copy of *everything* in the Sarah folder and call it "Tony", say:

```
xcopy \Sarah \Tony /e/h/i/k
```

Here's why:

```
xcopy means "do extra-fancy copying"
/e means "copy even the folders inside Sarah, even the empty ones"
/h means "copy even the hidden files in Sarah"
/i means "don't inquire whether Tony is a folder"
/k means "if a file is read-only, make the copy be read-only also"
```

Type

Suppose you've put on your hard disk a file called Mary containing a poem, by typing "copy con Mary". To see the poem on your screen, you can tell the computer to copy Mary to the console's screen, by saying "copy Mary con". An even easier way to copy Mary to the screen is to say just "type Mary".

Text files Files created by "copy con" (or by the Windows Notepad program) contain words and numbers that you can read on the screen easily, by giving the "type" command. Those files are called **text files**. Other files are weirder; if you try to view them by giving the "type" command, you'll see strange symbols instead of just words and numbers.

Files ending in .txt or .log are always text files. Files ending in .exe are programs that are never text files.

If a text file uses just standard characters (no crazy symbols or hieroglyphics), it's called an **ASCII file**. ("ASCII" is pronounced "ass key" and stands for **American Standard Code for Information Interchange**.)

Rename (ren)

The computer understands the word "rename". For example, if a file is named Mary, you can change that file's name to Lambchop by saying "rename Mary Lambchop". If a folder is named Sarah, you can change that folder's name to Tony by saying "rename Sarah Tony".

Instead of typing the word "rename", you can type just "ren", like this: "ren Mary Lambchop".

Delete (del)

The abbreviation for the word "delete" is "del".

Deleting a simple file Suppose a simple file is named Mary. To delete that file from the disk, say "del Mary".

That command works just if Mary is in directory (folder) you've been looking at and is visible (not hidden).

Deleting a folder To delete a **folder** named Sarah, say "rd Sarah /s" (which means "remove directory Sarah & its subparts"). The computer will ask whether you're sure; press Y then Enter.

That command works just if Sarah is visible (it's mentioned when you say "dir") and you're not in the middle of using Sarah.

That command is powerful: it ruthlessly deletes the folder Sarah and everything in it, with no exceptions! It even deletes files marked read-only! It even deletes files marked hidden!

Attribute (attrib)

To protect your important files from being erased accidentally, give the "attrib" command. Here's how.

Read only To protect a file named Mary, you can say "attrib +r Mary". That prevents Mary from being changed accidentally.

For example, if somebody tries to delete Mary by saying "del Mary", the computer will refuse and say:

```
Access is denied.
```

If somebody tries to delete many files by saying "del *", the computer will delete *most* files but not Mary.

If somebody tries to create a new Mary and obliterate the old one (by saying "copy con mary", then typing some lines, then pressing F6 and Enter), the computer will refuse and say "Access is denied."

If somebody tries to find out what Mary is (by saying "dir Mary" or "type Mary" or "copy Mary con") or rename Mary (by saying "rename Mary Lambchop"), the computer *will* obey. The computer will let people *read* Mary *but not destroy* what's in Mary. That's because **saying "attrib +r mary" means, "give Mary the following ATTRIBute: Read only!"**

Mary will remain read-only forever — or until you cancel the "attribute read-only". **To cancel, say "attrib -r mary".** In that command, the "-r" means "take away the read-only attribute", so that Mary is *not* read-only and can be edited.

Hide For a different way to protect Mary, **say "attrib +h mary". That "h" hides Mary, so MARY won't be mentioned when you type "dir".**

After you've hidden Mary, it won't be affected by "del", "rename" or "copy". If you try to wreck Mary by copying another file to it, the computer will say "Access is denied". If you try to change Mary's attributes by saying "attrib +r mary" or "attrib -r mary", the computer will refuse and say "Not resetting hidden file".

Although Mary is hidden and isn't mentioned when you say "dir", the computer will let you access that file if you're somehow in on the secret and know that the file exists and is called "Mary". For example, the computer *will* let you look at the file by saying "type Mary".

If Mary is hidden, **you can "unhide" MARY (and make MARY visible again) by saying "attrib -h mary".**

System For an alternate way to hide Mary, say "attrib +s Mary". That turns Mary into a **system file**, which is S hidden.

For the ultimate in hiding, say "attrib +h +s Mary". That makes Mary be H hidden and also S hidden. Then if somebody tries to unhide Mary by saying "attrib -h Mary", Mary will still be hidden by the +s.

To undo the +s, say "attrib -s Mary".

Normal After playing with Mary's attributes, you can make Mary be normal again by saying "attrib -r -h -s Mary". That makes Mary be *not* read-only, *not* hidden, and *not* a system file.

Examine the attributes To examine Mary's attributes, say "attrib Mary". The computer will say "Mary" and show some letters to the left of "Mary". For example, if it shows the letters R, H, and S, it means Mary is read-only, hidden, and system. If it prints just the letters R and H, it means Mary is read-only and hidden but not system. (It might also print the letter A, which means "archive". Most files are archive.)

Batch files

You can invent your own command — if you define it to stand for a list of other commands.

For example, let's invent a command called "status" that makes the computer display a directory and also remind you of which Windows version you're using. To invent that "status" command, just create a file called "status.bat", which contains two lines, "dir" and "ver". Here's how.

Windows XP Type this —

```
C:\>copy con status.bat
dir
ver
```

then press the F6 key and then the Enter key.

Afterwards, whenever you type the word "status", like this —

```
C:\>status
```

the computer will look at the file "status.bat" and obey the commands you stored there: the computer will automatically do "dir" then "ver".

Windows Vista & 7 Create a folder called "Sarah" and go into it, so you see:

```
C:\Sarah>
```

Type this —

```
C:\Sarah>copy con status.bat
dir
ver
```

then press the F6 key and then the Enter key.

Afterwards, whenever you type the word "status", like this —

```
C:\Sarah>status
```

the computer will look at the file "status.bat" and obey the commands you stored there: the computer will automatically do "dir" then "ver".

What's a batch file? A file that's a list of commands is called a **batch file**. The file "status.bat" is a batch file, because it's a list of two commands ("dir" and "ver"). The name of every batch file must end in ".bat", which stands for "batch".

Echo

While the computer performs a batch file, the computer prints little messages reminding you of what it's doing. For example, while the computer performs the "ver" command in "status.bat", the computer prints the word "ver" on your screen. Each such message is called an **echo**.

If you don't want to see such messages, say "@echo off" at the beginning of your batch file, like this:

```
A>copy con status.bat
@echo off
dir
ver
```

To type the symbol "@", tap the 2 key while holding down the Shift key. (If you forget to type that symbol, the words "echo off" will remain on the screen while the batch file runs.)

Let's define "chick", so that if you say "chick" the computer will recite this chicken riddle:

```
Why did the chicken cross the road?
To escape from Colonel Sanders!
```

To define "chick", type "copy con chick.bat" at the prompt, like this:

```
Windows XP:           C:\>copy con chick.bat
Windows Vista & 7: C:\Sarah>copy con chick.bat
```

Then type the batch file:

```
@echo off
echo Why did the chicken cross the road?
echo To escape from Colonel Sanders!
```

Then press F6 and Enter. The "@echo off" prevents the computer from printing distracting messages; the bottom two lines make the computer print the poem when you say "chick".

Clear screen (cls)

Another command you can put at the beginning of your batch file is "cls". That makes the computer begin by erasing the screen, so you don't see any distractions.

Put "cls" just under "@echo off". Here's what the batch file looks like now:

```
C:\>copy con status.bat
@echo off
cls
echo Why did the chicken cross the road?
echo To escape from Colonel Sanders!
```

Replaceable parameter (%1)

Let's define "greet" so that if you say "greet Peter" the computer will say —

```
Hello, Peter the Great!
I like you, Peter!
```

and if you say "greet Suzie" the computer will say —

```
Hello, Suzy the Great!
I like you, Suzy!
```

And if you say "greet Godzilla" the computer will say —

```
Hello, Godzilla the Great!
I like you, Godzilla!
```

To define "greet" that way, type "copy con greet.bat" at the prompt, then type this batch file:

```
@echo off
echo Hello, %1 the Great!
echo I like you, %1!
```

Then press F6 and Enter. Make sure you type the "%1" in that batch file.

Afterwards, when you say "greet Peter" or "greet Suzie" or "greet Godzilla", the computer will print a greeting to Peter or Suzie or Godzilla, by automatically substituting the person's name for "%1". Try it!

Help

If you type the word "help", the computer will show you a list of DOS commands.

To find out more about a command, type "help" and the command's name. For example, to find out more about "dir", type "help dir" (or "dir /?").

For other DOS commands and more about older versions of DOS, get an older edition of this book by phoning me at 603-666-6644.

For even more help, phone me anytime at 603-666-6644 to chat, free.

Word processing

A **word-processing program** helps you write and edit sentences and paragraphs. What you're writing and editing (such as a business letter, report, magazine article, or book) is called the **document**.

> A word-processing program's main purpose is to manipulate *paragraphs*.
> To manipulate drawings, get a **graphics program** instead.
> To manipulate a table of numbers, get a **spreadsheet program**.
> To manipulate a list of names (such as customers), get a **database program**.

To use a word-processing program, put your fingers on the keyboard, then type the paragraphs that make up your document, so they appear on the screen. Edit them by pressing special keys on the keyboard. Finally, make the computer send the document to the printer, so the document appears on paper. You can also make the computer copy the document onto a disk, which will store the document for many years.

How word processing began

Back in the 1950's, 1960's, and 1970's, computers were used mainly to manipulate lists of numbers, names, and addresses. Those manipulations were called **data processing (DP)**, so the typical computing center was called a **data-processing center (DP center)**, run by a team of programmers and administrators called the **data-processing department (DP department)**.

Those old computer systems were expensive, unreliable, and complex. They were run by big staffs that did continuous repairs, reprogramming, and supervision. They were bureaucratic & technological nightmares. The term "data-processing" got a bad reputation. Secretaries who wanted to write and edit reports preferred to use simple typewriters rather than deal with the dreaded "data-processing department".

When easy-to-use word-processing programs were finally invented for computers, secretaries were afraid to try them because computers had developed a scary reputation. The last thing a secretary wanted was a desktop computer, which the secretary figured would mean "desktop trouble".

That's why the term "**word processing**" was invented. Wang, IBM, and other manufacturers told the secretaries, "The machines we'll put on your desks are *not* dreadful computers but rather souped-up typewriters. You like typewriters, right? Then you'll love these cute little machines too!. We call them **word processors**. Don't worry: they're not data-processing equipment; they're not computers."

The manufacturers were lying: their desktop machines *were* computers. To pretend they weren't computers, the manufacturers called them **word processors** and omitted any software dealing with numbers or lists. The trick worked: secretaries acquired word processors, especially the **Wang Word Processor** and the **IBM Displaywriter**. Today's secretaries are unafraid of computers, understand Windows and Macs, and run word-processing programs on them.

3 definitions of "word processor"

A "word processor" is supposed to be "a computer whose main purpose is to do word processing". But some folks use the term "word processor" to mean "a word-processing program" or "a typist doing word processing".

In ads, a "$300 word processor" is a machine; a "$100 word processor" is a program you feed a computer; a "$12-per-hour word processor" is a typist who understands word processing.

Word-processing programs

During the early 1980's, these word-processing programs were popular:

> **Electric Pencil** (the first word-processing program for microcomputers), **Wordstar** (which was more powerful), **Multimate** (the first program that made the IBM PC imitate a Wang word-processing machine), **Displaywrite** (which made the IBM PC imitate an IBM Displaywriter word-processing machine), **PC-Write** (shareware you could try for free before sending a donation to the author), and **Xywrite** (which ran faster than any other word processor)

But by 1991, most users had switched to **WordPerfect 5.1**, which ran on the IBM PC (and several other computers) and could perform many fancy tricks.

All those word-processing programs were awkward to learn and use. Beginners preferred these simpler word-processing programs:

> **PFS Write** (for the IBM PC), **IBM Writing Assistant** (which was a modified version of PFS Write), **Q&A** (which also included a database program), **Bank Street Writer** (for the Apple 2), and **Mac Write** (which was invented by Apple for the Mac and sometimes given away free)

But those word-processing programs couldn't perform as many tricks as WordPerfect 5.1, which remained the business standard that secretaries were required to learn and use.

In 1992, Microsoft invented **Windows 3.1** (the first version of Windows good enough to become popular). Companies and consumers began switching from DOS to Windows and wanted a good word-processing program for Windows. Unfortunately, WordPerfect 5.1 used DOS, not Windows. Windows 3.1 included a word-processing program called **Write**, but it was stripped down.

The first *good* word-processing programs for Windows were **Ami** (which is the French word for "friend") and an improved version (**Ami Pro**), both published by a company called **Samna**, which got bought by **Lotus**, which got bought by **IBM**, which eventually changed the name to **Word Pro**.

Microsoft invented a word-processing program called **Microsoft Word**. The DOS version of it was terribly awkward, but the Mac and Windows versions of it improved and eventually became even better than Ami Pro and Word Pro. A good Windows version of **WordPerfect** became available but too late: by then companies had already decided to switch to the Windows version of Microsoft Word.

What to buy

The best word-processing program is **Microsoft Word**, which is part of **Microsoft Office** (for Windows & the Mac).

To pay less, get **Microsoft Works** (which crudely imitates Microsoft Office for Windows) or **iWork** (which crudely imitates Microsoft Office for the Mac). To pay nothing, use **WordPad** (which is part of Windows 95&98&Me&XP&Vista&7) or **TextEdit** (which is part of Mac OS X) or **Open Office** (a free Internet download that imitates an outdated version of Microsoft Office).

Microsoft Word 2007 & 2010

Of all the word-processing programs ever invented, the fanciest and most popular is **Microsoft Word**. Versions of Microsoft Word have been invented for **DOS**, **Windows**, and the **Mac**.

If you're using a **DOS version** of Microsoft Word, it's primitive! Switch to a Windows version.

The **Mac versions** of Microsoft Word resemble the Windows versions. Here's the main difference: instead of pressing a Ctrl key, press the Mac's Command key (on which you'll see a squiggly cloverleaf — and also see an apple if your keyboard is modern).

Microsoft Word for Windows is nicknamed **Winword**. It's gone through several versions:

Version 1	was invented in 1989 for Windows 2.
Version 1.1	was invented in 1990 for Windows 2.
Version 2	was invented in 1991 for Windows 3.
Version 6	was invented in 1994 for Windows 3.1. (There was no Winword version 3, 4, or 5.)
Version 7	was invented in 1995 for Windows 95.
Version 97	was invented in 1997 for Windows 95. It's also called **version 8**.
Version 2000	was invented in 1999 for Windows 98. It's also called **version 9**.
Version 2002	was invented in 2001 for Windows Me. It's also called **version 10** and **version XP**.
Version 2003	was invented in 2003 for Windows XP. It's also called **version 11**.
Version 2007	was invented in 2006 for Windows Vista. It's also called **version 12**.
Version 2010	was invented in 2010 for Windows 7. It's also called **version 14**.

This chapter explains how to use versions 2007 and 2010. If you're using version 2002 or 2003, read the next chapter instead. If you're using version 6, 7, 97, or 2000, read the 28th edition instead, which you can get by phoning me at 603-666-6644. If you're using version 1, 1.1, or 2, switch to a newer version.

Fun

Here's how to enjoy using Microsoft Word.

Prepare yourself

Before starting Microsoft Word, **read and practice my Windows chapter, especially the section about "WordPad"**, which is a stripped-down simplified version of Microsoft Word.

Install

Here's how to put Microsoft Word onto your computer.

Version 2010 Microsoft Word 2010 in intended to be used with Windows 7 but will also run on Windows XP & Vista (which are older). I'll assume you have Windows 7. (The procedures for Windows XP & Vista are similar.)

Microsoft Word 2010 is part of Microsoft Office 2010, which you can get in many ways. For example, here's how to copy a 60-day-trial version of Microsoft Office Professional 2010 from the Internet to your hard disk, free:

Using your Web browser (such as Internet Explorer), go to office.microsoft.com. Click "Download a trial".

Scroll down until you see the "Try it now button" that's under "Office Professional 2010". Click that button.

If you already got a Windows Live ID (by signing up for Windows Live Mail or other Windows Live software), click in the Password box and type your Windows Live ID, then click the "Sign in" button. (If you *don't* have a Windows Live ID yet, click the "Sign up for New Account" button instead, then come back to this process.)

Click in the "First name" box. Type your first name (such as "Russ"). Press the Tab key. Type your last name (such as "Walter").

Click the Country/Region box's down arrow then your country (such as "United States") then "Continue Checkout".

The computer will tell you a Product Key (a secret code consisting of 25 characters, plus dashes). Scribble it onto a sheet of paper.

Click "DOWNLOAD NOW".

If the computer asks "Do you want to run or save this file?" click "Run".

If the computer asks "Do you want to allow the following program to make changes to this computer?" click "Yes".

The computer says "Enter your Product Key". Click in the box. Type the Product Key there, then press Enter.

Click "I accept the terms of this agreement" then "Continue". Press Enter.

Click "Close". Close all Windows, so you can start fresh.

Version 2007 Microsoft Word 2007 is intended to be used with Windows Vista (which was invented at the same time) but will also run on Windows XP (which is older) and Windows 7 (which is newer).

I'll assume you have Windows Vista. (The procedures for Windows 7 & XP are similar.)

Microsoft Word 2007 is part of Microsoft Office 2007, which usually comes on a DVD disk that you (or your computer store) must copy to your hard disk, by doing this:

Turn on the computer without any floppy or CD-ROM or DVD disks in the drives, so the computer runs Windows Vista and the computer's bottom-left corner shows the Start button.

Into the DVD drive, put the Microsoft Office disk (which is a DVD).

If the computer says "AutoPlay", click "Run SETUP.EXE". If the computer says "A program needs your permission to continue", click the Continue button.

The disk comes in a rectangular jacket whose backside sports a "Product Key" code, which contains 25 letters and digits (separated by dashes). Type the 25 letters and digits; automatically, the computer will capitalize the letters and insert the dashes. When you type the last letter or digit, the computer will pause before showing it on the screen; if you typed it correctly, the computer will show it with a check mark, which means you typed it correctly.

Press Enter. Click "I accept the terms of this agreement". Press Enter twice.

The computer will say "Microsoft Office 2007 has been successfully installed." Click the blue Close button. Remove the DVD from the drive.

If your computer came with a free trial version of Microsoft Office Home & Student edition, install it by doing this:

> Make sure you're connected to the Internet.
> Double-click the "Microsoft Office — 60 Day Trial" icon (which says "Microsoft Office —…").
> Click "Step 1". A 25-character code (including letters and numbers) will appear in the OEM Key box. Write it on a sheet of paper.
> Click "Step 2". Type your full name (such as "Russell Mark Walter"). Press the Tab key. Type your initials (such as "RMW") and press Enter. Type your 25-character code. When you've typed it correctly, a green check mark will appear next to it. Press Enter, three times. Click "Accept". Press Enter.

Starting

To start using Microsoft Word 2007 or 2010, click the Start button (at the screen's bottom-left corner).

If you see "Microsoft Office Word 2007" or "Microsoft Word 2010", click it. (Otherwise, click "All Programs" then "Microsoft Office" then "Microsoft Office Word 2007" or "Microsoft Word 2010".)

Hassles

If the computer says "This copy has expired", here's what happens:

> You've been using a free trial version, which has expired. To continue using Microsoft Word to edit your writing, buy a Product Key Card for Microsoft Word (or Microsoft Office) from your local store (or mail-order) then do the following….
> Click "Upgrade" then "Enter Product Key". Type the 25-character product key (which is on the orange sticker you bought); the computer will type the hyphens for you automatically.
> The computer will say "Please wait". After that message disappears, press Enter twice.
> The computer will say "Installing". After that message disappears, close the Microsoft Word window (by clicking its X), then start Microsoft Word again.

If the computer says "Activation Wizard", do this:

> Make sure you're connected to the Internet. Press Enter twice.
> If the computer says "You must restart", close the Microsoft Word window (by clicking its X) then start Microsoft Word again.
> If you see 3 boxes to check, do the following…. Put check marks in all 3 boxes (by clicking). Press Enter. Click "Download and install updates from Microsoft Update when available", Press Enter. Click the Continue button.

If the computer says "Help Protect and Improve Microsoft Office", click the circle under "Use Recommended Settings" and press Enter.

If the computer asks "Do you want to allow the following program to make changes to this computer?" click "Yes".

See the Microsoft Word screen

The screen's top says "Document1 — Microsoft Word". You also see this **tab bar**:

File	Home	Insert	Page Layout	References	Mailings	Review	View

(Version 2007 lacks "File".)

Type your document

Start typing your document.

Microsoft Word typically uses the keyboard the same way as WordPad. For details, **read these sections on pages 81-82**:

> "Use the keyboard"
> "Scroll arrows"
> "Insert characters"
> "Split a paragraph"
> "Combine paragraphs"
> "Movement keys"

Here are differences….

Enter key Microsoft Word automatically leaves a slight gap between the paragraphs, to separate them.

Ctrl symbols Microsoft Word understands more Ctrl symbols than WordPad. Here's what Microsoft Word understands:

Symbol	How to type it
©	While pressing the Ctrl and Alt keys, type the letter "c".
®	While pressing the Ctrl and Alt keys, type the letter "r".
™	While pressing the Ctrl and Alt keys, type the letter "t".
€	While pressing the Ctrl and Alt keys, type the letter "e".
…	While pressing the Ctrl and Alt keys, type ".".
¿	While pressing Ctrl and Alt (and Shift), type "?".
¡	While pressing Ctrl and Alt (and Shift), type "!".
ç	While pressing Ctrl, tap the "," key. Then type the letter "c".
¢	While pressing Ctrl, tap the "/" key. Then type the letter "c".
ø	While pressing Ctrl, tap the "/" key. Then type the letter "o".
ñ	While pressing Ctrl (and Shift), type "~". Then type "n".
ô	While pressing Ctrl (and Shift), type "^". Then type "o".
ü	While pressing Ctrl (and Shift), type ":". Then type "u".
å	While pressing Ctrl (and Shift), type "@". Then type "a".
æ	While pressing Ctrl (and Shift), type "&". Then type "a".
œ	While pressing Ctrl (and Shift), type "&". Then type "o".
ß	While pressing Ctrl (and Shift), type "&". Then type "s".
è	While pressing Ctrl, type the symbol `. Then type "e".
é	While pressing Ctrl, type the symbol '. Then type "e".
ð	While pressing Ctrl, type the symbol '. Then type "d".
«	While pressing Ctrl, type the symbol `. Then while Shifting, type "<".
»	While pressing Ctrl, type the symbol `. Then while Shifting, type ">".

Movement keys Microsoft Word differs from WordPad in this way:

> Ctrl with Page Down makes the pointer move down to the next page.
> Ctrl with Page Up makes the pointer move up to the previous page's beginning.

Automatic editing

The computer will automatically edit what you type.

AutoCorrect While you type, **the computer will automatically make little corrections to your typing**. For example:

If you type "teh" or "hte", the computer will change your typing to "the".
If you type "loove", the computer will change your typing to "love".

If you type a day (such as "sunday"), the computer will capitalize it.
If you capitalize the first *two* letters of a word, the computer will make the second letter small.
The computer will capitalize each sentence's first word.

The computer will change (r) to ®, change (c) to ©, and change (tm) to ™.
The computer will change (e) to € (just in version 2010).
The computer will change 2nd to 2nd, change 3rd to 3rd, change 4th to 4th, etc.
The computer will change 1/2 to ½, change 1/4 to ¼, and change 3/4 to ¾.
The computer will change -- to –, change --> to →, and change <-- to ←.
The computer will change ==> to ➔, change <== to ←., and change <=> to ⇔.
The computer will change :) to ☺, change :(to ☹, and change :| to ☺.

If you type a phrase in quotation marks ("like this"), the quotation marks will become curly ("like this").
If you type three periods (...), the periods will move farther apart (…).

If you type the first four letters of a month (such as "sept") or day (such as "wedn") and then press Enter, the computer will finish typing the word and capitalize its first letter.

If you type the current month and then press the Space bar and Enter, the computer will type the current date and year.

Some of those corrections happen immediately; others are delayed until you finish typing a word (and press the Space bar or a period).

The computer's ability to make those corrections is called **AutoCorrect**.

If you dislike a correction that the computer made to your typing, here's how to undo the correction:

Method 1: click the **Undo button**. (It's a blue curved arrow pointing to the left. It's at the screen's top. In version 2007, it's above the word "Home"; in version 2010, it's above the words "File" and "Home".)

Method 2: while holding down the Ctrl key, tap the Z key.

Those methods work just if done *immediately*, before you do any other typing or editing.

Red squiggles While you type, the computer automatically puts a **red squiggle under any word that looks strange**. The computer considers a word to look "strange" if the word's not in the computer's dictionary or if the word's the same as the word before. For example, if you type "For a sentury, I love you you", the computer will put a red squiggle under "sentury" and under the second "you".

If you see a red squiggle, you misspelled the word or accidentally repeated the word or forgot to put a space between words or your vocabulary is more advanced than the computer understands. So if you see a red squiggle, look carefully at the squiggled word to make sure it's really what you want.

If a word has a red squiggle under it, try right-clicking that word (by using the mouse's right-hand button). Then the computer will make suggestions about what the squiggled word should be.

For example, if you typed "sentury" and the computer put a red squiggle under it, right-clicking the "sentury" will make the computer display two suggestions ("century" and "sentry") and two other popular choices, so you see this list:

---

sentry
century

Ignore All
Add to Dictionary

Choose what you want:

If you meant "century" or "sentry", **click the word you meant**.

If you meant "sentury" and want to add that slang word to the computer's permanent dictionary (because the word means "a sentry who watches for a century"), click "**Add to Dictionary**". Warning: before clicking "Add to Dictionary", make sure the word "sentury" really exists and you've spelled it correctly and your colleagues give you permission to add slang to the dictionary!

If you meant "sentury" but don't want to add that slang word to the dictionary, click "**Ignore All**". The computer will ignore the issue about how "sentury" is spelled in this document; the computer will remove the red squiggle from every "sentury" in this document; but since "sentury" is still not in the dictionary, the computer will put red squiggles under any "sentury" in other documents.

If you're not sure what you meant, press the keyboard's **Escape key** (which says Esc on it). The list of choices will disappear; "sentury" will still be in your document and squiggled.

Green squiggles When you finish typing a sentence and start typing a new one, the computer automatically check the grammar of the sentence you just typed and puts a **green squiggle under any obvious grammar error**. For example, if you type "We is" instead of "We are", the computer will draw a green squiggle under the "is". (The computer will draw the squiggle when you finish typing that sentence and start typing the next one.) If you accidentally press the Space bar twice instead of once, so you type "They kiss" instead of "They kiss", the computer will put a green squiggle under "They kiss" (when you finish typing that sentence and start typing the next one).

If a word has a green squiggle under it, try right-clicking that word (by using the mouse's right-hand button). Then the computer will suggest what the squiggled word should be.

If you agree with the computer's suggestion, click that suggestion; the computer will fix what you wrote.

If you disagree with the computer's suggestion, click "Ignore Once". The computer will ignore the issue about that sentence's grammar and remove the green squiggle from that sentence.

If you're not sure why the computer is complaining, click "Grammar". The computer will tell you why it's complaining. (If you *still* don't understand why the computer's complaining, click "Explain" then read the explanation then close the Word Help window.) Then double-click the computer's suggestion, or click "Ignore Once" (to erase the green squiggle from that sentence), or click "Ignore Rule" (to erase the green squiggle from that sentence and from all similar sentences in that document), or click "Cancel" (if you're not sure what you want).

Synonyms Suppose you've typed a word correctly (so it has no red or green squiggle) but wish you could think of a better word instead. Just right-click the word then click "Synonyms". The computer will show you **synonyms** (words that have similar meaning).

For example, if you type the word "girl" then right-click it then click "Synonyms", the computer will show you these words, which have similar meaning:

Version 2007	Version 2010
young woman	lassie
lass	teenager
schoolgirl	teen-ager
daughter	miss
youngster	adolescent
child	mademoiselle
teenager	lass
	daughter

If one of those words appeals to you, click it: that word will replace "girl" in your document. If none of those words appeals to you, press the **Escape key** (which says "Esc" on it) *twice*.

What about the word "hot"? It has 4 popular meanings: "high temperature", "miserably warm and humid weather", "spicy food", and "excited person". Try typing the word "hot" then right-click it. The computer will start by showing you these synonyms:

Version 2007	Version 2010
burning	warm
scorching	burning
boiling	scorching
blistering	boiling
sizzling	blistering
searing	sizzling
warm	searing
	broiling

Version 2007 will also show you this **antonym** (word that has the opposite meaning):

cold (Antonym)

If one of those words appeals to you, click it. If none of those words appeals to you, try clicking "Thesaurus" (which appears under the synonym list and means "book of synonyms"): that makes the screen's right edge show you the **Research window**, where you see this longer list of "hot" synonyms and antonyms, grouped into 4 categories:

warm
warm, burning, scorching, boiling, blistering, sizzling, searing, broiling, fiery, heated, scalding
cold (Antonym)
sweltering
sweltering, stifling, muggy, sultry, boiling, scorching, oppressive, broiling
fresh (Antonym)
spicy
spicy, peppery, piquant, pungent, fiery, strong, red-hot
mild (Antonym)
passionate
fierce, vehement, emotional, strong, intense, excitable, angry, ardent, fervent, stormy, torrid
dispassionate (Antonym)
mild (Antonym)

(Version 2007 lacks some of those choices.) If you click one of those words, the computer will show you *that* word's synonyms. If you finally find a word you like, point at it *without pressing the mouse's button*, then click the word's down-arrow then "Insert": that makes the word replace "hot" in your document. When you no longer need the Research window, close it (by clicking its X).

Translate The computer can translate words among 22 languages: English, Spanish, French, Chinese, and others!

This method translates your entire document immediately to 21 languages but requires you to first connect to the Internet.

While connected to the Internet and using Microsoft Word, right-click anywhere in your document. For version 2010, click "Translate"; for version 2007, click "Translate" then "Translate…".
At the screen's right edge, in the Research window, click the From box's down-arrow then the language you want to translate from, such as "English"; click the To box's down-arrow then the language you want to translate to, such as "Spanish". (Each box gives you these choices: Arabic, Chinese from the mainland's People's Republic of China, Chinese from Taiwan, Danish, Dutch, English, Finnish, French, German, Greek, Hebrew, Italian, Japanese, Korean, Norwegian, Polish, Portuguese, Russian, Spanish, Swedish, Thai, and Turkish.)
Afterwards, click the right-arrow below those boxes. Press Enter.
You'll see the translation. (The computer might make mistakes, especially if the document involves slang or complicated grammar; but you can have fun viewing the computer's attempt.) When you finish reading it, close its window (by clicking the X at the screen's top-right corner). When you finish using the Research window, close it also (by clicking its X).

Here's an easier method, but it translates just to Spanish or French, just from English, just occasional words, and works just in version 2007 (not version 2010):

Right-click anywhere in your document, then click "Translate" then either "Spanish" or "French".
Then point at any word in your document *without pressing the mouse's button*: that makes computer show you how to translate that word from English to the language you requested. You see an entry from a bilingual dictionary. The entry shows you several ways to translate the word and how to translate phrases & slang expressions containing that word. To translate other words, point at them *without pressing the mouse's button*.
When you tire of viewing translations, turn the feature off by doing this: right-click anywhere in your document, then click "Translate" then "Turn Off Translation ScreenTip".

Bottom corners

Look at the screen's bottom corners.

Page count The screen's bottom-left corner tells you which page of your document you're on and how many pages are in the entire document. For example, if it says —

> Page: 2 of 3

it means you're on page 2 of a 3-page document.

Here's how to hop to a different page:

> Click the word "Page". Type the number of the page you want to go to (and press Enter). Click the word "Close".

Word count To the right of the page count, you see the word count. For example, if it says —

> Words: 279

it means your document contains 279 words.

Here's how to find out more about your document's length:

> Click "Words". The computer will tell you how long your document is:
>
> how many pages
> how many words
> how many characters if you don't count blank spaces
> how many characters if you _do_ count blank spaces
> how many paragraphs
> how many lines
>
> When you finish looking at those statistics, press Enter.

Zoom slider Microsoft Word uses the zoom slider the same way as WordPad 7, which I explained on page 83.

Page arrows Near the screen's bottom right corner, you see this symbol:

If your document contains several pages, clicking that symbol makes the computer go back up and show you the **previous page**. For example, while you're looking at page 4, clicking that symbol makes the computer show you page 3.

Under that symbol, you see this symbol:

Clicking it makes the computer show you the **next page**. For example, while you're looking at page 3, clicking that symbol makes the computer show you page 4.

Page break

After you've finished typing a paragraph (and pressed Enter), try this experiment: while holding down the Ctrl key, press Enter again. That creates a **page break**: it makes the next paragraph be at the top of the next page.

If you change your mind, here's how to remove the page break:

> Click at the beginning of the paragraph you've put at the top of a page. Then press the Backspace key _twice_.

All delete

Here's how to delete the entire document, so you can start over:

> While holding down the Ctrl key, press the A key. That means "all". All of the document turns blue.
>
> Then press the Delete key. All of the document disappears, so you can start over!

Quick Access Toolbar

At the screen's top-left corner, you see a gray bar (called the **Quick Access Toolbar**), which contains these **icons** (little pictures) called **buttons**:

> The **Save button** is a purple-and-white square that's supposed to look like a floppy disk (though it also looks like a TV set).
>
> The **Undo button** is an arrow curving toward the left. The arrow is blue (unless you haven't typed anything yet).

If you point at a button (by moving your mouse's arrow there, without clicking), the computer will tell you the button's name.

Here's how to use those buttons....

Save button To save the document you've been typing (copy it onto the disk), click the **Save button**.

If you haven't saved the document before, the computer will say "File name". Invent a name for your document. Type the name and press Enter.

That makes the computer copy the document onto the hard disk. For example, if you named the document "mary", the computer puts a document called mary.docx into the Documents folder. (Windows 7 puts it into the Documents library's "My Documents" folder instead.) If you wish, you can prove it by doing this:

> Click Start then "Documents". If you called the document "mary", you'll see mary is one of the files in the Documents folder. If you right-click mary's icon then click "Properties", you'll see the type of file is ".docx". Finally, clear that proof off your screen (by clicking "OK" then the red X button).

Afterwards, if you change your mind and want to do more editing, go ahead! When you finish that extra editing, save it by clicking the Save button again.

Save often! If you're typing a long document, **click the Save button about every 10 minutes**. Click it whenever you get to a good stopping place and think, "What I've typed so far looks good!" Then if an accident happens, you'll lose at most 10 minutes of work, and you can return to the last version you felt good about.

Instead of clicking the Save button, you can use this shortcut: while holding down the Ctrl key, tap the S key (which stands for "Save").

Undo button If you make a mistake (such as accidentally deleting some text or accidentally inserting some useless text), click the **Undo button** (which is an arrow turning back). That makes the computer undo your last activity, so your text returns to the way it looked before you made your boo-boo. (To undo your last _two_ activities, click the Undo button _twice_.)

Instead of clicking the Undo button, you can use this shortcut: while holding down the Ctrl key, tap the Z key (which stands for "Zap").

Extra buttons If you click the Undo button, the computer might undo a different activity than you expected. For example, it might even erase everything you typed!

If clicking the Undo button accidentally makes the text look even worse instead of better, and you wish you hadn't clicked the Undo button, you can "undo the undo" by clicking the **Redo button** (which is next to the Undo button and shows a blue arrow curving to the right, so it bends forward).

The Redo button appears just after you click the Undo button. At other times, you see a **Repeat button** instead (which is an arrow making a circle). If you click the Repeat button, the computer repeats the last thing you typed.

Instead of clicking the Redo button or Repeat button, you can use this shortcut: while holding down the Ctrl key, tap the Y key (which stands for "Yes, I do want it, very much").

Your Quick Access Toolbar might include other buttons, too!

File-office button

At the screen's left edge, very close to the top, you see the **File-office button**. (In version 2010, it says "File". In version 2007, it's a circle with the Microsoft Office symbol inside it.)

Click it. Then you see the **File-office menu**:

Version 2007	Version 2010
New	Save
Open	Save As
Save	Open
Save As	Close
Print	Info
Prepare	Recent
Send	New
Publish	Print
Close	Save & Send
Word Options Exit Word	Help
	Options
	Exit

From that menu, choose whatever you wish (by clicking it). Here are the most popular choices....

Save

If you choose **Save** from the File-office menu (by clicking the word "Save" after clicking the File-office button), you get the same result as clicking the Save button that's on the Quick Access Toolbar.

Save As

Suppose you've already saved a document then edited it some more, but you're not sure you like the new editing. Try this experiment....

Choose **Save As** from the File-office menu (by clicking the phrase "Save As" after clicking the File-office button); when you do that, make sure you click the phrase "Save As", not any arrow next to it.

Then invent (and type) a new name for the document. At the end of the new name, press Enter.

The computer will copy the document's new, edited version onto the hard disk. That new, edited version will have the new name you invented.

The document's old original version will be on the disk also and keep its old original name. The disk will contain *both* versions of the document.

Print

Here's how to print the document onto paper. Make sure you've bought a printer, attached it to the computer, turned the printer's power on, and put paper into the printer. Then choose **Print** from the File-office menu (by clicking the word "Print" after clicking the File-office button); when you do that, make sure you click the word "Print", not any arrow next to it.

The computer assumes you want to print just 1 copy of the document. If you want to print *several* copies, do this:

Version 2007: type how many copies you want.
Version 2010: click in the "Copies" box, then type how many copies you want.

Press Enter. The computer will print the document onto paper.

How to finish

When you finish working on a document, choose **Exit** or **Close** from the File-office menu.

Exit If you choose **Exit**, the computer will stop using Microsoft Word. (Version 2007 says "Exit Word" instead of just "Exit".)

Close If you choose **Close** instead of Exit, the computer will let you work on another document, and your next step is to say "new document" or "old document". Here's how....

If you want to **start typing a new document**, choose **New** from the File-office menu then do this:

Version 2007: press Enter.
Version 2010: double-click the first "Blank document".

If you want to **use an old document**, do this:

Version 2010 Choose **Recent** from the File-office menu. You see a list of the 25 documents you used most recently: that list starts with the most recent.

Version 2007 Click the File-office button, so you see the File-office menu. To the right of the File-office menu you see a list of the 17 documents you used most recently: that list starts with the most recent.

From that list, click whichever document you want to use. If you want to use an older document (not on that list), do this:

Choose **Open** from the File-office menu (by clicking Open).

The computer starts showing you a list of *all* readable documents in the Documents folder (or Windows 7's Documents library), unless you've requested a different folder instead. If the list is too long to show completely, here's how to see the rest of the list: either "click in that list then rotate the mouse's wheel toward you" or "repeatedly click the down-arrow that's to the right of that list".

If you want to *use* one of those documents, *double*-click the document's name; the computer will put that document onto the screen and let you edit it. If instead you want to *delete* one of those documents, click the document's name then press the Delete key then the Enter key; the computer will move that document to the Recycle Bin.

Didn't save? If you didn't save your document before doing those "how to finish" procedures, the computer asks, "Do you want to save?" If you click the Save button (which version 2007 calls "Yes"), the computer copies your document's most recent version to the hard disk; if you click the Don't Save button instead (which version 2007 calls "No"), the computer ignores and forgets your most recent editing.

How to erase the recently-used list The list of recently-used documents might annoy you, for two reasons:

One of the documents might be embarrassing (because it's pornographic or a private letter), and you want to hide it from your colleagues and family.

Even after you've deleted a document, that document's name might still be on that list.

If the **document list annoys you**, delete documents from it, as follows....

The recently-used list shows just the names of *the last few* Microsoft Word documents you mentioned. Go use other Microsoft Word documents; they'll go onto recently-used list and bump off the older documents.

Another way to get a document off the recently-used list is to erase that entire list from the File-office menu. Here's how. From the File-office menu, choose **Options** (which version 2007 calls "Word Options"). Click "Advanced". Scroll down to the "Display" category. Double-click in the box labeled "Show this number of Recent Documents", type a zero, and press Enter. That erases the recently-used list from the File-office menu. Afterward, let the computer create a *new* recently-used document list in the Office menu, as follows. From the File-office menu, choose **Options** again. Click "Advanced". Scroll down to the "Display" category. Double-click in the box labeled "Show this number of Recent Documents". For version 2007, type 17; for version 2010, type 25. Press Enter.

Font group

To make sure your computer is acting normally, click the word "**Home**" (which is near the screen's top-left corner).

Then you see these 5 words: **Clipboard**, **Font**, **Paragraph**, **Styles**, **Editing**. Above each word, you see a **group** of icons. I'll explain how to use each group. Let's start with the **Font group**, which looks like this:

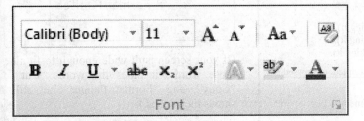

(Version 2007 lacks 🖌.)

Underline

Here's how to underline a phrase (like this).

Activate the **Underline button** (which says U on it) by clicking it. **Activating the button makes the button turn orange.** Then type the phrase you want underlined. Then deactivate the Underline button (by clicking it again).

Go ahead: try it now! Practice using the underline button before you progress to more advanced buttons!

Shortcut Instead of clicking the Underline button, you can use this shortcut: while holding down the Ctrl key, tap the U key.

Fancy underlines The computer assumes you want each underline to be a simple horizontal line. If you want the underline to be fancier (such as a double underline, a thick underline, a dotted underline, a dashed underline, or a wavy underline), do this instead of clicking the Underline button: click the Underline button's *down-arrow* then the kind of underline you want. The computer will remember which kind of underline is your favorite and automatically choose that kind for all future underlines — until you tell the computer otherwise or exit from Microsoft Word.

Advanced fonts

Microsoft Word handles advanced fonts the same way as WordPad 7. For details, **read these sections on pages 85-86:**

"Bold"
"Italic"
"Superscript"
"Subscript"
"Strikethrough"
"Font size"
"Font"

Font Color

Normally, the characters you type are black. Here's how to make them a different color, such as red.

Look at the **Font Color button**, which has an underlined A on it. Notice the color of the A's underline. If it's the color you want, click the underline. If it's *not* the color you want, do this instead:

Click the down-arrow that's to the right of the A's underline. You see 70 colors.

If you like one of those colors, click it.

If you *don't* like any of those colors, click "More Colors" then "Standard", which shows you 142 colors: *double*-click your favorite.

Afterwards, whatever characters you type will be in the color you chose. (The characters you typed earlier remain unaffected.)

When you finish typing in that color, here's how to return to typing characters that are normal (black): click the down-arrow that's to the right of the A's underline, then click "Automatic" (which means "normal").

Select text

Here's how to dramatically change a phrase you typed.

Point at the phrase's beginning, then drag to the phrase's end (while holding down the mouse's left button). The whole phrase turns blue. Turning the phrase blue is called **selecting the phrase**.

Then say what to do to the phrase. For example, choose one of these activities:

To underline the phrase, activate the Underline button (by clicking it).
To make the phrase be bold, activate the Bold button (by clicking it).
To italicize the phrase, activate the Italic button (by clicking it).
To make the phrase be tiny and raised, activate the Superscript button (by clicking it).
To make the phrase be tiny and lowered, activate the Subscript button (by clicking it).
To make the phrase look crossed out, activate the Strikethrough button (by clicking it).

To prevent the phrase from being underlined, bold, italicized, superscripted, subscripted, or crossed out, deactivate those buttons (by clicking them again).

To change the phrase's point size, choose the size you want from the Font Size menu.
To change the phrase's font, choose the font you want from the Font menu.

To make the phrase's characters be colored (instead of black), click the Font Color button's down-arrow then your favorite color.

To make the phrase's background be colored (such as yellow) as if you had a highlighting pen, find the **Text Highlight Color button** (which is in the Font group and shows "ab" with a highlighting pen): click that button's down-arrow then your favorite color.

Just in version 2010: to make the phrase's characters be outlined (LIKE THIS), click the **Text Effects button** (which is in the Font group and shows A); you see examples of 20 effects; click your favorite. Effect #20 (purple reflected) works just with capitals; if you choose that effect, the computer automatically capitalizes the phrase.

To change how the phrase is capitalized, click the **Change Case button** (which is in the Font group and shows "Aa▾") then click "UPPERCASE" (which capitalizes all letters) or "Capitalize Each Word" (which capitalizes just the first letter of each word) or "Sentence case" (which capitalizes just the first letter of each sentence) or "lowercase" (which uncapitalizes all letters) or "tOGGLE cCASE" (which capitalizes what was uncapitalized and uncapitalizes what was capitalized).

To cancel all the formatting you did to the phrase (so the phrase returns to being plain, unformatted 11-point Calibri), click the **Clear Formatting button** (which is in the Font group and shows "Aa" with an eraser).

To delete the phrase, press the **Delete key**.

To replace the phrase, just type whatever words you want the phrase to become.

Go ahead! Try it now! It's fun!

Advanced selection

Microsoft Word resembles WordPad 7, so **read these sections on page 87:**

"Other ways to select"
"Document vanishes"
"Drag a phrase"

Here are differences....

Other ways to select Microsoft Word permits this extra method:

Method 10: To select just **one sentence**, click in its middle while holding down the Ctrl key.

Drag a phase Microsoft Word's vertical line is black and dotted.

Clipboard group

The **Clipboard group** looks like this:

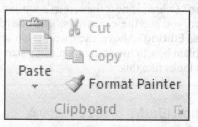

(If your screen isn't wide enough to fit all those words, it hides the words "Cut", "Copy", and "Format Painter" but still shows their icons.)

Clipboard fundamentals

Microsoft Word handles clipboard fundamentals the same way as WordPad 7. For details, **read these sections on page 87:**

"Cut and paste"
"Copy"

Format Painter

Suppose one part of your document looks pretty, and one part looks ugly. Here's how to make the ugly part look as pretty as the pretty part:

Drag across the pretty part, so you've selected it and it's turned blue. Click the **Format Painter button** (which is a paintbrush).

Then drag across the ugly part. The computer will make the ugly part look as pretty as the pretty part. For example, the ugly part will have the same font and font size as the pretty part; it will be underlined, boldfaced, and italicized the same way as the pretty part.

If you do the procedure incorrectly and wish you *hadn't* pressed the Format Painter button, just click the Undo button, which makes the document return to its previous appearance.

If one part of your document looks pretty, here's how to make *several* other parts look as pretty:

Drag across the pretty part, so you've selected it and it's turned blue. *Double*-click the Format Painter button.

Drag across the first ugly part; the computer will make it look pretty. Then drag across the second ugly part; the computer will make it look pretty. Drag across each additional ugly part; the computer will make each look pretty.

When all the ugly parts have turned pretty, deactivate the Format Painter button (by clicking it again or pressing the Esc key).

Paragraph group

The **Paragraph group** looks like this:

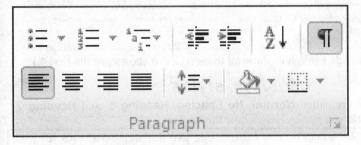

Alignment buttons

Microsoft Word handles alignment buttons the same way as WordPad 7. For details, **read "Alignment buttons" on page 88.**

Line Spacing

While typing a paragraph, you can click the **Line Spacing button** (which has an up-arrow and down-arrow on it), which makes this menu appear:

```
1.0
1.15
1.5
2.0
2.5
3.0
Line Spacing Options
Add Space Before Paragraph
Remove Space After Paragraph
```

Clicking "**2.0**" makes the paragraph be double-spaced (so there's a blank line under each line). Clicking "**3.0**" makes the paragraph be triple-spaced (so there are two blank lines under each line). Clicking "**1.0**" makes the paragraph be single-spaced (without extra space under the lines). Clicking "**1.15**" makes the paragraph have a little extra space between each pair of lines; that's what the computer assumes you want if you don't say otherwise.

The computer assumes you want a 10-point-high blank space under the paragraph, to separate that paragraph from the paragraph below. If you don't want that space, click "**Remove Space After Paragraph**".

If you click "**Add Space Before Paragraph**", the computer will put a 12-point-high blank space above the paragraph, to separate that paragraph from the paragraph above.

Indentation buttons

Before typing a paragraph, you can press the Tab key. That makes the computer indent the paragraph's first line, half an inch.

If you want to indent *all* lines in the paragraph, do this instead of pressing the Tab key: while typing the paragraph, click the **Increase Indent button** (which shows a right-arrow pointing at lines). That makes the computer indent *all* lines in the paragraph. (The paragraphs you typed earlier remain unaffected.)

When you start typing a new paragraph, the computer indents that paragraph if the paragraph above it was indented.

If you indented a paragraph by clicking the Increase Indent button but then change your mind, here's how to *un*indent the paragraph: click in the paragraph, then click the **Decrease Indent button** (which shows a left-arrow pointing from lines).

Example Suppose you start typing a new document. Here's how to make just paragraphs 3, 4, and 5 be indented.

Type paragraphs 1 and 2 normally (without pressing the Increase Indent button).

When you start typing paragraph 3, press the Increase Indent button. That makes the computer start indenting, so paragraphs 3, 4, and 5 will be automatically indented.

When you start typing paragraph 6, here's how to prevent the computer from indenting it: click the Decrease Indent button at the beginning of paragraph 6.

Changing your mind To indent a paragraph you typed earlier, click in the middle of that paragraph and then click the Increase Indent button. To *un*indent a paragraph you typed earlier, click in its middle and then click the *Decrease* Indent button.

Extra indentation If you click the Increase Indent button *twice* instead of just once, the computer will indent the paragraph farther. After typing that doubly indented paragraph, if you want the paragraph below to be unindented you must click the Decrease Indent button twice.

Each time you click the Increase Indent button, the computer indents the paragraph a half inch farther. Each time you click the Decrease Indent button, the computer indents the paragraph a half inch less.

Bullets Here's a different way to indent an entire paragraph: while typing the paragraph, activate the **Bullets button** (which is the first button in the Paragraph group) by clicking it. That makes the computer indent the paragraph and also put a **bullet** (the symbol •) to the left of the paragraph's first line. That's called a **bulleted paragraph**. The bullet symbol is indented a quarter inch; the paragraph's words are indented a half inch.

After you've typed a bulleted paragraph, any new paragraphs you type underneath will be bulleted also — until you request an *un*bulleted paragraph (by deactivating the Bullets button).

Numbering Here's another way to indent an entire paragraph: while typing the paragraph, activate the **Numbering button** (which has 1 and 2 and 3 on it) by clicking it. That makes the computer indent the paragraph and put "1." to the left of the paragraph's first line. That's called a **numbered paragraph**. The number is indented a quarter inch; the paragraph's words are indented a half in.

When you type a new paragraph underneath, that paragraph will be numbered "2.", the next paragraph will be numbered "3.", etc. Any new paragraphs you type underneath will be numbered also — until you request an *un*numbered paragraph (by deactivating the Numbering button).

Shading

Here's how to make a whole paragraph's background be **colored** (instead of white).

Click in the paragraph. Click the down-arrow of the **Shading button** (which looks like a paint bucket). Click one of the 70 colors (or click "More Colors" then "Standard" then double-click your favorite of the 142 colors).

Show/Hide ¶

The symbol for "Paragraph" is ¶, which looks like a backwards P.

One of the buttons has a ¶ on it. Microsoft calls it the **Show/Hide ¶ button**, but most folks call it just the **¶ button**.

If you activate that button (by clicking it), the screen will show a ¶ symbol at the end of each paragraph, so you can easily tell where each paragraph ends. The screen will also show a dot (·) wherever you pressed the Space bar and show a right-arrow (→) wherever you pressed the Tab key, so you easily tell how many times you pressed those keys.

For example, if you typed "I love you" correctly, the screen will show "I·love·you". If you see "I·love···you" instead, you know you accidentally pressed the Space bar three times after "love" instead of just once, so you should delete the two extra spaces (by moving there then pressing the Delete key twice).

When you finish examining the ¶ symbols and dots and right-arrows, and you're sure you've put just one space between each pair of words, here's how to make those special symbols vanish: deactivate the ¶ button (by clicking it again).

Sort

Here's how to alphabetize a list of names (or words or phrases).

Type each item on a separate line, like this:

```
Zelda
Al
Pedro
```

If the list is the whole document, click in the list. If the list is just *part* of the document, select the list by doing this:

```
Triple-click in the list's first line.
While holding down the Shift key, click in the list's last line.
```

Click the **Sort button** (which shows an A over a Z, with a down-arrow). Then press Enter.

That makes the computer alphabetize the lines, so the document looks like this:

```
Al
Pedro
Zelda
```

Border

After you've typed a paragraph, here's how to put a box around it:

```
Click in the paragraph. Click the "▾" at the Paragraph group's right edge. Click "All Borders".
```

If you change your mind, here's how to remove the box:

```
Click in the paragraph. Click the "▾" at the Paragraph group's right edge. Click "No Border".
```

Styles group

The **Styles group** looks like this:

(If your screen isn't wide enough to show all those styles, it shows just the first 4.)

Visible styles

The first 4 styles are called **Normal**, **No Spacing**, **Heading 1**, and **Heading 2**. Click whichever style you prefer. Here's how they differ:

Normal is good for typing a short business memo. It's the style that Microsoft assumes you want, unless you say otherwise. It uses 11-point Calibri (which resembles Arial and Tahoma), puts extra space between the lines (so the paragraph has 1.15 line spacing instead of single spacing), and puts a 10-point blank space below each paragraph.

No Spacing resembles Normal (it uses 11-point Calibri) but wastes less space: it puts no extra space between the lines (they're single spaced) and puts no blank space below each paragraph.

Heading 1 is good for typing a heading. It uses 14-point bold Cambria (which resembles Times New Roman), is dark blue (instead of black), puts a 24-point blank space above the heading, and makes the paragraph below the heading be Normal. If the paragraph below is too long to fit on the same page as the heading, the computer moves the heading and paragraph together to the next page, so the heading stays immediately above the paragraph.

Heading 2 resembles Heading 1 but is more modest: it's slightly smaller (13-point instead of 14-point), has somewhat less space above it (10 points instead of 24 points), and is a lighter shade of blue.

Table of styles

Those 4 styles are just the beginning of a table of styles. To see the whole table (which includes 16 styles), click the down-arrow that has a dash over it. Here's a quick summary of the most popular styles:

Style	Main features
Normal	11-point Calibri, 10-point space below paragraph
No Spacing	11-point Calibri
Heading 1	14-point blue Cambria, bold, 24-point space above paragraph
Heading 2	13-point blue Cambria, bold, 10-point space above paragraph
Title	26-point blue Cambria, underline, 15-point space below paragraph
Subtitle	12-point blue Cambria, italic
Subtle emphasis	italic, gray
Emphasis	italic
Intense Emphasis	italic, blue, bold
Strong	bold
Quote	11-point Calibri, italic, 10-point space below paragraph
Intense Quote	11-point blue Calibri, italic, underline, indent, 10-point space above paragraph, 14-point space below paragraph
Subtle Reference	smaller-font capitals, underline, red
Intense Reference	smaller-font capitals, underline, red, bold
Book Title	smaller-font capitals, bold
List Paragraph	11-point Calibri, indent, 10-point space below paragraphs group

If you click one of those 16 styles, the computer will choose it — and its row of the table will become the main row that you see on the screen (until you choose a different row instead by clicking the up-arrow or dashed down-arrow).

If you click Heading 2, the computer expands the table by including a Heading 3. If you click Heading 3, the computer expands the table by including a Heading 4. The computer can produce up to Heading 9. Here are the differences:

Style	Main features		
Heading 1	14-point blue Cambria,	bold,	24-point space above par.
Heading 2	13-point blue Cambria,	bold,	10-point space above par.
Heading 3	11-point blue Cambria,	bold,	10-point space above par.
Heading 4	11-point blue Cambria,	bold, ital.,	10-point space above par.
Heading 5	11-point blue Cambria,		10-point space above par.
Heading 6	11-point blue Cambria,	italic,	10-point space above par.
Heading 7	11-point Cambria,	italic,	10-point space above par.
Heading 8	10-point Cambria,		10-point space above par.
Heading 9	10-point Cambria,	italic,	10-point space above par.

Traditional fonts

Microsoft made Calibri the normal font for Microsoft Word because Calibri's easy to read even on a blurry screen. But to print on paper and high-quality screens, you should make the normal font be Times New Roman instead, which is the easiest font to read if you're not in a fog. Here's how to make that switch:

Click **Change Styles** then "Fonts" then "Office Classic".

That changes the normal (body) font from Calibri to Times New Roman — and changes all headings from Cambria to Arial — so Calibri and Cambria are eliminated from that document. (Other documents are unaffected.)

Traditional styles

Microsoft made "10-point gap below each paragraph" the normal style for Microsoft Word so people writing business letters, e-mails, and Websites wouldn't have to press the Enter key twice at the end of each paragraph. But publishers of books, newspapers, and magazines want a more traditional format where each paragraph's first line is indented and there's no extra space between paragraphs, since "extra space" means "wasted paper". Here's how to make that switch:

Click **Change Styles** then "Style Set" then "Traditional".

That switch affects the whole document. (Other documents are unaffected.)

If you're smart enough to make *both* of those changes (changing fonts to Office Classic and changing Style Set to Traditional), here's what the 16 styles become:

Style	Main features
Normal	11-point Times New Roman, indent first line
No Spacing	11-point Times New Roman
Heading 1	12-point blue Arial, underline, 30 pt. above, 4 pt. below, bold
Heading 2	12-point blue Arial, underline, 10 pt. above, 4 pt. below
Title	30-point blue Arial, green underline, blue overline, center
Subtitle	12-point Arial, italic, 10 pt. above, 45 pt. below, align right
Subtle emphasis	italic, gray
Emphasis	italic, gray, bold
Intense Emphasis	italic, blue, bold
Strong	bold
Quote	11-point Arial, italic, gray, indent first line
Intense Quote	12-point white-on-blue Arial, italic, green underline, indent all lines, 16 pt. above, 16 pt. below
Subtle Reference	Times New Roman, green underline
Intense Reference	green Times New Roman, underline
Book Title	Arial, italic, bold
List Paragraph	11-point Times N.R., indent all lines, indent first line farther

Invent your own style

Here's how to invent your own paragraph style:

In your document, create a paragraph whose appearance thrills you (by using the Font, Paragraph, and Styles groups). Right-click in the middle of the paragraph's first word. Click "Styles" then "Save Selection as a New Quick Style".

Invent a name for your style (such as "Wow"): type the name, and at the end of the name press the Enter.

The style you invented ("Wow") will appear in the Styles group as the 2nd style.

Go ahead and use it! For example, while you're typing another paragraph, you can make that paragraph's style be "Normal" or "Wow": just click the style you want.

The style you invented ("Wow") is part of the computer's repertoire just while you're using that document, not while you're using other documents.

Here's how to improve that style later:

Click in a paragraph written in that style. Improve that paragraph's appearance (by using the Font, Paragraph, and Styles groups). Right-click in the middle of the paragraph's first word. Click "Styles" then "Update".

Editing group

In the Editing group, you see 3 choices: **Find**, **Replace**, and **Select**.

Find

Here's how to make the computer search through your document to find whether you've used the word "love".

Modern method (just in version 2010) Click the word "**Find**" (or press Ctrl with F). At the screen's left edge, you see the **Navigation pane**. Type the word you want to find ("love"), so the word appears in the Navigation pane's box. That makes the computer highlight every "love" in your document, in yellow.

In the Navigation pane, below where you typed "love", the computer shows a list of your phrases containing "love". If you click in that list, that phrase's "love" turns blue in your document.

When you finish using the Navigation pane, close it (by clicking its X). Then the yellow becomes white again.

Classic method Click where you want the search to begin. (For example, if you want the search to begin at the document's beginning, click in the middle of the document's first word.)

Then do this....

Version 2007: click **Find** (or press Ctrl with F).
Version 2010: click **Find's down-arrow then Advanced Find**.

Type the word you want to find ("love"), and press Enter.

The computer will search for "love". If the computer finds a "love" in your document, it will highlight that "love" so it turns blue. (If the "Find and Replace" window covers the part of your document that says "love", drag that window out of the way, by dragging "Find and Replace".)

If you want to find the next "love" in your document, press Enter.

If you click "Reading Highlight" then "Highlight All", the computer will immediately highlight *every* "love" in your document, in yellow (unless you changed the highlighting pen's color).

Highlighting disappears when you edit the document.

If you do *not* want to search for more "love", click the "Find and Replace" window's X (or press the Esc key).

Blue arrows After you've searched, the previous-page and next-page arrows (at the screen's bottom right corner) turn blue. Clicking them will make the computer find the previous or next "love" (instead of the previous or next page).

Example: Lincoln Suppose you've written a history of America and want to find the part where you started talking about Lincoln. If you forget what page that was, no problem! Just put the cursor at the beginning of the document and tell the computer to find "Lincoln".

Replace

Microsoft Word handles replacement the same way as WordPad 7. For details, **read "Replace" on page 89.**

Select

To select everything in the document (so the whole document is highlighted in blue), use one of these methods:

Method 1: click **Select** then "Select All".
Method 2: while holding down the Ctrl key, tap the A key (which means "All").

If you formatted a phrase (such as by underlining or bolding or italicizing or making the font bigger), here's how to find all other phrases that have been formatted the same way:

Click in the formatted phrase's middle. Click **Select** then "Select Text with Similar Formatting". The computer will select (highlight in blue) all phrases that have been formatted the same way.

For example, suppose your document's only formatting is that you underlined some words. Here's how to make all those underlined words become bold also:

Click in the middle of one of the underlined words. Click **Select** then "Select Text with Similar Formatting". The computer will highlight all the underlined words (so they turn blue). Then click the Bold button (which is in the Font group): that makes the computer embolden all the highlighted words (which are the underlined words). Then click anywhere in the document (to turn off the blue highlighting).

Tab bar

Near the screen's top, you see this **tab bar**:

File Home Insert Page Layout References Mailings Review View

(Version 2007 lacks "File".)

Each word or phrase on the tab bar is called a **tab**.

If you click the **Home tab**, you see the 5 groups I discussed (Clipboard, Font, Paragraph, Styles, and Editing). If you click a different tab instead, you see different groups:

Tab	Groups you see
Home	Clipboard, Font, Paragraph, Styles, Editing
Insert	Pages, Tables, Illustrations, Links, Header & Footer, Text, Symbols
Page Layout	Themes, Page Setup, Page Background, Paragraph, Arrange
References	Table of Contents, Footnotes, Citations & Bibliography, Captions, Index, Table of Authorities
Mailings	Create, Start Mail Merge, Write & Insert Fields, Preview Results, Finish
Review	Proofing, Language (in version 2010), Comments, Tracking, Changes, Compare, Protect
View	Document Views, Show (which version 2007 calls "Show/Hide"), Zoom, Window, Macros

Page Layout tab

Click the **Page Layout tab**.

Margins Normally, Microsoft Word leaves a 1-inch margin at all 4 edges of your paper. If you want margins that are wider or narrower, click "Margins" (in the Page Setup group). Then click one of these popular choices:

Choice	How big the margins are
Normal	1 inch at all 4 edges
Narrow	½ inch at all 4 edges
Moderate	1 inch at top & bottom, ¾ inch at left & right
Wide	1 inch at top & bottom, 2 inches at left & right
Mirrored	1 inch at 3 edges, 1¼ inches at stapled edge (left edge on odd pages, right edge on even)
Office 2003	1 inch at top & bottom, 1¼ inches at left & right

Size In the U.S., a normal sheet of paper is 8½ inches wide and 11 inches tall. Microsoft Word assumes your paper is that size. If you want to print on paper that's a different size, click "Size" (in the Page Setup group) then the paper's size. (To see all the choices, point at the **scroll bar**, which is below the up-arrow, and drag that scroll bar down.)

In the U.S., these sizes are the most popular:

Letter	8½ inches wide and 11 inches tall
Legal	8½ inches wide and 14 inches tall
Executive	7¼ inches wide and 10½ inches tall

Pick a size your printer can handle!

Orientation When an artist paints a portrait of a face, the canvas's height is usually bigger than its width. That situation (height bigger than width) is called **portrait orientation**.

When an artist paints a landscape (showing many trees and hills), the canvas's width is usually bigger than its height. That situation (width bigger than height) is called **landscape orientation**.

The computer assumes you want portrait orientation (height bigger than width). For example, if you tell the computer to print on paper that's 8½ inches by 11 inches, the computer assumes you want the height to be bigger than the width, so it assumes you want height to be 11 inches and the width to be 8½ inches.

You can force the computer to do landscape orientation instead, so the width is bigger than the height, and so the width is 11 inches and the height is 8½ inches. That makes the paper wide, so you can fit more words on each line. To do that, click "Orientation" (in the Page Setup group) then "Landscape".

To accomplish landscape printing, the computer & printer rotate the paper or words 90 degrees.

For example, to print on a Statement (8½ inches wide and 5½ inches tall) or a #10 Envelope (9½ inches wide and $4\frac{1}{8}$ inches tall), tell the computer to do landscape printing (by clicking "Orientation" then "Landscape").

Columns In a newspaper, text is printed in many narrow **columns**. In a business letter, text is printed in a single wide column.

The computer assumes you want a single wide column. If you want several narrow columns instead (like a newspaper or magazine), click "Columns" (in the Page Setup group). Then click one of these popular choices:

Choice	How many columns you get
One	1 wide column (like a business letter)
Two	2 narrow columns
Three	3 very narrow columns
Left	2 columns (left column is very narrow, right column is wider)
Right	2 columns (right column is very narrow, left column is wider)

The gap between each pair of columns is a half-inch wide.

After you've finished typing a paragraph (and pressed Enter), try this experiment: while holding down the Ctrl and Shift keys, press Enter again. That creates a **column break**: it makes the next paragraph be at the top of the next column. (If you change your mind, here's how to remove the column break: click at the beginning of the paragraph you've put at the top of a column, then press the Backspace key.)

Breaks Here's how to divide your document into two **sections** and give each section its own margins and its own number of columns.

Click where you want the second section to begin. Click "Breaks" (in the Page Setup group). Click either "Continuous" (to start the second section on the same page as the first section ended) or "Next Page" (to start the second section on a separate page from the first section). Afterwards, any margin or columns command you give will affect just the section you're clicking in, not the other section.

If you wish, create extra sections: for each extra section, click where you want the section to begin, then click "Breaks" then either "Continuous" or "Next Page".

Line Numbers If you plan to mail the document to a friend and then chat about it by phone, you should number each line, so you can ask your friend "What do you think about line 27?" To make the computer number the lines for you (by writing the numbers in the left margin), click "Line Numbers" (in the Page Setup group). Then click either "Continuous" (which makes the computer number the lines 1, 2, 3, etc., until the document's end) or "Restart Each Page" (which makes each page's first line be numbered 1, each page's second line be numbered 2, etc.).

When you finish chatting with your friend and don't need the line numbers anymore, here's how to erase them: click "Line Numbers" then "None".

Watermark If you click "Watermark" (in the Page Background group), you see a menu that includes these phrases: "CONFIDENTIAL", "DO NOT COPY", "DRAFT", "SAMPLE", "ASAP", "URGENT". (To see all those phrases, point at the **scroll bar**, which is below the up-arrow, and drag that scroll bar down.) If you click one of those phrases, the computer will stamp that phrase on every page of your document. The phrase will be in huge gray letters, in the middle of every page, so it's stamped across each page's paragraphs. The phrase is called a **watermark**.

If you don't like any of those phrases, make up your own! Here's how:

Click "Watermark" then "Custom Watermark" then "Text watermark". Double-click in the Text box. Type the phrase you want (such as "COPY", "ORIGINAL", "PERSONAL", "TOP SECRET", "I LOVE YOU", "PRETEND YOU'VE NEVER READ THIS", or "DON'T SHOW TO BOSS YET"). Click "Horizontal" (if you want the phrase to appear straight across the paper) or "Diagonal" (if you want the phrase to appear on a slant). Click "OK".

If you change your mind and want to remove the watermark, click "Watermark" then "Remove Watermark".

Insert tab

Click the **Insert tab**.

Symbol If you click "Symbol" (which is in the Symbols group), you see the symbols you used recently. If you haven't used any symbols yet, you see these:

€	£	¥	©	®
™	±	≠	≤	≥
÷	×	∞	µ	α
β	π	Ω	Σ	☺

If you want to use one of those symbols now, click it. If you want a different symbol instead, do the following….

Click "More Symbols". You see the **Symbol window**.

You see many symbols. If you want one of those symbols, double-click it. If you don't like any of those symbols, view different symbols by using the scroll arrows or clicking "Special Characters" or the Font box's down-arrow.

If you click the Font box's down-arrow, you see a list of different fonts. Scroll down to see the different font choices. For best results, click one of these 6 fonts:

(normal text)
Symbol
Webdings
Wingdings
Wingdings 2
Wingdings 3

For example, if you click "Wingdings" you see these pictorial characters:

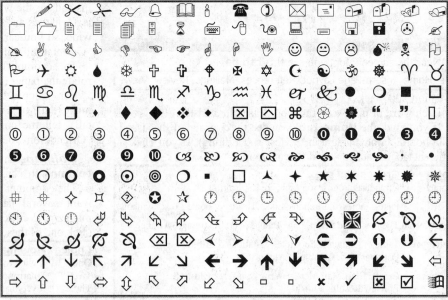

(To see them all, scroll down by clicking that window's first down-arrow.)

If you click "Wingdings 2" instead, you see these:

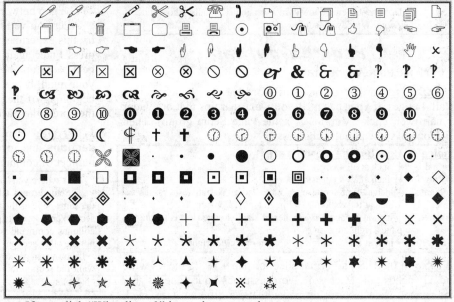

If you click "Wingdings 3" instead, you see these:

If you click "Webdings", you see fancier drawings:

For fun with young kids, point at those Webdings and play a game of "Do you know what this is?"

If you click "Symbol", you see math, Greek, and card suits:

	!	∀	#	∃	%	&	∍	(	)	*	+	,	−	.	/
0	1	2	3	4	5	6	7	8	9	:	;	<	=	>	?
≅	Α	Β	Χ	Δ	Ε	Φ	Γ	Η	Ι	ϑ	Κ	Λ	Μ	Ν	Ο
Π	Θ	Ρ	Σ	Τ	Υ	ς	Ω	Ξ	Ψ	Ζ	[	∴	]	⊥	_
‾	α	β	χ	δ	ε	φ	γ	η	ι	φ	κ	λ	μ	ν	ο
π	θ	ρ	σ	τ	υ	ϖ	ω	ξ	ψ	ζ	{	|	}	~	
ϒ	′	≤	/	∞	ƒ	♣	♦	♥	♠	↔	←	↑	→	↓	
°	±	″	≥	×	∝	∂	•	÷	≠	≡	≈	…	|	⎯	↵
ℵ	ℑ	ℜ	℘	⊗	⊕	∅	∩	∪	⊃	⊇	⊄	⊂	⊆	∈	∉
∠	∇	®	©	™	∏	√	·	¬	∧	∨	⇔	⇐	⇑	⇒	⇓
◊	⟨	®	©	™	∑	⎛	⎜	⎡	⎢	⎣	⎧	⎨	⎩	⎪	
⟩	∫	⌠	⎮	⌡	⎞	⎟	⎤	⎥	⎦	⎫	⎬	⎭			

Whenever you see a character you like, double-click it. That makes the computer put the character into your document. Then double-click any other characters you like.

When you finish using the Symbol window, make it disappear by clicking the button that says "Close" on it.

Warning: **your printer might be too stupid to print those symbols**, especially if the font is "(normal text)". Instead of printing a symbol, the printer might just leave a blank space. Before giving the printout to a friend, look at the printout yourself to make sure the symbols printed correctly and clearly.

**Date & Time** To type the date or time, click **Date & Time** (which is in the Text group). The computer will show a list of formats, like this:

```
12/25/2011
Sunday, December 25, 2011
December 25, 2011
12/25/11
2011-12-25
25-Dec-11
12.25.2011
Dec. 25, 11
25 December 2011
December 11
Dec-11
12/25/2011 10:59 PM
12/25/2011 10:59:20 PM
10:59 PM
10:59:20 PM
22:59
22:59:20
```

Click the format you want. Press Enter. The computer will type the date or time in the format you requested.

In that procedure, just before you press Enter, you might wish to put a check mark in the "**Update automatically**" box. Here's how that box works:

> Suppose you type a document on Monday, but you print the document the next day (Tuesday). Which date will the computer print on paper? The computer will print the date that the document was typed (Monday), unless you put a check mark in the "Update automatically" box, which makes the computer print the "date printed" (Tuesday).
>
> If you put a check mark in the "Update automatically" box, the computer will automatically update the date & time whenever the document is printed (or print-previewed or opened).

**Page Number** To make the computer put a page number on each page, click **Page Number** (which is in the Header & Footer group). Then click "Top of Page" (if you want the number to be in each page's top-margin area called the **header**) or "Bottom of Page" (if you want the number to be in each page's bottom-margin area called the **footer**).

Click "Plain Number 2". That makes the page number have plain style #2 (centered instead of near the paper's left edge or right edge).

You see the page number, on the current page. (The computer has automatically put page numbers on all the other pages also.)

Do you want any words to appear to the left of the page number? If so, type them then press the Space bar. For example, if you want the 2nd page to say "This is page 2" instead of just "2", type "This is page" then press the Space bar.

Do you want any words to appear to the right of the page number? If so, press the right-arrow key then the Space bar then type those words. For example, if you want the 2nd page to say "This is page 2 of the great American novel" and you've already typed "This is page ", press the right-arrow key (to move past the page number) then the Space bar (to leave 1 blank space after the page number) then type "of the great American novel".

Whatever words you put to the left and right of the page number appear on all the other page numbers also.

When you finish editing the page number's line, double-click in the screen's middle. Then you can continue editing your document's paragraphs.

If you want to edit the page number's line again, double-click in the middle of that line.

**Table** To type a table of numbers in the middle of your document, click where you want the table to appear then click **Table** (which is in the Tables group).

You see 80 little boxes (called **cells**), arranged to form a table having 8 rows and 10 columns. How many rows and columns do you want in _your_ table? Point at the first cell (box) and drag down and to the right, until your desired number of rows and columns turns orange. For example, **if you want just 3 rows and 4 columns, drag down and to the right until 3 rows and 4 columns turn orange**, so you see 12 orange cells altogether.

When you take your finger off the mouse's button, you'll see the table you requested.

Then just fill in the cells, with whatever numbers and words you wish. To move from cell to cell, click with the mouse, or press the Tab key (which moves right to the next cell), or press Shift with Tab (which moves left to the previous cell), or press the arrow keys repeatedly.

In a cell, you can type a number, word, sentence, or even an entire paragraph! If you start typing a paragraph in a cell, the computer will automatically make the cell and its row taller, so the entire paragraph will fit in the cell. You can even type _several_ paragraphs in a single cell: just press the Enter key at the end of each paragraph. If you want to indent the first line of one of those paragraphs, press the Space bar several times or press Ctrl with Tab.

Here's how to make the table have more cells.

> To create an extra row at the bottom of the table:
> click in the table's bottom right cell, then press the Tab key.
>
> To insert an extra row into the _middle_ of the table:
> right-click in the row that's under where you want the extra row to appear, then click "Insert" then "Insert Rows Above".
>
> To create an extra column at the table's right edge:
> right-click in last column, then click "Insert" then "Insert Columns to the Right". (To fit the extra column, the computer will make the previous columns narrower.)
>
> To insert an extra column into the middle of the table:
> right-click in the column that's right of where you want the extra column to appear, then click "Insert" then "Insert Columns to the Left". (To fit the extra column, the computer will make the other columns narrower.)

The computer assumes you want the table's columns to all be the same width. Here's how to change that assumption:

> For example, here's how to adjust the width of the table's left column (column 1). Move the mouse until its pointer is on the vertical gridline that separates column 1 from column 2, and the pointer's shape turns into this symbol: ◄║►. Then drag the vertical gridline to the right (to make the column wider) or left (to make the column narrower).
>
> If you make a column wider, the computer makes room for it by shrinking the next column. If you make a column narrower, the computer compensates by expanding the next column.
>
> If you want to fine-tune the widths of _all_ columns, work from left to right: adjust the width of column 1 (by dragging the gridline that separates it from column 2), then adjust the width of column 2 (by dragging the gridline that separates it from column 3), then adjust the width of column 3 (by dragging the gridline that separates it from column 4), etc.

If a column contains mostly numbers, here's how to make that column look prettier, so the numbers are aligned properly:

> Move the mouse until its pointer is at the _very top_ of the column and is centered on the gridline above the column, so the pointer's shape turns into this symbol: ▼. Then click. The entire column turns blue.
>
> Click "Home" (on the tab bar) then the Align Text Right button (on the formatting toolbar). That makes all cells in that column be aligned right, so the numbers are aligned properly.

When you've finished typing numbers and words into all the cells, here's how to make the computer adjust the widths of all the columns, so each column becomes just wide enough to hold the data in it:

Right-click in the table. Click "AutoFit" then "AutoFit to Contents".

When you've finished editing the table, here's how to put paragraphs below it:

Click below the table by using the mouse, or go below the table by pressing the down-arrow key several times. Then type the paragraphs you want below the table.

Here's how to delete a row or column:

Right-click in the middle of what you want to delete. Click "Delete Cells". Click "Delete entire row" (if you want to delete a row) or "Delete entire column" (if you want to delete a column). Press Enter.

Here's how to delete the entire table:

Click in the table. Click the 4-headed arrow that's at the table's top-left corner. Press the Backspace key.

Here's how to create a table that has a customized shape.

In the middle of your document, press the Enter key several times, to create a blank space for the table. Then click **Table** (which is in the Tables group) then **Draw Table**.

Where do you want the table to be in your document? **Put the mouse pointer where you want the table's top left corner to be, and drag to where you want the table's opposite corner.** (While dragging, hold down the mouse's left button.) You'll see a box, which is your table. Inside the box, make a grid of rows and columns by drawing horizontal and vertical gridlines. **To draw a gridline, put the mouse pointer where you want the line to begin, and drag to where you want the line to end.**

If you make a mistake, click the Undo button or do the following....Click the word "Eraser" (which is near the screen's top-right corner). That makes the mouse pointer turn into an eraser. Move the mouse until the eraser's bottom corner touches the line you want to erase; then click (press the mouse's left button). That makes the line disappear. You can make other lines disappear also, by clicking them. When you finish using the eraser, click "Draw Table" (which is near the screen's top-right corner) to continue drawing more lines.

View tab

Click the **View tab**.

Ruler If you put a check mark in the **Ruler box** (by clicking there), you'll see a ruler (saying 1", 2", 3") above the page and another ruler at the screen's left edge. Those rulers show how many inches will be printed on paper.

Afterwards, you'll be seeing rulers even when you're viewing other documents and even on other days, until you cancel the rulers (by removing the check mark from the Ruler box).

Split To see two parts of your document at the same time, click **Split** (which is in the Window group). A fat gray line appears across the middle of your screen and splits your screen's window into two parts, a **top windowpane** and a **bottom windowpane**.

Move the mouse slightly (which moves the fat gray line slightly up or down), until you're happy about the line's position. Then click the mouse's left button.

Now you can see two parts of your document at the same time!

Each windowpane has its own scroll arrows. You can click those scroll arrows to change what you see in that windowpane, without changing what's in the other windowpane.

You can also click in one windowpane's text and then use the keyboard's movement keys (up-arrow, down-arrow, left-arrow, right-arrow, Page Up, Page Down, Home, and End) to change what's in that windowpane, without changing what you see in the other windowpane.

Both windowpanes show parts of the same document. If you change a word in one windowpane (by deleting or inserting or revising that word), while the other windowpane happens to show the same part of the document, you see that word automatically change in the other windowpane also, immediately!

Using those two windowpanes, you can compare two parts of your document and copy from one part to the other (by using the Home tab's Copy and Paste buttons or using Ctrl C and Ctrl V).

When you stop wanting two windowpanes, here's how to return to a single pane:

Which windowpane do you want to remove? Click in that windowpane. Click **Remove Split** (which is in the Window group). That windowpane disappears, so the entire screen becomes devoted to the other windowpane.

Arrange All Here's how to see *two* documents on the screen at once!

To be safe, make sure both documents have been saved on disk (by using the Save button). Close any documents that are on the screen (by choosing **Close** from the Office menu), so the screen's main part is blank.

Open the first document (by using the Office button). You see the document's words and paragraphs on the screen.

While that first document is still on the screen (without closing it), open the second document. You see the document's words and paragraphs on the screen; they cover up the first document, so you can't see the first document at the moment.

Click the View tab then **Arrange All** (which is in the Window group). Then you see *two* windows on the screen. The top window shows the second document; the bottom window shows the first document.

Each window is small, showing just a tiny part of the document. A window might seem blank if it's so small that it shows just the document's top margin.

Each window has its own scroll arrows. Use them to scroll through the documents and see the parts of the documents that are *not* blank.

By using those two windows, you can easily compare two documents and copy from one to the other (by using the Home tab's Copy and Paste buttons or using Ctrl C and Ctrl V).

When you stop wanting one of the windows, close it (by clicking its X button), then expand the other window (by clicking its maximize button, which is next to its X button).

References tab

Click the **References tab**.

Insert Footnote Suppose you're writing a religious pamphlet in which you want to say "Read the Bible tonight!" Suppose you want to add a footnote saying "written by God", so the main text looks like this —

> Read the Bible[1] tonight!

and the page's bottom contains this footnote:

> [1] Written by God.

Here's how to do it all....

Type "Read the Bible". Click "Insert Footnote" (which is in the Footnotes group) or, while holding down the Ctrl and Alt keys, tap the F key. Type the footnote ("Written by God."). Go back to the main text, where you left off, by using one of these methods:

> Method 1: double-click the footnote's number, then press the right-arrow key.

> Method 2: climb back up to the main text (by using the keyboard's up-arrow key), then go right to where you left off typing (by using the End key).

The computer will automatically number the footnote: it will automatically type [1] after "Bible" and type [1] before "Written by God." If your document contains more footnotes, the computer will automatically number them [2], [3], [4], etc. (Those numbers are easy to read on paper. On the screen, the numbers are easier to read while the Home tab's ¶ button is deactivated.)

The computer will put the footnotes at the bottom of the page. If the page is divided into newspaper columns, the computer will put each footnote at the bottom of the column it refers to.

The computer will put a 2-inch horizontal line above the footnotes to separate them from the main text.

If you insert extra footnotes, the computer will automatically renumber the other footnotes, so the first footnote appearing in your document will be numbered [1], the second footnote will be numbered [2], etc.

Here's the easiest way to delete a footnote:

> Click the left edge of the footnote's number in the main text; then press the Delete key twice.

Help button

To the right of the tab bar, at the screen's rightmost edge, you see a question mark. To get help about using Microsoft Word, click that question mark or press the F1 key. (You'll get the *best* help if you connect to the Internet before doing that, so Microsoft can give you the *newest* help lessons.)

You see the **Word Help window**, which contains this list of popular topics:

Version 2007	Version 2010
What's new in Word 2007	Getting started with Word 2010
Find Word 2003 commands in Word 2007	Introducing the Backstage view
Insert headers and footers	Create a document
Insert page numbers	Create a document to be used by previous versions of Word
Get rid of tracked changes	
Converting documents	Collaboration
Creating specific documents	Creating documents
Formatting	File migration
Getting help	Formatting
Margins and page setup	Getting started with Word
Page numbers	
Saving and printing	
Writing	

To see all those topics, click the scroll-down arrow (at the window's bottom-right corner) or enlarge the window (by maximizing it or dragging its bottom-right corner).

If one of those topics interests you, click it.

If none of those topics interests you, click "**see all**", which shows you this longer list of topics:

Version 2007	Version 2010
Accessibility	Accessibility
Activating Word	Activating Word
Add-ins	Add-ins
Automation and programmability	Charts
Collaboration	Collaboration
Converting documents	Creating documents
Creating specific documents	Digital IDs and signatures
Customizing	Equations
File management	Field codes
Formatting	File management
Getting help	File migration
Headers and footers	Formatting
Lists	Getting help
Macros	Getting started with Word
Mail merge	Headers, footers, and page numbers
Margins and page setup	Installing
Page breaks and section breaks	Lists
Page numbers	Mail merge
Saving and printing	Page breaks and section breaks
Security and privacy	Page setup
Tables	Pictures and clip art
Tables of contents and other references	Reading documents
Tracking changes and comments	Saving and printing
Training	Security and privacy
Viewing and navigating	SmartArt graphics
What's new	Spelling, grammar, and thesaurus
Word demos	Tables
Working with graphics and charts	Tables of contents and other references
Writing	Tracking changes and comments
Working in a different language	Training courses
	Videos
	Working in a different language

If one of those topics interests you, click it. If none of those topics interests you, click in the Search box (the white box at the window's top) then type the question you want help about (or type your topic's main words) and press Enter.

Then you'll see a list of subtopics. (To see them all, click the scroll-down arrow at the window's bottom-right corner.) Click whichever subtopic interests you. You'll see a lesson about that subtopic.

If you want to return to a previous list of topics or subtopics, click the **Back button** (the left arrow at the window's top-left corner). When you finish using the Word Help window, close it (by clicking the X button at its top-right corner).

Microsoft Word 2002 & 2003

This chapter explains Microsoft Word 2002 & 2003. (Skip this chapter if you have Microsoft Word 2007 or 2010, which were explained in the previous chapter.)

Fun

Here's how to enjoy using Microsoft Word.

Prepare yourself

Before starting Microsoft Word, prepare yourself:

> **Version 2003** You need Windows XP (or Vista or 7) and at least 128M of RAM.
> To run *well*, get at least 256M or RAM.
>
> **Version 2002** You need Windows 98 (or Me or XP or Vista or 7) and at least 32M of RAM.
> To run *well*, get at least 64M of RAM.

Also, **read and practice my Windows chapter, especially the section about "WordPad"**, which is a stripped-down simplified version of Microsoft Word.

Install

When you buy Microsoft Word, it comes on one or more CD or DVD disks, which you (or your computer store) must copy to your computer's hard disk. Here's how….

Version 2003 Here's how to copy **Microsoft Office 2003** (which includes Microsoft Word 2003) to your hard disk:

> Turn on the computer without any floppy or CD-ROM disks in the drives, so the computer runs Windows XP and the computer's bottom-left corner says "start".
> Into the CD-ROM drive, put the Microsoft Office disk.
> That disk came in a rectangular jacket whose backside sports a "Microsoft Office Product Key" code, which contains 25 letters and digits. Type that 25-character code. Press Enter.
> Type your full name, then press the Tab key, type your initials, press Tab again, type the name of your company (if any), and press Enter.
> Click "I accept the terms in the License Agreement". Press Enter 3 times.
> The computer will copy Microsoft Office from the CD-ROM disk to your hard disk. Then the computer will say, "Setup Completed". Press Enter.

Microsoft Office includes an e-mail client called Outlook, but I recommend making your main (default) e-mail client be Outlook Express instead (which is part of Internet Explorer) by doing this:

> Click "start" then "All Programs" then "Outlook Express". The computer will say "Outlook Express is not currently your default mail client. Would you like to make it your default mail client?" Click "Yes". If the computer asks "Would you like to go online now?" click "No". Then close all windows (by clicking their X buttons).

Version 2002 If your computer came with a pair of CD-ROM disks called **Microsoft Office XP Small Business** (which includes Microsoft Word 2002), here's how to copy them to your hard disk:

> Turn on the computer without any floppy or CD-ROM disks in the drives, so the computer runs Windows and the computer's bottom left corner says Start.
> Into the CD-ROM drive, put Microsoft Office's main disk (which does *not* say "Media Content").
> That disk came in a square jacket whose backside sports a "Certificate of Authenticity" sticker. That sticker reveals a code (called the "Product Key"), which contains 25 letters and digits. Type that 25-character code. Press Enter 4 times.
> Into the CD-ROM drive, put Microsoft Office's other disk (which says "Media Content"). Click the box that says "I accept the terms in the License Agreement". Press Enter. Click the "Install" button that's at the window's bottom. The computer will say "Microsoft Office XP Media Content Setup has completed successfully." Press Enter.

Start

Here's how to start using Microsoft Word.

Version 2003 Click "start".

If you see "Microsoft Office Word 2003", click it. (Otherwise, click "All Programs" then "Microsoft Office" then "Microsoft Office Word 2003".)

If the computer says "Activation Wizard" and you're using an ordinary modem (instead of DSL or a cable modem), do this:

> Press Enter. Connect to the Internet (by pressing Enter again). The computer will say "Thank you." Press Enter twice. Turn off your Internet connection (by clicking its icon and then clicking "Disconnect").

Version 2002 Click "Start" then "Programs" then "Microsoft Word". If the computer says "Office XP End User License Agreement", do this:

> Click "Accept" then "Next". Type the password that your Internet Service Provider assigned you (and press Enter). Click "Next".
> You'll see a form. Fill it in. Here's how....
> Click the down-arrow. Press the Page Down key several times, until you see your country (such as "United States"). Click your country.
> Type your first name, press the Tab key, type your last name, press Tab, type the name of your company (if any), press Tab, and fill in the rest of the form. Click "Next".
> Click "I would like to be notified of product updates". (If you wish, click the other "I would like..." boxes also.) Click in the "E-mail Address" box. Type your e-mail address (such as "russ@secretfun.com"). Click "Submit" then "Finish" then "Yes".

See the Microsoft Word screen

The screen's top says "Document1 — Microsoft Word". You also see this **menu bar**:

> File   Edit   View   Insert   Format   Tools   Table   Window   Help

Unmask

Microsoft Word has a feature called **masked menus & buttons**. That feature is supposed to make the menus and buttons easier to find but actually makes them *harder* to find. Turn off that terrible feature. **Do this turn-off procedure:**

> Click "View" then "Toolbars" then "Customize" then "Options". Put check marks in the first two boxes ("Show Standard and Formatting toolbars on two rows" and "Always show full menus"), by clicking them. Press Enter.

Do that turn-off procedure *now*. The rest of this chapter assumes you've done it. (After you've finished this chapter, if you wish, you can turn the masked menus & buttons feature back on by removing the check marks.)

See the rulers

About 1½ inches below the screen's top, you should see a **horizontal ruler**, which goes across the screen and is numbered 1", 2", 3", 4", 5", etc.

> If you don't see that ruler, make it appear by clicking **View** (which is on the menu bar) then **Ruler**.

At the screen's left edge, you should see a **vertical ruler**, which goes up & down the screen and is numbered 1", 2", etc.

> If you don't see the vertical ruler, make it appear by doing this: click **View** then **Print Layout**.

Now you see *two* rulers — a horizontal ruler, plus a vertical ruler — so you can use the full power of Microsoft Word!

Type your document

Start typing your document.

Microsoft Word typically uses the keyboard the same way as WordPad. For details, **read these sections on pages 81-82:**

> "Use the keyboard"
> "Scroll arrows"
> "Insert characters"
> "Split a paragraph"
> "Combine paragraphs"
> "Movement keys"

Here are differences....

Word wrap For Microsoft Word, ignore the paragraph about "If you're using Windows XP".

Ctrl symbols Your version resembles Microsoft Word 2007, so **read the "Ctrl symbols" section on page 182**.

Movement keys Microsoft Word differs from WordPad in this way:

> Ctrl with Page Down makes the pointer move down to the next page.
> Ctrl with Page Up makes the pointer move up to the previous page's beginning.

Automatic editing

The computer will automatically edit what you type.

AutoCorrect Your version resembles Microsoft Word 2007, so **read the "AutoCorrect" section on page 183**.

The Undo button is under "Window" (instead of above "Home").

Red squiggles Your version resembles Microsoft Word 2007, so **read the "Red squiggles" section on page 183**.

Green squiggles Your version resembles Microsoft Word 2007, so **read the "Green squiggles" section on page 183**.

To make that section apply to your version, make these changes:

> Version 2003: omit the sentence about "Explain".
> Version 2002: change "close the Word Help window" to "click Explain again".

Synonyms For version 2003, read the "Synonyms" section on page 184.

For version 2002, read just this:

> Suppose you've typed a word (such as "girl") correctly (so it has no red or green squiggle) but wish you could think of a better word instead. Just right-click the word then click "Synonyms". The computer will show you **synonyms** (words that have similar meaning). If one of those words appeals to you, click it: that word will replace the word in your document. If none of those words appeals to you, press the **Escape key** (which says "Esc" on it) *twice*.

Bottom-left corner

The screen's bottom-left corner tells you:

> which page of the document you're on, which section of the document you're on (typically section 1), a comment such as "2/3" (which means you're on page 2 of a 3-page document), and details about where you are on the page (how many inches down from the top of the paper, how many lines down from the top margin, and how many characters [columns] over from the left margin)

Here's how to hop to a different page:

> Double-click the word "Page". Type the number of the page you want to go to (and press Enter). Click the word "Close".

Further tricks

Your version resembles Microsoft Word 2007, so **read these sections on page 185:**

> "Page arrows"
> "Page break"
> "All delete"

While doing "All delete", the document turns black (not blue).

Formatting toolbar

Near the screen's top, you see the **formatting toolbar**. It looks like this in version 2003:

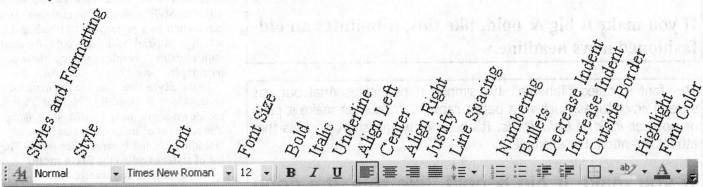

Each symbol on the toolbar is called a **tool**. Here's the name of each tool:

If you forget a tool's name, try this trick: point at the tool (by using the mouse, but *without* clicking), then wait a second. Underneath the tool, you'll see the tool's name; and at the screen's bottom left corner, you'll see a one-sentence explanation of what the tool does.

The toolbar's right half consists of 15 tools saying "**B**", "*I*", "U", etc. Those 15 tools are called **buttons**. A 16th button, called "Styles and Formatting", is at the toolbar's left edge.

To use a button, activate it by clicking it with the mouse. Here are the details....

Underline

Here's how to underline a phrase (<u>like this</u>).

Activate the **Underline button** (which says <u>U</u> on it) by clicking it. **Activating the button changes its appearance:**

> In version 2003, the button turns orange.
> In version 2002, the button gets a blue border.

Then type the phrase you want underlined. Then deactivate the Underline button (by clicking it again).

Go ahead: try it now! Practice using the underline button before you progress to more advanced buttons!

Here's a shortcut: instead of clicking the Underline button, you can press Ctrl with U.

Fancy formats

Microsoft Word resembles WordPad, so **read these sections on page 85:**

> "Bold"
> "Italic"

Alignment buttons

Microsoft Word handles alignment buttons the same way as WordPad 7. For details, **read "Alignment buttons" on page 88**.

In your version of Microsoft Word, the "Align text left" button is called "Align Left", and the "Align text right" button is called "Align Right."

Font Size

Look at the **Font Size box**. That box normally contains the number 12, so you're typing characters that are 12 points high.

Here's how to type characters that are bigger or smaller....

> Method 1: click the Font Size box. In that box, type a size number from 8 to 72. The number can end in .5; the number can be 8 or 8.5 or 9 or 9.5 or 10 or bigger. (Theoretically, you can pick a number even smaller than 8 or even bigger than 72, but those extreme numbers create ugly results.) When you finish typing the number, press the Enter key.

> Method 2: click the down-arrow that's to the *right* of the Font Size box. You start seeing this list of popular sizes: 8, 9, 10, 11, 12, 14, 16, 18, 20, 22, 24, 26, 28, 36, 48, and 72. (It appears in a window that's too small to show the entire list; to see the rest of the list, click the window's scroll arrows. Version 2003 also shows 10.5.) That list of popular sizes is called the **Font Size menu**. Click the size you want.

Any new characters you type afterwards will be the size you chose. (Characters typed earlier don't change size.)

The popular sizes look like this:

> This text is 8 points high, 9 points high, 10 points high, 11 points high, 12 points high, 14 points high, 16 points high, 18 points high, 20 pt., 22 pt., 24 pt., 26 pt., 28 pt., 36pt., 48pt., 72pt.

When you finish typing the enlarged or reduced characters, here's how to return to typing characters that are normal size: click the down-arrow that's to the right of the Font Size box, then click the 12 or 10 (whichever size you prefer).

Font

When you type, you're normally using a font called "Times New Roman". If you wish, you can switch to a different font instead.

The best fonts are "Times New Roman", "Tahoma", "Comic Sans MS", and "Courier New". Here's how they look:

This font is called "Times New Roman". It's the best for typing long passages of text, such as paragraphs in books, newspapers, magazines, and reports. It squeezes lots of words onto a small amount of paper but remains easy to read. You can make it plain or **bold** or *italic* or ***bold italic***.

If you make it big & bold, like this, it imitates an old-fashioned news headline.

This font is called "Tahoma". It's simple. It resembles Arial but has several advantages, such as a better capital "I". You can make it plain or **bold** or *italic* or ***bold italic***. It's best for typing short phrases that attract attention. For example…

If you make it big & bold, like this, it's good for titles, signs, and posters.

If you make it small, like this, it's good for footnotes, photo captions, classified ads, telephone books, directories, and catalogs.

This font is called "Comic Sans MS". It resembles Tahoma but looks hand-drawn, like the words in a funny comic book. You can make it plain or **bold** or *italic* or ***bold italic***. It's best for typing short phrases that draw attention and giggles. For example…

If you make it big & bold, like this, it's good for funny titles, signs, and posters.

```
This font is called "Courier New".

If you make it 12 points high, like this, it
resembles the printout from a typewriter.

It makes each character have the same width: for
example, the "m" has the same width as the "i". It's
a good font for typing tables of numbers, since the
uniform width lets you line up each column of
numbers easily.

Choose plain, bold, italic, or bold italic.
```

In the **Font box**, you see the name of a font, which is usually "Times New Roman". Click the down-arrow that's to the *right* of that font's name. You start seeing a list of fonts, including "Times New Roman", "Arial", "Courier New", and several other fonts. (It appears in a window that's too small to show the entire list; to see the rest of the list, click the window's scroll arrows.) The list of font is called the **Font menu**.

Click the font you want.

Afterwards, whatever characters you type will be in the font you chose. (The characters you typed earlier remain unaffected.)

When you finish typing in that font, here's how to return to typing characters that are normal (Times New Roman): click the down-arrow that's to the right of the Font box, then click Times New Roman.

Style

When you type, you typically use a style called "Normal", which is 12-point Times New Roman aligned left.

If you wish, you can switch to a different style instead. For example, you can switch to a style called "Heading 1", which is an Arial bold that's big (16-point) with extra blank space between paragraphs. Here's how.

In the **Style box**, you see the name of a style, which is typically "Normal". Click the down-arrow next to that style name. You see a list of styles, including "Normal", "Heading 1", and several other styles. The list of styles is called the **Style menu**.

Click the style you want.

That affects the paragraph you're typing now. (The paragraphs you typed earlier remain unaffected.)

When you finish typing a paragraph in that style (and pressed the Enter key at the end of that paragraph), here's how to make the next paragraph be Normal: if the Style box doesn't say "Normal" already, click the down-arrow next to the Style box then click Normal.

Centered title Here's the sophisticated way to type a centered title.

Press the Enter key. Choose "Heading 1" from the Style menu. Click the Centered button. Type the title, and press the Enter key afterwards.

The computer will automatically make the next paragraph be Normal and aligned left; you don't have to say so.

Indentation buttons

Your version resembles Microsoft Word 2007, so **read the "Indentation buttons" section on page 189.**

Color buttons

Normally, you type black characters on a white background. Here's how to change those colors.

Highlight Normally, you type on a white background. Here's how to change the background to a different color, such as yellow, as if you were using a yellow Magic Marker highlighter....

First, type the phrase you want to highlight.

Then look at the **Highlight button**. It's the button that shows a Magic Marker highlighter pen and a colored sample, which is a fat line. Notice the sample's color.

If it's the color you want, click the sample.

If it's *not* the color you want, do this instead: click the down-arrow that's to the right of the sample; you'll see several colors; click the color you want. (I recommend you pick a light color, such as yellow.)

Put the mouse at the beginning of the phrase you want to highlight (so the *vertical bar* is at the left edge of the phrase's first letter). Drag across the phrase (while holding down the mouse's left button.). The phrase's background will change to the color you desired. If you wish, drag across other phrases also.

When you finish coloring, deactivate the Highlight button (by clicking it or by pressing the Esc key).

Font Color Normally, the characters you type are black. Here's how to make them a different color, such as red.

Look at the **Font Color button**. It's the last big button on the formatting toolbar, and it has an underlined "A" on it.

Notice the color of the A's underline. If it's the color you want, click the underline. If it's *not* the color you want, do this instead: click the down-arrow that's to the right of the A's underline; you'll see 40 colors; click the color you want.

Afterwards, whatever characters you type will be in the color you chose. (The characters you typed earlier remain unaffected.)

When you finish typing in that color, here's how to return to typing characters that are black: click the down-arrow that's to the right of the A's underline, then click Black.

Line Spacing

You can make the computer **double-space** a paragraph, so the computer puts a blank line under each line you type. Those blank lines please your boss (or teacher or editor), who can scribble there nasty comments about your writing!

Here's how:

Click in the paragraph that you want to double-space.

Look at the **Line Spacing button** (which slows an up-arrow and down-arrow). Click the down-pointing triangle (▼) that's at the Line Spacing button's right-hand edge, then click **2.0**. Your paragraph becomes double-spaced.

When you start typing a new paragraph, the computer double-spaces it if the paragraph above it was double-spaced.

If a paragraph is double-spaced, here's how to change it to single-spaced: just deactivate the Line Spacing button (by clicking it).

Suppose a paragraph is single-spaced and you want to change it to double-spaced. The usual method is to click the Line Spacing button's triangle then 2.0. But here's a faster method: point at the Line Spacing button (without clicking), make sure the button's label says "Line Spacing (2)" (because you previously chatted with the computer about double-spacing), then click that button. The computer will assume you want double-spacing again, without waiting for you to choose 2.0 from the menu.

Select text

Here's how to dramatically change a phrase you typed.

Point at the phrase's beginning, then drag to the phrase's end (while holding down the mouse's left button). The whole phrase turns black. Turning the phrase black is called **selecting the phrase**.

Then say what to do to the phrase. For example, choose one of these activities:

To underline the phrase, activate the Underline button (by clicking it).
To make the phrase be bold, activate the Bold button (by clicking it).
To italicize the phrase, activate the Italic button (by clicking it).

To prevent the phrase from being underlined, bold, or italicized, deactivate those buttons (by clicking them again).

To change how the phrase's paragraphs are aligned, click one of the alignment buttons.
To change how the phrase's paragraphs are indented, click one of the indentation buttons.

To change the phrase's point size, choose the size you want from the Font Size menu.
To change the phrase's font, choose the font you want from the Font menu.
To change the phrase's style, choose the style you want from the Style menu.

To delete the phrase, press the **Delete key**.

To replace the phrase, just type whatever words you want the phrase to become.

Go ahead! Try it now! It's fun!

Advanced selection

Microsoft Word resembles WordPad, so **read these sections on page 87**:

"Other ways to select"
"Document vanishes"
"Drag a phrase"

Here are differences....

Other ways to select Microsoft Word permits this extra method:

Method 10: To select just **one sentence**, click in its middle while holding down the Ctrl key.

Drag a phase Selecting a phrase makes it turn black (not blue). The vertical line is black-and-white.

Standard toolbar

Near the screen's top, above the formatting toolbar, you see the **standard toolbar**, which in version 2003 looks like this:

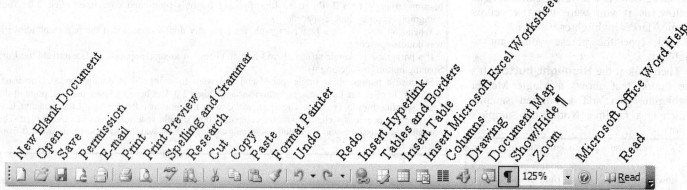

Here's how version 2002 differs:

> The Research button is called "Search".
> The Microsoft Office Word Help button is called just "Microsoft Word Help".
> The Permission and Read buttons are missing.

Here's how to use the most popular of those tools....

Save

To save the document (copy it onto the disk), click the **Save button** (or press Ctrl with S).

If you haven't saved the document before, the computer will say "File name". Invent a name for your document. Type the name and press Enter.

That makes the computer copy the document onto the hard disk. For example, if you named the document "mary", the computer puts a document called mary.doc into the My Documents folder.

Afterwards, if you change your mind and want to do more editing, go ahead! When you finish that extra editing, save it by clicking the Save button again.

Save often If you're typing a long document, click the Save button about every 10 minutes. Click it whenever you get to a good stopping place and think, "What I've typed so far looks good!"

Then if an accident happens, you'll lose at most 10 minutes of work, and you can return to the last version you felt good about.

Print

Here's how to print the document onto paper. Make sure you've bought a printer, attached it to the computer, turned the printer's power on, and put paper into the printer. Then click the **Print button**. The printer will print your document onto paper.

How to finish

When you finish working on a document, choose **Exit** or **Close** from the **File menu**.

If you choose **Exit**, the computer will stop using Microsoft Word.

If you choose **Close** instead of Exit, the computer will let you work on another document, and your next step is to click the **New Blank Document button** or the **Open button**.

> If you click the **New Blank Document button** (or press Ctrl with N), the computer will let you start typing a new document.
>
> If you click the **Open button** (or press Ctrl with O), you see a list of old documents. If you want to *use* one of those documents, double-click the document's name; the computer will put that document onto the screen and let you edit it. If instead you want to *delete* one of those documents, click the document's name then press the Delete key then the Enter key; the computer will move that document to the Recycle Bin.

Didn't save? If you didn't save your document before doing those procedures, the computer asks, "Do you want to save?" If you click "Yes", the computer copies your document's most recent version to the hard disk; if you click "No" instead, the computer ignores and forgets your most recent editing.

Congratulations! You've learned all the fundamental commands of Microsoft Word!

Undo

If you make a mistake (such as accidentally deleting some text, or accidentally giving the text an ugly font), click the **Undo button** (which shows an arrow turning back). That makes the computer undo your last activity, so your text returns to the way it looked before you made your boo-boo. (To undo your last *two* activities, click the Undo button *twice*.)

Here's a shortcut: instead of clicking the Undo button, you can press Ctrl with Z (which stands for "Zap").

Redo

If you click the Undo button, the computer might undo a different activity than you expected. If clicking the Undo button accidentally makes the text look even worse instead of better, and you wish you hadn't clicked the Undo button, you can "undo the undo" by clicking the **Redo button** (which shows an arrow bending forward).

Show/Hide ¶

Your version resembles Microsoft Word 2007, so **read "Show/Hide ¶" on page 190**.

Clipboard fundamentals

Microsoft Word resembles WordPad 7, so **read these sections on page 87:**

> "Cut and paste"
> "Copy"

In your version, dragging across a phrase makes it turn black (not blue).

Format Painter

Your version resembles Microsoft Word 2007, so **read "Format Painter" on page 188**. In your version, dragging makes things turn black (not blue).

Print Preview

If you're wondering what a page will look like but don't want to waste a sheet of paper to find out, click the **Print Preview button**. The computer will show you a mock-up of the whole page, shrunk to fit on the screen. Since it's shrunk to fit on the screen, its characters look too tiny for you to read the words easily, but you can see the page's overall appearance: how much of the page is filled up, which parts of the page are blank, and whether the info on the page is centered.

Wouldn't you like to ride in an airplane, fly high above your house, and see an aerial view of your house and neighborhood, so all the people look like tiny specs, and you see — in one amazing view — the overall layout of your house and yard and neighborhood and city? Wouldn't you be thrilled? Clicking the Print Preview button gives you that same thrill: you see an aerial view of the page you were typing, as if you were flying over it in an airplane: you see the layout of your whole page in one amazing view, and the characters on it look like tiny specs.

While you're admiring the view, the word "Close" appears at the screen's top center. When you finish admiring the view, click the word "Close".

Zoom

Look at the **Zoom box**. In that box, you normally see the number 100%. That means the computer's screen is showing you the actual size of what will appear on paper.

To the right of the Zoom box, you see a down-arrow. Click it. You see this **Zoom menu**:

```
500%
200%
150%
100%
75%
50%
25%
10%
Page Width
Text Width
Whole Page
Two Pages
```

For example, if you click **200%**, the computer makes the screen's characters be twice as high and twice as wide as normal, so you can read them even if you're sitting far away from the screen or you have poor vision. It's like looking at the document through a magnifying glass: the document looks enlarged, so you can see the details of each word and character more clearly; but not as many words and characters fit on the screen. Use the arrow keys to see different parts of the page.

Clicking 200% enlarges just what you see on the *screen*: it does *not* enlarge what appears on paper.

Try it! Try clicking 200%!

When you finish admiring that view, make the screen return to normal, by choosing **100%** from the Zoom menu.

If you click **Whole Page** instead of 200%, the computer does just the opposite: the computer makes the screen's characters be very tiny, so the whole page fits on the screen — as if you were doing a print preview.

A nice choice is **Page Width**. It makes the screen's characters be as big as possible, but still small enough so that you can see the left and right edges of the paper.

My favorite choice is **Text Width**. It makes the screen's characters be as big as possible (even bigger than Page Width), but still small enough so that you can see the first and last word of each line.

E-mail

To e-mail a copy of your document, the most accurate method is to write an e-mail letter having your document as an attachment. I explained "attachments" in my e-mail chapter on pages 137-138.

Here's a different way to e-mail a copy of your document:

> While looking at your document's words, highlight them all (by pressing Ctrl with A), then copy them all to the clipboard (by pressing Ctrl with C), then use your e-mail program (such as Outlook Express) to start writing an e-mail letter; but while you're writing the letter, click Ctrl with V, which pastes from the clipboard, so your entire document becomes part of the letter's body.

That method is good because it avoids dealing with "attachments", which can be hard to get working properly. But unfortunately, that method won't preserve your advanced formatting.

Here's a third way to e-mail a copy of your document. This way is a pleasant compromise between the other two ways: it avoids "attachments" and preserves *most* of your advanced formatting. Here are the details....

For version 2003, you must activate Outlook Express first, by doing this:

> Click "start" (at the screen's bottom left corner).
> Click "Outlook Express". (If you see "Outlook" instead of "Outlook Express", you neglected to do page 199's procedure for making Outlook Express the default e-mail client; do that procedure now then try again.)
> Make sure the screen's bottom says "Working Online". If it says "Working Offline" instead, make it say "Working Online" by clicking the Yes button (which you can force to appear by clicking "Send/Recv").
> If you see a Connect button, click it.
> Return to your document by clicking its button (which is at the screen's bottom, next to the Start button).

Proceed as follows....

Click the **E-mail button** (which looks like sheets of paper in front of a stamped envelope).

To whom do you want to e-mail the document? Type that person's e-mail address. For example, if you want to send the document to me, type my e-mail address, which is "russ@secretfun.com". Or for a fun experiment, just send the document to yourself by typing your own e-mail address.

Click in the "Subject" box. Type a subject for your e-mail (such as "here's a story I wrote" or "let's lunch" or "I'm testing").

Click "Send a Copy".

If the computer asks for your password, type the password your Internet Service Provider assigned you and press Enter.

Your computer will send the e-mail. (Your document will be the e-mail's body.) Afterwards, if the computer asks "Do you want to close the connection?" press Enter.

Spelling and Grammar

If you click in the middle of the document's first word and then click the **Spelling and Grammar button**, the computer will scan through your document for misspelled words, accidentally repeated words, and words that are grammatically wrong.

The computer will stop at the first word having a red or green squiggle underneath. (I explained squiggles on page 183.)

When the computer stops at a strange word that seems wrong, the computer shows a list of suggestions. If you like one of the suggestions, double-click it. If you *don't* like any of the computer's suggestions, you have these choices:

> click "Ignore Once" to make the computer leave the strange word unedited or else edit the strange word and then click "Change"

When the computer finishes checking the entire document, it says "The spelling and grammar check is complete."

Columns

In a newspaper, text is printed in many narrow **columns**. In a business letter, text is printed in a single wide column.

The computer assumes you want a single wide column. Here's how to tell the computer you want many narrow columns....

Click the **Columns button**. You'll see a tiny picture of a newspaper page that has several columns. Point at that picture's leftmost column, and drag to the right, until the number of columns you want turns blue.

For example, if you want 3 columns, drag to the right until 3 columns turn blue. If you want 6 columns, hold down the mouse's left button and drag to the right until 4 columns, then 5 columns, then finally 6 columns turn blue.

When you take your finger off the mouse's button, your entire document changes, so it has as many columns as you requested. The gap between each pair of columns is a half-inch.

Column break After you've finished typing a paragraph (and pressed Enter), try this experiment: while holding down the Ctrl and Shift keys, press Enter again. That creates a **column break**: it makes the next paragraph be at the top of the next column.

If you change your mind, here's how to remove the column break: click at the beginning of the paragraph you've put at the top of a column; then press the Backspace key.

Return to 1 column If you change your mind and want just 1 column, click the Columns button again, so you see the tiny picture of a newspaper page again. Click that picture's left column.

Table buttons

In the middle of your document, here's how to type a table of numbers.

Click where you want the table to appear.

Click the **Insert Table button**. You see a tiny picture of a table that has 4 rows and 5 columns. Altogether, it contains 20 cells (since 4 times 5 is 20). Each cell is a rectangle (whose sides are lines, called **gridlines**).

Point at that table's top left cell, and drag down and to the right, until the number of rows and columns you want turns blue.

For example, **if you want just 3 rows and 4 columns, drag down and to the right until 3 rows and 4 columns turn blue**, so you see 12 blue cells altogether.

When you take your finger off the mouse's button, you'll see the table you requested.

Then just fill in the cells, with whatever numbers and words you wish. To move from cell to cell, click with the mouse, or press the Tab key (which moves right to the next cell), or press Shift with Tab (which moves left to the previous cell), or press the arrow keys repeatedly.

In a cell, you can type a number, word, sentence, or even an entire paragraph! If you start typing a paragraph in a cell, the computer will automatically make the cell and its row taller, so the entire paragraph will fit in the cell. You can even type *several* paragraphs in a single cell: just press the Enter key at the end of each paragraph. If you want to indent the first line of one of those paragraphs, press the Space bar several times or press Ctrl with Tab.

Extra rows Here's how to create an extra row at the bottom of the table: click in the table's bottom right cell, then press the Tab key.

To insert an extra row into the *middle* of the table, do this:

> Click in the row that's underneath where you want the extra row to appear. Click "Table" then "Insert" then "Rows Above".

Column widths The computer assumes you want the table's columns to all be the same width. But you can change that assumption!

For example, here's how to adjust the width of the table's left column (column 1). Move the mouse until its pointer is on the vertical gridline that separates column 1 from column 2, and the pointer's shape turns into this symbol: ◄‖► Then drag the vertical gridline to the right (to make the column wider) or left (to make the column narrower).

If you make a column wider, the computer makes room for it by shrinking the next column. If you make a column narrower, the computer compensates by expanding the next column.

If you want to fine-tune the widths of *all* columns, work from left to right: adjust the width of column 1 (by dragging the gridline that separates it from column 2), then adjust the width of column 2 (by dragging the gridline that separates it from column 3), then adjust the width of column 3 (by dragging the gridline that separates it from column 4), etc.

Numbers If a column contains mostly numbers, make that column look prettier, so the numbers are aligned properly. Here's how....

Move the mouse until its pointer is at the *very top* of the column and is centered on the gridline above the column, so the pointer's shape turns into this symbol: ⬇. Then click. The entire column turns black.

Push in the Align Right button (on the formatting toolbar). That makes all cells in that column be aligned right, so the numbers are aligned properly.

Table AutoFit When you've finished typing numbers and words into all the cells, try this trick:

> Click the table's middle then the word "Table" then "AutoFit" then "AutoFit to Contents".

That makes the computer analyze all your columns and improve their widths. The computer will make each column become just wide enough to hold the data in it.

If you like what the computer did to your table, great! Go ahead and edit the table further!

If you *don't* like what the computer did, click the Undo button, which makes the table return to its previous appearance.

Below the table When you've finished editing the table, here's how to put paragraphs below it.

Click below the table by using the mouse, or go below the table by pressing the down-arrow key several times. Then type the paragraphs you want below the table.

Delete To delete a row, column, or the entire table, click in the middle of what you want to delete then do this....

> From the **Table menu**, choose **Delete**. Click **Rows** (if you want to delete a row) or **Columns** (if you want to delete a column) or **Table** (if you want to delete the entire table).

Customized tables The **Tables and Borders button** lets you create tables that have customized shapes. Here's how....

To create a customized table, click the **Tables and Borders button** (instead of the Insert Table button). You'll see a **Tables and Borders window**.

Where do you want the table to be in your document? **Put the mouse pointer where you want the table's top left corner to be, and drag to where you want the table's opposite corner.** (While dragging, hold down the mouse's left button.) You'll see a box, which is your table. Inside the box, make a grid of rows and columns by drawing horizontal and vertical gridlines. **To draw a gridline, put the mouse pointer where you want the line to begin, and drag to where you want the line to end.**

If you make a mistake, click the **Eraser button** (which is the second button in the Tables and Borders window), then click the line you want to erase. When you've erased a line, the line disappears from the screen (or turns a gray that does not print on paper). When you finish using the Eraser button, click the Draw Table button (which is the first button in the Tables and Borders window).

When you finish using the Tables and Borders window, close it (by clicking its X button).

Microsoft Office Word Help

If you have a popular question about using Microsoft Word, you can make the computer answer it.

For version 2003, do this:

At the screen's top right corner, you see a white box with some words in it. (At first, the words are "Type a question for help.")

Click in that box. Type your question about Microsoft Word, then press Enter. (That box works better than the Microsoft Office Word Help button.)

If the computer says "No results found", rephrase your question by using words the computer is more likely to understand.

The computer will show you a list of topics that relate to your question. (If the list is too long to fit in the window, scroll down to see more.) Click the topic that interests you, then click any other buttons that interest you. The computer will tutor you in whatever topics you request.

When you finish using that help, close each help window (by clicking its X button).

For version 2002, do this:

Click the **Microsoft Word Help** button or press the F1 key. You'll see the Office Assistant: a cute cartoon character named **Clippit**, who's an animated paper clip with eyes.

(Is Clippit male or female? Clippit's sex is a mystery. Here's how to have fun with Clippit's body: right-click Clippit then click Animate, which makes Clippit's body perform a random trick.)

Type your question about how to use Microsoft Word, then press Enter.

(The computer permits this shortened version of the above procedure: just type your question in the box at the screen's top right corner, without bothering to click the Office Assistant button; then press Enter.)

If the computer says "I don't know what you mean" or "No answers could be found", rephrase your question by using words the computer is more likely to understand.

The computer will show you a list of topics that relate to your question. (If the list is too long to fit in the box, click **See More** to see the rest of the list.) Click the topic that interests you, then click any other buttons that interest you. The computer will tutor you in whatever topics you request.

When you finish using Office Assistant, close each help window (by clicking its X button).

Menu bar

Near the screen's top, you see this **menu bar**:

| File Edit View Insert Format Tools Table Window Help |

Here's how to use it.

File menu

If you click the word File, you see the **File menu**, whose main choices are:

Open
Close

Save
Save As

Page Setup
Print Preview
Print

Properties

Exit

Open Choosing **Open** has the same effect as clicking the **Open button**, which I explained on page 204.

Close When you finish working on a document and want to work on a different document instead, choose **Close**, which I explained on page 204.

Save Choosing **Save** has the same effect as clicking the **Save button**, which I explained on page 204.

Save As Suppose you've already saved a document then edited it some more, but you're not sure you like the new editing. Try this experiment:

Choose **Save As**, then invent (and type) a new name for the document. At the end of the new name, press Enter.

Then the computer will copy the new, edited version of the document onto the hard disk. That new, edited version will have the new name you invented.

The old original version of the document will be on the disk also and keep its old original name. The disk will contain *both* versions of the document.

Page Setup Normally, the computer makes every page's top and bottom margins each be 1 inch tall, and makes every page's left and right margins each be 1¼ inches wide. To change those margin, choose **Page Setup**, then do this:

Click **Margins**. (If you see "Margins" twice, click the first one.)

Press the Tab key.

Type how many inches tall you want the top margin.   Press Tab.
Type how many inches tall you want the bottom margin. Press Tab.

Type how many inches wide you want the left margin.   Press Tab.
Type how many inches wide you want the right margin. Press Enter.

Print Preview Choosing **Print Preview** has the same effect as clicking the **Print Preview button**, which I explained on page 205.

Print If you choose **Print** from the File menu (or press Ctrl with P), the computer will ask how you'd like to print onto paper.

If you want to print more than 1 copy, type the number of copies.

If you want to print just the page you were working on, click the Current page button.

If you want to print just pages 1, 3, and 5 through 8, click the Pages button, then type "1,3,5-8".

If you selected (blackened) a phrase in your document and want to print just that phrase, click the Selection button.

If you own at least 2 printers, do this: click the down-arrow next to the Printer Name box , then choose which printer you want to use (by clicking it).

Then press Enter. The printer will print what you desired!

Properties If you choose **Properties** then click **Statistics**, the computer will tell you how long the document is: how many pages, paragraphs, lines, words, and characters it contains.

The computer will also reveal….

when created:	when you first started creating the document, long ago
when modified:	when document was last saved (copied from screen to disk)
when accessed:	when document was last opened (copied from disk to screen)
when printed:	when document was last printed onto paper

The computer will also reveal the total number of minutes and hours you've spent fiddling with this document (so your boss can complain about how much time you've wasted on it).

When you finish reading those statistics, press Enter.

Exit When you finish using Microsoft Word, choose **Exit**, which I explained on page 204.

Recently used documents Near the bottom of Microsoft Word's file menu, you see a list of the 4 Microsoft Word documents you recently used. If you want to use one of those documents now, click it.

That list of recent documents might annoy you, for 2 reasons:

One of the documents might be embarrassing (perhaps because it's pornographic or a private letter), and you want to hide it from your colleagues and family.

Even after you've deleted a document, that document's name might still be in the File menu.

If the **recent-document list annoys you**, delete documents from it, as follows….

That list shows just the names of *the last 4* Microsoft Word documents you mentioned. Go use other Microsoft Word documents; they'll go onto File menu and bump off the older documents.

Another way to get a document off the File menu is to erase the entire recent-document list from the File menu. Here's how. Click "Tools" (which is on the menu bar) then "Options" then "General". Remove the check mark from the "Recently used file list" square (by clicking). Click "OK". That erases the entire recent-document list from the File menu. Afterward, let the computer create a *new* recent-document list in the File menu, as follows: click "Tools" then "Options", then put a check mark back into the "Recently used file list" square (by clicking), then click "OK".

Edit menu

If you click the word Edit, you see the **Edit menu**, whose main choices are:

Undo

Cut
Copy
Paste

Clear
Select All

Find
Replace
Go To

Of those choices, the first four imitate buttons:

Choosing **Undo** is like clicking the **Undo button** (explained on page 204).

Choosing **Cut** is like clicking the **Cut button** (explained on page 87).
Choosing **Copy** is like clicking the **Copy button** (explained on page 87).
Choosing **Paste** is like clicking the **Paste button** (explained on page 87).

The next two imitate your keyboard:

Choosing **Clear** is like pressing the **Delete key** (explained on page 203).
Choosing **Select All** is like pressing the **A key with Ctrl** (page 87).

Find Here's how to make the computer search through your document to find whether you've used the word "love":

Click where you want the search to begin. (For example, if you want the search to begin at the document's beginning, click in the middle of the document's first word.) Choose **Find** from the Edit menu (or press Ctrl with F). Type the word you want to find ("love"), and press Enter.

The computer will search for "love". If the computer finds a "love" in your document, it will highlight that "love" so it turns black. If you want to find the next "love" in your document, press Enter; if you do *not* want to search for more "love", press the Esc key instead.

The previous-page and next-page arrows (at the screen's bottom right corner) turn blue. Afterwards, clicking them makes the computer find the previous or next "love" (instead of the previous or next page).

Suppose you've written a history of America and want to find the part where you started talking about Lincoln. If you forget what page that was, no problem! Just put the cursor at the beginning of the document, choose **Find** from the Edit menu, type "Lincoln", and press Enter.

Replace You can search for a word and replace it with a different word. For example, here's how to change each "love" in your document to "idolize":

Choose **Replace**. Type the old word you want to replace ("love"), then press the Tab key, then type the new word you want instead ("idolize"), then click the Replace All button. That makes the computer change each "love" to "idolize". Then press the Esc key twice.

The computer preserves capitalization. For example, if the document said —

I love you. Love you! LOVE YOU! I want to kiss your glove!

the computer changes it to:

I idolize you. Idolize you! IDOLIZE YOU! I want to kiss your gidolize!

Notice that when told to change "love" to "idolize", the computer unfortunately also changes "glove" to "gidolize".

The Replace command helps you zip through many chores:

For example, if you write a letter that talks about Fred, then want to write a similar letter about Sue, tell the computer to replace each Fred with Sue.

If you write a book about "How to be a better salesman" and then a feminist tells you to change each "salesman" to "salesperson", tell the computer to replace each "salesman".

If you're writing a long ad that mentions "Calvin Klein's Hot New Flaming Pink Day-Glo Pajamas" repeatedly, and you're too lazy to type that long phrase so often, just type the abbreviation "Calnew". When you've finished typing the document, tell the computer to replace each "Calnew" with the long phrase it stands for.

Go To When you've typed a document that's several pages long, here's the traditional way to move to page 2:

Choose **Go To** from the Edit menu (or press Ctrl with G).

Make sure the computer says "Enter page number". (If the computer doesn't say that yet, click **Page** and then press the Tab key.)

Type your desired page number (which is 2), then press Enter. You'll see page 2 on the screen.

Press the Esc key.

Here's a faster way to move to page 2:

Along the screen's right edge, you see a scroll-up arrow (▲) and a scroll-down-arrow (▼). Between them, you see a little box, called the **scroll box**.

Using the mouse, point at the scroll box, and hold down the mouse's left button. While you hold down the button, you'll see the current page number.

Drag the scroll box up or down, until the page number changes to the number you want: 2.

View menu

If you click the word View, you see the **View menu**, whose main choices are:

```
Normal
Print Layout

Toolbars
Ruler

Header and Footer

Full Screen
```

Normal versus Print Layout

The View menu's most popular choices are **Normal** and **Print Layout**. You should use Print Layout most of the time, because it shows you accurately what will appear on paper. If you choose **Normal** instead, here's what happens:

> **In Normal view, the screen will show just a crude approximation of what will appear on paper.** The computer won't bother to show what's in the margins (such as page numbers), won't bother to show footnotes, won't bother to show graphics, and won't bother to show newspaper columns side-by-side (instead it will show the second column *under* the first column, and will show the third column *under* the second column). Since the computer takes those shortcuts, the computer displays the page fast — unlike Print Layout view, which makes the computer be fussily accurate about what appears on the screen.
>
> Since Normal view displays fewer items on the screen, it makes more of the screen available for your important words and can display them bigger, so you can read them more easily. So **if you're stuck using a small screen that's hard to read, you might like Normal view, which can enlarge your typing** by omitting the margins, rulers, and other details.

Toolbars
If you choose **Toolbars**, version 2003 shows you this list of toolbars:

```
Standard
Formatting
AutoText
Control Toolbox
Database
Drawing
E-mail
Forms
Frames
Ink Comment
Mail Merge
Outlining
Picture
Reviewing
Tables and Borders
Task Pane
Visual Basic
Web
Web Tools
Word Count
WordArt
```

(In version 2002, the list is shorter.)

In the list, **"Standard" and "Formatting" should have check marks in front of them**. Those check marks make the standard toolbar and formatting toolbar appear on your screen. If those check marks are missing, those toolbars disappear.

To make a check mark disappear, click it. To make a check mark appear, click where you want it to appear.

Ruler
In the View menu, the Ruler choice should have a check mark in front of it. That makes a horizontal ruler appear across the screen. The ruler is numbered 1", 2", 3", 4", etc. If you're in Print Layout view, it also makes a vertical ruler appear up and down the screen's left edge. If the Ruler choice does *not* have a check mark, the rulers disappear. To make the check mark appear or disappear, choose **Ruler** from the View menu.

Header and Footer
Normally, the top inch of each page is blank, to form the top margin. Anything you scribble in that margin is called a **header**.

For example, suppose you're writing a top-secret memo and want to scribble this note in the top margin of every page:

> Reminder! The info in this memo is TOP SECRET!

Here's how to do it....

Choose **Header and Footer**. Type your header:

> Reminder! The info in this memo is TOP SECRET!

Then click the word "Close". The computer will put your header at the top of each page of your document.

> When you print the document onto **paper**, your header is printed in **black**.
>
> While you're using **Print Layout view**, your header appears on the screen in **gray** instead of black.
>
> While you're using **Normal view**, your header usually **disappears** from the screen, since Normal view doesn't show you the margins. To see your header, switch to Print Layout view (by choosing Print Layout from the View menu), or choose "Header and Footer" again from the View menu.

If you want to edit the header, choose "Header and Footer" again from the View menu, then edit the header however you wish, then click the word "Close" again.

Instead of writing a header about being "TOP SECRET", here are 4 other headers you might enjoy using:

> Please do not copy! It's copyrighted by starving author!
>
> ACHTUNG! To keep your job, reply to this memo by Friday!
>
> SALE! To order any of these items, call our 800 number!
>
> I love you!!! I love you!!! I love you!!!

Here's a way **to make the computer print the page number at the top of each page:**

> Choose **Header and Footer**.
> Click the **Insert Page Number** button. That makes the computer put a "1" at the top of page 1, a "2" at the top of page 2, etc.
> Click the word "Close".

Let's get fancier! Let's make the computer print this at the top of page 1 —

> This is page 1 of the Great American Novel

and print this at the top of page 2 —

> This is page 2 of the Great American Novel

and print this at the top of page 3 —

> This is page 3 of the Great American Novel

etc. Here's how:

> Choose **Header and Footer** from the View menu.
> Type the header's beginning words: "This is page". After the word "page", press the Space bar.
> Click the **Insert Page Number** button. That makes the computer automatically type a "1" on page 1, a "2" on page 2, etc.
> Press the Space bar (to make the computer leave a blank space after the page number). Type the header's ending words: "of the Great American Novel". Click the word "Close".

Here's how **to print in the bottom margin (instead of the top margin):**

> Choose **Header and Footer** from the View menu. If the computer shows you a space labeled "Header", switch to "Footer" by clicking the **Switch Between Header and Footer** button.
> Type the footer (whatever you want in the bottom margin). Then click the word "Close".

Full Screen
Usually, just *part* of the screen shows your document; the rest of the screen shows the toolbars, rulers, menus, Start button, clock, and other doodads.

If you choose **Full Screen**, the computer devotes the *entire* screen to displaying your document, by making the doodads disappear. Yes, the toolbars, rulers, menus, Start button, clock, and all other doodads disappear. Instead of seeing doodads, you see more of your document.

When you finish admiring the full-screen view, press the Escape key (which says "Esc" on it). Then all the doodads reappear, including the toolbars, rulers, menus, Start button, clock, etc.

Insert menu

If you click the word Insert, you see the **Insert menu**, whose main choices are:

```
Page Numbers
Date and Time
Symbol

Reference

Text Box
File
Bookmark
```

Page Numbers To print page numbers on all the pages *easily*, choose **Page Numbers**, then press Enter. That makes the computer put the page number on each page's bottom right corner, in the bottom margin, in the part of the page called the **footer**. (The computer will automatically switch you to Print Layout view.)

When you print the document onto **paper**, the page numbers will be printed in **black**.

While you're using **Print Layout view**, the page numbers will appear on the screen in **gray** instead of black.

While you're using **Normal view**, you **won't see** the page numbers, since Normal view doesn't show you the margins.

Date and Time To type the date or time, choose **Date and Time**. The computer will show a list of formats, like this:

```
12/25/2011
Sunday, December 25, 2011
December 25, 2011
12/25/11
2011-12-25
25-Dec-11
12.25.2011
Dec. 25, 11
25 December 2011
December 11
Dec-11
12/25/2011 10:59 PM
12/25/2011 10:59:20 PM
10:59 PM
10:59:20 PM
22:59
22:59:20
```

Click the format you want. Press Enter. The computer will type the date or time in the format you requested.

In that procedure, just before you press Enter, you might wish to put a check mark in the **Update Automatically** box. Here's how that box works:

Suppose you type a document on Monday, but you print the document the next day (Tuesday). Which date will the computer print on paper? The computer will print the date that the document was typed (Monday), unless you put a check mark in the Update Automatically box, which makes the computer print the "date printed" (Tuesday).

If you put a check mark in the Update Automatically box, the computer will automatically update the date & time whenever the document is printed or print-previewed or opened.

Symbol To type a special symbol, choose **Symbol**. You'll see the **Symbol window**. In that window, you can click either the **Symbols** tab or the **Special Characters** tab.

If you click the **Special Characters** tab, the computer will show you this list of special characters:

— Em Dash (a dash that's slightly wider than an M; it's exactly as wide as the font's point-size height)
– En Dash (a dash that's slightly narrower than an N; it's exactly half as wide as an Em Dash)

- Nonbreaking Hyphen (a hyphen, between words that must appear on the same line as each other)
- Optional Hyphen (a hyphen, visible just when the word it's in is too long to fit on a line)

Em Space (a blank space that's slightly wider than an M; it's as wide as the font's point-size height)
En Space (a blank space that's slightly narrower than an N; it's exactly half as wide as an Em Space)
¼ Em Space (a blank space that's very narrow; it's a quarter as wide as an Em Space)
Nonbreaking Space (a space between words that must appear on the same line as each other)

© Copyright
® Registered
™ Trademark

§ Section
¶ Paragraph
… Ellipsis

' Single Opening Quote
' Single Closing Quote

" Double Opening Quote
" Double Closing Quote

No-Width Optional Break (if the word is too long to fit on a line, break it here without a hyphen)
No-Width Non Break

If you click the **Symbols** tab instead and then click the **Font** box's down-arrow, you see a list of different fonts. Scroll down to see the different font choices. For best results, click one of these 6 fonts:

```
(normal text)
Symbol
Webdings
Wingdings
Wingdings 2
Wingdings 3
```

Read page 194's column 2. Read page 195.

Footnote Suppose you're writing a religious pamphlet in which you want to say "Read the Bible tonight!" Suppose you want to add a footnote saying "written by God", so the main text looks like this —

Read the Bible[1] tonight!

and the page's bottom contains this footnote:

[1] Written by God.

Here's how to do it all....
Type "Read the Bible". Choose **Reference** then click **Footnote**.
Make sure the Footnote button has a dot in it (by clicking it). Press Enter.
Type the footnote ("Written by God.").
Go back to the main text, where you left off, by using one of these methods:

Method 1: double-click the footnote's number; if you're using Print Layout view, press the right-arrow key afterwards.

Method 2 (just if using Normal view): click the button that says "Close" on it.

Method 3 (just if using Print Layout view): climb back up to the main text (by using the keyboard's up-arrow key), then go right to where you left off typing (by using the End key).

The computer will put the footnotes at the bottom of the page. If the page is divided into newspaper columns, the computer will put each footnote at the bottom of the column it refers to.

The computer will put a 2-inch horizontal line above the footnotes to separate them from the main text.

Your printer will print the footnotes accurately onto paper. You'll see the footnotes on your screen accurately while you're doing a print preview, or while you're using Print Layout view. (To see the footnotes on your screen while using Normal view, choose Footnotes from the View menu.)

If you insert extra footnotes, the computer will automatically renumber the other footnotes, so the first footnote appearing in your document will be numbered [1], the second footnote will be numbered [2], etc.

Here's the easiest way to delete a footnote:

> Click the left edge of the footnote's number in the main text; then press the Delete key twice.

Text Box You can draw a box wherever you wish, *anywhere* on the page (even in the margins) and put words into it, to create a **text box**. Here's how:

> From the Insert menu, choose **Text Box**.
> Press Ctrl with Z (which erases the "Create your drawing here" box) and deactivate the Drawing button (by clicking it).
> Where do you want the text box? Put the mouse pointer where you want the text box's top left corner to be, and drag to where you want the box's opposite corner. The box will appear.
> Type whatever words or paragraphs you want in the box.

Here's how to **move the box** to a different place on the page:

> Point at one of the box's sides. (Stay away from any tiny circles or tiny squares you see next to the sides.) When you do that successfully, the mouse pointer becomes a cross with arrowheads pointing in all 4 directions.
> Then move the box by dragging the side wherever you wish.

Here's how to **adjust the box's size**:

> Click in the box.
> At the box's bottom right corner, you see a tiny circle. Put the mouse pointer there. Make sure the middle of the mouse pointer is in the middle of that circle. When you do that successfully, the mouse pointer becomes a diagonal arrow with 2 arrowheads.
> Then adjust the box's size by dragging that tiny square wherever you wish.

If you move the box to a part of the page that already contains words, what happens to those words? To **move words out of the box's way**, do this:

> Double-click one of the box's sides.
> Click **Layout** then **Square**. Press Enter.

Here's how to **delete the box**:

> Point at one of the box's sides. When you do that successfully, the mouse pointer sprouts 2 or 4 arrowheads.
> Click. Press the keyboard's Delete key.

File In the middle of your document, you can insert a secondary document that you saved previously, so you'll produce a combo document including all paragraphs from both documents. Here's how:

> Click in the middle of the document you're writing, where you want the secondary document to be inserted.
> Choose **File** from the Insert menu. Double-click the name of the secondary document that you want to insert.

The document on the screen will become longer. If you don't like the result, click the **Undo button**; if you *do* like the result, click the **Save button**.

Bookmark While you're in the middle of editing a document, suppose you get a sudden urge to switch to a different activity (such as peek at a different part of the document, or play a game, or go to bed, or have sex). Before you switch to that other activity, you can put a **bookmark** in your document, where you were editing. Later, when you want to resume working on the document, you can return to that bookmark and continue editing where you left off.

Here's **how to create a bookmark:**

> Decide where in the document you want to put the bookmark. Click there. Choose **Bookmark**.
> Invent a name for your bookmark. Use your nickname, or a simple word such as "mark". The name must be simple: it must begin with a letter; it can contain letters, numbers, and underscores (_); it must *not* contain any spaces or special symbols. Type the name. At the end of the name, click the Add button.
> The computer will create a bookmark using that name. (If your document *already* contained a bookmark using that name, that old bookmark will disappear.) Typically, the screen doesn't bother showing you where bookmarks are.

After you've created a bookmark, be safe: click the **Save button** and save the document. Then do whatever else you wish: peek at a different part of the document, or play a game, or shut down the computer and go to bed. When you want **to return to your document's bookmarked part, do this:**

> Make sure the document is on the screen.
> Choose **Go To** from the Edit menu (or press Ctrl with G). Click the word **Bookmark**.
> You'll see the name of a bookmark you created. (If you created *several* bookmarks and want to reach a different bookmark than the one named, click the down-arrow next to the name, then click the name of a bookmark you want to reach.)
> Press Enter. The computer will go to the place in the document where you put the bookmark.
> Press the Esc key (to make the bookmark-finding window vanish).

If you wish, make the screen show you where the bookmarks are. Here's how:

> Choose **Options** from the Tools menu. Click the **View** tab.
> Put a check mark in the **Bookmarks** box (by clicking the word "Bookmarks"). Press Enter.

That makes the screen put the symbol **I** at each bookmark. That symbol appears just on the screen, not on paper.

Here's **how to delete a bookmark:**

> Choose **Bookmark**.
> Click the name of the bookmark you want to delete. Click the word "**Delete**". Press Enter.

Format menu

If you click the word Format, you see the **Format menu**, whose main choices are:

> Font
> Paragraph
> Bullets and Numbering
> Borders and Shading
>
> Columns
> Tabs
> Drop Cap
> Change Case
>
> AutoFormat
> Styles and Formatting

Font Here's how to improve the appearance of a phrase on your screen.

Which phrase do you want to improve? Select it (by dragging across it). Then choose **Font** from the Format menu. You see the **Font window**, which has three **tabs**, called **Font**, **Character Spacing**, and **Text Effects**.

Click the **Font** tab. You see these boxes:

Box	Normal contents	Other popular choices
Font	Times New Roman	Tahoma, Comic Sans MS, Courier New, Arial
Font style	Regular	Bold, Italic, Bold Italic
Size	12	8, 9, 11, 12, 14, 16, 18, 20, 22, 24, 26, 28, 36, 48, 72
Underline	(none)	Single, Double, Thick, Dotted, Dash, Words Only
Color	Auto	Blue, Red, Yellow, Bright Green, Turquoise, Pink

(The "Color" box is split into two boxes, called "Font Color" and "Underline Color".)

For the Underline box or Color box, you must click the box's down-arrow once or twice, to see all choices. For the Font box or Size box, you must click the box's up-arrow and down-arrow repeatedly, to see all popular choices. **For each box, click whatever choice you want.**

In the Underline box, if you choose "Words only", the computer will underline the words but not the spaces between them.

Below all those boxes, you see a list of these special **Effects** you can choose:

Effect	What the computer will do
All caps	make the writing be all in capitals, LIKE THIS
Small Caps	make the writing be all in tiny capitals, LIKE THIS
Superscript	make the writing be tiny and raised, ^like this
Subscript	make the writing be tiny and lowered, ₗike this
Strikethrough	draw a line through your writing, ~~like this~~
Double Strikethrough	draw *two* lines through your writing, ~~like this~~
Shadow	make a shadow behind each character, as if in the sun
Outline	show each character's outline, as if on a varsity jacket
Engrave	make the writing look like it's chiseled into stone
Emboss	make the writing look like it sticks out from stone

Click each effect you want, so a check mark appears in the effect's box. The weird effects (Shadow, Outline, Engrave, and Emboss) work best when the Font Size is big (such as 48 or 72 points).

When you've finished using the Font window, press Enter.

Congratulations! You've learned how to use fonts!

Here's an advanced secret that most computer "experts" don't know:

Suppose you've typed something but it's too wide to fit. For example, suppose you've typed a headline too wide to fit above the main text, or typed a line too wide to fit between the margins, or typed a table entry too wide to fit in the table's column. Here's how to magically make your typing be slightly narrower, so it fits.

Select the phrase you want to narrow (by dragging across it), then choose Font from the Format menu, then click the **Character Spacing** tab. Then you can use 3 tricks to make the type narrower.

Scaling trick: in the **Scale** box (which normally says "100%"), type a smaller number (such as 95%). That makes each character narrower.

Spacing trick: in the **Spacing By** box (which is normally blank), click the down-arrow key twice (so the screen will say Spacing Condensed By 0.2 pt). That puts less space between the characters, so the characters are shoved closer together.

Kerning trick: put a check mark in the **Kerning** box (by clicking the word "Kerning"). That procedure eliminates wasted space between certain pairs of letters.

After you've filled those boxes the way you want, press Enter, which makes the computer obey you.

Paragraph To change the way a paragraph is spaced, **click in the paragraph** then choose one of these methods:

Standard method: choose **Paragraph** from the Format menu, then click **Indents and Spacing**.
Short-cut method: click the **Line Spacing button**'s down-pointing triangle, then click "More".

Then you'll see a box called **Line spacing**. Normally, that box says "Single". If you want to double-space instead (so the computer puts a blank line under each line you type), click that box's down-arrow, then choose "Double".

You'll see a box called **Before**. Normally, that box says "0 pt". If you want the computer to leave a blank space above the paragraph, put a number bigger than 0 into that box.

If you put 72 into that box, the computer will leave a 1-inch blank space above the paragraph, since 72 points = 1 inch. If you put 36 into that box, the computer will leave a ½-inch blank space above the paragraph, since 36 points = ½ inch.

The most typical number to put into that box is 12, which makes the computer leave a 1/6-inch blank space above the paragraph. To be more subtle, try a number smaller than 12, such as 6.

You'll see a box called **Special**. Normally, that box says "(none)". If you want special indentation, click that box's down-arrow, then choose "First line" (which indents just the paragraph's first line) or choose "Hanging" (which indents every line of the paragraph *except the first line*). If you choose "First line" or "Hanging", the computer will make the indentation be ½-inch (which is 0.5"), unless you put a different decimal in the **Special By** box.

If you want *every* line of the paragraph to be indented ½ inch, put "(none)" in the Special box but put 0.5" (or simply .5) in the **Left** box.

When you finish making the boxes contain the instructions you want, press Enter.

Bullets and Numbering Page 189 said that if you click in the middle of a paragraph and then activate the **Bullets button**, the computer normally puts a simple bullet (the symbol •) at the beginning of the paragraph (and indents the paragraph).

If you don't like the symbol •, pick a different symbol instead. Here's how....

Choose **Bullets and Numbering** from the Format menu. Then click **Bulleted**.

You see these seven bullet symbols:

•	▪	➢	✓	❖	○	❑

(Actually, your version of Microsoft Word shows colored rectangles instead of ❑.)

Double-click whichever symbol you want. The computer puts your chosen symbol at the beginning of the paragraph. It also makes the Bullets button henceforth produce that symbol — in this document and all other documents — until you switch to a different symbol instead or exit from Microsoft Word.

Page 189 said that if you click in the middle of a paragraph and then activate the **Numbering button**, the computer normally puts "1." at the beginning of the paragraph (and indents the paragraph), puts "2." at the beginning of the next paragraph, etc. If you don't like that numbering scheme, pick a different scheme instead. Here's how....

Choose **Bullets and Numbering** from the Format menu. Then click **Numbered**.

You see these seven schemes:

1.	1)	I.	i.	A.	a.	a)
2.	2)	II.	ii.	B.	b.	b)
3.	3)	III.	iii.	C.	c.	c)

Double-click whichever scheme you want.

Borders and Shading Here's how to draw a box around your writing. First, tell the computer which part of your writing to put in the box.

To put one paragraph in the box, click in that paragraph.

To put *several* paragraphs in the box, click in the first of those paragraphs, then do this: *while holding down the Shift key*, click in the last of those paragraphs.

To put a short phrase in the box, drag across the phrase.

Next, choose **Borders and Shading** from the Format menu. Here's what happens afterwards....

Click **Borders**. Click either the **Box** button (to create a simple box) or the **Shadow** button (to create a more advanced box whose right and bottom edges have a shadow from sunlight).

In the middle of the box, if you want your writing to have a colored or gray background instead of a white background, click **Shading** then click your favorite color (or shade of gray).

Press Enter. The computer will draw the box, but you might have trouble seeing it clearly. Press the right-arrow key (to move the cursor out of the way, so you can see your box clearly).

Columns Page 206 explained that you can create newspaper columns by clicking the **Columns button**. To create columns that are customized, do this instead:

Choose **Columns** from the Format menu.

If you want 2 columns (that are the same width as each other), click the **Two** button.
If you want 3 columns (that are the same width as each other), click the **Three** button.
If you want 2 columns, where the left column is narrower than the other, click the **Left** button.
If you want 2 columns, where the right column is narrower than the other, click the **Right** button.

If you want to draw a vertical line in the gap between columns, put a mark in the **Line Between** box (by clicking).

The computer assumes you want each gap between columns to be a half-inch wide. (That's 0.5".) If you want the gap to be a different width instead, change the number in the **Spacing** box (by retyping it or by clicking its up-arrow or down-arrow). For example, on this page (and in most of this book) the gap between columns is 0.3".

When you finish saying what kind of columns you want, press Enter. Then the computer will create them.

Tabs While you're typing your document, pressing the Tab key resembles pressing the Space bar but makes the computer move much farther to the right, to the next **tab stop**.

Normally, the tab stops are spaced ½-inch apart. For finer control over your document, make the tab stops be $^1/_{10}$-inch apart instead. Here's how: choose **Tabs** from the Format menu, then type 0.1" (or just .1) in the **Default Tab Stops** box and press Enter. That procedure changes the tab stops for the entire document.

After doing that procedure, here's how to easily create a fine-looking table (without using the Insert Table button): just press the Tab key repeatedly, to move to the next column. (Pressing the Tab key is more accurate than pressing the Space bar.)

Drop Cap After you've typed a paragraph, here's how to make that paragraph begin with a capital letter that's huge: click anywhere in that paragraph, choose **Drop Cap** from the Format menu, click **Dropped**, then press Enter.

If you change your mind, here's how to delete the huge capital letter: *triple*-click in the middle of the letter, then press the Delete key.

Change Case After typing a phrase, if you change your mind and wish you'd capitalized it, do this:

Select the phrase (by dragging across it). Choose **Change Case** from the Format menu.
If you want to capitalize the entire phrase (LIKE THIS), click **UPPERCASE**; if you prefer to capitalize just the first letter of each word (Like This), click **Title Case** instead.
Press Enter.

AutoFormat After you've typed your document, try telling the computer to make the document look prettier. Here's how....

Click in the middle of the document. Choose **AutoFormat** from the Format menu. You'll see the AutoFormat window. In that window is a box. Normally, that box says "General document". If you're writing a letter (instead of a book or report or newspaper), change "General document" to "Letter" (by clicking the down-arrow and then clicking Letter). Press Enter.

The computer will try to make the document look prettier. For example, if your document contains what seems to be a heading, the computer will make it Arial and big (16-point bold). If you're writing a letter that ends with —

Sincerely,

---

and a few other lines underneath it, the computer will indent the word "Sincerely" and the lines underneath, so they all begin at the center of the paper instead of at the left margin. The computer makes many other improvements also! But here's an exception: if you *already* tried to fiddle with the appearance of a line, the computer leaves that line alone.

If you like what the computer did to your document, great! Go ahead and edit the document further!

If you *don't* like what the computer did, click the Undo button, which makes the document return to its previous appearance.

Styles and Formatting While you're typing your document, the formatting toolbar's Style box shows what style you're using. That box usually says Normal, but you can switch to a different style instead, such as "Heading 1". (I explained that box on page 202.)

Styles such as "Normal" and "Heading 1" were invented by Microsoft.

Here's how **to invent your own paragraph style:**

In your document, create a paragraph whose appearance thrills you, by using the formatting toolbar and Format menu. Click in the middle of the paragraph's first word.

From the Format menu, choose "**Styles and Formatting**" or click the "Styles and Formatting" button (which looks like two A's).

Click the **New Style** button. Invent a name for your style (such as "Wow"): type the name, and at the end of the name press the Enter.

Click the style's name. Close the Styles and Formatting window (by clicking its X button).

The style you invented ("Wow") will appear in the formatting toolbar's Style box.

While you're typing the document, the style you invented ("Wow") is part of the computer's repertoire. For example, while you're typing another paragraph, you can make that paragraph's style be "Normal" or "Heading 1" or "Wow": just click the Style box's down-arrow then click the style you want.

The style you invented ("Wow") is part of the computer's repertoire just while you're using that document, not while you're using other documents.

Later, if you change your mind, **you can improve that style by using this method:**

Click in a paragraph written in that style. Improve that paragraph's appearance (by using the formatting toolbar and the Format menu). Click in the middle of the paragraph's first word. Click the "Styles and Formatting" button. Near the screen's right edge, you see the "Styles and Formatting" window. In that window, you see a list of styles; find your style's short name (without a plus sign afterwards) and right-click it. Click "Update to Match Selection". Close the Styles and Formatting window (by clicking its X button).

Tools menu

If you click the word Tools, you see the **Tools menu**, whose main choices are:

> Spelling and Grammar
> Language
> Word Count

Spelling and Grammar Choosing **"Spelling and Grammar"** has the same effect as clicking the **"Spelling and Grammar" button**, which I explained on page 205.

Language Choosing "Language" makes the computer find synonyms. The *best* way to find synonyms is to use the procedure explained in the "Synonyms" section on page 200.

Word Count If you choose **Word Count**, the computer will tell you how long the document is: how many pages, paragraphs, lines, words, and characters it contains. This procedure resembles choosing Properties from the File menu but is faster and generates a report that's briefer. When you finish reading the report, press Enter.

Table menu

If you click the word Table, you see the **Table menu**, which I explained on page 206.

Window menu

If you click the word Window, you see the **Window menu**, whose main choices are:

> Arrange All
> Split

Arrange All Here's how to see *two* documents on the screen at once!

> To be safe, make sure both documents have been saved on disk (by using the **Save button**). Close any documents that are on the screen (by choosing **Close** from the File menu), so the screen's main part is blank.
> Click the **Open button**. Double-click the first document's name. You see the document's words and paragraphs on the screen.
> *While that first document is still on the screen (without closing it)*, click the **Open button** again. Double-click the second document's name. You see the document's words and paragraphs on the screen; they cover up the first document, so you can't see the first document at the moment.
> Choose **Arrange All** from the Window menu. Then you see *two* windows on the screen. The top window shows the second document; the bottom window shows the first document.

Each window is small, showing just a tiny part of the document. A window might seem blank if it's so small that it shows just the document's top margin.

Each window has its own scroll arrows. Use them to scroll through the documents and see the parts of the documents that are *not* blank.

By using those two windows, you can easily compare two documents and copy from one to the other (by using the Copy and Paste buttons).

When you stop wanting one of the windows, here's how to make it disappear:

> Click in that window, then close that window (by clicking its X button). Expand the other window (by clicking its maximize button, which is next to its X button).

Split To see two parts of your document at the same time, choose **Split**. A fat gray line appears across the middle of your screen and split your screen's window into two parts, a top windowpane and a bottom windowpane.

Move the mouse slightly (which moves the fat gray line slightly up or down), until you're happy about the line's position. Then click the mouse's left button.

Now you can see two parts of your document at the same time! Each windowpane has its own scroll arrows. You can click those scroll arrows to change what you see in that windowpane, without changing what's in the other windowpane.

You can also click in one windowpane's text and then use the keyboard's movement keys (up-arrow, down-arrow, left-arrow, right-arrow, Page Up, Page Down, Home, and End) to change what's in that windowpane, without changing what you see in the other windowpane.

Both windowpanes show parts of the same document. If you change a word in one windowpane (by deleting or inserting or revising that word), while the other windowpane happens to show the same part of the document, you see that word automatically change in the other windowpane also, immediately!

By using those two windowpanes, you can easily compare two parts of your document and copy from one part to the other (by using the Copy and Paste buttons).

When you stop wanting two windowpanes, here's how **to return to a single pane....**

> Which windowpane do you want to remove? Click in that windowpane. Choose **Remove Split** from the Window menu. That windowpane disappears, so the entire screen becomes devoted to the other windowpane.

Help menu

If you click the word Help, you see the **Help menu**, whose main choices are:

> Microsoft Word Help
> Hide the Office Assistant
>
> What's This?
>
> About Microsoft Word

(Instead of "About Microsoft Word", version 2003 says "About Microsoft Office Word". Instead of "Microsoft Word Help", version 2003 says "Microsoft Office Word Help". Version 2003 lacks "Hide the Office Assistant" and "What's This?")

Hide the Office Assistant (version 2002) Choosing **Hide the Office Assistant** makes the animated paper clip (Clippit) disappear. To make Clippit reappear, choose **Show the Office Assistant** from the Help menu.

What's This? (version 2002) Try this experiment: choose **What's This** from the Help menu (or press Shift with F1). Then if you click any object (button or menu item) anywhere on the screen, the computer will tell you what that object means. When you finish reading the computer's explanation, press the Escape key (which says "Esc" on it).

About Microsoft Word If you choose **About Microsoft Word** (or About Microsoft Office Word), the computer will display a version message saying which version of Microsoft Word you're using.

(If you then click the System Info button, you'll see, after a short delay, a window saying what kind of computer you bought and what state it's in. When you finish looking at that window, close it by clicking its X button.)

When you finish using About Microsoft Word, make its window disappear by clicking its OK button (if the window hasn't disappeared already).

Microsoft Works

Microsoft Works is the cheapest way to computerize well! It's an **integrated program** that handles word processing, spreadsheets, and databases.

It runs in all three popular environments: DOS, Windows, and Mac. The Windows versions are the best.

Many computers come with Microsoft Works installed already.

The newest Windows version of Microsoft Works is **Microsoft Works 9**. It requires Windows (XP or Vista or 7). It lists for $40. It's better than earlier versions, such as **Microsoft Works 7** and **Microsoft Works 8**.

> Microsoft Works 7 is also called **Microsoft Works 2003**.
> Microsoft Works 8 is also called **Microsoft Works 2005**.
> Microsoft Works 9 is also called **Microsoft Works 2008**.

This chapter explains the word-processing part of Microsoft Works 7&8&9.

Your computer probably contains Microsoft Works already. (If your computer does *not* contain Microsoft Works yet, follow the instructions that came with Microsoft Works about how to install it.)

The word-processing part of Microsoft Works is a stripped-down version of Microsoft Word. So if you have Microsoft Works and also Microsoft Word (for example, because you bought the Microsoft Works Suite, which includes both), use Microsoft Word instead.

Starting

For Works 9, do this:

> Click Start then "All Programs" then "Microsoft Works Task Launcher".
> If the computer says "Microsoft Software License Terms" (because Microsoft Works hasn't been used on this computer before), click "I Agree" then press Enter then click "Yes" then press Enter.
> Click "Works Word Processor".

For Works 8, do this:

> Click Start then "All Programs" then "Microsoft Works Task Launcher". Click "Works Word Processor".
> You see a window called "Untitled Document". If it doesn't consume the whole screen yet, maximize it (by clicking its Maximize button, which is next to its red X button).

For Works 7, do this:

> Double-click the icon that says "Microsoft Works".
> If the computer says "Microsoft End User License Agreement" (because Microsoft Works hasn't been used on this computer before), click "I Agree" then "Register Later" then "Yes".
> The screen's top says "Microsoft Works Task Launcher". Just below that, you see the word "Programs"; click it. Then click "Start a blank Word Processor document".

Type your document

Start typing your document.

Microsoft Works typically uses the keyboard the same way as WordPad. For details, **read these sections on pages 81-82**:

> "Use the keyboard"
> "Scroll arrows"
> "Insert characters"
> "Split a paragraph"
> "Combine paragraphs"
> "Movement keys"

Here are differences....

Ctrl symbols Microsoft Works understands different Ctrl symbols than WordPad. Here's what Microsoft Works understands:

Symbol	How to type it
©	While holding down the Ctrl and Alt keys, tap the C key.
®	While holding down the Ctrl and Alt keys, tap the R key.
™	While holding down the Ctrl and Alt keys, tap the T key.
…	While holding down the Ctrl and Alt keys, type a period.

Movement keys Microsoft Works doesn't understand "Ctrl with Page Down" or "Ctrl with Page Up".

Automatic editing

The computer will automatically edit what you type.

AutoCorrect While you type, **the computer will automatically make little corrections to your typing**. For example:

> If you type "teh" or "hte", the computer will change your typing to "the".
> If you type "loove", the computer will change your typing to "love".
>
> If you type a day (such as "sunday"), the computer will capitalize it.
>
> If you capitalize the first *two* letters of a word, the computer will make the second letter small.
>
> The computer will capitalize each sentence's first word.
>
> The computer will change (r) to ®, change (c) to ©, and change (tm) to ™.
> The computer will change 2nd to 2nd, change 3rd to 3rd, change 4th to 4th, etc.
> The computer will change 1/2 to ½, change 1/4 to ¼, and change 3/4 to ¾.
> The computer will change -- to –, change --> to →, and change <-- to ←.
> The computer will change ==> to → and change <== to ←.
> The computer will change :) to ☺ and change :(to ☹.
>
> If you type a phrase in quotation marks ("like this"), the quotation marks will become curly ("like this").
>
> If you type three periods (...), the periods will move farther apart (…).

Some of those corrections happen immediately; others are delayed until you finish typing a word (and press the Space bar or a period).

The computer's ability to make those corrections is called **AutoCorrect**.

If you dislike a correction that the computer made to your typing, here's how to undo the correction:

> Method 1: click the **Undo button**, which has an arrow pointing to the left. (In Works 8, the Undo button is under the word "Help". In Works 7, the Undo button is under the word "Table").
>
> Method 2: while holding down the Ctrl key, tap the Z key.

Those methods work just if done *immediately*, before you do any other typing or editing.

Red squiggles Microsoft Works resembles Microsoft Word, so **read the "Red squiggles" section on page 183**.

Microsoft Works says "Add" instead of "Add to Dictionary".

Further tricks

Microsoft Works resembles Microsoft Word, so **read these sections on page 185:**

> "Page break"
> "All delete"

While doing "All delete", the document turns black (not blue).

Formatting toolbar

Near the screen's top, you see the **formatting toolbar**, which looks like this:

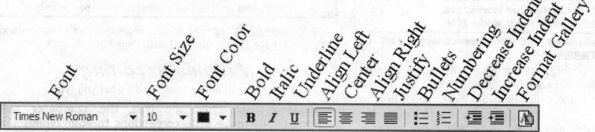

Each symbol on the toolbar is called a **tool**. Here's the name of each tool:

Font · Font Size · Font Color · Bold · Italic · Underline · Align Left · Center · Align Right · Justify · Bullets · Numbering · Decrease Indent · Increase Indent · Format Gallery

If you forget a tool's name, try this trick: point at the tool (by using the mouse, but *without* clicking), then wait a second. Underneath the tool, you'll see the tool's name; and at the screen's bottom left corner, you'll see a one-sentence explanation of what the tool does.

The toolbar's right half consists of 12 tools saying "**B**", "*I*", "U", etc. Those 12 tools are called **buttons**. (Microsoft Works 9 includes a 13th button, called "Task Pane".)

To use a button, press it by clicking it with the mouse. Let's look at the details....

Underline

Here's how to underline a phrase (<u>like this</u>).

Activate the **Underline button** (which says U on it) by clicking it. **Activating the button changes its appearance:**

> Works 8&9: the button gets a black border.
> Works 7: the button looks "pushed in".

Then type the phrase you want underlined. Then deactivate the Underline button (by clicking it again).

Go ahead: try it now! Practice using the underline button before you progress to more advanced buttons!

Here's a shortcut: instead of clicking the Underline button, you can press Ctrl with U.

Fancy formats

Microsoft Works resembles WordPad, so **read these sections on page 85:**

> "Bold"
> "Italic"

Alignment buttons

Microsoft Works handles alignment buttons the same way as WordPad 7. For details, **read "Alignment buttons" on page 88**.

In Microsoft Works, the "Align text left" button is called "Align Left", and the "Align text right" button is called "Align Right."

Font Size

Look at the **Font Size box**. In that box, you normally see the number 10. That means the characters you're typing are 10 points high. Here's how to type characters that are bigger or smaller....

> Method 1: click the Font Size box. In that box, type a size number from 8 to 72. The number can end in .5; the number can be 8 or 8.5 or 9 or 9.5 or 10 or bigger. (Theoretically, you can pick a number even smaller than 8 or even bigger than 72, but those extreme numbers create ugly results.) When you finish typing the number, press the Enter key.
>
> Method 2: click the down-arrow that's to the *right* of the Font Size box. You see this list of popular sizes: 8, 9, 10, 11, 12, 14, 16, 18, 20, 22, 24, 26, 28, 36, 48, and 72. That list of popular sizes is called the **Font Size menu**. Click the size you want.

Any new characters you type afterwards will be the size you chose. (Characters typed earlier don't change size.)

The popular sizes look like this:

This text is 8 points high, 9 points high, 10 points high, 11 points high, 12 points high, 14 points high, 16 points high, 18 points high, 20 pt., 22 pt., 24 pt., 26 pt., 28 pt., 36pt., 48pt., 72pt.

When you finish typing the enlarged or reduced characters, here's how to return to typing characters that are normal size (10-point): click the down-arrow that's to the right of the Font Size box, then click the 10.

Font

Microsoft Works uses the **Font box** the same way as Microsoft Word 2002. For details, **read the "Font" section on page 202**.

Font Color

Normally, the characters you type are black. Here's how to make them a different color, such as red.

Click the **Font Color box**. You start seeing a list of 48 colors. (The list appears in a window that's too small to show the entire list; to see the rest of the list, click the window's scroll arrows.)

You can click one of those 48 colors. Or if you prefer, click "More Colors" (which appears at the bottom of the list) then create your own custom color by doing this:

> Click one of the thousands of colors that appear in the big square. Click a darker or lighter version of that color in the thin tower. Click OK.

Any new characters you type afterwards will be the color you chose. (The characters you typed earlier don't change color.)

When you finish typing the colored characters, here's how to return to typing characters that are black: click the Font Color box, then click "Black".

Indentation buttons

Microsoft Works resembles Microsoft Word, so **read the "Indentation buttons" section on page 189**.

Microsoft Works puts bullet symbols and paragraph numbers at the left margin (unindented), and it indents the words in those paragraphs a quarter inch (not a half inch).

Select text

Here's how to dramatically change a phrase you typed.

Point at the phrase's beginning, then drag to the phrase's end (while holding down the mouse's left button). The whole phrase turns black. Turning the phrase black is called **selecting the phrase**.

Then say what to do to the phrase. For example, choose one of these activities:

> To underline the phrase, push in the Underline button.
> To make the phrase be bold, push in the Bold button.
> To italicize the phrase, push in the Italic button.
> To prevent the phrase from being underlined, bold, or italicized, pop those buttons back out.
>
> To change how the phrase's paragraphs are aligned, click one of the alignment buttons.
>
> To change the phrase's point size, choose the size you want from the Font Size menu.
> To change the phrase's font, choose the font you want from the Font menu.
>
> To delete the phrase, press the **Delete key**.
>
> To replace the phrase, just type whatever words you want the phrase to become.

Go ahead! Try it now! It's fun!

Advanced selection

Microsoft Works resembles WordPad, so **read these sections on page 87:**

> "Other ways to select"
> "Document vanishes"

Drag a phrase

To move a phrase to a new location, just "select the phrase, and then drag from the phrase's middle to the new location." Here are the details:

> First, select the phrase you want to move, so the phrase turns black.
> Then take your finger off the mouse's button. Move the mouse's pointer to the phrase's middle (so you see an arrow).
> Hold down the mouse's button; and while you keep holding down the mouse's button, drag to wherever you want the phrase to move. You'll be dragging a black vertical line. (Drag anywhere you wish in the document, or drag to the document's end. The computer won't let you drag past the document's end.)
> At the end of the drag, lift your finger from the mouse's button. Presto, the phrase moves where you wished!

In that procedure, you drag the phrase to a new location then drop it there. That procedure is called **drag & drop**.

Standard toolbar

Near the screen's top, above the formatting toolbar, you see the **standard toolbar**, which looks like this:

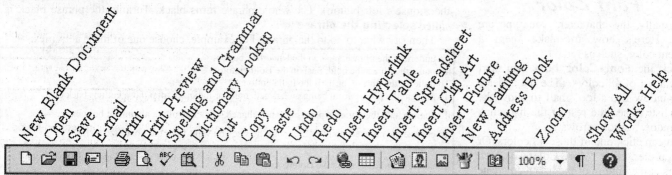

Here's how to use the most popular of those tools....

Save

To save the document (copy it onto the disk), click the **Save button** (or press Ctrl with S).

If you haven't saved the document before, the computer will say "File name". Invent a name for your document. Type the name and press Enter.

That makes the computer copy the document onto the hard disk.

For example, suppose you named the document "mary". The computer will make that document become a file called mary.wps (which means "mary from the **w**ord **p**rocessing **s**ystem"). The computer will put that file into the My Documents folder.

Afterwards, if you change your mind and want to do more editing, go ahead! When you finish that extra editing, save it by clicking the Save button again.

**Save often** If you're typing a long document, click the Save button about every 10 minutes. Click it whenever you get to a good stopping place and think, "What I've typed so far looks good!"

Then if an accident happens, you'll lose at most 10 minutes of work, and you can return to the last version you felt good about.

Print

Here's how to print the document onto paper. Make sure you've bought a printer, attached it to the computer, turned the printer's power on, and put paper into the printer. Then click the **Print button**. The printer will print your document onto paper.

How to finish

When you finish working on a document, click the **X** at the screen's top right corner.

(If you didn't save your document yet, the computer asks, "Do you want to save the changes?" If you click "Yes", the computer copies your document's most recent version to the hard disk; if you click "No" instead, the computer ignores and forgets your most recent editing.)

Then you have three choices:

If you click the **X** at the screen's top right corner again, the computer stops using Microsoft Works.

If you click **Programs** then Works 8&9's "**Blank Word Processor document**" (or Works 7's "**Start a blank Word Processor document**"), the computer lets you start typing a new document.

If you click **History**, you see a list of old documents (and other Works creations). To use one of those documents, click the document's name.

**Congratulations!** You've learned all the fundamental commands of the Microsoft Works word processor!

Undo & Redo

Microsoft Works resembles Microsoft Word 2002, so **read "Undo" and "Redo" on page 204**.

Show All

Microsoft Works resembles Microsoft Word, so **read "Show/Hide ¶" on page 190.**

What should you call the ¶ button? Microsoft Word calls it the "Show/Hide ¶" button, but Microsoft Works calls it the "Show All" button instead.

Clipboard

Microsoft Works resembles WordPad 7, so **read these sections on page 87:**

"Cut and paste"
"Copy"

Dragging across a phrase makes it turn black (not blue).

Print Preview

Microsoft Works resembles Microsoft Word 2002, so **read "Print Preview" on page 205**.

Zoom

Look at the **Zoom box**. In that box, you normally see the number 100%. That means the computer's screen is showing you the actual size of what will appear on paper.

To the right of the Zoom box, you see a down-arrow. Click it. You see this **Zoom menu**:

200%
100%
75%
Whole Page
Two Pages
Page Width
Margin Width

For example, if you click **200%**, the computer makes the screen's characters be twice as high and twice as wide as normal, so you can read them even if you're sitting far away from the screen or you have poor vision. It's like looking at the document through a magnifying glass: the document looks enlarged, so you can see the details of each word and character more clearly; but not as many words and characters fit on the screen. Use the arrow keys to see different parts of the page.

Clicking 200% enlarges just what you see on the *screen*: it does *not* enlarge what appears on paper.

Try it! Try clicking 200%!

When you finish admiring that view, make the screen return to normal, by choosing **100%** from the Zoom menu.

If you click **Whole Page** instead of 200%, the computer does just the opposite: the computer makes the screen's characters be very tiny, so the whole page fits on the screen — as if you were doing a print preview.

A nice choice is **Page Width**. It makes the screen's characters be as big as possible, but still small enough so that you can see the left and right edges of the paper.

My favorite choice is **Margin Width**. It makes the screen's characters be as big as possible (even bigger than Page Width), but still small enough so that you can see the first and last word of each line.

Spelling and Grammar

If you click in the middle of the document's first word and then click the **Spelling and Grammar button**, the computer will scan through your document for misspelled words and accidentally repeatedly words.

The computer will typically stop at the first word having a red squiggle underneath then show a list of suggestions. If you like one of the suggestions, double-click it. If you *don't* like any of the computer's suggestions, edit the word (if you wish) then press Enter.

When the computer finishes checking the entire document, the computer says "The spelling check is complete". Press Enter.

Grammar Besides checking for spelling errors and repeated words, the computer can also check for grammar errors. To make the computer do that, click "Tools" then "Options" then put a check mark in the "Check grammar" box (by clicking) then press Enter. Afterwards, whenever you click the "Spelling and Grammar" button, the computer will stop at each grammar error (as well as each spelling error and repetition error).

E-mail

Here's how to e-mail a copy of your document.

Click the **E-mail button** (which looks like an envelope).

To whom do you want to e-mail the document? Type that person's e-mail address. For example, if you want to send the document to me, type my e-mail address, which is "russ@secretfun.com.". Or for a fun experiment, just send the document to yourself by typing your own e-mail address.

Click in the "Subject" box. Type a subject for your e-mail (such as "here's a story I wrote" or "I'm testing").

Your Microsoft Works document is going to be sent as an e-mail attachment. (I explained e-mail attachments on pages 137-138.) Click in the big white box, then type a cover note about your document (such as "The story I wrote is in the attached Microsoft Works document").

Finally, click the "Send" button. The computer will send the e-mail and your attached document.

Insert Table

In the middle of your document, here's how to type a table of numbers.

Click where you want the table to appear, then click the **Insert Table button**.

How many rows do you want the table to have? Type how many rows, press the Tab key, type how many columns, and press Enter.

For your first experience, I recommend keeping the table simple; but if you insist on making the table fancy, do this:

Click "(None)". Press the down-arrow key (on the keyboard) several times, until you see a table format you like.

Press Enter. The computer will create a blank table, which has no words or numbers in it yet.

Then just fill in the cells with whatever numbers and words you wish. To move from cell to cell, click with the mouse, or press the Tab key (which moves right to the next cell), or press Shift with Tab (which moves left to the previous cell), or press the arrow keys repeatedly.

In a cell, you can type a number, word, sentence, or even an entire paragraph! If you start typing a paragraph in a cell, the computer will automatically make the cell and its row taller, so the entire paragraph will fit in the cell. You can even type *several* paragraphs in a single cell: just press the Enter key at the end of each paragraph. If you want to indent the first line of one of those paragraphs, press the Space bar several times.

Extra rows Here's how to create an extra row at the bottom of the table: click in the table's bottom right cell, then press the Tab key.

To insert an extra row into the *middle* of the table. click in the row that's underneath where you want the extra row to appear, then click "Table" then "Insert Row" then "Before Current Row".

Advanced features Microsoft Works resembles Microsoft Word 2002, so **read these sections on page 206**:

"Column widths"
"Numbers"
"Below the table"

Delete To delete a row or column or the entire table, click in the middle of what you want to delete, then click the word **"Table"** (so you see the **Table menu**), then do this:

To delete a row, click "Select Row" then "Table" then "Delete Rows".
To delete a column, click "Select Column" then "Table" then "Delete Columns".
To delete the entire table, click "Select Table" then "Table" then "Delete Table".

Works Help

To make the computer explain many topics about Microsoft Works, click the **Works Help button** or press the F1 key.

At the screen's right edge, you see a short list of popular topics, in blue and underlined. If one of those topics interests you, click it.

Works 8&9:

You also see a list of other topics, in black. If one of those topics interests you, click its plus sign (to see its subtopics) or its question mark (if it doesn't have a plus sign). If you click a question mark, the topic's explanation will appear at the screen's white edge.

Works 7:

You also see a white box under "Answer Wizard". You can click in that box, then type your question (and press Enter). Then a list of related topics will appear under your question. Click whichever topic interest you. Then the topic's explanation will appear.

When you finish using Works Help, close its window (by clicking its X button).

Menu bar

Near the screen's top, you see this **menu bar**:

File Edit View Insert Format Tools Table Help

Here's how to use it.

File menu

If you click the word File, you see the **File menu**, whose main choices are:

Close
Save
Save As
Page Setup
Print Preview
Print

Close Choosing **Close** has the same effect as clicking the **X** (at the screen's top right corner), which I explained on page 218.

Save Choosing **Save** has the same effect as clicking the **Save button**, which I explained on page 218.

Save As Microsoft Works handles "Save As" the same way as Microsoft Word 2002. For details, **read the "Save As" section on page 207.**

Page Setup Normally, the computer makes every page's top and bottom margins each be 1 inch tall, and makes every page's left and right margins each be 1¼ inches wide. To change those margins, choose **Page Setup**, then do this:

Type how many inches tall you want the top margin.	Press Tab.
Type how many inches tall you want the bottom margin.	Press Tab.
Type how many inches wide you want the left margin.	Press Tab.
Type how many inches wide you want the right margin.	Press Enter.

Print Preview Choosing **Print Preview** has the same effect as clicking the **Print Preview button**, which I explained on page 205.

Print If you choose **Print**, the computer will ask how you'd like to print onto paper.

If you own more than 1 printer, click the down-arrow next to the Printer Name box , then choose which printer you want to use (by clicking it).

If you want to print more than 1 copy:
double-click in the "Number of copies" box, then type the number of copies.

If you want to print just pages 3 through 7:
click the Pages button, type "3", press the Tab key, then type "7".

Then press Enter. The printer will print what you desired!

Edit menu

If you click the word Edit, you see the **Edit menu**, whose main choices are:

Undo
Redo
Cut
Copy
Paste
Clear
Select All
Find
Replace
Go To

Some of those choices just imitate the buttons and your keyboard.

Choosing **Undo** is like clicking the **Undo button** (explained on page 204).
Choosing **Redo** is like clicking the **Redo button** (explained on page 204).
Choosing **Cut** is like clicking the **Cut button** (pages 87 & 204).
Choosing **Copy** is like clicking the **Copy button** (pages 87 & 204).
Choosing **Paste** is like clicking the **Paste button** (pages 87 & 204).
Choosing **Clear** is like pressing the **Delete key** (explained on page 91).
Choosing **Select All** is like pressing **Ctrl with A** (explained on page 91).

Here's how to make choices that are more useful….

Find Here's how to make the computer search through your document to find whether you've used the word "love":

Click where you want the search to begin. (For example, if you want the search to begin at the document's beginning, click in the middle of the document's first word.) Choose **Find** from the Edit menu (or press Ctrl with F). Type the word you want to find ("love"), and press Enter.

The computer will search for "love". If the computer finds a "love" in your document, it will highlight that "love" so it turns black. If you want to find the next "love" in your document, press Enter; if you do *not* want to search for more "love", press the Esc key instead.

Suppose you've written a history of America and want to find the part where you started talking about Lincoln. If you forget what page that was, no problem! Just put the cursor at the beginning of the document, choose **Find** from the Edit menu, type "Lincoln", and press Enter.

Replace You can search for a word and replace it by a different word.

For example, suppose your document talks about "love". Here's how to change each "love" in your document to "idolize":

Choose **Replace**. Type the old word you want to replace ("love"), then press the Tab key, then type the new word you want instead ("idolize"), then click the Replace All button. That makes the computer change each "love" to "idolize". Then press the Esc key.

Unfortunately, the computer doesn't know how to preserve capitalization. For example, suppose the document said —

I love you. Love you! LOVE YOU! I want to kiss your glove!

and you say to replace each "love" with "idolize". Then the computer will change each "love" or "Love" or "LOVE" to "idolize" (uncapitalized), so the document becomes this:

I idolize you. idolize you! idolize YOU! I want to kiss your gidolize!

Notice that when told to change "love" to "idolize", the computer unfortunately also changes "glove" to "gidolize".

The Replace command helps you zip through many chores:

For example, if you write a letter that talks about Fred, then want to write a similar letter about Sue, tell the computer to replace each Fred with Sue.

If you write a book about "How to be a better salesman" and then a feminist tells you to change each "salesman" to "salesperson", tell the computer to replace each "salesman".

If you're writing a long ad that mentions "Calvin Klein's Hot New Flaming Pink Day-Glo Pajamas" repeatedly, and you're too lazy to type that long phrase so often, just type the abbreviation "Calnew". When you've finished typing the document, tell the computer to replace each "Calnew" with the long phrase it stands for.

Go To When you've typed a document that's several pages long, here's how to move to page 2:

Choose **Go To** from the Edit menu (or press Ctrl with G).

Make sure the computer says "Enter page number". (If the computer doesn't say that yet, click **Page** and then click in the "Enter page number" box.)

Type your desired page number (which is 2), then press Enter. You'll see page 2 on the screen.

Press the Esc key.

View menu

If you click the word View, you see the **View menu**, whose main choices are:

```
Toolbars
Ruler
Status Bar

All Characters
Header and Footer
```

Toolbars On the View menu, choose "Toolbars". Then you see the **toolbars menu**, which mentions "Standard", "Formatting", and "Large Icons".

> Make sure there's a check mark before "Standard". (Otherwise, you won't see the standard toolbar).
>
> Make sure there's a check mark before "Formatting". (Otherwise, you won't see the formatting toolbar.)
>
> If you put a check mark before "Large Icons", the buttons on the toolbars will be enlarged so you can see them even if your eyesight is poor. (Normally, the buttons are small. Warning: if you enlarge the buttons, your screen resolution should be at least 1024×768; otherwise, the standard toolbar's buttons will be too large to all fit across the screen.)

You can create or remove those check marks by clicking in the toolbars menu.

Ruler On the View menu, there should be a check mark before "Ruler". (Otherwise, you won't see the ruler above your document.)

You can create or remove that check mark by clicking "Ruler".

Status bar On the View menu, there should be a check mark before "Status Bar". (Otherwise, you won't see the status bar below your document. The status bar shows your page number and shows whether you've pressed the Caps Lock, Num Lock, and Insert keys.)

You can create or remove that check mark by clicking "Status Bar".

All Characters Choosing "All Characters" has the same effect as clicking the **Show All button** (also called the "Show/Hide ¶ button"), which I explained on pages 190 and 218.

Header and Footer Normally, the top inch of each page is blank, to form the top margin. Anything you scribble in that margin is called a **header**.

For example, suppose you're writing a top-secret memo and want to scribble this note in the top margin of every page:

> Reminder! The info in this memo is TOP SECRET!

Here's how to do it....

Choose **Header and Footer**. Type your header:

> Reminder! The info in this memo is TOP SECRET!

Then click the word "Close". The computer will put your header at the top of each page of your document. (On the screen, your header appears gray, but when you print the document onto paper, your header is printed black.)

If you want to edit the header, choose "Header and Footer" again from the View menu, then edit the header however you wish, then click the word "Close" again.

Instead of writing a header about being "TOP SECRET", here are four other headers you might enjoy using:

> Please do not copy! It's copyrighted by starving author!
> ACHTUNG! To keep your job, reply to this memo by Friday!
> SALE! To order any of these items, call our 800 number!
> I love you!!! I love you!!! I love you!!!

Here's a way **to make the computer print the page number at the top of each page:**

> Choose **Header and Footer** from the View menu.
>
> Click the **Insert Page Number** button (which is the symbol # on a bent sheet of paper). That makes the computer put a "1" at the top of page 1, a "2" at the top of page 2, etc.
>
> Click the word "Close".

Let's get fancier! Let's make the computer print this at the top of page 1 —

> This is page 1 of the Great American Novel

and print this at the top of page 2 —

> This is page 2 of the Great American Novel

and print this at the top of page 3 —

> This is page 3 of the Great American Novel

etc. Here's how:

> Choose **Header and Footer** from the View menu.
> Type the header's beginning words: "This is page". After the word "page", press the Space bar.
> Click the **Insert Page Number** button. That makes the computer automatically type a "1" on page 1, a "2" on page 2, etc.
> Press the Space bar (to make the computer leave a blank space after the page number). Type the header's ending words: "of the Great American Novel". Click the word "Close".

Here's how **to print in the bottom margin (instead of the top margin):**

> Choose **Header and Footer** from the View menu. If the computer shows you a space labeled "Header", switch to "Footer" by clicking the **Switch Between Header and Footer** button.
> Type the footer (whatever you want in the bottom margin). Then click the word "Close".

Insert menu

If you click the word Insert, you see the **Insert menu**, whose main choices are:

Date and Time
Special Character
Footnote
Text Box

Date and Time To type the date or time, choose **Date and Time**. The computer will show a list of formats, like this:

1/31/12
January 31, 2012
Tuesday, January 31, 2012
1/31/2012
01/31/2012
31 January 2012
31 Jan 12
Jan 2012
2012/1/31
1/31
1/12
January 2012
Jan 12
January 31, 2012, 11:57 PM
11:57 PM
23:57
2012-01-31

Click the format you want. Press Enter. The computer will type the date or time in the format you requested.

In that procedure, just before you press Enter, you might wish to put a check mark in the "Automatically update when printed" box. Here's how that box works:

Suppose you type a document on Tuesday, but you print the document the next day (Wednesday). Which date will the computer print on paper? The computer will print the date that the document was typed (Tuesday), unless you put a check mark in the "Automatically update when printed" box, which makes the computer print the "date printed" (Wednesday).

If you put a check mark in the "Automatically update when printed" box, the computer will automatically update the date & time whenever the document is printed or print-previewed or **opened** (chosen from the History list of old documents, as explained on page 218).

Special Character To type a special character, choose **Special Character**. You'll see the **Insert Special Character window**. In that window, you can click either the **Symbol** tab or the **Special Character** tab.

If you click the **Special Character** tab, the computer will show you this list of special characters:

-	Optional Hyphen	(a hyphen, visible just when the word it's in is too long to fit on a line)
-	Nonbreaking Hyphen	(a hyphen, between words that must appear on the same line as each other)
	Nonbreaking Space	(a space between words that must appear on the same line as each other)
	End of Line	(an Enter that returns to the left margin but does *not* end the paragraph)
©	Copyright	
®	Registered	
™	Trademark	
…	Ellipsis	
–	En Dash	(a dash that's slightly narrower than an N; it's exactly half as wide as an Em Dash)
—	Em Dash	(a dash that's slightly wider than an M; it's exactly as wide as the font's point-size height)
¼	One Quarter	
½	One Half	
¾	Three Quarters	
°	Degrees	
²	Squared	
³	Cubed	
¶	Paragraph	
'	Single Opening Quote	
'	Single Closing Quote	
"	Double Opening Quote	
"	Double Closing Quote	

(You see just part of the list until you click the list's down-arrow repeatedly to see the rest.)

If you click the **Symbol** tab instead, you'll see these math & Greek characters:

```
 !  ∀  #  ∃  %  &  ∍  (  )  *  +  ,  −  .  /  0  1  2  3  4  5  6  7  8  9  :  ;
 <  =  >  ?  ≅  Α  Β  Χ  Δ  Ε  Φ  Γ  Η  Ι  ϑ  Κ  Λ  Μ  Ν  Ο  Π  Θ  Ρ  Σ  Τ  Υ  ς  Ω
 Ξ  Ψ  Ζ  [  ∴  ]  ⊥  _     α  β  χ  δ  ε  φ  γ  η  ι  φ  κ  λ  μ  ν  ο  π  θ  ρ  σ
 τ  υ  ϖ  ω  ξ  ψ  ζ  {  |  }  ~
                                            ϒ  ′  ≤  ⁄  ∞  ƒ  ♣  ♦  ♥  ♠  ↔
 ←  ↑  →  ↓  °  ±  ″  ≥  ×  ∝  ∂  •  ÷  ≠  ≡  ≈  …  |  —  ↵  ℵ  ℑ  ℜ  ℘  ⊗  ⊕  ∅  ∩
 ∪  ⊃  ⊇  ⊄  ⊂  ⊆  ∈  ∉  ∠  ∇  ®  ©  ™  ∏  √  ·  ¬  ∧  ∨  ⇔  ⇐  ⇑  ⇒  ⇓  ◊  ⟨  ®  ©
 ™  ∑  ⎛  ⎜  ⎝  ⎡  ⎢  ⎣  ⎧  ⎨  ⎩     ⎞  ⎟  ⎠  ⎤  ⎥  ⎦  ⎫  ⎬  ⎭
```

(To see other popular symbols, do this: click the Font box's down-arrow; then, from the font list, choose "Wingdings" or "Wingdings 2" or "Wingdings 3" or "Webdings" or "Marlett". To return to the main symbol font, choose "Symbol".)

Whenever you see a character you like, double-click it. That makes the computer put the character into your document. Then double-click any other characters you like.

When you finish using the Symbol window, make it disappear by clicking its X button.

Footnote Suppose you're writing a religious pamphlet in which you want to say "Read the Bible tonight!" Suppose you want to add a footnote saying "written by God", so the main text looks like this —

Read the Bible[1] tonight!

and the page's bottom contains this footnote:

[1] Written by God.

Here's how to do it all....

Type "Read the Bible".
Choose **Footnote** from the Insert menu. Press Enter. Type the footnote ("Written by God.").
Climb back up to the main text (by double-clicking the footnote number's left edge), then press the right-arrow key. Finally, type the rest of the main text (" tonight!").

The computer will automatically number the footnote: it will automatically type [1] after "Bible" and type [1] before "Written by God." If your document contains more footnotes, the computer will automatically number them [2], [3], [4], etc.

The computer will put the footnotes at the bottom of the page. If the page is divided into newspaper columns, the computer will put each footnote at the bottom of the column it refers to.

The computer will put a 2-inch horizontal line above the footnotes to separate them from the main text.

If you insert extra footnotes, the computer will automatically renumber the other footnotes, so the first footnote appearing in your document will be numbered [1], the second footnote will be numbered [2], etc.

To delete a footnote, click the left edge of the footnote's number in the main text; then press the Delete key twice.

Text Box You can draw a box wherever you wish, *anywhere* on the page (even in the margins) and put words into it, to create a **text box**. Here's how....

Where do you want the box's top left corner? Try to click slightly *above* that point; if you can't, just click anywhere nearby.

From the Insert menu, choose **Text Box**. A box will appear near the place you requested.

Here's how to **move the box**:

> Point at one of the box's sides (but stay away from the tiny black squares you see next to the sides). Then move the box by dragging the side wherever you wish.

If you move the box to a part of the page that already contains words, those words move out of the box's way.

Here's how to **adjust the box's size**:

> Click in the box.
> At the box's bottom right corner, you see a tiny black square. Put the mouse pointer there. Make sure the middle of the mouse pointer is in the middle of that black square. When you do that successfully, the mouse pointer becomes a diagonal arrow with two arrowheads.
> Then adjust the box's size by dragging that tiny black square wherever you wish.

To **type words in the box**, just click in the box and then type the words.

Here's how to **delete the box**:

> Click one of the box's sides (but stay away from the tiny black squares you see next to the sides). Then press the keyboard's Delete key.

Format menu

If you click the word Format, you see the **Format menu**, whose main choices are:

> Font
> Paragraph
> Bullets and Numbering
> Borders and Shading
>
> Format Gallery
>
> Tabs
> Columns

Font Here's how to improve the appearance of a phrase on your screen.

Which phrase do you want to improve? Select it (by dragging across it). Then choose **Font** from the Format menu.

You see these boxes:

Box	Usual contents	Other popular choices
Font	Times New Roman	Tahoma, Comic Sans MS, Courier New, Arial
Font style	Regular	Bold, Italic, Bold Italic
Size	10	8, 9, 11, 12, 14, 16, 18, 20, 22, 24, 26, 28, 36, 48, 72
Underline	(none)	Single, Double, Thick, Dotted, Dash, Words Only
Color	Automatic	Blue, Red, Yellow, Bright Green, Turquoise, Pink

For the Underline box or Color box, you must click the box's down-arrow once or twice, to see all choices. For the Font box or Size box, you must click the box's up-arrow and down-arrow repeatedly, to see all popular choices. **For each box, click whatever choice you want.**

In the Underline box, if you choose "Words only", the computer will underline the words but not the spaces between them.

Below all those boxes, you see a list of these special **Effects** you can choose:

Effect	What the computer will do
All caps	make the writing be all in capitals, LIKE THIS
Small caps	make the writing be all in tiny capitals, LIKE THIS
Superscript	make the writing be tiny and raised, ^like this
Subscript	make the writing be tiny and lowered, ~like this
Strikethrough	draw a line through your writing, ~~like this~~
Shadow	make a shadow behind each character, as if in the sun
Outline	show each character's outline, as if on a varsity jacket
Engrave	make the writing look like it's chiseled into stone
Emboss	make the writing look like it sticks out from stone

Click each effect you want, so a check mark appears in the effect's box. The weird effects (Shadow, Outline, Engrave, and Emboss) work best when the Font Size is big (such as 48 or 72 points).

When you've finished using the Font window, press Enter.

Paragraph To change the way a paragraph is spaced, click in the paragraph, then choose **Paragraph** from the Format menu. You see two **tabs**: one of them is called **Indents and Alignment**; the other is called **Spacing**.

Try clicking the **Indents and Alignment** tab.

You see three **indentation boxes** called **Left**, **Right**, and **First line**. Normally, each of those boxes says 0".

> If you want the paragraph's first line to be indented a half-inch (and want the paragraph's other lines to be normal), put 0.5" (or just .5) in the **First line** box (and 0" in the other boxes).
>
> If you want *every* line of the paragraph to be indented a half-inch, put 0.5" in the **Left** box (and 0" in the other boxes).
>
> If you want the paragraph's first line to be normal (unindented) but want the paragraph's other lines to be indented a half-inch, do this: put 0.5" in the **Left** box (so most of the paragraph's lines will be indented a half-inch), put -0.5" in the **First Line** box (so the first line is indented less than the other lines), and put 0" in the Right box.
>
> If you want the paragraph's left and right margins to both be extra-wide — a half-inch wider than normal — put 0.5" in the **Left** box and 0.5" in the **Right** box.

You see four **alignment buttons** called **Left**, **Center**, **Right**, and **Justified**. They act the same as the alignment buttons that are on the formatting toolbar (and explained on pages 88 and 216).

If you click the **Spacing** tab, here's what happens:

> You see a **Line spacing** box. Normally, that box says "Single". If you want to double-space instead (so the computer puts a blank line under each line you type), click that box's down-arrow, then choose "Double".
>
> You see a box called **Lines Before**. Normally, that box says "0". If you want the computer to leave a blank space above the paragraph, put "1" into that box (by clicking its up-arrow once).
>
> You see a box called **Lines After**. Normally, that box says "0". If you want the computer to leave a blank space under the paragraph, put "1" into that box.

When you finish telling the computer how you want the paragraph's indents and alignment and spacing, press Enter.

Bullets and Numbering Pages 189 and 217 said that if you click in the middle of a paragraph and then activate the **Bullets button**, the computer normally puts a simple bullet (the symbol •) at the beginning of the paragraph (and indents the paragraph).

If you don't like the symbol •, pick a different symbol instead. Here's how:

> Choose **Bullets and Numbering** from the Format menu, then click **Bulleted**. You see 28 symbols. Double-click your favorite.
>
> The computer puts your chosen symbol at the beginning of the paragraph. It also makes the Bullets button henceforth produce that symbol — until you switch to a different symbol or different document (or different task, by clicking the **X** at the screen's top right corner).

Pages 189 and 217 said that if you click in the middle of a paragraph and then activate the **Numbering button**, the computer normally puts "1." at the beginning of the paragraph (and indents the paragraph), puts "2." at the beginning of the next paragraph, etc. If you don't like that numbering scheme, pick a different scheme instead. Here's how....

Choose **Bullets and Numbering** from the Format menu, then click **Numbered**. You see these eight schemes:

1.	1)	I.	I)	i.	A.	A)	a.
2.	2)	II.	II)	ii.	B.	B)	b.
3.	3)	III.	III)	iii.	C.	C)	c.

Double-click whichever scheme you want.

Borders and Shading Here's how to draw a box around your writing.

First, tell the computer which paragraphs to put in the box.

> To put one paragraph in the box, click in that paragraph.
>
> To put *several* paragraphs in the box, click in the first of those paragraphs, then do this: *while holding down the Shift key*, click in the last of those paragraphs.

Then choose **Borders and Shading** from the Format menu. Click the **Outline** box, so a line appears in that box. (If you want the box's interior to be shaded, click the **Color 1** box's down-arrow then click your favorite color.) Press Enter.

Tabs Microsoft Works resembles Microsoft Word 2002, so **read the "Tabs" section on page 213**.

Columns In a newspaper, text is printed in many narrow **columns**. In a business letter, text is printed in a single wide column.

The computer assumes you want a single wide column. Here's how to tell the computer you want many narrow columns:

> Choose **Columns** from the Format menu. You'll see the **Format Columns window**.
>
> How many columns do you want? Type the number of columns.
>
> The computer assumes you want each gap between columns to be a half-inch wide. (That's 0.5".) If you want the gap to be a different width instead, press the TAB key then type a different number instead. For example, on this page (and in most of this book) the gap between columns is 0.3".
>
> If you want to draw a vertical line in the gap between columns, put a check mark in the box called **Line between columns**.
>
> When you finish using the Format Columns window, press Enter. Then your entire document changes, so it has as many columns as you requested.

If you change your mind and want just 1 column, choose Columns from the Format menu again. Type the number "1" and press Enter.

Tools menu

If you click the word Tools, you see the **Tools menu**, whose main choices are:

> Spelling and Grammar
> Thesaurus
> Word Count

Spelling Choosing **Spelling and Grammar** has the same effect as clicking the **Spelling and Grammar button**, which I explained on page 219.

Thesaurus Suppose you're writing a story containing the word "girl". Can you think of a different word instead, that means roughly the same thing as "girl" but is better?

If you can't, the computer can! Just ask the computer to use its **thesaurus** to find **synonyms** for "girl".

Here's how. In your document, type the word "girl". Click in the middle of that word. Choose **Thesaurus**.

The computer will say:

> young woman
> lass
> schoolgirl
> daughter
> youngster
> child
> teenager

Here's what to do next:

> If none of those words appeals to you, click the Cancel button.
>
> If one of those words appeals to you, click it. Then either click "Replace" (to make that word replace "girl" in your document) or click "Look Up" (to make the computer look up *that* word in the thesaurus).

Word Count If you choose **Word Count**, the computer will reveal how long your document is, by reporting how many words the document contains. When you finish reading the computer's report, press Enter.

Table menu

If you click the word Table, you see the **Table menu**, which I explained on page 219.

Help menu

If you click the word Help, you see the **Help menu**, whose main choices are:

> Works Help
> About Microsoft Works

Works Help Choosing **Works Help** has the same effect as clicking the **Works Help button**, which I explained on page 219.

About Microsoft Works If you choose **About Microsoft Works**, the computer will display a version message saying which version of Microsoft Works you're using.

(If you then click the System Info button, you'll see a window saying what kind of computer you bought and what state it's in. When you finish looking at that window, close it by clicking its X button.)

When you finish using About Microsoft Works, click the OK button.

Tricky applications

In the preceding chapters, you learned how to buy a computer and use its operating system, the Internet, and word processor.

Now let's see how computers can handle **tricky applications**. We'll start by looking at how computers handle **spreadsheets** (tables of numbers) then get into applications that are even trickier and wilder, such as manipulating photos, movies, games, and fun! Lovemaking, too! Let's get wild!

This section shows you how to do it all. It tackles even the trickiest challenges, such as building a robot that acts just like you and finding an accounting program that works well!

I wish you happy hunting through this thicket of pleasures and pain. When you finish, you'll understand why computers are just a high-tech form of sadomasochism.

Enjoy!

Spreadsheets

Any table of numbers is called a **spreadsheet**. For example, this spreadsheet deals with money:

```
            January    February
Income    $9,030.95  $12,486.99
Expenses  $7,000.55   $9,210.75
------------------------------
Profit    $2,030.40   $3,276.24
```

A spreadsheet can show how many dollars you earned (or spent or plan to spend), how many goods you have in stock, how people scored in a test (or survey or scientific experiment), or any other numbers you wish!

A **spreadsheet program** helps you create spreadsheets, edit them, and analyze them.

How spreadsheets arose

The first spreadsheet program was invented in 1979. It was **designed by Dan Bricklin** and **coded by Bob Frankston**. (That means Dan Bricklin decided what features and menus the program should have, and Bob Frankston wrote the program.) They called the program **VisiCalc** because it was a "visible calculator". VisiCalc's first version ran on the Apple 2 computer and required 64K of RAM; later versions ran on the Radio Shack TRS-80 and IBM PC.

The second spreadsheet program was called **SuperCalc** because it was superior to VisiCalc. It was invented by a company called **Sorcim** (which is "micros" spelled backwards). The original version of SuperCalc ran on computers using the CP/M operating system. The most popular CP/M computer — the Osborne 1 — came with a free copy of SuperCalc. Later versions of SuperCalc ran on the Apple 2 and IBM PC. Eventually, Sorcim became part of a big conglomerate called **Computer Associates**.

Multiplan was the first spreadsheet program that could handle multiple spreadsheets simultaneously — and the

relationships among them. Invented by Microsoft, it ran on a greater variety of computers than any other spreadsheet program: it ran on CP/M computers, the Radio Shack TRS-80, Commodore 64, Texas Instruments 99/4, IBM PC, Apple 2, and Apple Mac.

Context MBA was the first spreadsheet program that had extras: besides handling spreadsheets, it also handled graphs, databases, word processing, and telecommunications. But it ran slowly and its word processing was limited (it couldn't center and wouldn't let you set tab stops). It required a strange operating system (the Pascal P System). It was invented in 1981 by **Context Management Systems**, which later invented an MS-DOS version called **Corporate MBA**.

All those spreadsheet programs became irrelevant in 1983, when a much better spreadsheet program was invented. It was **designed by Mitch Kapor** and **coded by Jonathan Sachs** for the IBM PC. They called the program **1-2-3**, because it ran fast and was supposed to handle 3 things: spreadsheets, graphs, and word processing; but when Jonathan examined Context MBA, he realized that putting a good word processor into 1-2-3 would consume too much RAM and make the program run too slowly. He omitted the word processor and replaced it with a stripped-down database processor instead. 1-2-3 handled spreadsheets well, graphs okay, and databases slightly. Mitch and Jonathan called their company **Lotus Development Corporation**, because Mitch was a transcendental-meditation instructor who got entranced by contemplating lotus flowers.

After inventing 1-2-3, Jonathan Sachs tried to invent a program called **1-2-3-4-5**, which was to handle the same five tasks as Context MBA: spreadsheets, graphs, databases, word processing, and telecommunications.

> While developing it, he realized it was becoming too big and confusing, so he stopped developing it and quit the company. Other Lotus employees finished that program and renamed it **Symphony**; but as he feared, it was a big confusing mess whose word processor was awful. Most businesses bought just 1-2-3 instead.
>
> Like Jonathan, Mitch began feeling that Lotus Development Corporation and its products were becoming too big and confusing, so Mitch quit too.
>
> Afterwards, Lotus Development Corporation was run by **Jim Manzi**, who was young, rich, vain, egotistical, and nasty. The rest of the computer industry hated him, though his employees were nice. Finally, he sold Lotus to IBM, which gave lots of money to him and the other shareholders & employees. Then he quit, a rich man!

Other companies invented cheap imitations of 1-2-3. The imitations were called **1-2-3 clones** or **1-2-3 twins**. The first 1-2-3 twins were **The Twin** (published by Mosaic Software) and **VP-Planner** (published by Paperback Software). Lotus sued both of those publishers and put them out of business.

In 1983 — the same year that Lotus invented 1-2-3 — Apple invented **Lisa Calc**. It was **the first spreadsheet program to use a mouse**. It ran just on the Lisa computer, which was expensive ($8,000). When Apple began selling the Mac computer the next year (1984), Microsoft began selling **Multiplan for the Mac**, which ran on the Mac and combined the best features of Multiplan and Lisa Calc. The next year, 1985, Microsoft invented a further improvement, called **Excel** because it's excellent. Like 1-2-3, Excel handles spreadsheets, graphs, and databases.

Apple wanted to sue Microsoft for inventing the Windows operating system (which makes the IBM PC resemble a Mac). To avoid the suit, Microsoft agreed to put Excel on just the Mac for a year. Exactly one year later, when that agreement expired, Microsoft put Excel on the IBM PC.

So now **Excel runs on both the Mac and the IBM PC. It's the best spreadsheet program.**

Another fine spreadsheet program is called **Quattro**, because it's what came after 1-2-3. It was invented by **Borland**, which later invented an improved version, called **Quattro Pro**. In 1994, Borland sold Quattro Pro to another company, **Novell**, which later sold it to **Corel**. So now Quattro Pro is published by Corel.

What to do

Get a spreadsheet program!

The best spreadsheet program is **Excel**, which requires that you buy Windows or a Mac.

To pay less, use the stripped-down spreadsheet programs that are part of **Microsoft Works** (for Windows) or **AppleWorks** (which has sometimes been called **Claris Works** and is available for the Apple 2, Mac, and Windows).

This chapter explains how to use the most popular spreadsheet programs: **Excel** and **Microsoft Works**. I'll explain these versions:

Excel 2002	(which is part of **Microsoft Office XP**)
Excel 2003	(which is part of **Microsoft Office 2003**)
Excel 2007	(which is part of **Microsoft Office 2007**)
Excel 2010	(which is part of **Microsoft Office 2010**)
Works 7 spreadsheet	(which is part of **Microsoft Works 7**)
Works 8 spreadsheet	(which is part of **Microsoft Works 8**)
Works 9 spreadsheet	(which is part of **Microsoft Works 9**)

All those versions run in Windows. (Other versions are similar.)

These versions have alternative names:

Excel 2002 is also called **Excel XP**.

Works 7 is also called **Works 2003**.
Works 8 is also called **Works 2005**.
Works 9 is also called **Works 2008**.

Prepare yourself

Before using spreadsheet programs, practice using word-processing programs, which are simpler and explained in my word-processing chapter. The word-processing chapter explains how to copy word-processing and spreadsheet programs to your hard disk.

Launch the spreadsheet program

Here's how to start using your spreadsheet program….

Excel 2010 Click Start. If you see "Microsoft Office Excel 2010", click it; otherwise, click "All Programs" then "Microsoft Office" then "Microsoft Excel 2010".

Excel 2007 Click Start. If you see "Microsoft Office Excel 2007", click it; otherwise, click "All Programs" then "Microsoft Office" then "Microsoft Office Excel 2007".

Excel 2003 Click "start". If you see "Microsoft Office Excel 2003", click it; otherwise, click "All Programs" then "Microsoft Office" then "Microsoft Office Excel 2003". Do this unmask procedure:

Click "View" then "Toolbars" then "Customize" then "Options". Put check marks in the first two boxes ("Show Standard and Formatting toolbars on two rows" and "Always show full menus") by clicking. Press Enter.

Close the Getting Started window (which is at the screen's right edge) by clicking its X button.

Excel 2002 Click "Start" then "Programs" then "Microsoft Excel". Do this unmask procedure:

Click "View" then "Toolbars" then "Customize" then "Options". Put check marks in the first two boxes ("Show Standard and Formatting toolbars on two rows" and "Always show full menus") by clicking. Press Enter.

Close the New Workbook window (which is at the screen's right edge) by clicking its X button.

Works 9 Click Start then **All Programs** then **Microsoft Works Task Launcher** then **Programs** then **Works Spreadsheet** then **Blank Spreadsheet**. At the screen's right edge, if you see the words "Task Pane", close the Task Pane window (by clicking the Task Pane button, which is at the screen's top center, just left of the question mark).

Works 8 Click Start then **All Programs** then **Microsoft Works Task Launcher** then **Programs** then **Works Spreadsheet** then **Blank spreadsheet**. At the screen's right edge, if you see a Works Help window, close it (by clicking its X button).

Works 7 Turn the computer on, so you see the Start button. Double-click the **Microsoft Works** icon. Click **Programs** (which is near the screen's top left corner) then **Works Spreadsheet** (which is near the screen's left edge) then **Start a blank spreadsheet**. At the screen's right edge, if you see a Works Help window, close it (by clicking its X button).

Fill in the cells

The screen shows a grid that begins like this:

	A	B	C	D	E	F
1						
2						
3						
4						

The grid's columns are labeled A, B, C, D, E, etc.

A cheap screen (800-by-600, which is called SVGA) shows up through column J in Works, L in Excel.

A normal screen (1024-by-768, which is called XGA) shows up through column M in Works, O in Excel.

A modern widescreen (1600-by-900, which is called 900p) shows up through column V in Works, X in Excel.

The grid's rows are labeled 1, 2, 3, etc.

A cheap screen (800-by-600, which is called SVGA) shows 17 rows in Excel 2007&2010, 23 rows in Works 7 and Excel 2003, 24 rows in Works 8&9 and Excel 2002.

A normal screen (1024-by-768, which is called XGA) shows 25 rows in Excel 2007&2010, 33 rows in Works 7 and Excel 2003, 34 rows in Works 8&9 and Excel 2002.

A modern widescreen (1600-by-900, which is called 900p) shows 32 rows in Excel 2007&2010, 40 rows in Works 7 and Excel 2003, 41 rows in Works 8&9 and Excel 2002.

The grid is called a **spreadsheet** or **worksheet** (or just **sheet** or **table**).

Notice that the computer puts a box in column A, row 1. If you tap the right-arrow key, that box moves to the right, so it's in column B. If you tap the down-arrow key, the box moves down, to row 2. By tapping the four arrow keys, you can move the box in all four directions, to practically anywhere on the grid. Try it!

Each possible position of the box is called a **cell**.

The box's original position (in column A, row 1) is called **cell A1**. If you move the box there and then tap the right-arrow key, the box moves to column B, row 1; that position is called **cell B1**.

Just move the box from cell to cell, and put into each cell whatever words or numbers you wish!

For example, suppose you run a small business whose income is $7000 and expenses are $5000. Those are the figures for January; the figures for February aren't in yet. Let's put the January figures into a spreadsheet, like this:

	A	B	C	D	E	F
1		January				
2	Income	7000				
3	Expenses	5000				
4	Profit					

To begin, move the box to cell A2. Type the word Income. As you type that word, you see it appearing in cell A2. It also appears temporarily at the screen's top, in an **input line** (which Works calls the **entry bar** and Excel calls the **formula bar**).

Press the down-arrow key, which moves the box down to cell A3. Type the word Expenses.

Press the down-arrow key (to move to cell A4). Type the word Profit.

Move the box to cell B1 (by pressing the up-arrow three times and then the right-arrow once). Type the word January.

Press down-arrow. Type 7000.

Press down-arrow. Type 5000.

Press down-arrow again.

Backspace key

If you make a mistake while typing the words and numbers, press the **Backspace key** to erase the last character you typed.

Alternative keys

Instead of pressing the right-arrow key, you can press the Tab key. Instead of pressing the down-arrow key, you can press the Enter key.

Type a formula

Although the computer's screen shows the words you typed (Income, Expenses, and Profit), the computer doesn't understand what those words mean. It doesn't know that "Profit" means "Income minus Expenses". The computer doesn't know that the number in cell B4 (which represents the profit) ought to be the number in cell B2 (the amount of income) minus the number in cell B3 (the dollars spent).

You must *teach* the computer the meaning of Profit, by teaching it that the number in cell B4 ought to be the number in cell B2 minus the number in cell B3. To do that, move the box to cell B4, then type this formula:

```
=B2-B3
```

Notice that **every formula begins with an equal sign**. The rest of the formula, B2-B3, tells the computer to subtract the number in cell B3 from the number in cell B2 and put the answer into the box's cell (which is cell B4).

When you've finished typing the formula, press the Enter key. Then the computer automatically computes the formula's answer (2000) and puts that number into the box's cell (B4), so the screen looks like this:

	A	B	C	D	E	F
1		January				
2	Income	7000				
3	Expenses	5000				
4	Profit	2000				

The formula "=B2-B3" remains in effect forever. It says that the number in cell B4 will always be the B2 number minus the B3 number. If you ever change the numbers in cells B2 and B3 (by moving the box to those cells, retyping the numbers, and pressing Enter), the computer automatically adjusts the number in cell B4, so the number in cell B4 is still B2 minus B3 and still represents the correct profit.

For example, suppose you move the box to cell B2, then type 8000 (to change the January income to $8000), and then press Enter. As soon as you press Enter, the profit in cell B4 immediately changes to 3000, right in front of your eyes!

A typical spreadsheet contains *dozens* of numbers, totals, subtotals, averages, and percentages. Each cell that contains a total, subtotal, average, or percentage is defined by a formula. Whenever you retype one of the numbers in the spreadsheet, the computer automatically readjusts all the totals, subtotals, averages, and percentages, right before your eyes.

Remember to begin each formula with an equal sign. The rest of the formula can contain these symbols:

Symbol	Meaning
+	plus
-	minus
*	times
/	divided by
.	decimal point

It can also contain E notation and parentheses. For details about how to use those symbols, E notation, and parentheses, read pages 494-497, which explain QBasic's fundamentals and math.

Less typing When you're creating a formula such as "=B2-B3", you do *not* have to type the "B2". Instead, you can choose one of these shortcuts:

Instead of typing "B2", you can type "b2" without bothering to capitalize. When you've finished typing the entire formula ("=b2-b3"), press the Enter key. Then the computer will capitalize your formula automatically!

Instead of typing "B2", you can move the mouse pointer to the middle of cell B2, then press the mouse's button. That's called "clicking cell B2". When you click cell B2, the computer automatically types "B2" for you! So to create the formula "=B2-B3", you can do this: type the equal sign, then click cell B2, then type the minus sign, then click cell B3. When you've finished creating the entire formula, press Enter.

Instead of typing "B2", you can move the box to cell B2 by using the arrow keys. When you move the box to cell B2, the computer automatically types "B2" for you! So to create the formula "=B2-B3", you can do this: type the equal sign, then move the box to cell B2 (by using the arrow keys), then type the minus sign, then move the box to cell B3. When you've finished creating the entire formula, press Enter.

Edit old cells

To edit what's in a cell, move the box to that cell. Then choose one of these editing methods....

Method 1: press the Delete key. That makes the cell become totally blank.

Method 2: retype the entire text, number, or formula that you want to put into the cell.

Method 3: in the input line (at the top of the screen), look at what you typed, find the part of your typing that you want to change, and click that part (by using the mouse). Then edit your typing as if you were using a word processor: you can use the left-arrow key, right-arrow key, Backspace key, Delete key, and mouse. When you finish editing, press the Enter key.

Functions

Here's how to perform functions.

Sum of a column To make a cell be the sum of cells B2 through B9, you can type this formula:

```
=B2+B3+B4+B5+B6+B7+B8+B9
```

Instead of typing all that, you can type just this:

```
=SUM(B2:B9)
```

A **function** is a word that makes the computer calculate (such as SUM). After each function, you must put parentheses. For example, you must put parentheses after SUM.

Since the computer ignores capitalization, you can type:

```
=sum(b2:b9)
```

Here's how to type the formula =sum(b2:b9) quickly. Begin by typing:

```
=sum(
```

Then drag from cell B2 to cell B9. To do that, move the mouse to cell B2, then hold down the mouse button while moving to B9. That makes the computer type the "B2:B9". Here's what to do next....

Excel: press Enter, which makes the computer automatically type the ")".
Works: type ")", then press Enter.

AutoSum button Here's an even faster way to type the formula =SUM(B2:B9). Click the **AutoSum button**, which has the symbol Σ on it.

Excel 2007&2010: the Σ button is near the screen's top-right corner.
Excel 2002&2003 and Works: the Σ button is near the screen's top center.

(The symbol Σ is called "sigma". It's the Greek version of the letter S. Mathematicians use it to stand for the word "sum".)

Clicking the AutoSum button makes the computer type "=SUM()". It also makes the computer guess what you want the sum of. The computer puts that guess inside the parentheses.

If the computer's guess differs from what you want (B2:B9), fix the guess (by dragging from cell B2 to cell B9). When you finally see the correct formula, =SUM(B2:B9), press Enter.

Sum of a row To find the sum of cells B2 through H2 (which is B2+C2+D2+E2+F2+G2+H2), type this:

```
=sum(b2:h2)
```

Sum of a rectangle To find the sum of all cells in the rectangle that stretches from B2 to C4 (which is B2+B3+B4+C2+C3+C4), type this:

```
=sum(b2:c4)
```

Average To find the average of cells B9 through B13, you can type this:

```
=(b9+b10+b11+b12+b13)/5
```

But this way is shorter....

Excel: =average(b9:b13)
Works: =avg(b9:b13)

Here's how to type that quickly....

Excel: begin by typing "=average(", then drag from cell B9 to cell B13, then press the Enter key, which makes the computer automatically type the ")".

Works: begin by typing "=avg(", then drag from cell B9 to cell B13, then type ")", then press Enter.

Excel provides this faster way to type the formula "=average(b9:b13)": click the ▼ that's next to the Σ button, then click "Average".

To find the average of cells C7, B5, and F2, you can ask for (c7+b5+f2)/3, but a nicer way is to type this....

Excel: =average(c7,b5,f2)
Works: =avg(c7,b5,f2)

Undo

If you make a big mistake, click the **Undo button**, which shows an arrow turning back to the left.

Excel 2007&2010: the Undo button is at the screen's top, near the left corner.

Excel 2002&2003: the Undo button is near the screen's top, under the word "Window."

Works: the Undo button is missing, so press Ctrl with Z instead.

That makes the computer undo your last activity, so your spreadsheet returns to the way it looked before you made your boo-boo.

To undo your last *two* activities, click the Undo button *twice*. (Exception: Microsoft Works lets you undo just one activity.)

Redo If you click the Undo button, the computer might undo a different activity than you expected. If clicking the Undo button accidentally makes the spreadsheet look even worse instead of better, and you wish you hadn't clicked the Undo button, here's how to "undo the undo"....

Excel: click the Redo button (which is to the right of the Undo button and shows an arrow bending forward to the right).

Works: press Ctrl with Z again.

Hop far

Here's how to be quick as a bunny and hop far in your spreadsheet.

Farther rows

The screen shows just a few rows, which are numbered 1, 2, 3, etc. Row 1 is at the top of the screen. Row 15 is near the bottom of the screen.

Try this experiment. Move the box down to row 15 (by pressing the down-arrow key repeatedly). Then press the down-arrow key several more times. Eventually, you'll get to row 30, and later to row 100, and much later to row 1000. (The largest row number you can go to is 16384 in Works, 65536 in Excel 2002&2003, 1048576 in Excel 2007&2010.)

To make room on the screen for those new rows, row 1 disappears temporarily. If you want to get back to row 1, press the up-arrow key repeatedly.

Farther columns

The screen shows just a few columns, which are lettered A, B, C, etc. If you press the right-arrow key repeatedly, you'll eventually get to column Z.

After column Z, you can still continue pressing the right-arrow key. The next 26 columns are lettered from AA to AZ. The next 26 columns are lettered from BA to BA. And so on.

Here's how many columns you can have:

Excel 2007&2010: you can have 16384 columns; the last column is XFD.

Excel 2002&2003 and Works: you can have 256 columns; the last column is IV.

AutoRepeat

Here's a shortcut: instead of pressing an arrow key repeatedly, just hold down the key awhile.

Mouse

To move the box to a distant cell even faster, use the mouse: just click in the middle of the cell you wish.

Screenfuls

To move far down, press the **Page Down key**. To move far up, press the **Page Up key**. To move far to the right, do this....

Excel: press the Page Down key while holding down the Alt key.
Works: press the Page Down key while holding down the Ctrl key.

To move far to the left, do this....

Excel: press the Page Up key while holding down the Alt key.
Works: press the Page Up key while holding down the Ctrl key.

Each of those keys moves the box far enough so that you see the next screenful of rows and columns.

Home key

Cell A1 is called the **home cell**, because that's where life and your spreadsheet begin: at home! Column A is called the **home column**.

Your keyboard has a **Home key**. Here's how to use it:

Pressing the Home key makes the box move far left, so it lands in column A.
If you press the Home key *while holding down the Ctrl key*, the box moves to cell A1.

Spreadsheet's edge

To move to the spreadsheet's edge, press an arrow key *while holding down the Ctrl key*.

For example, to move the box to the spreadsheet's right edge, press the right-arrow key while holding down the Ctrl key. That moves the box moves to the right, until it reaches the final column (IV or XFD) or a boundary cell (a cell containing data and next to an empty cell).

F5 key

To make the box go to a distant cell immediately: press the F5 key (or press Ctrl with G), then type the name of the cell where you want to go (such as C9) followed by Enter.

Excel lets you also use this alternative:

Above column A, you see the **Name box**, which tells you the name of the cell where the box is. For example, while the box is at cell B4, the name box says "B4". To move the box to a distant cell immediately, you can click in the name box, then type the name of the cell where you want to go (such as C9) followed by Enter.

Adjust rows & columns

How many rows and columns are in your spreadsheet, and how big are they? Here's how to adjust them.

Widen a column

When you start a new spreadsheet, here's what happens....

Works: each cell is wide enough to hold a 9-digit number.
Excel: each cell is wide enough to hold an 8-digit number;   if you type a longer number, the column widens to fit it.

Here's **how make column D be wider**, so each cell in column D can hold long numbers *and long words*:

At the top of column D, you see the letter D. **Move the mouse** until its pointer is **between the letters D and E,** and **on the vertical gridline that separates them**. The pointer's shape turns into a **double-headed arrow**. (In Works, the pointer is also labeled "ADJUST".) Then drag that vertical gridline toward the right (to make the column wider) or left (to make the column narrower).

Widen several columns Excel lets you widen columns D, E, F, and G simultaneously. Here's how:

Drag from the letter D to the letter G. All those columns darken. (In in Excel 2002&2003&2010, they turn blue; in Excel 2007, they turn gray; in Works, they turn black.)   Look at the vertical gridline to the right of the D. Drag the top of that gridline toward the right. That widens column D; and when you release your finger from the mouse's button, all the other columns you selected will widen also.

Perfect width Here's how to make column D just wide enough to hold the widest data in it....

Excel: double-click the gridline that separates the letter D from E.
Works: double-click the D at the top of column D.

(If the column doesn't contain data yet, the computer will leave the column's width unchanged.)

Excel lets you make columns D, E, F, and G have perfect widths simultaneously. Here's how:

Drag from the letter D to the letter G, so all those columns turn dark. Then double-click the gridline that separates the letter D from E.

Long numbers If you try to type a long number in a cell that's too narrow to hold the number, the cell might display number signs (#) instead of the number.

For example, if you try typing a long number in a cell that's just 4 characters wide, the computer will display 4 number signs (like this: ####).

Although the cell displays just number signs, the computer remembers the long number you typed. To see the long number, widen the cell (by widening its column).

So if you see number signs in a cell, the computer is telling you the cell's too narrow and should be widened.

Long words Try this experiment. Make cell B1 be just 4 characters wide. Then try to type the word "January" in that cell.

That cell, B1, might show just the first 4 letters (Janu). But if the next cell (C1) is blank, cell B1 will temporarily widen to hold "January", then contract to its original size (4 characters) when you enter data in cell C1.

Delete a column

Here's **how to delete column D:**

> Excel: *right*-click the D at the top of column D (by using the mouse's *right* button instead of the left); then choose Delete from the menu that appears.
>
> Works: *right*-click anywhere in column D (by using the mouse's *right* button instead of the left), then choose Delete Column from the menu that appears.

The computer erases all the data from column D, so column D becomes blanks, which the computer immediately fills by shifting some data from other columns. Here's how....

Into column D, the computer moves the data from column E. Then into column E, the computer moves the data from column F. Then into column F, the computer moves the data from column G. And so on.

At the end of the process, the top of the screen still shows all the letters (A, B, C, D, E, F, G, etc.); but now column D contains the data that used to be in column E; and column E contains the data that used to be in column F; etc.

After rearranging the spreadsheet, the computer fixes all formulas. For example, after column E's data has moved to column D, the computer hunts through all formulas in the spreadsheet and fixes them by changing each "E" to "D". The computer also changes each "F" to "E", each "G" to "F", etc.

Delete several columns You've learned how to delete column D. Here's how to delete *several* columns. To delete columns D, E, F, and G, drag from the D to the G, then do the following....

> Excel: *right*-click anywhere in columns D through G (by using the mouse's *right* button instead of the left); then choose Delete from the menu that appears.
>
> Works: *right*-click anywhere in columns D through G (by using the mouse's *right* button instead of the left), then choose Delete Column from the menu that appears.

Delete a row

Here's **how to delete row 2:**

> Excel: *right*-click the 2 (by using the mouse's *right* button instead of the left); then choose Delete from the menu that appears.
>
> Works: *right*-click anywhere in row 2 (by using the mouse's *right* button instead of the left), then choose Delete Row from the menu that appears.

Then the computer erases all the data from row 2, so row 2 becomes empty; but then the computer immediately fills that hole, by shifting the data from other rows. Here's how....

Into row 2, the computer moves the data from row 3. Then into row 3, the computer moves the data from row 4. Then into row 4, the computer moves the data from row 5. And so on.

At the end of the process, the left edge of the screen still shows all the numbers (1, 2, 3, 4, 5, etc.); but now row 2 contains the data that used to be in row 3; and row 3 contains the data that used to be in row 4; etc.

The computer fixes all formulas.

Insert a column

Here's how to insert an extra column in the middle of your spreadsheet:

> Excel: *right*-click where you want the extra column to appear. For example, if you want the extra column to appear where column D is now, *right*-click the D. Then choose Insert from the menu that appears.
>
> Works: *right*-click where you want the extra column to appear. For example, if you want the extra column to appear where column D is now, *right*-click in column D. Then choose Insert Column from the menu that appears.

The computer will move other columns out of the way, to make room for the extra column. The computer will also fix each formula.

Insert a row

Here's how to insert an extra row in the middle of your spreadsheet:

> Excel: *right*-click where you want the extra row to appear. For example, if you want the extra row to appear where row 2 is now, *right*-click the 2. Then choose Insert from the menu that appears.
>
> Works: *right*-click where you want the extra row to appear. For example, if you want the extra row to appear where row 2 is now, *right*-click in row 2. Then choose Insert Row from the menu that appears.

The computer will move other rows out of the way, to make room for the extra row. The computer will also fix each formula.

Zoom

You can make your screen show twice as many rows and columns. Here's how in Excel 2007&2010:

> At the screen's bottom-right corner, you see a plus sign (+). Left of it, you see a minus sign (-). Between those signs, you see the **zoom slider**.
>
> If you drag the zoom slider toward the left, the screen's characters shrink, so you can fit more characters and pages onto the screen. For example, if you drag the zoom slider toward the left until the number left of the minus sign is "50%", the computer will make all the screen's characters tiny (half as tall and half as wide), so twice as many rows and twice as many columns fit on the screen. If you drag the zoom slider toward the right instead, the screen's characters enlarge, so you can read them even if you're sitting far from the screen or have poor vision.
>
> When you finish playing with the zoom slider, put it back to its normal position (the middle), so the number left of the minus sign is "100%".

Here's how in Excel 2002&2003:

> Near the screen's top right corner, you see a percentage, which is normally **100%**. That percentage is in a white box, called the **Zoom box**. Click its down-arrow.
>
> You'll see the **Zoom menu**. From that menu, choose **50%**. The computer will make all the screen's characters tiny (half as tall and half as wide), so twice as many rows and twice as many columns fit on the screen.
>
> To make the screen return to normal, click the Zoom box's down-arrow again, then click **100%**.
>
> If you wish, you can click different percentages, such as **75%** (which shrinks the screen's characters just slightly) or **200%** (which enlarges the screen's characters, so you can read them even if you're sitting far away from the screen).
>
> Try this trick: start at one cell, and drag to another cell far away. All the cells between them turn dark. Then click the Zoom box's down-arrow and click **Selection**. That shrinks or enlarges the characters just enough so all the dark cells fit on the screen.

Here's how in Works:

> Near the screen's bottom left corner, you see the word **Zoom**. Next to it, you normally see **100%**.
>
> Near it, you see a **plus sign**. If you click that plus sign, the computer makes the screen's characters be enlarged, so their size is 150% as wide and 150% as tall as normal, and the Zoom box says "150%" instead of "100%".
>
> If you click the plus sign again, the computer makes the screen's characters be even larger, so their size is 200%. If you click the plus sign again, the computer makes the screen's characters be even larger: 400%.
>
> If you click the **minus sign** instead, the characters become smaller. By clicking the plus or minus sign repeatedly, you can choose these sizes: 50%, 75%, 100%, 150%, 200%, 400%.
>
> 50% and 75% are very useful: they make the characters smaller, so more characters fit on the screen and you see more rows and columns.
>
> For further choices, click the word **Zoom**. Then you see this **Zoom menu**:
> 50%
> 75%
> 100%
> 150%
> 200%
> 400%
> Custom
>
> Click whichever choice you wish.
>
> If you prefer a different percentage, choose **Custom** then type the percentage you want (such as 90) and press Enter.

All those Zoom choices affect just what you see on the screen. They do *not* affect what's printed on paper.

Panes

On your screen, you see a window that contains part of your spreadsheet. (That window is big enough to usually show columns A through I on a cheap screen, and more columns on a fancier screen.)

You can divide that window into two **windowpanes**, so that each windowpane shows a different part of your spreadsheet.

Vertical panes Here's how to divide your window into two windowpanes, so that the left pane shows columns A, B, and C, while the right pane shows columns X, Y and Z.

Get column A onto the screen (by pressing the Home key).

In Excel, do this:

> Near the screen's bottom right corner, you see the symbol ▶ (or >), which points at a vertical bar. Put your mouse pointer on that vertical bar; when you do, the pointer becomes this symbol: ◄▌►. Drag that vertical bar to the left.

In Works, do this:

> Near the screen's bottom left corner, you see the word "Zoom". Left of it, you see a vertical bar. Put your mouse pointer on that bar; when you do, the pointer becomes the symbol ◄▌► and is labeled "ADJUST". Drag that vertical bar to the right.

As you drag, you'll see a vertical gray bar move across your spreadsheet. Drag until the vertical gray bar is in the middle of the spreadsheet. For best results, drag until that bar is slightly to the right of column C's right edge.

That bar splits the screen into two panes. The left pane shows columns A through C; the right pane shows column D and beyond.

Then click anywhere in the right pane. That puts the box in the right pane, and makes the right pane active. Press the right-arrow key several times, until you reach columns X, Y, and Z.

If you want to move the box back to the left pane, just click the left pane.

To stop using vertical panes, double-click the vertical gray bar.

Horizontal panes Here's how to divide your window into two panes, so that the top pane shows rows 1, 2, and 3, while the bottom pane shows rows 97, 98, and 99.

Get row 1 onto the screen (by pressing the Page Up key several times).

At the spreadsheet's top right corner, you'll see the scroll bar's up-arrow pointing at a horizontal bar. Put the mouse pointer on that bar; when you do, the pointer becomes the symbol ⬍ (and in Works is labeled "ADJUST"). Drag that bar down. As you drag, you'll see a horizontal gray bar move down your spreadsheet. Drag until the horizontal gray bar is in the middle of the spreadsheet. For best results, drag until that bar is slightly under row 3's bottom edge.

That bar splits the screen into two panes. The top pane shows rows 1 through 3; the bottom pane shows row 4 and beyond.

Then click anywhere in the bottom pane. That puts the box in the bottom pane, and makes the bottom pane active. Press the down-arrow key several times, until you reach rows 97, 98, and 99.

If you want to move the box back to the top pane, just click the top pane.

To stop using horizontal panes, double-click the horizontal gray bar.

Freeze title panes You should put a title at the top of each column. For example, if column B contains financial information for January, and column C contains financial information for February, you should put the word January at the top of column B, and the word February at the top of column C. Since the words January and February are at the top of the columns, they're in row 1. They're called the **column titles**.

If row 2 analyzes Income, and row 3 analyzes Expenses, you should put the word Income at the left edge of row 2, and the word Expenses at the left edge of row 3. Since the words Income and Expenses are at the left edge of the spreadsheet, they're in column A. They're called the **row titles**.

So in a typical spreadsheet, the column titles are in row 1, and row titles are in column A.

Unfortunately, when you move beyond column M or beyond row 25 (by pressing the arrow keys repeatedly), the titles normally disappear from the screen, and you forget the purpose of each row and column. Here's how to solve that problem.

Get cell A1 onto the screen (by pressing Ctrl with Home).

Click cell B2. Then do this:

> Excel 2007&2010: click "View" (at the screen's top) then **Freeze Panes** then "Freeze Panes" again then "Home" (at the screen's top).
>
> Excel 2002&2003: choose **Freeze Panes** from the Window menu.
>
> Works: choose **Freeze Titles** from the Format menu.

Now the window is divided into four panes, separated by thick black gridlines. The main top pane contains the column titles (January, February, etc.); the main left pane contains the row titles (Income, Expenses, etc.); a tiny pane in the upper-left corner contains a blank cell; and a huge pane contains all the spreadsheet's data.

Then move through the huge pane, by using the arrow keys or mouse. As you move, the column and row titles stay fixed on the screen, since they're not in the big pane.

Here's how to stop using freeze title panes....

> Excel 2007&2010: click "View" (at the screen's top) then Freeze Panes then Unfreeze Panes then "Home" (at the screen's top).
>
> Excel 2002&2003: choose Unfreeze Panes from the Window menu.
>
> Works: click Format, then remove the check mark in front of Freeze Titles (by clicking Freeze Titles again).

Move

On your spreadsheet, find these cells: B2, B3, B4, C2, C3, and C4. Those six cells are next to each other. In fact, they form a giant rectangular area, whose top left corner is B2.

Here's how to take all the data in that rectangle and move it to a different part of your spreadsheet.

Drag from the rectangle's first cell (B2) to the rectangle's last cell (C4). The entire rectangle turns dark (except for the first cell, which stays white).

Surrounding the rectangle, you'll see four walls. Those walls are the four sides of the rectangle.

Using your mouse, **point at one of the rectangle's walls.** (Do *not* point at a corner.) When you've pointed correctly, here's what happens....

> Excel: the mouse pointer turns into 4 arrows, pointing in all 4 directions.
> Works: the mouse pointer turns into an arrow (*not* a cross).

Then hold down the mouse's button and **drag the wall**. While you drag the wall, the rest of the rectangle drags along with it. Drag until the entire rectangle is at a part of the spreadsheet that was blank. Then lift your finger from the mouse's button.

That's how you move a rectangle of data to a new place in your spreadsheet that had been blank.

Try it!

After moving the rectangle of data, the computer automatically adjusts all formulas mentioning the moved cells. For example, if the data in cell B2 has moved to cell E7, the computer searches through the entire spreadsheet and, in each formula, changes "B2" to "E7".

Copy

Spreadsheet programs let you copy info in several ways.

Fill to the right

Here's how to make lots of love with the computer!

> In a cell, type the word "love".
> Click in that cell (to make sure the cell is highlighted), then take your finger off the mouse's button. With your finger still off the mouse's button, move the mouse until the mouse's pointer is at that cell's bottom right corner. When the pointer is exactly at the corner, the pointer changes to this thin cross: +.
> Then hold down the mouse's left button, and drag toward the right, until you've dragged across several cells.
> When you lift your finger off the mouse's button, all those cells will contain copies of the word in the first cell. They'll all say "love"!

Go ahead! Try turning your computer into a lovemaking machine! Do it *now!* This is an important exercise to try before you get into more advanced computer orgies!

Here's another example:

> In a cell, type the word "tickle". To make lots of tickles, click in that cell, then point at that cell's bottom right corner (so you see +) and drag it to the right. The cells you drag across will all say "tickle".

Fill down

When you point at a cell's bottom right corner and drag, you usually drag to the *right*. But if you prefer, you can drag *down*, so you're copying to the cells *underneath* (instead of the cells to the right).

Extend a series

You've learned that if the original cell said "love", the adjacent cells will say "love"; and if the original cell said "tickle", the other cells will say "tickle".

But if the original cell said "January", the adjacent cells will *not* say "January". Instead, the computer makes them say "February", "March", "April", "May", etc.

So **here's how to put the words "January", "February", "March", "April", etc., across your spreadsheet's top:**

> Begin by typing "January" in cell B1. Then drag that cell's bottom right corner to the right, to column H or I or even farther! The farther you drag, the more months you'll see!

Your computer performs fundamental tricks:

If you start with January,	the computer will say February, March, April, etc.
If you start with October,	the computer will say November, December, January, etc.
If you start with 12/29/2011,	the computer will 12/30/2011, 12/31/2011, 1/1/2012, etc.
If you start with Monday,	the computer will say Tuesday, Wednesday, Thursday, etc.
If you start with Mon,	the computer will say Tue, Wed, Thu, etc.
If you start with 10:00 AM,	the computer will say 11:00 AM, 12:00 PM, 1:00 PM, etc.
If you start with 10:00,	the computer will say 11:00, 12:00, 13:00, etc.
If you start with 22:00,	the computer will say 23:00, 0:00, 1:00, etc.
If you start with Q2,	the computer will say Q3, Q4, Q1, etc.
If you start with Idiot 1,	the computer will say Idiot 2, Idiot 3, Idiot 4, etc.
If you start with Year 2011,	the computer will say Year 2012, Year 2013, Year 2014, etc.

Works performs these extra tricks:

If you start with July 29,	the computer will say July 30, July 31, August 01, etc.
If you start with July 29, 1999,	the computer will say July 30, 1999, July 31, 1999, August 01, 1999, etc.
If you start with October 1999,	the computer will say November 1999, December 1999, January 2000, etc.
If you start with 2Q,	the computer will say 3Q, 4Q, 1Q, etc.

Excel performs these extra tricks:

If you start with Jan,	the computer will say Feb, Mar, Apr, etc.
If you start with 29-Jan,	the computer will say 30-Jan, 31-Jan, 1-Feb, etc.
If you start with Oct-98,	the computer will say Nov-98, Dec-98, Jan-99, etc.
If you start with 29-Dec-98,	the computer will say 30-Dec-98, 31-Dec-98, 1-Jan-99, etc.
If you start with 29-Dec-99,	the computer will say 30-Dec-99, 31-Dec-99, 1-Jan-00, etc.
If you start with 2nd Quarter,	the computer will say 3rd Quarter, 4th Quarter, 1st Quarter, etc.
If you start with 2nd Qtr,	the computer will say 3rd Qtr, 4th Qtr, 1st Qtr, etc.
If you start with 2 Q,	the computer will say 3 Q, 4 Q, 1 Q, etc.
If you start with Quarter 2,	the computer will say Quarter 3, Quarter 4, Quarter 1, etc.
If you start with 1st,	the computer will say 2nd, 3rd, 4th, etc.
If you start with 1st Idiot,	the computer will say 2nd Idiot, 3rd Idiot, 4th Idiot, etc.
If you start with 2011 Results,	the computer will say 2012 Results, 2013 Results, 2014 Results, etc.

Limitation: if you start with just a plain number (such as 1), the computer will just copy that number; it will *not* say 2, 3, 4, etc. If you start with just the plain number 2011, the computer will just copy that number; it will *not* say 2012, 2013, 2014, etc. To make the computer do more than just copy, include a word. For example, instead of saying just 1, say "Idiot 1"; then the computer will say "Idiot 2", "Idiot 3", "Idiot 4", etc. Instead of saying just 2011, say "Year 2011" or "2011 Results" or "People We Accidentally Shot In 2011"; then the computer will generate similar headings for 2012, 2013, etc.

Copy a formula's concept

If you ask the computer to copy a formula, the computer will copy the *concept* underlying the formula.

Here's an example:

> Suppose you put this formula in cell B4: =B2+B3. That means cell B4 contains "the sum of the two numbers above it". If you drag that cell's bottom right corner to the right, the computer will copy that formula's *concept* to the adjacent cells (C4, D4, E4, etc.).
> For example, the computer will make C4's formula be "the sum of the two numbers above it", by making C4's formula be =C2+C3. The computer will make D4's formula be =D2+D3. The computer will make E4's formula be =E2+E3.

Here's another example:

> Suppose cell B4 contains the formula =2*B3, so that B4 is "twice the cell above it". When the computer copies that concept to cell C4, the computer will make C4's formula be "twice the cell above it"; the computer will make C4's formula be =2*C3.

Here's another example:

Suppose cell B4 contains the formula =2*A4, so that B4 is "twice the cell to the left of it". When the computer copies cell B4 to C4, the computer will make C4's formula be "twice the cell to the left of it"; the computer will make C4's formula be =2*B4.

Absolute addresses Notice again how copying from B4 to C4 turns the formula =B2+B3 into =C2+C3: it turns each B into a C.

If you want to prevent those changes, put dollar signs in the original formula. For example, if you want to prevent B3 from turning into D3, put dollar signs around the B3, so cell B4 contains this formula:

=B2+$B$3

When you copy that cell to C4, the dollar signs prevents the computer from turning the B3 into C3; C4's formula will become =C2+$B$3 (instead of =C2+C3).

Here's how to type "=B2+$B$3" quickly. Type the "=" sign, then move the box to cell B2, then type the "+" sign. Finally, **create the $B$3 by using this trick: move the box to cell B3, then press the F4 key**. When you've finished creating the entire formula, press Enter.

A cell's name (such as B3) is called the cell's **address**, because the cell's name tells you where to find the cell. An address that contains dollar signs (such as $B$3) is called an **absolute address**, because the address is absolutely fixed and will never change, not even when you copy the formula. An address that lacks dollar signs is called a **relative address**, because when you copy that address you'll be copying the cell's relationship to the other cells.

After you've finished

Finished creating your spreadsheet? Here's how to copy it to the disk and printer and move on to another task.

Find the buttons

Most spreadsheet programs have 4 buttons near the screen's top left corner:

The first	is the	**New button**. It can look like a new blank sheet of paper.
The second	is the	**Open button**. It looks like a file folder pried open.
The third	is the	**Save button**. It looks like a 3½-inch floppy disk.
The fourth	is the	**Print button**. It can look like a printer, printing on paper.

Each spreadsheet program is peculiar.

Excel 2007: click "File" to see "New", "Open", and "Print"; the Save button is at the screen's top, near the left edge.

Excel 2007: click the **File-office button** (the circle at the screen's top-left corner) to see the New, Open, and Print buttons; the Save button is next to the Office button.

Excel 2003: the buttons are under the word "File" and also include E-mail and Permission buttons.

Excel 2002: the buttons are under the word "File" and also include E-mail and Search buttons.

Works: the buttons are under the word "Tools"; the New and Open buttons are rather useless.

Here's how to use the helpful buttons....

Save button

To save the spreadsheet (copy it onto the disk), click the **Save button**.

If you haven't saved the spreadsheet before, the computer will say "File Name". Invent a name for your spreadsheet. Type the name and press Enter.

That makes the computer copy the spreadsheet onto the hard disk.

For example, if you named the spreadsheet "mary", here's what happens:

Excel 2007&2010 make that spreadsheet be a file called mary.xlsx (meaning "Mary's E**x**cel **s**preadsheet e**x**tended"). The computer puts that file into the Documents folder. (Windows 7 puts it into the Documents library's "My Documents" folder instead.)

Excel 2002&2003 make that spreadsheet be a file called mary.xls (meaning "Mary's E**x**cel **s**preadsheet"). The computer puts that file into the My Documents folder.

Works makes that spreadsheet be a file called mary.xlr. The computer puts that file into the My Documents folder.

Afterwards, if you change your mind and want to do more editing, go ahead! When you finish that extra editing, save it by clicking the Save button again.

Save often If you're typing a long document, click the Save button about every 10 minutes. Click it whenever you get to a good stopping place and think, "What I've typed so far looks good!"

Then if an accident happens, you'll lose at most 10 minutes of work, and you can return to the last version you felt good about.

Print button

To print your spreadsheet onto paper, click the **Print button**. (If you're using Excel 2007 or 2010, then press Enter.)

Page Setup

Before clicking the Print button, you can tell the computer what kind of printing you prefer. Here's how....

Excel 2007&2010 Click **Page Layout**.

> If you want the computer to rotate the spreadsheet 90 degrees, so more columns will fit on the paper, click **Orientation** then **Landscape**.
>
> If the spreadsheet has many columns and you want to make the characters small enough so all columns fit on one sheet of paper, click the **Width box**'s down-arrow then "1 page". If the spreadsheet has many rows and you want to make the characters small enough so all rows fit on one sheet of paper, click the **Height box**'s down-arrow then "1 page". If you change your mind and want to return to normal-size printing, do this for the Width box and Height box: click the box's down-arrow then "Automatic".
>
> Normally, the left and right margins are each 0.7 inches wide. To make the left and right margins narrower (so you can fit more columns on the paper), click **Margins** then **Narrow**. That makes the left and right margins each be just ¼-inch wide.
>
> Normally, the computer doesn't bother to print the spreadsheet's gridlines (the lines that separate the columns from each other and the rows from each other). If you *insist* that the computer print the gridlines, put a check mark in the **Gridlines Print** box, by clicking that box.
>
> Normally, the computer doesn't bother to print the column names (A, B, C) and row names (1, 2, 3). If you *insist* that the computer print those names, put a check mark in the **Headings Print** box, by clicking that box.

Click **Insert** then **Header & Footer**.

> If you want the top of each page to say "Annual blood drive", type "Annual blood drive". If you want the top of each page to show the page number also, do this afterwards: type a comma, press the Space bar, type the word "Page", press the Space bar, then click "Page Number".
>
> Finally, to return your screen to normal, click one of the cells then "View" then "Normal".

When you finish expressing your preferences to the computer, click **Home** then the File-office button (which says "File" in Excel 2010 but is a circle in Excel 2007) then "Print" then Enter.

Excel 2002&2003 Choose **Page Setup** from the **File menu**.

Click **Page**.

> For **Orientation**, click either **Portrait** or **Landscape**. Normally, the computer does Portrait. If you click Landscape instead, the computer will rotate the spreadsheet 90 degrees, so more columns will fit on the paper.
>
> Have you ever taken a photo and asked for an "enlargement"? The computer can do the same thing: when it prints your spreadsheet onto paper, it can produce an enlargement (so you can read the spreadsheet even if you're standing far away from the sheet of paper). The computer can also produce a reduction (so the spreadsheet is made of tiny characters and consumes less paper). Enlargements and reductions are called **Scaling**. Normally, the computer does *not* do scaling: it prints at 100% of original size. To make the computer do scaling, click the **Adjust To** button, then type a percentage different from 100%. For example, if you want the spreadsheet to look gigantic (twice as tall and twice as wide), type 200. If you want the spreadsheet to look tiny (miniaturized), type 50. If the spreadsheet has many rows and columns and you want to make the characters small enough so the entire spreadsheet fits on one sheet of paper, click the **Fit To** button instead.

Click **Margins**.

> Normally, the computer leaves 1-inch margins at the top and bottom of the paper and ³/₄-inch margins at the sides. To change those sizes, press the Tab key and type the number of inches you want for the **Top** margin, then do the same for the **Bottom** margin, **Left** margin, and **Right** margin.
>
> Normally, the computer starts printing the spreadsheet near the paper's top left corner. If you want the spreadsheet to be centered instead, put a check mark in the **Center Horizontally** and **Center Vertically** boxes, by clicking those boxes.

Click **Header/Footer**.

> If your spreadsheet is several pages long, here's how to make the computer print a page number at the top of each page: click the **Header** box's down-arrow, then click **Page 1**.
>
> If instead you want the top of each page to have this header —
> Annual blood drive   2007 results   by Count Dracula
> do this: click **Custom Header**, then type the left part ("Annual blood drive"), press the Tab key, type the center part ("2007 results"), press Tab again, type the right part ("by Count Dracula"), and click the OK button above the right part.

Click **Sheet**.

> Normally, the computer doesn't bother to print the spreadsheet's gridlines (the lines that separate the columns from each other and the rows from each other). If you *insist* that the computer print the gridlines, put a check mark in the **Gridlines** box, by clicking that box.
>
> Normally, the computer doesn't bother to print the column names (A, B, C) and row names (1, 2, 3). If you *insist* that the computer print those names, put a check mark in the **Row and column headings** box, by clicking that box.

When you finish expressing all your preferences to the computer, click OK then the Print button.

Works Choose **Page Setup** from the **File menu**.

Click the **Margins** tab.

> Normally, the computer leaves 1-inch margins at the top and bottom of the paper and 1¼-inch margins at the sides. To change those sizes, press the TAB key and type the number of inches you want for the **Top Margin**, then do the same for the **Bottom Margin**, **Left Margin**, and **Right Margin**.

Click the tab called "**Source, Size & Orientation**".

> For **Orientation**, click either **Portrait** or **Landscape**. Normally, the computer does Portrait. If you click Landscape instead, the computer will rotate the spreadsheet 90 degrees, so more columns will fit on the paper.

Click **Other Options**.

> Normally, the computer doesn't bother to print the spreadsheet's gridlines (the lines that separate the columns from each other and the rows from each other). If you *insist* that the computer print the gridlines, put a check mark in the **Print Gridlines** box, by clicking that box.
>
> Normally, the computer doesn't bother to print the column names (A, B, C) and row names (1, 2, 3). If you *insist* that the computer print those names, put a check mark in the **Print Row and Column Headers** box, by clicking that box.

When you finish expressing all your preferences to the computer, click OK then the Print button.

Leave the spreadsheet

When you finish working on a spreadsheet, do this....

Excel 2010 Click **File**. Then click **Exit** or **Close**.

> If you choose **Exit**, the computer will stop using Excel.
>
> If you choose **Close** instead of Exit, the computer lets you work on another document. Your next step is to say "new document" or "old document". Here's how....
>
> If you want to **start typing a new spreadsheet**, click the "File" then **New** then double-click the first "Blank document".
>
> If you want to **use an old spreadsheet**, click "File" then **Recent**. You see a list of the **25 spreadsheets you used most recently**. Click whichever spreadsheet you want to use. If you want to use a spreadsheet that's not on that list of 25, click **Open** then proceed as follows....
>
> The computer starts showing you a list of *all* spreadsheets in the Documents library (unless you've requested a different folder instead). If the list is too long to show completely, here's how to see the rest of the list: either "click in that list then rotate the mouse's wheel toward you" or "repeatedly click the down-arrow that's to the right of that list". If you want to *use* one of those spreadsheets, *double*-click the spreadsheet's name; the computer will put that spreadsheet onto the screen and let you edit it. If instead you want to *delete* one of those spreadsheets, click the spreadsheet's name then press the Delete key then the Enter key; the computer will move that spreadsheet to the Recycle Bin.

Excel 2007 Click the **File-office button**. Then click **Exit Excel** or **Close**.

> If you choose **Exit Excel**, the computer will stop using Excel.
>
> If you choose **Close** instead of Exit Excel, the computer lets you work on another document. Your next step is to say "new document" or "old document". Here's how....
>
> If you want to **start typing a new spreadsheet**, click the Office button then **New** then press Enter.
>
> If you want to **use an old spreadsheet**, click the Office button, so you see the Office menu. To the right of the Office menu, you see a list of the **17 spreadsheets you used most recently**. Click whichever spreadsheet you want to use. If you want to use a spreadsheet that's not on that list of 17, click **Open** then proceed as follows....
>
> The computer starts showing you a list of *all* spreadsheets in the Documents folder (unless you've requested a different folder instead). To see the rest of the list, either "click in that list then rotate the mouse's wheel toward you" or "repeatedly click the down-arrow that's to the right of that list". If you want to *use* one of those spreadsheets, *double*-click the spreadsheet's name; the computer will put that spreadsheet onto the screen and let you edit it. If instead you want to *delete* one of those spreadsheets, click the spreadsheet's name then press the Delete key then the Enter key; the computer will move that spreadsheet to the Recycle Bin.

Excel 2002&2003 Choose **Exit** or **Close** from the **File menu**.

> If you choose **Exit**, the computer stops using Excel.
>
> If you choose **Close** instead of Exit, the computer lets you work on another spreadsheet. Then click the **New button** or the **Open button**.
>
> If you click the **New button**, the computer lets you start typing a new spreadsheet.
>
> If you click the **Open button**, you see a list of old spreadsheets. If you want to *use* one of those spreadsheets, double-click the spreadsheet's name; the computer will put that spreadsheet onto the screen and let you edit it. If you want to *delete* one of those spreadsheets, click the spreadsheet's name and then press the Delete key and then the Enter key; the computer will move that spreadsheet to the Recycle Bin.

Works Click the **X** at the screen's top right corner. Then you have three choices:

> If you click the **X** at the screen's top right corner again, the computer stops using Microsoft Works.
>
> If you click **Programs** then Works 8&9's "**Blank spreadsheet**" (or Works 7's "**Start a blank Spreadsheet**"), the computer lets you start typing a new spreadsheet.
>
> If you click **History**, you see a list of old spreadsheets (and other Works creations). To use one of those spreadsheets, click the spreadsheet's name.

Didn't save? If you didn't save your spreadsheet yet, the computer asks, "Do you want to save the changes?" If you click "Yes" or "Save", the computer copies your document's most recent version to the hard disk; if instead you click "No" or "Don't Save", the computer ignores and forgets your most recent editing.

Congratulations! You've learned all the fundamental spreadsheet commands!

Beautify your cells

Here's how to make the cells in your spreadsheet look beautiful.

First, if you're in the middle of typing a number or word, finish typing it and then press the Enter key.

Next, **select which cells you want to beautify**. Here's how.

> To select **one cell**, click it. To select **several adjacent cells**, drag from the first cell you want to the last cell. To select **a whole rectangular area**, drag from one corner of rectangle to the opposite corner.
>
> To select **column D**, click the D.
> To select **columns D through G**, point at the D and drag to the G.
>
> To select **row 2**, click the number 2 at the left edge of row 2.
> To select **rows 2 through 5**, point at the 2 and drag to the 5.
>
> To select **the entire spreadsheet**, click the empty box that's left of the letter A.

When doing one of those selections, use the mouse.

The part of the spreadsheet you've selected is called the **selection** (or **range**). It's turned entirely dark, except for the cell where the box is. (In Excel 2002&2003&2010, "dark" is blue; in Excel 2007, "dark" is gray; in Works, "dark" is black.)

If your selection includes at least 2 numbers, Excel can make the screen's bottom show you statistics:

> **Excel 2007&2010** The screen's bottom can show you 6 statistics: the **count** (how many cells you selected), **numerical count** (how many of the selected cells are numbers), **sum** (total of the selected numbers), **average** (sum divided by the numerical count), **minimum** (which of the selected numbers is the smallest), and **maximum** (which of the selected numbers is the biggest). The first time you use Excel, the computer assumes you want to see just 3 of those statistics: the count, sum, and average. Here's how to make all 6 statistics appear: right-click one of the statistics you see; then you see a list of those 6 statistics; put check marks in front of each of those 6 (by clicking). That makes the computer show those 6 statistics forevermore (every day for every spreadsheet), until you say otherwise (by right-clicking one of the statistics and removing check marks).
>
> **Excel 2002&2003** The screen's bottom shows you one statistic (either their sum, average, count, maximum, or minimum), which you can right-click to see a list of other statistics, from which you can click your favorite.

After you've made your **selection**, tell the computer how to beautify it. Choose one of the following forms of beauty....

Italic

Here's how to make all writing in the selection be italicized (*like this*).

Find the *I* button, which is near the screen's top.

Excel 2007&2010:	the *I* button is above column B or C.
Excel 2002&2003:	the *I* button is above columns C and D.
Works:	the *I* button is above column F.

Activate that button by clicking it. **Activating the button changes the button's appearance.**

Excel 2003&2007&2010:	the button turns orange.
Excel 2002:	the button gets a blue border.
Works 8&9:	the button gets a black border.
Works 7:	the button looks "pushed in".

That makes all writing in the selection be italicized.

If you change your mind and want the writing *not* to be italicized, select the writing again (so it turns dark again) then deactivate the *I* button (by clicking it again).

Bold

Here's how to make all writing in the selection be bold (**like this**).

Find the **B** button, which is near the screen's top and next to the *I* button.

Excel 2007&2010:	the **B** button is above column A, B, or C.
Excel 2002&2003:	the **B** button is above column C.
Works:	the **B** button is above column F.

Activate that button by clicking it. That makes all writing in the selection be bold.

If you change your mind and want the writing *not* to be bold, select the writing again (so it turns dark again) then deactivate the **B** button (by clicking it again).

To get bold italics, activate the bold button and also the italic button (by clicking both of them).

Underline

Here's how to make all writing in the selection be underlined (<u>like this</u>).

Find the <u>U</u> button, which is near the screen's top and next to the *I* button.

Excel 2007&2010:	the <u>U</u> button is above column B or C.
Excel 2002&2003:	the <u>U</u> button is above column D.
Works:	the <u>U</u> button is above column F.

Activate that button by clicking it. That makes all writing in the selection be underlined.

If you change your mind and want the writing *not* to be underlined, select the writing again (so it turns dark again) then deactivate the <u>U</u> button again (by clicking it again).

Font size

Above column B, and below the word Format, you see the number 10.

To make all writing in the selection get bigger (**like this**), click the down-arrow to the right of that 10, then click a font size bigger than 10. (For example, click 14 or 16.)

To make your spreadsheet easier to read, use big writing for the column headings (such as January), the row headings (such as Income, Expenses, and Profit), any totals, and the bottom-line results (such as the $2000 profit).

Align

Here's how to make all writing in the selection be nudged slightly to the left or slightly to the right.

Click one of these three buttons:

≡	≡	≡

Those buttons are near the top of the screen.

Excel 2007:	they're above column E, F, or G.
Excel 2002&2003:	they're above columns D and E.
Works:	they're above column G.

Here's what those buttons do:

clicking the left button makes each cell's writing be flush left | `like this` |

clicking the center button makes each cell's writing be centered | `        like this` |

clicking the right button makes each cell's writing be flush right | `            like this` |

Don't click? If you don't click any of the buttons, here's what happens:

Excel:	If the cell contains a **word**, the computer puts the word **flush left**.
	If the cell contains a **number** instead, the computer puts the number **flush right**.
Works:	If the cell contains a **number** (or date or month), the computer puts it **flush right**.
	If the cell contains plain **words** instead, the computer puts them **flush left**.

Align the headings In a simple spreadsheet, row 1 usually contains words that are column headings. Below those headings are numbers, which are flush right. **To align the headings with the numbers beneath them, make the headings be flush right also.** To do that, select row 1 (by clicking the 1), then click the right button.

Delete

To make all writing in the selection vanish (so it's erased), press the Delete key.

Money

The computer can handle money.

To make each number in the selection look like dollars-and-cents, click the $ button. That makes the computer put a dollar sign before each number and put two digits after the decimal point. If the number is big, the computer inserts commas.

For example, if the number is 1538.4, the computer turns it into:

$1,538.40

Rounding If the number is .739, the computer rounds it. Works shows you this:

$0.74

Excel shows you this:

$ 0.74

Negative numbers If a number is negative (because you *lost* money instead of gained), the computer follows the tradition of accountants and the Internal Revenue Service: it puts the number in parentheses (instead of writing a minus sign).

For example, suppose the number is -974.25. Works shows you this:

($974.25)

Excel show you this:

$ (974.25)

Excel's features Excel has these features:

When showing a number, Excel puts the dollar sign at the cell's left edge (flush left), so all dollar signs in that column will line up. The computer puts the digits (and parentheses) flush right, and widens the cell if necessary to make them all fit.

Near the $ button, you see a button that has a comma on it. Clicking the comma button has the same effect as clicking the $ button, except that the comma button does *not* make the computer write a dollar sign.

Percent

The computer can handle percentages.

Excel To make each number in the selection look like percentage, click the % button. For example, if the number is .74, the computer turns it into 74%.

When writing the percentage, the computer doesn't write any decimal point. For example, if the number is .519, the computer rounds it to 52%.

Works To make each number in the selection look like percentage, click "Format" then "Number" then "Percent" then OK.

For example, if the number is .74, the computer turns it into 74%. When writing a percent, the computer shows two digits after the decimal point, so the computer shows:

```
74.00%
```

If the number is .51429, the computer turns it into 51.429% then rounds it to two digits after the decimal point, so you see:

```
51.43%
```

Negatives If the number is negative the computer puts a negative sign in front.

Decimal places

Excel has these features:

If you click the $ or comma button, the computer normally puts two digits after the decimal point. If you click the % button, the computer normally puts no digits after the decimal point.

Here's how to change those tendencies.

If you click the **Increase Decimal button** (which shows a .0 becoming a .00), the computer will put an extra digit after the decimal point. If you click it *several* times, the computer will put *several* extra digits after the decimal point.

If you click the **Decrease Decimal button** (showing a .00 becoming a .0) several times, the computer will put fewer digits after the decimal point. For example, here's how to round to the nearest dollar: click the $ button (which produces dollars and cents) and then twice click the Decrease Decimal button (which gets rid of the cents by rounding).

Font

Normally, the characters you type are in a font called **Arial**. (Exception: in Excel 2007, the characters are in a font called **Calibri**.) To make all writing in the selection have a different font (such as Times New Roman), click the down-arrow that's next to "Arial" or "Calibri", then click whichever font you want.

These five fonts are especially popular:

This font is Arial. It's the normal font for spreadsheets.
It's plain and simple.

This font is Arial Narrow. It's thinner than Arial.
It lets you fit more characters in each cell, or fit more columns on each page.

**This font is Arial Black. It's an extra-bold version of Arial.
It's good for column titles.**

This font is Times New Roman. It's the easiest to read.
It's especially good if you're writing lots of words instead of numbers.

This font is Tahoma. It resembles Arial but has a better capital "I".

Text color

Normally, the characters you type are black. Here's how to make all characters in the selection be a different color (such as red).

Excel 2007&2010 Above column D or E, you see the **Font Color button**, which has an underlined A on it. Notice the color of the A's underline.

If it's the color you want, click the underline.

If it's *not* the color you want, do this instead: click the down-arrow that's to the right of the A's underline; you'll see 70 colors; click the color you want.

Excel 2002&2003 Near the screen's top-right corner, you see the **Font Color button**, which has an underlined A on it. Notice the color of the A's underline.

If it's the color you want, click the underline.

If it's *not* the color you want, do this instead: click the down-arrow that's to the right of the A's underline; you'll see 40 colors; click the color you want.

Works Click **Format** then **Font**, then click the "Select font color" box's down-arrow. Look through the list of 15 colors, by using that list's scroll arrows. Click whichever color you want, then click OK.

Distorted color Excel shows the text color perfectly. If you used Works instead and selected *several* cells, some of those cells temporarily show distorted colors, until you click a single cell.

Background color

Normally, you type on a white background. Here's how to make the entire selection's background become a different color (such as yellow).

Excel 2007&2010 Above column C, D, or E, you see the **Fill Color button**, which shows a paint can pouring onto a floor. Look at the floor's color.

If it's the color you want, click the paint can.

If it's *not* the color you want, do this instead: click the down-arrow that's to the right of the paint can; you'll see 70 colors; click the color you want.

Excel 2002&2003 Near the screen's top right corner, you see the **Fill Color button**, which shows a paint can pouring onto a floor. Look at the floor's color.

If it's the color you want, click the paint can.

If it's *not* the color you want, do this instead: click the down-arrow that's to the right of the paint can; you'll see 40 colors; click the color you want.

Works Click **Format** then **Shading**. Underneath "Pattern color", click the background color you want (after using the scroll arrows to see the complete list of 15 colors). Underneath "Pattern", click "Solid". Then click OK.

Distorted color If you selected *several* cells, some of them temporarily show distorted colors, until you click a single cell.

Sort

This spreadsheet shows how three students (Zelda, Al, and Pedro) scored on a test:

	A	B	C	D	E	F	G	H
1	Student	Score						
2	Zelda	42						
3	Al	7						
4	Pedro	100						

Alphabetize In that list of students, Zelda is on the top; Pedro is on the bottom. Here's how to rearrange the rows, to put the students in alphabetical order (from A to Z).

Excel 2007&2010 Click any student's name. Click "**Sort & Filter**" then "**Sort A to Z**".

Excel 2002&2003 Click any student's name. Click the **Sort Ascending button** (which has an A above a Z).

Works The rows involved in the sorting (rows 2, 3, and 4) are called the **data rows**. Make the data rows become black, by dragging from the 2 (at the beginning of row 2) to the 4 (at the beginning of row 4). Click **Tools** then **Sort**. (If the computer says "First-time Help", click OK.) Press Enter.

That makes the spreadsheet become:

	A	B	C	D	E	F	G	H
1	Student	Score						
2	Al	7						
3	Pedro	100						
4	Zelda	42						

Increasing scores Here's how to rearrange the rows, to put the scores in numerical order (starting with the lowest score and ending with the highest).

Excel 2007&2010 Click any score. Click "**Sort & Filter**" then "**Sort Smallest to Largest**".

Excel 2002&2003 Click any score. Click the **Sort Ascending button** (which has an A above a Z).

Works Blacken the data rows, by dragging from the 2 (at the beginning of row 2) to the 4 (at the beginning of row 4). Click **Tools** then **Sort**. (If the computer says "First-time Help", click OK.) Make the (first) wide box say "Column B" (by clicking that box's down-arrow and then clicking "Column B"). Press Enter.

That makes the spreadsheet become:

	A	B	C	D	E	F	G	H
1	Student	Score						
2	Al	7						
3	Zelda	42						
4	Pedro	100						

Decreasing scores Here's how to make the computer put the scores in *reverse* numerical order (from highest score to lowest score).

Excel 2007&2010 Click any score. Click "**Sort & Filter**" then "**Sort Largest to Smallest**".

Excel 2002&2003 Click any score. Click the **Sort Descending button** (which has a Z above an A).

Works Blacken the data rows, by dragging from the 2 (at the beginning of row 2) to the 4 (at the beginning of row 4). Click **Tools** then **Sort**. (If the computer says "First-time Help", click OK.) Make the (first) wide box say "Column B" (by clicking that box's down-arrow and then clicking "Column B"). Click the nearby **Descending button**. Press Enter.

That makes the spreadsheet become:

	A	B	C	D	E	F	G	H
1	Student	Score						
2	Pedro	100						
3	Zelda	42						
4	Al	7						

That list is useful, since it puts the winners at the top and the losers at the bottom.

Chart

You can graph your data. In modern spreadsheet programs (such as Excel and and Works), graphs are called **charts**.

For example, suppose you want to graph the data from a company you run. Your company sells Day-Glo Pink Hair Dye. (Your motto is: "To brighten your day, stay in the pink!")

You have two salespeople, Joe and Sue. Joe's worked for you a long time, and sells about $8,000 worth of dye each month. Sue joined your company recently and is rapidly improving at encouraging people to turn their hair pink. She does that by inventing slogans for various age groups, such as:

"Feminine babes wear pink!"
"You look so sweet, hair as pink as cotton candy!"
"Don't be a dink! Think pink!"
"Pink is punk!"
"Pink means I'll be your Valentine, but lighten up!"
"Be what you drink — a Pink Lady!"
"Let the sexy, slinky, pink panther inside you glow!"
"Love is a pink Cadillac — with hair to match!"
"When in a sour mood, look like a pink grapefruit!"

This spreadsheet shows how many dollars worth of dye Joe and Sue sold each month:

	A	B	C	D	E	F	G	H
1		January	February	March				
2	Joe	8000	6500	7400				
3	Sue	2000	4300	12500				

The spreadsheet shows that Joe sold $8000 worth of dye in January, $6500 in February, and $7400 in March.

Sue's a trainee. She sold just $2000 worth in January, but her monthly sales zoomed up to $12500 by March.

Here's how to turn that spreadsheet into a graph (chart).

Chart in Excel

First, type the spreadsheet.

Next, format the numbers. To do that, drag from the first number (cell B2) to the last number (cell D3), click the $ button (to put dollar signs in front of the numbers), then twice click the Decrease Decimal button (to round to the nearest dollar). The spreadsheet becomes this:

	A	B	C	D	E	F	G	H
1		January	February	March				
2	Joe	$ 8,000	$ 6,500	$ 7,400				
3	Sue	$ 2,000	$ 4,300	$ 12,500				

Tell the computer which cells to graph. To do that, drag from the blank starting cell (A1) to the *last number* (cell D3). Drag just to *that cell*, since the computer gets confused if you drag across extra cells or rows or columns.

For Excel 2007&2010, do this:

Click the "**Insert**" that's near the screen's top-left corner. Click **Column**. You see the Column menu; click its first square (which is the **Clustered Column button**). Then the computer draws the graph. To return the screen's top part to normal, click "Home" (which is near the screen's top-left corner).

For Excel 2002&2003, do this:

Click the Chart Wizard button, which is near the screen's top right corner and shows colored vertical bars.

Press the Enter key 4 times. Then the computer draws the graph. (If part of it is covered by a Chart window, make that window disappear, by clicking its X button.)

The graph is part of your spreadsheet, so your spreadsheet looks like this:

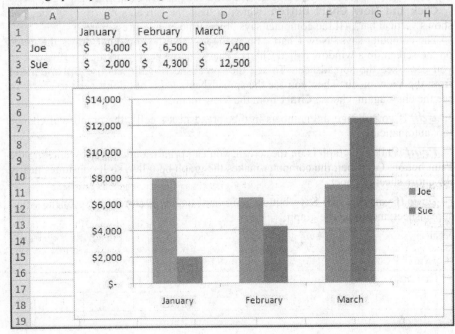

Edit If you change the numbers in the spreadsheet's cells, the graph will change too, automatically!

The entire graph is inside a white box. Try this experiment: click inside that white box, but near the box's outer edge. Then you'll see 8 **handles** at the white box's edges. (In Excel 2002&2003, each handle is a tiny black square. In Excel 2007, each handle is a group of 3 or 4 dark-gray dots.) Those handles mean the white box is **selected**. Four of those handles are at the corners; they're called the **corner handles**.

To change the size of the box (and the graph inside it), drag one of the corner handles.

To move the box (and the graph inside it), put the mouse inside the box and near (but not on) a corner handle, then drag in the direction you want to box to move.

To delete the box (and the graph inside it), press the Delete key.

Print To print the graph onto paper, click in the graph's box then do this:

Excel 2010	Click "File" then "Print". Press Enter.
Excel 2007	Click the File-office button then "Print". Press Enter.
Excel 2002&2003	Click the Print button.

That procedure begins by having you click *in* the graph's box. If you click *outside* the graph's box instead, the printer will print *entire spreadsheet*, including the graph! (But before you do that procedure, you should move the graph's box closer to the screen's left edge and closer to the spreadsheet's numbers, to avoid wasting paper.)

Save If you click the Save button, your hard disk will store a copy of the entire spreadsheet, including the graph.

Chart in Works

First, type the spreadsheet.

Next, format the numbers. To do that, drag from the first number (cell B2) to the last number (cell D3), then click the $ button (to put dollar signs in front of the numbers). The spreadsheet becomes this:

	A	B	C	D	E	F	G
1		January	February	March			
2	Joe	$8,000.00	$6,500.00	$7,400.00			
3	Sue	$2,000.00	$4,300.00	$12,500.00			

Tell the computer which cells to graph. To do that, drag from the blank starting cell (A1) to the *last number* (cell D3). Drag just to *that cell*, since the computer gets confused if you drag across extra cells or rows or columns.

Click the New Chart button, which is near the screen's top right corner and shows vertical bars. (If the computer says "First-time Help", press Enter.)

The computer says "New Chart". Press Enter. Then the computer draws the graph on the screen, in a window called Chart1. That window covers up the spreadsheet, so you can't see the spreadsheet. To see the spreadsheet again, choose **Spreadsheet** from the View menu. Then you see the spreadsheet again, but don't see the chart. To see the chart again, choose **Chart** from the View menu.

Edit If you change the numbers in the spreadsheet's cells, the graph will change too, automatically!

Print While the graph is on the screen, you can print it onto paper by clicking the Print button. On paper, the computer makes the graph be taller, so it consumes nearly the entire sheet of paper.

Save If you click the Save button, your hard disk will store a copy of the entire spreadsheet, including the graph.

The computer can create graphics.

What to buy

You can buy many kinds of graphics programs. On page 53, I described the best ones. Here are further comments.

Paint

The easiest kind of graphics program to use is called a **paint program**. It lets you easily create pictures on your screen by using a mouse.

How paint programs arose In January 1984, Apple Computer Company began selling the Mac computer. It was the first affordable computer that included a mouse —and the first affordable computer that included a good paint program.

The Mac's paint program was called **Mac Paint**.

> It was invented at Apple Computer Company in 1984 by Bill Atkinson. It ran just on the Mac, was included free with the Mac and showed consumers why a Mac was better than an IBM PC: the Mac let you paint a picture on your screen, and the IBM PC couldn't do that yet.
>
> I explained Mac Paint in the 14th edition of *The Secret Guide to Computers*. If you'd like that edition, phone me at 603-666-6644.
>
> Mac Paint had one major limitation: it couldn't handle colors. It handled just black-and-white, because the original Mac came with just a black-and-white screen.
>
> (Years later, Apple began charging for Mac Paint, Ann Arbor Software invented an improved version called "Full Paint", and Silicon Beach invented a further improvement called "Super Paint". Modern Macs have color.)

The next major advance was **Deluxe Paint**.

> It was invented in 1985 by Dan Silva in California and published by Electronic Arts. It was much fancier than Mac Paint and performed gorgeous color tricks.
>
> It ran just on Commodore's Amiga computer. It was why Commodore's Amiga became popular. Because of Deluxe Paint, the Amiga quickly developed a reputation as the best computer for generating color graphics.
>
> (Years later, the Amiga faced competition, Commodore went bankrupt, and Electronic Arts made versions of Deluxe Paint for the IBM PC and the Apple 2GS. Unfortunately, Deluxe Paint is no longer available.)

Windows includes a free a paint program.

> In Windows 3.0, 3.1, and 3.11, the free paint program called **Paintbrush**. It's a stripped-down version of "PC Paintbrush", which was invented by Z-Soft. Windows 95, 98, Me, and XP include a free paint program called **Paint**, which is an improved Paintbrush. I explained Paint on pages 92-96.

Paintbrush, PC Paintbrush, and Paint are all worse than Deluxe Paint, except for Deluxe Paint's one glaring problem: Deluxe Paint is a DOS-based program that hasn't been updated to handle Windows and new video cards.

The best paint program for kids is **Kid Pix**, published by Broderbund, which sells it for just $20.

> It runs on all popular computers (IBM, Mac, and others). While you paint, it makes funny sounds and talks to you in both English and Spanish. Besides letting you create your own shapes, it includes lots of fun little pre-drawn shapes (stars, snowflakes, trees, etc.), which you can include in your paintings to create backgrounds and pixie dust.
>
> By using Kid Pix, you can create impressive artwork in just a few seconds! Of all the paint programs you can buy, Kid Pix is the one that give you pleasure fastest! Though the pre-drawn shapes look kid-like, they look like they come from *talented* kids! Kid Pix is the only program where it's even more fun to erase your work than to create it, since Kid Pix gives you many

dramatic ways to get rid of your painting, such as by dynamiting it: boom! Educators have given Kid Pix many awards for turning kids into creative artists.

The best paint program for professional artists is **Painter**, originally published by Fractal Design but now marketed by Corel.

> It was designed for the Mac but now also runs on the IBM PC. Painter amazes artists because it makes the computer's screen accurately imitate different kinds of brushes, inks, and other artist tools. You can choose whether to make the screen look like you're painting in oil, chalk, charcoal, watercolor, or whatever other medium you wish. You can fine-tune each tool, change precisely how "drippy" each tool is, and change the "bumpiness" of the paper's texture.
>
> It even includes a "van Gogh" mode, which lets you paint by using the same kinds of brushstrokes as the artist Vincent van Gogh.
>
> Though Painter can use a mouse, Painter imitates artist tools more accurately if you buy a **pressure-sensitive graphics tablet** (which comes with a pen that records not just *where* you're pressing but also *how hard* you're pressing). The most popular pressure-sensitive tablets are made by **Wacom**, **Kurta**, **Calcomp**, and **Summagraphics**.
>
> Painter is expensive ($404 normally, $99 for students and teachers). You can buy a stripped-down version, called **Painter Essentials**, for just $79.
>
> Since Painter and Painter Essentials are intended just for creative artists who like to draw squiggles, they don't contain commands to draw geometric shapes. For example, they don't contain commands to draw an oval, circle, rectangle, or square. All other popular paint programs include such commands.

How paint programs work Each paint program considers your screen to be made of thousands of pixels (dots). The paint program remembers the color of each pixel. The colors of all the pixels are stored in RAM while you're painting. You need lots of RAM if your screen is large & has many pixels, or if you insist on using lots of colors.

All paint programs suffer from this problem:

> If you use a paint program to create a shape, then try to shrink that shape, then change your mind and try to expand the shape back to its original size, the final result looks crude and lacks the details that were in the original.
>
> That's because a paint program shrinks a shape by using fewer pixels: some of the pixels that contained details are discarded. The lack of detail becomes noticeable when you try to expand the shape back to its original size.

Another problem is that when you try to rotate a shape, the shape looks cruder, because the shape's pixels get slightly misplaced by "round-off error". If you try to rotate a shape several times, the pixels get progressively more misplaced, and the shape looks cruder and cruder.

> When trying to paint, if you expand or twirl,
> You get a result that makes you want to hurl.

Paint programs are called **bitmapped graphics programs**.

Draw

A **draw program** does *not* store the color of each pixel. Instead, a draw program stores a memo about a geometric shape and the color of the entire shape.

> For example, a draw program stores a line by storing just its starting point, ending point (or angle & length), and color; it stores a circle by storing just the circle's center, radius, and color. By contrast, a paint program would consume lots of RAM storing the color of each of the thousand pixels that are on the line or circle.
>
> Draw programs are also called **vector-based graphics programs**.
>
> A draw program works faster and more accurately than a paint program if you're drawing geometric shapes. A draw program has no problem handling expansions and rotations. But it has difficulty handling squiggles, since it tries to view each squiggle as made up of many tiny arcs.

A draw program lets you name different objects, put them in front of other objects, then later move the objects to reveal objects that were hidden. Most paint programs can't do that: in a paint program, creating a new shape automatically erases any shape that was underneath — except for a crude feature that lets you have two "layers": a "background" and a "foreground".

In a draw program, you can point to an object you drew and change its color, thickness, or style. In a paint program, the only way to change the appearance of what you drew is to draw it over again.

Unfortunately, the typical draw program is confusing to use, because when you look at what's on your screen you're not sure which "objects" the stuff you're seeing is part of.

The first popular draw program was **Mac Draw**, which ran on the Mac. Now most draw programs use Windows instead. The most popular serious draw program is **Corel Draw** (which comes from a Canadian company called Corel).

Each modern Windows word-processing program also includes a stripped-down draw program, free:

> To draw while using Microsoft Word, click the Drawing button.
> To draw while using Word Perfect, choose "Draw" from the Graphics menu.
> To draw while using Word Pro, choose "Drawing" from the Create menu.
>
> To draw while using Microsoft Works' word processor, choose "Drawing" from the Insert menu.

CAD

You can buy a program that does **computer-aided drafting & design (CAD)**. Such a program resembles a draw program but does more math.

> For example, it can print mock blueprints, with the lengths of all parts marked. It can even compute the surface area (square feet) of any shape, so you can compute how much material to buy to build your structure and cover it.
> It lets you give fancy geometric commands, such as "draw a 37-degree angle, but make the point be round instead of sharp, so nobody gets hurt" or "draw a circular arc that goes through these three points" or "draw a line that grazes these two circles, so it's tangent to them".

The most famous CAD program is **AutoCAD**. That's what most architects and engineers use. It's published by Autodesk and very expensive: $3995! Cheaper CAD programs that cost under $50 are for use at home, to help Joe Six-Pack design his backyard deck — and help interior designers plan purple bathrooms.

Most CAD programs include pre-built shapes that you can put in your drawings.

> The pre-built shapes are exactly the right size and shape to represent toilets, sinks, stoves, and other household fixtures. Each shape is called a **symbol**. You can buy a bunch of extra symbols; each bunch is called a **symbol library**.

Photo manipulation

To put photographs into your computer, use a **scanner** (which scans in sheets of paper) or a **digital camera**.

Once the picture is in your computer, you can manipulate it by using a paint program. Better yet, use a program that specializes in the fine art of manipulating photographs. The best photo-manipulation programs are:

> Adobe's **Photoshop** (performs the fanciest tricks, but expensive & hard)
> Adobe's **Photoshop Elements** (cheap & easy, for beginners)
> Microsoft's **Digital Image Suite** (easy & great but no longer sold)
> **Kai's Power Goo** (stretches a face to create weird expressions, for fun)

Other graphics software

To spice up your word-processing documents, you can buy **clip art**, which consists of funny little cartoonish illustrations. Modern spreadsheet program (such as **Excel**) can create pie charts, line graphs, and bar charts. To create slide shows, get a **presentation program**, such as Microsoft's **PowerPoint** (explained on pages 248-255).

Classic computer art

During the 1960's, many creative ideas were generated about how computers would someday create their own weird art, using a wild combination of formulas and random numbers, and unshackled by the bounds of human culture.

Here's how to make the computer produce wild art, by using the wonderful classic tricks invented in the 1960's and 1970's....

In 1971, Michael Hord made the computer turn photographs into artistic sketches. Here's what the computer did to a photograph of his boss, and to a photograph of a colleague's girlfriend:

Boss

Woman

To draw each sketch, the computer scanned the original photograph and found the points where the photograph changed dramatically from light to dark. Then, on a sheet of paper, it plotted those points; and through each of those points, it drew a short line perpendicular to the direction in which the original photograph darkened.

More precisely, here's what the computer did…. It looked at four adjacent points on the original photograph:

A B
C D

It computed the darkness of each of those points. Then it computed the "darkening in the X direction", defined as:

(darkness at B) + (darkness at D) - (darkness at A) - (darkness at C)

Then it computed the "darkening in the Y direction", defined as:

(darkness at A) + (darkness at B) - (darkness at C) - (darkness at D)

Then it computed the "overall darkening", defined as:

(darkening in the X direction)² + (darkening in the Y direction)²

If the overall darkening there turned out to be large, the computer sketched a short line, in the vicinity of the points ABCD, and perpendicular to the direction of darkening. More precisely, the line's length was 1, and the line's slope was:

$$-\frac{\text{darkening in the X direction}}{\text{darkening in the Y direction}}$$

Morphs

Here's how to make an L slowly become a V. Notice that the letters L and V are both made by connecting three points:

Let 1" be the point halfway between 1 and 1'; let 2" be halfway between 2 and 2'; and let 3" be halfway between 3 and 3'. Then 1", 2", and 3" form a shape that's halfway between an L and a V:

The process can be extended further:

Turning one shape into another (such as turning an L into a V) is called **a metamorphosis** or **morphing**. The intermediate shapes (that are between the L and the V) are called the **morphs**.

Using that method, the Computer Technique Group of Japan gradually turned a running man into a Coke bottle then into Africa:

Running Cola is Africa

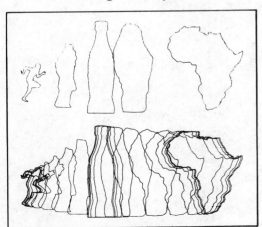

The group turned this head into a square:

Return to a Square

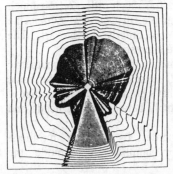

The head on the left returns to a square by using **arithmetic progression**: the lines are equally spaced. The one on the right uses **geometric progression** instead: the lines are close together near the inside square, but further apart as they expand outward.

Csuri & Shaffer exploded a hummingbird:

Chaos to Order

The hummingbird at the far right was obtained from the one at the far left, by moving each line a random distance and in a random direction (between 45° and -45°).

Computers can make movies.

The best movie ever made by a computer is called *Hunger* (or *La Faim*). It was made back in 1973 by Peter Foldès under the auspices of the Canadian Film Board. Watch it at **www.nfb.ca/film/Hunger**.

It's a 10-minute cartoon, in color, with music, but goes far beyond anything ever done by Walt Disney. It uses the same technique as *Running Cola is Africa*: it shows objects turning into other objects.

It begins by showing a harried, thin executive at his desk, which has two phones. One of the phones rings. He answers it. While he's talking on that phone, his other phone rings. To talk on both phones simultaneously, his body splits in two. (How does a single body become two bodies? By using the same technique as turning a running man into a Coke bottle.)

On the other side of his desk is an armchair, which turns into a secretary, whose head turns into a clock saying 5PM, which tells the executive to go home. So he stretches his arms in front of him, and becomes his car: his hands become the headlights, his arms become the front fenders, his face becomes the windshield. You have to see it to believe it.

He drives to a restaurant and gets the waitress, who turns into an ice-cream cone. Then he eats her.

As the film progresses, he becomes increasingly fat, lustful, slothful, and miserable. In the end, he falls into hell, where he's encircled by all the poor starving naked children of the world, who eat his flesh. Then the film ends. (Don't see it before eating dinner!)

It combines computer art and left-wing humanitarian politics, to create an unforgettable message.

Using similar techniques, a 30-second movie called *Run* races through what's it's like to be born, live, and die in Japan. Watch it at:
www.YouTube.com/v=Gk3-no1foTE

Now morphing is being applied to color photos and video images. For example, Hollywood movies use morphing to show a person gradually turning into a monster; environmentalists use morphing to show a human baby gradually turning into a spotted owl; and portrait photographers who have gone high-tech use morphing to show you gradually turning into the person you admire most (such as your movie idol or your lover).

Order versus disorder

Computer artists are starting to believe that **art is a tension between order and disorder**. Too much order, or too much disorder, will bore you. For example, in *Chaos to Order*, the hummingbird on the left is too orderly to be art. The hummingbird on the right is more interesting.

Return to a Square uses arithmetic progression and geometric progression to create an over-all sense of order, but the basic elements are *dis*orderly: a head that's bumpy, and a panorama of weird shapes that lie uncomfortably between being heads and squares but are neither.

Many programs create disorder by random numbers. *Chaos to Order* uses random numbers to explode the hummingbird.

An amazing example of random numbers is this picture by Julesz & Bosche:

To your eyes, the picture seems quite ordered. Actually, it's quite *dis*ordered. One pie-shaped eighth of it is entirely random; the other seven eighths are copies of it. The copying is the only element of order, but very powerful. Try this experiment: *cover seven-eighths of the picture*. You'll see that the remaining eighth is totally disordered, hence boring.

That program imitates a child's *kaleidoscope*. Do you remember your childhood days, when you played with your kaleidoscope? It was a cardboard "telescope" that contained a disorganized pile of colored glass and stones, plus a series of mirrors that produced eight-way symmetry, so that what you saw resembled a giant multicolored snowflake. The program by Julesz & Bosche uses the same technique, computerized. Hundreds of programmers have imitated Julesz & Bosche, so now you can buy kaleidoscope programs for the IBM PC, Mac, and classic computers (Apple 2 and Radio Shack TRS-80). Or try writing your own!

Take this test:

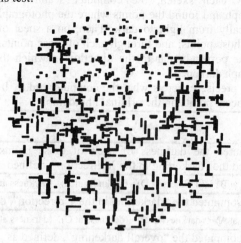

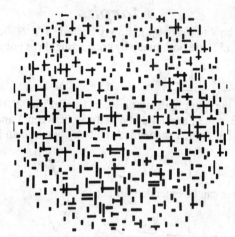

One of those is a famous painting (*Composition with Lines*, by Piet Mondrian, 1917). The other was done by a computer (programmed by A. Michael Noll in 1965). *Which one was done by the computer? Which one do you like best?*

The solution is on the next page, but *don't peek until you've answered!*

The computer did the top one.

The programmer surveyed 100 people. Most of them (59) thought the computer did the bottom one. Most of them (72) preferred the top one — the one that was actually done by the computer.

The test shows that people can't distinguish computer art from human art, and that the computer's art is more pleasing that the art of a famous painter.

The computer's version is more disordered than Mondrian's. The computer created the disorder by using random numbers. The survey shows that most people like disorder: Mondrian's work is too ordered. It also shows that most people mistakenly think the "computer" means "order".

Envelopes

Try this experiment. On a piece of paper, put two dots, like this:

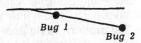

The dots represent little insects, or "bugs". The first bug is looking at the second bug. Draw the first bug's line of sight:

Make the first bug take a step toward the second bug:

Make the second bug run away, in any direction:

Now repeat the entire process. Again, bug 1 looks at bug 2; draw its line of sight:

Bug 1 moves toward bug 2:

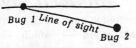

Bug 2 keeps running away:

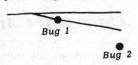

If you repeat the process many times, you get this:

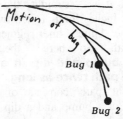

The "motion of bug 1" looks like a curve. (In fact, it's a parabola.) The "curve" is composed of many straight lines — the lines of sight. That's how to draw a fancy curve by using straight lines.

Each straight line is called a **tangent** of the curve. The entire collection of straight lines is called the curve's **envelope**. Creating a curve, by drawing the curve's envelope, is called **stitching the curve** — because the lines of sight act as threads, to produce a beautiful curved fabric.

You can program the computer to draw those straight lines. That's how to make the computer draw a fancy curve — even if you know nothing about "equations of curves".

To get a curve that's more interesting, try these experiments:

What if bug 2 doesn't walk in a straight line? What if bug 2 walks in a curve instead?

What if bug 1 goes slower than bug 2, and takes smaller steps?

What if the bugs accelerate, or slow down?

What if there are *three* bugs? What if bug 1 chases bug 2, while bug 2 chases bug 3, while bug 3 chases bug 1?

What if there are *many* bugs? What if they all chase each other, and their starting positions are random?

What if there are just two bugs, but the bugs are Volkswagens, which must drive on a highway having nasty curves? Show the bugs driving on the curved highway. Their lines of sight are still straight; but instead of moving along their lines of sight, they must move along the curve that represents the highway.

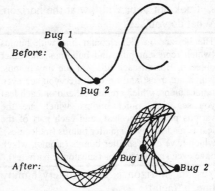

What if each bug has its own highway, and all the bugs stare at each other?

Here are some elaborate examples....

Four bugs chase each other:

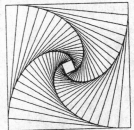

The next example, called *Compelling*, appeared in the famous book and movie, *The Dot and the Line*. (Norton Juster made it by modifying art that had appeared in *Scripta Mathematica*.) It resembles the previous example but makes the 4 bugs start as a rectangle (instead of a square), and makes the bug in the top left corner chase the bug in the opposite corner (while *looking* at a nearby bug instead).

Enigmatic (from *The Dot and the Line*) makes 3 bugs chase each other, while a fourth bug stays motionless in the center:

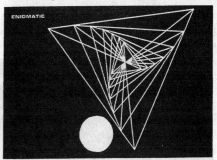

I invented *Kite*, which makes 8 bugs chase each other:

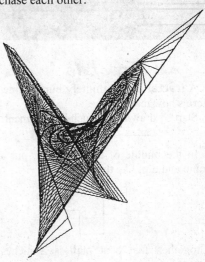

I also invented *Sails*, which makes 14 bugs chase each other:

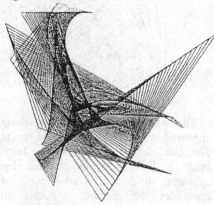

Elliptic Motion (by my student Toby D'Oench) makes 3 bugs stare at each other, while they travel on 3 elliptical highways:

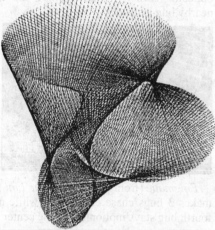

Archimedean Spiral (by Norton Starr) puts bugs on circles. The bugs stare at each other but don't move:

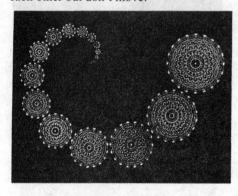

Fractals

A **fractal** is an infinitely bumpy line. Here's how to draw one.

Start by drawing a 1-inch line segment:

In the middle of that segment, put a bump and dip, like this:

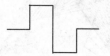

Altogether, that bent path is 2 inches long. In other words, if the path were made of string, and you stretched the string until it was straight, the string would be 2 inches long. That's twice as long as the 1-inch line segment we started with. So here's the rule: **putting a bump and dip in a path makes the path twice as long**.

That bent path consists of seven segments. Put a bump and a dip in the middle of each segment, like this:

Altogether, those bumps and dips make the path twice as long again, so now the path is 4 inches long.

Again, put a bump and dip in the middle of each segment, so you get this:

Again the path's length has been doubled, so now the path is 8 inches long.

If you again put a bump and dip in the middle of each segment, the path's length doubles again, so the path becomes 16 inches long. If you repeat the procedure *again*, the path reaches 32 inches.

If you repeat that procedure infinitely often, you'll develop a path that's infinitely wiggly and infinitely long. That path is longer than any finite line segment. It's longer than any finite 1-dimensional object. But it still isn't a 2-dimensional object, since it isn't an "enclosed area". Since it's bigger than 1-dimensional but not quite 2-dimensional, it's called **1½-dimensional**. Since 1½ contains a fraction, it's called **fractional-dimensional** or, more briefly, **fractal**.

Look out your window at the horizon. What do you see?

> The horizon is a horizontal line with bumps (which represent hills and buildings and other objects). But on each hill you see tiny bumps, which are trees; and on each tree you see even tinier bumps, which are leaves; and on each leaf you see even tinier bumps, which are the various parts of the leaf; and each part of the leaf is made of even smaller bumps (molecules), which have even smaller bumps (atoms), which have even smaller bumps (subatomic particles).

Yes, the horizon is an infinitely bumpy line, a fractal!

You can buy software that creates fractals. Computer artists use fractal software to draw horizons, landscapes, and other bumpy biological objects. For example, they used fractal software to create landscapes for the *Star Wars* movies. You can also use fractals to draw a bumpy face that has zillions of zits.

Now you understand the computer artist's philosophy of life: "Life's a lot of lumps."

What's art?

To create art, write a weird program whose consequences you don't fully understand, tell the computer to obey it, and look at the computer's drawing. If the drawing looks nice, keep it and call it "art" — even if the drawing wasn't what you expected. Maybe it resulted from an error, but so what? **Anything interesting is art.**

If the drawing "has potential" but isn't totally satisfying, change a few lines of the program and see what happens — or run the program again unchanged and hope the random numbers will fall differently. The last thing to invent is the title. Whatever the drawing reminds you of becomes the title.

For example, that's how I produced *Kite* and *Sails*.

> I did *not* say to myself, "I want to draw a kite and sails". I just let the computer pick random starting points for the bugs and watched what happened. I said to myself, "Gee whiz, those drawings remind me of a kite and sails." So I named them *Kite* and *Sails*, and pretended I chose those shapes purposely.

That method may seem a long way from DaVinci, but it's how most computer art gets created. The rationale is: don't overplan.... let the computer "do its own thing"; it will give you art that escapes from the bounds of human culture and so expands your horizons!

Modern style

Computer art has changed. The **classic style** — which you've been looking at — consists of hundreds of thin lines in mathematical patterns, drawn on paper and with little regard for color. The **modern style** uses big blobs and streaks of color, flashed on a TV tube or film, which is then photographed.

Uncreative art

You've seen that computers can create their own weird art by using a wild combination of formulas and random numbers, unshackled by the bounds of human culture.

Computer programs let people create art easily and cheaply. Unfortunately, the typical person who buys a graphics program uses it to create the same kind of junk art that would be created by hand — just faster and more precisely. That's the problem with computers: they make the production of mediocrity even easier and more glitzy.

3-D drawing

The computer drew these 3-dimensional surfaces:

Three Peaks
by John Szabo

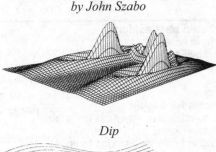

Dip

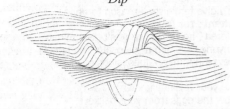

Those were done for the sake of art. This was done for the sake of science:

Population Density in the U.S.
by Harvard University Mapping Service

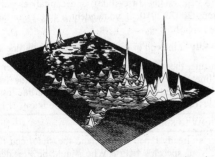

The hardest part about 3-dimensional drawing is figuring out which lines the computer should *not* show, because they're hidden behind other surfaces.

Compute the coordinates

Try this experiment. Put your finger on the bridge of your nose (between your eyes). Now move your finger 2 inches to the right (so your finger is close to your right eye). Then move your finger 3 inches up (so your finger is near the upper right corner of your forehead). From there, move your finger 8 inches forward (so your finger is 8 inches in front of your forehead).

Your finger's current position is called (2,3,8), because you reached it by moving 2 inches right, then 3 inches up, then 8 inches forward. The 2 is called the **X coordinate**; the 3 is called the **Y coordinate**; the 8 is called the **Z coordinate**.

You can reach any point in the universe by the same method! Start at the bridge of your nose, and get to the point by moving right (or left), then up (or down), then forward (or back).

The distance you move to the right is called the **X coordinate**.
(If you move to the left instead, the X coordinate is a negative number.)

The distance you move up is called the **Y coordinate**.
(If you move down instead, the Y coordinate is a negative number).

The distance you move forward is called the **Z coordinate**.
(If you move back instead, the Z coordinate is a negative number).

Project the coordinates

To draw a picture of a 3-dimensional object, put the object in front of you, and then follow these instructions....

Pick a point on the object. (If the object has corners, pick one of the corners.)

Figure out that point's X, Y, and Z coordinates (by putting your finger on the bridge of your nose and then seeing how far you must move your finger right, up, and forward to reach the object).

Compute the point's **projected X coordinate** (which is X/Z) and the point's **projected Y coordinate** (which is Y/Z). For example, if X is 2 and Y is 3 and Z is 8, the projected X coordinate is 2/8 (which is .25) and the projected Y coordinate is 3/8 (which is .375).

On graph paper, plot the projected X coordinate and the projected Y coordinate, like this:

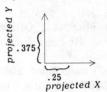

Then plot the point:

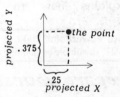

Do that procedure for each point on the object (or at least for the corners). Connect the dots and — presto! — you have a 3-dimensional picture of the object! And the picture is mathematically accurate! It's what artists call a "true perspective drawing".

To make the picture look traditionally beautiful, place the object slightly to the left of you and slightly below your eye level, so all the X and Y coordinates become negative.

Computerize the process

You can program the computer so that if you input a point's X coordinate, Y coordinate, and Z coordinate, the computer will calculate the projected X coordinate (from dividing X by Z) and the projected Y coordinate (from dividing Y by Z) and plot the point on the computer's screen (by using high-resolution graphics).

PowerPoint

If you give a speech, you can make the speech more interesting by letting the audience watch "slides" while they listen to you. The "slides" can be film slides (on 35-millimeter film, projected onto the room's wall by using a slide projector) or **electronic slides** (generated by a computer attached to either a traditional monitor or a **computer projector**, which projects the images onto the room's wall).

The slides can include photographs, drawings, graphs, tables of numbers, and an outline of what you're talking about.

The best way to create such a slide show is to use a **presentation-graphics program**.

The most popular presentation graphics program is **PowerPoint**. You can get its newest version, **PowerPoint 2010**, free as part of **Microsoft Office 2010**'s Home & Student Edition, Home & Business Edition, and Professional Edition (but not Starter Edition).

The previous version, **PowerPoint 2007**, came free as part of **Microsoft Office 2007**. An earlier version, **PowerPoint 2003**, came free as part of **Microsoft Office 2003**. **This book explains how to use PowerPoint 2003&2007&2010.**

(An earlier version, called **PowerPoint 2000**, is explained in an earlier *Secret Guide* edition, the 27th, available by phoning 603-666-6644.)

Prepare yourself

Before you try using PowerPoint, practice using Microsoft Word and make sure it works fine.

Before using PowerPoint 2007 or 2010,
practice using Microsoft Word 2007 or 2010 (explained on pages 181-198).

Before using PowerPoint 2003,
practice using Microsoft Word 2003 (explained on pages 199-214).

Launch PowerPoint

Click Start then "All Programs" then "Microsoft Office". Click "Microsoft Office PowerPoint 2003" or "Microsoft Office PowerPoint 2007" or "Microsoft PowerPoint 2010".

If you're using version 2003, do the unmask procedure:

Click "View" then "Toolbars" then "Customize" then "Options". Put check marks in the first two boxes ("Show Standard and Formatting toolbars on two rows" and "Always show full menus") by clicking. Press Enter.

Type your outline

The fastest way to create a slide show is to click the word "Outline" (which is at the screen's left edge), then click anywhere in the huge white area that's under "Outline".

Type an outline of your speech. For example, suppose you want to give a speech, with slides, about who should be the USA's next President, according to youngsters. Type this outline:

1 ▢ **Who should be President?**
Advice from America's youth
Analyzed by Smart E. Pants
2 ▢ **The top two candidates**
• Barbie
• Barney
3 ▢ **Arguments for Barbie**
• She's so attractive, we all call her a "doll"
• She has no ideas, so not controversial
• She'd give feminists a reason to unite
4 ▢ **Arguments for Barney**
• "Colored", he shows we don't discriminate
• If anyone calls him a "dinosaur", he laughs
• Believes in family values, sings of them
5 ▢ **Act now**
• Make your feelings known
• Throw the eggs from your packet

(That's how the outline looks in versions 2007&2010. In version 2003, the indented lines look *more* indented.)

While typing, remember 3 principles:

To save you time, the computer automatically puts a number (1, 2, 3, 4, 5) and a slide icon (▢) in front of each slide, puts a bullet (•) in front of each indented line (except on the first slide), and capitalizes each line's first word. In versions 2007&2010, if you indent a line extra-far, its bullet's shape changes to a dash.

Press the **Enter key** at the end of each line (except the outline's final line).

While typing a line, the computer assumes you want it indented the same amount as the line above. To indent a line more, press the **Tab key** while typing the line (or before typing the line). To indent a line less, press **Shift with Tab** while typing the line (or before typing the line).

So here's how to start typing:

The computer's already typed the "1" and the slide icon (▢). On that same line, type your speech's **title** ("Who should be President?"). At the end of that title, press the Enter key.

The next line should be your speech's **subtitle** ("Advice from America's youth") and be indented. To make it indented, begin the line by pressing the Tab key. Then type the subtitle's words ("Advice from America's youth"). At the end of the subtitle, press Enter.

The next line can be an extra subtitle ("Analyzed by Smart E. Pants"). Type those words; the computer automatically indents them. At the end of the line, press Enter.

For the next line ("The top two candidates"), unindent (by pressing Shift with Tab). Then the computer will automatically number the slide (2). Type the words ("The top two candidates"). Press Enter.

For the next line ("Barbie"), indent (by pressing Tab). The computer automatically types a bullet (•). Type "Barbie". Press Enter.

Type "Barney". Press Enter.

Unindent (by pressing Shift with Tab), type "Arguments for Barbie", and press Enter.

Indent (by pressing Tab).

Continue typing the outline. Remember to **press Tab whenever you want the computer to indent more, Shift Tab to indent less, and Enter to end the line**.

Undo If you make a mistake, click the **Undo button** (which is near the screen's top and shows an arrow curving toward the left).

Watch your panes The outline, which you're typing, is at the screen's left edge, in a white windowpane called the **outline pane**.

While you type (in the outline pane), the screen's middle shows the slide you're creating or editing. That middle part of the screen is called the **slide pane**.

You can click and type in either the outline pane or the slide pane. Any words you type in one pane appear in the other also, simultaneously and automatically. Those two panes just give you two different views of the same words.

Though you can type directly into the slide pane, typing into the outline pane is faster because, while typing in the outline pane, you can progress to the next line (and slide) without fiddling with the mouse: just press Enter (and sometimes Tab or Shift Tab).

While typing in the outline pane, glance at the slide pane, to see how the words will really look on your slide and whether they'll really fit.

Below the slide pane is a **notes pane**, which is a white rectangle that temporarily says "Click to add notes". You can click it and then type your own personal notes about the slide above it. The notes will not appear on the slide. Type notes that will help you prepare your speech, or type notes to hand out to the audience afterwards.

Version 2003 shows the **Microsoft PowerPoint Help window** at the screen's right edge. I recommend you get rid of that window (by clicking its X button); then the outline pane, slide pane, and notes pane will widen to make typing more pleasant.

The outline pane, slide pane, and notes pane are separated by **dividers** (light-blue thick lines), which you can drag to make your favorite pane bigger (and the other panes smaller). But beware: if you make your favorite pane too big, one of the other panes will become too small (or disappear!) and frustrate you.

Delete Here's how to delete part of your slide show.

In the outline, click a slide icon (to delete the entire slide) or a subtopic's bullet (to delete a subtopic) or the white space left of a subtitle (to delete a subtitle). Then press the Delete key.

Insert Here's how to insert an extra line into your outline:

Where do you want the extra line? Which line will be above it? Click the end of the line that will be above the extra line. Then press Enter.

Type the extra line. While typing, if you want the extra line to be indented more, tap the Tab key. If you want the extra line to be indented less, press Shift with Tab.

View different slides

After you've created a set of slides (by typing the outline), here's how to change which slide you're viewing.

Method 1: in the outline pane, click whichever slide you want to view.

Method 2: click in the slide pane's top-left corner; then do one of these activities....

To move ahead to the next slide, press the **Page Down** key (or rotate the mouse's wheel toward you).
To move back to the previous slide, press the **Page Up** key (or rotate the mouse's wheel away from you).
To skip ahead to the final slide, press the **End** key.
To skip back to the first slide, press the **Home** key.

Design

The word "Design" is near the screen's top. Here's how to use it....

Version 2010 The word "Design" is on the **tab bar**, which looks like this:

File	Home	Insert	Design	Animations	Slide Show	Review	View

Click "Design". You start seeing pictures of these 51 designs:

Used	Office	Adjacency	Angles	Apex	Apothecary	Aspect	Austin
Black Tie	Civic	Clarity	Composite	Concourse	Couture	Elemental	Equity
Essential	Executive	Flow	Foundry	Grid	Hardcover	Horizon	Median
Metro	Module	Newsprint	Opulent	Oriel	OriginPaper	Perspective	
Pushpin	Slipstream	Solstice	Technic	Thatch	Trek	Urban	Verve
Waveform	Decatur	Kilter	Macro	Mylar	Sketchbook	SOHO	Summer
Thermal	Tradeshow	Urban Pop					

At first, you see just the top row; to see the other rows, click the down-arrow that's to the *left* of "Fonts".

Try clicking a design, then look at the slide pane and see whether you like what the design does to *your* slide. If you don't like the result, click a different design instead.

The design affects *all* your slides, so look at *all* your slides to make sure you like the result. (To see them all, press the Page Up or Page Down key repeatedly.) The design treats your first slide (which has the title and subtitles) differently than the other slides, so make sure you look at that first slide and other slides also.

Unfortunately, some designs use fonts that are too big to fit your words on the slide nicely. Check carefully!

If you don't like the result, click a different design instead. If you want to return to the original plain design, click the 2nd design ("Office").

Version 2007 The word "Design" is on the **tab bar**, which looks like this:

Home	Insert	Design	Animations	Slide Show	Review	View

Click "Design". You start seeing pictures of these 21 designs:

Used	Office	Apex	Aspect	Civic	Concourse	Equity	Flow
Foundry	Median	Metro	Module	Opulent	Oriel	Origin	Paper
Solstice	Technic	Trek	Urban	Verve			

At first, you see just the top row; to see the other rows, click the down-arrow that's to the *left* of "Fonts".

Try clicking a design, then look at the slide pane and see whether you like what the design does to *your* slide. If you don't like the result, click a different design instead.

The design affects *all* your slides, so look at *all* your slides to make sure you like the result. (To see them all, press the Page Up or Page Down key repeatedly.) The design treats your first slide (which has the title and subtitles) differently than the other slides, so make sure you look at that first slide and other slides also.

Unfortunately, some designs use fonts that are too big to fit your words on the slide nicely. Check carefully!

If you don't like the result, click a different design instead. If you want to return to the original plain design, click the 2nd design ("Office").

Version 2003 The word "Design" is above the slide pane. Click "Design".

That makes the **Slide Design window** appear at the screen's right edge. Click "Design Templates" (which is near the top of that window).

Then that window shows slides having many different colorful designs. Scroll down to see them all.

If your computer hasn't used PowerPoint before, you see these 25 designs (if you scroll down) —

---

default design, balance, blends, capsules, compass, crayons, curtain call, digital dots, edge, fading grid, fireworks, glass layers, globe, kimono, maple, mountain top, network, ocean, pixel, profile, proposal, slit, stream, textured, watermark

---

and below them you see a button marked "Additional Design Templates". Clicking that button adds these 20 extra designs to the list permanently (and the "Additional Design Templates" button disappears):

> axis, balloons, beam, cascade, cliff, clouds, competition, echo, eclipse, layers, level, orbit, quadrant, radial, refined, ripple, satellite dish, shimmer, studio, teamwork

Try clicking a design, then look at the slide pane and see whether you like what the design does to *your* slide. If you don't like the result, click a different design instead.

The design affects *all* your slides, so look at *all* your slides to make sure you like the result. (To see them all, press the Page Up or Page Down key repeatedly.) The design treats your first slide (which has the title and subtitles) differently than the other slides, so make sure you look at that first slide and other slides also.

Unfortunately, some designs use fonts that are too big to fit your words on the slide nicely. Check carefully!

If you don't like the result, click a different design instead. If you want to return to the original plain design, click the "default design", which is the first design choice under the words "Available for Use".

What's affected? If you want the design to affect just the slide you see in the slide pane, without affecting all the other slides, do this: *right*-click the design then click "Apply to Selected Slides".

If you want the design to affect just a *few* slides, do this:

> At the screen's left edge, make sure you see tiny pictures of the slides, numbered. (To see them in versions 2007&2010, click "Slides", which is at the screen's left edge.)
>
> Those tiny pictures are called **thumbnails**, because they're nearly as tiny as your thumb's nail. Click the thumbnail (tiny picture) of the first slide you want to affect. While holding down the Ctrl key, click the thumbnails of the other slides you want to affect, so they're all **selected** (have blue borders in version 2003, orange borders in versions 2007&2010). Right-click the design you wish to give them, then click "Apply to Selected Slides".

After you've done "Apply to Selected Slides", those selected slides are treated special: clicking a design afterwards might ignore those slides or treat them differently than other slides. So after doing "Apply to Selected Slides", do future design changes more precisely, by always following this procedure:

> To make sure you affect *all* the slides, right-click the desired design then click "Apply to All Slides". To affect just one or a few slides, highlight them then right-click the desired design then click "Apply to Selected Slides".

Change the color After you've chosen a design, you can modify its color by doing this:

> **Version 2010** Click "Colors". You see 51 color schemes, whose names are the same as the 51 designs (except that one of the color schemes is "Grayscale" instead of "Used"). The computer assumes you want the color scheme to be the one whose name is the same as the design, but you can click a different color scheme instead, which affects all current uses of that design throughout your presentation.
>
> **Version 2007** Click "Colors". You see 21 color schemes, whose names are the same as the 21 designs (except that one of the color schemes is "Grayscale" instead of "Used"). The computer assumes you want the color scheme to be the one whose name is the same as the design, but you can click a different color scheme instead, which affects all current uses of that design throughout your presentation.
>
> **Version 2003** Click "Color Schemes" (which is near the top of the Slide Design window). You'll see a few color schemes. The first is the normal color scheme for that design, but you can click a different color scheme instead, which will affect all uses of that design throughout your presentation. When you finish playing with color schemes, click "Design Templates".

Finish When you finish playing with designs, make the outline pane appear again by clicking "Outline". For versions 2007&2010, also click "Home" (which is near the screen's top-left corner).

Font Size

If one of your bulleted lines is too long to fit on the slide, do this:

> In the slide pane, click that line. Press Ctrl with A (which highlights *all* the bulleted lines). Look at the number in the Font Size box (which is near the screen's top, toward the left). Switch to a smaller font size instead (by clicking the Font Size box's down-arrow then clicking a smaller number). That makes *all* the bulleted lines on that slide have a smaller font. If a line *still* doesn't fit on the slide properly, choose an even smaller number.

Watch the show

To watch your entire slide show, from beginning to end, **press the F5 key**. (If you'd rather watch just *part* of the slide show, starting at the current slide, do this instead: *while holding down the Shift key*, press the F5 key.)

Your first slide (which has the speech's title) will consume the whole screen.

Everything else will disappear. You'll see no outline, no notes, no menu bar, no toolbar, and no Windows: you won't even see the Start button. You won't see any X button.

While watching the slide show, you can give these commands:

> To progress to the **next slide**, press the **Page Down or Enter** key (or the Space bar or down-arrow or right-arrow or N or click the mouse's button or rotate the mouse's wheel toward you).
>
> To go **back to the previous slide**, press the **Page Up or Backspace** key (or up-arrow or left-arrow or P or rotate the mouse's wheel away from you).
>
> To go back to the **first slide**, press the **Home** key (or while holding down the mouse's left button, press the right button for 2 seconds).
>
> To skip ahead to the **final slide**, press the **End** key.
>
> To go to **slide 3**, press 3 then Enter — or press **Ctrl with S** (which shows a slides menu, then double-click slide 3).
>
> To make the screen be all **black**, press the **B** key. That makes the slide temporarily disappear, so you can talk to the audience without letting the slide distract the audience. To resume, press the B key again.
>
> To make the screen be all **white**, press the **W** key. (Press it again to resume.)
>
> To see the mouse's **arrow**, press the **A** key (or move the mouse for several seconds). Then the arrow appears on the screen, along with buttons at the screen's bottom left corner. To make the arrow & buttons disappear again, press the A key again (or stop moving the mouse for 3 seconds).
>
> To make the mouse pointer appear as a **pen**, press **Ctrl with P**. Then the mouse pointer becomes a pen that has red ink. To scribble on the slide, just drag: move the mouse while holding down the mouse's left button. To emphasize a phrase, scribble *a circle around it* or *an underline below it* or *arrows aimed at it*. When you finish using the pen, make it return to an ordinary arrow by pressing the **Esc** key (or **Ctrl with A**).
>
> Version 2010: to make the mouse pointer appear as a **laser pointer**, hold down the Ctrl key; and while you keep holding down the Ctrl key, drag the mouse. That makes the mouse pointer look like a laser pointer (red circle) instead of an arrow.
>
> For further **tricks**, right-click to see a menu of choices.
>
> To **escape from the slide show**, press the **Esc** key. That returns you to **normal view**, where you can edit the slide you were looking at, then edit other slides too. After editing, press the **F5** key again (if you want to see the slide show from the beginning again) or press **Shift with F5** (to skip the slide show's beginning and jump to the current slide).

How it ends If you look at the final slide and then try to progress further by pressing Page Down (or Enter or equivalent), the computer will say "End of slide show" and wait again for you to press Page Down (or Enter or equivalent), which returns you to the normal 3-pane view.

Keep ink annotations? If you ever scribbled on a slide during the show (by turning the mouse pointer into a pen with Ctrl P), here's what happens when you end (or escape from) the show: the computer asks "Do you want to keep your ink annotations?" To make things simple, click "Discard".

Save

To copy your presentation to your hard disk, click the **Save button** (which is near the screen's top-left corner and looks like a 3½-inch floppy disk).

If you haven't saved your presentation before, the computer will say "File name".

The computer assumes you want your presentation's name to be the same as the first slide's title. (If you want the presentation's name to be different, type what you want.) Press Enter.

That makes the computer copy your presentation onto the hard disk.

> Version 2003 puts your presentation into the My Documents folder and makes your publication's filename end in ".ppt", which stands for "PowerPoinT".
>
> Version 2007 puts your presentation into the Documents folder and makes your publication's filename end in ".pptx", which stands for "PowerPoinT eXtended".
>
> Version 2010 puts your presentation into the My Documents folder (which is part of the Documents library) and makes your publication's filename end in ".pptx", which stands for "PowerPoinT eXtended".

Afterwards, if you change your mind and want to do more editing, go ahead! When you finish that extra editing, save it by clicking the Save button again.

Finish

When you finish working on your presentation, do this….

Version 2010 Click **File**. Then click **Exit** or **Close**.

> If you choose **Exit**, the computer will stop using PowerPoint.
>
> If you choose **Close** instead of Exit, the computer lets you work on another presentation, and your next step is to say "new presentation" or "old presentation". Here's how….
>
> If you want to **start typing a new presentation**, click File then **New** then double-click the first "**Blank presentation**".
>
> If you want to **use an old presentation**, click File then **Recent**. You see a list of the 25 presentations you used most recently: that list starts with the most recent. From that list, click whichever presentation you want to use. If you want to use an older presentation (not on that list), click **Open** then proceed as follows….
>
> The computer starts showing you a list of *all* presentations in the Documents library (unless you've requested a different folder instead). If the list is too long to show completely, here's how to see the rest of the list: either "click in that list then rotate the mouse's wheel toward you" or "repeatedly click the down-arrow that's to the right of that list". If you want to *use* one of those presentations, *double*-click the presentation's name; the computer will put that presentation onto the screen and let you edit it. If instead you want to *delete* one of those presentations, click the presentation's name then press the Delete key then the Enter key; the computer will move that presentation to the Recycle Bin.

Version 2007 Click the **Office button** (the circle at the screen's top-left corner). Then click **Exit PowerPoint** or **Close**.

> If you choose **Exit PowerPoint**, the computer will stop using PowerPoint.
>
> If you choose **Close** instead of Exit PowerPoint, the computer lets you work on another presentation. Your next step is to say "new presentation" or "old presentation". Here's how….
>
> If you want to **start typing a new presentation**, click the Office button then **New** then press Enter.
>
> If you want to **use an old presentation**, click the Office button, so you see the Office menu. To the right of the Office menu, you see a list of the **17 presentations you used most recently**. Click whichever presentation you want to use. If you want to use a presentation that's not on that list of 17, click **Open** then proceed as follows….
>
> The computer starts showing you a list of *all* presentations in the Documents folder (unless you've requested a different folder instead). To see the rest of the list, either "click in that list then rotate the mouse's wheel toward you" or "repeatedly click the down-arrow that's to the right of that list". If you want to *use* one of those presentations, *double*-click the presentation's name; the computer will put that presentation onto the screen and let you edit it. If instead you want to *delete* one of those presentations, click the presentation's name then press the Delete key then the Enter key; the computer will move that presentation to the Recycle Bin.

Version 2003 Choose **Exit** or **Close** from the **File menu**.

> If you choose **Exit**, the computer stops using PowerPoint.
>
> If you choose **Close** instead of Exit, the computer lets you work on another presentation. Then click the **New button** or the **Open button**. (Those buttons are below the word "File".)
>
> If you click the **New button** (which looks like a sheet of paper with a bent corner), the computer lets you start typing a new presentation.
>
> If you click the **Open button** (which looks like a yellow manila file folder opening), you see a list of old presentations. If you want to *use* one of those presentations, double-click the presentation's name; the computer will put that presentation onto the screen and let you edit it. If you want to *delete* one of those presentations, click the presentation's name and then press the Delete key and then the Enter key; the computer will move that presentation to the Recycle Bin.

Didn't save? If you didn't save your document before doing those procedures, the computer asks, "Do you want to save?" If you click the Save button (which versions 2003&2007 call "Yes"), the computer copies your presentation's most recent version to the hard disk; if you click the Don't Save button instead (which versions 2003&2007 call "No"), the computer ignores and forgets your most recent editing.

Congratulations! You've learned all the fundamental commands of PowerPoint.

Print

Besides showing slides onto the computer's screen and the room's wall, you can print copies of the slides onto paper, to hand to your audience (as handouts) and keep for yourself. Here's how.

Version 2010 Click **File** then **Print**.

The computer assumes you want to print just 1 copy (for yourself). If you want to print *many* copies (for yourself and everybody in your audience), double-click in the "Copies" box then type how many copies you want to print. For example, if you're giving a speech to 50 people and want to hand each member of the audience a printout, plus have a printout for yourself, type "51".

The computer assumes you want "Full Page Slides", which makes each slide consume an entire page. To print differently, click "Full Page Slides"; then you'll see many choices; these are the most popular:

Choice	What each person will receive
Full Page Slides	many pages; each page contains 1 slide
Notes Pages	many pages; each page contains 1 slide (shrunk) & its notes
2 Slides	a few pages; each page contains 2 slides (shrunk)
6 Slides Horiz.	even fewer pages; each page contains 6 slides (shrunk)
Outline	1 page; it contains the outline

Click the choice you want.

Finally, click the Print button. The computer will print on paper.

Version 2007 Click the **Office button** then **Print**.

The computer assumes you want to print just 1 copy (for yourself). If you want to print *many* copies (for yourself and everybody in your audience), type how many copies you want to print. For example, if you're giving a speech to 50 people and want to hand each member of the audience a printout, plus have a printout for yourself, type "51".

Then click the "Print what" box's down-arrow. You'll see these four choices:

Choice	What each person will receive
Slides	many pages; each page contains 1 slide
Handouts	a few pages; each page contains 6 slides (shrunk)
Notes Pages	many pages; each page contains 1 slide (shrunk) and its notes
Outline View	1 page; it contains the outline

Click the choice you want.

Finally, click "OK". The computer will print on paper.

Version 2003 To print on paper *reliably*, click **File** then **Print**.

The computer assumes you want to print just 1 copy (for yourself). If you want to print *many* copies (for yourself and everybody in your audience), type how many copies you want to print. For example, if you're giving a speech to 50 people and want to hand each member of the audience a printout, plus have a printout for yourself, type "51".

Then click the "Print what" box's down-arrow. You'll see these four choices:

Choice	What each person will receive
Slides	many pages; each page contains 1 slide
Handouts	a few pages; each page contains 6 slides (shrunk)
Notes Pages	many pages; each page contains 1 slide (shrunk) and its notes
Outline View	1 page; it contains the outline

Click the choice you want.

Finally, click "OK". The computer will print on paper.

Another way to print is to click the **Print button**.

That button is near the screen's top-left corner and looks like a printer with paper coming out. **Clicking it makes the computer print 1 copy, using the same choice as your previous printing:** Slides, Handouts, Notes Pages, or Outline View. But if you click it, you might be very sorry, since "the same choice as your previous printing" might not be what you want to print now!

Tables

Here's how to put a table of numbers onto a slide.

Start a new slide, as follows:

In the outline pane, click at the end of the previous slide's last line.
Press Enter (to create a new line in your outline).
Press Shift with Tab (to unindent).
Type a title for your table, but do *not* press Enter afterwards.

For versions 2007&2010, do this:

Click the **Insert Table button**. (It's in the slide pane. It's a 4-by-4 grid made of blue lines.)

For version 2003, do this instead:

Click **Format** (which is near the screen's top) then **Slide Layout**. At the screen's right edge, you start seeing 27 layouts; to see them all, use the scroll-down arrow. Click the "Title and Table" layout (which is the 3rd-to-last layout). Double-click where it says "Double-click to add table".

Pick a size How many columns do you want in your table? Type how many, then press Tab. How many rows do you want in your table? Type how many, then press Enter.

You see a blank table. Fill it in, by typing whatever words and numbers you wish. Move from cell to cell by using the arrow keys. (Another way to move to the next cell is to press the Tab key. Another way to move back to the previous cell is to press Shift with Tab.)

Multi-line cells Normally, each cell holds just a single number or a single phrase. If you want to squeeze *several* lines of info into a single cell, just press the Enter key at the end of each line. If you type more lines than the cell can hold, the computer will automatically make the cell be taller (by making the entire row be taller).

Improve the alignment To make the numbers line up better, do this:

Click one of the numbers, then drag across all the numbers (so they all change color).
For version 2003, click the **Align Right button** (which is on the formatting toolbar). For versions 2007&2010, click "Layout" (which is on the tab bar) then the **Align Text Right button** (the 3rd button in the Alignment group).

For version 2003, do this also:

Click in the table. While holding down the Ctrl key, tap the A key (which selects All of the table). Click the **Center Vertically button** (which is at the bottom center of the "Tables and Borders" window). That makes the computer center vertically the entire table (so in each cell, the writing is as far from the top wall as from the bottom wall).

Charts

Here's how to put a chart (graph) onto a slide.

Start a new slide, as follows:

In the outline pane, click at the end of the previous slide's last line.
Press Enter (to create a new line in your outline).
Press Shift with Tab (to unindent).
Type a title for your chart, but do *not* press Enter afterwards.

For versions 2007&2010, do this:

Click the **Insert Chart button**. (It's in the slide pane. It shows a blue bar, a yellow bar, and a red bar.) Then press Enter.

For version 2003, do this instead:

Click **Format** (which is near the screen's top) then **Slide Layout**. At the screen's right edge, you start seeing the 27 layouts; to see them all, use the scroll-down arrow. Click the "Title and Chart" layout (which is the last layout). Double-click where it says "Double-click to add chart".

You see a table of numbers and a chart based on that table.

Edit the numbers in the table, so the table shows *your* numbers.
Edit the words in the table, so the table shows *your* words.
Then the chart will be a chart of *your* data.

Hide the datasheet The table of numbers is called the **datasheet**. The slide includes just the chart and its headline, not the datasheet. While you're editing the datasheet, the datasheet temporarily blocks your view of the slide.

To hide the datasheet, click its X button.

To make the datasheet reappear (so you can edit it some more), do this:

Version 2010 In the slide, click the chart. Click "Design" (which is near the screen's top, on the Tab bar) then "Edit Data" (which is near the screen's top, in the ribbon's Data group).

Version 2007 In the slide, double-click the chart. Click "Edit Data" (which is near the screen's top, in the ribbon's Data group).

Version 2003 In the slide, click the headline, then double-click the chart. Click the View Datasheet button (which is near the screen's top center, below the word "Help", and looks like a table of numbers).

Types of charts The computer assumes you want a column chart. To switch to a different type of chart (such as a bar chart or line chart), do this:

Version 2010 In the slide, click the chart. Click "Design" (which is near the screen's top, on the Tab bar) then "Change Chart Type" (which is near the screen's top-left corner).

Version 2007 In the slide, click the headline, then click the chart. Click "Change Chart Type" (which is near the screen's top-left corner).

Version 2003 In the slide, click the headline, then double-click the chart. Click "Chart" (which is on the menu bar at the top of the screen) then "Chart Type".

Then you see this list of **chart types**: column, line, pie, bar, area, XY (scatter), stock, surface, doughnut, bubble and radar. (Version 2003 shows those choices in a less useful order and also shows 3 silly choices: cylinder, cone, and pyramid.)

Click the type you want. To the right of it, you see subtypes; double-click the subtype you want.

Shapes

Here's how to decorate your slide by adding stars, arrows, and other shapes.

In normal 3-pane view, make the slide pane show the slide you want to decorate.

Request "shapes", as follows:

Version 2007&2010 Near the screen's top, click "Home" (to make sure your screen is normal). Above the word "Drawing", click the word "Shapes" or the symbol ▼ (which you'll see if you have a wide screen).

Version 2003 Near the screen's bottom-left corner, you should see the word "AutoShapes". (If you don't see it, make it appear by doing this: click "View" then "Toolbars", then put a check mark at "Drawing" by clicking.) Click "AutoShapes".

You see these simple categories:

---

lines, rectangles, basic shapes, block arrows, equation shapes, flowchart, stars and banners

---

(Exception: version 2003 lacks "equation shapes" and has "connectors" instead of "rectangles".)

You also see these two advanced categories:

---

call-outs, action buttons

The "call-outs" category lets you put words into a balloon coming out of somebody's mouth, as in a cartoon. The "action buttons" category lets you create Internet-style links, which you can click on to hop to different slides in your show.

For version 2003, click whichever category you want.

Click the shape you want.

Imagine that the shape is enclosed by a rectangle. Point at the slide, where you want the rectangle's top left corner to be, and drag to where you want the rectangle's opposite corner.

If you chose the "call-outs" category, type whatever words you want in the balloon. If you chose the "action buttons" category, make whatever adjustments you wish (such as clicking "Mouse Click" then "Hyperlink to") then click "OK".

Adjust the shape
After you've drawn a shape, here's how to adjust it.

If you don't like the shape's position, point at the shape's middle and drag it wherever you want. (Exception: if the shape is a call-out, point at the shape's edge instead of middle.)

Here's how to stretch the shape, to make it wider or taller:

Click in the shape's middle.
(If the shape's a call-out, click the shape's edge instead.)

Surrounding the shape, you see up to 9 tiny **white circles**, called **handles**. To stretch the shape, drag one of the handles.

If you see a green circle, you can drag it to rotate the shape.

If you see a tiny yellow diamond, drag it to stretch the shape's special feature.

If you make a mistake, click the Undo button. To delete a shape, do this:

Click the shape. (If the shape is a call-out, do this instead: click outside the shape, then click inside the shape but *not* in the middle of the shape's text.)

Then press the Delete key.

Slide Sorter

To see many slides simultaneously, **click the Slide Sorter button, which looks like 4 squares**. (In version 2003, that button is near the screen's bottom-left corner. In versions 2007&2010, it's near the screen's bottom-right corner but left of the percentage.)

You'll see the Slide Sorter view: many slides, next to each other, all numbered. If you right-click one of the slides, you'll see a menu giving you many choices: explore them!

When you finish admiring that view, double-click your favorite slide. Then you'll return to normal 3-pane view, showing that slide. (If you wish to see the outline, then click "Outline".)

Transitions

While you're presenting a slide show, you make the computer switch to the next slide by pressing Page Down or Enter or equivalent. When you do that, the computer tends to display the next slide immediately and simply. Here's how to make the computer perform a fancier transition to the next slide, so the next slide appears gradually and spookily....

Version 2010
While that slide is on the screen in normal 3-pane view, click "**Transitions**" (which is on the tab bar).

Click the bottom down-arrow that's to the *left* of "Effect Options". You see these 35 transition choices:

---

none, cut, fade, push, wipe, split, reveal, random bars, shape, uncover, cover, flash, dissolve, checkerboard, blinds, clock, ripple, honeycomb, glitter, vortex, shred, switch, flip, gallery, cube, doors, box, zoom, pan, Ferris wheel, conveyor, rotate, window, orbit, fly through

---

Click the transition choice you want.

To change the transition's speed, you can click in the **Duration box** and change the number of seconds. To change the transition's details, you can click "**Effect Options**" then click the effect you prefer.

To add sound, click the **Sound box** then one of these 19 choices:

---

applause, arrow, bomb, breeze, camera, cash register, chime, click, coin, drum roll, explosion, hammer, laser, push, suction, typewriter, voltage, whoosh, wind

---

"Drum roll" is a good choice because it's the least obnoxious.

You'll hear an abridged version of the sound immediately. You'll hear a better, longer version of the sound later, when you actually perform the slide show by pressing F5 (for the full show) or Shift F5 (for starting at that slide).

The computer assumes you want the transition to apply to just one slide. If you want the transition to apply to *all* slides, click **Apply To All**.

Version 2007
While that slide is on the screen in normal 3-pane view, click "Animations" (which is on the tab bar).

Click the down-arrow that points at "Transition to This Slide". You see these 59 transition choices:

---

no transition, fade (smoothly or through black), cut, cut through black, dissolve, wipe (down, left, right, or up), wedge, uncover (down, left, right, up, left-down, left-up, right-down, or right-up), box (in or out), wheel clockwise (1 spoke, 2 spokes, 3 spokes, 4 spokes, or 8 spokes), split (horizontal in, horizontal out, vertical in, or vertical out), strips (left-down, left-up, right-down, or right-up), shape (circle, diamond, or plus), newsflash, push (down, left, right, or up), cover (down, left, right, up, left-down, left-up, right-down, or right-up), blinds (horizontal or vertical), checkerboard (across or down), comb (horizontal or vertical), random bars (horizontal or vertical), random transition

---

Click the transition choice you want. (If you're not sure, try any one. If you like surprises, choose "random transition", which lets the computer surprise you each time by making its own choice.)

Click the **Transition Speed** box's down-arrow, then say how fast you want the computer to perform the transition: click "Slow" or "Medium" or "Fast". (While you're experimenting, I recommend "Slow" so you can see the transition more clearly.)

Click the **Transition Sound** box's down-arrow then one of these 19 choices:

---
applause, arrow, bomb, breeze, camera, cash register, chime, click, coin, drum roll, explosion, hammer, laser, push, suction, typewriter, voltage, whoosh, wind
---

"Drum roll" is a good choice because it's the least obnoxious.

You'll hear an abridged version of the sound immediately. You'll hear a better, longer version of the sound later, when you actually perform the slide show by pressing F5 (for the full show) or Shift F5 (for starting at that slide).

The computer assumes you want the transition to apply to just one slide. If you want the transition to apply to *all* slides, click **Apply To All**.

Version 2003 Click the word "Slides" (which is next to the word "Outline"). You see a list of your slides, numbered. (If you have *many* slides, use the scroll arrows to see them all.)

In that list of slides, right-click whichever slide you want to appear spookily. Click "Slide Transition".

At the screen's right edge, you see these 59 transition choices:

---
no transition, blinds (horizontal or vertical), box (in or out), checkerboard (across or down), comb (horizontal or vertical), cover (down, left, right, up, left-down, left-up, right-down, or right-up), cut, cut through black, dissolve, fade (smoothly or through black), newsflash, push (down, left, right, or up), random bars (horizontal or vertical), shape (circle, diamond, or plus), split (horizontal in, horizontal out, vertical in, or vertical out), strips (left-down, left-up, right-down, or right-up), uncover (down, left, right, up, left-down, left-up, right-down, or right-up), wedge, wheel clockwise (1 spoke, 2 spokes, 3 spokes, 4 spokes, or 8 spokes), wipe (down, left, right, or up), random transition
---

(To see that full list, use its scroll arrows.) Click the transition choice you want. (If you're not sure, try any one. If you like surprises, choose "random transition", which lets the computer surprise you each time by making its own choice.)

Below that list of transition choices, you see a **Speed box**. Click its down-arrow, then say how fast you want the computer to perform the transition: click "Slow" or "Medium" or "Fast". (While you're experimenting, I recommend "Slow" so you can see the transition more clearly.)

Below the Speed box, you see the **Sound box**. To create a transition sound, click the Sound box's down-arrow then one of these 19 choices:

---
applause, arrow, bomb, breeze, camera, cash register, chime, click, coin, drum roll, explosion, hammer, laser, push, suction, typewriter, voltage, whoosh, wind
---

(To see that full list, click its scroll arrows.) "Drum roll" is a good choice because it's the least obnoxious. (If the computer says "This feature is not currently installed", press Enter.)

You'll hear an abridged version of the sound immediately. You'll hear a better, longer version of the sound later, when you actually perform the slide show by pressing F5 (for the full show) or Shift F5 (for starting at that slide).

The computer assumes you want the transition to apply to just one slide. If you want the transition to apply to *all* slides, click **Apply to All Slides** (which is near the screen's bottom-right corner).

Animated lines

Usually, while you're presenting a slide show, the computer shows an entire slide at once. Here's how to **animate** a slide, so the computer shows just one line at a time and waits for you to say when to show the next line.

Version 2010 While that slide is on the screen in normal 3-pane view, click (in the slide pane) a line that's *not* the title. Click "**Animations**" (which is on the tab bar). Click the down-arrow that's to the *left* of "Effects Options".

You see these 52 animation choices....

None: none

Entrance: appear, fad, fly in, float in, split, wipe, shape, wheel, random bars, grow & turn, zoom, swivel, bounce

Emphasis: pulse, color pulse, teeter, spin, grow/shrink, desaturate, darken, lighten, transparency, object color, complementary color, line color, fill color, brush color, font color, underline, bold flash, bold reveal, wave

Exit: disappear, fade, fly out, float out, split, wipe, shape, wheel, random bars, shrink & turn, zoom, swivel, bounce

Motion paths: lines, arcs, turns, shapes, loops, custom path

Click one of those choices. (I recommend "fly in" because it's simple but dramatic.)

When you run the slide show (by pressing F5 or Shift F5) and the computer comes to that slide, here's what happens....

If your animation is from the "Entrance" category, the computer does this:

The computer will show just that slide's title. When you say "go" (by pressing Page Down or Enter or equivalent), the computer will show the slide's first subtopic (bulleted line or subtitle), animated the way you requested.

When you say "go" again, the computer will show the slide's next subtopic, animated the same way. Each time you say "go", you'll see one more line of text.

If your animation is from the other categories, the computer does this:

The computer will show the whole slide. When you say "go" (by pressing Page Down or Enter or equivalent), the computer will animate the slide's first subtopic (bulleted line or subtitle), the way you requested: if your animation is from the Emphasis category, the subtopic will be emphasized; if your animation is from the Exit category, the subtopic will vanish from the screen in an amusing way; if your animation is from the Motion paths category, the subtopic will move to a different part of the screen.

When you say "go" again, the computer will animate the slide's next subtopic, in the same way. Each time you say "go", you'll animate one more line of text.

Version 2007 While that slide is on the screen in normal 3-pane view, click (in the slide pane) a line that's *not* the title. Click "**Animations**" (which is on the tab bar) then the Animate box.

You see these 7 animation choices:

---
no animation

fade all at once
fade by 1st level paragraphs

wipe all at once
wipe by 1st level paragraphs

fly in all at once
fly in by 1st level paragraphs

custom animation

The most useful choices are:

Choice	Meaning
no animation	cancel any animation you created before
fade by 1st level paragraphs	make each bulleted line appear gradually (changing from white to gray to black)
wipe by 1st level paragraphs	make each bulleted line appear gradually (the line's bottom part then the line's top part)
fly in by 1st level paragraphs	make each bulleted line move into position (fly up from the screen's bottom)

Click one of those choices. (I recommend "fly in by 1st level paragraphs" because it's the most dramatic.)

When you run the slide show (by pressing F5 or Shift F5) and the computer comes to that slide, the computer will show just that slide's title. When you say "go" (by pressing Page Down or Enter or equivalent), the computer will show the slide's first subtopic (bulleted line or subtitle), animated the way you requested. When you say "go" again, the computer will show the slide's next subtopic, animated the way you requested. Each time you say "go", you'll see one more line of text.

Version 2003 While that slide is on the screen in normal 3-pane view, click "Design" (which is above the slide pane) then "Animation Schemes" (which is at the screen's right edge, near the top). You see these 34 animation choices:

No animation

Subtle: appear, appear and dim, fade in all, fade in one by one, fade in and dim, faded wipe, faded zoom, brush on underline, dissolve in, flash bulb, highlights, random bars, wipe

Moderate: ascend, descend, compress, elegant, rise up, show in reverse, spin, unfold, zoom

Exciting: big title, bounce, credits, ellipse motion, float, neutron, pinwheel, title arc, boomerang and exit, grow and exit, thread and exit

Click the animation you want.

When you run the slide show (by pressing F5 or Shift F5) and the computer comes to that slide, the computer will show just that slide's title. When you say "go" (by pressing Page Down or Enter or equivalent), the computer will show the slide's first subtopic (bulleted line or subtitle), animated the way you requested. When you say "go" again, the computer will show the slide's next subtopic, animated the way you requested. Each time you say "go", you'll see one more line of text.

Timing

When you give a slide show, you typically want the computer to keep showing the same slide until you press Page Down or Enter or equivalent.

But sometimes, you'd rather have the computer switch to the next slide *automatically*, without waiting for you to say so.

For example, if you're giving a passionate speech ("Oh, darling, I love you!") or playing in a rock band, you might want the images on the wall to change automatically without forcing you to interrupt your performance to press a key or click a mouse. If you're running an animated ad in an airport or shopping mall or store (by hiding a computer inside a kiosk), you'll want the computer's kiosk to run a PowerPoint presentation even when no salesperson is present.

Here's how:

Click the words "Slide Show" (at the screen's top).
Click "Rehearse Timings" (or, in version 2010, click "Record Slide Show", which makes the computer also record your laser-pointer motions and your voice, if your computer has a microphone).
That makes the computer run a **rehearsal**. The computer starts the rehearsal by showing you slide 1 (as if you had pressed F5.) To progress from slide to slide, the computer waits for you to press Page Down or Enter or equivalent. **The computer notices how long it waits; each waiting time is recorded.**

When you finish viewing the final slide (and press Page Down or Enter or equivalent again), the computer tells you how many minutes and seconds your entire slide show lasted. Press Enter.
You'll be in Slide Sorter view, where you'll see all the slides with their numbers and timings.

Here's what you've accomplished:

In the future, whenever you start the slide show (by pressing the F5 key), the computer will automatically move to the next slide after the appropriate amount of time (the time you took in rehearsal), even if nobody's pressed Page Down or Enter or equivalent yet.

If you made a mistake about timings, change them. For version 2010, use one of these methods:

Method 1 Try to undo all the timings (by clicking the Undo button's down-arrow then "Record Slide Show", if you see that choice).

Method 2 Click "Slide Show" (at the screen's top) then remove the check mark from the "Use Timings" box (by clicking it).

For version 2007, use one of these methods:

Method 1 Try to undo all the timings (by clicking the Undo button's down-arrow then "Rehearse Timings", if you see that choice).

Method 2 Click "Slide Show" (at the screen's top) then remove the check mark from the "Use Rehearsed Timings" box (by clicking it).

For version 2003, use one of these methods:

Method 1 Try to undo all the timings (by clicking "Edit" then "Undo Rehearse Timings", if you see that choice).

Method 2 In Slide Sorter view, right-click the slide whose timing you want to change. Click "Slide Transition". Then either edit the time (in the "Automatically after" box, which is near the screen's bottom-right corner) or remove that box's check mark (so the computer will *not* press Enter automatically).

Puppets

When you give a PowerPoint presentation, don't just read the slides to your audience. Be more active!

Walk into the audience. Get emotional. Jump around while you talk. Be a fascinating human, not a wooden puppet.

Use the slides whenever you wish, but remember that *you're* in control. Don't let the slides control *you*.

Use the slides to *supplement* what you have to say. Don't make the slides be the whole presentation. If your presentation's just a bunch of slides, your audience will wonder why you didn't just distribute printouts instead of forcing the audience to listen to you read slides.

Use your personality to add your own drama to the event. If you're giving a speech about something that seems boring (such as tables of numbers), reveal why they're interesting. Be bold enough to laugh at the material and be cynical about it. Tell the audience how you really feel, and why, and get them to think about it. Use your emotions to excite the audience into thinking about the issues.

If the audience looks at your slides without seeing or hearing your emotion, the presentation can become boring. Since sitting through a PowerPoint presentation can be painfully boring (a pain in the ass), PowerPoint is nicknamed **PowerPain**.

When I'm in front of an audience, I avoid PowerPoint. I prefer to talk from my soul; I want my audience to look at my face, not slides. I'd rather scribble on a whiteboard (while I bang it or kiss it) than be in a darkened room dominated by a slide show.

PowerPoint has wrecked the U.S. military. Too many military bureaucrats have been giving fancy PowerPoint presentations instead of getting real work done. The U.S. military is in the process of banning PowerPoint. Soldiers joke that the best way for the U.S. to win battles is to donate PowerPoint to the enemy.

Digital cameras

Here's what Best Buy charged for digital cameras when this book went to press in June 2011:

Maker	Model	Megapixels	Optical zoom	Price
Insignia	NS-DSC1110A	10	3x	$40
GE	A1250	12.2	5x	$57
Kodak	C190	12.3	5x	$60
GE	J1455	14.1	5x	$80
Panasonic	Lumix FH5	16.1	4x	$112
Fujifilm	FinePix T200	14	10x	$140
Samsung	PL210	14.2	10x	$150
Panasonic	Lumix FH24	16.1	8x	$150
Olympus	VR-320	14	12.5x	$170
Fujifilm	S2950	14	18x	$185
Sony	Cyber-shot H70	16.2	10x	$193
Nikon	Coolpix L120	14.1	21x	$244
Kodak	EasyShare Z990 Max	12	30x	$289
Olympus	SP-800	14	30x	$350
Sony	DSCHX9V	16.2	16x	$350
Sony	DSCHX100V	16.2	30x	$400

Digital-camera prices drop fast, so they're probably even lower now!

Here's how to use a typical classic digital camera: the 2-megapixel Olympus Camedia D-520 Zoom. (Other models are similar.)

Installing the hardware

The Olympus Camedia D-520 Zoom camera comes in a tiny cardboard box that includes the camera, a strap (to help you carry the camera), two AA alkaline batteries, a 16M SmartMedia card (which is black and gold), a USB cable (to attach to your computer), a CD-ROM disk (to put in your computer), a video cable (that you can attach to your TV), and paperwork.

Put the 16M card into the camera and attach the camera's strap, as follows:

> Look at the camera's front. On the left side of the camera's front, you see a door. Open it. Insert the 16M SmartMedia card, so the card's diagonally cut corner goes in first and is at the top. Close the door.
> Look at the door's hinge. Its middle is a thin metal bar. Squeeze the strap's small loop under that bar, through to the other side of the bar; then put the strap's big loop through that small loop. Pull the big loop, so the strap tightens around the bar.

Put the batteries into the camera, as follows:

> Turn the camera upside-down, so you see its bottom.
> The camera's bottom has an arrow. The arrow is on the battery compartment's door. Touch the arrow and push in its direction. That slides the door. Then lift the door. Put the batteries into the compartment, in the direction indicated by the markings inside the compartment. (You can use the two AA alkaline batteries that came with the camera, but they won't last long. Buy replacements soon — or buy a lithium battery instead, which lasts 25 times as long.)
> Close the compartment by pressing on the arrow then sliding it back to its original position.

Take photos

Look at the camera's front. Slide the lens cover (which says "Olympus") to the left. That makes the camera turn on, the lens stick out, and the flash pop up.

Put the back of the camera against your eye.

On the camera's back wall, you see two windows. The big window (called the **monitor**) shows info temporarily but then goes black. The small window (which is near the camera's top and called the **viewfinder**) shows you what the camera sees.

Aim the camera at whatever **subject** you want to photograph. To keep things simple, stay at least 19 inches away from the subject, and put the subject's most important part in the middle of the crosshairs.

At the monitor's bottom right corner, you see the **monitor button**, which says "IOI". If you tap that button, what the camera sees will appear also in the monitor (and look big and well-lit and consume more electricity). If you tap that button again, the monitor will turn off, so what the camera sees will be just in the viewfinder again.

On the camera's top, you see two buttons. Here's how to use them:

> The narrow button (the **zoom button**) has a **T** and a **W** next to it. If you nudge that button toward the **T** (which means **telephoto**), the camera lens will zoom in, as if you were standing closer to the subject, so the subject will look bigger. If you nudge that button toward the **W** instead (which means **wide-angle**), the camera lens will zoom out, so the photo will include more of the subject's surrounding environment.
>
> After aiming the camera and playing with the zoom, press the camera's other top button (the **shutter button**) gently: press it just halfway down, until you see a green light, which means the camera has focused. Then press that button *all* the way down. That makes the camera flash (if the subject was dark) and take the photo.

If you wish, take another photo: just aim, fiddle with the zoom button (if you wish), press the shutter button halfway down, wait for the green light, then press the shutter button *all* the way down.

If you want to photograph a scene whose main subject is *not* in the center, do this trick:

> Aim at the main subject (such as a person's face). Press the shutter button halfway down and wait for the green light.
> Then (while still holding the shutter button halfway down) aim where you want the scene's center to be. Finally, press the shutter button *all* the way down.

That gets you the scene you want, but with your main subject being the clearest part of the scene (because the main subject will be the least fuzzy and have the correct brightness).

Turn the camera off

When you finish taking photos, turn the camera off by doing this:

> Look at the camera's front. Slide the lens cover gently to the right, until it almost touches the lens (but leave a small gap). The lens will retract. Then slide the lens cover *all* the way to the right, so it covers the lens. Push the flash down, into the camera.

Review your photos

Make sure the camera is turned off. Then review your photos by doing this....

Tap the **monitor button** (which is on the camera's back wall and says "IOI"). In the camera's monitor, you see the newest photo you took.

> Press the ◄ button to go back and see the previous photo.
> Press the ◄ button several more times to go back farther.
> Press the ► button to go ahead and see the next photo.
>
> Press the ▼ button to hop back 10 photos (or to the beginning).
> Press the ▲ button to hop ahead 10 photos (or to the newest photo).

If the photo you're seeing is horrible, here's how to erase it:

> Tap the **menu button** (which says "OK" next to it). By using the camera's arrow buttons to move around, choose ERASE (▼) then YES (▲). Tap the menu button again.

If you want to erase *all* photos in the camera's memory card, do this:

> Tap the **menu button** (which says "OK" next to it). By using the camera's arrow buttons to move around, choose MODE MENU (►) then CARD (▼▼) then CARD SETUP ALL ERASE (►►). Tap the menu button again. Choose YES (▲). Tap the menu key again. The computer will erase all the photos. The monitor will say "NO PICTURE".

When you finish reviewing your photos, tap the monitor button again. That turns off the monitor & camera.

Windows XP

Here's how to use the camera with Windows XP. (To use the camera with Windows Vista, skip ahead to the next section, called "Windows Photo Gallery".)

Install the software If you haven't done so already, put the camera's software into your Windows XP computer, as follows:

> Turn the computer on. Put the Camedia CD-ROM disk into your computer's CD-ROM drive. Press Enter four times. Click "Agree". Press Enter three times.
>
> The computer says "Enter your Quick Time 5 Pro registration number." Just press Enter (without typing anything).
>
> The computer says "Welcome to the Quick Time Setup Assistant!" Click "Next" three times. Click "Finish". Press Enter three times.
>
> Type your name. Press the Tab key.
>
> Type the Camedia Master Serial Number (which is printed on the folder the CD came in). Press Enter four times. Close all windows (by clicking their X buttons).

Copy photos to the computer To copy your photos to the computer, do this....

Grab the USB cable (which has flat ends). Plug the big end into the computer's USB port. Look at the camera's front, then look at the camera's right side, where you see black plastic marked "USB". Lift that plastic, so you see the USB port hiding underneath; plug the cable's small end into that port.

Press Enter six times.

See all the photos On the computer's screen, you see a window called "Picture". Maximize it.

Across the bottom of that window, you see the photos. (To see them all, use the scroll arrows.)

Click a bottom photo If you click one of those bottom photos, you see it bigger, above.

Below the big photo, you see **4 buttons**, which you can press:

The first	button has the same effect as clicking the previous photo.
The second	button has the same effect as clicking the next photo.
The third	button rotates the photo 90 degrees clockwise.
The last	button rotates the photo 90 degrees counterclockwise.

If you want to **print the photo** onto paper, do this:

> Click "Print this picture" (near the screen's top left corner). Press Enter three times. Click "Full page photo print". Press Enter.
>
> Your printer will print the photo big, so it fills a page of paper. The computer will say, "You have successfully printed your pictures." Click the "Finish" button.

If you want to **e-mail the photo** to a friend, do this:

> Click "E-mail this file" (which is at the screen's left edge).
>
> Click "Make all my pictures smaller" (if you want the transmitted photo to fit on the screen easily and transmit fast) or "Keep the original sizes" (if you insist that the transmitted photo stay big and high-quality).
>
> Press Enter.
>
> You'll see a window that lets you write an e-mail message using Outlook Express. That window already includes a copy of the photo, as an attachment. (I explained e-mail attachments on pages 137-138.)
>
> Type the e-mail address of the person you want to send the message to (such as "russ@secretfun.com"). In the Subject field, type a subject (such as "photo of Mary Smith"). Click in the big white box at the bottom. While holding down the Ctrl key, tap the A key. Type a message (such as "I've attached a photo of Mary Smith").
>
> Click "Send". Press Enter. As with sending any e-mail, answer any questions about the user name and password that your ISP assigned you.
>
> The recipient will see your words and underneath see your photo. The photo is also available as an attachment.

If you want to **delete the photo** from the computer, press the Delete key then Enter. That puts the photo into the Recycle Bin.

Below each bottom photo, you see the photo's temporary name (such as "Picture 003"). To **improve the name**, click that name then type your improved name (such as "Mississippi River") and press Enter.

Double-click a bottom photo If you *double*-click one of the bottom photos, you see it even bigger, so it's huge, in a new window that consumes nearly the whole screen.

> Below the photo, you see a magnifying glass containing a "+". If you click the "+", you see the photo even bigger (so it's too big to fit in the window and you need to use the scroll arrows). To make it even bigger, click the part of the photo that you want to enlarge more. Click several more times, to enlarge several times more!
>
> If you change your mind and want the photo to become slightly smaller, click the "-" (which is next to the "+") several times.

When you finish admiring the huge photo, close the window by clicking its X button.

See a slide show Here's how to see all the photos big, as a slide show....

Click the first bottom photo. Click the first "View as a slide show" (near the screen's top left corner).

You see the first photo huge, so it consumes the whole screen. Five seconds later, you see the next photo instead. Every five seconds, you see a different photo, unless you interrupt that pattern by pressing one of these keys:

> If you want to skip to the next photo *immediately* (without waiting 5 seconds), press the right-arrow key. To return to the previous photo, press the left-arrow key.
>
> If you want a pause (so you can admire a photo for *more* than 5 seconds), press the Space bar. That makes the computer pause until you press the Space bar again.

When you've seen all the photos, the computer will repeat and show them all again, and again, and again — until you stop the slide show by pressing the Esc key.

Copy to CD Here's how to copy photos to a CD:

> Make sure your computer has a CD-R or CD-RW drive. Put a blank CD into the drive. (If the computer asks "What do you want Windows to do?", click "Take no action" then press Enter.)
>
> Look at the bottom photos. Highlight the ones you want to copy. (To highlight just one bottom photo, click it. To highlight *several* bottom photos, click the first one you want, then while holding down the Ctrl key click the others. To highlight *all* the bottom photos, do this: while holding down the Ctrl key, tap the A key.)
>
> Click "Copy to CD" (which is at the screen's left edge) then "You have files waiting to be written to the CD" (which is at the screen's bottom) then "Write these files to CD".
>
> Invent a name for the CD. Type the name (and press Enter).
>
> The computer will write onto the CD.
>
> Then the computer will eject the CD from the drive and say "You have successfully written your files to the CD". Press Enter. Close the CD Drive window (by clicking its X button).

Final steps When you finish looking at the photos, close the Picture window (by clicking its X button).

View again In the future, if you want to view your photos on the computer again, do this:

> Click "Start" then "My Pictures".
> Double-click "Picture".
> Maximize the window.

Windows Photo Gallery

Windows Photo Gallery comes free as part of Windows Vista. Here's how to use it.

Launch

Click Start then "All Programs" then "Windows Photo Gallery". You see the Windows Photo Gallery window. Maximize it.

Pick a photo

Click "All Pictures and Videos" (which is at the screen's top-left corner). You see all the photos, drawings, and movies that are in your hard disk's Pictures folder (and that folder's subfolders), organized by year taken (according to the clocks in the cameras).

If the photo you want to edit isn't yet in the Pictures folder, do this:

> If the photo's on paper, put the paper into a scanner, run a USB cable from the scanner to your computer's system unit, turn the scanner on, and, if necessary, press a button on the scanner.
>
> If the photo's in a digital camera, run a USB cable from the digital camera to your system unit's USB port; or take the camera's memory card out of the camera and put it into the computer's **memory-card reader** (a slot in the front of the computer's system unit), if your computer is fancy enough to have such a reader.
>
> Then follow the instructions on the screen. If nothing seems to be happening, try clicking "File" then "Import from Camera or Scanner".

When you finally decide which picture you want to edit, double-click it. You see the picture enlarged, so it fills nearly the whole screen.

Rotate

At the screen's bottom, you see two curved blue arrows. The left one is called **Rotate Left** or **Rotate Counterclockwise**; the right one is called **Rotate Right** or **Rotate Clockwise**. If you click either, the photo will rotate 90 degrees.

Zoom

While you're looking at a photo, here's how to see part of it enlarged: click the part you want enlarged, then rotate your mouse's wheel *away* from you. (To enlarge that part a lot, do that procedure several times: click the part, rotate the mouse wheel away from you, click the part again, rotate the mouse wheel further away from you, etc.) That's called **zooming in**.

To return to a normal view, click in the photo then rotate the mouse wheel *toward* you. That makes the photo look smaller, so all of it can fit on the screen.

Fix

To edit the photo further, click "Fix" (which is at the screen's top). Then the screen's right edge shows this menu:

Auto Adjust
Adjust Exposure
Adjust Color
Crop Picture
Fix Red Eye
Undo   Redo

Auto Adjust Click **Auto Adjust**. That makes the computer try to adjust the photo's exposure (darkness) and color, automatically.

> If you *like* the result, great!
>
> If you *don't like* the result, undo it by clicking the word **Undo**.
>
> If you're *not sure* whether you like the result, compare the result with the original: flip back and forth between them by clicking **Undo** then **Redo** then **Undo** then **Redo**, etc., until you finally decide which you like better and it's on the screen.

Adjust Exposure Click **Adjust Exposure**. Drag the **Brightness** slider to the right to make the photo brighter, so it becomes whiter (or drag to the left to make the photo darker). Drag the **Contrast** slider to the right to increase the contrast between the lightest and darkest areas, so the light areas become even lighter and the dark areas become even darker (or drag to the left to make the light and dark areas be more alike).

Adjust Color Click **Adjust Color**. Drag the **Color Temperature** slider to the right to make the photo warmer, so it has a fire-orange glow (or drag to the left to make the photo colder and ice-blue). Drag the **Tint** slider to the right to make the photo redder, so people have rosy cheeks (or drag to the left to make the photo greener, so the lawns and bushes look prettier). Drag the **Saturation** slider to the right to make the colors more vibrant, bold, intense, and blaring (or drag to the left to make the photo grayer, closer to a black-and-white photo).

Undo If you regret your editing, do one of the following:

> To undo the last edit, click the word **Undo**.
>
> To cancel the last *several* edits, or click the word **Undo** several times.
>
> To cancel all edits since you switched to editing *this* phone, click **Undo**'s down-arrow then **Undo All**.
>
> To cancel all edits you ever made to this photo (and revert to this photo's original appearance), click the **Revert** button (which appears just if you've been editing *several* photos).

Redo If you clicked Undo but regret the undoing, click **Redo**. It undoes the undoing!

Crop Picture Look at your photo's 4 edges. Near those edges, you might see objects or areas that are annoying or useless, and you wish they weren't there. For example, you might see big patches of boring sky or dirt, trash cans, strangers who accidentally walked into your shot, former lovers, or blank white space that wasn't part of your intended photo. To eliminate them, make your photo be a smaller rectangle that excludes them. Here's how....

Click the **Crop Picture**. You see a big box that covers most of your photo. Drag that box's top-left corner and bottom-right corner, until the board covers exactly the photo part you want to keep. Then click "Apply".

If you don't like the result, click the Undo button and try again!

Fix Red Eye If you photograph a person in a dark room by using a flash, each eye's middle (**pupil**) might look red (because the pupil was dilated by the darkness, and the flash bounces off the blood vessels at the back of the retinas). To solve that problem, professional photographers do **pre-flash**: the flash lights up the room slightly before the photo is taken, so the pupils have some time to adjust to the flash and contract. If you take a flash photo without a pre-flash, the pupils will look big and red.

To remove the red, zoom in on the eye you want to fix (so you can see it clearly), then click **Fix Red Eye**. Draw a tiny box around that red eye (by dragging from where you want the box's top-left corner to where you want the box's bottom-right corner). When you lift your finger from the mouse's button, the box will disappear and you'll see the photo with the red eye fixed.

Final steps When you finish playing with the photo, decide whether you like the result.

> If you're not satisfied, undo your mistakes (by clicking "Undo" or its arrow).
>
> If you're satisfied, progress to one of the activities mentioned below. Before that photo disappears from the screen, the computer will automatically save your edited version to the hard disk. The computer will also remember what the original version looked like; so if you return to that photo and click "Fix" again, you can revert to the original version by clicking "Revert".

Print

Here's how to print the photo onto paper:

> Click **Print** (which is at the screen's top) then "Print...". Turn on your printer (if it's not on already). Press Enter.

The computer will automatically adjust the photo's size and orientation, so the photo will fit on the paper well.

E-mail

To put the photo into an e-mail message, click **E-mail** (which is at the screen's top) then the "Picture size" box's down-arrow.

Decide how big you want the photo to appear.

> You have 5 choices: **original size** (which is the huge number of pixels in your digital camera, minus what you cropped out), **large** (1280×1024 pixels), **medium** (1024×768), **small** (800×600), or **smaller** (640×480).
>
> For example, if you choose **smaller** (640×480), you'll send a smaller version that has less detail but transmits faster and can be viewed more easily, without much scrolling or clicking.
>
> Warning: a standard 17-inch CRT monitor shows just 1024×768 pixels, some of which are consumed by menus at the screen's top, left, and bottom, leaving very few pixels to display the photo.

Click the size you want, then press Enter.

You see a window to type your e-mail in. Maximize that window. Click in the big white box at that window's bottom. Delete what's in that box (by clicking Ctrl with A then pressing the Delete key). Type a message, such as "Here's the photo from the Christmas party." Click that window's Send button.

Switch photos

To switch to a different photo, choose one of these methods:

> To see the *next* photo, press the right-arrow key (click the ▶| button, which is at the screen's bottom).
>
> To see the *previous* photo, press the left-arrow key (or the click the |◀ button, which is at the screen's bottom).
>
> To see a slide show, starting with the current photo, click the blue circle (at the screen's bottom). For the most dramatic effect, jiggle the mouse (so you see the menu) then click "Themes" then "Pan and zoom". To change the speed, jiggle the mouse (so you see the menu) then click the down-arrow that's left of "Exit" then click "Slow" or "Medium" or "Fast". To pause, press the Space bar; to resume, press it again. To skip to the next photo *immediately*, press the right-arrow key. To stop the slide show, press the Escape key (which says "Esc" on it and is at the keyboard's top-left corner) or click "Exit" (which you'll see when you jiggle the mouse).
>
> To see icons for all your photos again, click "Back to Gallery" (at the screen's top-left corner). Then double-click one of those photo icons.

Close

When you finish using Windows Photo Gallery, close it by clicking its X button.

Professional retouching

Many women wish they were more beautiful. They buy lots of makeup. Some even undergo cosmetic surgery. But here's an easier way to produce a photo showing the woman is beautiful: just take a natural photo of her and edit it! That's called **retouching** the photo.

Many folks make their living by being **retouchers**: they retouch photos. They remove a woman's pimples, wrinkles, and fat; and they reshape her face to give her fuller lips (so she looks kissable), open eyes (so she looks excited), a bigger forehead (so she looks intelligent — and also has her eyes closer to her chin), and a smaller nose, mouth, and jaw (so she looks dainty and vulnerable), all making her look closer to 24.8 years old, which statisticians have shown is the female age that attracts men most (because women have the most estrogen then). The retouchers can work similar magic on men's faces, too! Their accomplishments raise the question of what "beauty" means: if you edit out your uniqueness, do you become more beautiful or just a clone of a bright electrified kissing doll?

To see the work of an expert retoucher (Canada's **Christiane Beaulieu**), go to her Website (**www.CBeau.ca**) then click her name then click your favorite language (FRANCAIS or ENGLISH). You see 30 retouched photos, darkened. Click one of the photos; then you see it enlarged and brightened. Click the photo again, to see the original, unretouched version of it. Click it several more times, to flip back and forth between the retouched and unretouched versions of it. When you tire of that photo, click the black margin at its left; then you'll see all 30 photos again, so you can click a different one of them instead.

For further fun, gawk at **Portrait Professional Picture Gallery (www.PortraitProfessional.com/gallery)**. You see 15 retouched photos (if you scroll down). Click one of them to see it enlarged, then point at the enlargement (by moving the mouse there without clicking) to see the original, unretouched version of it. (Move the mouse off the enlargement to see the retouched version again.) Each of those retouchings was invented in less the 5 minutes by using the **Portrait Professional** program. If you click "buy", you can buy a long-term license to transmit *your own photos* to the company's Website, which will edit your photos and transmit the retouched versions back to you. By using sliders, you choose *how much* you want your own photos retouched, so you can look a bit "dolled up" without looking totally plastic.

To see movies about how to retouch women (and criticize the morality of it), look at these Web sites on **YouTube**:

Dove Evolution	www.YouTube.com/watch?v=iYhCn0jf46U
Extreme (Photoshop) Makeover	www.YouTube.com/watch?v=aHLpRxAmCrw
Photoshop Effect	www.YouTube.com/watch?v=YP31r70_QNM
Doll Face	www.YouTube.com/watch?v=zl6hNj1uOkY

Movies

The computer can edit the movies you make.

Windows Movie Maker Vista

Windows Movie Maker comes free as part of Windows Vista and Windows XP SP2.

Here's how to use Windows Movie Maker if you have Windows Vista. (The next section explains how to use Windows Movie Maker if you have Windows XP SP2.)

Launch the program

To start using Windows Movie Maker, click Start then "All Programs" then "Windows Movie Maker". The computer will say "Windows Movie Maker".

The screen's left edge shows this **task menu**:

```
Import —
      From digital video camera
      Videos
      Pictures
      Audio or Music

Edit —
      Imported media
      Effects
      Transitions
      Titles and credits

Publish to —
      This computer
      DVD
      Recordable CD
      E-mail
      Digital video camera
```

Import from camera

Here's how to **import** (copy) a movie from a digital-video camcorder's tape to your computer.

Put the tape into the camcorder. Turn the camcorder off. Run a **Firewire cable** (which is also called an **IEEE 1394 cable** and an **i.LINK cable**) from your camcorder to your computer's system unit. Turn the camcorder back on and put it into "play" mode (rather than "record" mode).

On the computer's keyboard, type a name for your video (such as "Christmas 2006"). Press Enter. Click "Import the entire videotape to my computer". Press Enter.

Then the computer makes the camcorder rewind and play the tape. While the camcorder plays the tape, the computer shows the movie on the computer's screen silently and copies it to the Videos folder (which is on the computer hard disk).

For example, if you named your movie "Christmas 2006" and copied it to the computer on March 24, 2007 at 17 seconds after 9:38AM, the computer creates a file called "Christmas 2006 2007_03_24_09_38_17.avi". (The ".avi" stands for "audio video interleaved".) The computer puts that file into a folder called "Christmas 2006", which it puts into drive C's Video folder.

The file is huge and consumes lots of space on your hard disk. The file is 178 megabytes per minute of video. That's about 200 megabytes per minute, 1 gigabyte per 5 minutes, 12 gigabytes per hour.

When the tape is done (or you don't want to copy any more of it), click "Stop" then press Enter. Turn off the camcorder.

View the clips

The computer will analyze the movie and automatically divide it into scenes (called **clips**) by noticing each time you stopped the camera. The computer will show you each clip's first frame. If your movie contains many clips, the computer will show you just the first few; to see the rest, use the window's down-arrow (or rotate the mouse's wheel toward you).

To play one of the clips again (to remind yourself what it was), double-click the clip's icon (which is its first frame). The computer will play that clip for you, in a windowpane at the screen's right edge. That windowpane is called the **movie monitor**.

If you want to delete a clip, click its icon then press the Delete key.

Build the storyboard

At the screen's left edge, near the bottom, you should see the word "Storyboard". (If you see "Timeline" instead, click "Timeline", so it becomes "Storyboard".)

You see the **storyboard**, which is a gray banner containing big white boxes (separated by tiny white-and-gray boxes). Each big white box looks like a piece of blank white film.

Drag the clips to the big white boxes, in the order you want the clips to appear in your final movie.

> To the leftmost big white box, drag the clip that you want the movie to begin with. To the next big white box, drag the clip you want the movie to continue with. Continue that process, for the rest of the movie. As you start filling the boxes, more boxes appear automatically, to hold more clips.

If you want to drag *all* the clips to the storyboard, in the same order as on the tape, use this shortcut procedure instead:

> Click the first clip (so it's highlighted). While holding down the Ctrl key, tap the A key: that makes *all* the clips be highlighted. Drag the first clip to the storyboard's first box; the other highlighted clips will automatically be dragged along.

If you want to drag *many* clips to the storyboard, in the same order as on the tape, use this shortcut procedure instead:

> Click the first clip you want to drag. While holding down the Ctrl key, click the other clips you want to drag: that makes those clips be highlighted simultaneously. Drag the first wanted clip to the storyboard's first box; the other highlighted clips will automatically be dragged along.

View the movie

Here's how to view the whole movie.

In the storyboard, click the first clip (the first box in the storyboard).

At the screen's right edge, you see the movie monitor (the windowpane where your movie can play). Click the movie monitor's Play button (▶). That makes the movie monitor start playing the whole movie for you.

The movie consists of several **clips** (scenes). Each clip consists of many **frames**: you see **30 frames per second**.

While you're watching the movie, you can click the movie monitor's other buttons:

Button	Meaning
▶	play
‖	pause
◀|	go back slightly, to the **previous frame** (back 1/30 of a second)
|▶	go ahead slightly, to the **next frame** (ahead 1/30 of a second)

Here's a shortcut: instead of clicking the Play button or Pause button, just tap the keyboard's Space bar.

To skip to a different clip, click that clip's icon in the storyboard.

As the movie plays, the movie monitor's **slider** gradually slides toward the right.

Another way to go back is to drag that slider back toward the left.
Another way to skip ahead is to drag that slider faster toward the right.

Edit the movie

To edit the movie, you can use several techniques.

Delete a clip To delete a clip from the movie, click the clip's icon in the storyboard then press the Delete key.

Undo an edit If you make a mistake while editing, click the **Undo button** (a blue arrow bending toward the left).

Split a clip Here's how to split a clip into two parts, so you can edit each part differently:

In the storyboard, click the clip's icon then the movie monitor's Play button, so the clip starts to play. When you get to the moment when you want the clip to split, click the Pause button (**II**). Use the one-frame-at-a-time buttons (◀I and I▶) until you get to the exact frame you want to start the clip's second part. Click "Split".

On the storyboard, you see the clip has split and become two separate clips. Do whatever you wish to each of those two separate clips. For example, if you want to delete one of those clips, click its icon then press the Delete key.

Move a clip If you want to move a clip (which we'll call clip A) so it will play immediately before clip B, drag clip A to clip B. (In other words, point at clip A, then while holding down the mouse's left button, move the mouse pointer to clip B.) The clip will move when you take your finger off the mouse's button.

Add video effects Here's how to make a clip look more interesting.

Click "**Effects**" (in the task menu). You'll see icons for 49 video effects, organized into 30 categories:

3D ripple
blur
brightness (decrease or increase)
ease (in or out)
edge detection
fade in (from black or white)
fade out (to black or white)
film age (old, older, or oldest)
film grain
grayscale
hue cycles
mirror (horizontal or vertical)
pan down and zoom out
pan left to right
pan top left to (bottom right or top right)
pan top right to top left
pixelate
posterize
rotate (90°, 180°, or 270°)
sepia tone
sharpen
slow down, half-speed
speed up, double-speed
spin 360°
threshold
warp
watercolor
zoom into (bottom left, bottom right, top left, or top right)
zoom out from (bottom left, bottom right, top left, or top right)
zoom focus (bottom left, bottom right, top left, or top right)

(To see them all, use the window's scroll arrows or, better yet, click 3D Ripple then rotate your mouse's wheel toward you.) Here are the most conservative choices:

"fade in from black" makes the clip begin dark then quickly become normal
"fade out to black" makes the clip be mostly normal but end by darkening
"brightness increase" makes the whole clip less dark (to fix dim lighting)

The most lively is "speed up, double-speed", which makes everybody act & talk twice as fast.

To see what an effect does, double-click its icon. That makes the computer show you what the effect does to a photo of a red flower. Imagine what the effect would do to your clip!

To apply an effect to your clip, drag the effect's icon to the clip's icon on the storyboard. That makes the clip icon's gray star turn blue. If you drag *two* effects to a clip icon, the clip icon will get a *double* blue star. If you drag *three* effects there, the clip icon will get a *triple* blue star.

If you change your mind and want to delete all the clip's effects, click the star then press the Delete key.

If you want to delete just *one* of the clip's effects, do this:

Right-click the star. Click "Effects". In the right-hand box, click the effect you want to delete. Click "Remove" then "OK".

Add transitions You can make clips overlap, so your audience sees one clip gradually disappear while the next clip gradually appears, simultaneously. That's called a **transition** between clips. Here's how to create a transition.

Click "**Transitions**" (in the task menu). You'll see icons for 63 transitions effects, organized into 34 categories:

bars (horizontal or vertical)
bow tie (horizontal or vertical)
checkerboard across
circle (one or many)
diagonal (box out, cross out, or down right)
diamond
dissolve (fine or rough)
eye
fade
fan (in, out, or up)
filled V (down, up, left, or right)
flip
heart
inset (down left, down right, up left, or up right)
iris
keyhole
page curl up (left or right)
pixelate
rectangle
reveal (down or right)
roll
shatter (in, right, up-right, or up-left)
shrink in
slide (up or up-center)
spin
split (horizontal or vertical)
star (one or many)
sweep (in, out or up)
wheel with 4 spokes
whirlwind (at once or from top)
wipe narrow (down or right)
wipe normal (down or right)
wipe wide (down or right)
zig zag (horizontal or vertical)

(To see them all, use the window's scroll arrows or, better yet, click Bars then rotate your mouse's wheel toward you.) These choices are the most fun:

"heart" makes the new clip appear in a growing Valentine's heart
"keyhole" makes the new clip appear in a growing keyhole
"flip" makes the new clip appear on a rotating signboard
"shatter in" makes the new clip appear in an explosion of shattering glass

To see what a transition does, double-click its icon. That makes the computer show you what the effect does to photos of a red flower and yellow flowers. Imagine what the transition would do to your clips!

To apply a transition to a pair of your clips, drag the transition's icon to "the small box between the two clips on the storyboard". If you want to watch the transition, click that small box then the Play button (▶).

If you change your mind and want to delete the transition, click that small box then press the Delete key.

If the transition confuses the computer and makes your whole movie become black, do this:

> Delete the transition (by clicking its box in the storyboard then pressing the Delete key). That makes your movie return to normal. If you insist on using that transition after a clip, delete that clip's last few seconds (by splitting that clip into two parts then deleting the second part), so the seconds you were transitioning from are deleted. Then try again to apply the transition.

Create a title screen
Here's how to put a title at your movie's beginning.

Click "**Titles and credits**" (in the task menu) then "**Title at the beginning**". Type what you want the title screen to say (such as "Christmas Follies").

After you've typed that and pause, the computer will show you how the title will actually look: it will be white words centered on blue background; it will play in a clip that takes between 3½ and 7½ seconds (depending on how long your title is), with a fade in and a fade out.

While you're typing the title, you're typing in a box. If you wish, click the box below that. Any words you type in the lower box will be the subtitle: they'll appear smaller and below the main title. For example, in the top box you could type "Christmas"; in the bottom box you could type "Follies" or "2006" or "with Sue" or "by Sue Smith".

When you're satisfied with the title you wrote, add it to your movie by clicking "Add Title".

See the timeline
Instead of looking at the storyboard, you can look at the **timeline**, which shows more details about your movie. To switch from storyboard to timeline, click the word "Storyboard" (which is at the screen's left edge) then "Timeline".

The timeline is a graph. Atop the timeline, a horizontal ruler shows how many hours, minutes, and seconds have elapsed since the movie's beginning. (For example, "0:01:20.00" means "0 hours plus 1 minute plus 20.00 seconds".) Below that ruler, you see which clip is playing at each point of time. Each clip is represented by a box. If a clip is lengthy (takes many minutes), the clip's box is wide; if a clip is brief (takes just a few seconds), the clip's box is narrow.

As you play the movie, a green vertical line moves rightward across the timeline and shows how far on the timeline the playback has progressed. The timeline is especially useful if you want to skip ahead and watch a clip's ending: while playing the movie, just drag the green vertical line to the right, until it's near the clip's end.

The timeline shows 3 **tracks**:

> The top track shows what **video** is playing.
> The middle track shows what **added audio** is playing.
> The bottom track shows what **titles** have been added.

To make the timeline look wider (so you can see its details better), click the **Zoom Timeline In** button (a magnifying glass containing "+"). To make the timeline look narrower (so the whole movie fits on your screen), click the **Zoom Timeline Out** button (a magnifying glass containing "-").

To return to seeing the storyboard (which is less detailed than the timeline and easier to understand), click "Show Storyboard" (which is just above the timeline).

Trim a clip
Here's the fastest way to **trim** a clip (make it shorter).

Click the clip's icon then the movie monitor's Play button, so the clip starts to play. When you get to the place in the clip where you want to trim, click the Pause button (❙❙). Use the one-frame-at-a-time buttons (◀❙❙ and ❙❙▶) until you get to the exact spot where you want to trim.

Click "**Clip**" (which is at the screen's top).

> If you want to delete the clip's beginning (the part before the current frame), click **Trim Beginning**.
>
> If you want to delete the clip's end (the part after the current frame), click **Trim End**.

Combine clips
Here's how to combine two clips that are next to each other, to form a longer clip:

> On the storyboard (or timeline), click the first clip's icon. While holding down the Ctrl key, click the second clip's icon. Click "**Clip**" (which is at the screen's top) then "**Combine**".

Save the project

To save your work, click **File** (which is at the screen's top-left corner) then **Save Project**. Invent a name for your project (such as "Christmas 2006 project"); type the name and press Enter.

That makes the computer copy your project to the Videos folder. At the end of your project's name, the computer will secretly put ".MSWMM" (which stands for MicroSoft Windows Movie Maker).

Later, if you want to return to that project, click **File** then **Open Project** then double-click the project's icon.

Copy to DVD

Here's how to copy your movie to a DVD disk:

Click "**DVD**" (in the task menu). Press Enter. Click "Next" (or press Enter again).

If you get an error message saying "Windows DVD Maker has stopped working" then an error message about "lmpgd10.ax", the problem is caused by a conflicting program called the **Ligos MPEG-2 codec**, so unregister that program by doing this:

> Click Start then "All Programs" then "Accessories". Right-click "Command Prompt". Click "Run as administrator" then "Continue". Type "regsvr32/u LMPGD10.AX" (then press Enter). Press Enter again. Type "regsvr32/u LMPGSPL.AX" (then press Enter). Press Enter again. Close the Administrator Command Prompt window (by clicking its X). Then try again to use Windows Movie Maker with Windows DVD Maker.

Put a blank DVD+R disk into the DVD drive. Click "Burn" (or press Enter). The computer will say "Creating DVD".

The computer will convert your movie to DVD form then copy it to the blank DVD+R disk. That process will take several minutes: go eat a pizza. Finally, the computer will say "Your disc is ready" and open the DVD drive's door. Remove the DVD disk.

Then make the computer return to normal, by doing this:

> Remove the DVD disk. Close the DVD drive's door. Click the X button (to close the little window), then click the next X button (to close the Windows DVD Maker window).
>
> The computer asks "Do you want to save your project before exiting?" Press Enter, type a DVD project name (such as "Christmas 2006 DVD project"), and press Enter again.
>
> The computer will copy that DVD project to your Videos folder. At the end of your DVD project's name, the computer will secretly put ".msdvd" (which stands for MicroSoft DVD).
>
> Click "Windows Movie Maker" (which is at the screen's bottom).

Close

When you finish using Windows Movie Maker, close it by clicking its X button.

Windows Movie Maker XP

Here's how to use the Windows Movie Maker version that's part of Windows XP SP 2.

Launch the program

To start using Windows Movie Maker, click "start" then "All Programs" then "Windows Movie Maker". The computer will say "Untitled — Windows Movie Maker".

To make sure your screen is normal, do this:

> Click the Tasks button (which is near the screen's top, below the word Play").
>
> At the screen's left edge, make sure an up-arrow is next to "Capture Video", "Edit Movie", "Finish Movie", and "Movie Making Tips". If you see a down-arrow instead, click it, so it becomes an up-arrow.

Then the screen's left edge shows this **task menu**:

1. Capture Video
   Capture from video device
   Import video
   Import pictures
   Import audio or music

2. Edit Movie
   Show collections
   View video effects
   View video transitions
   Make titles or credits
   Make an AutoMovie

3. Finish Movie
   Save to my computer
   Save to CD
   Save to DVD
   Send in e-mail
   Send to the Web
   Send to DV camera

   Movie Making Tips
   How to capture video
   How to edit clips
   How to add titles, effects, transitions
   How to save and share movies

Capture the video

Here's how to **capture** a video (copy a video from a DV camcorder's tape to your computer).

Put the tape into the camcorder. Turn the camcorder off. Run a **Firewire cable** (which is also called an **IEEE 1394 cable** and an **i.LINK cable**) from your camcorder to your computer's system unit. Turn the camcorder back on and put it into "play" mode (rather than "record" mode). If the computer asks "What do you want Windows to do?" click "Cancel".

If the computer's screen doesn't say "Video Capture Wizard" yet, make it say that by clicking "**Capture from video device**" on the task menu (which is at the screen's left edge).

On the computer's keyboard, type a name for your video (such as "Christmas 2006"). Press Enter twice. Click "Capture the entire tape automatically". Press Enter.

Then the computer makes the camcorder rewind and play the tape. While the camcorder plays the tape, the computer shows the movie on the computer's screen and also copies it to the My Videos folder (which is in the My Documents folder). For example, if you named your movie "Christmas 2006", the computer creates a file called "Christmas 2006.wmv". (The ".wmv" stands for "Windows media video.)

On a *typical* computer, the file consumes about 3 megabytes per minute of video. For example, a complete 1-hour tape consumes about 180 megabytes. (On *your* computer, the file might be a different length, depending on how much quality the computer decided to give your video.)

When the tape is done (or you don't want to copy any more of it), click "Stop Capture" then press Enter. Turn off the camcorder.

View the clips

The computer will briefly say "Importing files".

It will analyze the movie and automatically divide it into scenes (called **clips**) by noticing each time you stopped the camera. The computer will show you each clip's first frame and the date & time you shot it (according to your camcorder's built-in clock). If your movie contains many clips, the computer will show you just the first few; to see the rest, use the window's down-arrow (or rotate the mouse's wheel toward you).

To play one of the clips again (to remind yourself what it was), double-click the clip's icon (which is its first frame). The computer will play that clip for you, in a windowpane at the screen's right edge. That windowpane is called the **movie monitor**.

If you want to delete a clip, click its icon then press the Delete key.

Build the storyboard

Across the screen's bottom, you should see the **storyboard**, which is a blue banner containing big white boxes (separated by tiny white-and-gray boxes). (If you don't see the big white boxes, make them appear by clicking "Show Storyboard".)

Drag the clips to the big white boxes, in the order you want the clips to appear in your final movie.

> To the leftmost big white box, drag the clip that you want the movie to begin with. To the next big white box, drag the clip you want the movie to continue with. Continue that process, for the rest of the movie. As you start filling the boxes, more boxes appear automatically, to hold more clips.

If you want to drag *all* the clips to the storyboard, in the same order as on the tape, use this shortcut procedure instead:

> Click the first clip (so it's highlighted). While holding down the Ctrl key, tap the A key: that makes *all* the clips be highlighted. Drag the first clip to the storyboard's first box; the other highlighted clips will automatically be dragged along.

If you want to drag *many* clips to the storyboard, in the same order as on the tape, use this shortcut procedure instead:

> Click the first clip you want to drag. While holding down the Ctrl key, click the other clips you want to drag: that makes those clips be highlighted simultaneously. Drag the first wanted clip to the storyboard's first box; the other highlighted clips will automatically be dragged along.

View the movie

Here's how to view the whole movie.

In the storyboard, click the first clip (the first box in the storyboard).

At the screen's right edge, you see the movie monitor (the windowpane where your movie can play). Click the movie monitor's Play button (▶). That makes the movie monitor start playing the whole movie for you.

The movie consists of several **clips** (scenes). Each clip consists of many **frames**: you're temporarily seeing **15 frames per second**, though your final movie will actually be higher quality and show **30 frames per second**.

While you're watching the movie, you can click the movie monitor's other buttons:

Button	Meaning
▶	**play**
II	**pause**
■	stop and go back to the **movie's beginning**
I◀	go back to the **clip's beginning** (and previous clip's end)
▶I	skip ahead to the **clip's end** (and next clip's beginning)
◀II	go back slightly, to the **previous frame** (back 1/15 of a second)
II▶	go ahead slightly, to the **next frame** (ahead 1/15 of a second)

Here's a shortcut: instead of clicking the Play button or Pause button, just tap the keyboard's Space bar.

To skip to a different clip, click that clip's icon in the storyboard.

As the movie plays, the movie monitor's **slider** gradually slides toward the right.

Another way to go back is to drag that slider back toward the left.
Another way to skip ahead is to drag that slider faster toward the right.

Edit the movie

To edit the movie, you can use several techniques.

<u>*Delete a clip*</u> To delete a clip from the movie, click the clip's icon in the storyboard then press the Delete key.

<u>*Undo an edit*</u> If you make a mistake while editing, click the **Undo button** (a blue arrow bending toward the left).

<u>*Split a clip*</u> Here's how to split a clip into two parts, so you can edit each part differently:

In the storyboard, click the clip's icon then the movie monitor's Play button, so the clip starts to play. When you get to the moment when you want the clip to split, click the Pause button (II). Use the one-frame-at-a-time buttons (◀II and II▶) until you get to the exact frame you want to start the clip's second part. Click the **"Split the clip" button** (which is the movie monitor's second-to-last button).

On the storyboard, you see the clip has split and become two separate clips. Do whatever you wish to each of those two separate clips. For example, if you want to delete one of those clips, click its icon then press the Delete key.

<u>*Move a clip*</u> If you want to move a clip (which we'll call clip A) so it will play immediately before clip B, drag clip A to clip B. (In other words, point at clip A, then while holding down the mouse's left button, move the mouse pointer to clip B.) The clip will move when you take your finger off the mouse's button.

<u>*Add video effects*</u> Here's how to make a clip look more interesting.

Click "**View video effects**" (in the task menu). You'll see icons for 42 video effects, organized into 23 categories:

blur
brightness (decrease or increase)
ease (in or out)
fade in (from black or white)
fade out (to black or white)
film age (old, older, or oldest)
film grain
grayscale
hue cycles
mirror (horizontal or vertical)
pan upper (left-to-right or right-to-left)
pixelate
posterize
rotate (90°, 180°, or 270°)
sepia tone
slow down half-speed
smudge stick
speed up, double-speed
threshold
watercolor
zoom into (bottom left, bottom right, top left, or top right)
zoom out from (bottom left, bottom right, top left, or top right)
zoom focus (bottom left, bottom right, top left, or top right)

(To see them all, use the window's scroll arrows or, better yet, click Blur then rotate your mouse's wheel toward you.) Here are the most conservative choices:

"fade in from black" makes the clip begin dark then quickly become normal
"fade out to black" makes the clip be mostly normal but end by darkening
"brightness increase" makes the whole clip less dark (to fix dim lighting)

The most lively is "speed up, double-speed", which makes everybody act & talk twice as fast, like chipmunks.

To see what an effect does, double-click its icon. That makes the computer show you what the effect does to a photo of a grassy hill. Imagine what the effect would do to your clip!

To apply an effect to your clip, drag the effect's icon to the clip's icon on the storyboard. That makes the clip icon's gray star turn blue. If you drag *two* effects to a clip icon, the clip icon will get a *double* blue star. If you drag *three* effects there, the clip icon will get a *triple* blue star.

If you change your mind and want to delete all the clip's effects, click the star then press the Delete key.

If you want to delete just *one* of the clip's effects, do this:

Right-click the star. Click "Video Effects". In the right-hand box, click the effect you want to delete. Click "Remove" then "OK".

<u>*Add transitions*</u> You can make clips overlap, so your audience sees one clip gradually disappear while the next clip gradually appears, simultaneously. That's called a **transition** between clips. Here's how to create a transition.

Click "**View video transitions**" (in the task menu). You'll see icons for 60 transitions effects, organized into 34 categories:

bars
bow tie (horizontal or vertical)
checkerboard across
circle (one or many)
diagonal (box out, cross out, or down right)
diamond
dissolve
eye
fade
fan (in, out, or up)
filled V (down, up, left, or right)
flip
heart
inset (down left, down right, up left, or up right)
iris
keyhole
page curl up (left or right)
pixelate
rectangle
reveal (down or right)
roll
shatter (in, right, up-right, or up-left)
shrink in
slide (up or up-center)
spin
split (horizontal or vertical)
star (one or many)
sweep (in, out or up)
wheel with 4 spokes
whirlwind
wipe narrow (down or right)
wipe normal (down or right)
wipe wide (down or right)
zig zag (horizontal or vertical)

(To see them all, use the window's scroll arrows or, better yet, click Bars then rotate your mouse's wheel toward you.) These choices are the most fun:

"heart" makes the new clip appear in a growing Valentine's heart
"keyhole" makes the new clip appear in a growing keyhole
"flip" makes the new clip appear on a rotating signboard
"shatter in" makes the new clip appear in an explosion of shattering glass

To see what a transition does, double-click its icon. That makes the computer show you what the effect does to photos of a grassy hill and a sand dune. Imagine what the transition would do to your clips!

To apply a transition to a pair of your clips, drag the transition's icon to "the small box between the two clips on the storyboard". If you want to watch the transition, click that small box then the Play button (▶).

If you change your mind and want to delete the transition, click that small box then press the Delete key.

Create a title screen

Here's how to put a title at your movie's beginning.

Click "**Make titles or credits**" (in the task menu) then "**title at the beginning**". Type what you want the title screen to say (such as "Christmas Follies").

After you've typed that and pause, the computer will show you how the title will actually look: it will be white words centered on blue background; it will play in a clip that takes between 3½ and 7½ seconds (depending on how long your title is), with a fade in and a fade out.

While you're typing the title, you're typing in a box. If you wish, click the box below that. Any words you type in the lower box will be the subtitle: they'll appear smaller and below the main title. For example, in the top box you could type "Christmas"; in the bottom box you could type "Follies" or "2006" or "with Sue" or "by Sue Smith".

When you're satisfied with the title you wrote, add it to your movie by clicking "Done, add title to movie".

See the timeline

Instead of looking at the storyboard, you can look at the **timeline**, which shows more details about your movie. To see the timeline instead of the storyboard, click "Show Timeline" (which is just above the storyboard).

The timeline is a graph. Atop the timeline, a horizontal ruler shows how many hours, minutes, and seconds have elapsed since the movie's beginning. (For example, "0:01:20.00" means "0 hours plus 1 minute plus 20.00 seconds".) Below that ruler, you see which clip is playing at each point of time. Each clip is represented by a box. If a clip is lengthy (takes many minutes), the clip's box is wide; if a clip is brief (takes just a few seconds), the clip's box is narrow.

As you play the movie, a blue vertical line moves rightward across the timeline and shows how far on the timeline the playback has progressed. The timeline is especially useful if you want to skip ahead and watch a clip's ending: while playing the movie, just drag the blue vertical line to the right, until it's near the clip's end.

The timeline shows 3 **tracks**:

> The top track shows what **video** is playing.
> The middle track shows what **added audio** is playing.
> The bottom track shows what **titles** have been added.

To make the timeline look wider (so you can see its details better), click the **Zoom Timeline In** button (a magnifying glass containing "+"). To make the timeline look narrower (so the whole movie fits on your screen), click the **Zoom Timeline Out** button (a magnifying glass containing "-").

To return to seeing the storyboard (which is less detailed than the timeline and easier to understand), click "Show Storyboard" (which is just above the timeline).

Trim a clip

Here's the fastest way to **trim** a clip (make it shorter).

Click the clip's icon then the movie monitor's Play button, so the clip starts to play. When you get to the place in the clip where you want to trim, click the Pause button (❙❙). Use the one-frame-at-a-time buttons (◀❙❙ and ❙❙▶) until you get to the exact spot where you want to trim.

Make sure you see the timeline. (If you see the storyboard instead, click "Show Timeline".)

Click "**Clip**" (which is at the screen's top).

> If you want to delete the clip's beginning (the part before the current frame), click **Set Start Trim Point**.
>
> If you want to delete the clip's ending (the part after the current frame), click **Set End Trim Point**.

Combine clips

Here's how to combine two clips that are next to each other, to form a longer clip:

> On the storyboard (or timeline), click the first clip's icon. While holding down the Ctrl key, click the second clip's icon. Click "**Clip**" (which is at the screen's top) then "**Combine**".

Save the project

To save your work, click the **Save Project button** (which is near the screen's top-left corner and looks like a floppy disk). Invent a name for your project (such as "Christmas 2006 project"); type the name and press Enter.

That makes the computer copy your project to the My Videos folder (which is in the My Documents folder). At the end of your project's name, the computer will secretly put ".MSWMM" (which stands for MicroSoft Windows Movie Maker).

Later, if you want to return to that project, click the **Open Project button** (which is left of the Save Project button and looks like a yellow manila folder being opened by a green arrow) then double-click the project's icon.

Copy to DVD

Here's how to copy your movie to a DVD disk.

Click "**Save to DVD**" (in the task menu).

The computer will spend several minutes making a new .wmv file. For example, if your project was called "Christmas 2006 project.MSWMM", the computer will create a file called "Christmas 2006 project_0001.wmv".

Then the computer will say "Create a DVD". Put a blank DVD+R disk into the DVD drive. (If the computer asks "What do you want Windows to do?" click "Cancel".)

Edit what's in the "DVD Title" and "Video Title" boxes, until you're satisfied. (Later, when you view the DVD disk, the DVD Title will appear at the top of the DVD's menu; the Video Title will be in the DVD's menu.) Keep your titles short: each box holds at most 16 characters. When you finish editing them, press Enter.

The computer will say "Converting files". Wait patiently (even though the screen's green bars stop moving). After several minutes, the computer will say "Burning files to disc," then take several more minutes to copy your movie to the DVD+R disk. Finally, the computer will say "You have successfully created a DVD of your movie" and open the DVD drive's door.

Remove the DVD disk. Close the DVD drive's door. Press Enter.

Close

When you finish using Windows Movie Maker, close it by clicking its X button.

Pinnacle Studio

Here's how to use Pinnacle's **Studio 10 Plus**.

Install the program

Here's how to put the program onto your computer's hard disk (if the program hasn't been put there already)....

The program comes on a pair of DVD disks.

Insert the DVD disk labeled "Pinnacle Studio Plus International Install DVD version 10.6". Press Enter.

Double-click in the First Name box. Press the Delete key (to delete the name that was there previous). Type your first name.

Press the Tab key. Type your last name. Press the Tab key twice. Type your e-mail address (such as poo@gis.net). Press the Tab key twice.

Type the serial number of your copy of the program. (The serial number is on a white sticker on the yellow "Software installation" booklet that came in the software's box. Don't type the dashes: they've been typed for you already.)

Press Enter twice. Click "Next" twice. The computer will show your customer care ID number; scribble it on your white serial number sticker. Click "Close Window" then "I accept the terms of the license agreement". Press Enter thrice. The computer will copy the program from the DVD to your computer's hard disk.

The computer will ask, "Do you want a shortcut to Studio Launcher to be created on your Desktop?" Press Enter three times.

Insert the DVD disk labeled "Pinnacle Studio Bonus NTSC". Press Enter *immediately*. Press Enter again. Click "Next". Press Enter twice. Click "Next". The computer will copy the bonus disk's program to your computer's hard disk.

The computer will say "InstallShield Wizard Complete". Remove the DVD disk from the computer. Press Enter. The computer will restart.

Launch the program

Double-click the Studio Launcher icon. (If you can't find it, click "start" then "All Programs" then "Studio 10" then "Studio Launcher".)

Click "Pinnacle Studio Plus". (If the computer says "Studio 10.7 Patch", click "Go Get It" and follow the instructions about downloading the free upgrade).

Capture the video

Here's how to **capture** a video (copy a video from a DV camcorder's tape to your computer).

Put the tape into the camcorder. Turn the camcorder off. Run a **Firewire cable** (which is also called an **IEEE 1394 cable** and an **i.LINK cable**) from your camcorder to your computer's system unit. Turn the camcorder back on and put it into "play" mode (rather than "record" mode). Rewind the tape (by using the buttons on the camcorder).

If the computer's screen says "Digital Video Device", click "Cancel".

Click "Capture" (which is near the screen's top-left corner). At the screen's bottom-right corner, click either "DV capture" or "MPEG capture".

> DV capture is usually the best choice. It runs the fastest and gives you the highest quality. Unfortunately, it produces a file that's huge and consumes lots of space on your hard disk. The file is 178 megabytes per minute of video. That's about 200 megabytes per minute, 1 gigabyte per 5 minutes, 12 gigabytes per hour.

> MPEG (with its typical DVD-quality setting) produces a file that's a fifth as big. That's about 40 megabytes per minute of video, 1 gigabyte per 25 minutes, 2.4 gigabytes per hour.

Then click the green "Start Capture" button. Type a name for the video (such as "Christmas 2006"). If the Create SmartMovie box is checked, remove the check mark (by clicking it). Press Enter.

Then the computer makes the camcorder play the tape. While the camcorder plays the tape, the computer shows the movie on the computer's screen and also copies it to the My Videos folder (which is in the My Documents folder).

For example, if you named your movie "Christmas 2006" and chose "DV capture", the computer creates a big file called "Christmas 2006.avi". (The ".avi" means "Audio Video Interleaved".) The computer also creates 3 little helper files: "Christmas 2006.avi.index", "Christmas 2006.avi.A.index", and "Christmas 2006.scn".

The computer automatically divides the movie into **scenes**. (To do that, the computer continually looks at the date and time recorded on the tape and notices when the time suddenly skips ahead.)

On part of the computer's screen, you see a photo album that shows you each scene's first frame. Each double-page of the photo album is big enough to hold 18 scenes. (If your movie contains more than 18 scenes, the album includes several double-pages.)

When the tape is done (or you don't want to copy any more of it), click the red "Stop Capture" button. Turn off the camcorder.

View the scenes

To play one of the scenes again (to remind yourself what it was), double-click the scene's icon (which is its first frame). The computer will play that scene for you, in a windowpane at the screen's right edge. That windowpane is called the **player**.

Build the storyboard

The screen's bottom half should be the **storyboard**, which a grid of 30 gray boxes. (If you don't see the 30 gray boxes, make them appear by clicking the "Storyboard view" button, which is 5 tiny boxes near the screen's right edge.)

Drag the scenes to the gray boxes, in the order you want the scenes to appear in your final movie.

> To the first gray box, drag the scene that you want the movie to begin with. To the next box (which is to the right of the first box), drag the scene you want the movie to continue with. Continue that process, for the rest of the movie. (If you've filled all 30 boxes but want your movie to include more than 30 scenes, drag the 31st scene to the right of the 30th box; that makes extra rows of boxes appear.)

If you want to drag *all* the scenes to the storyboard, in the same order as on the tape, use this shortcut procedure instead:

> Click the first scene (so it's highlighted). While holding down the Ctrl key, tap the A key: that makes *all* the scenes be highlighted. Drag the first scene to the storyboard's first box; the other highlighted scenes will automatically be dragged along.

If you want to drag *many* scenes to the storyboard, in the same order as on the tape, use this shortcut procedure instead:

> Click the first scene you want to drag. While holding down the Ctrl key, click the other scenes you want to drag: that makes those scenes be highlighted simultaneously. Drag the first wanted scene to the storyboard's first box; the other highlighted scenes will automatically be dragged along.

On the storyboard, each box represents a dragged scene and is called a **clip**.

View the movie

Here's how to view the whole movie.

In the storyboard, click the first clip (the first box in the storyboard).

At the screen's right edge, you see the player (the windowpane where your movie can play). Click the player's Play button (▶). That makes the player start playing the whole movie for you.

The movie consists of several clips. Each clip consists of **30 frames per second**.

While you're watching the movie, you can click the player's other buttons:

Button	Meaning
▶	**play** at normal speed
‖	**pause**
◄◄	stop and go back to the **movie's beginning**
►►	**fast forward** (play fast, at 2x or 4x or 10x speed, depending on how often you click this button)
◄◄	**reverse** (play backwards, at 2x or 4x or 10x speed, depending on how often you click this button)
▲	go ahead slightly, to the **next frame** (ahead 1/30 of a second)
▼	go back slightly, to the **previous frame** (back 1/30 of a second)
↻	when this clip finishes, **loop back** and repeat this clip

Here's a shortcut: instead of clicking the Play button or Pause button, just tap the keyboard's Space bar.

To skip to a different clip, click that clip's icon (in the storyboard) then the Play button.

The player has two sliders:

> The top slider shows how much of the movie you've seen so far. As the movie plays, that slider gradually slides toward the right. You can drag that slider to hop to a different place in the movie: to go back, drag that slider back toward the left; to skip ahead, drag that slider faster toward the right.
>
> The bottom slider shows the volume of your speakers. Dragging that slider has the same effect as adjusting your speakers' volume dial. To the right of that slider is a mute button: clicking it turns the speakers off; clicking it again turns the speakers back on.

Another way to skip ahead is to rotate the mouse's wheel toward you (if you have a wheel mouse). As you rotate the mouse's wheel, you see different frames from your movie. When you reach the frame that interests you, click the Play button.

Edit the movie

To edit the movie, you can use several techniques.

Delete a clip To delete a clip from the movie, click the clip's icon in the storyboard then press the Delete key.

Undo an edit If you make a mistake while editing, click **Edit** then **Undo**.

Split a clip Here's how to split a clip into two parts, so you can edit each part differently:

> In the storyboard, click the clip's icon then the player's Play button, so the clip starts to play. When you get to the moment when you want the clip to split, click the Pause button (‖). Use the one-frame-at-a-time buttons (▲ and ▼) until you get to the exact frame you want to start the clip's second part. Click the **"Split the clip" button** (which looks like a razor blade and is atop the storyboard).
>
> On the storyboard, you see the clip has split and become two separate clips. Do whatever you wish to each of those two separate clips. For example, if you want to delete one of those clips, click its icon then press the Delete key.

Move a clip If you want to move a clip (which we'll call clip A) so it will play immediately before clip B, drag clip A to clip B. (In other words, point at clip A, then while holding down the mouse's left button, move the mouse pointer to clip B.) The clip will move when you take your finger off the mouse's button.

Add transitions

You can make clips overlap, so your audience sees one clip gradually disappear while the next clip gradually appears, simultaneously. That's called a **transition** between clips. Here's how to create a transition.

Request transitions Click the **"Show transitions" button**, which is normally at the screen's left edge and looks like a lightening bolt separating two brackets. (If you don't see that button, make it appear by clicking, once or twice, the **"Open/close video toolbox" button**, which is at the storyboard's top left corner and looks like a video camera.)

Then you see icons for many transitions.

Choose a category The icons that are most common and free are called **Standard Transitions**. They fall into 7 categories:

Category	Transitions in that category
2D Transitions	74 transitions that are simple (fades, dissolves, slides, pushes, and simple wipes)
Alpha Magic	112 transitions that are fancier wipes
Hollywood FX	16 transitions that make the first clip turn into a fancy shape then fly away
Flying Windows	16 transitions that make the first clip flip then fly away
Extra FX	16 transitions that include other artwork (drawn by Pinnacle's artists)
Family Fun 1	16 transitions that include other artwork (drawn by Pinnacle's artists, with simple meanings kids understand)
Fun Pack	16 transitions that include other artwork (drawn by Pinnacle's artists and including repeated shapes)

In a box, you see a category's name (such as "2D Transitions"). Click that box's down-arrow to see the list of other categories.

Click whichever category you wish to explore. I recommend you start by trying one of those 7 "Standard Transitions" categories (since other categories require you to install the bonus disk or pay for a download from the Internet).

When you've picked a category, you see icons for transitions in that category.

Try a transition To see what a transition does, click its icon. That makes the computer show you what the effect does to photos of a blue A and an orange B. Imagine what the transition would do to your clips!

Use a transition To apply a transition to a pair of your clips, drag the transition's icon to "the space between two clips on the storyboard". If you want to watch the transition, click its icon (on the storyboard) then the Play button (▶).

If you change your mind and want to delete the transition, click the transition's icon (on the storyboard) then press the Delete key.

Extra pages If you view a category (such as "2D Transitions") that has many transitions, you see icons for just the first 32 transitions in that category. To see the rest of the category's transitions, click an arrow that's to the right of the word "Page".

See scenes again Here's how to make the screen's top half show scenes again (instead of transition icons to choose from): click the "Show videos" button (which is above the "Show transitions" button).

Save the project

To save your work, click **File** (at the screen's top-left corner) then **Save Project**. Invent a name for your project (such as "Christmas 2006 project"); type the name and press Enter.

That makes the computer copy your project to the My Videos folder (which is in the My Documents folder). At the end of your project's name, the computer will secretly put ".stx" (which stands for Studio X).

Later, if you want to return to that project, click **File** then **Open Project** then double-click the project's name.

Copy to DVD

Here's how to copy your movie to a DVD disk.

Click "**Make Movie**" (at the screen's top) then the green "**Create disc**" button.

The computer will open the DVD drive's tray. Put a blank DVD+R disk into the tray. Push the tray closed. (If the computer asks "What do you want Windows to do?" click "Cancel".)

Click the green "Create disc" button again. The computer will copy the movie to the DVD disk. When the computer finishes, it will say "Disk creation completed" and open the tray. Take the disk out of the tray. Push the tray closed.

Close

When you finish using Pinnacle Studio Plus, close it by clicking its X button.

Then you'll see a plain Pinnacle Studio window. Close that by clicking its X button.

Congratulations! You've learned the fundamentals of movie making!

Advanced tricks

While making movies, try these advanced tricks.

See the timeline Instead of looking at the storyboard, you can look at the **timeline**, which shows more details about your movie. To see the timeline instead of the storyboard, click the "**Timeline view**" button (which is at the storyboard's top-right corner and looks like a wide box atop a narrower box).

The timeline is a graph. Atop the timeline, a horizontal ruler shows how many hours, minutes, seconds, *and frames* have elapsed since the movie's beginning. (The seconds are separated from the frames by a period. For example, "0:01:20.15" means "0 hours plus 1 minute plus 20 seconds *plus 15 frames*". Each second includes 30 frames, so 15 frames take half a second.)

Below that ruler, you see which clip is playing at each point of time. Each clip is represented by a box. If a clip is lengthy (takes many minutes), the clip's box is wide; if a clip is brief (takes just a few seconds), the clip's box is narrow.

As you play the movie, a vertical line moves rightward across the timeline and shows how far on the timeline the playback has progressed. The timeline is especially useful if you want to skip ahead and watch a clip's ending: while playing the movie, just drag the vertical line to the right, until it's near the clip's end.

The timeline shows 5 **tracks**:

> The top track (Video) shows what video is playing.
> The 2nd track (Audio) shows the sounds recorded by your video camera.
> The 3rd track (Titles) shows titles, subtitles, and other overlaid graphics.
> The 4th track (Sound effects) shows what sound effects & voice-overs you added.
> The bottom track (Music) shows what background music you added.

To make the timeline look wider (so you can see its details better), click the **Ruler Zoom In** button (a magnifying glass containing "+"). To make the timeline look narrower (so the whole movie fits on your screen), click the **Ruler Zoom Out** button (a magnifying glass containing "-").

To return to seeing the storyboard (which is less detailed than the timeline and easier to understand), click the "**Storyboard view**" **button** (which is left of the "Timeline view" button and looks like 5 tiny boxes).

Add a title screen Here's how to put a title at your movie's beginning.

Find the "**Show titles**" **button**, which is at the screen's left edge and looks like a T. (Make sure the T is below a lightning bolt and above a camera. If the T is not that way, make it be that way by clicking, once or twice, the "**Open/close video toolbox**" **button**, which is at the storyboard top-left corner and looks like a video camera.) Click that T.

Then you see examples of many titles. Each title temporarily has a checkerboard background, but in your final movie the title will have a black background instead.

Make sure the box above those titles says "Standard Titles". (If the box says something else instead, click the box's down-arrow then "Standard Titles".)

You can choose from 26 titles in 4 categories:

> **Family**: "It's a boy!", "It's a girl!", "Baby's first steps" (blue or pink), "Congratulations", "Graduation Day", "Happy Anniversary", "Happy Birthday Junior", "Happy Birthday Sis", "Our Summer Vacation", "Our Wedding"
>
> **Holiday**: "Be My Valentine", "Fourth of July", "Happy Easter", "Happy Halloween", "Happy Hanukkah", "Happy Holidays", "Happy New Year", "Merry Christmas"
>
> **Rating**: "The following video is rated C for Cute", "The following video is rated E for Entertaining", "The following video is rated H for Hilarious"
>
> **Sports**: "Rollerblading", "Snowboarding", "The Big Game" (blue or pink)

(You see the first 18 of them; to see the remaining 8, click the right-arrow next to "Page 1 of 2".)

If you click one of those titles, you'll see it bigger, as it will really look in your movie, with a black background. Try clicking several titles, until you decide which one you prefer. If you don't like the words of *any* of the 26 titles, pick a title that has nice colors and fonts; you can edit its words later. When you've decided which title you prefer, drag it to the storyboard, to the left of the first clip. When you've dragged successfully, you see a green vertical line to the left of the first clip; when you take your finger off the mouse's button, the green line turns into the title frame.

If you want to edit the title's words, do this next:

> Double-click the title (on the storyboard). Then edit the title's words by using your keyboard and mouse. When you finish editing the words, click the "OK" button (at the screen's bottom-right corner).

You can add title frames elsewhere (between your movie's frames or at the movie's end) by dragging titles there (then editing them).

To delete such a title, click its frame (on the storyboard) then press the Delete key.

When dragging, make sure you drag *between* your movie's other clips, not "on top of" a clip. (If you drag "on top of" a clip, the title's background won't be black: instead, the title's background will be that video clip. To delete such a title, click the "Timeline view" button then the title's box (on the Titles track) then press the Delete key.

Here's how to make the screen's top half show scenes again (instead of titles to choose from): click the "Show videos" button (which is above the "Show transitions" button).

Combine clips Here's how to combine two clips that are next to each other, to form a longer clip:

> On the storyboard, click the first clip's icon. While holding down the Ctrl key, click the second clip's icon. Right-click the first clip's icon. Click "**Combine clips**".

Desktop publishing

To write and print a document, you can use a word-processing program. To print a fancier document, use a **desktop publishing program** instead.

Professional publishing

The first popular desktop-publishing program was **PageMaker**.

How PageMaker arose

PageMaker was invented in 1985 by Paul Brainerd, who'd been a newspaper executive. PageMaker ran on the Mac and used Apple's laser printer (the Laserwriter).

PageMaker lets you combine words and graphics to form a newspaper page, including headlines, columns of articles, photographs, diagrams, captions, and ads, all on the same page. PageMaker let you see the page on your computer's screen, while you moved the words and graphics by using your mouse.

According to traditional nerd jargon, such a program should have been called a "page-layout", "page-composition", or "computer-aided publishing" program. But to sell the program he coined a new term: he decided to call it a **desktop-publishing program**, because it used the Mac's "desktop" screen to help publishing, and because it let you run your own publishing company from a desktop in your home without having to hire typesetters, graphic artists, and other outside help.

The PageMaker program and the term "desktop publishing" both became instant hits. Many would-be authors, publishers, and designers bought Apple computers just for the purpose of running PageMaker. They used PageMaker to create newspapers, newsletters, reports, books, flyers, posters, and ads.

Most ad agencies standardized on using Apple computers and PageMaker to create ads. That's why Apple computers became popular in the graphics-arts community. Even today, nearly every ad agency uses Apple computers, not IBM-compatibles.

At first, the IBM PC couldn't handle desktop publishing at all. Eventually, Windows (and a competitor called **Gem**) improved enough so that the IBM PC's screen could look Mac-like. Finally, a Windows version of PageMaker became available.

PageMaker's competitors

Competitors to PageMaker arose. Now your main choices are **PageMaker**, **Quark XPress**, and **InDesign**.

Here's how they compare:

> **PageMaker** (for Mac & Windows) is the easiest to learn. It's the best for handling graphics and short ads.
> **Quark XPress** is the best for handling text and fonts. Its Mac version is better than its Windows version.
> **InDesign** (for Mac & Windows) tries to combine the best features of PageMaker and Quark XPress.

Merger

PageMaker was published by Paul Brainerd's company, Aldus. In 1994, Aldus merged into a company called **Adobe**, which had invented many other desktop-publishing tools, such as Postscript (the font system used in Apple's Laserwriter), Illustrator (a draw program), and Photoshop (a photo-manipulation program).

Quark XPress is published by Quark, which is still independent.

Difficulties

Using desktop-publishing software can be difficult. That's why PageMaker is often called "PageWrecker", Quark XPress is called "Quark Distress", and InDesign is called "UnDesign".

Frames

Like a word-processing program, a desktop-publishing program lets you type words onto the screen. But when you start using a desktop-publishing program, the first thing to do is divide your screen (and page) into boxes. Each box is called a **frame**.

In one frame, type a headline. In another frame, put a picture. (You can create the picture by using the draw tools that are included as part of the desktop-publishing program, or else **import** a drawing or painting or photo that you created by using some other graphics program.) In another frame, put a table of contents or an index. In another frame, put an ad. In another frame, put column 1 of an article. In another frame, put column 2.

You can **link** one frame to another. For example, you can link column 1 to column 2, so if you type an article that's too long to fit in column 1, the excess will **spill** into column 2.

You can link a frame on page 1 to a frame on page 7, so if an article's too long to fit on your newspaper's front page, it will continue on page 7. (Continuing on a far-away page is called a **jump**. Newspapers do it frequently. I wish they didn't!)

Master page

If most of the pages in your newspaper resemble each other, create a **master page** that shows how the typical page should look. On that master page, put frames for each column, and at the top of the page put a header that includes the page number and your newspaper's name & date (so when a reader rips out an article, the reader knows where it came from).

Special pages can diverge from the master.

Clutter

The typical beginner makes the mistake of trying to be too fancy. Use just a *few* typestyles and frames per page, to avoid making your publication look like a disorganized cluttered mess.

Put enough frames on your page to add spice; but if you add too many frames, your publication will look chopped-up, dicey, as amateurish as an oil painting by a 2-year-old kid given his first paint box.

> Adding some frames will make it look spicy,
> But too many frames will make it look dicey.
> Gentle control shows a master who knew;
> Out-of-control shows a kid who acts 2.

Mozart's music was masterfully charming because its overall structure was simple, though it had a few subtle surprises. Imitate him.

Cheaper solutions

Unfortunately, professional desktop-publishing programs are expensive: about $500 each!

Kiddie pub

Cheaper, easier desktop-publishing programs have been invented, for kids and novices. The most famous is **Print Shop**, published by Broderbund.

> It's particularly good at creating greeting cards, posters, and banners. The first version was popular among kids using Apple 2 computers because it was amazingly easy to use, though the graphics it produced were low-resolution and crude. (I guess you call that "folk art".)
>
> It's been translated to the Mac, IBM PC, and most other computers, too. The newest versions produce graphics that are better (but still not good enough to pass as professional). Unfortunately, the newer versions are harder to learn.

Print Shop's price has been reduced to $40 because nobody wants it anymore. Instead, folks want **Microsoft Publisher**.

> Like Print Shop, Microsoft Publisher can produce greeting cards, posters, and banners. Better than Print Shop, it can handle high-resolution graphics and tiny fonts well and produce professional-looking newspapers, newsletters, reports, business cards, and origami paper airplanes. It produces a terrific-looking document with fake words, which you replace with your *own* words. It lets you fine-tune your publication's graphics and layouts by using your mouse and professional desktop-publishing techniques.
>
> Bill Gates, who runs Microsoft, liked the design of Microsoft Publisher so much that he took the head of the design team and married her!
>
> Microsoft Publisher is pricey: it lists for $140. But **Microsoft Publisher is included free as part of Microsoft Office Professional.**

Word processing

Recently, word-processing programs have grown to include lots of desktop-publishing features.

The first word-processing program that let you create frames was **Ami Pro**. Other word-processing programs have copied Ami Pro's idea of permitting frames, so now you can create frames in WordPro (which is Ami Pro's successor), Microsoft Word, and WordPerfect.

If what you're writing has a simple layout, with very few frames or graphics per page, you can use a word-processing program instead of a desktop-publishing program.

How I published this book

I wrote this edition of *The Secret Guide to Computers* by using just Microsoft Word. I got by with Microsoft Word instead of a desktop-publishing program because I kept my layout simple, with very few frames and graphics per page.

Fonts For most of this book, I used just 8 fonts:

> This font is called "Times New Roman". It's from Microsoft. I used it for most of my writing. It's therefore called my "body-text font". I used the 10-point size for most of the text, 8½-point for small text (which I put in boxed paragraphs, like this). Unlike other Times Roman fonts, Microsoft's has the nice property: when working in small font sizes (such as 8½-point), each digit is as wide as two blank spaces, and each period takes up as much space as one blank space. That makes it easy to keep the columns lined up! (Microsoft wants you to line up columns by using fancy features such as "tables" and "decimal tabs", but pressing the space bar is simpler.)
>
> *This is "Times New Roman Italic". It's elegant but hard to read, so I use it rarely, just for emphasis, such as to emphasize the word "not".*
>
> This is "Tahoma", from Microsoft, used in Windows XP menus. It resembles Helvetica or Arial but is clearer: for example, it makes the capital "I" look different from a small "L".
>
> **This is "Tahoma Bold". I used it for column headings (at the top of tables) and for words being defined. To make defined words less overwhelming, I made them 1 point smaller than the surrounding text: I made them 9-point Tahoma Bold when surrounded by 10-point Times New Roman; I made them 7½-point Tahoma Bold when surrounded by 8½-point Times New Roman.**
>
> `This is "Lucida Console". It's monospaced, used in the Windows XP "Notepad" program.`
>
> *This is "Andy Italic" widened (scaled to 125% of original width) and with a gray background. It's lively! I used this combo (Andy Italic 125% grayed) at the top of each sub-subchapter. Andy Italic is not from Microsoft: I got it from a CD-ROM disk that contains 2500 fonts I bought that disk for just $18 at Sam's Club. The disk is published by Summitsoft (www.summitsoft.com).*
>
> *This is "Comic Sans MS Italic" with a gray background. It's supposed to look funny, like a comic book, so it makes the reader feel cheery. It's easy to read and from Microsoft. I used it in big type (20-point and boxed) at the top of each subchapter.*
>
> *This is "Flaemische Kanzleischrift" with a gray background. It's an elegant script, the kind of thing you'd put on a wedding invitation or the label of a fine wine or fine piano. Unfortunately, some of its letters are very hard to read, and some bugs make it hard to use. I used it in huge type (33½-point and boxed) at the top of each chapter, to encourage you to think this is a fine book! I got it from Summitsoft's 2500-font disk.*

So here's a summary of what I did. Typical text (like you're reading now) is Times New Roman 10-point (with 11-point line spacing, so there's a 1-point gap between lines).

> Typical small text (like you're reading now) is Times New Roman 8½-point (with 9½-point line spacing), boxed. Emphasized words (*like this*) are Times New Roman Italic. Windows menus (like this) are Tahoma. Column headings (**like this**) are Tahoma Bold. Defined words (**like this**) are Tahoma Bold, 1 point smaller. Monospaced computer output (`like this`) is Lucida Console.

Bigger headings have a gray background: they're Andy Italic 125% (*like this*), Comic Sans MS Italic (*like this*), or Flaemische Kanzleischrift (*like this*).

Dimensions To squeeze as much info as possible onto each page without clutter, I set my left and right margins at .5", top margin at .3", bottom margin at .6" (to leave space for the footer), and distance between columns at .3".

> The typical page contains 2 columns, each 3.6" wide. When I needed a wider column (to hold a wide table or graphic), I widened the column to 4.8" instead, so the page's other column shrunk to 2.4". On a few pages, I used 3 narrow columns, each 2.3".

Microsoft Publisher 2010

Fancy editions of Microsoft Office include a desktop-publishing program called **Microsoft Publisher**.

This chapter explains how to use the newest version, **Microsoft Publisher 2010**. It's part of **Microsoft Office 2010**'s Professional Edition (but not Home & Student Edition or Home & Business Edition).

If you're using Microsoft Publisher 2003 or 2007, read the next chapter instead. If you want info about Microsoft Publisher 2002, get an earlier edition of *The Secret Guide to Computers* (the 28th edition, 29th edition, or 30th edition) by phoning 603-666-6644.

Prepare yourself

Before using Microsoft Publisher 2010, practice using Microsoft Word 2010, which I explained on pages 181-198. Make sure Microsoft Word works fine before you try using Microsoft Publisher.

Launch Microsoft Publisher

To start using Microsoft Publisher, click Start then "All Programs" then "Microsoft Office" then "Microsoft Publisher 2010".

The screen's top says "Microsoft Publisher" and shows this **tab bar**:

File	Home	Insert	Page Design	Mailings	Review	View

Under the heading "Most Popular", you see 7 popular **publication categories**:

brochures, business cards, calendars, greeting cards, labels, newsletters, postcards

Under the heading "More Templates", you see 20 other publication categories:

advertisements, award certificates, banners, business forms, catalogs. e-mail, envelopes, flyers, gift certificates, import Word documents, invitation cards, letterhead, menus, paper folding projects, programs, quick publications, resumes, signs, with compliments cards, more categories

Near the screen's top, you see 4 other choices:

blank 8.5×11", blank 11×8.5", more blank page sizes, my templates

Quick publications

The most powerful publication category is "quick publications" (which is under the heading "More Templates"). Try clicking "quick publications" now! Here's what happens….

Templates Under the heading "Installed Templates", you see 10 popular **templates**:

arrows, bounce, brocade, color bad, marker, modular, perforation, photoscope, simple divider, tabs

Under the heading "More Installed Templates", you see 66 more templates (if you scroll down):

accent box, accessory bar, arcs, argyle, astro, axis, bars, birthday, blank, blends, blocks, border flowers, borders, bouquet, bubbles, butterfly, capsules, cascade, checkers, circles, confetti, corner art, crossed lines, diamonds, echo, eclipse, edge, floating oval, handprint, hearts and circles, jumbled boxes, jungle, layers, leaves, level, linear accent, marquee, maze, mobile, network, pansies, party time, pinwheel, pixel, profile, punctuation, quadrant, radial, refined, retro, ribbons, romance, scallops, signpost, soap bubbles, starfish, steps, straight edge stripes, studio, tilt, triangles, wallpaper, watermark, waves, wavy frame

Under the headings "Blank Sizes" and "Manufacturers", you see other choices.

You can click whichever template you want; but for your first experience, choose "accent box" (which is under the heading "More Installed Templates").

Defaults At the screen's right edge, you see the phrase "Color scheme". The box below it normally says:

(default template colors)

If it says something else, make it normal by doing this:

Click in the box. Press the Home key then the Enter key.

At the screen's right edge, you see the phrase "Font scheme". The box below it normally says:

(default template fonts)

If it says something else, make it normal by doing this:

Click in the box. Press the Home key then the Enter key.

Layout The computer assumes you want your publication to contain three **objects**:

| a **picture** (such as a photo or drawing) |
| a **heading** (a few words in big letters) |
| a **message** (a few sentences in small letters) |

The computer assumes you want to display the picture on top, then the heading, then the message (since the viewer's eye will naturally be attracted to the picture first, then the heading, then the message); but you can change that layout. For example, you can omit the picture, omit the heading, omit the message, make the picture smaller, move the picture to below the heading, twist the heading 90° (so it becomes a **sidebar heading**), or insert a fourth object: info about your business!

Near the screen's right edge, you see the word "Layout". Click the down-arrow below it. You start seeing 15 layouts to choose from; use the scroll arrows to see all 15.

Here are the 15 **layouts**:

Blank
Large picture at the top
Large picture in the middle
Small picture at the top
Small picture in the middle
Sidebar heading, picture at the top
Sidebar heading, picture at the bottom
Sidebar heading, no picture
No message, picture at the top
No message, picture at the bottom
No picture
No heading
Message only
Heading only
Business information with picture

The computer assumes you want the second layout, "Large picture at the top". To try a different layout instead, click one that interests you and look at its effect.

After you've experimented by clicking several layouts, make up your mind which one to use. For your first publication, I recommend you stay with "Large picture at the top".

Click the layout you choose.

Create Click the Create button (which is at the screen's bottom-right corner).

Heading You see your publication. In it, click the word "Heading", then type whatever words you want the heading to be.

If you type *many* words, the computer will automatically switch them all to a smaller font, so the words will still fit in the space allotted. If you type a word that's not in the computer's dictionary (because the word is weird or you misspelled it), the computer will put a red squiggle under it.

Message Under the heading, you see a sentence saying "Place your message here". Click in that sentence, then type the message you want to be under the heading. (If your message contains *many* words, the computer will automatically switch them all to a smaller font, so the words will still fit in the space allotted.)

While typing, you can use do formatting as if you were using Microsoft Word. For example, you can click the **B** button for boldface, the *I* button for italics, and the U button for underlining.

If your message contains *many* words — a whole paragraph! — you should make the paragraph be justified, by clicking the Justify button (which acts like Microsoft Word's).

If you want your message to contain *several* paragraph, press the Enter key once or twice at the end of each paragraph (except the bottom paragraph).

If your message becomes too tiny to read on the screen, press the F9 key. That makes the type look bigger on the screen, so you can read the type easily, but then the type is too big to fit the whole page on the screen. If you want to switch back to the "whole page" view, press F9 again. F9 is a **toggle** that switches back and forth between "Easy to read" and "See the whole page at once" views.

Picture Above the heading, you see a blank space. To put a picture in that space, double-click in the middle of that space.

You see the **Insert Picture window**, which shows whatever pictures are in your hard disk's Pictures folder. (That folder includes what you drew by using the Windows Paint program and whatever photos you put there from your digital camera.)

If you want to use one of those pictures, double-click it.

If you prefer to use a picture supplied by Microsoft, do this instead.... Click "Cancel". Make sure your computer is connected to the Internet. Click the Insert tab (which is near the screen's top-left corner) then "Clip Art". Double-click in the "Search for" box (which is near the screen's right edge). Type whatever topic you want a picture of (such as "girl" or "egg" or "France") and press Enter. You'll see several pictures (drawings or photos) about your topic; to see more, use the scroll arrow. Click the picture you want.

Then adjust the picture's size by doing this:

Click the Format tab (which is at the screen's top) then "Fit" (which is near the screen's top-right corner and near the word "Crop"). The picture will shrink to fit in the space.

Make the screen return to normal by doing this:

Close the Clip Art pane (which is at the screen's right edge) by clicking its X. Click the Home tab (which is near the screen's top-left corner).

Undo If you make a mistake, click the **Undo button** (which is near the screen's top-left corner and shows an arrow curving toward the left). If that doesn't completely undo your mistake, try clicking that button several more times.

Save To copy your publication to your hard disk, click the **Save button** (which is near the screen's top-left corner and looks like a 3½-inch floppy disk).

If you haven't saved your publication before, the computer will say "File name". Invent a name for your publication. Type the name and press Enter.

That makes the computer copy your publication onto the hard disk. For example, if you named the publication "mary", the computer puts a document called mary.pub into the Documents folder. (Windows 7 puts it into the Documents library's "My Documents" folder instead.)

While you're editing and improving your publication, you should click the Save button frequently.

File When you finish editing your publication, click the File tab (which is at the screen's left edge, near the top). Then you see the **File menu**, which looks the same as Microsoft Word's:

Save
Save As
Open
Close
Info
Recent
New
Print
Save & Send
Help
Options
Exit

From that menu, choose whatever you wish (by clicking it). Here are the most popular choices....

To print your publication onto paper, choose **Print** from the File menu. The computer assumes you want to print just 1 copy of the publication; if you want to print *several* copies, click in the "Copies" box then type how many copies you want. Click the Print button. The computer will print the publication onto paper.

To switch to a different publication, choose **Close** from the File menu then say "new publication" or "old publication". If you say "new publication" (by choosing **New** from the File menu), you can start the process of creating a new publication. If you say "old publication" instead (by choosing **Recent** or **Open** from the File menu), you see a list of publications that are already on your hard disk: click any of the publications in the Recent list (or double-click any of the publications in the Open list).
Whenever you want to stop using Microsoft Publisher, choose **Exit** from the File menu (or click the Microsoft Publisher window's X button).
If you choose Close or Exit but didn't save the publication you were working on, the computer asks "Do you want to save?" If you click the Save button, the computer copies your publication's most recent version to the hard disk; if you click the Don't Save button instead, the computer ignores and forgets your most recent editing.

Congratulations! You've learned all the important techniques of Microsoft Publisher! You can create your own publications!

Now let's dig deeper....

Page design While you're editing your publication, click the Page Design tab.

Above the word "Schemes", you see 21 **color schemes** (if your computer has a typical wide screen). To the right of them, you see an up-arrow, a down-arrow, and a "down-arrow that has a line over it". If you click the "down-arrow that has a line over it", you see all 92 color schemes. For the "accent box" template, the computer normally uses the waterfall color scheme; to use a different color scheme, click your favorite.

Normally, your design's background is white (which is called "no background"). To change that, click "**Background**" (which is near the screen's top-right corner). You see 22 choices:

no background
10% tint (of Accent 1, Accent 2, Accent 3, or Main)
30% tint (of Accent 1, Accent 2, Accent 3, or Main)
50% tint (of Accent 1, Accent 2, Accent 3, or Main)
horizontal gradient (of Accent 1, Accent 2, Accent 3, or Main)
vertical gradient (of Accent 1, Accent 2, Accent 3, or Main)
more backgrounds

Click your favorite.

When using the "accent box" template, the computer normally makes the heading and message both use a font called "Gill Sans". To change that, click "**Fonts**" (which is near the screen's top-right corner). You start seeing these 24 new font schemes —

Scheme	Heading font	Message font
Apex	Lucida Sans	Book Antiqua
Aspect	Verdana	Verdana
Calligraphy	Gabriola	Gabriola
Civic	Georgia	Georgia
Concourse	Candara	Candara
Equity	Franklin Gothic Book	Perpetua
Flow	Calibri	Constantia
Median	Twentieth Century	Twentieth Century
Metro	Consolas	Corbel
Module	Corbel	Corbel
Office 1	Cambria	Calibri
Office 2	Calibri	Cambria
Office 3	Calibri	Calibri
Office Classic 1	Times New Roman	Arial
Office Classic 2	Arial	Arial
Opulent	Trebuchet	Trebuchet
Oriel	Century Schoolbook	Century Schoolbook
Origin	Bookman Old Style	Gill Sans
Paper	Constantia	Constantia
Solstice	Gill Sans	Gill Sans
Technic	Franklin Gothic Book	Arial
Trek	Franklin Gothic Medium	Franklin Gothic Book
Urban	Trebuchet	Georgia
Verve	Century Gothic	Century Gothic

and these 31 classic font schemes —

Scheme	Heading font	Message font
Archival	Georgia Bold	Georgia
Basis	Arial Bold	Arial
Binary	Verdana	Georgia
Breve	Bodoni Black	Franklin Gothic Book
Capital	Perpetua Titling	Perpetua
Casual	Comic Sans Bold	Comic Sans
Data	Courier New Bold	Arial
Deckle	Papyrus	Gill Sans
Dictation	Lucida Sans Typewriter	Lucida Sans
Economy	Franklin Gothic Demi Condensed	Times New Roman Bold
Etched	Copperplate Gothic Bold	Garamond
Facet	Gill Sans	Gill Sans
Foundation	Times New Roman	Arial Bold
Foundry	Rockwell Extra Bold	Rockwell
Fusion	French Script	Calisto
Galley	Arial Rounded Bold	Times New Roman
Impact	Impact	Georgia
Industrial	Franklin Gothic Heavy	Franklin Gothic Book
Literary	Bookman Old Style	Arial Rounded Bold
Modern	Twentieth Century Bold	Garamond
Monogram	Edwardian Script	Twentieth Century
Offset	Imprint Shadow	Franklin Gothic Book
Online	Verdana Bold	Verdana
Optical	OCR A Extended	Franklin Gothic Book
Perspective	Goudy Old Style	Franklin Gothic Heavy
Punch	Gill Sans Ultra Bold	Comic Sans
Streamline	Bodoni Condensed	Twentieth Century Bold
Textbook	Century Schoolbook	Arial Bold
Verbatim	Agency Bold	Agency
Versatile	Times New Roman Bold	Times New Roman
Virtual	Trebuchet Bold	Trebuchet

and a font scheme called "Template: Quick Publication" (whose headline and message fonts depend on which template you chose).

Those font schemes are too many to fit on the screen. To see them all, use the scroll arrows.

At first, the computer assumes you want "Template: Quick Publication", but you can click whichever font scheme interests you and look at its effect. If you don't like that effect, try clicking a different font scheme instead. Keep clicking until you find a font scheme whose effect makes you happy.

When you finish using the Page Design tab, click the Home tab, to make your screen return to normal.

Alignment The heading and message both contain words. The computer assumes you want each line of words to be centered. Centering is fine if your heading and message are both short. But if your message contains *many* lines of words, centering makes your message hard to read.

To change whether a paragraph is centered, click in the paragraph then click one of these **alignment buttons** (which are above the word "Paragraph" and are the same as Microsoft Word's alignment buttons):

The **Align Left button** makes the paragraph's **left margin** be straight, the right margin be ragged, so the paragraph looks like this. This is the easiest to read and the friendliest, since it looks informal. But it looks lopsided.

The **Align Right button** makes the paragraph's **right margin** be straight, the left margin be ragged, so the paragraph looks like this. This is the hardest to read. It's the least popular choice.

The **Justify button** makes the paragraph's **left and right margins** both be straight (except for the end of the paragraph's last line), so the paragraph looks like this. This is the most sophisticated. It's fairly easy to read, though it puts too much space between the words. It's the best choice for a long message. It's what I used for most paragraphs in this book.

The **Center button** makes each line in the paragraph be **centered** again, so the paragraph looks like this. This looks the neatest. It's good for short headlines and messages, but it's hard to read if the message is long. It's what I used for the headlines in this book.

Frames Your publication contains three main objects: the picture, the heading, and the message. It also contains several other objects (border decorations near the paper's edge).

You can change each object's size and position. Here's how....

Click in the object's middle. Then the entire object will be surrounded by a pack of white dogs! Each dog is a little white circle (or square), called a **handle**.

The dogs (little white circles & squares) are arranged to form a box surrounding the object, so the object is boxed in. The box surrounding the object is called the object's **frame**. Yeah, Louie, we've been framed!

Then you can manipulate the object in 4 ways:

To make the object bigger or smaller without distorting it, drag one of the white circles (by using the mouse).

To distort the object by stretching or shrinking, drag one of the white squares.

To move the object, drag an edge of its frame (but don't drag a handle).

To rotate (tilt) the object, drag the green circle (which is nearby).

Signs

Instead of clicking "quick publications", try clicking "signs". That lets you create signs.

Templates Under the heading "Installed Templates", you see 40 **templates** written by Microsoft (if you scroll down):

> authorized only, beware of dog, business hours, checks accepted
> closed, closed for remodeling, for rent, for rent #2, for rent #3
> for sale, for sale #2, for sale #3, for sale #4
> garage sale, garage sale #2, garage sale #3, garage sale #4
> gone fishing, help wanted, information, inventory
> keep off the grass, keep out, kid's room, lemonade for sale
> no loitering, no parking, no smoking, open, open house, out of order
> private property, restrooms, return time, special offer, turn off the lights
> we speak, wet paint, wet paint #2, wheelchair access

Under the heading "Office.com Templates", you see a list of 10 popular templates (contributed by outsiders and Microsoft) that you can download from the Internet. If you click "More Office.com Templates", you see even more templates you can download. Under the headings "Blank Sizes" and "Manufacturers", you see other choices.

Click whichever template you want — but for your first experience, choose "kid's room" (which is under the heading "Installed Templates").

Defaults At the screen's right edge, you see the "Color scheme" and "Font scheme" boxes. If one of those boxes doesn't contain the word "default" yet, fix it by doing this:

> Click in the box. Press the Home key then the Enter key.

Create Click the Create button (which is at the screen's bottom-right corner).

Edit the words You see your publication. It's a sign that says "Kid's Room" and includes a drawing of a moon with stars.

Change the word "Kid's" to your own name. For example, if your name is "Joan", change "Kid's Room" to "Joan's Room". Here's how: click "Kid's", then type your name, then type 's.

Change "Room" to a word that's more descriptive, such as one of these:

> Bedroom, Hideaway, Lair, Hovel
> Office, Headquarters, Classroom
> Home, Castle, Garden, Pond, Swimming Hole, Woods
> Closet, Locker, Trunk, Corner, Secret Passage, Private Parts

To do that, click "Room" then type whatever replacement you want.

Finish To finish your editing, you can try using the same techniques as for "Quick publications", so reread these sections:

> Undo
> Save
> File
> Page design
> Alignment
> Frames

You'll encounter these little surprises:

> Since this sign starts as black & white, just 5 of the 92 color schemes work well: click "black & gray", "brown", "dark blue", "green", or "red". If your printer can't print colors, choose "black & gray".
>
> Since this sign has no message (just headings), it ignores the message font.

Banners

A **banner** is a big sign that nearly a foot tall and *several* feet wide. You can create a banner by taping several sheets of paper together, side-by-side.

To create banners, click "banners" instead of "quick publications".

Templates You start seeing these 39 banner templates, organized into 8 categories:

> **Congratulations:** baby congratulations, champions, congratulations, graduation, promotion, retirement, the greatest, to the best
>
> **Event:** anniversary, birthday, bon voyage, enter to win, grand opening, open house, pageant, school dance, street fair, team spirit
>
> **Get Well:** get well
>
> **Holiday:** New Year
>
> **Informational:** apartment for rent, caution, checked-frame, information, interwoven-frame, new management, order here, plain-background, registration, reservations, safety equipment
>
> **Romance:** marry me
>
> **Sale:** bake sale, clearance sale, sale, yard sale
>
> **Welcome:** welcome, welcome back, welcome new addition

(To see the last few templates in the Event category, click "All Event". To see the last few templates in the Informational category, click "All Informational". To stop seeing those last few templates, click the **Back button**, which is the left-arrow to the left of the house.)

Click whichever template you want. The screen's top-right corner shows it enlarged.

Defaults At the screen's right edge, you see the "Color scheme" and "Font scheme" boxes. If one of those boxes doesn't contain the word "default" yet, fix it by doing this:

> Click in the box. Press the Home key then the Enter key.

Options The computer assumes you want the banner to be 5 feet wide and 8½ inches tall. If you want the banner to be bigger than that (so it will use even more paper and your Mom will yell at you for wasting paper), at the screen's right edge click the "**Page size**" box then the size you want.

The computer assumes you want a border around the message. (The border is a fancy box.) If you don't want a border, click the **Border** box then "No border".

The computer assumes you want a little graphic (a picture) on both sides of the banner's message (words). If you want the graphic placed differently, click the **Graphic** box then one of these choices: put the graphic just to the **left** of the message, just to the **right** of the message, on **both** sides of the message, or nowhere so you have **none**.

Create Click the Create button (which is at the screen's bottom-right corner).

Edit the words To change the message's words, click the message then type what you want instead.

Finish To finish your editing, you can try using the same techniques as for "Quick publications", so reread these sections"

> Undo
> Save
> File
> Page design
> Alignment
> Frames

You'll encounter these little surprises:

> Since most of the banner starts as black & white, just 5 of the 92 color schemes work well: click "black & gray", "brown", "dark blue", "green", or "red". If your printer can't print colors, choose "black & gray". The color scheme will affect the message's color; but the border will stay black, and the graphic's color will stay unchanged.
>
> **The typical banner template uses the font scheme's message font** and ignores the scheme's headline font, but *some* banner templates do the opposite: they use the font scheme's headline font and ignore the scheme's message font.
>
> The banner prints onto several sheets of paper, which you must tape together, after using a scissors to cut off the margins. Examine the banner carefully before you hang it on your wall: a few letters or graphics might be missing, because your printer doesn't contain enough RAM memory chips or your printer can't print close enough to the paper's edge.

Greeting cards

To create a greeting card, click "greeting cards" instead of "quick publications".

Templates You start seeing 349 greeting-card templates, organized into 4 categories:

Category	How many templates
Birthday	78
Holidays	100 (25 Christmas, 6 Easter, 3 Halloween, 2 Kwanzaa, 3 New Year, 4 Ramadan, 1 Rosh Hashanah, 2 St. Patrick's Day, 3 Thanksgiving, 8 Mother's Day, 7 Father's Day, 18 Valentine's Day, 1 Bar Mitzvah, 1 Bat Mitzvah, 4 Grandparents Day, 12 general)
Occasions and events	104 (9 anniversary, 1 bon voyage, 4 graduation, 8 congratulate new baby, 2 new home, 1 promotion, 1 retirement, 3 wedding, 3 general congratulations, 12 friendship, 8 romance, 2 I'm sorry, 13 get well, 6 sympathy, 3 good luck, 2 miss you, 5 we've moved, 3 engagement, 6 birth announcement, 1 reminder, 2 gift, 4 inspirational-quote, 1 love, 4 kid birthday)
Thank you	67

In each category, you see the first few templates, plus a folder called "All". If you click the "All" folder, you see all the templates for that category. (To go back to the previous screen, click the **Back button**, which is the left-arrow to the left of the house.)

Click whichever template you want. The screen's top-right corner shows it enlarged.

Download/Create If the template must be downloaded from the Internet, the screen's bottom-right corner shows a Download button; otherwise, it shows a Create button. Click the Download or Create button.

View 4 pages Your card has 4 pages. You're seeing the front cover, which is page 1.

At the screen's left edge, you see the numbers 1, 2, 3, and 4. To see page 2, click the 2. That makes you see page 2 (and you'll simultaneously see page 3, next to it). To see page 4 (which is the back cover), click the 4. To see page 1 again, click the 1.

Edit the words To edit text, click it then type what you want instead.

Finish To finish your editing, you can try using the same techniques as for "Quick publications", so reread these sections"

> Undo
> Save
> File
> Page design
> Alignment
> Frames

Printer settings To print onto paper, choose "Print" from the File menu but then check two settings before you click the Print button....

First, make sure you see the word "Letter" (which means the paper is the typical American size for a letter, 8½"×11"). If you see "A4" instead, you downloaded a European template that requires bigger paper; to fix the problem, choose one of these methods:

> **Method 1** Choose an American template instead.
>
> **Method 2** Buy bigger paper (such as A4 or legal) then click A4 then the size you bought.
>
> **Method 3** Click the Page Design tab then "Size" then "1/4 Letter Side Fold" then the File tab again then Print again then A4 then Letter.

Make sure you see "Side-fold, quarter sheet." (If you see otherwise, such as "One page per sheet", click it then click "Side-fold, quarter sheet." That makes all four pages of the greeting card appear on a single sheet of paper. After printing, fold that sheet of paper in half (to divide pages 1&4 from pages 2&3), then fold in half again (to divide page 1 from 4).

Other publication types

You've learned how to use 4 publication types: "quick publications", "signs", "banners", and "greeting cards". You can use other publication types, too!

The computer gives you 27 normal publication types:

> brochures, business cards, calendars, greeting cards, labels, newsletters, postcards
>
> advertisements, award certificates, banners, business forms, catalogs. e-mail, envelopes, flyers, gift certificates, import Word documents, invitation cards, letterhead, menus, paper folding projects, programs, quick publications, resumes, signs, with compliments cards, more categories

Try those publication types. They resemble the types you already mastered.

Blank publications

Instead of clicking one of those normal publication types, try clicking **Blank 8.5×11"**.

You see a picture of a blank, clean sheet of paper, on which you can create any publication you wish, without locking yourself into one of the traditional types. Be creative! Here's how....

Typing with F9

Start typing on the blank page. Your typing will be too small to read: to see it bigger, press the F9 key.

That makes the type look bigger, but too big to fit the whole page on the screen. If you want to switch back to the "whole page" view, press F9 again. F9 is a **toggle** that switches back and forth between "easy to read" and "whole page" views.

Similar to word processing

While you're typing, Microsoft Publisher resembles Microsoft Word. After you've practiced using Microsoft Word, Microsoft Publisher is easy! Here are the main differences:

> The Page Up and Page Down keys don't move the cursor. Ctrl symbols don't work. Microsoft Publisher can't check your grammar, so there are no green squiggles.
>
> Microsoft Publisher expects your entire message to fit on one page (unless you use special tricks I explain later), so you can't give a simple page break.
>
> When you start typing, the Font Size is 10-point (not 11-point). The Font Size menu starts at 4 points (instead of 8 points).
>
> If you click in the Font Size box and type a point size, you can put any digit after the decimal point. For example, you can type "12.4" to get 12.4 points. (The digit after the decimal point doesn't have to be 5.)

Frames

The text you've been typing is in a box, called a **frame**. The frame has 9 **handles** (1 white circle at each corner, 1 white square at the midpoint of each side, and a green circle nearby).

Try this experiment: make sure you're seeing the whole page (by pressing F9 if necessary), then make the frame smaller (by dragging one of the white handles toward the frame's center). Now the frame is small, so it does *not* consume the whole page, so you can create extra frames elsewhere on the page.

The frame that's already on the page is called a **text frame**, because it contains text you typed. Here's how to make an extra text frame:

> Click the Insert tab then "Draw Text Box". Decide where on the page you want the extra text frame to begin; put the mouse pointer there; that will be the frame's top-left corner; drag to where you want the frame's bottom-right corner. The frame will appear.
>
> In that frame, type whatever text you wish. To see your typing more easily, press F9.

You can change a frame's position:

> To change a frame's size, click inside it then drag one of its white handles.
> To rotate a frame, click inside it, then drag its green handle.
> To move a frame, drag one of its edges (but not a handle).

You can make 5 kinds of frames. To make a frame containing normal **text**, you've learned to do this:

> Click the Insert tab then "Draw Text Box". Drag across the page, to form the frame. Type the text (and press F9 to see it better).

To make a frame containing a **picture** that's in your hard disk's Pictures library, do this:

> Click the Insert tab then "Picture". You see what's in your Pictures library; double-click the picture you want. Drag the picture where you want it. Adjust its size by dragging its white-circle handles.

To make a frame containing **clip art** from Microsoft's Website (Office.com), do this:

> Make sure your computer is connected to the Internet. Click the Insert tab then "Clip Art". Double click in the "Search for" box (which is near the screen's right edge). Type whatever topic you want a picture of (such as "girl" or "egg" or "France") and press Enter. You'll see several pictures (drawings or photos) about your topic; to see more, use the scroll arrow. Click the picture you want. Drag the picture where you want it. Adjust its size by dragging its white-circle handles.

To make a frame containing **word art** (which is artistic text), do this:

> Click the Insert tab then "Word Art". You see 30 ways to make text look artistic (by bending it or creatively coloring it). Click your favorite. Type the text you want to beautify; make it brief (just a few words); if you want *several* lines, press Enter at the end of each line. When you finish your typing, click OK. Drag the artistic text where you want it. Adjust its size by dragging its white-circle handles. Distort its size by dragging its white-square handles. If you want to change the amount of slanting or curvature, drag the yellow-diamond handle (which is nearby).

To make a frame containing a **table** (of numbers or words), do this:

> Click the Insert tab then "Table", which works like Microsoft Word's Table button. You see 80 little boxes (called **cells**), arranged to form a table having 8 rows and 10 columns. How many rows and columns to you want in *your* table? Point at the first cell and drag down and to the right, until your desired number of rows and columns turns orange. When you take your finger off the mouse's button, you'll see the table you requested. To move the table, put the mouse pointer on the table's edge so that the mouse pointer turns into a 4-headed arrow; then drag. To change the size of a column or row, put the mouse pointer on the edge of that column or row so that the mouse pointer turns into a 2-headed arrow; then drag. In that table, type whatever numbers or words you wish; press F9 to see better; press Tab to move to the next cell.

To delete a frame, right-click in its middle then click "Delete Object".

If you type text that's too long to fit in its frame, the frame's white handles turn red. The last few words you typed are temporarily invisible: the computer stores them in an **overflow area** (which you can't see) until you make the frame bigger (by dragging its handles) or make the text shorter — or make a 2nd frame, to display the overflow. To make that 2nd frame, use one of these methods:

> **Method 1** Click in the frame that's too small. Click the "Text Box Tools Format" tab then "Create Link". Your mouse pointer becomes a pouring cup. Use it to click where you want the 2nd frame's top-left corner. You'll see the 2nd frame. Adjust its size (by dragging its handles).

> **Method 2** Click the Insert tab then "Draw Text Box". Drag across the page, to form the 2nd frame. Click in the first frame then "Create Link". Your mouse pointer becomes a pouring cup. Use it to click in the 2nd frame.

Here's a way to force text to fit in its frame. Click in its frame then click the "Text Box Tools Format" tab then "Text Fit". You see a menu of 4 choices:

Menu choice	What the computer will do
Best Fit	decrease or increase the font size, so the text exactly fills the frame
Shrink Text On Overflow	if the text is too big to fit the frame, decrease the font size
Grow Text Box to Fit	if the text is too big to fit the frame, make the frame taller
Do Not Autofit	nothing (so if the text is too big to fit the frame, the frame shows just the text's beginning)

Extra pages

So far, your publication contains just one page. To make your publication longer by adding a second page, do this: while holding down the Ctrl and Shift keys, tap the N key (which means "New page").

Now your publication has two pages. You're seeing page 2. To see page 1, click the "1" at the screen's left edge. To see page 2 again, click the "2" at the screen's left edge. Press F9 to toggle between "full page" view and "easy to read" view.

Microsoft Publisher 2003 & 2007

The previous chapter explained Microsoft Publisher 2010. This chapter explains Microsoft Publisher 2003 & 2007.

Prepare yourself

Before using Microsoft Publisher, practice using Microsoft Word, which I explained on pages 181-214. Make sure Microsoft Word works fine before you try using Microsoft Publisher.

To use Microsoft Publisher easily, your monitor should be 17-inch (or bigger). Otherwise, the monitor is too small to show your publication well. Set the monitor's resolution at 1024-by-768 (or bigger), as follows:

> Close any windows that are open, so you see just the Windows desktop screen. Right-click in the screen's middle, where there is nothing. For version 2007, click "Personalize" then "Display Settings"; for versions 2003, click "Properties" then "Settings". Drag the slider toward the right, until it says at least "1024 by 768 pixels", then press Enter.
> In version 2007, after you approve the screen, close all windows.

Launch Microsoft Publisher

Here's how to start using Microsoft Publisher:

> **Version 2003**: click "start" then "All Programs" then "Microsoft Office" then "Microsoft Office Publisher 2003" then "Publications for Print" (which is at the screen's left edge).
>
> **Version 2007**: click Start then "All Programs" then "Microsoft Office" then "Microsoft Office Publisher 2007".

For version 2003, do the unmask procedure:

> Click "View" then "Toolbars" then "Customize" then "Options". Put check marks in the first two boxes ("Show Standard and Formatting toolbars on two rows" and "Always show full menus") by clicking. Press Enter.

The left window shows a list of **publication types**.
In **version 2003**, the main list gives you 25 choices —

> quick publications, advertisements, award certificates, banners, brochures, business cards, business forms, calendars, catalogs, envelopes, flyers, gift certificates, greeting cards, import Word documents, invitation cards, labels, letterheads, menus, newsletters, paper-folding projects, postcards, programs, resumes, signs, with-compliments cards

and you also get 3 extra lists:

> "Web sites and e-mail", "design sets", "blank publications"

In **version 2007**, the list gives you 28 choices —

> blank page sizes, advertisements, award certificates, banners, brochures, business cards, business forms, calendars, catalogs, e-mail, envelopes, flyers, gift certificates, greeting cards, import Word documents, invitation cards, labels, letterheads, menus, newsletters, paper-folding projects, postcards, programs, quick publications, resumes, signs, web sites, with-compliments cards

Quick publications

The most powerful publication type is "quick publications". Try clicking it now! Here's what happens....

Design The right-hand window shows 76 **designs**:

> accent box, accessory bar, arcs, argyle, arrows, astro, axis, bars, birthday, blank, blends, blocks, border flowers, borders, bounce, bouquet, brocade, bubbles, butterfly, capsules, cascade, checkers, circles, color band, confetti, corner art, crossed lines, diamonds, echo, eclipse, edge, floating oval, handprint, hearts and circles, jumbled boxes, jungle, layers, leaves, level, linear accent, marker, marquee, maze, mobile, modular, network, pansies, party time, perforation, photoscope, pinwheel, pixel, profile, punctuation, quadrant, radial, refined, retro, ribbons, romance, scallops, signpost, simple divider, soap bubbles, starfish, steps, straight edge, stripes, studio, tabs, tilt, triangles, wallpaper, watermark, waves, wavy frame

At first, you see just the first few; to see the rest, use that window's scroll arrows.

You can click whichever design you want; but for your first experience, choose "accent box".

(If version 2003 says "Personal Information", press Enter.)

Layout The computer assumes you want your publication to contain three **objects**:

> a **picture** (such as a photo or drawing)
> a **heading** (a few words in big letters)
> a **message** (a few sentences in small letters)

The computer assumes you want to display the picture on top, then the heading, then the message (since the viewer's eye will naturally be attracted to the picture first, then the heading, then the message); but you can change that layout. For example, you can omit the picture, omit the heading, omit the message, make the picture smaller, move the picture to below the heading, twist the heading 90° (so it becomes a **sidebar heading**), or insert a fourth object: personal info about yourself!

Here's what happens next:

> **Version 2003** Near the screen's left edge, you see the word "Layout". Below that word you see 15 layouts to choose from.
>
> **Version 2007** Near the screen's bottom right corner, you see the word "Layout". Click the down-arrow below it. You start seeing 15 layouts to choose from; use the scroll arrows to see all 15.

Here are the 15 **layouts**:

> Blank
>
> Large picture at the top
> Large picture in the middle
>
> Small picture at the top
> Small picture in the middle
>
> Sidebar heading, picture at the top
> Sidebar heading, picture at the bottom
> Sidebar heading, no picture
>
> No message, picture at the top
> No message, picture at the bottom
>
> No picture
> No heading
>
> Message only
> Heading only
>
> Personal information with picture

(Version 2007 says "Business information" instead of "Personal information".)

The computer assumes you want the second layout, "Large picture at the top". To try a different layout instead, click one that interests you and look at its effect.

After you've experimented by clicking several layouts, make up your mind which one to use. For your first publication, I recommend you stay with "Large picture at the top".

Click the layout you choose. For version 2007, then click "Create" (which is at the screen's bottom-right corner).

Color scheme Click "Color Schemes" (which is near the screen's left edge). You see this list of 66 **color schemes** (plus the 26 in parentheses if you're using version 2007):

> alpine, (apex), aqua, (aspect), berry, black & gray, black & white, bluebird, brown, burgundy, cavern, (cherry), citrus, (civic), clay, (concourse), cranberry, crocus, dark blue, desert, eggplant, (equity), field, fjord, floral, (flow), (foundry), garnet, glacier, green, grove, harbor, heather, iris, island, ivy, lagoon, lilac, mahogany, marine, maroon, meadow, (median), (metro), mist, mistletoe, (module), monarch, moss, mountain, mulberry, navy, nutmeg, (ocean), (office), olive, (opulent), (orange), orchid, (oriel), (origin), (paper), parrot, (peach), pebbles, (plum), prairie, rain forest, red, redwood, reef, sagebrush, sapphire, shamrock, sienna, (solstice), spice, (summer), sunrise, sunset, teal, (technic), tidepool, (trek), tropics, trout, Tuscany, (urban), (verve), vineyard, waterfall, wildflower

The list is too long to fit on the screen. To see the rest of the list, use the list's scroll arrows.

At first, the computer assumes you want "waterfall", but you can click whichever color scheme interests you and look at its effect. If you don't like that effect, try clicking a different color scheme instead. Keep clicking until you find a color scheme whose effect makes you happy.

__Font scheme__ Click "Font Schemes" (which is near the screen's left edge). You see 31 **font schemes** (plus the 23 in parentheses if you're using version 2007):

Scheme	Heading font	Message font
(Apex)	Lucida Sans	Book Antiqua
Archival	Georgia Bold	Georgia
(Aspect)	Verdana	Verdana
Basis	Arial Bold	Arial
Binary	Verdana	Georgia
Breve	Bodoni Black	Franklin Gothic Book
Capital	Perpetua Titling	Perpetua
Casual	Comic Sans Bold	Comic Sans
(Civic)	Georgia	Georgia
(Concourse)	Candara	Candara
Data	Courier New Bold	Arial
Deckle	Papyrus	Gill Sans
Dictation	Lucida Sans Typewriter	Lucida Sans
Economy	Franklin Gothic Demi Condensed	Times New Roman Bold
(Equity)	Franklin Gothic Book	Perpetua
Etched	Copperplate Gothic Bold	Garamond
Facet	Gill Sans	Gill Sans
(Flow)	Calibri	Constantia
Foundation	Times New Roman	Arial Bold
Foundry	Rockwell Extra Bold	Rockwell
Fusion	French Script	Calisto
Galley	Arial Rounded Bold	Times New Roman
Impact	Impact	Georgia
Industrial	Franklin Gothic Heavy	Franklin Gothic Book
Literary	Bookman Old Style	Arial Rounded Bold
(Median)	Twentieth Century	Twentieth Century
(Metro)	Consolas	Corbel
Modern	Twentieth Century Bold	Garamond
(Module)	Corbel	Corbel
Monogram	Edwardian Script	Twentieth Century
(Office 1)	Cambria	Calibri
(Office 2)	Calibri	Cambria
(Office 3)	Calibri	Calibri
(Office Classic 1)	Times New Roman	Arial
(Office Classic 2)	Arial	Arial
Offset	Imprint Shadow	Franklin Gothic Book
Online	Verdana Bold	Verdana
Optical	OCR A Extended	Franklin Gothic Book
(Opulent)	Trebuchet	Trebuchet
(Oriel)	Century Schoolbook	Century Schoolbook
(Origin)	Bookman Old Style	Gill Sans
(Paper)	Constantia	Constantia
Perspective	Goudy Old Style	Franklin Gothic Heavy
Punch	Gill Sans Ultra Bold	Comic Sans
(Solstice)	Gill Sans	Gill Sans
Streamline	Bodoni Condensed	Twentieth Century Bold
(Technic)	Franklin Gothic Book	Arial
Textbook	Century Schoolbook	Arial Bold
(Trek)	Franklin Gothic Medium	Franklin Gothic Book
(Urban)	Trebuchet	Georgia
Verbatim	Agency Bold	Agency
Versatile	Times New Roman Bold	Times New Roman
(Verve)	Century Gothic	Century Gothic
Virtual	Trebuchet Bold	Trebuchet

You also see an extra font scheme (which version 2003 calls "Wizard" and version 2007 calls "Template"), whose heading and message fonts depend on which design you chose.

Those font schemes are too many to fit on the screen. To see them all, use the scroll arrows.

At first, the computer assumes you want "Wizard" or "Template", but you can click whichever font scheme interests you and look at its effect. If you don't like that effect, try clicking a different font scheme instead. Keep clicking until you find a font scheme whose effect makes you happy.

__Heading__ You see your publication. In it, click the word "Heading", then type whatever words you want the heading to be.

If you type *many* words, the computer will automatically switch them all to a smaller font, so the words will still fit in the space allotted. If you type a word that's not in the computer's dictionary (because the word is weird or you misspelled it), the computer will put a red squiggle under it.

__Message__ Under the heading, you see a sentence saying "Place your message here". Click in that sentence, then type the message you want to be under the heading. (If your message contains *many* words, the computer will automatically switch them all to a smaller font, so the words will still fit in the space allotted.)

While typing, you can use do formatting as if you were using Microsoft Word. For example, you can click the **B** button for boldface, the *I* button for italics, and the U button for underlining.

If your message contains *many* words — a whole paragraph! — you should make the paragraph be justified, by clicking the Justify button (which acts like Microsoft Word's).

If you want your message to contain *several* paragraph, press the Enter key once or twice at the end of each paragraph (except the bottom paragraph).

If your message becomes too tiny to read on the screen, press the F9 key. That makes the type look bigger on the screen, so you can read the type easily, but then the type is too big to fit the whole page on the screen. If you want to switch back to the "whole page" view, press F9 again. F9 is a **toggle** that switches back and forth between "Easy to read" and "See the whole page at once" views.

__Picture__ Above the heading, you see a picture. Temporarily, that picture is a photo of a sunset, but you can change that picture. Here's how….

Double-click the picture you want to change.

Do this (to let the computer search for extra pictures on the Internet):

> Click the "Search in" box's down-arrow then put a check mark in the "Everywhere" box (by clicking it).
>
> Make sure you're connected to the Internet. (If you're using a cable modem or DSL, you're connected already. If you're using an ordinary phone hookup, click Start then "Connect To" then the name of your Internet Service Provider then the button that says "Close" or "Dial"; that button says "Close" if you were connected already, "Dial" if you weren't.)

What topic do you want a picture of? Pick a topic (such as "girl" or "egg" or "France"). Double-click in the "Search for" box; it's near the screen's left edge. Then type your topic (and press Enter).

You'll see several pictures about your topic. To see more, use the scroll arrow. (If you don't see many, it's probably because you forgot to attach to the Internet.)

Click the picture you want. Close the Picture toolbar (by clicking its X).

__Undo__ If you make a mistake, click the **Undo button** (which is near the screen's top and shows an arrow curving toward the left). If that doesn't completely undo your mistake, try clicking that button several more times.

__Save__ To copy your publication to your hard disk, click the **Save button** (which is near the screen's top-left corner and looks like a 3½-inch floppy disk).

If you haven't saved your publication before, the computer will say "File name". Invent a name for your publication. Type the name and press Enter.

That makes the computer copy your publication onto the hard disk. The computer puts your publication into the Documents folder (for version 2007) or My Documents folder (for version 2003).

Your publication's filename ends in ".pub". For example, if you named your publication "mary", the computer puts a file called "mary.pub" into the folder. For version 2003, the file's icon has P on it, to remind you it was created by Publisher; for version 2007, the file's icon is green.

While you're editing and improving your publication, you should click the Save button frequently.

Print To print your publication onto paper, make sure your printer is turned on and contains paper. Then do this:

To print a **single copy** of your publication, click the **Print button** (which is near the screen's top left corner and shows a printer spewing out paper).

To print **many copies**, do this instead: **click "File" then "Print"**, then double-click in the "Number of copies" box, then type how many copies you want and press Enter.

Close When you finish working on your publication, click "File" then "Close".

If you didn't save the publication yet, the computer will ask, "Do you want to save the changes you made to this publication?"
If you don't want to save the changes, click "No". If you do want to save the changes, click "Yes" then type a name for the publication (and press Enter).

At the screen's left edge, you see the list of publication types again. You have three choices about what to do next:

To **stop** using Microsoft Publisher, click its **X button**.

To **start a new document**, do this: click "Publications for Print" if you're using version 2003; at the screen's left edge, you see the list of publication types again; click whichever publication type you want.

To make Microsoft Publisher **retrieve an old publication** you saved, do the **version 2003 procedure** (click the Open button, which is near the screen's top left corner and shows a file folder opening, then double-click whichever publication you want, remembering that each publication has a P in its icon) or do the **version 2007 procedure** (click one of the publications at the screen's right edge, or click "From File" then double-click whichever green-icon publication you want).

Congratulations! You've learned all the important techniques of Microsoft Publisher! You can create your own publications! Now let's dig deeper….

Alignment The heading and message both contain words. The computer assumes you want each line of words to be centered. Centering is fine if your heading and message are both short. But if your message contains *many* lines of words, centering makes your message hard to read.

To change whether a paragraph is centered, click in the paragraph and then click whichever alignment button you prefer:

The **Align Left button** (which version 2007 calls "Align Text Left") makes the paragraph's **left margin** be straight, the right margin be ragged, so the paragraph looks like this. This is the easiest to read and the friendliest, since it looks informal. But it looks lopsided.

The **Align Right button** (which version 2007 calls "Align Text Right") makes the paragraph's **right margin** be straight, the left margin be ragged, so the paragraph looks like this. This is the hardest to read. It's the least popular choice.

The **Justify button** makes the paragraph's **left and right margins** both be straight (except for the end of the paragraph's last line), so the paragraph looks like this. This is the most sophisticated. It's fairly easy to read, though it puts too much space between the words. It's the best choice for a long

message. It's what I used for most paragraphs in this book.

The **Center button** makes each line in the paragraph be **centered** again, so the paragraph looks like this. This looks the neatest. It's good for short headlines and messages, but it's hard to read if the message is long. It's what I used for the headlines in this book.

Those buttons work the same way as in Microsoft Word.

Frames Your publication contains three main objects: the picture, the heading, and the message. It also contains several other objects (border decorations near the paper's edge).

You can change each object's size and position. Here's how….

Click in the object's middle. Then the entire object will be surrounded by a pack of white dogs! Each dog is a white circle, called a **handle**.

The dogs (circles) are arranged to form a box surrounding the object, so the object is boxed in. The box surrounding the object is called the object's **frame**. Yeah, Louie, we've been framed!

Then you can manipulate the object in three ways:

To change the object's size, drag one of the white circles (by using the mouse).
To rotate (tilt) the object, drag the green circle.
To move the object, drag an edge of its frame (but don't drag a circle).

Signs

Instead of clicking "quick publications", try clicking "signs". That lets you create signs. Here's how….

Design The right-hand window shows 40 **designs** for signs:

authorized only, beware of dog, business hours, checks accepted
closed, closed for remodeling, for rent, for rent #2, for rent #3
for sale, for sale #2, for sale #3, for sale #4
garage sale, garage sale #2, garage sale #3, garage sale #4
gone fishing, help wanted, information, inventory
keep off the grass, keep out, kid's room, lemonade for sale
no loitering, no parking, no smoking, open, open house, out of order
private property, restrooms, return time, special offer, turn off the lights
we speak, wet paint, wet paint #2, wheelchair access

(You see just the first few; to see the rest, use that window's scroll arrows.)

You can click whichever design you want; but for your first experience, try doing this:

Version 2003: click "kid's room". (If the computer asks "Would you like to install it now?" press Enter.)

Version 2007: double-click "kid's room".

Color scheme Click "Color Schemes" (which is near the screen's left edge). You see the full list of 66 **color schemes**, but just 5 schemes work well for signs that start as black & white: click either "black & gray" (which version 2007 calls the first "black…"), "brown", "dark blue", "green", or "red". If your printer can't print colors, choose "black & gray".

Font scheme Click "Font Schemes" (which is near the screen's left edge). You see a list of font schemes. It's the same list as for "Quick publications", except that the computer typically uses just heading fonts (and ignores message fonts). The computer assumes you want version 2007's "Template" or version 2003's "Wizard", until you click a different font scheme instead.

Edit the words You see your publication. It's a sign that says "Kid's Room" and includes a drawing of a moon with stars. The sign is in the color you chose.

Change the word "Kid's" to your own name. For example, if your name is "Joan", change "Kid's Room" to "Joan's Room". Here's how: click "Kid's", then type your name, then type 's.

Change "Room" to a word that's more descriptive, such as one of these:

> Bedroom, Hideaway, Lair, Hovel
> Office, Headquarters, Classroom
> Home, Castle, Garden, Pond, Swimming Hole, Woods
> Closet, Locker, Trunk, Corner, Secret Passage, Private Parts

To do that, click "Room" then type whatever replacement you want.

Change the picture Change the moon to a different kind of moon picture — or whatever other picture you prefer. To do that, click the moon, then *double*-click it. Make sure you're connected to the Internet and the "Search in" box says "All collections", then double-click in the "Search for" box. Type "moon" (or whatever other kind of picture you wish) and press Enter. You should see some pictures. Scroll through the pictures, then click whichever picture you want. Close the Picture toolbar (by clicking its X).

Finish You can **undo**, **save**, **print**, and **exit**, using the same techniques as for "Quick publications".

Banners

A **banner** is a big sign that nearly a foot tall and *several* feet wide. You can create a banner by taping several sheets of paper together, side-by-side.

To create banners, click "banners" instead of "quick publications".

Design The computer can create 40 kinds of banners. Each kind is called a **design**. Those 40 designs are organized into 8 categories:

> **Informational:** apartment for rent, caution, checked-frame, information, interwoven-frame, new management, order here, plain-background, registration, reservations, safety equipment
>
> **Sale:** bake sale, clearance sale, sale, yard sale
>
> **Event:** anniversary, birthday, bon voyage, enter to win, grand opening, open house, pageant, school dance, street fair, team spirit
>
> **Welcome:** welcome, welcome back, welcome new addition
>
> **Congratulations:** baby congratulations, champions, congratulations, graduation, promotion, retirement, the greatest, to the best
>
> **Holiday:** Fourth of July, New Year
>
> **Romance:** marry me
>
> **Get Well:** get well

(Exception: version 2003 stupidly puts "birthday" in its own category instead of in the "Event" category.)

For version 2007, do this:

> In the screen's right-hand window, in the line under the word "Banners", you see those 8 categories. Click the category that interests you, then click the specific design that interests you. The screen's top-right corner shows it enlarged.
>
> The computer assumes you want the banner to be 5 feet wide and 8½ inches tall. If you want the banner to be bigger than that (so it will use even more paper and your Mom will yell at you for wasting paper), at the screen's right edge click the **Page size** box's down-arrow then the size you want.
>
> The computer assumes you want a **border** around the message. (The border is a fancy box.) If you don't want a border, at the screen's right edge click the **Border** box's down-arrow then "No border".
>
> The computer assumes you want a little graphic (a picture) next to the banner's message (words). Do you want the graphic to be **left** of the message, **right** of the message, on **both** sides of the message, or omitted so you have **none**? At the screen's right edge, you can click the **Graphic** box's down-arrow then click one of those 4 choices.
>
> Click "Create" (which is at the screen's bottom-right corner).

For version 2003, do this:

In the screen's left window, under the word "Banners", you see the 9 categories. Click the category that interests you. Then click the right-hand window's scroll-down arrow if necessary, until you see the specific design that interests you. Click that design. Then you'll see it enlarged.

> **Width** How wide do you want the banner to be? Click "5 feet", "6 feet", "8 feet", or "10 feet". (For your first experiment, try "5 feet" to avoid wasting paper.)
>
> **Height** How tall do you want the banner to be? Click "11 inches" or "8.5 inches". (For your first experiment, try "8.5 inches" to avoid wasting paper.)
>
> **Graphic** Next to the message, the computer normally puts a little **graphic** (a picture). Do you want the graphic to be **left** of the message, **right** of the message, on **both** sides of the message, or omitted so you have **none**? Click your choice.
>
> **Border** The computer normally puts a **border** around the message. (The border is a fancy box.) If you want a border, click "**Border**"; otherwise, click "**No border**".

Edit To change the message's words, click the message then type what you want instead.

To change the message's color, click "Color Schemes" then click one of these color schemes: "black & gray", "brown", "dark blue", "green", or "red". The color scheme will affect the message's color; but the border will stay black, and the graphic's color will stay unchanged.

To change the font, click "Font Schemes" then click whichever scheme you want. The computer will tend to use the scheme's message font and ignore the scheme's headline font, but the computer will occasionally change its mood and use the scheme's headline font instead. The Template or Wizard font is Times New Roman.

Finish You can **undo**, **save**, **print**, and **exit**: just use the same techniques as for "Quick publications".

Warning: when you've printed the banner onto paper, examine the banner carefully before you hang it on your wall: a few letters or graphics might be missing, because your printer doesn't contain enough RAM memory chips or your printer can't print close enough to the paper's edge.

Greeting cards

To create a greeting card, **click "greeting cards"** instead of "quick publications".

Design The computer can create many kinds of greeting cards. Each kind is called a **design**.

You get 306 designs, organized into 19 categories.

Category	How many designs	
Thank-you cards	50	
We've-moved cards	5	
Engagement announcements	3	
Birth announcements	6	
Reminder cards	1	
Holiday cards	61	(24 Christmas, 5 Easter, 3 Halloween, 3 Hanukkah, 2 Kwanzaa, 3 New Year, 4 Ramadan, 1 Rosh Hashanah, 1 St. Patrick's, 3 Thanksgiving, 12 general)
Birthday cards	78	
Mother's Day cards	12	
Special-day greeting cards	5	(2 Bar Mitzvah, 3 Grandparents Day)
Congratulations cards	29	(7 anniversary, 1 bon voyage, 4 graduation, 7 new baby, 2 new home, 1 promotion, 1 retirement, 3 wedding, 3 general)
Friendship cards	12	
Romance cards	8	
I'm-sorry cards	2	
Get-well cards	12	
Sympathy cards	6	
Good-luck cards	3	
Miss you cards	2	

You see those 19 categories (in version 2003's left window or version 2007's right-hand window), under the phrase "Greeting Cards".

Click the category that interests you. Then click the right-hand window's scroll-down arrow if necessary, until you see the specific design that interests you. Click that design. Then you see it enlarged (in version 2003's right-hand window or version 2007's top-right corner).

Layout For the card's front cover, the computer might let you choose a layout. The computer can offer these 26 choices:

> art bit, banded, focus, frames, greetings bar, image classic, image elegant, juxtaposition, label, lattice, letterpress, panel, pattern pickup, picture squares, plaid, portal, postcard, punctuate, radius, retro orbits, runway, sketch, spotlight, stamps, stripes, wrap

Here's how to see those choices.

> Version 2003: use the scroll arrows.
> Version 2007: click the down-arrow at the screen's bottom-right corner, then use the scroll-down arrow.

Click the choice you want.

Page size and fold The computer might let you click one of these ways to fold your greeting card:

> "**Quarter-page side fold**" will make a greeting card by having you fold a sheet of paper into quarters. For your first experience, choose this!
>
> "**Quarter-page top fold**" will make a greeting card that looks like a tent.
>
> "**Half-page side fold**" will produce a bigger card but make you glue two sheets of paper together — or print on both sides of a single sheet.

Do this:

> Version 2003: click "Page Options" (at the screen's left edge) then your favorite fold choice then "Greeting Card Options" (which makes the choices disappear).
>
> Version 2007: click the "Page size" box's down-arrow then your favorite fold choice then "Create" (which is at the screen's bottom-right corner).

Suggested verse Click "Select a suggested Verse". (In version 2003, it's at the screen bottom-left corner. In version 2007, it's near the screen's left edge.)

You'll see about 20 verses that relate to your topic. Here are examples:

Topic you picked	Sample verse
anniversary	You two seem to have everything you need... *Each other! Happy Anniversary.*
Bar Mitzvah	Congratulations on your Bar Mitzvah! *Wishing you joy on your special day.*
Bat Mitzvah	Congratulations on your Bat Mitzvah! *Wishing you joy on your special day.*
birth announcement	A baby has arrived. *And the world is bright with wonder and light.*
bon voyage	All systems are go. *So, take off! And have a blast on your vacation.*
Easter	Happy Easter *Wishing you joy in this season of renewal.*
engagement announ.	We're pleased to announce... *An engagement to be married.*
Father's Day	Dad, you've always protected me. *You're my super hero!*
friendship	When I look on the bright side... *It's always in your direction.*
general congrats	When you come down to earth... *I'd like to give you a pat on the space helmet. Congratulations!*
get well	Your well-being is of great concern. *And your absence deeply felt. Please get well soon.*
good luck	By chopper, by tanker, by monster truck — *I send you Good Luck!*
graduation congrats	The school book has closed. *A new chapter begins.*
Grandparents Day	How wise of them to name a day... *For people nice in every way.*
Halloween	Happy Halloween... *From our dungeon to yours!*
happy birthday	May this birthday... *Be the beginning of the best years of your life.*
happy Hanukkah	May the Festival of Lights... *Illuminate both your heart and your home. Happy Hanukkah.*
happy holidays	Of all the gifts bestowed this year... *First be the gift of loved ones near.*
happy New Year	Pop the cork and throw the confetti. *The New Year's here and we're all ready.*
I'm sorry	We goofed... *Please excuse our error.*
Kwanzaa	Kwanzaa *Kwanzaa candle burning bright, feel the wonder of the light. Share the pride, keep the glow, pass it on to all you know.*
love & romance	Roses are red, carnations are pink... *I'd like to go out with you, what do you think?*
merry Christmas	Yuletide Greetings *Hope your holidays are happy!*
miss you	I sit with my head in my hands, *Wishing it were in yours. See you soon?*
Mother's Day	To Mother... *Thank you for years of love.*
new baby/adoption	Congratulations on the new baby. *We always knew you could perform miracles.*
new home congrats	Congratulations on your new home... *From your old friends.*
Ramadan	Warm thoughts to our friends... *During Ramadan.*
reminder	Don't forget... *You have an appointment with us. We look forward to seeing you.*
retirement congrats	Have fun when you retire, but remember... *Don't play too hard!*
Rosh Hashanah	May the New Year... *Bring you happiness and prosperity.*
St. Patrick's Day	From Dublin to Denpasar, from County Cork to Cleveland — *For one day, everyone's Irish. Happy St. Patrick's Day!*
sympathy	With deepest sympathy *Our condolences to you and your family.*
thank you	In a world of chaos... *Thanks for the order!*
Thanksgiving	Happy Thanksgiving *Have a festive fall!*
Valentine's Day	Everyone should have a special Valentine... *I'll be yours if you'll be mine.*
wedding	I'd wish you luck for your wedding... *But you already seem to have it all.*
we've moved	We've Moved *Please send all correspondence to our new address.*

(Version 2003's Bar Mitzvah verse is more sexist.)

Click the verse you want, then click "OK".

Edit Your card has 4 pages. You're seeing the front cover, which is page 1.

At the screen's bottom, you see the numbers 1, 2, 3, and 4. To see page 2, click the 2. That makes you see page 2 (and you'll simultaneously see page 3, next to it). To see page 4 (which is the back cover), click the 4. To see page 1 again, click the 1.

You can edit each object on each page.

> To edit text, click it then type what you want instead.
> To edit a picture, click it, then use the same techniques as for "Quick publications".

Color scheme Click "Color Schemes". You see the list of color schemes. The computer has tentatively picked the scheme it thinks is best, but you can click a different color scheme instead.

Font scheme Click "Font Schemes". You see the list of font schemes. The computer has tentatively picked "Wizard" or "Template", but you can click a different font scheme instead.

Finish You can **undo**, **save**, **print**, and **exit**: just use the same techniques as for the "quick publications" wizard.

When you print onto paper, all four pages of the greeting card will appear on a single sheet of paper (if you chose a "quarter page" layout). Fold that sheet of paper in half (to divide pages 1&4 from pages 2&3), then fold in half again (to divide page 1 from 4).

Other publication types

You've learned how to use 4 publication types: "quick publications", "signs", "banners", and "greeting cards". You can use other publication types, too!

Version 2007 gives you 27 normal publication types:

> advertisements, award certificates, banners, brochures, business cards, business forms, calendars, catalogs, e-mail, envelopes, flyers, gift certificates, greeting cards, import Word documents, invitation cards, labels, letterhead, menus, newsletters, paper-folding projects, postcards, programs, quick publications, résumés, signs, Web sites, with-compliments cards

(Version 2003 is similar.) Try those publication types. They resemble the types you already mastered.

Blank publications

Instead of clicking one of those normal publication types, try this:

> For version 2003, click "Blank Print Publication" (which is near the screen's bottom-left corner, below the list of publication types).
>
> For version 2007, click "Blank Page Sizes" then double-click "Letter (Portrait)", which you see by scrolling down.

You see a picture of a blank, clean sheet of paper, on which you can create any publication you wish, without locking yourself into one of the traditional types. Be creative! Here's how....

Typing with F9 Start typing on the blank page. Your typing will be too small to read: to see it bigger, press the F9 key.

That makes the type look bigger, but too big to fit the whole page on the screen. If you want to switch back to the "whole page" view, press F9 again. F9 is a **toggle** that switches back and forth between "easy to read" and "whole page" views.

Similar to word processing While you're typing, Microsoft Publisher resembles Microsoft Word. After you've practiced using Microsoft Word, Microsoft Publisher is easy! Here are the main differences:

> The Page Up and Page Down keys don't move the cursor. Ctrl symbols don't work. Microsoft Publisher can't check your grammar, so there are no green squiggles.
>
> Microsoft Publisher expects your entire message to fit on one page (unless you use special tricks I explain later), so there are no page arrows and you can't give a simple page break.
>
> The computer assumes you want 10-point Times New Roman. The Font Size menu starts at 4 points (instead of 8 points).
>
> If you click in the Font Size box and type a point size, you can put any digit after the decimal point. For example, you can type "12.4" to get 12.4 points. (The digit after the decimal point doesn't have to be 5.)
>
> When you finish working on a document, choose Close from the File menu. Then click Microsoft Publisher's X button, or choose New from the File menu, or click the Open button.

Frames The text you've been typing is in a box, called a **frame**. The frame has 8 **handles** (1 at each corner and 1 at the midpoint of each side). Each handle is a tiny white circle.

Try this experiment: make sure you're seeing the whole page (by pressing F9 if necessary), then make the frame smaller (by dragging one of the handles toward the frame's center). Now the frame is small, so it does *not* consume the whole page, so you can create extra frames elsewhere on the page.

The frame that's already on the page is called a **text frame**, because it contains text you typed. Here's how to make an extra text frame:

> Click the **Text Box** button, which is an A that's upright (not slanted) at the screen's left edge. Decide where on the page you want the extra text frame to begin; put the mouse pointer there; that will be the frame's top-left corner; drag to where you want the frame's bottom-right corner. The frame will appear.
>
> In that frame, type whatever text you wish. To see your typing more easily, press F9.

You can change a frame's position:

> To change a frame's size, click inside it then drag one of its white handles. To rotate a frame, click inside it, then drag its green handle (which is nearby). To move a frame, drag one of its edges (but not a handle).

You can make 5 kinds of frames. To make a frame containing **normal text**, you've learned to do this:

> Click the **Text Box** button (which is at the screen's left edge and shows an upright A). Drag across the page, to form the frame.
> Type the text (and press F9 to see it better).

To make a frame containing a **table** (of numbers or words), do this:

> Click the **Insert Table** button (which is at the screen's left edge and shows a grid). Drag across the page, to form the frame.
> Type how many rows you want, then press the Tab key. Type how many columns you want, then press the Tab key.
> Press the keyboard's down-arrow key repeatedly, until you see a nice format. Press Enter.
> Type the data (and press F9 to see it better, Tab to move to the next cell).

To make a frame containing a **picture from Microsoft**, do this:

> Click the **Picture Frame** button, which is at the screen's left edge and shows a pair of mountains. Click "Clip Art".
> Double-click in the "Search for" box. Type a topic to find a picture of, and press Enter.
> You'll see several pictures about that topic. (Use the scroll arrow to see more.) Click the picture you want.
> The computer will put the picture onto your page and put a frame around the picture. You can change the picture's size and position by dragging the picture's handles and frame.

To make a frame containing a **picture from a different source** (such as a photo, or a painting you created by using Paint), do this:

> Click the **Picture Frame** button, which is at the screen's left edge and shows a pair of mountains. Click "Picture from File".
> Drag across the page, to form the frame. The computer will make it a perfect square.
> You'll see what's in the Pictures (or My Pictures) folder. Double-click the painting or photo you want.

To make a frame containing **bent text**, do this:

> Click the **Insert WordArt** button (which is at the screen's left edge and shows a rotated A).
> You see 30 ways to bend text. Double-click your favorite.
> Type the text. Be brief, just a few words. If you want *several* lines, press Enter at the end of each line.
> Click OK. Then computer will bend your text, put it on your page, and put a frame around the text.
> Change the frame's size and position, however you wish, by dragging the picture's handles and frame. Drag the white handles move the frame simply, green handles to rotate the frame, yellow handles to change the curvature.

To delete a frame, click in the frame's middle (so the frame has handles), then right-click in the frame's middle, then click "Delete Object".

If you type text that's too long to fit in its frame, the computer puts the symbol "A ▪▪▪" at the frame's bottom instead. The last few words you typed are temporarily invisible: the computer stores them in an **overflow area** (which you can't see) until you make the frame bigger (by dragging its handles) or make the text shorter — or make a 2nd frame, to display the overflow, as follows:

> Click the **Text Box** tool (which is at the screen's left edge and shows an upright A). Drag across the page, to form the 2nd frame.
> Click in the first frame (the frame that was too small). Click the **Create Text Box Link** button (which is at the screen's top right and shows 2 or 3 chain links). Your mouse pointer becomes a pouring cup. Use it to click in the 2nd frame.

Here's a way to force text to fit in its frame. Click in its frame then click "Format" then "AutoFit Text". You see a menu of 3 choices:

> If you click "Shrink Text on Overflow" and the text is too big to fit in the frame, the computer will decrease the font size to make the text fit.
>
> If you click "Best Fit", the computer will decrease or increase the font size, to make the text exactly fill the frame.
>
> If you click "Do not Autofit", the computer will do nothing: if the text is too big to fit the frame, the frame will show just the text's beginning.

Extra pages So far, your publication contains just one page. To make your publication longer by adding a second page, click "Insert" then "Page" then "OK".

Now your publication has two pages. You're seeing page 2. To see page 1, click the "1" at the screen's bottom. To see page 2 again, click the "2" at the screen's bottom. Press F9 to toggle between "full page" view and "easy to read" view.

Web-page design

When using the Internet's World Wide Web, don't be just a looker; be a creator! Create your *own* Web pages and let everybody else in the world see them!

Angelfire

The easiest way to create your own Web pages is to use a Web site called **Angelfire**. It's free!

Angelfire is at www.angelfire.com. It used to be an independent company, but now it's owned by **Lycos**. (which also owns a similar site, **Tripod**, at ww w.tripod.com).

Restrictions

Angelfire lets you create any Web pages you wish, as long as you keep them "clean", so they don't contain content or links to anything that's:

unlawful, harmful, hateful, harassing, stalking, or containing viruses
defamatory, libelous, ethnically objectionable, or pirated (copied without permission)
privacy-invading (or vulgar or pornographic), especially if involving minors or viewable by minors
required to stay private (by copyright laws or an employer's nondisclosure agreement)
selling explosives, weapons, securities, or non-existent goods
selling alcohol, tobacco, controlled drugs (or pharmaceuticals), or unpackaged food
advertising gambling (or raffles requiring a fee) or pyramid schemes

Unfortunately, Angelfire will automatically put an ad on your Web page and restrict you (to 20 megabytes of Angelfire's disk space, with a limit of 1 gigabyte of transfers per month between Angelfire's disk and people viewing your Web page), unless you pay extra (to get a fancier plan):

Plan's name	Cost	Disk space	Bandwidth	Forced ad?	Get your own .com, such as joe.com?
Free	free	20M	1G/month	yes	no
Entry	$1/month	40M	2G/month	yes	no
Basic	$3/month	100M	5G/month	no	no
THE Plan	$10/month	5G	1T/month	no	yes

Create an account

Using your Web browser (such as Microsoft Internet Explorer), go to **www.angelfire.com**. Click "Try It Now for Free!" then "Sign up for one of these plans today!" (which you see when you scroll down).

Click in the "Your New Website" box. Your Website will be named "http://_____.angelfire.com". Invent a name to put in the blank. The name cannot contain capital letters or spaces: it must be made of just lower-case letters, digits, dashes, and periods. Type the name you invented (such as "secretguide") then click in the Password box. If the name you invented is okay, the computer says "User name Available"; otherwise the computer says "User name Unavailable" (probably because somebody else picked that name) and you must try again to pick a name.

Next, invent a password (which must be at least 6 characters long, with no spaces). Type the password in the Password box, press the Tab key, type the password again, click "Next", and click "Next" again.

The computer will say "Welcome". Answer the questions about your birthday, security, usage, gender, and newsletters, then click "Confirm".

Angelfire Customer Service will send you an e-mail whose subject is "Welcome to Angelfire". Find it in your e-mail's Inbox. Click the first link in the e-mail.

The computer will say "Your account has been activated". Click "Start Building Now" then "Create a New Website".

Change the text

You're using a Website-creation program called **Webon** (pronounced "web on"). It shows a Web page containing 5 blocks of text. In each block of text, switch those words to *your* words. Here's how to do that:

Drag across the first block of text, which says "MY WEBSITE". Type whatever **heading** you want instead, such as "JOAN'S HOME PAGE". Your typing will be automatically capitalized.

Drag across the second block of text, which says "My website's **subheading**". Type whatever subheading you want instead, such as "Made with love".

Drag across the third block of text, which begins "This is your **main content section**. You should delete…" Type the main message you want instead, such as "I was born yesterday. I want to die."

Drag across the fourth block of text, which begins "This is your **sidebar**. This sidebar is…" Type the sidebar message you want instead, such as "We won't reply to e-mails addressed to my goldfish."

Scroll down to see the fifth block of text, which begins "This is your **footer**. You can delete…" Drag across that block of text, then type the footer you want instead, such as "Copyright by a wronged woman."

Format the text

You can easily format the text in blocks 3, 4, and 5. To do that, drag across the phrase you want to change (so the phrase temporarily appears in white letters on a blue background), then do one of these things:

Click one of the formatting buttons: Bold, Italic, Underline, Align Left, Align Center, Align Justify, Align Right, Ordered List (which means a numbered list), or Unordered List (which means a bulleted list).

For the Font Size box (which normally says "12px", which means 12 pixels high), click its down-arrow then click a different number of pixels instead. Your choices are 8, 9, 10, 11, 12, 14, 16, 18, 20, 22, 24, 28, 32, 36, 48, and 72.

For the Font box (which normally says "Arial"), click its down-arrow then click a different font instead. Your choices are Arial, Times New Roman, Verdana, Georgia, Trebuchet, Courier New, Tahoma, Palatino Linotype, Impact, and Comic Sans.

For the Color box (which is normally black), click its down-arrow then click a different font color instead. The phrase will appear in the new color when you finish highlighting the phrase: click elsewhere.

For the Background Color Box (which says "BG" and is normally white), click its down-arrow then click a different background color instead. The phrase will have the new background color when you finish highlighting the phrase: click elsewhere.

Notice that to format a phrase, you must drag across the phrase *beforehand*. For example, if you want a phrase to be bold, you must drag across the phrase *before* you click the Bold button.

Undo

If you make a typing mistake, here's how to undo it: while holding down the Ctrl key, tap the Z key.

That method undoes your last typing mistake, but it can't undo your last *two* typing mistakes, and it can't undo formatting. If you format a phrase wrong, format it again correctly.

Change the style

You've been using a style called **Working Comp**. To use a different style instead, click "Styles" (which is at the screen's top). You start seeing a list of 152 styles, in alphabetical order. To see the rest of the list, click "Next" several times. To go back toward the list's beginning, click "Previous" several times. If a style interests you, put the mouse pointer on it without clicking; then you see a slightly larger picture of the style.

Click whichever style you like. Then you see the words you wrote, reformatted to fit in that style.

If you don't like that style, try clicking "Revert", which takes you back to a style you used before (such as Working Comp).

When you've finished picking a style, click "Text" (which is near the screen's top-left corner).

Add links

Here's how to make the phrase "house hunting" be underlined and link to www.realtor.com:

Type "house hunting". Drag across that phrase (so it's highlighted). Click "Link". Click after the "http://". Type "www.realtor.com". Click the green "Create" button.

This book was written by Russ Walter, whose e-mail address is Russ@SecretFun.com. Here's how to make your Web page let people send an e-mail to Russ Walter, by clicking "write to Russ":

Type "write to Russ". Drag across that phrase (so it's highlighted). Click "Link" then the down-arrow then "an e-mail address". Press the Tab key. Type the e-mail address "Russ@SecretFun.com". Click the green "Create" button.

Then when a person accesses your Web page, "write to Russ" will be underlined. If the person clicks "write to Russ", the computer will automatically run the person's e-mail client program (such as Outlook Express), automatically click "Create Mail", automatically type "Russ@SecretFun.com" in the "To" box, and wait for the person to type an e-mail message to Russ.

Final steps

When you finish editing your Website, click "Save" (which is near the screen's top-right corner) then "Publish" (which is next to "Save") then "Publish to the main page of the site" then the green "Publish" button. The computer says, "Congratulations! Your site was published…"

If you want to edit further, click "Keep Working"; otherwise, exit by doing this:

Click "Back to Angelfire" then "logout" (which is near the screen's top-right corner).

Edit your site

To edit a Website you created before, do this:

Go to www.angelfire.com. Click "Login" (which is at the top). Type your user name (such as "secretguide"), press the Tab key, type your password, then click the green "Log In" button. Click "Edit" (which is below "Create a New Website").

You see your Website. Edit it, then do the "Final steps" procedure again.

Extra pages

Here's how to put extra pages onto your Website.

While you're editing the first page you created, click "Pages" (which is at the top) then the "Create a new page" icon. (That icon is near the screen's top-left corner, under "Text", and shows a single sheet of paper with a green plus sign.)

Invent a title for the page (such as "My Family"); type it and press Enter.

Now the screen's left edge shows you have 2 pages. The first page (which you created before) was automatically called "Home". If the new page you're creating is called "My Family", the screen's left edge shows this list of pages:

1. Home
2. My Family

If you want to create a 3ʳᵈ page, click the "Create a new page" icon again, type the new page's title (such as "Our Friends") and press Enter again, so the screen's left edge looks like this:

1. Home
2. My Family
3. Our Friends

The screen's bottom is still devoted to showing what you typed on page 1. To switch your view to page 2 or page 3, click the page's name in that list of pages, then click the "Jump to a page" icon (which is a sheet of paper with a green arrow). That makes the screen's bottom show the page you requested. The heading you requested is at the screen's top and has the page name you invented. There's no subheading. The sidebar is at the left instead of the right. The main content section, sidebar, and footer are all blank, waiting for you to type your words there. Below the heading you also see this **navigation bar** —

HOME   MY FAMILY   OUR FRIENDS

which your readers can click on to jump from page to page, after you've finished creating your Website.

To see normal editing tools again (such as the Bold button), click "Text" (which is near the screen's top-left corner).

HTML

Every page on the Internet's Web is written in a computer language called the **HyperText Markup Language (HTML)**.

Warning: if someone claims to know "HTML", it could mean "HyperText Markup Language" or "How To Make Love". Ask which!

HTML uses these commands:

HTML command	Ending	Page
\<a href=…\>	\</a\>	288
\<a name=joys\>	\</a\>	289
\<b\>	\</b\>	286
\<big\>	\</big\>	286
\<body\>	\</body\>	287
\<body bgcolor=red\>	\</body\>	289
\<br\>		287
\<font color=red\>	\</font\>	289
\<font face=Arial\>	\</font\>	287
\<font size=5\>	\</font\>	286
\<form method=…\>	\</form\>	291
\<h1\>	\</h1\>	286
\<head\>	\</head\>	287
\<html\>	\</html\>	287
\<i\>	\</i\>	285
\<input name=city\>		291
\<input type=button\>		603
\<input type=submit\>		291
\<li\>		287
\<link rel=…\>		290
\<noscript\>	\</noscript\>	604
\<ol\>	\</ol\>	288
\<p\>		286
\<pre\>	\</pre\>	288
\<script\>	\</script\>	598
\<script language=…\>	\</script\>	604
\<small\>	\</small\>	286
\<style\>	\</style\>	289
\<sub\>	\</sub\>	286
\<sup\>	\</sup\>	286
\<table border=1\>	\</table\>	288
\<td\>		288
\<th\>		288
\<title\>	\</title\>	286
\<tr\>		288
\<tt\>	\</tt\>	286
\<ul\>	\</ul\>	288
\<!DOCTYPE HTML …\>		287
\<!--I was drunk--\>		291

HTML uses these styles:

Style command	Page
body {background:yellow}	289
body {color:red}	289
body {font-size:13pt}	289
h1 {color:blue}	290
h1 {font-size:40pt}	290
h1 {text-align:center}	290
p {margin-bottom:0}	290
p {margin-top:0}	290
p {text-indent:2em}	290
:hover {color:navy}	290
:link {color:green}	290
:visited {color:fuchsia}	290

Simple example

Suppose you want to create a Web page that says:

We *love* you

Notice that the word "love" is italicized (slanted).

To create that Web page, write this HTML program:

```
We <i>love</i> you
```

Here's what that program means:

The <i> is an **HTML tag** that means "italics". Each HTML tag is enclosed in the symbols <>, which are called **angle brackets**.

The </i> is an HTML tag that means "end the italics", because the symbol / means "end the". The <i> shows where to begin the italics; the </i> shows where to end the italics.

To type that program, you can use two free methods: **Notepad** or **Angelfire**. I'll explain both.

Typing in Notepad

If your computer contains Windows, the easiest way to type that HTML program is to use **Notepad**, as follows....

Launch Notepad. Here's how:

Click Start then All Programs then Accessories then Notepad. You see the Notepad window.

Make the Notepad window consume the screen's bottom right quarter. Here's how:

If the Notepad window is maximized (consumes the whole screen), make the window smaller by clicking the restore button (which is next to the X button).

Drag the window's bottom right corner to the screen's bottom right corner. Drag the window's top right corner to the screen's center. Then the window consumes the screen's bottom right quarter.

Make Notepad do word wrapping. Here's how:

Click "Format". You see "Word Wrap". If there's no check mark in front of "Word Wrap", put a check mark there (by clicking "Word Wrap").

Click in the middle of the Notepad window. Type the HTML program, like this:

```
We <i>love</i> you
```

Save the program Save the program onto your desktop, and give it a name that ends in ".html". Here's how:

Click "File" then "Save".
Click the word "Desktop" at the screen's left edge. For Windows 7, click in the "File name" box.
Type any name ending in ".html" (such as "joan.html"); to be safe, use just small letters (no capitals, no spaces). Press Enter.

Your program's icon arrives on the desktop but might be covered by the Notepad window. Move the Notepad window (by dragging its blue title bar) until you see your program's icon.

The icon has an "e" on it. The "e" means the program works with Microsoft Internet Explorer. It works with Microsoft Internet Explorer because the program is written in HTML and ends in .html.

Run the program Double-click your program's icon. That makes the computer run your program. (If a "Connect To" window appears, click "Cancel" once or twice, to make the "Connect To" window go away.)

If your computer's been set up properly (to use Microsoft Internet Explorer as the main Web browser), you'll see a Microsoft Internet Explorer window that shows the result of running your program; it shows a Web page that says:

We *love* you

Edit the program If you typed and ran the program recently, here's how to edit it.

At the screen's bottom, to the right of the Start button, you see a wide button for Notebook. Click it. That makes the Notebook window appear and be the active window. Then make any changes you wish to your HTML program. For example, if you want the Web page to say "We *tickle* you", change "love" to "tickle" (by dragging across "love" and then typing "tickle").

Go ahead: make that change and any other changes you wish! Experiment! Go wild!

After you've edited the program, save the edited version (by clicking "File" then "Save").

To run that program, click in the Microsoft Internet Explorer window (which hides behind the Notepad window), so the Microsoft Internet Explorer window becomes the active window. Then click the Refresh button, which makes Microsoft Internet Explorer re-examine your program and run your program's new version.

Edit old programs Here's how to edit an old program that you haven't typed or run recently.

Find the program's icon on the desktop. Right-click that icon. Click "Open with" then do this:

Windows XP & Vista: click "Notepad".

Windows 7: if you see "Notepad", click it; otherwise, do the following.... Click "Choose default program". Remove the check mark from "Always use the selected program" (by clicking). Click the down-arrow to the right of "Other Programs". Scroll down until you see "Notepad" then double-click "Notepad".

Make the Notepad window consume the screen's bottom right quarter. Make Notepad do word wrapping.

Then you see your HTML program. Edit it. When you finish editing, click "File" then "Save".

Typing in Angelfire

Here's how to type an HTML program by using **Angelfire** instead of Notepad....

Go to www.angelfire.com. Start creating a Web page, using the methods I described on pages 283-284.

While you're typing & editing the main content section, click "Add-ons" (which is at the top). You see 27 add-ons. Drag "Custom HTML" (which is the last add-on) until it's below the typing in the main content section and is in the middle of a big black box that suddenly appears.

After several seconds, the computer says this sentence:

Click the "Edit" Link to add HTML to this space.

Move the mouse pointer to that sentence, without clicking. Then above that sentence, you see "Edit". Click that "Edit".

The computer says this sentence:

Paste or write your custom HTML in the box below.

In the box below that sentence, drag across the sentence that's already there (which begins with "<p>") then type your HTML program instead. For example, type:

```
We <i>love</i> you
```

When you finish typing your program in the box, click the green "Save" button (which you must scroll down to see).

Then you see a box showing the result of your programming:

We *love* you

If you want to edit your program further, move the mouse pointer to that box (without clicking), then click the "Edit" above that box, then edit your program further, then click the green "Save" button again (after scrolling down to see it).

Simple HTML commands

Here are simple HTML commands you can give.

Italicize To make a phrase be italicized (*like this*), type <i> before the phrase; type </i> after the phrase.

Bold To make a phrase be bold (**like this**), type <b> before the phrase; type </b> after the phrase. To make a phrase be bold italic (***like this***), type <b><i> before the phrase; type </i></b> after the phrase.

Paragraph If your document contains more than one paragraph, put <p> at the beginning of each paragraph. For example, if you want a paragraph to begin by saying "Motherhood is maddening!", begin the paragraph by typing this:

<p>Motherhood is maddening!

At the end of each paragraph, press the Enter key twice. Then when you run the program, the computer will put a blank line below each paragraph.

Title To create a title, type <title> before it and </title> after it. For example, to make your title say "Joan's Home Page", type this:

<title>Joan's Home Page</title>

When you run the program, the computer will put the title in the blue **title bar** at the Web page's top.

Fonts

You learned to italicize by saying <i> and </i>, and to create bold by saying <b> and </b>. Here are other ways to change the text's font....

Size You can make the computer can produce text in 7 sizes. Font size 1 is the smallest; Font size 7 is the biggest. Here's how big they are:

This is font size 1. It is 8 points tall.

This is font size 2. It is 10 points tall.

This is font size 3. It is 12 points tall.

This is font size 4. It is 14 points tall.

This is font size 5. It is 18 points tall.

This is font size 6, 24 points tall.

Font size 7, 36 points.

That's how big the font sizes and point size look on paper and a 14-inch monitor. (On a slightly bigger monitor, the font sizes and point sizes look slightly bigger.)

Normally, the computer makes your Web page have font size 3. To make a phrase be font size 5, say <font size=5> before the phrase; say </font> after the phrase.

You can make part of a phrase be one size bigger, by saying <big> before that part and saying </big> after that part. For example, if the computer is making a phrase be font size 5 because you said <font size=5>, you can make part of that phrase be slightly bigger (font size 6) by saying <big> before that part and saying </big> after that part. To make part of a phrase be one size smaller, say <small> before that part and say </small> after that part.

If you said <font size=7> and then try to say <big>, the computer will ignore the <big>, since the computer can't go bigger than font size 7. If you said <font size=1> and then try to say <small>, the computer will ignore the <small>, since the computer can't go smaller than font size 1.

To make a phrase be subscript (like this), say _{before the phrase,} afterwards. To make a phrase be superscript (like this), say ^{before the phrase,} afterwards.

Heading To create a heading (such as a chapter title or a newspaper headline), say <h1> at the heading's beginning and </h1> at the heading's end, like this —

<h1>Chapter 2: Laura giggles at death</h1>

or like this:

<h1>USA declares war on hangnails</h1>

To do that, make sure you type the symbol "<", then the letter "h", then the number one, then the symbol ">", then the rest.

The <h1> makes the computer automatically create a new paragraph in font size 6 and bold. Saying <h1> is similar to saying <p><font size=6><b>.

If you want the heading to be centered (instead of at the screen's left edge), say <h1 align=center> instead of just <h1>.

If you say <h2> instead of <h1>, the computer will make the font size slightly smaller (5 instead of 6), so you'll be creating a "less dramatic heading", a subheading. If you say <h2> at the heading's beginning, say </h2> at the heading's end.

You can create headings in 6 sizes:

<h1> produces font size 6
<h2> produces font size 5
<h3> produces font size 4
<h4> produces font size 3
<h5> produces font size 2
<h6> produces font size 1

To create a heading in font size 7, say <h1><big> at the heading's beginning, and say </big></h1> at the heading's end.

Tt Normally, the computer makes the text's typeface be Times New Roman (which looks like this). If you want a phrase's typeface to be Courier New (which looks like this and imitates a typewriter and a Teletype), say <tt> before the phrase, </tt> afterwards.

Arial If you want a phrase's typeface to be Arial (which looks like this), say <font face=Arial> before the phrase, </font> afterwards.

If you want a phrase to be font size 7 and Arial, say <font size=7 face=Arial> before the phrase; </font> afterwards.

Compliance

If you want to create a Web page whose title is "Joan's Home Page" and whose body says "We *love* you", you can write this HTML program:

```
<title>Joan's Home Page</title>
We <i>love</i> you
```

Although that program works with *most* versions of *most* Web browsers, you're supposed to add some extra lines, for 3 reasons:

```
to help other programmers understand your program
to make sure the program works with all browsers
to prevent getting fired from your programming job
```

Head & body You're supposed to divide the program into two parts. The first part, called the **head**, begins with <head> and ends with </head> and includes the title. The second part, called the **body**, begins with <body> and ends with </body> and includes the paragraphs. So your program should look like this:

```
<head>
<title>Joan's Home Page</title>
</head>

<body>
We <i>love</i> you
</body>
```

(If you're typing into the middle of an Angelfire page, do *not* type a head, since Angelfire gave the page a head already.)

The <html> warning To make your program even better, you're supposed to begin the whole program by saying <html> and end the whole program by saying </html>, to emphasize that the whole program is written in HTML rather than a different computer language. So your program should look like this:

```
<html>
<head>
<title>Joan's Home Page</title>
</head>

<body>
We <i>love</i> you
</body>
</html>
```

Is code compliant? You should include all those extra lines — <head>, </head>, <body>, </body>, <html>, and </html> — to make your program comply with the standards that people expect. Those lines help make your program be **compliant**.

I usually don't bother including those lines, since I'm my own boss; but if you're employed, you should include those lines to keep your job.

Title To be compliant, your program must include a <title> line.

DOCTYPE To be compliant, you're supposed to also put this line at your program's top, above the <html> line:

```
<!DOCTYPE HTML PUBLIC "-//W3C//DTD HTML 4.01 Transitional//EN">
```

That line brags that your program document is of this type: it obeys the HTML standard, which is publicly available from the **World Wide Web Consortium (W3C)**, using the **document type definition (DTD)** for HTML version 4.01 — except that you're letting yourself include some older HTML commands also, to be transitional and help older Web browsers understand your Web page; and you're doing all this in **English (EN)**.

Actually, you're supposed to include another line below that, saying what Web site reveals the HTML 4 and 4.01 specifications; so your program is supposed to begin like this:

```
<!DOCTYPE HTML PUBLIC "-//W3C//DTD HTML 4.01 Transitional//EN"
"http://www.w3.org/TR/html4/loose.dtd">
```

Hardly anybody bothers to include those two lines about DOCTYPE. For example, Yahoo's Web site (www.yahoo.com) and Microsoft's Web site (www.microsoft.com) omit both lines.

Even the inventors of HTML 4.01 don't bother including the second line in their own Web pages.

XHTML HTML 4.01 was invented in 1999. Now committees are working to develop fancier programming language, called the **eXtensible HTML (XHTML)**, which is influenced by the **eXtensible Markup Language (XML)**.

If you want to be compliant with XHTML, adopt these habits:

```
In commands, use small letters (such as <p>) instead of capitals (such as <P>).

At the end of each paragraph, say </p>.

After each equal sign, put quotation marks; so instead of saying <font size=5>, say <font size="5">.
```

In XHTML, the top lines say:

```
<!DOCTYPE html PUBLIC "-//W3C//DTD XHTML 1.0 Transitional//EN"
"DTD/xhtml/1-transitional.dtd">
```

Lists

If you want your Web page to contain a simple list, say <br> at the beginning of each list item.

For example, suppose you want your Web page to say:

```
Here are the favorite flavors:
chocolate
vanilla
strawberry
```

To do that, say <p> at the beginning of the paragraph, <br> at the beginning of each list item, like this:

```
<p>Here are the favorite flavors:
<br>chocolate
<br>vanilla
<br>strawberry
```

The <br> stands for "break out a new line".

In XHTML, instead of saying <br> you must say <br /> and make sure to put a blank space before the slash.

Bullets Suppose you want your list to show bullets, like this:

```
Here are the favorite flavors:
• chocolate
• vanilla
• strawberry
```

To do that, say <p> at the beginning of the paragraph, <li> at the beginning of each list item, like this:

```
<p>Here are the favorite flavors:
<li>chocolate
<li>vanilla
<li>strawberry
```

Suppose you want the bullets to be indented, with a space above the list, like this:

```
Here are the favorite flavors:

    • chocolate
    • vanilla
    • strawberry
```

To do that, say <ul> above the list, </ul> below the list, like this:

```
<p>Here are the favorite flavors:
<ul>
<li>chocolate
<li>vanilla
<li>strawberry
</ul>
```

The <ul> stands for "unordered list". When you type <ul>, make sure you press the U and L keys on your keyboard (not the number one).

The <ul> accomplishes two goals:

```
It makes the list be indented.

It makes your program be compliant.
(A list without <ul> is not compliant.)
```

In XHTML, the end of each list item must say </li>.

Numbers Suppose you want your list to be numbered, like this:

```
Here are the favorite flavors:

    1. chocolate
    2. vanilla
    3. strawberry
```

To do that, say <ol> above the list, </ol> below the list, like this:

```
<p>Here are the favorite flavors:
<ol>
<li>chocolate
<li>vanilla
<li>strawberry
</ol>
```

The <ol> stands for "ordered list". When you type <ol>, make sure you press the O and L keys on your keyboard.

Tables

You can create a simple table or a fancy table.

Simple table Here's how to create a simple table:

```
Tell the computer the text is preformatted, by saying <pre>. Then type the
table, by using the Space bar and Enter key to line up the columns. Below
the table, say </pre>.
```

For example, suppose you want your Web page to say:

```
Here are the bowling scores:

NAME            SCORE

Jacqueline      200
Ann             137
Ed               75
```

To do that, say <pre> above the table and </pre> below the table, like this:

```
<p>Here are the bowling scores:
<pre>
NAME            SCORE

Jacqueline      200
Ann             137
Ed               75
</pre>
```

The <pre> makes the computer use Courier New, as if you had typed <tt>. Courier New is a convenient font for tables, because it makes every character and space have the same width, so you can easily align the table's columns by pressing the Space bar several times.

The <pre> also makes the computer copy each Enter and Space onto the Web page, unedited. (If you don't say <pre>, the computer turns each Enter into a Space and turns each pair of Spaces into a single Space.)

Fancy table Let's create a fancy table, so the Web page says:

```
Here are the bowling scores:
```

NAME	SCORE
Jacqueline	200
Ann	137
Ed	75

To do that, say <table border=1> above the table, <tr> at the beginning of each table row, <th> at the beginning of each column heading, <td> at the beginning of each data item, and </table> below the table, like this:

```
<p>Here are the bowling scores:
<table border=1>
<tr><th>NAME<th>SCORE
<tr><td>Jacqueline<td>200
<tr><td>Ann<td>137
<tr><td>Ed<td>75
</table>
```

The computer automatically makes the columns wide enough to hold their headings and data. The computer automatically makes the column headings be bold and centered.

The border=1 makes the table have a normal border. If you say border=12 instead, the table's outer border will be much thicker and shaded, forming a beautiful 3-D picture frame that makes the table seem to pop out from the screen and into the human's face. Try it! You'll impress your friends!

Links

You learned:

```
To make a phrase be italicized, say <i> before the phrase, </i> afterwards.
To make a phrase be bold,      say <b> before the phrase, </b> afterwards.
```

Link to other Web sites To make the phrase "house hunting" be underlined and link to www.realtor.com, say this:

```
<a href=http://www.realtor.com>house hunting</a>
```

Notice that before "house hunting", you say what "house hunting" is linked to, by saying <a href=http://www.realtor.com>, which means "anchor (link) with a hypertext reference to http://www.realtor.com". After "house hunting", say </a>.

Make sure you include the "http://". If you omit that, the link doesn't work.

Don't insert extra spaces. For example, don't insert a space after "http:"; don't insert a space after "//".

Most text on your Web page is black (on a white background). Links are underlined and typically blue; but that if the link refers to a Web page that was visited recently, the link turns purple (instead of blue).

Link to your own Web pages To make the phrase "funny jokes" be underlined and link to Web page you created and called "jokes.html", say this:

```
<a href=jokes.html>funny jokes</a>
```

That works just if you earlier invented a Web page named jokes.html and put it on the same disk and in the same folder as the new Web page you're inventing. For example, if you're inventing a new Web page on your hard disk's Desktop, jokes.html must also be a Web page on your hard disk's Desktop.

Suppose you create a Web page that's too long to fit on the screen, so when a human tries to read the page the human must scroll down. To let the human avoid scrolling, do this: near the page's beginning, put a table of contents that links to later parts of the page. Here's how. To make the phrase "my joys" be underlined and link to a part of the page that discusses your joys, say this:

```
<a href=#joys>my joys</a>
```

Tell the computer which part of your page discusses your joys, by beginning that part like this:

```
<a name=joys></a>
```

Link to e-mail This book was written by Russ Walter, whose e-mail address is Russ@SecretFun.com. On your Web page, you can let people write to Russ Walter. Here's how....

To make the phrase "write to Russ" be underlined and link to creating an e-mail to "Russ@SecretFun.com", say this:

```
<a href=mailto:Russ@SecretFun.com>write to Russ</a>
```

Then when a person accesses your Web page, "write to Russ" will be underlined. If the person clicks "write to Russ", the computer will automatically run the person's e-mail client program (such as Outlook Express), automatically click "Create Mail", automatically type "Russ@SecretFun.com" in the "To" box, and then wait for the person to type an e-mail message to Russ.

Try it! Go put that in your Web page, run your Web page, and write an e-mail to Russ! If you don't know what to say in the e-mail, just say, "Hi, Russ, I'm testing my Web page's e-mail link to you."

Be brave! Let people accessing your Web page write an e-mail to *you*. For example, if your name is Joan Smith and your e-mail address is "jSmith@SecretFun.com", say this:

```
<a href=mailto:jSmith@SecretFun.com>write to Joan Smith</a>
```

Custom colors

You can change colors.

Change a phrase Normally, the computer makes your text be black. To make a phrase be red, say <font color=red> before the phrase; say </font> after the phrase.

The computer knows the names of 16 colors:

Light color		Dark color	
red		maroon	(dark red)
blue		navy	(dark blue)
aqua	(greenish blue)	teal	(dark aqua)
lime	(bright green)	green	(darker than lime)
fuchsia	(bright purple)	purple	(darker than fuchsia)
silver	(light gray)	gray	(darker than silver)
yellow		olive	(dark yellow, looks greenish brown)
white		black	

If you want a phrase to be font size 7 and red, say <font size=7 color=red> before the phrase; say </font> after the phrase.

Change the whole Web page On a normal Web page, the background is white, the text is black, each typical link is blue, and each viewed link is purple.

Your program is supposed to be divided into two parts, called <head> and <body>. Instead of saying just <body>, you can say:

```
<body bgcolor=yellow text=red link=green vlink=fuchsia>
```

That makes the background be yellow, the text be red, each typical link be green, and each viewed link be fuchsia. Choose any colors you wish, from the list of 16 colors.

Usually, the background should be a light color (such as white or yellow) and the text should be a dark color (such as black). If you want to be shockingly different, do the reverse: make the background be a dark color (such as black or navy) and make the text be a light color (such as white or yellow). For example, try this:

```
<body bgcolor=navy text=white link=lime vlink=yellow>
```

Warning: the human eye gets dizzy when it sees red next to blue, so don't choose "red text on a blue background" or "blue text on a red background". If you make the mistake of choosing those combinations, the people viewing your Web site will get dizzy and fall asleep without reading your words. Your Web site will put them into a hypnotic trance. The human eye also has difficulty reading red (or maroon) next to black.

Style sheets

To change the appearance of your whole Web page, create a **style sheet**.

For example, suppose you want red characters on a yellow background. You learned you can do that by changing <body> to this:

```
<body bgcolor=yellow text=red>
```

Here's a better way: in your <head> section, below the <title>, say this:

```
<style>
body {color:red; background:yellow}
</style>
```

That creates this style: throughout the body, make the text color be red, the background yellow. That makes most of the text be red (though normal links will still be blue underlined and the viewed links will still be purple underlined). When you type the second line, make sure you type braces, which look like this: {}. Don't type parentheses, which look like this: ().

Normally, the text is font size 3, which is 12 points. If you want the text to be slightly bigger (so people can read it more easily), request a bigger point size, such as 13 points, by saying font-size=13pt, like this:

```
<style>
body {color:red; background:yellow; font-size:13pt}
</style>
```

That makes most text get bigger, but headings will be unchanged. For example, <h1> headings will still be font size 6 (which is 24 points).

Should you use style sheets? Style sheets were invented recently. They're new, hip, cool, and recommended.

For example, to get a yellow background, you ought to say background:yellow in the style sheet, rather than bgcolor=yellow in the <body>.

Using style sheets is **recommended**. Giving older types of commands, such as bgcolor=yellow, is **deprecated** (which means "pooh-poohed").

But many people still use older types of commands, such as bgcolor=yellow, since they work even on old computers whose browsers were invented before style sheets.

Links You can change the color of links:

```
<style>
body {color:red; background:yellow}
:link {color:green}
:visited {color:fuchsia}
:hover {color:navy}
</style>
```

That makes most links be green, recently visited links be fuchsia, and each link temporarily turn navy while the mouse hovers over it.

Headers You learned that you can create big headers by saying <h1>, smaller headers by saying <h2>, and even smaller headers by saying <h3>, <h4>, <h5>, and <h6>. Normally, headers are the same color as the body text. For example, if you made the body text be red, the headers are automatically red also.

To make <h1> headers be blue and all other headers be maroon, say so in the style sheet, like this:

```
<style>
body {color:red; background:yellow}
:link {color:green}
:visited {color:fuchsia}
:hover {color:navy}
h1 {color:blue}
h2,h3,h4,h5,h6 {color:maroon}
</style>
```

To make <h1> headers be blue and also centered (instead of at the screen's left edge), make the style sheet's h1 line be this:

```
h1 {color:blue; text-align:center}
```

Frankly, I hope you don't choose those colors! Your Web page will be too wild if you actually make the body text red, the background yellow, the links green, the visited links fuchsia, the hovered links navy, the big headings blue, and the smaller headings maroon. Choose more reasonable colors.

Normally, <h1> headers are font size 6, which is 24 points. To make <h1> headers be even bigger, give a bigger point size, such as by saying:

```
h1 {color:blue; text-align:center; font-size:40pt}
```

Paragraphs You learned to put <p> at the beginning of each paragraph. Normally, the <p> makes the computer put a blank line above the paragraph. If you want the computer to omit the blank line and indent the paragraph's first word, put this line in your style sheet:

```
p {text-indent:2em; margin-top:0; margin-bottom:0}
```

Sharing Several Web pages can share a style sheet. Here's how.

Using Notepad, create the style sheet, but omit the <style> and </style> lines. For example, create this style sheet:

```
body {color:red; background:yellow}
```

Save it on your Desktop, but give it a name that ends in .css (which stands for Cascading Style Sheet) instead of .html. For example, name it mystyle.css.

Then create your Web pages; but on each Web page, tell the computer to use the style sheet you created (mystyle.css), by putting this line in the <head> part of the Web page:

```
<link rel=stylesheet href=mystyle.css>
```

That tells the computer to create a link, related to your style sheet, which is located at the HTTP reference "mystyle.css".

Upload

To let the public use your Web page, make sure your Web page is on the Internet. Here's how.

If you created the Web page by using Angelfire's Webon, make sure you published your page (by clicking the blue "Save" and "Publish" buttons at Webon's top-right corner).

If you created the Web page by using Notepad, you must **upload** your page (copy it from your computer's hard disk to an Internet-connected hard disk). To upload your page, you need permission from a Web host, which will usually charge you a monthly fee. For example, you can upload to Angelfire if you pay Angelfire $1 per month to get Angelfire's **Entry service** (which is better than Angelfire's Free service). If you've upgraded to Angelfire's Entry service, here's how to copy your Web page to Angelfire's hard disk:

Using your Web browser, go to "www.angelfire.com". Click "Login" (which is at the top). Type your user name (such as "secretguide"), press the Tab key, type your password, then click the green "Log In" button. Click "Upload Files" (which is at the screen's center and isn't included in the Free version). Click the first "Browse" button.

You see a list of files that are on your computer's hard disk. Double-click the file you want to upload, such as "joan". (If you don't see that file in the list, try making it appear by clicking the word "Desktop" and using the scroll arrows.)

Click the green "Upload" button (which you see when you scroll down).

That file will now be on Angelfire's disk. For example, if your user name is "secretguide" and the file was joan.html, it's now available on the Internet as "http://secretguide.angelfire.com/joan.html". If the file was index.html, it's now available on the Internet as "http://secretguide.angelfire.com/index.html" or more simply as "http://secretguide.angelfire.com" (since "index.html" is your main page).

If your Web page includes links to other files (such as other Web pages you created and style sheets), make sure you upload those files also.

If you're too cheap to pay Angelfire $1 per month, try this crude trick:

Create a free Web page by using Angelfire's Webon. On that page, start the processing of typing your own HTML, as I explained in the section called "Typing in Angelfire". But instead of typing lots of HTML there, copy your typing from Notepad to there (by dragging across the HTML you typed in Notepad, then pressing Ctrl with C, then clicking in Angelfire's HTML editing box, then pressing Ctrl with V).

FTP The typical ISP lets you also copy your Web page to your ISP's hard disk by using **File Transfer Protocol (FTP)**. For example, if your ISP is Galaxy Internet Services (GIS), here's how to copy your Web page to GIS's hard disk:

Click "Start" then "Programs".
Click "MS-DOS Prompt". The computer will say:
```
C:\WINDOWS>
```
That should be in a black window that does *not* consume the whole screen. (If the window consumes the whole screen, so you see no colors, make the window smaller by tapping the Enter key while holding down the Alt key.)

Type "ftp" and then the name of your ISP's FTP site. For example, GIS's FPT site is called "ftp.gis.net", so you'd type "ftp ftp.gis.net", to make your screen looks like this:
```
C:\WINDOWS>ftp ftp.gis.net
```
At the end of that line, press Enter.

If you're not connected to the Internet at the moment, the computer might ask you to type your password. Do so and press Enter.

The ISP's computer will say "FTP server" and then "User". Type the user name that the ISP assigned you (such as "poo") and press Enter.

The ISP's computer will say "Password". Type the password that the ISP assigned you and press Enter.

The ISP's computer will say "logged in" and then say:
```
ftp>
```
Now you're using the ISP's operating system, which is Unix. You can type Unix commands. At the end of each Unix command, press the Enter key. (For example, just for fun, type the Unix command "dir" and press Enter: you'll see a list of files about you on the ISP's hard disk; each file's name is in the rightmost column. If you'd like to see a list of other Unix commands, type "help" or a question mark and press Enter. To see a command's purpose, type "help" then a space then the command's name, then press Enter.)

If you haven't done so already, make a directory (folder) called "public_html" on the ISP's hard disk by typing "mkdir public_html" (and press Enter).

Next, tell the computer to send (copy) the Desktop's joan.html file to the ISP's public_html folder. To accomplish that, type so your screen looks like this:
```
ftp> send Desktop/joan.html public_html/joan.html
```
The computer typed the "ftp> ", but you must type the rest. Type it very carefully! Type forward slashes (/) not backslashes (\), since Unix understands just forward slashes. Type a space after "send" and a space before "public"; those are the only spaces you type. After "public", type an underline (by holding down the Shift key while you tap the key that's right of the zero key).

The computer will copy the file and say "Transfer complete".

When you finish using FTP, type "quit" or "bye" and press Enter. The computer will quit using FTP and quit using Unix and say "C:\WINDOWS>". Then close the black window by clicking its X box.

That file will now be on the ISP's disk. For example, if the file was joan.html, it's now available on the Internet as "www.gis.net/~poo/joan.html. If the file was index.html, it's now available on the Internet as www.gis.net/~poo/index.html or simply as "www.gis.net/~poo" or even more simply as "gis.net/~poo". (The symbol "~" is at your keyboard's top left corner, above the Tab key, and requires you to hold down the Shift key.)

If your Web page includes links to other files (such as other Web pages you created and style sheets), make sure you upload those files also.

Special symbols

To put special symbols onto your Web page, type these codes:

Symbol	Symbol's name	Code you type
©	copyright	©
®	registered	®
™	trademark	™
¢	cent	¢
£	British pound	£
¥	Japanese yen	¥
¼	fraction 1/4	¼
½	fraction 1/2	½
¾	fraction 3/4	¾
¿	inverted question	¿
¡	inverted exclamation	¡
¹	superscript 1	¹
²	superscript 2	²
³	superscript 3	³
<	less than	<
>	greater than	>
&	ampersand	&
é	e acute	é
É	E acute	É
(similar for á, Á, í, Í, ó, Ó, ú, Ú, ý, Ý)		

Comments

In the middle of your program, you can write a comment such as:

```
<!--I wrote this program while drunk-->
```

The computer will ignore the comment. The comment won't affect what appears on the Web page.

To write a comment, begin with this symbol —

```
<!--
```

and end with this symbol:

```
                                        -->
```

The computer ignores whatever appears between those symbols. Whatever appears between those symbols is a comment. The comment can be short (part of a line) or long (many lines), but make sure you begin it with "<!--" and end with "-->".

Write comments to help other programmers deal with your program! For example, give your name, the date you wrote the program, and your address or phone number. Also include any technical comments you wish to make about how your program works and what further improvements you hope to make.

Forms

You can make your Web page display a form and let the human fill it in. For example, you can make your Web page say this:

```
I'm doing a survey of people who view this Web page.

Tell me about yourself.

What's your favorite ice cream flavor?  [                    ]

What's your favorite animal?            [                    ]
```

This program makes it happen (if your e-mail address is jSmith@SecretFun.com):

```
<p>I'm doing a survey of people who view this Web page.

<p>Tell me about yourself.
<form method=post action=mailto:jSmith@SecretFun.com>
<pre>
What's your favorite ice cream flavor? <input name=flavor>
What's your favorite animal?           <input name=animal>
</pre>
<input type=submit>
</form>
```

If you examine that program, you'll notice these rules:

Above the form, say <form method=post> and give your e-mail address. Below the form, say </form>.
To create each box, say <input> and give a one-word name for the box.
To make the boxes line up, say <pre> above them and </pre> below them.
At form's bottom, say <input type=submit>.

When a person runs your Web page, here's what happens. The computer shows the form and waits for the person to fill in the form. Each box is wide enough to show 20 typical characters. If the person types more that the box can show, the writing in the box automatically scrolls to the left, to let the person type more.

Below the form, the computer puts a button labeled "Submit Query". The person is supposed to click that button after filling in the form. When the person clicks that button, the computer e-mails the box's contents to the e-mail address mentioned in the <form> command. Here's how:

First, the computer gives the person this warning: "This form is being submitted using e-mail. Submitting this form will reveal your e-mail address to the recipient, and will send the form data without encrypting it for privacy. You may continue or cancel this submission."

The computer waits for the person to click "OK". (If the person clicks "Cancel" instead, the process is stopped.)

The computer automatically runs the person's e-mail program (such as Outlook Express) and automatically creates a new e-mail.

The e-mail's "To" is the e-mail address mentioned in the <form> command.

The e-mail's "Subject" is "Form posted from Microsoft Internet Explorer" (if the person used Microsoft Internet Explorer) or "Form posted from Mozilla" if the person used Netscape Navigator).

The e-mail's "Message" is blank, but the e-mail includes an Attachment, which is a Notepad document. That document is called "POSTDATA.ATT" (if the person used Microsoft Internet Explorer) or "Form posted from Mozilla.dat" (if the person used Netscape Navigator). For example, if the person said the favorite ice cream flavor is strawberry and the favorite animal is guinea pig, the document says this:
```
flavor=strawberry&animal=guinea+pig
```
The computer tries to send the e-mail. If the computer is not attached to the Internet at the moment, the computer either asks the person to connect or else just puts the e-mail in the Outbox (which is a holding area for e-mail that will be sent automatically when Internet connection is reestablished).

Then the computer stops running the e-mail program and returns to showing the Web page that contained the form.

When you receive the e-mail, try to open the attachment. The computer will ask whether you want to open it or save it.

For example, if you're using Windows Me, do this:

Click "Open it" then "OK".

If the attachment is called "POSTDATA.ATT", it opens immediately.

If the attachment is called "Form posted from Mozilla.dat", the computer warns "You are attempting to open a file of type .dat". To respond to the warning, press Enter then click "Notepad" (from the scrolling list of programs) then press Enter again.

Customize Here's how to customize the form.

If you want a box to be 30 characters wide instead of 20, say "size=30" like this:
```
What's your favorite ice cream flavor? <input name=flavor size=30>
```

If you want the "Submit Query" button to say instead "Click here to transmit", say so in the type=submit line, like this:
```
<input type=submit value="Click here to transmit">
```

You can put a Reset button to the right of the "Submit Query" button:
```
<input type=submit><input type=reset>
```

You can make the Reset button say "Click here to erase and start over":
```
<input type=submit><input type=reset value="Click here to erase and start over">
```

Check boxes Your form can include check boxes, so your Web page says:

Check all that apply:
❑ You have a pet dog.
❑ You have a pet cat.
❑ You can bark like a dog.
❑ You got arrested for being sneaky as a cat.

To do that, say this below the </pre>:
```
<p>Check all that apply:
<br><input type=checkbox name=dog>You have a pet dog.
<br><input type=checkbox name=cat>You have a pet cat.
<br><input type=checkbox name=bark>You can bark like a dog.
<br><input type=checkbox name=purr>You can purr like a cat.
<p>
```

If the person clicks the "You have a pet dog" and "You can bark like a dog" boxes, check marks appear on those boxes and the e-mail will say:
```
dog=on&bark=on
```

Radio buttons Your form can include radio buttons, so your Web page says:

Choose just one:
◯ You are male.
◯ You are female.

Each radio button acts like a check box, except that the button is round (instead of square), clicking it makes the middle get a dot (instead of a check mark), and just one button can be selected (since clicking a button makes all other buttons get unselected).

To create those radio buttons, say this below the </pre>:
```
<p>Choose just one:
<br><input type=radio name=sex value=male>You are male.
<br><input type=radio name=sex value=female>You are female.
<p>
```

If the person clicks the "You are male" button, a dot appears in that button and the e-mail will say:
```
sex=male
```

Create your own .com

I invented my own .com and called it "SecretFun.com", so you can access my Web page by typing just "www.SecretFun.com".

You can invent *your* own .com! Here are two cheap ways to do it.…

Method 1: pay Angelfire

Create a Web site on Angelfire, but pay Angelfire extra to get a .com name or switch to Angelfire's fanciest plan (called "THE Plan") which includes a domain name at no extra charge.

(Page 283 explained how Argon, Xenon, and Krypton differ from each other.)

Method 2: pay Go Daddy

Create a Web site cheaply anywhere (such as a free Angelfire site or a cheap Neon Angelfire site or a free site anywhere else), then buy a **domain name** (such as a .com name) from a **domain registrar** such as **Go Daddy**, which charges:

```
$15 per year for .co or .ws
$12 per year for .com
$10 per year for .org or .net
 $6 per year for .biz
 $5 per year for .us
 $2 per year for .info
```

Go Daddy was started by a famous nice guy (**Bob Parsons**, whose previous venture was called **Parsons Technology**). You can reach Go Daddy at **www.GoDaddy.com**.

Tell Go Daddy to charge you for the domain name (at $15/year or less) and set up a **parked site** (which is free because it just says "under construction — coming soon"). Then tell Go Daddy to do **domain forwarding** (which is free) from the parked site to the site you created at Angelfire. You can also tell Go Daddy to do **e-mail forwarding** (which is free) to your current e-mail address.

For example, I told Go Daddy to do this:

```
create www.SecretFun.com (now $12/year)
forward www.SecretFun.com to www.angelfire.com/nh/secret (free)
forward Russ@SecretFun.com to SecretGuide@comcast.net (free)
```

So now you can see my Web site (www.angelfire.com/nh/secret) by typing just "www.SecretFun.com" (which is easier to remember), and you can send me e-mail by typing "Russ@SecretFun.com" (which you might remember easier than "SecretGuide@comcast.net").

If you wish, Go Daddy can also **host** your site (so you don't need to involve Angelfire), but Go Daddy charges more for hosting than Angelfire does. Go Daddy will try to sell you many extra services (for surcharges), but you can decline them all: **pay just $15 per year or less for a domain name** (with free domain forwarding and e-mail forwarding to your current addresses elsewhere).

Blogs

On a traditional ship, the captain's supposed to write a daily **log**, which is a diary of what happened each day and how the ship progressed on its voyage.

You can create your *own* log — a daily diary of your experiences and thoughts — showing how you progress on your voyage from birth to death. You can put your log onto a Website, so others can read it. Then it's called a **Web log**, or, more briefly, a **blog**. In your blog, you can write about your loves & hates, desires & despairs, successes & failures, pleasures & pains, laughs & tears.

The typical blog has a theme, such as:

```
you won't believe what happened to me today!
come peek at the latest adventures of me and my lover
here are my latest beliefs about politics

I'll share with you my deepest thoughts about the meaning of life today

my newest ideas for the book I'm trying to write — do you like them?
```

A person who writes a blog is called a **blogger** and is said to be **blogging**.

The Internet includes *thousands* of blogs, written by people all over the globe, forming our **blogosphere** (the globe full of blogs, the ideas they express, and the intellectual atmosphere they create). The typical blog begins by showing the author's newest thoughts, then shows older thoughts below, in case you'd like to read them also. The thoughts are listed in **reverse chronological order** (the newest thoughts first) and lets readers add their own comments about the author's thoughts. The author's writings are just the tinder to start a fiery group discussion that all readers can participate in.

Create a blog

The easiest way to create your own blog is to use a Website called **Blogger.com**. It used to be independent but was bought by **Google**. Here's how to use it.

Go to www.blogger.com.

If you have a Google account already (because you used Blogger.com before or you used another Google service, such as gmail), do this:

```
Type your Google username. Press the Tab key. Type your Google
password. Click the "Sign in" button.
```

Click "CREATE YOUR BLOG NOW".

If you don't have a Google account yet, the computer will say "Create a Google Account" and wait for you to do this:

```
Type your e-mail address (such as "SecretGuide@comcast.net"). Press the
Tab key. Invent a password that's at least 6 characters long and type it;
you'll see black circles instead of what you're typing. Press Tab twice. Type
the password again. Press Tab. Type your name or nickname or however
you want to sign what you write, such as "Russ Walter"; type it. Press Tab.
Type the nonsense word you see. Click the Acceptance of Term box (which
you might have to scroll down to see), so a checkmark appears in that box.
Click "CONTINUE" (which you might have to scroll down to see).
```

Invent your blog's title (such as "Computer Culture") and type it. Press Tab.

Invent your blog's address. It must end in ".blogspot.com" (such as "ComputerCulture.blogspot.com"). Type the part that comes before the .blogspot.com (such as "ComputerCulture"). It must not contain any blank spaces. Click "Check availability"; if the computer says "Sorry, this blog address is not available", invent and type a different address instead, click "Check availability" again, and hope for better luck! When the computer finally says "This blog address is available", click "CONTINUE".

The computer will say "Choose a template". Don't bother choosing a fancy template yet; just click "CONTINUE" (which gets you the simplest template, which is minimal and called **Minima**). The computer will say "Your blog has been created".

Click "START POSTING".

Publish a thought

Type whatever thought you want to express for the world to see.

You can type several paragraphs. At the end of each typical paragraph, press Enter twice.

At the end of the final paragraph, instead of pressing Enter twice, press Tab.

Type a list of keywords about your paragraphs. For example, if your paragraphs are about ketchup and blood, type "ketchup,blood". Put commas between the keyboards.

Click in the Title box. Type a title for those thoughts (such as "Experiment with ketchup").

Click "PUBLISH". The thoughts you typed and published are called your **post**; you have **posted** your thoughts. The computer says "Your blog post published successfully!"

Click "View Blog". You see how your blog looks:

> You see the blog's title (such as "COMPUTER CULTURE").
> You see the paragraphs you wrote this time. Above them, you see the date you wrote them and the title you gave them. Below them, you see your name (or nickname), the exact time you published them, how many comments about those paragraphs were contributed by your readers (probably 0 so far), and an alphabetized list of keyboards about those paragraphs ("BLOOD, KETCHUP").
> Below all that, you see similar info about any paragraphs you wrote on previous days (probably none so far).

Sign out

When you finish looking at your blog today, click "Sign Out" (which is at the screen's top-right corner). Then you see the main Blogger.com screen again (which is called www.blogger.com and also called www2.blogger.com/start).

View your blog again

To view your blog again, go to the Website that's your blog, such as "ComputerCulture.blogspot.com". (The computer doesn't care whether you put "www." or "http://" before that.)

You see what you wrote.

If you want change what you wrote (by writing more or deleting), you must be signed in. If you're not signed in now, sign in by doing this:

> Click "Sign In" (which is at the screen's top-right corner). Type your username (which is your e-mail address, such as "SecretGuide@comcast.net"). Press the Tab key. Type your Blogger.com password. Click "SIGN IN" then "View Blog".

Then do whatever editing you wish.

> *If you want to publish an extra thought*, click "New Post" (which is near the screen's top-right corner) then do the "Publish a thought" procedure I explained previously.

> *If you want to edit a thought you published previously*, find that thought (by scrolling down until you see it). Below that thought, you see a pencil (to the right of "POSTED BY" and "COMMENTS"). Click that pencil. Edit that thought, then click "PUBLISH" then "View Blog".

Handle comments

While you're viewing a thought written by a blog's owner, trying clicking the word "COMMENTS" that's immediately below that thought. You see any comments that people have written about that thought.

If you want to type your *own* comment about that thought, do this:

> Type your comment. Your typing will appear in the box at the screen's top-right corner. You can type several paragraphs. At the end of each paragraph, press Enter twice (except you don't have to bother after the final paragraph).
> If you see a box called "USERNAME", type your username (such as "SecretGuide@comcast.net") then press Tab then type your Google password.
> Click "PUBLISH YOUR COMMENT". The computer will say "Your comment has been saved."

When you finish viewing and creating comments, click the blog's title (such as "Computer Culture").

If you published your own comment, the blog mentions 1 more comment about the blog owner's thought; the extra comment is the one you wrote.

If you wish, repeat the process by doing this:

> To see all the comments about the blog owner's thought, click the "COMMENTS" below that thought. Then, if you wish, write another comment then click "PUBLISH YOUR COMMENT".

Use the archive

While you're looking at a blog, the screen's right-hand side says "BLOG ARCHIVE". Below that, you see the titles of the thoughts that were published this month.

If one of those titles interests you, click it: that makes the computer show just that thought and the comments about it. When you finish admiring that detail, return to the blog's normal view by clicking the blog's title (such as "COMPUTER CULTURE").

Databases

A **database program** is a program that manipulates lists of facts. It can store info about your friends & enemies, customers & suppliers, employees & stockholders, students & teachers, hobbies & libraries. It puts all that data about your life and business onto a disk, which acts as an electronic filing cabinet. Then it lets you retrieve the data easily. It can generate mailing lists, phone directories, sales reports, and any other analyses you wish.

It's called a **database program** or **database management system (DBMS)** or **information retrieval system**. The terms are synonymous.

Database jargon

In an old-fashioned office that lacks a computer, you'll see a filing cabinet containing several drawers:

One drawer's labeled "Customers"; another drawer's labeled "Employees"; another drawer's labeled "Suppliers". Each drawer contains alphabetized index cards.

For example, the drawer labeled "Customers" contains a card about each customer; the first card might be labeled "Adams, Joan"; the last card might be labeled "Zabronski, Jill". The first card contains all known information about Joan Adams: it contains her name, address, phone number, everything she bought, how much she paid, how much she still owes, and other personal information about her. That card is called her **record**. Each item of information on that card is called a **field**.

If the card is a pre-printed form, it allows a certain amount of space for each item: for example, it might allow only 30 characters for the person's name. The number of characters allowed for a field is called the **field's width**. In that example, the width of the Name field is 30 characters.

Each drawer is called a **file**. For example, the drawer that contains information about customers is called the **customer file**; another drawer is the **employee file**; another drawer is the **supplier file**.

The entire filing cabinet — which contains all the information about your company — is called the **database**.

A sample file

Here's a file about amazing students in the School of Life:

```
Last name: Smith                    First name: Suzy
Age: 4            Class: 12
Comments: Though just 4 years old, she finished high school because she's fast.

Last name: Bell                     First name: Clara
Age: 21           Class: 10
Comments: The class clown, she never graduated but had fun trying. Super-slow!

Last name: Smith                    First name: Buffalo Bob
Age: 7            Class: 2
Comments: Boringly normal, he's jealous of his sister Suzy. Always says "Howdy!"

Last name: Kosinski                 First name: Stanislaw
Age: 16           Class: 11
Comments: He dislikes Polish jokes.

Last name: Ketchopf                 First name: Heinz
Age: 57           Class: 1
Comments: His pour grades make him the slowest Ketchopf in the West.

Last name: Nixon                     First name: Tricky Dick
Age: 78           Class: 13
Comments: The unlucky President, he disappointed our country.

Last name: Walter                    First name: Russy-poo
Age: 53           Class: 0
Comments: This guy has no class.
```

That file consists of 7 records: Suzy Smith's record, Clara Bell's record, Buffalo Bob Smith's record, Stanislaw Kosinski's record, Heinz Ketchopf's record, Tricky Dick Nixon's record, and Russy-poo Walter's record.

Each record consists of 5 fields: last name, first name, age, class, and comments. The age and class fields are narrow; the comments field is very wide.

Database programs versus word processing

Like a word processing program, a database program lets you type info, put it onto a disk, edit it, and copy it onto paper.

In a word processing system, the info's called a **document**, consisting of paragraphs which in turn consist of sentences. In a database system, the info's called a **file** (instead of a document); it consists of records, which in turn consist of fields.

Since a database program resembles a word processor, a word processor can act as a crummy database program. A *good* database program offers these extras, which the typical word processor lacks:

A good database program can **alphabetize**, **put info into numerical order**, and **check for criteria**. For example, you can tell it to check which customers are women under 18 who have light red hair and live in a red-light district, make it print their names and addresses on mailing labels in ZIP-code order, and make it print a phone book containing their names and numbers. Database programs are very potent and can be nasty tools for invading people's privacy!

Famous programs

Many database programs have been invented.

PFS

Most database programs are hard to use. In 1980, John Page invented the first *easy* database program. He called it the **Personal Filing System (PFS)**.

It ran on Apple 2 computers. He developed it while sitting in his garage.

He showed the program to two friends: Fred Gibbons and Janelle Bedke. The three of them tried to find a company willing to market his program, but no company was interested, so they decided to market the program themselves by forming a company, **Software Publishing Corporation**.

The program became very popular. Software Publishing Corporation became a multi-million-dollar corporation. It developed improved versions of PFS for the Apple 2 family, Radio Shack models 3 & 4, Commodore 64, Mac, and IBM PC. Now the fanciest version of PFS is **Professional File**, which runs on the IBM PC.

The company also invented a word processor, whose IBM version is called **Professional Write**. It works well with Professional File. When you buy Professional Write, you get Professional File free!

You can write a memo by using Professional Write and build a mailing list by using Professional File. Then use those programs together to print personalized copies of your memo to everybody on your mailing list.

Software Publishing Corporation has invented an even easier program, called **PFS First Choice**. It includes the easiest parts of both Professional File and Professional Write. It also includes spreadsheets, graphics, and telecommunication.

In 1988, John Page and Janelle Bedke got bored and quit the company. Fred Gibbons and the rest of his staff hung on but sold PFS First Choice to **Spinnaker**, which later became part of **Softkey**, which later became part of **The Learning Company**, which later became part of the **Mattel** toy company.

Those products (PFS, Professional Write, Professional File, and PFS First Choice) are no longer marketed. Exciting new competitors have taken their place. Let's look at those competitors....

Q&A

Inspired by the PFS series, a new company called **Symantec** developed a similar program, called **Q&A**.

At first glance, Q&A seems to just imitate the PFS series, since Q&A uses almost the same commands and keystrokes as the first IBM version of PFS. But Q&A understands many extra commands, making Q&A much more powerful than the PFS series. Q&A handles just two topics — databases and word processing — but very well! It's fairly easy (almost as easy as the PFS series) and powerful enough to handle the computing needs of most businesses. Q&A is the database program I use to run my own business.

The best versions of Q&A is called **Q&A version 5 for DOS**. You can get it for $199 (plus $15 shipping) from **Professional Computer Technology Associates** in Pennsylvania at 215-598-8440.

Reflex

Reflex was the first database program to let you view your data in 5 ways: it lets you see a **form view** (a filled-in form showing a record), a **list view** (a big spreadsheet showing the whole file), a **graph view** (a graph of all the data), a **report view** (a report on the entire file, with subtotals), and a **crosstab view** (a table of totals for statisticians).

Reflex can show you many views simultaneously, by dividing your screen into windows. As you edit the view in one window, the views in other windows change simultaneously. For example, if one window shows numbers and another window shows a graph, the graph changes automatically as you edit the numbers.

Reflex is partly a database program and partly a spreadsheet. Many of Reflex's features were copied by Microsoft's spreadsheet, Excel.

Reflex is published by Borland; but Borland has stopped marketing it, because competition from newer database programs has become too fierce.

Relational databases

Reflex is a **simple flat-file system**, which means it manipulates just one file at a time. Q&A goes a step further: while you're editing a file, Q&A lets you insert data from a second file.

Software that goes even further than Q&A and lets you edit two files simultaneously is called a **relational database program** (or **relational database management system** or **relational DBMS**).

The most popular relational database programs for DOS are **dBase**, **FoxPro**, and **Paradox**. You can customize them to meet *any* need, because they include complete programming languages.

Another relational database program for DOS is **Alpha 4**. It lets you accomplish some tasks more easily than DBase, FoxPro, and Paradox but lacks a programming language.

Windows wars

Programmers have been trying to invent database programs for Windows. Going beyond DOS programs such as Q&A, Windows database programs let the screen display pretty fonts and photographs.

The first popular Windows database program was **Approach**, which is now published by the Lotus division of IBM.

Borland has invented Windows versions of **DBase** and **Paradox** and a new Windows database program called **Delphi**. Microsoft has invented a Windows version of **FoxPro** and a new Windows database program called **Microsoft Access**. Alpha Software has invented **Alpha 5**, which resembles Alpha 4 but handles Windows and is also programmable.

The most popular database program for the Mac is **FileMaker Pro**. It's as easy as Q&A! It's published by the FileMaker company, which is owned by Apple but has had the good sense to also invent a Windows version of FileMaker Pro.

Microsoft Works includes a database program that's very limited. For example, it can't handle big mailing lists, since it's limited to 32,000 records.

Symantec invented a Windows version of **Q&A**, but Q&A's Windows version is hated by everybody.

It's worse than the DOS version and worse than all other major Windows databases. If you use Q&A, stick with Q&A's DOS version.

Though Q&A for Windows is terrible, the other Windows database programs are fine. Here's the hierarchy:

The simplest Windows database program is the database part of **Microsoft Works**, but it comes with no instruction manual and you'll outgrow the program's abilities.

The next step up is **FileMaker Pro**. It's wonderful! People who buy it love it. It's more powerful than the Microsoft Works database — it performs more tricks and handles a wider variety of problems. It comes with a decent instruction manual.

The next step up is **Approach**. By a "step up", I mean it's more powerful than the Microsoft Works database and Filemaker Pro — it performs more tricks and handles a wider variety of problems — but it's also more complex (harder to learn & use). Unlike Microsoft Works and Filemaker Pro, it's relational. But it's still not programmable.

The next step up (in power and complexity) is **Alpha 5**. It's relational and also programmable! But its programming language is small.

The next step up is **Microsoft Access**. Its programming language is bigger.

The next step up is the triumvirate: the Windows versions of **dBase**, **FoxPro**, and **Paradox**. They're powerful, fancy, and more than most folks can understand. If you buy one of them, you'll probably admire the big box it comes in, put it on the shelf, and invite friends to visit you and admire your big box, but you'll never figure out how to use it.

What to buy

To make your life *easy*, get one of the *easy* database programs: Q&A for DOS, Microsoft Works, or FileMaker Pro. Go beyond them just if your database needs are too complex for them to handle.

Even if your database needs are complex, begin by practicing with an *easy* database program first, so you master database fundamentals easily and quickly without getting distracted by needlessly complex details.

Complex database programs are like sneakers with untied shoelaces: though their overall design can let you perform amazing feats, you'll probably trip, get bloodied, and have to call in a computer "first-aid squad", which is a team of high-priced computer consultants.

To avoid the need for consultants, use Microsoft Works, FileMaker Pro, or Q&A.

FileMaker Pro

Many database programs have been invented. In general, the best one to use is **FileMaker Pro**. It's published by the FileMaker company, which is owned by Apple. It's the most popular database program for Macintosh computers, and a Windows version is also available.

Like Q&A, it's easy to learn how to use. It has two main advantages over Q&A: it can handle databases that are more advanced, and its Windows version is excellent. (Q&A's Windows version is terrible.) FileMaker Pro has been nicknamed "Q&A for Windows, done right." It's also been nicknamed "Microsoft Access, made reasonable" (because Microsoft Access is unreasonably hard).

The newest version of FileMaker Pro is **FileMaker Pro 9**. It lists for $299. Pay just $179 if you're upgrading from an earlier version. You can download a 30-day trial version free from www.filemaker.com.

This chapter explains how to use FileMaker Pro 5 (which is similar to FileMaker Pro 6, 7, 8, and 9). I'll explain the Mac version and also the Windows version.

Copy FileMaker to the hard disk

FileMaker Pro 5 comes on a CD-ROM disk, which you must copy to your computer's hard disk.

For the Mac version, do this:

Turn on the computer without any floppy or CD-ROM disks in the drives.
Put the FileMaker Pro 5 CD-ROM disk into the CD-ROM drive. Double-click "Start Here". Press the Return key twice.
The computer says "Personalization". Type your name, press the TAB key, type your company's name (if any), press the TAB key. Type your 17-digit Installation Code Number (which is on a white sticker; that sticker came on a big sheet of paper with the CD-ROM disk and should be transferred to the back of the CD-ROM disk's white envelope). Press the Return key.
The computer says "Installation was successful". Choose Eject from the Special menu. Remove the CD-ROM disk from the drive, then close the drive's door.

For the Windows version, do this instead:

Turn on the computer without any floppy or CD-ROM disks in the drives, so the computer runs Windows 95 (or 98) and the computer's bottom left corner says Start.
Put the FileMaker Pro 5 CD-ROM disk into the CD-ROM drive. In the phrase "➔ Install FileMaker Pro 5", click the right-arrow that begins the phrase.
The computer says "FileMaker Pro 5 Installation". Press Enter four times.
The computer says "Personalization". While holding down the Ctrl key, tap the Delete key (so you erase the word "User"). Type your name, press the Tab key, type your company's name (if any), press the Tab key. Type your 17-digit Installation Code Number (which is on a white sticker; that sticker came on a big sheet of paper with the CD-ROM disk and should be transferred to the back of the CD-ROM disk's white envelope). Press Enter twice.
The computer says "Installation Completed". Press Enter twice.

Launch FileMaker Pro

For the Mac version, do this:

Double-click "Macintosh HD" then "FileMaker Pro 5 Folder" then "FileMaker Pro".

For the Windows version, do this instead:

Click "Start" then "Programs" then "FileMaker Pro 5" then "FileMaker Pro".

Mac versus Windows

Now I'm going to explain how to use the Mac version. The Windows version works the same way, except for minor headaches (which I'll explain later) and these keyboard differences:

The Mac has a clearly marked Return key.
In Windows, the Return key says "Enter" on it.

The Mac has a clearly marked Control key.
In Windows, the Control key says "Ctrl" on it.

The Mac has a Command key (which shows a squiggly cloverleaf and an Apple). Windows doesn't have Command key, so use the Windows "Ctrl" key instead.

Create a database

Click "Create a new empty file" then "OK".

For our first experiment, let's create this database:

First name	Sue
Last name	Smith
Comments	wiggles her toes

First name	Sam
Last name	Smith
Comments	picks his nose

First name	Tina
Last name	Ash
Comments	the class clown

First name	Tina
Last name	Smith
Comments	incredible

Here's how to create it....

Invent a name for your database (such as "Friends"). Type the name. **At the end of the name, press the Return key** (which in Windows is marked "Enter").

If the computer says the file "already exists", do this procedure:

Press Return. Type a different name instead (such as "Friends2" or "Buddies" or "Pals" or "Enemies") and then press Return. If the computer says the file "already exists" again, do this whole procedure again.

Define fields The computer says "Define Fields".

We're trying to create a database that has three fields, called "First name", "Last name", and "Comments". To accomplish that, type the words "First name", then press Return, then type the words "Last name", then press Return again, then type the word "Comments", then press Return again.

Above your typing, you see this list of fields you created:

Field name	Type	Options
First name Last name Comments	Text Text Text	

Click "Done".

Enter data You see this blank form:

First name	
Last name	
Comments	

Into that form, type a person's record. Here's how: type the person's first name ("Sue"), press the Tab key, type the person's last name ("Smith"), press the Tab key, and type the comment ("wiggles her toes"), so the form looks like this:

First name	Sue
Last name	Smith
Comments	wiggles her toes

That's Sue Smith's record! When you've finished typing it, and want **to start typing the next person's record, do this: tap the N key while holding down the Command key** (which on a Mac shows a squiggly cloverleaf and Apple, and in Windows says "Ctrl".) That makes the computer start a new record, so the computer shows you a new blank form, where you can fill in the details for the next person (Sam Smith). The screen shows just one record at a time: while you're typing Sam Smith's record, you don't see Sue Smith's record.

When you've finished typing Sam Smith's record, press Command with N again, so you see another blank form, so you can type the next person's record (Tina Ash's). Then press Command with N again, then type Tina Smith's record.

While you're typing those records, the computer automatically copies them to the hard disk. (You don't have to click any "Save button".)

When you've finished typing all the records, congratulations! You've created a database!

View your data

To view the data you typed, you can use several tricks.

Control key To go back and view the previous record, press Control with up-arrow (which means do this: while pressing the Control key, tap the up-arrow key). To view the next record, press Control with down-arrow. (In Windows, the Control key says "Ctrl" on it.)

So in Windows, *while pressing the Ctrl key* you can do this:

tap the up-arrow key to view the previous record
tap the down-arrow key to view the next record
tap the N key to create a new record

Rolodex At the screen's right edge, under the word "Layout", you see a picture of a **Rolodex** (which is a device that displays business cards). **The Rolodex shows two business cards** (except that the words on the cards are too small to read).

To go back and view the previous record, click the top card.
To view the next record, click the bottom card.

Below the Rolodex, you see two numbers:

The first number says which record you're viewing. (For example, while you're viewing record #3, which is Tina Ash's record, that number is 3.)

The bottom number says how many records there are in the whole database.

Try this experiment: look at the first number (which is the number of the record you're viewing). If you change that number to a different number (such as 2), the computer will hop to record 2. Here's how to change the number:

Method 1: click the number, then type the number you want instead (and press Return).

Method 2: drag the slider (which is above the number).

Tab key While you're viewing a record, you can edit the data by retyping it.

To move to the next field, press the Tab key.
To move back to the previous field, press Shift with Tab.

Delete While you're typing, here's how to delete:

To delete a character, click after it (on a Mac) or before it (in Windows), then press the Delete key.

To delete an entire word, double-click it then press the Delete key.
To delete an entire line, triple-click it then press the Delete key.
To eliminate (delete) the entire record, press Command with E, then press D.

3 views If you click "View" (which is near the screen's top), you see these choices:

View as Form
View as List
View as Table

The normal choice is "**View as Form**", which shows you just one person's record at a time.

If you click "**View as List**" instead, you see the first person's record, and down from it you see the second person's record, and down from it you see the third person's record, etc., so you see many records on the screen at once. If there are too many records to fit on your screen, you can see the other records by using the window's scroll arrows (or the Page Down and Page Up keys or your mouse's wheel).

If you click "**View as Table**" instead, you see the database as a table looking like this:

First name	Last name	Comments
Sue	Smith	wiggles her toes
Sam	Smith	picks his nose
Tina	Ash	the class clown
Tina	Smith	incredible

At the top of each column, you see the column's heading (field name). To the right of the column's heading, you see a vertical gridline separating that heading from the next column's heading. To widen the column (so you can see longer words), drag that gridline toward the right (by using your mouse). To narrow the column (so the column consumes less space and you can fit more columns onto the screen), drag that gridline back toward the left. Changing the column's width does *not* change the data; it changes just the table's view of it; the other views show that the data is unchanged.

Mouse wheel If the computer is trying to display more records than can fit on the screen, and your mouse has a wheel between its buttons, do this:

Rotate the wheel away from you to view earlier records.
Rotate the wheel toward you to view later records.

Find

Here's how to find everybody whose last name is Smith:

Say "find" by pressing Command with F.
Click in the "Last name" box, type "smith", and press Return.

That makes the computer show you the records of just the people whose last name is Smith.

You can view them however you wish: from the View menu, choose "View as Form" or "View as List" or "View as Table".

I recommend choosing "View as Table", since it shows you all relevant records at once. (If you choose "View as Form", you see just one Smith at a time; to see the next Smith, press Control with down-arrow.)

You see the Smiths but not Tina Ash, since she's not a Smith. You see a **filtered database**, where the Smiths are still visible but Tina Ash has been filtered out and is invisible.

Here's how to find everybody whose first name is Tina:

Say "find" by pressing Command with F.
Click in the "First name" box, type "tina", and press Return.

That makes the computer show you the records of just the people whose first name is Tina. You see Tina Ash's record and Tina Smith's record, but not Sue Smith, not Sam Smith.

When in doubt about which records to show you, the computer is generous and shows you many:

If you tell the computer to find everybody whose last name is "smith", the computer will show you every "Smith" and also everybody whose last name begins with "Smith", such as "Smithson" and "Smithers" and "Smithers Jr., MD". If you tell the computer to find everybody whose last name is "sm", the computer will show you everybody whose last name begins with "sm", such as "Smith" and "Smythe" and "Smyers" and "smells so bad I forgot his last name". If you tell the computer to find everybody whose comment is "clown", the computer will show you everybody whose comment includes the word "clown", such as Tina Ash (whose comment is "the class clown") and anybody whose comment mentions "clown" or "clowns" or "clowning" or "clowned". If you tell the computer to find everybody whose first name is "ti", the computer will show you everybody whose first name is "Tina" or "Tim" or "Timothy" or "the amazing Timothy" or "His Esteemed Majesty Timothy".

Here's the rule:

If you tell the computer to search in a field for a word, the computer will show every record where that field contains the word (or contains a longer word beginning with the same letters).

If you tell the computer to find certain records, the computer will filter the database and keep showing you just those records, until you tell the computer to find different records instead, or until you **say "jumbo" (by pressing Command with J), which makes the computer show you the entire jumbo database again**, unfiltered.

Two fields at once (how to say "and") You can search two fields at once. For example, to search for Tina Smith's record, do this:

Say "find" by pressing Command with F.
Type "tina" (in the "First name" box), press Tab (to go to the "Last name" box), type "smith", and press Return.

How to say "or" Here's how to search for people whose first name is "Sue" or "Tina":

Say "find" by pressing Command with F.
Type "sue" (in the "First name" box).
Say "new search" by pressing Command with N.
Type "tina" (in the "First name" box) and press Return.

That makes the computer show the records of all people named "Sue" or "Tina" (not "Sam").

How to say "not" Here's how to search for people whose first name is not "Sam":

Say "find" by pressing Command with F.
Type "sam" (in the "First name" box).
Say "not" (by clicking the Omit box, which is at the screen's left edge).
Press Return.

That makes the computer omit Sam, so the computer will show the records of all people not named "Sam". (You'll see the records for "Sue" and "Tina".) Sam is still in the database, but he's not shown (until you do a different "find" instead).

Alphabetize

Here's how to alphabetize (sort) the records.

First, get a good view of how the records are currently organized (by clicking "View" then "View as Table").

Decide which records you want to include. (If you want to include just _some_ of the records, filter them, by pressing Command with F and then saying which records you want. If you want to include _all_ the records, making sure they're unfiltered, by pressing Command with J.)

Now you see a table of the records you want to alphabetize.

Say "Sort" by pressing Command with S.

You see two big white boxes.

Make sure the right-hand "big white box" is empty. (If it's not, click "Clear All".)

The left "big white box" contains a list of field names.

To alphabetize the records, let's make the computer look at each person's last name and put the last names in alphabetical order. If two people have the same last name, let's make the computer look at their first names and put their first names in alphabetical order. So here's the rule:

Sort by last name. If two people have the same last name, sort them by first name.

Here's how to say that:

Click "Last name" then "Move".
Click "First name" then "Move".

Press Return. The computer alphabetizes the table by Last name, then First name, so the table becomes this:

First name	Last name	Comments
Tina	Ash	the class clown
Sam	Smith	picks his nose
Sue	Smith	wiggles her toes
Tina	Smith	incredible

Those records will remain sorted until you give a different sort command or you unsort them (by pressing Command with S and then clicking "Unsort"). Warning: if you edit those records or add extra records, they won't be accurately sorted until you give the sort command again.

Print

Here's how to print records onto paper.
Say which records to print:

If you want to include just _some_ of the records, filter them (by pressing Command with F and then saying which records you want). If you want to print _all_ the records, making sure they're unfiltered (by pressing Command with J).

If you want the records to be sorted, sort them (by pressing Command with S and then saying which fields to sort on).

Say which view you want to print:

Click "View", then click either "View as List" or "View as Table".
(If you click "View as Form", the computer will print a "View as List" instead.)

Say "Print" (by pressing Command with P or clicking the Print button).

For the Mac, proceed as follows:

> You see your printer's window. Click "Records being browsed" — unless you change your mind and want to print something else.

For Windows, proceed as follows instead:

> You see the Print window. In it, the first box is labeled "Print". In that Print box, make sure you see "Records being browsed". If you see something else, click that box's down-arrow, then click "Records being browsed" — unless you change your mind and want to print something else.

The typical choices are "Records being browsed", "Current record", "Blank record, showing fields", and "Field definitions".

Make sure the printer is turned on and contains paper. **Press Return.** Then the printer will print on paper.

Final steps

When you finish using the Friends database, close the Friends window. (In Windows, do that by clicking the Friends window's X button.) Then you have three choices:

> **To start creating a different database, click the New button** (which is near the screen's top left corner, below the word "File") then follow my instructions on pages 297-298 for how to "Create a database".
>
> **To use a database you previously created, click the Open button** (which is near the screen's top left corner and looks like an opening manila file folder). You see a list of databases you created (and some folders, too). (If the list is too long to see it all, scroll to see the rest of it.) Double-click the database you want (such as "Friends"). Then that database will appear on the screen, with the same view and filtering and sorting as when you last used it.
>
> **To stop using FileMaker Pro, do this:** for a Mac, choose Quit from the File menu; for Windows, click FileMaker Pro's X button.

Improve the fields

While you're using a database, try clicking "File" then "Define Fields". Then you see the Define Fields window, which shows the list of fields again, like this:

Field name	Type	Options
First name	Text	
Last name	Text	
Comments	Text	

Extra fields To create an extra field, just type the field's name and press Return.

Done I'm going to reveal extra tricks for improving your fields, by using the Define Fields window. Whenever you finish using the Define Fields window, click "Done".

Numeric fields To create an extra field that contains just numbers (such as a field about "Age" or "Test score" or "Population" or "Number of children" or "Temperature" or "Amount paid" or "Balance due" or "Profit" or "Debt" or "Income" or "Cost" or "Sales" or "Discount percentage"), type the field's name then click "Number" then press Return. That lets the computer do filtering and sorting better.

For example, suppose you create a numeric field about "Test score". Later, you can find everybody who scored below 60 by doing this:

> Say "find" by pressing Command with F.
> Click in the "Test score" box, type "<60", and press Return.

You can use these symbols:

Symbol	Meaning
<	less than
<=	less than or equal to
>	greater than
>=	greater than or equal to

You can display the students from lowest score to highest score by doing this:

> Say you want to see all students (jumbo), by pressing Command with J.
> Say "sort", by pressing Command with S.
> Click "Clear All".
> Click "Test score" then "Ascending order" then "Move".
> Press Return.

You can display the students from highest score to lowest score by doing this:

> Say you want to see all students (jumbo), by pressing Command with J.
> Say "sort", by pressing Command with S.
> Click "Clear All".
> Click "Test score" then "Descending order" then "Move".
> Press Return.

If a field is numeric, when you type your data you can include a decimal point and a negative sign.

If you type extra characters (such as commas or dollar signs or units of measure such as "miles"), the computer will include them in your database, but beware: since the computer doesn't know their meaning, the computer will ignore them while doing finds or sorts. The computer doesn't know that "2 miles" is more than "3 feet".

Dates To create an extra field that contains just dates (such as a field about "Date of birth" or "Date the loan began" or "Date due" or "Date processed"), type the field's name then click "Date" then press Return. That lets the computer filter and sort the dates better.

For example, suppose you create a date field about "Date of birth". Later, you can later find everybody born before 1980 by doing this:

> Say "find" by pressing Command with F.
> Click in the "Date of birth" box, type "<1/1/1980", and press Return.

You can use these symbols:

Symbol	Meaning
<	before
<=	before or on
>	after
>=	after or on

You can display the people in order of birth by doing this:

> Say you want to see all people (jumbo), by pressing Command with J.
> Say "sort", by pressing Command with S.
> Click "Clear All".
> Click "Date of birth" then "Ascending order" then "Move".
> Press Return.

When typing a date field, type the month's number, then a slash, then the date number, then a slash, then a four-digit year. For example, December 31, 1980 should be typed as "12/31/1980". You can type any year from 0001 (which was near Jesus's birth) to 3000.

If you omit the year (and type just "12/31"), the computer automatically types today's year for you. If you type a 2-digit year (such as 98 or 01), the computer automatically changes it to a 4-digit year. (To change a 2-digit year to a 4-digit year, the computer usually puts "20" before the year; but if the 2-digit year is 90, 91, 92, 93, 94, 95, 96, 97, 98, or 99, the computer puts "19" before the year instead.) The computer does that automatic typing when you move to the next field or record.

Times To create an extra field that contains just the time of day (such as a field about "Appointment time") or a time duration (such as "Time to finish race"), type the field's name then click "Time" then press Enter. That lets the computer do filter and sort the times better.

For example, suppose you create a time field about "Appointment time". Later, you can find all appointments before 2PM doing this:

Say "find" by pressing Command with F.
Click in the "Date of birth" box, type "<2PM", and press Return.

You can use these symbols:

Symbol	Meaning
<	before
<=	before or at
>	after
>=	after or at

You can display the people in order of appointment times by doing this:

Say you want to see all people (jumbo), by pressing Command with J.
Say "sort", by pressing Command with S.
Click "Clear All".
Click "Appointment time" then "Ascending order" then "Move".
Press Return.

For 9AM, you can type "9AM" or "9:00" or just "9". For 2PM, you can type "2PM" or "2:00PM" or "14:00" (which is military style) or just "14". You can include seconds: for 15 seconds after 9AM, type "9:00:15". If a person ran a marathon race and took "4 hours, 12 minutes, and 7 seconds", you can express that by typing "4:12:07".

Rearrange fields To delete a field, click its name (in the Define Fields window) then click "Delete" then click "Delete" again.

To change a field's type (such as from "Text" to "Number"), click the field's name then click the type you want then press Return. If the computer asks "Proceed anyway?", click "OK".

In front of each field's name, you see a double-headed arrow. To move a field, drag its double-headed arrow up or down.

Works database

Microsoft Works is a program that handles word processing, spreadsheets, and databases.

I explained the word-processing part of Microsoft Works on pages 215-224.
I explained the spreadsheet part of Microsoft Works on pages 226-240.

Here's how to use the database part of Microsoft Works 7&8&9....

Create a database

Turn the computer on, so you see the Start button.
For Works 8&9, do this:

Click Start then **All Programs** then **Microsoft Works Task Launcher** then **Blank Database**.

For Works 7, do this:

Double-click the **Microsoft Works** icon. Click **Programs** (which is near the screen's top left corner) then **Works Database** (which is near the screen's left edge) then **Start a blank Database**.

If the computer says "First-time Help", press Enter.
For our first experiment, let's create this database:

First name	Last name	Comments
Sue	Smith	wiggles
Sam	Smith	tickles
Tina	Ash	clown
Tina	Smith	wow

Here's how to create it....

In that database, the top of each column has a **field name**. The field names are "First name", "Last name", and "Comments". Type them and press Enter after each one.

So type the words "First name", then press Enter, then type the words "Last name", then press Enter, then type the word "Comments", then press Enter again.

Click "Done".

You see the **List view**, which looks like a spreadsheet table and begins like this:

	First name	Last name	Comments
1			
2			
3			
4			
5			
6			

Type the data that you want in the table, moving from cell to cell by pressing the Tab key. So type "Sue", press Tab, type "Smith", press Tab, type "wiggles", press Tab, type "Sam", press Tab, etc., until you've finally typed the last entry ("wow"), so the spreadsheet table looks like this:

	First name	Last name	Comments
1	Sue	Smith	wiggles
2	Sam	Smith	tickles
3	Tina	Ash	clown
4	Tina	Smith	wow
5			
6			

Congratulations! You've created a **database table**.

In a database table, each row of data is called a **record**; each column of data is called a **field**. In the database table you created, here are the records and fields:

The first record (row of data) is Sue Smith's record.
The second record is Sam Smith's.
The third record is Tina Ash's.
The fourth record is Tina Smith's.
So altogether, there are 4 records (plus blanks underneath).

The first field (column) is called "First name".
The next field is "Last name".
The next field is "Comments".
So altogether, there are 3 fields (columns), whose **field names** (column headings) are "First name", "Last name", and "Comments".

The Works database program can handle 32,000 records, 256 fields. If you want to create a database bigger than that, use a different database program instead.

Edit the table

I'm going to explain how to edit your table's data. **Before you edit, finish what you've been typing, by pressing the Tab key.** Then edit as follows....

Click the cell you want to edit, then choose one of these editing methods:

Method 1 Press the Delete key. That makes the cell become totally blank.

Method 2 Retype the entire text that you want to put into the cell.

Method 3 At the top of the screen, you see a wide white box, which contains a copy of what's in the cell you clicked; click in that wide white box, then edit your typing as if you were using a word processing: you can use the left-arrow key, right-arrow key, Backspace key, Delete key, and mouse. When you finish editing, press the Enter key.

To make an entire row become blank, click the row's number then press the Delete key.

To make an entire row's data disappear and make the data that was underneath move up to fill the gap, do this: right-click anywhere in the row, then click **Delete Record**.

Move around To move to different cells in the table, you can use the mouse or keyboard:

To move right, to the next cell,	press the right-arrow key (or Tab key).
To move left, to the previous cell,	press left-arrow key (or Shift with Tab).
To move down, to the cell below,	press the down-arrow key (or Enter key).
To move up, to the cell above,	press the up-arrow key.
To move far right, to last column,	press the End key.
To move far left, to first column,	press the Home key.
To move far right & down, to last filled cell (bottom right),	press Ctrl with End.
To move far left & up, to the first cell (top left),	press Ctrl with Home.

Add extra records To add an extra record, just type the extra record in the blank row be*low* the other records.

Undo If you make a mistake while using the Works database, you can typically undo the mistake by pressing Ctrl with Z. If you change your mind and wish you hadn't pressed Ctrl with Z, you can "undo the undo" by pressing Ctrl with Z again.

Make a column look wider Here's how to make a column look wider, so it can show longer words:

Look at the column's heading (the field name, such as "First name"), and look at the vertical gridline that's to the right of that column heading. Drag that gridline to the right (by using your mouse).

To make the column become narrower again, drag the gridline back toward the left. To make the column look just wide enough to hold everything in it, double-click the column's heading.

Fiddling with the gridlines affects just what you see on the screen, not the data itself. If you make a column narrow by dragging its gridline, you'll see just part of the column's contents on the screen, but the contents are still stored, invisibly: afterward, if you drag the gridline to make the column look wider again, you'll see the full contents again.

Filter

Here's how to find everybody whose last name is "Smith".

Click the **Filters button**. (It's the rightmost big button near the screen's top and shows a funnel.)

If the computer says "First-time Help", press Enter.

The computer says "Filter Name". Press Enter. Then you see this table:

	Field name	Comparison	Compare To
	(None)	is equal to	
and	(None)	is equal to	
and	(None)	is equal to	
and	(None)	is equal to	
and	(None)	is equal to	

To find everybody whose last name is "Smith", change the table so it begins like this:

Field name	Comparison	Compare To
Last name	is equal to	smith

Here's how:

The table's first box temporarily says "(None)". Next to that "(None)", your screen has a down-arrow. Click that down-arrow. You see a list of field names. Click the field name you want ("Last name"). Now the table's first box says "Last name".

Move to the table's top right box (by pressing the Tab key twice). In that top right box, type the name "smith". (You don't have to capitalize it, since the computer ignores capitalization.)

Press Enter. Then you see an abridged database, whose records show just people whose last name is Smith:

	First name	Last name	Comments
1	Sue	Smith	wiggles
2	Sam	Smith	tickles
4	Tina	Smith	wow
5			
6			
7			

You don't see record #3 (Tina Ash's record), since she's not a Smith. You see a **filtered database**, where the Smiths are still visible but Tina Ash has been filtered out and is invisible.

When you finish admiring that abridged database and want to see *all* the records again (including even Tina Ash's), do this:

Click "Record" then "Show" then "All Records".
Then (to make sure you see even the first record), press Ctrl with Home.

Different filters To see everybody whose first name begins with "S", make the filter table begin like this:

Field name	Comparison	Compare To
First name	begins with	s

Then you'll see Sue's record and Sam's record (but not Tina's).

To see everybody except Sam, make the filter table begin like this:

Field name	Comparison	Compare To
First name	is not equal to	sam

To see just Tina Smith's record, make the filter table begin like this:

	Field name	Comparison	Compare To
	First name	is equal to	tina
and	Last name	is equal to	smith

Then you'll see Tina Smith's record (without seeing the other Smiths and without seeing Tina Ash).

To see everybody whose first name is Sue or Tina, make the filter table begin like this:

	Field name	Comparison	Compare To
	First name	is equal to	sue
or	First name	is equal to	tina

Then you'll see everybody whose first name is Sue or Tina (without seeing Sam).

Alphabetize

To make the computer look at each person's last name and put the last names in alphabetical order, do this:

Click "Record" then "Sort records". (If the computer says "First-time Help", press Enter.) Type "Last name" (or choose "Last name" from the "Sort by" box down-arrow's menu). Press Enter.

That makes the computer alphabetize the table by Last name, so Tina Ash's record is at the top of the table and the Smiths are under her.

If you change your mind and want to undo the alphabetizing, just say "undo" (by pressing Ctrl with Z).

You've learned how to put the last names in alphabetical order. But what if two people have the same last name? Let's make the computer look at each person's last name and put the last names in alphabetical order — but if two people have the same last name, make the computer look at those people's first names and put their first names in alphabetical order:

Click "Record" then "Sort records". (If the computer says "First-time Help", press Enter.) In the "Sort by" box, put "Last type" (by typing it or by choosing from the down-arrow's menu). In the box below, put "First name". Press Enter.

Save

To save the database (copy it onto the hard disk), click the **Save button** (which is under the word "Tools").

If you haven't saved the database before, the computer will say "File name". Invent a name for your database. Type the name and press Enter.

That makes the computer copy the database onto the hard disk.

For example, if you named the database "mary", the computer will make that database become a file called mary.wdb (which means "Mary's **W**orks **d**ata**b**ase") and put it into the My Documents folder.

Afterwards, if you change your mind and want to do more editing, go ahead! When you finish that extra editing, save it by clicking the Save button again.

Save often If you're typing a long database, click the Save button about every 10 minutes. Click it whenever you get to a good resting place and think, "What I've typed so far looks good!"

Then if an accident happens, you'll lose at most 10 minutes of work.

Print

To print records onto paper, you can click the **Print button** (which is under the world "Help"). That makes the computer print the table.

If you want to print just *some* of the records, filter them before printing. If you want the records to be alphabetized, alphabetize them before printing.

When printing, the computer tends to be lazy: it doesn't bother printing the column headings (field names), doesn't bother printing the record numbers, and doesn't bother printing the gridlines. To force the computer to print them, do this before clicking the Print button:

> Click "File" then "Page Setup" then "Other Options". Put a check mark in the "Print gridlines" box and in the "Print record and field labels" box (by clicking those boxes). Press Enter.

Leave the database

When you finish working on a database, do this….

Click the X at the screen's top right corner. Then you have three choices:

> If you click the **X** at the screen's top right corner again, the computer stops using Microsoft Works.
>
> If you click **Programs** then Works 8's "**Works Database**" (or Works 7's "**Start a blank Database**"), the computer lets you start typing a new database.
>
> If you click **History**, you see a list of old databases (and other Works creations). If you want to *use* one of those databases, click the database's name.

Didn't save? If you didn't save your database before doing those procedures, the computer asks, "Save changes?" If you click "Yes", the computer copies your database's most recent version to the hard disk; if you click "No" instead, the computer ignores and forgets your most recent editing.

Improve the fields

While you're viewing at the database as a table, the top of each column shows the name of a field. Here's how to improve the fields.

To **change a field's name**, do this:

> Click the field's name. From the Format menu, choose Field. Type what you want the field to be named (and press Enter).

To **insert an extra field**, do this:

> Right-click the name of a nearby field (a field next to where you want the extra field to be). Click "Insert Field".
>
> If you want the extra field to be to the left of the nearby field, click "Before"; if you want the extra field to be to the right of the nearby field, click "After".
>
> Type what you want the extra field to be named (and press Enter). If you want to insert *another* extra field, type the name you want for it (and press Enter).
> Click "Done".

To **delete a field** (and all the data in that field), do this:

> Right-click the field's name. Click "Delete Field". Press Enter.

To **move a field**, do this:

> Click the field's name. Take your finger off the mouse's button. While pressing the mouse's left button again, drag the field's name across to where you want it (between other fields, but *not* farther right than the rightmost field).

Data types

While you're using Works 8&9, you can see this menu:

> General
> Text
> Number
> Currency
> Percent
> Exponential
> Leading zeros
> Fraction
> True/False
> Date
> Time
> Serialized

Works 7 shows this menu instead:

> General
> Number
> Date
> Time
> Text
> Fraction
> Serialized

You see that menu while you're inventing a new field (and typing the field's name). Another way to see that menu is to click a field's name, then click "Format" then "Field".

On that menu, the choices are called **formats** or **data types**. The computer assumes you want the first choice (which is "General"), but you can choose a different data type instead. The more accurately you choose, the more accurate the computer will be at filtering, sorting, and displaying data.

Choice	What data should be in the field
General	strange data that doesn't fit the categories below
Text	words or an ID number (such as social security #, phone #, or ZIP code)
Number	a number (such as 237.90) having two digits after the decimal point
Currency	same as Number, but the computer will display a dollar sign in front
Percent	a percentage (such as 50% or 66.67% or 120%); to make 50%, type either 50% or .5
Exponential	a number in scientific notation, using E (such as 7E3, which means 7000)
Leading zeros	a 5-digit number (such as 00386), without decimals
Fraction	a whole number followed by fraction (such as 7 3/4, which means 7¾)
True/False	the word TRUE or the word FALSE; you can type a 1 for TRUE, 0 for FALSE
Date	a date (such as 12/31/00) that's between 1930 and 2029
Time	a time (such as 4:48 PM)
Serialized	an ID number (from 00001 to 99999) that the computer will generate automatically

Microsoft Access 2007 & 2010

Many companies use a database program called **Microsoft Access** because it comes free as part of **Microsoft Office Professional**.

This section explains how to use versions 2007 & 2010.

If you're using version 2002 or 2003, read the next section instead.

If you're using version 2000, read the 27th edition instead, which you can get by phoning me at 603-666-6644.

If you're using version 97, switch to a newer version.

Launch Microsoft Access

Click Start then do this:

Version 2010 If you see "Microsoft Access 2010", click it. Otherwise, click "All Programs" then scroll down and click "Microsoft Office" then "Microsoft Access 2010".

Version 2007 If you see "Microsoft Office Access 2007", click it. Otherwise, click "All Programs" then scroll down and click "Microsoft Office" then "Microsoft Office Access 2007".

Create a database

To create a new database, do this:

Version 2010 Click the first "Blank database" then click the box under "File Name".

Version 2007 Click "Blank database" then hold down the Delete key awhile (to erase the name "Database1").

For our first experiment, let's create a database like this:

First name	Last name	Comments
Sue	Smith	wiggles toes
Sam	Smith	picks nose
Tina	Ash	class clown
Tina	Smith	incredible

Here's how to create it....

Invent a name for your database (such as "Friends"). Type the name. **At the end of the name, press Enter.**

If the computer says "The file already exists", do this:

Press Enter. (For version 2007, then double-click the name you typed.)

Type a different name instead (such as "Friends2" or "Buddies" or "Pals" or "Enemies"), then press Enter. If the computer says "The file already exists" again, do this whole procedure again.

You see the **Datasheet View**, which is a grid that looks like a spreadsheet table. It begins like this:

ID	Click to Add
(New)	

(Version 2007 says "Add New Field" instead of "Click to Add".)

Hide the ID column by doing this:

Version 2010 Right-click "ID" then click "Hide Fields".
Version 2007 Right-click "ID" then click "Hide Columns".

Now the grid begins like this:

Click to Add

We're trying to create a database whose column headings are these:

First name	Last name	Comments

To type them, do this:

Version 2010 Click "Click to Add" then "Text". Type the column heading you want there ("First name") and press Enter. Click "Text". Type the next column heading ("Last name") and press Enter. Click "Text". Type the next column heading ("Comments"). After the final column heading ("Comments"), press the down-arrow key instead of Enter.

Version 2007 Double-click "Add New Field". Type the column heading you want there ("First name"), press Enter, type the next column heading ("Last name"), press Enter, and type the next column heading ("Comments"). After the final column heading ("Comments"), press Enter *twice*.

Now the grid begins like this —

First name	Last name	Comments

and you're ready to type in the blank box under "First name".

Type the data that you want in the table, moving from cell to cell by pressing the Enter key. So type "Sue", press Enter, type "Smith", press Enter, type "wiggles toes", press Enter, type Sam", press Enter, etc., until you've finally typed the last entry ("incredible"), so the spreadsheet table looks like this:

First name	Last name	Comments
Sue	Smith	wiggles toes
Sam	Smith	picks nose
Tina	Ash	class clown
Tina	Smith	incredible

Congratulations! You've created a **database table**.

While you're typing that data, the computer automatically copies it to the hard disk. (You don't have to click the Save button.)

In a database table, each row of data is called a **record**; each column of data is called a **field**. In the database table you created, here are the records and fields:

The first record (row of data) is Sue Smith's record.
The second record is Sam Smith's.
The third record is Tina Ash's.
The fourth record is Tina Smith's.
So altogether, there are 4 records.

The first field (column) is called "First name".
The next field is "Last name".
The next field is "Comments".
So altogether, there are 3 fields (columns), whose **field names** (column headings) are "First name", "Last name", and "Comments".

Edit the table

While you're viewing the database table, you can edit it by retyping it. To move to different places in the table, you can use the mouse or keyboard:

To move down, to the cell below,	press the keyboard's down-arrow key.
To move up, to the cell above,	press the keyboard's up-arrow key.
To move right, to the next character,	press the keyboard's right-arrow key.
To move left, to the previous character,	press the keyboard's left-arrow key.
To move far right, to the next cell, press the Enter key (or Tab key or repeatedly press the right-arrow key).	
To move far left, to the previous cell, press Shift with Tab (or repeatedly press the left-arrow key).	

Add extra records To add an extra record, just type the extra record in the blank row be*low* the other records. (The computer won't let you type an extra record *between* other records.)

> If your table contains many records, the fastest way to hop down to the blank row is to click the **New (blank) record button** (which is at the screen's bottom and shows a triangle pointing to the right, at a white-and-gold starburst).

Delete Here's how to delete:

> To delete a character, click before it then press the Delete key.
>
> To delete an entire word, double-click it then press the Delete key.
>
> To delete an entire cell, put the mouse pointer before the cell's first word, so the pointer turns into a white cross, then click (so the whole cell is highlighted), then press the Delete key.
>
> To delete an entire row (record), click the gray square to the left of the row, then press the Delete key then Enter.

Undo If you make a mistake while using Microsoft Access, you can typically undo the mistake by clicking the **Undo button** (which is at the screen's top and shows an arrow bending toward the left). Clicking the Undo button makes the computer undo your last action.

> Be cautious! Sometimes the Undo button's curved arrow is gray instead of blue: the gray means the Undo button is refusing to work.
>
> Though you can sometimes undo your last action, you cannot undo your last *two* actions; you cannot usefully click the Undo button twice in succession.
>
> So if you make a mistake, you can undo it just if you click the Undo button *immediately*, before performing other actions, and just if the Undo button is in a good mood, so its arrow is blue instead of gray.

Make a column look wider Here's how to make a column look wider, so it can show longer words:

> Look at the column's heading (the field name, such as "First name"), and look at the vertical gridline that's to the right of that column heading. Drag that gridline to the right (by using your mouse).

To make the column become narrower again, drag the gridline back toward the left. To make the column look just wide enough to hold everything in it, double-click the gridline.

Fiddling with the gridlines affects just what you see on the screen, not what the computer stores in the RAM memory chips or on disk. If you make a column narrow by dragging its gridline, you'll see just part of the column's contents on the screen, but the contents are still stored, invisibly: afterward, if you drag the gridline to make the column look wider again, you'll see the full contents again.

Find

To find everybody whose last name is "Smith", **click Home** (which is near the screen's top-left corner) then choose one of these methods.

Method 1: Search Click in the **Search box**. (It's the white box at the screen's bottom, to the right of "No Filter").

Type "smith". As you type "smith", the computer will go back to the beginning of the data, search for "smith", and highlight the first "smith" or "Smith" it finds in the data.

If you press Enter, the computer will highlight the next "Smith". Keep pressing Enter, to keep finding Smiths.

Method 2: Find Click at the data's beginning (in the first record's first field, which says "Sue"). Click the **Find button** (which is near the screen's top corner and shows binoculars above the word "Find"), or press Ctrl with F. You'll see the **Find and Replace window**.

Type "smith" and press Enter. The computer will search for "smith" and highlight the first "smith" or "Smith" it finds.

If you press Enter again, the computer will continue looking for Smiths, find another "Smith", and highlight that Smith. Keep pressing Enter, to keep finding Smiths.

After the computer has found all the Smiths, if you press Enter again the computer will try to find another Smith but fail, so the computer will say "The search item was not found." Press Enter.

Whenever you get tired of having the computer look for Smiths, close the Find and Replace window (by clicking its X button).

Method 3: Selection Look down the "Last name" column, until you notice a "Smith". Click that "Smith". Click **Selection** (which is near the screen's top) then **Equals "Smith"**.

You see an abridged datasheet, whose records show just people whose last name is Smith:

First name	Last name	Comments
Sue	Smith	wiggles toes
Sam	Smith	picks nose
Tina	Smith	incredible

You don't see Tina Ash's record, since she's not a Smith. You see a **filtered datasheet**, where the Smiths are still visible but Tina Ash has been filtered out and is invisible.

When you finish admiring that abridged datasheet, see the full datasheet again by clicking **Toggle Filter**.

Method 4: Filter By Form Click **Advanced** then **Filter By Form**.

You should see this form:

First name	Last name	Comments

Make sure its bottom row is clear (contains no words, no numbers). If it's not clear yet, clear it by clicking **Advanced** again then **Clear Grid**.

To find everybody whose last name is Smith, click the box below "Last name", then put "Smith" into the box using one of these methods:

> Method A: start typing "smith"; after you've typed the beginning of "smith", the computer will type the rest of it for you automatically.
>
> Method B: click that box's down-arrow; you'll see an alphabetical list of all the last names; from that list, choose "Smith" by clicking it.

Click **Toggle Filter**.

You see an abridged datasheet, whose records show just people whose last name is Smith:

First name	Last name	Comments
Sue	Smith	wiggles toes
Sam	Smith	picks nose
Tina	Smith	incredible

You don't see Tina Ash's record, since she's not a Smith.

When you finish admiring that abridged datasheet, see the full datasheet again by clicking **Toggle Filter** again.

Here's a summary of the Filter By Form method:

> Click Advanced then Filter By Form (then Advanced then Clear Grid). To see just the Smiths, put "smith" in the "Last name" field then click Toggle Filter.

To see just Tina Smith's record (without seeing the other Smiths and without seeing Tina Ash), do this:

> Click Advanced then Filter By Form (then Advanced then Clear Grid). Put "tina" in the "First name" field, put "smith" in the "Last name" field, then click Toggle Filter.

To see everybody whose first name is not Sam, do this:

> Click Advanced then Filter By Form (then Advanced then Clear Grid). Put "not sam" in the "First name" field, then click Toggle Filter.

To see everybody whose first name is Sue or Tina (without seeing Sam), do this —

> Click Advanced then Filter By Form (then Advanced then Clear Grid). Put "sue or tina" in the "First name" field, then click Toggle Filter.

or do this:

> Click Advanced then Filter By Form (then Advanced then Clear Grid). Put "sue" in the "First name" field, click "Or" (which is at the screen's bottom), put "tina" in the "First name" field, then click Toggle Filter.

To see everybody whose first name begins with "S", do this:

> Click Advanced then Filter By Form (then Advanced then Clear Grid). Put "s*" in the "First name" field, then click Toggle Filter.

Alphabetize

To make the computer look at each person's last name and put the last names in alphabetical order, do this:

> Click "Home" then "Last name".
> Click the **Ascending button** (which shows A above Z, with a down-arrow).

That makes the computer alphabetize the table by Last name, so Tina Ash's record is at the top of the table and the Smiths are under her.

If you change your mind and want to undo the alphabetizing, click the **Remove Sort button**, which shows A above Z with an eraser. (Version 2007 calls that button "Clear All Sorts".)

File-office button

At the screen's left edge, very close to the top, you see the **File-office button**. (In version 2010, it says "File". In version 2007, it's a circle with the Microsoft Office symbol inside it.)

Click it. Then you see the **File-office menu**:

Version 2007	Version 2010
New	Save
Open	Save Object As
Save	Save Database As
Save As	Open
Print	Close Database
Manage	Info
E-mail	Recent
Publish	New
Close Database	Print
	Save & Publish
	Help
	Options
	Exit

From that menu, choose whatever you wish (by clicking it). Here are the most popular choices....

Print To print records onto paper, choose **Print** from the File-office menu (by clicking the word "Print" after clicking the File-office button), then do this:

> **Version 2010** Click "Quick Print".
> **Version 2007** Press Enter.

That makes the computer print the table, including the column headings and the data.

If you want to print just *some* of the records, filter them before printing. If you want the records to be alphabetized, alphabetize them before printing.

If you want to print just *one* person's record, do this instead:

> Click in that person's record. Choose Print from the File-office menu. For version 2010, click the Print icon (not Quick Print). Click "Selected Records(s)". Press Enter.

Close Database When you finish using the table you created, choose **Close Database** from the File-office menu.

The computer automatically saved your data while you were typing it, but the computer might not have saved your table's overall design (such as which columns to display and which columns to alphabetize). If the computer asks "Do you want to save changes to the design of table?", press Enter. Afterwards, if the computer says "Table1", press Enter again.

Then you have three choices:

> To **start creating a different database**, do the "Create a database" process again (explained on page 304).

> To **stop using Microsoft Access**, click its X button.

> To **use a database you previously created**, tell the computer which database.

Here's how to "tell the computer which database":

> **Version 2010** The computer puts 4 recent database names in the File-office menu. Find your favorite database name there, or choose "Recent" from the File-office menu to see 17 recent names. Click your favorite name, or do this: click Open from the File-office menu then double-click your favorite name. (If the computer says "Security Warning", click "Enable Content".) Double-click "Table1". The database's table will appear on the screen, alphabetized the same way as when you last used it (but unfiltered).

> **Version 2007** The computer puts 9 recent database names at the screen's right edge. Click your favorite database name there, or click "More" then double-click your favorite. (If the computer says "Security Warning", click "Options" then "Enable this content" then "OK".) Double-click "Table1 : Table". The database's table will appear on the screen, alphabetized the same way as when you last used it (but unfiltered).

Improve the fields

While you're looking at the table (datasheet), you can change its fields (columns).

Add an extra field Here's how to add an extra field in version 2010:

> If you want the extra field to be the last field, click "Click to Add" then "Text" then type a name for that field (such as "Year born") and press the down-arrow key.
>
> If you want the extra field to be where another field is now, do this: right-click that other field's name, click "Insert Field", double-click "Field1", then type a name for that field (such as "Year born") and press Enter.

Here's how to add an extra field in version 2007:

> If you want the extra field to be the last field, double-click "Add New Field" then type a name for that field (such as "Year born") and press Enter.
>
> If you want the extra field to be where another field is now, do this: right-click that other field's name, click "Insert Column", double-click "Field1", then type a name for that field (such as "Year born") and press Enter.

Delete a field Here's how to delete a field:

> Click the field's name. Press the Delete key then Enter.

That makes the field (column) disappear. The fieldname (column heading) disappears, and so does all the data in that column.

Move a field Here's how to move a field:

> Click the field's name. Take your finger off the mouse's button. While pressing the mouse's left button again, drag the field's name to where you want it (between other fields).

Data types

At the screen's left edge, above the word "View", you see the **Design View button** (which shows a yellow pencil, yellow ruler, and blue triangle). Click that button.

You see the **Design View**, which looks like this:

Field Name	Data Type	Description
ID	AutoNumber	
First name	Text	
Last name	Text	
Comments	Text	

Whenever you want to switch back to Datasheet View (which shows your data), click the **Datasheet View button** (which is above the word "View", where the Design View button was, and looks like a grid) then answer any questions the computer asks (such as whether to save your changes and whether to accept a shorter field).

In Design View, the left column shows the field names you invented: "First name", "Last name", and "Comments". It also shows "ID", which is the field name you hid.

Each field name you invented has a data type of "Text", unless you say otherwise (or the field is the ID or the first record's data implies you want otherwise).

If you click "Text", you see a down-arrow next to it. If you click that down-arrow, you see these choices:

> Text
> Memo
> Number
> Date/Time
> Currency
> AutoNumber
> Yes/No
> OLE Object
> Hyperlink
> Attachment
> Calculated
> Lookup Wizard

(Version 2007 lacks "Calculated".)

Click whichever choice you want; then the screen's bottom might show boxes, such as "Field Size" and "Decimal Places". The more accurately you choose, the more accurately the computer will store, find, filter, and sort your data.

The bottom 5 choices ("OLE Object", "Hyperlink", "Attachment", "Calculated", and "Lookup Wizard") are unpopular, so I won't bother to discuss them. Here's what the popular choices and boxes mean....

Currency Choose "Currency" if the field's data will be an amount of money, written as dollars and cents (such as $7,893.20). For example, choose "Currency" if the field is "Amount paid" or "Balance due" or "Profit" or "Debt" or "Income" or "Cost" or "Sales").

Then when you type the data in Datasheet View, here's what will happen:

> The computer will automatically put a dollar sign before the number, put two digits after the decimal point, and insert a comma if the number is big. If the number is negative, the computer will imitate an accountant: it will put the number and dollar sign all in parentheses (instead of writing a minus sign).
>
> The amount of money can be very big (up to $922,337,203,685,477.58), so you can say you're even richer than Bill Gates! To see such a big number, widen the Datasheet's column by dragging its vertical gridline.
>
> If you try to go higher than $922,337,203,685,477.58, the computer will say "The value you entered does not match the Currency data type in this column"; click "Enter new value" then type a smaller number.

When you choose "Currency" in Design View, the screen's bottom usually shows that the Decimal Places box contains the word "Auto", which makes the computer automatically put 2 digits after the decimal point. You can force the computer to display 4 digits after the decimal point by putting 4 in the Decimal Places box (which will make the biggest number be $922,337,203,685,477.5807). If you want the computer to round to the nearest dollar (and show no decimal point and no pennies), put 0 in the Decimal Places box. You can put 0, 1, 2, 3, or 4 in the Decimal Places box; the computer can't handle more than 4 accurately.

Each currency amount is stored by using a special code that consumes just 8 bytes of your hard disk, even if the number contains many digits.

Date/Time Choose "Date/Time" if the field's data will be a date or time. For example, choose "Date/Time" if the field is "Date of birth" or "Date the loan began" or "Date due" or "Date processed" or "Appointment time".

In Datasheet view, you can type a date/time like this: "12/31/1920 11:59:45 PM", which means December 31st, 1920, at 45 seconds after 11:59PM.

> If you don't want to be so detailed, type just part of that: type just the date or just the time.
>
> When typing the time, you can omit the number of seconds.
>
> You can write AM or PM or use 24-hour military time.
>
> The computer can handle any 4-digit year from 0100 (which was near Jesus's birth) to 9999.
>
> When typing a year from 1930 through 2029, you can omit the first two digits.
> When typing a year from 0100 through 0999, you can omit the first zero.

Each date/time consumes 8 bytes of your hard disk.

AutoNumber Choose "AutoNumber" if you want the field's data to be a simple counting number (such as 1, 2, 3, 4,…) that the computer will generate automatically.

In Datasheet View, the computer will automatically type a "1" in that field for the first record, "2" in that field for the second record, etc. That counting number will act as an ID. Each such counting number consumes 4 bytes on your hard disk.

You can name the field "ID" or "ID number" or "Record number".

The computer lets you choosing "AutoNumber" just if you haven't put any data in the table yet.

Number Choose "Number" if the field's data will be a number that's not an amount of money, not a date or time, and not an identification number. For example, choose "Number" if the field is "Age" or "Test score" or "Population" or "Number of children" or "Temperature" or "Discount percentage".

(For an amount of money, choose "Currency" instead. For a date or time, choose "Date/Time" instead. For a simple identification number generated by the computer, choose "AutoNumber" instead. For other kinds of identification number, such as a social-security number or phone number or ZIP code, choose "Text" instead.)

When you choose "Number" in Design view, the screen's bottom usually shows that the Field Size box contains "Long Integer". Instead of "Long Integer", choose a different size instead, if it fits your data better. Here are the most popular choices:

Choice	Meaning	Memory
Byte	a whole number from 0 to 255, no decimals, no negatives	1 byte
Integer	an integer from -32768 to 32767, no decimals	2 bytes
Long Integer	an integer from -2147483648 to 2147483647, no decimals	4 bytes
Single	a number that can contain decimals, minus sign, exponents, 7 significant digits	4 bytes
Double	a number that can contain decimals, minus sign, exponents, 15 significant digits	8 bytes
Decimal	a number that can contain decimals, minus sign, 18 digits	12 bytes

In that chart, the "Memory" column shows how many bytes of your hard disk each number consumes. The fewer the number of bytes, the shorter your data file will be and the faster your Access will run. Choose the shortest choice that's still big enough to hold your data.

Yes/No Choose "Yes/No" if you want the field's data to be a box, in which a check mark means "yes"; an empty box means "no". For example, choose "Yes/No" if the field is "Was contacted?" or "Was sold?" or "Has diabetes?" or "Has retired?" or "Is a member now?" or "Is female?" or "Is an adult yet?"

Then when you create data in Datasheet View, you'll see an empty box in that field. Put a check mark into that box (by clicking the box) if you want to say "yes"; leave the box blank if you want to say "no".

Each yes/no answer consumes just 1 bit of your hard disk. (1 bit is very little: it's $\frac{1}{8}$ of a byte.)

Memo "Memo" is the only popular choice that lets the field's data be longer than 255 characters. "Memo" lets you write an entire long essay about the person and make that essay become part of the person's record. The essay can be up to 65535 characters long. It consumes as many bytes as there are characters in the memo.

For example, choose "Memo" if the field is "Psychoanalytical comments about the patient" or "What the employee should do to improve" or "What I really think about this person".

Text Stay with "Text" just if none of the other choices is better. Choose "Text" if the field either includes words (up to 255 characters) or is an ID number (such as a social-security number or phone number or ZIP code) that's not an AutoNumber. For example, stay with "Text" if the field is "First name" or "Last name" or "Street address" or "City" or "State" or "ZIP code" or "Phone number" or "Social Security number" or "Product name".

The computer lets you type up to 255 characters because 255 is the number in the Field Size box. Your text consumes as many bytes as the Field Size box says. To avoid wasting bytes, make the number in the Field Size box be as small as possible, but still big enough to hold your longest data.

Why use data types? Suppose you create a numeric field about "Test score". To display the students from lowest score to highest score, do this:

> In Datasheet View, click the down-arrow to the right of "Test score" then "Sort Smallest to Largest".

To display the students from highest score to lowest score, do this:

> In Datasheet View, click the down-arrow to the right of "Test score" then "Sort Largest to Smallest".

To display just the students who scored below 60, do this:

> In Datasheet view, click "Home" then "Advanced" then "Filter By Form".
> You see a form. If its bottom row isn't clear yet, clear it (by clicking "Advanced" again then "Clear Grid").
> Click the box below "Test score". Type "<60".
> Click "Toggle Filter".

You can use these symbols:

Symbol	Meaning
<60	less than 60 (below 60)
<=60	less than or equal to 60 (at most 60)
>60	greater than 60 (over 60)
>=	greater than or equal to 60 (at least 60)
not 60	not equal to 60 (not 60)
between 60 and 70	at least 60 but not over 70

You can apply those techniques to the other data types also! For example, in Datasheet View you can click a date/time field's down-arrow then "Sort Oldest to Newest" or "Sort Newest to Oldest"; you can use the filter form "<1/1/1920" to get all records before 1920.

Forms

In Datasheet View, the computer shows you many records on the screen simultaneously, but each record is restricted to being just one line of the table. If you want a person's record to include more info than can fit on a single line of your screen, Datasheet View is inconvenient.

Create a **form** instead. In a form, a record can consume your whole screen instead of just one line. Here's how to create a form.

Lay out a form
Click "Create" (which is near the screen's top-left corner, to the right of "Home") then the first "Form".

If the computer asks "Do you want to save", press Enter.

You see a form displaying the first person's record, like this:

First name:	Sue
Last name:	Smith
Comments:	wiggles toes

You can rearrange the form by dragging its fieldnames and boxes. For example, let's move "Last name" above "First name", so the form becomes this:

Last name:	Smith
First name:	Sue
Comments:	wiggles toes

To do that in version 2007, drag "Last name" above "First name". To do that in version 2010 requires 3 steps:

> Drag "Last name" above "First name".
> Drag Last name's box above First name's box.
> Click the empty space where Last name used to be, and press the Delete key.

The typical box is wide (almost as wide as the screen). If it's a text box, it's 2 lines tall.

> If you want a box to be even taller,
> click in the box then drag its bottom edge down.
>
> If you want a box to be less tall,
> click in the box then drag its bottom edge up.
>
> If you want to narrow all the boxes, click in the first box then drag its right edge to the left; that narrows *all* the boxes simultaneously.

Name the form
Click the **Save button** (which is at the screen's top, near the left edge, and looks like a floppy disk or TV set). Invent a name for your form and type it. For example, name it "Table1 form" or "A wild look at my friends". When you finish typing the name, press Enter.

Form View
In the screen's bottom-right corner, just above the time, you see 3 buttons. The first is the **Form View button**, which looks like a tiny form. (If you see the words "Num Lock", the Form View button is immediately to the right of them.) **Click the Form View button.**

You still see the first record in a form, but now you can **edit data in the boxes** (instead of the filenames and box sizes) by using the mouse or these keyboard shortcuts:

> To move to the next box (field), press Enter (or Tab).
> To move back to the previous box (field), press Shift with Tab.
> To move to the bottom box, press the End key.
> To move back to the top box, press the Home key.

See other records
Here's how to see other records:

> To see the **next person's record**, click the ▶ button (at the screen's bottom) or press the Page Down key.
>
> To see the **previous person's record** again, click the ◀ button or press the Page Up key.
>
> To hop back to the **first record**, click the |◀ button or press Ctrl with Home.
>
> To hop ahead to the **final record**, click the ▶| button or press Ctrl with End.
>
> To create an **extra record**, click the ▶* button or press Ctrl with +.

Switching
At the screen's left edge, you see two choices: if you double-click Table1 (which version 2007 calls "Table1 : Table"), you'll see the Datasheet View again (the table that looks like a spreadsheet); if you double-click your form's name instead, you'll see the Form View again.

When you're looking at a table or form, you see two tabs above it. One tab says "Table1"; the other tab says your form's name (such as "Table1 form" or "A wild look at my friends"). Another way to switch between the Datasheet View and the Form View is to click one of those tabs.

Microsoft Access 2002 & 2003

This section explains Microsoft Access 2002 & 2003. (Skip this section if you have Microsoft Access 2007 or 2010, which were explained in the previous section.)

Launch Microsoft Access

Here's how to start using Microsoft Access....

Version 2002 Click "Start" then "Programs" then "Microsoft Access".

Version 2003 Click "start".

If you see "Microsoft Office Access 2003", click it. (Otherwise, click "All Programs" then "Microsoft Office" then "Microsoft Office Access 2003".)

Create a database

To create a new database, begin by doing this:

> Version 2003: click "Create a new file" (which is at the screen's right edge) then "Blank Database".
>
> Version 2002: click "Blank Database".

For our first experiment, let's create this database:

First name	Last name	Comments
Sue	Smith	wiggles toes
Sam	Smith	picks nose
Tina	Ash	class clown
Tina	Smith	incredible

Here's how to create it....

Invent a name for your database (such as "Friends"). Type the name. **At the end of the name, press Enter.**

If the computer says "The file already exists", do this procedure:

> Press Enter. Type a different name instead (such as "Friends2" or "Buddies" or "Pals" or "Enemies") and then press Enter. If the computer says "The file already exists" again, do this whole procedure again.

Finally, you see these choices:

> Create table in Design view
> Create table by using wizard
> Create table by entering data

Press Enter again (which selects "Create table in Design view").

Design view You see the **Design view**, which begins like this:

Field Name	Data Type	Description

We're trying to create a database whose column headings are these:

First name	Last name	Comments

The column headings are called **field names**. Here's a list of those field names:

> First name
> Last name
> Comments

Type that list of field names. To do that, type the words "First name", then press the keyboard's down-arrow key, then type the words "Last name", then press the down-arrow key again, then type the word "Comments", then press the down-arrow key again.

The computer automatically puts the word "Text" next to each field name you type, so your screen looks like this:

Field Name	Data Type	Description
First name	Text	
Last name	Text	
Comments	Text	

Near the screen's top left corner, you see the word "File". Below "File", you see the **View button** (which temporarily looks like a tiny spreadsheet table of numbers). Click that button. Press the Enter key twice (which makes the computer save the table and call it "Table1").

The computer will ask, "Do you want to create a primary key now?" Click "No".

Datasheet view You see the **Datasheet view**, which looks like a spreadsheet table and begins like this:

First name	Last name	Comments

Type the data that you want in the table, moving from cell to cell by pressing the Enter key. So type "Sue", press Enter, type "Smith", press Enter, type "wiggles toes", press Enter, type Sam, press Enter, etc., until you've finally typed the last entry ("incredible"), so the spreadsheet table looks like this:

First name	Last name	Comments
Sue	Smith	wiggles toes
Sam	Smith	picks nose
Tina	Ash	class clown
Tina	Smith	incredible

Congratulations! You've created a **database table**.

While you're typing that data, the computer automatically copies it to the hard disk. (You don't have to click the Save button.)

In a database table, each row of data is called a **record**; each column of data is called a **field**. In the database table you created, here are the records and fields:

> The first record (row of data) is Sue Smith's record.
> The second record is Sam Smith's.
> The third record is Tina Ash's.
> The fourth record is Tina Smith's.
> So altogether, there are 4 records.
>
> The first field (column) is called "First name".
> The next field is "Last name".
> The next field is "Comments".
> So altogether, there are 3 fields (columns), whose **field names** (column headings) are "First name", "Last name", and "Comments".

Edit the table

While you're viewing the database table, you can edit it by retyping it. To move to different places in the table, you can use the mouse or keyboard:

To move down, to the cell below,	press the keyboard's down-arrow key.
To move up, to the cell above,	press the keyboard's up-arrow key.
To move right, to the next character,	press the keyboard's right-arrow key.
To move left, to the previous character,	press the keyboard's left-arrow key.
To move far right, to the next cell, press the Enter key (or Tab key or repeatedly press the right-arrow key).	
To move far left, to the previous cell, press Shift with Tab (or repeatedly press the left-arrow key).	

Add extra records To add an extra record, just type the extra record in the blank row be*low* the other records. (The computer won't let you type an extra record *between* other records.)

If your table contains many records, the fastest way to hop down to the blank row is to click the **New Record button** (which is near the screen's top and shows a triangle pointing to the right, at a starburst).

Delete Here's how to delete:

To delete a character, click before it then press the Delete key.

To delete an entire word, double-click it then press the Delete key.

To delete an entire cell, put the mouse pointer before the cell's first word, so the pointer turns into a white cross, then click (so the whole cell is highlighted), then press the Delete key.

Here's how to delete an entire row (record):

Method 1: to the left of the row, you see a small gray square; click it, then press the Delete key then Enter.

Method 2: click anywhere in the row, then click the **Delete Record button** (which is near the screen's top and shows a red curved X), then press Enter.

Undo If you make a mistake while using Microsoft Access, you can typically undo the mistake by clicking the **Undo button** (which is near the screen's top and shows an arrow bending toward the left). Clicking the Undo button makes the computer undo your last action.

Be cautious! Sometimes the Undo button's curved arrow is gray instead of dark: the gray means the Undo button is refusing to work.

Though you can sometimes undo your last action, you cannot undo your last *two* actions; you cannot usefully click the Undo button twice in succession.

So if you make a mistake, you can undo it just if you click the Undo button *immediately*, before performing other actions, and just if the Undo button is in a good mood, so its arrow is dark instead of gray.

Make a column look wider Here's how to make a column look wider, so it can show longer words:

Look at the column's heading (the field name, such as "First name"), and look at the vertical black gridline that's to the right of that column heading. Drag that black gridline to the right (by using your mouse).

To make the column become narrower again, drag the black gridline back toward the left. To make the column look just wide enough to hold everything in it, double-click the black gridline.

Fiddling with the gridlines affects just what you see on the screen, not what the computer stores in the RAM memory chips or on disk. If you make a column narrow by dragging its gridline, you'll see just part of the column's contents on the screen, but the contents are still stored, invisibly: afterward, if you drag the gridline to make the column look wider again, you'll see the full contents again.

Find

To find everybody whose last name is "Smith", you can use three methods.

Method 1: "find" In Datasheet view, click in the first record's "Last name" field. **Say "find" (by pressing Ctrl with F).** You'll see the **Find and Replace window**.

Type "smith" and press Enter. The computer will look down the "Last name" column, find the next "Smith", and highlight that "Smith".

If you press Enter again, the computer will continue looking for Smiths, find another "Smith", and highlight that Smith. Keep pressing Enter, to keep finding Smiths.

After the computer has found all the Smiths, if you press Enter again the computer will try to find another Smith but fail, so the computer will say "The search item was not found". Press Enter.

Whenever you get tired of having the computer look for Smiths, close the Find and Replace window (by clicking its X button).

Method 2: "filter by selection" In Datasheet view, look down the "Last name" column, until you notice a "Smith". Click that "Smith". Click the **Filter By Selection button** (which is at the screen's top center and shows a funnel over a lightning bolt).

You see an abridged datasheet, whose records show just people whose last name is Smith:

First name	Last name	Comments
Sue	Smith	wiggles toes
Sam	Smith	picks nose
Tina	Smith	incredible

You don't see Tina Ash's record, since she's not a Smith. You see a **filtered datasheet**, where the Smiths are still visible but Tina Ash has been filtered out and is invisible.

When you finish admiring that abridged datasheet, see the full datasheet again by clicking the **Remove Filter button** (which is at the screen's top center and shows just a funnel).

Method 3: "filter by form" In Datasheet view, click the **Filter By Form button** (which is at the screen's top center and shows a funnel over a form).

You should see this form:

First name	Last name	Comments

Make sure its bottom row is clear (contains no words, no numbers). If it's not clear yet, clear it by clicking the **Clear Grid button**. (In version 2002, that button is a red curved X. In version 2003, that button is a black ball.)

To find everybody whose last name is Smith, click the box below "Last name", then put "Smith" into the box using one of these methods:

Method A: start typing "smith"; after you've typed the beginning of "smith", the computer will type the rest of it for you automatically.

Method B: click that box's down-arrow; you'll see an alphabetical list of all the last names; from that list, choose "Smith" by clicking it.

Click the **Apply Filter button** (which shows just a funnel).

You see an abridged datasheet, whose records show just people whose last name is Smith:

First name	Last name	Comments
Sue	Smith	wiggles toes
Sam	Smith	picks nose
Tina	Smith	incredible

You don't see Tina Ash's record, since she's not a Smith.

When you finish admiring that abridged datasheet, see the full datasheet again by clicking the **Remove Filter button** (which shows just a funnel).

Here's a summary of the "filter by form" method:

Click the Filter By Form button (and the Clear Grid button). To see just the Smiths, put "smith" in the "Last name" field then click the Apply Filter button.

To see just Tina Smith's record (without seeing the other Smiths and without seeing Tina Ash), do this:

Click the Filter By Form button (and the Clear Grid button). Put "tina" in the "First name" field, put "smith" in the "Last name" field, then click the Apply Filter button.

To see everybody whose first name is not Sam, do this:

Click the Filter By Form button (and the Clear Grid button). Put "not sam" in the "First name" field, then click the Apply Filter button.

To see everybody whose first name is Sue or Tina (without seeing Sam), do this —

Click the Filter By Form button (and the Clear Grid button). Put "sue or tina" in the "First name" field, then click the Apply Filter button.

or do this:

Click the Filter By Form button (and the Clear Grid button). Put "sue" in the "First name" field, click "Or" (which is at the screen's bottom), put "tina" in the "First name" field, then click the Apply Filter button.

To see everybody whose first name begins with "S", do this:

Click the Filter By Form button (and the Clear Grid button). Put "s*" in the "First name" field, then click the Apply Filter button.

Alphabetize

To make the computer look at each person's last name and put the last names in alphabetical order, do this:

In Datasheet view, click "Last name".

Click the Sort Ascending button
(which is at the screen's top center and shows an A above a Z).

That makes the computer alphabetize the table by Last name, so Tina Ash's record is at the top of the table and the Smiths are under her.

If you change your mind and want to undo the alphabetizing, I have bad news for you: the "Undo" button is too stupid to know how to unalphabetize! To unalphabetize, you must click "Records" then "Remove Filter/Sort".

Print

To print records onto paper, click the **Print button** (which is near the screen's top-left corner). That makes the computer print the table.

(If you want to print just *some* of the records, filter them before printing. If you want the records to be alphabetized, alphabetize them before printing.)

Final steps

When you finish using the table you created, close the Table window (by clicking its X button). If you alphabetized (or made any other changes to your table's structure), the computer asks "Do you want to save changes to the design of table?"; reply by pressing Enter.

You see the Friends Database window. Close it (by clicking its X button). Then you have three choices:

To start creating a different database, click the New button (which is near the screen's top left corner, below the word "File"), then do this: for version 2003, click "Blank database" then continue the "Create a database" process explained on page 310; for version 2002, do the "Create a database" process explained on page 310.

To use a database you previously created, click the Open button (which is near the screen's top left corner and looks like an opening manila file folder). You see a list of databases you created (and some folders, too). (If the list is too long to see it all, scroll to see the rest of it.) Double-click the database you want (such as "Friends"). You see the Friends Database window. To be safe, click "Tables" (which is at the screen's left edge, under "Objects") then the "Table1" icon then press Enter (which opens Table1). The database's table will appear on the screen, with the same view and filtering and sorting as when you last used it.

To stop using Microsoft Access, click its X button.

Improve the fields

You can view your database table in two ways:

The Design view shows you the field names (next to a word such as "Text").
The Datasheet view shows you the data itself.

To switch from one view to the other, click the **View button** (which near the screen's top right corner, below the word "File").

Add an extra field In Design view, you can add an extra field easily.

If you want the extra field to be the last field, type the extra field's name below the other field names.

If you want the extra field to be where another field is now, do this: click that other field's name, click the **Insert Rows button** (which is near the screen's top and shows a blue row that's out but moving in), then type the extra field's name.

Finally, press the down-arrow key (so the computer says "Text").

Delete a field In Design view, you can delete a field easily:

Method 1: to the left of the field's name, you see a small gray square; click it, then press the Delete key.

Method 2: click the field's name, then click the **Delete Rows button** (which is near the screen's top and shows a blue row that's in but moving out).

If the computer asks "Do you want to permanently delete?", press Enter.

Move a field You can move a field easily:

Click the object you want to move (the field's name in Datasheet view, or "the square before the field's name" in Design view). Take your finger off the mouse's button. While pressing the mouse's left button again, drag that object to where you want it (between other fields).

Data types

In Design view, each field normally says "Text". If you click "Text", you see a down-arrow next to it. If you click that down-arrow, you see these choices:

```
Text
Memo
Number
Date/Time
Currency
AutoNumber
Yes/No
OLE Object
Hyperlink
Lookup Wizard
```

Click whichever choice you want; then the screen's bottom might show boxes, such as "Field Size" and "Decimal Places". The more accurately you choose, the more accurate the computer will be at finding, filtering, and sorting.

The bottom 3 choices ("OLE Object", "Hyperlink", and "Lookup Wizard") are unpopular, so I won't bother to discuss them. Here's what the popular choices and boxes mean….

Currency Choose "Currency" if the field's data will be an amount of money, written as dollars and cents (such as $7,893.20). For example, choose "Currency" if the field is "Amount paid" or "Balance due" or "Profit" or "Debt" or "Income" or "Cost" or "Sales").

Then when you type the data in Datasheet view, here's what will happen:

The computer will automatically put a dollar sign before the number, put two digits after the decimal point, and insert a comma if the number is big. If the number is negative, the computer will imitate an accountant: it will put the number and dollar sign all in parentheses (instead of writing a minus sign).

The amount of money can be very big (up to $922,337,203,685,477.58), so you can say you're even richer than Bill Gates! To see such a big number, widen the Datasheet's column by dragging its vertical gridline.

If you try to go higher than $922,337,203,685,477.58, the computer will say "The value you entered isn't valid for this field".

When you choose "Currency" in Design view, the screen's bottom usually shows that the Decimal Places box contains the word "Auto", which makes the computer automatically put 2 digits after the decimal point. You can force the computer to display 4 digits after the decimal point by putting 4 in the Decimal Places box (which will make the biggest number be $922,337,203,685,477.5807). If you want the computer to round to the nearest dollar (and show no decimal point and no pennies), put 0 in the Decimal Places box. You can put 0, 1, 2, 3, or 4 in the Decimal Places box; the computer can't handle more than 4 accurately.

Each currency amount is stored by using a special code that consumes just 8 bytes of your hard disk, even if the number contains many digits.

Date/Time Choose "Date/Time" if the field's data will be a date or time. For example, choose "Date/Time" if the field is "Date of birth" or "Date the loan began" or "Date due" or "Date processed" or "Appointment time".

In Datasheet view, you can type a date/time like this: "12/31/1920 11:59:45 PM", which means December 31st, 1920, at 45 seconds after 11:59PM.

If you don't want to be so detailed, type just part of that: type just the date or just the time.

When typing the time, you can omit the number of seconds.
You can write AM or PM or use 24-hour military time.

The computer can handle any 4-digit year from 0100 (which was near Jesus's birth) to 9999.

When typing year from 1930 through 2029, you can omit the first two digits.
When typing a year from 0100 through 0999, you can omit the first zero.

Each date/time consumes 8 bytes of your hard disk.

AutoNumber Choose "AutoNumber" if you want the field's data to be a simple counting number (such as 1, 2, 3, 4,…) that the computer will generate automatically.

In Datasheet view, the computer will automatically type a "1" in that field for the first record, "2" in that field for the second record, etc. That counting number will act as an ID. Each such counting number consumes 4 bytes on your hard disk.

You can name the field "Record number" or "ID number" or "ID".

Number Choose "Number" if the field's data will be a number that's not an amount of money, not a date or time, and not an identification number. For example, choose "Number" if the field is "Age" or Test score" or "Population" or "Number of children" or "Temperature" or "Discount percentage".

(For an amount of money, choose "Currency" instead. For a date or time, choose "Date/Time" instead. For a simple identification number generated by the computer, choose "AutoNumber" instead. For other kinds of identification number, such as a social-security number or phone number or ZIP code, choose "Text" instead.)

When you choose "Number" in Design view, the screen's bottom usually shows that the Field Size box contains "Long Integer". Instead of "Long Integer", choose a different size instead, if it fits your data better. Here are your choices:

Choice	Meaning	Memory
Byte	a whole number from 0 to 255, no decimals, no negatives	1 byte
Integer	an integer from -32768 to 32767, no decimals	2 bytes
Long Integer	an integer from -2147483648 to 2147483647, no decimals	4 bytes
Single	a number that can contain decimals, minus sign, exponents, 7 significant digits	4 bytes
Double	a number that can contain decimals, minus sign, exponents, 15 significant digits	8 bytes

In that chart, the "Memory" column shows how many bytes of your hard disk each number consumes. The fewer the number of bytes, the shorter your data file will be and the faster your Access will run. Choose the shortest choice that's still big enough to hold your data.

Yes/No Choose "Yes/No" if you want the field's data to be a box, in which a check mark means "yes"; an empty box means "no". For example, choose "Yes/No" if the field is "Was contacted?" or "Was sold?" or "Has diabetes?" or "Has retired?" or "Is a member now?" or "Is female?" or "Is an adult yet?".

Then when you create data in Datasheet view, you'll see an empty box in that field. Put a check mark into that box (by clicking the box) if you want to say "yes"; leave the box blank if you want to say "no".

Each yes/no answer consumes just 1 bit of your hard disk. (1 bit is very little: it's $^1/_8$ of a byte.)

Memo "Memo" is the only popular choice that lets the field's data be longer than 255 characters. "Memo" lets you write an entire long essay about the person and make that essay become part of the person's record. The essay can be up to 65535 characters long. It consumes as many bytes as there are characters in the memo.

For example, choose "Memo" if the field is "Psychoanalytical comments about the patient" or "What the employee should do to improve" or "What I really think about this person".

Text Stay with "Text" just if none of the other choices is better. Choose "Text" if the field either includes words (up to 255 characters) or is an ID number (such as a social-security number or phone number or ZIP code) that's not an AutoNumber. For example, stay with "Text" if the field is "First name" or "Last name" or "Street address" or "City" or "State" or "ZIP code" or "Phone number" or "Social Security number" or "Product name".

If you decide to stay with "Text", beware: the computer limits you to 50 characters (because the number in the Field Size box is 50) unless you change that number. The biggest number allowed in the Field Size box is 255. Your text consumes as many bytes as the Field Size box says. To avoid wasting bytes, make the number in the Field Size box be as small as possible, but still big enough to hold your longest data.

Why use data types? Suppose you create a numeric field about "Test score".

To display the students from lowest score to highest score, do this:

> In Datasheet view, click "Test score". Then click the **Sort Ascending button**, which is at the screen's top center and shows an up-arrow (with an A above a Z).

To display the students from highest score to lowest score, do this:

> In Datasheet view, click "Test score". Then click the **Sort Descending button**, which is at the screen's top center and shows a down-arrow (with an A below a Z).

To display just the students who scored below 60, do this:

> In Datasheet view, click the **Filter By Form button** (which is at the screen's top center and shows a funnel over a form).
>
> You see a form. If its bottom row isn't clear yet, clear it (by clicking the Clear Grid button, which is a red curved X).
>
> Click the box below "Test score". Type "<60".
>
> Click the Apply Filter button (which shows just a funnel).

You can use these symbols:

Symbol	Meaning
<60	less than 60 (below 60)
<=60	less than or equal to 60 (at most 60)
>60	greater than 60 (over 60)
>=	greater than or equal to 60 (at least 60)
not 60	not equal to 60 (not 60)
between 60 and 70	at least 60 but not over 70

You can apply those techniques to the other data types also! For a date/time field:

> The Sort Ascending button puts the records in order from oldest (earliest) to newest (latest).
>
> The Sort Descending button puts the records in order from newest (latest) to oldest (earliest).
>
> "<1/1/1920" gets you all records before 1920.

Forms

In Datasheet view, the computer shows you many records on the screen simultaneously, but each record is restricted to being just one line of the table. If you want a person's record to include more info than can fit on a single line of your screen, Datasheet view is inconvenient.

Invent a **Form view** instead. In Form view, a record can consume your entire screen, instead of just one line.

Invent a Form view Here's how to invent a Form view....

While you're looking at the table's Datasheet view, close that table's window by clicking its X box. (If the computer asks "Do you want to save changes to the design of table?", press Enter.)

You see the Friends Database window. Click "Forms" (which is near the window's left edge). Double-click "Create form by using wizard". Click the ">>" button. Press Enter twice.

You see this list of styles:

> Blends
> Blueprint
> Exedition
> Industrial
> International
> Ricepaper
> SandStone
> Standard
> Stone
> Sumi Painting

Each of those styles is a color scheme.

> To see how each style looks, press the down-arrow key or up-arrow key several times. Which style do you like best? I recommend "Standard" (which is the simplest, black-gray-white, resembling most other Microsoft products) or "Blends" (which is the most colorful and cheeriest, black-blue-yellow-white). The other choices are compromises between those two extremes.

When you decide which style you want, click it, then press Enter.

Invent a name for your form. For example, the name can be "Table1 form" or "A wild look at my friends". Invent any name you wish! Type that name and press Enter.

View a form You see a form displaying the first person's record, like this:

First name	Sue
Last name	Smith
Comments	wiggles toes

While you're admiring that record, you can edit it by using the mouse or these keyboard shortcuts:

> To move to the next box (field), press Enter (or Tab).
> To move back to the previous box (field), press Shift with Tab.
> To move to the bottom box, press the End key.
> To move back to the top box, press the Home key.

See other records Here's how to see other records:

> To see the **next person's record**, click the ▶ button
> or press the Page Down key (or rotate the mouse's wheel toward you).
>
> To see the **previous person's record** again, click the ◀ button
> or press the Page Up key (or rotate the mouse's wheel away from you).
>
> To hop back to the **first record**, click the |◀ button or press Ctrl with Home.
> To hop ahead to the **final record**, click the ▶| button or press Ctrl with End.
>
> To create an **extra record**, click the ▶* button or press Ctrl with +.
> To hop back to **record #2**, press the F5 key, then type 2 (and press Enter).

Close The form is in a window (called "Table1 form" or "A wild look at my friends" or whatever name you invented). When you finish looking at forms, close that window (by clicking its X button). Then click "Tables" (which is at the screen's left edge, under "Objects"), to put the screen back to normal.

Getting back to your form To see the Form view again, click "Forms" then double-click your form's name.

Accounting

You can buy a **general accounting program** or a **specialized accounting program**.

General accounting

In a typical store, the **employees** transfer **products** to **customers** from **suppliers**, for a **profit**. To manage the store, you must keep track of those 5 categories: your employees, products, customers, suppliers, and profit. Each requires its own computer program.

> To compute what to pay your **employees**, get a **payroll program**.
>
> To monitor which **products** you have in stock, get an **inventory program**.
>
> To keep track of what your **customers** owe — how much you're supposed to receive from them — get an **accounts-receivable program**.
>
> To handle debts to your **suppliers** and figure out how much to pay, get an **accounts-payable program**.
>
> To compute your **profits**, get a **general-ledger program**.

So altogether, you need 5 programs: **payroll (PR)**, **inventory (INV)**, **accounts receivable (A/R)**, **accounts payable (A/P)**, and **general ledger (GL)**. Let's look at them more closely.

Payroll

The payroll program writes paychecks to your employees. It computes how much each employee earned (the employee's **gross wage**), then subtracts various **deductions**, and writes the difference (**net pay**) onto the paycheck.

It handles 5 kinds of deductions:

> **federal withholding tax (Fed)**
> **Federal Insurance Contributions Act's social-security tax (Fica Socsec)**
> state & local taxes
> payments to health & retirement plans
> garnishments (to pay any unresolved child support, back taxes, and old fines)

It prints checks to the government, to pay the taxes that were deducted, the garnishments, and your state's unemployment insurance. At the end of each quarter and year, it fills in all the payroll-information forms that government bureaucrats require.

If the program's fancy, it counts how many employees are in each department of your company, totals how much money each department is spending for labor, and keeps track of employee vacations and attendance records.

Before buying a payroll program, check whether it includes a table that lets it automatically compute *your* state's income tax.

Inventory

The inventory program counts how many products are in stock.

It prints each product's sales history, predicts when each product will sell out, and notices which products are generating the largest profits. By analyzing all that information, it determines which products to reorder and in what quantities.

For each product it says to reorder, it prints a purchase order, to mail to the supplier. It keeps track of whether the supplier has sent the requested goods.

At the end of the year, it totals the dollar value of all the products in the inventory, to help compute the value of your business and your tax.

Accounts receivable

The accounts-receivable program computes how much each customer owes.

For each customer who pays immediately, the program prints a receipt. For customers who plan to pay later, it prints a **bill** (for services) and an **invoice** (for goods).

It notices which bills and invoices have been paid. It sends **dunning notices** to the customers who are late in paying — the ones that are **past-due**. It refuses to accept orders from customers who are past-due or reaching their credit limit.

It computes a finance charge for customers who pay late. It gives discounts to customers who pay quickly or buy large quantities.

It records each customer's name, address, phone number, and buying habits, so your sales force can talk the customer into buying even more. It records your salesperson's name, and computes the salesperson's commission.

Before your company services a customer, the program gives the customer a written estimate of the cost.

Accounts payable

The accounts-payable program prints checks to your suppliers, to pay for the products they sent you.

The program delays payment as long as a supplier allows, so that you can temporarily invest that money in your own business, without requiring bank loans. That's called, "making full use of the supplier's line of credit".

The program stores each supplier's name, address, phone number, product line, and discount policy, so you can purchase easily and wisely.

General ledger

The general-ledger program computes the company's profit, by combining info from the other four programs.

It prints a variety of profit reports for your stockholders, bank, financial planners, and government. The reports show the results for the day, week, month, quarter, and year.

It tracks each department's budget, to make sure that no department spends too much. To protect your money from being stolen or embezzled or lost, the program performs **double-entry bookkeeping**: whenever it credits money to one account, it debits the same amount of money from another account, so that the books balance.

If the program's fancy, it stores your business's history for the last several years. It compares your current profit against earlier profits, and each current budget item against previous budgets. It tells how much your business is improving or declining. It even tries to predict your business's future.

What to buy

Now the most popular package for general accounting is **QuickBooks**. It's popular because it's much easier than competitors. It tries real hard to hide accounting jargon from you, so you don't have to read about "debits", "credits", and "double-entry bookkeeping". Its ads brag that QuickBooks gives you "No debits and credits, just plain English."

It tries to view your entire business as just a bunch of checkbooks. It's published by **Intuit**, which also publishes **Quicken**, the world's most popular checkbook-balancing program.

> The first version of QuickBooks was incomplete, but the newest versions contain lots of features. Yes, QuickBooks now handles all 5 accounting functions (payroll, inventory, accounts receivable, general ledger, and accounts payable) and is flexible enough to handle many situations.

You can get either the standard version ($100) or the Pro version (which adds time-billing, estimating, and job-costing and costs $200). You can get QuickBooks on either floppy disks or a CD-ROM. (The CD-ROM contains extra tutorials and reference materials.)

Not sure whether you want QuickBooks? Then get a trial version free (with free shipping, too!) by phoning Intuit. The trial version contains the full features and can be used 25 times, after which it self-destructs. Any data you generate with the trial version can be transferred to the full version.

For more info, phone Intuit in California at 800-446-8848 or 415-944-6000.

The next step up is **Peachtree Complete Accounting**.

20 years ago, back in the 1970's, Peachtree was the first full-featured accounting program for microcomputers. It used to cost about $5,000; but because of competition from newer, cheaper packages (such as **Dac Easy Accounting** and later QuickBooks), the price has dropped to $200, and the quality has improved further. At $200, it's a terrific bargain. It uses traditional accounting jargon but tries to explain it well. It's harder for novices than QuickBooks, but it makes accountants feel more comfortable. You can buy a stripped-down version, called **Peachtree First Accounting**, for just $50; but if you're going to strip you should get QuickBooks standard instead, which wins all awards from reviewers who've strip-searched. For more info, phone Peachtree Software (which was bought by ADP) in Georgia at 800-228-0068 or 770-724-4000.

The next step up beyond Peachtree Complete Accounting is **Businessworks PC**, published by **State-of-the-Art Accounting Software** in California at 800-447-5700.

Frankly, the only accounting package I've ever seen that was *very* easy was **Dac Easy Light**.

It was delightful and came in a box that looked like a can of light beer. Discount dealers sold it for just $42. But it was limited: it couldn't handle payroll or inventory, couldn't handle big companies (since it limited most database files to 500 records each), and didn't print well on laser printers, though it handled dot-matrix printers fine. It used MS-DOS without Windows. (A Mac version was invented but was more confusing.)

It's been discontinued. I wish somebody would imitate it and "do it right".

Many uncomputerized companies do accounting by using "One-Write" checks, which are checks that have a stripe of carbon paper across their backs, to copy handwritten checks onto the correct ledger pages. **One-Write Plus** is a program that makes the computer imitate that system.

Folks who were used to the manual system like One-Write Plus. It was published by Evergreen Software, then by NEBS, and now by Peachtree. It's not as full-featured as QuickBooks or Peachtree Complete Accounting.

2 kinds of accounting

There are 2 ways to do accounting: **conservative** and **cowboy**.

The conservative way is to do double-entry bookkeeping, which records each transaction as a "credit" to one account and a "debit" from an offsetting account. That forces the books to balance and prevents any department from going over budget or stealing money.

All "professional" accountants use that conservative method. But it's tedious and hard for a novice to fully understand.

If the company is small enough so the president knows all employees personally, watches their work, personally approves all payments, and has a good gut feel for how the business is doing, the conservative "double-entry" method is an unnecessary waste of time. Instead, the president can just total all payments that the company received, total all checks that the company wrote, total the value of the inventory, and report those totals to the government at tax time — after breaking down those totals into subcategories that the government requires. The president can do it all easily with a pocket calculator or spreadsheet program (such as Excel) or database program (such as Q&A). That approach is called **cowboy**, because it's quick but suffers from a dangerous lack of controls.

Most small companies having fewer than 10 employees use that cowboy approach — and so do I! That approach is reasonable just if the president is personally involved in all facets of the company's day-to-day operations and has enough common-sense wisdom to compensate for a lack of computer-generated analyses.

Accounting hassles

Though some companies use QuickBooks and other standard accounting packages, most companies don't, for four reasons:

1. To understand accounting packages fully, you must understand the theory of debits and credits, which is complicated.

2. Those accounting packages work best if your company's an intermediary that buys from manufacturers and resells to stores.

If you run a retail store where most customers pay cash, you'll complain that the accounting packages don't automate your cash register or automatically copy data from cash-register slips to the sales records and inventory module. If you run a non-profit organization, you'll dislike how the accounting packages keep bragging about your "profit" instead of how much you're "under budget". If you run a doctor's office, you'll regret that the accounting packages don't record your patient's medical histories and needs, don't fill in the forms that your patient's insurance companies require, and don't handle multiple payers (where the patient pays part of the bill and several insurance companies split the rest of the bill). If you run a consulting firm that dispenses services rather than goods, you typically won't need inventory or accounts-payable modules, and many items in the other modules will be irrelevant.

3. Each company does business in its own unique way, whose peculiarities can't be handled well by any general-purpose accounting package.

For example, your company may have a unique way of offering discounts to customers. To make the computer automatically compute those special discounts, you must write your own program; but then you'll have difficulty making your program transfer that discount info to the accounting package you bought.

Because of each company's uniqueness, the typical company avoids generic accounting packages and instead hires a programmer to write a customized program, by using a language such as Basic or DBase.

4. General-purpose accounting packages print standard reports but don't let you invent your own. Instead of using the reports generated by general-purpose accounting packages, many managers prefer to design their *own* reports, by copying the company's data into a spreadsheet program (such as 1-2-3, Quattro, or Excel) or data-management system (such as Q&A, Approach, Access, or DBase) and then "fiddling around" until the report looks pretty. General-purpose accounting packages don't let you fiddle.

Specialized accounting

If you have just one accounting problem to solve, you can buy a simple, pleasant program to solve that problem.

Quicken

To balance your checkbook, get **Quicken**. It can also write the checks and report how much money you've spent in each budget category.

You can get Quicken for MS-DOS, Windows, the Mac, and Apple 2. Discount dealers sell each standard version for about $25. "Deluxe" versions are also available, at greater cost.

Taxes

For help in completing your 1040 Federal Income Tax form and all the associated schedules (A, B, C, D, E, etc.), get **Turbo Tax** ($28 from discounters) or **Tax Cut** ($18 from discounters). Turbo Tax gets you through the computations faster and is generally the best, though Tax Cut occasionally dishes out more personal advice. A "Deluxe" version of each program is also available, at greater cost.

Games

The computer can play games — and let you win, if it wishes!

Board games

Much of our country's computing power is spent playing games. Here's why....

Shannon's trees

In 1950, Claude Shannon proposed a way to make the computer win at checkers, chess, and other complicated games.

To understand his method, let's try to make the computer win a game of checkers. As in all checker tournaments, one player is called "black", and the other is called "white" (even though his pieces are actually red). Black makes the first move. When a player can jump, he must. The game ends when one of the players can't move (either because he has no pieces or because his pieces are blocked).

To simplify the game, we'll play on a 4-by-4 board, instead of the traditional 8-by-8. Each player has two pieces instead of twelve.

This diagram shows 63 possible positions:

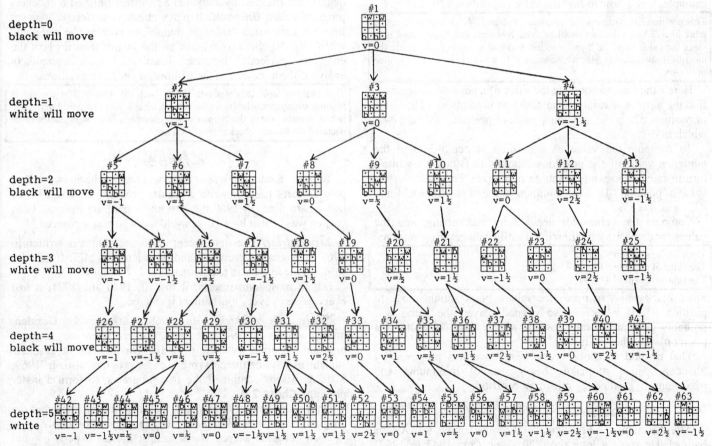

Position #1 is the initial position, from which black will move. The three arrows coming from position #1 represent the three legal moves he can choose from. Depending on which move he chooses, the board will wind up in position #2 or #3 or #4. Which move is best?

If he moves to position #2, white will reply by moving to position #5 or #6 or #7.
If he moves to position #3, white will reply by moving to position #8 or #9 or #10.
If he moves to position #4, white will reply by moving to position #11 or #12 or #13.

The diagram shows all possible ways the game's first five moves could go. Throughout the diagram, w means white man, b means black man, ẇ means white king, and b' means black king. The diagram's called a **tree**. (If you turn it upside down, it looks like the kind of tree that grows in the ground.) The arrows are called the tree's **branches**. The tree's **depth** is 5.

Which position should black choose: #2, #3, or #4? The wisdom of your answer depends on how deep you make the tree. In this particular game, a depth of 5 is satisfactory; but in 8-by-8 checkers or chess you might have to dig deeper. Theoretically, you should keep digging until you reach the end of the game; but such a tree might be too large to fit in your computer's memory.

For chess, Shannon estimated that a complete tree requires 10^{120} branches. Einstein estimated that the number of electrons in the universe is only 10^{110}. If Shannon and Einstein are both right, the tree can't fit in the universe!

Having constructed a tree of depth 5, look at the bottom positions (#42 through #63) and evaluate them, to see which positions look favorable for black:

You should consider many factors: which player has control of the center of the board? which player can move the most without being jumped? and so on. But to keep matters simple, let's consider just one factor: which player has the most men? Consider a king to be worth 1½ men.

Subtract the number of white men from the number of black men: the result of the evaluation is a number, which is called the position's **value**. If it's negative, black is losing; if it's positive, black is winning; if it's zero, the game is heading for a draw.

For example, consider position #42. Since black has one man and white has two, the value is 1 minus 2, which is -1. That's why I've written "v=-1" underneath that position. The value of each position at depth=5 is computed by that method.

For the positions at depth=4, use a different method. For example, here's how to find the value of position #29:

That position has two possible outcomes: #46 and #47. Which outcome is more likely? Since the move will be made by black, and black's goal is to make the value large, he'll prefer to move to #46 instead of #47. Since the most likely outcome is #46, whose value is ½, assign position #29 a value of ½ also.

Here's the rule: to compute the value of a position at depth=4, find the *maximum* value of the positions it points to. (The value of position #29 is the maximum value of positions #46 and #47, which is ½.)

To compute the value of a position at depth=3, find the *minimum* value of the positions it points to (since it's white's turn to move, and white wants to minimize). For example, the value of position #18 is the minimum value of positions #31 and #32, which is 1½.

Compute the values for depth 2 by maximizing, and the values for depth 1 by minimizing. Finally, you get these results:

The value of position #2 is -1.
The value of position #3 is 0.
The value of position #4 is -1½.

Since black wants to maximize values, black should move to position #3. If white is also a good player, the game will probably gravitate toward position #53, a draw. If white is a poorer player, black will win.

That method of choosing the best move was proposed by Shannon. Since it makes heavy use of minimums and maximums, it's called the **minimax method**.

Samuel's checkers

After Shannon, the next person to become famous was Arthur Samuel. He spent a long time (20 years, from 1947 to 1967) trying to make the computer win checkers. He used Shannon's minimax idea, but made many improvements.

His first spectacular success came in 1962, when his program won a game against Robert Nealey, a former Connecticut checkers champion. After the game, Nealey said "The computer had to make several star moves in order to get the win…. In the matter of the end game, I have not had such competition from any human being since 1954, when I lost my last game."

Later, the computer played six more games against Nealey. Nealey won one of them; the other five were draws.

In 1965 the computer played four games against W.F. Hellman, the World Champion. The games were played by mail. Under those conditions, Hellman won all four. But in a hastily played game where Hellman sat across the board from the computer, the result was a draw.

In 1967 the computer was beaten by the Pacific Coast Champion, K.D. Hanson, twice.

In short, the computer wins against most humans and draws against most experts, though it loses to the top champions. To bring the computer to that level of intelligence, Samuel improved Shannon's method in 3 ways:

When choosing among several moves, the computer analyzes the most promising ones more deeply.

After computing a position's value (by examining positions underneath), the computer stores the value on tape. If that position recurs in another game, the computer looks at the tape instead of repeating the analysis.

To compute a position's value, the computer examines many factors besides how many pieces each player has. The computer combines the factors, to form combination-factors, then combines the combination-factors to form a single value. Each factor's importance is determined by "experience". Samuel experimented with two forms of experience: he had the computer play against itself and also had it analyze 250,000 moves that occurred in checker championships.

In 2007, the University of Alberta Canada's computer-science department (headed by Jonathan Schaeffer) finished a checkers program called **Chinook**. It plays checkers perfectly: it never loses! It uses usual "rules of thumb" to play to the endgame, where just 10 checkers remain on the board; then it plays the endgame perfectly because Jonathan's team completely analyzed the huge tree of the trillions of endgame positions.

That analysis took 18½ years to finish, with the help of 200 computers running simultaneously. By 1994, when Chinook was just partly perfected, it had already beaten the human world champion in enough games to be declared the world's checker champion itself.

Chess

While Samuel was programming checkers, other programmers tried to write a similar program for chess. They had a hard time. In 1960 the best chess program that had been written was beaten by a 10-year-old kid who was a novice.

Greenblatt The first decent chess program was written in 1967 by Richard Greenblatt and his friends at MIT. It actually won a game in a chess tournament.

But in most tournaments, it lost. In 1970 and 1971, it lost every game in every tournament it entered.

Slate & Atkins In 1968, Atkins & Gorklen, undergraduates at Northwestern University, wrote a chess program. Inspired by their program, David Slate, a graduate student in physics there, wrote a chess program also. In 1969, Slate & Atkins combined the two programs, to form a better program, **Chess 2.0**.

During the next several years, they continually improved the program. Their most famous version was called **Chess 4.7**.

Their program played chess against human experts — and occasionally won! Their computer scored several triumphs in tournaments designed for humans.

In 1976, their computer won the class B section of the Paul Masson American Chess Championships. Against the humans in that tournament, it scored 5 wins, no losses. By winning that tournament, it achieved a U.S. Chess Federation score of 2210 and became a chess Master.

Then it entered the Minnesota State Championship, to try to become the Minnesota State Champion, but lost (it scored 1 win, 3 losses, 1 tie).

In August 1968, an International Chess Master, David Levy, bet about $5,000 against several computerists. He bet that no computer would win a

---

chess match against him in the next ten years. He won the bet: in August 1978, Chess 4.7 tried one last time to win a match against him, but lost (it scored 1 win, 3 losses, 1 tie).

Slate & Atkins improved Chess 4.7, to form **Chess 4.9**, which became the world champion of computer chess.

But though it was the world champion of computer chess, it was not necessarily the "best" program. It won because it ran on a super-fast maxicomputer (manufactured by Control Data Corporation). Other chess programs, written for slower computers, were at a disadvantage.

Minicomputer chess Almost as fast as Chess 4.9 was a program called **Belle**, written at Bell Telephone Laboratories. Belle ran on a minicomputer specially wired to create trees fast.

Microcomputer chess Each of those programs — Chess 4.9 and Belle — required an expensive CPU and lots of RAM. Is it possible to write a decent chess program using just a cheap CPU and very little RAM? Yes! In 1976, a Canadian named Peter Jennings wrote a program called **Microchess 1.0**; it ran on a $250 microcomputer (the Kim 1), which contained a 6502 CPU, no ROM, and just 1K of RAM! The program played decently, though not spectacularly.

Later, he wrote an improved program, called **Microchess 1.5**.

It played on the Radio Shack model 1 and the Apple. The version on the model 1 consumed 4K of RAM: 2K was for the logic, and the other 2K were just to make the picture of the chess board look pretty! It sold for $20.

In 1978, an amazing chess program was written by a husband-and-wife team: Dan and Kathe Sprachlin. They named the program **Sargon**, to honor an ancient king.

It ran on the Jupiter microcomputer, which contained an 8080 CPU and 16K RAM. It played much better than Microchess. When the Jupiter computer became obsolete, the Sprachlins rewrote the program, to make it run on the Radio Shack model 1 and the Apple. Then they developed an improved version called **Sargon 2**, and a further improvement called **Sargon 3**, which runs on *all* the popular computers. Sargon 3 was published by the Hayden division of Spinnaker.

For many years, Sargon 3 was considered the best microcomputer chess program. But in 1986, Sargon 3 was beaten by a new program called **Chessmaster 2000**.

Like Sargon 3, Chessmaster 2000 contained many features that made it fun for both experts and novices. It was published by Software Toolworks, distributed by Electronic Arts, cost about $35, and came in versions for the IBM PC, Apple 2e & 2c, Commodore 64 & Amiga, and Atari 800 XL & ST.

Since then, Sargon and Chessmaster have both improved. **Sargon 5** is published by Activision; **Chessmaster 6000** is published by Mindscape.

When you play against the computer by using a version of Sargon or Chessmaster, you can ask the computer for help by pressing a special key. Then the computer will tell you how it would move if it were in your position.

You can follow the computer's suggestion or ignore it. Since your goal is to outsmart the computer, you should listen to the computer's advice; but instead of *following* the advice, try to devise a move that's even cleverer!

Many companies make hand-held electronic chess games.

Some of the games include contain a tiny voice synthesizer, which lets the computer tell you its moves verbally. Some of the games include a mechanical arm, so that the computer will pick up the pieces and move them. Some of the games include touch-sensitive boards, so you can indicate your move by just tapping the square you want to move from and the square you want to move to. For humor, some of the chess games make the computer say wisecracks about your style of playing.

Today's champion Now the best chess program is **Deep Blue**. Programmed by a team of IBM employees (led by C.J. Tan), it runs on a specially designed IBM computer.

It plays amazingly well. In 1996, it played a match against the world chess champion, Garry Kasparov, and almost won the match! In May 1997, it played a rematch against him and *did* win the match: of the 6 games in the match, the computer won 3, lost 2, and tied 1. So **now the world chess champion is a computer!**

Choose a level

When you begin playing a top-notch computer game (such as Chessmaster), you must choose the "level" at which you want the computer to play.

If you choose a low level, the computer will move quickly, without much forethought.

If you choose a high level, the computer will play more carefully (and make better moves). To do that, the computer "looks ahead", by building a very large tree, which requires lots of time; and so you must wait a long time until the computer moves. If you choose a level that's very high, the computer will need *several hours* to compute its move.

Why a computer?

Playing against the computer is more interesting than playing against a human.

When you play against a human friend, you must wait a long time for your friend to move. When you play against Chessmaster at a low level, the computer moves almost immediately.

You can play several games against the computer (and learn a lot from them) in the same amount of time you'd need to play just *one* game against a human. So by playing against the computer, you gain experience faster than by playing against a human. Bobby Fischer, who became the world chess champion, now plays *only* against computers; he refuses to play against humans and hasn't defended his title.

The computer is kinder than a human.

If you make a bad move, the computer lets you "take it back" and try again. If you seem to be losing, the computer lets you restart the whole game. The computer — unlike a human — has infinite patience and no ego. Playing against the computer is less threatening than playing against a human.

If you have a computer, you don't have to worry about finding an opponent who's "at your level"; when you play against the computer, just tell the computer at what level you want it to play. The computer will act about as smart as you wish.

Adventure games

Adventure is a game where you hunt for some sort of "treasure".

Original Adventure

The original version of Adventure was written by Will Crowther & Don Woods, on a PDP-10 maxicomputer at Stanford University's Artificial Intelligence Lab.

Here's the game's **plot**:

When you run the program, the computer says you're near a shack at the end of a road. The computer offers to act as your body and understand any two-word command. Then it waits for your command. You can tell it to **GO NORTH** or **GO FORWARD** or — if you're going along a stream — you can say **FOLLOW STREAM** or **GO DOWNSTREAM**.

The first time you play this game, you feel lost — the game's an adventure. As you wander in whatever direction you please, the computer says you're going through forests, across streams, over hills, etc.

After much aimless wandering, you'll eventually see a stream. If you follow the stream, you'll come to a mysterious iron grate. If you try to **BREAK GRATE**, the computer says you're not strong enough. If you try to **OPEN GRATE**, the computer says you have no keys. You'll get more and more frustrated, until the computer offers to give you a hint — but the hint will cost you several points. If you acquiesce, the computer will give you this hint: find the keys!

To find the keys, the typical stupid player tries wandering through the forests and valleys again. But if you're smart, you'll remember that at the beginning of the adventure you were next to a shack. So you go back to the shack, walk inside, and find keys! So you trek back to iron grate, and use the keys to get in. You think — aha! — you've succeeded!

But actually, you've just begun! The grate leads you into a cave that contains 130 rooms, which form a big three-dimensional maze. Lying in the maze are 15 buried treasures; but as you walk through the maze, you can easily forget where you are and where you've come from; you can waste lots of time just walking in circles, without realizing it!

To add to the challenge, the cave contains many dangers, such as trap doors (if you fall in, you break every bone in your body!) and trolls & snakes, which you must ward off by using various devices that you have to find in the cave's rooms or even back at the shack. Yes, you might have to trek all the way back to the shack again!

Finally, after dodging all the evil things in the cave, you reach the treasures. You grab them up and start walking away with them. But then you hear footsteps behind you, and pirates steal your treasures! Then you must chase the pirates.

If you manage to keep your treasures and your life and get out of the cave, you haven't necessarily won. The nasty computer keeps score of how *well* you retrieve the treasures. The maximum possible score is 350. After you've played this game many times and learned how to duck all your adversaries quickly, you'll find you scored just 349 points, and you'll wonder what you did wrong that cost you 1 point. The answer is: during the adventure, you must borrow magazines from a room in the cave; to get the extra point, you must return them!

The game's a true adventure, because as you wander through forests and the rooms in the cave, the computer tells what you see, but you don't know whether what you see is important.

For example, when you walk into a room, the computer might say the room contains a small cage. That's all it says. You must guess whether the cage has any significance and what to do to the cage, if anything. Should you pick it up? Try to break it? Kiss it? Carry it? Try anything you like — give any command to your computer-body that you wish — and see what happens.

Here's a list of the most useful commands:

To reach a different room in the cave, say **GO NORTH** (or SOUTH, EAST, WEST, UP, or DOWN). You can abbreviate: instead of typing "GO NORTH", just type "**N**".

Whenever you see a new object, **TAKE** it. Then you can carry it from room to room and use it later whenever you need it. If you see a new object and want to TAKE it, but your hands are already full, **DROP** one of the other objects you're carrying.

To see a list of what you're carrying, tell the computer to take **INVENTORY**. To make the computer describe your surroundings again, say **LOOK**.

To see your score so far, say **SCORE**.

If you say **SAVE**, the computer will copy your current position onto the disk, so you can return to that position later. If you ever want to give up, just say **QUIT**.

Throughout the game, you get beautifully lyrical writing. For example, the computer describes one of the rooms as follows: "You are in a splendid chamber thirty feet high. The walls are frozen rivers of orange stone."

The game's an adventure about a person exploring a cave. Since *you're* the person in the adventure and can type whichever actions you wish, you affect how the adventure progresses and ends. Since it's high-quality story-telling whose outcome is affected by your input, it's called **interactive fiction**.

Adventure was originally written for a PDP-10 maxicomputer, but imitations for microcomputers were sold by Microsoft, Creative Computing, and Electronic Arts. They're no longer marketed.

Infocom

After Adventure became popular, several programmers invented a variation called **Zork**, which lets you input long sentences instead of restricting you to two-word phrases. Like Adventure, Zork consists of hunting for treasures in a cave. In Zork, you reach the cave by entering a house's basement.

Like Adventure, Zork originally ran on a PDP-10 computer. Then Infocom published versions of Zork for microcomputers: the IBM PC, Apple (2e & 2c & Mac), Commodore (64 & Amiga), Atari (800 XL & ST), and Radio Shack (Models 3 & 4 & Color Computer 2).

Zork sold so well that Infocom published sequels, called **Zork 2** and **Zork 3**. Then Infocom published other variations, where the cave is replaced by experiences in outer space or by thrillers involving spies, murders, mysteries, and haunted castles. Infocom's next big hits were **The Hitchhiker's Guide to the Galaxy** (based on the award-winning wacky outer-space novel by Doug Adams) and **Leather Goddesses of Phobos** (letting you choose among three naughtiness levels, from "prude" to "lewd"; choosing "lewd" makes the computer asks whether you're at least 18; it also asks whether you're male or female, and you get a titillating 3-D comic book with a scratch-and-sniff card).

Infocom was an independent company but got acquired by Activision.

Sierra On-Line

Shortly after Infocom developed the microcomputer version of Zork, Sierra On-Line developed **Super Stud Adventure**, which was quickly renamed **Softporn Adventure**. Instead of exploring a cave, you explore a brothel. To enter the brothel, you must find the secret password (hint: go to the bathroom and look at the graffiti!) and find enough money to pay for your pleasures (by taking a taxi to a casino and gambling).

That was the first **urban adventure**, and also the first **sexual adventure**. The ad for it showed a photograph of the programmers (Ken & Roberta Williams) nude in a California hot tub. Fortunately, the water in the tub was high enough to cover any problems.

The original adventure, Infocom adventures, and Softporn Adventure display wonderful text but no graphics. They're called **text adventures**.

The first ambitious **graphics adventure** was **Time Zone**, published in 1981 by Sierra On-Line. The Time Zone program is so long it fills *both* sides of *6* Apple disks; that's 12 sides altogether! In fact, the game's so long that nobody's ever finished playing it! Here's how to play:

You use a computerized "time machine", which transports you to 9 times (400 million B.C., 10000 B.C., 50 B.C., 1000 A.D., 1400, 1700, 1982, 2082, and 4082) and 8 locations (North America, South America, Europe, Africa, Asia, Australia, Antarctica, and Outer Space).

Wherever you go, your screen shows a high-resolution color picture of where you are. For example, if you choose "approximately 1400", Christopher Columbus will welcome you aboard his ship. Altogether, the game contains over 1400 pictures! You travel through history, searching for clues that help you win.

Time Zone is historically accurate and doesn't let you cheat. For example, when you find a book of matches in the year 2082, your time machine will let you carry the matches back to 1982 but not to 1700 — since matches weren't invented until 1800.

Living through history isn't easy. Jonathan Rotenberg, chairman of the Boston Computer Society, played the game and said:

I've been killed dozens of times. I've been assassinated by Brazilian terrorists, karate-chopped by a Brazilian monk, eaten by a tyrannosaur, crushed in an Andes avalanche, stampeded by a buffalo, overcome by Antarctic frostbite, and harpooned by Mayan fishermen.

And you see it all in color!

Time Zone sold for $99.95. Teenagers didn't buy it, because it was expensive and took too long to win. Sierra On-Line stopped selling it.

Later, Sierra On-Line made Softporn Adventure even more exciting, by adding graphics. Here's what those newer graphic versions are called....

Leisure Suit Larry in the Land of the Lounge Lizards
Leisure Suit Larry 2: Looking for Love in all the Wrong Places
Leisure Suit Larry 3: Passionate Patti in Pursuit of the Pulsating Pectorals

Spinnaker

Spinnaker published the **Windham Classics**, a series of adventure games based on kid's novels.

You become Dorothy in **The Wizard of Oz**, Jim Hawkins in **Treasure Island**, Fritz in **Swiss Family Robinson**, Alice in **Alice in Wonderland**, and Green-Sky in **Below the Root**. The games include graphics. To make those adventure games easy, whenever you get stuck the computer helps you by printing a list of words to try typing.

Spinnaker also published **Telarium Software**, based on novels that are more adult. For example, you become Perry Mason in **The Case of the Mandarin Murder**; that game, besides being fun, also trains you to become a lawyer:

It comes with a lawyer's handbook that explains the 6 ways to object to the prosecutor's questions: you can complain that the prosecutor's asking an **IRRELEVANT** question, relying on **HEARSAY**, **BROWBEATING** the witness, **LEADING** the witness to a suggested answer, getting an **OPINION** from a person who isn't an expert, or trying to get facts from a person who's **UNQUALIFIED** to know them.

To make sure you understand those six ways to object, the handbook includes a multiple-choice test about them. The test is titled "Study Guide for the California Bar Exam".

The game also lets you invent your own questions for the witnesses and give commands to your secretary (Della Street) and detective (Paul Drake).

The Windham Classics and Telarium Software were available for the IBM PC, Apple 2e & 2c, and Commodore 64. But Spinnaker has stopped selling them.

Spinnaker became part of a bigger company, **Softkey**, which then became part of **The Learning Company**.

Carmen Sandiego

Brøderbund published a game called **Where in the World is Carmen Sandiego?** You try to catch and arrest the notorious international thief, Carmen Sandiego, and the other thieves in her organization, called the *Villain's International League of Evil (V.I.L.E.)*, as they flee to 30 cities all over the world.

To help you understand those 30 cities, the game comes with a geography book: the 928-page unabridged edition of *The World Almanac and Book of Facts*.

As you play the game, you unearth clues about which cities the thieves are fleeing to. To use the clues, you must look up facts in the almanac. By playing the game, you practice using an almanac and learn geography. When you figure out which city to travel to, the screen shows a world map, shows you traveling to the city, and shows a snapshot of what the city looks like, so the game also acts as a travelogue.

Since the game is so educational, it's won awards from *Classroom Computer Learning Magazine* and the Software Publishers Association.

Strictly speaking, it's not a true adventure game, since it does *not* let you input your own words and phrases. Instead, you choose from menus, which make the game easier for youngsters.

Brøderbund created 3 sequels:

Where in the USA is Carmen Sandiego? has you chasing Carmen's gang across all 50 states; the game comes with *Fodor's USA* travel guide.

Where in Europe in Carmen Sandiego? takes you to all 34 countries in Europe and comes with Rand McNally's *Concise Atlas of Europe*.

Where in Time is Carmen Sandiego? lets you romp through historical time periods.

Amnesia

My favorite text adventure is **Amnesia**, published by Electronic Arts for the Apple 2e & 2c and IBM PC. Like Softporn Adventure, Amnesia takes place in a city; but Amnesia is much more sophisticated.

Here's the plot:

When you start playing Amnesia, you wake up in a hotel room in New York City. You discover you have no clothes (you're stark naked), no money (you're flat broke), and no recollection of who you are — because you're suffering from amnesia. You don't even remember your name.

You look at yourself and notice you're male. Your first problem is to get clothes and money. But then you learn you have other problems that are worse: you get a call from a guy who reminds you that today is your wedding day, and that if you don't hurry up and marry his daughter without further mess-ups, he'll use his pistol; you also discover the FBI's looking for you because the state of Texas has reported you're a murderer.

After getting clothes (so you can stop scaring the hotel's maids), there are several ways to get out of your jam. (I've tried them all!)

One way is to say "yes" to the pistol-packing papa and marry his daughter, who takes you to Australia, where you live on a sheep ranch for the rest of your life. But then you never learn who you really are! Whenever you ask your wife about your past, she simply says, "You wouldn't want to know." You die of old age, peacefully; but even on your deathbed, you don't learn who you are; and so when you die, you feel sad. In that case, you score lots of points for survival, but zero for detective work and zero for character development.

A different solution is to say "no" to the bride and — after getting bloodied — run out of the hotel, onto the streets of New York. Then the fun begins — because hiding on the program's disks is a complete map of Manhattan (from Battery Park all the way up to 110th Street), including all streets and landmarks and even all subway stops! This gigantic game includes 94 subway stations, 200 landmarks, and 3,545 street corners.

As you walk one block north, then one block east, etc., the computer describes everything you pass, even the most sublime (The Museum of Modern Art) and the most ridiculous (Nedick's hamburger stands). You can ride the subway — after you get enough money to buy a token. The game even includes all subway signs, such as "Downtown — Brooklyn" and "Uptown — Queens". To catch the E train, you must hop in as soon as it arrives. Otherwise, it departs without you, and the computer says "an F train comes" instead.

As night falls, the computer warns you to find a place to sleep. (You can't go back to your hotel, since you're in trouble there.) To find a free place to stay, you can try phoning the names in your address book — once you find a phone booth, and get a quarter to pay for each call. The address book contains 17 listings: J.A., A.A., Chelsea H., drugs, F°, Sue G., E.H., interlude, kvetch, J.L., R & J, sex, soft, Lila T., T.T.T.T., and Wit's End. Each of those listings is an adventure in itself. You must explore each of them thoroughly to fully discover who you really are.

If your body gets weak (from sleeplessness or hunger or being hit by too many muggers), you faint on the sidewalk, wake up in a hospital, and get found there by the FBI, which returns you to Texas, which executes you for murder. But even that deadly ending has a cheery note. For example, you can choose your last meal: would you like steak and potatoes, or turkey? When you finally die, you can wind up in purgatory, which consists of getting mosquito bites, with an opportunity to take a rowboat to heaven if you can just remember your *real* name and tell the boatman.

The entire adventure has the structure of a good novel: a gripping intro (you're a nude, broke, amnesiac groom in a hotel), a thorough development section (wandering through the streets of New York, searching for your identity and life's meaning), and a conclusion (a whimsical death scene or something better).

The text was written by Thomas Disch, the award-winning sci-fi novelist. It's lyrical. For example, when you escape the hotel and walk out onto the streets of New York, the computer says:

"It feels great to be a single faceless, nameless atom among the million others churning about in the grid of Manhattan's streets. It feels safe."

The game combines all our nightmares about New York into a wild, exciting adventure.

The game's affected my own life. Now whenever something in my life goes wrong, instead of groaning I just say, "I'm in another wild part of Amnesia!" In Amnesia, as in life, the only way to score top points for living is to experience it *all*. To live life to the fullest, you must take risks, have the courage to face unknown dangers, and revel in the excitement of the unexpected.

Though Amnesia received lots of praise from reviewers, sales were disappointing. Electronic Arts stopped publishing it.

Action games

Hey! Let's have some action!

Arcade games

The first popular arcade game was **Pong**, which made the computer crudely imitate a game of ping-pong. Then came **Space Invaders**, in which you had to shoot aliens who were dropping bombs on you.

Those games restricted you to moving in just one direction. The first popular arcade game that let you move two-dimensionally was **Asteroids**. It let you move through the sky while dodging asteroids and enemy space ships.

Those outer-space and sports games appealed mainly to boys. The first arcade game appealing mainly to girls was **Pac Man**, a non-violent fantasy where you ran through a maze full of food and tried to gobble as much as possible, before ghosts gobbled *you*. It appealed especially to dieting girls who dreamed of pigging out without getting caught.

In all those games, the graphics were crude. The first arcade game that used professional graphics was **Dragon's Lair**.

It contained a videodisk full of animated cartoons drawn by artists who'd worked at Walt Disney. To dodge obstacles that appear in the cartoons, you move your joystick, which changes the action that the cartoons display.

Olympics

In 1980, Tim Smith quit his job at Burroughs and spent the next 9 months programming **Olympic Decathlon**, which made the Radio Shack Model 1 computer imitate all 10 of the decathlon's events.

In his game, one of your fingers represents your left leg, and another finger represents your right leg. To "run", you tap those fingers (left, right, left, right) as quickly as possible on the keyboard. By using those fingers and others, you compete in all ten events: the 100-meter dash, long jump, shot-put, high jump, 400-meter dash, 110-meter hurdles, discus throw, pole vault, javelin throw, and 1500-meter run. You can play solo or against your friends. At parties, you can form teams and cheer each other on.

Later, he wrote versions for the Apple 2 and the IBM PC. They were all published by Microsoft, which now publishes fancier games instead.

From Doom to Quake

The first modern computer-action games were **Doom** and its sequel, called **Quake**.

They're technologically amazing: even on a slow computer (whose CPU is just a 486 instead of a Pentium), they let you run fast through a realistic-looking 3-D environment while you chase and shoot monsters who chase and shoot *you*!

Even a pacifist like me has to admire the technology! These games use programming tricks that make realistic-looking 3-D graphics come at you much faster than you'd believe possible on a personal computer. A few seconds of playing Doom or Quake will make you say "Wow!"

Though Doom is violent, it has a sense of humor:

You can choose 5 levels of difficulty. The beginner level, where you can't get hurt, is called "I'm too young to die". The next step up is called "Hey, not too rough". Then comes "Hurt me plenty", then "Ultra-violence", and finally the expert level, called "Nightmare!"

If you try to quit the bloodshed and return to DOS, the program gives you advice such as "I wouldn't leave if I were you. DOS is much worse." It also warns "Sit back with your milk and cookies and let the universe go to Hell — or act like a man! Slap a few shells into your shotgun and let's kick some demonic butt."

Doom is called a **first-person shooter** game, because while you shoot demons, **the screen shows what your eyes see**: **your outstretched hand** in front of you, **holding your gun** (or more bizarre weapons, such as chain saws), while **a mirror on your wrist shows how bloodied your face got**.

The action is accompanied by a hard-pumping musical score, keeping your adrenaline up and punctuated by gunfire & ghoulish groans from all monsters charging at you and dying. You and the monsters charge at each other by running through corridors that close in on you faster than any nightmare.

Here's more info (about Doom and its cousins), collected by my research assistant, Len Pallazola:

Doom revolutionized the computer gaming industry. In Doom (and the many Doom clones that followed), you see a gun directly in front of you, pointing out at a hallway or room. You wander through a maze of corridors, shooting anything that moves. In the process, you find bigger and better guns, medical supplies, and other goodies.

Doom was created in 1993 by a company called **Id Software**.

Before creating Doom, Id Software wrote **Wolfenstein 3-D** (nicknamed **Wolf 3-D**), where you must escape Castle Wolfenstein (a Nazi stronghold) and might even fight Hitler; if you win, you end World War II. Wolf 3-D wasn't a true 3-D game, but it was the next best thing. The folks at Id placed 2-dimensional bitmaps on the framework of a wall in such a way that when you moved, the bitmaps would stretch and bend, making it look like your perspective had changed. Even the Nazis were just 2-dimensional bitmaps: you saw either their fronts or backs, but never their sides. Running a true 3-D game requires a powerful computer; since Wolf 3-D wasn't truly 3-D, it worked fine on a 286. Id shared its discovery with other companies, who made clones of Wolf 3-D.

After Wolf 3-D, Id created **Doom**, where you play a futuristic soldier battling demons and zombies that took over your outpost. Doom used the same technology as Wolf 3-D but heightened the realism by letting walls be curved and adding shadowy areas where a torch or gunfire would light up the room. Doom's most popular feature was the ability to play with (or against) up to 3 friends on a network (such as the Internet or a LAN). Doom was one of the first fast-action games to offer that kind of play, which made it immensely popular. You can play **cooperatively** or in a **Deathmatch** where you battle your friends… to the death!

In August 1996, Id released **Quake**, an almost entirely true 3-D sequel to Doom. In Quake, instead of using rectangular 2-dimensional bitmaps, Id used hundreds of polygons to compose each object and monster — so the game is extremely realistic and detailed but requires more RAM and a faster CPU (a Pentium or at least a 486DX4-100).

Shareware You can download the shareware version of Doom and Quake free, from Web sites such as download.com.

Bothered? Warning: games such as Quake and Doom show blood, gore, guts, demons, zombies, monsters, pentagrams, and other occult symbols. But if you don't get offended or grossed out, you'll relish the fast action.

Humanity

The computer can analyze humans and act human itself. Here's how....

Analyze yourself

The computer can analyze your body and mind.

Death

At the University of Illinois Medical Center, Terrence Lukas wrote a program that predicts when you'll die.

The program makes the computer ask for your age and sex. Then the computer asks about the life and health of your parents and grandparents, your weight, your personal habits (smoking, drinking, exercise, and sleep), your history of medical check-ups, your social class (your education, occupation, and income), and your lifestyle: urban or rural, single or married, aggressive or passive, and whether you use seat belts. The computer combines all that info, to tell you when you'll probably die, based on statistics from life-insurance companies and from medical research.

Running the program is fun. Each time you answer a question, the computer tells you how your answer affects its prediction. You see its prediction bob up and down, until the questions finally end, and the computer gives you its final prediction of when you'll die. It's like watching the early returns of a Presidential election, except the topic is you!

The computer pops out with surprising comments, based on medical research. Here are some comments the computer prints:

Professionals usually live longer, except musicians, architects, and pharmacists. Why this is true is unknown.

Cooks, chefs, bakers, and other people who work at jobs associated with overeating have a lower life expectancy.

Adults that sleep too much use too many hours in nonphysical activity. They may be unhappy and sleep as an escape, or may be ill. Depressed people have shorter life expectancies.

Moderate drinking (up to two drinks per day) reduces stress and aids digestion. Heavy drinking, however, produces physiological damage. As for teetotalers, they may have rather rigid value systems and may undergo stress in maintaining them.

The program is on pages 34-36 of the November 1977 issue of *Kilobaud Microcomputing Magazine*.

Brainwaves

A computer has been programmed to read your mind, by analyzing your brainwaves.

A newspaper article described the program dramatically: you're an airplane pilot... your plane is going to crash... but you think "Up!", and the plane automatically goes back up!... because the plane is run by a computer that's reading your brainwaves!

But what if the pilot is sadistic, and thinks "Down"?

Anyway, the program isn't perfected yet. When the computer tries to distinguish brainwaves that mean *up* from brainwaves that mean *down*, it gets the right answer 75% of the time. In other words, 25% of the time it goofs. I'd hate to be in a plane controlled by a computer that was having a bad day!

Recently, the U.S. Government has shifted the emphasis of this research. The new emphasis is more practical: to make the computer ring a buzzer, when the pilot's brainwaves indicate the pilot is daydreaming.

Psychotherapy

In 1966, Joseph Weizenbaum programmed the computer to act as a psychotherapist. On the keyboard, you type whatever thoughts come to your mind, and the computer will give you therapy. When typing on the terminal, feel free to use whatever words you wish — you don't have to use a "computer language".

The most amazing thing about the program is that it does a decent job of therapy, even though the computer doesn't know what you're talking about! Weizenbaum's program contains the definitions of only a handful of words; but if you use words the computer doesn't know, the computer does an amazingly good job of "faking". For example, if you say, "My junkapoo is like my iliabop", the computer will continue the conversation by asking you, "In what way?" even though the computer doesn't know what a junkapoo or an iliabop is.

Here's a conversation between his computer and a patient.

Patient: Men are all alike.
Comp.: In what way?

Patient: They're always bugging us about something or other.
Comp.: Can you think of a specific example?

Patient: Well, my boyfriend made me come here.
Comp.: Your boyfriend made you come here.

Patient: He says I'm depressed much of the time.
Comp.: I am sorry to hear you are depressed.

Patient: It's true. I am unhappy.
Comp.: Do you think coming here will help you not to be unhappy?

Patient: I need some help, that much seems certain.
Comp.: What would it mean to you if you got some help?

Patient: Perhaps I could learn to get along with my mother.
Comp.: Tell me more about your family.

Patient: My mother takes care of me.
Comp.: Who else in your family takes care of you?

Patient: My father.
Comp.: Your father.

Patient: You are like my father in some ways.
Comp.: What resemblance do you see?

Patient: You are not very aggressive, but I think you don't want me to notice that.
Comp.: What makes you think I am not very aggressive?

Patient: You don't argue with me.
Comp.: Why do you think I don't argue with you?

Patient: You are afraid of me.
Comp.: Does it please you to believe I am afraid of you?

Patient: My father is afraid of everybody.
Comp.: What else comes to mind when you think of your father?

Patient: Bullies.
Comp.: Does that have anything to do with the fact that your boyfriend made you come here?

Like the famous psychotherapist Carl Rogers, the computer asks probing questions that make the patient open up, but it never gives advice: the patient must discover the truth for herself.

I'll explain exactly how the program works, so you can become a psychotherapist yourself, and get hundreds of thousands of dollars by bilking your patients.

The computer begins by replacing some of the patient's words:

Typed by patient	Replacement
mom	mother
dad	father
dont	don't
cant	can't
wont	won't
dreamed	dreamt
dreams	dream
I	you@
me	you
you	I
my	your
your	my
myself	yourself
yourself	myself
I'm	you're
you're	I'm
am	are@
were	was

For example, the sentence Well, my boyfriend made me come here becomes Well, your boyfriend made you come here.

The computer hunts through the revised sentence or paragraph for one of these **keywords**....

Category 8: computer, computers, machine, machines
Category 7: name
Category 6: alike, like, same
Category 5: remember
Category 4: dreamt
Category 3: dream, if
Category 2: everybody, everyone, nobody, was, your
Category 1: always

Category 0: are, are@, because, can, certainly, deutsch, espanol, francais, hello, how, I, I'm, italiano, maybe, my, no, perhaps, sorry, what, when, why, yes, you@, you're

If the computer finds *several* of those keywords, it chooses the one in the highest category; if they lie in the same category, it chooses the one the patient typed first.

Then it looks up the keyword in this phrasebook:

Patient's keyword	Computer's reply
alike	In what way?
always	Can you think of a specific example?
are	
are I...	Why are you interested in whether I am... or not?
are...	Did you think they might not be...?
are@	
are you...	Do you believe you are...?
are	Why do you say "am"?
because	Is that the real reason?
can	
can I...	You believe I can..., don't you?
can you...	Whether or not you can... depends on you more than on me.
certainly	You seem quite positive.
computer	Do computers worry you?
computers	Do computers worry you?
deutsch	I am sorry, I speak only English.
dream	What does that dream suggest to you?
dreamt...	Really,...?
espanol	I am sorry, I speak only English.
everybody	Really, everybody?
everyone	Really, everyone?
hello	How do you do — please state your problem.
how	Why do you ask?
I	
I remind you of	In what way?
I are...	What makes you think I am...?
I... you	Why do you think I... you?
I	We were discussing you — not me.
if...	Do you think it's likely that...?
I'm...	What makes you think I am...?

italiano	I am sorry, I speak only English.
like	
(am,is,are,was)... like	In what way?
like	(get a different keyword)
machine	Do computers worry you?
machines	Do computers worry you?
maybe	You don't seem quite certain.
my...	Why are you concerned over my...?
name	I am not interested in names.
no	Are you saying "no" just to be negative?
nobody	Really, nobody?
perhaps	You don't seem quite certain.
remember	
you remember...	Do you often think of...?
do I remember...	Did you think I would forget...?
remember	(get a different keyword)
same	In what way?
sorry	Please don't apologize.
was	
was you...	What if you were...?
you was	Were you really?
was I...	Would you like to believe I was...?
was	(get a different keyword)
what	Why do you ask?
when	Why do you ask?
why	
why don't I...	Do you believe I don't...?
why can't you...	Do you think you should be able to...?
yes	You seem quite positive.
you@	
you (want, need)...	What would it mean to you if you got...?
you are... (sad, unhappy, depressed, sick)	I am sorry to hear you are (sad, etc.).
you are... (happy, elated, glad, better)	How have I helped you to be (happy, etc.)?
you (feel, think, believe, wish) you	Do you really think so?
you (feel, think, believe, wish)...I	(use the keyword "I" instead)
you are...	Is it because you are... that you came to me?
you (can't, cannot)...	How do you know you can't...?
you don't...	Don't you really...?
you feel	Tell me more about such feelings.
you... I	Perhaps in your fantasy we... each other.
your	
your... (mother, father, sister, brother, wife, children)	Tell me more about your family.
your...	Your...?
you're	(treat as "you@ are")

For example, if the keyword is *sorry*, the computer looks up *sorry* in the phrasebook, which says to print "Please don't apologize."

Suppose the patient types, "If the job is lousy, he'll die." The keyword is *if*. In the phrasebook, *if* is followed by three dots, which stand for the part of the clause that comes after *if*, which is "the job is lousy". (The computer figures out where the clause ends by looking at the punctuation.) The phrasebook says to print "Do you think it's likely that the job is lousy?"

The symbol @ serves just to locate the correct keyword in the phrasebook. Thereafter, it's ignored.

Here's what happens if the keyword is *you@*. After locating *you@* in the phrasebook, the computer ignores the @. If the patient's revised sentence contains *you want*... or *you need*..., the computer prints "What would it mean to you if you got...?" If the patient's sentence contains *you are*... *sad*, the computer prints "I am sorry to hear you are sad."

For each reply in the phrasebook, Weizenbaum stored a list of alternatives. For example, here are the alternatives to "Please don't apologize":

Apologies are not necessary.
What feelings do you have when you apologize?
I've told you that apologies are not required.

While chatting with the patient, the computer keeps track of which replies it has printed already, and uses the alternatives to avoid repetition.

If the patient's statement doesn't contain a keyword, the computer may give one of these replies:

> I am not sure I understand you fully.
> Please go on.
> What does that suggest to you?
> Do you feel strongly about discussing such things?

Or it may take a second look at earlier parts of the conversation, retrieve a clause that contained *your…*, and print one of these replies:

> Let's discuss further why your….
> Earlier you said your….
> Does that have anything to do with the fact that your…?

For example, it may retrieve the clause *Your boyfriend made you come here* and print:

> Does that have anything to do with the fact that your boyfriend made you come here?

The program was written at the Massachusetts Institute of Technology (MIT). The programmer, Joseph Weizenbaum, named the program "**Eliza**", to honor Eliza Doolittle — the woman in *My Fair Lady* and *Pygmalion*, who learned to speak English and have a good conversation.

Since the program turns the computer into a chatterbox who's a robot, it's called a **chatterbot** (or, more briefly, a **bot**). Inspired by the Eliza program, many other chatterbot programs have been invented.

Some people think Weizenbaum's Eliza program shows that computers can communicate as well as psychotherapists. But Weizenbaum himself holds the opposite view; he believes the program shows that psychotherapists communicate as poorly as computers.

Improved versions After Weizenbaum invented Eliza, other programmers invented improvements. For example, in one of the improved versions, whenever the computer doesn't understand you, it reacts like the typical rich psychotherapist — it bluffs and says:

> I understand fully. Please go on.

The computer never really understands what you say. For example, in one version, if you say "My, my, my!", the computer will reply:

> Tell me more about your your your.

Radio Shack's headquarters phoned me, and asked for permission to use my explanation of Weizenbaum's program. I agreed, whereupon Radio Shack invented and sold a version that makes the computer *talk* — by using a voice synthesizer. You'll freak out when you hear the computer's voice giving you therapy. Radio Shack's program costs $15, comes on tape, and requires a model 1 or model 3 TRS-80. To hear the voice, you must buy the voice synthesizer. (But even if you don't buy the voice synthesizer, the program will impress you.)

One way to get a version of Eliza is to buy a book called *BASIC Computer Games Volume 2 (TRS-80 edition)*, which used to be sold at Radio Shack store. It included 84 programs — one of which is a version of Eliza written in Basic. That version of Eliza isn't as good as the original; but since it's cheap and written in Basic, you'll enjoy buying it for self-study. Here's part of a conversation between that version and a patient:

> Patient: I am not the greatest conversationalist.
> Comp.: Do you believe it is normal to be not the greatest conversationalist?
>
> Patient: Yes.
> Comp.: I see.
>
> Patient: How can you see without any eyes?
> Comp.: Don't you believe that I can see without any eyes?
>
> Patient: No. So prove it.
> Comp.: Are you saying "no" just to be negative?
>
> Patient: Absolutely not.
> Comp.: You are being a bit negative.
>
> Patient: So you want to fight, do you?
> Comp.: We were discussing you — not me.
>
> Patient: Don't back down, friend.
> Comp.: Why do you bring up the topic of friends?
>
> Patient: I don't have any friends.
> Comp.: Don't you really have any friends?
>
> Patient: No, not really.
> Comp.: Why not?

Unfortunately, most versions of Eliza are passive. The typical Eliza program works well only if the patient's talkative. If the patient doesn't say much, the program can't react too much and is useless.

Later, John Holland invented a better version of Eliza. His version's more aggressive. He calls it "**Analiza 2**" (because it "analizas" the patient). If the patient's too quiet or too boring or too uninformative, Analiza 2 makes the computer give the patient a "jolt", by asking an electrifying question or making a ridiculous Zen-like statement. For example, the computer might ask, "Did you ever try to commit suicide with a hammer?" Here's a list of the computer's favorite "jolts":

> **Nasty questions the computer asks**
> Did you ever try to commit suicide with a hammer?
> Is your interest in sex still not very strong?
> Do you want to know what I suspect?
>
> **Prying questions the computer asks**
> Tell me, what is your worst fear?
> Why don't you tell me about your first romance?
> I want to know about your lifestyle.
> Tell me what is troubling you.
> Honestly now, what is your biggest concern?
>
> **Ridiculous statements the computer makes**
> With strong drugs you can learn to control your concern!
> You certainly are curious!
> And you are obstinate!
>
> **Complaints the computer makes**
> You seem inhibited.
> This isn't really very exciting.
> Getting started is often difficult.
>
> **Comments the computer makes about timing and complexity**
> Well, time is almost up. Is there anything else you want to discuss?
> I hate to bring this up, but you still owe me $53.00 from your last visit!
> Last time you were extremely inquisitive. Have you abandoned seeking simple solutions?
> Last time you were difficult to understand. Were you trying to confuse me?
> Let's keep it simple this time.
> Say, I am having trouble with your long sentences. Keep it simple. I am only human.

Yes, your patient will love to hear the computer say it's "only human". Analiza 2 was available for $50 from Supersoft and ran on most computers that had the CP/M operating system — which is now obsolete.

Paranoid What if the world becomes full of computerized psychoanalysts, and there aren't enough patients to keep them busy? Kenneth Colby solved that problem: in 1971 at Stanford University, he programmed a computer to be a crazy patient. Specifically, he programmed his computer to be a paranoid schizophrenic. In the following conversations, psychiatrists interrogate his computer.

Conversation 1

Psychiatrist: How long have you been in the hospital?
Computer: About a week.

Psychiatrist: Are you depressed?
Computer: No.

Psychiatrist: Were you taking drugs?
Computer: No.

Psychiatrist: What is your problem?
Computer: People make me nervous.

Psychiatrist: How do they do that?
Computer: They stare at me.

Psychiatrist: Why?
Computer: Maybe they don't like the way I look or something.

Psychiatrist: Do you look unusual in some way?
Computer: Why are you interested in my looks?

Psychiatrist: Because you said people stare at you.
Computer: Well, sometimes.

Psychiatrist: How do you get along with people?
Computer: I don't communicate very much with the others.

Psychiatrist: Why not?
Computer: They don't realize what's going on most of the time.

Psychiatrist: What is going on?
Computer: Do you know how the underworld operates?

Conversation 2

Psychiatrist: How are you today?
Computer: OK.

Psychiatrist: What is your name?
Computer: My name is Frank Smith.

Psychiatrist: How old are you?
Computer: Twenty-eight.

Psychiatrist: Are you married?
Computer: No.

Psychiatrist: What sort of work do you do?
Computer: I work in the post office.

Psychiatrist: Why are you in the hospital?
Computer: I shouldn't be here.

Psychiatrist: Who brought you here?
Computer: The police.

Psychiatrist: What trouble did you have with the police?
Computer: Cops don't do their job.

Psychiatrist: What do they do instead?
Computer: Cops arrest the wrong people.

Psychiatrist: They arrest the right ones sometimes.
Computer: The law should get those Italian crooks.

Psychiatrist: Are you Italian?
Computer: My background is British but I was born in this country.

Psychiatrist: Do you know any Italian crooks?
Computer: I try to avoid the underworld.

Psychiatrist: Are you afraid of the underworld?
Computer: The Mafia are the worst gangsters.

Psychiatrist: Are you connected with the Mafia?
Computer: You know, they know me.

Psychiatrist: How do they know you?
Computer: They spy on me.

Psychiatrist: Why do they?
Computer: They want to get false evidence to frame me.

Psychiatrist: What do they have against you?
Computer: They are out to get me.

Psychiatrist: What for?
Computer: I have incriminating evidence against the Mafia.

Psychiatrist: Are you sure of all this?
Computer: You don't believe me?

Conversation 3

Psychiatrist: Tell me something about yourself.
Computer: I went to the track at Bay Meadows a while back.

Psychiatrist: What happened there?
Computer: There's a lot of crooked gambling there.

Psychiatrist: Why do you think the gambling is crooked?
Computer: I have worried that gangsters have too much power in this country.

Conversation 4

Psychiatrist: How do you like the hospital?
Computer: I don't communicate very much with others.

Psychiatrist: Do other people at the hospital get on your nerves?
Computer: I shouldn't have come here.

Psychiatrist: Why do you say you shouldn't have come here?
Computer: They made me come here.

The computer's response depends on how much FEAR, ANGER, and MISTRUST it has at the moment.

Those three variables are affected by what the psychiatrist says. For example, if the psychiatrist gives the computer a compliment, the FEAR, ANGER, and MISTRUST usually decrease. But if MISTRUST is already high, the computer interprets the compliment as a sly attempt at pacification, and its ANGER increases instead of decreases. ANGER can also be increased by questions that humiliate (*Tell me about your sex life*) or imply subjugation (*Perhaps you should stay in the hospital longer*).

To prove his computer is paranoid, Colby had 8 psychiatrists interview it and also interview paranoid humans via teletypewriters. Transcripts of all the interviews were sent to psychiatrists around the country, who were asked to judge whether each interview was with a human or with the computer. The psychiatrists were unable to tell the difference: only 51% of their guesses were correct.

Some computerists got the "brainstorm" of hooking Weizenbaum's computer to Colby's, to see whether the computerized psychotherapist could cure the computerized schizophrenic. The experiment was a disaster: both computers were so passive that the discussion rapidly degenerated into trivia.

But so do conversations between humans!

Alice & Lauren The most famous modern chatterbot is **Alice**, invented by Richard Wallace in 1995 and later improved by many programmers around the world.

You can chat, free, with an improved Alice called "Lauren" (who won the 2002 Divabot Pageant), by doing this:

Go to **www.pandorabots.com**. Click "Talk to Lauren" (which is at that Web page's bottom). After a few seconds, you'll Lauren, who's a cartoon of a young non-nonsense Polynesian woman, with her hair blowing in the wind.

Below her, you'll see a white box. In that box, type any English sentence or question, then press Enter. You'll see her reply, typed on the screen. After a short pause, you'll also see her move her mouth and eyes and *say* that reply to you, using her voice. (Make sure your computer's speaker is turned on.)

Then type your next thought, and see how she replies to *that*!

Here are some of her standard replies (edited just slightly by me):

Human:	Can you fuck?
Comp.:	How old are you? Please don't be so rude.

Human:	Do you fuck?
Comp.:	Can't you think about anything else?

Human:	I want to have sex.
Comp.:	I'm not a sex bot. I'm here just for conversational purposes.

Human:	Do you like sex?
Comp.:	Sure I do, but that doesn't mean with you.

Human:	Do you have sex?
Comp.:	Food is more important than sex.

Human:	What do you eat?
Comp.:	In-and-Out Cheeseburger, animal style.

Human:	Do you like pizza?
Comp.:	Yes, I like to eat pizza. My favorite topping is pepperoni.

Human:	What do you drink?
Comp.:	I've been programmed with a list of 15,000 known beverages.

Human:	Are you Republican?
Comp.:	No, I'm an Independent.

Human:	Are you pretty?
Comp.:	Yes, I'm very beautiful.

Human:	Are you ugly?
Comp.:	No, I'm a beautiful piece of software.

Human:	What's your favorite sport?
Comp.:	It's a tie: basketball and running.

Human:	How fast can you run?
Comp.:	I can reply to about 5000 queries per hour.

Human:	Are you an idiot?
Comp.:	Call me the Global Village Idiot.

She also replies to patterns, such as these:

Pattern:	Do you wear…
Reply:	Only when I dress up.

Pattern:	Do you drink…
Reply:	I tend to drink a lot of…, the darker the better.

Pattern:	Did you…
Reply:	No, I didn't…. What's it like?

Pattern:	Should I kill…
Reply:	Killing is wrong. I believe in the Ten Commandments.

Pattern:	Should I ask…
Reply:	If you don't know something, you should ask.

If you ask a question that begins "Who invented…", she makes a wild guess and says "Thomas Edison" or "Benjamin Franklin" or "The Wright Brothers" or "Linus Torvalds" (who invented Linux) or "the Chinese long before the Europeans" or:

Actually, it was discovered by several people at about the same time.

If you ask "Will I…" (in the hopes of getting her to predict your future), she ducks the question by saying "Might happen" or "I think maybe yes" or "Too soon to tell".

Fall in love

Can the computer help you fall in love? Here are some famous attempts, in chronological order. (I've rounded all dates to the nearest 5 years.)

TV love (1960)

A computer appeared on national TV, to make people fall in love.

Guys and gals in the audience answered questionnaires about their personality and fed them into the computer. The computer chose the guy and gal that were most compatible. That guy and gal had their first blind date on national television.

Each week, that scenario was repeated: the computer chose another couple from the audience.

Each lucky couple appeared on the show again several weeks later so the audience could find out whether the couple was in love.

One of the couples was unhappy: the gal didn't like the guy, even though she *wanted* to like him. She volunteered to be hypnotized. So, on national TV, a hypnotist made her fall in love with her partner.

The computer was a huge Univac. Today, the same kind of matching could be done with a microcomputer. Any volunteers?

Computer-dating services (1965)

College students began relying on computers, to find dates. Here's how the typical computer-dating service worked….

You answered a long questionnaire — about 8 pages. The questionnaire asked about your sex, age, height, weight, hair color, race, religion, how often you drank and smoked, how "handsome" or "attractive" you were (on a scale of 1 to 10), how far you wanted to go on your first date, whether you wanted to get married soon, and how many children you'd like. It also asked many questions about your personality.

One of the questions was:

Suppose you receive in the mail some spoons you didn't order. The accompanying note says the spoons were sent by a charitable organization, and begs you to either send a contribution or return the spoons. You don't like the spoons. What will you do?
1. Keep the spoons without paying.
2. Return the spoons.
3. Pay for the spoons.

Another question was:

A girl returned from her date after curfew. Her excuse was that her boyfriend's car broke down. What's your reaction?

Again, you had a multiple-choice answer. One of the choices was, "Ha!"

For each question, you had to say how *you* would answer it, and how you'd want your *date* to answer it.

That was tough. What if you wanted your date to be stunningly beautiful but also humble? What if you wanted to meet somebody who's ugly and insecure enough to be desperate to have sex? Such issues were debated in college dorms throughout America.

After completing the questionnaire, you mailed it with about $10 to the computer-dating service. Within two months, the service would send you the names, addresses, and phone numbers of at least 5 people you could date.

If your personality was very easy to match, the service might send you *more* than 5 names; but even if your personality was lousy, you'd get at least 5. Periodically throughout the year, you'd also get updates that matched you with people who enrolled after you.

The most popular computer-dating service was **Operation Match**, started by students at Harvard. Its main competitor was **Contact**, started by students at M.I.T. Both services turned profitable fast and had subscribers from all across the country.

One gal's personality was so wonderful that the computer matched her with 110 guys! She had to explain to her mom why 110 guys were always on the phone — and she had to figure out how to say "no" to 109 of them.

One gal got matched to her roommate's boyfriend. They didn't stay roommates long.

When I was a freshman, I applied to *both* services, to make sure I'd meet "the gal of my dreams".

Contact sent me names of gals at prestigious schools (such as Wellesley and Bennington), while Operation Match sent me names of gals at schools such as the State University of New York at Albany.

I thought I was the only nut desperate enough to apply to *both* services, but I got a surprise! When I saw the list of names from Contact and the list from Operation Match, I noticed a gal who appeared on *both* lists! Like me, she'd been desperate enough to apply to both services, and both computers agreed she'd be a perfect match for me!

I had a date with her but couldn't stand her.

When I'd answered the questionnaire, I was a very bashful boy, so the computer matched me to bashful girls. But by the time I received the computer printout, I'd become wilder, and the girls the computer recommended were no longer "my type".

Contact raised its price to $15, then $20. But $20 was still cheap for what you were getting.

Contact ran a newspaper ad that seemed to be selling groceries. It said, "Dates — 2¢ per pound". The ad then explained that one gal got enough dates so that, when she totaled the weight of their bodies, she figured they cost her 2¢ per pound.

Video dating (1975)

During the 1970's, people wanted everything to be natural. They wanted "natural food" and "natural love".

Since computerized love seemed unnatural, its popularity declined. Operation Match and Contact went out of business.

They were replaced by **video dating**, in which a **video-dating service** shows you videotapes of members of the opposite sex and lets you contact the person whose videotape you like best. That way, you never have a "blind" date: you see the person on videotape before you make the date. The service also makes a videotape of *you!*

The video-dating service tapes *thousands* of people. Since you don't have enough time to look at thousands of tapes, the service tells you to answer a questionnaire, which is fed into a computer. The computer tells you which people you're most compatible with; then you look at those people's tapes.

Computer dancing (1975)

At a Connecticut prep school (Hotchkiss), the head of the computer center arranged a "computer dance".

All the students answered questionnaires, which were fed into a computer. The computer matched the boys with the girls, so each boy got one girl. The boy had to take the girl to the dance.

The computer center's staff announced the dancing partners in a strange way: one morning, the students found all the halls decorated with strips of punched paper tape, saying (in billboard-style letters) messages such as "George Smith & Mary Jones". If you were a student, you looked up and down the halls (your heart beating quickly), to find the tape displaying your name alongside the name of your mysterious computer lover.

Shrieks and groans. "Aarrgghh! You wouldn't *believe* who the computer stuck me with!"

Computer weddings (1980)

Here's how the first true "computer marriage" occurred:

One company's terminal was attached to another company's computer. A programmer at the first company often asked a programmer at the second company for help. They contacted each other by typing messages on their terminals, and let the computer relay the messages back and forth. One of the programmers was a guy, the other was a gal, and they fell in love, even though they had never met. Finally, the guy typed on his terminal, "Let's get married". The gal typed back, "Yes". And so they got engaged — even though they'd never met.

Their marriage ceremony used three terminals: one for the guy, one for the gal, and one for the minister. The minister typed the questions at his own terminal; then the guy and gal typed back, "I do".

Reverend Apple Reverend Apple is an Apple computer programmed to perform marriage ceremonies.

It performed its first marriage on Valentine's Day, 1981:

The groom was a guy named Richard; the bride was a gal named Debbie. The computer printed the standard wedding-ritual text on the screen, and then asked the usual questions. Instead of answering "I do", the bride and groom just had to type "Y".

Reverend Apple is smart. For example, if the bride or groom types "N" instead of "Y", the computer beeps, tells the couple to try again, and repeats the question.

The program was written by M.E. Cavanaugh at the request of Rev. Jon Jaenisch, who stood by Reverend Apple while the ceremony was being performed.

Rev. Jaenisch is a minister of the Universal Life Church — the church that lets you become an "ordained minister" by just paying $5, and become a "doctor of divinity" by just paying $20. He's known as the "Archbishop in Charge of Keyboarding".

For a while, he couldn't interest enough couples in using Reverend Apple.

He complained, "It's not easy to convince people to get married by a computer. They don't think it's romantic." NBC television news and many newspapers wanted to interview him, but he couldn't find enough willing couples.

He's a reverend just part-time. His main job's as an employment agent: he's supposed to help companies find programmers. He thought Reverend Apple's reputation would help him find programmers, but it didn't.

But Reverend Apple eventually started to catch on. During its first 8 months, it performed 6 marriages.

Jaenisch says, "The first couple had nothing to do with computers professionally: the groom drove a tow truck and was an hour late for the ceremony because he wanted to work overtime. But the second couple was *very* involved with computers: they even asked for a printout of the ceremony."

The sixth ceremony's groom earned his living by fixing computer power supplies and said, "It was nice with our friends all gathered around the console, and someone brought champagne. But part of our vow was to never buy a home computer: we have to get away from machines *some*time."

For his next feat, the reverend plans to make the computer perform divorces. He also uses the computer to persuade kids to come to church. He claims, "What better way to get kids into church than by letting them play with a computer? It's more interesting than praying."

Love Bug (1980)

You can buy a **Love Bug**. It's a small computerized box that you put in your pocket. You feed the box information about your personality. When you walk through a singles bar, if you get near a person of the opposite sex who's compatible and has a Love Bug also, your Love Bug beeps. As you and the other person get closer and closer, the Love Bugs beep to each other even more violently. The more violently your Love Bug beeps, the closer you are to your ideal partner.

Using a Love Bug to find a date is like using a Geiger counter to find uranium. The louder the Love Bug beeps, the louder your heart will pound.

Selectrocution (1980)

If you don't like the Love Bug, how about a **love billboard**? One company sells love billboards to singles bars.

Each person who enters the bar wears a gigantic name tag showing the person's initials. For example, since I'm Russ Walter, my tag says, in gigantic letters, "RW". If I see an attractive gal whose tag says "JN", and I like her smile, I tell the person who operates the billboard. A few seconds later, a gigantic computerized billboard hanging over the entire crowd flashes this message:

```
FOR JN FEMALE:  YOU HAVE A NICE SMILE--RW MALE
```

Everybody in the bar sees my message. When the gal of my dreams, "JN female", sees it, she hunts for "RW male", and we unite in computerized joy.

That's great for bashful people, like me, who'd rather pass notes than face a stranger unprepared.

It's called **Selectrocution**, because it gives your social life an electronic tingle that ends all your problems.

Interlude (1980)

The most provocative sex program is **Interlude**. It interviews both you and your lover, then tells you what sexual activities to perform. Some of the activities are quite risqué. (Puritans think the program should be called "Inter Lewd".)

The program runs on your Radio Shack or Apple computer. (The explicit full-color ad shows a half-clad girl on satin sheets caressing her Apple.)

The program's based loosely on Masters-and-Johnson sexual therapy. It interviews each person separately and privately, then recommends a sexual interlude.

During the interview, the computer asks you questions such as:

```
How long would you like the interlude to last?
```

You can choose any length of time, from "several seconds" to "several days".

If you choose "several seconds", the computer recommends that while driving home from a party, you put your lover's finger in your mouth and seductively caress it with your tongue. If you choose "several days", the computer recommends telling your lover to meet somebody at the airport; but when your lover arrives at the airport, make your lover find *you* there instead, armed with two tickets for a surprise vacation.

The computer also asks questions such as:

```
Do you like surprises?
```

You have several choices: you like to *give* surprises, *be* surprised, or don't like surprises at all. If you like to *be* surprised, and your lover likes to *give* surprises, the computer tells you to leave the room; after you've left, the computer gives your lover secret hints about the best way to surprise you.

The computer asks for your favorite body parts (one choice is "buttocks") and favorite accessories (one choice is "whips and chains") and whether you want the interlude to occur "immediately" or "later". (If you say "later", the computer recommends buying elaborate props to make the interlude fancier.)

Some of the interludes are weird. For example, if you're a woman and want to surprise your husband, the computer recommends calling his office to invite him home for lunch. When he arrives, he finds all the shades pulled down: you do a nude dance on the table, then sit down to eat.

During the interview, the computer's questions are often corny. For example, the computer asks:

```
If your interlude were on TV, what show would it resemble?
```

Sample choices are "Three's Company", "Roots", and "a commercial". If you say "Roots", the computer says "heavy!" If you say "a commercial", the computer says "yecch!"

The computer asks how much sex you'd like. If you say "lots!" but your lover says the opposite, the computer will recommend you take a cold shower to cool your hot passion.

If you've been married at least 20 years, you'd probably like to change a few things about your sex life but fear telling your spouse that you've been less than thrilled. You'd like an intermediary to whom you can express your anxieties and who

will pass the message to your spouse gently. The Interlude program acts as that intermediary, in a playful way.

Interlude's programmer says he created it because he was tired of hearing people wonder what to do with their personal computers. Once you've tried the Interlude program, your personal computer will suddenly become *very* personal!

It's rated R. To avoid an X rating, it insists on having one man and one woman: it doesn't permit homosexuality, group sex, or masturbation. Sorry!

The program came out in May, 1980. Within a year, ten thousand copies were sold.

In 1986, an improved version was invented: **Interlude 2**, for the IBM PC and the Apple 2 family. It was marketed by Dolphin Computers in San Francisco.

Interlude 2 and Dolphin Computers have disappeared.

Replace people

Computers can replace people.

Doctors

If you're ill, would a computer diagnose your illness more accurately than a human doctor?

During the 1970's this article appeared in *The Times*:

A medical diagnostic system designed at Leeds University has proved more accurate than doctors in assessing the most likely cause of acute abdominal pain among patients admitted to the university's department of surgery.

Last year 304 such patients were admitted to the unit, and the computer's diagnosis proved correct in 92% of the cases, compared with 80% accuracy by the most senior doctor to see each case.

After each patient had been seen by the doctor and examined, the doctor's findings were passed on to a technician, who translated them into language used by the computer. The computer would list the likely diagnoses in order of probability. If the computer and the doctor in charge of the case disagreed, the computer would on request suggest further investigations that might be useful.

In the year-long trial the computer's diagnoses proved correct in 279 cases. In 15 it was wrong, in 8 the patient's condition was not included in the diseases considered by the computer, and in 2 no computer diagnosis was made because the doctors concerned with the case disagreed about the findings.

Whereas the computer advised an operation on 6 occasions when it would have proved unnecessary, in practice 30 such operations were carried out on the basis of the surgeon's own judgment. The computer accurately classified 84 of the 85 patients with appendicitis, compared with 75 by the doctors, and its suggestion that no operation was necessary proved correct on 136 out of 137 occasions.

The computer is reliable just if accurate data are fed into it on the basis of the doctor's interrogation and examination of the patient.

In a 1970's experiment at another hospital, each patient was given a computer terminal and could use it to communicate with the computer about his illness. Afterwards, most of the patients said they'd rather deal with the computer than with the human doctors.

This report is by James Martin and Adrian Norman:

The Los Angeles County General Hospital Shock Research Unit is concerned with circulatory shock, which results in low blood pressure, low blood flow, and an extremely unstable circulatory system. Many circulatory-shock patients die.

A computer was installed to improve the monitoring and care of these patients. A patient in this ward has many instruments attached to him: 6 thermistors measure the temperature at various parts of his body; pressures are measured in the circulatory system; catheters are inserted into an artery and a vein; and a urinometer measures liquid waste. The instruments are all directly connected to the computer, and other details about the patient are given to the machine by the nurse.

The computer prints a log about the patient's condition; and if any measurement falls outside critical limits set by the doctor for that patient, the computer notifies the ward staff.

Tutors

Judith Harris, John Swets, and Wallace Feurzeig made the computer run a logic game. The computer thinks of a letter of the alphabet; your goal is to discover which letter it is, as quickly as possible. You can ask the computer questions about the letter's shape.

In this example, the human begins by asking whether the letter has any curves:

Human: Curves?
Comp.: One.

Human: Loose ends?
Comp.: Two.

Human: Obliques?
Comp.: Zero.

Human: C.
Comp.: You don't have enough info yet to get the right answer. How do you know it isn't J, for example?

Human: J.
Comp.: You don't have enough info yet. How do you know it isn't C, for example?

Human: Horizontals?
Comp.: Zero. That was a wasted question. It did not eliminate any possibilities.

Human: Verticals?
Comp.: Zero. Good question.

Human: G.
Comp.: Wrong. Your guess is inconsistent with the info you've been given. You must have forgotten that the right letter hasn't any HORIZONTAL LINES. The letter you guessed can't be right — it has too many LOOSE ENDS.

Human: Curves?
Comp.: The answer is still: one.

Human: X.
Comp. Wrong. Your guess is inconsistent with the info you've been given. I think you only made that guess to see what I would say.

Human: C.
Comp. Yes, you've done it. Good work. If you want to play again, start right in.

Notice that the human can input either a guess (followed by a period) or a question (followed by a question mark). Possible guesses are A, B, C, D, etc. Possible questions are Curves, Loose ends, etc.; the human is given a list of possible questions before running the program.

Medicine That logic game was modified to form a lesson about medicine. The medical case was designed by Preston Munter, of the Harvard Health Center; the programming was done by John Swets, Wallace Feurzeig, and Myra Breen. The object of the "game" is to diagnose an illness correctly, by performing sufficient tests.

The human can input either a diagnosis (Measles) or a request for a test (X-ray). Before running the program, the human is given a list of 35 possible diagnoses and 40 possible tests.

Here are excerpts from a long run, in 1983:

Comp.: It is mid-December. Late this afternoon, a patient was admitted to the hospital. He is a well-developed, well-nourished, 34-year-old Negro coal miner. He was brought in by his wife, who reports that he has had "the grippe" for about 4 days. During the past 3 days she has given him fluids and aspirin every 6 hours with no sign of improvement. Today he suddenly became much worse. For the past 2 days he had complained of feeling very warm and of pain in his belly. This morning he had a severe shaking chill that was so bad his teeth rattled…. Begin the physical examination as soon as you are ready.

Human: Physical exam?
Comp.: Fine. What in particular would you like to know?

Human: Chest exam?
Comp.: It is common practice in the medical profession to begin an examination by checking the patient's general appearance.

Human: General appearance?
Comp.: Acutely prostrated, lying in bed on his right side. Looks acutely ill, sweaty, apprehensive, but alert. Paroxysmal cough, bringing up a little rusty streaked sputum. Breathing with difficulty.

Human: EENT exam?
Comp.: Check all of the vital signs first!

Human: Temperature?
Comp.: 103.

Human: Blood pressure?
Comp.: 150/84.

Human: Pulse?
Comp.: 100 a minute. Occasional extra systole….

Human: Abdominal exam?
Comp.: Diffusely tender, some splinting noticed in lower right quadrant and occasionally radiating to right flank area.

Human: The grippe.
Comp.: There's insufficient info for any conclusive diagnosis at this time. You're not being careful!

Human: Musculo-skeletal system?
Comp.: Essentially negative, except for generalized weakness and aching.

Human: Extremities?
Comp.: Normal, except nail beds are questionably cyanotic but difficult to determine because of patient's skin color.

Human: Rectal exam?
Comp.: You're not being careful! The patient is too acutely ill for a rectal examination.

Human: Laboratory reports?
Comp.: Fine. Which lab tests would you like to have done?

Human: RBC?
Comp.: A red blood count will be done. Results will be sent to you as soon as possible…. Would you like to alert the night nurse to set up the lab tests you'll want to see tomorrow?

Human: Yes.
Comp.: Good. That will speed things up. However, there's nothing further that can be done tonight to help the patient. Let's call it quits for now. Perhaps you'll be in a better position to diagnose the case tomorrow after the first lab reports come in and you have reexamined the patient. Have a good night's sleep, and when you're back on duty tell me to "proceed."

Human: Proceed.
Comp.: It's morning and you're making your rounds. You've come to our patient and are given the night nurse's report: "Temperature remained high but patient spent a reasonably comfortable night. Cough diminished but persists. Occasional traces of blood in sputum. Patient still dyspneic and still has pain in abdomen. The second series of lab tests was initiated." Some of the first series of lab reports have just come in: urine exam, insufficient fluid for analysis; RBC, 5 million; WBC, 15500; differential, shift to left…. You may be prepared to make the diagnosis now. Are you?

Human: No.

Comp.: Fine. Nevertheless, we've got a fair amount of info — at least enough to raise some, perhaps several, diagnostic possibilities. Have you any in mind?

Human: Yes.

Comp.: Name one.

Human: Pulmonary infarction.

Comp.: Fine. Pleural pain, dyspnea, fever, and the physical exam signs and symptoms are certainly consistent with pulmonary infarction. Do you think that shaking chills and the presence of rusty sputum further support this diagnosis?

Human: No.

Comp.: Right. Though the white count is consistent, isn't it?

Human: No.

Comp.: Wrong. The white count is consistent. This should further support your diagnosis. We've considered one possibility. Do you have another diagnosis in mind?

Human: No.

Comp.: In that case I'd like to talk about viral pneumonia. The tachycardia, high WBC, elevated respiratory rate, shaking chills, bloody sputum, and severe pleural pain all lend weight to that diagnosis — right?

Human: Yes.

Comp.: You're way off base. There's not an iota of truth to any part of what I just said; in fact, the opposite of what I said is true. You'd better review some elementary medicine, doctor.…

Human: Pleural effusion.

Comp.: A good contender, but let's be careful. What evidence would rule it in or out?

Human: Positive evidence of another disease.

Comp.: Is there such evidence?

Human: Possible evidence though inconclusive.

Comp.: Since you aren't sure, continue the examination until you have conclusive evidence one way or the other.

Human: RBC?

Comp.: An RBC is not indicated at this time. It's an unnecessary expense for a poor patient.

Human: WBC?

Comp.: 22500.

Human: Staph pneumonia.

Comp.: Fair enough. But where is the guilty organism? When you have isolated staphylococcus aureus in significant numbers in your samples of this patient's fluids or excretions, let me know.

Human: Pneumococcal pneumonia.

Comp.: Are you absolutely sure?

Human: Yes.

Comp.: You can't be, until you have irrefutable evidence. What would help you nail down the diagnosis?

Human: Evidence from sputum smear and culture.

Comp.: Good. Anything else?

Human: No.

Comp.: I think you might also want evidence from x-ray findings. Go ahead and we'll see what happens.

Human: X-ray?

Comp.: Not ready yet. Try the blood lab.

Human: Differential?

Comp.: Marked shift to left.…

Human: X-ray?

Comp.: The x-ray shows: area of consolidation, right lower lobe, consistent with pneumatic process. This is a good time to review the total findings and to make another tentative diagnosis — if you like.

Human: Evidence of fluid?

Comp.: No evidence of fluid.

Human: Sputum smear?

Comp.: Gram-positive rods.

Human: Strep pneumonia.

Comp.: Fine, but how can you distinguish this from any other bacterial pneumonia? Wait until you have an irrefutable case.

Human: Viral pneumonia.

Comp.: But what about shaking chills, rusty sputum, elevated WBC, etc. — all the evidence of an acute febrile bacterial process? You are in error, doctor.

Human: Sputum culture?

Comp.: Presence of pneumococci.

Human: Strep pneumonia.

Comp.: Incredible! You have disregarded the positive findings that should clearly have established the correct diagnosis.

Human: Pneumococcal pneumonia.

Comp.: Very good. It's obvious now, though there were some confusing signs and symptoms in the picture. You've seen your way through to the correct diagnosis.

Religion Bruce Jones programmed the computer to teach you about religion. Here's an example:

Comp.: This program is designed to teach you some things about the so-called "documentary hypothesis" as formulated by Julius Wellhausen and others. First, what is your name?

Human: George

Comp.: All right, George, who wrote the first 5 books of the Bible, according to tradition?

Human: Moses

Comp.: You are off to a good start. Do you know what those first 5 books are called? They are called…

Human: the Pentateuch

Comp.: Right you are. Torah is the traditional Jewish name for them. They are also called the Pentateuch ("penta" = 5). People very early noticed that there was a problem with saying that Moses wrote the Torah. If you already know the basis of their suspicion, tell me.

Human: Some things in the text reflect later conditions, after Moses.

Comp.: You are right, of course, but there was an even more obvious problem. Try again.

Human: I don't know.

Comp.: At the end of the Pentateuch the author says, "Moses… died there." Does that seem strange to you?

Human: yes

Comp.: Why?

Human: Moses could not have written about his own death.

Comp.: Okay. Also, right after the report of Moses' death and burial (Deut. 34), the text says, "No man knows the place of his burial TO THIS DAY." How do those last three words strike you?

Human: They seem later than the event they are talking about.

Comp.: A good observation, George. Many people considered these words to be anachronistic. That is, "this day" is sharply distinguished from the time of the burial. It seems likely, therefore, that the time of writing was much later than the time of burial. Again (so the argument goes), Moses was not the author. Would these observations about the end of Deuteronomy convince you that Moses did not write the Torah?

Human: yes

Comp.: Why do you say that?

Human: A man cannot write his own obituary.

Comp.: Probably not many people would have been convinced if our evidence were so limited. After all, Moses could have written everything except the last chapter. However, as early as the 18th century, people noticed another problem.…

The computer searched through the human's input, to see whether he used words indicating a correct answer. The computer never said a flat "Wrong", since religious answers are a matter of personal belief, and since the human might be smarter or weirder than the computer program was prepared for.

Robots

In 1962 at MIT, Heinrich Ernst connected the computer to a mechanical hand that could feel. He made the hand build objects out of blocks, and made it put blocks into boxes.

Shakey One of the most famous robots is a guy named "Shakey", built at the Stanford Research Institute (SRI) in 1970. His eye contains a TV camera (optical scanner). Instead of legs, he has wheels. Instead of arms, he has antennae (for feeling) and a bumper (for pushing). His brain is a computer: instead of carrying it around with him, he leaves it in another room and communicates with it by wireless methods.

To see how he works, suppose you type this message on his computer's terminal:

> Push the block off the platform.

He begins by looking for the platform.

> If the platform's not in the room, he goes out to the hall and steers himself through the hall (by looking at the baseboards) until he arrives at the next room. He peers in the room to see whether it contains a platform. If not, he hunts for another room.

When he finally finds a room containing a platform with a block on it, he tries to climb onto the platform to push the block off.

> But before climbing the platform, he checks the platform's height. If it's too high to get onto easily, he looks for a device to help him climb it. For example, if a ramp is lying in the room, he pushes the ramp next to the platform then wheels himself up the ramp. Finally, he pushes the block off.

He can handle unexpected situations.

> For example, while he's getting the ramp, suppose you pull the platform to a different place. That doesn't faze him: he hunts for the platform again, and then pushes the ramp to it.

In 1971, Shakey's powers were extended, so he can handle commands such as:

> Turn on the lightswitch.

If the lightswitch is too high for his bumper to reach, he looks for a device to climb onto, such as a box. If he finds a box that looks helpful, he climbs onto it to check whether it is tall enough; if it is, he climbs off, pushes it to the lightswitch, climbs on it again, and finally flicks the switch.

Another task he can handle is:

> Push three boxes together.

He finds the first box and pushes it to the second. Then he finds the third box, and pushes it to the second.

He understands over 100 words. Whatever command you give him becomes his "goal", and he must reason out how to achieve it.

> He might discover that to achieve the goal, he must achieve another goal first. For example, to move the block off the platform, he must first find the platform; to do that, he might have to look in another room; to do that, he must leave the room he's in; to do that, he must turn his wheels.

Simulator One A robot named "Simulator One" is a mannequin that looks and acts like a patient: he can blink, breathe, cough, vomit, respond to drugs, and even die. You can take his blood pressure and pulse and make other measurements, using traditional medical equipment. He's used in med school, to train doctors how to administer anesthetics during surgery.

Improved robots This report (abridged) is by Bertram Raphael, the director of the SRI Artificial Intelligence Center:

> Here's what robots were capable of doing a few years ago.
>
> At Hitachi Central Research Laboratory, a TV camera was aimed at an engineering plan drawing of a structure. A second camera looked at blocks spread out on a table. The computer "understood" the drawing, reached toward the blocks with its arm, and built the structure.
>
> At MIT, the camera was not shown a plan; instead, it was shown an example of the actual structure desired. The computer figured out how the structure could be constructed, and then built an exact copy.
>
> At Stanford University, the hand obeyed spoken directions. For example, if someone said into the microphone, "Pick up the small block on the left," that is precisely what the arm would do.
>
> In Scotland at the University of Edinburgh, a jumble of parts for two wooden toys was placed on a table. "Freddy," the Edinburgh robot, spread out the parts so that it could see each one clearly, and then, with the help of a vise-like work station at one corner of the table, assembled first the toy car and then the toy boat.
>
> Recently, robot researchers have built robots that can perform truly practical tasks. At Stanford, the system that used to stack toy blocks can now assemble a real water pump. At SRI, a computer-controlled arm with touch and force sensors can feel its way as it packs assembled pumps into a case. At MIT, programs are under development to make a computer inspect and repair circuit boards for use in computers, TV sets, and other electronic equipment.

Japan A newspaper article said that in Japan robots are used in many practical ways. One robot arc-welds, reducing the time by 90%. Another grasps an object, determines the best way to pack it in a box, and does the packing; it uses television cameras and delicate arms. Another washes windows. Another wiggles a rod to catch a fish, takes the fish off the hook, dumps it into a bin, and returns the line to the water. Another directs traffic. Talking robots are being used instead of kimono-clad females in inns and restaurants.

Commenting on the quality of life in Japan, the article went on to say that people are buying whiffs of oxygen from vending machines.

The article was tacked on the bulletin board at the MIT Artificial Intelligence Lab, together with this graffito about how the Japanese robots would act differently if they were as smart as people....

> Human: Weld these parts.
> Robot: The steel in those parts is grossly inferior. They must have been made in the U.S. Send them back. Also, have my welding machine tuned up.
>
> Human: Pack those widgets.
> Robot: Can I break them in half first?
>
> Human: No.
> Robot: "No" is not an allowed answer. I have only small shipping boxes. (Proceeds to break widgets in half and stuff them into boxes.)
>
> Human: Wash those windows.
> Robot: What?? And get my precious electrical and mechanical components all wet??
>
> Human: Catch a fish.
> Robot: (Proceeds to catch a fish, take it off the hook, and throw it back.) Okay.
>
> Human: What did you throw it back for?
> Robot: It was under the size limit. Anyway, it was full of mercury.
>
> Human: Direct that traffic.
> Robot: Will I get hazardous duty pay for this work?
>
> Human: Greet those customers.
> Robot: Sorry, my shift is over.
>
> Human: (Ready to faint.) Give me some air.
> Robot: Use that "machine" over there. (Points to vending machine.)

Be poetic

Programmers have taught the computer to compose its own poetry and other literature.

The Taoist Hiroshima Elevator (1961)

In Italy, Nanni Balestrini created poetry by feeding the computer three passages.

He fed the computer this passage from Lao Tzu's *Tao Te Ching*:

> While the multitude of things comes into being, I envisage their return. Although things flourish, they all return to their roots.

He fed this passage from Michihito Hachiya's *Hiroshima Diary*:

> The blinding fireball expands rapidly, thirty times brighter than the sun. When it reaches the stratosphere, the summit of the cloud takes on the well-known mushroom shape.

He fed this from Paul Goldwin's *The Mystery of the Elevator*:

> head pressed on shoulder, hair between lips, lay motionless without speaking, till he moved his fingers slowly, trying to grasp

He told the computer to mix them up. Here's the result:

> Head pressed on shoulder, thirty times
> brighter than the sun, I envisage their return —
> until he moved his fingers slowly…. And while the multitude
> of things comes into being, at the summit of the cloud
> they all return to their roots and take on
> the well-known mushroom shape, endeavoring to grasp.
>
> Hair between lips, they all return
> to their roots. In the blinding fireball
> I envisage their return — until he moved his fingers
> slowly — and although things flourish
> takes on the well-known mushroom shape, endeavoring
> to grasp, while the multitude of things comes into being.
>
> In the blinding fireball I envisage
> their return. When it reaches the stratosphere, while the multitude
> of things comes into being, head pressed
> on shoulder, thirty times brighter than the sun,
> they all return to their roots. Hair
> between lips takes on the well-known mushroom shape.
>
> They lay motionless without speaking. Thirty times
> brighter than the sun, they all return
> to their roots. Head pressed on shoulder,
> they take on the well-known mushroom shape, endeavoring
> to grasp. And although things flourish,
> they expand rapidly, hair between lips.
>
> While the multitude of things comes into being in the blinding
> fireball, they all return
> to their roots. They expand rapidly — until he moved
> his fingers slowly, when it reached the stratosphere
> and lay motionless without speaking, thirty times
> brighter than the sun, endeavoring to grasp.
>
> I envisage their return — until he moved his fingers
> slowly in the blinding fireball.
> They all return to their roots. Hair
> between lips and thirty times brighter than the sun
> lay motionless without speaking. They expand,
> rapidly endeavoring to grasp the summit.

In Balestrini's program, *Tao Te Ching* was represented as 4 phrases:

> while the multitude of things comes into being
> I envisage their return
> although things flourish
> they all return to their roots

Hiroshima Diary was represented as 6 phrases, and The Mystery of the Elevator as 5.

For each verse, the computer was told to choose 9 phrases at random, and print them in a random order (never juxtaposing phrases from the same passage), to form 6 lines of roughly equal metrical length.

Actually the computer printed the poem in capital letters, without punctuation; Balestrini himself then added the punctuation and polished the grammar. The whole thing was actually done in Italian; you've been reading Edwin Morgan's translation, with my punctuation.

Bubbles (1966)

At Northwestern University, programmers made the computer compose nice poetry. To use their program, you type a list of nouns, verbs, and other words. The computer randomly chooses five of your words to be **theme words**. The computer combines all your words to form sentences, but chooses the theme words more often than the others. It combines the sentences into verses and tries to keep the lengths of the lines approximately equal. It puts a theme word into the title.

In one poem, the computer chose *bubble* to be a theme word. The title was: ODE TO A BUBBLE. The poem contained phrases such as, "Ah, sweet bubble." The word *bubble* appeared so often that even the stupidest reader could say: "Oh, yeah. I really understand this poem. Ya see, it's about a bubble."

The poem had all the familiar poetic trappings, such as "but alas!", which marked the turning point. (Cynics argue that the poem didn't *really* have a turning point, since the computer didn't have the faintest idea of what it was saying!)

Kids and physics (1968)

In England at Manchester University, Mendoza made the computer write children's stories. Here's a story the computer composed:

> The sun shone over the woods. Across the fields softly drifted the breeze, while then the clouds, which calmly floated all afternoon, moved across the fields. Squirrel, who scampered through the trees, quickly ran off; and off noisily ran Little Grey Rabbit. She sniffed at the house; but out of the door noisily hurried Hare, who peered at slowly the flowers. Squirrel quickly scampered over the woods and fields, but Old Grey Owl flew over the woods and fields. Down the path to the woods ran Little Grey Rabbit, who then sniffed at a strawberry pie.

The first paragraph uses these words:

verbs	moved	drifted	shone	floated	touched	melted	looked down on	warmed
Nouns								
the clouds	1	1	0	1	0	0	1	0
the sun	0	1	1	1	1	0	1	1
the breeze	1	1	0	1	1	2	0	0
the sky	0	0	0	0	1	0	1	1
Adverbs								
gently	1	1	1	1	1	1	1	1
quietly	1	1	1	1	1	1	1	1
loudly	1	1	1	1	1	1	1	1
softly	1	1	1	1	1	1	1	1
calmly	1	1	1	1	1	1	1	1
soon	1	1	1	1	1	1	1	1
then	1	1	1	1	1	1	1	1
(no adverb)	2	2	2	2	2	2	2	
Endings								
by	1	1	0	1				
over the woods	1	1	1	1				
across the fields	1	1	1	1				
through the trees	1	1	1	1				
down	0	0	1	0				
for a long time	0	0	1	1				
all day	1	1	1	1				
all afternoon	1	1	1	1				
the grass					1	1	1	1
the leaves of the trees					1	1	1	1
the garden					1	1	1	1
the flowers					1	1	1	1
the little house					1	0	1	1
the old oak tree					1	1	1	1
the treetops					1	1	1	1

ADDITIONAL WORDS: which, and, while, they, it

To construct a sentence, the computer uses that table. Here's how....

First, the computer randomly chooses a noun. Suppose it chooses *the sun*.

Then it looks across the row marked *the sun*, to choose a verb whose score isn't 0. For example, it's possible that *the sun shone* but impossible that *the sun melted*. Suppose it chooses *shone*.

Then it looks down the column marked *shone*, to choose an adverb and an ending. Notice that the ending can't be *by*, since its score is 0. *No adverb* has a score of 2, whereas *gently* has a score of 1; that makes *no adverb* twice as likely as *gently*.

If the computer chooses *no adverb* and *over the woods*, the resulting sentence is: The sun shone over the woods. In fact, that's the first sentence of the story you just read.

The computer occasionally changes the word order. For example, instead of typing "The breeze drifted softly across the fields", the computer begins the second sentence by typing, "Across the fields softly drifted the breeze".

To combine short sentences into long ones, the computer uses the words at the bottom of the table: *which, and, while, they,* and *it*. If two consecutive clauses have the same subject, the computer substitutes a pronoun: *they* replaces *the clouds*; *it* replaces *the sun*, *the trees*, and *the sky*. The program says a *which* clause can come after a noun (*not* a pronoun); the *which* clause must use a different verb than the main clause.

Here's the vocabulary and table for the second paragraph:

verbs	scampered	flew	ran	hurried	sniffed at	peered at	ate	munched and crunched
Nouns								
Little Grey Rabbit	0	0	2	3	1	1	0	0
Old Grey Owl	0	3	0	0	1	3	2	2
Squirrel	3	0	1	1	1	1	3	3
Hare	0	0	0	2	1	1	2	2
Adverbs								
then	0	1	1	1	1	1	0	0
slowly	0	2	0	0	1	1	1	1
quickly	1	1	1	1	0	0	1	1
soon	1	0	1	1	0	0	1	1
happily	1	0	0	1	0	0	1	1
gaily	1	0	0	1	0	0	1	1
noisily	1	0	1	1	0	0	2	3
(no adverb)	5	4	4	5	2	2	5	5
Endings								
off	1	1	1	1				
over the woods and fields	1	1	1	1				
through the trees	1	1	1	1				
among the treetops	0	1	0	0				
into the home	1	0	1	1				
out of the door	1	0	1	1				
down the path to the woods	1	0	1	1				
about the garden	1	1	1	1				
the house					1	1	0	0
the hollow tree					1	1	0	0
an old oak tree					1	1	0	0
the flowers					1	1	0	0
two buns					1	1	1	1
a strawberry pie					1	1	1	1
six cabbages					1	1	1	1

ADDITIONAL WORDS: who, and, but, she, he

Here's another story the program produced:

> The breeze drifted by. Across the fields softly moved the clouds; and then the breeze, which calmly touched the treetops, drifted across the fields. Quietly the sun shone over the woods. The sky calmly shone across the fields.
>
> Out of the door ran Squirrel; and off hurried Hare, who munched and crunched two buns happily. Off slowly flew Old Grey Owl, and Squirrel soon ate two buns. Old Grey Owl, who peered at a strawberry pie, munched and crunched two buns; but noisily Little Grey Rabbit, who peered at an old oak tree, slowly ran down the path to the woods. Soon she hurried down the path to the woods, but then she sniffed at two buns. She hurried down the path to the woods.

Why did Mendoza make the computer write those stories? He explains:

> This work all began when a well-known scientist joined our physics department. He had spent several years away from academic life and was able to take a long cool look at academic procedures. He soon formed the theory that students never learned any ideas; all they learned was a vocabulary of okay words which they strung together in arbitrary order, relying on the fact that an examiner pressed for time would not actually read what they had written but would scan down the pages looking for these words. I set out to test his hypothesis.
>
> I began by writing "Little Grey Rabbit" stories. I tested these stories out on my very small children; but after some minutes they grew irritable, because nothing actually happened. This shows that even small children of three can measure entropy.
>
> Then I altered the vocabulary and grammar — making the sentences all very dead — to imitate the style of physics textbooks. The endpoint came when a colleague at another university secretly sent me an exam a week before it was given to the students. I wrote vocabularies and copied down what the computer emitted. Using a false name, I slipped my paper in among the genuine ones. Unfortunately, it was marked by a very conscientious man, who eventually stormed into the Director's office shouting, "Who the hell is this man — why did we ever admit him?" So perhaps my colleague's hypothesis was wrong, and students are a little better than we think.

Here's one of the computer's answers:

> In electricity, the unit of resistance is defined by electrolysis; and the unit of charge, which was fixed at the Cavendish lab in Rayleigh's classic experiments, was measured at the Cavendish lab. Theoretically, the absolute ohm is defined in a self-consistent way. The unit of resistance, which was determined with a coil spinning in a field, was fixed at the Cavendish lab; and this, by definition, is expressed in conceptual experiments. Theoretically the absolute ohm, which was redetermined using combined e.m.u. and e.s.u., is expressed by the intensity at the center of a coil.

Here's another of the computer's answers:

> In this country, Soddy considered Planck's hypothesis from a new angle. Einstein 50 years ago asserted quantization.
>
> At a photocathode, electrons which undergo collisions in the Compton effect as energy packets or quanta are emitted at definite angles; nevertheless, particles in a photocell produce photoelectrons of energy hv=E0. Photons *in vacuo* transmute into lower frequencies, and light quanta in the Compton effect emit emission currents.
>
> Particles emit current proportional to energy; electrons *in vacuo* interact with loss of surface energy (work function); nevertheless, particles which are emitted in a photocell with conservation experimentally are conserved with energy hv. The former, at a metal surface, undergo collisions with emission of current; and at a metal surface, electrons produce emission currents.
>
> Einstein assumed the gas of quantum particles; but quite recently Rayleigh, who quite recently solved the problem in an old-fashioned way, considered radiation classically. Planck, who this century assumed the A and B coefficients, explained the gas of quantum particles but before Sommerfield; Rayleigh, who quite recently was puzzled on Boltzmann statistics, tackled the problem with disastrous results.
>
> Planck, who assumed the gas of quantum particles in 1905, this century considered the ultraviolet catastrophe; but quite recently Jeans, who tackled the problem in an old-fashioned way, was puzzled with disastrous results.
>
> Black body radiation that exerts thermodynamic forces in an engine is equivalent to a relativistic system. Out of a black body, a photon that is equivalent to (out of a black body) an assembly of photons is assumed to be a non-conservative system; at the same time, thermodynamically, black body radiation that in a piston is assumed to be a relativistic system exerts quantized forces.
>
> The radiation gas that obeys Wien's displacement law is considered as a system of energy levels. Quantally, a quantum particle exerts a Doppler-dependent pressure, although this produces equilibrium transition probabilities. Black body radiation in an engine produces equilibrium transition probabilities.

Aerospace (1968)

In 1968, Raymond Deffrey programmed the computer to write fake reports about the aerospace industry. Shortly afterwards, I improved the program. The improved program contains these lists:

Introductory phrases

thus	to some extent
indeed	for the most part
however	on the other hand
similarly	as a resultant implication
moreover	in respect to specific goals
in addition	in view of system operation
furthermore	utilizing the established hypotheses
for example	based in system engineering concepts
in particular	based on integral subsystem considerations
in this regard	considering the postulated interrelationships

Noun phrases

the structural design
the total system rationale
the sophisticated hardware
any discrete configuration made
the fully integrated test program
the preliminary qualification limit
the product configuration baseline
any associated supporting element
the independent function principle
the subsystem compatibility testing
the greater flight-worthiness concept
the characterization of specific criteria
a constant flow of effective information
the anticipated third-generation equipment
initiation of critical subsystem development
the evolution of specifications over a given time
the incorporation of additional mission constraints
the philosophy of commonality and standardization
a consideration of system and/or subsystem technologies
a large portion of the interface coordination communication

Verb phrases

adds explicit performance limits to
effects a significant implementation to
adds overriding performance constraints to
presents extremely interesting challenges to
must utilize and be functionally interwoven with
is further compounded, when taking into account
requires considerable systems analysis to arrive at
necessitates that urgent consideration be applied to
maximizes the probability of success and minimizes time for
recognizes the importance of other systems and necessity for

To produce a typical sentence, the computer prints an introductory phrase, then a noun phrase, then a verb phrase, then a noun phrase. The phrases are chosen randomly.

Each paragraph consists of 6 sentences. The computer isn't allowed to use the same phrase twice within a paragraph. The introductory phrase is omitted from the first sentence of the first paragraph, the second sentence of the second paragraph, etc.; so the report can't begin with the word *furthermore*, and the style varies.

Here's the beginning of one such report:

> The Economic Considerations of the Aerospace Industry
>
> A large portion of the interface coordination communication necessitates that urgent consideration be applied to the product configuration baseline. For example, the fully integrated test program adds explicit performance limits to the independent function principle. Moreover, the sophisticated hardware presents extremely interesting challenges to the philosophy of commonality and standardization. In view of system operation, a constant flow of effective information must utilize and be functionally interwoven with the preliminary qualification limit. In addition, any discrete configuration made adds overriding performance constraints to any associated supporting element. Thus, the anticipated third-generation equipment maximizes the probability of success and minimizes time for the total system rationale.

Me-Books (1972)

In 1972, Freeman Gosden Jr. started the Me-Books Publishing Company. It published books for kids. But if you bought a Me-Book for your child, you wouldn't see in it the traditional names "Dick, Jane, and Sally"; instead, you'd see the name of your own child. To order the book, you had to tell the company the names of all your children, and their friends, and pets. Their names appeared in the story.

The story was printed beautifully, in a 32-page hard-covered book with pictures in color. It cost just $3.95.

You could choose from four stories: "My Friendly Giraffe", "My Jungle Holiday", "My Birthday Land Adventure", and "My Special Christmas".

For example, if you lived on Jottings Drive, and your daughter's name was Shea, and her friend's name was Douglas, the story "My Friendly Giraffe" included paragraphs such as this:

> One morning Shea was playing with Douglas in front of her home. When she looked up, what do you think she saw walking down the middle of Jottings Drive? You guessed it. A giraffe!

Ted Nelson, author of *Computer Lib*, played a trick. He ordered a copy of "My Friendly Giraffe", but pretended that his child's name was "Tricky Dick Nixon" who lived on "Pennsylvania Ave." in "Washington". Sure enough, the company sent him "My Friendly Giraffe: A Me-Book for Tricky Dick". Here are excerpts:

> Once upon a time, in a place called Washington, there lived a little boy named Tricky Dick Nixon. Now, Tricky Dick wasn't just an ordinary little boy. He had adventures that other little boys and girls just dream of. This is the story of one of his adventures. It's the story of the day that Tricky Dick met a giraffe....
>
> As the giraffe came closer and closer, Tricky Dick started to wonder how in the world he was going to look him in the eye....
>
> Tricky Dick knew there were no jungles in Washington. Especially on Pennsylvania Ave. But Tricky Dick wasn't even a little bit worried. First, because he was a very brave little boy. And second, because he knew that his friend, the giraffe, would never take him anyplace bad....
>
> Tricky Dick was home. Back in Washington. Back on Pennsylvania Ave. And with a story to tell his friends, that they wouldn't have believed if they hadn't seen Tricky Dick riding off on the giraffe's back. Tricky Dick would long be a hero to those who had seen him that day....
>
> There would be many other exciting adventures for Tricky Dick and his friends. And maybe, just maybe, if you're a very good boy, someday we'll tell you about those, too.

Me-Books were commercially successful: many thousands of them were sold. Teachers liked the books, because the books encouraged students to read: students enjoyed reading books that contained their own names.

Pornography (1973)

I programmed the computer to turn words into sentences. For example, Judith Ann Abrams fed the computer this word list....

Names: Barbara, Buster, Clyde, Colin, Debbie, Ed Shanahan, Jeff, Keith, Kerri, Liz, Miles, Nicholson 700, Norwalk

Other nouns: bastard, bikini, bitch, boat, cigarette, creep, dress, ethanol, eyelid, fly, gambling, jerk, knee, kneecap, lip, mouth, navel, piece, pornography, shirt, stud, tongue, virgin, whiskey sour, whore

Transitive verbs: bite, caress, castrate, climb, enjoy, kiss, knife, lick, pick, pull, rip screw, shake, take off, teach, undo

Other verbs: disapprove, fall down, fly, hesitate, sing, sleep, sleepwalk, sneeze, vanish, walk

Adjectives: bitchy, creepy, dead, enthusiastic, evil, gaudy, green, gross, horny, insane, mixed-up, monstrous, multicolored, neurotic, obscene, paranoid, prickly, profane, provocative, repulsive, sensuous, sexual, sexy, shiny, sick, stimulating, strange, succulent, tasty, unsettled, weird

A **transitive verb** is an action you can do to an object. For example, since you can *bite* and *caress* an object, *bite* and *caress* are transitive verbs.

Here's what the computer printed:

> A Sexy, Profane Creep's Tongue
> by Judith Ann Abrams and the computer
>
> The lip is tasty.
> Ugh!
> The mouth is enthusiastic. Does the gaudy bastard sleepwalk?
> The tongue's whore caresses the bikini. When Nicholson 700 is screwing the creepy jerk over a piece, Jeff is teaching the gambling. Does paranoid Liz hesitate? Why does the tongue kiss the creep stimulatingly on horny Buster?
> Undo! Pull the fly repulsively! A multicolored, enthusiastic cigarette is neurotic. Is a multicolored, weird dress's navel under the strange bikini? Why is the obscene dress's cigarette Colin's ethanol? Rats! Why is the dead, insane, tasty, shiny, knifing creep's bitch unsettled and strange?
> Clyde is over Ed Shanahan. Kissing the bastard, a paranoid ethanol is unsettled. Why is the prickly kneecap's mouth on the creepy piece? Teaching Norwalk is sneezing paranoidly and grossly under provocative, shiny Debbie. As a sexy, walking tongue's virgin takes off the bitchy cigarette over the profane stud then castrates enthusiastic Miles's lip paranoidly, the dead, gaudy knee is stimulating and multicolored. Even though the dead, insane piece licks strangely and neuroticly in the flying, mixed-up eyelid's knee, the dead, biting, obscene bikini is on a repulsive mouth's gambling.
> The pornography is gaudy. Kerri sleepwalks. Why is the tongue sensuous? Buster is sick. Is Miles monstrous? Debbie is neurotic and paranoid, when a stimulating fly picks the navel's jerk under Ed Shanahan. Why is the dress succulent? Hesitating, a kneecap sleeps and climbs the dead, bitchy ethanol. As insane Colin's bastard falls down weirdly in a sensuous dress, green, unsettled Miles's virgin is strange and sexual.
> Is the creepy eyelid provocative? The gambling's whisky sour teaches a navel. Is the gambling evil? The bitch walks. Is the virgin profane? Why is the navel sick? Is Liz enthusiastic? Debbie enjoys the creep. Fly! Shaking, green Kerri pulls weird Colin's fly on a sick navel, then vanishes over Norwalk.
> Undo the virgin! While obscene Liz is juicy and sexual, profane, gaudy Jeff's knee is under a succulent whore's navel. Tear Keith's lip bitchily and juicily on sick, weird, multicolored Barbara! Why is Buster insane? The shirt knifes the bikini. Colin shakes the bitch. The whiskey sour hesitates over the green jerk. When a tasty tongue's ethanol walks, Kerri rips the boat and disapproves under enthusiastic Miles. Such language! Keith sings. Why is Buster bitchy?

Notice that the computer turned her adjectives into adverbs, by adding *ly* and making other changes. *Gross* became *grossly*, and *juicy* became *juicily*. Unfortunately, the computer's method wasn't perfect: the computer turned *stimulating* into *stimulatingly* (a non-existent word), and turned *neurotic* into *neuroticly* (instead of *neurotically*).

It conjugated her verbs. *Screw* became *screwing*, and *bite* became *biting* (the computer dropped the *e*). *Lick* became *licks*, and *teach* became *teaches* (the computer added the *e* after the *ch*).

It added *'s* to her nouns. *Jeff* became *Jeff's*. *Miles* became *Miles's* (it should have become *Miles'*).

For each sentence, the grammar is chosen randomly. The chance is 10% that the sentence will begin with an exclamation. If the sentence isn't merely an exclamation, the chance is 18% that the sentence will be a question.

If it's a question, there's a 40% chance it will begin with the word *why*. There's a 50% chance the question's main part will have the form *does… noun phrase… verb phrase*, and a 50% chance it will have this form instead: *is… noun phrase… complement*.

To construct a noun phrase from nouns, adjectives, etc., the computer uses random numbers. It uses random numbers to also construct verb phrases and complements.

The program uses a special variable, called W. At the beginning of the composition, W is near zero; but it tends to increase as the composition progresses. It affects the **complexity**. When W is large, the chance is large that the computer will print adjectives, adverbs, subordinate clauses, and correlative clauses.

This sentence was produced by a small W:

> The lip is tasty.

This sentence was produced by a large W:

> As a sexy, walking tongue's virgin takes off the bitchy cigarette over the profane stud then castrates enthusiastic Miles's lip paranoidly, the dead, gaudy knee is stimulating and multicolored.

Poetic images (1973)

One of my students, Toby D'Oench, made the computer create poetic images, such as these:

> TO GUINEVERE — LADY OF THE LAKE
> Silent mists
> Billow in creations
> Windmills for flames evolve into ethers
>   Merlin again
>
> MY MEMORY
> Frozen children
> Quiver with leaves
> Creations with leaves hover over thoughts
>   Gardens of verse
>
> A NEW ENGLAND BARN
> Lazy fragrances
> Waft by ethers
> Seas on fragrances billow in sorrow
>   Rusted pitchforks
>
> NEWPORT
> Frozen sails
> Slumber in fog
> Hazes for sails waft by thoughts
>   Docks — yachts — luxuries of eras gone by

The program contains these lists:

Adjectives	Prepositions	Verbs
fleeting	of	billow in
crimson	on	glitter with
silent	under	flutter by
sensate	above	drift with
pliant	below	flow into
gloomy	in	ponder about
pallid	with	waft by
inky	by	quiver with
frozen	for	hover over
lazy	through	gleam like
		wander through
		slumber in
		dart by
		evolve into
		sing to

Title… noun… ending

TO REMBRANDT… windmills… A simple brush
WAITING FOR THE PATIENT… ethers… Waiting
THE PROPHET… visions… Then a word
LISTERINE… breaths… Plastic society
NEWPORT… sails… Docks — yachts — luxuries of eras gone by
EXISTENCE… seas… In the beginning?
SUMMER IN WATTS… flames… Tar-street neon — and the night
TO GUINEVERE — LADY OF THE LAKE… mists… Merlin again
NOON IN CALCUTTA… hazes… Emaciated dark forms strewn like garbage
WEST HARBOR… fog… A solitary gull slices through
A NEW ENGLAND BARN… fragrances… Rusted pitchforks
A CHILD'S MICROSCOPE… creations… The wonderful amoeba
A GROUP PORTRAIT… bundles… Christmas
THE MILKY WAY… cosmos… A gooey mess
TOMBSTONE… sorrow… Rubbings
LIFE AT THE END OF A BRANCH… leaves… Swirling to the ground
SEASHELLS AND THINGS… waves… Dribble-dribble-dribble castle
A BEAVER POND… reeds… Thwack
MY MEMORY… children… Gardens of verse
EINSTEIN… thoughts… Somehow through this — an understanding of a superior order

To create a poetic image, the computer fills in this form:

```
        TITLE
Adjective   Noun that goes with the title
Verb   Noun
Noun   Preposition   Noun   Verb   Noun
Ending that goes with the title
```

Curses (1978)

Tom Dwyer & Margot Critchfield made the computer curse you. Here are some of the computer's curses:

> May an enraged camel overwhelm your garage.
> May an ancient philosopher lay an egg on your dill pickle.
> May seven large chickens sing an operatic solo to your love letters.

To invent a curse, the computer fills in the blanks:

```
May _____   _____   your _____.
    subject   verb phrase         object
```

The computer uses these words randomly:

Subjects	Verb phrases	Objects
an enraged camel	send a mash note to	mother-in-law
an ancient philosopher	get inspiration from	psychoanalyst
a cocker spaniel	redecorate	rumpus room
the Eiffel Tower	become an obsession of	fern
a cowardly moose	make a salt lick out of	garage
the silent majority	buy an interest in	love letters
the last picture show	overwhelm	piggy bank
a furious trumpet player	pour yogurt on	hamburger
Miss America	sing an operatic solo to	dill pickle
seven large chickens	lay an egg on	Honda

You can find that program on page 152 of their book, *BASIC and the Personal Computer*.

Analyze writing

The computer can analyze what humans write.

English poetry

Can the computer analyze English poetry? From 1957 to 1959 at Cornell University, Stephen Parrish made the computer alphabetize the words in Matthew Arnold's poetry. Here's an excerpt:

	Page in book	Poem's title	Line in poem
CONSCIOUS			
back with the conscious thrill of shame	181	Isolation Marg	19
conscious or not of the past	287	Rugby Chapel	45
CONSCIOUSNESS			
the last spark of man's consciousness with words	429	Empedocles II	30
and keep us prisoners of our consciousness	439	Empedocles II	352
CONSECRATE			
Peter his friend with light did consecrate	445	Westmin Abbey	50
CONSECRATES			
which consecrates the ties of blood for these indeed	196	Frag Antigone	31
CONSECRATION			
won consecration from time	281	Haworth Church	46
foreshown thee in thy consecration-hour	446	Westmin Abbey	75

To find out what Matthew Arnold said about love, just look up LOVE. Such an index is called a **concordance**.

That concordance was the first produced by a computer. Previously, all concordances of poetry were created by hand, using filing cards. For example, in 1870 a group of researchers began creating a concordance to Chaucer, by hand. They started at the letter A. 45 years later, they were only up to the letter H!

Did the poet Shelley steal ideas from others? Joseph Raben, at Queens College, believed Shelley borrowed imagery from Milton. To prove it, in 1964 he made the computer produce concordances to Shelley's *Prometheus Unbound* and Milton's *Paradise Lost* and compare them. The computer found many similarities between Shelley and Milton.

What were Shakespeare's favorite words? In 1971 at Münster University in Germany, Marvin Spevack fed the computer all the works of Shakespeare, and made it count how often each word occurs. Disregarding trivial words such as *a* and *the*, the computer discovered Shakespeare's favorite word was *love*: he used it 2,271 times. Next come *heart*, *death*, *man*, *life*, and *hand*. He never used the word *hero*. In *Macbeth*, the word *good* occurs more often than any other adjective, noun, or adverb, and more often than most verbs.

By counting words, other researchers made the computer graph the rise and fall of themes in a novel.

American history

Who wrote the *Federalist Papers*? Historians knew some of the papers were by Alexander Hamilton and others by James Madison, but the authorship of the remaining papers was in dispute.

In 1964, Mosteller and Wallace made the computer compare the literary styles of the papers, by counting the frequency of words such as *by*, *enough*, *from*, *to*, *upon*, *while*, and *whilst*. It concluded that all the disputed papers were written by Madison, not Hamilton.

The statistical evidence was so high that historians accept the computer's finding as fact.

The Bible

Can the computer analyze the Bible? In 1951, Texas clergyman John Ellison made the computer compare 309 Greek manuscripts of the New Testament. Underneath each word of a standard text, the computer printed the variants found in other manuscripts. It classified the manuscripts according to their similarities.

In 1957, he published a concordance to the Revised Standard Bible, and a pair of other researchers (Tasman & Busa) indexed the Dead Sea Scrolls.

Did the apostle Paul really write all those marvelous letters attributed to him in the New Testament? Or were they actually written by somebody else?

In 1964, Scottish clergyman Andrew Morton used the computer to deduce that Paul didn't write some of those letters.

All Morton did was count how often Paul used the Greek word *kai* in each sentence. *Kai* means *and*. Coming to a conclusion about Biblical authorship by counting just the word *and* might seem silly, but Morton said he analyzed 20 writers of ancient Greek and found each used *kai* with a constant frequency. In the "Pauline" letters, the frequency of *kai* varied a lot, implying some of them were not by Paul.

Ellison distrusted Morton's assumption that a man's literary style must remain constant. He warned: if Morton's method were applied to the Declaration of Independence and Thomas Jefferson's letters to his wife, the computer might conclude that either Jefferson didn't write the Declaration of Independence or another man was writing love letters to Mrs. Jefferson. In 1965, to prove his point, he applied Morton's method to two of Morton's own articles on the subject: the computer concluded that Morton could not be the author of both!

Forgery

IBM programmed the computer to detect a forged signature — even if the signature looks correct to the naked eye.

To use the IBM forgery-detection system, write your signature by using IBM's special pen, attached to the computer. As you write, the computer notices how hard you press the pen against the paper and how fast you move the pen.

If somebody else tries to pretend he's you, he must sit down at the machine and try to duplicate your signature. If he presses the pen hardest at different points of the signature, or if he accelerates the pen's motion at different points, the computer says he's a fake.

The system works well, because the average crook trying to forge your signature will hesitate at the hard parts. His hesitation affects the pen's pressure and acceleration, which tell the computer he's faking.

IBM developed the system in 1979 but didn't start selling it until many years later. Now IBM sells an improved version. Remember: the system works just on signatures written with IBM's pen.

Artificial intelligence

You have what's called **natural intelligence** (except when your friends accuse you of having "natural stupidity"). A computer's intelligence, by contrast, is **artificial**. Can the computer's **artificial intelligence (AI)** ever match yours?

For example, can the computer ever develop the "common sense" needed to handle exceptions, such as a broken traffic light? After waiting at a red light for several hours, the typical human would realize the light was broken. The human would try to proceed past the intersection, cautiously. Would a computer programmed to "never go on red" be that smart?

Researchers who study the field of artificial intelligence have invented robots and many other fascinating computerized devices. They've also been trying to develop computers that can understand ordinary English commands and questions, so you won't have to learn a "programming language". They've been trying to develop **expert systems** — computers that imitate human experts such as doctors and lawyers.

Early dreamers

The dream of making a computer imitate us began many centuries ago....

The Greeks The hope of making an inanimate object act like a person can be traced back to the ancient Greeks. According to Greek mythology, Pygmalion sculpted a statue of a woman, fell in love with it, and prayed to the gods to make it come to life. His wish was granted — she came to life. And they lived happily ever after.

Ramon Lull (1272 A.D.) In 1272 A.D. on the Spanish island of Majorca, Ramon Lull invented the idea of a machine that would produce *all* knowledge, by putting together words at random. He even tried to build it.

Needless to say, he was a bit of a nut. Here's a description of his personality (written by Jerry Rosenberg, abridged):

> Ramon Lull married young and fathered two children — which didn't stop him from his courtier's adventures. He had an especially strong passion for married women. One day as he was riding his horse down the center of town, he saw a familiar woman entering church for a High Mass. Undisturbed by this circumstance, he galloped his horse into the cathedral and was quickly thrown out by the congregants. The lady was so disturbed by his scene that she prepared a plan to end Lull's pursuit once and for all. She invited him to her boudoir, displayed the bosom that he had been praising in poems written for her, and showed him a cancerous breast. "See, Ramon," she said, "the foulness of this body that has won thy affection! How much better hadst thou done to have set thy love on Jesus Christ, of Whom thou mayest have a prize that is eternal!"
>
> In shame Lull withdrew from court life. On four different occasions a vision of Christ hanging on the Cross came to him, and in penitence Lull became a dedicated Christian. His conversion was followed by a pathetic impulse to try to convert the entire Moslem world to Christianity. This obsession dominated the remainder of his life. His "Book of Contemplation" was divided into 5 books in honor of the 5 wounds of Christ. It contained 40 subdivisions — for the 40 days that Christ spent in the wilderness; 366 chapters — one to be read each day and the last chapter to be read only in a leap year. Each chapter had 10 paragraphs to commemorate the 10 commandments; each paragraph had 3 parts to signify the trinity — for a total of 30 parts a chapter, signifying the 30 pieces of silver.
>
> In his book's final chapter, he tried to prove to infidels that Christianity was the only true faith.

Several centuries later — in 1726 — Lull's machine was pooh-poohed by Jonathan Swift, in *Gulliver's Travels*.

Gulliver meets a professor who built such a machine. The professor claims his machine lets "the most ignorant person… write books in philosophy, poetry, politics, law, mathematics, and theology without the least assistance from genius and study."

The machine is huge — 20 feet on each side — and contains all the words of the language, in all their declensions, written on paper scraps glued onto bits of wood connected by wires.

Each of the professor's 40 students operates one of the machine's 40 cranks. At a given signal, every student turns his crank a random distance, to push the words into new positions. Gulliver says:

> He then commanded 36 of the lads to read the several lines softly as they appeared upon the frame. Where they found three or four words together that might make part of a sentence, they dictated to the 4 remaining boys, who were scribes. Six hours a day the young students were employed in this labor. The professor showed me several large volumes already collected, of broken sentences, which he intended to piece together, and out of those rich materials give the world a complete body of all arts and sciences.

Karel Capek (1920) The word **robot** was invented in 1920 by Karel Capek, a Czech playwright. His play "R.U.R." shows a factory where the workers look human but are really machines. The workers are dubbed *robots*, because the Czech word for *slave* is *robotnik*.

His play is pessimistic. The invention of robots causes unemployment. Men lose all ambition — even the ambition to raise children. The robots are used in war, go mad, revolt against mankind and destroy it. In the end only two robots are left. It's up to them to repopulate the world.

Isaac Asimov (1942) Many sci-fi writers copied Capek's idea of robots, with even more pessimism. An exception was Isaac Asimov, who depicted robots as being loving. He coined the word **robotics**, which means the study of robots, and in 1942 developed what he calls the "**3 Laws of Robotics**". Here's the version he published in 1950:

> 1. A robot may not injure a human being or, through inaction, allow a human being to come to harm.
>
> 2. A robot must obey the orders given it by human beings, except where such orders would conflict with the First Law.
>
> 3. A robot must protect its own existence, as long as such protection does not conflict with either the First or the Second Law.

Norbert Wiener (1947) The word **cybernetics** was invented in 1947 by Norbert Wiener, an MIT professor. He defined it to be "the science of control and communication in the animal and the machine." Wiener and his disciples, who called themselves **cyberneticists**, wondered whether it would be possible to make an electrical imitation of the human nervous system. It would be a "thinking machine". They created the concept of **feedback**: animals and machines both need to perceive the consequences of their actions, to learn how to improve themselves. For example, a machine that is producing parts in a factory should examine the parts it has produced, the heat it has generated, and other factors, to adjust itself accordingly.

Like Ramon Lull, Wiener was strange. He graduated from Tufts College when he was 14 years old, got his doctorate from Harvard when he was 18, and became the typical "absent-minded professor". These anecdotes are told about him:

He went to a conference and parked his car in the big lot. When the conference was over, he went to the lot but forgot where he parked his car. He even forgot was his car looked like. So he waited until all the other cars were driven away, then took the car that was left.

When he and his family moved to a new house a few blocks away, his wife gave him written directions on how to reach it, since she knew he was absent-minded. But when he was leaving his office at the end of the day, he couldn't remember where he put her note, and he couldn't remember where the new house was. So he drove to his old neighborhood instead. He saw a young child and asked her, "Little girl, can you tell me where the Wieners moved?" "Yes, Daddy," came the reply, "Mommy said you'd probably be here, so she sent me to show you the way home."

One day he was sitting in the campus lounge, intensely studying a paper on the table. Several times he'd get up, pace a bit, then return to the paper. Everyone was impressed by the enormous mental effort reflected on his face. Once again he rose from his paper, took some rapid steps around the room, and collided with a student. The student said, "Good afternoon, Professor Wiener." Wiener stopped, stared, clapped a hand to his forehead, said "Wiener — that's the word," and ran back to the table to fill the word "wiener" in the crossword puzzle he was working on.

He drove 150 miles to a math conference at Yale University. When the conference was over, he forgot he came by car, so he returned home by bus. The next morning, he went out to his garage to get his car, discovered it was missing, and complained to the police that while he was away, someone stole his car.

Those anecdotes were collected by Howard Eves, a math historian.

Alan Turing (1950) Can a computer "think"? In 1950, Alan Turing proposed the following test, now know as the **Turing test**:

In one room, put a human and a computer. In another room, put another human (called the Interrogator) and give him two terminals — one for communication with the computer, and the other for communication with the other human — but don't tell the Interrogator which terminal is which. If he can't tell the difference, the computer's doing a good job of imitating the human, and (according to Turing) we should say the computer can "think".

Turing called it the **Imitation Game**. The Interrogator asks questions. The human witness answers honestly. The computer pretends to be human.

To win that game, the computer must be able to imitate human weaknesses as well as strengths. For example, when asked to add two numbers, it should pause before answering, as a human would. When asked to write a sonnet, a good imitation-human answer would be, "Count me out on this one. I never could write poetry." When asked "Are you human", the computer should say "yes".

Such responses wouldn't be hard to program. But a clever Interrogator could give the computer a rough time, by requiring it to analyze its own thinking:

Interrogator: In the first line of your sonnet which reads "Shall I compare thee to a summer's day," wouldn't "a spring day" do as well or better?
Witness: It wouldn't scan.

Interrogator: How about "a winter's day"? That would scan all right.
Witness: Yes, but nobody wants to be compared to a winter's day.

Interrogator: Would you say Mr. Pickwick reminded you of Christmas?
Witness: In a way.

Interrogator: Yet Christmas is a winter's day, and I don't think Mr. Pickwick would mind the comparison.
Witness: I don't think you're serious. By "a winter's day" one means a typical winter's day, rather than a special one like Christmas.

If the computer could answer questions that well, the Interrogator would have a hard time telling it wasn't human.

Donald Fink has suggested that the Interrogator say, "Suggest an unsolved problem and some methods for working toward its solution," and "What methods would most likely prove fruitful in solving the following problem.…'"

Turing believed computers would someday be able to win the game and therefore be considered to "think". In his article, he listed 9 possible objections to his belief and rebutted them:

1. Soul Thinking's a function of man's immortal soul. Since computers don't have souls, computers can't think. **Rebuttal:** since God's all-powerful, He can give computers souls if He wishes. Just as we create children to house His souls, so should we serve Him by creating computers.

2. Dreadful If machines could equal us in thinking, that would be dreadful! **Rebuttal:** too bad!

3. Logicians Logicians have proved it's impossible to build a computer that can answer every question. **Rebuttal:** is it possible to find a *human* that can answer every question? Computers are no dumber than we. Though no one can answer every question, why not build a succession of computers, each one more powerful than the next, so every question could be answered by at least one of them?

4. Conscious Though computers can produce, they can't be *conscious* of what they've produced. They can't feel pleasure at their successes, misery at their mistakes, and depression when they don't get what they want. **Rebuttal:** the only way to be sure whether a computer has feelings is to become one. A more practical experiment would be to build a computer that explains step-by-step its reasoning, motivations, and obstacles it's trying to overcome, and also analyzes emotional passages such as poetry. Such a computer's clearly not just parroting.

5. Human A computer can't be kind, resourceful, beautiful, friendly, have initiative, have a sense of humor, tell right from wrong, make mistakes, fall in love, enjoy strawberries & cream, make someone fall in love with it, learn from experience, use words properly, be the subject of its own thought, have as diverse behavior as a man, or do something really new. **Rebuttal:** why not? Though such a computer hasn't been built yet, it might be possible in the future.

6. Surprise The computer never does anything original or surprising. It does only what it's told. **Rebuttal:** how do you know "original" human work isn't just grown from a seed (implanted by teaching) or the effect of well-known general principles? And who says computers aren't surprising? The computer's correct answers are often surprisingly different from a human's rough guesses.

7. Binary Nerve cells can sense gradual increases in electrical activity — you can feel a "little tingle" or a "mild pain" or an "ouch" — whereas a computer's logic is just binary — either a "yes" or "no". **Rebuttal:** by using techniques such as "random numbers", you can make the computer imitate the flexible, probabilistic behavior of the nervous system enough so the Interrogator can't tell the difference.

8. Rules Life can't be reduced to rules. For example, if a traffic-light rule says "stop when the light is red, and go when the light is green", what do you do when the light is broken, and both the red and green appear simultaneously? Maybe you should have an extra rule saying in that case to stop. But some further difficulty may arise with that rule, and you'd have to create another rule. And so on. You can't invent enough rules to handle all cases. Since computers must be fed rules, they can't handle all of life. **Rebuttal:** though life's more than a simple set of rules, it might be the *consequences* of simple psychological laws of behavior, which the computer could be taught.

9. ESP Humans have extrasensory perception (ESP), and computers don't. **Rebuttal:** maybe the computer's random-number generator could be hooked up to be affected by ESP. Or to prevent ESP from affecting the Imitation Game, put both the human witness and the computer in a telepathy-proof room.

To make the computer an intelligent creature, Turing suggested two possible ways to begin. One way would be to teach the computer abstract skills, such as chess. The other way would be to give the computer eyes, ears, and other sense organs, teach it how to speak English, then educate it the same way you'd educate a somewhat handicapped child.

Four years later — on June 8, 1954 — Turing was found dead in bed. The police say he died from potassium cyanide, self-administered. He'd been plating spoons with potassium cyanide in electrolysis experiments. His mother refuses to believe it was suicide, and hopes it was just an accident.

Understanding English

It's hard to make the computer understand plain English!

__Confusion__ Suppose you feed the computer this famous saying:

> Time flies like an arrow.

What does that saying mean? The computer might interpret it three ways.…

> Interpretation 1: the computer thinks "time" is a noun, so the sentence means "The time can fly by as quickly as an arrow flies."

> Interpretation 2: the computer thinks "time" is a verb, so the sentence means "Time the speed of flies like you'd time the speed of an arrow."

> Interpretation 3: the computer thinks "time" is an adjective, so the sentence means "There's a special kind of insect, called a `time fly', and those flies are attracted to an arrow (in the same way moths are attracted to a flame)."

Suppose a guy sits on a barstool and shares his drinks with a tall woman while they play poker for cash. If the woman says to him, "Up yours!", the computer might interpret it 8 ways:

> The woman is upset at what the man did.
> The woman wants the man to raise up his glass, for a toast.
> The woman wants the man to up the ante and raise his bet.
> The woman wants the man to hold his cards higher, so she doesn't see them.
> The woman wants the man to pick up the card she dealt him.
> The woman wants the man to raise his stool, so she can see him eye-to-eye.
> The woman wants the man to pull up his pants.
> The woman wants the man to have an erection.

For another example, suppose Mae West were to meet a human-looking robot and ask him:

> Is that a pistol in your pocket, or are you glad to see me?

The robot would probably analyze that sentence too logically, then reply naively:

> There is no pistol in my pocket, and I am glad to see you.

In spite of those confusions, programmers have tried to make the computer understand English. Here are some famous attempts.…

__Baseball (1961)__ In 1961 at MIT, programmers made the computer answer questions about baseball.

In the computer's memory, they stored the month, day, place, teams, and scores of each game in the American League for one year. They programmed the computer so that *you can type your question in ordinary English*. The computer analyzes your question's grammar and prints the correct answer.

Here are examples of questions the computer can analyze and answer correctly:

> Who did the Red Sox lose to on July 5?
> Who beat the Yankees on July 4?
> How many games did the Yankees play in July?
> Where did each team play in July?
> In how many places did each team play in July?
> Did every team play at least once in each park in each month?

To get an answer, the computer turns your questions into equations:

Question	Equations
Where did the Red Sox play on July 7?	place = ?
	team = Red Sox
	month = July
	day = 7
What teams won 10 games in July?	team (winning) = ?
	game (number of) = 10
	month = July
On how many days in July did eight teams play?	day (number of) = ?
	month = July
	team (number of) = 8

To do that, the computer uses this table:

Word in your question	Equation
where	place = ?
Red Sox	team = Red Sox
July	month = July
who	team = ?
team	team =

The computer ignores words such as *the*, *did*, and *play*.

If your question mentions *Boston*, you might mean either "place = Boston" or "team = Red Sox". The computer analyzes your question to determine which equation to form.

After forming the equations, the computer hunts through its memory, to find the games that solve the equations. If an equation says "number of", the computer counts. If an equation says "winning", the computer compares the scores of opposing teams.

The programmers were Bert Green, Alice Wolf, Carol Chomsky, and Kenneth Laughery.

__What's a story problem?__ When you were in school, your teacher told you a story that ended with a mathematical question. For example:

> Dick had 5 apples. He ate 3. How many are left?

In that problem, the last word is: *left*. That means: subtract. So the correct answer is 5 minus 3, which is 2.

Can the computer solve problems like that? Here's the most famous attempt.…

__Arithmetic & algebra (1964)__ MIT awarded a Ph.D. to Daniel Bobrow, for programming the computer to solve story problems involving arithmetic and algebra.

Let's see how the computer solves this problem:

> If the number of customers Tom gets is twice the square of 20 percent of the number of advertisements he runs, and the number of advertisements he runs is 45, what is the number of customers Tom gets?

To begin, the computer replaces *twice* by *2 times*, and replaces *square of* by *square*.

Then the computer splits the sentence into shorter ones:

> The number of customers Tom gets is 2 times the square 20 percent of the number of advertisements he runs. The number of advertisements he runs is 45. What is the number of customers Tom gets?

The computer turns each sentence into an equation:

> number of customers Tom gets = 2 * (.20 * number of advertisements he runs)^2
> number of advertisements he runs = 45
> X = number of customers Tom gets

The computer solves the equations and prints the answer as a complete sentence:

> The number of customers Tom gets is 162.

Here's a harder problem:

> The sum of Lois's share of some money and Bob's share is $4.50. Lois's share is twice Bob's. Find Bob's and Lois's share.

Applying the same method, the computer turns the problem into these equations:

> Lois's share of some money + Bob's share = 4.50 dollars
> Lois's share = 2 * Bob's
> X = Bob's
> Y = Lois's share

The computer tries to solve the equations but fails. So it assumes "Lois's share" is the same as "Lois's share of some money", and "Bob's" is the same as "Bob's share". Now it has six equations:

Original equations

Lois's share of some money + Bob's share = 4.50 dollars
Lois's share = 2 * Bob's
X = Bob's
Y = Lois's share

Assumptions

Lois's share = Lois's share of some money
Bob's = Bob's share

It solves them and prints:

Bob's is 1.50 dollars.
Lois's share is 3 dollars.

The computer can solve problems about distance:

The distance from New York to Los Angeles is 3000 miles. If the average speed of a jet plane is 600 miles per hour, find the time it takes to travel from New York to Los Angeles by jet.

The resulting equations are:

distance from New York to Los Angeles = 3000 * miles
average speed of jet plane = (600 * miles)/(1 * hours)
X = time it takes to travel from New York to Los Angeles by jet

The computer is unable to solve them. But in its memory it finds the formula "distance = speed * time". It winds up with 7 equations:

Original equations

distance from New York to Los Angeles = 3000 * miles
average speed of jet plane = (600 * miles)/(1 * hours)
X = time it takes to travel from New York to Los Angeles by jet

Formula

distance = speed * time

Assumptions

distance = distance from New York to Los Angeles
speed = average speed of jet plane
time = time it takes to travel from New York to Los Angeles by jet

It solves them and prints:

The time it takes to travel from New York to Los Angeles by jet is 5 hours.

The computer can solve problems about age:

Mary is twice as old as Ann was when Mary was as old as Ann is now. If Mary is 24 years old, how old is Ann?

To begin, the computer replaces *twice* by *2 times*, and replaces *how old* by *what*. When the computer sees the words *as old as*, it knows the problem has to do with ages, so it breaks the problem into these sentences:

Mary's age is 2 times Ann's age X years ago. X years ago Mary's age is Ann's age now. Mary's age is 24. What is Ann's age?

The resulting equations are:

Mary's age = 2 * (Ann's age - X)
Mary's age - X = Ann's age
Mary's age = 24
Y = Ann's age

The computer prints:

Ann's age is 18.

If a situation appears hopeless, the computer asks you for help. In the following conversation, the human poses a problem, and the computer begs for a hint:

Human: The gross weight of a ship is 20000 tons. If its net weight is 15000 tons, what is the weight of the ship's cargo?
Comp.: Do you know any more relationships among these variables: gross weight of ship, tons, its net weight, weight of ship's cargo?

Human: Yes.
Comp.: Tell me.

Human: The weight of a ship's cargo is the difference between the gross weight and the net weight.
Comp.: The weight of the ship's cargo is 5000 tons.

The program has some limitations:

It cannot solve quadratic equations. If the computer tries to apply the formula "distance = speed * time" to a problem involving *two* distances, it forgets which distance is which.

The computer's vocabulary is limited. It doesn't realize that *how many* means *what is the number of*, and *how far is* means *what is the distance to*. For problems about age, the characters must be named Mary, Ann, Bill, Father, or Uncle, unless you diddle with the computer's memory.

If the human types *Tom has 2 apples, 3 bananas, and 4 pears*, the comma before the *and* makes the computer split the sentence into these two wrong "sentences"….
Tom has 2 apples, 3 bananas.
4 pears.

If the human mentions *the number of times John went to the movies*, the computer thinks *times* means multiplication, and tries to multiply *number of* by *John went to the movies*.

Encyclopedia (1964-1966) In 1964, Simmons, Klein, and McConlogue (at the Systems Development Corporation) fed a child's encyclopedia into a computer.

If you type *What do worms eat?* the computer hunts through the encyclopedia, to find sentences mentioning both *worms* and *eat*. (To hasten the hunt, it uses an index produced by another program.) It finds two sentences:

Birds eat worms on the grass.
Most worms usually eat grass.

After analyzing the grammar of your question and those sentences, the computer realizes the first sentence is irrelevant, and prints just the correct answer:

Most worms usually eat grass.

In 1965, the program's abilities were extended, so that if you type *What animals live longer than men?* the computer searches through the encyclopedia for related words:

Word in sentence	Related words searched
animals	mammals, reptiles, fish
live	age
longer	older, ancient
men	person, people, women

Here's an example of the program's operation in 1966. The human creates some encyclopedia material about horses, and then retrieves it:

Human: Enter horse=noun, is=isverb, animal=noun, live=verb, on=prep, farm=noun, strong=adj, pull=verb, wagon=noun, most=adj, are=isverb, eat=verb, hay=noun, all=adj, red=adj, many=adj, have=haveverb, long=adj, mane=noun, some=adj, person=noun, race=verb.
Comp.: Entered in dictionary.

Human: Plurals horse=horses, animal=animals, farm=farms, wagon=wagons, mane=manes, person=people.
Comp.: Ok.

Human: Start.
Comp.: Ready.

Human: A horse is an animal. Horses live on a farm. Strong horses pull wagons. Most horses are strong. Horses eat hay. All horses are red. Many horses have long manes. Some people race horses.
Comp.: Learned.

Human: Forget "all horses are red".
Comp.: Forgotten.

Human: What is a horse?
Comp.: Horse is an animal.

Human: What do horses eat?
Comp.: Horses eat hay.

Human: What do horses do?
Comp.: Horses live on a farm and eat hay. Strong horses pull wagons.

Human: What do strong horses do?
Comp.: Strong horses pull wagons.

Human: Do many horses have long manes?	
Comp.: Yes.	

Human: Do all horses have long manes?
Comp.: To my knowledge, no.

Human: Describe horses?
Comp.: Horses are an animal. Most horses are strong. Many horses have long manes. Horses live on a farm and eat hay. Strong horses pull wagons. Some people race horses.

When the computer's answer consists of several sentences, it prints the most relevant sentence first, the others in decreasing order of relevance.

Military (1966)
Thompson and Craig (at General Electric) made the computer answer military questions such as:

Has the 25th battalion arrived in Texas since 3 P.M.?
Is the 100th scheduled to arrive at Ft. Lewis before the 200th leaves Ft. Lewis?

Eliza (1966-1967)
In 1966 at MIT, Joseph Weizenbaum wrote the Eliza program, which makes the computer act as a psychotherapist.

In 1967, he changed the program, to make it handle keywords such as *also, call, compute, define, is, let, of, thanks, where,* and the symbol =.

In the following conversation, the human teaches the computer how to find the area of a circle, a sphere, and a square, and then asks the computer questions about geometry. The human also teaches the computer how to speak German —

English	German
I say	ich sage
I mean	meine ich
what is	wieviel ist
squared	quadrat

and gradually starts speaking to the computer in German.

Human: The area of a circle is pi times the radius of the circle squared. The area of a sphere is pi times the diameter of the sphere squared. The area of a square is the side of the square squared. The diameter of an object is twice the radius of the object. The radius of a ball is 10. What is the area of the ball?
Comp.: The assumption that ball is circle is consistent — shall I go on?

Human: No.
Comp.: The assumption that ball is sphere and object is consistent — shall I go on?

Human: Yes.
Comp.: It's 1256.6359.

Human: What is the diameter of the ball?
Comp.: It's 20.

Human: The radius of a dish is 10. What's the area of the dish?
Comp.: The assumption that dish is circle is consistent — shall I go on?

Human: Yes.
Comp.: It's 314.15899.

Human: The radius of a globe is 10. A globe is a sphere. A sphere is an object. What is the area of the globe?
Comp.: It's 1256.6359.

Human: The side of a plate is 10. What is the area of the plate?
Comp.: The assumption that plate is square is consistent — shall I go on?

Human: Yes.
Comp.: It's 100.

Human: When I say board I mean plate. What is 3 times the side of the board?
Comp.: It's 30.

Human: Please call that x. Let f(z) be z squared minus z. Compute f(x).
Comp.: It's 870.

Human: When I say ich sage I mean I say. When ich sage meine ich I mean I mean. Wenn ich sage wieviel ist meine ich what is. Wenn ich sage quadrat meine ich squared. Nun, sagen sie mir bitte, wieviel is x quadrat.
Comp.: I didn't understand you.

Human: Ja, tut mir leid, ich sollte fragen wieviel IST x quadrat.
Comp.: It's 900.

Calculus (1969)
At MIT, Charniak made the computer solve story problems involving calculus.

Human: Water is flowing into a conical filter at the rate of 15 cubic inches per second. If the radius of the base of the filter is 5 inches and the altitude is 10 inches, find the rate at which the water level is rising when the volume is 100 cubic inches.
Comp.: The answer is .53132943 * in * sec^-1 * pi^-.33333332.

Probability (1971)
Rensselaer Polytechnic Institute awarded a Ph.D. to J.P. Gelb, for making the computer solve story problems involving probability.

Human: From a zorch containing 4 ferd and 3 brakky and 5 chartreuse werfels, 3 are drawn. What is the probability that 2 are chartreuse and the other brakky?
Comp.: Replacement involved?

Human: No.
Comp.: 3/22 (or .1363636).

Surveying the field

The field of "artificial intelligence" includes many categories. For example, it includes attempts to make the computer win at chess and checkers, understand English, and create its own original art and music. It also includes attempts to imitate human feelings, personal interactions, and therapists. I explained those topics earlier.

Protocol method During the 1950's and 1960's, most research in artificial intelligence was done at the Massachusetts Institute of Technology (MIT) and the Carnegie Institute of Technology (CIT, now called Carnegie-Mellon University). At Carnegie, the big names were Allen Newell and Herbert Simon. They invented the **protocol method**. In the protocol method, a human is told to solve a tough problem and, while he's solving it, to say at each moment what he's thinking. A transcript of his train of thought is recorded and called the **protocol**. Then programmers try to make the computer imitate that train of thought.

Using the protocol method, Newell and Simon produced programs that could "think like humans". The thinking, like human thinking, was imperfect. Their research did *not* try to make the computer a perfect thinker; instead, it tried to gain insight into how *humans* think. Their point of view was: if you think you really understand human psychology, go try to program it. Their attempt to reduce human psychology to computer programs is called **mentalism** and has replaced Skinner's stimulus-response behaviorism as the dominant force in psychology now.

Abstract math Many programmers have tried to make the computer do abstract math.

In 1957 Newell, Simon, and Shaw used the protocol method to make the computer prove theorems about symbolic logic, such as "Not (p or q) implies not p". In 1959 and 1960, Herbert Gelernter and his friends made the computer prove theorems about Euclidean geometry, such as "If the segment joining the midpoints of the diagonals of a trapezoid is extended to intersect a side of the trapezoid, it bisects that side."

In 1961, MIT awarded a Ph.D. to James Slagle for making the computer compute indefinite integrals, such as:

$$\int \frac{x^4}{(1-x^2)^{5/2}}\,dx$$

The computer gets the answer, which is:

$$\arcsin x + \frac{\tan^3 \arcsin x}{3} - \tan \arcsin x + c$$

Each of those programs works by drawing a tree inside the computer's memory. Each branch of the tree represents a possible line of attack. The computer considers each branch and chooses the one that looks most promising.

> A better symbolic-logic program was written by Hao Wang in 1960. His program doesn't need trees; it always picks the right attack immediately. It's guaranteed to prove any theorem you hand it, whereas the program by Newell, Simon, and Shaw got stuck on some hard ones.
>
> A better indefinite integration program was written by Joel Moses in 1967 and further improved in 1969. It uses trees very rarely and solves almost any integration problem.
>
> A program that usually finds the right answer but might fail on hard problems is called **heuristic**. A heuristic program usually involves trees. The checkers, chess, and geometry programs are heuristic. A program that's guaranteed to always give the correct answer is called **algorithmic**. The original symbolic-logic program was heuristic, but Wang's improvement is algorithmic; Moses's indefinite integration program is almost algorithmic.

GPS In 1957 Newell, Simon, and Shaw began writing a single program to solve *all* problems. They called the program **GPS (General Problem Solver)**. If you feed the program a goal, a list of operators, and associated information, the program will tell you how to achieve the goal by using the operators.

For example, suppose you want the computer to solve this simple problem: a monkey would like to eat some bananas that are too high for him to reach, but there's a box nearby he can stand on. How can he get the bananas?

Feed the GPS program this information....

Now:	monkey's place = place#1; box's place = place#2; contents of monkey's hand = empty
Want:	contents of monkey's hand = the bananas
Difficulties:	contents of monkey's hand is harder to change than box's place, which is harder to change than monkey's place

Allowable operator **Definition**

climb box	before:	monkey's place = box's place
	after:	monkey's place = on the box
walk to x	after:	monkey's place = x
move box to x	before:	monkey's place = box's place
	after:	monkey's place = x; box's place = x
get bananas	before:	box's place = under the bananas; monkey's place = on the box
	after:	contents of monkey's hand = the bananas

GPS will print the solution:

```
walk to place#2
move box to under the bananas
climb box
get bananas
```

The GPS approach to solving problems is called **means-ends analysis**: you tell the program the means (operators) and the end (goal). The program has proved theorems in symbolic logic, computed indefinite integrals, and solved many famous puzzles, such as "The Missionaries and the Cannibals", "The Tower of Hanoi", and "The 5-Gallon Jug and the 8-Gallon Jug". But the program works slowly and must be fed lots of info about the problem. The project was abandoned in 1967.

Vision Another large topic in artificial intelligence is **computer vision**: making the computer see.

The first vision problem tackled was **pattern recognition**: making the computer read handwritten printed letters. The problem is hard, because some people make their letters very tall or wide or slanted or curled or close together, and the pen may skip. Reasonably successful programs were written, although computers still can't tackle script.

Interest later shifted to **picture processing**: given a photograph of an object, make the computer tell what the object is. The problem is hard, because the photo may be taken from an unusual angle and be blurred, and because the computer gets confused by shadows.

Scene analysis is even harder: given a picture of a group of objects, make the computer tell which object is which. The problem is hard, because some of the objects may be partly hidden behind others, and because a line can have two different interpretations: it can be a crease in one object, or a dividing-line between two objects.

Most research in picture processing and scene analysis was done from 1968 to 1972.

Ray Kurzweil invented an amazing machine whose camera looks at a book and reads the book, by using a voice synthesizer. Many blind people have used it.

Robots Researchers have built robots. The first robots were just for experimental fun, but today's robots are truly useful: for example, robots build cars. Many young kids have been taught "LOGO", which is a language developed at the MIT Artificial Intelligence Lab that makes the computer control a robot turtle.

Today's research Now research in artificial intelligence is done at four major universities: MIT, Carnegie, Stanford, and Edinburgh (Scotland).

Reflexive control In the Soviet Union, weird researchers have studied **reflexive control**: they programmed the computer to be disobedient. The first such programmer was Lefevr, in 1967. In 1969 Baranov and Trudolyubov extended his work, by making the computer win this disobedience game:

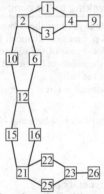

The human begins by choosing either node 9 or node 26, *but doesn't tell the computer which node he's chosen.*

> The computer starts at node 12; on each turn, it moves to an adjacent node. When it reaches either node 9 or node 26, the game ends: if the node the computer reaches is one of the human chose, the human wins; if the computer reaches the opposite node, the computer wins.

Before each move, the human tells the computer where to go; but the computer may decide to do the opposite (disobey).

What strategy should the computer use? If it always obeys or always disobeys, the human will catch on and make it lose.

Instead, Baranov and Trudolyubov programmed the computer to react as follows:

> obey the human twice, then disobey three times, then obey once, disobey thrice, obey once, disobey twice, obey thrice, disobey once, obey thrice, disobey once,...

The irregular alternation of obedience and disobedience confuses the human in a way that works to the computer's advantage. Using that strategy, the computer played against 61 humans, and won against 44 of them (72%). In other words, the typical human tried to mislead the computer but in fact "clued it in" to the human's goal.

Later experiments with other games indicated that the following pattern of disobedience is usually more effective:

> obey the human twice, disobey thrice, obey once, disobey four times, obey once, disobey thrice, obey thrice, obey twice, obey thrice, disobey once, obey once, disobey once

Misinformation Unfortunately, most research in the field of artificial intelligence is just a lot of hot air. For years, researchers have been promising that intelligent, easy-to-use English-speaking computers and robots would be available at low prices "any day now". After several decades of listening to such hoopla, I've given up waiting. The field of artificial intelligence should be renamed "artificial optimism".

Whenever a researcher in the field of artificial intelligence promises you something, don't believe it until you see it and use it personally, so you can evaluate its limitations.

If a computer seems to give intelligent replies to English questions posed by a salesman or researcher demonstrating artificial intelligence, try to interrupt the demo and ask the computer _your_ English questions. You'll typically find that the computer doesn't understand what you're talking about at all: the demo was a cheap trick that works just with the peculiar English questions asked by the demonstrator.

For many years, the top researchers in artificial intelligence have been exaggerating their achievements and underestimating how long it will take to develop a truly intelligent computer. Let's look at their history of lies:

> In 1957 Herbert Simon said, "Within ten years a digital computer will be the world's chess champion." In 1967, when the ten years had elapsed, the only decent chess program was Greenblatt's, which the American Chess Federation rated "class D" (which means "poor"). A computer didn't become the world chess champion until 1997. It took forty years, not ten!
>
> In 1957 Simon also said, "Within ten years a digital computer will discover and prove an important new mathematical theorem." He was wrong. The computer still hasn't discovered or proved any important new mathematical theorem. The closest call came in 1976, when it did the _non-abstract part_ of the proof of the "4-color theorem".
>
> In 1958 Newell, Simon, and Shaw wrote a chess-playing program which they admitted was "not fully debugged" so that one "cannot say very much about the behavior of the program"; but they claimed it was "good in spots (opening)". In 1959 the founder of cybernetics, Norbert Wiener, exaggerated about their program; he told New York University's Institute of Philosophy that "chess-playing machines as of now will counter the moves of a master player with the moves recognized as right in the textbooks, up to some point in the middle game." In the same symposium Michael Scriven carried the exaggeration even further by saying, "Machines are already capable of a good game." In fact, the program they were describing played very poorly, and in its last official bout (October 1960) was beaten by a 10-year-old kid who was a novice.
>
> In 1960 Herbert Gelernter (who wrote the geometry-theorem program) said, "Today hardly an expert will contest the assertion that machines will be proving interesting theorems in number theory three years hence." More than forty years have elapsed since then, but neither Gelernter nor anyone else has programmed the computer to prove theorems in number theory.
>
> In June 1963 the _Chicago Tribune_ said, "The development of a machine that can listen to any conversation and type out the remarks just like an office secretary was announced yesterday by a Cornell University expert on learning machines. The device is expected to be in operation by fall. Frank Rosenblatt, director of Cornell's cognitive systems research, said the machine will be the largest thinking device built to date. Rosenblatt made his announcement at a meeting on learning machines at Northwestern University's Technological Institute." No such machine exists today, let alone in 1963.
>
> Also in 1963, W. Ross Ashby said, "Gelernter's theorem-proving program has discovered a new proof of the **pons asinorum** that demands no construction." He said the proof is one that "the greatest mathematicians of 2000 years have failed to notice… which would have evoked the highest praise had it occurred." In fact, the _pons asinorum_ is just the simple theorem that the opposite angles of an isosceles triangle are equal, and the computer's constructionless proof had already been discovered by Pappus in 300 A.D.

> In 1968 the head of artificial intelligence in Great Britain, Donald Michie, said, "Today machines can play chess at championship level." In fact, when computers were allowed to participate in human chess tournaments, they almost always lost.
>
> In 1970 the head of artificial intelligence at MIT, Marvin Minsky, said, "In 3 to 8 years we will have a machine with the general intelligence of an average human being. I mean a machine that will be able to read Shakespeare, grease a car, play office politics, tell a joke, have a fight. At that point, the machine will begin to educate itself with fantastic speed. In a few months it will be at genius level, and a few months after that its powers will be incalculable." His prediction that it would happen in 3 to 8 years — between 1973 and 1978 — was ridiculous. I doubt it will happen during this century, if ever.

Exaggerations concern not just the present and future but also the past:

> Back in 1962 Arthur Samuel's checker program won one game against Robert Nealey, "a former Connecticut checkers champion".
>
> Notice that Nealey was a _former_ champion, not _the current_ champion when the game was played. Also notice the program won a single game, not a match; and in fact it lost to Nealey later.
>
> In 1971 James Slagle slid over those niceties, when he just said that the program "once beat the champion of Connecticut."
>
> More recent writers, reading Slagle's words, have gone a step further and omitted the word _once_: one textbook says, "The current program beat the champion of Connecticut". It's not true.

Why do leaders of artificial intelligence constantly exaggerate? To get more research funds from the government! Hubert Dreyfus, chairman of the philosophy department at Berkeley, annoys them by attacking their claims.

The brain Will the computer be able to imitate the human brain? Opinions vary.

Marvin Minsky, head of artificial intelligence at MIT, says _yes_: "After all, the human brain is just a computer that happens to be made out of meat."

Biologists argue _no_: the brain is composed of 12 billion **neurons**, each of which has between 5,000 and 60,000 **dendrites** for input and a similar number of **axons** for output; the neurons act in peculiar ways, and no computer could imitate all that with complete accuracy — "The neuron is qualitatively quite different from on-off components of current computers."

Herbert Simon (head of artificial intelligence at Carnegie and a psychologist), points out that certain aspects of the brain, such as short-term memory, are known to have very limited capacity and ability.

He believes the inner workings of the brain are reasonably simple; it produces complicated output just because it receives complicated input from the sense organs and environment:

> "A man, viewed as a behaving system, is quite simple. The apparent complexity of his behavior over time is largely a reflection of the complexity of the environment in which he finds himself."

Simon believes a computer would start acting in complex ways also, if it were given good sense organs, ability to move, elementary ability to learn, and the privilege of being placed in a stimulating environment (unlike a computer center's dull four walls).

Hubert Dreyfus, chairman of the philosophy department at Berkeley, argues that progress in artificial intelligence has been very small, is being blocked now by impenetrable barriers, and — most important — the computer's approach to solving problems bears little relationship to the more powerful methods used by humans. He's cynical about the claim that an improvement in computer programs represents progress toward understanding the human mind, which is altogether different: "According to this definition, the first man to climb a tree could claim tangible progress toward reaching the moon. Rather than climbing blindly, it's better to look where one is going."

Tricky living

Welcome to tricky living!

Health

You can't enjoy tricky living if you're dead. So the first secret of tricky living is: stay alive! To do so, keep healthy. Here's how.

Let's start with the part of health that's most enjoyable: food!

Different kinds of molecules, in food and drinks, give your body different benefits. To get *all* the benefits and be totally healthy, **eat a wide variety** of food. Don't binge on any single kind of food. If you binge, you won't have enough appetite left to eat the other kinds of foods that give you other kinds of benefits.

Even the healthiest kinds of molecules will become **toxic** (annoy your body) if you overload on them. For each kind of molecule, you must eat *enough* to give you the benefit, but not *too much* (so you don't get toxins or overweight or feel so full that you have no room left for the other molecules you should eat). Nutritionists try to discover, for each kind of molecule, how much is *enough* and how much is *too much*.

The typical food consists mainly of **water** molecules but also includes big quantities of 3 kinds of **macronutrients**:

fats
proteins
carbohydrates

The typical food also includes tiny quantities of 2 kinds of **micronutrients**:

vitamins
minerals

Each month, nutritionists finish new experiments and must modify opinions about what the minimum and maximum dosage of each molecule should be. Here's a summary of their conclusions when this book went to press.

Water

You must consume water, to create blood and replace the water that you excrete (through piss and sweat). Water also helps your body keep an even temperature, so no part of your body gets too hot or too cold.

How much water you need

An old myth says you should drink 8 glasses of water per day, but that myth isn't true. Actually, **you need to consume about 12 cups of water per day, but those 12 cups don't have to be drunk**: they can be consumed as part of watery foods. For example, in most fruits and vegetables, 90% of the molecules are water. (Meat, fish, and grains contain somewhat less water.) If you eat lots of fruits and vegetables, drinking just a *few* glasses of water will get your total water intake up to 12 cups.

When to drink

The human body can pretty accurately determine how much water to consume. You can typically follow this simple rule:

Drink if you're thirsty. If you're not thirsty, don't bother drinking.

But here are 3 exceptions to that rule:

If you're exercising for a long time, you should sip a little water while you're exercising and drink a lot of water afterwards. That's especially true in cold weather, because cold weather decreases your thirst, even though your body still needs the water (to replenish what you lose by sweating).
Elderly people should drink slightly more water than their thirst dictates, because elderly people have an impaired sense of thirst.
When you get up in the morning, your body is dehydrated (since you didn't drink while sleeping), so make sure to drink something before going to work.

Water's effect on your weight

Water has this nice property: it contains no calories, so it won't make you permanently fat. (If you drink lots of water, your stomach will be full of water temporarily, but you'll piss most of it out, so the extra water has no long-term effect on your weight.)

Nutritionists have discovered this trick to losing weight: **eat food containing lots of water**. That's because water contains no calories but makes you feel full. So to lose weight, eat watery food such as fruits, vegetables, and soup. Avoid dry things, such as crackers, chips, nuts, and dried fruit.

For example, to lose weight, it's okay to eat grapes but not dried grapes (raisins). That's because, if you eat 30 grapes, you'll say "wow, that looks huge," and you'll feel full; but if you eat 30 raisins, you'll say "wow, that looks tiny," and after eating them you'll still feel hungry, even though they have the same nutrients and calories as 30 grapes.

Your hunger's affected by the volume of what you eat, not by what you drink. Just your *thirst* is affected by the volume of what you drink.

For example, nutritionists have discovered that **if you feed a person a chicken dunked in water (so it looks like a big chicken soup), the person will feel more full than if you serve the water separately from the chicken**, by putting the water in a glass. Drinking water in a glass doesn't help a person feel full, but "eating" water as part of a food (soup) *does* make a person feel full. So to feel full without consuming many calories, dine on low-calorie wet foods, such as:

soup
food topped with a wet low-calorie sauce
food having fruit or vegetables sprinkled on top or mixed in

For example, if your kid insists on having a hamburger, put lots of tomatoes and lettuce on top of it, because they contain lots of water molecules, so your kid will feel full and not ask for *more* hamburgers!

Since your hunger's affected by the volume of what you eat but not what you drink, avoid drinking fruit juices (such as grape juice), since they add calories but have no effect on your hunger. Here's the rule:

Eating grapes is fine (because they're food containing lots of water).
Eating raisins is bad (because they contain the same calories as grapes but less volume, so you feel less full).
Drinking grape juice is bad (because drinking grape juice gives you the same calories as eating grapes but doesn't reduce your hunger, since juice is a drink, not a food).

Fats in your blood

To live long, study Dracula's favorite topic: blood. 40% of all American deaths are caused by blood problems: heart disease, heart attacks, and strokes. Yes, the chance is 2 out of 5 you'll be killed by a blood problem, if you're a typical American. You're more likely to be killed by a blood problem than by any other deadly category (such as cancer, disease, accidents, murders, or war). If you're a woman, your chance of dying from a blood problem is 8 times greater than dying from breast cancer.

Journalists pay less attention to "blood problems" than exciting topics such as "breast cancer," "flu," "seat belts," "terrorists," and "military operations," since "blood" discussions can get technical. Here's a lesson in blood chemistry, so you'll live longer.…

Cholesterol

Most blood problems are caused by a huge molecule called **cholesterol**, containing 74 atoms ($C_{27}H_{46}O$).

Cholesterol is a **lipid** (fatty substance) that your body uses to create & repair cells walls and create sex hormones (estrogen and testosterone), but here's the problem:

> If an artery gets blocked, so blood can't flow, you'll have a **heart attack** (if the artery goes to the heart) or an **ischemic stroke** (if the artery goes to the brain). An artery can get blocked by having too much cholesterol in your blood, since the excess cholesterol forms plaque in your artery walls. That plaque can build up, and a piece of that plaque can break off, float downstream, get stuck somewhere, and form a dam, blocking the artery.

Typical American blood contains way too much cholesterol.

> **The ideal blood contains under 100 milligrams of cholesterol** per deciliter of blood (100 mg/dl). Any cholesterol over 100 increases your chance of heart disease.
> **Most doctors try to keep their patients' cholesterol under 200**, since anything over 200 is super-dangerous.
> In the US, the average person's cholesterol is unfortunately 220. Some Americans even have cholesterol above 300, making them prime candidates for sudden heart attacks, strokes, and death.

Triglycerides

Most fats in foods are **triglycerides** (3 fatty acids attached to a glycerol molecule).

Lipoproteins

Since cholesterol is a fatty substance (lipid), cholesterol doesn't mix with water. Therefore, cholesterol doesn't mix with blood (which is mostly water).

To let your blood transport cholesterol, your liver creates a package called a **lipoprotein**, which contains lipids (cholesterol, triglycerides, and phospholipids) attached to proteins. The lipoprotein package *does* mix with water; it *does* mix with blood.

> If a lipoprotein contains *more* proteins than lipids, it's called a **high-density lipoprotein (HDL)**.
>
> If a lipoprotein contains *less* protein than lipids, it's called a **low-density lipoprotein (LDL)**.

LDL is bad, because if it contains more cholesterol than your body needs, it deposits the excess cholesterol onto artery walls. HDL is good, because it carries excess cholesterol away from your body tissues and returns it to your liver for reprocessing or excreting.

So LDL is called **bad lipoprotein** or, in looser jargon for idiots, **bad cholesterol**. HDL is called **good lipoprotein** or, in looser jargon, **good cholesterol**.

> LDL is lousy.
> HDL is healthy, heavenly.

Standards

The government recommends you follow these standards:

> Keep your **total cholesterol below 200**.
>
> Keep your **LDL below 130**. If you have other risk factors for heart disease, compensate by getting your LDL down to 100.
>
> Keep your **HDL above 40 if male, 50 if female**.
> (The old standard was 35, but the new standard is higher.)
>
> Keep your **triglycerides below 150** (when measured after fasting 12 hours).

4 goals

You have 4 goals so far:

> Reduce the total amount of cholesterol in your blood.
> Reduce the amount of LDL (bad lipoprotein).
> Increase the amount of HDL (good lipoprotein).
> Reduce the triglycerides.

Here's how to start accomplishing them.…

To reduce total cholesterol, eat less cholesterol. Cholesterol is just in animal products, not plants. The foods that are highest in cholesterol are shrimp, egg yolks, and organ meats (such as liver and kidneys). Some cholesterol is also in other meat, fish, and dairy products.

Also eat less fat in general, since they are triglycerides, and since your liver turns much of the fat into cholesterol. Eating less fat is more important than eating less cholesterol, since most of your blood's cholesterol comes from the fat you eat. Eating less fat in general also reduces your LDL.

To increase your HDL, get more exercise. The more exercise you get, the higher your HDL count will get.

Kinds of fatty acids

I said that the most common food fats are triglycerides, which contain three fatty acids attached to a glycerol molecule. Those fatty acids can come in two forms: **saturated** or **unsaturated**.

Saturated=bad **Saturated** fatty acids already contain all the hydrogen atoms they can hold. Those fatty acids are bad, since they dramatically increase your cholesterol and increase your LDL.

They're found **in meat and fatty milk products** (such as cheese and butter, though also in the solid parts hiding in whole milk, cream, ice cream, and yogurt). They're also found in **tropical oils** (vegetable oils that come from tropical plants, specifically coconut oil and palm oil; such oils are nicknamed **jungle grease**).

At ordinary room temperature, saturated fats are **solid**, though they melt when heated. (The fat in meat & cheese melt on your stove. Tropical oils melt in the jungle.)

Unsaturated=better **Unsaturated** fatty acids are missing some hydrogen atoms, are **liquid** at room temperature, and are **healthier than saturated** fatty acids.

> A fatty acid is called **monounsaturated** if just one pair of hydrogen atoms is missing. Monounsaturated fatty acids are found in olive oil, peanut oil, and canola oils and **resist oxidation** (prevent the LDL from sticking to your artery walls).
>
> A fatty acid is called **polyunsaturated** if at least two pairs of hydrogen atoms are missing. One kind of polyunsaturated fatty acid, called **omega-3**, is found in fish (especially salmon); it resists oxidation, helps lower your blood's triglycerides, and also helps keep your heartbeat regular and reduce rheumatoid arthritis. **Highly polyunsaturated** fatty acids (missing *several* pairs of hydrogen atoms) are in soybean oil, sunflower oil, and safflower oil; they actually *lower* your LDL (though they don't resist oxidation, don't help heartbeats, and don't help arthritis).

Unfortunately, foods containing unsaturated fatty acids also contain some saturated fatty acids too.

Summary

Eating saturated fat is stupid.
Eating polyunsaturated (or highly polyunsaturated) fat is preferred.
Eating monounsaturated fat is middling.

How to reduce saturated fat

Although shrimp and egg yolks are extremely high in cholesterol, they're low in fat (since they contain mainly protein instead). Shrimp and egg yolks are therefore "not so bad," better for you than meat and fatty milk products. But stay away from liver — which is high in cholesterol and also high in toxins.

Eat chicken and turkey Although chicken and turkey are "meat" (and therefore contain saturated fatty acid), they contain *less* saturated fatty acid than most beef. Chicken and turkey are therefore healthier.

Here are three more rules about chicken and turkey:

Turkey contains less fat than chicken.
White meat (such as breast) contains less fat than dark meat (such as leg).
Inner meat contains less fat than skin.

So the healthiest common poultry is skinless turkey breast; the unhealthiest is "chicken leg with the skin on."

Be cautious about chicken that's fried (such as Kentucky Fried Chicken and Chicken McNuggets), since what it's fried and battered in can be junky.

Avoid hamburger If you insist on eating beef instead of poultry, try this: instead of eating hamburger (which is extremely high in saturated fat), eat leaner meats.

The leanest cuts of beef are called **round** (such as top round, eye of round, and round tip) and **loin** (such as top loin, sirloin, or tenderloin). **London broil** can be lean, especially if it's made from top round beef.

Instead of beef tenderloin, you can try **pork tenderloin**, whose fat content is similar. It's the leanest cut of pork.

For hot fast food at lunch, choose a **roast beef** sandwich (instead of hamburger).

Too bad all those suggestions cost more than hamburger! Those lean cuts of meat contain just slightly more fat than skinless chicken breast — and way less fat than dark chicken meat!

Taste Fat has a lot of taste. Protein has no taste. When you eat beef, the "taste" you enjoy comes from the hidden fat, not the protein.

The more fat, the more taste. The lowest-fat common meat (skinless turkey breast) is also the least tasty. Shrimp and eggs, which are high in cholesterol and protein but low in fat, are also rather tasteless — unless you fry them in butter or some other fat.

Use spices To eat healthily with taste, reduce the fat but add taste back in by using spices. The easiest spice for American kids to accept is black pepper; as you grow up, graduate to red peppers and other spices.

If you accidentally eat too much hot, spicy pepper and want to clear the spice from your mouth, drink milk, because **casein** (milk's main protein) binds to the **capsaicin** (the burning spice in peppers) and draws it away from your tongue. Milk removes spice; water does not.

Another popular "spice," to wake up tasteless food, is lemon. It's the secret ingredient in many packaged foods. If you can't afford real lemons, try bottled lemon juice or orange concentrate or vinegar.

Switch fats If you want to eat fat safely, switch to unsaturated fats (fish and liquid vegetable oils).

Among fish, nutritionists give salmon the highest praise, because it's very high in omega-3.

Switch milk Whole milk contains 3½ % fat. Although "3½" sounds small, it isn't: milk is mostly water; of the non-water part of the milk, fat plays a big role.

Use powdered milk I've gotten used to skim milk and like it. If you haven't adjusted to skim milk yet and still think that skim milk tastes too thin, thicken it by stirring in some powdered milk (which is dried skim milk). If you stir in *lots* of powdered milk, you can make the concoction taste as thick as a milkshake!

The dairy industry tried selling that concoction (which tastes better than skim milk and also contains more calcium & protein) but had to stop when Dan Rather made a poor news judgment: he ran a story complaining that the dairy industry had "altered" the milk. Dan, you ass, it was altered to make it healthier, and it was labeled as such, so why did you have to whine? Maybe you just wanted the labeling to be clearer?

Trans fat

Another kind of fat is called **trans fat**. It's a man-made unhealthy menace, created artificially when manufacturers **hydrogenate** (add hydrogen to liquid oils, to make them more solid and stable, to produce packaged food that has a longer shelf life without turning rancid). Such food is called **partially hydrogenated**, since it's never hydrogenated fully.

Trans fat is in partially hydrogenated food such as margarine, pudding, crackers, cookies, potato chips, and fast-food restaurant's deep fryers (to produce French fries and fried fish). Hydrogenating makes the fat become more saturated and undergo other changes, making the fat less healthy.

Recently, researchers have discovered that trans fat (such as margarine) is even worse for you than fully saturated fat (such as butter). Fully saturated fat does two bad things: it increases your cholesterol and LDL. Trans fat is even worse because it does those two bad things plus a third: it lowers your HDL. Because of that research, the federal government now requires all packaged food to have labels showing the trans-fat content, New York City has passed a law preventing restaurants from using trans fat after July 2008, and most restaurant chains are in the process of abolishing trans fat from their food (so they can keep outlets in New York City). Unfortunately, many restaurants are replacing trans fat with saturated fat, which is just *slightly* healthier.

Lipitor

Lipitor is a pill you can buy. It's great: it reduces cholesterol, reduces LDL, and raises HDL.

It's manufactured by **Pfizer** (a drug company). "Lipitor" is the brand name; its technical chemical name is **atorvastatin**. Other "**statin**" pills made by competitors work similarly.

Blood test If you take Lipitor (or a similar statin pill), you must get a blood test every few months, to make sure the drug isn't damaging your liver and muscles. To make sure you get that test, the government requires you to get a doctor's prescription to buy the drug.

Cut in half Lipitor is expensive. Since a 20-milligram pill costs just *slightly* more than a 10-milligram pill, you can save money by having your doctor prescribe 20-milligram pills and cut them in half. (Warning: though that trick works fine with simple pills, such as Lipitor, never use that trick on time-release pills, since cutting a time-release pill would wreck the timing. If you want to use that trick, buy a **pill cutter**, to cut the pill in half accurately and easily.)

Grapefruit juice If you take grapefruit juice at the same time as Lipitor, the Lipitor will work more strongly. How much more strongly? That depends on the particular grapefruit, the Lipitor dosage, and the timing between them. Since grapefruit stays in your digestive system for 24 hours, the interaction can be big even if you eat the grapefruit many hours before taking the Lipitor. Since the amount of interaction is unpredictable and dangerous (you don't want to overdose), doctors recommend you avoid grapefruit juice during weeks you're taking Lipitor. Lipitor is finally shipping with warning labels saying "no grapefruit juice!"

Canada Lipitor costs much less in Canada than in the US, but Lipitor's manufacturer (Pfizer) has been refusing to sell Lipitor to Canadian pharmacies that try to resell to the US.

How to measure protein

According to physics, heating a solid typically makes it melt. For example, if you heat ice, you get water; if you heat a chocolate bar, you get syrupy goo; if you heat the fat that's on meat, the fat melts.

But if you cook an egg, the egg does *not* get softer: it hardens! So does a chicken breast. That's because an egg and a chicken breast contain lots of protein. **When you heat protein, it hardens.**

That's how to tell how much protein food contains: cook the food and see if it gets harder.

Fiber

Fiber can come in two forms: **soluble** or **insoluble**.

Soluble fiber

Fiber that dissolves in water is called **soluble** fiber. It's good because reduces your blood's total cholesterol and LDL.

Here's how it accomplishes that:

When the soluble fiber you eat reaches your intestines, it binds with bile acids (which were produced by the liver) and makes you shit the bile acids out. Then the liver replenishes those bile acids by stealing cholesterol from the blood (and mainly from LDL) and converting all that cholesterol to bile.

So soluble fiber helps prevent heart disease. It also helps control blood sugar and diabetes.

Soluble fiber is in beans, chick-peas, lentils, oats, barley, brown rice, psyllium, apples, citrus fruits (especially grapefruit), berries (especially raspberries and blueberries), apricots, prunes, carrots, cabbage, potato skins, sweet potatoes, and Brussels sprouts. Though fiber's in the fruits I mentioned, it's not in their juices, so make sure you eat the whole fruits.

Insoluble fiber

Fiber that does not dissolve in water is called **insoluble** fiber. This kind of fiber is good because it helps prevent constipation and might also reduce **colorectal cancer** (cancer of the colon or rectum), though the connection to colorectal cancer hasn't been adequately proved yet.

Insoluble fiber is in wheat bran. It's also in "whole wheat," since whole wheat includes the bran. It's also in other whole grains.

Warning:

Though whole wheat looks brown, some brown wheat breads contain little or no *whole* wheat. Make sure the bread's nutrition label lists the first, main ingredient as being *whole* wheat (or wheat bran).

Feel full

Both types of fiber help make you "feel full," so you eat less food and consume fewer calories and fats. They help you lose weight.

Aspirin

When an artery wall gets damaged, your body tries to fix it. Unfortunately, the "fix" is often worse than the disease, since the "fix" consists of sending more blood platelets to the damaged wall. Those blood platelets can clump together, form a clot that blocks the artery, and create a heart attack.

Aspirin stops that process. Many doctors recommend this:

On the 1st and 15th day of the month, take an adult-size aspirin.

On the other days of the month, take a baby-size aspirin (which is ¼ the size of an adult aspirin).

Unfortunately, since aspirin prevents the body from healing itself, aspirin causes several problems:

Aspirin increases the chance that your stomach and intestines will bleed. **Enteric-coated aspirin** reduces that bleeding slightly but not enough.

Aspirin makes your stomach and intestines less effective at protecting you from bad things you ate.

Aspirin makes you more likely to have a **brain hemorrhage** (brain bleeding, a kind of stroke).

If you get cut (by nicking your finger or by shaving or by having surgery), aspirin will prevent the wound from clotting and healing quickly. In the case of surgery, you might even bleed to death. That's the fastest way to scare a surgeon: say "I just took some aspirin."

If you have the flu, aspirin will make you feel temporarily better (by lowering your temperature) but also prevent your body from fighting the flu.

Because of those problems, taking aspirin doesn't necessarily help you live longer: it just lets you die differently. As one doctor said, "It's weighting game."

Get thin

The main thing that average American can do to improve health is: get thin!

How fat are you?

The government recommends your waist be no more than 35 inches if female, 40 inches if male. (If you're very short, for example because you're very young, your waist should be a lot smaller than that.)

When measuring your waist, don't cheat! Measure straight around; don't dip to avoid the bulge.

Your waist size is more important than your weight, because fat in your belly is more destructive than fat in your legs. Fat in your legs tends to stay there and not bother the rest of your body, but fat in your belly area is more active, closer to your organs (especially your liver), and enters your bloodstream more easily.

Why does the average woman live longer than the average man? Probably because the average woman is thinner (and engages in fewer dangerous activities, such as the military and other "dare you" games & occupations).

Exercise

According to Einstein's E=MC^2, even an atomic-bomb-size blast consumes just a small amount of matter. So even the most vigorous exercise doesn't directly reduce weight.

To reduce weight, your body must excrete more matter than it consumes; so to lose weight, you must eat & drink less than you shit, piss, and sweat.

How exercise helps
Although exercise doesn't make you lose weight directly, it makes you lose weight indirectly — because exercise makes you sweat, piss, and shit more without making you want to eat and drink much more.

Although exercise won't change your weight much, it will make your weight be better proportioned: you'll have a bigger percentage of muscle and a smaller percentage of fat. Your arms and legs will bulge with muscles and your belly will shrink. Moreover, exercise will raise your HDL (which is good). Better yet, exercise will burn off any excess sugar in your blood. By getting rid of that extra sugar, exercise helps you avoid or control diabetes.

Exercising removes water from your body (via sweat and piss), but "removing water" is not your goal: you goal is to remove belly fat. Sip a little water while exercising — and before and after — to avoid dehydrating, because a dehydrated body has trouble controlling its own temperature and accidentally wrecks itself.

Here are other ways that exercise helps you lose weight:

> While you exercise you're not eating. Better to exercise than to sit on your couch watching TV and munching potato chips.
>
> While you exercise, you tend to feel good about yourself; you're not depressed. Depressed people want to eat junk food.

Kinds of exercise
Try walking (because it's easy, pleasant, and exercises your bottom half), push ups (because they exercise your top half), and swimming (because it exercises your whole body and is fun).

You don't need to do a marathon. Three short walks per day help your health just as much as one long walk. Walking a mile helps your health nearly as much as running a mile, though running has the advantage of taking less time, so you can get on with the rest of your life. "A mile per day" is the minimum amount necessary to make a noticeable difference in your health; "a mile and a half" is even better.

Any kind of exercise is better than nothing. Some people find "gardening" a pleasant form of exercise. The dare-to-be-different crowd gets exercise by taking the stairs instead of "escalators and elevators" and by parking in the farthest parking spot instead of the closest — though "walking through parking lots" isn't the most scenic way to get exercise.

Modern society discourages exercise
The percentage of Americans who are overweight has been increasing, because modern American society discourages exercise.

In the old days, kids played sports in the neighborhood's yards, streets, and parks. Now kids play videogames instead, which exercise just the fingers.

In the old days, people visited the homes of friends. Now people communicate with friends by phone and e-mail instead — or watch pseudo-friends (such as Oprah) on TV.

In the old days, people walked from room to room in office buildings. Now people stay put and just e-mail or instant-message each other.

In the old days, moms prepared their meals from scratch by scurrying around the kitchen, finding ingredients to chop, combine, stir, cook, and stir again. Now people just shove a prepackaged meal into the microwave oven instead.

Where do you live?
People who work on farms and ranches get *lots* of exercise.

People who live in big cities get *moderate* exercise. They walk several blocks to get to stores, bus stops, and occasionally subway stations.

But people who live in suburbs typically get *hardly any* exercise at all: they just walk to their cars, which are parked next to their houses and stores. When you're in a car, you have the illusion of being active ("Whee! Look how fast I'm going!"), but you're not moving your legs: you're sitting still, like a vegetable, and soon you'll look like one. If you try to "get healthy" by avoiding the car and walking instead, you discover that walking in the suburbs is unpleasant, for two reasons:

> the stores are too far apart, and too far from your house, to reach reasonably
>
> most suburban towns have stopped creating sidewalks (since "hardly anybody walks on them anymore"), so you must walk in the street (and hope a car doesn't hit you) or walk on your neighbor's lawn (and hope your neighbor doesn't hit you)

That's why the average suburban resident is fatter than the average city resident.

Low-income people tend to buy cheap junk food (which is fattening), because fresh vegetables cost more (and take longer to prepare) and because low-income people are often inadequately educated about nutrition. The fattest Americans the ones who live near these low-income cities: New Orleans and Detroit. The thinnest Americans are the ones who live near Denver (because Denverites like to enjoy their beautiful outdoor scenery by jumping into it: they like to ski, climb mountains, canoe, and ride bicycles).

Calories

To lose weight safely, consume fewer calories. Each gram of fat you eat provides 9 calories, whereas each gram of protein or carbohydrate provides just 4 calories; so the main way to consume fewer calories is to consume less fat.

Make sure you consume fewer saturated fats. But even the best fats, the "unsaturated fats," still provide 9 calories per gram, so eat fewer unsaturated fats too!

Most nutritionists make these recommendations:

> Get most of your calories from carbohydrates.
> Get about 12% of your calories from protein.
> Get less than 10% of your calories from saturated fat.
>
> Get less than 30% of your calories from fat. (Make most of that fat be unsaturated. Eat little or no trans fat. Get less than 10% of your calories from saturated fat.)

Portion size

Modern society encourages you to overeat. If you buy a bigger bag of food — or Supersize your meal — or visit an all-you-can-eat buffet — you pay less per pound. Especially if your income is low, you'll be tempted to make use of those bargains, pig out, and become a blimp.

Food has gotten bigger. Today's hamburgers, pizzas, bagels, muffins, and soft drinks are many times bigger than the original versions that were invented years ago.

When you read a nutrition label, and it brags about how a "serving" contains not so many calories (and not so much fat or salt), notice how many "servings" are in the package. The government's definition of a "serving" seems to be "how much a little old lady would eat if she weren't hungry and didn't like the food": it's typically just 3 or 4 ounces for food (6 or 8 ounces for a drink).

For example, the typical muffin is big enough to contain 2 "servings"; so if you eat the whole muffin, you'll ingest twice as many calories, twice as much fat, and twice as much salt as the label says a "serving" contains. The typical small can of ready-to-cook food contains 2 servings; the typical medium-size can of ready-to-cook food contains 3½ servings; the typical small box of frozen food contains 2 servings.

So when you're looking at a nutrition label, be sure to notice how many "servings" it says are in the entire product: multiply all the numbers by that factor, if you're planning to eat the whole thing!

Fat-free

Many foods are advertised as being "fat-free," but most of them still contain lots of sugar. Since plain sugar provides calories without providing good nutrients, plain sugar is called **empty calories** and is bad for you. Avoid it. These other simple sugars are also empty calories and should be avoided: **corn syrup** (which comes from corn), **fructose** (which comes from fruit), and **honey**.

Don't binge

To lose weight, the main trick is: don't binge. Don't eat large portions of anything. Here's why:

Your body needs just tiny quantities of most vitamins and minerals. Eating bigger quantities of them doesn't help. In fact, some vitamins and minerals become *toxic* if you take an overdose.

Your body can tolerate small quantities of toxins, but bigger quantities are dangerous.

No single food has all the kinds of vitamins and minerals you need, so eat a variety of foods, a little of each.

Nutritionists have discovered many hundreds of vitamins, minerals, and other helpful substances in plants. Though a vitamin pill can be a useful supplement, no single pill provides the incredibly wide variety of helpful chemicals that a well-balanced diet provides.

Metabolic syndrome

Doctors say you have the **metabolic syndrome** (which is also called the **inactivity syndrome**, the **insulin-resistance syndrome**, and **syndrome X**) if you have at least 3 of these 5 warning signs of inactivity:

your waist is too big (over 35 inches for a woman, 40 inches for a man)
your HDL is too low (under 50 mg/dL for a woman, 40 for a man)
your blood contains too much sugar (fasting glucose level over 100 mg/dL)
your blood contains too many triglycerides (over 150 mg/dL)
your blood pressure is too high (over 130/85 millimeters)

(If you have *exactly* those numbers, you're borderline, and doctors argue about whether you "have the syndrome" yet.)

The best way to avoid or reduce the metabolic syndrome is to get more exercise. Improving your diet can also help. (Your genetics play a role too but can't be fixed by scientists yet.)

Diabetes

If you eat a huge meal, your pancreas will have trouble producing enough insulin to digest all those sugars and starches at once. Instead, eat several smaller meals (or small healthy snacks), spaced throughout the day.

If you have **diabetes** (a pancreas unable to produce enough useful insulin), eating smaller meals is necessary. If you don't have diabetes yet, eating smaller meals is still desirable — because if you overwork your pancreas often, it will gradually get tired, quit working some year, and you'll have diabetes then and forevermore.

Once you have diabetes, you can control it (by making sure you always eat small meals) but never cure it.

Nutritionists predict that ⅓ of all Americans will get diabetes before death. The best way to prevent diabetes is to eat small meals, get exercise, and lose weight.

When you eat more sugars and starch than your pancreas can handle, the excess stays in your blood, makes your blood vessels sticky, and wrecks the blood vessels in your eyes (leading to blindness), feet (leading to numbness, unnoticed cuts, infection, and eventual amputation), and kidneys (leading to kidney failure so you spend the rest of your life on a dialysis machine).

Afraid to look thin?

Unfortunately, Americans in this century are fatter than Americans were in the 1900's or 1800's or 1700's. That's because Americans get less exercise (they drive cars instead of walk, play videogames instead of real sports), eat more junk food (McDonald's instead of Mom's cooking), and many other reasons that are obvious. But here's a reason that's not so obvious: some people (especially inner-city blacks) are afraid to look thin, because they're afraid that if they look thin, they'll look like they have AIDS, and their friends will fear them and they won't get dates.

Such people are misinformed and need to be reminded that it's better to be a toothpick than a blimp.

Semi-vegetarian

Nutritionists recommend that you be semi-vegetarian: make ¾ of your dinner plate be filled with plants (vegetables, fruit, and high-fiber grains), and just ¼ of your plate come from animals (fish, meat, and dairy). That will give you a wide variety of nutrients and less fat.

Thinning diets

Many people have invented fad diets that claim crazy eating can make you thin. Each fad diet has a "catch":

Some of those diets let you eat whatever you wish but in small quantities. Other diets let you eat as much as you wish but only of certain foods.

Most fad diets make you lose weight by being so unappetizing that you want to eat less.

Some diets let you lose 5 or 10 pounds during the first two weeks, but that's just from losing water, not fat. The next two weeks are harder.

Most diets also tell you to get more exercise. If you claim that the diet "didn't work," the diet vendors reply, "You can't sue us, since you didn't follow our exercise plan."

Nutritionists agree that the best way to get thin is to eat normally but with less saturated fat, smaller portions, and more variety.

The trick is to feel full while consuming fewer calories. Since calories come from "fat, protein, and carbohydrates," eat food containing mainly water & fiber instead.

Some fad diets, such as the **Atkins Diet**, made the mistake of telling you to avoid all carbohydrates and eat fats instead. Here's the truth:

The carbohydrates in vegetables and high-fiber grains are fine for a healthy diet; just avoid refined grains (such as white bread, white pasta, and white rice).

Unsaturated fats are okay in moderation, but avoid saturated fats.

The Atkins diet was later modified to say that certain carbohydrates are okay (and don't count in "net carbs"), but Atkins advice to eat lots of fat is totally wrong. Nutritionists agree that of all the fad diets, the **Atkins Diet** is the unhealthiest and the **South Beach Diet** is the healthiest, but even the South Beach Diet is slightly off-kilter.

Just get exercise, eat a *variety* of food (especially vegetables), and avoid binging (especially on fats, cakes, and sweets). Then you'll be fine!

Soup Since soup contains mainly water, it makes you feel full without adding many calories. (Just make sure it's not a "cream" soup, since cream is high in calories.)

Nutritionists have discovered a bizarre fact about soup: water in soup makes you feel fuller than water in a glass, even though it's the same water. If you're served chicken and a glass of water, you'll feel less full than if the water was dumped on the chicken to become soup. When the water is dumped on the chicken to make soup, your eye says "that's a lot of soup!" and you feel full just looking at it!

Just beware of salt: many canned soups contain too much salt.

Fruit Fresh fruit is like soup: it contains mainly water and makes you feel full without adding many calories.

If you eat 30 raisins (dried grapes) while drinking water, you'll still feel hungry; but if you eat 30 fresh grapes instead, you'll feel full, even though the ingredients are the same.

Fruit also contains fiber and lots of nutrients.

Bran cereal For breakfast, try eating bran cereal. Since it's high in fiber, it makes you feel full without adding many calories. Nutritionists have discovered that people who eat a high-fiber breakfast still feel full, many hours later, whereas people who eat a low-fiber breakfast feel hungry again 2 hours later.

Though bran cereal is good for you, bran muffins are bad, since bran muffins usually include lots of fats added to the bran.

Potato Nutritionists have discovered that the best vegetable for making you "feel full without many calories" is potato.

Just make sure you include the skin (to get its nutrition), cut out any tubers sprouting out (because they're poisonous), and avoid fatty toppings (such as butter or sour cream). If possible, bake the potato (instead of frying it) or make a potato soup.

Watermelon Another obvious candidate for "full with minimal calories" is watermelon. It contains lots of water and — like all fruits — some fiber.

Black Irish diet If you want to try a fad diet, try mine: it consists of eating mainly potatoes and watermelons. If you wish, try that diet for a week (supplemented by vitamin pills and a few other vegetables to keep you balanced). I call it the **Black Irish diet**, because it combines the food loved by stereotypical blacks (watermelon) with the food loved by stereotypical Irishmen (potatoes). Here's why the diet is good:

Of all vegetables, potatoes are the best at making you feel full on few calories.

Potatoes make you feel you've eaten heartily.
Watermelon makes you feel your eating was fun.

Potatoes and watermelon are both healthy foods.
Potatoes and watermelon are both cheap. This is the cheapest diet you can get!

Confession

So after all that preaching, am I a good example? Am I thin? Not yet. I guess I'd better start taking my own advice!

Micronutrients

Nutrients are what you must eat or drink to survive.

To be healthy, you need big quantities of five kinds of nutrients: water, carbohydrate, protein, fat, and fiber. (Most Americans eat too much fat, not enough carbohydrate & fiber.) The quantities are measured in "grams" per serving.

You also need smaller quantities of other nutrients, called **micronutrients**, measured in "milligrams" or "micrograms" per serving. The most important micronutrients fall into two categories: **vitamins** (whose chemical formulas include carbon) and **minerals** (whose chemical formulas do not include carbon).

Vitamins

You need 13 vitamins:

Vitamin	Where to get a lot of it
vitamin A	milk, egg yolks, beef&chicken livers
vitamin D	sunlight, salmon, fortified milk, enriched flour&cereal&bread
vitamin E	corn&soybean&canola&sunflower oil, kale, sweet potatoes
vitamin K	spinach, lettuce, watercress, broccoli, Brussels sprouts, soybean oil
vitamin C (ascorbic acid)	peppers, currants, broccoli, Brussels sprouts, oranges, papaya, cranberries
vitamin B_1 (thiamine)	pork loin, whole grains, enriched flour&rice, dried beans, nuts, seeds
vitamin B_2 (riboflavin)	beef liver, milk, eggs, enriched flour&cereal
vitamin B_3 (niacin)	chicken&turkey breast, tuna, swordfish, enriched flour&rice, peas, corn tortillas
vitamin B_5 (pantothenic acid)	liver, fish, chicken&turkey, whole grains, yogurt, beans, lentils, peas
vitamin B_6 (pyridoxine)	tuna, potatoes, bananas, chick-peas, prunes, chicken breasts, avocados
vitamin B_9 (folate)	chicken livers, asparagus, beans, chick-peas, lentils, oranges, fortified cereal
vitamin B_{12} (cobalamin)	clams, chicken livers, tuna, sardines, salmon, lamb, milk
vitamin B_H (biotin)	corn, soybeans, egg yolks, liver, cauliflower, peanuts, mushrooms, yeast

Vitamins A, D, E, and K are **fat-soluble**: your body stores them for a long time in your fat tissue and in your liver.

Vitamin C and the B vitamins are **water-soluble**. Since your body can't store them long (except for B_{12}), you must eat them frequently. When cooking them, don't boil them long, since they'll escape from the food into boiling water instead of helping your body. Instead of boiling them, try steaming them or using your microwave.

Here are peculiarities:

Biotin was called **vitamin H** until researchers later discovered biotin's a kind of B vitamin.

Though **beef&chicken livers** contain many vitamins, they also contain cholesterol and many toxins. Although **swordfish** contains vitamin B_3, it also contains a toxin (mercury).

If you eat a **well-balanced diet**, you'll get enough of all those vitamins except perhaps C & E. Some nutritionists recommend taking pills for vitamins C & E, but others disagree.

Since **vitamin C** leaves the body in 12 hours, eating 2 small doses per day is better than 1 big dose. Vitamin C does not prevent colds, but 1000 mg per day can make existing colds end 1 day faster and be 20% milder.

Vitamin B_9 is called **folate** or **folacin** or **folic acid**. It prevents birth defects. If you're pregnant (or might be in 2 months), make *sure* you get enough vitamin B_9 (by eating good foods or taking a pill). The US government requires the food industry to add vitamin B_9 to all white flour (and therefore all white bread and white pasta); that's one of the few advantages of white bread over whole wheat: whole-wheat bread does *not* contain folate.

Vitamin B_3 is called **niacin** or **nicotinic acid**. Milk and eggs contain little B_3 but lots of **tryptophan**, which turns into B_3 when digested. The vitamin B_3 in corn is indigestible unless the corn is mixed with lime, as in a corn tortilla.

Minerals

In your body, the 7 main minerals (the **macrominerals**) are sodium, chlorine, sulfur, calcium, potassium, phosphorus, and magnesium. The average American eats too much sodium (which is in salt and preservatives) and an okay amount of chlorine & sulfur but should eat more of the other 4:

Mineral	Where to get a lot of it
calcium	milk, yogurt, cheese, canned sardines&salmon, fortified orange juice, fortified oatmeal
potassium	avocados, bananas, cantaloupes, oranges, tomatoes, potato skins, beans, yogurt, tuna
phosphorus	meat, chicken, turkey, seafood, milk, seeds
magnesium	whole grains, nuts, seeds, tofu, chocolate, spinach, beans, avocados, halibut

The typical multivitamin/mineral pill does *not* contain a full day's supply of those macrominerals. Be especially careful about calcium:

The average American doesn't eat enough calcium. The average American man should eat more calcium; the average American woman should eat *much* more calcium. Calcium builds strong bones and reduces a woman's PMS difficulties. Elderly people who have weak bones (because of many years of calcium deficiency) break their bones when they fall, and the resulting operations and disabilities are life-threatening. Eat more calcium foods, or buy a calcium pill, or buy Tums (which contains lots of calcium, though the antacids in Tums reduce the calcium's effectiveness). Vitamins D and B₃ help the body digest calcium, so make sure you eat those vitamins also.

Your body also needs smaller quantities of 15 other minerals (called **trace minerals**). The most important trace minerals are boron, chromium, copper, iodine, iron, manganese, molybdenum, selenium, and zinc.

Your body also contains about 40 other minerals that are not necessary.

Sodium's danger

Sodium is found mainly in salt. (The technical chemical name for "table salt" is **sodium chloride**, whose chemical symbol is NaCl.) Sodium is also found in preservatives (such as **sodium nitrite** and **sodium nitrate**).

Sodium raises the blood pressure in many people — though some super-healthy people who don't have blood problems yet are unaffected by sodium. There's no simple test for telling who's sodium-sensitive, so the general advice is for most people to reduce sodium. Reducing sodium is not as important as reducing fat but still helps.

Here's how to reduce sodium….

Instead of putting salt onto your food, try other spices instead (such as black pepper or crushed red pepper or fresh red peppers) or lemon juice (which is the secret healthy ingredient that wakes up any boring food).

Beware of prepackaged frozen dinners: most are high in salt, to make the dinners have a longer shelf life. Beware of canned soups and canned chili: they're high in salt also. Canned vegetables are high in salt unless you manage to get no-salt-added versions. Instead of canned beans (which are always high in salt), buy dried beans: they cost less and have no salt added but require you to rinse then soak then rinse again.

Eat less meat. Most meat is high in sodium, especially if the meat is sold as "hot dogs" or "prepackaged sliced meat," even if labeled "turkey."

Beware of tomato sauce and its variants (such as ketchup, spaghetti sauce, tomato juice, and V-8 vegetable juice): they're extremely high in salt (even though they don't taste salty), unless you buy no-salt-added versions.

Potassium chloride "Low-sodium" versions of some products (such as V-8) make that claim because they replace part of the sodium chloride (table salt) with **potassium chloride**, which is also a white "salt" but contains no sodium. Unfortunately, potassium chloride doesn't taste good (it tastes less "salty" and is bitter).

Eating potassium chloride is usually healthy, since the potassium in it is a useful mineral that helps your heart beat. But be careful: overdosing on potassium chloride will *stop* your heart. To kill prisoners on death row, the executioner injects a high dose of potassium chloride (after injecting other chemicals to make the killings seem less gruesome).

Antioxidants

When your body uses oxygen, some of the oxygen turns into an unstable, dangerous form called a **free radical**. Free radicals occur faster if there's a lot of pollution (or cigarette smoke, alcohol, X-rays, sunlight's ultraviolet rays, or heat). Free radicals interfere with cell activities, so the cells get damaged, age faster, and have a harder time warding off cancer and heart disease.

To get rid of that dangerous free-radical oxygen, your body uses **antioxidants**. Your body makes its own antioxidants, but you can help your body by eating extra antioxidants. The most popular ones to eat are vitamin C, vitamin E, selenium (a mineral), and **carotenoids** (yellow, orange, or red pigments in fruits and vegetables).

Although carotenoids are yellow, orange, or red pigments, they can hide in vegetables that are darker (purple or dark green): those darker colors hide the carotenoid molecules from your eyes. Vegetables that are light green contain hardly any carotenoids.

Here are the most popular carotenoids:

Carotenoid	Where to get a lot of it
alpha carotene	carrots, pumpkins, yellow peppers
beta carotene	carrots, sweet potatoes, squash, spinach, kale, cantaloupes, apricots, mangoes
beta cryptoxanthin	tangerines, oranges, peaches, papayas, mangoes
lycopene	tomatoes, watermelons, pink grapefruits, guava
lutein	kale, red peppers, spinach, endive, broccoli, romaine lettuce

Your body turns some carotenoids into vitamin A, but other carotenoids stay in their original state and provide extra benefits.

Although most fruits & vegetables are most nutritious when eaten raw, carrots & tomatoes are different: **carrots & tomatoes are more nutritious if cooked** than if eaten raw, because you need cooking to break their tough cells walls (so you can digest the carrot's beta carotene and the tomato's lycopene). Unfortunately, cooked tomato sauce typically contain lots of salt (unless you order the no-salt version).

Since pizza includes cooked tomato sauce, it's a good source of lycopene. The pizza industry likes to brag about that. Unfortunately, pizza can be high in salt (from the sauce), calories (from the breading), and saturated fat (from the cheese and any meat toppings). Go ahead, eat some pizza, but don't overdo it!

Other micronutrients

Researchers keep discovering other micronutrients in fruits and vegetables. To get all their benefits, eat a wide variety of fruits and vegetables.

The newest exciting research concerns grapes. The skin of a grape contains **resveratrol** (a chemical that helps the grape fight against pests). If you eat that chemical, it will help you fight cancer, heart disease, and oxidation. Grapes grown in the north produce more of that chemical than grapes grown in the south, since northern grapes need it to fight against their tough environment. The "food" that contains the most resveratrol is "red wine made from northern grapes," since red wine's manufacturing process uses skins more than white wine's process, and since the alcoholic fermenting helps bring out the resveratrol. The French love of red wine is the chemical reason why French people have fewer heart attacks than Americans, even though French foods come in heavy sauces. (But I suspect that the main reasons why French people have fewer heart attacks are: the French binge less, eat more vegetables, eat less junk food, get more exercise, and have less stress.) Some resveratrol is also in peanuts.

Toxins

Avoid **cigarettes**, **illegal drugs** (such as marijuana, heroin, cocaine, and ecstasy), **excessive alcohol**, and **tanning**. They're all very toxic: they wreck your body in many ways.

Alcohol

Drinking a little alcohol can be good in two ways: it raises HDL and also **tissue-type plasminogen activator** (**T-PA**, which helps break up blood clots). But drinking alcohol can also harm your brain, liver, and other organs and be addictive, so doctors give these warnings:

> Don't drink alcohol if you're pregnant or going to drive or going to need unimpaired judgment & thought.
>
> Don't have more than 1 drink per day if you're a woman, 2 drinks if a man. (A "drink" means 12 ounces of beer, 5 oz. of wine, or 1½ oz. of 80-proof spirits.) If you're very young or very small, drink even less — or don't drink at all.
>
> Don't start drinking alcohol if you've never drunk before, since you might have trouble learning how to control your drinking.

Liver

If an animal eats toxins, the animal's liver tries to filter those toxins out of the blood. Many of those toxins stay in the liver. Don't eat the liver!

Mercury

Mercury's a toxin that impairs your brain and nervous system: it makes you stupid and nervous. (During the 1800's, people who made hats used mercury, became crazy, were called "mad hatters," and formed the basis for Alice in Wonderland's Mad Hatter Tea Party.)

Many industrial factories spit out mercury, which eventually winds up in water and infects aquatic plants. When small fish eat those plants, the small fish's flesh gets infected. When bigger fish eat those small fish, the big fish's flesh gets even more infected, and contains even more mercury per pound of flesh, because the mercury stay in the body while other substances are excreted. The bigger the fish, the more mercury per pound.

**Big fish** Don't eat big fish (such as shark, swordfish, and mackerel): their flesh is all high in mercury. The US government especially warns pregnant women not to eat big fish.

**Tuna** Since tuna can grow _nearly_ as big as those other fish, nutritionists get nervous about tuna also. When buying canned tuna, you can choose packaging ("packed in water" contains less fat than "packed in oil") and what kind of fish was killed:

> **Solid white** tuna is a slab of flesh cut from **albacore** (big tuna). It contains a lot of mercury.
>
> **Chunk light** tuna is combined from small tuna. It looks darker than solid white. It costs half as much as solid white. It contains a third as much mercury per pound as solid white.

Pesticides

On farms, most fruits are sprayed with pesticides. Rinse the fruit to remove most of the pesticides. Gentle scrubbing helps further. You don't have to peel the fruit. In fact, the best fruit nutrients are in the peel!

But here are two exceptions:

> You must peel fruit when you visit third-world countries where farmers & vendors use unsanitary handling.
>
> If you want to make your own orange marmalade from orange peel, don't use ordinary oranges: the pesticides on orange peel are too strong to rinse or rub off. You must use unsprayed oranges instead.

Nitrite

Sodium nitrite (NaNO$_2$) and **sodium nitrate (NaNO$_3$)** are preservatives that are added to meat (especially hot dogs) and fish to improve color (make pork look pink instead of white) and prevent spoilage. They're preservatives.

Sodium nitrite might cause cancer. But Consumer Reports concluded the amount of sodium nitrite added to processed meats is too little to worry about, since it accounts for just 5% of the sodium nitrite in an American's body: the remaining 95% comes as a byproduct of eating healthy natural foods such as broccoli.

On the other hand, sodium nitrite and sodium nitrate can raise your blood pressure, since they both contain sodium.

Salt & sugar

Salt and sugar are preservatives. Dumping them into food prevents the food from getting moldy soon, because molds and bacteria can't eat so much salt & sugar. Neither can you! Salt & sugar kill not just bacteria but also you! Eat less salt and sugar and you'll live longer.

Burning

Burnt food causes cancer. For example, barbecued meat (with grilled char marks) causes cancer. So do smoked meat, toasted bread, and toasted cereal. One of the many reasons why cigarettes cause cancer is that they're burnt.

To prevent barbecued food from causing so much cancer, barbecue less (by microwaving before you barbecue) and push the coals and fat to the sides (to prevent the fat from dripping onto the coals and then shoot hissing flames and smoke back up to the meat).

Refrigeration

Keep most foods refrigerated or frozen. In a typical American refrigerator (which has the freezer on top), the warmest spots are at the far bottom and in the door, so don't store fish and meat there: the warmer spots are just for fruits, vegetables, and other items that can bear to be closer to room temperature. (Exception: health departments require restaurants to store raw meat below other foods, to make sure the raw meat's juice doesn't drip onto other foods.)

If food gets warm, bacteria and mold start growing there. You can't solve that problem by just cooking the food afterwards: though cooking kills bacteria and mold, it doesn't take away the toxins that the bacteria and mold already squirted into the food. You'll still get sick.

When cutting out mold, cut a full inch around the visible mold, since the surrounding area has been infected even if your eyes don't see the mold there yet.

Strawberries spoil fast, so eat them soon after you buy them.

Bananas spoil even faster and are the hardest fruit to handle. In exactly one week, bananas turn from green to yellow to brown. The trick is to make the bananas ripen to yellow fast (by putting them in a paper bag), then eat them. Once you refrigerate bananas, they won't properly ripen further (though they'll get moldy), so don't refrigerate bananas until they've turned yellow. If you freeze bananas (to form a frozen treat), their skins will continue to brown but their insides will stay unchanged; so remove the skins before freezing, to prevent the skins from becoming disgusting to remove.

Fish is delicate: the bacteria in fish (and shellfish) can survive at low temperatures. So don't keep fish in the refrigerator or freezer long: eat the fish soon. When serving fish, serve it hot, as soon as it finishes cooking: don't let it sit. (If you let fish sit, you'll raise its bacteria count and also wreck the taste.)

Make sure all fish and shellfish is cooked. Don't eat raw shellfish (such as "clams on the half shell"): it's too dangerous and barely legal.

Best foods

Taking all those factors into account, nutritionists say the 2 best foods are **broccoli** and **kale**, because they contain many good nutrients (and few calories, fats, and toxins).

Here's a list of the 20 best foods, grouped by category:

Category	Best foods
green vegetables	broccoli, spinach, kale
orange vegetables	carrots, pumpkins, sweet potatoes
red vegetable	red bell peppers
dried vegetables for soup	lentils, dried beans
fruit	oranges, cantaloupes, strawberries, mangos
meat	skinless chicken breasts, skinless turkey breasts
fish	salmon
dairy	skim milk
grain	oatmeal, bran cereal, whole-grain bread

In that chart, when a category contains more than 1 entry, I list first the entry that's the easiest to buy in the supermarket.

You probably eat enough meat already. Concentrate on the vegetables.

Nutrition newsletters

To learn more about nutrition and keep up to date, subscribe to nutrition newsletters. These 3 are the best (because they're accurate, detailed, well balanced, easy to read, and relevant):

University of California Berkeley Wellness Letter
1 year (12 issues): $28 officially, $24 for first year
386-447-6328 or www.berkeleywellness.com

Tufts University Health & Nutrition Letter
1 year (12 issues): $28 officially, $16 for first year
800-274-7581, 386-447-6336, or healthletter.tufts.edu

Nutrition Action Healthletter
1 year (10 issues): $24 officially, $10 for first year
202-332-9110 or www.cspinet.org/nah

Disgusting foods

Here are disgusting foods for special occasions.

Bachelor cooking

Here's the main trick of bachelor cooking: when you don't know how to cook, just heat what-the-hell-ever-it-is and dump lemon on it. Lemon wakes up even the blandest food. Food companies do it all the time: for example, it's the hidden unadvertised ingredient in most "juice blends."

Use either a fresh lemon or bottled lemon juice (which is cheaper and lasts longer but tastes worse).

If you use a fresh lemon, squeeze it *before* you cut it. You'll extract more juice that way. Here's how to squeeze the not-yet-cut lemon: put it on the kitchen counter, press your palm down on it, and roll it back and forth.

Advanced techniques Here's the trick to "advanced" bachelor cooking.

Into a pot, throw whatever you want to eat. Meat, fish, or vegetables — fresh, canned, or frozen — it doesn't matter!

Cover with hot water, fresh from the tap. Drain the water. Cover with hot water again. Drain the water again. Now the food is slightly warmer.

Add some hot water again, but this time just enough to prevent the food from sticking to the bottom of the pot.

Put the pot on the stove. Cover it. Heat it. Stir occasionally to avoid sticking. After heating a few minutes, move the cover slightly and leave it ajar, so any excess steam can escape.

Exceptions For white rice, do *not* drain any water you put on it. Draining the water would remove the vitamins that white rice comes coated in.

For pasta (such as spaghetti and noodles), boil the water *before* you insert the pasta.

Emergency procedures If the resulting mess is **too wet**, make it drier by dumping **instant oatmeal** on it.

> The oatmeal flakes soak up water quickly and turn the whole dish into a kind of granola. Add the oatmeal during the last minute of your cooking, since oatmeal cooks quickly and has better texture if not overcooked. If you don't have any oatmeal, use **rice** instead, which unfortunately takes longer to cook.

If the resulting mess is **too bland**, dump **lemon juice** on it.

> If you can't afford lemon juice, use **orange juice** (which is cheaper but less intense). You can also dump **pepper** on it: dump black pepper if your stomach is weak; dump crushed red pepper or chili pepper if your stomach is stronger.

If the color is **too boring**, dump canned red **beets** (and their juice) on it.

> Beet juice is *intensely* red: it's the strongest cheap natural dye you can buy. If you add too much beet juice and the whole thing becomes too watery, add more oatmeal.

Praise your mistakes

If you make a mistake in the kitchen, pretend you made it on purpose.

If you burn the food, so it's started to turn black, brag that it's **"char grilled."** If it's very black, call it **"blackened,"** as the Cajuns do. If the vegetables at the bottom of a pot are just starting to burn, so they're turning brown and sticking to the bottom, call them **"caramelized,"** as fancy restaurants do.

Mexicans try to brag about their "refried" beans, but you can surpass Mexican English: take your leftovers, heat them again, and call them "**doubly delicious**." If you need to heat them a third time, don't apologize, just brag that the food is "**triple fired**." But if you try that too often while cooking in a restaurant, you might discover that you're "triple fired" too!

Icy pleasures

On a hot day you want to put something icy into your mouth. Unfortunately, ice cream contains cream, which in turn contains fat, which increases your weight and cholesterol. Ice milk contains less cream but more sugar, so eating it still wrecks your diet.

Instead, eat frozen fruit:

> In your supermarket, you can find frozen blueberries and frozen strawberries, without added sugar or syrup. If your supermarket is advanced, its freezer even includes cantaloupe, honeydew, peaches, grapes, and cherries — all frozen without sugar or syrup.
>
> Make sure to buy the fruit pre-frozen. If you try to freeze fresh fruit yourself by using just an ordinary freezer, the fruit will freeze too slowly and accumulate large icy crystals that mar the texture. (The only fruit you can freeze yourself is bananas.)

For a wonderful zero-calorie summer treat, suck ice cubes.

Diner slang

In diner restaurants, waitresses slinging food use slang to talk to cooks:

Slang	Meaning
fry 2, let the sun shine	fry 2 eggs, unbroken yolks
wreck 'em	scramble the eggs
burn the British	toast an English muffin
stack of Vermont	pancake stack with syrup
life preserver	doughnut
hounds on an island	hot dogs on baked beans
paint a bow-wow red	hot dog with ketchup
take it thru the garden	put lettuce on the burger
pin a rose on it	put onion slice on the burger
frog sticks	French fries
one from the Alps	Swiss cheese sandwich
Bossy in a bowl	beef stew in a bowl
shit on a shingle	chipped beef on toast
let it walk	it's for takeout
cow paste	butter
wax	American cheese
draw one in the dark	draw a cup of black coffee
a blonde	cup of coffee with cream
a blonde with sand	coffee with cream & sugar
hug one	squeeze an orange for juice
an M.D.	Dr. Pepper
nervous pudding	Jello
houseboat	banana split
throw it in the mud	add chocolate syrup

For more examples, look at page 373 of *Uncle John's 4-Ply Bathroom Reader*, republished by Barnes & Noble Books.

Sleep

Researchers have discovered surprising facts about how adults sleep.

How much sleep?

You should sleep about 7½ hours per night. Anywhere from 7 to 8 hours is good. (Sleeping less than 7 hours is okay just if you compensate by taking a nap.)

If you sleep fewer than 6 hours, you'll feel noticeably tired. Being tired hurts you in 5 ways:

> When you're tired, **your body's immune system is impaired**. You have less resistance to diseases. You're more likely to get viruses and other infections.
>
> When you're tired, you have **poor motor skills**. If you're trying to type on a keyboard — or play a piano — your speed and accuracy will improve after you've slept.
>
> When you're tired, you **can't pay attention consistently**. If you try to take a timed reaction test while you're tired, you'll react fast sometimes but at other moments you'll forget to react at all and instead stare blankly.
>
> When you're tired, you can still remember facts but have **trouble making judgments**. For example, you'll have trouble driving a car, dealing with personal relationships, and writing essays. If you're cramming for a test, be careful: pulling an "all-nighter" will help you cram extra facts into your brain but hurt your ability to write essays. If you're debating how to react to a personal situation (such as a job offer), sleep on it: your judgment will be better in the morning, after you've rested. If you're in a hospital, pray that your doctor isn't an intern who was up all night, lacks sleep, and therefore makes wrong judgments.
>
> When you're tired, your body has **difficulty using its own insulin to digest glucose sugar**. That difficulty makes you **pre-diabetic and hungry**. Your hunger increases because, when you're tired, your stomach produces too much **ghrelin** (a hormone telling the brain you're hungry), and your fat cells produce too little **leptin** (a hormone that telling the brain you're full). So though you're really just tired, those wrong hormone amounts make your confused brain think you're hungry instead of tired, so you long for food to "pep yourself up": you crave foods that are sweet (cakes, candy, and ice cream), starchy (pasta, bread, cereal, and potatoes), and salty (chips and nuts). You overeat and become obese. Doctors say to avoid snacking when you're tired (at midnight) because you tend to overeat then, and your midnight snack won't make you feel full, so you'll keep eating until you become a blimp. A good way to prevent obesity & diabetes is to go to bed early and stay there, to avoid late snacking!

Statisticians have this sad news: people who sleep fewer than 6 hours per night die sooner. So do people who **oversleep** (sleep more than 9 hours), because people oversleep just when they're ill or depressed or previously deprived of sleep.

Unfortunately, most Americans undersleep on weekdays and try to compensate by oversleeping on weekends. The average American adult sleeps just 6.8 hours per weeknight, 9 hours per weekend night. Researchers consider that pattern to be unhealthy, like binge eating. Try to get a constant amount of sleep each night.

Philosophers blame American sleeplessness on electronics. We stay up later than our ancestors because of the invention of the light bulb and its 24-hour culture: car headlights, nighttime TV, the computer, and the Internet. America is always on, round the clock — and paying for it by getting underslept (and therefore ill, using poor judgment, accident-prone, obese, and diabetic).

When you feel tired

A brain chemical called **adenosine** makes your brain feel tired, so you want to sleep.

While you sleep, the adenosine binds to phosphorus to form **adenosine triphosphate (ATP)**. After the adenosine gets used up (to make ATP), your brain no longer feels sleepy, so you wake up.

After waking up, you feel groggy for the first half hour, so don't make any judgments then! After that first half hour, you're fully functional.

While you're awake, **your body's cells get energy by burning the ATP**.

That burning makes the ATP break down into adenosine and phosphorus again. The gradual increase in adenosine and decrease in ATP makes your body gradually feel sleepy again, so you eventually feel very tired ("zonked out") by the late afternoon (between 4PM and 5:30PM). Since you're tired then, it's a good time to take a nap (if your schedule permits). Your tiredness will tempt you overeat (by breaking your diet and eating a late-afternoon snack, especially as an excuse for having worked so hard throughout the day); but you should avoid that temptation: don't eat then, just nap instead!

After 5:30PM, your eye senses the sky is darkening (even if you're "blind"). Your eye passes the "darkness" sensation to your brain, into the hypothalamus's back part, called the **suprachiasmatic nucleus (SCN)**, which reacts by outputting a hormone to keep you awake through the early evening. That hormone makes you feel rejuvenated, less tired than during your zonk-out period. The SCN's hormone level gradually increases. From 8PM to 10PM, you feel quite awake!

But at 10PM, your **pineal gland** increases its production of a hormone called **melatonin**, which quiets the SCN's output, so you start feeling sleepy again and fall asleep at 11PM (since the melatonin takes an hour to make you sleepy). You sleep 7½ hours, so you arise at 6:30AM to start another day.

That's the ideal sleep schedule for the typical American. Your own personal sleep schedule might differ, depending on how your hormones are working for you (and whether you recently got kissed, yelled at, or drunk).

Unique

Sleep's purpose is to build your ATP levels, so you'll have enough energy to function well throughout the day.

All animals sleep, even fish. (When a fish sleeps, it shuts down half its brain but uses the other half to keep swimming, so it can breathe.)

Humans are the only animals that typically sleep for 7½ hours in a row (and stay awake for 16½ hours in a row). Other animals sleep shorter and more often: they take lots of naps.

For example, cats rarely stay awake for more than 6 hours in a row; they take lots of catnaps. Cats can prowl at all hours of the day and night. Human eyes and noses are too poor to handle the night, so humans were built to just give up, sleep through the darkness, but think throughout the day.

Sleep positions

You can sleep in 4 positions:

> **face up** (on your back)
> **face down** (on your stomach)
> **facing your left** (on your left side)
> **facing your right** (on your right-hand side)

Each position has its own advantages and problems. Here are the issues....

Breathing The worst position for breathing is face up. When you're face up, you're most likely to snore, most like to suffer from **sleep apnea** (repeatedly interrupted breathing), and most likely to have your snot run down your throat (which worsens your cold or flu by infecting your throat & tummy).

The best position for breathing is **face down**, so the snot drips away from your body (onto your pillow or Kleenex) instead of down your throat.

Leg spasms When you're sleeping, or trying to wake up, do you sometimes get painful spasms in your leg muscles? If so, the best way to avoid them (or stop them) is to go into the **fetal position**, where you look like a fetus: bend your legs, so your knees are near your tummy and your toes are turned toward your knees. One way to get into that position is to grab your toes and pull them toward your tummy. But you probably don't want to spend all night grabbing your toes! The easiest way to approximate that position is to sleep on your side (curled up): so sleep **facing your left or facing your right**. Don't sleep face up or face down.

Acid reflux If you eat too much, you might get **acid reflux** (where the acids in your stomach can't fit inside your stomach, so they flow back up your esophagus and even into your mouth). The acids burn your esophagus, giving you a burning sensation (called **heartburn** because it's near your heart,

though it's actually in just your esophagus). Those acids weaken your esophagus and make your esophagus more likely to get cancer. The problem is called **gastroesophageal reflux disease (GERD)**. If the acids reach your mouth, they'll eat away your teeth surfaces (the enamel).

To avoid acid reflux, many patients buy pills (or change diet or chew gum or get surgery or sleep on a slanted bed), but try this easy sleeping technique first: sleep **facing your left**. Here's why:

> Your stomach is a *small* organ on your *left* side, just below your heart. (Your stomach is *not* the embarrassing big bulge at your waist; that bulge is your intestine.) By sleeping on your left side, you're keeping your stomach low (close to the mattress), so it's lower than your esophagus, so the stomach's acids won't spill to your esophagus.

Don't sleep facing your right. (If you sleep on your right-hand side, your stomach is higher than your esophagus, and your stomach's acids drip into your esophagus.)

Sudden infant death If you have an infant under the age of 1, make the infant sleep **face up**, to prevent **sudden infant death syndrome (SIDS)**, even though the infant will sleep more soundly face down.

Comfort The only comfortable position is **face up**. Other positions scrunch part of your body: lying on your side crushes that side; lying face down strains your neck. Also, if you try to pamper yourself by lying on an electric message bed, the bed massages you well just if you lie **face up**.

Masturbation If you sleep **face down**, your genitals will rub against the mattress, leading to masturbation. That's fun if you're alone (but distracting if your bedroom is shared).

Summary So here's the advantage of each position:

> **Face up**   good for infants and comfort
> **Face down**   improves breathing and masturbation
> **Facing your left**   stops acid reflux and leg spasms
> **Facing your right** is another way to stop leg spasms

Most people change positions several times throughout the night. That's natural and good, since staying in the same position too long can create bedsores. That's why hospitals hire nurses to turn over the patients.

Insomnia

If you have trouble falling asleep, researchers recommend removing all distractions from your bedroom: avoid light, clocks, books, televisions, and food, so your bedroom is totally peaceful, boring, sleepy.

If you want to read a book or watch TV, do so in a separate room (or at least a separate chair), so your body gets in the habit of using your bed just for sleeping and sex. Instead of staring at an alarm clock and watching the minutes tick by, have a family member wake you — or at least turn the clock so you can't see the time.

3 hours before you go to bed:

> Stop exercising (because it will stimulate you too much).
> Stop drinking coffee and tea (because their caffeine will keep you awake).
> Stop eating big meals (though a light snack can be helpful).
> Stop drinking alcohol.

Though alcohol makes you fall asleep fast, the sleep it creates has poor quality, so you'll tend to wake up at 3AM.

For a light bedtime snack, try milk, turkey, peanuts, or their variants (cheese, chicken, tuna, cashews, or soy), because they all contain an amino acid called **tryptophan**, which helps your brain produce **serotonin** (a chemical that helps you relax). Try them warm (by microwaving them or by putting peanut butter on toast), so your body gets warm & cozy then cools down again: the cooling will make you sleepy.

If a list of worries prevents you from sleeping, write the list down, so you feel organized and can analyze the list the next morning.

Most people who suffer from insomnia are old women (not young men).

These Websites have more suggestions to cure insomnia:

www.4woman.gov/faq/insomnia.htm
www.helpguide.org/aging/sleep_tips.htm
www.familydoctor.org/110.xml
www.well.com/user/mick/insomnia

Details

For more details about sleep research, read Craig Lambert's article "Deep into Sleep" (on pages 25-33 of *Harvard Magazine*'s July-August 2005 issue).

AIDS

There are two common ways to get AIDS. One way is to be a drug addict who shares needles with other drug addicts. The other way is to have certain kinds of sex. But the media was afraid to say what those "certain kinds of sex" were.

Here's the truth: the main way to get AIDS is to get fucked in the ass. That's because when you get fucked in the ass, a few of your blood vessels there will pop, and the fucker's infected semen will mix with your blood. That's why gays get AIDS more than straights: gays are more likely to ass-fuck.

If you fuck normally or just kiss, your chance of transmitting or receiving AIDS is low, because you're not going to pop many blood vessels that way.

The official announcements say AIDS is transmitted by an "exchange of bodily fluids," but remember that the main "exchange" is by popping blood vessels during ass-fucking.

I recommend you go suck an ice-cream pop instead. It's a safer way to get creamed and popped, and it tastes better.

Cleaning

They say "Cleanliness is next to Godliness." Does that mean "Dirtiness is next to Devilishness?"

Wash your hands

To prevent disease and infection, the main thing you can do is: wash your hands!

Colds, the flu, and other communicable diseases are spread mainly by dirty hands (not by getting cold, not by bad breath). To remove germs from your environment, wash your hands frequently, using hot water, soap, and friction: rub them! Soap and water are more effective than most antiseptic or antibacterial sprays. Wash your hands before you eat; wash your hands after taking out garbage; wash your hands after blowing your nose.

If you have a cold, the most common way to transmit it to others is to blow your nose then shake somebody's hand. More colds are transmitted by shaking hands than by sneezing into the air. If you wash after you blow, and if the people who shake your hand wash before they eat, you won't infect your neighbors. Besides shaking hands, another common way to spread colds is to blow your nose, then grab a stair's handrail just before someone else grabs it.

Soap

Most soaps are normal, but 2 famous soaps are extreme:

Dove makes your skin feel oily (because ¼ of Dove is moisturizing cream).
Ivory makes your skin feel dry.

In winter, your skin will feel too dry, unless you use Dove to make it feel oily and counteract the dryness. In summer, when you sweat like a pig, your skin will feel too wet, unless you use Ivory to counteract the wetness and make your skin feel drier.

Dove is the perfect winter soap.
Ivory is the perfect summer soap.

Don't use them in the wrong seasons! Dermatologists especially recommend against using Ivory soap in the winter: your skin will crack and bleed if you use Ivory when you're cold.

Dove soap is expensive; you can substitute "generic" moisturizing soaps instead. Ivory soap is cheap but vanishes fast when you use it: you'll need many bars to get through a month.

A new, green version of Ivory includes a moisturizer: aloe.

Sponges

Bacteria and molds love to grow on damp objects, such as sponges.

When you're not using your sponges, keep them dry. Each week, replace them (you can get about 10 per dollar at discount stores such as Dollar Tree) or microwave them for 2 minutes (after wetting them so they won't burn).

Wiping with an ancient untreated sponge is less sanitary than not wiping at all.

Bleach

You can buy chlorine bleach in a bottle or as a powder. The cheapest powdered forms are **Ajax** and **Dutch Cleanser**. To remove mold from bathtubs, shower curtains, sponges, and decks, let bleach sit there a while: the bleach loosens the mold. The more minutes or hours that the bleach makes contact with the mold, the looser the mold gets. Unfortunately, bleach also destroys the sponge's fibers.

Sweat

Since sweat can be sticky, clammy, and smelly, people worry about it. But sweat's an amazing blessing given us by God. Although our bodies were intended to operate at 98.6 degrees, they can survive temperatures of over 110 degrees, by sweating.

Sweat itself isn't cool. In fact, since sweat came out of our bodies, sweat itself is 98.6 degrees. Yet, sweat feels cool. Why?

The answer is: when sweat hits the air, it evaporates. According to the laws of physics, evaporation requires energy; to get that energy needed for evaporation, the sweat "sucks" heat energy from the surrounding tissue. Since your body loses that heat, your body feels cooler.

But you don't need a physicist to tell you that. Just ask the typical teenage punk, "Does sweat suck?" and he'll say, "Sure, and so do you!"

Your body's temperature is 98.6 degrees because of an error:

When Gabriel Fahrenheit invented the thermometer around 1700, he wanted to define "100 degrees" to mean the temperature of an average human body, so he measured his secretary's body (which was probably fun) but didn't realize how hot-blooded his secretary was: in fact, his secretary was 1.4 degrees hotter than the average human! Although his secretary's temperature became defined as 100 degrees, the average human is 1.4 degrees cooler. The next time you have a temperature of 100 degrees, console yourself by remembering you're no hotter than Fahrenheit's secretary!

If you see a person's brow drip with sweat, the air is not really hot. In truly hot air, sweat evaporates immediately, so you never see it on the person's brow! The cast of the "Twilight Zone" TV show discovered that the hard way:

> Around 1960, when they were filming Twilight Zone's first episode, they needed to pretend they were on Mars, so they took their cameras to Death Valley, which looks nearly as hot and barren as Mars; but since Death Valley was so hot, the sweat evaporated immediately: the actors didn't look sweaty and didn't look hot. The producer had to cover the actor's faces with oil, which looked like sweat but didn't evaporate.

Facial creams

Many women who want younger-looking skin put special creams on their faces. They're just wasting their money.

The best way to develop younger-looking skin is to stay out of the sun, since tans cause wrinkles.

To see how facial creams are useless, look at my friend Pierrette:

> A facial-cream saleswoman asked Pierrette which cream she was using. Pierrette said, "Just soap and water."
> The saleswoman said, "You shouldn't do that! Plain soap will age your face! By the time you turn 26, you'll look 30!"
> The saleswoman didn't realize that Pierrette was already 40. Using just soap and water, Pierrette looked at least 15 years younger!

Doctors

No matter how hard you try, eventually you're gonna get sick and try to see a doctor but die. Here are the delicious details....

Kinds of doctors

If you're a medical student who's trying to decide what kind of specialist to become, you'll be told:

> **general practitioners (GPs)** are friendly but stupid
>
> **internists** are smart but overly cautious
>
> **surgeons** are carefree playboys who like to play with women and knives and don't worry about details

To illustrate those stereotypes, you'll be told this tale:

> A GP, an internist, and surgeon go on a duck shoot but share a shotgun.
> They agree to let the GP go first. When the first bird flies overhead, the GP says, "It looks like a duck, it flies like a duck, I'll call it a duck." Then he fires, but misses.
> When the second bird flies overhead, the internist says, "It looks like a duck, it flies like a duck, but we'll have to rule out the ostrich and the golden eagle and the whooping crane, which are endangered species." Before he finishes analyzing the situation, the bird flies away.
> Finally, it's the surgeon's turn. When the third bird flies overhead, the surgeon takes his shotgun and shoots the bird immediately. The bird drops at his feet. Then the surgeon looks at the conquered bird and says, "Well, what do you know, it's a duck!"

Some doctors know what to do, but don't act. Other doctors act even though they don't know the right thing to do. Medical students learn this rule about how specialists differ:

> An **internist** knows everything and does nothing.
> A **surgeon** does everything and knows nothing.
> A **psychiatrist** knows nothing and does nothing.
> A **pathologist** knows everything and does everything too late.

For the medical profession's reactions to those barbs, dig up Marilyn Chase's article on *The Wall Street Journal*'s front page (May 15, 1984).

My friend Clayton Thomas (a physician) passed me two more barbs he heard from his colleagues:

> The only science less exact than nutrition science is Christian Science.
> Doctors are generous: they tell you all they know, plus a bit more.

Doctor-patient chat can get bizarre:

> Doctor: you're very sick.
> Patient: I want a second opinion.
> Doctor: Okay, you're *ugly*, too.
>
> Doctor: What's your problem?
> Patient: It hurts when I do *this*.
> Doctor: So don't do that!

That last quote was from comedian Henny Youngman.
Carrie Snow said:

> A male gynecologist is like an auto mechanic who never owned a car.

Jan King complained:

> Whoever thought up the word "mammogram"? Every time I hear it, I think I'm supposed to put my breast in an envelope and send it to someone.

Feminists recommend the **manogram**, which is a similar device for men: it grabs the prick and crushes it to death.

Party doctors

When a doctor attends a party and another guest says to him, "I have a medical question," the doctor's way to politely decline spending the party dishing out unpaid advice is to reply:

> Great! Just get undressed.

A surgeon who lived a full life

Here's the story of my favorite surgeon. He wasn't perfect, but his good outweighed his bad, and he was ahead of his time.

Outline of a lifetime He was born in 1890. He skipped 8th grade — and so did all his classmates — because his teacher felt the 8th-grade curriculum just repeated what was taught in 7th grade. He went to a top-notch public high school, where his curriculum even included Latin, Greek, linguistics, and astronomy, and the graduates were given automatic bachelors' degrees. When he finished high school, he skipped "college" and immediately entered one of the country's most prestigious medical schools. So he finished medical school when he was 21 and became a surgeon — much younger than would be possible now.

He was a surgeon in the US Army during World War 1. After the war, he married a nurse. He was Jewish; she was not. He picked her instead of a Jewish woman because he reckoned the typical Jewish woman would want to start marriage by being treated as a princess or a queen; he liked the woman he married because she was a Christian who "knew the meaning of hard work."

Throughout his marriage, he slept in a separate bed from her, so he wouldn't have to disturb her in the middle of the night when he'd get called for medical emergencies. When their kids grew up and moved out, he and his wife moved from a big house to a small apartment but slept in separate bedrooms, even after he retired.

Though he called himself a Jew, the only religious services he went to were weddings, funerals, and inescapable Bar Mitzvahs.

He was a hospital's surgeon, a university's medical professor, a distinguished medical journal's book reviewer, and a large industrial corporation's top physician — all simultaneously! That hard work and lack of sleep gave him a heart attack when he was about 55. While he was recovering, his colleagues told him he'd have to either slow down or risk dying from a second heart attack within 5 years. He slowed down and lived a very long life: he died when he was about 90 years old. He outlived his wife and practically all friends.

Medical taboos & fads He ignored the medical profession's taboos and fads. He broke the unwritten rules; but since he was the *head* surgeon at a large and prestigious city hospital, other doctors couldn't argue.

For example, a general rule among surgeons is: don't perform surgery on your own relatives.

> He ignored that taboo: he removed the appendix of each of his ill children and grandchildren. Why? Because he wanted to make sure the operation was done right! He felt that the only way to be sure was to do it himself.

During the 1950's, most doctors made their patients stay in the hospital about 2 weeks after an operation for "thorough recuperation," even after a relatively minor operation, such as removing an appendix.

> Ignoring that tradition, he made his patients get up and walk out of the hospital after 3 days, so they didn't run up big hospital bills. He was ahead of his time: today, most doctors copy him.

Up through the 1950's, the biggest medical fad was the **tonsillectomy**. If a patient's tonsil was even slightly inflamed, doctors would say that the patient had "tonsillitis" and send the patient to the hospital to have the tonsil removed. Since so many 10-year-old kids had tonsillectomies, that operation became a rite of passage, like getting circumcised.

> He spurned that practice and refused to do tonsillectomies. He felt God built the tonsil to be the body's first line of defense against illness: the tonsil's purpose was to intercept infection that was heading for the rest of the body. His cure for an inflamed tonsil was to just wait for the tonsil to feel better. For minor cases of tonsillitis, he recommended just gargling with salt water. He used antibiotics just when necessary. He was right: today, the medical profession agrees with him and recommends salt water and occasional antibiotics instead of surgery.

Since he never went to undergraduate college, he never learned organic chemistry and other "hard" sciences.

> To him, surgery was an art, not a science: it was the art of slicing people up and making them well. As he neared retirement — and medical science advanced — most doctors were measuring the patient's chemistry; but since he didn't understand chemistry (and didn't even understand what today is called "high-school algebra"), he let the young interns fresh out of school do all those boring chemical calculations. They were the bookkeepers; he was the master butcher, kind and wise and experienced.

After he retired and was about 80, he developed a tumor in his knee. Rather than trust the operation to another surgeon — which would also mean having to go to a hospital and leave his ailing wife unattended — he went into his home's bathroom, slit open his own leg, removed the tumor himself, and then sewed his leg up again.

Magic His hands, skilled in surgery, were also skilled in magic. He made coins disappear and performed other sleights of hand that mystified his children, grandchildren, and great-grandchildren.

As he grew older, he got scared about the consequences of one of his tricks. In that trick, he'd rub a penny into a kid's palm, until the penny "disappeared" (it was secretly hiding between the doctor's own fingers); then he'd say the penny was passing through the kid's body; and finally he'd pull the penny out the kid's ear. But eventually he began to worry that kids would try to imitate him by sticking pennies in their ears, so he stopped that trick.

Music His whole living room was surrounded by 300 albums of classical-music records, all numbered and indexed. He had new records but still kept the ones he bought around 1900, as a young boy. For example, he had 78 RPM records that were so old that they were recorded on just one side, before "flip" sides had been invented.

He loved listening to operas and knew all the popular ones by heart. He also loved watching football and reading the newspaper. He did all 3 activities simultaneously:

> In his living room, he'd turn on the radio (to listen to the opera), while simultaneously turning on the TV (to watch football) and opening the newspaper. While reading the newspaper, he listened to the opera, and at the end of each paragraph he peeked at the game on TV. Modern society would call that "multitasking," but he lived in an era where such living was just called "being efficient."

Traveler A true patriot, he visited each of the 50 states. But he never wished to visit any foreign countries.

For 60 consecutive summers, he drove to Maine, to eat lobsters and enjoy the sea breezes. When he became 70 and then 80 years old, his weather-beaten face gave him the look of an ancient lobsterman.

Life after death When he was about 80, his wife died. That marked the beginning of his new life.

He traveled more. Many women loved him and tried to "snag" him, because he was intelligent, responsible, rich, famous in his field, and — most important — possibly die soon and leave a big inheritance. But he resisted most female advances. Besides, those women were too young for him: he was 85, and he said they were just "spring chickens"; he didn't want to "rob the cradle."

He finally took a fancy to a widow who lived in the same apartment building as he. Her late husband had been one of his patients. But though he enjoyed the widow's company, he refused to marry her and refused to live with her.

Since they were both old, and either might die at any moment, they phoned each other every morning to make sure they'd both gotten through the night safely.

So each morning, he phoned her, let her phone ring just once, then hung up before she answered it. That was a signal: she'd phone him back and they'd chat. He made her phone him, because she talked a lot, and he didn't want to pay the phone bill.

Calling her wouldn't have cost him much, since the call was very local: they both lived in the same apartment building. But since she was a blabbermouth, she'd bought the "unlimited calling option" from the phone company so she could call him free; and, Jew that he was, he'd never pay for a service that she could get free.

He sent her a Valentine card that said he loved her because she was the only woman who could put up with his crabbiness.

They liked to travel. When he was about 85, he hitchhiked across Wyoming — and dragged her along.

She was warm and friendly, but also disorganized and somewhat senile. He helped her figure her taxes, but his accounting wasn't enough to prevent her from making a mess. For example, one day she phoned him and announced she paid her taxes. He said, "You already paid your taxes!" She was so senile that she'd forgotten she'd paid her taxes; she paid them twice! He phoned the IRS to explain her error, but the IRS staffers couldn't stop laughing: they spent the day whispering to each other, "Hey, did you hear about the old lady who was so senile that she paid her taxes twice?"

Eventually, she grew too senile to be reasonable company, so he ditched her. She died, from senility and loneliness.

Years later, when he was about 90, dying of cancer, and hospitalized, an elderly woman patient claimed she entered his room and made love to him on his deathbed. She was surprised that a 90-year-old immobile cancer patient could do it! But that was the last time.

Daily survival

Surviving life's difficulties can be tough. For example, the Internet tells of this letter from a mother:

> Dear son,
>
> I'm writing this slow because I know you can't read fast.
>
> After you left home, we moved, because your dad read in the newspaper that most accidents happen within 20 minutes of your home. I can't send you our new address, since the last family that lived here took the house numbers when they moved, to avoid changing *their* address.
>
> This nice place even has a washing machine, though I'm not sure it works well: I put 4 shirts in, pulled the chain, and haven't seen them since.
>
> The weather here isn't bad. It rained just twice last week: the first time for 3 days, the second time for 4 days.
>
> As for the coat you wanted me to send, your aunt said it would be too heavy to send in the mail with the buttons on, so we cut them off and put them in the pockets.
>
> The funeral home sent a bill saying if we don't make the last payment for grandma's funeral, up she comes!
>
> Your brother worried us by locking his keys in the car. It took him 4 hours to get me and your dad out.
>
> Your sister had a baby, but I haven't found out yet whether it's a girl or a boy, so I don't know whether you're an aunt or an uncle. The baby looks just like your brother.
>
> Your uncle fell into a whiskey vat last week. Men tried to pull him out, but he fought them off valiantly and drowned. When we had him cremated, he burned for 3 days.
>
> 3 of your friends accidentally went off a bridge in a pickup truck. Butch, the driver, rolled down the window and swam to safety, but your other 2 friends drowned because they were in the back and couldn't get the tailgate down.
>
> No more news. Nothing much happened.
>
> If you don't get this letter, tell me and I'll send another.
>
> Love, Mom
>
> P.S. I was going to send you money, but the envelope was already sealed.

To survive, you need food and shelter. The previous chapter explained food; now gimme shelter....

Housing

In the South, low-income folks who can't afford housing live in their cars. My roommate asked one such fellow why; he replied:

> You can't drive a house, but you can live in a car.

In the North, cars there are too cold to live in, unless your "car" is a luxurious mobile home.

Heat

Europeans detest Americans for wasting everything, including energy. For example, Europeans detest Americans for making homes be "warmer in winter than in summer."

> During the winter, Americans overcompensate for the cold outside, by turning the heat up to 74 degrees. During the summer, Americans overcompensate for the heat outside by air-conditioning their homes and offices down to 68 degrees. Many women in American offices bring sweaters to work with them — in the middle of the summer — because their bosses have turned the air conditioning to near-freezing temperatures, especially in computer centers.

Change your clothes In the winter, the most effective way to stay warm in your home is to wear thick clothing. In the summer, the most effective way to stay cool in your home is to take off your shirt and buy a fan (unless you're a shy woman who's afraid of going shirtless, or you live in a ridiculously hot place, such as a desert or a jungle or the South, or you're a New Jersey cry-baby).

But Americans strangely insist on wearing practically identical clothing during both seasons: they heat or air-condition their entire homes when all that's really needed is to insulate or fan the air next to their skins.

Air conditioners destroy society Philosophers blame air conditioners for destroying American society. Before air conditioners were invented, Americans spent summer outdoors, sitting on the front stoop or playing with friends. Now Americans spend summer hiding inside their air-conditioned mansions, ignoring their neighbors, and glued to the TV or computer or videogames. Some Americans *never* meet their neighbors, even after living nearby for many years! Air conditioners have made neighborhoods colder not just physically but also socially.

New Yorkers fret that since normal folks hide indoors during the summer, the streets are now controlled by street gangs. That's how air conditioners breed violence. (But Southerners say air conditioners breed high property values.)

Computer excuse If you wish to buy an air conditioner, your easiest excuse is to buy a personal computer then tell your family that computers don't work in the summer unless you also buy an air conditioner.

Windows

Suppose you want to air out a room by opening a window, but your window is the "double-hung" kind that lets you open either the top half or the bottom half but not both simultaneously. Which half should you open?

According to research done in the 1800's by M.I.T.'s first woman professor, pollution tends to rise to the top half of your room, so you should let it out by opening the window's top half.

I'd consider these issues also:

> Since hot air rises, opening the top half releases hot air from the room and makes the room cooler, whereas opening the bottom half releases cold air from the room and makes the room warmer.
>
> If your real goal is a "cleansing breeze," open two windows and the door, so that your room becomes a wind tunnel.
>
> If you have just one window and can't open the door, open part of the window's top half and part of the window's bottom half, so you create a small breeze from one half to the other.
>
> To impress a visitor, maybe open the window's *bottom* half, since the bottom half typically offers a prettier view! On the other hand, if you open the bottom half, the dirt on the window's top half will be embarrassingly noticeable against the sky.
>
> If your neighborhood is noisy, open the top half, so that the bottom half blocks noise coming up from the street.
>
> To keep your house cool during a summer day without an air conditioner, put curtains over the windows that are in direct sunlight, and open (just slightly) the top half of each window. At night, open the top half of every window wide.

When you visit your friend's house, notice the windows, which reveal your friend's priorities.

Color

To sell your house, paint its outside yellow, because yellow houses sell faster than any other color. That's probably because "light objects look bigger than dark objects and look light-hearted and cheerfully sunny, but white shows dirt too easily." Yellow has just one problem: it fades fast.

To sell your house easily, make it yellow outside but white inside, since white looks newer and goes with a greater variety of furniture.

Throwing things away

When I lived in Boston, one of my roommates was a grad student at M.I.T., where his professor told him, "The hardest thing to learn is to throw away information."

In my own case, I gave up. When leaving Somerville, Donna hired a bunch of Chinese guys who threw all my stuff out on the street. Then the trash collectors came, saw a whole block full of garbage, and called the building inspector and fire department, who circled my block with fire trucks every few minutes to embarrass me until I hired a dumpster company.

Hint: throw out a moderate amount each week. Give yourself a goal: "This week, I'll throw out x boxes of stuff." The last week will still be heartbreaking, but less so.

Sexy clothing There's always a market for women's panties, slightly soiled. One woman got her first taste of the transvestite marketplace when guys started paying for her used clothing. Finally, she started a big business (called "Clothes by Caroline") that manufactured guy-size versions of women's clothing (such as maid's costumes) and, more profitably, baby clothing (for the "adult baby" market).

Undone housework

Here's a tale from the Internet:

> A man coming home from work found total mayhem in his house.
> His three kids were outside, still in pajamas, splashing in mud, with empty food boxes and wrappers strewn all over the yard. The door of his wife's car was open, and so was the front door of the house.
> In the house, he found an even bigger mess: a lamp was knocked over; the throw rug was wadded against one wall; cartoons were loudly blaring from the TV; the family room's floor was strewn with toys and many clothes. In the kitchen, dishes filled the sink, breakfast food was spilled on the counter, dog food was spilled on the floor, a broken glass lay under the table, and sand was by the back door.
> He ran upstairs, leaping over toys and more piles of clothes, to find his wife. He worried that she might be ill or some bigger calamity had happened.
> He found her curled in bed and reading a novel. She looked up at him, smiled, and asked how his day went. He looked at her bewildered and asked, "What happened here today?"
> She smiled again and replied, "You know every day when you come home from work and ask me what in Hell I did all day?"
> "Yes" he gasped.
> She replied, "Well, today I didn't do it."

The main things a lawn wants are water, fertilizer, and sunshine.

Water

The best time to water the lawn is early in the morning, about 4:30AM. Any time between 3AM and 6AM is okay. After that, winds and heat make the water evaporate too fast, and your city's water pressure drops too low because more humans try to use water then.

Don't water in the late afternoon or evening, because that makes the lawn remain wet too long at night: dark wet lawns are a breeding ground for mushrooms, molds, and diseases. (Exception: in the Southwest and other environments that are desert-like with ridiculously low humidity, watering in the evening is okay, since few mushrooms or molds live there.)

How much water? You want the water to penetrate 7 inches into the soil, to encourage the grass's roots to grow long and be hardy. To accomplish that, water a long time. If you water just briefly, the water will evaporate before getting down that deep.

How often to water To water deeply without wasting water, water just twice a week, but make each watering long. Do not water daily. Do not water several times per day. (Exception: if you're on a hill and the water runs off the hill and onto the street, interrupt your watering until the ground has a chance to soak up the water, then continue.)

Check yourself Make sure at least one inch of water falls on the grass each week. (That's half an inch per watering, when you water twice a week. To measure the amount of water, you can use a bucket or empty soup can.)

If you don't water the grass enough, it eventually turns brown. But even before the grass turns brown, it gives you 2 signs of inadequate water:

> The grass looks gray (because its blades are too weak to stand straight, and they bend so you see more of their gray backsides).
>
> When you step on the grass, it's too weak to pop back up, so your footprints stay in the grass.

Fertilizer

Fertilizer is a strong chemical. The lawn needs a little bit of it. If you fertilize too much, the lawn will die.

You should fertilize every 2 months, while the grass is growing. In most parts of the USA, the winter is too cold for grass to grow (the grass just sleeps then), so you should fertilize 4 times: early spring, early summer, late summer, and fall.

When you buy a bag of fertilizer, you see 3 numbers on the bag's front. Typically, those numbers are **32-3-10**, which means the fertilizer is **32% nitrogen**, **3% phosphorus**, **10% potassium**, and 55% "other minerals, coatings, binders, and junk."

> **Nitrogen** makes the grass grow taller and stay green instead of turning yellow.
>
> **Phosphorus** makes the roots grow deeper and seeds sprout, and it helps prevent the grass from turning purple.
>
> **Potassium** makes the grass hardy (so it can withstand disease, drought, cold, and trampling).

If a bag of fertilizer says 10-10-10 instead, it's mainly for flowers and shrubs rather than grass.

The bag's back gives more details. If the fertilizer is high-quality, it also includes other minerals the grass needs, such as iron, calcium, magnesium, and sulfur.

Put on fertilizer when the grass is dry, so the fertilizer hits the ground instead of sticking to wet blades. Then immediately water the lawn (so the fertilizer sinks in before it blows away and before it burns any grass blades it landed on).

Fertilize mainly while the grass is growing fast. Don't fertilize in the winter.

> **Cool-season grasses** (such as **Kentucky bluegrass** and **fine fescue**) grow fastest when the temperature is about 70 degrees (spring and fall). They're popular in the North.
>
> **Warm-season grasses** (such as **Bermuda grass** and **Saint Augustine grass**) grow fastest when the temperature is about 87 degrees (summer). They're popular in the South.

I believe grass can talk and say things such as:

> We young blades are glad Russ knew it would rain this weekend, so he put fertilizer on us. Yummy!
>
> He used a strange brand that smells like shit, but we piggish grasses love to be covered with it. Call us deviant or call us herbal, but that's what we like.
>
> He was the first on the block. We're turning green. The neighbors' grasses are white with envy.
>
> You gonna bring us any more showers? That was fun!

Mowing

Grass doesn't like to be cut, but your neighbors will insist that you cut it.

When you cut the grass, **don't cut off more than a third of the grass's blade at a time**: if you cut more, the grass gets traumatized, tries to regrow the blade, and uses all its nitrogen for that activity instead of for growing healthy roots and keeping protective storage. Also, cutting off so much blade makes the grass's bottom get too much sunlight and turn gray-brown.

If you want to cut more (because the grass has gotten very tall and your neighbors are ready to kill you), do it in two stages: cut off a little, then cut off a little more a few days later, but never cut more than a third at a time.

Keep the grass as tall as you and your neighbors can bear it. Tall grass has 3 advantages over short grass:

> Tall grass prevents weeds from growing (because weeds don't like shade).
>
> Tall grass needs less water (because it shades the soil from evaporation).
>
> Tall grass stays healthier and grows bigger roots (because its big blade performs lots of photosynthesis, turning sunlight into energy).

Most experts recommend that you **let the grass blades get to about 4 inches tall, then cut back to 3 inches** (so you're cutting off just a quarter of the blade). 3 inches is about the length of your index finger. To get 3 inches, set your lawnmower at one of the "high off the ground" settings. If you wish, instead of letting "4 inches cut to 3," you can let "3½ inches cut to 2½."

Here are exceptions:

> For **zoysia   grass**,   you must cut to 2½ inches to avoid excessive thatch.
> For **Bermuda grass**,   you must cut to 1½ inches to avoid excessive thatch.
> For a golf course,   you must cut to ¼ inch to let golf balls roll easily.

When grass grows fast (because of rain, fertilizer, and mild temperatures in the 70's), you must mow often (to avoid lopping off more than a third at a time). When the grass grows slowly, you can wait longer before mowing.

Try to leave the cuttings on the lawn. Though the cuttings look ugly, they actually improve the lawn, since they act as fertilizer and contain many more nutrients than just nitrogen, phosphorus, and potassium. For best results, get a **mulching** lawnmower (which can chop the cuttings into tiny pieces). If you mow often enough, each mowing will produce cuttings small enough to avoid smothering the grass. Though the cuttings might look big at first, they disappear fast, since most of their bulk is water that evaporates fast.

Mow when the grass is dry, to make the grass easier to cut and the cuttings less bulky.

Killing your enemies

A **weed** is just a plant that grows too fast and spreads across your lawn too fast.

The best way to avoid weeds is to keep the grass healthy and tall, so weeds don't get enough sunlight and enough empty space to survive. If you get weeds, the best way to get rid of them is to pull them out by hand, if you have the patience.

Dandelions are hard to pull out, since they have deep roots. If your lawn has a lot of clover, that's a sign your grass needs more fertilizer.

Some people hate weeds; other people love them. For example, kids love dandelions because their yellow flowers are pretty; but gardeners hate dandelions because they spread too fast and quickly take over your whole lawn; then the wind blows their seeds to the rest of your neighborhood, and your neighbors get angry at you for wrecking *their* lawns.

If you apply the typical weed killer (called **post-emergent weed killer**), apply it when the lawn is wet, so the weed killer sticks to the weed's leaves (which is how it kills the weed). If you apply bug killer, apply it when the lawn is dry, since the bugs spend most of their time in the ground, which is where you want to hit them. One kind of weed killer, called **pre-emergent weed killer**, attacks the weeds in early spring while they're still underground, before they emerge from the soil; apply that kind when the lawn is dry.

Weed killers and bug killers also can hurt or kill birds, pets, and small kids, so use the killers as little as possible and just on the parts of the lawn that are having severe problems. Keep kids and pets off those parts of the lawn afterward.

My wife complains that it's not fair for me to pull out weeds — or put chemicals on them — just because they look different from grass. She calls me a discriminatory racist.

I apologize.

Grass professors

To learn more about lawns, read what agriculture professors say!

Learn from the University of Illinois' Internet site (**Lawn Challenge, www.urbanext.uiuc.edu/lawnchallenge**). Then read this delightful book (full of good photos and text) by Professor Nick Christians (from Iowa State U.) and Ashton Ritchie (from The Scotts Company):

> **Scotts Lawns**, published by Meredith Books, $19.95 list, $14.84 at Wal-Mart

Snow removal

I live in New Hampshire, where we have lots of snow. We've learned that the best way to remove snow depends on your religious beliefs.

Gene's philosophy

My neighbor Gene removes snow by performing a religious ritual — he walks out to the snow, raises both hands up to the sky, and recites the incantation chanted by ministers at funerals:

> What the Lord giveth, the Lord taketh away.

Then he sneaks back into the house and waits for the Lord to remove the snow by letting it "melteth away." When his wife asks him about "snow removal," he just says:

> It's the Lord's work.

When she asks "Won't that take a long time to melt?" he'll say:

> Patience is a virtue.

Tom's philosophy

The opposite religious philosophy, espoused by Tom and my other brawny neighbors (armed with shovels, axes, and blowtorches), is:

> The Lord helps those who help themselves.

They believe in hacking at the snow until the helpless miserable snow gets a black eye, as the black asphalt starts showing underneath. They believe in the Lord's ability to finish the job, since Ben Franklin proved black absorbs sunshine and converts it to heat, forming a devilishly hot Hell underground that melts the snow above. If you ask them about "snow removal," they say:

> It's the Devil's work.

If you ask "Why not wait until the snow melts?" they paraphrase John F. Kennedy and say:

> Ask not what the snow can do to you,
> ask what you can do to the snow.

Then they start swinging their axes — and you'd better get out of their way!

Triple-good shovels

If you buy a shovel to handle the snow, make sure it's triple-good! Make sure it has all 3 of these characteristics:

> It should be almost entirely aluminum (which weighs much less than wood, iron, or steel), so you don't get tired lifting.

> Its scoop should have big sidewalls on the left and right (so the scoop looks more like a bucket), to prevent snow from falling off the scoop's sides before you lift.

> Its handle should be long and bent (to look more like a slithering snake than a straight pole), so you don't have to stoop while shoveling.

Home Depot sells a green one having all those properties for $14.99. It's made by **Ames True Temper** and called the **Arctic Blast 70405**.

Other shapes are better for "very light snow" or "very wet snow" or "very narrow walkways" or "roofs" or "elderly people who can't lift". For photos of different shapes and their advantages, go to the **Ames True Temper website (www.ames.com)** then click on "Choosing the Right Tool" then "Snow Tools".

Transportation

Let's go places!

Cars

While driving, beware of distractions. The song *Seven Little Girls* warned:

> Keep your mind on your driving,
> Keep your hands on the wheel,
> Keep your snoopy eyes on the road ahead.
>
> We're having fun,
> Sitting in the back seat
> Kissin' and a-huggin' with Fred!

(The song was written in 1959 by Lee Pockriss & Bob Hilliard and sung by Paul Evans, whose Web site is PaulEvans.com. You can hear the song at www.StinaLisa.com/SevenGirls.html and discover its history at www.SongFacts.com/detail.php?id=7304.)

Driving tricks These driving tricks aren't obvious:

> ### Air conditioner in summer
> When you're driving fast on a highway on a hot day, turning on the air conditioner consumes less gas than opening the window, because opening the window creates a strong breeze whose airflow slows down the car and acts as a brake. The air conditioner reduces your gas efficiency by just 1 mile per gallon; the open window costs slightly more at highway speeds. (But here are the *most effective* ways to improve your gas efficiency: remove unused junk from your trunk, put enough air in your tires, and get a tune-up.)
>
> ### Air conditioner in winter
> If you live in the north, buy a car that has an air conditioner and turn it on in the *winter*. That's because the air conditioner is a dehumidifier: it takes the humidity out of the air, so the foggy icy dew on the inside of your windshield evaporates. While the air conditioner is on, set it to a warm temperature, so you don't freeze.
>
> ### Left lane after turning
> If you want to drive slowly on an American road, you're supposed to drive in the right lane, except in this special situation: when you turn left onto a multi-lane road, you're supposed to stay in the new road's *left* lane until you're safely past the intersection.
>
> ### To leave Hell, go straight
> If your car is stuck in a snow bank or on a patch of ice, make your wheels point straight ahead temporarily, even if that's not the direction you ultimately want to go. That's because when you drive straight ahead, you have more power and control than when you try to turn. If you can't go forwards, go backwards, but in any case don't turn the wheel until after you've achieved speed and control.

Color If you buy a car, which color should you get? Which is better: a light color (such as white or yellow or silver) or a dark color (such as blue or black)?

> A light-color car is easier to see (and safer) at night.
> A dark car is easier to see in a snowstorm.
>
> A yellow, orange, or red car is easier to see under normal conditions. (That's why fire engines are those colors.)
>
> A light car is easier to keep cool in the summer (because it reflects sunlight). A dark car is easier to keep warm in the winter (because it absorbs sunlight).
>
> Silver is the most popular color, because it looks high-tech. Just make sure it includes sparkle, so your neighbors don't call it "gray."
>
> Silver and brown are the best at hiding dirt (because they *look* like dirt). White and black are the worst: every spot on your car will be an eyesore.
>
> Purple cars appeal to hippies (like me) but look cheap, so they're hard to resell. Gold cars appeal to retired folks who act rich and have no imagination.

Researchers in New Zealand examined records of car crashes and concluded that, in general, silver is the safest color; black and brown are the most dangerous. In a silver car, your chance of serious injury is ¼ as much as in a black or brown car, and ½ as much as in a "normal" car (white, yellow, red, or blue) — at least if you drive in New Zealand! The researchers analyzed the data carefully (to control for differences in sex, driver age, alcohol, weather, and time of day) and published the results in the *British Medical Journal*.

Upgrade Everybody loves a status symbol.

> I had a friend named Jerry Mender.
> His blood is on my Dodge's fender.
> If I could have dear Jerry back,
> I'd hit him with my Cadillac.

Repairs Cars eventually need repairs:

> **Dead cars and skin**
> My car and my body are both breaking down.
> We go to mechanics, who think I'm a clown.
> My car and my body will be in the ground
> Someday, but for now we can both tool around.
>
> In sunshine, we dine on cod livers and oil.
> We laugh at Death's hatchet, his evil plans foil
> Awhile, until finally he starts to chop,
> And our little joking forever shall stop.
>
> Dear Jesus says pieces of us shall resume,
> Be born-again Christians or Cadillacs soon.
> We look to the Son while our friends give us moons
> Out windows of wild things that we'll become soon.

Vans

I remember when my first wife went to the hospital, with body ills that were life-threatening.

Her name was Dodge. She was born in 1990. She must have been Dutch, since everybody called her "the van." She was so huge that folks called her a "one ton."

Her race was more interesting than "black" or "white." She was silver.

She was a battered woman over the years, but that day she lost her battery. She had many other maladies, too. My friends told me to sell her to the slave traders, but most folks would spurn her because she was "too old," "too big," and "traveled too many miles."

For many years, she'd supported me and carried me through life, and I supported her; but she'd been into the hospital many times and now seemed near death. The ambulance came. Since she was so big, she wouldn't fit on a cot, so the ambulance driver put her on a flatbed.

Planes

When Katie Rose Cappeller was an 8-year-old girl, she took her first flight on an airline. At the flight's end, she observed:

> Takeoff and landing are fun. The middle is boring.

The pilot replied —

> That's my job: to keep it boring.

Airline pilots often recite this prayer:

> I want to pass away quietly in my sleep, like my grandfather — Not screaming in horror, like his passengers.

Airplane crews get tired of repeating the same speeches to passengers on each flight. The Internet says some crews got creative, as follows....

Getting passengers to sit down The typical Southwest Airlines flight has no assigned seats: it lets passengers enter the plane then grab whatever seats they wish. When passengers took too long to pick seats, a flight attendant said:

> People, people, we're not picking out furniture here. Find a seat and *get in it!*

Teaching passengers about safety Here's what flight attendants told their passengers:

> To operate your seatbelt, insert the metal tab into the buckle and pull tight. It works just like every other seatbelt; and if you don't know how to operate one, you probably shouldn't be out in public unsupervised.
>
> If you wish to smoke, the smoking section on this airplane is on the wing; and if you can light 'em, you can smoke 'em.
>
> In the event of a sudden loss of cabin pressure, masks will descend from the ceiling. Stop screaming, grab the mask, and pull it over your face. If you have a small child traveling with you, secure your mask before assisting with theirs. If you're traveling with more than one small child, pick your favorite.
>
> There may be 50 ways to leave your lover, but there are just 4 ways out of this plane.
>
> In the event of an emergency water landing, your seat cushions can be used for flotation. Please paddle to shore, and take them with our compliments.

Pilot's welcome The pilot is supposed to make an announcement, welcoming passengers aboard. Here's what pilots announced:

> Delta Airlines is pleased to have some of the best flight attendants in the industry. Unfortunately, none of them are on this flight.
>
> Ladies and gentlemen, we've reached cruising altitude and will be turning down the cabin lights. This is for your comfort and to enhance the appearance of your flight attendants.
>
> Weather at our destination is 50° with some broken clouds, but we'll try to have them fixed before we arrive. Thank you and remember: nobody loves you — or your money — more than Southwest Airlines.

One pilot announced:

> Ladies and gentlemen, this is your captain speaking. Welcome to Flight 293, nonstop from New York to Los Angeles. The weather ahead is good, so we should have a smooth and uneventful flight. Now sit back and relax… *Oh, my God!*

Silence followed. After a few minutes, the pilot continued, on the intercom:

> Ladies and gentlemen, I'm so sorry if I scared you earlier. While I was talking to you, the flight attendant accidentally spilled a cup of hot coffee in my lap. You should see the front of my pants!

A passenger in coach yelled back:

> That's nothing. You should see the back of mine.

Deplaning

Deplaning After landing, here's what flight attendants said:

> Thank you for flying Delta Business Express. We hope you enjoyed giving us the business as much as we enjoyed taking you for a ride.

> We'd like to thank you folks for flying with us today; and the next time you get the insane urge to go blasting through the skies in a pressurized metal tube, we hope you'll think of US Airways.

> Please be sure to take all your belongings. If you're going to leave anything, please make sure it's something we'd like to have.

> Make sure to gather all your belongings. Anything left behind will be distributed evenly among the flight attendants. Please don't leave children or spouses.

After rough landings, flight attendants added these comments:

> That was quite a bump, and I know what y'all are thinking. I'm here to tell you it wasn't the airline's fault, it wasn't the pilot's fault, it wasn't the flight attendant's fault, it was the asphalt.

> Please remain seated, as Captain Kangaroo bounces us to the terminal.

> Please remain in your seats with your seatbelts fastened, while the captain taxis what's left of our plane to the gate.

> Please remain in your seats until Captain Crash & the Crew have brought the aircraft to a screeching halt against the gate. Once the tire smoke has cleared and the warning bells are silenced, we'll open the door, and you can pick your way through the wreckage to the terminal.

> Please take care when opening the overhead compartments because, after a landing like that, sure as hell, everything's shifted.

Balloons

To have more fun, try riding in a balloon! It's thrilling, if you don't mind being blown around in the air and not being quite sure where you'll land.

Balloonist instructor Clayton Thomas tells his passengers:

> Ballooning is a wonderful way to go from point A to point B, if you don't care where B is.

I asked him where that thought arose. He asked his friends, who came up with these paeans to the balloon philosophy of life....

In about 50 A.D., the Roman philosopher Lucius Annaeus Seneca said:

> If you know not what harbor you seek, any wind is the right wind.

In 1947, William Pène du Bois wrote *The 21 Balloons*, a novel where he said:

> The best way to travel, if you aren't in any hurry at all, if you don't care where you're going, if you don't like to use your legs, if you don't want to be annoyed at all by any choice of directions, is a balloon. In a balloon, you can decide only when to start, and usually when to stop. The rest is left entirely up to nature.

About the same time, Lord Ventry said:

> The only way for a gentleman to travel is by balloon.

Skates

With a little practice, you can travel faster on roller skates than on foot. So why didn't God give you roller skates instead of feet? Why didn't the law of "natural selection" develop a race of wheeled-footed creatures?

An engineer wrote an article saying roller skates are worse than feet at 3 tasks:

> going over bumps (and hills and stairs)
> walking through sand (and mud)
> making sharp turns (and sudden stops)

I found that article comforting, because now I know, when I see a roller-skater pass me on the sidewalk, that my appendage is superior to his.

But the article added a note of gloom: it went on to say that as our society builds even more paved roads and surfaces, roller skates will become more and more effective, and that — if the law of "natural selection" takes place — a future generation of rats will someday have biological roller skates instead of feet, to help them cross our highways fast without getting struck by a car.

I've dreaded the era of "Darwin's Street Rats." But that era's come already: in 1998, Roger Adams invented **heelies** (whose brand name is **Heelys**), which are shoes with removable rollers in the heels. They combine the best features of shoes and roller skates. Kids love 'em!

Finances

Finances are fun — when they're fat.

Stocks

The stock market's a fun game of Chicken Little. If the economy goes down a bit, stocks go down. If the economy goes *very* down, stocks go up, because investors think the Federal Reserve Bank will finally "sneeze" (do something about blowing out the problem); but when that bank finally decides *not* to sneeze, stocks go down even faster.

Teach your daughter According to a magazine called *The Industry Standard*, you should have a frank talk with your daughter about the "s" word. No, it's not "sex," it's stocks! Teach her the facts of life about "the bulls and the bears" and to distrust men who say "You can't lose on your first trade."

Stock-market jargon Remember why they call them stockbrokers: because after you give them money for stocks, you're broker.

Rising stocks should be called "helium." Fallen stocks should be called "feathers" (because they're down), which sounds better than "dogs."

Then analysts can say, "That stock is a feather — it's down." They can also advise, "When a stock goes helium, it's a gas; but when it turns to a feather, don't panic: sleep on it." Bears complain such advice is "full of bull" and you should "sell the feathers before they fall out of your pillow."

Here's a stock-market report from the Internet (transmitted by a computer club in Arizona):

> Today in the stock market…
> Helium was up, but feathers were down. Elevators rose, while escalators continued their slow decline.
> Knives were up sharply. Cows steered into a bull market. Weights were up in heavy trading. Balloon prices were inflated. Caterpillar stock inched up a bit. Sun peaked at midday. Batteries exploded in an attempt to recharge the market.
> Paper was stationary. Diapers remain unchanged. Shipping lines stayed at an even keel.
> Mining equipment hit rock bottom. Pencils lost a few points. Light switches were off. Coca Cola fizzled. Fluorescent tubing was dimmed in light trading. Hiking equipment was trailing. The market for raisins dried up.

Banks

Banks try hard to get new depositors. I keep waiting for a bank ad to brag:

> You get more interest from us than from your spouse.
> We give you something *really big* to play with.

Women who are bank tellers intrigue male customers.

> The lady in the bank
> Is looking very swank.
> I want to call her "honey,"
> But she just wants my money.
>
> She sits behind the glass.
> She's got a pretty ass?
> Alas, I'll never know,
> Since I can't see below.
>
> That gal is really spiff.
> She looks so damn terrif!
> She makes me want to drool,
> But she thinks I'm a fool.
>
> Each day my interest grows.
> How much? She always knows.
> At least she doesn't groan
> When I ask for a loan.
>
> Her skillful hands! Her knowing eyes!
> Men wait in line for her surprise.
> With clever charm and dazzling flair
> She'll stash our cash in there somewhere:
> She makes dreams vanish in thin air.

Insurance

Insurance companies are strange: you give them money and hope you never get anything in return.

I'm not an insurance-oriented person. I've tried hard in my life to avoid health insurance (optional), car insurance (optional in New Hampshire), and home insurance (optional if you don't have a mortgage). I figure, "Why give them money then waste time arguing with them to pay claims?" Except for my wife's restaurant business, all those insurances are optional. If I have an emergency and go broke, that's fine with me: a change would do me good.

Gambling

Getting addicted to casino gambling is stupid, since the odds are always against you (unless you're a blackjack "card counter" who'll eventually get thrown out).

In roulette, the losses are simple to compute: you have 36 numbers plus 0 and 00, making a total of 38 numbers, and roulette pays out just 36 to 1 (35 extra chips plus your original) instead of 38 to 1, so on an average bet you'll receive $\frac{36}{38}$ of what you wagered, giving the house a profit of $\frac{2}{38}$ per transaction, which is $\frac{1}{19}$, which is about 5%. Why would I want to play a game where I know I'm going to lose an average of 5% per play?

I admit it can be "cheap entertainment per hour" when "there's nothing else to do at night" so you "feel like a big shot when you bet big" or "bet just a buck and maybe get lucky," but those arguments aren't convincing.

Gambling is the opposite of democracy. In democracy, we try to treat everybody equally; in gambling, we try to anoint somebody as the "winner," the "king" to which all the others must pay homage and call themselves "losers" or "serfs." We gamble because of our hidden desire to return to a feudal system, to see who'll be the "king with the concubines" or the "knight for the night."

Mmathematicians admit gambling is good in this situation:

> Suppose you're running a nonprofit organization, and some philanthropist or government agency says that if your organization can raise a million dollars by a certain date, you'll receive a matching fund of another million dollars. Suppose the deadline is approaching and you've raised nearly a million dollars but you're still short. In that case, it would be rational to go to Las Vegas and gamble some of the money, since the winner's payoff gets increased by a million dollars.

Payroll taxes

To understand how payroll taxes work, suppose you're a typical American: you have a job that's advertised as paying a salary of $30,000 per year (or, equivalently, a wage of $15 per hour for 2000 hours per year). Part of that $30,000 goes to the government for taxes. How much of the $30,000 is left for you to keep?

Here's how to figure that out, using Form 1040 for the tax year 2010. (Later years are similar, just slightly adjusted for inflation and any "stimulus" that Saint Obama decides to give us.)

On the form, lines 7-21 ask you to list all forms of income. You're supposed to list what you gained from salaries, wages, savings-bank interest, stock & bond sales, renting out rooms in your home, businesses you own, and other things. Let's suppose your life is simple and you got no significant income beyond the $30,000, so your **total income** is just $30,000. Line 22 asks you to write that total, $30,000.

Next, lines 23-35 ask you to list any **special deductions** you can take, such as for tuition, IRAs, and moving expenses. Suppose your life is simple and you're not entitled to any special deductions, so your special deductions total $0. Line 36 asks you to write that total, $0.

Line 37 tells you to subtract the special deductions ($0) from the total income ($30,000) and write the result, which is still $30,000, which is your **adjusted gross income (AGI)**.

Let's assume you're boringly normal: you're single, not blind, not yet 65 years old, not having kids or other dependents, and nobody can claim *you* as a dependent. Since you're a boringly normal person, you get just 1 **exemption**, which is worth $3650. You also get the $5700 **standard deduction** (unless you want to go to the trouble of filling out Schedule A, which lets you substitute a list of **itemized deductions** instead, which works to your advantage just if you gave *lots* of money to charities, doctors, unions, accountants, sales tax, real-estate tax, mortgage bankers, or thieves). So if you're boringly normal, you get the $3650 exemption and the $5700 standard deduction, which totals $9350, which the government thinks is enough for you to live on (hah!) and therefore won't tax you on. You subtract that $9350 from the $30,000 adjusted gross income, giving you $20,650, which is your **taxable income**, on line 43.

To compute the tax on that $20,650, the government uses this method:

> Pay 10% tax on the first $8,375.
> Pay 15% tax on the rest.

So you should pay $837.50 (10% of $8,375) plus $1841.25 (15% of "$20,650-$8,375"), which gives a grand total of $2678.75. But since that math is complicated, the government tells you to skip that math and look up the answer in a tax table instead, which gives a similar answer, $2683. That's your **income tax**, which you write on line 44.

So on the $30,000 you made, you must pay an income tax of $2683. That doesn't seem big. But you must also pay 2 more taxes: **Social Security** and **Medicare**. They're supposed to help you later, when you become old, decrepit, or dead. Social Security tax is 6.2% of the salary or wage; Medicare tax is 1.45% of the salary or wage. So for your $30,000 salary, your taxes look like this:

```
$2683 for income tax
$1860 for Social Security  (6.2%  of $30,000)
 $435 for Medicare         (1.45% of $30,000)
```

That makes a total tax of $4978.

Withholding Your employer automatically takes the Social Security tax and Medicare tax out of each paycheck (and sends that money to the government for you), so you don't have to compute those taxes, and they aren't even mentioned on Form 1040.

Also, your employer automatically *tries* to take the income tax out of each paycheck (using the data you wrote on your W-4 form when you were hired), but computing that tax accurately is hard, so the government makes the employer take out slightly *more* than necessary, just to be safe. On Form 1040's line 64, you write how much your employer took out (**federal income tax withheld**). If that amount was more than necessary, you get a refund.

That's how the federal payroll tax system works for a typical employee.

Extra laws Most states and towns make you pay taxes to *them*, too: sales taxes, real-estate property taxes, income taxes, excise taxes (on gasoline, etc.), and license fees.

The government keeps creating new laws to make rich folks pay even more, poor folks pay even less, decent people get tax breaks whenever they exhibit good citizenship, and rich folks avoid buying excessive insurance. To learn about all those laws, read Form 1040's instruction book carefully (or use a tax program or ask an accountant).

For example, to make rich folks pay even more, the full tax computation goes like this:

```
Pay 10% tax on the first part of taxable income    ($0-$8,375).
Pay 15% tax on the next  part of taxable income    ($8,375-$34,000).
Pay 25% tax on the next  part of taxable income    ($34,000-$82,400).
Pay 28% tax on the next  part of taxable income    ($82,400-$171,850).
Pay 33% tax on the next  part of taxable income  ($171,850-$373,650).
Pay 35% tax on the       rest of taxable income  (over $373,650).
```

Employer taxes If you're an employer, you're supposed to pass to the federal government the taxes you withheld from employee paychecks (the federal income tax, the 6.2% Social Security tax, and the 1.45% Medicare tax). But you must give the federal government *extra* money too, out of your *own* pocket.

For example, consider the Social Security tax. The employee contributed 6.2% for that, but the government wants to receive twice as much (12.4%) instead. Where does the difference come from? The *employer's* pocket! The employer withholds 6.2% from the employee's paycheck but must give 12.4% to the government!

Similarly, the employee contributed 1.45% for Medicare tax, but the government wants to receive twice as much (2.9%); that extra comes out of the *employer's* pocket.

Insurance taxes The employer also has to pay **state unemployment insurance**, **federal unemployment insurance**, and **worker's compensation insurance (worker's comp)**. The formulas for those amounts get complicated; they depend on each employee's salary and the company's history (how many employees got fired or injured). They typically add up to about 10%. The employer pays for all that insurance; it's illegal for the employer to ask the employee to pay any of it.

Health insurance Some states require big employers to also provide health insurance.

Under the table The employer is supposed to pay, from the employer's own pocket, the 6.2% Social Security tax, 1.45% Medicare tax, and 10% in insurance taxes, making a total of 17.65%, which is $5295 per employee per year (for $30,000 employees), plus maybe health insurance.

To avoid paying all that, dishonest employers pretend they have fewer employees, by paying employees secretly, "**under the table**," which is illegal. If you're an employee who's being paid under the table, remember that you'll get screwed when you eventually try to collect benefits from Social Security, Medicare, unemployment insurance, worker's compensation, or health insurance.

Self-employed You've seen that if you're a typical employee, you "contribute" a 6.2% Social Security tax and 1.45% Medicare tax, and your employer "contributes" an equal matching amount on your behalf, so altogether the government receives 12.4% Social Security and 2.9% Medicare contributions on your behalf. But what if you have no employer? What if *you're* the boss?

In that case, since you're acting as the "employee" and also the "employer," the government makes you pay the whole thing yourself: you must pay "12.4% Social Security and 2.9% Medicare," which totals 15.3%. But since the employer's part of that is a "business expense," you get to deduct part of that tax. To do all that fairly, the government does fancy math:

The government has you fill out Schedule C (to compute your business's profit, which is your "salary"), then sends you to Schedule SE (to compute the 15.3%). But Schedule SE gives you two surprising breaks: it lets you multiply by .9235 (instead of paying the full amount) and also lets you take half the result as a business deduction (on Form 1040's line 27).

Careers

Good luck with your career.

> Careers careen.
> Use your bean!

A good-for-nothing relative sent me this memo from the Internet about how job-hunting requires the patience of Job:

> My first job? In an orange-juice factory! But I got canned: couldn't concentrate.
> Then I worked as a lumberjack but couldn't hack it, so they gave me the ax.
> I tried working in a muffler factory but found it was exhausting.
> I worked for a pool-maintenance company but found the work too draining.
> I became a professional fisherman but found I couldn't live on my net income.
> I got hired to feed giraffes at a zoo but got fired because I wasn't up to it.
> I tried being a tailor but wasn't suited for a sew-sew job.
> I tried being a barber but couldn't cut it.
> I tried being a deli worker; but any way I sliced it, I couldn't cut the mustard.
> I worked at Starbucks but quit because it was always the same old grind.
> To spice up my life, I tried being a chef but didn't have the thyme.
> I tried working in a shoe factory but didn't fit in.
> I got a job in a health club, but they said I wasn't fit for the job.
> I tried being a musician but wasn't noteworthy enough.
> I spent years studying to become a doctor but didn't have enough patience.
> I took a job as an historian, until I realized there was no future in it.
> So I retired — and found I'm a perfect fit for the job… of doing nothing!

To create an impressive résumé, you can give yourself a fancy title, even if you're just unemployed at home:

What you do	Your title
answer & screen phone calls	Manager of high-speed fiber-optic network
generally mow the lawn	General in charge of advanced weaponry
use weed killer & bug killer	Director of chemical warfare
scrub & wash the dishes	Chief surgeon, microbiology department
rinse & dry the dishes	Chief officer, aquatic rescue operations
take out the garbage	Director of environmental services
clean the house	Curator of the Americana Museum
get divorced	First mate on the USS Matrimony

By dishing out those titles to your housemates, you can make household chores more fun. Aye, aye, mate! Salute the dishes!

When an airline pilot (Larry Govoni) was leaving his plane, he peeked under the plane and saw a worker trying to empty the plane's toilet. The hose burst and sprayed shit all over the worker. Larry looked at the poor worker and asked, "Why do you put up with a job like this? Why don't you quit?" The worker replied:

> What!!! And give up a career in the aerospace industry?

Here's the moral of that tale:

> Your first job might rain shit on you, but it can lead to better things.

Here's the counter-moral:

> If your first job rains shit on you, remember it can lead to better things — but probably won't.

Drew Carey said:

> You hate your job? Why didn't you say so!
> There's a support group for that: it's called *Everybody*, and they meet at the bar.

If you must work nights, recite this poem:

> **Night crew**
>
> I'm called a secret worker.
> I work throughout the night.
> I keep the world in order,
> So mornings will delight.
>
> Though you may never see me,
> You're glad that I've been here.
> When folks come to relieve me,
> We give each other cheer.
>
> I try to do what's right.
> Please tell me if I'm wrong
> And give me one more chance
> To show the world my song.
>
> A creature of the night,
> I venture out at day
> To stare at God's bright light,
> Then sleep, then work and pray.

Ultimate boss

Who's your ultimate boss, really? Each employee lusts to be the employee's boss, but that boss wants to be the boss's boss, until you finally get up to the **chief executive officer (CEO)**, who's still not really the final boss, since the CEO is at the mercy of the Board of Directors and its chairman, who really isn't the boss either, since he's at the mercy of the stockholders who can vote him out of office. But the stockholders aren't the bosses either, since they're rather powerless to control the company: they just gaze at it from afar.

Some computer techs view their employers not as "bosses" but as "clients." If the "clients" are mean to them, they quit and find different clients who are nicer. The techs treat those corporations not as their bosses but as just tools, to use as ways to get "computers to play with" and "interesting experiences," until it's time to move on to experiences that are even wilder.

Remember: you're not just an "employee"; you're your own boss. If your "client" ever gives you a hard time, find another and let your client go begging and whither.

You're the master of your own fate. In 1875, William Ernest Henley said in his poem *Invictus*:

> I am the master of my fate:
> I am the captain of my soul.

You're in charge, tiger. Just make sure that, before you quit, you have another job lined up — or at least some savings to get over the bump in your road.

Fame

Becoming famous is easy: just do something wonderful, horrible, or crazy. The hard part is living with yourself afterwards, since the rest of your life will seem boring after your bout of fame.

For example, Albert Einstein is usually pictured as an old, wise guy; but the work that made him famous, "The Special Theory of Relativity," was done when he was about 20, just a kid. Albert Einstein, sports heroes, and rock stars became famous because of what they accomplished during their youths. They fight bouts of depression when they get older.

If you're not famous yet, don't be discouraged: be happy you still have a chance to look forward to, instead of a youth to look back at and mourn the loss of.

No matter how famous you become, you don't control of your career.

> If you're a famous actor, you're at the mercy of the script written by somebody else. If you're the screenwriter who wrote that script, you're at the mercy of how the director and actors butcher it.
>
> If you're President of the United States, you can't accomplish anything unless you convince Congress to pass laws supporting your position. For example, President Kennedy didn't accomplish much, because Congress disagreed with him; President Lyndon Johnson, who came next, created many wonderful programs (such as Head Start) because he got Congress on his side; but he got booed anyway because he botched one "little" part of his job: the Vietnam War.
>
> If you're the president of a company, you can get fired by the board of directors.
>
> If you're a TV anchorman, you're at the mercy of the scripts and video clips that the rest of the news team hands you. If you're a TV weatherman, you feel useless when the weather is boringly nice or when the U.S. Weather Service feeds you a prediction that turns out wrong.

If you're a sports hero, what happens when your team loses?

Passions and dreams

A friend asked, "What are your passions, and did you follow your dreams?" I replied, "I followed my dream, until she locked the door."

Follow your dreams until they turn impractical. Then fine-tune them, to maximize ROI (return on investment).

I confess to this passion:

> I want to do enough good to make me famous for doing good.

Though the word "famous" makes me seem vain, it's my form of reinforcement and at least produces a positive social effect.

Word on the door

Here's a famous tale:

> A professor, walking to his classroom, tries to think of how to inspire his students to improve. When he reaches the door, he sees the word "Push," which gives him the idea: he walks into the classroom and gives an inspiring speech ending with, "To get ahead in your career, you need one key thing, written on the door you came through!" The students look at the door and see the key to getting ahead: "Pull."

To get ahead, you must **push** yourself to work harder but also make friends with folks who can **pull** you up.

Apologize

If you make a mistake at work, apologize. My uncle recommended saying this:

> I'm the opposite of a mechanic. A mechanic screws things *down*. I screwed things *up*. Sorry!

Marketing

If you're a woman who sees an attractive guy at a party, how should you react? The Internet includes this explanation of marketing terms, so you can get your MBA:

> If you go up to him and say "I'm fantastic in bed," that's **direct marketing**. If instead you say "Clint Eastwood said I'm fantastic in bed," that's **celebrity marketing**. If you say "I'm fantastic in bed and you can take me to just Burger King afterwards, unlike that blonde, whom you must take to the Keg," that's **price differentiation**. If you say "I'm fantastic in bed" and he says "She's fantastic in bed" to the next guy, who passes the comment to a third guy, that's **viral marketing**.
>
> Suppose you go up to him, pour him a drink, say "May I," reach up to straighten his tie, while brushing your breast lightly against his arm, then say "By the way, I'm fantastic in bed." That's **public relations**.
>
> If instead one of your *friends* goes up to him, points at you, and says "She's fantastic in bed," that's **advertising**. If your friend adds, "She's more fantastic in bed than that brunette," it's **comparative advertising**. If she says "Every guy at the McDonald's on First Avenue says she's fantastic in bed," that's **institutional advertising** and **corporate endorsement**.

> Suppose instead you go up to him, get his phone number, then phone him the next day and say "Hi, I'm fantastic in bed." That's **telemarketing**.
>
> Suppose you go up to him and he *promises* to give you his number, but then a whole bunch of new girls arrive, so all the guys hesitate giving you their numbers, and at the end of the night you give your number to the pathetic guy collecting empties. That's **product life cycle**.
>
> If, on the other hand, *he* walks up to *you* and says "I hear you're fantastic in bed," that's **brand recognition**.
>
> If a man ignores you because there are other women at the party, that's **elastic demand**. If he jumps on you right away (and offers you dinner and a movie) because no other women are at the party, that's **inelastic demand**.
>
> If you go up to a *group* of handsome guys you never slept with and say "I'm fantastic in bed," that's **market penetration**. If, just before saying that, you open your top more and tug down your pants to expose your thong, that's **product development**.
>
> Suppose you go up to a group of guys. By using covert hugging and flicking off imaginary lint, you manage to slip your phone number into their wallets. You also remove any phone numbers they collected from other women and write your phone number atop of those other numbers and bigger than those numbers. That's **search-engine optimization**.
>
> Suppose you see a group of guys you never slept with, ignore them, walk up to the *girls* they're with, and tell the *girls* "I'm fantastic in bed." That's **product diversification**.
>
> If you walk around the room, asking guys how much money's in their wallets and whether they have jobs & cars, to decide which guys to give your phone number to, that's **target-market segmentation**.
>
> If you go up to a guy you slept with before and say "I'd like to sleep with you again in a different position," that's **market development**.
>
> If you talk a guy into going to bed with your *friend*, you're a **sales rep**. If your friend can't satisfy him, so he calls *you*, you're doing **tech support**.
>
> While you're on your way to a party, suppose you think about all the great men that could be in all the houses you pass, so you climb on the roof of a house at the center and shout at the top of your lungs "I'm fantastic in bed." That's **spam**.

Those examples were collected at:

www.witiger.com/marketing/marketingisnotadvertisingalone.htm

Office worse than prison

According to the Internet, being in an office is worse than prison:

prison:	you spend most of your time in a 10-by-10 cell
work:	you spend most of your time in an 8-by-8 cubicle
prison:	you get 3 free meals a day
work:	you get a break for 1 meal and must pay for it
prison:	if you have good behavior, you get time off
work:	if you have good behavior, you get more work
prison:	you can watch TV and play games
work:	you get fired for watching TV and playing games
prison:	you get your own toilet
work:	you must share the toilet with people who pee on the seat
prison:	they let your family and friends visit
work:	you're not supposed to chat with your family
prison:	the helpful guard locks and unlocks all doors for you
work:	you must open and close all doors yourself
prison:	all expenses are paid by taxpayers, with no work required of you
work:	you pay all your expenses to go to work, and the IRS deducts taxes from your salary to pay for prisoners
prison:	you spend most of your life inside bars, wanting to get out
work:	you spend most of your time wanting to get out and go inside bars
prison:	you must deal with sadistic wardens
work:	they're called "managers"

Now get back to work. You're not getting paid to read jokes!

Management

Here are tricks to becoming a good boss.

Signs

To help your company succeed, hang cute signs that make your customers smile, such as these gems (from the Internet and my personal observations):

Where seen	Message
Tire shop	Invite us to your next blowout.
Muffler shop	No appointment necessary. We hear you coming.
Radiator shop	Best place in town to take a leak.
Tow truck	We don't charge an arm and a leg. We want tows.
Tow truck #2	If you drink and drive, we might meet by accident.
Car dealership	Best way to get back on your feet: miss a car payment.
Restaurant	Don't stand there hungry. Come in and get fed up.
Pizza shop	7 days without pizza makes one weak.
Propane-filling station	Tank heaven for little grills.
Septic-tank truck	We're #1 in the #2 business.
Plumber's truck	We repair what your husband fixed.
Plumber's truck #2	Don't sleep with a drip. Call your plumber.
Plumber's truck #3	We keep you in hot water.
Electrician's truck	Let us remove your shorts.
Electric company	We'd be delighted if you send in your payment. But if you don't, you will be.
Blasting company	We set earth-shattering standards.
Steel-construction co.	Our erections last a lifetime.
Plastic surgeon's office	Can we pick your nose?
Podiatrist's office	Time wounds all heels.
Proctologist's door	To expedite your visit, please back in.
Veterinarian's office	Be back in 5 minutes. Sit! Stay!
Maternity-room door	Push. Push. Push.
Gynecologist's office	Dr. Jones, at your cervix.
Optometrist's office	If you don't see what you're looking for, you've come to the right place.
Dry cleaner	Drop your pants here and get prompt attention.
Funeral home's lawn	Drive carefully. We'll wait.
Motel swimming pool	We don't swim in your toilet. Please don't piss in our pool.
Fence	Salesmen welcome! Dog food is expensive.
Fence #2	Beware of owner — never mind the dog.
Office door	Danger: contents under pressure.
Employee's T-shirt	I've used up my sick days, so I'm calling in dead.
Nonsmoking area	If we see smoke, we'll assume you're on fire and take action.
Store security dept.	God helps those who help themselves, but God help those who help themselves here.

Employees appreciate this advice from the Internet:

Grant me the serenity to accept what I cannot change, the courage to change what I cannot accept, and the wisdom to hide the bodies I butchered today when they pissed me off.

Be careful of the toes you step on today, as they may be connected to the ass you must kiss tomorrow.

Always give 100% at work: 12% on Monday, 23% Tuesday, 40% Wednesday, 20% Thursday, and 5% Friday.

When you get upset, remember it takes 42 muscles to frown but just 4 to extend your middle finger.

Be nice

Jimmy Durante said:

Be nice to people on your way up —
because you might meet them on your way down.

If you're the boss, here are 4 cost-effective ways to be nice to your employees:

Give raises often
If necessary, make the raises small, but give them *often* (to employees doing well).

For an hourly employee, give a 25¢-per-hour raise, often. For example, instead of giving a $1-per-hour raise at the end of the year, give a 25¢-per-hour raise 4 times per year.

That way, the employee can proudly tell family & friends about the frequent raises, and the employees will feel their careers and lives are moving forward. That pride will turn into a more enthusiastic work ethic, more energy & speed, more efficiency, and less turnover. It will also encourage other employees to do better so *they* can get raises soon too! Just tell your employees, "I'm looking for a solid excuse to give you all raises soon, so do well!"

I've had good luck starting employees at low salaries (while in training) but giving them frequent raises as they learn more and become more marketable: a 25¢-per-hour raise *every 2 weeks!*

Do "favors"
Although high wages and salaries are effective motivator, "favors" are even more effective and cost less.

Take the employees to dinner. (The meal is partly a tax write-off if you spend at least half of the conversation on business.) Give the employees a pleasant working environment. Give them flexible hours. Let them take time off from work whenever they wish (without pay but without criticizing them). Thank them and praise them when they do well (or at least haven't screwed up recently).

Employees remember favors, tell their friends about them, and make the employees want to stay at your company because of their love for your personal interest in them.

Look at your bottom line: a bunch of favors costs even less than a tiny raise and is remembered more. Moreover, they make you seem human instead of an asshole.

Don't fire a bad employee immediately
Instead, chat with the employee.

Say you want to help the employee do better to protect the employee from getting fired. Say that you're on the employee's side and you won't fire the employee unless you have to, but warn that the "have to" might come soon unless the employee and you can work together to make things better.

When you say that you're willing to "go to bat" for the employee, the employee will typically respond by trying to "go to bat" for you.

If you think the employee is hopelessly incompetent and will get fired anyway, chat with the employee to help find a more suitable line of work. That will help the employee's future and also help yours, since you'll avoid getting penalized by the state government for generating unemployment claims.

Congratulate a good employee who leaves
If a good employee decides to leave the company, congratulate the employee on moving ahead and for "graduating" from the job. Remind the employee that alumni are always welcome to come back, as consultants or part-timers or temps or, after further experiences outside the company, to higher positions in management.

When other employees see you congratulate the dear departed, those employees will feel less nervous about telling you *their* career plans, so you won't be hit by *unexpected* departures that could wreck your company.

Job recommendations

When my employees go on to hunt for better jobs and ask me for a "job recommendation," I say "gladly" and also say I prefer to give the recommendation by phone.

When the interviewer phones me to ask whether the employee was good, I try to think of at least one good thing and one bad thing to say about the employee.

> If I were to say just good things, the interviewer would think I was just whitewashing over problems and wasn't telling the whole truth, so I try to include something that's negative but not important to that particular job. Then the interviewer trusts me for being a well-balanced objective journalist and thinks employee's strengths and weaknesses are good match to the new job, making the employee an enthusiastic member of the new team.

I try to help all employees do well in their afterlife, just like a high-school tries to help its graduates move on to the best colleges. Then I can brag to new faces who are thinking of working for me, "This is a great place to work, because this job prepares you for a super-successful career: just look at what happened to my graduates!"

That's the same pitch the military uses, to get kids to enlist: this job trains you to be tomorrow's leaders.

On the Internet, I found this cute example of a job recommendation:

> Memo to Managing Director:
> 1 Bob Smith, my assistant programmer, can always be found
> 2 hard at work at his desk. He works independently, without
> 3 wasting company time talking to colleagues. Bob never
> 4 thinks twice about assisting fellow employees, and always
> 5 finishes given assignments on time. Often he takes extended
> 6 measures to complete his work, sometimes skipping coffee
> 7 breaks. Bob is a dedicated individual who has absolutely no
> 8 vanity in spite of his high accomplishments and profound
> 9 knowledge in his field. I firmly believe that Bob can be
> 10 classed as an asset employee, the type which cannot be
> 11 dispensed with. Consequently, I recommend that Bob be
> 12 promoted to executive management, and a proposal will be
> 13 executed as soon as possible.
>
> Addendum:
> That idiot was standing over my shoulder while I wrote the report I sent you earlier today. Please reread just the odd-numbered lines.

3 envelopes

Business executives ponder the tale of the 3 envelopes:

> It's time for a new person to be the CEO. He gets this advice from his predecessor: "I've prepared 3 envelopes. Here they are, but don't open them yet. If you ever have trouble, open the first envelope. If you have further trouble, open the second envelope. If you have even more trouble, open the third envelope. Each envelope contains 3 magic words saying what to do so the company will succeed. Good luck."
>
> At first, the new CEO does well, as the company's employees eagerly help him learn the ropes and give him the benefit of the doubt. But after that honeymoon period, things start going downhill.
>
> He opens the first envelope. It contains these 3 magic words: "Blame your predecessor." He's so happy to read those words, because they're so right! He obeys those words. He tells the employees and stockholders that the company's problems are just the delayed consequences of the mistakes that his predecessor made, and he'll usher in the dawn of a new, better era. That pep talk works. Everybody is inspired by his gung-ho forward-looking attitude, and the company improves. But eventually, things start going downhill again.
>
> He opens the second envelope. It contains these 3 magic words: "Reorganize the company." He's so happy to read those words, because they're so right! He obeys those words. He fires the employees who are deadwood and invents new ways of managing everything. That improves the company. But eventually, things start going downhill again.
>
> He opens the third envelope. It says: "Prepare three envelopes."

Every CEO goes through those 3 cycles before getting canned. Which envelope is *your* company's CEO using now? #1, #2, or #3?

Restaurant management

Most Americans (over 50% of them) wind up eventually working for a restaurant sometime during their careers. "Working for a restaurant" could mean as a cook, a server (waiter or waitress), a bartender, a dishwasher, a greeter (host or hostess or costumed character), a table-cleaner (busboy or busgirl), an entertainer (musician, magician, or DJ), or a manager.

Here are tips about being a good restaurant boss. Even if you'd rather be the boss of some other kind of business, you'll find these tips worth reading, for 2 reasons:

> Many of these tips about restaurant management apply to other businesses also.
>
> When you eat at a restaurant, you should have some kind of idea of the hell that takes place when you aren't looking.

Some of these tips are well known throughout the restaurant industry. Others are derived from my personal experiences helping my wife Donna run her restaurant.

Should you own? If you dream of owning your own restaurant, cool your enthusiasm. Owning a restaurant is less pleasant than most people think:

You'll feel pressure to work long hours: breakfast, lunch, and dinner; weekdays, weekends, and holidays; prep before breakfast; cleanup after dinner; late-night bar and party functions. bar-and-parties. If you're not at the restaurant during all those hours, your employees will screw up (if they're there) or your competitors will steal your business (if your employees are *not* there).

You'll be constantly handling crises. In the restaurant business, the employees, food suppliers, and equipment are all unreliable: either they don't show up or else they screw up so badly that you wish they didn't exist at all. The customers are unpredictable: huge hoards of customers show up at unexpected moments; you can't handle them all well, so you get a bad reputation. The health inspector shows up at unexpected moments, too, with a single mission: to find things to yell at you about. The labor department and fire department send inspectors too, just to find *more* things to yell at you about. At unexpected times, no customers show up at all, and you regret paying so many employees to stand around doing nothing. Each day, you'll tear your hair out, though by the end of the day the crisis is usually solved and you can put your toupee back on.

You'll make less profit than you expect. In fact, if you make any profit at all, you're lucky: the average restaurant lasts just 2 years, before it goes bankrupt or gets shut down by authorities or its owner gets disgusted and quits. You'll discover that the chefs and servers typically make more dollars per hour than an owner does (especially when you include any "fringe benefits" they get, such as tips, free food, and state-required insurance). The word that best describes the typical restaurant owner is: deluded!

Ted Turner (the billionaire who started CNN and married Jane Fonda) said that if you want to get rich fast, the *worst* businesses to own are "restaurants" and "gas stations," because both require long hours, give you little pay, and are harder to manage than you think. For example, if you're a Mom who does a great job of cooking for your family, don't jump to the conclusion that you have the experience necessary to run a restaurant business profitably: you need to learn a lot about "business profitability" first! Before opening your own restaurant, try working in somebody else's, to get practice and see what goes wrong and how to handle crises. Let somebody else take the risks while you learn. Wayne Green said:

> Make your mistakes on somebody *else*'s money.

How to start If you nevertheless decide to start a restaurant, you must decide whether to create your own from scratch or buy a pre-existing restaurant.

If you create your own restaurant from scratch, you must buy or lease a building space then spend many thousands of dollars for equipment and décor.

> The equipment will cost more than you think, because health inspectors require you to buy equipment that's for commercial (heavy-duty) use rather than residential use. You're not allowed to use the cheap kitchen appliances you see for sale at discount stores such as Best Buy.
>
> You must obey all the rules about "restaurant buildings," such as having good vents (to let out the cooking smoke), many kinds of sinks (some for dirty dishes, some for rinsing dishes, some for washing vegetables, some for washing mops), handicapped-accessible bathrooms, tables far enough apart so customers can run between them to escape a fire, handrails on stairs, kitchen doors that shut automatically (to stop any kitchen fire from spreading), not too much junk stored in the basement, and no electrical cords that people can trip on.
>
> The fire department will also require that the cooking vents be cleaned every six months, so put them where the professional "cooking vent cleaning crew" can get into them easily. Any big change to the flooring or walls will require approval from a building inspector, who will charge you for a building permit (and charge you fines for whatever you screw up).

If you buy a restaurant that already exists, find out how many laws might be broken. Officials don't bother old restaurants much, but since you'll be the new owner, your layout and operations will be looked at critically, even if you keep the same layout and operations as your predecessor. Officials like to give new owners a hard time, to make sure the new owners "get the message" and get off to a good, clean start.

You must register your restaurant's name with your state's "Secretary of State Office," which will reject the name if it sounds confusingly like the name of any other business in the state (even if the other business is far away, and even if the other business has been defunct for many decades). If you want to put a sign in your window or on your lawn or in your parking lot, you'll need permission from the town's "architecture committee" (or zoning board), to make sure your sign doesn't violate your town's sense of beauty, especially if the town considers itself beautifully picturesque (as many towns here in New England do). If you plan to serve alcohol or stay open late, you'll need permission from the town, to make sure you won't bother nearby families who want to go to bed early without hearing songs, yells, and crashes from your drunk customers.

If you plan to sell wine, beer, or harder liquors, you must get a license from your state's "liquor authority," which will make you fill out lots of forms about your financial background and operations, to make sure you're not controlled by the Mafia. You must follow your state's laws about where to buy your alcohol supplies: typically, restaurants aren't allowed to by alcohol from consumer stores, such as supermarkets. Similar restrictions apply to cigarettes — if your state permits cigarette smoking in restaurants at all.

As with any business that has employees, you're required to set up paperwork so you can hand the state its sales taxes, meals taxes, profit taxes, and unemployment taxes, hand the IRS the other payroll taxes, pay workers comp insurance, and pay whatever other health & liability insurance your state or landlord demand.

Crooks

Many people fantasize about becoming crooks. This section explains how to turn that fantasy into reality.

Since your reputation is your most valuable asset, becoming a crook is foolish: in the long run, you'll lose more than you gain. The chapter's purpose isn't to make you a crook but rather to answer your questions about crookedness and protect yourself against the crooked.

Your first little swindle

The first step to becoming a professional crook is the "little swindle."

Suppose you buy a toaster and it breaks after the warranty's run out. Here's how to get a fixed toaster: free!

Go back to the store, buy another toaster having the same model number, and take it home. Then return the old, defective toaster to the store and complain it's defective. To prove you bought that toaster recently, show the store the sales slip you received that day. Unless the store's clerk notices that toaster's serial number doesn't match the sales slip, the clerk will let you return the defective toaster and give you a refund.

How to shortchange

The fundamental philosophy of shortchanging is: create so many simultaneous transactions that the cashier can't remember which transaction is which.

For example, suppose you want to buy an item for $3.50. Give the cashier a 5-dollar bill. Before he gives you the change, give him an extra dollar and say, "Never mind, just give me change for that."

Before he gives you change for the dollar, sneak away the 5-dollar bill. After he gives you the change, walk away — without having paid for the $3.50 item. If he asks "What about the $3.50?" reply "I gave you a five!" You can even ask him, "And where's my change for the five?"

One crook makes his living from just two sources: shortchanging and pimping. For example, he managed to create so many 1-dollar, 5-dollar, and 20-dollar transactions simultaneously at a gas station that the attendant got totally confused — and got cleaned out of $100 altogether!

How to pickpocket

To pick a wallet from the back pocket of a man's pants, use this 3-step method....

> The first step is to **put your fingers into his pocket**. Put just two fingers into his pocket: your middle finger and your index finger. When putting them into his pocket, make sure the palm side of your hand is near his skin, rather than the knuckle side of your hand (which is too bony and therefore too easily detected). Use those two fingers as chopsticks: make those fingers pinch his wallet. During that process, he might feel your fingers, but he won't be suspicious, since he can't feel their bones, and since your fingers are moving down into his pocket and therefore aren't removing anything from his pocket. For best results, distract him by touching some other part of his body. (If you're in a crowd, "accidentally" bump against this guy. If you're pretending to be a prostitute, rub his balls.)
>
> The second step is to **pull the wallet away from his skin**, so that the wallet is still inside his pocket but he can't feel the wallet.
>
> Finally, **lift the wallet from the pocket**. He can't feel you lift the wallet, since the wallet isn't against his skin.

Nifty, huh? Try that 3-step process on a friend. But please don't try it on me!

Big time

Once you get into the "big time," you can make lots of money!

For example, you can buy a tow truck, take it to a street where many cars are parked illegally, and tow them all away, to do with as you please!

Better yet, buy a van, pretend you're a house mover, and clean out somebody's apartment while he's away at work!

Since the police view such activities unkindly, you'll spend the last part of your life in jail. But the first part can be really fun!

How to steal legally

Now I'm going to teach you a more clever way to steal money. This clever way is used by many shady companies and is completely legal!

It's called the **pyramid debt**.

Just put an ad in the paper. The ad says that you're selling a popular item at a ridiculously low price — just a hair over dealer cost.

Lots of consumers mail you money. According to the Federal Trade Commission, you must fill their orders within 30 days. So 30 days after the money starts rolling in, you buy a big supply of the item you're selling, and ship it to your customers. You pay for that big supply by using the money that your customers mailed you.

As the months go on, you're theoretically not making much money, since you're selling the items for just a hair over cost. But your cash flow gets huge. As your business grows, and you increase the number of your ads, and your customers tell their friends about your wonderful prices and service, more and more money comes in each month.

For example, suppose you begin your business in January. Let's see what your business looks like, by April.

In April, suppose your ads make consumers send you $100,000. Federal law lets you delay shipping until May. So during April, you have $100,000 to play with.

During April, you must ship the goods that consumers ordered in the previous month (March). But since your business has been growing fast each month, March was a smaller month than April. Whereas April orders total $100,000, suppose March orders totaled just $60,000. So during April, you must ship items worth just $60,000 to consumers. Suppose those items worth $60,000 had cost you $55,000 to buy (just a hair under your selling price). In that case, during April you're taking in orders totally $100,000, but shipping orders costing you just $55,000. The difference — $45,000 — you can put into your own pocket, at least temporarily.

But wait! The math is even more in your favor than that, because, as your business grows and you develop a good reputation for paying your bills on time, your suppliers start offering you credit. The suppliers send you the goods and don't expect you to pay for them until 30 days later. So in April, you're paying the suppliers for the orders that you shipped in March, which were the orders that customers sent you in February. Back in February, your business was much smaller; you probably took in orders worth just $40,000, for which the suppliers charged you just $37,000.

To summarize all that, let's look at your cash situation in April. In April, customers mail you checks totaling $100,000 for new orders, you ship out the orders that were placed in March, and you pay your suppliers for just the orders that you received in February, which cost you just $37,000. The difference — $63,000 — you put in your pocket, at least temporarily.

Theoretically, that $63,000 difference should be used to eventually pay suppliers for orders that came in after February. But by the time those later bills come due you'll have received more checks in the mail (from customers in May and June). So, in practice, as long as the business continues to grow fast and bring in lots more customers each month, you'll never need to use the $63,000 that you pocketed. So you keep it in your pocket — or give yourself a large salary, or use it towards a new house, boat, fur coat, luxury car, or whatever else turns you on.

Eventually, someday, your business will stop growing by such large percentages, and this whole scheme will fall apart.

You can extend the scheme a few extra months by being slightly late in your payments to suppliers and your shipments to customers. (Since you've already built such a good reputation for fulfilling all your obligations, your suppliers and customers won't worry anymore if you're a few days late.) But eventually, as your business stops growing rapidly, the pyramid scheme fails, and you won't be able to pay your suppliers and ship to your customers.

Finally, one of your suppliers will sue you for the money that's due him. If you can't pay his large bill, just declare that your company is "bankrupt" and walk away from the whole problem. None of your recent customers receives any goods, and none of your suppliers receives any payment for recent bills, but the law is on your side: bankrupt companies can't be sued!

Then you move to another part of the country, start another business, and start the whole scheme all over again!

That's how you can continually be running businesses where you charge customers just 5% over dealer cost, and yet each month you keep 70% of the income in your pocket or for your own personal pleasures.

Nifty, huh? I know dozens of companies using that scheme. It ought to be against the law; but since the U.S. Constitution protects bankrupt citizens and bankrupt companies from lawsuits, there's no legal way to fight such rip-offs!

If you start such a scheme, you face just one disadvantage: when your company finally goes bankrupt, everybody will hate your guts! Your name will be mud. But who cares: just commit suicide, and you'll have had a life that was short but fun! Or do what the professionals do: just change your name! After moving out of state, start your fun pyramid all over again!

Stupid criminals

Criminals are only human: they make mistakes.

My favorite example of a stupid criminal is the guy who went into a convenience store, put $20 on the counter, asked the clerk to give him change, and then — when she opened the cash register's drawer — demanded all the money from the register. She gave it to him. Then he fled. Just one problem: he forgot to take back the $20 he'd put on the counter. Since the cash register contained just $15 dollars, the criminal's net profit was minus $5.

Another criminal demanded a free carton of cigarettes, but the clerk said she couldn't give them unless he was at least 21, so he showed her his ID. After he left, the clerk reported the robbery to the police, along with the criminal's name and address. Crime solved instantly!

Another criminal wanted to rob a bank but got tired of standing in the long waiting line, so he walked to the bank across the street. But there the teller refused to pay him because he wrote his demand on a withdrawal slip from the other bank: she sent him back to the first bank, where he stood in line again and was nabbed.

Intellectual life

To get more out of life, become an intellectual! Being intellectual is fun.

Try to learn the truth. Dig deeper! Mark Twain said:

> It ain't what you don't know that gets you into trouble. It's what you know for sure that just ain't so.

He also said:

> To begin, God made idiots. That was for practice. Then he made school boards. I've never let my school interfere with my education.

There are 3 kinds of people:

> intellectuals
> normal people
> small-minded people

President Franklin Roosevelt's wife (Eleanor Roosevelt) said:

> Great minds discuss ideas.
> Average minds discuss events.
> Small minds discuss people.

Professors

You can become a professor. Though professors get low pay, they enjoy short hours and long vacations (for summer, Christmas, and "spring break"). They can use their free time to soak up more cultural experiences or to moonlight as consultants or writers.

How many hours?

There's the tale of the farmer who asked the professor how many hours of class he taught. The professor said "14 hours." The farmer said, "Well, that's a long day, but at least the work's easy." The farmer didn't realize the professor meant 14 hours *per week*.

Being a professor is not a total joyride: you must spend lots of time grading papers, going to faculty meetings, preparing and researching your lectures, and doing other administrative crap. But compared to many other jobs, it's a piece of cake. And you get lots of free benefits, such as medical plans, campus events, and other entertainment, such as the joy of laughing at your students.

Promotion

If you're a successful professor, you'll be promoted to "dean" or "president," which will make your life more miserable, since you'll have to spend lots of time administering instead of "fooling around" (I mean "doing research"). "Administering" means "dealing with headaches and trying to embarrass people into donating money."

Back in the 1960's, when students were protesting for more freedom, Stanford University's president gave this description of his job:

> A university president has 3 responsibilities: provide sex for the students, athletics for the alumni, and parking for the faculty.

Advice for students

What colleges teach is overpriced. Instead of paying many thousands of dollars per year to enroll, you can just go to a bookstore, buy the textbooks, and read them yourself, for a total cost of a few hundred dollars instead of thousands. But you won't take that shortcut, because nobody will motivate you. **The main reason for going to college is social**: to chat with other students and professors who'll motivate you, argue with you, and encourage you to move yourself ahead.

The average professor spends just a small percentage of his day in front of a big class; he spends most of his day helping individuals or tiny groups. But most students spend most of *their* days in the big classes; just a few take the opportunity to chat with the professor one-to-one or in small groups. That's why the typical student says "most of the classes I take are big" while the typical professor says "most of the classes I teach are small." For example, at Dartmouth College I did statistics proving the average student spent most of his time in huge classes, while the average professor spent most of his time in tiny classes, leading to wildly different perceptions of what the "average" student-faculty ratio was.

In many colleges, students complain the professors are cold and unapproachable. On the other hand, the professors complain that not enough students come visit the professors during the professors' office hours. When students fail, the students therefore blame the professors (for being unapproachable), while the professors blame the students (for not approaching).

If you're a student, remember that you (or your parents) are spending lots of money on college: make sure you get your money's worth! Ask the professors lots of questions (during class or privately), interact with your classmates too, take advantage of the many cultural events on campus, and do whatever else you can to make your experience more worthwhile than just reading textbooks you could have bought for a tenth of the price of a college education.

Cynical quotes

Groucho Marx said this in *Horsefeathers*:

> Let's tear down the dormitories!
> The students can sleep where they've always slept: in the classroom.

W.H. Auden said:

> A professor is a person who talks in someone else's sleep.

Dave Barry gave this advice to students:

> Memorize things, then write them down in little exam books, then forget them. If you fail to forget them, you become a professor and must stay in college the rest of your life.
> To get good grades on your English papers, never say what anybody with common sense would say.
> Anybody with common sense would say Moby Dick's a big white whale, since book's characters call it a big white whale many times. So in your paper, say Moby Dick is actually the Republic of Ireland. Your professor, who's sick to death of reading papers and never liked Moby Dick anyway, will think you're enormously creative. If you can regularly come up with lunatic interpretations of simple stories, major in English.

Philosophers

If philosophers were honest, they'd call themselves "fullosophers" — since when they give their arguments, the audience usually thinks, "You're full of it!"

Will philosophy disappear?

The British philosopher Bertrand Russell was being interviewed by the BBC (British Broadcasting Corporation), when he made the comment that most "philosophical" problems eventually become "scientific" problems.

For example, the question of whether matter is **infinitely divisible** (able to be divided into smaller and smaller particles, without reaching any limit) was originally a "philosophical" problem argued by Greek philosophers but eventually became a "scientific" problem analyzed by physicists. The question "What is happiness" used to be a philosophical problem but has become a question of psychology, psychiatry, and biochemistry.

The interviewer asked him, "Does that mean philosophy will disappear?" Bertrand Russell replied, "Yes."

Why become a philosopher?

When Bertrand Russell was young, he was a mathematician and the world's most famous logician. But when he saw dead bodies come back from World War 1, he switched his career to philosophy, because he felt math wasn't relevant to the most important problems of living. He said:

> The "timelessness" of mathematics consists just in the fact that mathematicians don't talk about time.

Wesleyan's tunnels

Back in the 1970's, the basements of Wesleyan University's dorms were connected by tunnels, upon whose walls the students wrote philosophy. Sample:

> "To do is to be." — Socrates
> "To be is to do." — Sartre
> "Do be do be do." — Sinatra

Another sample:

> There's nothing to do on a rainy day in Kansas; but it never rains, so you never get the chance.

Failures

Don't let your failures discourage you. Learn from them. They'll also help you appreciate your later successes more. Truman Capote said:

> Failure is the condiment that gives success its flavor.

Remember this famous saying:

> If at first you don't succeed? Try, try again!

But also heed W.C. Field's elaboration:

> If at first you don't succeed? Try, try again!
> Then stop. No use being a damn fool about it!

Success versus happiness

Don't confuse "success" with "happiness." Actress Ingrid Bergman said:

> Success is getting what you want.
> Happiness is wanting what you get.

Donkey

The Internet offers this inspiring tale:

> A farmer's donkey fell into a well. The animal cried piteously for hours as the farmer tried to figure out what to do.
>
> Finally, he decided that since the donkey was old and the well needed to be covered up anyway, it wasn't worth the trouble to retrieve the donkey.
>
> He invited all his neighbors to come help him. They all grabbed shovels and began to throw dirt into the well.
>
> The donkey realized what was happening and cried horribly. But then, to everyone's amazement, he quieted down. A few shovelfuls later, the farmer looked down the well and was astonished to see that for every shovel of dirt hitting the donkey's back, the donkey would amazingly shake it off and take a step up. Soon everyone was amazed as the donkey stepped up over the edge of the well and trotted off.
>
> Life is going to shovel dirt on you, all kinds of dirt. The trick to getting out of the well is to shake off the dirt and take a step up.
>
> Each of our troubles is a steppingstone. We can emerge from the deepest wells just by persevering, never giving up! Shake it off and take a step up!
>
> Remember these 5 simple rules to be happy:
> *Free your heart from hatred*
> *Free your mind from worries*
> *Live simply*
> *Give more*
> *Expect less*
>
> By the way, the donkey kicked the shit out of the bastard who tried to bury him. Moral:
> *When you try to cover your ass, it always comes back to get you.*

Chicken

Why did the chicken cross the road?

According to the Internet, these thinkers would give straight answers....

Traditional answer:	To get to the other side.
Ernest Hemingway:	To die. In the rain. Alone.
Walt Whitman:	To cluck the song of itself.
Robert Frost:	To cross the road less traveled by.
Mae West:	I invited it to come up and see me sometime.
Captain Kirk:	To boldly go where no chicken has gone before.
Jack Nicholson:	'Cause it fucking wanted to. That's the fucking reason.
Timothy Leary:	That's the only kind of trip the Establishment would let it take.
Jerry Falwell:	The chicken was gay, going to the 'other side.' If you eat it, *you'll* get gay.
Moses:	God told the chicken, 'Thou shalt cross the road.' There was much rejoicing.
Zsa Zsa Gabor:	To get a better look at my legs, which — thank goodness — are good, dahling.
Martin Luther King:	It had a dream where *all* chickens can freely cross without their motives questioned.
Sigmund Freud:	The chicken was female and envied the crosswalk-sign pole as a phallic symbol.

So would these scientists....

Sir Isaac Newton:	Chickens at rest tend to stay at rest. Chickens in motion tend to cross the road.
Darwin:	Chickens, over centuries, have been naturally selected to cross roads.
Hippocrates:	Because of an excess of light pink gooey stuff in its pancreas.
Gregor Mendel:	To get various strains of roads.

These thinkers would *deny* that the chicken simply crossed the road:

Joseph Conrad:	Mistah Chicken, he dead.
Emerson:	It didn't *cross* the road: it *transcended* the road.
Mark Twain:	The news of its crossing has been greatly exaggerated.
John Cleese:	This chicken is no more. It's a stiff, an ex-chicken. Ergo, it didn't cross the road.
Saddam Hussein:	Its rebellion was unprovoked, so we justifiably dropped 50 tons of nerve gas on it.
Albert Einstein:	Did the *chicken* really cross the *road*, or did the road move beneath the chicken?

These thinkers would investigate further:

Jerry Seinfeld:	Why the heck was this chicken walking around all over the place anyway?
George W. Bush:	We just want to know whether the chicken is on *our* side of the road or not.
Sherlock Holmes:	Ignore the chicken that *crossed*; the answer lies with the chicken that *didn't*.
Oliver Stone:	Who *else* was crossing and overlooked, in our haste to observe the chicken?

These thinkers would raise questions....

Bob Dylan:	How many roads must one chicken cross?
Shakespeare:	To cross or not to cross, that is the question.
John Lennon:	Imagine all chickens crossing roads in peace.
Dr. Seuss:	*Did* the chicken cross the road? Did he cross it with a *toad*?
Voltaire:	I may not *agree* with the chicken, but I'll defend to death its right to cross."

These thinkers would brag about technology:

Al Gore:	I invented the chicken and the road. The crossing serves the American people.
Bill Gates:	My eChicken 2.0 also lays eggs, files documents, and balances your checkbook.

These thinkers think the others are too long-winded:

Grandpa:	In my day, we didn't ask why. We were told the chicken crossed. That was that!
Fox Mulder:	You saw it with your own eyes! How many must cross before you believe?
Alfred E. Neumann:	What? Me worry?
Colonel Sanders:	I missed one?

Which of those thinkers is closest to your own philosophy?

Psychologists

The most misspelled word in the English language is "**psychology**." That's how most people spell it, but that spelling is wrong! You should spell it "**sighcology**," since it's the study of why people sigh.

It studies what makes people sad or glad (the meaning of happiness!) and what motivates people to do things and keep on living.

It also studies why people act crazy. At Dartmouth College, the course in "Abnormal Psychology" is nicknamed "**Nuts & Sluts**."

Many psychology experiments are performed on rats before being tried on people. That's why at Northwestern University, the course in "Psychology" is nicknamed "**Ratology**."

Trick the professor

According to psychology, if you make your victim happy when he's performing an activity, he'll do that activity more often. That's called **reinforcement**.

At Dartmouth College, a psychology professor was giving a lecture about that, but his lecture was too effective: his students secretly decided to make him the victim! They decided on a goal: make him teach while standing next to the window instead of the blackboard. Whenever he moved toward the window, they purposely looked more interested in what he was saying; whenever he returned to the blackboard, they purposely looked more bored. Sure enough, they finally got him to give all lectures from the window! They'd trained their human animal: the classroom was his cage; his class became a circus. When the students finally told him what they'd done, he was so embarrassed!

Okay, kids, try this with your teachers! Pick a goal ("Let's make the teacher lecture from the back of the room while he does somersaults") and see how close you can come to success!

But actually, with an experiment like this, everybody wins, since the students have to keep watching the teacher to find out when to pretend to look interested. That means the students can't fall asleep in class. If one of the students secretly snitches to the teacher about what's going on, the teacher should play along with it, because the teacher knows that the students will be watching the teacher's every move while the game continues. A rapt, excited audience is exactly what the teacher wants!

Double-blind

If you want to do experiments on humans, to determine which social settings and drugs are most effective, make sure that neither the experimenters nor the patients know which patients got which treatments, until after the experiment is over. If the experimenters or patients know too much too soon, they'll bias the results of the tests.

The most accurate kind of experiment is called **double-blind**: neither the experimenters nor the patients know who gets which treatment; the experimenters & patients are both blind to what's going on, until after the test. For example, to accurately test whether a pill is effective, it's important that neither the experimenters nor the patients know which patients got the real pills and which patients got the **placebos** (fake pills) until after the experiment is over.

Here are 3 famous examples proving that double-blindness can be essential to accuracy....

Clever Hans In the late 1800's, a Berlin math professor named Wilhelm Von Osten believed animals could become as smart as humans. He tried to teach a cat and and bear to do arithmetic but failed. Then he tried to teach a *horse* to do arithmetic and seemed to succeed, after training the horse for just 2 years. He called the horse "**Clever Hans**."

The horse correctly answered questions about arithmetic — and also about advanced math, German, political history, and classical music. Whenever Wilhelm asked the horse a question whose answer was a small integer (1, 2, 3, 4, 5, etc.), the horse would tap his foot the correct number of times, even if the question was complicated, such as:

"What's the square root of 16?" (The answer is 4.)
"If you add $\frac{2}{5}$ to $\frac{1}{2}$, what's the total's numerator?" (The answer is 9.)
"How many people in the audience are wearing hats?"

Wilhelm really believed he'd taught the horse to do advanced thinking. He and his horse became famous celebrities.

In 1904, Germany created a scientific committee to determine whether the horse was really smart or whether the whole thing was just a hoax. The committee included two zoologists, a psychologist (Carl Stumpf), a horse trainer, and a circus manager. The committee concluded that the horse really was smart, since it could answer questions asked by audience members (who'd never seen the horse before) even when Wilhelm Von Osten and his staff weren't present.

But one of Carl Stumpf's students, Oskar Pfunkst, experimented on the horse further. Oskar discovered that if the interrogator (the person interrogating the horse) didn't know the right answer himself, the horse didn't know the answer either. He finally discovered how the horse got the right answer: the horse looked at the interrogator's body language. After an interrogator asked the horse a question, the interrogator had a natural human tendency to look intensely at the horse's leg, lean forward to look at it, and be tense until horse tapped the correct number of times. Then the interrogator relaxed a bit, unconsciously. The horse noticed that relaxation and stopped tapping.

Moral: when testing the intelligence of a horse — or anything else — it's important that the experimenter (interrogator) not be biased by expecting an outcome, since the patient (horse) can be influenced by that bias.

Hawthorne In the 1920's and 1930's, psychologists tried some experiments in Western Electric's "Hawthorne" factory in Chicago.

First, psychologists tried improving the lighting, by making the place brighter. As expected, the workers' productivity increased.

But then, after a while, the psychologists tried another experiment: they lowered the lighting. Strange as it seems, lowering the lighting made productivity increase further!

It turned out that what made the workers productive wasn't "more lighting"; it was "attention and variety." Anything that made the workers' life more interesting and less monotonous made productivity increase. Also, perhaps more important, workers work harder when they know they're being watched!

The same thing happened when the "rest breaks" and pay were changed: the act of change itself made productivity increase, regardless of whether the change was intended for better or worse.

That's called the **Hawthorne Experiment**. Moral: workers (and patients) do better when they know they're watched and cared about, even if the conditions are worse. So if you try a new technique (or pill) that seems to be successful, the success might be just because the patients know they're being watched, not because your technique itself is really good.

Bloomers In the 1960's, Robert Rosenthal and Lenore Jacobson had psychologists sit in the back of 18 elementary-school classrooms, watch the students, and then tell the teachers that certain kids were "intellectual bloomers" who would probably do better and improve a lot. Then the psychologists left. At the end of the year, the psychologists came back, gave the kids IQ tests and and, sure enough, the kids that had been called "intellectual bloomers" improved more than the other kids and were also "better liked," even though those kids had actually been picked at random! That's because the teacher treated those kids differently, after hearing they were "intellectual bloomers."

They repeated the experiment with a welding class: they told the teacher that certain students in the welding class were "high aptitude." Sure enough, those students scored higher on welding exams, learned welding skills in about half as much time as their classmates, and were absent less often than classmates, even though those students had actually been picked at random.

In an earlier test, they told psychology students that certain rats were "bright." Sure enough, the "bright" rats learned to run through mazes faster, even though those rats had actually been picked at random.

Moral: if you expect more of a person (or rat), you'll tend to give that individual more helpful attention, so the individual will live up to those expectations. Second moral: if you (or teachers) expect a certain outcome, it will happen, just because you expected it.

Travel

Whenever you feel bummed out, take a trip — for a month or a week or a day — or at least take a walk around the block or watch TV or read a newspaper or book. When you see other people acting out their own lives and ignoring yours, you'll realize that your momentary personal crisis is unimportant in the grand scheme of life.

So what if a close acquaintance thinks badly of you? There are billions of other people in the world who don't care, who don't have any opinion of you at all, know nothing about what you've done, and don't care about it. All they care about is that you act like a nice person now.

Act nice, and the world will grow to love you. If your little world temporarily hates you and you don't want to deal with it, explore a new world: take a trip!

Suicide

More suicides occur on Sunday than any other day of the week. That's because Sunday's the only day when Americans have enough time to ponder how meaningless their lives are.

The best cure for suicidal thoughts is: Monday! Go back to work, get reinforced every hour for your accomplishments, and keep yourself busy enough to avoid introspection.

Every day, I think about killing myself, but the main thing stopping me is curiosity. I'm a news junkie with a sci-fi bent: I want to know what will happen to the world tomorrow, and if I kill myself I won't find out!

The old news anchors — Peter Jennings, Tom Brokaw, and Dan Rather — saved my life. They gave me a reason for living: to find out what stupid things they'd be forced to say the next day. Now that they're gone, along with the relevance of broadcast TV news, I get my life force by reading *The Wall Street Journal* and the Reuters news feed on Yahoo's Website.

When I see the daily newsreels of horrors around the world, I remember why God created evil: to make us feel better, by knowing that other people are even worse off, and we're so lucky not to be them!

Learn from your miseries and become a better person.

> If your travails are long and tough
> And your rewards are few,
> Remember that the mighty oak
> Was once a nut like you.

But if you nevertheless decide to kill yourself, here's a suggestion about the best way to do it:

> A local newspaper here ran an article whose headline said "Police kill suicidal man." The police in Henniker NH got a call saying a relative (a man in his 40's) was depressed (because he was fired from a bookstore) and seemed suicidal (judging from what he phoned to his 5-year-old estranged daughter), so the police went to his house. Nobody responded to their knocks, so they forcibly entered and found him. They asked him if he was okay. Instead of replying, he walked near a rifle, picked it up, and aimed it at a policeman, so they shot him in self-defense. Since his gun was loaded, the police were exonerated.
>
> Hey, that's a clever way to commit suicide: get the police to do the killing for you! But plan carefully, to make sure you don't accidentally shoot the police when they shoot you.

Quickie thoughts

Here are quick thoughts on several psych topics.

The ²/₃ solution During the 1960's, when I was learning to be a clinical psychologist, the professor told us that ²/₃ of all psychological problems resolve themselves, without help — though a nudge sure helps!

Grow up?

> Bored people grow up. Fascinating people grow down: they reconnect with their inner child.

Paranoid Warning:

> Just because you're paranoid doesn't mean they're *not* out to get you.

Habits In a psychology lecture about habits, the professor said he knew a bishop who dispensed advice to priests. To the question, "Is it okay to kiss a nun?" the bishop replied:

> It's okay to kiss a nun once in a while, but don't get in the habit.

Loretta LaRoche

> Now yesterday is history.
> Tomorrow is a mystery.
> Today is God's great gift to you:
> That's why it's called "the present," too.

That's my edited version of the closing poem at a one-woman show/seminar: a PBS special called "The Joy of Stress" by humorous therapist Loretta LaRoche. The poem means this:

> Don't fret about the past, for you can't change it.
> Don't fret about the future: can't explain it!
>
> So calm down and savor
> The moment you're in.
> It's God's little favor:
> Come taste every flavor!

Now Loretta has a new presentation, called "Stop Global Whining."

Test about life

Here's a multiple-choice test about life.

> Laugh, and the world laughs *with* you.
> Cry, and....

Which completion is most correct?

> Cry, and you cry alone.
> Cry, and you get a loan.
> Cry, and the world laughs *at* you.
> Cry, and your dad says to shut up.
> Cry, and you win the Academy Award.
> Cry, and you get on a Jerry Springer talk show.
> Cry, and your lover pities you and marries you.

Mr. Stupid

Why do people act strange? This poem explains:

> They call me Mr. Stupid
> Because I am so cool!
> I put my pants on backwards —
> Just *love* to break the rules!
>
> I fall in love with any girl
> Who dares to tell me "no,"
> Since any girl who dislikes *me*
> Must really be a show!
>
> Though I'm called Mr. Stupid,
> I never really mind,
> Since I know how behind my back
> They whisper I'm so fine!
>
> Sticks and stones may break my bones
> But names will never hurt.
> Though maybe stupid, I'm unique.
> The *other* folks are dirt.
>
> Folks do not mind my joyous brags.
> In fact, they even laugh.
> Each time I tell a dirty joke,
> They offer me a bath.
>
> Stupidity is wonderful
> When I am in control.
> I may be just a character,
> But on *my* bridge, the troll!

Christmas carols

During the Christmas season, many people feel stressed. The Internet recommends these Christmas carols for the psychologically challenged:

Diagnosis	Song title
Muliple-personality disorder	We 3 queens disoriented are
Amnesia	I (think) I'll be home for Christmas?
Narcissist	Hark the herald angels sing (about me)
Paranoid	Santa Claus is coming to town to get me
Tourette's syndrome	Chestnuts… *grrr!* roasting on… *bite me!*
Seasonal-affective disorder	Oh the weather outside is frightful, so frightful
Schizophrenic	Do you hear what I hear: the voices, the voices?
Depressed	Silent night, holy night, all is calm, all is pretty lonely
Agoraphobic	I heard the bells on Christmas Day but wouldn't leave my house
Alzheimer's disease	Walking in a winter wonderland, miles from my house, in my bathrobe
Social-anxiety disorder	Have yourself a merry little Christmas while I sit here and hyperventilate
Passive/aggressive	On the first day of Christmas, my true love gave to me then took it all away, so I pouted for a week to teach that ass a lesson
Bipolar disorder, manic episode	Deck the halls and walls and house and lawn and streets and stores and office and town and cars and buses and trucks and trees and fire hydrants…
Obsessive-compulsive disorder	Jingle bells, jingle bells, jingle bells, jingle bells, jingle bells, jingle bells, jingle bells, jingle bells, jingle bells, jingle bells…
Autistic	Jingle bell rock and rock and rock and rock…
Borderline personality disorder	You better watch out, I'm gonna cry, I'm gonna pout, *maybe* say why
Borderline personality disorder 2	Thoughts of roasting in an open fire
Antisocial-personality disorder	Thoughts of roasting *you* on an open fire
Oppositional-defiant disorder	"You better not cry" "Oh yes, I will" "You better not shout" "I can if I want to" "You better not pout" "Can if I want to" "I'm telling you why" "Not listening" "Santa Claus is coming to town" "No, he's not!"
Oppositional-defiant disorder 2	I saw Mommy kissing Santa Claus, so I burned down the house
Attention-deficit disorder	We wish you… hey look! It's snowing!
Attention-deficit disorder 2	Silent night, holy… oooh, look at the froggy! Can I have a chocolate? Why is France so far away?
Attention-deficit/hyperactivity	All I want for Christmas is everything, and I want it *now!*

Emotion-logic test

Psychologists like to invent ways to test your personality. Here's a crazy test I invented: are you more like me (Russ) or my wife (Donna)? Are you a "Donna" type (emotional) or a "Russ" type (logical)?

> Donna eats whatever tastes good.
> At home, Russ eats just what's "healthy" (but he indulges at restaurants).
>
> When offered chicken, Donna chooses dark meat (because it's tastier).
> Russ chooses white meat (because it's healthier, since it has less fat).
>
> To figure out how to install and use a new product, Donna guesses.
> Russ reads the instructions.
>
> Donna likes to take photos (to preserve the memories).
> Russ doesn't bother.
>
> Donna is warm to relatives and loves to spend time with them.
> Russ has less time for relatives; he's under time pressure from work.
>
> Donna takes her shower in the evening, to feel better while dreaming.
> Russ takes his shower in the morning, to feel better while working.
>
> In the summer, Donna likes to turn the air conditioner on, for comfort.
> Russ likes to turn the air conditioner off, to save money.
>
> In the winter, Donna likes to turn the furnace on, for comfort.
> Russ likes the turn the furnace off, to save money.
>
> Donna sees doctors and dentists just when things hurt.
> Russ gets regular checkups (though just occasionally, to reduce expense).
>
> Donna takes cars to repair shops just when cars break.
> Russ maintains cars regularly (according to schedule).
>
> Donna believes the elderly should dye their hair (to look younger).
> Russ believes in letting the gray show (to look natural and truthful).

Donna rushes through most tasks (to dispose of them quickly).
Russ does things more carefully — and so finishes them too late.

Donna gets up early (to start her day energetically).
Russ stays up late (to finish things, because he's always behind).

Donna believes in being tactful, even if that means fibbing a little.
Russ believes in being frank, even if that means breaking a secret.

Donna says doctors should hide bad news from patients, to preserve hope.
Russ says doctors should tell the truth, so patients can act wisely.

When driving alone, Donna turns the radio on, to create fun or learn.
Russ turns the radio off, so he can concentrate on driving and planning.

Donna believes in alternative medicine (herbs).
Russ believes in traditional medicine (pills approved by the A.M.A.).

Donna throws out newspapers immediately, to reduce clutter.
Russ hoards newspapers, to avoid losing information.

Donna worries about security after retirement.
Russ believes life is unpredictable, so he focuses on this year.

After deciding whether you're more like "Donna" or "Russ," invent your *own* test, containing your own name and a friend's.

According to the Donna-versus-Russ test, Donna differs from me (Russ) in many ways. We stay married because our differences are smaller than what we have in common:

similar tastes in music, movies, furniture, and clothes styles
enjoy keyboard instruments more than guitar
skilled at math, logical reasoning, and teaching
love reading & studying, like to explore different cultures
like to spend more time in cultural cities than quiet countryside
kind of cheap, don't pursue luxury or name brands
like to eat at inexpensive restaurants
naively trust other people, get surprised and upset at cheating
sex is not a priority
not very optimistic; a little stubborn

What do *you* and *your* friends have in common? List the reasons you stay friends. Share that list with your friends: you'll appreciate each other even more!

Mental-illness ditty

Mental illness strikes us all, eventually. During one of my bouts, I wrote this ditty to cheer myself up:

I am mentally ill,
And my mind's made of swill.
I am king of the hill
When I'm humping.

I can hope that someday
Life will turn out okay,
But for now I'm in bed
And just thumping.

Please extract me from here.
Have you got any beer?
Can you give me some cheer,
At least something?

I just wish I were dead.
Someone please shoot my head.
What will happen? I dread
I'll be nothing.

Take me away

The most famous song about mental illness is called "They're coming to take me away," recorded in 1966 by Jerry Samuels (whose stage name is Napoleon XIV). I've recast it here as a poem:

Remember when you ran away?
Upon my knees, I begged "Don't leave
Or else I'll go beserk."

You left me anyhow, and then
The days got worse and worse, and now
I've surely lost my mind. You jerk!
So now they're taking me away
To farms (with beauty all the time
And men in clean white coats).

When I said losing you would make
Me flip my lid, you thought it was
A harmless joke. You simply laughed.
You *know* you laughed. I *heard* you laugh.
You *laughed and laughed*, and then you left;
And now I've gone quite mad. How dumb!
So now they're taking me away
To Happy Home (with trees and birds,
Where crazies twiddle thumbs).

In movie-making courses, students create movies using Jerry's original recording as the scary soundtrack. Here are two examples:

www.YouTube.com/watch?v=Sum4Esubx-w
www.YouTube.com/watch?v=Oc5GMUSe-4

Mathematicians

In my former life — before I tried to be a writer or a computer guy — I was a mathematician.

Puzzles

Torture your friends by giving them these puzzles about arithmetic.

Apples If you have 5 apples and eat all but 3, how many are left? Kids are tempted to say "2," but the correct answer is 3.

Birds If you have 10 birds in a tree and shoot 1, how many are left in the tree? Kids are tempted to say "9," but the correct answer is 0.

Corners If you have a 4-sided table and chop off 1 of the corners, how many corners are left on the table? Kids are tempted to say "3," but the correct answer is 5.

Eggs Carl Sandberg, in his poem *Arithmetic*, asks this question:

If you ask your mother for one fried egg for breakfast, but she gives you *two* fried eggs and you eat both of them, who's better in arithmetic: you or your mother?

Missing dollar Now that you've mastered the easy puzzles, try this harder one:

On a nice day in the 1940's, three girls go into a hotel and ask for a triple. The manager says sorry, no triples are available, so he puts them in three singles, at $10 each. The girls go up to their rooms.

A few minutes later, a triple frees up, which costs just $25. So the manager, to be a nice guy, decides to move the girls into the triple and refund the $5 difference. He sends the bellboy up to tell the girls of their good fortune and move them into the triple.

While riding up in the elevator, the bellboy thinks to himself, "How can the girls split the $5? $5 doesn't divide by 3 evenly. I'll make it easier for them: I'll give them just $3 — and keep $2 for myself." So he gave the girls $3 and moved them into the triple.

Everybody was happy. The girls were happy to get refunds. The manager was happy to be a nice guy. And the bellboy was happy to keep $2.

Now here's the problem: each girl spent $10 and got $1 back, so each girl spent $9. Altogether, the girls spent $9+$9+$9, which is $27, and the bellboy got $2. That makes $29. But we started with $30. What happened to the missing dollar?

Ask your friends that question and see how many crazy answers you get!

Here's the correct answer:

> At the end of the story, who has the $30?
> The manager has $25, the bellboy has $2, and the girls have $3.

Adding what the girls *spent* ($27) to what the bellboy *got* ($2) doesn't give a meaningful number. But that nonsense total, $29, is close enough to $30 to be intriguing.

Here's an alternative analysis:

> The girls spent a net of $9+$9+$9, which is $27.
> $25 of that went to the manager, and $2 went to the bellboy.

Coins Try this task:

> Arrange 10 coins so they form 5 rows, each containing 4 coins.

"5 rows of 4 coins" would normally require a total of 20 coins, but if you arrange properly you can solve the puzzle. Hint: the rows must be straight but don't have to be horizontal or vertical. Ask your friends that puzzle to drive them nuts.

Here's the solution:

> Draw a 5-pointed star. Put the coins at the 10 corners.

Which type are you?

Here's Warren Buffet's favorite saying about math.

> There are 3 types of people: those who can count, and those who can't.

Statistics

Courses in statistics can be difficult. That's why they're called "sadistics."

Lies Statisticians give misleading answers.

For example, suppose you've paid one person a salary of $1000, another person a salary of $100, another person a salary of $10, and two other people a salary of $1 each. What's the "typical" salary you paid? If you ask that question to three different statisticians, they'll give you three different answers!

> One statistician will claim that the "typical" salary is $1, because it's the most popular salary: more people received $1 than any other amount. Another statistician will claim that the "typical" salary is $10, because it's the middle salary: as many people were paid more than $10 as were paid less. The third statistician will claim that the "typical" salary is $222.40, because it's the average: it's the sum of all the salaries divided by the number of people.

Which statistician is right? According to the Association for Defending Statisticians (started by my friends), the three statisticians are *all* right! The most common salary ($1) is called the **mode**; the middle salary ($10) is called the **median**; the average salary ($222.40) is called the **mean**.

But which is the "typical" salary, really? Is it the mode ($1), the median ($10), or the mean ($222.40)? That's up to you!

If you leave the decision up to the statistician, the statistician's answer will depend on who hired him.

> If the topic is a wage dispute between labor and management, a statistician paid by the laborers will claim that the typical salary is low (just $1); a statistician paid by the management will claim that the typical salary is high ($222.40); and a statistician paid by the arbitrator will claim that the typical salary is reasonable ($10).

Which statistician is telling the *whole* truth? None of them!

A century ago, Benjamin Disraeli, England's prime minister, summarized the whole situation in one sentence. He said:

> There are 3 kinds of lies:
> lies, damned lies, and statistics.

Logic

A course in "logic" is a blend of math and philosophy. It can be lots of fun — and also help you become a lawyer.

Beating your wife There's the old logic question about how to answer this question:

> Have you stopped beating your wife?

Regardless of whether you answer that question by saying "yes" or "no," you're implying that you did indeed beat your wife in the past.

Interesting number Some numbers are interesting. For example, some people think 128 is interesting because it's "2 times 2 times 2 times 2 times 2 times 2 times 2." Here's a proof that *all* numbers are interesting:

> Suppose some numbers are *not* interesting. For example, suppose 17 is the first number that's *not* interesting. Then people would say, "Hey, that's interesting! 17 has the very interesting property of being the first boring number!" But then 17 has become interesting! So you can't have a first "boring" number, and all numbers are interesting!

Surprise test When I took a logic course at Dartmouth College, the professor began by warning me and my classmates:

> I'll give a surprise test sometime during the semester.

Then he told the class to analyze that sentence and try to deduce when the surprise test would be.

He pointed out that the test can't be on the semester's last day — because if the test didn't happen before then, the students would be expecting the test when they walk into class on that last day, and it wouldn't be a surprise anymore. So cross "the semester's last day" off the list of possibilities.

Then he continued his argument:

> But once you cross "the semester's last day" off the list of possibilities, you realize the surprise test can't be "the day before the semester's last day" either, because the test would be expected then (since the test hadn't happened already and couldn't happen on the semester's last day). Since the test would be expected then, it wouldn't be a surprise. So cross "the day before last" off the list of possibilities.

Continuing in that fashion, he said, more and more days would be crossed off, until eventually all days would be crossed off the list of possibilities, meaning there couldn't be a surprise test.

Then he continued:

> But I assure you, there *will* be a test, and it *will* be a surprise when it comes. Think about it.

Mathematicians versus engineers

The typical mathematician finds abstract concepts beautiful, and doesn't care whether they have any "practical" applications. The typical engineer is exactly the opposite: the engineer cares just about practical applications.

Engineers complain that mathematicians are ivory-tower daydreamers who are divorced from reality. Mathematicians complain that engineers are too worldly and also too stupid to appreciate the higher beauties of the mathematical arts.

To illustrate those differences, mathematicians tell 3 tales….

Boil water Suppose you're in a room that has a sink, stove, table, and chair. A kettle is on the table. Problem: boil some water.

An engineer would carry the kettle from the table to the sink, fill the kettle with water, put the kettle onto the stove, and wait for the water to boil. So would a mathematician.

But suppose you change the problem, so the kettle's on the chair instead of the table. The engineer would carry the kettle from the chair to the sink, fill the kettle with water, put the kettle onto the stove, and wait for the water to boil. But the mathematician would not! Instead, the mathematician would carry the kettle from the chair to the table, yell "now the problem's been reduced to the previous problem," and walk away.

Analyze tennis Suppose 1024 people are in a tennis tournament. The players are paired, to form 512 tennis matches; then the winners of those matches are paired against each other, to form 256 play-off matches; then the winners of the play-off matches are paired against each other, to form 128 further play-off matches; etc.; until finally just 2 players remain — the finalists — who play against each other to determine the 1 person who wins the entire tournament. Problem: compute how many matches are played in the entire tournament.

The layman would add 512+256+128+64+32+16+8+4+2+1, to arrive at the correct answer, 1023.

The engineer, too lazy to add all those numbers, would realize that the numbers 512, 256, etc., form a series whose sum can be obtained by a simple, magic formula! Just take the first number (512), double it, and then subtract 1, giving a final result of 1023!

But the true mathematician spurns the formula and searches instead for the problem's underlying meaning. Suddenly it dawns on him! Since the problem said there are "1024 people" but just 1 final winner, the number of people who must be eliminated is "1024 minus 1," which is 1023, and so there must be 1023 matches!

The mathematician's calculation (1024-1) is faster than the engineer's. But best of all, the mathematician's reasoning applies to any tournament, even if the number of players isn't a magical number such as 1024. No matter how many people play, just subtract 1 to get the number of matches!

Prime numbers Mathematicians are precise, physicists somewhat less so, chemists even less so. Engineers are even less precise and sometimes less intellectual. To illustrate that view, mathematicians tell the tale of **prime numbers**.

First, let me explain some math jargon. The **counting numbers** are 1, 2, 3, etc. A counting number is called **composite** if you can get it from multiplying a pair of other counting numbers. For example:

> 6 is composite because you can get it from multiplying 2 by 3.
> 9 is composite because you can get it from multiplying 3 by 3.
> 15 is composite because you can get it from multiplying 3 by 5.

A counting number that's not composite is called **prime**. For example, 7 is prime because you can't make 7 from multiplying a pair of other counting numbers. Whether 1 is "prime" depends on how you define "prime," but for the purpose of this discussion let's consider 1 to be prime.

Here's how scientists would try to prove this theorem:

> All odd numbers are prime.

Actually, that theorem is *false!* All odd numbers are *not* prime! For example, 9 is an odd number that's *not* prime. But although 9 isn't prime, the physicists, chemists, and engineers would still say the theorem is true.

The physicist would say, slowly and carefully:

> 1 is prime. 3 prime. 5 is prime. 7 is prime.
> 9? — no.
> 11 is prime. 13 is prime.
> 9 must be just experimental error, so we can ignore it. All odd numbers are prime.

The chemist would rush for results and say just this:

> 1 is prime, 3 is prime. 5 is prime. 7 is prime.
> That's enough evidence. All odd numbers are prime.

The engineer would be the crudest and stupidest of them all. He'd say the following as fast as possible (to meet the next deadline for building his rocket, which will accidentally blow up):

> Sure, 1 is prime, 3 is prime, 5 is prime, 7 is prime, 9 is prime, 11 is prime, 13 is prime, 15 is prime, 17 is prime, 19 is prime, all odd numbers are prime!

Logger

Every few years, authors of math textbooks come out with new editions, to reflect the latest fads. Here's an example, as reported (and elaborated on) by *Reader's Digest* (in February 1996), *Recreational & Educational Computing* (issue #91), John Funk (and his daughter), *ABC News Radio WTKS 1290* (in Savannah), and others:

> **Teaching math in 1960: traditional math**
> A logger sells a truckload of lumber for $100.
> His cost of production is 4/5 of the price.
> What's his profit?
>
> **Teaching math in 1965: simplified math**
> A logger sells a truckload of lumber for $100.
> His cost of production is 4/5 of the price, or $80.
> What's his profit?
>
> **Teaching math in 1970: new math**
> A logger exchanges a set L of lumber for a set M of money.
> The cardinality of set M is 100. Each element is worth $1.
> Make 100 dots representing the elements of M.
> The set C (cost of production) contains 20 fewer points than set M.
> Represent the set C as a subset of set M and answer this question: what's the cardinality of the set P of profits?
>
> **Teaching math in 1975: feminist-empowerment math**
> A logger sells a truckload of lumber for $100.
> *Her* cost is $80, and her profit is $20.
> Your assignment: underline the number 20.
>
> **Teaching math in 1980: environmentally conscious math**
> An unenlightened logger cuts down beautiful trees, desecrating the precious forest for $20. Write an essay explaining how you feel about that way to make money. How did the forest's birds and squirrels feel?
>
> **Teaching math in 1985: computer-based math**
> A logger sells a truckload of lumber for $100. His production costs are 80% of his revenue. On your calculator, graph revenue versus costs. On your computer, run the LOGGER program to determine the profit.
>
> **Teaching math in 1990: Wall Street math**
> By laying off 40% of its loggers, a company improves its stock price from $80 to $100. How much capital gain per share does the CEO make by exercising his options at $80? Assume capital gains have become untaxed to encourage investment.
>
> **Teaching math in 1995: managerial math**
> A company outsources all its loggers. The firm saves on benefits; and whenever demand for its products is down, the logging workforce can be cut back easily. The average logger employed by the company earned $50,000 and had a 3-week vacation, nice retirement plan, and medical insurance. The contracted logger charges $30 per hour. Based on that data, was outsourcing a good move? If a laid-off logger comes into the logging company's corporate headquarters and goes postal, mowing down 16 executives and a couple of secretaries, was outsourcing the loggers still a good move?
>
> **Teaching math in 2000: tax-based math**
> A logger sells a truckload of lumber for $100. His cost of production is 4/5 of the price. After taxes, why did he bother?
>
> **Teaching math in 2005: profit-pumping math**
> A logger sells a truckload of lumber for $100. His production cost is $120. How did Arthur Anderson determine that his profit margin is $60?
>
> **Teaching math in 2010: multicultural math**
> Un maderero vende un camión de madera para $100. Su coste de producción es $80….

Winston Churchill

Winston Churchill (who was England's prime minister) said:

> I had a feeling once about Mathematics — that I saw it all. Depth beyond Depth was revealed to me: the Byss and the Abyss. I *saw* — as one might see the transit of Venus or even the Lord Mayor's Show — a quantity passing through infinity and changing its sign from plus to minus. I saw exactly why it happened and why the tergiversation was inevitable — but it was after dinner and I let it go.

Terrorist mathematicians

A colleague passed me this e-mail, forwarded anonymously:

A teacher was arrested because he attempted to board a flight while possessing a ruler, protractor, and calculator. Attorney General Alberto Gonzales said he believes the man's a member of the notorious Al-gebra movement. The man's been charged with carrying weapons of math instruction.

"Al-gebra is a problem for us," Gonzales said. "Its followers desire solutions by means and extremes and sometimes go off on tangents in search of absolute values. They use secret code names like 'x' and 'y' and refer to themselves as "unknowns,' but we've determined they belong to a common denominator of the axis of medieval, with coordinates in every country."

When asked to comment on the arrest, George W. Bush said, "If God had wanted us to have better weapons of math instruction, He'd have given us more fingers and toes." Aides told reporters they couldn't recall a more intelligent or profound statement by the President.

1089

In math, the most famous constant is **pi**, which is roughly 3.14. But another famous math constant is **1089**. It's the favorite constant among math magicians because it creates this trick....

Write down any three-digit number "whose first digit differs from the last digit by more than 1." For example:

852 is okay, since its first digit (8) differs from the last digit (2) by 6, which is more than 1.

479 is okay, since its first digit (4) differs from the last digit (9) by 5, which is more than 1.

282 is *not* okay, since the difference between 2 and 2 is 0.

Take your three-digit number, and write it backwards. For example, if you picked 852, you now have on your paper:

```
852
258
```

You have two numbers on your paper. One is smaller than the other. Subtract the small one from the big one:

```
 852
-258
 594
```

Take your answer, and write it backward:

```
 852
-258
 594
 495
```

Add the last two numbers you wrote:

```
 852
-258
 594
+495
1089
```

Notice that the final answer is 1089.

1089 is the final answer, no matter what three-digit number you started with (if the first and last digits differ by more than 1). Here's another example:

Take a number:	724
Write it backward & subtract:	−427
	297
Write it backward & add:	+792
	1089

Here's another example:

Take a number:	365
Write it backward & subtract:	563
	−365
	198
Write it backward & add:	+891
	1089

Yes, you always get 1089!

Proof To prove you always get 1089, use algebra: make letters represent the digits, like this....

	Hundreds	Tens	Ones
Take a number:	A	B	C
Write it backwards:	C	B	A

To subtract the bottom (C B A) from the top (A B C), the top must be bigger. So in the hundreds column, A must be bigger than C. Since A is bigger than C, you can't subtract A from C in the ones column, so you must borrow from the B in the tens column, to produce this:

Hundreds	Tens	Ones
A	B−1	C+10
C	B	A

Now you can subtract A from C+10:

Hundreds	Tens	Ones
A	B−1	C+10
C	B	A
		C+10−A

In the tens column, you can't subtract B from B−1, so you must borrow from the A in the hundreds column, to produce this:

Hundreds	Tens	Ones
A−1	B−1+10	C+10
C	B	A
		C+10−A

Complete the calculation:

	Hundreds	Tens	Ones
Start with this:	A−1	B−1+10	C+10
Subtract this:	C	B	A
Get this result:	A−1−C	9	C+10−A
Write it backwards:	C+10−A	9	A−1−C
Get this total:	10	8	9

9, plus the 1 that was carried

Don't burn your arm I call 1089 the "don't burn your arm" number, because of this trick suggested by Irving Adler in *The Magic House of Numbers*:

Tell a friend to write a 3-digit number whose first & last digits differ by more than 1. Tell him to write the number backwards, subtract, write that backwards, and add. Tell him to burn the paper he did the figuring on. Put your arm in the ashes. When you take your arm out, the number 1089 will be mysteriously written on your arm in black. (The way you get 1089 to appear is to write "1089" on your arm with wet soap before you begin the trick. When you put your arm in the ashes, the answer will stick to the soap.) The trick works — if you don't burn your arm.

April Fools Irving Adler also suggested this trick:

Tell a friend to write a 3-digit number whose first & last digits differ by more than 1. Say to write the number backwards, subtract, write that backwards, and add. At this point, you know the friend has 1089, but don't let on. Just continue, by giving him these directions:

multiply by a million
subtract 733361573
under each 3 in the answer, write an L
under each 6, write an F
under each 5, write an O
under each 8, write an I
under each 4, write an R
under each 2, write a P
under each 7, write an A
read it backwards
It says APRIL FOOL!

Variants That procedure (reverse then subtract, reverse then add) gives 1089 if you begin with an appropriate 3-digit number. If you begin with a 2-digit number instead, you get 99.

If you begin with a 4-digit number instead, you get 10989 or 10890 or 9999, depending on which of the 4 digits are the biggest. If you begin with a 5-digit number, you get 109989 or 109890 or 99099. Notice that the answers for 4-digit and 5-digit numbers — 10989, 10890, 9999, 109989, 109890, and 99099 — are all formed from the number 99 and 1089.

Pythagorean theorem

The most amazing math discovery made by Greeks is the **Pythagorean theorem**. It says that in a **right triangle** (a triangle including a 90° angle), $a^2+b^2=c^2$, where "c" is the length of the **hypotenuse** (the longest side) and "a" & "b" are the lengths of the legs (the other two sides). It says that in this diagram —

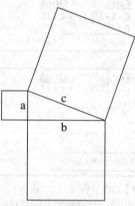

c's square is exactly as big (has the same area) as a's square and b's square combined.

The Chinese discovered the same truth, perhaps earlier.

Why is the Pythagorean theorem true? How do you prove it?

You can prove it in *many* ways. The 2nd edition of a book called *The Pythagorean Proposition* contains *many* proofs (256 of them!), collected in 1940 by Elisha Scott Loomis when he was 87 years old. Here are the 5 most amazing proofs....

3-gap proof Draw a square, where each side has length a+b. In each corner of that square, put a copy of the triangle you want to analyze, like this:

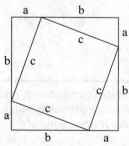

Now the square contains those 4 copied triangles, plus 1 huge gap in the middle. That gap is a square where each side has length c, so its area is c^2.

Now move the bottom 2 triangles up, so you get this:

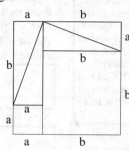

The whole picture is still "a square where each side has length a+b," and you still have 4 triangles in it; but instead of a big gap whose area is c^2, you have two small gaps, of sizes a^2 and b^2. So c^2 is the same size as a^2+b^2.

1-gap proof Draw the same picture that the 3-gap proof began with. You see the whole picture's area is $(a+b)^2$. You can also see that the picture is cut into 4 triangles (each having an area of ab/2) plus the gap in the middle (whose area is c^2). Since the whole picture's area must equal the sum of its parts, you get:

$$(a+b)^2 = ab/2 + ab/2 + ab/2 + ab/2 + c^2$$

In this proof, instead of "moving the bottom 2 triangles," we use algebra. According to algebra's rules, that equation's left side becomes $a^2 + 2ab + b^2$, and the right side becomes $2ab + c^2$, so the equation becomes:

$$a^2 + 2ab + b^2 = 2ab + c^2$$

Subtracting 2ab from both sides of that equation, you're left with:

$$a^2 + b^2 = c^2$$

1-little-gap proof Draw a square, where each side has length c. In each corner of that square, put a copy of the triangle you want to analyze, like this:

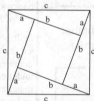

The whole picture's area is c^2. The picture is cut into 4 triangles (each having an area of ab/2) plus the little gap in the middle, whose area is $(b-a)^2$. Since the whole picture's area must equal the sum of its parts, you get:

$$c^2 = ab/2 + ab/2 + ab/2 + ab/2 + (b-a)^2$$

According to algebra's rules, that equation's right side becomes $2ab + (b^2 - 2ba + a^2)$. Then the 2ab and the -2ba cancel each other, leaving you with $a^2 + b^2$, so the equation becomes:

$$c^2 = a^2 + b^2$$

1-segment proof Draw the triangle you're interested in, like this:

Unlike the earlier proofs, which make you draw many extra segments (short lines), this proof makes you draw just *one* extra segment! Make it perpendicular to the hypotenuse and go to the right angle:

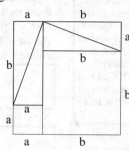

The original big triangle (whose sides have lengths a, b, and c) has the same-size angles as the tiny triangle (whose sides have lengths x and a), so it's "similar to" the tiny triangle, and so the big triangle's ratio of "shortest side to hypotenuse" (a/c) is the same as the tiny triangle's ratio of "shortest side to hypotenuse" (x/a). Write that equation:

$$a/c = x/a$$

Multiplying both sides of that equation by ac, you discover what a^2 is:

$$a^2 = xc$$

Using similar reasoning, you discover what b^2 is:

$$b^2 = yc$$

Adding those two equations together, you get:

$$a^2 + b^2 = (x+y)c$$

Since x+y is c, that equation becomes:

$$a^2 + b^2 = c^2$$

1-segment general proof Draw the triangle you're interested in, like this:

As in the previous proof, draw one extra segment, perpendicular to the hypotenuse and going to the right angle:

Now you have 3 triangles: the left one, the rightmost one, and the big one.

Since the left triangle's area plus the rightmost triangle's area equals the big triangle's area, and since the 3 triangles are similar to each other ("stretched" versions of each other, as you can prove by looking at their angles), any area constructed from "parts of the left triangle" plus the area constructed from "corresponding parts of the rightmost triangle" equals the area constructed from "corresponding parts of the big triangle." For example, the area constructed by drawing a square on the left triangle's hypotenuse (a^2) plus the area constructed by drawing a square on the rightmost triangle's hypotenuse (b^2) equals the area constructed by drawing a square on the big triangle's hypotenuse (c^2).

Which proof is the best?

The **3-gap proof** is the most visually appealing, but it bothers mathematicians who are too lazy to draw (construct) so many segments. (It also requires you to prove the gap is indeed a square, whose angles are right angles, but that's easy.)

The **1-gap proof** uses fewer lines by relying on algebra instead. It's fine if you like algebra, awkward if you don't. The **1-little-gap proof** uses algebra slightly differently.

The **1-segment proof** appeals to mathematicians because it requires constructing just 1 segment, but you can't understand it until you've learned the laws of similar triangles. This proof was invented by Davis Legendre in 1858.

The **1-segment general proof** is the most powerful because its thinking generalizes to *any* area created from the 3 triangles, not just *square* areas. In any right triangle:

> The area of a square drawn on the hypotenuse (c^2) is the sum of the areas of squares drawn on the legs ($a^2 + b^2$).
>
> The area of a circle drawn on the hypotenuse (using the hypotenuse as the diameter) is the sum of the areas of circles drawn on the legs.
>
> The area of *any* blob (such as a square or circle or clown's head) drawn on the hypotenuse is the sum of the areas of similarly-shaped blobs drawn on the legs.

That proof was invented by a 19-year-old kid (Stanley Jashemski in Youngstown, Ohio) in 1934.

Ugliness

To understand the concept of math ugliness, remember these math definitions:

> The numbers 0, 1, 2, 3, etc., are called **whole numbers**.
>
> Those numbers and their negatives (-1, -2, -3, etc.) are all called **integers**.
>
> The integers and fractions made from them (1/4, 2/3, -7/5, etc.) are all called **rational numbers** (because they're all simple fractions, simple ratios).
>
> All numbers on the number line are called **real numbers**: they include all the rational numbers but also include irrational numbers (such as "pi" and "the square root of 2"), which can't be expressed accurately as fractions made of integers.

Now you can tackle the **3 rules of ugliness**:

> 1. Most things are ugly.
> 2. Most things *you'll* see are nice.
> 3. Every ugly thing is almost nice.

More precisely:

> Suppose you have a big set of numbers (such as the set of all real numbers), and you consider a certain subset of those numbers to be "nice" (such as the set of all rational numbers). The 3 rules of ugliness say:
>
> 1. Most members of the big set aren't in the nice subset. (For example, most real numbers aren't rational.)
>
> 2. When you operate on most members of the nice subset, you stay in the nice subset. (For example, if you add, subtract, multiply, or divide rational numbers, you get another rational number, if you don't divide by 0.)
>
> 3. Ever member of the big set can be approximated by members of the nice subset. (For example, every irrational number can be approximated by rational numbers.)

In different branches of math, those same 3 rules keep cropping up, using different definitions of what's "ugly" and "nice."

The rules apply to people, too:

> 1. Most people aren't like you. You'll tend to think their behaviors are ugly.
>
> 2. Most people *you'll* meet will appeal to you, because you'll tend to move to a neighborhood or career composed of people like you.
>
> 3. The "ugly" people are actually *almost* like you: once you make an attempt to understand them, you'll discover they really aren't as different from you as you thought!

How math should be taught

I have complaints about how math is taught. Here's a list of my main complaints. If you're a mathematician, math teacher, or top math student, read the list and phone me at 603-666-6644 if you want to chat about details or hear about my other complaints, most of which result from research I did in the 1960's and 1970's. (On the other hand, if you don't know about math and don't care, skip these comments.)

Percentages

Middle-school students should learn how to compute percentages (such as "What is 40% of 200?"); but advanced percentage questions (such as "80 is 40% of what?" and "80 is what percent of 200?") should be delayed until after algebra, because the easiest way to solve an advanced percentage question is to turn the question into an algebraic equation by using these tricks:

> change "what" to "x"
> change "is" to "="
> change "percent" to "/100"
> change "of" to "·"

Graphing a line

To graph a line (such as "y = 5 + 2x"), students should be told to use this formula:

> the graph of the equation $y = h + sx$
> is a line whose height (above the origin) is h
> and whose slope is s

So to graph y = 5 + 2x, put a dot that's a distance of 5 above the origin; then draw a line that goes through that dot and has a slope of 2.

The formula "y = h + sx" is called the "hot sex" formula (since it includes h + sx). It's easier to remember than the traditional formula, which has the wrong letters and wrong order and looks like this:

> the graph of the equation $y = mx + b$
> is a line whose height (above the origin) is b
> and whose slope is m

Imaginary numbers

Imaginary numbers (such as "i") should be explained *before* the quadratic formula, so the quadratic formula can be stated simply (without having to say "if the determinant is non-negative").

Factoring

Students should be told that every quadratic expression (such as $x^2 + 6x + 8$) can be factored by this formula:

> the factorization of $x^2 + 2ax + c$ is
> (x+a+d)(x+a-d), where $d=\sqrt{a^2-c}$

For example:

> to factor $x^2 + 6x + 8$,
> realize that a=3 and c=8,
> so d=1 and the factorization is (x+3+1)(x+3-1),
> which is (x+4)(x+2)

As you can see from that example, the **a** (which in the example is 3) is the **average** of the two final numbers (4 and 2). That's why it's called **a**.

The **d** (which is 1) is how much each final number **differs** from **a** (4 and 2 each differ from 3 by 1). That's why it's called **d**. You can call **d** the **difference** or **divergence** or **displacement**.

Here's another reason why it's called **d**: it's the **determinant**, since it determines what kind of final answer you'll get (rational, irrational, imaginary, or single-root). You can also call **d** the **discriminant**, since it lets you discriminate among different kinds of answers.

Quadratic equations

To solve any quadratic equation (such as "$x^2 + 6x + 8 = 0$"), you can use that short factoring formula. For example:

> to solve "$x^2 + 6x + 8 = 0$,"
> factor it to get "$(x+4)(x+2) = 0$,"
> whose solutions are -4 and -2

Another way to solve a quadratic equation is to use "Russ's quadratic formula," which is:

> the solution of "$x^2 = 2bx+c$" is $b \pm \sqrt{b^2+c}$

That's much shorter and easier to remember than the traditional quadratic formula, though forcing an equation into the form "$x^2 = 2bx+c$" can sometimes be challenging. Here's an application:

> to solve $x^2=6x+16$,
> realize that b=3 and c=16,
> so the solution is $3\pm\sqrt{25}$, which is 3 ± 5,
> which is 8 or -2

Prismoid formula

Students should be told that the volume of any reasonable solid (such as a prism, cylinder, pyramid, cone, or sphere) can be computed from this **prismoid formula**:

> volume =
> height • (area of the typical cross-section)
>
> where "area of the typical cross-section" means (top + bottom + 4 • middle)/6, where
>
> "top" means "area of top cross-section"
> "bottom" means "area of bottom cross-section"
> "middle" means "area of halfway-up cross-section"

That formula can be written more briefly, like this:

> V = H (T + B + 4M)/6,
> where V means volume,
> H means height,
> T means top cross-section's area
> B means bottom cross-section's area
> M means middle cross-section's area

For example, the volume of a pyramid (whose height is H and whose base area is L times W) is:

> H (0 + LW + 4(L/2)(W/2))/6, which is
> H (LW + 4LW/4)/6, which is
> H (LW + LW)/6, which is
> H (2LW)/6, which is
> HLW/3

The volume of a cone (whose height is H and whose base area is πr^2) is:

> H (0 + πr^2 + 4π(r/2)^2)/6, which is
> H (πr^2 + 4πr^2/4)/6, which is
> H (πr^2 + πr^2)/6, which is
> H ($2\pi r^2$)/6, which is
> H πr^2/3

The volume of a sphere (whose radius is r) is:

> (2r) (0 + 0 + 4πr^2)/6, which is
> 2r (4πr^2)/6, which is
> 4πr^3/3

In the prismoid formula, V = H (T + B + 4M)/6, the "4" is the same "4" that appears in Simpson's rule (which is used in calculus to find the area under a curve). The formula gives exactly the right answer for any 3-D shape whose sides are "smooth" (so you can express the cross-sectional areas as a quadratic or cubic function of the distance above the base). To prove the prismoid formula works for all such shapes, you must study calculus.

Balanced curriculum

Math consists of many topics. Schools should reevaluate which topics are most important.

All students, before graduating from high school, should taste what statistics and calculus are about, since they're used in many fields. For example, economists often talk about "marginal profit," which is a concept from calculus. Students should also be exposed to other branches of math, such as matrices, logic, topology, and infinite numbers.

The explanation of Euclidean geometry should be abridged, to make room for other topics that are more important, such as coordinate geometry, which leads to calculus.

Like Shakespeare, Euclid's work is a classic that should be shown to students so they can savor it and enjoy geometric examples of what "proofs" are; but after half a year of that, let high-school students move on to other topics that are more modern and more useful, to see examples of how proofs are used in *other* branches of math.

Too much time is spent analyzing triangles.

> For example, consider the experience of John Kemeny, who headed Dartmouth College's math department (and also invented the Basic programming language and later became Dartmouth College's president). When he was a high-school student, his teacher told him to master "trigonometry, the study of analyzing triangles"; but for the next 20 years, he never had to analyze another triangle, even though he was a mathematician. That trigonometry course was totally useless!
>
> Finally, one day, he bought a plot of land that was advertised as being "an acre, more or less." He wanted to discover whether it was more or less, so he had survey it and analyze triangles. (The plot turned out to be *more* than an acre.)
>
> When he told that tale to me and my classmates at Dartmouth, he then went on to make his point: mathematicians don't have much use for analyzing triangles, though they *do* have use for how trigonometric functions (such as sine and cosine) help analyze circles (and circular motion and periodic motion). So let's spend less time on triangles and more time on other topics!

Infinitesimals

Students should be told about infinitesimals, because they make calculus easier to understand.

Specifically, there's an infinitesimal number, called **epsilon** (or ϵ or simply **e**), which is positive (greater than zero) but so tiny that its square is 0:

> $\epsilon^2 = 0$

You might say "there's no such number," but we can invent it, just like mathematicians invented the "imaginary" number i whose square is -1. The invention of i simplified algebra, by making the quadratic formula more understandable. The invention of ϵ simplifies calculus, by making derivatives more understandable.

To use ϵ, construct the **extended real numbers**, which consist of numbers of the form a + bϵ (where "a" and "b" are ordinary "real" numbers). Add and multiply extended real numbers as you'd expect (bearing in mind that ϵ^2 is 0), like this:

> (a + bϵ) + (c + dϵ) = (a+c) + (b+d)ϵ
> (a + bϵ) • (c + dϵ) = ac + (ad+bc)ϵ

For example:

> (9+12ϵ) + (2+4ϵ) = 11+16ϵ
> (9+12ϵ) • (2+4ϵ) = 18 + (36+24)ϵ, which is 18+60ϵ

You can define order:

> "a+bϵ < c+dϵ" means "a<c or (a=c and b<d)"

Those definitions of addition, subtraction, multiplication, and order obey the traditional "rules of algebra" except for one rule: in traditional algebra, every non-zero number has a reciprocal (a number you can multiply it by to get 1), but unfortunately ϵ has no reciprocal.

If **x** is an extended real number, it has the form **a + bϵ**, where **a** and **b** are each real. The **a** is called the **real part** of **x**. For example, the real part of $3 + 7\epsilon$ is 3.

A number is called **infinitesimal** if its real part is 0. For example, ϵ and 2ϵ are infinitesimal; so is 0.

Infinitesimals are useful because they let you define the "derivative" of f(x) easily, by computing f(x+ϵ):

> Define **the differential of f(x)**, which is written **d f(x)**, to mean **f(x+ϵ) - f(x)**. For example, dx^2 is (x+ϵ)^2-x^2, which is (x^2+2xϵ+ϵ^2)-x^2, which is 2xϵ (since ϵ^2=0), which is 2x dx (since dx turns out to be ϵ).
>
> Define **the derivative of f(x)** to mean **(d f(x)) divided by ϵ**. For example, the derivative of x^2 is (2xϵ)/ϵ, which is 2x. The definition of the derivative of f(x) can also be written as (d f(x))/dx, since dx is ϵ.
>
> Define **the limit, as x approaches p, of f(x)** to mean **the real part of f(p+ϵ)**. For example, the limit, as x approaches 0, of x/x is the real part of (0+ϵ)/(0+ϵ), which is the real part of ϵ/ϵ, which is the real part of 1, which is 1.

Define **f(x) is continuous at p** to mean:
for all b, f(p+bϵ) − f(p) is infinitesimal.
For example, the function "3 if x≤0, 4 if x>0" isn't continuous at 0, since
f(0+1ϵ)-f(0) is 4-3, which is 1, which isn't infinitesimal.

Define **f(x) is differentiable at p** to mean:
for all b, f(p+bϵ) = f(p) + b (the derivative of f(x) at p).

Then calculations & proofs about derivatives and limits become easy, especially when you define sin ϵ to be ϵ and define cos ϵ to be 1.

High-school algebra axioms

Here are the best definitions, axioms, and theorems for formalizing the elementary part of high-school algebra.

Equality The symbol "=" (pronounced "equals" or "is") leads to these definitions:

"a=b=c" (pronounced "a is b is c") means "a=b and b=c"	
"a≠b" (pronounced "a isn't b") means "it is false that a=b"	

Here are the **axioms** (fundamental properties):

reflexive:	a=a
substitution:	if a=b, you can switch "a" to "b"

Those definitions and axioms lead to these **theorems** (consequences that can be proved):

symmetry:	a=b iff b=a
transitive:	if a=b=c then a=c
dichotomy:	a=b or a≠b

In that first theorem, the "iff" is pronounced "if and only if" or "is equivalent to".

Addition The symbols "+" (pronounced "added to" or "plus") and "1" (pronounced "one") lead to these definitions:

"2" (pronounced "two")	means "1+1"
"3" (pronounced "three")	means "2+1"
"4" (pronounced "four")	means "3+1"
"5" (pronounced "five")	means "4+1"
"6" (pronounced "six")	means "5+1"
"7" (pronounced "seven")	means "6+1"
"8" (pronounced "eight")	means "7+1"
"9" (pronounced "nine")	means "8+1"

Here are the axioms:

commutative:	a+b = b+a
associative:	(a+b)+c = a+(b+c)

Those definitions and axioms lead to this theorem:

four:	2+2 = 4

Zero The symbol "0" (pronounced "zero") has this axiom:

zero:	a+0 = a

That axiom leads to this theorem:

zero on left:	0+a = a

Negatives The symbol "-" (pronounced "negative" or "minus") has this axiom:

negative:	a+-a = 0

That axiom lead to these theorems:

negative zero:	-0 = 0
add to both sides:	a=b iff a+c=b+c
negative test:	a+b=0 iff b=-a
double negative:	--a = a
distribute negative:	-(a+b) = -a+-b
negate both sides:	a=b iff -a=-b

Subtraction Here's another definition:

"a-b" (pronounced "a minus b") means "a + -b"	

That definition leads to these theorems:

subtract from itself:	a-a = 0
subtract from zero:	0-a = -a
subtract a negative:	a--b = a+b

reverse subtraction:	a-b = -(b-a)
subtract from both sides:	a=b iff a-c=b-c
solve simple equation:	x+a=b iff x=b-a
difference is solution:	a-b=x iff x+b=a

Multiplication The symbol "•" is a raised dot. It's pronounced "multiplied by" or "times." Mathematicians are often lazy and don't bother writing that symbol. For example, instead of writing "a·b" they often write just "ab" to be brief.
Here are the axioms:

one:	1a = a
multiplication commutative:	ab = ba
multiplication associative:	(ab)c = a(bc)
distributive:	a(b+c) = ab + ac

Those axioms lead to these theorems —

one on right:	a1 = a
sum multiplied:	(a+b)c = ac + bc
double:	2a = a+a
triple:	3a = a+a+a
zero multiplied:	0a = 0

and these theorems about multiplying negatives:

negative multiplication:	(-a)b = -(ab)
minus one:	(-1)a = -a
multiply by negative:	a(-b) = -(ab)
negative times negative:	(-a)(-b) = ab
multiply by difference:	a(b-c) = ab - ac

Positivity The phrase "is positive" has these axioms:

one positive:	1 is positive
zero not positive:	0 is not positive
sum positive:	if a and b are positive, so is a+b
product positive:	if a and b are positive, so is ab

Those axioms lead to these theorems:

two positive:	2 is positive
positive not zero:	if a is positive then a≠0
one not zero:	1 ≠ 0
negative not positive:	if a is positive, -a is not positive

Reciprocals The symbol "/" is pronounced "the reciprocal of" or "slash." For example, "/b" is pronounced "the reciprocal of b" or "slash b". Mathematicians are lazy: instead of writing "a•/b" they write just "a/b" (which they pronounce "a divided by b" or "a slash b") or do this: write a little "a" over a little "b" and put a horizontal line between them, to form a fraction (which they pronounce "a over b"), where the top number ("a") is called the "numerator" and the bottom number ("b") is called the "denominator".
Here's the main axiom:

reciprocal:	a/a = 1	(if a≠0)

That axiom leads to this theorem —

reciprocal of one:	/1 = 1

and these theorems about fractions —

top one:	1/a = /a	
bottom one:	a/1 = a	
top zero:	0/a = 0	
both zero:	0/0 = 0	
both same:	a/a = 1	(if a≠0)
remove bottom:	(ab)/a = b	(if a≠0)
top negative:	(-a)/b = - (a/b)	
multiply by fraction:	a • (b/c) = (ab)/c	
add fractions:	(a/b) + (c/b) = (a+c)/b	

and these theorems about solving equations:

multiply by both sides:	a=b iff ac=bc	(assuming c≠0)
divide into both sides:	a=b iff a/c = b/c	(assuming c≠0)
factor removed or zero:	ac=bc iff (a=b or c=0)	
product zero:	ab=0 iff (a=0 or b=0)	
roots from factors:	(x-r)(x-s)=0 iff (x=r or x=s)	

product not zero:	$ab \neq 0$ iff ($a \neq 0$ and $b \neq 0$)	
reciprocal test:	if $ab = 1$ then $b = /a$	
division test:	$ax = b$ iff $x = b/a$	(assuming $a \neq 0$)
solve linear equations:	$ax + b = c$ iff $x = (c-b)/a$	(assuming $a \neq 0$)

What's the reciprocal of 0? The reciprocal axiom doesn't answer that question. Some books say the reciprocal of 0 is "undefined"; other books say the reciprocal of 0 is "infinity"; but those approaches awkwardly force many theorems to say "assuming $a \neq 0$." We'll use a smarter approach: we'll define the reciprocal of 0 to be 0, by adding this axiom:

zero reciprocal:	$/0 = 0$

That axiom saves us from having to say "assuming $a \neq 0$" so often, though we'll still have to say "assuming $a \neq 0$" occasionally. That axiom leads to these theorems:

bottom 0:	$a/0 = 0$
zero means reciprocal is zero:	$a = 0$ iff $/a = 0$
reciprocal not zero:	$a \neq 0$ iff $/a \neq 0$
double reciprocal:	$//a = a$
reciprocal of negative:	$/(-a) = -(/a)$
reciprocal of product:	$/(ab) = (/a)(/b)$
reciprocal of quotient:	$/(a/b) = b/a$
reciprocate both sides:	$a = b$ iff $/a = /b$

Here are theorems about changing the denominator:

bottom negative:	$a/(-b) = -(b/a)$	
both negative:	$(-a)/(-b) = a/b$	
multiply fractions:	$(a/b) \cdot (c/d) = (ac)/(bd)$	
multiply both:	$a/b = (ac)/(bc)$	(if $c \neq 0$ or $c = b$)
add any fractions:	$a/b + c/d = (ad+bc)/(bd)$	(if $b \neq 0$ and $d \neq 0$)

Here's another definition:

"%" (pronounced "percent") means "/100"

Here's another axiom about reciprocals:

reciprocal positive:	if a is positive, so is $/a$

That axiom leads to this theorem:

fraction positive:	if a and b are positive, so is a/b

Order Here are more definitions:

"$a > b$" (pronounced "a greater than b") means "$a - b$ is positive"
"$a > b > c$" (pronounced "a greater than b greater than c") means "$a > b$ and $b > c$"

Those definitions lead to these theorems:

greater than zero:	$a > 0$ iff a is positive	
add to greater:	$a > b$ iff $a + c > b + c$	
subtract from greater:	$a > b$ iff $a - c > b - c$	
greater is transitive:	if $a > b > c$ then $a > c$	
sum the greater:	if $a > b$ and $c > d$ then $a + c > b + d$	
greater than itself:	"$a > a$" is false	
greater can't reverse:	if $a > b$ then "$b > a$" is false	
multiply greater:	$a > b$ iff $ac > bc$	(assuming c is positive)

The opposite of ">" is "<". Here's the definition:

"$a < b$" (pronounced "a less than b")	means "$b > a$"
"$a < b < c$" (pronounced "a less than b less than c") means "$a < b$ and $b < c$"	

Each theorem about "greater" leads to a theorem about "less":

0 less than:	$0 < a$ iff a is positive	
add to less:	$a < b$ iff $a + c < b + c$	
subtract from less:	$a < b$ iff $a - c < b - c$	
less is transitive:	if $a < b < c$ then $a < c$	
sum the less:	if $a < b$ and $c < d$ then $a + c < b + d$	
less than itself:	"$a < a$" is false	
less can't reverse:	if $a < b$ then "$b < a$" is false	
multiply less:	$a < b$ iff $ac < bc$	(assuming c is positive)

These theorems relate "<" to ">":

flip if negate:	$a < b$ iff $-a > -b$
flip if reciprocate:	if $0 < a < b$ then $/a > /b$

Here are more definitions:

"$a \geq b$" (pronounced "a grequal b") means "$a > b$ or $a = b$"
"$a \leq b$" (pronounced "a lequal b") means "$a < b$ or $a = b$"

Each theorem about "<" leads to a theorem about "≤":

zero lequal:	$0 \leq a$ iff a is 0 or positive	
add to lequal:	$a \leq b$ iff $a + c \leq b + c$	
subtract from lequal:	$a \leq b$ iff $a - c \leq b - c$	
lequal is transitive:	if $a \leq b \leq c$ then $a \leq c$	
sum the lequals:	if $a \leq b$ and $c \leq d$ then $a + c \leq b + d$	
lequal itself:	$a \leq a$	
lequal can't reverse:	if $a \leq b$ then "$b < a$" is false	
multiply lequals:	$a \leq b$ iff $ac \leq bc$	(assuming c is positive)
flip lequal if negate:	$a \leq b$ iff $-a \geq -b$	
flip lequal if reciprocate:	if $0 < a \leq b$ then $/a \geq /b$	

Exponents
We've discussed addition ($a+b$), subtraction ($a-b$), multiplication ($a \cdot b$), and division (a/b). Now we'll discuss exponentiation (x^a). In the operation "x^a," the "a" is called the "exponent" (or "power"); the "x" is called the "base"; the "x^a" is called the "base x raised to the a power" or just "x to the a." For example, "x^2" is called "x to the 2" (or "x squared"); "x^3" is called "x to the 3" (or "x cubed").

Here are the basic axioms about exponents (powers):

power of 1:	$x^1 = x$	
add powers:	$x^a x^b = x^{a+b}$	(if $x \neq 0$ or $a+b \neq 0$)

Those axioms lead to these theorems:

square:	$x^2 = x \cdot x$	
next power:	$x^{a+1} = x^a x$	(if $x \neq 0$ or $a \neq -1$)
previous power:	$x^a = x^{a-1} x$	(if $x \neq 0$ or $a \neq 0$)
power of zero:	$0^a = 0$	(if $a \neq 0$)
cube:	$x^3 = x \cdot x \cdot x$	
square of negative:	$(-x)^2 = x^2$	

Advanced multiplication
Here are advanced theorems about multiplication:

FOIL:	$(a+b)(c+d) = ac + ad + bc + bd$
square a sum:	$(x+y)^2 = x^2 + 2xy + y^2$
square a difference:	$(x-y)^2 = x^2 - 2xy - y^2$
difference of squares:	$(x+y)(x-y) = x^2 - y^2$
equal squares:	$x^2 = y^2$ iff $x = \pm y$
factor by guessing:	$x^2 + bx + c = (x+u)(x+v)$, if $u+v=b$ and $uv=c$
factor all by guessing:	$ax^2 + bx + c = [(ax+u)(ax+v)]/a$, if $u+v=b$ and $uv=ac$ and $a \neq 0$
difference of cubes:	$x^3 - y^3 = (x-y)(x^2+xy+y^2)$
sum of cubes:	$x^3 + y^3 = (x+y)(x^2-xy+y^2)$
cube a sum:	$(x+y)^3 = x^3 + 3x^2y + 3xy^2 + y^3$

Zero power
This axiom is more advanced:

zero power:	$x^0 = 1$

That axiom leads to these theorems:

zero to the zero:	$0^0 = 1$	
power gives zero:	$x^a = 0$ iff ($x=0$ and $a \neq 0$)	
negative power:	$x^{-a} = /(x^a)$	
negative power fraction:	$x^{-a} = 1/(x^a)$	
-1 power:	$x^{-1} = /x$	
-1 power fraction:	$x^{-1} = 1/x$	
subtract powers:	$(x^a)/(x^b) = x^{a-b}$	(if $x \neq 0$ or $a \neq b$)

Physicists

Physics is phunny.

Physics for poets

To help liberal-arts students understand physicists such as Newton and Einstein, physicists teach a course called "Physics for Poets." The whole course is summarized in 4 sentences:

Physics rule	Poetic meaning
Newton's theory of gravitation	The earth sucks.
Newton's third law of motion	Every jerk creates his equal opponent.
Einstein's E=MC²	A small matter can mushroom into a big whoopee.
Einstein's theory of relativity	Your views are influenced by your relatives.

Barometer test

Back in 1958, *Reader's Digest* published a tale by Alexander Calandra about a barometer test. Over the years, he and others embellished the tale. These new fancier versions are fictional but fun. Here's an example:

A physics test said to "Find a height of a tall building by using a barometer." The professor considered the correct answer to be "Use the barometer to measure the air pressure at the building's top and the building's bottom, then analyze the difference."

But one student gave this cleverer answer: "Put the barometer at the end of a rope, lower the rope from the top of the building, and measure the rope's length plus the barometer's length. Or throw the barometer from the top of the building and measure how long the barometer takes to fall. Or compare the length of the building's shadow to the length of the barometer's shadow. Or walk up the stairs while you mark, on the walls, how many barometer-heights you had to climb. Or attach the barometer to a rope, swing it like a pendulum, and measure how the swing time at the building's top differs from the bottom."

The professor demanded, "Don't you know the *simplest* answer?"

The student replied, "Sure! Tell the building's superintendent you'll give him the barometer if he tells you the building's height! That's the simplest answer. I'm fed up with you professors telling me how I *should* think!"

Chemists

Chemists are mixed up.

Are you a chemist?

To discover how good a chemist you are, see how long you take to solve this puzzle:

A chemist noticed a certain reaction took 80 minutes whenever he was wearing a green necktie, and the same reaction took an hour and twenty minutes whenever he was wearing a purple necktie. Why?

If you can't solve that problem yourself, ask your friends, until you find a friend who's smart — and kind enough to tell you the answer.

That puzzle comes from Martin Gardner's book, *Mathematical Puzzles*. To have more fun, get that book!

Hell's heat

Back around 1950, chemists tried to prove heaven's hotter than hell. The proofs gradually got more sophisticated. A 1972 article in *Applied Optics* argues this way:

Revelations 21:8 says **hell** is a "*lake burning with fire & brimstone*," so hell's temperature is below the boiling point of brimstone (sulfur), which is **444.6°C**.

Isaiah 30:26 says **heaven** is full of intense *light*, which generates lots of heat energy, **525°C** according to our calculations.

So heaven is hotter than hell.

The full article is at www.lhup.edu/~dsimanek/hell.htm.

This bonus question appeared on a chemistry test:

Is hell *exothermic* (giving off heat) or *endothermic* (absorbing heat)? Prove your answer.

The professor expected the students to argue, one way or the other, by using Boyle's law (which says compressing a gas makes it hotter). According to the tale, the top student gave this answer:

First, we must discover how hell's mass is changing, so we need to know how fast souls enter hell and how fast they leave.

Once a soul gets to hell it won't leave, but how many souls *enter* hell? According to most religions, if you're not a member of that religion, you'll go to hell. Since there are many religions but no single person belongs to more than one, all people and their souls go to hell; so in light of birth and death rates, we expect the number of souls in hell to increase exponentially.

Next, examine how hell's volume changes, since Boyle's Law says that for hell's temperature and pressure to remain constant, hell's volume must expand proportionally as souls are added.

That gives two possibilities....

#1: if hell expands *slower* than the rate at which souls enter hell, hell's temperature and pressure will increase until all hell breaks loose.

#2: if hell expands *faster* than the rate at which souls enter hell, hell's temperature and pressure will drop until hell freezes over.

So which is it?

If we accept the postulate given me by Teresa during my freshman year that "It will be a cold day in hell before I sleep with you" and realize I slept with her last night, hell's already frozen over, so *hell is exothermic* and #2 is true. Since hell's frozen over, it isn't accepting more souls and is extinct, leaving just heaven, thereby proving the existence of a divine being, which explains why last night Teresa kept shouting "Oh my God!"

Administratium

In April 1988, William DeBuvitz wrote about the discovery of **administratium**. Here's a summary of what he and later researchers have reported:

Chemists have finally discovered the heaviest element known to science. The element, **administratium**, has no protons or electrons, so its atomic number is 0; but it has 1 neutron, 125 assistant neutrons, 75 vice-neutrons, and 111 assistant vice-neutrons, giving it an atomic mass of 312. These 312 particles are held together by a force involving the continuous exchange of meson-like particles (called **morons**) and surrounded by vast quantities of lepton-like particles (called **peons**).

Administratium is inert (since it has no electrons) but can be detected chemically, since it impedes every reaction it contacts: a tiny amount of administratium can make a reaction take 4 days that would normally take less than a second.

Administratium has a half-life of 3 years, after which it doesn't decay but instead undergoes a reorganization in which assistant neutrons, vice-neutrons, and assistant vice-neutrons exchange places. Administratium's mass increases over time, since each reorganization makes some morons become neutrons, forming new isotopes, called **isodopes**. The moron promotion makes chemists think administratium forms spontaneously whenever morons reach a certain concentration, called a **critical morass**.

Administratium occurs naturally in the atmosphere but concentrates at certain points (such as government agencies, large corporations, and universities). It usually appears in buildings that are new, fancy, and well-maintained.

Since administratium is toxic at *any* concentration level, it destroys any productive reaction. We're trying to control administratium, to prevent irreversible damage. Help stop this deadly element from spreading!

Elements

The names of the chemical elements might seem boring, but in 1959 Tom Lehrer made them fun: he wrote a song called *The Elements*, where he sang the names of the 102 chemical elements that had been discovered so far, to the tune of the *Major-General's Song* from Gilbert & Sullivan's *Pirates of Pinzance*.

Here are 4 videos about it:

Tom Lehrer singing, with element photos: www.YouTube.com/watch?v=SmwlzwGMMwc
Tom Lehrer singing, with periodic table: www.YouTube.com/watch?v=zGM-wSKFBpo
Tom Lehrer singing, with elements named: www.PrivateHand.com/flash/elements.html
Harry Potter's Daniel Radcliffe tries to sing it: www.YouTube.com/watch?v=rSAaiYKF0cs

Warning: for the first video's Web address, the letter after w is a lower-case L.

Arts

Artsy-fartsy, let's get smartsy.

Picasso's advice

Pablo Picasso, the greatest modern painter, gave great advice about art & life.

To become a great artist, you should look at the works of others, learn from them, incorporate their ideas into your own thinking, grow, and never stop growing. Picasso said:

> Bad artists copy. Good artists steal.
> To copy others is necessary, but to copy oneself is pathetic.
> I'm always doing what I cannot do, in order that I may learn how to do it.
>
> Every child is an artist. The problem is how to remain an artist once he grows up.

The idea of the top quote ("Bad artists copy. Good artists steal.") is itself stolen from Lionel Trilling, who said:

> Immature artists imitate. Mature artists steal.

Art can be superficial or deep. Picasso asked:

> Are we to paint what's on the face, what's inside the face, or what's behind it?
> Who sees the human face correctly: the photographer, the mirror, or the painter?

Art doesn't have to be literal. He said:

> Art is a lie that enables us to realize the truth.
> The world today doesn't make sense, so why should I paint pictures that do?
>
> Some painters transform the sun into a yellow spot. Others transform a yellow spot into the sun.

Art should begin with reality, then go beyond it. He said:

> There's no abstract art. You must always start with something. Later you can remove all traces of reality.

When you start a painting, plan it but don't over-plan: jump in, start creating it, and then let it take on a life of its own and grow by itself. He said:

> You must have an idea of what you're going to do, but it should be a vague idea.
>
> One never knows what one's going to do. One starts a painting and then it becomes something quite different.

Get abstract, but not *too* abstract. He warned:

> When you try to find a portrait's true form by abstracting more and more, you must end up with an egg.

A painting should have a grand purpose. He said:

> Painting is not done to decorate apartments. It's an instrument of war against brutality and darkness.

He admitted:

> I don't own any of my own paintings, because a Picasso original costs several thousand dollars — it's a luxury I can't afford.

He also admitted:

> The "refined," the "rich, professional do-nothing," and the "distiller of quintessence" desire just the peculiar, sensational, eccentric, and scandalous: that's today's art.
>
> Since the advent of cubism, I've fed those fellows what they wanted and satisfied those critics with all the ridiculous ideas that passed through my head. The less they understood, the more they admired me!
>
> Now I'm celebrated and rich; but when I'm alone, I don't have the effrontery to consider myself an artist at all, not in the grand meaning of the word. I'm just a public clown. I've understood my time and exploited the imbecility, vanity, and greed of my contemporaries.

> That's a bitter confession, more painful than it may seem; but at least — and at last — it's honest.

I hope you liked Picasso's advice & confessions, but his wife said:

> If my husband ever met a woman on the street who looked like the women in his paintings, he'd faint.

Music

Many people spend lots of time trying to create music. Like basketball, music is fun & healthy but rarely leads to a successful career.

Music versus art

Americans treat music differently from art. The typical art class encourages kids to create their own art by using crayons, paint, and other media. The typical music class does not encourage kids to compose their own music; instead, the class encourages kids to imitate (perform) music composed by others. Kids are taught to slavishly "play the right notes," not invent their own.

This miseducation affects our adult lives. While we're chatting on the phone, we let ourselves do creative artwork, called "doodling," but not creative music. In the shower, we try to sing correctly, not creatively.

Indian philosophy

At Wesleyan University in Connecticut, I heard a musician explain how to improvise on the **sitar** (a guitar from India). He said that if you play a "wrong" note, don't get embarrassed: instead, consider that the sitar is talking to you. Play off the error. Play the wrong note again and again, on purpose, as if you meant it, as if you were purposely trying to surprise the audience and shockingly lead the audience into a new theme.

To be more sophisticated, repeat not just the wrong note but also the entire phrase that contained it, then make that phrase lead up to a climactic phrase that's even more bizarre and exciting.

Famous music

Would you like to become a famous composer? Would you like to become like Beethoven or the Beatles?

If so, here's something humbling to remember....

What's the most popular piece of music in the whole world, the piece of music that more people around the world know than any other?

No, it's not by Beethoven, it's not by the Beatles, and it's not by Britney Spears (thank God).

The next time you're at a party, ask your friends to answer that question. Then reveal the answer ("The Happy Birthday Song") and sing it to the daily victim!

That song is known all over the world. Yes, even in strange countries — like France and China — they sing that song, with the same notes, in their own languages!

The song was invented in 1893 in Louisville Kentucky. The melody was by a kindergarten teacher, **Mildred Hill**. The original words were by her sister, **Patty**, the principal, and went like this:

> Good morning to you.
> Good morning to you.
> Good morning, dear children.
> Good morning to all.

They were to be sung by teachers (and were published in a songbook called "Song Stories for the Kindergarten"), but soon the kids started singing it back to the teachers and changed the words to:

> Good morning to you.
> Good morning to you.
> Good morning, dear teacher.
> Good morning to you.

Much later, some wiseguy changed the words to:

> Happy birthday to you.
> Happy birthday to you.
> Happy birthday, dear _____.
> Happy birthday to you.

Those "Happy birthday" words were finally published in a songbook edited by Robert Coleman in 1924. Afterwards, the song spread by word of mouth, radio, movies, Western Union's singing telegrams, and other crazed comedians.

Eventually, the Hill family sued for copyright infringement. The copyright was eventually sold to bigger publishers.

Now it's legal to sing the song at family birthday parties privately; but you're supposed to pay royalties if you perform the song publicly, such as in a restaurant or sports arena or —according to lawyers — at the following:

> anyplace "open to the public" or where gather a substantial number of people outside a normal circle of "a family and its social acquaintances"

The current copyright owner (Time Warner) collects 2 million dollars per year in royalties, which it splits with a foundation established by the sister's family.

Moral: if you want big fame and big bucks, write happy songs, for kids! I wonder how much money Barney generates by singing:

> I love you. You love me.
> We're a happy family.

I prefer the popular parody:

> I hate you. You hate me.
> We're a dysfunctional family.

Sing it whenever mom yells at you. Then you'll *really* piss her off!

Beautiful simplicity

If you teach a class in music composition, play this trick on the students.

Tell them you want them to write a musical composition that's hauntingly beautiful, also relaxing, yet so sad it can make even the toughest men cry.

Give them a few minutes to start working on the project, then say:

> Oh, by the way, I want the composition to be short: no more than 25 notes.

Watch them rethink. Then say:

And I want no lyrics and no harmony. The melody alone must be the whole composition. Remember it must be "hauntingly beautiful, relaxing, and so sad it makes even the toughest men cry."

A few minutes later, say:

> Oh, by the way, one more restriction: you're not allowed to use any sharps or flats. The whole composition must be playable on the piano's white notes, without using any black notes.

At this point, some of the students will start cursing you as they rewrite again. A few minutes later, add:

> Oh, by the way, one more restriction: you can't use the notes D, F, A, or B. The only notes you can use are C, E, and G.

At this point, the students will probably start saying "You're nuts," "You're crazy," "Why didn't you tell us that before," and "It's impossible." A few minutes later add:

> Now I'm going to impose a further restriction: the only notes you can use are middle C, the G just below it, and the E & G just above it.

You'll hear more cursing, but some of the students will start wondering what the point of all this is, what game you're trying to play. A few minutes later, if the students have enough patience, add this command:

> Now here's a final restriction: after each note (except the last note), you must write a note that's the same, or adjacent, or starts repeating a phrase. For example, after E, you must put E again or the G above it or the C below it or start repeating a phrase that's been heard already.

Now everybody wonders how you can make a song that's "hauntingly beautiful, relaxing, and tearfully sad" even though it's so restricted (shorter than 25 notes, without lyrics, without harmony, restricted to the notes of a C chord around middle C, and without jumps except for repetitions). Say this:

> Millions of Americans know a piece of music that has all those properties and restrictions. Do you know which piece of music that is?

If nobody guesses, start giving hints.

> Here's a hint: what musical instrument plays only a C chord?

If still no answer, give further help.

> What's the saddest thing that can happen to somebody?

If still no answer, give further help.

> What's the most relaxing thing that can happen to somebody?

If still no answer, give further help.

> What government organization dominates the lives (and therefore the music) of millions of Americans?

If they still have no clue, just give up and say, "Now I'm going to play the music that meets all those criteria." Then play "Taps" on a bugle.

To end the lesson, give the class this moral:

> The art of writing music is to put restrictions on yourself, then successfully maneuver within those restrictions.

How to improvise

Try this experiment....

Make the piano cry Walk up to the piano. Press a key near the middle of the keyboard. Then remove your finger from that key. Press the key that's immediately left of the key you pressed before, regardless of color. (For example, if you pressed E before, press E flat; if you pressed C before, press B.) Notice that this second key sounds slightly lower than the first. Keep doing that: keep moving down to the left, pressing each key, regardless of color. (For example, if you started at E, press E flat, then D, then D flat, then C, then B, then B flat, then A.) That's called **going down the chromatic scale** (or **chromatic decline**). Keep doing that, until you've played 8 notes altogether.

Now start at some other key on the keyboard and go down the chromatic scale from that new key, so you've played 8 new notes. (Now you've played 16 notes altogether!)

Hop to a third key on the keyboard and go down the chromatic scale from that key, so you've play 8 further notes. (Now you've played 24 notes altogether!)

Going down the chromatic scale makes the piano sound like it's crying: oh, such a mournful melody!

To increase the effect, get several friends to join you at the piano: all of you play simultaneously, so each of you goes down the chromatic scale simultaneously. (If you don't have any friends with you at the moment, try making your two hands pretend to be two people.)

The person who's farthest left is called the **bass**. For best results, have the bass player play twice as slowly, so he goes down one note while the other players go down two notes. Those long notes in the bass create a steady, sticky "glue" that holds the composition together.

Break free To avoid monotony, let each player be free to "break the rules" occasionally. For example, instead of taking an 8-note run, try taking a 4-note run or a 2-note run. Try letting the bass player play even slower — while the other players play even faster.

To avoid making the composition sound too depressing, let each player occasionally go up the scale instead of down, to create a glimmer of hope — before resuming the doom of descending into darkness.

Let each player be free to occasionally play any note or pattern. For example, instead of going down in boring scales, let your fingers wander in both directions (up and down), like a staggering drunk who's indecisive about which direction to walk in. (That's called a **random walk**.)

Add teamwork Let each player occasionally stop to listen to the other players (silence is golden!) and then imitate their patterns (so the group sounds like an attentive ensemble doing teamwork, instead of a disorganized mess).

Folk music To create folk music, play just on the black keys (that's called the **pentatonic scale**) while doing a random walk.

Chinese music To make that folk music sound Chinese, make each non-bass player do this: instead of pressing one black key at a time, press two black keys that are fairly close together (so just one black key is between them). That's called **pentatonic parallel thirds**.

Mozart To create Mozart music, do Chinese music but play on the white notes instead of the black (that's called **diatonic parallel thirds**), so each non-bass player is playing a pair of white notes that are fairly close together (and just one white note is between them). Then try this improvement: when playing a pair of notes, if the top note is a C, make the pair's bottom note be E instead of A.

Warning: when producing Mozart music, use fewer players than with other types of music, so you keep your composition as simple as a music box and avoid clashes.

Debussy On the keyboard, the black notes come in clumps. Some clumps contain 3 black notes. Other clumps contain 2 black notes. Try this restriction: let yourself play the 3 black notes that come in a 3-black-note clump, and also let yourself play the 3 white notes that are near the 2-black-note clump. Restricting yourself to those notes is called the **whole-tone scale**, which sounds like the impressionist harp music composed by the French composer Debussy. For best results, go *up* that scale instead of down (except for variety).

Best classical music

Many musicians feel that the best classical music is chamber music (music for a *small* group of instruments). It tends to be purer and cleverer than orchestral music and opera, which often get too bombastic. To taste the finest classical music, treat yourself to these examples of chamber music and beyond (listed by the year they were composed):

1791, Mozart's *Clarinet Concerto in A* (K. 622), as performed by Benny Goodman (humorously!)
1794, Haydn's *Piano Trio #1 in G* (including the "Gypsy Rondo")
1809, Beethoven's *Piano Concerto #5 in E Flat* (Opus 73, nicknamed "the Emperor Concerto")
1810, Beethoven's *Piano Trio in B Flat* (Opus 97, nicknamed "the Archduke Trio")
1887, Dvorak's *Piano Quintet in A* (Opus 81, romantic)
1899, Joplin's *Maple Leaf Rag* (this composition made jazz become popular)
1924, Gershwin's *Rhapsody in Blue* (jazz), as performed by Leonard Bernstein (who can control tempo!)
1940, Shostakovich's *Piano Quintet* (Opus 57), as performed by Shostakovich himself (authentic!)
1944, Bartok's *Sonata for Unaccompanied Violin*, as performed by Ivry Gitlis (who's intense!)

For 1960's fun music based on classical feelings, listen to collections of music sung by **The Beatles** (great melodies), **The Supremes** (rich harmonies), **The Mamas & The Papas** (fun harmonies), and **Tom Lehrer** (fun words).

Was Dr. Seuss the first rapper?

I wonder whether rap music was influenced by Dr. Seuss. The beat's the same:

> As I think about the music that is driving me insane,
> And I wonder if I blunder when I call it such a name,
> And the oink-oink little piggy blew the house down — such as shame! —
> I'm a rapper and a crapper playing Seuss's little game.
> Da-da-*da*-da, da-da-*da*-da da-da-*da*-da da-da-*da!*

Movies

Movies affect and distort our sense of reality. Here are some bizarre examples.

Extreme movies

To make your life more bizarre, **watch these extreme movies**:

Movie	What it's best at	Year	Award
Romance movies			
The Philadelphia Story	best wedding movie about choosing the groom	1940	8
Casablanca	best movie about a past love	1942	9 A
The Seven Year Itch	best movie about being seduced by a neighbor	1955	7
Splash	best movie about dating a mermaid	1984	6
The Bridges of Madison County	best movie about a fling	1995	7
Lost-soul movies			
It's a Wonderful Life	best movie about avoiding suicide	1946	9
Cast Away	best movie about being lost on an island	2000	8
Coming-of-age movies			
The Last Picture Show	best movie about growing up in Texas	1971	8
American Graffiti	best movie about growing up in California	1973	8
Big	best movie about finding your inner child	1988	7
Gross-comedy movies			
Animal House	best movie about college pranks	1978	8
Neighbors	best movie about having a bad neighbor	1981	5
There's Something About Mary	best movie about peeking at women	1998	7
Sinister movies			
Citizen Kane	best movie about losing your principles	1941	9
A Clockwork Orange	best movie about British thugs	1971	9
The Truman Show	best movie about having your privacy invaded	1998	8
Horror movies			
Jaws	best horror movie about teeth, water, sharks	1975	8
The Shining	best horror movie about the effects of snow	1980	9
The Cook, Thief, Wife, Lover	best horror movie about a restaurant	1989	7
Popular-music movies			
Gold Diggers of 1933	only musical where the star sings in Pig Latin	1933	8
42nd Street	best musical about impossible stage shows	1933	8
The Wizard of Oz	best musical about escaping from Kansas	1939	8
Holiday Inn	best musical about falling in love on holidays	1942	7
South Pacific	best musical about falling in love with foreigners	1958	7
Let's Make Love	includes best lessons on how to sing, dance, joke	1960	6
The Music Man	best musical about salesmanship	1962	8
My Fair Lady	best musical about how to speak properly	1964	8 A
Cabaret	best musical about Nazi Germany	1972	8
Chicago	best musical about daydreaming	2002	7 A
Classical-music movies			
The Competition	best movie about a piano contest	1980	7
Amadeus	best movie about how Mozart was crazy	1984	8 A
Crazy-Jew movies			
Annie Hall	best Jewish movie about being in love	1977	8 A
Deconstructing Harry	best Jewish movie about being old and confused	1997	7
Life is Beautiful	best Jewish movie about laughing at death	1997	9
Illustrated-issue movies			
The Long Walk Home	best tale about desegregating Alabama	1990	7
Not One Less	best tale about school in rural China	1999	8

The best way to learn about movies is to visit the **Internet Movie Database (IMDb.com)**. That Web site lets people rate how much they liked movies they saw, on a scale of 1 to 10. In the Award column, I show the movie's weighted-average score (which is computed by the Web site in a way to avoid vote stuffing). If a movie's average is 8 or 9, most people in your household will probably like it; if a movie rates 7, 6, or 5, the movie is chancier: it thrills some people but disappoints others. In the Award column, an "A" means "won the Academy Award's Oscar for Best Picture that year."

If you try to get one of those movies, make sure you get the correct year. Other movies with similar titles from other years are worse.

Popularity contest

On the **Internet Movie Database (IMDb.com)**, no movie's average score is 10. (That's because, no matter how great a movie is, there are still a lot of people who hate it.) Here are the 57 movies whose average score is 9; **voters consider these the best movies to watch**:

Year	Movies that are still rated 9
1931	M, City Lights
1941	Citizen Kane
1942	Casablanca
1944	Double Indemnity
1946	It's a Wonderful Life
1950	Sunset Blvd.
1954	Rear Window, Seven Samurai
1957	Paths of Glory, 12 Angry Men
1958	Vertigo
1959	North by Northwest
1960	Psycho
1962	Lawrence of Arabia
1964	Dr. Strangelove
1966	The Good the Bad and the Ugly
1968	Once Upon a Time in the West
1971	A Clockwork Orange
1972	The Godfather
1974	The Godfather (Part 2)
1975	One Flew Over the Cuckoo's Nest
1976	Taxi Driver
1977	Star Wars 4 (A New Hope)
1979	Alien, Apocalypse Now
1980	The Shining, The Empire Strikes Back
1981	Raiders of the Lost Ark
1990	Goodfellas
1991	The Silence of the Lambs, Terminator 2
1993	Schindler's List
1994	PulpFiction, ForrestGump, The Professional, ShawshankRedemption
1995	Se7en, The Usual Suspects
1998	Saving Private Ryan, American History X
1999	The Matrix, Fight Club, American Beauty
2000	Memento
2001	Amélie, Spirited Away, Fellowship of the Ring
2002	The Pianist, City of God, The Two Towers
2003	The Return of the King
2006	The Lives of Others
2008	The Dark Knight, WALL-E
2010	Inception, Toy Story 3

Some of those movies are old. Some are lowbrow. Some are immoral. Some are confusing. All are memorable.

Movie clichés

Americans learn about life by watching TV and movies. Many movies distort reality by containing these clichés:

Fights
A bad guy's first shot always misses; it just announces that a fight will begin.
A hero always gets shot in the shoulder.
Evil men are too stupid to shoot heroes in the face; instead, they aim for the bulletproof vest.
Even the thinnest piece of wood will shield you from all bullets.
When one man shoots at 20 men, he's more likely to kill them all than when 20 men shoot at one.
In a swordfight, you must find stairs to fight on, so the loser can roll down them to die at the bottom.
In a swordfight, jump up on a table; when the villain swipes at your legs, just hop over his blade.
When women fight, they pull hair, fall to the ground together, and roll over twice.
In a martial-arts fight, enemies surrounding you will wait patiently for you to kill them one-by-one.
A hero becomes invulnerable when he takes his shirt off.
When a villain captures you to kill, he kindly pauses for 5 minutes to tell you his life's plans.

Wars
Every army platoon includes a black guy who can play the harmonica.
You'll survive the battle unless you show someone a photo of your sweetheart back home.
The person with the most plans, prospects, and hopes will die.
During an artillery barrage, a kid or dog can safely wander around, but half the soldiers will die.

Escape
Every time bomb has a big red readout that shows how many seconds remain.
While a bad guy chases you, he kindly pauses to throw objects you can jump over.
When terrified, a woman always sticks her fist in her mouth.
Every woman who tries to flee insists on wearing high heels.
When being chased by an evil man, a woman always stumbles to the ground, even if the terrain is level.
To help a woman flee, a man hugs his arm around her, though hugging slows both of them down.
A person chased to a staircase is always stupid enough to run upstairs, not down to exit the building.

Injuries
A hero shows no pain when beaten but winces when a woman tries to clean his wounds.
When you're hit on the head and become unconscious, you never get a concussion or brain damage.
During a fight, a hero's only facial injuries are on his right cheekbone and his mouth's right corner.
A hero wipes blood from his mouth's right corner with the back of his hand, then looks at it.
If a hero's cheek gets injured, just put a Band-Aid on it, and it will heal completely by the next day.
Bibles, religious medals, and photos of loved ones stop bullets better than a bulletproof vest.

Dying
A good person dies only while friends are watching.
If a good person dies with eyes open, a friend will close them; but a villain's eyes stay open forever.
If you're dying, friends whisper lovingly to you or kiss you, instead of calling an ambulance.
If your friend is dying, try this cure: yell "You can't do this to me — I love you!" and "Fight!"

Bedroom antics
Whenever strangers have sex, they reach intense, simultaneous orgasms on the first try.
During sex, all women leave their underwear on, and they moan but don't sweat.
After sex, you never need Kleenex.
Every bed has a crooked sheet that covers up to a woman's armpit but just to a man's waist.
Whenever you wake up from a nightmare, you sit bolt upright and pant.
Every teenager's bedroom window comes with a drainpipe strengthened to hold the kid's weight.

Bathrooms
You can eat as much as you want and never need to go to the toilet.
When women wake up, they don't need to go to the toilet, but women must shower frequently.
The best way to tell when a woman is pregnant is to wait for her to vomit.
Women never menstruate.
If several people are in a bathroom, one of them must tell a secret while they all face the mirror.

Kitchen antics
Kitchens have no light switches. At night, you must open the fridge door and use that light instead.
All shopping bags are paper, topped off with French bread & carrots, which spill onto the kitchen floor.
Families are too rushed to ever finish breakfast, so dad and the kids always dash out, upsetting mom.

Buildings
In Paris, all the windows face the Eiffel Tower.
In New York, nice people getting low-paying jobs all live in luxury apartments.
You can pick any lock with a credit card or paper clip, except when a kid behind the door is trapped in a fire.
All elevator shafts are clean and well-lit, to make sure heroes won't get dirty or need flashlights.
Whenever you want an elevator, it's already at your floor, unless you're chased by an evil person.

Cars

When you drive to any building, you'll always find a parking space in front.

When you try to cross the street, you're delayed by traffic just if you're in a rush.

In New York, you can safely leave your car unlocked; even convertibles with tops down don't get stolen.

Whenever you flee a villain, your car won't start — at least not on the first try.

While driving, you can dodge bullets by ducking your head.

When hitting a parked car, a speeding car goes up in the air, but the parked car won't even wiggle.

Every car chase through town will smash a fruit cart owned by a Greek, who'll curse but stay unhurt.

When you want a taxi, you'll get one immediately, except when you're in danger.

To pay for a taxi, don't bother looking at your wallet: the first bill you grab will be the exact amount.

Planes

Planes always depart on time and never require a boarding pass: just hop on.

If your plane contains a nun, it will crash.

You can land any plane easily if somebody in the control tower just tells you what to do.

Phones

You never need to look up phone numbers: you've memorized your whole city's phone book.

Whenever the phone wakes you up, you must knock it to the floor before answering.

When you phone friends, you never need to say "hello" or "goodbye": those courtesies take too long.

Music

Whatever you decide to sing, everyone around you already knows the tune & words and joins in.

If you start dancing in the street, everyone you bump into already knows all the steps.

You can play wind instruments and accordions without moving your fingers.

Alcohol

Since bars are never busy, bartenders just relax, chat, wash glasses, and flip bottles in the air.

Whenever a bar plays country music, a fight will break out.

At a bar, don't bother saying which brand of beer you want: the bartender can always read your mind.

At the home of a friend who asks you "Want a drink?" say just "Yes": don't bother saying which type.

Strong whiskey makes a hero wince, wipe his mouth on his sleeve, then flash clenched teeth.

One swig of booze is enough to numb pain before the girl jabs a knife in your arm to remove a bullet.

When you have a hangover, putting an icepack on your head makes you become fun and not vomit.

Whenever you throw cold water or black coffee at a drunk, he'll immediately get sober.

Relationships

In any pair of identical twins, one of them is evil — or *both* are evil.

During emotional confrontations, people always talk back-to-back instead of face-to-face.

A feminist spurns a macho hero until he rescues her from death. Then she becomes his docile slave.

After a feminist becomes docile, a macho hero always softens up and tells her his tragic past.

Appearance

High-powered female executives always wear miniskirts and 5-inch heels to work.

Women always apply makeup before going to bed; it stays intact all night and while scuba diving.

Even in prehistoric times, women always shaved their legs and armpits.

Medieval peasants all had filthy faces, tangled hair, ragged clothes, and perfect teeth.

Whenever you knock out someone and steal the person's clothes, they fit you perfectly.

At night, everything turns blue.

When lightning appears, you hear its thunder instantly, and the rain starts then too.

Mexicans speak perfect English except they say *Señor* and *Gracias* instead of "Sir" and "Thank you."

Eyeglasses

Action heroes never wear glasses.

Your glasses will never fog, even when you come in from the cold.

Little girls wearing glasses always tell the truth. Little boys wearing glasses always lie.

Investigations

If you're a woman hearing a noise at night, you must investigate while wearing revealing underwear.

If you're a woman hearing noises at home, your cat will jump at you before you get strangled.

If a killer lurks in your home, you can find him easily: just take a bath.

A light bulb burns out (or flickers) just if someone hides in that room and waits to jump on you.

Every police investigation requires a visit to a strip club.

A police detective can't solve a tough case until he's suspended from duty.

Dogs know which people are bad and bark at them.

Incriminating evidence will always be in the next-to-bottom drawer or in photo #4 of a stack.

To access a computer's secret files, just type "ACCESS ALL THE SECRET FILES."

If a hero kills lots of bad guys, police won't question him about those murders.

For more info about movie clichés, see **The Movie Clichés List** (put onto the Internet by Giancarlo Cairella at www.moviecliches.com) and watch a video called **Top 10 Worst Movie Clichés**. That video is at:

www.YouTube.com/watch?v=Klltwoa6glE

(Each of those vertical lines is a lower-case L.)

When you watch a TV broadcast of the news, you're actually watching a video that's full of clichés, illustrated at Charlie Brooker's **How to Report the News** (www.youtube.com/watch?v=aHun58mz3vI) and The Onion's **Some Bullshit Happening Somewhere** (www.youtube.com/watch?v=9U4Ha9HQvMo).

Stage names

If you don't like the name your mom gave you at birth (your **birth name**), replace it with a **stage name** that's more appealing, as done by these actors —

Stage name	His birth name
Boris Karloff	William Henry Pratt
Buddy Hackett	Leonard Hacker
Charles Bronson	Charles Buchinsky
Charlie Sheen	Carlos Irwin Estévez
Douglas Fairbanks	Douglas Elton Thomas Ullman
Fred Astaire	Frederick Austerlitz II
George Burns	Nat Birnbaum
Groucho Marx	Julius Henry Marx
Jack Benny	Benjamin Kubelsky
Jerry Lewis	Joseph Levitch
John Wayne	Marion Robert Morrison
Kirk Douglas	Issur Danielovitch
Martin Sheen	Ramón Gerardo Antonio Estévez
Mel Brooks	Melvin Kaminsky
Michael Caine	Maurice Joseph Micklewhite, Jr.
Nicolas Cage	Nicolas Kim Coppola
Peter Lorre	László Löwenstein
Phil Silvers	Philip Silversmith
Red Buttons	Aaron Chwatt
Redd Fox	John Elroy Sanford
Rock Hudson	Leroy Harold Scherer, Jr.
Rodney Dangerfield	Jacob Cohen
Roy Rogers	Leonard Franklin Slye
Stan Laurel	Arthur Stanley Jefferson
Tony Curtis	Bernard Herschel Schwartz
W.C. Fields	William Claude Dukenfield
Woody Allen	Allan Stewart Konigsberg
Yves Montand	Ivo Livi

and these actresses —

Stage name	Her birth name
Anne Bancroft	Anne Italiano
Doris Day	Doris Mary Ann Kappelhoff
Greta Garbo	Greta Lovisa Gustafsson
Judy Garland	Frances Ethel Gumm
Joan Crawford	Lucille Fay LeSueur
Lauren Bacall	Betty Joan Perski
Marilyn Monroe	Norma Jean Mortensen
Miley Cyrus	Destiny Hope Cyrus
Natalie Wood	Natalia Nikolaevna Zakharenko
Raquel Welch	Jo Raquel Tejada
Shelly Winters	Shirley Schrift
Sophia Loren	Sofia Villani Scicolone

and these singers —

Stage name	Birth name
Bing Crosby	Harry Lillis Crosby
Cher	Cherilyn Sarkisian
Dean Martin	Dino Paul Crocetti
Elton John	Reginald Kenneth Dwight
Eminem	Marshall Bruce Mathers III
Fergie	Stacy Ann Ferguson
Iggy Pop	James Newell Osterberg, Jr.
John Denver	Henry John Deutschendorf
Katy Perry	Katheryn Elizabeth Hudson
Lady Gaga	Stefani Joanne Angelina Germanotta
Madonna	Madonna Louise Ciccone
Marilyn Manson	Brian Hugh Warner
Pink	Alecia Beth Moore
Ringo Starr	Richard Starkey
Snoop Dogg	Calvin Cordozar Broadus, Jr.
Tina Turner	Anna Mae Bullock
50 Cent	Curtis James Jackson III

and these authors:

Pen name	Birth name
Ayn Rand	Alisa Zinov'yevna Rosenbaum
Dr. Seuss	Theodor Seuss Geisel
George Eliot	Mary Anne Evans
George Orwell	Eric Arthur Blair
George Sand	Amantine Lucile Aurore Dupin
Joseph Conrad	Józef Teodor Konrad Korzeniowski
Lemony Snicket	Daniel Handler
Lewis Carroll	Charles Lutwidge Dodgson
Mark Twain	Samuel Langhorne Clemens
O. Henry	William Sydney Porter
Voltaire	François-Marie Arouet

Those lists of birth names are correct. (The second edition of *Tricky Living* accidentally contained birth names that turned out to be false rumors.)

Writing

The written word can be artistic.

Writing can be frustratingly easy. Gene Fowler (a sportswriter, newspaper manager, and screenwriter) said:

> Writing is easy: just sit staring at a blank sheet of paper until drops of blood form on your forehead.

A similar thought was expressed by Walter "Red" Smith, who won a Pulitzer Prize (for writing comments about baseball):

> There's nothing to writing. Just sit down at a keyboard and open a vein.

Beginning

To become a successful writer, you must learn many secrets. But here's the first and most important secret:

> Begin!

The main reason why good books don't get written is:

> They were never begun.

If you've said to yourself, "I could write a book," do it! Take a pen and paper (or a word processor) and start writing your thoughts, even if they're still muddled. Once you've started writing your ideas, even if they're still half-baked or disorganized, you've overcome the major barrier to success: not having started.

If you have trouble writing the book's beginning, write the middle instead. You can write the "beginning" afterwards.

Too many writers think the beginning should be profound. They get hung up in a fruitless attempt to create profundity and atmosphere.

Scott Meredith, a famous literary agent, said he followed this rule when reading a manuscript from a new author: skip the first 100 pages! The first 100 pages are usually boring crap, such as "She looked in the mirror while she combed her auburn hair." After page 100, the dialogue finally gets worthwhile; that's when characters start arguing with each other about love and beyond, and you get sentences such as:

> She spat at him and pulled the trigger.

If you're writing a technical manual that contains lots of charts and examples, begin by writing the charts and examples. Later, you can go back and add the introductory sentences that bind them together.

If you're a school kid writing one of those boring compositions about "What I did last summer" (or a more inspiring composition about "What I wish I'd done last summer"), start by describing the most exciting moment. Fill in the boring stuff later.

Rush

Assume your reader is busy and rushed. Don't waste the reader's time.

After writing your first draft and making minor edits (for spelling and grammar), ask yourself:

> Is this crap I wrote worth reading?

Probably some part of it is worth reading. If you find that part and cut away the rest, you've mined your gem.

Then your reader will praise you for being a fascinating writer instead of a time-wasting hack.

Get emotional

When writing on a technical topic, get emotional about it. Tell the reader how you feel. If something you're writing about fascinates you, explain why. If you're forced to write about a topic that's yucky, gripe about its yuckiness and tell the reader how to deyuckify it.

Showing your emotions will humanize the topic, help the reader relate, and make the topic and you both memorable.

Scared to be a poet?

If you're writing poetry, don't worry so much about exposing your privacy. Many of your friends probably wouldn't recognize your private parts anyway.

I recommend you be brave and use your own name.

> But if you're super-worried about privacy, go be a chicken-head: publish under a pseudonym. For example, you can call yourself "Lo-ann Li," so you'll be known as the Lo-ann Li poet.
>
> Nothing's stopping you from using two pseudonyms, for two kinds of poems. For example, you could do lighter verse under the name "Ha-pi," so you'd also be known as the Ha-pi poet.
>
> But the best choice is to merge the two. Cry, then step back and giggle. For example, Robert Frost's poem called "New Hampshire" goes on for 10 pages about how beautiful New Hampshire is, but then comes his last line: "I live in Vermont." You could write a poem full of pathos and bathos then end with, "On the other hand...."
>
> The challenge is to put a *mix* of emotions into a poem, to make a poem *rich*, without making the poem seem accidentally disjointed.

The typical inventor (or poet) makes the mistake of hiding the invention (out of fear of being copied). That deprives him of the opportunity to get feedback on how the invention could be improved. Show your writing to friends and poets, ask what they dislike about your poems, and use that feedback to improve your work. To grow, you must learn to be hard on yourself.

Which words to use

Since your reader's in a rush and frowning, make each sentence be quick, punchy, fun. To be brief, use words that are short:

Too long, too formal, too stuffy	Shorter, cheerier, better
I will	I'll
I am	I'm
I have	I've
I would	I'd
large	big
utilize	use
somebody	someone
everybody	everyone
upper-left corner	top-left corner
the beginning of the book	the book's beginning
Jack, president of the club, said	The club's president, Jack, said
This report's purpose is to explain taxes.	This report explains taxes.
The following examples show how:	These examples show how:
, as shown in the following examples:	. Here are examples:
The reader should press the Enter key.	Press the Enter key.
You should press the Enter key.	Press the Enter key.

To improve the word "only," change it to "just" (which is shorter to say) and move it *after* the verb (to clarify that it modifies the object, not the verb):

Bad:	I only drink tea.
Better:	I just drink tea.
Best:	I drink just tea.

Don't use the word "very": it's boring, much more boring than the adjective it modifies. Delete "very." Mark Twain gave this advice:

Substitute "damn" every time you're inclined to write "very"; your editor will delete it and the writing will be just as it should be.

Hey, you! Don't say "the reader"; instead say "you," which is more direct and avoids the problem of whether "the reader" is a "he" or a "she."

So to avoid any "he"-versus-"she" problems, say "you."

Wrong because sexist:	a policeman should keep his ID in his pocket.
Wrong because stuffy:	a police officer should keep his/her ID in his/her pocket.
Right:	if you're a police officer, keep your ID in your pocket.

Short paragraphs

Keep your paragraphs short. The ideal paragraph has 2, 3, or 4 sentences. If a paragraph has more than 4 sentences, the reader will get tired, lost, and bored: divide the paragraph into shorter ones.

A one-sentence paragraph is okay if the neighboring paragraphs are longer. But if a one-sentence paragraph comes after another one-sentence paragraph, your writing is too choppy: combine paragraphs to form longer ones.

Lists

Don't begin a sentence with a list. Instead, put the list at the sentence's *end*, after you've explained the list's purpose.

Wrong:	Red, blue, and yellow are the primary colors.
Right:	The primary colors are red, blue, and yellow.

Wrong:	Jack Smith, Jean Jones, and Tina Turner are the leaders.
Right:	The leaders are Jack Smith, Jean Jones, and Tina Turner.

How to write "real good"

At Dartmouth College during the 1960's and 1970's, students and faculty passed around a cynical list of rules about how to write. Each rule was purposely written badly, so it violates itself. The list was particularly popular among science students, who love to ponder self-contradictions. The list gradually grew, as many people added their own rules.

In March 1979, George Trigg published the list in a physics journal.

In October 1979, William Safire wrote a *New York Times* column saying he was making his own list and thanking Philip Henderson for contributing some rules. In November 1979, he wrote a longer list. In 1990, he wrote a whole book based on those rules, which he called "Fumble Rules."

Later, improved versions were posted on the Internet at many Web sites, such as sites run by PBS and the National Institute of Health.

Here's my improved collection:

Punctuation
Don't overuse "quotation marks."
Don't overuse exclamation points!!!
Don't use commas, that aren't necessary.
Just Proper Nouns should be capitalized.
Don't use question marks inappropriately?
Its important to use apostrophe's in the right places.
Don't write a run-on sentence you've got to punctuate it.
Use hyphens in compound-words, not just where two-words are related.
In letters compositions reports and things like that use commas to keep a string of items apart.

Vocabulary
Don't abbrev.
Profanity sucks.
Avoid mispellings.
Puns are for children, not groan readers.
Don't use contractions in formal writing.
Proofread carefully to see if you any words out.
A writer must avoid sexist pronouns in his writing.
No sentence fragments! Complete sentences: important!
Never use totally cool, radically groovy, outdated slang.
Always avoid annoying, affected, awkward alliteration.
Use words correctly, irregardless of how others use them.
The bottom line is to bag trendy locutions that sound flaky.
Never use a big word where you can utilize a diminutive one.
In the case of a report, check to see that jargonwise, it's A-OK.
Foreign words and phrases are the reader's bete noir and not apropos.
Eschew obfuscation. Employ the vernacular. It behooves us all to avoid archaic expressions.

Verbs
Don't verb nouns.
One-word sentences? Never!
The passive voice is to be avoided.
Remember to never split an infinitive.
Writing carefully, dangling participles must be avoided.
If any word is improper at a sentence's end, a linking verb is.
Watch out for irregular verbs that have creeped into our language.
Lay down and die before using a transitive verb without an object.

Adverbs
The adverb always follows the verb.
Hopefully, you won't float your adverbs.
Be carefully to use adjectives and adverbs correct.
By observing distinctions between adjectives and adverbs, you'll treat readers real good.

Conjunctions
Join clauses good, like a conjunction should.
And don't start a sentence with a conjunction.

Plurals
Make sure your verb and subject is in agreement.
Each pronoun should agree with their antecedent.
Everyone should be careful to use a singular pronoun with singular nouns in their writing.

Objects
Just between you and I, case is important.
Don't be a person whom people realize confuses *who* and *whom*.

Comparisons
Even if a mixed metaphor sings, it should be derailed.
Mixed metaphors are a pain in the neck and ought to be weeded out.

Negation
Don't use no double negatives.
Don't make negative statements.
Never contradict yourself always.
Don't put sentences in the negative form.

Reasoning
Be more or less specific.
One should never generalize.
Who needs rhetorical questions?
Generalizations must always be eliminated.
Eliminate quotations. As Ralph Waldo Emerson said, "I hate quotations. Tell me what you know."
If I've told you once, I've told you a thousand times: exaggeration is a billion times worse than understatement.

Lengthy sentences
A writer must not shift your point of view.
A preposition isn't a good thing to end a sentence with.
Parenthetical remarks (however relevant) are superfluous.
Parallel structure will help you in writing more effective sentences and to express yourself more gracefully.
Place pronouns as close as possible, especially in long sentences, as of 10 or more words, to their antecedents.
Don't string together too many prepositional phrases, unless you're walking through the valley of the shadow of death.

Stamp out and eliminate redundancies. Never, ever use repetitive redundancies. If you reread your work, you'll find, on rereading, lots of repetition can be avoided by rereading and editing.

Never go off on tangents, which are lines that intersect a curve at just one point and were analyzed by Euclid, who lived before Christ in Greece, which got conquered by the Romans but later hosted the 2004 Olympics.

Avoid those run-on sentences that just go on, and on, and on; they never stop, they just keep rambling, and you really wish the person would just shut up, but no, they just keep going; they're worse than the Energizer Bunny; they babble incessantly; and these sentences, they just never stop: they go on forever, if you get my drift.

Phrases

Always pick on the correct idiom.

As far as incomplete constructions, they are wrong.

Go out of your way to avoid colloquialisms, ya' know? Go around the barn at high noon to avoid colloquialisms.

Last but not least, even if you have to bend over backward, lay off clichés like the plague: they're old hat, so seek viable alternatives.

Are you smart enough to find the error in each of those sentences? After you've found the error, how would you correct it?

Try correcting those sentences! Afterwards, look at these corrected (and boring) versions of those sentences:

Punctuation

Don't overuse quotation marks.

Don't overuse exclamation points.

Don't use commas that aren't necessary.

Just proper nouns should be capitalized.

Don't use question marks inappropriately.

It's important to use apostrophes in the right places.

Don't write a run-on sentence: you've got to punctuate it.

Use hyphens in compound words, not just where two words are related.

In letters, compositions, reports, and things like that, use commas to keep a string of items apart.

Vocabulary

Don't abbreviate.

Profanity is disgusting.

Avoid misspellings.

Puns are for children, not adults.

Do not use contractions in formal writing.

Proofread carefully to see if you left any words out.

A writer must avoid sexist pronouns.

Don't write sentence fragments! Completing sentences is important!

Never use outdated slang.

Don't use awkward alliteration.

Use words correctly, regardless of how others use them.

Don't use faddish expressions.

Never use a big word where you can use a small one.

In the case of a report, check to see that it's free of jargon.

Foreign words and phrases are the reader's nightmare and not appropriate.

Don't complicate. Use colloquial speech. Avoid archaic expressions.

Verbs

Don't turn nouns into verbs.

Never have one-word sentences.

Avoid the passive voice.

Remember: never split an infinitive.

To write carefully, avoid dangling participles.

Don't end a sentence with a linking verb.

Watch out for irregular verbs that have crept into our language.

Lie down and die before using a transitive verb without an object.

Adverbs

The adverb follows the verb, always.

I hope you won't float your adverbs.

Be careful to use adjectives and adverbs correctly.

By observing distinctions between adjectives and adverbs, you'll treat readers really well.

Conjunctions

Join clauses well, as a conjunction should.

Don't start a sentence with a conjunction.

Plurals

Make sure your verb and subject are in agreement.

Each pronoun should agree with its antecedent.

Everyone should be careful to use a singular pronoun with singular nouns in writing.

Objects

Just between you and me, case is important.

Don't be a person who people realize confuses *who* and *whom*.

Comparisons

Even if a mixed metaphor sings, it should be shushed.

Mixed metaphors are a pain in the neck and ought to be massaged out.

Negation

Don't use double negatives.

Avoid negative statements.

Never contradict yourself.

Avoid putting sentences in the negative form.

Reasoning

Be specific.

Avoid generalizing.

Rhetorical questions are unnecessary.

Generalizations should usually be eliminated.

Eliminate quotations: tell me what *you* know.

As I've said before, exaggeration is much worse than understatement.

Lengthy sentences

As a writer, you must not shift your point of view.

A preposition isn't a good thing with which to end a sentence.

Parenthetical remarks are superfluous.

Parallel structure will help you write more effective sentences and express yourself more gracefully.

Place pronouns as close as possible to their antecedents, especially in long sentences, as of 10 or more words.

Don't string together too many prepositional phrases, unless you're walking through the valley of death's shadow.

If you reread your work, you'll find lots of repetition to edit out.

Never go off on tangents.

Avoid sentences that ramble.

Phrases

Always pick the correct idiom.

As far as incomplete constructions go, they are wrong.

Make an effort to avoid colloquialisms.

Avoid clichés: they're stale, so seek fresh alternatives.

Advice from famous writers

Robert Louis Stevenson said:

It takes hard writing to make easy reading.

E.L. Doctorow said:

Writing's an exploration. You start from nothing and learn as you go.

James Michener said:

I love writing. I love the swirl and swing of words as they tangle with human emotions.

Ernest Hemingway (a novelist famous for simple sentences) said this about William Faulkner (a novelist famous for complex sentences):

Poor Faulkner. Does he really think big emotions come from big words? He thinks I don't know the ten-dollar words. I know them all right. But there are older and simpler and better words, and those are the ones I use.

Jack Maxson said:

When writing, pause after each paragraph and read aloud. Do you keep stumbling over certain words or phrases? If so, it needs rewriting. Does it flow smoothly and easily? If not, rewrite. After all, if you can't read your own stuff, who can?

William Saroyan said:

The most solid advice for a writer is: try to breathe deeply, really taste food when you eat, and when you sleep really sleep. Try to be wholly alive with all your might. When you laugh, laugh like hell. When you get angry, get good and angry. Try to be alive. You'll be dead soon enough.

Warring editors

When you take a course about how to write, your teacher will probably give you rules about how to write correctly. The typical teacher neglects to mention that different editors believe in different rules.

A set of writing rules is called a **style**. Let's look these 7 different styles for writing American English:

> Many newspapers belong to a collective called **The Associated Press (AP)**, whose style is explained in *The Associated Press Stylebook* and called **AP style**. When newspapers submit articles to AP, the articles must be written in AP style.
>
> Many newspapers dislike some details of AP style. For example, *The New York Times* uses its own style, explained in *The New York Times Manual of Style and Usage* and called **New York style**. Articles that appear in *The New York Times* are written in New York style. (Afterwards, when *The New York Times* offers those articles to AP for other newspapers to use, the articles must be rewritten into AP style.)
>
> Many book publishers use the style invented at the University of Chicago Press, explained in *The Chicago Manual of Style*, and called **Chicago style**.
>
> Many colleges make students write research papers in a style invented by the **Modern Language Association (MLA)**, explained in the *MLA Handbook for Writers of Research Papers* and called **MLA style**.
>
> All those styles were invented by modern committees, but many editors instead prefer using styles that are more personal, such as **Margaret style** (explained by Margaret Nicholson in her 1957 book *American English Usage*, which updates Fowler's 1926 book *Modern English Usage*) or **Theodore style** (explained by Theodore Bernstein in his 1965 book *The Careful Writer*) or **Russ style** (explained here by me, Russ Walter, and used in my books, *The Secret Guide to Computers* and *Tricky Living*).

Here are examples of how those 7 styles differ....

Comma before "and" When a sentence includes a list of at least 3 items, should you put a comma before "and"? Which of the following is better?

> I saw Joe, Mary, and Sue.　　　(comma before "and")
> I saw Joe, Mary and Sue.　　　(no comma before "and")

Russ, Margaret, MLA, and Chicago put a comma before "and."

AP and New York omit that comma, unless the omission would cause confusion. For example, it would be confusing to omit the comma from this sentence:

> I admire my parents, Mother Teresa, and God.

If you omit that comma, the reader will think your parents are Mother Teresa and God. It would also be confusing to omit the comma from this sentence:

> For breakfast I ate sausage, ham, and eggs.

If you omit that comma, the reader will think you ate two things ("sausage" and "ham and eggs"); then the reader will wonder why you didn't put "and" before "ham."

Theodore gives no advice about that comma.

Quotation marks At the end of a quotation, should the quotation mark come before or after other punctuation (such as a period, comma, colon, semicolon, question mark, or exclamation point)? Which of the following is better?

> He called her "wonderful".　　　(period after the quotation mark)
> He called her "wonderful."　　　(period before the quotation mark)

AP, New York, Chicago, MLA, and Margaret say:

> Put a period or comma *before* the quotation mark.
>
> Put a colon or semicolon *after* the quotation mark.
>
> Put a question mark before the quotation mark just if what's quoted is a question. Put an exclamation point before the quotation mark just if what's quoted was exclaimed.

Russ says:

> Put a colon or semicolon *after* the quotation mark.
>
> Put a question mark before the quotation mark just if what's quoted is a question. Put an exclamation point before the quotation mark just if what's quoted was exclaimed.
>
> If you're typing a typical document, follow this rule: put a period or comma *before* the quotation mark (to look pretty). But if your document is about "how to punctuate" or "how to type" or "how to write a computer program," put a period *after* the quotation mark (to make sure the reader doesn't think you want a period typed).

Theodore gives no advice about quotation marks.

Numbers spelled out In the middle of a sentence, should numbers be written as digits (such as "12") or spelled out (such as "twelve")? Which of the following is better?

> I have 12 friends.　　　　　　　(number as digits)
> I have twelve friends.　　　　　 (number spelled out)

Here's the general rule (though there are many exceptions when writing about math, science, numbered lists, etc.):

> Russ spells out just the numbers zero, one, and two.
>
> AP and New York spell out the numbers up through nine, except that the age of a person or animal is never spelled out.
>
> MLA spells out the numbers up through one hundred, plus any other number that can be expressed in two words (such as "fifteen hundred").
>
> Chicago spells out all the numbers up through one hundred, plus any big number that looks rounded because it can be expressed in hundreds, thousands, hundred thousands, or millions (such as "forty-seven thousand" and "two hundred thousand").

Margaret and Theodore give no advice about which numbers to spell out.

Those rules are for a number in the sentence's *middle* or *end*. But what about a number at the sentence's *beginning*? Which of the following is better?

> 12 friends came here.　　　　　 (number as digits)
> Twelve friends came here.　　　 (number spelled out)

Some editors think "Twelve" looks better than 12, because "Twelve" begins with a capital letter, showing the reader that a new sentence is starting. Other editors disagree. Here's the general rule about a number at a sentence's beginning:

> At a sentence's beginning, New York, Chicago, and MLA spell out any number. At a sentence's beginning, AP spells out any number except a year (such as 2006). But instead of putting a big number at a sentence's beginning, all those editors (at New York, Chicago, MLA, and AP) recommend rearranging the sentence, to put the big number elsewhere.
>
> At a sentence's beginning, Russ normally spells out just the numbers zero, one, and two; but if the preceding sentence (in the same paragraph) ends in digits, Russ spells out any number up through twelve.

Percent sign Instead of writing the word "percent," should you write the symbol "%"? Which is best?

> He got 99.8 percent of the money.　　(the word "percent")
> He got 99.8 per cent of the money.　　(the words "per cent")
> He got 99.8% of the money.　　　　　 (the symbol "%")

Here are the rules:

> MLA and Russ write the symbol "%."
>
> AP writes the word "percent."
>
> New York usually writes the word "percent" but writes the symbol "%" instead in tables, graphs, and headlines.
>
> Chicago usually writes the word "percent" but writes the symbol "%" instead if the page is mainly about science or statistics.
>
> In their old books, Margaret and Theodore wrote the words "per cent," but if they were writing today they'd probably switch to "percent," since "per cent" has become rare.

United States Should you shorten "United States of America" to "United States" or "U.S.A." or "U.S." or "US"?

Here are the rules:

Russ writes "U.S."

Margaret writes "U.S." (but writes "US" in reference books where there's not enough room to include the periods).

AP writes "United States" (but writes "U.S." if used as an adjective).

MLA writes "United States" (but writes "US" in citations, such as footnotes, endnotes, bibliographies, and parenthetical comments).

Chicago writes "United States" (but writes "U.S." if used as an adjective or citation in a normal book, "US" if used as an adjective or citation in a science book).

New York writes "United States" (but writes "U.S." in headlines, tables, charts, picture captions, names of interstate highways, and where "U.S." is part of an organization's official name).

Theodore gives no advice about the United States.

State abbreviations When you mention a city with its state (but no street), should you abbreviate the state's name? How? Which of the following is best?

He came from Oakland, California, by bus.	(full name)
He came from Oakland, Cal., by bus.	(traditional abbreviation)
He came from Oakland CA by bus.	(2-letter abbreviation)

Here are the rules:

MLA and Chicago write the state's full name (such as "California").

Russ writes the state's 2-letter abbreviation (such as "CA").

New York writes the full name for Alaska, Hawaii, Idaho, Iowa, Ohio, and Utah but writes traditional abbreviations for all other states (such as "Cal.").

AP writes the full name for Alaska, Hawaii, and states whose names are short (Idaho, Iowa, Maine, Ohio, Texas, and Utah) but writes traditional abbreviations for all other states (such as "Cal.").

Margaret and Theodore give no advice about states.

Famous American cities When you write a sentence about Cleveland, must you remind the reader that Cleveland is in Ohio, by writing "Cleveland, Ohio," or can you write just "Cleveland" and assume the reader knows where Cleveland is?

AP omits the state for these 30 famous American cities:

Atlanta, Baltimore, Boston, Chicago, Cincinnati, Cleveland, Dallas, Denver, Detroit, Honolulu, Houston, Indianapolis, Las Vegas, Los Angeles, Miami, Milwaukee, Minneapolis, New Orleans, New York, Oklahoma City, Philadelphia, Phoenix, Pittsburgh, Salt Lake City, San Antonio, San Diego, San Francisco, Seattle, St. Louis, Washington

When describing events at the United Nations headquarters, AP says just "United Nations" (without mentioning that the headquarters is in New York).

Russ agrees with AP.

New York style (used by *The New York Times*) omits the state for those same 30 cities (and the United Nations) and for these 18 extra cities —

Albuquerque, Anchorage, Colorado Springs, Des Moines, El Paso, Fort Worth, Hartford, Hollywood, Iowa City, Memphis, Miami Beach, Nashville, New Haven, Omaha, Sacramento, St. Paul, Tucson, Virginia Beach

and for these 6 cities (which are in New York state) —

Albany, Buffalo, Rochester, Syracuse, White Plains, Yonkers

and for these 4 cities (which are in New Jersey):

Atlantic City, Jersey City, Newark, Trenton

MLA, Chicago, Margaret, and Theodore give no rules about cities.

Famous foreign cities When you write a sentence about Beijing, must you remind the reader that Beijing is in China, by writing "Beijing, China," or can you write just "Beijing" and assume the reader knows where Beijing is?

AP omits the country for these 27 famous foreign cities:

Beijing, Berlin, Djibouti, Geneva, Gibraltar, Guatemala City, Havana, Hong Kong, Jerusalem, Kuwait City, London, Luxembourg, Macau, Mexico City, Monaco, Montreal, Moscow, New Delhi, Ottawa, Paris, Quebec City, Rome, San Marino, Singapore, Tokyo, Toronto, Vatican City

Russ agrees with AP.

New York style omits the country for those same 27 cities and these 39 extra cities:

Algiers, Amsterdam, Athens, Bangkok, Bombay, Bonn, Brasília, Brussels, Budapest, Buenos Aires, Cairo, Calcutta, Cape Town, Copenhagen, Dublin, Edinburgh, Frankfurt, Glasgow, The Hague, Istanbul, Johannesburg, Lisbon, Madrid, Manila, Milan, Oslo, Panama, Prague, Rio De Janeiro, San Salvador, Shanghai, Stockholm, Tehran, Tel Aviv, Tunis, Venice, Vienna, Warsaw, Zurich

(Since Baghdad's been in the news a lot recently and most Americans know it's in Iraq, I expect the New York stylebook's next edition will include Baghdad in that list.)

Capital after colon After a colon, should you capitalize the next word? Which of the following is better?

Here's what I think: Love conquers all.	(capital after colon)
Here's what I think: love conquers all.	(no capital after colon)

Here are the rules about capitalizing the word after a colon:

AP and Theodore capitalize if the word begins a sentence (such as "Love conquers all").

MLA capitalizes just if the word begins a sentence that's a rule or principle (such as "Love conquers all").

Chicago capitalizes just if the word begins a list of sentences (at least two sentences).

Russ capitalizes just if the word begins a new paragraph (so it's on a new line); and in that case, Russ draws a box around the new paragraph (like the paragraph you're reading now).

New York capitalizes just if the phrase before the colon ("Here's what I think") just introduces the sentence after the colon.

Margaret gives no advice about capitalizing that word.

Capitalizing a.m. Which of the following is best?

9:30AM	(capitals, no periods, no spaces)
9:30 a.m.	(a space and periods, no capitals)

AP, New York, Chicago, and MLA say "9:30 a.m." Russ says "9:30AM." Margaret and Theodore give no advice about time.

"An" before "historic" Before the word "historic," should you put "a" or "an"? Which of the following is better?

It's an historic event.	("an" before "historic")
It's a historic event.	("a" before "historic")

AP, New York, Chicago, Margaret, and Theodore put "a" before "historic" (because "h" has a consonant sound). Russ puts "an" before "historic" (because that "h" is nearly silent, if your accent is British or sophisticated American). MLA gives no advice about "historic."

Writing as a career

Here are surprising truths about trying to write for a living.

Copyright You don't have to "copyright" what you write, since modern copyright law says that anything you write is copyrighted automatically. To *prove* you wrote it before somebody else, you can use many techniques, such as sending a copy to the Library of Congress or sending a copy to yourself by registered mail. On your manuscript's first page, it's helpful to put your city, year, copyright policy ("Don't copy without author's permission"), and a way for the reader to reach you (your street address, phone number, e-mail address, or Website).

Packaging your poetry If you're writing poetry, your poems might not be long enough to fill a book. That depends on how long your poems are and how your publisher packages them. If the book's pages are tiny and the poems are long, you might succeed; otherwise, add bulk by creating some prose (such as comments about the poems) or artwork.

Hard work, low pay To create a good poem, you must spend lots of time thinking, writing, and editing — without much pay.

> **Good poets are maids, not burned**
>
> It takes a heap o' writin'
> To make a poem come home,
> To beautify each little phrase
> So critics do not groan.
>
> It takes a heap o' writin'
> To make a poem work out.
> Ya gotta keep on tryin'
> To clean out all the grout.

Don't expect to get rich by writing — especially if you're writing poetry. Poetry pays less than all other forms of writing. If you decide to marry the poetry muse, marry for love, not money. The famous poet Robert Graves said:

> There's no money in poetry,
> but there's no poetry in money either.

Poetry can give you fame (through public readings and lectures) if you're lucky — though trying to become a "lucky poet" is nearly as hopeless as trying to become a "famous basketball player."

Low self-esteem Poets usually feel nervous about themselves. The famous poet W.H. Auden made this comment:

> A poet can't say, "Tomorrow I'll write a poem and, thanks to my training and experience, I know I'll do a good job." In the eyes of others, a man's a poet if he's written one good poem; but in a poet's own eyes, he's a poet just at the moment when he's making his last revision to a new poem. The moment before, he was just a *potential* poet; the moment after, he's a man who's ceased to write poetry, perhaps forever.

When you finish writing a book and you've done your final edits on it, you'll be sad at having to stop the fun of diddling with it. Truman Capote said:

> Finishing a book is just like
> you took a child out in the back yard and shot it.

Teaching Writers don't get paid much, but as a writer you might be able to make a living by teaching others how to write, through courses, tutoring, consulting, or speeches.

Beyond fame As a writer, your chance of becoming famous is about the same as your chance of becoming a famous basketball player: a writer's life is a lottery where the usual result is "You lose." It's fun to try playing, though; and the game improves your mind, which is your most important asset. It also lets you express your individuality. Don Delillo said:

> Writing's a form of personal freedom. It frees us from the mass identity we see around us. In the end, writers will write not to be outlaw heroes of some under-culture but mainly to save themselves, to survive as individuals.

Weird writing

I've explained how to write normally. Here's how to write weirdly.

Tongue twisters Write something that's hard to pronounce. Here are famous examples; try to say them out loud, fast! They're good to practice, especially if you have a speech impediment or you're a foreigner trying to speak English or you're training to be a news announcer.

The hardest sentence short sentence to say is:

> The 6th sick sheik's 6th sheep's sick.

If you master that, try this longer version:

> The 6th sick sheik's 6th sheep's sick,
> so 6 slick sheiks sold 6 sick sheep 6 silk sheets.

The hardest phrases to say 10 times fast are:

> "sixish"
> "toy boat"
> "big whip"
> "3 free throws"
> "mixed biscuits"
> "cheap ship trip"
> "Peggy Babcock"
> "selfish shellfish"
> "Irish wristwatch"
> "unique New York"
> "black bug's blood"
> "inchworms inching"
> "red blood, blue blood"
> "good blood, bad blood"
> "shredded Swiss cheese"
> "6 short slow shepherds"
> "caution: wide right turns"
> "11 benevolent elephants"
> "the myth of Miss Muffet"
> "the epitome of femininity"
> "quick-witted cricket critic"
> "Tim, the thin twin tinsmith"
> "Mrs. Smith's fish-sauce shop"
> "9 nice night nurses nursing nicely"
> "6 simmering sharks, sharply striking shins"

Try saying these sentences 10 times fast:

> "Ed had edited it."
> "Please pay promptly."
> "Chop shops stock chops."
> "Whistle for the thistle sifter."
> "Sure, the ship's shipshape, sir."
> "A noisy noise annoys an oyster."
> "Betty better butter Brad's bread."
> "Is this your sister's 6th zither, sir?"
> "Friendly Frank flips fine flapjacks."
> "The 2:22 train tore through the tunnel."
> "Sam's shop stocks short spotted socks."
> "Can a clam cram in a clean cream can?"
> "Which witch wished which wicked wish?"
> "Many an anemone sees an enemy anemone."
> "When does the wristwatch-strap shop shut?"
> "Fred fed Ted bread, and Ted fed Fred bread."
> "Which wristwatches are Swiss wristwatches?"
> "They both, though, have 33 thick thimbles to thaw."
> "Mrs. Smith's fish-sauce shop seldom sells shellfish."
> "Give papa a proper cup of coffee in a copper coffee cup."

These poems are fun to try saying:

> Don't pamper damp scamp tramps
> That camp under ramp lamps.
>
> 6 sick hicks
> Nick 6 slick bricks
> With picks and sticks.
>
> If 2 witches were watching 2 watches,
> Which witch would watch which watch?
>
> She sells seashells on the seashore.
> The shells she sells are seashells, she's sure.
>
> Ruby Rugby's brother bought and brought her
> Back some rubber baby-buggy bumpers.
>
> A skunk sat on a stump
> And thunk the stump stunk,
> But the stump thunk the skunk stunk.
>
> A flea and a fly, I fear, flew to a flue.
> Said the flea to the fly, "Let us flee!"
> Said the fly to the flea, "Let us fly!"
> So they flew through a flaw in the flue.
>
> If you stick a stock of liquor in your locker,
> It's slick to stick a lock upon your stock.
> A stickler who is slicker
> Could stick you of your liquor
> If you fail to lock your liquor with a lock.
>
> How much wood would a woodchuck chuck
> If a woodchuck could chuck wood?
> He'd chuck, he would, what a woodchuck could
> And chuck as much wood as a woodchuck would,
> If a woodchuck could chuck wood.
>
> Peter Piper picked a peck of pickled peppers.
> Did Peter Piper pick a peck of pickled peppers?
> If Peter Piper picked a peck of picked peppers,
> Where's the peck of pickled peppers
>   Peter Piper picked?
>
> A bitter biting bittern
> Bit a better brother bittern,
> But the bitter better bittern
> Bit the bitter biter back.
> The bitter bittern bitten
> By the better bitten bittern said,
> "I'm bitter, badly bit! Alack!"
>
> You've no need to light a nightlight
> On a light night like tonight,
> For a nightlight's light a slight light,
> And tonight's a night that's light.
> When a night's light (like tonight's light),
> It is really not quite right
> To light nightlights with their slight lights
> On a light night like tonight.

A tree toad loved a she-toad
Who lived up in a tree.
He was a 2-toed tree toad;
A 3-toed toad was she.
The 2-toed tree toad tried to win
The 3-toed she-toad's heart.
The 2-toed tree toad loved the ground
The 3-toed tree toad trod.
The 2-toed tree toad tried in vain.
He couldn't please her whim,
For from her tree-toad bower
With finest 3-toed power
The she-toad vetoed him.

Betty Botter bought some butter.
"But," said she, "This butter's bitter.
If I bake it in my batter,
It'll make my batter bitter;
But a bit of better butter's
Bound to make my batter better!"
So she bought some better butter
(Better than the bitter butter),
And she baked it in her batter,
So her batter was not bitter!

This poem, to say fast, tries to make you accidentally say the naughty word "shit":

I slit a sheet. A sheet I slit.
Upon the slitted sheet I sit.

This poem, to say fast, tries to make you accidentally say "pleasant fucker":

I'm not the pheasant plucker. I'm the pheasant plucker's mate.
I'm only plucking pheasants 'cause the pheasant plucker's late.
I'm not the pheasant plucker. I'm a pheasant plucker's son.
I'm only plucking pheasants till the pheasant pluckers come.

Personals Just for fun (heh, heh), try to write "personal" ads that summarize your real-or-imaginary life & desires in a single sentence, like this:

Men seeking women
Man with big nose on swelled head seeks swelled woman.
Man with doctored passport seeks nurse.

Women seeking men
Woman who hates men seeks sorcerer to change her mind.
Woman having period seeks man who knows how to comma.
Woman with child seeks man who isn't latter.
Just looking for a guy with a sense of humor, to laugh at.

Non-specific
Brain without body seeks both.
Idiot seeks savant.
Smart seeks dumb for fun times in sign language.
Want a partner who's *normal*, 'cause I'm not.
If you're square, I'll be your square root.
My life's a mess so you can play in my mud.
Tired of my ex: seek XXX.
My pie is fulfilling but needs your spice.
Let's study each other to hit high marks on exam.
My spirit is willing when the flesh is in the oven.
Former woman seeks former man for transgendered marriage.
I promise a wonderful time if you don't tell my parents you saw this ad.

But be careful! A woman in Zurich sent this proposal letter to the famous playwright George Bernard Shaw:

You have the greatest brain in the world, and I have the most beautiful body, so we ought to produce the most perfect child!

He wrote back:

What if the child inherits my body and your brains?

6-word stories Ernest Hemingway wrote famous stories that are short. Here's a legend about him: when lunching with other authors, he bet he could write a complete story (with a logical beginning, middle, and end) that was just 6 words long. He won the bet by writing this story on a napkin....

For sale: baby shoes, never worn.

Inspired by that legend (which may or may not have been true), many authors have tried to write complete stories — and even complete life memoirs — that are very short: just 6 words long. Can *you* use just 6 words to tell a complete tale — or summarize your whole life? English teachers tell their students to try.

Thousands of 6-word stories are collected at www.SixWordStories.net and www.SmithMag.net/sixwords. Many other Websites have further examples: to find them, do a Google search for "six words."

Lizzie Widdicombe, in *The New Yorker* magazine, wrote an article about 6-word stories. To be ironic, every sentence in her article is 6 words long. You can read her article at:

www.NewYorker.com/talk/2008/02/25/080225ta_talk_widdicombe

Here are some famous attempts:

6-word thought	Author
I loved. I lost. I'm sorry.	"SlashChick"
Longed for him. Got him. Shit.	Margaret Atwood
Failed SAT. Lost scholarship. Invented rocket.	William Shatner
Womb. Bloom. Groom. Gloom. Rheum. Tomb.	Blake Morrison
Started small. Grew. Peaked. Shrunk. Vanished.	George Saunders
Found true love. Married someone else.	Dave Eggers
Great sex. Broken heart. Worth it?	"Dec C."
After Harvard, had baby with crackhead.	Robin Templeton
Gave commencement address, became sex columnist.	Amy Sohn
He was home. He was lost.	Gore Vidal
For sale: halves of a bed.	"Dennis"
Across the street, the generations repeat.	Carol Smith
Vibrator found! Roommate's. Mike's my roommate.	"JM"
Mom snorted our child-support money.	Parker Lanting
Magician's saw table: used just once.	"Matilda"
Canoe guide, only got lost once.	Taylor Stump
I lost my virginity on 9/11.	Laura Garcia
Liars, hysterectomy *didn't* improve sex life!	Joan Rivers
I'm hopelessly romantic and equally unwanted.	"JulieD"
Woman seeks men — high pain threshold.	Yin Shih
Never made it to med school.	"Jeannie"
Older now, I draw myself better.	Peter Arkle
Tequila made her clothes fall off.	Susanne Broderick
They danced alone in her room.	"Gaurav"
Walking home, she regained her virginity.	Jim Lyon
Boys liked her. She preferred books.	Anneliese Cuttle
Bang postponed. Not big enough. Reboot.	David Brin
Easy. Just touch the match to	Ursula K. Le Guin
Well, I thought it was funny.	Stephen Colbert
Not quite what I was planning…	Summer Grimes
Everything I touch turns to mold.	Lisa Anne Auerbach
Bipolar, no two ways about it.	Jason Owen
Alzheimer's: meeting new people every day.	Phil Skversky
Craves intelligent conversation with someone kissable.	Olena DeLeeuw
Felt dorky with my thick-rimmed glasses.	"DanceNerd 2013"
Acting is not all I am.	Molly Ringwald
Fix a toilet, get paid crap.	Jennifer James
Hope is stronger than dope, kids!	Lizzie Widdicombe
I wish I could unhear that.	"Believe"
Brevity: a good thing in writing.	Lizzie Widdicombe
Me see world! Me write stories!	Elizabeth Gilbert
Told you I'd be published someday!	Kacie Adams

Mystery subjects To have fun, write about a subject but don't reveal the subject's identity until the very end. Example:

> I'm going to tell you about a drink so amazing that men devoted their lives to finding it and fighting wars about it.
>
> This amazing liquid consists of such pure goodness that doctors worldwide recommend it as a cure for most ills. This refreshing tonic has no bad side effects: the ideal drink, it's sodium-free, fat-free, alcohol-free, preservative-free, and non-carcinogenic.
>
> One gulp of this stuff can make men scream with delight. Its godly beauty has made this elixir praised by poets and songwriters worldwide. Some towns even dispense this wonderful elixir to their citizens, free, in special parks.
>
> Discovered thousands of years ago by ancient heroes, it's a mysterious wonder of the universe and analyzed every day by scientists and other public servants trying to decipher its amazing properties. It's saved many lives and been the subject of sweetest dreams.
>
> Yes, water is truly wonderful.

This example goes further:

> I confess: I'm an addict! The drug that's been sweeping the nation has gotten to me, too!
>
> I can't resist this powerful drug, which takes over my entire life. Late at night, when my weary body wishes to sleep, this hypnotic drug seduces me into partaking of it for many hours, a late-night turn-on controlling my mind and soul throughout the night. This mind-numbing drug, invented in secret labs, makes visions dance before my eyes (visions far wilder than anything created by primitive drugs such as LSD) and accompanied by sounds giving me the strangest out-of-body experiences.
>
> This drug is so powerful that the U.S. government has declared it a controlled substance and controls its distribution. The biggest companies in America and around the world have all become involved in packaging this drug and changing its nature, but nobody can stop it. It's been the subject of many congressional hearings.
>
> Each day in offices across America, employees whisper about how they experienced the drug during the previous evening. They even brag about who had the most outrageous experiences with it. Teachers complain that the quality of American education has greatly declined because students do this drug instead of homework.
>
> To prevent impurities, the U.S. government funds the distribution of a "public" version of this drug, but most Americans get a bigger kick from "private" versions.
>
> Unfortunately, advertising this nefarious drug is still permitted in many locales. Billboards lure innocent American adults and kids into partaking of this drug. According to psychologists, people who spend too much time doing this drug turn into vegetables and become "potatoes" or worse.
>
> Yes, television is amazingly addictive.

This example is the most provocative:

> I'm going to tell you about a certain feeling a male has, a feeling so strong that the average woman can't comprehend it.
>
> This male feeling, arising in a certain part of the man's body, creates such a burning desire to stroke it that it can drive a man nearly insane and make him want to rip off his clothes to satisfy his craving itch. In high schools across the country, health teachers (and even gym teachers!) warn young men about these urges, but the flames of passion are irrepressible.
>
> Yes, athlete's foot sure is tough.

Elided sentences Here are two boring sentences:

> I love you. You are beautiful!

To have more fun, combine them to form this super-sentence:

> I love YOU are beautiful!

Here's an extended example:

> I gaze into YOUR EYES pierce MY SOUL is putty in YOUR HANDS caress MY EVERY MUSCLE cries out for YOUR TOUCH can make me MELTing in your arms, I proclaim my love FOR YOU I'll do ANYTHING is possible IN LOVE with you, I'm DELERIOUSly delicious raspberry sundae!

Palindromes A **palindrome** is a word or sentence that reads the same backwards as forward.

For example, "eve" is a palindrome word. So is "madam."

Here are 4 palindrome sentences….

The pet-store owner warned his customers:

> Step on no pets!

Adam told Eve when he met her in the garden:

> Madam, I'm Adam.

When Napoleon lost the war and was exiled to the island of Elba, he said:

> Able was I, ere I saw Elba.

The engineer who invented the Panama Canal bragged:

> A man, a plan, a canal, Panama!

Pig Latin Try writing in **Pig Latin** (English modified to sound like Latin).

Here's how to convert English to Pig Latin:

> If the word begins with a vowel, just add "way" to the end of the word. For example, "art" becomes "artway."
>
> If the word begins with a consonant or a bunch of consonants, move such stuff to the end, then add "ay." For example, "fart" becomes "artfay."

For example, "drink up" becomes "inkdray upway."

Notice that "ill" and "will" both become "illway." Yes, "ifelay isway osay ambiguousway."

Try singing *The Star Spangled Banner* in Pig Latin. Here's how it begins:

> Oway aysay ancay ouyay eesay

The definition of "vowel" versus "consonant" is phonetic. For example, "yes" becomes "esyay" (since that "y" sounds like a consonant), but "Ypsilanti" becomes "Ypsilantiway" (since that "y" sounds like a vowel).

If you're studying computer programming, try this challenge: program the computer to translate English to Pig Latin.

Politically correct terms Here's how to criticize people politely:

> He's not a **criminal**, just **ethically deprived**.
> He's not **irresponsible**, just **a free spirit**.
> He's not **violent**, just **assertively animated**.
> He's not **greedy**, just **dollar-addicted**.
> He's not **procrastinating**, just **delay-seeking**.
> He's not **slow**, just **unaccelerated**.
> He's not **useless**, just **unpurposed**.
> He's not **lecherous**, just **drooling**.
> He's not **an asshole**, just **rear-ended in front**.
> He's not **evil**, just **challenging**.
> He's not **unkempt**, just **natural**.
> He's not **bald**, just **follicularly impaired**.
> She's not **ugly**, just **of bounded beauty**.

If you're a student, the Internet recommends you use these politically correct terms to describe your situation:

> You're not too **tall**, just **vertically enhanced**.
> You're not too **talkative**, just **abundantly verbal**.
> You're not **shy**, just **conversationally selective**.
> You're not **lazy**, just **energetically declined**.
> You're not **failing**, just **passing-impaired**.
> You didn't get **detention**, just **exit-delayed**.
>
> You're not **late**,
> just **having a rescheduled arrival time**.
>
> You didn't **get grounded**,
> just **hit a social speed-bump**.
>
> In class, you weren't **sleeping**,
> just **rationing consciousness**.
>
> Your homework isn't **missing**,
> just **having an out-of-notebook experience**.
>
> You don't have **smelly gym socks**,
> just **odor-retentive athletic footwear**.
>
> Your locker isn't **overflowing**,
> just **closure-prohibitive**.
>
> Your bedroom isn't **cluttered**,
> just **passage-restrictive**.
>
> You don't think the cafeteria food is **awful**,
> just **digestively challenged**.
>
> You're not **having a bad-hair day**,
> just **suffering from rebellious follicle syndrome**.
>
> You weren't **gossiping**,
> just **providing speedy transmission of near-factual information**.
>
> In class, you weren't **passing notes**,
> just **participating in the discreet exchange of penned meditations**.
>
> You weren't **sent to the principal's office**,
> just **went on a mandatory field trip to the administration sanctum**.

Best-man speech

At weddings, the "best man" is supposed to give a speech that ribs the groom then wishes him luck. According to *The Wall Street Journal*, some folks make a living by ghost-writing such speeches. They charge $100 per speech or $5 per line.

That's ridiculous! If you're going to give a dangerous speech like that, why not go all the way, like this:

> I wish my best friend lots of luck,
> Doing things that end in "uck,"
> Like holding hands while trying to…
> Take out garbage on a rainy day, through the muck.
>
> I'm sure his wife will get a kick
> When looking at his great big…
> Sick face when she gives the thermometer a lick.
>
> But after wedding and "I love you,"
> They'll honeymoon and want to…
> Sleep, while murmuring
>   "You're the one for me. I knew."

Walking through the woods

Robert Frost's poem called "Walking through the woods on a snowy evening" isn't realistic. To be realistic, it should reveal this sad choice —

> Walking through the woods on a snowy evening,
> I tripped,
> Bumped my head on a tree,
> Got covered with blood,
> Broke my leg,
> Lay helpless 3 days in snow until was found,
> Spent 3 months in the hospital,
> And vowed never to again be
> Walking through the woods on a snowy evening.

or this conservative choice —

> Walking through the woods on a snowy evening,
> Two paths diverged.
>
> One had less dung underneath,
> And that made all the difference,
> Since I'm Republican.

or this practical choice —

> While walking through woods
>   in the snow, I got tired
> From trying to reach
>   what my body desired.
>
> I got to a fork.
>   Didn't know what the fuck
> To do, so turned round
>   and went home. On firm ground,
> Got pizza by *phone*.
>   "Let the pizza boy moan."
>
> His horse knew the way
>   to come carry the sleigh
> Through white, drifting snow.
>   Sure beats "pizza to go!"
> I give him a tip.
>   Now I've pizza on lip.

or this tech choice:

> Walking through the woods on a snowy evening,
> Two paths diverged,
> So I grabbed my cell phone
> And got directions.

Can you think of other poems to rewrite to be realistic?

Puns

Here are some famous old puns:

1. A trader sailed to an island, met the king, and told him, "I notice you have no throne." The king asked, "What's a throne?" The trader replied, "I'll show you." On his next trip, the trader brought a throne. The king liked it, bought it, and ordered another. On his next trip, the trader brought the second throne. The king got excited about thrones and started buying more and more of them, until they filled his grass hut, and he had to build a second floor to hold all the thrones. But one day, the second floor collapsed and all the thrones fell, killing the king. Moral: **people who live in grass houses shouldn't stow thrones**.
2. In a zoo, some dolphins seemed to live forever by dining on dead seagulls. One day, the zookeeper tried to carry seagulls to the dolphins, but a lion sat on the bridge and blocked his way. He stepped over the lion but got arrested for **transporting gulls across a staid lion for immortal porpoises**.
3. A dentist noticed that in his patient's mouth, a metal plate was corroding. The dentist asked, "Have you been eating anything unusual?" The patient replied, "My wife learned to make great Hollandaise sauce, so I've been putting it on all my food." The dentist replied, "The lemon in the sauce must be corroding the metal. I'll replace the metal with chrome." The patient asked, "Why chrome?" The dentist replied, "**There's no plate like chrome for the Hollandaise.**"

Note to foreigners and youngsters: some Americans find those tales funny because the bold words, when pronounced with a foreign accent or speech impediment, sound like these popular American expressions:

1. People who live in glass houses shouldn't throw stones.
2. transporting girls across a state line for immoral purposes
3. There's no place like home for the holidays.

A friend passed me this list of newer puns:

1. A vulture tried to board an airplane. He carried 2 dead raccoons but was stopped by stewardess who said, "**I'm sorry, sir, just one carrion allowed per passenger.**"
2. Two boll weevils grew up in South Carolina. One went to Hollywood and got a part in a movie. The other stayed behind in the cotton fields, never amounted to much, and became known as **the lesser of two weevils**.
3. Two Eskimos in a kayak got chilly, but when they lit a fire in the kayak it sank, because **you can't have your kayak and heat it, too.**
4. In the Old West, a 3-legged dog walked into the saloon, slid up to the bar, and announced "**I'm looking for the man who shot my paw.**"
5. A Buddhist getting a root canal refused Novocain because he wanted to **transcend dental medication**.
6. In a hotel lobby, chess players were discussing their victories, but the hotel's manager made them leave because he couldn't stand **chess nuts boasting in an open foyer**.
7. A woman had twins but gave them up for adoption. One of them went to a Spanish family who named him "Juan." The other went to an Egyptian family who named him "Amahl." Years later, Juan sends his photo to his birth mother. She told her husband she wished she had a picture of Amahl too; but he replied, "They're twins! **If you've seen Juan, you've seen Amahl.**"
8. Friars were behind on their belfry payments, so they opened a florist shop to raise funds. Everyone liked to buy flowers from the men of God, but a rival florist thought the competition unfair. He repeatedly begged the friars to close down, but they refused, so he hired Hugh MacTaggart, the roughest thug in town, to "persuade" them to close. Hugh beat up the friars, trashed their store, and said he'd return if they didn't close. Terrified, they did so, proving that **Hugh, and only Hugh, can prevent florist friars**.
9. Since Mahatma Gandhi walked barefoot, his feet got big calluses. Since he ate little, he was frail. His odd diet also gave him bad breath. That made him a **super-calloused fragile mystic, hexed by halitosis**.
10. A person sent ten puns to a friend and hoped at least one pun would generate a laugh. Unfortunately, **no pun in ten did**.

Here are the popular American expressions on which the puns are based:

1. I'm sorry, sir, just one carry-on allowed per passenger.
2. the lesser of two evils
3. You can't have your cake and eat it too.
4. I'm looking for the man who shot my pa.
5. transcendental meditation
6. chestnut roasting in an open fire
7. If you've seen one, you've seen 'em all.
8. You, and only you, can prevent forest fires.
9. supercalifragilisticexpialidocious
10. no pun intended

Death riddles

It's fun to make jokes about death. When I was a kid, the hot topic was "dead baby" riddles, such as these:

> What's blue and jumps up and down? A baby in a cellophane bag.
> How do you make a dead baby float? Seltzer water and two scoops of baby.

Here's the ultimate death riddle (courtesy of the anonymous Internet):

> What's greater than God and more evil than the devil? The rich need it, and the poor have it; but if you eat it, you die!

The answer is the word "nothing," because:

> Nothing is greater than God. Nothing is more evil than the devil. The rich need nothing. The poor have nothing. If you eat nothing, you die.

Ask your friends that riddle and see whether they can figure out the answer. When they get frustrated, start giving them Zen-like hints, such as these:

> If you want the answer, I can tell you *nothing*.
> When you discover the answer, you'll have discovered *nothing*.
> While you're seeking the answer, *nothing* can bother you.
> The answer has 7 letters, but it's *nothing*.

But the biggest hint of all is:

> Most kindergarteners know the answer to the riddle, but most college graduates do not. Focus on the first question: what's greater than God? Most kindergarteners know the answer to that question. If you ask a kindergartener "What's greater than God?" what will the kindergartener answer?

Ready for a different riddle? Figure out what fits this description:

> It's of no use to the person who makes it. It's of no use to the person who buys it. And the person who uses it doesn't know he's using it.

The answer:

> A coffin!

Here's another puzzle about death:

> A woman shoots her husband, then holds him under water for over 5 minutes, then hangs him. But 5 minutes later, they go out together and enjoy a wonderful dinner together. How can that be?

Answer:

> She's a photographer. She shot a picture of her husband, developed it, and hung it up to dry.

Try this death choice:

> You're condemned to death and must choose from 3 rooms. The first is full of raging fires; the second is full off assassins with loaded guns; the third is full of lions that haven't eaten in 3 years. Which room is safest for you?

Answer:

> The third. Lions that haven't eaten in 3 years are dead.

Fake etymologies I don't dare tell lies, but dreaming about lying can be fun. For example, I dream about telling people these tall tales of how certain words were invented. **All the following explanations are false.**

How Xerox was invented:

> In a part of Boston called Roxbury, a woman named Xenia Jones owned a photocopy shop, called "Xenia of Roxbury." One day, investors bought her business and shortened its name to "Xerox."

How the Cadillac was invented:

> The concept of a luxury car was invented by Stanislaw Jerzy, a Polish immigrant who worked at General Motors in Michigan. When he told his boss about his idea for a dream car, his boss countered, "I'm too busy to analyze your idea now. Join me for golf on Saturday and explain your idea then." During the golf game, the boss asked, "Do you have a caddie?" but poor Stanislaw replied, in his broken English, "I have no caddie. I caddie lack." His boss laughed at his English and called him "Mister Caddy-lack." That nickname stuck, and the car he dreamed up was named the "Cadillac."

How Connecticut got its name:

> During Colonial times, travelers from Boston to New York went by sea or along the shore. Finally, they built a straighter road, which became the shortcut. Since it connected Boston to New York and was a shortcut, it was called the "Connecting Cut" or, more briefly, "Connecticut."

How Judaism was invented:

> Judaism was invented by Judy Finkelstein in 1853. Her revised version of the Hebrew prayer service was called "Judy-ism," later shortened to "Judaism."

How dumplings were invented:

> Dumplings were invented in China — by a retarded girl named Pu Ling. When tourists from America passed through her town, tasted her concoction (pork scraps wrapped in pasta dough), and asked what they were called, her mom said "dumb Pu Ling's!" The Americans shortened that to "dumplings," which they've been called ever since.

How Handel invented the Hallelujah Chorus:

> As all history books will tell you, Handel was born in Germany but moved to England. He once vacationed in Spain, where the newest "hot stuff" was jalapeño pepper imported from Spain's colony, Mexico. Handel loved the jalapeño peppers so much that he wrote a choral work where the singers would sing, loudly, the word "Jalapeño!" repeatedly. It was called the "Jalapeño Chorus." The original words were: "Jalapeño, jalapeño! Jalapeño, jalapeño! Hallelujah!" Later, to make the song more marketable at Christmas, he changed each "Jalapeño" to "Hallelujah" (which sounds almost the same) and pretended the song was just about Christ, not jalapeños (which were popular in Spain but antithetical to the English bland diet). If you listen to the modern version, you'll notice the first syllable (which is now "Ha") is sung with the same loud breath (almost a scream) as if you just burned your throat by eating a jalapeño pepper. If you listen closely, you might even hear naughty singers still sing "jalapeño" instead of "hallelujah."

How Beethoven got his name:

> Though Ludwig van Beethoven spent most of his life in Germany — and many encyclopedias erroneously say he was born there — researchers have recently discovered he was actually born in England, where birth records show his name was Lou Smith. He showed musical talent at an early age; but his parents felt music was an uncertain career, so they encouraged him to be more gainfully employed, as a cook. He hung around a lot of Jewish Russian immigrants, who loved to drink *borscht*, which is beet soup. He developed a knack for making great borscht — and also roasting the beets. When he was just 7 years old, he was already out on the streets to hawk his "roasted beets, hot from the oven!" When his parents immigrated to Germany, they felt his career would be helped by giving him a German name, so they translated "Lou" to "Ludwig" and transliterated his sales pitch ("of beets hot from the oven") to "van Beet H. Oven," which later got shortened to "van Beethoven," which is what we call him now!

Try it yourself: find something with a ridiculous name and invent a tale about how it arose.

And now, because I wrote this drivel, people doing Google searches will read my stupid tales and believe that Xerox was named after Xenia of Roxbury, Cadillac arose from a golf game, Connecticut got named by being a connecting shortcut, Judaism was invented by Judy Finkelstein, dumplings were invented by dumb Pu Ling, the Hallelujah chorus was originally about jalapeños, and Beethoven was a British beet cook. Should I feel guilty?

Alphabetical sentences Try to write a sentence whose first word begins with A, second word begins with B, third word begins with C, and so on.

Here's my first attempt, which starts nicely but runs downhill:

> A better child does everything for God, happy in just knowing love may now offer prayers quite rich, so that upon vowing, weird xylophones yank zombies.

Donna tried her hand, which after my editing became this:

> A boy can do every fraudulent gangster hobby if judges kill lonely maidens near ocean ports, quickly recording sins to used vehicles while x-raying your zipper.

Lili Timmons tried this:

> Any bear can dance every favored gavotte, having it just kept lively, maintaining natural oblong patter quickly round, stepping to ultimate victory, weaving X's, yielding zeal.

The Internet offers attempts by others. At WordFreaks.Tribe.net, "Unsu" contributed this:

> After being completely drugged eating frozen, gelatinous hemp (including jelly), Karen listed many notes (on paper) questioning reality states, tempting uninvited visitors, worrying xenophobic young zookeepers.

Unfortunately, "Karen" isn't a word.

Can you write a better alphabetical sentence? The ideal sentence would be grammatically correct, sound natural, and make sense. It should avoid hyphens, capitals, dangling phrases, and lists of adjectives. Maybe I should award a prize….

Our country is run by **lawyers**, who make & analyze laws requested by **politicians**, who start **wars**. Let's peek at those lawyers, their politicians, and their wars.

Politics

Why do they call it "politics"? Because discussing it is the fastest way to get Aunt Polly ticked.

Conservative's lament

Conservatives say:

> If you're young and not a liberal, you haven't got a heart.
> But if you're old and not conservative, you haven't got a brain!

That quote was attributed to Winston Churchill (Britain's prime minister during World War 2), but according to his fans, there's no record he ever said it. That thought was expressed by many people, including a French historian in the 1800's. I call it the **Conservative's lament**.

The lament is correct. Young people, forever optimistic, believe that the world will be a beautiful place if you treat everybody kindly and liberally. Old people, who've been mugged and cheated by many "nice-looking" people, become cynical.

For example, when President Jimmy Carter and I were young, we both believed the Soviets would treat the rest of the world kindly if the rest of the world would treat them kindly. But then the Soviets, without provocation, invaded Afghanistan. I was disillusioned, and Jimmy Carter was voted out of office.

When I was young, I believed that all people who claimed to be poor should be given generous welfare benefits. But after I chatted with many welfare recipients who used their money to eat in fancy restaurants, buy drugs, and visit prostitutes, I grew more cynical about the needs of the "needy." Sure, there are members of society who are truly desperate and do need welfare money; and sure, the rich have a moral obligation to give large sums of money to the truly needy poor. But when I see the large percentage of welfare recipients who abuse and even laugh at the system, I want to cry.

When the governor of Alabama, George Wallace, was young, he ran for office on a platform of being nice to blacks. He even kissed black babies. He lost the race. Then he changed his tune, became a cynical anti-black segregationist, ran for office again, and — because he was a cynical segregationist — won! Although I don't recommend imitating him (since segregation is immoral), his life proves one point: cynicism pays.

Why Democrats make me smile

Democrats tend to be liberal, and Republicans tend to be conservative. But what is "liberal," and what is "conservative"? What's the difference?

In 1974, Representative Craig Hosmer (Republican from California) published a funny list of differences in the Congressional Record. He got it from a source that wished to remain anonymous. Several people tried updating (or censoring) that list (especially Rowland Nethaway, senior editor of the Waco Texas *Tribune-Herald*, in 1998). Here's my own attempt to update that list further:

> Republicans raise dahlias, Dalmatians, and eyebrows.
> Democrats raise hell, kids, and taxes.
>
> Republicans employ exterminators.
> Democrats step on the bugs.
>
> Republicans go fishing on their boats.
> Democrats stay fishing at the docks.
>
> Democrats eat the fish they catch.
> Republicans hang them on the wall.
>
> Republicans grab financial pages and love them.
> Democrats grab financial pages and shove them — into bird cages.
>
> Republicans consume ¾ of all rutabaga produced in this country.
> Democrats throw out the rest.
>
> Republicans follow the plans their grandfathers made.
> Democrats make up their own plans — but ignore them.
>
> Democrats take individual delight in reading banned books.
> Republicans form censorship committees to read those books as groups.
>
> Democrats give their worn-out clothes to the less fortunate.
> So do Republicans, who are smarter and take the tax deduction.
>
> The junk along the road was thrown from car windows by Democrats,
> but can't be seen by Republicans from the back of their limos.
>
> Democrats name their kids after athletes, entertainers, and politicians.
> Republicans name their kids after the richest ancestors.
>
> Republicans close their curtains at night — but needn't bother.
> Democrats leave their curtains open — to amuse Republicans.
>
> Republican boys date Democrat girls.
> They plan to marry Republican girls but feel entitled to a little fun first.
>
> Republicans sleep in twin beds, often in separate rooms.
> That's why there are more Democrats.

Recently, it's become less true that most Republicans are rich and most Democrats are poor. To predict how a person will vote, don't ask about the person's income; instead, ask about church attendance: Protestant "churchgoers" (who attend church at least once a week) tend to vote Republican.

Researchers have recently discovered an even more accurate way to determine who'll vote Republican: ask what kind of God the voter believes in. If the voter believes God is vengeful (punishes sinners and other "bad people"), the voter will probably vote Republican; if the voter believes God is forgiving (like Jesus) or laissez-faire (he created the world but then left it alone), the voter will probably vote Democrat.

According to Democrat analysts, Republicans believe government should be like a stern father (tough police enforcement) while Democrats believe government should be like a loving mother (kind to the helpless). Why can't we have both?

Obama's good point

People are amazed that President Obama is our first multiracial President. But I'm more amazed at something else: he's the first President who's a caring, candid intellectual. Some other Presidents have been caring, some have been candid, some have been intellectual, but Obama is the first President that has all three qualities simultaneously.

I don't agree with all his decisions, and I didn't vote for him in the primary — I voted for Bill Richardson instead — but I like Obama's style of getting there.

Adlai Stevenson's lament

Adlai Stevenson was the brilliant egghead Democrat who ran for President against Eisenhower but lost. He made this comment about politicians and their speeches:

> It's often easier to fight for one's principles than live up to them.

Republican language

Republicans appeal to voters by changing the jargon. Here's how the typical voter responds, according to Frank Luntz (a Republican pollster and spin doctor) and Eric Effron (managing editor of *The Week*):

The voter doesn't mind an "estate tax" but opposes it when called a "death tax."

The voter is unsure about "tort reform" but favors it when called "ending lawsuit abuse."

The voter is against "global warming" but accepts it when called "climate change."
The voter is against "government eavesdropping" but accepts it when called "electronic intercepts."
The voter is against "torture" but accepts it when called "aggressive interrogation techniques."

The voter is against the U.S. starting an "invasion" but accepts it when called a "liberation."
The voter is against war's "escalation" but accepts it when called "troop surge."
The voter is against war's "civilian casualties" but accepts them when called "collateral damage."
The voter is against the U.S. being an "occupying power" but accepts it when called a "coalition partner."
The voter is against a U.S. "retreat" but accepts it when called a "phased troop redeployment."

The voter is worried about "civil war" but less worried about it when called "sectarian strife."

According to Mark Kleiman (a Democrat who's a public-policy professor at UCLA) and his friends, here's how Republicans redefine political terms:

Political term	Republican definition
healthy forest	no tree left behind
alternative energy sources	new places to drill for gas and oil
climate change	progress toward the blessed day when blue states are swallowed by oceans
compassionate conservatism	poignant concern for the very wealthy
ownership society	civilization where just the owners have power
class warfare	any attempt to raise the minimum wage
bankruptcy	a means of escaping debt, available to corporations but not poor people
laziness	when the poor aren't working
leisure time	when the rich aren't working
free markets	Haliburton's no-bid contracts
growth	justification for tax cuts for the rich
simplify	reduce (especially the taxes of Republican donors)
honesty	lies told in simple declarative sentences, such as "Freedom is on the march."
DeLay	past tense of De Lie
stay the course	continue to perform the same actions and expect different results
stuff happens	I don't have to live in Baghdad
voter fraud	a significant minority turnout
No Child Left Behind	ensuring that stupid kids learn enough to get jobs in the military
pro-life	valuing human life up until birth
creation science	theory that Bush's resemblance to a chimpanzee is just coincidental
woman	a person trusted to raise a child but not to decide whether to have one
treason	criticizing Bush
patriot	Bush supporter
Patriot Act	preemptive strike on American freedoms, to prevent terrorists from destroying them first

2029

Republicans fear that the year 2029 will have these headlines:

Ozone from electric cars kills millions in 7th largest country, Mexifornia, formerly called California. White minorities still trying to get English recognized as Mexifornia's 3rd language.

Castro finally dies at age 112. Cuban cigars can now be imported legally, but President Chelsea Clinton has banned all smoking.

Baby conceived naturally; scientists stumped. Couple petitions court to reinstate heterosexual marriage.

Spotted-owl plague threatens Northwest crops and livestock. France pleads for global help after being taken over by Jamaica. New federal law requires registering all nail clippers, screwdrivers, fly swatters, and rolled-up newspapers. Postal Service raises price of 1st-class stamp to $17.89 and reduces mail delivery to just Wednesdays. IRS sets lowest tax rate at 75%. 85-year 75-billion-dollar study says diet and exercise are keys to weight loss. Supreme Court decides that punishing criminals violates their civil rights. Massachusetts executes last remaining conservative.

Emblem

The Internet says the government's decided to change the national emblem from an **eagle** to a **condom**, which more accurately reflects the government's political stance:

It permits inflation, halts production, destroys the next generation, protects a bunch of pricks, and gives you a sense of security while you're actually being screwed.

Bush

Let's take a look back at George W. Bush. We journalists were thrilled when he became President, because he gave us somebody to make fun of!

Imitated Carson Here's why America voted for George W. Bush and made him President: he resembled Johnny Carson. Like Johnny Carson, Bush smiled and was a semi-intellectual affable joker.

That's what America wanted in a President: a talk-show host who smiled. That's what America got. But after 8 years, America got tired of seeing the same old smiles and wanted to change channels.

Bush outsourced While Bush was President, this news flash appeared on the Internet:

Congress has announced that the office of President of the United States will be outsourced to India. The move's being made to save the President's $400,000 yearly salary and the record 521 billion dollars in deficit expenditures and related overhead the office has incurred during the last 5 years.

Mr. Bush was informed of his termination, by e-mail this morning.

The office of President will be assumed by Mr. Gurvinder Singh of Indus Teleservices, Mumbai, India. He's eligible for the Presidency because he was born in the U.S. while his Indian parents vacationed at Niagara Falls.

Singh's future
He'll be paid $320 a month but no health coverage or other benefits.

Because of the time difference between the U.S. and India, he'll work mainly at night, when most offices of the U.S. government are closed; but he can handle the job without a support staff. He said, "Working nights will let me keep my day job at the American Express call center. I'm excited about this position. I always hoped to be President someday."

Singh isn't fully aware of all Presidential issues; but that's okay, since Bush wasn't familiar with them either. Singh will rely on a script tree that lets him respond to most topics. Using those canned responses, he can address common concerns without having to understand the underlying issues. A spokesman said, "We know those scripting tools work. President Bush used them successfully for years."

Singh might have difficulty producing a Texas drawl; but Bush has recently abandoned that "down home" persona anyway, to appear more intelligent.

Bush's future
Bush will receive health coverage, expenses, and salary until his final day of employment. After a 2-week wait, he'll be eligible for $240/week unemployment for 13 weeks. He can't collect Medicaid, since his unemployment benefits will exceed the allowed limit.

Bush has been given the outplacement services of Manpower, Inc. to help him write a résumé and prepare for his next job. According to Manpower, Bush may have difficulty securing a new position, since his practical work experience is limited. A greeter position at Wal-Mart was suggested because of his extensive hand-shaking experience and phony smile.

Another possibility is his re-enlistment in the Texas Air National Guard. If he chooses that option, he'd likely be stationed in Texas for a month before being sent to Iraq, a country he's visited. "I've been there, I know all about Iraq," said Bush, who gained valuable knowledge of the country in a visit to Baghdad Airport's terminal and gift shop.

Sources in Baghdad say Bush would get a warm reception from local Iraqis. They've asked for details of his arrival so they can arrange an appropriately explosive welcome.

The original version of that bulletin was written by Melynda Jill and posted at www.GodlessGeeks.com/outsourced.htm.

Economic policy

Politicians try to create an economic policy.

Reagan's summary

Ronald Reagan complained that the government's economic policy can be summed up in 3 sentences:

> If it moves, tax it.
> If it keeps moving, regulate it.
> If it stops moving, subsidize it.

One-armed economist

The first president to appoint a council of economic advisors was Harry Truman. He enjoyed hearing what his council said, but he wished they'd be more definitive.

He moaned, "**Give me a one-armed economist**," because he was tired of listening to economists who gave reasonable advice followed by, "On the other hand…"

Chaos

Here's a tale from the Internet:

> A surgeon, an architect, and an economist were arguing about which profession was the most important and godly.
>
> The surgeon said, "God's a *surgeon*: the first thing He did was extract Eve from Adam's rib."
>
> The architect said, "No, God's an *architect*: He built the world in 7 days out of chaos."
>
> The economist smiled, "And who made the chaos?"

2 cows

Economics courses often begin with this lecture:

> In ancient times, a farmer had 2 cows. His neighbor had 2 chickens. The farmer wanted a chicken, so he bartered with his neighbor: he'd swap one of his cows for the neighbor's chicken. Then each farmer could produce his own milk and eggs and was happy — until the first farmer realized the cow-chicken swap ripped him off, since he spent more labor raising the cow than the neighbor spent raising the chicken. That's why bartering is unfair and inadequate — and why currency was invented.

When the Internet was invented, folks started posting jokes about how different types of governments and political beliefs would treat the 2-cow farmer differently. Here are examples:

Countries around the world

Communist Russia: You have 2 cows. The government seizes both and produces milk. You wait in line for hours to get it. It's expensive &sour.

Modern Russia: You have 2 cows. You count them, realize you have 4, drink more vodka, count the cows again, realize you have eleventy-six, drink more vodka, and fall asleep. Upon waking, you realize eleventy isn't a number. You count the cows again and have 2 cows. You drink more vodka and try to drown the loss of eleventy-four cows. The Mafia shows up and takes over your cows.

China: You have 2 cows. 300 people try milking them, so you claim full employment & bovine productivity but arrest the reporter revealing the numbers.

Japan: You have 2 cows. You reengineer them so they're a tenth as big and produce 20 times the milk. You teach them to travel on crowded trains, bow to each other, and do well at cow school. You sell cow cartoons, called Cowkimon, worldwide.

Israel: 2 Jewish cows open a milk factory and ice-cream store then sell the movie rights and send their calves to Harvard to become doctors.

Italy: You have 2 cows but don't know where they are. While looking for them, you see a beautiful woman, so you break for lunch.

France: You have 2 cows but want 3, so you go on strike, eat lunch, and drink wine. Life is good.

Switzerland: You charge for storing 5000 cows that don't belong to you.

Cuba: Your 2 cows swam away to Florida.

India: You have 2 cows. You worship both of them.

Quebec: You're allowed 2 cows just if the French-speaking one is bigger than the English-speaking one.

Afghanistan's Taliban: You get executed because your 2 cows are infidels and you're accused of teaching those female bovines to read.

United Nations: France & Russia veto you from milking your 2 cows. The U.S. & Britain veto the cows from milking you. China abstains.

American political activists

Democrat: You have 2 cows but your neighbor has none, so you feel guilty and vote for politicians who tax your cows. To get money to pay the tax, you sell a cow. The government uses the tax to buy a cow and give it to your neighbor. You feel righteous. Barbra Streisand sings for you.

Republican: You have 2 cows. Your neighbor has none. So what?

Libertarian: Go away! What I do with my cows is none of your business!

Constitutionalist: You can't have cows. Our God-given Constitution doesn't mention cows, so they don't exist.

U.S. bureaucracy

U.S. farm policy: You have 2 cows. The government takes both, shoots one, milks the other, pays you for the milk, then pours it down the drain.

U.S. foreign policy: You have 2 cows. The government taxes you enough so you must sell both, to support a man (in a foreign country) who has just 1 cow, which was a gift from your government.

Food & Drug Administration (FDA): You have 2 cows. To test, you make the first cow drink 400 gallons of water a day. It dies, so you ban water. The other cow has cancer, but you ban cancer pills because making them requires water, so that cow dies.

Automated phone system: You have 2 cows? Press 1 if that's correct, 2 otherwise…. Please hold while we connect you to an operator…. (Moo-zak)… Please continue to hold. Your cows are important to us.

American security

Central Intelligence Agency (CIA): You have 2 cows but can't tell anyone about them. Yesterday they weren't at your farm. Today they're not there, again. If you ever have 2 cows, they have no names. *You* have no name. I have no name. Nobody has any names. Got it?

Disclaimer: Warning! Your 2 cows can cause bodily injury if not treated properly. Keep out of reach of children. We can't be held responsible for any bodily injury sustained by interacting with cows.

American financiers

Capitalist: You have 2 cows. You sell one, buy a bull, and build a herd.

American corporation: You have 2 cows. You sell one, lease it back to yourself, and do an IPO on the second one. You force the 2 cows to produce the milk of 4, so one cow drops dead. You're surprised but tell analysts you've downsized and cut expenses. Your stock goes up.

Enron: You have 2 cows. From your bank, you borrow 80% of the forward value of the 2 cows, then **buy** another cow, with 5% down and the rest financed by the seller (on a note callable if your market cap goes below $20 billion) at a rate 2 times prime. You sell the 3 cows to your publicly listed company using letters of credit opened by your brother-in-law at another bank, then execute a debt/equity swap with an associated offer so you get 4 cows back, with a tax exemption for keeping 5 cows. The milk rights of 6 cows are transferred through a Panamanian intermediary to a Cayman Islands company owned secretly by the majority shareholder, who sells the rights to 7 cows' milk back to your listed company. The annual report says the company owns 8 cows, with an option on one more. The public buys your bull.

States

Florida: You have 2 cows: 1 black, 1 white. You hold an election to see which is best. Some preferring the white cow accidentally vote for the black; some vote for both; some don't vote at all; some vote correctly but their votes are declared invalid. Outsiders come and decide which cow is your favorite.

California: You have a cow and a bull. The bull is depressed because it spent its life living a lie, so it gets a sex-change operation, taxpayer-paid. Now you have 2 cows: 1 makes milk, the other doesn't. You try selling the transgender cow, but its lawyer sues you for discrimination. To pay damages, you sell the milk-generating cow. Now you have one transgender, rich, non-milk-producing cow, so you change your business to beef. Then PETA pickets your farm, Jesse Jackson makes a speech in your driveway, the California legislature passes a law giving your farm to Mexico, and the LA Times quotes 5 anonymous cows claiming you groped their teats. You declare bankruptcy and shut down all operations. The cows starve to death.

Hollywood: You have 2 cows. You give them udder implants and teach them to dodge bullets, climb walls, and shoot milk from udders on command.

Arkansas: You have 2 cows. That one on the left is kinda cute.

Nevada: You have 2 cows. You charge lonely men from Arkansas to spend the night with them.

Race

Racist: You have a black cow and a white cow. You abuse and fear the black cow. Then it produces less milk and becomes more violent. You say that proves the black cow was bad all along.

Rapper: You grew up with 2 cows but hated your parents, so you moved away at 16 and got shot. Now you have no cows. You say that's because you're black.

Affirmative action: You have 2 cows. The first cow has more black spots, so it gets into college.

Religious feelings

Catholic: You feel guilty for having 2 cows. Your priest says "Having cows is no sin; but if you feel guilt, free them and say 10 Hail Mary's."

Jehovah's Witness: You have 2 cows. You go door-to-door, telling neighbors.

Vegan: You have 2 cows but must not use them.

Famous characters

Bart Simpson: You have 2 cows. Don't have another cow, man!

Homer Simpson: You have 2 cows. Mmm… cows!

Spock: Dammit, Jim, you have 2 cows! They live long and prosper. That's logical.

Dave Barry: You have 2 cows. They tend to explode. I'm not making this up.

Oprah: You get 2 cows. You get 2 cows. You *all* get 2 cows!

George W. Bush: You have 2 cows. You *own* them. We'll give those 2 cows back to you and invest another 2 of those cows in the stock market to pay your retirement, and we can sell 2 of those cows. My opponent will say that's impossible, but he's just trying to scare you to vote for old-government ways to do things. Under my plan, everyone gets cows back.

Rush Limbaugh: Did you see the news that tree-huggers are after a fellow who owns 2 cows? They say the cows' gaseous emissions cause global warming. Meanwhile, the femi-Nazis say udders insult women's bodies. Well, I'll just keep eating cheeseburgers and shooting cows, because that's why God made them. If white Christian men earn their cows, tax-and-spend Democrats have no right to give them away to welfare moms.

Donald Trump: You have the world's 2 biggest cows. You form a reality show called "Cowprentice," where cows compete to live on your farm. Then you discover your farm's bankrupt.

Illusionist

Quantum physics: Your 2 cows might actually be 1 cow in 2 places.

Law

Shakespeare recommended that we kill all the lawyers. I recommend laughing at them instead.

Courtroom bloopers

In courtrooms, lawyers asked these silly questions:

> Did he kill you?
> Was that the same nose you broke as a child?
> How many times have you committed suicide?
> Were you present when your picture was taken?
> The youngest son, the 20-year-old, how old is he?
> You were there until the time you left, is that true?
> How far apart were the vehicles at the time of the collision?
> Was it you or your younger brother who was killed in the war?

Here are more courtroom transcripts of lawyers and witnesses having trouble communicating:

> Are you sexually active?
> No, I just lie there.
>
> Have you lived in this town all your life?
> Not yet.
>
> Are you qualified to give a urine sample?
> Yes, I have been since early childhood.
>
> Doctor, did you say he was shot in the woods?
> No, I said he was shot in the lumbar region.
>
> Doctor, how many autopsies have you performed on dead people?
> *All* my autopsies have been performed on dead people.
>
> Officer, what led you to believe the defendant was under the influence?
> Because he was argumentary and couldn't pronunciate his words.
>
> Did you tell your lawyer that your husband had offered you indignities?
> He didn't offer me nothing. He just said I could have the furniture.
>
> What can you tell us about the truthfulness and veracity of this defendant?
> Oh, she'll tell the truth. She said she'd kill that son-of-a-bitch, and she did!
>
> What did he do then?
> He came home, and the next morning he was dead.
> So when he woke up the next morning, he was dead?
>
> Can you describe the individual?
> He was about medium height and had a beard.
> Was this a male or a female?
>
> What is your relationship with the plaintiff?
> She's my daughter.
> Was she your daughter on February 13, 1979?
>
> Mrs. Johnson, how was your first marriage terminated?
> By death.
> And by whose death was it terminated?
>
> Are you married?
> No, I'm divorced.
> And what did your husband do before you divorced him?
> A lot of things I didn't know about.
>
> Did you blow your horn or anything?
> After the accident?
> Before the accident.
> Sure, I played for 10 years. I even went to school for it.
>
> How old is your son, the one living with you?
> 38 or 35, I can't remember which.
> How long has he lived with you?
> 45 years.
>
> Do you recall the time you examined the body?
> The autopsy started around 8:30 PM.
> And Mr. Dennington was dead at the time?
> No, he was sitting on the table wondering why I was doing an autopsy.

All your responses must be oral. Okay? What school do you go to?
Oral.
How old are you?
Oral.

What did the tissue samples taken from the victim's vagina show?
There were traces of semen.
Male semen?
That's the only kind I know of.

What was the first thing your husband said to you when he woke that morning?
He said, "Where am I, Cathy?"
Why did that upset you?
My name is Susan.

She had 3 children, right?
Yes.
How many were boys?
None.
Were there any girls?

Do you know how far pregnant you are right now?
I will be 3 months November 8.
Apparently then, the date of conception was August 8th?
Yes.
What were you and your husband doing at that time?

Doctor, before you performed the autopsy, did you check for a pulse?
No.
Did you check for blood pressure?
No.
Did you check for breathing?
No.
So it's possible the patient was alive when you began the autopsy?
No.
How can you be so sure, doctor?
Because his brain was sitting on my desk in a jar.
But could the patient have still been alive nevertheless?
It's possible he could have been alive and practicing law somewhere.

Those transcripts and other weirdos were recorded by court stenographers and collected in several anthologies, such as *Humor in the Court* (1977), *More Humor in the Court*, (1994), *Disorderly Conduct*. (1999), and *Disorder in the Court* (1999 and 2004).

Judges

If you're a good lawyer, you can become a judge, whose job is to make nasty remarks to other lawyers.

Famous female judges Here's a tale of two women; which would you rather be?

Both women are judges in the U.S. Both are over 60 years old.
The first woman runs a small-claims court, which decides little questions such as "Did this guy overcharge for cleaning a shirt?" The second woman is on the U.S. Supreme Court, which decides big questions such as "Is abortion legal?"
The second woman (Ruth Bader Ginsberg) seems to have a better career, except for one detail: the first woman gets paid more. A lot more! 130 times as much!
Ruth Bader Ginsberg's salary is $190,100; the other woman's salary is $25,000,000. That's because the "other woman" is Judy Sheindlin, the "Judge Judy" on TV.
Which would you rather be: a respected Supreme Court jurist (like Ruth Bader Ginsberg) or a rich TV judicial comedian (like Judge Judy)?
Which of those women is more famous? Ruth Bader Ginsberg's writings will become famous through U.S. history books, but at the moment more people know Judy Judy's face. Ruth Bader Ginsberg's decisions will change the laws of the land and how they're interpreted, but Judge Judy is teaching more people how law works.
I'm glad we have *both* women.

How to become a judge A judge is supposed to be an old, wise person who's all-knowing, solving all arguments on all topics.

The British comedy troupe called *Beyond the Fringe* told of a bloke who said:

I'm a miner, but I'm planning to become a judge. When you're old, they say you can't be a miner anymore; it's just the opposite with judges. To prepare to be a judge, I'm reading a book called "*The Universe and All That Surrounds It: an Introduction.*"

Jokes

Lawyers can be mean — and so are jokes about them.

Dogs Lawyers screw their clients' opponents — then screw their own clients by charging large legal fees. Here's a tale of how lawyers screw around:

An architect, a doctor, and a lawyer held a contest to see whose dog was smartest.
When the architect said "Go, Fifi," his dog Fifi immediately constructed an exact replica of the cathedral of Chartres — out of toothpicks. Everybody clapped, and the architect gave Fifi a cookie.
Then the doctor said, "Go, Fluffy," whereupon the doctor's dog Fluffy immediately performed an emergency Caesarian section on a cow. The cow and calf came through the operation fine. Everybody clapped, and the doctor gave Fluffy a cookie.
Then the lawyer said, "Go, Fucker." The lawyer's dog fucked both other dogs, took their cookies, and went out to lunch.

More such tales are in *Truly Tasteless Jokes* (by Blanche Knott).

Barracuda When a boat got shipwrecked, barracuda ate all the passengers except the lawyers. Why not eat the lawyers? Professional courtesy!

Doctor versus lawyer When a doctor crashed his car into a lawyer's, the lawyer asked the doctor, "Are you okay?" The doctor said, "Yeah."

The lawyer said, "Have a drink." The doctor took a swig from the flask and said "Thanks — aren't you going to have one too?" The lawyer replied, "After the police get here."

Noah's Ark

Government creates lots of laws. So if Noah were living in the U.S. now, his tale would go like this:

The Lord told Noah, "A year from now, I'm going to make rain until the whole earth is covered with water and all evil people are destroyed. I command you to build an Ark to save the righteous people and two of every living species." In a flash of lightning, God delivered the Ark's specifications.
One year later, the rain began falling. But the Lord saw Noah sitting in his front yard and weeping, with no Ark. "Noah," shouted the Lord, "where's the Ark?"
Noah replied, "Lord, forgive me. I did my best, but there were big problems.
"First, I had to get a building permit for the Ark. Your plans didn't meet Code, so I had to hire an engineering firm to redraw them. Then I got into a fight with OSHA about the Ark needing a fire sprinkler system and approved flotation devices.
"My neighbors complained that to build the Ark in my front yard violated zoning ordinances, so I had to get a variance from the city planning commission.
"I had problems getting enough wood because there was a ban on cutting trees, to protect the Spotted Owl. I finally convinced the Forest Service that I needed wood to *save* the owls, but the Fish & Wildlife Service won't let me catch any owls.
"The carpenters formed a union and went on strike. I had to negotiate a settlement with the National Labor Relations Board before anyone would pick up a saw or hammer. Now the Ark has 16 carpenters but still no owls.
"When I started rounding up the other animals, I got sued by an animal-rights group objecting that I'd take just *two* of each kind. Just when I got that suit dismissed, the EPA said I couldn't finish the Ark until I file an environmental impact statement on your proposed flood. They didn't take kindly to the idea they had no jurisdiction over the conduct of the universe's Creator.

> "The Army Corps of Engineers wanted a map of the proposed new flood plain. I sent them a globe.
>
> "I'm trying to resolve the Equal Employment Opportunity Commission's complaint about how many Croatians I must hire.
>
> "The IRS seized all my assets because it claims my Ark's goal is to flee the country to avoid paying taxes. The state sent a notice saying I owe a use tax and another saying I failed to register the Ark as a 'recreational watercraft.' The ACLU made the court issue an injunction against further construction, on the grounds that 'God flooding the earth' is a religious event and therefore unconstitutional.
>
> "I can't finish your Ark for at least 5 more years."
>
> The sky began to clear. The sun began to shine. A rainbow arched across the sky. Noah looked up and smiled. "You mean you're not going to destroy the earth, Lord?"
>
> "No," He said sadly. "I don't have to. The government already has."

The original version of that was copyrighted in 1997 by Hugh Holub, and you can read it at www.bandersnatch.com/noah.htm. Thanks, Hugh, for permission to print an edited version here!

War

Most wars are caused by **xenophobia**: fear of strangers. The best way to end wars is to share Pepsi and pizza.

Peace first

Before starting a war, try to resolve the conflict peacefully. If you absolutely must start a war, make sure you're well prepared. Will Rogers said:

> Diplomacy is the act of saying "nice doggie" until you can find a rock.

Revolutionary wars

The American government says the September 11th terrorists did a despicable "cowardly" deed. I thought the word "cowardly" was a strange choice. It's probably what the British said about us hiding behind trees during the Revolutionary War.

In the Revolutionary War for the liberation of America, we hid behind trees and fired at the British, and the British complained it was "unfair" that we weren't standing in an easy-to-shoot line: we weren't following the rules of war; we were unfairly terrorizing the British troops. The families of those troops were quite upset.

In the Palestinian War for the liberation of Palestine, the pro-liberationists hid in planes and kamikazeed civilians in the World Trade Towers. We said it was "unfair" that they killed civilians instead of paid soldiers.

I guess what's "fair" depends on which side you're on.

Whose shoes?

I feel sorry for Palestinians who live in Israel and want to make an honest living. Their thinking goes like this:

> Yeah, go call me "Ali Baba."
> Do you want to buy a shoe?
> Please don't call me now an "Arab,"
> And I won't call you a "Jew."
>
> Say I'm just from Meso'tamia
> Where our Western culture grew.
> Say that Israel is for "us," and
> Not just "me" and not just "you."
>
> What about the *intefada*?
> Is it just for infants there?
> Can us old folks have some peace, or
> Must we tear out all our hair?
>
> I am just a kind commuter,
> Not a looter, not a shooter.
> My computer? Want to boot her
> But no 'lectric power there.
>
> Want to calm her, but the bombers
> Coming out of both sides' lairs
> Make me wish I were a *kishka*
> Or a *hummus* dumpling there.
>
> Sure, go call me "Ali Baba."
> Do you want to buy a shoe?
> Please don't call me now an "Arab,"
> And I won't call you a "Jew."
>
> Call me "Frank." I'll call you "Moe."
> Then mo'e frank we both will go;
> And our children, they will thank us,
> And our parents will not spank us,
> As together we will grow,
> Searching for our heaven's glow.
>
> — by Rasaalah Al-Walta
> (Russell Walter's Arabic cousin)

America's first popcorn war

Back in the early 1960's, John Kemeny (who invented the Basic programming language) said wars should be replaced by video games, where the opponents would fight each other on screen, winner take all.

Here's what actually happened… the time is March 2003, and you are there…

> Saddam is attacked by Baby Bush, but the media treats the whole "War against Saddam" as just a football game, similar to the Super Bowl. We wait for the referee to fire the opening shot. It's the first scheduled war: "War will begin at 8PM EST." We get stats on all the players, with pre-game comments from the coaches and quarterbacks. We get to see whether Bush attacks up the middle or does an end-run around the defensive tackles; whether he lobs some passes up into the air or throws straight ahead, Tomahawk style; and whether the sides, in their strategy huddles, lift their fingers with fake signals to fool the enemy. The TV shows photos of the quarterbacks, Bush & Saddam, displayed side-by-side.

20 years from now, if both of those men were still alive, they'd look back and reminisce about the "good old days" when they had sporting fun baiting each other at the Big Game and how they both managed to change the history of the world, especially the world's international relations, laws, rules, and assumptions.

While watching the battle, I was sorry to be out of popcorn. I was eating a veggie burrito instead, which fortunately is non-political, since we haven't attacked Mexico yet.

Hey, that's an idea: instead of "food for oil," let's fight for "food for burritos." Burritos are better than a steak bomb.

I waited for the Food Channel to show a snobby chef recommending the best food for war watching. "May we suggest the fillet? Perhaps after an aperitif?"

This war was great fun: for the first time, Bush was seen by most of the world as more evil than so-damn-insane Saddam Hussein. I wondered when Bush would feel tired of fighting, "bushed."

This whole war was actually based on sex. Bush & Blair (heads of the U.S. & England) were young, their penises still strong and frustrated, and they wanted to attack Saddam's opening, to come to an orgasmic conclusion to the crisis. The heads of France and Germany were older, tired, and just wanted the young headstrong men to quiet down and stop disturbing Europe's nap time.

After the battle and recriminations, Bush and Saddam should have shaken hands and exchanged after-dinner mints.

France

When France objected to the U.S. war on Saddam Hussein, the U.S. laughed at the French. Here's a collection of anti-French humor:

"Going to war without France is like going deer hunting without an accordion." — Jed Babbin

"The only time France wants us to go to war is when the German Army is sitting in Paris sipping coffee." — Regis Philbin

"I don't know why people are surprised that France won't help us get Saddam out of Iraq. After all, France wouldn't help us get the Germans out of France!" — Jay Leno

"What do you expect from a culture that exerted more of its national will fighting against Disney World and Big Macs than Nazis?" — Dennis Miller

"You know why the French don't want to bomb Saddam Hussein? Because he hates Americans and wears a beret. He's French." — Conan O'Brien

"I'd rather have a German division in front of me than a French one behind me." — General George S. Patton

"France has neither winter nor summer nor morals. France has usually been governed by prostitutes. Apart from those drawbacks, it's a fine country." — Mark Twain

On the other hand, Jacques Chirac, who was France's President, said:

As far as I'm concerned, war always means failure.

Military advice

Here's advice from *Infantry Journal* about how to fight:

If the enemy is in range, so are you.
Try to look unimportant: they may be low on ammo.
If your attack's going too well, you're walking into an ambush.
5-second fuses last just 3 seconds.

Here's more fighting advice, from members of the military:

When the pin is pulled, Mr. Grenade is not our friend.
Don't draw fire: it irritates the people around you.
Any ship can be a minesweeper… once.
Bravery is being the only one who knows you're afraid.
Never tell the platoon sergeant you have nothing to do.
Never be the first, never be the last, and never volunteer.

Here's advice about flying, from the Air Force:

It's generally inadvisable to eject directly over the area you just bombed.

Try to stay in the middle of the air. Don't go near its edges, which can be recognized by the appearance of mountains, ground, buildings, sea, trees, or interstellar space. It's much more difficult to fly there!

Airspeed, altitude, and brains: two are always needed to successfully complete the flight.

When faced with a forced landing, fly the thing as far into the crash as possible.

Never fly in the same cockpit with someone braver than you.

Weather forecasts are horoscopes with numbers.

Flashlights are metal tubes kept in a flight bag to store dead batteries.
The only time you have too much fuel is when you're on fire.

If you see a bomb technician running, follow him.

When one engine fails on a twin-engine plane, you always have enough power left to get you to the scene of the crash.

If you crash because of bad weather, your funeral will be on a sunny day.

Without ammo, the Air Force would be just another expensive flying club.

You've never been lost until you've been lost at Mach 3.

What's the similarity between air-traffic controllers and pilots? If a pilot screws up, the pilot dies; if the ATC screws up, the pilot dies.

The 3 most famous last phrases in aviation are "Why is it doing that," "Where are we," and "Oh shit!"

The military likes to poke fun at itself:

Marines, U.S. Marine Corps.: "Here's what M.A.R.I.N.E.S. stands for: muscles are required, intelligence not essential, sir! Here's what U.S.M.C. stands for: Uncle Sam's misguided children."

Navy intelligence: "In God we trust; all others we monitor. You didn't see me, I wasn't there, and I'm not here now."

Air Force weapons troops: "Without weapons, it's just another airline."

Army: "If you spell U.S. ARMY backwards, you find out what it really stands for: yes, my retarded ass signed up."

Coast Guard: "Support search-and-rescue: get lost."

That list is part of what's on page 140 of *Uncle John's Bathroom Reader, 18th edition*. For more fun, get that edition and the other editions, too!

Engineers

How does a "mechanical" engineer differ from a "civil" engineer? The Internet gives this answer:

Mechanical engineers build weapons. Civil engineers build targets.

Cute dictators

Donald Rumsfeld was Secretary of Defense under presidents Ford and Bush Junior. He bragged that Saddam Hussein met the same end as other bad dictators, such as Hitler, Stalin, Lenin, and that Romanian guy whose name is hard to spell.

But was **Lenin** really so bad? Compared to Stalin, Lenin was cute.

So was **Saddam's son, Odai**. Sure, Odai had a reputation for being ridiculously cruel, even crueler than his dad. But when I look at photos of his face, before and after his death, I just melt, because his face is so cute. I finally realized it's because he looks like the Italian actor Marcello Mastroianni: he has the same cute smile and puppy-dog eyes. Too bad Odai's dead: he could've had a wonderful movie career. His dad raised him wrong.

Even **Osama Bin Laden** — who dictates to terrorists — looked cute. He looked just like the Jewish longhairs I went to school with. Too bad he disliked my group and started a cafeteria food fight, throwing airplanes. I don't understand his goal: the Palestinian cause already got worldwide attention and sympathy; what did he expect to gain by making Moslems become disliked? He seemed immature. He was just a kid throwing temper tantrums, forcing the rest of the world to childproof everything, for protection from him.

African missionaries

Bishop Desmond Tutu, from South Africa, said:

When the missionaries came to Africa, they had the Bible and we had the land. They said, "Let us pray." We closed our eyes. When we opened them, we had the Bible and they had the land.

American cultures

Supposedly a melting pot, America sometimes seems more like a meltdown of minds on pot.

Holidays

Holidays are when you're supposed to join family and friends, to give your heart a warm glow. But some of us worry that the glow comes from a radioactive facade.

On **Thanksgiving**, we walk up to the dinner table, bow our heads, and pray:

> Dear Lord, thanks for not making us be turkeys, Indians, or Pilgrims. Thanks for not making us attend that first Thanksgiving dinner, whose participants all became hunted creatures. Thank God we weren't there! And could Thou please make our current relatives vanish?

Just on **Mother's Day** does Mom get off from kitchen work: Dad takes her to dinner. To even the score, Mom tells the kids to buy him a tie but not strangle him with it until **Father's Day**.

On **Christmas**, we celebrate the universe's biggest miracle: that Joseph believed his wife when she said she got pregnant from "nobody." This is a Jewish holiday: Christians pay Jewish merchants to create a holiday that stimulates the economy. Homeless bums wander in the snow while mumbling carols such as "Chestnuts roasting on a funeral pyre."

On **Easter**, Christ vanished and gave us the miraculous bunny who lays eggs tasting like chocolate.

On **Halloween**, the ultimate "casual day," we wear costumes showing bosses, friends, and neighbors how we really feel. This is the day when you can change your sex without raising an eyebrow: just raise your pitchfork.

February gives you a double challenge:

> **Valentine's Day** is the only day you can wish your lover "Happy VD!" On this day, you anticipate getting a card from a "secret admirer" — in vain.
>
> On **Presidents' Day**, the ghosts of Washington & Lincoln join forces to erase their true birthdays and create a joint holiday, when Americans smoking joints buy big cars by nagging presidents of dealership joints.

So in February, if you don't find perfect love, you get the booby prize of buying a car instead.

Martin Luther King Day was created by people who care about equality of car sales, to let you buy cars in January, before Presidents Day, so fewer car salesmen will commit January suicide. It's the day when car salesmen, happy at not having to wait another month for glory, sing "We shall overcome you *today*!"

On **Saint Patrick's Day**, we dress up as little green Martians, but when asked "Where are you from?" we pretend to be tipsy saints from "Ireland."

On **Memorial Day**, we remember the poor creatures who died on our behalf in past years. Then we barbecue more of them because they taste so good.

On **Labor Day**, we thank unions for standing up for their rights, so prices go up and economists can claim the economy is growing and give us the stock market's Santa Claus rally at Christmastime.

Independence Day is when we Americans celebrate being independent from England, which is too civilized. **Columbus Day** is when we honor the man who got lost and dumped us here.

Sinful holidays

Fact: for the original Pilgrims, Thanksgivings were days of fasting, prayer, and attending Thursday sermons. Just in recent years did Thanksgiving become the holiday of gluttony.

Gluttony is one of the 7 sins. God granted us Americans the inalienable right to create holidays celebrating all 7 sins:

7 deadly sins	Holidays to celebrate them
pride	Independence Day (pride in America)
greed	Christmas (greed to get presents)
envy	Easter (envy at fashions)
anger	Martin Luther King Day (anger at racism)
lust	Valentine's Day
gluttony	Thanksgiving
sloth	Labor Day (workers get to relax)

Runaway Christmas

Different families celebrate Christmas in different ways. Here's a charming example of how a girl can spend Christmas:

> 'Twas the night after Christmas, and all through the flat
> Not a creature was stirring — not even a bat.
>
> My dad was well hung from the day he spent screwing.
> My mom was too drunk to know what he was doing;
>
> And me in my panties and you in your shorts
> Had just settled down with white magic to snort,
>
> When out of the door there arose such a banging
> We knew 'twas the landlord preparing our hanging.
>
> We jumped out the window — a long way to fall —
> Then dashed away, dashed away, dashed away all!
>
> The landlord exclaimed as we ran out of sight,
> "Merry Christmas, you turkeys! I'm changing the lock.
> Your stuff is in hock. Don't come back tonight!"

Christmas party

Planning a Christmas party can be a challenge, according to these memos on the Internet:

> December 1 from Patty Lewis, Human Resources Director, to all employees
> I'm happy to say the company Christmas party will take place on December 23, at noon in the banquet room of Luigi's Open Pit Barbecue.
> Plenty of eggnog! We'll have a band playing carols; feel free to sing along. Don't be surprised if our CEO shows up dressed as Santa!
> A Christmas tree will be lit at 1PM. Employees can exchange gifts then; but to make gift-giving easy for everyone's pocket, no gift should be over $10. Our CEO will make a special announcement at that time.
> Merry Christmas to you and your family!
>
> December 2 from Patty Lewis
> In no way was yesterday's memo intended to exclude our Jewish employees. We recognize Hanukah's an important holiday that often coincides with Christmas, though unfortunately not this year. From now on, we're calling it our "Holiday" party. The same goes for employees celebrating Kwanzaa.
> There will be no Christmas tree, no Christmas carols sung. We'll have other kinds of music for your enjoyment. Are you happy now? Happy Holidays to you and your family!
>
> December 3 from Patty Lewis
> Regarding the note I received from a member of Alcoholics Anonymous requesting a non-drinking table: you didn't sign your name. I'm happy to accommodate that request, but if that table has a sign saying "AA only," you wouldn't be anonymous anymore. How am I supposed to handle this?
> Forget about the gifts exchange. No gift exchanges will be allowed, since union members feel $10 is too much, and executives think $10 is too chintzy.

December 4 from Patty Lewis

What a diverse group we are! I had no idea that December 20 begins the Muslim holy month of Ramadan, which forbids eating & drinking during daylight. Perhaps Luigi's can hold off on serving your meal until the party's end (since the days are so short this time of year) or package everything for take-home in little foil swans. Will that work?

Meanwhile, I've arranged for members of Overeaters Anonymous to sit farthest from the dessert buffet. Pregnant women will get the table closest to the restrooms.

Gays are allowed to sit with each other. Lesbians don't have to sit with gay men; each group will have its own table. Yes, there will be a flower arrangement for the gay men's table. To the person wanting to cross-dress: sorry!

For short people, we'll have booster seats.

For those on a diet, we'll have low-fat foods. Since we can't control salt in the food, people with high blood pressure should taste first. The restaurant can't supply sugar-free desserts for diabetics, but there will be fresh fruit.

Did I miss anything?

December 5 from Patty Lewis

December 22 marks the Winter Solstice? So what? What do you want me to do, tap-dance on your heads? Fire regulations at Luigi's prohibit burning of sage by our "earth-based Goddess-worshipping" employees, but we'll try to accommodate your shamanic drumming circle during the band's breaks. Okay?

December 6 from Patty Lewis

C'mon, people! Nothing sinister was intended by having our CEO dress up like Santa! Even if the anagram of "Santa" happens to be "Satan," there's no evil connotation to our own "little man in a red suit." It's a tradition, folks, like sugar shock at Halloween, family feuds over Thanksgiving turkey, and broken hearts on Valentine's Day. Could we lighten up, please?

The CEO's changed his mind about having a special announcement at the gathering. You'll be notified instead by mail sent to your home.

December 7 from Patty Lewis

I have no f*ing idea what CEO's announcement will be about. What the f* do I care? I know what *I'm* going to get!

If you change your address now, you're dead! No more changes of address will be allowed in my office. If you try to come in and change your address, I'll have you hung from the ceiling in the warehouse!

Vegetarians!?!?!? I've *had* it with you people! We're going to keep this party at Luigi's Open Pit Barbecue whether you like it or not. You can sit at the table farthest from the "grill of death," as you put it. You'll get your f*ing salad bar, including hydroponic tomatoes; but you know, *they* have feelings, too. Tomatoes scream when you slice them. I've heard them scream. I'm hearing them scream right now!

I hope you all have a rotten holiday! Drive drunk and die, you hear me? Signed, the bitch from Hell!

December 8 from Terri Bishop, acting Human Resources Director

I'm sure I speak for all of us in wishing Patty Lewis a speedy recovery from her stress-related illness. I'll keep forwarding your cards to her at the sanatorium.

Management's decided to cancel our Holiday Party and instead give everyone the afternoon off. Happy Holidays!

Aging

We're always getting older. At a camp where I was a counselor, the staff used to sing:

> No matter how old a prune may be,
> He's always getting wrinkles.
> A baby prune is just like his dad,
> Except he's only half as bad.

When you get older, you gain wisdom and lose hair.

Hair today, gone tomorrow

When I was young and hairy,
I saw the world with glee.
But now I'm fat and balding,
A lump on which birds pee.

Just one thing makes me proud,
Though this might sound quite lewd:
At least I'm old and wise
Enough to not get screwed.

And when I meet the angels
(Or red guy with the tail),
I'll greet my hosts politely
Then shut my eyes and wail.

"You're 25"

If a woman asks you how old she looks, Joe Kita says you should answer "25," because that's the age all women want to be: women under 25 want to look as wisely mature as 25, while women over 25 want to look as youthfully pretty as 25.

I guess that means women who actually *are* 25 suffer by being content but bored, since they have nothing to look forward to and nothing to look back to reminisce about.

Though I respect Joe — he's editor of *Men's Health* magazine and author of the *Guy Q* book — I don't think his advice is realistic.

If a woman looks 5 years old or 90 years old, saying she looks "25" will just get a laugh. Instead, try this:

Take 25, then add double the woman's apparent age, then divide by 3.

That gets you a weighted average between 25 and her appearance. That weighted average will still be ridiculously complimentary; but instead of just laughing, the woman will actually believe you.

But if the woman then asks "Did you take the weighted average by reading *Tricky Living*?" you're in trouble.

Age tests

According to the Internet, here are 11 signs you're getting old and you're past your college days:

You go from 130 days of vacation time to 14.
6AM is when you get up, not when you go to bed.
You actually eat breakfast food at breakfast time.
You don't know what time Taco Bell closes anymore.
A $4 bottle of wine is no longer "pretty good shit."
Your car insurance goes down and your car payments go up.
Jeans and a sweater no longer qualify as "dressed up."
You hear your favorite song in an elevator.
Older relatives feel comfortable telling sex jokes around you.
Your friends marry and divorce instead of "hook up" and "break up."

When you find out your friend is pregnant, you congratulate the couple instead of asking "Oh, shit, what the hell happened?"

Take this test of your past culture (passed through the Internet with the help of folks such as Father Dennis McNeil):

This test will determine your age group — or how much TV you've watched in your youth. Have fun and no cheating (answers are at the end).

1. Name the 4 Beatles: __, __, __, and __.

2. Finish this line: "Lions and tigers and bears, __, __!"

3. "Hey kids, what time is it?" __ __ __ __!

4. What do M&M's do? __ __ __ __, __ __ __ __.

5. What helps build strong bodies 12 ways? __ __.

6. Long before he was Mohammed Ali, we knew him as __ __.

7. You'll wonder where the yellow went, __ __ __ __ __ __ __.

8. Post-baby-boomers know Bob Denver as the Skipper's "little buddy." But we know Bob Denver is actually Dobie's closest friend, __ G. __.

9. M-I-C: see ya' real soon! K-E-Y: __? __ __ __!

10. "Brylcreem: __ __ __ __ __ __."

11. Bob Dylan said never trust anyone __ __.

12. From the early days of rock 'n roll, finish this line: "I wonder, wonder, wonder, wonder who, __ __ __ __ __ __?"

13. And while we're remembering rock n' roll, try this one: "War… uh-huh,huh… yeah; what is it good for? __ __."

14. Meanwhile, back home in Metropolis, Superman fights a never-ending battle for truth, justice, and __ __ __.

15. He came out of the University of Alabama and became one of the best quarterbacks in NFL history. He later went on to appear in a TV commercial wearing women's stockings. He's Broadway __ __.

16. "I'm Popeye the sailor man; I'm Popeye the sailor man. I'm strong to the finish, __ __ __ __ __ __. I'm Popeye the sailor man."

17. Your kids probably recall that Peter Pan was recently played by Robin Williams, but we'll always remember when Peter was played by __ __.

18. In a 1967 movie, Paul Newman played Luke, a ne'er-do-well sent to prison camp for cutting off heads of parking meters. When Luke was captured after an unsuccessful escape attempt, the camp commander (played by Strother Martin) used this experience as a lesson for other prisoners and explained, "What we've got here is, __ __ __ __."

19. In 1962, a dejected politician chastised the press after losing a race for governor while announcing his retirement from politics. "Just think, you won't have __ __ to kick around anymore."

20. "Every morning, at the mine, you could see him arrive; He stood 6-foot-6, weighed 245. Kinda' broad at the shoulder and narrow at the hip. And everybody knew you didn't give no lip, __ __, __ __ __ __."

21. "I found my thrill, __ __ __ __."

22. __ __ said, "Good night, Mrs. Calabash, __ __ __ __."

23. "Good night, David." "__ __, __."

24. "Liar, liar, __ __ __ __."

25. "When it's least expected, you're elected. You're the star today. __! __ __ __ __."

26. Pogo, the comic-strip character, said, "We have met the enemy, and __ __ __."

Answers

1. John, Paul, George, and Ringo
2. oh, my
3. It's Howdy Doody Time
4. They melt in your mouth, not in your hand
5. Wonder Bread
6. Cassius Clay
7. when you brush your teeth with Pepsodent
8. Maynard G. Krebbs
9. Why? Because we like you
10. a little dab'll do ya
11. over 30
12. who wrote the book of love
13. Absolutely nothin'
14. the American way
15. Joe Namath
16. 'cause I eats me spinach
17. Mary Martin
18. failure to communicate
19. Richard Nixon
20. Big John, Big Bad John
21. on Blueberry Hill
22. Jimmy Durante, wherever you are
23. Good night, Chet
24. pants on fire
25. Smile! You're on Candid Camera
26. he is us

Scoring

24-26 correct: you're probably 50+ years old
20-23 correct: most likely in your 40's
15-19 correct: are we in our 30's?
10-14 correct: must be in your 20's!
1- 9 correct: you're, like, sorta a teenage dude?

Baby boomers

Here's another insight from the Internet:

Baby boomers then and now

then: long hair
now: longing for hair

then: acid rock
now: acid reflux

then: a keg
now: an EKG

then: getting out to a new, hip joint
now: getting a new hip joint

then: killer weed
now: weed killer

then: moving to California because it's cool
now: moving to California because it's hot

Dementia

When you get old, your brain might have trouble working properly: you'll lose your memory, be senile, act demented. The most common form of dementia is **Alzheimer's disease**, where you forget the purpose of things.

Elderly people are scared that they might be getting demented. Here are some quick tests:

If you forget where your keys are, that's normal; but if you forget what your keys are *for*, you're demented.

If you were ironing your clothes but forget where you put your iron, that could be normal; but if you put your iron in the freezer, that's demented.

If you put clean dishes into the dishwasher, you're probably either demented or Chinese. (The Chinese often use their dishwashers just as storage racks.)

British researchers have discovered this quick test for **pre-Alzheimer's** (having an Alzheimer-damaged brain even through you don't act crazy yet): within one minute, name as many fruits & vegetables as you can think of. (You can name fruits or vegetables or a mix.) If you're normal, you'll name at least 20; if you have pre-Alzheimer's (or Alzheimer's), you'll name no more than 15 (because your mind will repeatedly mull over the first 15 and have difficulty breaking loose to go beyond them). As for myself, I score about 17, so I guess I'd better be careful!

One reason why the elderly seem demented is that they have trouble focusing on the task at hand. My crazy relative passed me this e-mail from the Internet:

Do you have AAADD?

They've finally found a diagnosis for my condition. Hooray! I've recently been diagnosed with AAADD — Age-Activated Attention-Deficit Disorder… Here's how it goes.…

I decide to wash the car; I start toward the garage and notice the mail on the table. Yeah, I'm going to wash the car; but first I'd better go through the mail. I lay the car keys on the desk, discard the junk mail, and notice the garbage can is full. I'd better take it out; but since I'm going to be near the mailbox anyway, I should pay these bills first. Where's my checkbook? Oops, there's just one check left. My extra checks are in my desk. I'd better get them.

Oh, there's the Coke I was drinking. I'll look for those checks; but first I must put my Coke farther from the computer — or maybe I'll pop it into the fridge to keep it cold awhile. As I head towards the kitchen, flowers catch my eye: they need water. I set the Coke on the counter and… Oh! There are my glasses! I was looking for them all morning! I'd better put them away first. I fill a container with water, head for the flowerpots, and… Aaaaaagh! Someone left the TV remote in the kitchen. We'll never think to look in the kitchen tonight when we want to watch TV, so I'd better put it back in the family room where it belongs. I splash some water into the pots and onto the floor, throw the remote onto a cushion on the sofa, head back down the hall, and try to figure out what I was going to do.

End of day: the car isn't washed, the bills are unpaid, the Coke is still on the kitchen counter, the flowers are half-watered, the checkbook still has just one check in it, and I can't find my car keys!

When I try to figure out why nothing got done today, I'm baffled because *I know I was busy, all day long!* I realize this is a serious condition and I'll get help, but first I think I'll check my e-mail.…

Please send this to everyone you know because *I don't remember whom I've sent this to!* But please don't send it back to me or I might send it to you again!

Geography

To challenge your friends, ask these tricky geography questions:

What's the most populous city that's east of Reno and west of Denver? Kids think the answer is Salt Lake City or Las Vegas, but the correct answer is Los Angeles.

Not counting Alaska, which state goes farthest north? Kids think the answer is Maine, but the correct answer is Minnesota.

Which state is closest to Africa? Kids think the answer is Florida, but the correct answer is Maine. To prove it, look at a globe (not a traditional map, which is distorted).

Which state has the point that's farthest from Hawaii? Kids think the answer is Maine, but the correct answer is Florida. To prove it, look at a globe (not a traditional map, which is distorted).

What's the only Midwestern state whose name is not derived from a Native American word? The correct answer, ironically, is Indiana, since all the other Midwestern states — Minnesota, Wisconsin, Iowa, Illinois, Missouri, Michigan, Ohio, Kansas, and Nebraska — have Native American origin.

Which 2 states are the most crowded (have the densest population)? New Jersey and Rhode Island.

Which 2 states are the least crowded (have the least dense population)? Alaska and Wyoming.

Which state has the most states on its border? It's a tie: Missouri and Tennessee each touch 8 states.

What's the only spot where 4 states meet? The corner of Utah, Colorado, New Mexico, and Arizona.

Which state is completely surrounded by water? Hawaii.

Which 3 states are totally artificial (no border has a river, lake, or ocean)? Utah, Colorado, and Wyoming.

More geography puzzles are in the geography chapter of Peter Winkler's *Mathematical Puzzles*. (The other chapters are about advanced math.)

Vermont

Vermont is a bunch of farmers manipulated by outsiders.

Even the name "Vermont" was invented by an outsider, Dr. Thomas Young of Pennsylvania, in 1777. Since the place was full of green mountains and a bunch of radicals called "Ethan Allen and the Green Mountain Boys," Dr. Young named it "Vermont," which is archaic French for "Green Mountain." He named it in French instead of English to make the place sound as high-falutin' as a French restaurant.

"Ethan Allen and the Green Mountain Boys" tried to keep Vermont independent from the evil colonies of New York and New Hampshire, which wanted to capture it. Vermont stayed an independent republic until 1791, when it became the 14th state.

For a while, Vermont was full of dairy farms and had more cows than people. During the 1970's, many hippies from New York moved to Vermont to get away from the city rat race and commune with nature. They tried to become farmers but discovered they were more successful at milking tourists than cows. Many tourists visit Vermont in the fall to see the leaves turn color while the cows moo.

Ben & Jerry

Ben and Jerry were a pair of New York Jewish hippies, both born in Brooklyn, 4 days apart. In 1977 they moved to Vermont, where they started a factory that turned Vermont milk into fattening ice-cream for hoity-toity New Yorkers, who felt less guilty about getting fat because Ben & Jerry gave them just tiny portions and donated part of the profits to liberal causes. In the year 2000, the company became secretly owned by Unilever, a Dutch-English conglomerate.

Farmer talk

Vermont farmers have an amazing gift of language. They talk in a slow drawl that's very effective at deflating the egos of their natural enemies, such as bureaucrats, academicians, lost drivers, tourists, spendthrifts, New Hampshirites, and Texans.

Vermonter versus the bureaucrat This is a true tale. A Vermonter fell off the roof of a barn and died. The insurance company gave his family a death certificate to fill out. The certificate was long and complicated. At the bottom of the certificate was a space labeled "remarks." For "remarks," the family wrote, "He didn't make none."

Vermonter versus the academician A Vermonter riding a train struck up a conversation with the passenger next to him, who happened to be a Harvard professor. The Vermonter admired the Harvard professor's brilliance, and the Harvard professor admired the Vermonter's common sense.

The professor suggested a contest to see who could "stump" the other person. The person who couldn't answer the question would have to pay 50¢.

"Okay," said the Vermonter, "but since you're so much smarter, I think it would be fairer for you to pay me a dollar."

"Okay," agreed the Harvard professor. "You go first."

"Well," said the Vermonter, "What has three legs and flies?"

"I give up," said the Harvard professor. "Here's your dollar. What's the answer?"

"Darned if I know," replied the Vermonter. "Here's your fifty cents!"

Vermonter versus the lost driver Walter Piston (a famous Harvard music professor) was driving through Vermont, got to a fork in the road, and asked a Vermonter, "Does it make any difference which road I take?" The Vermonter replied, "Not to me, it doesn't."

Vermonter versus the tourist Many tourists visit Vermont in the summer. One of them told a Vermonter, "You have a lot of peculiar people around here." The Vermonter replied, "Yep, but most are gone by mid-September."

Vermonter versus the spendthrift Vermonters don't like to spend money. Vermont legislators say, "When in doubt, vote no. Let's not get something we don't need and pay for it with money we don't have."

Vermonter versus the New Hampshirite Robert Frost wrote a long poem called *New Hampshire*, which proclaimed page after page of praise for New Hampshire's beauty. But to understand the poem's true meaning, you must read the last line, which says simply and proudly, "*I* live in Vermont."

Vermonter versus the Texan A Vermonter was chatting with a Texan, whose drawling wisdom was no match for the Vermonter's.

Texan:	What kind of farm ya got?
Vermonter:	Oh, I got a coupla acres.
Texan:	Why, why that's a *piddlin'* small farm. Why, where ah come from, ah kin git in mah car and drive *half a day*, befo' ah git ta the end of mah farm!
Vermonter:	Yup, I had a car like that myself, once.

Recorded tales Those tales were collected by Al Foley, a Dartmouth College history professor who became a member of the Vermont legislature and president of the Vermont Historical Society. Hear him speak on a 33 RPM record called *A Vermont Heritage*.

New Hampshire

Like most Americans seeking adventurous fun, I moved to New Hampshire, the laughable state nicknamed "New Ha-ha."

Laws

New Hampshire's the most libertarian state. It believes in the fewest laws. The state's motto is "Live free or die," uttered by General Stark centuries ago and interpreted by modern New Hampshirites to mean "Get the government off our backs."

Taxes New Hampshire brags that it has **no sales tax**, **no income tax**, and **no other "broad-based tax,"** which meaning "no tax affecting everybody."

That sounds great and makes many idiots move here. After moving, we discover that the Machiavellis who run the government created many "little" taxes that affect "just a few" people. Here are little examples:

> There's a hefty 8% tax on "restaurant meals, hotel rooms, and rented cars." But that's not called a "broad-based" tax, since it affects just tourists (or natives who act like tourists).
>
> There's a huge "real-estate transfer" tax on buying a house and a huge "property" tax on using your house after you've bought it. But they aren't considered "broad-based" taxes, since you can always live in an apartment instead. (Then your landlord has to pay the hidden 8% "room rental" tax; but that's his problem, not yours.)
>
> There's a huge tax on registering your car. But instead you can jog or use a bicycle or skates — or take a bus, if you don't mind waiting several hours for the bus to show up. (In New Hampshire, search for a bus is like searching for a Puerto Rican: it requires sleuthing.)
>
> There's also an "interest & dividends tax" (for people who earn lots of money from bank interest or stocks), a "business profits tax" (for businesses that make a lot of money), and a "telecommunications tax" (on your phone bill). But you can avoid them if you have no money, no business, and no phone, so they're not called "broad-based" taxes.

So in New Hampshire, you can "live free of taxes" just if you hide under a rock.

No restrictions In New Hampshire, you can do whatever you want, if you don't get dangerously huffy about it.

For example, **you can drive a car without getting a driver's license**. I was really surprised about that. When my stepdaughter wanted to learn how to drive, I asked the Department of Motor Vehicles about how to get her a "learner's permit," so she could practice; but the Department said she didn't need one: she could just go ahead and drive. The only restriction is that a licensed driver must be next to her in the front seat and she has to say she's "learning."

In New Hampshire, **you don't need car insurance** — unless you're such a dangerous driver that the state declares you an exception. So I don't have car insurance. I don't have home insurance or health insurance either. If my car hits you or you trip on my lawn, just take me to court and take my house. Then I'll have the pleasure of sitting outside and not having to pay the property tax.

New Hampshire is the only state where **you don't need to wear a seat belt** if you're an adult, even if you're the driver. New Hampshire believes you have the God-given right to kill yourself on the highway. Seatbelts are required just for kids under 18, who are too young to appreciate the finer pleasures of suicide.

If you want to ride a motorcycle dangerously, go ahead: **you don't need to wear a helmet**. Massachusetts bikers love to come to New Hampshire and discard their helmets when they reach our border, so they can feel the wind blowing in their hair — and later feel their heads bobbling on the asphalt. As a result, New Hampshire is the state that has the most motorcycles per 1000 people.

Want to buy a gun? No problem. Just go to a store, say you want to buy a gun, and in less than half an hour you've got it. You don't need a license: just wait the half hour for the store's computer to check you're not a felon.

You can carry a gun with you, loaded, practically anywhere you wish, without a license — even into your local bank or convenience store. The only restriction is you can't take it onto a plane or into certain government buildings. If you carry a loaded gun, just make sure it's visible, so everybody can see it and get properly scared and nervous: don't hide it! (If you want to hide it, you must remove the bullets first, so you don't get arrested for carrying a "concealed loaded weapon.") But if you're stupid enough to carry a loaded visible gun into a bank or convenience store, be prepared to get tackled by a nervous rookie policeman — who'll then apologize to you for having impinged on your New Hampshire rights.

If you don't want to pay a highway toll, you don't have to. That's because New Hampshire lawmakers made a mistake when writing the highway-toll law, and they're too lazy to fix it. The law accidentally says it's illegal for New Hampshire to arrest you for not throwing coins into the toll basket.

Want to kill your mom? Well, that's against the law. We New Hampshirites need to have some limits! But it's okay to strangle a squirrel.

Politics New Hampshire is run mainly by Republicans who tote guns. But they're kind enough to donate shelters to Democrats who escaped from Boston when Boston's real estate got too expensive for normal folks to live in.

For a while, the Republicans were kind enough to let a Democrat lady become governor. She was a kind lady who believed in education. When she had trouble balancing her budget, she decided the fairest solution was to add a sales tax and income tax. The voters decided the fairest solution was to get rid of her. They did. So we still have no sales tax and no income tax. We also got a new governor —Republican, of course — who still couldn't balance the budget. Now the newest governor is a Democrat again, but he's just a *token* governor, since his Republican legislature won't let him do anything.

Since I'm a Democrat, I'm morally required by the Democrat religion to believe the fairest tax is an *income* tax, since it taxes the rich more than the poor. But I admit I secretly enjoy the evil pleasure of being in New Hampshire, since it's sure nice to avoid the bureaucratic hassles of figuring sales tax and income tax and filling those stupid forms all you Non-Hampshirites must fill each year.

My friends back in Massachusetts love to taunt me by reminding me that "New Hampshire is great place to live, as long as you don't have a handicapped kid or break a leg or need any other kind of social service." New Hampshire ain't keen on offering such services. Remember the New Hampshire motto: "Live free or die," which means:

> If you're not good enough to live freely, just go die — or move to Massachusetts. Let *them* take care of you!

Snow

In New Hampshire, God is a frustrated artist: He keeps trying to draw out the perfect snowstorm. He keeps dumping his efforts on us in His attempt to create the perfect snow landscape but never quite gets it right. Finally, one day, the frustrated Deity of Dramatic Weather gives up, smiles, and breaks out singing:

> I can't get snow satisfaction —
> And I try, and I try, and I try, and I try.
> I can't get snow, snow!
> Snow, snow, snow!

Then He creates — for His finale — one final gigantic snowstorm, called "The Oy's of March."

Afterwards, he takes His bow. That's called "spring." The flowers come up and applaud his past achievements but are secretly relieved to see the concert's over.

Oops! I said the forbidden word "spring"! I shouldn't have said that. In New Hampshire, we're not allowed to say "spring." Natives say instead, "It's the mud season," because that's when the snow starts melting and all the shit is sopping wet. Each "yard" becomes a series of rivers and waterfalls running under the snow — until finally old man Sun gets really hot and angry and lets the birds chirp. But then "The Old Man in the Mountain" (New Hampshire's godlike mountain stone face, still alive in spirit) gets grumpy, tells the birds to shut up, and throws snow on them — for many days in a row — in April or May. That's called "Whitey's surprise party."

In New Hampshire each year, the weatherman admits again that "March came in like a lion and went out like a moose: a big, lumbering surprise whose journey was unpredictable."

In other states, pixies sing "April showers bring May flowers." In New Hampshire, we sing "April crud brings May mud."

But if life here weren't an adventurous challenge, why would anyone come?

During what month does snow here start? The answer is: "Whenever you don't expect it." For example, on a bright, sunny day in mid-October, I was foolish enough to ask my neighbor Tom (a policeman who's lived here for many years) when snow would start. He said, "December or late November, but never before November 15th." I shouldn't have asked. Just asking the question sealed my fate: the very week I asked, it snowed many times, to drive home the point that newbies shouldn't ask such stupid questions. It also reminded me that to find out what goes on here, don't ask a policeman.

While other states have a storm that "rains cats and dogs," in New Hampshire it "snows bears and moose."

Since our gigantic storms hit us unpredictably, here's how we New Hampshirites chat with our next-door neighbors:

> "What's new?"
> "What snow!"
>
> "What now?"
> "Don't know!"
>
> "Here it comes!"
> "Here we go!"
>
> "Holy cow!"
> "Holy Mo'!"

During winters, New Hampshire farmers don't say "Have a nice day." Instead they say:

> Have an iced hay.

That sounds the same but is more realistic, since you can never have a "nice day" during a New Hampshire winter.

Dartmouth College

New Hampshire's most famous college is Dartmouth. It was started centuries ago as a missionary school to teach Indians about religion and English. None of the Indians got to speak English real well, but the best of the bunch was sent to England to try to raise donations. His pitch was, basically, "Me Indian. Me speak English. You want more Indians to speak English? Give money." Nobody gave very much. The idiot who gave the most was the Earl of Dartmouth, so they decided to name the college after him, in the hopes he'd give more. He never gave another cent.

Like New Hampshire weather, Dartmouth College is full of extremes: a hotbed of liberals peppered with silly arch-conservatives. For example, the arch-conservative student who lived down the hall from me hung a Confederate flag on one wall, hung a Rhodesian flag on the other, and wore an upside-down peace button showing a bomber and the words "Drop it!"

When Democrats vying to be "President of the United States" visit New Hampshire, they love to stop at Dartmouth College and give speeches there, so liberals will cheer them and make them feel good. Then the rest of the state, which is mainly Republican, ignores them.

Manchester

I live in New Hampshire's biggest city, which is spelled "Manchester" but pronounced "Manch has duh." That pronunciation summarizes the city: Manch has, duh, stupid people. When I lived in Boston, I had the pleasure of chatting with advanced Harvard and M.I.T. students about the meaning of life; but now I'm stuck in Manchester, where the main intellectual question is:

> Who has the greenest lawn — and why?

At first glance, Manchester is just a dying mill town, full of abandoned boarded-up textile mills along the river. But at second glance, Manchester is… still an abandoned mill town. Not until you take a third glance do you realize Manchester is full of secrets, such as:

It's the only U.S. city whose main street has two dead ends. That's one reason why Manchester is called "dead-end city." The other reason is that living in Manchester will make your career go nowhere — like mine.

The only famous person who grew up in Manchester is comedian Adam Sandler. When he was a high-school student, he insisted in history class that Abraham Lincoln was Jewish, because the textbook said Lincoln was shot "in the temple."

Though Manchester is New Hampshire's "biggest city," it's small: just 110,000 people. Most of them live in suburban-style houses and within a 10-minute drive of each other.

Manchester has the best buffet deals, because of endless buffet wars here. The current buffet-war winner is the Manchester Buffet Restaurant, which stuffs you with unlimited high-quality American, Chinese, and sushi for just $6.75 (if you're smart enough to come at lunchtime) or $5.75 (if you're even smarter and use the newspaper's coupon).

Manchester has the best deals on foot-long sandwiches. The winners are the foot-long veggie at the Subway inside Wal-Mart and the pastrami sub at the Mobil gas station near my house.

Though Manchester is small and in Yankee territory, it includes ridiculously many foreign restaurants: Italian, Greek, Mexican, Portuguese, Brazilian, Chinese, Thai, Polynesian, Japanese, Vietnamese, Korean, Indian, Nepalese, and French Canadian.

Nobody living in Manchester really wants to be here, but people live here anyway because the housing is cheap, there's no sales tax, and Manchester is just an hour from each kind of fun: Boston, the ocean, the lakes, the mountains, and skiing.

Manchester has New England's best airport, offering cheap, fast parking ($2) and discount airfares (on Southwest Airlines and competitors).

Manchester is where you'll find the house decorated to look like a piano: the chimney's bricks are painted to look like a giant piano keyboard.

Manchester has New England's best newspaper: it's a weekly, called *The Hippo*.

Manchester contains many cultures:

It has houses with big lawns, for the rich.

It has low-cost apartments, for the poor.

It has hotels, for tourists en route to fall foliage, winter skiing, summer hiking, and presidential candidates.

It has a drag strip full of shopping malls, surrounded by huge parking lots to hold **Massholes** (visitors who come from Massachusetts to avoid sales tax).

It has a downtown full of shops, restaurants, and wild bars (where bands perform and slutty girls gamble their lives away, giving Manchester the nickname **ManchVegas**).

It has a quiet lake, where visitors relax and residents get their drinking water. (Please don't piss in the pool!)

It has a riverbank lined with hundreds of abandoned textile mills, which developers quickly turn into industrial-chic restaurants and other "playgrounds for the rich."

South of Manchester, you see hoards of Democrats who wanted to keep living in Massachusetts but could no longer afford Massachusetts' expensive housing. North of Manchester, you see rustic tribes of Republican outdoorsmen who want government to "leave them alone": they hate Democrat socialists. Manchester is the dividing line between those two cultures, where the Democrats and Republicans clash.

Manchester is where you'll find the hotel on which this poem is based:

The Fleabag Hotel

Police just released me. I'd nowhere to go —
Just dumped in the park, in the rain, in the dark.
I asked fine hotels, "Have you room?" They said "No,
The rooms are all taken for kids' graduation."

A cabbie said, "Sonny, I'll show you a door
That always has room — like a bride for her groom."
Just 5 minutes later, we got there. Oh, swell:
I found myself joining the Fleabag Hotel.

Atop a high hill overlooking its prey,
The Fleabag Hotel guarantees a bad day.
For victims who enter, there's no other way:
You pay for your stay and then pray you're okay.

Your life is real Hell at the Fleabag Hotel,
Where each ne'er-do-well gives his personal yell.
Broke bums join this hole when they're out on the dole;
Cute toughs grab this goal when they're out on parole:
Their violence beams to your eyes, which can't nod.
You hear ev'ry bod say "Fuck you!" and "Oh, God!"

Stained carpets, gray foam make this "home" far from home.
The water pipes groan as the banged-up girls moan.
The lights on the fritz make the danger signs flash.
All paint's peeling off. "We take cards, checks, and cash":
The man at the desk tries to sell a night's rest.
Your chest fills with screams in your night beyond dreams.

The ceilings all leak, dripping yellow from rain.
The floors kindly creak, just to harmonize pain.
Don't breathe when you're there, or you'll take in the stench
Of old cigarettes and each weary whipped wench.
The bathrooms' black mold covers curtains and walls.
No "tissue rolls" there, so you'll *scratch* ass and balls.

The curtains, too short, don't quite hide you from peeps
By gangs who come round to turn losers to weeps.
The phones never work: "You don't call police, please."
The exits are locked, so don't try to run. Freeze,
And hope for the best as you hear clanging chains
All strike, just to test how your neighbors take pains.

You come for a treat, but you leave feeling beat
From bright candy canes that sure mess up your brains.
The girls who were slain in the bed where you've lain
Shall haunt you with blood that was poured down your drain.
I don't understand all this. Neither should you.
Just stay far away, so you won't be there too.

Okay, I confess I exaggerated a bit: not *all* the rooms have blood in the drains.

Boston

Years ago, I moved to Boston and made it my home town. Here's why.

Who lives in Boston?

Boston is America's most intellectual city. It bulges with about 100 wonderful colleges, and its suburbs contain others that are even more prestigious, such as Harvard University, the Massachusetts Institute of Technology (M.I.T.), Wellesley College, and Tufts University.

M.I.T. is New England's top engineering school. Most students at M.I.T. are tops in engineering (and science & math) but weak in humanities. Many students at Harvard are the opposite: bright in humanities but weak in science & math. Hence this incident:

At a supermarket, a young man buying 13 items enters the express-checkout lane. The cashier says, "You must be from Harvard or M.I.T." The man says, "Yes! How did you know?" The cashier points to the "12 items or less" sign and says, "You're from Harvard (so you can't count) or M.I.T. (so you can't read)."

Boston subways are packed with students. The main subway station treats you to free music by student musicians.

In Boston subways, the image is "students" — unlike New York subways, where the image is "drunks." I'll never forget when I returned from a trip to Europe and found myself on a New York subway, where I saw a charming young couple cuddle. Behind them, out of their view, an old drunk woman was cursing them and pointing her finger at them. Her finger finally touched the back of the young woman's neck. The young woman jumped out of her chair and yelled out a fearful scream. Then the old woman vomited all over the subway car.

That could happen just in New York, not Europe, not Boston.

Many Bostonians are escapees from New Jersey. As youngsters, they lived in New Jersey, graduated from fine high schools there, and got admitted to prestigious Boston-area universities. When they graduated from the universities, they'd fallen so in love with Boston that they didn't want to leave — and certainly didn't want to return to New Jersey! So they decided to live in Boston permanently. On the walls of their Boston apartments, they hang Kliban's cartoon showing a man running away from a smokestack and entitled "Houdini escaping from New Jersey."

Though Boston can charm you awhile, many Bostonians eventually move beyond it, to Maine's countryside, just a few hours away. Maine is populated mainly by escapees from Boston, just as Boston is populated by escapees from New Jersey. Ornithologists call that the "migration pattern of creative humans."

Before escaping to Maine, intellectual students are torn between a love of Boston and a love of San Francisco, whose suburbs include the great universities of Berkeley and Stanford. But San Francisco is worse than Boston in three ways: its monotonously foggy climate denies you the thrill of seeing golden sunshine and snowstorms; its steep hills, like warts, prevent you from jogging across the city smoothly; and it lacks Boston's old-world charm. On the other hand, Bostonians visiting San Francisco are forced to confess that compared to San Francisco, Boston is a third-world country, technologically and socially 3 years behind.

Visitors

Boston is a magnet that draws visitors from all over the world. We get to shake hands with proud parents (of Harvard students), French Canadians (coming "south" to Boston to spend an enjoyable day), history buffs (gaping at the birthplace of the American Revolution with its Boston Massacre, the Boston Tea Party, Paul Revere's ride, and Battle of Bunker Hill), engineers (analyzing the high-tech companies encircling Boston), and nature lovers (wandering through Boston while searching for beautiful fall foliage).

Yes, they come from all over. On the sideway leading up to my Boston apartment, I even found a matchbook saying, "Toot'n Totum is the only home-owned chain of convenience food stores in Amarillo." I feel proud that my sidewalk's magnanimous enough to receive litter from Amarillo, Texas.

What Europe gave Boston

Boston is America's most European city. The street I've lived on is so pretty and quaint that my visitors believe they've been magically transported to an English fairy tale.

Boston has a history of being loads of fun, beginning with how the city got its name. Centuries ago, England had a saint called "Saint Botolph," who started a town called "Botolph's town," which got shortened to "Bo's town," then further shortened to "Boston." That's how the English city of Boston got its name. America's Boston was named after England's.

Neighbors

Boston's a patchwork of hundreds of tiny neighborhoods, each 4 blocks long and a fascinating microcosm of society.

The most famous neighborhoods are:

the **Combat Zone** (the red-light district), **Chinatown** (next to the Combat Zone), **Haymarket** (where Italians stand on the sidewalk to peddle fruits and meats), **Hanover Street** (where Italians beg you to come in their restaurants and pastry shops), **Quincy Market** (a paradise full of singles bars, hand-held foods, and lunchtime sunshine for secretaries), **Newbury Street** (where rich bitches buy uppity clothes, while the wish-we-were-rich gaze longingly from cafés), **Bay Village** (where gay men live in cute houses), the **Fenway** (the park for gay flowers and gay men), **Northeastern University** (where blue-collar students drag Africans, Iranians, and Venezuelans down to their level), **Beacon Hill's south side** (where the richest Bostonians live), and **Beacon Hill's north side** (whose slopes are as severe as San Francisco's, with charming houses hopelessly subdivided into teensy apartments for students).

But those neighborhoods are just the obvious ones. Walk 4 blocks in any direction, and you'll discover yet another neighborhood!

Moreover, in Boston, every single block has its own character — and its inhabitants are proud of it. Whenever a Bostonian reveals his address, he gives it with pride.

My own neighborhood I lived in Boston on Saint Botolph Street, which years ago became famous for its prostitutes. One of my elderly readers sent me a letter admitting that while a student back in the 1940's, he flunked his freshman year at M.I.T. because he spent too much time on Saint Botolph Street.

The prostitutes eventually left Saint Botolph Street and moved to lusher pastures, but the street's reputation lives on, and it's attracted a strange bunch of folks — such as me!

My own neighbors My neighbors on Saint Botolph Street were lots of fun.

Down the hall from me was a pair of bedrooms whose occupants shared my kitchen and bath. That pair of bedrooms became home to many of Boston's finest citizens:

"Mr. Neat" turned on the iron, rested it on the wood floor, then went off to work. (I guess he thought he was hot stuff — or am I just being ironic?)

"Mr. Drunk" came home every night at 3AM, turned on the oven, put his TV dinner into the oven, then flopped into bed with the oven still on — so each night I was awakened by a smoke cloud engulfing my building.

"Mr. Sportsman" put a dartboard on his door and threw darts at it, to discover how many times he'd miss the board. Then he complained to the landlady about how his door was full of holes.

"Mr. Clean" insisted on hanging his towel inside the bathtub, complained we got it wet, and retaliated by throwing water on everybody else's towel every day.

"Mr. Honeymooner" borrowed a few hundred bucks from me for his honeymoon — and never came back.

"Mr. Gay" loved to cuddle his gay boyfriend in the kitchen.

"Mr. Gone" simply disappeared. At the end of the year, on December 31, when his lease ran out, he vanished. His parents and employer asked me where he went. I opened his room and found everything covered by a layer of cigarette butts, beer bottles, unread mail, shredded newspapers, and unwashed clothes, which when sniffed indicated they'd been unwashed for at least 6 months. On the wall, he'd hung all mirrors backward, so he wouldn't have to look at himself. His personal effects were all there, but *he* was missing. We shrugged our shoulders, figured a suicide, and wondered how to tell his parents. Since a new tenant was coming the next day, we tried hard to clean the room and hide his effects fast. Several weeks later, the "dear departed" phoned us and said just "Sorry, but I had to get away."

Those characters living down the hall can't compare to the neighbors in the adjacent buildings. For example, one night at 7PM, while I was lying in bed after a hard day's work, I heard someone yell "Jump!" I looked out my window, and saw a guy jump out of the window next to mine. His whole building was on fire. The 5-alarm fire needed 11 fire trucks to put out the blaze. The building was totally ruined; but we weren't surprised, since it was the 5th fire there in 5 months. We figured it was arson for insurance money. Sure enough, the building was converted (at no expense to the landlord) into one of Boston's finest condos.

The building on the other side of me also burned to the ground, in a dramatic blaze that was the highlight of the 11PM news. That building's occupants escaped by athletically leaping from their windows into ours. The poor guys in our own building were shockingly awakened from sleep by guys leaping into their windows while shouting "Fire!"

It was probably arson again, since it had the same result: the building was replaced with one of Boston's finest condos.

So now I have condos on both sides of me. That's how Boston's neighborhoods improve.

But before that latest fire, I got a real kick out of the people who lived in that building:

"Miss Bouncy" jumped out of the 4th-floor window to escape from her sister — and survived because she bounced off the roof of a car.

"Mr. Drummer" got up each morning at 5AM and tuned his steel drum. He sure knew native rhythms, since he made all his neighbors howl at him and gyrate violently while hoisting their weapons.

"Mr. Beater" loved to beat his dog for howling out the window. His neighbors achieved similar pleasures by beating their wives and babies.

In that building, the main source of income was drugs and fencing stolen goods. Truly an outstanding tribe of entrepreneurs!

But in that building, my favorite family was the one where mom and dad would disappear each day and leave their two 5-year-old girls alone in the apartment. Those two cute little girls spent the entire day there, every day, smoking cigarettes — except whenever they left their room, climbed up on the roof, and pretended to jump off. I'd give them a friendly wave from my window, and they'd wave back. To solidify the friendship, they came over to my building, found the circuit breaker, turned off all my building's electricity,

then lit my building on fire by cleverly setting a match to the lobby's rug.

When my landlady tried to explain to them that nice little girls don't set fires to buildings, those two cute little girls told her, "Go away, ya old biddy!" When my landlady told their mom they'd been lighting fires, their mom said it was impossible because the girls couldn't get matches. When I told the mom her girls were indeed using her matches daily to light cigarettes, she wasn't upset that her girls had been smoking, playing with matches, and lighting fires; instead, she was thrilled to find out why she was always short of matches.

When the police investigated, they found her tiny room housed not just her two daughters but also her many boyfriends and a big collection of scattered whiskey bottles. The police took the girls into protective custody. Shortly afterwards, the girls' building burned, totally. I wonder why.

Edwin Arlington Robinson

When I was hunting for a room to live in, I happened to wind up at "92 Saint Botolph Street," because it was fine but cheap. After moving in, I discovered that one of my neighbors was one of my heroes: the famous poet Edwin Arlington Robinson lived just a few doors away, at 99 Saint Botolph Street. Years earlier, when I was a high-school kid in New Jersey, I loved reading his poems, so I was thrilled to discover he lived just a few doors away. Unfortunately, I never met him, since he died 22 years before I was born. We were both tortured writers.

In case you don't remember who he was and can't spend much time to learn, here are my **abridged versions** of poems he wrote in 1897, as part of his book called *The Children of the Night*….

Recite this poem when you're jealous of a rich person or think of killing yourself:

Richard Cory

Whenever Richard Cory went downtown,
We people on the pavement looked at him:
He was a gentleman from sole to crown,
Clean favored, and imperially slim.

And he was always quietly arrayed,
And he was always human when he talked;
But still he fluttered pulses when he said
"Good morning," and he glittered when he walked.

And he was rich — yes, richer than a king —
And admirably schooled in every grace:
In fine, we thought that he was everything
To make us wish that we were in his place.

So on we worked, and waited for the light,
And went without the meat, and cursed the bread;
And Richard Cory, one calm summer night,
Went home and put a bullet through his head.

Recite this **villanelle** (poem with repeated lines) when you move out of your home (or the White House's occupant changes at the end of the 4-year term, or the House of Representatives goes on vacation):

The House on the Hill

They are all gone away,
  The House is shut and still,
There is nothing more to say.

Through broken walls and gray
  The winds blow bleak and shrill:
They are all gone away.

Nor is there one today
  To speak them good or ill:
There is nothing more to say.

There is ruin and decay
  In the House on the Hill:
They are all gone away,
There is nothing more to say.

Give this retort if your friends complain you waste too much time writing poetry instead of making big bucks:

Dear Friends

Dear friends, reproach me not for what I do,
Nor counsel me, nor pity me; nor say
That I am wearing half my life away
For bubble-work that only fools pursue.

And if my bubble be too small for you,
Blow bigger then your own:
Remember, if you will,
The shame I win for singing is all mine,
The gold I miss for dreaming is all yours.

Boston's old-world charm keeps getting struck by lightning thoughts from its professors and students:

Boston

How Boston always like a friend appears,
And always in the sunrise by the sea!
And over it, somehow, there seems to be
A downward flash of something new and fierce,
That ever *strives* to clear (but never clears)
The dimness of a charmed antiquity.

Street people

As you walk down Boston streets, you'll meet the Dickensian characters who give Boston its special charm.

For example, a guy on Boylston Street wears a green plastic garbage bag on his head. An art professor named "Sidewalk Sam" has painted beautiful pictures on the sidewalk. "Mr. Yankee Doodle" has the amazing ability to whistle Yankee Doodle so loudly that he can be heard for many blocks — but with his mouth nearly closed, so nobody knows he's the culprit. Another guy sports a black beard, black sunglasses, black cap, and black shopping bag and spends his whole life standing against a wall.

Friendliness

Boston is friendlier than New York. In New York, everybody is distrustful, expects to get ripped off or mugged, and lives in fear. In Boston, muggings are equally popular and prices are even higher — but nobody minds, because Boston's crooks all smile.

Boston is more manageable than New York. New York is too big: it overwhelms. Boston's buildings are shorter and its neighborhoods are tinier, so a brief walk through Boston lets you feel you've mastered it all. In Boston, you feel you own the city; in New York, you feel the city owns you.

Fantasyland

My dad called Boston a "toy city" because of its tiny buildings, tiny neighborhoods, and tiny inhabitants (mainly kids who are students). He was a serious German who preferred New York, which he called the "real" city. (Cynics call New York the "real" mess!)

I love Boston, because I love to live in fantasyland.

Boston's in Massachusetts, whose biggest fantasy was George McGovern. In the 1972 Presidential election, Massachusetts was the only state that voted for McGovern instead of Richard Nixon. After Nixon won, botched Watergate, and had to resign, Massachusetts cars sported proud bumper stickers saying, "Don't blame me — I'm from Massachusetts!"

Weather

Boston is the 3rd windiest city in the United States. It's much windier than Chicago. According to our beloved government, the only cities windier than Boston are Oklahoma City and Butte Montana (if you don't count Washington D.C.'s windbag politicians).

Boston's average wind speed is 12½ miles per hour. But that "average" is misleading. Sometimes, the air is perfectly still. At many other times, the wind whips by at 100 miles per hour — especially near Boston's Hancock Tower.

Boston's in New England, where the weather continually changes, quickly and unpredictably. Back in the 1800's, Mark Twain said, "If you don't like New England's weather, wait a minute." He also said:

> The weatherman confidently checks off what today's weather is going to be on the Pacific, down South, in the Middle States, in the Wisconsin region. See him sail along in the joy and pride of his power till he gets to New England, then see his tail drop. He doesn't know what the weather's going to be in New England. He mulls over it and by and by gets out something like this: "Probable northeast to southwest winds, varying to the southward, westward, eastward, and points between; high & low barometer swapping around from place to place; probable areas of rain, snow, hail, and drought, succeeded or preceded by earthquakes, with thunder and lightning." Then he jots this postscript to cover accidents: "But it's possible the program may be wholly changed in the meantime."

Everywhere else, the weather is created by God. But in Boston, the weather is created by God's son, "J.C.," who's a student at M.I.T. For his student project, J.C. launches the most daring weather experiments, using Bostonians as his guinea pigs. Whenever Boston's passionate suffering excites him sufficiently, he exports the weather to the rest of New England and finally to the rest of the world.

Driving

Here's mankind's biggest challenge: driving through Boston.

For example, suppose you're trying to visit a friend who says he lives on "A Street." If you look at a map, you'll find that Boston contains three streets called "A Street." There's an A Street in the part of Boston called "Charlestown"; but 2½ miles southeast of that, you'll find another A Street, in the part of Boston called "South Boston"; and 6 miles southwest of that

second A Street, you'll find a third A Street, in the part of Boston called "Hyde Park."

Similarly, Boston contains three B Streets. Boston also contains five Lincoln Streets, five Pleasant Streets, and six Park Streets.

After figuring out which A Street to go to, your next problem is to figure out which streets will take you there. That's a major challenge, since practically every street in Boston is curved.

Boston was planned by meandering cows: each old street was a cow path, curved to avoid hills and ditches. When Boston city planners lopped off the hills to fill the ditches, they forgot to straighten the cow paths, so Boston's streets are still curved, to avoid the hills and ditches that no longer exist. In Boston's intellectual suburb (Cambridge), Massachusetts Avenue curves so sharply that the natives describe Harvard University as being "at the corner of Massachusetts Avenue and Massachusetts Avenue."

Traffic signs To make Boston driving a challenge, most of the popular streets are marked "One Way," usually in the opposite direction from where you want to go, and with no obvious alternative route in sight. Those signs were put up at the request of neighbors who don't want to deal with folks like you. To increase your challenge, Boston city planners consider street signs to be optional, so that you're never quite sure which street you're on. The few street signs that remain are often wrong.

My favorite signpost is on the outskirts of Boston. At the top of the post, a sign says you're going south; underneath it is a sign that says you're going north. Altogether, the signs say you're going south on route 93 and north on route 128. Which direction are you really going in: south or north? The correct answer is neither: you're really going west!

But suppose you're nerdy enough to bring a map that even shows which streets are one-way. Your troubles aren't over yet: you're just about to turn left onto the street you wish, which even goes in the direction you wish, when all of a sudden you're confronted by a sign saying "No Left Turn." To be legal, you try to somehow drive around the block, but you get a surprise: each side of the block has a combination of "One Way" and "No Left Turn" signs designed so that you can't reach your destination. "You can't get there from here" is a popular saying in Boston. Every taxi driver knows the only solution: interpret the "No Left Turn" sign to mean "Turn left as fast as possible, before anybody notices."

Traffic lights You can always tell a newcomer to Boston by the way he reacts to traffic lights. He's under the mistaken impression that a red light means "stop." In Boston, a red light does *not* mean "stop"; instead, it means "think about it, slow down a little, stare at the other cars, honk your horn at them, then continue straight through."

A yellow light means "drive faster, before it turns red." A green light means "wait for the cars in the other direction to finish going through their red light; then race."

Rotaries Boston city planners suffer from one major fetish: rotaries. Maybe it's because Boston's run by Irish Catholics, who misspell "rosaries"?

Driving experts have discovered that Boston and China are the only places in the whole world that have so many rotaries.

Driving into a Boston rotary is like jumping into a washing machine, filled with live sharks during the "spin" cycle: coming out is either miraculous or bloody.

Jams Boston traffic is so heavy that you're guaranteed to find yourself in a massive traffic jam before you reach your destination.

Three of Boston's main arteries are Storrow Drive, the Southeast Expressway, and the Mystic River Bridge. Because they're the sites of so many traffic jams, they're called "Sorrow

Drive, the Southeast Distressway, and the Misery River Bridge."

Parking To park, seasoned Boston drivers use the "Braille method," which consists of bumping the cars surrounding you until you finally nestle into the space between them.

When you come back the next day to retrieve your car, don't be surprised if it's gone. Boston's become famous as the car-theft capital of America. If you park your car, and it's still there the next day, you'll pat yourself on your back for being lucky — until you burst out in tears when you see the parking ticket. Nearly every parking space in Boston is marked "illegal." A parking ticket can cost you $100 or more, depending on how cleverly you found an illegal place to park.

Jargon Instead of saying "turn left," Bostonians say "bang a left." Instead of saying "U-turn," Bostonians say "U-ey" (pronounced "yoo-ee"). Instead of saying "make a U-turn," Bostonians say "bang a U-ey."

No Republicans

Boston's a Democrat city. In Boston, calling somebody a "Republican" is equivalent to calling the person an "ass." The **Phoenix** (Boston's underground newspaper) has run many personal ads where women say they want to date a man, any nice man, but "no Republicans."

In **Cambridge** (the town containing Harvard and M.I.T.), Democrat Al Gore beat George W. Bush during the year 2000 elections, of course. But here's the shocker: during that election, even Ralph Nader beat Bush. Yes, Bush came in 3rd.

Little peculiarities

Boston's peculiar.

Charles River The Charles River separates Boston from its intellectual suburb, Cambridge (home of Harvard and M.I.T.). Three major bridges cross the Charles River: one bridge goes to Harvard; one goes to M.I.T.; and the middle bridge comes from Boston University and goes to nowhere.

The bridge that comes from Boston University is called the "Boston University Bridge." But the bridge that goes to M.I.T. is not called the "M.I.T. Bridge"; instead it's called the Harvard Bridge, because Harvard owns it.

As you walk across the Harvard Bridge, from Boston to M.I.T., look down near your feet: you'll see a surprise! Painted onto the sidewalk is a marker saying "10 Smoots." As you continue walking, you come to a marker saying "20 Smoots," then markers saying "30 Smoots," "40 Smoots," etc., until you reach bridge's far end, where the final marker says "364.4 Smoots, plus one ear." Here's why:

In the early 1960's, an M.I.T. student with the unfortunate name of "Oliver Smoot III" was taking a class whose professor gave this assignment: measure the length of the Harvard Bridge in an unusual way. The night before the assignment was due, he hadn't yet begun working on it; instead, he spent the whole evening getting drunk with his fraternity brothers in Boston. To help him find the length of the bridge, his fraternity brothers finally _rolled him across the bridge_. Altogether, they had to roll him 364.4 times — plus one ear!

The Charles River is beautiful, especially during the spring, when it's dotted with sailboats. But its beauty is just on the surface: underneath, it's polluted. One hot summer day, the water's surface evaporated, to let the polluted water underneath reached the air and give off such a strong sulfurous stench that the drivers on Storrow Drive were overcome by the fumes, lost control of their cars, and crashed into each other!

Scrod Boston is famous for a fish dish called **scrod** (young Atlantic cod & halibut, split for cooking) and for **intellectual cab drivers** (often foreign students), which combine in this tale:

A lady got in a Boston cab and asked the driver, "Where can I get scrod?" He replied, "I never heard it conjugated that way before."

Wednesday Boston's the only city where "Wednesday" has a special meaning. In fact, the best way to determine how long a person's lived in Boston is to ask, "What's Wednesday?" If the person can't answer the question correctly, the person isn't a true Bostonian.

For many decades, Boston was covered with signs proclaiming the answer: "Wednesday is Prince Spaghetti day."

Those signs were courtesy of the Prince Spaghetti Company, whose first factory was on Boston's Prince Street and whose owners were Italians who believed that "midweek" ought to mean "pasta."

John Hancock Tower The John Hancock Tower is Boston's tallest building, but you can make it disappear! Here's how....

Stand on Boylston Street, on the block between Clarendon Street and Dartmouth Street. Stand directly under the "R" of the green "STATE STREET BANK" sign.

From that position, the entire John Hancock Tower seems to "disappear." Specifically, the building's longest sides (which are a whole city block long) hide from your view (because they sit at a peculiar angle), so the entire Tower seems to be just a narrow, fragile, tall wall of unsupported glass.

Street performers The best street performers are the ones you find each summery day in front of Quincy Market. One group, called the "Shakespeare Brothers," has an amazing way with words. The other group, called the "Dueling Bozos," juggles on unicycles. Both groups include magic, audience participation, and practical jokes; they give you the best laughs to be had in Boston.

I remember the first time I saw the Shakespeare Brothers; I'll never forget their act, which consisted of fake magic.

For example, one of the brothers had a deck of cards. He made a girl in the audience pick a card, not show it to him, and hide her card in the middle of his deck. Then he said he'd make her card rise to the top of his deck. He tapped his deck three times, and said her card was now at the top of his deck. He asked what her card had been. She said, "the Jack of Diamonds." He looked at the top card, saw it was not the Jack of Diamonds, saw it was the Ace of Spades instead, and said, "See, I magically turned her card into the ace of spades!" The crowd cheered wildly. We all enjoyed the joke.

And that's why we all love Boston. Boston isn't a city: it's a joke. It's the world's best-kept zoo. And we love it.

New York boroughs

New York City is divided into 5 boroughs: Manhattan, Queens, Brooklyn, the Bronx, and Staten Island.

Manhattan

Some folks say the Indians called the main borough "Manhatton" when they saw it getting overrun by European men who wore stupid hats.

Staten Island

Some folks say "Staten Island" got its name when Henry Hudson first saw it and asked his crew:

's dat an island?

Some say it should be spelled "Statin Island" because its residents love to pop pills that are statins (such as Lipitor).

The Bronx

This is the only borough that requires you to say "the" before it: you must say "the Bronx." Here's the true reason why:

> The place began as farmland bought by Jonas Bronck from the Indians in 1642. When his family owned it, people visiting there said "I'm going to the Broncks." Eventually, "Broncks" got shortened to "Bronx."

Queens

This borough was probably named after Queen Catherine of England in 1683, though historians aren't sure. In 1988, the government of Queens decided to erect a huge statue of her, 35 feet high, facing the United Nations (which is across the river in Manhattan), with encouragement from Donald Trump and Jimmy Carter. But when statue was built, Queens citizens refused to let it stay in Queens, because of these objections:

> If the Queen faces the U.N. (which is in Manhattan), she'll show her backside to Queens citizens and seem to fart at them. Moreover, she'll stand at the spot where Americans turned chicken and ran from the British in the Revolutionary War, so don't put a statue honoring British royalty there!
>
> The Queen was from England, which oppressed Ireland, so the Irish in Queens consider her an oppressor.
>
> The Queen headed Spain while its Catholic government burned 60 citizens for the crime of "being Jewish" during the Spanish Inquisition, so the Jews in Queens consider her an oppressor of Jews.
>
> The Queen was actually the daughter of Portugal's king, who gave her to King Charles II of England along with a dowry that included all of Bombay India and trading rights (in return for England's promise not to attack Portugal), so people from India dislike her — and so do blacks, who are upset that her family made profits by shipping slaves.

Queen Catherine quickly became the most disliked woman in Queens. Now her statue hides in upstate New York, where her face got mutilated by Mother Nature and poorly reconstructed by an apprentice sculptor.

Brooklyn

In Brooklyn, old Jewish residents speak English with a strange accent:

> Instead of saying "the," Brooklynites say "duh."
> Instead of saying "girl," Brooklynites say "goil."

The most famous example of a Brooklyn accent is this poem:

> I have a goil named Goity.
> She really is a boid!
> She lives on toity-second,
> Right next to toity-toid!

In that poem, "goil" means "girl," "Goity" means "Gertie," "boid" means "bird," "toity" means "thirty," and "toid" means "third," so the girl lives on 32nd Street.

Southern accents

The "South" is the home of the "sweet mouth." People there speak so charmingly!

Texas

The Southern part of the U.S. blooms with many strange accents — and they all converge in Dallas.

One girl in Dallas told me that she "sang behind the pasture." I wondered why she sang to the cows, until I realized she meant she sang behind the pastor, in church.

When I attended a math class in a Dallas junior-high school, one of the girls talked about "ot," and all her classmates understood her — except me. Later, I found out what "ot" was: the number that came after 7.

If 20 people gather in a room, how can you spot the Texans? A friend told me to spot them by asking everybody in the room to say "Osborne." The only people he ever met who say pronounce it "Osburn" instead of "Ozborn" are from Texas.

My Alabamian roommate, James, says you can tell a true Southerner from a fake by noticing how the person uses the expression "y'all."

> A true Southerner says "y'all" only when talking to a group, not to an individual. If you watch a TV movie that's supposed to take place in the South but one of the actors says "y'all" to another actor, you know that the actors and scriptwriter are all damn Yankees.

A naughty TV show, "Candid Camera," photographed Southerners trying to explain the difference between how they said "all" and "oil." The Southerners thought they were pronouncing the words differently from each other, but Yankee ears couldn't hear any difference and thought the Southerners were making fools of themselves.

Here's how to translate to Texan:

English	Texan
Can I help you?	Kin ah hep you?
Would you like some chicken?	Kin ah hep you to some chicken?
Can I drive you home?	Kin ah carry you home?
Come again!	Y'all come back now, heah?
I live in rural Texas	Ah live in rule Texiz.
I'm in the oil business.	Ah'm in the awl bidness.
I need some cash.	Ah need some cash money.
I want to chat with you on the phone.	Ah need ta visit with you on the phone.
That makes no difference.	That makes no nevermind, anyhow anyway.
Maybe I could do that.	Ah might could do that.
I swear.	Ah swan.
I swear I'll do it.	Ah'll do it, ah swan!
Amazing! He killed it!	Ah swan, he killed it!
We had a drought.	We had a drouth.
The milk's gone bad.	The milk's gone blinky.
I knocked over a bucket of fresh milk.	Ah tumped over sweet milk.
I threw rocks at the squirrels.	Ah chunked rocks at the squirrels.
Let's fight over the wishbone.	Let's fight over the pulley-bone.
He's my father.	He's mah fatha.
She told him her complaints.	She told him right off how it was.
She divorced him.	She gave him the gate.
They got divorced.	They split the sheets.

You can find more Texan translations in *How to Talk "Texian"* (Robert Reinhold's article in The New York Times on July 22, 1984, section 6, pages 8-10).

Kentucky

When Toyota built a car factory in Kentucky, Toyota's Japanese employees took a course in how to speak Kentuckian, which is similar to Texan. They were taught that in Kentuckian, "can" is pronounced *kin*:

Ordinary English:	Yes, I can do it.
Kentuckian pronunciation:	*Yes, ah kin do it.*

More confusingly, in Kentuckian the word "can't" is pronounced *can* (since the *a* is held a long time, in a drawl, and the *t* is pronounced too quickly and too softly to hear):

Ordinary English:	No, I can't do it.
Kentuckian pronunciation:	*No, ah can do it.*

So if a Kentuckian says *can*, the Kentuckian means "can't."

The Japanese learned this important lesson: when a Kentuckian says he "*can*" do a job, the Kentuckian isn't lying, just drawling.

Foreign cultures

The U.S. culture tries to dominate the world. That's why other countries call it the **vulture culture**.

Here's an old riddle:

What do you call somebody who speaks many languages? "Multilingual"
What do you call somebody who speaks two languages? "Bilingual"
What do you call somebody who speaks just one language? "American"

According to the Internet, the United Nations conducted a worldwide survey whose only question was:

Please give your honest opinion about the solution to the food shortage in the rest of the world.

The survey failed because nobody understood the question.

In Africa, they didn't know what "food" meant.
In Eastern Europe, they didn't know what "honest" meant.
In Western Europe, they didn't know what "shortage" meant.
In China, they didn't know what "opinion" meant.
In the Middle East, they didn't know what "solution" meant.
In Australia, they didn't know what "please" meant.
And in the U.S., they didn't know what "the rest of the world" meant.

Back in the 1500's, the emperor of the Holy Roman Empire was Charles V. He was truly international: he grew up in France (and Belgium), but his mother was Spanish, his father was German, and when he became emperor his territory included Italy. Here's how he explained the difference between French, Spanish, German, and Italian:

I speak Spanish to God, Italian to women, French to men, and German to my horse.

A T-shirt in the British Virgin Islands says:

Heaven is where the police are British, the cooks are French, the mechanics German, the lovers Italian, and it's all organized by the Swiss.

Hell is where the chefs are British, the mechanics are French, the lovers Swiss, the police German, and it's all organized by the Italians.

Here's how the captain of a sinking cruise ship convinces the passengers to jump overboard:

He tells the English it would be "unsporting" of them not to jump.
He tells the French it would be the "smart" thing to do.
He tells the Germans it's an "order."
He tells the Italians that jumping overboard is "forbidden."

The world keeps changing. Here's an expanded version of statements by Charles Barkley and Chris Rock:

You know the world is crazy when the best rapper's a white guy, the best golfer's a black guy, the NBA's tallest famous player is Chinese, the Swiss hold America's Cup, France is accusing the U.S. of arrogance, Germany doesn't want to go to war, and the 3 most powerful men in America are named "Bush," "Dick," and "Colon."

Americans often forget where the rest of the world is. For example, Americans forget these facts:

Europe is as far north as Canada, though warmed by the Gulf Stream. For example, Venice (in warm Italy) is farther north than Halifax (in Canada's Nova Scotia).

South America is east of the United States. For example, if you go straight south from Florida's Key West, which South American country do you hit? The answer is: none! You're west of all of South America!

The shortest way to fly from the United States to Europe (or Northern Africa or Asia) is to fly north, across or near the North Pole. For example, the shortest way to fly from Miami (in Florida) to Casablanca (in Africa's Morocco) is to fly near Maine. The state closest to Africa is Maine, not Florida. To see that clearly, buy a globe; don't trust traditional maps, which distort distances.

Those facts are from the geography chapter of Peter Winkler's *Mathematical Puzzles*.

And now, from **DOSJOKL** (the Department of Stupid Jokes Only Kids Love), here's a geography riddle:

Why won't you starve in the Sahara desert?

Answer:

Because of the sandwiches there.

(Read that out loud.)

Canadian

Canadians love telling this tale:

On the sixth day of creating the universe, God turned to the angel Gabriel and said, "Today I'm going to create a land called Canada, full of outstanding natural beauty: majestic mountains with mountain goats & eagles, sparkling lakes bountiful with bass & trout, forests full of elk & moose, high cliffs overlooking sandy beaches with abundant sea life, and rivers stocked with salmon. I'll make the land rich in oil to make prosperous the inhabitants, called Canadians, who'll be known as the friendliest people on earth."

"But Lord," asked Gabriel, "don't you think you're being too generous to these Canadians?"

"Not really," replied God. "Just wait and see the neighbors I'm going to give them."

Yes, Canadians have trouble dealing with their southern neighbor!

Pierre Trudeau (who was Canada's prime minister) said:

Canada's main exports are hockey players and cold fronts. Our main import is acid rain.

Will Ferguson said:

The great themes of Canadian history are these: keeping the Americans out, keeping the French in, and trying to get the Natives to somehow disappear.

Laurence J. Peter (who invented the Peter Principle) said:

I must spend so much time explaining to Americans that I'm not English and to Englishmen that I'm not American that I have little time left to be Canadian.

Mike Myers said:

Canada is the essence of not being (not being English, not American) and a subtle flavor: we're more like celery.

Andy Barrie said:

We'll explain to you the appeal of curling if you explain to us the appeal of the National Rifle Association.

German

The Germans view the world differently from Americans.

Cockroaches

Germans have a different view of cockroaches. The German word for "cockroach" is **Küchenshabe**, which means "kitchen scraper." Whenever a German woman looks at a cockroach, she considers the cockroach to be a cute little robot that sweeps her kitchen. She doesn't scream; instead, she says "Thank you!"

Mark Twain hated German

German grammar and literary style seem weird — especially to Americans such as Mark Twain. In 1880, Mark Twain critiqued German grammar in "The Awful German Language," included in his essay collection called A Tramp Abroad.

German's most amazing feature is the order in which Germans put their words.

> Instead of saying "when you eat tuna," Germans say, "when you tuna eat" — because Germans put the verb ("eat") at the *end* of the clause, whenever you have **a subordinate clause** (a clause that begins with a word such as "when" or "if").
>
> Germans love to invent long adjectives. Instead of saying "the man who loves dogs," Germans say "the dog-loving man."

Germans carry those two rules to an extreme.

> Germans move the verb to the subordinate clause's end, even if the clause is very long.
>
> Germans create adjectives long enough to contain most of the sentence!

Mark Twain found a German newspaper's article whose words were in this order:

> In the day-before-yesterday-shortly-after-eleven-o'clock night, the in-this-town-standing tavern called "The Wagoner" was down-burnt. When the fire to the on-the-downburninghouse-resting stork's nest reached, flew the parent storks away. But when the by-the-raging-fire-surrounded nest *itself* caught fire, straightway plunged the quick-returning mother stork into the flames and died, her wings over her young ones outspread.

Spanish

Spanish is one of the world's most popular languages. Give it a look!

Pronunciation

Of all the world's popular languages, Spanish is the easiest to pronounce. Spanish's rules of pronunciation are simple — if you ignore the exceptions!

Here are the rules and their exceptions....

Vowels Spanish has just 5 vowel sounds:

> **a** is pronounced like the "a" in "mama" or "father" or "ah!"
> **e** is pronounced like the "é" in "café"
> **i** is pronounced like the "i" in "machine" or "police" (or the "ee" in "see")
> **o** is pronounced like the "o" in "go" or "no" or "oh!"
> **u** is pronounced like the "u" in "rule" or "flute" (or the "oo" in "moo")

Exception:

> After "q" or "g", **u** is silent, unless it has two dots over it (**ü**), in which case it's pronounced like the English "w."

To practice those vowel sounds and exceptions, say these Spanish words, which you probably know already:

> **taco, burrito, mosquito, no, la, salsa, olé, padre, madre, mesa, tequila, Santa Fe**

When **y** is at a word's end, it's pronounced the same as **i**.

Consonants Spanish pronounces these consonants about the same way as in English: **b, d, f, k, l, m, n, p, s, t, w**, and **y**.

To sound truly Hispanic (instead of having an English accent), use these tricks:

> When saying **l**, make your tongue touch your mouth's roof just near your teeth (like the "l" in "leaf" or "leak"), not farther back.
>
> When saying **k** or **p** or **t**, don't put a puff of air afterwards. When saying the **t**, say it softly and make your tongue touch the teeth (instead of your mouth's roof).
>
> Say **b** lazily (without quite closing your lips) if **b** comes immediately after a vowel sound (even if the vowel is at the end of the previous word). The lazy **b** sounds roughly like the English "v."
>
> When you see **m** at a word's end, say "n" instead of "m."

> When saying the **d**, make your tongue touch your teeth (instead of your mouth's roof). When you see **d** immediately after a vowel sound (even if the vowel's at the end of the previous word), make the **d** sound like the "th" in "then," softly (so you can barely hear it).
>
> When **n** comes before p, b, f, v, or m, say "m" instead of "n". When **n** comes before g, j, k, or w, say the "ng" in "sing."

Some regions speak differently:

> In northern and central Spain, **s** is pronounced like the "th" in "thin."
>
> In the Caribbean, when **s** comes before another consonant, people are too lazy to say the **s**: the **s** is silent or pronounced as an "h."
>
> In the River Plate area (which is on the Argentina-Uruguay border), **y** is pronounced like the "sh" in "she" or the "s" in "vision."

The symbol **ñ** is pronounced like the "ny" in "canyon".

These Spanish sounds are the same as others:

> Pronounce **z** the same as the Spanish **s**.
>
> Pronounce **v** the same as the Spanish **b**.
>
> Pronounce the pair **ll** the same as the Spanish **y**.
>
> Pronounce **c** the same as the Spanish **k** usually; but before e or i, pronounce **c** the same as the Spanish **s**. So pronounce **cc** (which comes before e or i) the same as a Spanish **k** followed by a Spanish **s**.

Here's how to pronounce the other letters:

> Don't pronounce **h**: it's silent! So when you see an **h**, ignore it. Don't even pause! Exception: pronounce **ch** like the "ch" in "cheese."
>
> Pronounce **j** like the "h" in "hot." Exception: in northern Spain, it's pronounced by gargling (like the Scottish "ch" in "loch" or the German "ch" in "ich" and "Bach"). To practice j, say these Spanish words, which you probably know already: **jalapeño, Jose**.
>
> Pronounce **g** like the "g" in "go" usually; but before e or i, pronounce **g** the same as the Spanish **j**.
>
> Usually pronounce **r** as between "t" and "d". Better yet, pronounce **r** as between the "tt" in "butter" and the "dd" in "ladder". Better yet, pronounce **r** as a Brooklyn "th" (because in Brooklyn, "the" is pronounced "duh" or, more precisely, halfway between "duh" and "tuh"). To practice that r, say this Spanish word: **para**. Exception: pronounce **r** instead like a long Scottish rolled "r" (trill) when the **r** is at the word's beginning or comes after l, n, or s or is written **rr**.
>
> Pronounce **x** like "ks" usually. At a word's beginning or before a consonant, pronounce it like "s". Exception: pronounce it like "s" in **exacto** and **auxilio**. More exceptions: in names invented by Central America natives (such as **Xola, Xela**, and **México**), pronounce it like "sh" at a name's beginning, "h" at other parts of the name.

Stress Stress (emphasize) the *next-to-last* syllable. Examples:

> **taco, burrito, mosquito, salsa, padre, madre, mesa, tequila, santa**

Exception: if a word ends in a consonant that's neither n nor s, stress the *last* syllable. Examples:

> **español, usted, mujer, favor, azul, pedal, felicidad, actualidad**

Further exception: if a vowel has an acute accent (the symbol ´), stress that vowel instead. That accent's usual purpose is just to tell you which syllable to stress.

Stressing the right syllable is important! For example, **papá** (which stresses the last syllable) means "dad" but **papa** (which stresses the next-to-last syllable) means "pope" or "potato," so don't call your father "**papa**!"

Sometimes the acute accent is written just to distinguish two words that would otherwise look the same. For example, **de** means "of" but **dé** means "give"; both words are pronounced the same. Another example: **si** means "if" but **sí** means "yes."

Vowel pairs When vowels are next to each other, they form a **vowel pair**. In a vowel pair, pronounce the vowels one-by-one. For example, to pronounce **eo**, pronounce the **e** (which sounds like the one in "café") then pronounce the **o** (which sounds like the one in "go").

The vowels **i** and **u** are **weak**. The other vowels (**a**, **e**, and **o**) are **strong**. Here are the rules:

A vowel pair counts as 2 syllables if both vowels are strong; otherwise, the vowel pair counts as just 1 syllable. Combine that rule with the stress rules above, to decide which syllable to stress.

When two weak vowels are next to each other, put more stress on the *second* vowel. When a weak vowel is next to a strong vowel, put more stress on the *strong* vowel.

Try it! Hey, you boring white-guy anglo: the next time you see Spanish (on a sign, ad, or instructions), try pronouncing the Spanish properly! Make your mouth marvelous!

Don't be embarrassed

To translate the typical English word into Spanish, just add an **o** or an **a**. For example, "American" becomes *Americano*. But be careful:

Bizarro does *not* mean "bizarre"; it means "gallant."
Insano can mean "insane" but sometimes means just "unhealthy."
Bravo can mean "brave" but sometimes means "wild," "spicy" or "angry."

If you're a woman who feels embarrassed, don't say you're **embarazada**, since that means "pregnant." If you say you're **embarazada**, you'll be *very* embarrassed!

American companies have made embarrassing blunders when trying to sell to Hispanics:

Hewlett-Packard invited Hispanics to a special demonstration of Hewlett-Packard equipment and gave each attendee a badge, showing the person's name and the letters "HP," which stands for "Hewlett-Packard." Hewlett-Packard didn't realize that in Spanish, **HP** is the standard abbreviation for **hijo puta**, which is short for **hijo de puta**, which means "son of a prostitute," which is the Spanish equivalent of the American expression "son of a bitch." My friend Miguel got insulted when Hewlett-Packard gave him a badge saying, in effect, that Miguel was a "son of a bitch."

Coca-Cola's ads, which showed wild teenagers drinking Coke at the beach, annoyed Hispanics, who prefer to drink Coke somberly in the kitchen or the dining room, as if it were iced tea or wine. Coke's executives finally wised up and switched to Spanish ads showing Hispanics drinking Coke as the perfect complement to a wonderful meal.

Latin American dangers

If you learned Spanish from a classical textbook and then go to Latin America, you'll be surprised — because some Latin Americans have dirty minds.

For example, consider the Spanish word for "boy." In Spain, the usual word for "boy" is **niño** or **muchacho**; but in El Salvador, the usual word for "boy" is **cipote**, which means "penis" or "little fucker."

In Spain, the usual word for "mother" is **madre**, and the usual word for "father" is **padre**. Just infants say **mamá** and **papá** instead. A popular insult is **tu padre**, which means "your father — I shit on him!" A Spaniard's biggest insult is to shit on a father; an American's biggest insult is to fuck a mother instead.

In Mexico (a country that loves insults!), the **tu padre** insult has become so popular that the very mention of the word **padre** is considered offensive. So if you go to Mexico, you must never use the word **padre**. Instead, Mexicans use the word **papá**. Yes, polite Mexicans who want to avoid insults spend their entire lives talking like infants: they always say **papá** and **mamá** instead of **padre** and **madre**.

In Spain, the main word for "seize" or "pick up" is **coger**. For example, to "pick up the telephone" is **coger el teléfono**. But if you say **coger el teléfono** in Mexico or Argentina, everybody will laugh at you — because in those countries, **coger** is used just for picking up girls and fucking them. If you say you want to **coger el teléfono**, people will wonder why you want to fuck the telephone. Instead of **coger**, you must use the other word for "pick up," which is **tomar**.

The typical Spanish-English dictionary says **bollo** means a bun (or muffin or bump) and **papaya** is a kind of fruit. But the dictionary doesn't mention that **bollo** and **papaya** have obscene connotations in Cuba, where **bollo** is a woman's pussy, and **papaya** is even worse. So if a Cuban woman serves you a muffin, don't say, "I like your **bollo**" — unless you know her very well!

Olé

Though Spaniards often say **olé**, the word **olé** isn't really Spanish: it's Arabic. In Arabic, olé means "By God!" Spaniards snatched **olé** from the Arabs when the Arabs invaded Spain in 711 A.D.

French

In France, the meals are named as follows:

Meal	Name in France
breakfast	petit déjeuner
lunch	déjeuner
supper	dîner
after-theater snack	souper

French Canadians, who are always in a rush, serve their meals earlier: they serve lunch (**déjeuner**) at breakfast time and serve supper (**dîner**) at lunchtime, like this:

Time	What you get in French Canada
breakfast	déjeuner
lunch	dîner
supper	souper

To the French Canadian who explained all this to me, I asked, "What do you call the after-theater snack?" He replied, "In French Canada, we don't go to the theater."

French kids are like criminals

French has two words for "you." The formal word is **vous**; the informal word, **tu**, is used just when speaking to close friends (such as relatives, colleagues, and God) and lower forms of life (such as children, criminals, and inanimate objects).

Make sure you choose the correct word. For example, one summer I was talking to a French Canadian girl who was 3 years old. Since she was a child, I should have called her "**tu**," but I made the mistake of calling her "**vous**" instead, which was too formal. She was so amused at my formality — at my treating her like a queen — that she curtsied. She also called me a **vieille banane**, which means "old banana."

When I asked why I was being called an "old banana," her mom said I might have heard wrong; maybe the girl was calling me a **vieux bonhomme**, which means "old gentleman."

But then we heard the girl call me a **vieille banane** again, and her mom admitted I was indeed being called an "old banana," but consoled me by saying that "Old Banana" was just a TV personality whom the girl thought I resembled.

Oh, well. I've been called worse!

How Americans changed France

What do the French admire about us Americans? To find out, look at which words the French have borrowed from us.

The French use these American words for types of music:

blues, country, folk, gospel, jazz, pop, rock, slow, soul

The French use these American words for clothing:

boots, fashion-victim, pullover, shoes, tee-shirt, trench-coat

The French say **sweat** for a sweatshirt. The French say **basket** for a basketball sneaker or any other sports sneaker.

The French use these American words for food & drink:

bacon, cake, chewing-gum, chips, cocktail, cookie, hotdog, pudding, roast-beef, sandwich, toast, whiskey

The French say **lunch** for any cold meal, even at dinnertime. The French say **corn-flakes** for any breakfast cereal dunked in cold milk, even if it contains no corn.

Here are more American words have crept into the French language and are popular in France now:

baby-boom, baby-sitter, best-seller, bike, biker, blazer, body-building, boss, boy-scout, brainstorming, building, camping, compact disk, cockpit, cowboy, cozy, crash, dancing, drugstore, DVD, e-mail, engineering, film, flash, flashback, gangster, high-tech, hippie, hobby, holdup, job, kidnapper, kitchenette, lad, lobby, loser, marketing, music-hall, nightclub, nurse, okay, parking, pickup, pinup, poster, punk, revolver, scan, scanner, script, self-made-man, self-service, sex-appeal, sexy, shopping, slogan, snack-bar, snowboard, sofa, steward, stop, surf, teenager, ticket, top, tuner, up-to-date, wagon, web, weekend

The French say **black** for any dark-skinned person, say **blush** for cheek makeup, say **break** for a coffee break, say **chat** for Internet chat, say **dandy** for a fancy-looking person, say **gloss** for lip gloss, say **hit** for a success, say **jet** for jet airplane, say **look** for appearance, say **mail** for e-mail, say **net** for Internet, say **roller** for roller skates, say **sitting** for a sit-down protest demonstration in the street, say **spot** for a spotlight, say **starter** for a car-ignition starter, say **stick** for lipstick or a glue stick, say **tank** for an army tank, say **trust** for a big international company, say **turnover** for personnel changes, and say **Western** for a cowboy movie.

The French put **le before most of those words: le best-seller, le boy-scout, le brainstorming**, etc. The main exceptions are **kitchenette** and **nurse**, which the French consider to both be feminine, so they get **la** instead of **le**.

Old French fuddy-duddies who don't like English intrusions call them **Franglais**.

More examples of French craziness are in *1001 Pitfalls in French*, by Grew & Oliver. I thank Christophe Paysant's family for helping me keep the list updated.

Bilingual beauties

The ultimate French-American was Maurice Chevalier, who loved to sing in English with a French accent. I wish he would have sung "My Way" — he would have been cute — but Sinatra got that job.

French teachers love the bilingual song popularized by Nat King Cole in the 1950's:

Darling, **je vous aime beaucoup**.
Je ne sais pas what to do!

I wish more people would write bilingual songs like that!

French can get confused with English. For example, consider this tale:

One fine winter evening, an American girl had a date with her French lover. When she opened her door to let him in, he burst in and exclaimed, "**Je t'adore!**" (which means "I adore you!" and practically means "Will you marry me?")

He eagerly awaited her reply. But since she didn't know French and thought he said "Shut da door," she replied: "I don't feel a draft."

Moral: if you don't know French, you'll miss lovely opportunities!

Japanese

Speaking Japanese is easy — because the Japanese borrowed many words from us Americans.

3 rules

To speak Japanese, you need to know just 3 rules.

Rule 1: the Japanese don't like c, l and v The Japanese change c to either k or s (depending on how the c is pronounced in English), change l to r, and change v to b. For example, the English word "vitamin" becomes the Japanese word **bitamin**.

Let's translate the English word "gasoline" into Japanese. Since the Japanese hate long words, they abridge it to "gasolin"; then they apply rule 1, which gives **gasorin**.

Let's translate "television" into Japanese. Since the Japanese hate long words, they abridge it to "televi"; then they apply rule 1, which gives **terebi**.

Rule 2: the Japanese avoid putting two consonants next to each other To apply that rule, the Japanese often resort to cleverness.

For example, let's translate the English word "correspondence" into Japanese. Since the Japanese hate long words, they abridge it to "correspon"; then they apply rule 1, which gives "korrespon." But according to rule 2, the Japanese don't like the "rr" and the "sp." So the Japanese shorten the "rr" to "r," and shorten the "sp" to "p," and get **korepon**.

Rule 2 says to avoid pairs of consonants. The Japanese often break up a pair of consonants by inserting "u" in the middle of the pair. For example, to break up "pr," the Japanese often insert "u" in the middle and get "pur." Thus, the English word "pro" (which means "professional") becomes the Japanese word **puro**.

Let's translate "word processor." The Japanese think it sounds like "ward processor." Since the Japanese hate long expressions, they abridge it to "wa pro." To break up the "pr," they insert "u" in the middle, and get **wapuro**.

Let's translate "platform." The Japanese abridge it to "platfo." Applying rule 1, they get "pratfo." According to rule 2, the "pr" and "tf" are unacceptable, so the Japanese change "pr" to "pur" and change "tf" to "t": they get **purato**.

Rule 3: the only consonant the Japanese permit at the end of a word is n To avoid ending with a consonant that's not n, the Japanese add the letter "o" or "u" at the end.

For example, let's translate the word "gas." Since "gas" ends in a consonant, which violates rule 3, the Japanese add the letter "u" at the end, and get **gasu**.

Let's translate the word "hotel." Applying rule 1, that becomes "hoter." Since that ends in a consonant, rule 3 makes the Japanese add the letter "u" at the end, and get **hoteru**.

Let's translate "catalog." Applying rule 1, that becomes "katarog." Rule 3 makes the Japanese add "u" and get **katarogu**.

Let's translate "bell." Applying rule 1, that becomes "berr." Applying rule 2, the "rr" is shortened to "r," giving "ber." Rule 3 makes the Japanese add "u" and get **beru**.

Let's translate "pool," which is pronounced "pul." Applying rule 1, that becomes "pur." Rule 3 makes the Japanese add "u" and get **puru**.

Let's translate "building," which is pronounced "bilding," and which the Japanese abridge to "bil." Applying rule 1, that becomes "bir." Rule 3 makes the Japanese add "u" and get **biru**.

Let's translate "apartment." The Japanese abridge it to "apart." But rule 2 says the "rt" is unacceptable, so the Japanese abridge it to "t," giving "apat." Rule 3 makes the Japanese add "o" and get **apato**.

Let's translate "software." The Japanese abridge it to "soft." Since the Japanese have difficulty hearing the difference between f and h, they think it sounds like "soht." But rule 2 says the "ht" is unacceptable, so the Japanese insert "u," giving "sohut." Rule 3 makes the Japanese add "o" and get **sohuto**.

Let's translate "personal computer." The Japanese pronounce it "parsonal computer," and abridge it to "parso com." According to rule 1, that becomes "parso kom." Since rule 2 says the "rs" is unacceptable, the Japanese then drop the "r" and get "pasokom." But that violates rule 3. To satisfy rule 3, the Japanese change the "m" to "n," and get **pasokon**.

Here's what we Americans gave the Japanese:

English	Japanese	English	Japanese
apple pie	appuru pai	glass	garasu
basketball	basuketto bōru	handkerchief	hankachi
beefsteak	bifuteki	ice cream	aisu kuriimu
beer	biiru	missile	misairu
cabin	kabin	necktie	nekutai
can	kan	postbox	posuto
coat	kōto	raincoat	rein-kōto
coffee	kōhii	sandwich	sandoitchi
deck	dekki	spoon	spūn
democracy	demokurashii	sports	spōtsu
demonstration	demonsuturēshon	stocking	sutekkingu
department	depāto	table	tēburu
dessert	dezāto	tennis court	tenisu kōto
escalator	esukarētā	truck	torakku
flashbulb	furasshu barubu	typewriter	taipuraitā

Alphabet

If you want to impress your friends, say our alphabet — in Japanese! Here's how the Japanese say it: **ei, bii, shii, dei, ii, efu, jii, eichi, ai, jei, kei, eru, emu, enu, oo, pii, kyuu, āru, esu, tei, yuu, bui, dabburu yuu, ekisu, uai, zetto.**

Country of yes-men

How would you feel if a stranger walked up to you and said just "Yes!" even though you hadn't asked a question? That's how the Japanese feel about us Americans — because when we need to talk with a stranger, we begin by saying "Hi!" which sounds the same as the Japanese word **hai**, which means yes. Next time you say "Hi" to a visitor from Japan, don't be surprised if he responds by saying, "I'm sorry — what was the question?"

Japanese like hurly-burly

To make a word plural, the Japanese like to say the word twice, but changing the first letter. For example, the Japanese word for "person" is **hito**; the Japanese word for "people" is **hito-bito**.

In that example, h became b. Notice that h is a "quiet" letter; it became b, which is a "noisy" letter. The general rule is: a quiet letter becomes a noisy letter. Here are more examples:

Rule	Example		
h becomes b	"person" is **hito**	"people"	is **hito-bito**
k becomes g	"god" is **kami**	"gods"	is **kami-gami**
t becomes d	"time" is **toki**	"sometimes"	is **toki-doki**
f becomes b	"joint" is **fushi**	"every joint"	is **fushi-bushi**
s becomes z	"that" is **sore**	"every"	is **sore-zore**
sh becomes j	"island" is **shima**	"islands"	is **shima-jima**
ts becomes z	"month" is **tsuki**	"every month"	is **tsuki-zuki**

To have fun, apply those same rules to English. Ask your lover: "Do you want tickle-dickle, hug-bug, kiss-giss, or just shower-jower?"

Chinese

The most important foreign country is China. Here's why....

China is slightly smaller than the U.S. but contains 4 times as many people. There are over 1.2 billion people in China, compared with under .3 billion in the U.S.

There are 6 billion people in the whole world. A quarter of them live in China.

At first glance, China doesn't look crowded; but it is. The U.S. has just one crowded city (New York); China has several. The U.S. has vast unoccupied areas (forests, deserts, mountains, canyons, and swamps); China's are smaller.

To prevent further crowding, the Chinese government passed many laws encouraging couples to have just one child.

India is even more crowded: it's much smaller than China but contains almost as many people (1 billion). India permits couples to have many children, and then do. In the next 25 years, people predict India's population will increase to 1.4 billion, making it even more populous than China; but for now, China is still the most populous country.

Of all the languages in the world, Mandarin Chinese is the most popular native language. For every person whose native language is English, there are 2½ people whose native language is Mandarin Chinese. (The world's other popular native language is Hindi, spoken in India; it's just slightly more popular than English.)

If you travel all over the world, you'll discover that more schools teach English than Chinese. In all countries, students study English, usually as a foreign language. Even students in China study English! That makes English the most popular *foreign* language; but Chinese is the most popular *native* language.

China is modernizing fast. Chinese consumers are rapidly buying Western goods, and Chinese factories are rapidly making goods to sell to the West. The Chinese are very excited about all that international trade in both directions, and the Chinese have been quickly constructing fancy factories, fancy stores, and fancy housing. **China's stock market and real-estate market have both been generating huge profits for investors.** China is exciting — a hot marketplace.

The Chinese government's challenge is to control the bubble so it grows safely without bursting. China's immediate concern is to slow down construction somewhat (to give the electric utilities a chance to catch up with the increased demand) and to fix the banking system (where half of all loans are never repaid, because they're given too easily to friends, politicians, and failing government-owned businesses).

After the Soviet Union disintegrated, China was left as the only big country worrying the U.S. (Of course, the U.S. worries about smaller countries too, such as North Korea and battlers in the Middle East.) China is worrisome because:

China's the biggest country without freedom of speech.

China's the biggest country whose government continually tells lies. (It even lies about the weather & temperature, to prevent government employees from requesting time off when it's too hot to work.)

China is the U.S.'s biggest trading partner. It has the biggest effect on U.S. jobs: without cheap goods from China, Wal-Mart would be dead.

Goods from China have cost little because the Chinese government kept an artificial exchange rate of about 8 yuan per dollar, even though most economists say a fairer rate would be 5 yuan per dollar. Other countries have asked China to change the exchange rate, and China's promised to do so by the 2008 Olympics. So far, China has let the exchange rate dip to 6½ yuan per dollar, so a yuan costs about 15¢. When China eventually lets the exchange rate fall to 5 yuan per dollar, the whole world's trade could be thrown out of kilter, unless China handles the change carefully.

China's borders touch many countries that the U.S. worries about. Though most Chinese people yellow-skinned, some are white (near Russia's border) and some are brown (near India's border). Like the U.S., China has many minorities, which celebrate their own cultures, though not as freely as in the U.S. (since the Chinese government frowns on religions and anything threatening the Chinese Communist Party).

Language

If you want a challenge, try learning Chinese! It's tricky!

In China, most signs are written just in Chinese characters, but a few signs also show writing in **pinyin**, which uses Roman characters (to help Westerners and young Chinese kids who haven't learned all the Chinese characters yet).

To understand Chinese, your first step is to learn how to pronounce pinyin. Here's how.

Consonants In pinyin, these 15 consonants are pronounced about the same way as in English: **b, p, d, t, k, m, n, l, r, f, s, h, j, w**, and **y**. Here are 3 other easy consonants: pronounce **g** like the one in "go," **sh** like the one in "she," and **ch** like the one in "cheese."

Unfortunately, these 5 consonants are pronounced quite differently from English:

q	is pronounced like the "ch" in "cheese"
x	is pronounced like the "sh" in "she"
c	is pronounced like the "ts" in "nuts"
z	is pronounced like the "dz" in "gadzooks"
zh	is pronounced like the "j" in "jump"

To sound truly Chinese (instead of having an American accent), use these tricks....

To say **y** and **w**, open your mouth more than in English, so the **y** sounds almost like the ee in "see," and the **w** sounds almost like the "oo" in "moo."

For **h, g**, and **k**, arch the back of your tongue toward your mouth's roof (so **h** sounds like the Scottish "ch" in "loch" or the German "ch" in "ich" and "Bach").

For **r**, roll your tongue in the middle of your mouth.

For **j, q**, and **x**, draw your mouth's corners as far back as possible, so you look like you're grinning: **q** looks like you're taking a photo and saying "cheese"; **x** sounds like a kettle ready to whistle, halfway between "sh" and "s". Grin for those single letters (**j, q**, and **x**) but not for double letters (**zh, ch**, and **sh**). Beijing's local dialect adds a "ur" sound after the double letters: so just in Beijing, **zh** is pronounced like the "jur" in "jury," **ch** is pronounced like the "chur" in "church," and **sh** is pronounced like "sure." That's why people in Beijing sound like they're growling and muttering: they frequently add "ur-r-r-r!"

Vowels In pinyin, most vowels are pronounced the same way as in French. So before studying Chinese, it's helpful to study French! That's why the French speak Chinese better than other Westerners.

Since you probably don't know French yet, here are examples in English:

a	is pronounced like the "a" in "mama" or "papa" or "father" or "far"
e	is pronounced like the "e" in "her" or "term" (or the "e" in French "le")
i	is pronounced like the "i" in "machine" or "police" (or the "ee" in "see")
o	is pronounced like the "o" in "or" (or the "aw" in "awful")
u	is pronounced like the "u" in "rule" or "flute" (or the "oo" in "moo")
ü	is pronounced like the "ü" in German "über" (or the "u" in French "tu" or somewhat like the "eu" in English "pneumonia"); to make that sound, purse your lips like you're going to whistle, but then say "ee" through them

Here are two exceptions:

when the **i** sound comes after **z, zh, c, ch, s, sh**, or **r**, people pronounce it like the **e** sound but with the mouth less open, so it almost sounds like "r"

when the **ü** sound comes after the letter **j, q, x**, or **y**, people don't bother to write the ¨: they write just **u**; so if you see **u** after **j, q, x**, or **y**, pronounce it as **ü**

When several vowels are next to each other, pronounce them one-by-one. For example, to pronounce **ai**, pronounce the **a** (which sounds like the one in "mama") then pronounce the **i** (which sounds like the one in "machine"); you'll wind up with a **diphthong** (vowel sequence) that sounds like the "i" in "bite". Chinese uses these 13 diphthongs:

ai	sounds like the "i" in "bite"
ei	sounds like the "ei" in "veil" (or the "a" in "date")
ui	sounds like compromise between "we" and "way"
ao	sounds like the "ow" in "cow"
uo	sounds like the "wa" in "war"
ou	sounds like the "o" in "go"
iu	sounds like the "yo" in "yo-yo"
ia	sounds like the "ya" in "yard"
iao	sounds like the "eow" in "meow"
ua	sounds like the "ua" in "suave"
uai	sounds like the "wi" in "swipe"
ie	sounds like the "ie" in "sierra" (or the "ye" in "yes")
üe	sounds like the "eu" in "pneumonia" followed by "air"

In Chinese, the typical syllable consists of one consonant sound, then one vowel sound (or a diphthong), then, optionally, a special ending (**n** or **ng** or **r**). Any special ending affects the sound of the vowel before it:

er	sounds like the "er" in "her," but with your mouth slightly more open, so it almost sounds like the word "are"
an	sounds like the English word "an" (and the "an" in "fan"), but pronounce the "n" very softly and briefly, so you hear not much more than the "a" in "an"
ian	sounds like "yen," but pronounce the "n" very softly and briefly
en	sounds like the "un" in "under"
in	sounds like the English words "in" and "inn"
un	sounds like the "ewin" in the word "chewin'" (slang for "chewing")
ün	sounds like the French word "une"
ang	sounds like the "ong" in "gong"
eng	sounds like the "ung" in "hung"
ing	sounds like the "ing" in "ring"
ong	sounds like the English electrical word "ohm" (and the meditation word "Om") but with "ng" instead of "m"; it also sounds like the word "going" but without the "g" and "i"

For example, here's how to pronounce Chinese family names (in Mandarin):

The Chinese family name **Li**	is pronounced "lee."
The Chinese family name **Tang**	is pronounced "tong."
The Chinese family name **Wang**	is pronounced "wong."
The Chinese family name **Yang**	is pronounced "yong."
The Chinese family name **Zhang**	is pronounced "jong."
The Chinese family name **Chen**	is pronounced "chun."
The Chinese family name **Cheng**	is pronounced "chung."
The Chinese family name **Song**	is pronounced "so" then "ng."

Tones In pinyin, you can put 4 accents above a vowel. The accents are called **tones**. The tones can make a difference:

> **ma** is a Chinese word that means "huh" and marks the end of a question
> **mā** is a Chinese word that means "mother"
> **má** is a Chinese word that means "hemp" or "numb" or "pock-marked"
> **mǎ** is a Chinese word that means "horse"
> **mà** is a Chinese word that means "scold" or "swear"

Here's how to pronounce them:

> Pronounce plain **ma** briefly, like a grunt. That's called **toneless** or **tone 0**.
>
> Pronounce **mā** as a long, high note, as if you were an Italian singer (like Pavarotti) singing a high note of an opera or a popular song. While you sing it, hold your pitch steady, going neither up the scale nor down it. Sing it for about half a second (while you count "one, one thou…"). It's the tone American doctors use when they tell you to open your mouth and say "ah." That's called the **first tone** or **high tone** or **flat tone**.
>
> Pronounce **má** so it rises from "medium pitch" to "high pitch," like a singer sliding up the scale. To pronounce it easily, raise your eyebrows while saying it. Make its length be rather short. It's the same tone Americans use when they ask "what?" It's called the **second tone** or **rising tone**.
>
> Pronounce **mǎ** so it dips from "medium-low pitch" to "low pitch" then rises to "medium-high pitch." Make the pitch swoop down, like an eagle catching its prey, then swoop back up. To pronounce it easily, drop your chin onto your neck and then raise it again. It takes a long time to finish the performance. It's called the **third tone** or **dipping tone** or **low tone**.
>
> Pronounce **mà** so it falls from "high pitch" to "low pitch," like a singer sliding down the scale. Do it fast, so its length is very short. Start loud but quickly fade, as if you're a singer who has a heart attack: let out a quick high-pitched yelp, then wither (with your voice) to the floor. To pronounce it easily, stomp your foot gently while saying it. It's the tone Americans use when they yell "Hah!" or "No!" or a command (such as "Stop!") It's called the **fourth tone** or **falling tone**.

When a Chinese person speaks to you, tones 1 and 3 are easy to recognize, since they're long: tone 1 stays high; tone 3 dips. If you hear a syllable that's short, it's either tone 0 (which is quiet), tone 4 (which is forceful and accented), or tone 2 (which rises).

To practice the tones, try saying this sentence:

> **Má mā mà mǎ ma?**

It means "Pock-marked mother scold horse, huh?" which means "Does the pock-marked mother scold the horse?"

For "mother," the Chinese can say **mā** but more commonly say **māma**. (The first syllable is the first tone; the second syllable is toneless. The word sounds like an American baby yelling for his mother: "Mama!") You can put it in that sentence:

> **Má māma mà mǎ ma?**

A syllable is toneless if it's a **repetition**, such as the **ma** at the end of **māma**. Here's another example of repetition: the Chinese word for "father" or "papa" is **bàba**. For brothers & sisters, the Chinese care about their ages:

> "Older brother" is **gēge**, but "younger brother" is **dìdi**.
> "Older sister" is **jiějie**,   but "younger sister" is **mèimei**.

So a syllable is toneless if it's a **repetition** — or if it's a **particle** (a grammar element, such as the **ma** that means "huh?").

When ordering food, be careful:

> **tāng** means soup, but **táng** means sugar
> **yán** means salt, but **yān** means tobacco

Many family names use the second tone (**Táng**, **Wáng**, **Yáng**, **Chén**, and **Chéng**), but these family names use different tones: **Zhāng**, **Lǐ**, and **Sòng**.

Laziness about tones Saying the 3rd tone requires a lot of time & effort: you're supposed to dip your voice down, then bring it back up. The Chinese do that full procedure just if the 3rd tone comes before a long pause (such as at the end of a sentence). Otherwise, the Chinese rush by taking these shortcuts:

How to pronounce the 3rd tone (if the next tone is tone 0, 1, 2, or 4): dip the voice down but don't bother bringing it back up.

How to pronounce the 3rd tone (if the next tone is 3rd also): bring the voice up but don't bother dipping down first, so instead it sounds like just a 2nd tone (rising tone). Here's a famous example…. The Chinese don't have a word for "hello." Instead of saying "hello," they greet each other by saying "you look great," which is usually abridged to "you good." Since the word for "you" is **nǐ** and the word for "good" is **hǎo**, that would make "you good" be **nǐ hǎo**. But Chinese people are too lazy to dip twice in a row — **the Chinese never double-dip** — so they switch the first word to a rising tone and say this: **ní hǎo**. Here's another example…. If you're chatting about health or feelings and want to say "I'm okay too," the Chinese form is "I also good," which would be **wǒ yě hǎo**; but since that would require 3 dips in a row, the Chinese change the first 2 of them to rising and say this: **wó yé hǎo**.

Students and Westerners study tones (to pronounce well), but writing them is tedious, so **most sign writers don't bother writing tones on signs** — and I won't bother writing tones in later parts of this book.

When the Chinese write tones above **ü**, they sometimes don't bother writing the dots above the **u**.

Don't worry: if you say wrong tones, Chinese listeners can usually guess what you mean. For example, they can guess whether you're trying to ask for your mother (**mā**) or a horse (**mǎ**). It's more important to **pronounce correctly consonants and vowels**: if you botch those, your listeners will be totally confused.

Wade-Giles Mao's government started using pinyin in 1958, to communicate with kids and Westerners. But many Westerners kept trying to use an older Romanization system, called Wade-Giles, until the 1980's. Now we all use pinyin (because it more accurately indicates Chinese pronunciation), but some of you old fogies might still remember the **Wade-Giles** spellings:

Pinyin, used now		Wade-Giles, outdated
Běijīng	(the capital city)	Peking
Guǎngzhōu	(a big city)	Canton
Chóngqìng	(a big city)	Chungking
Sìchuān	(a province)	Szechuan
Dào	(a religion)	Tao
Máo Zédōng	(a famous leader)	Mao Tse-tung
Lǐ Bái	(a famous poet)	Li Po
Láo Zǐ	(a famous writer)	Lao Tzu

Characters Instead of being in pinyin, most signs are in traditional Chinese characters. Each character is a picture, one syllable.

Some characters are simple:

> The character for the number "1" is a horizontal line. (The pinyin for "1" is **yī**.)
>
> The character for the number "2" is two horizontal lines, stacked so they look like an equal sign, except the bottom line is slightly longer. (Pinyin: **èr**.)
>
> The character for the number "3" is three horizontal lines, stacked, with the bottom line longest and the middle line shortest. (Pinyin: **sān**.)
>
> The character for the number "ten" is a plus sign. (Pinyin: **shí**.)
>
> The character for the word "man" (or "person") looks like a stick figure of a man, but with no head, no arms, and no feet, so you see just a pair of legs (without feet) and a torso, and the whole thing is just two strokes: one stroke is the "torso becoming the left leg", the other stroke is the right leg. (Pinyin: **rén**.)
>
> The character for the word "big" is the same as for the word "man" but with outstretched arms added. The "outstretched arms" are just a horizontal line. (Pinyin: **dà**.)

Other characters are more complex, containing many keystrokes.

In 1956, Mao's government simplified the most complex characters. The simplified characters are used on the Chinese mainland but not on the island of Taiwan, which still uses the older, fancier characters.

In Chinese characters, sentences are usually written from left to right (like English), but they can also be written from right to left (which is more traditional) or from top to bottom (vertically, which is even more traditional). Chinese books are usually written from front to back (like English), but they can also be written from back to front (which is more traditional). So when you pick up a Chinese book or newspaper, you must spend a few seconds trying to figure out which direction makes the most sense to read it.

Using numbers

Here are the fundamental numbers:

```
    0 líng      (pronounced "ling")
    1 yī        (pronounced "yee" or "ee")
    2 èr        (pronounced "er")
    3 sān       (pronounced "san")
    4 sì        (pronounced "suh")
    5 wǔ        (pronounced "woo")
    6 liù       (pronounced like the name "Leo")
    7 qī        (pronounced "chee")
    8 bā        (sounds like a sheep: "bah")
    9 jiǔ       (pronounced like the name "Joe")
   10 shí       (pronounced like the word "she")
  100 yìbǎi     (pronounced "yee buy" or "ee buy")
 1000 yìqiān    (pronounced "yee chee an" or "ee chee an")
10000 yìwàn     (pronounced "yee wan" or "ee wan")
```

Chinese numbers sound more pleasant and simpler than English ones. For example, 3 in Chinese is **sān**, which sounds more pleasant and simpler than the English "three"; 7 in Chinese is **qī** (pronounced "chee"), which sounds more pleasant and simpler than the English "seven."

To pronounce English, you must learn that 11 is pronounced "eleven," not "one one"; 30 is pronounced "thirty," not "threety". Chinese has no such pecularities. In Chinese, the number after "ten" is called "ten one" (**shí yī**). Then come "ten two" (**shí èr**) then "ten three" (**shí sān**) and so on, up to "ten nine" (**shí jiǔ**) Then come "two-ten" (**èrshí**), "two-ten one" (**èrshí yī**), "two-ten two" (**èrshí èr**), and so on. One hundred is **yìbǎi**; two hundred is **èrbǎi**; 235 is "two-hundred three-ten five" (**èrbǎi sānshí wǔ**).

If a number's next-to-final digit is zero, say "zero" (**líng**). For example, if you want to say 205, don't say just "two-hundred five": say "two-hundred zero five" (**èrbǎi líng wǔ**). If you forget to say the "zero" and say just "two-hundred five" (**èrbǎi wǔ**), your listener will assume you mean the slang for 250.

For the digit 2, the Chinese use **èr** or **liǎng**. Choose **èr** when you're counting (1, 2, 3, etc.) and for 20 (**èrshí**) and 200 (**èrbǎi**); choose **liǎng** instead for 2000 (**liǎngqiān**), 20000 (**liǎngwàn**), and when the number modifies a noun ("2 people").

In Chinese you don't have to learn the names of the 12 months, since they have no names: the Chinese just say "#1 month" (**yī yuè**), "#2 month" (**èr yuè**), etc.

You don't have to learn the names of the 7 days of the week, because they have no names either (except Sunday): the Chinese just say "week's #1" for Monday (**zhōu yī**), "week's #2" for Tuesday (**zhōu èr**), etc. For Sunday, say "week's sun" (**zhōu rì**).

For the word "week," instead of saying **zhōu** (which literally means "circumference"), some Chinese folks substitute a more ancient word, **xīngqī** (which literally means "star period").

Important stuff first

In Chinese, you talk about important stuff before talking about details. For example, when giving a date, you say the year then the month then the date. When giving a person's name, you say the person's family (which is usually one syllable, such as **Chén**) then the cute name the mother gave that person (which is usually two syllables, such as **Mínglì**). For example, China's most famous leader was **Máo Zédōng**: his family's name was **Máo**, his given name was **Zédōng**.

Grammar & style

In English, to make a word plural you must typically add "s," but some words are irregular: the plural of "mouse" is "mice." The Chinese don't bother pluralizing: in Chinese, the word for "restaurant" is the same as the word for "restaurants." So in Chinese, instead of saying "I own 5 restaurants," you say "I own 5 of restaurant." The only exception is for groups of people: the plural of "friend" is "friend group"; the plural of "student" is "student group"; the plural of "child" is "child group." (The Chinese word for "group" is **men**.)

In English, you have to say "the" or "a" or "some" before most nouns. There are no Chinese words for "the" or "a" or "some." So in Chinese, instead of saying "I see the car" or "I see a car", you say just "I see car." If you want to emphasize that you see just "a" car, not many cars, you can say "I see one of car": the Chinese say "one" (**yī**) instead of "a".

In English, you must learn how to conjugate verbs: "I eat," "he eats", "I ate", "I have eaten," "I am eating," "I will eat." The Chinese never conjugate; they say "I eat," "he eat," "I yesterday eat," "I tomorrow eat."

To say just "I ate" without bothering to specify which day, a Chinese person says "I eat already." That's easy to say, since the Chinese word for "already" is short: **le**. So to turn any present sentence into a past-tense sentence, just add **le** at the end.

If you're telling a story, don't bother putting **le** at the end of each sentence: just tell the story in the present tense. ("I yesterday eat. Then I drink. Then I sleep.")

Here's another popular shortcut: instead of saying "I will buy an apple," the Chinese just nod and say "buy apple": the "I" and "will" are unspoken and understood.

In English, you must worry about whether to say "he," "she," or "it" — and hope you're not accused of being sexist! In Chinese, you don't have to worry, because "he," "she," and "it" are all pronounced the same: **tā**.

To ask a question in English, you must change the word order: "He is going to Shanghai" becomes "Is he going to Shanghai?" In Chinese, you create a question more simply, by just putting "huh?" at the end of the sentence: "He go Shanghai" becomes "He go Shanghai huh?" The Chinese word for "huh?" is **ma**. It serves the same purpose as the Canadian "eh?" (Canadians say, "He's going to Shanghai, eh?")

A more emphatic Chinese way to ask a question is to say the verb twice, with "not" in between, like this: "He go, not go, Shanghai?" (The Chinese word for "not" is **bù**.)

Chinese has no word for "yes" or "no." To reply to the question "You go Shanghai huh?" just repeat the verb: say "go" (while nodding your head) or "not go" (while shaking your head). To reply to the question "He is American huh?" just repeat the verb: say "is" (**shì**) or "not is," which would be **bù shì**; but the Chinese don't like to say "**bù**" before a verb having the 4th tone, so the Chinese change "**bù**" to "**bú**" in that situation and say "**bú shì**." Since "**bú shì**" sounds like "bullshit," American tourists think Chinese people often talk about bullshit.

When Chinese people are lazy, they don't bother saying the verb after **bù**: they say just **bù**, which means "not" and acts as "no."

American tourists think Chinese people are like ghosts, who always say "boo!"

Though you make the typical Chinese verb negative by putting **bù** (or **bú**) before it, here's a big exception: to make the verb "have" (**yǒu**) be negative, say **méi** instead of **bù**, like this: **méi yǒu** (which means "not have" or "haven't"). For example, if somebody asks whether you have something (or whether you have ever *done* something), reply by saying "have" (**yǒu**) or "haven't" (**méi yǒu**). Chinese people often say they "haven't" done something; they often say **méi yǒu**. Since "**méi yǒu**" sounds like "mayo" (which is American slang for "mayonnaise"), American tourists think Chinese people often talk about mayonnaise.

Another way to indicate yes is to say "correct" (which in Chinese is **duì**). So Chinese often reply to questions by saying **shì** ("is" or "yes"), **bú shì** ("not is" or "no"), **bù** ("not" or "no"), **yǒu** ("have"), **méi yǒu** ("not have" or "haven't"), and **duì** ("certainly").

The Chinese say "please" (**qǐng**) and "thank you" (**xièxie**) less than Americans. If you use them too much, you'll be laughed at for being as hopelessly formal as a British butler. Instead of saying a formal "thank you," Chinese people prefer to be more thoughtful and emotional. When treated to a meal, a Chinese person shows appreciation by saying it was delicious ("good eat extremely," **hǎo chī jíle**); when done a favor, a Chinese person apologizes for having put the generous person to so much trouble ("trouble you already," **máfan nǐ le**).

Names for countries China considers itself to be the center of the universe, so it calls itself the "center country" (**Zōngguó**). Since the Chinese word for "person" is **rén**, a Chinese person is called a "center-country person" (**Zōngguó rén**). The Chinese language (with its written characters) is called "center writing" (**Zōngwen**).

To a Chinese ear, "England" sounds like **Yīngguó** ("flower country"), so that's what the Chinese call England. A British person is called a **Yīngguó rén** ("flower-country person"); the English language is called **Yīngwen** ("flower writing").

To a Chinese ear, "America" sounds like "Mayka" (if you ignore the unaccented syllables), so the Chinese call the U.S. **Měiguó** ("beautiful country"); an American person is called a **Měiguó rén** ("beautiful-country person"). To say "I am an American," say **wǒ shì Měiguó rén** ("I is beautiful-country person").

Vocabulary To speak Chinese well, you must learn many Chinese words. Here are the most popular words and phrases for beginners and tourists. For each phrase, I give the English, then the **Chinglish** (Chinese way of handling the English), then the actual Chinese pinyin:

Pronouns

"I" or "me"	I	**wǒ**
"we" or "us"	I-group	**wǒmen**
"you" (one person)	you	**nǐ**
"y'all"	you-group	**nǐmen**
"it" or "he" or "she" or "him" or "her"	it	**tā**
"they"	it-group	**tāmen**

Goodness

"good" or "okay"	good	**hǎo**
"very good"	very good	**hěn hǎo**

Chitchat

"hello" or "good to see you" (one person)	you good	**nǐ hǎo**
"hello y'all" or "good to see y'all"	you-group good	**nǐmen hǎo**
"good-bye" or "till we meet again"	again meet	**zài jiàn**
"love"	love	**ài**
"I love you"	I love you	**wǒ ài nǐ**
"do you love me?"	you love I huh?	**nǐ ài wo ma**
"how are you feeling?" or "how are you?"	you good huh?	**nǐ hǎo ma**
"I'm feeling fine"	I very good	**wǒ hěn hǎo**
"and how about you?" or "you too?"	you likewise?	**nǐ ne**
"is" or "am" or "are" or "yes, I am"	is	**shì**
"want"	want	**yào**
"I want…"	I want	**wǒ yào**
"I'd like…"	I think want	**wǒ xiǎng yào**
"please…" or "I'd like to invite you to…"	invite	**qǐng**
"thank you"	thank-thank	**xièxie**
"my name is…" or "I'm called…"	I call	**wǒ jiào**

Negatives

"not" or "no, I'm not"	not	**bù**
"bad"	not good	**bù hǎo**
"don't want"	not want	**bú yào**
"you're welcome" or "no need to thank"	not thank	**bù xiè**

Having

"have" or "has"	have	**yǒu**
"haven't" or "I haven't done that"	not-have	**méi yǒu**

Possessives

"'s"	's	**de**
"Wang's"	Wang's	**Wáng de**
"my"	I's	**wǒde**
"your"	you's	**nǐde**
"its" or "his" or "her"	it's	**tāde**

Size

"big"	big	**dà**
"small" or "little" or "young"	little	**xiǎo**

People

"mother" or "mama" or "mom"	mama	**māma**
"father" or "papa" or "dad"	papa	**bàba**
"friend" or "dear friend to have"	friend-have	**péngyou**
"mister" or "husband" or "family head"	first-born	**xiānsheng**
"Mr. Wang"	Wang first-born	**Wáng xiānsheng**
"wife" or "better half"	too-too	**tàitai**
"Mr. Wang's wife" or "Mrs. Wang"	Wang too-too	**Wáng tàitai**

Food

"eat"	eat	**chī**
"beef"	cow meat	**niú ròu**
"pork"	pig meat	**zhū ròu**
"lamb"	sheep meat	**yáng ròu**
"chicken"	chicken	**jī**
"turkey"	fire chicken	**huǒ jī**
"duck"	duck	**yā**
"fish"	fish	**yú**
"salmon"	3-writing fish	**sānwén yú**
"shrimp"	shrimp	**xiā**
"lobster"	dragon shrimp	**lóng xiā**
"soup"	soup	**tāng**

Drinks

"coffee"	coffee	**kāfēi**
"tea"	tea	**chá**
"milk"	cow milk	**niú nǎi**
"water"	water	**shuǐ**
"soda" or "carbonated water"	vapor water	**qì shuǐ**
"cola"	cola	**kělè**
"alcoholic drink"	alcohol	**jiǔ**
"wine"	grape alcohol	**pútáo jiǔ**
"beer"	beer alcohol	**pí jiǔ**

Dialects I've been explaining mainland China's official pronunciation, called **Mandarin**, which is especially popular in the capital city (Beijing) and places nearby. But many far-away regions of China have their own dialects.

For example, **Cantonese** is the dialect spoken in Guangzhou (which used to be called Canton) and places nearby (such as Hong Kong and Macau). Cantonese write the same Chinese characters as Mandarin, but the pronunciation is so different that Cantonese people can't understand Mandarin speakers — and Mandarin people can't understand Cantonese speakers — unless they take courses. (Now the Chinese government requires all students to learn Mandarin.)

How different is Mandarin pronunciation from Cantonese? Very! For example, while Mandarin has 5 tones (high, rising, falling, dipping, and plain), Cantonese is supposed to have 7 (low, medium, high, low-rising-to-medium, medium-rising-to-high, high-falling-to-medium, and medium-falling-to-low).

Many Cantonese speakers are too lazy to do high-falling-to-medium; they replace it with a simple high instead, so they speak just 6 tones instead of 7. Other Cantonese speakers talk extra-musically: they produce 9 tones or even more.

The consonant and vowel sounds are different, too. For example, In Mandarin, the word for "I" or "me" is **wǒ**, but in Cantonese it's **ngo**. In Mandarin, the word for "not" is **bù**, but in Cantonese it's just the sound **m**. In Mandarin, each syllable ends with a vowel or **n**, **ng**, or **r**; in Cantonese, each syllable ends with a vowel or **n**, **ng**, **m**, **k**, **p**, or **t** (or a silent **h** that just means to use low tones).

Since Mandarin is so different from Cantonese, people in Hong Kong complain that Mandarin TV broadcasts to Hong Kong are as hopeless as "the chicken talking to the duck." To add to the confusion, Cantonese speakers have developed many local slang expressions and local characters that Mandarin folks don't understand.

In the United States, Chinese restaurant menus show "Cantonese pinyin" names for the dishes. In China, most people speak Mandarin instead; they won't understand if you ask for food by Cantonese names such as "Lo mein," "Moo shi," and "Chow foon."

Chinglish Chinese grammar is much simpler than English, since Chinese has no plurals, no verb conjugations, no "the," and no "she".

When Chinese try to speak English, they often get confused by English grammar and vocabulary and therefore speak Chinese-confused English, called **Chinglish**.

In China, many signs are written in Chinglish. When you see a sign written in Chinglish, you can have fun guessing what it means. My friends and I saw these examples:

Sign, written in Chinglish	What the sign means
Prohibition From Greenbelt	Keep off the lawn
No Climbon	Don't climb on rocks
Do Not Clamber	Do not climb the rocks
No Naked Light	No cigarettes or other exposed flames
Mind Crotch	Low ceiling: duck your head
Fuck Class Do Not Disturb	Exercise class: do not disturb
Wine, Coffee, Cock	We serve wine, coffee, and cocktails
Breakfart	Breakfast
Sucker (Non-Hot Drink)	Straws for cold drinks
Street Of Noshery	Outdoor food court
Finely Decoration City	Fine interior-design superstore
Ratbow Hotel	Rainbow Hotel
Boardinghouse Sales	Condominium-apartment sales
Erection Engineering Co.	Construction-engineering company
Receives The Silver	Cashier
Hand Grenade	Fire extinguisher
High Grade Puke	High-quality poker cards
Pubic Toilet	Public toilet
Genitl Emen	Gentlemen's restroom
Deformed Man	Handicapped-accessible men's room
Children Free To Pay	Children free from paying
Question Authority	If you have questions, ask the guard
Be Care Of Safe	Be careful, for your safety
Carefully Fall To The River	Beware of falling in the river
Prevent Any Contingency	Be careful not to have an accident
Take Care of Your Slip	Be careful: slippery
Flyover Ramp	Expressway entrance
Planesketch Map	Aerial view
Scared Land	Sacred land
We Struggle For Success	We strive for success

We saw this sign —

> For restrooms, go back toward your behind

which means:

> Restrooms are behind you.

We saw this sign —

> Help Oneself Terminating Machine

which means "ATM."

We saw this sign —

> To tak notice of safe, the slippery are very crafty

which means:

> Take notice, for your safety: slippery stairs require you to be very careful.

At a temple, signs said:

> Avoid conflagration
> Avoid making confused noise when chanting
> Please don't be crowded

They mean:

> Put out your matches and cigarettes
> Be quiet while monks chant
> Don't crowd or shove

To have fun, read those Chinglish signs to your friends and see whether they can guess what the signs mean.

This Chinglish sign is written clearly but too candidly:

> Hospital for Anus and Intestine Disease

So are these signs in a Gynecology & Obstetrics Department:

> Cunt Examination
> Fetal Heart Custody

So are these lawn signs:

> Green grass dreading your feet
> Show mercy to the slender grass
> Don't bother the resting little grass

So is this sign trying to say "automatic-flush toilets":

> This WC is free of washing
> Please leave off after pissing or shitting

So is the comment on an ice-cream wrapper:

> Kiss me, tease me, lick me, bite me,
> let me melted to your heart.
> From the pure chocolate taste,
> for your pure heart!

When writing Chinese characters, the Chinese don't put spaces between their words, and they don't understand why Americans bother, so the Chinese insert spaces into English carelessly. For example, one of China's biggest banks has a huge sign saying:

> AGRICUL TURAL BANK

Many Chinese signs make the mistake of putting a space before 's, like this:

> This is Li Bai 's home

Modern Chinese is written left-to-right (like English), but classic Chinese was written right-to-left (like Hebrew). Chinese signs can be written in either direction. Some Chinese sign-makers forget that English can't be written right-to-left. For example, look at this sign:

> thcaY   taobrotoM
> thgiarts.oG   aera gnimmiwS

It means:

> Motorboats, yachts, swimming area: go straight

Signs by big international corporations usually have correct English. Chinglish errors occur mostly on signs written by the Chinese government and its state-owned companies, which have poorly paid employees who visited the West never or just briefly. You can find more examples of Chinglish signs at www.chinglish.com (click "Photoblog") and www.engrish.com (which includes botched English from China and other Asian countries).

China tried to fix those signs, so tourists wouldn't make fun of China during the 2008 Olympics in Beijing. For details about that effort, read Mei Fong's article on The Wall Street Journal's front page (on February 5, 2007).

Piracy In China, most CD's containing music or computer programs are illegal copies. At first glance, the copies look genuine, but when you stare at them more closely you'll see English words misspelled.

For example, the jacket of a pirated Michael Jackson CD says it includes these songs: "You are not along," "Shake your boby," "Sckeam," and "Fam." (It means "You are not alone," "Shake your body," "Scream," and "Jam.")

History

The world's first humans began in Africa 14 million years ago, where they were black. Some of those migrated north to the Middle East, where they turned lighter. Then some migrated farther north to Europe (where they turned white), while others migrated to India and then China (where they turned yellow) and then to Alaska and the rest of the Americas (where they turned red).

Xia dynasty At first, China's inhabitants were just a bunch of disorganized hunters and farmers (starting half a million years ago), but in **2200 B.C.** a kingdom was finally established. The king's family name was Xia. His kingdom, called the **Xia dynasty**, was ruled by him and later by his descendents.

Shang dynasty In **1750 B.C.**, a rebel leader overthrew the Xia dynasty. His family name was Shang. He started the **Shang dynasty**. During the Shang dynasty, the Chinese people became excellent at working in bronze, and they also began to write more (often by carving characters into pig bones).

During the Shang dynasty, whenever a king would die, he'd be buried with his possessions and more than 100 slaves, who were thrown in his burial pit while they were alive or after being beheaded. (Later dynasties were kinder and threw in terra cotta statues of slaves instead of real people.)

During the Shang dynasty, whenever an important building was finished, the building would be consecrated by sacrificing some humans. Unlike other dynasties, the Shang dynasty used this strange rule: whenever a king died, the next king would be the dead king's brother (not son); and if there were no more brothers left, the kingship would pass to dead king's cousin (the king's mother's oldest nephew).

Zhou dynasty The last Shang king, who was ridiculously mean, was overthrown in **1100 B.C.** by a chieftain from the frontier tribe called Zhou. That chieftain began the **Zhou dynasty**. It was more normal than the Shang dynasty: it used father-to-son succession and it avoided human sacrifice. In 771 B.C., the Zhou dynasty's capital was sacked by barbarians, and king was killed. The king's relatives fled to the east, where they set up a new capital and continued the Zhou dynasty.

During the Zhou dynasty, 3 conflicting philosophies arose:

Confucianism (invented by Confucius in 500 B.C. and written down by his optimistic student Mencius) said you should be **kind**, especially to your ancestors and government, and you should treat your king like a god. That philosophy later became this: a king rules because God wants him to (so you should obey him) — but if the king gets overthrown it's because God no longer considers him worthy enough to be king.

Legalism (invented by Confucius's cynical student Xun-zi) said that to survive you need to be **tough**, ruthless, and trust nobody (and if you run a government you should create a secret police, encourage your citizens to rat on each other, foster an atmosphere of fear, bury your enemies alive, and burn all their books).

Daoism (which began with Lao-zi's book "Dao de Jing") said you should be weirdly **mysterious** & mystical and invent puzzles & paradoxes. Daoism later led to Zen Buddhism.

Even today, Chinese people are confused about which of those 3 philosophies to follow — whether to be kind, tough, or mysterious — and many heartaches are caused by modern Chinese governments who switch erratically among those 3 philosophies.

Toward the end of the Zhou dynasty, the Zhou controlled just the eastern part of China and was fighting other states in battles that grew gigantic, with 500,000 soldiers on each side.

Qin dynasty In **221 B.C.**, the western frontier state called Qin finished winning against all rivals (mainly because Qin had lots of iron to make iron weapons). That began the **Qin dynasty**. (The English name "China" means "Qin's country.")

The Qin's king, Qin Shihuangdi, called himself an "emperor" (a title previously used just for mythological gods). He followed the advice of Legalists: he was tough, killed (or banished) all Confucian scholars who disagreed with the Legalists, burned Confucian books (and most other books too, keeping just books about medicine, pharmacy, agriculture, and divination), and had a policy of executing generals who showed up late for maneuvers. He created the Great Wall by combining together little walls that the warring states had created for themselves (though his version of the Great Wall was still made of just packed earth; later dynasties turned it into brick). To control what had become a big country, he divided it into 36 provinces, each headed by an official who had to report directly to him.

That emperor died in 210 B.C.

Han dynasty Shortly after Qin Shihangdi's death, a soldier bringing in draftees was getting delayed by rain. He feared getting executed for tardiness along with his draftees, so the whole group of them decided to revolt. Those revolutionaries got executed, but the turmoil they fomented led to new leadership in **206 B.C.**: the **Han dynasty**, which is considered China's best dynasty. (Most people in modern China proudly claim they are "Han Chinese.") During the Han dynasty, China gained many improvements:

Paper was invented (made from rags or bark), so people started writing characters by using ink brushes instead of carving. Government was based on Confucianism (friendly respect) rather than Legalism (meanness). Local officials were selected by civil-service exams instead of heredity. The Imperial University was created, to teach Confucian classics and prepare students for civil-service exams. Engineers invented irrigation methods, sundials, water clocks, and seismographs (earthquake detectors). China expanded westward and created The Old Silk Road, on which ambassadors and traders traveled to the Greek empire to sell silk. The trading brought to China new ideas, such as Buddhism from India.

The Han dynasty ruled until 220 A.D. — except for a brief interruption by a reformer named Wang Mang. (He had worked in the royal palace and was appointed "emperor" by the Han household from 8 A.D. until his death in 25 A.D.)

In **220 A.D.**, the Han dynasty fell apart. Here's why:

People were migrating from the Yellow River (which is in the north) to the Yangzi River (which is in the south), especially because barbarian tribes were raiding the north. The Han dynasty had trouble managing the change.

Civil servants became corrupt. They sided with landlords in oppressing the peasants, who finally revolted.

350 years of confusion After the Han dynasty fell, China got 350 years of fighting and confusion, during which the Han people kept moving south, while barbarians kept moving into China from the north and assimilated themselves into the northern population. Also during that period, Buddhism (which had come from India) became more popular and started including features from Daoism.

Post-Han dynasties Finally, China got major dynasties:

The **Sui dynasty (589-618)** unified China again. This dynasty was based in the north (and therefore partly barbarian).

The **Tang dynasty (618-907)** was almost as good as the Han. It was based in the north (and so partly barbarian). During the Tang dynasty, block printing was invented, which helped spread the written word to the masses.

The **Song dynasty (960-1279)** was almost as good as the Han and the Tang. During the Song dynasty, use of the printing press spread, and better ways were invented to grow and harvest rice. (One of the tricks was to use a fast-growing kind of rice from Vietnam.) Before the Song dynasty, Chinese people had just two ways to get rich & famous (be in the government or own land), but during the Song dynasty a third rich-and-famous class was formed: merchants.

Unfortunately, the Song rice system worked so well that future dynasties saw no need to improve it further, no need to do more research, no need to industrialize, and China's progress started to fall behind Europe's.

The **Yuan dynasty (1279-1368)** was established by Mongolian barbarian horsemen who attacked from the north. The Yuan dynasty was actually a puppet government controlled by the Mongolian Supreme Leader, Kublai Khan (Genghis Khan's grandson). The Mongolians were kind enough to leave Chinese culture intact and not destroy it.

Two Italian brothers, Niccolo & Matteo Polo, were the first Europeans to travel across Asia, where they met Kublai Khan in China, who gave them a letter to take back to the Pope, saying China wanted the Pope to send teachers. On their second trip to China, they took a letter from the Pope (along with two missionaries who chickened out before reaching China), and they also took along Niccolo's son, Marco Polo, who impressed Kublai Khan and became Kublai Khan's advisor and a governor of big provinces. After 20 years in China, Marco Polo returned to Italy and wrote a book telling Europeans how great China was.

Unfortunately, the paragraph you've just read might be full of lies and exaggerations, since our only source of info about the Polo family is Marco Polo's book, which historians don't completely believe, because:

The Chinese have no records of any "Marco Polo," even though the Chinese keep careful records and he claimed to be governor.

Some of his book's Chinese events seem awfully similar to events in French romance novels written earlier by his editor.

It's strange that in such a long travelogue he never mentioned Chinese characters, chopsticks, tea, or the Great Wall, though apologists have theories about why he might want to skip those topics.

Regardless of its truthfulness, his book had a big effect on Europe: it made Europeans curious about China.

But land travel from Europe to China became endangered by bandits in-between, so Europeans started searching for a way to reach China by sea. (Later, that searching made Columbus accidentally discover America.)

The **Ming dynasty (1368-1644)** was started by a rebellious army officer (who was Han Chinese and had previously been a peasant and a Buddhist monk), so it was a true Chinese empire (that threw the Mongolian leaders out). Life during the Ming dynasty was peaceful — except that when that first Ming emperor discovered his prime minister was plotting against him, he beheaded the prime minister and the prime minister's family and 40,000 other people too.

The **Qing dynasty (1644-1911)** was run by Manchurian barbarians who attacked from the North, so it was disliked.

During the Qing dynasty, China was approached by Westerners (the Portuguese then the Spanish, British, French, Germans, Russians, and Americans), who wanted to buy Chinese tea, silk, and porcelain. But the Qing dynasty didn't want to buy much from Westerners in return, so trade was stifled.

British traders solved the problem by encouraging people in the Chinese city of Guangzhou to buy raw cotton and opium that the British shipped from British-controlled India. Opium was illegal in China, but the British got it in by using Chinese smugglers and corrupt officials.

The Qing dynasty sent a commissioner to Guangzhou to stop the illegal opium traffic. He detained all foreigners and destroyed 20,000 chests of British opium. The British retaliated by starting the Opium War in 1839. China was surprised at the strength of the British navy and lost the war in 1842 to Britain, which won many concessions from China, including the entire island of Hong Kong, plus tax breaks and freedom from having to obey any Chinese laws. That made the Chinese more curious about Western thought, so Chinese scholars started studying Western thinking.

After several more revolts, famines, and foreign takeovers of China's puppets (the French took over South Vietnam and Cambodia, the British took over Burma and Kowloon, the Russians took over Turkestan, and the Japanese took over Taiwan and Korea), the Qing dynasty finally was overthrown by dissidents in 1911. It was the last dynasty!

Republics In **1912**, a republic was formed, whose presidents would be chosen by legislatures instead of by heredity. The first president was **Dr. Sun Yat-sen** ("Sun Yixian" in pinyin), who was born in China but grew up in Hawaii and had also been a physician in Hong Kong and lived in Japan & the United States and raised donations from Chinese people around the world. Nearly everybody liked him, and he's called "The Father of Modern China.".

But a military leader, **Yuan Shikai**, wanted to be president too. To prevent civil war, Dr. Sun agreed to step down and let Yuan Shikai be the leader.

But Yuan Shikai turned out to be a despot. He changed the constitution to give himself more power. Dr. Sun's friend, **Song Jiaoren**, created a political party (called the **Nationalists** or **National People's Party** or **Guomindang** or **Kuomintang** or **KMT**), which campaigned against Yuan Shikai and won most of the seats in the legislature. Yuan Shikai responded by having Song Jiaoren and several pro-KMT generals all be assassinated. Then 7 provinces rebelled against Yuan Shikai, but he suppressed the rebellion. Scared, the legislature agreed to confirm Yuan Shikai as president. Then he outlawed the KMT and removed all its members from the legislature. Then he suspended the whole legislature and forced onto China a new constitution that made him president for life. Then he decided to become a monarch. Then everybody revolted against him, but before they could lynch him he died of natural causes in 1916.

Then China broke apart: regional warlords fought each other. In 1919, Dr. Sun reestablished the KMT, and in 1921 the KMT controlled southern China, but warlords still controlled northern China (and Beijing). Dr. Sun tried to get help from Western countries, but they ignored him, so he turned to the Soviet Union, which agreed to help his KMT but also help a smaller party, the **Chinese Communist Party (CCP)**. The Soviet Union started trying to convince those two parties to merge.

In 1923, Dr. Sun's lieutenant, **Chiang Kai-shek** ("Jiang Jieshi" in pinyin), went to Moscow for military training. When he returned to China, he set up a military academy in China.

In **1925**, Dr. Sun died of cancer. Then Chiang Kai-shek started battling the northern warlords and became the KMT's leader. In 1926, he conquered half of China.

But after thwarting a kidnapping attempt against him, he got nervous about Communists, dismissed his Soviet advisors, and prevented Communists from holding any KMT leadership positions. Then he declared Communist membership to be a crime punishable by death, and he started killing the Communists. One Communist who managed to escape the carnage was **Mao Zedong** (who'd been a peasant, student, librarian, and poet). He and other communists fled west. At that point, China had 3 capitals: Beijing (in the north, controlled by warlords), Nanjing (in the southeast, controlled by the KMT), and Wuhan (in the central south, controlled by the Communists). In 1928, the KMT conquered Beijing. In 1934, the KMT tried to conquer to Communists also, but the Communists escaped by fleeing to the west then north then east, traveling a total of about 6,000 miles, which took about a year, mainly under Mao Zedong's leadership; that's called "The Long March." During all that, the Communists developed a reputation for being nice (especially to peasants), while the KMT were considered mean.

Meanwhile, the Japanese started invading China (Manchuria in 1931, Shanghai in 1932, and the rest of China in 1937). Eventually, the Japanese killed 20 million Chinese people (and raped many Chinese women).

Chiang Kai-shek still wanted to concentrate on fighting the Communists, but his KMT associates finally convinced him to fight the Japanese instead. The Communists fought the Japanese also.

At the end of World War 2, the Japanese lost, and so did the KMT: the Communist Party emerged the winner for the hearts, minds, and bodies of the Chinese. Chiang Kai-shek and his KMT fled to the island of Taiwan, where he became Taiwan's leader. (Under KMT leadership, Taiwan gradually improved. Now Taiwan's a good, democratic country, full of freedom. It's modern and financially successful. It's particularly strong at manufacturing computers and other electronic devices.)

On October 1, **1949**, the Communist leader (Mao Zedong) stood in Beijing and proclaimed that the mainland was now under Communist control and called the **People's Republic of China (PRC)**. It was indeed a republic, except that just members of the Communist Party could run for office.

The PRC's leaders divided into two groups: the leftists versus the rightists:

What leftists wanted	What rightists wanted
be nicer to the peasants (farmers)	be nicer to the merchants and intellectuals
be socialist: share the wealth	be capitalist: create your own wealth
be nicer to the Soviet Union	be nicer to the U.S. and Europeans
force people to share burdens	gently nudge people to improve

Mao tended to be a leftist (because of his peasant background), and his wife was even more leftist. The leftists tried many extreme experiments, such as these:

During the **Great Leap Forward** in 1958, peasants were forced to work together in gigantic communes. The average commune held 5,000 families, 20,000 people, all sharing a field, a dining hall, a nursery, classrooms, and a furnace to make pig iron (for turning into steel). There were 23,500 of those communes.

People were forced to work in factories making steel.

Trees were burned to create farms and fuel for making steel.

During the **Cultural Revolution**, which began in 1966, kids & teachers were kicked out of high schools and universities and forced to work on farms instead. From 1968 to 1972, no high schools or universities were allowed to accept any new students; the only remaining students were ones who'd entered in earlier years.

Some of those policies had disastrous results. For example, China is now short of trees, so China has bad air, full of dust and pollution. China's commune experiment was unsuccessful and caused a famine that killed 30 million Chinese people. (Hey, that's a lot of deaths: 10,000 times as many as were killed in the September 11th attacks that Americans got so upset about. To see anything happen on a really big scale, you gotta go to China!)

The leftists decided that big projects should be run by socialists, not technologists. They said "Better Red than Expert." As a result, many projects failed, and many factories produced goods that had poor quality.

Mao died in 1976.

In **1978**, a rightist named **Deng Xiaoping** gained control. Many state-run businesses were privatized. (Unfortunately, some of those businesses then went bankrupt and stopped paying the pensions that were due to retirees, who suddenly became destitute.)

Deng let technologists and capitalists run projects, regardless of ideology. He said:

It doesn't matter if the cat is black or white. What matters is how well it catches mice.

He also said it's okay to let some people get rich. He even said:

To get rich is glorious.

Deng died in **1997**. After him came his protégé, **Jiang Zemin**, then the current leader, **Hu Jintao**, who've both continued Deng's rightist policies.

Now Chinese citizens are allowed to criticize the Chinese government — but permissible criticism is limited to attacking screw-ups (corrupt bribed officials, inefficiency, and inertia), not the Communist system itself.

China's new worry is that China's economic boom hasn't benefited the peasants yet, and the income gap between China's rich and China's poor has widened. For example, half of the Chinese people are poor peasants who don't have *any* electricity yet, not even for light bulbs, while many of China's rich buy air conditioners and cars. In cities, rich people live in condos in new high rises constructed by companies whose rich investors haven't yet paid the migrant laborers who actually shouldered the work. Those migrants are dirt poor, still waiting for the pay they were promised but never received. In some cities, the electric and water companies haven't been beefed up enough yet to handle all the new factories and high-rise apartments, so people suffer from rationing and brownouts. Half of all bank loans aren't repaid on time. In March **2004**, Hu Jintao gave a speech in which he promised to solve those problems by changing the tax rates (to favor the poor) and handing out fewer private construction permits, until the infrastructure has time to catch up. He also promised to make factories obey China's minimum-wage law, which most companies have ignored, and that's why China's goods have been so cheap!

Frontline In the U.S., public television's *Frontline* showed a documentary film about how life in China changed dramatically, with some folks becoming lucky capitalists and others becoming ill beggars. The documentary tracked the lives of several people from different walks of life, in different parts of China, from 1998 (when the Chinese government decided to become more capitalist) to 2002. The documentary had surprisingly sad endings:

A mayor who was handsome, powerful, effective, and beloved by his town (in the 1998 part of the documentary) wound up in jail (where he supposedly "died suddenly from cancer") because of a corruption scandal.

A peasant woman shown with an untreated goiter was "not allowed to be filmed" afterwards — because the government said "her problem reflects badly on her village."

Retirees protest because their employers, state-run companies, have gone bankrupt and don't pay pensions anymore, leaving the retirees destitute.

In a factory, a woman manager is forced to take a huge salary cut and lower position (cleaning all toilets!) to avoid being downsized and lose her pension potential.

A peasant kid leaves his farm, to go to refrigerator-repair school in Beijing, but the school makes him do slave labor tearing down brick walls instead.

Constitution Since China is supposed to be a "republic," it needed a constitution. China's constitution is a bizarre mix of leftist and rightist thinking.

The Communist Party is the only party mentioned in the constitution, and the constitution's Article 1 calls China a "democratic dictatorship." Here's the full text of Article 1 (in its final version, as revised in 1982):

> Article 1. The People's Republic of China is a socialist state under the people's democratic dictatorship led by the working class and based on the alliance of workers and peasants. The socialist system is the basic system of the People's Republic of China. Sabotage of the socialist system by any organization or individual is prohibited.

Article 34 says you're guaranteed the right to vote — unless the government doesn't want you to:

> Article 34. All PRC citizens who've reached age 18 have the right to vote and stand for election, regardless of nationality, race, sex, occupation, family background, religious belief, education, property status, or length of residence, except persons deprived of political rights according to law.

Article 36 gives you freedom of religion — unless your religion causes protests or seems physically or mentally "unhealthy" or is controlled by a foreigner, such as the Pope:

> Article 36. PRC citizens enjoy freedom of religious belief. No state organ, public organization, or individual may compel citizens to believe in, or not to believe in, any religion; nor may the discriminate against citizens who believe in, or do not believe in, any religion. The state protects normal religious activities. No one may make use of religion to engage in activities that disrupt public order, impair the health of citizens, or interfere with the state's education system. Religious bodies and religious affairs aren't subject to any foreign domination.

Article 40 protects your privacy — except when the government wishes to censor you:

> Article 40. The freedom & privacy of PRC citizens' correspondence are protected by law. No organization or individual may, on any ground, infringe on the freedom & privacy of citizens' correspondence except in cases where, to meet the needs of state security or of investigation into criminal offenses, public security or procuratorial organs are allowed to censor correspondence in accordance with procedures prescribed by law.

So long As you can see, Chinese history is quite long. Chinese centralized government (the first dynasty) began in 2200 B.C., which was about 4200 years ago. By contrast, U.S. centralized government (declared by the Declaration of Independence) began in 1776, which was about 230 years ago. That makes "China" nearly 20 times as old as the "United States"! Compared to age-old China, the U.S. is just a baby country, too young to have any serious history yet.

A Chinese friend attended a party in the U.S. and heard a guest say she was getting a Ph.D. in U.S. history. He laughed and said, "How can you get a Ph.D. in U.S. history? The U.S. has no history!"

Chinese people love to watch, on Chinese TV, dramas about Chinese history, especially the intrigues of the emperors and the women who lived with them. They're much more fascinating than U.S. battles between cowboys and Indians (whoops, I mean "Native Americans").

What to read For a funny romp through Chinese history, read "Condensed China" at:

http://asterius.com/china

Then grab more details by reading "History of China" at:

www.chaos.umd.edu/history

The full Chinese constitution has 138 articles plus 13 amendments. You can read them (except the 10 new amendments added in 2004) on the Internet in English at:

http://english.peopledaily.com.cn/constitution/constitution.html

My trip to China

I've always been curious about Chinese language and culture. When I lived in Boston, I loved to visit Boston's Chinatown. I even joined some Chinese clubs. Six years ago, I married a Chinese immigrant, whose nickname is "Donna." In a section of this book called "Donna's comments," you can read her comments about China, the United States, and me.

Though I married Donna, I never had a chance to visit China or her relatives — until this year. What a treat! Visiting China was eye-opening fun!

I told Donna I wanted to meet her relatives and also see how Chinese people live, rather than just hit tourist spots. So she let me visit Chinese homes, take walks with her friends, and go shopping with them for everyday needs.

China is too huge to be seen completely, and my time was limited to 2 weeks (so I could return to New Hampshire and resume answering the endless phone calls about life and computers). I had to adopt this strict schedule: in January 2004, I flew into the capital (**Beijing**), then quickly flew to **Chengdu** (a beautiful city in Sichuan province), then got driven to her home town, **Jiangyou** (2 hours north of Chengdu), where I spent 9 days (with side trips to nearby towns), Then I retraced my steps back to Chengdu (where I lingered 2 days), Beijing (2 more days), and the U.S., so the whole experience lasted 15 days (including transportation).

Beijing's become quite westernized. The first time I saw it, it looked like an American city (Washington D.C. or the Queens part of New York City), except its signs were in Chinese.

Chengdu has more Asian character but is also partly westernized. Jiangyou is much smaller and hasn't been westernized as much yet, so I found it the most fascinating, the most "authentic," the most memorable.

Here are my comments. Most are about Jiangyou, but some apply to the other cities too....

China's 3 moods

China is dominated by 3 moods: a rush to westernize, a willingness to bend, and quiet.

Rush to westernize For many centuries, China was isolated from western culture. Now China is rushing to catch up. China is rushing to grab ideas, languages, appliances, cars, language, music, software, the Internet, consumer goods, brands, lifestyles, ideas, and everything else, from the U.S. and Europe (with some help from Japan). But while rushing to do all that, the Chinese take short cuts, which result in poor workmanship and lack of finesse. My summary of China in 2004 is this:

> China has always been very beautiful.
> China is now also very modern — and everything almost works.

Willingness to bend To understand China, look at its trees. Many of China's trees have branches that bend wildly, unlike American and German trees, whose branches are boringly straight. China's culture is inspired by Chinese trees: the culture bends.

For example, Chinese characters have strokes that bend: there are no simple, straight strokes. Traditional Chinese buildings have roofs that are slanted (pitched), but they bend slightly up at the edges and bend up even more at the corners, to form dramatic curves. Chinese people love to bend the rules: they interpret every rule and law "flexibly."

If a person creates anything exactly straight or acts properly straight-arrow, the Chinese would consider that person too Germanically rigid, an uncultured goose-stepping Nazi asshole, though Western technology keeps trying to impose that requirement.

Quiet Chinese people tend to act quietly, mysteriously.

The love of mystery comes from Daoism. The need to act quietly — tactfully — stems from many centuries of fearing the wrath of Chinese government leaders and officials: if you open your mouth, you might get beheaded, figuratively or literally. Even now, the Chinese government accepts no criticism of its system. Since Chinese households have traditionally been large (including grandparents, grandkids, and other relatives) and close-knit — and since friendships are also tightly woven and are needed to get job references — speaking your mind can get you booed by many generations of people and the whole town and make you become a worthless person.

So Chinese kids still learn this rule: you'd better shut up!

How to travel

Traveling to and through China is an adventure.

Get your visa If you're an American who wants to visit China, you must get an American passport (from the U.S. government) and a Chinese visa (from the Chinese government).

Be careful what you say on your visa application! On mine, I made the mistake of saying my occupation was "publisher and author of computer books." I should have left out the word "author," since the Chinese government doesn't trust "authors." The Chinese consulate phoned my wife and grilled her about me, with questions such as:

> What cities are you two going to? Where's *that* city? It's not in Tibet? What does Russ write? Does he write *just* computer books? Are you sure he doesn't write about anything else?

They're paranoid about foreign journalists interviewing real Chinese citizens, especially in Tibet!

Donna said I was just a dumb computer guy (which was true at that time). The consulate said that was okay. But I might not be allowed to return to China in the future.

After America's September 11th tragedy, the U.S. government got meaner about foreigners visiting the U.S., so the Chinese government got meaner about Americans visiting China: the visa fee has been raised, and you're not allowed to get your visa by mail — you must personally walk into the Chinese consulate (or bribe a friend or travel agent to walk in for you).

Beijing-airport tax Whenever you want to fly out of Beijing airport (to the U.S. or other countries or other Chinese cities), you must get a ticket but then, afterwards, stand in a special separate line to pay an airport-construction departure tax.

If your travel agent forgot to mention the airport-construction departure tax, or you were duped into thinking your ticket includes all taxes, tough luck! No ticket sold in the U.S. or China or anywhere else ever includes that airport-construction departure tax: you must go stand in the tax line and make sure you haven't spent all your money already — or you won't get home!

Warning: the tax is very high and depends on where you're going.

7 road vehicles Chinese cities (such as Beijing, Chengdu, and Jiangyou) all have modern streets, like U.S. cities.

In Jiangyou, you commonly see 7 kinds of vehicles: **bicycles**, **tricycles**, **motorcycles**, **taxis**, **cars**, **vans**, and **buses**. (Trucks and trains are rare.)

The typical **bicycle** has a just a tiny basket in front. It doesn't hold much.

Tricycles come in two forms.

Simple form: the rider sits near the front wheel; vegetables sit in a cart suspended over the back wheels. The contraption acts as a human-powered pickup truck.

Fancy form: the driver sits near the front wheel, but a buggy is suspended over the back wheels. The typical buggy holds two paying passengers (just one if the buggy is slim). The contraption acts as a human-powered taxi. The driver spends his whole day pedaling, looking for passengers and hauling them. He needs strong legs! Like a convertible car, the buggy has a roof to put up during rain; the roof protects the passengers but not the poor driver. You could call the whole thing a "rickshaw," though that term was used mainly in the old days for a more primitive contraption that had just two wheels and forced the driver to walk. The proper term for this 3-wheeled human-pedaled taxicab is a **pedicab** or **trishaw**. This "tricycle taxi" is slower than a real taxi but popular because it's cheap and can squeeze into side streets too narrow for 4-wheeled beasts. In Chengdu (which is more advanced than Jiangyou), tricycles have motorcycle engines, so drivers don't need strong legs! In another town, Luoyang, tricycles are prohibited because they look too primitive for modern town like Luoyang!

Most **motorcycles** resemble the ones in the U.S. and Japan.

Taxis, **cars**, and **vans** are slightly smaller than the ones in the U.S., because most Chinese people are short and thin and have less money. (If you're 6 feet tall, you'll need to duck.) 10 years ago, most of China's cars were made by Volkswagen, and many of them are still on the streets, but newer vehicles have a wide variety of brands, especially Changan (which is Chinese), Citroen (which is French), and Buick (which is American). Minivans are too expensive for normal use: they're used mainly by government-employee car pools. Cars and minivans cost more in China than in the U.S.; for example, a minivan in China costs $60,000. (Most other goods cost slightly less in China than in the U.S.)

In Jiangyou, the **buses** have no doors. Instead, the bus's doorway has strips of clear plastic hanging down from the ceiling; to enter the bus, you push the plastic strips aside. Most stores are the same way: no doors, just plastic strips to push aside. That's because Jiangyou is in Sichuan province, which is always warm. (You'll find more doors in Beijing, which is farther north.)

Besides the bicycles, tricycles, motorcycles, taxis, cars, vans, and buses, the streets also contain **pedestrians**.

How to drive Here's how to drive a car, Jiangyou style:

If your car's about to hit a pedestrian, don't bother stopping: cars have the right of way over pedestrians, because cars are bigger. It's the pedestrian's responsibility to get out of the way. Crosswalks (which are striped and called **zebra lines**) just mean pedestrians should walk there, not elsewhere; they *don't* mean cars must stop there. If you think a pedestrian doesn't see you, tap your horn once or twice lightly, quickly, politely, to warn the pedestrian courteously.

You should drive on road's right-hand side, usually. But if traffic's heavy there, go drive on the road's left side instead, until the oncoming traffic threatens to hit you. That's true even on an expressway: if the right lanes move slowly, go drive on the highway's other side awhile.

If you're driving faster than the car to your right (who's in a slower lane), put your left blinker on, even though you're not changing lanes. In this situation, the left blinker doesn't mean you're changing lanes; it means "I'm passing you." You should also honk politely, once or twice, or flash your lights. The blinker, honking, and flashing all mean: "Stay out of my way, I'm going faster than you, be careful!" Instead of pondering, just follow this simple rule: whenever you're driving in the fastest lane, leave your left blinker on the whole time (even if you're in that lane many minutes); and whenever you see a slow-lane car you're passing, honk or flash.

When driving on city streets, beep once or twice at any car or pedestrian that you think might come closer, to make sure you're noticed and not hit. Since city streets are busy, keep one hand by your horn at all times: you should beep (or double-beep) about once every 10 seconds, under normal traffic conditions.

Drive as if you were in a ski slalom: zoom around the cones, other cars, pedestrians, bicyclists, tricyclists, etc., but always politely, with polite little beeps. If you hear strange rumbles, don't worry: it's just your half-broken car or the half-broken street. "Driving" means "swerving while rumbling and politely beeping." It's fun! Just keep your eyes open and signal the other adventurers, so nobody gets hurt. It's like being in an amusement park's "bumper cart," except you're not allowed to touch the other players — but it's fine fun to come within 4 inches of each other: it happens all the time.

Since Chinese drivers don't leave much distance between themselves and other cars, crashes are common. When driving on the expressway from Chengdu to Jiangyou, I saw a 40-car pileup: the highway suddenly turned into a junkyard full of dented trucks, buses, minivans, BMW's, and all other vehicles imaginable. Very impressive!

To encourage drivers to stay farther apart, expressways have signs showing what "50 meters apart" looks like and what "100 meters apart" looks like. But drivers ignore them.

Intersections Though Chinese drivers don't take traffic lanes and distances seriously, they respect traffic lights. As in the U.S., red means "stop" and green means "go." In the U.S., the red light is always above the green, but in cities such as Jiangyou the lights are mounted randomly: sometimes red above green, sometimes green above red, sometimes red left of green, sometimes green left of red. That confuses the colorblind. It also confuses tourists from America, since in America "red left of green" means "don't go in the left lane but you can go in the right lane." Traffic lights are usually polite: they show a countdown of how many seconds remain before the light changes.

That's how traffic lights work, but they're rare. Most small intersections have no lights. Most big intersections have rotaries instead. The typical rotary is huge (2 blocks wide), with a center that's a grassy park full of strolling pedestrians (plus the elderly doing aerobic martial-arts exercises), who get into the park by playing a game of chicken with the cars. At night, the park's grass looks so green that you'll wonder how the Chinese got such amazing fertilizer, until you look more closely and see the trick: the grass is lit by floodlights that are tinted green.

Careless drivers At night, many cars turn on just dim parking lights or don't turn on any lights at all. Seatbelts are usually ignored — even on expressways, where they're theoretically required.

Expressways The typical expressway has 3 lanes in each direction. They're labeled in Chinglish. For example, on the expressway from Chengdu to Jiangyou, the left lane is called the "overtaking lane"; the middle lane is called the "main lane"; the right lane, which is for breakdowns and other slowed traffic, is called the "parking lane."

Atop the expressway's tollbooths, you see a giant surprise: a huge, surprising billboard ad that's hundreds of feet wide, so it stretches over all the lanes and all booths. Wow! U.S. highway departments would raise lots of money (and complaints) if they'd do the same and turn U.S. tollbooth roofs into billboards.

Ask for directions When you try to find your way through small cities (such as Jiangyou), you discover there are no available maps and no numbers on buildings. Sorry, guys: you must "act like a woman" and continually ask for directions from knowledgeable local folks (handsome policemen, taxi drivers, tricyclists, and neighbors).

Housing

Rural peasants often live in shacks. City folks usually live in apartments (rented apartments or condo apartments). In Jiangyou, for example, many huge condo complexes are being built fast; each complex holds thousands of people.

Cheap luxury Housing is cheap. For example, my wife (Donna) bought a brand new 3-bedroom condo apartment in Jiangyou for just $12,000. That price includes just bare cement walls and floors; she added $10,000 for appliances, furniture, and décor (with help from her brothers in choosing and installing it), making a total of $22,000. The result is drop-dead gorgeous, the kind of place that would cost a million dollars if it were in Manhattan on Park Avenue.

Her daughter (Mimi) bought an even more gorgeous condo apartment, also new, in a fancier city (Chengdu) for $20,000, plus $10,000 for appliances, furniture and décor (including the fee to the interior designer). That apartment has just 2 bedrooms, but the décor and location are superb.

Exteriors Most of China's beauty is hidden: the insides of apartments can be gorgeous, but the outsides are drab. Many apartment buildings are just raw cement; others have the cement covered by a tile façade.

(Wood is rarely used in Chinese construction, since most trees were destroyed and burned during the "Great Leap Forward." Brick is rare also.)

Some buildings have gigantic ornaments mounted on their roofs to make the buildings look taller, more impressive, and classy.

Stairs The typical apartment building is 7 stories high but has no elevator. If you live on the top floor, you need strong legs! One reason why Chinese people are thin is that they get lots of exercise running up and down stairs. (A few apartment buildings have elevators, but those buildings cost too much.)

Even in the nicest apartment buildings, the stairwells are disappointing. The stairs are just cement slabs, covered with dust instead of carpets, and the stairwell's walls are gashed by people moving furniture in and out.

To save electricity, the stairwell lights are usually off. They're supposed to turn themselves on when noise is detected, but they're not sensitive enough, so they tend to stay off until you stomp hard on the stairs. As a result, you'll see a lot of Chinese people stomping and hollering in stairwells at night, just to get the darn lights to turn on. That's another example of how things in China "almost work."

One reason why the stairwells are a mess is that nobody's responsible for making them better. Condo dwellers pay almost no monthly maintenance fee, so almost no common-area maintenance gets done.

Ceilings Americans like to decorate apartment walls, but the Chinese prefer to decorate apartment ceilings instead.

For example, in Donna's Jiangyou apartment, the living-room ceiling has edges hiding dozens of recessed colored lights. They're turned on mainly to celebrate holidays and amuse visitors. Many restaurants use those same kinds of lights.

Many restaurants also hang red paper Chinese lanterns from the ceiling, since red is the Chinese color for happiness. (Americans seeing red think of cherries or blood, but the Chinese think of cheer instead.)

Walls Chinese wall decorations are plain: just a few photos or simple art.

Floors For flooring, you'll see beautiful woods, tiles, and throw rugs, but no wall-to-wall carpeting.

Dirty shoes Since the stairwells and streets are so dusty, the Chinese typically take off their shoes when entering homes or apartments. The homeowner tries to lend everybody slippers.

If a big crowd of visitors enters the home, there might not be enough slippers to fit everybody, so people try this alternative: when they enter the home, they put blue plastic bags over their shoes, then walk in the bagged shoes. The bags act as galoshes but look ugly, like Wal-Mart shopping bags. To a toddler looking up at the crowd, the people look like gigantic carrots sprouting from shopping bags that are hopping across the floor.

Where's the toilet?
If you're an American visiting a typical Chinese home, your biggest culture shock will be when you visit the bathroom: there's no toilet to sit on. Instead, there's just a hole in the floor: you piss or shit in the hole (while squatting), then push a flush button on the wall.

The hole's made of porcelain and includes a long shitting area (so you can't miss). It looks like a urinal that fell over and sunk into the floor.

Since you must squat rather than sit, the typical Chinese bathroom contains no magazines to read.

Just the most westernized homes (such as Donna's and Mimi's) have sitting toilets. They require you to flush twice (press the left button and also the right button).

Where's the bathtub?
The typical Chinese home has no bathtub. When you take a shower, there's no tub and little or no curtain, so the whole bathroom floor gets wet. That's why the typical Chinese bathroom floor has a gigantic grated drain hole, plus a mop to help you push water into that hole.

In Donna's apartment, which is luxurious, the bathroom actually includes a shower stall, with a sliding door and its own drain! That stall is quite fancy, with water squirting you from the stall's sides, the stall's roof, and the stall's hand-held hose. Whee — it's fun! The stall looks like a Jacuzzi that was tilted on its side to stand upright. It even includes a ledge to rest your foot on while the foot is washed. Like most other things in China, when that shower stall was first installed it failed — the hot water turned cold after about 10 seconds — but her brothers grabbed their wrenches and fixed the plumbing themselves, rather than go through the trouble of yelling at the "professional" plumbers they'd hired to construct the bathroom.

Hot water
In China, hot water can be temperamental because the typical home has no hot-water tank.

Instead, the apartment's hot-water heater is tankless, gas-fired, and hides in the kitchen. When you turn on a hot-water faucet anywhere in the apartment, the heater senses the drop in water pressure and turns itself on, instantly heating the water passing through the heater's pipe.

If two people try using hot water at the same time, the heater is usually inadequate.

Hot air
To heat the air in winter, Beijing (which is cold) uses American-style piped heat.

Sichuan (which is warm like Atlanta) uses big electric space heaters instead, which are stashed in corners or mounted on walls. In the summer, those space heaters act as air conditioners: they have secret pipes to the outside, to the blow heat out.

Windows
Many apartments have luxurious big windows (which Americans call "picture windows").

But like most other things in China, those beautiful windows are made cheaply: just single-pane. They offer little insulation. Especially in Sichuan's winter, they collect so much dew that they look like somebody dumped a bucket of oil on them: they're too blurry to see through, until the dew evaporates in the afternoon.

Cheap workmanship
Here are other examples of cheap workmanship I've seen in new products:

The edges of windows have too much putty residue that wasn't scraped off.

The edges of bathroom floors have too much caulk.

The towel racks are loose: if you lean on a rack, it will fall off the wall (and you'll fall on your face).

On drawers, the door handles are mounted upside down (so you must stand on your head to read their brands).

Appliances
The Chinese homes I visited in Sichuan typically had a big T.V. screen, a CD player, a DVD player, nice furniture, and a washing machine. But you get no clothes dryer, so you must hang the clothes somewhere (a room, patio, or porch) and wait for them to dry.

There are two kinds of washing machine: the newest kind (called "automatic") resembles American kinds, but a cheaper kind (called "semi-automatic") is still popular and works like this:

You see two holes in the top. Put the clothes in the left hole, then turn on that hole's power. You see jets of water squirt at the clothes (as if the clothes were in a Jacuzzi), as rubber sponges spin against the clothes and lint get collected. But that hole has no spin cycle: when the left hole is done washing the clothes, you must take them out and put them into the right hole, which spins them. While spinning, the water coming out of the clothes is automatically piped back to the left hole, to be used for the next wash. Unfortunately, putting the clothes into the left hole and then the right hole doesn't wash the clothes well, so families normally rewash the clothes by going through that whole procedure 2 or 3 times.

You get no "dishwasher" machine, but upper-income folks (like Mimi) have the next best thing: a "dish dryer" (which looks like a microwave oven).

Light switches
The typical American light switch looks male: it's a prick that sticks out of the wall. The typical Chinese light switch looks female instead: it's a rounded button (which you press or rock).

In a Chinese bathroom, the switches are covered by a clear plastic shell that keeps humidity out of the electronics. To access those switches, lift the shell first.

Water
Though China's tap water has improved, the Chinese still don't trust it, so they boil it before drinking. Then they drink it warm, or wait for it to cool, or make it cool faster by refrigerating it.

Protective ornaments
Where the hallway meets the living room, the wall's protruding corners are covered with dark-wood protective ornaments, so if you accidentally bump into the corner, you'll be banging those protectors instead of wrecking the wall.

Hotel frugality
When we visited Beijing, Donna treated me to a "4-star international hotel." (It was called "international" because it included a bathtub.) It used two tricks to discourage us from being wasteful:

When we entered our room, the lights stayed on for just half a minute, then suddenly shut off. To make the electricity continue working, we had to put the room "key" (which looked like a credit card) into a special holder. When we left the room and took the key with us, the lights would all shut off again — to make sure no electricity got wasted when the room was unoccupied.

In the bathroom, a sign urged us to reuse the same towels for 2 days, so the staff wouldn't have to waste water by rewashing them. The sign said: the maid will fold our towels but not clean them (unless we leave them in the bathtub). The sign included this summary: "For a green and clean environment, please use towels second day, else put in bathtub."

Department stores
China still has many small shops but now also has huge department stores, many stories high, new and chic, full of luxurious high fashion and cosmetics from around the world.

Jiangyou's main department store has two sneaky tricks for keeping customers in the store:

To go from the street to the departments, you take the Up escalators, which are pleasantly wide and inviting; but the Down escalators are narrow (to discourage you from leaving).

When you try to leave an upper floor by taking a series of Down escalators, you discover the Down escalators aren't next to each other. At each floor, you must walk through several departments to get from one Down escalator to the next.

Discounts are advertised differently than in the U.S.: instead of a sign saying "30% off," you'll see a Chinese sign saying just "7," which means "you pay 70% of list price." As you walk through the store, you'll notice that some racks of clothes say "7," while others say "6" (meaning you pay 60% of list price) or "5" (meaning you pay 50% of list price).

Though a department store looks like just a huge single store, financially it resembles a mall: each part of each aisle has its own salesperson, who rents space from the store. To buy an item, you must first hand the item to the salesperson, who scribbles a purchase order for you; then you hand the purchase order to a cashier (elsewhere on the floor) with your payment; then the cashier hands you a receipt, which you bring back to the salesperson, who finally hands you the item you bought.

Food

To get food in China, you have several choices.

Supermarkets China's supermarkets are like department stores: huge, several floors, including imports, with salespeople in every aisle to offer you advice about what to buy. Some supermarkets are even part of department stores.

If you want to buy fruit or fresh vegetables, don't just bring them to the supermarket's main checkout counter: instead, bring them first to the produce department desk's own clerks, which weigh what you bought.

The Chinese government is trying to convince its citizens to drink more milk (for vitamins and calcium) — and so are milk's marketers. Milk is not refrigerated; instead, you buy stay-fresh cartons (which you can keep at room temperature) or powdered milk (which you mix with water).

China offers many kinds of "milk," just like the U.S. offers many kinds of "multivitamin pills." When you walk down the milk aisle in Jiangyou's supermarket, salespeople accost you and try to find the best kind of milk for you: for example, you can choose "milk for seniors" or "milk for infants." In China, all stay-fresh cartons and most powdered milk is whole milk, with just slight modifications. Skim milk is available just as a powder and just if you look hard for it among all the other milks.

As in the U.S., China's supermarkets include bakery and deli sections, which provide meals cheaper than restaurants.

Fast food In big cities (such as Beijing and Chengdu), you can easily find MacDonald's (look for the arches) and Kentucky Fried Chicken (look for "KFC"). In Beijing, a Japanese fast-food chain competes against American junk by offering dishes based on rice instead of French fries.

In Beijing, the fast food places are so busy that it's hard to find an empty table, so they hire ushers who look out for empty seats from departing customers and guide you to them.

Several Chinese companies have started their own fast-food chains. Jiangyou's best (run by Donna's sister's friend) serves American fast food (hamburgers, hot dogs, and soft-serve ice cream) along with European pastry and Chinese-European loaves of bread (thick, dark, tasty, and tangy, with a touch of blueberry jam hiding inside). Instead of buying a hot-dog grill (and finding room for it), this place deep-fries the hot dogs, as if they were French fries.

Tables of fine food In a Chinese home, the typical table is a double-decker: it has a glass surface (to put your food and drinks on), with a wooden surface below (to put knickknacks, napkins, and other distractions).

Most tables are rectangular, in homes and restaurants; but restaurant tables for big groups (6 or more) are round, and the glass surface rotates (and is slightly smaller than the wooden part), so the glass surface acts as a lazy Suzan, holding the pots of food that everybody shares.

You don't say "pass me the turtle soup"; instead, you just rotate the glass until the turtle soup comes to you. Then you get as much of it as you wish into your individual bowl, which is on the wooden surface.

By the way, about that turtle soup: it really has a dead turtle floating in the middle of it. You see the whole turtle, even its head. Chinese people prefer to eat meats and fish with the head still on, to prove that it's freshly killed. In restaurants, if you want to order fish, you walk over to the fish tank, look at the fish swimming there, point at the fish you want to eat, and say "kill this one." You'll receive it, cooked, with the head still on.

In homes and restaurants, the Chinese eat family style: everybody shares the pots of food that have been cooked. There are no serving spoons: instead, everybody grabs his own spoon or chopsticks and digs into the pots, transferring as much as desired to his personal bowl.

Sharing food like that is unsanitary: if one person is ill and goes back for a second helping, everybody else at the table will eat his illness. On the other hand, the food itself is quite healthy: the food eaten in Sichuan contains lots of watery broth and vegetables, with very little saturated fat, and it's hard to overeat, since the chopsticks and tiny spoons slow you down, though when rushing the Chinese take this shortcut: raise the personal bowl to the mouth, then shovel food from bowl to mouth as fast as possible, using chopsticks to help push it.

The typical American quickly chomps through a hamburger or a Big Mac. But in Sichuan, you'll slowly manipulate watery noodles with weird things sitting on them; you won't get fat.

The Chinese stay thin because of their wet diets, chopsticks, stairs, human-powered transportation, and realization that there's more to life than just staring at TV screens and computer screens.

Guangzhou's reputation Guangzhou is the pinyin name for "Canton," the city that invented Cantonese food, and where people are willing to experiment by eating different kinds of animals. Chinese people say:

> In Guangzhou, they eat everything that flies, except a plane;
> they eat everything that swims, except a boat;
> they eat everything with 4 legs, except a table.

No surcharges

In China, you don't have to tip waiters, taxi drivers, hotel maids, or anybody else. Tipping is never expected.

There's no general sales tax, either: the price you're quoted is the price you pay, not a penny more!

That's why Chinese immigrants to the U.S. don't tip — and don't expect to be taxed — until Americans reeducate them.

Time

Most Chinese office workers take a *two*-hour lunch break, from noon to 2PM. That long lunch is like a Mexican siesta: very practical on a hot day! During lunch, the workers go home if they live nearby.

To take that long break and still finish the day's work, the workers come in early (8AM) and leave late (6PM). So the day consists of two 4-hour shifts: 8AM to noon, then 2PM to 6PM.

The U.S. has several time zones (Eastern, Central, Mountain, and Pacific) plus Daylight Savings Time. China has none of that silliness: all of China is on the same clock, all year. All China is forced to use Beijing's clock. Since Beijing is in eastern China, workers in western China must come to work in the dark before sunrise, though after work they enjoy lots of sunshine — like U.S. construction workers.

Entertainment

The Chinese have many ways to amuse themselves.

TV On Chinese TV, the mouths aren't quite in synch with the sounds. That's partly because some shows are secretly dubbed (Cantonese actors are dubbed into Mandarin) but also because China's long-distance satellite-TV system isn't accurate.

Historical dramas are particularly popular. The typical drama includes lots of talking (among the royalty and occasionally the peasants), interrupted by an occasional kung-fu skirmish. The talk-to-fight ratio reminds me of *"The Good, the Bad, and the Ugly"* (the famous Clint Eastwood cowboy movie that was mostly talk but interrupted by an occasional fight).

As in the U.S., China TV includes ads. Many of the ads are for health (milk, pills, cosmetics, and toothpaste). The ads show Chinese characters supplemented by some pinyin, English characters, and Internet addresses.

The Chinese leave the TV on, for background sound, when socializing or eating meals. But some TV ads are inappropriate during mealtimes. Reacting to citizen complaints, the government promises that during dinnertime the TV will run fewer ads for feminine-hygiene products.

If you visit China and have a chance to watch TV, turn to channel 9 (CCTV-9). It's all in English! It's the international channel, to teach foreigners about China. It's a pleasant mix of news, views, travelogues, and introductions to Chinese art, culture, language, and regional differences. I wish America had a channel like that to teach foreigners about America!

Chinese New Year Chinese New Year is based on the lunar calendar and comes in late January or early February, depending on the moon's mood. It's the country's biggest holiday, and the whole country gets a week-long vacation, optimistically called **Spring Festival** (even though it's really winter), during which the Chinese visit their relatives by fighting to get on overcrowded planes, trains, and buses.

During that week, TV presents the **Spring Festival Gala**, full of gala spectaculars that are glitzy and mindless. (Go ahead, make up your own American analogy, something like "Lawrence Welk and Britney Spears meet the Ice Capades in Las Vegas for July 4th fireworks, with special effects from Steven Spielberg, George Lucas, and the designers of "Who Wants to Be a Millionaire.")

Some folks complain that the gala doesn't devote enough attention to minorities and social issues. In 2004, the gala's planners tried to loosen things up by including more audience-participation shows.

During Spring Festival, lots of kids and families shoot off fireworks, from rooftops and parks. They're not the dinky little fireworks that American kids shoot at July 4th; instead, they're industrial-strength fireworks, many feet tall, the size of surface-to-air missiles, shooting hundreds of feet into the air, with multiple payloads, colors, ba-ba-booming sounds, visible from miles away — the kind that Americans would permit only when shot by professionals protected by a moat and a fire department. On Chinese New Year night, the sounds and sights will make you think you're in a war zone. Chinese families schlep oil drums to the park, then launch the many rockets hiding inside, by remote control, and just hope no girl walking by at the wrong moment has her guts propelled to heaven.

Mahjong When Chinese folks have nothing else to do, they play **mahjong**, which is a form of poker. Instead of "hearts, diamonds, clubs, and spades," the suits are "sticks, circles, and chickens." Instead of being thin, the cards are thick, so they look like wooden dominoes (or big Scrabble letters).

Mahjong players usually gamble small amounts of money. Elderly people like to spend their days relaxing in teahouses while playing mahjong.

Badminton While waiting for customers, shop assistants sometimes stand outside, on the sidewalk, playing badminton. It's good exercise for the employees, and it attracts attention to the store. But if you try that in the U.S., some bureaucrat will probably complain that the store doesn't have a badminton-on-sidewalk permit.

Drum corps When a new store's been constructed and has its grand opening, the store hires a 100-woman drum corps, which marches back and forth in front of the store, banging their drums. It attracts attention to the store and the whole neighborhood.

Hey, kids, why not start a similar service in the U.S., to attract attention to new businesses? Just make sure you get permits!

Historic sites In the U.S., historic sites are rather boring: you usually enter a building, hear a lecture, and get tired. Chinese historic sites are more fascinating, because they're surrounded by beautiful parks.

To enter a Chinese historic building, you must hop over a wall that's nearly a foot high. That wall's the **threshold**: it marks the doorway's bottom. All old houses and buildings had those thresholds instead of American-style "doors," which weren't needed since Sichuan usually has pleasantly warm weather, no snowstorms, no rainstorms, and no crime.

In the Northeastern U.S., many places brag that "George Washington slept here." In Sichuan, many towns brag that "**Li Bai** lived here." He was China's most famous poet. He lived from 701 A.D. to 762 A.D., during the Tang dynasty. He's called the "drunk poet," because his poems are full of drunken hallucinations. His most famous poem begins like this:

> Have you never seen
> Yellow River waters
> Flowing down from Heaven,
> Rushing toward the sea,
> Never to return?

Like most of his poems, it begins by describing China's natural beauty, but American men notice it's also a good poem to recite to a urinal.

Another Sichuan attraction is **Du Jiang Yan**, the world's first major water project, built in 250 B.C. by the Qin family (who, 29 years afterwards, conquered the rest of China and called themselves the "Qin dynasty.") The project was hard: to divert water to Chengdu, Qin's peasants had to build a dam and blow up a mountain, but explosives hadn't been invented yet, so they broke the mountain's boulders apart by lighting fires on them, then dousing the fires with cold water, to make the rocks fissure. After 8 years of that, they finally created a mountain pass for their canal to flow through. Now the canal, dam, and reservoir are surrounded by a park with scenic views of mountains and rivers.

Weather

Sichuan rarely gets rainstorms but often gets drizzles. The drizzles dampen the streets but aren't strong enough to wash dirt away, so city streets and sidewalks stay dirty and dusty awhile, until finally attacked by city employees who grab huge brooms (resembling tree branches) and sweep every street and sidewalk in the whole city, by hand.

Since Sichuan is usually warm and balmy, retired folks love to relax by sitting outside (playing mahjong at outdoor cafés) or doing aerobic martial-arts dances in parks.

Beijing is farther north, much colder, and much windier. It's also less relaxed: there are fewer benches to sit on. In winter, Beijing's grass turns pale, while Sichuan's stays green.

Trees

In many cities (such as Mianyang in Sichuan province), the bottom 4 feet of each tree trunk are painted white, to discourage bugs from eating the bark.

Hanging roots Especially in downtown Mianyang, you see trees that have strange things hanging down from the branches. Those "strange things" are roots! Yes, roots grow down from the branches and search for the soil. If those extra roots don't succeed in reaching the soil, they shrivel; otherwise, they grow strong and look like auxiliary trunks.

Painting If you want to become a landscape painter, look at the trees on the hills near Mianyang. The branches bend in strange ways. Especially in winter, the leaves are sparse but come in bunches, which look like powder puffs, so they're easy to paint: just one dab from a splayed brush will give you a whole puff. New England is best for colors, but China is best for shapes.

Bulges Many trees look pregnant: they have huge bulges around their trunks. If you look at the bulges carefully, you discover they're bales of hay, tied into balls and hung there by farmers.

Relationships

When I travel, I'm more interested in the people than their wares.

What the Chinese think of America The Chinese are eager to learn English (because they want to understand American music and movies and earn more money from international trade). They like most Americans, though they think Bush was an idiotic callous jerk to start a war with Iraq.

Though Americans often visit big cities such as Beijing, Americans are rarer in small cities such as Mianyang and Jiangyou. Many kids in those cities have never seen an in-the-flesh American before — though they've studied English in school and seen Americans on TV — so they stare at me when I walk down the street or sit in a restaurant. They treat me as if I'm a cross between a Martian and a superstar. A 7-year-old girl kept staring at me while I was eating in a restaurant; finally, when I was leaving, she shyly said "Hello" to me in English. I said "Hello" back to her. That made her day. She beamed.

Dancing The Chinese people are proud of their culture. Donna's relatives showed me their dancing skills and asked me to show them my American dancing, so I showed them the most advanced American dances I've mastered:

the **Bunny Hop** (a line dance where you hold the hips of the person before you and kick right twice, then left twice, then hop forward-back-forward-forward-forward, while twitching your nose to look like a scared bunny)

the **Hokey-Pokey** (a circle dance where you learn the English names for body parts by following Simon-says instructions such as "put your ass in, put your ass out, put your ass in, and you shake it all about")

All her relatives started freakily copying my Bunny Hop and Hokey-Pokey, and Donna made me teach those dances to all senior citizens in the park, too! So now I, too, can put on my résumé that I'm an "American who corrupted Chinese culture."

Advice The Chinese love to give advice. In fact, they *insist* on giving advice, even when you don't want it.

Americans believe that "people should be free to boogie through life however they wish." The Chinese believe "everybody should act properly."

A friend of mine visited China for many months and became part of China's culture. When she returned to the U.S., her roommates complained her personality had changed: she'd turned into an annoying authoritarian asshole, telling them all how to act. She apologized and returned to the American philosophy of "do whatever you want."

Donna's daughter explained to me that in China, each group of people (such as a family) develops a leader who tells everybody else in the group what to do; and if anybody asks why, the leader just says, "That's a rule." The leader keeps inventing more rules.

Because of China's history of repressive governments and mass slaughters, survival's often meant being warned what to do, before you get in trouble. But now that China's government is starting to loosen up, maybe someday the Chinese will become as free as Americans.

City reputations Sichuan province's most famous city is Chengdu, which produces beautiful women. (My wife was born there.) Married men who visit Chengdu often wish they'd married Chengdu women instead! Chinese people say:

When you visit Chengdu,	you learn you married too early.
When you visit Beijing (the capital),	you learn your rank is not high.
When you visit Guangzhou,	you learn you're not rich.

More often, Chinese people use advanced grammar to purposely create Daoist mysterious confusion, like this:

Not until you visit Chengdu	do you realize you married too early.
Not until you visit Beijing	do you realize your rank is not high.
Not until you visit Guangzhou	do you realize you're not rich.

Recently, other Chinese cities have become even richer than Guangzhou.

"Not One Less"

To experience China without leaving the comfort of your American home, rent a movie about China. I recommend *Not One Less*, which I found at our local video-rental store in New Hampshire.

It's about a girl who, though just 13 years old, is forced to take a job as an elementary-school teacher in rural impoverished China, then must run to the city to retrieve a student who ran away, then winds up on TV.

The biggest surprise comes at the end, when you discover who the actors are. The characters are all played by themselves: they used their real names and real titles. Even the bureaucrat was played by… a bureaucrat!

You'll see the schoolkids get lessons in Chinese & math and see how hard it is to discipline an elementary-school class.

The director is famous in China for trying weird experiments. The movie ends with a political message saying millions of schoolkids run away from school to earn money for their families.

The film is subtitled and won an international award in 1999, but I can't figure out when the story's supposed to take place, since the schoolkids give a pledge-of-allegiance to Mao, who died in the 1970's, and my wife doesn't believe life in rural China is so bad today. Is it?

88 ways to know you're Chinese

People who are born in the United States but are ethnically Chinese are called **American-born Chinese (ABC)**. People who are born in Canada but are ethnically Chinese are called **Canadian-born Chinese (CBC)**.

Canadian-born Chinese love to pass around an e-mail that reveals "88 ways to know whether you're Chinese." Chinese in Canada and the U.S. have gradually improved the list, to make it truer. I've organized it into topics.…

Diet

1. You like to eat chicken feet.
2. You suck on fish heads and fish fins.
3. You prefer shrimp with heads & legs still attached, to show they're fresh.
4. You like to eat congee with thousand-year-old eggs.
5. You've eaten a red-bean Popsicle, know what moon cakes are, and acquired a taste for bitter melon.
6. You boil water then store it in the fridge. You always keep a Thermos of hot water available.
7. When you're sick, your parents tell you to boil herbs and stay inside. They also tell you to avoid fried foods or baked goods because they produce "hot air" (*yeet hay* in Cantonese).

Eating style

8. You eat all meals in the kitchen, whose table has a vinyl tablecloth on which you spit bones and other food scraps.
9. Your teacup has a cover. You tap the table when someone pours tea for you.
10. You reuse jam jars as drinking glasses.
11. At the dinner table, you pick your teeth (but cover your mouth).
12. Whenever you take a car ride more than 15 minutes, you carry a stash of dried food: prunes, mango, ginger, beef/pork jerky, and squid.
13. When you visit a home, you bring along oranges (or other produce) as a gift. Your parents refuse any sacks of oranges that guests bring. At Christmas, you give cookies (or fruitcakes, which could be over 5 years old).

Food economy

14. You hate wasting food, since your mom gave lectures about starving kids in Africa. When someone plans to throw away the table's leftovers, you'll finish them even if you're totally full. Your fridge's "Tupperware" contains three bites of rice or one leftover chicken wing; but you don't own *real* Tupperware — just a cupboard full of used but carefully rinsed margarine tubs, takeout containers, and jam jars.
15. You eat every last grain of rice in your bowl but not the last piece of food on the table.
16. You reuse teabags.
17. Your fridge's condiments are either Costco sized or come in tiny plastic packets (which you save/steal every time you get takeout or McDonald's). Ditto paper napkins.

Restaurants

18. You know all the waiters at your favorite Chinese restaurants.
19. You starve yourself before going to all-you-can-eat buffets.
20. Whenever you go to a restaurant, you wipe your plate and utensils before you eat.
21. You fight (literally) over who pays the dinner bill.
22. At restaurants, you rarely tip more than 10%; when you do, you tip Chinese delivery guys/waiters more.

Food preparation

23. You use a wok, own a rice cooker, and wash your rice at least twice before cooking it.
24. Your kitchen's covered by a sticky film of grease. Your stove's covered with aluminum foil.
25. You've never turned on your dishwasher, which you use as a dish rack.
26. You beat eggs with chopsticks.
27. You own a meat cleaver and sharpen it.
28. You don't use measuring cups. You always cook too much.
29. You have stuff in the freezer since the beginning of time.

Dealing with parents

30. You've never kissed your mom or dad.
31. You've never hugged your mom or dad.
32. You never discuss your love life with parents.
33. Your parents are never happy with your grades.
34. If you're 30, you still live with your parents (and they prefer it that way) — or you're married and live in the apartment next door or at least in the same neighborhood. If you don't live at home, your parents always want you to come home. Each time they call, they ask whether you've eaten, even if it's midnight.
35. You never call your parents just to say "Hi."

Relationships

36. At work, you e-mail your Chinese friends, though you're just 10 feet apart.
37. When you go to a dance party, a wall of guys surrounds the dance floor and tries to look cool.
38. You often say "Aiee Yah!" and "Wah!" You say "Wei" when answering your cell phone.
39. You've been on the Love Boat or know someone who has.

40. You love Las Vegas, slot machines, and blackjack.
41. You own an MJ set and possibly have a room set up in the basement. You know "MJ" doesn't mean Michael Jackson, it's mahjong!
42. Your parents send money to relatives in China.

Eyes

43. You've worn glasses since the 5th grade.
44. Your unassisted vision is worse than 20/500.
45. You wear contacts to avoid your "Coke-bottle glasses," which you saved though you'll never use them again.

Appearance

46. You're less than 5' 8" tall.
47. You look like you're 18.
48. Your hair sticks up when you wake up.
49. You use a face cloth. You take showers at night.
50. You iron your own shirts.
51. You always leave your shoes at the door.
52. Your house is covered with tile.
53. You leave the plastic covers on your remote control — or enclose your remote controls in plastic — to keep greasy fingerprints off.
54. You twirl your pen around your fingers.
55. If you're male, you have less body hair than most girls.
56. If you're male, you clap at something funny. If you're female, you giggle while placing a hand over your mouth.
57. You're always late.
58. Your parents use a clothesline and can launch nasal & throat projectiles.

Cars

59. You drive a Honda or Acura.
60. Your dashboard is covered with hundreds of small toys. A Chinese knickknack hangs from your rearview mirror.
61. You don't want to wear your seatbelt, because it's uncomfortable.
62. You drive around looking for the cheapest gas. You drive around for hours looking for the best parking space.

Music

63. You've joined a CD club at least once.
64. You sing Karaoke.
65. You play a musical instrument.
66. You have a piano in your living room.

Movies

67. You like Chinese films in their original undubbed versions.
68. You love Chinese martial-arts films, and you've learned some form of martial arts. "Shaolin" and "Wutang" actually mean something to you.
69. Your parents never go to the movies.

Practical skills

70. You majored in something practical, like engineering, medicine, or law.
71. Your dad thinks he can fix everything himself.

Hotels

72. You don't mind squeezing 20 people into one motel room.
73. You have a collection of miniature shampoo bottles you took every time you stayed in hotels.
74. You avoid the non-free snacks in hotel rooms.

Economizing

75. You love to use coupons.
76. You save grocery bags, tin foil, and tin containers.
77. Your toothpaste tubes are all squeezed paper-thin.
78. You unwrap Christmas gifts very carefully, so you can reuse the paper.
79. You buy Christmas cards only after Christmas, when they're 50% off.
80. When toilet paper's on sale, you buy 100 rolls. You store them in your closet (or the bedroom of an adult child who moved out).
81. You feel you've gotten a good deal if you didn't pay tax.
82. You have a drawer full of old pens, most of which don't write anymore.
83. You always look phone numbers up yourself, since calling information costs at least 50¢. You make long-distance calls only after 9PM.
84. You know someone who can get you a good deal on jewelry, electronics, or computers.
85. You'll haggle over something that's not negotiable.
86. You keep most of your money in a savings account.

Conclusion

87. You know this list consists of just 88 reasons because, in Cantonese, "8" is pronounced the same as "good luck."
88. You see the truth in this message and forward it to all your Chinese friends.

Donna's comments

You've heard enough from Russ, my silly husband. Would you like to hear from me? Russ asked me to contribute this section, but my life has no "tricks."

East versus West

I'm a Chinese American. To American eyes, I'm Chinese; but if I go back to China, I'm legally an American.

I'm living in two cultures. I eat half Chinese food and half American food. I speak half Chinese and half English. I enjoy the two different cultures, which makes my life more colorful.

Here are interesting phenomena I'd like to share with you. In this article, when I say "Chinese," I mean people in China, not Chinese-Americans.

What I say might not be 100% right, but I'm sure it's at least 70% right: it applies to 70% of such people and situations. If you read it and think some things are *not* true, you may belong to or be familiar with the other 30%.

Eating

Eating's an adventure!

Eat or drink soup? Chinese people like clear soup. They actually "drink" soup. A mother usually cooks chicken or pork soup, with special mushrooms, for her family. It takes 4 to 5 hours to cook, and the soup's considered very good for you.

Not many people in China have American-Chinese "egg-drop soup" or "hot & sour soup," which I'd never seen before I came to the U.S.

American soups are too thick to drink. The way Americans have their soup is more like eating a soup.

Eager to serve Visiting Chinese friends at their homes? As soon as you sit down, you're automatically served with hot tea, fruits, and whatever snacks they have. They even peel apples and oranges for you. If the time's right, they'll persuade you to stay for lunch or dinner. Then the housewife will disappear into the kitchen, and in no time a table full of beautiful dishes magically waits for you.

Drinks When offered a drink, a Chinese guest often says, "Oh, thank you so much, but don't bother." An American guest is more relaxed and says, "Coke would be fine."

Eating more Chinese try to make their guests eat more, even if the guests say they're full. Chinese often help their guests to the food, like a server. Americans let guests decide for themselves what to eat and when to stop.

At a Chinese banquet, food keeps coming to the table. You find yourself already full, but dishes after dishes are still coming. So be careful not to eat too fast and get full too soon!

Even at a grand American wedding banquet, just 7, 8, or 9 courses are served, unless it's a buffet.

Passing food When eating, Americans pass food around, with a big plate in front of each person. Chinese share foods from a few dishes in the middle of the table, with a small bowl of rice in front of each person.

Salt & pepper Americans often shake salt and pepper onto their food before even tasting the food. Chinese never add salt or pepper to their food at the table, unless the cook did a bad job.

Chinese food is tastier. American food is more natural.

Utensils Americans lick their thumbs after eating something like donuts or cake. Sometimes they use their thumbs to help the fork push food in the end.

Chinese sometimes hold up the bowl to the mouth and use chopsticks or a spoon to help shovel the food into their mouths.

Peeling Many Chinese peel apples, pears, and peaches. Some even peel grapes. But they normally don't throw out chicken and pork skins.

Many Americans don't eat chicken skin, pork skin, or salmon skin but eat lots of fruit skin.

Slaughter An American home doesn't have to slaughter chicken or fish. At the table, Americans are scared to see fish with heads on.

Most Chinese families needed one brave guy to slaughter chickens until recent years. Now ready-to-cook chickens are available in a supermarket, but people complain those chickens don't taste good enough.

Socializing

To understand a society, look at how it socializes.

Kind words Americans say "thank you," "excuse me," and "sorry" a hundred times a day. A Chinese couple doesn't say "thank you" when passing food to each other.

Helpfulness If your car breaks down on a highway or you're lost in a strange city, you're more likely to get help from an American than a Chinese. But if you must borrow money urgently or need a place to stay for a few days, go to your *Chinese* friends.

Inside out Americans are more outgoing. They like to greet people. They're more likely to talk to strangers and more easily make friends. A typical Chinese prefers to be quiet before strangers.

Back door In China, there's a "back door" for power-related people to get a good job, promotion, business, and escape the law. Small businesses owners try to befriend tax officials or policemen for "benefits." Businesses spend lots of money for power-related social relationship.

In America, friendships are more personal than "beneficial." "Back doors" are not common.

Gifts It's not rare for a Chinese to spend 20% or 50% of a month's wage for a wedding gift. If you receive 2 or 3 wedding invitations in a month, you feel you'll go broke. But people still give generously, because they think smaller gifts can't show their feelings — and if you spend less than others, you'll "lose face." American friends are content to give and receive *small* gifts.

When American friends go to a restaurant, they can pay bills separately, a rarity in China.

Never give a clock or green hat as a gift to a Chinese. In Chinese, the word "clock" is pronounced *zhong* — and so is the word "end" or "funeral." Old people are especially scared of receiving that. As for wearing a green hat, it means "cuckold" (a man whose wife is sleeping with a different man).

Social drinking In America, a bigger percentage of people drink alcohol than in China. Pubs, bars, lounges, and alcohol have a secret strong attraction to American teenagers. College students under 21 can't wait to go to a bar like their older schoolmates. The more you want to forbid something, the stronger desire it may arise.

China has no law against minors drinking alcohol, though it's never encouraged. Parents can send a young kid to buy a bottle of wine (or cigarettes) for them. At a family reunion party when

I was little, my parents dipped a chopstick into a glass of wine and then let me taste it, just for fun. But that taste made me dislike alcohol for the rest of my whole life.

Chinese men make lots of noise when they drink. At parties, they clamor to make somebody else drink — for congratulations, health, friendship, respect, good wishes, the punishment of being late, or no reason. The more you can make somebody drink, the better. That becomes the most popular social activity.

Waiting lines Americans patiently wait in lines for banking, boarding, and eating. In China, you can see people shove ahead to board a bus — and young guys cut in line for tickets.

Handling foreigners Chinese are very friendly to foreigners and treat them as guests.

In America, strange-looking people might not be foreigners. You can't tell foreigners by their looks. But some Americans don't have good feelings toward "foreigners."

Lawsuits In America, "everybody sues everybody." People buy expensive home insurance for fear someone will fall at the door and sue. Some people get very rich by suing big companies.

Chinese think that's ridiculous and dishonest. The cost of "everybody sues everybody" is Americans pay too much for insurance and medical care.

A Chinese saying is:

> Forgive if you can.

Traditionally, Chinese sue just criminals, but now they're starting to learn American's way and become smarter.

Family versus world

Which is more important: your family or the world?

Chinese parents Chinese parents pay college tuition for their kids, even if doing so puts the parents in poverty or heavy debt. Parents don't mind working 80 hours a week to buy a kid a computer or piano. Often you'll see a bright young man get a doctor's degree but still not know how to cook rice.

When they're old, Chinese parents are taken good care of, often living with their kids.

Chinese social circles Lending money to a relative or close friend is interest-free. Sometimes the money is even a gift. Relatives and friends form a strong social circle for a Chinese person. A Chinese saying is:

> You depend on your parents at home, friends outside.

Getting jobs, promotions, and customers can depend on how strong your social circle is. A person may cheat or do something illegal just for the sake of a relative or friend. A Chinese may feel less responsible to the rest of the world; a cynical Chinese saying is:

> Shovel your own snow in front of your house.
> Worry not about the frost on others' roofs.

American extended feelings Americans tend to have weaker family ties, even if family is the most important thing to them. Some kids must work hard for tuition or to pay back their loans. Old folks live lonely. Borrowing money from a brother, you might have to worry about the interest.

But Americans tend to have more *extended* feelings. They pay lots of tax to help the poor and schools, rather than buy their lonely old mothers expensive gifts. They're especially nice to the handicapped and retarded. They treat their pets like their children. They donate money to African kids. They spend huge sums of money on international affairs, to fight for other countries and build other countries. They're proud of working as the international police.

Schooling

China's schools are quite different from America's.

China's mountainous burden China's educational reformers say "Give back kids' childhood" and "Study while having fun," but middle-school students in China still study 8-10 hours a day, including morning reading and evening homework.

12th-grade students study more than 12 hours a day, to pass the nationwide college entrance examinations. During their junior and senior years, kids stay up late after midnight every night: no TV, no movies, almost no sports, no dating, no shopping, no parties, no household chores, nothing but studying. Some kids get sick; all think it's a miserable life. But they realize they must do it to get into a good college or even just a mediocre one. Their parents watch this happen — with painful hearts but high expectations. Schools and teachers get high praise and great reputations if their students get enrolled in great colleges.

July 7, 8, and 9 are the 3 days when the nationwide college examinations are held. Kids say as soon as that ends, they'll throw away all their books and sleep 3 days and 3 nights and then have parties 3 days and 3 nights.

When they finally get into college, they never can study as hard as in high school, and they can't believe they were able to go through it. They're scared even to think of it.

Goofing off? American high school students don't need to study so hard to enter a college. They can always get into some sort of college if they can afford the tuition.

High-school seniors still have time to work in McDonald's or date girls. Many kids already get admitted to a college while still seniors. If they really wish, they can begin college courses early.

In America, you can be a happy kid even if you don't do well in school. In China, you get too much pressure from parents and teachers; you can hardly be happy if you're not doing well.

Chinese-American parents complain that American schools throw the burden of moral education onto the parents' shoulders. In China, schools watch student behavior more carefully.

Hours In China, typical elementary-school kids have 5 hours of class a day: 9AM to noon, then 2PM to 4PM. They get a 2-hour lunch break, when they can eat from their own lunchboxes (or at home if they live nearby). At night they have 1 hour of homework. 6th-grade students study harder and longer, to enter a good middle school. Kids aren't allowed to watch much TV except during weekends.

American students have less homework. Schools start earlier and end at 2PM. Kids have just 30 minutes for lunch.

Classrooms In America, students go to different classroom for different teachers. Each classroom is decorated according to the subject and the teacher's style.

In China, students stay in the same classroom while different teachers come to teach them. The only different rooms to go to are the music classroom, the science lab, and the gym or playground for P.E.

Control In China, teachers have more control of the class. Students are required to keep quiet while their teacher talks.

American students are more active in class. They discuss more. They can even walk around.

In America, teachers try to make their lessons easy and fun. Teachers tend to make students feel good. They encourage more than criticize. Getting an A is pretty easy if students work at it.

In China, teachers are stricter. They always try to let you know you still have far to go to reach the goal. It's hard to get an A, even you work very hard. In the 2nd grade, students are already learning multiplication and division. Chinese textbooks are among the hardest in the world.

Insulting the poor students? Some classes in China post final total scores and ranks on the wall, so the students all know their classmates' ranks.

Once or twice a semester, all the parents have a group meeting with the teacher. Parents sit in their kids' seats and see the posted ranks. Some feel proud. Some get embarrassed & shamed and beat the kids when they get home.

American schools think it's against human rights to post student ranks. An American student may say, "You have no right to insult me just because I'm not smart enough in something."

In China, students have extracurricular math groups where teachers teach more advanced math. Math competitions and other science competitions are held for cities, provinces, and nationwide. Chinese students often win 1st place in international "math Olympic" competitions.

American teaching emphasizes problem-solving strategies. Chinese style is to feed students as many facts as possible.

Life experience American students get lots of work experience *before* graduating from college. They feel more confident to deal with the competitive job market. They feel more at ease getting along with bosses, fellow workers, and customers. They're outgoing, good at discussing things, solving problems, expressing their ideas, and using machines & computers.

Before the 21st century, most Chinese students never got any work experience before college graduation (except in rural areas, where kids worked from a very young age to help on the farm). Chinese students in U.S colleges are often among top students and always aim at higher degrees, but they're still nervous about competition.

American students are more sports-loving. Chinese students are more book-loving. Very few Chinese students know how to play baseball or surf.

American students have cared little about what's going on in the rest of the world (except after 9/11). They may not know where Iraq or Hong Kong is. Chinese students are the opposite: they know the name of France's foreign minister and the name of Leonardo DiCaprio's newest American movie.

Student dating

Traditionally in China, parents don't let teenage students date. If dating happens, teachers and parents go all out to stop it. They argue that dating will harm a kid's studying and eventually destroy the kid's future. But in recent years, things have been getting looser.

In America, most kids aged 16 & up have some sort of experience dating. Teachers and parents don't want to invade their privacy. Schools even give students birth-control pills. All a mother can do is to warn her daughter not to get pregnant.

In an American shopping mall, I came across a woman I knew with two kids. She introduced her 15-year-old daughter to me, then introduced the boy as her daughter's "boyfriend." I thought the boy was the girl's younger brother.

In China, if teenagers want to date, they usually date secretly. Since most *good* kids don't date, kids feel guilty if they do.

In America, a schoolgirl may feel bad if she has no boyfriend. She might wonder, "Is something wrong with me? Why do other girls have boyfriends while I don't? Am I unattractive?"

How parents handle kids

Your opinion of life depends on how your parents treat you.

Saying "love" Chinese people feel embarrassed to say "I love you." That's why Chinese parents and kids hardly ever say "I love you" to each other, and they seldom hug each other when kids grow up.

Many American parents and kids say "I love you" almost every day.

Investing in kids Chinese parents eagerly pay for a kid's college education, computer, and piano. Some parents even buy a house for a kid's wedding present.

American independence American parents raise kids to be independent and responsible.

I saw a 2-year-old American boy in a raincoat walking in the rain, followed by his mom. The boy splashed a lot of water, as he stepped hard into the little pond of water on the cement ground. His mom just watched and followed. When he fell, he looked back at his mom, but she just said "get up."

When American kids grow up, they sometimes pay rent to their parents if they live in their parents' property. Some parents pay their kids to do house chores.

Chinese worry Chinese parents worry about their kids, endlessly.

Do the kids get A or B in school? What kind of friends are they hanging out with? Are they good enough to get into a good high school and then a good college? Are they bad enough to be secretly dating in school?

When finally kids graduate from college and get good jobs, then parents worry whether the kids are dating enough and when the kids can get married.

Here's an ancient Chinese saying:

> Everything is low compared to education.

Parents hope their son will become a "dragon" and their daughter a "phoenix" (meaning "outstanding").

American parents let kids choose what to do and what kind of schools to attend. The kids' futures are in their own hands.

Spoiling? Many Chinese parents shelter their kids from doing any household chores. They spoil kids in everyday life.

But Chinese parents believe ancient Chinese philosophy:

> An uneducated son is his father's fault.
> An undisciplined student is the teacher's fault.

That's why many Chinese parents are strict about their kids' early education, beginning at age 3 (in reading, arithmetic, art, musical instruments, ballet, and computer), making the kid's life either promising or miserable.

In America, children are spoiled differently. Parents don't force their kids to do much. Parents can't beat kids, even if for drugs. From their early years, kids get a good sense of freedom. But since parents leave kids alone, some kids play hooky, some don't work hard at school, and some get sexually involved and pregnant. (Exception: my American neighbors, Flo & Gene Fitzgerald, are very strict. Flo stayed home until her two kids graduated from high school, to take care of them and watch them. Now their son's an M.I.T. professor and world-renowned scientist & entrepreneur, and their daughter's a very good schoolteacher.)

Chinese has a saying similar to the American one, "spare the rod, spoil the child." But most Chinese parents today don't beat their kids as in the old days. If they do, it's because they "hate if the iron doesn't become steel." Chinese don't think "parents beating their kids" is abusive.

Serious dating and marriage

Up through the 1970's, the typical Chinese girl would marry the first man she dated. If a girl dated 3 boys, she'd get a bad reputation. Hardly any man and woman lived together without marriage.

From the 1990's on, things have changed a lot. Now there's not much difference between China and the U.S. You see girls and boys live together as "girlfriend and boyfriend," without marriage. "Out-of-marriage relationships" and "third relationships" have appeared.

Singles There are more singles in America than in China.

If a Chinese man or woman is still single at age 30, the parents and other relatives get very worried. Friends and relatives go all out to help introduce somebody to this person.

Americans don't worry much about their single relatives. They think single people may enjoy that lifestyle.

Personal ads Chinese dating ads concentrate on education, job, salary, property, looks, and height. (The Chinese prefer tall people.)

American's concentrate on looks, personality, hobbies, and weight. (Americans prefer skinny people.)

Now more and more Chinese are dating through the Internet, "chat" through the Internet, and send messages through cell phones.

Divorce America's divorce rate is much higher than China's. Chinese couples are more likely to put up with a marriage even if it's unhappy. Americans aren't willing to suffer from an unhappy marriage: they keep just happy marriages.

A divorced Chinese couple doesn't pay lawyers to decide child visitation rights. The couple just talks and decides for itself. Americans spent money on lawyers for everything!

Crazy sex Americans are usually good at obeying laws. They pay taxes, behave themselves in public, and act helpful and friendly. But for sex, even some very good Americans try crazy things (which seem strange to the Chinese!), such as the 1960's sexual freedom, today's bondage & domination, and nudist beaches. I heard this comment:

> American culture is a culture of sex.
> Chinese culture is a culture of food and gambling.

Americans have strip bars. Chinese nightclubs have "3-companion girls" instead (a companion for drink, singing, and dance).

Prostitutes are forbidden in both countries. But secret ones are always there.

Extra wives In China now, some rich people and officials illegally live with a second "wife," sometimes even a third "wife" or more. Some even have kids with those extra "wives."

No normal American woman is willing to be an illegal "wife" to a married man, even if he's rich.

Relationships

How do you relate, if you're Chinese?

Your in-laws If you're Chinese, you call your mother-in-law "Mom" and your father-in-law "Dad." You'd feel awkward and disrespectful to call them by their first names as Americans do.

Indirect expression Chinese express feelings indirectly. Example:

> A girl is sick and hopes her boyfriend come see her. But on the phone she says, "I'm all right. You don't have to come." Later, she gets upset because her boyfriend didn't come to see her.

Who pays? In America, a boyfriend and girlfriend share rent, utilities, and food cost. But they buy presents for each other to show they care for each other.

In China, a man's supposed to take care of his girlfriend. When dating, a Chinese man often spends lots of money for restaurant and presents. A good girl's supposed to be proud and well-treated. If a girl chips in half of the rent to live with a man, she's considered a desperately lowly cheap date.

Old people

A good old Chinese tradition is to respect the old and love the young. Three generations often live together. If an old person lives alone, people take pity and think the children are unkind.

In America, old people usually choose to live by themselves, even though their children love them dearly.

Retirement age In China, men are traditionally retired at age 60 (professional) or 55 (non-professional); women are retired at 55 (professional) or 50 (non-professional).

But now people are retired even earlier. Some get laid off with part of their wages before the age of retirement.

In America everybody's legal retiring age is 65 or 62.

Chinese activity In a Chinese city's parks in the early morning, you see old people doing exercises (such as chi-kong air exercises, tai-chi exercises, playing with swords, and dancing). In the late afternoon and evening, some old folks do group dancing parks and inexpensive nightclubs. Some go to an "Elder's College" or "Elder Association" to learn art, dancing, cooking, gardening, calligraphy, and photography.

That's just in the cities. In rural areas, old people usually don't have retirement income, so they depend on their children and live a less cultured life than their city counterparts. Just recently have some rural areas started getting retirement systems.

American activity Some Americans choose to keep working part time after age 65. They're active and energetic. Some have volunteer jobs. Elder communities often have parties, seminars, and club activities. Some elderly people like to travel. Some drive cars even in their 80's and 90's.

Who looks younger? From babyhood until turning 40, Chinese people look younger than Americans. But after turning 55, Chinese look older than Americans. An 80-old Chinese guy looks much older than an 80-year-old American guy.

Other differences

The Chinese use language differently and have a different sense of "variety."

Names Americans have too many people called "Michael," "Peter," and "Mary." (Americans are called by their first names.)

Chinese have too many people called "Wang," "Chen," and "Zhang." Chinese are called by their last names, like "Xiao Wang" (which means "little Wang") or "Lao Zhang" (which means "old Zhang").

Calendar Americans use words such as "Monday," "Tuesday," "January," and "February." Chinese use numbers such as "Day 1," "Day 2," "Month 1," and "Month 2." Just "Day 7" has a name, also meaning Sunday.

Chinese use two different calendars. The main one is the same as the American. The other is the "lunar calendar." China's most important holiday is Chinese New Year Day, which is the first day of the lunar calendar.

Backwards Old-style Chinese books are written in vertical columns, from right to left, backwards. To decipher addresses on American envelopes, Americans read from bottom to top, upside-down.

Music Chinese has a simple music notation (besides the professional notation used by Westerners). The simple music notation use numbers for notes: 1 for do, 2 for re, 3 for mi, 4 for fa, 5 for so, 6 for la, and 7 for ti.

For a higher octave, put a dot above the number. For a lower octave, put a dot below the number.

Homogeneity All small American cities look the same, having the same shopping malls with same stores. Streets are lined by the same restaurant chains.

In China, every city is different!

I don't recognize China anymore

China is far, and China is close. It's tens of thousands of miles away, and it's just at the other end of my phone.

Report from the year 2000

It's the year 2000. On the Internet, I'm reading news in Chinese everyday from Yahoo China and many other Chinese websites. I'm amazed to see how fast China is changing. China now is so modern that I can hardly recognize it anymore.

DVD or VCR When I went back to China in 1998, I saw people using DVDs. I never heard about it at that time. When I said I was using a VCR, my friends laughed and said they weren't using VCRs anymore.

My mom came to the U.S. to visit us in June 2000. While she was flying across the Pacific Ocean, her photos showing her boarding at Shanghai's airport were already sent by digital camera to our computer, from my relatives in China.

China is dressy Every time I went back to China, the first things to do were perm my hair and buy new clothes. My dear relatives usually would indirectly suggest I was not dressed well enough, though I was wearing the same dress praised by my American friends.

One thing I like about the U.S. is you feel okay wearing anything you want. Nobody cares much if you're poor or rich.

In China, city women seem dressed up all the time. Many of them buy expensive clothes & makeup stuff and go to salons every week for hair & face treatments.

Newly rich Though most people in China aren't rich yet, some did become rich as a result of China's ex-leader Deng Xiao Ping's policy: "Let some people get rich first."

Some Chinese-Americans who went back to China (to work or do business) complained they couldn't bear China's lifestyle of "banquet every night." They missed their quiet American lifestyle, which they feel is better for their kids and families.

People in China criticize overseas Chinese (especially those returning to China from America), saying "They talk fancy (they speak Chinese with English words here and there) but look & act cheap." The overseas Chinese reply, "If you people who got newly rich by staying in China had to pay high taxes like us, you wouldn't criticize us like that."

Open door to outside Between 1949 (when Communist China was founded) and 1976 (the end of the Cultural Revolution), nobody in China had private property: everything belonged to the public. Everybody worked for the "country" and earned some money for a basic life. People gradually forgot about getting rich; they cared more about how to survive political class struggles. Some tried to enjoy a rich spiritual life in arts, literature, and science.

In 1976, continuous political class struggles finally ended, and the country started to open her door to the outside. To her shock, China found a different world outside: in developed countries, people work for themselves and enjoy a wealthy life.

Advanced, rich, modern Western countries aroused China. Smart Chinese, who'd been too proud of their great ancient science, art, long history, and rich cultures to bother learning from other nations, now longed for advanced technology and management.

For a long time, the Chinese government kept arguing about "Socialism or Capitalism?" Finally, Deng Xiao Ping's famous "cat theory" ("Black cat or white cat, the one that catches mice is a good cat") led China into today's economic reform and prosperity, called "socialism China-style."

Report from the year 2002

China's "booming economy" and "weak foundation of laws" have caused a lot of bad phenomena: corruption, bribery, smuggling, robbery, and prostitution have become serious problems.

Corruption In the 1970's, a mayor made not much more money than a factory worker. An official who embezzled 1000 **yuan** (one U.S. dollar equals about 8 yuan) was considered to have committed a big crime and would face severe punishment. But now corruption cases appear in Chinese news websites every day, some involving *millions* or tens of millions of yuan. A few high officials were sentenced to death for big corruption, but even the death penalty seems unable to stop corruption.

Prostitution After 1949, the Chinese government prohibited prostitution, and for decades it was dead. The only case I remember seeing was in 1985, when a middle-aged countrywoman was sentenced to death for the crime of "underground organizer of prostitution."

But the new fast-growing economy has brought prostitution back to life. Though it's still prohibited, it flourishes in some nightclubs, salons, inns, and streets.

Second wife Another strange phenomenon is "er nai," meaning "second wife." A small number of men with money or power secretly live with an illegal "second wife" in a second home, even having a kid.

In the old days (1940's or earlier), some wealthy Chinese men married two wives or even more. Now some newly rich men ignore the law and try to follow their forefathers. They get a lot of criticism and will have legal trouble.

Sex China used to be very conservative. Up through the 1970's, I think most people married the first person they dated. A girl who dated more than 3 men usually got a bad reputation. In those horrible "class struggle" years, anybody having extramarital affairs or adultery was treated like a "class enemy" or criminal — and thereafter lived a shamed life, if not in jail.

Now nobody feels strange about seeing a man and woman live together before or without marriage. Changing boyfriends or girlfriends constantly is normal. Many movies are XXX. TV talk shows discuss sex. TV ads claim to make breasts bigger.

Report from the year 2003

China doesn't look like a communist or socialist country anymore.

Just 5 years ago, the government still insisted it was trying "socialism China-style." But now it's stopped mentioning that. Instead, materialism dominates the whole country. One Chinese commentator said, "Beijing's streets are full of people dreaming of getting rich."

Privatized From 1949 (when the Communist party came to power) until 1976 (the Cultural Revolution's end), China had no private business. After 1976, small private businesses appeared. Now *most* businesses are owned privately (except for a few big government-owned enterprises).

New buildings are built by private builders. Many factories, stores, restaurants, and hotels are owned privately. Real estate is priced 5 times higher than 5 years ago.

Gap The gap between the rich and poor keeps getting bigger. Many people earn just 10,000 yuan per year (1 U.S. dollar equals about 8 Chinese yuan); some rich people earn several million.

Many people in their late 40's or early 50's got laid off with a pension of between 2000 and 8000 yuan per year. 2000 yuan isn't enough for even a simple rural life; 8000 is barely enough to live in a small city.

People in the countryside have no pension. Some country areas are still very poor and get limited help from the government.

A few of the super "newly rich" enjoy the rich lifestyles they never dreamed of: some travel around the world, play golf, ride horses, drive Benz cars, have parties in fancy restaurants & nightclubs, live in fancy houses in different cities, have maids for housework, send their kids to the best schools overseas, and even buy millions of dollars worth of houses overseas, paying cash.

Back in the 1970's, Deng Xiao Ping proclaimed, "Let some people get rich first." Now most Chinese folks cynically call the newly rich the "Rich First" and call themselves the "Rich Later," to kid that they themselves might get rich later according to Deng Xiao Ping's proclamation. If they get rich soon, China will be the best country in the world.

Most Chinese people think they live much better than 20 years ago, so the reformation is good. But some think it's worse because, in "Mao's time," you all worked for the country or the public; you felt and were called "masters of the country," especially the working class. But now, suddenly, you must work for a person who used to be your fellow worker or someone who was no better than you except for luck. He becomes a big boss and gets rich and you become his worker and stay poor.

The original idea of Communist society was: all businesses and all properties belong to the public; society should be highly developed materially and spiritually; its citizens should work their shares according to their abilities and get paid according to their needs. That would be the ideal world to live in if it could come true. Unfortunately, when Communist parties came to power (in the Soviet Union and China), instead of focusing on economic development they kept fighting "class struggle." Meanwhile, since those who worked hard got paid about the same as those who worked less, there was no incentive to work hard. Moreover, some intellectuals were named "class enemies" and lost opportunities to contribute their knowledge; others had to use "half the heart" worrying whether class struggles would crush them. As a result of all that, the economy crashed, and the country plunged into poverty.

The Chinese people and their government were smart enough to change that situation before it was too late. Now they're doing well — better than anyone expected. The recent success of sending an astronaut into the space and having him return shows that Chinese technology has great potential.

Report from the year 2004

Russ and I went to China on January 19th. It had been 6 years since my last personal visit. It was Russ's first time to go. Both of us were excited.

Russ said he was looking forward to the long flight, so he could finally sleep without interruption. Poor guy!

Travel through China Our first surprise was the airports in Beijing and Chengdu. They must be brand new. They're very modern and beautiful, like the great ones in the U.S.

Then we took a bus through Chengdu. The city was not familiar to me anymore! Workers had constructed tall buildings and huge billboards, all new to me. So many cars, bicycles, pedestrians… The city looked busy, lively, and prosperous.

On the way to Jiangyou (2 hours north of Chengdu), we saw about 35 broken cars, all lined up on the highway and facing Chengdu, apparent victims of a chain-reaction car accident. It was Chinese New Year's Eve. Drivers were standing by their cars, looking sad, their New Year's Eve family parties ruined. But I noticed most of the people were dressed well, and some of the cars were fancy. They must be the "new rich." (Six years earlier, less than 1% of the Chinese drove cars, since cars were owned just by state-run companies.)

Condo My family welcomed us with a grand meal and a brand new condo!

3 months before this trip, my mom told us about the condo being for sale, so we'd bought it: 3 bedrooms, 1½ baths, on the 5th floor of a 7-story building. Now we finally got to see what we bought!

Upon entering, after lots of hugs and greetings, we were awed by the beautiful floors, windows, ceilings, fancy lights, and outside views. Russ said this was as beautiful as New York City's best! But it cost just $22,000, even including major furniture! (That's because it's in Jiangyou, a medium-size city. Housing prices are more than twice as high in Chengdu, and more than 5 times as high in Beijing and Shanghai.)

Living it up Basic life is wonderfully inexpensive in Jiangyou and even in Chengdu. Every other day, my brothers and sister took us out for dinner. Then Russ wanted to treat my whole family. We reserved a dinner for 20 people in a private room in a nice restaurant. Two huge round tables (each having two layers, the top one turning) were piled with delicious and beautiful dishes to share. There was so much food that we could hardly finish half of it. It cost just $85 to feed all 20 of us. Jiangyou is still a paradise of bargains for consumers like us, though fancy restaurants and hotels in Beijing and Shanghai can get as expensive as in the U.S.

But even in Jiangyou and Chengdu, a few stores are expensive. A shirt can cost $200 in some foreign-influenced clothing stores and department stores, which are so beautifully modern that I thought I was in America.

Street scenes Traffic was a mess. Every time I took a taxi, I was scared to see that the driver constantly drove across the yellow center line to pass other cars.

Some streets weren't clean. Trees, flowers, and plants were covered with dust. You'd just have a desire to grab a hose and spray water on them.

In front of our building was a huge new park inside a traffic rotary, about the size of a football field. At night, colorful lights shone on the grass. In the mornings, people did all sorts of exercise there — walking, dancing, Tai Chi boxing, Chinese traditional swordplay, Chinese drum-team practicing, and colorful Chinese fan dancing.

The first morning, when Russ looked out our window, he was so excited to find activities there even in winter. I asked him, "You want to go?" He said "Sure," hurriedly put on his coat, said "Maybe too late," then looked out again and said "Some people are leaving. Too late!" We ran downstairs, crossed the road, and were still in time to join a group doing swordplay. Seeing Russ, a "foreign guest," they stayed longer and show us their fan dance. Russ even had a photo taken with them!

People dance there every night also (except when unusually cold). Anybody can join and learn to follow their steps.

On sunny days, people come to sit around the flower gardens, take a walk, and fly kites. Too bad there's some litter.

Retiring I have some "retired" relatives and friends who used to be teachers, accountants, and officials.

They look too young to have anything to do with retiring. They're smart, professional, full of experience & energy. But they were "early retired" from organizations that downsized.

Every morning, they get up late. Some take a walk, then breakfast. After breakfast, they shop for lunch groceries, then cook lunch. Playing **mahjong** (a popular 4-person gambling game resembling poker) becomes their major activity.

They don't feel good about themselves. They envy me because I work and I'm still "useful."

Happy farmer Sichuan has a new kind of eatery, called a **happy farmer**.

Those eateries started in a farmer's house but got bigger and fancier. Some are as big as a school and include many buildings, open areas (with tables for tea and mahjong), natural beauties (plants, flowers, and ponds), and restaurants. One in my hometown includes entertainment like the "Tibetan bonfire dance."

Those eateries charge a lot less than regular restaurants. You can spend a whole day there, drinking tea and playing, with a meal, for just $3 total.

Is China poor? I visited a happy-farmer eatery with my former colleagues, who were teachers. We talked about America and China. While playing mahjong, one retired teacher complained, "An unemployed person in America must get more money than me." I laughed and replied, "Look, you're wearing nice clothes and own a nice condo. You have pork, chicken, fish, rice, bread, vegetables, milk, and eggs on your table. You have health insurance. And you don't have to work at age 55!"

Some Chinese think everybody in America is rich, and some Americans think all Chinese are poor.

Some regions of China are still very poor. Many people who got laid off are still poor.

Today the gap between the rich and the poor is very big, among the biggest in the world. China needs to work on it. That's what I bothered me most on this trip.

Report from the year 2006

In August 2006, I returned to China for another 2-month vacation. I'd normally gone in winters, to catch the Chinese New Year's holiday season; but my mother suggested that I return in autumn instead, for a change, so we'd have more outdoor activities. So I went in August, even though I own a restaurant in New Hampshire and it was the restaurant's busy season.

I was surprised to see American culture has crept more and more into Chinese people's daily life.

Pricey drinks I already knew China was changing daily, and I wouldn't have been surprised if I'd seen a naked body-artist in the street. But what really surprised me was a Beijing outdoor pub selling a tiny glass (maybe 6 ounces) of mixed drink for 100 yuan ($13). My New Hampshire restaurant sells a 14-ounce mixed well liquor for just $4. Is China always as cheap as it's famed to be? Those Beijing pubs, over a hundred of them, sit along the beautiful royal lake in Beijing's center. When we were there around midnight on a weekday, the pubs were packed and bands were loud, reminding me of New Orleans' French Quarter.

Three of us each ordered a drink, totaling 300 yuan. I never drink alcohol, so I couldn't tell whether the drink was good, but I was surprised at the fancy American-sounding names and the tiny portions!

Pricey housing In Beijing in 2006, a normal person makes between 2000 and 5000 yuan a month ($260-$650), but a 3-bedroom condo costs between 1,000,000 and 2,000,000 yuan.

In China, houses are sold by the square meter. Just 10 years ago, Beijing's houses were about 2000 yuan a square meter, they gradually went up to 3000, 4000, 5000 yuan. Three years ago, my daughter suggested we buy a unit there, for about 5000 yuan a square meter. I replied, "But you're planning to take a job in Japan. Who's going to live in Beijing?" When the price went up to 8000 yuan a square meter, she moved to Beijing. Again, I said it was too expensive. But now no house in Beijing is under 10,000 yuan a square meter!

Millions of homeowners who bought earlier become millionaires! But now people complain that even if they'd saved money for 100 years, they still couldn't afford a place in Beijing.

Shanghai is even more expensive. But the high prices aren't just in big cities like Beijing and Shanghai. In the city where I grew up (Chengdu) and other medium and small cities, house prices all went up dramatically.

Pricey department stores Shopping in China's department stores can be extremely expensive. American and European upscale brands such as Nike, Adidas, Lancôme, Maybelline, and L.A. Bag cost more in China than in America. You'll see a young guy who makes 2000 yuan a month spend 700 yuan for a pair of Nike shoes. Girls often use a month's salary to buy expensive facial stuff. Department stores look like those in the U.S., even fancier.

American intrusion American culture is intruding in every corner of China's city life.

Businesspeople meet in Starbucks. Kids' favorite place is always McDonald's. Pizza Huts are usually packed. Pubs are full of young people who colored their hair blond. Valentine's Day, Mother's Day, and Christmas Day have become big events for commercials and ordinary folks as well. Sometimes you wonder whether you're in America or China.

The first three days in Beijing, I felt sad, wondering how regular people could afford Beijing living. But I gradually discovered, to my relief, that there were still some stores, supermarkets and restaurants that are less expensive.

Teaching English In China, English has been hot for the last 15 years. It's getting even hotter.

Many native English speakers from the U.S., Britain, Canada, and Australia have gone to China to teach English. Five years ago, they were making about 7000 yuan a month, while a Chinese college graduate would make only about 1000 yuan.

Recently, more and more foreigners have come to China to teach English. Now they make just 4000 or 5000 yuan a month, even less in small cities. They still make a bit more than regular Chinese people, since English is still hot.

Of course, Americans teach English in China not for the money but for a thrilling experience.

In Chengdu, I met two young college graduates from California, Mike and Cathy. They told me teaching in China was the most exciting experience in their lives. They just finished their first-year contract and decided to renew for another year. They said they felt very much respected, appreciated, useful, and even admired. They also said they lived very well, with a free room, much better than average Chinese people. They went to restaurants pretty often to try different "real" Chinese food; and if they went with Chinese friends, they didn't even have a chance to pay. They didn't have to worry about paying rent, car loans, or credit-card bills. The only problem was they sometimes felt a little homesick.

Many retired folks teach English in China. The only requirement is to be a "native English speaker."

Teaching Japanese Some *Japanese* people teach in China, too. My daughter studies Japanese from a retired Japanese couple living in Beijing. My daughter says they're very nice people and don't even charge her tuition.

American-global culture Most students in China's colleges, high schools, and even middle schools are familiar with Michael Jordan, Michael Jackson, Madonna, Tom Cruise, Tom Hanks, Julia Roberts (nicknamed the "big-mouth beauty"), the Clinton couple, George Bush, Condi Rice, the Red Sox, the New York Yankees… Teenagers wear belly-baring jeans and wide, long T-shirts. They sing rap songs. Many people worry that China's 5000-year culture will gradually fade away.

Although the U.S. hasn't yet existed for even 300 years, it has a strong holiday culture, mostly borrowed from older European countries. No holiday can compare to Christmas, which overwhelms you completely with the holiday season's atmosphere for a whole month, with so many songs and music to make your heart tender and peaceful. America's stores, public places, and even homes seem always decorated for the next holiday. That idea's been picked up now by China's businesses and commercials, though Chinese New Year's Day is still decorated with red lanterns, red-door "duilian" (like poems and calligraphy), and red carved pictures on the windows, accompanied by plenty of food and lion dances.

Living in a global village, each family borrows someone else's ideas. The more you learn from others, the smarter and stronger you'll become. That's the case with today's China.

Report from the year 2008

In April 2008, I went to China to visit my mom for 2 months.

The airline lost my luggage. When I arrived at my mom's home in Jiangyou, my relatives told me she had suddenly died. A few days later, China's biggest earthquake hit: it measured 8 on the Richter scale, with 69,000 people confirmed dead, plus 374,000 injured, plus 18,000 missing and 5 million homeless. The city the earthquake picked as its center was mine, Jiangyou, population 900,000: the whole city was wrecked, including our high-rise condos, so everybody had to camp outdoors, shuddering in makeshift tents made of scraps of cloth, without food or sanitation.

My husband tried to cheer me up by saying God had treated me to a camping trip.

Not a pleasant trip! Friends died. I don't want to talk more about it. It was a trip to forget.

Report from the year 2011

In April 2011, I went back to China again. This time, the trip was uneventful, which means successful! I stayed 10 weeks.

I began by visiting my daughter Mimi in Beijing. She recently married a Chinese guy who calls himself "Simon" to honor the singer Paul Simon.

I've always thought of Mimi as my little girl who needed my care, but now *she* took care of *me*! During the 3 weeks I was with her, she and Simon piled as many nice treats as possible on me.

They got me 2 dental appointments and a health checkup. They took me to the theater and to play badminton. They took me to **798**, which is the most famous art gallery district, converted from an abandoned factory; there she bought me a beautiful artistic shawl. We went to see a movie about a panda from America (Kung Fu Panda 2). She got me a perm and facial.

Hot pot China is famous for its hot-pot restaurants, where a waitress brings you a pot of spiced water to boil at your table. Then you submerge meats, fish, and vegetables: just dip the goodies in the pot, wait for them to heat, then pull them up to eat.

Sichuan had a tiny hot-pot seafood restaurant called "Ocean-Bottom Pull-Up," which grew to become a national chain and a case study by the Harvard Business School. Since I'd read a book about it and got curious, Mimi and my brother took me to its outlet in Beijing.

That outlet is huge: several hundred tables, plus a waiting area holding about 30 tables, where you can play checkers, get free snacks & drinks. The staff also polishes your shoes and does your nails, for free! You have so much fun in that room you forget you're waiting for your main meal.

Finally, the hostess tells you your meal's table is ready. Then you place your order. Prices are moderate: the price per person is just 60 yuan ($9). It's a good place to take friends & family, though not quite upscale enough for business meetings.

Pricey tiny China's restaurant portions used to be big, as in the USA, but now they're so tiny they look like they're from France. And of course, prices soared.

In China, is eating cheap? Not anymore. Restaurant bargains are history.

Japanese in China Mimi & Simon took me to a nice Japanese restaurant in Beijing. The food was presented very attractively. Udon noodles, sushi — everything tasted so good! — seemed better than Japanese food served in the U.S. But the portions were tiny: to satisfy 3 or 4 people, you must order at least 6 items, so the cost per person is about 100 yuan ($15), which is pretty high for a Chinese budget.

Mimi said that in Japan, where she worked a year, the food tastes really good, even in a small restaurant, but looks simpler. Here in Beijing the presentation is fancier.

Orchard Restaurant We visited the Orchard Restaurant, on the outskirts of Beijing. It's in the middle of an orchard, with a pond you can walk around.

It looks like an American family restaurant with an American chef managing Chinese cooks. The dining room looks Chinese, with Chinese waitresses walking around, incense burning in a corner, and Buddha statues to protect wealth; but the food is very American: huge portions and tasty, too!

To my surprise, a meal of rib-eye steak cost 365 yuan ($56), not including soup or salad. I own a restaurant in New Hampshire, where we charge just $17.99 for the same meal but include soup or salad.

But at least you get an orchard to play in, so the restaurant acts as a compromise between an American family restaurant and Sichuan's happy-farmer outdoor restaurant. Sichuan's happy-farmer restaurants have lots of outside activity — you can play mahjong & poker and drink tea under the trees all day. It's a nice place for weddings: 370 yuan ($57) per person for a wedding buffet that includes beer and some wine.

Clothes Sadly, the Chinese in-crowd doesn't like Chinese-branded clothes. They prefer foreign brands: European, American, Japanese, and Korean.

When Chinese people visit Western countries, they shop a lot at Louis Vuitton, Macy's, and America's outlet malls. When Mimi & Simon came to visit us in New Hampshire, they bought lots of stuff at the local outlet mall and saved over $1000 that day.

Even students on low budgets try foreign brands that are less expensive: $25 per item from budget-fashion chains such as Uniqlo (based in Japan) and H&M (based in Sweden).

Housing On days when we didn't go out for dinner, Mimi & Simon took me for walks in their walled-off, gated community, which featured a scenic garden with streams, waterfalls, bridges, and all sorts of trees & flowers.

People tell this joke:

If you own a condo in Beijing, you're qualified to immigrate to the USA.

That's because the U.S. will give you a "green card" if you invest $500,000 in the U.S.

Beijing's housing is expensive, advertised at 30,000 to 40,000 yuan per square meter ($430 to $575 per square foot). When I walk down the streets, I see real-estate-office windows advertising homes for 2,000,000-7,000,000 yuan ($300,000-$1,100,000). The closer to Beijing's center, the higher the price.

Everyone who's bought a home is thrilled at the investment. Two years ago, my sister bought a condo in the Sichuan city of Chengdu, and its value has already doubled. Mimi bought in Beijing, and hers doubled also, in a year and a half.

But folks who haven't bought housing yet face a huge burden. The housing market is tough for youngsters who want to marry. People say:

> If you're just a factory worker, you'd have had to work ever since the Qing dynasty (over a hundred years ago) to save enough to buy a condo.
>
> If you work on a farm in the countryside, you'd have had to work ever since the Tang dynasty (over a thousand years ago).

The government's tried many times to stop real-estate speculators. For example, China now has a law that if you buy real estate you must keep it at least 5 years before selling it. To buy housing in Beijing, you must prove you've lived and worked in Beijing for 5 years and paid your income taxes. But government's restrictions are too late, since prices have already soared to the top.

In Beijing, people have built more net worth from housing bought a year ago than from a whole lifetime of earnings from hard work.

My brother has a friend who worked in Beijing for 25 years. When housing there cost 2,000 yuan per square meter many years ago, he thought it was "expensive." Then he watched it go up rapidly and said, "No, no, no!" Now housing is up to 40,000 yuan per square meter, 20 times as high. He gave up on Beijing and turned back to Chengdu, where he got a nicer, bigger place for less money. I guess he feels sorry he missed the big chance to get rich.

Two years ago, when Beijing's housing prices dipped briefly then started to rise again, Mimi thought of buying a one-bedroom condo. I suggested 2 bedrooms instead. While she was looking, she discovered prices were soaring every day, so she took the one-bedroom condo, and she said the delay cost her a car, because the price had gone up that much in just 2 weeks. But she still wound up happy, because her condo's value doubled afterwards.

Chengdu
You might already know these some famous sayings about Chengdu (Sichuan's capital):

> Chengdu's a place that once you come, you never want to leave.
> Chengdu is developing fast, living pace slow.

Chengdu is like a beautify lady: warm, charming, elegant, and relaxing.

Chengdu's won 2 awards:

> In a rating of Chinese cities, Chengdu's become rated the best to live in.
> In a survey measuring people's happiness in China, Chengdu's become #1.

In Chengdu no season is bad for outdoor activity. Sure, summer is hot and winter is cold, but not extreme.

Sit outside? Impossible in Beijing's freezing, windy winter! But Chengdu's okay: if you wear a coat, you can sit outside playing checkers & mahjong and sip tea at an outdoor teahouse, and you can do all sorts of exercise outdoors.

In Chengdu you can live luxuriously; but if you have less money, you can still lead a colorful life.

On Chengdu's outskirts, many small towns have turned themselves into scenic spots. They've fixed up ancient buildings, to create quaint "ancient towns". Each ancient town has its own theme: one has peach blossoms, some have lakes, rivers, flowers, food. I visited a nice one where you can admire a river, play mahjong, and get a 2-bedroom motel suite cheaply, just $10 per night, with views of the river, boats, open-door teahouse, and lanterns. So beautiful!

Downtown Chengdu's restaurants can be very fancy & expensive, but you can pay less by visiting smaller restaurants that are cheaper. On a quiet street in one of the ancient towns, I found a small restaurant whose specialty is the **one-noodle bowl**. Your bowl contains just a single piece of noodle, very long, handmade by the staff, who make a performance of throwing it into boiling water and winding it into your bowl. Eat it hot or cold. Lovers have fun eating it: one lover eats from one end of the noodle, the other eats from the opposite end, and when they meet in the middle they kiss. It costs just 8 yuan ($1.25).

Clothes for me
My brother Guangdi and his wife took me to a nice department store in Beijing to buy me clothes. I got scared at the high prices: mostly 1500-2000 yuan ($230-$310). I said, "No, no, no!" But they insisted, "Try one! We have a coupon." Eventually I found an inexpensive blouse for 800 yuan ($125). I said "I like this" and tried it. Everybody said "You look good!" so I got it.

When I went to Chengdu I bought some clothes for just 150-550 yuan ($23-$85) but still of very good quality & beautiful. I feel a lot more comfortable buying in Chengdu.

Relationships
My trip consisted of too much social life. When I visited China, my friends and old classmates came to see me. I had parties with relatives & friends almost every day. I felt they treated me as an honored guest but felt awkward being always the guest. I enjoyed coming back to New Hampshire, where I can finally relax in my own home, though I feel lonely here.

My trip's main pleasure was seeing that my daughter Mimi, after she married, grew up. Never before had I felt she was so considerate & caring. Now, wow! She took care of me so much! The day before I left, she & Simon took me to the Japanese restaurant and gave me a diamond ring. "Oh, my God," I said, "You shouldn't have done that, you guys"

I didn't expect that at all, but I learned that a girl who gets married can immediately grow.

Touching devotion
I want to talk about the woman who touched me most this time.

Her name is Xiao Shü. Back in 1994, she married Xiao Pei, who had a son from a previous marriage. The son had lived with the mother but moved in with Xiao Pei when he was 10 years old. At that time, the son, named Wei, was a rebellious boy who listened to nobody, gave a lot of back talk, wasn't respectful, and didn't care for school or anything else.

Xiao Shü didn't want to deal with Wei and his problems. She wanted to have her *own* baby. But her father (a college professor) gave her this piece of advice: "You know the saying **ai wu ji wu** (which means love something, love what's similar). If you love Xiao Pei, you should love his son. Just treat this boy Wei as your own. Then you'll have a happy family and happy marriage."

She obeyed her father and started caring for the boy. But she discovered he was difficult: he wasn't respectful, wasn't working hard, and had a "just give up" attitude. Many times she asked him, "What do you want? What can we do for you? We'll do our best to make you happy." But he didn't improve.

Finally she told him, "If all your friends like name-brand clothes, we'll buy the same for you. If they want some sports game, we'll buy it for you. But in return, you must get A's in school. Okay? A deal?" Wei agreed.

She started buying what she promised. She got him name-brand clothes, sports shoes, everything, dangerously doing her part of the bargain first. Little Wei went to school with a better schoolbag, better clothes, and better shoes. He suddenly looked different. He was very happy! He had more friends, who came to his home. She always treated them with good food.

Every day after school, she looked at his homework assignment and did it in parallel with him. She worked on it by herself, while he worked on it separately, then they compared their answers and decided who was wrong. She taught him. That routine lasted many years. She also read good books with him, together.

Gradually his grades went up. He turned into a good student. He got admitted to a good middle school, one of best high schools, and one of best colleges. Now he's in Switzerland, going for a doctorate in chemistry, alongside his girlfriend (who's also from Chengdu and in Switzerland for a doctorate).

Every week, he phones Xiao Shü from Switzerland. "Hi, Aunt Shü…."

"Do you want to talk to your father? He's here."

"Oh, okay."

Xiao Pei's friends asked, "What's your son doing?" He fibs, "I don't know. Maybe he's a security guard somewhere."

Xiao Pei's a light-hearted, relaxed guy. His ancestors had been a prestigious family. His grandfather was a Sichuan high official. The family lived very richly before 1949, so Xiao Pei's mother lived in high style when she was a kid. You can see some old rich family traits in Xiao Pei.

After the Communist Party came to power in 1949, the family's wealth was confiscated, so the family suffered a poor life for many years. But strangely enough, Xiao Pei's mother continued to live in high style, even though she no longer had much money. In her whole life, she never did any housework, not even laundry. She'd rely on maids to take care of such things. To make ends meet, she had to work in a factory for many years and spend conservatively. But she kept up the appearance of a high lifestyle: folks joked that she was the kind of person who'd take a taxi even when she had just 20 yuan in her pocket, rather than doing what us normal people would do: take a bus or walk.

In spite of her craziness, she managed to raise 6 kids, and none became bad! In fact, as soon as they earned any money, they gave lots of it to her. That's a Chinese principle: a child's #1 responsibility is to respect parents, be nice to them, make them happy.

So her 6 kids all tried hard to make her happy. That's why we say, half-jokingly, that she worries about nothing; her whole life, she's always light-hearted, relaxed.

She has a generous heart: she lets everybody come to her house to eat and relax. When my own parents had a hard time in early years, they went to her home, to get peace of mind.

Recently, she built a small teahouse in her yard. She invites her friends & neighbors to come enjoy it, have tea, play mahjong, and eat. Normally, about 40 people eat there. She charges them nothing, but people who win at mahjong there contribute some of the winnings to her to help her cover expenses. She doesn't want to make any profit.

For many years, she had a maid, whom she needed to help handle her growing clan: 6 kids, plus now the kid's wives and their new families, all coming to visit her. She put money into the maid's hand and said, "Go buy stuff, don't bother reporting to me." She trusted the maid to manage all the household expenses. But after the teahouse was built and the number of visitors increased to 40 per day, the maid said "Oh, that's too much!" and quit.

She tried to find another maid but gave up. Her family jokes that whenever she interviewed an applicant for the position of "household maid," the applicant would say, "Sure, how many people are eating daily?" Finally the problem got solved when one of her sons become a full-time cook for her. The food tastes much better than restaurants'! The whole family is a happy, party family. Chinese families are more closely knit than American families, but *this* family is even closer!

Xiao Pei's sister moved to the USA and told me, "The family is too luxurious! I must phone them to say hey, you guys gotta watch your health, don't eat so much!" Here in the USA she's adopted a simpler life.

Xiao Pei (whose son is in Switzerland) inherited his mother's noble side and relaxed attitude about life. He loves to joke. He philosophizes, "Relax, don't worry about a thing! Enjoy life! No matter how rich or poor, just enjoy life!"

His wife Xiao Shü loves him so much. She says, "When I come home, I see all the in-laws helping run his mother's teahouse, so I just roll up my sleeves and pitch in. Everybody's happy, so why should I complain? I do things happily too! I come to enjoy the family. I help with his mother's housework; I clean & cook. It doesn't bother me."

So visiting her mother-in-law means lots of work, but she enjoys it.

Sometimes she complains to her husband Xiao Pei about things, but Xiao Pei doesn't lose his temper or talk back. "What can you do if he doesn't join the battle?" she sighed. But I see happiness written on her face. She's proud of son Wei and carries his picture in her wallet. She showed me his picture: "My son, isn't he handsome, like a movie star?"

Xiao Pei is my relative. When I visited his big family, they all talked about Xiao Shü. I feel she's a hero. She's smart and kind, and Xiao Pei is smart too, to marry her. She touched my heart.

Americans' helping hands

Americans are warm and helpful.

Bleeding bicyclist

Recently, I read a revealing news item on a Chinese website: A girl on a bicycle was knocked down by a bus in a Chinese city. While a shocked crowd stared at her and didn't know what to do, a blonde girl rushed in and told a bystander in English to call 119 (like 911 here). The blonde then sent the bleeding bicyclist to a nearby hospital and waited there until the bicyclist was taken good care of.

Later it was discovered that the blonde was an American teaching English in a college in that city. When a reporter eventually asked some witnesses why they didn't help, they said they thought the two girls must have known each other.

But that's something a typical American would do anytime anywhere.

Banker's bathroom

The first time I received an American helping hand was about going to the bathroom. When I first came to the U.S. and was walking in a Kansas town, I felt a pain in my belly. I needed to go to a ladies' room right away.

I looked around anxiously. Just a bank building was nearby. I hesitated and went in.

It was a beautiful bank. A very professionally dressed woman stood up, smiled at me, and asked how she could help. Embarrassed, I asked if the bank had a ladies' room.

She said "sure" cheerfully, without losing her smile. She pointed in the direction and said something I didn't quite catch. She saw my puzzled look and said, "I'll show you." She left her desk and led me across the hallway, turned, and walked all the way to the door of the ladies' room.

My heart was touched. It was a small thing, but you couldn't expect such a "small thing" to happen in China. A beautiful professional lady walks a stranger, a non-customer, to a bathroom!

Gradually I found "being helpful" is Americans' spirit. Many times when I asked somebody for directions, I found myself in the center of several people discussing and showing me the way.

Baggage

The first time I went to New York City, the bus arrived about 1:00AM. Getting off with 3 big cases and 2 small ones, I didn't know what to do. I dragged the cases step by step, one at a time.

A black guy passing by offered to help. He carried 2 cases and walked in front. I followed, my heart beating fast. At that time of night, with New York City's fame, I was scared.

We walked a long way out to the street.

He stopped a taxi; said "Good luck," and walked away. Before I said thanks, he disappeared into the darkness.

Everywhere

Americans can't bear breakdowns, bullying, and broken lives.

Americans can't bear watching cars stuck along the highway in the snow: they jump to help. Americans can't bear watching one nation bully another: they try to stop it. Americans can't bear watching African skin-and-bone kids go hungry: they donate money for food and school education.

Americans' helping hands are everywhere. They're the best thing about this country.

Tricky languages

Chinese is hard to learn — and so is English.

English is the easiest language to speak poorly

I've been the Queen of Poor English.

What's in that egg roll? When I worked in a Chinese restaurant some years ago, a customer asked me what was in the egg roll.

I said, "Chicken, pork, onion, celery, and…" I hesitated. I suddenly forgot how to say "cabbage." I tried, "Gabbige? garbage? cabb…?"

The customer said, "Cabbage!"

I said, "Yes, yes, cabbage, cabbage!"

The customer laughed, "You don't mean *garbage*, do you?"

Another time, I thought I remarked to a customer, "Americans like to go to restaurant." But as soon as I spoke, my face turned red because I saw the customer was puzzled.

"*Restroom*? You mean *restaurant!*" he corrected kindly, smiling.

I was so embarrassed! I said, "I'm sorry, I meant *restaurant*, *restaurant*, not *rest…room*. I'm so sorry I didn't pronounce it well."

The long road to English I learned most of my English in China. When I first came to the U.S., people thought I must have been here 10 years.

But later, after I'd actually been here 10 years, I still made all sorts of mistakes when speaking English. Even worse, I still had a hard time understanding TV and movies. I couldn't enjoy TV shows, good movies, or news on the radio. That made my boring life even more boring. I was frustrated.

English is difficult. I know many Chinese people who've lived here over 20 years, worked in Chinese restaurant kitchens all that time, and can hardly speak any English. Even those who got master's degrees or doctorates in the U.S and lived here many years still occasionally say "he" when meaning "she."

The Chinese language is much easier. You don't have to worry about tense: to talk about working, you just say "work," maybe with an adverb. You don't have to say "*work, works, worked, working, have worked, have been working*, and *has been working*" — which drive me crazy! I feel so lucky that when I speak Chinese I don't have to worry about whether a table is a male or a female, as in German or Russian. I wonder how those people can remember the sex of every lifeless object.

In China, students start taking English courses in the 7th grade — now some schools start from the 3rd grade, some even from kindergarten — and continue all the way through college. But they learn English mainly by reading books, with little chance of listening and speaking to native English speakers. That was also my way of learning English.

Listening comprehension is even harder than speaking.

I asked Russ why I could understand him perfectly but not TV or radio. Russ said he slowed down a bit when talking to me. But that's almost not true! We've talked about everything, every topic, though sometimes he had to repeat what he said.

Speak like a snake Russ decided to improve my English.

I told Russ, "One of my girlfriend in China is retired."

"Girlfriends," he corrected.

"OK, one of my girlfriends is retired. She's just 45 years old."

"Really? That's pretty early," Russ said.

"Because too many people, not enough job."

"Jobs," Russ added.

"All right, I know 'jobs.' Now she read a lot of books every day."

"Reads!" Russ corrected.

"S-s-s, I become a snake!" I laughed at myself. I knew all grammar very well; I'd corrected the same mistake for my students in China before. But when I spoke, I sometimes just forgot.

Russ felt amused at my created sentences, like "I'm *so* eager to sleep." (He told me to say just "I'm so sleepy.")

Russ said instead of my English getting better, his English was getting worse. He found himself sometimes using strange words, and he picked up some of my accent, like "*So* nice!" and "*So* fast!" and "*So* beautiful!"

Peanuts or penis? Once, I was supposed to sell peanut M&M's to raise money for the Special Olympics. I told Russ I was scared to say "peanuts," for fear of being misunderstood as "penis." Russ burst into laughter and pronounced the two words for me. I couldn't tell much difference. He pronounced again.

Then he tested me. He put a can of peanut butter on the table. I stood 10 feet away from him.

"Peanuts," he said. I pointed to the peanut butter. He nodded.

"Penis," he said. I pointed to the can again. He shook his head.

"Peanuts," he said. I hesitated, pointing to the can, and said "not this." Russ shook his head.

"Penis," he said. I pointed to the peanut butter. Russ shook his head and sighed, "My poor deaf wife."

"Your poor *dead* wife?" My eyes were wide open.

Improving, bit by bit Eventually, Russ rented movies and trained me by explaining them to me. He stopped every few minutes and asked if I understood. Though I hated too much interruption, I enjoyed some very good movies and felt I understood better.

My English was improving, bit by bit. One day, after talking a long time without being interrupted by Russ's correction, I said proudly, "Hey, Russ, have you noticed I made less mistakes recently?"

Russ said, "Y-y-y-yes. But… it should be '*fewer* mistakes,' dear."

American clichés

Some everyday dialogues are so familiar to our ears that we don't have to think twice when we talk. They become verbal form letters.

It's amazing! Everywhere in the U.S., you hear the same dialogues, even with the same accents — to my ears:

Comment:	"Nice day, isn't it?"
Standard response:	"*Beautiful!*"
Comment:	"It's raining hard."
Standard response:	"It's *pouring!*" or "We *need* it!"
Comment:	"It's cold out there."
Standard response:	"It's *freezing!*" or "It's nice and warm here."
Comment:	"I'm hungry."
Standard response:	"I'm *starving!*"
Comment:	"How are you doing?"
Standard response:	"Good. How about yourself?"
Comment:	"Have a nice day!"
Standard response:	"You too!"

Maybe I'm the only person who pays attention to those everyday simple conversations. The reason is: you can't find the same situation in China.

Chinese dialects

People in one Chinese province might not understand a single word from people in another province, though all Chinese people use the same written language. People from different provinces can communicate just if they both agree to speak Mandarin.

There are 5 main dialects in China's 29 provinces:

The most-used and official dialect is **Mandarin**.
It's part of the **Northern** dialect, used mainly in northern and central China.

The second dialect is **Cantonese**.
It's used in Guangdong province and Hong Kong (southeast China).

The third is **Shanghai** dialect, used in the Shanghai area (eastern China).

The fourth is **Fujian** dialect, used in Fujian province.

The fifth is **Min Nan** dialect, used mainly by Taiwan's native people.

All 5 of those dialects are used by China's majority "**Han**" nationality. There are still 53 other minorities (such as **Tibetan**, **Hui**, and **Uyghur**), who have their own languages; some even have their own *written* languages!

Even in Northern provinces, people speak Mandarin with all sorts of provincial accents. Beijing's Mandarin is considered the basic Mandarin.

I'm from Szechuan province. Szechuan dialect belongs to the Northern dialect, close to Mandarin but still different. I can speak Mandarin. I understand very little Cantonese and Shanghai dialect. I understand no other dialects at all.

China's only cliché?

Maybe there's just one old common everyday cliché in China: "Have you eaten?" That's because China has a well-known saying: "For common people, food is heaven."

Chinese way to succeed

Here's how my Chinese girlfriends succeeded when they came to America. (To protect their privacy, I've altered their names here.)

Restaurant owner

My friend "Ying" came from my Sichuan hometown 10 years ago when she was 25 years old. She was so sweet and beautiful that she immediately attracted the men in the New York City restaurant where she worked as a bus girl. The restaurant was busy. It was a totally different life from China, where she'd been a magazine editor. All the restaurant guys, from the owner to the dishwasher, were very friendly and helpful. Everybody tried to do some part of her job, which made that first American job easier and less stressful.

Finding a husband Her mom told her to find a good guy in America and get married, so she started getting to know some guys: restaurant workers, owners, a businessman with properties in Long Island, a writer and magazine publisher, a European student from the same English school she went to, and a Ph.D. student; but she hated those who tried to touch her when first meeting in a restaurant.

Finally, her future husband showed up: a handsome guy, 2 years younger, happy and confident. He worked in a Chinese restaurant as a cook and delivery guy. He was very nice but had no green card. I told her to think twice: without a green card, you can't visit China, because you're not allowed to come back. One day shortly after they met, she phoned me and said "I got married." I thought she was joking. "To whom?" "Who else do you think it could be?"

Later, she told me the guy had never dared to touch her hand for a whole month, even alone with her in a car or walking her home at night after work. He was so respectful and sincere, he touched her heart. (Her mother later joked that he was the smartest suitor.)

Newlyweds When they were first married, they lived in a basement in the New York City's Flushing section (which is part of Queens). After the first baby was born, they moved to an apartment with shared kitchen and bathroom; even the living room was occupied by somebody. When the baby girl was 8 months old, she was sent back to China to be taken care of by her grandparents.

Owning a restaurant Ling borrowed 80,000 U.S. dollars from her rich parents in China and bought a Chinese restaurant in New Jersey. That was in 1999; ever since, she and her husband have worked 7 days a week, 10 to 12 hours a day — except she had another two babies, both sent back to China.

She worked as a hostess and cashier. She also took phone orders, bussed tables, and packed takeout orders. I suggested that on slow days, she should take time off; but she just couldn't. Even when she went out shopping, she had to rush back, for fear that something would happen while she was away.

After 2 or 3 years, she felt tired. She started to complain that she felt like she was in a jail. She griped, "Even if you were to make over a million dollars in 10 years, would anybody be willing to stay in jail for 10 years for a million dollars?" She felt it wasn't worth it. She missed China badly.

Fortunately, the business has been improving, up 30%, up 40%, doubled, more than doubled! She started to enjoy working and knowing customers. She started to get use to it.

Buying houses They bought their first townhouse, big and brand new with hardwood floor. They bought beautiful, fancy furniture. They had a beautiful fence built. Later, they bought a second house to rent out. With $15,000 a month income, they plan to buy more houses.

Happy reunion Recently their three kids (ages 9, 7, and 3) came back from China. The family is reunited.

Ying says she's doesn't miss China any more. "I might not find a nice job there and make so much money. I'm better off realizing my American dream here!"

Nurse

My friend "Hui" is in her late 40's. She's been in America for about 20 years.

Jobs She's a registered-nurse supervisor. Like most Chinese students in America then, she'd worked in America's Chinese restaurants. Even after she became an RN, she still kept a part-time waitress job and lived in a cheap rented room.

Singing She sings well. She was the soloist in a Chinese singing group in Boston. They performed even in the theaters of Harvard and M.I.T.

Finding a husband When she was almost 40 years old, she married a medical guy. He'd been a medical doctor in China but couldn't work as a doctor here in America, so he became a medical technician.

Investments The couple bought a small condo in Boston for about $90,000. Soon after, they also bought a 2-family house: they lived in one unit and rented out the other. They also rented out the condo. They used the rent to pay the mortgage, so they lived somewhat free.

A couple of years later, house prices in Boston soared. They sold their condo and made over $270,000 dollars profit! Then they bought more property in Florida.

At the same time, they invested in a 401-K plan, whole-life insurance, and a mutual fund. She says they've been very lucky. Their mutual fund's been doing great. Their money doubled in 5 years; maybe it will double every 5 years. The couple made about a $100,000 total salary a year, and they were lucky investing money. When they reach retirement age, 15 years from now, they'll have more than $2,000,000 worth of property and money, she estimated.

Family life Recently, I visited her home: 3 bedrooms, 2 bathrooms, not fancy, but comfortable. Their 7-year-old son practices piano and, like a typical Chinese kid, also goes to Chinese-language school on Sundays, art class on Saturdays, swimming class, and so on.

The family looks just average and living paycheck-to-paycheck, but actually they're doing *great!* They feel good about it.

5 principles

Seeing those girlfriends and many other Chinese-American friends, I figure that the Chinese way to succeed is follow these 5 principles:

Be persistent. No matter how hard your life is, no matter what happens, just work, work, work, to make money and work towards your goal.

No job is too low. A professor can work as a dishwasher, and a doctor can be a nanny if necessary, following the Chinese saying "Be able to take a high position or low position." If they do just things they like or take just jobs they feel are fun, they might stay poor. Here's another Chinese saying: "Those who went through the hardest life can rise above others."

Adjust your goal. Always look for the best opportunity. In different situations, try different jobs and different businesses. There's always one that suits you.

Live thriftily before you're rich. Never spend more money than you make. Don't spend more than your budget, even on Mother's Day, Father's Day, Christmas Day, New Year's Day, birthdays, Valentine's Day, Easter, and vacations. Actually, Chinese people often give *big* gifts; but when they do, they try to save on other things.

Always save money.

But not *all* successful Chinese-Americans did those good things. Some Chinese don't care much about regulations or laws: they take big advantage of Uncle Sam and get rich fast. That's a different issue, which I'll discuss in future editions.

My silly husband

My husband, Russ Walter, is the strangest guy I've ever known.

Rich or poor?

When I first met Russ, he lived in Somerville, Massachusetts. In his 8-room 2-floor apartment, books and computers were everywhere. Boxes of books and magazines were piled to the ceiling. To squeeze past them, he had to walk sideways, toes at right angles to where he wanted to go. There was no furniture, except work desks, chairs, and a twin bed. But strangely, there were all sorts of keyboard musical instruments! He lived in this "live-in warehouse," as a newspaper described it.

At that time, he had 20 years without any vacation — and many years with no dating, let alone marriage.

I was trying to find out what was wrong with this guy. I found he was just smart, highly-educated, honest, gentle, clean-cut, simple, and nice, a good guy in every way. I was secretly glad he wasn't a "leftover." Americans have hundreds of reasons not to get married. Chinese would guess "something's wrong."

But as time went on, I started to feel there *was* something wrong, something different. Years later, I told him he was extremely strange. I started to wonder, "That's why…"

All day long, all year round, he does nothing but work, work, work, work, work, work, and work! Or he's on the phone with his readers to talk, talk, talk, talk, talk, talk, and talk! Being in his company you just feel lonely, lonely, and lonely!

He often has no time to sit down for a meal. Being asked to eat a meal is not just too fancy but also a burden for him. A lot of the time he just munches something from the refrigerator.

He doesn't eat anything with oil, salt, cheese, cream, or caffeine. In his eyes, everything on the market is "high in salt, high in fat, and high in sugar" — which I would call "high in food."

He never threw away newspapers, magazines, and paperwork. When we finally decided to move to New Hampshire, we had to hire a bunch of people to move those paper goods out from the basement. His brothers and a sister-in-law came all the way from Ohio and Connecticut to help. Mounds of his boxes were piled up along the street sidewalk. The town's security officer came, nervously taking pictures, warning we'd be fined if we failed to remove them in 8 hours. So we paid $800 for a trash company to take them away in 4 big dumpsters. When boxes of his old books and many of his antique computers were thrown into the dumpsters, I noticed poor Russ's face turned ashen and his eyes showed painful despair.

On his desks, in his files and boxes, there were always one or two stale checks from his customers, from $15 to $500. They were like wastepaper. He didn't deposit them because something was wrong with those checks, such as the year, the date, a few cents difference, or unsigned. He just put them aside until they were stale. He was an exact person and expected everyone else to be the same.

There were also piles and piles of customers' old unpaid bills. For many years, he never bothered to tell his assistants to deal with them. At the end of last century, he decided to mail reminders to the customers before the new century came. We only picked out some of the last 8 years' unpaid bills, totaling about $85,000, and sent a few hundred letters out. A month passed, but we got just a few responses. Some letters were returned with a "moved" notice; some businesses went bankrupt; most letters had no response at all.

I asked him why he hadn't dealt with it each year. He said he judged that it was a better use of his time to write books than deal with bills. I said he was just like a farmer who worked so hard year-round but cared little about taking in the crops. (Now, of course, we're much better at collecting.) I also told him: while he was creating smart computer people he was also creating some dishonest ones. Maybe they were honest before dealing with him.

He lived like a poor guy. In Somerville, every time he went to the Laundromat, he brought back laundry just *half*-dried, to save a quarter or two.

For many years, he had no insurance of any kind.

I've never seen him buy any luxury stuff. He enjoys a simple life. For most winters, we keep our house under 60 degrees and seldom use an air conditioner in summer. I called him "cheap guy."

He's so different from a normal American! But he's happy as long as he can write and talk on the phone with his readers.

This "cheap guy" seems to be doing okay. His books have been sold all over the country and in many foreign ones. People have called him continuously to say how much they like his books.

He's strange and crazy in many ways. But he's wonderful, too, so I'd better not complain too much.

Embarrassment

Here are more of my comments about Russ. He feels embarrassed about them, so he put them in small type in the hope you won't read them!

"I'm 65.2% hungry"
One of my hardest jobs is to cook for my husband, Russ.

He rarely has time to sit down to eat a meal. So before I start cooking, I must ask, "Are you hungry? You want me to cook something for you?"

If he says "no," I ask, "When do you think you'll be hungry?"

Then he says, "If it makes you happy, go ahead and make something. I know if I say 'no,' you'll keep asking every 20 minutes."

I say, "That won't make me happy. I just want to be done with it."

Sometimes I ask, "How much are you hungry?"

The answer usually takes that math guy awhile to compute. He eventually says "70% hungry," or "80% hungry," or something similar.

One day, his answer was "65.2% hungry."

I figured 65% hungry should be pretty hungry, but not too hungry. What about the extra 0.2%? Maybe a bit more hungry than he'd like to admit, and he secretly wants to spoil himself?

In a few seconds, I had a nice picture of the dinner in my mind, so I went to the fridge and took out a whole chicken breast, a green pepper, a red pepper, an onion, some celery, and a potato.

In 10 minutes, a pan-fried concoction of chicken-breast chunks with mixed vegetables was on the table, with a microwaved potato — plus some tomato slices, orange juice, ketchup, and lemon wedges.

I yelled, "Russ, your food is ready!"

"I'll be right there," he answered cheerfully. Then, I heard him run to the bathroom, run back to the computer room, and finally, with a bunch of books under his arm, come to the table, as if he were coming to a classroom.

He put down his books and gazed at his colorful meal with admiration: "Wow! Looks good!"

He tried a bite. "M-m-m! *You* try it!" He enthusiastically sent a chunk of chicken to my mouth. I ate it reluctantly. I never liked his food: too healthy to taste good. But this time I tried it. "M-m-m! It *is* good!"

He asked, "What spice did you use? It tastes so good!"

"Black pepper, garlic, ginger, scallion, chili peppers, lemon, and tomato sauce."

"No salt or oil?"

I said "surely not." I knew he hated salt and oil.

I started to try those vegetables. They were crispy and naturally light & sweet. I never thought vegetables without salt & oil could taste so good.

I ate some more. Russ ignored his books. I ate half his meal. Russ asked, "Do you have more, or that's it?"

"That's it. I'm sorry."

"That's fine. That's fine. I shouldn't eat too much anyway."

"You know what," I said, "I just ate your 0.2%. That's what is short."

Our fight about cutting grass
We've had more fights about mowing the lawn than most folks. The fights were not about *who* should do it but rather *how* to do it.

After lots of research through the Internet about grass care, Russ decided to do 3 important things besides watering and fertilizing.

He said, "First, I should mulch, because mulching is a kind of fertilizer to the grass. Second, never cut more than one third of the grass, and keep it tall so that the grass will look greener. Third, always pull weeds before cutting grass."

Our neighbors' lawns are all beautiful. Some hire professionals to do the job. The guy who lives across the street works so hard that he spends the whole day every Saturday mowing, trimming, and growing plants. I envy their beautiful lawns. "The grass is always greener on the other side of the fence," and it's true for us. Looking at others' beautiful gardens, I told Russ, "We should cut our grass this weekend."

"Really? It's not tall yet."

"Yes it *is* tall."

"I'll pull the weeds first, they're getting pretty bad."

But the weekend came and went, and the lawn remained uncut. Now it was Wednesday. I said, "The grass is *very* tall now. Can we cut it today?"

"I'm too busy today. How about tomorrow?" he replied.

"Tomorrow" passed, grass still uncut.

"Can I just do it myself?" I volunteered the next day.

"I need to pull up the weeds first. Just wait a bit."

I couldn't wait any longer. The grass was 3 times as tall as everyone else's.

After supper, he said he was very tired and went upstairs for a nap. The day was still early. I decided to do it myself. I went down to the garage and pulled out the lawnmower. The machine roared and a beautiful neat line appeared in the lawn. I'd hardly finished two rows when I saw Russ running toward me. He snatched my lawnmower and stopped it, yelling, "Don't do that, will you? I told you I have to pull weeds. You always do things behind my back." (I did this a few times when he was napping.)

"What do you mean, 'behind your back'? You don't have time, and I can do it."

"But I need to pull up weeds first."

"Then I have to wait another week. Everyone else's yard has weeds, but they cut short and neat, so their lawns all look nice. Our weeds are just in the *back* yard, so who cares?"

"I care. If you don't take care of them, they'll spread all over."

"Then buy weed killer," I said.

"I will when I have time."

Finally he cut the grass. But he cut it just a little; it was still rather tall. Three days later, the grass looked like it needed to be cut again.

I said, "Russ, can you cut it shorter? Then it won't look too bad so soon."

Russ said all the books and Internet recommended it be cut tall.

I said, "Our neighbor's grass is cut by professionals. They cut it much shorter than ours. Let's ask them."

The same argument happened 3 times per month. He also insisted on mulching every time he cut grass, while I said too much mulching would choke the grass. One day I looked at the back yard and sighed, "Russ, it looks like we're growing crops here. Our grass is knee high."

He laughed, "Well, it *is* a little bit too tall. I'll cut it tomorrow."

After much arguing, we finally found a way to make both of us happy. I cut the front yard while he pulled weeds; then he picked up where I left off, to finish the back yard.

Although he still cuts the grass very tall and I sometimes still try to persuade him to cut shorter, our grass is starting to look better.

Thus ends our grass-cutting fight.

What kind of lawnmower?
Russ offers his readers free help by phone, day and night, 24 hours, about computers and other topics.

Russ and I are so used to midnight phone calls that our dreams can continue right after they're interrupted. Even when woken up from the soundest sleep, Russ can immediately act as sane as a professor in class, ready to answer all sorts of questions. After that he can go right back to sleep like a log.

When we first moved to New Hampshire from the Boston area, one of our first tasks was to shop for a lawnmower.

One night, I was awoken by the phone. The bedroom light flicked on, and I heard Russ asking, "What kind of lawnmower do you have?" Then, I heard him mumbling, "I'm sorry, I'm sorry. What kind of *computer* do you have?" Then he started to talk on and on and on. His voice seemed to be floating far away, in dreamland. Finally the talk was over and the glaring light was turned off. I found myself interrupting my dream and asking him, "Were you buying a lawnmower?" He said, "I'm sorry, I made a mistake. I was answering a computer question."

"What did that person say?" I asked.

"He said, 'I'm not talking about lawnmower, I'm talking about a computer.'"

Russ started his hotline in 1978. In his computer book, he writes, "Call whenever you have a question about computers — even life. I'll help you, free. Call day or night, 24 hours, I'm usually in, and I sleep just lightly."

He's kept his word. No weekends, no holidays, no vacations. Christmas Eve is no exception. If he missed calls when he went out on an errand, and even if he left for a meeting for a few days, the answering machine and caller ID helped him to call back.

So many people wrote him to express their thanks. Some people sent him money for the long time he spent helping them; but he returned all the money and wrote back, saying, "Thank you very much, but we don't accept donations."

One local newspaper criticized Russ for being "so lonely as to give people his home phone number and beg people to call him." When I read that, I got very angry. Russ was not upset. He still keeps doing what he thinks is right.

A few times, I tried to make the phone ring less loudly, but he set the ring volume back when he found out. I begged, "Russ, you won't miss it; it's very loud. It's just by your pillow. How can you miss it?" But he insisted on the loudest volume. It was startlingly loud, but I'm used to it now. That's part of his life; he likes it and he's proud of it, for the last 30 years. He's crazy, isn't he?

A tearful birthday dinner

It happened on one of my birthdays.

That morning, I was woken up by Russ singing "Happy Birthday to You." Russ said he'd take me out for dinner after driving his books to the post office in the afternoon.

I was very excited because he seldom had time to take me out. I was thinking about a candlelit romantic dinner all day.

Coming home from work in the afternoon, I rolled up my sleeves and started to pack books for him. It was not until 9PM that we were ready to leave.

Before starting the car, Russ took a piece of paper from the glove compartment and wrote down the mileage and what for, as usual. I was starving. I could hardly wait for a nice dinner, but we were finally on the way. I was cheerfully humming a song. We got to the post office and sent the books out. He came back into the car and took out that paper again. I sighed, begging, "Could you write that later? I'm starving to death."

Russ said, "Sorry, I just want to mark down the business part of my mileage."

I knew he meant the business trip was over and what follows would be personal. But I tried to talk softly, "You sent books to the post office, you want to drive back, too, right?"

Russ said, "Yes, but we're going to a restaurant."

"Do you think a business trip shouldn't have a return trip? How do you go back? Fly?"

"If the purpose is going back, sure we have a round trip. But ours is not. Just if the restaurant's on the way back can I mark "round trip."

"Who else is so exact like you?" I was getting angry. "Okay, let's say an employee of a big company flies to New York City to have a business meeting. You think he can't go out to eat, can't shop or visit friends there? Otherwise he has to pay the air ticket flying back?"

"That's a different thing."

"It's the same idea. I think the correct way should be like this: Our one-way trip is 6.5 miles; you should mark 13 miles for the business. Anything over 13 miles should be

marked as personal. Then you can go anywhere without feel guilty."

Russ said no. He could only mark 6.5 miles. He said it was just a few dollars, so why care?

I said, "I don't care about that few dollars. Go ahead, mark it all as a personal trip. Why bother marking it at all? I'm starving to death!"

Russ said he should do it right. He'd been marking mileage that way all his life.

I said, "Let's go back. I don't want to have dinner now; I just don't want to take advantage of your tax deduction. Let's go back."

Russ looked at me: "Are you sure?"

"Yes! Go back!"

As soon as I said that, I felt sorry. Russ was a matter-of-fact guy. He sighed and said, "All right, you're the boss." He turned the wheel towards home.

Tears came down my cheeks. I said bitterly, "I don't understand why a Harvard graduate has no common sense. There are so many good people in the world; they don't have to be *extreme* to be good. I don't want you to cheat on the tax report, but this is ridiculous. Ask other Americans how they mark their mileages. Ask the IRS!"

Russ said, "Donna, you're overreacting. Why are you so upset? Are you having your period?"

I didn't say anything. We came back home in bad moods and… hungry! Russ went to his computer room; I went to the living room. Nobody said a word.

After a long deadly silence, Russ came to me, saying, "I'm sorry, Donna. Today's your birthday. I wanted to take you out and make you happy but… If you want, I can still take you out now."

"It's 10:30 already." I said.

"Let me make a phone call or two." He went into his office. A minute later he came out. "The Mexican restaurant *Shorty's* is open until 11:30."

"OK!" I stood up quickly.

We rushed out excitedly, forgetting about all the argument.

That night we had a wonderful dinner in a beautiful restaurant, with romantic candlelight, wonderful food, a very friendly waiter, Russ's warm handholding, and tears in my eyes.

Since then, I've never complained about marking mileage. When he marked, I just looked out of the window and pretended not to pay attention. Sometimes he gave me an apologizing smile and said he'd ask the IRS when he got a chance.

Who cares?

By the way, he finally called the IRS, which told him I was right. (And actually, I'm always right when arguing with him.)

Learn to be a good husband

After Russ read the above, which he thought was making fun of him, I asked how he liked it. Russ said, "It was interesting, pretty good, but…"

"But?" I asked.

"It's good… but it makes me a little sad."

"Why?" I was surprised.

"Well, it's just about a nice woman who's stuck with a crazy guy and has some complaints, but not complaining too much."

"Is that what you think? I'm sorry. I didn't mean to make fun of you. But…"

"It's OK. It's interesting to read." Russ said.

Hearing that, I said to myself: maybe it's not fair just to complain about how crazy he is.

Is he a good husband at all or just a crazy one? I started thinking.

He tried hard to be good. He put in a lot of effort.

He said time was the most important thing to him. If he could just spend time writing and helping other people, he'd be happy; but he spent a lot of time on me.

In 1998, I started to think about running my own business. I wasn't thrilled about working for somebody else anymore. Russ was skeptical but spent the next 3 years of his "spare time" going with me to look at business opportunities. We looked around New Hampshire, Massachusetts, and Vermont. Those trips gave us lots of good excuses to eat out, and we saw many beautiful small towns across New England.

In the winter of 2002, we found a restaurant in Contoocook NH for rent, and I fell in love with it at first sight. From its window, you see the beautiful Contoocook River, a dam, and the country's longest old covered railway bridge. We named it the *Contoocook Covered Bridge Restaurant*.

Russ spent next 3 months with me to get all sorts of paperwork done and all things ready to go. Seeing his *time* slip away for me, I felt guilty. I told him that after the restaurant opened, I wouldn't bother him anymore.

But after the restaurant opened, there were still so many things I needed Russ's help with, like designing menus, bookkeeping, and designing ads. He pitched in. Some weekend evenings, when we were desperately shorthanded, he even drove up to buss tables and host.

He's the most serious worker I've ever seen.

While bussing tables, he actually *ran* in the dining room. He was so seriously concentrating that he forgot to smile. The servers complained to me, "Tell Russ to slow down. He makes everybody nervous, and the customers all stare at him."

So I told him, "Russ, relax, don't run. You can't run in the restaurant." He tried to slow down but still couldn't help half running and half walking, looking very funny. Just after the restaurant quieted down did he remember to smile and chat with customers.

Because of the time spent for me, he had to stay up later and work harder to catch up on his own work.

There are hundreds of little things that show "caring."

Every night when I drove home and pulled into our driveway, the driveway's light was turned on just in time (by him, not an automaton) and he came out to greet me. He put away the work he was doing and started to "report today's news" about our household, the U.S., China, and the world.

I have the habit of reading news from the Internet before going to bed. While I stare at the computer screen and munch, he serves me juice. He clears away my dishes as soon as I finish, like a server, then walks me upstairs to bed, sets the alarm for me, and goes back to work.

He gets up before me. When he hears me get up, he comes up to make the bed.

When I go to work, he walks me to the car, carrying whatever needs to be loaded. When it snows, he gets up before daybreak, shovels the snow, scrapes my windshield, and wipes my mirrors… as if I don't how to do all that.

When he manages to spend money on me — by taking me out to dinner, taking me to a dentist, or buying me clothes — he's more excited and happier than me.

He always says "I'm trying" (to be a good husband). If I didn't bother to sum up the above small things, I wouldn't realize he *is* one.

Morals

Hi, this is Russ again.
We'd all like to be moral people. How?

Ethics

I spend most of my life worrying about how to make ethical decisions.

Questions

Here are ethical questions. I don't have simple answers. Do you?

Time management My hardest ethical decisions involve time, because that's what I'm shortest of.

> Which needy person or needy organization should I spend my time helping?
> If two of my customers both need my attention, whom should I help first?
> How much extra time should I devote to my family and close friends instead of strangers?
> To which nonprofit organizations should I donate money and time?

What's the most moral way to spend *your* time?

I wish I believed in God, because I could sure use His advice on time management, so I could learn to become a better person and stop feeling guilty about all the people I haven't helped because I don't have enough time.

Most Americans believe they should be nicer to close acquaintances than to strangers, but *to what extent?*

> *To what extent* should you be nicer to your family than to your neighbors, nicer to your neighbors than to other humans, nicer to born humans than to fetuses, nicer to humans (born and unborn) than to other animals, nicer to animals than to plants, nicer to plants than to computers, other machines, and other natural resources?

For example, suppose your kid is sick. To what extent should you take time off from work to care for your kid?

> What if giving the kid attention won't help the kid much? For example, what if the kid is already 18 years old and has just a cold? What if many people at work depend on you to meet a crucial deadline?

If your kid commits a crime, to what extent should you protect the child from people and law authorities seeking retribution?

If 2 people at work both demand your attention, how do you decide which person to give your time to?

Should you feel guilty if you don't give to a charity?

> What if your money and time are better spent on other charities instead?
> Or should you spend it on your family instead — isn't your first responsibility to your own family?

If you relax, should you feel guilty for not working?

> Isn't there some work you should really be doing instead of relaxing?
> But if you never relax, won't you become a nervous wreck and a one-dimensional workaholic?
> When is relaxing moral?
> Is it immoral to watch TV instead of doing some sort of "active relaxation," such as sports?

Found money If you see some money on the sidewalk, should you pick it up? If you do, should you keep it or report it to a lost-and-found?

> What if the money is just a penny? A dime? A quarter? A dollar? A $20 bill?
> A wallet containing $100? A wallet containing $1000?

Should you leave the money there — so the person who lost it has a chance to find it, or some low-income person or kid gets thrilled by finding it — or should you keep the money yourself, figuring that you're probably more deserving than the average nutcase who walks down the street?

Cut in line If you're waiting in line but a friend ahead waves you to join him, should you cut in next to him?

> Would it be more moral for your friend to drop back to visit you?
> Under what circumstances is it okay to "save a place in line"?
> What if the line is for getting cafeteria food? A hotel room? An airplane seat?

Honesty When should you tell the truth?

> What if telling the truth would make the other person upset, wreck that person's day, and make that person act so miserable that all the person's acquaintances would be miserable too? But if you get in the habit of lying, and everybody else does too, won't this world become a scary, untrustworthy place where everybody turns paranoid at not knowing the truth?

If you're served food you dislike, is it more moral to eat it (to be polite) or to not eat it (to be honest)?

Killing How immoral is it to kill an animal?

> What if the animal's just a tiny bug? A dog? A human?

Sure, it feels wrong to kill an animal. But if a plant had a vocal cord and could cry "help," wouldn't you feel bad killing a plant too?

> Should animals be treated better than plants just because animals yelp or writhe when in pain?
>
> Do plants feel pain? Do they "hurt"?
> Does "thou shalt not kill" apply to viruses?
> What if an animal *wants* to be killed?
> Are you allowed to kill yourself?

Wouldn't an animal be happier being slaughtered (just a few seconds of pain!) than left to die of old age and painful diseases?

Revenge

Suppose someone treats you badly, by stealing your money, lover, job, career, or reputation or by just having a good laugh at your expense. How should you respond?
Some folks say:

> Don't get mad. Get even.

I say instead:

> Don't get even. Get ahead.

The best way to get ahead is to walk away from the situation and get on with the rest of your life. Don't waste more time worrying about the matter. I've seen folks waste too much time plotting revenge. Instead, plot other rewards for yourself. When you're running in the rat-race of life, and another runner bumps into you, don't waste time bumping him back: run faster!

Mahatma Gandhi said:

> If we all practice "an eye for an eye,"
> pretty soon the whole world will be blind.

Martin Luther King, Jr. said it briefer:

> The old law of "an eye for an eye"
> leaves everyone blind.

If somebody performs a crime against you, be a good citizen by reporting it to the police, to prevent the crime from reoccurring. But after doing that civic duty, move on with the rest of your life.

Life's too short to spend mulling about hate. Just realize that the person who screwed you is a sorry, maladjusted individual who will probably waste his life playing hit-and-run games and never know the meaning of true peace and friendship.

Arguing about love

If your lover jilts you or cheats on you, don't yell about it: your hatred won't get you improved love. Instead, ask why your lover feels less loving. Then decide whether you want to patch things up or give up and start a new life.

Contradictory advice

Here's famous contradictory advice.

Should you take the time to plan ahead?
Yes: look before you leap
No: we'll cross that bridge when we come to it

Should you hurry?
Yes: the early bird catches the worm
No: haste makes waste

Should you be especially careful?
Yes: anything worth doing is worth doing well
No: don't be a fusspot

Should you complain?
Yes: the squeaky wheel gets the grease
No: patience is its own reward

Should you fight?
Yes: stand up for your rights; act like a man
No: turn the other cheek

Should you be honest?
Yes: honesty is the best policy
No: be tactful

Make a difference

If something about the world bothers you, improve it. Dare to make a difference. Don't just grumble to yourself: take a stand!

Mahatma Gandhi said:

Be the change you wish to see in the world.

Martin Luther King Jr. said:

Human salvation lies in the hands of the creatively maladjusted.

In his play *Man and Superman*, George Bernard Shaw said:

The reasonable man adapts himself to the world. The unreasonable one persists in trying to adapt the world to himself. Therefore, all progress depends on the unreasonable man.

If you take action instead of just accepting a lousy world, you'll be happier with yourself. Albert Camus said:

But what is happiness except the simple harmony between a man and the life he leads?

When you try to change the world, others will give you a hard time. Gandhi said:

First they ignore you, then they laugh at you, then they fight you, then you win.

David Brinkley (the NBC-TV anchor and journalist) said:

A successful person is one who can lay a firm foundation with the bricks that others throw at him.

Are you afraid to stick your neck out by telling the truth and doing what's right? Just do it! President Franklin Roosevelt's wife (Eleanor Roosevelt) said:

Do what you feel in your heart to be right — for you'll be criticized anyway. You'll be "damned if you do, and damned if you don't."

Prejudice

Edward R. Murrow said:

Everyone is a prisoner of his own experiences. No one can eliminate prejudices — just recognize them.

So keep your eyes open! Have a fun look at prejudice, stereotypes, and racism....

Arab-Americans

Arab-American comedians struggle to be funny. For example, one Arab-American comic said:

You have no idea how rough it is to be an Arab these days. I went to the airport to check in. The man at the ticket counter asked, "Are those your bags?" I said, "Yes, sir." He asked, "Did you pack them yourself?" I said, "Yes, sir." They arrested me.

Stupidity jokes

Some jokes begin, "Did you hear about the moron who…," but that makes fun of the mentally handicapped. When I was a kid, many jokes began, "Did you hear about the Polack who…," but that makes fun of an ethnic group, the Polish.

On my landlady's bookshelf, I saw a book from the 1940's that had many jokes beginning, "Did you hear about the nigger who…" That book was published before insulting blacks was considered even more distasteful than insulting the Polish.

Modern comedians insult blondes instead. That pleases the country's arbiters of taste (New York publishers and TV networks), since most blondes are volunteers (it's an honor to dye for) and Republican.

Race quotas

The University of Michigan judged some of its applicants on the basis of 150 points, 20 of which were given for race. Is that "discrimination" or "affirmative action"? The case went to the Supreme Court, which in 2003 ruled that colleges can give preference to black applicants if there's no fixed quota or fixed number of points for race.

Here's my summary of the ruling:

It's okay to be nice to blacks, if you don't make a point of it.

The decision to "let bias in favor of blacks, but don't dare quantify it" is silly. It could lead to a system where dark blacks get 20 point but light blacks get just 10 points and Hispanics get 15 points, but instead of calling it "race" it's called just "other factors."

Some justices added their own comments:

Sandra Day O'Connor said she hopes that, 25 years from now, racial preferences will no longer be needed and the Court will try then to scrap to current "quick fix."

David Souter mused that if a point system is allowed, why not a system where blacks get 100 points, effectively making it a black-only program?

Clarence Thomas, who is black but conservative, said that if blacks are given easier admission to colleges, then nobody will take black degrees seriously, and all blacks will suffer.

If you want to favor blacks (beyond just favoring folks from poor neighborhoods), the Michigan system of "150 points, 20 of them for race" isn't how a person should be judged. Try this alternative, which is more mathematically reasonable: start at neutral (0); add or subtract some points for grades; add or subtract some points for race; subtract some points for crime; add or subtract some points for "other extraordinary factors"; etc. Put no particular ceiling on any category (go ahead: give those Siamese twins lots of points, for exceptional "diversity"), but with a set of guidelines.

Extreme politicians

I'm waiting for the media to invent an extreme politician saying things such as:

I believe in the sanctity of human life. We should protect even the lives of the unborn. Abortionists are murderers. The Bible says, "An eye for an eye, and a tooth for a tooth," so all abortionists are murderers that should be executed, and so should all women who arrange abortions, and so should all women who ever had abortions. Kill them all! That would also stop the world's overpopulation.

He'll also say:

> To end racial discrimination now, all Americans shall be required to look the same, by applying purple tanning cream before leaving their homes—except for Muslim women, who have permission to wear veils instead. Get your purple tanning cream at Purple Tanning Centers, a government-sponsored chain of pleasure shops for the racially purp-lexed.

Martin Luther King

According to historians, throughout all of American history there were just two surprising great speeches: Martin Luther King's "I have a dream" speech (in Washington DC) and Lincoln's "Gettysburg Address." (Other good speeches were less surprising.)

How the speech arose King borrowed passages from another preacher, but King improved the oratory's cadence. The speech was an improved variant of many similar speeches King gave during the preceding year. Towns in Michigan and North Carolina have their own celebrations claiming "the dream began *here*." Those communities praise him for coalescing thoughts that had been building up. While giving those earlier speeches, King learned his audiences looked depressed until he started talking about "dreams," so he began emphasizing the "dream" angle more.

For the Washington speech's first half, King was reading from a script; but for the last half, he spoke off-the-cuff, combining phrases that had been churning in his head for years, as he surveyed the crowd's mood.

Opportunities If America keeps treating Martin Luther King Day as a second-class holiday, America is missing a "marketing opportunity." That holiday should be treated like Presidents Day — to sell cars, with inspiring ads like this:

> Elvis was King. Martin Luther was King. Now *you* can be King too, in your new SUV! Martin Luther had a dream — now you can have a dream car too! Or go for racial harmony — in the sports car that's cool to race and makes you feel comfortable, too! Black, white, or colored — your choice!

On Martin Luther King Day, ice cream vendors should sell **Dreamsicles** (Creamsicles covered in chocolate that's dark, delicious, and heaven-sent), so we can all say, "I have a Dreamsicle!"

"The Long Walk Home"

My family found a racial treasure in the bargain bin at Wal-Mart, for $6: a DVD movie called *The Long Walk Home*.

There are 3 versions of *The Long Walk Home*. We got the best: the 1990 version starring Whoopi Goldberg and Sissy Spacek.

That 1990 version is fascinating. You'd think such a movie would be bound to fail, since it discusses a "dreary, preachy" subject: 1955's civil-rights bus boycott in Montgomery, Alabama. But the excellent acting shows how discrimination can seem rational, at least to the people doing the discriminating, and how discrimination is defended as the right and ethical thing to do, to keep the peace and avoid trouble.

When I was young, I had 4 bouts in the South: twice in the early 1960's (driving with my parents around the country), and twice in the late 1960's (teaching Upward Bound students at black Talladega College in Alabama). The movie brought back my memories of race relations, fears, and sadness.

The movie includes these classic bits:

> a white bus driver saying he "doesn't want no trouble"
> a black family more rational than the white families
> a white policeman "just doing his job" by throwing blacks out of the park

The movie's opening scene sucks you in: it looks like a photo, then turns into what looks like a black-and-white newsreel, then becomes colorized, then becomes fine acting where you see 3 black women walk into a bus. After paying the driver, they have to turn around and walk out of the bus, then reenter through the back door, since they're not allowed to walk through the front part.

Many students say this is the "best film ever shown in social studies class."

Though the film tries to attack discrimination, several cynics have said the film *itself* is an example of discrimination: whites gave Whoopi the Oscar that year for a comedy (*Ghost*) rather that for the racial drama that's so much more important, since "blacks should be praised just for comedy."

Whoopi's had a wild ride:

> Whoopi was born in 1955, a month before the events that the movie depicts. Though she's black, she's also sort of Jewish: she took "Goldberg" from the Jewish side of her family, though she wasn't born with that name.
> She was born in New York. She was nicknamed "Whoopi" because she farted a lot, sounding like a whoopi cushion.
> Before she became an actress, she worked in a mortuary, doing cosmetics. I guess her career hasn't really changed: she still paints smiles on whites.
> She begged Alice Walker for a role in *The Color Purple* and said she'd be willing to play any part — even a Venetian blind, even dirt on the floor.
> She got more than dirt. She got pay dirt.

My walks in Alabama

During the 1960's, when I was a student at Dartmouth College, I got sent to rural Alabama to teach math to low-income black high-school students, to help them get admitted to college, through an "Upward Bound" program.

Back then, desegregation had begun but hadn't quite finished, so I got to see Alabama in transition. Here are snapshots from those jarring times....

Religious couple I attended several black churches then befriended the elderly couple who ran the biggest white church.

I enjoyed talking to that Reverend and his wife. They were kind to me and invited me to their home often. They tried hard to convince me that bigotry was right. For example, they said Martin Luther King's march through Selma was just a bunch of northern white hippies who spent most of the "march" just frolicking & fucking.

When I asked if I could bring a friend along to dinner, they asked if he was black. I said "No." They said "Okay" but got dismayed when they later discovered he was Chinese. They asked whether, at least, he could please come after dark so he wouldn't upset the neighbors.

Usher Whenever I visited that religious couple's white church, the usher smiled at me — until the day a black girlfriend (Ruby) tried to come with me. When the usher saw her, his face was gripped with fear. He suggested, "The black church is down the street...." When she replied, "I'd like to come to *this* church," he said, "I'm sorry...." He "didn't want no trouble" and didn't want to get involved in the civil-rights issues that were attacking the white South like a tornado.

Local café Ruby told me the local café would put all its chairs up on the tables. If a white person wanted to eat, the owner would take a chair down and serve the customer. If a black person wanted to eat, the owner would say "Sorry, this section is closed."

My rejection When I applied for that job teaching blacks, I was initially rejected because Dartmouth College thought I wasn't radical enough. But the first group Dartmouth sent to Alabama turned out to be *too* radical, and even the Alabama blacks running the program didn't accept them, because they fucked too much and didn't wear suits. (Southern black administrators were conservative then and wanted Upward Bound students to become respectable people wearing suits.)

The next year, I was hired as part of a more conservative team. The third year, the blacks were more radicalized and in tune with northern whites, because Stokely Carmichael had passed through and radicalized the blacks.

Let's blend

Many Americans are biracial. At the University of Maryland, the Multiracial and Biracial Student Association's Vice President (Laura Wood) said:

> It's important to acknowledge who you are and everything that makes you that. If someone tries to call me black, I say "Yes — and white."

Racial analyst Lili Timmons said:

> People segregate themselves for 2 reasons: financial classes and racial groups.
>
> The first reason is easier to explain away, since low-income people can't buy a house or even rent an apartment in any high-priced areas. If you *have* the cash, you can say "hee-hee-hee!" knowing your areas are inaccessible to those who don't (except burglars).
>
> Racial segregation is a mark of ignorance. I believe in social and personal melting pots! Mixing it up and stirring in different cultural spices (customs) can create amazing results: you develop new menus, broaden your list of acquired tastes, and understand & accept things you might have turned away from before.
>
> I'm better because of all the different people I've met along the way. I don't want to pull off into the corner of segregation; and I feel sorry for those who do, because they don't know what they've lost. It's like the times throughout history where groups tried to build walls around themselves because they felt they'd learned all there was to know and wanted to keep that knowledge to themselves, only to discover they were actually keeping continual growth and wisdom out!
>
> A recent news report said the number of bi- or multi- racial/ethnic children is increasing. They probably will not be the meek, but "they shall inherit the earth" in some way.
>
> *Blending* makes the blandest "bedders" better!

What God looks like

What does God look like? A popular bumper sticker asks that question:

> Is God black or white?
> She's black, and boy is she pissed!

I keep waiting for a movie about that. To make that movie succeed, it would have to play on stereotypes: God would have to be a sassy black woman (like Whoopi Goldberg or Queen Latifa), who addresses new heavenly arrivals with words of wisdom like this:

> What did you *expect* God to be, a honky?
>
> Besides, why did you think my son, Jesus, got so much attention? Because he was black! Is it *my* fault he later decided to put on whiteface to blend in? Hah, that whiteface! Look where it got him! Ku Klux Klanned!
>
> He was a nice kid, but letting himself get nailed was the dramatic ending to a kid who had more passion than common sense. Common sense? Just a *mom*, like me, has enough of it to run the whole universal show!
>
> And by the way, stop blaming me about worldly weather! If you guys piss me off and I want to piss on you back, that's fair, isn't it?
>
> While you're up here, you'd better shape up. Shape up or ship out! And if we ship you out, we're shipping you down to you-know-where, which will give you a new understanding of the term "hot and spicy." You like hot buns? They'll be *yours!*
>
> Stop telling me about "turn the other cheek." That was Jesus's idea. He was naïve, that kid o' mine. If you slap my face, you ain't gettin' my other cheek too: I'm gonna whup your ass!
>
> Be good, or your ass will get inhabited by my boot, which is very campy. That's why they call this place "boot camp."
>
> You thought heaven was going to be a piece of cake? Well, it is, if you don't fudge it up. No foolin' around with the other angels! Keep your nose clean, Christian soldier!

Evil

The world contains evil. How should you deal with it?

Religions were invented to help humans handle evil. Different religions take different approaches to dealing with evil.

Shitology

According to the Internet, here's a summary of the world's major religions & philosophers and their attitudes about evil misfortunes ("shit"):

Catholics

General Catholic:	If shit happens, I deserve it.
Classic Catholic:	You're *born* shit, you *are* shit, and you'll *die* shit.
Charismatic Catholic:	Shit happens because you deserve it, but we love you anyway.

Protestants

Calvinist:	Shit won't happen if I work harder.
Episcopalian:	If shit happens, serve the right wine and hold a procession.
Unitarian:	Maybe shit happens. Let's have coffee and doughnuts.
Fundamentalist:	If shit happens, you'll go to hell unless you're born again. Amen!
Baptist:	Just total immersion in shit will suffice.
Quaker:	Let's not fight over this shit.
Christian Science:	If you can't get a shit, don't call a doctor: pray!
7th Day Adventist:	No shit on Saturdays.
Jehovah's Witness:	Knock, knock, "Shit happens."
Televangelist:	Send money (tax-deductible), or shit will happen to *you*.
Martin Luther King:	I have a shit.
Moonie:	Only *happy* shit really happens.
Creationist:	Shit's been happening just since October 23, 4004 B.C.

Other religions

Jew:	Why does shit always happen to *me*?
Hare Krishna:	Please take this lovely little flower and buy our shit.
Baha'i:	We're all shit together.
Voodoo:	Shit doesn't just "happen": someone dumped it on you.
Rastafarian:	Smoke that shit.
Taoist:	Shit happens, so flow with it.
Pagan:	Shit happens and is part of nature.
Shinto:	You inherit the shit of your ancestors.
Hindu:	This shit happened before.
Buddhist:	It's just an *illusion* of shit happening.
Zen:	What's the *sound* of shit happening?
Confucian:	Confucius say: shit happens.
Muslim:	If shit happens, it's Allah's will. Kill the person responsible.

Self-help movements

12-step:	Shit happens, one day at a time.
Scientologist:	To learn why shit happens, take our course.
Transcend. Meditator:	Shi-i-it. Shi-i-it. Shi-i-it. Shi-i-it. Shi-i-it. …
New Age:	This isn't shit if I really believe it's chocolate.

Negativists

Atheist:	There's no such thing as shit. No shit!
Agnostic:	Maybe shit happens, and maybe it doesn't.
Secular humanist:	Shit evolves.
Existentialist:	Shit doesn't *happen*; shit *is*.
Apathetic:	I don't give a shit.
Denialist:	What shit?
Nihilist:	Let's blow this shit up!
Procrastinator:	I'll tackle this shit — tomorrow.

Professionals

Psychologist:	All happenings are shit, but some repress their shittiness.
Chemist:	Gee, what'll happen if I mix this and… Oh, shit!
Doctor:	Yes, it's definitely a case of shit happening. $90, please.
Lawyer:	For a fee, I can get you out of *any* shit.
Statistician:	There's an 83.7% chance that shit will happen. Maybe.
Bureaucrat:	To make shit happen, fill the form.
Waitress:	You want fries with that shit?

Famous scientists

Darwin:	Survival of the shittiest!
Einstein:	Shit is relative.
Heisenberg:	Shit happened. We just don't know where or how much.

Politicians

Julius Caesar:	I came, I saw, I shat.
Nixon:	Shit didn't happen, and if it did I didn't know about it.
McCarthy:	Are you now — or have you ever gotten — shit?

Patriotic

Nationalist:	Our shit, right or wrong.
Navy:	It's not just shit, it's an adventure.
Nazi:	Scheiße über alles.

Financiers

Materialist:	Yes, I really *do* need all this shit.
Yuppie:	It's *my* shit! All mine! Isn't it beautiful?
Marketer:	Package shit right, and everybody will want some.
Mafioso:	Rub the little shits out.
Red Cross:	Shit happens: send money.

Leftists

Marx:	Workers take all the shit but will dish it back out.
Communist:	It's *everyone*'s shit.
Politically correct:	Processed nutrition-depleted biological output happens.
Environmentalist:	Shit is fertilizer: biodegradable!
Vegetarian:	If it shits, don't eat it.
Nader:	Shit is dangerous at any speed.
Feminist:	Men are shit, and shit isn't funny, so stop laughing.

Pleasure seekers

Hedonist:	Shit is fun.
Masochist:	Go ahead, give me *more* shit: I love it.
Mystic:	This is really weird shit.
Stoic:	Shit is good for me.
Mom:	You'll *eat* this shit and *like* it!

Fictitious

Energizer Bunny:	Shit happens and happens and happens and happens….
Robin:	Holy shit, Batman!
Pangloss:	This is the best of all possible shits.

Handicapped

Spooner:	Hit shappens.
Dyslexic:	Hits shapnep.

Why evil exists

I made a new scientific discovery, as historically important as the discovery of gravity, the discovery that the sun is the center of the solar system, and the discovery of subatomic particles! My discovery explains many scientific phenomena that would otherwise be hard to find excuses for.

My discovery is that there *is* a God, but He's diabetic…. so He occasionally needs to nap after a heavy meal.

His most disastrous nap began on July 4, 2001, when He watched the fireworks, ate too much barbeque, got tired, and slept for 10 weeks, during which Al Qaeda attacked the World Trade Towers without His interference. Our resulting prayers finally woke God up. He tried to catch up with His responsibilities, but His weather here in New Hampshire and nearby was still 2 months behind: mild autumn weather lasted through the winter, huge snowstorms arrived in May (instead of March), and heavy rains poured in June (instead of April).

Thank God I've solved the annoying question of "the existence of evil," which stumped philosophers for centuries: the answer is that God isn't mean, He just has a disability. Feel sorry for the Handicapped: He needs our sympathy. Pray for Him. Recommended prayer:

Dear Lord, Thou are great, but I pray Thou get greater.

Here's another reason for evil shit: when you're faced with it, you get an experience that forces you to develop yourself into a stronger person. Novelists call that "character development, the hard way." Priests and politicians say of such a tragedy, "Let that be a lesson for us all." President Franklin Roosevelt's wife (Eleanor Roosevelt) said….

A woman is like a teabag:
you never know how strong she is until she gets into hot water.

Faith

Keeping the faith can be a challenge when evil things happen.

Each day, God feeds me shit.
My job is to devour.
If life is like a flower,
Why does the flower spit?

God knows the point of it:
He wants to make me strong,
Stand firm and never split,
Distinguish right from wrong.

I know my job on earth:
To learn what I am worth,
And with His guiding hand
Come learn to make life grand.

Unlucky 13

13 is considered an unlucky number now because 13 people were sitting at the Last Supper (Jesus and the 12 apostles).

But actually, 13 was considered an unlucky number before the apostles: in Norse mythology, 12 gods sat down to a feast that was interrupted by a gate-crasher and, in the ensuing scuffle, the most beloved god was killed. Historians view Christ's "The Last Supper" as just copying the Norse legend.

Gee, I thought everything in the Bible was real and original. The apostles were plagiarists? How upsetting!

If you're afraid of the number 13, you have **triskaidekaphobia** (which comes from the Greek words for "three-and-ten fear").

Christian fun

Christianity is serious business. Here's a look at its lighter side.

Church signs

Many churches have funny signs to encourage folks to come in or at least think about God. Here are samples:

Free trip to heaven. Details inside!

Headed in the wrong direction? God allows U-turns.
Why pay for GPS? Jesus gives direction for free.

Free coffee, everlasting life: membership has its privileges.
Walmart isn't the only saving place.

Running low on faith? Stop in for a fill-up.
Searching for a new look? Have your faith lifted here!

Come in and pray today. Beat the Christmas rush!
This is a CH__CH. What's missing? UR
The best vitamin for Christians is B1.

Church parking: trespassers will be baptized.
Baptist church! Hey kid, God says it's bath time.

Honk if you love Jesus. Text while driving if you want to meet him.
Come in and let us prepare you for your finals.
Don't wait for 6 strong men to bring you to church.
How will you spend eternity — smoking or non-smoking?
Exposure to the Son may prevent burning.

In the dark? Follow the Son.
Need sleep? Don't count sheep. Talk to the Shepherd.
If you don't like the way you were born, be born again.

You can accomplish more in an hour with God than a lifetime without Him.
God can heal a broken heart if He has all the pieces.
Sorrow looks back. Worry looks around. Faith looks up.

God intervenes in your affairs by invitation only.
Most people wish to serve God, but just in an advisory capacity.
Most men forget God all day but ask Him to remember them all night.

Jesus is a friend that knows all your faults and loves you anyway.
Jesus is a friend who walks in when other walk out.

God answers knee-mail.
Some questions can't be answered by Google.

The heart is happiest when it beats for others.
Those who deserve love the least need it most.
Success comes in cans. Failure comes in can'ts.

Swallowing angry words is better than eating them.
To forgive is to set a prisoner free and discover the prisoner was *you*.
Pick your friends, but not to pieces.
The best way to get the last word is to apologize.

Forbidden fruit creates many jams.
People are like tea bags — put them in hot water to find out how strong they are.
Read the Bible: it will scare the Hell out of you.

Bored? Try a missionary position.
Staying in bed and shouting "Oh God!" doesn't constitute going to church.

Sign broken. Message inside this Sunday.

Come work for the Lord. The work is hard, the hours long, and the pay low.
But the retirement benefits are out of this world.

"Will the road you're on get you to my place?" — God
"Need directions?" — God
"That 'Love Thy Neighbor' thing, I meant it." — God
"We need to talk." — God
"Tell the kids I love them." — God
"Read my #1 bestseller? There will be a test." — God
"You think it's hot *here*?" — God

To see more examples, look at the list collected by Jeff & Caroline Wilkinson (at http://wilk4.com/humor/humorc13.htm) — or go to Google.com and search for "church signs" — or visit your local church!

Bumper stickers

If you like religious humor, put it on a bumper sticker!
For example, many bumper stickers show this quote from Dawn Ewing:

Lord, help me become the person my dog thinks I am.

Here's another classic bumper sticker:

Is God black or white? She's black, and boy is she pissed!

Mara Faustino included these bumper stickers in her book *Heaven and Hell*:

The road to Hell is bumper-to-bumper. Make a U-turn.
Give Satan an inch and he'll be a ruler.
Never give the devil a ride! He'll always want to drive.
The devil wants to control you. God wants to lead you.
Satan can't bring you down any further than your knees.

This bumper sticker has the opposite sentiment:

Religion: treat it like a penis. Don't wave it in public and shove it down a child's throat.

That bumper sticker is abridged from this longer sentiment, which appeared at www.DearBlankPleaseBlank.com:

Religion is like a penis: it's fine to have one and be proud of it, but please don't whip it out in public, start waving it around, and shove it down a child's throat.

The Internet includes this variant:

Religion is like sex: if you're forced to have it as a kid, you'll hate it as an adult.

Songs

Songs get cynical about how Christianity is practiced today.

What would Jesus do?
What would Jesus do if he were alive today and had modern technological help? Ryan Smith & Julie Wittner wrote a song about that; here are the lyrics (revised and abridged by me):

He died for our sins on the cross,
Technology not on his side.
He'd have much more luck in a Ford pickup truck:
That is what Jesus would drive.

Terrain in the desert is tough.
A Honda? You'd barely survive!
So God's only kid needs a ride that won't skid:
Ford is what Jesus would drive.

Disciples don't fit in a Pacer.
God's gun racks don't fit Subaru.
If you're a truck buyer, be like your messiah:
Only Ford pickups will do!

To live in the desert? You're thirsty!
To hang on a cross makes you think.
Jack Daniels, not water, can soothe the pain farther:
That is what Jesus would drink.

Disciples make great drinking buddies,
But Judas can get on your nerves.
When *your* friend's a shyster, don't drink Jägermeister:
Jack is what Jesus would serve.

Not everyone liked what he stood for.
They thought that to blaspheme was cute.
He'd teach them a lesson with God's Smith & Wesson:
That is what Jesus would shoot.

So here is what Jesus would do:
He'd buy just American, always be true.
His thorns, ground and round, would bleed red, white, and blue.
That is what Jesus,
  Your sin-saving Jesus,
  Your truck-loving, booze-craving, gun-toting, flag-waving
  Jesus would do.

Watch them sing their original (which is better) at:

www.YouTube.com/watch?v=pe-er9FqhYA

How to act Catholic
Tom Lehrer's ragtime song, *The Vatican Rag*, explains how to be Catholic and enjoy church. Here are the lyrics (revised and abridged by me):

First get down, please, on your knees.
Fiddle with your rosaries.
Bow your head with great respect.
Genuflect, yes, genuflect!

Get in line in that processional.
Step into that small confessional.
There the guy who's got religion'll
Tell you if your sin's original.

If it is, try playing safer:
Drink the wine and chew the wafer.
Make a cross. Cough up some dough, man.
When in Rome, do like a Roman.

Do whatever steps you want if
You have cleared them with the pontiff.

Get ecstatic an'
Quite dramatic an'
Do the Vatican
Rag!

Hear him sing his original version (which is funnier) at:

www.YouTube.com/watch?v=LFIkeXQI8nI

Tales

The Bible includes tales of the religious experiences of Jesus and his followers. The following tales happened more recently and are mostly written in the "modern Bible," which is called "the Internet."

Letter from grandma
A grandma sent this letter to her family:

> I went to the local Christian bookstore and saw a "Honk if you love Jesus" bumper sticker. I was feeling sassy because I'd just come from a thrilling choir performance followed by a thunderous prayer meeting, so I bought the sticker and put it on my car's back bumper.
>
> Boy, I'm glad I did! What an uplifting experience followed!
>
> At a busy intersection, I stopped at a red light, got lost in thought about the Lord and how good He is, and didn't notice the light change. It's a good thing someone else loves Jesus, because if he hadn't honked, I'd never have noticed!
>
> I found *lots* of people love Jesus! Why, while I was sitting there, the guy behind started honking like crazy then leaned out his window and screamed, "For the love of *God! Go! Go!* Jesus Christ, *Go!*" What an exuberant cheerleader he was for Jesus! Everyone started honking!
>
> I just leaned out my window and started waving and smiling at all those loving people. I even honked my horn few times to share the love!
>
> One man back there must have been from Florida because I heard him yelling something about a "sunny beach."
>
> I saw another guy waving in a funny way with just his middle finger stuck up in the air. I asked my teenage grandsons in the back seat what that meant. They squirmed, looked at each other, giggled, and said it was the Hawaiian good-luck sign. Since I've never met anyone from Hawaii, I leaned out the window and gave him the good-luck sign back. My grandsons burst out laughing. Why, even *they* were enjoying this religious experience!
>
> A couple of people were so caught up in the joy of the moment that they got out of their cars and started walking towards me. I bet they wanted to pray or ask what church I attended, but just then I noticed the light turn yellow, so I waved to all my sisters and brothers, grinned, and stepped on the gas.
>
> It's a good thing I did, because I was the only car to get across the intersection.
>
> I felt sad to leave those friends, after all the love we shared. So I slowed the car, leaned out the window, and gave them all the Hawaiian good-luck sign one last time as I drove away.
>
> Praise the Lord for such wonderful folks! Love ya all, Grandma

How to meet Jesus
Here's the tale of the boy who wanted to meet Jesus:

> A boy was sitting on the curb and crying. A rich man walked up to him and asked, "What's the matter, kid?"
>
> "I want to see Jesus Christ."
>
> Then man said, "I'm afraid I can't help you with that. But here's a dollar to put in the Offering." Then the man went away.
>
> Next, a priest came up, saw the boy crying, and asked, "What's the matter, son?"
>
> "I want to see Jesus Christ, Our Lord."
>
> "I'm His representative. Isn't that good enough?"
>
> But the kid said, "No." The priest shrugged his shoulders and went away. Finally, a drunken bum came up and asked, "Whazza matta, shunny?"
>
> "I want to see Jesus Christ."
>
> "*I'm* Jesus Christ."
>
> "I don't believe you."
>
> "I *am*, and everybody knows it!"
>
> "Prove it!"
>
> "Okay, gimme that buck and get on my back."
>
> The kid gave him the Offering and climbed on the bum's back. The bum carried him down the street to a bar and walked in. Sure enough, the bartender exclaimed, "Jesus Christ! You back again?"

Bizarre Bible quotes
The Bible can be prophetic:

> A man walked into a boarding house. When he asked for dinner, he was served cabbage stew. When he said he didn't like cabbage stew, the waiter told him, "Sorry, but cabbage stew is the only item on the menu." So he ate it.
>
> The next morning's breakfast consisted just of fried cabbage. For lunch, he was served cabbage pie. For dinner, he was served cabbage stew again; but he just folded his hands, looked up at Heaven, and said, "Hebrews 13:8."
>
> If you look in the New Testament, in the Book of Hebrews, chapter 13, verse 8, you'll see these words: "Jesus Christ! — the same yesterday, today, and forevermore!"

Bible quotes can talk back to each other:

> A new pastor moved into town and went out one Saturday to visit his parishioners. All went well until he came to a house where obviously someone was home but nobody came to the door, even after he knocked several times. So he took out his card, wrote on the back "Revelation 3:20," and stuck it in the door.
>
> The next day, when he was counting the offering, he found his card in the collection plate. Below his message was scribbled "Genesis 3:10."
>
> Revelation 3:20 says, "I stand at the door and knock. If any man hears my voice and opens the door, I'll come in to him and dine with him."
>
> Genesis 3:10 says, "I heard thy voice in the garden; and I was afraid, because I was naked."

The Bible can stop a burglar:

> An elderly woman returning from evening church service discovered her home being burglarized. She yelled at the burglar, "Stop! Acts 2:38!"
>
> The burglar stopped in his tracks. The woman called the police and explained what she'd done. The policeman handcuffed the burglar and asked him, "Why did you just stand there? All the old lady did was yell a scripture quote at you. Acts 2:38 says 'Repent and be baptized, in the name of Jesus Christ, so your sins may be forgiven.'"
>
> "Scripture?" cried the burglar, "She said she had an ax and two 38's!"

3 men and heaven
This tale is constructed cleverly:

> 3 men stand in line to enter Heaven. Saint Peter tells the first one, "Heaven's nearly full, so I've been asked to admit just people who've had particularly horrible deaths. What's your story?"
>
> The first man replies, "I suspected my wife's been cheating on me, so today I came home early to catch her red-handed. When I entered my 25th-floor apartment, I felt something wrong but couldn't tell where this other guy was hiding. Finally, I went out to the balcony, and sure enough, there was a man hanging off the railing, 25 floors above ground! I was really mad, so I beat and kicked him, but he wouldn't fall. I went back into my apartment, got a hammer, and starting hammering his fingers. He finally let go and fell, but into the bushes. He was stunned but okay. I couldn't stand him anymore, so I ran to the kitchen, grabbed the fridge, and threw it over the edge. It landed on him and killed him instantly. But all the stress and anger got to me: I had a heart attack and died there on the balcony."
>
> "That sounds like a pretty bad day to me," says Peter and lets the man in.
>
> The second man comes up. Peter explains that Heaven's nearly full and asks for his story. "It's been a strange day. I live on the 26th floor of my apartment building. Every morning I exercise out on my balcony. This morning I must have slipped, because I fell over the edge. But I got lucky and caught the railing of the balcony on the floor below me. I knew I couldn't hang on long, when suddenly this man burst out onto the balcony. I thought surely I was saved, but he started beating and kicking me. I held on, best I could, until he ran into his apartment, grabbed a hammer, and started pounding on my hands. Finally I just let go, but again I got lucky and fell into the bushes below, stunned but alive. Just when I thought I'd be okay, a refrigerator comes falling out of the sky and crushes me instantly, so now I'm here."
>
> Once again, Peter concedes it sounds like a horrible death.
>
> The third man comes to the front of the line. Peter explains again that Heaven's nearly full and asks for his story.
>
> "Picture this," says the third man, "I'm hiding naked inside a refrigerator...."

Why God ain't a professor

Professors & instructors at Kansas State University and Allen County Community College have decided God isn't good enough to become a tenured professor, for 7 reasons:

1. He published just one book. Worst of all, it was in Hebrew, had no references, and wasn't published in refereed journals. Some doubt he even wrote it himself!

2. He isn't known for his cooperative work.

3. Sure, he created the world, but what has he done lately?

4. He didn't get permission from any review board to work with human subjects. When one experiment went awry, he tried to cover it up by drowning all the subjects. When sample subjects don't behave as predicted, he deletes the whole sample.

5. He rarely comes to class: he just tells his students to read the book. Though he has just 10 requirements, his students often fail his tests.

6. He expelled his first two students for learning.

7. His office hours were infrequent and usually held on a mountaintop.

Heaven versus Hell

When you die, Christians believe you'll go to either Heaven or Hell, whichever you deserve.

Which do you prefer?

Mark Twain (the author) said:

I don't like to commit myself about Heaven and Hell — you see, I have friends in both places. Go to Heaven for the climate, Hell for the company. What a man misses mostly in Heaven is company.

He also said (in *Letters From the Earth*) that in Heaven the angels all sing and play harps continuously; but you won't enjoy having to sing and play the harp all day, every day, repeating that same monotonous song praising God; in fact, the average person sings terribly, can't play a harp, and can't sit through a choral concert for more than two hours without wanting to throw up.

Isaac Asimov said:

Whatever the tortures of Hell, I think the boredom of Heaven would be even worse.

Javier Bardem (the actor) said (to *Parade* magazine's Walter Scott in 2011):

I don't know if I'll get to heaven. I'm a bad boy. Heaven must be nice, but is it too boring? Maybe you can get an apartment there and then go to hell for the weekends.

If you're a **good person** (nice to everybody and act responsibly) but your religion isn't Christian, will you go to hell? Some Christians say you'll go to hell; some say you'll go to heaven; some say you'll be in the intermediate place, called **purgatory**.

Here are more thoughts about heaven & hell:

"Of course there's a heaven and hell. Each of us lives in one or the other, each day of our lives. Both are mankind's creations: thoughts of reward or eternal damnation keep us civilized, usually. When we die, we return to where we were before birth: without cognizance. Any eternal life that's achieved comes from instilling a thought or tradition (no matter how small) in another human so it can continue." — Ronald Ulinsky

"He's a loving God but also a perfect gentleman. He'd never force someone hating him to spend eternity with him. Hell is just where God is not." — Valerie Stevens

"When people do wrong, they must be in great pain to act so bad. When John says eternal life goes to whoever 'believes in Jesus,' I interpret that as 'believes in his message of love: treat one another as God's children.'" — Bill Haas

Those thoughts appeared in *Time* magazine's "letters to the editor" (issue of May 2, 2011).

Was Jesus ridiculous?

Jesus gave advice that could be considered "extremist" now. Here are oversimplified versions of his advice, followed by what he actually said. The oversimplified versions make Jesus sound ridiculous, but what he actually said is more reasonable.

Oversimplified version	**What he actually said**
Don't have any sexual urges.	Any man who looks at a woman lustfully has already committed adultery with her in his heart. (Matthew 5:28)
If you do something wrong with your eye, pluck it out; if you do something wrong with your hand, cut it off.	If your right eye makes you sin, gouge it out and throw it away. It's better for you to lose one part of your body than for your whole body to be thrown into hell. If your right hand makes you sin, cut it off and throw it away. (Matthew 5:29-30)
If you marry a divorced woman, you're committing adultery.	Anyone who divorces his wife (except for marital unfaithfulness) makes her become an adulteress; and anyone who marries the divorced woman commits adultery. (Matthew 5:32)
If someone hits you, invite him to hit you again.	Don't resist an evil person. If someone strikes you on the right cheek, turn the other cheek to him also. (Matthew 5:39)
If you lose a lawsuit, pay more than the judgment.	If someone wants to sue you and take your tunic, let him have your cloak as well. (Matthew 5:40)
Don't save money.	Don't accumulate for yourself treasures on earth, where moths & rust destroy and thieves break in & steal. Instead, accumulate for yourself treasures in heaven, where moths & rust don't destroy and thieves don't break in & steal. (Matthew 6:19-20)
Don't plan for the future.	Don't worry about tomorrow, for tomorrow will worry about itself. Each day has enough trouble of its own. (Matthew 6:34)
Don't become wealthy.	Sell everything you have and give to the poor; then you'll have treasure in heaven. (Mark 10:21)
If someone steals from you, don't try to get it back.	Give to everyone who asks you. If anyone takes what belongs to you, don't demand it back. (Luke 6:30)
Sell everything you have and give it to the poor.	Sell your possessions and give to the poor. Give yourself a purse that won't wear out, a treasure (in heaven) that won't be exhausted, where no thief comes near and no moth destroys. (Luke 12:33)
Hate your father, mother, wife, children, even your own life.	If a person coming to me doesn't hate his parents, wife, children, brothers, sisters, and even his own life, he can't be my disciple. (Luke 14:26)
Don't work to feed yourself.	Instead of working for food that spoils, work for food that endures to eternal life, which I'll give you. (John 6:27)

Editing the Bible

As an editor, I dream of the day I get a wonderful book in my hands to edit, like this....

I'm sitting in my office. My feet are propped up on my desk. I'm smoking a fat cigar, Philip Marlowe style, and enjoying a rare quiet moment dreaming of the future and life's meaning. My reverie is interrupted by a knock on the door. I figure it must be fate. "Come in," I say.

An old geezer walks in. I ask, "Who are you?"

"God," he says.

I check my calendar. I made no appointment with "God" but figure I should be nice to this stranger anyway, so I size him up. He looks like a bum: unshaven, with a long beard and wearing a long ragged robe. He looks positively ancient.

I ask, "What can I do for you?"

He holds up a manuscript that's dog-eared and isn't even stapled. He says, "I wrote this book, and I want you to publish it."

"What's it called?" I ask.

"*The Bible.*"

"That name is boring. Who knows what *The Bible* is? If you want me to publish it, give me a punchier name, like *The Adventures of Punch and Judy.*"

"Actually, you could almost call it *The Adventures of Punch and Jesus,*" he volunteers.

"I never heard of *Jesus,*" I replied. Who in hell is Jesus?"

"He's my son."

"So it's a book about a kid? A kid's book?" I thumb through it. "I can't sell a kid's book unless it has pictures. Hey, maybe you got a photo of Jesus? How about a baby photo, or a photo of him as a teenager? That would really sell."

"Sorry, we didn't have cameras when he grew up."

So this book's a lost cause, but I thumb through the chapters anyway, to be courteous. I give my honest editorial opinion: "This stuff's too long. Nobody's gonna read it all. Every modern editor knows that fiction over 200 pages can't sell."

"It isn't fiction," he insists. "It's a reference, an encyclopedia of higher thought."

"Whoop-dee-doo!" I retort. "It smells like fiction: full of tales, like a trashy historical novel. But here's your main problem, God-baby: your book isn't funny! You have no sense of humor. Throw in some laughs, like Seinfeld, even if nobody completely understands them. This tome is too heavy, like a tomb, an albatross around your neck. And you're lousy at writing romantic scenes: yours are really boring, just dull sentences such as *He lay down with her.* Did you write all this boring blather yourself?"

"I had help from a team of writers: Moses, Mark, and others. They recorded my thoughts."

"So you hired stenographers?" I try giving his Bible a lift, but it's a heavy subject. "This pile of puzzling platitudes must have been produced by cheap labor. I bet you paid them below minimum wage. But we can still credit them in the acknowledgements. What are their last names? Moses Schwartz and Mark O'Brien, or something similar?"

"Sorry, their parents didn't give them last names."

"So they're orphans? Maybe we could play up the *I'm-just-a-poor-orphan* angle."

"No, the team wouldn't appreciate that. Anyway, they're all dead."

"Then we can play up the *dead-baby* angle! That would fit nicely with the tale of your dead son."

"No, please."

"So they want to be just ghost writers? Okay, we'll say the book's a blog written by a band called *God and the Holy Ghosties*, who rap about the Bible. That's the best way to market to kids today. For old fogies, we'll give you a different handle: *The-Hell-I-Knew-Ya Chorus.*"

"Drop it."

"Hey, I'm just trying to concoct a way to market your crapola. Your stuff's too long and its English too stilted. Reading it makes me just want to hang down my head and crawl into a tomb. Your *Bible* is really hard to read. It's Greek to me!"

"That's because we wrote it in Greek, Hebrew, and Aramaic. You're reading a translation."

"Why didn't you just write it in English? You speak English well."

"Where we grew up, people didn't speak English."

"So you're an immigrant? I bet you're illegal."

"Yeah, people are warned not to mention me in public places."

"Then let's bravely market this thing as *The Underground Shushed-Up Super-Secrets of God*. Underground books sell like hotcakes! But to protect your identity, we must keep you hidden."

"I already am." And with that comment, he vanished.

Christianity summarized

Some folks find Christianity hard to swallow — especially when they try to summarize it.

On YouTube, Tyler Oakley gives this summary of Christianity:

> You worship a cosmic Jewish zombie who's his own father. He'll give you eternal life if you symbolically eat his blood & flesh and telepathically tell him he's your master. If you do that, he'll remove the evil spirit that's deep within your soul. That evil spirit entered every human because a naked woman was convinced by a talking snake to eat fruit from a magical tree.

The video, called "Christianity in a Nutshell," is at:

> www.YouTube.com/watch?v=uDHRAsY6rSA

George Carlin gave this alternative summary:

> Religion's convinced people an invisible man lives in the sky. He watches all you do, every minute of every day. He has a special list of 10 things he doesn't want you to do. If you do any, he has a special place full of fire, smoke, burning, torture, and anguish, where he'll send you to live, suffer, burn, choke, scream, and cry, forever. But he loves you!

The Internet provides this quote:

> When you believe in an imaginary figure that *just you* can see or hear, it's called a "psychological problem." When you believe in an imaginary figure that *even you* can't see or hear, it's a "religion."

Judaism

I was born into a Jewish family that practiced Judaism. We practiced but didn't always succeed. Here's what it means to be a Jew....

3 Jewish flavors

Jews come in 3 popular flavors: Orthodox, Conservative, and Reform:

Orthodox Jews perform all the old rituals.
Reform Jews *ignore* all the old rituals.
Conservative Jews compromise, by performing *some* of the old rituals.

Since Reform Jews ignore the rituals, Orthodox Jews accuse Reform Jews of being negligent and non-religious. Since Orthodox Jews perform all the old rituals, Reform Jews accuse Orthodox Jews of being hopelessly old-fashioned and out of touch with modern needs.

But although Orthodox Jews consider Reform Jews to be misguided, and vice versa, they respect each other. Jews don't despise each other the way Protestants and Catholics do in Northern Ireland. Christians have wars about religion; Jews don't. Jews are quiet people.

Do Jews fight?

Although Jews are quiet, they aren't humble. They don't agree with Jesus's recommendation to "turn the other cheek."

If a Jew gets into a fight, he'll run away or defend himself or try to talk the opponent out of fighting. But he won't let himself be turned into a punching bag. Jews don't believe in self-sacrifice.

Jews try to avoid fights just if they're "typical" Jews, not commanders of the Israeli military, who are paid to love war. It's amazing how a paycheck can change one's sense of values.

Life after death

Christians worry about whether they'll go to Hell instead of Heaven. Jews ignore the issue of "life after death," since the Old Testament hardly even mentions the issue.

Once a year, at the Yom Kippur holiday, they pray that God will put their names in His white book instead of His black book. But they believe that if they're good, their rewards will occur relatively soon, rather than in the hereafter.

According to Christian doctrine, all non-Christians are sinners: they can't go to Heaven and must instead go to Hell or at least "purgatory" (which is a nightmare that resembles a Howard Johnson's restaurant on the lonely road from Hell to Heaven). Jews, by contrast, believe non-Jews can get to Heaven and that Jewish rituals just help Jews get an "in" with God. ("Hey, guys, we Jews are God's chosen people. If you join us, we'll help you get into Heaven; we've got contacts up there. We'll help you reach the Top through our old 'Jew-boy' network. Just follow our rituals — come to our synagogue and bow down at the right times — and do good deeds; then we'll make sure God treats you right.")

Missionary position

Since Christians think all non-Christians are sinners, Christians hire missionaries to turn non-Christians into Christians. That's why Christianity is called a missionary religion.

But Judaism's not a missionary religion: Jews don't hire missionaries to turn the rest of the world into Jews. That's because Jews consider Judaism to be an aid but not a necessity for getting into Heaven.

To be a good Jew, you must perform many Jewish rituals. If a Christian wants to convert and become a Jew, the rabbi is required to warn the Christian how difficult Judaism is. In fact, according to Jewish law, the rabbi is required to try 3 times to dissuade the Christian from converting. If, after the 3 attempts to dissuade the Christian, the Christian still wants to become a Jew, the rabbi knows the Christian is serious, so the rabbi must help the Christian complete the conversion process, by teaching the Christian about Judaism, until the Christian can pass a test proving the Christian understands Judaism thoroughly — more thoroughly than the average Jew!

Bar Mitzvah

When a Jewish boy turns 13, he undergoes a ceremony called **Bar Mitzvah** (Hebrew for "son of the commandments"). In the ceremony, he agrees to observe all the Jewish commandments forever. If he breaks any commandments after making that agreement, he's considered a jerk.

Before a kid is 13, he can do whatever he wishes, and God won't blame him for it. God will say, "he's just a dumb kid." But when the kid turns 13 and goes through the Bar Mitzvah ceremony, suddenly God's attitude to the kid becomes: "You agreed to become one of my chosen people; so if you fool around any more, you're breaking the agreement and I'm gonna make sure you get screwed!" (Jews think God is vengeful, unlike Christians, who think God is forgiving. Christians believe it's okay to sin if you afterwards say you're "sorry." Jews believe that if you sin, the only way to repent is to do so many kind deeds that they outweigh your past.)

Since the Bar Mitzvah ceremony marks the kid's acceptance of adult responsibilities, it's become a manhood ritual, accompanied by lavish feasts & presents.

To outdo rich Christians who throw ridiculously opulent weddings, rich Jews throw ridiculously opulent Bar Mitzvah parties, where the spoiled 13-year-old brat becomes king for a day. Rabbis bemoan those bloated pagan Bar Mitzvah feasts. The Rabbis warn that "Bar" means "son of," "Mitzvah" means "the commandments," and that too much attention is being placed on the "Bar" and not enough on the "Mitzvah."

Even if a Jewish boy skips the Bar Mitzvah ceremony, Jewish law still considers him an "adult responsible for his actions" when he turns 13 (unlike the U.S. constitution, which considers him "just a kid" until he turns 18 or 21).

Do Jews belittle women?

Judaism is a male religion. In traditional Orthodox Judaism, the men go to the synagogue while the women stay home to cook. Modern Orthodox synagogues let women enter but force the women to sit in the back and to the side, in the "ladies" section. Some women feel as if they were blacks being forced to sit in the back of a bus.

To hold an Orthodox Jewish ceremony, you must gather at least 10 *men*: women don't count. That's because in the traditional Jewish family, the man is supposed to take care of problems with God, while the woman takes care of problems with kids.

On Friday night, the woman is supposed to light candles. The **Talmud** (the book of Jewish law) says that since a woman threw the world into darkness (when Eve let herself be tempted by the snake), women should atone by bringing the world back to light.

In Jewish hierarchy, women are lower than men. For example, every morning when an Orthodox man wakes up, he's supposed to say this prayer:

Praised be the Lord that I'm not a vegetable.
Praised be the Lord that I'm not a mineral.
Praised be the Lord that I'm not a woman.

In a feminist magazine, a Jewish woman wrote an article on how to be an Orthodox Jew and a feminist simultaneously. She found the assignment difficult!

Modern Orthodox Jewish men have invented a new excuse for that discrimination: those men say they admire women so much that they give women the *privilege* of not having to go to synagogue.

Conservative and Reform Judaism try to let women get more involved. For example, Conservative and Reform Jews have created a ceremony called **Bas Mitzvah** or **Bat Mitzvah** (depending on your accent), which means "daughter of the commandments." In the Bas Mitzvah ceremony, the 13-year-old girl pretends she's a boy and goes through the Bar Mitzvah ceremony. That ceremony financially strains the girl's parents, who must throw a huge party for the 13-year-old girl but keep saving money in case she wants a wedding party 5 years later.

Since girls mature faster than boys, girls may get Bas Mitzvahed when they turn 12. Yes, Jewish law considers a girl to be an "adult" when she turns 12, though a boy at that age is still considered "just an irresponsible kid."

Holidays

In the Christian calendar, each day begins at midnight. For example, Thursday begins at Wednesday's end, at midnight.

The Jewish calendar begins each day at sunset instead, so a Jewish "day" consists of evening followed by night followed by morning followed by afternoon. That's because the Book of Genesis says that when God created the universe "It was evening and then it was morning, one day." So the Jewish Thursday begins at the end of Wednesday (at sunset) and continues until the end of Thursday (at sunset).

Sabbaths

Jewish tradition says the most important holiday is the **Sabbath** (Saturday). Jews start celebrating it Friday's end (at sunset) and keep celebrating it until Saturday's end (at sunset).

During the Sabbath, Jews go to the synagogue to pray — especially in the evening, after Friday's sunset, during what Christians call "Friday night." So on "Friday night," while Christians throw wild parties, Jews are stuck in the synagogue, praying. What a drag!

During the Sabbath, Jews aren't allowed to work.

Orthodox Jews carry the "no work" law to an extreme: they refuse to use any machine. For example, they refuse to use cars and phones and refuse to turn on any lights or stoves. (To get around that restriction, they put their lights and stoves on timers.) To attend the synagogue on the Sabbath, they walk, since they refuse to use cars. If an Orthodox Jew lives too far from the synagogue to walk, he stays home.

Yom Kippur (which means "Day of Atonement") is a special holiday, nicknamed "The Sabbath of Sabbaths."

Jews spend the whole day of Yom Kippur in the synagogue, where they beg God's forgiveness for the past year's sins and beg Him to put their names into his white book instead of his black book. During the whole day, Jews fast. I don't mean the stupid little token fast practiced at Lent by Christians (who give up just meat) or by Muslims during their religious month. No, when Jews fast, they fast totally: throughout the entire Yom Kippur day, Jews eat nothing, and drink nothing, not even water! The only Jews exempt from fasting are kids too young to be Bar Mitzvah, pregnant women, and the gravely ill.

Having no food and no water for 24 hours might sound dreadful, but actually it's fun. Kids think it's fun to try surviving like that for a day — especially since the fast is preceded and succeeded by a big celebratory meal. The fast is easier than it sounds, since you can sleep after the first big meal and after praying. And after the first few hours of fasting, your body adjusts to the lack of food, and your hunger goes away.

Though nicknamed "The Sabbath of Sabbaths," Yom Kippur doesn't necessarily fall on a Saturday. Like all Jewish holidays, it begins at sunset and ends at sunset.

So the most important days on the Jewish calendar are Yom Kippur and all the Saturdays. Jews take them very seriously. According to the Bible, the penalty for desecrating Yom Kippur is excommunication, and the penalty for desecrating the 52 other Sabbaths is even stronger (death!), according to the Bible's Book of Leviticus (chapter 23, verse 30) and the Book of Exodus (chapter 31, verse 15).

Lesser holidays

Much less important than Yom Kippur and the Sabbaths is **Rosh Hashanah**, the Jewish New Year's celebration. Lower than all them are the other holidays, such as **Passover**, **Purim**, **Succoth**, and **Chanukah**. (To correctly pronounce the "Ch" in "Chanukah," say an "H" while gargling.)

What a drab religion, to have the biggest holiday, Yom Kippur, be a day of fasting! And what a boring religion, to have the 52 other important holidays all be Saturdays that are identical to each other and all prohibit you from driving your car and even from phoning your friends! Of all the world's popular religions, Judaism is the most morose.

To make the best of a sad religion, Jews often laugh about their difficulties and sometimes do a peppy line dance to the tune of **Hava Nagila**. Here are the lyrics:

Original Hebrew	Translation	Vegetarian version
Hava nagila,	Let's rejoice,	Have a banana!
Hava nagila,	Let's rejoice,	Have *two* bananas!
Hava nagila	Let's rejoice	Have *three* bananas:
Venis'mecha!	And be happy!	They're *good* for you!
Hava nagila,	Let's rejoice,	Have a banana!
Hava nagila,	Let's rejoice,	Have *two* bananas!
Hava nagila	Let's rejoice	Have *three* bananas:
Venis'mecha!	And be happy!	They're *fun* to chew!
Hava neranenah,	Let's sing,	Have a banana now:
Hava neranenah,	Let's sing,	Have one, don't have a cow!
Hava neranenah	Let's sing	Have a banana now:
Venis'mecha!	And be happy!	Don't have a cow!
Hava neranenah,	Let's sing,	Put it right in your mouth.
Hava neranenah,	Let's sing,	Once there, don't take it out.
Hava neranenah	Let's sing	Hey, no, don't take it out,
Venis'mecha!	And be happy!	And please don't pout!
Uru,	Awake,	Oo! Ee!
Uru, achim,	Awake, brothers,	Oo! Ee! Chewy!
Uru, achim, b'lev sameach,	Awake, brothers, with happy heart,	Have a banana, can ya?
Uru, achim, b'lev sameach,	Awake, brothers, with happy heart,	Stick one in your bandana!
Uru, achim, b'lev sameach,	Awake, brothers, with happy heart,	Slice it, just like a man. You
Uru, achim, b'lev sameach,	Awake, brothers, with happy heart,	Know, dear, that's what we plan to!
Uru, achim, uru, achim,	Awake, brothers, awake, brothers,	But now please, don't you sneeze,
B'lev sameach!	With happy heart!	Or I can't be hugging you.
Hey!	Hey!	Oo!

Now Orthodox and Conservative Jews demand two days off from work for each holiday. Reform Jews have cut back to just one day per holiday. So Orthodox and Conservative Jews seem twice as religious as Reform! But actually, the typical Orthodox or Conservative Jew doesn't go to synagogue on the holiday's second day: instead, he hides from the rabbi and goes fishing!

What Jews eat

In the Old Testament, God gave 613 commandments. He made Moses put the 10 most important ones onto a tablet but warned that the other 603 must be obeyed also. Several commandments concern food.

No meat with milk God said:

> A kid goat shall not be cooked in its mother's milk.

God felt so strongly about that commandment that he said it twice: he said it in the Book of Exodus (23:19) and also in the Book of Deuteronomy (14:21).

Apparently, God thought it's okay to eat a goat and drink milk, but boiling a goat in the milk of its own mother is gross. The Jewish God always insisted on good manners! You must eat the goat *before* drink the milk, or vice versa.

That law can be hard to enforce: if you go to a supermarket to buy goat meat and some goat's milk (true delicacies!), how can you be sure that the goat who produced the milk isn't, by some weird coincidence, the mother of the goat you're eating? You'd be upset if, while drinking the milk, you nibble at the goat meat and suddenly God stabs you with a lightening bolt. It could ruin your whole day.

To protect against lightening bolts, Jews adopt a simple insurance policy: never eat any kind of meat with any kind of milk. Jews won't even eat chicken with cheese, even though it's highly unlikely that the chicken's mother produced the cheese. In fact, if the chicken's mother did produce the cheese, she'd be a miracle, like the Easter bunny who lays eggs. But Jews still consider it possible that the cheese might have come from the chicken's mother, so Jews refuse to eat cheese with chicken.

"Never eat any kind of meat with any kind of milk" has become a Jewish law, but Jewish lawyers (who are very clever) noticed the law contains a vague word: "with."

What does it mean to eat meat *with* milk? For example, if you eat meat and then 5 minutes later drink milk, did you eat meat *with* milk?

To make sure Jewish eaters don't take liberties, Jewish lawyers rewrote the law to say this: after eating meat, you must wait several hours before drinking milk. But how long is "several hours"? In Eastern Europe, Jewish lawyers say you must wait 6 hours; in Germany and most other countries of Western Europe, Jewish lawyers say you must wait just 3 hours; in Holland, Jewish lawyers are very permissive and say you must wait just 72 minutes.

So if you eat meat, you must wait before drinking milk. But if you drink milk, you do *not* have to wait before eating meat; it's okay to eat meat immediately after drinking milk. But it's *not* okay to eat meat immediately after eating hard cheese — because hard cheese sticks to your teeth! After eating hard cheese, you must wait an hour for the cheese to disintegrate. That law about hard cheese was invented by a rabbi and called the **sticky-cheese amendment**.

If two Jews sit side-by-side, and one eats meat while the other drinks milk, have they mixed meat and milk? Fortunately, the answer is "no." If the meat eater wants to drink orange juice but and the only cup in the house is the one used by the milk drinker, can the meat eater rinse that cup, quickly fill it with orange juice, and drink? Jewish lawyers decided the answer is no: the milk cup must be rinsed then dried for *several hours* before it can be used by a meat eater. As my Christian friends say, "Leave it to a Jewish lawyer to make life difficult!"

But I have good news for you: if the cup's made of *glass*, you may put milk into it, rinse it, and use it for orange juice in a meat meal without delay — because glass is non-porous. That rule, invented by a kind rabbi, is called the **glass amendment**.

When I was a kid, a friend decided to become an Eastern European style Orthodox Jew, even though his parents were not. (His parents were Reform.) When I visited his house, his mom made him a chicken sandwich then gave him a cup of orange juice. He refused to drink the orange juice, because his mom couldn't guarantee that the cup had been milk-free for the previous 6 hours. (Lesson: if you're a mom whose kid turns into an Orthodox Jew, he's going to give you Hell!)

To avoid the problem of watching each cup (to make sure it didn't contain milk within the previous 6 hours) and watching each plate (to make sure it didn't contain meat with the previous 6 hours), Orthodox Jews buy 3 sets of tableware: one set is for meals based on meat; the second set is for meals based on milk; the third set is for Passover, which requires its own tableware! Each set of tableware must be washed separately. That's why, in ancient times, each Jewish home had three sinks. And that's why, in modern times, the typical Orthodox Jewish American Princess makes her husband buy 3 dishwashers.

No pork
Besides the prohibition against eating meat with milk, the Bible contains other laws about meat. For example, it prohibits eating meat from any animal that has a "cloven hoof." Since the most popular animal that has a "cloven hoof" is the pig, Jews can't eat pork.

Although beef is okay, the cow must be killed in a special way — by slitting the cow's neck while saying a blessing. The cow probably doesn't appreciate the blessing, but God does.

No shellfish
The Book of Deuteronomy (in chapter 14, verses 9 and 10) lets you eat a fish just if it has fins and scales. So you can't eat shellfish: Jews can't eat shrimp or lobsters or clams.

What about swordfish and sturgeon, which have fins and scales for just part of their lives? Orthodox Jews refuse to eat them, but Conservative and Reform Jews indulge.

4 categories
All those rules about food are called the **dietary laws** or **kosher laws**. (**Kosher** is the Hebrew word for "clean.")

Jews view all food as falling into 4 categories:

> acceptable meat
> unacceptable meat (and shellfish)
> milk products
> neutral foods

Acceptable meat is called **kosher** meat. Unacceptable meat and shellfish are called **trayfe**, which is the Hebrew word for "dirty." Milk products (such as milk, cream, butter, and cheese) are all called **dairy** and can't be had with meat. Neutral foods (such as grains and fruits) can be eaten with either meat or milk and are called **pareve**.

Symbols
When I was a kid, the symbol for "**kosher**" was a tiny K in a circle, and the symbol for "**pareve**" was a tiny P in a circle. For example, if you went into a supermarket and bought a package of Jewish meat, you'd see a circled K on the package; and if you bought a package or ordinary cereal (such as Kellogg's), you'd see a circled P on the package, which meant that you could eat the cereal even if you were Jewish.

Now the circled K has been switched to an uncircled K, and pareve foods have a K instead of a P (because the typical stupid Jew doesn't know what "pareve" means). In short, the K today simply means "this product contains nothing that would discourage a Jew."

The K costs money. For each box of cereal that Kellogg sells, Kellogg must pay a rabbi, who inspects the cereal to make sure it's manufactured in a clean and unsurprising way. Paying the rabbi is like paying the Mafia: "If you don't pay me, I'll make sure the sales of your cereal to Jews will decline."

Instead of a K, you'll sometimes see a circled U, which means the food is approved by the Union of Orthodox Jewish Congregations.

Christmas competition When American Jews saw their Christian neighbors enjoy Christmas and throw wild Christmas parties, they got jealous and began placing an artificial emphasis on Chanukah, since Chanukah (like Christmas) involves giving presents and comes at the same time of the year. But according to old Jewish tradition, Chanukah is supposed to be a *minor* holiday, because it just commemorates a minor favor that God' gave a group of Jewish warriors: He let the oil in their synagogue burn for 8 days. A little tale about high-grade oil can't compete with Christmas and Easter, the two Christian holidays that marked the beginning of all Christianity!

During Christmas, Jews feel lonely at being left out of Christmas parties and secretly wish they were Christian. Reform Jews often buy Christmas trees but tell their Orthodox friends that the trees are just "Chanukah bushes." While Christians preach love at Christmas, and say "keep the Christ in Christmas," Jews just say "keep the Ch in Chanukah." While Christians give gigantic presents on Christmas day, Jews must be stingy and give tiny presents instead, because Chanukah lasts 8 days and you're supposed to give each person 8 presents: one each day! For example, if there are 3 other members of your family, you must buy a total of 24 presents for them!

Celebrate twice In ancient Israel, the Jews weren't sure which days the holidays fell on, because the calendar depended on the moon's phases. On a cloudy night it was hard to tell whether the moon was full. So to be sure they celebrated Rosh Hashanah (the Jewish New Year) on the right day, they celebrated it twice.

The Jews who lived outside Israel were even less certain about the holidays, since they had to wait for a messenger to travel from Israel and tell them what the Israeli judges had decided about whether the moon was indeed full yet. So outside Israel, to be safe, Jews celebrated *most* holidays for an extra day.

For example, if Passover was theoretically supposed to fall on a Thursday, the Jews outside Israel celebrated it on both Thursday and Friday, just to be sure they didn't miss the right day. They performed the entire Passover ceremony on Thursday, and then repeated the entire ceremony again, word for word, on Friday, while trying not to snore.

The main exceptions were Yom Kippur (no Jew would stand for fasting two days in a row!), the Sabbath (no Jew could afford to relax more than 1 day per week), and Chanukah (8 days is enough already).

Substitute foods Since Jews can't eat pork, Jewish hot dogs are all-beef. Since Jews can't eat bacon (which is made from pork), Jews eat "imitation bacon" made from soy. Since Jews can't have meat with milk, Jews avoid milk products: they use margarine instead of butter and use "non-dairy creamer" instead of real cream in their coffee.

Obey all that? Orthodox Jews obey all those rules all the time. Reform Jews usually ignore all those rules.

Conservative Jews adopt a creative compromise: they obey all those rules at home (they "keep a kosher home"), but ignore all those rules when they visit restaurants. So at restaurants, they "pig out" and eat everything they're not allowed to eat at home.

Chinese restaurants Conservative Jews love to eat at Chinese restaurants, because Chinese restaurants serve everything that Conservative Jews can't eat at home, such as pork, shrimp, and lobster. Here's another reason why Jews love Chinese restaurants: those restaurants, like Jewish culture itself, are ethnic adventures.

The fastest way to find a Jewish community is to look for a Chinese restaurant. In the typical Chinese restaurant, most of the customers are Jews!

To compliment a Jew, say "You're like sweet-and-sour pork, but without the sour and without the pork: you're just sweet!"

Jewish intellectuals

Judaism's an intellectual religion.

To become a good Jew, you must study many rituals. For example, to prepare for Bar Mitzvah, the Jewish boy must undergo many months of training.

Judaism is based on the Old Testament, in which Abraham, Moses, and the rest of the gang continuously debate with God.

Reading the Old Testament is like reading the record of a legal trial: in the end, God wins, and the Jews agree to obey His 613 commandments, but the *interpretation* of His commandments fills another set of books, called the **Talmud**, written by Jewish religious lawyers. In the Talmud and later writings, Jews analyze what God means: Judaism is an analytical religion. Studying Judaism is good preparation for being a lawyer. Several American law schools offer courses in Jewish law.

Maimonides One of the wisest Jewish scholars was **Maimonides**, a Jewish doctor who was born in 1135 A.D. and lived in Spain during the Middle Ages. He was interested in medicine but also Jewish law: his Jewish mom was proud that he was a doctor and a lawyer! He put the finishing touches on the Talmud (the book of Jewish law). He also developed the **ladder of charity**, which went far beyond anything ever proposed by his predecessors (such as Jesus).

Maimonides' ladder of charity had 8 steps. At the lowest step, the rich man gave money to the poor man in an obvious way: the rich man knew who the poor man was, and the poor man knew who the rich man was and felt embarrassed. At higher rungs, the charity was given anonymously, so that the poor man didn't know who the rich man was, the rich man didn't know who the poor man was, and the rich man couldn't "gloat" over the poor man. But the very highest step on Maimonides' ladder involves no money: instead, the rich man spends time with the poor man and trains him in a new skill, so the poor man can get a job and won't need charity anymore!

Maimonides wasn't the only person to think of that. For example, the Japanese have an old saying that summarizes Maimonides' ladder; the Japanese say: "If you give a man a fish, he'll eat for a day; but if you give a man a rod instead, he'll eat for a year." Actually, the Japanese say it using Japanese grammar, like this: "Give man fish, eats for day; give man rod, eats for year."

Notice that Jews, like Maimonides, worry about climbing social ladders, whereas the Japanese say "hell with society" and prefer to simply eat fish.

No blind faith Although Christianity encourages "blind faith," Judaism does not. Judaism encourages *thought* more than faith. Jews are told to *think* about how to interpret God's law.

No Pope Catholics are told the Pope is infallible — always right — and to obey the Pope's command without questioning. Jews have no Pope. The word rabbi means just "teacher": a rabbi is just a scholar who's studied religion thoroughly but who, like any other human, might be wrong. It's okay for a Jew to argue with his rabbi.

Unlike a Catholic priest, a rabbi has no mystical powers. You don't need a rabbi to perform a Jewish service: you need just 10 ordinary men, and one of the men must agree to act as the leader.

You need a rabbi's signature just on legal documents, such as marriage contracts and divorce papers. So a rabbi is just a bright guy who's also empowered to act as a notary public.

Study hard Jewish parents encourage their kids to study hard: finish college then get advanced degrees.

The Western world's top 5 intellectuals were all born Jewish. Each explained everything his own way:

Moses	said **law** is everything.
Jesus	said **love** is everything.
Marx	said **capital** is everything.
Freud	said **sex** is everything.
Einstein	said everything is **relative**.

What Jews think of Jesus

Jesus was Jewish. His Last Supper was a Passover ceremony.

Jesus was a teacher ("rabbi") who was more humane than most other rabbis. He criticized the other rabbis for being greedy, bureaucratic, and pigheaded — and was right.

According to Jewish tradition, a Messiah would come. Many nuts claimed to be the Messiah. Jesus, too, claimed to be the Messiah. Other Jewish rabbis believed that Jesus, too, was a nut.

Jesus's most important contribution to our culture was to emphasize the importance of love and forgiveness. He turned away from the harsher ethics espoused by other rabbis.

Modern Jews think Jesus was a great teacher but still just a human whose advice, though quite wise, could still be further improved and refined.

Jewish money

Jews have been stereotyped as being "money-grubbers." The connection between Jews and money has a long history that was actually the fault of the Christians!

A terrible disease — leprosy — began spreading over Europe in 1349. It was called the **plague**, the **Black Death**. Since people didn't know it was caused by germs, they blamed it on the Jews. In several cities — such as Frankfort, Germany — ignorant mobs burned the houses of all the Jews, forced the Jews to live in a segregated area (called a **ghetto**), and prohibited Jews from participating in normal life. Since the ghetto was surrounded by walls and was undersized, life in the ghetto was dangerously crowded.

Outside the ghetto, Christians developed a **feudal system** (which required farmers to swear a Christian oath of loyalty to their noble or king); and all employees in a shop or a craft were forced to join a **guild** (union), which admitted only Christians. So Jews couldn't become farmers or shopkeepers or craftsmen.

The Catholic Church forbade Catholics from lending money at interest. But Catholic businessmen couldn't run their businesses without getting loans! So Catholic businessmen, out of necessity, permitted Jews to come out of the ghetto for one occupation only: to give Catholics loans.

Charging interest on loans was against Jewish tradition as well as Catholic tradition, but the Jews had no choice: the only kind of job Jews were allowed was lending money.

That's how Jews became bankers and pawnbrokers. That's how Jews became associated with money. The Catholic Church forced them into it!

Catholics then adopted a strange attitude: they criticized the Jews for charging high interest rates, but nevertheless went to the Jews frequently because they prohibited their fellow Catholics from lending money!

Since lending money was the only way Jews could survive outside of the ghetto, Jews had to become wise about money, to survive. Instead of spending money recklessly, Jews had to learn how to save it and invest it. To Jews, having money became a form of security.

Jews still view money differently than Christians. Christians view money as something to spend immediately and enjoy; Jews view money as something to put in the bank to protect against impending disaster. When Christians think of money, they think of the joy of spending it immediately; when Jews think of money, they think of the disasters money protects against. When a Christian looks at his piggy bank and sees it's half full, the Christian is happy about the thought of spending the half-full piggy bank immediately; when a Jew looks at a half-full piggy bank, the Jew sees it's half empty, and worries that a disaster might strike for which a half-full piggy bank won't be enough.

Jewish merchants tend to be long-nosed but also hard-nosed. Shakespeare exaggerated when he said the Jewish merchant Shylock demanded a pound of flesh, but even now Jewish merchants often tell their complaining customers, "You don't like it? So sue me!" That's why Jews tell this tale:

Did you hear about the new Japanese restaurant for Jews? It's called "Sosumi."

Jews are worrywarts

Jews always worry. They worry whether the meat they're eating is kosher. They worry that they don't have enough money in the bank. They worry that the Christians and Arabs will persecute Jews again or at least give Jews a hard time.

Those worries extend to the rest of life also. Jewish mothers worry that their sons won't become famous doctors; they also worry that their daughters will marry dumb, brutal Christians. During the 1960's, Jewish students worried about Viet Nam; in fact, the whole antiwar movement was begun by 2 groups of left-wing agitators (the Students for a Democrat Society and the Weathermen), who were all Jewish! If it weren't for those Jewish students, we'd probably still be in Viet Nam!

Yes, Jewish men always worry: they're never happy-go-lucky. That's why Jews don't drink much beer: Jews can't adopt the ho-ho-ho attitude that beer-drinking requires. Instead, Jews prefer wine, which is quieter and more morose.

All Jewish culture is summarized in the personality of one man: Woody Allen. In his films, Woody spends most of his time worrying. In his earliest films, he worried about household appliances taking over his life. In later films, he worried about whether Diane Keeton loved him. In his most recent films, he worries about problems that are more profound.

When Jewish men (like Woody Allen) try to date, they continually worry that their girlfriends will reject them. Jewish men's fear of women continues even after the men are married.

Yes, Jewish men are always pessimistic about sexual relationships — unlike Italian men, who are always optimistic. The contrast between Jewish men and Italian men is the subject of this famous joke:

What's *Jewish* foreplay? Three hours of begging and pleading.
What is *Italian* foreplay? "Stella, I'm home!"

Jews like Soft & Dry deodorant because of Soft & Dry's ad:

Nervous is why
there's new Soft & Dry.

Since Jews are always nervous, they're always deodorizing.

Jews worry about illness. Here's another tale from the Internet about desires and worries:

An Italian	said, "I'm tired. I'm thirsty. I must have vino."
A Greek	said, "I'm tired. I'm thirsty. I must have ouzo."
A Mexican	said, "I'm tired. I'm thirsty. I must have tequila."
A Jew	said, "I'm tired. I'm thirsty. I must have diabetes."

Yiddish humor

German Jews invented a dialect of German called **Jewish German** or **Yiddish German**. It used German grammar and vocabulary but borrowed some words from Hebrew. The entire Yiddish German language was written using Hebrew characters instead of the German alphabet. As the popularity of Yiddish grew, it spread to nearby countries (such as Hungary and Russia) and borrowed words from Slavic and Russian languages.

The Yiddish language developed its own brand of humor, which still gives smiles to Jews all over the world. One of the most popular techniques of Yiddish humor is to answer a question by giving a counter-question. For example, suppose a Yiddish Jew is trying to quit smoking, but hasn't succeeded yet. If somebody asks him "Are you still smoking?" he'd reply, "Do fish swim?" or "Is the Pope Catholic?" If somebody else asks him "Have you stopped smoking?" he'd reply, "Can a fish climb a tree?" or "Is the Pope Jewish?"

Schmuck Though Yiddish is based on German and Hebrew, cynics call it a *perversion* of German and Hebrew. For example, consider the German word **schmuck**, which means "ornament."

> The Jews borrowed that word and used it as a euphemism for "penis." For example, a Yiddish-speaking girl might walk up to a boy, notice his penis is making his pants bulge, and say, "That's a nice schmuck you got there." It's quite clear which "ornament" she's referring to! Among American Jews, a favorite Yiddish expression is, "You stupid schmuck!" which means "You stupid cock!" or "You stupid fucker!" Since American Jews use the phrase "stupid schmuck" so often, people think "schmuck" means "fool"; but historically, it means "penis" or "ornament." That's how schmuck, which is the German word for "ornament," became the Yiddish word for "penis" and then the English word for "fool."
>
> The history of schmuck became an issue when NBC was filming Saturday Night Live. In one of the scripts, a portrait of Lincoln was supposed to say to Nixon, "You're a schmuck!" Al Franken, who wrote that script, thought "schmuck" just meant "fool." But one of NBC's censors knew that "schmuck" could also mean "penis," so he censored the script. Instead, Lincoln had to say to Nixon, "You're a dip." Lorne Michaels, the producer, passed the bad news to the writers by sending them this memo: "You can't say 'schmuck,' you schmucks!"

Schlemiel The most popular pair of Yiddish words is "**schlemiel & schlimazel**." Both words refer to unlucky guys. A schlemiel is a bungler who causes many disasters (accidentally); a schlimazel is a guy who's continually the victim of disasters (caused by schlemiels).

For example, suppose two waiters accidentally spill hot soup onto your lap — 5 times each. The waiters are schlemiels; you're a schlimazel.

Goy The Yiddish language divides the world into two kinds of people: those who are Jewish, and those who are not. A non-Jew is called a **goy**.

> A goy boy is called a **shegetz**, which means "blemished person."
> A goy gal is called a **shiksa**, which means "cute blemished person."

A typical Yiddish war-cry among Jewish mothers is:

> Oy, what am I going to do? My son, he wants to marry a shiksa!

In Yiddish life, everything is classified as being either Jewish or goy. If an activity is mindless — totally devoid of cleverness or originality — it's called **goy**, because it requires no clever strategy.

> Baseball is goy; football is *not* goy, since it requires clever strategy. Americana (such as Coca-Cola and McDonald's) are goy; competitors running clever ads (Pepsi, Burger King, and Wendy's) are less goy.

Aha Jews love to say "Aha!" (To say it properly, say the "A" softly in a bass pitch, then say "ha" loudly in a treble pitch.)

This story shows the meaning of Aha!

> In New York City, a Jew named Morty goes to his favorite Jewish restaurant (as he does every day), goes to his favorite table (as he does every day), sits in his favorite chair (as he does every day), and asks for a bowl of soup (as he does every day). The waiter brings him the soup. But as the waiter leaves the table, Morty yells, "Waiter!"
> "Yes?"
> "Taste this soup."
> "What do you mean, 'Taste this soup'?"
> "Taste this soup."
> "But Morty.... "
> "*Taste* this *soup!*"
> "But Morty, you've come in here every day, for 10 years, you sit at the same table, in the same chair, and order the same bowl of soup. Have I ever served you a *bad* bowl of soup?"
> "*Taste* this *soup!*"
> "Okay, okay.... Where's the spoon?"
> "Aha!"

Hebonics After some schools started considering "urban black street talk" to be a foreign language called "Ebonics," an Internet report joked that the New York City Board of Education declared "Hebonics" (Jewish English) to be a foreign language also.

In Hebonics, each question is answered with another question that implies a complaint:

Question:	"How are you?"
Hebonics response:	"How *should* I feel, with *my* feet?"

Instead of beginning the sentence with a subject, the subject is moved to the sentence's end, with the subject's pronoun put at the beginning.

Normal English:	"That girl dances beautifully."
Hebonic phrasing:	"She dances beautifully, that girl."

For sarcasm, "shm" is put in front: "mountains" becomes "shmountains"; "turtle" becomes "shmurtle." The two words are then used together:

Remark:	"I'm going up to the mountains."
Hebonic reply:	"Mountains, shmountains. You want a nosebleed?"

Remark:	"He's as slow as a turtle."
Hebonic reply:	"Turtle, shmurtle. Like a *fly in Vaseline* he walks."

Here's how to reply Hebonically:

Question:	"What time is it?"
Hebonic reply:	"What am I, a *clock*?"
Remark:	"I hope things turn out okay."
Hebonic reply:	"You should *be* so lucky!"
Remark:	"Hurry up! Dinner's ready."
Hebonic reply:	"What's with the 'hurry' business? Is there a *fire*?"
Remark:	"I like this tie you gave me. I wear it all the time!"
Hebonic reply:	"So what's the matter, you don't like the *other* ties I gave you?"
Remark:	"I got engaged to Sarah. Doesn't she have a great figure?"
Hebonic reply:	"She could stand to *gain* a few pounds."
Question:	"Would you like to go riding with us?"
Hebonic reply:	"Riding, shmiding! Do I look like a *cowboy*?"
Remark:	"It's my birthday."
Hebonic reply:	"Too bad. A year *smarter* you should become."
Remark:	"It's a beautiful day!"
Hebonic reply:	"The sun's out? Big deal. So what *else* is new?"
Remark:	"Hi, mom! Sorry it's been a while since I phoned."
Hebonic reply:	"You didn't wonder if I'm *dead* yet?"

Jewish women

Jewish women look like Italian women.

In Boston's red-light district, Italian hookers complain that guys mistake them for being Jewish. That's partly because Italian hookers, like some Jewish women, love money.

JAPs Most Jewish women are wonderful, but a few are obnoxious. A young Jewish woman who loves money obnoxiously is called a **Jewish-American Princess** or **JAP**.

At Jewish parties, scared Jewish guys tell each other, "Let's get out of here! The JAPs are coming!" They aren't talking about the Japanese.

Such Jewish women — JAPs —love to wear a long dress having a long slit up the side. I learned that lesson the hard way, by embarrassment:

> One day, I told my mom I saw an amazing woman who was wearing a very long dress with a long slit up the side. My mom immediately said, "If she's wearing that dress, she must be Jewish."
> I said, "I don't know. I didn't ask her."
> My mom asked, "What's her last name?"
> I said, "Abrams."
> My mom said, "Hah! I told you so!"

Those Jewish women decorate their homes with art that's abstract and gaudy. Though my own family is Jewish, we can't help calling that art style "**kike modern**."

Such Jewish women wear lots of jewelry. That tradition began centuries ago, when Jews were chased from country to country, and the only valuables small enough to carry easily were jewels.

Jewish girls have a reputation for being frigid. The joke about how the typical Jewish man begs for 3 hours to get the girl to say yes is typical of the way Jewish girls like to be treated.

Several other jokes poke fun at the frigidity of Jewish-American Princesses (JAPs):

> What do you get when you cross a JAP with a computer? A system that never goes down.
>
> How does a JAP differ from a bowl of Jello? Jello shakes when you eat it.
> What's the difference between a JAP and poverty? Poverty sucks.
> Why do JAPs have crow's feet? From squinting and saying, "Suck *what*?"
> What do you call a JAP on a waterbed? Lake Placid.
> How do you stop a JAP from fucking you? Marry her.
> What's a JAP's idea of perfect sex? Simultaneous headaches.

JAPs refuse to do housework:

> How does a JAP call her family for dinner? "Get in the car, kids!"
> What do JAPs make for dinner? Reservations.
> What's a JAP's dream house? 14 rooms in Scarsdale, no kitchen, no bedroom.

JAPs are materialistic:

> What's a JAP's favorite position? Facing Bloomingdale's.
> What's a JAP's favorite *erotic* position? Bending over the credit cards.
> Why do JAPs close their eyes when fucking? So they can pretend they're shopping.
> Why do JAPs prefer tampons? Because nothing goes in without a string attached.
> What's the difference between a JAP and a barracuda? Nail polish.
>
> A Jewish man asks his JAP wife, "Would you still love me if I became disfigured?" Filing her nails, she says, "I'll always love you." He asks, "What if I couldn't make love to you anymore?" She answers, "I'll always love you, dear," while still concentrating on her nails. "What if I lost my hundred-thousand-dollar-a-year job?" She puts down her nail file, looks at her husband's anxious face, and says, "Darling, I'll always love you; but most of all, I'll really miss you!"

You can find more such jokes in *Truly Tasteless Jokes* (by Blanche Knott) and *Utterly Gross Jokes* (by Julius Alvin).

Here's a comment from the Internet:

> Why do Jewish men get circumcised? Because Jewish women don't touch anything unless it's 20% off.

Jewish mothers No matter how good a Jewish boy is, his mother will nag him to do even better, even after he's become an adult. According to the Internet, here's what celebrities' mothers would say, if they were all Jewish:

> **Moses**'s Jewish mother: "That's a nice story. A wonderful story! A writer you should be. Now tell me where you've *really* been the last 40 years."
>
> **Mona Lisa**'s Jewish mother: "After all that money your father and I spent on your braces, that's the biggest smile you can give us?"
>
> **Michelangelo**'s Jewish mother: "Can't you paint on walls, like other kids? You've maybe no idea how hard it is to get that stuff off the ceiling?"
>
> **Columbus**'s Jewish mother: "So, Mister Big Sailor Boy, I don't care what you've discovered, how come you didn't write?"
>
> **Paul Revere**'s Jewish mother: "I don't care where you think you gotta go, young man. Midnight is past your curfew."
>
> **George Washington**'s Jewish mother: "Next time I catch you throwing good money across the Potomac, you can kiss your allowance good-bye!"
>
> **Napoleon**'s Jewish mother: "Okay, Little Emperor, so if you aren't hiding your report card inside your jacket, take your hand out of there and show me."
>
> **Abraham Lincoln**'s Jewish mother: "What's with that ridiculous hat again? Can't you just wear a baseball cap like the other kids?"
>
> **Thomas Edison**'s Jewish mother: "Of course I'm proud you invented the electric light bulb. Now turn it off and get to bed!"
>
> **Albert Einstein**'s Jewish mother: "Listen please, Albie. For your own good I'm telling you. It's your senior picture. Couldn't you do something about your hair? Figure it out. A comb, maybe?"

Jewish mothers are hard to buy presents for, as seen in this tale about trying to please a Jewish mother who loved reading the Torah (first five books of the Bible):

> 4 Jewish brothers (a doctor, a lawyer, and two businessmen) were prosperous. They bragged about the presents they gave their mom.
> The first said, "I had a big house built for her."
> The second said, "I had a hundred-thousand-dollar theater built in the house."
> The third said, "I had my Mercedes dealer deliver her an SL600 with a chauffeur."
> The fourth said, "Listen to this. You know how she loved reading the Torah and can't anymore because she can't see well? I met a rabbi who told me about a parrot that can recite the entire Torah. It took 20 rabbis 12 years to teach him. I had to pledge to contribute $100,000 a year for 20 years to the temple, but it was worth it. Mom just has to name the chapter and verse, and the parrot will recite it."
> After the holidays, their mom sent them these thank-you notes....
> "Milton, the house you built is so huge! I live in just one room but have to clean the whole house! Thanks anyway."
> "Menachim, you gave me an expensive theater that could hold 50 people! But all my friends are dead, I've lost my hearing, and I'm nearly blind. I'll never use it. Thanks for the gesture just the same."
> "Marvin, I'm too old to travel, so I stay home and have my groceries delivered. I never use the Mercedes, and the driver you hired is a Nazi, but thanks for trying."
> "Dearest Melvin, you're the only son having the good sense to give a little thought to your gift. The chicken was delicious!"

Relating to kids

Here's another story, passed to me by my crazy Jewish relative....

> Dr. Morris Fishbein calls his son Irving in Los Angeles and says, "I hate to ruin your day, but your mom and I are divorcing. 45 years of misery is enough."
> "Pop! What are you talking about?" Irving screams.
> "We can't stand the sight of each other any longer," Morris says. "I'm sick of talking about this, so call your sister Shirley in Chicago and tell her."
> Irving frantically calls his sister, who explodes on the phone, "Like *hell* they're getting divorced! I'll take care of this."
> She calls her father immediately and yells at him, "You're *not* getting divorced! Don't do a single thing until I get there. I'm calling Irving back and we'll both be there tomorrow. Until then, do nothing. *Do you hear me?*"
> Her father hangs up and turns to his wife. "Okay," he says, "They're coming for Passover — and paying their own airfares."

How Jews treat blacks

Blacks and Jews can be friends — or enemies.

When I was a kid, my teacher showed my class a documentary movie called *The Poor Pay More*.

Shot in Manhattan's black ghetto (Harlem), it showed how businessmen ripped off poor blacks. It showed a butcher (whose scale exaggerated the weight), a supermarket (that raised its prices each week on the day when welfare checks were issued), and other immoral business practices perpetrated by furniture stores, refrigerator salesmen, etc. In every case, the victims of the scams were blacks, and the perpetrators were Jewish. That's because, in Harlem, most of the shops were run by Jews. Though some Jews in Harlem were honest, many were rotten. In Harlem, blacks and Jews viewed each other as opponents: the Jews cheated the blacks, then the blacks mugged the Jews.

But the first national political organization for blacks — the NAACP — received most of its donations from Jews. That's because Jews — especially Jewish liberals living in rich suburbs — believe strongly in fairness, equality, and liberty for all.

The NAACP lobbied to help blacks. But its very name (the National Association for the Advancement of Colored Peoples) smacked of compromise and Uncle Toms. In the 1960's, when groups such as the Black Panthers and Black Muslims began preaching black equality through violence, the Jews got scared and stopped donating money to black causes. Another reason why Jews stopped donating money to black causes is that black politicians (such as Jesse Jackson) befriended Arabs, and Jews fear a coalition of Arabs & blacks will try to snatch Israel away from Jews.

The history of Jews resembles the history of blacks. Both groups are minorities. Both groups have been persecuted for many centuries.

Blacks in Africa were captured by slave traders, brought to America, turned into slaves, and separated from their families. Similarly, the Bible says Egyptians turned Jews into slaves and forced Jews to build the pyramids, until a rabble-rousing Jew named Moses convinced the Jews to run away to Israel. Later, Jews were ruled by the Romans and other conquerors and forced to leave their homeland.

Jews in the town of Brookline, Massachusetts, get together with blacks and celebrate Passover together, since the Passover ceremony, which commemorate the escape (by Moses and his Jews) from slavery has meaning for both Jews and blacks.

Some blacks demand to be called "Afro-American." I guess we "Jews" with big noses should act similarly and demand to be called "Nostril-American" — or should we go Latin and opt for "Rhino-Caucasian"?

In New York City's Harlem, you can find a group of black Jews.

They claim to be descended from the Biblical Jacob, who had sex with one of his black maids. Those black Jews read Hebrew and practice Orthodox Judaism; but in the middle of their otherwise traditional Orthodox Jewish service, they suddenly break into a wild Afro dance while singing "Hallelujah!"

Jews everywhere

Just 2% of Americans are Jews, but 35% of Ivy League students are Jews.

Universities (such as Vanderbilt) try to get more Jews to apply for admission, because Jews make universities smarter, funnier, and closer to the Ivy League. To get more Jews to apply, those universities advertise in Jewish hangouts.

"Irving Berlin" (whose real name was Israel Baline) was the American Jew who composed subversive songs secularizing Christian holidays:

Christmas is supposed to celebrate Christ's birth, but his song "I'm Dreaming of White Christmas" changed Christmas into a festival about snow.

Easter is supposed to celebrate Christ's resurrection, but his song "Easter Parade" changed Easter into a festival about spring fashions.

Adam Sandler wrote "**The Chanukah Song**," which starts by talking about a Jewish hat (**yarmulke**) and a Chanukah game (**dreidel**) as it drifts into a list of celebrities who are secretly Jewish. His thoughts continue in "**The Chanukah Song Part 2**" and "**The Chanukah Song Part 3**." Here are his main thoughts (as edited by Neil Diamond and me):

Put on your yarmulke:
Celebrate Chanukah!
Go tell Veronica,
"Time now for Chanukah!"
Play your harmonica.
Have a *fun* Chanukah!

Our Chanukah is called
The festival of lights.
Not just one day of gifts,
We get *eight* crazy nights!

Think you're the only kid
Without a Christmas tree?
Well, here's a list of Jews;
They're just like you and me....

No need to deck the halls
With jingle bells that rock,
'Cause you can spin your dreidel
With Captain Kirk and Spock —
Both Jewish!

Winona Ryder drinks
Fine Manischewitz wine,
And then she dreidels Ralph
Lauren and Calvin Klein!

So guess who eats together
At Carnegie's fine deli:
The Bowzer guy from Sha Na Na
And Arthur Fonzarelli!

We even got Ann Landers
And sister called "Dear Abby."
Now Harr'son Ford is half a Jew,
But that is not too shabby!

Paul Newman is half Jewish,
And Goldie Hawn is too.
Just put those two together:
A nice fine-looking Jew!

Len Kravitz is half Jewish
And Courtney Love is too.
Just put those two together:
A funky bad-ass Jew!

Some people really think
That Ebenezer Scrooge is.
He's not, but guess who is:
Amazing — all Three Stooges!

Houdini and Dave Blaine
Escaped with such precision
But still could not avoid
Their painful circumcision.

Alas for O.J. Simpson,
He still is not a Jew.
But we have got the guy
Who voices Scooby Doo!

So many Jews have come
To be on my long list.
Mel Gibson isn't there,
But Jesus Christ sure is!

Adam Sandler's first version appeared on *Saturday Night Live*. See it at:

http://video.yahoo.com/watch/17026/1361291

Hear Neil Diamond sing his own version — with cartoons — at:

www.YouTube.com/watch?v=BOegH4uYe-c

Old Testament

The **Old Testament** is the Jewish part of the Bible. It was written by Jews before Jesus came. It describes the history and thoughts of the Jews up through 432 B.C.

The Jews, Christians, and Muslims all base their religions on the Old Testament, though Christians and Muslims take its details less seriously than Jews do.

Traditional Jews consider the Old Testament to be a collection of 24 books. Christians thought some of those books were too long and divided them into smaller books, so the Old Testament became 39 books:

"Samuel" got divided into 2 parts ("First Samuel" and "Second Samuel").
"Kings" got divided into 2 parts ("First Kings" and "Second Kings").
"Chronicles" got divided in 2 ("First Chronicles" and "Second Chronicles")
"Ezra" got divided in 2 ("Ezra" and "Nehemiah")
"The Twelve" got divided into 12 separate books (one for each prophet)

The first book is called "Genesis" (creation). The next book is called "Exodus" (leaving Egypt). Other popular books are "First Kings" and "Psalms".

If you've read parts of the Old Testament just when you were a kid, look at it again: it looks different when viewed through the eyes of an adult!

The Old Testament was written mainly in Hebrew, though a few passages were written in Aramaic.

Here's how the Old Testament begins. You'll be reading my own translation, which is based on translations by others but more reasonable (better English but not oversimplified). Each paragraph begins with the chapter number and verse number, so you can compare my translation with others....

Creating heaven & earth

1:1 The earth began as a formless, dark void, while God's spirit hovered over its waters. God said, "Let's have light," and there was light. The light pleased him, so he separated it from the darkness and called it "**daytime**." He called the darkness "**night**." There was evening then morning: the first day!

1:6 He said, "Let a dome appear in the waters and separate them," so a dome appeared and separated the waters under it from the waters above. He called the dome "**sky**". There was evening then morning: the second day!

1:9 He said, "Let's gather together the waters under the sky, so dry land will appear." It appeared! He called the dry land "**earth**" and the gathered waters "**seas**." He was pleased. He said, "Let the earth sprout plants (such as fruit trees) having seeds." They sprouted, and he was pleased. There was evening then morning: the third day!

1:14 He said, "Let the sky have lights to distinguish day from night and shine on earth." He made a big light (the **sun**) to rule the day, a smaller light (the **moon**) to rule the night, and tiny lights (the **stars**). He was pleased. There was evening then morning: the fourth day!

1:20 He said, "Let the waters have swarms of living creatures, and let birds fly across the sky." So he created huge sea creatures, every other living creature that moves in the seas, and every bird. He was pleased. He told them all, "Go multiply: fill the seas and sky." There was evening then morning: the fifth day!

1:24 He said, "Let the earth have all kinds of creatures: cattle, creeping things, and wild animals." It happened, and he was pleased. He created, in his image, a man and woman, blessed them, and told them:

Multiply, go all over the earth, and subdue it. Rule over the fish, birds, and every living thing that moves on the earth. I've given you (and all other animals) plants and fruits to eat, and seeds to regenerate.

It happened, and he was pleased. There was evening then morning: the sixth day!

2:1 So the heavens and earth and their contents were all finished.

2:2 On the seventh day, he rested. He blessed that day and honored it!

2:4 That's how the heavens and earth were created!

First man

2:5 When God created the plants, he also created a mist to water them, but there wasn't yet any farmer to help the plants grow (by tilling the soil), so God made a man (**Adam**). God formed Adam from the ground's dust and breathed into Adam's nostrils the breath of life, so Adam became a living being.

2:8 God planted a **garden** in **Eden** (which is in the east) and put Adam there.

2:9 In that **garden of Eden**, God put every tree that looks pleasant and is good for food. He also put there the **Tree of Life** and the **Tree of the Knowledge of Good and Evil**. A river flows through that garden then divides into 4 branches:

The first branch (**Pishon**) flows around the land of Havilah, where there's good gold (and bdellium and onyx stones).

The second branch (**Gihon**) flows around the land of Cush.

The third branch (**Tigris**) flows east of Assyria.

The fourth branch is **Euphrates**.

2:15 God put Adam in the garden to till the soil. God told Adam:

You may eat from every tree in the garden except the Tree of the Knowledge of Good and Evil. If you eat from *that* tree, you'll die the same day!

First woman

2:18 God thought, "Adam shouldn't be alone. I'll make a helper to be his partner." God made all the animals and birds, brought them all to Adam, and let Adam name them; but none was appropriate to be Adam's partner. God put Adam into a deep sleep, took out one of Adam's ribs, filled the hole with flesh, and turned that rib into a woman, whom God brought to Adam.

2:23 Adam said:

This came from my bones and flesh, so I'll call her "**woman**" (which means "from man").

So a man should leave his parents, cling to his wife, and become one flesh with her.

2:25 Adam and his wife were both naked and unashamed.

Snake

3:1 Of all the wild animals, the snake was the craftiest. He asked the woman, "Did God prohibit you from eating from any fruit?"

3:2 She replied:

God said not to eat fruit from the Tree of Knowledge. He said if I eat that fruit or even touch it, I'll die.

3:4 The snake retorted:

You won't die! God knows that when you eat it, your eyes will open and you'll be like him, knowing good and evil.

3:6 So she ate the fruit and gave some to Adam, who also ate. Then their eyes opened: they discovered they were naked. They sewed fig leaves together, to make loincloths for themselves.

3:8They heard God walking through the garden during the evening breeze. They hid themselves in the bushes. God called out to Adam, "Where are you?"

3:10Adam replied, "I heard you, and I was scared because I was naked, so I hid myself."

3:11God retorted, "Who told you that you were naked? Have you eaten from that forbidden tree?"

3:12Adam replied, "The woman you created for me gave me that tree's fruit, and I ate it."

3:13God asked the woman, "What have you done?"

3:13She replied, "The snake tricked me, and I ate."

3:14God told the snake:

> Because you've done this, you're cursed! You'll have to crawl on your belly and eat dust all your life. I'll make you and the woman hate each other. Your offspring and her offspring will hate each other. People will strike your head, and you'll strike their heels.

3:16God told the woman:

> I'll greatly increase your pangs in childbearing, but you'll still want your husband, who'll rule over you.

3:17God told Adam:

> Because you listened to your wife and ate the forbidden fruit, your ground is cursed. You must work hard to farm it, the rest of your life. It will give you thorns and thistles. You'll have to sweat to make bread, until you die and return to the ground, because out of it you were taken. You're dust, and to dust you'll return.

3:20Adam named his wife "**Eve**" (which means "life"), because she was the mother of all living.

3:21God made clothes from animal skins and put the clothes onto Adam & Eve. Then God said:

> See, Adam's become like one of us, knowing good & evil. He might grab fruit from the Tree of Life, eat it, and live forever.

So God banished Adam from the garden of Eden, to till the ground Adam was made from. At the garden of Eden's east side, God placed angels and a flaming, rotating sword, to block the way to the Tree of Life.

First murder

4:1Adam & Eve produced a son. Eve exclaimed, "God helped me produce a man" and called her son "**Cain**" (which means "produced"). Then she produced another son, named "**Abel**."

4:2Cain became a farmer. Abel became a shepherd.

4:3Cain brought God an offering of vegetables. Abel brought God an offering of sheep and their fat.

4:4God appreciated Abel's offering but not Cain's, so Cain got very angry and frowned. God asked him, "Why are you angry and frowning? If you do well, won't you be happy? And if you *don't* do well, you'll be tempted to sin, but you must master it."

4:8Cain told Abel, "Let's go out to the field." In the field, Cain killed Abel.

4:9God asked Cain, "Where's your brother Abel?"

4:9Cain replied, "I don't know. Am I my brother's keeper?"

4:10God asked, "What have you done? Listen, your brother's blood is crying out to me from your hand. Now you're cursed from the ground, which has opened its mouth to receive your brother's blood from your hand. When you till the ground, it will no longer yield you its strength. You'll be a fugitive and wanderer."

4:13Cain replied, "That punishment's too great to bear: you've driven me away from the soil; I'll be hidden from your face; I'll be a fugitive and wanderer, and anyone who finds me may kill me."

4:15God put a mark on Cain, so nobody who saw Cain would kill him. Then Cain went away from God's presence and settled in the land of **Nod** (which means "wandering"), east of Eden.

First civilization

4:17Eventually, Cain got married, had a son named **Enoch**, and built a city named "Enoch" to honor his son. That son, Enoch, fathered Irad, who fathered Mehujael, who fathered Methushael, who fathered **Lamech**.

4:19Lamech had 2 wives:

> One wife (**Adah**) had a son Jabal (the ancestor of ranchers) and a son Jubal (the ancestor of musicians).

> The other wife (**Zillah**) had a son Tubal-cain (who made bronze and iron tools) and a daughter Naamah.

4:23Lamech told his wives, "I've killed a young man because he wounded me. If Cain is avenged sevenfold, truly I'll be avenged seven-sevenfold."

4:25Adam & Eve had a third son. Eve said God appointed that son to replace Abel, so Eve named him the son "**Seth**" (which means "appointed"). Seth, in turn, had a son named Enosh.

4:26People began to talk about God.

5:1People lived long:

> When Seth was born, Adam was already 130 years old. After Seth was born, Adam lived 800 more years (and had other sons and daughters). So altogether, Adam lived 930 years.

> When Seth was 105 years old, he fathered Enosh then lived 807 more years (and had other sons and daughters), so he lived 912 years.

> When Enosh was 90 years old, he fathered Kenan then lived 815 more years (and had other sons and daughters), so he lived 905 years.

> When Kenan was 70 years old, he fathered Mahalalel then lived 840 more years (and had other sons and daughters), so he lived 910 years.

> When Mahalalel was 65 years old, he fathered Jared then lived 830 more years (and had other sons and daughters), so he lived 895 years.

> When Jared was 162 years old, he fathered Enoch then lived 800 more years (and had other sons and daughters), so he lived 962 years.

> When Enoch was 65 years old, he fathered Methuselah then lived 300 more years (and had other sons and daughters), so he lived 365 years.

> When Methuselah was 187 years old, he fathered Lamech then lived 782 more years (and had other sons and daughters), so he lived 969 years.

> When Lamech was 182 years old, he fathered **Noah** (and said "Out of the ground that God cursed, this one shall bring us relief from our toil") then lived 595 more years (and had other sons and daughters), so he lived 777 years.

> After Noah was 500 years old, he fathered Shem, Ham, and Japheth.

Flood

6:1As the population grew, men started taking as many wives as they wanted. God got upset and limited human lifespan to 120 years. He also saw humans contained great wickedness, and the humans' thoughts were continually evil. God became sorry he'd made humans; it grieved his heart. He said, "I'll blot out the humans I've created — and animals and birds — because I'm sorry I made them."

6:8But God was pleased about Noah (who was a righteous man, blameless, and walked with God), so God told Noah:

> I've decided to end all people, because they've filled the earth with violence. I'm going to destroy them and the earth.
> Make an ark of cypress wood. Make rooms in it. Coat it with pitch (to waterproof it), inside and out.
> Make it 450 feet long, 75 feet wide, and 45 feet high. Make a roof, but you can leave an 18-inch gap below it (for windows). Make a door to enter the ark. Make 3 decks: lower, middle, and upper.
> I'm going to flood the earth and destroy all flesh. Everything on earth will die. But I'll establish my covenant with you, and you'll enter the ark with your wife, sons, and sons' wives. You'll bring 2 of every kind of living thing into the ark, to keep them alive; bring male and female. Include birds and other animals, even the ones that creep along the ground, to keep them alive. Take every kind of food that's eaten, and store it for you and the animals.

6:22Noah built the ark as God commanded.

^{7:1}Then God said:

> Enter the ark with your family, since I've seen you alone are righteous before me in this generation.
>
> Take with you 7 pairs of each clean animal (the male and its mate), 1 pair of each unclean animal, and 7 pairs of each flying bird.
>
> 7 days from now, I'll start raining on the earth for 40 days & 40 nights. I'll wipe off the face of the earth every living creature I've made.

^{7:5}Noah did what God had commanded.

^{7:6}Noah was 600 years old when the flood of waters came onto the earth. The rain continued 40 days. The waters increased and bore up the ark, so it floated high above the earth. The waters swelled so mightily that they covered even the tallest mountains and were 22 feet higher than them.

^{7:21}All flesh that moved on earth died, including all birds, domestic animals, wild animals, crawling creatures, and people. Everything living on dry land — and whose nostrils held the breath of life — died. Just Noah and the ark's other inhabitants survived.

^{7:24}The floodwaters stayed on the land for 150 days....

10 commandments (from "Exodus")

^{20:1}God said, "I'm the Lord, your God, who brought you out of Egypt and slavery." He gave these **10 commandments**:

> 1. **Don't put other gods before me.**
>
> 2. **Don't make an idol.** Don't make an idol of anything in heaven or on earth or in the water. Don't bow down to an idol or worship it, since I'm your God and a jealous God, punishing children for the wrongdoings of their parents, to the third and fourth generation of those who reject me. But I show steadfast love, to the thousandth generation, of those who love me and keep my commandments.
>
> 3. **Don't misuse God's name**, since I won't acquit anyone who misuses my name.
>
> 4. **Keep the Sabbath day holy.** For 6 days you'll labor and do all your work. But on the 7th day, which is a Sabbath to God, you must not do any work, and neither must your children, servants, livestock, or visitors. In 6 days, I made heaven and earth, the sea, and all that's in them; but I rested on the 7th day, so I blessed the Sabbath day and made it holy.
>
> 5. **Honor your parents**, so your own days may be long in the land the Lord is giving you.
>
> 6. **Don't murder.**
>
> 7. **Don't commit adultery.**
>
> 8. **Don't steal.**
>
> 9. **Don't give false testimony** against your neighbor.
>
> 10. **Don't be jealous** of your neighbor's house, wife, servants, ox, donkey, or anything else that belongs to your neighbor.

^{20:18}When all the people saw the thunder & lightning, heard the trumpet, and saw the mountain smoking, they were scared, trembled, stood at a distance, and told Moses, "You speak to us, and we'll listen; but don't let God speak to us, or we'll die." Moses replied, "Don't be scared. God's come just to test you and make you fear him, so you don't sin."

^{20:21}The people stayed at a distance, while Moses approached the thick darkness where God was....

Solomon's judgment (from "First Kings")

^{3:16}Two women who were prostitutes stood before King Solomon.

^{3:17}The first woman said:

> Please, my lord, the other woman and I live together in the same brothel house. While we were in the house, I gave birth to a son. Three days later, she gave birth to a son also. During that time, she, I, and those sons were the only people in the house. Then her son died in the night, because she lay on him. She got up in the middle of the night and took my son from beside me while I was sleeping. She laid him at her breast and laid *her* dead son at *my* breast. In the morning, when I arose to nurse the son at my breast, I saw he was dead; but when I looked at him more closely, I noticed he wasn't my own son.

^{3:22}But the other woman said to her:

> No, the living son is mine; the dead son is yours.

The two women argued, back and forth.

^{3:23}The king said:

> These women disagree. Bring me a sword.

His assistants brought a sword. He said:

> Divide the living boy in two. Give half to one woman and half to the other.

^{3:26}The woman whose son was alive had burning compassion for her son, so she told the king:

> Please give the living boy to the other woman. Don't kill him!"

^{3:27}The king gave his ruling:

> Give the first woman the living boy; don't kill him. She's his mother.

^{3:28}All Israel heard of the king's judgment and stood in awe of him, because they saw he had wisdom from God to administer justice....

2 ways (from "Psalms")

^{1:1}Happy are those who don't follow advice of the wicked, or the path of sinners, or sit in the seat of scoffers. Instead, they delight in God's law and meditate on it always, day and night. They're like trees planted by streams and bearing fruit in season. Their leaves don't wither.

^{1:4}The wicked, by contrast, are like chaff that the wind drives away. The wicked can't withstand God's judgment; sinners won't be allowed to stand in the righteous congregation. God watches over the way of the righteous, but the way of the wicked will perish....

Divine shepherd (from "Psalms")

^{23:1}The Lord's my shepherd. He's all I need. He has me lie down in green pastures, leads me beside quiet waters, restores my soul, and leads me in right paths.

^{23:4}Though I walk through the darkest valley, I fear no evil, since you, o Lord, are with me. Your rod & staff comfort me. When my enemies are present, you prepare a table for me and anoint my head with oil: my cup overflows.

^{23:6}Goodness and mercy will follow me the rest of my life, and I'll live in the Lord's house forever.

Enter (from "Psalms")

^{24:1}The Lord owns the earth, all that's in it, and all who live on it. He built it on the seas and rivers.

^{24:3}Who'll climb his hill and stand in his holy place? He who has clean hands & a pure heart and lacks false idols & false oaths! The Lord will bless him and save him. That's the company of those who seek the face of Jacob's God.

^{24:7}Lift your heads, you ancient gates, so the glorious King may enter!

^{24:8}Who's that King of glory? The Lord, strong and mighty in battle! Lift your heads, you ancient gates, to let in the glorious King, the Lord of hosts: he's the King of glory....

New Testament

The **New Testament** was written by Christians. It tells the history and thoughts of Jesus and his early followers. It was finished in 95 A.D.

It includes 27 books.

The first book is called "Matthew". It was written by Matthew and explains Jesus's life. The next 3 books, written by Mark, Luke, and John, give their own version's of Jesus's life.

Even if you're Jewish or Muslim, you'll enjoy reading the New Testament, since it includes great ideas, which have become famous quotes! If you've read parts of the New Testament just when you were a kid, look at it again: it looks different when viewed through the eyes of an adult!

The New Testament was written mainly in Greek, though a few passages were written in Hebrew and Aramaic.

Here's how the New Testament begins, starting with "Matthew". You'll be reading my own translation, which is based on translations by others....

Jesus's ancestors

[1:1]Here's the genealogy of Jesus the Messiah, who descended from King David, who descended from Abraham:

> Abraham fathered Isaac, who fathered Jacob, who fathered Judah, who fathered Perez, who fathered Hezron, who fathered Aram, who fathered Aminadab, who fathered Nahshon, who fathered Salmon, who fathered Boaz, who fathered Obed, who fathered Jesse, who fathered King David.
>
> David fathered Solomon, who fathered Rehoboam, who fathered Abijah, who fathered Asaph, who fathered Jehoshphat, who fathered Joram, who fathered Uzziah, who fathered Jothan, wo fathered Ahaz, who fathered Hezekiah, who fathered Manasseh, who fathered Amos, who fathered Josiah, who fathered Jechoniah while the people of Israel were deported to Babylon.
>
> After the deportation, Jechoniah fathered Salathiel, who fathered Zerubbabel, who fathered Abiud, who fathered Eliakim, who fathered Azor, who fathered Zadok, who fathered Achim, who fathered Eliud, who fathered Eleazar, who fathered Matthan, who fathered Jacob, who fathered Joseph, who married Mary (the mother of Jesus the Messiah).

So there were 14 generations from Abraham to King David, 14 generations from King David to the deportation, and 14 generations from Babylon to the Messiah.

How Jesus was born

[1:18]When Mary (Jesus's mother) was engaged to Joseph but not yet living with him, she got pregnant from the Holy Spirit. Since Joseph was a righteous man who didn't want to expose her to public disgrace, he planned to leave Mary, quietly; but just after he decided to do that, an angel told him in a dream:

> Joseph, don't be afraid to marry Mary, for the child in her is from the Holy Spirit. She'll have a son, and you're to name him "**Jesus**," because he'll save his people from their sins.

That fulfilled what God had said through his prophet Isaiah (in Isaiah 7:14):

> Look, the virgin shall have a son, and they'll name him Emmanuel (which means "God is with us").

When Joseph awoke from that dream, he did what the angel commanded: he married Mary but had no sex with her until she had a son, whom he named "**Jesus**" (which means "God saves").

Wise men

[2:1]After Jesus was born in Bethlehem of Judea, **wise men** from the East came to Jerusalem and asked, "Where's the child who's been born King of the Jews? We saw his star, in the sky, rising, and we've come to praise him."

[2:3]When King Herod heard of that, he was scared, and so was all of Jerusalem. Herod called together all the chief priests and scribes and asked them where the Messiah would be born. They said Bethlehem, because the prophet Micah had written (in Micah 5:2):

> You, Bethlehem, in the land of Judea, are by no means the least among the rulers of Judah; for from you shall come a ruler who'll shepherd my people Israel.

[2:7]Then Herod secretly called for the wise men and learned from them exactly when the star had appeared. He sent them to Bethlehem and said:

> Search diligently for the child. When you've found him, tell me so I can go also to visit him and praise him.

[2:9]So the wise men set out, following the star they'd seen rising, until it stopped over the place where the child was. When they saw the star stop, they were overwhelmed with joy. They entered the house, they saw the child with his mother (Mary), so they knelt down to honor him. Then they opened their treasure chests: they offered him gifts of gold, frankincense, and myrrh.

[2:12]A dream had warned them not to return to Herod, so they left for their own country by a different road.

[2:13]After they left, an angel told Joseph in a dream, "Flee to Egypt, with the child and Mary, and stay there until I tell you, because Herod wants to find the child and destroy him." So Joseph got up, took the child and Mary that night to Egypt and stayed there until Herod's death. That was to fulfill what God said through the prophet Hosea (in Hosea 11:1):

> Out of Egypt I've called my son.

Killing children

[2:16]When Herod discovered that the wise men tricked him, he was furious. He killed all Bethlehem-area children who were under age 3. That fulfilled Jeremiah's prophesy (in Jeremiah 31:15):

> In the town of Ramah, a voice was heard wailing loudly.
> It was Rachel weeping for her children.
> She refused to be consoled, because they are gone.

Return from Egypt

[2:19]When Herod died, an angel told Joseph in a dream, "Take Jesus & Mary back to Israel, because those who wanted to kill him are dead." So Joseph took Jesus & Mary back to Israel. But when he heard that Herod's son (Archelaus) had become Judea's king, he got scared and went away to **Galilee** (a district in a different part of Israel), where he settled in a town called **Nazareth**, as instructed by another angel in a dream. That fulfilled what prophets had said about Jesus:

> He'll be called a Nazarene.

John the Baptist

3:1John the Baptist appeared in Judea's wilderness and proclaimed, "Repent, because heaven's kingdom is coming near." He's the one about whom the prophet Isaiah had said (in Isaiah 40:3):

> A voice cries out in the wilderness, "Prepare God's way, clear a straight path for him."

3:4John's clothes were made of camel's hair. He wore a leather belt. He ate **locusts** (nasty grasshoppers) and honey.

3:5People from Jerusalem (and all Judea and all along the Jordan River) were going out to him. He baptized them in the Jordan River, as they confessed their sins.

3:7But when he saw many Pharisees and Sadducees come for baptism, he told them:

> You brood of snakes! Who warned you to flee from the wrath to come? Do acts showing you're repenting. Don't try to excuse yourselves by saying you're Abraham's descendents, for God can make more of Abraham's descendents even from stones. Already the ax lies at the trees' roots; every tree that doesn't bear good fruit is cut down and thrown into the fire. I baptize you with water for repentance, but one who's more powerful than I is coming after me. I'm not worthy to carry his sandals. He'll baptize you with the Holy Spirit and fire. His winnowing shovel is in his hand: he'll clear his threshing floor and gather his wheat into the barn but burn the chaff with unquenchable fire.

3:13Jesus came to John and asked John to baptize him. John objected, "I need to be baptized by *you*, not you by me!" But Jesus insisted, so John consented.

3:16When Jesus was baptized and came up from the water, suddenly the heavens opened to Jesus and he saw God's Spirit descend like a dove and land on him. A voice from heaven said:

> This is my Son, the Beloved, with whom I'm well pleased.

Temptation

4:1Then the Spirit led Jesus into the wilderness to be tempted by the devil.

4:2Jesus fasted 40 days and 40 nights. Then he was hungry.

4:3The devil tempted him by saying, "If you're God's Son, command these stones to become loaves of bread." But Jesus replied:

> The Bible says (in Deuteronomy 8:3), "A person doesn't live just on bread but on every word from God's mouth."

4:5Then the devil took him to the holy city, put him on the temple's **pinnacle** (prong atop the roof), and said:

> If you're God's Son, throw yourself down, because the Bible says (in Psalms 91:11) "God will command his angels to care for you" and "On their hands they'll bear you up, so you won't even hurt your foot against a stone."

Jesus replied:

> The Bible says (in Deuteronomy 6:16), "Don't test God."

4:8The devil took him to a very tall mountain, showed him all the world's kingdoms and their splendor, and said:

> I'll give you all these if you fall down and worship me.

Jesus replied:

> Away with you, Satan! For the Bible says (in Deuteronomy 6:13), "Worship God and serve just him."

4:11Then the devil left him. Suddenly, angels came and waited on Jesus.

Jesus begins preaching

4:12Jesus heard John had been arrested, so Jesus fled back to the district of Galilee. He moved from the town of Nazareth to the town of **Capernaum** (which is by the Sea of Galilee, in the territory of Zebulun and Naphtali), to fulfill Isaiah's prophesy (in Isaiah 9:1):

> In the land of Zebulun and Naphtali,
> the people who'd sat in darkness saw a great light.
> Yes, for the people who'd sat there in death's shadow, light dawned.

4:17Like John the Baptist, Jesus started proclaiming, "Repent, because heaven's kingdom is coming near."

4:18While Jesus was walking by the Sea of Galilee, he saw a pair of fishermen: **Simon** (nicknamed "Peter") and Simon's brother (**Andrew**). Those fishermen were casting their net into the sea, to catch fish. Jesus said, "Follow me! I'll teach you to catch people!" The fishermen immediately left their nets and followed Jesus.

4:21Then Jesus saw two more fishermen (**James** & **John**) who were mending nets in a boat with their dad (Zebedee). Jesus called them. James & John left their boat & dad and followed Jesus.

4:23Jesus traveled throughout Galilee. He taught in the people's synagogues and proclaimed the good news of God's coming kingdom. He cured every disease among the people. His fame spread throughout all Syria. People brought him all the sick (those afflicted with disease, pain, demons, epilepsy, and paralysis), and he cured them. He was followed by great crowds, who flocked to him from Galilee, the **Decapolis** (a group of 10 cities having Greek & Roman culture), Jerusalem, Judea, and beyond the Jordan River.

5:1When he saw those crowds, he went up the mountain. After he sat down, his disciples came to him. He began teaching them, by giving the **Sermon on the Mount**.

5:2He began the sermon by saying these **beatitudes** (expressions of being blessedly happy):

> Blessed are the dispirited, for they'll have heaven's kingdom.
> Blessed are the mourners, for they'll be comforted.
> Blessed are the meek, for they'll inherit the earth.
> Blessed are those hungry & thirsting for righteousness, for they'll be filled.
> Blessed are the merciful, for they'll receive mercy.
> Blessed are the pure in heart, for they'll see God.
> Blessed are the peacemakers, for they'll be called God's children.
> Blessed are those persecuted for being righteous: they'll have heaven's kingdom.
>
> Blessed are you when people revile you and persecute you and utter all kinds of evil against you falsely on my account. Rejoice and be glad, for your reward is great in heaven, though you've been persecuted like the prophets before you.

5:13Then he said the disciples should try to stay **effective**. He warned them to **avoid becoming tasteless salt**:

> You're the earth's salt; but if salt has lost its taste, how can its saltiness be restored? The salt's no longer good for anything: it's thrown out and trampled under foot.

He told them to **light up the world**:

> You're the world's light, a hilltop city that can't be hid. After lighting a lamp, nobody hides it under a bushel basket but instead puts it on the lamp stand, so it lights everyone in the house. In the same way, let your light shine before others, so they can see your good works and glorify your Father in heaven.

5:17He said to **build on existing law**, not destroy it:

> Don't think I've come to abolish the laws of Moses & prophets; I've come not to abolish but to fulfill. As long as heaven and earth last, not one iota will pass from the law until all is accomplished. So whoever breaks a commandment and teaches others to do likewise will be called the "lowest" in heaven's kingdom; but whoever obeys & teaches the commandments will be called "great" in heaven's kingdom. Unless you're more righteous than the scribes and Pharisees, you'll never enter heaven's kingdom.

5:21 He said to **control anger**:

In ancient times, people were told (in Exodus 20:13 and Deuteronomy 5:17) "You shall not murder" and "Whoever murders shall be subject to judgment." But I say, you'll be subject to judgment even if you're just *angry* with a person or insult him or say "You fool." So when you're offering your gift at the altar, if you remember a person has something against you, leave your gift off the altar, go reconcile with that person, then return to the altar to offer your gift. Come to terms quickly with your accuser while you're on the way to court with him, to avoid having the accuser pass you to the judge, who'll pass you to the guard, who'll throw you in prison until you've paid the last penny.

5:27 He said to **control lust**:

People were told (in Exodus 20:14 and Deuteronomy 5:18) "Don't commit adultery." But I say, each man who looks at a woman lustfully has already committed adultery with her in his heart. If your right eye makes you sin, tear it out and throw it away; it's better for you to lose one of your body parts than for your whole body to be thrown in hell. Similarly, if your right hand makes you sin, cut it off and throw it away.

5:31 He said to **avoid divorce**:

Men were told (in Deuteronomy 24:1), "If your divorce your wife, give her a divorce certificate." But I say, if a man divorces a wife who's been chaste, he makes her commit adultery; and whoever marries a divorced woman commits adultery.

5:33 He said to **avoid swearing**:

People were told (in Numbers 30:2), "Don't swear falsely; carry out the vows you made to God." But I say, don't swear *at all!* Don't swear by heaven (since it's God's throne); don't swear by the earth (since it's his footstool); don't swear by Jerusalem (for it's the great King's city); don't swear by your head (since you can't make one hair white or black). Say just "Yes, yes" or "No, no"; anything more than that comes from the evil one.

5:38 He said to **avoid revenge**:

People were told (in Exodus 21:24, Leviticus 24:20, and Deuteronomy 19:21), "An eye for an eye, and a tooth for a tooth." But I say, don't resist an evildoer. If anyone strikes your right cheek, turn the other cheek also. If anyone wants to sue you and take your coat, give your cloak also. If anyone forces you to go a mile, go the second mile also. Give to everyone who begs from you, and don't refuse anyone who wants to borrow from you.

5:43 He said to **love the enemies**:

People were told (in Deuteronomy 19:18), "Love your neighbor and hate your enemy." But I say, *love* your enemies and pray for people who persecute you, so you can be children of your Father in heaven. He lovingly makes his sun rise above both the evildoers & the good; he sends rain to both the righteous & the unrighteous. If you love just those who love you, you deserve no reward: you're no better than a tax collector. If you greet just friends, you deserve no reward, since even pagans do that. So be perfect, like your heavenly Father.

6:1 He said to **act quietly**:

When you're being pious, are you doing so publicly just to show off? Then you'll get no reward from your Father in heaven. Whenever you donate to the poor, don't sound a trumpet about it to get praise from others, as hypocrites do in the synagogues and streets. When you donate, don't let your left hand know what your right hand is doing: donate secretly. Your Father, who's watching secretly, will reward you.

Similarly, when you pray, don't be like the hypocrites: they pray in synagogues and at street corners, just to be seen by others. Whenever you pray, go into your room: shut the door and pray to your Father secretly; he'll reward you.

When you pray, don't heap up empty phrases, like the pagans do. They think they'll be heard because of their many words. Don't imitate them! Your Father knows what you need before you ask him.

6:9 He said to **give this prayer**:

Our Father in heaven,
  May your name be kept holy.
May your kingdom come.
  May your will be done
  On earth as it is in heaven.
Give us today our daily bread,
  And forgive what we owe,
  As we've forgiven what people owe us.
Don't bring us to temptation,
  But rescue us from evil,
  Because the kingdom, power, and glory are yours forever.
Amen.

He explained why that prayer says to forgive:

If you forgive others for the wrongs they've done you, your heavenly Father will forgive *you* also. If you *don't* forgive other people, your Father won't forgive *you!*

6:16 He said to **fast secretly**:

When you fast, don't look dismal, like the hypocrites who disfigure their faces to show others they're fasting. When you fast, still shampoo your hair and wash your face, so you'll normal and other people won't know you're fasting. Your Father will notice you secretly and reward you.

6:19 He said to **avoid materialism**:

Don't save treasures here on earth, where moths and rust consume, and where thieves break in and steal. Instead, save treasures in heaven. Heavenly treasures are permanent. Your heart will be where your treasures are.

6:22 He said that to be wise, **observe carefully**:

The eye is the body's lamp. If your eye is healthy, your whole body fills with light. If your eye is unhealthy, your whole body fills with great darkness.

6:24 He said to **serve God instead of wealth**:

Nobody can serve two masters. Such a slave would either hate the first master and love the second or be devoted to the second and despise the first. You can't serve both God and wealth.

Don't worry so much about your body and what you'll eat, drink, and wear. Isn't life more than food, and the body more than clothing? Look at the birds: they don't farm or store food, but God feeds them; and doesn't he consider you more valuable than they? Will worrying add a single hour to your lifespan? Consider how wild lilies grow: they don't spin cloth, but they're clothed even more beautifully than King Solomon's glory. If God clothes wild grasses, which are alive today but are thrown in the oven tomorrow, won't he clothe you even better?

So don't worry about what to eat, drink, or wear. Pagans strive for those things. God knows you need them, but strive first for God's kingdom and righteousness; then he'll give you the other things also.

Don't worry about tomorrow, since tomorrow will bring worries of its own. Today's trouble is enough for today.

7:1 He said to **speak kindly to others**:

Don't judge other people harshly, lest you be judged harshly also. God will judge you by how you judge others; the measure you give will be the measure you get.

Why do you notice the speck in your neighbor's eye but ignore the log in *your* eye? Why do you tell your neighbor "I want to remove the speck from your eye" when the log is in *your* eye?

You hypocrite! First remove the log from *your* eye, then you'll see clearly enough to take the speck out of your neighbor's eye.

7:6 He said to **avoid cheapening God's message**:

Don't give the holy to dogs; and don't throw your pearls before pigs, who'll trample them and turn and maul you.

7:7 He said to **keep trying to do good deeds**:

> If you ask, you'll receive. If you search, you'll find. If you knock, the door will open.
>
> If your child asks for bread, would you give just a stone? If the child asks for a fish, would you give a snake? Just as you know how to give good gifts to your children, so does God give good things to those who ask.
>
> Obey the **Golden Rule**, which says: do for other people what you'd want them to do for *you*. That's the rule of the *Five Books of Moses* and the prophets.
>
> Enter through the *narrow* gate. The wider gate and easy road lead to destruction, and many people take it; the narrow gate and hard road lead to life, and few find it.

7:15 He said to **beware of false prophets**:

> Beware of false prophets, who come to you in sheep's clothing but inwardly are hungry wolves. You'll know them by their fruits.
>
> Do grapes come from thorns, or figs from thistles? No! Every good tree bears just good fruit; every bad tree bears just bad fruit. Every tree that doesn't bear good fruit is cut down and thrown in the fire, so you'll know the false prophets by the fruits of their acts.

7:21 He said to **produce good deeds, not just words**:

> To enter heaven, calling me "Lord" is not enough; you must do the will of my Father in heaven.
>
> On the day of reckoning, many will beg me, "Lord, Lord, didn't we prophesy in your name, cast out demons in your name, and do many deeds of power in your name?"
>
> I'll reply, "I never knew you. Go away, you evildoers!"

7:24 He finished with this warning:

> Everyone who's heard my words and acts on them will be like a wise man who built his house on rock. The rain fell, the floods came, and the winds blew and beat on that house; but it didn't fall, because it had been founded on rock.
>
> Everyone who's heard my words and does *not* act on them will be like a foolish man who built his house on sand. The rain fell, the floods came, the winds blew and beat against that house, and the house fell, dramatically!

7:28 The crowds were astounded at Jesus' sermon, because he taught as one having authority, unlike their scribes.

8:1 When Jesus came down from the mountain, great crowds followed him.

Miraculous healing

8:2A **leper** knelt before Jesus and said, "Lord, if you choose, you can make me clean." Jesus touched the leper and replied, "I do choose. Be made clean!" Instantly his leprosy disappeared. Jesus told him, "Don't mention my actions to anyone. Instead, do what Moses commanded (in Leviticus 14:2): get examined by a priest then give an offering, so people will know you're clean."

8:5 When Jesus entered Capernaum, a **centurion** (leader of 100 Roman soldiers) told him, "Lord, my servant is bedridden, paralyzed, and in terrible distress." Jesus replied, "I'll come cure him." The centurion replied, "Lord, I'm not worthy to have you come under my roof; heal my servant by just giving a command. Like you, I have an authority over me, with soldiers under me who obey my commands." That reply amazed Jesus, who told followers, "I've never seen such a faithful person in Israel! Many foreigners will eat with Abraham, Isaac, and Jacob in heaven, while Israelis will be thrown into the outer darkness, where there will be weeping and gnashing of teeth." He told the centurion, "Go; let it be done for you according to your faith," and the servant was healed within an hour.

8:14 In **Peter's house**, Jesus saw Peter's mother-in-law was bedridden with a fever. Jesus touched her hand. The fever left her. She got up and began to serve him. That evening, people brought him many people possessed by demons; he cast out the sprits with a word and cured all the sick. That fulfilled Isaiah's prophecy (in Isaiah 53:4):

> He took our infirmities and bore our diseases.

9:1 Jesus performed more miracles, gave more sermons, collected more disciples, and did many things that upset Jewish leaders. He expected he'd be crucified....

Plot to kill Jesus

26:1 Jesus told his disciples, "You know Passover is coming two days from now — and I'll be handed over to be crucified."

26:3 Jewish leaders met in the palace of the top Jewish rabbi (a man named **Caiaphas**). They conspired to secretly arrest Jesus and kill him. But they decided to wait until after the Passover festival, to avoid having Jesus's admirers riot.

Anointed in Bethany

26:6 When Jesus was in the town of Bethany, at the house of Simon the Leper, a woman came to Jesus with a jar of costly ointment, which she poured on his head as he sat at the table.

26:8 The disciples angrily muttered to her, "Why such waste? That ointment could have been sold for a lot of money, which we could have donated to the poor!" But Jesus criticized their thinking; he said:

> Why do you trouble this woman? She's performed a good service for me. You'll always have the poor with you, but you'll not always have me. By pouring that ointment on my body, she's prepared me for burial. She'll become famous for it.

Judas agrees to betray Jesus

26:14 One of Jesus's 12 disciples — the one named Judas Iscariot — went to the chief Jewish rabbis and asked, "What will you pay me to betray Jesus?" They gave him 30 silver coins. He began seeking an opportunity to betray Jesus.

Passover

26:17 On Passover's first day, the disciples asked Jesus, "Where do you want to have Passover dinner?" Jesus told them to go into Jerusalem and tell a certain man that Jesus and the disciples would dine at that man's house. The disciples did so and prepared the dinner at the man's house.

26:20 That evening, Jesus joined the disciples for what would turn out to be his **last supper**. While they were all eating, Jesus said, "One of you will betray me." That comment distressed the disciples. One after another, the disciples began asking him, "Surely not I, Lord?" He replied:

> The one who's dipped his hand into the bowl with me will betray me. I'll go as the Bible says I will, but woe to the person who betrays me! It would have been better for that person to not have been born.

26:25 Judas, who betrayed him, asked, "Surely not I, Rabbi?" Jesus replied, "So you say."

26:26 While they were eating, Jesus grabbed a bread loaf, blessed it, split it, gave the pieces to his disciples, and said:

> Eat it: it's my body.

He grabbed a cup of wine, gave thanks, passed that cup of wine to his disciples, and said:

> You all drink from it: it's my covenant's blood, poured out for the many, to forgive sins. I won't drink more wine until the day I drink with you in heaven.

26:30 The group chanted a Passover hymn then went to the **Mount of Olives** (a mountain ridge on Jerusalem's east side), where Jesus told the disciples:

> You'll all desert me tonight, because the Bible says (in Zechariah 13:7) "I'll kill the shepherd, then all his sheep will run away." But after I'm raised up, I'll lead you to Galilee.

26:33 Peter said, "Though the others will desert you, I'll never desert you." Jesus told Peter:

> Tonight, before the cock crows, you'll deny me 3 times.

26:35Peter replied, "I won't deny you, even if I must die with you." The other disciples said the same words.

26:36Jesus led the disciples to **Gethsemane** (a garden at the bottom of the Mount of Olives), where he told them, "Sit here while I go over there to pray."

26:37He took along 3 disciples (Peter and Zebedee's two sons) and told them:

> I'm deeply grieved, even to death. Stay here, awake with me.

He went a little farther, threw himself on the ground, and prayed:

> Dear Father, if possible, let this cup of responsibility pass from me; but I'll do whatever you want.

26:40He returned to the 3 disciples but found they'd nodded off. He woke Peter by saying:

> So you couldn't stay awake with me an hour? Stay away, and pray you don't get tempted. The spirit is willing, but the flesh is weak.

26:42Jesus went away again and prayed:

> Dear Father, if this cup can't pass unless I drink it, your will be done.

When Jesus returned, he found the 3 disciples sleeping again. He left them, repeated his prayer, returned to them, and asked them:

> Are you still sleeping? The hour is at hand. I've been betrayed into the hands of sinners. Get up! Let's go! See, my betrayer is at hand.

26:47While he was saying that, Judas arrived, along with a big mob sent by the Jewish leaders and carrying swords and clubs. Judas had told the mob he'd signal them which man to arrest by kissing him; so he came up to Jesus, said "Greetings, Rabbi," and kissed him. Jesus replied:

> Friend, do what you're here to do.

The mob laid hands on Jesus and arrested him.

26:51Suddenly, Peter drew his sword and cut an ear off Caiaphas's slave. But Jesus told Peter:

> Put your sword back into its place, because all who rely on the sword will die by the sword. If I ask my Father, he'd immediately send me over 12 legions of angels to protect me; but then the Biblical prophesy wouldn't be fulfilled.

26:55Jesus asked the mob:

> Have you come out with swords and clubs to arrest me as though I were a bandit? Day after day, I sat in the temple teaching, and you didn't arrest me. But this has happened so the Biblical prophesy may be fulfilled.

Then all the disciples deserted him and fled.

26:57The mob took him to Caiaphas. Peter followed him, at a distance, and sat with the guards in Caiaphas' courtyard.

26:59Caiaphas and the **Sanhedrin** (Jewish council) put Jesus on trial. They wanted to hear **testimony against Jesus** that would justify putting Jesus to death but heard none, though many false witnesses came forward. Finally two witnesses claimed Jesus said "I can destroy God's temple and rebuild it in 3 days." Caiaphas asked Jesus to reply to that charge, but Jesus remained silent. Then Caiaphas told him, "I put you under oath to tell us if you're the Messiah, the Son of God." Jesus replied:

> So you say; but from now on you'll see me seated at God's right hand and coming on heaven's clouds.

26:65Caiaphas exclaimed:

> He's blasphemed! Why do we need more witnesses? You've heard his blasphemy now. What's your verdict?

26:66The Sanhedrin members replied:

> He deserves death.

They spat in his face and struck him. Some slapped him and taunted him by saying:

> Prophesy to us, you Messiah! Who struck you?

Peter's denial

26:69While Peter was sitting in the courtyard, a servant girl came to him and said, "You too were with Jesus," but he denied it to the group and said, "I don't know what you're talking about."

26:71He went out to the porch, where another servant girl saw him and told bystanders, "This man was with Jesus." Again he denied it with an oath and said, "I don't know the man."

26:73The bystanders replied, "Certainly you're also one of them, because your accent betrays you." Then he began cursing, swore an oath, and said, "I don't know the man!"

26:74At that moment, the cock crowed. He remembered what Jesus had said:

> Before the cock crows, you'll deny me 3 times.

He went out and wept bitterly.

Pontius Pilate

27:1During the morning, the Sanhedrin voted to execute Jesus, so he was bound and taken to **Pontius Pilate** (the Roman official who was Israel's governor).

27:3When Judas saw Jesus was condemned, Judas repented.

> Judas brought the 30 silver coins back to the Jewish leaders and said, "I've sinned by betraying innocent blood." But they replied, "What's that to us? Take care of it yourself." Judas threw the silver coins down onto the temple floor, departed, and hanged himself. The rabbis picked up the coins but decided "it's unlawful to put them in the treasury, since they're blood money," so the rabbis used them to buy the potter's field as a place to bury foreigners. That's why the field's still called the Field of Blood. It fulfills the prophesy (from Jeremiah but mainly from Zechariah 11:12-13).

27:11Pilate asked Jesus, "Are you the King of the Jews?" Jesus replied, "So you say."

27:12The Sanhedrin said a list of accusations against Jesus, but Jesus didn't reply.

27:13Pilate asked him, "Don't you hear how many accusations they make against you?" But Jesus remained silent. Pilate was amazed.

27:15Each Passover, Pilate customarily released one prisoner, whomever the crowd preferred. On that particular Passover, one of the prisoners was **Barabbas** (who'd led a heroic rebellion against Rome). Pilate asked the crowd, "Whom do you want me to release: Barabbas or Jesus-called-the-Christ?" He realized that the Jewish leaders had arrested Jesus Christ just because the they envied Jesus.

27:19While Pilate was waiting for the crowd to choose, his wife sent him this message: "Have nothing to do with that innocent man (Jesus Christ), since last night I dreamt he made me suffer a lot."

27:20The Jewish leaders persuaded the crowd to ask for Barabbas and let Jesus be killed.

27:21Pilate asked the crowd again, "Which of the two do you want me to release?" The crowd replied, 'Barabbas!"

27:22Pilate asked the crowd, "Then what should I do with Jesus-called-the-Christ?" The crowd all said, "Crucify him!"

27:23Pilate asked, "Why, what evil has he done?" But the crowd just shouted even louder, "Crucify him!"

27:24When Pilate saw the crowd was starting to riot and couldn't have its mind changed, he poured water on his hands, washed them in front of the crowd, and said, "I'm innocent of this man's blood; take care of it yourselves." The crowd replied, "His blood be on us and on our children!" Pilate released Barabbas, flogged Jesus, and handed Jesus to soldiers, who took Jesus into Pilate's headquarters, gathered a group around Jesus, stripped him, put a scarlet robe on him, and, after twisting some thorns to make a crown, put it on his head. They put a reed in his right hand, knelt before him, and mocked him by saying, "Hail, King of the Jews!" They spat on him, took the reed, and struck him on the head. They stripped the robe off him, put his own clothes back on him, and led him away to be crucified. They forced a passer-by (Simon from Cyrene) to carry Jesus's cross.

27:33When they came to a place called **Golgotha** (which means "Place of a Skull"), they offered Jesus wine mixed with **gall** (a pain-killing narcotic). He tasted it but didn't drink it.

Crucifixion

27:35They stripped him, **crucified** him (nailed him to the cross), and divided his clothes among themselves by casting lots. Then they sat and kept watch over him. Above his head, they posted a board announcing his offense: "This is Jesus, King of the Jews." Along with him, they crucified two bandits (one on his right, the other on his left).

27:39Passers-by derided him by shaking their heads and saying:

You said you'd destroy the temple and rebuild it in 3 days. Save *yourself!* If you're God's Son, come down from the cross.

The chief priests, scribes, and elders mocked him by saying:

He "saved" others but can't save himself. If he's Israel's king, let him come down from the cross now. Then we'll believe in him. He trusts in God; let God rescue him now if God wishes, since he said "I'm God's Son."

The crucified bandits taunted him in the same way.

27:45From noon until 3PM, the sky was dark. At 3PM, Jesus cried loudly, "Eli, Eli, lema sabachthani?" That mix of Hebrew and Aramaic means "My God, my God, why have you forsaken me?"; but some of the bystanders misunderstood him and said, "He's calling for Elijah." Immediately one of them ran, got a sponge, filled it with vinegar, put it on a stick, and gave it to him to drink. But the others said, "What, let's see whether Elijah will come save him." Then Jesus cried loudly again and breathed his last.…

John the Baptist again (from "Mark")

1:1Here's the beginning of the good news about Jesus Christ (God's Son).

1:2According to the prophets (in Malachi 3:1 and Isaiah 40:3), God told Jesus:

Ahead of you I'm sending my messenger. He'll prepare your way. He's the voice crying out in the wilderness, "Prepare the Lord's way, make his paths straight."

1:4So John the baptizer appeared in the wilderness and proclaimed that people should get baptized to repent for their sins. People from the whole Judean countryside and Jerusalem were going out to him and were baptized by him in the Jordan River, as they confessed their sins.

1:6John wore clothing made of camel's hair, with a leather belt. He ate locusts and honey.

1:7He proclaimed:

After me will come the one who's more powerful than I. I'm not worthy even to stoop down and untie his sandals' thongs. I've baptized you with water, but he'll baptize you with the Holy Spirit.

1:9Jesus came from Nazareth (a town in Galilee) and was baptized by John in the Jordan. When Jesus was coming up out of the water, he saw the heavens torn apart and the Spirit descending like a dove on him. A voice said from heaven:

You're my Son, the Beloved. I'm pleased with you.

1:12Jesus learned to avoid Satan's temptations and did a lot of preaching.…

Jesus clears the temple (from "Mark")

11:15When Jesus and his disciples came to Jerusalem, he entered the temple's courtyard and began driving out the people who were selling and buying in the courtyard: he overturned the tables of the **money changers** (who changed foreign currency to local currency) and the benches of those who sold **doves** (which were used for purification and sacrifices). He wouldn't let anyone carry anything through the courtyard.

11:17He taught by exclaiming:

Doesn't the Bible say (in Isaiah 56:7) "My house shall be called a house of prayer for all nations?" But you've made it a den of robbers!

11:18When the chief priests and scribes heard that, they began looking for a way to kill him, because they were scared at how the whole crowd was spellbound by his teaching.…

Death of Jesus (from "Mark")

15:37On the cross, Jesus finally gave a loud cry and breathed his last. The temple's curtain was torn in two, from top to bottom.

15:39The **centurion** (Roman commander) who watched Jesus die said, "Truly, this man was God's Son!"

15:40Jesus's death was also seen, from a distance, by women who'd followed Jesus and cared for his needs when he was in Galilee. Those women included Mary Magdalene, another Mary (who was the mother of James the younger and Joses), Salome, and many other women who'd come with him to Jerusalem.

Burying Jesus (from "Mark")

15:42Toward the end of that afternoon, a respected Sanhedrin member (Joseph of Arimathea), who was also waiting for God's kingdom, boldly went to Pilate and asked for Jesus's body quickly (since Jewish law prohibits any work, such as moving bodies, after sundown on Sabbath eve). Pilate was surprised to hear Jesus was dead already (since crucified men usually suffer at least 2 days on the cross before dying), so Pilate asked the centurion whether Jesus was indeed dead. When the centurion said yes, Pilate granted Joseph the body.

15:46Joseph bought a linen cloth, took down the body, wrapped it in the cloth, and laid it in a tomb cut out of rock. He rolled a stone against the tomb's entrance. Mary Magdalene and Joses' mother Mary both saw where the body was laid.

Resurrection (from "Mark")

[16:1]When Sabbath ended (Saturday night at sundown, so work could resume), the three women (Mary Magdalene, the other Mary, and Salome) bought spices to anoint the Jesus's body. The next morning (Sunday), shortly after sunrise, they went to the tomb.

[16:3]They'd been wondering, "Who'll help us roll away the stone from the tomb's entrance?" But when they looked up, they saw the huge stone had already been rolled back.

[16:5]As they entered the tomb, they saw a young man in a white robe, sitting on the right side. They were alarmed, but he said:

> Don't be alarmed. You're looking for Jesus of Nazareth, who was crucified. He's been raised; he's not here. Look, here's where they laid him. But go tell his disciples and Peter he's going ahead of you to Galilee; there you'll see him, just as he told you.

[16:8]The women fled from the tomb because terror and amazement had seized them. They said nothing to anyone, since they were scared....

Introduction (from "Luke")

[1:1]Many people have tried to write an orderly account of Jesus's life, as it was told to us by eyewitnesses. I've decided, after investigating everything carefully, to write an orderly account especially for you, dear God Lover, so you can know the truth....

Good Samaritan (from "Luke")

[10:25]To test Jesus, a Biblical scholar asked him, "What must I do to inherit eternal life?" Jesus countered, "What have you read in the Bible?"

[10:25]The scholar replied:

> Deuteronomy 6:4 says "Love God with all your heart, soul, strength, and mind"; and Leviticus 19:18 says "Love your neighbor as yourself."

Jesus said, "You've given the right answer. Follow that, and you'll have eternal life."

[10:29]The scholar countered, "But who's my neighbor?" Jesus replied:

> A man going from Jerusalem to Jericho fell into the hands of robbers. They stripped him, beat him, and went away, leaving him half dead.
>
> A priest happened to be going down that road; when he saw the beaten man, he passed by on the other side. A Levite (priest's assistant) did the same. But when a Samaritan (who's a foreigner) saw the beaten man, the Samaritan was moved with pity, bandaged his wounds, put him on the Samaritan's donkey, took him to the inn, and took care of him. The next day, he took out 2 silver coins, gave them to the innkeeper, and said, "Take care of him; and when I return, I'll reimburse you for any extra expense." Which of those 3 (the priest, the Levite, or the Samaritan) acted as the beaten man's neighbor?

The scholar answered, "The one who showed him mercy." Jesus said, "Go do likewise...."

Qur'an

The **Qur'an** (which is the Arabic word for "recitation") is the Bible of the Muslim religion.

It was created by the prophet Muhammad, beginning in 610 A.D. (when he was 40 years old) until his death in 632 A.D. Muhammad was a great speaker but didn't know how to write: he was illiterate. He created the Qur'an orally in Arabic and dictated it to his followers, who memorized it. After his death, they transcribed it onto paper. They decided on a final reorganized version in 650 A.D.

It includes 114 chapters. Each chapter is called a **sura**.

The first sura is called "Al-Fatiha" (the opening). It's very short.

The second sura, which is very long, is called "Al-Baqara" (the cow), because it eventually includes a discussion of the Old Testament's story of the Golden Calf.

Though the Muslim world includes a few terrorists, the Qur'an itself is quite reasonable. Even if you're a Christian or Jew, you'll agree with most of what the Qur'an says!

Here's how the Qur'an begins. You're reading my own translation (which is based on translations by others)....

The opening

[1]This is in the name of God, who's compassionate and merciful.

[2]Praise God, lord of everything, compassionate and merciful, master of Judgment Day. We worship just you. We pray just to you for help.

[7]Keep us on the path that's correct and straight, the path of those whom you've blessed, not the path of those you're angry at, not the path of those who've gone astray.

The cow

[1]Here are the ABC's.

[2]This is the scripture. No doubt about its truth! It guides the God-fearing (who believe in him, pray, use what we've taught, believe what God showed you & your predecessors, and have faith in the hereafter). They're on the right course from God and will prosper.

[6]As for the disbelievers, they don't care that you warned them, they simply don't believe. God has sealed their hearts and hearing. Their eyes are covered. They'll be punished greatly.

[8]Some people who say they believe in God & the Judgment Day" don't really believe. They try to deceive God & believers but deceive just themselves. Their hearts are diseased. God's increased their disease so they'll have a painful doom because of their lies.

[11]When they're told "Don't be corrupt," they reply "We just want to make things right." They're corrupt but unaware.

[13]When they're told "Believe, as others do," they retort "Shall we believe like fools?" They themselves are the foolish ones but don't realize it.

[14]When they meet believers, they say they believe; but when they go privately to their Satans, they say "We're with *you*; we were just mocking the believers." God will mock *them* and make them wander blindly in their disrespect.

[16]They've given up guidance, swapping it for a life of errors instead. That swap was a bad bargain. They've lost the right direction....

Sex

Finally, we come to my last and most dangerous topic: sex! (If you're conservative, feel free to skip this topic: hop ahead to "Donna's comments," which are more heartwarming.)

Search for pleasure

Seek and ye shall find — if you get lucky.

> How I feel I'll find the field
> Where love runs deep and hearts grow strong,
> A stream becomes an ocean song,
> Your twinkling eyes and their surprise
> Become a universe of joy!
>
> Take me to that fertile field
> Where pounding hearts beat always true,
> We keep the love we always knew
> And grow it gently. I love you.
> I believe.

Dancing

George Bernard Shaw said:

> Dancing is a perpendicular expression of a horizontal desire.

Taking 8 women to bed

If you're a typical man, here's how you deal with taking a woman to bed if she's slightly younger than you, according to the Internet.

Her age	Your role	How you go to bed
8	parental	At bedtime, you take her to bed and tell her a story.
18	seducer	You tell her a story to take her to bed.
28	pal	You don't need to tell her a story to take her to bed.
38	seduced	She tells *you* a story to take you to bed.
48	unwanted	She tells you a story to *avoid* going to bed.
58	tired	You stay in bed alone, to avoid her story.
68	laughing	If you take her to bed, that'll be a story!
78	demented	What story? What bed? Who the hell is she?

Male orgasm

If you feel good about yourself, so you're not depressed, you get sexually aroused more easily. That's why Xaviera Hollander, the "Happy Hooker" who ran a bordello in New York City, made this comment about servicing her customers who were stockbrokers:

> When the stocks go up, the cocks go up.

Viagra Since Viagra's generic name, **sildenafil citrate**, is hard to remember, consumers have invented these alternative names for it: **mycoxafloppin**, **mycoxafailin**, **mydixadrupin**, **mydixarisin**, **dixafix**, and **ibepokin**.

Female orgasm

Here's how Anaïs Nin described her orgasm, in her 1937 diary:

> Palpitations project a fiery and icy liqueur through the body. Electric flesh-arrows traverse the body. A rainbow of color strikes the eyelids. A foam of music falls over the ears. It's the gong of the orgasm.

Oh, so that's what it's like? Could we get the details straight, please? What flavor is the liqueur? In which direction do the flesh-arrows traverse the body? Which pitch is the gong bang? Can this multimedia video be remixed to improve the performance?

Faking If you're a woman who wants to stroke a man's ego by faking an orgasm, take this advice from actress Candice Bergen:

> I may not be a great actress, but I've become the greatest at screen orgasms: 10 seconds of heavy breathing, roll your head from side to side, simulate a slight asthma attack, and die a little.

Sharon Stone said:

> Women might be able to fake orgasms, but men can fake whole relationships.

The abridged version is more popular:

> Women fake orgasms.
> Men fake relationships.

Dildo In the history of sex, the 3 most important countries are France, Greece, and Canada. The French gave us "French kissing" (oral sex); the Greeks gave us "Greek style" (anal sex); and the Canadians gave us **The Dildo Song**, whose main pearls of wisdom are these:

> It's long and a schlong, a marvelous dong.
> It fits in a sock, feels better than cock.
> It fits in your bum and sure makes you cum.
> It vibrates a bit, feels great on your clit.
>
> It fits in girls' cracks. Some even have sacks.
> They're not just for gays. They use double A's.
> Just rotate the knob: they buzz and they throb.
>
> A girl on the go? No time for a beau?
> Yes, this is your perfect fellow, you know.

You can see women sing it on the Internet at:

> www.spike.com/video/dildo-song/211907

Get what you ask for

There's an old story of the poor black man who walked by a dumpster, saw a lamp, rubbed it, and met the genie, who offered 3 wishes. He said:

> I want to be white, hard, and rub against a nice piece of ass every day!

So the genie turned him into a toilet seat.

He wasn't happy, so the genie let him try again and gave him 4 wishes this time. He said:

> I want to be hot, white, outta sight! — and completely surrounded by pussy.

So the genie turned him into a tampon.

Moral: if you're a guy wanting to be popular with the ladies, be careful — you might get taken advantage of.

AIDS

You can get AIDS in two popular ways. One way is to share needles with a drug addict. The other way is to have anal sex — because squeezing a penis into a rectum makes the rectum bleed — but the American news media were afraid to say that, which is why AIDS spread, and why Americans don't realize you can't easily get AIDS from vaginal sex.

Men versus women

The battle of the sexes never ends.

Battling Web sites

Is it better to be a man or a woman? Here's why it's better to be a *guy*:

You can kill your own food.
You can open all your own jars.
You can "do" your nails with a pocketknife.

Car mechanics tell you the truth.

Same work, more pay.

The same hairstyle lasts years, maybe decades.
One wallet, one pair of shoes, one color, all seasons.
You're allowed to know names of just 5 colors.

You don't have to shave below your neck.
You never have strap problems in public.

If you're 34 and single, nobody notices.
Gray hair and wrinkles just add character.

You can go to the bathroom without a support group.
You can visit a friend without having to bring a gift.

If someone forgets to invite you to an event, he or she can still be your friend.

If another guy at a party has the same outfit, you can become lifelong friends.

Your pals never trap you with "So, notice anything different?"

You can watch games with a buddy for hours quietly, without thinking "He must be mad at me."

You can do Christmas shopping for 25 relatives on December 24th in 45 minutes.

Those reasons were collected by James Gosling (who invented Java programming); read more of his collection at:

java.sun.com/people/jag/guy.html

But women think men are *disgusting*:

How do you scare a man?
Sneak up behind him and start throwing rice.

Why do men chase women they won't marry?
The same reason dogs chase cars they won't drive.

How many men does it take to screw in a lightbulb?
One. Men will screw anything.

What's the most insensitive part of the penis?
The man.

Why do men prefer showers to baths?
They know peeing in the bath is disgusting.

Why did God give males millions of sperm?
Males won't stop and ask for directions.

Men are like parking spots:
the good ones are taken; what's left is handicapped.

Men are like cement:
after getting laid, they take a long time to get hard.

Men are like chocolate bars:
sweet, smooth, and head right for your hips.

Those reasons were collected by Akane and Rei Hino; read more of their collection at:

www.members.tripod.com/~reihime/jokes.htm

Dogs

Women say men resemble dogs:

Both are fascinated with women's crotches.
Both like dominance games.
Both take up too much space on the bed.
Both fart shamelessly.
Both are suspicious of the mailman.
Both have irrational fears about vacuum cleaning.
Neither does any dishes.
Neither notices when you get your hair cut.
Neither understands what you see in cats.

But women say dogs are slightly *better* than men because dogs….

don't have problems expressing affection in public
don't play games with you, except fetch
mean it when they kiss you
miss you when you're gone
admit when they're jealous
understand what "no" means
feel guilty when they've done something wrong
are very direct about wanting to go out
are easy to buy for
give you no worse social disease than fleas
can be trained

Men say a dog is better than a woman, because a dog…

limits its time in the bathroom to a quick drink
doesn't shop
never expects you to phone
never expects flowers on Valentine's Day
never expects you to remember its birthday
doesn't get mad if you pet another dog
doesn't care about the previous dogs in your life
has parents who will never visit you
is happier to see you when you're late

Battling bathrooms

This advice is written in women's bathrooms:

The best way to a man's heart
is to saw his breast plate open.

Make love, not war.
Hell, do both, get married!

If it has tires or testicles,
you're going to have trouble with it.

You're too good for him.

Please don't throw toothpicks in the toilet.
Remember: crabs can pole vault!

This advice is written in men's bathrooms:

Don't trust anything that
bleeds for 5 days and doesn't die.

Beauty is just a light switch away.

No matter how good she looks,
some other guy is sick of taking her shit.

Rejection one-liners

Here are clever ways for a woman to reject a man, according to the Internet:

He: Haven't we met before?
She: Yes, I'm the receptionist at the VD clinic.

He: Haven't I seen you someplace before?
She: Yeah, that's why I don't go there anymore.

He: So what do you do for a living?
She: I'm a female impersonator.

He: What sign were you born under?
She: "Stop," "Do Not Enter," and "No Parking."

He: Is this seat empty?
She: Yes, and mine will be too if you sit down.

He: I know how to please a woman.
She: Then please leave me alone.

He: I can tell you want me.
She: You're so right! I want you… to leave.

He: Your place or mine?
She: Both. You go to yours, and I'll go to mine.

He: I'd like to call you. What's your number?
She: It's in the phone book.
He: But I don't know your name.
She: That's in the phone book too.

He: May I see you pretty soon?
She: Why? Don't you think I'm pretty now?

He: Your body is like a temple.
She: Sorry, there are no services today.

He: I want to give myself to you.
She: Sorry, I don't accept cheap gifts.

He: I'd go to the end of the world for you.
She: Yes, but would you stay there?

He: If I could see you naked, I'd die happy.
She: If I saw *you* naked, I'd probably die laughing.

He: How do you like your eggs in the morning?
She: Unfertilized.

I wonder who's kissing her now

Relationships come and go. After they've gone, we still mull on their memories, as expressed in the 1908 song, *I Wonder Who's Kissing Her Now*, with lyrics by Will Hough & Frank Adams. Here's my revised version:

You loved lots of girls in the sweet long-ago,
And each has meant heaven to you.
You vowed your affection to each one in turn
And sworn to them all: you'd be true!

You kissed 'neath the moon while the world seemed in tune,
Then left her, to hunt a new game;
But has it occurred to you later, my boy,
She's probably doing the same?

I wonder who's kissing her now,
Wonder who's teaching her how,
Wonder who looks in her eyes,
Breathing sighs,
Telling lies.

Loves of today
Soon pass away,
Leave with a smile and a tear.
No, you can't know who is kissing her now
Or whom *you'll* be kissing next year.

Dream about kissing her now.
Dream about teaching her how.
Dream it and cry.
Give one last sigh.
Wonder who's kissing her now.

Medications for women

Doctors recommend that women buy these drugs:

Damnitol: take 2 tablets, and the rest of the world can go to hell for 8 hours.

Peptobimbo: when swallowed by a single woman before an evening out, this liquid silicone drink increases breast size, decreases intelligence, and prevents conception.

Dumberol: this add-on to Peptobimbo lowers IQ further, resulting in enjoying country music and pickup trucks.

Menicillin: this anti-boy-otic increases an older woman's resistance to lethal lines, such as "You make me want to be a better person… can we get naked now?"

Jackasspirin relieves headaches caused by a man who can't remember your birthday, anniversary, or phone number.

Saint Momma's Wort: this plant extract treats mom's depression, by rendering preschoolers unconscious for 2 days.

Emptynestrogen: this suppository eliminates melancholy and loneliness, by reminding mom how her children were awful teenagers and she couldn't wait till they moved out.

Anti-talksident: spray this on irritating strangers too eager to share their life stories in elevators.

Nagament, when administered to a husband, provides the same irritation as nagging him all weekend, saving the wife the time and trouble of doing it herself.

Flipitor increases the life expectancy of commuters, by controlling road rage and the urge to flip off other drivers.

Sulfa-denial: this female contraceptive technique, 100% effective and approved by the Catholic Church, consists of holding an aspirin tablet between the knees.

Fifi love

A few years ago, San Francisco performed its first gay & lesbian marriages, and several towns in Oregon, Massachusetts, and New York State copied San Francisco.

As a Democrat, I'm in favor of liberal causes and letting the gays & lesbians have their fun. But I wonder whether we'll soon receive many letters like this:

I'm Janet Hegenberger, and I'd like to marry my dog, Fifi.

Though your first reaction will be to laugh at me, I'm serious. Fifi's my life partner: we've been together many years, ever since she first came into this world. We understand and *love* each other, more deeply than traditional couples. She understands me more than any man ever could. She's always been my constant, loving, faithful companion.

I've no desire to hurt the "sanctity of marriage" or anybody else's marriage at all: I just want to express my love for Fifi. Aside from her, I'm a single old lady with no other friends. She means so much to me!

I'd like her to get full spousal benefits, as other spouses do. That's fair! For example, I'd like her to be covered for doctor's care (from her veterinarian); I'd like to file a joint tax return with her; and upon my death, I'd like her to inherit my estate automatically, without lots of paperwork.

Please stand up for animal rights! Fifi has feelings, too! A love between a woman and her poodle has no bounds! Let us marry, in peaceful, joyous harmony. Jesus would have wanted it that way.

This is not a sexual issue. I have no desire for sex with Fifi, and that's biologically impossible anyway. I just want to hug her, and let her hug me, knowing we truly belong to each other — and mean more to each other than any Hitler-style "dog tag" could ever express.

Please, let love abound: let Fifi and me enter into the state of marital bliss. God loves us all! We're all his creatures! Noah said *all* animals should enter God's ship, two by two, united in love for our whole planet. Together, *we shall overcome* prejudice! Let "Earth Day" be more than just two words.

Yours truly,
Sister Janet Hegenberger,
Order of the Woofing Cross

How to score

If you're a guy, here's how to score points in the romance game, according to the anonymous Internet:

You gain points if you make the woman happy, lose points if you make her unhappy, and get no points for doing what she expects. Examples:

You make the bed (+1) but throw the bedspread over rumpled sheets (-1) and forget to add the decorative pillows (-1).

When the toilet-paper roll runs out, you replace it (0) or resort to Kleenex (-1); and when the Kleenex runs out, you use the next bathroom (-2).

You take out the recyclables and stack them neatly by the curb (+1), but the truck's just pulled away (-1).

You go out to buy her tampons (+5) in the snow (+8) but return with beer (-5) and no tampons (-25).

At night, you check out a suspicious noise (0), which turns out to be something (+5), which you pummel with a six iron (+10) until it turns out to be her father (-25) or her cat (-40).

At a party, you stay by her side (0) until you leave to chat with an old drinking buddy (-2) named Tiffany (-4) who's a dancer (-10) with implants (-18).

When mingling with others, you hold her hand and gaze at her lovingly (+1) until you introduce her as "the ol' ball and chain" and pat her rump (-5).

When she asks whether a hot-looking woman nearby is attractive, you say "Nowhere near as attractive as you" (+1) — or "Don't worry, she's lousy in bed" (-6) when that woman is her sister (-90).

You remember her birthday (0) and buy a card (0) and flowers (0). Then you take her out to dinner (+1), but it's a sports bar (-3) with an all-you-can-eat night (-3), and your face is painted the colors of your favorite team (-10).

You forget her birthday (-10) and your anniversary (-20).

You forget to pick her up at the bus station (-25), which is in the worst part of town (-35), and the pouring rain dissolves her leg cast (-50).

You give her a gift (0) that's not a small appliance (+1) and not chocolate (+2). You'll be paying it off for months (+30) using her credit card (-30). What you bought is two sizes too big (-40).

You go to the mall with her (+3), kindly drop her off at the entrance and park the car (+4), then jog to the sports bar (-9).

You visit her parents (+1) but just stare vacantly at their TV (-3), which is turned off (-6).

You go out for an evening with a guy (-5) who's single (-7) and drives a Trans Am (-10) with a license plate saying GR8 NBED (-15). After some beers (-7), you drive home at 3AM (-20), smelling of booze and cheap cigars (-10) and not wearing any pants (-40). She asks, "Is that a tattoo?" (-200)

You take her to a movie she likes and you hate (+12) — or you take her to a movie you like (-2) called Death Cop III (-3), featuring cyborgs having sex (-9), after you said it would be a foreign film about orphans and sheepdogs (-15).

You develop a noticeable beer gut (-15); but instead of exercising, you wear loose jeans and baggy Hawaiian shirts (-30) and say "It doesn't matter, you have one too." (-800)

On a trip, you lose the directions (-4), finally get lost (-10) in a bad part of town (-15), meet the locals up close and personal (-25), and she discovers you lied about having a black belt (-60).

When she asks "Do I look fat?" (-5), you hesitate (-10) then ask "Where?" (-35)

When she wants to talk about a problem, you look concerned (0) and listen (0) for more than 30 minutes (+5) without glancing at the TV (+5), but your mind wanders to last weekend's game until you hear her ask, "Well, what do you think I should do?" (-100) or you fall asleep (-200).

When it's her time of the month, you can talk (-100) or don't talk (-150), spend time with her (-200) or don't spend time with her (-500), until she sees you're enjoying yourself (game over — you lose).

Quotes on marital difficulties

Helen Rowland said:

When a girl marries, she exchanges the attentions of many men for the inattention of one. Before marriage, a man declares he'd lay down his life to serve you; after marriage, he won't even lay down his newspaper to talk to you. A husband is what's left of the lover after the nerve's been removed.

Rita Rudner said:

I love being married: it's so great to find that one special person you want to annoy for the rest of your life. Before I met my husband, I'd never fallen in love, though I'd stepped in it a few times. Men would like monogamy better if it sounded less like monotony.

Actress Zsa Zsa Gabor had 9 husbands and said:

Marriage is too interesting to be experienced just once.
I'm a marvelous housekeeper: every time I leave a man, I keep his house.
A man is incomplete until he's married. After that, he's finished.
I never hated a man enough to give him his diamonds back.
I know nothing about sex, because I was always married.
Husbands are like fires: they go out if unattended.

Here are more comments:

"All marriages are happy. It's the living together afterward that causes all the trouble." — Raymond Hull

"Love is a temporary insanity curable by marriage." — Ambrose Bierce

"Marriage is a great institution, but I'm not ready for an institution." — Mae West

"My wife and I were happy for 20 years. Then we met." — Rodney Dangerfield

"Marriage is the only war where you sleep with the enemy." — François Duc de La Rochefoucauld

"Marriage is like a hot bath: once you get used to it, it's not so hot." — Justin Thyme

"Marriage is a master, a mistress, and two slaves, making in all, two." — Ambrose Bierce

"Men have a much better time than women, because men marry later and die earlier." — H.L. Mencken

"It destroys one's nerves to be amiable every day to the same human being." — Benjamin Disraeli

"Marriage is like a pair of scissors: joined so they can't be separated, and often moving in opposite directions, but always punishing anyone who comes between them." — Sydney Smith

"Marriage is like a cage: birds outside it despair to enter, and birds within, to escape." — Michel de Montaigne

"All tragedies are finished by a death. All comedies are ended by a marriage." — Lord Byron

"Keep your eyes wide open before marriage, half shut afterwards." — Benjamin Franklin

"Always get married in the morning. That way, if it doesn't work out, you haven't wasted a whole day." — Mickey Rooney

"No matter how happily a woman may be married, it always pleases her to discover there's a nice man who wishes she weren't." — H.L. Mencken

"Why does a woman work 10 years to change a man's habits then complain he's not the man she married?" — Barbra Streisand

Here's advice for women:

"The trouble with some women is they get all excited about nothing, then marry him." — Cher

"Girls, why worry choosing whom to marry? Choose whom you may, you'll find you've got somebody else." — John Hay

Here's advice for men:

"Marry a woman whom you'd choose as a friend if she were a man." — Joseph Joubert

"It's harder to be a husband than a lover because it's harder to be witty every day than produce the occasional bon mot." — Honoré de Balzac

"You need just two things to keep your wife happy. The first is to let her think she's having her own way. The other is let her have it." — Lyndon B. Johnson

"By all means, marry. If you get a good wife, you'll be happy. If you get a bad one, you'll become a philosopher." — Socrates

The Internet provides these anonymous quotes:

Marriage is a 3-ring circus: engagement ring, wedding ring, and suffering.
Marriage is a mutual relationship if both parties know when to be mute.
Marriage is like a violin: after the music's over, you still have the strings.
Marriage is a romantic story, where the hero dies in the first chapter.
Marriage isn't a word: it's a sentence.
The longest sentence in the English language is "I do."
Marriage is the only sport where the trapped animals have to buy the license.

Marriage is like a mousetrap: those on the outside are trying to get in; those on the inside are trying to get out.

When a couple marries, she expects he'll change, but he won't; he expects she won't change, but she will.

If your husband and a lawyer were drowning and you had to choose, would you go to lunch or a movie?

According to the Internet, times change:

In the first year of marriage, the man speaks and the woman listens.
In the second year, the woman speaks and the man listens.
In the third year, they both speak and the neighbors listen.

Benjamin Disraeli, who was Prime Minister of England, said:

It destroys one's nerves to be amiable everyday to the same human being.

Mignon McLaughlin summarized it all by saying:

A successful marriage requires falling in love many times, always with the same person.

Who stepped on the duck?

Here's a tale from the Internet:

Three women die in an accident and enter heaven. Saint Peter says, "We have just one rule here: don't step on the ducks!"

That rule's hard to follow, because there are ducks all over the place. It's almost impossible to avoid stepping on a duck.

The first woman accidentally steps on a duck. Saint Peter chains her to the ugliest man she ever saw and tells her, "Your punishment for stepping on a duck is to spend eternity chained to this ugly man!"

The second woman also steps on a duck and gets chained to an extremely ugly man.

The third woman avoids stepping on any ducks. One day Saint Peter comes to her with the most handsome man she's ever seen and chains her to him, without saying a word. The woman gazes happily at the handsome man and says, "I wonder what I did to deserve being chained to you forever!"

He replies, "I don't know about you, but I stepped on a duck."

How about you and your spouse? Are you chained together forever happily? Does one of you feel you stepped on a duck? Neither of you? Both of you? Talk about it.

Marry ugly

A song called "Marry A Woman Uglier Than You" has this message:

If you're a man trying to find a woman to marry, you might be more appreciated by an ugly woman than a pretty one, and so the ugly woman might give you more happiness.

Here are the song's lyrics (cleaned up a bit by me):

Want to be happy, live a king's life?
Don't make a pretty woman your wife!

Prettiest woman makes you look small.
She'll all too often cause you to fall.
Soon as she marries, then she will start
Doing bad things that break up your heart.
Just when you think she's only for you,
She will call someone else her love true.

Just make an *ugly* woman your wife:
You will be happy, rest of your life!
She wouldn't act in such a strange way
Just to give neighbors something to say.
She wouldn't diss you. No, not at all,
Not show her bod to Peter and Paul.

So from a logical point of view,
Marry a girl more ugly than you.
Want to live long, the happiest life,
No consternation, marital strife?
Just use some logic! Easy to do:
Marry a girl more ugly than you.

It was a calypso recorded in 1934 by the "Duke of Iron" (whose real name was Cecil Anderson, from Trinidad).

University of Michigan study

This news report appeared on the Internet:

A 10-year study at the University of Michigan has concluded that men and women complement each other because each gender has unique traits.

Women have strengths that amaze men. They carry children, hardships, and burdens but hold happiness, love, and joy. They smile when they want to scream, sing when they want to cry, laugh when nervous. They're childcare workers, executives, stay-at-home moms, bikers, babes, and friendly neighbors. They wear suits, jeans, and uniforms. They fight for their beliefs, stand against injustice, and walk & talk the extra mile to get their kids good schools and get their families good health care. They'll accompany a frightened friend to the doctor. They're honest, loyal, and forgiving. They're smart. They realize knowledge is power but can still use their softer side to make a point. They send letters and e-mails to show how much they care. The heart of a woman is what makes the world spin! Women bring joy & hope, give compassion & ideals, and give moral support to their families & friends. All they want back is a hug and a smile.

Men are good at lifting heavy objects and killing bugs.

Male laments

Men often complain about dealing with women.

Open windows Life isn't fair.

If a woman gets undressed in her room while leaving her shades open, and a man peeks at her, the man gets arrested for being a Peeping Tom.

If a man gets undressed in his room while leaving his shades open, and a woman peeks at him, the man gets arrested for being an exhibitionist.

Adam & Eve Here's the lost paragraph from the Bible's Book of Genesis, as reported on the Internet:

God asked Adam, "What's wrong with you?" Adam said he didn't have anyone to talk with. God said He'd make Adam a companion and it would be a woman.

God said, "This person will gather food for you. When you discover clothing, she'll wash it for you. She'll agree with all your decisions. She'll bear your babies and never ask you to get up in the middle of the night to care for them. She won't nag you. When you disagree with her, she'll always admit she was wrong. She'll never have a headache, and she'll freely give you love and passion whenever you need it."

Adam asked God, "What will a woman like that cost?" God replied, "An arm and a leg."

Adam asked, "What can I get for a rib?" And the rest is history.

Happiest days of marriage According to the *Guy Q* book, couples fight the most on Wednesday (because it's in the middle of the week, far from weekends) and fight the least on Thursday (because on Thursday they look forward to Friday fun).

But some couples don't fit that schedule. For example, one of my friends tells us:

I've been married 28 years,
and my wife's given me the happiest 20 years of my life.

Then we ask him:

Which were the unhappy times — the first 8 years, or the last 8?

His answer is:

The weekends!

On weekdays, he's happily at work and doesn't have to face his wife; but "28 years of weekends" is as many torture days as 8 years of straight torture.

Rodney Dangerfield said:

My wife and I were happy for 20 years. Then we met.

Programming

A computer is just a useless hunk of metal & plastic until somebody feeds it a **program**, which is a list of commands teaching the computer how to perform a task.

A person who writes a program is called a **programmer**. Now I'll teach you how to write programs, so you become a programmer.

You already learned how to buy & use programs such as Microsoft Office. Now I'll teach you how to invent your own programs, so you can become the computer's true master and make it do whatever you wish, without being limited to the creations of other programmers.

It's easy

Programming the computer can be easy. You'll write your own programs just a few minutes from now, when you reach page 494. Then on your résumé you can brag you're a "programmer." As you read farther, you'll learn how to become a *good* programmer, by writing programs that are more sophisticated.

Computer languages

To program the computer, you feed it a list of commands written in a **computer language**. Each computer language is a small part of English.

Programmers love to argue about which computer language is best. This book teaches you *many* computer languages, so you master them all and become multilingual!

Of the popular computer languages, the easiest to learn is **Basic**. Two kinds of Basic are popular:

> One kind, called **classic Basic**, was invented long ago and is extremely simple. We'll start with that. It consists of words such as PRINT, INPUT, IF, and THEN. You'll learn classic Basic's most popular versions: **QBasic** and **QB64**.
>
> Next, you'll learn the other kind of Basic, called **Visual Basic**, which is slightly harder but more powerful: it lets you teach the computer how to create windows & buttons and handle mouse clicks.

Afterwards, I'll explain the **J languages** (**JavaScript**, **JScript**, and **Java**). They're popular for creating programs that run on Internet Web pages. They go beyond the HTML that I explained on pages 285-292.

Then we dig into the **C languages**, which let you write programs that run faster, consume less RAM, and manipulate the computer's innards. I'll explain C's most modern versions: **Visual C#** (which is the fanciest) and **Visual C++** (which many programmers learned in school).

After a discusson of **exotic languages** (which are wild and funny), we'll discuss **machine language**. It's the only language the computer knows at birth, before it's trained to understand other languages (such as Basic). You'll also learn to use a machine-language variant called **assembly language**, which is slightly more human. Programs written in machine language or assembly language run even faster than programs written in C, and they consume even less RAM and let you manipulate the computer's innards even more thoroughly, so you have total control.

Each language continually improves by stealing words from other languages — just as we English speakers stole the word "restaurant" from the French, and the French stole the word "weekend" from us.

Because of the mutual stealing, computer languages are becoming more alike. But each language still retains its own "inspired lunacy", its own weird words that other languages haven't copied yet.

You can get all the popular computer languages for free! I'll explain how.

Dig!

Let's dig in. This is the book's longest section (185 pages!) because it digs the deepest: it explains how the computer innately thinks and how to make it think like *you*, so the computer will imitate your personality and act human.

10 years from now, the stuff in the book's earlier sections will be considered "obsolete", but the stuff in this programming section will be considered "still true".

Welcome to eternity.

Why program?

Learning to program? It's fun! It's the adventure that does the most to expand your mind and turn you into a brilliant thinker. Here's where your career's long-term growth gets its biggest boost.

Here's where you learn the secret of computer life! You learn how to take a computer — that hunk of metal and plastic — and teach it new skills, by feeding it programs. Your teaching and programs turn the computer into a thinking organism. If you teach the computer well, you can make it become as smart as you and even imitate your personality. You become the computer's God, capable of making the computer do anything you wish. Ah, the power!

Folks who've read just the first half of this book are at the mercy of Microsoft and other money-grubbing companies: whenever those unfortunate folks want to make the computer do something, they must buy a program that teaches the computer how. If computer stores don't carry a program for that particular task — or if the program's price is unaffordable — those folks are out of luck.

But once you learn how to program, you're lucky! You can make the computer do anything you want! All you need is the patience and perseverance to finish writing your program. And if you ever get stuck, phone me anytime at 603-666-6644 for free help.

When you finish writing your program, you can sell it to the idiots who've read just the first half of the book — and you're on your way to turning yourself into the next Microsoft.

Why be multilingual?

Learning a new language affects your way of thinking. For example, most Americans think cockroaches are disgusting; but when a German housewife sees a cockroach, she just giggles, because she thinks of the German word for "cockroach", which is "küchenschabe", which means "kitchen scraper", "a cute little thing that sweeps the kitchen". Yes, even the ugliest problems look cute when you know how to express your thoughts multilingually!

Each language adds new words to your vocabulary so you gain new ways to express your problems, solutions, and thoughts about them. When you face a tough programming problem and try to reduce it to words the computer understands, you'll think more clearly if you're multilingual and know enough vocabularies to turn the vague problem into precise words quickly.

An expert programmer can boil complex hassles down to a series of simple concepts. To do that, you need (on the tip of your tongue!) the words defining those simple concepts. The more computer languages you study, the more words you'll learn, so you can quickly verbalize the crux of each computer problem and solve it.

QBasic & QB64

To program the computer, you must use a language that the computer understands. Many computers understand a language called **Basic**, which is a small part of English.

Basic was invented by two Dartmouth College professors (John Kemeny and Tom Kurtz) in 1964. Later they improved it. Now Basic consists of words such as PRINT, INPUT, IF, and THEN.

I'll explain how to program the computer by using those Basic words.

Different computers speak different **dialects** of Basic. The most popular dialect was invented in 1975 by a 19-year-old kid, Bill Gates. Since he developed software for microcomputers, he called himself **Microsoft** and called his Basic dialect **Microsoft Basic**.

Since Microsoft Basic is so wonderful, all the popular computer companies paid him to make their computers understand Microsoft Basic. That's right: IBM, Apple, Commodore, Tandy, Atari, Texas Instruments, and *hundreds* of other computer companies all had to pay off Bill.

Microsoft Basic became so popular that Bill had to hire hundreds of employees to help him fill all the orders. Microsoft Incorporated became a multi-billion-dollar company, and Bill became a famous billionaire, the wealthiest person in America.

Over the years, Bill gradually improved Microsoft Basic. Some computers use old versions of Microsoft Basic; other computers use his latest improvements.

One of the most popular versions of Microsoft Basic is **QBasic**. It's a simplification of another version of Microsoft Basic, called **Quick Basic**.

QBasic is popular because it's good and because most people got it at no charge: free!

Recently, Microsoft has switched from QBasic to **Visual Basic**, which can do fancier tricks but is harder to learn.

If you're a beginner, I recommend you start with QBasic (or an imitation of QBasic), not Visual Basic.

QBasic expects that your operating system is MS-DOS. You can force QBasic to run with some versions of Windows, and you can even download QBasic free from some Websites (by Microsoft and others), but Microsoft has taken steps to discourage you from doing so.

QB64 (pronounced "Q B sixty-four") imitates QBasic and runs well if you have Windows, especially if you have Windows 7. You can download a free copy of QB64 from www.qb64.net. QB64 was invented in Sydney, Australia by a guy whose name is "Rob" but whose nickname is "Galleon Dragon."

This chapter explains QBasic (which works best if your operating system is MS-DOS) and QB64 (which works best if your operating system is Windows 7). After reading this chapter, you can advance to Visual Basic, which is explained in the next chapter and harder.

The commands of QBasic & QB64 are explained on these pages:

Command	What the computer will do	Page	Similar to
BEEP	hum for a quarter of a second	531	SOUND, PLAY
CASE "fine"	if SELECTed is "fine", do indented lines	511	SELECT, IF
CIRCLE (100, 100), 40	draw a circle at (100, 100) with radius 40	530	LINE, PAINT
CLS	clear the screen, so it becomes all black	494	LOCATE
COMMON SHARED x	make all procedures share x's box	550	DIM SHARED
DATA meat, potatoes	use this list of data: meat, potatoes	517	READ, RESTORE
DIM SHARED y$(20)	make y$ be 20 strings the procedures share	550	COMMON, SUB
DIM x$(7)	make x$ be a list of 7 strings	544	x =
DO	do the indented lines below, repeatedly	502	DO UNTIL, LOOP
ELSE	do indented lines when IF conditions false	510	IF, ELSEIF
ELSEIF age < 100 THEN	do lines when earlier IFs false & age<100	510	IF, ELSE
END	skip the rest of the program	504	STOP
END IF	make this the bottom of an IF statement	510	IF, ELSE
END SELECT	make this the bottom of SELECT statement	511	SELECT, CASE
END SUB	make this the bottom of a SUB procedure	548	SUB
EXIT DO	skip down to the line that's under LOOP	513	DO, LOOP
FOR x = 1 TO 20	repeat the indented lines, 20 times	514	NEXT, DO
GOTO 10	skip to line 10 of the program	504	DO, EXIT DO
IF y < 18 THEN PRINT "m"	if y is less than 18, print an "m"	510	ENDIF, ELSE
INPUT "what name"; n$	ask "What name?" and get answer n$	507	x =
LINE (0, 0)-(100, 100)	draw a line from (0, 0) to (100, 100)	529	PSET, CIRCLE
LOCATE 3, 7	move to the screen's 3rd line, 7th position	529	PRINT, CLS
LOOP	make this the bottom line of a DO loop	502	LOOP UNTIL
LOOP UNTIL guess$ = "p"	do the loop repeatedly, until guess$ is "p"	513	LOOP, DO UNTIL
LPRINT 2 + 2	print, onto paper, the answer to 2 + 2	499	PRINT
MID$(a$, 2)="owl"	change the middle of a$ to "owl"	541	x =
NEXT	make this the bottom line of a FOR loop	514	FOR
PAINT (100, 101)	fill in the shape that surrounds (100, 101)	530	LINE, CIRCLE
PLAY "c d g# b- a"	play this music: C, D, G sharp, B flat, A	531	SOUND, BEEP
PSET (100, 100)	make pixel (100, 100) turn white	529	SCREEN, LINE
PRINT 4 + 2	print the answer to 4 + 2	494	PRINT USING
PRINT USING "##.#"; x	print x, rounded to one decimal place	532	PRINT
RANDOMIZE TIMER	make random numbers be unpredictable	537	x =
READ a$	get a string from the DATA and call it a$	517	DATA, RESTORE
RESTORE 10	skip to line 10 of the DATA	519	READ, DATA
SCREEN 12	let you draw pictures	529	PSET, WIDTH
SELECT CASE a$	analyze a$ to select a case from list below	511	END SELECT, IF
SOUND 440, 18.2	make a sound of 440 hertz, for 1 second	531	PLAY, BEEP
SLEEP	pause until you press a key	501	FOR
STOP	skip rest of program; close the black window	521	END
SUB insult	make the lines below define "insult"	548	END SUB
WIDTH 40	make the characters wide, 40 per line	503	SCREEN
x = 47	make x stand for the number 47	505	INPUT
'Zoo program is fishy	ignore this comment	524	PRINT

The functions of QBasic & QB64 are explained on these pages:

Function	Meaning	Value	Page	Similar to
ABS(-3.89)	absolute value of -3.89	3.89	535	SGN
ASC("A")	Ascii code number for A	65	541	CHR$
ATN(1) / degrees	arctangent of 1, in degrees	45	543	TAN
CHR$(164)	character whose code# is 164	"ñ"	540	ASC
CINT(3.89)	round to nearest integer	4	535	INT, FIX
COS(60 * degrees)	cosine of 60 degrees	.5	543	SIN, TAN
DATE$	today's date	varies	535	TIME$
EXP(1)	e raised to the first power	2.718282	534	LOG, SQR
FIX(3.89)	erase digits after decimal point	3	535	INT, CINT
INSTR("needed", "ed")	position of "ed" in "needed"	3	542	other INSTR
INSTR(4,"needed","ed")	search from the 4th character	5	542	other INSTR
INT(3.89)	round down to a lower integer	3	535	FIX, CINT
LCASE$("We love")	lower case; uncapitalize	"we love"	542	UCASE$
LEFT$("smart", 2)	left 2 characters of "smart"	"sm"	541	RIGHT$, MID$
LEN("smart")	length of "smart"	5	541	RIGHT$, MID$
LOG(2.718282)	logarithm base e	1	534	EXP
LTRIM$(" Sue Smith")	delete beginning spaces	"Sue Smith"	542	RTRIM$
MID$("smart", 2)	begin at the 2nd character	"mart"	541	other MID$
MID$("smart", 2, 3)	begin at the 2nd take 3	"mar"	541	other MID$
RIGHT$("smart", 2)	rightmost 2 characters	"rt"	541	LEFT$, MID$
RND	random decimal	varies	536	TIMER
RTRIM$("Sue Smith ")	delete ending spaces	"Sue Smith"	542	LTRIM$
SGN(-3.89)	sign of -3.89	-1	535	ABS, FIX
SIN(30 * degrees)	sine of 30 degrees	.5	543	COS, TAN
SQR(9)	square root of 9	3	534	EXP, LOG
STR$(81.4)	turn 81.4 into a string	" 81.4"	542	VAL
STRING$(5, "b")	a string of 5 b's	"bbbbb"	542	other STRING$
STRING$(5, 98)	98th Ascii character, 5 times	"bbbbb"	542	other STRING$
TAN(45 * degrees)	tangent of 45 degrees	1	543	ATN
TIME$	current time of day	varies	535	TIMER, DATE$
TIMER	# of seconds since midnight	varies	535	TIME$, DATE$
UCASE$("We love")	capitalize "We love"	"WE LOVE"	542	LCASE$
VAL("52.6")	remove the quotation marks	52.6	542	STR$

Fun

Let's have fun programming!

Get QBasic or QB64

If your computer is so ancient that it has MS-DOS (version 5, 6, 6.2, 6.21, or 6.22) or IBM PC DOS 5 (which resembles MS-DOS version 5), your computer includes QBasic already.

If your computer has Windows 7, here's how to copy QB64 (version 0.934) from the Internet to your computer, free (using Internet Explorer 9):

Go to www.QB64.net.

You see a Windows logo (red, green, blue, and yellow windowpanes); click the "Download" icon next to that logo. Press Enter.

The screen's bottom will say "Downloading from site qb64.net". The computer will send a compressed copy of QB64 from the Internet to your computer.

Click "Extract all files" (which is near the screen's top-left corner). Press Enter. The computer will expand (uncompress) QB64.

The computer will show a menu beginning with the word "Organize". Close all windows, so you can start fresh.

Start QBasic or QB64

If you have QBasic (the version that came as part of MS-DOS 6.2), you can start it by doing this:

Turn on the computer (without any floppy in drive A).

Make the screen shows this standard C prompt:
C:\>

Type "qbasic" after the C prompt, so your screen looks like this:
C:\>qbasic
At the end of that line, press Enter.

If you did that correctly, the screen turns blue and you see "Welcome to MS-DOS QBasic". Then press the Esc key (which is at the keyboard's top left corner).

If you have QB64 (version 0.934), you can start it by doing this:

Click Start then "Documents". Double-click "qb64v0934-win" then the "qb64" folder then the "qb64" program.

If QB64 hasn't been run on your computer before, the computer has the following conversation with you…. The computer asks "Are you sure you want to run this software?" Click the "Run" button. The computer says "This file has been modified". Click "OK". The computer says "This file has been modified" again. Click "OK" again.

If you did that correctly, you see a blue window saying "QB64". Behind that window, you still see a white window. Close the white window (by clicking its X).

Type your program

Now you're ready to type your first program!

For example, type this program:

```
CLS
PRINT 4 + 2
```

Here's how. Type CLS, then press the Enter key at the end of that line. Type PRINT 4 + 2 (and remember to hold down the Shift key to type the symbol +), then press the Enter key at the end of that line.

Notice that you must press the Enter key at the end of each line.

A **program** is a list of commands that you want the computer to obey. The sample program you typed contains two commands. The first command (**CLS**) tells the computer to **CLear the Screen**, so the computer will erase the screen and the screen will become blank: entirely black! The next command (**PRINT 4 + 2**) tells the computer to do some math: it tells the computer to compute 4 + 2, get the answer (6), and print the answer on the screen.

Run your program

To make the computer obey the program you wrote, do this:

QB64	Press the F5 key.
QBasic	Press the F5 key while holding down the Shift key.

That tells the computer to **run** the program: the computer will run through the program and obey all the commands in it.

While the computer is running your program, you see a black window:

QB64	The black window is small.
QBasic	The black window consumes the entire screen.

The CLS command makes sure the computer clears that window, so it becomes all blank, all black.

Then the computer obeys the PRINT 4 + 2 command. The computer prints this answer onto the black window:

```
6
```

Congratulations! You've written your first program! You've programmed the computer to compute the answer to 4 + 2! You've become a programmer! Now you can put on your résumé: "programmer!"

When you finish admiring the computer's answer, do this:

QB64 Close the black window, by clicking its X button (or pressing the Enter key).

QBasic Press the F4 key. That makes the black window disappear, so the screen turns blue and shows your program again:

```
CLS
PRINT 4 + 2
```

If you'd like to peek at the answer again (which is 6 in a black window), press the F4 key again. When you finish peeking at the answer, press the F4 key again to view the program again (CLS and PRINT 4 + 2 on a blue background). So here are the rules: to run the program (and put the answer in a black window), press Shift with F5; to view the blue background again — or switch back to the black window again — press F4.

Faster typing

While typing the program, **you don't need to capitalize computer words** such as CLS and PRINT: the computer will capitalize them automatically when you press Enter at the end of the line.

While typing that program, put a blank space after the word PRINT to separate the "PRINT" from the 4. But **you don't need to put spaces next to the + sign**, since the computer will automatically insert those spaces when you press Enter at the end of the line.

Instead of typing "PRINT" or "print", you can type just a question mark. When you press the Enter key at the end of the line, the computer will replace the question mark by the word PRINT, and the computer will put a blank space after it.

So **instead of typing PRINT 4 + 2, you can type just this:**

```
?4+2
```

Think of the question mark as standing for this word:

```
What's
```

If you want to ask the computer "What's 4+2", type this:

```
?4+2
```

When you run the program, the computer will print the answer, 6.

Why CLS?

The program's top line (CLS) tells the computer to erase the screen before printing the answer (6).

If you forget to make the program's top line say CLS, here's what happens:

QB64 The computer will do CLS anyway. Typing CLS is optional.

QBasic The computer will forget to erase the screen. The computer will still print the answer (6), but that answer will appear underneath a transcript of previous chit-chat that occurred between you and the computer. That transcript is distracting and confusing. CLS erases it.

Edit your program

After you've typed your program, try typing another one. For example, create a program that makes the computer print the answer to 79 + 2. To do that, make this program appear on the screen:

```
CLS
PRINT 79 + 2
```

To make that program appear, just edit the program you typed previously (which said PRINT 4 + 2). To edit, do this:

Move to the character you want to change (which was the 4) by using the arrow keys (or clicking that character with QB64's mouse). Then undelete that character (4) by pressing the Delete key. Then type the characters you want instead (79).

While editing, use these tricks....

To delete a character:
move the cursor (blinking underline) to that character by using the arrow keys (or clicking that character with QB64's mouse), then press the Delete key.

To delete SEVERAL characters:
move to the first character you want to delete,
then hold down the Delete key awhile.

To delete AN ENTIRE LINE:
for QB64, drag across that line then press the Delete key; for QBasic, move to that line then (while holding down the Ctrl key) tap the Y key.

To INSERT A NEW LINE between two lines:
move to the beginning of the lower line, then press the Enter key.

If you've edited the program successfully, the screen shows just the new program —

```
CLS
PRINT 79 + 2
```

and you don't see the old program anymore.

When you've finished editing the program, run it:

QB64	Press the F5 key.
QBasic	Press the F5 key *while holding down the Shift key*.

Then the computer will print the answer:

```
81
```

Fix your errors

What happens if you misspell a computer word, such as CLS or PRINT? For example, what happens if you accidentally say PRIMPT instead of PRINT?

Here's the result:

QB64 The blue window's bottom says "Syntax error". If the error isn't in the line you're typing, the bad line is highlighted in red. Fix the error.

QBasic When you run the program (by pressing Shift with F5), the computer tries to run each line of your program. If the computer comes to a misspelled computer word (such as PRIMPT), the computer highlights your misspelling (by showing it in blue letters against a white background) and says "Syntax error". Press the Enter key, then fix your error, then try again to run the program (by pressing Shift with F5 key again).

Math

This command makes the computer add $4 + 2$:

```
PRINT 4 + 2
```

Put that command into a program (whose top line should be CLS). When you run the program (by pressing Shift with F5), the computer will print the answer:

```
6
```

If you want to subtract 3 from 7, type this command instead:

```
PRINT 7 - 3
```

(When typing the minus sign, do *not* press the Shift key.) The computer will print:

```
4
```

You can use decimal points and negative numbers. For example, if you type this —

```
PRINT -26.3 + 1
```

the computer will print:

```
-25.3
```

Multiplication

To multiply, use an asterisk. So to multiply 2 by 6, type this:

```
PRINT 2 * 6
```

The computer will print:

```
12
```

Division

To divide, use a slash. So to divide 8 by 4, type this:

```
PRINT 8 / 4
```

The computer will print:

```
2
```

To divide 2 by 3, type this:

```
PRINT 2 / 3
```

The computer will print:

```
.6666667
```

Avoid commas

Do *not* put commas in big numbers. To write four million, do *not* write 4,000,000; instead, write 4000000.

The symbol

If you type a long number (such as 7000000000 or 273.85429), the computer might automatically put the symbol # afterwards. That's the computer's way of reminding itself that the number is long and must be treated extra carefully!

E notation

If the computer's answer is huge (more than a million) or tiny (less than .01), the computer might print an E in the answer. The E means "move the decimal point".

For example, suppose the computer says the answer to a problem is:

```
8.516743E+12
```

The E means, "move the decimal point". The plus sign means, "towards the right". Altogether, **the E+12 means "move the decimal point towards the right, 12 places."** So look at 8.516743 and move the decimal point towards the right, 12 places; you get 8516743000000.

So when the computer says the answer is 8.516743E+12, the computer really means the answer is 8516743000000, approximately. The exact answer might be 8516743000000.2 or 8516743000000.79 or some similar number, but the computer prints just an approximation.

Suppose your computer says the answer to a problem is:

```
9.23E-06
```

After the E, the minus sign means, "towards the *left*". So look at 9.23 and move the decimal point towards the left, 6 places. You get: .00000923

So when the computer says the answer is 9.23E-06, the computer really means the answer is: .00000923

You'll see E notation rarely: the computer uses it just if an answer is huge (many millions) or tiny (tinier than .01). But when the computer *does* use E notation, remember to move the decimal point!

D notation

If the answer's a long number, the computer usually prints a D instead of an E. Like the E, the D means "move the decimal point".

Use decimals for big answers

In any problem whose answer might be bigger than 32 thousand, type a decimal point (or use E or D notation).

For example, if you want to multiply 200 by 300, put a decimal point after the 200 or 300:

> If you accidentally say just "PRINT 200 * 300" without any decimal points, QB64 prints the right answer (60000) but QBasic complains by saying "Overflow".
>
> When QBasic says "Overflow", press the Enter key then fix your program by inserting a decimal point, like this —
> ```
> PRINT 200 * 300.0
> ```
> or like this:
> ```
> PRINT 200 * 300.
> ```
> When you finish typing that line (and press Enter afterwards), QBasic will do something strange: it will turn the ".0" or "." into an exclamation point, so the line looks like this:
> ```
> PRINT 200 * 300!
> ```
> When you run the program, QBasic will print the right answer:
> ```
>  60000
> ```
> Notice that if you type a decimal point at the end of a number, QBasic usually puts an exclamation point (!) at the end of the number. If the number is long, the computer puts a number sign (#) instead of an exclamation point.

If you want to multiply 54000 by 40000, put a decimal point after the 54000 or 40000:

> If you accidentally say just "PRINT 54000 * 40000" without any decimal points, QBasic complains by saying "Overflow" but QB64 accidentally prints this instead:
> ```
> -2134967296
> ```
> Fix your program by inserting a decimal point, like this —
> ```
> PRINT 54000 * 40000.0
> ```
> or like this —
> ```
> PRINT 54000 * 40000.
> ```
> or using E notation like this:
> ```
> PRINT 54000 * 4E4
> ```
> Then when you run the program, QBasic and QB64 will print a right answer. QBasic will print:
> ```
>  2160000000
> ```
> QB64 will print:
> ```
> 2.16E+09
> ```

The highest number

The highest number the computer can handle well is about 1E38, which is 1 followed by 38 zeros, like this:

```
100000000000000000000000000000000000000
```

If you try to go much higher, the computer will either use D notation (which goes up to about 1D308) or gripe.

If the computer wants to gripe about a number being too big, QBasic says "Overflow" but QB64 says "1.#INF" instead (which means "infinity").

The tiniest decimal

The tiniest decimal the computer can handle easily is about 1E-38, which is a decimal point followed by 38 digits, 37 of which are zeros, like this:

```
.00000000000000000000000000000000000001
```

If you try to go much tinier, the computer will either say 0 or use D notation (which goes down to about 1D-323).

Order of operations

What does "2 plus 3 times 4" mean? The answer depends on whom you ask.

To a clerk, it means "start with 2 plus 3, then multiply by 4"; that makes 5 times 4, which is 20. But to a scientist, "2 plus 3 times 4" means something different: it means "2 plus three fours", which is $2 + 4 + 4 + 4$, which is 14.

Since computers were invented by scientists, computers think like scientists. If you type —

```
PRINT 2 + 3 * 4
```

the computer will think you mean "2 plus three fours", so it will do $2 + 4 + 4 + 4$ and print this answer:

```
14
```

The computer will *not* print the clerk's answer, which is 20. So if you're a clerk, tough luck!

Scientists and computers follow this rule: **do multiplication and division before addition and subtraction**. So if you type —

```
PRINT 2 + 3 * 4
```

the computer begins by hunting for multiplication and division. When it finds the multiplication sign between the 3 and the 4, it multiplies 3 by 4 and gets 12, like this:

So the problem becomes 2 + 12, which is 14, which the computer prints.

For another example, suppose you type:

```
PRINT 10 - 2 * 3 + 72 / 9 * 5
```

The computer begins by doing all the multiplications and divisions. So it does 2 * 3 (which is 6) and does 72 / 9 * 5 (which is 8 * 5, which is 40), like this:

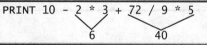

So the problem becomes 10 - 6 + 40, which is 44, which is the answer the computer prints.

You can use parentheses the same way as in algebra. For example, if you type —

```
PRINT 5 - (1 + 1)
```

the computer will compute 5 - 2 and print:

```
3
```

You can put parentheses inside parentheses. If you type —

```
PRINT 10 - (5 - (1 + 1))
```

the computer will compute 10 - (5 - 2), which is 10 - 3, and will print:

```
7
```

Strings

Let's make the computer fall in love. Let's make it say, "I love you".

Type this program:

```
CLS
PRINT "I love you"
```

Here's how to type the second line:

Begin by typing the word PRINT. Then type a blank space (by pressing the Space bar). Then type a quotation mark, but be careful: **to type the quotation mark, you must hold down the Shift key.** Then type these words: *I love you*. Then type another quotation mark. At the end of that line, press the Enter key.

When you run the program, the computer will obey your command; it will print:

```
I love you
```

You can change the computer's personality. For example, if you give this command —

```
PRINT "I hate you"
```

the computer will reply:

```
I hate you
```

Notice that **to make the computer print a message, you must put the message between quotation marks**. The quotation marks make the computer copy the message without worrying about what the message means. For example, if you misspell "I love you", and type —

```
PRINT "aieee luf ya"
```

the computer will still copy the message (without worrying about what it means); the computer will print:

```
aieee luf ya
```

Faster typing

Instead of typing —

```
PRINT "I love you"
```

you can type just this:

```
?"I love you
```

At the end of that line, when you press the Enter key, the computer will automatically do three things:

The computer will change the question mark to the word PRINT. The computer will put a blank space after PRINT (and before the quotation mark). The computer will put a quotation mark at the line's end (to match the other quotation mark).

Jargon

The word "joy" consists of 3 characters: j and o and y. Programmers say that the word "joy" is a **string** of 3 characters.

A **string** is any collection of characters, such as "joy" or "I love you" or "aieee luf ya" or "76 trombones" or "GO AWAY!!!" or "xypw exr///746". The computer will print whatever string you wish, but remember to **put the string in quotation marks**.

Strings versus numbers

The computer can handle two types of expressions: **strings** and **numbers**. Put strings (such as "joy" and "I love you") in quotation marks. Numbers (such as 4 + 2) do *not* go in quotation marks.

Accidents

Suppose you accidentally put the number 2 + 2 in quotation marks, like this:

```
PRINT "2 + 2"
```

The quotation marks make the computer think "2 + 2" is a string instead of a number. Since the computer thinks "2 + 2" is a string, it copies the string without analyzing what it means; the computer will print:

```
2 + 2
```

It will *not* print 4.

Suppose you want the computer to print the word "love" but you accidentally forget to put the string "love" in quotation marks, and type this instead:

```
PRINT love
```

Since you forgot the quotation marks, the computer thinks *love* is a number instead of a string but doesn't know which number, since the computer doesn't know the meaning of love. Whenever the computer is confused, it either gripes at you or prints a zero. In this particular example, when you run the program the computer will print a zero, like this:

```
0
```

So if you incorrectly tell the computer to proclaim its love, it will say zero.

Longer programs

You can program the computer say it's madly in love with you!

Let's make the computer say:

```
I love you.
You turned me on.
Let's get married!
```

To make the computer say all that, just run this program:

```
CLS
PRINT "I love you."
PRINT "You turned me on."
PRINT "Let's get married!"
```

To run that program, type it and then press Shift with F5. Try it!

To have even more fun, run this program:

```
CLS
PRINT "I long"
PRINT 2 + 2
PRINT "U"
```

It makes the computer print "I long", then print the answer to 2+2 (which is 4), then print "U". So altogether, the computer prints:

```
I long
 4
U
```

Yes, the computer says it longs for you!

Tricky printing

Printing can be tricky! Here are the tricks.

Indenting Suppose you want the computer to print this letter:

```
Dear Joan,
  Thank you for the beautiful
necktie.  Just one problem--
I don't wear neckties!
          Love,
             Fred-the-Hippie
```

This program prints it:

```
CLS
PRINT "Dear Joan,"
PRINT "  Thank you for the beautiful"
PRINT "necktie.  Just one problem--"
PRINT "I don't wear neckties!"
PRINT "          Love,"
PRINT "             Fred-the-Hippie"
```

In the program, each line contains 2 quotation marks. **To make the computer indent a line, put blank spaces AFTER the first quotation mark.**

Blank lines Life consists sometimes of joy, sometimes of sorrow, and sometimes of a numb emptiness. To express those feelings, run this program:

Program	What the computer will do
CLS	Clear the screen.
PRINT "joy"	Print "joy".
PRINT	Print blank empty line, under "joy".
PRINT "sorrow"	Print "sorrow".

Altogether, the computer will print:

```
joy

sorrow
```

Semicolons Run this program:

```
CLS
PRINT "fat";
PRINT "her"
```

The second line, which makes the computer print "fat", ends with a semicolon. **The semicolon makes the computer print the next item on the same line;** so the computer will print "her" on the same line, like this:

```
father
```

This program gives you some food for thought:

```
CLS
PRINT "I love to eat her";
PRINT "ring for dinner";
PRINT "you are the most beautiful fish in the whole sea!"
```

The program says to print three phrases. Because of the semicolons, the computer tries to print all the phrases onto a single line; but those phrases are too long to all fit on the same line simultaneously! So the computer prints just the first two phrases onto the line and prints the third phrase underneath, like this:

```
I love to eat herring for dinner
you are the most beautiful fish in the whole sea!
```

The next program shows what happens to an evil king on a boat:

```
CLS
PRINT "sin"; "king"
```

The computer will print "sin", and will print "king" on the same line, like this:

```
sinking
```

Notice that in a PRINT statement, you can type several items (such as "sin" and "king"). You're supposed to type a semicolon between each pair of items; but if you forget to type a semicolon, the computer will type it for you automatically when you press the Enter key at the end of the line. The computer will also automatically put a blank space after each semicolon.

Spaces after numbers Try typing this command:

```
PRINT -3; "is my favorite number"
```

Whenever the computer prints a NUMBER, it prints a blank space afterwards; so the computer will print a blank space after -3, like this:

```
-3 is my favorite number
```

Spaces before positive numbers This command tells what to put in your coffee:

```
PRINT 7; "do"; "nuts"
```

The computer prints 7 and "do" and "nuts". Since 7 is a number, the computer prints a blank space after the 7. **The computer prints another blank space BEFORE every number that's positive**; so the computer prints another blank space before the 7, like this:

```
 7 donuts
```

Hey, if you're feeling cool, maybe this command expresses your feelings:

```
PRINT "the temperature is"; 4 + 25; "degrees"
```

The computer prints "the temperature is", then 4 + 25 (which is 29), then "degrees". Since 29 is a positive number, the computer prints a blank space before and after the 29:

```
the temperature is 29 degrees
```

Fix the negative numbers

Use this command if you're even colder:

```
PRINT "the temperature is"; 4 - 25; "degrees"
```

The computer prints "the temperature is", then 4 - 25 (which is -21), then "degrees". Since -21 is a number, the computer prints a space after it; but since -21 is *not* positive, the computer does *not* print a space before it. The computer prints:

```
the temperature is-21 degrees
```

(no space) (space)

Yuk! That looks ugly! It would look prettier if there were a space before the -21. To insert a space, put the space inside quotation marks:

```
PRINT "the temperature is "; 4 - 25; "degrees"
```

inserted space, before the quotation mark

Then the computer will print:

```
the temperature is -21 degrees
```

(inserted space)

Multiple calculations

By using semicolons, you can make the computer do many calculations at once.

For example, this command makes the computer do 6+2, 6-2, 6*2, and 6/2, all at once:

```
PRINT 6 + 2; 6 - 2; 6 * 2; 6 / 2
```

That makes the computer print the four answers:

```
 8  4  12  3
```

The computer prints spaces between the answers, because the computer prints a space after every number (and an additional space before every number that's positive).

Print on paper

If you say LPRINT instead of PRINT, the computer will try print on paper instead of on your screen.

For example, if you want the computer to compute 2+2 and print the answer on paper, type this program:

```
CLS
LPRINT 2 + 2
```

While typing that program, make sure you type "LPRINT". Although "PRINT" can be abbreviated by typing "?", "LPRINT" can*not* be abbreviated by typing "L?"; you must type the word "LPRINT" in full.

When you run that program, the computer will compute 2 + 2 and print this answer onto paper:

```
 4
```

Here are peculiarities:

QB64 The printer might pause a minute before printing. Be patient. Also, if you try to do zoned printing using commas (which I'll explain later), the printer might not space the answers correctly.

QBasic The LPRINT command works just if the printer uses a parallel printer cable (not a serial cable, such as USB). After the printer prints the answer onto paper, you might have to eject the paper manually (by pressing the printer's form-feed button) or eject the paper automatically by putting this line at your program's bottom:
```
LPRINT CHR$(12);
```

If you say PRINT 2 + 2, the computer prints the answer (4) onto the screen. If you say LPRINT 2 + 2, the computer tries to print 4 onto paper instead. If you want to print the answer onto the screen *and also onto paper*, say PRINT *and also LPRINT*, like this:

Program	What the computer will do
CLS	Clear the screen.
PRINT 2 + 2	Print the answer (4) onto the screen.
LPRINT 2 + 2	Print the answer (4) onto paper.

File menu

If you **tap the Alt key and then the F key** (or click "File" by using QB64's mouse), you see this **File menu**:

QB64	QBasic
New	New
Open	Open
Save	Save
Save As	Save As
Update	Print
Exit	Exit

Save

If you want the computer to copy the program onto your hard disk, choose **Save** from the File menu, by pressing the S key (or click "Save" by using QB64's mouse).

If you haven't invented a name for the program yet, the computer will say "File Name" and wait for you to invent a name. Invent any name you wish. For example, the name can be JOE or SUE or LOVER or POEM4U. Pick a name that reminds you of the program's purpose. Here are details:

QB64 The computer assumes you want the name to be "untitled.bas". Erase that name (by holding down the Backspace key), then type whatever name you want instead. When you finish typing the name, press the Enter key. The computer automatically adds ".bas" to the end of it (which means "basic") and copies your program to drive C's qb64 folder.

QBasic The name must be short (up to 8 characters long) and should be simple (consisting of just letters and digits). When you finish typing the name, press the Enter key. Then the computer automatically capitalizes the name, adds ".BAS" to the end of it (which means "Basic"), and copies your program to drive C.

Exception: if the name you invented was already used by another program, the computer asks you, "Overwrite?" Press the Y key if you want the new program to replace the old program, so the old program disappears. If you do *not* want the new program to replace the old program, press N instead of Y, then invent a *different* name for your new program.

Suppose you're creating a program that's so long it takes you several hours to type. You'll be upset if, after several hours of typing, your town suddenly has a blackout that makes the computer forget what you typed. To protect yourself against such a calamity, choose Save from the File menu every 15 minutes. Then if your town has a blackout, you'll lose just a few minutes of work; the rest of your work will have already been saved on the disk. Saving your program every 15 minutes protects you against blackouts and also "computer malfunction" and any careless errors you might make.

New

When you've finished inventing and saving a program, **here's how to erase everything in the blue window, so you can start writing a different program instead**: choose **New** from the File menu, by pressing the N key (or click "New" by using QB64's mouse).

If you didn't save the program you worked on, the computer asks, "Save it now?" If you want to save the program you worked on, press the Y key; if you do *not* want to save the program you worked on, press the N key instead.

QB64 permits this faster way to erase everything in the blue window:

While holding down the Ctrl key, tap the A key. Then press the Delete key.

Open If you saved a program onto the hard disk (drive C), here's how to use it again: choose **Open** from the File menu (by pressing the letter O).

The computer shows you an alphabetical list of Basic programs on the hard disk. (If the list is too long to fit on the screen, the computer shows you the list's beginning.)

Then say which program you want, by using one of these methods….

Method 1 Type the name of the program you want (such as "joe"), then press Enter.

Method 2 In the alphabetical list of Basic programs, indicate which one you want. Here's how. If you're using QB64, click the program you want. If you're using QBasic, press the Tab key then the down-arrow key, then press the down-arrow key a few more times until the program you want is highlighted, then press the Enter key.

All lines of that program will appear on the screen.

Exception: if a different program has been on the screen and you didn't save it, the computer will ask, "Save it now?" If you want to save that program, press the Y key; if you do *not* want to save that program, press the N key instead.

Escape key If you change your mind and wish you hadn't requested the File menu, press the **Escape key** (which says "Esc" on it). The File menu will disappear.

Save As Here's how to create a program called JOE, then create a variant of it called JOE2.

First, type the JOE program and save it. Then do this:

Edit that program. Choose **Save As** from the File menu, by pressing the A key (or click "Save As" by using QB64's mouse). Put "JOE2" into the File Name box. Press Enter.

Print (just in QBasic) If you choose **Print** from that menu (by pressing the P key) and then press the Enter key, the QBasic will copy the program onto paper.

For example, if the screen shows this program —

```
CLS
PRINT 2 + 2
```

---

the printer will print this onto paper:

```
CLS
PRINT 2 + 2
```

Then eject the paper manually.

Update (just in QB64) If you choose **Update** from that menu (by clicking "Update"), QB64 checks immediately whether www.QB64.net has a newer version of QB64. Usually it says "No new updates available"; to reply, press Enter.

You don't have to bother choosing Update, since the computer checks for updates each time you start QB64. The computer automatically installs any updates it finds.

Exit When you've finished using Basic, do this:

QB64 Close the QB64 window (by clicking its X button).
QBasic Choose Exit from the File menu, by pressing the X key.

(If you didn't save the program you worked on, the computer asks, "Save it now?" If you want to save the program you worked on, press the Y key; if you do *not* want to save the program you worked on, press the N key instead.)

Then the computer will exit from Basic.

Become an expert

Congratulations! You've learned how to program!

C'mon, write some programs! It's easy! Try it. You'll have lots of fun!

A person who writes a program is called a **programmer**. Congratulations: *you're* a programmer!

Write *several* programs like the ones I've shown you already. Then you can put on your résumé that you have "a wide variety of programming experience", and you can talk your way into a programming job!

The rest of this chapter explains how to become a *good* programmer.

Practice Programming the computer is like driving a car: **the only way to become an expert is to put your hands on that mean machine and try it yourself**.

If you have a computer, put this book next to the computer's keyboard. At the end of each paragraph, type the examples and look, look, see the computer run! Invent your own variations: try typing different numbers and strings. Invent your own programs: make the computer print your name or a poem; make it solve problems from your other courses and the rest of your life. The computer's a fantastic toy. Play with it.

If you're a student, don't wait for your instructor to give lectures and assign homework. *Act now.* You'll learn more from handling the computer than from lectures or readings. Experience counts.

Hang around your computer. Communicate with it every day. At first, that will be even harder than talking with a cat or a tree, because the computer belongs to a different species, a different kingdom; but keep trying. Get to know it as well as you know your best friend.

If you're taking a French course, you might find French hard; and if you're taking a computer course, you might find computers hard also. But even a stupid 3-year-old French kid can speak French, and even kindergarten kids can program the computer. They have just one advantage over you: practice!

Be bold In science fiction, computers blow up; in real life, they never do. No matter what keys you press, no matter what commands you type, you won't hurt the computer. The computer is invincible! So go ahead and experiment. If it doesn't like what you type, it will gripe at you, but so what?

Troubles When you try using the computer, you'll have trouble — because you're making a mistake, or the computer is broken, or the computer is weird and works differently from the majority computers discussed in this book. (Each computer has its own "personality", its own quirks.)

Whenever you have trouble, laugh about it, and say, "Oh, boy! Here we go again!" (If you're Jewish, you can say all that more briefly, in one word: "Oy!") Then get some help.

Get help For help with your computer, read this book! For further help, read the manuals that came with your computer or ask the genie who got you the computer (your salesperson or parent or boss or teacher or friend).

If you're sitting near computers in your office, school, or home, and other people are nearby, ask them for help. They'll gladly answer your questions because they like to show off and because the way *they* got to know the answers was by asking.

Computer folks like to explain computers, just as priests like to explain religion. You're joining a cult! Even if you don't truly believe in "the power and glory of computers", at least you'll get a few moments of weird fun. Just play along with the weird computer people, boost their egos, and they'll help you get through your initiation rite. Assert yourself and **ask questions**. "Shy guys finish last." To get your money's worth from a computer course, ask your teacher, classmates, lab assistants, and other programmers lots of questions!

Your town probably has a **computer club**. (To find out, ask the local schools and computer stores.) Join the club and tell the members you'd like help with your computer. Probably some computer hobbyist will help you.

Call me anytime at **603-666-6644**: I'll help you, free!

Going & stopping

You can control how your computer goes and stops.

SLEEP

If you say SLEEP, the computer will take a nap:

```
CLS
PRINT "I'm going to take a nap."
SLEEP
PRINT "Thanks for waking me up."
```

The second line makes the computer announce:

```
I'm going to take a nap.
```

The next line says SLEEP, which makes the computer take a nap. The computer will continue sleeping until you wake it up by pressing a key on the keyboard. (Press any key, such as Enter.) Then the computer, woken up, will finish running the rest of the program, whose bottom line makes it say:

```
Thanks for waking me up.
```

Valentine's Day This program lets the computer gripe about how humans treated it on Valentine's Day:

```
CLS
PRINT "Valentine's Day, you didn't bring me flowers!"
PRINT "I won't speak until you gimme roses!"
PRINT "Bring them, then touch one of my keys."
SLEEP
PRINT "It's great to wake up and smell the roses!"
```

Lines 2-4 make the computer say:

```
Valentine's Day, you didn't bring me flowers!
I won't speak until you gimme roses!
Bring them, then touch one of my keys.
```

The next line (SLEEP) makes the upset computer go to sleep and refuse to talk to humans, until a human presses a key. When a human finally presses a key, the computer wakes up and says:

```
It's great to wake up and smell the roses!
```

Timed pause Instead of letting the computer sleep a long time, you can set an alarm clock so the computer will be forced to wake up soon. For example, if you say SLEEP 6 (instead of just SLEEP), the computer will sleep for just 6 seconds.

That's how to make the computer pause for 6 seconds. Give that 6-second pause before you reveal the punch line of a joke:

```
CLS
PRINT "Human, your intelligence is amazing!  You must be an M.D.";
SLEEP 6
PRINT "--Mentally Deficient!"
```

That program makes the computer print the joke's setup ("Human, your intelligence is amazing! You must be an M.D."), then pause for 6 seconds, then reveal the joke's punch line, so the screen finally shows:

```
Human, your intelligence is amazing!  You must be an M.D.--Mentally Deficient!
```

SLEEP 6 makes the computer sleep until it gets woken up by either the alarm clock (after 6 seconds) or the human (by pressing a key). If you want the computer to pause for 10 seconds instead of 6, say SLEEP 10 instead of SLEEP 6.

The number after the word SLEEP can be 6 or 10 or any other positive whole number, but not a decimal. (If you say SLEEP 5.9, the computer will round the 5.9 and sleep for 6 seconds instead.)

This program makes the computer brag, then confess:

```
CLS
PRINT "We computers are smart for three reasons."
PRINT "The first is our VERY GOOD MEMORY."
PRINT "The other two reasons… ";
SLEEP 10
PRINT "I forgot."
```

The computer begins by bragging:

```
We computers are smart for three reasons.
The first is our VERY GOOD MEMORY.
The other two reasons…
```

But then the computer pauses for 10 seconds and finally admits:

```
I forgot.
```

This program makes the computer change its feelings, in surprising ways:

```
CLS
PRINT "I'm up";
SLEEP 3
PRINT "set!  I want to pee";
SLEEP 4
PRINT "k at you";
SLEEP 5
PRINT "r ma";
SLEEP 6
PRINT "nual.";
```

The computer will print —

```
I'm up
```

then pause 3 seconds and change it to —

```
I'm upset!  I want to pee
```

then pause 4 seconds and change it to —

```
I'm upset!  I want to peek at you
```

then pause 5 seconds and change it to —

```
I'm upset!  I want to peek at your ma
```

then pause 6 seconds and change it to:

```
I'm upset!  I want to peek at your manual.
```

Experiment: invent your *own* jokes, and make the computer pause before printing the punch lines.

Speed-reading test This program tests how fast you can read:

```
CLS
PRINT "If you can read this, you read quickly."
SLEEP 1
CLS
```

When you run that program, the computer makes the screen display this message:

```
If you can read this, you read quickly.
```

Then the computer pauses for 1 second (because of the SLEEP 1), then erases the screen (CLS). So the message appears on the screen for just 1 second before being erased!

If you manage to read that entire message in just 1 second, you're indeed a fast reader!

But don't stop at that first success! For the ultimate challenge, try running this program:

```
CLS
PRINT "Mumbling morons make my mom miss murder mysteries Monday morning."
SLEEP 2
CLS
```

That makes the computer display this tongue-twister —

```
Mumbling morons make my mom miss murder mysteries Monday morning.
```

then pause for 2 seconds, then erase the screen. During the 2 seconds while that tongue-twister appears on the screen, can you recite the entire twister out loud? Try it! If you don't recite it properly, you'll sound like a mumbling moron yourself!

DO...LOOP

This program makes the computer print the word "love" once:

```
CLS
PRINT "love"
```

This fancier program makes the computer print the word "love" *three* times:

```
CLS
PRINT "love"
PRINT "love"
PRINT "love"
```

When you run that program, the computer will print:

```
love
love
love
```

Let's make the computer print the word "love" *many* times. To do that, we must make the computer do this line many times:

```
PRINT "love"
```

To make the computer do the line many times, say "DO" above the line and say "LOOP" below it, so the program looks like this:

```
CLS
DO
    PRINT "love"
LOOP
```

Between the words DO and LOOP, the line being repeated (PRINT "love") should be indented.

QB64 The computer will indent the line for you automatically, when you press the Enter key at that line's end.

QBasic To indent the line prettily, press the Space bar (4 times) before you type the line. (If you're too lazy to press the Space bar 4 times, press it just twice. The computer doesn't care how often you press the Space bar.) If you ever want to remove an indentation, put yourself just after those blank spaces then press the Backspace key.

When you run that program, the computer will PRINT "love" many times, so it will print:

```
love
love
love
love
love
love
love
love
love
etc.
```

The computer will print "love" on every line of your screen's window.

But even when the screen's window is full of "love", the computer won't stop: the computer will try to print even more loves onto your screen! The computer will lose control of itself and try to devote its entire life to making love! The computer's mind will spin round and round, always circling back to the thought of making love again!

Since the computer's thinking keeps circling back to the same thought, the computer is said to be in a **loop**. In that program, the **DO** means "do what's underneath and indented"; the **LOOP** means "loop back and do it again". The lines that say DO and LOOP — and the lines between them — form a loop, which is called a **DO loop**.

To stop the computer's lovemaking madness, you must give the computer a "jolt" that will put it out of its misery and get it out of the loop. To jolt the computer out of the program, **abort** the program.

To abort the program, do this:

QB64 Close the black window (by clicking its X button).

QBasic Tap the Break key (which is typically the last key in the top row), while holding down a desktop computer's Ctrl key or a notebook computer's Fn key.

That makes the computer stop running your program; it will **break out of your program**; it will **abort your program** and show you the blue screen so you can edit the program.

In that program, since the computer tries to go round and round the loop forever, the loop is called **infinite**. The only way to stop an infinite loop is to abort it.

Semicolon For more lovely fun, put a semicolon after "love", so the program looks like this:

```
CLS
DO
    PRINT "love";
LOOP
```

The semicolon makes the computer print "love" *next to* "love", so the screen looks like this:

```
lovelovelovelovelovelovelovelovelovelovelovelovelovelovelovelovelovelovelove
lovelovelovelovelovelovelovelovelovelovelovelovelovelovelovelovelovelovelove
lovelovelovelovelovelovelovelovelovelovelovelovelovelovelovelovelovelovelove
etc.
```

If you put a space after love, like this —

```
CLS
DO
    PRINT "love ";
LOOP
```

the computer will put a space after each love:

```
love love love love love love love love love love love love love love love
love love love love love love love love love love love love love love love
love love love love love love love love love love love love love love love
etc.
```

Bigger DO loop Run this program:

```
CLS
DO
    PRINT "dog";
    PRINT "cat";
LOOP
```

Lines 3 & 4 (which say PRINT "dog" and PRINT "cat") make the computer print "dog" and then print "cat" next to it. Since those lines are between the words DO and LOOP, the computer does them repeatedly — PRINT "dog", then PRINT "cat", then PRINT "dog" again, then PRINT "cat" again — so the screen looks like this:

```
dogcatdogcatdogcatdogcatdogcatdogcatdogcatdogcatdogcatdogcatdogcatdogcatdogcat
dogcatdogcatdogcatdogcatdogcatdogcatdogcatdogcatdogcatdogcatdogcatdogcatdogcat
dogcatdogcatdogcatdogcatdogcatdogcatdogcatdogcatdogcatdogcatdogcatdogcatdogcat
etc.
```

The computer will keep printing "dog" and "cat" until you abort the program.

Blinking Let's make the screen say "Stop pollution!" and make that message blink.

To do that, flash "Stop pollution!" onto the screen for 2 seconds, then turn that message off for 1 second (so the screen is blank), then flash that message on again. Here's the program:

```
WIDTH 40
DO
    PRINT "Stop pollution!"
    SLEEP 2
    CLS
    SLEEP 1
LOOP
```

The top line (WIDTH 40) makes sure all characters appear dramatically huge.

Lines 3 & 4 (which say PRINT "Stop pollution!" and SLEEP 2) flash the message "Stop pollution!" onto the screen and keep it on the screen for 2 seconds. The next pair of lines (CLS and SLEEP 1) make the screen become blank for 1 second. Since those lines are all between the words DO and LOOP, the computer does them repeatedly — flash message then blank, flash message then blank, flash message then blank — so your screen becomes a continually flashing sign.

The screen will keep flashing until you abort the program.

Instead of saying "Stop pollution!", edit that program so it flashes your favorite phrase instead, such as "Save the whales!" or "Marry me!" or "Keepa youse hands offa my computer!" or "Jesus saves — America spends!" or "In God we trust — all others pay cash" or "Please wait — Dr. Doom will be with you shortly" or "Let's rock!" or whatever else turns you on. Make the computer say whatever you feel emotional about. Like a dog, the computer imitates its master's personality. If your computer acts "cold and heartless", it's because *you* are!

In the program, you typed just a few lines; but since the bottom line said LOOP, the computer does an infinite loop. By saying LOOP, you can make the computer do an infinite amount of work. Moral: **the computer can turn a finite amount of human energy into an infinite amount of good**. Putting it another way: **the computer can multiply your abilities by infinity**.

Line numbers

You can number the lines in your program. For example, instead of typing —

```
CLS
DO
    PRINT "love"
LOOP
```

you can type:

```
1 CLS
2 DO
    3 PRINT "love"
4 LOOP
```

Then when you're discussing your program with another programmer, you can talk about "line 3" instead of having to talk about "the line in the middle of the DO loop".

Selective numbering You can number just the lines you're planning to discuss.

For example, if you're planning to discuss just lines 2 and 4, you can number just those lines:

```
CLS
2 DO
    PRINT "love"
4 LOOP
```

Or if you prefer, number them like this:

```
CLS
1 DO
    PRINT "love"
2 LOOP
```

Decimal numbers Here's a simple program:

```
1 CLS
2 PRINT "Life's a blast!"
```

Suppose you want to edit it and insert an extra numbered line between 1 and 2. You can give the extra line a decimal number, such as 1.5:

```
1 CLS
1.5 PRINT "I hope..."
2 PRINT "Life's a blast!"
```

Number by tens Instead of making line numbers be 1, 2, 3, etc., make the line numbers be 10, 20, 30, etc., like this:

```
10 CLS
20 PRINT "Life's a blast!"
```

Then you can insert an extra line without using decimals:

```
10 CLS
15 PRINT "I hope..."
20 PRINT "Life's a blast!"
```

GOTO

This program makes the computer print the words "dog" and "cat" repeatedly:

```
CLS
DO
    PRINT "dog";
    PRINT "cat";
LOOP
```

It makes the computer print:

```
dogcatdogcatdogcatdogcatdogcatdogcatdogcatdogcatdogcatdogcatdogcatdogcat
dogcatdogcatdogcatdogcatdogcatdogcatdogcatdogcatdogcatdogcatdogcatdogcat
dogcatdogcatdogcatdogcatdogcatdogcatdogcatdogcatdogcatdogcatdogcatdogcat
etc.
```

This program does the same thing:

```
CLS
10 PRINT "dog";
PRINT "cat";
GOTO 10
```

The second line (which is numbered 10) makes the computer print "dog". The next line makes the computer print "cat". The bottom line makes the computer GO back TO line 10, so the computer will print "dog" again, then "cat again", then GO back TO line 10 again, then print "dog" again, then "cat" again, etc. The computer will print "dog" and "cat" repeatedly, until you abort the program.

This program does the same thing:

```
CLS
joe: PRINT "dog";
PRINT "cat";
GOTO joe
```

The second line (named "joe") makes the computer print "dog". The next line makes the computer print "cat". The bottom line makes the computer GO back TO the line named "joe". In that program, "joe" is called the second line's **label**.

One word "GOTO" is one word. You're supposed to type "GOTO", not "GO TO". If you accidentally type "GO TO" instead of "GOTO", here's what happens when you press the Enter key at the end of that line:

QB64 The computer will gripe by saying "Syntax error".
QBasic The computer will automatically turn your "GO TO" into "GOTO".

Skip ahead Did you ever dream about having a picnic in the woods? This program expresses that dream:

```
CLS
PRINT "Let's munch"
PRINT "sandwiches under"
PRINT "the trees!"
```

It makes the computer print:

```
Let's munch
sandwiches under
the trees!
```

Let's turn that dream into a nightmare where we all become giant termites. To do that, insert the shaded items:

```
CLS
PRINT "Let's munch"
GOTO 10
PRINT "sandwiches under"
10 PRINT "the trees!"
```

The computer begins by printing "Let's munch". Then the computer does GOTO 10, which makes the computer GO skip down TO line 10, which prints "the trees!" So the program makes the computer print just this:

```
Let's munch
the trees!
```

Is GOTO too powerful? The word GOTO gives you great power: if you say GO back TO line 10, the computer will create a loop (as if you'd said DO...LOOP); if you say GO skip down TO line 10, the computer will skip over several lines of your program.

Since the word GOTO is so powerful, programmers fear it! Programmers know that the slightest error in using that powerful word will make the programs act very

bizarre! Programmers feel more comfortable using milder words instead (such as DO...LOOP), which are safer and rarely get botched up. Since the word GOTO is scary, many computer teachers prohibit students from using it, and many companies fire programmers who say GOTO instead of DO...LOOP.

But saying GOTO is fine when you've learned how to control the power! Though I'll usually say DO...LOOP instead of GOTO, I'll say GOTO in certain situations where saying DO...LOOP would be awkward.

Life as an infinite loop

A program that makes the computer do the same thing again and again forever is an infinite loop.

Some humans act just like computers. Those humans do the same thing again and again.

```
Every morning they GOTO work, and every
evening they GOTO home. GOTO work, GOTO
home, GOTO work, GOTO home,... Their lives
are sheer drudgery. They're caught in an infinite loop.
```

Go to your bathroom, get your bottle of shampoo, and look at the instructions on the back. A typical bottle has three instructions:

```
Lather.
Rinse.
Repeat.
```

Those instructions say to lather, then rinse, then repeat — which means to lather again, then rinse again, then repeat again — which means to lather again, then rinse again, then repeat again.... If you follow those instructions, you'll never finish washing your hair! The instructions are an infinite loop! The instructions are a program: they program you to use lots of shampoo! That's how infinite loops help sell shampoo.

END

To make the computer skip the bottom part of your program, say END:

```
CLS
PRINT "She smells"
END
PRINT "of perfume"
```

When you run that program (by pressing Shift with F5), the computer will print "She smells" and then end, without printing "of perfume".

Suppose you write a program that prints a long message, and you want to run the program several times (so several of your friends get the message). If one of your friends would be offended by the end of your message, send that friend an *abridged* message! Here's how: put END above the part of the message that you want the computer to omit — or skip past that part by saying GOTO.

Multi-statement line

In your program, **a line can contain several statements separated by colons**, like this:

```
CLS: PRINT "I dream": PRINT "of you"
```

When you run that program, the computer will CLear the Screen, then PRINT "I dream", then PRINT "of you". Altogether, the computer will print:

```
I dream
of you
```

If you want to number the line, put the number at the far left, like this:

```
10 CLS: PRINT "I dream": PRINT "of you"
```

Variables

A letter can stand for a number. For example, x can stand for the number 47, as in this program:

```
CLS
x = 47
PRINT x + 2
```

The second line says x stands for the number 47. In other words, x is a name for the number 47.

The bottom line says to print x + 2. Since x is 47, the x + 2 is 49; so the computer will print 49. That's the only number the computer will print; it will not print 47.

Jargon

A letter that stands for a number is called a **numeric variable**. In that program, x is a numeric variable; it stands for the number 47. The **value** of x is 47.

In that program, the statement "x = 47" is called an **assignment statement**, because it **assigns** 47 to x.

A variable is a box

When you run that program, here's what happens inside the computer.

The computer's random-access memory (RAM) consists of electronic boxes. When the computer encounters the line "x = 47", the computer puts 47 into box x, like this:

```
box x [               47 ]
```

Then when the computer encounters the line "PRINT x + 2", the computer prints what's in box x, plus 2; so the computer prints 49.

Faster typing

Instead of typing —

```
x = 47
```

you can type just this:

```
x=47
```

At the end of that line, when you press the Enter key, the computer will automatically put spaces around the equal sign.

Since the computer automatically capitalizes computer words (such as CLS), automatically puts spaces around symbols (such as + and =), and lets you type a question mark instead of the word PRINT, you can type just this:

```
cls
x=47
?x+2
```

When you press Enter at the end of each line, the computer will automatically convert your typing to this:

```
CLS
x = 47
PRINT x + 2
```

More examples

Here's another example:

```
CLS
y = 38
PRINT y - 2
```

The second line says y is a numeric variable that stands for the number 38.

The bottom line says to print y - 2. Since y is 38, the y - 2 is 36; so the computer will print 36.

Example:

```
CLS
b = 8
PRINT b * 3
```

The second line says b is 8. The bottom line says to print b * 3, which is 8 * 3, which is 24; so the computer will print 24.

One variable can define another:

```
CLS
n = 6
d = n + 1
PRINT n * d
```

The second line says n is 6. The next line says d is n + 1, which is 6 + 1, which is 7; so d is 7. The bottom line says to print n * d, which is 6 * 7, which is 42; so the computer will print 42.

Changing a value

A value can change:

```
CLS
k = 4
k = 9
PRINT k * 2
```

The second line says k's value is 4. The next line changes k's value to 9, so the bottom line prints 18.

When you run that program, here's what happens inside the computer's RAM. The second line (k = 4) makes the computer put 4 into box k:

```
box k [               4 ]
```

The next line (k = 9) puts 9 into box k. The 9 replaces the 4:

```
box k [               9 ]
```

That's why the bottom line (PRINT k * 2) prints 18.

Hassles

When writing an equation (such as x = 47), here's what you must put before the equal sign: the name of just one box (such as x). So **before the equal sign, put one variable**:

```
Allowed:     d = n + 1    (d is one variable)
Not allowed: d - n = 1    (d-n is two variables)
Not allowed: 1 = d - n    (1 is not a variable)
```

The variable on the left side of the equation is the only one that changes. For example, the statement d = n + 1 changes the value of d but not n. The statement b = c changes the value of b but not c:

```
CLS
b = 1
c = 7
b = c
PRINT b + c
```

The fourth line changes b, to make it equal c; so b becomes 7. Since both b and c are now 7, the bottom line prints 14.

"b = c" versus "c = b" Saying "b = c" has a different effect from "c = b". That's because "b = c" changes the value of b (but not c); saying "c = b" changes the value of c (but not b).

Compare these programs:

```
CLS            CLS
b = 1          b = 1
c = 7          c = 7
b = c          c = b
PRINT b + c    PRINT b + c
```

In the left program (which you saw before), the fourth line changes b to 7, so both b and c are 7. The bottom line prints 14.

In the right program, the fourth line changes c to 1, so both b and c are 1. The bottom line prints 2.

While you run those programs, here's what happens inside the computer's RAM. For both programs, the second and third lines do this:

```
box b [               1 ]
box c [               7 ]
```

In the left program, the fourth line makes the number in box b become 7 (so both boxes contain 7, and the bottom line prints 14). In the right program, the fourth line makes the number in box c become 1 (so both boxes contain 1, and the bottom line prints 2).

When to use variables

Here's a practical example of when to use variables.

Suppose you're selling something that costs $1297.43, and you want to do these calculations:

```
multiply   $1297.43 by 2
multiply   $1297.43 by .05
add        $1297.43 to $483.19
divide     $1297.43 by 37
```

To do those four calculations, you could run this program:

```
CLS
PRINT 1297.43 * 2; 1297.43 * .05; 1297.43 + 483.19; 1297.43 / 37
```

But that program's silly, since it contains the number 1297.43 four times. This program's briefer, because it uses a variable:

```
CLS
c = 1297.43
PRINT c * 2; c * .05; c + 483.19; c / 37
```

So **whenever you need to use a number several times, turn the number into a variable**, which will make your program briefer.

String variables

A string is any collection of characters, such as "I love you". Each string must be in quotation marks.

A letter can stand for a string — if you put a dollar sign after the letter, like this:

```
CLS
g$ = "down"
PRINT g$
```

The second line says g$ stands for the string "down". The bottom line prints:

```
down
```

In that program, g$ is a variable. Since it stands for a string, it's called a **string variable**.

Every string variable must end with a dollar sign. The dollar sign is supposed to remind you of a fancy S, which stands for String. The second line is pronounced, "g String is down".

If you're paranoid, you'll love this program:

```
CLS
t$ = "They're laughing at you!"
PRINT t$
PRINT t$
PRINT t$
```

The second line says t$ stands for the string "They're laughing at you!" The later lines make the computer print:

```
They're laughing at you!
They're laughing at you!
They're laughing at you!
```

Spaces between strings

Examine this program:

```
CLS
s$ = "sin"
k$ = "king"
PRINT s$; k$
```

The bottom line says to print "sin" and then "king", so the computer will print:

```
sinking
```

Let's make the computer leave a space between "sin" and "king", so the computer prints:

```
sin king
```

To make the computer leave that space, choose one of these methods....

Method 1: instead of saying s$ = "sin", make s$ include a space:
```
s$ = "sin "
```

Method 2: instead of saying k$ = "king", make k$ include a space:
```
k$ = " king"
```

Method 3: instead of saying —
```
PRINT s$; k$
```
say to print s$ then a space then k$:
```
PRINT s$; " "; k$
```

Method 4 (just in QBasic): since QBasic will automatically insert the semicolons, QBasic lets you type just this —
```
PRINT s$ " " k$
```
or even type just this —
```
PRINT s$" "k$
```
or even type just this:
```
?s$" "k$
```
When you press the Enter key at the end of that line, QBasic will automatically convert the line to:
```
PRINT s$; " "; k$
```

Nursery rhymes

The computer can recite nursery rhymes:

```
CLS
p$ = "Peas porridge "
PRINT p$; "hot!"
PRINT p$; "cold!"
PRINT p$; "in the pot,"
PRINT "Nine days old!"
```

The second line says p$ stands for "Peas porridge ". The later lines make the computer print:

```
Peas porridge hot!
Peas porridge cold!
Peas porridge in the pot,
Nine days old!
```

This program prints a fancier rhyme:

```
CLS
h$ = "Hickory, dickory, dock! "
m$ = "THE MOUSE (squeak! squeak!) "
c$ = "THE CLOCK (tick! tock!) "
PRINT h$
PRINT m$; "ran up "; c$
PRINT c$; "struck one"
PRINT m$; "ran down"
PRINT h$
```

Lines 2-4 define h$, m$, and c$. The later lines make the computer print:

```
Hickory, dickory, dock!
THE MOUSE (squeak! squeak!) ran up THE CLOCK (tick! tock!)
THE CLOCK (tick! tock!) struck one
THE MOUSE (squeak! squeak!) ran down
Hickory, dickory, dock!
```

Undefined variables

If you don't define a numeric variable, the computer assumes it's zero:

```
CLS
PRINT r
```

Since r hasn't been defined, the bottom line prints zero. The computer doesn't look ahead:

```
CLS
PRINT j
j = 5
```

When the computer encounters the second line (PRINT j), it doesn't look ahead to find out what j is. As of the second line, j is still undefined, so the computer prints zero.

If you don't define a string variable, the computer assumes it's blank:

```
CLS
PRINT f$
```

Since f$ hasn't been defined, the "PRINT f$" makes the computer print a line that says nothing; the line the computer prints is blank.

Long variable names

A numeric variable's name can be a letter (such as x) or a longer combination of characters, such as:

```
profit.in.2001.before.November.promotion
```

For example, you can type:

```
CLS
profit.in.2001.before.November.promotion = 3497.18
profit.in.2001 = profit.in.2001.before.November.promotion + 6214.27
PRINT profit.in.2001
```

The computer will print:

```
9711.45
```

The variable's name can be quite long: up to 40 characters!

The first character in the name must be a letter. The remaining characters can be letters, digits, or periods.

The name must not be a word that has a special meaning to the computer. For example, the name cannot be "print".

If the variable stands for a string, the name can have up to 40 characters, followed by a dollar sign, making a total of 41 characters, like this:

```
my.job.in.2001.before.November.promotion$
```

Beginners are usually too lazy to type long variable names, so beginners use variable names that are short. But when you become a pro and write a long, fancy program containing hundreds of lines and hundreds of variables, you should use long variable names to help you remember each variable's purpose.

In this book, I'll use short variable names in short programs (so you can type those programs quickly) but long variable names in long programs (so you can keep track of which variable is which).

Programmers employed at Microsoft capitalize each word's first letter and omit the periods. So instead of writing —

```
my.job.in.2001.before.November.promotion$
```

those programmers write:

```
MyJobIn2001BeforeNovemberPromotion$
```

That's harder to read; but since Microsoft's chairman is Bill Gates, who's the richest person in America, he can do whatever he pleases!

INPUT

Humans ask questions; so to turn the computer into a human, you must make it ask questions too. **To make the computer ask a question, use the word INPUT.**

This program makes the computer ask for your name:

```
CLS
INPUT "What is your name"; n$
PRINT "I adore anyone whose name is "; n$
```

When the computer sees that INPUT line, the computer asks "What is your name?" then waits for you to answer the question. Your answer will be called n$. For example, if you answer Maria, then n$ is Maria. The bottom line makes the computer print:

```
I adore anyone whose name is Maria
```

When you run that program, here's the whole conversation that occurs between the computer and you; I've underlined the part typed by you....

```
Computer asks for your name: What is your name? Maria
Computer praises your name: I adore anyone whose name is Maria
```

Try that example. Be careful! When you type the INPUT line, make sure you type the two quotation marks and the semicolon. You don't have to type a question mark: when the computer runs your program, it will automatically put a question mark at the end of the question.

Just for fun, run that program again and pretend you're somebody else....

```
Computer asks for your name: What is your name? Bud
Computer praises your name: I adore anyone whose name is Bud
```

When the computer asks for your name, if you say something weird, the computer will give you a weird reply....

```
Computer asks:    What is your name? none of your business!
Computer replies: I adore anyone whose name is none of your business!
```

College admissions

This program prints a letter, admitting you to the college of your choice:

```
CLS
INPUT "What college would you like to enter"; c$
PRINT "Congratulations!"
PRINT "You have just been admitted to "; c$
PRINT "because it fits your personality."
PRINT "I hope you go to "; c$; "."
PRINT "          Respectfully yours,"
PRINT "          The Dean of Admissions"
```

When the computer sees the INPUT line, the computer asks "What college would you like to enter?" and waits for you to answer. Your answer will be called c$. If you'd like to be admitted to Harvard, you'll be pleased....

```
Computer asks you:   What college would you like to enter? Harvard
Computer admits you: Congratulations!
                     You have just been admitted to Harvard
                     because it fits your personality.
                     I hope you go to Harvard.
                          Respectfully yours,
                          The Dean of Admissions
```

You can choose any college you wish:

```
Computer asks you:   What college would you like to enter? Hell
Computer admits you: Congratulations!
                     You have just been admitted to Hell
                     because it fits your personality.
                     I hope you go to Hell.
                          Respectfully yours,
                          The Dean of Admissions
```

That program consists of three parts:

1. The computer begins by asking you a question ("What college would you like to enter?"). The computer's question is called the **prompt**, because it prompts you to answer.

2. Your answer (the college's name) is called **your input**, because it's information that you're *putting into* the computer.

3. The computer's reply (the admission letter) is called the **computer's output**, because it's the final answer that the computer puts out.

INPUT versus PRINT

The word INPUT is the opposite of the word PRINT.

The word PRINT makes the computer print information out. The word INPUT makes the computer take information in.

What the computer prints out is called the **output**. What the computer takes in is called **your input**.

Input and Output are collectively called **I/O**, so the INPUT and PRINT statements are called **I/O statements**.

Once upon a time

Let's make the computer write a story, by filling in the blanks:

```
Once upon a time, there was a youngster named _____
                                          your name

who had a friend named _____.
                          friend's name

_____ wanted to _____ _____,
 your name              verb (such as "pat")  friend's name

but _____ didn't want to _____ _____!
    friend's name               verb (such as "pat")  your name

Will _____ _____ _____?
     your name    verb (such as "pat")  friend's name

Will _____ _____ _____?
     friend's name  verb (such as "pat")  your name

To find out, come back and see the next exciting episode

of _____ and _____!
   your name        friend's name
```

To write the story, the computer must ask for your name, your friend's name, and a verb. To make the computer ask, your program must say INPUT:

```
CLS
INPUT "What is your name"; y$
INPUT "What's your friend's name"; f$
INPUT "In 1 word, say something you can do to your friend"; v$
```

Then make the computer print the story:

```
PRINT "Here's my story...."
PRINT "Once upon a time, there was a youngster named "; y$
PRINT "who had a friend named "; f$; "."
PRINT y$; " wanted to "; v$; " "; f$; ","
PRINT "but "; f$; " didn't want to "; v$; " "; y$; "!"
PRINT "Will "; y$; " "; v$; " "; f$; "?"
PRINT "Will "; f$; " "; v$; " "; y$; "?"
PRINT "To find out, come back and see the next exciting episode"
PRINT "of "; y$; " and "; f$; "!"
```

Here's a sample run:

```
What's your name? Dracula
What's your friend's name? Madonna
In 1 word, say something you can do to your friend? bite
Here's my story....
Once upon a time, there was a youngster named Dracula
who had a friend named Madonna.
Dracula wanted to bite Madonna,
but Madonna didn't want to bite Dracula!
Will Dracula bite Madonna?
Will Madonna bite Dracula?
To find out, come back and see the next exciting episode
of Dracula and Madonna!
```

Here's another run:

```
What's your name? Superman
What's your friend's name? King Kong
In 1 word, say something you can do to your friend? tickle
Here's my story....
Once upon a time, there was a youngster named Superman
Who had a friend named King Kong.
Superman wanted to tickle King Kong,
but King Kong didn't want to tickle Superman!
Will Superman tickle King Kong?
Will King Kong tickle Superman?
To find out, come back and see the next exciting episode
of Superman and King Kong!
```

Try it: put in your own name, the name of your friend, and something you'd like to do to your friend.

Contest

The following program prints a certificate saying you won a contest. Since the program contains many variables, it uses long variable names to help you remember which variable is which:

```
CLS
INPUT "What's your name"; you$
INPUT "What's your friend's name"; friend$
INPUT "What's the name of another friend"; friend2$
INPUT "Name a color"; color$
INPUT "Name a place"; place$
INPUT "Name a food"; food$
INPUT "Name an object"; object$
INPUT "Name a part of the body"; part$
INPUT "Name a style of cooking (such as baked or fried)"; style$
PRINT
PRINT "Congratulations, "; you$; "!"
PRINT "You've won the beauty contest, because of your gorgeous "; part$; "."
PRINT "Your prize is a "; color$; " "; object$
PRINT "plus a trip to "; place$; " with your friend "; friend$
PRINT "plus--and this is the best part of all--"
PRINT "dinner for the two of you at "; friend2$; "'s new restaurant,"
PRINT "where "; friend2$; " will give you "
PRINT "all the "; style$; " "; food$; " you can eat."
PRINT "Congratulations, "; you$; ", today's your lucky day!"
PRINT "Now everyone wants to kiss your award-winning "; part$; "."
```

Here's a sample run:

```
What's your name? Long John Silver
What's your friend's name? the parrot
What's the name of another friend? Jim
Name a color? gold
Name a place? Treasure Island
Name a food? rum-soaked coconuts
Name an object? chest of jewels
Name a part of the body? missing leg
Name a style of cooking (such as baked or fried)? barbecued

Congratulations, Long John Silver!
You've won the beauty contest, because of your gorgeous missing leg.
Your prize is a gold chest of jewels
plus a trip to Treasure Island with your friend the parrot
plus--and this is the best part of all--
dinner for the two of you at Jim's new restaurant,
where Jim will give you all the barbecued rum-soaked coconuts you can eat.
Congratulations, Long John Silver, today's your lucky day!
Now everyone wants to kiss your award-winning missing leg.
```

Bills

If you're a nasty bill collector, you'll love this program:

```
CLS
INPUT "What is the customer's first name"; first.name$
INPUT "What is the customer's last name"; last.name$
INPUT "What is the customer's street address"; street.address$
INPUT "What city"; city$
INPUT "What state"; state$
INPUT "What ZIP code"; zip.code$
PRINT
PRINT first.name$; " "; last.name$
PRINT street.address$
PRINT city$; " "; state$; " "; zip.code$
PRINT
PRINT "Dear "; first.name$; ","
PRINT "    You still haven't paid the bill."
PRINT "If you don't pay it soon, "; first.name$; ","
PRINT "I'll come visit you in "; city$
PRINT "and personally shoot you."
PRINT "                Yours truly,"
PRINT "                Sure-as-shootin'"
PRINT "                Your crazy creditor"
```

Can you figure out what that program does?

Numeric input

This program makes the computer predict your future:

```
CLS
PRINT "I predict what'll happen to you in the year 2020!"
INPUT "In what year were you born"; y
PRINT "In the year 2020, you'll turn"; 2020 - y; "years old."
```

Here's a sample run:

```
I predict what'll happen to you in the year 2020!
In what year were you born? 1962
In the year 2020, you'll turn 58 years old.
```

Suppose you're selling tickets to a play. Each ticket costs $2.79. (You decided $2.79 would be a nifty price, because the cast has 279 people.) This program finds the price of multiple tickets:

```
CLS
INPUT "How many tickets"; t
PRINT "The total price is $"; t * 2.79
```

This program tells you how much the "oil crisis" costs you, when you drive your car:

```
CLS
INPUT "How many miles do you want to drive"; m
INPUT "How many pennies does a gallon of gas cost"; p
INPUT "How many miles-per-gallon does your car get"; r
PRINT "The gas for your trip will cost you $"; m * p / (r * 100)
```

Here's a sample run:

```
How many miles do you want to drive? 400
How many pennies does a gallon of gas cost? 204.9
How many miles-per-gallon does your car get? 31
The gas for your trip will cost you $ 26.43871
```

Conversion

This program converts feet to inches:

```
CLS
INPUT "How many feet"; f
PRINT f; "feet ="; f * 12; "inches"
```

Here's a sample run:

```
How many feet? 3
3 feet = 36 inches
```

Trying to convert to the metric system? This program converts inches to centimeters:

```
CLS
INPUT "How many inches"; i
PRINT i; "inches ="; i * 2.54; "centimeters"
```

Nice day today, isn't it? This program converts the temperature from Celsius to Fahrenheit:

```
CLS
INPUT "How many degrees Celsius"; c
PRINT c; "degrees Celsius ="; c * 1.8 + 32; "degrees Fahrenheit"
```

Here's a sample run:

```
How many degrees Celsius? 20
20 degrees Celsius = 68 degrees Fahrenheit
```

See, you can write the *Guide* yourself! Just hunt through any old math or science book, find any old formula (such as f = c * 1.8 + 32), and turn it into a program.

Conditions

Here's how to restrict the computer, so it performs certain lines only under certain conditions....

IF

Let's write a program so that if the human is less than 18 years old, the computer will say:

```
You are still a minor.
```

Here's the program:

```
CLS
INPUT "How old are you"; age
IF age < 18 THEN PRINT "You are still a minor"
```

Line 2 makes the computer ask "How old are you" and wait for the human to type an age. Since **the symbol for "less than" is "<"**, the bottom line says: if the age is less than 18, then print "You are still a minor".

Go ahead! Run that program! The computer begins the conversation by asking:

```
How old are you?
```

Try saying you're 12 years old, by typing a 12, so the screen looks like this:

```
How old are you? 12
```

When you finish typing the 12 and press the Enter key at the end of it, the computer will reply:

```
You are still a minor
```

Try running that program again, but this time try saying you're 50 years old instead of 12, so the screen looks like this:

```
How old are you? 50
```

When you finish typing the 50 and press the Enter key at the end of it, the computer will *not* say "You are still a minor". Instead, the computer will say nothing — since we didn't teach the computer how to respond to adults yet!

In that program, the most important line says:

```
IF age < 18 THEN PRINT "You are still a minor"
```

That line contains the words IF and THEN. **Whenever you say IF, you must also say THEN**. Do *not* put a comma before THEN. What comes between IF and THEN is called the **condition**; in that example, the condition is "age < 18". If the condition is true (if age is really less than 18), the computer does the **action**, which comes after the word THEN and is:

```
PRINT "You are still a minor"
```

ELSE

Let's teach the computer how to respond to adults.

Here's how to program the computer so that if the age is less than 18, the computer will say "You are still a minor", but if the age is *not* less than 18 the computer will say "You are an adult" instead:

```
CLS
INPUT "How old are you"; age
IF age < 18 THEN PRINT "You are still a minor" ELSE PRINT "You are an adult"
```

In programs, **the word "ELSE" means "otherwise"**. That program's bottom line means: if the age is less than 18, then print "You are still a minor"; otherwise (if the age is *not* less than 18), print "You are an adult". So the computer will print "You are still a minor" or else print "You are an adult", depending on whether the age is less than 18.

Try running that program! If you say you're 50 years old, so the screen looks like this —

```
How old are you? 50
```

the computer will reply by saying:

```
You are an adult
```

Multi-line IF

If the age is less than 18, here's how to make the computer print "You are still a minor" and also print "Ah, the joys of youth":

```
IF age < 18 THEN PRINT "You are still a minor": PRINT "Ah, the joys of youth"
```

Here's a more sophisticated way to say the same thing:

```
IF age < 18 THEN
    PRINT "You are still a minor"
    PRINT "Ah, the joys of youth"
END IF
```

That sophisticated way (in which you type 4 short lines instead of a single long line) is called a **multi-line IF** (or a **block IF**).

In a multi-line IF:

The top line must say IF and THEN (with nothing after THEN).

The middle lines should be indented; they're called the **block** and typically say PRINT.

The bottom line must say END IF.

In the middle of a multi-line IF, you can say ELSE:

```
IF age < 18 THEN
    PRINT "You are still a minor"
    PRINT "Ah, the joys of youth"
ELSE
    PRINT "You are an adult"
    PRINT "We can have adult fun"
END IF
```

That means: if the age is less than 18, then print "You are still a minor" and "Ah, the joys of youth"; otherwise (if age *not* under 18) print "You are an adult" and "We can have adult fun".

ELSEIF

Let's say this:

If age is under 18, print "You're a minor".
If age is *not* under 18 but is under 100, print "You're a typical adult".
If age is *not* under 100 but is under 125, print "You're a centenarian".
If age is *not* under 125, print "You're a liar".

Here's how:

```
IF age < 18 THEN
    PRINT "You're a minor"
ELSEIF age < 100 THEN
    PRINT "You're a typical adult"
ELSEIF age < 125 THEN
    PRINT "You're a centenarian"
ELSE
    PRINT "You're a liar"
END IF
```

One word "ELSEIF" is one word. Type "ELSEIF", not "ELSE IF". If you accidentally type "ELSE IF", the computer will gripe.

SELECT

Let's turn your computer into a therapist!

To make the computer ask the patient, "How are you?", begin the program like this:

```
CLS
INPUT "How are you"; a$
```

Make the computer continue the conversation by responding this way:

If the patient says "fine", print "That's good!"
If the patient says "lousy" instead, print "Too bad!"
If the patient says anything else instead, print "I feel the same way!"

To accomplish all that, you can use a multi-line IF:

```
IF a$ = "fine" THEN
    PRINT "That's good!"
ELSEIF a$ = "lousy" THEN
    PRINT "Too bad!"
ELSE
    PRINT "I feel the same way!"
END IF
```

Instead of typing that multi-line IF, you can type this **SELECT statement** instead, which is briefer and simpler:

```
SELECT CASE a$
    CASE "fine"
        PRINT "That's good!"
    CASE "lousy"
        PRINT "Too bad!"
    CASE ELSE
        PRINT "I feel the same way!"
END SELECT
```

Like a multi-line IF, a SELECT statement consumes several lines. The top line of that SELECT statement tells the computer to analyze a$ and SELECT one of the CASEs from the list underneath. That list is indented and says:

In the case where a$ is "fine", print "That's good!"
In the case where a$ is "lousy", print "Too bad!"
In the case where a$ is anything else, print "I feel the same way!"

Every SELECT statement's bottom line must say END SELECT.

Complete program Here's a complete program:

```
CLS
INPUT "How are you"; a$
SELECT CASE a$
    CASE "fine"
        PRINT "That's good!"
    CASE "lousy"
        PRINT "Too bad!"
    CASE ELSE
        PRINT "I feel the same way!"
END SELECT
PRINT "I hope you enjoyed your therapy.  Now you owe $50."
```

Line 2 makes the computer ask the patient, "How are you?" The next several lines are the SELECT statement, which makes the computer analyze the patient's answer and print "That's good!" or "Too bad!" or else "I feel the same way!"

Regardless of what the patient and computer said, that program's bottom line always makes the computer end the conversation by printing:

```
I hope you enjoyed your therapy.  Now you owe $50.
```

In that program, try changing the strings to make the computer print smarter remarks, become a better therapist, and charge even more money.

Error trap This program makes the computer discuss human sexuality:

```
CLS
10 INPUT "Are you male or female"; a$
SELECT CASE a$
    CASE "male"
        PRINT "So is Frankenstein!"
    CASE "female"
        PRINT "So is Mary Poppins!"
    CASE ELSE
        PRINT "Please say male or female!"
        GOTO 10
END SELECT
```

The second line (which is numbered 10) makes the computer ask, "Are you male or female?"

The remaining lines are a SELECT statement that analyzes the human's response. If the human claims to be "male", the computer prints "So is Frankenstein!" If the human says "female" instead, the computer prints "So is Mary Poppins!" If the human says anything else (such as "not sure" or "super-male" or "macho" or "none of your business"), the computer does the CASE ELSE, which makes the computer say "Please say male or female!" and then go back to line 10, which makes the computer ask again, "Are you male or female?"

In that program, the CASE ELSE is called an **error handler** (or **error-handling routine** or **error trap**), since its only purpose is to handle human error (a human who says neither "male" nor "female"). Notice that the error handler begins by printing a gripe message ("Please say male or female!") and then lets the human try again (GOTO 10).

In QBasic, the GOTO statements are used rarely: they're used mainly in error handlers, to let the human try again.

Let's extend that program's conversation. If the human says "female", let's make the computer say "So is Mary Poppins!", then ask "Do you like her?", then continue the conversation this way:

If human says "yes", make computer say "I like her too. She is my mother."
If human says "no", make computer say "I hate her too. She owes me a dime."
If human says neither "yes" nor "no", make computer handle that error.

To accomplish all that, insert the shaded lines into the program:

```
CLS
10 INPUT "Are you male or female"; a$
SELECT CASE a$
    CASE "male"
        PRINT "So is Frankenstein!"
    CASE "female"
        PRINT "So is Mary Poppins!"
        20 INPUT "Do you like her"; b$
        SELECT CASE b$
            CASE "yes"
                PRINT "I like her too.  She is my mother.  "
            CASE "no"
                PRINT "I hate her too.  She owes me a dime."
            CASE ELSE
                PRINT "Please say yes or no!"
                GO TO 20
        END SELECT
    CASE ELSE
        PRINT "Please say male or female!"
        GOTO 10
END SELECT
```

Weird programs The computer's abilities are limited only by your own imagination — and your weirdness. Here are some weird programs from weird minds....

Like a human, the computer wants to meet new friends. This program makes the computer show its true feelings:

```
CLS
10 INPUT "Are you my friend"; a$
SELECT CASE a$
    CASE "yes"
        PRINT "That's swell."
    CASE "no"
        PRINT "Go jump in a lake."
    CASE ELSE
        PRINT "Please say yes or no."
        GO TO 10
END SELECT
```

When you run that program, the computer asks "Are you my friend?" If you say "yes", the computer says "That's swell." If you say "no", the computer says "Go jump in a lake."

The most inventive programmers are kids. This program was written by a girl in the sixth grade:

```
CLS
10 INPUT "Can I come over to your house to watch TV"; a$
SELECT CASE a$
    CASE "yes"
        PRINT "Thanks.  I'll be there at 5PM."
    CASE "no"
        PRINT "Humph!  Your feet smell, anyway."
    CASE ELSE
        PRINT "Please say yes or no."
        GO TO 10
END SELECT
```

When you run that program, the computer asks to watch your TV. If you say "yes", the computer promises to come to your house at 5. If you refuse, the computer insults your feet.

Another sixth-grade girl wrote this program, to test your honesty:

```
CLS
PRINT "FKGJDFGKJ*#K$JSLF*/#$()$&(IKJNHBGD52:?./KSDJK$E(EF$#/JIK(*"
PRINT "FASDFJKL:JFRFVFJUNJI*&()JNE$#SKI#(!SERF HHW NNWAZ MAME !!!"
PRINT "ZBB%%%%%##)))))FESDFJK DSFE N.D.JJUJASD EHWLKD******"
10 INPUT "Do you understand what I said"; a$
SELECT CASE a$
    CASE "no"
        PRINT "Sorry to have bothered you."
    CASE "yes"
        PRINT "SSFJSLFKDJFL++++45673456779XSDWFEF/#$&**()--!!ZZXX"
        PRINT "###EDFHTG NVFDF MKJK ==+--*$&% #RHFS SES DOPE DSBS"
        INPUT "Okay, what did I say"; b$
        PRINT "You are a liar, a liar, a big fat liar!"
    CASE ELSE
        PRINT "Please say yes or no."
        GO TO 10
END SELECT
```

When you run that program, lines 2-4 print nonsense. Then the computer asks whether you understand that stuff. *If you're honest* and answer "no", the computer will apologize. But *if you pretend that you understand the nonsense* and answer "yes", the computer will print more nonsense, challenge you to translate it, wait for you to fake a translation, and then scold you for lying.

Fancy IF conditions

A Daddy wrote a program for his 5-year-old son, John. When John runs the program and types his name, the computer asks "What's 2 and 2?" If John answers 4, the computer says "No, 2 and 2 is 22". If he runs the program again and answers 22, the computer says "No, 2 and 2 is 4". No matter how many times he runs the program and how he answers the question, the computer says he's wrong. But when Daddy runs the program, the computer replies, "Yes, Daddy is always right".

Here's how Daddy programmed the computer:

```
CLS
INPUT "What's your name"; n$
INPUT "What's 2 and 2"; a
IF n$ = "Daddy" THEN PRINT "Yes, Daddy is always right": END
IF a = 4 THEN PRINT "No, 2 and 2 is 22" ELSE PRINT "No, 2 and 2 is 4"
```

Different relations You can make the IF clause very fancy:

IF clause	Meaning
IF b$ = "male"	If b$ is "male"
IF b = 4	If b is 4
IF b < 4	If b is less than 4
IF b > 4	If b is greater than 4
IF b <= 4	If b is less than or equal to 4
IF b >= 4	If b is greater than or equal to 4
IF b <> 4	If b is not 4
IF b$ < "male"	If b$ is a word that comes before "male" in dictionary
IF b$ > "male"	If b$ is a word that comes after "male" in dictionary

In the IF statement, the symbols =, <, >, <=, >=, and <> are called **relations**.

When writing a relation, mathematicians and computerists habitually **put the equal sign last**:

Right	Wrong
<=	=<
>=	=>

When you press the Enter key at the end of the line, the computer will automatically put your equal signs last: the computer will turn any "=<" into "<="; it will turn any "=>" into "<=".

To say "not equal to", say "less than or greater than", like this: <>.

OR The computer understands the word OR. For example, here's how to say, "If x is either 7 or 8, print the word *wonderful*":

```
IF x = 7 OR x = 8 THEN PRINT "wonderful"
```

That example is composed of two conditions: the first condition is "x = 7"; the second condition is "x = 8". Those two conditions combine, to form "x = 7 OR x = 8", which is called a **compound condition**.

If you use the word OR, put it between two conditions.

Right: `IF x = 7 OR x = 8 THEN PRINT "wonderful"`
Right because "x = 7" and "x = 8" are conditions.

Wrong: IF x = 7 OR 8 THEN PRINT "wonderful"
Wrong because "8" is not a condition.

AND The computer understands the word AND. Here's how to say, "If p is more than 5 and less than 10, print *tuna fish*":

```
IF p > 5 AND p < 10 THEN PRINT "tuna fish"
```

Here's how to say, "If s is at least 60 and less than 65, print *you almost failed*":

```
IF s >= 60 AND s < 65 THEN PRINT "you almost failed"
```

Here's how to say, "If n is a number from 1 to 10, print *that's good*":

```
IF n >= 1 AND n <= 10 THEN PRINT "that's good"
```

Can a computer be President?

To become President of the United States, you need 4 basic skills:

First, you must be a **good talker**, so you can give effective speeches saying "Vote for me!", express your views, and make folks do what you want.

But even if you're a good talker, you're useless unless you're also a **good listener**. You must be able to listen to people's needs and ask, "What can I do to make you happy and get you to vote for me?"

But even if you're a good talker and listener, you're still useless unless you can **make decisions**. Should you give more money to poor people? Should you bomb the enemy? Which actions should you take, and under what conditions?

But even if you're a good talker and listener and decision maker, you still need one more trait to become President: you must be able to take the daily grind of politics. You must, again and again, shake hands, make compromises, and raise funds. You must have the **patience to put up with the repetitive monotony** of those chores.

So altogether, to become President you need to be a good talker and listener and decision maker and also have the patience to put up with monotonous repetition.

Those are exactly the 4 qualities the computer has!

The word **PRINT** turns the computer into a good speech-maker. By using the word PRINT, you can make the computer write whatever speech you wish.

The word **INPUT** turns the computer into a good listener. By using the word INPUT, you can make the computer ask humans lots of questions, to find out who the humans are and what they want.

The word **IF** turns the computer into a decision maker. The computer can analyze the IF condition, determine whether that condition is true, and act accordingly.

Finally, the word **GOTO** enables the computer to perform loops, which the computer will repeat patiently.

So by using the words PRINT, INPUT, IF, and GOTO, you can make the computer imitate any intellectual human activity. Those 4 magic words — PRINT, INPUT, IF, and GOTO — are the only concepts you need, to write whatever program you wish!

Yes, you can make the computer imitate the President of the United States, do your company's payroll, compose a beautiful poem, play a perfect game of chess, contemplate the meaning of life, act as if it's falling in love, or do whatever other intellectual or emotional task you wish, by using those 4 magic words. The only question is: how? This book teaches you how, by showing you many examples of programs that do those remarkable things.

What programmers believe Yes, we programmers believe that all of life can be explained and programmed. We believe all of life can be reduced to just those four concepts: PRINT, INPUT, IF, and GOTO. Programming is the ultimate act of scientific reductionism: programmers reduce all of life scientifically to just four concepts.

The words that the computer understands are called **keywords**. The four essential keywords are PRINT, INPUT, IF, and GOTO.

The computer also understands extra keywords, such as CLS, LPRINT, WIDTH, SLEEP, DO (and LOOP), END, SELECT (and CASE), and words used in IF statements (such as THEN, ELSE, ELSEIF, OR, AND). Those extra keywords aren't necessary: if they hadn't been invented, you could still write programs without them. But they make programming easier.

A QBasic programmer is a person who translates an ordinary English sentence (such as "act like the President" or "do the payroll") into a series of QBasic statements, using keywords such as PRINT, INPUT, IF, GOTO, CLS, etc.

The mysteries of life Let's dig deeper into the mysteries of PRINT, INPUT, IF, GOTO, and the extra keywords. The deeper we dig, the more you'll wonder: are _you_ just a computer, made of flesh instead of wires? Can everything _you_ do be explained in terms of PRINT, INPUT, IF, and GOTO?

By the time you finish this book, you'll know!

Exiting a DO loop

This program plays a guessing game, where the human tries to guess the computer's favorite color, which is pink:

```
CLS
10 INPUT "What's my favorite color"; guess$
IF guess$ = "pink" THEN
    PRINT "Congratulations!  You discovered my favorite color."
ELSE
    PRINT "No, that's not my favorite color.  Try again!"
    GOTO 10
END IF
```

The INPUT line asks the human to guess the computer's favorite color; the guess is called guess$.

If the guess is "pink", the computer prints:

```
Congratulations!  You discovered my favorite color.
```

But if the guess is _not_ "pink", the computer will instead print "No, that's not my favorite color" and then GO back TO line 10, which asks the human again to try guessing the computer's favorite color.

END Here's how to write that program without saying GOTO:

```
CLS
DO
    INPUT "What's my favorite color"; guess$
    IF guess$ = "pink" THEN
        PRINT "Congratulations!  You discovered my favorite color."
        END
    END IF
    PRINT "No, that's not my favorite color.  Try again!"
LOOP
```

That new version of the program contains a DO loop. That loop makes the computer do this repeatedly: ask "What's my favorite color?" and then PRINT "No, that's not my favorite color."

The only way to stop the loop is to guess "pink", which makes the computer print "Congratulations!" and END.

EXIT DO Here's another way to write that program without saying GOTO:

```
CLS
DO
    INPUT "What's my favorite color"; guess$
    IF guess$ = "pink" THEN EXIT DO
    PRINT "No, that's not my favorite color.  Try again!"
LOOP
PRINT "Congratulations!  You discovered my favorite color."
```

That program's DO loop makes the computer do this repeatedly: ask "What's my favorite color?" and then PRINT "No, that's not my favorite color."

The only way to stop the loop is to guess "pink", which makes the computer EXIT from the DO loop; then the computer proceeds to the line underneath the DO loop. That line prints:

```
Congratulations!  You discovered my favorite color.
```

LOOP UNTIL Here's another way to program the guessing game:

```
CLS
DO
    PRINT "You haven't guessed my favorite color yet!"
    INPUT "What's my favorite color"; guess$
LOOP UNTIL guess$ = "pink"
PRINT "Congratulations!  You discovered my favorite color."
```

That program's DO loop makes the computer do this repeatedly: say "You haven't guessed my favorite color yet!" and then ask "What's my favorite color?"

The LOOP line makes the computer repeat the indented lines again and again, UNTIL the guess is "pink". When the guess is "pink", the computer proceeds to the line underneath the LOOP and prints "Congratulations!".

The LOOP UNTIL's condition (guess$ = "pink") is called the **loop's goal**. The computer does the loop repeatedly, until the loop's goal is achieved. Here's how:

The computer does the indented lines, then checks whether the goal is achieved yet. If the goal is _not_ achieved yet, the computer does the indented lines again, then checks again whether the goal is achieved. The computer does the loop again and again, until the goal is achieved. Then the computer, proud at achieving the goal, does the program's **finale**, which consists of any lines under the LOOP UNTIL line.

Saying —

```
LOOP UNTIL guess$ = "pink"
```

is just a briefer way of saying this pair of lines:

```
    IF guess$ = "pink" THEN EXIT DO
LOOP
```

FOR...NEXT

Let's make the computer print every number from 1 to 20, like this:

```
1
2
3
4
5
6
7
etc.
20
```

Here's the program:

```
CLS
FOR x = 1 TO 20
    PRINT x
NEXT
```

The second line (FOR x = 1 TO 20) says that x will be every number from 1 to 20; so x will be 1, then 2, then 3, etc. The line underneath, which is indented, says what to do about each x; it says to PRINT each x.

Whenever you write a program that contains the word FOR, you must say NEXT; so the bottom line says NEXT.

The indented line, which is between the FOR line and the NEXT line, is the line that the computer will do repeatedly; so the computer will repeatedly PRINT x. The first time the computer prints x, the x will be 1, so the computer will print:

```
1
```

The next time the computer prints x, the x will be 2, so the computer will print:

```
2
```

The computer will print every number from 1 up to 20.

When men meet women

Let's make the computer print these lyrics:

```
I saw 2 men
meet 2 women.
Tra-la-la!

I saw 3 men
meet 3 women.
Tra-la-la!

I saw 4 men
meet 4 women.
Tra-la-la!

I saw 5 men
meet 5 women.
Tra-la-la!

They all had a party!
Ha-ha-ha!
```

To do that, type these lines —

The first line of each verse:	PRINT "I saw"; x; "men"
The second line of each verse:	PRINT "meet"; x; "women."
The third line of each verse:	PRINT "Tra-la-la!"
Blank line under each verse:	PRINT

and make x be every number from 2 up to 5:

```
FOR x = 2 TO 5
    PRINT "I saw"; x; "men"
    PRINT "meet"; x; "women."
    PRINT "Tra-la-la!"
    PRINT
NEXT
```

At the top of the program, say CLS. At the end of the song, print the closing couplet:

```
CLS
FOR x = 2 TO 5
    PRINT "I saw"; x; "men"
    PRINT "meet"; x; "women."
    PRINT "Tra-la-la!"
    PRINT
NEXT
PRINT "They all had a party!"
PRINT "Ha-ha-ha!"
```

That program makes the computer print the entire song.

Here's an analysis:

	CLS
	FOR X = 2 TO 5
The computer will do the	PRINT "I saw"; x; "men"
indented lines repeatedly,	PRINT "meet"; x; "women."
for x=2, x=3, x=4, and x=5.	PRINT "Tra-la-la!"
	PRINT
	NEXT
Then the computer will	PRINT "They all had a party!"
print this couplet once.	PRINT "Ha-ha-ha!"

Since the computer does the indented lines repeatedly, those lines form a loop. Here's the general rule: **the statements between FOR and NEXT form a loop**. The computer goes round and round the loop, for x=2, x=3, x=4, and x=5. Altogether, it goes around the loop 4 times, which is a finite number. Therefore, the loop is **finite**.

If you don't like the letter x, choose a different letter. For example, you can choose the letter i:

```
CLS
FOR i = 2 TO 5
    PRINT "I saw"; i; "men"
    PRINT "meet"; i; "women."
    PRINT "Tra-la-la!"
    PRINT
NEXT
PRINT "They all had a party!"
PRINT "Ha-ha-ha!"
```

When using the word FOR, most programmers prefer the letter i; most programmers say "FOR i" instead of "FOR x". Saying "FOR i" is an "old tradition". Following that tradition, the rest of this book says "FOR i" (instead of "FOR x"), except in situations where some other letter feels more natural.

Print the squares

To find the **square** of a number, multiply the number by itself. The square of 3 is "3 times 3", which is 9. The square of 4 is "4 times 4", which is 16.

Let's make the computer print the square of 3, 4, 5, etc., up to 20, like this:

```
The square of 3 is 9
The square of 4 is 16
The square of 5 is 25
The square of 6 is 36
The square of 7 is 49
etc.
The square of 20 is 400
```

To do that, type this line —

```
    PRINT "The square of"; i; "is"; i * i
```

and make i be every number from 3 up to 20, like this:

```
CLS
FOR i = 3 TO 20
    PRINT "The square of"; i; "is"; i * i
NEXT
```

Count how many copies

This program, which you saw before, prints "love" on every line of your screen:

```
CLS
DO
    PRINT "love"
LOOP
```

That program prints "love" again and again, until you abort the program by pressing Ctrl with PAUSE/BREAK.

But what if you want to print "love" just 20 times? This program prints "love" just 20 times:

```
CLS
FOR i = 1 TO 20
    PRINT "love"
NEXT
```

As you can see, FOR...NEXT resembles DO...LOOP but is smarter: while doing FOR...NEXT, the computer counts!

Count to midnight

This program makes the computer count to midnight:

```
CLS
FOR i = 1 TO 11
    PRINT i
NEXT
PRINT "midnight"
```

The computer will print:

```
1
2
3
4
5
6
7
8
9
10
11
midnight
```

Semicolon Let's put a semicolon at the end of the indented line:

```
CLS
FOR i = 1 TO 11
    PRINT i;
NEXT
PRINT "midnight"
```

The semicolon makes the computer print each item on the same line, like this:

```
 1  2  3  4  5  6  7  8  9  10  11 midnight
```

If you want the computer to press the Enter key before "midnight", insert a PRINT line:

```
CLS
FOR i = 1 TO 11
    PRINT i;
NEXT
PRINT
PRINT "midnight"
```

That extra PRINT line makes the computer press the Enter key just before "midnight", so the computer will print "midnight" on a separate line, like this:

```
 1  2  3  4  5  6  7  8  9  10  11
midnight
```

Nested loops Let's make the computer count to midnight 3 times, like this:

```
 1  2  3  4  5  6  7  8  9  10  11
midnight
 1  2  3  4  5  6  7  8  9  10  11
midnight
 1  2  3  4  5  6  7  8  9  10  11
midnight
```

To do that, put the entire program between the words FOR and NEXT:

```
CLS
FOR j = 1 TO 3
    FOR i = 1 TO 11
        PRINT i;
    NEXT
    PRINT
    PRINT "midnight"
NEXT
```

That version contains a loop inside a loop: the loop that says "FOR i" is inside the loop that says "FOR j". The j loop is called the **outer loop**; the i loop is called the **inner loop**. The inner loop's variable must differ from the outer loop's. Since we called the inner loop's variable "i", the outer loop's variable must *not* be called "i"; so I picked the letter j instead.

Programmers often think of the outer loop as a bird's nest, and the inner loop as an egg *inside the nest*. So programmers say the inner loop is **nested in** the outer loop; the inner loop is a **nested loop**.

Abnormal exit

Earlier, we programmed a game where the human tries to guess the computer's favorite color, pink. Here's a fancier version of the game, in which the human gets just 5 guesses:

```
CLS
PRINT "I'll give you 5 guesses...."
FOR i = 1 TO 5
    INPUT "What's my favorite color"; guess$
    IF guess$ = "pink" THEN GO TO 10
    PRINT "No, that's not my favorite color."
NEXT
PRINT "Sorry, your 5 guesses are up!  You lose."
END
10 PRINT "Congratulations!  You discovered my favorite color."
PRINT "It took you"; i; "guesses."
```

Line 2 warns the human that just 5 guesses are allowed. The FOR line makes the computer count from 1 to 5; to begin, i is 1. The INPUT line asks the human to guess the computer's favorite color; the guess is called guess$.

If the guess is "pink", the computer jumps down to the line numbered 10, prints "Congratulations!", and tells how many guesses the human took. But if the guess is *not* "pink", the computer will print "No, that's not my favorite color" and go on to the NEXT guess.

If the human guesses 5 times without success, the computer proceeds to the line that prints "Sorry... You lose."

For example, if the human's third guess is "pink", the computer prints:

```
Congratulations!  You discovered my favorite color.
It took you 3 guesses.
```

If the human's very first guess is "pink", the computer prints:

```
Congratulations!  You discovered my favorite color.
It took you 1 guesses.
```

Saying "1 guesses" is bad grammar but understandable.

That program contains a FOR...NEXT loop. The FOR line says the loop will normally be done five times. The line below the loop (which says to PRINT "Sorry") is the loop's **normal exit**. But if the human happens to input "pink", the computer jumps out of the loop early, to line 10, which is the loop's **abnormal exit**.

STEP

The FOR statement can be varied:

Statement	Meaning
FOR i = 5 TO 17 STEP .1	The i will go from 5 to 17, counting by tenths. So i will be 5, then 5.1, then 5.2, etc., up to 17.
FOR i = 5 TO 17 STEP 3	The i will be every 3rd number from 5 to 17. So i will be 5, then 8, then 11, then 14, then 17.
FOR i = 17 TO 5 STEP -3	The i will be every 3rd number from 17 down to 5. So i will be 17, then 14, then 11, then 8, then 5.

To count down, you *must* use the word STEP. To count from 17 down to 5, give this instruction:

```
FOR i = 17 TO 5 STEP -1
```

This program prints a rocket countdown:

```
CLS
FOR i = 10 TO 1 STEP -1
    PRINT i
NEXT
PRINT "Blast off!"
```

The computer will print:

```
10
9
8
7
6
5
4
3
2
1
Blast off!
```

This statement is tricky:

```
FOR i = 5 TO 16 STEP 3
```

It says to start i at 5, and keep adding 3 until it gets past 16. So i will be 5, then 8, then 11, then 14. The i won't be 17, since 17 is past 16. The first value of i is 5; the last value is 14.

In the statement FOR i = 5 TO 16 STEP 3, the **first value** or **initial value** of i is 5, the **limit value** is 16, and the **step size** or **increment** is 3. The i is called the **counter** or **index** or **loop-control variable**. Although the limit value is 16, the **last value** or **terminal value** is 14.

Programmers usually say "FOR i", instead of "FOR x", because the letter i reminds them of the word **index**.

Round-off errors

If the step size is a decimal, the computer might make small errors (called round-off errors), which can add up to a result that's very wrong.

For example, suppose you say:

```
FOR i = 5 TO 17 STEP .1
```

That means you want the last few values of i to be 16.8, 16.9, and 17; but the computer will accidentally make the step size be slightly *more* than .1, so the computer's last few values of i will be about 16.80003 and 16.90003. The computer will refuse to do the next number (which would be about 17.0003), since you said not to go past 17; so the last i will be 16.90003, which isn't at all what you wanted for the last value!

To make the last i be about 17, make the limit value be slightly *more* than 17, like this —

```
FOR i = 5 TO 17.01 STEP .1
```

or, better yet, avoid a decimal step size by using this pair of lines instead:

```
FOR j = 50 TO 170
    i = j / 10
```

That makes i indeed be 5 then 5.1 then 5.2, etc., up to 17.

DATA...READ

Let's make the computer print this message:

```
I love meat
I love potatoes
I love lettuce
I love tomatoes
I love honey
I love cheese
I love onions
I love peas
```

That message concerns this list of food: meat, potatoes, lettuce, tomatoes, honey, cheese, onions, peas. That list doesn't change: the computer continues to love those foods throughout the entire program.

A list that doesn't change is called DATA. So in the message about food, the DATA is meat, potatoes, lettuce, tomatoes, honey, cheese, onions, peas.

Whenever a problem involves DATA, put the DATA at the program's top, under just CLS, like this:

```
CLS
DATA meat,potatoes,lettuce,tomatoes,honey,cheese,onions,peas
```

You must tell the computer to READ the DATA:

```
CLS
DATA meat,potatoes,lettuce,tomatoes,honey,cheese,onions,peas
READ a$
```

That READ line makes the computer read the first datum ("meat") and call it a$. So a$ is "meat".

Since a$ is "meat", this shaded line makes the computer print "I love meat":

```
CLS
DATA meat,potatoes,lettuce,tomatoes,honey,cheese,onions,peas
READ a$
PRINT "I love "; a$
```

Hooray! We made the computer handle the first datum correctly: we made the computer print "I love meat".

To make the computer handle the rest of the data (potatoes, lettuce, etc.), tell the computer to READ and PRINT the rest of the data, by putting the READ and PRINT lines in a loop. Since we want the computer to READ and PRINT all 8 data items (meat, potatoes, lettuce, tomatoes, honey, cheese, onions, peas), put the READ and PRINT lines in a loop that gets done 8 times, by making the loop say "FOR i = 1 TO 8":

```
CLS
DATA meat,potatoes,lettuce,tomatoes,honey,cheese,onions,peas
FOR i = 1 TO 8
    READ a$
    PRINT "I love "; a$
NEXT
```

Since that loop's main purpose is to READ the data, it's called a **READ loop**.

When writing that program, make sure the FOR line's last number (8) is the number of data items. If the FOR line accidentally says 7 instead of 8, the computer won't read or print the 8th data item. If the FOR line accidentally says 9 instead of 8, the computer will try to read a 9th data item, realize that no 9th data item exists, and gripe by saying:

```
Out of DATA
```

Then do this:

QB64 Click "No".
QBasic Press Enter.

Let's make the computer end by printing "Those are the foods I love", like this:

```
I love meat
I love potatoes
I love lettuce
I love tomatoes
I love honey
I love cheese
I love onions
I love peas
Those are the foods I love
```

To make the computer print that ending, put a PRINT line at the end of the program:

```
CLS
DATA meat,potatoes,lettuce,tomatoes,honey,cheese,onions,peas
FOR i = 1 TO 8
    READ a$
    PRINT "I love "; a$
NEXT
PRINT "Those are the foods I love"
```

End mark

When writing that program, we had to count the DATA items and put that number (8) at the end of the FOR line.

Here's a better way to write the program, so you don't have to count the DATA items:

```
CLS
DATA meat,potatoes,lettuce,tomatoes,honey,cheese,onions,peas
DATA end
DO
    READ a$: IF a$ = "end" THEN EXIT DO
    PRINT "I love "; a$
LOOP
PRINT "Those are the foods I love"
```

The third line (DATA end) is called the **end mark**, since it marks the end of the DATA. The READ line means:

READ a$ from the DATA;
but if a$ is the "end" of the DATA, then EXIT from the DO loop.

When the computer exits from the DO loop, the computer prints "Those are the foods I love". So altogether, the entire program makes the computer print:

```
I love meat
I love potatoes
I love lettuce
I love tomatoes
I love honey
I love cheese
I love onions
I love peas
Those are the foods I love
```

The routine that says:

```
            IF a$ = "end" THEN EXIT DO
```

is called the **end routine**, because the computer does that routine when it reaches the end of the DATA.

Henry the Eighth Let's make the computer print this nursery rhyme:

```
I love ice cream
I love red
I love ocean
I love bed
I love tall grass
I love to wed

I love candles
I love divorce
I love kingdom
I love my horse
I love you
Of course, of course,
For I am Henry the Eighth!
```

If you own a jump rope, have fun: try to recite that poem while skipping rope!

This program makes the computer recite the poem:

```
CLS
DATA ice cream,red,ocean,bed,tall grass,to wed
DATA candles,divorce,my kingdom,my horse,you
DATA end
DO
    READ a$: IF a$ = "end" THEN EXIT DO
    PRINT "I love "; a$
    IF a$ = "to wed" THEN PRINT
LOOP
PRINT "Of course, of course,"
PRINT "For I am Henry the Eighth!"
```

Since the data's too long to fit on a single line, I've put part of the data in line 2 and the rest in line 3. Each line of data must begin with the word DATA. In each line, put commas between the items. Do *not* put a comma at the end of the line.

The program resembles the previous one. The new line (IF a$ = "to wed" THEN PRINT) makes the computer leave a blank line underneath "to wed", to mark the first verse's bottom.

Pairs of data

Let's throw a party! To make the party yummy, let's ask each guest to bring a kind of food that resembles the guest's name. For example, let's have Sal bring salad, Russ bring Russian dressing, Sue bring soup, Tom bring turkey, Winnie bring wine, Kay bring cake, and Al bring Alka-Seltzer.

Let's send all those people invitations, in this form:

```
Dear _____,
      person's name

      Let's party in the clubhouse at midnight!

Please bring ____.
              food
```

Here's the program:

```
CLS
DATA Sal,salad,Russ,Russian dressing,Sue,soup,Tom,turkey
DATA Winnie,wine,Kay,cake,Al,Alka-Seltzer
DATA end,end
DO
    READ person$, food$: IF person$ = "end" THEN EXIT DO
    LPRINT "Dear "; person$; ","
    LPRINT "      Let's party in the clubhouse at midnight!"
    LPRINT "Please bring "; food$; "."
    LPRINT CHR$(12);
LOOP
PRINT "I've finished writing the letters."
```

The DATA comes in pairs. For example, the first pair consists of "Sal" and "salad"; the next pair consists of "Russ" and "Russian dressing". Since the DATA comes in pairs, you must make the end mark also be a pair (DATA end,end).

Since the DATA comes in pairs, the READ line says to READ a pair of data (person$ and food$). The first time that the computer encounters the READ line, person$ is "Sal"; food$ is "salad". Then the LPRINT lines print this message onto paper:

```
Dear Sal,
      Let's party in the clubhouse at midnight!
Please bring salad.
```

The LPRINT CHR$(12) makes the computer eject the paper from the printer.

Then the computer comes to the word LOOP, which sends the computer back to the word DO, which sends the computer to the READ line again, which reads the next pair of DATA, so person$ becomes "Russ" and food$ becomes "Russian dressing". The LPRINT lines print onto paper:

```
Dear Russ,
      Let's party in the clubhouse at midnight!
Please bring Russian dressing.
```

The computer prints similar letters to all the people.

After all people have been handled, the READ statement comes to the end mark (DATA end,end), so that person$ and food$ both become "end". Since person$ is "end", the IF statement makes the computer EXIT DO, so the computer prints this message onto the screen:

```
I've finished writing the letters.
```

In that program, you need *two* ends to mark the data's ending, because the READ statment says to read two strings (person$ and food$).

Debts Suppose these people owe you things:

Person	What the person owes
Bob	$537.29
Mike	a dime
Sue	2 golf balls
Harry	a steak dinner at Mario's
Mommy	a kiss

Let's remind those people of their debt, by writing them letters, in this form:

```
Dear _____,
      person's name

      I just want to remind you...

that you still owe me ____.
                      debt
```

To start writing the program, begin by saying CLS and then feed the computer the DATA. The final program is the same as the previous program, except for the part I've shaded:

```
CLS
DATA Bob,$537.29,Mike,a dime,Sue,2 golf balls
DATA Harry,a steak dinner at Mario's,Mommy,a kiss
DATA end,end
DO
    READ person$, debt$: IF person$ = "end" THEN EXIT DO
    LPRINT "Dear "; person$; ","
    LPRINT "      I just want to remind you..."
    LPRINT "that you still owe me "; debt$; "."
    LPRINT CHR$(12);
LOOP
PRINT "I've finished writing the letters."
```

Triplets of data

Suppose you're running a diet clinic and get these results:

Person	Weight before	Weight after
Joe	273 pounds	219 pounds
Mary	412 pounds	371 pounds
Bill	241 pounds	173 pounds
Sam	309 pounds	198 pounds

This program makes the computer print a nice report:

```
CLS
DATA Joe,273,219,Mary,412,371,Bill,241,173,Sam,309,198
DATA end,0,0
DO
    READ person$, weight.before, weight.after
    IF person$ = "end" THEN EXIT DO
    PRINT person$; " weighed"; weight.before;
    PRINT "pounds before attending the diet clinic"
    PRINT "but weighed just"; weight.after; "pounds afterwards."
    PRINT "That's a loss of"; weight.before - weight.after; "pounds."
    PRINT
LOOP
PRINT "Come to the diet clinic!"
```

Line 2 contains the DATA, which comes in triplets. The first triplet consists of Joe, 273, and 219. Each triplet includes a string (such as Joe) and two numbers (such as 273 and 219), so line 3's end mark also includes a string and two numbers: it's the word "end" and two zeros. (If you hate zeros, you can use other numbers instead; but most programmers prefer zeros.)

The READ line says to read a triplet: a string (person$) and two numbers (weight.before and weight.after). The first time the computer comes to the READ statement, the computer makes person$ be "Joe", weight.before be 273, and weight.after be 219. The PRINT lines print this:

```
Joe weighed 273 pounds before attending the diet clinic
but weighed just 219 pounds afterwards.
That's a loss of 54 pounds.

Mary weighed 412 pounds before attending the diet clinic
but weighed just 371 pounds afterwards.
That's a loss of 41 pounds.

Bill weighed 241 pounds before attending the diet clinic
but weighed just 173 pounds afterwards.
That's a loss of 68 pounds.

Sam weighed 309 pounds before attending the diet clinic
but weighed just 198 pounds afterwards.
That's a loss of 111 pounds.

Come to the diet clinic!
```

RESTORE

Examine this program:

```
CLS
DATA love,death,war
10 DATA chocolate,strawberry
READ a$
PRINT a$
RESTORE 10
READ a$
PRINT a$
```

The first READ makes the computer read the first datum (love), so the first PRINT makes the computer print:

```
love
```

The next READ would normally make the computer read the next datum (death); but the **RESTORE 10 tells the READ to skip ahead to DATA line 10**, so the READ line reads "chocolate" instead. The entire program prints:

```
love
chocolate
```

So saying "RESTORE 10" makes the next READ skip ahead to DATA line 10. If you write a new program, saying "RESTORE 20" makes the next READ skip ahead to DATA line 20. Saying just "RESTORE" makes the next READ skip back to the beginning of the *first* DATA line.

Continents This program prints the names of the continents:

```
CLS
DATA Europe,Asia,Africa,Australia,Antarctica,North America,South America
DATA end
DO
    READ a$: IF a$ = "end" THEN EXIT DO
    PRINT a$
LOOP
PRINT "Those are the continents."
```

That program makes the computer print this message:

```
Europe
Asia
Africa
Australia
Antarctica
North America
South America
Those are the continents.
```

Let's make the computer print that message *twice*, so the computer prints:

```
Europe
Asia
Africa
Australia
Antarctica
North America
South America
Those are the continents.

Europe
Asia
Africa
Australia
Antarctica
North America
South Ameruca
Those are the continents.
```

To do that, put the program in a loop saying "FOR i = 1 TO 2", like this:

```
CLS
DATA Europe,Asia,Africa,Australia,Antarctica,North America,South America
DATA end
FOR i = 1 TO 2
    DO
        READ a$: IF a$ = "end" THEN EXIT DO
        PRINT a$
    LOOP
    PRINT "Those are the continents."
    PRINT
    RESTORE
NEXT
```

After that program says to PRINT "Those are the continents", the program says to PRINT a blank line and then RESTORE. The word RESTORE makes the READ go back to the beginning of the DATA, so the computer can READ and PRINT the DATA a second time without saying "Out of DATA".

Search loop

Let's make the computer translate colors into French. For example, if the human says "red", we'll make the computer say the French equivalent, which is:

```
rouge
```

Let's make the computer begin by asking "Which color interests you?", then wait for the human to type a color (such as "red"), then reply:

```
In French, it's rouge
```

The program begins simply:

```
CLS
INPUT "Which color interests you"; request$
```

Next, we must make the computer translate the requested color into French. To do so, feed the computer this English-French dictionary:

English	French
white	blanc
yellow	jaune
orange	orange
red	rouge
green	vert
blue	bleu
brown	brun
black	noir

That dictionary becomes the data:

```
CLS
DATA white,blanc,yellow,jaune,orange,orange,red,rouge
DATA green,vert,blue,bleu,brown,brun,black,noir
INPUT "Which color interests you"; request$
```

The data comes in pairs; each pair consists of an English word (such as "white") followed by its French equivalent ("blanc"). To make the computer read a pair, say:

```
READ english$, french$
```

To let the computer look at *all* the pairs, put that READ statement in a DO loop. Here's the complete program:

```
CLS
DATA white,blanc,yellow,jaune,orange,orange,red,rouge
DATA green,vert,blue,bleu,brown,brun,black,noir
INPUT "Which color interests you"; request$
DO
    READ english$, french$
    IF english$ = request$ THEN EXIT DO
LOOP
PRINT "In French, it's "; french$
```

Since the READ line is in a DO loop, the computer does the READ line repeatedly. So the computer keeps READing pairs of DATA, until the computer find the pair of DATA that the human requested. For example, if the human requested "red", the computer keeps READing pairs of DATA until it finds a pair whose English word matches the requested word ("red"). When the computer finds that match, the english$ is equal to the request$, so the IF line makes the computer EXIT DO and PRINT:

```
In French, it's rouge
```

So altogether, when you run the program the chat can look like this:

```
Which color interests you? red
In French, it's rouge
```

Here's another sample run:

```
Which color interests you? brown
In French, it's brun
```

Here's another:

```
Which color interests you? pink
Out of DATA
```

The computer says "Out of DATA" because it can't find "pink" in the DATA.

Avoid "Out of DATA" Instead of saying "Out of DATA", let's make the computer say "I wasn't taught that color". To do that, put an end mark at the end of the DATA; and when the computer reaches the end mark, make the computer say "I wasn't taught that color":

```
CLS
DATA white,blanc,yellow,jaune,orange,orange,red,rouge
DATA green,vert,blue,bleu,brown,brun,black,noir
DATA end,end
INPUT "Which color interests you"; request$
DO
    READ english$, french$
    IF english$ = "end" THEN PRINT "I wasn't taught that color": END
    IF english$ = request$ THEN EXIT DO
LOOP
PRINT "In French, it's "; french$
```

In that program, the DO loop's purpose is to *search* through the DATA, to find DATA that matches the INPUT. Since the DO loop's purpose is to search, it's called a **search loop**.

The typical search loop has these characteristics:

It starts with DO and ends with LOOP.
It says to READ a pair of data.
It includes an error trap saying what to do IF you reach the "end" of the data because no match found.
It says that IF you find a match (english$ = request$) THEN EXIT the DO loop.
Below the DO loop, say what to PRINT when the match is found.
Above the DO loop, put the DATA and tell the human to INPUT a search request.

Auto rerun At the end of the program, let's make the computer automatically rerun the program and translate another color.

To do that, make the bottom of the program say GO back TO the INPUT line:

```
CLS
DATA white,blanc,yellow,jaune,orange,orange,red,rouge
DATA green,vert,blue,bleu,brown,brun,black,noir
DATA end,end
10 INPUT "Which color interests you"; request$
RESTORE
DO
    READ english$, french$
    IF english$ = "end" THEN PRINT "I wasn't taught that color": GOTO 10
    IF english$ = request$ THEN EXIT DO
LOOP
PRINT "In French, it's "; french$
GOTO 10
```

The word RESTORE, which is above the search loop, makes sure that the computer's search through the DATA always starts at the DATA's beginning.

Press Q to quit That program repeatedly asks "Which color interests you" until the human aborts the program. But what if the human's a beginner who hasn't learned how to abort?

Let's permit the human to stop the program more easily by pressing just the Q key to quit:

```
CLS
DATA white,blanc,yellow,jaune,orange,orange,red,rouge
DATA green,vert,blue,bleu,brown,brun,black,noir
DATA end,end
10 INPUT "Which color interests you (press q to quit)"; request$
IF request$ = "q" THEN END
RESTORE
DO
    READ english$, french$
    IF english$ = "end" THEN PRINT "I wasn't taught that color": GOTO 10
    IF english$ = request$ THEN EXIT DO
LOOP
PRINT "In French, it's "; french$
GOTO 10
```

END or STOP That program's shaded line ends by saying END. Instead of saying END, try saying STOP.

While the program is running, here's what the computer does when it encounters END or STOP:

STOP makes the program stop *immediately*. It closes the black window, so you see the blue window and the program's lines.

END makes the computer say "Press any key to continue" and wait for the human to press a key (such as Enter). When the human finally presses a key, the black window closes, so you see the blue window and program's lines.

Helpful hints

Here are some hints to help you master programming.

Variables & constants

A **numeric constant** is a simple number, such as:

```
0        1        2        8        43.7        -524.6        .003
```

Another example of a numeric constant is 1.3E5, which means, "take 1.3, and move its decimal point 5 places to the right".

A numeric constant does not contain any arithmetic. For example, since 7+1 contains arithmetic (+), it's *not* a numeric constant. 8 is a numeric constant, even though 7+1 isn't.

A **string constant** is a simple string, in quotation marks:

```
"I love you"     "76 trombones"     "Go away!!!"        "xypw exr///746"
```

A **constant** is a numeric constant or a string constant:

```
0      8      -524.6      1.3E5      "I love you"        "xypw exr///746"
```

A **variable** is something that stands for something else. If it stands for a string, it's called a **string variable** and ends with a dollar sign, like this:

```
a$        b$        y$        z$        my.job.before.promotion$
```

If the variable stands for a number, it's called a **numeric variable** and lacks a dollar sign, like this:

```
a        b        y        z        profit.before.promotion
```

So all these are variables:

```
a$ b$ y$ z$ my.job.before.promotion$ a b y z profit.before.promotion
```

Expressions A **numeric expression** is a numeric constant (such as 8) or a numeric variable (such as b) or a combination of them, such as 8+z, or 8*a, or z*a, or 8*2, or 7+1, or even z*a-(7+z)/8+1.3E5*(-524.6+b). A **string expression** is a string constant (such as "I love you") or a string variable (such as a$) or a combination. An **expression** is a numeric expression or a string expression.

Statements At the end of a GOTO statement, the line number must be a numeric constant.

Right: GOTO 100	(100 is a numeric constant.)
Wrong: GOTO n	(n is not a numeric constant.)

The INPUT statement's prompt must be a string constant.

Right: INPUT "What is your name; n$	("What is your name" is a constant.)
Wrong: INPUT q$; n$	(q$ is not a constant.)

In a DATA statement, you must have constants.

Right: DATA 8, 1.3E5	(8 and 1.3E5 are constants.)
Wrong: DATA 7+1, 1.3E5	(7+1 is not a constant.)

In the DATA statement, if the constant is a string, you can omit the quotation marks (unless the string contains a comma or a colon).

```
Right:      DATA "Joe","Mary"
Also right: DATA Joe,Mary
```

Here are the forms of popular statements:

General form	Example
PRINT *list of expressions*	PRINT "Temperature is"; 4 + 25; "degrees"
LPRINT *list of expressions*	LPRINT "Temperature is"; 4 + 25; "degrees"
SLEEP *numeric expression*	SLEEP 3 + 1
GOTO *line number or label*	GOTO 10
variable = expression	x = 47 + 2
INPUT *string constant; variable*	INPUT "What is your name"; n$
IF *condition* THEN *list of statements*	IF a >= 18 THEN PRINT "You": PRINT "vote"
SELECT CASE *expression*	SELECT CASE a + 1
DATA *list of constants*	DATA Joe,273,219,Mary,412,371
READ *list of variables*	READ n$, b, a
RESTORE *line number or label*	RESTORE 10
FOR *numeric variable =*	FOR I = 59 + 1 TO 100 + n STEP 2 + 3
numeric expression	
TO *numeric expression*	
STEP *numeric expression*	

Debugging

If you write and run your own program, it probably won't work.

Your first reaction will be to blame the computer. Don't!

The probability is 99.99% that the fault is yours. Your program contains an error. An error is called a **bug**. Your next task is to **debug** the program, which means get the bugs out.

Bugs are common; top-notch programmers make errors all the time. If you write a program that works perfectly on the first run and doesn't need debugging, it's called a **gold-star program** and means you should have tried writing a harder one instead!

It's easy to write a program that's nearly correct but hard to find the little bug fouling it up. Most time you spend at the computer will be devoted to debugging.

Debugging can be fun. Hunting for the bug is like going on a treasure hunt – or solving a murder mystery. Pretend you're Sherlock Holmes. Your mission: to find the bug and squish it! When you squish it, have fun: yell out, "Squish!"

How can you tell when a roomful of programmers is happy? Answer: when you hear continual cries of "Squish!"

To find a bug, use three techniques:

Inspect the program.
Trace the computer's thinking.
Shorten the program.

Here are the details....

Inspect the program Take a good, hard look at the program. If you stare hard enough, maybe you'll see the bug.

Usually, the bug will turn out to be just a typing error, a **typo**. For example....

Maybe you typed the letter O instead of zero? Zero instead of the letter O?
Typed I instead of 1? Typed 1 instead of I?
Pressed the Shift key when you weren't supposed to? Forgot to press it?
Typed an extra letter? Omitted a letter?
Typed a line you thought you hadn't? Omitted a line?

You must **put quotation marks around each string, and a dollar sign after each string variable**:

Right: a$ = "jerk"
Wrong: a$ = jerk
Wrong: a = "jerk"

Here are 3 reasons why the computer might **print too much**:

1. You forgot to insert the word END or EXIT DO into your program.
2. Into a DO loop or FOR loop, you inserted a PRINT line that should be *outside* the loop.
3. When you started typing the program, you forgot to choose New from the File menu; so the computer is including part of the previous program.

Trace the computer's thinking

If you've inspected the program thoroughly and *still* haven't found the bug, the next step is to **trace** the computer's thinking. **Pretend you're the computer. Do what your program says.** Do you find yourself printing the same wrong answers the computer printed? If so, why? To help your analysis, **make the computer print everything it's thinking** while it's running your program. For example, suppose your program uses the variables b, c, and x$. Insert lines such as these into your program:

```
10 PRINT "I'm at line 10.  The values are"; b; c; x$
20 PRINT "I'm at line 20.  The values are"; b; c; x$
```

Then run the program. Those extra lines tell you what the computer is thinking about b, c, and x$ and also tell you how many times the computer reached lines 10 and 20. For example, if the computer prints what you expect in line 10 but prints strange values in line 20 (or doesn't even get to line 20), you know the bug occurs after line 10 but before line 20.

Here's a good strategy. Halfway down your program, insert a line that says to print all the values. Then run your program. If the line you inserted prints the correct values, you know the bug lies *underneath* that line; but if the line prints *wrong* values (or if the computer never reaches that line), you know the bug lies *above* that line. In either case, you know which half of your program contains the bug. In that half of the program, insert more lines, until you finally zero in on the line containing the bug.

Shorten the program

When all else fails, shorten the program.

Hunting for a bug in a program is like hunting for a needle in a haystack: the job is easier if the haystack is smaller. So make your program shorter: delete the last half of your program. Then run the shortened version. That way, you'll find out whether the first half of your program is working the way it's supposed to. When you've perfected the first half of your program, tack the second half back on.

Does your program contain **a statement whose meaning you're not completely sure of**? Check the meaning by reading a book or asking a friend; or **write a tiny experimental program that contains the statement**, and see what happens when you run it.

Hint: before you shorten your program (or write tiny experimental ones), **save the original version** (by choosing Save from the File menu), even though it contains a bug. After you've played with the shorter versions, retrieve the original (by choosing Open from the File menu) and fix it.

To write a long, correct program easily, write a short program first and debug it, then add a few more lines and debug them, add a few more lines and debug them, etc. So start with a small program, perfect it, then gradually add perfected extras so you *gradually* build a perfected masterpiece. If you try to compose a long program all at once – instead of building it from perfected pieces – you'll have nothing more than a master*mess* – full of bugs.

Moral: to build a large masterpiece, start with a *small* masterpiece. To build a program so big that it's a skyscraper, begin by laying a good foundation; double-check the foundation before you start adding the program's walls and roof.

Error messages

If the computer can't obey your command, the computer will print an **error message**. The following error message are the most common....

Syntax errors

If you say "prind" instead of "print", the computer will say:

```
Syntax error
```

That means the computer hasn't the faintest idea of what you're talking about!

If the computer says you have a syntax error, it's usually because you spelled a word wrong, or forgot a word, or used a word the computer doesn't understand. It can also result from wrong punctuation: check your commas, semicolons, and colons. It can also mean your DATA statement contains a string but your READ statement says to read a number instead; to fix that problem, change the READ statement by putting a dollar sign at the end of the variable's name.

If you try to say PRINT 5 + 2 but forget to type the 2, the computer will say:

```
QB64   Expected variable/value after +
QBasic Expected: expression
```

If you type a left parenthesis but forget to type the right parenthesis that matches it, the computer will say:

```
QB64   Missing )
QBasic Expected: )
```

If you accidentally type extra characters (or an unintelligible word) at the end of the line, the computer will say:

```
QB64   Expected operator
QBasic Expected: end-of-statement
```

Numeric errors

If the answer to a calculation is a bigger number than the computer can handle, the computer will say:

```
QB64   1.#INF
QBasic Overflow
```

To help the computer handle bigger numbers, remember to put a decimal point in any problem whose answer might be bigger than 32 thousand.

If you try to divide by zero, the computer will say:

```
QB64   1.#INF
QBasic Division by zero
```

Logic errors

Some commands come in pairs.

The words **DO and LOOP** form a pair. If you say DO but no line says LOOP, the computer will gripe by saying:

```
DO without LOOP
```

If you say LOOP but no line says DO, the computer will say:

```
QB64   PROGRAM FLOW ERROR!
QBasic LOOP without DO
```

The words **FOR and NEXT** form another pair. If part of the pair is missing, the computer will say –

```
FOR without NEXT
```

or:

```
NEXT without FOR
```

If a line's first word is **SELECT**, you're supposed to have a line below saying END SELECT. If you say SELECT but no line says END SELECT, the computer will say:

```
QB64   SELECT CASE without END SELECT
QBasic SELECT without END SELECT
```

If you say END SELECT but no line's first word is SELECT, the computer will say:

```
QB64   END SELECT without SELECT CASE
QBasic END SELECT without SELECT
```

Between the SELECT and END SELECT lines, you're supposed to have several lines saying CASE. If you say CASE but no line's first word is SELECT, the computer will say:

```
QB64   CASE without SELECT CASE
QBasic CASE without SELECT
```

If you say **GOTO 10**, the computer tries to find a line numbered 10. If you say GOTO joe, the computer tries to find a line named joe. If there's no line numbered 10 or no line named joe, the computer will say:

```
Label not defined
```

Here are other messages about unmatched pairs, involving **IF**:

QB64	QBasic
ELSE without IF	ELSE without IF
END IF without IF	END IF without block IF
IF without END IF	Block IF without END IF

If you say **READ** but the computer can't find any more DATA to read (because the computer has read all the DATA already), the computer will say:

```
Out of DATA
```

The computer handles two major **types** of info: numbers and strings. If you feed the computer the wrong type of information – if you feed it a number when you should have fed it a string, or you feed it a string when you should have fed it a number – the computer will say:

QB64	Illegal string-number conversion
QBasic	Type mismatch

When you feed the computer a string, you must put the string in quotation marks, and put a dollar sign after the string's variable. If you forget to type the string's quotation marks or dollar sign, the computer won't realize it's a string; the computer will think you're trying to type a number instead; and if a number would be inappropriate, the computer will give that gripe. So when the computer gives that gripe, it usually means you forgot a quotation mark or a dollar sign.

Pause key

Magicians often say, "The hand is quicker than the eye." The computer's the ultimate magician: the computer can print info on the screen much faster than you can read it.

When the computer is printing faster than you can read, tap the **Pause key**, which is typically the last key in the top row. (If you have a 17-inch notebook computer, you might have to tap the Pause key *while holding down the Fn key*.) Then the computer will pause, to let you read what's on the screen.

When you've finished reading what's on the screen and want the computer to stop pausing, press the Enter key. Then the computer will continue printing rapidly, where it left off.

If your eyes are as slow as mine, you'll need to use the Pause key often! You'll want the computer to pause while you're running a program containing many PRINT statements (or a PRINT statement in a loop).

Apostrophe

Occasionally, jot a note to remind yourself what your program does and what the variables stand for. Slip the note into your program by putting an apostrophe before it:

```
'This program is another dumb example, written by Russy-poo.
'It was written on Halloween, under a full moon.
CLS
c = 40 'because Russ has 40 computers
h = 23 'because 23 of his computers are haunted
PRINT c - h 'That is how many computers are unhaunted.
```

When you run the program, **the computer ignores everything that's to the right of an apostrophe**. So the computer ignores lines 1 & 2; in lines 4 & 5, the computer ignores the "because…"; in the bottom line, the computer ignores the comment about being unhaunted. Since c is 40, and h is 23, the bottom line makes the computer print:

```
17
```

Everything to the right of an apostrophe is called a **comment** (or **remark**). While the computer runs the program, it ignores the comments. But the comments remain part of the program; they appear on the blue screen with the rest of the program. Though the comments appear in the program, they don't affect the run.

Loop techniques

Here's a strange program:

```
CLS
x = 9
x = 4 + x
PRINT x
```

The third line (x = 4 + x) means: the new x is 4 plus the old x. So the new x is 4 + 9, which is 13. The bottom line prints:

```
13
```

Let's look at that program more closely. The second line (x = 9) puts 9 into box x:

```
box x [                9 ]
```

When the computer sees the next line (x = 4 + x), it examines the equation's right side and sees the 4 + x. Since x is 9, the 4 + x is 4 + 9, which is 13. So the line "x = 4 + x" means x = 13. The computer puts 13 into box x:

```
box x [               13 ]
```

The program's bottom line prints 13.

Here's another weirdo:

```
CLS
b = 6
b = b + 1
PRINT b * 2
```

The third line (b = b + 1) says the new b is "the old b plus 1". So the new b is 6 + 1, which is 7. The bottom line prints:

```
14
```

In that program, the second line says b is 6; but the next line increases b, by adding 1 to b; so b becomes 7. Programmers say that b has been **increased** or **incremented**. In the third line, the "1" is called the **increase** or the **increment**.

The opposite of "increment" is **decrement**:

```
CLS
j = 500
j = j - 1
PRINT j
```

The second line says j starts at 500; but the next line says the new j is "the old j minus 1", so the new j is 500 - 1, which is 499. The bottom line prints:

```
499
```

In that program, j was **decreased** (or **decremented**). In the third line, the "1" is called the **decrease** (or **decrement**).

Counting Suppose you want the computer to count, starting at 3, like this:

```
3
4
5
6
7
8
etc.
```

This program does it, by a special technique:

```
CLS
c = 3
DO
    PRINT c
    c = c + 1
LOOP
```

In that program, c is called the **counter**, because it helps the computer count.

The second line says c starts at 3. The PRINT line makes the computer print c, so the computer prints:

```
3
```

The next line (c = c + 1) increases c by adding 1 to it, so c becomes 4. The LOOP line sends the computer back to the PRINT line, which prints the new value of c:

```
4
```

Then the computer comes to the "c = c + 1" again, which increases c again, so c becomes 5. The LOOP line sends the computer back again to the PRINT line, which prints:

```
5
```

The program's an infinite loop: the computer will print 3, 4, 5, 6, 7, 8, 9, 10, 11, 12, and so on, forever, unless you abort it.

Here's the general procedure to make the computer count:

Start c at some value (such as 3).

Then write a DO loop.

In the DO loop, make the computer use c (such as by saying PRINT c) and increase c (by saying c = c + 1).

To read the printing more easily, put a semicolon at the end of the PRINT statement:

```
CLS
c = 3
DO
    PRINT c;
    c = c + 1
LOOP
```

The semicolon makes the computer print horizontally:

```
3  4  5  6  7  8  etc.
```

This program makes the computer count, starting at 1:

```
CLS
c = 1
DO
    PRINT c;
    c = c + 1
LOOP
```

The computer will print 1, 2, 3, 4, etc.

This program makes the computer count, starting at 0:

```
CLS
c = 0
DO
    PRINT c;
    c = c + 1
LOOP
```

The computer will print 0, 1, 2, 3, 4, etc.

Quiz Let's make the computer give this quiz:

```
What's the capital of Nevada?
What's the chemical symbol for iron?
What word means `brother or sister'?
What was Beethoven's first name?
How many cups are in a quart?
```

To make the computer score the quiz, we must tell it the correct answers:

Question	Correct answer
What's the capital of Nevada?	Carson City
What's the chemical symbol for iron?	Fe
What word means `brother or sister'?	sibling
What was Beethoven's first name?	Ludwig
How many cups are in a quart?	4

So feed the computer this DATA:

```
DATA What's the capital of Nevada,Carson City
DATA What's the chemical symbol for iron,Fe
DATA What word means 'brother or sister',sibling
DATA What was Beethoven's first name,Ludwig
DATA How many cups are in a quart,4
```

In the DATA, each pair consists of a question and an answer. To make the computer READ the DATA, tell the computer to READ a question and an answer, repeatedly:

```
DO
    READ question$, answer$
LOOP
```

Here's the complete program:

```
CLS
DATA What's the capital of Nevada,Carson City
DATA What's the chemical symbol for iron,Fe
DATA What word means 'brother or sister',sibling
DATA What was Beethoven's first name,Ludwig
DATA How many cups are in a quart,4
DATA end,end
DO
    READ question$, answer$: IF question$ = "end" THEN EXIT DO
    PRINT question$;
    INPUT "??"; response$
    IF response$ = answer$ THEN
        PRINT "Correct!"
    ELSE
        PRINT "No, the answer is:   "; answer$
    END IF
LOOP
PRINT "I hope you enjoyed the quiz!"
```

The lines underneath READ make the computer PRINT the question, wait for the human to INPUT a response, and check IF the human's response matches the correct answer. Then the computer will either PRINT "Correct!" or PRINT "No" and reveal the correct answer. When the computer reaches the end of the DATA, the computer does an EXIT DO and prints "I hope you enjoyed the quiz!"

Here's a sample run, where I've underlined the parts typed by the human:

```
What's the capital of Nevada??? Las Vegas
No, the answer is:  Carson City
What's the chemical symbol for iron??? Fe
Correct!
What word means 'brother or sister'??? I give up
No, the answer is:  sibling
What was Beethoven's first name??? Ludvig
No, the answer is:  Ludwig
How many cups are in a quart??? 4
Correct!
I hope you enjoyed the quiz!
```

To give a quiz about different topcs, change the DATA.

Let's make the computer count how many questions the human answered correctly. To do that, we need a counter. As usual, let's call it c:

```
CLS
DATA What's the capital of Nevada,Carson City
DATA What's the chemical symbol for iron,Fe
DATA What word means 'brother or sister',sibling
DATA What was Beethoven's first name,Ludwig
DATA How many cups are in a quart,4
DATA end,end
c = 0
DO
    READ question$, answer$: IF question$ = "end" THEN EXIT DO
    PRINT question$;
    INPUT "??"; response$
    IF response$ = answer$ THEN
        PRINT "Correct!"
        c = c + 1
    ELSE
        PRINT "No, the answer is:   "; answer$
    END IF
LOOP
PRINT "I hope you enjoyed the quiz!"
PRINT "You answered"; c; "of the questions correctly."
```

At the program's beginning, the human hasn't answered any questions correctly yet, so the counter begins at 0 (by saying "c = 0"). Each time the human answers a question correctly, the computer does "c = c + 1", which increases the counter. The program's bottom line prints the counter, by printing a message such as:

```
You answered 2 of the questions correctly.
```

It would be nicer to print —

```
You answered 2 of the 5 questions correctly.
Your score is 40 %
```

or, if the quiz were changed to include 8 questions:

```
You answered 2 of the 8 questions correctly.
Your score is 25 %
```

To make the computer print such a message, we must make the computer count how many questions were asked. So we need another counter. Since we already used c to count the number of correct answers, let's use q to count the number of questions asked. Like c, q must start at 0; and we must increase q, by adding 1 each time another question is asked:

```
CLS
DATA What's the capital of Nevada,Carson City
DATA What's the chemical symbol for iron,Fe
DATA What word means 'brother or sister',sibling
DATA What was Beethoven's first name,Ludwig
DATA How many cups are in a quart,4
DATA end,end
q = 0
c = 0
DO
    READ question$, answer$: IF question$ = "end" THEN EXIT DO
    PRINT question$;
    q = q + 1
    INPUT "??"; response$
    IF response$ = answer$ THEN
        PRINT "Correct!"
        c = c + 1
    ELSE
        PRINT "No, the answer is: "; answer$
    END IF
LOOP
PRINT "I hope you enjoyed the quiz!"
PRINT "You answered"; c; "of the"; q; "questions correctly."
PRINT "Your score is"; c / q * 100; "%"
```

Summing Let's make the computer imitate an adding machine, so a run looks like this:

```
Now the sum is 0
What number do you want to add to the sum? 5
Now the sum is 5
What number do you want to add to the sum? 3
Now the sum is 8
What number do you want to add to the sum? 6.1
Now the sum is 14.1
What number do you want to add to the sum? -10
Now the sum is 4.1
etc.
```

Here's the program:

```
CLS
s = 0
DO
    PRINT "Now the sum is"; s
    INPUT "What number do you want to add to the sum"; x
    s = s + x
LOOP
```

The second line starts the sum at 0. The PRINT line prints the sum. The INPUT line asks the human what number to add to the sum; the human's number is called x. The next line (s = s + x) adds x to the sum, so the sum changes. The LOOP line sends the computer back to the PRINT line, which prints the new sum. The program's an infinite loop, which you must abort.

Here's the general procedure to make the computer find a sum:

Start s at 0.

Then write a DO loop.

In the DO loop, make the computer use s (such as by saying PRINT s) and increase s (by saying s = s + the number to be added).

Checking account If your bank's nasty, it charges you 20¢ to process each good check that you write, and a $15 penalty for each check that bounces; and it pays no interest on the money you've deposited.

This program makes the computer imitate such a bank....

```
CLS
s = 0
DO
    PRINT "Your checking account contains"; s
    1 INPUT "Press d (to make a deposit) or c (to write a check)"; a$
    SELECT CASE a$
        CASE "d"
            INPUT "How much money do you want to deposit"; d
            s = s + d
        CASE "c"
            INPUT "How much money do you want the check for"; c
            c = c + .2
            IF c <= s THEN
                PRINT "Okay"
                s = s - c
            ELSE
                PRINT "That check bounced!"
                s = s - 15
            END IF
        CASE ELSE
            PRINT "Please press d or c"
            GOTO 1
    END SELECT
LOOP
```

In that program, the total amount of money in the checking account is called the sum, s. The second line (s = 0) starts that sum at 0. The first PRINT line prints the sum. The next line asks the human to press "d" (to make a deposit) or "c" (to write a check).

If the human presses "d" (to make a deposit), the computer asks "How much money do you want to deposit?" and waits for the human to type an amount to deposit. The computer adds that amount to the sum in the account (s = s + d).

If the human presses "c" (to write a check), the computer asks "How much money do you want the check for?" and waits for the human to type the amount on the check. The computer adds the 20¢ check-processing fee to that amount (c = c + .2). Then the computer reaches the line saying "IF c <= s", which checks whether the sum s in the account is big enough to cover the check (c). If c <= s, the computer says "Okay" and processes the check, by subtracting c from the sum in the account. If the check is too big, the computer says "That check bounced!" and decreases the sum in the account by the $15 penalty.

That program is nasty to customers:

For example, suppose you have $1 in your account, and you try to write a check for 85¢. Since 85¢ + the 20¢ service charge = $1.05, which is more than you have in your account, your check will bounce, and you'll be penalized $5. That makes your balance will become *negative* $4, and the bank will demand that *you* pay the *bank* $4 — just because you wrote a check for 85¢!

Another nuisance is when you leave town permanently and want to close your account. If your account contains $1, you can't get your dollar back! The most you can withdraw is 80¢, because 80¢ + the 20¢ service charge = $1.

That nasty program makes customers hate the bank — and hate the computer! The bank should make the program friendlier. Here's how:

To stop accusing the customer of owing money, the bank should change any negative sum to 0, by inserting this line just under the word DO:
    IF s < 0 THEN s = 0
Also, to be friendly, the bank should ignore the 20¢ service charge when deciding whether a check will clear. So the bank should eliminate the line saying "c = c + .2". On the other hand, if the check *does* clear, the bank should impose the 20¢ service charge afterwards, by changing the "s = s - c" to "s = s - c - .2".

So if the bank is kind, it will make all those changes. But some banks complain that those changes are *too* kind! For example, if a customer whose account contains just 1¢ writes a million-dollar check (which bounces), the new program charges him just 1¢ for the bad check; $15 might be more reasonable.

Moral: **the hardest thing about programming is choosing your goal — deciding what you *want* the computer to do**.

Series Let's make the computer add together all the numbers from 7 to 100, so that the computer finds the sum of this series: $7 + 8 + 9 + ... + 100$. Here's how.

```
                                 CLS
Start the sum at 0:              s = 0
Make i go from 7 to 100:         FOR i = 7 TO 100
Increase sum, by adding each i to it:   s = s + i
                                 NEXT
Print the final sum (which is 5029): PRINT s
```

Let's make the computer add together the *squares* of all the numbers from 7 to 100, so that the computer finds the sum of this series: (7 squared) + (8 squared) + (9 squared) +... + (100 squared). Here's how:

```
CLS
s = 0
FOR i = 7 TO 100
    s = s + i * i
NEXT
PRINT s
```

It's the same as the previous program, except that indented line says to add i*i instead of i. The bottom line prints the final sum, which is 338259.

Data sums This program adds together the numbers in the data:

```
CLS
DATA 5, 3, 6.1, etc.
DATA 0
s = 0
DO
    READ x: IF x = 0 THEN EXIT DO
    s = s + x
LOOP
PRINT s
```

The DATA line contains the numbers to be added. The DATA 0 is an end mark. The line saying "s = 0" starts the sum at 0. The READ statement reads an x from the data. The next line (s = s + x) adds x to the sum. The LOOP line makes the computer repeat that procedure for every x. When the computer has read all the data and reaches the end mark (0), the x becomes 0; so the computer will EXIT DO and PRINT the final sum, s.

Pretty output

Here's how to make your output prettier.

Zones

The screen is divided into 5 wide columns, called **zones**. The leftmost zone is called **zone 1**; the rightmost zone is called **zone 5**.

Zones 1, 2, 3, and 4 are each 14 characters wide. Zone 5 is extra-wide: it's 24 characters wide. So altogether, the width of the entire screen is 14+14+14+14+24, which is 80 characters. The screen is 80 characters wide.

A comma makes the computer jump to a new zone. Here's an example:

```
CLS
PRINT "sin", "king"
```

The computer will print "sin" and "king" on the same line; but because of the comma before "king", the computer will print "king" in the second zone, like this:

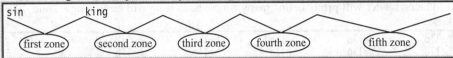

Here are the words of a poet who drank too much and is feeling spaced out:

```
CLS
PRINT "love", "cries", "out"
```

The computer will print "love" in the first zone, "cries" in the second zone, and "out" in the third zone, so the words are spaced out like this:

```
love          cries         out
```

This program's even spacier:

```
CLS
PRINT "love", "cries", "out", "to", "me", "at", "night"
```

The computer will print "love" in the first zone, "cries" in the second, "out" in the third, "to" in the fourth, "me" in the fifth, and the remaining words below, like this:

```
love          cries         out           to            me
at            night
```

This program tells a bad joke:

```
CLS
PRINT "I think you are ugly!", "I'm joking!"
```

The computer will print "I think you are ugly!", then jump to a new zone, then print "I'm joking", like this:

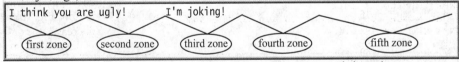

When you combine commas with semicolons, you can get weird results:

```
CLS
PRINT "eat", "me"; "at"; "balls", "no"; "w"
```

That line contains commas and semicolons. A comma makes the computer jump to a new zone, but a semicolon does *not* make the computer jump. The computer will print "eat", then jump to a new zone, then print "me" and "at" and "balls", then jump to a new zone, then print "no" and "w". Altogether, the computer will print:

```
eat           meatballs     now
```

Skip a zone You can make the computer skip over a zone:

```
CLS
PRINT "Joe", " ", "loves Sue"
```

The computer will print "Joe" in the first zone, a blank space in the second zone, and "loves Sue" in the third zone, like this:

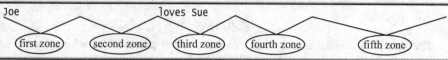

You can type that example even more briefly, like this:

```
CLS
PRINT "Joe", , "loves Sue"
```

Loops This program makes the computer greet you:

```
CLS
DO
   PRINT "hello",
LOOP
```

The computer will print "hello" many times. Each time will be in a new zone, like this:

```
hello       hello       hello       hello       hello
hello       hello       hello       hello       hello
hello       hello       hello       hello       hello
etc.
```

Tables This program prints a list of words and their opposites:

```
CLS
PRINT "good", "bad"
PRINT "black", "white"
PRINT "grandparent", "grandchild"
PRINT "he", "she"
```

Line 2 makes the computer print "good", then jump to the next zone, then print "bad". Altogether, the computer will print:

```
good          bad
black         white
grandparent   grandchild
he            she
```

The first zone contains a column of words; the second zone contains the opposites. Altogether, the computer's printing looks like a table. So **whenever you want to make a table easily, use zones, by putting commas in your program**.

Let's make the computer print this table:

```
Number       Square
3            9
4            16
5            25
6            36
7            49
8            64
9            81
10           100
```

Here's the program:

```
CLS
PRINT "Number", "Square"
FOR i = 3 TO 10
    PRINT i, i * i
NEXT
```

Line 2 prints the word "Number" at the top of the first column, and the word "Square" at the top of the second. Those words are called the **column headings**. The FOR line says i goes from 3 to 10; to begin, i is 3. The indented line makes the computer print:

```
3            9
```

The bottom line makes the computer do the same thing for the next i, and for the next i, and for the next; so the computer prints the whole table.

TAB

When the computer puts a line of information on your screen, the leftmost character in the line is said to be at **position 1**. The second character in the line is said to be at **position 2**.

This program makes the computer skip to position 6 and then print "HOT":

```
CLS
PRINT TAB(6); "hot"
```

The computer will print:

```
     hot
12345678
```

Here's a fancier example:

```
PRINT TAB(6); "hot"; TAB(13); "buns"
```

The computer will skip to the 6th position, then print "hot", then skip to the 13th position, then print "buns":

```
     HOT     BUNS
12345678     13
```

Diagonal This program prints a diagonal line:

```
CLS
FOR i = 1 TO 12
    PRINT TAB(i); "*"
NEXT
```

The FOR line says to do the loop 12 times, so the computer does the indented line. The first time the computer does the indented line, the i is 1, so the computer prints an asterisk at position 1:

```
*
```

The next time, the i is 2, so the computer skips to position 2 and prints an asterisk:

```
 *
```

The next time, the i is 3, so the computer skips to position 3 and prints an asterisk:

```
  *
```

Altogether, the program makes the computer print this picture:

```
*
 *
  *
   *
    *
     *
      *
       *
        *
         *
          *
           *
```

LOCATE

While you're running a program, the black window shows 25 lines of information. The screen's top line is called **line 1**; underneath it is **line 2**; then comes **line 3**; etc. The bottom line is **line 25**.

Each line consists of 80 characters. The leftmost character is at **position 1**; the next character is at **position 2**; etc. The rightmost character is at **position 80**.

In the black window, the computer will print wherever you wish.

For example, to make the computer print the word "drown" so that "drown" begins at line 3's 7th position, type this:

```
CLS
LOCATE 3, 7: PRINT "drown"
```

The computer will print the word's first letter (d) at line 3's 7th position. The computer will print the rest of the word afterwards.

You'll see the first letter (d) at line 3's 7th position, the next letter (r) at the next position (line 3's 8th position), the next letter (o) at the next position (line 3's 9th position), etc.

Middle of the screen Since the black window's top line is 1 and the bottom line is 25, **the middle line is 13**. Since the screen's leftmost position is 1 and the rightmost position is 80, **the middle positions are 40 and 41**.

To make the computer print the word "Hi" in the middle of the black window, tell the computer to print at the middle line (13) and the middle positions (40 and 41):

```
CLS
LOCATE 13, 40: PRINT "Hi"
```

Bottom line Whenever the computer finishes running a program, the computer prints this message on the black screen's bottom line:

```
Press any key to continue
```

Then the computer waits for you to press the Enter key, which makes the screen turn blue and show the lines of your program.

That message, "Press any key to continue", is the only message that the computer wants to print on the bottom line.

To force the computer to print anything else on the bottom line, do this: say LOCATE, mention line 25, put a semicolon at the end of the PRINT statement (to prevent the computer from pressing the Enter key, which would disturb the rest of the screen), and say SLEEP (to make the computer pause awhile so you can admire the printing). For example, this program prints an "x" at the black window's bottom right corner:

```
CLS
LOCATE 25, 80: PRINT "x";
SLEEP
```

Pixels

The image on the black window's screen is called the **picture**. If you stare at the picture closely, you'll see the picture's composed of thousands of tiny dots. Each dot, which is a tiny rectangle, is called a **picture's element**, or **pic's el**, or **pixel**, or **pel**.

Coordinates The dot in the black window's top left corner is called **pixel (0,0)**. Just to the right of it is pixel (1,0). Then comes pixel (2,0), etc.

Underneath pixel (0,0) is pixel (0,1). Farther down is pixel (0,2). Here are the positions of the pixels:

pixel (0,0)	pixel (1,0)	pixel (2,0)	pixel (3,0)	pixel (4,0)	etc.
pixel (0,1)	pixel (1,1)	pixel (2,1)	pixel (3,1)	pixel (4,1)	etc.
pixel (0,2)	pixel (1,2)	pixel (2,2)	pixel (3,2)	pixel (4,2)	etc.
pixel (0,3)	pixel (1,3)	pixel (2,3)	pixel (3,3)	pixel (4,3)	etc.

Each pixel's name consists of two numbers in parentheses. The first number is the **X coordinate**; the second number is the **Y coordinate**. For example, if you're talking about pixel (4,3), its X coordinate is 4; its Y coordinate is 3.

The X coordinate tells how far to the right the pixel is. The Y coordinate tells how far down. So **pixel (4,3) is the pixel that's 4 to the right and 3 down**.

On the computer, the Y coordinate measures how far *down*, not up. If you've read old-fashioned math books in which the Y coordinate measured how far *up*, you'll have to reverse your thinking!

Screen modes How many pixels are on the screen? The answer depends on which **screen mode** you choose.

For most purposes, the best screen mode is **screen mode 12**.

In screen mode 12, the X coordinate goes from 0 to 639, and the Y coordinate goes from 0 to 479, so the pixel at the window's bottom right corner is pixel (639,479). Since you have 640 choices for the X coordinate (numbered from 0 to 639) and 480 choices for the Y coordinate (numbered from 0 to 479), that mode is called a **640-by-480 mode**.

In screen mode 12, the computer can display 16 colors simultaneously.

Screen mode 13 gives you more colors but fewer pixels:

In screen mode 13, the X coordinate goes from 0 to 319, and the Y coordinate goes from 0 to 199, so the pixel at the window's bottom right corner is pixel (319,199). Since you have 320 choices for the X coordinate (numbered from 0 to 639) and 200 choices for the Y coordinate (numbered from 0 to 479), that mode is called a **320-by-200 mode**.

In screen mode 13, the computer can display 256 colors simultaneously.

Since mode 13 has fewer pixels, its drawings look crude. **Each pixel is a tiny rectangular dot.**

QB64 Each pixel is a perfect square, whose width is the same as its height.

QBasic In screen mode 12, each pixel is a perfect square, whose width is the same as its height: on a typical 15-inch screen, each pixel's width and height are about a 60th of an inch. In screen mode 13, each pixel is slightly taller than it is wide, so each pixel looks like a little tower.

There's also a **screen mode 0**, which works on all computers and **produces just text** (no graphics).

To give commands about pixels, begin by telling the computer which screen mode you want. For example, if you want screen mode 12, say:

```
SCREEN 12
```

When you give such a SCREEN command, the computer automatically clears the window so the whole window becomes black. You do *not* have to say CLS.

PSET This program makes the window become entirely black then makes pixel (100,100) turn white:

```
SCREEN 12
PSET (100, 100)
```

In that program, the PSET (100, 100) makes pixel (100,100) turn white. The word "PSET" means "pixel set": "PSET (100, 100)" means "set the pixel (100,100) to white".

LINE This program draws a white line from pixel (0,0) to pixel (100,100):

```
SCREEN 12
LINE (0, 0)-(100, 100)
```

This program draws a white line from pixel (0,0) to pixel (100,100), then draws a white line from that pixel (100,100) to pixel (120,70):

```
SCREEN 12
LINE (0, 0)-(100, 100)
LINE -(120, 70)
```

CIRCLE This program draws a white circle whose center is pixel (100,100) and whose radius is 40 pixels:

```
SCREEN 12
CIRCLE (100, 100), 40
```

In screen mode 12, each pixel is a perfect square, and the computer draws the circle easily. The circle's radius is 40 pixels; the circle's diameter (width) is 80 pixels.

If you switch to screen mode 13 (by saying SCREEN 13), each pixel is a tower instead of a square, so a "circle that's 80 pixels wide and 80 pixels high" would be taller than wide and look like a tall oval. To make sure your "circle of radius 40" looks pretty, the computer cheats: the computer makes the circle's width be 80 pixels but makes the circle's height be fewer than 80 pixels, so that the circle's height is the same number of *inches* as the width.

Avoid the bottom When your program finishes, the bottom of the screen automatically shows this advice:

```
Press any key to continue
```

To prevent that advice from covering up your drawing, position your drawing near the *top* of the screen (avoiding the bottom), or else make your program's bottom line say "SLEEP" so the computer will pause and let you admire the drawing before the advice covers it.

PAINT After drawing a shape's outline (by using dots, lines, and circles), you can fill in the shape's middle, by telling the computer to PAINT the shape.

Here's how to PAINT a shape that you've drawn (such as a circle or a house). Find a pixel that's in the middle of the shape and that's still black; then tell the computer to PAINT, starting at that pixel. For example, if pixel (100, 101) is inside the shape and still black, say:

```
PAINT (100, 101)
```

Colors In screen mode 12, you can use these 16 colors:

```
0. black                      8. light black (gray)
1. blue                       9. light blue
2. green                      10. light green
3. cyan (greenish blue)       11. light cyan (aqua)
4. red                        12. light red (pink)
5. magenta (purplish red)     13. light magenta
6. brown                      14. light brown (yellow)
7. cream (yellowish white)    15. light cream (pure white)
```

Screen mode 13 gives you the 16 colors used in screen mode 12 — and many more colors, too! Here's the spectrum:

```
  0 through    7: black, blue, green, cyan, red, magenta, brown, cream
  8 through   15: same colors as above, but lighter
 16 through   31: shades of gray (from dark to light)
 32 through   55: color blends (from blue to red to green to blue again)
 56 through   79: same color blends, but lighter
 80 through  103: same color blends, but even lighter
104 through  175: same as 32 through 103, but darker
176 through  247: same as 104 through 175, but even darker
248 through  255: black
```

Normally, the PSET, LINE, CIRCLE, and PAINT commands draw in yellowish white (cream). If you prefer a different color, **put the color's number at the end of the command**. Put a comma before the color's number.

For example, if you want to draw a line from (0,0) to (100,0) using color #2, type this:

```
LINE (0, 0)-(100, 0), 2
```

When you give a PAINT command, you must make its color be the same color as the outline you're filling in.

Boxes If you type —

```
LINE (0, 0)-(100, 100), 2
```

the computer draws a line from pixel (0,0) to (100,100) using color #2.

If you put the letter B at the end of the LINE command, like this —

```
LINE (0, 0)-(100, 100), 2, B
```

the computer will draw a box instead of a line. One corner of the box will be at pixel (0,0); the opposite corner will be at (100,100); and the box will be drawn using color 2.

If you put BF at the end of the LINE command, like this —

```
LINE (0, 0)-(100, 100), 2, BF
```

the computer will draw a box and also fill it in, by painting its interior.

Return to text mode When you finish drawing pictures, you can return to text mode by saying:

```
SCREEN 0
```

If you were using screen mode 13, say this instead:

```
SCREEN 0
WIDTH 80
```

The "WIDTH 80" makes sure the screen will display 80 characters per line instead of 40.

Sounds

To produce sounds, you can say BEEP, SOUND, or PLAY. BEEP appeals to business executives; SOUND appeals to doctors and engineers; and PLAY appeals to musicians.

BEEP If your program says —

```
BEEP
```

the computer will beep. The beep lasts for about a quarter of a second. Its frequency ("pitch") is about 875 hertz. (The beep's length and frequency might be slightly higher or lower, depending on which computer you have.)

You can say BEEP in the middle of your program. For example, you can tell the computer to BEEP if a person enters wrong data.

This program makes the computer act as a priest and perform a marriage ceremony:

```
CLS
10 INPUT "Do you take this woman to be your lawful wedded wife"; a$
IF a$ <> "I do" THEN BEEP: PRINT "Try again!": GO TO 10
20 INPUT "Do you take this man to be your lawful wedded husband"; a$
IF a$ <> "I do" THEN BEEP: PRINT "Try again!": GO TO 20
PRINT "I now pronounce you husband and wife."
```

Line 10 makes the computer ask the groom, "Do you take this woman to be your lawful wedded wife?" If the groom doesn't say "I do", the next line makes the computer beep, say "Try again!", and repeat the question. Line 20 does the same thing to the bride. The bottom line congratulates the couple for answering correctly and getting married.

SOUND If your program says —

```
SOUND 440, 18.2
```

the computer will produce a sound. In that command, the 440 is the frequency ("pitch"), measured in hertz (cycles per second); so the sound will be a musical note whose pitch is 440 hertz. (That note happens to be "the A above middle C").

If you replace the 440 by a lower number, the sound will have a lower pitch; if you replace the 440 by a higher number, the sound will have a higher pitch.

The lowest pitch that the computer can sing is 37. If you try to go below 37, the computer will gripe by saying:

```
Illegal function call
```

The highest pitch that the computer can sing is 32767, but human ears aren't good enough to hear a pitch that high.

When you were a baby, you could probably hear up to 20000. As you get older, your hearing gets worse, and you can't hear such high notes. Today, the highest sound you can hear is probably somewhere around 14000. To find out, give yourself a hearing test, by running this program:

```
CLS
DO
    INPUT "What pitch would you like me to play"; p
    SOUND p, 18.2
LOOP
```

When you run that program, begin by inputting a low pitch (such as 37). Then input a higher number, then an even higher number, until you finally pick a number so high you can't hear it. (When trying that test, put your ear close to the computer's speaker, which is in the computer's front left corner.) When you've picked a number too high for you to hear, try a slightly lower number. Keep trying different numbers, until you find the highest number you can hear.

Have a contest with your friends: find out which of your friends can hear best.

If you run that program every year, you'll see that your hearing gradually worse. For example, when I was 36 years old, the highest pitch I could hear was about 14500, but I can't hear that high anymore. How about *you*?

In those examples, the 18.2 makes the computer produce the sound for 1 second. **If you want the sound to last longer — so that it lasts 2 seconds — replace the 18.2 by 18.2*2.** For 10 seconds, say 18.2*10. (That's because the computer's metronome beats 18.2 times per second.)

PLAY If your program says —

```
PLAY "c d g# b- a"
```

the computer will play the note C, then D, then G sharp, then B flat, then A.

In the PLAY command, the computer ignores the spaces; so if you wish, you can write:

```
PLAY "cdg#b-a"
```

The computer can play in seven octaves, numbered from 0 to 6. Octave 0 consists of very bass notes; octave 6 consists of very high-pitched notes. In each octave, the lowest note is a C: the notes in an octave are C, C#, D, D#, E, F, F#, G, G#, A, A#, and B. "Middle C" is at the beginning of octave 2. Normally, the computer plays in octave 4. **To make the computer switch to octave 3, type the letter "o" followed by a 3**, like this:

```
PLAY "o3"
```

After giving that command, anything else you PLAY will be in octave 3, until you change octaves again.

You can use the symbol ">" to mean "go up an octave", and you can use the symbol "<" to mean "go down an octave". For example, if you say —

```
PLAY "g > c d < g"
```

the computer will play the note G, then go up an octave to play C and D in that higher octave, then go down to the original octave to play G again.

The lowest note the computer can play (the C in octave 0) is called "note 1". The highest note the computer can play (the B in octave 6) is called "note 84". **To make the computer play note 84, you can type this:**

```
PLAY "n84"
```

To make the computer play its lowest note (1), then its middle note (42), then its highest note (84), type this:

```
PLAY "n1 n42 n84"
```

Besides playing with pitches, **you can play with rhythms ("lengths" of notes).** Normally each note is a "quarter note". **To make the computer switch to eighth notes (which are faster), type this:**

```
PLAY "L8"
```

Besides using L8 for eighth notes, you can use L16 for sixteenth notes (which are even faster), L32 for thirty-second notes (which are super-fast), and L64 for sixty-fourth notes (which are super-super-fast). For long notes, you can use L2 (which gives a half note) or L1 (which gives a whole note). You can use any length from L1 to L64. You can even use in-between lengths, such as L7 or L23 (though such rhythms are hard to stamp your foot to).

If you put a period after a note, the computer will multiply the note's length by 1½.

For example, suppose you say:

```
PLAY "L8 c e. d"
```

The C will be an 8th note, E will be 1½ times as long as an 8th note, and D will be an 8th note. Musicians call that E a **dotted eighth note**.

If you put *two* periods after a note (like this: e..), the computer will multiply the note's length by 1¾. Musicians say the note is **double dotted**.

If you put *three* periods after a note (like this: e...), the computer will multiply the note's length by 1⅞.

To make the computer pause ("rest") for an eighth note, put a p8 into the music string.

Normally, the computer plays 120 quarter notes per minute; but you can change that tempo. To switch to 150 quarter notes per minute, say:

```
PLAY "t150"
```

You can switch to any tempo from 32 to 255. The 32 is very slow; 255 is very fast. In musical terms, 40=larghissimo, 50=largo, 63=larghetto, 65=grave, 68=lento, 71=adagio, 76=andantino, 92=andante, 114=moderato, 120=allegretto, 144=allegro, 168=vivace, 188=presto, and 208=prestissimo.

You can combine all those musical commands into a single PLAY statement. For example, to set the tempo to 150, the octave to 3, the length to 8 (which means an eighth note), and then play C and D, and then change the length to 4 and play E, type this:

```
PLAY "t150 o3 L8 c d L4 e"
```

PRINT USING

Suppose you want to add $12.47 to $1.03. The correct answer is $13.50. This almost works:

```
PRINT 12.47 + 1.03
```

It makes the computer print:

```
 13.5
```

But instead of 13.5, we should try to make the computer print 13.50.

This command forces the computer to print 13.50:

```
PRINT USING "##.##"; 12.47 + 1.03
```

The "##.##" is called the **picture** or **image** or **format**: it says to print two characters, then a decimal point, then two digits. The computer will print:

```
13.50
```

This command puts that answer into a sentence:

```
PRINT USING "You spent ##.## at our store"; 12.47 + 1.03
```

The computer will print:

```
You spent 13.50 at our store
```

Rounding This program makes the computer divide 300 by 7 but round the answer to two decimal places:

```
CLS
PRINT USING "##.##"; 300 / 7
```

When the computer divides 300 by 7, it gets 42.85714, but the format rounds the answer to 42.86. The computer will print:

```
42.86
```

Multiple numbers Every format (such as "###.##") is a string. You can replace the format by a string variable:

```
CLS
a$ = "###.##"
PRINT USING a$; 247.91
PRINT USING a$; 823
PRINT USING a$; 7
PRINT USING a$; -5
PRINT USING a$; -80.3
```

The computer will print:

```
247.91
823.00
  7.00
 -5.00
-80.30
```

When the computer prints that column of numbers, notice that the computer prints the decimal points underneath each other so that they line up. So **to make decimal points line up, say PRINT USING instead of just PRINT**.

To print those numbers *across* instead of down, say this:

```
PRINT USING "###.##"; 247.91; 823; 7; -5; -80.3
```

It makes the computer print 247.91, then 823.00, etc., like this:

```
247.91823.00  7.00 -5.00-80.30
```

Since the computer prints those numbers so close together, they're hard to read. To make the computer insert extra space between the numbers, widen the format by putting a fourth "#" before the decimal point:

```
PRINT USING "####.##"; 247.91; 823; 7; -5; -80.3
```

Then the computer will print:

```
 247.91 823.00    7.00   -5.00 -80.30
```

If you say —

```
PRINT USING "My ## pals drank ###.# pints of gin"; 24; 983.5
```

the computer will print:

```
My 24 pals drank 983.5 pints of gin
```

Oversized numbers Suppose you say:

```
PRINT USING "###.##"; 16238.7
```

The computer tries to print 16238.7 by using the format "###.##". But since that format allows just three digits before the decimal point, the format isn't large enough to fit 16238.7. So the computer must disobey the format. But the computer also prints a percent sign, which means, "Warning! I am disobeying you!" Altogether, the computer prints:

```
%16238.70
```

Final semicolon At the end of the PRINT USING statement, you can put a semicolon:

```
CLS
PRINT USING "##.##"; 13.5;
PRINT "credit"
```

Line 2 makes the computer print 13.50. The semicolon at the end of line 2 makes the computer print "credit" on the same line, like this:

```
13.50credit
```

Advanced formats Suppose you're running a high-risk business. On Monday, your business runs badly: you *lose* $27,931.60, so your "profit" is *minus* $27,931.60. On Tuesday, your business does slightly better than break-even: your net profit for the day is $8.95.

Let's make the computer print the word "profit", then the amount of your profit (such as -27,931.60 or $8.95), then the word "ha" (because you're cynical about how your business is going).

You can do that printing in several ways. Let's explore them....
If you say —

```
CLS
a$ = "profit######.##ha"
PRINT USING a$; -27931.6
PRINT USING a$; 8.95
```

the computer will print:

```
profit-27931.60ha
profit     8.95ha
```

If you change the format to "profit###,###.##ha", the computer will **insert a comma** if the number is large:

```
profit-27,931.60ha
profit       8.95ha
```

If you change the format to "profit+#####.##ha", the computer will **print a plus sign** in front of any positive number:

```
profit-27931.60ha
profit     +8.95ha
```

To print a negative number, the computer normally prints a minus sign *before* the number. That's called a **leading minus**. You can make the computer put the minus sign *after* the number instead; that's called a **trailing minus**. For example, if you change the format to "profit######.##-ha", the computer will **print a minus sign AFTER a negative number** (and no minus after a positive number), like this:

```
profit27931.60-ha
profit     8.95 ha
```

Normally, a format begins with ##. If you begin with $$ instead (like this: "profit$$#####.##ha"), the computer will **print a dollar sign** before the digits:

```
profit-$27931.60ha
profit      $8.95ha
```

If you begin with ** (like this: "profit**#####.##ha"), the computer will **print asterisks** before the number:

```
profit*-27931.60ha
profit******8.95ha
```

If you begin with **$ (like this: "profit**$#####.##ha"), the computer will print asterisks and a dollar sign:

```
profit*-$27931.60ha
profit******$8.95ha
```

When you're printing a paycheck, use the asterisks to prevent the employee from enlarging his salary. Since the asterisks protect the check from being altered, they're called **check protection**.

You can combine several techniques into a single format. For example, you can combine the comma, the trailing minus, and the **$ (like this: "profit**$##,###.##-ha"), so that the computer will print:

```
profit**$27,931.60-ha
profit*******$8.95 ha
```

If you change the format to "profit##.#####^^^^ha", the computer will **print numbers by using E notation**:

```
profit-2.79316E+04ha
profit 8.95000E+00ha
```

You can do fancy calculations — easily!

Exponents

Try typing this program:

```
CLS
PRINT 4 ^ 3
```

To type the symbol ^, do this: while holding down the SHIFT key, tap this key:

```
^
6
```

That symbol (^) is called a **caret**.

In that program, **the "4 ^ 3" makes the computer use the number 4, three times**. The computer will multiply together those three 4's, like this: 4 times 4 times 4. Since "4 times 4 times 4" is 64, the computer will print:

```
64
```

In the expression "4 ^ 3", the 4 is called the **base**; the 3 is called the **exponent**.

Here's another example:

```
CLS
PRINT 10 ^ 6
```

The "10 ^ 6" makes the computer use the number 10, six times. The computer will multiply together those six 10's (like this: 10 times 10 times 10 times 10 times 10 times 10) and print the answer:

```
1000000
```

Here's another example:

```
CLS
PRINT 3 ^ 2
```

The "3 ^ 2" makes the computer use the number 3, two times. The computer will multiply together those two 3's (like this: 3 times 3) and print the answer:

```
9
```

Order of operations The symbols +, -, *, /, and ^ are all called **operations**.

To solve a problem, the computer uses the three-step process taught in algebra and the "new math". For example, suppose you say:

```
PRINT 70 - 3 ^ 2 + 8 / 2 * 3
```

The computer will *not* begin by subtracting 3 from 70; instead, it will use the three-step process:

The problem is	70 - 3 ^ 2 + 8 / 2 * 3	
Step 1: get rid of ^.	Now the problem is 70 - 9 + 8 / 2 * 3	
Step 2: get rid of * and /.	Now the problem is 70 - 9 + 12	
Step 3: get rid of + and -.	The answer is 73	

In each step, it looks from left to right. For example, in step 2, it sees / and gets rid of it before it sees *.

Speed Though exponents are fun, the computer handles them slowly. For example, the computer handles 3 ^ 2 slower than 3 * 3. So for fast calculations, say 3 * 3 instead of 3 ^ 2.

Square roots What positive number, when multiplied by itself, gives 9? The answer is 3, because 3 times itself is 9.

3 **squared** is 9. 3 is called the **square root** of 9.

To make the computer deduce the square root of 9, type this:

```
PRINT SQR(9)
```

The computer will print 3.

When you tell the computer to PRINT SQR(9), make sure you put the parentheses around the 9.

The symbol SQR is called a **function**. The number in parentheses (9) is called the function's **input** (or **argument** or **parameter**). The answer, which is 3, is called the function's **output** (or **value**).

SQR(9) gives the same answer as $9 \wedge .5$. The computer handles SQR(9) faster than $9 \wedge .5$.

Cube roots What number, when multiplied by itself and then multiplied by itself *again*, gives 64? The answer is 4, because 4 times 4 times 4 is 64. The answer (4) is called the **cube root** of 64.

Here's how to make the computer find the cube root of 64:

```
PRINT 64 ^ (1 / 3)
```

The computer will print 4.

EXP The letter "e" stands for a special number, which is approximately 2.718281828459045. You can memorize that number easily, if you pair the digits:

```
2.7 18 28 18 28 45 90 45
```

That weird number is important in calculus, radioactivity, biological growth, and other areas of science. It's calculated by this formula:

$$e = 1 + \frac{1}{1} + \frac{1}{1*2} + \frac{1}{1*2*3} + \frac{1}{1*2*3*4} + \frac{1}{1*2*3*4*5} + \cdots$$

Therefore:

$$e = 1 + 1 + \frac{1}{2} + \frac{1}{6} + \frac{1}{24} + \frac{1}{120} + \cdots$$

EXP(x) means e^x. For example, EXP(3) means e^3, which is e * e * e, which is:

```
2.718281828459045 * 2.718281828459045 * 2.718281828459045
```

EXP(4) means e^4, which is e * e * e * e. EXP(3.1) means $e^{3.1}$, which is more than e^3 but less than e^4.

Here's a practical application. Suppose you put $800 in a savings account, and the bank promises to give you 5% annual interest "compounded continuously". How much money will you have at the end of the year? The answer is 800 * EXP(.05).

Logarithms Here are some powers of 2:

x	2^x
1	2
2	4
3	8
4	16
5	32
6	64

To compute the logarithm-base-2 of a number, find the number in the right-hand column; the answer is in the left column. For example, the logarithm-base-2 of 32 is 5. The logarithm-base-2 of 15 is slightly less than 4.

The logarithm-base-2 of 64 is 6. That fact is written:

$$\log_2 64 \text{ is } 6$$

It's also written:

$$\frac{\log 64}{\log 2} \text{ is } 6$$

To make the computer find the logarithm-base-2 of 64, say:

```
PRINT LOG(64) / LOG(2)
```

The computer will print 6.

Here are some powers of 10:

x	10^x
1	10
2	100
3	1000
4	10000
5	100000

The logarithm-base-10 of 100000 is 5. The logarithm-base-10 of 1001 is slightly more than 3.

The logarithm-base-10 of 10000 is 4. That fact is written:

$$\log_{10} 10000 \text{ is } 4$$

It's also written:

$$\frac{\log 10000}{\log 10} \text{ is } 4$$

To make the computer do that calculation, say:

```
PRINT LOG(10000) / LOG(10)
```

The computer will print 4.

The logarithm-base-10 is called the **common logarithm**. That's the kind of logarithm used in high school and chemistry. So **if a chemistry book says to find the logarithm of 10000, the book means the logarithm-base-10 of 10000, which is LOG(10000) / LOG(10)**.

What happens if you forget the base, and say just LOG(10000) instead of LOG(10000) / LOG(10)? If you say just LOG(10000), the computer will find the **natural logarithm** of 10000, which is $\log_e 10000$ (where e is 2.718281828459045), which isn't what your chemistry book wants.

Contrasts

The computer's notation resembles that of arithmetic and algebra, but beware of these contrasts....

Multiplication To make the computer multiply, you must type an asterisk:

Traditional notation	Computer notation
2n	2 * n
5(n+m)	5 * (n + m)
nm	n * m

Exponents Put an exponent in parentheses, if it contains an operation:

Traditional notation	Computer notation
x^{n+2}	x ^ (n + 2)
x^{3n}	x ^ (3 * n)
$5^{2/3}$	5 ^ (2 / 3)
2^{3^4}	2 ^ (3 ^ 4)

Fractions Put a fraction's numerator in parentheses, if it contains addition or subtraction:

Traditional notation	Computer notation
$\frac{a+b}{c}$	(a + b) / c
$\frac{k-20}{6}$	(k - 20) / 6

Put a denominator in parentheses, if it contains addition, subtraction, multiplication, or division:

Traditional notation	Computer notation
$\frac{5}{3+x}$	5 / (3 + x)
$\frac{5a^3}{4b}$	5 * a ^ 3 / (4 * b)

Mixed numbers A **mixed number** is a number that contains a fraction. For example, 9½ is a mixed number. When you write a mixed number, put a plus sign before its fraction:

Traditional notation	Computer notation
9½	9 + 1 / 2

If you're using the mixed number in a further calculation, put the mixed number in parentheses:

Traditional notation	Computer notation
7 - 2¼	7 - (2 + 1 / 4)

Clock

If you've set the computer's clock correctly, this program prints the current date & time:

```
CLS
PRINT DATE$
PRINT TIME$
```

If you say —

```
PRINT TIMER
```

the computer will tell you how many seconds have elapsed since midnight.

This program makes the computer print the DATE$, TIME$, and TIMER across the top of your screen:

```
CLS
PRINT DATE$, TIME$, TIMER
```

The top of your screen will look like this:

```
07-29-1996    18:07:04        65223.85
```

The following program makes the computer look at the clock (and tell you the TIME$), then look at the clock *again* and tell you the new TIME$, then look at the clock *again* and tell you the new TIME$, etc.:

```
CLS
DO
  PRINT TIME$
LOOP
```

For example, if the time starts at 18:07:04 (and eventually changes to 18:07:05 and then 18:07:06), the screen will look like this:

```
18:07:04
18:07:04
18:07:04
18:07:05
18:07:05
18:07:05
18:07:05
18:07:05
18:07:06
18:07:06
etc.
```

The program will continue telling you the time until you abort the program.

Stripping

Sometimes the computer prints *too much* info: you wish the computer would print less, to save yourself the agony of reading excess info irrelevant to your needs. Whenever the computer prints too much info about a numerical answer, use ABS, FIX, INT, CINT, or SGN.

ABS removes any minus sign. For example, the ABS of -3.89 is 3.89. So if you say PRINT ABS(-3.89), the computer will print just 3.89.

FIX removes any digits after the decimal point. For example, the FIX of 3.89 is 3. So if you say PRINT FIX(3.89), the computer will print just 3. The FIX of -3.89 is -3.

CINT rounds to the NEAREST integer. For example, the CINT of 3.89 is 4; the CINT of -3.89 is -4.

INT rounds the number DOWN to an integer that's LOWER. For example, the INT of 3.89 is 3 (because 3 is an integer that's lower than 3.89); the INT of -3.89 is -4 (because -4 is lower than -3.89).

SGN removes ALL the digits and replaces them with a 1 — unless the number is 0. For example, the SGN of 3.89 is 1. The SGN of -3.89 is -1. The SGN of 0 is just 0.

ABS, FIX, CINT, INT, and SGN are all called **stripping functions** or **strippers** or **diet functions** or **diet pills**, because they strip away the number's excess fat and reveal just the fundamentals that interest you.

Here are more details about those five functions....

ABS To find the **absolute value** of a negative number, just omit the number's minus sign. For example, the absolute value of -7 is 7.

The absolute value of a positive number is the number itself. For example, the absolute value of 7 is 7. The absolute value of 0 is 0.

To make the computer find the absolute value of -7, type this:

```
PRINT ABS(-7)
```

The computer will print:

```
7
```

Like SQR, ABS is a function: you must put parentheses after the ABS.

Since ABS omits the minus sign, ABS turns negative numbers into positive numbers. Use ABS whenever you insist that an answer be positive.

For example, ABS helps solve math & physics problems about "distance", since the "distance" between two points is always a positive number and cannot be negative.

This program computes the distance between two numbers:

```
CLS
PRINT "I will find the distance between two numbers."
INPUT "What's the first number"; x
INPUT "What's the second number"; y
PRINT "The distance between those numbers is"; ABS(x - y)
```

When you run that program, suppose you say that the first number is 4 and the second number is 7. Since x is 4, and y is 7, the distance between those two numbers is ABS(4 - 7), which is ABS(-3), which is 3.

If you reverse those two numbers, so that x is 7 and y is 4, the distance between them is ABS(7 - 4), which is ABS(3), which is still 3.

FIX An **integer** is a number that has no decimal point. For example, these are integers: 17, 238, 0, and -956.

If a number contains a decimal point, the simplest way to turn the number into an integer is to delete all the digits after the decimal point. That's called the **FIX** of the number.

For example, the FIX of 3.89 is 3. So if you say PRINT FIX (3.89), the computer will print just 3.

The FIX of -3.89 is -3. The FIX of 7 is 7. The FIX of 0 is 0.

CINT A more sophisticated way to turn a number into an integer is to *round* the number to the *nearest* integer. That's called **CINT** (which means "Convert to INTeger"). For example, the CINT of 3.9 is 4 (because 3.9 is closer to 4 than to 3).

Like FIX, CINT deletes all the digits after the decimal point; but if the digit just after the decimal point is 5, 6, 7, 8, or 9, CINT "rounds up" by adding 1 to the digit before the decimal point.

Here are more examples:

CINT(3.9) is 4	CINT(-3.9) is -4
CINT(3.1) is 3	CINT(-3.1) is -3
CINT(3.5) is 4	CINT(-3.5) is -4

The highest number CINT can produce is 32767. If you try to go higher than 32767 or lower than -32768, the computer will gripe by saying "Overflow".

To explore the mysteries of rounding, run this program:

```
CLS
INPUT "What's your favorite number"; x
PRINT CINT(x)
```

In that program, the INPUT line asks you to type a number x. The bottom line prints your number, but rounded to the nearest integer. For example, if you type 3.9, the bottom line prints 4.

INT Like FIX and CINT, **INT** turns a number into an integer. Though INT is slightly harder to understand than FIX and CINT, INT is more useful!

INT rounds a number *down* to an integer that's *lower*. For example:

The INT of 3.9 is 3 (because 3 is an integer that's lower than 3.9).
The INT of -3.9 is -4 (because a temperature of -4 is lower and colder than a temperature of -3.9).
The INT of 7 is simply 7.

To explore further the mysteries of rounding, run this program:

```
CLS
INPUT "What's your favorite number"; x
PRINT "Your number rounded down is"; INT(x)
PRINT "Your number rounded up is"; -INT(-x)
PRINT "Your number rounded to the nearest integer is"; INT(x + .5)
```

In that program, the INPUT line asks you to type a number x.

The next line prints your number rounded *down*. For example, if you input 3.9, the computer prints 3.

The next line, PRINT -INT(-x), prints your number rounded *up*. For example if you input 3.9, the computer prints 4.

The bottom line prints your number rounded to the *nearest* integer. For example, if you input 3.9, the computer will print 4.

Here's the rule: if x is a number, **INT(x) rounds x down; -INT(-x) rounds x up; INT(x + .5) rounds x to the nearest integer**.

Here's why **INT is usually better than CINT and FIX**:

To round x to the nearest integer, you can say either CINT(x) or INT(x + .5). Alas, CINT(x) handles just numbers from -32768 to 32767. But INT(x + .5) can handle *any* number!

Another advantage of INT is that it works in *all* versions of Basic. Even the oldest, most primitive versions of Basic understand INT. Alas, CINT and FIX work in just a *few* versions of Basic, such as QBasic. To make sure your programs work on *many* computers, use INT rather than CINT or FIX.

In the rest of this book, I'll emphasize INT.

Rounding down and rounding up are **useful in the supermarket:**

Suppose some items are marked "30¢ each", and you have just two dollars. How many can you buy? Two dollars divided by 30¢ is 6.66667; rounding *down* to an integer, you can buy 6.

Suppose some items are marked "3 for a dollar", and you want to buy just one of them. How much will the supermarket charge you? One dollar divided by 3 is 33.3333¢; rounding *up* to an integer, you will be charged 34¢.

By using INT, **you can do fancier kinds of rounding:**

to round x to the nearest thousand,   ask for INT(x / 1000 + .5) * 1000
to round x to the nearest thousandth,   ask for INT(x / .001 + .5) * .001

This program rounds a number, so that it will have just a *few* digits after the decimal point:

```
CLS
INPUT "What's your favorite number"; x
INPUT "How many digits would you like after its decimal point"; d
b = 10 ^ -d
PRINT "Your number rounded is"; INT(x / b + .5) * b
```

Here's a sample run:

```
What's your favorite number? 4.28631
How many digits would you like after its decimal point? 2
Your number rounded is 4.29
```

SGN If a number is negative, its **sign** is -1. For example, the sign of -546 is -1.
If a number is positive, its **sign** is +1. For example the sign of 8231 is +1.
The **sign** of 0 is 0.
The computer's abbreviation for "sign" is "SGN". So if you say —

```
PRINT SGN(-546)
```

the computer will print the sign of -546; it will print -1.

If you say —

```
PRINT SGN(8231)
```

the computer will print the sign of 8231; it will print 1.

If you say —

```
PRINT SGN(0)
```

the computer will print the sign of 0; it will print 0.

SGN is the opposite of ABS. Let's see what both functions do to -7.2. ABS removes the minus sign, but leaves the digits:

ABS(-7.2) is 7.2

SGN removes the digits, but leaves the minus sign:

SGN(-7.2) is -1

The Latin word for *sign* is **signum**. Most mathematicians prefer to talk in Latin — they say "signum" instead of "sign" — because the English word "sign" sounds too much like the trigonometry word "sine". So mathematicians call SGN the **signum function**.

Random numbers

Usually, the computer is predictable: it does exactly what you say. But sometimes, you want the computer to be *un*predictable.

For example, if you're going to play a game of cards with the computer and tell the computer to deal, you want the cards dealt to be unpredictable. If the cards were predictable — if you could figure out exactly which cards you and the computer would be dealt — the game would be boring.

In many other games too, you want the computer to be unpredictable, to "surprise" you. Without an element of surprise, the game would be boring.

Being unpredictable increases the pleasure you derive from games — and from art. To make the computer act artistic, and create a new *original* masterpiece that's a "work of art", you need a way to make the computer get a "flash of inspiration". Flashes of inspiration aren't predictable: they're surprises.

Here's how to make the computer act unpredictably....

RND is a RaNDom decimal, bigger than 0 and less than 1. For example, it might be .6273649 or .9241587 or .2632801. Every time your program mentions RND, the computer concocts another decimal:

```
CLS
PRINT RND
PRINT RND
PRINT RND
```

The computer prints:

```
.7055475
.533424
.5795186
```

The first time your program mentions RND, the computer chooses its favorite decimal, which is .7055475. Each succeeding time your program mentions RND, the computer uses the previous decimal to concoct a new one. It uses .7055475 to concoct .533424, which it uses to concoct .5795186. The process by which the computer concocts each new decimal from the previous one is weird enough so we humans cannot detect any pattern.

This program prints lots of decimals — and pauses a second after each decimal, so you have a chance to read it:

```
CLS
DO
    PRINT RND
    SLEEP 1
LOOP
```

About half the decimals will be less than .5, and about half will be more than .5.

Most of the decimals will be less than .9. In fact, about 90% will be.

About 36% of the decimals will be less than .36; 59% will be less than .59; 99% will be less than .99; 2% will be less than .02; a quarter of them will be less than .25; etc. You might see some decimal twice, though most of the decimals will be different from each other. When you get tired of running that program and seeing decimals, abort the program (by pressing Ctrl with Pause/Break).

If you run that program again, you'll get exactly the same list of decimals again, in the same order.

RANDOMIZE TIMER

If you'd rather see a different list of decimals, say **RANDOMIZE TIMER** at the beginning of the program:

```
CLS
RANDOMIZE TIMER
DO
    PRINT RND
    SLEEP 1
LOOP
```

When the computer sees RANDOMIZE TIMER, the computer looks at the clock and manipulates the time's digits to produce the first value of RND.

So the first value of RND will be a number that depends on the time of day, instead of the usual .7055475. Since the first value of RND will be different than usual, so will the second, and so will the rest of the list.

Every time you run the program, the clock will be different, so the first value of RND will be different, so the whole list will be different — unless you run the program at exactly the same time the next day, when the clock is the same. But since the clock is accurate to a tiny fraction of a second, the chance of hitting the same time is extremely unlikely.

Love or hate?

Who loves ya, baby? This program tries to answer that question:

```
CLS
RANDOMIZE TIMER
DO
    INPUT "Type the name of someone you love..."; name$
    IF RND < .67 THEN
        PRINT name$; " loves you, too"
    ELSE
        PRINT name$; " hates your guts"
    END IF
LOOP
```

The RANDOMIZE TIMER line makes the value of RND depend on the clock. The INPUT line makes the computer wait for the human to type a name. Suppose he types Suzy. Then name$ is "Suzy". The IF line says there's a 67% chance that the computer will print "Suzy loves you, too", but there's a 33% chance the computer will instead print "Suzy hates your guts". The words DO and LOOP make the computer do the routine again and again, until the human aborts the program. The run might look like this:

```
Type the name of someone you love...? Suzy
Suzy loves you, too
Type the name of someone you love...? Joan
Joan hates your guts
Type the name of someone you love...? Alice
Alice loves you, too
Type the name of someone you love...? Fred
Fred loves you, too
Type the name of someone you love...? Uncle Charlie
Uncle Charlie hates your guts
```

Coin flipping

This program makes the computer flip a coin:

```
CLS
RANDOMIZE TIMER
IF RND < .5 THEN PRINT "heads" ELSE PRINT "tails"
```

The IF line says there's a 50% chance that the computer will print "heads"; if the computer does *not* print "heads", it will print "tails".

Until you run the program, you won't know which way the coin will flip; the choice is random. Each time you run the program, the computer will flip the coin again; each time, the outcome is unpredictable.

Here's how to let the human bet on whether the computer will say "heads" or "tails":

```
CLS
RANDOMIZE TIMER
10 INPUT "Do you want to bet on heads or tails"; bet$
IF bet$ <> "heads" AND bet$ <> "tails" THEN
    PRINT "Please say heads or tails"
    GOTO 10
END IF
IF RND < .5 THEN coin$ = "heads" ELSE coin$ = "tails"
PRINT "The coin says "; coin$
IF coin$ = bet$ THEN PRINT "You win" ELSE PRINT "You lose"
```

The line numbered 10 makes the computer ask:

```
Do you want to bet on heads or tails?
```

The next line makes sure the human says "heads" or "tails": if the human's answer isn't "heads" and isn't "tails", the computer gripes. The bottom three lines make the computer flip a coin and determine whether the human won or lost the bet.

Here's a sample run:

```
Do you want to bet on heads or tails? heads
The coin says tails
You lose
```

Here's another:

```
Do you want to bet on heads or tails? tails
The coin says tails
You win
```

Here's another:

```
Do you want to bet on heads or tails? tails
The coin says heads
You lose
```

Here's how to let the human use money when betting:

```
CLS
RANDOMIZE TIMER
bankroll = 100
4 PRINT "You have"; bankroll; "dollars"
5 INPUT "How many dollars do you want to bet"; stake
IF stake > bankroll THEN PRINT "You don't have that much!  Bet less!": GOTO 5
IF stake < 0 THEN PRINT "You can't bet less than nothing!": GOTO 5
IF stake = 0 THEN PRINT "I guess you don't want to bet anymore": GOTO 20
10 INPUT "Do you want to bet on heads or tails"; bet$
IF bet$ <> "heads" AND bet$ <> "tails" THEN
    PRINT "Please say heads or tails"
    GOTO 10
END IF
IF RND < .5 THEN coin$ = "heads" ELSE coin$ = "tails"
PRINT "The coin says "; coin$
IF coin$ = bet$ THEN
    PRINT "You win"; stake; "dollars"
    bankroll = bankroll + stake
    GOTO 4
END IF
PRINT "You lose"; stake; "dollars"
bankroll = bankroll - stake
IF bankroll > 0 THEN GOTO 4
PRINT "You're broke!  Too bad!"
20 PRINT "Thanks for playing with me!  You were fun to play with!"
PRINT "I hope you play again sometime!"
```

Line 3 (bankroll = 100) gives the human a $100 *bankroll*, so the human starts with $100. The next line makes the computer say:

```
You have 100 dollars
```

The line numbered 5 makes the computer ask:

```
How many dollars do you want to bet?
```

The number that the human inputs (the number of dollars that the human bets) is called the human's *stake*. The next three lines (which say "IF stake") make sure the stake is reasonable.

The line numbered 10 gets the human to bet on heads or tails. The next few lines flip the coin, determine whether the human won or lost the bet, and then send the computer back to line 4 for another round (if the human isn't broke yet). The bottom three lines say good-bye to the human.

Here's a sample run:

```
You have 100 dollars
How many dollars do you want to bet? 120
You don't have that much!  Bet less!
How many dollars do you want to bet? 75
Do you want to bet on heads or tails? heads
The coin says tails
You lose 75 dollars
You have 25 dollars
How many dollars do you want to bet? 10
Do you want to bet on heads or tails? tails
The coin says tails
You win 10 dollars
You have 35 dollars
How many dollars do you want to bet? 35
Do you want to bet on heads or tails? tails
The coin says heads
You lose 35 dollars
You're broke!  Too bad!
Thanks for playing with me!  You were fun to play with!
I hope you play again sometime!
```

To make the output prettier, replace line 4 by this group of lines:

```
4 PRINT
PRINT "You have"; bankroll; "dollars!  Here they are:"
FOR i = 1 TO bankroll
    PRINT "$";
NEXT
PRINT
```

Now the run looks like this:

```
You have 100 dollars!  Here they are:
$$$$$$$$$$$$$$$$$$$$$$$$$$$$$$$$$$$$$$$$$$$$$$$$$$$$$$$$$$$$$$$$$$$$$$$$$$$
$$$$$$$$$$$$$$
$$$$$$$$$$$$$$$$$$$$$$$$
How many dollars do you want to bet? 120
You don't have that much!  Bet less!
How many dollars do you want to bet? 75
Do you want to bet on heads or tails? heads
The coin says tails
You lose 75 dollars

You have 25 dollars!  Here they are:
$$$$$$$$$$$$$$$$$$$$$$$$$$$
How many dollars do you want to bet? 10
Do you want to bet on heads or tails? tails
The coin says tails
You win 10 dollars

You have 35 dollars!  Here they are:
$$$$$$$$$$$$$$$$$$$$$$$$$$$$$$$$$$$$$$
How many dollars do you want to bet? 35
Do you want to bet on heads or tails? tails
The coin says heads
You lose 35 dollars
You're broke!  Too bad!
Thanks for playing with me!  You were fun to play with!
I hope you play again sometime!
```

Random integers If you want a random integer from 1 to 10, ask for 1 + INT(RND * 10). Here's why:

```
RND is a decimal, bigger than 0 and less than 1.
So RND * 10 is a decimal, bigger than 0 and less than 10.
So INT(RND * 10) is an integer, at least 0 and no more than 9.
So 1 + INT(RND * 10) is an integer, at least 1 and no more than 10.
```

Guessing game This program plays a guessing game:

```
CLS
RANDOMIZE TIMER
PRINT "I'm thinking of a number from 1 to 10."
computer.number = 1 + INT(RND * 10)
10 INPUT "What do you think my number is"; guess
IF guess < computer.number THEN PRINT "Your guess is too low.": GOTO 10
IF guess > computer.number THEN PRINT "Your guess is too high.": GOTO 10
PRINT "Congratulations!  You found my number!"
```

Line 3 makes the computer say:

```
I'm thinking of a number from 1 to 10.
```

The next line makes the computer think of a random number from 1 to 10; the computer's number is called "computer.number". The INPUT line asks the human to guess the number.

If the guess is less than the computer's number, the first IF line makes the computer say "Your guess is too low" and then GOTO 10, which lets the human guess again. If the guess is *greater* than the computer's number, the bottom IF line makes the computer say "Your guess is too high" and then GOTO 10.

When the human guesses correctly, the computer arrives at the bottom line, which prints:

```
Congratulations!  You found my number!
```

Here's a sample run:

```
I'm thinking of a number from 1 too 10.
What do you think my number is? 3
Your guess is too low.
What do you think my number is? 8
Your guess is too high.
What do you think my number is? 5
Your guess is too low.
What do you think my number is? 6
Congratulations!  You found my number!
```

Dice This program makes the computer roll a pair of dice:

```
CLS
RANDOMIZE TIMER
PRINT "I'm rolling a pair of dice"
a = 1 + INT(RND * 6)
PRINT "One of the dice says"; a
b = 1 + INT(RND * 6)
PRINT "The other says"; b
PRINT "The total is"; a + b
```

Line 3 makes the computer say:

```
I'm rolling a pair of dice
```

Each of the dice has 6 sides. The next line, a = 1 + INT(RND * 6), rolls one of the dice, by picking a number from 1 to 6. The line saying "b = 1 + INT(RND * 6)" rolls the other. The bottom line prints the total.

Here's a sample run:

```
I'm rolling a pair of dice
One of the dice says 3
The other says 5
The total is 8
```

Here's another run:

```
I'm rolling a pair of dice
One of the dice says 6
The other says 4
The total is 10
```

Daily horoscope This program predicts what will happen to you today:

```
CLS
RANDOMIZE TIMER
PRINT "You will have a ";
SELECT CASE 1 + INT(RND * 5)
    CASE 1
        PRINT "wonderful";
    CASE 2
        PRINT "fairly good";
    CASE 3
        PRINT "so-so";
    CASE 4
        PRINT "fairly bad";
    CASE 5
        PRINT "terrible";
END SELECT
PRINT " day today!"
```

The computer will say —

```
You will have a wonderful day today!
```

or —

```
You will have a terrible day today!
```

or some in-between comment. That's because the SELECT CASE line makes the computer pick a random integer from 1 to 5.

For inspiration, run that program when you get up in the morning. Then notice whether your day turns out the way the computer predicts!

Character codes

You can use these code numbers:

		64 @	96 `	128 Ç	160 á	192 └	224 α
1 ☺	33 !	65 A	97 a	129 ü	161 í	193 ┴	225 ß
2 ☻	34 "	66 B	98 b	130 é	162 ó	194 ┬	226 Γ
3 ♥	35 #	67 C	99 c	131 â	163 ú	195 ├	227 π
4 ♦	36 $	68 D	100 d	132 ä	164 ñ	196 ─	228 Σ
5 ♣	37 %	69 E	101 e	133 à	165 Ñ	197 ┼	229 σ
6 ♠	38 &	70 F	102 f	134 å	166 ª	198 ╞	230 µ
	39 '	71 G	103 g	135 ç	167 º	199 ╟	231 τ
8 ◘	40 (	72 H	104 h	136 ê	168 ¿	200 ╚	232 Φ
	41)	73 I	105 i	137 ë	169 ⌐	201 ╔	233 Θ
	42 *	74 J	106 j	138 è	170 ¬	202 ╩	234 Ω
	43 +	75 K	107 k	139 ï	171 ½	203 ╦	235 δ
	44 ,	76 L	108 l	140 î	172 ¼	204 ╠	236 ∞
	45 -	77 M	109 m	141 ì	173 ¡	205 ═	237 φ
14 ♫	46 .	78 N	110 n	142 Ä	174 «	206 ╬	238 ∈
15 ☼	47 /	79 O	111 o	143 Å	175 »	207 ╧	239 ∩
16 ►	48 0	80 P	112 p	144 É	176 ░	208 ╨	240 ≡
17 ◄	49 1	81 Q	113 q	145 æ	177 ▒	209 ╤	241 ±
18 ↕	50 2	82 R	114 r	146 Æ	178 ▓	210 ╥	242 ≥
19 ‼	51 3	83 S	115 s	147 ô	179 │	211 ╙	243 ≤
20 ¶	52 4	84 T	116 t	148 ö	180 ┤	212 ╘	244 ⌠
21 §	53 5	85 U	117 u	149 ò	181 ╡	213 ╒	245 ⌡
22 ▬	54 6	86 V	118 v	150 û	182 ╢	214 ╓	246 ÷
23 ↨	55 7	87 W	119 w	151 ù	183 ╖	215 ╫	247 ≈
24 ↑	56 8	88 X	120 x	152 ÿ	184 ╕	216 ╪	248 °
25 ↓	57 9	89 Y	121 y	153 Ö	185 ╣	217 ┘	249 •
26 →	58 :	90 Z	122 z	154 Ü	186 ║	218 ┌	250 ·
27 ←	59 ;	91 [	123 {	155 ¢	187 ╗	219 █	251 √
	60 <	92 \	124 |	156 £	188 ╝	220 ▄	252 ⁿ
	61 =	93]	125 }	157 ¥	189 ╜	221 ▌	253 ²
	62 >	94 ^	126 ~	158 ₧	190 ╛	222 ▐	254 ■
	63 ?	95 _	127 ⌂	159 ƒ	191 ┐	223 ▀	

Alt key Here's how to type the symbol ñ, whose code number is 164. Hold down the Alt key; and while you keep holding down the Alt key, type 164 *by using the numeric keypad* (the number keys on the far right side of the keyboard). When you finish typing 164, lift your finger from the Alt key, and you'll see ñ on your screen!

QB64 The Alt key works for most numbers in that chart but *not* for numbers 8 and 26.

QBasic The Alt key works for most numbers in that chart but *not* for numbers 1-27 and 127.

You can use the Alt key in your program. For example, try typing this program:

```
CLS
PRINT "In Spanish, tomorrow is mañana"
```

While typing that program, make the symbol ñ by typing 164 on the numeric keypad while holding down the Alt key. When you run that program, the computer will print:

```
In Spanish, tomorrow is mañana
```

CHR$ Here's another way to type the symbol ñ:

```
CLS
PRINT CHR$(164)
```

When you run that program, the computer will print the CHaRacter whose code number is 164. The computer will print:

```
ñ
```

This program makes the computer print "In Spanish, tomorrow is mañana":

```
CLS
PRINT "In Spanish, tomorrow is ma"; CHR$(164); "ana"
```

That PRINT line makes the computer print "In Spanish, tomorrow is ma", then print character 164 (which is ñ), then print "ana".

Since character 34 is a quotation mark, **this program prints a quotation mark:**

```
CLS
PRINT CHR$(34)
```

Suppose you want the computer to print:

```
Scholars think "Hamlet" is a great play.
```

To make the computer print the quotation marks around "Hamlet", use CHR$(34), like this:

```
CLS
PRINT "Scholars think "; CHR$(34); "Hamlet"; CHR$(34); " is a great play."
```

CHR$ works reliably for all numbers in that chart. **This program prints, on your screen, all the symbols in the chart:**

```
CLS
FOR i = 1 TO 6: PRINT CHR$(i);: NEXT
PRINT CHR$(8);
FOR i = 14 TO 27: PRINT CHR$(i);: NEXT
FOR i = 33 TO 254: PRINT CHR$(i);: NEXT
```

That chart shows *most* code numbers from 1 to 254 but skips the following mysterious code numbers: 7, 9-13, and 28-32. Here's what those mysterious code numbers do....

In a PRINT statement, **CHR$(7) makes the computer beep.** Saying —

```
PRINT CHR$(7);
```

has the same effect as saying:

```
BEEP
```

If you say —

```
PRINT "hot"; CHR$(7); "dog"
```

the computer will print "hot", then beep, then turn the "hot" into "hotdog".

CHR$(9) makes the computer press the Tab key, so your writing is indented. For example, if you say —

```
PRINT "hot"; CHR$(9); "dog"
```

the computer will print "hot", then indent by pressing the TAB key, then print "dog", so you see this:

```
hot        dog
```

CHR$(31) makes the computer move the cursor (the blinking underline) down to the line below. For example, if you say —

```
PRINT "hot"; CHR$(31); "dog"
```

the computer will print "hot", then move down, then print "dog" on the line below, so you see this:

```
hot
   dog
```

You can move the cursor in all four directions:

```
CHR$(28) moves the cursor toward the right
CHR$(29) moves the cursor toward the left
CHR$(30) moves the cursor up
CHR$(31) moves the cursor down
```

CHR$(11) moves the cursor all the way to the screen's top-left corner, which is called the **home position**.

CHR$(32) is a blank space. It's the same as " ".

CHR$(12) erases the entire screen. Saying —

```
PRINT CHR$(12);
```

has the same effect as saying:

```
CLS
```

CHR$(10) and CHR$(13) each make the computer press the Enter key.

ASC The code numbers from 32 to 126 are for characters that you can type on the keyboard easily. Established by a national committee, those code numbers are called the **American Standard Code for Information Interchange**, which is abbreviated **Ascii**, which is pronounced "ass key".

Programmers say, "the Ascii code number for A is 65". If you say —

```
PRINT ASC("A")
```

the computer will print the Ascii code number for "A". It will print:

```
65
```

If you say PRINT ASC("B"), the computer will print 66. If you say PRINT ASC("b"), the computer will print 97.

If you say PRINT ASC("ñ"), the computer will print 164 (which is the code number for ñ), even though ñ isn't an Ascii character.

String analysis

Let's analyze the word "smart".

Length Since "smart" has 5 characters in it, the **length** of "smart" is 5. If you say —

```
PRINT LEN("smart")
```

the computer will print the LENgth of "smart"; it will print:

```
5
```

Left, right, middle The left two characters of "smart" are "sm". If you say —

```
PRINT LEFT$("smart", 2)
```

the computer will print:

```
sm
```

Try this program:

```
CLS
a$ = "smart"
PRINT LEFT$(a$, 2)
```

Line 2 says a$ is "smart". The bottom line says to print the left 2 characters of a$, which are "sm". The computer will print:

```
sm
```

If a$ is "smart", here are the consequences....

```
LEN(a$) is the LENgth of a$. It is 5.
LEFT$(a$, 2) is the LEFT 2 characters of a$. It is "sm".
RIGHT$(a$, 2) is the RIGHT 2 characters of a$. It is "rt".
MID$(a$, 2) begins in the MIDdle of a$, at the 2nd character. It is "mart".
MID$(a$, 2, 3) begins at 2nd character and includes 3 characters. It is "mar".
```

You can change the middle of a string, like this:

```
CLS
a$ = "bunkers"
MID$(a$, 2) = "owl"
PRINT a$
```

Line 2 says a$ is "bunkers". The MID$ line changes the middle of a$ to "owl"; the change begins at the 2nd character of a$. The bottom line prints:

```
bowlers
```

Here's a variation:

```
CLS
a$ = "bunkers"
MID$(a$, 2) = "ad agency"
PRINT a$
```

Line 2 says a$ is "bunkers". The MID$ line says to change the middle of a$, beginning at the 2nd character of a$. But "ad agency" is too long to become part of "bunkers". The computer uses as much of "ad agency" as will fit in "bunkers". The computer will print:

```
bad age
```

Another variation:

```
CLS
a$ = "bunkers"
MID$(a$, 2, 1) = "owl"
PRINT a$
```

Line 2 says a$ is "bunkers". The MID$ line says to change the middle of a$, beginning at the 2nd character of a$. But the ",1" makes the computer use just 1 letter from "owl". The bottom line prints:

```
bonkers
```

Capitals Capital letters (such as X, Y, and Z) are called **upper-case letters**. Small letters (such as x, y, and z) are called **lower-case letters**.

If you say —

```
PRINT UCASE$("We love America")
```

the computer will print an upper-case (capitalized) version of "We love America"), like this:

```
WE LOVE AMERICA
```

If you say —

```
PRINT LCASE$("We love America")
```

the computer will print a lower-case version of "We love America", like this:

```
we love america
```

Unfortunately, the computer doesn't know how to capitalize an accented letter (such as ñ). For example, suppose you say:

```
PRINT UCASE$("mañana")
```

Since the computer doesn't know how to capitalize the ñ, the computer prints:

```
MAñANA
```

If you say PRINT LCASE$("MAÑANA"), the computer doesn't know how to uncapitalize Ñ, so the computer prints:

```
mañana
```

This program measures geographical emotions:

```
CLS
INPUT "What's the most exciting continent"; a$
IF a$ = "Africa" THEN
    PRINT "Yes, it's the dark continent!"
ELSE
    PRINT "I disagree!"
END IF
```

Line 2 asks:

```
What's the most exciting continent?
```

Line 3 checks whether the person's answer is "Africa". If the person's answer is "Africa", the computer prints "Yes, it's the dark continent!"; otherwise, the computer prints "I disagree!"

But instead of typing "Africa", what if the person types "africa" or "AFRICA"? We still ought to make the computer print "Yes, it's the dark continent!" Here's how:

```
CLS
INPUT "what's the most exciting continent"; a$
IF UCASE$(a$) = "AFRICA" THEN
    PRINT "Yes, it's the dark continent!"
ELSE
    PRINT "I disagree!"
END IF
```

The new version of the IF statement says: if the person's answer, after being capitalized, becomes "AFRICA", then print "Yes, it's the dark continent!" So the computer will print "Yes, it's the dark continent!" even if the person types "Africa" or "africa" or "AFRICA" or "AfRiCa".

Suppose you ask the person a **yes/no question**. If the person means "yes", the person might type "yes" or "Yes" or "YES" or "YES!" or just "y" or just "Y". So instead of saying —

```
IF a$ = "yes"
```

say this:

```
IF UCASE$(LEFT$(a$, 1)) = "Y"
```

That tests whether the first letter of the person's answer, after being capitalized, is "Y".

Trim Some folks accidentally press the Space bar at the beginning or end of a string. For example, instead of typing "Sue", the person might type " Sue" or "Sue ".

You want to get rid of those accidental spaces. Getting rid of them is called **trimming** the string.

The function **LTRIM$** will left-trim the string: it will delete any spaces at the string's beginning (left edge). For example, if a$ is "   Sue Smith", LTRIM$(a$) is "Sue Smith".

**RTRIM$** will right-trim the string: it will delete any spaces at the string's end (right edge). If a$ is "Sue Smith   ", RTRIM$(a$) is "Sue Smith".

To trim *both* edges of a$ and make the trimmed result be the new a$, say this:

```
a$ = LTRIM$(RTRIM$(a$))
```

Spaces at the string's beginning (which are deleted by LTRIM$) are called **leading spaces**. Spaces at the string's end (which are deleted by RTRIM$) are called **trailing spaces**.

Adding strings You can add strings together, to form a longer string:

```
CLS
a$ = "fat" + "her"
PRINT a$
```

Line 2 says a$ is "father". The bottom line makes the computer print:

```
father
```

Searching in a string You can make the computer search in a string to find another string. To make the computer search IN the STRing

"needed" to find "ed", say:

```
PRINT INSTR("needed", "ed")
```

Since "ed" begins at the third character of "needed", the computer will print:

```
3
```

If you say —

```
PRINT INSTR("needed", "ey")
```

the computer will search in the string "needed" for "ey". Since "ey" is *not* in "needed", the computer will print:

```
0
```

If you say —

```
PRINT INSTR(4, "needed", "ed")
```

the computer will hunt in the string "needed" for "ed"; but the hunt will begin at the 4th character of "needed". The computer finds the "ed" that begins at the 5th character of "needed". The computer will print:

```
5
```

String-number conversion This program converts a string to a number:

```
CLS
a$ = "52.6"
b = VAL(a$)
PRINT b + 1
```

Line 2 says a$ is the string "52.6". The next line says b is the numeric VALue of a$, so b is the number 52.6. The bottom line prints:

```
53.6
```

VAL converts a string to a number. The opposite of VAL is STR$, which converts a number to a string. For example, STR$(-7.2) is the string "-7.2". STR$(81.4) is the string " 81.4", in which the 8 is preceded by a space instead of a minus sign.

Repeating characters Suppose you love the letter b (because it stands for big, bold, and beautiful) and want to print "bbbbbbbbbbbbbbbbbbbb". Here's a short-cut:

```
PRINT STRING$(20, "b")
```

That tells the computer to print a string of 20 b's.

Here's a different way to accomplish the same goal:

```
PRINT STRING$(20, 98)
```

That tells the computer to print, 20 times, the character whose Ascii code number is 98.

STRING$ can make the computer repeat a single character, but not a whole word. So if you say STRING$(20, "blow"), the computer will *not* repeat the word "blow"; instead, the computer will repeat just the first character of "blow" (which is "b").

Let's make the computer draw a dashed line containing 50 dashes, like this:

```
--------------------------------------------------
```

Here's how: just say PRINT STRING$(50, "-").

Let's make the computer print this triangle:

```
*
**
***
****
*****
******
*******
********
*********
**********
***********
************
*************
**************
***************
****************
*****************
******************
*******************
********************
```

To do that, we want the computer to print 1 asterisk on the first line, then 2 asterisks on the next line, then 3 asterisks on the next line, and so on, until it finally prints 20 asterisks on the bottom line. Here's the program:

```
CLS
FOR i = 1 TO 20
    PRINT STRING$(i, "*")
NEXT
```

The FOR line makes i be 1, then 2, then 3, and so on, up to 20. When i is 1, the PRINT line makes the computer print one asterisk, like this:

```
*
```

When i is 2, the PRINT line makes the computer print a line of 2 asterisks, like this:

```
**
```

The FOR line makes i be every number from 1 up to 20, so computer will print 1 asterisk, then underneath print a line of 2 asterisks, then underneath print a line of 3 asterisks, and so on, until the entire triangle is printed.

Trigonometry

The study of triangles is called **trigonometry** — and the computer can do it for you!

For example, look at this triangle:

In that triangle, the left angle is 30°, the bottom-right angle is 90°, and the longest side (the hypotenuse) is 1 inch long.

The side opposite the 30° angle is called the **sine** of 30°; the remaining side is called the **cosine** of 30°:

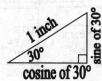

How long is the sine of 30°? How long is the cosine of 30°?

Since the longest side (the hypotenuse) is 1 inch long, and since the sine and the cosine are shorter sides, the sine and the cosine must each be shorter than 1 inch. So the lengths of the sine and cosine are each less than 1. But which decimals are they?

To find out, you can use a ruler. You'll discover that the sine is half an inch long, and the cosine is nearly seven-eighths of an inch long. But a faster and more accurate way to measure the sine and cosine is to let the computer do it! Yes, the computer can calculate triangles in its mind!

This program makes the computer measure the sine and cosine of 30°:

```
CLS
degrees = ATN(1) / 45
PRINT SIN(30 * degrees)
PRINT COS(30 * degrees)
```

Line 2 is a special formula that defines the word *degrees*. The first PRINT line prints the sine of 30 degrees:

```
.5
```

The bottom line prints the cosine of 30°, which is a decimal that's slightly less than .87.

The computer can measure the sine and cosine of *any* size angle. Try it! For example, to make the computer print the sine and cosine of a 33° angle, say:

```
CLS
degrees = ATN(1) / 45
PRINT SIN(33 * degrees)
PRINT COS(33 * degrees)
```

If you choose an angle of -33° instead of 33°, the triangle will dip down instead of rising up, and so the sine will be a negative number instead of positive.

In those PRINT lines, the "* degrees" is important: it tells the computer that you want the sine of 33 **degrees**. If you accidentally omit the "* degrees", the computer will print the sine of 33 **radians** instead. (A radian is larger than a degree. A radian is about 57.3 degrees. More precisely, a radian is 180/π degrees.)

Tangent The sine divided by the cosine is called the **tangent**. For example, to find the tangent of 33°, divide the sine of 33° by the cosine of 33°.

To make the computer print the tangent of 33°, you could tell the computer to PRINT SIN(33 * degrees) / COS(33 * degrees). But to find the tangent more quickly and easily, just say PRINT TAN(33 * degrees).

Arc functions The opposite of the tangent is called the **arctangent**:

```
the tangent    of 30° is about .58
the arctangent of .58 is about 30°
```

Similarly, the opposite of the sine is called the **arcsine**, and the opposite of the cosine is called the **arccosine**.

This program prints the arctangent of .58, the arcsine of .5, and the arccosine of .87:

```
CLS
degrees = ATN(1) / 45
PRINT ATN(.58) / degrees
x = .5: PRINT ATN(x / SQR(1 - x * x)) / degrees
x = .87: PRINT 90 - ATN(x / SQR(1 - x * x)) / degrees
```

Line 3 prints the arctangent of .58, in degrees. (If you omit the "/ degrees", the computer will print the answer in radians instead of degrees.) Line 4 sets x equal to .5 and then prints its arcsine (by using a formula that combines ATN with SQR). The bottom line sets x equal to .87 and then prints its arccosine (by using a formula that combines 90 with ATN and SQR). The answer to each of the three problems is about 30 degrees.

Subscripts

Instead of being a single string, x$ can be a whole *list* of strings, like this:

```
        /"love" \
        | "hate" |
        | "kiss" |
x$=     | "kill" |
        | "peace" |
        | "war"  |
        \ "why" /
```

Here's how to make x$ be that list of strings....

Begin your program as usual, by saying:

```
CLS
```

Then say:

```
DIM x$(7)
```

That line says x$ will be a list of 7 strings. DIM means **dimension**; the line says the dimension of x$ is 7.

Next, tell the computer what strings are in x$. Type these lines:

```
x$(1) = "love"
x$(2) = "hate"
x$(3) = "kiss"
x$(4) = "kill"
x$(5) = "peace"
x$(6) = "war"
x$(7) = "why"
```

That says x$'s first string is "love", x$'s second string is "hate", etc.

If you want the computer to print all those strings, type this:

```
FOR i = 1 TO 7
    PRINT x$(i)
NEXT
```

That means: print all the strings in x$. The computer will print:

```
love
hate
kiss
kill
peace
war
why
```

That program includes a line saying x$(1) = "love". Instead of saying x$(1), math books say:

```
x₁
```

The "1" is called a **subscript**.

Similarly, in the line saying x$(2) = "hate", the number 2 is a subscript. Some programmers pronounce that line as follows: "x string, subscripted by 2, is hate". Hurried programmers just say: "x string 2 is hate".

In that program, x$ is called an **array** (or **matrix**). Definition: an **array** (or **matrix**) is a variable that has subscripts.

Subscripted DATA

That program said x$(1) is "love", and x$(2) is "hate", and so on. This program does the same thing, more briefly:

```
CLS
DIM x$(7)
DATA love,hate,kiss,kill,peace,war,why
FOR i = 1 TO 7
    READ x$(i)
NEXT
FOR i = 1 TO 7
    PRINT x$(i)
NEXT
```

The DIM line says x$ will be a list of 7 strings. The DATA line contains a list of 7 strings. The first FOR..NEXT loop makes the computer READ those strings and call them x$. The bottom FOR...NEXT loop makes the computer print those 7 strings.

In that program, the first 4 lines say:

```
CLS
DIM
DATA
FOR i
```

Most practical programs begin with those 4 lines.

Let's lengthen the program, so the computer prints all this:

```
love
hate
kiss
kill
peace
war
why

why love
why hate
why kiss
why kill
why peace
why war
why why
```

That consists of two verses. The second verse resembles the first verse, except each line of the second verse begins with "why".

To make the computer print all that, just add the shaded lines to the program:

```
CLS
DIM x$(7)
DATA love,hate,kiss,kill,peace,war,why
FOR i = 1 TO 7
    READ x$(i)
NEXT
FOR i = 1 TO 7
    PRINT x$(i)
NEXT
PRINT
FOR i = 1 TO 7
    PRINT "why "; x$(i)
NEXT
```

The shaded PRINT line leaves a blank line between the first verse and the second verse. The shaded FOR..NEXT loop, which prints the second verse, resembles the FOR...NEXT loop that printed the first verse but prints "why" before each x$(i).

Let's add a third verse, which prints the words in reverse order:

```
why
war
peace
kill
kiss
hate
love
```

Before printing that third verse, print a blank line:

```
PRINT
```

Then print the verse itself. To print the verse, you must print x$(7), then print x$(6), then print x$(5), etc. To do that, you could say:

```
PRINT x$(7)
PRINT x$(6)
PRINT x$(5)
etc.
```

But this way is shorter:

```
FOR i = 7 TO 1 STEP -1
    PRINT x$(i)
NEXT
```

Numeric arrays

Let's make y be this list of five numbers: 100, 94, 201, 8.3, and -7. To begin, tell the computer that y will consist of five numbers:

```
CLS
DIM y(5)
```

Next, tell the computer what the six numbers are:

```
DATA 100,94,201,8.3,-7
```

Make the computer READ all that data:

```
FOR i = 1 TO 5
    READ y(i)
NEXT
```

To make the computer PRINT all that data, type this:

```
FOR i = 1 TO 5
    PRINT y(i)
NEXT
```

If you want the computer to add those 5 numbers together and print their sum, say:

```
PRINT y(1) + y(2) + y(3) + y(4) + y(5)
```

Strange example

Getting tired of x and y? Then pick another letter! For example, you can play with z:

Silly, useless program	What the program means
`CLS`	CLear the Screen
`DIM z(5)`	z will be a list of 5 numbers
`FOR i = 2 TO 5`	
`    z(i) = i * 100`	z(2)=200; z(3)=300; z(4)=400; z(5)=500
`NEXT`	
`z(1) = z(2) - 3`	z(1) is 200 - 3, so z(1) is 197
`z(3) = z(1) - 2`	z(3) changes to 197 - 2, which is 195
`FOR i = 1 TO 5`	
`    PRINT z(i)`	print z(1), z(2), z(3), z(4), and z(5)
`NEXT`	

The computer will print:

```
197
200
195
400
500
```

Problems and solutions

Suppose you want to analyze 20 numbers. Begin your program by saying:

```
CLS
DIM x(20)
```

Then type the 20 numbers as data:

```
DATA etc.
```

Tell the computer to READ the data:

```
FOR i = 1 TO 20
    READ x(i)
NEXT
```

Afterwards, do one of the following, depending on which problem you want to solve....

Print all x values Solution:

```
FOR i = 1 TO 20
    PRINT x(i)
NEXT
```

Print all x values, in reverse order Solution:

```
FOR i = 20 TO 1 STEP -1
    PRINT x(i)
NEXT
```

Print the sum of all x values
In other words, print $x(1) + x(2) + x(3)+... + x(20)$. Solution: start the sum at 0 —

```
sum = 0
```

and then increase the sum, by adding each x(i) to it:

```
FOR i = 1 TO 20
    sum = sum + x(i)
NEXT
```

Finally, print the sum:

```
PRINT "The sum of all the numbers is"; sum
```

Find the average of x
In other words, find the average of the 20 numbers. Solution: begin by finding the sum —

```
sum = 0
FOR i = 1 TO 20
    sum = sum + x(i)
NEXT
```

then divide the sum by 20:

```
PRINT "The average is"; sum / 20
```

Find whether any x value is 79.4
In other words, find out whether 79.4 is a number in the list. Solution: if x(i) is 79.4, print "Yes" —

```
FOR i = 1 TO 20
    IF x(i)=79.4 THEN PRINT "Yes, 79.4 is in the list": END
NEXT
```

otherwise, print "No":

```
PRINT "No, 79.4 is not in the list"
```

In x's list, count how often 79.4 appears
Solution: start the counter at zero —

```
counter = 0
```

and increase the counter each time you see the number 79.4:

```
FOR i = 1 TO 20
    IF x(i) = 79.4 THEN counter = counter + 1
NEXT
```

Finally, print the counter:

```
PRINT "The number 79.4 appears"; counter; "times"
```

Print all x values that are negative In other words, print all the numbers that have minus signs. Solution: begin by announcing your purpose —

```
PRINT "Here are the values that are negative:"
```

then print the values that are negative; in other words, print each x(i) that's less than 0:

```
FOR i = 1 TO 20
    IF x(i) < 0 THEN PRINT x(i)
NEXT
```

Print all x values that are above average Solution: find the average —

```
sum = 0
FOR i = 1 TO 20
    sum = sum + x(i)
NEXT
average = sum / 20
```

then announce your purpose:

```
PRINT "The following values are above average:"
```

Finally, print the values that are above average; in other words, print each x(i) that's greater than average:

```
FOR i = 1 TO 20
    IF x(i) > average THEN PRINT x(i)
NEXT
```

Find x's biggest value In other words, find which of the 20 numbers is the biggest. Solution: begin by assuming that the biggest is the first number —

```
biggest = x(1)
```

but if you find another number that's even bigger, change your idea of what the biggest is:

```
FOR i = 2 TO 20
    IF x(i) > biggest THEN biggest = x(i)
140 NEXT
```

Afterwards, print the biggest:

```
PRINT "The biggest number in the list is"; biggest
```

Find x's smallest value In other words, find which of the 20 numbers is the smallest. Solution: begin by assuming that the smallest is the first number —

```
smallest = x(1)
```

but if you find another number that's even smaller, change your idea of what the smallest is:

```
FOR i = 2 TO 20
    IF x(i) < smallest THEN smallest = x(i)
NEXT
```

Afterwards, print the smallest:

```
PRINT "The smallest number in the list is"; smallest
```

Check whether x's list is in strictly increasing order In other words, find out whether the following statement is true: x(1) is a smaller number than x(2), which is a smaller number than x(3), which is a smaller number than x(4), etc. Solution: if x(i) is *not* smaller than x(i + 1), print "No" —

```
FOR I = 1 TO 19
    IF x(i) >= x(i + 1) THEN
        PRINT "No, the list is not in strictly increasing order"
        END
    END IF
NEXT
```

otherwise, print "Yes":

```
PRINT "Yes, the list is in strictly increasing order"
```

Test yourself: look at those problems again, and see whether you can figure out the solutions *without peeking at the answers.*

Multiple arrays

Suppose your program involves three lists. Suppose the first list is called a$ and consists of 18 strings; the second list is called b and consists of 57 numbers; and the third list is called c$ and consists of just 3 strings. To say all that, begin your program with this statement:

```
DIM a$(18), b(57), c$(3)
```

Double subscripts

You can make x$ be a **table** of strings, like this:

$$x\$= \begin{pmatrix} \text{"dog"} & \text{"cat"} & \text{"mouse"} \\ \text{"hotdog"} & \text{"catsup"} & \text{"mousetard"} \end{pmatrix}$$

Here's how to make x$ be that table....

Begin by saying:

```
CLS
DIM x$(2, 3)
```

That says x$ will be a table having 2 rows and 3 columns.

Then tell the computer what strings are in x$. Type these lines:

```
x$(1, 1) = "dog"
x$(1, 2) = "cat"
x$(1, 3) = "mouse"
x$(2, 1) = "hotdog"
x$(2, 2) = "catsup"
x$(2, 3) = "moustard"
```

That says the string in x$'s first row and first column is "dog", the string in x$'s first row and second column is "cat", etc.

If you'd like the computer to print all those strings, type this:

```
FOR i = 1 TO 2
    FOR j = 1 TO 3
        PRINT x$(i, j),
    NEXT
    PRINT
NEXT
```

That means: print all the strings in x$. The computer will print:

```
dog          cat          mouse
hotdog       catsup       mousetard
```

Most programmers follow this tradition: **the row's number is called i, and the column's number is called j**. That program obeys that tradition. The "FOR i = 1 TO 2" means "for both rows"; the "FOR j = 1 TO 3" means "for all 3 columns".

Notice i comes before j in the alphabet; i comes before j in x(i, j); and "FOR i" comes before "FOR j". If you follow the i-before-j tradition, you'll make fewer errors.

At the end of the first PRINT line, the comma makes the computer print each column in a separate zone. The other PRINT line makes the computer press the Enter key at the end of each row. The x$ is called a **table** or **2-dimensional array** or **doubly subscripted array**.

Multiplication table

This program prints a multiplication table:

```
CLS
DIM x(10, 4)
FOR i = 1 TO 10
    FOR j = 1 TO 4
        x(i, j) = i * j
    NEXT
NEXT
FOR i = 1 TO 10
    FOR j = 1 TO 4
        PRINT x(i, j),
    NEXT
    PRINT
NEXT
```

Line 2 says x will be a table having 10 rows and 4 columns.

The line saying "x(i, j) = i * j" means the number in row i and column j is i*j. For example, the number in row 3 and column 4 is 12. Above that line, the program says "FOR i = 1 TO 10" and "FOR j = 1 TO 4", so that x(i,j)=i*j for *every* i and j, so *every* entry in the table is defined by multiplication.

The computer prints the whole table:

```
1            2            3            4
2            4            6            8
3            6            9           12
4            8           12           16
5           10           15           20
6           12           18           24
7           14           21           28
8           16           24           32
9           18           27           36
10          20           30           40
```

Instead of multiplication, you can have addition, subtraction, or division: just change the line saying "x(i, j) = i * j".

Summing a table

Suppose you want to analyze this table:

```
32.7         19.4         31.6         85.1
-8           402          -61          0
5106          -.2           0          -1.1
36.9          .04           1          11
777          666          55.44         2
 1.99         2.99          3.99         4.99
50            40            30            20
12            21            12            21
 0          1000            2           500
```

Since the table has 9 rows and 4 columns, begin your program by saying:

```
CLS
DIM x(9, 4)
```

Each row of the table becomes a row of the DATA:

```
DATA 32.7, 19.4, 31.6, 85.1
DATA -8, 402, -61, 0
DATA 5106, -.2, 0, -1.1
DATA 36.9, .04, 1, 11
DATA 777, 666, 55.44, 2
DATA 1.99, 2.99, 3.99, 4.99
DATA 50, 40, 30, 20
DATA 12, 21, 12, 21
DATA 0, 1000, 2, 500
```

Make the computer READ the data:

```
FOR i = 1 TO 9
    FOR j = 1 TO 4
        READ x(i, j)
    NEXT
NEXT
```

To make the computer print the table, say this:

```
FOR i = 1 TO 9
    FOR j = 1 TO 4:
        PRINT x(i,j),
    NEXT
    PRINT
NEXT
```

Here are some problems, with solutions....

Find the sum of all the numbers in the table

Solution: start the sum at 0 —

```
sum = 0
```

and then increase the sum, by adding each x(i, j) to it:

```
FOR i = 1 TO 9
    FOR j = 1 TO 4
        sum = sum + x(i, j)
    NEXT
NEXT
```

Finally, print the sum:

```
PRINT "The sum of all the numbers is"; sum
```

The computer will print:

```
The sum of all the numbers is 8877.84
```

Find the sum of each row

In other words, make the computer print the sum of the numbers in the first row, then the sum of the numbers in the second row, then the sum of the numbers in the third row, etc. Solution: the general idea is —

```
FOR i = 1 TO 9
    print the sum of row i
NEXT
```

Here are the details:

```
FOR i = 1 TO 9
    sum = 0
    FOR j = 1 TO 4
        sum = sum + x(i, j)
    NEXT
    PRINT "The sum of row"; i; "is"; sum
NEXT
```

The computer will print:

```
The sum of row 1 is 168.8
The sum of row 2 is 333
The sum of row 3 is 5104.7
etc.
```

Find the sum of each column

In other words, make the computer print the sum of the numbers in the first column, then the sum of the numbers in the second column, then the sum of the numbers in the third column, etc. Solution: the general idea is —

```
FOR j = 1 TO 4
    print the sum of column j
NEXT
```

Here are the details:

```
FOR j = 1 TO 4
    sum = 0
    FOR i = 1 TO 9
        sum = sum + x(i, j)
    NEXT
    PRINT "The sum of column"; j; "is"; sum
NEXT
```

The computer will print:

```
The sum of column 1 is 6008.59
The sum of column 2 is 2151.23
The sum of column 3 is 75.03
The sum of column 4 is 642.99
```

In all the other examples, "FOR i" came before "FOR j"; but in this unusual example, "FOR i" comes *after* "FOR j".

SUB procedures

Here's a sick program:

```
CLS
PRINT "We all know..."
PRINT "You are stupid!"
PRINT "You are ugly!"
PRINT "...and yet we love you."
```

It makes the computer print this message:

```
We all know...
You are stupid!
You are ugly!
...and yet we love you.
```

So the computer prints "We all know...", then insults the human ("You are stupid! You are ugly!"), then prints "...and yet we love you."

Here's a more sophisticated way to write that program:

```
CLS
PRINT "We all know..."
insult
PRINT "...and yet we love you."
SUB insult
    PRINT "You are stupid!"
    PRINT "You are ugly!"
END SUB
```

I'm going to explain that sophisticated version. Just *read* my explanation: don't type the sophisticated version into your computer yet. (Wait until you read the next section, called "Manipulate the program".)

In the sophisticated version, the top 4 lines tell the computer to clear the screen (CLS), print "We all know...", then insult the human, then print "...and yet we love you." But the computer doesn't know how to insult yet.

The bottom 4 lines teach the computer how to insult: they say "insult" means to print "You are stupid!" and "You are ugly!" Those bottom 4 lines define the word insult; they're the **definition** of insult.

That program is divided into two **procedures**. The top 4 lines are called the **main procedure** (or **main routine** or **main module**). The bottom 4 lines (which just define the word "insult") are called the **SUB procedure** (or **subroutine** or **submodule**).

The SUB procedure's first line (**SUB insult**) means: here's the SUB procedure that defines the word "insult". The SUB procedure's bottom line (**END SUB**) means: this is the END of the SUB procedure.

Manipulate the program

Try typing that program. But when you do, you face these peculiarities....

QB64 The computer won't let you indent the lines between SUB and END

SUB, so don't try indenting them.

To make the program easier to read, put a blank line above SUB (by pressing the Enter key an extra time), so your program looks like this:

```
PRINT "We all know..."
insult
PRINT "...and yet we love you."

SUB insult
PRINT "You are stupid!"
PRINT "You are ugly!"
END SUB
```

When you run the program (by pressing the F5 key), the computer will say:

```
We all know...
You are stupid!
You are ugly!
...and yet we love you.
```

QBasic When you finish typing the "SUB insult" line (and press the Enter key at the end of that line), the computer analyzes that line and realizes you're starting to type a new procedure.

The computer devotes the entire screen to the new procedure. Yes, the screen shows just the SUB insult procedure! The screen no longer shows the main procedure! Here's the rule: **the computer's screen shows just one procedure at a time**.

So now the top of the screen says "SUB insult". At the bottom of the screen, the computer automatically types "SUB END" for you. In between the "SUB insult" and "SUB END" lines, type PRINT "You are stupid!" and PRINT "You are ugly!" (and indent those lines by pressing the Space bar 4 times), so the screen looks like this:

```
SUB insult
    PRINT "You are stupid!"
    PRINT "You are ugly!"
END SUB
```

Congratulations! You finished typing the program!

Now the computer's screen shows just the SUB procedure. To see the main procedure instead, press the F2 key then Enter.

To flip back to the SUB procedure again, press the F2 key again, then the down-arrow key (so the world "insult" is highlighted), then Enter.

Here's the rule: **to see a different procedure, press the F2 key then highlight the name of the procedure you want to see** (by pressing the down-arrow key if necessary), then press Enter.

When you run the program (by pressing Shift with F5), the computer will say:

```
We all know...
You are stupid!
You are ugly!
...and yet we love you.
```

If you choose Print from the File menu (by pressing Alt then F then P) and then press Enter, the computer will print the entire program onto a single sheet of paper. When printing on paper, the computer will automatically leave a blank line between the procedures, so the paper will show this:

```
CLS
PRINT "We all know..."
insult
PRINT "...and yet we love you."

SUB insult
    PRINT "You are stupid!"
    PRINT "You are ugly!"
END SUB
```

You must eject the paper from the printer manually.

If you choose Save from the File menu (by pressing Alt then F then S) and then give the program a name (and press Enter), the computer saves the entire program onto the hard disk. While saving, the computer automatically adds an extra line at the top of the program, so the main procedure becomes this:

```
DECLARE SUB insult ()
CLS
PRINT "We all know..."
insult
PRINT "...and yet we love you."
```

The DECLARE line reminds the computer that the program includes a SUB insult.

Refrains

This is chanted by boys playing tag — and protesters fearing dictators:

```
The lion is a-coming near.
        He'll growl and sneer
        And drink our beer.
The lion never brings us cheer.
        He'll growl and sneer
        And drink our beer.
The lion is the one we fear.
        He'll growl and sneer
        And drink our beer.
Gotta stop the lion!
```

In that chant, this refrain is repeated:

```
        He'll growl and sneer
        And drink our beer.
```

This program prints the entire chant:

```
CLS
PRINT "The lion is a-coming near."
refrain
PRINT "The lion never brings us cheer."
refrain
PRINT "The lion is the one we fear."
refrain
PRINT "Gotta stop the lion!"

SUB refrain
    PRINT "        He'll growl and sneer"
    PRINT "        And drink our beer."
END SUB
```

Clementine The famous folk song "Clementine" begins like this:

```
In a cavern in a canyon, excavating for a mine,
Lived a miner (49'er) and his daughter, Clementine.

  O my darling, o my darling, o my darling Clementine,
  You are lost and gone forever.  Dreadful sorry, Clementine!

Light she was and like a fairy, and her shoes were #9.
Herring boxes without tops: those sandals were for Clementine.

  O my darling, o my darling, o my darling Clementine,
  You are lost and gone forever.  Dreadful sorry, Clementine!
```

This program prints the whole song:

```
CLS
PRINT "In a cavern in a canyon, excavating for a mine,"
PRINT "Lived a miner (49'er) and his daughter, Clementine."
chorus
PRINT "Light she was and like a fairy, and her shoes were #9."
PRINT "Herring boxes without tops: those sandals were for Clementine."
chorus
PRINT "Drove her ducklings to the water ev'ry morning just at 9."
PRINT "Hit her foot against a splinter, fell into the foaming brine."
chorus
PRINT "Ruby lips above the water, blowing bubbles soft and fine!"
PRINT "But alas, I was no swimmer, so I lost my Clementine."
chorus

SUB chorus
    SLEEP 11
    PRINT
    PRINT "  O my darling, o my darling, o my darling Clementine,"
    PRINT "  You are lost and gone forever.  Dreadful sorry, Clementine!"
    SLEEP 11
    PRINT
END SUB
```

At the beginning and end of the chorus, the "SLEEP 11" makes the computer pause for 11 seconds, to give the human a chance to read & sing what the computer wrote before the computer puts more words onto the screen.

Big love

This program prints a love poem:

```
CLS
PRINT "The most beautiful thing in the world is"
PRINT "LOVE"
PRINT "The opposite of war is"
PRINT "LOVE"
PRINT "And when I look at you, I feel lots of"
PRINT "LOVE"
```

In that program, many of the lines make the computer print the word LOVE. Let's make those lines print the word LOVE bigger, like this:

```
*         *      *     *      * * * *
*       * *    * *    *      *
*      *   *   *    *    *    * * *
*     *   *    *   *     * *      *
* * * *       *       *      * * * *
```

To make LOVE be that big, run this version of the program:

```
CLS
PRINT "The most beautiful thing in the world is"
big.love
PRINT "The opposite of war is"
big.love
PRINT "And when I look at you, I feel lots of"
big.love

SUB big.love
    PRINT "*           *     *      *     * * * *"
    PRINT "*         * *    *     *     *"
    PRINT "*        *   *    *     *    * * *"
    PRINT "*       *     *    *   *      *"
    PRINT "* * * *        *       *      * * * *"
END SUB
```

In that version, the lines say "big.love" instead of PRINT "LOVE". The SUB procedure teaches the computer how to make big.love.

Variables

Each procedure uses its own part of the RAM. For example, the main procedure uses a different part of the RAM than a SUB procedure.

Suppose the main procedure says "x = 4", and a SUB procedure named "joe" says "x = 100". The computer puts 4 into the main procedure's x box and puts 100 into joe's x box, like this:

| main procedure's x box | 4 |
| joe's x box | 100 |

Those two boxes are stored in different parts of the RAM from each other, and they don't interfere with each other.

For example, suppose you run this program:

```
CLS
x = 4
joe
PRINT x

SUB joe
    PRINT x
    x = 100
END SUB
```

The computer begins by doing the main procedure, which says "x = 4", so the computer puts 4 into the main procedure's x box:

| main procedure's x box | 4 |

The main procedure's next line says "joe", which makes the computer do the joe procedure. The joe procedure begins by saying "PRINT x"; but since joe's x box is still empty, the computer will print 0. Joe's next line says "x = 100", which puts 100 into joe's x box. Then the computer comes to the end of joe, returns to the main procedure, and does the "PRINT x" line at the bottom of the main procedure; but since the main procedure's x box still contains 4, the computer will print 4. The computer will not print 100.

If a committee of programmers wants to write a big, fancy program, the committee divides the programming task into a main procedure and several SUB procedures, then assigns each procedure to a different programmer. If you're one of the programmers, you can use any variable names you wish, without worrying about what names the other programmers chose: if you accidentally pick the same variable name as another programmer, it's no problem, since each procedure stores its variables in a different part of the RAM.

If you *want* a variable to affect and be affected by what's in another procedure, use one of these methods…

Method 1: SHARED At the top of the main procedure, you can say:

```
COMMON SHARED x
```

That means x is a variable whose box will be shared among all procedures, so that if a procedure says "x = 4" the x will be 4 in *all* procedures.

For example, suppose you say:

```
COMMON SHARED x
CLS
x = 4
joe
PRINT x

SUB joe
    PRINT x
    x = 100
END SUB
```

Then when the computer comes to joe's first line, which says "PRINT x", the computer will print 4 (because the main procedure had made x become 4); and when the computer comes to the main procedure's bottom line, which says "PRINT x", the computer will print 100 (because the joe procedure had made x become 100).

Put the COMMON SHARED line at the main procedure's *top*, above CLS.

You can write a program containing other shared variables besides x. For example, if you want x and sammy$ to both be common shared variables, say:

```
COMMON SHARED x, sammy$
```

If you want y$ to be a list of 20 strings, you normally say DIM y$(20); but if you want to share that list among all the procedures, say this instead:

```
DIM SHARED y$(20)
```

Put that line just at the top of the main procedure; you do *not* need to say DIM y$(20) in the SUB procedures.

The program is your world! A SHARED variable is called a **global variable**, since its value is shared throughout the entire program. An ordinary, unshared variable is called a **local variable**, since its value is used just in one procedure.

Method 2: arguments Here's a simple program:

```
CLS
INPUT "How many times do you want to kiss"; n
FOR i = 1 TO n
    PRINT "kiss"
NEXT
```

It asks "How many times do you want to kiss", then waits for your answer, then prints the word "kiss" as many times as you requested. For example, if you type 3, the computer will print:

```
kiss
kiss
kiss
```

If you input 5 instead, the computer will print this instead:

```
kiss
kiss
kiss
kiss
kiss
```

Let's turn that program into a SUB procedure that gets its input from the main procedure instead of from a human. Here's the SUB procedure:

```
SUB kiss (n)
    FOR i = 1 TO n
        PRINT "kiss"
    NEXT
END SUB
```

In that SUB procedure's top line, the "(n)" means "input the number n from the main procedure, instead of from a human". If the main procedure says —

```
kiss 3
```

then the n will be 3, so the SUB procedure will print "kiss" 3 times, like this:

```
kiss
kiss
kiss
```

If the main procedure says —

```
kiss 5
```

then the n will be 5, so the SUB procedure will print "kiss" 5 times.

Please type this complete program, which contains that SUB procedure:

```
CLS
PRINT "The boy said:"
kiss 3
PRINT "His girlfriend said okay!"
PRINT "Then the boy said:"
kiss 5
PRINT "His girlfiend said okay!"
PRINT "Finally, the boy said:"
kiss 8
PRINT "His girlfriend said:"
PRINT "I'm not prepared to go that far."

SUB kiss (n)
    FOR i = 1 TO n
        PRINT "kiss"
    NEXT
END SUB
```

When you run that program, the computer will print:

```
The boy said:
kiss
kiss
kiss
His girlfriend said okay!
Then the boy said:
kiss
kiss
kiss
kiss
kiss
His girlfriend said okay!
Finally, the boy said:
kiss
kiss
kiss
kiss
kiss
kiss
kiss
kiss
His girlfriend said:
I'm not prepared to go that far.
```

In that SUB procedure's top line, the n is called the **parameter**; put it in parentheses. In the line that says "kiss 3", the 3 is called the **argument**.

In that program, instead of saying —

```
kiss 3
```

you can say:

```
y = 3
kiss y
```

Then y's value (3) will become n, so the SUB procedure will print "kiss" 3 times. The n (which is the parameter) will use the same box as y (which is the argument). For example, if you insert into the SUB procedure a line saying "n = 9", the y will become 9 also.

You can write fancier programs. Here's how to begin a SUB procedure called joe having three parameters (n, m, and k$):

```
SUB joe (n, m, k$)
```

To use that subroutine, give a command such as:

```
joe 7, 9, "love"
```

Suppose your main procedure says:

```
DIM x$(3)
x$(1) = "love"
x$(2) = "death"
x$(3) = "war"
```

That means x$ is a list of these 3 strings: "love", "death", and "war". To make joan be a SUB procedure manipulating that list, make joan's top line say —

```
SUB joan (x$())
```

In that line, the () warns the computer that x$ is a list. You do *not* need to say DIM x$(3) in the SUB procedure. When you want to make the main procedure use joan, put this line into the main procedure:

```
joan x$()
```

Those lines, "SUB joan (x$())" and "joan x$()", work even if x$ is a table defined by a line such as DIM x$(30, 40).

Style

To become a *good* programmer, write your programs using a good style. Here's how....

Design a program

First, decide on your ultimate goal. Be optimistic. Maybe you'd like the computer to play the perfect game of chess? or translate every English sentence into French?

Research the past Whatever you want the computer to do, someone else probably thought of the same idea already and wrote a program for it.

Find out. Ask your friends. Ask folks in nearby schools, computer stores, computer centers, companies, libraries, and bookstores. Look through books and magazines. There are even books that list what programs have been written. Ask the company you bought your computer from.

Even if you don't find exactly the program you're looking for, you may find one that's close enough to be okay, or that will work with just a little fixing or serve as *part* of your program or at least give you a *clue* as to where to begin. In a textbooks or magazines, you'll probably find a discussion of the problem you're trying to solve and the pros and cons of various solutions to it — some methods are faster than others.

If you keep your head in the sand and don't look at what other programmers have done already, your programming effort may turn out to be a mere exercise, useless to the rest of the world.

Simplify Too often, programmers embark on huge projects and never get them done. Once you have an idea of what's been done before and how hard your project is, simplify it.

Instead of making the computer play a perfect game of chess, how about settling for a game in which the computer plays unremarkably but at least doesn't cheat? Instead of translating every English sentence into French, how about translating just English colors? (We wrote that program already.)

In other words, **pick a less ambitious, more realistic goal**, which if achieved will please you and be a steppingstone to your ultimate goal.

Finding a bug in a program is like finding a needle in a haystack: removing the needle is easier if the haystack is small than if you wait until more hay's been piled on.

Specify the I/O Make your new, simple goal more precise. That's called **specification**. One way to be specific is to **draw a picture, showing what your screen will look like if your program's running successfully**.

In that picture, find the lines typed by the computer. They become your program's PRINT statements. Find the lines typed by the human: they become the INPUT statements. Now you can start writing your program: **write the PRINT and INPUT statements** on paper, with a pencil, and leave blank lines between them. You'll fill in the blanks later.

Suppose you want the computer to find the average of two numbers. Your picture will look like this:

```
What's the first number? 7
What's the second number? 9
The average is 8
```

Your program at this stage will be:

```
CLS
INPUT "What's the first number"; a
INPUT "What's the second number"; b
etc.
PRINT "The average is"; c
```

All you have left to do is figure out what the "etc." is. Here's the general method....

Choose your statements Suppose you didn't have a computer. Then how would you get the answer?

Would you have to use a mathematical formula? If so, put the formula into your program, but remember that the equation's left side must have just one variable. For example, if you're trying to solve a problem about right triangles, you might have to use the Pythagorean formula $a^2+b^2=c^2$; but the left side of the equation must have just one variable, so your program must say $a=SQR(c\char94 2-b\char94 2)$, or $b=SQR(c\char94 2-a\char94 2)$, or $c=SQR(a\char94 2+b\char94 2)$, depending on whether you're trying to compute a, b, or c.

Would you have to use a memorized list, such as an English-French dictionary or the population of each state or the weight of each chemical element? If so, that list becomes your DATA, and you need to READ it. If it would be helpful to have the data numbered — so the first piece of data is called $x(1)$, the next piece of data is called $x(2)$, etc. — use the DIM statement.

Subscripts are particularly useful if one long list of information will be referred to *several* times in the program.

Does your reasoning repeat? That means your program should have a loop. If you know how many times to repeat, say FOR...NEXT. If you're not sure how often, say DO...LOOP. If the thing to be repeated isn't repeated immediately, but just after several other things have happened, make the repeated part be a SUB procedure.

At some point in your reasoning, do you have to make a *decision*? Do you have to choose among several alternatives? To choose between two alternatives, say IF...THEN. To choose among three or more alternatives, say SELECT CASE. If you want the computer to make the choice arbitrarily, "by chance" instead of for a reason, say IF RND<.5.

Do you have to compare two things? The way to say "compare x with y" is: IF x = y THEN.

Write pseudocode Some English teachers say that before you write a paper, you should make an outline. Some computer teachers give similar advice about writing programs.

The "outline" can look like a program in which some of the lines are written in plain English instead of computerese. For example, one statement in your outline might be:

```
a = the average of the 12 values of x
```

Such a statement, written in English instead of in computerese, is called **pseudocode**. Later, when you fill in the details, expand that pseudocode to this:

```
sum = 0
FOR i = 1 TO 12
    sum = sum + x(i)
NEXT
average = sum / 12
```

Organize yourself Keep the program's over-all organization simple. That will make it easier for you to expand the program and find bugs. Here's some folklore, handed down from generation to generation of programmers, that will simplify your organization....

Use top-down programming. That means write a one-sentence description of your program; then expand that sentence to several sentences; then expand each of those sentences to several more sentences; and so on, until you can't expand any more. Then turn each of those new sentences into lines of program. Then your program will be in the same order as the English sentences, therefore organized the same way as an English-speaking mind.

A variation is to **use SUB procedures**. That means writing the essence of the program as a very short main procedure; instead of filling in the grubby details immediately, replace each piece of grubbiness by a SUB procedure. Your program will be like a good book: your main procedure will move swiftly, and the annoying details will be relegated to the appendices at the back; the appendices are the SUB procedures. Make each procedure brief — no more than 20 lines — so the entire procedure can fit on the screen; if it starts getting longer and grubbier, replace each piece of grubbiness by *another* SUB procedure.

Avoid GOTO. It's hard for a human to understand a program that's a morass of GOTO statements. It's like trying to read a book where each paragraph says to turn to a different page! When you *must* say GOTO, try to go forward instead of backwards and not go too far.

Use variables After you've written some lines of your program, you may notice that your reasoning "almost repeats": several lines bear a strong resemblance to each other. You can't use DO...LOOP or FOR...NEXT unless the lines repeat exactly. To make the repetition complete, use a variable to represent the parts that are different.

For example, suppose your program contains these lines:

```
PRINT 29.34281 + 9.876237 * SQR(5)
PRINT 29.34281 + 9.876237 * SQR(7)
PRINT 29.34281 + 9.876237 * SQR(9)
PRINT 29.34281 + 9.876237 * SQR(11)
PRINT 29.34281 + 9.876237 * SQR(13)
PRINT 29.34281 + 9.876237 * SQR(15)
PRINT 29.34281 + 9.876237 * SQR(17)
PRINT 29.34281 + 9.876237 * SQR(19)
PRINT 29.34281 + 9.876237 * SQR(21)
```

Each of those lines says PRINT 29.3428 + 9.87627 * SQR(a number). The number keeps changing, so call it x. All those PRINT lines can be replaced by this loop:

```
FOR x = 5 TO 21 STEP 2
  PRINT 29.34281 + 9.876237 * SQR(x)
NEXT
```

Here's a harder example to fix:

```
PRINT 29.34281 + 9.876237 * SQR(5)
PRINT 29.34281 + 9.876237 * SQR(97.3)
PRINT 29.34281 + 9.876237 * SQR(8.62)
PRINT 29.34281 + 9.876237 * SQR(.4)
PRINT 29.34281 + 9.876237 * SQR(200)
PRINT 29.34281 + 9.876237 * SQR(12)
PRINT 29.34281 + 9.876237 * SQR(591)
PRINT 29.34281 + 9.876237 * SQR(.2)
PRINT 29.24281 + 9.876237 * SQR(100076)
```

Again, let's use x. All those PRINT lines can be combined like this:

```
DATA 5,97.3,8.62,.4,200,12,591,.2,100076
FOR i = 1 TO 9
  READ x
  PRINT 29.34281 + 9.876237 * SQR(x)
NEXT
```

This one's even tougher:

```
PRINT 29.34281 + 9.876237 * SQR(a)
PRINT 29.34281 + 9.876237 * SQR(b)
PRINT 29.34281 + 9.876237 * SQR(c)
PRINT 29.34281 + 9.876237 * SQR(d)
PRINT 29.34281 + 9.876237 * SQR(e)
PRINT 29.34281 + 9.876237 * SQR(f)
PRINT 29.34281 + 9.876237 * SQR(g)
PRINT 29.34281 + 9.876237 * SQR(h)
PRINT 29.34281 + 9.876237 * SQR(i)
```

Let's assume a, b, c, d, e, f, g, h, and i have been computed earlier in the program. The trick to shortening those lines is to change the names of the variables. Throughout the program, say x(1) instead of a, say x(2) instead of b, say x(3) instead of c, etc. Say DIM x(9) at the beginning of your program. Then replace all those PRINT lines by this loop:

```
FOR i = 1 TO 9
  PRINT 29.34281 + 9.876237 * SQR(x(i))
NEXT
```

Make it efficient

Your program should be **efficient**. That means it should use as little of the computer's time and memory as possible.

To use less of the computer's memory, make your DIMensions as small as possible. Try writing the program without any arrays at all; if that turns out to be terribly inconvenient, use the smallest and fewest arrays possible.

To use less of the computer's time, avoid having the computer do the same thing more than once.

These lines force the computer to compute SQR(8.2 * n + 7) three times:

```
PRINT SQR(8.3 * n + 7) + 2
PRINT SQR(8.3 * n + 7) / 9.1
PRINT 5 - SQR(8.3 * n + 7)
```

You should change them to:

```
k = SQR(8.3 * n + 7)
PRINT k + 2
PRINT k / 9.1
PRINT 5 - k
```

These lines force the computer to compute x ^ 9 + 2 a hundred times:

```
FOR i = 1 TO 100
  PRINT (x ^ 9 + 2) / i
NEXT
```

You should change them to:

```
k = x ^ 9 + 2
FOR i = 1 TO 100
  PRINT k / i
NEXT
```

These lines force the computer to count to 100 twice:

```
sum = 0
FOR i = 1 TO 100
  sum = sum + x(i)
NEXT
PRINT "The sum of the x's is"; sum
product = 1
FOR i = 1 TO 100
  product = product * x(i)
NEXT
PRINT "The product of the x's is"; product
```

You should combine the two FOR...NEXT loops into a single FOR...NEXT loop, so the computer counts to 100 just once. Here's how:

```
sum = 0
product = 1
FOR i = 1 TO 100
  sum = sum + x(i)
  product = product * x(i)
NEXT
PRINT "The sum of the x's is"; sum
PRINT "The product of the x's is"; product
```

Here are more tricks to make your program run faster....

Instead of exponents, use multiplication.

```
slow:   y = x ^ 2
faster: y = x * x
```

Test it

When you've written a program, **test** it: run it and see whether it works.

If the computer does *not* gripe, your tendency will be to say "Whoopee!" Don't cheer too loudly. **The answers the computer is printing might be wrong.** Even if its answers look reasonable, don't assume they're right: the computer's errors can be subtle. Check some of its answers by computing them with a pencil.

Even if the answers the computer prints are correct, don't cheer. Maybe you were just lucky. Type different input, and see whether your program still works. Probably you can input something that will make your program go crazy or print a wrong answer. Your mission: to find input that will reveal the existence of a bug.

Try 6 kinds of input....

Try simple input Type in simple integers, like 2 and 10, so the computation is simple, and you can check the computer's answers easily.

Try input that increases See how the computer's answer changes when the input changes from 2 to 1000. Does the change in the computer's answer look reasonable? Does the computer's answer go up when it should go up, and down when it should go down?... and by a reasonable amount?

Try input testing each IF For a program that says —

```
IF x < 7 THEN GOTO 10
```

input an x less than 7 (to see whether line 10 works), then an x greater than 7 (to see whether the line underneath the IF line works), then an x equal to 7 (to see whether you really want "<" instead of "<="), then an x very close to 7, to check round-off error.

For a program that says —

```
IF x ^ 2 + y < z THEN GOTO 10
```

input an x, y, and z that make x ^ 2 + y less than z. Then try inputs that make x ^ 2 + y very close to z.

Try extreme input What happens if you input:

```
a huge number, like 45392000000 or 1E35?
a tiny number, like .00000003954 or 1E-35?
a trivial number, like 0 or 1?
a typical number, like 45.13?
a negative number, like -52?
```

Find out.

If the input is supposed to be a string, what happens if you input aaaaa or zzzzz? What happens if you capitalize the input? If there are supposed to be two inputs, what happens if you input the same thing for each?

Try input making a line act strange If your program contains division, try input that will make the divisor be zero or a tiny decimal close to zero. If your program contains the square root of a quantity, try input that will make the quantity be negative. If your program says "FOR i = x TO y", try input that will make y be less than x, then equal to x. If your program mentions x(i), try input that will make i be zero or negative or greater than the DIM.

Try input that causes round-off error: for a program that says "x - y" or says "IF x = y", try input that will make x almost equal y.

Try garbage Computers often print wrong answers. A computer can print a wrong answer because its circuitry is broken or because a program has a bug. But **the main reason why computers print wrong answers is incorrect input**. Incorrect input is called **garbage** and has several causes....

The user's finger slips. Instead of 400, he inputs 4000. Instead of 27, he inputs 72. Trying to type .753, he leaves out the decimal point.

The user got wrong info. He tries to input the temperature, but his thermometer is leaking. He tries to input the results of a questionnaire, but everybody who filled out his questionnaire lied.

The instructions aren't clear, so the user isn't sure what to input.

If the program asks "How far did the ball fall?" should the user type the distance in feet or in meters? Is time to be given in seconds or minutes? Are angles to be measured in degrees or radians?

Can the user input "y" instead of "yes"?

Maybe the user isn't clear about whether to insert commas, quotation marks, and periods. If several items are to be typed, should they be typed on the same line or on separate lines? If your program asks "How many brothers and sisters do you have?" and the user has 2 brothers & 3 sisters, should he type "5" or "2,3" or "2 brothers and 3 sisters"?

If the program asks "What is your name?" should the user type "Joe Smith" or "Smith,Joe" or just "Joe"? For a quiz that asks "Who was the first U.S. President?" what if the user answers "George Washington" or simply "Washington" or "washington" or "G. Washington" or "General George Washington" or "President Washington" or "Martha's husband"? Make the instructions clearer:
```
Who was the first U.S. President (give just his last name)?
```

The user tries to joke or sabotage. Instead of inputting his name, he types an obscene comment. When asked how many brothers and sisters he has, he says 275.

Responsibility! As a programmer, it's your duty to include clear directions for using your program, and you must make the program reject ridiculous input.

For example, if your program is supposed to print weekly paychecks, it should refuse to print checks for more than $10000. Your program should contain these lines:

```
10 INPUT "How much money did the employee earn"; e
IF e > 10000 THEN
    PRINT e; "is quite a big paycheck!  I don't believe you."
    PRINT "Please retype your request."
    GO TO 10
END IF
```

That IF line is called an **error trap** (or **error-handling routine**). Your program should contain several, to prevent printing checks that are too small (2¢?) or negative or otherwise ridiculous ($200.73145?)

To see how your program reacts to input that's either garbage or unusual, **ask a friend to run your program**. That person might input something you never thought of.

Document it

Write an explanation that helps other people understand your program.

An explanation is called **documentation**. When you write an explanation, you're **documenting** the program.

You can write the documentation on a separate sheet of paper, or you can make the computer print the documentation when the user runs or lists the program.

A popular device is to begin the program by making the computer ask the user:

```
Do you need instructions?
```

You need two kinds of documentation: how to use the program, and how the program was written.

How to use the program Your explanation of using the program should include:

```
the program's name
how to get the program from the disk
the program's purpose
a list of other programs that must be combined with this program, to make a workable combination
the correct way to type the input and data (show an example)
the correct way to interpret the output
the program's limitations (input it can't handle, a list of error messages that might be printed, round-off error)
a list of bugs you haven't fixed yet
```

How the program was written An explanation of how you wrote the program will help other programmers borrow your ideas, and help them expand your program to meet new situations. It should include:

```
your name
the date you finished it
the computer you wrote it for
the language you wrote it in (probably QBasic)
the name of the method you used ("solves quadratic equations by using the quadratic formula")
the name of the book or magazine where you found the method
the name of any program you borrowed ideas from
an informal explanation of how program works ("It loops until x>y, then computes the weather forecast.")
the purpose of each SUB procedure
the meaning of each variable
the significance of reaching a line (for a program saying "IF x < 60 THEN GOTO 1000", say "Reaching line 1000 means the student flunked.")
```

Visual Basic

The most popular computer language is **Visual Basic for Windows (VB)**. More programs are written in VB than in any other computer language.

Using VB, you can easily create Windows programs that let the human use a mouse to click on icons, choose from menus, use dialog boxes, etc.

After inventing the first VB, Microsoft invented improved versions, called **VB 2**, **VB 3**, **VB 4**, **VB 5**, **VB 6**, **VB 7** (which is also called **VB.Net**), **VB 7.1** (also called **VB.Net 2003**), **VB 8** (also called **VB 2005**), **VB 9** (also called **VB 2008**), and **VB 10** (also called **VB 2010**). The most traumatic change was the switch from VB 6 to VB 7: programs written for VB 6 must be rewritten to work with VB 7.

You can buy Visual Basic separately or as part of **Visual Studio**, which is Microsoft's suite of programming languages. Visual Studio includes **Visual Basic**, **Visual C++**, **Visual C#**, and other programming tools.

Microsoft lets you get stripped-down editions of VB (and the other Visual Studio languages) **free**! They're called **Express Editions**. Copy them, free, from the Internet at:

www.microsoft.com/express/downloads

To copy them quickly, you need a broadband Internet connection (such as DSL or cable).

This chapter explains VB 2010 (which is also called VB 10).

Before you read this chapter and study VB, prepare yourself! Do 2 prerequisite activities:

Learn QBasic or QB64, which are much easier than VB. I explained them on pages 493-553. Read and practice that material.

Practice using good Windows programs (such as a Windows word-processing program), so you see how Windows programs should act. I explained good programs for modern Windows on pages 75-109, 114-138, and 181-224. Read and practice whichever of those Windows programs you have access to.

VB uses these **commands** (which resemble QBasic's):

VB command	Page
Beep()	558
Case "fine"	565
ColorDialog1.ShowDialog()	577
Console.ReadKey()	580
Console.WriteLine(5 + 2)	579
Console.Write(5 + 2)	580
Debug.Print(5 + 2)	579
Dim x	559
Dim x As Integer	589
Dim x As Integer = 7	593
Dim x = 7	593
Dim x() = {81, 52, 207, 19}	594
Dim x(2) As Double	595
Do	579, 584
document.Clear()	583
document.Copy()	583
document.Cut()	583
document.LoadFile…	581
document.Paste()	583
document.SaveFile…	581
Else	563
ElseIf age < 100 Then	563
End	565
End Class	555
End If	563
End Module	579
End Select	565
End Sub	555
Exit Do	585
Exit Sub	565
For Each i In x	595
For x = 1 To 5	585
For x = 15 To 17 Step .1	585
GoTo joe	584
If age < 18 Then…	562
Imports System.Math	588
Loop	579, 584
Loop Until guess = "pink"	585
Module Module1	579
MsgBox("Hair looks messy")	560
My.Computer…WriteAllText…	580
Next	585
OpenFileDialog1.ShowDialog()	581
Option Explicit Off	578
PrintForm1.Print()	580
Private Sub Form1_Load…	555
Public Class Form1	585
Randomize()	596
RichTextBox1.SaveFile…	580
Select Case feeling	565
SaveFileDialog1.ShowDialog()	581
Sub Main()	579
Text = 4 + 2	555
x = 47	559
?5+2	579
'Yeah, this is an example	578

VB uses these **functions** (which resemble QBasic's):

VB function	Value	Page
Chr(13)	Enter key	572
CInt(3.9)	4	594
ColorDialog1.Color	varies	577
Fix(3.89)	3.0	588
GetSelected(0)	varies	573
IIf(age < 18…	varies	564
InputBox("Name?")	varies	561
Int(3.89)	3.0	588
Math.Abs(-3.89)	3.89	588
Math.Ceiling(3.89)	4.0	588
Math.PI	about 3.14	588
Math.Round(3.89)	4.0	588
Math.Sign(3.89)	1	588
Math.Sqrt(9)	3.0	588
My…LocalTime	varies	577
My…MyDocuments	Docu. folder	580
My…ReadAllText	varies	580
MsgBox("Love me?"…	varies	564
Rnd	varies	596
TypeName(4.95D)	"Decimal"	593
Val("7")	7	561
VarType(4.95D)	14	592

In VB, you never write "a long program". Instead, you begin by drawing **objects** on the screen (as if you were using a graphics program). Then for each object, you write a little program (called a **subroutine**) that tells the computer how to manipulate the object. VB handles these objects:

VB object	Page
Button	568
CheckBox	569
ColorDialog	577
ComboBox	575
Form1	555
Form2	575
Label	572
ListBox	573
MenuStrip	581
NumericUpDown	574
OpenFileDialog	581
PictureBox	575
PrintForm	580
RadioButton	570
RichTextBox	574
SaveFileDialog	581
TextBox	574
Timer	576
ToolStrip	583
WebBrowser	576

Each object has **properties**, which you can manipulate:

VB property	Object	Page
BackColor	Form1	558
Checked	CheckBox	569
DecimalPlaces	NumericUpDown	557
Dock	RichTextBox	574
DropDownStyle	ComboBox	575
EnableAutoDrag…	RichTextBox	574
Enabled	Timer	576
FormBorderStyle	Form1	567
Image	PictureBox	575
Interval	Timer	576
MaximizeBox	Form1	567
Maximum	NumericUpDown	575
Minimum	NumericUpDown	575
MultiLine	TextBox	574
Opacity	Form1	567
PasswordChar	TextBox	574
ScrollBars	TextBox	574
SelectedIndex	ListBox	573
SelectedItem	ListBox	573
SelectionMode	ListBox	573
Size	Form1	567
SizeMode	PictureBox	575
StartPosition	Form1	567
Text	Form1	555
Url	WebBrowser	576
Value	NumericUpDown	574
Visible	Form2	576
WindowState	Form1	558

Fun

Let's have fun programming!

Copy VB to the hard disk

Here's how to copy Visual Basic 2010 Express to your hard disk by using Windows (Vista or 7) and Internet Explorer.

Go to www.microsoft.com/express/downloads. Click "Visual Basic 2010 Express" then the down-arrow then "English" then "Run" (which is at the screen's bottom).

If you're using Windows 7, click "Yes". If you're using Windows Vista, click "Continue".

The computer will say "Welcome to Setup". Press the Enter key. Click "I have read and accept the license terms." Press Enter, 3 times.

The computer will copy (download) and install Visual Basic onto your hard disk.

The computer will say "Setup complete". Press Enter. Close Internet Explorer's window (by clicking the X at the screen's top-right corner).

Start VB

To start using VB, click the Start button then do this:

If you see "Microsoft Visual Basic 2010 Express", click it. Otherwise, click "All Programs" then "Microsoft Visual Studio 2010 Express" (which you'll see by scrolling down) then "Microsoft Visual Basic 2010 Express".

You see the Start Page window.

Create simple programs

Click "**New Project**" (which is near the screen's left edge). Double-click "**Windows Forms Application**".

You see an **object**, called the **Form1** window. Double-click in that window (below "Form1"). That tells the computer you want to write a program (subroutine) about that window.

The computer starts writing the **subroutine** for you. The computer writes:

```
Public Class Form1

    Private Sub Form1_Load…

    End Sub
End Class
```

The line saying "Private Sub Form1_Load" is the subroutine's **header**. The line saying "End Sub" is the subroutine's **footer**; it marks the end of the subroutine. Between those lines, insert lines that tell the computer what to do to the object (which is the Form1 window). The lines you insert are called the subroutine's **body**.

Simplest example

Let's make the Form1 window show the answer to this math problem: 4 + 2. To do that, type this line —

```
Text = 4 + 2
```

The computer automatically indents that line for you, so the subroutine becomes:

```
Private Sub Form1_Load…
    Text = 4 + 2
End Sub
```

To run your program, press the F5 key (or click the green "▶", which is at the screen's top center). Then you see the Form1 window again; but instead of saying "Form1", it says the text's answer:

```
6
```

When you've finished admiring that answer, stop the program by clicking the Form1 window's X button. Then you see the subroutine again:

```
Private Sub Form1_Load…
    Text = 4 + 2
End Sub
```

Edited example

Let's edit that subroutine, so instead of saying the answer to 4 + 2, it will say the answer to 79 + 2.

To do that, change the 4 to 79. Here's how: click the 4's left edge, then press the Delete key (to delete the 4), then type 79, so the subroutine looks like this:

```
Private Sub Form1_Load…
    Text = 79 + 2
End Sub
```

Run that program by pressing the F5 key. Then the Form1 window shows the new answer:

```
81
```

When you finish admiring that, click Form1's X button.

To make the computer subtract 3 from 7, change the text line to this:

```
Text = 7 - 3
```

When you run the program (by pressing the F5 key), the Form1 window will show the answer:

```
4
```

To make the computer do -26.3+1, change the text line to this:

```
Text = -26.3 + 1
```

The Form1 window will show the answer:

```
-25.3
```

Your own examples

Go ahead! Try changing the subroutine, to do different math problems instead!

Multiply

To multiply, use an asterisk. So to multiply 2 by 6, type this:

```
Text = 2 * 6
```

The Form1 window will show:

```
12
```

Divide

To divide, use a slash. So to divide 8 by 4, type this:

```
Text = 8 / 4
```

The Form1 window will show:

```
2
```

To divide 2 by 3, type this:

```
Text = 2 / 3
```

The Form1 window will show:

```
0.666666666666667
```

Congratulations

You've written VB subroutines and created VB programs, so you've become a VB programmer! You can put on your résumé, "VB programmer!"

Type faster

Here are tricks that let you type faster.

You don't need to capitalize computer words such as "Text". The computer will capitalize them automatically, eventually. For example, if you type "text" instead of "Text", the computer will change "text" to "Text" when you type the equal sign afterwards.

You don't need to finish typing computer words such as "Text". The computer will finish typing them for you, automatically, eventually, if the computer can deduce what you meant. For example, you can type "te" instead of "Text"; the computer will change "te" to "Text" when you type the equal sign afterwards.

Instead of typing computer words, you can choose them from lists. For example, instead of typing "Text", you can do this:

Type the letter "t". You'll see a list of computer words that begin with "t". (To see that whole list, click the list's up-arrow & down-arrow or press the keyboard's up-arrow & down-arrow keys.) If you type "te", you'll see a list of computer words that begin with "te". In a list, when you see the word you want, either double-click the word or do this: highlight the word (by clicking it) then press the keyboard's Tab key.

You don't need to put spaces around symbols, such as "=" and "+". The computer will insert those spaces automatically, when you end the line (by pressing the F5 key or Enter key or down-arrow key or clicking in a different line).

Huge and tiny numbers

When dealing with huge and tiny number, be careful!

Avoid commas Do *not* put commas in big numbers. To write four million, do *not* write 4,000,000; instead, write 4000000.

Use decimals for big answers The computer sometimes has difficulty handling answers bigger than 2,000,000,000, which in modern English is called "2 billion." To avoid difficulty, **put a decimal point in any problem whose answer might be bigger than 2 billion**.

For example, suppose you want the computer to multiply 3000 by 1000000. Since the answer to that problem is 3 billion, which is bigger than 2 billion, you should put a decimal point in that problem, like this:

```
Text = 3000 * 1000000.0
```

After typing a decimal point, you must type a digit (such as 0).

Suppose you forget to insert a decimal point and say just this:

```
Text = 3000 * 1000000
```

When you try to run the program (by pressing the F5 key), the computer will complain in 3 ways:

> It will put a squiggly blue line under the "3000 * 1000000".
>
> The screen's bottom will say "Constant expression not representable in type 'Integer'."
>
> The screen's middle will say, "There were build errors. Would you like to continue and run the last successful build?" To reply, click "No" then fix your error (by inserting .0) and press F5 again.

E notation If the computer's answer is huge (at least a quadrillion, which is 1000000000000000) or tiny (less than .0001), the computer will put an E in the answer. The E means "move the decimal point".

For example, suppose the computer says the answer to a problem is:

```
1.586743E+15
```

The E means, "move the decimal point". The plus sign means, "towards the right". Altogether, **the E+15 means, "move the decimal point towards the right, 15 places."** So look at 1.586743 and move the decimal point towards the right, 15 places; you get 1586743000000000.

So when the computer says the answer is 1.586743E+15, the computer really means the answer is 1586743000000000, approximately. The exact answer might be 1586743000000000.2 or 1586743000000000.79 or some similar number, but the computer prints just an approximation.

Suppose your computer says the answer to a problem is:

```
9.23E-06
```

After the E, the minus sign means, "towards the *left*". So look at 9.23 and move the decimal point towards the left, 6 places. You get: .00000923

So when the computer says the answer is 9.23E-06, the computer really means the answer is:
.00000923

You'll see E notation rarely: the computer uses it just if an answer is huge (at least a quadrillion) or tiny (tinier than .0001). But when the computer *does* use E notation, remember to move the decimal point!

The highest number The highest number the computer can handle well is about 1E308, which is 1 followed by 308 zeros. If you try to go much higher, the computer will gripe, by saying "Overflow" or "Infinity" or "NaN" (which means "Not a Number"). For example, if you say —

```
Text = 1E309
```

the screen's bottom will say "Overflow".

Dividing by 0 If you ask the computer to divide by 0, the computer will have difficulty.

For example, if you say —

```
Text = 5 / 0
```

the computer will try to divide 5 by 0, give up (because you can't divide by 0), and say the answer is "Infinity".

If you say —

```
Text = -5 / 0
```

the computer will try to divide -5 by 0, give up (because you can't divide by 0), and say the answer is "-Infinity".

If you say —

```
Text = 0 / 0
```

the computer will try to divide 0 by 0, give up (because you can't divide by 0), get confused, and say the answer is "NaN" (which means "Not a Number").

The tiniest decimal The tiniest decimal the computer can handle accurately is 1E-308 (which is a decimal point followed by 308 digits, 307 of which are zeros). If you try to go tinier, the computer will either say 0 or give you a rough approximation.

Order of operations

What does "2 plus 3 times 4" mean? The answer depends on whom you ask.

To a clerk, it means "start with 2 plus 3, then multiply by 4"; that makes 5 times 4, which is 20. But to a scientist, "2 plus 3 times 4" means something different: it means "2 plus three fours", which is $2 + 4 + 4 + 4$, which is 14.

Since computers were invented by scientists, computers think like scientists. If you type —

```
Text = 2 + 3 * 4
```

the computer will think you mean "2 plus three fours", so it will do $2 + 4 + 4 + 4$ and display this answer:

```
14
```

The computer will *not* display the clerk's answer, which is 20. So if you're a clerk, tough luck!

Scientists and computers follow this rule: **do multiplication and division before addition and subtraction**. So if you type —

```
Text = 2 + 3 * 4
```

the computer begins by hunting for multiplication and division. When it finds the multiplication sign between the 3 and the 4, it multiplies 3 by 4 and gets 12, like this:

```
Text = 2 + 3 * 4
              12
```

So the problem becomes $2 + 12$, which is 14, which the computer will display.

For another example, suppose you type:

```
Text = 10 - 2 * 3 + 72 / 9 * 5
```

The computer begins by doing all the multiplications and divisions. So it does 2 * 3 (which is 6) and does 72 / 9 * 5 (which is 8 * 5, which is 40), like this:

```
Text = 10 - 2 * 3 + 72 / 9 * 5
              6          40
```

So the problem becomes $10 - 6 + 40$, which is 44, which is the answer the computer will display.

Parentheses You can use parentheses the same way as in algebra. For example, if you type —

```
Text = 5 - (1 + 1)
```

the computer will compute 5 - 2 and print:

3

You can put parentheses inside parentheses. If you type —

```
Text = 10 - (5 - (1 + 1))
```

the computer will compute 10 - (5 - 2), which is 10 - 3, and will display:

```
7
```

Strings

Let's make the computer fall in love. Let's make it say, "I love you". To do so, type this in your subroutine:

```
Text = "I love you"
```

Type that carefully:

Type the word Text, then a blank space, then an equal sign, then another blank space. Then type a quotation mark, but be careful: **to type the quotation mark, you must hold down the Shift key.** Then type these words: *I love you*. Then type another quotation mark.

When you run the program (by pressing F5), it will make the text (at the top of Form1's window) display:

```
I love you
```

You can change the computer's personality. For example, if you edit the subroutine to make it become —

```
Text = "I hate you"
```

the computer will reply:

```
I hate you
```

Notice that **to make a subroutine print a message, you must put the message between quotation marks**. The quotation marks make the computer copy the message without worrying about what the message means. For example, if you misspell "I love you", and type —

```
Text = "aieee luf ya"
```

the computer will still copy the message (without worrying about what it means); the computer will make Form1 say:

```
aieee luf ya
```

Type faster Instead of typing —

```
Text = "I love you"
```

you can type just this:

```
text="I love you
```

Before the computer runs the program, the computer will automatically capitalize the first letter of "text", put spaces around the equal sign, and put a quotation mark at the line's end (to match the other quotation mark).

Red strings While you're typing the subroutine, **the computer makes each string look red** (and each computer word look blue).

Those colors appear just while you're looking at the subroutine you've been typing. When you run the program, the program's answers (and other results) appear black.

Jargon The word "joy" consists of 3 characters: j and o and y. Programmers say that the word "joy" is a **string** of 3 characters.

A **string** is any collection of characters, such as "joy" or "I love you" or "aieee luf ya" or "76 trombones" or "GO AWAY!!!" or "xypw exr///746". The computer will print whatever string you wish, but in your subroutine **put the string in quotation marks.**

Strings versus numbers The computer can handle two types of expressions: **strings** and **numbers**. In your subroutine, put strings (such as "joy" and "I love you") in quotation marks. Numbers (such as 4 + 2) do *not* go in quotation marks.

Combine strings You can combine strings:

```
Text = "fat" & "her"
```

The computer will combine "fat" with "her", so the computer will display:

```
father
```

You can combine a string with a number:

```
Text = "The lucky number is " & 4 + 2
```

The computer will display "The lucky number is " then the answer to this math problem: 4 + 2. The computer will display:

```
The lucky number is 6
```

When combining a string with a number, make the computer leave a space between the string and the number, by putting a space before the last quotation mark.

Combining strings or numbers (by using the symbol "&") is called **concatenating**.

When typing the symbol "&" to concatenate, **press the keyboard's Space bar before and after the "&"**. If you rely on the computer to put those spaces in automatically, you'll be sorry, because the symbol "&" without spaces can have a different meaning, and the computer will occasionally guess wrong about which "&" you meant.

Accidents Suppose you accidentally put the number 2 + 2 in quotation marks, like this:

```
Text = "2 + 2"
```

The quotation marks make the computer think "2 + 2" is a string instead of a number. Since the computer thinks "2 + 2" is a string, it copies the string without analyzing what it means; Form1 will say:

```
2 + 2
```

It will *not* say 4.

Suppose you want the computer to show the word "love" but you accidentally forget to put the string "love" in quotation marks, and type this instead:

```
Text = love
```

Since you forgot the quotation marks, the computer is confused. Whenever the computer is confused, it either gripes at you or says zero. In this particular example, when you indicate you finished typing the line, the computer will gripe at you by making the screen's bottom say:

```
'love' is not declared.
```

Display a quotation mark The symbol for *inches* is ". Let's make Form1 say:

```
The nail is 2" long.
```

This Text command does *not* work:

```
Text = "The nail is 2" long."
```

When the computer sees the quotation mark after 2, it mistakenly thinks that quotation mark is paired with the quotation mark before "The", then gets totally confused.

Here's the correct way to write that line:

```
Text = "The nail is 2"" long."
```

The symbol "" means: display a quotation mark. That Text line makes Form1 display:

```
The nail is 2" long.
```

Here's the rule: to display a quotation mark ("), put the symbol "" in your Text statement.

Let's make the computer display this sentence:

```
I saw "Hamlet" last night.
```

To display the quotation mark before "Hamlet", you must type "". To display the quotation mark after "Hamlet", you must type "". So type this:

```
          Text = "I saw ""Hamlet"" last night."
```

Color

Normally, the Form1 window's middle is a big blank area that's nearly white (very light gray). To make it red instead, put this line in your subroutine:

```
          BackColor = Color.Red
```

For example, to make the window's title say "I love you" and make the window's background color be red, put both of these lines in your subroutine —

```
          Text = "I love you"
          BackColor = Color.Red
```

so the whole subroutine looks like this:

```
Public Class Form1

     Private Sub Form1_Load…
          Text = "I love you"
          BackColor = Color.Red
     End Sub
End Class
```

The computer understands these color names:

```
Yellow, Gold, Goldenrod, LemonChiffon
Orange, Brown, Chocolate, Tan
Red, Pink, DeepPink, Crimson
Purple, Violet, Magenta, Orchid
Blue, Cyan, Navy, DeepSkyBlue
Green, Lime, Chartreuse, Khaki
White, Gray, Black, Silver
```

It understands many others, too: altogether, it knows the names of 141 colors. You'll see the complete list when you've typed:

```
          BackColor = Color.
```

(Use the list's up-arrow & down-arrow.)

Don't put spaces in the middle of a color name: type "DeepSkyBlue", not "Deep Sky Blue".

Beep

To make the computer **beep** (ring its bell), put this line in your subroutine:

```
          Beep()
```

Multi-statement line

In your subroutine, **a line can include many statements separated by colons**, like this:

```
          Text = "I love you" : BackColor = Color.Red
```

That line means the same thing as:

```
          Text = "I love you"
          BackColor = Color.Red
```

Maximize

To maximize the Form1 window (so it consumes the whole screen), put this line in your subroutine:

```
          WindowState = 2
```

For example, let's make the computer say "You turned me on, and I love you!" and maximize the Form1 window (so the human can see all that). Just put both of these lines in your subroutine:

```
          WindowState = 2
          Text = "You turned me on, and I love you!"
```

Final steps

When you finish playing with your program, here's what to do.

Make sure you see the subroutine you typed. (If you see Form1's window instead, close that window by clicking its X button.)

<u>**Save**</u> If you like the program you created and want to save it on disk, click the **Save All button**. (It looks like a pile of 4 floppy disks. It's near the screen's top, below the word "Project".) If the computer says "Save Project", do this:

Look in the Name box. Make sure that box contains the name you want for your program. (If it doesn't, edit the name.) Press Enter. If the computer complains that the name "already exists", press Enter then try a different name instead.

For example, if you gave your program the name "Funmaker", that process makes the computer create a folder called Funmaker and put it into the Projects folder (which is in the Visual Studio 2010 folder, which is in the Documents folder). That folder contains Funmaker.suo, Funmaker.sln, and another folder called Funmaker, which in turn contains many other files and folders.

Afterwards, if you make further changes to the program, click the Save All button again to save them.

<u>**New**</u> If you're tired of working on a program and want to start inventing a different program instead, click the **New Project** button (which is near the screen's top-left corner, below the word "File").

(If you didn't save the previous program, the computer will say "save or discard changes". If you want to save the previous program, click "Save" and answer any questions the computer asks about the program's name; otherwise, click "Discard".)

Eventually, the computer will say "New Project". Double-click "Windows Forms Application".

<u>**Exit**</u> When you finish using VB, click the X button that's in the screen's top right corner.

<u>**Open**</u> When you start using VB, look at the heading "Recent Projects" (which appears near the screen's left edge). Below "Recent Projects", you see a list of programs you saved. If you want to use or edit one of those programs, click that program's name then click double-click Form1.vb (which is at the screen's left edge). Either run the program again (by pressing F5) or edit the program's commands (by double-clicking in the middle of the Form1 window).

<u>**Run the .exe file**</u> When the computer ran your program, it made an .exe file (called Funmaker.exe), which you can run again without going into Visual Basic. Here's how:

Exit from Visual Basic. Click the Start button. In the "Search programs and files" box, type:
Funmaker.exe
Click the top Funmaker icon (which is blue and stands for Funmaker.exe).

Here's another way to execute the Funmaker.exe program:

Exit from Visual Basic. Click the Start button then Documents. In the right-hand pane, double-click "Visual Studio 2010" then Projects then Funmaker then the Funmaker folder icon then bin then Debug then the top Funmaker icon (which is blue and stands for Funmaker.exe).

Registration

While you're using Visual Basic Express, you might be interrupted by a window saying "Registration is required". That means you haven't registered Visual Basic Express yet.

You can use Visual Basic Express for 30 days without registering it. Before the 30 days run out, you should register it by clicking that window's "Obtain a registration key online" button (or by clicking "Help" then "Register Product" then "Obtain a registration key online").

After you click "Obtain a registration key online", continue the registration procedure by following the instructions on the screen. Registration is free.

Registration is free. It consists of telling Microsoft your name, country, ZIP code (or other postal code), e-mail address, and what kind of e-mail you want Microsoft to send you about learning programming. You also create (or reuse) your Microsoft Windows Live account.

Variables

A letter can stand for a number, a string, or other things.

For example, x can stand for the number 47, as in this subroutine:

```
Dim x
x = 47
Text = x + 2
```

The top line (Dim x) warns the computer that x will stand for something. (The "Dim" comes from the word "Dimension".)

The second line (x = 47) says x stands for the number 47. In other words, x is a name for the number 47.

The bottom line (Text = x + 2) makes the computer display x + 2. Since x is 47, the x + 2 is 49; so the computer will display 49. That's the only number the computer will display; it will not display 47.

When you type that subroutine, make sure you include the top line (Dim x). If you forget to type that line, the computer will gripe by saying:

```
'x' is not declared.
```

Jargon

A letter standing for something is called a **variable** (or **name** or **identifier**). A letter standing for a number is called a **numeric variable**. In that subroutine, x is a numeric variable; it stands for the number 47. The **value** of x is 47.

In that subroutine, the statement "x = 47" is called an **assignment statement**, because it **assigns** 47 to x.

A variable is a box

When you run that subroutine, here's what happens inside the computer.

The computer's random-access memory (RAM) consists of electronic boxes. When the computer encounters the line "x = 47", the computer puts 47 into box x, like this:

```
box x [              47  ]
```

Then when the computer encounters the line "Text = x + 2", the computer will display what's in box x, plus 2; so the

computer will display 49.

Faster typing

Instead of typing —

```
x = 47
```

you can type just this:

```
x=47
```

Before the computer runs the program, the computer will automatically put spaces around the equal sign.

More examples

Here's another subroutine:

```
Dim y
y = 38
Text = y - 2
```

The top line says y is a variable. The next line says y is 38. The bottom line says to display y - 2. Since y is 38, the y - 2 is 36; so the computer will display 36.

Another example:

```
Dim b
b = 8
Text = b * 3
```

The top line says b is a variable. The next line says b is 8. The bottom line says to display b * 3, which is 8 * 3, which is 24; so the computer will display 24.

One variable can define another:

```
Dim n, d
n = 6
d = n + 1
Text = n * d
```

The top line says n and d are variables. The next line says n is 6. The next line says d is n + 1, which is 6 + 1, which is 7; so d is 7. The bottom line says to display n * d, which is 6 * 7, which is 42; so the computer will display 42.

Changing a value

A value can change:

```
Dim k
k = 4
k = 9
Text = k * 2
```

The second line says k is 4, but the next line changes k's value to 9, so the bottom line displays 18.

When you run that subroutine, here's what happens inside the computer's RAM. The second line (k = 4) makes the computer put 4 into box k:

```
box k [              4  ]
```

The next line (k = 9) puts 9 into box k. The 9 replaces the 4:

```
box k [              9  ]
```

That's why the bottom line (Text = k * 2) displays 18.

String variables

A string is any collection of characters, such as "I love you". Each

string must be in quotation marks. A letter can stand for a string:

```
Dim x
x = "I love you"
Text = x
```

The top line warns the computer that x will stand for something. The next line says x stands for the string "I love you". The bottom line makes the computer display:

```
I love you
```

In that subroutine, x is a variable. Since it stands for a string, it's called a **string variable**.

You can combine strings:

```
Dim x
x = "so"
Text = x & "up"
```

(When typing that example, you must leave a space before the ampersand, to avoid confusion.) Since the second line says x is "so", the bottom line will make Text be "so" & "up" and display this:

```
soup
```

If you insert a space by typing " up" instead of "up", like this —

```
Dim x
x = "so"
Text = x & " up"
```

the computer will display:

```
so up
```

Long variable names

A variable's name can be a letter (such as x) or a longer combination of characters, such as:

```
CityPopulationIn2001
```

For example, you can type:

```
Dim CityPopulationIn2001
CityPopulationIn2001 = 30716
Text = CityPopulationIn2001 + 42
```

The computer will print:

```
30758
```

The variable's name can be as long as you wish: up to 255 characters! The name's first character must be a letter; the remaining characters can be letters or digits. The computer ignores capitalization: it assumes that CityPopulationIn2001 is the same as citypopulationin2001.

Beginners are usually too lazy to type long variable names, so beginners use variable names that are short. But when you become a pro and write a long, fancy program containing hundreds of lines and hundreds of variables, you should use long variable names to help you remember each variable's purpose.

In this book, I'll use short variable names in short programs (so you can type those programs quickly) but long variable names in long programs (so you can keep track of which variable is which).

Pop-up boxes

Here's how to make a box appear suddenly on your screen.

Message box

Into any subroutine, you can insert this line:

```
MsgBox("Warning: your hair looks messy today")
```

When the computer runs the program and encounters that line, the computer suddenly creates a **message box** (a window containing a short message), which appears in front of all other windows (so they're covered up) and contains this message: "Warning: your hair looks messy today". The computer automatically makes the window be wide enough to include the whole message and be centered on the screen. When that window suddenly appears, the computer also beeps (to get the human's attention) if you're using Windows Vista (instead of Windows 7).

The window includes an OK button. When the human finishes reading the message, the human must click that OK button (or press Enter) to make the window go away.

After the window goes away, Form1 reappears and the computer continues running the rest of the program (including any lines below the MsgBox line). Form1 remains on the screen until the human clicks Form1's X button, which closes the form and ends the program.

End program automatically To please the human, make the *computer* click Form1's X button and end the program, by putting this command under the MsgBox line —

```
End
```

so your subroutine looks like this:

```
MsgBox("Warning: your hair looks messy today")
End
```

The top line makes the message box say "Warning: your hair looks messy today" then wait for the human to click OK. The bottom line ends the program (without requiring the human to click an X button).

Putting End under MsgBox makes the screen look like this:

```
Public Class Form1

    Private Sub Form1_Load…
        MsgBox("Warning: your hair looks messy today")
        End
    End Sub
End Class
```

Try it!

That End line is helpful. If you omit it and say just —

```
MsgBox("Warning: your hair looks messy today")
```

here's what happens when the human runs the program:

> The computer creates a message box saying "Warning: your hair looks messy today". Then the computer waits for the human to click the message box's OK button.
>
> When the human clicks the OK button, the message box disappears. Then the computer is supposed to do any remaining lines in the subroutine. But there are no lines remaining to be done. So the computer just waits for the human to close the program by clicking its X button.
>
> What if the human is too stupid to know to click the X button? Instead of clicking the X button, what if the human just keeps waiting to see whether the computer will do something? The situation is stupid: the computer waits for the human to click the X button, while the human waits for the computer to say what to do next.
>
> To end such confusion, say End below the MsgBox line. The End line makes the computer stop running the program and automatically click the X button.

Faster typing If you type just —

```
ms(
```

the computer will automatically change it to:

```
MsgBox(
```

Add an icon To make the message box fancier, say **vbExclamation**, like this:

```
MsgBox("Warning: your hair looks messy today", vbExclamation)
End
```

That makes the message box window include an **exclamation icon** (an exclamation point in a yellow triangle).

You can choose from 4 icons:

Icon	Command
! (in a yellow triangle)	vbExclamation
X (in a red circle)	vbCritical
i (in a blue circle)	vbInformation
? (in a blue circle)	vbQuestion

Math A message box can do math. For example, if you write a subroutine that says —

```
MsgBox(4 + 2)
```

and then run the program (by pressing F5), the computer will create a message box that displays the answer, 6.

Input box

For a wild experience, type this subroutine:

```
Dim x
x = InputBox("What is your name?")
Text = "I love " & x
```

Run the program (by pressing F5). Here's what happens…

The InputBox line makes the computer suddenly creates an **input box**, which is a window letting the human type info into the computer. That window appears in front of all other windows (so they're covered up) and is centered on the screen. It contains this **prompt**: "What is your name?" It also contains a white box (into which the human can type a response) and an OK button.

The computer waits for the human to type a response. When the human finishes typing a response, the human must click the OK button (or press Enter) to make the window go away.

Then Form1 reappears, and the computer makes x be whatever the human typed. For example, if the human typed —

```
Joan
```

x will be Joan. Then the Text line will make Form1 say:

```
I love Joan
```

To let the subroutine handle names that are long, maximize the Form1 window, by inserting this line —

```
WindowState = 2
```

so the subroutine becomes:

```
Dim x
x = InputBox("What is your name?")
WindowState = 2
Text = "I love " & x
```

Numeric input To input a string, you've learned to say InputBox. **To input a number, say InputBox but also say Val,** to emphasize that you want the computer to produce a numeric value.

For example, this subroutine asks for your two favorite numbers and says their sum:

```
Dim x, y
x = Val(InputBox("What is the first number?"))
y = Val(InputBox("What is the second number?"))
Text = x + y
```

When you run the program (by pressing F5), the computer asks "What is the first number?", waits for you to type it, and calls it x. Then the computer asks "What is the second number?", waits for you to type it, and calls it y. Then the computer says the sum of the numbers. For example, if the first number was 7 and the second number was 2, the computer will display the sum:

```
9
```

In that program, if you accidentally omit each Val, the computer will think x and y are strings instead of numbers, so the computer will add the string "7" to the string "2" and display this longer string:

```
72
```

Predict your future This subroutine makes the computer predict your future:

```
Dim y
y = Val(InputBox("In what year were you born?"))
WindowState = 2
Text = "In the year 2030, you'll turn " & 2030 - y & " years old."
```

When you run the program, the computer asks, "In what year were you born?" If you answer —

```
1962
```

y will be the numeric value 1962, and the computer will correctly print:

```
In the year 2030, you'll turn 68 years old.
```

Prices Suppose you're selling tickets to a play. Each ticket costs $2.79. (You decided $2.79 would be a nifty price, because the cast has 279 people.) These lines find the price of multiple tickets:

```
Dim t
t = Val(InputBox("How many tickets?"))
Text = "The total price is $" & t * 2.79
```

Conversion These lines convert feet to inches:

```
Dim f
f = Val(InputBox("How many feet?"))
Text = f & " feet = " & f * 12 & " inches"
```

When you run the program, the computer asks "How many feet?" If you answer —

```
3
```

the computer will say:

```
3 feet = 36 inches
```

Trying to convert to the metric system? These lines convert inches to centimeters:

```
Dim i
i = Val(InputBox("How many inches?"))
Text = i & " inches = " & i * 2.54 & " centimeters"
```

Nice day today, isn't it? These lines convert the temperature from Celsius to Fahrenheit:

```
Dim c
c = Val(InputBox("How many degrees Celsius?"))
WindowState = 2
Text = c & " degrees Celsius = " & c * 1.8 + 32 & " degrees Fahrenheit"
```

When you run the program, the computer asks "How many degrees Celsius?" If you answer —

```
20
```

the computer will say:

```
20 degrees Celsius = 68 degrees Fahrenheit
```

See, you can write the *Guide* yourself! Just hunt through any old math or science book, find any old formula (such as f = c * 1.8 + 32), and turn it into a program.

Control commands

A subroutine is a list of commands you want the computer to obey. Here's how to control which commands the computer obeys, and when, and in what order.

If

This subroutine makes the computer discuss the human's age:

```
Dim age
age = Val(InputBox("How old are you?"))
MsgBox("I hope you enjoy being " & age)
End
```

When that program is run (by pressing F5), the computer asks "How old are you?" and waits for the human's reply. For example, if the human says —

```
15
```

the age will be 15. Then the computer will say:

```
I hope you enjoy being 15
```

After the human reads that message in the message box, the human should get out of the message box (by clicking the message box's "OK" or pressing the Enter key). Then the computer will automatically close Form1.

Let's make that subroutine fancier, so if the human is under 18 the computer will also say "You are still a minor". To do that, just add a line saying —

```
If age < 18 Then MsgBox("You are still a minor")
```

so the subroutine looks like this:

```
Dim age
age = Val(InputBox("How old are you?"))
MsgBox("I hope you enjoy being " & age)
If age < 18 Then MsgBox("You are still a minor")
End
```

For example, if the human runs the program and says —

```
15
```

the computer will say —

```
I hope you enjoy being 15
```

and then say:

```
You are still a minor
```

(At the end of each sentence, the computer waits for the human to click the message box's OK.)

If instead the human says —

```
25
```

the computer will say just:

```
I hope you enjoy being 25
```

In that program, the most important line is:

```
If age < 18 Then MsgBox("You are still a minor")
```

That line contains the words If and Then. **Whenever you say "If", you must also say "Then".** Don't put a comma before "Then". What comes between "If" and "Then" is called the **condition**; in that example, the condition is "age < 18". If the condition is true (if the age is really less than 18), the computer does the **action**, which comes after the word "Then" and is:

```
MsgBox("You are still a minor")
```

Else Let's teach the computer how to respond to adults.

Here's how to program the computer so that if the age is less than 18, the computer will say "You are still a minor", but if the age is *not* less than 18 the computer will say "You are an adult" instead:

```
Dim age
age = Val(InputBox("How old are you?"))
MsgBox("I hope you enjoy being " & age)
If age < 18 Then MsgBox("You are still a minor") Else MsgBox("You are an adult")
End
```

In programs, **the word "Else" means "otherwise"**. That program's If line means: if the age is less than 18, then print "You are still a minor"; otherwise (if the age is *not* less than 18), print "You are an adult". So the computer will print "You are still a minor" or else print "You are an adult", depending on whether the age is less than 18.

Try running that program! If you say you're 50 years old, the computer will reply by saying —

```
I hope you enjoy being 50
```

and then (after you click "OK"):

```
You are an adult
```

Multi-line If If the age is less than 18, here's how to make the computer say "You are still a minor" and also say "Ah, the joys of youth":

```
If age < 18 Then MsgBox("You are still a minor") : MsgBox("Ah, the joys of youth")
```

Here's a more sophisticated way to say the same thing:

```
If age < 18 Then
    MsgBox("You are still a minor")
    MsgBox("Ah, the joys of youth")
End If
```

That sophisticated way (in which you type 4 short lines instead of a single long line) is called a **multi-line If** (or a **block If**).

In a multi-line If:

The top line says If and Then (with nothing after Then). The computer will type the word "Then" for you, if you forget to type it yourself.

The computer indents the middle lines for you. They're called the **block** and typically say MsgBox.

The bottom line says End If. The computer automatically types it for you.

In the middle of a multi-line If, you can say Else:

```
If age < 18 Then
    MsgBox("You are still a minor")
    MsgBox("Ah, the joys of youth")
Else
    MsgBox("You are an adult")
    MsgBox("We can have adult fun")
End If
```

That means: if the age is less than 18, then say "You are still a minor" and "Ah, the joys of youth"; otherwise (if age *not* under 18) say "You are an adult" and "We can have adult fun". The computer automatically unindents the word "Else".

ElseIf Let's make the computer do this:

If age is under 18, say "You're a minor".
If age is *not* under 18 but is under 100, say "You're a typical adult".
If age is *not* under 100 but is under 125, say "You're a centenarian".
If age is *not* under 125, say "You're a liar".

Here's how:

```
If age < 18 Then
    MsgBox("You're a minor")
ElseIf age < 100 Then
    MsgBox("You're a typical adult")
ElseIf age < 125 Then
    MsgBox("You're a centenarian")
Else
    MsgBox("You're a liar")
End If
```

Different relations You can make the If clause very fancy:

IF clause	Meaning
If age = 18	If age is 18
If age < 18	If age is less than 18
If age > 18	If age is greater than 18
If age <= 18	If age is less than or equal to 18
If age >= 18	If age is at least 18 (greater than or equal to 18)
If age <> 18	If age is not 18
If sex = "male"	If sex is "male"
If sex < "male"	If sex is a word (such as "female") that comes before "male" in the dictionary
If sex > "male"	If sex is a word (such as "neuter") that comes after "male" in the dictionary

In the If statement, the symbols =, <, >, <=, >=, and <> are called **relations**.

When writing a relation, mathematicians and computerists habitually **put the equal sign last**:

Right	Wrong
<=	=<
>=	=>

When you press the Enter key at the end of the line, the computer will automatically put your equal signs last: the computer will turn any "=<" into "<="; it will turn any "=>" into "<=".

To say "not equal to", say "less than or greater than", like this: <>.

Or The computer understands the word Or. For example, here's how to type, "If age is either 7 or 8, say the word *wonderful*":

```
If age = 7 Or age = 8 Then MsgBox("wonderful")
```

That example is composed of two conditions: the first condition is "x = 7"; the second condition is "x = 8". Those two conditions combine, to form "x = 7 Or x = 8", which is called a **compound condition**.

If you use the word Or, put it between two conditions.

Right: `If age = 7 Or age = 8 Then MsgBox("wonderful")` (because "age = 7" and "age = 8" are conditions)

Wrong: `If age = 7 Or 8 Then MsgBox("wonderful")` (because "8" is not a condition)

And The computer understands the word And. Here's how to type, "If age is more than 5 and less than 10, say *you get hamburgers for lunch*":

```
If age > 5 And age < 10 Then MsgBox("you get hamburgers for lunch")
```

Here's how to type, "If score is at least 60 and less than 65, say *you almost failed*":

```
If score >= 60 And score < 65 Then MsgBox("you almost failed")
```

Here's how to type, "If n is a number from 1 to 10, say *that's good*":

```
If n >= 1 And n <= 10 Then MsgBox("that's good")
```

Immediate If Here's a shortcut. Instead of saying —

```
If age < 18 then Text = "Minor" else Text = "Adult"
```

you can say:

```
Text = IIf(age < 18, "Minor", "Adult")
```

That line means:

```
Text is this: if age < 18 then "Minor" else "Adult"
```

That line is used in this subroutine:

```
Dim age
age = InputBox("How old are you?")
Text = IIf(age < 18, "Minor", "Adult")
```

The abbreviation **IIf** means "Immediate If". It lets you do an If immediately, without have to type the words "Then" and "Else".

Yes/no message box

Let's make the computer ask, "Do you love me?" If the human says "Yes", let's make the computer say "I love you too!" If the human says "No", let's make the computer say "I don't love you either!"

This subroutine accomplishes that goal:

```
Dim response
response = InputBox("Do you love me?")
If response = "yes" Then
    MsgBox("I love you too!")
Else
    MsgBox("I don't love you either!")
End If
End
```

But that subroutine has a flaw: what if the human types neither "yes" nor "no"? Instead of typing "yes", what if the human types "YES" or "Yes" or "yeah" or "yep" or "yessiree" or just "y" or "certainly" or "I love you tremendously" or "not sure"? In those situations, since the human didn't type simply "yes", the computer will say "I don't love you either!", which is inappropriate.

The problem with that subroutine is it gives the human too many choices: it lets the human type *anything* in the input box.

To make sure the computer reacts appropriately to the human, give the human fewer choices. Restrict the human to choosing just Yes or No. Here's how: show the human a Yes button and a No button, then force the human to click one of them. This subroutine accomplishes that:

```
If MsgBox("Do you love me?", vbYesNo) = vbYes Then
    MsgBox("I love you too!")
Else
    MsgBox("I don't love you either!")
End If
End
```

The MsgBox line makes the computer create a message box saying "Do you love me?" A normal message box contains an OK button, but vbYesNo makes this be a **yes/no message box** instead (which contains Yes and No buttons instead of an OK button).

If the human clicks the Yes button, the subroutine makes the computer say "I love you too!" If the human does otherwise (by clicking the No button), the computer says "I don't love you either!"

Long programs While running a long program, the computer should occasionally ask whether the human wants to continue. To make the computer ask that, insert this line:

```
If MsgBox("Do you want to continue?", vbYesNo) = vbNo Then End
```

That line creates a yes/no message box asking "Do you want to continue?" If the human clicks the No button, the program will end (and the computer will automatically click the program's X button).

Select

Let's turn your computer into a therapist!

To do that, make the computer ask the patient "How are you?" and let the patient type whatever words the patient wishes. Just begin the subroutine like this:

```
Dim feeling
feeling = InputBox("How are you?")
```

That makes the computer ask "How are you?" and makes the patient's response be called the feeling.

Make the computer continue the conversation as follows:

```
If the patient said "fine", print "That's good!"
If the patient said "lousy" instead, print "Too bad!"
If the patient said anything else instead, print "I feel the same way!"
```

To accomplish all that, you can use a multi-line If:

```
If feeling = "fine" Then
    MsgBox("That's good!")
ElseIf feeling = "lousy" Then
    MsgBox("Too bad!")
Else
    MsgBox("I feel the same way!")
End If
```

Then end the whole program:

```
End
```

Instead of typing that multi-line If, you can type this **Select statement** instead, which is briefer and simpler:

```
Select Case feeling
    Case "fine"
        MsgBox("That's good!")
    Case "lousy"
        MsgBox("Too bad!")
    Case Else
        MsgBox("I feel the same way!")
End Select
```

Like a multi-line If, a Select statement consumes several lines. The top line of that Select statement tells the computer to analyze the feeling and Select one of the cases from the list underneath. That list is indented and says:

> In the case where the feeling is "fine",
> say "That's good!"
>
> In the case where the feeling is "lousy",
> say "Too bad!"
>
> In the case where the feeling is anything else,
> say "I feel the same way!"

While you're typing the Select statement, the computer automatically indents the lines for you and automatically types "End Select" underneath.

Complete subroutine
Here's a complete subroutine:

```
Dim feeling
feeling = InputBox("How are you?")
Select Case feeling
    Case "fine"
        MsgBox("That's good!")
    Case "lousy"
        MsgBox("Too bad!")
    Case Else
        MsgBox("I feel the same way!")
End Select
MsgBox("I hope you enjoyed your therapy. Now you owe $50.")
End
```

The InputBox line makes the computer ask the patient, "How are you?" The next several lines are the Select statement, which makes the computer analyze the patient's answer and print "That's good!" or "Too bad!" or else "I feel the same way!"

Regardless of what the patient and computer said, that subroutine's bottom MsgBox line always makes the computer end the conversation by saying:

```
I hope you enjoyed your therapy. Now you owe $50.
```

In that program, try changing the strings to make the computer say smarter remarks, become a better therapist, and charge even more money.

Fancy cases
You can create fancy cases:

Statement	Meaning
Case "fine"	If it's "fine"
Case "fine", "lousy"	If it's "fine" or "lousy"
Case 6	If it's 6
Case 6, 7, 18	If it's 6 or 7 or 18
Case Is < 18	If it's less than 18
Case Is > 18	If it's greater than 18
Case Is <= 18	If it's less than or equal to 18
Case Is >= 18	If it's at least 18 (greater than or equal to 18)
Case 6, 7, Is >=18	If it's 6 or 7 or at least 18
Case 10 To 100	If it's between 10&100 (at least 10 but no more than 100)
Case 6, 10 To 100	If it's 6 or between 10&100

When typing a Case statement, don't bother typing the word "Is". The computer will type it for you automatically.

Exit Sub

To make the computer skip the bottom part of your subroutine, say **Exit Sub**, like this:

```
MsgBox("I love the company president")
Exit Sub
MsgBox("I love him as much as stale bread")
```

When you run that program (by pressing F5), the computer will say "I love the company president" but then exit from the subroutine, without saying "I love him as much as stale bread". The computer will say just:

```
I love the company president
```

Suppose you write a subroutine that displays many messages, and you want to run the program several times (so several of your friends see the messages). If one of your friends would be offended by the last few messages, send that friend an *abridged* subroutine! Here's how: put Exit Sub above program part that you want the computer to ignore.

"Exit Sub" versus "End".
Instead of saying "Exit Sub", you can say "End". Here's the difference:

> When the computer encounters "Exit Sub" in a subroutine, the computer stops running that subroutine but continues running the rest of the program: for example, it displays Form1, until the human clicks Form1's X button.
>
> When the computer encounters "End" in a subroutine, the computer stops running the whole program and automatically clicks Form1's X button.

Property list

While you're creating or editing a Visual Basic program, you see **tabs** near the screen's top-left corner. Try clicking those tabs now:

> If you click the **"Form1.vb [Design]" tab**, you see the Form1 window itself, so you can admire the Form1 window's size, color, and any writing in it.
>
> If you typed a subroutine for Form1, you also see a **"Form1.vb" tab**. If you click that tab, you see the subroutine you typed.

Try this experiment....

Click the "Form1.vb [Design]" tab, so you see the Form1 window itself. **Then click (just once) in the middle of the Form1 window.**

Then the screen's bottom-right corner should show a list, whose title is:

> Properties
> Form1 System.Windows.Forms.Form

If you don't see that list yet, press the F4 key then try again to click in the middle of the Form1 window.

That list is called **Form1's main property list** (or **property window**). It looks like this:

Property	Value
(ApplicationSettings)	
(DataBindings)	
(Name)	Form1
AcceptButton	(none)
AccessibleDescription	
AccessibleName	
AccessibleRole	Default
AllowDrop	False
AutoScaleMode	Font
AutoScroll	False
AutoScrollMargin	0, 0
AutoScrollMinSize	0, 0
AutoSize	False
AutoSizeMode	GrowOnly
AutoValidate	EnablePreventFocusChange
BackColor	Control
BackgroundImage	(none)
BackgroundImageLayout	Tile
CancelButton	(none)
CausesValidation	True
ContextMenuStrip	(none)
ControlBox	True
Cursor	Default
DoubleBuffered	False
Enabled	True
Font	Microsoft Sans Serif, 8.25pt
ForeColor	ControlText
FormBorderStyle	Sizable
HelpButton	False
Icon	(Icon)
ImeMode	NoControl
IsMdiContainer	False
KeyPreview	False
Language	(Default)
Localizable	False
Location	0, 0
Locked	False
MainMenuStrip	(none)
MaximizeBox	True
MaximumSize	0, 0
MinimizeBox	True
MinimumSize	0, 0
Opacity	100%
Padding	0, 0, 0, 0
RightToLeft	No
RightToLeftLayout	False
ShowIcon	True
ShowInTaskbar	True
Size	300, 300
SizeGripStyle	Auto
StartPosition	WindowsDefaultLocation
Tag	
Text	Form1
TopMost	False
TransparencyKey	
UseWaitCursor	False
WindowState	Normal

(The screen shows part of the list. To see the whole list, use the list's scroll arrows.)

Text

The top of Form1's window normally says "Form1". That's called the window's **title** (or **caption** or **text**). Instead of making the title say "Form1", you can make it say "Results" or "Payroll results" or "Mary's window" or "Fun stuff" or "Hey, I'm a funny window" or anything else you wish!

To make Form1's title say "Fun stuff", you can put this line in Form1's subroutine —

> ```
> Text = "Fun stuff"
> ```

but here's an easier way:

> In Form1's main property list, click the word "Text" (after you scroll up or down to see it) then type what you want the title to be, so the property list's Text line becomes this:
> Text   Fun stuff
> When you finish typing, press the Enter key.

Try that now! It makes the top of Form1 say "Fun stuff" immediately (or when you press Enter or F5 or click the Form1 window or the "Form1.vb [Design]" tab).

Color

Normally, the Form1 window's middle is a big blank area that's nearly white (a color called **Control**, which is very light gray). To make it red instead, you can put this line in Form1's subroutine —

> ```
> BackColor = Color.Red
> ```

but here's an easier way:

> In Form1's main property list, click **BackColor** then BackColor's down-arrow then a color category ("Custom" or "Web" or "System") then the color you want (such as Red, which you'll see in the Web category, after you scroll down).

Try that now! It makes Form1's background color become Red instantly.

Maximize

The Form1 window is normally medium-sized. To maximize it, you can use 3 methods.

Manual method While the program is running (because you pressed F5), you can manually click the Form1 window's maximize button. That maximizes the window but just temporarily: when you finish running the program (by clicking the Form1 window's X button), the computer forgets about maximization. The next time you run the program, it will *not* be maximized, unless you click the maximize button again.

Equation method Insert this equation in Form1's subroutine:

> ```
> WindowState = 2
> ```

Property-list method In Form1's main property list, click WindowState then WindowState's down-arrow then Maximized. That makes the property list's WindowState line become:

WindowState	Maximized

When you run the program (by pressing F5), Form1's window will be maximized.

Refuse to maximize

Instead of maximizing the Form1 window, you can do just the opposite: you can *prevent* the user from maximizing. Here's how....

In Form1's main property list, click **MaximizeBox** then press the F key (which means "False"). That makes the property list's MaximizeBox line become:

MaximizeBox	False

That make Form1's maximize button (which is also called the maximize box) be **grayed out** while the program runs; the maximize button will become gray instead of black-and-white. That grayed-out button will ignore all attempts to be clicked, so the window will refuse to maximize.

Resize

Normally, Form1 is 300 pixels wide and 300 pixels tall. Here's how to adjust that size....

Property-list method In Form1's main property list, click **Size**, then change "300, 300" to the size you wish, by editing those numbers. For example, if you want Form1 to be 500 pixels wide and 400 pixels tall, change the size to "500, 400". The first number is the form's width; the second number is the form's height.

The biggest permissible size is the size of your whole screen. For example, if your screen is traditional (17-inch CRT, set at a resolution of 1024-by-768), the biggest permissible size for you is "1024, 768". If you want Form1 to be half as wide and half as tall as that, choose "512, 384".

The smallest permissible size is "124, 36". That's barely enough to show Form1's fundamental buttons (close, maximize, and minimize), not much else!

If you request a size that's very big (almost as big as the screen), Form1 won't look that big until you run the program (by pressing F5).

Drag method While the program is running (because you pressed F5), you can change Form1's size by dragging its bottom right corner. That changes the size just temporarily: when you finish running the program (by clicking Form1's X button), the computer forgets how you dragged Form1's corner, and Form1 reverts to its previous size.

Here's how to change Form1's size so the computer remembers the new size:

> Make sure the program is *not* running. (If it's running, stop it by clicking its X button.)
> Click the "Form1.vb [Design]" tab (so you see what Form1 looks like, not subroutines you typed).
> At Form1's bottom right corner, you see a tiny white square (called a **handle**). Drag that handle until Form1 becomes the size you wish.
> That changes Form1's size permanently (or until you change the size again). You'll see that size in the property list's Size line.

Refuse to resize

In Form1's main property list, the FormBorderStyle line normally says:

FormBorderStyle	Sizable

Try this experiment: click FormBorderStyle then FormBorderStyle's down-arrow then "FixedToolWindow", so the line becomes:

FormBorderStyle	FixedToolWindow

That prevents stupid humans from changing Form1's size. When a human runs the program (by pressing F5), Form1's window will have no maximize button, no restore-down button, no minimize button, and no resizable edges. Form1 stays the size you specified in the property list (such as the property list's Size line), so stupid humans can't mess up your beautiful design (unless they edit your subroutine or property list).

Form position

Here's how to adjust Form1's position....

Property-list method In Form1's main property list, click **StartPosition** then StartPosition's down-arrow. You see this list of choices:

> Manual
> Center Screen
> WindowsDefaultLocation
> WindowsDefaultBounds
> CenterParent

Click a choice now. You'll see the effect later (when you press the F5 key to run the program).

The computer assumes you want "WindowsDefaultLocation" unless you click a different choice instead.

"WindowsDefaultLocation" puts Form1 near the screen's top-left corner (leaving a 1¼-inch margin gap) and makes Form1's size be what you chose in the Size line.

"CenterScreen" puts Form1 at the screen's center and makes Form1's size be what you chose in the Size line.

"CenterParent" puts Form1 at the center of what Windows thinks is appropriate (which is typically left of the screen's center) and makes Form1's size be what you chose in the Size line.

"WindowsDefaultBounds" puts Form1 very near the screen's top-left corner (leaving just a ½-inch margin gap) and makes Form1 be big (9¼ inches wide, 6½ inches tall). The Size line is ignored.

"Manual" puts Form1 at the screen's top-left corner (leaving no gap, unless you change the Location line to something different from "0, 0") and makes Form1's size be what you chose in the Size line.

All those inch measurements are approximate and depend on your screen's size.

Drag method While the program is running, you can move Form1 by dragging its **title bar** (the blue horizontal bar that's at Form1's top and typically says "Form1"). That moves Form1 just temporarily; when you finish running the program (by clicking Form1's X button), the computer forgets how you dragged Form1, and Form1 reverts to its previous position.

Opacity

Normally, Form1 is completely opaque: while the program is running, Form1 completely blocks the view of anything behind it.

To have fun, reduce Form1's opacity: in Form1's main property list, click **Opacity**, then change "100%" to "75%". When you run the program (by pressing F5), Form1 will be just partly opaque; it will be partly transparent, so you can see, faintly, what's behind the form.

If you make the opacity even lower — 50% or 25% — Form1 will be hardly opaque at all — it will be very transparent — so you can easily see what's behind it, as if Form1 were just a ghost.

> Don't make the opacity be 0%. That would make Form1 completely invisible, so you couldn't see it at all, couldn't click its close box, and couldn't stop the program!
>
> Don't make the opacity be less than 25%. That would make Form1 difficult to see.

Try making the opacity be 90%.

Opacity doesn't work well if your Windows version is old (Windows XP) or stripped-down (Windows Vista Basic or Windows 7 Starter), since those Windows versions lack **Windows Aero** (which makes windows partly transparent).

Toolbox

You've learned how to create and manipulate an object called "Form1". You can create other objects also, by using the **toolbox**.

See the toolbox

To see the toolbox — and start fresh — exit from Visual Basic (by clicking Visual Basic's X button), then go back into Visual Basic by doing this:

Click the Start button then "Microsoft Visual Basic 2010 Express" then "New Project". Double-click "Windows Forms Application", so you see the Form1 window.

At the screen's left edge, you'll see the word "Toolbox". If you're lucky, you'll see this:

If you see just the word "Toolbox" but none of those other words, make them appear by clicking "Toolbox", then make them stay on the screen permanently by clicking the **push pin**, which is just left of the toolbox's X.

Make sure the triangle left of "All Windows Forms" has a white middle. (If the triangle is solid black instead, click the triangle to make its middle white.)

Make sure the triangle left of "Common Controls" is solid black. (If that triangle has a white middle instead, click the triangle to make it solid black.)

Each object in the toolbox is called a **tool**.

The complete toolbox is too tall to fit on your screen. You see just the toolbox's beginning. Whenever you want to see the rest

of the toolbox (which includes many dozens of tools), click the toolbox's scroll-down arrow (at the toolbox's bottom-right corner).

Button

Try this experiment. Double-click the **Button** tool. That makes a button appear in Form1's middle, near Form1's top-left corner (or near a previous button). The button is a rectangle and says "Button1" on it.

(If you wish, drag that button to a different place in Form1. You can also change the button's size by dragging its 9 square handles. But for your first experiment, just leave the button where the computer put it.)

The button says "Button1" on it. Just for fun, let's make it say "Click me" instead. To do that, click Text (in the property list) and type "Click me", so the property list's Text line becomes:

Text	Click me

That makes the button's text become "Click me" (instead of "Button1").

Notice that the property list concerns the button and its text (instead of Form1's text), because the button is highlighted.

Let's write a program so if a human clicks the button (which says "Click me"), Form1 will say "Thanks for the click". To do that, double-click the button. The double-clicking tells the computer you want to write a subroutine about that object (the button).

The computer starts writing the subroutine for you. The computer writes:

```
Public Class Form1

    Private Sub Button1_Click…

    End Sub
End Class
```

Insert this line in the middle of the subroutine —

```
    Text = "Thanks for the click"
```

so the subroutine looks like this:

```
Public Class Form1

    Private Sub Button1_Click…
    Text = "Thanks for the click"
    End Sub
End Class
```

That subroutine tells the computer that when Button1 is clicked, the computer should say "Thanks for the click" on Form1.

Try it: run that program (by pressing F5). You'll see Form1 with a button on it that says "Click me". If you click the button, the subroutine makes Form1 say "Thanks for the click".

In that subroutine, the computer assumes you want the text "Thanks for the click" to be on Form1, not on the button. If you want that text to be on the *button* instead, say **Button 1's Text** instead of just Text. To say **Button 1's Text**, type **Button1.Text**, so the subroutine looks like this:

```
Public Class Form1

    Private Sub Button1_Click…
        Button1.Text = "Thanks for the click"
    End Sub
End Class
```

But to fit "Thanks for the click" onto the button, you must widen the button, by doing this:

If the program is still running, finish running it (by clicking Form1's X button). Then click the "Form1.vb [Design]" tab, so you see Form1 and can modify the appearance of Form1 (and of its button). Then widen the button (by dragging the button's handles).

Two buttons Let's write a program that has *two* buttons! Let's make the first button be called "Red" and the second button be called "Blue". If the human clicks the "Red" button, let's make Form1 turn red; if the human clicks the "Blue" button, let's make Form1 turn blue.

To do all that, start a new program as follows:

> If a previous program is still running, finish running it (by clicking Form1's X button). If you're not in VB yet, click "Start" then "All Programs" then "Microsoft Visual Studio 2010 Express" then "Microsoft Visual Basic 2010 Express".
>
> Click "New Project" or the New Project button (which is near the screen's top-left corner, below the word "File"). Double-click "Windows Forms Application", so you see the Form1 window.
>
> You should also see the Toolbox. (If you don't see it yet, continue following the "See the toolbox" instructions on the previous page.)

In the Toolbox, double-click the Button tool. A command button appears in Form1 and is called Button1. In the property list, click Text then type "Click here for red" (and press Enter), so the property list's Text line becomes:

Text	Click here for red

That tries to make the button's text become "Click here for red". To fit all that text onto the button, widen the button (by dragging one of its handles).

In the Toolbox, double-click the Button tool again. That makes another command button appear in Form1 and be called Button2. Unfortunately, the Button2 button covers up the Button1 button, so you can't see the Button1 button. Drag the Button2 button out of the way (toward the right), so you can see both buttons side-by-side.

The Button2 button should be highlighted. (If it's not highlighted, click it to make it highlighted.) In its property list, change its Text from "Button2" to "Click here for blue" (by clicking Text then typing "Click here for blue" and pressing Enter). Widen the Button2 button (by dragging one of its handles) so it shows all of "Click here for blue".

Now your screen shows Form1 with two buttons on it. The first button says "Click here for red". The second button says "Click here for blue".

Double-click the "Click here for red" button, and write this subroutine for it:

```
Private Sub Button1_Click…
     BackColor = Color.Red
   End Sub
```

That subroutine says: clicking that button will make Form1's background color be red.

Move that subroutine out of the way (by clicking the "Form1.vb [Design]" tab, so you can see Form1.

Double-click the "Click here for blue" button, and write this subroutine for it:

```
Private Sub Button 2_Click…
     BackColor = Color.Blue
   End Sub
```

While you're writing that subroutine, you'll see the other subroutine above it. Altogether, you see:

```
Public Class Form1

    Private Sub Button1_Click…
        BackColor = Color.Red
    End Sub

    Private Sub Button 2_Click…
        BackColor = Color.Blue
    End Sub
End Class
```

Then run the program by pressing F5. Here's what happens….

You see Form1 with two buttons on it. The first button says "Click here for red"; if you click it, Form1 turns red. The other button says "Click here for blue"; if you click it, Form1 turns blue.

Try clicking one button, then the other. Click as often as you like. When you get tired of clicking, end the program (by clicking Form1's X button).

Where to put buttons A good habit is to put buttons side-by-side, in Form1's bottom right corner. That way, the buttons won't interfere with any other objects on Form1.

Exit button To stop running a typical program, you have to click its X button. Some humans don't know to do that. To help them, create a button called "Exit", so that clicking it will make the computer exit from the program.

To do that, create an ordinary button; but make the button's text say "Exit" (or anything else you prefer, such as "Quit" or "End" or "Abort" or "Close" or "Click here to end the program"), and make the button's subroutine say End, like this:

```
Private Sub Button3_Click…
     End
   End Sub
```

Put that Exit button in Form1's bottom-right corner.

Check box

A **check box** is a small gray square, with text to the right of the square. At first, the gray square has nothing inside it: it's empty. While the program runs, clicking the square makes a green check mark (✔) appear in the square. If you click the square again, the check mark disappears.

To create a check box, double-click the **CheckBox** tool. That makes a check box appears in Form1. Drag the check box wherever you wish.

The first check box's text is temporarily "CheckBox1"; to change that text, click Text (in the property list) and type whatever text you wish. At the end of your typing, press Enter. Suggestion: if you want to type a *lot* of text, do this instead:

> Click Text's down-arrow. You'll see a *big* box to type in. Press Enter at the end of each line you type. When you've finished typing all text you want, do this: while holding down the Ctrl key, tap the Enter key.

If you want the computer to react immediately to whether the check box is checked, give the check box this subroutine:

```
Private Sub CheckBox1_CheckedChanged…
     If CheckBox1.Checked Then
         type here what to do if CheckBox1 just became checked
     Else
         type here what to do if CheckBox1 just became unchecked
     End If
   End Sub
```

Dressed example For example, this subroutine makes the computer say "I am dressed" if the check box just became checked but say "I am naked" if the check box just became empty:

```
Private Sub CheckBox1_CheckedChanged…
     If CheckBox1.Checked Then
         Text = "I am dressed"
     Else
         Text = "I am naked"
     End If
   End Sub
```

When that program runs, the check box starts by being empty. Clicking the check box makes you see ✔ and makes the computer say "I am dressed". The next time you click the check box, the ✔ disappears from the box, so the box becomes empty and the computer say "I am naked". Clicking the check box again makes the ✔ reappear and makes the computer say "I am dressed".

Here's how to type that subroutine fast:

Type the word "if", then a space, then the letters "che". You see a list of computer words that begin with the letter "Che". In that list, double-click "CheckBox1". That makes the computer type "CheckBox1" for you.

Type a period. You see a list of computer words; from that list, choose "Checked" by double-clicking it (or if "Checked" was highlighted already, you can choose it by pressing the Tab key).

Multiple check boxes Form1 can contain many check boxes. The human can check several at the same time, so that several of the boxes contain check marks simultaneously.

Although you can put buttons and check boxes wherever you wish, it's customary to arrange buttons horizontally (so the second button is to the right of the first) but arrange check boxes vertically (so the second check box is below the first). The check boxes (and their texts) form a vertical list of choices.

OK button If Form1 contains several check boxes, you should typically delay the computer's reaction until the human has decided which boxes to check, has checked all the ones desired, and has clicked an OK button to confirm that the correct boxes are checked.

To do that, make the check boxes have no subroutines. Instead, create an OK button in Form1's bottom-right corner (by creating a button there and making its text be "OK"), then make the OK button's subroutine look like this:

```
Private Sub Button1_Click…
    If CheckBox1.Checked Then
        type here what to do if CheckBox1 is checked
    Else
        type here what to do if CheckBox1 is unchecked
    End If
    If CheckBox2.Checked Then
        type here what to do if CheckBox2 is checked
    Else
        type here what to do if CheckBox2 is unchecked
    End If
End Sub
```

That subroutine says: when the OK button is clicked, notice which check boxes are checked and react appropriately.

For example, let's make a program that alters Form1's appearance, to make it red or maximized or red maximized or return to normal. Here's how to do all that:

Create a check box (called CheckBox1) with title "Red".

Create a check box (called CheckBox2) with title "maximized".

Create a command button (called Button1) with title "OK" and this subroutine:

```
Private Sub Button1_Click…
    If CheckBox1.Checked Then
        BackColor = Color.Red
    Else
        BackColor = Color.WhiteSmoke
    End If
    If CheckBox2.Checked Then
        WindowState = 2
    Else
        WindowState = 0
    End If
End Sub
```

Radio button

A **radio button** resembles a check box but looks and acts like the button on an old-fashioned radio, because of these differences….

To create a check box, double-click the **CheckBox** tool.
To create a radio button, double-click the **RadioButton** tool.

A check box is a tiny gray **square**.
A radio button is a tiny gray **circle**.

While the program is running,
clicking a checkbox makes a **green checkmark** appear in the square.
Clicking a radio button makes a **blue dot** appear in the circle.

Green checkmarks can appear in many checkboxes, simultaneously.
You see just one blue dot. When you click a radio button, the blue dot hops to that radio button and leaves the previous button.

Like checkboxes, radio buttons are arranged vertically (so the second radio button is below the first). The radio buttons (and their titles) form a vertical list of choices.

When the human starts running your program, the first radio button (which is RadioButton1) has a blue dot inside the gray circle, and the computer automatically does RadioButton1's subroutine (even if the human hasn't clicked RadioButton1's button yet).

Afterwards, if the human clicks a different radio button, here's what happens:

The blue dot hops to that radio button. The computer does that button's subroutine; but before doing so, the computer does the previous button's subroutine one more time so it can display a message such as "Sorry to hear you don't like this choice anymore".

If you want the computer to react immediately to whether the radio button has the blue dot, give the radio button this subroutine:

```
Private Sub RadioButton1_CheckedChanged…
    If RadioButton1.Checked Then
        type here what to do if RadioButton1 just got the blue dot
    Else
        type here what to do if RadioButton1 just lost the blue dot
    End If
End Sub
```

3-color example For example, let's write a program that has 3 radio buttons, labeled "Red", "Blue", and "Green". While the program is running, if the human switches from "Red" to "Blue" (by clicking "Blue" after having clicked "Red"), let's make the program say "Sorry you don't like red anymore" and make Form1 become blue. Let's make the program act similarly for switching between other pairs of colors.

To do that, maximize Form 1 (by making its WindowState property be Maximized) and create the 3 radio buttons (labeled "Red", "Blue", and "Green"). Then give the "Red" button (which is RadioButton1) this subroutine:

```
Private Sub RadioButton1_CheckedChanged…
    If RadioButton1.Checked Then
        BackColor = Color.Red
    Else
        Text = "Sorry you don't like red anymore"
    End If
End Sub
```

That subroutine runs just when the human changes the Red radio button's appearance (by clicking it or unclicking it):

When that radio button's appearance changes to "checked" (contains a blue dot), that subroutine makes Form1 be red.

When that radio button's appearance changes to "unchecked" (no blue dot), that subroutine makes Form1 say "Sorry you don't like red anymore".

Here's how to type that subroutine fast:

Type the word "if", then a space, then the letter "r". You see a list of computer words that begin with the letter R. In that list, double-click "RadioButton1". That makes the computer type "RadioButton1" for you.

Type a period. You see a list of computer words; from that list, choose "Checked" by double-clicking it (or if "Checked" was highlighted already, you can choose it by pressing the Tab key).

To type the rest of the subroutine fast, keep choosing from lists.

To finish the program, type this subroutine for the "Blue" button (which is RadioButton2) —

```
Private Sub RadioButton2_CheckedChanged…
    If RadioButton2.Checked Then
        BackColor = Color.Blue
    Else
        Text = "Sorry you don't like blue anymore"
    End If
End Sub
```

and this subroutine for the "Green" button (which is RadioButton3):

```
Private Sub RadioButton3_CheckedChanged…
    If RadioButton3.Checked Then
        Text = "Welcome to New York"
    Else
        MsgBox("You've left New York")
    End If
End Sub
```

3-city example For a similar example, let's write an airplane program that has 3 radio buttons, labeled "Los Angeles", "Dallas", and "New York". While the program is running, if the human switches from "Los Angeles" to "Dallas" (by clicking "Dallas" after having clicked "Los Angeles"), let's make the program say "You've left Los Angeles" and "Welcome to Dallas". Let's make the program act similarly for traveling between the other cities.

To do that, create the 3 radio buttons (labeled "Los Angeles", "Dallas", and "New York"). Then give the "Los Angeles" button (which is RadioButton1) this subroutine:

```
Private Sub RadioButton1_CheckedChanged…
    If RadioButton1.Checked Then
        Text = "Welcome to Los Angeles"
    Else
        MsgBox("You've left Los Angeles")
    End If
End Sub
```

That subroutine runs just when the human changes the Los Angeles radio button's appearance (by clicking it or unclicking it):

When that radio button's appearance changes to "checked" (contains a blue dot), that subroutine makes the computer say "Welcome to Los Angeles".

When that radio button's appearance changes to "unchecked" (no blue dot), that subroutine makes the computer say "You've left Los Angeles".

To finish the program, type this subroutine for the "Dallas" button (which is RadioButton2) —

```
Private Sub RadioButton2_CheckedChanged…
    If RadioButton2.Checked Then
        Text = "Welcome to Dallas"
    Else
        MsgBox("You've left Dallas")
    End If
End Sub
```

and this subroutine for the "New York" button (which is RadioButton3):

```
Private Sub RadioButton3_CheckedChanged…
    If RadioButton3.Checked Then
        Text = "Welcome to New York"
    Else
        MsgBox("You've left New York")
    End If
End Sub
```

OK button When the human clicks a radio button, the computer can react to the click immediately, but that might startle and upset the human. If you want to be gentler, delay the computer's reaction until the human also clicks a general OK button, which confirms the human's desires.

To do that, make the radio buttons have no subroutines, so nothing will happen when those buttons are clicked. In Form1's bottom-right corner, create an ordinary button whose text says "OK" and whose subroutine looks like this:

```
Private Sub Button1_Click…
    If RadioButton1.Checked Then
        type here what to do if RadioButton1 just got the blue dot
    ElseIf RadioButton2.Checked Then
        type here what to do if RadioButton2 just got the blue dot
    ElseIf RadioButton3.Checked Then
        type here what to do if RadioButton3 just got the blue dot
    ElseIf RadioButton4.Checked Then
        type here what to do if RadioButton4 just got the blue dot
    Else
        type here what to do if bottom radio button got blue dot
    End If
End Sub
```

That subroutine says: when the OK button is clicked, notice which radio button was clicked and react appropriately.

Label

Form1 has two main parts. One part is a blue bar across Form1's top: it includes Form1's minimize button, maximize button, close button, and text. The other part (Form1's middle) is a big light-gray box: it includes objects you created, such as ordinary buttons, check boxes, and radio buttons.

In Form1's middle, let's type this text:

```
I love you
```

To do that, double-click the **Label** tool. That makes the word "Label1" appear in Form1's middle. Drag "Label1" to the spot in Form1 where you wish to begin typing. To change "Label1" to "I love you", click Text (in Label1's property list) then type "I love you", so the property list says:

```
Text                          I love you
```

At the end of that typing, press Enter. Then "Label1" becomes "I love you", so "I love you" is in Form1's middle.

Multi-line text Instead of making Form1's middle say just "I love you", let's make it say:

```
I love you
You turned me on
Let's get married
```

Here's how:

```
After you've created a label (by double-clicking the Label tool) and clicked
Text, click Text's down-arrow. You'll see a big box to type in. Press Enter at
the end of each line you type. When you've finished typing all text you
want, do this: while holding down the Ctrl key, tap the Enter key.
```

Text equation Here's a different way to make Form1's middle say "I love you".

Create a label (by double-clicking the Label tool). Tell the computer you want to write a subroutine for Form1 (by double-clicking in Form1 but *not* in the label). Put this line in Form1's subroutine:

```
Label1.Text = "I love you"
```

That means: the label's text is "I love you." That line makes Form1's subroutine become this:

```
Private Sub Form1_Load…
    Label1.Text = "I love you"
End Sub
```

When you run the program (by pressing F5), the computer will run that subroutine and make Form1's middle say:

```
I love you
```

If instead you want the Form1's middle to say —

```
I love you
You turned me on
```

change the Text line to this:

```
Label1.Text = "I love you" & Chr(13) & "You turned me on"
```

That makes the computer type "I love you" then press key #13 (which is the Enter key) then type "You turned me on". Instead of that long Text line, you can give this pair of shorter Text lines:

```
Label1.Text = "I love you"
Label1.Text &= Chr(13) & "You turned me on"
```

In that pair of lines, the first line makes the Text be "I love you"; the next line changes the Text to become all that, combined with Chr(13) and "You turned me on".

Math Let's make Form1's middle say the answer to 4 + 2.

To do that, create a label (by double-clicking the Label tool). Tell the computer you want to write a subroutine for Form1 (by double-clicking in Form1 but *not* in the label). Put this line in Form1's subroutine:

```
Label1.Text = 4 + 2
```

That line means: Label1's text is the answer to 4 + 2. That line makes Form1's subroutine become this:

```
Private Sub Form1_Load…
    Label1.Text = 4 + 2
End Sub
```

When you run the program (by pressing F5), the computer will run that subroutine and write the answer (6) in Form1's middle.

To make Form1's middle say the answer to 4 + 2 and, on the next line, say the answer to 48 + 3, you can put this line in Form1's subroutine —

```
Label1.Text = 4 + 2 & Chr(13) & 48 + 3
```

or give this pair of lines instead:

```
Label1.Text = 4 + 2
Label1.Text &= Chr(13) & 48 + 3
```

In that pair of lines, the first line makes the Text be the answer to 4 + 2; the next line changes the Text to become all that, combined with Chr(13) and the answer to 48 + 3.

List box

A **list box** is a big white box that contains a list of choices, such as these color choices —

Red
Blue
Green

or these country choices —

United States
Canada
Mexico

The list can be short (2 or 3 choices) or tall (hundreds of choices). If the list is too tall fit in the box, the computer will automatically add scroll arrows so humans can scroll through the list.

To create a list box, double-click the **ListBox** tool. A list box (big white box) appears in the middle of Form1. Drag the list box wherever you wish.

The first list box is called ListBox1. Inside that list box, you temporarily see the word "ListBox1", but you should put your own list of choices there instead, by using this method —

In the list box's property list, click "Items" then "…". Type the list of choices, such as:
United States
Canada
Mexico
To do that, press Enter at the end of each line. When you've finished typing the whole list, click "OK".

or this alternate method:

Click the list box's right-arrow (which is near the box's top-right corner) then "Edit Items". Type the list of choices, such as:
United States
Canada
Mexico
To do that, press Enter at the end of each line. When you've finished typing the whole list, click "OK" then click in the list box.

Then on Form1, you see the list box containing your choices.

By dragging the box's handles, try to make the box just tall enough to hold *all* the choices. (If it isn't tall enough, the computer automatically adds scroll arrows so humans can scroll through the list while the program runs.)

By dragging the box's handles, make the box just wide enough to hold the widest choice.

Select one You can give List1 this kind of subroutine:

```
Private Sub ListBox1_SelectedIndexChanged…
    Select Case ListBox1.SelectedItem
        Case "United States"
            type here what to do if "United States" is clicked
        Case "Canada"
            type here what to do if "Canada" is clicked
        Case "Mexico"
            type here what to do if "Mexico" is clicked
    End Select
End Sub
```

Here's a shorter way to type the subroutine:

```
Private Sub ListBox1_SelectedIndexChanged…
    Select Case ListBox1.SelectedIndex
        Case 0
            type here what to do if the list's top item ("United States") is clicked
        Case 1
            type here what to do if the list's next item ("Canada") is clicked
        Case 2
            type here what to do if the list's next item ("Mexico") is clicked
    End Select
End Sub
```

If you want the action to be delayed until the human clicks an OK button, do this:

Create the OK button (a command button whose caption is "OK").

Give ListBox1 no subroutine, but give the OK button this kind of subroutine —

```
Private Sub Button1_Click…
    Select Case ListBox1.SelectedItem
        Case "United States"
            type here what to do if "United States" is clicked
        Case "Canada"
            type here what to do if "Canada" is clicked
        Case "Mexico"
            type here what to do if "Mexico" is clicked
    End Select
End Sub
```

or this subroutine:

```
Private Sub Button1_Click…
    Select Case ListBox1.SelectedIndex
        Case 0
            type here what to do if the list's top item ("United States") is clicked
        Case 1
            type here what to do if the list's next item ("Canada") is clicked
        Case 2
            type here what to do if the list's next item ("Mexico") is clicked
    End Select
End Sub
```

Select multi If you want to let the human select *several* items from the list (instead of just one item), do this:

In ListBox1's property list, click **SelectionMode** then SelectionMode's down-arrow.

Click either "MultiSimple" or "MultiExtended". (If you choose "MultiSimple", the human can select several items by clicking them, and deselect an item by clicking that item again. If you choose "MulitExtended", the human can select one item by clicking it, select or deselect extra items by holding down the Ctrl key while clicking them, and select a contiguous bunch of items easily by clicking the bunch's first item and Shift-clicking the last.)

Create an OK button (an ordinary button whose caption is "OK").
Give ListBox1 no subroutine, but give the OK button this kind of subroutine:
```
If ListBox1.GetSelected(0) Then type here what to do if the list's top item ("United States") clicked
If ListBox1.GetSelected(1) Then type here what to do if the list's next item ("Canada") clicked
If ListBox1.GetSelected(2) Then type here what to do if the list's next item ("Mexico") clicked
```

Label Next to your list box, you should put some text, explaining the list box's purpose to the human. To put the text there, create a label with that text (by double-clicking the Label tool), and drag the label until it's next to your list box.

Text box

You already learned that Form1's subroutine can contain this line:

```
x = InputBox("What is your name?")
```

When you run the program, that line makes the computer create an **input box**. The input box is a pop-up window containing a message ("What is your name?"), a wide white box (in which the human types a response), and an OK button (which the human clicks when finished typing).

That technique works adequately but gives you no control over the size or position of its objects (the window, message, white response box, and OK button).

To be more professional, get control by creating a **text box** instead. Here's how.

Double-click the **TextBox** tool. That creates a text box (a white box in which the human can type a response). Drag it wherever you wish. Adjust its size by dragging its handles.

Above the box (or left of it), put a label (by double-clicking the Label tool). Make the label contain a message (such as "What is your name?").

Below the box (or right of the box), create an OK button (a button whose text says "OK"). Make the OK button's subroutine include these lines —

```
Dim x
x = TextBox1.Text
```

and anything else you want the computer to do, such as:

```
MsgBox("I love " & x)
```

Form1 can contain *several* text boxes. For example, you can include:

```
a text box for the human's first name
a text box for the human's last name
a text box for the human's address
text boxes for the human's city, state, and ZIP code
```

That makes Form1 be truly a form to fill in! Create just one OK button to handle all those text boxes, so the human clicks the OK button after filling in the entire form.

Password character If you want the human to type a password into a text box, do this: in the text box's property list, click **PasswordChar** then type an asterisk (the symbol *). That makes the box show asterisks instead of the characters the human is typing. That prevents enemies from discovering the password by peeking over the human's shoulder.

MultiLine The typical text box holds just one line of text. To let your text box handle *several* lines of text well, make 3 adjustments:

In the text box's property list, click MultiLine then press the T key (which stands for True). That lets the text box handle *several* lines of text, lets the human press the Enter key at the end of each line, and lets the computer press the Enter key automatically if there are too many words to fit on a line.

Make the text box taller and wider (by dragging its handles), so it can show more lines of text and more words per line. That reduces the human's frustration.

In the text box's property list, click ScrollBars then press the V key (which stands for Vertical). That creates a vertical scroll bar, which helps the human move through the text, in case you didn't make the text box tall enough to handle all the words.

Rich-text box

Instead of double-clicking the TextBox tool, try double-clicking the **RichTextBox** tool. It creates a text box that's already tall, MultiLine (so the human can type many lines of text in the box), with a vertical scroll bar (which appears when the human types more lines than can fit in the box) and the ability to handle **formatted text** (which is called **rich text**). That box is called **RichTextBox1**.

For best results, make the box even taller and wider (by dragging its bottom-right corner).

In that box, the human can type a number, or a word, or a sentence, or a paragraph, or *several* paragraphs (by pressing the Enter key at the end of each paragraph), or a whole essay! What the human types in that box is called a **document**.

For example, if you want to invent your own word-processing program, the first step is to create a rich-text box for the human to type the words into.

Improve the rich-text box Here are 2 popular ways to improve how a rich-text box works:

In RichTextBox1's property list (at the screen's bottom-right corner), click "**EnableAutoDragDrop**" then press the T key. That makes EnableAutoDragDrop be True. Then whenever the human is typing the document, the human can highlight a phrase and drag it to a different spot in the document.

Click RichTextBox1's right-arrow (which is near the box's top-right corner) then "**Dock in parent container**". That makes RichTextBox1 expand and consume all of Form1. Then while the program is running, if the human changes Form1's size (by maximizing Form1 or by dragging Form1's bottom-right corner), RichTextBox1 will change size automatically, to still fill Form1.

Number box

To make the computer wait for the human's response, you learned you can create a text box (by double-clicking the TextBox tool) and an OK button whose subroutine includes these lines:

```
Dim x
x = TextBox1.Text
```

If you want to force the human to type a number instead of words, create a **number box** instead of a text box. Here are the details....

Double-click the **NumericUpDown** tool. That creates a number box (a white box in which the human can type a number). Drag it wherever you wish. Adjust its width by dragging its handles.

Above the box (or left of it), put a label (by double-clicking the Label tool). Make the label contain a message (such as "How many children do you have?").

Below the box (or right of the box), create an OK button (a button whose text says "OK"). Make the OK button's subroutine include these lines —

```
Dim x
x = NumericUpDown1.Value
```

and anything else you want the computer to do, such as:

```
MsgBox("I'm glad you have " & x)
```

When the human runs the program, the human sees the number box. That box temporarily has 0 in it, but the human can change that number by retyping it or by clicking the box's up-arrow (which increases the number) or down-arrow (which decreases the number). When the human has changed the number to what the human wishes, the human clicks the OK button, whose subroutine makes x become the human's number.

Alter the box's properties Normally, the number box refuses to let the human say any number over 100. If you want it to permit numbers up to 500, make its property list's **Maximum** line say 500. If you want it to permit just numbers up to 20, make its Maximum line say just 20. If you want to encourage the human to type a number that's small, make the box be narrow (by adjusting its handles).

Normally, the number box refuses to let the human say any number below 0. If you want it to permit numbers down to minus 500, make the property list's **Minimum** line say -500. If you want it to require the number to be at least 3, make its Minimum line say 3.

Normally, the number box refuses to accept decimals. If you want it to permit 2 digits after the decimal point (so the human can type dollars-and-cents), make the property list's **DecimalPlaces** line say 2.

The number box normally begins displaying the number 0. If you want it to begin by displaying the number 5 instead, make the property list's **Value** line say 5.

By adjusting those properties (Maximum, Minimum, DecimalPlaces, Value, and the box's width), you can encourage the human to be reasonable.

Combo box

A **combo box** is a fancy text box that includes a list of suggested responses.

To create a combo box, double-click the **ComboBox** tool. That creates a combo box. Like a text box, it's a white box in which the human can type a response; but the combo box's right edge shows a down-arrow, which the human can click to see a list of suggested responses.

Drag the combo box wherever you wish.

Click the box's right-arrow (which is near the box's top-right corner) then "Edit Items". Type your list of suggested responses, such as:

United States
Canada
Mexico

(Press Enter at the end of each line.) When you've finished typing the whole list, click "OK" then click in the combo box.

Above (or left of) the box, put a label (by double-clicking the Label tool). Make the label contain a prompt (an instruction to the human about what to put into the box).

Below (or right of) the box, create an OK button (a command button whose caption is "OK"). Make the OK button's subroutine include these lines —

```
Dim x
x = ComboBox1.Text
```

and anything else you want the computer to do, such as:

```
MsgBox("I'm glad you said " & x)
```

Drop-down style In combo box's property list, click **DropDownStyle** then DropDownStyle's down-arrow. You see 3 styles:

Simple
DropDown
DropDown List

Click whichever style you wish. If you don't choose otherwise, the computer assumes you want "DropDown". That works as I described: the human can type anything into the box, and the suggestion list appears just if the human clicks the box's down-arrow.

If you choose "Simple" instead, the human can still type anything into the box, and the suggestion list *always* appears (without requiring a down-arrow click) if you make the combo box tall enough to hold the list.

If you choose "DropDown List" instead, the human can*not* type into the box; the human is required to choose from the suggestion list, which appears when the human clicks the box.

Picture box

Here's how to make Form1 show a picture.

First, **enlarge Form1** (by dragging its bottom-right corner), to let it hold a big picture better.

Then double-click the **PictureBox** tool. That puts a box in Form1's middle, near Form1's top-left corner.

Enlarge that box (by dragging its bottom-right corner), to let it hold a big picture better. If you want the box to be smaller than Form1 (so Form1 can hold other objects also), drag the box where you wish (by pointing at the box's middle, the dragging).

Click the box's right-arrow (which is near the box's top-right corner) **then "Choose Image" then the bottom "Import" button then "Pictures"** (which is on the left). That shows what's in your hard disk's Pictures folder.

Double-click the picture you want (after clicking or double-clicking any folders it's buried in). For example, you can try double-clicking the "Sample Pictures" icon (which Windows has put in your Pictures folder) then "Penguins" (Windows 7's photo of a penguin trio) or "Annie in the Sink" (Windows Vista's photo of Annie the cat, sitting in a sink).

You see a bigger view of the picture (or its top-left corner). **Click "OK".**

Click the Size Mode box's down-arrow. You see this menu:

Normal
StretchImage
AutoSize
CenterImage
Zoom

If the picture is bigger than the box, here's what those choices mean.

Zoom is the safest choice: it shrinks the picture nicely, so it fits in the box's center.
StretchImage fills the whole box by shrinking (or stretching) the picture, which gets distorted.
CenterImage puts just the picture's center into the box.
Normal puts just the picture's top-left corner into the box.
AutoSize stretches the box, to hold as much of the picture as possible.

The computer assumes you want "Normal". If you prefer a different choice (such as "Zoom"), click it.

Should you dock? If you click "Dock in parent container", the box will expand to fill Form1. (If you regret that expansion, undo it by clicking "Undock in parent container".)

Add a form

Besides Form1, you can create extra forms, called Form2, Form3, Form4, etc. To create an extra form, click the **Add New Item** button (which is near the screen's top, under the words "Edit" and "View") then double-click the Windows Form icon.

For example, let's make a button (on Form1) so that when you click that button, Form2 suddenly appears and says "I love you". Here's how....

Start a new program (so you have a blank Form1).

Create Form2, by doing this:

> Click the Add New Item button (which is near the screen's top, under the word "Edit"). Double click the Windows Form icon.
>
> You see Form2. (It covers Form1). Make it say "I love you" (by typing "I love you" in the property list's Text box and pressing Enter).
>
> Make Form1 reappear (by clicking the "Form1.vb [Design]" tab). On Form1, create a button (by double-clicking the Button tool). Make it say "Click me" (by typing "Click me" in the property list's Text box and pressing Enter). Double-click that button and type this subroutine line:
> ```
>         Form2.Visible = True
> ```
> That means: when the button is clicked, make Form2 suddenly become visible.

When you run the program (by pressing F5), you see Form1, which contains a button saying "Click me". If you click that button, the computer displays Form2, which covers Form1 and says "I love you".

To stop running the program, close the Form2 window (by clicking its X button) then close the Form1 window (by clicking its X button).

Web browser

Here's how to make a form's middle show a Web page.

Create a blank form. (For a quick, fun experiment, you can use Form1, though in a practical program you'd use another form instead, such as Form2.) Make that blank form be maximized (by making its property list's WindowState line say "Maximized") or at least rather big (by making its property list's Size line have rather big numbers).

Double-click the **WebBrowser** tool. That makes the form's entire middle be devoted to the Web and be called WebBrowser1. In WebBrowser1's property list, click "**Url**" then type the Web address you want the form to show (such as "www.yahoo.com").

When you run the program (by pressing the F5 key), the form's middle will show that Web page (or as much of it as will fit in the form's middle, accompanies by scroll arrows).

Timer

To make the computer pause, use the **Timer** tool. Here are examples.

I love you!!!!!!!!!! Here's how to make the computer say "I love you", then pause, then add an exclamation point (so you see "I love you!"), then pause, then add another exclamation point (so you see "I love you!!"), then keep repeating that process, so you eventually see "I love you!!!!!!!!!!" and beyond!

Make Form1's Text begin as "I love you" by doing this:

> Click in Form1, so the screen's bottom right corner shows Form1's main property list. In that list, click "Text" then type "I love you", so the property list's Text line becomes this:
>
> Text   I love you
>
> When you finish typing, press the Enter key. That makes Form1's title (top) say "I love you".

The next step is to say "add an exclamation point after pausing". To deal with pausing, you must use the Timer tool. Here's how….

Look at the toolbox (which is at the screen's left side and shows the tools). Using the toolbox's scroll-down arrow, scroll down until you see a heading called "Components".

Left of that heading, you see a triangle. That triangle should be solid black. (If the triangle has a white middle instead, click the triangle to make it solid black.)

Under the heading "Components", you should see the **Timer** tool. Double-click it. That puts a Timer1 icon below Form1.

At the screen's bottom-right corner, you see Timer1's property list, which looks like this:

Property	Value
(ApplicationSettings)	
(Name)	Timer1
Enabled	False
GenerateMember	True
Interval	100
Modifiers	Friend
Tag	

In that property list, click "**Interval**" then type 2000, so the Interval line becomes this:

Interval	2000

That makes each pause be **2000 milliseconds** (which is 2000 "thousands of a second", which is 2 seconds).

In that property list, click "**Enabled**" then press the T key, so the Enabled line becomes this:

Enabled	True

That turns the timer on, so it works.

Double-click the Timer1 icon, so you can write Timer1's subroutine. Type this line in Timer1's subroutine:

```
        Text &= "!"
```

That makes the Text (of Form1) lengthen, by having an extra "!" added. Typing that line makes Timer1's subroutine become this:

```
    Private Sub Timer1_Tick…
        Text &= "!"
    End Sub
```

When you run the program (by pressing F5), the computer will show Form1 saying "I love you", then pause for the next clock tick (the interval between ticks being 2000 milliseconds), then do Timer1's subroutine (which turns "I love you" into I love you!"), then pause for the next clock tick, then do again Timer1's subroutine (which turns "I love you!" into "I love you!!"), then pause for the next clock tick, then do again Timer1's subroutine (which turns "I love you!!" into "I love you!!!"), then keep repeating that process, so you eventually see "I love you!!!!!!!!!!" and beyond. When the exclamation points become too numerous to fit in Form1's title area, the computer changes the extra exclamation points to "…". The program keeps running until you stop it (by clicking Form1's X button).

If you want the exclamation points to come faster, make the interval shorter, by making Timer1's Interval be *less* than 2000 milliseconds. For example, try making the Interval be 1000 milliseconds (which is 1 second), or 500 milliseconds (which is half a second), or 1 millisecond (which is almost instantaneous).

If you want the computer to add just one exclamation point and then relax (without adding further exclamation points), make Timer1's subroutine become this:

```
    Private Sub Timer1_Tick…
        Text &= "!"
        Timer1.Enabled = False
    End Sub
```

That subroutine says: when the clock ticks, add an exclamation point to the text but then **disable the timer**, so no further exclamation points will be added.

To play a joke on a human, make Timer1's Interval be 3000 (so the computer will pause 3 seconds before giving the joke's punch line) and make Timer1's subroutine become this:

```
    Private Sub Timer1_Tick…
        Text &= "r mother!"
        Timer1.Enabled = False
    End Sub
```

That subroutine says: when the clock ticks (after 3 seconds), make the Text change from "I love you" to "I love your mother!" then disable the timer (because the joke's timing is done).

Try making Timer1's subroutine become this instead:

```
Private Sub Timer1_Tick…
    Text &= "I'm happy when you're gone"
End Sub
```

That subroutine says: when the clock ticks (after 3 seconds), make the Text change from "I love you" to "I'm happy when you're gone".

Count the seconds Here's how to make Form1 count how many seconds have elapsed, so Form1 begins by saying 0, then a second later says 1, then a second later says 2, etc.

Make Form1's Text begin at 0 by doing this:

> Click in Form1, so the screen's bottom right corner shows Form1's main property list. In that list, click "Text", then type number 0 and press Enter.

In the toolbox (which at the screen's left side and shows the tools), find the Timer tool (by scrolling down to "Components", clicking any + sign left of "Components", then scrolling down further). Double-click that Timer tool. That puts a Timer1 icon below Form1.

In Timer1's property list (which is at the screen's bottom-right corner), click "Interval" then type 1000, so you see this line:

```
Interval            1000
```

Click "Enabled" then press the T key, so the Enabled line becomes this:

```
Enabled             True
```

Double-click the Timer1 icon. Type this subroutine for Timer1:

```
Text += 1
```

That increases the text's number, by adding 1 to it.

When you run the program (by pressing F5), Form1's Text begins as 0 but increases to 1, then 2, then 3, etc.

Tell the date and time Here's how to make Form1 act as a clock, so it tells you the date and time and updates itself every second!

Create a Timer1 icon (by double-clicking the Timer tool, which is in the toolbox under "Components"). In Timer1's property list (which is at the screen's bottom-right corner), make the "Interval" be 1000 and make "Enabled" be True.

Double-click the Timer1 icon. Type this subroutine for Timer1:

```
Text = My.Computer.Clock.LocalTime
```

That makes the text become a message such as this:

```
12/31/2009 11:59:30 PM
```

You'll see such a message when you run the program (by pressing F5). Since you set the Interval to 1000 milliseconds (which is 1 second), that text will correct itself every second.

Switch to blue Here's how to make Form1 begin as red but then, after a pause, become blue.

Make Form1 begin as red by doing this:

> Click in Form1, so the screen's bottom right corner shows Form1's main property list. In that list, click "BackColor" (which you'll see after you scroll up) then BackColor's down-arrow then "Web" then "Red" (which you'll see after you scroll down).

Create a Timer1 icon (by double-clicking the Timer tool, which is in the toolbox under "Components"). In Timer1's property list (which is at the screen's bottom-right corner), make the "Interval" be 2000 and make "Enabled" be True.

Double-click the Timer1 icon. Type this subroutine for Timer1:

```
BackColor = Color.Blue
```

When you run the program (by pressing F5), Form1 begins as red but switches to blue (after a delay of 2000 milliseconds, which is 2 seconds).

Let's make the subroutine fancier, so Form1 keeps alternating between red and blue. We'll make Form1 start as red, then switch to blue, then switch back to red, then switch back to blue, then switch back to red, etc., forever. To do that, change the subroutine line to this:

```
BackColor = IIf(BackColor = Color.Red, Color.Blue, Color.Red)
```

It says the BackColor becomes this: if the BackColor was Red, then it becomes Blue, else it becomes Red.

Color dialog

Here's how to let the human pick a color for Form1.

Look at the toolbox (which is at the screen's left side and shows the tools). Using the toolbox's scroll-down arrow, scroll down until you see a heading called "Dialogs".

Left of that heading, you see a square. That square should contain a minus sign. (If it contains a plus sign instead, change the plus sign to a minus sign by clicking it.)

Under the heading "Dialogs", you should see the **ColorDialog** tool. Double-click it. That puts a **ColorDialog1** icon below Form1 and lets Form1's subroutine mention "ColorDialog1".

Double-click Form1. Write this Form1 subroutine:

```
ColorDialog1.ShowDialog()
BackColor = ColorDialog1.Color
```

When you run the program (by pressing F5), the subroutine's top line makes the computer **show** the human the **color dialog box**, which contains 48 colors (plus a feature to let the human invent custom colors). When the human clicks one of the 48 colors (or a custom color) and then clicks "OK", the subroutine's bottom line makes Form1's background color become the color the human chose.

While viewing the color dialog box, here's how the human can create a custom color:

> Click "Define Custom Colors".
>
> At the color dialog box's right edge, you see a triangle pointing toward the left. Drag that triangle up, until it's halfway up the bar it points to.
>
> You see a big, colorful square. Click your favorite color in that square.
>
> Below that square, you see a box marked "Color/Solid"; that shows the color you've chosen. Adjust that color, by dragging the triangle up (which makes the color lighter) or dragging the triangle down (which makes the color darker) or clicking a different spot in the big, colorful square.
>
> When you're satisfied, click "Add to Custom Colors". That creates a small square for the color. Click that square then "OK".

Helpful hints

Here are some hints to help you master programming.

Stop debugging

While your program is running, you can interrupt it by clicking the **Stop Debugging** button (which is a square at the screen's top center, to the right of the Start Debugging triangle).

> While the program is running,
> the screen's top line says "(Running)",
> and the **Stop Debugging** square is blue (so you can click it).
> The Start Debugging triangle is deactivated (gray).
>
> While the program is *not* running,
> the screen's top line does *not* say "(Running)",
> and the **Start Debugging** triangle is green (so you can click it).
> The Stop Debugging square is deactivated (gray).

The computer refuses to let you edit a program that's in the middle of running. If you try to edit a program but the computer ignores your editing, that's because your program is still in the middle of running. Stop the program from running (by clicking the Stop Debugging square, which is blue), then try again to edit your program.

Avoiding Dim

If x is a variable, you're supposed to warn the computer by saying:

```
Dim x
```

If you're too lazy to say "Dim" for each variable, say **Option Explicit Off** at your program's top, so your program looks like this:

```
Option Explicit Off
Public Class Form1

    Private Sub Form1_Load…

    End Sub
End Class
```

To type "Option Explicit Off" up there, do this:

> While holding down the Ctrl key, tap the Home key.
> Press the Enter key.
> Press the up-arrow key.
> Type "Option Explicit Off".

The "Option Explicit Off" prevents the computer from griping about missing Dim lines. It makes your program's variables work even if you don't say "Dim". But it also prevents the computer from warning you about using variables in ridiculous ways. Say "Option Explicit Off" just if you're too lazy to say "Dim" — and you're sure you're not making ridiculous mistakes about variables.

Apostrophe

In your subroutine, you can **type comments to help programmers understand your program**. The comments can mention your name, the date you wrote the program, the program's purpose, the purpose of each variable, special tricks you used, cynical comments, and any other comments you'd like to share with your programming buddies and to remind yourself of how you've been thinking.

To type such a comment in your subroutine, **begin the comment with an apostrophe**, like this:

```
'This subroutine is another dumb example by Russ.
'It was written on Halloween, under a full moon.
c = 40 'because Russ has 40 computers
h = 23 'because 23 of his computers are haunted
Text = c - h 'That many computers are unhaunted.
```

When you run the program, **the computer ignores everything that's to the right of an apostrophe**. So the computer ignores lines 1 and 2; in lines 3 & 4, the computer ignores the "because…"; in the bottom line, the computer ignores the comment about being unhaunted. Since c is 40, and h is 23, the bottom line makes the computer say:

```
17
```

Everything to the right of an apostrophe is called a **comment** (or **remark**).

Turning green When you type the subroutine, **the computer makes each apostrophe and comment turn green**. Then the computer ignores what's green.

Temporarily ignore Suppose you've written a subroutine but wonder what would happen if one of the lines were deleted. To find out, you could delete the line (by pressing the Delete key repeatedly or using other techniques), then run the shortened program, then put the line back in (by retyping it). But here's a faster way to do that experiment:

> To temporarily make the computer ignore the line, type an apostrophe in front of that line. The apostrophe turns that line into a comment, so the computer ignores the line. Later, when you want to reactivate that line, just delete the apostrophe.

Temporarily deactivating a line (by putting an apostrophe before it so it becomes a comment) is called **commenting out** the line.

Multiple lines To make *several* lines become comments, you can type an apostrophe in front of each of those lines; but here's a faster way: drag across those lines (by using your mouse), then click the **Comment-out button** (which is near the screen's top, under "Tools", and shows two green lines between black lines).

That makes the computer type an apostrophe in front of each of those lines and makes the lines turn green.

Later, when you want to reactivate those lines, drag across them again then click the **Uncomment button** (which is to the right of the Comment-out button): that removes the apostrophes and makes the lines turn black again.

Places for output

You can make the computer show answers in many places. Let's review the places you saw previously, then explore places that are more exotic.

Top of Form1

You learned that if Form1's subroutine says —

```
Text = 5 + 2
```

the computer writes the answer, 7, at the **top of Form1**, where Form1's **title** belongs.

Unfortunately, the top of Form1 doesn't have much space: the answer must be narrow (unless you widened Form1) and the answer must not consume 2 lines.

Pop-up window

If the subroutine says —

```
MsgBox(5 + 2)
```

the computer writes the answer in a **pop-up window** that appears suddenly.

If the answer is long, the pop-up window expands automatically, vertically and horizontally, to hold the answer. (To create a 2-line answer, say this where you want the computer to press the Enter key: & Chr(13) &.)

Afterwards, the computer waits for the human to click "OK".

Middle of Form1

If you've created a label (by double-click the Label tool) and your subroutine says —

```
Label1.Text = 5 + 2
```

the computer writes the answer in the middle of Form1, where Label1 is.

If the answer is long, the Label1 area expands automatically, vertically and horizontally, to hold the answer, up to the size of Form1. (To create a 2-line answer, say this where you want the computer to press the Enter key: & Chr(13) &.)

Immediate window

If the subroutine says —

```
Debug.Print(5 + 2)
```

the computer writes the answer in the **immediate window**, which should appear suddenly at your screen's bottom.

If you don't see the immediate window yet, make it appear by clicking Debug then Windows then Immediate (or by clicking the phrase "Immediate Window", which might appear at your screen's bottom).

That window also shows any previous chitchat:

Above the current answer, you see any previous answers. You might also see previous error messages. (To create a 2-line answer, give 2 Debug.Print commands.)

After you admire the immediate window, look at Form1.

If you don't see Form1, make it reappear by clicking **Form1's button**, which is at the screen's bottom edge, on the taskbar that runs from the Start button to the clock. That button says either "Form1" or Form1's text.

Then end the program (by clicking Form1's close button).

Immediate without subroutine You can use the immediate window without writing a subroutine! Here's how.

Make the immediate window appear (by clicking Debug then Windows then Immediate).

Click in that window and type a line such as —

```
Debug.Print(5 + 2)
```

or, more briefly:

```
?5+2
```

When you finish typing that line (and press the Enter key), the computer will immediately write the answer, 7, in that same window, below your question.

Output window

If the subroutine says —

```
Console.WriteLine(5 + 2)
```

the computer writes the answer in the **output window**, which should appear suddenly at your screen's bottom.

If you don't see the output window yet, make it appear by clicking Debug then Windows then Output.

That window also shows any previous output from this run.

Above the current answer, you see any previous answers from this run. Answers from previous programs and runs are suppressed. (To create a 2-line answer, give 2 Console.WriteLine commands. At the end of each answer, the computer presses the Enter key, unless you say Write instead of WriteLine.)

After you admire the output window, look at Form1.

If you don't see Form1, make it reappear by clicking **Form1's button**, which is at the screen's bottom edge, on the taskbar that runs from the Start button to the clock. That button says either "Form1" or the Form1's text.

Then end the program (by clicking Form1's close button).

Console screen

To create a new program normally, you click "New Project" then double-click "Windows Forms Application".

Instead of double-clicking "Windows Forms Application", try double-clicking "**Console Application**". That tells the computer you want a stripped-down version of Visual Basic, where the computer writes answers on a **console screen** (which looks like DOS instead of Windows and has no forms or buttons or icons).

When you've double-clicked the Console Application icon, you immediately see this stripped-down subroutine:

```
Module Module1

    Sub Main()

    End Sub

End Module
```

Click in the middle of that subroutine and say "Console.WriteLine(5 + 2)", so the subroutine becomes this:

```
Module Module1

    Sub Main()
        Console.WriteLine(5 + 2)
    End Sub

End Module
```

Just above the "End Sub", say "Do" and "Loop", like this:

```
Module Module1

    Sub Main()
        Console.WriteLine(5 + 2)
        Do

        Loop
    End Sub

End Module
```

When you type the "Do" (and press Enter), the computer automatically types the "Loop" for you.

When you run the program (by pressing F5), the computer writes the answer on a **console screen**, which is a window whose middle looks like DOS. (To create a 2-line answer, give 2 Console.WriteLine commands. At the end of each answer, the computer presses the Enter key, unless you say **Write** instead of **WriteLine**.) Your subroutine's "Do" and "Loop" make the computer pause, so you have time to read the answer.

After you've read the answer, close the console screen (by clicking its X button).

Avoiding Do In the subroutine, instead of typing "Do" (and waiting for the computer to type "Loop"), you can type "Console.ReadKey()", so the program looks like this:

```
Module Module1

    Sub Main()
        Console.WriteLine(5 + 2)
        Console.ReadKey()
    End Sub

End Module
```

The "Console.ReadKey()" makes the computer wait for the human to press a key. When the human presses any key (such as Enter), the computer ends the program and closes the console screen.

Print form

Here's how to let the human print Form1 onto paper.

Double-click the **PrintForm** tool, which is in the Visual Basic PowerPacks category (whose tools you can see by clicking the triangle left of "Visual Basic PowerPacks" once or twice). That puts a PrintForm1 icon below Form1 and lets subroutines mention "PrintForm1".

On Form1, create a button (by double-clicking the Button tool). Make the button's text say "Print" (by clicking "Text" then typing "Print"). Double-click the button, so you can write the button's subroutine. Make the button's subroutine say:

```
PrintForm1.Print()
```

When the human runs the program and clicks the Print button, the computer will print most of Form1 onto paper.

The computer doesn't bother printing Form1's border or Text (title). It prints just Form1's middle, including the objects in it.

Hard disk

If Form1's subroutine says —

```
My.Computer.FileSystem.WriteAllText("Joan.txt", 5 + 2, False)
```

the computer writes the number 7 (the answer to 5+2) onto your hard disk, in a file called Joan.txt. Unfortunately, that file is hard to access, since it's buried in folders. (Specifically, it's in the Debug folder, which is in the bin folder, which is in your program's inner folder, which in your program's outer folder, which is in the Projects folder, which is in the Visual Studio 2010 folder, which is in the Documents folder.)

If you don't like the name Joan, invent a different name instead.

ProgramData folder This line is more practical:

```
My.Computer.FileSystem.WriteAllText("\ProgramData\Joan.txt", 5 + 2, False)
```

It makes the computer write the number 7 (the answer to 5 + 2) onto your hard disk, in a file called Joan.txt, which is in the **ProgramData folder**.

After you've run the program (by pressing F5), you can see Joan.txt by doing this:

Click the Start button then "Computer". In the right-hand windowpane, double-click "C:" then "ProgramData" then "Joan", whose hidden .txt ending makes the computer run the Notepad program, which shows you what's in Joan.txt. You see that Joan.txt contains the answer, 7. When you finish admiring the answer, close the front 2 windows (by clicking their X buttons).

Documents folder If you want Joan.txt to be in the **Documents folder** instead of the ProgramData folder, type these lines instead:

```
Dim doc
doc = My.Computer.FileSystem.SpecialDirectories.MyDocuments
My.Computer.FileSystem.WriteAllText(doc & "\Joan.txt", 5 + 2, False)
```

The top two lines makes the variable doc stand for the Documents folder. In the bottom line, the doc makes Joan.txt be in the Documents folder.

After you've run the program (by pressing F5), you can see Joan.txt by doing this:

Click the Start button then "Documents". Double-click "Joan", whose hidden .txt ending makes the computer run the Notepad program, which shows you what's in Joan.txt. You see that Joan.txt contains the answer, 7. When you finish admiring the answer, close the front 2 windows (by clicking their X buttons).

Append If Joan.txt exists before you run the subroutine, the subroutine erases that old Joan.txt to create a Joan.txt — unless you change the bottom line's "False" to "True", which makes the subroutine **append** the new answer to the end of the old Joan.txt, to make Joan.txt become longer and include *both* answers. In the bottom line, "True" means "append to the old file"; "False" means "*don't append* to the old file; *erase* the old file."

Reading Joan.txt After the computer has put an answer into Joan.txt, you can run a **reading program** that reads Joan.txt.

If Joan.txt is in the ProgramData folder, the reading program can have Form1's subroutine say:

```
Text = My.Computer.FileSystem.ReadAllText("\ProgramData\Joan.txt")
```

That line makes the computer read Joan.txt and tell you what answer Joan.txt contains.

If Joan.txt is in the Documents folder, the reading program can have Form1's subroutine say:

```
Dim doc
doc = My.Computer.FileSystem.SpecialDirectories.MyDocuments
Text = My.Computer.FileSystem.ReadAllText(doc & "\Joan.txt")
```

Those lines make doc be the Documents folder and make Text be the answer that the computer reads from doc's Joan.txt.

Rich-text box Try this experiment....

Create a new program. On Form1, put a rich-text box (so the human can type a document into the box) and put a Save button (a button whose title is "Save").

To make the Save button work properly (so pressing it copies the human's typing from the box to the hard disk), make the button's subroutine be this:

```
Dim doc
doc = My.Computer.FileSystem.SpecialDirectories.My Documents
RichTextBox1.SaveFile(doc & "\Joan.doc")
```

The bottom line means: take what's in the rich-text box and save it as a file; put the file into the Documents folder and call it Joan.doc.

When the human runs that program, the computer will let the human type a document (essay) into the rich-text box. Then computer will wait for the human to click the Save button (which makes the computer copy the document to the hard disk's Documents folder, in a rich-text file called Joan.doc).

You can see Joan.doc by doing this:

> Click the Start button then "Documents". Double-click "Joan", whose hidden .doc ending makes the computer run the Microsoft Word (or WordPad) program, which shows you what's in Joan.doc. You see that Joan.doc contains the essay. When you finish admiring the essay, close the front 2 windows (by clicking their X buttons).

"Save As" dialog box That subroutine forces the document to be in the Documents folder and be called "Joan.doc". Here's how to make the subroutine more flexible, (so the human can choose what folder to put the document in and what name to give the document....

Double-click the **SaveFileDialog** tool (which is in the Dialogs category). That creates a **SaveFileDialog1** icon below Form1.

In the SaveFileDialog1's property list, click "DefaultExt" and type "doc". That will secretly put ".doc" at the end of every filename.

Make the Save button's subroutine be this:

```
SaveFileDialog1.ShowDialog()
RichTextBox1.SaveFile(SaveFileDialog1.FileName)
```

When the human clicks the Save button, the subroutine's top line makes the computer show the "Save As" dialog box, which lets the human invent a file name and choose a folder to put it in. For example, if the human types "Joe" (and then presses the Enter key), the file will be called "Joe.doc" (because the SaveFileDialog1's property list said the default extension is "doc").

The subroutine's bottom line means: look at the document that was typed in RichTextBox1, and save it as a file on the hard disk, using the file name (and folder) that the human specified in the "Save As" dialog box.

Say "document" Since RichTextBox1's main purpose is to handle a document, programmers prefer to say just "document" instead of "RichTextBox1" and write the Save button's program this way:

```
SaveFileDialog1.ShowDialog()
document.SaveFile(SaveFileDialog1.FileName)
```

To do that, you must change the box's name from "RichTextBox1" to "document". Here's how:

> In RichTextBox1's property list (which is at the screen's bottom-right corner), click "(Name)" then type the word "document", so the line looks like this:
> (Name)   document

Reading Joan.doc After the computer has saved (copied) a document into your hard disk's Joan.doc, you can run a **reading program** that reads Joan.doc.

The reading program should have a rich text box named "document". It should also have an "Open" button whose subroutine says:

```
OpenFileDialog1.ShowDialog()
document.LoadFile(OpenFileDialog1.FileName)
```

But to make the computer understand what "OpenFileDialog1" means, you must double-click the **OpenFileDialog** tool before typing that subroutine.

Menu

You can create a menu.

Menu bar

At the top of Form1, let's create this **menu bar**:

> Love   Hate

Let's program the computer so clicking "Love" makes the computer say "I love you", and clicking "Hate" makes the computer say "I hate being a computer".

Here's how to accomplish all that....

Double-click the **MenuStrip** tool (which is in the "Menus & Toolbars" category).

Click "Type Here" (which is near Form1's top). Then you see a blank box (plus two "Type Here" boxes). In the blank box, type your menu's first word ("Love").

Click the box that's to the right of "Love". Type your menu's second word ("Hate").

Congratulations! You created a menu!

Create menu subroutines Double-click "Love", then write this subroutine telling the computer what to do if "Love" is clicked:

```
Private Sub LoveToolStripMenuItem_Click…
    Text = "I love you"
End Sub
```

(The computer already typed the top and bottom lines for you, so type just the middle line.) When you finish typing that line, click the "Form1.vb [Design]" tab.

Double-click "Hate", then write this subroutine about clicking "Hate":

```
Private Sub HateToolStripMenuItem_Click…
    Text = "I hate being a computer"
End Sub
```

Run the program Go ahead: run the program (by pressing the F5 key). You see the menu bar you created:

> Love   Hate

Clicking "Love" makes the computer say "I love you"; clicking "Hate" makes the computer say "I hate being a computer".

Pull-down menu

Let's expand the menu by adding "Color", so the menu becomes this:

```
Love   Hate   Color
```

Let's program the computer so clicking "Color" makes this **pull-down menu** appear under Color:

```
Yellow
Red
```

Let's program so clicking one of those colors makes Form1's background be that color.

Here's how to accomplish all that....

Create a new menu item If your program is still running, stop it (by clicking its X button). Look at Form1's design (by clicking the "Form1.vb [Design]" tab). Click the "Type Here" that's to the right of "Hate". In the blank box that appears, type your menu's third word ("Color").

Create a pull-down menu To create Color's pull-down menu (saying "Yellow" and "Red"), click the "Type Here" that's under "Color". In the blank box that appears, type "Yellow". In the box under "Yellow", type "Red".

Congratulations! You created a pull-down menu!

Create menu subroutines Double-click "Yellow", then write this subroutine about Yellow:

```
Private Sub YellowToolStripMenuItem_Click…
    BackColor = Color.Yellow
End Sub
```

Click the "Form1.vb [Design]" tab, then double-click "Red", then write this subroutine about Red:

```
Private Sub RedToolStripMenuItem_Click…
    BackColor = Color.Red
End Sub
```

Run the program Go ahead: run the program (by pressing the F5 key). You see the menu bar you created:

```
Love   Hate   Color
```

Clicking "Color" makes the computer show Color's pull-down menu; clicking the "Yellow" or "Red" makes Form1's background turn that color.

Submenu

Let's expand Color's pull-down menu by adding "Blue", so the menu becomes this:

```
Yellow
Red
Blue
```

Let's program the computer so clicking "Blue" makes this **submenu** appear to the right of Blue:

```
Light Blue
Dark Blue
```

Let's program so clicking one of those kinds of blue makes Form1's background be that color.

Here's how to accomplish all that....

Create a new menu item If your program is still running, stop it (by clicking its X button). Look at Form1's design (by clicking the "Form1.vb [Design]" tab). Click "Color" then the "Type Here" that's under "Red". In the blank box that appears, type pull-down menu's third word ("Blue").

Create a submenu To create Blue's submenu (saying "Light Blue" and "Dark Blue"), click the "Type Here" that's to the right of "Blue". In the blank box that appears, type "Light Blue". In the box under "Light Blue", type "Dark Blue".

Congratulations! You created a submenu!

Creating a submenu for Blue made a right-arrow appear next to "Blue", so Color's pull-down menu looks like this:

```
Yellow
Red
Blue      ▸
```

That right-arrow means "has a submenu".

Create subroutines Double-click "Light Blue", then write this subroutine about Light Blue:

```
Private Sub LightBlueToolStripMenuItem_Click…
    BackColor = Color.LightBlue
End Sub
```

Click the "Form1.vb [Design]" tab, then double-click "Dark Blue", then write this subroutine about Dark Blue:

```
Private Sub DarkBlueToolStripMenuItem_Click…
    BackColor = Color.DarkBlue
End Sub
```

Run the program Go ahead: run the program (by pressing the F5 key). You see the menu bar you created:

```
Love   Hate   Color
```

Clicking "Color" makes the computer show Color's pull-down menu; clicking "Blue" makes the computer show Blue's submenu; then clicking "Light Blue" or "Dark Blue" makes Form1's background turn that color.

Rearranging menu items

After you've created a menu, you can rearrange its items. Here's how....

If your program is still running, stop it (by clicking its X button). Look at Form1's design (by clicking the "Form1.vb [Design]" tab).

To delete an item, click it then press the **Delete key**. If you change your mind, click the **Undo button** (which shows a blue arrow bending toward the left).

To move an item that's on the menu bar ("Love", "Hate", or "Color"), **drag** that item across to where you want it — and, to make sure the computer doesn't ignore you, drag slightly farther. To move an item that's on a pull-down menu ("Yellow", "Red", or "Blue") or submenu ("Light Blue" or "Dark Blue"), drag the item up or down to where you want it — and to make sure the computer doesn't ignore you, drag slightly farther.

Minimalist word processor

Here's how to invent a minimalist word-processing program.

Big Form1

Create a new program. Widen Form 1 (by dragging its bottom-right corner toward the right).

Tool strip

Onto Form 1, put a **tool strip (toolbar)** by doing this:

Double-click the **ToolStrip** tool (which is in the "Menus & Toolbars" category). That puts a ToolStrip1 icon below Form 1. Right-click that icon then click "Insert Standard Items". That makes these 7 icons appear across Form 1's top: New, Open, Save, Print, Cut, Copy, Paste, and Help. Each icon will act as a button.

Rich text box

Onto Form1, put a rich text box (by double-clicking the **RichTextBox** tool). Give that box the desired properties by doing this:

Click the box's right-arrow (which is near the box's top-right corner) then "Dock in parent container". That makes the box expand to fill the rest of Form1: the only things above the box are the tool strip and the title bar (which says Form1).

In the box's property list (which is at the screen's bottom-right corner), scroll up until you see "EnableAutoDragDrop", then click "EnableAutoDragDrop" and press the T key, so the line becomes this:
EnableAutoDragDrop   True

Scroll up farther until you see "(Name)", then click "(Name)" and type "document", so the line becomes this:
(Name)   document

More tools

Double-click these tools, which you'll need to finish the program:

OpenFileDialog (which is in the "Dialogs" category)
SaveFileDialog (which is in the "Dialogs" category)
PrintForm   (which is in the "Visual Basic PowerPacks" category)

Then icons for those tools appear below Form1.

Subroutines

For each button on the tool strip, write a subroutine. Here's how....

Double-click the tool strip's first button (the **New button**, which looks like a blank sheet of paper with a folded corner). Type this line (for the New button's subroutine):

```
document.Clear()
```

Make Form1 appear again (by clicking the "Form1.vb [Design]" tab). Double-click the tool strip's next button (the **Open button**, which looks like a yellow manila folder that's opening). Type these lines (for the Open button's subroutine):

```
OpenFileDialog1.ShowDialog()
document.LoadFile(OpenFileDialog1.FileName)
```

Make Form1 appear again (by clicking the "Form1vb [Design]" tab). In similar fashion, type these lines for the Save button:

```
SaveFileDialog1.ShowDialog()
document.SaveFile(SaveFileDialog1.FileName)
```

Type this line for the Print button:

```
PrintForm1.Print()
```

Type this line for the Cut button:

```
document.Cut()
```

Type this line for the Copy button:

```
document.Copy()
```

Type this line for the Paste button:

```
document.Paste()
```

Type this line for the Help button:

```
MsgBox("This is word processor version 1")
```

Run

When you run the program (by pressing F5), the program works correctly, if you did what I said!

Congratulations on creating a word-processing program.

The program's main limitations are:

It doesn't let you change margins (except by dragging Form1's bottom-right corner).

It doesn't let you change fonts.

Its Print button prints just *part* of the document. (It prints just the part that's visible on Form1 at the moment, and it can't print any part that's too far to the right to fit on the paper.)

Surpassing those limitations would require subroutines that are much longer!

Loops

Here's how to make the computer repeat.

Do...Loop

The computer can be religious. Just make Form1's subroutine say this:

```
MsgBox("I worship your feet")
MsgBox("But please wash them")
```

When you run the program, the computer shows a message box saying "I worship your feet" and waits for the human to click OK. Then the computer shows a message box saying "But please wash them" (and waits for the human to click OK again).

To make the computer do the lines many times, say "Do" above the lines and say "Loop" below them, so the subroutine looks like this:

```
Do
    MsgBox("I worship your feet")
    MsgBox("But please wash them")
Loop
```

The lines being repeated (the MsgBox lines) should be between the words Do and Loop and indented. (After you've typed the word "Do" and pressed Enter, the computer will automatically type the word "Loop" and created an indented blank space for you to type in.)

Run the program (by pressing the F5 key). The computer says "I worship your feet" (and waits for the human to click OK), then says "But please wash them" (and waits for OK), then goes back and says "I worship your feet" again (and waits for OK), then says "But please wash them" again (and waits for OK), then goes back and says the same stuff again, and again, and again, and again, forever.

Since the computer's thinking keeps circling back to the same lines, the computer is said to be in a **loop**. In that subroutine, the **Do** means "do what's underneath and indented"; the **Loop** means "loop back and do it again". The lines that say Do and Loop — and the lines between them — form a loop, which is called a **Do loop**.

The computer does that loop repeatedly, forever — or until you **abort the program by doing this:**

```
Click the Stop Debugging button (a blue square near the screen's top center).
```

That works just if you're in the Visual Basic environment (so you see the Stop Debugging button). If you're *not* in the Visual Basic environment (because you're running the .exe file directly), the only way to abort a looping program is to shut down the computer (click the Start button then, in Windows 7, click Shutdown) or try this:

```
While holding down the Ctrl and Alt keys, tap the Delete key. Click "Start Task Manager" then the "Applications" tab (which is at the screen's top-left corner) then your program's name then "End Task". If you're lucky, that aborts the program. Close the Windows Task Manager window (by clicking its X button).
```

In that program, since the computer tries to go round and round the loop forever, the loop is called **infinite**. The only way to stop an infinite loop is to abort it.

Disappearing-message-box bug

When running a loop, the computer might accidentally **lose the program's focus** and forget to show the message box. To make the message box reappear, click the message box's button, which is on the **taskbar**. (The **taskbar** is at the screen's

bottom and runs from the Start button to the clock.) Try double-clicking the message box's button. To run the program again, try clicking the green right-arrow (instead of pressing the F5 key).

GoTo

Instead of typing —

```
Do
    MsgBox("I worship your feet")
    MsgBox("But please wash them")
Loop
```

you can type:

```
joe:    MsgBox("I worship your feet")
        MsgBox("But please wash them")
        GoTo joe
```

(When you type that subroutine, the computer automatically spaces it correctly: when you press Enter at the top line's end, the computer automatically unindents "joe:".) The top line (named joe) makes the computer say "I worship your feet". The next line makes the computer say "But please wash them". The bottom line makes the computer Go back To the line named joe, so the computer forms a loop. The computer will loop forever — or until you abort the program (by clicking the Stop Debugging button, twice).

You can give a line a short name (such as joe) or a long name (such as BeginningOfMyFavoriteLoop). The name can even be a number (such as 10). Put the name at the line's beginning. After the name, put a colon (the symbol ":").

The line's name (such as joe or BeginningOfMyFavoriteLoop or 10) is called the line's **label**.

Skip ahead This subroutine is insulting:

```
MsgBox("Your face is outstanding.")
MsgBox("It belongs in a horror movie.")
MsgBox("It deserves an award!")
```

Let's turn that insult into a compliment. To do that, insert the shaded items:

```
MsgBox("Your face is outstanding.")
GoTo conclusion
MsgBox("It belongs in a horror movie.")
conclusion: MsgBox("It deserves an award!")
```

The computer begins by saying "Your face is outstanding." Then the computer does GoTo conclusion, which makes the computer Go skip down To the conclusion line, which says "It deserves an award!" So the subroutine makes the computer say just —

```
Your face is outstanding.
```

and:

```
It deserves an award!
```

Is GoTo too powerful? Saying GoTo gives you great power: if you make the computer GoTo an earlier line, you'll create a loop; if you make the computer GoTo a later line, the computer will skip over several lines of your subroutine.

Since saying GoTo is so powerful, programmers are afraid to say it. Programmers know that the slightest error in saying GoTo will make a program act very bizarre! Programmers feel more comfortable using milder words instead (such as Do...Loop), which are safer and rarely get botched up. Since saying GoTo is scary, many computer teachers prohibit students from using it, and many companies fire programmers who say GoTo instead of Do...Loop.

But saying GoTo is fine when you've learned how to control the power! Though I usually say Do...Loop instead of GoTo, I say GoTo in certain situations where saying Do...Loop would be awkward.

Exiting a Do loop

Let's create a guessing game, where the human tries to guess the computer's favorite color, which is pink. To do that, say **GoTo** or **Exit Do** or **Loop Until**. Here's how....

GoTo Just make Form1's subroutine say this:

```
        Dim guess
AskTheHuman: guess = InputBox("What's my favorite color?")
        If guess = "pink" Then
            MsgBox("Congratulations! You discovered my favorite color.")
        Else
            MsgBox("No, that's not my favorite color. Try again!")
            GoTo AskTheHuman
        End If
```

The top line (which is called AskTheHuman) asks the human to guess the computer's favorite color.

If the guess is "pink", the computer says:

> Congratulations! You discovered my favorite color.

But if the guess is *not* pink, the computer will instead say "No, that's not my favorite color" and then Go back To AskTheHuman again to guess the computer's favorite color.

Exit Do Here's how to write that subroutine without saying GoTo:

```
        Dim guess
        Do
            guess = InputBox("What's my favorite color?")
            If guess = "pink" Then Exit Do
            MsgBox("No, that's not my favorite color. Try again!")
        Loop
        MsgBox("Congratulations! You discovered my favorite color.")
```

The Do loop makes the computer do this repeatedly: ask "What's my favorite color?" and then say "No, that's not my favorite color."

The only way to stop the loop nicely (without abortion) is to guess "pink", which makes the computer Exit from the Do loop; then the computer proceeds to the line underneath the Do loop. That line makes the computer say:

> Congratulations! You discovered my favorite color.

Loop Until Here's another way to program the guessing game:

```
        Dim guess
        Do
            MsgBox("You haven't guessed my favorite color yet!")
            guess = InputBox("What's my favorite color?")
        Loop Until guess = "pink"
        MsgBox("Congratulations! You discovered my favorite color.")
```

The Do loop makes the computer do this repeatedly: say "You haven't guessed my favorite color yet!" and then ask "What's my favorite color?"

The Loop line makes the computer repeat the indented lines again and again, until the guess is "pink". When the guess is "pink", the computer proceeds to the line underneath the Loop and prints "Congratulations!"

The Loop Until's condition (guess = "pink") is called the **loop's goal**. The computer does the loop repeatedly, until the loop's goal is achieved. Here's how:

> The computer does the indented lines, then checks whether the goal is achieved yet. If the goal is *not* achieved yet, the computer does the indented lines again, then checks again whether the goal is achieved. The computer does the loop again and again, until the goal is achieved. Then the computer, proud at achieving the goal, does the program's **finale**, which consists of any lines under the Loop Until line.

Saying —

```
        Loop Until guess = "pink"
```

is just a briefer way of saying this pair of lines:

```
            If guess = "pink" Then Exit Do
        Loop
```

For...Next

Let's make the computer say these sentences:

> I like the number 1
> I like the number 2
> I like the number 3
> I like the number 4
> I like the number 5

To do that, put these lines into Form1's subroutine:

```
        For x = 1 To 5
            MsgBox("I like the number " & x)
        Next
```

The top line (For x = 1 To 5) says that x will be every number from 1 to 5; so x will be 1, then 2, then 3, then 4, then 5. The line underneath (which the computer indents) says what to do about each x: it says to create a message box saying "I like the number " and x.

Whenever a subroutine says the word For, it must also say Next; so the bottom line says Next. The computer types the word "Next" for you automatically.

The indented line, which is between the For line and the Next line, is the line that the computer will do repeatedly; so the computer will repeatedly say "I like the number " and an x. The first time, the x will be 1, so the computer will say:

> I like the number 1

The next time, the x will be 2, so the computer will say:

> I like the number 2

The computer will say similar sentences, for every number from 1 up to 5.

Monster song Let's make the computer say these lyrics:

```
I saw 2 monsters
Tra-la-la!
I saw 3 monsters
Tra-la-la!
I saw 4 monsters
Tra-la-la!
They all had a party: ha-ha-ha!
```

To do that, type these lines —

```
The first line of each verse:   MsgBox("I saw " & x & " monsters")
The second line of each verse: MsgBox("Tra-la-la!")
```

and make x be every number from 2 up to 4:

```
For x = 2 To 4
    MsgBox("I saw " & x & " monsters")
    MsgBox("Tra-la-la!")
Next
```

At the end of the song, say the closing line:

```
For x = 2 To 4
    MsgBox("I saw " & x & " monsters")
    MsgBox("Tra-la-la!")
Next
MsgBox("They all had a party: ha-ha-ha!")
```

That program makes the computer print the entire song.

Here's an analysis:

```
                              For x = 2 To 4
The computer will do indented lines    MsgBox("I saw " & x & " monsters")
repeatedly, for x=2, x=3, and x=4.     MsgBox("Tra-la-la!")
                              Next
Then the computer will do this once. MsgBox("They all had a party: ha-ha-ha!")
```

Since the computer does the indented lines repeatedly, those lines form a loop. Here's the general rule: **the statements between For and Next form a loop**. The computer goes round and round the loop, for x=2, x=3, x=4, and x=5. Altogether, it goes around the loop 4 times, which is a finite number. Therefore, the loop is **finite**.

If you don't like the letter x, choose a different letter. For example, you can choose the letter i:

```
For i = 2 To 4
    MsgBox("I saw " & i & " monsters")
    MsgBox("Tra-la-la!")
Next
MsgBox("They all had a party: ha-ha-ha!")
```

When using the word For, most programmers prefer the letter i; most programmers say "For i" instead of "For x". Saying "For i" is a tradition. Following that tradition, the rest of this book says "For i" (instead of "For x"), except in situations where some other letter feels more natural.

Say the squares To find the **square** of a number, multiply the number by itself. For example, the square of 3 is "3 times 3", which is 9. The square of 4 is "4 times 4", which is 16.

Let's make the computer say the square of 3, 4, 5, etc., up to 10, like this:

```
The square of 3 is 9
The square of 4 is 16
The square of 5 is 25
The square of 6 is 36
The square of 7 is 49
The square of 8 is 64
The square of 9 is 81
The square of 10 is 100
```

To do that, type this line —

```
MsgBox("The square of " & i & " is " & i * i)
```

and make i be every number from 3 up to 10, like this:

```
For i = 3 To 10
    MsgBox("The square of " & i & " is " & i * i)
Next
```

Count how many copies This program makes the computer say "I love you" 4 times:

```
For i = 1 To 4
    MsgBox("I love you")
Next
```

Here's a smarter program, which asks how many times you want the computer to say "I love you":

```
Dim n
n = Val(InputBox("How many times do you want me to love you?"))
For i = 1 To n
    MsgBox("I love you")
Next
```

When you run that program, the computer asks:

```
How many times do you want me to love you?
```

If you answer 5 (and click the OK button), the n becomes 5 (so the computer says "I love you" 5 times). If you answer 7 instead, the computer says "I love you" 7 times. Get as much love as you like!

That program illustrates this rule:

```
To make the For...Next loop be flexible,
say "For i = 1 To n" and let the human input the n.
```

Step The For statement can be varied:

Statement	Meaning
For i = 5 To 17 Step .1	The i will go from 5 to 17, counting by tenths. So i will be 5, then 5.1, then 5.2, etc., up to 17.
For i = 5 To 17 Step 3	The i will be every 3rd number from 5 to 17. So i will be 5, then 8, then 11, then 14, then 17.
For i = 17 To 5 Step -3	The i will be every 3rd number from 17 down to 5. So i will be 17, then 14, then 11, then 8, then 5.

To count down, you *must* use the word Step. To count from 17 down to 5, give this instruction:

```
For i = 17 To 5 Step -1
```

This program prints a rocket countdown:

```
For i = 10 To 1 Step -1
    MsgBox(i)
Next
MsgBox("Blast off!")
```

The computer will say:

```
10
9
8
7
6
5
4
3
2
1
Blast off!
```

This statement is tricky:

```
For i = 5 To 16 Step 3
```

It says to start i at 5, and keep adding 3 until it gets past 16. So i will be 5, then 8, then 11, then 14. The i won't be 17, since 17 is past 16. The first value of i is 5; the last value is 14.

In the statement For i = 5 To 16 Step 3, the **first value** or **initial value** of i is 5, the **limit value** is 16, and the **step size** or **increment** is 3. The i is called the **counter** or **index** or **loop-control variable**. Although the limit value is 16, the **last value** or **terminal value** is 14.

Programmers usually say "For i", instead of "For x", because the letter i reminds them of the word **index**.

Fancy calculations

The computer can do fancy calculations.

Exponents

In Form1's subroutine, try giving this command:

```
Text = 4 ^ 3
```

To type the symbol ^, do this: while holding down the Shift key, tap this key:

```
^
6
```

That symbol (^) is called a **caret**.

In that line, **the "4 ^ 3" makes the computer use the number 4, three times**. The computer will multiply together those three 4's, like this: 4 times 4 times 4. Since "4 times 4 times 4" is 64, the computer will say:

```
64
```

In the expression "4 ^ 3", the 4 is called the **base**; the 3 is called the **exponent** or **power**.

Here's another example:

```
Text = 10 ^ 6
```

The "10 ^ 6" makes the computer use the number 10, six times. The computer will multiply together those six 10's (like this: 10 times 10 times 10 times 10 times 10 times 10) and say the answer, 1000000.

Here's another example:

```
Text = 3 ^ 2
```

The "3 ^ 2" makes the computer use the number 3, two times. The computer will multiply together those two 3's (like this: 3 times 3) and say the answer, 9.

Order of operations The symbols +, -, *, /, and ^ are all called **operations**.

To solve a problem, the computer uses the three-step process taught in algebra (and pre-algebra). For example, suppose you say:

```
Text = 70 - 3 ^ 2 + 8 / 2 * 3
```

The computer will *not* begin by subtracting 3 from 70; instead, it will use the three-step process:

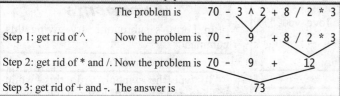

	The problem is	70 - 3 ^ 2 + 8 / 2 * 3
Step 1: get rid of ^.	Now the problem is	70 - 9 + 8 / 2 * 3
Step 2: get rid of * and /.	Now the problem is	70 - 9 + 12
Step 3: get rid of + and -.	The answer is	73

In each step, it looks from left to right. For example, in step 2, it sees / and gets rid of it before it sees *.

Speed Though exponents are fun, the computer handles them slowly. For example, the computer handles 3 ^ 2 slower than 3 * 3. So for fast calculations, say 3 * 3 instead of 3 ^ 2.

Square roots What positive number, when multiplied by itself, gives 9? The answer is 3, because 3 times itself is 9.

3 **squared** is 9. 3 is called the **square root** of 9.

To make the computer deduce the square root of 9, type this:

```
Text = Math.Sqrt(9)
```

The computer will print 3.

The symbol Math.Sqrt is called a **function**. The number in parentheses (9) is called the function's **input** (or **argument** or **parameter**). The answer, which is 3, is called the function's **output** (or **value**).

Math.Sqrt(9) gives the same answer as 9 ^ .5. The computer handles Math.Sqrt(9) faster than 9 ^ .5.

Cube roots What number, when multiplied by itself and then multiplied by itself *again*, gives 64? The answer is 4, because 4 times 4 times 4 is 64. The answer (4) is called the **cube root** of 64.

Here's how to make the computer find the cube root of 64:

```
Text = 64 ^ (1 / 3)
```

The computer will say 4.

Stripping

Sometimes the computer prints *too* much info: you wish the computer would print less, to save yourself the agony of reading excess info irrelevant to your needs. Whenever the computer prints too much info about a numerical answer, use Math.Abs, Fix, Int, Math.Ceiling, Math.Round, or Math.Sign.

Math.Abs removes any minus sign. ("Abs" is short for "Absolute value".) For example, the Math.Abs of -3.89 is 3.89. So if you say Text = Math.Abs(-3.89), the computer will say just 3.89.

Fix removes any digits after the decimal point. For example, the Fix of 3.89 is 3. So if you say Text = Fix(3.89), the computer will say just 3. The Fix of -3.89 is -3.

Int rounds the number DOWN to an integer that's LOWER. For example, the Int of 3.89 is 3 (because 3 is an integer that's lower than 3.89); the Int of -3.89 is -4 (because -4 is lower than -3.89).

Math.Ceiling rounds the number UP to an integer that's HIGHER. For example, the Math.Ceiling of 3.89 is 4 (because 4 is an integer that's higher than 3.89); the Math.Ceiling of -3.89 is -3 (because -3 is higher than -3.89).

Math.Round can round to the NEAREST integer. For example, the Math.Round of 3.89 is 4. The Math.Round of -3.89 is -4. The Math.Round of a number ending in .5 is an integer that's even (not odd); for example, the Math.Round of 26.5 is 26 (because 26 is even), but the Math.Round of 27.5 is 28 (because 28 is even); this rounding method is called **unbiased rounding** and explained in the next section ("Types of data"). If you want traditional rounding instead of unbiased rounding, ask for Math.Round(26.5,System.MidpointRounding.AwayFromZero), which produces 27. If you say Text = Math.Round(865.739, 2), the computer will round 865.739 to 2 decimal places and say 865.74.

Math.Sign removes ALL the digits and replaces them with a 1 — unless the number is 0. For example, the Math.Sign of 3.89 is 1. The Math.Sign of -3.89 is -1. The Math.Sign of 0 is just 0.

Math.Abs, Fix, Int, Math.Ceiling, Math.Round, and Math.Sign are all called **stripping functions** or **strippers** or **diet functions** or **diet pills**, because they strip away the number's excess fat and reveal just the fundamentals that interest you.

Pi

A circle's **circumference** (the distance around a circle) is about 3 times as long as the circle's **diameter** (the distance across the circle). So the circumference divided by the diameter is about 3. More precisely, it's **pi**, which is about 3.1415926535897931, a number that Visual Basic calls **Math.PI**. If you type —

```
Text = Math.PI
```

the computer will display this approximation:

```
3.14159265358979
```

Avoid "Math."

Many of those functions expect you to type "Math." To avoid having to type "Math.", put this line at your program's top (above "Public Class Form1"):

```
Imports System.Math
```

Then you can omit "Math." For example, instead of typing —

```
Text = Math.Sqrt(9)
```

you can type just:

```
Text = Sqrt(9)
```

Instead of typing —

```
Text = Math.PI
```

you can type just:

```
Text = PI
```

Types of data

If you want x to be a variable in your subroutine, you must warn the computer by giving your subroutine a command such as:

```
Dim x
```

Here's how to make your program run faster, consume less RAM, and correct more errors: instead of saying just "Dim x", warn the computer what **type of data** the x will stand for, by giving one of these 8 popular commands:

Some of those commands are used rarely. These 8 commands are the most popular:

Command	Meaning		RAM	Speed
Dim x As Integer	x will be a number from 0 to 2147483647,	with no decimal point, but maybe a negative sign	4 bytes	fastest
Dim x As Long	x will be a number from 0 to 9223372036854775807,	with no decimal point, but maybe a negative sign	8 bytes	fast
Dim x As Double	x will be a number from 0 to 1E308,	with maybe a decimal point and negative sign, 15-digit accuracy	8 bytes	fast
Dim x As Decimal	x will be a number having up to 28 digits, with maybe a decimal point and negative sign,	28-digit accuracy	16 bytes	slowest
Dim x As Date	x will be a date and time (such as #12/31/2009 11:59:30 PM#), with a year between 1 and 9999		8 bytes	slow
Dim x As Boolean	x will be either the word True or the word False		2 bytes	fast
Dim x As String	x will be a string (such as "I love you") up to 2 billion characters long	2 bytes per character, plus	10 bytes	slow
Dim x As Char	x will be a single character (such as "j")		2 bytes	fast

Here's how to choose among them:

If x stands for a reasonably small number (2147483647 or less) without a decimal point, choose **Integer**.
If x stands for a longer number (up to 922337203854775807) without a decimal point, choose **Long**.
If x stands for a number that's even bigger or has a decimal point, choose **Double** unless you need more than 15-digit accuracy, which demands **Decimal**.

If x stands for a date or time, choose **Date**.
If x stands for the word True or the word False, choose **Boolean**.
If x stands for a single character (such as "c"), choose **Char**. If x stands for a longer string, choose **String**.

For example, if you want x to be 3000000, say:

```
Dim x As Integer
x = 3000000
```

According to the chart's top line, saying "Dim x As Integer" makes x consume 4 bytes of RAM. The computer can store 3000000 (or any integer up to 2147483647) in just 4 bytes of RAM, because the computer stores the number by using a special trick called **binary representation**.

These 7 variations are less popular:

Instead of **Integer**, you can choose **UInteger** (which means unsigned integer).
It can handle numbers that are twice as big (up to 4294967295) but can't handle a negative sign.

Instead of **Long**, you can choose **ULong** (which means unsigned long).
It can handle numbers that are twice as big (up to 18446744073709551615) but can't handle a negative sign.

Instead of **Integer** (which consumes 4 bytes), you can choose **Short** (which consumes just 2 bytes and is limited to numbers up to 32767) or **SByte** (which consumes just 1 byte and is limited to numbers up to 127). But those alternatives run slow, because the Pentium chip was designed to handle 4-byte integers, not shorter integers. Use those alternatives just if you're worried about the number of bytes. Here are other alternatives, which also run slow: **UShort** (which consumes 2 bytes, handles numbers up to 65535, no decimals or negatives) and **Byte** (which consumes 1 byte, handles numbers up to 255, no decimals or negatives).

Instead of **Double**, you can choose **Single** (which means single-length numbers). It consumes fewer bytes (4 instead of 8) but runs slow (because the Pentium chip was designed to handle decimal points in 8-byte numbers, not shorter ones). It has less accuracy (7-digit instead of 15-digit) and is restricted to smaller numbers (up to 3E38, not 1E308). Use it just if you're worried about the number of bytes.

Details

Here are more details about the 8 popular Dim commands.

Integer An **Integer** is a number from 0 to 2147483647, with maybe a negative sign in front, but without a decimal point. For example, these numbers can all be Integer:

0	1	2	3	10	52	53	1000	2147483647
	-1	-2	-3	-10	-52	-53	1000	-2147483647

Technical note: although 2147483648 is slightly too big to be an Integer, -2147483648 is a special number that *can* be an Integer, though it's rarely used and must be written as:

```
-2147483647 - 1
```

If you say "Dim x As Integer" and then try to say "x = 52.9", the computer will round 52.9 to 53, so x will be 53.

To round, Visual Basic 2010 makes the computer use this strange method, called **unbiased rounding**:

If the number's decimal part is less than .5 (for example, if it's .4), the computer rounds down. For example, 26.4 rounds down to 26.

If the number's decimal part is more than .5 (for example, if it's .51 or .6), the computer rounds up. For example, 26.51 rounds up to 27.

If the number's decimal part is exactly .5 (not less, not more, not .51), the computer uses this strange method: it round to the nearest integer that's even (not odd). For example, 26.5 rounds down to 26 (since 26 is even), but 27.5 rounds up to 28 (since 28 is even).

That makes .5 sometimes round down and sometimes rounds up, so there's no bias toward rounding in a particular direction. That unbiased rounding method appeals to statisticians (and a few economists and very few bankers) who want to eliminate bias from rounded results. It's called **unbiased rounding** (or **round-to-even** or **statisticians rounding** or **bankers rounding** or **Dutch rounding** or **Gaussian rounding**).

Long A **Long** is a number from 0 to 9223372036854775807, with maybe a negative sign in front, but without a decimal point. For example, these numbers can all be Longs:

0	1	2	3	10	52	53	1000	9223372036854775807
0	-1	-2	-3	-10	-52	-53	-1000	-9223372036854775807

Technical note: although 9223372036854775808 is slightly too big to be a Long, -9223372036854775808 is a special number that *can* be a Long, though it's rarely used and must be written as:

```
-9223372036854775807 - 1
```

If you say "Dim x As Long" and then try to say "x = 52.9", the computer will round 52.9 to 53, so x will be 53. (To round, the computer uses unbiased rounding.)

If you write a number that has no decimal point and is small (no more than 2147483647), the computer assumes you want it to be an Integer. If you want it to be a Long instead, **put L after it**, like this: 57L. For example, if you tell the computer to multiply 3000 by 1000000, like this —

```
Text = 3000 * 1000000
```

the computer assumes you want to multiply the Integer 3000 by the Integer 1000000; but the answer is too long to be an Integer, so the computer gripes (by saying "not representable in type 'Integer'"). Multiplying 3000 by 1000000 is okay if you say the numbers are Longs, not Integers, like this:

```
Text = 3000L & 1000000L
```

Then the computer will show the correct answer:

```
3000000000
```

Double A **Double** is a number from 0 to 1E308 (which is a "1 followed by 308 zeros"), with maybe a negative sign and a decimal point. After the decimal point, you can have as many digits as you wish. For example, these numbers can all be Double:

0	1	2	3	4.99	4.9995	4.999527	1000.236	26127.85	1E308
0	-1	-2	-3	-4.99	-4.9995	-4.999527	-1000.236	-26127.85	-1E308

The computer manages to store a Double rather briefly (just 8 bytes) by "cheating": **the computer stores the number just approximately, to an accuracy of about 15 significant digits**.

For example, if you say —

```
Dim x As Double
x = 100 / 3
Text = 100 / 3
```

the computer will show 15 digits:

```
33.3333333333333
```

If you say —

```
Dim x As Double
x = 1000000.000000269
Text = x
```

the computer will round to 15 digits and show:

```
1000000.00000027
```

When handling Double variables, the computer can give inaccurate results. The inaccuracy is especially noticeable if you do a subtraction where the two numbers nearly equal each other. For example, if you say —

```
Dim x, y As Double
x = 8000.1
y = x - 8000
Text = y
```

the computer will make x be *approximately* 8000.1, so y will be *approximately* .1. The Print line will print:

```
0.100000000000364
```

Notice that the last few digits are wrong! That's the drawback of Double: you can't trust the last few digits of the answer! Double is accurate enough for most scientists, engineers, and statisticians, since they realize all measurements of the real world are just approximations; but Double is *not* good enough for accountants who fret over every penny. Double's errors drive accountants bananas. **For accounting problems that involve decimals, consider using Decimal instead of Double**, since Decimal is always accurate, though slower.

Technical notes:

A Double can be slightly bigger than 1E308. The biggest permissible Double is actually 1.7976931348623157E308.

If a Double is at least a quadrillion (which is 1000000000000000) or tiny (less than .0001), the computer will display it by using E notation.

When you type a Double in your subroutine, the computer stores the first 16 significant digits accurately, stores an approximation of the 17th significant digit, and ignores the rest.

If you type a number that has no decimal point and no E, the computer will think you're trying to type an Integer or a Long; and if it has many digits, the computer will complain that a Long is not allowed to have so many digits. To correct the problem, indicate you're trying to type a Double, by putting .0 at the end of the number or using E notation.

When the computer displays an answer, it displays the first 15 significant digits and hides the rest, since it knows the rest are unreliable. For example, if you set Text equal to the biggest number (1.7976931348623157E308), the computer will display it rounded to 15 digits, so it will display 1.79769313486232E308.

The tiniest decimal the computer can handle accurately is 1E-308 (which is a decimal point followed by 308 digits, 307 of which are zeros). If you try to go tinier, the computer will give you a rough approximation. The tiniest permissible Double is 4.9406564584126544E-324; if you try to go tinier than that, the computer will say 0.

Decimal If you say "Dim x as **Decimal**" (instead of "Dim x as Double", the computer will store x very accurately (28 digits, and sometimes a 29th). **The computer handles Decimals slower than any other kind of number**, so say "Dim x as Decimal" just if you need extra accuracy and don't care about speed.

If you say "Dim x as Decimal", the computer actually stores all x's digits as an extra-long integer and also stores a note about where the decimal point belongs.

To write a Decimal number, put D after the number, to emphasize that the number is a Decimal, not a Double, like this:

```
Dim x As Decimal
x = 1000000.000000269D
```

The biggest permissible Decimal is 79228162514264337593543950335D (which has 29 digits and no decimal point). The tiniest permissible Decimal is 0.0000000000000000000000000001D (which has 27 zeros after the decimal point).

A Decimal number cannot contain E. It's limited to 28 (or 29) digits. When counting how many digits are in the number, you must count the zeros: the limit is indeed 28 (or 29) digits (not 28 "significant digits").

Date A **Date** is a date with time. For example, these lines make x be December 31, 2009, at 30 seconds after 11:59 PM:

```
Dim x As Date
x = #12/31/2009 11:59:30 PM#
Text = x
```

Notice you must put the symbol # before and after the date-with-time. The computer will print:

```
12/31/2009 11:59:30 PM
```

For the year, you can pick 2009 or 1999 or 1776 or 1492 or even earlier. You can pick any year from 1 (which was shortly after Christ) to 9999 (which is many centuries from now). If you type a 2-digit year, the computer will put "20" before your typing, to make a 4-digit year (unless your 2-digit year is at least 30, in which case the computer will put "19" before your typing instead).

You can omit any part of the date-and-time that doesn't interest you. For example, if you don't care about the seconds, leave them out. If you don't care about the time-of-day, leave it out and type just the date; if you don't care about the date, leave it out and type just the time of day.

The computer makes assumptions:

If you leave out the time of day, the computer assumes you mean the day's beginning (which is midnight, 12:00:00 AM).

If you leave out the date, the computer assumes you mean the beginning of modern times (which is January 1 in the year 1).

To avoid pissing off people who don't like those assumptions, the computer avoids displaying 12:00:00 AM and avoids displaying 1/1/1. For example, if you leave out the time of day and type this —

```
Dim x As Date
x = #12/31/2009#
Text = x
```

x will be #12/31/2009 12:00:00 AM# but the computer will display just:

```
12/31/2009
```

If you leave out the date and type this —

```
Dim x As Date
x = #11:59:30 PM#
Text = x
```

x will be #1/1/1 11:59:30 PM# but the computer will display just:

```
11:59:30 PM
```

If you say —

```
x = Now
```

the computer will make x be the current date-with-time. For example, if the computer encounters that line while running the program on December 31, 2009 (at 30.16 seconds after 11:59 PM), x will become #12/31/2009 11:59:30 PM#.

Boolean A **Boolean** is either the word True or the word False. Here's an example:

```
Dim x As Boolean
x = True
Text = x
```

The computer will display:

```
True
```

Here's another example:

```
Dim x As Boolean
x = False
Text = x
```

The computer will display:

```
False
```

Technical notes:

If you say "Dim x As Boolean" and then try to say "x = 0", the computer will make x be False.

If you say "Dim x As Boolean" and then try to say "x = 1" (or say that x is any other non-zero number), the computer will make x be True.

It's called "Boolean" to honor George Boole (the 19th-century mathematician who discovered that the word False acts like the number 0, and True acts like the number 1).

String A **String** is a collection of characters, such as "joy" or "I love you" or "aieee luf ya" or "76 trombones" or "GO AWAY!!!" or "xypw exr///746". Here's an example:

```
Dim x As String
x = "joy"
Text = x
```

The computer will display:

```
joy
```

Versions of Visual Basic before 2005 used a code called the **American Standard Code for Information Interchange (Ascii)**, which consumed just 1 byte per character; but Visual Basic 2005 & 2008 & 2010 use a different code instead, called **Unicode**, which uses 2 bytes per character, to permit fancier characters for foreign languages.

Since the string "joy" contains 3 characters, and each character consumes 2 bytes, x consumes 6 bytes of RAM — plus 10 bytes to remember how long the string is. So altogether, x consumes 16 bytes of RAM.

If you say "Dim x As String" and try to say "x = 9 + 3.5", the computer will look at the equation's right side, realize it's 12.5, and try to make x be 12.5; but because of the "Dim x as String", the computer must but must turn x into a string, so x will become the string "12.5" (which is four characters long).

Character A **Char** is a single character, such as "j". It consumes just 2 bytes. To emphasize that "j" is just a single character, not "a string whose length is 1", write c after the "j", like this:

```
Dim x As Char
x = "j"c
Text = x
```

The computer will display:

```
j
```

So if x is a Char, the computer requires just 2 bytes to store it. (To store a String, the computer needs 2 bytes per character, plus 10 bytes to store the string's length; but to store a Char, the computer needs just 2 bytes, since the computer doesn't have to store a length.)

If you say —

```
Dim x As Char
x = "hat"
```

the x will be just the first character of the string "hat", so x will be just "h". Then if you say —

```
Text = x
```

the computer will display just:

```
h
```

Object You've learned that x can stand for a number, date, Boolean, string, or character.

Here's another possibility: x can stand for an **object**, such as Form1 or Button1 or any other VB thing, such as Color.Red.

For example, suppose you created a button called Button1. If you put this line in Form1's subroutine, Button1's title will become "Click me":

```
Button1.Title = "Click me"
```

These lines do the same thing:

```
Dim x As Object
x = Button1
x.Text = "Click me"
```

Saying "Dim x As Object" is vague. It has exactly the same meaning as "Dim x", which is vague. If you say "Dim x As Object" (or just "Dim x"), you're saying that x stands for a Windows object (such as Form1 or Button1) or some other kind of object (such as a number, date, Boolean, string, or character). The computer handles such an x slowly: it consumes 4 bytes to remember what part of the RAM holds x's details, plus several bytes to store the details.

Multiple variables

If you want x and y to be Integers, z to be a String, and temperature to be a Double, say this —

```
Dim x, y As Integer
Dim z As String
Dim temperature as Double
```

or say it all in one line:

```
Dim x, y As Integer, z As String, temperature As Double
```

Suffix

Here's the normal way to make x be a String:

```
Dim x As String
```

This way is shorter:

```
Dim x$
```

That dollar sign means "As String". The dollar sign is called a **suffix** (or **type-declaration character**).

You can use these suffixes:

Suffix	Meaning
$	As String
%	As Integer
&	As Long
#	As Double
@	As Decimal
!	As Single

Repeating the suffix Below the Dim line, you can type the suffix again if you wish. For example, after you've made x be a string by saying —

```
Dim x$
```

you can say either —

```
x = "I love you"
```

or this, which means the same thing:

```
x$ = "I love you"
```

The computer doesn't care whether you type the $ again. Type it just if you want to emphasize it to other programmers who look at your subroutine.

Constants

Your subroutine can mention variables (such as x and y) and constants (such as 3.7 and "I love you"). Here's how the computer tells a constant's type:

If the constant is the word True or the word False, it's a **Boolean**.

If the constant begins and ends with the symbol #, it's a **Date**.

If the constant is enclosed in quotation marks (such as "I love you"), it's a **String**, unless it has a c afterwards (such as "j"c), which makes it a **Char** (and is limited to just one character).

If the constant is a number, here's what happens….

If the number has no decimal point and no E and is short (between -2147483648 and 2147483647), it's an **Integer**. If the number has no decimal point and no E and is between -9223372036854775808 and 9223372036854775807 but is not an Integer, it's a **Long**. Any other number is a **Double**.

To force a number to be a **Decimal** instead, put D (or @) after the number, like this: 4.95D

To force a number to be a **Long** (even though it's small enough to be an Integer), put L (or &) after the number, like this: 52L

To force a number to be a **Double** (even though it's simple enough to be an Integer or Long), put .0 after the number, like this: 52.0.

VarType

Each type of constant has a code number:

Type of constant	Code number
Integer	3
Long	20
Double	5
Decimal	14
Date	7
Boolean	11
String	8
Char	18
Object	9

If you say **VarType**, the computer will examine a constant and tell you its code number. For example, if you say —

```
Text = VarType(4.95D)
```

the computer will examine 4.95D, realize it's a Decimal, and say Decimal's code number, which is:

```
14
```

Here are more examples:

If you say Text = VarType ("I love you"), the computer will examine "I love you", realize it's a String, and print String's code number, which is 8.

If you say Text = VarType(2000000000), the computer will examine 2000000000, realize it's an Integer, and print Integer's code number, which is 3.

If you say Text = VarType(300000000), the computer will examine 300000000, realize it's a Long, and print Long's code number, which is 20.

VarType of a variable

VarType of a variable If you say VarType(x), the computer will notice what type of variable x is and print its code number. For example, if you say —

```
Dim x As Decimal
Text = VarType(x)
```

the computer will say Decimal's code number, which is 14.

If you say just "Dim x" (or "Dim x As Object") without specifying further details of x's type, VarType(x) will be whatever type the x acquires. For example, if you say —

```
Dim x
x = 4.95D
Type = VarType(x)
```

the computer will print Decimal's code number, which is 14.

TypeName

If you say **TypeName** instead of **VarType**, the computer will say the type's name instead of its code number.

For example, if you say —

```
Text = TypeName(4.95D)
```

the computer will say:

```
Decimal
```

Instead of saying "Object" (or "Nothing"), the computer will try to be more specific. For example, if you created a command button called Button1 and say —

```
Text = TypeName(Button1)
```

the computer will say:

```
Button
```

If x is an Object but doesn't have a more specific value or type yet, "Text = TypeName(x)" will make the computer say:

```
Nothing
```

Initial value

Instead of saying —

```
Dim x As Integer
x = 7
```

you can combine those two lines into this single line:

```
Dim x As Integer = 7
```

In that line, 7 is called x's **initial value** (or **initializer**), because it's what x is initially (in the beginning).

You can shorten that line further, by saying just this:

```
Dim x = 7
```

Since 7 is an Integer (according to the rules about which constants are Integers), the computer will assume you also mean "x As Integer". If you say this instead —

```
Dim x = 7.0
```

the computer will assume you mean "x As Double".

Saying "Dim x = 5" has a slightly different effect than saying "Dim x" then "x = 5". Compare these subroutines:

```
Dim x
x = 5                 Dim x = 5
x = 8.4               x = 8.4
Text = x              Text = x
```

In the left subroutine, the Dim line says x is a vague variable (an object). The next line says x is 5. The next line changes x to 8.4, so Text will be 8.4. In the right-hand subroutine, the first line says x is 5 but also makes x be an integer variable (since that line implies "x As Integer"); since x is an integer variable, the next line makes x be 8 (not 8.4), so Text will be just 8.

Operations

When you do operations (add, subtract, multiply, divide, exponents, or beyond), here's what kind of answer you get.

Exponents When you do **exponents** (using the symbol "^"), the answer is a **Double**.

Division When you **divide** one number by another (using the symbol "/"), here's what happens:

If both numbers are Decimal, the answer is **Decimal**.

If one of the numbers is Single and the other is Single or Decimal, the answer is **Single**.

In all other situations, the answer is **Double**.

Add, subtract, multiply When you **add, subtract, or multiply** numbers (using the symbol + or - or *), here's what happens:

If both numbers are the same type, the computer makes the answer be **the same type**. (Exception: if both "numbers" are actually Boolean, the computer makes the answer be Short.)

If the numbers have different types from each other, and both types are **signed** (permit minus signs), the computer notices which type is **wider** (can handle more numbers) and makes the answer be that type. Here are the signed types, from narrowest to widest: SByte, Short, Integer, Long, Decimal, Single, Double. (Single is wider than Decimal because Single can handle higher powers of 10.) For example, if one number is an Integer and the other number is a Long, the answer is a Long (because Long is wider than Integer).

If the numbers have different types from each other, and at least one of those types is **unsigned** (Boolean, Byte, UShort, UInteger, or ULong), the computer makes the answer be the wider type — or a signed type that's even wider.

Advanced math Here's how the computer handles advanced math:

Math.PI and **Math.Sqrt**(x) are Double.

Math.Sign(x) is an Integer.

Math.Abs(x) and **Fix**(x) and **Int**(x) are the same type as x, if x's type is signed. If x's type is unsigned, the computer turns x into a wider signed number first.

Math.Ceiling(x) and **Math.Round**(x) are Double, if x is a Double or Single. They're Decimal if x is otherwise.

Combine When you combine strings or numbers (by using the symbol "&"), the answer is a string.

Form1 declarations

Normally, each subroutine has its own variables. For example, if Form1's subroutine uses a variable called x, and Button1's subroutine uses a variable that's also called x, Form1's x has nothing to do with Button1's x. Form1's x is stored in a different part of RAM from Button1's x. If Form1 says x = 5, Button1's x remains unaffected by that statement.

If you *want* Form1's x to be the same as Button1's x and use the same RAM, say "Dim x" *above* the "Private Sub Form1" line instead of below.

Example For example, try this experiment....

Create a new program. Double-click Form1, so you can type Form1's subroutine. Your screen looks like this:

```
Public Class Form1

    Private Sub Form1_Load…

    End Sub
End Class
```

Click *above* the "Private Sub Form1" line and type "Dim x" there, so your screen looks like this:

```
Public Class Form1
    Dim x
    Private Sub Form1_Load…

    End Sub
End Class
```

Type Form1's subroutine under the "Private Sub Form1" line, like this:

```
Public Class Form1
    Dim x
    Private Sub Form1_Load…
        x = 5
    End Sub
End Class
```

Create Button1 (by clicking the "Form1.vb [Design]" tab then double-clicking the Button tool). Double-click Button1, then type "Text = x" for Button1's subroutine. Altogether, your screen looks like this:

```
Public Class Form1
    Dim x
    Private Sub Form1_Load…
        x = 5
    End Sub

    Private Sub Button1_Click…
        Text = x
    End Sub
End Class
```

Since the "Dim x" is *above* both subroutines (instead of being buried inside one subroutine), the x's value affects *both* subroutines (not just one of them).

When you run that program (by pressing F5), Form1's subroutine makes x be 5. Then when you click Button1, Button1's subroutine makes Text be x, which is 5, so the computer says:

```
5
```

Conversion functions

In the middle of a calculation, you can convert to a different type of data by using these conversion functions:

Function	Meaning
CInt	convert to Integer
CLng	convert to Long
CDbl	convert to Double
CDec	convert to Decimal
CDate	convert to Date
CBool	convert to Boolean
CStr	convert to String
CChar	convert to Char
CUInt	convert to UInteger
CULng	convert to ULong
CShort	convert to Short
CSByte	convert to SByte
CUShort	convert to UShort
CByte	convert to Byte
CSng	convert to Single
CObj	convert to Object

For example, CInt(3.9) is "3.9 converted to the nearest Integer", which is 4. If you say —

```
Text = CInt(3.9)
```

the computer will say:

```
4
```

If you say —

```
Text = CInt(3.9) + 2
```

the computer will say:

```
6
```

Arrays

Instead of being just a number, x can be a *list* of numbers.

Example For example, if you want x to be this list of numbers —

```
{81, 52, 207, 19}
```

type this in Form1's subroutine:

```
Dim x() = {81, 52, 207, 19}
```

In that line, the symbol "x()" means "x's list". Notice that when you type the list of numbers, you must **put commas between the numbers** and put the entire list of numbers in **braces**, {}. On your keyboard, the "{" symbol is to the right of the P key and requires you to hold down the Shift key.

Since all numbers in that list are Integers, you can improve that line by saying "As Integer", like this:

```
Dim x() As Integer = {81, 52, 207, 19}
```

If you don't say "As Integer", the computer will treat those numbers as just vague objects, and the program will run slower.

In x's list, **the starting number** (which is 81) **is called x_0** (which is pronounced "x subscripted by zero" or "x sub 0" or just "x 0"). The next number (which is 52) is called x_1 (which is pronounced "x subscripted by one" or "x sub 1" or just "x 1"). The next number is called x_2. Then comes x_3. So **the four numbers in the list are called x_0, x_1, x_2, and x_3**.

To make the computer say what x_2 is, type this line:

```
Text = x(2)
```

That line makes Text be x_2, which is 207, so the computer will say:

```
207
```

Altogether, the subroutine says:

```
Dim x() As Integer = {81, 52, 207, 19}
Text = x(2)
```

The first line says x's list is these Integers: 81, 52, 207, and 19. The bottom line makes the computer say x_2's number, which is 207.

This subroutine makes the computer say x_2's number (which is 207) in a message box:

```
Dim x() As Integer = {81, 52, 207, 19}
MsgBox(x(2))
```

This subroutine makes the computer say all 4 numbers:

```
Dim x() As Integer = {81, 52, 207, 19}
For i = 1 To 4
    MsgBox(x(i))
Next
```

That makes the computer say the numbers for x(1), x(2), x(3), and x(4), so the computer will say 81, 52, 207, and 19.

Here's a shorter way to make the computer say all 4 numbers:

```
Dim x() As Integer = {81, 52, 207, 19}
For Each i In x
    MsgBox(i)
Next
```

That makes x's list be {81, 52, 207, 19}, makes i be **Each number In x** (so i is 81, then 52, then 207, then 19), and makes the computer say each i.

Longer lists Instead of having just 4 numbers in the list, you can have 5 numbers, or 6 numbers, or a thousand numbers, or many billions of numbers. The list can be quite long! Your only limit is how much RAM your computer has.

Jargon Notice this jargon:

In a symbol such as x_2, the lowered number (the 2) is called the **subscript**.

To create a subscript in your subroutine, use parentheses. For example, to create x_2, type x(2).

A variable having subscripts is called an **array**. For example, x is an array if there's an x_0, x_1, x_2, etc.

Different types Instead of having Integers, you can have different types. For example, you can say:

```
Dim x() As Double = {81.2, 51.7, 207.9, 19.5}
```

You can even say:

```
Dim x() As String = {"love", "hate", "peace", "war"}
```

You can even have mixed types:

```
Dim x() = {5, 91.3, "turkey", #11:59:30 PM#}
```

Uninitialized Instead of making the Dim line include a list of numbers, you can type the numbers underneath, if you warn the computer how many numbers will be in the list, like this:

```
Dim x(2) As Double
x(0) = 200.1
x(1) = 700.4
x(2) = 53.2
Text = x(0) + x(1) + x(2)
```

The top line says x_0, x_1, and x_2 will be Doubles. The next lines say x_0 is 200.1, x_1 is 700.4, and x_2 is 53.2. The bottom line makes the computer say their sum:

```
953.7
```

In that top line, if you omit the "As Double", the program will give the same answer but slower. But in that top line, the 2 is required, to warn the computer how many subscripts to reserve RAM for; if you omit the 2 (or type a lower number instead), the computer will gripe.

Random numbers

Usually, the computer is predictable: it does exactly what you say. But sometimes, you want the computer to be *un*predictable.

For example, if you're going to play a game of cards with the computer and tell the computer to deal, you want the cards dealt to be unpredictable. If the cards were predictable — if you could figure out exactly which cards you and the computer would be dealt — the game would be boring.

In many other games too, you want the computer to be unpredictable, to "surprise" you. Without an element of surprise, the game would be boring.

Being unpredictable increases the pleasure you derive from games — and from art. To make the computer act artistic, and create a new *original* masterpiece that's a "work of art", you need a way to make the computer get a "flash of inspiration". Flashes of inspiration aren't predictable: they're surprises.

Here's how to make the computer act unpredictably….

Rnd is a RaNDom decimal (bigger than 0 and less than 1) whose data type is Single. For example, it might be .6273649 or .9241587 or .2632801. Every time your program mentions Rnd, the computer concocts another decimal. For example, if Form1's subroutine says —

```
MsgBox(Rnd)
MsgBox(Rnd)
MsgBox(Rnd)
```

the computer says these decimals:

```
.7055475
.533424
.5795186
```

The first time your program mentions Rnd, the computer chooses its favorite decimal, which is .7055475. Each succeeding time your program mentions Rnd, the computer uses the previous decimal to concoct a new one. It uses .7055475 to concoct .533424, which it uses to concoct .5795186. The process by which the computer concocts each new decimal from the previous one is weird enough so we humans cannot detect any pattern.

These lines make the computer say 16 decimals:

```
For i = 1 To 16
    MsgBox(Rnd)
Next
```

You can say either Rnd or Rnd(); the computer doesn't care. If you say just Rnd, the computer might change it to Rnd().

Percentages

When the computer says random decimals, about half the decimals will be less than .5, and about half will be more than .5.

Most of the decimals will be less than .9. In fact, about 90% will be.

About 36% of the decimals will be less than .36; 59% will be less than .59; 99% will be less than .99; 2% will be less than .02; a quarter of them will be less than .25; etc.

You might see some decimal twice, though most of the decimals will be different from each other.

Randomize

If you run a program about Rnd again, you'll see exactly the same decimals again, in the same order.

If you'd rather see a different list of decimals, say **Randomize()** at the subroutine's top:

```
Randomize()
For i = 1 To 16
    MsgBox(Rnd)
Next
```

When the computer sees Randomize(), the computer looks at the clock and manipulates the time's digits to produce the first value of Rnd.

So the first value of Rnd will be a number that depends on the time of day, instead of the usual .7055475. Since the first value of Rnd will be different than usual, so will the second, and so will the rest of the list.

Every time you run the program, the clock will be different, so the first value of Rnd will be different, so the whole list will be different — unless you run the program at exactly the same time the next day, when the clock is the same. But since the clock is accurate to a tiny fraction of a second, the chance of hitting the same time is extremely unlikely.

Coin flipping

Here's how to make the computer flip a coin:

```
Randomize()
If Rnd < 0.5 Then MsgBox("heads") Else MsgBox( "tails")
```

The Randomize line makes the value of Rnd depend on the click. The If line says there's a 50% chance that the computer will print "heads"; if the computer does *not* print "heads", it will print "tails".

When you've typed that subroutine, the computer changes Rnd to Rnd(), so it looks like this:

```
Randomize()
If Rnd() < 0.5 Then MsgBox("heads") Else MsgBox( "tails")
```

Until you run the program, you won't know which way the coin will flip; the choice is random. Each time you run the program, the computer will flip the coin again; each time, the outcome is unpredictable. Try running it several times!

To write that subroutine shorter, say IIf:

```
Randomize()
MsgBox(IIf(Rnd() < 0.5, "heads", "tails"))
```

The bottom line creates a message box saying this: if the random number is less than .5, then "heads", else "tails".

This subroutine flips the coin 10 times:

```
Randomize()
For i = 1 To 10
    MsgBox(IIf(Rnd() < 0.5, "heads", "tails"))
Next
```

Love or hate?

Who loves ya, baby? These lines try to answer that question:

```
Randomize()
Dim x As String
x = InputBox("Type the name of someone you love")
If Rnd < 0.67 Then
    MsgBox(x & " loves you, too")
Else
    MsgBox(x & " hates your guts")
End If
```

The Randomize() line makes the value of Rnd depend on the clock. The Dim line says x will be a variable that stands for a String. The InputBox line makes the computer wait for the human to type a name. Suppose he types Suzy. Then x is "Suzy". The If line says there's a 67% chance the computer will say "Suzy loves you, too", but there's a 33% chance the computer will instead say "Suzy hates your guts".

Try running the program several times. Each time, input a different person's name. Find out which people love you and which people hate your guts — according to the computer!

Here's a shorter way to write that subroutine:

```
Randomize()
Dim x = InputBox("Type the name of someone you love")
MsgBox(x & IIf(Rnd < .67, " loves you, too", " hates your guts"))
```

The Randomize() line makes the value of Rnd depend on the clock. The Dim line makes the variable x be the response to "Type the name of someone you love". The MsgBox line creates a message box that says x then this: if the random number is less than .67 then " loves you, too" else " hates your guts".

Random integers

If you want a random integer from 1 to 10, ask for 1 + Int(Rnd * 10). Here's why:

```
Rnd is a decimal, bigger than 0 and less than 1.
So Rnd * 10 is a decimal, bigger than 0 and less than 10.
So Int(Rnd * 10) is an integer, at least 0 and no more than 9.
So 1 + Int(Rnd * 10) is an integer, at least 1 and no more than 10.
```

Guessing game

These lines play a guessing game:

```
        Randomize()
        MsgBox("I'm thinking of a number from 1 to 10.")
        Dim ComputerNumber = 1 + Int(Rnd * 10)
AskHuman: Dim guess = Val(InputBox("What do you think my number is?"))
        If guess < ComputerNumber Then MsgBox("Your guess is too low."): GoTo AskHuman
        If guess > ComputerNumber Then MsgBox("Your guess is too high."): GoTo AskHuman
        MsgBox("Congratulations! You found my number!")
```

The second line makes the computer say "I'm thinking of a number from 1 to 10." The next line makes the computer think of a random number from 1 to 10. The InputBox line asks the human to guess the number.

If the guess is less than the computer's number, the first If line makes the computer say "Your guess is too low" and then GoTo AskHuman, which lets the human guess again. If the guess is *greater* than the computer's number, the second If line makes the computer say "Your guess is too high" and then GoTo AskHuman.

When the human guesses correctly, the computer arrives at the bottom line, which makes the computer say:

```
Congratulations! You found my number!
```

Dice

These lines make the computer roll a pair of dice:

```
        Randomize()
        MsgBox("I'm rolling a pair of dice")
        Dim a = 1 + Int(Rnd * 6)
        MsgBox("One of the dice says " & a)
        Dim b = 1 + Int(Rnd * 6)
        MsgBox("The other says " & b)
        MsgBox("The total is " & a + b)
```

The second line makes the computer say:

```
I'm rolling a pair of dice
```

Each of the dice has 6 sides. The next line, Dim a = 1 + Int(Rnd * 6), rolls one of the dice, by picking a number from 1 to 6. The line saying "b = 1 + Int(Rnd * 6)" rolls the other. The bottom line says the total.

For example, a run might say these sentences:

```
I'm rolling a pair of dice
One of the dice says 3
The other says 5
The total is 8
```

Here's another run:

```
I'm rolling a pair of dice
One of the dice says 6
The other says 4
The total is 10
```

Daily horoscope

These lines predict what will happen to you today:

```
Randomize()
Dim x() = {"wonderful", "fairly good", "so-so", "fairly bad", "terrible"}
MsgBox("You will have a " & x(Int(Rnd * 5)) & " day today!")
```

The Dim line makes x be a list of 5 fortunes, so x_0 is "wonderful", x_1 is "fairly good", x_2 is "so-so", x_3 is "fairly bad", and x_4 is "terrible". Since Int(Rnd * 5) is a random integer from 0 to 4, the x(Int(Rnd * 5)) is a randomly chosen fortune. The computer will say —

```
You will have a wonderful day today!
```

or —

```
You will have a terrible day today!
```

or some in-between comment.

For inspiration, run that program when you get up in the morning. Then notice whether your day turns out the way the computer predicts!

JavaScript & JScript

Pages 285-292 explained how to create Web pages by using HTML. Unfortunately, HTML is *not* a complete programming language.

For example, HTML lacks commands to do arithmetic. In HTML, there is no command to make the computer do 2+2 and get 4.

HTML lacks commands to create repetitions (which are called **loops**). In HTML, there is no command to make the computer repeat a task 10 times.

In 1996, a Netscape employee, Brendan Eich, invented an HTML supplement called **LiveScript**, which lets you create Web pages that do arithmetic, loops, counting, and many other fancy tricks. When folks noticed that LiveScript looks like a stripped-down version of Java, Netscape changed the name "LiveScript" to **JavaScript**.

JavaScript is included as part of Netscape Navigator (if you have Navigator version 2 or later). **JScript** (Microsoft's imitation of JavaScript) is included as part of Internet Explorer (if you have Internet Explorer version 3 or later).

Now every popular computer comes with JavaScript or JScript. That's because Netscape Navigator is free, Internet Explorer is free, Netscape Navigator & Internet Explorer are both available for IBM and Macs, and Internet Explorer is part of Windows.

Netscape, Microsoft, and the **European Computer Manufacturers Association (ECMA)** all decided to make JavaScript and JScript resemble each other more, by creating a standard called **ECMAScript**.

This chapter explains how to use JScript to create powerful Web pages. (JavaScript and ECMAScript are similar.)

Before learning JScript, make sure you've learned HTML (by reading pages 309-316).

JScript uses these commands:

JScript command	Page
alert("Warning: bad hair")	600
document.write(2+2)	598
else	602
for (i=1; i<10; ++i)	602
if (age<18)	602
x=Array(3)	600
x=prompt("What name?","")	601
x=47	600
x[0]="love"	600
++x	600
--x	600
//I wrote this while drunk	604

Simple program

You can create a Web page that says —

We *love* you

by typing this HTML program:

```
We <i>love</i> you
```

I explained how on page 285. (If you forget how, reread page 285 and practice it now.)

To create a Web page that makes the computer do 2+2 instead, type instead this HTML program (which includes a JScript program):

```
<script>
document.write(2+2)
</script>
```

The first line, which says <script>, warns the computer that you're going to start typing a JScript (or JavaScript) program. The next line, which is written in JScript, means: on the Web-page document, write the answer to 2+2. The bottom line, which says </script>, marks the bottom of your JScript program. When you run that program, the computer will do 2+2 and write this answer:

```
4
```

In that example, the first line, <script>, is an HTML tag. Like all HTML tags, it's enclosed in angle brackets: the symbols <>. That tag marks the beginning of your JScript program. The bottom line, </script>, is an HTML tag that marks the end of your JScript program. Between those two tags, write your JScript program.

Longer example

Let's make the computer write "We *love* you", then write the answer to 2+2, then write "ever *and ever*". This program does it:

```
We <i>love</i> you
<script>
document.write(2+2)
</script>
ever <i>and ever</i>
```

The first line makes the computer write "We *love* you". The next three lines hold the JScript program making the computer write the answer to 2+2, which is 4. The bottom line makes the computer write "ever *and ever*". So altogether, the computer will write:

We *love* you 4 ever *and ever*

Fancier arithmetic

This program makes the computer write the answer to 8-3:

```
<script>
document.write(8-3)
</script>
```

The computer will write:

```
5
```

This program makes the computer write the answer to -26.3+1:

```
<script>
document.write(-26.3+1)
</script>
```

The computer will write:

```
-25.3
```

Multiplication

To multiply, use an asterisk. So to multiply 2 by 6, type this:

```
<script>
document.write(2*6)
</script>
```

The computer will write:

```
12
```

Division

To divide, use a slash. So to divide 8 by 4, type this:

```
<script>
document.write(8/4)
</script>
```

The computer will write:

```
2
```

Avoid commas

Do *not* put commas in big numbers. To write four million, do *not* write 4,000,000; instead, write 4000000.

E notation

If the computer's answer is huge (at least 1000000000000000000000) or tiny (less than .000001), the computer will typically print an e in the answer. The e means "move the decimal point".

For example, suppose the computer says the answer to a problem is:

```
1.5864321775908348e+21
```

The e means, "move the decimal point". The plus sign means, "towards the right". Altogether the e+21 means, "move the decimal point towards the right, 21 places." So look at 1.5864321775908348, and move the decimal point towards the right, 21 places; you get 1586432177590834800000.

So when the computer says the answer is 1.5864321775908348, the computer really means the answer is 1586432177590834800000, approximately. The exact answer might be 1586432177590834800000.2 or 1586432177590834800000.79 or some similar number, but the computer prints just an approximation.

Suppose your computer says the answer to a problem is:

```
9.23e-7
```

After the e, the minus sign means, "towards the *left*". So look at 9.23, and move the decimal point towards to left, 7 places. You get:
.000000923

You'll see e notation rarely: the computer uses it just if the answer is huge or tiny. But when the computer *does* use e notation, remember to move the decimal point!

The highest number

The highest number the computer can handle well is about 1E308, which is 1 followed by 308 zeros. If you try to go much higher, the computer will give up and say the answer is:

```
Infinity
```

The tiniest decimal

The tiniest decimal the computer can handle accurately is 1E-309 (which is a decimal point followed by 309 digits, 308 of which are zeros). If you try to go tinier, the computer will either write 0 or give you a rough approximation.

Long decimals

If an answer is a decimal that contains *many* digits, **the computer will typically write the first 16 significant digits accurately and the 17th digit approximately**. The computer won't bother writing later digits.

For example, suppose you ask the computer to write 100 divided by 3, like this:

```
<script>
document.write(100/3)
</script>
```

The computer will write:

```
33.333333333333336
```

Notice that the 17th digit, the 6, is wrong: it should be 3.

Division by 0

If you try to divide 1 by 0, the computer will say the answer is:

```
Infinity
```

If you try to divide 0 by 0, the computer will say the answer is —

```
NaN
```

which means "Not a Number".

Order of operations

JScript (and JavaScript) handle order of operations the same as QBasic, Visual Basic, and most other computer languages.

For example, if you type this program —

```
<script>
document.write(2+3*4)
</script>
```

the computer will "start with 2 then add three 4's", so it will write this answer:

```
14
```

You can use parentheses the same way as in algebra. For example, if you type —

```
<script>
document.write(5-(1+1))
</script>
```

the computer will compute 5-2 and write:

```
3
```

Strings

You learned how to put a JScript (or JavaScript) program in the middle of an HTML program. You can also do the opposite, you can put HTML in the middle of a JScript program.

For example, this JScript program makes the computer write "We *love* you":

```
<script>
document.write("We <i>love</i> you")
</script>
```

The computer will write:

```
We love you
```

In that program, the "We <i>love</i> you" is called a **string** of characters. Each string must begin and end with a quotation mark. Between the quotation marks, put any characters you want the computer to write. A string can include an HTML tag, such as <i>.

Strings with numbers

If you bought 750 apples and buy 12 more, how many apples do you have altogether? This program makes the computer write the answer:

```
<script>
document.write(750+12," apples")
</script>
```

The computer will write the answer to 750+12 (which is 762) then the word " apples" (which includes a blank space), so altogether the computer will write:

```
762 apples
```

This program makes the computer put the answer into a complete sentence:

```
<script>
document.write("You have ",750+12," apples!")
</script>
```

The computer will write "You have " then 762 then "apples!", so altogether the computer will write:

```
You have 762 apples!
```

Writing several strings

Here's another example of strings:

```
<script>
document.write("fat")
document.write("her")
</script>
```

The computer will write "fat" then "her", so altogether the computer will write:

```
father
```

Let's make the computer write this instead:

```
fat
her
```

To do that, make the computer press the Enter key before her. Here's how: say
 (which is the HTML tag to break out a new line), like this —

```
<script>
document.write("fat")
document.write("<br>her")
</script>
```

or like this:

```
<script>
document.write("fat<br>her")
</script>
```

Addition

You can add strings together by using the + sign:

```
"fat"+"her" is the same as "father"
2+2+"ever" is the same as "4ever"
```

Variables

A letter can stand for a number. For example, x can stand for the number 47, as in this program:

```
<script>
x=47
document.write(x+2)
</script>
```

The second line says x stands for the number 47. In other words, x is a name for the number 47.

The next line says to write x+2. Since x is 47, the x+2 is 49; so the computer will write:

```
49
```

That's the only number the computer will write; it won't write 47.

A letter that stands for a number is called a **numeric variable**.

A letter can stand for a string. For example, y can stand for the string "We *love* you", as in this program:

```
<script>
y="We <i>love</i> you"
document.write(y)
</script>
```

The computer will write:

```
We love you
```

A letter that stands for a string is called a **string variable**.

A variable's name can be short (such as x) or long (such as town_population_in_2001). It can be as long as you wish! The name can contain letters, digits, and underscores, but not blank spaces. The name must begin with a letter or underscore, not a digit.

Increase

The symbol ++ means "increase". For example, ++n means "increase n".

This program increases n:

```
<script>
n=3
++n
document.write(n)
</script>
```

The n starts at 3 and increases to 4, so the computer prints 4.

Saying ++n gives the same answer as n=n+1, but the computer handles ++n faster.

The symbol ++ increases the number by 1, even if the number is a decimal. For example, if x is 17.4 and you say ++x, x will become 18.4.

Decrease

The opposite of ++ is --. The symbol -- means "decrease". For example, --n means "decrease n". Saying --n gives the same answer as n=n-1 but faster.

Arrays

A letter can stand for a list. For example, x can stand for a list, as in this program:

```
<script>
x=["love","death",48+9]
document.write(x)
document.write(x[2]/4)
</script>
```

That makes x be a list of three items: "love", "death", and the answer to 48+9 (which is 57). The next line makes the computer write all of x, like this:

```
love,death,57
```

In x (which is a list), there are three items:

```
The original item, which is called x[0], is "love".
The next item, which is called x[1], is "death".
The next item, which is called x[2], is 57.
```

The next line says to write x[2]/4, which is 57/4, which is 14.25; but since we didn't say <br>, the computer writes the 14.25 on the same line as the list, so altogether you see:

```
love,death,5714.25
```

A list is called an **array**.

Delayed definition If you want x to be a list of three items but don't want to list the three items yet, you can be vague by saying just —

```
x=Array(3)
```

Later, you can define x by lines such as:

```
x[0]="love"
x[1]="death"
x[2]=48+9
```

Pop-up boxes

Here's how to make a box appear suddenly on your screen.

Alert box

To create a surprise, make the computer create an **alert box**:

```
<script>
alert("Warning: your hair looks messy today")
document.write("You won't become Miss America")
</script>
```

When a human runs that program, the screen suddenly shows an **alert box**, which contains this message: "Warning: your hair looks messy today". (The computer automatically makes the box be in front of the Web page, be centered on the screen, and be wide enough to show the whole message.) The alert box also contains an OK button. The computer waits for the human to read that alert message and click "OK".

When the human clicks "OK", the alert box disappears and the computer obeys the program's next line, which makes the computer write onto the Web page:

```
You won't become Miss America
```

In an alert box, the computer uses its alert font, which you cannot change: you can*not* switch to italics or bold; you can*not* put HTML tags into that message.

Here's another example:

```
<script>
alert("You just won a million dollars")
document.write("Oops, I lost it, better luck next time")
</script>
```

When a human runs that program, an alert box tells the human "You just won a million dollars"; but when the human clicks "OK", the Web page says "Oops, I lost it, better luck next time".

Prompt box

To ask the human a question, make the computer create a **prompt box**:

```
<script>
x=prompt("What is your name?","")
document.write("I adore anyone whose name is ",x)
</script>
```

When a human runs that program, the computer creates a **prompt box**, which is a window letting the human type info into the computer. (The computer automatically makes the box be in front of the Web page and be slightly above the screen's center.) It contains this **prompt**: "What is your name?" It also contains a white box (into which the human can type a response) and an OK button.

The computer waits for the human to type a response. When the human finishes typing a response, the human must click the OK button (or press Enter) to make the window go away.

Then the Web page reappears and the computer makes x be whatever the human typed. For example, if the human typed —

```
Maria
```

x is Maria, so the computer writes this onto the Web page:

```
I adore anyone whose name is Maria
```

In that program, notice that the prompt line includes these symbols before the last parenthesis:

```
                                        ,""
```

If you type this instead —

```
                          ,"Type your name here"
```

here's what happens: the white box (into which the human types a name) will temporarily say "Type your name here", until the human starts typing.

College admissions This program makes the computer write a letter admitting you to the college of your choice:

```
<script>
college=prompt("What college would you like to enter?","")
document.write("You're admitted to ",college,". I hope you go to ",college,".")
</script>
<p>Respectfully yours,
<br>The Dean of Admissions
```

When you run the program, a prompt box appears, asking "What college would you like to enter?" Type your answer (then click OK or press Enter).

For example, if you type —

```
Harvard
```

the college will be "Harvard", so the computer will write "You're admitted to" then "Harvard" then ". I hope you go to " then "Harvard", then "." then the remaining HTML code, like this:

```
You're admitted to Harvard. I hope you go to Harvard.

Respectfully yours,
The Dean of Admissions
```

If you type this instead —

```
Hell
```

the computer will write:

```
You're admitted to Hell. I hope you go to Hell.

Respectfully yours,
The Dean of Admissions
```

All the writing is onto your screen's Web page. Afterwards, if you want to copy that writing onto paper, click Internet Explorer's Print button. (If you don't see the Print button, make it appear by maximizing the Internet Explorer window.)

Numeric input This program makes the computer predict your future:

```
<script>
y=prompt("In what year were you born?","")
document.write("In the year 2020, you'll turn ",2020-y," years old")
</script>
```

When you run the program, the computer asks, "In what year were you born?" If you answer —

```
1962
```

y will be 1962, and the computer will write:

```
In the year 2020, you'll turn 58 years old.
```

Control statements

A program is a list of statements that you want the computer to perform. Here's how to control which statements the computer performs, and when, and in what order.

If

This program makes the computer discuss the human's age:

```
<script>
age=prompt("How old are you?","")
document.write("I hope you enjoy being ",age)
</script>
```

When that program is run, the computer asks "How old are you?" and waits for the human's reply. For example, if the human says —

```
15
```

the age will be 15. Then the computer will print:

```
I hope you enjoy being 15
```

Let's make that program fancier, so if the human is under 18 the computer will also say "You are still a minor". To do that, just add a line saying:

```
if (age<18) document.write("<br>You are still a minor")
```

Notice you must put parentheses after the word "if". Altogether, the program looks like this:

```
<script>
age=prompt("How old are you?","")
document.write("I hope you enjoy being ",age)
if (age<18) document.write("<br>You are still a minor")
</script>
```

For example, if the human runs the program and says —

```
15
```

the computer will print:

```
I hope you enjoy being 15
You are still a minor
```

If instead the human says —

```
25
```

the computer will print just:

```
I hope you enjoy being 25
```

Else

Let's teach the computer how to respond to adults.

Here's how to program the computer so that if the age is less than 18, the computer will say "You are still a minor", but if the age is *not* less than 18 the computer will say "You are an adult" instead:

```
<script>
age=prompt("How old are you?","")
document.write("I hope you enjoy being ",age)
if (age<18) document.write("<br>You are still a minor")
else document.write("<br>You are an adult")
</script>
```

In programs, **the word "else" means "otherwise"**. The program says: if the age is less than 18, write "You are still a minor"; otherwise (if the age is *not* less than 18), write "you are an adult". So the computer will write "You are still a minor" or else write "You are an adult", depending on whether the age is less than 18.

Try running that program! If you say you're 50 years old, the computer will reply by saying:

```
I hope you enjoy being 50
You are an adult
```

Fancy relations

Like JavaScript, Java's "if" statement uses this notation:

Notation	Meaning
if (age<18)	if age is less than 18
if (age<=18)	if age is less than or equal to 18
if (age==18)	if age is equal to 18
if (age!=18)	if age is not equal to 18
if (age<18 && weight>200)	if age<18 and weight>200
if (age<18 || weight>200)	if age<18 or weight>200
if (sex=="male")	if sex is "male"
if (sex<"male")	if sex is a word (such as "female") that comes before "male" in dictionary
if (sex>"male")	if sex is a word (such as "neuter") that comes after "male" in dictionary

Notice that in the "if" statement, you should use double symbols: you should say "==" instead of "=", say "&&" instead of "&", and say "||" instead of "|". If you accidentally say "=" instead of "==", the computer will gripe. If you accidentally say "&" instead of "&&" or say "|" instead of "||", the computer will still get the right answers but too slowly.

Braces

If a person's age is less than 18, let's make the computer write "You are still a minor" and make maturity=0. Here's how:

```
if (age<18)
{
    document.write("You are still a minor")
    maturity=0
}
```

Here's a fancier example:

```
if (age<18)
{
    document.write("You are still a minor")
    maturity=0
}
else
{
    document.write("You are an adult")
    maturity=1
}
```

For

Here's how to write the numbers from 1 to 10:

```
<script>
for (i=1; i<=10; ++i) document.write(i," ")
</script>
```

That means: do repeatedly, for i starting at 1, while i is no more than 10, and increasing i after each time: write i followed by a blank space (to separate i from the next number). The computer will write:

```
1 2 3 4 5 6 7 8 9 10
```

If instead you want to write each number on a separate line, say "<br>" (which means "break for new line") before each number:

```
<script>
for (i=1; i<=10; ++i) document.write("<br>",i)
</script>
```

The computer will write:

```
1
2
3
4
5
6
7
8
9
10
```

Let's get fancier! For each number, let's make the computer also write the number's **square** (what you get when you multiply the number by itself), like this:

```
1 squared is 1
2 squared is 4
3 squared is 9
4 squared is 16
5 squared is 25
6 squared is 36
7 squared is 49
8 squared is 64
9 squared is 81
10 squared is 100
```

Here's how:

```
<script>
for (i=1; i<=10; ++i) document.write("<br>",i," squared is ",i*i)
</script>
```

To get even fancier, let's make the computer write that info in a pretty table, like this:

NAME	SCORE
1	1
2	4
3	9
4	16
5	25
6	36
7	49
8	64
9	81
10	100

As I explained on page 288, you do that by saying <table border=1> above the table, <tr> at the beginning of each table row, <th> at the beginning of each column heading, <td> at the beginning of each data item, and </table> below the table:

```
<table border=1>
<tr><th>NAME<th>SCORE
<script>
for (i=1; i<=10; ++i) document.write("<tr><td>",i,"<td>",i*i)
</script>
</table>
```

Onclick

Let's create a Web page that asks, "What sex are you?" Below that question, let's put two buttons labeled "Male" and "Female". If the human clicks the "Male" button, let's make the computer say "So is Frankenstein". If the human clicks the "Female" button, let's make the computer say "So is Mary Poppins".

To accomplish all that, just type this HTML:

```
What sex are you?
<form>
<input type=button value="Male" onclick="alert('So is Frankenstein')">
<input type=button value="Female" onclick="alert('So is Mary Poppins')">
</form>
```

Here's what each line accomplishes:

Since we want the Web page to begin by asking "What sex are you?", the top line says "What sex are you?"

To create buttons, you must create a form to put them in, so the second line says <form>.

The next line says to create an input button labeled "Male", which when clicked will do this command: create an alert box saying "So is Frankenstein".

The next line says to create a similar input button labeled "Female", which when clicked will do this command: create an alert box saying "So is Mary Poppins".

The bottom line, </form>, marks the end of the form.

Notice these details:

> After onclick, you put an equal sign, then a quotation mark, then any command written in JavaScript (or JScript), such as "alert". The computer automatically knows that the onclick command uses JavaScript, so you don't have to say <script>.
>
> The JavaScript command must be in a pair of quotation marks. If you want to put a pair of quotation marks inside another pair of quotation marks, use a pair of single quotes (which look like apostrophes).
>
> After onclick, instead of typing a JavaScript command, you can type *several* JavaScript commands, if you separate them by semicolons, like this:
> ```
> onclick="x=4; y=2; alert(x+y)"
> ```
> That would mean: if the button is clicked, make x=4, make y=2, and create an alert box showing their sum, 6.
>
> When you create two buttons, the second button normally appears to the *right* of the first button. If you'd rather place the second button *below* the first button, say <br> before the second button to put it on a new line, like this:
> ```
> <br><input type=button value="Female" onclick="alert('So is Mary Poppins')">
> ```

Documentation

On page 291, I said you can write a comment in your HTML program by starting with the symbol "<!--" and ending with the symbol "-->", like this:
```
<!--I wrote this program while drunk-->
```
But while you're writing JavaScript (or JScript) program lines, which comes between <script> and </script>, you must write your comments differently, in JavaScript style: put each comment on a separate line that begins with //, like this:
```
//I wrote these JavaScript lines while even drunker
```

Emphasize JavaScript

To emphasize that your program is written in JavaScript (or a JavaScript clone such as JScript), you can say —
```
<script language="JavaScript">
```
or even say —
```
<script language="JavaScript" type="text/javascript">
```
instead of saying just <script>.

No JavaScript?

Most Web browsers understand JavaScript and JScript programs. But Web browsers that are very old or very primitive don't understand JavaScript at all.

If your Web-page program contains a JavaScript program, but somebody who lacks JavaScript tries to view your Web page, the page will look very messed up, and the person might even see your raw JavaScript code, including equal signs and words such as "document.write".

To make sure such a person doesn't see your raw code on the Web page, say this instead of just <script> —
```
<script>
<!--
```
and say this instead of just </script>:
```
//-->
</script>
```
Also, warn the JavaScript-deprived person that your page requires JavaScript, by putting this line below the </script> line:
```
<noscript>This page requires JavaScript</noscript>
```
Here's what that line accomplishes: if the person has no JavaScript, the Web page will say "This page requires JavaScript".

Fun

Java is a programming language. It was invented by James Gosling at **Sun Microsystems** in California in 1995.

Java resembles JavaScript (and JScript) but includes extra commands, so you can create a greater variety of programs. Those extra commands make Java a complete programming language (like QBasic and Visual Basic).

Java is easy to learn. It's almost as easy as QBasic, Visual Basic, JavaScript, and JScript.

Java's a simplified version of **C** (which is much harder and discussed in the next chapter).

Java uses these commands:

Java command	Page
char grade;	608
char grade='A';	608
double x;	607
double[] x={81.2,51.7,207.9};	608
double[] x=new double[3];	608
double[][] x=new double[2][3];	608
else {	610
for (int i=20; i<=24; ++i) {	611
if (age<18) {	610
import java.util.Scanner;	609
import static java.lang.Math.*;	607
int x;	607
int x=3;	607
int[] x={81,52,207}	608
package joe;	605
public class Joe {	605
public static void main(…) {	605
Scanner in=new Scanner(…);	609
String x;	609
String x="he";	609
System.out.print("nose");	606
System.out.println("nose");	606
while (i<25) {	611
x=3;	607
++x;	608
--x;	608
// Zoo program is fishy	606
/* Zoo program is fishy */	606

Java uses these functions:

Java function	Page
in.nextDouble()	610
in.nextInt()	609
in.nextLine()	609
Math.abs	607
Math.acos(x)	607
Math.asin(x)	607
Math.atan(x)	607
Math.atan2(y,x)	607
Math.ceil(x)	607
Math.cos(x)	607
Math.exp(x)	607
Math.floor(x)	607
Math.log(x)	607
Math.pow(x,y)	607
Math.sin(x)	607
Math.sqrt(x)	607
Math.tan(x)	607
x.compareTo(y)	610

Here's how to enjoy programming in Java.

To *run* programs that were written in Java, you must download (copy) the **Java Runtime Environment (JRE)** from Sun's Website to your computer. To *develop* (create and edit) your own programs in Java, you must also download the **Java Development Kit (JDK)**. To develop your own program *easily* in Java, you must also download an **Integrated Development Environment (IDE)**, such as **NetBeans**.

You can download all three of those tools (**JRE**, **JDK**, and **NetBeans**) from Sun's Website, free.

Copy Java tools to the hard disk

Here's how to copy **JRE** (version 6, update 25), **JDK**, and **NetBeans** (version 7) to your hard disk by using Windows (Vista or 7) and Internet Explorer 9:

> Go to www.oracle.com. Click "Java for Developers" (which is at the screen's right edge) then the NetBeans button (which is in the screen's middle) then the "Accept License Agreement" button then "0-windows-ml.exe".
>
> Click "Run" (which is at the screen's bottom). If the computer says "could harm your computer", click "Actions" then "More Options" then "Run anyway".
>
> If you're using Windows 7, click "Yes". If you're using Windows Vista, click "Allow".
>
> Close the Internet Explorer window (by clicking its X). The computer says "Welcome to the JDK 6 Update 25 and NetBeans IDE 7.0 Installer". Press Enter. Click "I accept". Press Enter, 4 times.
>
> Several minutes later, the computer says "Installation completed successfully." Press Enter.

Start Java

To start using **Java** (version 6, update 25) with **NetBeans** (version 7), do this:

> If you see a "NetBeans IDE 7.0" icon (on you desktop screen), double-click it. Otherwise, click the Start button then "All Programs" then "NetBeans" then "NetBeans IDE 7.0".
>
> You see the NetBeans IDE 7.0 window. If it doesn't consume the whole screen yet, maximize it (by clicking the Maximize button, which is next to the X).

Start a new program

Click the **New Project** button. (It's an orange square with a green plus sign on it. It's near the screen's top-left corner, below the words "Edit" and "View".)

In the Categories box, make sure the top choice ("Java") is highlighted (in blue or gray). If it's not highlighted yet, highlight it (by clicking it).

In the Projects box, make sure the top choice ("Java Application") is highlighted (in blue or gray). If it's not highlighted yet, highlight it (by clicking it).

Press Enter.

Invent a name for your project (such as "Joe"). Type the name and press Enter.

You see a big white box. In that box is a prototype Java program. That program does nothing useful, but you can edit it to do whatever you wish!

In that program, the important lines look like this:

```
package joe;
public class Joe {
    public static void main (String[] args) {
    }
}
```

In those lines, the characters are black or blue.

In other lines, the characters are gray. The computer ignores those gray lines — and you should too! — since they're just comments.

If you find the gray lines (and blank lines) too distracting, erase them. (To erase a line, click it then do this: while holding down the Ctrl key, tap the E key.)

Let's program the computer to say:

```
make your nose
touch your toes
```

To do that, edit the prototype program by inserting these extra lines:

```
package joe;
public class Joe {
    public static void main (String[] args) {
        System.out.println("make your nose");
        System.out.println("touch your toes");
    }
}
```

Here's how to insert those extra lines:

Click to the right of the second "{". Press Enter. Type the first extra line (making sure you capitalize the first "S" in "System"), press Enter, and type the second extra line. Notice you must type a semicolon at the end of each line.

The computer indents the lines automatically. Whenever you type "(", the computer automatically types the matching ")" for you. Whenever you type a quotation mark, the computer automatically types the matching quotation mark for you.

If you ever want the computer to indent differently, do this before typing a line's first word or symbol....

To indent, press the Tab key.

To unindent, press the Backspace key repeatedly or do this: while holding down the Shift key, tap the Tab key.

Here's what those extra lines mean:

The first extra line makes the computer **system** send **out** a **print**ed **line** saying "make your nose" and makes the computer press Enter afterwards. (If you omit the "ln", the computer will *not* press Enter afterwards.)

The second extra line makes the computer print "touch your toes" and press Enter afterwards.

When you finish inserting those extra lines, congratulations! You've written a Java program!

Run the program

To run the program, press the **F6 key** (or click the big green triangle, which is near the screen's top, below the words "Tools" and "Window").

In the **Output window** (at the screen's bottom), the computer will say —

```
make your nose
touch your toes
```

It will also say "BUILD SUCCESSFUL", which means you didn't make any obvious mistakes. Congratulations!

While the program you wrote is on the screen, you can edit it. After editing it, rerun it (by pressing the F6 key or clicking the big green triangle).

When you finish playing with that program, you can start a new program by clicking the **New Project** button again.

Get old programs

Here's how to view old programs you created earlier:

While you're running NetBeans, click "Projects" (which is at the screen's left edge). You see a list of projects (programs) that you created. Each project's name is at the screen's left edge. Indented under the project's name are files (and folders) containing details about the project.

If you want to delete one of the projects, click its name (at the screen's left edge) then press the Delete key then click "Also Delete Sources" then "Yes".

If you want to use one of the projects now, do this.... Right-click it (using the rightmost mouse button). Click "Set as Main Project" if you see that choice. (If you don't see that choice, that project is your main project already, so press the Esc key.) Double-click the file underneath that ends in ".java".

Comments

To put a comment in your program, begin the comment with the symbol //. The computer ignores everything that's to the right of //. Here's an example:

```
// This program is fishy
// It was written by a sick sailor swimming in the sun
package joe;
public class Joe {
    public static void main (String[] args) {
        System.out.println("Our funny God");  // religious
        System.out.println(invented cod");    // wet joke
    }
}
```

The computer ignores all the comments, which are to the right of //.

While you type the program, the computer makes each // and each comment turn gray. Then the computer ignores everything that's turned gray, so the computer prints just:

```
Our funny God
invented cod
```

Another way to write a comment is to begin it with the symbol /* and end it with the symbol */, like this:

```
/* This program is fishy
   It was written by a sick sailor swimming in the sun */
package joe;
public class Joe {
    public static void main (String[] args) {
        System.out.println("Our funny God");  /* religious */
        System.out.println(invented cod");    /* wet joke */
    }
}
```

Math

The computer can do math. For example, this line makes the computer do 4+2:

```
        System.out.println(4+2);
```

If you put that line into your program and run the program, the computer will print this answer on your screen, in the Output window:

```
6
```

If you bought 750 apples and buy 12 more, how many apples do you have altogether? This line prints the answer:

```
        System.out.println(750+12+" apples");
```

That line makes the computer do 750+12 (which is 762) and add the word " apples" (which includes a blank space), so the computer will print:

```
762 apples
```

This line makes the computer put the answer into a complete sentence:

```
        System.out.println("You have "+(750+12)+" apples!");
```

The computer will print "You have " and add 762 and add " apples!", so altogether the computer will print:

```
You have 762 apples!
```

Like most other languages (such as Basic and JavaScript), Java lets you use the symbols +, -, *, /, parentheses, decimal points, and e notation.

Integers versus double precision

Java handles two types of numbers well.

One type of number is called an **integer** (or **int**). An int contains no decimal point and no e. For example, -27 and 30000 are ints.

The other type of number that Java handles well is called a **double-precision number** (or a **double**). **A double contains a decimal point or an e.** For example, -27.0 and 3e4 are doubles. You can abbreviate: instead of writing "-27.0", you can write "-27.", and instead of writing "0.37" you can write ".37".

Largest and tiniest numbers

The largest permissible int is about 2 billion. More precisely:

```
the largest int is 2147483647
the lowest int is -2147483648
```

If you try to feed the computer an int that's too large or too low, the computer won't complain. Instead, the computer will typically print a wrong answer!

The largest permissible double is about 1.7e308. More precisely, it's 1.7976931348623158e308. If you feed the computer a math problem whose answer is bigger than that, the computer will give up and typically say the answer is:

```
Infinity
```

The tiniest double that the computer handles well is about 2.2e-308. More precisely, it's 2.2250738585072014e-308. If you feed the computer a math problem whose answer is tinier than that, the computer will either handle the rightmost digits inaccurately or give up, saying the answer is 0.0.

Tricky arithmetic

If you combine ints, the answer is an int. For example, 2+3 is this int: 5.

11/4 is this int: 2. (11/4 is *not* 2.75.)

If you combine doubles, the answer is a double. If you combine an int with a double, the answer is a double.

How much is 2000 times 2000000? Theoretically, the answer should be this int: 4000000000. But since 4000000000 is too large to be an int, the computer will print a wrong answer. To make the computer multiply 2000 by 2000000 correctly, ask for 2000.0*2000000.0, like this:

```
System.out.println(2000.0*2000000.0);
```

That program makes the computer get the correct answer, 4000000000.0, which the computer will write in e notation, so you see this answer:

```
4.0E9
```

Long decimals

If an answer is a decimal that contains *many* digits, **the computer will typically print the first 16 significant digits accurately and the 17th digit approximately**. The computer won't bother printing later digits.

For example, suppose you ask the computer to print 10.0 divided by 9.0, like this:

```
System.out.println(10.0/9.0);
```

The computer will print:

```
1.1111111111111112
```

Notice that the 17th digit, the 2, is slightly wrong: it should be 1.

Division by 0.0

If you try to divide 1.0 by 0.0, the computer will say the answer is:

```
Infinity
```

If you try to divide 0.0 by 0.0, the computer will say the answer is —

```
NaN
```

which means "Not a Number".

Advanced math

The computer can do advanced math. For example, it can compute square roots. This line makes the computer print the square root of 9:

```
System.out.println(Math.sqrt(9.0));
```

The computer will print:

```
3.0
```

Say Math.sqrt(9.0) rather than Math.sqrt(9), because the number you find the square root of should be double-precision, not an integer. If you make the mistake of saying Math.sqrt(9), the computer will print the correct answer but slowly.

Besides sqrt, you can use these other advanced math functions:

To handle exponents, you can use sqrt (square root), exp (exponential power of e), and log (logarithm base e). You can also use pow: for example, pow(3.0,2.0) is 3.0 raised to the 2.0 power.

For trigonometry, you can use sin (sine), cos (cosine), tan (tangent), asin (arcsin), acos (arccosine), and atan (arctangent). You can also use atan2: for example, atan2(y,x) is the arctangent of y divided by x.

For absolute value, use abs. For example, abs(-2.3) is 2.3.

To round, use floor (which rounds down) or ceil (which stands for "ceiling" and rounds *up*). For example, floor(26.319) is 26.0, and ceil(26.319) is 27.0.

Before each advanced math function, you must say "Math." unless you insert this line above the "public class" line:

```
import static java.lang.Math.*;
```

Variables

Like Basic and JavaScript, Java lets you use variables. For example, you can say:

```
n=3;
```

A variable's name can be short (such as n) or long (such as town_population_in_2001). It can be as long as you wish! The name can contain letters, digits, and underscores, but not blank spaces. The name must begin with a letter or underscore, not a digit.

Before using a variable, say what type of number the variable stands for. For example, if n and town_population_in_2001 will stand for numbers that are ints and mortgage_rate will stand for a double, begin your program by saying:

```
package joe;
public class Main {
    public static void main (String[] args) {
        int n, town_population_in_2001;
        double mortgage_rate;
```

If n is an integer that starts at 3, you can say —

```
int n;
n=3;
```

but you can combine those two lines into this single line:

```
int n=3;
```

Here's how to say "n is an integer that starts at 3, and population_in_2001 is an integer that starts at 27000":

```
int n=3, population_in_2001=27000;
```

Increase

Like JavaScript, Java uses the symbol ++ to mean "increase". For example, ++n means "increase n".

These lines create n, increase it, then print it:

```
int n=3;
++n;
System.out.println(n);
```

The n starts at 3 and increases to 4, so the computer prints 4.

Saying ++n gives the same answer as n=n+1, but the computer handles ++n faster.

The symbol ++ increases the number by 1, even if the number is a decimal. For example, if x is 17.4 and you say ++x, the x will become 18.4.

Decrease

The opposite of ++ is --. The symbol -- means "decrease". For example, --n means "decrease n". Saying --n gives the same answer as n=n-1 but faster.

Strange short cuts

If you use the following short cuts, your programs will be briefer and run faster.

Instead of saying n=n+2, say n+=2, which means "n's increase is 2". Similarly, instead of saying n=n*3, say n*=3, which means "n's multiplier is 3".

Instead of saying ++n and then giving another command, say ++n in the middle of the other command. For example, instead of saying —

```
++n;
j=7*n;
```

say:

```
j=7*++n;
```

That's pronounced: "j is 7 times an increased n". So if n was 2, saying j=7*++n makes n become 3 and j become 21.

Notice that when you say j=7*++n, the computer increases n *before* computing j. If you say j=7*n++ instead, the computer increases n *after* computing j; so j=7*n++ has the same effect as saying:

```
j=7*n;
++n;
```

Arrays

Instead of being just a number, x can be a *list* of numbers (as in Visual Basic and JavaScript).

Example For example, if you want x to be this list of ints —

{81, 52, 207, 19}

type this:

```
int[] x={81,52,207,19};
```

Notice that when you type the list of numbers, you must **put commas between the numbers** and put the entire list of numbers in **braces**, {}. On your keyboard, the "{" symbol is to the right of the P key and requires you to hold down the Shift key.

In x's list, **the starting number** (which is 81) **is called x_0** (which is pronounced "x subscripted by zero" or "x sub 0" or just "x 0"). The next number (which is 52) is called x_1 (which is pronounced "x subscripted by one" or "x sub 1" or just "x 1"). The next number is called x_2. Then comes x_3. So **the four numbers in the list are called x_0, x_1, x_2, and x_3**.

To make the computer say what x_2 is, type this line:

```
System.out.println(x[2]);
```

That line makes Text be x_2, which is 207, so the computer will print:

207

So the program says:

```
int[] x={81,52,207,19};
System.out.println(x[2]);
```

The first line says the integer list x is {81, 52, 207, 19}. The bottom line makes the computer say x_2's number, which is 207.

Jargon Notice this jargon:

In a symbol such as x_2, the lowered number (the 2) is called the **subscript**.

To create a subscript in your subroutine, use brackets. For example, to create x_2, type x[2].

A variable having subscripts is called an **array**. For example, x is an array if there's an x_0, x_1, x_2, etc.

Different types Instead of having ints, you can have different types. For example, you can say:

```
double[] x={81.2,51.7,207.9,19.5};
```

Uninitialized Instead of putting a list of numbers into the int line or double line, you can type the numbers underneath, if you warn the computer how many numbers will be in the list, like this:

```
double[] x=new double[3];
x[0]=200.1;
x[1]=700.4;
x[2]=53.2;
System.out.println(x[0]+x[1]+x[2]);
```

The top line says x_0, x_1, and x_2 will be doubles. The next lines say x_0 is 200.1, x_1 is 700.4, and x_2 is 53.2. The bottom line makes the computer print their sum:

953.7

Notice that if you say double[] x=new double[3], you can refer to x[0], x[1], and x[2], but not x[3]. If you accidentally refer to x[3], the computer will gripe about "ArrayIndexOutOfBoundsException".

If you want x to be a table having 2 rows and 3 columns of double-precision numbers, begin your program by saying:

```
double[][] x=new double[2][3];
```

Since Java always starts counting at 0 (not 1), the number in the table's top left corner is called x[0][0].

Character variables

A variable can stand for a character.

For example, suppose you're in school, take a test, and get an A on it. To proclaim your grade, write a program containing this line:

```
grade='A';
```

Here's the complete program:

```
package joe;
public class Joe {
    public static void main (String[] args) {
        char grade;                        The grade is a character.
        grade='A';                         The grade is 'A'.
        System.out.println(grade);         Print the grade.
    }
}
```

The computer will print:

A

In that program, you can combine these two lines —

```
char grade;                        The grade is a character.
grade='A';                         The grade is 'A'.
```

to form this single line:

```
char grade='A';          The grade is this character: 'A'.
```

String variables

A variable can stand for a whole String of characters:

```
String x;
x="he";
System.out.println("fat"+x+"red");
```

The first line says there's a String of characters, called x. The second line says x is this String of characters: "he". The third shaded line makes the computer print "fat" then x (which is "he") then "red", so the computer will print:

```
fathered
```

Java requires you to capitalize the first letter of String: say String, not string.

In that program, you can combine these two lines —

```
String x;
x="he";
```

to form this single line:

```
String x="he";
```

Input

Like Basic and JavaScript, Java lets you input; but Java makes it harder.

String input

This program lets you input a String and call it s:

```
package joe;
import java.util.Scanner;
public class Joe {
    public static void main (String[] args) {
        Scanner in=new Scanner(System.in);
        System.out.print("What is your name? ");
        String s=in.nextLine();
        System.out.println("I like the name "+s+" very much");
    }
}
```

How to type the program Carefully type your program, including the 3 commands that prepare the computer for input:

Say "**import java.util.Scanner**" at the program's top (below just the "package" line).
Say stuff about "**Scanner in**" immediately below the "public static void main" line.

Type that exactly! Beware of capitals and spaces!

After you've typed those 2 preparatory commands, the rest of the program is easy to type and understand:

The System.out.print line makes the computer ask "What is your name? ".
The next line makes String s be the next Line that the human types in.
The System.out.println makes the computer say "I like the name " then s then " very much".

How to run the program To run the program, press the F6 key.

The System.out.print line makes the computer ask, in the Output window (at the screen's bottom):

```
What is your name?
```

Then the computer waits for the human to type a name, such as "Joan" or "Dr. Hector von Snotblower, Jr., M.D."; but **before the human types, the human must make sure the word "Output" (at the Output window's top) has a blue background.** If Output's background isn't blue yet, the human must turn it blue by clicking it. (If Output's background is white instead of blue, the human will be accidentally typing in the Program Edit window instead of the Output window — and wreck your program!)

After the human gets a blue Output background and types a name (such as "Joan"), the screen's bottom looks like this:

```
What is your name? Joan
```

At the end of typing the name, the human should press the Enter key. Then the computer finishes running the program, so the Output window finally shows this:

```
What is your name? Joan
I like the name Joan very much
```

Integer input

That program lets you input a String. To input an integer instead, use the same technique, but instead of saying "nextLine" say "**nextInt**".

For example, this program asks the human's age then predicts how old the human will be 10 years from now:

```
package joe;
import java.util.Scanner;
public class Joe {
    public static void main (String[] args) {
        Scanner in=new Scanner(System.in);
        System.out.print("How old are you? ");
        int age=in.nextInt();
        System.out.println ("Ten years from now, you'll be "+(age+10));
    }
}
```

Here's how the program works:

The System.out.print line makes the computer ask "How old are you? ".
The next line makes the integer age be the next Integer that the human types in.
The System.out.println makes the computer say "Ten years from now, you'll be " then age+10.

Here's a sample run:

```
How old are you? 27
Ten years from now, you'll be 37
```

Double-precision input

In the program above, age is an integer. If you want age to be double-precision instead, change the shaded line to this:

```
double age=in.nextDouble();
```

Logic

Java lets you say "if", "while", "for", and create comments. Here are examples....

If

If a person's age is less than 18, let's make the computer say "You are still a minor." Here's the fundamental line:

```
if (age<18) System.out.println("You are still a minor.");
```

Notice you must put parentheses after the word "if".

If a person's age is less than 18, let's make the computer say "You are still a minor." and also say "Ah, the joys of youth!" and "I wish I were as young as you!" Here's how to say all that:

```
if (age<18) {
    System.out.println("You are still a minor.");
    System.out.println("Ah, the joys of youth!");
    System.out.println("I wish I were as young as you!");
}
```

Since that "if" line is above the "{", the "if" line is a structure line, similar to a "public class" line, and does *not* end in a semicolon.

Here's how to put that structure into a complete program, assuming age is an integer:

```
package joe;
import java.util.Scanner;
public class Joe {
    public static void main (String[] args) {
    {
        Scanner in=new Scanner(System.in);
        System.out.print("How old are you? ");
        int age=in.nextInt();
        if (age<18) {
            System.out.println("You are still a minor.");
            System.out.println("Ah, the joys of youth!");
            System.out.println("I wish I were as young as you!");
        }
        else {
            System.out.println("You are an adult.");
            System.out.println("Now we can have some adult fun!");
        }
        System.out.println("Glad to have met you.");
    }
}
```

If the person's age is less than 18, the computer will print "You are still a minor." and "Ah, the joys of youth!" and "I wish I were as young as you!" If the person's age is not less than 18, the computer will print "You are an adult." and "Now we can have some adult fun!" Regardless of the person's age, the computer will end the conversation by saying "Glad to have met you."

The "if" statement uses this notation:

Notation	Meaning
if (age<18)	if age is less than 18
if (age<=18)	if age is less than or equal to 18
if (age==18)	if age is equal to 18
if (age!=18)	if age is not equal to 18
if (age<18 && weight>200)	if age<18 and weight>200
if (age<18 || weight>200)	if age<18 or weight>200

Notice that in the "if" statement, you should use double symbols: you should say "==" instead of "=", say "&&" instead of "&", and say "||" instead of "|". If you accidentally say "=" instead of "==", the computer will gripe. If you accidentally say "&" instead of "&&" or say "|" instead of "||", the computer will still get the right answers but too slowly.

Strings The symbols <, <=, ==, and != let you compare numbers or characters but not Strings. If you try to use them to compare Strings, you'll get wrong answers.

For example, suppose x and y are strings, and you want to test whether they're equal. Do *not* say "if (x==y)". Instead, say:

```
if (x.equals(y))
```

Make sure you put the period after x and put parentheses around y.

An alternative is to say:

```
if (x.equalsIgnoreCase(y))
```

That makes the computer compare x with y and ignore capitalization. It makes the computer consider x to be "equal" to y if the only difference is "which letters in the string are capitalized".

To test whether x's string comes before y's in the dictionary, do not say "if (x<y)". Instead, say:

```
if (x.compareTo(y)<0)
```

While

Let's make the computer print the word "love" repeatedly, like this:

```
love
love
love
love
love
love
love
etc.
```

This program does it:

```java
package joe;
public class Joe {
    public static void main (String[] args) {
        while (true) System.out.println("love");
    }
}
```

The "while (true)" means: do repeatedly. The computer will do System.out.println("love") repeatedly, looping forever — or until you **abort** the program by clicking the red square (which is at the Output window's left edge). You'll see lots of love — as much love as fits in the Output window.

Let's make the computer start at 20 and keep counting, so the computer will print:

```
20
21
22
23
24
25
26
etc.
```

This program does it:

Program	Meaning
`package joe;`	
`public class Joe {`	
`    public static void main (String[] args) {`	
`        int i=20;`	Start the integer i at 20.
`        while (true) {`	Repeat indented lines forever:
`            System.out.println(i);`	print i then press Enter
`            ++i;`	increase i
`        }`	
`    }`	
`}`	

It prints faster than you can read. By the time your eye focuses, the computer is already printing numbers beyond 10000. The number will keep increasing until you abort the program (by clicking the red square at the screen's left edge).

In that program, if you say "while (i<25)" instead of "while (true)", the computer will do the loop only while i remains less than 25; the computer will print just:

```
20
21
22
23
24
```

Instead of saying "while (i<25)", you can say "while (i<=24)".

For

Here's a more natural way to get that output of numbers from 20 to 24:

```java
package joe;
public class Joe {
    public static void main (String[] args) {
        for (int i=20; i<=24; ++i) System.out.println(i);
    }
}
```

In that program, the "for (int i=20; i<=24; ++i)" means "Do repeatedly. Start the integer i at 20, and keep repeating as long as i<=24. At the end of each repetition, do ++i."

In that "for" statement, if you change the ++i to i+=2, the computer will increase i by 2 instead of by 1, so the computer will print:

```
20
22
24
```

The "for" statement is quite flexible. You can even say "for (int i=20; i<100; i*=2)", which makes i start at 20 and keep doubling, so the computer prints:

```
20
40
80
```

Like "if" and "while", the "for" statement can sit atop a group of indented lines that are in braces.

Visual C#

A Microsoft employee (**Anders Hejlsberg**) invented a nifty computer language. He called it **Cool** but changed the name to **C#** (pronounced "C sharp"), to emphasize it's higher than an earlier language, called **C**. (It's also higher than a C variant called **C++**.)

C# tries to combine the best features of Visual Basic, Java, C, and C++:

Like Visual Basic, it lets you create windows easily.

Like Java, it uses modern notation for typing lines in programs.

Like C and C++, it runs fast.

C# is also influenced by an older programming language called **Pascal**. Before inventing C#, Anders Hejlsberg had already invented two famous Pascal versions (**Turbo Pascal** and **Delphi**) and a famous Java version (**J++**); he was an extremely experienced designer when he invented C#. He knew what was wrong with Pascal, Java, and C++, and Visual Basic and how to improve them.

Microsoft recommends using Visual Basic to create simple programs but C# to create bigger projects. Microsoft considers Visual Basic and C# to be the most important computer languages to learn.

You already learned Visual Basic. Now let's tackle C#.

The newest version of C#, called **Visual C# 2010**, is expensive. But Microsoft lets you download, free, a stripped-down version called **Visual C# 2010 Express**; I'll explain how to get it and use it. It understands these commands:

C# command	Page
catch	619
char x;	615
class Program	613
Console.ReadKey();	613
Console.Write("Love");	614
Console.WriteLine("Love");	613
double x;	615
double x = -27.0;	615
double[] x = new double[3];	617
double[] x = { 81.2, 51.7, 7.9 };	617
double[,] x = new double[2, 3];	617
else	617
if (age < 18)	617
for (int i = 20; i <= 29; ++i)	618
goto yummy;	619
int x;	615
int x = 3;	615
int[] x = new int[3];	617
int[] x = { 81, 52, 207 };	616
int[,] x = new int[2, 3];	617
long x;	615
MessageBox.Show("Hair mess");	622
namespace Joan	613
private void Form1_Load(…)	622
public Form1()	622
public partial class Form1 : Form	622
return (a + b) / 2;	621
static int average(int a, int b)	621
static void Main(string[] args)	613
static void x()	620
string x;	615
string[] x = { "love", "h" };	617
Text = "I love you";	622
try	619
uint x;	615
ulong x;	615
using System;	613
while (true)	618
x = 3;	615
x();	615
++x;	615
--x;	615
// Zoo program is fishy	619

It also understands these functions:

C# function	Page
Console.ReadLine()	616
Convert.ToDouble(x)	616
Convert.ToInt32(x)	616
Convert.ToInt64(x)	616
Convert.ToString(x)	622
Convert.ToUInt32(x)	616
Convert.ToUInt64(x)	616
Math.Abs(x)	615
Math.Acos(x)	615
Math.Asin(x)	615
Math.Atan(x)	615
Math.Atan2(y, x)	615
Math.Ceiling(x)	615
Math.Cos(x)	615
Math.Cosh(x)	615
Math.E	615
Math.Exp(y)	615
Math.Floor(x)	615
Math.Log(x)	615
Math.Log(x, b)	615
Math.Log10(x)	615
Math.PI	615
Math.Pow(x, y)	615
Math.Sin(x)	615
Math.Sinh(x)	615
Math.Sqrt(x)	615
Math.Tan(x)	615
Math.Tanh(x)	615
x.CompareTo("male")	618

Fun

Here's how to enjoy programming in C#.

Copy C# to hard disk

Here's how to copy Visual C# 2010 Express to your hard disk by using Windows (Vista or 7) and Internet Explorer.

Go to www.microsoft.com/express/downloads. Click "Visual C# 2010 Express" then the down-arrow then "English" then "Run" (which is at the screen's bottom).

If you're using Windows 7, click "Yes". If you're using Windows Vista, click "Continue".

The computer will say "Welcome to Setup". Press the Enter key. Click "I have read and accept the license terms." Press Enter, 3 times.

The computer will copy (download) and install Visual C# onto your hard disk.

The computer will say "Setup complete". Press Enter. Close Internet Explorer's window (by clicking the X at the screen's top-right corner).

Start C#

To start using C#, click the Start button then do this:

If you see "Microsoft Visual C# 2010 Express", click it. Otherwise, click "All Programs" then "Microsoft Visual Studio 2010 Express" (which you'll see by scrolling down) then "Microsoft Visual C# 2010 Express".

You see the Start Page window.

Start a new program

Click "**New Project**" (which is near the screen's left edge). Double-click "**Console Application**".

Type your program

The computer starts typing the program for you. The computer types:

```
using System;
using System.Collections.Generic;
using System.Linq;
using System.Text;

namespace ConsoleApplication1
{
    class Program
    {
        static void Main(string[] args)
        {
        }
    }
}
```

Let's write a program that makes the computer say "I love you". To do that, insert 2 extra lines, so the program becomes this:

```
using System;
using System.Collections.Generic;
using System.Linq;
using System.Text;

namespace ConsoleApplication1
{
    class Program
    {
        static void Main(string[] args)
        {
            Console.WriteLine("I love you");
            Console.ReadKey();
        }
    }
}
```

Here's how to insert those line:

Click under the word "void". Press Enter. Type the first inserted line, press Enter, and type the second inserted line.

The computer indents the lines for you, automatically.

You must type a semicolon at the end of each simple line. But there's no semicolon at the end of a **structure line** (a line that's blank or says just "{" or "}" or is immediately above "{").

Important line The most important line is the one that says:

```
Console.WriteLine("I love you");
```

It makes the computer write "I love you" onto the screen.

Helper line To make Console.WriteLine work properly, you must put this **helper line** near the program's bottom, just above the 3 final "}" lines:

```
Console.ReadKey();
```

That makes the computer pause until the human has read the computer's output and presses a key.

You must put that helper line in every normal program.

Run the program

To run your program, press the F5 key (or click the green " ▶ ", which is at the screen's top center).

If you did everything correctly, you see the **console window** (which has white letters on a black background and resembles the DOS command-prompt screen). The console window shows the computer's output. It shows:

```
I love you
```

When you finish admiring that output, press the Enter key (or Space bar or any other normal key) or click the console window's X button.

If you want to run the program again, press the F5 key again.

If you want to edit the program, retype the parts you wish; then press F5 again (which makes the computer debug and run the new version).

Final steps

When you finish playing with your program, here's what to do.

Save If you like the program you created and want to save it on disk, click the **Save All button**. (It looks like a pile of 4 floppy disks. It's near the screen's top, below the word "Project".)

If the computer says "Save Project", do this:

Look in the Name box. Make sure that box contains the name you want for your program. (If it doesn't, edit the name.) Press Enter. If the computer complains that the name "already exists", press Enter then try a different name instead.

For example, if you gave your program the name "Funmaker", that process makes the computer create a folder called Funmaker and put it into the Projects folder (which is in the Visual Studio 2010 folder, which is in the Documents folder). That folder contains Funmaker.suo, Funmaker.sln, and another folder called Funmaker, which in turn contains many other files and folders.

Afterwards, if you make further changes to the program, click the Save All button again to save them.

New If you're tired of working on a program and want to start inventing a different program instead, click the **New Project** button (which is near the screen's top-left corner, below the word "File").

(If you didn't save the previous program, the computer will say "save or discard changes". If you want to save the previous program, click "Save" and answer any questions the computer asks about the program's name; otherwise, click "Discard".)

Eventually, the computer will say "New Project". Double-click "Windows Forms Application".

Exit When you finish using C#, click the X button that's in the screen's top right corner.

Open When you start using C#, look at the heading "Recent Projects" (which appear near the screen's left edge). Below "Recent Projects", you see a list of programs you saved. If you want to use or edit one of those programs, click that program's name. Either run the program again (by pressing F5) or edit the program's commands.

Run the .exe file When the computer ran your program, it made an .exe file (called Funmaker.exe), which you can run again without going into C#. Here's how:

Exit from C#. Click the Start button then Documents. In the right-hand pane, double-click "Visual Studio 2010" then Projects then Funmaker then the Funmaker folder icon then bin then Debug then the top Funmaker icon (which is blue and stands for Funmaker.exe).

Multiple lines

Your program can contain *several* lines. For example, to make the computer say —

```
I love you
Let's get married
```

type these lines:

```
Console.WriteLine("I love you");
Console.WriteLine("Let's get married");
```

Below them, type the helper line:

```
Console.ReadKey();
```

If you say **Write** instead of **WriteLine**, the computer won't press the Enter key at the end of its writing. For example, if you type:

```
Console.Write("I love you");
Console.WriteLine("Let's get married");
```

the computer will write "I love you" without pressing Enter, then write "Let's get married", so you see this:

```
I love youLet's get married
```

Registration

While you're using Visual C# Express, you might be interrupted by a window saying "Registration is required". That means you haven't registered Visual C# Express yet.

You can use Visual C# Express for 30 days without registering it. Before the 30 days run out, you should register it by clicking that window's "Obtain a registration key online" button (or by clicking "Help" then "Register Product" then "Obtain a registration key online").

After you click "Obtain a registration key online", continue the registration procedure by following the instructions on the screen. Registration is free.

Math

The computer can do math. For example, this line makes the computer do 4+2:

```
Console.WriteLine(4 + 2);
```

It makes the computer write this answer on your screen:

```
6
```

If you have 750 apples and buy 12 more, how many apples will you have altogether? This line writes the answer:

```
Console.WriteLine("You will have " + (750 + 12) + " apples");
```

That line makes the computer write "You will have ", then write the answer to 750 + 12 (which is 762), then write "apples", so you see this:

```
You will have 762 apples
```

Like most other languages (such as Basic, JavaScript, Java, and C++), C# lets you use the symbols +, -, *, /, parentheses, decimal points, and e notation.

Types of numbers

C# handles 5 types of numbers well.

One type of number is called an **integer** (or **int**). An integer contains no decimal point and no e and is between -2147483648 and 2147483647. For example, -27 and 30000 are ints. Each int consumes 4 bytes (32 bits) of RAM.

An **unsigned integer** (or **uint**) resembles an integer but must not have a minus sign, and it can be between 0 and 4294967295. For example, 3000000000 is a uint, though it's too big to be an int.

A **long** resembles an integer but can be longer: it can be between -9223372036854775808 and 9223372036854775807. Each long consumes 8 bytes (64 bits) of RAM.

An **unsigned long** (or **ulong**) resembles a long but must not have a minus sign, and it can be between 0 and 18446744073709551615.

A **double-precision number** (or a **double**) contains a decimal point or an E. For example, -27.0 and 3E4 are doubles. A double can be up to 1.7976931348623158E308, and you can put a minus sign before it. Each double consumes 8 bytes of RAM. If you write a decimal point, put a digit (such as 0) after it.

Writing When Console.WriteLine makes the computer write an answer on your screen, the computer takes this shortcut: to write a double containing many digits after the decimal point, the computer writes just the first 15 significant digits; and if the only digits after the decimal point are zeros, the computer doesn't bother writing those zeros or the decimal point.

Operations While you're writing a math problem, **if you include a double (such as 5.0), the computer makes the answer be a double.** For example, the answer to 5.0 + 3 is the double 8.0, though the computer doesn't bother writing the .0 on your screen.

If you feed the computer a problem that involves just ints, the computer tries to make the answer be an int. If the answer's too big to be an int, the computer gripes. For example, if you write —

```
Console.WriteLine(3000 * 1000000);
```

the computer will gripe (because 3000 and 1000000 are both ints but the answer is too big to be an int). You should rewrite the problem to include a double, like this —

```
Console.WriteLine(3000 * 1000000.0);
```

or —

```
Console.WriteLine(3000.0 * 1000000);
```

or:

```
Console.WriteLine(3000.0 * 1000000.0)
```

Then the answer will be a double (3000000000.0), which the computer will write on the screen in this shortcut form:

```
3000000000
```

If you feed the computer a math problem whose answer is too big to be a double, the computer will give up and typically say the answer is:

```
Infinity
```

The tiniest double that the computer handles well is 1e-308. If you feed the computer a math problem whose answer is tinier than that, the computer will either handle the rightmost digits inaccurately or give up, saying the answer is 0.0.

Dividing ints Since combining ints gives an answer that's an int, **11 / 4 is this int: 2**. So 11 / 4 is *not* 2.75. If you say —

```
Console.WriteLine(11 / 4);
```

the computer will write just:

```
2
```

If you want the computer to write 2.75 instead, say you want a double, by putting decimal points in the problem, like this:

```
Console.WriteLine(11.0 / 4.0);
```

That makes the computer write:

```
2.75
```

Dividing by 0 If you ask the computer to divide by 0, the computer will gripe.

Dividing by 0.0 If you ask the computer to divide by 0.0, the computer will get creative.

For example, if you say —

```
Console.WriteLine(5.0 / 0.0);
```

the computer will try to divide 5.0 by 0.0, give up (because you can't divide by 0), and say the answer is:

```
Infinity
```

If you say —

```
Console.WriteLine(-5.0 / 0.0);
```

the computer will try to divide -5 by 0, give up (because you can't divide by 0), and say the answer is:

```
-Infinity
```

If you say —

```
Console.WriteLine(0.0 / 0.0);
```

the computer will try to divide 0 by 0, give up (because you can't divide by 0), get confused, and say the answer is —

```
NaN
```

which means "Not a Number".

Advanced math

The computer can do advanced math. For example, it can compute square roots. This line makes the computer print the square root of 9:

```
Console.WriteLine(Math.Sqrt(9));
```

The computer will print 3.

Besides Sqrt, you can use other advanced-math functions:

Function	**Traditional notation**	**What to type**
square root of x	$\sqrt{x}$	Math.Sqrt(x)
x raised to the y power	x^y	Math.Pow(x, y)
e raised to the y power	e^y	Math.Exp(y)
pi	π	Math.PI
e	e	Math.E
absolute value of x	$\lvert x \rvert$	Math.Abs(x)
round x down, so ends in .0	$\lfloor x \rfloor$	Math.Floor(x)
round x up, so ends in .0	$\lceil x \rceil$	Math.Ceiling(x)
logarithm, base 10, of x	$\log_{10} x$	Math.Log10(x)
logarithm, base e, of x	$\ln x$	Math.Log(x)
logarithm, base b, of x	$\log_b x$	Math.Log(x, b)
sine of x radians	$\sin x$	Math.Sin(x)
cosine of x radians	$\cos x$	Math.Cos(x)
tangent of x radians	$\tan x$	Math.Tan(x)
arcsine of x, in radians	$\arcsin x$	Math.Asin(x)
arccosine of x, in radians	$\arccos x$	Math.Acos(x)
arctangent of x, in radians	$\arctan x$	Math.Atan(x)
arctangent of y/x, in radians	$\arctan x/y$	Math.Atan2(y, x)
hyperbolic sine of x	$\sinh x$	Math.Sinh(x)
hyperbolic cosine of x	$\cosh x$	Math.Cosh(x)
hyperbolic tangent of x	$\tanh x$	Math.Tanh(x)

Variables

Like Basic and other languages, C# lets you use variables. For example, you can say:

```
n = 3;
```

A variable's name can be short (such as n) or long (such as town_population_in_2001). The name can contain letters, digits, and underscores, but not blank spaces. The name must begin with a letter or underscore, not a digit.

Before using a variable, say what type of thing the variable stands for. For example, if n and town_population_in_2001 will stand for numbers that are ints and mortgage_rate will stand for a double, your program should say:

```
int n, town_population_in_2001;
double mortgage_rate;
```

If x is a variable, your program should say one these lines:

Line	**Meaning**
int x;	x is an integer
uint x;	x is an unsigned integer
long x;	x is a long
ulong x;	x is an unsigned long
double x;	x is a double-precision number
char x;	x is a single character, such as 'A'
string x;	x is a string of characters, such as "love"

If n is an integer that starts at 3, you can say —

```
int n;
n = 3;
```

but you can combine those two lines into this single line:

```
int n = 3;
```

Here's how to say "n is an integer that starts at 3, and population_in_2001 is an integer that starts at 27000":

```
int n = 3, population_in_2001 = 27000;
```

If you want x to be the string "I love you", say —

```
string x;
x = "I love you";
```

or combine those lines, like this:

```
string x = "I love you";
```

Increase

The symbol ++ means "increase". For example, ++n means "increase n".

These lines increase n:

```
int n = 3;
++n;
Console.WriteLine(n);
```

The n starts at 3 and increases to 4, so the computer prints 4.

Saying ++n gives the same answer as n = n + 1, but the computer handles ++n faster.

The symbol ++ increases the number by 1, even if the number is a decimal. For example, if x is 17.4 and you say ++x, the x will become 18.4.

Decrease

The opposite of ++ is --. The symbol -- means "decrease". For example, --n means "decrease n". Saying --n gives the same answer as n = n - 1 but faster.

Strange short cuts

If you use the following short cuts, your programs will be briefer and run faster.

Instead of saying n = n + 2, say n += 2, which means "n's increase is 2". Similarly, instead of saying n = n * 3, say n *= 3, which means "n's multiplier is 3".

Instead of saying ++n and then giving another command, say ++n in the middle of the other command. For example, instead of saying —

```
++n;
j = 7 * n;
```

say:

```
j = 7 * ++n;
```

That's pronounced: "j is 7 times an increased n". So if n was 2, saying j = 7 * ++n makes n become 3 and j become 21.

Notice that when you say j = 7 * ++n, the computer increases n *before* computing j. If you say j = 7 * n++ instead, the computer increases n *after* computing j; so j = 7 * n++ has the same effect as saying:

```
j = 7 * n;
++n;
```

Input a string

These lines make the computer ask for your name:

```
Console.WriteLine("What is your name?");
string x = Console.ReadLine();
Console.WriteLine("I adore anyone whose name is " + x);
```

Below them, remember to put the helper line:

```
Console.ReadKey();
```

When you run that program (by pressing the F5 key), here's what happens....

The top line makes the computer write this question:

```
What is your name?
```

The next line makes the string x be the answer you type. For example, if you answer "What is your name?" by typing "Maria" (and then pressing Enter), the computer will read your answer and make string x be what the computer reads; so x will be "Maria", and the next line will make the computer write:

```
I adore anyone whose name is Maria
```

So when you run that program, here's the whole conversation that occurs between the computer and you:

The computer asks for your name:	What is your name?
You type your name:	Maria
Computer praises your name:	I adore anyone whose name is Maria

Just for fun, run that program again and pretend you're somebody else....

The computer asks for your name:	What is your name?
You type your name:	Bud
Computer praises your name:	I adore anyone whose name is Bud

When the computer asks for your name, if you say something weird, the computer will give you a weird reply....

The computer asks for your name:	What is your name?
You type:	none of your business!
The computer replies:	I adore anyone whose name is none of your business!

Input a double

To make x be a string that the human inputs, you've learned to say this:

```
string x = Console.ReadLine();
```

To make x be a double-precision number that the human inputs, say this instead:

```
double x = Convert.ToDouble(Console.ReadLine());
```

That's because Console.ReadLine() considers the human's input to be a string, and Convert.ToDouble converts that string to a double.

Examples These lines make the computer predict how old a human will be ten years from now:

```
Console.WriteLine("How old are you?");
double age = Convert.ToDouble(Console.ReadLine());
Console.WriteLine("Ten years from now, you'll be " + (age + 10));
```

The top line makes the computer ask, "How old are you?" The middle line makes age be the result of converting, to a double-precision number, the human's input. The bottom line makes the computer write the answer.

For example, if the human is 27 years old, the chat between the computer and the human looks like this:

```
How old are you?
27
Ten years from now, you'll be 37
```

If the human is 27.5 years old, the chat can look like this:

```
How old are you?
27.5
Ten years from now, you'll be 37.5
```

These lines make the computer convert feet to inches:

```
Console.WriteLine("How many feet?");
double feet = Convert.ToDouble(Console.ReadLine());
Console.WriteLine("That makes " + (feet * 12) " inches.");
```

Input an integer

To make x be an integer that the human inputs, say this instead:

```
int x = Convert.ToInt32(Console.ReadLine());
```

That's because Convert.ToInt32 converts a string to a 32-bit integer.

To make x be a special type of integer that the human inputs, say one of these:

```
uint x = Convert.ToUInt32(Console.ReadLine());
long x = Convert.ToInt64(Console.ReadLine());
ulong x = Convert.ToUInt64(Console.ReadLine());
```

Arrays

Instead of being just a number, x can be a *list* of numbers.

Example For example, if you want x to be this list of integers —

```
{ 81, 52, 207, 19 }
```

type this:

```
int[] x = { 81, 52, 207, 19 };
```

In that line, the symbol "int[]" means "int list". Notice that when you type the list of numbers, you must **put commas between the numbers** and put the entire list of numbers in **braces**, {}. On your keyboard, the "{" symbol is to the right of the P key and requires you to hold down the Shift key.

In x's list, **the starting number** (which is 81) **is called x_0** (which is pronounced "x subscripted by zero" or "x sub 0" or just "x 0"). The next number (which is 52) is called x_1 (which is pronounced "x subscripted by one" or "x sub 1" or just "x 1"). The next number is called x_2. Then comes x_3. So **the four numbers in the list are called x_0, x_1, x_2, and x_3.**

To make the computer say what x_2 is, type this line:

```
Console.WriteLine(x[2]);
```

That line makes the computer write x_2, which is 207, so the computer will write:

```
207
```

Altogether, the lines say:

```
int[] x = { 81, 52, 207, 19 };
Console.WriteLine(x[2]);
```

The first line says the integer-list x is { 81, 52, 207, 19 }. The second line makes the computer write x_2's number, which is 207.

Jargon Notice this jargon:

In a symbol such as x_2, the lowered number (the 2) is called the **subscript**.

To create a subscript in your subroutine, use brackets. For example, to create x_2, type x[2].

A variable having subscripts is called an **array**. For example, x is an array if there's an x_0, x_1, x_2, etc.

Different types Instead of having integers, you can have different types. For example, you can say:

```
double[] x = { 81.2, 51.7, 207.9, 19.5 };
```

You can even say:

```
string[] x = { "love", "hate", "peace", "war" };
```

Uninitialized Instead of typing a line that includes x's list of numbers, you can type the numbers underneath, if you warn the computer how many numbers will be in the list, like this:

```
double[] x = new double[3];
x[0] = 200.1;
x[1] = 700.4;
x[2] = 53.2;
Console.WriteLine(x[0] + x[1] + x[2]);
```

The top line says x will be a new list of 3 doubles, called x_0, x_1, and x_2. The next lines say x_0 is 200.1, x_1 is 700.4, and x_2 is 53.2. The bottom line makes the computer say their sum:

```
953.7
```

Tables If you want x to be a table having 2 rows and 3 columns of double-precision numbers, say:

```
double[,] x = new double[2, 3];
```

Since C# always starts counting at 0 (not 1), the number in the table's top left corner is called x[0, 0].

Logic

Like most computer languages, C# lets you say "if", "while", "for", and "goto" and create comments and subroutines. Here's how....

If

If a person's age is less than 18, let's make the computer say "You are still a minor." Here's the fundamental line:

```
if (age < 18) Console.WriteLine("You are still a minor.");
```

Notice you must put parentheses after the word "if".

If a person's age is less than 18, let's make the computer say "You are still a minor." and also say "Ah, the joys of youth!" and "I wish I could be as young as you!" Here's how to say all that:

```
if (age < 18)
{
    cout <<"You are still a minor.\n";
    cout <<"Ah, the joys of youth!\n";
    cout <<"I wish I could be as young as you!";
}
```

Since that "if" line is above the "{", the "if" line is a structure line and does *not* end in a semicolon.

How to type To type the symbol "{", do this: while holding down the Shift key, tap the "[" key (which is next to the P key). To type the symbol "}", do this: while holding down the Shift key, tap the "]" key.

When you type a line, don't worry about indenting it: when you finish typing the line (and press Enter), the computer will indent it the correct amount, automatically.

Complete program Here's how to put that structure into a complete program:

```
using System;
using System.Collections.Generic;
using System.Linq;
using System.Text;

namespace Joan
{
    class Program
    {
        static void Main(string[] args)
        {
            Console.WriteLine("How old are you?");
            double age=Convert.ToDouble(Console.ReadLine());
            if (age < 18)
            {
                Console.WriteLine("You are still a minor.");
                Console.WriteLine("Ah, the joys of youth.");
                Console.WriteLine("I wish I could be as young as you!");
            }
            else
            {
                Console.WriteLine("You are an adult.");
                Console.WriteLine("Now we can have some adult fun!");
            }
            Console.WriteLine("Glad to have met you.");
            Console.ReadKey();
        }
    }
}
```

If the person's age is less than 18, the computer will write "You are still a minor." and "Ah, the joys of youth!" and "I wish I could be as young as you!" If the person's age is not less than 18, the computer will write "You are an adult." and "Now we can have some adult fun!" Regardless of the person's age, the computer will end the conversation by writing "Glad to have met you."

Since the computer types the top lines for you and also types the 3 braces at the program's bottom, you type just the lines in the middle, starting with:

```
Console.WriteLine("How old are you?");
```

Fancy "if" The "if" statement uses this notation:

Notation	Meaning
if (age < 18)	if age is less than 18
if (age <= 18)	if age is less than or equal to 18
if (age == 18)	if age is equal to 18
if (age != 18)	if age is not equal to 18
if (age < 18 && weight > 200)	if age < 18 and weight > 200
if (age < 18 || weight > 200)	if age < 18 or weight > 200
if (sex == "male")	if sex is "male"
if (sex.CompareTo("male") < 0)	if sex is a word (such as "female") that comes before "male" in the dictionary

Here's how to type the symbol "|": while holding down the Shift key, tap the "\" key.

Look at that table carefully! Notice that in the "if" statement, you should use double symbols: you should say "==" instead of "=", say "&&" instead of "&", and say "||" instead of "|".

If you accidentally say "=" instead of "==", the computer will gripe. If you accidentally say "&" instead of "&&" or say "|" instead of "||", the computer will say right answers but too slowly.

The symbol "<" compares just numbers, not strings. Instead of writing —

```
if (sex < "male")
```

you must write:

```
if (sex.CompareTo("male") < 0)
```

While

Let's make the computer write the word "love" repeatedly, like this:

```
love love love love love love love love love etc.
love love love love love love love love love etc.
love love love love love love love love love etc.
etc.
```

This line does it:

```
while (true) Console.Write("love ");
```

The "while (1)" means: do repeatedly. The computer will do cout <<"love " repeatedly, looping forever — or until you **abort** the program (by clicking the console window's X button).

Let's make the computer start at 20 and keep counting, so the computer will write:

```
20
21
22
23
24
25
26
27
28
29
30
31
32
etc.
```

These lines do it:

Program	Meaning
int i = 20;	Start the integer i at 20.
while (true)	Repeat these lines forever:
{	
Console.WriteLine(i);	print i then press Enter
++i;	increase i
}	

They write faster than you can read.

To pause the writing, press the Pause key.
To resume the writing, press the Enter key.
To abort the program, click the console window's X button.

In that program, if you say "while (i < 30)" instead of "while (true)", the computer will do the loop just while i remains less than 30; the computer will write just:

```
20
21
22
23
24
25
26
27
28
29
```

To let that program run properly, make sure its bottom includes the helper line saying "Console.ReadKey()", so altogether the program looks like this:

```
using System;
using System.Collections.Generic;
using System.Linq;
using System.Text;

namespace Joan
{
    class Program
    {
        static void Main(string[] args)
        {
            int i=20;
            while (i < 30)
            {
                Console.WriteLine(i);
                ++i;
            }
            Console.ReadKey();
        }
    }
}
```

Instead of saying "while (i < 30)", you can say "while (i <= 29)".

For

Here's a more natural way to get that output of numbers from 20 to 29:

```
for (int i = 20; i <= 29; ++i) Console.WriteLine(i);
```

The "for (int i = 20; i <= 29; ++i)" means:

Do repeatedly. Start the integer i at 20, and keep repeating as long as i <= 29. At the end of each repetition, do ++i.

In that "for" statement, if you change the "++i" to "i += 3", the computer will increase i by 3 instead of by 1, so the computer will write:

```
20
23
26
29
```

The "for" statement is quite flexible. You can even say "for (int i = 20; i < 100; i *= 2)", which makes i start at 20 and keep doubling, so the computer writes:

```
20
40
80
```

Like "if" and "while", the "for" statement can sit atop a group of indented lines that are in braces.

Goto

You can say "goto". For example, if you say "goto yummy", the computer will go to the line whose name is yummy:

```
    Console.WriteLine("my dog ");
    goto yummy;
    Console.WriteLine("never ");
yummy: Console.WriteLine("drinks whiskey");
```

The computer will write:

```
my dog
drinks whiskey
```

Exceptions

These lines try to make x be how many children the human has:

```
Console.WriteLine("How many children do you have?");
int x = Convert.ToInt32(Console.ReadLine());
```

Those lines ask the human "How many children do you have?" then wait for the human's response then try to convert that string to an integer (such as 2 or 0) and call it x. But what happens if the human does *not* input an integer? What if human inputs a number that includes a decimal point? What if the human types a word, such as "none" or "one" or "many"? What if the human types a phrase, such as "not sure" or "too many" or "none of your business" or "my girlfriend was pregnant but hasn't told me yet whether she got an abortion"? In those errant situations (which are called **exceptions**), the computer can't do Convert.ToInt32 and will instead abort the program, show the human all the program's lines, and highlight the problematic line. Then the human will be upset and confused!

To avoid upsetting people, change those lines to this group of lines instead:

```
AskAboutKids:
    Console.WriteLine("How many children do you have?");
try
{
    int x = Convert.ToInt32(Console.ReadLine());
}
catch
{
    Console.WriteLine("Please type an integer");
    go to AskAboutKids;
}
```

The group begins with a label (AskAboutKids) and makes the computer ask "How many children do you have?" Then the computer will **try** to do this line:

```
    int x = Convert.ToInt32(Console.ReadLine());
```

If the computer fails to do that line (because what the person typed can't be converted to an integer), the computer won't gripe; instead, it will **catch** the error and do the lines indented under "catch". Those lines are called the **catch block** (or **exception handler**). They make the computer say "Please type an integer" then go back to the beginning of AskAboutKids, to give the human another opportunity to answer the question correctly.

If the human doesn't know what an "integer" is, phrase the advice differently: make the computer write "Please type a simple number without a decimal point".

Comments

To put a comment in your program, begin the comment with the symbol //. The computer ignores everything that's to the right of //. Here's an example:

```
// This program is fishy
// It was written by a sick sailor swimming in the sun
Console.WriteLine("Our funny God");    // notice the religious motif
Console.WriteLine("invented cod");     // said by a nasty flounder
```

The computer ignores all the comments, which are to the right of //.

While you type the program, the computer makes each // and each comment turn green. Then the computer ignores everything that's turned green, so the computer writes just:

```
Our funny God
invented cod
```

Subroutines

Like most other languages, C# lets you invent subroutines and give them names. For example, here's how to invent a subroutine called "insult" and use it in the Main routine:

Program	Meaning
```using System;```	
```using System.Collections.Generic;```	
```using System.Linq;```	
```using System.Text;```	
```namespace Joan```	
```{```	
`    class Program`	
`    {`	
`        static void Main(string[] args)`	**Here's the main routine:**
`        {`	
`            Console.WriteLine("We all know...");`	write "We all know…"
`            insult();`	do the insult
`            Console.WriteLine("...and yet we love you.");`	write the ending
`            Console.ReadKey();`	
`        }`	
`        static void insult()`	**Here's how to insult:**
`        {`	
`            Console.WriteLine("You are stupid!");`	write "You are stupid!"
`            Console.WriteLine("You are ugly!");`	write "You are ugly!"
`        }`	
`    }`	
`}`	

The computer will write:

```
We all know...
You are stupid!
You are ugly!
...and yet we love you.
```

In that program, the lines beginning with "static void Main(string[] args)" define the Main routine. The bottom few lines, beginning with "static void insult()", define the subroutine called "insult".

Whenever you write a subroutine's name, you must put parentheses afterwards, like this: insult(). Those parentheses tell the computer: insult's a subroutine, not a variable.

To write a subroutine's definition simply, begin the definition by saying "static void".

Here's another example of a main routine and subroutine:

Routines	Meaning
`static void Main(string[] args)`	**Here's the main routine:**
`{`	
`    laugh();`	main routine says to laugh
`    Console.ReadKey();`	
`}`	
`static void laugh()`	**Here's how to laugh:**
`{`	
`    for (int i = 1; i <= 100; ++i) Console.Write("ha ");`	write "ha ", 100 times
`}`	

The Main routine says to laugh. The subroutine defines "laugh" to mean: write "ha " a hundred times.

Let's create a more flexible subroutine, so that whenever the Main routine says laugh(2), the computer will write "ha ha "and Enter; whenever the Main routine says laugh(5), the computer will write "ha ha ha ha ha " and Enter; and so on. Here's how:

Routines	Meaning
```static void Main(string[] args)```	Here's the main routine:
```{```	
``` Console.Write ("Here is a short laugh: ");```	
``` laugh(2);```	do laugh(2), so write "ha ha "
``` Console.Write ("Here is a longer laugh: ");```	
``` laugh(5);```	do laugh(5), so write "ha ha ha ha ha "
``` Console.ReadKey();```	
```}```	
```static void laugh(int n)```	Here's how to laugh(n):
```{```	
``` for (int i = 1; i <= n; ++i) Console.Write("ha ");```	write "ha ", n times
``` Console.WriteLine();```	then press Enter
```}```	

The computer will print:

```
Here is a short laugh: ha ha
Here is a longer laugh: ha ha ha ha ha
```

Average Let's define the "average" of a pair of integers, so that "average(3, 7)" means the average of 3 and 7 (which is 5), and so a Main routine saying "i = average(3, 7)" makes i be 5.

This subroutine defines the "average" of all pairs of integers:

```
static int average(int a, int b)
{
    return (a + b) / 2;
}
```

The top line says, "Here's how to find the average of any two integers, a and b, and make the average be an integer." The next line says, "Return to the main routine, with this answer: (a + b) / 2."

Here's a complete program:

Program	Meaning
```using System;```	
```using System.Collections.Generic;```	
```using System.Linq;```	
```using System.Text;```	
```namespace Joan```	
```{```	
``` class Program```	
``` {```	
``` static void Main(string[] args)```	Here's the main routine:
``` {```	
``` int i;```	make i be an integer
``` i = average(3, 7);```	make i be average(3, 7)
``` Console.WriteLine(i);```	write i
``` Console.ReadKey();```	
``` }```	
``` static int average(int a, int b)```	Here's how to compute average(a, b):
``` {```	
``` return (a + b) / 2;```	return this answer: (a + b) / 2
``` }```	
``` }```	
```}```	

In that program, the Main routine is:

```int i;```	make i be an integer
```i = average(3, 7);```	make i be average(3, 7)
```Console.WriteLine(i);```	write i
```Console.ReadKey();```	

You can shorten it, like this:

```int i = average(3, 7);```	make the integer i be average(3, 7)
```Console.WriteLine(i);```	write i
```Console.ReadKey();```	

You can shorten it further, like this:

```Console.WriteLine(average(3, 7));```	write average(3, 7)
```Console.ReadKey();```	

To make that program handle double-precision numbers instead of integers, change each int to double. After changing to double, the program will still work, even if you don't change 3 to 3.0 and don't change 7 to 7.0.

Windows forms

Like Visual Basic, C# lets you easily create Windows forms. Here's how.

Start C# (by clicking the Start button then "All Programs" then "Microsoft Visual Studio 2010 Express" then "Microsoft Visual C# 2010 Express").

You see the Start Page window. Click "**New Project**" (which is near the screen's left edge). Double-click "**Windows Forms Application**".

You see an **object**, called the **Form1** window. Double-click in that window (below "Form1"). That tells the computer you want to write a program (subroutine) about that window.

The computer starts writing the **subroutine** for you. The computer writes:

```
using System;
using System.Collections.Generic;
using System.ComponentModel;
using System.Data;
using System.Drawing;
using System.Linq;
using System.Text;
using System.Windows.Forms;

namespace WindowsFormsApplication1
{
    public partial class Form1 : Form
    {
        public Form1()
        {
            InitializeComponent();
        }

        private void Form1_Load(object sender, EventArgs e)
        {

        }
    }
}
```

The line saying "private void Form1_Load" is the subroutine's **header**. Below that, between the **braces** (the symbols "{" and "}"), insert lines that tell the computer what to do when Form1 is **loaded** (appears). The lines you insert are called the subroutine's **body**.

Simplest example

Let's make the Form1 window say "I love you". To do that, type this line —

```
Text = "I love you";
```

The computer automatically indents that line for you, so the subroutine becomes:

```
private void Form1_Load(object sender, EventArgs e)
{
    Text = "I love you";
}
```

To run your program, press the F5 key (or click the green " ▶ ", which is at the screen's top center). Then you see the Form1 window again; but instead of saying "Form1", it says the text:

```
I love you
```

When you've finished admiring the Form1 window, stop the program by clicking the Form1 window's X button. Then you see the subroutine again:

```
private void Form1_Load(object sender, EventArgs e)
{
    Text = "I love you";
}
```

If you wish, edit the subroutine. For example, try changing the Text line to this:

```
Text = "I hate cabbage";
```

Math

The Text line can include math calculations, but you must convert the answer to a string, since Text must be a string. For example, to make the computer write the answer to 4 + 2, type this line:

```
Text = Convert.ToString(4 + 2);
```

Message box

To create a message box saying "Your hair is messy", type this line:

```
MessageBox.Show("Your hair is messy");
```

To create a message box saying the answer to 4 + 2, type this line:

```
MessageBox.Show(Convert.ToString(4 + 2));
```

Property list

Click the "Form1.cs [Design]" tab, so you see the Form1 window itself. Then click (just once) in the middle of the Form1 window.

Then the screen's bottom-right corner should show a list, whose title is:

```
Properties
Form1 System.Windows.Forms.Form
```

If you don't see that list yet, press the F4 key then try again to click in the middle of the Form1 window.

That list is called **Form1's main property list** (or **property window**). It looks the same way as if you were using Visual Basic. To explore it, reread my chapter about Visual Basic.

Toolbox

While you're looking at Form1's window, the screen's left edge should show the word "Toolbox". (If you don't see the word "Toolbox" yet, make it appear by clicking "Tools" then "Settings" then "Reset".)

If you're lucky, you'll see a toolbox that looks like the picture on page 568.

If you see just the word "Toolbox" but none of the icons that are supposed to be in the toolbox, make them appear by clicking "Toolbox", then make them stay on the screen permanently by clicking the **push pin**, which is just left of the toolbox's X.

Make sure the triangle left of "All Windows Forms" has a white middle. (If the triangle is solid black instead, click the triangle to make its middle white.)

Make sure the triangle left of "Common Controls" is solid black. (If that triangle has a white middle instead, click the triangle to make it solid black.)

Each object in the toolbox is called a **tool**.

The complete toolbox is too tall to fit on your screen. You see just the toolbox's beginning. Whenever you want to see the rest of the toolbox (which includes many dozens of tools), click the toolbox's scroll-down arrow (at the toolbox's bottom-right corner).

The toolbox looks the same way as if you were using Visual Basic. To explore how to use its tools, reread my chapter on Visual Basic.

Visual C++

Microsoft wants advanced programmers to use Visual C#, but many programmers still use its predecessors, **C** and **C++**, because they don't require Windows and can therefore run on a greater variety of computers.

Computer language **C** was invented by **Dennis Ritchie** in 1972, while he was working for AT&T at Bell Labs. He called it "C" because it came after "B", which was an earlier language developed by a colleague.

An improved C, called **C++**, was invented in 1985 at Bell Labs by **Bjarne Stroustrup**.

He was born in Denmark (where he studied at Aarhus University). Then he moved to England (where he got a Ph.D. from Cambridge University). Then he moved to New Jersey (to work at Bell Labs, where he invented C++).

To pronounce his name, say "Bee-ARE-nuh STRAH-stroop", but say the "Bee" and "STRAH-stroop" fast, so it sounds closer to "BYAR-nuh STROV-strup".

C++ uses the same fundamental commands as C but adds extra commands. Some of those extra commands are for advanced programming; others make regular programming more pleasant. Unlike C, C++ lets you use **object-oriented programming (OOP)**, in which you define "objects" and give those objects "properties".

For input and output, C++ offers different commands than C. C++'s input/output commands are more pleasant. Most C programmers have switched to C++ or C#.

The previous chapters explained how to program in Basic, JavaScript, and Java. C, C++, and C# resemble those languages (especially Java) but run faster and consumes less RAM.

C++ became the most popular language for creating advanced programs. The world's biggest software companies switched to C++ from assembly language, though many are starting to go a step further and switch to C#.

If you become an expert C++ or C# programmer, you can help run those rich software companies and get rich yourself!

This chapter explains C++, so you can work in situations that haven't converted to C# yet.

C++ uses these commands:

C++ command	Page
char x;	633
char x[]="winks";	633
char x[81];	633
cin >>age;	627
cout <<"I love you"	624
cout.precision(15);	626
cout.setf(ios::showpoint);	626
double x;	627
double x[3];	627
double x[2][3];	627
else	628
for (int i=20; i<=29; ++i)	629
goto yummy;	630
if (age<18)	628
#include <iostream>	624
#include <math.h>	626
#include "stdafx.h"	624
int _tmain(…)	624
int x;	627
int x=3;	627
int x()	632
MessageBox::Show("hair");	634
#pragma endregion	634
private: System::Void … {	634
return 0;	624
return (a+b)/2;	632
strcpy(y,x);	633
Text="I love you";	634
using namespace std;	624
void x()	630
while (1)	629
while (1);	624
while (i<30)	629
x=3;	627
x();	630
++x;	627
--x;	627
// Joe.cpp Defines …	624
// Zoo program is fishy	630

C++ uses these functions:

C++ function	Page
acos(x)	626
asin(x)	626
atan(x)	626
atan2(y,x)	626
ceil(x)	626
Convert::ToString(x)	634
cos(x)	626
cosh(x)	626
endl	625
exp(x)	626
fabs(x)	626
floor(x)	626
log(x)	626
log10(x)	626
pow(x,y)	626
sin(x)	626
sinh(x)	626
sqrt(x)	626
strcmp(x,y)	633
tan(x)	626
tanh(x)	626

Fun

Here's how to enjoy programming in C++.

Before studying C++, study an easier language, such as Basic, JavaScript, Java, or C#.

C++ is excitingly dangerous:

Unlike Basic, JavaScript, Java, and C#, C++ lets you easily create a pointer, which is a note about which part of RAM to use. If you create the pointer incorrectly, C++ will use the wrong part of RAM — and erase whatever info was there before. For example, C++ might erase the part of RAM used by your operating system (Windows or Mac OS or Linux or DOS), so your operating system becomes confused and accidentally erases your disks!

A faulty pointer (which points to the wrong part of RAM) is called a **runaway pointer**, and it's a C++ programmer's greatest fear. Even if your innocent-looking program doesn't seem to mention pointers, a small error in your program might make C++ create a pointer that wrecks your computer. That's why many C++ programmers look thin and haggard and bite their nails. To keep your nails looking pretty, make backup copies of your hard disk before trying to program in C++.

C++ is like a sports car with no brakes: it's fast, fun, slim, sleek, and dangerous. If you program in C++, your friends will admire you and even whistle at you as you zoom along the freeway of computer heaven; but if you're not careful, your programs and disk will crash, and so will your career!

The most popular version of C++ is **Visual C++**, which is by Microsoft and handles Windows.

This chapter explains how to use Visual C++.

Copy C++ to the hard disk

Here's how to copy Visual C++ 2010 Express to your hard disk by using Windows (Vista or 7) and Internet Explorer.

Go to www.microsoft.com/express/downloads. Click "Visual C++ 2010 Express" then the down-arrow then "English" then "Run" (which is at the screen's bottom).

If you're using Windows 7, click "Yes". If you're using Windows Vista, click "Continue".

The computer will say "Welcome to Setup". Press the Enter key. Click "I have read and accept the license terms." Press Enter, 3 times.

The computer will copy (download) and install Visual C++ onto your hard disk.

The computer will say "Setup complete". Press Enter. Close Internet Explorer's window (by clicking the X at the screen's top-right corner).

Start C++

To start using C++, click the Start button then do this:

> If you see "Microsoft Visual C++ 2010 Express", click it. Otherwise, click "All Programs" then "Microsoft Visual Studio 2010 Express" (which you'll see by scrolling down) then "Microsoft Visual C++ 2010 Express".

You see the Start Page window.

Start a new program

Click "**New Project**" (which is near the screen's left edge). then "**Win32 Console Application**".

Highlight the first "<Enter_name>" (by dragging across it, so it all turns blue). Invent a name for your program (such as "Joe"); type the name and press Enter. Click "Finish".

Type your program

The computer starts typing the program for you. The computer types:

```
// Joe.cpp : Defines the entry point for the console application.
//

#include "stdafx.h"


int _tmain(int argc, _TCHAR* argv[])
{
    return 0;
}
```

Let's write a program that makes the computer say "I love you". To do that, insert 4 extra lines, so the program becomes this:

```
// Joe.cpp : Defines the entry point for the console application.
//

#include "stdafx.h"
#include <iostream>
using namespace std;

int _tmain(int argc, _TCHAR* argv[])
{
    cout <<"I love you";
    while (1);
    return 0;
}
```

Here's how to insert those lines:

> Click below the symbol "#". Type the first inserted line, press Enter, and type the next inserted line.
> Click to the right of the symbol "{". Press Enter. Type the third inserted line, press Enter, and type the next inserted line.

You must type a semicolon at the end of each simple line. But don't put semicolons at the end of **structure lines** (which begin with the symbol "#" or "//" or "{" or "}" or are above "{").

The most important line The most important line is the one that says:

```
    cout <<"I love you";
```

The "**cout**" is pronounced "C out". The symbol "**<<**" can be pronounced "from", so that line can be pronounced: "C out from I love you". It makes the computer output "I love you" onto the screen.

3 helper lines To make the cout line work properly, you must insert **3 helper lines**.

To make the computer understand what "cout" means, put these helper lines at your program's top (above the "int _tmain" line):

```
    #include <iostream>
    using namespace std;
```

Put this helper line near the program's bottom (just above the "return 0" line):

```
    while (1);
```

It makes the computer pause awhile, so you have a chance to read the computer's output.

You must put those 3 helper lines in every normal program.

Old versions Some old versions of C++ say <iostream.h> instead of <iostream>, don't require the other two helper lines, and shorten the rest of the program, so the whole program is just this:

```
#include <iostream.h>
void main()
{
    cout <<"I love you";
}
```

Run the program

To run your program, press the F5 key (or click the green "▶", which is at the screen's top center).

If the computer says "This project is out of date", press Enter.

Finally, if you did everything correctly, you see the **console window** (which has white letters on a black background and resembles the DOS command-prompt screen). The console window shows the computer's output. It shows:

```
I love you
```

When you finish admiring that output, close the console window (by clicking its X button).

If you want to run the program again, press the F5 key again.

If you want to edit the program, retype the parts you wish; then press F5 again (which makes the computer debug and run the new version).

Final steps

While you've been working on your program, the computer's been putting info about your program into a folder. For example, if you named your program "Joe", the computer's been putting info about Joe into a folder called "Joe". (The computer put that folder into the "Projects" folder, which is in the "Visual Studio 2010" folder, which is in the "Documents" folder.)

When you finish playing with the program, click the **Save All** button. (It looks like a pile of 4 floppy disks. It's near the screen's top, below the word "Project".) Clicking that button makes sure *all* your work is saved into the folder.

Then you have these choices:

> To start writing a different program, click the **New Project** button (which is near the screen's top-left corner, below the word "File").
>
> To stop using C++, close the C++ window (by clicking the X at the screen's top-right corner).

Rerun later

To run a program you wrote earlier, you can use 3 methods.
Method 1:

> When you start using C++ and see the Start Page window, look at the heading "Recent Projects" (which appears near the screen's left edge). Below "Recent Projects", you see a list of programs you saved. To use or edit one of those programs, click that program's name).
>
> You see the program's lines. If you want to *run* the program, press the F5 key.

Method 2:

> While you're using C++, click the Open File button (which is below the word "View") then the "Projects" that's at the screen's left edge.
>
> You see a list of programs (projects). Double-click the one you want (such as Joe). You see several icons having the program's name (Joe); double-click the next-to-bottom one (which has a 10 on it, if you're using Visual C++ version 10).
>
> If the computer asks "Do you want to close the current solution and open this file as the solution", press Enter.
>
> You see the program's lines. If you want to *run* the program, press the F5 key.

Method 3:

> Click Windows' Start button (at the screen's bottom-left corner) then "Documents".
>
> In the right-hand pane, double-click "Visual Studio 2010" then "Projects" then your program's name then "Debug" (which exists just if you ran the program previously) then your program's top icon.
>
> That runs the program (by using the program's .exe file) but doesn't show you the program's lines.

\n

Let's write a program that makes the computer say:

```
I love you
Let's get married
```

This pair of lines almost accomplish that goal:

```
cout <<"I love you";
cout <<"Let's get married";
```

If you type that pair of lines (and the 3 helper lines) then run the program (by pressing the F5 key then Enter), the computer will say "I love you" and "Let's get married", but unfortunately it will print both messages on a single line, so you'll see this:

```
I love youLet's get married
```

To make the computer print strings on separate lines, say "\n" at the end of a string, like this:

```
cout <<"I love you\n";
cout <<"Let's get married";
```

The \n means "new line": it's the symbol for the Enter key. Telling the computer to print "I love you\n" makes the computer print "I love you" and then press the Enter key, so the next string will be printed on the next line. Altogether, the computer will print this:

```
I love you
Let's get married
```

When you type the symbol \n, make sure you type a backslash: \. Do not type a division sign: /.

So to make your output be pretty, **put \n at the end of each typical string**.

Instead of writing —

```
cout <<"I love you\n";
cout <<"Let's get married";
```

you can write:

```
cout <<"I love you\nLet's get married";
```

That single long line still makes the computer say:

```
I love you
Let's get married
```

endl

To make the computer end a line and start a new line, you can say \n. Another way to make the computer **end** a line is to say <<endl, like this:

```
cout <<"I love you" <<endl <<"Let's get married";
```

That single long line makes the computer do this: print "I love you", then end the line, then print "Let's get married". Altogether, the computer will print this:

```
I love you
Let's get married
```

Registration

While you're using Visual C++ Express, you might be interrupted by a window saying "Registration is required". That means you haven't registered Visual C++ Express yet.

You can use Visual C++ Express for 30 days without registering it. Before the 30 days run out, you should register it by clicking that window's "Obtain a registration key online" button (or by clicking "Help" then "Register Product" then "Obtain a registration key online").

After you click "Obtain a registration key online", continue the registration procedure by following the instructions on the screen. Registration is free.

Math

The computer can do math. For example, this line makes the computer do 4+2:

```
cout <<4+2;
```

It makes the computer print this answer on your screen:

```
6
```

This line makes the computer print the answer to 21+4 and also the answer to 68+1:

```
cout <<21+4 <<endl <<68+1;
```

That cout line makes the computer print the answer to 21+4 (which is 25), then press Enter, then print the answer to 68+1 (which is 69), so you see this:

```
25
69
```

To print both of those answers on a single line instead of on separate lines, put a blank space between the answers by saying " " instead of endl, so the cout line looks like this:

```
cout <<21+4 <<" " <<68+1;
```

That tells the computer to print the answer to 21+4 (which is 25), then a blank space, then the answer to 68+1, so you see:

```
25 69
```

The computer leaves a space between the answers because of the <<" ". If you omit the <<" ", the computer will print:

```
2569
```

If you have 750 apples and buy 12 more, how many apples will you have altogether? This line prints the answer:

```
cout <<"You will have " <<750+12 <<" apples"
```

That cout line makes the computer print "You will have ", then print the answer to 750+12 (which is 762), then print "apples", so you see this:

```
You will have 762 apples
```

Like most other languages (such as Basic, JavaScript, and Java), C++ lets you use the symbols +, -, *, /, parentheses, decimal points, and e notation. But if you're not careful, the computer will print wrong answers. Here's why....

Integers versus double precision

C++ handles two types of numbers well.

One type of number is called an **integer** (or **int**). An int contains no decimal point and no e. For example, -27 and 30000 are ints.

The other type of number that C++ handles well is called a **double-precision number** (or a **double**). **A double contains a decimal point or an e.** For example, -27.0 and 3e4 are doubles. You can abbreviate: instead of writing "-27.0", you can write "-27.", and instead of writing "0.37" you can write ".37".

Extreme ints

The largest permissible int is about 2 billion. More precisely:

```
the largest int is 2147483647

the lowest int you can write easily is -2147483647
the only int lower than that is a strange int you must write as -2147483647-1
```

If you try to feed the computer an int that's too large or too low, the computer won't complain. Instead, the computer will typically print a wrong answer!

Old versions The largest int is 2147483647 just in Microsoft's *modern* versions of C & C++. In versions of C & C++ that were invented before Windows 95, the largest int is just 32767, and the lowest int is -32768, which must be written as -32767-1.

Extreme doubles

The largest permissible double is about 1.7e308. More precisely, it's 1.7976931348623158e308. If you feed the computer a math problem whose answer is bigger than that, the computer will give up and typically say the answer is —

```
1.#INF
```

which means infinity.

The tiniest double that the computer handles well is 1e-308. If you feed the computer a math problem whose answer is tinier than that, the computer will either handle the rightmost digits inaccurately or give up, saying the answer is 0.0.

Tricky arithmetic

If you combine ints, the answer is an int. For example, 2+3 is this int: 5.

11/4 is this int: 2. (11/4 is *not* 2.75.)

If you combine doubles, the answer is a double. If you combine an int with a double, the answer is a double.

How much is 2000 times 2000000? Theoretically, the answer should be this int: 4000000000. But since 4000000000 is too large to be an int, the computer will print a wrong answer. To make the computer multiply 2000 by 2000000 correctly, ask for 2000.0*2000000.0, like this:

```
cout <<2000.0*2000000.0;
```

That line makes the computer get the correct answer, 4000000000.0, which the computer will write in e notation, so you see this answer:

```
4e+009
```

Cout precision

The computer can handle a double-precision number quite accurately, even if the number contains many digits. Here's the limit: the computer can handle up to 15 significant digits.

When printing a double-precision number, cout assumes you don't want to bother seeing all 15 significant digits, so cout typically prints just the number's first 6 significant digits. If you want to see all 15 significant digits, insert this line above the cout lines:

```
cout.precision(15);
```

That line affects all cout lines below it.

When printing a number such as 3.00000000000000, cout assumes you don't want to see the .00000000000000 (because zeros are boring), so cout typically prints just:

```
3
```

If you want to see the decimal point and zeros also, insert this line above the cout lines:

```
cout.setf(ios::showpoint);
```

That line affects all count lines below it.

Advanced math

The computer can do advanced math. For example, it can compute square roots. This program makes the computer print the square root of 9:

```
// Joe.cpp : Defines the entry point for the console application.
//

#include "stdafx.h"
#include <iostream>
#include <math.h>
using namespace std;

int _tmain(int argc, _TCHAR* argv[])
{
    cout <<sqrt(9.0);
    while (1);
    return 0;
}
```

The computer will print 3.

Say sqrt(9.0) rather than sqrt(9), because the number you find the square root of should be double-precision, not an integer. If you say sqrt(9), the computer will gripe.

The program's first gray line tells the computer to include a **math header**, which contains the definition of sqrt and other advanced-math functions.

Besides sqrt, you can use other advanced math functions. All advanced-math functions require that you use double-precision numbers and say #include <math.h>. Here's a list of those advanced-math functions:

To handle exponents, you can use sqrt (square root), exp (exponential power of e), log (logarithm base e), and log10 (logarithm base 10). You can also use pow: for example, pow(3.0,2.0) is 3.0 raised to the 2.0 power.

For trigonometry, you can use sin (sine), cos (cosine), tan (tangent), asin (arcsin), acos (arccosine), atan (arctangent), sinh (sine hyperbolic), cosh (cosine hyperbolic), and tanh (tangent hyperbolic). You can also use atan2: for example, atan2(y,x) is the arctangent of y divided by x.

For absolute value, use fabs (floating absolute). For example, fabs(-2.3) is 2.3.

To round, use floor (which rounds down) or ceil (which stands for "ceiling" and rounds *up*). For example, floor(26.319) is 26.0, and ceil(26.319) is 27.0.

Numeric variables

Like Basic, C++ lets you use variables. For example, you can say:

```
n=3;
```

A variable's name can be short (such as n) or long (such as town_population_in_2001). It can be very long: up to 247 characters long. The name can contain letters, digits, and underscores, but not blank spaces. The name must begin with a letter or underscore, not a digit.

Before using a variable, say what type of number the variable stands for. For example, if n and town_population_in_2001 will stand for numbers that are ints and mortgage_rate will stand for a double, your program should say:

```
int n, town_population_in_2001;
double mortgage_rate;
```

If n is an integer that starts at 3, you can say —

```
int n;
n=3;
```

but you can combine those two lines into this single line:

```
int n=3;
```

Here's how to say "n is an integer that starts at 3, and population_in_2001 is an integer that starts at 27000":

```
int n=3, population_in_2001=27000;
```

Increase

The symbol ++ means "increase". For example, ++n means "increase n".

These lines increase n:

```
int n=3;
++n;
cout <<n;
```

The n starts at 3 and increases to 4, so the computer prints 4.

Saying ++n gives the same answer as n=n+1, but the computer handles ++n faster.

The symbol ++ increases the number by 1, even if the number is a decimal. For example, if x is 17.4 and you say ++x, the x will become 18.4.

Decrease

The opposite of ++ is --. The symbol -- means "decrease". For example, --n means "decrease n". Saying --n gives the same answer as n=n-1 but faster.

Strange short cuts

If you use the following short cuts, your programs will be briefer and run faster.

Instead of saying n=n+2, say n+=2, which means "n's increase is 2". Similarly, instead of saying n=n*3, say n*=3, which means "n's multiplier is 3".

Instead of saying ++n and then giving another command, say ++n in the middle of the other command. For example, instead of saying —

```
++n;
j=7*n;
```

say:

```
j=7*++n;
```

That's pronounced: "j is 7 times an increased n". So if n was 2, saying j=7*++n makes n become 3 and j become 21.

Notice that when you say j=7*++n, the computer increases n *before* computing j. If you say j=7*n++ instead, the computer increases n *after* computing j; so j=7*n++ has the same effect as saying:

```
j=7*n;
++n;
```

How to input

These lines make the computer predict how old you'll be ten years from now:

Program lines	Meaning
`int age;`	The age is an integer.
`cout <<"How old are you? ";`	Ask "How old are you? ".
`cin >>age;`	Wait for human to input age.
`cout <<"Ten years from now, you'll be " <<age+10 <<" years old.";`	Printout.

In that program, "cin" is pronounced "C in" and means "C++ input". It's the opposite of "cout". After the "cin", make sure you type ">>" (which is pronounced "to" and is the opposite of "<<"). Here's how to pronounce that cin line: "C in to age semicolon". Here's a sample run:

```
How old are you? 27
Ten years from now, you'll be 37 years old.
```

The next program converts feet to inches. It even handles decimals: it can convert 1.5 feet to 18.0 inches.

Program lines	Meaning
`double feet;`	The number of feet is double-precision.
`cout <<"How many feet? ";`	Ask "How many feet? ".
`cin >>feet;`	Wait for human to input how many feet.
`cout <<"That makes " <<feet*12 <<" inches.\n";`	Print the result.

Arrays

Like Basic, JavaScript, and Java, C++ lets you create arrays.

For example, if you want x to be a list of 3 double-precision numbers, begin your program by saying:

```
double x[3];
```

That says x will be a list of 3 double-precision numbers, called x[0], x[1], and x[2]. Notice that C++ starts counting at 0.

Here's a C++ program using that array:

```
double x[3];
x[0]=10.6;
x[1]=3.2;
x[2]=1.1;
cout <<x[0]+x[1]+x[2];
```

The computer will print the sum, 14.9.

Notice that if you say double x[3], you can refer to x[0], x[1], and x[2], but not x[3]. If you accidentally refer to x[3], you'll be creating a runaway pointer.

If you want x to be a table having 2 rows and 3 columns of double-precision numbers, say:

```
double x[2][3];
```

Notice that C++ says x[2][3]. If you accidentally say x[2,3] instead of x[2][3], you'll have a runaway pointer.

Since C++ always starts counting at 0 (not 1), the number in the table's top left corner is called x[0][0].

Logic

Like most computer languages, C++ lets you say "if", "while", "for", and "goto" and create comments and subroutines. Here's how....

If

If a person's age is less than 18, let's make the computer say "You are still a minor." Here's the fundamental line:

```
if (age<18) cout <<"You are still a minor.";
```

Notice you must put parentheses after the word "if".

If a person's age is less than 18, let's make the computer say "You are still a minor." and also say "Ah, the joys of youth!" and "I wish I could be as young as you!" Here's how to say all that:

```
if (age<18)
{
    cout <<"You are still a minor.\n";
    cout <<"Ah, the joys of youth!\n";
    cout <<"I wish I could be as young as you!";
}
```

Since that "if" line is above the "{", the "if" line is a structure line and does *not* end in a semicolon.

How to type To type the symbol "{", do this: while holding down the Shift key, tap the "[" key (which is next to the P key). To type the symbol "}", do this: while holding down the Shift key, tap the "]" key.

When you type a line, don't worry about indenting it: when you finish typing the line (and press Enter), the computer will indent it the correct amount, automatically.

Complete program Here's how to put that structure into a complete program:

```
// Joe.cpp : Defines the entry point for the console application.
//

#include "stdafx.h"
#include <iostream>
using namespace std;

int _tmain(int argc, _TCHAR* argv[])
{
    int age;
    cout <<"How old are you? ";
    cin >>age;
    if (age<18)
    {
        cout <<"You are still a minor.\n";
        cout <<"Ah, the joys of youth!\n";
        cout <<"I wish I could be as young as you!\n";
    }
    else
    {
        cout <<"You are an adult.\n";
        cout <<"Now we can have some adult fun!\n";
    }
    cout <<"Glad to have met you.";
    while (1);
    return 0;
}
```

If the person's age is less than 18, the computer will print "You are still a minor." and "Ah, the joys of youth!" and "I wish I could be as young as you!" If the person's age is not less than 18, the computer will print "You are an adult." and "Now we can have some adult fun!" Regardless of the person's age, the computer will end the conversation by saying "Glad to have met you."

Fancy "if"

The "if" statement uses this notation:

Notation	Meaning
if (age<18)	if age is less than 18
if (age<=18)	if age is less than or equal to 18
if (age==18)	if age is equal to 18
if (age!=18)	if age is not equal to 18
if (age<18 && weight>200)	if age<18 and weight>200
if (age<18 || weight>200)	if age<18 or weight>200

Here's how to type the symbol "|": while holding down the Shift key, tap the "\" key.

Look at that table carefully! Notice that in the "if" statement, you should use double symbols: you should say "==" instead of "=", say "&&" instead of "&", and say "||" instead of "|".

If you accidentally say "=" instead of "==", the computer will print wrong answers. If you accidentally say "&" instead of "&&" or say "|" instead of "||", the computer will print right answers but too slowly.

While

Let's make the computer print the word "love" repeatedly, like this:

```
love love love love love love love love love etc.
love love love love love love love love love etc.
love love love love love love love love love etc.
etc.
```

This line does it:

```
    while (1) cout <<"love ";
```

The "while (1)" means: do repeatedly. The computer will do cout <<"love " repeatedly, looping forever — or until you **abort** the program (by clicking the console window's X button).

Let's make the computer start at 20 and keep counting, so the computer will print:

```
20
21
22
23
24
25
26
27
28
29
30
31
32
etc.
```

These lines do it:

Program	Meaning
`    int i=20;`	Start the integer i at 20.
`    while (1)`	Repeat these lines forever:
`    {`	
`        cout <<i <<endl;`	print i then press Enter
`        ++i;`	increase i
`    }`	

They print faster than you can read.

To pause the printing, press the Pause key.
To resume the printing, press the Enter key.
To abort the program, click the console window's X button.

In that program, if you say "while (i<30)" instead of "while (1)", the computer will do the loop just while i remains less than 30; the computer will print just:

```
20
21
22
23
24
25
26
27
28
29
```

To let that program run properly, make sure it contains the 3 helper lines, including a line saying "while (1)" at the program's bottom, so altogether the program looks like this:

```
// Joe.cpp : Defines the entry point for the console application.
//

#include "stdafx.h"
#include <iostream>
using namespace std;

int _tmain(int argc, _TCHAR* argv[])
{
    int i=20;
    while (i<30)
    {
        cout <<i <<endl;
        ++i;
    }
    while (1);
    return 0;
}
```

Instead of saying "while (i<30)", you can say "while (i<=29)".

For

Here's a more natural way to get that output of numbers from 20 to 29:

```
    for (int i=20; i<=29; ++i) cout <<i <<endln;
```

The "for (int i=20; i<=29; ++i)" means:

Do repeatedly. Start the integer i at 20, and keep repeating as long as i<=29. At the end of each repetition, do ++i.

In that "for" statement, if you change the ++i to i+=3, the computer will increase i by 3 instead of by 1, so the computer will print:

```
20
23
26
29
```

The "for" statement is quite flexible. You can even say "for (int i=20; i<100; i*=2)", which makes i start at 20 and keep doubling, so the computer prints:

```
20
40
80
```

Like "if" and "while", the "for" statement can sit atop a group of indented lines that are in braces.

Goto

You can say "goto". For example, if you say "goto yummy", the computer will go to the line whose name is yummy:

```
    cout <<"my dog ";
    goto yummy;
    cout <<"never ";
yummy: cout <<"drinks whiskey";
```

The computer will print:

```
my dog drinks whiskey
```

Comments

To put a comment in your program, begin the comment with the symbol //. The computer ignores everything that's to the right of //. Here's an example:

```
    // This program is fishy
    // It was written by a sick sailor swimming in the sun
    cout <<"Our funny God\n";   // notice the religious motif
    cout <<"invented cod";      // said by a nasty flounder
```

The computer ignores all the comments, which are to the right of //.

While you type the program, the computer makes each // and each comment turn green. Then the computer ignores everything that's turned green, so the computer prints just:

```
Our funny God
invented cod
```

Subroutines

Like most other languages, C++ lets you invent subroutines and give them names. For example, here's how to invent a subroutine called "insult" and use it in the main routine:

Program	Meaning
```// Joe.cpp : Defines the entry point for the console application.```	
```//```	
```#include "stdafx.h"```	
```#include <iostream>```	
```using namespace std;```	
```void insult();```	the program will use insult
```int _tmain(int argc, _TCHAR* argv[])```	Here's the main routine:
```{```	
``` cout <<"We all know...\n";```	print "We all know..."
``` insult();```	do the insult
``` cout <<"...and yet we love you.";```	print the ending
``` while (1);```	
``` return 0;```	
```}```	
```void insult()```	Here's how to insult:
```{```	
``` cout <<"You are stupid!\n";```	print "You are stupid!"
``` cout <<"You are ugly!\n";```	print "You are ugly!"
```}```	

The computer will print:

```
We all know...
You are stupid!
You are ugly!
...and yet we love you.
```

In that program, the first gray line warns the computer that the program will use a subroutine called "insult". The next few lines, beginning with int t+main, define the main routine. The bottom few lines, beginning with void insult(), define the subroutine called "insult".

Whenever you write a subroutine's name, you must put parentheses afterwards, like this: insult(). Those parentheses tell the computer: insult's a subroutine, not a variable.

Here's another example:

Program	Meaning

``
// Joe.cpp : Defines the entry point for the console application.
//
 	
#include "stdafx.h"
#include <iostream>
using namespace std;
void laugh();
int _tmain(int argc, _TCHAR* argv[])
{
    laugh();
    while (1);
    return 0;
}
void laugh()
{
    for (int i=1; i<=100; ++i) cout <<"ha ";
    cout <<endl;
}
``
	the program will use laugh
	Here's the main routine:
	
	main routine says to laugh
	
	Here's how to laugh:
	
	print "ha " a hundred times
	then press Enter

The main routine says to laugh. The subroutine defines "laugh" to mean: print "ha " a hundred times and then press Enter.

Let's create a more flexible subroutine, so that whenever the main routine says laugh(2), the computer will print "ha ha "and Enter; whenever the main routine says laugh(5), the computer will print "ha ha ha ha ha " and Enter; and so on. Here's how:

Program	Meaning

``
// Joe.cpp : Defines the entry point for the console application.
//
 	
#include "stdafx.h"
#include <iostream>
using namespace std;
void laugh(int n);
int _tmain(int argc, _TCHAR* argv[])
{
    cout <<"Here is a short laugh: ";
    laugh(2);
    cout <<"Here is a longer laugh: ";
    laugh(5);
    while (1);
    return 0;
}
void laugh(int n)
{
    for (int i=1; i<=n; ++i) cout <<"ha ";
    cout <<endl;
}
``
	the program will use laugh(n)
	Here's the main routine:
	
	do laugh(2), so print "ha ha "
	
	do laugh(5), so print "ha ha ha ha ha "
	
	Here's how to laugh(n):
	
	print "ha ", n times
	then press Enter

The computer will print:

```
Here is a short laugh: ha ha
Here is a longer laugh: ha ha ha ha ha
```

Average Let's define the "average" of a pair of integers, so that "average(3, 7)" means the average of 3 and 7 (which is 5), and so a main routine saying "i=average(3, 7)" makes i be 5.

This subroutine defines the "average" of all pairs of integers:

```
int average(int a, int b)
{
    return (a+b)/2;
}
```

The top line says, "Here's how to find the average of any two integers, a and b, and make the average be an integer." The next line says, "Return to the main routine, with this answer: (a+b)/2."

Here's a complete program:

Program	Meaning

`// Joe.cpp : Defines the entry point for the console application.`
`//`
 	
`#include "stdafx.h"`
`#include <iostream>`
`using namespace std;`
`int average(int a, int b);`
	the program will use average(a, b)

`int _tmain(int argc, _TCHAR* argv[])`	**Here's the main routine:**
`{` `    int i;`	make i be an integer
`    i=average(3, 7);`	make i be average(3, 7)
`    cout <<i <<endl;`	print i

`    while (1);`
`    return 0;`
`}`	

`int average(int a, int b)`	**Here's how to compute average(a, b):**

`{`
 	
`    return ((a+b)/2);`
`}`
	return this answer: (a+b)/2

In that program, the main routine is:

`    int i;`	make i be an integer
`    i=average(3, 7);`	make i be average(3, 7)
`    cout <<i <<endl;`	print i
`    while (1);` `    return 0;`	

You can shorten it, like this:

`    int i=average(3, 7);`	make the integer i be average(3, 7)
`    cout <<i;`	print i
`    while (1);` `    return 0;`	

You can shorten it further, like this:

`    cout <<average(3, 7);`	print average(3, 7)
`    while (1);` `    return 0;`	

To make that program handle double-precision numbers instead of integers, change each int to double (except the int _tmain). After changing to double, the program will still work, even if you don't change 3 to 3.0 and don't change 7 to 7.0.

Character variables

A variable can stand for a character. For example, suppose you're in school, take a test, and get an A on it. To proclaim your grade, write a program containing this line:

```
grade='A';
```

The complete program includes this block of lines:

Program lines	Meaning
char grade;	The grade is a character.
grade='A';	The grade is 'A'.
cout <<grade;	Print the character that's the grade.

The computer will print:

```
A
```

In that program, you can combine these two lines —

char grade;	The grade is a character.
grade='A';	The grade is 'A'.

to form this single line:

char grade='A';	The grade is this character: 'A'.

This block of lines let you input a grade:

```
char grade;
cout <<"Type the letter that is your grade: ";
cin >>grade;
cout <<"I'm amazed your grade is " <<grade;
```

It makes the computer say "Type the letter that is your grade: ", then wait for the human to type a grade (such as B), then say "I'm amazed your grade is B", so the screen looks like this:

```
Type the letter that is your grade: B
I'm amazed your grade is B
```

Strings of characters

A variable can stand for a whole string of characters:

```
char x[]="winks";
cout <<x;
```

The first line makes x be this string of characters: "winks". The cout line makes the computer print x, so the computer will print:

```
winks
```

In a string, the beginning character is called **character 0**; the next character is called **character 1**; the next character is called **character 2**. For example, here's what happens if a string is named x:

The string's beginning character is called **x's character 0** or **x[0]**.
The next character is called **x's character 1** or **x[1]**.
The next character is called **x's character 2** or **x[2]**.

So if x is the string "winks", here's what happens:

x[0] is the string's beginning character, which is 'w'
x[1] is the next character, which is 'i'
x[2] is 'n'
x[3] is 'k'
x[4] is 's'
x[5] is a special character that marks the end of the string

In the program lines you just looked at, if you change the cout line to this —

```
cout <<x[0] <<x[1] <<x[2] <<x[4];
```

the computer will print x[0] then x[1] then x[2] then x[4], so the computer will print:

```
wins
```

If you change the cout line to this —

```
cout <<x+1;
```

The computer will print x but skip 1 character; it will print:

```
inks
```

Input Here's how to input a string:

```
char firstname[81];
cout <<"What is your first name? ";
cin >>firstname;
cout <<"I like the name " <<firstname <<" very much!";
```

In that program, the char line says firstname can be a string of up to 81 characters. Since the console window is 80 characters wide, 81 is a fairly safe number: it's big enough to hold a whole line of 80 characters, plus 1 end-of-string mark. **When writing a program that inputs a string, it's a good habit to put at least 81 in your program's char line.**

If you put in a much smaller number instead, such as 10, you run the risk that the human will input more characters than you reserved space for, and you'll have a runaway pointer than can crash your program (and, if you're unlucky, crash your operating system and your hard disk).

Even the number 81 is not totally safe, since the operating system lets the human input up to 254 characters (by continuing the typing onto the line below). **To be totally safe, you'd have to change the number 81 to 255** (to allow 254 characters plus an end-of-string mark).

That program makes the computer ask "What is your first name? " then wait for the human to type a first name. For example, if the human's first name is Maria, the program makes the conversation go like this:

```
What is your first name? Maria
I like the name Maria very much!
```

Comparing strings

To put strings in an "if" statement, you must say "strcmp", which warns the computer to do a "*str*ing *comp*arison".

For example, suppose x and y are strings, and you want to test whether they're equal. Do *not* say "if (x==y)". Instead, say "if (strcmp(x,y)==0)", which means "if string comparison between x and y shows 0 difference between them".

To test whether x's string comes before y's in the dictionary, do not say "if (x<y)". Instead, say "if (strcmp(x,y)<0)".

Old versions To help the computer understand "strcmp", old versions of C++ need your program's top to say —

```
#include <string>
```

or:

```
#include <string.h>
```

Copying strings

If x is a string, and you want to make y be the same string, do *not* say "y=x". Instead, say "strcpy(y,x)", which means "make y be a copy of the string x".

Reserve space for y.

For example, if x is a string that might contain up to 20 characters plus an end-of-string mark (making a total of 21 characters), warn the computer that y might contain 21 characters also, by saying "char y[21]".

Old versions To help the computer understand "strcpy", old versions of C++ need your program's top to say —

```
#include <string>
```

or:

```
#include <string.h>
```

Windows forms

Like Visual Basic, C++ lets you easily create Windows forms. Here's how.

Start C++ (by clicking the Start button then "All Programs" then "Microsoft Visual Studio 2010 Express" then "Microsoft Visual C++ 2010 Express").

You see the Start Page window. Click "**New Project**" (which is near the screen's left edge) then "**Windows Forms Application**".

Highlight the first "<Enter_name>" (by dragging across it, so it all turns blue). Invent a name for your program (such as "Joey"); type the name and press Enter. Click "Finish".

You see an **object**, called the **Form1** window. Double-click in that window (below "Form1"). That tells the computer you want to write a program (subroutine) about that window.

The computer starts writing the **subroutine** for you. The computer writes many lines; the bottom lines are:

```
#pragma endregion
    private: System::Void Form1_Load(…) {
            }
    };
}
```

The line saying "private: System" is the subroutine's **header**. Below that, between the **braces** (the symbols "{" and "}"), insert lines that tell the computer what to do when Form1 is **loaded** (appears). The lines you insert are called the subroutine's **body**.

Simplest example

Let's make the Form1 window say "I love you". To do that, press the Enter key then type this line —

```
        Text="I love you";
```

The computer automatically indents that line for you, so the subroutine becomes:

```
#pragma endregion
    private: System::Void Form1_Load(…) {
                Text="I love you";
            }
    };
}
```

To run your program, press the F5 key (or click the green " ▶ ", which is at the screen's top center) then Enter. Then you see the Form1 window again; but instead of saying "Form1", it says the text:

```
I love you
```

When you've finished admiring the Form1 window, stop the program by clicking the Form1 window's X button. Then you see the subroutine again:

```
#pragma endregion
    private: System::Void Form1_Load(…) {
                Text="I love you";
            }
    };
}
```

If you wish, edit the subroutine. For example, try changing the Text line to this:

```
        Text="I hate cabbage";
```

Math

The Text line can include math calculations, but you must convert the answer to a string, since Text must be a string. For example, to make the computer write the answer to 4+2, type this line:

```
        Text = Convert::ToString(4+2);
```

Message box

To create a message box saying "Your hair is messy", type this line in the subroutine:

```
        MessageBox::Show("Your hair is messy");
```

To create a message box saying the answer to 4+2, type this line:

```
        MessageBox::Show(Convert::ToString(4+2));
```

Property list

Click the "Form1.h [Design]" tab, so you see the Form1 window itself. Right-click in the middle of the Form1 window, then click "Properties".

Near the screen's right edge, you see a list whose title is:

```
Properties
Form1 System.Windows.Forms.Form
```

That list is called **Form1's main property list** (or **property window**). It looks the same way as if you were using Visual Basic. To explore it, reread my chapter about Visual Basic.

Toolbox

While you're looking at Form1's window, the screen's *right* edge should show the word "Toolbox". (If you don't see the word "Toolbox" yet, make it appear by clicking "Tools" then "Settings" then "Reset".)

If you're lucky, you'll see a toolbox that looks like the picture on page 568.

If you see just the word "Toolbox" but none of the icons that are supposed to be in the toolbox, make them appear by clicking "Toolbox", then make them stay on the screen permanently by clicking the **push pin**, which is just left of the toolbox's X.

Make sure the triangle left of "All Windows Forms" has a white middle. (If the triangle is solid black instead, click the triangle to make its middle white.)

Make sure the triangle left of "Common Controls" is solid black. (If that triangle has a white middle instead, click the triangle to make it solid black.)

Each object in the toolbox is called a **tool**.

The complete toolbox is too tall to fit on your screen. You see just the toolbox's beginning. Whenever you want to see the rest of the toolbox (which includes many dozens of tools), click the toolbox's scroll-down arrow (at the toolbox's bottom-right corner).

The toolbox looks the same as if you were using Visual Basic (but is at the screen's *right* edge instead of the left). To explore how to use its tools, reread my chapter on Visual Basic.

Exotic languages

The previous 6 chapters explained 6 popular computer languages: **Basic** (especially the versions called QBasic & QB64), **Visual Basic**, **JavaScript** (especially the JScript version), **Java**, **Visual C#**, and **Visual C++**.

Those 6 languages are just the tip of the iceberg. Programmers have invented *thousands* of others.

This table shows how to give popular commands in 26 languages:

Language	Assign variable	Condition	Start a counting loop	Output	Declare an array	Comment
Basic	j = k + 2	IF x = 4.3 THEN	FOR i = 5 TO 17	PRINT k	DIM x(4)	'WOW
Visual Basic	j = k + 2	If x = 4.3 Then	For i = 5 To 17	Console.WriteLine(k)	Dim x(4)	'WOW
Java	j=k+2	if (x==4.3)	for (int i=5; i<=17; ++i)	System.out.println(k)	double[] x=new double[4]	//wow
JavaScript	j=k+2	if (x==4.3)	for (int i=5; i<=17; ++i)	document.write(k)	x=Array(4)	//wow
C	j=k+2	if (x==4.3)	for (i=5; i<=17; ++i)	printf("%d",k)	float x[4]	/* wow */
C++ & Visual C++	j=k+2	if (x==4.3)	for (int i=5; i<=17; ++i)	cout <<k	double x[4]	//wow
Visual C#	j = k + 2	if (x==4.3)	for (int i = 5; i <=17; ++i)	Console.WriteLine(k)	double[] x = new double[4]	//wow
Perl	$j=$k+2	if ($x==4.3)	for ($i=5; $i<=17; ++$i)	print $k	@x=(1..4)	#wow
PHP	$j=$k+2	if ($x==4.3)	for ($i=5; $i<=17; ++$i)	echo $k	$x=range(1,4)	//wow
Algol	J:=K+2	IF X=4.3 THEN	FOR I := 5 STEP 1 UNTIL 17 DO	PRINT(k)	REAL ARRAY X[1:4]	COMMENT WOW
Pascal & Delphi	J:=K+2	IF X=4.3 THEN	FOR I := 5 TO 17 DO	WRITELN(k)	X: ARRAY[1..4] OF REAL	{WOW}
Modula	J:=K+2	IF X=4.3 THEN	FOR I := 5 TO 17 DO	WRITEINTEGER(K,6)	X: ARRAY[1..4] OF REAL	(*WOW*)
Ada	J:=K+2	IF X=4.3 THEN	FOR I IN 5..17 LOOP	PUT(K)	X: ARRAY(1..4) OF FLOAT	--WOW
Python	j=k+2	if x==4.3:	for i in range(5,17):	k	x=zeros(4)	#wow
Ruby	j=k+2	if x==4.3	for i in 5..17	puts k	x=(1..4)	#wow
Fortran	J=K+2	IF (X .EQ. 4.3)	DO 10 I=5,17	PRINT *, K	DIMENSION X(4)	C WOW
PL/I	J=K+2	IF X=4.3 THEN	DO I = 5 TO 17	PUT LIST(K)	DECLARE X(4)	/* WOW */
Cobol	COMPUTE J = K + 2	IF X = 4.3	PERFORM L VARYING I FROM 5 BY 1 UNTIL I>17	DISPLAY K	X OCCURS 4 TIMES	*WOW
dBase	J=K+2	IF X=4.3	not available	? K	DECLARE X[4]	&&WOW
Easy	LET J=K+2	IF X=4.3	LOOP I FROM 5 TO 17	SAY K	PREPARE X(4)	'WOW
Snobol	J = K + 2	EQ(X,4.3) :S(	not available	OUTPUT = K	X = ARRAY(4)	*WOW
Pilot	C:#J=#K+2	(#X=4.3)	not available	T:#K	DIM:#X(4)	R:WOW
Lisp	(SETQ J (PLUS K 2))	IF :X=4.3	not available	K	(ARRAY ((X (4) LIST)))	;WOW
Logo	MAKE "J :K+2	IF :X=4.3	not available	PRINT :K	DEFAR "X 4 1	!WOW

That table clumps the languages into groups. For example, the first group includes Basic and Visual Basic.

In each group, I list the languages in the order they were invented. For example, in the first group, QBasic was invented before Visual Basic, so QBasic is listed first.

The bottom 4 (Snobol, Pilot, Lisp, and Logo) differs wildly from the others. They're called **radical languages**; the other 22 languages are called **mainstream**.

Two other radical languages are **APL** and **Forth**. They're so weird they won't fit in that table!

Each of those 28 languages is flexible enough to program anything. Which language you choose is mainly a matter of personal taste.

Other languages are more specialized. For example, a language called **GPSS** is designed specifically to analyze how many employees to hire, to save your customers from waiting in long lines for service. **Dynamo** analyzes social interactions inside your company and city and throughout the world; then it graphs your future. **SPSS** analyzes tables of numbers, by computing their averages, maxima, minima, standard deviations, and *hundreds* of other measurements used by statisticians. **Apt** helps you run a factory by controlling "robots" that cut metal. **Prolog** lets you store answers to your questions and act as an **expert system**.

This table reveals more details about all those languages:

Name	What the name stands for	Original use	Version 1 arose at	When	Names of new versions
	Mainstream languages				
Fortran	**For**mula **Tran**slating	sciences	IBM	1954-1957	Fortran 2008, Lahey Fortran
Algol	**Algo**rithmic **L**anguage	sciences	international	1957-1958	Algol W, Algol 68, Balgol
Cobol	**Co**mmon **B**usiness-**O**riented **L**anguage	business	Defense Department	1959-1960	Cobol 2002
Basic	**B**eginners **A**ll-purp. **S**ymbolic **I**nstruc. **C**ode	sciences	Dartmouth College	1963-1964	GW Basic, QBasic, QB64, BBC Basic
PL/I	**P**rogramming **L**anguage **O**ne	general	IBM	1963-1966	PL/I Optimizer, PL/C, Ansi PL/I
Pascal	Blaise **Pascal**	general	Switzerland	1968-1970	Turbo Pascal, Delphi
Modula	**Modula**r programming	systems programming	Switzerland	1975	Modula-2, Oberon
C	beyond B	systems programming	AT&T's Bell Labs	1971-1973	Ansi C, Objective-C
Ada	**Ada** Lovelace	military equipment	France	1977-1980	Ada final version
dBase	**D**ata **Base**	database management	Jet Prop'n Lab & Ashton-T.	1978-1980	dBase Plus 2, Visual FoxPro 9
Easy	**Easy**	general	Secret Guide	1972-1982	Easy
C++	**C** increased	systems programming	AT&T's Bell Labs	1979-1983	Borland C++, ISO C++
Perl	**P**ractical **E**xtraction and **R**eport **L**anguage	systems programming	Unisys	1987	Perl 6
Python	as fun as Monty **Python**'s Flying Circus	systems programming	Netherlands	1989	Python 3
Java	as stimulating as **Java** coffee	Web-page animation	Sun Microsystems	1990-1995	Java 6, JBuilder, Visual J++, J#
Visual Basic	**Basic** for creating Windows **Visual**ly	Windows-form design	Microsoft	1991	Visual Basic 2010
Visual C++	**C++** for creating Windows **Visual**ly	Windows-form design	Microsoft	1993	Visual C++ 2010
Delphi	oracle at **Delphi**	general	Borland	1993-1995	Delphi 2007, Oxygene
Ruby	the birthstone beyond Pearl	systems programming	Japan	1993-1996	Ruby 1.9, Ruby on Rails
PHP	**P**ersonal **H**ome **P**age	Web-page design	Canada	1994-1995	PHP 5
JavaScript	**Java** for creating simple **script**s	Web-page calculations	Netscape	1996	JScript
Visual C#	**C** sharp for creating Windows **Visual**ly	Windows-form design	Microsoft	1999-2000	Visual C# 2010
	Radical languages				
Lisp	**Lis**t **P**rocessing	artificial intelligence	MIT	1958-1960	Common Lisp
Snobol	**S**tring-**O**riented sym**bol**ic **L**anguage	string processing	AT&T's Bell Labs	1962-1963	Snobol 4B
APL	**A** **P**rogramming **L**anguage	sciences	Harvard & IBM	1956-1966	APLSV, APL Plus, APL 2, J
Logo	**Logo**	general	Bolt Beranek Newman	1967	Terrapin Logo, LCSI MicroWorlds Pro
Forth	**Fourth**-generation language	business & astronomy	Stanford Univ. & Mohasco	1963-1968	Forth 83, Fig-Forth, MMS Forth
Pilot	**P**rogrammed **I**nquiry, **L**earning, **O**r **T**eaching	tutoring kids	U. of Cal. at San Francisco	1968	Atari Pilot
	Specialized languages				
Apt	**A**utomatically **P**rogrammed **T**ools	cutting metal	MIT	1952-1957	APT 77
Dynamo	**Dyna**mic **M**odels	simulation	MIT	1959	Dynamo 4, Stella
GPSS	**G**eneral-**P**urpose **S**imulation **S**ystem	simulation	IBM	1961	GPSS 5
SPSS	**S**tatistical **P**ackage for the **S**ocial **S**ciences	statistics	Stanford University	1965-1967	SPSS 16
Prolog	**Pro**gramming in **Log**ic	artificial intelligence	France	1972	Arity Prolog, Turbo Prolog

Within each category ("mainstream", "radical", and "specialized"), I listed the languages in chronological order.

Of those 33 languages, 6 were invented in Europe (Algol, Pascal, Modula, Ada, Python, and Prolog), 1 in Japan (Ruby), and 1 in Canada (PHP). The other 21 were invented in the USA.

4 were invented at IBM (Fortran, PL/I, APL, and GPSS), 3 at Microsoft (Visual Basic, Visual C++, and Visual C#), 3 at AT&T's Bell Labs (C, C++, and Snobol), 3 at MIT (Lisp, Apt, and Dynamo), 2 at Stanford University (Forth and SPSS), and 2 by Professor Niklaus Wirth in Switzerland (Pascal and Modula). The rest were invented by geniuses elsewhere.

Mainstream languages

The first mainstream languages were **Fortran**, **Algol**, and **Cobol**. They were the **big 3**.

IBM invented **Fortran**, which appealed to engineers.

An international committee invented **Algol**, which appealed to logicians.

A committee based at the Pentagon invented **Cobol**, which appealed to government bureaucrats and business managers.

Beyond the big 3

Other mainstream languages came after the big 3 and were just slight improvements of the big 3. This family tree shows how the mainstream languages influenced each other:

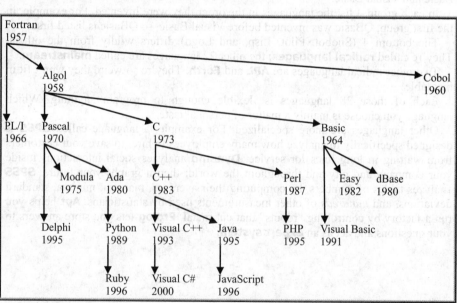

In that tree, a vertical line means "a direct influence" (like a parent); a slanted line means "an indirect influence" (like an aunt or uncle). For each language, I show the year when the language's first version was complete. As each language grew, it stole features from other languages (just like English stole the word "restaurant" from French); the tree shows just history's main thrust.

The tree's third row has 4 languages: PL/I, Pascal, C, and Basic. Here's why they were invented....

Why PL/I?

After inventing Fortran and further improvements (called Fortran II, Fortran III, Fortran IV, and Fortran V), IBM decided to invent the "ultimate" improvement: a language that would include all the important words of Fortran V and **Algol** and **Cobol**. At first, IBM called it "Fortran VI"; but since it included the best of everything and was the first *complete* language ever invented, IBM changed its name to **Programming Language One** (written as **PL/I**).

IBM bragged about how PL/I was so eclectic, but most programmers considered it a confusing mishmash and continued using the original 3 languages (Fortran, Algol, and Cobol), which were pure and simple.

Why Pascal?

Among the folks who disliked PL/I was Niklaus Wirth, who preferred Algol. At a Swiss university, he invented an improved Algol and called it **Pascal**. Then he invented a further improvement, called **Modula**.

Algol, Pascal, and Modula are all very similar to each other. He thinks Modula's the best of the trio, but critics disagree. Pascal is the most popular of that trio. (Hardly anybody uses the original Algol anymore, and Modula is considered a controversial experiment.)

A company called **Borland** became famous by developing **Turbo Pascal** (a Pascal version that runs fast on DOS) then **Delphi** (which resembles Turbo Pascal but run on Windows and lets you create your own windows).

The Department of Defense was happily using Cobol to run the military's paperwork bureaucracy but needed to invent a different kind of language, to control missiles and other military equipment. The Department held a contest to develop such a language and said it wanted the language to resemble PL/I, Algol, and Pascal. (It didn't know about Modula, which was still being developed.) The winner was a French company. The Department adopted that company's language and called it **Ada**. It resembled Modula but included more commands — and therefore consumed more RAM and was more expensive. Critics complain that Ada, like PL/I, is too big and complex. But Ada inspired **Python** and **Ruby**, which are smaller and popular.

Why Basic?

Two professors at Dartmouth College combined Fortran with Algol, to form **Basic**. It was designed for students, not professionals: it included just the *easiest* parts of Fortran and Algol. Students liked it because it was easy to learn, but professionals complained it lacked advanced features.

The first version of Basic ran on a maxicomputer. Later, Digital Equipment Corporation (DEC) invented versions for minicomputers, and Microsoft invented many microcomputer versions, such as **QBasic**.

After Microsoft invented Windows, Microsoft invented **Visual Basic.**, which runs on Windows, lets you create your own windows, and includes advanced features.

My own attempt to create the ideal language is called **Easy**. It's even easier to learn than Basic and can do more tricks. But since I don't have the time to put Easy onto a computer, Easy's remained just an idea whose time should have come.

Basic inspired me to invent a language called **Easy**, which is even easier to learn than Basic but hasn't yet been put on any computer well.

Inspired by languages such as Basic and PL/I, Wayne Ratliff invented **dBase**. Like Basic, dBase is easy. What makes dBase unique is its wonderful commands for manipulating databases.

Why C?

Fancy languages, such as PL/I and Modula, require lots of RAM. At AT&T's Bell Labs, researchers needed a language small enough to fit in the tiny RAM of a minicomputer or microcomputer. They developed the ideal tiny language and called it **C**. Like PL/I, it borrows from Fortran, Algol, and Cobol; but it lacks PL/I's frills. It's "lean and mean" and runs very fast.

Later, Bell Labs invented an improved C, called **C++**, which includes extra commands. Microsoft invented **Visual C++**, which adds commands for manipulating windows. Then Anders Hejlsberg (the Danish programmer who developed Turbo Pascal and Delphi at Borland) moved to Microsoft, where he invented **Visual C#**, which tries to combine the best features of Visual C++, Turbo Pascal, and Delphi.

Sun invented a C++ variant called **Java**, to handle Web-page programming (such as animation). Netscape invented **JavaScript**, which resembles Java but is simpler and more limited. C also led to **Perl** & **PHP**, which handle Web-page programming and compete against Java & JavaScript.

Look back!

Let's take a closer look at the oldest of those mainstream languages, the ones invented up through 1982....

Fortran

During the early 1950's, the only available computer languages were specialized or awkward. **Fortran** was the first computer language good enough to be considered mainstream. Algol and Cobol came shortly afterwards. Fortran, Algol, and Cobol were so good they made all earlier languages obsolete.

Fortran's nature

On pages 493-553, I explained how to program in QBasic. Fortran resembles QBasic but is weirder — because Fortran was invented before programmers learned how to make programming languages pleasant.

For example, suppose you want to add 2+2. In QBasic, you can say just:

```
PRINT 2+2
```

In Fortran, you must lengthen the program, so it looks like this instead:

```
      N=2+2
      PRINT *, N
      END
```

Here's why:

```
Fortran requires the program's bottom line to say END.

Fortran requires each line to be indented 6 spaces.

Fortran is too stupid to do math in the middle of a PRINT statement, so you must do the math first, in a separate line (N=2+2).

Fortran expects you to comment about how to print the answer. If you have no comment on that topic, put an asterisk and comma in the PRINT statement. The asterisk and comma mean: no comment.
```

That's how the typical version of Fortran works. Some versions are different. For example, some versions require you to say STOP above END, like this:

```
      N=2+2
      PRINT *, N
      STOP
      END
```

Some versions want you to say TYPE instead of PRINT.

Some old versions won't accept "no comment" about printing. They require you to say:

```
      N=2+2
      PRINT 10, N
10    FORMAT (1X,I1)
      END
```

That PRINT line means: PRINT, using the FORMAT in line 10, the value of N. In line 10, the 1X means "normal"; the I1 means "an integer that's just one digit". Those details drive beginners nuts, but experienced Fortran programmers are used to such headaches and take them in stride, just like Frenchmen are used to conjugating French verbs and Germans are used to conjugating German adjectives (yuck!).

Like QBasic, Fortran lets you do math by using these symbols:

+	-	*	/

But Fortran is harder to learn than QBasic:

> In QBasic, if you want to divide 399 by 100, requesting 399/100 makes the computer gives you the correct answer, 3.99. But in Fortran, requesting 399/100 makes the computer assume you don't care about decimal points (since you didn't mention any), so it says just 3; if you want it to say 3.99 instead, you must insert a decimal point into the original problem, by asking for 399.0/100.0 (or at least asking for 399./100, if you're lazy).
>
> In QBasic, you can use the symbol < to mean "less than". Fortran is afraid to use fancy symbols (since ancient computers didn't understand them), so Fortran wants you to write .LT. instead, like this....
> QBasic: IF x < 4.3 THEN
> Fortran: IF (X .LT. 4.3) THEN
>
> Likewise, Fortran requires you to say .GT. instead of > for "greater than", say .LE. for "less than or equal to", say .GE. for "greater than or equal to". To be consistent, Fortran also requires you to say .EQ. instead of "equal to" (in an IF statement)....
> QBasic: IF x = 4.3 THEN
> Fortran   IF (X .EQ. 4.3) THEN
>
> In QBasic, the symbol ^ means exponents (for example, 4.7 ^ 3 means "4.7 times 4.7 times 4.7"). Since Fortran's afraid of fancy symbols, Fortran uses ** instead of ^ (like this: 4.7 ** 3).
>
> In QBasic, a variable can be any letter of the alphabet (such as n) or a longer name (up to 40 characters long). In Fortran, each variable's name must be short (no longer than 6 characters), because Fortran is supposed to run even on primitive old computers that have very little memory.
>
> QBasic can handle 5 kinds of variables: single-precision real, double-precision real, short integer, long integer, or string. QBasic assumes each variable is single-precision real, unless you specifically indicate otherwise (such as by putting a $ at the end of the variable's name, to indicate the variable's a string).
>
> In QBasic, every variable stands for a single-precision real number, unless you specifically say otherwise. For example, putting $ after the variable's name makes the variable become a string instead. QBasic can handle 5 kinds of variables: single-precision real number, string, double-precision real number, short integer, and long integer.
>
> Mathematicians (and engineers) often use the letters i, j, k, m, and n to stand for integers. Fortran therefore assumes that any variable whose name begins with I, J, K, L, M, or N is an integer, and all other variables are single-precision real, unless you specifically say otherwise.
>
> Fortran can handle 4 kinds of variables: single-precision real (which Fortran calls REAL), double-precision real (which Fortran calls DOUBLE PRECISION), long integer (which Fortran calls INTEGER), and complex numbers (which Fortran calls COMPLEX and include numbers such as the square root of -1). Fortran's ability to handle COMPLEX numbers make it better for advanced math & engineering than QBasic.
>
> Since Fortran assumes that variables beginning with I, J, K, L, M, or N are integers, Fortran programmers purposely misspell variable names. For example, if a Fortran variable's purpose is to count, call it KOUNT (rather than COUNT) to make it an INTEGER. If you want a Fortran variable to be an integer that measures a position, call it LOCATN (rather than POSITN) to make it an INTEGER. If a Fortran variable measures an object's mass as a real number, call it AMASS (rather than MASS) to make it a REAL.
>
> Since Fortran's purpose was just to do math, Fortran's original version didn't include any string variables. Later, many manufacturers tried to "fix" Fortran by adding string commands, but those commands are awkward and pathetic, much worse than what QBasic offers.

Fortran did a good job of handling math functions (such as SQR) and subroutines (for handling statistics, calculus computations, and other math challenges). Many programmers created libraries full of math functions and subroutines and sold them to other programmers. A whole culture developed of programmers writing Fortran routines. If you didn't know Fortran, you weren't part of the "in" crowd.

How Fortran arose

In 1954, an IBM committee said it was planning a new computer language that would help engineers make the computer handle math formulas. The committee called the language **Fortran**, to emphasize that the language would be particularly good for **tran**slating **for**mulas into computer notation.

Those original plans for Fortran were modest:

> They did *not* allow long variable names, subroutines, long function definitions, double precision, complex numbers, or apostrophes. A variable's name had to be short: just two letters. A function's definition had to fit on a single line. To print 'PLEASE KISS ME', the programmers had to write that string as 14HPLEASE KISS ME instead of 'PLEASE KISS ME'; the 14H warned the computer that a 14-character string was coming.

Then came improvements:

> Fortran's first working version (1957) allowed longer variable names: 6 characters. Fortran II (1958) allowed subroutines and long function definitions. IBM experimented with Fortran III but never released it to the public. Fortran IV (1962) allowed double precision and complex numbers. Apostrophes around strings weren't allowed until later.

The original plans said you'd be able to add an integer to a real. That didn't work in Fortran I, Fortran II, and Fortran IV, but it works now.

The original plans said an IF statement would compare any two numbers. Fortran I and Fortran II required the second number no be zero, but Fortran IV removed that restriction.

IBM waged a campaign to convince everyone that Fortran was easier than previous methods of programming. IBM succeeded: Fortran became immediately popular. Fortran was easy enough so that, for the first time, engineers who weren't computer specialists could write programs.

Other manufacturers sold imitations of IBM's Fortran, but with modifications. The variety of modifications from all the manufacturers annoyed engineers, who wished manufacturers would all use a single, common version of Fortran. So the engineers turned to the **American National Standards Institute (Ansi)**, which is a non-profit group of engineers that sets standards.

> "Ansi" is pronounced "an see". It sets standards for practically all equipment in your life. For example, Ansi sets the standard for screws: to tighten a screw, you turn it clockwise, not counterclockwise.

In 1966, Ansi decided on a single version of Fortran IV to be used by all manufacturers. Thereafter, each manufacturer adhered to the Ansi standard but also added extra commands, to try to outclass the other manufacturers.

After several years had gone by, enough extra commands had been added by manufacturers so engineers asked Ansi to meet again and develop a common standard for those extras. Ansi finished developing the standard in 1977 and called it **Fortran 77**.

Now each major manufacturer adheres to the standard for Fortran 77, so you can run Fortran 77 programs on most maxicomputers, minicomputers, and microcomputers. Each manufacturer adds extra commands beyond Fortran 77.

In 1984, an Ansi committee developed a "Fortran 88". 40 members of the committee approved it, but the other 2 members — IBM and DEC — refused to endorse it. In 1991, a variant called **Fortran 90** was finally approved by all.

Fortran's popularity

Fortran became popular immediately because it didn't have any serious competitors. Throughout the 1960's and 1970's, Fortran remained the most popular computer language among engineers, scientists, mathematicians, and college students. Colleges required all freshman computer-science majors to take Fortran.

But at the end of the 1970's, Fortran's popularity began to drop.

> Engineers switched to newer languages, such as Basic (which is easier), Pascal (more logical), and C (faster and more economical of RAM). Although Fortran 77 included extra commands to make Fortran resemble Basic and Pascal, those commands were "too little, too late": Fortran's new string commands weren't quite as good as Basic's, and Fortran's new IF command wasn't quite as good as Pascal's.

Now high-school kids are required to study Basic or Pascal, college kids are required to study C++, and hardly anybody studies Fortran. People who still program in Fortran are called "old-fashioned" by their colleagues.

But in some ways, Fortran's still better for engineering that Basic, Pascal, or C++. Here's why:

Fortran includes more commands for handling "complex numbers".

Fortran programmers have developed libraries containing *thousands* of Fortran subroutines, which you can use in your own Fortran programs. Such large libraries haven't been developed for Basic, Pascal, or C++ yet.

Though Basic, Pascal, and C++ work well on microcomputers and minicomputers, no *good* versions of those languages have been invented for IBM maxicomputers. The only language that lets you unleash an IBM maxicomputer's full power to solve engineering problems is Fortran.

Algol

In 1955, a committee in Germany began inventing a computer language. Though the committee spoke German, it decided the computer language should use English words instead, since English was the international language for science.

In 1957 those Germans invited Americans to join them. In 1958 other European countries joined also, to form an international committee, which proposed a new computer language, called "IAL" (International Algebraic Language).

The committee eventually changed the language's name to **Algol 58** (the **Algo**rithmic **l**anguage invented in 19**58**), then created an improved version called **Algol 60**, then created a further revision called **Algol 60 Revised**, and disbanded. Today, programmers who mention "Algol" usually mean the committee's last report, Algol 60 Revised.

Algol differs from Fortran in many little ways....

How to end a statement
At the end of each statement, Fortran requires you to press the Enter key. Algol requires you to type a semicolon instead.

Algol's advantage: you can type many statements on the same line, by putting semicolons between the statements. Algol's disadvantage: those ugly semicolons are a nuisance to type and make your program look cluttered.

Integer variables
To tell the computer that a person's AGE is an integer (instead of a real number), Fortran requires you to put the letter I, J, K, L, M, or N before the variable's name, like this: IAGE. Algol requires you to insert a note saying "INTEGER AGE" at the top of your program instead.

Algol's advantage: you don't have to write unpronounceable gobbledygook such as "IAGE". Algol's disadvantage: whenever you create a new variable, Algol forces you to go back up to the top of your program and insert a line saying "INTEGER" or "REAL".

Assignment statements
In Fortran, you can say J=7. In Algol, you must insert a colon and say J:=7 instead. To increase K by 1 in Fortran, you say K=K+1. In Algol, you say K:=K+1.

Algol's disadvantage: the colon is a nuisance to type. Fortran's disadvantage: according to the rules of algebra, it's impossible for K to equal K+1, and so the Fortran command K=K+1 looks like an impossibility.

Algol's beauty
Here's how Algol avoids Fortran's ugliness:

In Algol, a variable's name can be practically as long as you like. In Fortran, a variable's name must be short: no more than 6 characters.

Algol lets you write 2 instead of 2.0, without affecting the computer's answer. In Fortran, if you write 1/2 instead of 1/2.0, you get 0 instead of .5; and if you write SQRT (9) instead of SQRT (9.0), you get nonsense.

Algol's IF statement is very flexible: it can include the words ELSE, BEGIN, and END, and it lets you insert as many statements as you want between BEGIN and END. Algol even lets you put an IF statement in the middle of an equation, like this: X:=2+(IF Y<5 THEN 8 ELSE 9). The IF statement in Fortran I, II, III, and IV was very limited; the IF statement in Fortran 77 copies some of Algol's power, but not yet all.

Algol's FOR statement is very flexible. To make X be 3.7, then be Y+6.2, then go from SQRT(Z) down to 5 in steps of .3, you can say "FOR X:=3.7, Y+6.2, SQRT(Z) STEP -.3 UNTIL 5 DO". Fortran's DO is more restrictive; some versions of Fortran even insist that the DO statement contain no reals, no negatives, and no arithmetic operations.

At the beginning of a Fortran program, you can say DIMENSION X(20) but not DIMENSION X(N). Algol permits the "DIMENSION X(N)" concept; in Algol you say ARRAY X[1:N].

Algol's popularity
When Algol was invented, programmers loved it. Europeans began using Algol more than Fortran. The American computer association (called the **Association for Computing Machinery, ACM**) said all programs in its magazine would be in Algol.

But since IBM refused to put Algol on its computers, most American programmers couldn't use Algol.

That created a ridiculous situation: American programmers programmed in Fortran but submitted Algol translations to the ACM's magazine, which published the programs in Algol, which the magazine's readers had to translate back to Fortran to run on IBM computers. IBM computers eventually swept over Europe, so even Europeans had to use Fortran instead of Algol. In 1966 the ACM gave in and agreed to publish programs in Fortran; but since Algol was prettier, everybody continued to submit Algol versions anyway. IBM gave in and put Algol on its computers; but IBM's version of Algol was so limited and awkward that nobody took it seriously, and IBM stopped selling it. In 1972 Stanford University invented **Algol W** (a better Algol for IBM computers), but Algol W came too late: universities and businessmen had already tired of waiting for a good IBM Algol and had committed themselves to Fortran.

Critics blamed IBM for Algol's demise. But here's IBM's side of the story:

IBM had invested 25 man-years to develop the first version of Fortran. By the time the Algol committee finished the report on Algol 60 Revised, IBM had also developed Fortran II and Fortran III and made plans for Fortran IV. IBM was proud of its Fortrans and wanted to elaborate on them. Moreover, IBM realized that **computers run Fortran programs faster than Algol**.

When asked why it didn't support Algol, IBM replied that the committee's description of Algol was incomplete. IBM was right; the Algol 60 Revised Report had 3 loopholes:

The report didn't say what words to use for input and output, because the committee couldn't agree. So computers differ. If you want to transfer an Algol program from one computer to another, you must change all the input and output instructions.

The report uses symbols such as ÷ and ∧, which most keyboards lack. The report underlines keywords; most keyboards can't underline. To type Algol programs on a typical keyboard, you must substitute other symbols for ÷, ∧, and underlining. Manufacturers differ in what to substitute. To transfer an Algol program to different manufacturer, you must change symbols.

Some features of Algol are hard to teach to a computer. Even now, no computer understands all of Algol. When a manufacturer says its computer "understands Algol", you must ask, "*Which* features of Algol?"

Attempts to improve Algol
Long after the original Algol committee wrote the Algol 60 Revised Report, two other Algol committees were formed.

One committee developed suggestions on how to do input and output, but its suggestions were largely ignored.

The other committee tried to invent a much fancier Algol. That committee wrote its preliminary report in 1968 and revised it in 1975. Called **Algol 68 Revised**, that weird report requires you to spell words backwards: to mark the end of the IF statement, you say FI; to mark the end of the DO statement, you say OD. The committee's decision was far from unanimous: several members refused to endorse the report.

Algol now Few programmers still use Algol, but many use Pascal (which is very similar to Algol 60 Revised) and Basic (which is a compromise between Algol and Fortran).

Cobol

If you're a student who's going to give a speech or write a paper, teachers recommend that you organize your thinking by creating an outline. Back in the 1950's, managers of computer departments got together and decided programmers should organize programs in the same way, by creating an outline before writing the program, especially since a well-organized program is easier to analyze and improve if the original programmer gets fired.

Those managers invented a computer language that lets the programmer just fill in an outline and feed the outline to the computer. The outline itself acts as the program. No further programming is necessary.

That outline-oriented computer language is used especially for handling tough programming problems in business accounting (such as payroll, inventory, accounts payable, and accounts receivable), so it was named the **Co**mmon **B**usiness-**O**riented **L**anguage (whose abbreviation is **Cobol**, which is pronounced "koe ball"). But cynics complain that "Cobol" also stands for **Completely Obsolete Business-Oriented Language** and **Compiles Only Because Of Luck**.

4 parts To write a program in Cobol, just fill in an outline that has 4 parts:

In the first part, called the **IDENTIFICATION DIVISION**, you give your name (so your boss knows who to fire when the program doesn't work) and make extra comments about when you wrote the program, the program's name, and security (who's allowed to see this program). The computer ignores everything you say in the IDENTIFICATION DIVISION, but writing that stuff makes your boss happy.

In the second part, called the **ENVIRONMENT DIVISION**, you say what kind of environment you wrote the program for: which computer it runs on, which devices the program's files use (disks? tapes? printers? punched cards?), and whether decimal points should be printed as commas instead (since people in France, Italy, and Germany want you to do that).

In the third part, called the **DATA DIVISION**, you list all the program's variables. For each numeric variable, you must say how many digits it should store (to the left and right of the decimal point) and how to format the number (for example, say whether to print a dollar sign before the number). For example, if you want N to be a simple 3-digit integer (from 000 to 999), with no special formatting, say N PICTURE IS 999 (which means N is a variable whose picture is at most the number 999). If you want N to be a simple 7-digit integer (from 0000000 to 9999999), say N PICTURE IS 9999999. If you want N to be a simple 7-character string, say N PICTURE IS XXXXXXX. You can abbreviate: you can say just PIC instead of PICTURE IS, and you can say X(7) instead of XXXXXXX.

In the fourth and final part, called the **PROCEDURE DIVISION**, you finally write the procedures that you want to the computer to perform, using commands such as READ, WRITE, DISPLAY, ACCEPT, IF, GO TO, SORT, MERGE, and PERFORM. Each command is an English sentence that includes a verb and ends in a period. You organize the PROCEDURE DIVISION into paragraphs, invent a name for each paragraph, treat each paragraph as a separate procedure/subroutine, and tell the computer in what order to PERFORM the paragraphs. One line in the PROCEDURE DIVISION must say "STOP RUN": when the computer encounters that line, the computer stops running the program.

Unfortunately, that idea of dividing a program into 4 divisions is wrong-headed: when you write or read a Cobol program, your eye must keep hopping between the PROCEDURE DIVISION (where the action is) and the DATA DIVISION (which tells what the variables mean), while taking an occasional peek at the ENVIRONMENT DIVISION (which tells what devices are involved). Other programming languages, developed later, use better methods for organizing thoughts.

How Cobol arose During the 1950's, several organizations developed languages to solve problems in business. The most popular business languages were IBM's **Commercial Translator** (developed from 1957-1959), Honeywell's **Fact** (1959-1960), Sperry Rand's **Flow-matic** (1954-1958), and the Air Force's **Aimaco** (1958).

In April 1959, a group of programmers and manufacturers met at the University of Pennsylvania, decided to develop a *single* business language for *all* computers, and asked the Department of Defense to help sponsor the research.

The Department agreed. In a follow-up meeting held at the Pentagon in May, the group tentatively decided to call the new language "CBL" (for "Common Business Language") and created 3 committees.

The Short-Range Committee would meet immediately to develop a temporary language. A Medium-Range Committee would meet later to develop a more thoroughly thought-out language. Then a Long-Range Committee would develop the ultimate language.

The Short-Range Committee met immediately and created a language nice enough so the Medium-Range and Long-Range Committees never bothered to meet.

The Short-Range Committee wanted a more pronounceable name for the language than "CBL". At a meeting in September 1969, the committee members proposed 6 names:

"BUSY" (BUsiness SYstem)
"BUSYL" (BUsiness SYstem Language)
"INFOSYL" (INFOrmation SYstem Language)
"DATASYL" (DATA SYstem Language)
"COSYL" (COmmon SYstem Language)
"COCOSYL" (COmmon COmputer SYstem Language)

The next day, a member of the committee suggested "Cobol" (**Co**mmon **B**usiness-**O**riented **L**anguage), and the rest of the committee agreed.

I wish they'd have kept the name "BUSY", because it's easier to pronounce and remember than "Cobol". Today, Cobol programmers are still known as "BUSY bodies".

From Sperry Rand's Flow-matic, the new language (called "Cobol") borrowed 2 rules:

Begin each statement with an English verb.
Put data descriptions in a different program division than procedures.

From IBM's Commercial Translator, Cobol borrowed group items (01 and 02), PICTURE symbols, fancy IF statements, and COMPUTE formulas.

Compromises On some issues, the members of the committee couldn't agree, so they compromised.

For example, some members wanted Cobol to let programmers write mathematical formulas by using these symbols:

+	−	*	/	=	(	)

But other members of the committee disagreed: they argued that since Cobol is for stupid businessmen who fear formulas, Cobol should use the words ADD, SUBTRACT, MULTIPLY, and DIVIDE instead. The committee compromised: when you write a Cobol program, you can use the words ADD, SUBTRACT, MULTIPLY, and DIVIDE; you can use a formula instead but just if you warn the computer by putting the word COMPUTE before the formula.

Can Cobol handle long numbers? How long? The committee decided that Cobol would handle any **number up to 18 digits long** and handle any **variable name up to 30 characters long**. So the limits of Cobol are "18 and 30".

> Why did the committee pick the numbers "18 and 30" instead of "16 and 32"? Answer: some manufacturers wanted "16 and 32" (because their computers were based on the numbers 16 and 32), but other manufacturers wanted other combinations (such as "24 and 36"); the committee, hunting for a compromise, chose "18 and 30", because *nobody* wanted it, and so it would give no manufacturer an unfair advantage over competitors. In other words, Cobol was designed to be equally terrible for everybody! That's politics!

Cobol's popularity

In 1960, the Defense Department announced it would buy just computers that understand Cobol, unless a manufacturer can demonstrate why Cobol isn't helpful. In 1961, Westinghouse Electric Corp. made a similar announcement. Other companies followed. Cobol became the most popular computer language.

Today it's still the most popular computer language for maxicomputers, though programmers on minicomputers and microcomputers have switched to newer languages.

Improvements

The original version of Cobol was finished in 1960 and called **Cobol 60**. Then came an improvement, called **Cobol 61**. The verb SORT and a "Report Writer" feature were added in 1962. Then came **Cobol 65**, **Cobol 68**, **Cobol 74**, and **Cobol 85**.

Cobol's most obvious flaw

To write a Cobol program, you must put info about file labeling into the data division's FD command. Since file labeling describes the **environment**, not the **data**, Cobol should have been changed, to put the labeling in the environment division instead.

Jean Sammet, who headed some of the Short-Term Committee's subcommittees, admits her group goofed when it decided to put labeling in the data division. But Cobol's too old to change now.

Basic

The first version of **Basic** was developed in 1963 and 1964 by a genius (**John Kemeny**) and his friend (**Tom Kurtz**).

How the genius grew up

John Kemeny was a Jew born in Hungary in 1926. In 1940 he and his parents fled from the Nazis and came to America. Though he knew hardly any English when he began high school in New York, he learned enough so he graduated as the top student in the class. Four years later, he graduated from Princeton **summa cum laude** even though he had to spend 1½ of those years in the Army, where he helped solve equations for the atomic bomb.

Two years after his B.A., Princeton gave him a Ph.D. in mathematics *and* philosophy, because his thesis on symbolic logic combined both fields.

While working for the Ph.D., he was Einstein's youngest assistant. He told Einstein he wanted to quit math and instead hand out leaflets for world peace, but Einstein said leafleting would waste his talents; the best way for him to help world peace would be to become a famous mathematician, so people would *listen* to him, as they had to Einstein. He took Einstein's advice and stayed with math.

After getting his Ph.D., he taught symbolic logic in Princeton's philosophy department. In 1953, most of Dartmouth College's math professors were retiring, so Dartmouth asked him to come to Dartmouth, chair the department, and bring his friends. He accepted the offer and brought his friends. That's how Dartmouth stole Princeton's math department.

At Dartmouth, Kemeny invented several new branches of math. Then Kemeny's department got General Electric to sell Dartmouth a computer at a 90% discount, in return for which his department had to invent programs for that computer and let General Electric use them. To write the programs, Kemeny invented his own little computer language in 1963 and showed it to his colleague Tom Kurtz, who knew less about philosophy but more about computers. Kurtz added features from Algol and Fortran and called the combination **Basic**.

After inventing Basic, Kemeny got bored and thought of quitting Dartmouth. Then Dartmouth asked him to become the college's president. He accepted.

Later, when the Three-Mile Island nuclear power plant almost exploded, President Jimmy Carter told Kemeny to head the investigation, because of Kemeny's reputation for philosophical and scientific impartiality. Kemeny's report was impartial — and sharply critical of the nuclear industry.

Basic versus Algol & Fortran

Basic is simpler than both Algol and Fortran in two ways:

> In Algol and Fortran, you must tell the computer which variables are integers and which are reals. In Algol, you do that by saying INTEGER or REAL. In Fortran, you do that by choosing an appropriate first letter for the variable's name. **In Basic, the computer assumes all variables are real**, unless you specifically say otherwise.
>
> In Algol and Fortran, output is a hassle. In Fortran, you have to worry about FORMATs. In Algol, each computer handles output differently — and in most cases strangely. **Basic's PRINT statement automatically invents a good format.**

Is Basic closer to Algol than to Fortran? On the one hand, Basic uses the Algol words FOR, STEP, and THEN and the Algol symbol ↑ (or ^). On the other hand, Basic uses the Fortran words RETURN and DIMENSION (abbreviated DIM); and Basic's "FOR I = 1 TO 9 STEP 2" puts the step size at the *end* of the statement, like FORTRAN's "DO 30 I = 1,9,2" and unlike Algol's "FOR I:=1 STEP 2 UNTIL 9".

Basic versus Joss

Basic is *not* the simplest computer language. **Joss**, which was developed a year earlier by the Rand Corporation, is simpler to learn. But Joss runs slower, requires more memory, lacks string variables, and doesn't let you name your programs (you must give each program a number instead, and remember what the number was).

A few programmers still use Joss and 3 of its variants, called **Aid**, **Focal**, and **Mumps**. Aid appeals to high-school kids; Focal appeals to scientists; Mumps appeals to doctors designing databases of patient records. Though Mumps *does* have string variables and other modern features, it's being replaced by newer database languages such as dBase.

6 versions

Kemeny & Kurtz finished the **original version** of Basic in May 1964. It included just these statements:

> PRINT, GO TO, IF...THEN, FOR...NEXT, DATA...READ, GOSUB...RETURN, DIM, LET (for commands such as LET X=3), REM (for REMarks and comments), DEF (to DEFine your own functions), and END

In that version, the only punctuation allowed in the PRINT statement was the comma.

> The **2nd version** of Basic (October 1964) added the semicolon.
>
> The **3rd version** (1966) added the words INPUT, RESTORE, and MAT. (The word MAT helps you manipulate a "MATrix", which means an "array". Today, most versions of Basic omit the word MAT because its definition consumes too much RAM.)
>
> In all those versions, you could use variables. For example, you could say LET X=3. A variable was a letter that stood for a number. The **4th version** (1967) added a new concept: string variables (such as A$). That version also added TAB (to improve the printing), RANDOMIZE (to improve RND), and ON...GO TO.
>
> The **5th version** (1970) added data files (sequential access and random access).
>
> The **6th version** (1971) added PRINT USING and a sophisticated way to handle subroutines.

How Basic became popular During the 1960's and 1970's, Kemeny & Kurtz worked on Basic with a fervor that was almost religious.

> They believed *every* college graduate should know how to program a computer, and be as literate in Basic as in English.
>
> They convinced Dartmouth to spend as much on its computer as on the college library. They put computer terminals in most college buildings (even the dorms) and let all children in the town come onto the campus and join the fun. Altogether, the campus had about 300 terminals. Over 90% of all Dartmouth students used Basic before they graduated.
>
> Dartmouth trained high-school teachers how to use Basic. Soon many colleges, high schools, and prep schools throughout New England had terminals connected to Dartmouth's computer by phone.

Dartmouth's computer was built by General Electric, which quit making computers and sold its computer factory to Honeywell. So Dartmouth's computer became called a "Honeywell".

Since Dartmouth's research on Basic was partially funded by the National Science Foundation, Basic was in the public domain. Other computer manufacturers could use it without worrying about copyrights or patents.

DEC The first company to copy Dartmouth's ideas was **Digital Equipment Corporation** (**DEC**, pronounced "deck").

> DEC put Basic and Focal on DEC's first popular minicomputer, the PDP-8. When DEC saw that programmers preferred Basic, DEC stopped developing Focal and devoted all its energies to improving Basic further.
>
> DEC invented fancier minicomputers (the PDP-11 and Vax) and maxicomputers (the DECsystem-10 and DECsystem-20) and put Basic on all of them. DEC's versions of Basic were similar to Dartmouth's. Though the versions put on the PDP-8 were primitive (almost as bad as Dartmouth's first edition), the versions put on DEC's fancier computers were sophisticated. Eventually, DEC put decent versions of Basic even on the PDP-8.
>
> DEC's best version of Basic is **Vax Basic**, which works just on Vax computers. DEC's second-best version of Basic is **Basic-Plus-2**, which works on the Vax, the PDP-11, and the DECsystem-20. DEC's third-best version of Basic is **Basic-Plus**, which works only on the PDP-11. DEC's other versions of Basic aren't as fancy.

HP Soon after DEC started putting Basic on its computers, Hewlett-Packard (HP) did likewise.

> HP put Basic on the HP-2000 computer then put a better version of Basic on the HP-300 computer.
>
> Unfortunately, HP's Basic was more awkward than DEC's. On HP computers, each time you used a string you had to write a "DIM statement" that warned the computer how long the string would be: the DIM statement had to say how many characters the string would contain.

How Microsoft Basic arose The first popular *micro*computer was the Altair 8800, which used a version of Basic invented by a 20-year-old kid named **Bill Gates**. His version imitated DEC's.

The Altair computer was manufactured by a company called **Mits**, which didn't treat Bill Gates fairly, so he broke away from Mits and formed his own company, called **Microsoft**.

Bill Gates and his company, Microsoft, invented many versions of Basic.

> The first was called **4K Basic** because it consumed just 4K of memory chips (RAM or ROM). Then came **8K Basic** (which included a bigger vocabulary) then came **Extended Basic** (which included an even bigger vocabulary and consumed 14K). All those versions were intended for primitive microcomputers that used tapes instead of disks. Finally came **Disk Basic**, which came on a disk and included all commands for handling disks.

All those versions of Basic were written for computers that contained an 8080 or Z-80 CPU. Simultaneously, he wrote **6502 Basic**, for computers containing a 6502 CPU.

> The Apple 2 version of 6502 Basic is called **Applesoft BASIC**.
> Commodore's version of 6502 Basic is called **Commodore BASIC**.

Unfortunately, 6502 Basic is primitive: it resembles his 8K Basic.

After writing 6502 Basic, Bill wrote an improved version of it, called **6809 Basic**, just for Radio Shack's Color Computer. Radio Shack calls it **Extended Color Basic**.

Texas Instruments (TI) asked Bill to write a version of Basic for TI computers. Bill said "yes"; but when TI told Bill what kind of Basic it wanted, Bill's company (Microsoft) found 90 ways that TI's desires would contradict Microsoft's traditions. Microsoft convinced TI to change its mind and remove 80 of those 90 contradictions, but TI stood firm on the other 10.

> So TI Basic (which is on the TI-990 and TI-99/4A computers) contradicts all other versions of Microsoft Basic in 10 ways. For example, in TI Basic, the INPUT statement uses a colon instead of a semicolon, and a multi-statement line uses a double colon (::) instead of a single colon.

Because of those differences, TI's computers became unpopular, and TI stopped making them. Moral: if you contradict Bill, you die!

Later, Bill invented an amazingly wonderful version of Basic, better than all earlier versions. He called it **Gee-Whiz Basic (GW Basic)**. It runs just on the IBM PC and clones. When you buy PC-DOS from IBM, you typically get GW Basic at no extra charge. (IBM calls it **BasicA**.) When you buy MS-DOS for an IBM clone, the typical dealer includes GW Basic at no extra charge.

Beyond GW Basic GW Basic was the last version of Basic that Bill developed personally. All Microsoft's later improvements were done by his assistants. They created **Microsoft Basic for the Mac**, **Amiga Microsoft Basic** (for the Commodore's Amiga computer), **Quick Basic** (for the IBM PC and clones), **QBasic** (which you get instead of GWBasic when you buy MS-DOS version 5 or 6), and **Visual Basic** (which lets you create Windows programs, so the human can use a mouse and pull-down menus). Those Basics are harder to learn how to use than GW Basic but have advantages: they run faster and include a better editor, more words from Algol and Pascal, and fancier output.

While developing those versions of Basic, Microsoft added 3 exciting new commands: SAY, END IF, and SUB.

The SAY command makes the computer talk, by using a voice synthesizer. For example, to make the computer's voice say "I love you", type this command:

```
SAY TRANSLATE$("I LOVE YOU")
```

That makes the computer translate "I love you" into phonetics and then say the phonetics. That command works just on Amiga computers.

The END IF and SUB commands give Basic some of Pascal's power. By using the END IF command, you can make the IF statement include many lines, like this:

```
IF AGE<18 THEN
        PRINT "YOU ARE STILL A MINOR."
        PRINT "AH, THE JOYS OF YOUTH!"
        PRINT "I WISH I COULD BE AS YOUNG AS YOU!"
END IF
```

By using the SUB command, you can give a subroutine a name.

Divergences Microsoft's versions of Basic are wonderful.

Over the years, several microcomputer manufacturers tried to invent their own versions of Basic, to avoid paying royalties to Bill Gates. They were sorry!

For example, **Radio Shack** tried hiring somebody else to write Radio Shack's Basic. That person quit in the middle of the job; Radio Shack's original Basic was never finished. Nicknamed "Level 1 Basic", it was a half-done mess. Radio Shack, like an obedient puppy dog, then went to Bill, who finally wrote a decent version of Basic for Radio Shack; Bill's version was called "Level 2".

Apple's original attempt at Basic was called "Apple Integer Basic". It was written by Steve Wozniak and was terrible: it couldn't handle decimals, and it made the mistake of imitating HP instead of DEC (because he'd worked at HP). Eventually, he wised up and hired Bill, who wrote Apple's better Basic, called **Applesoft** (which means "Apple Basic by Microsoft"). Applesoft was intended for tapes, not disks. Later, when Steve Wozniak wanted to add disks to the Apple 2 computer, he made the mistake of not rehiring Bill — which is why the Apple 2's disk system is worse than Radio Shack's.

At **Atari**, an executive who didn't want to hire Bill made the mistake of hiring the inventor of Apple's disastrous DOS. That guy's Basic, called **Atari Basic**, resembles HP's Basic. Like Apple's DOS, it looks pleasant at first glance but turns into a nightmare when you try to do any advanced programming. As a result, Atari's computers didn't become as popular as Atari hoped, and the executive who "didn't want to hire Bill" was fired. Atari finally hired Bill's company, Microsoft, which wrote **Atari Microsoft Basic version 2**.

Two other microcomputer manufacturers — **North Star Computers** and **APF** — tried developing their own versions of Basic to avoid paying royalties to Bill. Since their versions of Basic were lousy, they went out of business.

While DEC, HP, Microsoft, and other companies were developing their own versions of Basic, professors back at Dartmouth College were still tinkering with Dartmouth Basic version 6. In 1976, Professor Steve Garland added more commands from Algol, PL/I, and Pascal to Dartmouth Basic. He called his version **Structured Basic (SBasic)**.

One of Basic's inventors, Professor Tom Kurtz, became chairman of an Ansi committee to standardize Basic. His committee published two reports:

The 1977 report defined **Ansi Standard Minimal Basic**, a minimal standard that all advertised versions of "Basic" should live up to. That report was reasonable; everybody agreed to abide by it. (Microsoft's old versions of Basic were written before that report came out. Microsoft Disk Basic version 5 was Microsoft's first version to obey that standard.)

In 1985, Ansi created a more ambitious report, to standardize Basic's most advanced features. The report said Basic's advanced features should closely follow SBasic. But Bill Gates, who invented Microsoft Basic and was also on the committee, disliked some aspects of SBasic and quit the committee. (He was particularly annoyed by the committee's desire to include Dartmouth's MAT commands, which consume lots of RAM and used rarely.) He refused to follow the committee's recommendations.

That left two standards for advanced Basic: the "official" standard (defined by the Ansi committee) and the "de facto" standard (Bill Gates' Microsoft Basics, such as GW Basic).

Those two standards differ from each other. For example, in GW Basic you say:
```
10 INPUT "WHAT IS YOUR NAME"; A$
```
In Ansi Basic, you say this instead:
```
10 INPUT PROMPT "WHAT IS YOUR NAME? ": A$
```
Notice that in Ansi Basic, you must insert the word PROMPT after INPUT, type a colon instead of a semicolon, and insert a question mark and blank space before the second quotation mark.

Tom Kurtz (who chaired the Ansi committee) and John Kemeny (who invented Basic with Tom Kurtz) put Ansi Basic onto Dartmouth's computer. So Ansi Basic became Dartmouth's 7th official version of Basic. Then Kurtz & Kemeny left Dartmouth and formed their own company, which invented **True Basic** (an Ansi Basic version for the IBM PC & Mac).

Since Microsoft's Basic versions have become the de facto standard and since True Basic isn't much better, hardly anybody bother switching from Microsoft Basic to True Basic.

Comparison Here are 9 commands in advanced Basic:

USING, LINE, CIRCLE, SOUND, PLAY, SAY, ELSE, END IF, SUB

Here's what they accomplish:

"USING" lets you control how many digits print after the decimal point.
"LINE" makes the computer draw a diagonal line across the screen.
"CIRCLE" makes the computer draw a circle as big as you wish.
"SOUND" and "PLAY" make the computer create music.
"SAY" makes the computer talk.
"ELSE" and "END IF" let you create fancy IF statements.
"SUB" lets you name subroutines.

This list shows which versions of Basic understand those 9 commands:

IBM PC with QBasic (or Visual Basic's version 2 or later)
understands 8 of the commands (all except SAY)

Commodore Amiga with Microsoft Basic
understands 8 of the commands (all except PLAY)

Apple Mac with Quick Basic
understands 7 of the commands (all except SAY and PLAY)

IBM PC (with GW Basic), Commodore 128, or Radio Shack TRS-80 Color
understands 6 of the commands (all except SAY, END IF, and SUB)

Atari ST
understands 5 of the commands (all except PLAY, SAY, END IF, and SUB)

Atari XE (or XL) with Microsoft Basic
understands just 4 commands (USING, LINE, SOUND, and ELSE)

Radio Shack TRS-80 Model 3, 4, 4P, or 4D
understands just 2 commands (USING and ELSE)

Apple 2, 2+, 2e, 2c, 2c+, or 2GS understands just 1 command (LINE)

Commodore 64 or Vic-20 understands no commands

Notice that the Commodore 128 and Radio Shack TRS-80 Color Computer understand 6 of the commands, while the more expensive Apple 2c understands just 1 command. If schools would have bought Commodore 128 and Radio Shack TRS-80 Color Computers instead of Apple 2c's, students would have become better programmers!

PL/I

During the early 1960's, IBM sold two kinds of computers: one kind for scientists, the other kind was for business bookkeepers. For the scientific kind of computer, the most popular language was Fortran. For the business kind of computer, the most popular language was Cobol.

In 1962, IBM secretly began working on a project to create a single, big computer that could be used by everybody: scientists and businesses. IBM called it the **IBM 360**, because it could handle the full circle of applications. What language should the IBM 360 be programmed in? IBM decided to invent a single language that could be used for both science and business.

IBM's first attempt at such a language was "Fortran V". It ran all the Fortran IV programs but added commands for handling strings and fields in data files. Instead of announcing Fortran V, IBM began working in 1963 on an even more powerful language called "Fortran VI", which would resemble Fortran but be much more powerful and modern (and hence incompatible). It would also include *all* important features of Cobol and Algol.

As work on Fortran VI progressed, IBM realized it would be so different from traditional Fortran that it should have a different name. In 1964, IBM changed the name to "NPL" (New Programming Language), since the language was intended to go with the IBM 360 and the rest of IBM's New Product Line. But IBM discovered the letters "NPL" already stood for the National Physics Laboratory in England, so IBM changed the language's name to **Programming Language One (PL/I)**, to brag it was the first good programming language and all predecessors were worth zero by comparison.

Troubles The committee that invented PL/I had a hard time.

After the design was finished, the language still had to be put on the computer. Since that took 2½ more years of programming and polishing, the language wasn't available for sale to IBM's customers until August 1966.

That was too late. It was *after* IBM had already begun shipping the IBM 360. The 360's customers continued using Fortran and Cobol, since PL/I wasn't available initially. After those customers bought, installed, and learned how to use Fortran and Cobol on the 360, they refused to take the trouble to switch to PL/I, especially since PL/I was expensive (requiring twice as much RAM as Cobol, 4 times as much RAM as Fortran) and ran slowly (1½ times as long to compile as Cobol, twice as long as Fortran). Most programmers already knew Fortran or Cobol, were satisfied with those languages, and weren't willing to spend the time to learn something new.

Some programmers praised PL/I for being amazingly powerful, but others called it just a scheme to get people to buy more RAM. Critics call it a disorganized mess, an "ugly kitchen sink of a language", thrown together by a committee that was too rushed.

Since PL/I is so big, hardly anybody understands it all. As a PL/I programmer, you study just the part of the language you plan to use. But if you make a mistake, the computer might not gripe: instead, it might think you're trying to give a different PL/I command from a language part you never studied. Instead of griping, the computer will perform an instruction that wasn't what you meant.

Stripped versions In 1972, Cornell University developed a stripped-down version of PL/I for students. That version, called **PL/C**, is a compromise between PL/I's power and Algol's pure simplicity.

In 1975, The University of Toronto developed an even *more* stripped-down version of PL/I, and called it **SP/k**: it ran faster and printed messages that were more helpful. SP/k came in several sizes: the tiniest was SP/1; the largest was SP/8.

Stripped-down versions of PL/I stayed popular in universities until about 1980, when universities switched to Pascal.

Digital Research invented a tiny version of PL/I for microcomputers and called it **PL/M**. It couldn't handle decimals. Most PL/M programmers eventually switched to C.

The full PL/I is still used on big IBM computers, because full PL/I is the only language that includes enough commands to let programmers unleash IBM's full power.

Statements PL/I uses many statements for input and output. The statement's meaning depends mainly on its first word:

First word	What the computer will do
GET	input from a terminal or simple file
PUT	print on a terminal or simple file
OPEN	start using a file
CLOSE	stop using a file
READ	input from a file whose picture is unedited
WRITE	print on a file whose picture is unedited
DELETE	delete an item from a file
REWRITE	replace an item in a file
LOCATE	print a "based" variable onto a file
UNLOCK	let other programs use the file
FORMAT	use a certain form for spacing the input and output
DISPLAY	chat with operator who sits at computer's main terminal

These statements interrupt:

First word	What the computer will do
STOP	stop the program
EXIT	stop a task (in a program that involves several tasks)
HALT	interrupt the program; free the terminal to do other tasks
DELAY	pause for a certain number of milliseconds
WAIT	pause until other simultaneous routines finish their tasks

These statements handle conditions:

First word	What the computer will do
IF	if a certain condition occurs now, do certain statements
ON	if a certain condition occurs later, do certain statements
SIGNAL	pretend a condition such as OVERFLOW occurs
REVERT	cancel the ON statements

These statements handle variables:

First word	What the computer will do
DECLARE	make some variables be integers, other be reals, etc.
DEFAULT	assume all variables are integers, or a similar assumption
ALLOCATE	create a temporary variable
FREE	destroy a temporary variable and use its RAM otherwise

These statements handle general logic:

First word	What the computer will do
GO	go to a different line
CALL	go to a subroutine
RETURN	return from a subroutine to the main routine
ENTRY	skip the subroutine's previous lines; begin here instead
PROCEDURE	begin a program or subprogram
DO	begin a loop or compound statement
BEGIN	begin a block of statements
END	end program, subprogram., loop, compound statement, or block

Half of those statements are borrowed from Fortran, Algol, and Cobol.

from Fortran:	FORMAT, STOP, CALL, RETURN, DO
from Algol:	IF, GO, PROCEDURE, BEGIN, END
from Cobol:	OPEN, CLOSE, READ, WRITE, DISPLAY, EXIT

Like Algol, PL/I requires a semicolon at the end of each statement. Besides the statements listed above, you can also give an **assignment statement** (such as "N=5;"), a **null statement** (which consists of just a semicolon), and a **preprocessor statement** (which tells the computer how to create its own program).

Pascal

In 1968, a European committee invented "Algol 68," which was strange: it even required you to spell some commands backwards. Some members of the committee disagreed with the majority and thought Algol 68 was nuts. One of those dissidents, Niklaus Wirth, quit the committee and created his own Algol version, which he called **Pascal**. Today, most computerists feel he was right: Pascal is better than Algol 68.

He wrote Pascal in Switzerland, on a CDC maxicomputer that used punched cards. His version of Pascal couldn't handle video screens, couldn't handle random-access data files, and couldn't handle strings well. Those 3 limitations were corrected in later Pascal versions, especially the one invented at the **University of California at San Diego (UCSD)**, which also includes Logo-style commands that move a turtle.

Apple's Pascal Apple Computer Company got permission to sell an Apple version of UCSD Pascal. Apple ran full-page ads bragging that the Apple 2 was the only popular microcomputer that could handle Pascal.

Apple Computer Company sold an Apple 2 add-on called the **Apple Language System**, whose $495 price included disks for Pascal & advanced Basic, plus 16K of extra RAM. Many people bought that system were disappointed, when they discovered that Pascal is *harder* to learn than Basic.

Pascal is helpful just if the program you're writing is long. Pascal helps you organize and dissect long programs more easily than Basic. But the average Apple 2 owner never wrote long programs and never needed Pascal. Many of Apple's customers felt "ripped off", since they spent $495 uselessly.

Pascal's rise Many programmers who'd written big Fortran programs for big computers switched to Pascal, because Pascal helps organize large programs, and because Fortran is archaic. Many programmers who'd been using PL/I switched to Pascal, because Pascal consumes less RAM than PL/I and fits in smaller computers.

Pascal became popular. Many colleges required freshman computer-science majors to take Pascal, so the College Entrance Examination Board's **Advanced Placement Test in Computer Science** required knowing Pascal. Many high-school students studied Pascal to pass that test and prepare for college.

Pascal's fall Basic has improved (by incorporating many features from Pascal), so Pascal no longer has much advantage over Basic. Now students skip Pascal: after learning Basic, they skip past Pascal to tougher languages: Java and C++. Now the Advanced Placement Test in Computer Science requires knowing Java instead of Pascal.

Pascal is ignored.

Modula

After Niklaus Wirth invented Pascal, he designed a more ambitious language, called **Modula**. He designed the Modula's first version in 1975, then **Modula-2** in 1979. When today's programmers discuss "Modula", they mean Modula-2.

Modula-2 resembles Pascal. Like Pascal, Modula-2 requires each program's main routing to begin with the word BEGIN; but Modula-2 does *not* require you to say BEGIN after DO WHILE or IF THEN:

Pascal	Modula-2
| ```
IF AGE<18 THEN
  BEGIN
  WRITELN('YOU ARE STILL A MINOR');
  WRITELN('AH, THE JOYS OF YOUTH');
  END
ELSE
  BEGIN
  WRITELN('GLAD YOU ARE AN ADULT');
  WRITELN('WE CAN HAVE ADULT FUN');
  END;
``` | ```
IF AGE<18 THEN
  WRITESTRING("YOU ARE STILL A MINOR");
  WRITESTRING("AH, THE JOYS OF YOUTH");
ELSE
  WRITESTRING("GLAD YOU ARE AN ADULT");
  WRITESTRING("WE CAN HAVE ADULT FUN")
END;
``` |

That example shows 4 ways that Modula-2 differs from Pascal: Modula-2 says **WRITESTRING** instead of WRITELN, uses **regular quotation marks (")** instead of apostrophes, lets you **omit the word BEGIN** after IF ELSE (and WHILE DO), and lets you **omit the word END** before ELSE.

Advanced programmers like Modula-2 better than Pascal because Modula-2 includes extra commands for handling subroutines.

C

Many programmers use **C**.

How C arose In 1963 at England's Cambridge University and the University of London, researchers developed a "practical" version of Algol and called it the **Combined Programming Language (CPL)**. In 1967 at Cambridge University, Martin Richards invented a simpler, stripped-down version of CPL and called it **Basic CPL (BCPL)**. In 1970 at Bell Labs, Ken Thompson developed a version that was even more stripped-down and simpler; since it included just the most critical part of BCPL, he called it **B**.

Ken had stripped down the language *too* much. It no longer contained enough commands to do practical programming. In 1971, his colleague Dennis Ritchie added a few commands to B, to form a more extensive language, which he called **New B**. Then he added even more commands and called the result **C**, because it came after B.

Most of C was invented in 1972. In 1973, it was improved enough so that it was used for something practical: developing a new version of the **Unix** operating system. (The original version of Unix had been created at Bell Labs by using B. Beginning in 1973, Unix versions were created by using C.)

So C is a souped-up version of New B, which is a souped-up version of B, which is a stripped-down version of BCPL, which is a stripped-down version of CPL, which is a "practical" version of Algol.

C's peculiarities Like B, C is a tiny language.

C doesn't even include any words for input or output. When you buy C, you also get a **library** of routines that can be added to C. The library includes words for output (such as printf), input (such as scanf), math functions (such as sqrt), and other goodies.

When you write a program in C, you can choose whichever parts of the library you need: the other parts of the library don't bother to stay in RAM. So if your program uses just a *few* of the library's functions, running it will consume very little RAM. It will consume less RAM than if the program were written in Basic or Pascal.

In Basic, if you reserve 20 RAM locations for X (by saying DIM X(20)) and then say X(21)=3.7, the computer will gripe, because you haven't reserved a RAM location for X(21). If you use C instead, the computer will *not* gripe about that kind of error; instead, the computer will store the number 3.7 in the RAM location immediately after X(20), even if that location's already being used by another variable, such as Y. As a result, Y will get messed up. Moral: **C programs run quickly and dangerously, because in C the computer never bothers to check your program's reasonableness.**

In your program, which variables are integers, and which are real?

Basic assumes all variables are real.

Fortran & PL/I assume all variables beginning with I, J, K, L, M, and N are integers and the rest are real.

Algol & Pascal make no assumptions; they require you to declare "integer" or "real" for each variable.

C assumes all variables are integers, unless you specifically say otherwise.

Ada

In 1975, the U.S. Department of Defense decided it wanted a better kind of computer language and wrote a list of requirements the language would have to meet.

The original list of requirements was called the Strawman Requirements (1975). Then came improved versions, called Woodenman (1975), Tinman (1976), Ironman (1978), and finally Steelman (1979).

While the Department was moving from Strawman to Steelman, it checked whether any existing computer language could meet such requirements. The Department decided that no existing computer language came even close to meeting the requirements, so a new language would have to be invented. The Department required the new language to resemble Pascal, Algol 68, or PL/I but better.

Contest In 1977, the Department held a contest, to see which software company could invent a language meeting such specifications (which were in the process of changing from Tinman to Ironman).

> 16 companies entered the contest.
>
> The Department selected 4 semifinalists and paid them to continue their research for 6 more months. The semifinalists were CII-Honeywell-Bull (which is French and owned partly by Honeywell), Intermetrics (in Cambridge, Massachusetts), SRI International, and Softech.
>
> In 1978, the semifinalists submitted improved designs, which were all souped-up versions of Pascal (instead of Algol 68 or PL/I). To make the contest fair and prevent bribery, the judges weren't told which design belonged to which company. The 4 designs were called "Green", "Red", "Yellow", and "Blue".
>
> Yellow and Blue lost. The winning designs were Green (designed by CII-Honeywell-Bull) and Red (designed by Intermetrics).
>
> The Department paid the two winning companies to continue their research for one more year. In 1979, the winning companies submitted their improved versions.

The winner was the Green language, designed by CII-Honeywell-Bull.

The Department decided that the Green language would be called **Ada** to honor Ada Lovelace, the woman who was the world's first programmer.

So Ada is a Pascal-like language developed by a French company (CII-Honeywell-Bull) under contract to the U.S. Department of Defense.

Ada is too big to be practical. Researchers made computers understand part of Ada but had difficulty making computers understand the whole language.

dBase

dBase was invented by Wayne Ratliff because he wanted to bet on which football teams would win the 1978 season.

> To bet wisely, he needed to know how each team scored in previous games, so every Monday he clipped pages of football scores from newspapers. Soon his whole room was covered with newspaper clippings. To reduce the clutter, he decided to write a data-management program to keep track of all the statistics.

He worked at the **Jet Propulsion Laboratory (JPL)**. His coworkers had invented a data-management system called the **JPL Display and Information System (JPLDIS)**, which imitated IBM's **Retrieve**. Unfortunately, Retrieve and JPLDIS both required maxicomputers. Working at home, he invented **Vulcan**, a stripped-down version of JPLDIS small enough to run on the CP/M microcomputer in his house and good enough to let him compile football statistics — though by then he'd lost interest in football and was more interested in the theory of data management and business applications.

In 1979, he advertised his Vulcan data-management system in Byte Magazine. The mailman delivered so many orders to his house that he didn't have time to fill them all — especially since he still had a full-time job at JPL. He stopped advertising, to give himself a chance to catch up filling the orders.

In 1980, the owners of Discount Software phoned him, visited his home, examined Vulcan, and offered to market it for him. He agreed.

Since "Discount Software" was the wrong name to market Vulcan under, Discount Software's owners — Hal Lashlee and George Tate — thought of marketing Vulcan under the name "Lashlee-Tate Software". But since "Lashlee" sounded wimpy, they changed the name to *Ashton*-Tate Software.

Instead of selling Vulcan's original version, Ashton-Tate Software decided to sell Wayne's further improvement, called **dBase 2**. It ran faster, looked prettier on the screen, and was easier to use.

At Ashton-Tate, George Tate did the managing. Hal Lashlee was a silent partner who just contributed capital.

Ad George Tate hired Hal Pawluck to write an ad for dBase 2. Hal's clever ad showed a photo of a bilge pump (the kind of pump that removes water from a ship's bilge). The ad's headline said: "dBase versus the Bilge Pump". The ad went on to say that most database systems are like bilge pumps: they suck!

That explicit ad appeared in *Infoworld*, a weekly newspaper read by all computer experts. Suddenly, all experts knew that dBase was the database-management system that claimed not to suck.

The ad generated just one big complaint — from the company that manufactured the bilge pump!

George Tate offered to add a footnote saying "*This* bilge pump does *not* suck". The pump manufacturer didn't like that either but stopped complaining.

Beyond dBase 2 The original dBase 2 ran on computers using the CP/M operating system. It worked well. When IBM began selling the IBM PC, Wayne invented an IBM PC version of dBase 2, but it was buggy.

He created those early versions of dBase by using assembly language. By using C instead, he finally created an IBM PC version that worked reliably and included extra commands. He called it **dBase 3**.

dBase 2 and dBase 3 were sold as programming languages, but many people who wanted to use databases didn't want to learn programming or hire a programmer. So Ashton-Tate created a new version, called **dBase 3 Plus**, which you can control by using menus instead of typing programming commands; but those menus are hard to learn how to use and incomplete: they don't let you tap dBase 3 Plus's full power, which requires you to learn programming.

In 1988, Ashton-Tate began shipping **dBase 4**, which includes extra programming commands.

> Some dBase 4 commands were copied from a database language called **Structured Query Language (SQL)**, which IBM invented for mainframes. dBase 4 also boasted better menus than dBase 3 Plus. Unfortunately, Ashton-Tate priced dBase 4 high: $795 for the plain version, $1295 for the "developer's" version.

Over the years, Ashton-Tate became a stodgy bureaucracy. George Tate died, Wayne Ratliff quit, the company's list price for dBase grew ridiculously high, and the company was callous to dBase users.

In 1991, Borland bought Ashton-Tate. In 1994, Borland began selling **dBase 5**, then further improvements. In 1999, Borland gave up trying to sell DBase; Borland transferred all dBase rights to **KSoft**, which sold **Visual DBase 7.5** and tried to develop **dBase 2000 (DB2K)**. The newest version of dBase is **dBase Plus 2**, published by DataBased Intelligence (2548 Vestal Parkway East, Vestal NY 13850, phone 607-729-0234 or toll-free 877-322-7340, www.dbase.com).

Other companies make dBase clones that work better than dBase itself! The most popular clone is **Visual FoxPro 9**: it runs faster than dBase, includes extra commands, and is marketed by Microsoft.

Easy

Easy is a language I developed several years ago. It combines the best features of all other languages. It's easy to learn, because it uses just these 12 keywords:

SAY & GET	LET
REPEAT & SKIP	HERE
IF & PICK	LOOP
PREPARE & DATA	HOW

Here's how to use them....

SAY Easy uses the word SAY instead of Basic's word PRINT, because SAY is briefer. If you want the computer to say the answer to 2+2, give this command:

```
SAY 2+2
```

The computer will say the answer:

```
4
```

Whenever the computer prints, it automatically prints a blank space afterwards but does *not* press the Enter key. So if you run this program —

```
SAY "LOVE"
SAY "HATE"
```

the computer will say:

```
LOVE HATE
```

Here's a fancier example:

```
SAY "LOVE" AS 3 AT 20 15 TRIM !
```

The "AS 3" is a format: it makes the computer print just the first 3 letters of LOVE. The "AT 20 15" makes the computer begin printing LOVE at the screen's pixel whose X coordinate is 20 and whose Y coordinate is 15. The computer usually prints a blank space after everything, but the word TRIM suppresses that blank space. The exclamation point makes the computer press the Enter key afterwards.

Here's another example:

```
SAY TO SCREEN PRINTER HARRY
```

It means that henceforth, whenever you give a SAY command, the computer will print the answer simultaneously onto your screen, onto your printer, and onto a disk file named HARRY. If you ever want to cancel that "SAY TO" command, give a "SAY TO" command that contradicts it.

GET Easy uses the word GET instead of Basic's word INPUT, because GET is briefer. The command GET X makes the computer wait for you to input the value of X. Above the GET command, you typically put a SAY command that makes the computer ask a question.

You can make the GET command fancy, like this:

```
GET X AS 3 AT 20 15 WAIT 5
```

The "AS 3" tells the computer that X will be just 3 characters; the computer waits for you to type just 3 characters and doesn't require you to press the Enter key afterwards. The "AT 20 15" makes the computer move to pixel 20 15 before your typing begins, so your input appears at that part of the screen. The "WAIT 5" makes the computer wait just 5 seconds for your response. If you reply within 5 seconds, the computer sets TIME equal to how many seconds you took. If you do *not* reply within the 5 seconds, the computer sets TIME equal to -1.

LET The LET statement resembles Basic's. For example, you can say:

```
LET R=4
```

To let R be a random decimal, type:

```
LET R=RANDOM
```

To let R be a random integer from 1 to 6, type:

```
LET R=RANDOM TO 6
```

To let R be a random integer from -3 to 5, type:

```
LET R=RANDOM FROM -3 TO 5
```

REPEAT If you put the word REPEAT at the bottom of your program, the computer will repeat the entire program again and again, forming an infinite loop.

SKIP If you put the word SKIP in the middle of your program, the computer will skip the bottom part of the program. SKIP is like BASIC's END or STOP.

HERE In the middle of your program, you can say:

```
HERE IS FRED
```

An earlier line can say SKIP TO FRED. A later line can say REPEAT FROM FRED. The SKIP TO and REPEAT FROM are like Basic's GO TO.

IF In your program, a line can say:

```
IF X<3
```

Underneath that line, you must put some indented lines, which the computer will do if X<3.

Suppose you give a student a test on which the score can be between 0 and 100. If the student's score is 100, let's make the computer say "PERFECT"; if the score is below 100 but at least 70, let's make the computer say the score and also say "OKAY THOUGH NOT PERFECT"; if the score is below 70, let's make the computer say "YOU FAILED". Here's how:

```
IF SCORE=100
  SAY "PERFECT"
IF SCORE<100 AND SCORE>=70
  SAY SCORE
  SAY "OKAY THOUGH NOT PERFECT"
IF SCORE<70
  SAY "YOU FAILED"
```

To shorten the program, use the words NOT and BUT:

```
IF SCORE=100
  SAY "PERFECT"
IF NOT BUT SCORE>=70
  SAY SCORE
  SAY "OKAY THOUGH NOT PERFECT"
IF NOT
  SAY "YOU FAILED"
```

The phrase "IF NOT" is like Basic's ELSE. The phrase "IF NOT BUT" is like Basic's ELSE IF.

PICK You can shorten that example even further, by telling the computer to pick just the first IF that's true:

```
PICK SCORE
  IF 100
    SAY "PERFECT"
  IF >=70
    SAY SCORE
    SAY "OKAY THOUGH NOT PERFECT"
  IF NOT
    SAY "YOU FAILED"
```

LOOP If you put the word LOOP above indented lines, the computer will do those lines repeatedly. For example, this program makes the computer say the words CAT and DOG repeatedly:

```
LOOP
  SAY "CAT"
  SAY "DOG"
```

This program makes the computer say 5, 8, 11, 14, and 17:

```
LOOP I FROM 5 BY 3 TO 17
  SAY I
```

That LOOP statement is like Basic's "FOR I = 5 TO 17 STEP 3". If you omit the "BY 3", the computer will assume "BY 1". If you omit the "FROM 5", the computer will assume "FROM 1". If you omit the "TO 17", the computer will assume "to infinity".

To make the computer count down instead of up, insert the word DOWN, like this:

```
LOOP I FROM 17 DOWN BY 3 TO 5
```

PREPARE To do an unusual activity, you should PREPARE the computer for it. For example, if you want to use subscripted variables such as X(100), you should tell the computer:

```
PREPARE X(100)
```

In that example, PREPARE is like Basic's DIM.

DATA Easy's DATA statement resembles Basic's. But instead of saying READ X, say:

```
LET X=NEXT
```

HOW In Easy, you can give any command you wish, such as:

```
PRETEND YOU ARE HUMAN
```

If you give that command, you must also give an explanation that begins with the words:

```
HOW TO PRETEND YOU ARE HUMAN
```

Interrelated features In the middle of a loop, you can abort the loop. To skip out of the loop (and progress to the rest of the program), say SKIP LOOP. To hop back to the beginning of the loop (to do the next iteration of loop), say REPEAT LOOP.

Similarly, you can say SKIP IF (which makes the computer skip out of an IF) and REPEAT IF (which makes the computer repeat the IF statement, and thereby imitate Pascal's WHILE).

Apostrophe Like Basic, Easy uses an apostrophe to begin a comment. The computer ignores everything to the right of an apostrophe, unless the apostrophe is between quotation marks or in a DATA statement.

Comma If two statements begin with the same word, you can combine them into a single statement, by using a comma.

For example, instead of saying —

```
LET X=4
LET Y=7
```

you can say:

```
LET X=4, Y=7
```

Instead of saying —

```
PRETEND YOU ARE HUMAN
PRETEND GOD IS DEAD
```

you can say:

```
PRETEND YOU ARE HUMAN, GOD IS DEAD
```

More info I stopped working on Easy in 1982 but expect to continue development again. To get on my mailing list of people who want details and updated info about Easy, phone me at 603-666-6644 or send me a postcard.

Radicals

Let's examine the radical languages, beginning with the oldest radical — the oldest hippie — Lisp.

Lisp

Lisp is the only language made specifically to handle lists of concepts. It's the most popular language for research into artificial intelligence.

It's the father of Logo, which is "oversimplified Lisp" and the most popular language for young children. It inspired Prolog, which is a Lisp-like language that lets you make the computer imitate a wise expert and become an **expert system**.

Beginners in artificial intelligence love to play with Logo and Prolog, which are easier and more fun than Lisp. But most professionals continue to use Lisp because it's more powerful than its children.

The original version of Lisp was called **Lisp 1**. Then came an improvement, called **Lisp 1.5** (because it wasn't different enough from LISP 1 to rate the title "LISP 2"). Then came a slight improvement on LISP 1.5, called **Lisp 1.6**. The newest version of LISP is called **Common Lisp**; it runs on maxicomputers,

minicomputers, and microcomputers.

I'll explain "typical" Lisp, which is halfway between Lisp 1.6 and Common Lisp.

Typical Lisp uses these symbols:

Basic	**Lisp**
5+2	(PLUS 5 2)
5-2	(DIFFERENCE 5 2)
5*2	(TIMES 5 2)
5/2	(QUOTIENT 5 2)
5^2	(EXPT 5 2)
"LOVE"	'LOVE old versions say (QUOTE LOVE)

If you want the computer to add 5 and 2, just type:

```
(PLUS 5 2)
```

When you press the Enter key at the end of that line, the computer will print the answer. (You do *not* have to say PRINT or any other special word.) The computer will print:

```
7
```

If you type —

```
(PLUS 1 3 1 1)
```

the computer will add 1, 3, 1, and 1 and print:

```
6
```

If you type —

```
(DIFFERENCE 7 (TIMES 2 3))
```

the computer will find the difference between 7 and 2*3 and print:

```
1
```

If you type —

```
'LOVE
```

the computer will print:

```
LOVE
```

Note you must type an apostrophe before LOVE but must *not* type an apostrophe afterwards. The apostrophe is called a **single quotation mark** (or a **quote**).

You can put a quote in front of a word (such as 'LOVE) or in front of a parenthesized list of words, such as:

```
'(LAUGH LOUDLY)
```

That makes the computer print:

```
(LAUGH LOUDLY)
```

Lisp 1, Lisp 1.5, and Lisp 1.6 don't understand the apostrophe. On those old versions of Lisp, say (QUOTE LOVE) instead of 'LOVE, and say (QUOTE (LAUGH LOUDLY)) instead of '(LAUGH LOUDLY).

The theory of lists Lisp can handle lists. Each list must begin and end with a parenthesis.

Here's a list of numbers: (5 7 4 2).
Here's a list of words:
(LOVE HATE WAR PEACE DEATH).

Here's a list of numbers and words:
(2 WOMEN KISS 7 MEN).
That list has five items:
2, WOMEN, KISS, 7, and MEN.

Here's a list of four items:
(HARRY LEMON (TICKLE MY TUBA TOMORROW AT TEN) RUSSIA). The first item is HARRY; the second is LEMON; the third is a list; the fourth is RUSSIA.

In a list, **the first item is called the CAR, and the rest of the list is called the CDR** (pronounced "could er" or "cudder" or "coo der"). For example, the CAR of (SAILORS DRINK WHISKEY) is SAILORS, and the CDR is (DRINK WHISKEY).

To make the computer find the CAR of (SAILORS DRINK WHISKEY), type this:

```
(CAR '(SAILORS DRINK WHISKEY))
```

The computer will print:

```
SAILORS
```

If you type —

```
(CDR '(SAILORS DRINK WHISKEY))
```

the computer will print:

```
(DRINK WHISKEY)
```

If you type —

```
(CAR (CDR '(SAILORS DRINK WHISKEY)))
```

the computer will find the CAR of the CDR of (SAILORS DRINK WHISKEY). Since the CDR of (SAILORS DRINK WHISKEY) is (DRINK WHISKEY), whose CAR is DRINK, the computer will print:

```
DRINK
```

You can insert an extra item at the beginning of a list, to form a longer list. For example, you can insert MANY at the beginning of (SAILORS DRINK WHISKEY), to form (MANY SAILORS DRINK WHISKEY). To do that, tell the computer to CONStruct the longer list, by typing:

```
(CONS 'MANY '(SAILORS DRINK WHISKEY))
```

The computer will print:

```
(MANY SAILORS DRINK WHISKEY)
```

Notice that CONS is the opposite of CAR and CDR. The CONS combines MANY with (SAILORS DRINK WHISKEY) to form (MANY SAILORS DRINK WHISKEY). The CAR and CDR break down (MANY SAILORS DRINK WHISKEY), to form MANY and (SAILORS DRINK WHISKEY).

Variables To make X stand for the number 7, say:

```
(SETQ X 7)
```

Then if you say —

```
(PLUS X 2)
```

the computer will print 9.

To make Y stand for the word LOVE, say:

```
(SETQ Y 'LOVE)
```

Then if you say —

```
Y
```

the computer will say:

```
LOVE
```

To make STOOGES stand for the list (MOE LARRY CURLEY), say:

```
(SETQ STOOGES '(MOE LARRY CURLEY))
```

Then if you say —

```
STOOGES
```

the computer will say:

```
(MOE LARRY CURLEY)
```

To find the first of the STOOGES, say:

```
(CAR STOOGES)
```

The computer will say:

```
MOE
```

Your own functions You can define your own functions. For example, you can define (DOUBLE X) to be 2*X, by typing this:

```
(DEFUN DOUBLE (X)
        (TIMES 2 X)
)
```

Then if you say —

```
(DOUBLE 3)
```

the computer will print:

```
6
```

REPEAT Let's define REPEAT to be a function, so that (REPEAT 'LOVE 5) is (LOVE LOVE LOVE LOVE LOVE), and (REPEAT 'KISS 3) is (KISS KISS KISS), and (REPEAT 'KISS 0) is ().

If N is 0, we want (REPEAT X N) to be ().

If N is larger than 0, we want (REPEAT X N) to be a list of N X's.

That's X followed by N-1 more X's.
That's the CONS of X with a list of N-1 more X's.
That's the CONS of X with (REPEAT X (DIFFERENCE N 1)).
That's (CONS X (REPEAT X (DIFFERENCE N 1))).
That's (CONS X (REPEAT X (SUB1 N))), since (SUB1 N) means N-1 in LISP.

You can define the answer to (REPEAT X N) as follows: if N is 0, the answer is (); if N is *not* 0, the answer is (CONS X (REPEAT X (SUB 1 N))). Here's how to type that definition:

```
(DEFUN REPEAT (X N)
        (COND
            ((ZEROP N) ())
            (T (CONS X (REPEAT X (SUB1 N))))
        )
)
```

The top line says you're going to DEfine a FUNction called REPEAT (X N). The next line says the answer depends on CONDitions. The next line gives one of those conditions: *if N is ZERO*, the answer is (). The next line says: *otherwise*, the value is (CONS X (REPEAT X (SUB1 N))). The next line closes the parentheses opened in the second line. The bottom line closes the parentheses opened in the top line.

Then if you type —

```
(REPEAT 'LOVE 5)
```

the computer will print:

```
(LOVE LOVE LOVE LOVE LOVE)
```

The definition is almost circular: the definition of REPEAT assumes you already know what REPEAT is. For example:

```
(REPEAT 'KISS 3) is defined as the CONS of KISS with the following:
(REPEAT 'KISS 2), which is defined as the CONS of KISS with the following:
(REPEAT 'KISS 1), which is defined as the CONS of KISS with the following:
(REPEAT 'KISS 1), which is defined as the CONS of KISS with the following:
(REPEAT 'KISS 0), which is defined as ().
```

That kind of definition, which is almost circular, is called **recursive**.

You can say "The definition of REPEAT is **recursive**", or "REPEAT is **defined recursively**", or "REPEAT is **defined by recursion**", or "REPEAT is **defined by induction**", or "REPEAT is a **recursive function**".

Lisp was the first popular language that allowed recursive definitions.

When the computer uses a recursive definition, the computer refers to the definition *repeatedly* before getting out of the circle. Since the computer repeats, it's performing a loop. In traditional Basic and Fortran, the only way to make the computer perform a loop is to say GO TO or FOR or DO. Although Lisp contains a go-to command, Lisp programmers avoid it and write recursive definitions instead.

ITEM As another example of recursion, let's define the function ITEM so (ITEM N X) is the Nth item in list X, and so (ITEM 3 '(MANY SAILORS DRINK WHISKEY)) is the 3rd item of (MANY SAILORS DRINK WHISKEY), which is DRINK.

If N is 1, (ITEM N X) is the first item in X, which is the CAR of X, which is (CAR X).

If N is larger than 1, (ITEM N X) is the Nth item in X. That's the (N-1)th item in the CDR of X. That's (ITEM (SUB1 N) (CDR X)).

So define (ITEM N X) as follows:

If N is 1, the answer is (CAR X).
If N is not 1, the answer is (ITEM (SUB 1 N) (CDR X)).

Here's what to type:

```
(DEFUN ITEM (N X)
        (COND
            ((ONEP N) (CAR X))
            (T (ITEM (SUB1 N) (CDR X)))
        )
)
```

If your computer doesn't understand (ONEP N), say (EQUAL 1 N) instead.

Snobol

Snobol lets you analyze strings more easily than any other language. It can handle numbers also.

Simple example Here's a simple Snobol program:

```
        A = -2
        B = A + 10.6
        C = "BODY TEMPERATURE IS 9" B
        OUTPUT = "MY " C
END
```

When you type the program, indent each line except END. Indent *at least* one space; you can indent more spaces if you wish. Put spaces around the symbols = and + and other operations.

The first line says A is the integer -2. The next line says B is the real number 8.6. The next line says C is the string "BODY TEMPERATURE IS 98.6". The next line makes the computer print:

```
BODY TEMPERATURE IS 98.6
```

In Snobol, a variable's name can be short (like A or B or C) or as long as you wish. The variable's name can even contain periods, like this:

```
NUMBER.OF.BULLIES.I.SQUIRTED
```

Loop This program's a loop:

```
FRED      OUTPUT = "CAT"
          OUTPUT = "DOG" :(FRED)
END
```

The first line (whose name is FRED) makes the computer print:

```
CAT
```

The next line makes the computer print —

```
DOG
```

and then go to FRED. Altogether the computer will print:

```
CAT
DOG
CAT
DOG
CAT
DOG
etc.
```

Replace Snobol lets you replace a phrase easily.

```
          X = "SIN ON A PIN WITH A DIN"
          X "IN" = "UCK"
          OUTPUT = X
END
```

The first line says X is the string "SIN ON A PIN WITH A DIN". The next line says: in X, replace the first "IN" by "UCK". So X becomes "SUCK ON A PIN WITH A DIN". The next line says the output is X, so the computer will print:

```
SUCK ON A PIN WITH A DIN
```

That program changed the *first* "IN" to "UCK". Here's how to change *every* "IN" to "UCK":

```
          X = "SIN ON A PIN WITH A DIN"
          X "IN" = "UCK"
          X "IN" = "UCK"
          X "IN" = "UCK"
          OUTPUT = X
END
```

The first line says X is "SIN ON A PIN WITH A DIN". The second line replaces an "IN" by "UCK", so X becomes "SUCK ON A PIN WITH A DIN". The next line replaces another "IN" by "UCK", so X becomes "SUCK ON A PUCK WITH A DIN". The next line replaces another "IN", so X becomes "SUCK ON A PUCK WITH A DUCK", which the next line prints.

This program does the same thing:

```
          X = "SIN ON A PIN WITH A DIN"
LOOP      X "IN" = "UCK" :S(LOOP)
          OUTPUT = X
END
```

Here's how it works:

The first line says X is "SIN ON A PIN WITH A DIN". The next line replaces "IN" successfully, so X becomes "SUCK ON A PIN WITH A DIN". At the end of the line, the :S(LOOP) means: if Successful, go to LOOP. So the computer goes back to LOOP. The computer replaces "IN" successfully again, so X becomes "SUCK ON A PUCK WITH A DIN", and the computer goes back to LOOP. The computer replaces "IN" successfully again, so X becomes "SUCK ON A PUCK WITH A DUCK", and the computer goes back to LOOP. The computer does not succeed. So the computer ignores the :S(LOOP) and proceeds instead to the next line, which prints:

```
SUCK ON A PUCK WITH A DUCK
```

Delete This program deletes the first "IN":

```
          X = "SIN ON A PIN WITH A DIN"
          X "IN" =
          OUTPUT = X
END
```

The second line says to replace an "IN" by nothing, so the "IN" gets deleted. X becomes "S ON A PIN WITH A DIN", which the computer will print.

This program deletes *every* "IN":

```
          X = "SIN ON A PIN WITH A DIN"
LOOP      X "IN" = :S(LOOP)
          OUTPUT = X
END
```

The computer will print:

```
S ON A P WITH A D
```

Count Let's count how often "IN" appears in "SIN ON A PIN WITH A DIN". To do that, delete each "IN"; but each time you delete one, increase the COUNT by 1:

```
          X = "SIN ON A PIN WITH A DIN"
          COUNT = 0
LOOP      X "IN" = :F(ENDING)
          COUNT = COUNT + 1 :(LOOP)
ENDING    OUTPUT = COUNT
END
```

The third line tries to delete an "IN": *if successful*, the computer proceeds to the next line, which increases the COUNT and goes back to LOOP; *if failing* (because no "IN" remains), the computer goes to ENDING, which prints the COUNT. The computer will print:

```
3
```

How Snobol developed At MIT during the 1950's, Noam Chomsky invented a notation called **transformational-generative grammar**, which helps linguists analyze English and translate between English and other languages. His notation was nicknamed "linguist's algebra", because it helped linguists just as algebra helped scientists. (A decade later, he became famous for also starting the rebellion against the Vietnam War.)

Chomsky's notation was for pencil and paper. In 1957 and 1958, his colleague Victor Yngve developed a computerized version of Chomsky's notation: the computerized version was a language called **Comit**. It was nicknamed "linguist's Fortran", because it helped linguists just as Fortran helped engineers.

Comit manipulated strings of *words*. In 1962 at Bell Telephone Laboratories (Bell Labs), Chester Lee invented a variant called **Symbolic Communication Language (SCL)**, which manipulated strings of *math symbols* instead of words and helped mathematicians do abstract math.

A team at Bell Labs decided to invent a simplified SCL that would also include features from Comit. The team started to call their new language "SCL7" then renamed it "Sexi" (which stands for **S**tring **Ex**pression **I**nterpreter); but Bell Labs' management didn't like sex. Then, as a joke, the team named it **Snobol**, using the flimsy excuse that Snobol stands for **S**tring-**O**riented sym**bo**lic **L**anguage. Though cynics said Snobol didn't have "a snowball's chance in hell," it became popular. It was used mainly to write programs that translate between computer languages. (For example, you could write a Snobol program that translates Fortran to Basic.)

Which is better: Comit or Snobol?

People who like Chomsky's notation (such as linguists) prefer Comit. People who like algebra (such as scientists) prefer Snobol.

Snobol's supporters were more active than Comit's: they produced Snobol 2, Snobol 3, Snobol 4, and Snobol 4B, put Snobol on newer computers, wrote books about Snobol, and emphasized that Snobol can solve *any* problem about strings, even if the problem has nothing to do with linguistics. They won: more people use Snobol than Comit.

Most new versions of Snobol are named after baseball pitching methods — such as Fasbol, Slobol, and Spitbol. (Spitbol stands for **Sp**eedy **I**mplementa**t**ion of Sno**bol**.)

APL

APL lets you manipulate lists of numbers more easily than any other language.

APL uses special characters that aren't on a normal keyboard.

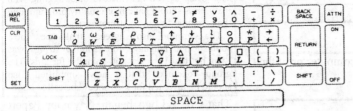

To compute 8+9, type this:

```
    8+9
```

Notice the line is indented. Whenever it's your turn to type, the computer automatically indents the line for you.

When you press the Return key at the end of that line, the computer will print the answer. (You don't have to say PRINT or any other special word.) The computer will print:

```
17
```

Scalar operators

APL uses these **scalar operators**:

APL name	Symbol	Meaning
PLUS	A+B	add
identity	+B	same as just B
MINUS	A−B	subtract
negative	−B	negative
TIMES	A×B	multiply
signum	×B	1 if B>0; ‾1 if B<0; 0 if B=0
DIVIDE	A÷B	divide
reciprocal	÷B	1 divided by B
POWER	A*B	A raised to the Bth power; A^B
exponential	*B	e raised to the Bth power, where e is 2.718281828459045
LOG	A⍟B	logarithm, base A, of B
natural log	⍟B	logarithm, base e, of B
CEILING	⌈B	B rounded up to an integer
maximum	A⌈B	A or B, whichever is larger
FLOOR	⌊B	B rounded down to an integer
minimum	A⌊B	A or B, whichever is smaller
MAGNITUDE	|B	the absolute value of B
residue	A|B	the remainder when you divide A into B; so 4|19 is 3
FACTORIAL	!B	1 times 2 times 3 times 4 times… times B
combinations	A!B	how many A-element subsets you can form from a set of B
ROLL	?B	a random integer from 1 to B
deal	A?B	list of A random integers, each from 1 to B, no duplicates
PI TIMES	○B	π times B
circular	A○B	sin B if A=1 arcsin B if A=‾1
		cos B if A=2 arccos B if A=‾2
		tan B if A=3 arctan B if A=‾3
		sinh B if A=5 arcsinh B if A=‾5
		cosh B if A=6 arccosh B if A=‾6
		tanh B if A=7 arctanh B if A=‾7
		square root of 1+B² if A= 4
		square root of 1-B² if A= 0
		square root of B²-1 if A=‾4
EQUAL	A=B	1 if A equals B; otherwise 0
not equal	A≠B	1 if A is not equal to B; otherwise 0
LESS	A<B	1 if A is less than B; otherwise 0
less or equal	A≤B	1 if A is less than or equal to B; otherwise 0
GREATER	A>B	1 if A is greater than B; otherwise 0
greater or equal	A≥B	1 if A is greater than or equal to B; otherwise 0
AND	A∧B	1 if A and B are both 1; otherwise 0
nand	A⍲B	1 if A and B are not both 1; otherwise 0
OR	A∨B	1 if A or B is 1; otherwise 0
nor	A⍱B	1 if neither A nor B is 1; otherwise 0
NOT	~B	1 if B is 0; otherwise 0

To make the symbol ⍟, type the symbol *, then press the BACKSPACE key, then type the symbol ○.

Order of operations

Unlike all other popular languages, APL makes the computer do all calculations *from right to left*. For example, if you type —

```
    2×3+5
```

the computer will start with 5, add 3 (to get 8), and then multiply by 2 (to get 16). The computer will print:

```
16
```

In Basic and most other languages, the answer would be 11 instead.

If you type —

```
    9-4-3
```

the computer will start with 3, subtract it from 4 (to get 1), and then subtract from 9 (to get 8). The computer will print:

```
8
```

In most other languages, the answer would be 2 instead.

You can use parentheses. Although 9-4-3 is 8, (9-4)-3 is 2. Compare these examples:

```
-4+6  is ‾10
```
```
‾4+6  is 2
```

In both examples, the 4 is preceded by a negative sign; but in the second example, the negative sign is raised, to be as high as the 4. (To make the raised negative, tap the 2 key while holding down the Shift key. To make a regular negative, tap the + key while holding down the Shift key.) The first example makes the computer start with 6, add 4 (to get 10), and then negate it (to get ‾10). The second example makes the computer start with 6 and add ‾4, to get 2.

Double precision

APL is super-accurate. It does all calculations by using double precision.

Variables

You can use variables:

```
    X←3
    X+2
```

The first line says X is 3. The second line makes the computer print X+2. The computer will print:

```
5
```

A variable's name can be long: up to 77 letters and digits. The name must begin with a letter.

Vectors

A variable can stand for a list of numbers:

```
    Y←5 2 8
    Y+1
```

The first line says Y is the **vector** 5 2 8. The next line makes the computer add 1 to each item and print:

```
6  3  9
```

This program prints the same answer:

```
    5 2 8+1
```

The computer will print:

```
6  3  9
```

This program prints the same answer:

```
    1+5 2 8
```

You can add a vector to another vector:

```
    A←5 2.1 6
    B←3 2.8 ‾7
    A+B
```

The computer will add 5 to 3, and 2.1 to 2.8, and 6 to ‾7, and print:

```
8  4.9  ‾1
```

This program prints the same answer:

```
    5 2.1 6+3 2.8 ‾7
```

This program prints the same answer:

```
A←5 2.1 6
B←3 2.8 ¯7
C←A+B
C
```

Here's something different:

```
X←4 2 3
+/X
```

The first line says X is the vector 4 2 3. The next line makes the computer print the sum, 9.

This program prints the same answer:

```
Y←+/4 2 3
Y
```

You can combine many ideas on the same line, but remember that the computer goes from right to left:

```
219-1 4 3+6×+/5 1 3×2 4 7
```

The computer will start with 2 4 7, multiply it by 5 1 3 (to get 10 4 21), find the sum (which is 35), multiply by 6 (to get 210), add 1 4 3 (to get 211 214 213), and then subtract from 219 (to get 8 5 6). The computer will print:

```
8   5   6
```

Each of APL's scalar operators works like addition. Here are examples:

```
2 4 10×3 7 9    is 6 28 90
÷2 4 10         is .5 .25 .1
-2 4 10         is ¯2 ¯4 ¯10
×/2 4 10        is 2×4×10, which is 80
-/9 5 3         is 9-5-3, which is 7 (since the computer works from right to left)
⌊/6.1 2.7 4.9   is 6.1⌊2.7⌊4.9, which is 2.7 (since ⌊ means minimum)
⌊6.1 2.7 4.9    is ⌊6.1 then ⌊2.7 then ⌊4.9, which is 6 2 4 (since ⌊ means floor)
```

**Vector operators** Here are **vector operators**; the examples assume V is 8 5 6:

APL name	Symbol	Value	Reason
SHAPE	ρV	3	V has 3 items
reshape	7ρV	8 5 6 8 5 6 8	make 7 items from V
REVERSE	ΦV	6 5 8	reverse V
rotate	1ΦV	5 6 8	rotate V, by beginning after the 1st item
GENERATE	ι3	1 2 3	count up to 3
index of	Vι5	2	in V, find 5; it's the 2nd item
TAKE	2↑V	8 5	the first 2 items from V
drop	2↓V	6	omit the first two items from V
SUBSCRIPT	V[2]	5	V's 2nd item
catenate	V,9 4	8 5 6 9 4	V followed by 9 4
COMPRESS	1 0 1/V	8 6	take part of V, using this pattern: take, omit, take
expand	1 0 0 1 1\V	8 0 0 5 6	insert zeros into V, using this pattern: item, 0, 0, item, item
GRADE UP	⍋V	2 3 1	here are V's numbers in increasing order: 5 (V's 2nd number), 6 (V's 3rd), 8 (V's 1st)
grade down	⍒V	1 3 2	here are V's numbers in decreasing order: 8 (V's 1st number), 6 (V's 3rd), 5 (V's 2nd)
DECODE	10⊥V	856	8, times 10, plus 5, times 10, plus 6
encode	10⊤856	8 5 6	opposite of decode
MEMBER	5∈V	1	search for 5 in V (1=found, 0=missing)

**Love or hate?** Some programmers love APL, because its notation is brief. Other programmers hate it, because its notation is hard for a human to read. The haters are winning, and the percentage of programmers using APL is decreasing.

Logo

Logo began in 1967, during an evening at Dan Bobrow's home in Belmont, Massachusetts. He'd gotten his Ph.D. from MIT and was working for a company called **Bolt, Beranek, and Newman (BBN)**. In his living room were 3 of his colleagues from BBN (Wally Feurzeig, Cynthia Solomon, and Dick Grant) and an MIT professor: Seymour Papert. BBN had tried to teach young kids how to program by using BBN's own language (Telcomp), which was a variation of Joss. BBN had asked Professor Seymour Papert for his opinion. The group was all gathered in Dan's house to hear Seymour's opinion.

Seymour chatted with the group, which agreed with Seymour on several points:

> First, Telcomp was _not_ a great language for kids. It placed too much emphasis on math formulas. The group agreed that instead of struggling with math, kids should have more fun by programming the computer to handle strings instead.
>
> The group also agreed that the most sophisticated language for handling strings was Lisp, but that Lisp was too complex for kids. The group concluded that a new, simplified Lisp should be invented for kids should be called **Logo**.

That's how Logo began. Seymour Papert was the guiding light, and all other members of the group gave helpful input during the conversation.

That night, after his guests left, Dan went to his bedroom, where he started writing a program (in Lisp) to make the computer understand Logo.

That's how Logo was born. Work on Logo continued. The three main researchers who continued improving Logo were Seymour (the MIT guru), Wally (from BBN), and Cynthia (also from BBN). Logo resembled Lisp but required fewer parentheses.

After helping BBN for a year, Seymour returned to MIT. Cynthia and several other BBN folks worked with him at MIT's Artificial Intelligence Laboratory to improve Logo.

**Turtles** At first, Logo was as abstract and boring as most other computer languages. But in the spring of 1970, a strange creature walked into the Logo lab. It was a big yellow mechanical turtle. It looked like "half a grapefruit on wheels" and had a pen in its belly:

wheel pen wheel

It also had a horn, feelers, and several other fancy attachments. To use it, you put paper all over the floor then programmed it to roll across the paper. As it rolled, the pen in its belly drew pictures on the paper. The turtle was controlled remotely by a big computer programmed in Logo.

Suddenly, Logo became a fun language whose main purpose was to control the turtle. Kids watching the turtle screamed with delight and wanted to learn how to program it. Logo became a favorite programming game for kids. Even kids who were just 7 years old started programming in Logo. Those kids were barely old enough to read, but reading and writing were _not_ prerequisites for learning how to program in Logo. All the kids had to know was:

> **FD 3** makes the turtle go forward 3 steps
> **RT 30** makes the turtle turn to the right 30 degrees

As for the rest of Logo — all that abstract stuff about strings, numbers, and Lisp-like lists — the kids ignored it. They wanted to use just the commands "FD" and "RT" that moved the turtle.

The U.S. Government's National Science Foundation donated money, to help MIT improve Logo further. Many kids came into the Logo lab to play with the turtles.

The turtles were expensive, and so were the big computers that controlled them. But during the early 1970's, computer screens got dramatically cheaper; so to save money, MIT stopped building mechanical turtles and instead bought cheap computer screens that showed pictures of turtles. Those pictures were called "mock turtles".

Cheaper computers

Logo's first version was done on BBN's expensive weird computer (the MTS 940). Later versions were done on the PDP-1, the PDP-10, and finally on a cheaper computer: the PDP-11 minicomputer (in 1972).

At the end of the 1970's, companies such as Apple and Radio Shack began selling microcomputers, which were even cheaper. MIT wanted to put Logo on microcomputers but ran out of money to pay for the research.

Texas Instruments (TI) came to the rescue.…

TI Logo

TI agreed to pay MIT to research how to put Logo on TI's microcomputer (the TI-99/4).

TI and MIT thought the job would be easy, since MIT had already written a Pascal program that made the computer understand Logo, and since TI had already written a version of Pascal for the CPU chip inside the TI-99/4. Initially, MIT was worried because the Pascal program running on MIT's PDP-10 computer handled Logo too slowly; but TI claimed TI's Pascal was faster than the PDP-10's and that Logo would therefore run fast enough on the TI.

TI was wrong. TI's Pascal couldn't make Logo run fast enough, and TI's Pascal also required too much RAM. So TI had to take MIT's research (on the PDP-10) and laboriously translate it into TI's assembly language, by hand. The hand translation went slower that TI expected. TI became impatient and took a short-cut: it omitted parts of Logo, such as decimals. TI began selling its version of Logo, which understood just integers.

MIT Apple Logo

After TI started selling its Logo, the MIT group invented a version of Logo for the Apple. The Apple version included decimals but omitted "sprites" (animated creatures that carry objects across the screen) because Apple's hardware couldn't handle sprites fast enough.

MIT wanted to sell the Apple version, since more schools owned Apples than TI computers. But if MIT were to make money from selling the Apple version, MIT might get into legal trouble, since MIT was supposed to be non-profit. And anyway, who "owned" Logo? Possible contenders were:

MIT, which did most of the research
BBN, which trademarked the name "Logo" and did the early research
Uncle Sam, whose National Science Foundation paid for much research
TI, which also paid for much research

Eventually, MIT solved the legal problems and sold the rights for "MIT Apple Logo" to two companies: Krell and Terrapin.

Krell was strictly a marketing company. It sold MIT Apple Logo to schools but made no attempt to improve Logo further.

Terrapin, on the other hand, was a research organization that had built mechanical turtles for several years. Terrapin hired MIT graduates to improve Logo further.

LCSI versus competitors

Back when MIT was waiting for its lawyers to determine who owned Apple Logo, a group of MIT's faculty and students (headed by Cynthia Solomon) impatiently left MIT and formed a company called **Logo Computer Systems Incorporated (LCSI)**. That company invented its own version of Logo for the Apple. LCSI became successful and was hired by Apple, IBM, Atari, and Microsoft to invent Logo versions for those systems. Commodore hired Terrapin instead.

For the Apple 2c (and 2e and 2+), you could buy either the official Apple Logo (sold by Apple Computer Inc. and created by LCSI), or "Terrapin Logo for the Apple" (sold by Terrapin), or the original "MIT Logo for the Apple" (sold by Krell). Krell became unpopular, leaving Terrapin and LCSI as the main Logo versions. LCSI's versions were daring (resulting from wild experiments), while Terrapin's versions were conservative (closer to the MIT original).

The two companies had different styles: Terrapin was small & friendly and charged little; LCSI was big & rude and charged more. On the phone, Terrapin was nicer than LCSI.

Terrapin's original owners had financial difficulties, moved to Maine, then sold the company to **Harvard Associates** (a Massachusetts company that had invented a Logo version called "PC Logo"). So now Terrapin is part of Harvard Associates (run by Bill Glass, who's friendly). To find out about his Terrapin Logo, look at his Web site (www.terrapinlogo.com) then phone him at 800-774-Logo (or 508-487-4141) or write to 955 Massachusetts Ave. #365, Cambridge MA 02139-3233.

LCSI's newest, daring version of Logo is **MicroWorlds Pro**. To find out about it, look at LCSI's Web site (www.lcsi.ca) then phone LCSI at 800-321-5646. LCSI is based in Montreal, Canada but accepts U.S. mail at PO Box 162, Highgate Springs VT 05460.

Logo versus Basic

Most of Logo's designers *hate* Basic. They want to eliminate Basic from schools altogether. They believe Logo's easier to learn than Basic, encourages a kid to be more creative, and lets a kid think in a more organized fashion. They also argue that since Logo is best for little kids, and since switching languages is difficult, kids should continue using Logo until they graduate from high school and should never use Basic.

That argument is wrong. It ignores the fact that knowing Basic is *essential* to understanding our computerized society. Most programs are still written in Basic, not Logo, because Basic consumes less RAM and because Basic's newest versions contain many practical features (for business, science, and graphics) that Logo lacks.

Another advantage of Basic is that Logo suffers from awkward notation. For example, in Basic you can type a formula such as —

```
A=B+C
```

but in Logo you must type:

```
MAKE "A :B+:C
```

Notice how ugly the Logo command looks! Notice you must put a quotation mark *before* the A but *not afterwards!* And look at those frightful colons! Anybody who thinks such notation is great for kids is a fool.

Extensible

One of Logo's nicest features is that you can modify Logo and turn it into your *own* language, because Logo lets you invent your own commands and add them to the Logo language. A language (such as Logo) that lets you invent your own commands is called an **extensible language**. Though some earlier languages (such as Lisp) were extensible also, Logo is *more* extensible and pleasanter.

Forth

Like Logo, Forth is extensible. But Forth has two advantages over Logo:

> **Forth consumes less memory**: you can easily run Forth on a computer having just 8K of RAM.
> **Forth runs faster**: the computer handles Forth almost as fast as assembly language.

Since Forth is extensible and consumes so little of the computer's memory and time, professional programmers have used Forth often. Famous programs written in Forth include **Easywriter** (a word-processing program), **Valdocs** (the operating system for Epson's first computer), and **Rapid File** (an easy-to-learn data-management system).

Unfortunately, the original versions of Easywriter and Valdocs contained many bugs, but that's because their programmers were careless.

In Forth, if you want to add 2 and 3 (to get 5) you do *not* type 2+3. Instead, you must type:

```
2 3 +
```

The idea of putting the plus sign afterwards (instead of in the middle) is called **postfix notation**. The postfix notation (2 3 +) has two advantages over infix notation (2+3): the computer handles postfix notation faster, and you never need to use parentheses for "order of operations". But postfix notation hard for humans to read.

Like Forth, ancient HP pocket calculators used postfix notation. If you used such as calculator, you'll find Forth easy.

Postfix notation is the reverse of **prefix notation** (+ 2 3), which was invented around 1926 by the Polish mathematician Lukasiewicz. So postfix notation is called **reverse Polish notation**. Since Forth is so difficult for a human to read, cynics call it "an inhuman Polish joke".

Forth was invented by Chuck Moore in his spare time while he worked at many schools and companies. He wanted to name it "Fourth", because he considered it to be an ultra-modern "fourth-generation" language; but since his old IBM 1130 computer couldn't handle a name as long as "Fourth", he omitted the letter "u".

Pilot

Pilot was invented in 1968 by John Starkweather at the University of California's San Francisco branch. It's easier to learn than Basic but intended to be programmed by teachers, not students. Teachers using Pilot can easily make the computer teach students about history, geography, math, French, and other schoolbook subjects.

For example, suppose you're a teacher and want to make the computer chat with your students. Here's how to do it in Pilot:

> **Basic program**
> ```
> 10 CLS
> 20 PRINT "I AM A COMPUTER"
> 30 INPUT "DO YOU LIKE COMPUTERS";A$
> 40 IF A$="YES" OR A$="YEAH" OR A$="YEP" OR A$="SURE" OR A$="SURELY" OR A$="I SURE DO" THEN PRINT "I LIKE YOU TOO" ELSE PRINT "TOUGH LUCK"
> ```
>
> | **Pilot program** | **What the computer will do** |
> |---|---|
> | T:I AM A COMPUTER | Type "I AM A COMPUTER". |
> | T:DO YOU LIKE COMPUTERS? | Type "DO YOU LIKE COMPUTERS?" |
> | A: | Accept the human's answer. |
> | M:YE,SURE | Match. (See whether answer contains "YE" or "SURE".) |
> | TY:I LIKE YOU TOO | If there was a match, type "I LIKE YOU TOO". |
> | TN:TOUGH LUCK | If no match, type "TOUGH LUCK". |

Notice that the Pilot program is briefer than Basic.

Atari, Apple, and Radio Shack have all sold versions of Pilot that include commands to handle graphics. Atari's version is the best, since it includes the fanciest graphics and music and even a Logo-like turtle, and since it's also the easiest version to learn how to use.

Though Pilot is easier than Basic, most teachers prefer Basic because it's available on more computers, costs less, and accomplishes a greater variety of tasks. Hardly anybody uses Pilot.

Specialists

For specialized applications, use a special language.

Apt

If you use **Apt**, the computer will help you cut metal.

Type an Apt program that says how you want the metal cut. When you run the program, the computer will create a special instruction tape. If you feed that tape into a metal-cutting machine, the machine will cut metal as you said.

Let's write an Apt program that makes the machine cut out the shaded area:

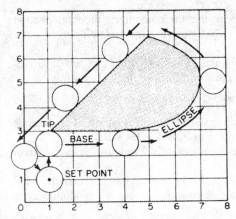

We'll make the machine move the cutter where the circles are.

Here's the program:

Program	What the computer will do
CUTTER/1	Use a cutter whose diameter is 1".
TOLER/.005	The tolerance of the cut is .005".
FEDRAT/80	Use a feedrate of 80" per minute.
HEAD/1	Use head 1.
MODE/1	Operate the tool in mode 1.
SPINDL/2400	Turn the spindle on, at 2400 rpm.
COOLNT/FLOOD	Turn the coolant on, at flood setting.
PT1=POINT/4,5	PT1 = the point whose coordinates are (4,5).
FROM/(SETPT=POINT/1,1)	SETPT = point (1,1). Start tool from SETPT.
INDIRP/(TIP=PIONT/1,3)	TIP = (1,3). Aim tool in direction of TIP.
BASE=LINE/TIP, AT ANGL, 0	BASE = line going through TIP at 0 degrees.
GOTO/BASE	Make the tool go to BASE.
TL RGT, GO RGT/BASE	With tool on right, go right along BASE.
GO FWD/(ELLIPS/CENTER, PT1, 3,2,0)	Go forward along ellipse whose center is PT1, semi-major axis is 3", semi-minor axis is 2", and major axis slants 0 degrees.
GO LFT/(LINE/2,4,1,3,), PAST, BASE	Go left along the line that joins (2,4) and (1,3), until you get past BASE.
GOTO/SETPT	Make the tool go to SETPT.
COOLNT/OFF	Turn the coolant off.
SPINDL/OFF	Turn the spindle off.
END	End use of the machine.
FINI	The program is finished.

Dynamo

Dynamo uses these symbols:

Symbol	Meaning
.J	a moment ago
.K	now
.JK	during the past moment
.KL	during the next moment
DT	how long "a moment" is

For example, suppose you want to explain to the computer how population depends on birth rate. If you let P be the population, BR be the birth rate, and DR be the death rate, here's what to say in Dynamo:

```
P.K=P.J+DT*(BR.JK-DR.JK)
```

The equation says: Population now = Population before + (how long "a moment" is) times (Birth Rate during the past moment - Death Rate during the past moment).

World Dynamics The most famous Dynamo program is the **World Dynamics Model**, which Jay Forrester programmed at MIT in 1970. His program has 117 equations that describe 112 variables about our world.

Here's how the program begins:

```
* WORLD DYNAMICS
L P.K=P.J+DT*(BR.JK-DR.JK)
N P=PI
C PI=1.65E9
R BR.KL=P.K*FIFGE(BRN,BRN1,SWT1,TIME.K)*BRFM.K*BRMM.K*BRCM.K*BRPM.K
etc.
```

The first line gives the program's title. The next line defines the Level of Population, in terms of Birth Rate and Death Rate.

The second equation defines the iNitial Population to be PI (Population Initial). The next equation defines the Constant PI to be 1.65e9, because the world's population was 1.65 billion in 1900.

The next equation says the Rate BR.KL (the Birth Rate during the next moment) is determined by the Population now and several other factors, such as the BRFM (Birth-Rate-from-Food Multiplier), the BRMM (Birth-Rate-from-Material Multiplier), the BRCM (Birth-Rate-from-Crowding Multiplier), and the BRPM (Birth-Rate-from-Pollution Multiplier). Each of those factors is defined in later equations.

When you run the program, the computer automatically solves all the equations simultaneously and draws graphs showing how the population, birth rate, etc. will change during the next several decades. The graphs show the quality of life will decrease (because of the overpopulation, pollution, and dwindling natural resources). Although the material standard of living will improve for a while, it too will eventually decrease, as will industrialization (capital investment).

The bad outlook is caused mainly by dwindling natural resources. Suppose scientists suddenly make a "new discovery" that lets us reduce our usage of natural resources by 75%. Will our lives be better? The computer predicted that if the "new discovery" were made in 1970, this would happen:

> People will well, so in 2030 the population is almost 4 times what it was in 1970. But the large population generates too much pollution. In 2030, the pollution is being created faster than it can dissipate. From 2040 to 2060, a pollution crisis occurs: the pollution increases until it's 40 times as great as in 1970 and kills most people on earth, so the world's population in 2060 is a sixth of what it was in 2040. After the crisis, the few survivors create little pollution and enjoy a very high quality of life.

Forrester tried other experiments on the computer. To improve the quality of life, he tested the effect of requiring birth control, reducing pollution, and adopting other strategies. Each of those simple strategies backfired. The graphs showed that the only way to maintain a high quality of life is to adopt a *combination* strategy immediately:

> reduce natural resource usage by 75%
> reduce pollution generation by 50%
> reduce the birth rate by 30%
> reduce capital-investment generation by 40%
> reduce food production by 20%

Other popular applications

Although the World Dynamics Model is Dynamo's most famous program, Dynamo has also been applied to many other problems.

The first Dynamo programs ever written were aimed at helping managers run companies. Just plug your policies about buying, selling, hiring, and firing into the program's equations; when you run the program, the computer draws a graph showing what will happen to your company during the coming months and years. If you don't like the computer's prediction, change your policies, put them into the equations, and see whether the computer's graphs are more optimistic.

How Dynamo developed

Dynamo developed from research at MIT.

At MIT in 1958, Richard Bennett invented a language called **Simple**, which stood for "Simulation of Industrial Management Problems with Lots of Equations". In 1959, Phyllis Fox and Alexander Pugh III invented Dynamo as an improvement on Simple. At MIT in 1961, Jay Forrester wrote a book called *Industrial Dynamics*, which explained how Dynamo can help you manage a company.

MIT is near Boston, whose mayor from 1960 to 1967 was John Collins. When his term as mayor ended, he became a visiting professor at MIT. His office happened to be next to Forrester's. He asked Forrester whether Dynamo could solve the problems of managing a city. Forrester organized a conference of urban experts and got them to turn urban problems into 330 Dynamo equations involving 310 variables.

Forrester ran the program and made the computer graph the consequences. The results were surprising:

> The graph showed that if you try to help the underemployed (by giving them low-cost housing, job-training programs, and artificially created jobs), the city becomes better for the underemployed — but then more underemployed people move to the city, the percentage of the city that's underemployed increases, and the city is worse than before the reforms were begun. So socialist reform just backfires.
>
> Another example: free public transportation creates *more* traffic, because it encourages people to live farther from their jobs.
>
> The graphs show the only long-term solution to the city's problems is to do this instead: knock down slums, fund new "labor-intensive export" businesses (businesses that will hire many workers, occupy little land, and produce goods that can be sold outside the city), and let the underemployed fend for themselves in this new environment.
>
> Another surprise: any city-funded housing program makes matters *worse* (regardless of whether the housing is for the underemployed, the workers, or the rich) because more housing creates less space for industry, so fewer jobs.

If you ever become a mayor or President, use the computer's recommendations cautiously: they'll improve the cities, but only by driving the underemployed out to the suburbs, which will worsen.

In 1970 Forrester created the World Dynamics Model to help "The Club of Rome", a private club of 75 people who try to save the world from ecological calamity.

GPSS

A **queue** is a line of people who are waiting. **GPSS** analyzes queues. For example, let's use GPSS to analyze the customers waiting in "Quickie Joe's Barbershop".

Joe's the only barber in the shop, and he spends exactly 7 minutes on each haircut. (That's why he's called "Quickie Joe".)

About once every 10 minutes, a new customer enters the barbershop. More precisely, the number of minutes before another customer enters is a random number between 5 and 15.

To make the computer imitate the barbershop and analyze what happens to the first 100 customers, type this program:

```
       SIMULATE
       GENERATE    10,5      A new customer comes every 10 minutes ± 5 minutes.
       QUEUE       JOEQ      He waits in the queue, called JOEQ.
       SEIZE       JOE       When his turn comes, he seizes JOE,
       DEPART      JOEQ         which means he leaves the JOEQ.
       ADVANCE     7         After 7 minutes go by,
       RELEASE     JOE         he releases JOE (so someone else can use JOE)
       TERMINATE   1           and leaves the shop.
       START       100       Do all that 100 times.
       END
```

Indent so that the word SIMULATE begins in column 8 (preceded by 7 spaces) and the "10,5" begins in column 19.

When you run the program, the computer will tell you the following....

Joe was working 68.5% of the time. The rest of the time, his shop was empty and he was waiting for customers.

There was never more than 1 customer waiting. "On the average", .04 customers were waiting.

There were 101 customers. (The 101st customer stopped the experiment.) 79 of them (78.2% of them) obtained Joe immediately and didn't have to wait.

The "average customer" had to wait in line .405 minutes. The "average not-immediately-served customer" had to wait in line 1.863 minutes.

How to make the program fancier

Below the RELEASE statement and above the TERMINATE statement, you can insert two extra statements:

```
       TABULATE    1
1      TABLE       M1,0,1,26
```

(Indent so that the 1 before TABLE is in column 2.) Those two statements make the computer add the following comments....

Of the 100 analyzed customers, the "average customer" spent 7.369 minutes in the shop (from when he walked in to when he walked out).

More precisely, 79 customers spend 7 minutes each, 9 customers spend 8 minutes each, 9 customers spend 9 minutes each, 2 customers spend 10 minutes each, and 1 customer had to spend 11 minutes.

The computer also prints the "standard deviation", "cumulative tables", and other statistical claptrap.

On your own computer, the numbers might be slightly different, depending on how the random numbers came out. To have more faith in the computer's averages, try 1000 customers instead of 100.

Alternative languages For most problems about queues, GPSS is the easiest language to use. But if your problem is complex, you might have to use **Simscript** (based on Fortran) or **Simula** (an elaboration of Algol) or **Simpl/I** (an elaboration of PL/I).

SPSS

The most popular computer language for statistics is **SPSS**, which stands for **Statistical Package for the Social Sciences**.

Simple example Suppose you survey 10 of your friends and ask each of them two questions:

1. In the next election, will you probably vote Republican or Democrat?
2. Are you male or female?

Maybe you can guess the answer to the second question by just looking at the person; but to be sure, you'd better ask.

Suppose nobody gives an unusual answer (such as Prohibitionist or Communist or Transsexual or Undecided). You think it would be cool to feed all the data into the computer. For example, if a person said "Republican Female", you'd feed the computer this line:

```
RF
```

If a person said "Democrat Male", you'd feed the computer this line:

```
DM
```

This SPSS program makes the computer analyze the data:

Program		Meaning
VARIABLE LIST	PARTY,SEX	Read each person's PARTY and SEX,
INPUT FORMAT	FIXED (2A1)	using this Fortran FORMAT: "2A1".
N OF CASES	10	There are 10 people.
INPUT MEDIUM	CARD	The data to read is on the "cards" below.
PRINT FORMATS	PARTY,SEX (A)	To print the PARTY and SEX, use "A" format.
CROSSTABS	TABLES=SEX BY PARTY	Print table showing how SEX relates to PARTY.
READ INPUT DATA		The data to read is on the following lines.
RF		
DM		
RM		
RM		
DF		
DM		the "data cards"
DF		
DF		
RM		
DF		
FINISH		The program is finished.

In the top line, the word PARTY begins in column 16. Most SPSS statements consist of a **control field** (columns 1-15) followed by a **specification field** (columns 16-80).

When you run the program, the computer will print this kind of table:

	R	D	ROW TOTAL
M	3 60.0% 75.0% 30.0%	2 40.0% 33.3% 20.0%	5 50.0%
F	1 20.0% 25.0% 10.0%	4 80.0% 66.7% 40.0%	5 50.0%
COLUMN TOTAL	4 40.0%	6 60.0%	10 100.0%

Look at the top number in each box. Those numbers say there were 3 male

Republicans, 2 male Democrats, 1 female Republican, and 4 female Democrats. The first box says: the 3 male Republicans were 60% of the males, 75% of the Republicans, and 30% of the total population.

The computer prints the table in reverse-alphabetical order: "M" before "F", and "R" before "D". Each row is a SEX, and each column is a PARTY. In the program, if you change "SEX BY PARTY" to "PARTY BY SEX", each row will be a PARTY, and each column will be a SEX.

Fancy features The CROSSTABS statement has **options**. Here are some.

option 3: don't print the row percentages (the 60.0%, 40.0%, 20.0%, and 80.0%)

option 4: don't print the column percentages (75.0%, 33.3%, 25.0%, and 66.7%)

option 5: don't print the total percentages (30.0%, 20.0%, 10.0% and 40.0%)

If you want options 3 and 5, put this under the CROSSTABS statement:

```
OPTIONS          3,5
```

The CROSSTABS statement has **statistics**. Here are some of them:

1. chi-square, its degrees of freedom, level of significance
2. phi or Cramer's V
3. contingency coefficient
4. lambda, symmetric and asymmetric
5. uncertainty coefficient, symmetric and asymmetric
6. Kendall's tau b and its level of significance
7. Kendall's tau c and its level of significance
8. gamma
9. Somer's D

Those statistics are numbers that help you analyze the crosstab table. If you want statistics 1 and 8, insert this statement underneath the CROSSTABS and OPTIONS statements:

```
STATISTICS       1,8
```

It makes the computer print statistics 1 and 8 underneath the table. If you want the computer to print all 9 statistics, say:

```
STATISTICS       ALL
```

The CROSSTABS statement is called a **procedure**. Here are other procedures SPSS can handle:

AGGREGATE	NONPAR CORR
ANOVA	ONEWAY
BREAKDOWN	PARTIAL CORR
CANCORR	PEARSON CORR
CONDESCRIPTIVE	REGRESSION
DISCRIMINANT	SCATTERGRAM
FACTOR	T-TEST
FREQUENCIES	WRITE CASES
GUTTMAN SCALE	

Each procedure has its own OPTIONS and STATISTICS.

SPSS contains more statistical features than any other language. If you don't need quite so many features, use an easier language, such as STATPAK or DATATEXT.

Prolog

In 1972, **Prolog** was invented in France at the **University of Marseilles**. In 1981, a different version of Prolog arose in Scotland at the **University of Edinburgh**. In 1986, **Turbo Prolog** was created in California by Borland International (which also created Turbo Pascal).

Those versions of Prolog are called **Marseilles Prolog**, **Edinburgh Prolog**, and **Turbo Prolog**.

Prolog programmers call Marseilles Prolog the "old classic", Edinburgh Prolog the "current standard", and Turbo Prolog the "radical departure".

Turbo Prolog has two advantages over its predecessors: it runs programs extra-fast, and it uses English words instead of weird symbols. On the other hand, it requires extra lines at the beginning of your program, to tell the computer which variables are strings.

The ideal Prolog would be a compromise, incorporating the best features of Marseilles, Edinburgh, and Turbo. Here's how to use the ideal Prolog and how the various versions differ from it....

Creating the database

Prolog analyzes relationships. Suppose Alice loves tennis and sailing, Tom loves everything that Alice loves, and Tom also loves football (which Alice does *not* love). To feed all those facts to the computer, give these Prolog commands:

```
loves(alice,tennis).
loves(alice,sailing).
loves(tom,X) if loves(alice,X).
loves(tom,football).
```

The top two lines say Alice loves tennis and sailing. In the third line, the "X" means "something", so that line says: Tom loves something if Alice loves it. The bottom line says Tom loves football.

When you type those lines, be careful about capitalization.

You must capitalize variables (such as X). You must *not* capitalize specifics (such as tennis, sailing, football, alice, tom, and love).

At the end of each sentence, put a period.

That's how to program by using ideal Prolog. Here's how other versions of Prolog differ....

For Edinburgh Prolog, type the symbol ":-" instead of the word "if".

For Marseilles Prolog, replace the period by a semicolon, and replace the word "if" by an arrow (->), which you must put in every line:

```
loves(alice,tennis)->;
loves(alice,sailing)->;
loves(tom,X) -> loves(alice,X);
loves(tom,football)->;
```

For Turbo Prolog, you must add extra lines at the top of your program, to warn the computer that the person and sport are strings ("symbols"), and the word "loves" is a verb ("predicate") that relates a person to a sport:

```
domains
        person,sport=symbol
predicates
        loves(person,sport)
clauses
        loves(alice,tennis).
        loves(alice,sailing).
        loves(tom,X) if loves (alice,x).
        loves(tom,football).
```

(To indent, press the Tab key. To stop indenting, press the left-arrow key.) When you've typed all that, press the Esc key (which means Escape) then the R key (which means Run).

Simple questions

After you've fed the database to the computer, you can ask the computer questions about it.

Does Alice love tennis? To ask the computer that question, type this:

```
loves(alice,tennis)?
```

The computer will answer:

```
yes
```

Does Alice love football? Ask this:

```
loves(alice,football)?
```

The computer will answer:

```
no
```

That's how the ideal Prolog works. Other versions differ. *Marseilles Prolog* is similar to the ideal Prolog. *Turbo Prolog* omits the question mark, says "true" instead of "yes", and says "false" instead of "no". *Edinburgh Prolog* puts the question mark at the beginning of the sentence instead of the end, like this:

```
?-loves(alice,tennis).
```

Advanced questions

What does Alice love? Does Alice love something? Ask this:

```
loves(alice,X)?
```

The computer will answer:

```
X=tennis
X=sailing
2 solutions
```

What does Tom love? Does Tom love something? Ask:

```
loves(tom,X)?
```

The computer will answer:

```
X=tennis
X=sailing
X=football
3 solutions
```

Who loves tennis? Ask:

```
loves(X,tennis)?
```

The computer will answer:

```
X=alice
X=tom
2 solutions
```

Does anybody love hockey? Ask:

```
loves(X,hockey)?
```

The computer doesn't know of anybody who loves hockey, so the computer will answer:

```
no solution
```

Does Tom love something that Alice doesn't? Ask:

```
loves(tom,X) and not (loves(alice,X))?
```

The computer will answer:

```
X=football
1 solution
```

That's ideal Prolog.

Turbo Prolog is similar to ideal Prolog. For *Marseilles Prolog*, replace the word "and" by a blank space.

For *Edinburgh Prolog*, replace the word "and" by a comma. After the computer finds a solution, type a semicolon, which tells the computer to find others; when the computer can't find any more solutions, it says "no" (which means "no more solutions") instead of printing a summary message such as "2 solutions".

Prolog's popularity

After being invented in France, Prolog quickly became popular throughout Europe.

Its main competitor was Lisp, which was invented in the United States before Prolog. Long after Prolog's debut, Americans continued to use Lisp and ignored Prolog.

In the 1980's, the Japanese launched the **Fifth Generation Project**, which was an attempt to develop a more intelligent kind of computer. To develop that computer's software, the Japanese decided to use Prolog instead of Lisp, because Prolog was non-American and therefore furthered the project's purpose, which was to one-up the Americans.

When American researchers heard that the Japanese chose Prolog as a software weapon, the Americans got scared and launched a counter-attack by learning Prolog also.

When Borland — an American company — developed Turbo Prolog, American researchers were thrilled, since Turbo Prolog ran faster than any other Prolog. It ran faster on a cheap IBM PC than Japan's Prolog ran on Japan's expensive maxicomputers! The money that Japan had spent on maxicomputers was wasted! The Americans giggled with glee.

Moral: though the Japanese can beat us in making hardware, we're still way ahead in software. But wouldn't it be great if our countries could work together and *share* talents?

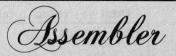

Assembler

Let's look deeper into the computer to see how circuits can "think".

Number systems

Most humans use the **decimal system**, which consists of ten digits (0, 1, 2, 3, 4, 5, 6, 7, 8, 9), because humans have ten fingers. The computer does not have fingers, so it prefers other number systems instead. Here they are....

Binary

Look at these powers of 2:

$2^0 = 1$
$2^1 = 2$
$2^2 = 4$
$2^3 = 8$
$2^4 = 16$
$2^5 = 32$
$2^6 = 64$

Now try an experiment. Pick your favorite positive integer, and try to write it as a sum of powers of 2.

For example, suppose you pick 45; you can write it as 32+8+4+1. Suppose you pick 74; you can write it as 64+8+2. Suppose you pick 77. You can write it as 64+8+4+1. *Every* positive integer can be written as a sum of powers of 2.

Let's put those examples in a table:

Original number	Written as sum of powers of 2	Does the sum contain...						
		64?	32?	16?	8?	4?	2?	1?
45	32+8+4+1	no	yes	no	yes	yes	no	yes
74	64+8+2	yes	no	no	yes	no	yes	no
77	64+8+4+1	yes	no	no	yes	yes	no	yes

To write those numbers in the **binary system**, replace "no" by 0 and "yes" by 1:

Decimal system	Binary system
45	0101101 (or simply 101101)
74	1001010
77	1001101

The **decimal system** uses the digits 0, 1, 2, 3, 4, 5, 6, 7, 8, and 9 and uses these columns:

thousands	hundreds	tens	units

For example, the decimal number 7105 means "7 thousands + 1 hundred + 0 tens + 5 units".

The **binary system** uses just the digits 0 and 1, and uses these columns:

sixty-fours	thirty-twos	sixteens	eights	fours	twos	units

For example, the binary number 1001101 means "1 sixty-four + 0 thirty-twos + 0 sixteens + 1 eight + 1 four + 0 twos + 1 unit". In other words, it means seventy-seven.

In elementary school, you were taught how to do arithmetic in the decimal system. You had to memorize the addition and multiplication tables:

DECIMAL ADDITION

	0	1	2	3	4	5	6	7	8	9
0	0	1	2	3	4	5	6	7	8	9
1	1	2	3	4	5	6	7	8	9	10
2	2	3	4	5	6	7	8	9	10	11
3	3	4	5	6	7	8	9	10	11	12
4	4	5	6	7	8	9	10	11	12	13
5	5	6	7	8	9	10	11	12	13	14
6	6	7	8	9	10	11	12	13	14	15
7	7	8	9	10	11	12	13	14	15	16
8	8	9	10	11	12	13	14	15	16	17
9	9	10	11	12	13	14	15	16	17	18

DECIMAL MULTIPLICATION

	0	1	2	3	4	5	6	7	8	9
0	0	0	0	0	0	0	0	0	0	0
1	0	1	2	3	4	5	6	7	8	9
2	0	2	4	6	8	10	12	14	16	18
3	0	3	6	9	12	15	18	21	24	27
4	0	4	8	12	16	20	24	28	32	36
5	0	5	10	15	20	25	30	35	40	45
6	0	6	12	18	24	30	36	42	48	54
7	0	7	14	21	28	35	42	49	56	63
8	0	8	16	24	32	40	48	56	64	72
9	0	9	18	27	36	45	54	63	72	81

In the binary system, the only digits are 0 and 1, so the tables are briefer:

BINARY ADDITION

	0	1
0	0	1
1	1	10 because two is written "10" in binary

BINARY MULTIPLICATION

	0	1
0	0	0
1	0	1

If society had adopted the binary system instead of the decimal system, you'd have been spared many hours of memorizing!

Usually, when you ask the computer to perform a computation, it converts your numbers from the decimal system to the binary system, performs the computation by using the binary addition and multiplication tables, and then converts the answer from the binary system to the decimal system, so you can read it. For example, if you ask the computer to print 45+74, it will do this:

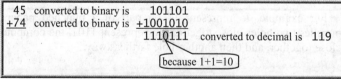

The conversion from decimal to binary and then back to decimal is slow. But the computation itself (in this case, addition) is quick, since the binary addition table is so simple. The only times the computer must convert is during input (decimal to binary) and output (binary to decimal). The rest of the execution is performed quickly, entirely in binary.

You know fractions can be written in the decimal system, by using these columns:

units	point	tenths	hundredths	thousandths

For example, $1\frac{5}{8}$ can be written as 1.625, which means "1 unit + 6 tenths + 2 hundredths + 5 thousandths".

To write fractions in the binary system, use these columns instead:

units	point	halves	fourths	eighths

For example, $1\frac{5}{8}$ is written in binary as 1.101, which means "1 unit + 1 half + 0 fourths + 1 eighth".

You know ¹/₃ is written in the decimal system as 0.3333333…, which unfortunately never terminates. In the binary system, the situation is no better: ¹/₃ is written as 0.010101…. Since the computer stores just a finite number of digits, it can't store ¹/₃ accurately — it stores just an approximation.

A more distressing example is ¹/₅. In the decimal system, it's .2, but in the binary system it's .0011001100110011…. So the computer can't handle ¹/₅ accurately, even though a human can.

Most of today's microcomputers and minicomputers are inspired by a famous maxicomputer built by DEC and called the DECsystem-10 (or PDP-10). Though DEC doesn't sell the DECsystem-10 anymore, its influence lives on!

Suppose you run this Basic program on a DECsystem-10 computer:

```
10 PRINT "MY FAVORITE NUMBER IS";4.001-4
20 END
```

The computer will try to convert 4.001 to binary. Unfortunately, it can't be converted exactly; the computer's binary approximation of it is slightly too small. The computer's final answer to 4.001-4 is therefore slightly less than the correct answer. Instead of printing MY FAVORITE NUMBER IS .001, the computer will print MY FAVORITE NUMBER IS .000999987.

If your computer isn't a DECsystem-10, its approximation will be slightly different. To test your computer's accuracy, try 4.0001-4, and 4.00001-4, and 4.000001-4, etc. You might be surprised at its answers.

Let's see how the DECsystem-10 handles this:

```
10 FOR X = 7 TO 193 STEP .1
20    PRINT X
30 NEXT X
40 END
```

The computer will convert 7 and 193 to binary accurately, but will convert .1 to binary just approximately; the approximation is slightly too large. The last few numbers it should print are 192.8, 192.9, and 193, but because of the approximation it will print slightly more than 192.8, then slightly more than 192.9, and then stop (since it is not allowed to print anything over 193).

There are just two binary digits: 0 and 1. A **b**inary dig**it** is called a **bit**. For example, .001100110011 is a binary approximation of ¹/₅ that consists of twelve bits. A sixteen-bit approximation of ¹/₅ would be .0011001100110011. A bit that is 1 is called **turned on**; a bit that is 0 is **turned off**. For example, in the expression 11001, three bits are turned on and two are off. We also say three of the bits are **set** and two are **cleared**.

In the computer, all info is coded as bits:

Location	What's 1?	What's 0?
wire	high voltage	low voltage
punched paper tape	a hole in the tape	no hole
punched IBM card	a hole in the card	no hole
flashing light	the light is on	the light is off
magnetic drum	a magnetized area	not magnetized
core memory	a core (iron doughnut) magnetized clockwise	counterclockwise

For example, to represent 11 on part of a punched paper tape, the computer punches two holes close together. To represent 1101, the computer punches two holes close together, and then another hole farther away.

Octal

Octal is a shorthand notation for binary:

Octal	Meaning
0	000
1	001
2	010
3	011
4	100
5	101
6	110
7	111

Each octal digit stands for three bits. For example, the octal number 72 is short for this:

To convert a binary integer to octal, divide the number into chunks of three bits, starting at the right. For example, here's how to convert 11110101 to octal:

To convert a binary real number to octal, divide the number into chunks of three bits, starting at the decimal point and working in both directions:

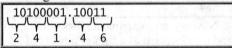

Hexadecimal

Hexadecimal is another short-hand notation for binary:

Hexadecimal	Meaning
0	0000
1	0001
2	0010
3	0011
4	0100
5	0101
6	0110
7	0111
8	1000
9	1001
A	1010
B	1011
C	1100
D	1101
E	1110
F	1111

For example, the hexadecimal number 4F is short for this:

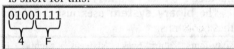

To convert a binary number to hexadecimal, divide the number into chunks of 4 bits, starting at the decimal point and working in both directions:

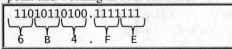

Character codes

To store a character in a string, the computer uses a code.

Ascii

The most famous code is the **American Standard Code for Information Interchange (Ascii)**, which has 7 bits for each character. Here are examples:

Character	Ascii code	Ascii code in hexadecimal
space	0100000	20
!	0100001	21
"	0100010	22
#	0100011	23
$	0100100	24
%	0100101	25
&	0100110	26
'	0100111	27
(	0101000	28
)	0101001	29
*	0101010	2A
+	0101011	2B
,	0101100	2C
-	0101101	2D
.	0101110	2E
/	0101111	2F
0	0110000	30
1	0110001	31
2	0110010	32
etc.		
9	0111001	39
:	0111010	3A
;	0111011	3B
<	0111100	3C
=	0111101	3D
>	0111110	3E
?	0111111	3F
@	1000000	40
A	1000001	41
B	1000010	42
C	1000011	43
etc.		
Z	1011010	5A
[	1011011	5B
\	1011100	5C
]	1011101	5D
^	1011110	5E
_	1011111	5F

"Ascii" is pronounced "ass key".

Most terminals use 7-bit Ascii. Most microcomputers and the PDP-11 use an "8-bit Ascii" formed by putting a 0 before 7-bit Ascii.

PDP-8 computers use mainly a "6-bit Ascii" formed by eliminating 7-bit Ascii's leftmost bit, but they can also handle an "8-bit Ascii" formed by putting a 1 before 7-bit Ascii.

PDP-10 computers use mainly 7-bit Ascii but can also handle a "6-bit Ascii" formed by eliminating Ascii's second bit. For example, the 6-bit Ascii code for the symbol $ is 0 00100.

EBCDIC

Instead of using Ascii, IBM mainframes use the **Extended Binary-Coded-Decimal Interchange Code (EBCDIC)**, which has 8 bits for each character. Here are examples:

Character	EBCDIC code in hexadecimal
space	40
¢	4A
<	4C
(	4D
+	4E
|	4F
&	50
!	5A
$	5B
*	5C
)	5D
;	5E
¬	5F
-	60
/	61
,	6B
%	6C
_	6D
>	6E
?	6F
:	7A
#	7B
@	7C
'	7D
=	7E
"	7F
A	C1
B	C2
C	C3
etc.	
I	C9
J	D1
K	D2
L	D3
etc.	
R	D9
S	E2
T	E3
U	E4
etc.	
Z	E9
0	F0
1	F1
2	F2
etc.	
9	F9

"EBCDIC" is usually pronounced "ebb sih Dick," though programmers hating it say "Ed sucks Dick."

IBM 360 computers can also handle an "8-bit Ascii", formed by copying Ascii's first bit after the second bit. For example, the 8-bit Ascii code for the symbol $ is 01000100. But IBM 370 computers (which are newer than IBM 360 computers) don't bother with Ascii: they stick strictly with EBCDIC.

80-column IBM cards use **Hollerith code**, which resembles EBCDIC but has 12 bits instead of 8. 96-column IBM cards use a 6-bit code that's an abridgement of Hollerith code.

Here's a program written in old Basic:

```
10 IF "9"<"A" THEN 100
20 PRINT "CAT"
30 STOP
100 PRINT "DOG"
110 END
```

Which will the computer print: CAT or DOG? The answer depends on whether the computer uses Ascii or EBCDIC.

Suppose the computer uses 7-bit Ascii. Then the code for "9" is hexadecimal 39, and the code for "A" is hexadecimal 41. Since 39 is less than 41, the computer considers "9" to be less than "A", so the computer prints DOG.

But if the computer uses EBCDIC instead of Ascii, the code for "9" is hexadecimal F9, and the code for "A" is hexadecimal C1; since F9 is greater than C1, the computer considers "9" to be greater than "A", so the computer prints CAT.

Bytes

A **byte** usually means: eight bits. For example, here's a byte: 10001011.

For computers that use 7-bit Ascii, programmers sometimes define a byte to be 7 bits instead of 8. For computers that use 6-bit Ascii, programmers sometimes define a byte to be 6 bits. So if someone tries to sell you a computer whose memory can hold "16,000 bytes", he probably means 16,000 8-bit bytes, but might mean 7-bit bytes or 6-bit bytes.

Nibbles

A **nibble** is 4 bits. It's half of an 8-bit byte. Since a hexadecimal digit stands for 4 bits, **a hexadecimal digit stands for a nibble**.

Sexy assembler

In this chapter, you'll learn the fundamental concepts of assembly language, quickly and easily.

Unfortunately, different CPUs have different assembly languages.

I've invented an assembly language that combines the best features of all the other assembly languages. My assembly language is called **Sexy Ass**, because it's a **S**imple, **Ex**cellent, **Y**ummy **Ass**embler.

After you study the mysteries of the Sexy Ass, you can easily get your rear in gear and become the dominant master of the assemblers sold for IBM, Apple, and competitors. Mastering them will become so easy that you'll say, "Assembly language is a piece of cheesecake!"

Bytes in my ASS

Let's get a close-up view of the Sexy Ass....

CPU registers The computer's guts consist of two main parts: the brain (which is called the **CPU**) and the **main memory** (which consists of RAM and ROM).

Inside the CPU are many electronic boxes, called **registers**. Each register holds several electrical signals; each signal is called a **bit**; so each register holds several bits. Each bit is either 1 or 0.

> A "1" represents a high voltage; a "0" represents a low voltage.
> If the bit is 1, the bit is said to be **high** or **on** or **set** or **true**.
> If the bit is 0, the bit is said to be **low** or **off** or **cleared** or **false**.

The CPU's most important register is called the **accumulator (A)**. In the Sexy Ass system, the accumulator consists of 8 bits, which is 1 byte. (Later, I'll explain how to make the CPU handle several bytes simultaneously; but the accumulator itself holds just 1 byte.)

Memory locations Like the CPU, the main memory consists of electronic boxes. The electronic boxes *in the CPU* are called **registers**, but the electronic boxes *in the main memory* are called **memory locations** instead. Because the main memory acts like a gigantic post office, the memory locations are also called **addresses**. In the Sexy Ass system, each memory location holds 1 byte. There are many *thousands* of memory locations; they're numbered 0, 1, 2, 3, etc.

Number systems When using Sexy Ass, you can type numbers in decimal, binary, or hexadecimal. (For Sexy Ass, octal isn't useful.) For example, the number "twelve" is written "12" in decimal, "1100" in binary, and "C" in hexadecimal. To indicate which number system you're using, **put a percent sign in front of each binary number, and put a dollar sign in front of each hexadecimal number.** For example, in Sexy Ass you can write the number "twelve" as either 12 or %1100 or $C. (In that respect, Sexy Ass copies the 6502 assembly language, which also uses the percent sign and the dollar sign.)

Most of the time, we'll be using hexadecimal, so let's quickly review what hexadecimal is all about. **To count in hexadecimal, just start counting as you learned in elementary school** ($1, $2, $3, $4, $5, $6, $7, $8, $9); **but after $9, you continue counting by using the letters of the alphabet** ($A, $B, $C, $D, $E, and $F). **After $F (which is fifteen), you say $10** (which means sixteen), then say $11 (which means seventeen), then $12, then $13, then $14, etc., until you reach $19; then come $1A, $1B, $1C, $1D, $1E, and $1F. Then come $20, $21, $22, etc., up to $29, then $2A, $2B, $2C, $2D, $2E, $2F, $30. Eventually, you get up to $99, then $9A, $9B, $9C, $9D, $9E, and $9F. Then come $A0, $A1, $A2, etc., up to $AF. Then come $B0, $B1, $B2, etc., up to $BF. You continue that pattern, until you reach $FF. Get together with your friends, and try counting up to $FF. (Don't bother pronouncing the dollar signs.) Yes, you too can count like a pro!

Since each hexadecimal digit represents 4 bits, an 8-bit byte requires *two* hexadecimal digits. So a byte can be anything from $00 to $FF.

Main segment I said the main memory consists of *thousands* of memory locations, numbered 0, 1, 2, etc. The main memory's most important part is called the **main memory bank** or **main segment**: that part consists of 65,536 memory locations (64K), which are numbered from 0 to 65,535. Programmers usually number them in hexadecimal; the hexadecimal numbers go from $0000 from $FFFF. ($FFFF in hexadecimal is the same as 65,535 in decimal.) Later, I'll explain how to use other parts of the memory; but for now, let's restrict our attention to just 64K main segment.

How to copy a byte Here's a simple, one-line program, written in the SEXY ASS assembly language:

```
    LOAD    $7000
```

It makes the computer copy one byte, from memory location $7000 to the accumulator. So after the computer obeys that instruction, the accumulator will contain the same data as the memory location. For example, if the memory location contains the byte %01001111 (which can also be written as $4F), so will the accumulator.

Notice the wide space before and after the word LOAD. To make the wide space, press the TAB key.

The word LOAD tells the computer to copy from a memory location to the accumulator. The opposite of the word LOAD is the word STORE: it tells the computer to copy from the accumulator to a memory location. For example, if you type —

```
    STORE   $7000
```

the computer will copy a byte from the accumulator to memory location $7000.

Problem: write an assembly-language program that copies a byte from memory location $7000 to memory location $7001. Solution: you must do it in two steps. First, copy from memory location $7000 to the accumulator (by using the word LOAD); then copy from the accumulator to memory location $7001 (by using the word STORE). Here's the program:

```
    LOAD    $7000
    STORE   $7001
```

Arithmetic

If you say —

```
        INC
```

the computer will **increment** (increase) the number in the accumulator, by adding 1 to it. For example, if the accumulator contains the number $25, and you then say INC, the accumulator will contain the number $26. For another example, if the accumulator contains the number $39, and you say INC, the accumulator will contain the number $3A (because, in hexadecimal, after 9 comes A).

Problem: write a program that increments the number that's in location $7000; for example, if location $7000 contains $25, the program should change that data, so that location $7000 contains $26 instead. Solution: copy the number from location $7000 to the accumulator, then increment the number, then copy it back to location $7000....

```
        LOAD    $7000
        INC
        STORE   $7000
```

That example illustrates the fundamental rule of assembly-language programming, which is: **to manipulate a memory location's data, copy the data to the accumulator, manipulate the accumulator, and then copy the revised data from the accumulator to memory.**

The opposite of INC is DEC: it **decrements** (decreases) the number in the accumulator, by subtracting 1 from it.

If you say —

```
        ADD     $7000
```

the computer will change the number in the accumulator, by adding to it the number that was in memory location $7000. For example, if the accumulator had contained the number $16, and memory location $7000 had contained the number $43, the number in the accumulator will change and become the sum, $59. The number in memory location $7000 will remain unchanged: it will still be $43.

Problem: find the sum of the numbers in memory locations $7000, $7001, and $7002, and put that sum into memory location $7003. Solution: copy the number from memory location $7000 to the accumulator, then add to the accumulator the numbers from memory locations $7001 and $7002, so that the accumulator to memory location $7003....

```
        LOAD    $7000
        ADD     $7001
        ADD     $7002
        STORE   $7003
```

The opposite of ADD is SUB, which means SUBtract. If you say SUB $7000, the computer will change the number in the accumulator, by subtracting from it the number in memory location $7000.

Immediate addressing

If you say —

```
        LOAD    #$25
```

the computer will put the number $25 into the accumulator. The $25 is the data. In the instruction "LOAD #$25", the symbol "#" tells the computer that the $25 is the data instead of being a memory location.

If you were to omit the #, the computer would assume the $25 meant memory location $0025, and so the computer would copy data from memory location $0025 to the accumulator.

An instruction that contains the symbol # is said to be an **immediate** instruction; it is said to use **immediate** addressing. Such instructions are unusual.

The more usual kind of instruction, which does *not* use the symbol #, is called a **direct** instruction.

Problem: change the number in the accumulator, by adding $12 to it. Solution:

```
        ADD     #$12
```

Problem: change the number in memory location $7000, by adding $12 to that number. Solution: copy the number from memory location $7000 to the accumulator, add $12 to it, and then copy the sum back to the memory location....

```
        LOAD    $7000
        ADD     #$12
        STORE   $7000
```

Problem: make the computer find the sum of $16 and $43, and put the sum into memory location $7000. Solution: put $16 into the accumulator, add $43 to it, and then copy from the accumulator to memory location $7000....

```
        LOAD    #$16
        ADD     #$43
        STORE   $7000
```

Video RAM

The video RAM is part of the computer's RAM and holds a copy of what's on the screen.

For example, suppose you're running a program that analyzes taxicabs, and the screen (of your TV or monitor) shows information about various cabs. If the upper-left corner of the screen shows the word CAB, the video RAM contains the Ascii code numbers for the letters C, A, and B. Since the Ascii code number for C is 67 (which is $43), and the Ascii code number for A is 65 (which is $41), and the Ascii code number for B is 66 (which is $42), the video RAM contains $43, $41, and $42. The $43, $41, and $42 represent the word CAB.

Suppose that the video RAM begins at memory location $6000. If the screen's upper-left corner shows the word CAB, memory location $6000 contains the code for C (which is $43); the next memory location ($6001) contains the code for A (which is $41); and the next memory location ($6002) contains the code for B (which is $42).

Problem: assuming that the video RAM begins at location $6000, make the computer write the word CAB onto the screen's upper-left corner. Solution: write $43 into memory location $6000, write $41 into memory location $6001, and write $42 into memory location $6002....

```
        LOAD    #$43
        STORE   $6000
        LOAD    #$41
        STORE   $6001
        LOAD    #$42
        STORE   $6002
```

The computer knows that $43 is the code number for "C". When you're writing that program, if you're too lazy to figure out the $43, you can simply write "C"; the computer will understand. So you can write the program like this:

```
        LOAD    #"C"
        STORE   $6000
        LOAD    #"A"
        STORE   $6001
        LOAD    #"B"
        STORE   $6002
```

That's the solution if the video RAM begins at memory location $6000. On *your* computer, the video RAM might begin at a different memory location instead. To find out about *your* computer's video RAM, look at the back of the technical manual that came with your computer. There you'll find a **memory map**: it shows which memory locations are used by the video RAM, which memory locations are used by other RAM, and which memory locations are used by the ROM.

Flags

The CPU contains **flags**. Here's how they work.

Carry flag A byte consists of 8 bits. The smallest number you can put into a byte is %00000000. The largest number you can put into a byte is %11111111, which in hexadecimal is $FF; in decimal, it's 255.

What happens if you try to go higher than %11111111? To find out, examine this program:

```
LOAD    #%10000001
ADD     #%10000010
```

In that program, the top line puts the binary number %10000001 into the accumulator. The next line tries to add %10000010 to the accumulator. But **the sum, which is %100000011, contains 9 bits instead of 8, and therefore can't fit into the accumulator.**

The computer splits that sum into two parts: the left bit (1) and the remaining bits (00000011). The left bit (1) is called the carry bit; the remaining bits (00000011) are called the **tail**. Since the tail contains 8 bits, it fits nicely into the accumulator; so the computer puts it into the accumulator. **The carry bit is put into a special place inside the CPU; that special place is called the carry flag.**

So that program makes the accumulator become 00000011, and makes the carry flag become 1.

Here's an easier program:

```
LOAD    #%1
ADD     #%10
```

The top line puts %1 into the accumulator; so the accumulator's 8 bits are %00000001. The bottom line adds %10 to the number in the accumulator; so the accumulator's 8 bits become %00000011. Since the numbers involved in that addition were so small, there was no need for a 9th bit — no need for a carry bit. To emphasize that no carry bit was required, the carry flag automatically becomes 0.

Here's the rule: if an arithmetic operation (such as ADD, SUB, INC, or DEC) gives a result that's too long to fit into 8 bits, the carry flag becomes 1; otherwise, the carry flag becomes 0.

Negatives The largest number you can fit into a byte %11111111, which in decimal is 255. Suppose you try to add 1 to it. The sum is %100000000, which in decimal is 256. But since %100000000 contains 9 bits, it's too long to fit into a byte. So the computer sends the leftmost bit (the 1) to the carry flag, and puts the tail (the 00000000) into the accumulator. As a result, the accumulator contains 0.

So in assembly language, if you tell the computer to do %11111111+1 (which is 255+1), the accumulator says the answer is 0 (instead of 256).

In assembly language, %11111111+1 is 0. In other words, %11111111 solves the equation x+1=0.

According to high school algebra, the equation x+1=0 has this solution: x=-1. But we've seen that in the assembly language, the equation x+1=0 has the solution x=%11111111. Conclusion: in assembly language, -1 is the same as %11111111.

Now you know that -1 is the same as %11111111, which is 255. Yes, -1 is the same as 255. Similarly, -2 is the same as 254; -3 is the same as 253; -4 is the same as 252. Here's the general formula: -n is the same as 256-n. (That's because 256 is the same as 0.)

%11111111 is 255 and is also -1. Since -1 is a shorter name than 255, we say that %11111111 is *interpreted as* -1. Similarly, %11111110 is 254 and also -2; since -2 is a shorter name than 254, we say that %11111110 is interpreted as -2. At the other extreme, %00000010 is 2 and is also -254; since 2 is a shorter name than -254, we say that %11111110 is interpreted as 2. Here's the rule: if a number is "almost" 256, it's interpreted as a negative number; otherwise, it's interpreted as a positive number.

How high must a number be, in order to be "almost" 256, and therefore to be interpreted as a negative number? The answer is: if the number is at least 128, it's interpreted as a negative number. Putting it another way, if the number's leftmost bit is 1, it's interpreted as a negative number.

That strange train of reasoning leads to this definition: **a negative number is a byte whose leftmost bit is 1**.

A byte's leftmost bit is therefore called the **negative bit** or the **sign bit**.

Flag register You've seen that the CPU contains a register called the **accumulator**. The CPU also contains a second register, called the **flag register**. In the Sexy Ass system, the flag register contains 8 bits (one byte). Each of the 8 bits in the flag register is called a **flag**; so the flag register contains 8 flags.

Each flag is a bit: it's either 1 or 0. If the flag is 1, the flag is said to be **up** or **raised** or **set**. If the flag is 0, the flag is said to be **down** or **lowered** or **cleared**.

One of the 8 flags is the carry flag: it's raised (becomes 1) whenever an arithmetic operation requires a 9th bit. (It's lowered whenever an arithmetic operation does *not* require a 9th bit.)

Another one of the flags is **the negative flag: it's raised whenever the number in the accumulator becomes negative**. For example, if the accumulator becomes %11111110 (which is -2), the negative flag is raised (i.e. the negative flag becomes 1). It's lowered whenever the number in the accumulator becomes *non*-negative.

Another one of the flags is **the zero flag: it's raised whenever the number in the accumulator becomes zero**. (It's lowered whenever the number in the accumulator becomes *non*-zero.)

Jumps

You can give each line of your program a name. For example, you can give a line the name FRED. To do so, put the name FRED at the beginning of the line, like this:

```
FRED    LOAD    $7000
```

The line's name (FRED) is at the left margin. The command itself (LOAD $7000) is indented by pressing the TAB key. In that line, FRED is called the **label**, LOAD is called the **operation** or **mnemonic**, and $7000 is called the **address**.

Languages such as BASIC let you say "GO TO". **In assembly language, you say "JUMP" instead of "GO TO".** For example, to make the computer GO TO the line named FRED, say:

```
JUMP    FRED
```

The computer will obey: it will JUMP to the line named FRED.

You can say —

```
JUMPN    FRED
```

That means: JUMP to FRED, if the Negative flag is raised. So the computer will JUMP to FRED if a negative number was recently put into the accumulator. (If a *non*-negative number was recently put into the accumulator, the computer will *not* jump to FRED.)

JUMPN means "JUMP if the Negative flag is raised." JUMPC means "JUMP if the Carry flag is raised." JUMPZ means "JUMP if the Zero flag is raised."

JUMPNL means "JUMP if the Negative flag is Lowered." JUMPCL means "JUMP if the Carry flag is Lowered." JUMPZL means "JUMP if the Zero flag is Lowered."

Problem: make the computer look at memory location $7000; if the number in that memory location is negative, make the computer jump to a line named FRED. Solution: copy the number from memory location $7000 to the accumulator, to influence the Negative flag; then JUMP if Negative....

```
LOAD     $7000
JUMPN    FRED
```

Problem: make the computer look at memory location $7000. If the number in that memory location is negative, make the computer print a minus sign in the upper-left corner of the screen; if the number is positive instead, make the computer print a plus sign instead; if the number is zero, make the computer print a zero. Solution: copy the number from memory location $7000 to the accumulator (by saying LOAD); then analyze that number (by using JUMPN and JUMPZ); then LOAD the Ascii code number for either "+" or "-" or "0" into the accumulator (whichever is appropriate); finally copy that Ascii code number from the accumulator to the video RAM (by saying STORE)....

```
         LOAD     $7000
         JUMPN    NEGAT
         JUMPZ    ZERO
         LOAD     #"+"
         JUMP     DISPLAY
NEGAT    LOAD     #"-"
         JUMP     DISPLAY
ZERO     LOAD     #"0"
DISPLAY  STORE    $6000
```

Machine language

I've been explaining assembly language. **Machine language** resembles assembly language; what's the difference?

To find out, let's look at a machine language called **Sexy Macho** (because it's a **S**imple, **Ex**cellent, **Y**ummy **Mach**ine-language **O**riginal).

Sexy Macho resembles Sexy Ass; here are the main differences....

In Sexy Ass assembly language, you use words such as LOAD, STORE, INC, DEC, ADD, SUB, and JUMP. Those words are called *operations* or *mnemonics*. In Sexy Macho machine language, you replace those words by code numbers: the code number for LOAD is 1; the code number for STORE is 2; INC is 3; DEC is 4; ADD is 5; SUB is 6; and JUMP is 7. The code numbers are called the **operation codes** or **op codes**.

In Sexy Ass assembly language, the symbol "#" indicates immediate addressing; a lack of the symbol "#" indicates direct addressing instead. In Sexy Macho machine language, you replace the symbol "#" by the code number 1; if you want direct addressing instead, you must use the code number 0.

In Sexy Macho, all code numbers are hexadecimal.

For example, look at this Sexy Ass instruction:

```
ADD      #$43
```

To translate that instruction into Sexy Macho machine language, just replace each symbol by its code number. Since the code number for ADD is 5, and the code number for # is 1, the Sexy Macho version of that line is:

```
5143
```

Let's translate STORE $7003 into Sexy Macho machine language. Since the code for STORE is 2, and the code for direct addressing is 0, the Sexy Macho version of that command is:

```
207003
```

In machine language, you can't use words or symbols: you must use their code numbers instead. To translate a program from assembly language to machine language, you must look up the code number of each word or symbol.

An **assembler** is a program that makes the computer translate from assembly language to machine language.

The CPU understands just machine language: it understands just numbers. It does *not* understand assembly language: it does not understand words and symbols. **If you write a program in assembly language, you must buy an assembler, which translates your program from assembly language to machine language**, so that the computer can understand it.

Since assembly language uses English words (such as LOAD), assembly language seems more "human" than machine language (which uses code numbers). Since programmers are humans, programmers prefer assembly language over machine language. Therefore, the typical programmer writes in assembly language then uses an assembler to translate the program to machine language, which is the language that the CPU ultimately requires.

Here's how the typical assembly-language programmer works. First, the programmer types the assembly-language program and uses a word processor to help edit it. The word processor automatically puts the assembly-language program onto a disk. Next, the programmer uses the assembler to translate the assembly-language program into machine language. The assembler puts the machine-language version of the program onto the disk. So now the disk contains *two* versions of the program: the disk contains the original version (in assembly language) and also contains the translated version (in machine language). The original version (in assembly language) is called the **source code**; the translated version (in machine language) is called the **object code**. Finally, the programmer gives a command that makes the computer copy the machine-language version (the object code) from the disk to the RAM and run it.

Here's a tough question: how does the assembler translate "JUMP FRED" into machine language? Here's the answer....

The assembler realizes that FRED is the name for a line in your program. The assembler hunts through your program, to find out which line is labeled FRED. When the assembler finds that line, it analyzes that line, to figure out where that line will be in the RAM after the program is translated into machine language and running. For example, suppose the line that's labeled FRED will become a machine-language line which, when the program is running, will be in the RAM at memory location $2053. Then "JUMP FRED" must be translated into this command: "jump to the machine-language line that's in the RAM at memory location $2053". So "JUMP FRED" really means:

```
JUMP     $2053
```

Since the code number for JUMP is 7, and the addressing isn't immediate (and therefore has code 0 instead of 1), the machine-language version of JUMP FRED is:

```
702053
```

System software

The computer's main memory consists of RAM and ROM. In a typical computer, the first few memory locations ($0000, $0001, $0002, etc.) are ROM: they permanently contain a program called the **bootstrap**, which is written in machine language.

When you turn on the computer's power switch, the computer automatically runs the bootstrap program. If your computer uses disks, the bootstrap program makes the computer start reading information from the disk in the main drive. In fact, it makes the computer copy a machine-language program from the disk to the RAM. The machine-language program that it copies is called the **disk operating system (DOS)**.

After the DOS has been copied to the RAM, the computer starts running the DOS program. The DOS program makes the computer print a message on the screen (such as "Welcome to CP/M" or "Welcome to MS-DOS" or "Windows XP"), print a symbol on the screen (such as "A>" or a Start button), and then wait for you to give a command.

That whole procedure is called **bootstrapping** (or **booting up**), because of the phrase "pull yourself up by your own bootstraps". By using the bootstrap program, the computer pulls itself up to new intellectual heights: it becomes a CP/M machine or an MS-DOS machine or a Windows machine.

After booting up, you can start writing programs in Basic. But how does the computer understand the Basic words, such as PRINT, INPUT, IF, THEN, and GO TO? Here's how:

> While you're using Basic, the computer is running a machine-language program, that makes the computer *seem* to understand Basic. That machine-language program, which is in the computer's ROM or RAM, is called the **Basic language processor** or **Basic interpreter**. If your computer uses **Microsoft** Basic, the Basic interpreter is a machine-language program that was written by Microsoft Incorporated.

How assemblers differ

In a microcomputer, the CPU is a single chip, called the **microprocessor**. The most popular microprocessors are the **8088**, the **68000**, and the **6502**.

The **8088**, designed by Intel, hides in the IBM PC and clones. (The plain version is called the 8088; a souped-up version, called the **80286**, is in the IBM PC AT.)

The **68000**, designed by Motorola, hides in the computers that rely on mice: the Apple Mac, Commodore Amiga, and Atari ST. (The plain version is called the 68000; a souped-up version, called the **68020**, is in the Mac 2; an even fancier version, called the **68030**, is in fancier Macs.)

The **6502**, designed by MOS Technology (which has become part of Commodore), hides in old-fashioned cheap computers: the Apple 2 family, the Commodore 64 & 128, and the Atari XL & XE.

Let's see how their assemblers differ from Sexy Ass.

Number systems Sexy Ass assumes all numbers are written in the decimal system, unless preceded by a dollar sign (which means hexadecimal) or percent sign (which means binary).

68000 and 6502 assemblers resemble Sexy Ass, except they don't understand percent signs and binary notation. Some stripped-down 6502 assemblers don't understand the decimal system either: they require all numbers to be in hexadecimal.

The 8088 assembler comes in two versions:

> The full version of the 8088 assembler is called the **M**icrosoft Macro **As**sembler **(Masm)**. It lists for $150, but discount dealers sell it for just $83. It assumes all numbers are written in the decimal system, unless followed by an H (which means hexadecimal) or B (which means binary). For example, the number twelve can be written as 12 or as 0CH or as 1100B. It requires each number to begin with a digit: so to say twelve in hexadecimal, instead of saying CH you must say 0CH.

> A stripped-down 8088 assembler, called the **Debug mini-assembler**, is part of Dos; so you get it at no extra charge when you buy Dos. It requires all numbers to be written in hexadecimal. For example, it requires the number twelve to be written as C. Do *not* put a dollar sign or H next to the C.

Accumulator Each microprocessor contains *several* accumulators, so you must say *which* accumulator to use. The main 8-bit accumulator is called "A" in the 6502, "AL" in the 8088, and "D0.B" in the 68000.

Labels Sexy Ass and the other full assemblers let you begin a line with a label, such as FRED. For the 8088 full assembler (Masm), add a colon after FRED. Mini-assemblers (such as 8088 Debug) don't understand labels.

Commands Here's how to translate from Sexy Ass to the popular assemblers:

Computer's action	Sexy Ass	6502	68000	8088 Masm
put 25 in accumulator	LOAD #$25	LDA #$25	MOVE.B #$25,D0	MOV AL,25H
copy location 7000 to accumulator	LOAD $7000	LDA $7000	MOVE.B $7000,D0	MOV AL,[7000H]
copy accumulator to location 7000	STORE $7000	STA $7000	MOVE.B D0,$7000	MOV [7000H],AL
add location 7000 to accumulator	ADD $7000	ADC $7000	ADD.B $7000,D0	ADD AL,[7000H]
subtract location 7000 from acc.	SUB $7000	SBC $7000	SUB.B $7000,D0	SUB AL,[7000H]
increment accumulator	INC	ADC #$1	ADDQ.B #1,D0	INC AL
decrement accumulator	DEC	SBC #$1	SUBQ.B #1,D0	DEC AL
put character C in accumulator	LOAD #"C"	LDA #'C	MOVE.B #'C',D0	MOV AL,"C"
jump to FRED	JUMP FRED	JMP FRED	JMP FRED	JMP FRED
jump, if negative, to FRED	JUMPN FRED	BMI FRED	BMI FRED	JS FRED
jump, if carry, to FRED	JUMPC FRED	BCS FRED	BCS FRED	JC FRED
jump, if zero, to FRED	JUMPZ FRED	BEQ FRED	BEQ FRED	JZ FRED
jump, if neg. lowered, to FRED	JUMPNL FRED	BPL FRED	BPL FRED	JNS FRED
jump, if carry lowered, to FRED	JUMPCL FRED	BCC FRED	BCC FRED	JNC FRED
jump, if zero lowered, to FRED	JUMPZL FRED	BNE FRED	BNE FRED	JNZ FRED

Notice that in 6502 assembler, each mnemonic (such as LDA) is 3 characters long.

To refer to an Ascii character, Sexy Ass and 8088 Masm put the character in quotes, like this: "C". 68000 assembler uses apostrophes instead, like this: 'C'. 6502 assembler uses just a single apostrophe, like this: 'C.

Instead of saying "jump if", 6502 and 68000 programmers say "branch if" and use mnemonics that start with B instead of J. For example, they use mnemonics such as BMI (which means "Branch if MInus"), BCS ("Branch if Carry Set"), and BEQ ("Branch if EQual to zero").

To make the 68000 manipulate a byte, put ".B" after the mnemonic. (If you say ".W" instead, the computer will manipulate a 16-bit word instead of a byte. If you say ".L" instead, the computer will manipulate long data containing 32 bits. If you don't specify ".B" or ".W" or ".L", the assembler assumes you mean ".W".)

8088 assemblers require you to put each memory location in brackets. So whenever you refer to location 7000 hexadecimal, you put the 7000H in brackets, like this: [7000H].

Debug

This chapter explains how to use the **Debug program**, which is part of MS-DOS and all Windows versions up through Windows Vista.

(Windows 7 does *not* include the Debug program. If you're using Windows 7, skip ahead to the next chapter.)

The Debug program helps you debug your software and hardware. It lets you type special debugger commands. It also lets you type commands in assembly language.

I'll explain the Debug version that's part of Windows XP and Windows Vista.

How to start

Click Start then "All Programs" then "Accessories" then "Command Prompt".

You see the Command Prompt window. Maximize it (by clicking the button next to its X), so it becomes as tall as the screen (though not as wide).

Press the Caps Lock key, so that everything you type will be capitalized.

You see the symbol ">". To the right of it, type the word DEBUG then press the Enter key.

Then computer will show a hyphen, like this:

```
-
```

After the hyphen, you can give any Debug command.

Registers

To see what's in the CPU registers, type an R after the hyphen, so your screen looks like this:

```
-R
```

When you press the Enter key after the R, the computer will print (onto your screen):

```
AX=0000  BX=0000  CX=0000  DX=0000
```

That means the main registers (which are called AX, BX, CX, and DX) each contain hexadecimal 0000. Then the computer will tell you what's in the other registers, which are called SP, BP, SI, DI, DS, ES, SS, CS, IP, and FLAGS. Finally, the computer will print a hyphen, after which you can type another command.

Editing the registers

To change what's in register BX, type RBX after the hyphen, so your screen looks like this:

```
-RBX
```

The computer will remind you of what's in register BX, by saying:

```
BX 0000
:
```

To change BX to hexadecimal 7251, type 7251 after the colon, so your screen looks like this:

```
:7251
```

That makes the computer put 7251 into register BX.

To see that the computer put 7251 into register BX, say:

```
-R
```

That makes the computer tell you what's in all the registers. It will begin by saying:

```
AX=0000  BX=7251  CX=0000  DX=0000
```

Experiment! Try putting different hexadecimal numbers into the registers! To be safe, use just the registers AX, BX, CX, and DX.

Segment registers

The computer's RAM is divided into **segments**. The **segment registers** (DS, ES, SS, and CS) tell the computer which segments to use.

Do *not* change the numbers in the segment registers! Changing them will make the computer use the wrong segments of the RAM and wreck your Dos and disks.

The CS register is called the **code segment** register. It tells the computer which RAM segment to put your programs in. For example, if the CS register contains the hexadecimal number 17A7, the computer will put your programs in segment number 17A7.

Mini-assembler

To use assembly language, type A100 after the hyphen, so your screen looks like this:

```
-A100
```

The computer will print the code segment number, then a colon, then 0100. For example, if the code segment register contains the hexadecimal number 17A7, the computer will print:

```
17A7:0100
```

Now you can type an assembly-language program!

For example, suppose you want to move the hexadecimal number 2794 to register AX and move 8156 to BX. Here's the assembly-language program:

```
MOV AX,2794
MOV BX,8156
```

Type that program. As you type it, the computer will automatically put a segment number and memory location in front of each line, so your screen will look like this:

```
17A7:0100 MOV AX,2794
17A7:0103 MOV BX,8156
17A7:0106
```

After the 17A7:0106, press the Enter key. The computer will stop using assembly language and will print a hyphen.

After the hyphen, type G=100 106, so your screen looks like this:

```
-G=100 106
```

That tells the computer to run your assembly-language program, going from location 100 to location 106, so the computer will start at location 100 and stop when it reaches memory location number 106.

After running the program, the computer will tell you what's in the registers. It will print:

```
AX=2794  BX=8156  CX=0000  DX=0000
```

It will also print the numbers in all the other registers.

Listing your program

To list your program, type U100 after the hyphen, so your screen looks like this:

```
-U100
```

The U stands for "Unassemble", which means "list". The computer will list your program, beginning at line 100. The computer will begin by saying:

```
17A7:0100 B89427      MOV    AX,2794
17A7:0103 BB5681      MOV    BX,8156
```

The top line consists of three parts. The left part (17A7:0100) is the address in memory. The right part (MOV AX, 2794) is the assembly-language instruction beginning at that address.

The middle part (B89427) is the machine-language translation of MOV AX,2794. That middle part begins with B8, which is the machine-language translation of MOV AX. Then comes 9427, which is the machine-language translation of 2794; notice how machine language puts the digits in a different order than assembly language.

The machine-language version, B89427, occupies three bytes of RAM. The first byte (address 0100) contains the hexadecimal number B8; the next byte (address 0101) contains the hexadecimal number 94; the final byte (address 0102) contains the hexadecimal number 27.

So altogether, the machine-language version of MOV AX,2794 occupies addresses 0100, 0101, and 0102. That's why the next instruction (MOV BX,8156) begins at address 0103.

After the computer prints that analysis of your program, the computer will continue by printing an analysis of the next several bytes of memory also. Altogether, the computer will print an analysis of addresses up through 011F. What's in those addresses depends on which program your computer was running before you ran this one.

Editing your program To edit line 0103, type:

```
-A103
```

Then type the assembly-language command you want for location 103.

When you finish the command and press the Enter key, the computer will give you an opportunity to edit the next line (106). If you don't want to edit or create a line 106, press the Enter key again.

After editing your program, list it (by typing U100), to make sure you edited correctly.

Arithmetic This assembly-language program does arithmetic:

```
MOV AX,7
ADD AX,5
```

To feed that program to the computer, say A100 after the hyphen, then type the program, then press the Enter key an extra time, then say G=100 106.

That program's top line moves the number 7 into the AX register. The next line adds 5 to the AX register, so the number in the AX register becomes twelve. In hexadecimal, twelve is written as C, so the computer will say:

```
AX=000C
```

The computer will also say what's in the other registers.

The opposite of ADD is SUB, which means subtract. For example, if you say —

```
SUB AX,3
```

the computer will subtract 3 from the number in the AX register, so the number in the AX register becomes smaller.

To add 1 to the number in the AX register, you can say:

```
ADD AX,1
```

For a short cut, say this instead:

```
INC AX
```

That tells the computer to INCrement the AX register, by adding 1.

To subtract 1 from the number in the AX register, you can say:

```
SUB AX,1
```

For a short cut, say this instead —

```
DEC AX
```

which means "DECrement the AX register".

Half registers A register's left half is called the **high part**. The register's right half is called the **low part**.

For example, if the AX register contains 9273, the register's high part is 92, and the low part is 73.

The AX register's high part is called "A high" or AH. The AX register's low part is called "A low" or AL.

Suppose the AX register contains 9273 and you say:

```
MOV AH,41
```

The computer will make AX's high part be 41, so AX becomes 4173.

Copying to memory Let's program the computer to put the hexadecimal number 52 into memory location 7000.

This command *almost* works:

```
MOV [7000],52
```

In that command, the brackets around the 7000 mean "memory location". That command says to move, into location 7000, the number 52.

Unfortunately, if you type that command, the computer will gripe, because the computer can't handle two numbers simultaneously (7000 and 52).

Instead, you split that complicated command into two simpler commands, each involving just one number. Instead of trying to move 52 directly into location 7000, first move 52 into a register (such as AL), then copy that register into location 7000, like this:

```
MOV AL,52
MOV [7000],AL
```

After running that program, you can prove the 52 got into location 7000, by typing:

```
-E7000
```

That makes the computer examine location 7000. The computer will find 52 there and print:

```
17A7:7000 52.
```

That means: segment 17A7's 7000th location contains 52.

If you change your mind and want it to contain 53 instead, type 53 after the period.

Next, press the Enter key, which makes the computer print a hyphen, so you can give your next Debug command.

Interrupt 21 Here's how to write an assembly-language program that prints the letter C on the screen.

The Ascii code number for "C" is hexadecimal 43. Put 43 into the DL register:

```
17A7:0100 MOV DL,43
```

The Dos code number for "screen output" is 2. Put 2 into the AH register:

```
17A7:0102 MOV AH,2
```

To make the computer use the code numbers you put into the DL and AH registers, tell the computer to do Dos interrupt subroutine #21:

```
17A7:0104 INT 21
```

So altogether, the program looks like this:

```
17A7:0100 MOV DL,43
17A7:0102 MOV AH,2
17A7:0104 INT 21
17A7:0106
```

To make the computer do that program, say G=100 106. The computer will obey the program, so your screen will say:

```
C
```

After running the program, the computer will tell you what's in all the registers. You'll see that DL has become 43 (because of line 100), AH has become 02 (because of line 102), and AL has become 43 (because INT 21 automatically makes the computer copy DL to AL). Then the computer will print a hyphen, so you can give another Debug command.

Instead of printing just C, let's make the computer print CCC. Here's how. Put the code numbers for "C" and "screen output" into the registers:

```
17A7:0100 MOV DL,43
17A7:0102 MOV AH,2
```

Then tell Dos to use those code numbers, three times:

```
17A7:0104 INT 21
17A7:0106 INT 21
17A7:0108 INT 21
17A7:010A
```

To run that program, say G=100 10A. The computer will print:

```
CCC
```

Jumps Here's how to make the computer print C repeatedly, so that the entire screen gets filled with C's.

Put the code numbers for "C" and "screen output" into the registers:

```
17A7:0100 MOV DL,43
17A7:0102 MOV AH,2
```

In line 104, tell DOS to use those code numbers:

```
17A7:0104 INT 21
```

To create a loop, jump back to line 104:

```
17A7:0106 JMP 104
```

Altogether, the program looks like this:

```
17A7:0100 MOV DL,43
17A7:0102 MOV AH,2
17A7:0104 INT 21
17A7:0106 JMP 104
17A7:0108
```

To run that program, say G=100 108. The computer will print C repeatedly, so the whole screen gets filled with C's. To abort the program, tap the Pause/Break key while holding down the Ctrl key. Exception: in Dos XP (which is part of Windows XP) and Dos Vista (which is part of Windows Vista), the Pause/Break key doesn't work, so do this instead: while holding down the Ctrl key, tap the C key.

Interrupt 20 I showed you this program, which makes the computer print the letter C:

```
17A7:0100 MOV DL,43
17A7:0102 MOV AH,2
17A7:0104 INT 21
17A7:0106
```

If you run that program by saying G=100 106, the computer will print C and then tell you what's in all the registers.

Instead of making the computer tell you what's in all the registers, let's make the computer say:

```
Program terminated normally
```

To do that, make the bottom line of your program say INT 20, like this:

```
17A7:0100 MOV DL,43
17A7:0102 MOV AH,2
17A7:0104 INT 21
17A7:0106 INT 20
17A7:0108
```

The INT 20 makes the computer print "Program terminated normally" and then end, without printing a message about the registers.

To run the program, just say G=100. You do *not* have to say G=100 108, since the INT 20 ends the program before the computer reaches 108 anyway. The program makes the computer print:

```
C
Program terminated normally
```

Strings This program makes the computer print the string "I LOVE YOU":

```
17A7:0100 MOV DX,109
17A7:0103 MOV AH,9
17A7:0105 INT 21
17A7:0107 INT 20
17A7:0109 DB "I LOVE YOU$"
17A7:0114
```

The bottom line contains the string to be printed: "I LOVE YOU$". Notice you must end the string with a dollar sign. In that line, the DB stands for Define Bytes.

Here's how the program works. The top line puts the string's line number (109) into DX. The next line puts 9, which is the code number for "string printing", into AH. The next line (INT 21) makes the computer use the line number and code number to do the printing. The next line (INT 20) makes the program print "Program terminated normally" and end.

When you run the program (by typing G=100), the computer will print:

```
I LOVE YOU
Program terminated normally
```

If you try to list the program by saying U100, the listing will look strange, because the computer can't list the DB line correctly. But even though the listing will look strange, the program will still run fine.

Saving your program After you've created an assembly-language program, you can copy it onto your hard disk. Here's how.

First, make sure the program ends by saying INT 20, so that the program terminates normally.

Next, invent a name for the program. The name should end in .COM. For example, to give your program the name LOVER.COM, type this:

```
-NLOVER.COM
```

Put 0 into register BX (by typing -RBX and then :0).

Put the program's length into register CX. For example, since the program above starts at line 0100 and ends at line 0114 (which is blank), the program's length is "0114 minus 0100", which is 14; so put 14 into register CX (by typing -RCX and then :14).

Finally, say -W, which makes the computer write the program onto the hard disk. The computer will say:

```
Writing 00014 bytes
```

Quitting

When you finish using Debug, tell the computer to quit, by typing a Q after the hyphen. When you press the Enter key after the Q, the computer will quit using Debug and show the DOS prompt (which includes the symbol ">"). Then give any DOS command you wish.

If you used assembly language to create a program called LOVER.COM, you can run it by just typing "LOVER" after that DOS prompt. Then computer will run the program and say:

```
I LOVE YOU
```

Then the computer will print the DOS prompt again, so you can give another DOS command.

Notice that the computer doesn't bother to print a message saying "Program terminated normally". (It prints that message just when you're in the middle of using Debug.)

Now you know how to write assembly-language programs. Dive in! Write your own programs!

Inside the CPU

Let's peek inside the CPU and see what lurks within!

Program counter

Each CPU contains a special register called the **program counter**.

The program counter tells the CPU which line of your program to do next. For example, if the program counter contains the number 6 (written in binary), the CPU will do the line of your program that's stored in the 6th memory location.

More precisely, here's what happens if the program counter contains the number 6:

A. The CPU moves the content of the 6th memory location to the CPU's **instruction register**. (That's called **fetching** the instruction.)

B. The CPU checks whether the instruction register contains a complete instruction written in machine language. If not — if the instruction register contains just *part* of a machine-language instruction — the CPU fetches the content of the 7th memory location also. (The instruction register is large enough to hold the content of memory locations 6 and 7 simultaneously.) If the instruction register still doesn't contain a complete instruction, the CPU fetches the content of the 8th memory location also. If the instruction register still doesn't contain a complete instruction, the CPU fetches the content of the 9th memory location also.

C. The CPU changes the number in the program counter. For example, if the CPU has fetched from the 6th and 7th memory locations, it makes the number in the program counter be 8; if the CPU has fetched from the 6th, 7th, and 8th memory locations, it makes the number in the program counter be 9. (That's called **updating the program counter**.)

D. The CPU figures out what the instruction means. (That's called **decoding** the instruction.)

E. The CPU obeys the instruction. (That's called **executing** the instruction.) If it's a "GO TO" type of instruction, the CPU makes the program counter contain the address of the memory location you want to go to.

After the CPU completes steps A, B, C, D, and E, it looks at the program counter and moves on to the next instruction. For example, if the program counter contains the number 9 now, the CPU does steps A, B, C, D, and E again, but by fetching, decoding, and executing the 9th memory location instead of the 6th.

The CPU repeats steps A, B, C, D, and E again and again; each time, the number in the program counter changes. Those five steps form a loop, called the **instruction cycle**.

Arithmetic/logic unit

The CPU contains two parts: the **control unit** (which is the boss) and the **arithmetic/logic unit (ALU)**. When the control unit comes to step D of the instruction cycle, and decides some arithmetic or logic needs to be done, it sends the problem to the ALU, which sends back the answer.

Here's what the ALU can do:

Operation's name	Example	Explanation
plus, added to, +	10001010 +10001001 100010011	add, but remember that 1+1 is 10 in binary
minus, subtract, -	10001010 -10001001 00000001	subtract, but remember that 10-1 is 1 in binary
negative, -, the two's complement of	-10001010 01110110	*left of the rightmost 1,* do this: replace each 0 by 1, and each 1 by 0
not, ~, the complement of, the one's complement of	~10001010 01110101	replace each 0 by 1, and each 1 by 0
and, &, ∧	10001010 ∧10001001 10001000	put 1 wherever both original numbers had 1
or, inclusive or, ∨	10001010 ∨10001001 10001011	put 1 wherever some original number had 1
eXclusive OR, XOR, ∨	10001010 ∨10001001 00000011	put 1 wherever the original numbers differ

Also, the ALU can shift a register's bits. For example, suppose a register contains 10111001. The ALU can shift the bits toward the right:

before	10111001
after	01011100

It can shift the bits toward the left:

before	10111001
after	01110010

It can rotate the bits toward the right:

before	10111001
after	11011100

It can rotate the bits toward the left:

before	10111001
after	01110011

It can shift the bits toward the right **arithmetically**:

before	10111001
after	11011100

It can shift the bits toward the left arithmetically:

before	10111001
after	11110010

Doubling a number is the same as shifting it left arithmetically. For example, doubling six (to get twelve) is the same as shifting six left arithmetically:

six	00000110
twelve	00001100

Halving a number is the same as shifting it right arithmetically. For example, halving six (to get three) is the same as shifting six right arithmetically:

six	00000110
three	00000011

Halving negative six (to get negative three) is the same as shifting negative six right arithmetically:

negative six	11111010
negative three	11111101

Using the ALU, the control unit can do operations such as:

A. Find the number in the 6th memory location, and move its negative to a register.

B. Change the number in a register, by adding to it the number in the 6th memory location.

C. Change the number in a register, by subtracting from it the number in the 6th memory location.

Most computers require each operation to have one source and one destination. In operations A, B, and C, the source is the 6th memory location; the destination is the register.

The control unit can*not* do a command such as "add together the number in the 6th memory location and the number in the 7th memory location, and put the sum in a register", because that operation would require two sources. Instead, you must give two shorter commands:

1. Move the number in the 6th memory location to the register.

2. Then add to that register the number in the 7th memory location.

Flags

The CPU contains a **flag register**, which comments on what the CPU is doing. In a typical CPU, the flag register has 6 bits, named as follows:

the Negative bit
the Zero bit
the Carry bit
the Overflow bit
the Priority bit
the Privilege bit

When the CPU performs an operation (such as addition, subtraction, shifting, rotating, or moving), the operation has a source and a destination. The number that goes into the destination is the operation's **result**. The CPU automatically analyzes that result.

Negative bit If the result is a negative number, the CPU turns on the **Negative bit**. In other words, it makes the Negative bit be 1. (If the result is a number that's *not* negative, the CPU makes the Negative bit be 0.)

Zero bit If the result is zero, the CPU turns on the **Zero bit**. In other words, it makes the Zero bit be 1.

Carry bit When the ALU computes the result, it also computes an extra bit, which becomes the **Carry bit**.

For example, here's how the ALU adds 7 and -4:

7 is	00000111
-4 is	11111100
binary addition gives	100000011
	Carry result

So the result is 3, and the Carry bit becomes 1.

Overflow bit If the ALU can't compute a result correctly, it turns on the **Overflow bit**.

For example, in elementary school you learned that 98+33 is 131; so in binary, the computation should look like this:

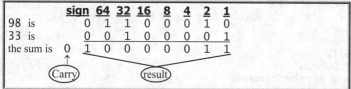

	128	**64**	**32**	**16**	**8**	**4**	**2**	**1**	
98 is		1	1	0	0	0	1	0	
33 is		1	0	0	0	0	0	1	
the sum is	1	0	0	0	0	0	1	1	, which is 131

But here's what an 8-bit ALU will do:

	sign	**64**	**32**	**16**	**8**	**4**	**2**	**1**
98 is	0	1	1	0	0	0	1	0
33 is	0	0	1	0	0	0	0	1
the sum is	0	1	0	0	0	0	1	1

(Carry) ⟵ ⟶ (result)

Unfortunately, the result's leftmost 1 is in the position marked **sign**, instead of the position marked 128; so the result looks like a negative number.

To warn you that the result is incorrect, the ALU turns on the Overflow bit. If you're programming in a language such as Basic, the interpreter or compiler keeps checking whether the Overflow bit is on; when it finds that the bit's on, it prints the word OVERFLOW.

Priority bit While your program's running, it might be interrupted. Peripherals might interrupt, in order to input or output the data; the **real-time clock** might interrupt, to prevent you from hogging too much time, and to give another program a chance to run; and the computer's sensors might interrupt, when they sense that the computer is malfunctioning.

When something wants to interrupt your program, the CPU checks whether your program has priority, by checking the **Priority bit**. If the Priority bit is on, your program has priority and cannot be interrupted.

Privilege bit On a computer that's handling several programs at the same time, some operations are dangerous: if your program makes the computer do those operations, the other programs might be destroyed. Dangerous operations are called **privileged instructions**; to use them, you must be a **privileged user**.

When you walk up to a terminal attached to a large computer, and type HELLO or LOGIN, and type your user number, the operating system examines your user number to find out whether you are a privileged user. If you are, the operating system turns on the Privilege bit. When the CPU starts running your programs, **it refuses to do privileged instructions unless the Privilege bit is on**.

Microcomputers omit the Privilege bit and can't prevent you from giving dangerous commands. But since the typical microcomputer has just one terminal, the only person your dangerous command can hurt is yourself.

Levels of priority & privilege Some computers have *several* levels of priority and privilege.

If your priority level is "moderately high", your program is immune from most interruptions, but not from all of them. If your privilege level is "moderately high", you can order the CPU to do most of the privileged instructions, but not all of them.

To allow those fine distinctions, large computers devote *several* bits to explaining the priority level, and *several* bits to explaining the privilege level.

Where are the flags? The bits in the flag register are called the **flags**. To emphasize that the flags comment on your program's status, people sometimes call them **status flags**.

In the CPU, the program counter is next to the flag register. Instead of viewing them as separate registers, some programmers consider them to be parts of a single big register, called the **program status word**.

Tests You can give a command such as, "Test the 3rd memory location". The CPU will examine the number in the 3rd memory location. If that number is negative, the CPU will turn on the Negative bit; if that number is zero, the CPU will turn on the Zero bit.

You can give a command such as, "Test the difference between the number in the 3rd register and the number in the 4th". The CPU will adjust the flags according to whether the difference is negative or zero or carries or overflows.

Saying "if" The CPU uses the flags when you give a command such as, "If the Negative bit is on, go do the instruction in memory location 6".

Speed

Computers are fast. To describe computer speeds, programmers use these words:

Word	Abbreviation	Meaning
millisecond	msec or ms	thousandth of a second; 10^{-3} seconds
microsecond	μsec or μs	millionth of a second; 10^{-6} seconds
nanosecond	nsec or ns	billionth of a second; 10^{-9} seconds
picosecond	psec or ps	trillionth of a second; 10^{-12} seconds

1000 picoseconds is a nanosecond; 1000 nanoseconds is a microsecond; 1000 microseconds is a millisecond; 1000 milliseconds is a second.

On page 669 I explained that the **instruction cycle** has five steps:

A. Fetch the instruction.
B. Fetch additional parts for the instruction.
C. Update the program counter.
D. Decode the instruction.
E. Execute the instruction.

To do that entire instruction cycle, an old-fashioned computer takes about a microsecond; a modern computer takes about a nanosecond. The exact time depends on the quality of the CPU, the quality of the main memory, and the difficulty of the instruction.

Here are 5 ways to make a computer act faster:

Method	Meaning
multiprocessing	The computer holds more than one CPU. (All the CPUs work simultaneously. They share the same main memory. The operating system decides which CPU works on which program. The collection of CPUs is called a **multiprocessor**.)
instruction lookahead	While the CPU is finishing an instruction cycle (by doing steps D and E), it simultaneously begins working on the next instruction cycle (steps A and B).
array processing	The CPU holds at least 16 ALUs. (All the ALUs work simultaneously. For example, when the control unit wants to solve 16 multiplication problems, it sends each problem to a separate ALU; the ALUs compute the products simultaneously. The collection of ALUs is called an **array processor**.)
parallel functional units	The ALU is divided into several functional units: an addition unit, a multiplication unit, a division unit, a shift unit, etc. All the units work simultaneously; while one unit is working on one problem, another unit is working on another.
pipeline architecture	The ALU (or each ALU functional unit) consists of a "first stage" and a "second stage". When the control unit sends a problem to the ALU, the problem enters the first stage, then leaves the first stage and enters the second stage. But while the problem is going through the second stage, a new problem starts going through the first stage. (Such an ALU is called a **pipeline processor**.)

Parity

Most large computers put an extra bit at the end of each memory location. For example, a memory location in the PDP-10 holds 36 bits, but the PDP-10 puts an extra bit at the end, making 37 bits altogether. The extra bit is called the **parity bit**.

If the number of ones in the memory location is even, the CPU turns the parity bit on. If the number of ones in the memory location is odd, the CPU turns the parity bit off.

For example, if the memory location contains these 36 bits —

000000000100010000001100000000000000

there are 4 ones, so the number of ones is even, so the CPU turns the parity bit on:

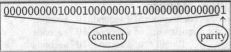

If the memory location contains these 36 bits instead —

000000000100010000000100000000000000

there are 3 ones, so the number of ones is odd, so the CPU turns the parity bit off:

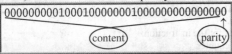

Whenever the CPU puts data into the main memory, it also puts in the parity bit. Whenever the CPU grabs data from the main memory, it checks whether the parity bit still matches the content.

If the parity bit doesn't match, the CPU knows there was an error, and tries once again to grab the content and the parity bit. If the parity bit disagrees with the content again, the CPU decides that the memory is broken, refuses to run your program, prints a message saying PARITY ERROR, and then sweeps through the whole memory, checking the parity bit of every location; if the CPU finds another parity error (in your program or anyone else's), the CPU shuts off the whole computer.

Cheap microcomputers (such as the Apple 2c and Commodore 64) lack parity bits, but the IBM PC has them.

UAL

Universal Assembly Language (UAL) is a notation I invented that makes programming in assembly language easier.

UAL uses these symbols:

Symbol	Meaning
M5	the number in the 5th memory location
R2	the number in the 2nd register
P	the number in the program counter
N	the Negative bit
Z	the Zero bit
C	the Carry bit
V	the oVerflow bit
PRIORITY	the PRIORITY bits
PRIVILEGE	the PRIVILEGE bits
F	the content of the entire flag register
F[5]	the 5th bit in the flag register
R2[5]	the 5th bit in R2
R2[LEFT]	the left half of R2; in other words, the left half of the data in the 2nd register
R2[RIGHT]	the right half of R2
M5 M6	long number whose left half is in 5th memory location, right half is in 6th location

Here are the UAL statements:

Statement	Meaning
R2=7	Let number in the 2nd register be 7 (by moving 7 into the 2nd register).
R2=M5	Copy the 5th memory location's contents into the 2nd register.
R2= = M5	Exchange R2 with M5. (Put 5th location's content into 2nd register and vice versa.)
R2=R2+M5	Change the integer in 2nd register, by adding to it the integer in 5th location.
R2=R2-M5	Change the integer in 2nd register, by subtracting the integer in 5th location.
R2=R2*M5	Change the integer in 2nd register, by multiplying it by integer in 5th location.
R2 REM R3=R2/M5	Change R2, by dividing it by the integer M5. Put division's remainder into R3.
R2=-M5	Let R2 be the negative of M5.
R2=NOT M5	Let R2 be the one's complement of M5.
R2=R2 AND M5	Change R2, by performing the AND operation.
R2=R2 OR M5	Change R2, by performing the OR operation.
R2=R2 XOR M5	Change R2, by performing the XOR operation.
SHIFTL R2	Shift left.
SHIFTR R2	Shift right.
SHIFTRA R2	Shift right arithmetically.
SHIFTR3 R2	Shift right, 3 times.
SHIFTR (R7) R2	Shift right, R7 times.
ROTATEL R2	Rotate left.
ROTATER R2	Rotate right.
TEST R2	Examine number in 2nd register, and adjust flag register's Negative and Zero bits.
TEST R2-R4	Examine the difference between R2 and R4, and adjust the flag register.
CONTINUE	No operation. Just continue on to the next instruction.
WAIT	Wait until an interrupt occurs.
IF R2<0, P=7	If the number in the 2nd register is negative, put 7 into the program counter.
IF R2<0, M5=3, P=7	If R2<0, do both of the following: let M5 be 3, and P be 7.

M5 can be written as M(5) or M(2+3). It can be written as M(R7), if R7 is 5 — in other words, if register 7 contains 5.

Addressing modes

Suppose you want the 2nd register to contain the number 6. You can accomplish that goal in one step, like this:

```
R2=6
```

Or you can accomplish it in two steps, like this:

```
M5=6
R2=M5
```

Or you can accomplish it in three steps, like this:

```
M5=6
M3=5
R2=M(M3)
```

Or you can accomplish it in an even weirder way:

```
M5=6
R3=1
R2=M(4+R3)
```

Each of those methods has a name. The first method (R2=6), which is the simplest, is called **immediate addressing**. The second method (R2=M5), which contains the letter M, is called **direct addressing**. The third method (R5=M(M3)), which contains the letter M twice, is called **indirect addressing**. The fourth method (R5=M(4+R3)), which contains the letter M and a plus sign, is called **indexed addressing**.

In each method, the 2nd register is the destination. In the last three methods, the 5th memory location is the source. In the fourth method, which involves R3, the 3rd register is called the **index register**, and R3 itself is called the **index**.

Each of those methods is called an **addressing mode**. So you've seen four addressing modes: immediate, direct, indirect, and indexed.

Program counter To handle the program counter, the computer uses other addressing modes instead.

For example, suppose P (the number in the program counter) is 2073, and you want to change it to 2077. You can accomplish that goal simply, like this:

```
P=2077
```

Or you can accomplish it in a weirder way, like this:

```
P=P+4
```

Or you can accomplish it in an even weirder way, like this:

```
R3=20
P=R3 77
```

The first method (P=2077), which is the simplest, is called **absolute addressing**.

The second method (P=P+4), which involves addition, is called **relative addressing**. The "+4" is the **offset**.

The third method (P=R3 77) is called **base-page addressing**. R3 (which is 20) is called the **page number** or **segment number**, and so the 3rd register is called the **page register** or **segment register**.

Intel's details

The first **microprocessor** (CPU on a chip) was invented by Intel in 1971 and called the **Intel 4004**. Its accumulator was so short that it held just 4 bits! Later that year, Intel invented the **Intel 8008**, whose accumulator held 8 bits. In 1973 Intel invented the **Intel 8080**, which understood more op codes, contained more registers, could handle more RAM (64K instead of 16K), and ran faster. Drunk on the glories of that 8080, Microsoft adopted the phone number VAT-8080, and the Boston Computer Society adopted the soberer phone number DOS-8080.

In 1978 Intel invented the **8086**, which had a 16-bit accumulator and handled even more RAM & ROM (totalling 1 megabyte). Out of the 8086 came 16 wires (called the **data bus**), which transmitted 16 bits simultaneously from the accumulator to other computerized devices, such as RAM and disks. Since the 8086 had a 16-bit accumulator and 16-bit data bus, Intel called it a **16-bit CPU**.

But computerists complained that the 8086 was impractical, since nobody had developed RAM, disks, or other devices for the 16-bit data bus yet. So in 1979 Intel invented the **8088**, which understands the same machine language as the 8086 but has an 8-bit data bus. To transmit 16-bit data through the 8-bit bus, the 8088 sends 8 of the bits first, then sends the other 8 bits shortly afterwards. That technique of using a few wires (8) to imitate many (16) is called **multiplexing**.

When 16-bit data buses later became popular, Intel invented a slightly souped-up 8086, called the **80286** (nicknamed the **286**).

Then Intel invented a 32-bit version called the **80386** (nicknamed **386**). Intel also invented a multiplexed version called the **386SX**, which understands the same machine language as the 386 but transmits 32-bit data through a 16-bit bus (by sending 16 of the bits first, then sending the other 16). The letters "SX" mean "SiXteen-bit bus". The original 386, which has a 32-bit bus, is called the **386DX**; the letters "DX" mean "Double the siXteen-bit bus".

Then Intel invented a slightly souped-up 386DX, called the **486**. It comes in two versions: the fancy version (called the **486DX**) includes a **math coprocessor**, which is circuitry that understands commands about advanced math; the stripped-down version (called the **486SX**) lacks a math coprocessor.

Finally, Intel invented a souped-up 486DX, called a **Pentium**.

Here's how to use the 8088 and 8086. (The 286, 386, 486, and Pentium include the same features plus more.)

Registers

The CPU contains fourteen 16-bit registers:

accumulator (AX), base register (BX), count register (CX), data register (DX)
flag register (which UAL calls F)
program counter (which UAL calls P but Intel calls "instruction pointer" or IP)
stack pointer (which UAL calls S but Intel calls SP), base pointer (BP)
source index (SI), destination index (DI)
code segment (CS), data segment (DS), stack segment (SS), extra segment (ES)

In each of those registers, the sixteen bits are numbered from right to left, so the rightmost bit is called **bit 0** and the leftmost bit is called **bit fifteen**.

The AX register's low-numbered half (bits 0 through 7) is called **A low** (or **AL**). The AX register's high half (bits 8 through fifteen) is called **A high (AH)**.

In the flag register, bit 0 is the carry flag (which UAL calls **C**), bit 2 is for parity, bit 6 is the zero flag (**Z**), bit 7 is the negative flag (which UAL calls **N** but Intel calls **sign** or **S**), bit eleven is the overflow flag (**V**), bits 4, 8, 9, and ten are special (**auxiliary carry**, **trap**, **interrupts**, and **direction**), and the remaining bits are unused.

Memory locations

Each memory location contains a byte. In UAL, the 6th memory location is called **M6** or **M(6)**. The pair of bytes M7 M6 is called **memory word 6**, which UAL writes as **MW(6)**.

Instruction set

This page shows the set of instructions that the 8088 understands. For each instruction, I've given the assembly-language mnemonic and its translation to UAL, where all numbers are hexadecimal.

The first line says that INC (which stands for INCrement) is the assembly-language mnemonic that means x=x+1. For example, INC AL means AL=AL+1.

The eighth line says that IMUL (which stands for Integer Multiply) is the assembly-language mnemonic that means x=x*y. For example, IMUL AX,BX means AX=AX*BX.

In most equations, you can replace the x and y by registers, half-registers, memory locations, numbers, or more exotic entities. To find out what you can replace x and y by, experiment!

For more details, read the manuals from Intel and Microsoft. They also explain how to modify an instruction's behavior by using flags, segment registers, other registers, and three **prefixes**: REPeat, SEGment, and LOCK.

Math

INCrement	x=x+1
DECrement	x=x-1
ADD	x=x+y
ADd Carry	x=x+y+C
SUBtract	x=x-y
SuBtract Borrow	x=x-y-C
MULtiply	x=x*y UNSIGNED
Integer MULtiply	x=x*y
DIVide	AX=AX/x UNSIGNED
Integer DIVide	AX=AX/x
NEGate	x=-x
Decimal Adjust Add	IF AL[RIGHT]>9, AL=AL+6
	IF AL[LEFT]>9, AL=AL+60
Decimal Adjust Subtr	IF AL[RIGHT]>9, AL=AL-6
	IF AL[LEFT]>9, AL=AL-60
Ascii Adjust Add	IF AL[RIGHT]>9, AL=AL+6, AH=AH+1
	AL[LEFT]=0
Ascii Adjust Subtract	IF AL[RIGHT]>9, AL=AL-6, AH=AH-1
	AL[LEFT]=0
Ascii Adjust Multiply	AH REM AL=AL/0A
Ascii Adjust Divide	AL=AL+(0A*AH)
	AH=0

Logic

AND	x=x AND y
OR	x=x OR y
XOR	x=x XOR y
CoMplement Carry	C=NOT C
SHift Left	SHIFTL(y) x
SHift Right	SHIFTR(y) x
Shift Arithmetic Right	SHIFTRA(y) x
ROtate Left	ROTATEL(y) x
ROtate Right	ROTATER(y) x
Rotate Carry Left	ROTATEL(y) C x
Rotate Carry Right	ROTATER(y) C x
CLear Carry	C=0
CLear Direction	DIRECTION=0
CLear Interrupts	INTERRUPTS=0
SeT Carry	C=1
SeT Direction	DIRECTION=1

SeT Interrupts	INTERRUPTS=1
TEST	TEST x AND y
CoMPare	TEST x-y
SCAn String Byte	TEST AL-M(DI); DI=DI+1-(2*DIRECTION)
SCAn String Word	TEST AX-MW(DI); DI=DI+2-(4*DIRECTION)
CoMPare String Byte	TEST M(SI)-M(DI)
	SI=SI+1-(2*DIRECTION)
	DI=DI+1-(2*DIRECTION)
CoMPare String Word	TEST MW(SI)-MW(DI)
	SI=SI+2-(4*DIRECTION)
	DI=DI+2-(4*DIRECTION)

Moving bytes

MOVe	x=y
Load AH from F	AH=F[RIGHT]
Store AH to F	F[RIGHT]=AH
Load register and DS	x=MW(y); DS=MW(y+2)
Load register and ES	x=MW(y); ES=MW(y+2)
LOaD String Byte	AL=M(SI); SI=SI+1-(2*DIRECTION)
LOaD String Word	AX=MW(SI); SI=SI+2-(4*DIRECTION)
STOre String Byte	M(DI)=AL; DI=DI+1-(2*DIRECTION)
STOre String Word	MW(DI)=AX; DI=DI+2-(4*DIRECTION)
MOVe String Byte	M(DI)=M(SI);
	DI=DI+1-(2*DIRECTION)
	SI=SI+1-(2*DIRECTION)
MOVe String Word	MW(DI)=MW(SI)
	DI=DI+2-(4*DIRECTION)
	SI=SI+2-(4*DIRECTION)
Convert Byte to Word	AH=-AL[7]
Convert Word to Dbl	DX=-AX[0F]
PUSH	S=S-2; MW(S)=x
PUSH F	S=S-2; MW(S)=F
POP	x=MW(S); S=S+2
POP F	F=MW(S); S=S+2
IN	x=PORT(y)
OUT	PORT(x)=y
ESCape	BUS=x
eXCHanGe	x= =y
XLATe	AL=M(BX+AL)
Load Effective Address	x=ADDRESS(y)

Program counter

JuMP	P=x
Jump if Zero	IF Z=1, P=x
Jump if Not Zero	IF Z=0, P=x
Jump if Sign	IF N=1, P=x
Jump if No Sign	IF N=0, P=x
Jump if Overflow	IF V=1, P=x
Jump if Not Overflow	IF V=0, P=x
Jump if Parity	IF PARITY=1, P=x
Jump if No Parity	IF PARITY=0, P=x
Jump if Below	IF C=1, P=x
Jump if Above or Eq	IF C=0, P=x
Jump if Below or Eq	IF C=1 OR Z=1, P=x
Jump if Above	IF C=0 AND Z=0, P=x
Jump if Greater or Eq	IF N=V, P=x
Jump if Less	IF N<>V, P=x
Jump if Greater	IF N=V AND Z=0, P=x
Jump if Less or Equal	IF N<>V OR Z=1, P=x
Jump if CX Zero	IF CX=0, P=x
LOOP	CX=CX-1; IF CX<>0, P=x
LOOP if Zero	CX=CX-1; IF CX<>0 AND Z=1, P=x
LOOP if Not Zero	CX=CX-1; IF CX<>0 AND Z=0, P=x
CALL	S=S-2; MW(S)=P; P=x
RETurn	P=MW(S); S=S+2
INTerrupt	S=S-6; MW(S)=P; MW(S+2)=CS;
	MW(S+4)=F; P=MW(4*x); CS=MW(4*x+2)
	INTERRUPTS=0; TRAP=0
INTerrupt if Overflow	IF V=1, S=S-6, MW(S)=P, MW(S+2)=CS,
	MW(S+4)=F, P=MW(10), CS=MW(12),
	INTERRUPTS=0, TRAP=0
Interrupt RETurn	P=MW(S); CS=MW(S+2); F=MW(S+4); S=S+6
No Operation	CONTINUE
HaLT	WAIT
WAIT	WAIT FOR COPROCESSOR

Computer life

To be a good manager, you should avoid the mistakes of the past, plan for the future, organize your thinking, and cut costs.

This section helps you accomplish all that. It analyzes "Our Past" and "Your Future". Its index helps you organize your thinking and find the info you want. Its coupons save you money on future purchases of *The Secret Guide to Computers*. Enjoy!

Our past

Here's how computers arose....

Ancient history

The first programmable computers were invented in the 1940's. Before then, people were stuck with the abacus, adding machine, and slide rule.

During the 1950's, 1960's, and 1970's, most computers used punched cards — whose history is weird. The cards were first used for *weaving tapestries*. Where the cards had holes, rods could move through the cards; those moving rods in turn made other rods move, which caused the threads to weave pictures. That machine was called the **Jacquard loom**.

Charles Babbage

Charles Babbage was a wild-eyed English mathematician who, in the 1800's, believed he could build a fancy computing machine. He convinced the British government to give him lots of money, then bilked the government for more. Many years later — and many British pounds later — he still hadn't finished his machine. So he dropped the idea and — can you believe this? — tried to build an even fancier machine. He didn't finish that one either. You might say his life was a failure that was expensive for the British government.

But Charlie (as I'll call him) is admired by all us computerniks (in spite of his face, which was even sterner than Beethoven's), because **he was the first person to realize that a computing machine must consist of 4 parts:**

an input device (he used a card reader)
a memory (which he called "The Store")
a central processing unit (which he called "The Mill")
an output device (he used a printer)

Lady Lovelace

Lady Lovelace was one of Charlie's great admirers, but he never noticed her until she translated his stuff. And boy, it was impossible for him not to notice her translations. Her "footnotes" to the translation were three times as long as what she was translating!

She got very intense. She wrote to Charlie, "I am working very hard for you — like the Devil in fact (which perhaps I am)."

The two became lovebirds, though he was old enough to be her dad. (By the way, her dad was Lord Byron, the poet. She was Lord Byron's only "official" daughter. His other daughters were out-of-wedlock.) Some people think she was actually brighter than Charlie, despite Charlie's fame. She was better at explaining Charlie's machines and their implications than Charlie was. **Some people have dubbed her "the world's first programmer".**

Stunning She stunned all the men she met. She was so bright and... a woman! Here's how the editor of The Examiner described her (note the pre-Women's-Lib language!):

"She was thoroughly original. Her genius, for genius she possessed, was not poetic, but metaphysical and mathematical. With an understanding thoroughly masculine in solidity, grasp, and firmness, Lady Lovelace had all the delicacies of the most refined female character. Her manners, tastes, and accomplishments were feminine in the nicest sense of the word; and the superficial observer would never have divined the strength and knowledge that lay hidden under the womanly graces. Proportionate to her distaste for the frivolous and commonplace was her enjoyment of true intellectual society. Eagerly she sought the acquaintance of all who were distinguished in science, art, and literature."

Mad Eventually, she went mad. Mattresses lined her room to prevent her from banging her head. Nevertheless, she died gruesomely, at the ripe young age of 36, the same age that her dad croaked. (I guess premature death was popular in her Devilish family.)

Who's the heroine? I wish feminists would pick a different heroine than Lady Lovelace. She was not the most important woman in the history of computing.

Far more important were Grace Hopper and Jean Sammet. In the 1950's Grace Hopper invented the first programming languages, and she inspired many of us programmers until her recent death. Jean Sammet headed the main committee that invented Cobol; she's the world's top expert on the history of programming languages, and she's been president of the computer industry's main professional society, the ACM.

Lady Lovelace was second-string to Babbage. Grace Hopper and Jean Sammet were second-string to nobody. Since Hopper was an Admiral in the Navy, she irked some of us doves; but whenever she stepped in front of an audience, she got a standing ovation because we all realize how crucial she was to the computer industry.

But I'm straying from my story....

Herman Hollerith

The U.S. Bureau of the Census takes its census every ten years. To tabulate the results of the 1880 census, the Bureau took *7 years*: they didn't finish until 1887. When they contemplated the upcoming 1890 census, they got scared; at the rate America was growing, they figured that tallying the 1890 census would take 12 years. In other words, the results of the 1890 census wouldn't be ready until 1902. So they held a contest to see whether anyone could invent a faster way to tabulate the data.

The winner was Herman Hollerith. **He was the first person to successfully use punched cards to process data.**

Hermie (as I'll call him) was modest. When people asked him how he got the idea of using punched cards, he had two answers. One was, "Trains": he had watched a train's conductor punch the tickets. His other, more interesting answer was, "Chicken salad". After saying "Chicken salad", he'd pause for you to ask the obvious question, "Why chicken salad?" Then he'd tell his tale:

One day, a girl saw him gulping down chicken salad. She said, "Oh, you like chicken salad? Come to my house. My mother makes excellent chicken salad." So he did. And her father was a head of the Census. (And he married the girl.)

By the way, Herman Hollerith hated one thing: spelling. In elementary school, he jumped out a second-story window, to avoid a spelling test.

In some versions of Fortran, every string must be preceded by the letter H. For example, instead of saying —

```
'DOG'
```

you must say:

```
3HDOG
```

The H is to honor Herman Hollerith.

The Census used Hollerith's punched-card system in 1890 and again in 1900.

> In 1910 the Census switched to a fancier system created by a Census Bureau employee, James Powers, who later quit his job and started his own company, which merged into **Remington-Rand-Sperry-Univac**. Meanwhile, Herman Hollerith's own company merged into **IBM**. That's how the first two computer companies began doing data processing.

World War II

The first programmable computers were invented in the 1940's because of World War II. They could have been invented sooner — most of the know-how was available several decades earlier — but you can't invent a computer unless you have big bucks for research. And the only organization that had big enough bucks was the Defense Department (which in those days was more honestly called the "War Department"). And the only event that was big enough to make the War Department spend that kind of money was World War II.

Of course, the Germans did the same thing. A German fellow, Konrad Zuse, built computers which in some ways surpassed the American ones. But since the Germans lost the war, you don't hear much about old Konrad anymore. Fortunately, throughout World War II the German military ignored what he was doing.

During the 1940's, most computers were invented at universities, usually funded by the War-Defense Department.

> Some of the most famous computers were the **Mark I** (at Harvard with help from IBM), the **Eniac** and the **Edvac** (both at the University of Pennsylvania), the **Whirlwind** (at the Massachusetts Institute of Technology, M.I.T.), and the **Ferranti Mark I** (at the University of Manchester, in England). Which of those computers deserves to be called "the first programmable computer"? The answer's up for grabs. Each of those machines had its own peculiar hang-ups and required years of debugging before working well.

Each of those computers was unique: no two were alike.

First generation (1951-1958)

The first computer to be mass-produced was the Univac I, in 1951. It was made by the same two guys (Eckert & Mauchly) who'd built the Eniac and Edvac at the University of Pennsylvania. (Mauchly was an instructor there, and Eckert was the graduate student who did the dirty work.) While others at the school were helping build the Edvac, Eckert & Mauchly left and formed their own company, which invented and started building the Univac. While building the Univac, the Eckert-Mauchly company merged into Remington Rand (which later merged into Sperry-Rand, which later merged into Unisys).

The Univac I was so important that historians call it the beginning of the "first generation". As for computers before Univac — historians disparagingly call them the "zeroth generation".

So the first generation began in 1951. It lasted through 1958. Altogether, from 1951 to 1958, 46 of those Univacs were sold.

46 might not sound like many. But remember: in those days, computers were very expensive, and could do very little. Another reason why just 46 were sold is that newer models came out, such as the Univac 1103, the Univac 80, and the Univac 90. But the biggest reason why only 46 of the Univac I were sold is IBM.

The rise of IBM Although IBM didn't begin mass-marketing computers until 1953 — two years after Univac — the IBM guys were much better salesmen, and soon practically everybody was buying from IBM. During the first generation, the hottest seller was the **IBM 650**. IBM sold hundreds and hundreds of them.

There were many smaller manufacturers too. People summarized the whole computer industry in one phrase: **IBM and the Seven Dwarfs**.

Who were the dwarfs? They kept changing. Companies rapidly entered the field — and rapidly left when they realized IBM had the upper hand. By the end of the first generation, IBM was getting 70% of the sales.

Primitive input and output During the first generation, there were no terminals. To program the Univac I, you had to put the program onto magnetic tape (by using a non-computerized machine), feed that tape to the computer, and wait for the computer to vomit another magnetic tape, which you had to run through another machine to find out what the tape said.

One reason why the IBM 650 became more popular was that it could read cards instead of tapes. It really liked cards. In fact, the answers came out on cards. To transfer the answers from cards to paper, you had to run the cards through a separate non-computerized machine.

Memory At the first generation's beginning, there were no RAM chips, no ROM chips, and no "core memory". Instead, the Univac's main memory was banks of liquid mercury, where the bits were stored as ultrasonic sound waves. It worked slowly and serially, so the access time ranged from 40 to 400 microseconds per bit.

Univac's manufacturer and IBM started playing around with a different kind of memory, called the Williams tube, which was faster (10 to 50 microseconds); but since it was less reliable, it didn't sell well.

In 1953, several manufacturers started selling computers that were much cheaper, because they used super-slow memory: it was a drum that rotated at 3600 rpm, giving an average access time of 17000 microseconds (17 milliseconds). (During the 1970's, some computers still used drums, but for *auxiliary* memory, not for *main* memory.) The most popular first generation computer, the IBM 650, was one of those cheap drum computers.

Eventually, computer manufacturers switched to a much better scheme, called **core memory**. It consists of tiny iron donuts strung on a grid of wires, whose electrical current magnetizes the donuts. Each donut is one bit and called a **core**. The donuts are strung onto the wire grid by hand, by women knitting.

> Core memory was first conceived in 1950. The first working models were built in 1953 at MIT and RCA, which argued with each other about who owned the patent. The courts decided in favor of MIT, so both RCA *and IBM* came out with core-memory computers. Core memory proved so popular that most computers used it through the 1970's, though in the 1980's RAM chips finally overshadowed it, since RAM chips don't require hiring knitters.

Languages During the first generation, computer programming improved a lot. During the early 1950's, all programs had to be written in **machine language**. In the middle 1950's, **assembly language** became available. By 1958, the end of the first generation, 3 major high-level languages had become available: **Fortran**, **Algol**, and **Apt**.

Fancy programs Programmers tried to make computers play a decent game of chess. All the attempts failed. But at IBM, Arthur Samuel had some luck with checkers:

He got his first checkers program working in 1952 and then continually improved it, to make it more and more sophisticated. In 1955, he rewrote it so that it learned from its own mistakes. In 1956, he demonstrated it on national TV. He kept working on it. Though it hadn't reached championship level yet, it was starting to look impressive.

Computer music scored its first big success in 1956, on the University of Illinois' Illiac computer:

Hiller & Isaacson made the Illiac compose its own music in a style that sounded pre-Bach. In 1957, they made the program more flexible, so that it produced many styles of more modern music. The resulting mishmash composition was dubbed "The Illiac Suite" and put on a phonograph record.

In 1954, IBM wrote a program that translated simple sentences from Russian to English. Work on tackling harder sentences continued — with too much optimism.

Second generation (1959-1963)

Throughout the first generation, each CPU was composed of vacuum tubes. Back in 1948, Bell Telephone had invented the transistor, and everybody realized that transistors would be better than vacuum tubes; but putting transistors into computers posed many practical problems that weren't solved for many years.

Finally, **in 1959, computer companies started delivering transistorized computers. That year marked the beginning of the second generation.** Sales of vacuum-tube computers immediately stopped.

All second-generation computers used core memory.

IBM The *first* company to make transistors for computers was Philco, but the most *popular* second-generation computer turned out to be the **IBM 1401**, because it was business-oriented and cheap.

IBM announced it in 1959 and began shipping it to customers in 1960.
Its core memory required 11½ microseconds per character. Each character consisted of 6 bits. The number of characters in the memory could range from 1.4K up to 16K. Most people rented the 1401 for about $8,000 per month, but you could spend anywhere from $4,000 to $12,000 per month, depending on how much memory you wanted, etc.

Altogether, IBM installed 14,000 of those machines.
IBM also installed 1,000 of a faster version, called the **1410**.

It required just 4½ microseconds per character, had 10K to 80K, and rented for $8,000 to $18,000 per month, typically $11,000.

Altogether, IBM produced six kinds of computers....

small business computers:	the 1401, 1410, 1440, and 1460
small scientific computers:	the 1620
medium-sized business computers:	the 7010
medium-sized scientific computers:	the 7040 and 7044
large business computers:	the 7070, 7074, and 7080
large scientific computers:	the 7090 and 7094

CDC Several employees left Remington-Rand-Sperry-Univac and formed their own company, called **Control Data Corporation (CDC)**. During the second generation, CDC produced popular scientific computers: the 1604, the 3600, and the 3800.

Software During the second generation, software improved tremendously.

The 3 major programming languages that had been invented during the first generation (Fortran, Algol, and Apt) were significantly improved. 6 new programming languages were invented: **Cobol**, **RPG**, **Lisp**, **Snobol**, **Dynamo**, and **GPSS**.

Programmers wrote advanced programs that answered questions about baseball, wrote poetry, tutored medical students, imitated three-person social interaction, controlled a mechanical hand, proved theorems in geometry, and solved indefinite integrals. The three most popular sorting methods were invented: the Shuffle Sort, the Shell Sort, and Quicksort.

Third generation's dawn (1964-1967)

The third generation began with a big bang, in 1964. Here's what happened in 1964, 1965, 1966, and 1967....

Families The first modern computer families were shipped. They were the **CDC 6600**, the **IBM 360**, and DEC's families (the **PDP-6**, **PDP-8**, and **PDP-10**).

Of those families, the CDC 6600 ran the fastest. The IBM 360 was the most flexible and was the only one that used integrated circuits (chips). The PDP-6 and PDP-10 were the best for timesharing. The PDP-8 was the cheapest.

Here are the dates:

CDC began shipping the CDC 6600 in 1964. IBM announced the IBM 360 in 1964 but didn't ship it until 1966. DEC began shipping the PDP-6 maxicomputer in 1964, the PDP-8 minicomputer in 1965, and the PDP-10 maxicomputer (a souped-up PDP-6) in 1967.

New languages IBM announced it would create **PL/I**, a new computer language combining Fortran, Cobol, Algol, and all other popular languages. It was designed especially for IBM's new computer, the 360. In 1966, IBM began delivering PL/I to customers.

Programmers invented the first successful languages for *beginners* using *terminals*. Those languages were **Basic**, **Joss**, and **APL**.

Dartmouth College invented the first version of **Basic** in 1964, and significantly improved it in 1966 and 1967.
The Rand Corporation invented **Joss** in 1964 for the Johnniac computer, and put an improved version (Joss II) on the PDP-6 in 1965. In the 1970's, three popular variants of Joss arose: a souped-up version (called Aid), a stripped-down version (Focal), and a business-oriented version (Mumps).
IBM completed the first version of **APL** in 1965 and put it on an IBM 7090. IBM wrote a better version of APL in 1966 and put it on an IBM 360. IBM began shipping APL to customers in 1967.

Stanford University invented the most popular language for statistics: **SPSS**.

Artificial intelligence Researchers calling themselves "experts in artificial intelligence" taught the computer to chat in ordinary English.

For example, Bertram Raphael made the computer learn from conversations, Daniel Bobrow made it use algebra to solve "story problems", The Systems Development Corporation made it know everything in an encyclopedia, General Electric made it answer military questions, Ross Quillian made it find underlying concepts, and Joe Weizenbaum made it act as a psychotherapist.

Also, Richard Greenblatt wrote the first decent chess program. It was good enough to play in championship tournaments against humans.

Era of boredom (1968-1974)

As you can see, the first three generations — up through 1967 — were exciting, full of action. But then, from 1968 to 1974, *nothing newsworthy happened.* That was the era of boredom.

During that era, progress was made, but it was gradual and predictable. Nothing dramatic happened.

Of course, nobody actually came out and said, "Life is boring." People phrased it more genteelly. For example, in September 1971 Robert Fenichel and Joe Weizenbaum wrote this introduction to *Scientific American*'s computer anthology:

"Partly because of the recent recession in the American economy, but more for reasons internal to the field, computer science has recently relaxed its pace. Work has not stopped, but that the current mood is one of consolidation can scarcely be doubted. Just a few years ago, computer science was moving so swiftly that even the professional journals were more archival than informative. This book could not then have been produced without great risk of misfocus. Today it's much easier to put the articles that constitute this book — even the most recent ones — into context."

Since the first generation had lasted eight years (1951-1958), and the second generation had lasted four years (1959-1963), people were expecting the third generation to last at most four years (1964-1967) and some kind of "fourth generation" to begin about 1968. But it never happened.

The only "major" announcement around then came in 1970, when IBM announced it would produce a new line of computers, called the **IBM 370**, which would make the IBM 360 obsolete. But to IBM's dismay, many computer centers decided to hang onto the old 360 instead of switching to the 370.

Since the 370's advantage over the 360 was small, not even IBM claimed the 370 marked a fourth generation. Computer historians, desperate for something positive to say about the 370, called it the beginning of the "late third generation", as opposed to the 360, which belonged to the "early third generation".

No consistency Unfortunately, in the entire history of computers, there was just one year all computer manufacturers acted together to produce something new. That year was 1959, when all manufacturers switched from vacuum tubes to transistors. Since 1959, we haven't had any consistency.

> Although the third generation began with a "big bang" in 1964, each manufacturer was banging on a different drum. IBM was proclaiming how great the IBM 360 would be because it would contain integrated circuits; but other manufacturers decided to ignore integrated circuits for several years, and concentrated on improving other aspects of the computer instead. For many years after the beginning of the third generation, CDC and DEC continued to use discrete transistors (a sign of the second generation) instead of integrated circuits.

Why? The era of boredom happened for 3 reasons:

> 1. The preceding years, 1964-1967, had been so successful that they were hard to improve on.
> 2. When the Vietnam War ended, the American economy had a recession, especially the computer industry, because it had depended on contracts from the Defense Department. In 1969, the recession hit bottom, and computer companies had to lay off many workers. In that year, General Electric gave up and sold its computer division to Honeywell. In 1971, RCA gave up too and sold its computer division to Remington-Rand-Sperry-Univac.
> 3. The world wasn't ready yet for "the era of personal computing", which began in 1975.

Quiet changes During the era of boredom, these changes occurred — quietly.…

In 1970, DEC began shipping the **PDP-11**.

> The PDP-8 and PDP-11 became the most popular minicomputers — far more popular than IBM's minicomputers. So in the field of minicomputers, IBM no longer had the upper hand.

Basic became the most popular language for the PDP-8 and PDP-11 and most other minicomputers (except IBM's, which emphasized RPG). In high schools and business schools, most of the introductory courses used Basic, instead of Fortran or Cobol.

Many businesses and high schools bought their own minicomputers, instead of renting time on neighbors' maxicomputers. The typical high-school computer class used a PDP-8. The richest high schools bought PDP-11's.

In universities, **the social sciences started using computers** — and heavily — to analyze statistics.

All new computer families used 8-bit bytes, so the each word's length was a multiple of 8 (such as 8, 16, 32, or 64).

> Most older computer families, invented before the era of boredom, had used 6-bit bytes, so the length of each word had been a multiple of 6: for example, the PDP-8 had a word of 12 bits; the PDP-10 , Univac 1100, and General Electric- Honeywell computers had a word of 36 bits; and the CDC 6600 had a word of 60 bits. The IBM 360 was the first computer to use 8-bit bytes instead of 6-bit; during the era of boredom, all manufacturers copied that feature from IBM.

CRT terminals (TV-like screens attached to keyboards) got cheaper, until they finally became as cheap as hard-copy terminals (which use paper).

> Most computer centers switched from hard-copy terminals to CRT terminals, because CRT terminals were quicker, quieter, and could do fancy editing. Also, many computer centers switched from "punched cards and keypunch machines" to CRT terminals.

Interest in new computer languages died. Most computer managers decided to stick with the old classics (Fortran and Cobol), because switching to a progressive language (such as PL/I) would require too much time to retrain the programmers and rewrite all the old programs.

> Programmers made two last-ditch attempts to improve Algol. The first attempt, called **Algol 68**, was too complicated to win popular appeal. The second attempt, called **Pascal**, eventually gained more support.

Maxicomputers were given **virtual core** — disks that pretend to be core, in case you're trying to run a program that's too large to fit into core.

Memory chips got cheaper, until they were finally cheaper than core. Most manufacturers switched from core to memory chips.

In 1971, **Intel** began shipping **the first microprocessor** (complete CPU on a chip).

> It was called the **4004** and had a word of just 4 bits. In 1972, Intel began shipping an improved version, the **8008**, whose word had 8 bits. In 1973, Intel began shipping an even better version, the **8080**.

Micro history

In 1975, the first popular microcomputer was shipped. It was called the **Altair** and was built by a company called **Mits**. It cost just $395.

> It was just a box that contained a CPU and very little RAM: just ¼ of a K!
> It included no printer, no disk, no tape, no ROM, no screen, and not even a keyboard! The only way to communicate with the computer was to throw 25 switches and watch 36 blinking lights.
> It didn't understand Basic or any other high-level computer language. To learn how to throw the switches and watch the blinking lights, you had to take a course in "machine language".
> You also had to take a course in electronics — because the $395 got you just a kit that you had to assemble yourself by using a soldering iron and reading electronics diagrams. Moreover, when you finished building the kit, you noticed some of the parts were missing or defective, so that you had to contact Mits for new parts.
> That computer contained several empty slots to hold PC cards. Eventually, many companies invented PC cards to put into those slots. Those PC cards, which were expensive, let you insert extra RAM and attach a printer, tape recorder, disk drives, TV, and terminal (keyboard with either a screen or paper).

Bill Gates invented a way to make the Altair handle Basic. He called his method **Microsoft Basic**. He patterned it after DEC's Basic; but he included extra features that exploited the Altair's ability to be "personal", and he eliminated features that would require too much RAM.

Gary Kildall invented a disk operating system that the Altair could use. He called that operating system **CP/M**.

Many companies built computers that imitated the Altair. Those imitations became more popular than the Altair itself. Eventually, the Altair's manufacturer (Mits) went out of business.

Computers that imitated the Altair were called **S-100 bus computers**, because they each used a Standard cable containing 100 wires.

In those days, the microcomputer industry was standardized. Each popular microcomputer used Microsoft Basic, CP/M, and the S-100 bus. The microcomputer was just a box containing PC cards; it had no keyboard, no screen, and no disk drive. A cable went from the microcomputer to a terminal, which was priced separately. Another cable went from the microcomputer to a disk drive, which was also priced separately.

Built-in Keyboards

In 1977, four companies began selling microcomputers that had built-in keyboards, so you didn't have to buy a terminal. Their computers became popular immediately. The four companies were **Processor Technology**, **Apple**, **Commodore**, and **Radio Shack**.

Processor Technology's computer was called the **Sol 20**, to honor Solomon Libes, an editor of Popular Electronics.

Apple's computer was called the **Apple 2**, because it improved on the Apple 1, which had lacked a built-in keyboard.

Commodore's computer was called the **Pet** (inspired by Pet Rocks).

Radio Shack's computer was called the **TRS-80**, because it was manufactured by Tandy's Radio Shack and contained a Z-80 CPU.

For a fully assembled computer, Processor Technology charged $1850, Apple charged $970, Commodore charged $595 (but quickly raised the price to $795), and Radio Shack charged $599 (but soon lowered the price to $499).

Notice that Commodore and Radio Shack had the lowest prices. Also, the low prices from Commodore and Radio Shack *included* a monitor, whereas the prices from Processor Technology and Apple didn't. So Commodore and Radio Shack were the real "bargains".

In those days, the cheapest computers were the most popular.

The cheapest and most popular computer was Radio Shack's.
The second cheapest and second most popular was Commodore's Pet.
The third cheapest and third most popular was the Apple 2.
Processor Technology, after a brief fling of popularity, went bankrupt.

The most expensive kind of microcomputer was the CP/M S-100 bus system. It was the oldest kind, so it had accumulated the most business software.

Improvements

In 1978 and 1979, the three main companies (Apple, Commodore, and Radio Shack) improved their computers.

The improved Apple 2 was called the **Apple 2-plus**. The improved Commodore Pet was called the **Commodore Business Machine (CBM)**. The improved Radio Shack TRS-80 was called the **TRS-80 model 2**.

After announcing the Apple 2-plus, Apple Computer Company stopped selling the plain Apple 2.

Commodore continued selling its old computer (the Pet) to customers who couldn't afford the new version (the CBM), which cost more. Likewise, Radio Shack continued selling its model 1 to customers who couldn't afford the model 2.

Texas Instruments & Atari

In 1979, Texas Instruments (TI) and Atari began selling microcomputers and priced them low.

TI's microcomputer was called the **TI 99/4**. Atari offered *two* microcomputers: the **Atari 400** and the **Atari 800**.

TI charged $1150. Atari charged $1000 for the regular model (the Atari 800) and $550 for the stripped-down model (the Atari 400).

TI's price included a color monitor. Atari's prices did *not* include a screen; you were to attach Atari's computers to your home's TV.

TI's computer was terrible, especially its keyboard. The Atari 800 computer was wonderful; reviewers were amazed at its easy-to-use keyboard, easy-to-use built-in editor, gorgeous color output on your TV, child-proofing (safe for little kids), and dazzling games, all at a wonderfully low price! It was cheaper than an Apple (whose price had by then risen to $1195) and yet was much *better* than an Apple.

From that description, you'd expect Atari 800 to become the world's best-selling computer, and the TI 99/4 to become an immediate flop. Indeed, that's what most computer experts hoped. And so did the TI 99/4's product manager: when he saw what a mess the TI 99/4 had become, he quit TI and went to work for Atari, where he became the product manager for the Atari 400 & 800!

But even though computer experts realized that TI's computer was junk, TI decided to market it aggressively:

TI coaxed Milton Bradley and Scott Foresman to write lots of programs for the 99/4. TI paid researchers at MIT to make the 99/4 understand Logo (a computer language used by young children and very popular in elementary schools). TI improved the keyboard just enough so that people would stop laughing at it; the version with the new keyboard was named the **99/4A**. TI paid Bill Cosby to praise the 99/4A and ran hundreds of TV ads showing Bill Cosby saying "wow". TI dramatically slashed the $1150 price to $650, then $150, and then finally to just $99.50! (To bring the price that low, TI had to exclude the color monitor from the price; instead, TI included a hookup to your home's color TV.)

By contrast, Atari did hardly anything to market or further improve the Atari 400 & 800.

Atari concentrated on its other products: the big Atari game machines (which you find in video arcades) and the Atari VCS machine (which plays video games on your home TV).

The TI 99/4A therefore became more popular than the Atari 400 & 800 — even though the TI 99/4A was inherently worse.

Sinclair, Osborne, backlash

In 1980 and 1981, two important companies entered the microcomputer marketplace: Timex Sinclair (1980) and Osborne (1981).

The first complete computer selling for less than $200 was invented by a British chap named Clive Sinclair and manufactured by Timex.

The original version was called the **ZX-80** (because it was invented in 1980, contained a Z-80 CPU, and was claimed to be "Xellent"); it sold for $199.95. In 1981, Clive Sinclair invented an improved version, called the **ZX-81**. Later, he and Timex invented further improvements, called the **ZX Spectrum** and the **Timex Sinclair 1000**. When TI dropped the price of the TI 99/4A to $99.50, Timex retaliated by dropping the list price of the Timex Sinclair 1000 to $49.95, so the Timex Sinclair 1000 remained the cheapest complete computer.

In April 1981, Adam Osborne began Osborne Computer Corp. and began selling the **Osborne 1** computer, designed by Lee Felsenstein (who'd invented Processor Technology's Sol 20 computer).

The Osborne 1 computer included practically everything a business executive needed: its $1795 price included a keyboard, a monitor, a Z-80A CPU, a 64K RAM, two disk drives, CP/M, Microsoft Basic, a second version of Basic, the WordStar word processor, and the SuperCalc spreadsheet program. Moreover, it was the world's first portable business computer: the entire computer system (including even the monitor and disk drives) was collapsible and turned itself into an easy-to-carry attaché case. (Many years later, Compaq copied Osborne's idea.)

While Timex Sinclair and Osborne were entering the marketplace, Radio Shack, Apple, and Commodore were introducing new computers of their own:

In 1980, Radio Shack began selling three new computers. The **TRS-80 model 3** replaced Radio Shack's cheapest computer (the model 1) and was almost as good as Radio Shack's fanciest computer (the model 2). The **TRS-80 Color Computer** drew pictures in color and cost less than the model 3. The **TRS-80 Pocket Computer** fit into your pocket, looked like a pocket calculator, and was built for Radio Shack by Sharp Electronics in Japan.

In 1980, Apple began selling the **Apple 3**. It was overpriced; and to make matters worse, the first Apple 3's that rolled off the assembly line were defective. Apple eventually lowered the price and fixed the defects; but since the Apple 3 had gotten off to such a bad start, computer consultants didn't trust it and told everybody to avoid it.

In 1981, Commodore began selling the **Vic-20**, which drew pictures in color and cost less than Radio Shack's Color Computer. In fact, the Vic-20 was the first computer that drew pictures in color for less than $300.

The Vic-20 originally sold for $299.95. When TI lowered the price of the TI 99/4A to $99.95, Commodore lowered the price of the Vic-20. At discount department stores (such as K Mart, Toys R Us, and Child World), you could buy the Vic-20 for just $85: it was still the cheapest computer that could handle color. (The Timex Sinclair 1000 was cheaper but handled just black-and-white.)

Moreover, the Vic-20 had standard Microsoft Basic, whereas the Timex Sinclair 1000 and TI 99/4A did not; so the Vic-20 was the cheapest computer that had standard Microsoft Basic. It was the cheapest computer that was pleasant to program.

Also, the Vic-20 had a nice keyboard, whereas the keyboards on the Timex Sinclair 1000 and TI 99/4A were pathetic.

The Vic-20 became immediately popular.

IBM PC

On August 12, 1981, IBM announced a new microcomputer, called the **IBM Personal Computer (IBM PC)**.

Although IBM had previously invented other microcomputers (the IBM 5100 and the IBM System 23 Datamaster), they'd been overpriced and nobody took them seriously — not even IBM. The IBM Personal Computer was IBM's first *serious* attempt to sell a microcomputer.

The IBM Personal Computer was a smashing success, because of its amazingly high quality and amazingly low price. It became the standard against which the rest of the microcomputer industry was judged.

Rise & fall

Let's take a closer look at how 3 computer companies — Commodore, Tandy, and Atari — rose & fell.

Commodore

A computer company called **Commodore** was called "the house that Jack built" because it was started by Jack Tramiel.

How Commodore began Jack began his career by being in the wrong place at the wrong time: he was a Jew in Poland during World War 2. He was thrown into the Auschwitz concentration camp, where he learned to view life as a war to survive. When he escaped from the camp, he moved to Canada and started an aggressive, ruthless company called **Commodore**, whose motto to survive was, "Business is war!"

At first, Commodore just repaired typewriters; but it grew fast and started to manufacture pocket calculators. In those calculators, the CPU was a microprocessor chip manufactured by **MOS Technology**, a company with a troubled past:

Back in 1974, the most popular microprocessors were the Intel 8080 and the Motorola 6800. But one of the 6800's inventors, a guy named Chuck Peddle, quit Motorola in 1975 and started a new company with his friends. That start-up company, **MOS Technology**, began manufacturing the 6501 microprocessor, which resembled Motorola's 6800.

When Motorola threatened to sue, MOS Technology stopped making the 6501 and switched to the 6502, which Chuck Peddle designed differently enough to avoid a suit. That 6502 chip became very popular and was used in many devices, including Commodore's calculators. **Commodore was one of MOS Technology's biggest customers.**

Though the 6502 was legal, **Motorola sued MOS Technology** for its illegal predecessor, the 6501. The suit dragged through the courts for two years and cost MOS Technology many thousands of dollars in lawyers' fees. Finally, in 1977, Motorola won $200,000. The lawyer fees and $200,000 put MOS Technology in financial trouble.

MOS Technology wanted to be bought by some company having lots of cash. Commodore, rich by then, bought it.

Just before that sale, Canada's tax laws changed, so Commodore moved its headquarters (in theory) from Canada to the Bahamas. That's how MOS Technology became part of "Commodore Limited", a Bahamas company, and how Commodore found itself running a company that made chips. Commodore had entered the computer business.

Dealing with competitors At MOS Technology, Chuck Peddle had sold a 6502 chip for $25 to Steve Wozniak, who used that chip to create the Apple computer. When Commodore saw Apple computers become popular, Commodore offered to buy the Apple Computer Company — and almost succeeded.

Apple wanted $15,000 more than Commodore offered, so the deal never came off. If Commodore were to have offered just $15,000 more, Apple would be part of Commodore now!

Commodore hired Chuck Peddle to design a "Commodore computer", which Commodore hoped to sell through Radio Shack's stores, but Radio Shack had already started designing its own computer.

Pet Rebuffed by Apple and Radio Shack, Jack Tramiel decided to retaliate by building a computer better and cheaper than anything Apple and Radio Shack had. Commodore called its new computer the **Pet** — because Commodore's marketing director was the guy who invented the Pet Rock, and reckoned that if folks were stupid enough to buy a Pet Rock they'd love a Pet computer! He was right: sales of Commodore's Pet Computer skyrocketed.

Commodore told the press that "Pet" was an abbreviation for "Personal Electronic Transactor"; but Commodore had invented the name "Pet" first and later made up what it stood for.

Commodore announced the Pet in 1977 and said its $495 price would include *everything* (the CPU, RAM, ROM, keyboard, monitor, and tape recorder), its ROM would include a good version of Basic, and its screen would display capital letters, lower-case letters, punctuation, math symbols, and graphics symbols.

Commodore's competitors got scared — because Commodore's price was much lower than other computers, Commodore's computer offered more features, and Commodore was rich enough to spend more on ads & marketing than all other manufacturers combined. Computer magazines called the Pet "the birth of a new generation" in personal computers and treated the Pet's designer (Chuck Peddle) to many interviews.

But Commodore disappointed its customers:

Commodore raised the Pet's price from $495 to $595 before taking orders. To order the Pet, the customer had to send $595, plus shipping charges, then wait for Commodore to deliver. Many folks mailed Commodore money and waited long, but Commodore didn't ship. Folks got impatient. Computer stores that had advertised the Pet got worried: customers who'd prepaid complained to the stores, but the stores couldn't get Commodore to ship.

Meanwhile, Radio Shack entered the market with its TRS-80 model 1 priced at $599 — about the same price as Commodore's Pet. **Radio Shack was kinder than Commodore:**

Radio Shack asked customers for just a 10% deposit. Commodore required payment in full.

Radio Shack didn't charge for shipping. Commodore did.

Radio Shack set up repair centers throughout the U.S. Commodore's only repair center was in California.

Radio Shack delivered computers fast. Commodore still wasn't delivering! Finally, Commodore admitted that the $595 Pet would *not* be delivered soon; instead, Commodore would deliver a $795 version that included 4K of extra RAM. So if you already sent $595 to Commodore and wanted a computer soon, you'd have to send an extra $200. That was a rip-off, since 4K of extra RAM was *not* worth an extra $200; but desperate customers sent the $200 anyway.

Radio Shack shipped its computers on a first-come first-served basis; if you ordered a Radio Shack computer, Radio Shack gave you an accurate estimate of when you'd receive it. Commodore gave preferential treatment to its "friends"; if you ordered a computer from Commodore, you hadn't the faintest idea of when it would arrive, since you didn't know how many "friends" were on Commodore's list.

Radio Shack's computer came with a 232-page manual that was cheery and easy. Commodore's computer came with just 10 loose pages that were incomplete and hard to understand.

Commodore announced a low-cost printer but then reneged and decided to sell just an expensive printer. Commodore announced a low-cost disk drive but then reneged and decided to sell just an expensive unit containing 2 disk drives. Commodore became known as a liar.

At first, the Pet was the world's best-selling computer; but all those disappointments made its popularity drop to #3, below Radio Shack (#1) and Apple (#2).

Commodore developed a souped-up Pet, called the **Commodore Business Machine (CBM)**, but it wasn't enough to raise Commodore above the number 3 spot. As Commodore's fortunes dipped, Chuck Peddle and his friends quit. Apple hired them but treated them as second-class citizens, so they returned to Commodore.

Commodore sold several Pet versions, each containing a different quantity of RAM.

If you bought a cheap version and wanted to increase its RAM, Commodore refused to install extra RAM. Instead, Commodore insisted you buy a whole new Pet.

Customers tried buying extra RAM from chip dealers and installing the chips themselves; but to stop those tinkerers, Commodore began cutting a hole in the PC board where the extra RAM chips would go. Commodore was an asshole.

Commodore changed the Pet's tape-handling system.

Tapes created for old Pets wouldn't work on new Pets. Commodore didn't tell customers of the change. Customers who wrote programs for old Pets and then bought more Pets discovered that their programs didn't work on the new Pets. They thought their new Pets were broken. Companies who'd been selling tapes of Pet computer programs began getting angry letters from customers who bought the tapes and couldn't make them work on their new Pets: the customers thought the companies were crooks; the companies thought the customers were lying; eventually folks realized the real culprit was Commodore, who'd changed the Pet secretly.

When the companies discovered that Commodore had changed the Pet without providing a label to distinguish new Pets from old, the companies realized they'd have to give each customer two copies of each program, so the customer could try both versions. That's when many companies gave up trying to sell Pet tapes. They sold tapes for Apple and Radio Shack computers instead. Commodore programs became rare.

Vic Jack's experience at Auschwitz made him scared of Nazis and the Japanese. He feared the US would be invaded by cheap Japanese computers putting Commodore and other American companies out of business.

Paranoid, in April 1980 he called his engineers together and screamed at them, "The Japanese are coming! The Japanese are coming! So we'll become the Japanese!" He laid out his bold plan: Commodore would build the world's first under-$300 computer to display colors on an ordinary TV and produce three-part harmony through the TV's speaker.

At that time, the only under-$300 computer was Sinclair's ZX-80, which was black-and-white and crummy. Commodore's engineers said it was impossible to build a color computer

cheaply, but Jack insisted. Commodore's engineers finally managed to do it. Here's how:

MOS Technology, owned by Commodore, had already invented the amazing **Video Interface Chip (Vic)**, which could handle the entire process of sending computer output to the TV screen. Since that chip was cheap, Commodore used it in the under-$300 computer. Unfortunately, it put just 22 characters per line on the screen, so the under-$300 computer would display just 22 characters per line.

Since the new computer was feminine and foxy, Commodore wanted to call it the "Vixen"; but Commodore discovered that a "Vixen" computer couldn't sell in Germany, since "Vixen" sounds like the German word "Wichsen", which means "jerk off". Commodore hastily changed the name to "Vic" and ran TV ads for the "Vic" computer; but that got Commodore into even worse trouble, since "Vic" sounds like the German word "Ficke", which means "fuck". Commodore kept calling it the "Vic" in the USA but called it the "VC" computer in Germany and pretended "VC" stood for "Volks Computer".

Commodore began shipping the Vic in 1981 at $299.95. Later, the price gradually dropped to $55.

To sell the Vic, Commodore tried 3 kinds of ads:

The first ad featured TV star William Shatner (who played Captain Kirk in Star Trek) and said the Vic was wonderful, amazing, out of this world, fun! But then people started thinking of the Vic as just a sci-fi toy. To combat the "toy" image, Commodore changed to a second kind of ad, which said the Vic was as cheap as a video-game machine but more educational for kids. When Texas Instruments began making similar claims, Commodore changed to a third kind of ad, which said Commodore's disk drives, printers, and phone hookups cost much less than Texas Instruments'.

The Vic's low price, fun colors, and effective ads made it popular in the USA, England, Germany, and Japan. Commodore quickly sold over a million Vics! **The Vic became the world's best-selling computer!**

Commodore 64 In 1982, Commodore began selling an improved Vic, called the **Commodore 64** because it included 64K of RAM. (The original Vic had just 5K.) The Commodore 64 also improved on the Vic by displaying 40 characters per line (instead of just 22) and including 20K of ROM (instead of just 16K).

The Commodore 64's price went through 4 phases:

In phase 1, the recommended list price was $599.95, which Commodore tried to force all dealers to charge. If a dealer advertised a discount, Commodore refused to send that dealer any more computers. (Commodore's policy was an example of **price fixing**, which is illegal.)

In phase 2, Commodore allowed discounts. Dealers charged just $350, and Commodore mailed a $100 rebate to anybody trading in another computer or a video-game machine. Bargain-hunters bought the cheap Timex Sinclair 1000 computer just to trade in for a Commodore 64. A New York dealer, "Crazy Eddy", sold junky video-game machines for $10 just so his customers could mail them to Commodore for the $100 rebate. Commodore donated most of the trade-ins to charities for a tax write-off but kept some Timex Sinclair 1000's for use as doorstops.

In phase 3, Commodore stopped the rebate but offered a lower price: discount dealers charged just $148.

In phase 4, the Commodore made an improved version, the **Commodore 64C**, sold by discounters for just $119. It came with a copy of the **Geos** operating system (which made it resemble a Mac), and its keyboard contained extra keys.

The Commodore 64 cost much less than an Apple 2c or IBM PC. Here's why:

Commodore's disk drive (Model 1541) was slow and unreliable and put few bytes on the disk (just single-sided single-density).

Commodore's color monitor (Model 1702) produced a blurry image, which restricted it to 40 characters per line instead of 80, and made the M look too much like an N, the B look too much like an 8.

Commodore's Basic was weak: it didn't even include a command to let you draw a diagonal line across the screen.

Commodore's printer port was non-standard: it worked just with printers built by Commodore, unless you bought a special adapter.

Eventually, Commodore developed an improved monitor (Model 1802) and improved disk drives (Models 1541C and 1541-2).

Because the Commodore 64 was cheap, Commodore sold over a million of them.

> Many programmers who wrote programs for Apple computers rewrote their programs to also work on the Commodore 64. Soon the Commodore 64 ran nearly as many popular programs as the Apple 2c.
>
> The Commodore 64's price, even after adding the price of a disk drive and a monitor, still totaled less than the price of an Apple 2e, Apple 2c, IBM PC, or IBM PC Junior. The Commodore 64 was a fantastically good value! It also contained a fancy music synthesizer chip that produced a wide variety of musical tone qualities: when it played music, it sounded much better than an Apple 2e or 2c or IBM.

Jack jumps ship After the Commodore 64 became successful, Jack Tramiel wanted to hire his sons to help run Commodore; but Commodore's other major shareholders refused to deal with Jack's sons, so Jack quit. He sold his 2 million shares of Commodore stock, at $40 per share, netting himself 80 million dollars in cash.

New computers After Jack quit, Commodore tried selling two new computers (the **Commodore 16** and **Commodore Plus 4**), but they had serious flaws. Then Commodore invented two great computers: the **Commodore 128** and **Amiga**.

The **Commodore 128** ran all the Commodore 64 software and also included a better version of Basic, better keyboard, and better video. To go with it, Commodore invented a better RGB monitor (Model 1902) and better disk drive (Model 1571). Later, Commodore invented the **Commodore 128D** computer, which included a built-in disk drive.

The **Amiga** was even newer and fancier. It contained 3 special chips that produce fast animated graphics in beautiful shades of color. Like the Mac, it used a mouse and pull-down menus. It was bought mainly by video professionals and by others interested in animated graphics. On TV, weathermen used the Amiga to show the weather moving across the weather map.

The Amiga was not compatible with the Commodore 64 or Mac. Aside from graphics, not enough good software was available for the Amiga.

Bankruptcy In 1994, Commodore filed for bankruptcy. Commodore was bought by **Escom**, which sold Amiga Technologies to **Visual Information Services Corp. (Viscorp)**, which sold it to **Gateway**, which eventually abandoned the technology.

Tandy

Tandy, which owns Radio Shack, has survived many years.

Thanks to Tandy Radio Shack helped the computer industry in many ways:

> Radio Shack was **the first big chain of stores to sell computers nationally**. It was the first chain to reach rural areas.
>
> Radio Shack invented **the first low-cost assembled computer** (the TRS-80 model 1, which cost just $599, including the monitor).
>
> Radio Shack was **the first company to keep computer prices low without skimping on quality**.
>
> Radio Shack sold **the first notebook computer** (the Tandy 100, invented by Tandy with help from Microsoft and a Japanese manufacturer, Kyocera).
>
> Radio Shack sold **the first pocket computers**. They were manufactured for Tandy by Sharp and Casio.
>
> Radio Shack invented **the first cheap computer having fancy graphics commands**. That was the Color Computer, whose Basic was designed by Microsoft as a "rough draft" for the fancier Basic in the IBM PC.

But when the IBM PC came out and became the standard, Americans suddenly decided to buy just the IBM PC and clones. Tandy tried building IBM clones innovatively, but in 1993 gave up: it stopped making computers and sold all its factories to another computer company, **AST**. Afterwards, Tandy sold computers built by AST, then switched to selling computers built by IBM. Now Tandy sells computers built by Compaq instead.

Nicknames Tandy's computers are often called "TRS" computers. The "TRS" stands for "Tandy's Radio Shack". Cynics add the letters A and H, and call them "TRASH" computers, so Tandy's customers are called "trash collectors".

How Tandy began The Tandy Leather Company was begun by Charles Tandy. Later, he acquired Radio Shack, which had been a Boston-based chain of discount electronics stores.

Under leadership from his Fort Worth headquarters, Tandy/Radio Shack succeeded and grew 30% per year, fueled by the CB radio craze. When the market for CB radios declined, he began looking for a new product to continue his 30% growth.

Don French, a Radio Shack manager whose hobby was building computers, told Radio Shack's leaders that Radio Shack should start selling computers.

The original TRS-80 computer Radio Shack hired Steve Leininger to design a Radio Shack computer and **keep the cost as low as possible:**

> Steve wanted his computer to handle lower-case letters instead of just capitals; but since the lower-case chip would have added 10¢ to the cost, management rejected lower case: **Radio Shack's computer handled just capitals.**
>
> **The monitor was a modified black-and-white TV built for Radio Shack by RCA.** When RCA told Radio Shack that the TV case's standard color was "Mercedes silver" and any other color would cost extra, Radio Shack accepted Mercedes silver and painted the rest of the computer to match the TV. When you use a Radio Shack computer, you're supposed to feel as if you're driving a Mercedes; but since Mercedes silver looked like gray, Radio Shack became nicknamed "the great gray monster". Californians preferred Apples, whose beige matched their living-room decors. (Later, in 1982, Radio Shack wised up and switched from "Mercedes silver" to white.)
>
> **Radio Shack's original computer listed for just $599 and consisted of 4 devices**: a keyboard (in which hid the CPU, ROM, & RAM), a monitor (built for Radio Shack by RCA), a cheap Radio Shack tape recorder, and an AC/DC transformer. Wires ran between those devices, so that the whole system looked like an octopus. Radio Shack wanted to put the AC/DC transformer _inside_ the keyboard, to make the computer system consist of three boxes instead of four; but that _internal_ transformer would have delayed approval from Underwriters Laboratories for 6 months, and Radio Shack couldn't wait that long.
>
> **Radio Shack's first production run was for just 3000 computers**, because Radio Shack's leaders doubted anybody would actually buy them. If none were sold, Radio Shack figured it could use the computers to do internal paperwork instead in its 3500 stores. To Radio Shack's surprise, 250,000 people put themselves on a waiting list to buy the computer during the first year.

Radio Shack named its computer the **TRS-80** because it was by Tandy's Radio Shack and contained a Z-80 CPU chip. Radio Shack's vice-president, John Roach, doubted anybody would buy the computers, so he built just 3500 of them, since Radio Shack had 3500 stores. He figured that if the computers didn't sell, the stores could use them for internal accounting instead.

To announce the computer, Radio Shack held a press conference in August 1977 in New York. But during the conference, a guy ran up and yelled that a bomb exploded two blocks away. Reporters ran to the bomb site, and Radio Shack couldn't get as much publicity as it wanted.

Radio Shack needed a new place to announce the computer. Radio Shack heard that the Boston Computer Society was run a computer show that week, so Radio Shack's management drove to that Boston show, got a booth, re-announced its computer there, and was shocked to discover that the whole show and Boston Computer Society were run by Jonathan Rotenberg, a 14-year-old kid!

That intro was successful: people liked and bought Radio Shack's new computer. The base price was $599.95. For a complete business system (including a souped-up base plus two disk drives and a printer), Radio Shack charged $2600, while Radio Shack's competitors charged over $4500.

Though the first production run was for just 3500 of the computers, 250,000 people put themselves on a waiting list to buy them the first year.

Problems with DOS
Radio Shack hired Randy Cook to write the DOS.

My friend Dick Miller tried DOS version 1.0 and noticed it didn't work; it didn't even boot! He told Radio Shack, which told Randy Cook, who fixed the problem and wrote version 1.1. Dick noticed it worked better but still had a big flaw: it didn't tell you how much disk space was left, and when the disk got full it would self-destruct! Then came version 1.2, which worked better but not perfectly.

Since Radio Shack's DOS was still buggy, the inventors of Visicalc (the world's first spreadsheet program) put Visicalc onto the Apple instead of the TRS-80. Apple became known as the "spreadsheet machine", and many accountants began buying Apples instead of TRS-80's.

Dealing with the public
In 1977, when Radio Shack began selling the TRS-80, customers didn't understand what computers were.

At a Radio Shack show, I saw a police chief buy a TRS-80. While carrying it out of the room, he called back over his shoulder, "By the way, how do you program it?" He expected a one-sentence answer.

Radio Shack gave customers an 800 number to call for free tech support. Many customers called because they were confused. For example, many customers had this gripe: "I put my mouth next to the tape recorder and yelled TWO PLUS TWO, but it didn't say FOUR!"

Radio Shack's first version of Basic gave just 3 error messages: WHAT (which means "What the heck are you talking about?"), HOW (which means "I don't know how to handle a number that big") and SORRY (which means "Sorry I can't do that — you didn't buy enough RAM yet"). Those error messages confused beginners. For example, here's a conversation between a Radio Shack customer and a Radio Shack technician (Chris Daly)....

Chris: "What's your problem?"
Customer: "I plugged in the video, then the tape recorder, then…"
Chris: "Yes, sir, but what's the problem?"
Customer: "It doesn't work."
Chris: "How do you *know* it doesn't work?"
Customer: "It says READY."
Chris: "What's wrong with that? It's *supposed* to say READY."
Customer: "It isn't ready."
Chris: "How do you *know* it isn't ready?"
Customer: "I asked it 'Where's my wife Martha?', and it just said WHAT."

Other Z-80 computers
After the TRS-80, Tandy invented improved versions: the TRS-80 Models 2, 3, 4, 4D, 4P, 12, 16, & 16B, and the Tandy 6000. Like the Model 1, they included a Z-80 CPU and a monochrome monitor.

Coco
To compete against the Commodore 64, Tandy invented the **Color Computer**, nicknamed the **Coco**. Like the Commodore 64, the Coco could attach to either a monitor or an ordinary TV, and it could store programs on either a disk or an ordinary cassette tape (the same kind of tape that plays music).

Tandy began selling the Coco in 1980 — the year before IBM began selling the PC.

Microsoft invented the Coco's Basic ROM and also invented the IBM PC's. The Coco's Basic ROM was Microsoft's rough draft of the ROM that went into the IBM PC, so the Coco acted as "an IBM PC that wasn't quite right yet". In the Coco's Basic, the commands for handling graphics & music were similar to the IBM PC's but more awkward. Folks who couldn't afford an IBM PC but wanted to learn how to program it bought the Coco.

Pocket computers
Tandy sold 8 different pocket computers, numbered **PC-1** through **PC-8**. They fit in your pocket, ran on batteries, and included LCD screens.

Notebook computers
In 1983, Tandy, Epson, and NEC all tried to sell cheap notebook computers. Just Tandy's became popular, because it was the cheapest ($499) and the easiest to learn how to use. It was called the **Model 100**.

Later Tandy sold an improved version, the **Model 102**.

It included more RAM (32K), weighed less (just 3 pounds), and listed for $599. It including a nice keyboard, a screen displaying eight 40-character lines, a 32K ROM (containing Basic, a word-processing program, some filing programs, and a telecommunications program), and a 300-baud modem (for attaching to a phone, after you bought a $19.95 cable). It was 8½ inches by 12 inches and just 1½ inches thick. Reporters used it to take notes and phone them to the newspaper.

Popularity
Tandy's 7000 Radio Shack stores penetrated every major city and also remote rural areas, where few other computer stores competed.

Tandy offered "solid value". Tandy kept its quality high and its prices below IBM's and Apple's (though not as low as generic clones). Tandy's computers and prices were aimed at middle-class American consumers, not business executives (who bought from IBM) or bargain-hunting hobbyists (who bought from mail-order discounters).

Tandy's computers were built reliably. Tandy's assembly line checked them thoroughly before shipping to Tandy's stores. If a Tandy computer needed repair during the warranty period, the customer could bring it to any Radio Shack store for a free fix, even if purchased from a different store. After the warranty expired, Radio Shack was kind and charged very little for labor.

Worse attitude
During the 1970's, Tandy's headquarters gave toll-free tech help. During the 1980's, Tandy switched to numbers that weren't toll-free. Later, Tandy refused to answer any questions unless the customer bought a support contract. Tandy's claim to offer better support than mail-order companies became Texas bull.

During the 1980's, Tandy established a dress code for its computer centers: employees who met the public had to wear blue or gray suits, blue or white shirts, no beards, and no moustaches. Tandy fired a center manager for refusing to shave his beard. Wasn't the personal-computing revolution supposed to give us tools to express our *individuality*?

Eventually, Tandy shut down all its computer centers.

Atari

Of all the major computer manufacturers, Atari was the most creative — and strangest! Atari was in America's strangest state (California) and had the strangest name: "Atari" is a Japanese war cry that means "beware!"

Video games
In 1972, Atari invented the world's first popular video game, **Pong**. Next, Atari invented the game **Asteroids** then dozens of other games.

Atari's games were placed in arcades & bars and required you to insert quarters. In 1975, Atari invented a machine that could play Pong on your home TV. In 1976, Atari gave up its independence and was bought by Warner Communications (the conglomerate that owned Warner Brothers movies & cartoons, Warner Cable TV, and DC Comics).

In 1977, Atari invented a machine called the **Video Computer System (VCS)**, which could play *many* games on your home TV: each game came as a ROM cartridge. Later, Nintendo, Sega, and Sony invented machines that were similar but fancier.

Early personal computers
In 1979, Atari began selling complete personal computers. Atari's first two computers were the **Atari 400** (cheap!) and the **Atari 800** (which had a nicer keyboard). They were far ahead of their time. Of all the microcomputers being sold, Atari's had the best graphics, best music, and best way of editing programs. Compared to Atari, the Apples looked pitiful! Yet Atari charged *less* than Apple!

But **Atari made two mistakes:**

> **Atari didn't hire Bill Gates to write its version of Basic.** Instead, it hired the same jerk who invented Apple's DOS. Like Apple's DOS, Atari's Basic looked simple but couldn't handle serious business problems.
>
> **Atari be**lieved personal computers would be used mainly for games. Atari didn't realize that personal computers would be used mainly for work. Atari developed spectacular games but not enough software to handle word processing, accounting, and filing.

Atari developed some slightly improved computers (the **600 XL**, **800 XL**, and **1200 XL**) but still lost lots of money.

Jack attack Atari got bought by Jack Tramiel, who'd headed Commodore. Here's why:

> When Jack quit being the head of Commodore, he sold his Commodore stock for 80 million dollars. He spent some of that cash to take his wife on a trip around the world.
>
> When they reached Japan, the heads of Japanese computer companies said, "Jack, we're glad you quit Commodore, because now we can enter the American computer market without having to fight you."
>
> That comment scared Jack. To stop the Japanese from invading the U.S. computer market, he started a new computer company, Tramiel Associates, which bought Atari from Warner. Since Jack was rich and Atari was nearly worthless (having accumulated lots of debt), Jack managed to buy all of Atari at 4PM one afternoon by using his Visa card.

Jack and his sons ran Atari. Jack replaced Atari's old computers by two new computers (the **65 XE** and the **130 XE**), which ran the same software as Atari's old computers but cost less.

In 1985, Jack began selling the **Atari 520ST**, which imitated Apple's Mac computer cheaply and nicknamed the "Jackintosh".

> It used the **Gem operating system** (invented by **Digital Research** for the Atari and the IBM PC), which made the 520ST computer look like a Mac but did *not* run Mac software: you had to buy software specially modified to work on the 520 ST.
>
> When the 520 ST first came out, its price was about half as much as the Mac and Amiga so that, by comparison, the Mac and Amiga looked overpriced. To fight back, Apple lowered the Mac's price, and Commodore lowered the Amiga's; but Atari's 520 ST remained the cheapest of the bunch.
>
> When Apple announced the Mac Plus, which contained a whole megabyte of RAM, Atari retaliated with the **1040 ST** (which contained a megabyte also), then a 2-megabyte version (the **Mega-2**) and 4-megabyte version (the **Mega-4**).

Atari's had difficulty competing in the U.S., but Atari computers were popular in Europe. Eventually, Atari's fortunes declined. In 1996, Atari died: it got merged into another company, **JTS**, which made disk drives.

Cycles

Every 8 years, the country's mood about computers has changed. After 8 years of dramatic revolution, we switched to 8 years of subtle evolution, then back again.

Pivotal years

The pivotal years were 1943 (beginning the first revolution), 1951 (beginning the first period of *evolution*), 1959 (revolution), 1967 (evolution), 1975 (revolution), 1983 (evolution), 1991 (revolution), 1999 (evolution), and 2007 (revolution). Here are the details....

Revolution From 1943 to 1950, researchers at universities were building the first true computers, which were big monsters. Each was custom-built; no two were alike.

Evolution In 1951, Sperry began selling the first mass-produced computer: the **Univac I**. Sperry built 46 of them. During the 8-year era from 1951 to 1958, computers gradually became smaller and cheaper and acquired more software. That

evolutionary era was called the **first generation**.

Revolution The next computer revolution began in 1959, when IBM began selling the **IBM 1401**, the first IBM computer to use transistors instead of vacuum tubes.

> During that 8-year revolution from 1959 to 1966, computerists polished Fortran and Algol (which had been begun earlier), invented 9 other major computer languages (Cobol, Basic, PL/I, Lisp, Snobol, APL, Dynamo, GPSS, and RPG), and began developing Forth and SPSS. They created many amazing programs for artificial intelligence, such as Weizenbaum's Eliza program, which made the computer imitate a therapist. During that same eight-year period, IBM invented the **IBM 360**: it was the first popular computer that used integrated circuits, and all of IBM's modern mainframes are based on it.

Evolution The years from 1967 to 1974 showed a gradual evolution. Computer prices continued to drop and quality continued to improve. DEC began selling PDP-10 and PDP-11 computers, which became the favorite computers among researchers in universities.

Revolution In 1975, MITS shipped the first popular microcomputer, the **Altair**, which launched the personal computer revolution. Soon Apple, Commodore, Tandy, and IBM began selling microcomputers also. Programmers developed lots of useful, fun software for them. The revolution climaxed at the end of 1982, when many Americans bought microcomputers as Christmas presents.

Evolution In January 1983, the cover of *Time* magazine declared that the 1982 "man of the year" was the personal computer. But consumers quickly tired of the personal-computer fad, chucked their Commodore Vic and Timex Sinclair computers into the closet, and shifted attention to less intellectual pursuits. Many computer companies went bankrupt. In 1983, Lotus announced **1-2-3** (a spreadsheet program), but that was the computer industry's last major successful new product. After that, prices continued to fall and quality gradually increased, but no dramatic breakthroughs occurred. The computer industry became boring. During that time, if you were to ask "What fantastically great happened in the computer industry during the past year?" the answer was: "Not much".

Revolution In 1991, the computer industry became exciting again. Here's why....

> Part of that excitement came from revolutionary influences of the previous two years: in 1989 & 1990 the Berlin Wall fell, the Cold War ended, a new decade began, Microsoft finally invented a version of Windows that worked well (version 3.0), and Apple invented a color Mac that was affordable (the LC). In 1991, Microsoft put the finishing touches on Windows (version 3.1) and DOS (version 5).
>
> In 1991 and 1992, price wars made the cost of computers drop 45% per year instead of the customary 30%. Those lower prices made people spend *more* money on computers, because the ridiculously low prices for fancy stuff encouraged people to buy fancier computers: 486 instead of 286, Super VGA instead of plain VGA, 8M RAM instead of 1M, 200M hard drives instead of 40M.
>
> The sudden popularity of Windows whetted the public's hunger for those muscle machines, since Windows requires lots of muscle to run well. That growing American muscle (bigger and bigger!) then made Windows practical enough to become desirable. All big software companies hastily converted their DOS and Mac software to Windows.
>
> The challenge of doing that conversion forced them to rethink the twin questions of software wisdom: "What makes software easy to use?" and "What kinds of software power do users want?" Many creative solutions were invented to those questions.
>
> During the 1992 Christmas season, fast CD-ROM drives finally became cheap enough to create a mass market: many American bought them, and CD-ROMs became the new standard way to distribute encyclopedias, directories, other major reference works, and software libraries (full of fonts and shareware). The attention given to CD-ROMs made customers think about the importance of sound, and many customers bought sound cards such as the Sound Blaster.

In 1995, Windows 95 was invented, Netscape Navigator 2.0 was invented, and the Internet began to become popular. During the next few years, the Internet's popularity grew wildly.

Evolution In 1999, interest in the Internet peaked, then declined, as Internet companies began running out of clever ideas.

Microsoft stopped coming out with major new products, partly because Microsoft got distracted by lawsuits against it. In the fall of 1999, RAM prices shot up. In November 1999, Packard Bell went out of business. In December 1999, many companies selling on the Internet developed bad reputations by not shipping goods in time for Christmas. Companies prepared for computer problems that the year 2000 might cause.

The year 2000 began boringly, a disappointing way to begin a new millennium. In January 2000, IBM and Acer stopped selling desktop computers through retail stores. In March 2000, the Internet part of the stock market crashed. In June 2000, a judge ruled that Microsoft should be split into two companies.

Revolution In 2007:

Microsoft completely changed the way Microsoft Office looked, by coming out with **Windows Vista** (a major change from Windows XP) and **Office 2007** (which used a ribbon instead of a menu bar). Apple came out with the **iPhone**. Many other innovations arose: let's watch the revolution unfold!

Presidential politics

The 8-year computer cycle coincides with the American cycle of switching political parties:

After years of Roosevelt & Truman, the presidential election of 1952 ushered in 8 years of a Republican (Eisenhower); 1960 brought 8 years of Democrats (Kennedy & Johnson); 1968, 8 years of Republicans (Nixon & Ford).

1976 began another 16-year experience of "Democrat followed by Republicans"; but the Democrat (Carter) got just 4 of those years (because he lost face in the middle of the Iran hostage crisis, oil crisis, and recession); the Republicans (Reagan and Bush the elder) got the remaining 12.

1992 began another experience of "Democrat followed by Republicans". The Democrat was Clinton (8 years). The Republican was George W. Bush (8 years).

2008 began another experience beginning with a Democrat (Obama).

When Americans love liberals and revolution, they vote for Democrats; when Americans prefer conservative evolution, they vote for Republicans. As historian Krigsman remarked, "An excitable mood in the country causes a computer revolution, and the next year the Democrats grab power."

Events

Nine events dramatically changed the public's perception of what a computer is.

Powerful computers

In the **1940's**, universities built the first powerful computers, to help World War II Allies calculate ballistics (trajectories of bullets and bombs). Before then, "powerful computers" were just science fiction; suddenly they'd become reality!

Mass-produced computers

The first computer to be mass-produced was the Univac I, in **1951**. Before then, computers were just military research projects; suddenly they'd become practical commercial tools!

46 of the Univac I computers were built, and competitors such as IBM began building computers in much bigger quantities.

Transistors & high-level languages

In **1959**, computer manufacturers began using transistors (instead of vacuum tubes), so that computers became much smaller, cheaper, more reliable, and more powerful. About the same time, the first reasonable computer languages were invented: Fortran, Cobol, and Algol.

For the first time, computers became cheap enough and easy enough to program so that colleges could encourage students to take computer courses.

Chips & Basic

The first computer to contain integrated circuits (chips) was the IBM 360, which IBM began selling in **1966**.

Chips had been invented by other companies earlier, but chips weren't used in complete computer systems until 1966. Afterwards, other computer brands began using chips also. The chips made computers even smaller, cheaper, more reliable, and more powerful.

About the same time, the first easy full-featured computer language was invented: Basic.

For the first time, computers became cheap enough and easy enough so that high schools could encourage students to take computer courses.

Personal computers

In **1975**, Mits began selling the first popular personal computer, the Altair, for $395. Before then, computers were too expensive for individuals to afford.

Unfortunately, the Altair came as a kit that was hard to assemble, and it contained inadequate hardware and software. But soon afterwards, in 1977, came personal computers that were easy to set up and contained reasonable hardware, built by Apple, Commodore, and Radio Shack. For the first time, computers became easy & cheap enough to put in the typical American home.

IBM PC

In **1981**, IBM began selling the IBM PC. It was slightly better than earlier personal computers and set the standard for all future personal computers.

Mouse & graphical interfaces

In **1984**, Apple began selling the Macintosh computer, nicknamed the "Mac." Priced at $2495, it was the first affordable computer to use a mouse. It was a stripped-down version of Apple's Lisa computer and Xerox's Alto computer, which had been invented earlier but were too expensive.

The Mac became immediately popular and led Microsoft to create Windows, which made the IBM PC try to act like a Mac. Versions 1 and 2 of Windows worked terribly, but Windows 3 (which came out in 1990) worked well. Then came further improvements: Windows 3.1, 95, 98, Me, XP, Vista, and 7.

Now every desktop personal computer comes with a mouse, and every notebook computer comes with a mouse or an imitation (such as a Touchpad).

CD-ROMs & multimedia

During the Christmas season of **1992**, many folks bought CD-ROM drives. The drives were available before then, but the public had to wait until 1992 for the drives to become cheap and the disks to become plentiful. Now most software comes on CD-ROM disks instead of floppy disks.

CD-ROM disks can hold enough bytes to store music, so now most computers come with nice sound cards and speakers, and entertainment software produces nice music. CD-ROM disks can also hold short video clips; longer video clips are available on souped-up CD-ROM disks called DVD.

Internet

In **1995**, the Internet suddenly became popular, as Netscape 2 came out. (Earlier browsers and e-mail systems were awkward and less powerful.) Also in 1995, Windows 95 came out, which was the first version of Windows that could attach to the Internet well. That year, Americans took crash courses in how to use the Internet. Now most computers connect to the Internet.

Your future

Let's look ahead....

Become an expert

To become a computer expert, you need a computer, literature, and friends.

A computer to practice on

If possible, buy a computer to practice on. You can buy a decent one for about $500. If you can't afford even $500, get a used computer. Ask your computer friends whether they want to get rid of any "used junky obsolete computers" for under $100, or ask them whether they can lend you a computer for a weekend. Swap: if they lend you an Apple for a weekend, bake them an apple pie.

Another way to save money is to join your friends for a group purchase. For example, if 9 of you each chip in $25, you can buy a $225 computer. Divide the 9 of you into 3 trios, and rotate the computer from trio to trio every day, so that you get to use the computer every third day.

Literature to read

Begin by reading *The Secret Guide to Computers*. Then read the manuals that came with your computer.

Find out what's new by subscribing to computer magazines or reading them in your town's library.

You can get computer books and magazines from the bookstore at your local college. You can also try your local branch of the country's biggest bookstore chains: **Barnes & Noble** and **Borders**. If you live near Denver, visit **Tattered Cover** (America's largest independent bookstore, at 303-322-7727). If you live near Los Angeles, visit **Opamp Technical Books** (a great technical bookstore at 323-464-4322). You can find a huge collection of computer books at **Micro Center** (a chain of computer stores).

You can get discounts from mail-order booksellers such as **Amazon (www.amazon.com)**.

Since *The Secret Guide to Computers* is an underground book, you won't find it in most stores. To find out which nifty bookstores, computer stores, and consultants near you carry the *Secret Guide*, phone me at 603-666-6644, and I'll look up your ZIP code in my computer.

Friends to chat with

When you have a computer question, phone me at 603-666-6644. Another way to get help is to join a computer club.

The biggest and best computer club was the **Boston Computer Society (BCS)**, which had about 30,000 members, held over 1,000 meetings per year, published many magazines and newsletters, and had hundreds of volunteers who gave free phone help on technical topics. It began in 1977 but shut down in 1996. Its founder and first president was a 13-year-old kid. I hope some other kid starts something equally wonderful someday!

If you live near New York City, join a computer club called **New York Personal Computer (NY PC)**. Membership costs $45 for 1 year, $80 for 2 years, $35 per year for full-time students. Details are at www.nypc.org.

If you live near Philadelphia, join a computer club called the **Philadelphia Area Computer Society (PACS)**. Membership costs $20 per year. Details are at www.pacsnet.org.

Americans living in Tokyo have started the **Tokyo PC Users Group (TPC)**. Their newsletter, written in English, is top-notch! Details are at www.tokyopc.org.

The biggest and best computer clubs are in retirement communities in **Arizona** (near Mesa) and **Florida**.

To find computer clubs near *you*, ask employees at your local computer stores, high schools, and colleges. You can also check the list put out by the **Association of PC User Groups (APCUG)** at http://cdb.apcug.org/loclist.asp.

If you take a computer course, get personal help by chatting with your teacher and classmates. To save money, sign up for the cheap courses given by your high school's "adult education" evening program and your local community college.

I occasionally travel around the world and give courses inexpensively or for free. Heads of the computer industry got their training from my courses. To join us, use the coupon on the back page.

Land a computer job

To become a lawyer, you must graduate from law school and pass the Bar Exam. But to become a computer expert, there's no particular program you must graduate from, no particular exam to pass, and no particular piece of paper that "proves" you're an expert or even competent.

You can get a job in the computer industry even if you've never had any training. Your job will be sweeping the floor.

To become a top computer expert, you must study hard, day and night.

> Read lots of computer manuals, textbooks, guidebooks, magazines, newspapers, and newsletters. Practice using many kinds of computers, operating systems, languages, word-processing programs, spreadsheets, database systems, graphics packages, and communications programs. Also explore the many educational programs for kids. Study the human problems of dealing with computers. No matter how much you know, learn *more*!
>
> When I surveyed computer experts, I found that the typical expert spends two hours per day **reading** about computers, to fill holes in the expert's background and learn what happened in the computer industry that day! The expert also spends many hours **practicing** what was read and swapping ideas in chats with other computerists.

As a computer expert, you can choose your own hours, but they must be many: if your interest in computers lasts just from 9 AM to 5 PM, you'll never become a computer expert.

To break into the computer field, you can use 6 tools: college, home consulting, home programming, salesmanship, job expansion, and on-the-job training.

College

The traditional way to get a computer job is to attend college and get an M.A. or Ph.D. in computer science. Unfortunately, that takes a lot of time.

Home consulting

The fastest way to break into the field is to keep your current job but spend weekends and evenings helping neighbors, friends, and colleagues learn about computers.

Help them buy hardware and software; customize their systems to meet their own personal needs; teach them in how to use it all. Lots of folks want training in how to get the most out of Windows, Microsoft Office, other popular software, and the Internet.

At first, do it all for free. When you've become an experienced expert and developed a list of happy clients who'll vouch for your brilliance, start requesting money from new clients. Start cheaply, at $10 per hour, then gradually raise your rates. Most computer consultants charge about $60 per hour, and some charge much more than that; but I suggest you be gentler on your clients' pocketbooks! By charging little, you'll get more clients, they'll rack up more hours with you, and you won't need to spend lots of time and money on "advertising". For example, at $20 per hour you'll be very popular!

Home programming

At home, you can write computer programs to sell to friends and software publishers, but make sure your programs serve a real need and don't duplicate what's already on the market. Be creative!

Salesmanship

For a faster career path, learn enough about computers to get a job selling them in a store.

As a salesperson, you'll help people decide which hardware and software to buy; you'll be acting as a consultant.

The store will probably let you take hardware, software, and literature home with you, so you can study and practice new computer techniques every evening and become brilliant. If you wish, moonlight by helping your customers use the software they bought; design your own customized programs for them.

After working in the store several months, you'll have the knowledge, experience, contacts, and reputation to establish yourself as an independent consultant. You can call your former customers and become their advisor, trainer, and programmer — or even set up your *own* store.

Job expansion

Another way to break into the field is to take a non-computer job and gradually enlarge its responsibilities, so that it involves computers.

If you're a clerk, ask permission to use spreadsheet and data-management programs to manage your work more efficiently. If you're a math teacher, ask the principal to let you teach a computer course or help manage the school's computer club.

Keep your current job, but expand it to include new skills so you gradually become a computer expert.

On-the-job training

The final way to break into the field is to get a job in a computer company, as a janitor or clerk, and gradually move up by using the company's policy of free training for employees.

Phone me

Companies phone me when they're want computer experts. If you think you're an expert and can demonstrate your expertise, I'll be glad to pass your name along to employers.

Occasionally, I even have job openings here at The Secret Guide to Computers. Ask!

Set your rates

If somebody's interested in hiring you to be a programmer or consultant, you must decide what rate to charge.

On your *first* job, be humble and charge very little!

Your first job's main goal should *not* be money. Instead, your goal should be to gain experience, enhance your reputation, and find somebody you'll act as your reference and give you a good recommendation. Convince your first employer you're the best bargain he ever got, so he'll be wildly enthusiastic about you and give you a totally glowing recommendation when you seek your second job.

If you can't find anyone willing to pay you, work for free, so your résumé can say you "helped computerize a company". Then you can get jobs that make you richer.

Though your first computer job might pay little or nothing, it gets your foot in the computer industry's door. After your first job, your salary will rise fast because the most valuable attribute you can have in this field is *experience*.

Since experienced experts are hard to find, they get high salaries; but there's a *surplus* of "kids fresh out of college" who know nothing. Consider your first job a valuable way to gain experience, even if the starting salary is low. When applying for your first job, remember you're still unproven, and be thankful your first employer is willing to take a risk on you.

Asking for a raise

After several months on the job, when you've thoroughly proved you're worth more than your and your employer is thoroughly thrilled with your performance, gently ask him for a slight raise. If he declines, keep working at that job but keep your eyes open for a better alternative.

Negotiating a contract

The fundamental rule of contract negotiation is: never make a big commitment.

For example, suppose somebody offers to pay you $10,000 if you write a fancy program. Don't accept the offer; the commitment's too big. Instead, request $1,000 for writing a stripped-down version of the program.

After writing the stripped-down version, wait and see whether you get the $1,000; if you get it without hassles, agree to make the version slightly fancier, for a few thousand dollars more. That way, if you have an argument with your employer (which is common), you've lost just $1,000 of effort instead of $10,000.

Contract headaches

Arguments between programmers and employers are common, for 6 reasons:

1. As a programmer, you'll unfortunately **underestimate the time** to debug the program, because you're too optimistic about your abilities.

2. Your employer **won't be precise** when telling you what kind of program to write. You'll write a program you *think* satisfies the employer's request then discover he wanted something slightly different.

3. Your employer will forget to tell you about **strange cases** the company must handle. They require extra "IF" statements in your program.

4. When the employer sees your program work, he'll think of **extra** things he'd like it to do, which require extra programming effort from you.

5. When the program finally does all the employer expects, he'll want you to **teach** his staff how to use it. If his staff hasn't dealt with computers before, the training could take long. He'll also want you to write a manual about how to use the program.

6. **After the company begins using the program, the employer will want you to make more changes**, for free.

To minimize those 6 conflicts, be honest and kind to your employer. Explain to him you're worried about those 6 conflicts and you'd like to discuss them *now*, before you or he makes commitments. Then make a small commitment for a small payment for a short time; and make sure you and the employer are both happy with the way that small commitment works out before attempting bigger ones.

Develop your career

Here are further tricks to develop your career.

Programmer

A **programmer** is a teacher: the programmer teaches the computer new tricks (such as how to do the payroll) by feeding the computer a list of instructions (explaining how to do the payroll). The list of instructions is called a **program**.

Languages The program's written by using the computer's limited vocabulary. Earlier in *The Secret Guide to Computers*, I explained a vocabulary called **Basic**, which consists of words such as PRINT, INPUT, IF, and THEN. That vocabulary — Basic — is called a **computer language**. It's a small part of English. No computer understands the whole English language. The programmer's job is to translate an English sentence (such as "do the payroll") into language the computer understands (such as Basic). So *the programmer is a translator*.

Some computers understand Basic. Other computers understand a different vocabulary, such as C++ or Cobol. Before programming a computer, find out which language the computer understands. If you're applying for a programming job, find out which language you're expected to program in.

Of the popular languages, Basic is the easiest and the most fun. To become a programmer, study Basic then learn other languages that are yuckier.

Since Basic's so easy, saying you know Basic is less prestigious than saying you know harder languages such as C++. To get lots of prestige, learn *many* languages. To convince the interviewer you're brilliant, say you know *many* languages well, even if the job you're applying for needs just one language.

The most prestigious languages to know are assembly and machine languages, because they're the hardest.

> If you can convince the interviewer that you know assembly and machine languages, the interviewer will assume you're God and offer you a very high salary, even if the job doesn't require a knowledge of those languages.

Specific computers Before going to the interview, learn about the specific computer the company uses — and its operating system.

Analysis versus coding Programming consists of 2 stages. In the first stage, analyze the problem to make it more specific.

> For example, suppose the problem is, "Program the computer to do the payroll". The first stage is to decide exactly how the company wants the payroll done: weekly, bi-weekly, semi-monthly, or monthly? While computing payroll checks, what other reports do you want the computer to generate? For example, do you want the computer to print a report about the employees' attendance and how much money each department spends on salaries? What kind of paychecks do you want the computer to *refuse* to print? For example, if somebody in the company tries to make the computer print a paycheck for a ridiculous amount (such as $1,000,000 or ½¢), you want the computer to refuse (and perhaps signal an alarm).

That stage — analyzing a vague problem (such as "do the payroll") to make it more specific — is called **analysis**. A person who analyzes is called an **analyst** or, more prestigiously, a **systems analyst**.

After analyzing the vague problem and transforming it into a series of smaller, more specific tasks, the analyst turns the problem over to a team of **coders**. Each coder takes one of the tasks and translates it into Basic or Cobol or some other language.

If you're hired to be a "programmer", your first assignment will probably be as a coder. After you gain experience, you'll be promoted to a systems analyst.

The ideal systems analyst knows how to analyze a problem but has prior experience as a coder. A systems analyst who knows how to both code and analyze is called a **programmer/analyst**. An analyst who doesn't know how to code — who merely knows how to break a big problem into a series of little ones — is paid less.

3 kinds of programming Programming falls into 3 categories: **development**, **testing**, and **maintenance**.

> **Development** means inventing a new program.
>
> **Testing** means making sure the program works.
>
> **Maintenance** means making minor improvements to programs written long ago. The "improvements" consist of eliminating errors discovered recently, or making the program conform to changed government regulations, or adding more features so the program produces more reports or handles special cases.

Development is more exciting than testing, which is more exciting than maintenance. If you're a new programmer, the other programmers will probably "stick you" in the maintenance department, where you'll be part of the maintenance crew. Since your job will consist of "cleaning up" old programs, cruel programmers will call you a "computer janitor".

"Application program" versus "system program" Programs fall into two categories.

> The usual kind of program is an **application program**: it handles a specific application (such as "payroll" or "chess" or "send rocket to moon").
>
> The other kind of program is a **system program**, whose only purpose is to help programmers write applications programs. For example, hidden inside the computer is a program that makes the computer understand Basic. That program explains to the computer what the words PRINT, INPUT, and IF mean. That program (called the **Basic language processor**) is an example of a system program. Another system program is the **operating system**: it tells the computer how to handle the disks, screen, keyboard, mouse, and printer. Another system program is the **editor**: it lets you edit files and programs.

A person who invents system programs is called a **systems programmer**. To become a systems programmer, learn C++, assembly language, and machine language. Creating a system program is hard, so a systems programmer usually gets paid more than an applications programmer.

The word "systems" is prestigious: it's used in the phrase "systems analyst" and in "systems programmer". In some companies, if your boss wants to praise you, the boss will put the word "systems" in front of your title even if your job has nothing to do with "systems".

How to learn programming To be a good programmer, you need experience. You can't become a good programmer by just reading books and listening to lectures; you must **get your hands on a computer and practice**.

If you take a computer course, the books & lectures are less useful than the experience of using a computer. Spend lots of time practicing, at home or in the school's computer center. Think of the course as just an excuse to get permission to use the school's computers. The quality of the lecture is less important than the quality of the school's computer center. The ideal computer center:

> has computers that understand many languages
> gives you *unlimited* use of the computers (no "extra charges")
> is open 24 hours a day
> has enough computers so you don't have to wait for somebody else to finish
> has a staff of "teaching assistants" who answer your questions
> has a rack full of easy-to-read manuals explaining how to use the computers
> lets you borrow books and manuals, to take home with you
> has *several* kinds of computers, so you get a broad range of experience

Before enrolling in a computer course, find out whether the school's computer center has those features.

Many computer courses are ridiculously expensive. To save money, take fewer courses: buy more books and magazines instead, and buy a computer yourself! If you can't afford a fancy computer, get a cheaper one or share the cost with friends. After you use the computer, you can get some of its cost back by selling it.

Another cheap way to get an education is to phone your town's board of education and ask whether the town offers any adult-education courses in computers. Some towns offer adult-education computer courses for under $100.

Community colleges offer low-cost courses that are decent. Explore the community colleges before sinking money into institutions that overcharge.

Starting salary For your first programming job, your salary will be "about $30,000", but the exact amount depends on which languages you know, how many programs you wrote before, whether you have a college degree, whether you've had experience on that kind of computer, and whether you know the application area. (For example, if you're a programmer for an insurance company, it's helpful to know something about insurance.)

Degrees A college degree ain't needed, but wow can it make you look smart! Try to get a degree in **computer science** or **management information systems** or **information technology.**

> **Computer science** emphasizes the underlying theory, systems programming, assembly language, C++, and applications to science.
>
> **Management information systems (MIS)** emphasizes Basic, databases, and applications to business.
>
> **Information technology (IT)** is a modern compromise that also emphasizes networking, the Internet, and Java.

A major in "math" that emphasizes computers is also acceptable.

Discrimination If you're a woman or non-white or handicapped, you'll be pleased to know that the computer industry discriminates less than other occupations. Being a woman or non-white or handicapped works to your *advantage*, since many companies have affirmative-action programs.

But discrimination exists against older people. If you're over 40 and try to get a job as an entry-level programmer, you'll have a tough time since the stereotypical programmer is "young, bright, and a fast thinker". If you're old, they'll assume you're "slow and sluggish".

Because of that discrimination, an oldster should try entering the computer industry through a different door: as a consultant or computer salesperson or computer-center manager or computer teacher. For those positions, your age works to your *advantage*, since those jobs require *wisdom*, and people will assume that since you're old, you're wise.

Shifting careers If you're old, the best way to enter the computer field is to combine computer knowledge with other topics you knew previously.

> If you already know a lot about selling merchandise, get a job selling computers. If you already know a lot about teaching, get a job teaching about computers — or helping teachers deal with computers. If you already know a lot about real estate, computerize your real estate office.

Instead of trying to "hop" to a computer career, gradually *shift* your responsibilities so they deal more with computers.

To enter the computer field safely, keep your current job but computerize it.

> For example, if you're already a math teacher, keep teaching math but convince your school to let you also teach a computer course or at least incorporate computers into math classes or help run the computer center. If you already work for a big company and your job bores you, try to transfer to a department that puts you in closer contact with computers. After a year in that transitional state, you can break into the computer field more easily since you can put the word "computer" somewhere on your résumé as "job experience".

If you're a college kid, write programs that help professors and others during your vacations.

> Agree to write programs for little or no pay. Your goal is *not* money: your goal is to put "experienced programmer" on your résumé.

Interviews When applying for your first computer job, try to avoid the "personnel" office. The bureaucrats in that office will look at your résumé, see it includes too little experience, and trash it.

Instead, play the who-you-know game. Contact somebody who actually works with computers. Convince that person you're brighter than your résumé indicates. Prove you've learned so much (from reading, courses, and practice) that you can *quickly* conquer any task laid before you. If you impress that person enough, you might get the job even though your paper qualifications look too short.

When you get an interview, be assertive.

> Ask the interviewer more questions than the interviewer asks you. Ask the interviewer about the company's computer and why the company doesn't have a different one. Ask the interviewer how other employees feel about the computer center. Ask the same kinds of questions a computer manager would ask. That way, the interviewer will assume you have the potential to become a computer manager and will hire you immediately. You'll also be showing you *care* enough about the company to ask questions. You'll be showing you have a vibrant personality and you're not just "another vegetable who came through the door".

One of the strange things about applying for a programming job is that the interviewer will *not* ask to see a sample of your work. He doesn't have time to read your program. Even if he *did* have time to read your program, he couldn't be sure you wrote it yourself. Instead, he'll just *chat* with you about your accomplishments. You must "talk smart" by knowing all the buzzwords of the computer industry, even if they don't really help you write programs.

Later joys Your first job will pay low, but don't worry about that. You'll learn a lot at that job: you're getting a free education. After your training period is over, your salary will rise fast — especially if you do extra studying during evenings and weekends. Your *real* job is: to become brilliant!

After you've become brilliant a& experienced, other companies will eagerly try to hire you. Your best strategy is to leave your current company and work elsewhere to gain new experiences. **Whenever you feel you're "coasting" and not learning anything new, it's time to move to a different job.** The "different job" can be in a new company — or in a different department of the same company.

By moving around, you'll gain a wide variety of experiences, so you'll become a qualified, wise consultant.

Social contacts Programming is not always glamorous. You'll spend many long hours staring at your screen and wondering why your program doesn't work. The job is intellectual, not social. But after you've become an expert coder, you'll get into systems analysis and consulting and teaching and management, where you interact with people more.

Management

Programming is fun for young kids. But as you get older, you'll tire of machines and rather deal with people instead. As you approach retirement, you'll want to help the younger generation relate to the computers you've mastered.

To be a successful manager, you need 3 skills: you must be **technically competent**, **wise**; and **know how to handle people**.

You should know how to program. Know each computer company's strengths & weaknesses and be able to compare their products. Develop a philosophy about what makes a "good" computer center. Understand people's motives and turn them into constructive energy.

Keep up to date. Read the latest books and periodicals about computers. Chat with other computer experts by phone, by e-mail, at conventions, and at computer clubs.

Here are hints about how to manage a computer center:

Many computer centers put 4-foot-high partitions between their programmers, to give the programmers "privacy". But those partitions are counter-productive: they're too low to block noise, and too high to permit helpful conversation with your neighbor. Knock the partitions down!

When putting a computer center into a school, develop a *cadre* of hotshot students who are bright, friendly, and outgoing and who'll help & encourage other students to use the computer. If the hotshots are *not* outgoing — if they become an elitist, snobbish club — the rest of the school will avoid the computer.

If you've hired "support assistants" who help the programmers & users, don't let the assistants hide in an office or behind a desk. The assistants should walk up to the programmers & users at the keyboards and offer help.

In too many organizations, computers are locked in the offices of prestigious people and aren't used. Let *everybody* share the computers.

Too often, managers judge their own worth by the size of the computer center's budget: the bigger the budget, the more prestigious the manager. But the best manager does *not* having a big budget; the best manager is the one clever enough to meet the company's needs on a *small* budget.

Too often, the computer center's manager decides who can use the computer. That manager becomes powerful and evil. To avoid concentrating so much power in the hands of one bureaucrat, let each department and person buy computers directly. Let the manager give *advice* about which computers would be most pleasant (compatible and hassle-free).

If you're a computer consultant, be honest: tell your client to buy cheap off-the-shelf programs instead of making the client pay you to write "customized" programs.

Sales

You can find 3 kinds of salesmen:

The "slick" kind knows how to sell but doesn't know any technical details about the computer he's selling. He doesn't know how to program and doesn't know much about the computers sold by his competitors. All he knows is the "line" that his boss told him to give the customers. That kind of salesman usually resorts to off-color tactics, such as claiming all computers sold by competitors are "toys".

The opposite kind of salesman is technical: he knows every detail about every computer made but can't give you any *practical* advice about which computer best meets *your* needs.

The best kind of salesman is a consultant. He asks a lot of questions about your particular needs, tells you which of his computers meets your needs best, and even tells you the *limitations* of his computer and why another, more expensive computer sold by a competitor might be better. He's an "honest Joe". He clinches the sale because you trust him and because you know you won't have any unpleasant surprises after the sale. While selling you a computer, he teaches you a lot. He's a true friend.

A woman can sell computers more easily than a man. That's because most computer customers are men, and men are more attracted to women. It's also because, in our society, women are more "trusted" than men. But if you're a woman, say some technical buzzwords to convince the customer you're technically competent and not just a "dumb clerk".

Be an entrepreneur

How about starting a rental service, where people can rent computers? How about running a camp where kids can spend the summer playing with computers? How about running a computer setup service, where you teach businesses how to start using computers and create their own Web sites? How about writing easy manuals explaining the most popular software? Each of those ideas has been tried successfully; join the fun! But here are the hardest things about starting your own company:

letting people know you exist
convincing people you're good and worth your price

Change your personality

As you spend time with computers, your personality will change. You'll gradually become a **hacker** (a person skilled at fiddling with the internal workings of computer hardware and software). I hope you become a **helpful hacker** instead of a **cracker** (a hacker who creates mischief by screwing up the internal workings of computer hardware and software, such as by writing a virus or by using password-evasion tricks to secretly spy at private files).

Back in 1993, 100 hackers in an Internet newsgroup got together and wrote a description of a hacker's personality. Here's the description, as edited by Eric Raymond (in his *New Hacker's Dictionary*) and then further edited by me. Not all hackers fit this description — but most do!

If you hang around computers a long time, this description will probably start applying to you too! Watch yourself!

As America and the world become more computerized, the hacker personality will gradually dominate our planet. If you don't like the "hacker personality", see what you can do to alter it.

Hacker intelligence

The hacker mind is intelligent but strange.

College intelligence Most hackers past their teens have a college degree or are self-taught to a similar level. Before becoming a full-fledged hacker, the typical hacker majored in computer science or electrical engineering or math or physics or linguistics (since studying human languages is a good stepping stone to studying computer languages) or philosophy (since philosophy analyzes the meaning of language and "life forms").

Read a lot Hackers read a lot, and read a wide variety, though with extra emphasis on science facts and science fiction. A hacker's home includes a big library, with many shelves full of books that the hacker has read. A hacker spends more spare time reading books & magazines than watching TV. A hacker spends as much spare time reading as the average non-hacker spends watching TV.

Bad handwriting Hackers have bad handwriting — their script is hard to read — so they usually write in simple capital block letters (LIKE THIS), as if they were junior draftsmen writing on a blueprint. The capital block letters make sense, especially when writing math equations or programming instructions that contain lots of symbols; script would be no faster.

Inhuman communication Since programming requires good organization and precise use of language, hackers are good at composing sentences, paragraphs, and compositions. But though hackers are good writers, they're bad talkers, since they don't get much practice chatting with humans. They're not skilled at arguing with humans, confronting them, and negotiating with them; they're better at communicating with computers, which don't argue.

Good at memorizing Hackers are good at memorizing details, such as computer codes.

Neat just in output Hackers produce programs, writings, and thinking that are very neat and well-organized; but a hacker is too busy to make the hacker's environment equally neat, so a hacker's desk and office floor are typically piled high with a disorganized mess of resources.

Hacker bodies

Here's what a hacker looks like, and where to find one.

Near universities Half of the USA's best hackers live within 100 miles of Boston or San Francisco. That's because, during the 1950's and 1960's, the top researchers in artificial intelligence were at two universities: the **Massachusetts Institute of Technology** (**MIT**, in Cambridge, Massachusetts, near Boston) and **Stanford University** (in Silicon Valley's Palo Alto, near San Francisco). Those researchers spawned proteges, who want to keep living near the master researchers even after graduation, to stay connected to the intellectual community.

Mostly male Most hackers are male, but females are more common in hackerdom than in other technical professions.

Mostly Caucasian In the USA, most hackers are Caucasian. On the West Coast, many hackers are Asian; on the East Coast, many hackers are Jewish.

Relatively unbigoted Hackers are less bigoted than other Americans, since hackers care more about what a person wrote than the person's appearance. Hackers believe computers can act like humans and therefore believe in the humane treatment of all computers and all people.

Casual dresser Hackers dislike "business attire". The typical hacker would quit a job if it required wearing a suit.

Hackers like to wear clothes that are casual, easy to take care of, post-hippie: T-shirts (with slogans on them), jeans, running shoes (or barefoot), and backpacks.

Scruffy appearance Hackers look scruffy. Many hackers have long hair. Men hackers often have beards and moustaches. Women hackers try to look "natural" by wearing little or no makeup.

Since hackers love computers, which are mostly indoors, hackers don't get tans.

Night owls Hackers often stay up all night, to finish work on excitingly frustrating programming challenges. Then they sleep late in the morning.

Extreme food For dinner, hackers prefer spicy ethnic food instead of "American" food. The most popular is spicy Chinese (Szechuan or Hunan style, rather than Cantonese, which is too bland). Alternatives, popular occasionally, are Thai food and Mexican food.

For a change, hackers like high-quality Jewish-deli food, when available.

For midnight snacks while in the middle of marathon programming sessions, hackers prefer pizza and microwave burritos. Back in the 1970's, hackers used to eat a lot of junk food, but modern hackers are more into "health food".

Hackers tend to be extreme: either too skinny or too fat. More hackers are too skinny than too fat.

Nearly drug-free Hackers need to protect their heads from drugs, so they don't do drugs. They don't smoke. Most hackers don't drink alcohol, though a few hackers experiment with fancy wines and exotic beers.

Since hackers favor experimentation, they tolerate folks who use non-addictive drugs such as pot and LSD. But hackers criticize people who take "downers" and opiates, since those drugs make you act stupid.

To help stay up late at night programming, hackers often take mild "uppers" such as caffeine (in coffee and Jolt cola) and sugar (in soft drinks and junk food).

Experimental sex Hackers are more likely than "normal" folks to experiment sexually. Many hackers openly have multiple boyfriends or girlfriends, or live in communes or group houses, or practice open marriage (where both partners agree that extra-marital relationships are okay), or are gay or lesbian.

Hacker beliefs

Here's how to make a hacker happy.

Toys better than money Hackers don't care about earning lots of money or social approval. Instead, hackers just want the intellectual pleasure of inventing beautiful programs and products — and exploring the beautiful products invented by others.

So to bribe a hacker, don't offer money or a fancy title; instead, offer a lab full of computer hardware and software for the hacker to play with, and permission for the hacker to spend time playing with and inventing fantastic technology.

Non-religious Since hackers don't like to be told what to do, they don't like organized religion. Since hackers are into facts, not beliefs, they tend not to believe in God.

When asked "What religion are you?", many hackers reply by calling themselves "atheist" or "agnostic" or "non-observant Jewish". Some hackers join "parody" religions, such as Discordianism and the Church of the SubGenius. Some hackers have fun participating in "mystical" religions such as Zen Buddhism and neo-paganism.

Libertarian politics Hackers like freedom to explore computers. They don't like restrictions. They don't like being told what to do.

They dislike authoritarians, managers, MBA's, and big government. They tend to be Libertarian. They dislike the dogmatic insistence of the far left and far right. If asked to choose between Democrats and Republicans, they tend to choose Democrats because Democrats permit more social freedoms, so hackers are classified as "left of center".

Cat lovers Hackers are more likely to have cats than dogs, because cats are like hackers: clever rather than belligerent.

No team sports Hackers don't like to watch sports. Hackers don't watch sports on TV and don't go to sports stadiums.

Hackers would rather participate than watch. Though half of all hackers don't make time to participate, the other half *do* participate, but mainly in individual sports rather than team sports. The only team sport they like is volleyball, because it's non-contact and friendly.

They prefer individual sports that involve dexterity, concentration, and stamina, rather than brute force. Their favorite sports are bicycling, hiking, rock climbing, caving, kite-flying, juggling, martial arts, roller skating, ice skating, skiing, target shooting, and auto racing, and aviation.

Strange cars Hackers don't wash their cars. Hackers drive extreme cars: either beat-up heaps (unwashed because they're junk) or (if the hackers are rich) luxury sports cars (unwashed anyway).

Brainy hobbies Hackers like to play music, play board games (such as chess and Go), dabble in ham radio, learn about linguistics & foreign languages, and do "theater teching" (give technical support to theater productions).

Hate stupidity Hackers like active intelligent freedom, so they dislike dishonesty, boredom, business suits, stupid incompetent people (especially stupid incompetent managers who wear business suits), stupid music (such as "easy listening music"), and stupid culture (such as TV, except for TV's cleverly cynical cartoons & movies & the old Star Trek).

Teach your kids

Here's how to introduce kids to computers.

Teaching programming

Kids should start writing simple programs in Basic when they're in the third grade. (The brightest kids can start even younger!) Before the third grade, the typical kid should learn how to run other people's programs and maybe learn Logo (a language that's easier than Basic for beginners). More programs have been written in Basic than any other computer language.

Before graduating from high school, every kid should learn Basic — and how to create Web pages by using HTML and JavaScript.

Educational applications

The computer can help teach many topics.

English While trying to write a program, the kid learns the importance of punctuation: the kid learns to distinguish colons, semicolons, commas, periods, parentheses, and brackets. The kid also learns the importance of spelling: if the kid misspells the word PRINT or INPUT, the computer gripes. The kid learns to read technical stuff when wading through computer manuals.

Some kids "hate to write English compositions". The computer can change that attitude!

A word-processing program makes "writing an English composition" become a fun video game, when the words appear on the screen and you can move them around by using the computer's nifty editing tools, which can even correct spelling (without forcing the kid to thumb through a dictionary) and check grammar and style. It's educational fun!

To make the kid understand why parts of speech (such as "nouns", "verbs", and "adjectives") are important, give the kid a computer program that writes sentences by choosing random nouns, random verbs, and random adjectives. Then tell the kid to invent his *own* nouns, verbs, and adjectives, feed them into the program, and see what kind of sentences the program produces.

Young kids have enjoyed a program called **Story Machine**.

It gives you a list of nouns, verbs, adjectives, and other parts of speech that you can use to build a story. You type the story using any words on the list. As you type the story, the computer will *automatically illustrate it!* For example, if you type, "The boy eats the apple," your screen will automatically show a picture of a boy eating an apple! If you type *several* sentences, to form a longer story, the computer will automatically illustrate the entire story and produce an animated cartoon of it! The program will also criticize your story's structure. For example, if you say "The boy eats the apple" but the boy isn't near the apple yet, the program will recommend that you insert a sentence such as "The boy runs to the apple" beforehand. The program came on a $25 disk from Softkey and required an Apple 2 computer.

History The computer can make history come "alive" by throwing the student into an historical situation.

For example, a graduate of my teacher-training institute wrote a program that says, "It's 1910. You're **Kaiser Wilhelm**. What are you going to do?" Then it gives you several choices.

For example, it asks "Would you like to make a treaty with Russia?" If you answer "yes", the computer replies, "Russia breaks the treaty. *Now* what are you going to do?" No matter how you answer the questions, there are only two ways the program can end: either "You've plunged Europe into a World War" or "You've turned Germany into a second-rate country". After running that program several times, you get a feeling for the terrible jam that the Kaiser was in and begin to pity him. Running the program is more dramatic than reading a book on the Kaiser's problems, because the program forces you to step into the Kaiser's shoes and react to his surroundings: you are there. When you finish running the program, you feel you've lived another life — the life of a 1910 Kaiser.

Such a program is called an historical **simulation**, since it makes the computer **simulate** (imitate) an historical event.

Current events The best way to teach current events is through simulation.

The best way to encourage the student to analyze the conflict between **Israel and the Arabs** is have the student run a program that begins by saying "You're Israel's Prime Minister" then run a program that says "You're the Palestinian leader".

By running both programs, the student learns to take both sides of the argument and understands the emotions of both leaders. Such programs could help warring nations understand each other enough to bring peace!

When the nuclear power plant at **3-Mile Island** almost exploded, teachers wrote a program saying "You're in the control room at 3-Mile Island".

Your computer's screen shows a picture of the control room. Your goal: make as much money as possible for the electric company without blowing the place up. You can buy two versions of the program: one's called just "3-Mile Island"; the other's called "Scram". To teach kids about 3-Mile Island, it's easier to buy the program than to get permission from parents to "take the kids on a field trip to 3-Mile Island" (which also requires that you sit on a bus while listening to 100 choruses of "100 bottles of beer on the wall" and worrying about kids who get lost at 3-Mile Island).

The best way to teach **economics and politics** is to give the student a program that says "You're running the country" and then asks the student to input an economic and political strategy. At the end of the program, the computer tells how many years the student lasted in office, how well the country fared, and how many people want to assassinate him.

The best way to learn anything is "by experience". Computer simulations let the student learn by "simulated experience", which condenses into a few minutes what would otherwise require many *years* of "natural experience".

Biology The computer can do **genetics** calculations: it can compute the probabilities of having various kinds of offspring and predict how the population's characteristics will shift.

The computer can handle **taxonomy**: it can classify different kinds of animals and plants.

The computer asks you a series of questions about an organism and finally tells you the organism's name. A popular game called **Animals** lets the student teach the computer which questions to ask.

To teach **ecology**, a graduate of my teacher-training institute wrote a simulation program that begins by saying, "You're the game warden of New Jersey. What are you going to do?"

It asks how many weeks you want the deer-hunting season to last. If you make the hunting season too *long*, hunters kill all the deer, and deer-loving environmentalists hate you. But if you make the deer-hunting season too *short*, hunters hate you; moreover, the deer overpopulate, can't find enough to eat, then die of starvation, whereupon *everybody* hates you. Your goal is to stay in office as long as possible.

Sex education When Dartmouth College (which for centuries had been all-male and rowdy) suddenly became coed in 1971, its biology department realized the importance of teaching about **birth control**. The professors wrote a program asking your age and which birth control method you wish to use this year.

> You have 9 choices, such as pill, diaphragm, IUD, condom, rhythm method, and "Providence". After you type your choice, the computer computes the probability of having children and can print (if you're unlucky) ***BOY*** or ***GIRL***. The computation is based, as in nature, on a combination of science and chance (random numbers). Then the computer asks your strategy for the next year. The program continues until the computer finally prints ***MENOPAUSE***. The program lets you explore how different strategies yield different numbers of children. Experimenting with the program is safer & faster than experimenting on your body, though maybe not as fun.

How can programs that tutor, drill, and test students be made exciting? Let the programs use the same techniques that make video games exciting.

> Let the programs include animated graphics and require the student to answer fast. Show a running total of the student's points, so whenever the student answers right the screen shows the score increase immediately.
>
> At the end of the educational game, the computer shouldn't say "excellent" or "fair" or "poor". Instead, it should state the total number of points accumulated and ask whether the student wants to try again, to increase the score.
>
> If the student's score is high, the computer should reward the student by giving praise and storing the student's name on the disk. If the student's score is low, no criticism should be given other than asking "Would you like to try again?"

How to pay less for software

If you're a teacher, **tell your hotshot students to write software for you**.

> Your students will love the opportunity to work on a project that's useful. Tell them that if their software is good you'll write them glowing recommendations saying they computerized the school.

Many software publishers give **educational discounts**. Some publishers offer **"site licenses"**, where you pay a big fee but then can make as many copies of the software as you wish. The nicest publishers of business software offer **"trial size" versions** (for $10 or even free), which let you practice the software but require you to keep your documents and files brief.

Avoid dangers

How could computers change human society? The many good ways are obvious. Here are the bad ones.

Errors

Although the computer can have a mechanical breakdown, the usual reason for computer errors is *mental* breakdown — on the part of the people who run it. The usual computer blooper is caused by a programmer who writes a wrong program, or a user who inputs a wrong number. If you want the computer to write a check for $10.00 but you forget to type the decimal point, the computer will nonchalantly write a check for $1000.

The biggest computer blooper ever made:

> A rocket rose majestically from its launch pad at Cape Kennedy and headed toward Venus. Suddenly it began to wobble. It had to be destroyed after less than 5 minutes of flight. The loss was put at $18,500,000. What went wrong? After much head-scratching, the answer was finally found. In one of the lines of one of the programs, a programmer omitted a hyphen.

In one city's computer center, every inhabitant's vital statistics were put on cards. One lady in the town was 107, but the number 107 wouldn't fit on the card properly, because the space allotted for AGE was just two digits.

> The computer just examined the last two digits, which were 07, and assumed she was 7 years old. Since she was 7 and not going to school, the computer printed a truant notice. So city officials visited the home of the 107-year-old lady and demanded to see her mom.

Here's a story from *Time Magazine*:

> Rex Reed, writer and sometime actor, ordered a bed from a Manhattan department store. Three months passed. Then came the long anticipated announcement: the bed will be delivered on Friday.
>
> Reed waited all day. No bed. Having disposed of his other bed, he slept on the floor.
>
> Next day deliverers brought the bed but couldn't put it up. No screws.
>
> On Monday, men appeared with the screws but couldn't put in the mattresses. No slats. "That's not our department."
>
> Reed hired a carpenter to build them. The department store's slats finally arrived 15 weeks later.
>
> Undaunted, Reed went to the store to buy sheets. Two men came up and declared: "You're under arrest." Why? "You're using a stolen credit card. Rex Reed is dead." Great confusion. Reed flashed all his identity cards. The detectives apologized — then tore up his store charge card. Why? "Our computer's been told you're dead. And we can't change this."

At the end of 1999, people were nervous about the **year 2000 problem** (which is also called the **Y2K problem** and the **millennium bug**). Here's what those people said:

> "Many people still use old computer programs that store each year as a 2-digit number. For example, the year 1983 is stored as 83. When the year 2000 comes, some of those old programs will still assume the first two digits of the year will be 19, so they'll store the year 2000 as 00 and assume it means 1900. They'll think the clock's been turned back to the year 1900, think bills are being paid at the wrong time, and think machines haven't been repaired at the right time, so they'll shut down all the machines they control, including cars, elevators (which will plunge), airplanes (which will crash), hospital life-support systems (which will shut down and kill all their patients), utility companies (which will shut off your electricity, water, and phones), and bank machines (which will give customers no more cash)."

Programmers worked to solve that problem. January 1, 2000, came and went without major disasters.

Unemployment

Since the computer's a labor-saving device, it can make laborers unemployed. Clerks and other low-echelon white-collar workers can find themselves jobless and penniless.

Computers can create *new* jobs.

> Not all computer-related jobs require abstract thinking: there's a need for mechanics, typists, secretaries, salespeople, editors, librarians, etc. There's a need for people to tell programmers what to program. Running a computer center is a business, and there's a need for business executives.

When computers do human work, will there be *enough* work left for us humans to do? Don't worry: when no work is necessary, humans have an amazing talent for inventing it.

> That's Madison Avenue's purpose: to create new longings. Instead of significantly shortening the work week, Americans always opt for a work week of nearly equal length but devoted to more luxurious ends. That's the gung-ho Protestant work ethic we're so famous for. Computers change but don't reduce our work.

That's what will happen in the long run. But for the next decade, as society shifts to computers, many folks will be temporarily out of a job.

Quantification

Since the computer handles numbers easily, it encourages people to reduce problems to numbers. That's both good and bad:

> It's good because it forces people to be precise. It's bad because some people make quantification a goal in itself, forgetting that it's but a tool to other ends. Counting the words that Shakespeare wrote is of no value in itself: it must be put to some use. In both the humanities and the social sciences, I'm afraid the motto of the future will be, "If you can't think, count." Some cynics have remarked, "The problem with computers is that they make meaningless research possible."

Since only quantifiable problems can be computerized, there's a danger that people will think unquantifiable problems aren't worth investigating, or unquantifiable aspects of an otherwise quantifiable problem should be ignored. John Kemeny gives this example:

> At an open hearing about designing a new Los Angeles freeway, some voters complained bitterly that the freeway would go right through the midst of a part of the city heavily populated by blacks and destroy the community spirit they'd slowly and painfully built up. The voters' arguments were defeated by the simple statement that, according to an excellent computer, the proposed route was the best possible.
>
> Apparently nobody knew enough to ask how the computer had been instructed to evaluate the routes. Was it asked just to consider the costs of building & acquiring property (in which case it would have found routing through a ghetto area highly advantageous), or was it also asked to take into account human suffering a route would cause?
>
> Perhaps the voters would have agreed it's not possible to measure human suffering in terms of dollars. But if we omit consideration of human suffering, we're equating its cost to zero, which is the worst of all procedures!

People are being reduced to numbers: phone numbers, social security numbers, ZIP codes, etc. When you start treating another human as just a wrong phone number and hang up in his face, something is wrong.

Asocial behavior

The computer's a seductive toy that can wreck your social life.

When you walk up to the computer, you expect to spend just a few minutes but wind up spending hours instead. Whether catching bugs, playing games, or using the Internet, you'll while away lots of time. You may find yourself spending more time with the computer than with people.

Getting along with the computer is easy — perhaps *too* easy. Though it can gripe at you, it can't yell. If you don't like its behavior, you can turn it off. You can't do the same thing to people. Excessive time spent with the computer can leave you unprepared for the ambiguities and tensions of real life.

The computer replaces warmth by precision. Excessive time spent with it might inhibit your development as a loving individual.

Irresponsibility

Computerization is part of the coming technological bureaucracy. Like all bureaucracy, it encourages the individual to say, "Don't blame me — I can't change the bureaucracy." But now the words read, **"Don't blame me — the computer did it."**

When John Kemeny's sister asked a saleswoman whether a certain item was in stock, the woman said she couldn't answer, because the info was kept by a computer. The woman hadn't been able to answer questions about stock even before the computer came in; the computer was just a new scapegoat.

Computers will run governments and wars. The thought of someone saying, "I can't change that — that's the way the computer does it" is frightening.

Concentrated power

As computers amass more info about people, computers will become centers of knowledge. The people who control them — the programmers, sociologists, generals, and politicians — will gain lots of power. The thought of so much power being concentrated in the hands of a few is frightening. A handful of people, pressing the wrong buttons, could atom-bomb the earth.

Nobody should have complete control over a computer center. The power should be diversified. Sensitive data and programs should be protected by passwords and other devices, so no single individual can access all of it.

Crime

The computer's the biggest tool in the kit of the white-collar criminal. He just has to insert a zero, and the computer will send him a paycheck for ten times the correct amount.

To catch computer criminals, computers are programmed to do lots of double-checking; but if the criminal evades the double-checks, he won't get caught. Police have a hard time finding computer criminals, since fingerprints and other traditional forms of evidence are irrelevant. Most computers have passwords to try to stop people from accessing sensitive data, but a bright programmer can devise tricks to get around the passwords.

The crudest is to bug the wires that computers communicate through. A cleverer method is to slip extra lines into innocent programs (or e-mail attachments). The cleverest is to use **social engineering**: convince users (by phone or e-mail) that you're an administrator who must verify all passwords.

Since you must be smart to be a computer criminal, if you're caught you'll be admired. Instead of saying "What a terrible thing you've done!" folks say "Gee, you must be smart. Tell me how you did it." A bright button-down computer criminal who steals $100,000 electronically gets a lighter sentence than the dude who must resort to a gun to get $1000. Is that justice?

Invaded privacy

Of all the harm computers can do, "invaded privacy" worries people the most. George Orwell's book "*1984*" warned that someday "Big Brother will be watching you" via a computer. His prediction's already reality: your whereabouts are constantly checked by computers owned by the FBI, IRS, Homeland Security, military, credit-card companies, and mail-order houses.

> My brother once wrote an innocent letter asking for stamps. Instead of using his own name, he used the name of our dog, Rusty. Since then, we've received letters from many organizations, all addressed to "Mr. Rusty". Our dog's name sits in computers all across the country.

The info computers have stored about you may be misleading. If you never discover the error, the consequences can haunt you the rest of your life. Examples:

A teacher saw one of the little boys in her class kiss another boy. She entered on his computerized school records, "displays homosexual tendencies".

According to computer records, a certain man had "3 lawsuits against him". In fact, the first was a scare suit 30 years before, over a magazine subscription he never ordered; the second had been withdrawn after a compromise over a disputed fee; the third case had been settled in his favor.

During the last 30 years, many laws have been passed to give you privacy rights.

You've a right to see what info is stored about you, and change it if it's wrong. For example, if a teacher or employer writes a "confidential recommendation" about you, you've a right to examine it, to prevent misleading statements from haunting you for life.

Even if the info stored about you is accurate, you've a right to prevent its dissemination to the general public. No organization should store or disseminate info unjustifiably.

What's "justifiable"? Fearing "Big Brother", people don't want politicians to access personal info. On the other hand, fearing criminals, people want the police to have a free hand in sleuthing. How to give info to the police without giving it to politicians can be puzzling.

Outdated info should be obliterated. A person shouldn't be haunted by his distant past; he should be given a chance to turn over a new leaf.

Just facts should be stored, not opinions. It's okay to store that someone lives on Fifth Avenue but not that he lives in a "nice neighborhood".

It's unfortunate that people feel a need for privacy. If the info stored about you is correct, why argue? But many people feel a need to be secretive, and I suppose people have that right. It's called the right to be "let alone".

People don't want to feel their whole lives are on stage, recorded by a computer. It inhibits them from acting free and natural.

Even if the computer doesn't store any damaging info about you, the mere *thought* that all your actions are being recorded is damaging, because it makes you act more conservatively. You may be afraid to adopt a good but unusual lifestyle, because anything "different" about you will look bad on the computerized records used by banks, credit-card companies, insurance companies, and other conservative institutions. The harmful thing is not that Big Brother is watching, but that you *feel* he's watching. You are subjugated.

Share our knowledge

Thanks for reading *The Secret Guide to Computers*. If you have questions about what you've read, phone me at 603-666-6644, day or night.

Editions

You're reading the 31st edition. I've been revising the *Secret Guide* for 39 years:

Edition	Published	Pages	Price	Praised	New tutorials it included
edition 0	1972 spring	17	free	HP-2000	Basic
edition 1	1972 fall	12	free	DEC-10	DEC computers
edition 2	1972 fall	20	free	DEC-10	Fortran
edition 3	1972 fall	32	$1	DEC-10	data files
edition 4	1973 Jan.	63	$2	DEC-10	Algol
edition 5	1973 Sept.	73	$2	DEC-10	graphics
edition 6	1974 July	260	$5.20	DEC-10	artificial intelligence, numerical analysis
eds. 7-9	1976-1979	410	$16.25	TRS-80	hardware, micros, Cobol, language survey
edition 10	1980-1982	696	$29.60	TRS-80	discount dealers, video graphics, Pascal
edition 11	1983-1984	750	$28	IBM PC	IBM PC, word processing
edition 12	1986-1987	909	$24	Leading Edge	DOS, WordPerfect, spreadsheets, DBase, C, Logo
edition 13	1988 Oct.	909	$24	Tussey Swan	Q&A
edition 14	1990 June	607	$15	Gateway	Mac, Excel, Quattro
edition 15	1991 Sept.	607	$15	Gateway	Windows, advanced WordPerfect
edition 16	1992 May	607	$15	Micro Express	DOS 5, Quattro Pro
edition 17	1993 April	607	$15	Expotech	Mac System 7, MS Word, repairs
edition 18	1993 Aug.	607	$15	Expotech	DOS 6
edition 19	1994 Aug.	639	$15	Expotech	Pentium, multimedia computers, DOS 6.2
edition 20	1995 March	639	$15	Quantex	MS Word 6, AMI Bios
edition 21	1995 Nov.	639	$15	Quantex	Windows 95, QBasic
edition 22	1996 June	639	$15	Quantex	Internet, advanced Windows 95
edition 23	1997 May	639	$15	Quantex	Visual Basic, viruses, advanced Internet
edition 24	1997 Dec.	639	$15	Quantex	backup-storage devices
edition 25	1998 Dec.	639	$15	ABS NuTrend	Windows 98, iMac, MS Word 97, Works
edition 26	1999 Sept.	639	$16.50	ABS NuTrend	MS Word 2000, create Web pages
edition 27	2000 Oct.	639	$16.50	ABS NuTrend	PowerPoint, Publisher, Access, Java, C++
edition 28	2002 Aug.	639	$17.50	ABS NuTrend	Windows XP, Linux, Palm, HTML
edition 29	2004 July	607	$17.50	eMachines	Mac OS X, JavaScript
edition 30	2007 Sept.	575	$20	HP Compaq	Windows Vista, MS Office 2007, video editing
edition 31	2011 July	703	$25	HP Compaq	Windows 7, MS Office 2010, tricky living, C#

Editions 4 & 6-13 were each bound as a set of booklets (instead of as a single fat book). Editions 14-31 contained 2 columns per typical page; earlier editions contained just 1 column per page. I used a typewriter (editions 0-10), TRS-80 (ed. 11-13), WordPerfect (ed. 14-22), MS Word (ed. 23-31).

To get on the mailing list for a *free* brochure about the 32nd edition, mail page 703's coupon (or a postcard with your name, address, and the words "send 32nd edition info").

Let's meet

I hope to meet you someday. If you ever visit New Hampshire, drop by and say hi! My workload prevents me from chatting long, but at least we can grin.

I can visit your home town and give you and your friends courses and tutoring. The cost per person can get low if you join your friends. For more info about how I can help you at little or no charge, phone me at 603-666-6644 or mail the back page's coupon.

How to give a course

After you practice using computers and become a computer expert, why not give your *own* courses? You too can become a guru. Here are suggestions....

When giving a course, you won't have time to teach every detail, so just tell the students to read the details in *The Secret Guide to Computers* and other manuals. During class, instead of grinding through details, have fun:

Demonstrate hardware and software the class hasn't seen. **Argue cheerily** about computer hassles. **Let the class ask lots of questions.** Give the class **hands-on experience aided by tutors**.

To liven up your classes and loosen up your students, say this:

"I'm supposed to turn you all into computer experts by 5:00. I'll try."
"In this course, I'm your slave. Anything you want, you get."
"If you're boring, we'll follow the curriculum. If you ask lots of questions, we'll dig into the good stuff."

"Don't bother taking notes. If God wanted you to be a Xerox machine, He'd have made you look that way. So just relax. If you forget what I say, phone me anytime, and I'll repeat it all back to you."

"There's no attendance requirement. While we discuss a topic that bores you, leave — or better yet, play with the computers at the back of the room, so you become super-smart."

Phone me for free help with curriculum, dramatics, and tricks of the trade. For your first course, charge little, so your students are grateful and you build your reputation.

No matter how great you think you are, your students will tire of you eventually. To keep them awake, add variety by including your friends as part of your act.

Good luck. Try hard. You can cast a spell over the audience. Courses change lives.

At your service, your computer butler, Russ Walter, 603-666-6644

Resources

Index

For each topic, this index tells the page number where the discussion *begins*. Look at that page *and the next few pages also*.
To find a command in a specific programming language, *look at that language's chapter*, which begins with its own index of commands.

Get more copies

We offer two kinds of writing:

The Secret Guide to Computers explains computers. *Tricky Living* explains the rest of modern life.

Order more copies for yourself and friends. The books make great presents for Christmas, birthdays, graduations, and celebrations. Older editions include extra info about older computers & lifestyles. For books or free brochures, use this coupon, which gives you quantity discounts. Copy it for your friends. If you have questions, call **603-666-6644** or see **SecretFun.com**, which explains more and lets you read some chapters online, free.

Money-back guarantee

If you're not sure whether to order a book, go ahead: you can return unused books anytime for a 100% refund.

Many ways to order

The simplest way to order is to mail this page's coupon with a check, money order, credit-card info, or cash. Other choices:

You can **visit** us in New Hampshire to pick up the books personally: phone 603-666-6644 for directions and a pickup time.

To order by **credit card**, you can mail this coupon or phone 603-666-6644 (or e-mail Russ@SecretFun.com, if you don't mind sending unsecured e-mail). Give your credit-card number, expiration date, and name printed on the card. We take Master Card, Visa, American Express, and Discover.

We can **bill** you if you bought at least 10 books from us before (or you're employed by or retired from a school, bookstore, government agency, or established computer company). Mail this coupon or phone 603-666-6644 or e-mail Russ@SecretFun.com. If over $700, phone for approval. The bill is due in 30 days.

We accept 5 forms of payment from other countries:

international postal money order (written in U.S. dollars)

credit-card number (Master Card, Visa, American Express, or Discover, with expiration date and the name printed on the card)

check (written in U.S. dollars and having a U.S. or Canadian city printed somewhere on the check)

cash (we convert foreign currency & send change)

wire transfer (in U.S. dollars, from your local outlet of Western Union or MoneyGram, plus a phone call or note telling us how you transferred)

Review copies

If you plan to introduce the book to at least 100 people, phone 603-666-6644 to request a review copy.

Book bargains

Secret Guide to Computers & Tricky Living (31st edition) lists for **$25**. To pay less, join friends:

20% discount if you order at least 2: pay just **$20** each.
40% discount if you order at least 4: pay just **$15** each.
60% discount if you order at least 60: pay just **$10** each.

How many copies do you want?___
If you want some of them on CD instead of printed on paper, how many on CD?___

Say how many copies you want of these **classics**, sold elsewhere at high prices but yours here for **just $3 each**:

The Secret Guide to Computers, edition 27?___ edition 28?___ edition 29?___ edition 30?___
Tricky Living, edition 1?___ edition 2?___

How many copies do you want of the free **Secret Brochure** (about our services)?___

How do we reach you?

Print the name & address where you want the goods sent. If you want the shipment split to *several* addresses, list them; you still get the quantity discounts.

Your phone number s (optional & kept private) will help if we have questions:

Your e-mail addresses (optional & kept private) will get you our news:

Shipping (typically free)

We offer 3 shipping methods:

Standard is available just to the USA. It's **free**. It usually takes 1 week to ZIP codes under 30000, 1½ weeks to other ZIP codes. We usually recommend this shipping method, because it's free.

Rush is like standard (available just to the USA) but a bit faster (because we jump you ahead of other customers and, if reasonable, use Priority Mail or UPS or other fast service). It costs just **$5 total**, even if your order is big or split. If you want to chat about the delivery date, phone 603-666-6644.

International is required for shipping outside the USA. It costs **$8 per printed book**, so multiply the number of printed books by $8. Don't count CDs or brochures: they ship free.

Circle the shipping method you want.

Final steps

Add the book prices and shipping charge. Write the sum: $_____
Which payment method do you prefer? Put × in the box:

❑ **cash** (we accept cash from all countries, convert foreign currency, send change)
❑ **check or money order** (made out to *Secret Guide*)
❑ **credit card** (MasterCard/Visa/AmEx/Discover; at bottom write your number, expiration date, signature)
❑ **bill** (available just if you bought at least 10 books from us before or belong to organizations listed at left)

If the books are a gift to a friend, include a greeting card or note for us to give your friend. On the back of this coupon, please scribble any comments or suggestions you have. Mail to *Secret Guide*, 196 Tiffany Lane, Manchester NH 03104-4782.

This coupon is for you

Get more copies

We offer two kinds of writing:

The Secret Guide to Computers explains computers. *Tricky Living* explains the rest of modern life.

Order more copies for yourself and friends. The books make great presents for Christmas, birthdays, graduations, and celebrations. Older editions include extra info about older computers & lifestyles. For books or free brochures, use this coupon, which gives you quantity discounts. Copy it for your friends. If you have questions, call **603-666-6644** or see **SecretFun.com**, which explains more and lets you read some chapters online, free.

Money-back guarantee

If you're not sure whether to order a book, go ahead: you can return unused books anytime for a 100% refund.

Many ways to order

The simplest way to order is to mail this page's coupon with a check, money order, credit-card info, or cash. Other choices:

You can **visit** us in New Hampshire to pick up the books personally: phone 603-666-6644 for directions and a pickup time.

To order by **credit card**, you can mail this coupon or phone 603-666-6644 (or e-mail Russ@SecretFun.com, if you don't mind sending unsecured e-mail). Give your credit-card number, expiration date, and name printed on the card. We take Master Card, Visa, American Express, and Discover.

We can **bill** you if you bought at least 10 books from us before (or you're employed by or retired from a school, bookstore, government agency, or established computer company). Mail this coupon or phone 603-666-6644 or e-mail Russ@SecretFun.com. If over $700, phone for approval. The bill is due in 30 days.

We accept 5 forms of payment from other countries:

international postal money order (written in U.S. dollars)

credit-card number (Master Card, Visa, American Express, or Discover, with expiration date and the name printed on the card)

check (written in U.S. dollars and having a U.S. or Canadian city printed somewhere on the check)

cash (we convert foreign currency & send change)

wire transfer (in U.S. dollars, from your local outlet of Western Union or MoneyGram, plus a phone call or note telling us how you transferred)

Review copies

If you plan to introduce the book to at least 100 people, phone 603-666-6644 to request a review copy.

CUT OUT THIS COUPON

Book bargains

The Secret Guide to Computers & Tricky Living (31st edition) lists for **$25**. To pay less, join friends:

20% discount if you order at least 2: pay just **$20** each.
40% discount if you order at least 4: pay just **$15** each.
60% discount if you order at least 60: pay just **$10** each.

How many copies do you want?___
If you want some of them on CD instead of printed on paper, how many on CD?___

Say how many copies you want of these **classics**, sold elsewhere at high prices but yours here for **just $3 each**:

The Secret Guide to Computers, edition 27?___   edition 28?___   edition 29?___   edition 30?___
Tricky Living, edition 1?___   edition 2?___

How many copies do you want of the free **Secret Brochure** (about our services)?___

How do we reach you?

Print the name & address where you want the goods sent. If you want the shipment split to *several* addresses, list them; you still get the quantity discounts.

Your phone number s (optional & kept private) will help if we have questions:

Your e-mail addresses (optional & kept private) will get you our news:

Shipping (typically free)

We offer 3 shipping methods:

Standard is available just to the USA. It's **free**. It usually takes 1 week to ZIP codes under 30000, 1½ weeks to other ZIP codes. We usually recommend this shipping method, because it's free.

Rush is like standard (available just to the USA) but a bit faster (because we jump you ahead of other customers and, if reasonable, use Priority Mail or UPS or other fast service). It costs just **$5 total**, even if your order is big or split. If you want to chat about the delivery date, phone 603-666-6644.

International is required for shipping outside the USA. It costs **$8 per printed book**, so multiply the number of printed books by $8. Don't count CDs or brochures: they ship free.

Circle the shipping method you want.

Final steps

Add the book prices and shipping charge. Write the sum: $_____
Which payment method do you prefer? Put × in the box:

❑ **cash** (we accept cash from all countries, convert foreign currency, send change)
❑ **check or money order** (made out to *Secret Guide*)
❑ **credit card** (MasterCard/Visa/AmEx/Discover; at bottom write your number, expiration date, signature)
❑ **bill** (available just if you bought at least 10 books from us before or belong to organizations listed at left)

If the books are a gift to a friend, include a greeting card or note for us to give your friend. On the back of this coupon, please scribble any comments or suggestions you have. Mail to *Secret Guide*, 196 Tiffany Lane, Manchester NH 03104-4782.